# Encyclopedia of Ukraine

*Encyclopedia of*

# UKRAINE

## VOLUME V
## St-Z

Edited by
## DANYLO HUSAR STRUK

under the auspices of
the Canadian Institute of Ukrainian Studies (University of Alberta),
the Shevchenko Scientific Society (Sarcelles, France), and
the Canadian Foundation for Ukrainian Studies

UNIVERSITY OF TORONTO PRESS INCORPORATED
Toronto Buffalo London

© University of Toronto Press Incorporated 1993
Toronto Buffalo London
Printed in Canada

ISBN 0-8020-3995-2
Collector's Edition: ISBN 0-8020-3010-6

**Canadian Cataloguing in Publication Data**
Main entry under title:
Encyclopedia of Ukraine

Revision of: Entsyklopediia ukraïnoznavstva.
Vols. 1–2 edited by Volodymyr Kubijovyč;
vols. 3–5 edited by Danylo Husar Struk.
Includes bibliographical references.
Contents: Map and gazetteer volume. –
V. 1. A–F – V. 2. G–K – V. 3. L–PF – V. 4. PH–SR – V. 5. ST–Z
ISBN 0-8020-3995-2 (v. 5)

1. Ukraine – Dictionaries and encyclopedias.
2. Ukraine – Gazetteers.
I. Kubijovyč, V. (Volodymyr), 1900–85.
II. Struk, Danylo Husar, 1940–.
III. Canadian Institute of Ukrainian Studies.
IV. Naukove tovarystvo imeny Shevchenka.
V. Canadian Foundation for Ukrainian Studies.
VI. Title: Entsyklopediia ukraïnoznavstva.

DK508.E52213 1984 fol     947'.71'003     C84-099336-6

Volodymyr Kubijovyč, *Editor-in-Chief, volumes 1, 2*

Danylo Husar Struk, *Editor-in-Chief, volumes 3, 4, 5*

The publication of this volume

has been made possible in part

through a grant from the Province of British Columbia

in recognition of the contribution of Ukrainian pioneers

to the development of the province.

EDITORIAL STAFF

# S

Yurii Stabovy

Jaroslaw Stachiw

**Stabovy, Yurii** [Stabovyj, Jurij], b 2 April 1894 in Kozelets, Chernihiv gubernia, d 10 July 1968 in Kiev. Film director, screenwriter, and playwright. He worked in the Odessa Artistic Film Studio (1924–34), where as a screenwriter he was associated with L. Kurbas's *Vendetta* (1924) and A. Lundin's *Lisovyi zvir* (A Forest Animal, 1927). He directed *Dva dni* (Two Days, 1927), *Eksponat z panoptykumu* (An Exhibit from a Panopticon, 1929), and the documentary *Vesnianyi bazar* (The Spring Bazaar, 1931) and wrote the plays *Dusha skhodu* (The Soul of the East) and *Vyr* (The Whirlpool, 1926). In 1934 he was accused of Ukrainian nationalism and arrested. After his release from prison he worked as a screenwriter in Moscow.

**Stachiw, Jaroslaw** (Jerry) [Staxiv, Jaroslav], b 23 May 1931 in Lviv. Ukrainian-American mechanical engineer and designer; fellow of the American Society of Mechanical Engineers (ASME) since 1983; son of M. and F. *Stakhiv. He graduated from Pennsylvania State University. He has been a researcher in the field of ocean engineering with the US Navy since 1951 and a marine materials research engineer with the ASME Ocean Engineering Division since 1970 (chairman in 1972–3). In 1970 he constructed the first transparent plastic submersible, the NEMO. He is a recognized authority on ceramic, glass, germanium, and zinc sulphide applications in the construction of structural components of external pressure housings. His design standards for acrylic plastic components were adopted in 1978 by the US Coast Guard, the American Bureau of Shipping, Det Norske Veritas, and Lloyd's Ships Register. Stachiw is the author of *Acrylic Plastic Viewports: Ocean Engineering and Other Hyperbaric Applications* (1982) and has published numerous technical papers on plastic and glass viewports for submersibles, diving bells, and hyperbaric chambers.

**Stadion, Franz Seraphim,** b 27 July 1806 in Vienna, d 8 June 1853 in Vienna. Austrian count and statesman. He began his career in the Austrian government as a senior civil servant in Stanyslaviv and Rzeszów. In the last years of his life he served as governor of Trieste and Istria (1841–7) and Galicia (1847–8) and as minister of the interior (1848–9). As governor of Galicia, in April 1848, months before the imperial law abolishing serfdom was announced, he abolished serfdom and 'hereditary tenancy' in Galicia. An opponent of Polish irredentism and the Polish National Council, he encouraged the creation of the *Supreme Ruthenian Council in Lviv and supported the Uniate clergy and the Ukrainians' demands for equal rights with the Poles and official use of Ukrainian in the schools and government. The Poles accused him of 'inventing' the Ukrainians.

**Stadnychenko, Yurii** [Stadnyčenko, Jurij], b 15 May 1929 in Kharkiv. Poet and translator. A former civil engineer and an editor of the journal *Prapor*, he has written the poetry collections *Stezhkamy iunosti* (Down the Paths of Youth, 1957), *Moie nespokiine sertse* (My Troubled Heart, 1961), *V okeani neskinchennosti* (In the Ocean of Infinity, 1965), *Smishynky z pertsem* (Peppered Jests, 1970), *Okhorontsi vohniu* (The Fire's Protectors, 1973), *Nadiia i virnist'* (Hope and Fidelity, 1977), *Zorianyi prybii* (The Stellar Breaker, 1980), *Pidkova i iakir* (The Horseshoe and the Anchor, 1982), and *Doroha kriz' dovhe lito* (The Road through a Long Summer, 1983). He has translated non-Russian Soviet and Polish literature into Ukrainian.

Sofiia Stadnyk

**Stadnyk, Sofiia** (Stadnykova; née Stechynska), b 13 September 1888 in Ternopil, Galicia, d 21 September 1959 in Lviv. Actress and singer (dramatic soprano); wife of Y. *Stadnyk. A teacher by training, she was an actress in the Ruska Besida Theater (1901–13), the Lviv Ukrainian People's Theater (1913–14), Sadovsky's Theater in Kiev (1916–18), Stadnyk's touring theaters (1919–39), the Lesia Ukrainka Theater (1939–41), and the Lviv Opera Theater (1941–4). In the 1928–9 season she was a guest actress in the Kiev Ukrainian Drama Theater. In 1946 she retired from the stage.

Stefaniia Stadnyk          Yosyp Stadnyk

**Stadnyk, Stefaniia** (Stadnykivna), b 20 September 1912 in Ternopil, Galicia, d 27 February 1983 in Lviv. Stage and film actress and singer (soprano); daughter of Y. and S. Stadnyk. She completed her education in a Warsaw drama school (1926) and then worked in Stadnyk's troupe (until 1939, with interruptions), the Lesia Ukrainka Theater (1939–41), the Lviv Opera Theater (1941–4), the Lviv Young Spectator's Theater (1944–8), the Kharkiv Ukrainian Drama Theater (1948–57), and the Lviv Ukrainian Drama Theater (1959–78). She acted in the film *Viter zi skhodu* (Wind from the East, 1941).

**Stadnyk, Yarema,** b 10 September 1903 in Zbarazh, Galicia, d 19 December 1946 in Lviv. Stage actor and singer; son of Y. and S. Stadnyk. He worked in various Ukrainian troupes in Galicia (1922–31 and 1935–7), the Kryve Zerkalo Theater (1932–4), the Lviv Operetta and variety theaters (1938–41), the Veselyi Lviv Theater (1942–4), and the Lviv Young Spectator's Theater (1945–6).

**Stadnyk, Yosyp,** b 18 March 1876 in Valiava, Peremyshl county, Galicia, d 8 December 1954 in Lviv. Theatrical director and actor. After completing a theatrical education he was an actor and director in the Ruska Besida Theater in Lviv (1894–1913), led it in 1906–13, and left it to lead his own troupe, the Lviv Ukrainian People's Theater (1913–14). He was interned by the Russian authorities during the First World War, and then worked in *Sadovsky's Theater in Kiev (1917–18) and, in 1919, led the Theater of the Western Ukrainian National Republic in Stanyslaviv. Stadnyk directed and administered the reborn *Ukrainska Besida Theater (1921–3); led various *touring theaters – the Union of Ukrainian Actors (1924–6), the co-operative Ukrainskyi Teatr (1927–31), and Stadnyk's Artistic Tour (1935–9) – in Western Ukraine; was appointed artistic director of the Lesia Ukrainka Ukrainian Drama Theater (1939–41); and worked as a director in the Tobilevych Theater (1933–5), the Lviv Opera Theater, the Drohobych Theater, and the Lviv Theater of Miniatures (1945–7). He was subsequently exiled by the Soviet authorities to Uglich, Russia (1947–54). Stadnyk played over 100 roles, mostly character roles in a realistic style, in plays by M. Starytsky, M. Kropyvnytsky, W. Shakespeare, Molière, F. Schiller, and N. Gogol. As a director he staged over 200 productions of dramas, operas, and operettas, including H. Heijermans's

*Good Hope*, E. Rostand's *Les Romanesques*, F. Grillparzer's *Des Meers und der Liebe Wellen*, F. Schiller's *Wilhelm Tell*, M. Lysenko's *Nocturne*, D. Sichynsky's *Roksoliana*, Ya. Lopatynsky's *Enei na mandrivtsi* (Aeneas on a Journey), J. Offenbach's *Tales of Hoffman*, K. Zeller's *Obersteiger*, F. Lehár's *Die Zigeunerliebe*, and J. Strauss's *Der Zigeunerbaron*. He translated numerous dramatic works into Ukrainian.

V. Revutsky

Georg Stadtmüller          Matvii Stakhiv

**Stadtmüller, Georg,** b 17 March 1909 in Bürstadt, Hessen, d 1 November 1985 in Munich. German historian of Eastern and Southeastern Europe and Byzantologist; full member of the Shevchenko Scientific Society from 1966. He was a professor at the universities of Leipzig (1938–45) and Munich (from 1950) and became director of the Eastern Europe Institute (1960–3) in Munich. From 1962 he served on the Scholarly Council and the board of trustees of the *Association for the Advancement of Ukrainian Studies in Munich. He wrote histories of Albania (1942), civil law (1951), Eastern Europe (1950), Eastern European studies (1963), and the Habsburg Empire (1966) and many other works, and received an honorary PH D from the Ukrainian Free University in 1979.

**Stafiniak, Volodymyr** [Stafinjak], b 1884, d 1920. Senior army officer. During the First World War he served in the Legion of Sich Riflemen as chief training officer (1915) and company commander (1917–18). In the Ukrainian Galician Army, he initially defended Rava Ruska and Uhniv against Polish forces and then commanded the Uhniv Brigade. In January 1919 he was promoted to captain, and in March he was put in charge of training. After being promoted to major in June 1919, he served as commander of the rear in the Red Ukrainian Galician Army (1920). He died of typhus.

**Stage design.** See Scenery, theatrical.

**Stahl, Pierre-Jules** (pseud of P.-J. Hetzel), b 18 January 1814 in Chartres, France, d 16 March 1886 in Monte Carlo. French children's writer and publisher. He befriended Marko *Vovchok in 1865 while she was living in Paris, and published nine of her stories in his journal *Magasin d'éducation et de récréation*. For many years Vovchok also served on the journal's editorial board and corresponded with Stahl. In 1869 Stahl coauthored *Le Chemin glissant* ... with Vovchok. The novella appeared in *Magasin* in 1871 and then in several separate editions. In 1878 Stahl published Vovchok's French adaptation of her novella *Marusia, Maroussia*, which gained great popularity in France, was reprinted more than 100 times, and received an award from the Académie Française. A Ukrainian translation appeared in Bratislava in 1965. Vovchok's relationship with Stahl is discussed in considerable detail in B. Lobach-Zhuchenko's *Pro Marka Vovchka* (About Marko Vovchok, 1979).

**Stained-glass windows.** The term used for windows filled with colored glass, usually built of panels in which the pieces of colored glass are held together with strips of lead. Generally the glass has been colored by such methods as the fusion of metallic oxides into the glass, the burning of pigment into the surface of white glass, or the joining of white with colored pieces of glass. In Ukraine no stained-glass windows from medieval times have survived, but there is mention of them in the Chronicle of 1259 and in the travel accounts of Paul of Aleppo in 1654 and 1656. In the 18th and 19th centuries the art of stained-glass windows declined in Europe and in Ukraine. It was revived at the beginning of the 20th century by such artists as P. Kholodny, Sr (The Dormition Church in Lviv, 1926). In Soviet Ukraine stained-glass windows were used from the 1960s on to decorate palaces of culture, museums, metro stations, pavilions, and hotel lobbies. Among the artists working in stained glass are V. Zadorozhny (*Shevchenko Triptych*, at Shevchenko University in Kiev) and O. Dubovyk (*Wandering Wind* and *Carnival Windows*, at the sanatorium in Teodosia).

Among the Ukrainian artists in the West, P. Kholodny, Jr, designed the stained-glass windows for the Ukrainian Catholic Church of St George in New York and Ya. Surmach-Mills designed the windows for St Demetrius's Church in Toronto. M. *Zubar gained national recognition in the United States for his numerous stained-glass windows in churches, synagogues, and community centres. He experimented with special effects achieved by a sandblasting technique used in conjunction with hand-blown glass and invented a new process of painting on glass. In Canada L. *Molodozhanyn has designed numerous stained-glass windows for churches in Manitoba, including 30 windows for the Ukrainian Catholic Cathedral of SS Volodymyr and Olha in Winnipeg. The windows of the chapel were designed by S. Lada. R. Kowal designed the stained-glass windows for St Andrew's and the Blessed Virgin Mary Ukrainian Catholic churches in Winnipeg, as well as others in rural Manitoba.

D. Zelska-Darewych

**Stakh, Ivan** [Stax], b 2 July 1918 in Blackwood, Pennsylvania, d 29 June 1972 in Philadelphia. Ukrainian Catholic bishop. He studied theology in Innsbruck, Switzerland, and Washington. After he was ordained in 1943, he served as a parish priest and then as secretary to Bishop K. Bohachevsky. In August 1946 he was sent by the Ukrainian Catholic Relief Committee to Germany to assist in the resettlement of Ukrainian displaced persons in Europe. When he returned to the United States in 1952, he was made chancellor of the exarchate (subsequently, eparchy) of Stamford, Connecticut. In 1971 he was consecrated bishop and named assistant to the metropolitan of Philadelphia, A. Senyshyn.

**Stakhanov, Aleksei** [Staxanov, Aleksej], b 21 December 1905 in Lugova, Orel gubernia, Russia, d 5 November 1977 in Torez, Donetske oblast. Miner. In 1927 he began working as a miner in Kadiivka (now Stakhanov, in Luhanske oblast). In August 1935 he allegedly set a personal record by mining 102 t of coal in a single shift of 5 hours and 45 minutes, thereby overfulfilling his quota by a factor of 14.5. In September of that year he set another record by mining 227 t of coal. These deeds were carefully staged by Party authorities and used extensively in propaganda to raise labor productivity (see *socialist competition). Afterward Stakhanov completed his education and occupied management positions in mining in Central Asia and, from 1957, in the Donbas.

**Stakhanov** [Staxanov]. V-19, DB II-5. A city (1990 pop 112,000) on the Kamyshuvakha River in Luhanske oblast. It originated in the mid-19th century, when coal mining was developed in the region, as the workers' settlement of Shubynka. From 1898 to 1978 it was called Kadiivka, and then it was renamed in honor of A. *Stakhanov. It was granted city status in 1932. Today the city has four coal mines and a central coal enrichment plant. It is also an important metallurgical and machine-building center with an iron-ore refinery, ferrous alloys plant, a machine-building factory, a railway-car plant, and a coke-chemical plant.

**Stakhanovite movement.** See Socialist competition.

**Stakhiv, Franka** [Staxiv] (née Nakonechna], b 3 October 1906 in Lviv. Civic and educational activist; wife of M. *Stakhiv and mother of J. *Stachiw. In the interwar period she was active in various Ukrainian organizations in Lviv, as secretary of the Union of Ukrainian Working Women (1931–9) and editor of its organ *Zhinochyi holos* (1931–9) and as secretary of the Samoosvita popular university (1930–9). In 1949, a refugee in Germany, she emigrated to the United States.

**Stakhiv, Matvii** [Staxiv, Matvij] (Stachiw, Matthew), b 30 November 1895 in Nushche, Zboriv county, Galicia, d 2 June 1978 in San Diego, California. Lawyer, historian, and political leader; full member of the Shevchenko Scientific Society from 1943. He served as an officer in the Ukrainian Galician Army (1918–20) and studied law at Prague University (LLD, 1924). After returning to Lviv he became active in the Ukrainian Radical party, in which he served as general secretary (1925–39) and editor of its weekly *Hromads'kyi holos* (1929–39). He also directed the Samoosvita popular university and edited its publications (1930–9). As a postwar émigré in Germany he lectured at the Ukrainian Free University and sat on the Ukrainian National Council. After settling in the United States (1949) he edited the weekly *Narodna volia* (1949–71), sat on the board of the United Ukrainian American Relief Committee, presided over the Shevchenko Scientific Society (1969–74), and was an executive member of the Ukrainian Congress Committee of America (1951–71) and the World Congress of Free Ukrainians (1967–72). In addition to numerous articles and pamphlets on political and historical subjects, he wrote *Zakhidnia Ukraïna* (Western Ukraine, 6 vols, 1958–61), *Ukraïna v dobi Dyrektoriï UNR* (Ukraine in the Period of the UNR Directory, 7 vols, 1962–8), and *Ukraine and Russia: An Outline of History of Political and Mil-*

*itary Relations* (1967). He also coauthored *Western Ukraine at the Turning Point of Europe's History, 1918–1923* (2 vols, 1969, 1971) and *Ukraine and the European Turmoil, 1917–1919* (1973).

Volodymyr Stakhiv          Danylo Stakhura

**Stakhiv, Volodymyr** [Staxiv] (pseud: Mek), b 1910 in Peremyshl, Galicia, d 25 October 1971 in Munich. Journalist and political activist. After joining the OUN in 1929, he worked in its Berlin office and at the Ukrainian Press Service (1930s). At the same time he studied at the Berlin Polytechnical Institute and was active in the Ukrainian student movement. In mid-1941 he was in charge of external relations for the Ukrainian State Administration before being imprisoned for three years at the Sachsenhausen concentration camp. After the war he settled in Munich, where he was one of the leaders of the External Units of the OUN and a member of the External Representation of the Ukrainian Supreme Liberation Council and of the Political Council of the OUN (Abroad). He also served as president of the Ukrainian Journalists' Association Abroad and of the League of Ukrainian Political Prisoners. He worked as chief editor of the weekly *\*Ukraïns'ka trybuna* and the biweekly *Suchasna Ukraïna* and as coeditor of *\*Suchasnist'*.

**Stakhiv, Yaroslav.** See Stachiw, Jaroslaw.

**Stakhovsky, Kostiantyn** [Staxovs'kyj, Kostjantyn], b 1882 in Podilia gubernia, d 11 May 1959 in Prague. Sculptor and ceramicist. He studied art in Warsaw, Paris, St Petersburg, Munich, and Berlin. An interwar émigré, in 1923 he settled in Prague, where he taught at the Ukrainian Studio of Plastic Arts. A specialist in the sculpture of bronze, clay, and plaster animals and busts, he displayed his works in London (1918–19) and in Paris at the Salon des Indépendants and the Salon d'Automne (1919–22).

**Stakhovsky, Lev** [Staxovs'kyj], b 1911 in Vinnytsia, Podilia gubernia, d 1968 in Caracas, Venezuela. Otolaryngologist and community leader; full member of the Shevchenko Scientific Society from 1955; son of M. \*Stakhovsky. A graduate of Prague University, he practiced medicine in Czechoslovakia and emigrated in 1947 to Venezuela. He was the founder and first president of the Ukrainian Hromada society in Caracas. His scientific publications included scientific articles on tuberculosis of the larynx.

**Stakhovsky, Mykola** [Staxovs'kyj], b 22 May 1879 in Volytsia, Starokostiantyniv county, Volhynia gubernia, d 7 December 1948 in Prague. Physician and civic activist. After graduating from Warsaw University (MD, 1904) he specialized in surgery in Kiev. During the Russo-Japanese War he served as an army surgeon in the Far East. The publisher of *Borot'ba*, an organ of the Ukrainian Social Democratic Workers' party, Stakhovsky was threatened with arrest in 1906 for writing an antigovernment article. He escaped to France. In 1908 he returned to Ukraine and opened a private practice in Vinnytsia. In 1917 he was appointed gubernial commissioner for Podilia under the Central Rada, and at the end of 1919 he headed the UNR diplomatic mission to Great Britain. In the interwar period he worked as a physician and cultural activist in Berehove, Transcarpathia.

**Stakhura, Danylo** [Staxura], b 19 December 1860 in Poliany, Krosno county, Galicia, d 20 December 1938 in Prague. Lawyer and civic and political leader. After graduating in law from Lviv University he worked as a lawyer in Ternopil, Peremyshl, and Sambir and was active in Ukrainian organizational life. In 1907 he was elected as a candidate of the National Democratic party to the Austrian parliament. After being deported by Russian authorities to Simbirsk in 1914, he returned to Sambir three years later and was elected mayor and member of the Ukrainian National Rada (1918–19). After emigrating to Czechoslovakia he served as judge of the provincial court in Berehove and worked with the Prosvita society in Uzhhorod. He was also a strong supporter of the Boikivskhchyna society in Sambir and provided it with a home for its ethnography museum.

**Stalin, Joseph** (real name: Yosif Dzhugashvili), b 21 December 1879 in Gori, Georgia, d 5 March 1953 in Moscow. Soviet political leader, first secretary of the CPSU, and absolute dictator of the USSR.

Stalin first emerged as a specialist on the nationality question. In 1914, under V. Lenin's guidance, he wrote *Natsionalnyi vopros i marksizm* (translated in 1942 as *Marxism and the National Question*), mostly a criticism of O. Bauer's and K. Renner's interpretation of nationalism, which had gained considerable popularity, especially among Georgian socialists. Because of this work and his Georgian origin he was appointed people's commissar of nationalities in the Bolshevik government (1917–22). In 1919 he also became people's commissar of state control. As commissar of nationalities, in 1920 he opposed the separation of the 'border' countries (Ukraine, Georgia, etc), which were important sources of raw materials and food for central Russia. In 1922 he rejected the concept of a union of independent and equal republics and advocated instead the incorporation of the national republics into the RSFSR as autonomous units. Although his idea was rejected, the Russian republic was made the cornerstone of the new union. Stalin relied on the Russian state bureaucracy to convert the USSR into a centralized, totalitarian empire (see \*Nationality policy).

His most important post, however, was the general secretaryship of the CC of the Russian Communist Party (Bol-

1

3

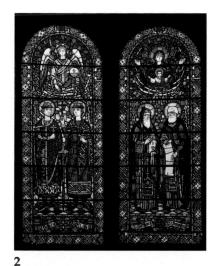

2

4

5

6

STAINED GLASS  1) M. Zubar: St Josaphat's Ukrainian Catholic Church in Rochester, New York. 2) L. Molodozhanyn: ss Volodymyr and Olha Ukrainian Catholic Cathedral in Winnipeg (1963). 3) M. Shkaraputa: *Movement towards Light* (Hungarian Consulate, Kiev, 1978). 4) M. Sosenko: St Michael's Church in Pidbereztsi, Galicia (1907–10). 5) O. Melnyk: *The Time of Yaroslav the Wise* (Historical Museum of Ukraine, Kiev, 1978). 6) I.-V. Zadorozhny: *People Save the Earth* (Palace of Culture, Bila Tserkva, Kiev oblast, 1978–9).

shevik) (RKP[B]), which he assumed in 1922. Although his authority was damaged somewhat by Lenin's strong reservations concerning his secretaryship, Stalin used this administrative post to build a firm power base in the Party. By placing his own supporters in key positions he was able to dominate the entire interlocking Party, state, military, and police bureaucracy. After Lenin's death he created a mass personality cult that glorified first Lenin and then himself as an all-powerful and all-knowing leader. One by one he expelled his allies and potential rivals – L. Trotsky, G. Zinovev, L. Kamenev, A. Rykov, and N. Bukharin – from the Party and then destroyed them. In the late 1920s he announced the policy of 'socialism in one country,' whereby he abandoned the *New Economic Policy and embarked on a program of rapid industrialization and *collectivization, which was enforced by means of widespread *terror. Millions of Ukrainian peasants were starved to death in 1932–3, millions of people were imprisoned in *concentration camps, and hundreds of thousands were executed by the secret police. Repeated *purges of the Party and government removed any possible source of opposition to his power. A favorite tactic was the show trials, such as those of 1936–8, in which former Bolshevik leaders confessed to treason and implicated many others in their crimes. Almost half of the Party membership was destroyed, and 139 members of the CC were executed. Of 1,966 delegates at the 17th Party Congress in 1934, 1,108 had been arrested by 1939. In the armed forces Stalin organized a major purge that destroyed most of the experienced senior officers on the eve of the Second World War.

In foreign affairs Stalin pursued an expansionist policy based, for a time, on an alliance with A. Hitler. He occupied Western Ukraine and the Baltic states, Bessarabia, and Bukovyna (see *Molotov-Ribbentrop Pact). Stalin failed to anticipate the German attack on the USSR in 1941, and the Soviets suffered heavy losses in the early stages of the war. At first many Soviet troops, including Ukrainians, had no desire to fight for the Stalinist regime and surrendered en masse. Later, taking advantage of the abominable treatment of the Soviet POWs by the Nazis and of the discontent among the nations subjugated by the Nazis, and playing up patriotism, Stalin succeeded in rallying his subjects and, assisted by the Allies, in emerging as a victor from the war. In the postwar settlement he extended Soviet influence to large new territories in Eastern Europe and the Far East and eventually turned them into Communist-ruled satellite states.

After the war Stalin encouraged the growth of Great Russian nationalism and discriminated against the other nationalities of the USSR. Some of the smaller nations, such as the Volga Germans, the Crimean Tatars, and the Chechens, were subjected to genocide for their alleged collaboration with the Germans. According to N. Khrushchev the Ukrainians were saved from mass deportation only by their large numbers. In 1939–41 and again after the war Stalin Sovietized the newly acquired Western Ukraine by deporting hundreds of thousands of people and destroying much of the intelligentsia. At the same time A. *Zhdanov imposed rigid control on Soviet cultural and intellectual life.

Stalin concentrated all political power in his own hands. From 1941 he was head of state, commissar of defence, and supreme commander of the armed forces (as-suming the title of 'generalissimo' in 1945). He built on the traditions of Russian oriental absolutism in creating a totalitarian state cemented together by terror. At the end of his life he began a major assault on the Jews, whom he characterized as 'rootless cosmopolitans.' Stalin was not a theoretical thinker, and Stalinism was not a political doctrine; it was a political system of ruthless, unrestricted dictatorship by the Party leader over a demoralized, helpless society.

After Stalin's death Khrushchev, in his 'secret speech' at the 20th Congress of the CPSU (1956), criticized to a degree the 'cult of personality' that had arisen around the dictator. This de-Stalinization campaign continued at the subsequent congress in 1961, when it was decided to remove Stalin's embalmed body from Lenin's mausoleum, rename all the places and institutions that had been named in his honor, and dismantle his statues. With L. Brezhnev's ascension to power in 1964, however, Stalin was partly rehabilitated, and some measures recalled the excesses of his regime – the personality cult, official Russification, closed trials, and repressions. In its final years the CPSU at last admitted the crimes against humanity committed under Stalin's rule, but it did not accept its responsibility for them.

BIBLIOGRAPHY
Souvarine, B. Stalin: A Critical Survey of Bolshevism (New York 1939)
Kostiuk, H. Stalinist Rule in the Ukraine: A Study of the Decade of Mass Terror, 1929–39 (New York 1960)
Wolfe, B. Three Who Made a Revolution, 4th edn (New York 1964)
Deutscher, I. Stalin: A Political Biography, 2nd edn (London 1967)
Conquest, R. The Great Terror: Stalin's Purge of the Thirties (London–New York 1968)
Tucker, R. Stalin as Revolutionary, 1879–1929 (New York 1973)
Ulam, A. Stalin: The Man and His Era (New York 1973)
Tucker, R. (ed). Stalinism: Essays in Historical Interpretation (New York 1977)

**Staline** or **Stalino.** See Donetske.

**Stalinsky, Oleh** [Stalins'kyj], b 16 January 1907 in Kiev, d 1991 in Lviv. Ballet dancer and ballet master. In 1920 he completed study at Z. Lange's ballet studio and choreographic training at Tsentrostudiia in Kiev. After working as an actor in Russian theaters, he danced as a soloist in the Kiev Theater of Opera and Ballet (1922–46, with interruptions in Odessa and Alma-Ata) and was a soloist and ballet master in the Lviv Theater of Opera and Ballet (1946–73).

**Stamford.** A city (1980 pop 102,000) at the mouth of the Rippowam River on Long Island Sound in the state of Connecticut. It is a residential suburb of New York with some industry and research laboratories. Ukrainians, who number about 400 today, began to settle there at the turn of the century. A Ukrainian Catholic parish was established in 1916. A minor seminary and high school were opened in Stamford in 1933; they were accredited and named St Basil's College and St Basil's Preparatory School respectively in 1939. The *Ukrainian Diocesan Museum of Stamford was founded in 1935. In 1942 Stamford became the seat of the auxiliary bishop of Philadelphia eparchy of the Ukrainian Catholic church, and later the seat of an exarchate (1956) and eparchy (1958) under A. Senyshyn. At Senyshyn's promotion to the office of archbishop of Philadelphia in 1961, his position was assumed by J. Schmondiuk and then B. Losten (1977). Today (1990) the eparchy has 55 parishes served by 57 priests and 20 monks.

**Stamp collecting.** See Ukraine-Philatelisten Verband, Ukrainian Philatelic and Numismatic Society, and Postage stamps.

*Stan.* In medieval Rus' a military encampment which was usually set up on elevated ground and surrounded by a makeshift barrier of carts or a palisade and sometimes by a ditch or earthworks. The term was also applied to stopover points on long routes and to places visited periodically by the prince's officials to collect tribute and to hold court over the local population. In the 19th century the *stan* was a police territorial unit within a county.

**Standard of living.** The goods and services enjoyed or aspired to by an individual or group. In the Soviet economy, where prices bore no relation to value, wages to labor, and consumer goods to quality of life, it was difficult to determine the real standard of living on the basis of statistical data. The task was complicated further by the fact that there were two different prices for goods, and that the buying power of the ruble varied with different categories of the population. Official statistics lacked a sound methodology and accurate measurements. Hence, the official data on the standard of living reflected propositions and tendencies rather than the real standard of living.

The standard of living is normally determined by the level of economic development or by the gross national product per capita. It is not to be confused with 'quality of life,' which also includes the cultural, spiritual, and social dimensions of life. In 1989 the gross national product of Ukraine was worth 271 billion rubles, or 29 percent of the Soviet Union's. The gross national products per capita in Ukraine and the Soviet Union were 5,211 and 3,208 rubles respectively. Ukraine's national income per capita was 2,078 rubles, whereas that of the Soviet Union was 2,281. Thus Ukraine's gross national product was 38 percent per capita higher, and its national income per capita was 9 percent lower, than the Union average.

The per capita output of basic industrial and agricultural products, such as coal, pig iron, steel, wheat, meat, milk, butter, sugar, and vegetables, in Ukraine exceeded the Union average. Soviet Ukraine's output of many products equaled that of the developed countries. Its per capita output of wheat, for example, was smaller than that of the United States and France but greater than that of Italy, the United Kingdom, and Germany. Its per capita output of butter and milk was second only to France's. Ukraine was ahead of the United Kingdom in electric power and ahead of every European country in pig iron and steel production. But in per capita consumption Ukraine lagged behind some developing countries. In 1989 the average monthly wage in Ukraine was 217.7 rubles and in the USSR, 240.4 rubles. In Ukraine expenditures from social funds were 619 rubles per person, in the USSR, 650 rubles, and in the United States, 5,200 dollars. The proportion of social consumption to the gross domestic product of the republic was 12 percent for Ukraine, 20 percent for the USSR, and 28 percent for the United States. The percentage of wages to national income did not exceed 37 percent in Ukraine, whereas in the developed countries it was 60–70 percent.

The per capita income from private plots was 11 rubles a month.

The structure of the Ukrainian population by income was as follows (1989): 3.1 million people (6 percent of the total population) received up to 75 rubles per month, 7.3 million (14.2 percent) received 75 to 100 rubles, 20.2 million (37.2 percent) received 101 to 150 rubles, 2.6 million (24.5 percent) received 151 to 200 rubles, and 3.6 million (6.9 percent) received over 250 rubles.

Until the dissolution of the USSR 75 rubles per month was regarded as the minimum living standard, but that figure was only a rough estimate without any scientific basis. According to criteria used in other countries, anyone with a monthly income of under 100 rubles, that is, 20 percent of the Ukrainian population, was below the poverty line. Another 10 million people, with an income of 100 to 125 rubles per month, were on the verge of poverty. According to the criterion of poverty adopted by the European Economic Commission of the United Nations (per capita income of under two-thirds of the country's average), 30.6 million Ukrainians, or 57.4 percent of the population, were poor in 1989 (average income = 153 rubles per month). As the economic situation in the USSR deteriorated in 1990–1, the number of people below the poverty line increased.

The group with an income of over 250 rubles per month was in the highest bracket. Those with an income of 151 to 250 rubles per month (35.7 percent of the population) could therefore have been regarded as constituting a middle class. In Japan, by contrast, the middle class consists of 90 percent of the population. In relation to private property, the well-to-do group (the equivalent of the American middle class) consists of those who own cars. In Ukraine 3.1 million people, or 6 percent of the population, belonged to that category, the same percentage that had an income of over 250 rubles a month. It was the only stratum of Soviet society that had the full range of consumer goods: an apartment or house, modern furniture, a car, and a summer cottage – all the attributes of the middle class.

The difference between Ukraine's per capita production and consumption was much higher than the Union average. The discrepancy was the result of the 'equalization' policy of the central government, which redistributed the gross national product among the unequally developed republics. The difference also reflected the structure of Ukrainian industry, in which heavy industry and the extractive and processing branches dominated the economy. The raw materials and products in those branches were priced low, and labor in them was poorly paid. The average wage in Russia was higher than that in Ukraine, not only because of regional compensations for severe climatic conditions (in the Far North or Kamchatka) but mostly because 80 percent of the defense industry was located in Russia. Income by itself does not indicate the real standard of living. It must be compared to the prices of consumer goods and to the structure of expenditures. In 1989 average Ukrainians spent a third of their income on food, another third on consumer goods, 3 percent on housing, and 20 percent on other needs, and saved about 10 percent. A family of four with two children spent 52 percent of its income on food, compared to 15.2 percent in the United States and 21 percent in Western Europe. To buy 1 kg of meat the average Ukrainian had to work 10 times longer than an American. Measured in that way, the price of butter was 8 times higher, of bread, 2 to 3 times higher; of a woolen suit, 15 times higher; of a color TV, 20 times higher; and of a car, 5 times higher in Ukraine than in the United States.

In 1989 the per capita food consumption in Ukraine was slightly higher than in the USSR; for example, meat, 69 kg (67 in the USSR); milk, 367 kg (359); sugar, 49 kg (41); vegetables, 125 kg (98); fruits, 47 kg (43); and baked goods, 138 kg (130). But the average Soviet citizen was better provided with consumer goods than the average Ukrainian. In the USSR there were 105 TV sets per 100 families, whereas in Ukraine there were only 100. Similarly, in the USSR there were 92 refrigerators and 72 washing machines, compared to 90 and 67 in Ukraine. For every thousand inhabitants there were 60 cars in Ukraine and 56 in the USSR (510 in the United States). The average living area per person was 7.6 sq m in Ukraine, 15.8 sq m in the USSR, 49 sq m in the United States, and up to 36 sq m in Western Europe. The average floor area of a house in Ukraine was 57 sq m, compared to 130–140 sq m in the developed countries. In the USSR there were 200 separate houses or flats per 1,000 inhabitants, in the United States there are 380, in Canada 351, and in the developed European countries over 400. In 1990, 2.5 million people in Ukraine were inadequately housed by Soviet standards, with less than 5–9 sq m per family member. A wait of about 10 years was required to get the living space guaranteed by the state. Population growth outpaced the building rate of the construction industry. The construction of private housing accounts for only 1 percent of the new housing in cities and 75 percent in rural areas.

In Soviet Ukraine only 3.9 percent of the gross national product was spent on health care. In most developed countries the figure is at least twice as high. The per capita medical service provided in Ukraine amounted to a third of that provided in the United States, although Ukraine had more medical personnel (44 physicians and 118 nurses per 10,000 people).

The statistical figures just cited cannot describe the real standard of living in Ukraine, because they do not take into account three important factors: (1) the quality of the consumer goods and services, (2) the hidden price inflation, and (3) the rapidly falling supply of consumer goods. The official statistics on meat consumption (69 kg per capita per year), for example, included by-products (over 10 kg) and losses in processing and transportation (10–15 percent). Thus, the real figure was 49 kg, which amounted to only 57 percent of Ukraine's meat output. In comparison Russia consumed 66 percent and Belarus 63 percent of their meat output. Some Ukrainian economists estimated that the real rate of meat consumption in the republic was closer to 25–32.9 kg per person. The housing statistics did not show that most of the stock had not been renovated or properly maintained for many years. Few of the new rural houses had modern conveniences. Only 5 percent of Ukrainian villages had natural gas. New apartments needed repairs at a cost of 9 rubles per sq m before people could move into them. The number of people waiting for their guaranteed share of living space was two or three times higher than the official number, because various formalities made it difficult to get on the waiting list.

As to medical care, an internal poll of 11,000 doctors showed that 4 percent of the polyclinics and 7 percent of the hospitals in Ukraine were in a critical condition. A third needed repair. Seven to 8 percent of them had no running water, and 10–14 percent had no sewage system or central heating. In 80 percent of the hospitals there were over six patients to a room. Only 2 percent of the polyclinics and 6 percent of the hospitals in Ukraine had ultrasound equipment. Over a third of Ukrainian villages did not even have first-aid stations.

The official figures on the standard of living in Soviet Ukraine did not take into account the high inflation created by the government in its last few years. In 1990 personal incomes grew by 18 percent. Most consumer goods at state-controlled prices disappeared from the shops, and prices on the collective-farm and black markets doubled and tripled. Prices were driven up also by the shortage of consumer goods and services, which intensified steadily for five years and reached alarming levels in 1990–1. Pent-up demand for goods, as well as individual savings, increased at a similar pace. The central government printed money without any backing in goods: 11 billion rubles in 1988, 18 billion in 1989, and 27 billion in 1990. In 1989 only 25 percent of the money supply was backed by consumer goods; in 1990, only 18 percent.

The causes of the sharp drop in the supply of consumer goods and the consumption level of the population in the former USSR lie primarily in the structure of the planned economy, which was designed to satisfy its own needs, not the demands of the consumer. In 1928, 60.5 percent of the industrial output was consumer goods, and 39 percent the means of production. In 1940 the proportion was 39:61, and in 1985, 25:75. Any improvement in productivity or any growth of national income, therefore, had little effect on the standard of living.

S. Voitovych

**Standard Ukrainian.** The standard, or literary, version of the Ukrainian *language evolved through three distinct periods: old (10th–13th centuries), middle (14th–18th centuries), and modern (19th–20th centuries). The cardinal changes that occurred were conditioned by changes in the political and cultural history of Ukraine.

Old Ukrainian is found in extant Kievan church and scholarly texts dating from the mid-11th century and the Kievan charter of 1130, in Galician church texts dating from the late 11th century, and in Galician charters dating from the mid-14th century. There are hardly any literary monuments from Chernihiv, Tmutorokan, and Pereiaslav; hence, we can only make conjectures about the literary language used in these principalities. In addition to church and scholarly texts, Old Ukrainian is represented by private letters, chronicles, and belles-lettres works. The language of all these genres is basically *Church Slavonic, with an ever-increasing admixture of local lexical, phonetic, morphological, and syntactic features. Although the language was not institutionally regulated, it remained quite stable, because of the patronage of the church and the concentration of literary life around religious centers. Thus, texts created in Kiev do not differ much from those transcribed from the Bulgarian. Some scholars, such as A. *Shakhmatov, have conjectured that this was also the koine of the most cultured intellectual strata. Hypotheses (by S. Obnorsky and, to a certain degree, L. Yakubinsky and I. Svientsitsky) about a local, urban-vernacular-based literary language that predated the widespread use of Church Slavonic have not been confirmed by known facts.

Only the language of the Galician charters reveals a local character, but data allowing us to date back that tradition do not exist.

The decline of Kievan Rus' and later the Principality of Galicia-Volhynia and the resulting annexation of most Ukrainian lands (except for Galicia, Bukovyna, and Transcarpathia) by the Grand Duchy of Lithuania interrupted the literary tradition of Old Ukrainian. This is particularly evident in the rift that occurred between the language of the church and that of government. The language of the religious genres and styles is characterized in the late 14th and 15th centuries by a renewed 'Church Slavonicization.' This so-called second wave of Church Slavonic influences stemmed from the linguistic reforms of Patriarch Euthymius of Tŭrnovo, who introduced artificial archaisms, a syntax and spelling closer to the Greek, and a rhetorical style. At the same time the language of government drew closer to the vernacular and was influenced also by the Latin, German, Czech, and Polish used in the central European chanceries. The political division of the Ukrainian lands between Poland and Lithuania led to the development of two variants of administrative language, Galician and Volhynian-Polisian. The Galician variant, which reflected the phonetics and morphology of the southwestern dialects and contained more Polonisms, became obsolete when the government adopted Latin or Polish (1433). The Volhynian-Polisian variant, with its center in Lutske, reflected the phonetics and morphology of the northern dialects and, after becoming the basis of the official language of the Lithuanian-Ruthenian state, absorbed more and more Belarusian features, especially those shared by the northern Ukrainian and southern Belarusian dialects (eg, the distinction between e and ě under stress, hardened r, ž, č, š). It became a distinctive koine which was used occasionally in Eastern Europe as a language of diplomacy.

The growth of towns, the rise of a Ukrainian burgher class, and the influence of the Reformation brought about a shift in the language of the higher genres toward the chancery and vernacular languages. There were even attempts at translating the Bible into a language approximating the vernacular (eg, the Peresopnytsia Gospel [1556–61] and Krekhiv Apostol [1563–72]). This trend was arrested, however, by the so-called third wave of Church Slavonicization. Polish cultural, political, and economic expansion after the 1569 Union of Lublin led to the Polonization of the Ukrainian nobility and the cultural and political decline of Ukrainian towns, thereby destroying the ground on which a vernacular-based Ukrainian literary language could rise. It was under these circumstances that the clergy assumed ideological leadership of the Ukrainian opposition and propagated the restoration and normalization of Church Slavonic as the vehicle of an older, Greco-Byzantine tradition. The *grammars and dictionaries produced by L. Zyzanii, M. Smotrytsky, P. Berynda, and others did not revive Church Slavonic in its pure form, but with an admixture of arbitrary changes and with some Ukrainian elements (eg, pronunciation of the nasal vowels ѧ, ѧ as u, ja; g as h; ѣ as i; and the nonpronunciation of *jers). The result of this policy was the opposite of what was intended: by severing the literary language from the vernacular and blocking the secularization of the literary language, the church in fact facilitated the Polonization process.

In practice even M. Smotrytsky's standards of Church Slavonic could not be maintained, and many vernacular elements and Western influences (especially Latinisms and Polonisms) crept into the literary language. Thus, an eclectic language based on Church Slavonic became the literary medium of the Cossack Hetman state of the 17th and early 18th centuries. Its variegated composition suited the prevailing style of the period, the baroque. The language was used in homiletics, scholarship, belles-lettres, and, with considerably fewer Church Slavonicisms, official communication and private correspondence. Given the artificial nature of the language, it is difficult to speak of its dialectal base; in general, however, southwestern dialectal elements prevailed over northern ones.

The decline of the Hetman state after the Russian victory at Poltava (1709) interrupted the normal development of the literary language. As baroque culture declined and became secularized, tsarist interference, as in the ukases of 1721, 1727–8, 1735, 1766, and 1772 censoring the language of Ukrainian printed books, as well as the Russification of education and the desire of certain strata of the Cossack starshyna and the higher Orthodox clergy to consolidate their position in the service of the Russian Empire, put an end to the printing of works in the literary language of the 17th century. In the second half of the 18th century the literary language used in Ukraine (eg, in the late Cossack chronicles, the writings of H. Skovoroda and V. Kapnist, and Istoriia Rusov) was, in fact, Russian. The vernacular was used only in satirical, humorous, intimate, or lyrical works, as prescribed by the classicist theory of low style. The authors of such works did not envision creating a new literary language, but merely recorded various 'Little Russian' dialects (eg, the northern in I. Nekrashevych, the Poltava in I. *Kotliarevsky, and the Kharkiv in H. Kvitka-Osnovianenko).

The attitude to the vernacular changed only with the rise of Romanticism, which in Ukraine acquired a distinctly populist flavor. Various writers, such as M. *Shashkevych, A. Metlynsky, and M. Kostomarov, raised the possibility of a serious, full-fledged literature based on the vernacular. They preferred folklore, which was associated with a historical tradition, to colloquial speech as a source of the literary language. Thus, the southeastern dialectal base of Modern Standard Ukrainian became established. But these efforts lacked historicity. Building on the achievements of his Romantic precursors from Poltava and Kharkiv, T. *Shevchenko first met the challenge of forging a synthetic, pan-Ukrainian literary language encompassing both the historical (eg, the use of archaisms and Church Slavonicisms) and the geographical dimension (the use of accessible dialects). P. *Kulish combined the same elements but in different proportions. Shevchenko's and Kulish's contemporaries and immediate successors failed to grasp the fact that historical and stylistic synthesis was the essence of language reform. The breadth of the geographic synthesis, however, secured a wide influence for the new literary language. This was the principle which gave direction to the linguistic strivings of the writers grouped around the journal *Osnova. Later it had a determining influence on the character of B. *Hrinchenko's dictionary, which, despite its apparent dialectal nature, played a major role in normalizing the literary language.

The new literary Ukrainian began to be used in scholarship and publicism in the early 1860s. This development was interrupted by P. *Valuev's circular (1863) forbidding Ukrainian-language printing within the Russian Empire. As Ukrainian publishing shifted to Austrian-ruled Galicia, the new literary language took root there, imposed the Middle Ukrainian–based literary language, and thereby undercut the attempts of local Russophiles to establish Russian as the literary language. In Galicia the new language became strongly influenced by the local vernacular. The impact of the northern dialects was not particularly evident, although they were used by writers living in Chernihiv gubernia (eg, P. Kulish, B. Hrinchenko, M. Kotsiubynsky). In the debate on Standard Ukrainian at the turn of the century, V. Mova, O. Pchilka, and M. Starytsky, and then M. Kotsiubynsky, Lesia Ukrainka, I. Franko, and M. Levytsky, favored a synthesis of the western and eastern vernaculars, while B. Hrinchenko, A. *Krymsky, and I. *Nechui-Levytsky argued for eliminating Western Ukrainian influences. When Standard Ukrainian 'returned' to Russian-ruled Ukraine after the lifting of the ban on the Ukrainian language in 1905, it already had a synthetic character. But its central Ukrainian foundation remained untouched.

The expansion of Standard Ukrainian into all social spheres and literary genres in the independent Ukrainian state of 1917–20 and in Soviet Ukraine in the 1920s necessitated its normalization and codification (see *Lexicology, *Orthography, and *Terminology). Two distinct currents of opinion arose in this regard. Supporters of a purist 'ethnographic' orientation (see *Purism), such as Ye. Tymchenko, S. Smerechynsky, O. Kurylo (at first), and V. Simovych, advocated the adoption of the popular vernacular as the standard. It was, however, the school led by O. *Syniavsky, which took into account not only tradition but also the development of the language, that gained the upper hand and determined the norms of orthography, orthoepy, morphology, and syntax.

Stalin's abolition of the policy of Ukrainization in the early 1930s and his suppression of Ukrainian national and cultural life were accompanied by bureaucratic attempts to restrict the use of Standard Ukrainian. It was totally eliminated from the military sphere and severely restricted in the scientific and technological spheres. Western Ukrainianisms and European loanwords existing in Ukrainian but not in Russian were expunged, and the language was reoriented toward the eastern Ukrainian dialects and Russian vocabulary and grammar. Changes in orthography, grammar, and lexicon were carried to such an extreme that some of them were to be rejected even in the official orthography adopted in 1946 and in the 1948 Kievan Russian-Ukrainian dictionary. The general direction of Soviet *language policy, however, has remained unchanged. Despite constantly increasing influence of the Russian language in Ukraine (see *Russian-Ukrainian linguistic relations), the general character of Standard Ukrainian as it was defined by Shevchenko and Kulish and codified by Hrinchenko, Syniavsky, and the VUAN dictionaries of the 1920s remains intact.

BIBLIOGRAPHY
Levchenko, H. Narysy z istorii ukrains'koi literaturnoi movy pershoi polovyny XIX st. (Kiev 1946)
Ilarion [Ohiienko, I.]. Istoriia ukrains'koi literaturnoi movy (Winnipeg 1950)
Bulakhovs'kyi, L. Pytannia pokhodzhennia ukrains'koi movy (Kiev 1956)
Lehr-Spławiński, T.; Zwoliński, P.; Hrabec, S. Dzieje języka ukraińskiego w zarysie (Warsaw 1956)
Bilodid, I. (ed). Kurs istorii ukrains'koi literaturnoi movy, 2 vols (Kiev 1958, 1961)
Pliushch, P. Narysy z istorii ukrains'koi literaturnoi movy (Kiev 1958)
Tymoshenko, P. (ed). Khrestomatiia materialiv z istorii ukrains'koi literaturnoi movy, 2 vols (Kiev 1959, 1961)
Shevelov, G.Y. Die ukrainische Schriftsprache, 1798–1965 (Wiesbaden 1966)
Chaplenko, V. Istoriia novoi ukrains'koi literaturnoi movy (XVII st.–1933 r.) (New York 1970)
Shevelov, G.Y. 'Evolution of the Ukrainian Literary Language,' in Rethinking Ukrainian History, ed I.L. Rudnytsky with the assistance of J.-P. Himka (Edmonton 1981)
– 'The Language Question in the Ukraine in the Twentieth Century (1900–1941),' HUS, 10–11 (1986–7) and as a separate publication (Cambridge, Mass 1989)

G.Y. Shevelov

**Stanimir, Osyp,** b 21 April 1890 in Ladychyn, Ternopil county, Galicia, d 13 February 1971 in Toronto. Military officer. After serving in the Austrian army during the First World War, he joined the Ukrainian Galician Army (UHA) in November 1918. During 1918–19, at the rank of captain, he commanded an infantry battalion of the Sambir Brigade. His unit was the first UHA force to enter Kiev on 30 August 1919. In the Red Ukrainian Galician Army he commanded the Third Brigade, which in April 1920 deserted the Soviet army. After escaping from Polish internment he joined the Kherson Division of the UNR Army and was briefly interned with it in Czechoslovakia. He graduated from the Commerce Academy in Vienna (1924) and was active in the co-operative movement in Galicia. After the Second World War he emigrated to Canada, where he wrote Moia uchast' u vyzvol'nykh zmahanniakh (My Participation in the Liberation Struggle, 1966).

**Stanishevsky, Yurii** [Staniševs'kyj, Jurij], b 28 October 1936 in Kharkiv. Theater historian and critic. He completed study at Kharkiv University in 1960, and since 1964 has worked in the AN URSR (now ANU) Institute of Fine Arts, Folklore, and Ethnography, from 1974 as head of the theater department. He is the author of many works on Ukrainian theater, including Opernyi teatr Radians'koi Ukrainy (The Opera Theater of Soviet Ukraine, 1988).

**Stanislaus I Leszczyński** (Stanisław), b 20 October 1677 in Lviv, d 23 February 1766 in Lunéville, France. Polish magnate and voivode of Poznań. In 1704, with the support of the Swedish king Charles XII, he replaced the deposed *Augustus II Frederick as king of Poland. As dissatisfaction with Muscovite rule increased in the Cossack Hetmanate, Stanislaus's negotiations with Hetman I. Mazepa (through Princess Anna Dolska) to ally with the Swedes in invading Russia culminated in a 1708 treaty. After Charles's defeat in the Battle of Poltava in 1709, Stanislaus left Poland for France. In 1733 he attempted, in vain, to reclaim the Polish throne. His son-in-law, Louis XV of France, granted him the Duchy of Lorraine in 1738. Stanislaus maintained relations with Hetmans P. and H. Orlyk.

**Stanislaus II Augustus Poniatowski** (Stanisław), b 17 January 1732 in Wołczyn, Poland, d 12 February 1798 in St Petersburg. Last king of Poland. He was elected in 1764 with the support of Catherine II of Russia, who later opposed his parliamentary reforms and pressed for the rights of non-Catholic religious dissenters in Polish territories. In 1768 Stanislaus faced a revolt by nobles grouped in the Confederation of *Bar, which sparked the *Koliivshchyna rebellion and the haidamaka movement in Right-Bank Ukraine. The weakened Polish state underwent partitioning by Russia, Austria, and Prussia in 1772, 1793, and 1795. Stanislaus then abdicated and lived in semicaptivity in Russia.

*Stanislavivs'ki visty* (Stanyslaviv News). A weekly newspaper published in Stanyslaviv (now Ivano-Frankivske) from January 1912 to May 1913 (a total of 69 issues). The publisher and editor was V. Ivanytsky.

**Stanislavova, Oleksandra,** b 16 November 1900 in Petropavlovsk, Akmolinsk province, d 20 March 1985 in Kiev. Opera singer (dramatic soprano). A graduate of the Technical School of Music in Moscow (1930), she was a soloist on Radio Moscow, with the Saratov Theater of Opera and Ballet, and with the Bolshoi Theater in Moscow (1936) before working at the Kiev Theater of Opera and Ballet (1938–52) and the Kiev Philharmonia (1952–7). Her operatic roles included the name-parts in M. Lysenko's *Natalka from Poltava*, G. Verdi's *Aida*, and G. Puccini's *Tosca*, and Hanna in M. Verykivsky's *Naimychka* (Servant Girl) and Varvara in K. Dankevych's *Bohdan Khmelnytsky*.

**Stanislavsky, Anatolii** [Stanislavs'kyj, Anatolij], b 9 September 1905 in Lubni, Poltava gubernia. Architect. He began to lecture at the Kiev Institute of Communal Economy in 1936 and obtained his candidate's degee from the Kharkiv Institute of Communal Economy in 1941. From 1947 he taught at the Kiev Civil-Engineering Institute. He prepared the general plans for the reconstruction and development of Lysychanske (1933), Poltava (1934), Artemivske (1935), Yasynuvata (1936), and Kramatorske (1937); designed residential subdivisions in Poltava (1936), Slovianske (1934), and Vologda, Russia (1936); and wrote studies and articles on architecture and construction.

**Stanislavsky, Vasyl** [Stanislavs'kyj, Vasyl'], 1870–1927. Literary scholar. In the 1920s he published articles in VUAN serials and collections about a duma on the Sorochyntsi events during the Revolution of 1905, T. Shevchenko's *Kobzar* of 1867, the life of S. Rudansky (with A. Krymsky and V. Levchenko), the unpublished works of A. Svydnytsky, P. Myrny's letters to M. Starytsky, and memoirs of Myrny.

**Stanisławski, Jan,** b 24 June 1860 in Vilshana, Zvenyhorodka county, Kiev gubernia, d 6 January 1907 in Cracow. Polish impressionist painter. He studied under W. Gersonin in Warsaw, at the Cracow School of Fine Arts (1883–5), and under E. Carolus-Duran in Paris (1885–8). From 1896 he taught at the Cracow Academy of Fine Arts, where he had a significant influence on his Ukrainian students M. Burachek, I. Trush, O. Novakivsky, and I. Severyn. He visited Ukraine often and painted many Ukrainian landscapes, such as *Dilapidated Windmill* (1883), *Bila Tserkva* (1890), *The Dnieper Limans at Dawn* (1902), *St Michael's Cathedral in Kiev* (1903), *The Dnieper below Kiev* (1905), *House by the Dnieper, Haystacks, Sunflowers,* and *Windmills*.

**Stankevych, Sofiia** [Stankevyč, Sofija], b 1862 in Ryzhiv, Zhytomyr county, Volhynia gubernia, d 1955 in Warsaw. Painter and graphic artist. She studied in Kharkiv, Warsaw, and Paris. She painted landscapes (eg, *Ukrainian Night* and *Kamianets at Night*) and still lifes. Later she created prints, including a series on the architecture of Warsaw and Pomerania.

**Stankovych, Vasyl** [Stan'kovyč, Vasyl'], b 25 April 1946 in Irshava, Transcarpathia oblast. Fencer. He was part of the USSR teams that won silver medals at the 1968 and 1972 Olympic Games in the team foil event, and the world championships in 1969, 1970, 1973, and 1974. He was also the 1971 foil world champion and the champion of Ukraine and the USSR many times.

Yevhen Stankovych

**Stankovych, Yevhen** [Stankovyč, Jevhen], b 19 September 1942 in Svaliava, Bereg county, Transcarpathia. Composer. He studied under B. Liatoshynsky and M. Skoryk and graduated in composition from the Kiev Conservatory (1970). He worked as an editor at the Muzychna Ukraina publishing house in 1970–6 and was deputy head of the Union of Composers of Ukraine. He has written five symphonies and the symphonic works *Overture, Sinfonietta,* and *Fantasia*; a concerto for violoncello and orchestra; three symphonies for chamber orchestra; and the triptych *In the Highlands* for violin and pianoforte. He has composed three sonatas for violoncello and piano. His other compositions include the folk opera *Tsvit paporoti* (The Fern Flower, 1980); the ballets *Ol'ha* (1982), *Iskra* (The Spark, 1983), and *Prometheus* (1986); the requiem *Babyn Yar* (1991); pieces for solo voice and for choir; and film scores.

**Stanove culture**. A late Bronze Age culture that existed in Transcarpathia in the 14th to 12th century BC. It was named in the 1930s after a site in the region. The people of this culture lived in surface and semi-pit dwellings and had crematory burial practices. Their major economic activities included agriculture and animal husbandry, although hunting and gathering were common. Site excavations revealed bronze and gold items, including implements, armor, and horse trappings, and well-polished stone items. Some Stanove pottery was distinctively decorated with spirals and meanders. Scholars believe that the people of the Stanove culture eventually played a role in the development of the *Thracian Hallstatt culture.

**Stanychno-Luhanske** [Stanyčno-Luhans'ke]. V-20. A town smt (1986 pop 16,100) on the Donets River and a raion center in Luhanske oblast. The settlement of Luhanske, founded in the second half of the 17th century, was destroyed by the Tatars in 1684. It was rebuilt and, to avoid the frequent floods, moved to higher ground in 1773. From then it was known as Stanytsia Luhanska, which name was later changed to its present form. The inhabitants were Don Cossacks, who served until the end of the 18th century as a frontier guard. Today the town has a food industry and a few enterprises serving the railway industry.

**Stanyslaviv.** See Ivano-Frankivske.

**Stanyslaviv Depression.** A land formation in Subcarpathia south of Ivano-Frankivske between the Bystrytsia Solotvynska River in the northwest and the Vorona River in the southeast. The depression is a tectonic formation overlain with thick alluvial deposits. Its elevation rises in a north–south direction from approx 250 to 500 m. The Bystrytsia Nadvirnianska River runs through the depression.

**Stanyslaviv eparchy.** An eparchy of Halych metropoly created from the eastern part of Lviv eparchy, with its see in Stanyslaviv (now Ivano-Frankivske). Although initial requests by Metropolitans A. Anhelovych and M. Levytsky to establish the eparchy were approved by the Austro-Hungarian authorities and the pope as early as 1850, it was only in 1885 that Yu. Pelesh was ordained and enthroned as the first bishop of Stanyslaviv. He was succeeded by Yu. *Kuilovsky-Sas, A. Sheptytsky (1899–1900), and H. *Khomyshyn (1904–45), with an auxiliary bishop, I. *Liatyshevsky (1929–45). By 1939 the eparchy had 419 parishes served by 541 priests, and over 1 million faithful. Various monastic orders were active in the eparchy, especially the Basilians (in 1938 there were 47 Basilian priests and monks, and 48 nuns), Sisters Servants of Mary Immaculate (157 nuns), Myronosytsi sisterhood (59 nuns), Redemptorists, Studites, Sisters of St Vincent de Paul, and Holy Family Sisterhood. An eparchial seminary and a theological lyceum were established in 1906. The eparchy's official organ was *Vistnyk Stanyslavivs'koï ieparkhiï*, published irregularly and then monthly from 1886 to 1939. The eparchy also copublished the religious quarterly *Dobryi pastyr*.

Under Khomyshyn, Stanyslaviv eparchy was the most Latinized of all eparchies of Halych metropoly. He introduced compulsory celibacy for all new priests in the eparchy in 1921 and attempted unsuccessfully to introduce the Gregorian calendar in 1916. His measures led to considerable dissension in the eparchy.

After the Second World War the territory of Stanyslaviv eparchy was incorporated into the Ukrainian SSR. The Soviet authorities arrested Bishops Khomyshyn (who was killed in a Kiev prison in 1947) and Liatyshevsky. The eparchy was forcibly converted to Orthodoxy, and A. Pelvelsky of the Russian Orthodox church was installed as bishop. The Ukrainian Catholic church survived in the underground until 1 December 1989, when it was again legalized. In 1989 S. Dmyterko was formally recognized as the ordinary of the eparchy (now called Ivano-Frankivske eparchy). He is assisted by Bishops P. Vasylyk and I. Bilyk. In March 1990 the eparchy had approx 530 parishes. At the same time the renewed Ukrainian Autocephalous

Orthodox church established its own eparchy of Ivano-Frankivske and Kolomyia.

BIBLIOGRAPHY
*Shematyzm vseho klyra hreko-katolyts'koï Eparkhiï Stanyslavivs'koï* (Stanyslaviv 1938)
Melnychuk, P. *Vladyka Hryhorii Khomyshyn* (Rome–Philadelphia 1979)

W. Lencyk

**Stanyslaviv Franko Ukrainian Drama Theater.** See Ivano-Frankivske Ukrainian Music and Drama Theater.

**Stanyslaviv oblast.** See Ivano-Frankivske oblast.

**Stanyslaviv Ukrainian Touring Theater** (Ukrainskyi peresuvnyi teatr). An ensemble founded in 1920 under the directorship of I. Kohutiak, with a cast from *Sadovsky's Theater. It toured Galicia and Volhynia, where it performed mainly Ukrainian ethnographic plays – notably S. Cherkasenko's *Kazka staroho mlyna* (A Tale of the Old Mill) – and H. Sudermann's *Johannisfeuer* and classical operettas, and helped to organize numerous amateur drama groups. In 1939 it was reorganized as a resident theater in Stanyslaviv (see *Ivano-Frankivske Ukrainian Music and Drama Theater).

*Stanyslavivs'ke slovo.* See *Ukraïns'ke slovo*.

**Stanyslavsky, Mykola** [Stanyslavs'kyj], b 29 August 1892 in Ozerne, Lokhvytsia county, Poltava gubernia, d ? Lexicographer. From 1926 he served as secretary of the Section of Administrative Language at the socioeconomic department of the VUAN *Institute of the Ukrainian Scientific Language. With M. Doroshenko and V. Strashkevych he compiled a normative Russian-Ukrainian dictionary of administrative language (1930). He also prepared a book of Russian-Ukrainian administrative and newspaper phraseology (unpublished) and wrote several reviews on contemporary Ukrainian orthographic and lexical issues and stylistics and an article on Ukrainian abbreviations (1930). He most likely perished during the terror of the 1930s.

*Stanytsia* (Russian: *stanitsa*). An administrative-territorial entity in Cossack territories within the Russian Empire (the Kuban, Don, and Terek regions) from the 18th century until 1920. A *stanytsia* consisted of several Cossack villages and *khutory*. Settlements which had fewer than 60 households were governed by *khutir administrations. Except for persons of non-Cossack status (*inohorodni*), all the inhabitants were members of the *stanytsia* community, which was governed by an assembly of householders. The assembly distributed the Cossack lands and obligations, and it managed the community storehouses and schools. It elected the *stanytsia* administration (an otaman, deputies, and a treasurer) and the *stanytsia* court. The *stanytsia* court ruled on petty criminal and civil suits. Non-Cossack residents paid a fee per *sazhen* for their home plot and for the use of farmland, pasture, and forest.

After 1929 the term *stanytsia* was used in the USSR to refer to a rural settlement on former Cossack territories. It was governed by a *stanytsia* soviet of workers' and peasants' deputies.

**Stará L'ubovňa.** IV-1. A village (1961 pop 2,900) on the Poprad River in the Prešov region of Slovakia, near the border of Ukrainian ethnic territory. Twenty-six villages out of 44 in the surrounding area have a predominantly Ukrainian (Lemko) population.

**Stara Sil** [Stara Sil']. IV-3. A town smt (1986 pop 1,300) in Staryi Sambir raion, Lviv oblast. It was founded in 1255, and it received the rights of *Magdeburg law in 1421, when it was called Zaltsbork. For many centuries it was an important salt-mining center. At its peak in the mid-18th century it produced 39,000 barrels of salt yearly. When the reserves ran out in 1853, the town declined. The wooden Church of the Resurrection dates back to the 17th century.

**Stara Syniava** [Stara Synjava]. IV-8. A town smt (1986 pop 6,500) on the Ikva River and a raion center in Khmelnytskyi oblast. The town of Syniava was founded at the beginning of the 16th century, and received the rights of *Magdeburg law in 1543. In the second half of the century, after Syniava was destroyed by the Tatars, the survivors built a new town and called it Stara Syniava. It was captured by M. Kryvonis in 1648, and belonged to Bratslav regiment before being returned to Poland in 1667. In 1672–99 it was occupied, along with the rest of Podilia, by the Turks. After the partition of Poland the town was annexed by Russia and assigned to Lityn county in Podilia gubernia. A sugar refinery was built there in 1875, and the local economy grew rapidly. In 1923 Stara Syniava was granted smt status. It is an agricultural town with a sugar refinery and the ruins of a 16th-century fortress.

*Stara Ukraïna*

***Stara Ukraïna.*** An illustrated monthly journal of history and culture, published in Lviv in 1924–5 by the Shevchenko Scientific Society. The journal was edited by I. *Krevetsky, and a total of 24 issues appeared. It featured articles by Galician and émigré authors, including the historians B. and O. Barvinsky, E. Borschak, D. Doroshenko, V. Karpovych, M. Korduba, I. Krevetsky, and I. Krypiakevych; the literary scholars Ya. Hordynsky, I. Ohiienko, K. Studynsky, M. Vozniak, and P. Zaitsev; the art scholars M. Holubets, P. Kholodny, V. Sichynsky, and V. Zalozetsky; and other contributors such as V. Hnatiuk, I. Nimchuk, and V. Zaikin. The journal also carried previously unpublished works by I. Franko and O. Konysky. Special thematic issues were devoted to the 350th anniversary of printing in Ukraine, the grave sites of noted Ukrainian activists, Ukrainian memoir writing from the 11th to 20th centuries, and T. Shevchenko. The journal provided a valuable chronicle of events, reviews, and bibliographies. It was the only Ukrainian historical journal in Western Ukraine. It ceased publication as a result of financial difficulties.

**Stara Ushytsia** [Stara Ušycja]. V-8. A town smt (1986 pop 2,200) near the junction of the Ushytsia and the Dniester rivers in Kamianets-Podilskyi raion, Khmelnytskyi oblast. It was first mentioned in the Hypatian Chronicle under the year 1144, as Ushytsia, a fortified town of Halych principality. In 1159 Ivan Rostyslavych Berladnyk laid siege to it and in 1199 it became part of the Principality of Galicia-Volhynia. Ushytsia's fortifications were dismantled on the demand of the Mongols in 1257. In the mid-14th century it fell under Lithuanian rule, and in the 1430s, under Polish rule. After being driven out by the rebellious townsmen in 1648, the Polish nobles avenged themselves by destroying the town in 1661. After the failed rebellion of 1702 many inhabitants of Ushytsia fled to Moldavia. Ushytsia was annexed by Russia in 1793, and served as a county center (1795–1826) of Podilia gubernia. It was subsequently renamed Stara Ushytsia. Its economy was dependent on farming and the river trade. The settlement was granted smt status in 1980.

**Starch-and-syrup industry.** A branch of industry that produces and processes starch, syrup, glucose, dextrose, and other products for use in the *food, chemical, paper, rubber, and other industries. The major raw materials for the industry are potatoes and corn, but wheat, sugar beets, sorghum, and rice are also used.

Starch has been extracted from potatoes since the 17th century and from wheat since the 18th century. Before the 1917 Revolution there were 186 enterprises producing starch and syrup in the Russian Empire. The industry has developed rapidly in the 20th century, and the USSR became the second-largest producer of starch and syrup in the world. In Ukraine in 1978 there were 18 specialized factories of the industry, the largest of which was the Verkhnodniprovske Starch-and-Syrup Complex (est in 1960). As well, some starch and syrup were produced as by-products at other food-processing plants. In total Ukraine produced 97,700 t of syrup, 57,300 t of starch, and 17,500 t of glucose. Ukraine was the second-largest producer of starch products and the largest producer of glucose in the USSR.

**Starchenko, Vasyl** [Starčenko, Vasyl'], b 20 March 1904 in Temriuk, Mariiupil county, Katerynoslav gubernia, d 17 July 1948 in Kiev. Agrochemist and political figure; corresponding member of the AN URSR (now ANU) from 1945. After graduating from the Ukrainian Scientific Research Institute of the Sugar Industry he served as director and research chief of the Myronivka Research and Selection Station (1934–8). From 1938 he was deputy premier of the Council of People's Commissars and then of the Council of Ministers of the Ukrainian SSR. His publications deal with problems of agrotechnology and selection, particularly with problems in increasing the yield of sugar beets.

**Starchenko, Yosyp** [Starčenko] (Startsev, Yosyf), b and d ? Ukrainian architect and builder in the 17th century. He worked in Moscow for Peter I during the 1680s and was recorded as a noted architect. On the special invitation of

Hetman I. Mazepa he came to Kiev, where he constructed the baroque cathedrals at the *Kiev Epiphany Brotherhood Monastery (1690–3) and the *Saint Nicholas's (so-called Military) Monastery (1690–6).

**Starchuk, Orest** [Starčuk], b 6 November 1915 in Toporivtsi, Bukovyna, d 14 February 1971 in Edmonton. Slavist; member of the Shevchenko Scientific Society. He graduated from Chernivtsi University (LLD, 1938). He emigrated to Germany in 1941 and worked for the British occupational administration in Hannover (1945–8). He settled in Canada in 1948, where he taught Russian and developed a program of Slavic studies emphasizing Ukrainian language and literature at the University of Alberta. He became the first chairman of the department of Slavic languages there in 1964. Starchuk was a founding member of the Canadian Association of Slavists and its president in 1958–9.

**Stare Lake.** VIII-14. One of the saltwater *Perekop lakes in the northern part of the Crimea. The lake is 6 km long and 2.5 km wide, with a prevailing depth of 0.2–0.45 m in the summer and 0.6–0.8 m in the spring. Its salinity averages about 28 percent. The deposits around the lake are used for extracting salts, calcium, bromine, and the like. The town of Krasnoperekopske is situated along the lake's southern shore.

The castle in Stare Selo

**Stare Selo.** IV-5. A village (1968 pop 2,300) in Pustomyty raion, Lviv oblast. It was first mentioned in historical documents in 1442. It was destroyed by the Turks in 1498 and by the Tatars in 1648. A fortress was built there by A. Prykhylny for the Ostrozky family in 1584–9 and was renovated in 1642 and 1654 in the late Renaissance style. Its walls (14–16 m high) and three towers are well preserved.

**Starkov, Arsenii,** b 1874 in the Voronezh region, d 18 December 1927 in Vienna. Anatomist. After being educated at Moscow University and abroad, he taught at Moscow and Kiev (from 1917) universities and was a member of the UAN in 1918. When the Soviets occupied Ukraine, he fled west. He served as a professor of biology at the Ukrainian Higher Pedagogical Institute in Prague (1923–5) and the Riga Polytechnic. Shortly before his death he was elected a fellow of the Ukrainian Scientific Institute in Berlin. He wrote the textbook *Zahal'na biolohiia* (General Biology, 1924).

**Starkova, Mariia,** b 1 August 1888 in Odessa, d 8 June 1970 in Odessa. Pianist and educator. After graduating from the St Petersburg Conservatory (1912), she lectured at the Odessa Conservatory, where she became a professor in 1926. In 1933 she was one of the organizers of a 10-year music school there, and in 1963 she became a consulting professor in its piano department. She was particularly noted for her methodological work in piano instruction.

**Starling** (Ukrainian: *shpak*). A chunky, metallic black, vocal bird of the family Sturnidae, especially *Sturnus vulgaris*, with a long, sharp bill, a body length reaching 20 cm, and a weight of 65–85 g. Starlings are found throughout Ukraine in thinned forests, orchards, and parks, where they nest in tree hollows, rock crevices, or ground holes, as well as in man-made bird houses. Starlings feed on insects on the ground and fly in tight flocks. They have been known to damage fruit and grain crops. The pink starling (*Pastor roseus*) can be found in Ukraine's southern steppes.

**Starobesheve** [Starobeševe]. VI-19, DB I-5. A town smt (1986 pop 7,400) on the Kalmiius River and a raion center in Donetske oblast. It was settled in 1779 by Greeks from the Crimea, who called it Besheve. The name was changed in 1896, when Novobesheve was founded nearby. In 1958 it attained smt status. The town is the center of an agricultural region. A thermoelectric power station (2,300,00 kW) was built nearby in 1954–8.

**Starobilske** [Starobil's'ke]. IV-19, DB I-5. A city (1989 pop 24,800) on the Aidar River and a raion center in Luhanske oblast. The site of the *sloboda* Bilska, founded in the 16th century, became deserted and was resettled by Cossacks from Ostrohozke regiment in 1683. The settlement was wiped out by the Russian army during K. Bulavin's rebellion in 1709. The new *sloboda*, established in 1732, was called Stara Bila. In 1797 it was promoted to city status, renamed Starobilske, and designated a county center in Slobidska Ukraine. From 1835 it was a county center in Kharkiv gubernia. Today the city has a food industry, a reinforced-concrete plant, a furniture factory, and a regional museum.

**Starodub.** I-13. A town (1975 pop 16,000) in the northern Chernihiv region and a raion center in Briansk oblast, RF. In medieval times it was a fortress on Siverianian territory. It was first mentioned in the Hypatian Chronicle under the year 1096, when it was part of Chernihiv principality. In 1239 it was destroyed by Batu Khan, and thereafter it was ruled successively by Lithuania, Poland, and Russia. In 1648 the town was taken by B. Khmelnytsky's Cossacks, and in 1654 *Starodub regiment was set up, first within Nizhen regiment and then (from 1663) separately. The town was destroyed in 1660 by the Tatars and in 1663 by the Poles. From 1782 Starodub was part of Novhorod-Siverskyi vicegerency, and then a county center of Little Russia (1797–1802) and Chernihiv gubernias. In the 19th century it was a major trading town dealing mostly in furs, honey, wax, oil, and hemp. By the end of the century its population was 26,000. During the revolutionary period (1917–18) Starodub was included in the territory of independent Ukraine. Today, the town has a food and a tobacco industry. Its chief architectural monuments are the Church of St John the Baptist (1720) and the Cathedral of the Nativity of Christ (built in 1617, burned down in 1677, and renovated at the end of the 17th century).

**Starodub regiment.** An administrative territory and military formation of the Hetman state. Before becoming a separate regiment in 1663, the Starodub region was an autonomous unit within Nizhen regiment. The regiment started with 7 companies and by the mid-18th century had 11 companies. Its male population in 1721 was 15,800, including 4,100 registered Cossacks. According to the 1764 census it had 172,800 male inhabitants, including 25,200 Cossacks. Its population had not experienced the Cossack rebellions of the 17th century; hence, it offered less resistance to enserfment than did other regiments. It was also under stronger Russian influence than the population of the rest of the Hetman state. A number of Starodub colonels rose to prominent offices in the Hetman state: I. Skoropadsky (1706–8) became hetman, and M. Myklashevsky (1689–1706) and H. Karpovych (1678–80) served on the general staff.

**Starodubov, Kyrylo,** b 19 April 1904 in Moscow, d 8 October 1984. Metallurgist; full member of the AN URSR (now ANU) from 1957. He studied at the Dnipropetrovske Mining Institute, and worked at the Dnipropetrovske Metallurgical Plant (1928–38). He held the chair of the thermal treatment of metal at the Dnipropetrovske Metallurgical Institute (1938–79) and headed a department at the ANU Institute of Ferrous Metallurgy (1948–74). During the Second World War he developed and put into operation in Magnitogorsk a highly efficient method of casting large metal parts.

Remains of the castle in Starokostiantyniv

**Starokostiantyniv** [Starokostjantyniv]. IV-8. A city (1989 pop 33,200) on the Sluch River and a raion center in Khmelnytskyi oblast. It was founded in the 1560s by K. *Ostrozky, who fortified Kolyshchentsi village and raised it to the status of a city with the rights of *Magdeburg law. Until the beginning of the 17th century the town was known as Kostiantyniv or Kostiantynivka. In the 16th and 17th centuries it was a major center of *Socinianism in Volhynia. Many battles between Cossack and Polish armies, especially during B. Khmelnytsky's rule, were fought in the vicinity of Starokostiantyniv. After the partition of Poland in 1793, the town was annexed by Russia. In the 19th century it was a county center of Volhynia gubernia and a manufacturer of tobacco products, oil, soap, beer, bricks,

and potash. By 1911 its population was about 20,000, including 11,800 Jews, 7,200 Ukrainians, and 1,200 Poles. During the war for Ukrainian independence the Ukrainian Galician Army fought the Bolshevik army near the town (13–14 August 1919), and later that year the UNR Army broke through the Bolshevik front there to launch its Winter Campaign. Today the city's main industries are food processing, machine building, and metalworking. Its architectural monuments include the remains of the old fortress (1571) and a 16th-century church.

*Starokursnyky.* See Russophiles.

**Starokyivska Hora.** A historically significant area of Kiev, situated on the plateau between the Dnieper and the Lybid rivers and the Khreshchatyi ravine, with an area of about 80 ha. It was settled fairly early in history (late Paleolithic), probably because of its naturally protected setting. The northwestern section is purported to be the site of the so-called Kyi's city, established in the late 6th century. By the late 10th century the hill was the location of the upper town, known as Volodymyr's city (approx 8 ha), where the prince's palace and the Church of the Tithes stood. In the 11th century all of Starokyivska Hora was settled as the upper town expanded and the city of Yaroslav the Wise was built up. It was encircled by high ramparts, which were 3.5 km in length and were studded with towers and gates. The Golden Gate, the St Sophia Cathedral, and St Michael's Golden-Domed Monastery were among the notable structures of the period. The district was almost completely destroyed by the Tatars in 1240. A partial reconstruction of it was effected in the 17th century, and since the 19th century it has been known as the Old Town district of Kiev. In 1945 it was declared a historical Preserve.

**Starosilia archeological site.** A Paleolithic Mousterian culture cave site along the Churuk-Su River near Bakhchesarai, Crimea. Excavations in 1952–6 uncovered a variety of flint tools and bones of wild animals (including mammoths). The site is best known for the recovery of a Neanderthal burial, one of a dozen such burials known worldwide.

**Starosolska, Dariia** [Starosol's'ka, Darija], b 3 January 1881 in Lviv, d 28 December 1941 in Georgievka, Kazakhstan. Musician and civic activist; daughter of V. and H.

Dariia Starosolska                Uliana Starosolska

*Shukhevych and wife of V. *Starosolsky. After studying piano at the Lviv Conservatory she taught at the Lysenko Higher Institute of Music (1907–40). She was a founding member and president of the Circle of Ukrainian Women in Lviv and editor of its journals *Meta* (1908) and *Nasha meta* (1919–20). She was also active in the Ukrainian Social Democratic party. Her articles, sketches, and verses appeared in the journal *Nasha khata* and the paper *Dilo*. In 1940 she was deported by the Soviet authorities to Kazakhstan, where she perished.

**Starosolska, Uliana** [Starosol's'ka, Uljana] (pseud: U. Liubovych), b 31 March 1912 in Lviv. Journalist and writer; daughter of V. Starosolsky and D. Starosolska. In 1936–9 she edited the Lviv periodicals *Nova khata, Na slidi*, and *Hospodars'ko-kooperatyvna chasopys*. In April 1940 she, her mother, and her brother Ihor were exiled by the Soviet authorities to Kazakhstan. After being released in May 1946, she was allowed to live in Poland, from which she emigrated to the United States in 1967. There she published her memoirs, *Rozkazhu vam pro Kazakhstan* (Let Me Tell You about Kazakhstan, 1969); edited the women's monthly *Nashe zhyttia* (1972–84, 1987–90); and contributed stories, essays, and sketches to the émigré press.

Ihor Starosolsky　　　　Volodymyr Starosolsky

**Starosolsky, Ihor** [Starosol's'kyj], b 3 August 1908 in Lviv, d 10 February 1988 in Lviv. Engineer and restorer; son of V. *Starosolsky and D. *Starosolska. A graduate of the Lviv Polytechnic, he was deported to Kazakhstan in May 1940 together with his mother and sister. In 1943–6 he was imprisoned in a labor camp in Siberia. He returned to Lviv in 1946, where he became an assistant in the department of urban construction at the Polytechnical Institute. In the fall of 1949 he was arrested for visiting his uncle, O. Shukhevych (father of R. *Shukhevych), and he languished in labor camps until June 1956. After his release he returned to Lviv. In 1957 he initiated the creation of a planning department for the restoration of architectural monuments, which eventually became a branch of the Kiev-based Ukrainian Restoration Planning Institute. He was involved in or supervised the restoration of many edifices, including churches in Drohobych, Lavriv, Lviv, Kamianka-Buzka, Potylych, Chervonohrad, Peremyshliany, Pidhirtsi, Horodok, Sambir, and Radekhiv; the castles in Nevytske, Olesko, Pidhirtsi, Svirzh, and Mukachiv; and the Maniava Hermitage.

**Starosolsky, Volodymyr** [Starosol's'kyj], b 8 January 1878 in Jarosław, Galicia, d 25 February 1942 in Mariinsk, Siberia. Lawyer, sociologist, and civic and political leader; member of the Shevchenko Scientific Society from 1923. He was a founding member of the Moloda Ukraina society and the editor of its journal. In 1902 he helped organize the *secession of Ukrainian students from Lviv University and the massive agrarian strike in Galicia. He belonged to the External Committee of the Revolutionary Ukrainian party and was a leading member of the *Ukrainian Social Democratic party. After completing his law studies in Vienna, Berlin, Graz, and Heidelberg he practiced law in Lviv and defended political activists (including M. *Sichynsky) in court. He was one of the organizers and the first president of the paramilitary Ukrainian Sich Riflemen society (1913). During the First World War he was a member of the Supreme Ukrainian Council, served on its Combat Board as liaison with the Sich Riflemen units at the front, and co-operated with the Union for the Liberation of Ukraine in Vienna. In 1918 he became a member of the Ukrainian Military Committee. In the fall of 1919 he was appointed deputy minister of foreign affairs in I. Mazepa's UNR government and served at the same time as a professor at the Ukrainian State University in Kamianets-Podilskyi. In the 1920s he lived as an émigré in Vienna and Prague, and taught state law at the Ukrainian Free University in Prague and the Ukrainian Husbandry Academy in Poděbrady. After returning to Lviv in 1927, he reopened his law office and gained prominence defending OUN members. During the Soviet occupation he was appointed a professor at Lviv University, but by December 1939 he had been arrested and sentenced to 10 years of hard labor in Siberia, where he perished.

In his scholarly work Starosolsky advocated the sociological approach to legal and political developments. His chief works include *Das Majoritätsprinzip* (1916), *Teoriia natsiï* (Theory of the Nation, 1921), *Metodolohichna problema v nautsi pro derzhavu* (The Methodological Problem in the Study of the State, 1925), *Do pytannia pro formy derzhavy* (On the Question of the Forms of the State, 1925), *Bohdan Kistiakowskyj und das russische soziologische Denken* (1929), and the textbook *Derzhava i polytychne pravo* (The State and Political Law, 2 vols, 1925).

**Starosolsky, Yurii** [Starosol's'kyj, Jurij], b 28 February 1907 in Lviv, d 21 October 1991 in Washington, DC. Lawyer and civic activist; son of V. Starosolsky; full member of

Yurii Starosolsky

the Shevchenko Scientific Society from 1949. After graduating from the law faculty of Lviv University (1931), he practiced law in his father's office in Lviv and was active in various political and civic organizations. He completed his doctorate at the Ukrainian Free University (UVU) in Prague (1940) and then taught criminal and procedural law. A displaced person in Germany after the Second World War, he emigrated to the United States in 1950, where he studied political science at the American University in Washington, DC (MA, 1953), lectured on the Soviet social and political system at the Institute of Adult Education of the Catholic University in Washington, DC, and was the longtime head of the Washington branch of the Ukrainian Catholic University. He was elected *nachalnyi plastun* (Head Scout) of the *Plast Ukrainian Youth Association in 1972. He wrote textbooks on criminal procedure (1947) and commercial law (1947); a monograph on Soviet criminal law (1954); numerous entries on law in the *Encyclopedia of Ukraine*; and *Velyka hra* (The Great Game, 1948), a scouting guide for Plast.

**Starosta.** In Kievan Rus' the starosta was a lower government official, usually in charge of a certain department of the princely household. In the Grand Duchy of Lithuania and Poland the starosta was a representative of the king or grand duke in a voivodeship. In Galicia and Podilia the general starosta was in charge of a whole voivodeship. By the end of the 16th century, as the power of the gentry had increased, the authority of the starosta diminished. In the Russian Empire the village starosta was the head of the lowest administrative unit, the village community. He was elected for three years by the village assembly. In Galicia and Bukovyna during Austrian rule a starosta was a county captain who supervised the county administration, conducted elections to the county council and the diet, headed the county school council, and oversaw the collection of direct taxes. Under the Hetman government in 1918, gubernial and county starostas were appointees of the central administration. In Polish-ruled Western Ukraine during the interwar period (1919–39), the starosta was an official of the state in the county and the head of the local administration. In Transcarpathia in 1919–39, the starosta was a village head or a city mayor. In addition, elected or appointed officers who conducted the affairs of any type of community (church, artel, etc) were known as starostas.

**Starostenko, Yurii,** b 16 August 1931 in Odessa. Painter, graphic artist, and scenery designer. After graduating from the Kharkiv Art Institute in 1958, he began teaching there. He has designed scenery for the Kharkiv Ukrainian Drama Theater and decorative wall panels for public buildings in Kharkiv and created line engraving series, such as 'The Carpathians' (1963), 'People and the Sea' (1962), and 'Capital Cities' (1967); engravings of Kharkiv; and book illustrations.

**Starostvo.** An administrative-territorial and economic unit of state lands in medieval Poland and the Grand Duchy of Lithuania and their Ukrainian and Belarusian territories. It usually included one or more cities or towns and some villages and was administered by a starosta, who was a high official of noble birth. In Western Ukraine under Austrian (1772–1918) and Polish (1919–39) rule, the starostvo was equivalent to a county.

**Starostvo estates** (*starostynski maietnosti*). In medieval Poland and Lithuania (14th–18th centuries), sections of crownlands granted by the ruler to magnates, nobles, or state officials for a fixed period or in perpetuity as a reward for services to the crown. The estates formed a part of the starostvos – hence their name. All income from the estates belonged to the starostas. Such estates were abolished in Left-Bank Ukraine after B. Khmelnytsky's uprising (1648), in Galicia after its annexation by Austria (1772), and in Right-Bank Ukraine after its annexation by Russia (1793).

**Starostvo peasants** (*starostynski seliany*). A category of peasants in Poland and Lithuania during the 14th to 18th centuries who were bound to *starostvo estates. They were obliged to fulfill various obligations to their lords. In the 16th century the crown established a special court to deal with their grievances, but that measure gave them little protection against their masters. With the abolition of the starostvo estates in Ukraine under Austrian and Russian rule, the starostvo peasants became either private or state serfs.

Marharyta Starovoit: woodcut (1974) of a wooden church built in 1724 in Loni (now in Peremyshliany raion, Lviv oblast)

**Starovoit, Marharyta** [Starovojt], b 9 June 1922 in Orenburg, Russia. Printmaker. A graduate of the Lviv Institute of Applied and Decorative Arts (1950), she has worked mostly in wood engraving, in which art she has produced bookplates, prints, and print series, such as 'Soviet Lviv' (1953–7), 'The Industrial Lviv Region' (1958–60), and 'The Hutsul Region under the Soviet Sun' (1962).

**Starowolski, Szymon** (Starovolscius), b 1588 in Starovolia, Brest county, Belarusia (then part of the Grand Duchy of Lithuania), d 6 April 1656 in Cracow. Polish writer and historian. A graduate of the Cracow Academy (1618), he traveled extensively in Europe, took part in the battles near Khotyn in 1620–1, and wrote approx 60 works on historical, political, theological, and other themes. His monographs on Polish history, notably a 1616 biography of Sigismund I and a 1632 survey history, give a favorable picture of the Zaporozhian Cossacks and their defense of the southeastern frontiers of the Commonwealth against the Crimean Tatars and the Ottoman Empire.

Michael Starr   Tymofei Starukh

**Starr, Michael** (Starchevsky), b 14 November 1910 in Copper Cliff, Ontario. Ukrainian-Canadian politician. Starr was an alderman (1944–9) and mayor (1949–52) of Oshawa, Ontario, before his election in 1952 to the federal House of Commons as the Progressive Conservative (PC) member for Oshawa constituency, which he represented until 1968. He was minister of labor (1958–63) in the J. Diefenbaker administration, the first Ukrainian to serve in a federal cabinet. Starr was PC House leader (1965–8) and a candidate for the PC party leadership in 1967. He was defeated in the 1968 general election. He served as a citizenship court judge (1968–72) and chairman of the Ontario Workers' Compensation Board (1973–80).

**Starsha Mohyla.** A kurhan located in a burial ground near Pustoviitivka, Romen raion, Sumy oblast. Excavated in 1888–9 by D. *Samokvasov, it revealed the remains of a Scythian chieftain under the 21 m mound. Among the grave goods recovered were a large number of weapons (sword, spears, dagger, gold coat of mail), 16 horse bits cast with Scythian-style zoomorphic figures, and objects of cult significance.

*Starshyna.* See Cossack *starshyna.*

*Start.* The main sports magazine in Ukraine, published monthly in Kiev since 1957 as the organ of the Committee on Physical Culture and Sports of the Council of Ministers. It succeeded the Russian magazine *Vestnik fizicheskoi kul'tury* (1922–9) and Ukrainian *Visnyk fizychnoï kul'tury* (1929–30) in Kharkiv, *Fizkul'turnyk Ukraïny* in Kharkiv (1931–4) and Kiev (1934–6), and *Sport* (1936–41) in Kiev. Until 1965 it was called *Fizkul'tura i sport*. Its circulation increased from 73,000 in 1965 to 109,000 in 1980.

**Startsev, Yosyf.** See Starchenko, Yosyp.

**Starukh, Antin** [Starux], b 1856 in Berezhnytsia Vyzhnia, Lisko county, Galicia, d 9 January 1938 in Berezhnytsia Vyzhnia. Farmer and civic and political activist; brother of T. *Starukh. He was elected as a candidate of the National Democratic party to the Galician Diet in 1901 and 1908. In 1918–19 he sat on the Ukrainian National Rada of the Western Ukrainian National Republic and served as commissioner of Lisko county.

**Starukh, Tymofei** [Starux, Tymofej], b 27 November 1860 in Berezhnytsia Vyzhnia, Lisko county, Galicia, d 21 April 1923 in Berezhany, Galicia. Civic and political activist. After serving in the Austrian army and gendarmerie he retired to a farm near Berezhany and became active in local Ukrainian organizations, such as the Prosvita society, and in the National Democratic party. He was elected to the Austrian parliament in 1907 and 1911 and to the Galician Diet in 1908 and 1913. In 1915, during the Russian occupation, he was arrested and deported to Siberia. After returning home through Kiev in 1917, he became a member of the Ukrainian National Rada (1918) and mayor of Berezhany. In January 1919 he attended the Labor Congress in Kiev. In 1920 he was arrested by the Poles, but he was released in January 1921 because of a serious illness.

Yaroslav Starukh

**Starukh, Yaroslav** [Starux, Jaroslav] (pseuds: Stiah, Stoian, Yarlan), b 1910 in Berezhnytsia Vyzhnia, Lisko county, Galicia, d 17 October 1947 near Liubachiv, Jarosław voivodeship, Poland. OUN political activist, insurgent, and publicist; son of T. *Starukh. He joined the OUN in 1930 and became a member of its executive committee in Galicia (and, later, Volhynia and Podilia) and a political instructor for its youth wing. At the same time he was an editor of several nationalist publications, notably the Lviv weekly *Nove selo*. In 1939 he was sentenced to a 13-year term during a major political trial of 23 Ukrainians which took place in Rivne. During the German occupation of Ukraine he was an OUN organizer in the Zhytomyr and Kiev regions, and S. *Bandera's chief of propaganda. He was arrested in Lviv by the Gestapo in December 1942, but in the fall of 1943 he was sprung from prison by OUN members and put to work as director of an underground OUN radio station located in the Carpathian Mountains. In 1945 Starukh (under the code name Stiah) became OUN regional chief for *Zakerzonnia and also led UPA troops in that area. He published *Opyr fashyzmu* (The Specter of Fascism), which was translated into Polish and English and widely distributed. He died in his command bunker after refusing to surrender to Polish military forces during *Operation Wisła.

**Starunia** [Starunja]. A village (1972 pop 1,900) on the Lukva River in Bohorodchany raion, Ivano-Frankivske oblast. It was first mentioned in historical documents in 1476. At the beginning of the 20th century an ozocerite mine operated there, in which well-preserved remains of a mammoth and a hairy rhinoceros were discovered in 1907 and 1928 respectively. They are displayed at the zoological museums in Cracow and Lviv.

**Starushych-Oksenovych, Ihnatii.** See Oksenovych-Starushych, Ihnatii.

**Staryi Chortoryisk** [Staryj Čortoryjs'k]. II-6. A village (1970 pop 2,600) on the Styr River in Manevychi raion, Volhynia oblast. It was first mentioned in the chronicles under the year 1100, when it was a fortified settlement called Chortoryisk. In 1228 it was taken by Danylo Romanovych, and 20 years later it was destroyed by the Mongols. From 1340 it belonged to Lithuania, and then to the Czartoryski family of Polish magnates (1442–1601) and Voivode K. Pac, a militant Roman Catholic who built a church and a Dominican monastery (1639) there. In 1795 it was annexed by Russia, and belonged to Lutske county of Volhynia gubernia. With the construction of the Kovel–Sarny railway line at the end of the 19th century, the station of Novyi Chortoryisk was built, and the old village was renamed Staryi Chortoryisk.

**Staryi Krym** [Staryj Krym]. VIII-16. A city (1989 pop 10,400) in Kirovske raion, Crimea. Artifacts dating back to the last few centuries BC have been found at the site of an ancient settlement called Kariia. In the 6th century it was known as Surkhat or Solkhat. Under the rule of the Golden Horde it was called Krym or Kerym and was the residence of the khan's viceregent. When the capital of the Crimean Khanate moved to Bakhchesarai in the 15th century, Krym declined and became known as Eski Krym (Old Crimea). It was annexed by Russia in 1783, was raised to city status in 1784, and was known as Levkopol for a few years thereafter. Today the town manufactures reinforced-concrete products, footwear, and furniture. A health resort just outside the town treats tuberculosis. The main architectural monuments are the remains of a 14th-century mosque, Armenian monastery, and caravansary.

**Staryi Krym graphite deposits.** Graphite deposits located on the right bank of the Kalchyk River near Staryi Krym, near Mariiupil, Donetske oblast. The graphite is found in veins 500 m long and 40–50 m wide in Precambrian gneisses. The deposits were discovered in 1881. In 1981 the recoverable reserves of graphite were estimated at 3.4 million t.

**Staryi Sambir** [Staryj Sambir]. IV-3. A city (1989 pop 6,200) on the Dniester River and a raion center in Lviv oblast. It was founded in the second half of the 11th century as Sambir and served as a residence of Lev Danylovych. After its destruction in 1241 and the founding of Novyi Sambir, it became known, toward the end of the 14th century, as Staryi Sambir. It was granted the rights of *Magdeburg law in 1553 (1500, according to some sources), when it was under Polish rule. The town was known for its manufacturing trades, particularly weaving. In the 16th century it also became a busy trading center: duty on livestock passing through the town on its way to markets in Peremyshl and Breslau (now Wrocław) was collected there, and strong economic ties with Transcarpathia, then under Hungary, were developed. In the second half of the 17th century the town declined. After the partition of Poland in 1772, it was annexed by Austria. In the interwar period (1919–39) it belonged to Poland. Today the city has a linen plant, a furniture-manufacturing complex, a lumber mill, and a branch of the Boryslav Sewing Consortium.

**Staryi Sambir oil field.** An oil field located near Staryi Sambir, Lviv oblast, at the edge of the *Drohobych-Boryslav Industrial Region. The field is approx 5.2 km long and 1.75 km wide. The oil, which dates from the Eocene and Paleocene epochs, is high in paraffin and resin. The field was discovered in 1969 and has been exploited since then. The oil is refined in Drohobych.

Steven Staryk

**Staryk, Steven,** b 28 April 1932 in Toronto. Violinist, concertmaster, and pedagogue of Ukrainian descent. He studied at the Royal Conservatory of Music in Toronto and then in New York with M. Mischakoff, O. Shumsky, and A. Schneider. Staryk has played as concertmaster with the Royal Philharmonic in London (1956–60), the Concertgebouw in Amsterdam (1960–3), the Chicago Symphony (1963–7), and the Toronto Symphony (1982–7). He has taught at the Amsterdam Conservatory (1960–3), at Northwestern University and the American Conservatory in Chicago (1963–7), at the Oberlin College Conservatory in Ohio (1968–72), and in a succession of Canadian cities (Victoria, Ottawa, London, and Toronto in 1973–8). Since 1987 he has been a professor at the University of Washington. His repertoire ranges from the baroque masters to works of contemporary composers. He has premiered the violin concertos of G. Fiala, T. Kenins, S.I. Glick, P. Hoffert, and L. Klein and has recorded more than 45 albums on a variety of labels.

**Starykov, Mykola** (Starikov, Nikolai), b 2 April 1897 in Edrovo, Novgorod gubernia, Russia, d 4 June 1961 in Kiev. Mining engineer; full member of the AN URSR (now ANU) from 1951. He studied in Leningrad and worked in Kryvyi Rih and in the Urals. He taught at mining institutes in Sverdlovske, Kryvyi Rih, and Dnipropetrovske and headed a laboratory of the ANU Institute of Mining (1958–61). His main contributions were methods of finding new metal-ore deposits, particularly at very great depths, and fire fighting in mines, especially copper mines.

**Starynkevych, Yelysaveta** [Starynkevyč, Jelysaveta], b 21 April 1890 in St Petersburg, d 1 December 1966 in Kiev. Literary critic and translator. She graduated from the historical-philological faculty of the Higher Courses for Women in Moscow (1917) and then moved to Ukraine. From 1945 she worked as a senior researcher for the Institute of Literature of the AN URSR (now ANU). She wrote on theoretical and practical translation and critical literary essays in journals and newspapers, mainly on issues of Ukrainian Soviet dramaturgy. Her published monographs include *Ukraïns'ka radians'ka dramaturhiia* (Ukrainian Soviet Dramaturgy, 1941), *Dramaturhiia Ivana Kocherhy* (The Dramaturgy of Ivan Kocherha, 1947), *Oleksander Korniichuk* (1954), and *Ukraïns'ka radians'ka dramaturhiia za 40 rokiv* (40 Years of Ukrainian Soviet Dramaturgy, 1957).

Mariia Starytska      Liudmyla Starytska-Cherniakhivska

**Starytska, Mariia** [Staryc'ka, Marija] (stage name: Yavorska), b 31 May 1865 in Kiev, d 20 December 1930 in Kiev. Actress, director, and theater pedagogue; daughter of M. Starytsky. She began her theatrical career in her father's troupe (1885), completed her theatrical education in the St Petersburg Theater College (1894, O. Fedotov's class), and played on the Russian stage in St Petersburg, Moscow, and Kiev. From 1898 she worked as a director and pedagogue in Ukrainian drama circles at regional People's Homes and in the Kiev Literary Artistic Society. She headed the drama faculty in the Lysenko Music and Drama School in Kiev (1904–18), participated in the organization of the Ukrainian National Theater (1917), and taught in the Lysenko Music and Drama Institute (1918–27). As director she premiered Lesia Ukrainka's play *Iohanna – zhinka Khusova* (Joanna, the Wife of Chuza).

**Starytska-Cherniakhivska, Liudmyla** [Staryc'ka-Černjaxivs'ka, Ljudmyla], b 29 August 1868 in Kiev, d 1941 on the way to exile in Kazakhstan. Writer, literary critic, and community activist; daughter of M. *Starytsky and sister of M. Starytska and O. Steshenko. Starytska-Cherniakhivska was a friend of Lesia Ukrainka, and together with other Ukrainian writers they took part in the activities of the literary group *Pleiada (1888–93). Starytska-Cherniakhivska began publishing her work in 1887 in the Lviv almanac *Pershyi vinok*, and then published in *Zoria*, *Pravda*, *Literaturno-naukovyi vistnyk*, and *Zhytie i slovo*. Her poetry was published in *Skladka* and other almanacs, in the anthology of recitations *Rozvaha* (Divertissement), and in the poetry anthologies *Akordy* (Chords) and *Ukraïns'ka muza* (The Ukrainian Muse). Starytska-Cherniakhivska's poetic works are similar to Lesia Ukrainka's in style and motif. She also wrote prose and drama, translated, and wrote literary criticism. Her most noteworthy dramatic works include *Het'man Petro Doroshenko* (1908), *Kryla* (Wings, 1913), *Ostannii snip* (The Last Sheaf, 1917), *Rozbiinyk Karmeliuk* (The Robber Karmeliuk, 1926), and *Ivan Mazepa* (1927). She also wrote many literary critical essays and memoirs, in particular about M. Kotsiubynsky (1913), L. Yanovska (1909), and H. Barvinok (1911).

One of Starytska-Cherniakhivska's best memoirs is 'Khvylyny zhyttia Lesi Ukraïnky' (Moments from the Life of Lesia Ukrainka, 1913). Noteworthy are her essays on the history of theater, 'Dvadtsiat'-p'iat' rokiv ukraïns'koho teatru' ('25 Years of Ukrainian Theater,' *Ukraïna*, 1907 nos 10–12). In 1917 Starytska-Cherniakhivska was elected to the Central Rada. In 1919 she was cofounder and deputy president of the National Council of Ukrainian Women in Kamianets-Podilskyi. In 1930 she was arrested in connection with the *Union for the Liberation of Ukraine trials and sentenced to five years of imprisonment, but after a few months she was released and exiled to Yuzivka instead. In 1936 Starytska-Cherniakhivska returned to Kiev. She was rearrested by the NKVD together with her sister, O. Steshenko, on 4 June 1941.

P. Odarchenko

**Starytsky** [Staryc'kyj]. A family of Cossack *starshyna* and Russian imperial nobility in the Poltava region. It was founded by Semen Starytsky in the early 17th century. His son, Luka Starytsky, was the archpriest of Poltava (1665–71). Luka's son, Zakhar Starytsky (d 1714), was a captain in Poltava regiment (1711–14). Zakhar's great-grandsons, Hryhorii (b 1731) and Vasyl (1737–95) Starytsky, founded two branches of the Starytsky family line. One branch was centered in Poltava; it included Heorhii (Yehor) Pavlovych Starytsky (b 27 November 1825, d 31 May 1899), a leading proponent of the 1864 judicial reform. He was an imperial senator (1867), a member of the State Council (1879), and head of the Department of Laws (1883–5). The other branch of the Starytsky family line was centered in Myrhorod; it included Mykhailo *Starytsky and his daughters, Mariia *Starytska and Liudmyla *Starytska-Cherniakhivska.

**Starytsky, Mykhailo** [Staryc'kyj, Myxajlo], b 14 December 1840 in Klishchyntsi, Zolotonosha county, Poltava gubernia, d 27 April 1904 in Kiev. Writer and theatrical and cultural activist. Orphaned in childhood, Starytsky was raised by his uncle, the father of M. *Lysenko. He studied at the Poltava gymnasium (until 1856) Kharkiv

Mykhailo Starytsky        Myroslav Starytsky

University (1858–60), and Kiev University (1860–6). From 1867 he lived in Kiev and worked with Lysenko. Starytsky collected and transcribed folk songs, which he published with music arranged by Lysenko. He wrote librettos for many of Lysenko's operas, such as *Harkusha*, *Chornomortsi* (The Black Sea Cossacks), *Rizdviana nich* (Christmas Night), *Taras Bul'ba*, and *Utoplena* (The Drowned Maiden). Owing to official tsarist hostility to his work after the Ems Ukase was introduced, Starytsky was forced to emigrate in 1878 and live abroad for some time. He returned to Ukraine in 1880 and resumed his publishing activities and theater work. In 1883 he headed the first Ukrainian professional theater. In 1885 he founded a new troupe with young actors. In 1895 he ceased his theatrical work altogether and devoted himself to literature.

Starytsky was first published in 1865. His translations of the tales of H.C. Andersen were published under the pseudonym Starchenko in Kiev in 1873. Also published in Kiev were his translations of Serbian folk dumas and songs (1876), the collection of poetry *Z davn'oho zshytku: Pisni ta dumy* (From an Old Notebook: Songs and Dumas, [2 parts, 1881, 1883]), and other works. Particularly noteworthy is his translation of W. Shakespeare's *Hamlet* (1882). An important part of Starytsky's literary legacy is his poetry on social issues, which is characterized by populist and patriotic motifs, glorification of the Ukrainian past, and protests against tsarism. Starytsky also wrote lyric poetry, exemplified by 'Monolohy pro kokhannia' (Monologues on Love.) Some of the lyric poems became folk songs, such as 'Nich iaka, Hospody, misiachna zoriana' (Lord, What a Moonlit, Starry Night). Starytsky's contribution to Ukrainian dramaturgy was large. He began by reworking prose for the stage and rewriting dramatic works, and proceeded to write many of his own, the most notable of which are the social dramas *Ne sudylos'* (It Was Not Destined, 1883), *U temriavi* (In the Darkness, 1892), and *Talan* (Destiny, 1894). His drama *Oi ne khody, Hrytsiu, ta i na vechornytsi* (Don't Go to Parties, Hryts!, 1892) became very popular. His historical dramas: *Bohdan Khmel'nyts'kyi* (1897) and *Marusia Bohuslavka* (1899) merit particular attention.

During the last years of his life Starytsky wrote the historical novel *Obloha Bushi* (The Siege of Busha, 1891), the novels *Pered bureiu* (Before the Storm, 1894) and *Razboinik Karmeliuk* (The Robber Karmeliuk, 1903), and other works in Russian. Collections of his works were published under the titles *Poezii* (Poems, 1908), *Dramatychni tvory* (Dramatic Works, 1907–10), *Vybrani Tvory* (Selected Works, 1954 and 1959), and *Tvory v vos'my tomakh* (Works in Eight Volumes, 1963–5).

BIBLIOGRAPHY
Kurylenko, I. *M.P. Staryts'kyi (Zhyttia i tvorchist')* (Kiev 1960)
Sokyrko, L. *M.P. Staryts'kyi: Krytyko-biohrafichnyi narys* (Kiev 1960)
Komyshanchenko, M. *Mykhailo Staryts'kyi* (Kiev 1968)
                                                            P. Odarchenko

**Starytsky, Myroslav** [Staryc'kyj] (Miro Skala-Starycky), b 13 June 1909 in Skala, Borshchiv county, Galicia, d 16 February 1969 in Paris. Opera and concert singer (lyric tenor), and teacher. He studied voice under A. Didur and L. Ulukhanova in Lviv and received a diploma from the Vienna Academy of Music (1942). He sang leading roles at theaters in Strasbourg (1943–4), Zurich (1950), Brussels (1954–7), and Paris (from 1949). He premiered the role of Igor in G. Bizet's opera *Ivan IV* in Le Grand-Théâtre in Bordeaux (1951) and toured throughout Europe and North America. His most famous roles were the name-part in C. Gounod's *Faust*, Rodolfo in G. Puccini's *La Bohème*, and the Duke of Mantua in G. Verdi's *Rigoletto*. In 1963 he founded a music-drama studio in Paris, where he taught until his death. He recorded several albums of art songs and of Ukrainian folk song arrangements.

**Stas, Anatolii** [Stas', Anatolij], b 5 May 1927 in Sushvalivka, Hlobyne raion, Poltava oblast. Writer and journalist. He has worked for the newpapers *Molod' Ukraïny*, *Robitnycha hazeta*, and *Literaturna Ukraïna* and the Moscow magazine *Ogonëk*. Since 1950 he has published essays, stories, and literary criticism, the novels *Pidzemnyi fakel'* (The Underground Torch, 1960), *Tovarysh Oleksa* (Comrade Oleksa, 1972), *Zelena pastka* (The Green Snare, 1972), *Sribliaste marevo* (The Silvery Phantom, 1974), and *Vulytsia chervonykh troiand* (The Street of Red Roses, 1977), and the prose collection *Taiemnytsia Ardel't-verke* (The Secret of Ardelt-Werke, 1970).

**Stashevsky, Yevhen** [Staševs'kyj, Jevhen], b 2 September 1884 in Zinkiv, Podilia gubernia, d 1938. Historian and economist. After graduating from Kiev University he lectured there as well as at the Kiev Commercial Institute and the Higher Courses for Women. After the Revolution of 1917 he served as a professor at the Kamianets-Podilskyi Ukrainian State University, as director of the All-Ukrainian Agricultural Museum in Kiev (1924–33), and as research associate of the Institute of Ukrainian History of the AN URSR (now ANU; 1936–7). He was arrested in 1938, and died in prison. Stashevsky's chief works deal with Russian political history and Ukrainian economic history: *Ocherki po istorii tsarstvovaniia Mikhaila Fedorovicha* (Outlines of the History of Mikhail Fedorovich's Reign, 1913), *Smolenskaia voina 1632–4* (The Smolensk War of 1632–4, 1919), *Sil's'kohospodars'kyi rynok Pravoberezhnoï Ukraïny za peredreformnoï doby* (The Agricultural Market of Right-Bank Ukraine in the Prereform Period, 1929), and *Istoriia dokapitalisticheskoi renty na Pravoberezhnoi Ukraine v XVIII–pervoi polovine XIX vv.* (The History of Precapitalist Rent in Right-Bank Ukraine from the 18th to the First Half of the 19th Century, 1968), which was unfinished and was published posthumously.

**Stashynsky trial.** The trial of Bohdan Stashynsky in Karlsruhe, West Germany, on 8–19 October 1962 for the assassination of the Ukrainian political figures L. *Rebet on 12 October 1957 and S. *Bandera on 15 October 1959. Stashynsky (b 1931 in the village of Borshchiv, near Lviv) confessed to killing the two nationalist leaders on the orders of the KGB chief A. Shelepin and provided a detailed account of how he had been recruited into the secret police and had carried out the assignments. He was sentenced to eight years' imprisonment. The trial was widely covered in the world press.

**Stasiuk, Ihor** [Stasjuk], b 29 September 1938 in Berezhany, Galicia. Theoretical solid-state physicist. A graduate of Lviv University (1958), he is a professor of physics there and head of the quantum statistics section of the Lviv division of the AN URSR (now ANU) Institute of Theoretical Physics. His extensive research covers several branches of solid-state theory, in particular the theory of phase transitions, theoretical electro-optics and piezo-optics, and superconductivity.

**Stasiuk, Mykola** [Stasjuk], b ? in the Katerynoslav region, d ? Political and co-operative leader. After studying at the St Petersburg Mining Institute (1903–5) he organized peasant associations and propagated populist socialism in Katerynoslav gubernia. He was active in the co-operative movement in Katerynoslav and Kiev. In 1917 he became a member of the Central Rada and the Little Rada, vice-president of the Peasant Association, and general secretary of food supplies in V. Vynnychenko's first cabinet. In 1919 he was put in charge of supplies for the UNR Army. In 1931 he was arrested by the NKVD, and disappeared. His articles on Ukraine's economy appeared in *Zapysky Naukovoho tovarystva v Kyievi* and *Literaturno-naukovyi vistnyk*.

**Stasiv, Iryna.** See Kalynets, Iryna.

Ivan Stasiv

**Stasiv, Ivan,** b 12 July 1895 in Liubachiv, Galicia, d 15 June 1986 in Paris. Community and political leader. He studied law at the university in Budapest (1922–4) and was cofounder of the Ukrainian Student Association in that city (1922). He was a diplomatic attaché and then secretary to the UNR diplomatic mission in Budapest (1919). From 1924 he lived in France. There he was closely involved with the Ukrainian Hromada (1924–8) and was an executive member of the Ukrainian National Union

(1932–40). During the German occupation (1941–4) he headed the French equivalent of the *Ukrainian Institution of Trust in the German Reich.

**State and Law Institute of the Academy of Sciences of Ukraine.** See Institute of State and Law of the Academy of Sciences of the Ukrainian SSR.

The State Banduryst Kapelle of Ukraine

**State Banduryst Kapelle of Ukraine** (Derzhavna kapelia bandurystiv Ukrainy). *Bandura ensemble of Ukraine. The group was formed in 1946 in Kiev from the remaining members of an earlier national bandura ensemble – the State Exemplary Banduryst Kapelle (the majority of whose members had emigrated to the United States and formed the *Ukrainian Bandurist Chorus in Detroit). Its conductors and directors have included O. Mikhnovsky (1946–74), H. Kuliaba (1974–7), and M. Hvozd (since 1977), and its repertoire consists of folk and historical songs, dumas, adaptations of classical or operatic works, and Soviet compositions. The ensemble helped to develop and adapt a chromatic bandura. It has also combined varieties of the bandura and tsymbaly, double-basses, and other instruments into a diverse orchestral section. The ensemble has traveled mainly in the Soviet Union and Eastern bloc countries, and it toured Japan in 1969 and North America in 1988.

**State Dance Ensemble of Ukraine** (Derzhavnyi akademichnyi ansambl tantsiu Ukrainy im P. Virskoho). A dance company, popularly called the Virsky Ensemble af-

Members of the State Dance Ensemble of Ukraine performing the *hopak*

ter P. *Virsky, who founded it in 1937 and was its artistic director to 1940 and again from 1955 to 1975. The company has attained international acclaim for its sophisticated choreography of traditional and modern Ukrainian and other dances, which it has performed throughout Europe and North America. The ensemble has a troupe of more than 80 dancers and an orchestra. Besides Virsky, V. Vronsky (1952–4), L. Chernyshova (1954–5), K. Vasylenko (1977–9), O. Homon (1979–80), and M. Vantukh (since 1980) have served as artistic director.

**State Drama Theater** (Derzhavnyi dramatychnyi teatr). A theater created on the initiative of N. *Doroshenko in Kiev by the Hetman government in August 1918. With O. Zaharov and B. Kryvetsky as artistic directors, the State Drama Theater debuted in the fall of 1918 with the premiere of Lesia Ukrainka's *Lisova pisnia* (The Forest Song). It performed modern Ukrainian and Western European plays by dramatists such as V. Vynnychenko, H. Ibsen, G. Hauptmann, and C. Goldoni. Its main cast was forced to merge with the State People's Theater in the spring of 1919 to form the *Shevchenko First Theater of the Ukrainian Soviet Republic.

**State Duma.** See Duma, State.

**State farm** (Ukrainian: *radianske hospodarstvo* or *radhosp*; Russian: *sovetskoe khoziaistvo* or *sovkhoz*). A state farming enterprise. According to Soviet theory the state farm was the highest and most fully socialist form of agricultural organization. State farms were agricultural 'factories,' where all the means of production were nationalized, and the labor was hired. In the latter respect state farms differed from other forms of socialist farming, including *collective farms, *associations for the joint cultivation of land, and *artels.

State farms were first introduced in the USSR in 1919–20, during the period of War Communism. The Bolshevik authorities forcibly took back the landowners' estates and equipment that had been divided among the peasants. By the summer of 1919 there were 1,256 state farms in Ukraine, with 1.3 million ha of land, more than in the Russian republic. Another 1.3 million ha had been taken over by sugar manufacturing and alcohol distilling enterprises. In practice the state farms were able to work only one-half of their land, because they lacked workers and other resources. The introduction of state farms was resisted strongly by the peasantry. Their resistance led the Party to adopt, at the Seventh Party Conference in December 1919, a slower tempo for establishing state farms throughout the USSR. Many state farms were also dissolved after that time. By the end of 1920 there were only 571 state farms, with 409,300 ha, in Ukraine. The decline continued, so that by 1923 there were only 423 farms, with 422,000 ha, or 0.65 percent of all arable land, in Ukraine. During the NEP period state farms were combined into large agricultural trusts. In addition some 100 state farms belonged to large factories and supplied their workers with food. Many of those farms were still plagued by a shortage of manpower and resources. In 1925 the Ukrainian State Farm Trust leased out, in return for one-half of the harvest, over 20 percent of its land to peasants, because it could not work the land on its own. In 1927, state farms accounted for only 1.8 percent of the capital funds in agriculture, 0.9 percent

of the livestock, and 4.9 percent of the farm inventory. But the regime favored the farms and gave them priority access to tractors and other machines, hoping to turn them into model farms.

During the *collectivization the political sections of state farms helped to force the peasants into joining collective farms. The Party considered transforming the collective farms into state ones but did not carry through the plan. By the beginning of 1934 there were 768 state farms organized into trusts, and many more belonged to various enterprises and institutions. In 1934, state farms in Ukraine owned 3.4 million ha of seeded land, 11,828 tractors, 309,000 draft animals, 703,000 cattle (including 292,000 cows), 1.2 million hogs, and 631,000 sheep and goats. Later, special suburban state farms were established to provide food for the urban population. Some state farms established by the NKVD were worked by prisoners.

State farms continued to operate in Ukraine under the Nazi occupation during the Second World War. In 1945 there were 784 state farms, with 1,172,000 ha of land, 198,000 workers, and 6,400 tractors. Their number continued to grow: to 902 in 1960, 1,605 in 1970, 2,110 in 1980, and 2,514 in 1987. Although state farms were usually much larger than collective farms, their average size was declining: whereas in 1958 the average farm had 6,500 ha of land, of which 4,200 ha were under cultivation, by 1980 the respective figures were 4,600 ha and 3,400 ha. On average they were approximately one-third larger than collective farms. State farms were most common in southern Ukraine and, after that, in central Ukraine; they were least common in Polisia and western Ukraine.

In 1987 approx 19.7 percent of the total land area and 23.9 percent of the agricultural land in Ukraine belonged to state farms. State farms had some 7.4 million ha under cultivation. Of that area, 3.5 million ha were seeded with grain crops; 0.6 ha with industrial crops; 0.3 ha with potatoes, vegetables, and melons; and 3 million ha with feed crops. In addition they owned 5 million head of cattle (including 1.6 million milk cows), 3.4 million hogs, and 1.9 million sheep and goats. State farms produced 0.9 million t of meat, 4.6 million t of milk, 7.9 billion eggs, and 6,800 t of wool. In total they employed 1.4 million people, including 1.1 million in agriculture. In 1970, when state farms accounted for over 21 percent of the agricultural land, they provided only 14.9 percent of the gross agricultural product in Ukraine. Productivity was somewhat higher than on collective farms, but much lower than on the small private plots. State farms supplied a higher proportion of their output to the state: in 1970 they turned over 38 percent of their grain to the state, compared to 33 percent for collective farms. More important, the state paid state farms lower procurement prices than other farms and thus realized a higher profit on the sale of their products. In response to the problems faced by collective farms, in the 1960s the average wage of their members was raised considerably and allowed to surpass the wage of state farm workers. The latter generally worked shorter hours, however, and were guaranteed a certain daily wage.

The prices of machinery, fuel, building materials, and fertilizer for state and collective farms were equalized in the 1960s. Since procurement prices for state farms remained a little lower than for collective farms, state farms ran larger deficits in their operation. The economic position of state farms was improved somewhat through

greater specialization. Most state farms began to specialize in milk and beef production, fruit and vegetable growing, poultry farming, or grain growing.

State farms were much more common and important
in the RSFSR than in Ukraine. There they accounted for
over 53 percent of all agricultural land in 1970. They were
paid higher prices by the government than state farms
in Ukraine, and their workers were paid higher wages.
There was no economic rationale for such discrimination.

BIBLIOGRAPHY
Sovkhozy k XV godovshchine Oktiabria (Moscow–Leningrad 1932)
Ievushenko, A. Radhospy Ukraïny za 50 rokiv Radians'koï vlady
   (Kiev 1967)
Sil's'ke hospodarstvo URSR: Statystychnyi zbirnyk (Kiev 1969)
Pohorielov, M.; Pakhomov, Iu. Ekonomichna reforma v radhospakh
   (Kiev 1970)
Zemnin, I.; Bogdenko, M. Sovkhozy SSSR: Kratkii istoricheskii ocherk
   1917–1975 (Moscow 1976)

V. Holubnychy

**State inspectorates** (derzhavni inspektury). In the UNR,
organs of political supervision established in the larger
military units in 1919. The government assigned representatives of the political parties to army units. The chief state
inspector at the staff of the UNR Army was V. Kedrovsky.
The UNR State Inspectorate was abolished in December
1919.

In the Soviet Union state inspectorates were special
control organs within government bodies, such as ministries and state committees. Their purpose was to supervise the implementation of laws and special regulations
pertaining to working and living conditions, sanitation,
safety, and commercial activity. Officials of the state inspectorates had the unrestricted power to inspect the operations and records of any organization, enterprise, or
institution and, in some cases, of individuals as well. Anyone guilty of violating regulations could be punished by
the inspectorates with a fine, suspension of occupational
rights, or dismissal from work.

**State Library of Ukraine** (Derzhavna biblioteka
Ukrainy). Founded in Kiev in 1866 as the Kiev Municipal
Public Library, it was renamed the State Library of the
Ukrainian SSR in 1957. Its holdings number over 3 million
items, including 200,000 periodicals, and its manuscript
division contains the collected works of T. Shevchenko, I.
Franko, Lesia Ukrainka, P. Myrny, M. Kotsiubynsky, and
others, as well as V. Modzalevsky's valuable collection of
archival documents pertaining to 17th- and 18th-century
Left-Bank Ukraine. The library also has a large catalog of
Ucrainica in foreign publications and periodicals.

**State loans.** Moneys borrowed by the state from the population or private corporations and repayable within a
specified time, usually with interest. Such loans are called
internal. Loans from foreign states or banks are called external.

The tsarist government in the Russian Empire began to
make internal loans in the 1860s and external loans in the
1870s. The latter were used to finance commercial and industrial enterprises. By the end of the 19th century the indebtedness of the imperial government exceeded 5 billion
gold rubles, the equivalent of the government's budget for
three years. Russia was the largest debtor state of the time.

To pay off its foreign debt the state encouraged a positive
trade balance by exporting raw material. A significant
portion of foreign loans was used for constructing a railroad network. That undertaking spurred the growth of
Ukraine's industry, particularly of its coal and metallurgical industry, and promoted the export of Ukraine's grain
and sugar.

Between 1908 and 1912 the tsarist government issued
5.2 billion rubles' worth of securities: 3.7 billion for sale at
home and 1.5 billion for sale abroad. Land mortgage credit constituted 44 percent of domestic securities, which
were used by the peasantry to purchase land from the
gentry, who in turn were able to pay off their own mortgage debts.

In January 1918 the new Soviet government canceled all
foreign debts. Internal state loans began in 1922 and
reached their peak during the First Five-Year Plan. Each
bond issue was identified with a particular economic campaign, such as the Loan of Economic Restoration, the Five-
Year-Plan-in-Four-Years Loan, and the Loan to Strength-
en the Peasant Economy. Bonds were purchased by individuals and, to a lesser extent, by savings banks and
enterprises. Political and administrative pressure was
used to sell the bonds, including direct deductions from
workers' wages and seizures of enterprises' bank accounts. In effect the bonds were a form of taxation that diverted part of the purchasing power of the population into
the state budget. Wage and salary workers were the main
individual purchasers of government bonds: by 1933 they
owned 69 percent of the bonds. Initially the peasantry
played a minor role, in purchasing only 5 percent of the
first industrialization loan; but, under pressure, by mid-
1931 they had subscribed 25 percent of the bonds. At the
same time the interest paid on the loans declined, from 12
percent during the mid-1920s to 4 percent and even 2 percent by the early 1930s, and the repayment term increased,
from between 2 and 8 to 10 and even 20 years.

Between 1927 and 1932 the population of Ukraine invested 1.3 billion rubles, or 23 percent of the all-Union
total, in state loans. The vast majority of revenues were retained by the central Union budget; the Ukrainian state
budget retained only 10.8 percent of such revenue. During
that period revenue from USSR state loans constituted 13
percent of all budgetary revenues from Ukraine. In the following decades Ukraine's participation in the Union state
debt remained at approx 19 percent. In 1957 compulsory
bond sales were abandoned, but a 20-year moratorium
was placed on the repayment of state loans. In 1960, state
loans raised from the population, mostly in the form of
lotteries, constituted 453 million rubles, or 1.2 percent of
the state revenues of the Ukrainian SSR. By 1988 such state
loans had declined to 128 million rubles, or 0.4 percent of
Ukraine's state revenues. Since 1989, with the advent of
economic reform, the importance of domestic government
bonds has increased.

Foreign debt has always been a monopoly of the Union
government in Moscow. By 1990 the USSR had a hard-cur-
rency foreign debt (owed to Western state and commercial institutions) estimated at over 60 billion dollars. That
year hard currency requirements for debt servicing were
estimated at up to 11 billion dollars. From 1988 individual
republican enterprises were free to establish foreign trade
ties, but hard currency obligations still had to be arranged
with the central State Bank in Moscow.

BIBLIOGRAPHY
Melnyk, Z. *Soviet Capital Formation: Ukraine, 1928/29–1932* (Munich 1965)

B. Somchynsky

**State peasants** (*derzhavni seliany*). A category of 'free persons' introduced by Peter I in the early 18th-century Russian Empire. Also known as treasury peasants, they lived on and farmed lands owned by the state, in exchange for which they were obliged to pay *quitrents, *poll taxes, and road taxes to the state treasury. They were also required to build and maintain roads and to perform other duties on demand. After the abolition of the Hetman state and the partition of Poland during the reign of Catherine II, peasants in Ukraine who lived on the former properties of the Polish crown, *economic peasants, free farmers, *Cossack helpers, rank-and-file Cossacks, foreign military colonists, single-homestead servitors (*odnodvirtsi) who could not prove noble descent, and Jewish farmers were all classified as state peasants. In Right-Bank Ukraine many state-owned lands were leased out to the gentry, and the state peasants on those lands (150,000 males during the reign of Paul I) were thus forced to perform corvée, and became serfs. From 1801, state peasants could buy uninhabited land from the state and have full property rights over it. Many were too poor to meet their steadily increasing financial obligations and were forced to migrate to Southern Ukraine in search of work or to hire themselves out to the landed gentry. Those unfortunate enough to become *work people in state-owned industrial enterprises or to live on lands incorporated into the *military settlements of Slobidska and Southern Ukraine in 1817–25 were brutally exploited. In 1837 corvée by state peasants was abolished, and the newly created Russian Ministry of State Domains under Count P. Kiselev introduced quitrent, tax, land-equalization, land-redistribution, administrative, and judicial reforms to improve the peasants' lives. Between 1839 and 1859, peasants who had been leased to the gentry were gradually transferred to paying cash quitrents to the state instead. By the mid-19th century the over four million male state peasants in Russian-ruled Ukraine made up 41 percent of all male peasants there. Sixty-seven percent of them were in Left-Bank Ukraine, 16 percent were in Right-Bank Ukraine, and 16.5 percent were in Southern Ukraine. In 1863 the state peasants in Right-Bank Ukraine were reclassified as proprietary peasants and forced to assume 49-year-term *redemption payments for their land allotments. In 1866 all other state peasants were allowed to purchase their allotments in full immediately, at grossly inflated prices, or to rent them permanently. In 1885 compulsory redemption payments were imposed on all peasants.

**State People's Theater.** See People's Theater.

**State Planning Committee of the Ukrainian SSR** (Derzhavnyi planovyi komitet URSR, or Derzhplan URSR). A Union-republican economic agency (est 1921) subordinated to both the Council of Ministers of the Ukrainian SSR and the USSR State Planning Committee. Its two chief functions were planning the economy of Ukraine and monitoring the implementation of the plans.

Its organizational structure consisted of three groups of departments, summary functional, summary resource, and branch. The summary functional departments set one or several plan targets (eg, labor investment) for all branches of the economy. The summary resource departments drafted material balances and plans for the distribution of material inputs and equipment. The branch departments were organized according to either the branch principle (coal, machine building, food) or the sector principle (agriculture, construction). The department heads were members of the committee, and the heads of the biggest departments, along with the committee chairman and deputy chairman, were members of the committee's collegium. The most important matters were discussed and decided by the collegium.

The Derzhplan drafted economic plans for the republic on the basis of control figures specifying the goals and constraints for a given period. Those figures were set by the USSR Planning Committee after consultations with the republican committees and ministries. The Derzhplan in turn communicated with the relevant ministries or directly with their enterprises and organizations. Its specialists were well acquainted with the methods, capacities, and technology used by the enterprises. Because of the traditional Soviet emphasis on material production, most of the committee staff were engineers and technicians, not economists.

Annual and five-year plans drafted by the Derzhplan were published in dozens of volumes, specifying outputs, investment, wages, employment, consumption, and so forth. Upon approval by the CPU Central Committee and Ukraine's Council of Ministers each plan was submitted to the USSR Planning Committtee, which then drafted the plan for the Soviet economy as a whole. As a result the plan approved for Ukraine could differ significantly from what had been proposed by the republic.

Decision-making in the USSR economy was centralized according to the vertical branch principle. The republics had a significant say in planning their social development but not their industrial production. The Derzhplan controlled material and financial flows only for the economic units subordinated to Ukraine's Council of Ministers: the enterprises of local industry, agriculture, and forestry, some enterprises of the construction, transportation, and communications industries, trade and public catering, and the 'nonproductive' sectors (education, medicine, etc). Enterprises of the oil, gas, chemical, and machine-building industries came only under the Union ministries. Enterprises of the coal, electric power, metallurgical, paper, construction-materials, light, and food industries were subordinated to both Union and republican ministries.

The economic restructuring begun in the last few years of the 1980s diminished the role of the Union and republican planning committees. Industrial enterprises became increasingly independent of government control, but at the same time republican governments assumed more and more powers formerly held by the Union authorities.

(See also *Economic planning.)

F. Kushnirsky

**State Publishing House of Ukraine** (Derzhavne vydavnytstvo Ukrainy [DVU], or Derzhvydav). The official publishing house of the Soviet Ukrainian state, founded by the All-Ukrainian Central Executive Committee in Kharkiv in May 1919 as the All-Ukrainian Publishing House (Vseukrvydav). It was renamed the All-Ukrainian State Publishing House in 1920, and DVU in 1922. In the second half of the 1920s, under the direction of Yu. Voi-tsekhivsky and S. Pylypenko, DVU was the largest and most important publisher in Soviet Ukraine – it produced over half of all its books – and the second-largest publisher in the USSR. It played a major role in the implementation of the *Ukrainization policy by publishing several hundred schoolbooks; several series of Ukrainian literary classics; works by contemporary Soviet Ukrainian authors; translations of European classics; political propaganda; sociopolitical, technical, and children's books; and 38 periodicals, including the literary journals *Chervonyi shliakh*, *Zhyttia i revoliutsiia*, *Literaturnyi iarmarok*, *Hart*, *Nova generatsiia*, *Ukraïna*, and *Pluh*. It also ran a Central Bibliographic Division (it became part of the Ukrainian *Book Chamber in 1922) and a network of 28 okruha branches, 75 bookstores, 15 kiosks, and 73 agencies. Its editorial staff was led by V. Shcherbanenko and included prominent writers, such as M. Khvylovy, M. Kulish, P. Panch, V. Svidzinsky, and P. Tychyna. From 1926 DVU came under increasing state control; in that year it was ordered by the CP(B)U Politburo to prepare and publish a scholarly edition of V. Lenin's works and to increase its output of political propaganda for the masses. In the period 1920–8 DVU published 6,624 titles with a combined pressrun of 81,471,000; 4,487 of the titles were in Ukrainian and had a pressrun of 63,254,000 copies. Approx 65 percent of the output consisted of schoolbooks. By 1929, 94 percent of its publications were in Ukrainian. In August 1930 DVU was replaced by the State Publishing Alliance of Ukraine (DVOU), an association of specialized publishers that was abolished in March 1934.

**State purchase of agricultural products.** See Agricultural procurement.

**State purchase prices.** See Prices.

**State Secretariat of the Western Ukrainian National Republic** (Derzhavnyi Sekretariiat Zakhidno-Ukrainskoi Narodnoi Respubliky). The executive organ of the government of Western Ukraine, established on 9 November 1918 as a provisional secretariat by the Ukrainian National Rada. Its first members were K. Levytsky, president and secretary of finance; V. Paneiko, secretary of foreign affairs; L. Tsehelsky, internal affairs; D. Vitovsky, the armed forces; S. Holubovych, justice; O. Barvinsky, education and religious affairs; S. Baran, agrarian affairs; Ya. Lytvynovych, trade and industry; I. Myron, highways; O. Pisetsky, post and telegraph; I. Makukh, public works; A. Chernetsky, labor and social welfare; I. Kurovets, public health; and S. Fedak, supplies. The first secretariat by its political composition was a coalition: all Galician parties were represented in it, although the National Democratic party was dominant. On 4 January 1919, after the reorganization of the Ukrainian National Rada in Stanyslaviv, a new secretariat was put together. Holubovych took over the presidency, finances, and trade and industry, and Paneiko, foreign affairs; Tsehelsky became acting secretary of foreign affairs (while Paneiko was at the Paris Peace Conference); Makukh took over internal affairs, Vitovsky, military affairs, O. Burachynsky, justice, A. Artymovych, education and religion, M. Martynets, agrarian affairs, Myron, highways and post and telegraph, and M. Kozanevych, public works. Some of the secretaries were

nonpartisan experts. In February 1919 Vitovsky and Tsehelsky left; V. Kurmanovych became secretary for military affairs, and P. Bubela became his deputy. M. Lozynsky was appointed deputy secretary of foreign affairs, and when he left for Paris in April 1919, the secretariat was directed by S. Vytvytsky. That secretariat functioned until June 1919, when the government of the Western Province of the Ukrainian National Republic was vested in the dictator Ye. Petrushevych. The secretariat's functions were taken over by a government consisting of the dictator's plenipotentiaries.

BIBLIOGRAPHY
Chubatyi, M. *Derzhavnyi lad na Zakhidnii oblasti UNR* (Lviv 1921)
Lozyns'kyi, M. *Halychyna v rr. 1918–1920* (Vienna 1922; repr, New York 1970)

**State Senate** (Derzhavnyi Senat). The highest judicial body in the court system of the *Hetman government of P. Skoropadsky. It was set up by an act of 8 July 1918 to replace the *General Court, which had functioned during the period of the Central Rada. The State Senate was organized on the model of the Russian State Senate, and it functioned temporarily according to the Russian procedural rules. There were 45 appointees to the Senate. The hetman appointed M. Vasylenko as president, and the chairmen of the general courts were D. Nosenko (administrative court), Husakivsky (civil court), and M. Chubynsky (criminal court). The Senate and each general court had its own procurator.

**Stations of young naturalists** (*stantsii yunykh naturalistiv*). Extracurricular educational institutions in the USSR which attempted to develop and encourage a love of nature, animal husbandry, and agriculture in the members of the Pioneer movement. The stations had groups of young plant scientists, stockbreeders, horticulturists, agricultural engineers, and the like.

**Stations of young technicians** (*stantsii yunykh tekhnikiv*). Extracurricular educational institutions in the USSR which increased the technical knowledge of Pioneers and young people in general. Stations helped the school system entrench the technical education of students, instill in them an interest in the subject, and encourage and develop young people's talents in construction. There were subgroups in the stations for those with interests in electronics, aeromodeling, photography, and the like.

**Statistics.** The gathering and analyzing of numerical data for the purpose of making inferences about mass phenomena, particularly social processes. Quantitative analysis has a long history, but it emerged as a modern science only in the 19th century and acquired important practical applications in science, economics, medicine, and other fields. The most common use of statistics is in the conduct and analysis of *censuses.

Statistically useful data began to be collected in Ukraine in the 16th and 17th centuries, when registries of the population of the Polish-Lithuanian state were compiled for the purposes of taxation. They contained general information on the population and real property. In the Hetman state more detailed surveys of economic life were compiled in census books (most notably in 1666), some of which have survived until today. From 1723 regular *re-

*vizii* were conducted, and the *Rumiantsev census of 1765–9 enumerated the entire population of the Hetmanate. Another important source of statistical data was the birth and death records which began to be kept by the Orthodox church in the first quarter of the 18th century.

In Russian-ruled Ukraine the Statistical Committee of the Police Ministry (est 1811) gathered some social statistics. In 1834 it was replaced by a statistics office of the Interior Ministry, which in 1858 was reorganized into the Central Statistical Committee. The purpose of the committee was to collect, with the help of its gubernial, county, and municipal committees, and to publish statistical materials. It issued several series, yearbooks, collections, and other publications. In 1897 it also administered the first general census of the Russian Empire. Various ministries and government departments and gubernial and municipal statistical offices also collected statistical data. Their publications contained much information about Ukraine, although they did not treat Ukraine as a separate entity.

From the first half of the 19th century gubernial committees and offices in Ukraine often published their materials in annual collections. The most prolific statistical offices were those of Kiev gubernia and Kuban. Eventually those of Poltava, Chernihiv, and Kherson gubernias gained recognition. The most important statistical publications on Ukraine in the 19th century included W. Marczyński's *Statystyczno-topograficzne i historyczne opisanie gub. Podolskiej* (Statistical-Topographic and Historical Survey of Podilia Gubernia, 2 vols, 1831), M. Arandarenko's *Zapiski o Poltavskoi gubernii, sostavlennye v 1846 godu* (Notes on Poltava Gubernia Taken Down in 1846, 3 vols, 1848–52), A. Skalkovsky's *Opyt statisticheskogo opisaniia Novorossiiskogo kraia* (An Attempt at a Statistical Description of the New Russia Region, 2 vols, 1850, 1853), and D. *Zhuravsky's *Statisticheskoe opisanie Kievskoi gubernii* (A Statistical Description of Kiev Gubernia, 3 vols, 1852). The commission for the study of the Kiev school district published four volumes of statistical materials and was active from 1851 to 1864. The Russian Army General Staff published its own statistical studies of the Ukrainian gubernias from the mid-19th century. At the same time the *Southwestern Branch of the Imperial Russian Geographic Society, the Free Economic Society (founded in St Petersburg in 1765), various church eparchies, and other organizations collected and published statistics on Ukrainian life.

In the mid-19th century chairs of statistics were established at Ukrainian universities (instruction in the discipline had been introduced earlier). The first statistics professor in Ukraine was O. Roslavsky-Petrovsky at Kharkiv University. Zhuravsky's *Ob istochnikakh i upotreblenii statisticheskikh svedenii* (On the Sources and Applications of Statistical Information, 1846) was an important contribution to the methodology of statistics.

After the emancipation of the peasants and the land reforms of the 1860s the zemstvos set up statistical offices to study the state of agriculture and the socioeconomic changes in their rural localities. Such offices were established by the Kherson (1873) and Chernihiv (1875) and then the Poltava, Kharkiv, Katerynoslav, and Tavriia zemstvos. The offices conducted censuses of peasant households and workshops and peasant cadastres. Initially the zemstvo statisticians studied entire peasant communities, but later they focused on selected aspects of small groups of representative households. Many noted Ukrainian statisticians and cultural figures worked in the zemstvo statistical offices in Ukraine. They tried to inform the government about the social and economic problems of the countryside. The work of the Chernihiv zemstvo statistical office, which was directed by O. *Rusov and staffed by P. *Chervinsky, V. *Varzar, M. Kotsiubynsky, and O. *Shlykevych, was particularly well known. It concentrated on land use and productivity, whereas the Moscow zemstvo office was interested mostly in demographic studies. When the Chernihiv statisticians showed that the local nobility had avoided taxes, the nobles succeeded in closing their office for several years. Moreover, statisticians were often accused of fomenting revolution among the peasantry. The charge was false, although many zemstvo staff were involved in political activities to raise the political and national consciousness of the common people. In the 1870s Shlykevych compiled combined statistical tables that were a major contribution to the statistical methodology of the time.

The statistical office of the Pereiaslav zemstvo, directed for a time by G. Rotmistrov, made some important contributions. It was one of the first institutions in the world to publish a survey of peasant household budgets (in 1898). Thanks to its efforts *Statisticheskii spravochnik po Iugu Rossii* (A Statistical Handbook for the South of Russia, 1890), which encompassed the Don Cossack province and Bessarabia as well as the nine Ukrainian gubernias, came out. Besides those already mentioned, the noted zemstvo statisticians in Ukraine included V. *Vasylenko, L. *Padalka, and F. *Shcherbyna. Altogether zemstvo statistical offices published over 100 volumes of materials on agriculture, cottage industries, peasant property, health care, and education. Most of the studies were restricted to individual gubernias or even counties. Only a few covered the entire Ukrainian territory – for example, *Statisticheskii spravochnik po Iugu Rossii* and *Ves' Iugo-Zapadnyi Krai* (The Entire South-Russian Region, 1913), supervised by M. Dovnar-Zapolsky, edited by A. Yaroshevych, and published by the Southwestern Branch of the Russian Export Chamber. Besides those already mentioned, the chief contributors to statistical research on Russian-ruled Ukraine in the late 19th and early 20th centuries were K. *Vobly, L. Lichkov, I. Myklashevsky (professor of statistics at Kharkiv University), S. *Podolynsky, V. Postnikov, H. Tsekhanovetsky, A. Borynevych, and M. *Ptukha.

In the Ukrainian territories of the Austro-Hungarian Empire, statistical research in the early 19th century was conducted by the Directorate of Administrative Statistics of the Ministry of Trade, Industry, and Public Works. In 1863 it was succeeded by the Central Statistical Commission in Vienna. Those agencies from 1842 through 1917 published statistical yearbooks that give information on population, agriculture, animal husbandry, industry, and commerce, broken down by crownland (and initially by circle as well). Later editions also provided data on education and the press. Several serials published by those bodies, including *Mitteilungen aus dem Gebiete der Statistik* (1852–74), *Monatsschrift* (1875–1917, 43 vols), and *Österreichische Statistik* (1882–1916, 111 vols), provided detailed and up-to-date statistical information. The Crownland Statistical Bureau for Galicia (est 1874) published a reference book titled *Rocznik Statystyki Galicyi* (Statistical Annual for Galicia, 1886–1900) and then *Podręcznik Statystyki*

*Galicyi* (Statistical Handbook for Galicia, 1901–13), which contained in addition to demographic and economic data considerable information on Ukrainian organizations and institutions, and the journal *Wiadomości statystyczne o stosunkach krajowych* (Statistical Information on Crownland Relations, 25 vols, 1874–1918), *Rocznik Statystyki Przemysłu i Handlu Krajowego* (Statistical Annual of Crownland Industry and Trade, 1885–93), and a special statistical serial devoted to the city of Lviv. The Crownland Statistical Bureau for the Duchy of Bukovyna published 17 volumes of *Mitteilungen des statistischen Landesamtes der Herzogthums Bukowina* (1892–1913). Previously the Bukovyna Chamber of Commerce had published several volumes of statistical materials, in 1851–72. Statistical information on Transcarpathia was published by the Hungarian statistical administration in Budapest from 1874.

Some statistical studies in Western Ukraine were conducted by Ukrainian institutions and scholars. The Statistical Commission of the Shevchenko Scientific Society published three volumes of *Studiï z polia suspil'nykh nauk i statystyky* (Studies in the Field of Social Sciences and Statistics, 1909–12), which included articles on statistical theory, on social relations in Russian-ruled Ukraine, and on the economy and society of Western Ukraine. Ukrainians who published statistical research included V. Navrotsky, I. Franko, M. Pavlyk, V. Okhrymovych, S. Dnistriansky, M. Korduba, and S. Rudnytsky. Polish scholars who made contributions to the statistical study of Galicia included J. Buzek, J. Kleczyński, and T. Pilat. S. Tomashivsky and V. Hnatiuk studied Ukrainian society in Transcarpathia. In 1914–20 several statistical surveys were published by the Union for the Liberation of Ukraine and other political and social organizations.

Centralized government statistical offices were established in Poland, Czechoslovakia, and Rumania in the 1920s. In the interwar period the Chief Statistical Office of Poland published much data relating to Galicia in its various serials and yearbooks, including *Statystyka Polski*, *Wiadomości Statystyczne*, and *Rocznik Statystyczny*. The Crownland Statistical Bureau for Galicia was abolished and replaced by several local statistical bureaus, which were not very active. The Shevchenko Scientific Society's Commission for the National Economy, Sociology, and Statistics issued two volumes of papers. The Ukrainian Scientific Institute in Warsaw published several statistical studies on Soviet Ukraine. Statistical works on Ukrainian demography and society were published by V. Kubijovyč, T. Olesiiuk, and V. Sadovsky; K. Kobersky, Yu. Pavlykovsky, and I. Vytanovych studied economic statistics. From 1933 the Ukrainian Economic Bureau in Warsaw published four yearbooks under the editorship of Kubijovyč, L. Lukasevych, and Ye. Glovinsky. The Polish scholars A. Krysiński and M. Feliński also wrote on Ukrainian topics. At the Ukrainian Free University in Prague and the Ukrainian Technical and Husbandry Institute in Poděbrady, Czechoslovakia, statistics courses were offered by Shcherbyna and L. Shramchenko. In the early 1920s Shcherbyna wrote several textbooks on statistical methodology and history.

The history of statistics in Soviet Ukraine, as in the entire USSR, can be divided into several periods. In the 1920s, statistical research was widely decentralized and well developed. The major institution was the Central Statistical Administration of Ukraine (TsSUU), directed by M. Avdi-

ienko. It published several periodicals and collections of statistical information (see *Central Statistical Administration of the Council of Ministers of the Ukrainian SSR). Its statistical studies and analyses were highly sophisticated for the time, and much important material on Ukrainian demographic, social, economic, and cultural topics was compiled. For the first time the essentially Ukrainian regions were treated as a single unit for statistical purposes. The USSR Central Statistical Administration in Moscow also published data on Ukraine, as did some local institutions. The VUAN Demography Institute, directed by the prominent demographer Ptukha, published 14 volumes of demographic materials. The main contributors to statistical research in the 1920s were the economists-statisticians Vobly, V. Kosynsky, H. Kryvchenko, Y. Paskhaver, and I. Shymonovych; the demographers Ptukha, O. Korchak-Chepurkivsky, Yu. Masiutyn, P. Pustokhod, S. Tomilin, M. Tratsevsky, and A. Khomenko; and the mathematicians M. Kravchuk and Ye. Slutsky. Annual all-Ukrainian conferences of statisticians were held from 1922 and congresses from 1925.

The second major period in Soviet statistical history lasted from approx 1930 to the late 1950s. In 1930, in connection with the introduction of the five-year plans and general economic planning, the TsSUU and its all-Union counterpart were abolished, and their functions were assumed by the All-Union State Planning Committee (Gosplan). In 1931 a special body in Gosplan, the USSR Central Economic Survey Administration, with its republican branches was given responsibility for gathering statistics. In reality, however, that body was hardly active, and statistical research was discontinued. In two major purges (1930–1 and 1937–8) many of the leading statisticians and related scholars, including Avdiienko, were imprisoned and even killed. Almost no statistical data on Ukraine were published in that period. In the mid- to late-1930s only a few guides or collections, edited by O. Asatkin, were issued, by the Ukrainian branch of the Central Economic Survey Administration: *Narodne hospodarstvo URSR* (The Economy of the Ukrainian SSR, 1935), a review of the results of the First and Second Five-year plans; *URSR v chyslakh* (The Ukrainian SSR in Figures, 1936); the highly propagandistic *Sotsialistychna Ukraïna* (Socialist Ukraine, 1937); and *Pratsia v URSR* (Work in the Ukrainian SSR, 1937). The quality of those works was poor. All of them contained little useful demographic information, because of attempts to hide the demographic costs of the 1932–3 famine and the terror. Typical for the period was the fact that the results of the 1937 census were completely suppressed, and only selected data from the 1939 census were released.

The revival of the All-Union Statistical Administration in 1941 did not lead to any practical changes. In 1948 it was separated from Gosplan and placed under the authority of the USSR Council of Ministers. The restored TsSUU was placed under the jurisdiction of the All-Union Statistical Administration, not under the Ukrainian government. Neither body published any detailed statistics. Some data were released occasionally in press articles or the speeches of Party leaders, but the information was not scientifically verified and was used mostly for propagandistic purposes.

A new period of statistical research in Ukraine began after J. Stalin's death. N. Khrushchev's decentralization of economic planning and administration required reliable statistical data. The TsSUU was reorganized to make it more responsible to the Ukrainian government, and statistical information began to be published again in 1957. An annual statistical yearbook containing the latest data and comparisons with earlier years was introduced in 1959. The All-Union Statistical Administration also began to publish Ukrainian statistical data, including the results of the 1959 census.

In general, statistical research in the USSR had a very specific character. The entire system of gathering, checking, and analyzing data was designed to monitor the fulfillment of state economic plans, the development of the economy and culture, changes in the standard of living, the expansion of productive forces, the introduction of technology, and the level of material and labor reserves in the economy. The state had a monopoly on statistical research, which played an important role in economic planning and political-economic administration. In the USSR all institutions and organizations filed standardized statistical reports according to a regular and specified schedule. Data fabrication was a typical feature of Soviet statistics and was especially prevalent in the 1930s to 1950s. The linkage of statistics with political and economic control induced enterprises to overstate production, understate resources, and hide the true state of affairs in other ways. Inconsistent pricing policies and changes in record-keeping and computing methods made it difficult to compare data from different years. Growth indexes of real domestic earnings, retail trade and commerce, labor productivity, and, to a certain degree, overall industrial and agricultural output were often unreliable. Demographic statistics were also unreliable and sometimes falsified, especially data on nationality, which tended to understate the number of non-Russians. As a rule, statistics were used as propaganda to exaggerate positive developments and downplay negative ones. Soviet authorities did not gather information that did not seem to have a direct political or economic purpose, and they published only a small part of the collected data. In the 1920s, for example, some data on morality (including crime) were published, but this stopped in the 1930s. Most data were classified as a state secret and not released to the public or to foreign scholars.

BIBLIOGRAPHY

Shcherbyna, F. *Statystyka: Istoriia statystyky ta statystychnykh ustanov* (Prague 1923)
Ptukha, M. *Ocherki po istorii statistiki XVII–XVIII vekov* (Moscow 1945)
– *Ocherki po istorii statistiki v SSSR*, 2 vols (Moscow 1955, 1959)
*Statisticheskii slovar'* (Moscow 1959)
Ptukha, M. *Ocherki po statistike naseleniia* (Moscow 1960)
Treml, V.; Hardt, J. (eds). *Soviet Economic Statistics* (Durham, NC 1972)

B. Balan, V. Kubijovyč

**Statute for the Armenians of Lviv.** A legal code that defined and regulated Armenian self-government in Lviv, Lutske, Ternopil, Sniatyn, Stanyslaviv (now Ivano-Frankivske), and other cities with large Armenian communities in Polish-ruled Ukraine. Based on an earlier Armenian code, it was adopted by the Diet in 1519 and ratified by King Sigismund I. In the second half of the 16th century a section on procedural law compiled in Lviv was added to the code. The statute remained in force until 1780–1.

**Statute of the Higher Administration of Ukraine** (Statut vyshchoho upravlinnia Ukrainy). The working constitution of autonomous Ukraine, adopted by the Little Rada on 29 July 1917. It arose out of an agreement between the *Central Rada and the Russian *Provisional Government, reached on 16 July, and it was consistent with the Second Universal of the Central Rada. According to this constitution the highest governing body (executive) in Ukraine was the *General Secretariat of the Central Rada, which was formed by the Executive Committee (the Little Rada) of the Central Rada and approved by the Provisional Government. The secretariat, composed of 14 general secretaries (ministers), controlled all the government organs of Ukraine and determined which of them would have direct relations with the Provisional Government. A state secretary for Ukrainian affairs, appointed by the Provisional Government and approved by the Central Rada, was to represent Ukraine's interests within the Provisional Government.

The statute further specified that the General Secretariat was responsible for obtaining the approval of the Provisional Government for laws and budgets passed by the Central Rada. The secretariat's activities were controlled by the Central Rada and (between its sessions) the Little Rada, and a nonconfidence vote by the Central Rada had the power to dissolve the secretariat. All bills passed by the Central Rada or Little Rada were countersigned by the secretariat. Laws passed by the Provisional Government became valid in Ukraine after being published in Ukrainian in the official government bulletin, *Vistnyk Heneral' noho Sekretariiatu Ukraïny. All laws and administrative decrees were to be published in Russian, Hebrew, and Polish as well as Ukrainian.

Among those who prepared the Statute of the Higher Administration of Ukraine was O. Shulhyn. It was approved by the Little Rada and presented to the Provisional Government by a delegation of the secretariat consisting of V. Vynnychenko, Kh. Baranovsky, and M. Rafes (who represented the national minorities). The statute was reviewed by representatives of the Provisional Government (including N. Nekrasov) and rejected. Instead the Provisional Government issued the 'Provisional Instruction to the General Secretariat' on 17 August 1917.

BIBLIOGRAPHY

Vynnychenko, V. *Vidrodzhennia natsiï*, vol 1 (Kiev–Vienna 1920; Kiev 1990)
Khrystiuk, P. *Zamitky i materiialy do istoriï ukraïns'koï revoliutsiï 1917–1920 rr.*, vol 1 (Vienna 1921; New York 1969)
Doroshenko, D. *Istoriia Ukraïny, 1917–1923*, vol 1 (Uzhhorod 1932; New York 1954)
Zozulia, Ia. *Velyka ukraïns'ka revoliutsiia* (New York 1967)

A. Zhukovsky

**Statute of Volodymyr Monomakh.** See Volodymyr Monomakh's Statute.

**Statutory deeds** (*ustavni hramoty*). Legal documents that indicated the relationship between peasants and landowners in the Russian Empire after the abolition of serfdom in 1861. Statutory deeds set out the obligations of the peasants and designated the amount of land allotted for their own use. The deeds were written up by the landlords, and their provisions were enforced by locally elected judicial representatives. The provisions often proved impossible to satisfy, and they were one of the main causes of the peasant rebellions throughout the empire during the 1860s, of which 660 took place in Ukraine.

**Stauropegion** (*stavropihiia*). Initially a Greek term referring to the placement of a cross by a bishop, symbolizing his approval of the construction of a church or monastery on the site. Later the term designated an autonomous Orthodox church body (church, monastery, brotherhood) that did not come under the jurisdiction of local hierarchs but was responsible directly to the patriarch (or the Holy Synod in the Russian Empire after 1721). The institution enjoyed special privileges, such as control over the local clergy and, in some cases, even over the local bishop.

In Ukraine stauropegion was conferred by the patriarchs of Constantinople (to 1686) and Moscow (to 1721) and then by the Holy Synod. It benefited many Orthodox *brotherhoods, which, during the religious struggles of the early 17th century, defended Orthodoxy and struggled against the corruption of local bishops and priests. The church hierarchy was generally opposed to the granting of stauropegion, and Archbishop M. Smotrytsky convinced the patriarch of Constantinople to issue a decree in 1626 canceling stauropegion status throughout Kiev metropoly. This decree, however, was later contradicted by new grants of stauropegion. In Ukraine institutions that were granted the right of stauropegion included the Kievan Cave Monastery and the Lviv Dormition Brotherhood (1586), the Kiev Epiphany Brotherhood and the Maniava Hermitage (1620), the Lutske Brotherhood of the Elevation of the Cross (1623), and the Mezhyhiria Transfiguration Monastery (1687). In the late 17th century stauropegion status lost its significance. The Lviv Dormition Brotherhood benefited from it longest, in that it remained Orthodox even after the conversion of the entire area to the Uniate church; the brotherhood finally accepted the union in 1709. It became the basis for the *Stauropegion Institute.

A. Zhukovsky

**Stauropegion Institute** (Stavropihiiskyi instytut u Lvovi). A cultural-educational institution in Lviv; it remained the only such institution in Galicia until the mid-1800s. It was founded in 1788 on the directive of Emperor Joseph II on the basis of the *Lviv Dormition Brotherhood. During the second half of the 19th century the institute was taken over by *Russophiles. It was under the control of Ukrainophile populists for a short time after 1915. In 1922 Polish control was established in Galicia, and the directorship of the institute was restored to the Russophiles, who were willing to support the Polish government.

The institute was well endowed, with parcels of land and buildings in Lviv. It had its own press, bindery, and bookstore. It was active in the fields of education, scholarship, and publishing. In 1788 the Stauropegion Institute reopened the *Lviv Dormition Brotherhood School and established a scholarship fund for elementary and secondary school students. In the early 19th century the institute published textbooks for elementary and secondary schools (including a spelling primer in 1807 and a Ukrainian grammar textbook) and for students of the *Studium Ruthenum.

The institute's museum and archives were a valuable resource for scholars. The museum was opened in 1889, through the efforts of A. *Petrushevych and I. *Shara-

nevych. Artifacts and documents dealing with the *Dormition Church in Lviv, the archives of the brotherhood, and monastic life in Galicia formed the basis of the museum's holdings. The most valuable of these were original manuscripts: the Krystynopil *Apostol* (see *Horodyshche *Apostol* [12th century]), the *Buchach (13th century) and Peremyshl (16th century) Gospels, the Nomocanon (15th century), P. Mohyla's *Knyha dushy, narytsaemaia zloto* (The Book of the Soul Named Gold), the *Lviv Chronicle, and *Perestoroha*. Other holdings of the museum included the archives of the Lviv Dormition Brotherhood; the original documents of Władysław Opolczyk (1375); grants, patents, and charters of Polish kings from the years 1522–1767; documents and letters of Moldavian princes concerning the Dormition Church in Lviv and the Lviv Dormition Brotherhood School and press from the years 1558–1694; charters of the patriarchs of Constantinople from the years 1586–1670; old printed books (of special note were church books from the 15th–17th centuries, and the grammar *Adelphotes*, published in 1591); and objects of religious art. The museum's holdings were described by I. Svientsitsky (1908) and I. Sharanevych (*Ruskie Muzeum Instytutu Stawropigijskiego we Lwowie*, 1937).

The institute gained control of the Lviv newspaper *Zoria halytska* in 1850 and continued to publish it until 1854, when it was once again taken over by Ukrainophiles. It published the valuable Ukrainian historical source *Vremennik Stavropigiskogo instituta* ... (1864–1915, 1923–39) and the *Zbirnyk Lvivskoï Stavropihiï* (1921). In the 19th century, publications of the Stauropegion Institute were written in *yazychiie; in the 20th century, in Russian.

The institute was administered by a council headed by a senior. I. Bachynsky (1801–16), I. Khomynsky (1861–6), V. Kovalsky (1871–84), and I. Sharanevych (1885–1901) were among those who headed the institute. The total membership of the Lviv Dormition Brotherhood and the Stauropegion Institute for the entire period of its existence was 726.

The institute did not survive the Soviet occupation of 1939–41. In 1940 the holdings of the institute's museum were transferred to the *Lviv Historical Museum, and its archives were taken over by the Central State Historical Archives of the Ukrainian SSR in Lviv.

**Stavka.** See *Ukraïns'ka stavka*.

**Stavnychy, Ivan** [Stavnyčyj] (pen name: Ivan Radyslavych), b 6 July 1891 in Tovste, Zalishchyky county,

Ivan Stavnychy

Galicia, d 2 October 1973 in Cleveland. Cultural and educational figure. In addition to translating G. Gama's textbook on folklore (1909), V. Hugo's *Quatrevingt-treize* (1913), and K. Hamsun's *Unter hoststjoernen* (1937) he worked as an editor and journalist. In 1909 he edited the weekly *Stanislavivs'ki visty*. During the period of Ukrainian independence he edited the semiweekly *Stanyslavivs'kyi holos* and the monthly *Prolom*. In the 1930s he edited *Fakhovyi vistnyk* (1933) and *Stanyslavivs'ki visti* (1937) and set up the Universalna Biblioteka publishers. Under the German occupation he was director of the Shevchenko Library in Stanyslaviv. Having fled to Germany in 1944, in 1950 he emigrated to the United States, where he was active in the Shevchenko Scientific Society and the Ridna Shkola society.

Roman Stavnychy

**Stavnychy, Roman** [Stavnyčyj], b May 1889 in Kuropatnyky, Berezhany county, Galicia, d 14 September 1959 in Buffalo. Choir conductor, teacher, and lawyer. He studied at Lviv University and at the Lysenko Higher Institute of Music, then became an Austrian army (then Ukrainian Galician Army) judge. In the 1920s he conducted the Boian choir in Kolomyia and taught at the local branch of the Lysenko Higher Institute of Music and in other schools. In 1944 he emigrated to Berchtesgaden, Germany, where he taught music theory and conducted the Boian choir (which was noted in Bavaria for its renditions of the religious music of D. Bortniansky and others). In 1949 he settled in Buffalo, where he continued to conduct and teach at the Ukrainian Music Institute of America.

**Stavnytsky, Semen** [Stavnyc'kyj], b ?, d 1697 in Lviv. Printer and writer. He directed the Lviv Dormition Brotherhood Press (1662–8, 1677–97) and Univ Press (1670–3, 1680), where he set and edited books and wrote introductions to them. He is also the author of a versified panegyric to Prince Volodymyr the Great, which is an adaptation of a poem by H. Smotrytsky from the Ostrih Bible. After Semen died his son Vasyl became director of the brotherhood press.

**Stavnytsky, Vasyl** [Stavnyc'kyj, Vasyl'], b ?, d 1730 in Lviv. Printer; son of S. Stavnytsky. He directed the press founded by Bishop Y. Shumliansky at St George's Cathedral in Lviv (1687–8). He then worked with his father at the Lviv Dormition Brotherhood Press and succeeded him as director in 1697.

**Stavropol.** VIII-23. A city (1989 pop 318,000) in the Stavropol Upland and the capital of Stavropol krai, RF. A fortress was built at the site in 1777 to defend the Russian Empire's southern borders. In 1822 it became the capital of Caucasia gubernia, and in 1847, of Stavropol gubernia. The main postal route linking Europe with Caucasia ran through Stavropol. According to the census of 1926, Ukrainians accounted for 10 percent of the city's population. The city was known as Voroshilovsk in 1935–43. Since then it has been the administrative, cultural, and economic center of Stavropol krai. The city is an industrial and transportation center. It has a large machine-building and chemical industry, a meat packing plant, a winery, a dairy, and leather and furniture factories. There are four higher educational institutions in Stavropol.

**Stavropol krai.** An administrative district in the RF that encompasses the central portion of the northern Caucusus region. The krai has an area of 80,600 sq km. It incorporates the historical *Stavropol region as well as the Karachai-Cherkess Autonomous Republic. Its population (1990) is 2,889,000, of whom 54 percent are urban dwellers. It has 34 raions, 22 cities and towns, 17 town smts, and almost 300 villages. Census figures show that Ukrainians formed approx 35 per cent of the Stavropol krai population in 1926 but only 2.3 per cent in 1979. A high degree of linguistic assimilation is indicated in the 1989 census, which shows that only 48.3 percent of the Ukrainians in the region claimed Ukrainian as their mother tongue.

**Stavropol region.** A historical-geographic region located in the central part of Subcaucasia, between the Kuban River (and region) to the west, the *Terek region to the southeast, the Don region to the north, the Kalmyk AR to the northeast, and the lands of the Caucasian mountain peoples to the south and southwest. The Stavropol region essentially corresponds in territory to the former Stavropol gubernia (within its 1861–1920 boundary, 59,500 sq km) and the present Stavropol krai, less the Karachai-Cherkess Autonomous Oblast (66,500 sq km). Until the 1930s the Stavropol region was settled by both Ukrainians and Russians, and constituted a part of contiguous, albeit mixed, Ukrainian ethnographic territory.

**Physical geography.** The major portion of the Stavropol region is occupied by the Stavropol Upland; the minor portion has parts of the Caspian Lowland in the east, the Kuma-Manych Depression in the north, and the foothills of the Caucasus Mountains in the southwest. The climate of the Stavropol region is transitional, from temperate continental in the west to drier and more continental in the east. The rivers in the region belong to the Sea of Azov and the Caspian Sea drainage basins. The larger ones include the Yegorlyk (which flows into the Manych), the Kalaus, the Kuma, and the Kuban and its upper tributaries, the Velykyi Zelenchuk and the Malyi Zelenchuk. River water is used for irrigation. Small, mostly saline lakes abound; the largest is the narrow but 160-km-long Lake Manych-Gudilo (Ukrainian: Manych-Hudylo).

The soils in the western and central part of the Stavropol region are various chernozems and chestnut soils; to the east and northeast they become light chestnut. The natural vegetation also changes eastward with declining humidity, from meadow fescue–feather grass steppe to dry fescue–feather grass steppe and then semidesert

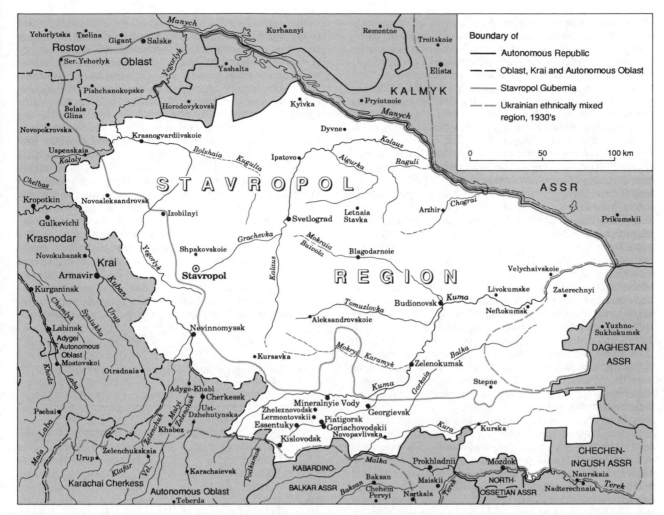

vegetation of wormwood, dry fescue, and feather grass. In the more humid part of the Stavropol Upland and in the Caucasus foothills the natural vegetation is forest-steppe with oak-hornbeam-beech forests. Today both the steppe and the forest-steppe are almost completely cleared for agriculture.

**History.** In the mid-16th century the Caucasus and the Stavropol region began to come into contact with Muscovite colonization. In the 16th and 17th centuries Subcaucasia experienced the beginnings of Cossack colonization (the Don Cossacks in the west and the Terek Cossacks in the east). Nevertheless the centrally located Stavropol region remained sparsely inhabited by the nomadic Nogay Tatars (a Turkic-speaking people) and Kalmyk people (a Mongol-speaking group), who together numbered about 80,000 Caucasian mountain peoples, the Karachai and the Cherkess, lived in the foothills of the region.

At the beginning of the 18th century the Stavropol region nominally became part of the Russian Empire. Permanent settlements, however, were not established until the last quarter of the century, when, in 1777–80, the Russian government built a line of forts, the Mozdok-Azov line, with headquarters at Stavropol, to contain the Caucasian mountain peoples. By 1785 the Stavropol region formed part of Caucasus oblast, which was redesignated a gubernia in 1802. Following several name changes it was

designated as Stavropol gubernia in 1847. Its boundaries were finally fixed in 1861, when it was separated from Terek oblast. In contrast to Kuban oblast and Terek oblast, Stavropol gubernia (since 1898) was not part of Caucasus krai.

The Russian government promoted the rapid colonization of the Stavropol region in order to establish a base for military campaigns in the Caucasus. Part of that aim was achieved by the granting of choice tracts of land to Russian noblemen, who settled them with their serfs. A more significant factor in colonization, however, was the spontaneous settlement by state peasants who were unimpeded by the central authorities. In fact the imperial government legalized extant claims with the ukase of 1804 and provided support to those who had settled in the Stavropol region. By the end of the 1850s the population of Stavropol gubernia had increased to 340,000 (5.5 persons per sq km). Its only city, Stavropol, grew from about 3,000 residents in 1800 to 17,600 residents in 1853. The most densely settled areas were the steppes between the Yegorlyk and the Kalaus rivers and the Kalaus River valley. The population of Stavropol gubernia (together with Terek oblast) in 1853 consisted of 48.7 percent Cossacks, 32 percent state peasants, 16.2 percent nomadic herders, and 3.1 percent serfs and others.

The region's population continued to grow after the abolition of serfdom in 1862 with the arrival of immigrants from Ukraine, particularly Left-Bank Ukraine and Katerynoslav gubernia. They were soon joined by settlers from the mixed Russian-Ukrainian gubernias of Voronezh and Kursk and then from the predominantly Russian Orel gubernia. By the beginning of the 20th century Ukrainians constituted 49.5 percent of all the immigrants to the Stavropol region, and Russians made up 36.6 percent. Stavropol gubernia's population had grown from 340,000 in 1867 to 873,000 by 1897 and to 1,150,000 by 1914. According to the 1897 census 9 percent of the population was urban. The ethnic composition was recorded as 55.3 percent Russian; Ukrainians constituted 36.6 percent of the total population and 39.9 percent of the rural population. The remaining 8.1 percent were mostly the pastoral Nogay, Kalmyk, and other Turkic peoples, who had been relegated to the dry eastern and northeastern steppes.

As the population grew, the area under the plow increased even faster, with the three-field system of cropping becoming a norm. The export of foodstuffs was facilitated by the construction of the railroads, notably the main line from Moscow through Rostov and Vladikavkaz to Baku (1875), a branch line from Kavkazskaia (renamed Kropotkin in 1921) to Stavropol (1897), and another from Pelagiada to Vinodelnoe (1916). Industry was poorly developed, and consisted almost exclusively of food processing.

During the civil war that followed the Revolution of 1917 the Stavropol region remained politically passive. Nevertheless, from the end of 1917 until the beginning of 1920, the region served as a battleground for Bolshevik and White forces. In January 1918 the Stavropol Soviet Republic was established as part of the RSFSR; from mid-1918 until the beginning of 1920 the Stavropol region was held by the Whites. The region finally was taken as a Soviet possession and became part of a large territorial-administrative region called North Caucasian krai. In 1924–30 the krai was subdivided into okrugs, and the former Stavropol gubernia became Stavropol okrug and parts of Terek, Armavir, and Salske okrugs. In 1937–43 the Stavropol region was the principal part of Ordzhonikidze krai, and in 1943 Stavropol krai was formed, to which the Karachai-Cherkess Autonomous Oblast was added as a subordinate part. After the Second World War the Stavropol region developed along much the same lines as other areas of the Soviet Union in general and the RSFSR in particular. A notable development was the rise to political prominence of one of the region's native sons, M. Gorbachev, who became the last leader of the USSR.

**Population.** After major population losses in 1917–20 and during the famine of 1922–3, the Stavropol region surpassed the prewar (1914) 1.15-million mark only in 1926 with a population of 1.2 million. The urban population, according to the 1926 census, remained at 8 percent; ethnic composition changed little, but there was a slight increase

in the proportion of Ukrainians and a decline in the share of the non-Slavic (other) population (see table 1). Among the other nationalities there were 21,000 Germans, 7,000 Armenians, and 3,000 Greeks. The distribution of Ukrainian settlement was uneven. Their lowest shares (5–10 percent) occurred in the southwestern part of the region along the line of former forts where the Don and Volga Cossacks and other Russian servitors were settled in the 18th century. Their largest presence, in the northeastern part, was established largely in the second half of the 19th century, when Ukrainian immigration was prevalent. The main basis for population growth in the early 20th century was natural increase, for immigration scarcely exceeded emigration. Among the immigrants, according to the 1926 census, the majority came from Ukrainian lands.

Demographic changes after 1926 in the Stavropol region indicated trends that were similar to though less pronounced than those in other Ukrainian regions: an average population growth until 1931 and in the period 1935–40 (reduced from high growth by the arrest of kulaks and by political purges), a decline during the manmade famine of 1932–3 and the hostilities of 1942–5, and revived growth after 1945. The share of urban population grew continuously (see table 2).

TABLE 2
Population changes in Stavropol krai (excluding the Karachai-Cherkess AO), 1926–90
(thousands; percentage in parentheses)

| Year | Total | Urban | Rural |
|------|-------|-------|-------|
| 1926 | 1,500 | 226 (15.2) | 1,274 |
| 1939 | 1,513 | 312 (20.6) | 1,201 |
| 1959 | 1,605 | 522 (32.5) | 1,083 |
| 1970 | 1,961 | 867 (44.1) | 1,094 |
| 1979 | 2,171 | 1,105 (50.9) | 1,066 |
| 1990 | 2,467 | 1,348 (54.6) | 1,119 |

Recent population growth has continued to be driven primarily by natural increase. The net migration in 1968–9 (as the 1970 census revealed) was only 14,900, or 0.76 percent of the total population. The largest number of immigrants came from other parts of North Caucasia, followed by the Volga and the Ural regions (all ethnically mixed territories).

The villages of the Stavropol region are large and populous and are located in river valleys. The greatest concentration of cities is in the region of the Caucasian mineral waters, including (1987 populations) Piatigorsk (121,000), Kislovodsk (110,00), Essentuky (84,000), Mineralnye Vody (75,000), and Georgievsk (62,000). Other, more dispersed, cities include Stavropol (306,000), Nevinnomyssk (116,000), and Budënnovsk (formerly Prikumsk, 54,000).

TABLE 1
Ethnic composition of the population in the Stavropol region, 1897–1989
(thousands; percentage in parentheses)

| Nationality | 1897 | | 1926 | | 1970 | | 1989 | |
|-------------|------|------|------|------|------|------|------|------|
| Russians | 482 | (55.2) | 700 | (56.9) | 1,760 | (90.0) | 2,024 | (84.0) |
| Ukrainians | 320 | (36.7) | 460 | (37.4) | 49 | (2.5) | 69 | (2.9) |
| Others | 71 | (8.1) | 70 | (5.7) | 152 | (7.5) | 317 | (13.1) |
| Total | 873 | (100.0) | 1,230 | (100.0) | 1,961 | (100.0) | 2,410 | (100.0) |

The current ethnic composition of the Stavropol region cannot be determined with certainty. Post–Second World War Soviet censuses claim that the Ukrainians have virtually disappeared. Statistics were manipulated to convey the impression that the contiguous Ukrainian ethnic territory did not extend beyond the borders of the Ukrainian SSR. According to the 1989 census, of the 69,200 Ukrainians in Stavropol krai, 33,400 (48.3 percent) reported Ukrainian as their mother tongue, 9,500 (13.7 percent) indicated their ability to speak it, and the remaining 26,200 (37.9 percent) did not know it.

**Economy.** Until the 1930s Stavropol was an agrarian region notable particularly for wheat and wool; now it has a mixed agricultural-industrial profile. Since 1914, industrial output has increased twentyfold; from 1940 to 1974 it increased twelvefold.

In the early 1950s about one-half of the land was cultivated, but during that decade more virgin steppe was broken. By 1974 plowland accounted for 63 percent of the total land area. Other land uses included pastures (22 percent), hayfields (3 percent), forests and scrublands (2 percent), orchards and vineyards (2 percent), and non-agricultural uses (10 percent). In most areas plowland accounted for 60–80 percent of total land uses. The mean annual harvest of all grains during the 1970–4 five-year period was 4.3 million t, of which 3 million t was wheat. Sunflower, occupying 70 percent of the sown area of all industrial crops, averaged an annual harvest of 206,000 t in the 1970–4 period. Orchards occupied 61,400 ha, mainly in the region's western and southwestern part; vineyards covered 17,500 ha, mostly in the Kuma valley.

The livestock sector provided 58 percent of agricultural production in 1974. The animals (in Stavropol krai outside the Karachai-Cherkess Autonomous Oblast) included 1.1 million cattle (40 percent of all standard animal units), 5.8 million sheep and goats (48 percent), 0.9 million pigs (6 percent), and nearly 10 million fowl (6 percent). Sheep raising was very important; it accounted for 11 percent of all the fine-fleeced merinos in the USSR.

Irrigation has gained great importance in Stavropol agriculture. The area irrigated increased from 44,000 ha in 1950 to 65,000 ha in 1960, 167,000 ha in 1970, and 234,000 ha in 1975. There were 1.5 million ha of water-supplied pastures.

Of the industries, food processing is the most important branch (contributing 29.3 percent of the industrial output in 1974); it is followed by light industry (21.8 percent). Since the 1950s the development of machine building and metalworking (17 percent) and the chemical branch (13.4 percent) as well as the fuel- and power-generating industries (about 3 percent in 1974) has diversified the industrial profile. In 1974 Stavropol krai produced 9,385 million kwh of electricity (compared to 58 million kwh in 1940), mostly at thermoelectric power stations at Nevinnomyssk and Stavropol as well as small hydroelectric power stations elsewhere.

Gas and oil extracting began in the region during the 1950s. By 1974 gas production had reached 13 billion cu m, or 5 percent of the USSR output (mostly in the northern part of Stavropol krai), and crude oil production had attained 7 million t, or 1.5 percent of the USSR output (in the east, along the Kuma river). At first the Stavropol gas was piped through Rostov-na-Donu to Ukraine, Moscow, and even Leningrad. Now, with its declining reserves, it has been overshadowed by gas from Orenburg and Western Siberia. Crude oil is transported by pipe from Zaterechnyi to refineries at Groznyi.

The food-processing industry is spread throughout the region, with major branches consisting of meat processing (Stavropol, Piatigorsk, Kislovodsk, and other cities), milling (Stavropol, Nevinnomyssk, Georgievsk, and elsewhere), canning (Georgievsk, Essentuky, Izobilnyi), oils (Nevinnomyssk and Georgievsk), and wine making.

Light industry is represented by the textile factory in Nevinnomyssk and garment making in Stavropol, Kislovodsk, Piatigorsk, and Essentuky. Reinforced-concrete products are made in Stavropol, Piatigorsk, and Mineralnye Vody, and wall construction materials and sound-proofing in Stavropol. Woodworking and furniture making are of small, local significance. Resorts based on the Caucasian mineral waters at Kislovodsk, Piatigorsk, Essentuky, Zheleznovodsk, and Mineralnye Vody had USSR-wide significance.

The Stavropol region is not generously supplied with railway lines (846 km, just short of 1 km/100 sq km). A major electrified trunk line from Rostov-na-Donu traverses the southwestern part of the region toward Baku. It links the Stavropol region with the Kuban and Ukraine to the west and northwest.

BIBLIOGRAPHY
Fadeev, A. *Ocherki ekonomicheskogo razvitiia stepnogo Peredkavkaz'ia v doreformennyi period* (Moscow 1957)
*Stavropolskii krai: Spravochnik* (Stavropol 1961)
Gnilovskii, V.; Babenysheva, G. *Geografiia Stavropolskogo kraia* (Stavropol 1972)
*Don i stepnoe Predkavkaz'e: XVIII–pervaia polovina XIX v.*, 2 vols (Rostov-na-Donu 1977)

V. Kubijovyč, I. Stebelsky

**Stavropol Upland.** A geographical formation in the central part of Subcaucasia between the Kuban Lowland in the west, the Caspian Lowland in the east, the Kuma-Manych Depression in the north, and the Caucasus Mountains in the south. The upland has prevailing elevations of 300–600 m and a maximum elevation of 831 m (Mt Stryzhament). It is composed largely of limestones, clays, and sandstones and is dissected by numerous river valleys into table mountains. The lower steppe regions in the area are under cultivation; forest-steppe and broad-leaved forest can be found in the upland's higher elevations. Water for the area is supplied by the Kuban-Yegorlyk system as well as the Great Stavropol Canal.

**Stavrovetsky-Tranquillon, Kyrylo** [Stavrovec'kyj-Trankvylijon], b ?, d 1646 in Chernihiv. Churchman, educator, poet, scholar, and printer. He taught at the Lviv Dormition Brotherhood School in the late 1580s and moved to Ostrih and Vilnius in 1592. At the beginning of the 17th century he returned to Lviv, where he resumed his activities with the brotherhood and defended it before Patriarch Jeremiah II of Constantinople. He served briefly as hegumen of the Univ Monastery (1618) and then at the Lubartów Monastery near Lublin (1618–9) before becoming a preacher in Zamość (1621–5). Stavrovetsky established his first printing press in 1618, to publish his *Zertsalo bohosloviia* (Mirror of Theology), an exposition of the theological doctrine concerning God, and his *didactic gospels (1619), which contained a collection of his sermons. Both of those works were republished several times (in Univ, Pochaiv, and Mohyliv) and circulated widely throughout Ukraine and Muscovy; his edition of the didactic gospels, however, was condemned in the early 1620s by a congress of Ukrainian Orthodox bishops headed by Metropolitan Y. Boretsky, and in 1627 Moscow church authorities ordered that it be burned. In 1626 Stavrovetsky joined the Uniate church and was appointed archimandrite of the Yeletskyi Dormition Monastery in Chernihiv. Just prior to his death there, he printed another collection of sermons and moralistic poems, *Perlo mnohotsinnoie* (The Priceless Pearl, 1646).

**Stavrovsky, Yulii** [Stavrovs'kyj, Julij] (pseud: Popradov), b 18 January 1850 in Sulyn, Szepes county, d 27 March 1899 in Chertizhne, Ung county, Prešov region. Russophile writer and cleric. In 1875, while studying at the Budapest Theological Seminary, he was ordained a Greek Catholic priest. He worked at the episcopal chancellery in Prešov and served as a pastor in Yarabina and, from 1879, Chertizhne. He published, in Russian, many lyrical and patriotic poems, and articles on ethnography, language, history, and civic affairs in the periodicals *Svit, Novyi svit, Karpat,* and *Listok.* He also contributed to Hungarian periodicals and prepared a primer. An edition of Stavrovsky's poems, written under his pseudonym, appeared in 1928.

**Stavyshche** [Stavyšče]. IV-11. A town smt (1986 pop 7,500) on the Hnylyi Tikych River and a raion center in Kiev oblast. It was first mentioned in historical documents in 1622, when it was under Polish rule. In 1635 it was granted the rights of *Magdeburg law. The town joined the Khmelnytsky uprising and became a company center of Bila Tserkva regiment. In 1655 B. Khmelnytsky engaged the Tatars in battle at Stavyshche. A decade later the town was the center of the Varenytsia Uprising. Its inhabitants did not accept the town's return to Polish rule (1667) and rebelled repeatedly in the course of the next century (1702–4, 1730s, 1750s). With the partition of Poland in 1793, Stavyshche was annexed by Russia, and became part of Tarashcha county in Kiev gubernia. In the 19th century it acquired a distillery, flour mill, and brick factory. By 1900 its population had reached 8,500. Today the town has an electric-instruments plant, a construction company, and a food industry.

**Stavysky, Iziaslav** [Stavys'kyj, Izjaslav], b 23 May 1927 in Zinovivske (now Kirovohrad). Film director. He completed study at the Kiev Pedagogical Institute (1953) and the State Institute of Cinema in Moscow (1959) and has worked in the Kiev Studio of Popular Science Films. Among his films are *Dumy pro khlib* (Thoughts about Bread, 1972) and *Piznavaty abetku roslyn* (Identifying the Alphabet of Plants, 1981).

**Steam-locomotive building.** See Locomotive industry.

**Steamship transportation.** See River transportation and Sea transportation.

**Stebelsky, Bohdan** [Stebel's'kyj] (pseuds: Vasyl Tkachenko, Ostap Khmurovych), b 15 March 1911 in Tomashivtsi, Kalush county, Galicia. Artist and community leader; full member of the Shevchenko Scientific Society

Bohdan Stebelsky (plaster portrait by Mykhailo Chereshnovsky, 1975)

(NTSh). Stebelsky studied at the Cracow Academy of Arts (1934–9), the Ukrainian Free University in Munich (PH D, 1959), and the University of Ottawa (MA, 1964). Prior to the Second World War he was director of the commercial art school in Yavoriv. After emigrating to Canada in 1949, he edited the literary-art page of the newspaper *Homin Ukraïny* (Toronto). He has had art exhibitions in Germany, the United States, and Canada, has headed the Ukrainian Canadian Artists' Association (1958–72), the Association of Ukrainian Cultural Workers (ADUK), and the Canadian section of the NTSh (since 1974), and has served on the national executive of the *Canadian League for Ukraine's Liberation (LVU). His works include *Pro iliustratsiiu dytiachoï knyzhky* (About the Illustration of Children's Books, 1966) and essays and articles on literary and art themes.

**Stebelsky, Hnat** [Stebel's'kyj, Hnat], b 1748? in Volhynia, d 1805. Basilian monk and church historian. He was the author of the life of SS Evfrosiniia and Paraskeviia and of a history of the Basilian monastery in Polatsk in which they lived, *Chronologia* (Chronology). These works provide much valuable information concerning the history of the Uniate church in Ukraine and Belarus. In addition Stebelsky prepared a third work, *Przydatek do Chronologii* (An Addendum to the Chronology), which contains a wealth of information about Catholic and Orthodox church hierarchs and notable Basilians. The first two manuscripts were not published until the 1870s; the addendum was published in 1781–3 and republished in 1866–7. An expanded and edited version of the *Chronologia* (to which the author continually added information) was published in 1878 as *Ostatnie prace Stebelskiego* (Stebelsky's Final Works).

**Stebelsky, Ihor** [Stebel's'kyj], b 6 September 1939 in Cracow, Poland. Geographer; member of the Shevchenko Scientific Society; son of B. *Stebelsky. Since graduating from the universities of Toronto and Washington (PH D, 1967), he has taught at the University of Windsor (head of the geography department since 1982). He is a coauthor of *Eurasia: Its Lands and Peoples* (1981) and the author of book chapters, articles, and encyclopedia entries on the economic, human, and physical geography of Ukraine and

Ihor Stebelsky                Oleksander Steblianko

the USSR. Since 1985 he has been the geography subject editor of the *Encyclopedia of Ukraine*.

**Stebelsky, Petro** [Stebel's'kyj], b 15 July 1857 in Nemyriv, Rava Ruska county, Galicia, d 24 September 1923 in Lviv. Jurist and legal historian; brother of V. Stebelsky. A graduate of Lviv University, from 1892 he lectured there on Austrian criminal and procedural law. His lectures and some of his publications were in Ukrainian. He supervised the translation of Austrian criminal law into Ukrainian and contributed to the development of Ukrainian legal terminology. Some of his articles appeared in *Chasopys' pravnycha*. O. Ohonovsky's work on the system of Austrian private law (1897) was edited and published by Stebelsky.

**Stebelsky, Stepan** [Stebel's'kyj] (nom de guerre: Khrin), b 18 October 1914 in Holyn, Kalush county, Galicia, d 9 November 1949 near Pohořelice, Czechoslovakia. UPA officer. A noncommissioned officer of the Polish army, in 1934 he joined the OUN, and in 1939 he was imprisoned for his activities by the Poles in Bereza Kartuzka. In September 1945 he organized a new combat unit, the Udarnyky 5 (95a) Company, in the Lemko region, and for two years he staged daring raids and other anti-Polish actions. On 28 March 1947 his company ambushed and killed the Polish deputy defense minister, Gen K. Świerczewski. Stebelsky received the Gold Cross of Combat Merit First Class for heroism and leadership in combat. From August 1947 to August 1949 he was commander of the Drohobych Tactical Sector (Makivka 24). After being put in charge of a special courier group in September 1949, he was killed en route to the west. He wrote *Zymoiu v bunkri* (Winter in a Bunker, 1950), *Kriz' smikh zaliza* (Through the Laughter of Iron, 1952), and other, unpublished, memoirs.

**Stebelsky, Volodymyr** [Stebel's'kyj] (pseuds: Volodko St, Ivan Iskra, Ruslan, Slavych, Bohdan iz Podolia), b 31 August 1848 in Mageriv, Zhovkva circle, Galicia, d 22 December 1891 in Warsaw. Writer and publicist. The son of a Ukrainian father and a Polish mother, he became a Ukrainophile populist while at the Sambir gymnasium (1863–5) and contributed publicistic articles and poems, in the style of T. Shevchenko, to *Meta* and *Nyva*. At Lviv University (1866–71), however, he was a leading Russophile. From 1870 to 1875 he contributed articles, poems (eg, the Byronic 'Morton'), and prose to *Boian, Slovo, Druh*, and *Strakhopud*. Published separately were the story *Monakh* (The Monk, 1870) and the more successful autobiographical poem *Molytva* (A Prayer, 1873). In the mid-1870s he abandoned the Russophile camp and thenceforth wrote mostly in Polish. His articles and humorous and satirical poems appeared in Polish periodicals in Lviv, St Petersburg, and Warsaw. In 1882 and 1883 he wrote a few Polonophile poems and stories in Ukrainian under the pseudonym Bohdan iz Podolia. From 1887 on he lived in Warsaw. After years of dissipation this 'first decadent in Galicia' committed suicide.

**Steblianko, Oleksander** [Stebljanko], b 24 May 1896 in Lebedyn, Sumy oblast, d 8 October 1977 in Kharkiv. Composer, pedagogue, and folklorist. A graduate in composition from the Kharkiv Institute of Music and Drama (1926) in the class of S. Bohatyrov, he taught at labor schools and the music tekhnikum (1920–30) before becoming the curator of the ethnomusicological department at the Kharkiv Conservatory (1936). In 1947 he was a member of the committee that composed the Soviet Ukrainian national anthem. His works include chamber pieces, incidental music, choruses, romances, and arrangements of folk songs. He collected over 2,000 Ukrainian folk songs, wrote *Ladova struktura i khromatyzm ukraïns'koï narodnoï pisni* (Modal Structure and Chromaticism of the Ukrainian Folk Song, 1946) and *Vykonannia narodnykh pisen' i ansambli narodnykh khoriv* (The Performance of Folk Songs and Ensembles of Folk Choruses, 1952), and edited *Ukraïns'ki narodni pisni* (Ukrainian Folk Songs, 1965).

**Steblin-Kamensky, Rostislav** [Kamenskij], b 16 July 1857 in Orel, Russia, d 29 July or 8 August 1894 in Irkutsk, Siberia. Russian revolutionary populist. In 1874 he was one of the organizers of Uniia, a clandestine populist circle in Poltava, to which Ukrainian figures such as D. Lyzohub, P. Myrny, and D. Pylchykov belonged. Uniia was uncovered in 1875, and most of its 70 members were imprisoned and exiled to Siberia. From 1877 Steblin studied at the Kharkiv Veterinary Institute while doing revolutionary work in Kharkiv and among the peasants of Zolotonosha county, Poltava gubernia. He was arrested in Kiev in February 1879 and sentenced to 10 years of hard labor in Siberia, where he committed suicide.

**Steblin-Kaminsky, Stepan** [Steblin-Kamins'kyj], b 8 May 1814 in Poltava, d 29 December 1885 in Poltava. Writer and gymnasium teacher in Poltava and Zolotonosha. He published the first biography of I. Kotliarevsky (*Severnaia pchela*, 1839, no. 146) and memoirs (Poltava 1869; 3rd edn 1883) and articles about Kotliarevsky in *Poltavskiia gubernskiia vedomosti*. He also wrote historical and ethnographic articles and religious poetry.

**Stebliv.** IV-12. A town smt (1986 pop 5,000) on the Ros River in Korsun-Shevchenkivskyi raion, Cherkasy oblast. In 1036 Yaroslav the Wise built a fortress at the site. Two centuries later it was destroyed by the Mongols. In the 16th century the town came under Polish rule and received the rights of Magdeburg law. In 1648 it took part in B. Khmelnytsky's uprising and became a company center in Korsun regiment. In 1664 it was destroyed by the Poles, and in 1667 transferred to them. At the partition of Poland in 1793, it was annexed by Russia, and became part of Kiev gubernia. In 1960 it was given smt status. Today Stebliv has a cotton and paper factory and a hydroelectric station. It is the birthplace of I. *Nechui-Levytsky and has a museum dedicated to him.

**Stebnyk.** IV-4. A city (1989 pop 21,400) under the jurisdiction of the Drohobych city council in Lviv oblast. It was first mentioned, as Izdebnyk, in a historical document in 1440, when it was granted the rights of *Magdeburg law. Since 1521 it has been known as Stebnyk. After the partition of Poland in 1772, it was annexed by Austria. In the interwar period (1919–39) the city was under Polish rule. Standing on one of the largest reserves of potassium salts in Ukraine, Stebnyk is known for its chemical industry. On 15 September 1983 one of the greatest chemical disasters in the USSR occurred at Stebnyk: the dam of the waste reservoir of the Potassium Fertilizer Manufacturing Complex collapsed, polluting large tracts of land and the Dniester, the Tysmenytsia, and the Bystrytsia rivers with brine.

A potassium salts refinery in Stebnyk in the early 20th century

**Stebnyk potassium salts deposit.** One of the largest potassium salts deposits in Ukraine, located near Stebnyk, Lviv oblast, in the *Drohobych-Boryslav Industrial Region. The deposit covers a territory of 30 sq km and has estimated recoverable reserves of 230 million t (1982). The salts lie in seams at depths of 90–1,000 m. The deposit was discovered in 1854, and began to be mined in 1922. The salts are processed for use in the soda industry and the making of *mineral fertilizers at the Stebnyk Potassium Complex, which has an annual capacity of 500,000 t of potassium-magnesium concentrate. In 1983 an accidental spill of the plant's chemical wastes caused extensive environmental damage.

**Stebnytsky, Petro** [Stebnyc'kyj] (pseuds: P. Smutok, A. Irpensky, Malorossiianin, Maloross, P. Khmara, P.S., S-ii), b 25 November 1862 in Horenychi, Kiev county, Kiev gubernia, d 14 March 1923 in Kiev. Community and political activist, writer, journalist, editor, and publicist. He graduated with a degree in mathematics and physics from Kiev University in 1886 and then moved to St Petersburg to work in various government positions, mainly with the finance ministry (1889–1904) and the Trade and Telegraph

Petro Stebnytsky

Agency (1904–17). He also wrote articles on economics for *Vestnik finansov, Torgovo-promyshlennaia gazeta*, and *Russkoe ekonomicheskoe obozrenie*. Even though he had previously been largely indifferent to Ukrainian affairs, Stebnytsky emerged as one of the leading figures of the Ukrainian community in St Petersburg. He helped organize the Society of Ukrainian Progressives and served as secretary and head of the *Philanthropic Society for Publishing Generally Useful and Inexpensive Books. He assisted with the publication of the periodicals *Ukrainskii vestnik* (1907) and *Ridna sprava-Dums'ki visti*, the first full *Kobzar* (1907), the Ukrainian encyclopedia *Ukrainskii narod v ego proshlom i nastoiashchem* (The Ukrainian People: Its Past and Present, 2 vols, 1914, 1916), the monographs *Ukrainskii vopros* (The Ukrainian Question, 1914) and *Galichina, Bukovina i Ugorskaia Rus'* (Galicia, Bukovyna, and Hungarian Rus', 1915), and (at his own expense) two volumes of O. Oles's poetry. In 1906 he began contributing to *Kievskaia starina, Hromads'ka dumka, Rada, Literaturno-naukovyi vistnyk, Ukrainskaia zhizn'*, and other periodicals.

After the February Revolution of 1917 he became head of the *Ukrainian National Council in Petrograd, a member of the Central Committee of the Ukrainian Party of Socialists-Federalists, and state secretary for Ukrainian affairs in the Russian Provisional Government from July to November 1917. In the spring of 1918 he moved to Kiev, where he joined a political commission in the Hetman government and later served as deputy leader of the Ukrainian delegation during negotiations with Soviet Russia (August 1918), senator in the administrative division of the State Senate, and minister of education in the cabinet of F. Lyzohub (19 October to 14 November 1918) as a representative of the Ukrainian National Union. While in Kiev in 1918–20, he contributed to *Nova rada, Literaturno-naukovyi vistnyk, Knyhar*, and *Nashe mynule*. He also headed the revived Kiev Prosvita society, served as the chief editor of the Chas publishing house, and sat on the Committee of the National Library of Ukraine (whose Ucrainica section he headed). In 1919 he became director of a commission for the compilation of a biographical dictionary of prominent figures in Ukraine and a member of a commission for preparing a Ukrainian encyclopedic dictionary at the All-Ukrainian Academy of Sciences.

In addition to his articles on culture and politics, Stebnytsky published *Pid steliamy Dumy* (Under the Ceilings of the Duma, 1907), *Ukraina i ukraintsy* (Ukraine and Ukrainians, 1917), *Ukraïns'ka sprava* (The Ukrainian Question, 1917), *Pomizh dvokh revoliutsii* (Between the Two Revolutions, 1918), and *Borys Hrinchenko* (1920). A commemorative volume about him was published in Kiev in 1926.

A. Zhukovsky

**Stebun, Illia** (pseud of I. Katsnelson), b 21 January 1911 in Horodnia, Chernihiv gubernia. Literary scholar, critic, and pedagogue. He graduated from the Chernihiv Institute of People's Education in 1930. From 1938 to 1941 he was managing editor of *Literaturna krytyka* and *Radians'ka literatura*. Until the Second World War he was considered one of the leading critics in Soviet Ukraine. In the initial stages of J. Stalin's anti-Jewish campaign against 'rootless cosmopolitans,' he was banished from Kiev. From 1959 to 1965 he worked at the Zaporizhia and Zhytomyr pedagogical institutes, and in 1966 he became a professor at Donetske University. He wrote, among other works, studies of I. Kotliarevsky, M. Shashkevych, T. Shevchenko, M. Kotsiubynsky, I. Franko, and Lesia Ukrainka. Some of his more notable works are *Mykhailo Kotsiubyns'kyi* (1938), *Pytannia realizmu v estetytsi I. Franka* (The Question of Realism in the Esthetics of I. Franko, 1958), *Mystetstvo, humanizm, suchasnist'* (Art, Humanism, Contemporaneity, 1965), *Dzherela khudozhn'oï istyny* (Sources of Artistic Truth, 1970), and *Shevchenko pro mystetstvo* (Shevchenko on Art, 1971, 1984).

Julian Stechishin    Michael Stechishin

**Stechishin, Julian** [Stečyšyn, Julijan], b 30 June 1895 in Hleshchava, Terebovlia county, Galicia, d 24 February 1971 in Saskatoon. Community leader; brother of Michael and Myroslav *Stechishin and husband of S. *Stechishin. Stechishin emigrated to Canada in 1910 and graduated from the Ruthenian Training School in Brandon, Manitoba, in 1915 and the University of Saskatchewan (BA, 1926). While rector of the *Mohyla Ukrainian Institute in Saskatoon (1921–9, 1931–3) he earned a law degree from the same university (1931). Stechishin was prominent in the formation of the *Ukrainian Self Reliance League (SUS) and served as its head (1940–2, 1952–8). He was also a member of the consistory of the Ukrainian Greek Orthodox Church of Canada (1951–74). He edited *Iuveleina knyha ukraïns'koho instytutu im. P. Mohyly v Saskatuni, 1916–1941* (Twenty-Five Years of the P. Mohyla Institute in Saskatoon, 1916–41, 1945) and was the author of *Ukrainian Grammar* (1951) and *Istoriia poselennia ukraïntsiv u Kanadi*

(History of Ukrainian Settlement in Canada, 1975). His biography was published by Rev H. Udod in 1978 as *Julian W. Stechishin: His Life and Work*.

**Stechishin, Michael** [Stečyšyn, Myxajlo], b 1 March 1888 in Hleshchava, Terebovlia county, Galicia, d 16 February 1964 in Saskatoon. Judge and community leader; brother of Myroslav and J. *Stechishin. He emigrated to Canada in 1905 and completed a teacher-training course (1910) and a law degree at the University of Saskatchewan (1920). In 1947 he was appointed a district court judge in Saskatchewan. Along with his brothers, Stechishin was prominent in the formation of the Mohyla Ukrainian Institute in Saskatoon, the Ukrainian Greek Orthodox Church of Canada, and the Ukrainian Self-Reliance League (SUS). He was coauthor of the Ruthenian-English primer used in the public schools of Manitoba in 1913–14 and the author of several children's books and books on religious themes.

Myroslaw Stechishin    Savella Stechishin

**Stechishin, Myroslaw** [Stečyšyn, Myroslav], b 24 July 1883 in Hleshchava, Terebovlia county, Galicia, d 18 November 1947 in Winnipeg. Editor and community leader; brother of Michael and J. *Stechishin. He emigrated to Canada in 1902 and then moved to Rev A. *Honcharenko's commune in California until 1905. Heavily influenced by Galician radicalism, he organized the Borotba society in Vancouver (1907) and became a leading figure (together with P. Krat) in the Ukrainian socialist movement in Canada. He served on the executive of the Socialist Party of Canada and was editor of *Robochyi narod* (Winnipeg, 1909–12) before breaking with the movement in 1912. He moved on to edit *Novyny* (Edmonton) and *Narodna volia* (Scranton, Pennsylvania) before serving as secretary to the diplomatic mission of the Ukrainian National Republic in Washington, DC, in 1920. In 1921 he became editor of *Ukraïns'kyi holos* in Winnipeg. He used his position (to 1946) to develop and refine the ideology of the *Ukrainian Self-Reliance League (SUS), which he had helped to establish in 1927. Stechishin was also a longtime member of the consistory of the Ukrainian Greek Orthodox Church of Canada.

**Stechishin, Savella** [Stečyšyn, Savelja] (née Vavryniuk), b 19 August 1903 in Tudorkovychi, Sokal county, Galicia. Pedagogue and community leader; wife of J.

*Stechishin. After being educated at the normal school in Saskatoon (1924) and the University of Saskatchewan (1930), Stechishin became a school teacher and taught Ukrainian classes at the University of Saskatchewan and the *Mohyla Ukrainian Institute in Saskatoon. A driving force behind the establishment of a Ukrainian women's movement in Canada, she was a founding member and the first president (1926–36) of the *Ukrainian Women's Association of Canada (SUK). She was also instrumental in promoting the presentation of Ukrainian folk art traditions in Canada and in the establishment of the *Ukrainian Museum of Canada in 1936. For many years she edited the women's page of *Ukraïns'kyi holos*. She is the author of *Traditional Ukrainian Cookery* (1957; 11th edn 1980). She received the Order of Canada in 1989.

**Stechynska, Eleonora** [Stečyns'ka] (née Blomberg), b 18 August 1852 in Cluj, Rumania, d 13 November 1924 in Lviv. Stage actress; wife of A. Stechynsky and grandmother of S. and Ya. Stadnyk. She worked in the Ruska Besida Theater in Lviv (with interruptions, 1879–1913), in Y. Stadnyk's troupe (1913–14), and in Yu. Kasinenko's and I. Moroz's troupes in Ukraine and Moscow (1896–7).

**Stechynsky, Andrii** [Stečyns'kyj, Andrij] (real surname: Muzhyk), b 16 December 1849 in Khreniv, Kaminka-Strumylova county, Galicia, d 5 April 1896 in Zolochiv, Galicia. Actor, stage director, and playwright. His theatrical career began in the Ruska Besida Theater (1867–96, with interruptions). Then he toured with O. Bachynsky's and A. Molentsky's troupes in eastern Ukraine (1868–9) and worked in T. Romanovych's troupe (1881–3). In 1893 he became a director in the Ruska Besida Theater, and in 1894–5 he was its administrative director. He is the author of the dramas *Mishchanka* (The Bourgeoise) and *Psotnytsia* (The Mischief Maker) and wrote librettos to I. Vorobkevych's operettas *Sadahurs'kyi diak* (The Precentor from Sadhora), *Vesillia na obzhynkakh* (A Wedding at Harvest), and *Dovbush*, an adaptation of V. Lozynsky's story *Chornyi Matvii* (Black Matthew). He also translated some vaudeville acts and N. Gogol's plays.

Col Mykola Stechyshyn

**Stechyshyn, Mykola** [Stečyšyn], b 19 December 1890 in Novosiiatske, Kherson region, d 7 August 1977 in Munich. Army officer and military writer. As an officer of the 105th Infantry Division of the Russian army, in 1917 he was active in its Ukrainianization. During 1918–20 he served in various staff positions of the UNR Army, including chief of staff of the Northern Group (1919), the Mohyliv Insurgent Group, and the Third Iron Rifle Division. During the interwar period he was active in émigré Ukrainian veterans' organizations, particularly in the Union of Ukrainian Veterans and the Union of Ukrainian War Invalids. His articles on military history appeared in *Tryzub*, *Za derzhavnist'*, and *Ukraïns'kyi invalid*. He also contributed entries to *Entsyklopediia ukraïnoznavstva* (Encyclopedia of Ukraine, 1955–88).

**Stechyshyn.** See Stechishin.

Ihor Stecura, architect: the Ukrainian Catholic Church of the Nativity of the Mother of God in Niagara Falls, Ontario

**Stecura, Ihor,** b 8 April 1932 in Lviv. Architect. A postwar émigré in Canada since 1948, he graduated from the University of Toronto (B ARCH) in 1963 and founded his own architectural firm in 1973. A specialist in Ukrainian wooden church architecture, he designed the wooden chapels at the Plast camp near Grafton, Ontario (1963); the Ukrainian Youth Association camp near Acton, Ontario (1973); and the Ukrainian Catholic wooden churches of St Volodymyr in the Ukrainian Park in Pike Lake, Saskatchewan (1982), of SS Volodymyr and Olha in Cawaja Beach, Ontario (1989), and of the Nativity of the Mother of God in Niagara Falls, Ontario (1988). For his designs of the churches in Pike Lake and Niagara Falls he was awarded first prize (1984) and the merit award (1988), respectively, by the Wood Council of Canada.

**Steel.** See Metallurgical industry.

**Stefan,** b ? in Medyka, near Peremyshl, d between 1678 and 1695. Painter. He lived and worked in Drohobych, where he supervised the painting of St George's Church (1651–78). He painted some icons of its iconostasis, such as *Akathyst of the Theotokos* (1659), *St George* (1662), and *Christ* (1663), and some of the murals in the nave. He also painted the icon of St John the Baptist (1669) for the Church of the Exaltation in Drohobych.

**Stefan of Kiev,** b 1040, d 7 April 1094. Churchman. A follower of St Theodosius of the Caves, he is mentioned in an early Kievan chronicle (ca 1047) as one of the first church singers in Rus'. He later became hegumen of the Kievan Cave Monastery and a bishop in Volodymyr-Volynskyi. The Ukrainian Orthodox church considers him a saint; his feast day falls on 10 May (27 April OS).

**Stefanchuk, Yurii** [Stefančuk, Jurij], b 17 January 1908 in Bila Tserkva, Vasylkiv county, Kiev gubernia. Scenery designer. He completed study at the Kiev State Art Institute (1931, pupil of V. Kasiian, F. Krasytsky, and F. Krychevsky) and then worked in the Donbas Ukrainian Theater of Musical Comedy (1931–4) and the Zaporizhia (later Lviv) Ukrainian Drama Theater (from 1934), where he created scenery for over 120 productions. He also designed scenery for productions of the Lviv Young Spectator's Theater, including M. Kropyvnytsky's *Poshylys' v durni* (They Made Fools of Themselves).

**Stefanis, Frants,** b 3 December 1865 in Odessa, Kherson gubernia, d 26 February 1917 in Kiev. Anatomist. A graduate of Kiev University (1893), he worked there (as professor from 1903) and organized an instructional museum in the anatomy department. His publications dealt with the lymphatic vessels of the abdominal organs, which he classified using a method of his own invention.

Gen Hnat Stefaniv          Klym Stefaniv

**Stefaniv, Hnat,** b 10 February 1886 in Toporivtsi, Horodenka county, Galicia, d 21 June 1949 in Regensburg, Germany. Senior army officer; brother of K. and Z. *Stefaniv. After being promoted to colonel he commanded the Ukrainian Galician Army from 10 November to 10 December 1918. Then he was transferred to the UNR Army, where he was chief of logistics and then commanded the marine infantry, a reserve brigade of the Third Iron Rifle Division, the Third Cavalry Regiment (in the First Winter Campaign), and the UNR Army rear area. In August 1920 he was appointed consul of the Western Ukrainian National Republic to Czechoslovakia, and headed the consulate in Uzhhorod. The UNR government-in-exile eventually promoted him to brigadier general.

**Stefaniv, Klym,** b 11 March 1890 in Toporivtsi, Horodenka county, Galicia, d 19 February 1963 in Yablunka, Bohorodchany raion, Ivano-Frankivske oblast. Galician civic figure; brother of H. and Z. Stefaniv. A former village teacher in Zalishchyky county and an officer in the Ukrainian Galician Army, after the First World War he was

active in the Galician co-operative and Prosvita movements, represented the Ukrainian Socialist Radical party in the Polish Sejm (1928–30), and served as a scribe and a rural district official in Porohy, Nadvirna county. Under Soviet rule he worked as a teacher in Yablunka until 1957.

**Stefaniv, Zenon,** b 22 July 1902 in Toporivtsi, Horodenka county, Galicia, d 1976 in Newark, New Jersey. Military historian and journalist; brother of H. and K. Stefaniv. After joining the Ukrainian Galician Army in 1918, he served in signal communications and became a platoon commander in the machine-gun company of the Uhniv Brigade. After the war he studied political science and worked as a journalist and an editor of *Zhyttia Pokuttia*. During the Second World War he served as captain in the Ukrainian National Army, and after the war he settled in the United States. He wrote a book of memoirs, *Vid Slov'ians'ka do Tukholi* (From Slovianske to Tuchola, 1935), and *Ukraïns'ki zbroini syly 1917–1921 rr.* (Ukrainian Armed Forces in 1917–21, 3 parts, 1934–5) and contributed to *Istoriia ukraïns'koho viis'ka* (History of the Ukrainian Armed Forces, 1936).

**Stefanivsky, Mykhailo** [Stefanivs'kyj, Myxajlo], b 1878 in Buzk, Kaminka-Strumylova county, Galicia, d 1945. Civic leader and trades organizer. As an independent locksmith in Lviv, he was a founder and longtime president of the Lviv Burgher Brotherhood, an insurance and mutual aid society. He was active in the Zoria trades association and a member of the Central Committee of the Ukrainian National Democratic Alliance as well as the executive committees of a number of Galicia-wide economic and cultural organizations.

Mykhailo Stefanovych

**Stefanovych, Mykhailo** [Stefanovyč, Myxajlo], b 14 February 1898 in Kiev, d 5 August 1970 in Kiev. Opera singer (bass), artistic director, and musicologist. A graduate of the Kiev Conservatory (1922), he studied singing under M. *Mykysha and Y. Zbruieva. His operatic career began at the Kiev Youth Opera Theater (1919), and from 1921 he was soloist of the Kiev, Odessa, Kharkiv, Perm, Saratov, and Novosibirsk opera theaters. His operatic roles included Taras Bulba, Ruslan, Boris Godunov, and Don Basilio in G. Rossini's *Il Barbiere di Siviglia*. From 1928 he was artistic director of opera theaters in Poltava, Dnipropetrovske, Kharkiv, Lviv, and Kiev (1947–54). He wrote biographies of the singers M. Donets, D. Hnatiuk, I. Patorzhynsky, and P. Bilynnyk.

Oleksa Stefanovych          Oleksander Stefanovych

**Stefanovych, Oleksa** [Stefanovyč], b 5 October 1899 in Myliatyn, Ostrih county, Volhynia gubernia, d 4 January 1970 in Buffalo, New York. Poet. A graduate (1919) of the Volhynia Theological Seminary in Zhytomyr, as an interwar émigré he studied at Prague University (1922–8; PH D diss on A. *Metlynsky as a poet, 1932) and the Ukrainian Free University (1928–30). His poetry appeared in Ukrainian journals in Prague, Lviv, and Chernivtsi and was published in Prague as the collections *Poeziï, zbirka I (1923–1926)* (Poems, Collection I [1923–6], 1927) and *Stephanos* (1939). Although Stefanovych belonged to the 'Prague school' of Ukrainian poets, the voluntarism characteristic of the works of its other members is absent in his poems. His creativity was inspired by elegiac memories of Volhynia's landscapes, by Ukrainian historical and mythological figures, and by tragic events in Ukraine's past and present. Paganism (with erotic overtones) and, in his later poems, Christianity (often of the mystical variety) were dominant forces in his oeuvre. His style is notable for the originality of his poetic language, with its archaisms, neologisms, and unique use of syntax. Neoromantic and symbolist elements and folklore-based imagery predominate in his early works. Later his language becomes abrupt and precise, and his rhythms frequently break in sharp, falling cadences to suggest a sense of fatalism and apocalypse. As a postwar refugee in Germany and, from 1949, Buffalo Stefanovych published a few poems in émigré periodicals. A posthumous edition of his collected works, including those previously unpublished, appeared in Toronto in 1975.

B. Boychuk

**Stefanovych, Oleksander** [Stefanovyč], b 17 July 1847 in Ozeriany, Stanyslaviv circle, Galicia, d 23 May 1933 in Lviv. Greek Catholic priest, educator, and civic and political leader. After completing his theological studies at Lviv and Vienna universities he served as catechist of both the men and women teachers' seminaries in Lviv (1873–1907). He was a founder and leading member of a number of important Ukrainian organizations, such as the newspaper *Dilo (1880), the *Ridna Shkola pedagogical society (1881), the *People's Council (1885) in Lviv, and the *National Democratic party (1899). After the First World War he was president of the Ukrainian Labor party (1922–3), and both the Prosvita and the Ridna Shkola societies elected him as an honorary member. In addition to contribut-

ing articles to *Dilo* and other newspapers he wrote a secondary-school textbook on the history of the Catholic church (1878; repr 1903) and the first prayer book in vernacular Ukrainian.

**Stefanovych, Vasyl** [Stefanovyč, Vasyl'], b 1697, d ca 1773. Jurist and government official of the Hetmanate. He studied at the Kievan Mohyla Academy and in Germany, Prague, Vienna, Rome, Milan, and Venice. In 1722 he obtained a master's degree in liberal arts and philosophy from Breslau University. In 1724 he became a translator in the chancellery of Peter I and a professor of rhetoric and philosophy at the theological seminary headed by T. Prokopovych in St Petersburg. In 1729 he was summoned to Hlukhiv by Hetman D. Apostol to head (until 1734) the commission that eventually produced the *Code of Laws of 1743. He was made a fellow of the standard, and served as a captain in Lokhvytsia (1729–51, with interruptions) and as regimental judge of Lubni (1751–73).

**Stefanovych, Yakiv** [Stefanovyč, Jakiv] (pseud: Dmytro Naida), b 10 December 1854 in Deptivka, Konotip county, Chernihiv gubernia, d 14 April 1915 in Krasnyi Koliadyn, Konotip county. Revolutionary populist. In 1873–4, while studying medicine at Kiev University, he belonged to the *Kiev Commune. He went underground in 1874 and organized the first circle of *Southern Rebels in 1875. In early 1877, using a fake charter from the tsar, he organized a conspiracy in Chyhyryn county, Kiev gubernia, in which approx 1,000 local peasants took part. The planned armed rebellion against the landed gentry and local officials was interrupted by mass arrests of the conspirators. Stefanovych was imprisoned in the Lukianivka Prison in Kiev in September 1877, but he escaped in May 1878 before his trial and fled abroad via St Petersburg. After returning to the Russian Empire in July 1879, he joined the revolutionary organization *Zemlia i Volia, became one of the leaders of the Black Partition anarcho-terrorist splinter organization, and spread revolutionary propaganda among the workers of Odessa. He fled abroad again in January 1880 but returned in November 1881 and became a member of the Executive Committee of *Narodnaia Volia. After being arrested in Moscow in February 1882, he was a defendant in the trial of 17 of its members held in St Petersburg in April–May 1883, at which he was sentenced to eight years of hard labor in eastern Siberia, followed (in 1890) by exile to Yakutia. After his return to Ukraine in 1905, he was politically inactive. His diary was published in St Petersburg in 1906. A detailed account of the Chyhyryn conspiracy is found in D. Field's *Rebels in the Name of the Tsar* (1976).

**Stefanovych-Dontsov, Mykhailo** [Stefanovyč-Doncov, Myxajlo], b 1753 in Kozly, near Chernihiv, d 18 March 1833 in Chernihiv. Physician. A graduate of Chernihiv College (1771) and the Medical School of the St Peterburg Military Hospital (1774), he obtained his physician's license in 1778 and took part in efforts to control epidemics in Ukraine and Russia. He was sentenced to 10 years of hard labor for protesting against abuse of power by the landlords. He invented a device for clearing the bronchopulmonary fistula of foreign bodies. His writings, which remain unpublished, deal with the plague, traumatic epilepsy, fractures, and tarantula bites.

**Stefanovych-Dontsov, Yakiv** [Stefanovyč-Doncov, Jakiv], b 1752 in Tserkovyshche, Chernihiv regiment, d 1829 in Mohyliv, Podilia gubernia. Physician. A graduate of Chernihiv College (1771) and the Medical School of the Moscow Hospital (1774), he obtained his license in 1777 and served as a military doctor in Kiev (1778–84), a county doctor in Oster, a lecturer in St Petersburg (1789–97), an inspector with the Voronezh Medical Board, and a quarantine doctor in Yevpatoriia and Mohyliv (1802–29). He wrote a doctoral dissertation on mass ergot poisoning (1793), studies of inflammation of the pleura and pathological childbirth, and a medico-topographic description of Voronezh gubernia (1798).

**Stefansky, Viacheslav** [Stefans'kyj, V'jačeslav], b 26 September 1867 in Odessa, d 7 May 1949. Epidemiologist and microbiologist. A graduate of Kiev University (1893), he worked in the Odessa Hospital for Infectious Diseases and (from 1897) the Odessa Bacteriological Station. He taught at Odessa University (from 1908) and at the Odessa Medical Institute (from 1921). He wrote numerous works, including a textbook on infectious diseases. During his research on the plague he discovered rat leprosy and its cause. Experimenting on himself, he showed that relapsing typhoid was transmitted by the louse (*Pediculus humanus*).

**Stefanyk, Semen,** b 1 March 1904 in Stetseva, Sniatyn county, Galicia, d 15 March 1981 in Lviv. Political activist; son of V. *Stefanyk. After graduating in law from Lviv University (1930) he worked as a lawyer. He was appointed vice-chairman of the executive committee of the Lviv Oblast Council of the People's Deputies in 1946 and deputy premier of the Ukrainian SSR in 1953. From 1954 to 1969 he was chairman of the Lviv Oblast Executive Committee and then director of the Franko Memorial Museum in Lviv.

Theodore Stefanyk    Vasyl Stefanyk

**Stefanyk, Theodore,** b 1880 in Hrytsovolia, Brody county, Galicia, d 21 March 1951 in Winnipeg. Community leader. Stefanyk, an electrician in Galicia, emigrated to Winnipeg in 1898. A prominent trade unionist, he was elected president of a local of the International Association of Engineers in 1902. Stefanyk supported the Conservative party and by 1907 had become its main 'Ukrainian' lieutenant for the province of Manitoba. He received an appointment as inspector and organizer of Ukrainian bilingual schools. He was the first Ukrainian elected to the Winnipeg city council (1912–14) and in 1913–15 was president of the Ruthenian Publishing Company, which produced a weekly called *Kanada* that was financed by the Conservative party.

**Stefanyk, Vasyl,** b 14 May 1871 in Rusiv, Sniatyn county, Galicia, d 7 December 1936 in Rusiv. Prose writer. In the course of his studies Stefanyk became aquainted with L. *Martovych and L. *Bachynsky, both of whom had an influence on his life: Martovych turned him to writing, and Bachynsky steered him toward community-political involvement. Later, while he was a student of medicine at Cracow University, Stefanyk was befriended by the Polish doctor W. *Moraczewski and his wife, S. Okunevska-Moraczewska, who aquainted him with contemporary European culture and literature and with the members of the then-fashionable Polish avant-garde group Młoda Polska, particularly with S. Przybyszewski and W. *Orkan. The hectic and interesting Bohemian life is reflected in Stefanyk's letters, in which references to the works of modernist authors, such as C.-P. Baudelaire, G. Keller, P. Verlaine, M. Maeterlinck, and P. Bourget, abound. Stefanyk's letters, full of poetic prose, lyricism, and introspection, also provide glimpses of the future master of the short story in the various narrative vignettes. Attempts to publish some of the introspective poetic prose in newspapers were unsuccessful, but in 1897 the terse narratives of scenes observed by Stefanyk appeared in *Pratsia* (Chernivtsi); they were followed by several novellas in *Literaturno-naukovyi vistnyk* (1898) and finally by Stefanyk's first collection of novellas, *Synia knyzhechka* (The Blue Book, 1899). With its appearance came immediate literary acclaim, and other collections followed: *Kaminnyi khrest* (The Stone Cross, 1900), *Doroha* (The Road, 1901), and *Moie slovo* (My Word, 1905).

In 1901 Stefanyk was at the height of his literary career, but for the next 15 years he wrote nothing. From 1908 until the collapse of the Austro-Hungarian Empire Stefanyk was a member of the Austrian parliament, elected as a substitute for V. Okhrymovych in 1907 from the *Ukrainian Radical party in Galicia. The horror of the First World War jolted him back into writing in 1916, and he produced one more collection, *Zemlia* (Earth, 1926). During the period of the Western Ukrainian National Republic, as a former member of parliament, Stefanyk became vice-president of the Ukrainian National Rada, and in 1919 he went to Kiev for the signing of the agreement on the unification of Ukraine. In 1922 he became a district head of the Radical party. Recognizing him as the greatest living writer in Western Ukraine, the government of Soviet Ukraine decreed a life pension for Stefanyk, which he turned down in protest against the repressions in Ukraine. In addition to his five collections of novellas, Stefanyk published stories, in several editions of collected works: an edition in 1927 in Soviet Ukraine; a jubilee edition (Lviv 1933); an émigré edition edited by his son, *Yu. Stefanyk (Regensburg 1948); and the three-volume 'academic' edition, published in Ukraine (1949–54). A 1964 edition of Stefanyk's selected works, edited by V. Lesyn and F. Pohrebennyk, complemented and corrected some of the lacunae and faults of the 'academic' edition.

Stefanyk's whole literary output consisted of 59 published novellas, most of them no longer than a couple of pages. In them he showed himself a master of a species of the short story genre, the Stefanyk novella, which is characterized by a succinct and highly dramatic form used to capture single crucial moments in the life of a hero. The dramatic quality of the novellas ensured their being successfully staged as plays by V. Blavatsky and adapted for film (*Kaminnyi khrest*, screenplay by I. Drach). The heroes of Stefanyk's stories are for the most part peasants from his native Pokutia. Against the general background of poverty or war (in the later stories) Stefanyk showed his heroes in a universal dilemma, confronting the pain at the heart of existence. Stefanyk concentrated on capturing the turbulence of the soul, the inner agon, which revealed the psychological complexity of the hero. His characterizations were achieved through the speech of the characters. Words spoken became important not only for their meaning but also for the elements of *skaz*, which throw direct light on the character's emotional state, personality, social position, and degree of literacy. The special blend of literary Ukrainian and the Pokutia dialect created a flavor not easily duplicated or translated. Nevertheless there have been several attempts to translate Stefanyk into Polish, German, and Russian. The French translation *La croix de pierre et autres nouvelles* appeared in 1975, and the following English translations have appeared: *The Stone Cross* (1971), *Maple Leaves and Other Stories* (1988), and some individual stories in anthologies.

BIBLIOGRAPHY

Lepky, B. *Vasyl' Stefanyk: Literaturna kharakterystyka* (Lviv 1903)

Hrytsai, O. *Vasyl' Stefanyk: Sproba krytychnoï kharakterystyky* (Vienna 1921)

Kryzhanivs'kyi, S. *Vasyl' Stefanyk: Krytyko-biohrafichnyi narys* (Kiev 1946)

Kostashchuk, V. *Volodar dum selians'kykh* (Lviv 1959)

Kushch, O. *Vasyl' Stefanyk: Bibliohrafichnyi pokazhchyk* (Kiev 1961)

Kobzei, T. *Velykyi riz'bar ukraïns'kykh selians'kykh dush* (Toronto 1966)

Lesyn, V. *Vasyl' Stefanyk – maister novely* (Kiev 1970)

Lutsiv, L. *Vasyl' Stefanyk – spivets' ukraïns'koï zemli* (New York–Jersey City 1971)

Struk, D. *A Study of Vasyl Stefanyk: The Pain at the Heart of Existence* (Littleton, Colo 1973)

Wiśniewska, E. *Wasyl Stefanyk w obliczu Młodej Polski* (Wrocław 1986)

Chernenko, O. *Ekspresionizm u tvorchosti Vasylia Stefanyka* (New York 1989)

Hnidan, O. *Vasyl' Stefanyk: Zhyttia i tvorchist'* (Kiev 1991)

D.H. Struk

**Stefanyk, Yurii** (pseuds: Yurii Klynovy and Yurii Hamorak), b 24 July 1909 in Stetseva, Sniatyn county, Galicia, d 25 April 1985 in Edmonton. Writer and community leader; son of V. *Stefanyk. Stefanyk studied law at the University of Lviv (LLB, 1935) and spent 1936–7 in Canada coediting *Ukraïns'ki visti* (Edmonton). After returning to Ukraine he worked on the magazine *Zhyttia i znannia* and the monthly *Novitnyi remisnyk* in Lviv. In 1940, after the Soviet occupation of Western Ukraine, he was arrested as a Ukrainian nationalist. He was released in 1941, left Ukraine in 1944, and settled in Edmonton in 1948. From 1971 he was president of the *Slovo Association of Ukrainian Writers in Exile and edited its irregular serial, *Slovo (1970–83). He wrote *Moïm synam, moïm pryiateliam* (To My Sons and to My Friends, 1981); edited *Vasyl' Stefanyk: Tvory* (Vasyl Stefanyk: Works, 1942; 2nd edn 1948), *Les' Mar-

Yurii Stefanyk                     Mariia Stefiuk

*tovych: Tvory I–III* (Les Martovych: Works I–III, nd), and *Nasha spadshchyna* (Our Heritage, 1979); and coedited (with J. Balan) *Yarmarok: Ukrainian Writing in Canada since the Second World War* (1987).

**Stefanyshyn, Myroslav** [Stefanyšyn], b 1 April 1927 in Bovshiv, Rohatyn county, Galicia. Composer, conductor, and folk song collector. After graduating from the Ivano-Frankivske Music School in 1949 and the Lviv Conservatory in 1954, he served as conductor of the Volhynia Folk Chorus and then as music director of the Volhynia Oblast Drama Theater (1959–60). He lectured at the Lutske Pedagogical Institute (1960–9) and then at the Lutske Music School. His compositions number about 400 and include songs for choir, arrangements of folk songs, and pieces for chamber orchestra. A selection of his works was published in 1966 as *Pisni onovlenoho kraiu* (Songs of a Renewed Land). As a folklorist he gathered over 1,000 Volhynian and Polisian folk songs and melodies and compiled several collections, including *Narodna tvorchist' Volyni* (The Folklore of Volhynia, 1957), *Pisni z Volyni* (Songs from Volhynia, 1970), and *Spivaie Lesyn krai* (Lesia [Ukrainka's] Land Sings, 1973).

**Stefanytsky, Ivan** [Stefanyc'kyj], b 19 March 1892 in Naluzhe, Terebovlia county, Galicia, d 24 April 1975 in Toronto. Journalist and Communist activist. After emigrating to the United States (1908) and then to Canada (1911) he became active in the *Ukrainian Labour-Farmer Temple Association, the Workers' Benevolent Association, the Communist Party of Canada (1923–75), and the Association of United Ukrainian Canadians. He edited the newspapers *Robochyi narod* and *Robitnyche slovo* (1914–18), and then *Svidoma syla*, *Ukraïns'ki robitnychi visti* (1930s), *Narodnia hazeta* (1930s), *Ukraïns'ke slovo* (1942–7), and *Ukraïns'ke zhyttia* (1947–66). For many years he fought for an independent political line in Ukrainian pro-Communist organizations.

**Stefiuk, Mariia** [Stefjuk, Marija], b 16 July 1948 in Rozhniv, Kosiv raion, Ivano-Frankivske oblast. Opera singer (lyric-coloratura soprano). A graduate of the Kiev Conservatory (1973), she studied under N. Zakharchenko and since 1972 has been a soloist of the Kiev Theater of Opera and Ballet. Her operatic roles include Marultsia in M. Lysenko's *Taras Bulba*, Mylusha in H. Maiboroda's *Yaroslav *the Wise*, Antonida in M. Glinka's *A Life for the Czar*, Marfa in N. Rimsky-Korsakov's *The Tsar's Bride*, and Violetta in G. Verdi's *La Traviata*. She has also sung abroad, in the United States (1975), in Canada (1976), and at Milan's La Scala (1981); in recital she often sings Ukrainian folk songs. She has recorded on the Melodiya label.

**Stefurak, Stepan,** b 16 January 1846 in Staryi Uhryniv, Kalush county, Galicia, d 25 September 1888 in Lviv. Actor. He worked in the Ruska Besida Theater (1869–88) and was renowned for his portrayal of characters in the Ukrainian ethnographic repertoire.

**Steklov, Vladimir**, b 9 January 1864 in Nizhnii Novgorod, Russia, d 30 May 1926 in Haspra, Crimea. Russian mathematician and mechanician; full member of the St Petersburg Academy from 1912 and of the VUAN from 1925. A student of A. Liapunov, he graduated from Kharkiv University (1887) and taught at the university (1889–1906) and the Kharkiv Technological Institute (1893–1905). In 1902 he was elected president of the Kharkiv Mathematics Society. Then he served as professor of St Petersburg University (1906–19), vice-president of the USSR Academy of Sciences in Moscow (1919–26), and director of the Physical-Mathematical Institute in Moscow, which was renamed in 1934 in his honor. Steklov had a considerable influence in both Ukraine and Russia on the application of mathematics to natural sciences. He made fundamental contributions to mathematical physics and various natural sciences as well as to pure mathematics, including a proof for the existence of Green's function and its analytical representations, new methods for the solution of basic differential equations in mathematical physics based on the completeness of the eigenfunctions, and some refinements of the theory of approximate integration, the theory of elasticity, and the theory of algebra.

**Steletska, Hanna** [Stelec'ka] (pseud: Hanna Suprunenko), b 1883 in Lubni, Poltava gubernia, d May 1962 in Kiev. Poet and teacher. A graduate of the Odessa Women's Pedagogical Courses, the Higher Courses for Women in Moscow, and the Moscow Archeological Institute (1914), from 1916 she worked as a teacher and orphanage director in Lubni and its environs. Her poems appeared in *Literaturno-naukovyi vistnyk* (1905) and the literary anthologies *Rozvaha* (Amusement, 1906), *Ternovyi vinok* (Crown of Thorns, 1908), and *Ukraïns'ka muza* (Ukrainian Muse, 1908). In 1923 she published the collection *Revoliutsiini pisni* (Revolutionary Songs). Manuscripts of her unpublished poetry are preserved at the ANU Institute of Literature.

**Stelletsky, Mykola** [Stellec'kyj], b 1862, d 1919. Priest and scholar. A graduate of the Kiev Theological Academy, he published articles on a variety of religious and philosophical topics – including the role of Kiev as a religious center, the history of Kharkiv College, and H. Skovoroda – in *Trudy Kievskoi dukhovnoi akademii*, *Vera i razum*, and other journals. He later became a professor at Kharkiv University. He was killed by the Bolsheviks in 1919.

**Stelmakh, Hryhorii** [Stel'max, Hryhorij], b November 1903 in Voitovychi, Pereiaslav county, Poltava gubernia. Ethnographer. After graduating from the Ukrainian Institute of Material Culture in Kharkiv (1931) he lectured at the Ukrainian Institute of Communist Education (1931–3)

and worked at the Ukrainian Institute of Material Culture (1932–4) and the Central Antireligious Museum in Moscow (1936–9). From 1946 he worked at the AN URSR (now ANU) Institute of Fine Arts, Folklore, and Ethnography. Besides articles on rural settlements and folk architecture he has written a monograph on the development of rural settlements in Ukraine (1964).

Mykhailo Stelmakh

**Stelmakh, Mykhailo** [Stel'max, Myxajlo], b 24 May 1912 in Diakivtsi, Letychiv county, Podilia gubernia, d 27 September 1983 in Kiev. Prose writer, poet, and dramatist; full member of the AN URSR (now ANU) from 1978. He graduated from the Vinnytsia Pedagogical Institute (1933) and taught in villages of the Kiev district until 1939. After the war he worked (1945–53) for the Institute of Fine Arts, Folklore, and Ethnography of the AN URSR. He was a deputy to the Supreme Soviet of the USSR and vice-chairman of the Council of Nationalities. His poetry was first published in 1936. His collections of poetry include *Dobryi ranok* (Good Morning, 1941), *Za iasni zori* (For the Bright Stars, 1942), *Provesin'* (Early Spring, 1942), *Shliakhy svitannia* (The Paths of Dawn, 1948), *Zhyto syly nabyraiet'sia* (The Rye is Growing in Strength, 1954), *Poeziï* (Poems, 1958), and *Mak tsvite* (The Poppies Are Blooming, 1968). From the 1940s he wrote mainly prose, such as the short-story collection *Berezovyi sik* (Birch Sap, 1944); the novel *Velyka ridnia* (The Large Family), published in two parts as *Na nashii zemli* (On Our Land, 1949) and *Velyki perelohy* (Large Fallow Fields, 1951); and the novels *Khlib i sil'* (Bread and Salt, 1959), *Pravda i kryvda* (Truth and Injustice, 1961), *Duma pro tebe* (A Duma about You, 1969), *Chotyry brody* (The Four Fords, 1979), *Nad Cheremoshem* (By the Cheremosh River, 1952), *Husy-lebedi letiat'* (The Geese and Swans Are Flying, 1964), and *Shchedryi vechir* (Eve of Epiphany, 1967). He wrote the plays *Zolota metelytsia* (The Golden Snowstorm, 1955), *Na Ivana Kupala* (On Midsummer's Night's Eve, 1966), *Zacharovanyi vitriak* (The Enchanted Windmill, 1967), and *Kum koroliu* (The Godfather of the King's Child, 1968).

Stelmakh wrote the script for the documentary film *Zhyvy Ukraïno!* (Long Live Ukraine!, 1958). He also wrote many children's books, mainly in verse: *Zhnyva* (Harvest, 1951), *Kolosok do koloska* (Ear of Grain to Ear of Grain, 1951), *Zhyvi ohni* (Live Fires, 1954), *Burundukova sim'ia* (The Chipmunk's Family, 1963), *Tsapkiv urozhai* (The Goat's Harvest, 1967), *Lito-liteplo* (The Lukewarm Summer, 1969), and others.

Stelmakh's prose is a typical example of *socialist realism. It shows the characteristic conformism to shifting Party policy (eg, the novel *Velyka ridnia* glorifies J. Stalin throughout and was awarded the Stalin Prize in 1951; later, criticized for succumbing to the Stalinist 'personality cult,' Stelmakh rewrote it under the new title *Krov liuds'ka – ne vodytsia* [Human Blood Is Not Water, 1957]). The characteristic socialist-realist glossing over of Soviet reality is present in Stelmakh's work even of the post-Stalinist era (eg, the novel *Pravda i kryvda*). Even Stelmakh's last novel, *Chotyry brody*, is distorted by the pressure of censorship. Stelmakh's prose is exceptionally rich in its folk lexicon. Stylistically it is reminiscent of Yu. Yanovsky's lyrical prose, with the influence of O. Dovzhenko clearly evident. Stelmakh's adherence to socialist realism, as well as his tendency toward sentimentalism (also characteristic of socialist realism), guaranteed him an upper niche in the literary hierarchy of the Ukrainian SSR. His collected works have been published (6 vols, 1972–3; 7 vols, 1982–3).

BIBLIOGRAPHY
Babyshkin, S. *Mykhailo Stel'makh* (Kiev 1961)
Burliai, Iu. *Mykhailo Stel'makh* (Kiev 1962)

I. Koshelivets

**Stempkovsky, Ivan** [Stempkovskij], b 1789 in Riazanovka, Saratov gubernia, Russia, d 18 December 1832 in Kerch. Russian archeologist and administrator. In 1814–15 he fought with the Russian forces in the Napoleonic Wars. Later he studied history and archeology in Paris (1815–19). He then returned to the Black Sea region, where he pursued a military career and worked in public administration. He was instrumental in establishing the *Odessa Archeological Museum (1825) and a regional museum in Kerch (1826). After becoming the city governor (*gradonachalnik*) of Kerch in 1828, he undertook a number of fruitful archeological expeditions at ancient Greek sites in the area. His best-known find is the *Kul Oba kurhan.

Stanisław Stempowski

**Stempowski, Stanisław,** b 27 January 1870 in Huta Cherlenovetska, eastern Podilia, d 11 January 1952 in Warsaw. Polish civic and political figure and writer. He developed an interest in Ukrainian affairs after meeting B. Kistiakovsky and other Ukrainian students at Dorpat University (1891). He became active in Ukrainian co-operative and educational work in Volhynia (1906–16) and was leader of the Polish Democratic Center party when it entered the Central Rada (1917). In 1920 he was minister of health

in the V. Prokopovych administration of the UNR. His memoirs were published as *Pamiętniki 1870–1914* (1953).

**Sten, Anna** (stage name of Anna Fesak), b 29 June 1908 in Kiev. Hollywood film and television actress of Ukrainian-Swedish origin. After appearing in Soviet and German films she moved to the United States (1932), where she made 17 films, including *We Live Again* (1934, with F. March), *The Wedding Night* (1935, with G. Cooper), and *Soldier of Fortune* (1955, with C. Gable and S. Hayward). Her last film was made in 1962.

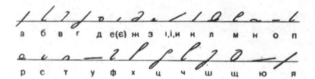

Ukrainian stenography

**Stenography,** or shorthand. A method of writing rapidly by using characters, abbreviations, or symbols in place of letters, words, and phrases. In Eastern Europe, the most widely used system was F.X. Gabelsberger's cursive shorthand (1824). In Western Ukraine it was adapted for Ukrainian by O. *Paneiko (1922). A state stenographic system was adopted in the USSR in 1933 on the basis of N. Sokolov's Russian version of the Gabelsberger system. In Soviet Ukraine it was adapted by O. Hershtansky and M. Lovshyn (author of a 1948 Ukrainian shorthand textbook).

**Step** (The Steppe). A 391-page Ukrainian and Russian literary miscellany published by writers living in Kherson under the leadership of D. Markovych and printed in St Petersburg in 1886. It contained poems by P. Tulub, Dniprova Chaika, A. Konoshchenko (Hrabenko), and P. Zalozny; stories by D. Mordovets, I. Nechui-Levytsky, A. Brauner, D. Markovych, M. Zavoloka (Hrushevsky), and Penchukivets; I. Karpenko-Kary's drama 'Bondarivna' (The Cooper's Daughter); and articles by M. Hanenko (on peasant family property relations in Yelysavethrad county), O. Markovych (on wedding songs in Yelysavethrad county, with the texts of 119 songs), K. Shram (Ivashchenko, on the Ukrainian village in the works of M. Starytsky and M. Kropyvnytsky), and O. Rusov (on the origin of zemstvo statistics).

**Step** (The Steppe). A 112-page miscellany published in Odessa in 1916 under the editorship of A. Nikovsky in place of the fourth issue of *Osnova. It included Nikovsky's obituary of V. Symyrenko, a historical article by L. Orlenko (pseud of O. Levytsky), and prose by P. Ustiak (pseud of S. Yefremov), I. Lypa, M. Pylypovych (pseud of Modest Levytsky), and Yu. Styzhavsky.

**Stepan** [Stepan']. II-7. A town smt (1986 pop 4,600) on the Horyn River in Sarny raion, Rivne oblast. It was first mentioned in the Hypatian Chronicle under the year 1292, as the capital of an appanage principality. It was destroyed by the Mongols and reappeared in historical documents in the 15th and 16th centuries, when it belonged to the Ostrozky family. They built a large fortress, the walls of which have been preserved, and St Michael's Monastery

(1572). During B. Khmelnytsky's uprising a large battle between the Polish army and the Cossacks took place at Stepan.

**Stepanenko, Arkadii,** b and d ? Political activist and member of the Central Rada. He was a member of the Ukrainian Party of Socialist Revolutionaries (UPSR) and of the Central Committee of the Peasant Association. As early as June 1917 he called on the Central Rada to secede from Russia and create an independent Ukrainian state. In December 1917 he was elected president of the All-Ukrainian Congress of Workers', Soldiers', and Peasants' Deputies, and at the beginning of 1918, vice-president of the Central Rada. He signed the bill introducing the new (Gregorian) calendar (25 February 1918). When the UPSR split into factions in May 1918, Stepanenko sided with the right wing and then the center. At the Labor Congress in January 1919 he demanded the UNR Directory's abdication and the formation of local labor councils. On 28 January he was elected to the Central Committee of the UPSR, and he acted as its representative in the Directory's government. In March 1919 he became vice-chairman of the Committee for the Defense of the Republic, and in August he joined Issac Mazepa's cabinet as minister of land affairs. In 1920 he tried to reach an understanding with the Soviet regime.

**Stepanenko, Borys,** b 15 March 1917 in Voitove, Pereiaslav county, Poltava gubernia. Ballet dancer. He completed ballet school in 1936 (pupil of I. Chystiakov). In 1937–8 he danced as a soloist in the Ensemble of Song and Dance of the Ukrainian SSR, and in 1939–61 he was a soloist in the Kiev Theater of Opera and Ballet.

**Stepanenko, Ihor,** b 10 October 1914 in Hlobyne, Kremenchuk county, Poltava gubernia. CPU and Soviet government leader. A former sugar-refinery engineer and head of the Cherkasy Sugar Trust, he served as deputy chairman of the Cherkasy Council of the National Economy (1960–1), chairman of the Cherkasy Oblast Executive Committee (1961–2) and the Podilia Council of the National Economy (1962–5), minister of the Ukrainian food industry (1965–?), deputy chairman of the Ukrainian Council of Ministers (1966–?), and CC CPU candidate (1961–6) and member (1966–?).

**Stepanenko, Mykhailo,** b 6 June 1942 in Semipalatinsk, Kazakh SSR. Composer, musicologist, pianist, and teacher. He graduated from the Kiev State Conservatory in the piano class of V. Nilsen and V. Tropinin (1966) and in the composition class of B. Liatoshynsky and A. Shtoharenko (1971). He has taught at the conservatory since 1967. His musical works include a symphony (1971); *Concert Allegro* (1977) for string quartet; piano and bandura compositions; pieces for flute, clarinet, and violin (all with piano); art songs; folk song arrangements; and music for theater, radio, and television. He has written articles for *Ukraïns'ka radians'ka entsyklopediiu* (Ukrainian Soviet Encyclopedia) and music journals and recorded works by D. Bortniansky, M. Berezovsky, O. Lyzohub, and M. Markevych for the Melodiya label.

**Stepanenko, Mykola,** b 6 December 1918 in Poltava, d 13 March 1993 in San Jose, California. Educator, literary scholar, and political activist; full member of the Shevchenko Scientific Society and the Ukrainian Acade-

Mykola Stepanenko

my of Arts and Sciences in the US. A graduate of the Poltava Pedagogical Institute (1938), he taught secondary school in Ukraine. A postwar refugee, after emigrating to the United States in 1949 he completed his studies at Syracuse University (PH D, 1963) and taught Slavic languages and literatures at Rutgers, George Washington, and Central Michigan universities. He coauthored a Ukrainian grammar and has contributed many articles to the Ukrainian émigré press and to Slavic studies journals. He has been active in Ukrainian émigré politics as a cofounder of the *Ukrainian Revolutionary Democratic party and the Ukrainian Democratic Youth Association, as a member of the board of directors of the Ukrainian Congress Committee of America (1950–4), and as a vice-president of the UNR government-in-exile (from 1967).

**Stepanenko, Oleh,** b 26 January 1916 in Chernihiv. Film set designer. He completed study in the Faculty of Architectural Design in the Leningrad Institute of Industrial Art (1934) and worked in various design firms (1935–41). From 1947 he worked as a film set designer in the Kiev Artistic Film Studio, where he designed the sets for over 20 films, including *Kyianka* (The Kiev Girl, 1958).

**Stepanenko, Oleksander,** b ? in Kremenchuk county, Poltava gubernia, d 1924 in Siberia. Co-operative and political leader. He joined the Revolutionary Ukrainian party (1900) and then the Ukrainian People's party (1902). After the February Revolution he became a member of the executive committee of Kiev gubernia, a representative of co-operatives in the Central Rada, and a member of the Ukrainian Party of Socialists-Independentists. Under the UNR Directory he was sent on an economic mission to Vienna. In 1922 he returned to Ukraine. During the Stalinist terror he was sent to a prison camp in Siberia. His further fate is unknown.

**Stepaniuk, Boryslav** [Stepanjuk], b 16 July 1923 in Kanivshchyna, Pryluka county, Poltava gubernia. Poet and translator. He graduated from Kiev University (1947) and was deputy chief editor of Radianskyi Pysmennyk publishers and editor of the quarterly *Poeziia*. Since 1948 he has published 20 books of lyric poetry and narrative poems, including the selected editions *Iasna dalechin'* (The Bright Distance, 1956), *Syn'ookyi mii lypen'* (My Blue-eyed July, 1973), and *Vybrani tvory* (Selected Works, 2 vols, 1983). He has translated Russian, Kirghiz, and Chuvash poetry into Ukrainian. He was awarded the first P. Tychyna Prize in 1974.

**Stepaniuk, Ivan** [Stepanjuk], b 19 April 1903 in Tsutsniv (now Petrove), Volodymyr-Volynskyi county, Volhynia gubernia, d 29 May 1934. Writer. From 1923 to 1924 he edited the Social Democratic weekly *Selians'ka dolia in Lutske. From 1925 on he lived in Soviet Ukraine, and in 1926 he began contributing poems, stories, and essays to journals (*Zoria, Zakhidnia Ukraïna*) and Dnipropetrovske newspapers as a member of the All-Ukrainian Association of Proletarian Writers and the writers' group Zakhidnia Ukraina. Published separately were the poetry collection *Strumuiut' dni* (The Days Stream, 1930) and a posthumous edition of his works with the same title (1965).

Olena Stepaniv                    Volodymyr Stepankivsky

**Stepaniv, Olena,** b 7 December 1892 in Vyshnivchyk, Peremyshliany county, Galicia, d 11 July 1963 in Lviv. Military and community figure and educator; wife of R. *Dashkevych. As a student at Lviv University she commanded a women's platoon in the Ukrainian Sich Riflemen Society (est 1913). During the First World War she joined the Legion of Ukrainian Sich Riflemen and fought in the battle for Makivka. She was decorated for bravery and promoted to second lieutenant. After being interned in a Russian POW camp in Tashkent (1915–17) she served on the legion's Supreme Military Board, which organized the November Uprising in Lviv, and commanded a platoon in the Ukrainian Galician Army (1918–19). In 1919 she was a press representative in the UNR Ministry of Foreign Affairs in Kamianets-Podilskyi. After the war she received a PH D in history and geography from Vienna University and then taught at the Basilian Sisters' gymnasium in Lviv. Forbidden to teach by the Polish authorities in 1935, she became director of the Ridna Shkola educational society's guidance department (1935–7) and director of the Secretariat of the Organizational Division of the Audit Union of Ukrainian Co-operatives. During the 1939–41 Soviet occupation she resumed teaching and headed the Statistical Administration in Lviv. In 1944–6 she lectured at Lviv University and oversaw the AN URSR (now ANU) Sector of Economics and Industry in Lviv. Incarceration in a Mordovian labor camp for being a Ukrainian patriot (1949–56) undermined her health. Stepaniv wrote over 75 works, including memoirs of the years 1912–14 (1930; repr 1968), a reference book on health co-operatives (1930), and a book on contemporary Lviv (1943; repr 1953).

**Stepankivsky, Volodymyr** [Stepankivs'kyj], b 1885 in eastern Podilia, d 1957 in the United States. Political activist and journalist. He was active in the Revolutionary Ukrainian party and an executive member of the Ukrainian Social Democratic Workers' party (USDRP). After emigrating in 1907 to Switzerland and then to France and England he contributed articles under various pseudonyms to *Rada, Dilo*, and the organs of the USDRP. In 1909 he founded the Ukrainian Hromada in London, and in 1911 he began to inform the European public about Ukraine. With M. *Tyshkevych he organized the Ucraina Information Society in Lausanne and edited its weekly L'*Ukraine (1915–20) and, irregularly, *The Ukraine*. His pamphlet *The Russian Plot to Seize Galicia (Austrian Ruthenia)* appeared in the United States in 1915. In Bern he collaborated with D. *Dontsov (1916–17) in publishing the bulletin of the Bureau of the Peoples of Russia. In the mid-1920s he emigrated to the United States and withdrew from Ukrainian public life.

**Stepankov, Kostiantyn,** b 3 June 1928 in Pechesky, near Proskuriv (now Khmelnytskyi). Stage, film, and television actor and pedagogue. He completed study at the Kiev Institute of Theater Arts (1953, pupil of A. Buchma) and then was an actor in the Kiev Ukrainian Drama Theater (1954–68) and the Kiev Artistic Film Studio (from 1968). He acted in the films *Kaminnyi khrest* (The Stone Cross, 1968, based on V. Stefanyk's story), *Zakhar Berkut* (1971, based on I. Franko's novel), and *Duma pro Kovpaka* (A Duma about Kovpak, 1975–8). Since 1953 he has taught in the Kiev Institute of Theater Arts.

**Stepanov, Dmytro,** b 1800, d 1856. Porcelain decorator. After graduating from the St Petersburg Academy of Arts (1817) he managed the engraving workshop of the Mezhyhiria Faience Factory. In 1826 he began to teach drawing and engraving at the factory's trade school. He produced about 200 original engravings that were reproduced on porcelain ware, including *The Four Seasons, The Golden Gate in Kiev, Kiev University*, and Ukrainian landscapes. He also drew floral ornamentation and illustrated books.

**Stepanov, Tikhon,** b 1795 in Voronezh, Russia, d 1847 in Kharkiv. Russian economist. After graduating from Kharkiv University (1824) he taught history there. In 1832 he was appointed a professor of political economy, and later, the rector, at Kharkiv University. He wrote works on economics, statistics, philosophy, and law, including the first original textbook of political economy published in the Russian Empire, *Zapiski o politicheskoi ekonomii* (Notes on Political Economy, 2 vols, 1844, 1848). It was based on the works of A. Smith and D. Ricardo.

**Stepanov, Vladimir,** b 14 December 1913 in Shchehlivka (now part of Makiivka), Bakhmut county, Katerynoslav gubernia. Astrophysicist; corresponding member of the USSR (now Russian) Academy of Sciences since 1968 and chairman of the presidium of its Eastern Siberian branch (1972–6). A graduate of Moscow University (1937), he worked at the Tashkent Astronomical Observatory (1937–41); the Lviv Astronomical Observatory (1946–53), where he became director in 1950; Moscow University (1953–5); the Crimean Astrophysical Observatory (1955–62); and, as deputy director (1962–4) and director (1964–

78), the Siberian Institute of the Earth's Magnetism, Ionosphere, and Dispersion of Radio Waves in Irkutsk. His scientific contributions have been mostly in solar physics and solar astronomy. Stepanov developed theories and equations explaining the interactions of solar magnetic fields, radiation, and plasma; studied the rotation of solar corona; and developed new astronomical instruments (a double-reflection spectroscope and a solar magnetometer).

**Stepanova, Galina**. See Prozumenshchikova, Galina.

*Stephanites kai Ichnelates.* An 11th-century Greek version of an 8th-century Arabic collection of animal fables, *Kalilah wa Dimnah*, which itself was a translation of an originally Sanskrit work, the *Panchatantra*, written between 100 BC and 500 AD. It was named after the two jackals that figure in the first fable and narrate the following fables, and was written in the form of an emperor's conversation with a philosopher. A Bulgarian translation of the Greek, *Stefanit i Ikhnalat*, circulated in Kievan Rus' in many interpolated copies from the mid-13th century on. It became a source of Ukrainian folk anecdotes and animal fables and was also used in belletristic works.

**Stephen III**, b 1457, d 1504. Hospodar of Moldavia. Under his rule Moldavia attained its greatest strength, and he became known as 'the Great.' He waged successful campaigns against Hungary (1467), Wallachia (1471, 1473), Turkey (1475; but he was later defeated, and conceded vassalage to the Porte), and Poland. He supported political, cultural, and economic ties with Ukraine and granted privileges to the merchants of Lviv. He also assisted in Ukrainian cultural development by arranging for Ukrainian chronicles and decrees as well as gospels from the Putna and Humora monasteries to be written in the Ukrainian variant of Church Slavonic. During his tenure several Ukrainians (Dazhboh, Andreiko, and Ya. Hudych) were members of the Moldavian boyar council. His first wife was Evdokiia, the daughter of the Kievan prince Semen Olelkovych. During his campaigns in Pokutia in 1491 and 1502, a number of Ukrainians resettled in Moldavia. Stephen was buried in the Putna monastery in southern Bukovyna.

**Stephen (István) Báthory** (Polish: Stefan Batory), b 27 September 1533 in Transylvania, d 12 December 1586 near Hrodna, Belarus. Transylvanian prince (1571–6) and Hungarian king (1576–86) of Poland. One of the most forceful and ambitious monarchs in the history of Poland, he attempted to form a great state from Poland, Muscovy, and Transylvania. To defend Poland's eastern Baltic provinces against Russian incursion (eg, in the war with Ivan IV, 1579–82), he strengthened the Polish army by increasing the numbers of *registered Cossacks and granting them privileges. In 1578 he allowed them to use the *Trakhtemyriv Monastery as a hospital and refuge.

**Stepniak, Myron** [Stepnjak], b 1902 in Oleksandrivske (now Zaporizhia), Katerynoslav gubernia, d ? Literary scholar and critic. In the 1920s he contributed articles about poetics and Galician and Soviet Ukrainian writers, as well as book reviews, to *Chervonyi shliakh* (*ChSh*), *Literaturnyi zhurnal*, *Hart*, and other journals. After his article about the Galician Modernist group Moloda Muza in *ChSh* was attacked by Party critics, he was expelled in his fourth year from the Kiev Institute of People's Education, and his work was no longer published. His further fate is unknown.

Sergius Stepniak

**Stepniak, Sergius** [Stepnjak] (pseud of Sergei Kravchinsky), b 13 July 1851 in Novyi Starodub, Oleksandriia county, Kherson gubernia, d 23 December 1895 in London. Russian populist revolutionary and writer. He edited the *Zemlia i Volia society's paper in St Petersburg in 1878. He worked as a translator and journalist in Geneva (1878–81, 1883–4) and Milan (1881–3). In Geneva he became a friend of M. *Drahomanov and a supporter of his federalist views.

In 1884 Stepniak settled in London, where he wrote most of his works and became the leading Russian revolutionary propagandist of his time. He founded the English Society of Friends of Russian Freedom (1890), its organ *Free Russia* (1890), and the Russian Free Press Fund (1891), which published, distributed, and smuggled back into the Russian Empire revolutionary and banned publications in Russian, Polish, and Ukrainian (eg, by Drahomanov, P. Myrny, S. Podolynsky, and T. Shevchenko [Stepniak's favorite author]).

Stepniak wrote populist booklets, such as *Skazka o kopeike* (Tale of a Kopeck, 1873) and *O pravde i krivde* (On Truth and Iniquity, 1875), and the books *La Russia sotterranea* (in Italian, 1882; English trans: *Underground Russia*, 1883; Ukrainian trans, 1901, 1979), *Russia under the Tzars* (2 vols, 1885), *The Russian Storm-Cloud; or, Russia in Her Relations to Neighbouring Countries* (1886), *The Russian Peasantry: Their Agrarian Condition, Social Life, and Religion* (2 vols, 1888), and *King Stork and King Log: A Study of Modern Russia* (2 vols, 1895), all of which provide information about political and social conditions in Ukraine. The most complete Russian editions of Stepniak's works were published in Petrograd (6 vols, 1906–8; 7 vols, 1917–19). Books about him have been written in Russian by L. Shishko (1903), L. Deich (1919), K. Berkova (1925), E. Taratuta (1967, 1970, 1987), and T. Maevskaia (1968), and in English by D. Senese (1987).

R. Senkus

**Stepnyi burial site.** An early Cimmerian and *Timber-Grave culture burial ground of the 11th to 10th century BC, found on the Stepnyi state farm near Zapovitne, Kamianka-Dniprovska raion, Zaporizhia oblast. Excavations in 1972 uncovered 14 graves in 13 kurhans. Among the objects recovered in the course of the excavations were earthenware goblets, bronze adornments, a bronze knife with an iron handle, and some of the oldest glass jewelry found in eastern Europe.

**Stepova-Karpiak, Mariia** [Karpjak, Marija], b 9 November 1903 in Pynske, Minsk gubernia, d 5 July 1984 in Philadelphia. Heroic character actress. She worked in various Ukrainian touring troupes in Galicia and Volhynia (1924–32), the Zahrava Theater (1932–8), the Kotliarevsky Theater (1938–9), the Lesia Ukrainka Theater (1939–41), and the Lviv Opera Theater (1941–4). She fled from Ukraine during the Second World War and then acted in the Ensemble of Ukrainian Actors in postwar Germany. After emigrating to the United States she continued with the ensemble (1949–53).

**Stepovy, Kostiantyn** [Stepovyj, Kostjantyn] (aka Blakytny, both noms de guerre of Kostiantyn Pestushenko), b 1897 in Hannivka, Kherson gubernia, d April 1921 in the Kryvyi Rih region. Partisan otaman. In 1918 he joined the Army of the UNR. When it retreated west in 1919, he returned to his native area and organized anti-Bolshevik partisan units. In May 1920 he united various insurgent units into the Steppe Division, and for the next six months he conducted guerrilla operations against the Red Army. Facing capture by a Cheka unit, he committed suicide.

Yakiv Stepovy          Dmytro Stepovyk

**Stepovy, Yakiv** [Stepovyj, Jakiv] (pseud of Yakiv Yakymenko), b 20 October 1883 in Pisky, near Kharkiv, d 4 November 1921 in Kiev. Composer, teacher, and music critic; brother of F. *Yakymenko. Recruited to sing with the St Petersburg court choir in 1895, he studied at the St Petersburg Conservatory in 1902–9 under N. Rimsky-Korsakov and A. Liadov. He lectured at the Kiev Conservatory from 1917 and was musical director of the Muzychna Drama theater and the State Vocal Ensemble from 1919. Stepovy played an important role in establishing a national school of Ukrainian music and is regarded (together with colleagues such as K. Stetsenko) as one of the luminaries of Ukrainian music. His compositions include numerous works for solo voice to the words of T. Shevchenko, I. Franko, Lesia Ukrainka, P. Tychyna, M. Rylsky, and others; the cycles *Barvinky* (Periwinkles) to the words of various poets and *Pisni nastroiu* (Songs of Mood, 1907–9) to the words of O. Oles; instrumental works such as sonatas,

rondos, a fantasia, a cycle of miniatures for piano (1909–13); and two suites for orchestra based on Ukrainian folk songs. Among his works for choir are 50 Ukrainian folk song arrangements, the children's vocal cycle *Prolisky* (Glades), a collection of songs for children to Shevchenko's *Kobzar*, and an unfinished opera based on Shevchenko's *Nevol'nyk* (The Captive). Biographies of Stepovy by M. Hrinchenko (1929 and 1959), V. Nadenenko (1950), Sh. Shvartsman (1951), T. Bulat (1980), and H. Stepanchenko (1987) have been published in Kiev.

R. Savytsky

**Stepovych, Andronyk** [Stepovyč] (né Dudka-Stepovych), b July 1857 in Lebedyntsi, Pryluka county, Poltava gubernia, d 1935 in Kiev. Slavist. He graduated from Galagan College (1875) and Kiev University (1879). He worked as a school inspector in Volhynia gubernia, taught Russian literature in several Kiev gymnasiums (1879–88), and taught Slavic philology at Kiev University (1895–1917). He was also director of Galagan College (1893–1906), and in 1907 he founded a private men's gymnasium in Kiev. In the Soviet period he was a professor of Slavic studies at the Kiev Institute of People's Education (1920–4), and he taught Slavic philology to graduate students at the VUAN until 1930. As a scholar he was influenced by his teacher O. Kotliarevsky and by P. Zhytetsky. From 1877 on he published many articles and Russian encyclopedia entries on Czech, Bulgarian, Serbian, Croatian, and Slovenian literature and translated into Russian West and South Slavic literary works (eg, by A. Jirásek, J. Vrchlický, and I. Vazov), thereby playing an important role in popularizing those literatures in the Russian Empire. His major contributions were a history of Czech literature (1886) and books of essays on the history of Slavic literatures (1893) and the history of Serbo-Croatian literature (1899). He also edited the annual of Galagan College (from 1894) and a few Slavist compendiums, published materials from the Galagan College archives, and wrote many studies and reviews in the fields of Ukrainian folk music, education, philology, and social and regional history in *Kievskaia starina* and the VUAN serials *Etnohrafichnyi visnyk, Za sto lit, Zapysky Istorychno-filolohichnoho viddilu*, and *Pervisne hromadianstvo ta ioho perezhytky na Ukraïni*.

R. Senkus

**Stepovyk, Dmytro**, b 7 October 1938 in Slobodyshche, Berdychiv raion, Zhytomyr oblast. Art historian and journalist. Since 1970 he has been a research fellow at the AN URSR (now ANU) Institute of Fine Arts, Folklore, and Ethnography in Kiev. He has written over 300 articles and reviews, and books on Ukrainian-Bulgarian artistic relations (1975); Ukrainian art (1976); Bulgarian art (1978); 16th- to 18th-century Ukrainian graphic art (1982); baroque master engravers, such as O. Tarasevych (1975), L. Tarasevych (1986), and I. Shchyrsky (1988); and Ukrainian art of the first half of the 19th century (1982). He has also edited an album of T. Shevchenko's paintings and graphic works (1984, 1986) and contributed entries to the *Encyclopedia of Ukraine*.

**Steppe**. A term, originally applied to the natural grasslands of *Southern Ukraine, which has been generalized to designate any natural grassland plain with a temperate, semiarid climate and chernozem or chestnut soils. The Ukrainian steppe encompasses most of the western segment of the Eurasian steppe that is known as the Black Sea (or Pontic) steppe province. The province forms a wedge, delimited by the forested foothills of the Crimean Mountains and the Caucasus Mountains in the south, the forest-steppe zone to the northwest, and the drier, more continental steppes east of the Volga. The border between the forest-steppe and the steppe is not distinct, but may be defined by the line Cahul–Tyraspil–Kirovohrad–Krasnohrad–Balakliia–Valuiky–Buturlynivka–Atkarsk–Samara. The steppe thus occupies about 240,000 sq km (40 percent) of Ukraine, nearly 300,000 sq km (40 percent) of the compact Ukrainian ethnographic territory, and 460,000 sq km (48 percent) of both compact and mixed Ukrainian national territory.

The steppe, endowed with the greatest heat resources in Ukraine, has the longest growing season, but receives the least precipitation and often suffers from drought. The mean January temperatures range from –2°C along the Black Sea coast to –10°C (Buturlynivka); the mean July temperatures are from 20°C in the north to 24°C in the eastern Stavropol region. The frost-free period ranges from 220 days in the southwest to 150 days in the northeast. The annual accumulation of degree-days above 10°C increases southward from 2,800 to 3,600, and the growing season increases from 210 to 245 days. The relatively moderate southern climate allows for the cultivation of heat-loving crops, relay cropping, and even double cropping. The annual precipitation, however, decreases southward from 450 mm along the forest-steppe margin to 300 mm at Perekop. The moisture deficit, generated by an average annual evaporation of 900–1,000 mm, is in part compensated for by an early summer precipitation maximum (when the plants need more water). Moisture accumulation in the soil is unstable, however, for the meager winter snow accumulation is often removed by thaws. The small rivers in the steppe tend to be seasonal and to dry up in the summer. The large rivers, such as the Dnieper and the Boh, carry their water in transit. The small lakes, often in *pody*, are seasonal; the large lakes are of the coastal, liman type, many with saline water.

The Ukrainian steppe is frequently differentiated according to climatic and soil conditions into three subzones, the northern steppe, the middle steppe, and the southern steppe. The northern subzone is characterized by a natural vegetation of meadow fescue and feather grass on ordinary, medium humus content (6–8 percent) chernozems. Its natural vegetation consisted of a luxuriant growth of tight-turfed, narrow-leaved grasses (such as feather grass and fescue), forbs (such as drooping sage, veronica, campion, steppe tulips), and shrubs (blackthorn, almond, steppe almond). The sandy river terraces were covered with pine forests. Some of the natural vegetation is preserved in the Luhanske Nature Reserve and the Ukrainian Steppe Nature Reserve.

The middle steppe, extending along the Black Sea coastal plain eastward toward the northern coast of the Sea of Azov, is characterized by narrow-leaved fescue and feather grass on southern chernozems (5–6 percent humus content) and dark chestnut soils (3–4 percent humus content). Its vegetation, dominated by narrow-leaved xerophytic grasses (such as feather grass, esparto grass, and several fescue grasses) with an admixture of xerophytic forbs (such as limonium) and spring ephemerals, is preserved in the Askaniia-Nova Nature Reserve.

The southern steppe, which straddles Perekop Bay and Syvash Lake, consists of dry wormwood-grassland steppe on chestnut and solonetz soils (2–3 percent humus content). The vegetation, containing wheat grass and fescue grass and occasionally esparto grass and several sages, is preserved in the Azov-Syvash Game Preserve.

The present fauna of the steppe is dominated by soil-boring rodents, who find sanctuary from inclement weather underground, and by their predators. Among the rodents are rabbits, marmots, hamsters, mice, and European mole rats; the predators are the polecat, the fox, and the wolf. Birds include larks, quail, yellow bunting, partridge, windhover, and, less commonly, bustards, owls, and eagles.

The Ukrainian steppe has been almost completely modified by human activity. Of the total land area in the steppe zone of Ukraine (1981), 64.9 percent is cultivated, 2.4 percent is under perennial plantings, 0.8 percent is hayfields, 10.8 percent is pastures, 4.2 percent is woodland (mostly riverbank and shelterbelt plantings), and the remaining 16.9 percent is devoted to other uses. Grains occupy one-half of the cropped area, among which winter wheat is prevalent. Among industrial crops sunflower and to a lesser degree sugar beets in the northeast and the Kuban are important. Heat-loving melons and vegetables such as tomatoes are produced in the Donbas, near Kherson, and near Odessa (in part for consumption in the northern cities). Vineyards are particularly common west of Odessa, near Kherson, and in the Crimea. Livestock densities are not high, but sheep are dominant on the dry pastures of the southern steppe. Moisture deficit, drought, and frequent *sukhovii* and dust storms have hindered agricultural production. Attempts to counter such climatic hazards have included shelterbelt afforestation and irrigation as well as the melioration of salinized soils following improper or careless irrigation.

BIBLIOGRAPHY

Dokuchaev, V. *Nashi stepi prezhde i teper* (St. Petersburg 1892)
Izmail'skii, A. *Kak vysokhla nasha step'* (Poltava 1893)
'Stepy, kamianysti vidslonennia, pisky,' in *Roslynnist' URSR* (Kiev 1973)
Pashchenko, V. 'Stepnaia zona,' in *Priroda Ukrainskoi SSR: Landshafty* (Kiev 1985)

I. Stebelsky

**Steppe dialects.** One of the three dialectal groups comprising the *southeastern dialects. The dialects evolved in the 17th to 20th centuries as a result of the intermingling of settlers in southern Ukraine speaking the Podilian, South Volhynian, Chernihiv, Poltava, and central Polisian dialects. They have also been influenced by the *Russian language in Ukraine. The dialects are spoken south of the line Uman–Novomyrhorod–Chyhyryn–Krasnohrad–Izium–Luhanske. They are divided into three subgroups: the western (in southern Bessarabia and Odessa and Mykolaiv oblasts between the Prut and Boh rivers), in which Podilian and Volhynian features are the most evident; the central (in Kirovohrad, Kryvyi Rih, Dnipropetrovske, and Zaporizhia oblasts); and the eastern (in Donetske and Luhanske oblasts).

The features of the steppe dialects are (1) the softened pronunciation of consonants before *i* derived from *ō* (eg, *st'il* SU *stil*] 'table'); (2) the retention of *o* derived from *ō* (eg, *odn'imá, stójte* [SU *vidnimáje, stíjte*] 'subtracts, stand [pl imp]'); (3) simplification of the group *ždž* in verbal forms of the type *odjižžát'* (SU *vid'jiždžáty*) 'to depart [by vehicle]';

(4) pronunciation of the group *m'ja* as *mn'a* (eg, *mn'áty* [Standard Ukrainian (SU) *m'játy*] 'to wrinkle'); (5) pronunciation of unstressed *o, e* as *u, i* before a subsequent stressed *u, i* (eg, *hudúj, min'í* [SU *hodúj, mení*] 'feed [sing impl], to me') and in endings of the type *slúxajiš* (SU *slúxaješ*) 'you listen'; (6) hardened pronunciation of *c'* in forms of the type *prósycca, prós'acca* (SU *prósyt'sja, prósjat'sja*) '(s)he/they plead', particularly in the west; (7) pronunciation of the type *d'it, t'aškė* (SU *did, tjažkė*) 'grandfather, heavy'; (8) influence of the endings of hard nouns on those of soft and mixed nouns (eg, *kon'óvi, koval'óm, nožóm, zeml'ój(u), dušój(u)* [SU *konévi, kovalém, nožém, zemléju, dušéju*] 'horse (dat), blacksmith, knife, land, soul (inst)'; (9) the endings *-oj/-ej* (in addition to *-oju/-eju*) in instrumental singular feminine nouns and *-iv* in genitive plural feminine and neuter nouns (eg, *žinkíŭ, nočíŭ, jáblukiŭ, poros'átiŭ* [SU *žinók, nočéj, jábluk, porosját*] 'women, nights, apples, piglets'), and, sporadically, forms such as *na ruk'í, na noh'í* (SU *na rucí, na nozí*) 'on the arm, on the leg' in dative and locative singular feminine nouns; (10) pronominal forms of the type *do jóho, kolo jéji, z jim, bez jíx* (SU *do n'óho, kolo néji, z nym, bez nyx*) 'to him, near her, with him, without them'; (11) verbal forms of the type *krut'ú, xod'ú, voz'ú, pokósynyj, pytá, pytát', pylác'c'a, pytájus', pytálas', pytáŭs'* (SU *kručú, xodžú, vožú, pokóšenyj, pytáje, pytáty, pytátysja, pytájusja, pytálasja, pytávsja*) 'I turn, I walk, I drive, mown, he asks, to ask, to enquire, I enquire, she enquired, he enquired'; (12) levelling of the *-y-/-ji-* and *-e-* conjugations in root-stressed verbs (eg, *krúte, krút'ut'* [SU *krútyt', krútjat'*] 'he turns, they turn'); (13) remnants of the archaic type of agreement of predicates with collective nouns used as subjects (eg, *naród zbíhlys', mólodiž pišlý* [SU *naród zbíhsja, mólod' pišlá*] 'the people gathered, the youth went').

Lexical *Turkisms are widespread, particularly in fishing and gardening terminology. *Rumanianisms are found in the western subgroup's sheepherding and gardening terminology. In the eastern subgroup, in southeastern Donetske oblast along the Azov littoral, the Russian influence has been quite strong and has resulted in mixed Ukrainian-Russian dialects. The Ukrainian dialects spoken in Rostov oblast, the Kuban, and the Stavropil region of Subcaucasia are similar to the steppe dialects.

The steppe dialects have been studied by linguists such as A. Berlizov, Y. Dzendzelivsky, A. Moskalenko. L. Tereshko. V. Drozdovsky, A. Mukan, T. Zavorotna, V. Karpova, Ya. Nahin, S. Samiilenko, V. Vashchenko, O. Horbach, and I. Matviias. Their grammatical and lexical elements can be found in the belletristic works of I. Tobilevych, V. Vynnychenko, and Yu. Yanovsky.

O. Horbach

**Steppe Ukraine.** See Southern Ukraine.

**Stepura, Hryhorii,** b 1881, d 1939 in Rivne, Volhynia. Civic and political activist. While practicing law in Kamianets-Podilskyi he was active in various local organizations. In 1917 he became a member of the Central Rada and gubernial commissioner for Podilia. From 1920 he lived in Rivne, where he was arrested and executed by the Soviets.

**Stercho, Petro** [Sterčo, Petro], b 14 April 1919 in Kuzmyne, Bereg county, Transcarpathia, d 18 June 1987 in Narberth, Pennsylvania. Economist, historian, and civic leader; full member of the Shevchenko Scientific Society. A graduate of the Ukrainian Higher School of Economics

Petro Stercho                    Metropolitan Volodymyr
                                 Sterniuk

in Munich (PH D, 1949), he emigrated to the United States in 1950 and taught at St Vincent's College (1955–63) while studying political science at the University of Notre Dame (PH D, 1959). From 1963 he lectured in economics at Drexel University in Philadelphia. He was a leading member of many Ukrainian organizations, such as the United Ukrainian American Relief Committee, the Ukrainian Congress Committee of America, the Ukrainian American Coordinating Council, the Carpathian Sich Brotherhood, and the *Ukrainian American Association of University Professors (president, 1967–71). Besides numerous articles in history and economics, he wrote *Carpatho-Ukraine in International Affairs, 1938–1939* (1959), *Karpato-ukraïns'ka derzhava* (The Carpatho-Ukrainian State, 1965), *Diplomacy of Double Morality: Europe's Crossroads in Carpatho-Ukraine, 1919–1939* (1971), and (with M. Stakhiv) *Ukraine and the European Turmoil, 1917–1919* (1973).

**Sterlet** (*Acipenser ruthenus*; Ukrainian: *sterliad, chechuha*). A fish of the *sturgeon family Acipenseridae, up to 125 cm in length and 16–17 kg in weight, with a life span of up to 22 years. In Ukrainian waters sterlet is found in the Black Sea, around the Danube delta, and in the Sea of Azov. It is a valuable commercial fish and is a source of caviar. Changing ecological conditions have diminished the number of sterlets, and artificial breeding and acclimatization are being experimented with in an attempt to increase their numbers. A productive hybrid crossed with white sturgeon (beluga) was recently obtained.

**Sterniuk, Volodymyr** [Sternjuk], b 12 February 1907 in Pustomyty, Lviv county, Galicia. Ukrainian Catholic metropolitan. He studied philosophy and theology in Belgium, where he entered the Redemptorist order in 1927. He was ordained a priest in Leuven in 1931 by Bishop V. Ladyka of Canada. After completing his theological studies in 1932, he returned to Galicia to do missionary work in Volhynia and the Ternopil and Stanyslaviv (now Ivano-Frankivske) regions, and then moved to Lviv, where he was consultator. In 1945 he was arrested in Lviv and exiled to Siberia. After being released in 1952, he returned to Lviv, where he worked in menial jobs and continued to be active in the underground church. In July 1964 he was consecrated bishop of Peremyshl by Bishop V. Velychkovsky, and in 1973 he was named deputy to Cardinal Y. Slipy and acting archbishop of Lviv and Halych metropoly. In August 1989, after the legalization of the Ukrainian Catholic church, he called a congress of all bishops of Halych metropoly. He has participated in negotiations with the Russian Orthodox church and the Vatican concerning the return of churches, monasteries, and other institutions confiscated from the Ukrainian Catholic church in 1946 and has helped preside over the rebirth of the church.

Iryna Steshenko    Ivan Steshenko (1873–1918)

**Steshenko, Iryna** [Stešenko], b 5 July 1898 in Kiev, d 30 December 1987 in Kiev. Actor and translator; daughter of I. and O. *Steshenko and granddaughter of M. *Starytsky. She graduated from the Higher Courses for Women (1918) and the Lysenko Music and Drama Institute (1920) in Kiev and performed in prominent roles with the Shevchenko First Theater of the Ukrainian Soviet Republic (1920–3) and *Berezil (1923–33) theater troupes under the direction of L. Kurbas in Kiev and Kharkiv. She gave up acting in 1949. Steshenko began translating in 1920. Her translations include comedies by Molière and C. Goldoni, several plays by W. Shakespeare, J.W. von Goethe's *Egmont*, F. Schiller's *Don Carlos*, F. Crommelynck's *Tripes d'or*, A. Berg's *Wozzeck*, Mark Twain's *Adventures of Huckleberry Finn*, and works by Jack London, M. Gorky, G. de Maupassant, and H. Ibsen. Several of her translations were used in Berezil's productions.

**Steshenko, Ivan** [Stešenko] (pseuds: I. Serdeshny, I. Sichovyk, I. Svitlenko, I. Stepura), b 24 June 1873 in Poltava, d 30 July 1918 in Poltava. Civic and political figure, literary scholar, writer, and translator; member of the Shevchenko Scientific Society from 1917; husband of O. and father of Iryna and Ya. Steshenko, and son-in-law of M. *Starytsky. While he was a student at Kiev University (1892-6), he was active in the Literary Hromada (the successor to *Pleiada). He published his first literary articles, poems, and translations in Lviv's *Pravda*, *Zoria*, and *Dzvinok*. He graduated from the historical-philological faculty (1896) and became a teacher at the Kiev women's gymnasium. Steshenko became politicized by M. Drahomanov's writings and through his friendship with M. Kovalevsky. In 1896, together with Lesia Ukrainka and others, he formed the first Ukrainian social-democratic circle and wrote the drama *Mazepa*. In 1897 he was imprisoned for four months, exiled from Kiev for three years, and prohibited from teaching. He occupied himself by preparing a Ukrainian dictionary (which was never published). He wrote the first book about I. Kotliarevsky's poetry (1898), published the poetry collections *Khutorni sonety* (Farmstead Sonnets, 1899) and *Stepovi motyvy* (Steppe Motifs,

1900), and began publishing articles and reviews in *Kievskaia starina*.

Steshenko returned to Kiev in 1900 and became a leading figure in the Ukrainian national movement. He was elected a member of the Hromada of Kiev, and collaborated with the General Ukrainian Non-Party Democratic Organization and its successor, the Society of Ukrainian Progressives. Steshenko continued publishing in many periodicals, delivered lectures in Kiev and elsewhere, and became secretary of the Kiev Literary-Artistic Society until its abolition in 1905. In 1902 he published the first major critical biography of I. Kotliarevsky. In 1905 he copublished the satirical magazine *Shershen'*. In 1906 he was reinstated as a teacher, and from 1907 until 1917 he taught literature at the First Commercial School in Kiev, the Higher Courses for Women, and the Lysenko Music and Drama School. He was secretary and deputy head of the Ukrainian Scientific Society, published a history of Ukrainian drama (1908) and edited the monthly *Siaivo* (1913–14), and directed a gymnasium for war refugees (1915–17).

After the February Revolution of 1917 Steshenko was elected a member of the Kiev Civic Executive Committee. He cofounded and headed the *Society of School Education and became a delegate to the Central Rada. He was appointed the UNR government's general secretary (June–December 1917) and minister of education (January–February 1918). He directed the Ukrainization of the national school curriculum and pedagogical education and founded the Ukrainian State Academy of Arts and the Ukrainian Pedagogical Academy. He was murdered by unknown assailants while on vacation. Steshenko was given a state funeral and buried in the Baikove Cemetery in Kiev.

Steshenko wrote many literary articles in addition to his books on Kotliarevsky and Ukrainian drama. He also contributed the chapter on 14th- to 18th-century Ukrainian literature to the encyclopedic compendium *Ukrainskii narod v ego proshlom i nastoiashchem* (The Ukrainian People: Its Past and Present, 2 vols, 1914, 1916) and translated works by Ovid (*Metamorphoses*), F. Schiller (*Die Jungfrau von Orleans*), G. Byron, A. Pushkin, F. Coppée, and P.-J. de Béranger into Ukrainian.

R. Senkus

**Steshenko, Ivan** [Stešenko] (Steschenko), b 24 January 1894 in Lebedyn, Kharkiv gubernia, d 3 May 1937 in Moscow. Opera and concert singer (bass). He studied at the Petrograd Conservatory and in Italy and won first prize in an international competition in Parma (1914). A soloist of the Kiev Opera (1917–21), he toured Poland, England, France, and Italy and in 1922–31 sang in American opera houses (Chicago, Philadelphia, Washington, DC, New York, and Boston), where he appeared with the conductors L. Stokowski and E. Goosens. After returning to Ukraine he was a soloist of the Kharkiv Opera (1931–4) and the Kharkiv Philharmonia (1934–7). His main roles were Zarastro in W. Mozart's *Die Zauberflöte*, Basilio in G. Rossini's *Il Barbiere di Siviglia*, Galitsky in A. Borodin's *Prince Igor*, and the name-parts in M. Lysenko's *Taras Bulba*, M. Mussorgsky's *Boris Godunov*, and A. Boito's *Mefistofele*. In recitals he performed art songs by M. Lysenko, Ya. Stepovy, and K. Stetsenko.

**Steshenko, Oksana** [Stešenko], b 1875 in Karpivka, Kremenchuk county, Poltava gubernia, d 1941. Writer; daughter of M. *Starytsky, and wife of Ivan and mother of Iryna and Ya. Steshenko. She compiled the children's anthology *Ridni kolosky* (Native Sheaves, 1924; 2nd edn, *Kolosky zhyttia* [Sheaves of Life, 1925]) and wrote the children's story collection *Iak Iurko podorozhuvav na Dniprovi porohy* (How Yurko Travelled to the Dnieper Rapids, 1929; rev edn 1942) and *Heroï zv'iazku* (Heroes of Communication, 1930). She also wrote literary criticism and translated Russian literature into Ukrainian. Steshenko and her sister, L. *Starytska-Cherniakhivska, were arrested by the NKVD. They were deported to Kazakhstan and died (were shot?) en route.

**Steshenko, Serhii** [Stešenko, Serhij], b 5 July 1902 in Nova Vodolaha, Valky county, Kharkiv gubernia. Scenery designer. He completed study at the Kharkiv Institute of Fine Arts (1929, pupil of S. Prokhorov and I. Padalka) and became a specialist in scenery and costumes for puppet theaters, particularly the Lviv Puppet Theater. He also designed for the Volhynian Ukrainian Music and Drama Theater.

**Steshenko, Yaroslav** [Stešenko, Jaroslav], b 6 April 1904 in Kiev, d 11 March 1939. Bibliographer; son of I. and O. *Steshenko. He graduated from the Kiev Institute of the National Economy (1928), and from 1929 he worked at the Ukrainian Scientific Institute of Bibliology in Kiev. He wrote articles on questions of bibliography and bibliology, on H. Narbut, and on S. Maslov and compiled several bibliographies, including an important systematic catalog of VUAN publications (1930, with M. Ivanchenko).

Fedir Steshko          Osyp Stetkevych

**Steshko, Fedir** [Steško], b 16 September 1877 in Kamianka, Sosnytsia county, Chernihiv gubernia, d 31 December 1944 in Prague. Musicologist. A lawyer by training, he worked as a judge for the Russian military court in Vladivostok before emigrating to Prague in 1920. There he completed his studies in musicology (PH D, Charles University, 1936) and lectured at the Ukrainian Free University and the Ukrainian Higher Pedagogical Institute. His published works include *Dzherela do istoriï pochatkovoï doby tserkovnoho spivu v Ukraïni* (Sources for the History of the Early Period of Religious Singing in Ukraine, 1929) and *Českí hudebníci v ukrajinské církevní hudbě* (Czech Musicians in Ukrainian Church Music, 1935) as well as articles on the history of Ukrainian music.

**Stetkevych, Osyp** [Stetkevyč] (Stetkewicz, Joseph), b 12 January 1876 in Plotycha Velyka, Berezhany county, Galicia, d 23 January 1942 in New York. Teacher, journalist, and civic figure. He completed study at a teachers' seminary and taught for several years until forced to emigrate to the United States in 1904 because of persecution by the Polish Galician authorities. He was active in Ukrainian educational work in the United States (he urged the development of nationwide structures and standard texts) and worked for an extended period with the newspaper *Svoboda* as an editor (1910 and 1912–19) and associate. He was also a cofounder of the American Ruthenian National Council.

Hryhorii Stetsenko's icon of the Theotokos in Romen

**Stetsenko, Hryhorii** [Stecenko, Hryhorij], b April 1710 in Romen, Lubni regiment, d 11 February 1781 in Romen. Painter. In the 1740s he painted murals at the mansion of K. and O. Rozumovsky on their estate, Pokorshchyna, near Kozelets. He painted murals and icons in the Church of the Resurrection (1748) in Hlukhiv and the Church of the Nativity of the Mother of God (1758) in Kozelets, and the iconostasis in the Transfiguration Cathedral in Pochep (1758–9). In the 1750s he served as Hetman K. Rozumovsky's official painter in Hlukhiv and painted portraits of the hetman and his brother Oleksii in 1753. He also painted other icons, such as the *Romen Theotokos, John* *the Theologian*, and *Lying in the Coffin*. In many of his icons he used typically Ukrainian figures in contemporary settings. He was promoted to the status of fellow of the banner in the Lubni Cossack Regiment in 1766 and lived thenceforth in Romen.

Kyrylo Stetsenko

**Stetsenko, Kyrylo** [Stecenko], b 24 May 1882 in Kvitky, Kaniv county, Kiev gubernia, d 29 April 1922 in Vepryk, Vasylkiv county, Kiev gubernia. Composer, conductor, teacher, and community activist. Stetsenko's musical talents were recognized while he was studying in Kiev by I. Apolonov, director of the St Michael's Golden-Domed Monastery choir. In 1899 he joined the Lysenko choir. After graduating from the Kiev Theological Academy in 1903 he began teaching music at the pedagogical institute and conducting church and secular choirs, continued studying composition under H. Liubomyrsky at the Lysenko Music and Drama School, and participated with leading Ukrainian musical figures in an unsuccessful attempt to establish an independent music publishing house. At the same time he compiled the songbook *Luna* (Echo). His activities led to his arrest and exile (1907–10) to a town in the Donbas, where he taught music in a local school. A year later he moved to Bila Tserkva, where he taught music in the gymnasium, and then to Tyvriv in the Vinnytsia region. Ordained in 1911, he became a pastor in a Podilian village near Tomashpil. He ceased virtually all his creative work until 1917, when he was recruited to the music department of the UNR Ministry of Education. Although many of his activities involved organizing and teaching (including the establishment of major choirs such as the *Ukrainian Republican Kapelle and Dniprosoiuz [later DUMKA]), he also returned to composing and conducting.

Stetsenko's compositions and pedagogical work continued the Ukrainian national music tradition established by M. *Lysenko. Rich melodies and harmonies are characteristic of his musical language. Songs for solo voice (more than 30) and settings of words of T. Shevchenko, I. Franko, Lesia Ukrainka, O. Oles, and others form a major part of his creative work. His compositions for choir are diverse in form: religious works (two liturgies, a requiem), cantatas, choral works both a cappella and with piano accompaniment, and arrangements of Ukrainian folk songs (including carols). He wrote scores for the plays *Svatannia na Honcharivtsi* (Matchmaking at Honcharivka, 1909) by H. Kvitka-Osnovianenko, *Pro shcho tyrsa shelestila* (What the Feather Grass Murmured About, 1916) by S. Cher-

kasenko, and *Buval'shchyna* (A True Tale) by A. Velisovsky. His operatic works include the unfinished *Polonianka* and *Karmeliuk* and the dramatic scene *Ifigeniia v Tavrii* (Iphigenia in Tauris, 1921), based on Lesia Ukrainka's play. He composed music to T. Shevchenko's poem *Haidamaky* (1919–21) and wrote two children's operas, *Lysychka, kotyk i pivnyk* (The Vixen, the Cat, and the Rooster, 1910) and *Ivasyk-Telesyk* (1911). Stetsenko also compiled songbooks for school and home use.

BIBLIOGRAPHY
Roshchakivs'kyi, M. 'Kyrylo Stetsenko,' *Nova Ukraïna*, 1923, no. 7–8
Hrinchenko, M. *Kyrylo Stetsenko – Kompozytor* (Kharkiv–Kiev 1930)
Parkhomenko, L. *Kyrylo Hryhorovych Stetsenko* (Kiev 1963)
Fedotov, Ie. *Kyrylo Hryhorovych Stetsenko – Pedahoh* (Kiev 1977)
Lisets'kyi, S. *Rysy styliu tvorchosti K. Stetsenka* (Kiev 1977)
Fedotov, Ie. (ed). *Kyrylo Stetsenko: Spohady, lysty, materialy* (Kiev 1981)

W. Wytwycky

**Stetsenko, Vasyl** [Stecenko, Vasyl'], b 27 December 1901 in Kozatske, Zvenyhorodka county, Kiev gubernia, d 9 December 1971 in Kiev. Graphic artist. In 1930 he graduated from the Kiev State Art Institute, where he studied under V. Kasiian and S. Nalepinska. He made posters, prints, and book illustrations, using mostly wood engraving. He did the print series 'The Dnieper' (1940) and a series of pencil sketches 'Crossing the Danube' (1943), and designed editions of the poetry of M. Rylsky, P. Tychyna, Lesia Ukrainka, A. Svydnytsky, and V. Samiilenko (1957); books of folk wisdom (1959), old Ukrainian humor and satire (1959), and contemporary Ukrainian humor (3 vols, 1960); and bookplates.

**Stetsenko, Yurii** [Stecenko, Jurij], b 11 April 1945 in Kiev. Canoeing competitor. World champion in doubles (with O. Shaparenko) at 1,000 m in 1966, and four-man canoes in 1970 and 1971 at the same distance. He was a gold medalist at the 1972 Olympics in the four-man 1,000 m. An eleven-time champion of the USSR, he was also champion of Ukraine many times over.

**Stetsiuk, Hryhorii** [Stecjuk, Hryhorij], b 13 October 1892, d autumn 1948 in Galicia. Galician journalist and community figure. He was chief editor of the Lviv newspaper *Nash prapor* (1932–9) and of *Visti* (1942–4), a paper published in Berlin for Ukrainians forced to work in Germany. He was arrested by the Soviet police in 1944 and imprisoned in a concentration camp in Kazakhstan until 1948. He died soon after returning home.

**Stetsiuk, Kateryna** [Stecjuk], b 23 November 1905 in Shpytky, Kiev county. Historian. A graduate of the Kiev Institute of People's Education (1928), she worked at the AN URSR (now ANU) Institute of History (from 1938) and taught at the Kiev Pedagogical Institute and the CC CPU Higher Party School (1938–53). She wrote *Vplyv povstannia Stepana Razina na Ukraïnu* (The Influence of S. Razin's Uprising on Ukraine, 1947), *Pereiaslavs'ke povstannia 1666 r.* (The Pereiaslav Uprising of 1666, 1958), and *Narodni rukhy na Livoberezhnii i Slobids'kii Ukraïni v 50–70-kh rokakh XVII st.* (Popular Movements in Left-Bank and Slobidska Ukraine in the 1650s to 1670s, 1960) and contributed to the collective works *Istoriia Ukraïns'koï RSR* (History of the

Ukrainian SSR, 2 vols, 1967) and *Istoriia selianstva Ukraïns'koï RSR* (History of the Peasantry of the Ukrainian SSR, 2 vols, 1967).

Vasyl Stetsiuk

**Stetsiuk, Vasyl** [Stecjuk, Vasyl'] (Steciuk, Basil), b 18 March 1910 in Hnylychky, Zbarazh county, Galicia, d 9 April 1975 in Jersey City, New Jersey. Classical philologist and pedagogue; member of the Shevchenko Scientific Society (NTSh) from 1950. He studied at Lviv University (1933; M ED, 1936). He lectured at the Ukrainian Free University in Munich after obtaining his PH D there (1946). After emigrating to the United States in 1950, he taught at the Ukrainian Technical Institute in New York (1955–63) and at Seton Hall University (1958–75). He was head of the NTSh Linguistic Commission and secretary of its Supreme Council (1970–5). He wrote a historical grammar of Latin (2 vols, 1950, 1953) in Ukrainian, a booklet on the Greek lexical fund in the Ukrainian language (1958), and various articles on classical philology.

**Stetsiuk, Yakiv** [Stecjuk, Jakiv], b 9 December 1922 in Mokre, Novohrad-Volynskyi okruha, Zhytomyr gubernia, d 15 October 1980 in Lviv. Writer. A former editor of *Zhovten'* (1951–5) and secretary responsible for the Lviv branch of the Writers' Union of Ukraine (1965–?), from 1952 on he published over 20 collections of stories and novelettes, the most recent of which are *Viriu* (I Believe, 1974), *Spalakh* (The Blaze, 1976), and *Des' tam syni zori* (Somewhere There Are Blue Stars, 1980). He also wrote the novels *Sovist'* (Conscience, 1964), *Zelenyi kut* (The Green Corner, 1965), and *Maidan* (The Square, 1970) and the historical novels *Honta* (1969) and *Ivan Pidkova* (1971). An edition of his selected works appeared in 1982.

**Stetsko, Dmytro** [Stec'ko], b 28 November 1943 in Polonna, Sianik county, Galicia. Avant-garde painter and sculptor. Since graduating from the Lviv School of Applied Art (1971) he has worked in Ternopil. His paintings are an amalgam of folk-art, Renaissance, and modernist influences. They include *Sunflowers* (1970), *Mowers* (1972), the triptych *Buckwheat Honey* (1980), the diptych *Cathedral* (1989), and the series 'Seasons of the Year' (1974–5), 'Sonata for Čiurlonis' (1978), 'Landmarks of History' (1981–90), and 'Peasant Frescoes' (1983); portraits of historical and cultural figures, such as Prince Volodymyr the Great (1984), Princess Olha (1987), T. Shevchenko (1986), Lesia Ukrainka (1986), I. Franko (1986), and D. Vyshnevetsky (1990); portraits of his mother (1976) and his wife (1978);

Dmytro Stetsko (self-portrait, oil, 1986)

and the self-portraits *Benefit* (1981), *White Portrait* (1984), and *Black Self-Portrait* (1985). More recently he has created cubist and abstract sculptures. He has also painted murals in several schools and institutes in Ternopil. The first solo exhibitions of Stetsko's works were held in Lviv and Kiev in 1989.

Slava Stetsko                          Yaroslav Stetsko

**Stetsko, Slava** [Stec'ko] (née Muzyka), b 14 May 1920 in Romanivka, Ternopil county, Galicia. Political leader and journalist; wife of Ya. *Stetsko. She studied at Lviv University and the Ukrainian Free University. She was a co-founder of the Red Cross units serving the Ukrainian Insurgent Army during the Second World War. She was imprisoned during the German occupation of Ukraine, and remained in Germany as an émigré in 1944. Stetsko became a member of the CC of the *Anti-Bolshevik Bloc of Nations (ABN). She edited the German edition of *ABN Correspondence (1948), the quarterly Ukrainian Review, and other ABN periodicals, and she organized and participated in a number of international anticommunist congresses. She served as a member of the central executive of the Ukrainian Youth Association (1948–53). From 1968 she was head of the external affairs sector of the OUN (Bandera faction). She was a co-organizer of the European Council of Liberty and became its vice-president in 1985. In 1986 she became president of the ABN and an executive member of the *World Anti-Communist League. In 1991, at the Seventh Great Assembly of the OUN, Stetsko was elected leader of the OUN Bandera faction.

**Stetsko, Yaroslav** [Stec'ko, Jaroslav] (pseuds: Z. Karbovych, E. Orlovsky, S. Osinsky, B. Ozersky, and Y. Pidlesetsky), b 19 January 1912 in Ternopil, d 5 July 1986 in Munich. Political leader and ideologue of the Ukrainian nationalist movement. As a youth he joined the underground Ukrainian Nationalist Youth organization and subsequently the *Ukrainian Military Organization and the *Organization of Ukrainian Nationalists. In 1932 he was appointed to the OUN executive with responsibility for ideology. The Polish authorities arrested him several times for his activities; in 1936 he was sentenced to five years' imprisonment, but he was released under a general amnesty in 1937. He was responsible for the preparations for the Great Assembly of the OUN held in Rome in 1939. He became one of the members of the Revolutionary Leadership of the OUN, which emerged in 1940 and was headed by S. *Bandera. At the Cracow Great Assembly he was elected Bandera's second-in-command. He participated in the organization of OUN expeditionary groups on the eve of the German-Soviet War. He prepared the *proclamation of Ukrainian statehood of 30 June 1941; at the National Assembly in Lviv where the renewal of Ukrainian statehood was officially proclaimed, he was chosen premier of the *Ukrainian State Administration. For refusing to annul the proclamation of statehood Stetsko was arrested by the Gestapo on 12 July 1941; he was first taken to Berlin and then incarcerated in the *Sachsenhausen concentration camp, until the fall of 1944. After his release he settled in Munich.

In 1945 Stetsko was elected to the Leadership of the OUN (Bandera faction). After the war he was active in the world anticommunist movement. In 1946 he was elected head of the *Anti-Bolshevik Bloc of Nations (ABN); he remained president of that organization until his death. In 1946 he was also chosen to head the foreign policy sector of the external units of the OUN. As head of the ABN Stetsko signed an agreement of co-operation with the Chinese Anti-Communist League in Taiwan (1955), which resulted in an ABN mission (1957–60) and later representation (until 1971) in Taipei. He also served on the executive of the *World Anti-Communist League (est 1967) and was a founder and life member of the honorary presidium of the European Freedom Council. At the Fourth Great Assembly of the Bandera faction in 1968, he was elected head, a position he retained until his death. A number of his works were published posthumously in Ukraïns'ka vyzvol'na kontsepsiia (The Ukrainian Liberation Concept, 1987) and Ukraine and the Subjugated Nations: Their Struggle for National Liberation (1989). He left an account of the events surrounding the proclamation of Ukrainian statehood, Trydtsiatoho chervnia 1941 (The 30th of June 1941, 1967).

B. Folusiewicz

**Stetsura, Ihor.** See Stecura, Ihor.

*Stiah* (Banner). A monthly journal of the Ukrainian Evangelical Church of the Augsburg Confession published in Stanyslaviv in 1932–9. It was published and edited by Pastor T. Yarchuk.

**Stieber, Zdzisław,** b 7 June 1903 in Szczakowa, Chrzanów county, Poland, d 12 October 1980 in Warsaw. Polish linguist and Slavic philologist; member of the Polish Academy of Sciences from 1954. After graduating from Cracow University (PH D, 1929), he conducted fieldwork on the Lemko and with S. Hrabec on the Boiko dialects (1934–9) and served as a professor at Lviv (1937–9, 1944–5), Łódź (1945–52), and Warsaw (1952–66) universities. He wrote numerous works on the history, dialects, and structure of Common Slavic, Polish, and other Slavic languages, including a number of important works in Ukrainian linguistics: a book on the toponomastics of the Lemko region (2 parts, 1948–9); a dialectal atlas of the Lemko region (8 fascicles with 416 maps, 1956–64), based on fieldwork in 72 settlements in 1934–5; and a posthumously published book on the phonetics and phonology of the Lemko dialect (1982). Many of his articles were reprinted as Świat językowy Słowian (1974). Articles about him and a bibliography of his works were published as Zdzisław Stieber (1903–1980) in 1982.

**Stih.** V-4. The tallest peak (elevation 1677 m) in the Svydivets Ridge in Transcarpathia oblast. It is composed largely of sandy clay deposits. Its northern slope is covered with coniferous forest, and the higher elevations have sloping meadows. Landscape formations caused by glaciation are evident on the mountain.

**Stilske fortified settlement.** A 10th-century Rus' fortress near Stilske, Mykolaiv raion, Lviv oblast. Discovered in 1984, the fort encompassed an area of approx 250 ha, and the total length of its defensive structures was nearly 10 km.

**Stilt, black-winged** (Himantopus h. himantopus; Ukrainian: khodulychnyk). An Old World shorebird of the family Recurvirostridae (order Charadriiformes), with long, thin, pink legs and a long, slender, black bill. In Ukraine it is found on the shores of the Black Sea and the Sea of Azov. There is also an island colony of stilts in the Poltava region. Stilts are listed as rare birds in Ukraine. Their fossils date back to the Pleistocene era.

**Stobensky** [Stobens'kyj]. A family of 17th- and 18th-century wood carvers and wood sculptors from Zhovkva, Galicia. Hnat (d 1742) learned his craft in the carpentry and wood carving guilds of Zhovkva. He carved the iconostases in the Trinity Church in Zhovkva with Yu. Shymanovych, S. Putiatytsky, and V. Sokovych and in the churches at the Krekhiv, Mezhyhiria, and Krasnopushcha monasteries. His son, Ivan (d after 1775), learned his craft from his father and helped him carve the iconostases in Zhovkva, Krekhiv, and Krasnopushcha. In 1746 he moved to Kiev, where he took part in rebuilding the campanile at the St Sophia Cathedral. Hnat's younger brother, Stepan (d late 18th century), was also taught by Hnat, and helped his nephew do the decorative carvings in the St Sophia campanile. In the 1750s he took part in the building of the Dormition Church in Poltava.

**Stock and commodity exchanges** (*birzhi*). Special markets for the sale and purchase of securities, such as stocks, shares, and bonds, or of commodity contracts. In Western Europe such exchanges arose in the 15th and 16th centuries. In the Russian Empire the first exchange opened in St Petersburg in 1703. The exchange, however, was not popular with the Russian merchants, who preferred to do business in the old manner. The second exchange opened in Odessa in 1796; it was followed by ones in Kiev (1815) Kharkiv (1818), and Kremenchuk (1834). The exchanges dealt primarily in commodities, particularly agricultural produce and raw materials, and often sold to foreign merchants. Only in the mid-19th century did exchanges in the Russian Empire begin to handle stocks and bonds. Stock trading grew rapidly with the rise of large *joint-stock companies, especially in the railway, mining, and metallurgical industries. In Ukraine the first stock exchanges were set up in Odessa (1848), Kiev (1865), and Kharkiv (1868). In the Soviet period commodity exchanges with departments handling securities were permitted to operate under the NEP in Kiev, Kharkiv, and Odessa. In the early 1930s all exchanges were closed down.

**Stockholm.** The capital of *Sweden (1990 pop 672,187, metropolitan area 1.2 million). References to Ukrainians in Stockholm before the First World War are sporadic. In 1654 Daniel Oliveberg de Graecani Atheniensis, an emissary of Hetman B. Khmelnytsky, arrived at the court of Charles X Gustav. P. *Orlyk lived in the city with an entourage of 24 men in 1715–20, and some of his correspondence with Swedish officials has been preserved in the local state archive.

During the First World War O. Nazaruk headed a representation of the Union for the Liberation of Ukraine in the city. In 1916 a Ukrainian press bureau headed by V. Stepankivsky was established there. In 1918–21 B. Bazhenov and then K. Losky headed the UNR mission in Stockholm. Its secretary, the painter O. Maidaniuk, later remained in the city. M. *Menzinsky sang with the Stockholm Royal Opera in 1904–10 (usually as a first tenor), returned to perform in 1914–17, and then settled in Stockholm in 1926. O. *Myshuha was another leading operatic tenor to perform in the city, where he also taught (1919–21).

The small Ukrainian community grew largely after the Second World War. At its height it numbered about 200; today it stands at approx 50. The Ukrainian Hromada in Sweden was established in 1947 and has been headed successively by V. Fedorchuk, V. Butko, K. Harbar, and B. Zaluha (since 1979). In 1949–55 the Ukrainian Press Bureau was headed by B. Kentrzhynsky. He also published *Stokhol'ms'kyi visnyk*. In 1950–60 Yu. Borys headed the Ukrainian Academic Club, and in 1948–61 the Hetman P. Orlyk Ukrainian Hromada was headed by V. Dekhtiar.

A. Zhukovsky

**Stoianov, Andrii** [Stojanov, Andrij], b 1830, d 15 June 1907. Jurist and legal historian. After graduating from Kharkiv University (MA, 1859) he studied abroad for two years and completed a doctoral dissertation on the history of the legal profession (1865). He taught legal history, international law, and Roman law at Kharkiv University (1865–85) and served as dean of the law faculty (1876–86). Besides articles on Western legal institutions, he wrote a book of recollections of D. Kachenovsky (1872) and *Ocherki istorii i dogmatiki mezhdunarodnogo prava* (Outlines of the History and Dogmatics of International Law, 1875).

Bishop Oleksander Stoika

**Stoika, Oleksander** [Stojka], b 16 October 1890 in Karachyn, Transcarpathia, d 31 May 1943 in Uzhhorod. Greek Catholic bishop. He studied theology in Budapest and was ordained in 1916, and then worked in the Transcarpathian church administration before being consecrated bishop of Mukachiv in 1932. He worked to improve the economic situation of his followers and initially patronized the 'Ru-thenian movement' in culture. After the Hungarian occupation of Transcarpathia in 1938, he moved his see to Uzhhorod and supported Hungarian policies and Magyarization.

**Stoika, Yosyp** [Stojka, Josyp], b ? in Chumaleve, Transcarpathia, d 1711. Orthodox bishop. He was a parish priest in Chumaleve and Bychkiv before he entered a monastery near Stryi. He was consecrated as the first bishop of Maramureş in 1690, after the eparchy was separated from Mukachiv eparchy because of fears that the entire region would be converted to the Uniate faith. Stoika was influenced by Calvinism and therefore met considerable opposition from the local Ukrainian and Rumanian clergy. He managed to retain his position for a time with backing from the Protestant Hungarian nobility but was finally deposed in 1705. His Rumanian successor proved totally unacceptable, and Stoika was returned as bishop in 1710. He died not long thereafter.

**Stoiko, Mykola** [Stojko], b 1881, d 1951. Pulmonary surgeon. A graduate of Odessa University (1909), he worked there until 1928. From 1932 he was director of the surgical clinic of the USSR Central Scientific Research Institute of Tuberculosis, and from 1939 he was a professor of surgery at the Central Institute for the Upgrading of Physicians (1939–51). His works include *Khirurgicheskoe lechenie legochnogo tuberkuleza* (The Surgical Treatment of Pulmonary Tuberculosis, 1949).

**Stojković, Atanasije** (Stoikovich, Afanasii), b 20 September 1773 in Ruma, Serbia, d 2 June 1832 in Kharkiv. Serbian novelist, physicist, and philosopher; one of the main representatives of Serbian sentimentalism and the author of the first systematic monograph on physics in Serbian (3 vols, 1801–3). After receiving his PH D from Göttingen University (1804) he became the first professor of physics at Kharkiv University (1805–13) and served as its rector (1807–8, 1811–13). He wrote books in Russian on the foundations of physics and physical astronomy.

**Stokhid River** [Stoxid]. A right-bank tributary of the Prypiat River that flows for 188 km through Volhynia oblast and drains a basin area of 3,125 sq km. The general width of the river is 5–15 m (60 m at its widest point). It is fed mainly by meltwaters, and freezes over from December to March. A large number of creeks and small tributaries flow into the river – hence its name, which can be understood literally as meaning 'one hundred ways.' During the First World War the Stokhid was the demarcation line between the Austro-Hungarian and Russian fronts from June 1916 to August 1917.

**Stoliarov, Yakiv** [Stoljarov, Jakiv], b 9 November 1878 in Moscow, d 3 December 1945 in Kharkiv. Scientist in the field of applied mechanics. He studied at the Kharkiv Polytechnical Institute and taught there and at other institutes in Kharkiv. He made contributions in the fields of construction mechanics, the strength of materials, and the theory of machines. He was a specialist in reinforced concrete and one of the scientists who first developed methods of calculating the breaking strength of reinforced-concrete structures.

**Stoliarsky, Petro** [Stoljars'kyj], b 30 November 1871 in Lypovets, Kiev gubernia, d 29 April 1944 in Sverdlovsk, Russia. Teacher and violinist. He studied at the Warsaw Conservatory with S. Barcewicz and at the Odessa Music School with E. Młynarski and Y. Karbulka (graduated in 1898). He then played in the Odessa Opera orchestra (1898–1914) and taught at his private music school. His exceptional ability as a teacher earned him a position at the Odessa Conservatory in 1920. In 1933 he founded the first 10-year special music school for talented children in the USSR. Stoliarsky is considered one of the founders of a noteworthy school of violin playing in the former USSR. His method of teaching children the whole range of professional and artistic skills that they would use as performers achieved striking results, as is illustrated by the list of his students, which includes D. Oistrakh, N. Milstein, and E. Gilels.

**Stolypin agrarian reforms.** A series of measures introduced by P. Stolypin, the head of the Council of Ministers of the Russian Empire, between 1906 and 1911 in order to restructure the peasant *land tenure system. They were instituted in the wake of the Revolution of 1905 in an effort to deal with the ongoing agrarian problem.

The legislation in which the reforms were introduced included the ukase 'Concerning the Fulfillment of Certain Existing Laws on Rural Land Ownership and Land Use' (22 November 1906) and a law passed by the State Duma on 27 June 1910. Those removed restrictions on landholding imposed by the peasant commune (*obshchina). All peasants were given the right to leave such communes along with the lands apportioned to them. Peasants also gained the right to demand that their allotments be consolidated into an integrated landholding, which could be farmed as a *khutir (if the household were settled on the property) or a vidrub (if the household remained in a village). The latter right marked a radical departure from the common practice of farming small, scattered strips of land. The *Peasant Land Bank provided loans for the purchase of land to establish vidrub or khutir holdings. The last reform was the Statute on Land Organization of 11 June 1911, which set a definite agenda for the land settlement commissions (at the gubernia and district volost levels) created by the ukase of 1906. In the Russian Empire in 1907–15 approx 26 percent of the total obshchina membership (2.5 million householders) took advantage of the reforms to acquire about 16.9 million desiatins of land (15 percent of total communal holdings).

In Ukraine the secession from communes was even more thoroughgoing, although it was also uneven because of the near-total absence of the obshchina in Right-Bank Ukraine and the Poltava region. As a result of the reforms about 42 percent of commune householders seceded in Southern Ukraine, 16.5 percent in Left-Bank Ukraine, and 48 percent in Right-Bank Ukraine. In Right-Bank Ukraine and Poltava gubernia virtually all of the land used by the peasantry became privately owned; in Chernihiv gubernia, the majority; and in Katerynoslav, Kharkiv, Kherson, and Tavriia gubernias, about half. In 1907–11 approx 225,000 Ukrainian householders established private vidruby and khutory consisting of 1.8 million desiatins of land. The most marked growth of such holdings occurred in the steppe gubernias and in Volhynia. Largely as a result of loans extended by the Peasant Land Bank peasants bought 385,000 desiatins of nobles' lands in 1906–9. By 1916 some 500,000 households in the nine Ukrainian gubernias, with 3.7 million desiatins of land, had been reorganized by land settlement commissions.

The new system encouraged peasants to show initiative and to improve their households. Assistance was provided by the Land Bank, agricultural associations, co-operatives, and zemstvo agronomists. Because of advancements in agricultural techniques (the alternation of crops) crop yields also improved (by 20 percent in 1904–12), and the value of farmsteads rose.

The intent of Stolypin's reforms was to improve the position of the wealthier peasantry and establish it as a base of support for the troubled imperial regime. Accordingly the reforms benefited only about 25 percent of the households. Poor and some middle-income peasants could not buy land because of high prices (400 to 700 rubles per desiatin in Right-Bank Ukraine) and were not given credit by the Land Bank. A substantial number of such peasants finally emigrated beyond the Urals to Asiatic Russia, a practice also encouraged by Stolypin to reduce rural overpopulation. Ultimately the reforms gave rise to an even greater social differentiation among peasants, with the largest peasant households growing larger and the number of middle-sized holdings shrinking. Stolypin's reforms were therefore harshly criticized by V. Lenin as well as by Russian and Ukrainian socialist parties.

BIBLIOGRAPHY
Pohrebil's'kyi, O. Stolypins'ka reforma na Ukraïni (Kharkiv 1931)
Iakymenko, M. 'Orhanizatsiia pereselennia selian z Ukraïny v

roky stolypins'koï ahrarnoï reformy (1906–1913),' *UIZh*, 1974, no. 7

Yaney, G. *The Urge to Mobilize: Agrarian Reform in Russia, 1861–1930* (Urbana 1982)

Atkinson, D. *The End of the Russian Land Commune, 1905–1930* (Stanford 1983)

B. Wynar

**Stomatology** or **Dentistry.** A branch of medicine dealing with the structure, functions, and diseases of the mouth and adjacent sections of the face and neck. In the Soviet Union dentists were known as stomatologists.

In 17th-century Ukraine barber-surgeons (*tsyrulnyky*) treated ailing teeth and performed minor surgical procedures. One of the first textbooks on dentistry in the Russian Empire, dealing with the diseases of the mouth and adjoining areas, was written by P. *Zablotsky-Desiatovsky. Schools for the treatment of teeth were established at the end of the 19th century in Odessa (1892), Kiev (1897), and Kharkiv (1897). The Odessa Scientific Research Institute of Stomatology was founded in 1928. Dentists are trained at 34 departments of stomatology in various *medical education institutions throughout the country. The status of a dentist in Ukraine is on a par with that of a physician. Dentists receive equal training plus training in oral surgery, for a total of five years.

**Stone Age.** The earliest phase of human development preceding the manufacturing and common use of metals, lasting in Ukraine from ca 300,000 to 2500 BC. The Stone Age in Ukraine is commonly divided into three phases – the *Paleolithic Period (300,000–8000 BC), the *Mesolithic Period (8000–5000 BC), and the *Neolithic Period (5000–2500 BC). The definition of the periods is based largely upon technological progress (nature of dwellings and number, function, and quality of implements) and social development (introduction of agriculture and permanent settlements, expansion of population and social groupings, growth of esthetic and religious consciousness). Each period can be further defined in terms of eras or individual cultural groupings. The periodization of this age is also closely linked with major geological changes, particularly the final retreat of glaciers from Ukraine (coinciding with the end of the Paleolithic), which increased temperatures, caused a change in fauna, and made agricultural activity (marking the start of the Neolithic) possible. The peoples of Stone Age Ukraine experienced social and technical development at differing paces and commonly coexisted at varying levels of development.

**Stone *baba*** (*kamiana baba*). An anthropomorphic stone statue, 1 to 4 m in height, found in the steppe belt of Europe and Asia from the Dniester River in the west to Mongolia in the east. Commonly used as grave markers, the *baby* were connected with cults of the dead among nomadic peoples. Those erected in Ukraine were left by Scythian and Sarmatian tribes of the 7th to 4th century BC and by Turkic peoples of the 6th to 13th century, particularly the *Cumans (Polovtsians). The figures are commonly in standing or sitting positions. In steppe Ukraine most of the *baby* are female figures that differ from their Asiatic counterparts in their more complex and varied dress. A large number of these monuments have been preserved in museums throughout Ukraine, and there is one at the *Niagara Falls Art Gallery.

A stone *baba*

**Stonecrop** (*Sedum*; Ukrainian: *ochytok, zaiacha kapusta*). A herbaceous-to-woody plant of the family Crassulaceae, 18 of the 250 species of which are found in Ukraine, in arid sandy regions and on cliffs. The most common is orpine (*S. telephium*), with pink or purple flowers, which was formerly used in folk medicine. The bitter stonecrop (*S. acre*) is an excellent nectariferous plant. Some *Sedum* species are cultivated as ornamentals.

*Stopa.* See Weights and measures.

**Stork** (*Ciconia*; Ukrainian: *leleka, buzko, chornohuz*). Large birds with long necks and legs of the family Ciconiidae (order Ciconiiformes). Storks range from about 60 cm to over 150 cm in height and weigh up to 4.5 kg. They are migratory birds that breed in Europe and winter in southern Africa. While breeding they nest on trees or, as in Ukraine, on buildings where a wagon wheel has been set up to serve as the base of the nest. Two species predominate in Ukraine: *C. nigra* or black stork (black with a white spot on the belly and red legs and bill) in the Carpathians and in Polisia, and *C. ciconia* or white stork (white with black wing feathers, a dark red bill, and reddish legs), found over the whole of Ukraine. Storks have become an endangered species and are now protected by law.

According to Ukrainian and other European folk belief the stork possesses magical powers to protect and help humans. A family with a stork's nest on its farm will live in peace, prosperity, and good health. A village with many storks can count on a bountiful harvest. The bird is believed to be capable of predicting the weather: restless behavior indicates the approach of bad weather, standing on one leg, cold weather, and clacking of the beak, a sunny day. In folktales and legends the stork always plays the role of a helper of humans.

**Storozhenko** [Storoženko]. A Cossack *starshyna* family, known from the early 17th century. Andrii Storozhenko was 'senior colonel of the Zaporozhian Army' in 1610. His descendant (possibly a grandson) Ivan Storozhenko (d 15 February 1693) was captain of Ichnia company (1670–87) and colonel of Pryluka regiment (1687–92); he was the first of a Storozhenko 'dynasty' of captains in the Cossack *company system. Among the Storozhenko captains of Ichnia company were Andrii Storozhenko (captain from 1700, d 1715); Andrii's son, Hryhorii Storozhenko (captain 1715–41, d 1745), who was often sent on diplomatic missions to Moscow (1722, 1727, 1729) and served on the commission that prepared the Code of Laws of 1743 (1735–7); and Andrii's grandson, Andrii Storozhenko (d 1753). Among the Storozhenko captains of Yabluniv company were Stepan Storozhenko (d 20 January 1758) and his son, Ivan Storozhenko. Among the Storozhenko captains of Ivanytsia company were Ivan Storozhenko (captain 1719–28, d 1733) and Hryhorii Storozhenko (captain 1770–81, d 16 June 1810 in Irzhavets, near Ichnia).

In the 19th century the Storozhenko family line included many civic and cultural leaders, notably the writer Oleksa *Storozhenko; the historian Andrii *Storozhenko (1791–1858) and his grandsons, the historians Andrii *Storozhenko (1857–?) and Mykola *Storozhenko (1862–1942); and the literary historian Mykola *Storozhenko (1836–1906). The Storozhenko family archive, partially published as *Storozhenki: Famil'nyi arkhiv* (The Storozhenkos: A Family Archive, 8 vols, 1902–10), is preserved in the Central State Historical Archives of Ukraine in Kiev.

A. Zhukovsky

**Storozhenko, Andrii** [Storoženko, Andrij] (pseud: Andrei Tsarynny), b 8 March 1791, d 4 July 1858 in Kiev. Historian and writer. He worked for the Russian Military Administration in Poland (1832–49) and became a senator (1842) and the director of internal and religious affairs (1845) there. Storozhenko possessed a large collection of Ukrainian antiquities and historical documents of the 17th and 18th centuries, including the original 1649 registers of the Zaporozhian Army. He wrote a history of Southern Russia (3 vols, unpub) which has not been preserved, as well as essays on B. Khmelnytsky and I. Mazepa and memoirs, of which fragments were published. His 1832 pseudonymous article 'Mysli malorossiianina' (Thoughts of a Little Russian) in the journal *Syn otechestva* criticized N. Gogol's *Vechera na khutore bliz Dikan'ki* (Evenings on a Farm near Dykanka). He wrote poetry in Ukrainian and Russian and the operetta *Zaporozhian Sich*. His literary works were published by his grandson, M. *Storozhenko (1836–1906), in *Kievskaia starina* (1886, nos 15–16). Storozhenko was a friend of T. Shevchenko, Ye. Hrebinka, P. Kulish, and O. Bodiansky. He was buried in Chevelcha, Lubni county, Poltava gubernia.

**Storozhenko, Andrii** [Storoženko, Andrij], b 24 August 1857 in Velyka Krucha, Pyriatyn county, Poltava gubernia, d ? Historian, ethnographer, and literary scholar. He studied at Kiev University (1879) under V. Antonovych. He worked as head of the Pereiaslav county zemstvo administration (1886–92), speaker of the Pereiaslav and Pyriatyn zemstvo assemblies (1892–1912), and marshal of the nobility in Pereiaslav county (1912–16). Storozhenko was a member of the Kiev Archeographic Commission,

vice-president of the Historical Society of Nestor the Chronicler, and associate of the journal *Kievskaia starina*, in which he published many documentary articles and notes. His main scholarly works examined the history of Ukraine and Poland from the 15th to 18th centuries. With his brother, M. *Storozhenko (1862–1942), he edited and published the Storozhenko family archives (8 vols, 1902–10), which included the first two volumes of V. Modzalevsky's *Malorossiiskii rodoslovnik* (Little Russian Genealogical Register; the two final volumes were also published by them, in 1912 and 1914).

Storozhenko sided with the conservative Ukrainian nobility in civic and political affairs. In his youth he was a liberal and a Ukrainophile, but later his position changed to one of Russian nationalism and anti-Ukrainianism, largely in reaction to 20th-century left-wing Ukrainian politics. He became one of the leaders of the Kiev Club of Russian Nationalists, and he wrote the anti-Ukrainian work *Proiskhozhdenie i sushchnost' ukrainofil'stva* (The Origin and Essence of Ukrainophilism, 1911). Storozhenko opposed the rebirth of Ukrainian statehood in 1917. He edited the collection of essays *Malaia Rus'* (Little Rus', 1917), and after emigrating, he published the pseudonymous anti-Ukrainian booklet *Ukrainskoe dvizhenie* (The Ukrainian Movement, 1926).

A. Zhukovsky

Mykola Storozhenko
(1836–1906)

**Storozhenko, Mykola** [Storoženko] (Nikolai), b 22 May 1836 in Irzhavets, Pryluka county, Poltava gubernia, d 25 January 1906 in Moscow. Literary scholar; corresponding member of the Russian Academy of Sciences from 1899. He graduated from Moscow University (1860) and taught at the Alexandrian Military School and the First Moscow Gymnasium. He was the first professor of the history of world literature at Moscow University (from 1872). He was also chief librarian at the Rumiantsev Museum (1893–1902) and chairman of the Society of Devotees of Russian Literature (1894–1901). An adherent of the cultural-historical school, he wrote on Western European, Russian, and Ukrainian literature and was the first Shakespearean scholar in the Russian Empire. Among his many works are books on J. Lilly and C. Marlowe (1872), R. Greene (1878; English trans 1881), and W. Shakespeare (1902), and 11 articles about T. Shevchenko, most of them in *Kievskaia starina*. A book of his selected literary articles and lectures appeared in Moscow in 1902, and an early Ukrainian version of his popular history of Western European literature to the end of the 18th century (1908; 4th edn 1916) was published in Lviv in 1905. A festschrift in his honor (1902) has a bibliography of his works. I. Borozdin's book about Storozhenko was published in Moscow in 1916.

**Storozhenko, Mykola** [Storoženko] (pseud: M. Tsarinny), b 29 May 1862 in Velyka Krucha, Pyriatyn county, Poltava gubernia, d 1942. Historian and pedagogue. He studied under V. Antonovych at Kiev University. He was a member of the Kiev Archeographic Commission and the Historical Society of Nestor the Chronicler and an associate of the journals *Kievskaia starina, Istoricheskii vestnik, Russkaia mysl'*, and others. He worked as a public school inspector in Chernihiv and Kiev gubernias (from 1889), as principal of Kiev gymnasiums No. 4 (from 1895) and No. 1, and as a zemstvo official in Pyriatyn county. Storozhenko wrote many works on the history of Ukraine in the 17th and 18th centuries, which were published in *\*Arkhiv Iugo-Zapadnoi Rossii, Kievskie universitetskie izvestia*, and, especially, *Kievskaia starina*. He also contributed historical, political, and pedagogical essays to *Istoricheskii vestnik, Russkaia mysl'*, and *Tserkov' i narod* and published the monograph *Zapadno-russkie provintsial'nye seimiki* (Western Russian Provincial Dietines, 1888). With his brother, A. *Storozhenko (1857–?), he edited and published the Storozhenko family archives (8 vols, 1902–10). He was a member of the Hromada of Kiev, a friend of P. Kulish, V. Horlenko, I. and P. Rudchenko, and O. Levytsky, and the pseudonymous author of the Ukrainian poetry collection *Litni krasy* (Summer Beauties, 1884).

After the Revolution of 1917 Storozhenko championed the Ukrainian cause and published works in Ukrainian in *Zbirnyk Istorychno-filolohichnoho viddilu VUAN*. He edited *Stoletie Kievskoi I gimnazii* (Centenary of Kiev Gymnasium No. 1, 3 vols, 1911) and published *Malorossiiskii rodoslovnik* (Little Russian Genealogical Register, 4 vols, 1902–14). While living as an émigré in Yugoslavia he wrote his memoirs (unpub), which remain a valuable source for the history of Ukrainian culture and of the Ukrainian movement in the later 19th century. The manuscript was housed in the Museum of Ukraine's Struggle for Independence in Prague.

A. Zhukovsky

**Storozhenko, Mykola** [Storoženko], b 24 September 1928 in Viazove, Konotip raion, now in Sumy oblast. Painter, mosaicist, and graphic artist. A graduate of the Kiev State Art Institute (1956), he has taught there since the early 1970s. He has created easel paintings and illustrated over 30 books, including Ye. Hutsalo's *Olen' Avhust* (Elk Avhust, 1965) and a 1987 edition of Ukrainian folk tales. He is best known for his mosaic wall panels *Kievan Academy* and *Science and Culture of the 16th and 17th Centuries* (1969–72), inside the building of the AN URSR (now ANU) Institute of Theoretical Physics, and his huge encaustic mural depicting over 20 of the world's most famous physicists, *Illuminated by Light* (1978–82), inside the building of the ANU Institute of Physics.

**Storozhenko, Oleksa** [Storoženko], b 24 November 1805 in Lysohory, Pryluka county, Poltava gubernia, d 19 November 1874 in Horishyn *khutir*, Brest county, Belarus. Writer, ethnographer, and artist. He began writing in Russian in the 1850s, by drawing on folktales, particularly those of the Zaporozhian M. Korzh, and on his military

Part of the mural by Mykola Storozhenko inside the ANU Institute of Physics

Oleksa Storozhenko

service (1824–50). His short stories were published in the journals *Severnaia pchela* and *Biblioteka dlia chteniia*. The latter was the vehicle for *Rasskazy iz krest'ianskogo byta malorossiian* (Stories from the Peasant Life of Little Russians, 1858) and the historical novel *Brat'ia bliznetsy* (Twin Brothers, 1857). When the journal *\*Osnova* first appeared, Storozhenko began writing in Ukrainian, and in 1863 he published a two-volume collection of stories titled *Ukrains'ki opovidannia* (Ukrainian Stories). The majority of his works consist of anecdotes, proverbs, and folktales, and their titles reflect their folkloric content and style: 'Vchy linyvoho ne molotom a holodom' (Teach the Lazy Man Not by Hammer but by Hunger), 'Mezhyhorods'kyi did' (The Old Man from Mezhyhorod), 'Vusy' (The Moustache), and 'Holka' (The Needle). A few of his stories were based directly on ethnographic and historical material, such as 'Matusyne blahoslovennia' (Mother's Blessing), 'Zakokhanyi chort' (A Devil in Love), and 'Marko Prokliatyi' (Damned Marko). His works are marked by earthy Ukrainian humor, a knowledge of folk myths, and picturesque language.

BIBLIOGRAPHY
Shamrai, A. 'O. Storozhenko,' in *O. Storozhenko: Vybrani tvory* (Kiev 1927)

Ishchuk, A. 'Oleksa Storozhenko,' in *O. Storozhenko: Tvory*, 2 vols (Kiev 1957)

P. Odarchenko

**Storozhova Mohyla.** A *Pit-Grave culture kurhan of the late 3rd millennium BC near Stari Kodaky, Dnipropetrovske raion. Excavations in 1949 by A. *Terenozhkin uncovered three corpses covered with red paint and buried in a crouched position. One of the graves also contained the first two-wheeled cart unearthed in Ukraine.

**Storozhuk, Oleksander** [Storožuk], b 1 January 1924 in Ivanivka, near Stavyshche, in Kiev gubernia, d 7 August 1988 in Kiev. Economist; corresponding member of the All-Union Academy of Agricultural Sciences. After graduating from the Kiev Finance and Economics Institute in 1951, he joined the staff of the AN URSR (now ANU) Institute of Economics and then of the Ukrainian Scientific Research Institute of the Economics and Organization of Agriculture, which he eventually headed. In his research Storozhuk specialized in the economics of agricultural production. He wrote a number of monographs, including *Rol' ekonomicheskikh stimulov v povyshenii kachestva sel'-skokhoziaistvennoi produktsii* (The Role of Economic Stimuli in Raising the Quality of Agricultural Production, 1984), and helped edit a Russian dictionary of the agricultural industry (1981).

**Storozhynets** [Storožynec']. V-6. A city (1989 pop 13,700) on the Seret River and a raion center in Chernivtsi oblast. The town was first mentioned in historical documents in 1448, when it was part of the Moldavian principality. In the 16th century it was under Turkish rule, and from 1774, under Austria. By the end of the 19th century the town had developed into a small manufacturing and trading center with a population of 7,000. In 1904 it was granted city status. After the First World War the city was occupied by Rumania, and in 1940 it was annexed by the Ukrainian SSR. Today it has a lumber-manufacturing complex and a large dendrological park.

**Stovbur, Oleksander,** b 1943 in Zaporizhia. Painter and muralist. He graduated from the Odessa Art School in 1971 and has lived in Odessa since then. His works were not exhibited publicly until 1986. They reveal the influence of medieval Rus' and Ukrainian icons. Stovbur has experimented with predominantly white compositions. His works include the semiabstract *Empress* (1984) and the nonobjective *Composition with Black Spot* (1983). He has also painted murals in Odessa, including ones in the Odessa Literary Museum and the Olimpiiets sports complex.

**Stove** (*pich*). Among the Slavs the stove replaced the open hearth probably in the 4th or 5th century AD. The traditional peasant stove in Ukraine was large and rectangular – 1.50 to 1.80 m long, 1.40 to 1.6 m wide, and 1.0 to 1.2 cm high – and occupied up to a quarter of a room. Two of its sides backed onto the room's walls, and two were freestanding. Built of clay, and, later, also of stone or brick, it was decorated on the outside in some regions with painted patterns or ceramic tiles. The opening (*cheliusty*) to the fire chamber, in which the fire was laid, was rectangular or semicircular. In front of it was a ledge (*prypik*), and

A peasant stove from the Dnipropetrovske region

above it was a smoke hood (*dymar*) consisting of a wattled frame covered with clay. From the hood the smoke was led by a duct (*tsivka*) through a wall into the antechamber, from which it escaped upward through a chimney. The stove was used for heating, baking bread, cooking meals, lighting the room, and drying fruits and mushrooms. In addition it provided a warm sleeping place on a ledge where the stove met the walls. Originally, food was cooked in pots placed next to the fire in the chamber. Later a small supplementary stove (*pudprypik*) with hot plates was built into the main stove. In recent times that cooking device has been replaced by an iron stove.

Because of its vital role in domestic life the stove occupied a prominent place in Ukrainian folkways. When a family moved to a new home, it often dismantled and took the stove with it. The mother blessed the stove before going to bed and upon rising. In the distant past the stove played an important role in the birth rites. Until recent times a midwife knocked on the stove to make the birth process easier, and a newborn infant was touched against the stove. A symbol of family unity, the stove figured prominently in wedding ceremonies. Before departing from her family the bride cuddled up to the stove and broke off several chips from it. The bridegroom's stove had to be cleaned and painted before the bride's arrival. The custom of touching the stove upon returning from a funeral was originally a purification ritual. The Hutsuls celebrated the feast of the stove on New Year's Eve.

**Strabo,** b ca 64 BC in Amaseia, Pontus (in present-day Turkey), d ca 23 AD. Greek geographer and historian. Although not widely traveled, he prepared a 17-volume *Ge-*

*ography* that encompassed most of the territories known in the ancient world. In volumes 11 and 14 he describes the tribes that inhabited the Crimea and the steppes along the northern coast of the Black Sea – their way of life and their commercial ties with the Greek city-states. The Ukrainian classical scholar H. Mishchenko translated the work into Russian (1879).

*Strakhopud*

**Strakhopud** (Scarecrow). A Russophile journal of satire and humor. It appeared first irregularly and then semi-monthly in Vienna in 1863–8, under the editorship of Y. Livchak. It was revived in Lviv and published with interruptions by I. Arsenych and V. Stebelsky (1872–3), S. Labash (1880–2), and O. Monchalovsky (1886–93); from 1887 it also issued a literary supplement, *Besida*. A journal with the same name was published as a supplement to *Russkoe slovo* in 1912 by H. Hanuliak.

A 1931 poster by Adolf          Volodymyr Strashkevych
Strakhov

**Strakhov, Adolf** [Straxov, Adol'f] (real name: Braslavsky), b 18 October 1896 in Katerynoslav, d 3 January 1979 in Kharkiv. Graphic artist, sculptor, and painter of Jewish origin. A graduate of the Odessa Art School (1915), he drew satirical sketches for Bolshevik newspapers in Katerynoslav (1919–22) and Bolshevik propaganda posters (eg, the lithograph series 'Alphabet of the Revolution' 1921). In 1919 in Katerynoslav he designed a triumphal arch with a 6 × 30 m poster dedicated to the Red Army and

an 8 × 40 m panel for a monument to those who died in the revolution. In 1922–5 he designed over 250 book covers for the State Publishing House of Ukraine and Proletar publishers in Kharkiv. In 1928 he designed decorative murals with folk-art motifs for the V. Blakytny Building in Kharkiv. From 1933 he worked also as a sculptor and created a popular bust of T. Shevchenko (1933), monuments to M. Glinka in Zaporizhia (1955) and S. Kirov in Makiivka (1959), and several monuments to V. Lenin. S. Raievsky has written two books about Strakhov's posters (1936, 1967).

**Strakhov, Tymofii** [Straxov, Tymofij], b 4 February 1890 in Luchki, Kursk gubernia, Russia, d 11 October 1960 in Kharkiv. Mycologist and phytopathologist; corresponding member of the AN URSR (now ANU) from 1948. A graduate of Kharkiv University (1916), he worked at the Kharkiv Agricultural Research Station (1913–30, from 1919 as department head), the Ukrainian Scientific Research Station of Plant Conservation (1930–2), and the ANU Institute of Genetics and Selection (1949–56). He lectured at the Kharkiv Agricultural Institute (from 1918) and at Kharkiv University (from 1921). He proposed a theory about the pathological process in plants and developed a number of immunization measures.

**Strakhsoiuz** (full name: Ukrainskyi kooperatyvnyi strakhovyi soiuz, or Ukrainian Co-operative Insurance Union). A central organization set up in the fall of 1918 in Kiev to organize insurance co-operatives. Its equity fund consisted of shares bought by various co-operatives and associations. Strakhsoiuz insured the property of co-operatives against fire and theft, transported goods against damage and theft, farm produce and crops against spoilage and damage, and farm animals against disease. The union planned to organize health and veterinary services, fire-fighting units, and the manufacture of fireproof building materials. Strakhsoiuz was dissolved by the Soviet authorities in 1922, but it was revived soon afterward with the introduction of NEP. It operated under its new name, Koopstrakh, or the All-Ukrainian Insurance Union, until 1930.

**Strashkevych, Volodymyr** [Straškevyč] (pseuds: V. P[otochny], V. Hamma, Ester), b 1875 in Vyshnevychi, Kiev gubernia, d ? Civic figure, writer, and lexicographer. A member of the Old Hromada of Kiev, in the 1900s and 1910s he worked for the Vik publishing house and contributed to *Literaturno-naukovyi vistnyk* and the Kiev periodicals *Svitlo*, *Kievskiia otkliki*, *Hromads'ka dumka*, and *Rada*. Under the UNR he was deputy director of a department in the Ministry of Religious Faiths. From 1926 he headed the professional (*dilova*) language section of the economics department at the *Institute of the Ukrainian Scientific Language. Together with M. Doroshenko and M. Stanyslavsky Strashkevych compiled the institute's Russian-Ukrainian dictionary of professional language (15,000 words and phrases, 1930). A defendant in the 1930 Stalinist show trial of the *Union for the Liberation of Ukraine, he was sentenced to three years in a labor camp. His subsequent fate is unknown.

**Stratii, Yaroslava** [Stratij, Jaroslava], b 1 September 1947 in Mukachiv, Transcarpathia oblast. Philosopher. After graduating from Lviv University she began working at the AN URSR (now ANU) Institute of Social Sciences in Lviv and received a candidate of philosophical sciences degree in 1978. A specialist in the history of Ukrainian philosophy, she has written *Problemy naturfilosofii v filosofskoi mysli Ukrainy XVII v.* (Problems of Natural Philosophy in the Philosophical Thought of 17th-Century Ukraine, 1981), cocompiled a collection of descriptions of the philosophy and rhetoric courses read by professors of the Kievan Mohyla Academy (1982), contributed two chapters to the first volume of the ANU history of philosophy in Ukraine (1987), and coauthored a book on humanistic and Reformation ideas in Ukraine (1990).

A bookplate by Mykola Stratilat

**Stratilat, Mykola**, b 6 June 1942 in Makiivka, Nosivka raion, Chernihiv oblast. Artist. He completed his studies in graphic arts at the Ukrainian Printing Institute (1966–72). Since 1976 he has been art editor for *Molod' Ukraïny* and, subsequently, *Narodna tvorchist' ta etnohrafiia*. Besides illustrations to numerous books, including M. Rylsky's *Iabluka dospili, iabluka chervoni* (Ripe Apples, Red Apples) and V. Sosiura's *Iakyi ia nizhnyi–takyi tryvozhnyi* (I Am So Gentle – So Skittish), he has done such graphic series as 'Song about Kiev' (1980–1) and 'In Memory of T.H. Shevchenko' (1985). His main strength, however, lies in the art of designing bookplates, which he fills with Cossack motifs, especially various representations of Kozak-Mamai.

Mykola Strazhesko

**Strazhesko, Mykola** [Straževsko], b 29 December 1876 in Odessa, d 27 June 1952 in Kiev. Internal medicine specialist; full member of the AN URSR (now ANU) from 1934, of the USSR Academy of Sciences from 1943, and of the USSR Academy of Medical Sciences from 1944. A graduate of Kiev University (1899), he worked under V. Obraztsov in the university's department of special pathology and in-

ternal medicine, studied in clinics in Paris, Berlin, and Munich, did research under I. Pavlov at the St Petersburg Military Medical Academy (1902–4) and wrote a dissertation on the physiology of the digestive tract, and worked in the clinic of internal medicine at Kiev University. He was a professor at the Kiev Women's Medical Institute (from 1907), Odessa University (1919–22), where he headed the internal medicine department, and the Kiev Medical Institute (1922–36). He was a fellow at the ANU Institute of Clinical Physiology (1934–6) and the founding director of the Ukrainian Scientific Research Institute of Clinical Medicine (1936, from 1952 the Ukrainian Scientific Research Institute of Cardiology).

Strazhesko published numerous works in clinical and theoretical medicine, dealing with angina pectoris, myocardial infarction, heart failure, rheumatic fever, and sepsis. He also prepared a classic manual on the physical diagnosis of abdominal diseases (1924). He described a number of symptoms associated with diseases of the digestive and circulatory organs, including the so-called cannon tone that results from heart blockage (1906). With Obraztsov he gave the first clear clinical description of coronary thrombosis (1909), thereby enabling practicing physicians to diagnose myocardial infarction. In 1934 he proved the streptococcal etiology of rheumatic fever. With V. Vasylenko he proposed a classification system of congestive heart failure (1935). The founder of a school of Ukrainian internal medicine specialists, Strazhesko also contributed to the development of functional cardiology in the former USSR. His collected works were published in two volumes (1957).

**Streetcar.** See Urban transit.

**Strelbytska, Oleksandra** [Strel'byc'ka], b 19 November 1905 in Odessa, Kherson gubernia, d 2 March 1980 in Kiev. Construction mechanics scientist. She studied at the Kiev Civil-Engineering Institute and taught there (1934–41). She also worked at the AN URSR (now ANU) Institute of Mechanics (from 1933). She studied the physics of the plastic deformation of metal structures and developed equations for predicting failures in such structures, and performed theoretical and experimental studies of thin-walled frames and trusses and of membranes under transverse loading.

**Strelbytsky, Ivan** [Strel'byc'kyj], b and d ? Copper engraver. From 1695 to 1709 he worked in Kiev and Chernihiv, where he created many portrait, mythological, and panegyrical engravings. His works include portraits of Hetman P. Doroshenko, Archimandrite M. Vuiakhevych of the Kievan Cave Monastery (1695), Archimandrite M. Lezhaisky (with a view of the Novhorod-Siverskyi Cathedral), and Metropolitan V. Yasynsky (1707). He illustrated I. Maksymovych's alphabet in rhymes (1705) and created 23 engravings for B. Hefden's *Tsarskii put' kresta Hospodnia* (The Royal Way of the Lord's Cross, 1709).

**Strelbytsky, Teodor** [Strel'byc'kyj, Teodor], b and d ? Copper engraver of the late 18th and early 19th centuries, in Pochaiv. He engraved icons, such as *Apostles Peter and Paul Carrying a Model of the Pochaiv Church*, *The Pochaiv Theotokos*, and *The Chernihiv Theotokos*. He also made the wood engraving *St John the Baptist* (1802) and copper-engraved prints in the folk style, including *The Knight and*

*Death* and *Two Paths of Life*. The influence of classicism is evident in his work.

**Strelkov, Ilia** [Strjelkov, Il'ja], b 9 August 1898 in Arkhangelskaia, Kuban, d 23 February 1954 in Kharkiv. Chemist; AN URSR (now ANU) corresponding member from 1948. A graduate of the Kharkiv Technological Institute (1925), he taught organic chemistry at various institutes in Kharkiv until 1941 and directed the Kharkiv Chemical-Technological Institute (1933–9) and the Kharkiv Technological Institute of Building Materials (1944–54). He also served as secretary of the Ukrainian Council of People's Commissars (CPC, 1921–4), as learned secretary to the CPC chairman (1924–30), and as learned secretary and then vice-chairman of the CPC committee in charge of the chemization of the national economy (1928–38). Strelkov's research dealt with thermochemistry and the thermodynamics of organic reactions. He introduced a simple method for approximating the entropy of organic compounds in liquid or solid phase.

Volodymyr Strelnikov in his studio in Munich

**Strelnikov, Volodymyr** [Strel'nikov], b 25 October 1939 in Odessa. Painter. He studied briefly at the Odessa Art School but was mostly self-taught. He worked as a muralist in Odessa and participated in and organized some of the exhibitions of nonconformist art there. Strelnikov has experimented with reduced shapes and the interrelationship between figures and architecture. In his later pictures architecture and figures have been reduced to simplified patterns within the larger contained form, so that a tension is sustained between the detailed, intricate shapes and the surrounding smooth areas of warm color (eg, *Autumnal* [1977]). Strelnikov participated in the 1975 and 1976 Moscow exhibitions of Ukrainian nonconformist artists and was consequently harassed by the Soviet authorities. In 1978 he was allowed to emigrate to Austria, and in 1979 he settled in Munich. Since that time he has exhibited in Western Europe, the United States, and Canada. He abandoned figuration in the late 1980s in favor of nonrepresentational compositions based on the interrelationship between form and color.

**Strelsky, Viacheslav** [Strel's'kyj, Vjačeslav], b 28 September 1910 in Kursk, Russia, d 11 August 1983 in Kiev.

Historian. After graduating from the Historical-Archival Institute in Moscow (1935) he was director of oblast archives and a teacher at the pedagogical institute (from 1937) in Mykolaiv. During the Second World War he worked in the NKVD archival division in Omsk and published two studies of Siberian political history. From 1944 he worked at Kiev University as archives director, head of the chair of archival studies at the department of history, and editor in chief of the university's scholarly collection *Naukovi zapysky Kyïvs'koho universytetu* (14 vols) and its historical series of *Visnyk Kyïvs'koho universytetu*. He wrote *Dzhereloznavstvo istoriï SRSR* (A Study of Sources for the History of the USSR, 1958; Russian edn 1962) and coauthored *Derzhavni arkhivy Ukraïns'koï RSR* (State Archives of the Ukrainian SSR, 1972).

**Striatyn Press** (Striatynska drukarnia). One of the earliest presses in Ukraine, established in Striatyn near Rohatyn, Galicia, by Bishop H. Balaban of Lviv and his nephew F. Balaban. From 1602 to 1606, under the direction of P. Berynda, it printed *Khyrotoniia: Poucheniie novostavlenomu iiereievi* (Chirotony: Instructions for a New Hierarch, 1602), a Missal (1604), a Euchologion (1606), and a few other books. The books are fine examples of Renaissance book ornamentation. The press's equipment was acquired by Ye. Pletenetsky and used to begin work at the Kievan Cave Monastery Press.

**Strichka, Ivan** [Strička], b ca 1800 in Berezivka, Pryluka county, Poltava gubernia, d ca 1833. Kobzar. The descendant of a long line of kobzars, he was one of the first to be studied seriously. His dumas about S. Kishka and I. Udovychenko-Konovchenko and his other dumas were written down and published by P. *Lukashevych.

**Strichka.** Part of the female folk dress, consisting of a wide band of patterned material in bright colors. It was worn differently in different parts of Ukraine. In the Kiev region, Right-Bank Ukraine, and most other regions the *strichky* were attached to a wreath and allowed to drop along the wearer's back. In the Chernihiv region they were worn like a cape, dropping down the back from a ribbon tied around the neck, and in the Poltava and Kharkiv regions they were inserted into a girl's braids and draped down the back. In Right-Bank Ukraine the *strichky* tended to be many-colored and decorated with woven designs; those in Left-Bank Ukraine were of one color and free of design.

**Strike.** A work stoppage by workers to enforce demands or protest against an act or condition, usually accompanied by demonstrations. Some strikes involve political demands. Local strikes are limited to one factory or region; general strikes can encompass an entire country.

In Russian-ruled Ukraine the earliest strikes were staged by serfs, who worked in tar, potash, saltpeter, and salt mines, distilleries, and fulling mills owned by landlords or the state. One of the most important strikes occurred in 1798 at the Hlushytsia manufactory. Some 9,000 workers and possessional serfs demanded higher wages and reduced feudal obligations. The protest was suppressed by troops, and its organizers were sentenced to long terms of forced labor. Other major strikes were staged by printers of the Kievan Cave Monastery (1805) and by the working peasants of the Pysarivka (1817) and Mashiv (1823) woolen-cloth manufactories.

After the emancipation a large strike took place in 1868 at the Horodok sugar mill in Kamianets-Podilskyi county. In 1870 the construction workers of the Kharkiv railway station went on strike. Strikes in the 1860s and 1870s were concerned with economic questions – low wages and poor working conditions. In 1860–79 there were 52 strikes in Ukraine, involving almost 16,000 workers. Industrial development meant an increase in strikes. In 1880–4 there were 26 strikes, involving 9,000 workers; in 1886–94, 71 strikes, with 20,000 workers; and in 1895–9, 212 strikes, with 120,000 workers. At first the work stoppages were localized, but in time they grew in geographical scope despite police repression. As political opposition to the regime grew, strikers began to raise political demands. The first strike in the Russian Empire to display political slogans took place in Ukraine in 1872.

The economic crisis of 1900–3 resulted in labor unrest that culminated in the first general strike in the Russian Empire. The so-called South Russian general strike demanded the introduction of the eight-hour workday and wage increases. In July and August 1903 it paralyzed almost all Ukraine and involved 150,000 workers. Some 100 workers were killed, 500 were injured, and over 2,000 were arrested. During the 1905–7 revolutionary period strikes took place throughout Ukraine, and many of them demanded democratic reforms. In December 1905, political strikes in the Donbas escalated into armed revolts. The biggest of them occurred in Horlivka on 30 December 1905.

The peasant strikes that engulfed Poltava and Kharkiv gubernias in 1902 were particularly serious. They were provoked by high redemption payments, excessive taxes, and the land shortage and were suppressed by troops. Over 800 peasants were arrested and sentenced to prison terms, and 800,000 rubles in fines were transferred to landlords as compensation. During those strikes demands for Ukraine's autonomy were also raised.

Strikes in the period of reaction 1907–10 did not have a mass character. They were mostly protests against deteriorating labor conditions and the erosion of gains won in 1905–7. There were 221 strikes in Ukraine, involving 98,000 workers. The economic recovery, which began in 1910, increased workers' confidence, and the number of strikes rose. In 1910–14 there were 958 strikes, with 323,000 participants.

With the outbreak of the First World War repression against the workers' movement increased, and strikes became rarer. As economic conditions deteriorated and impatience with the war grew, workers resorted to strikes. In 1916 there were 218 strikes in Ukraine, involving over 196,000 workers, mostly in metallurgy and mining. In the summer of 1917 strikes took place throughout Ukraine. As the Russian Empire disintegrated, strikes subsided. The all-Ukrainian railway strike against the German occupation of Ukraine in 1918 was a remarkable political action.

Under the tsarist regime strikes were illegal. An 1845 law treated strikes as revolts against established authority. A secret circular of 6 June 1870 authorized governors to deport strike organizers and leaders to remote parts of the empire. A secret circular of 1897 removed the requirement to allow such cases to be heard in court. Nevertheless, strikes were widely employed to improve working conditions and to force political change. The right to strike was won by the trade-union movement in Ukraine during the 1917 Revolution.

In Western Ukraine the first strikes took place in the 1870s. They were peasant protests against inadequate wages on estates. By 1902, peasant strikes had taken on a mass character. They were organized by Ukrainian political parties and were the first mass peasant strikes in Europe. Smaller strikes took place in 1901–2 in Transcarpathia and Bukovyna (see *Peasant strikes in Galicia and Bukovyna). Because Western Ukraine was underdeveloped, urban strikes were rare. The first strikes among urban workers were the printers' strike in Lviv in 1870, the bakers' strike in 1874, and the saddle makers' strike in 1875. In 1895–9 there were 35 strikes in Galicia, involving 3,500 people. The other significant industrial strikes were the 1904 strikes of oil workers in Boryslav and construction workers in Bukovyna. In the interwar period strikes in Western Ukraine (then divided among Poland, Czechoslovakia, and Rumania) were rare, because the urban working class was small, and there was widespread unemployment. The largest labor action in that period was the 1921 railway workers' strike in Galicia. There were work stoppages in some Lviv factories in 1929 and 1936 and a strike of forestry workers in Transcarpathia.

In Soviet Ukraine, although there were no laws against strikes, the militarization of labor under War Communism ruled out the right to strike. The Bolshevik-controlled trade unions worked to prevent any attempts to strike. It was argued that it was illogical for workers to strike against their own state. Yet strikes did take place under the Bolshevik regime in Ukraine. In many cases they were led by Mensheviks, who had led the Ukrainian trade unions before they were merged into all-Russian organizations by the Bolsheviks. In 1920–1 the Bolsheviks unleashed a wave of repression against their opponents within the working class and expelled over 200,000 people from the trade unions.

Under the NEP, strikes were allowed, and trade unions were instructed to obtain a speedy settlement. But Party members could not support strikes. As J. Stalin consolidated his power and the regime became totalitarian, strikes were banned as anti-Soviet actions, although there was no legislation against strikes. The Draconian labor laws of the 1930s ruled out any possibility of a strike. The official position was that in the USSR, where the state was controlled by the workers and acted in their interest, there was no social basis for strikes.

After Stalin's death a wave of strikes swept the labor camps of Norilsk (7 May to 2 August 1953), Vorkuta (July–August 1953), and Termir-Tau. Ukrainian political prisoners played a leading role in the strikes. The strikers demanded a shorter workday, of 9 instead of 12 hours, proper food, the removal of informers from the camps, unlimited correspondence with relatives, and guarantees against the arbitrary shooting of prisoners by guards. The strikes were brutally suppressed by the army.

Despite the massive apparatus for repressing discontent and opposition, there were surprisingly many strikes in Ukraine. The regime tended to accept quickly the demands of the strikers to avoid an escalation of the struggle. But once the strike was defused, its organizers were arrested and sentenced to long prison terms. If immediate concessions did not end the strike, force was used. The largest industrial action during N. Khrushchev's regime occurred in 1962. It started in Novocherkassk, RSFSR, and spread quickly to Ukrainian cities, such as Donetske and Zhdanov (Mariiupil). Its immediate cause was the announcement of price increases on meat and dairy products. Troops and KGB detachments were called in to suppress the strike, and scores of people were killed. In 1967 the workers of the Kharkiv Tractor Plant walked out, and a workers' protest in Pryluky raised political and national demands. The 1969 strike at the Kiev Hydroelectric Station was extensively reported in Ukrainian samvydav. During the 1970s many strikes were reported in Ukraine. The largest included actions in Dnipropetrovske and Dniprodzerzhynske in September and October 1972. Workers of several factories in Dnipropetrovske demanded higher wages, better food and living conditions, and the right to choose one's job. In Dniprodzerzhynske workers rioted and attacked police and Party headquarters in response to police repression. At the end of the 1970s, groups of workers in Ukraine attempted to establish free trade unions. The Association of Free Trade Unions (est 1978) was led by V. *Klebanov. One of its central demands was the right to strike. The activists of the group were arrested and incarcerated in special psychiatric hospitals or labor camps.

With the growth of the national and democratic movement in Ukraine in the late 1980s, the regime learned to tolerate strikes. As the economic and political crisis deepened, strikes become a common occurrence. From January to July 1990, 10 million man-days were lost through strikes in the USSR. In the summer of 1989 the workers at many Donbas mines went on strike. The strike committees that led and co-ordinated the actions became the nuclei of new trade unions. The strikers set forth a wide range of demands: higher wages, better food, improved safety, and the removal of Party organizations from the workplace. From 1989, strikers in Ukraine also raised political demands. Workers in Western Ukraine used strikes to defend democratic rights and national independence. Strikers demanded radical changes in labor legislation, including guarantees of the right to strike. In August 1989 the USSR Supreme Soviet passed the first law on strikes. That highly restrictive law permitted strikes only after the conciliation commission and the court of labor arbitration had failed to settle disagreements between labor and management. Strikes had to be approved by a majority of the general meeting consisting of at least three-quarters of the workers' collective. Management had to be given five days' notice of a strike. The Union or a republican supreme soviet or its presidium could postpone a strike or suspend it for a period of up to two months. Strikes in support of unconstitutional demands were illegal. Strikes in 'essential' sectors of the economy were not allowed. Strikers were entitled to state social insurance and pay from strike funds. Although the law did not permit political strikes, work stoppages in support of national and democratic demands occurred. In October 1990 strikes against the signing of a new union treaty took place in many cities of Ukraine. The strikers also demanded military service only on Ukrainian territory; the immediate closure of the Chornobyl Nuclear Power Station; the removal of the Party and the KGB from the army, government, and factories; workers' ownership of the factories and enterprises; and the nationalization of the Party's property.

BIBLIOGRAPHY
Horlach, M. *Virna opora partiï komunistiv: Profspilky Ukraïny u borot'bi za zdiisnennia lenins'koho planu komunistychnoho budivnytstva* (Kiev 1968)
Pospelovsky, D. *Russian Police Trade Unionism* (London 1971)
Haynes, V.; Semyonova, O. (eds). *Workers against the Gulag: The New Opposition in the Soviet Union* (London 1979)
Shumuk, D. *Life Sentence: Memoirs of a Ukrainian Political Prisoner* (Edmonton 1984)

B. Krawchenko

**Strikha, Edvard.** See Burevii, Kost.

*Strilets'* (Rifleman). A weekly paper for soldiers of the Ukrainian Galician Army, published in Stanyslaviv, Stryi, Kamianets-Podilskyi, and Borshchiv, from 1 January to 16 November 1919. A total of 95 issues appeared, some with a pressrun of 16,000 copies. The editors were V. Pachovsky, I. Krevetsky, H. Myketei, and O. Nazaruk.

Rev Yeronim Striletsky     Vasyl Striltsiv

**Striletsky, Yeronim** [Strilec'kyj, Jeronim], b 1732, d 1804. Basilian priest and scholar. He was raised in the Brody region and served in Zamość, Pidhirtsi, and Pochaiv after finishing his studies in Rome in 1761. From 1776 he was in Vienna as chaplain at the Barbareum and then as the first parish priest at St Barbara's Church (from 1784). He also served as a liaison between Ukrainian Catholic hierarchs and the imperial government in Vienna and the papacy. He wrote several religious studies and a Ukrainian grammar (in Polish). His extensive book collection later became the basis for eparchial libraries in Peremyshl and Lviv.

**Striletskyi Steppe** [Strilec'kyj step]. A division of the Luhanske Nature Reserve located in Milove raion, Luhanske oblast. The land was brought under administrative control in 1936 so that a remaining area of the Starobilske steppe and wild steppe fauna would be preserved. The reserve is 479 ha in area. It contains nearly 600 species of plants and nearly 200 types of birds and animals; most notably it provides shelter for the largest colony of marmots in Ukraine.

**Striletskyi Teatr.** See Theater of the Legion of Ukrainian Sich Riflemen.

**Striltsiv, Vasyl** [Stril'civ, Vasyl'], b 13 January 1929 in Zahvizdia, Stanyslaviv county, Galicia. Political prisoner. At the age of 15 he was sentenced in Stanyslaviv by the NKVD to 10 years in labor camps in the Soviet Arctic, for alleged contact with the Ukrainian Insurgent Army. After being freed in 1954 and rehabilitated in 1956, he studied at Chernivtsi University and then taught English in Ivano-Frankivske oblast. When his brother Pavlo was imprisoned for political reasons in 1972, he suffered persecution by the Soviet authorities. After losing his job in Dolyna, in September 1977 he renounced his Soviet citizenship, and in October he joined the *Ukrainian Helsinki Group. In January 1979 he was sentenced to three months' corrective labor without imprisonment for striking and applying to emigrate to England. He was arrested in October 1979 and sentenced in November in Dolyna to two years in a strict-regime labor camp in Poltava oblast. Before his sentence ended, he was rearrested in October 1981 and sentenced in April 1982 to six more years in a camp. He was released in 1987.

**Striltsov, Zosym** [Stril'cov], b 29 April 1831 in Slovianoserbske, Katerynoslav gubernia, d 27 May 1885 in Kharkiv. Embryologist. A graduate of Kharkiv University (1854), he practiced medicine in Katerynoslav gubernia and Katerynoslav (1857–74) and spent a year abroad working in pathological anatomy. From 1874 he worked in the department of embryology, histology, and comparative anatomy at Kharkiv University. His publications, in Russian, German, and French, dealt with the effects of ether on the animal organism, blood circulation, and the embryonic development of bone tissue.

**Stroev, Pavel,** b 27 July 1796 in Moscow, d 5 January 1876 in Moscow. Russian historian and archeographer; full member of the Russian Academy of Sciences from 1849. He studied at Moscow University (1812–16) and worked for the Imperial Russian Archeographic Commission. In 1828–34 he was in charge of its research expeditions to the libraries and archives of monasteries, which collected approx 3,000 items, including ancient monuments of *instructional literature, such as the *Izbornik* of Sviatoslav (1073), Ilarion's 'Slovo o zakoni i blahodati' (Sermon on Law and Grace), the *Sudebnik* of 1497, and works by Cyril of Turiv. Stroev also assisted in the preparation and publication of *Polnoe sobranie russkikh letopisei* (The Complete Collection of Russian Chronicles, 1843–71; repr 1908–10, 1962).

*Stroitel'stvo i arkhitektura* (Construction and Architecture). A Russian-language monthly organ of the State Committee for Construction of the Council of Ministers of Ukraine and the Union of Architects of Ukraine, published in Kiev from 1953. Until 1957 the journal was published six times a year and was called *Arkhitektura i budivnytstvo*. Until 1959 it appeared in both Russian and Ukrainian. The journal contained articles on urban planning, construction management, and the history and theory of architecture. In 1980 it had a pressrun of 5,500 copies.

**Strokach, Tymofii** [Strokač, Tymofij], b 4 March 1903 in Belotserkovka, Primorskaia oblast, in the Far East, d 15 August 1963 in Kiev. Senior NKVD and MVD official. Having served in the border guards for many years, in 1941 he was appointed deputy commissar for internal affairs of the Ukrainian SSR, and in 1942 chief of staff of the Ukrainian Partisan Headquarters. After being promoted to brigadier general (1943) and major general (1944) he returned to his deputy commissar's post (1945–6) and then rose to minister for internal affairs of the Ukrainian SSR (1946–56) and deputy minister for internal affairs of the USSR (1956–7). As chief of the MVD in Ukraine, he was responsible for the suppression of the UPA and the OUN underground after the war. His memoirs are titled *Nash pozyvnyi – Svoboda* (Our Call Is Freedom, 1975).

Nina Strokata

**Strokata, Nina,** b 31 January 1926 in Odessa. Political prisoner. A graduate of the Odessa Medical Institute (1947), she worked there as a microbiologist from 1952. From the mid-1960s she was persecuted by the KGB for her defense of her imprisoned husband, S. *Karavansky. She was fired from her job in May 1971, arrested in December, and sentenced in May 1972 to four years in a labor camp for women in the Mordovian ASSR for her active defense of political prisoners. In the camp she went on hunger strikes and participated in several prisoners' protests. In May 1974 she was elected a full member of the American Society for Microbiology. After her release in December 1975, she was forbidden to live in Ukraine and forced to settle in Tarusa, Kaluga oblast, RSFSR, where she was further persecuted and abused. In November 1976 she became a founding member of the *Ukrainian Helsinki Group. In November 1979 she and Karavansky were expelled from the Soviet Union, and received refuge in the United States. There she has remained active in the defense of human rights in Ukraine, and has compiled *Ukrainian Women in the Soviet Union: Documented Persecution* (1980), *A Family Torn Apart* (1981), and pamphlets about individual Ukrainian women political prisoners (1985).

**Stronin, Oleksander,** b 4 March 1826 in Rakitina *sloboda*, Belgorod county, Kursk gubernia, d 10 February 1889 in Yalta, Tavriia gubernia. Historian, sociologist, educator, and civic leader. After graduating from the philosophy faculty of Kiev University (1848) he taught secondary school (1848–62) in Kamianets-Podilskyi, Novhorod-Siverskyi, and Poltava. He had a significant influence on M. Drahomanov, who was his student. In Poltava he was active in the local hromada and organized Sunday schools. In 1862 he was arrested for 'disseminating Little

Russian propaganda,' held in the Peter and Paul Fortress in St Petersburg, and exiled to Arkhangelsk gubernia. After his release (1869) he held a government job in St Petersburg and then presided over the Lublin gubernia conference of civil judges and acted as a legal consultant to the Ministry of Communications in St Petersburg. He wrote a number of historical-sociological studies, such as *Istoriia i metod* (History and Method, 1869), *Politika kak nauka* (Politics as a Science, 1872), and *Istoriia obshchestvennosti* (History of Society, 1885), as well as some popular books for the masses under the pseudonym Ivanov, including *Priroda i liudi: Rasskazy o zemle i o nebe* (Nature and Men: Stories about the Earth and the Heavens, 1896). His memoirs (1826–62) and diary for 1848–88 have not been published, but extensive extracts from them appeared in the journal *Byloe* (vol 7) in 1907.

A. Zhukovsky

Ivan Stronsky

Danylo Husar Struk

**Stronsky, Ivan** [Strons'kyj], b 20 October 1864 in Zaraisko, Sambir county, Galicia, d 20 July 1935 in Lviv. Educator and civic leader. After graduating from the teachers' seminary in Lviv (1882) he worked as a teacher and principal in various villages of Lviv county (1891–1927). He was a founding member and president of the *Ukrainian Teachers' Mutual Aid Society and edited its organ *Uchytel's'ke slovo* (1925–9). He represented Ukrainian teachers at conferences of the Union of Slavic Teachers, the International Federation of Teachers' Associations, and the Federation of Teachers' Unions of Slavic Nations.

**Structural mechanics** (*budivelni nauky*). Before 1917, research in structural mechanics (or construction science) was conducted by S. *Timoshenko, O. Dynnyk, K. Siminsky, and S. *Prokofiev, in bridge building, by Ye. *Paton, and in building materials, by K. Dementiev. In 1919 the Institute of Technical Mechanics was founded within the Ukrainian Academy of Sciences. In 1929 it was renamed the Institute of Structural Mechanics, and in 1959, the *Institute of Mechanics of the AN URSR (now ANU). Other research institutions that dealt with construction were the *Institute for Problems of Materials Science, the *Institute of Electric Welding, and the Academy of Construction and Architecture of the Ukrainian SSR (1956–64). Research institutes specializing in construction included the Institute of Building Production of the State Committee for Construction (Derzhbud URSR), the Kiev branch of the All-

Union Scientific Research Institute of New Materials, the Institute of Typical and Experimental Design of Residential and Civic Buildings, and the Ukrainian Roads and Transportation Institute of the Ukrainian Ministry of Automotive Transport and Highways. Construction research is also conducted by the relevant faculties of various higher schools, civil-engineering institutes in Kiev, Kharkiv, and Odessa, and railway-engineering institutes in Kiev and Kharkiv. Ukrainian scientists have made some important contributions in the field, among them B. *Lysin, P. *Budnikov, H. *Pysarenko, Yu. Kozub, Yu. Rodychev, and H. *Slobodianyk. They studied the use of raw materials such as silicates and kaolins in the manufacture of glass, cement, ceramics, perlite, and slag pumice. Reinforced concrete was studied by Ya. *Stoliarov, V. *Yaryn, Y. Ulytsky, and I. Kyreienko (see *Reinforced concrete industry). F. *Bieliankin and M. Afanasiev studied covering for industrial buildings; S. *Serensen and Afanasiev researched repeated-changing loads, M. *Kornoukhov, B. Gorbunov, I. Amiro, M. Dluhach, V. Zarutsky, and V. Yatsenko analyzed the strength and stability of skeletal systems and rib cylindrical coverings; and Gorbunov, D. Vainberg, V. *Chudnovsky, and O. *Strelbytska calculated frame estimates. Budnikov, O. Harmash, and O. *Nerovetsky applied assembly line methods in the *construction industry, and P. *Neporozhnii and P. *Slipchenko developed the mechanization of constructing hydraulic structures. In sanitation technology Ukrainian scientists researched the aeration of industrial buildings, ventilation, air conduction, new heating systems, and air-conditioning (B. Lobaev), the heating and gasification of cities (P. Kolobkov), water purification and water supply (L. *Kulsky), and hydromechanics (M. *Lavrentev and H. *Sukhomel). In transportation construction O. Burulia, O. Frolov, M. Volkov, and Gorbunov proposed new bridge designs, rails, and road surfacing. The different branches of construction science have had their own periodicals, among them *Budivnychi materialy i konstruktsiï, Stroitel'stvo i arkhitektura, Promyshlennoe stroitel'stvo i inzhenernye sooruzheniia, Sil's'ke budivnytstvo, Mis'ke hospodarstvo Ukraïny,* and the bimonthly of the ANU Institute of Mechanics *Prikladnaia mekhanika* (which in 1955–65 came out in Ukrainian as *Prykladna mekhanika*).

**Struk, Danylo Husar,** b 5 April 1940 in Lviv. Literary scholar; member of the Shevchenko Scientific Society since 1988 and foreign member of the ANU since 1992; son of E. *Struk. A graduate of Harvard University (1963) and the universities of Alberta (1964) and Toronto (PH D, 1970), he has taught Ukrainian language and literature at Toronto since 1967 (full professor since 1981). He has been managing editor (1982–90) and, since 1989, editor-in-chief of the *Encyclopedia of Ukraine*. Struk is the author of *A Study of Vasyl Stefanyk: The Pain at the Heart of Existence* (1973), the textbook *Ukrainian for Undergraduates* (1978; 2nd edn 1982; 3rd edn 1988), and articles on Ukrainian writers (M. Khvylovy, V. Vynnychenko, E. Andiievska, I. Kalynets, H. Chubai, and others) in North American scholarly journals and collections, *Suchasnist', Novi dni,* and other émigré periodicals. He wrote many literature entries for the *Encyclopedia of Ukraine*. His Ukrainian poems have appeared in *Suchasnist'* and *Pivnichne siaivo* and in the collection *Gamma Sigma* (1963). Struk has translated Ukrainian writers (Stefanyk, L. Kostenko, V. Symonenko, Chubai, Vynnychenko) into English and T.S. Eliot, W. Kinsella, and T. Galay into Ukrainian.

**Struk, Evstakhii (Stanko),** b 22 September 1909 in Synevidsko Vyzhnie, Stryi county, Galicia, d end of June 1941 in Lviv. Civic leader; father of D.H. Struk. After completing a business and trade degree at Lviv University (1936) he worked for *Tsentrosoiuz in Lviv. For his activities as a member of the OUN he was arrested by the Polish authorities in 1939 and incarcerated in the Bereza Kartuzka concentration camp. He was sentenced to be shot, but escaped en route to the execution. After the Soviet occupation of Galicia Struk became director of the Medical Institute in Lviv and continued to serve as a clandestine liaison officer for couriers from the OUN leadership abroad. Because he ordered that the students of the Medical Institute detained by Soviet security forces be set free, he was arrested by the NKVD. His brutally mutilated body was later discovered in the cellars of Lontskyi prison, among those of thousands of other Ukrainians murdered by the Soviet secret police on the eve of Soviet-Nazi hostilities.

**Strukhmanchuk, Yakiv** [Struxmančuk, Jakiv], b 10 August 1884 in Rosokhovatets, Pidhaitsi county, Galicia, d 1933. Graphic artist and portraitist. He studied at the Cracow Academy of Fine Arts (1906–10) and L'Ecole des beaux arts in Paris (1911–19). He contributed caricatures to satirical magazines, such as *Zerkalo* and *Zhalo*, in Lviv and illustrated books, such as M. Arkas's history of Ukraine (1908), O. Makovei's *Revun* (The Bawler, 1910), and works by P. Kozlaniuk. In 1920 he moved to Kiev, where he joined the literary and artistic group Zakhidnia Ukraina. There he painted portraits of the group's members (V. Atamaniuk, D. Zahul, M. Kozoris, M. Kichura, M. Marfiievych, and A. Turchynska). He also wrote articles on art for *Dilo* (1909–12) and *Svit* (1926–9) and published his recollections in *Zakhidnia Ukraïna*. He was arrested under P. Postyshev's Stalinist regime in Ukraine, and perished in prison.

**Struminsky, Bohdan** [Strumins'kyj] (pseud: Demonodor Baiursky), b 7 March 1930 in Białystok, Poland. Linguist and philologist. He studied Polish and Ukrainian philology at Warsaw University (PH D, 1974). Since his arrival as a refugee in the United States (1975), he has taught Ukrainian at Harvard University and has been a research fellow, translator, and editor at the Harvard Ukrainian Research Institute. He has contributed numerous articles and reviews to Polish and North American scholarly periodicals, such as *Slavia Orientalis, Harvard Ukrainian Studies,* and *Journal of Ukrainian Studies,* and to the *Encyclopedia of Ukraine* and Ukrainian periodicals in Poland and abroad. He is the author of *Pseudo-Meleško: A Ukrainian Apocryphal Parliamentary Speech of 1615–1618* (1984), satirical and humorous short prose, and literary translations into Polish, Ukrainian, and English.

**Strusiv.** IV-6. A village (1973 pop 1,800) on the Seret River in Terebovlia raion, Ternopil oblast. The village of Pidbohorodyshche, which is mentioned in 15th-century documents, began to be called Strusiv (after its owner, the Strus family) at the end of the 16th century. A castle built there in the 16th century has been lost, but a palace of the 18th century has been preserved. There was a Basilian monastery with a grotto church and stone altar near the village. In the 18th century St Michael's Church was built above the grotto. The monastery burned down in 1893.

Mariia Strutynska          Mykhailo Strutynsky

**Strutynska, Mariia** [Strutyns'ka, Marija] (pseud: V. Marska), b 9 September 1897 in Dolyna, Galicia, d 6 May 1984 in Philadelphia. Writer, journalist, translator, and civic figure; daughter of Rev V. Navrotsky and wife of M. *Strutynsky. In Lviv she worked as a teacher and was a member of the national executive of the Union of Ukrainian Women (1922–39). She published articles and prose in Lviv periodicals (eg, *Dilo, Novyi chas*), coedited the union's biweekly *Zhinka* (1935–8), and edited the union's monthly *Ukraïnka* (1937–9) and the Lviv literary monthly *Nashi dni* (1941–4). In the 1930s she also contributed translations of French literature (eg, R. Rolland) to *Vistnyk*. As a postwar refugee she lived in Austria and, from 1950, Philadelphia. A founding member of the *Slovo Association of Ukrainian Writers in Exile and a member of its presidium, she published articles, prose, translations, and plays in Ukrainian-American periodicals and was a coeditor of *Notatky z mystetstva*. Published separately were her reportage novel *Buria nad L'vovom* (The Storm over Lviv, 1944; 2nd edn 1952), the story collection *Pomylka doktora Varets'koho* (Dr Varetsky's Mistake, 1964), the play *Amerykanka* (An American Woman, 1973), and the book of autobiographical stories, reminiscences, and diary notes *Daleke zblyz'ka* (The Distant Close Up, 1975).

**Strutynsky, Mykhailo** [Strutyns'kyj, Myxajlo], b 3 December 1888 in Pidmykhailia, Kalush county, Galicia, d end of June 1941 in Lviv. Journalist and civic and political leader; husband of M. *Strutynska. He studied at Vienna and Lviv universities and was active in Galician politics as an executive member of the National Democratic party, Ukrainian Labor party (1922–5), and Ukrainian National Democratic Alliance. In 1928 he was elected to the Polish Sejm, and he served on its communications committee. He edited or helped edit many Galician papers or journals, among them *Shliakhy, Zhyttia i mystetstvo, Dilo, Nash prapor,* and *Novyi chas* (1930–9). He also held important positions in Ukrainian organizations: he was a member of the board of trustees for Ukrainian postsecondary schools, member of the presidium of Ridna Shkola, and executive member of the Shevchenko Scientific Society. He was executed by Soviet security forces retreating from the invading German army.

**Strutynsky, Mykola** [Strutyns'kyj], b 1898, d 22 March 1943 in Hrubeshiv, Kholm region. Civic and political activist. He practiced law in Buzk and then Hrubeshiv. After being elected president of the Ukrainian Relief Committee in Hrubeshiv in 1943, he was instrumental in establishing a regional defense force called *Samooborona. He was murdered by Polish partisans.

**Strutynsky, Vilen** [Strutyns'kyj], b 16 October 1929 in Danylova Balka, now in Ulianivka raion, Kirovohrad oblast. Theoretical physicist; AN URSR (now ANU) corresponding member since 1972. A graduate of Kharkiv University (1952), he worked at the Atomic Energy Institute in Moscow (1953–70). Since 1970 he has headed the theoretical physics department of the ANU Institute for Nuclear Research in Kiev. Strutynsky has made significant contributions to the theory of nuclear structure and nuclear-reaction mechanisms. For his contribution to the understanding of the shell structure of deformed nuclei, in 1978 he was awarded the Tom W. Bonner Prize of the American Physical Society.

**Struve, Liudvig** (Ludwig), b 1 November 1858 in Pulkovo, St Petersburg gubernia, d 4 November 1920 in Symferopil, Crimea. Astronomer. A graduate of Dorpat (Tartu) University (PH D, 1887), he was a professor at Kharkiv University from 1897 and director of the Kharkiv Astronomical Observatory from 1898. His main contributions were in the area of binary stars. He also developed a method of measuring the moon's radius using stellar occlusions by the lunar disk.

**Struve, Otto**, b 12 August 1897 in Kharkiv, d 6 April 1963 in Berkeley, California. Astronomer; member of the Royal Society (London) from 1952. He studied at Kharkiv University and emigrated to the United States in 1920, where he worked at the University of Chicago. From 1932 to 1962 he headed a series of important American astronomic observatories, including the Yerkes Observatory in Wisconsin, the McDonald Observatory in Texas, and the National Radio Astronomy Observatory in Green Bank, West Virginia. He served as vice-president (1948–52) and president (1952–5) of the International Astronomic Union. His main scientific contributions were in the field of stellar spectroscopy, particularly the interactions of close binary stars. Many of his scholarly articles were published in *Astrophysical Journal* and *Astronomical Journal*; he also contributed to *Popular Astronomy*.

**Strviazh River.** See Stryvihor River.

**Stryboh.** The pagan god of the wind, one of the chief gods worshiped by early Ukrainians and other Eastern Slavs. He was the counterpart of the Greek god Aeolus. Stryboh is mentioned in early monuments of Ukrainian literature, including the Primary Chronicle and *Slovo o polku Ihorevi* (The Tale of Ihor's Campaign). The cult of Stryboh left many traces in Ukrainian toponymy – the village of Strybizh, in the Zhytomyr region, for example, and the Strybizka River, in the Kiev region. There are different theories concerning the etymology of the name Stryboh. It may have come from *strybaty* 'to leap' or from *sterty* 'to erase.' Some scholars contend that the first syllable (*stry-*) shares a common root with the universal Slavic word *strila*

or *strika* 'arrow', which relationship suggests that an ancient poetic trope comparing the wind to an arrow may be reflected here.

**Stryhun, Fedir,** b 1 November 1939 in Tomashivka (now in Uman raion, Cherkasy oblast). Stage and film actor. He completed study at the Kiev Institute of Theater Arts (1961, class of V. Nelli) and joined the Zaporizhia (later Lviv) Ukrainian Music and Drama Theater, where he was leading actor from 1965 and artistic director from 1987. His stage roles varied from that of Don Juan in Lesia Ukrainka's *Kaminnyi hospodar* (The Stone Host) to the title role in Shakespeare's *Richard III*. He also acted in the films *Khaziaïn* (The Master, 1976, based on I. Karpenko-Kary's drama) and *Poïzd nadzvychainoho pryznachennia* (The Train of Special Designation, 1979).

**Stryi** [Stryj]. IV-4. A city (1990 pop 67,000) on the Stryi River and a raion center in Lviv oblast. It was first mentioned in historical documents in 1385, when Galicia was under Polish rule. In 1460 the town was granted the rights of *Magdeburg law. Stryi's economic development can be attributed largely to its strategic location on the main trade route to Mukachiv through the Carpathian Mountains. Under Austrian rule (1772–1918) Stryi became a county center and the seat of a circuit court. It developed into an industrial and commercial town, and its population grew from 8,000 in 1843 to 12,600 in 1880, 23,200 in 1900, and 30,900 in 1910.

The town hall in Stryi

By the end of the 19th century Stryi was an important center of the Ukrainian national movement in Galicia. The town's chief civic leaders were Ye. Olesnytsky and O. Nyzhankivsky. Stryi was one of the first centers of the Ukrainian women's movement: the first women's rally was held there in 1891, and the first edition of the women's almanac *Nasha dolia* (Our Fate, 1893) was published there. Stryi was an important center of the Ukrainian cooperative movement: the Provincial Dairy Union (later *Maslosoiuz) was founded there in 1907, and the first Ukrainian provincial exhibition was held there in 1909. A Ukrainian gymnasium was opened in Stryi in 1906, and the newspapers *Stryis'kyi holos* (1894–5), *Hospodar i promyslovets'* (1909–11), and *Pidhirs'ka rada* (1910–11) appeared there. During the Ukrainian-Polish War in 1919, the headquarters of the Third Corps of the Ukrainian Galician Army were located in Stryi.

Under Polish occupation (1919–39) the city's economy hardly grew, and by 1931 its population was only 30,900. In 1939 about 28 percent of the inhabitants were Ukrainian, 34.5 percent were Polish, and 35.6 percent were Jewish. Stryi became a leading center of Ukrainian resistance: its cells of the Ukrainian Military Organization and the OUN were among the most active in Galicia. The Ukrainian state gymnasium (1918–23) was replaced by Ukrainian departments in the Polish gymnasium, but a private Ukrainian women's seminary and a gymnasium run by the Ridna Shkola society were opened in the 1920s. After Lviv, Stryi had the largest Plast organization in Galicia. A branch of the Lysenko Higher Institute of Music, the Verkhovyna Museum (est 1932), and many other cultural institutions served the Ukrainian community. The city's Ukrainian newspapers included *Stryis'ka dumka* (1933–9) and *Ukraïns'ka muzyka* (1937–9).

Under the Soviet regime the city's industry was developed rapidly. Large machine-building, metalworking, and reinforced-concrete plants were set up. Light industry (fur and footwear) and the food industry were expanded. The city became an important railway and highway junction. The city's population grew to 36,200 in 1959 and 48,000 in 1970, and its ethnic profile changed sharply: in 1959, 68 percent of the population was Ukrainian, and 30 percent was Russian. There is a regional studies museum in Stryi.

BIBLIOGRAPHY
Prichaska, A. *Historja miasta Stryja* (Lviv 1926)
V. Kubijovyč, Ya. Padokh

**Stryi Brigade of the Ukrainian Galician Army** (Stryiska [11] brygada UHA). A unit in the Third Corps of the UHA, organized in June 1919 from some units previously assigned to the Krukenychi and Hlyboka combat groups. It consisted of four infantry battalions, one artillery regiment, and reserve units. Its peak strength, in August 1919, was 2,400. Under Maj K. Schlosser's command the brigade became a leading fighting unit. In August 1919 it was assigned to the UNR Army to assist its Third Iron Rifle Division against the 45th and 47th Red Army divisions. In February 1920 it was reorganized into the Ninth Infantry Regiment of the Red Ukrainian Galician Army, and in late April it joined other UHA units in Polish internment camps.

**Stryi Regional Studies Museum Verkhovyna** (Stryiskyi kraieznavchyi muzei 'Verkhovyna'). A museum founded in Stryi in 1932 through the efforts of R. Dombchevsky, I. Siletsky (its principal collector), O. Bachynska, T. Zalesky, and I. Maksymchuk. In 1937 it had 2,000 items on exhibit. It was nationalized by the Soviet occupying authorities in 1939 and reorganized after the Second World War. The museum has natural science and history divisions and holds 14,000 artifacts (1971), including local archeological finds, 15th- to 20th-century historical documents, 17th- and 18th-century Cossack and opryshok weapons, 14th- to 16th-century coins, late-19th- to early-20th-century Boiko and Hutsul Easter eggs, 19th-century folk musical instruments, 18th- to 20th-century traditional clothing, and 19th- and 20th-century books and periodicals.

The Stryi River

**Stryi River** [Stryj]. A right-bank tributary of the Dniester River that flows for 232 km through southern Lviv oblast and drains a basin area of 3,055 sq km. The river originates in the High Beskyds and initially has a mountainous character. It is 30–50 m wide in its upper reaches and up to 150 m wide downstream. The river is fed by meltwater and has been known to flood. It is used for industrial and water-supply purposes. A hydroelectric station and water reservoir (200 million cu m) have been built on the waterway. Some major centers located along the river are Turka, Stryi, and Zhydachiv.

**Stryi Ukrainian Music and Drama Theater** (Stryiskyi ukrainskyi muzychno-dramatychnyi teatr). A theater founded in 1944 as a *touring theater on the basis of the Kiev troupes under I. *Sahatovsky and K. *Luchytska. It was joined by actors from the Sambir Touring Theater in 1948 and was active until 1964. It performed mostly Ukrainian classical dramas and toured Moldavia and the Russian SFSR. Luchytska was the director, and V. Borysovets was the stage designer; among the actors were S. Koval and Ye. Khoroshun.

*Stryis'ka dumka* (Stryi Thought). A newspaper in Stryi, published twice a week in 1933–5, and then twice a month to 1939 as *Dumka*, by A. Kozak. The newspaper carried mostly news from and information about Subcarpathia, the Boiko region, and Pokutia. Among the contributors were Ya. Padokh, J. Rudnyckyj, and Z. Lysko.

**Stryisky, Ivan** [Stryjs'kyj], b 1884, d 28 January 1935 in Chernivtsi, Bukovyna. Civic and political leader in the Kitsman region. A practicing lawyer, he was active in politics as deputy leader (from 1927) of the Ukrainian National party in Rumania. He contributed articles on legal issues and other matters to Ukrainian papers, such as *Ridnyi krai* and *Chas*.

**Stryjek, Dmytro**, b 5 November 1899 in Lanivtsi, Borshchiv county, Galicia, d 7 March 1991 in Saskatoon. Painter; one of the most prominent primitive artists in Canada. A resident of Canada since 1923, he began painting seriously after his retirement in 1965. After moving to

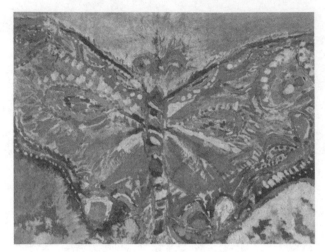

Dmytro Stryjek: *Butterfly*

Saskatoon in 1967, he began exhibiting and attracted the attention of curators and art historians. His subjects include landscapes, flowers, birds, and religious and historical events, often those remembered from his youth in Ukraine. His portraits include some famous Ukrainians, such as T. Shevchenko, Lesia Ukrainka, Hetman I. Mazepa, S. Petliura, and Cardinal Y. Slipy, and world leaders, such as Queen Elizabeth II, I. Ghandi, and P.E. Trudeau. Although Stryjek has lived most of his life in Canada, his vision is deeply rooted in his Ukrainian environment and the Ukrainian community in Saskatoon. His paintings are astonishingly inventive and hauntingly lyrical (eg, the series 'Hill of Flowers'). A brilliant colorist, Stryjek achieves a freshness that seems inexhaustible, and challenges accepted ideas of untutored painting as separate from mainstream art. A monograph about him by P. Millard was published in 1988 in conjunction with a cross-Canada traveling exhibition of Stryjek's paintings.

D. Zelska-Darewych

**Stryjkowski, Maciej** (Matys Strycovius; pseud: Osostevitius), b ca 1547 in Stryków, near Warsaw, d ca 1582–93. Polish historian and poet; author of the first printed history of Lithuania. He studied at the Cracow Academy (1567–70) and worked in the Lithuanian military and diplomatic service. He used Lithuanian, Polish, Ukrainian, and Russian chronicles and other records collected during his travels to prepare *Kronika polska, litewska, żmudzka i wszystkiej Rusi* (Chronicle of Poland, Lithuania, Samogitia, and All of Rus'), which covered events until 1572. Written in Polish, in places in an epic style, it provided an overview history of Lithuania with a Lithuanian political attitude and interpretation of events. It was published in 1582 in Königsberg and translated into Belarusian (1584) and Russian (17th century); some of its original sources have since then been lost. The chronicle was used by Ukrainian (S. Velychko, H. Hrabianka, T. Safonovych), Polish (A. Mickiewicz, J. Słowacki, J. Kraszewski), and Lithuanian (A. Kojelavičius) writers and historians.

**Strypa River.** A left-bank tributary of the Dniester River that flows southward for 147 km through Ternopil oblast and drains a basin area of 1,610 sq km. The river is generally approx 30 m wide and has a sharply defined valley.

Its waters are used for industry and agriculture. A small water reservoir has been built on it. The major centers located along the river include Zboriv and Buchach.

Hiiador Strypsky          Mykola Stsiborsky

**Strypsky, Hiiador** [Stryps'kyj, Hijador] (pseuds: Yador Bilenky, Beloň Rusinský), b 19 March 1875 in Shelestove, Bereg komitat, Transcarpathia, d 9 March 1949 in Budapest. Civic figure, ethnographer, librarian, and publicist; member of the Hungarian Academy of Sciences from 1913 and the Shevchenko Scientific Society from 1914. After being educated in Budapest, Lviv, and Cluj he worked as a librarian at the Transylvanian Museum in Cluj (1888–1908) and as a curator at the National Museum in Budapest (from 1910). He associated with V. Hnatiuk, I. Franko, and A. Voloshyn, contributed to the publications *Nauka* and *Selo* (1907), and published the journal \**Ukránia* (1916–17) in Budapest. In 1918 he was appointed section head of Ruthenian affairs in the Hungarian Ministry of Culture and Education and adviser to the Ministry of National Minorities. In 1919 he organized a chair of Ruthenian studies at Budapest University. Among his scholarly publications are *Starsha rus'ka pys'mennost' na Uhorshchyni* (Old Ruthenian Writing in Hungary, 1907), *Naistarshyi rumuns'kyi druk latynkoiu* (The Oldest Rumanian Incunabula in the Latin Alphabet, 1913), and *Gde dokumenti starshoi istorii Podkarpatskoi Rusi?* (Where Are the Documents of the Ancient History of Subcarpathian Ruthenia?, 1924), as well as an ethnographic description of Hungarian Ruthenia (1911), translations of Ukrainian literary works into Hungarian, and an annotated edition of M. Teodorovych's 1791 guide to home management and etiquette (1919).

**Stryvihor Museum.** A museum founded in Peremyshl in 1932 on the initiative of O. Kulchytsky and through the efforts of I. Shpytkovsky (its custodian) and B. Zahaikevych (its director). In 1937 it had 2,500 archeological, historical, religious, and ethnographic artifacts in its exhibits, including many rare icons. After the Second World War many of its holdings that were not destroyed or stolen were transferred to the Polish Regional Museum in Peremyshl.

**Stryvihor River** (also Strviazh). A left-bank tributary of the Dniester River. It is 94 km long and drains a basin area of 955 sq km. The river originates in the Middle Beskyds and flows through Poland and Ukraine (Lviv oblast). Part of it is used for industrial purposes.

**Strzałków.** A town in Poznań voivodeship, Poland, which after the First World War was the site of an internment camp. In 1919–20 almost 7,000 Ukrainians from Galicia were held in the camp, and in 1921–3 UNR Army internees were transferred there from Łańcut. The latter group brought with them a number of educational programs that had been set up in Łańcut (a popular university with four faculties, a gymnasium, and a primary school for children), several cultural societies (a Ukrainian language association, a choir, an opera, and three drama groups), a sports gymnasium supported by the YMCA, a chess club, and several papers (*Nasha zoria, Budiak, Zaporozhs'ka dumka, Blokha, Promin'*, and *Students'kyi vistnyk*).

**Strzyżów culture.** An Early Bronze Age culture that existed in western Volhynia and the upper Buh region. It was named after a Polish site excavated in the 1930s. The people of this culture, a subgroup of the Corded-Ware Pottery culture, engaged in agriculture, animal husbandry, hunting, and fishing. In addition, they had a well-developed flint industry that produced items for trade. They lived in semi-pit dwellings and buried their dead both in pit graves and in kurhans. An extensive flint inventory and bronze, stone, and bone items were found at excavation sites. In addition, pottery decorated with distinctive rope impressions and bladelike lines was also common. The Strzyżów culture eventually had a role in the development of the *Komariv and *Trzciniec cultures.

**Stsiborsky, Mykola** [Scibors'kyj] (pseuds: Zhytomyrsky, Orhansky, Rokosh), b 28 March 1897 in Zhytomyr, d 30 August 1941 in Zhytomyr. Nationalist publicist and ideologue. A captain in the UNR cavalry during the Ukrainian-Soviet War, he was interned in 1920–2 with other UNR soldiers in a Polish camp, where he received special training and was promoted to the rank of lieutenant colonel. In 1922 he emigrated to Bohemia. There he was one of the leaders of the *League of Ukrainian Nationalists (1925–9) and studied engineering at the Ukrainian Husbandry Academy in Poděbrady. A member from 1926 of the Leadership of Ukrainian Nationalists (PUN) in charge of organizational affairs and then propaganda, and a founding member of the clandestine OUN (est 1929), from 1930 he lived in Paris and organized OUN branches in Ukrainian émigré centers in Central and Western Europe.

Stsiborsky elaborated the ideology of 'solidarism' and state corporatism in official OUN publications, contributed many articles to nationalist periodicals, such as *Derzhavna natsiia, Rozbudova natsiï, Samostiina dumka, Surma, Ukraïns'ke slovo*, and *Proboiem!*, and coauthored the 1940 OUN draft constitution for an independent Ukrainian state. Published separately were his book *Natsiokratiia* (Natiocracy, 1935, 3 edns) and brochures and booklets on the OUN and the peasantry (1933), the OUN and the working class (1935), Bolshevik nationality policy in Ukraine (1938; trans into English [*Ukraine and Russia: A Survey of Soviet Russia's Twenty-Year Occupation of Eastern Ukraine*, 1940], French, and German), democracy, Stalinism (1938, 1941, 1947), Ukraine and Soviet nationality policy (1944), the land question (1939), and Ukraine's population and economy (1940; German edn 1944). Stsiborsky's article 'La question ukrainienne' appeared in *La revue économique internationale* (March 1940).

After moving to Cracow in late 1939 to run the clandes-

tine OUN political training school, Stsiborsky compiled the OUN white book on the 1940 split and remained loyal to A. Melnyk. He and O. *Senyk organized and initially led the *OUN expeditionary groups of the Melnyk faction that penetrated into central and eastern Ukraine during the Nazi invasion of the USSR in 1941. They were assassinated by B. Kozii, a member of the rival OUN Bandera faction and a former Communist.

R. Senkus

**Stubazka River** (also Stubelka or Stubla). A left-bank tributary of the Horyn River that flows northward for 86 km through southern Rivne oblast and drains a basin area of 1,350 sq km. The river is about 5 m wide at mid-course and has a valley that is 4 km wide. It supplies water for industrial purposes and is used as part of a regional drainage system. The old Rus' city of Peresopnytsia was once situated in its valley.

**Stubla River.** See Stubazka River.

*Studens'kyi visnyk.* See *Students'kyi visnyk*.

*Student*. A Ukrainian-Canadian student newspaper published irregularly from 1968 to the late 1980s. Established as the official publication of the *Ukrainian Canadian Students' Union (SUSK), the newspaper dealt with the concept and politics of multiculturalism, community affairs, the defense of human rights in Ukraine, and contemporary Ukrainian cultural phenomena in a spirited and occasionally provocative manner. Its most notable years of publication were in 1977–82, when it came out of Edmonton under the editorship of N. Makuch and became the first ethnic student newspaper to be accepted into the Canadian University Press association. From 1982 *Student* was formally independent of SUSK but maintained a working arrangement with it.

**Student Battalion** (Studentskyi kurin im. Ukrainskykh sichovykh striltsiv). A military unit organized in Kiev during January 1918 to defend Kiev and the Central Rada against Bolshevik insurgents within the city and the approaching Red Army. It consisted of university and senior secondary-school students, with a total of about 550 volunteers. After only one week of military training one of its companies left Kiev to reinforce the cadets of the Khmelnytsky Officer School. Thirty of its soldiers died in the Battle of *Kruty. The other units of the battalion remained in Kiev to resist the Bolsheviks. Most of the battalion's surviving soldiers later joined the Haidamaka Battalion of Slobidska Ukraine.

**Student fraternities** (*korporatsii*). Student organizations for the promotion of patriotism, fortitude, and discipline within small groups held together by friendship and enjoyment. Fraternities appeared in Germany during the Napoleonic Wars and inculcated a high concept of honor which demanded dueling as a response to insult. Eventually members of fraternities developed an inclination for a carefree and even dissipate life. Among Ukrainian students the first fraternities were organized in 1906, but they became popular only in the interwar period, particularly among students studying abroad. The Ukrainian fraternities were based on the original forms and ideas of honor, freedom, and fatherland. The richest traditions were developed by the fraternities in Chernivtsi, which adopted Cossack names – *Zaporozhe (1906–40) and *Chornomore (Black Sea 1913–40). In Danzig (now Gdańsk) Ukrainian fraternities were founded in 1924 (Chornomore, Halych, and Zarevo); they spread from there to other Ukrainian student centers, such as Lviv, Vienna, Prague, Berlin, Rome, Warsaw, Poznań, and Cracow. Fraternities of the same name from various centers formed associations, with their own ideological principles and statutes. After the Second World War Zaporozhe branches were re-established in New York, Vienna, and Munich, and Chornomore branches in Philadelphia and Montreal.

**Student movement.** See Students, postsecondary.

**Student press.** The first Ukrainian-language student periodicals were handwritten and circulated clandestinely among members of the Kiev Student Hromada: 'Samostaine slovo' (1861–2), which defended the Ukrainian culture, and the humorous 'Pomyinytsia' (1863–4). The first printed publications put together primarily by students were *Druh (1874–7) and *Hromads'kyi druh (1878) in Austrian-ruled Lviv; both were under the influence of M. Drahomanov and socialist in orientation. Also published in Lviv decades later were the first exclusively student journal, *Moloda Ukraïna (1900–3); *Shliakhy, the literary-cultural organ of the Ukrainian Student Union in 1913–14; and the journal *Vidhuky (1913), which advocated that students undergo military training in preparation for war. In the early 20th century there were attempts to establish Ukrainian student papers in the Russian Empire; these included Vistnyk Ukraïns'koï kyïvs'koï students'koï hromady (one issue in 1903, two in 1905) in Kiev and Ukraïns'kyi student (two issues in 1913, one in 1914) in St Petersburg.

During the First World War and the subsequent struggle for Ukrainian independence, conditions did not allow a student press to develop. Only a few periodicals appeared: Sterno (1917) in Kiev, Vistnyk Drahomanivs'koï orhanizatsiï (1917) in Lviv, and Nova dumka (1920) in Kamianets-Podilskyi.

Under Soviet rule, student newspapers in Ukraine were completely subordinated to the regime and their function as carriers of new ideas has been replaced by their adherence to and advocacy of the Party line. The first journal to appear was the short-lived Russian-language Studentcheskii vestnik (1919) in Kiev. The most important journal of the interwar period was the Central Union of Proletarian Students' *Student revoliutsiï (1922–33). Student journals at institutes of people's education, such as Molodi zahony in Kiev and Robitnyk osvity and Studenty zhovtnia in Kharkiv, were published or copublished by the Communist Youth League of Ukraine (Komsomol) and were therefore directed at a much wider audience of young people than just students. Since the Second World War the only republican periodical directed specifically at students has been Students'kyi hart (est 1969), a supplement (30 times a year) to the Komsomol paper Molod' Ukraïny. Only since the late 1980s has a student press not controlled by the regime been able to develop. In neighboring Poland, Ukrainian students in Warsaw have published the quarterly Zustrichi since 1984.

In interwar Lviv in the early 1920s, the lithographed periodicals Nash shliakh (1922), Students'ki visty (1923, 1926),

Informatsiinyi lystok (organ of the Ukrainian Provincial Student Council), and Istorychnyi visnyk (1923) were circulated secretly. They promoted the Lviv (Underground) Ukrainian University and Ukrainian political aspirations. The sanctioned Catholic monthly *Postup (1921–30) was called a student herald until 1927. Russophile students published four issues of the semiannual Razsvet (1923–4, ed B. Trush and Ya. Kmitsikevich) in Russian.

Many student journals were established in the major centers of Ukrainian émigré life in the 1920s, especially in Czechoslovakia. Their number in that country was a reflection of the dynamism of Ukrainian student and political life there, which was not subject to the restrictions imposed by the Polish authorities in Western Ukraine. *Students'kyi visnyk (1923–31), the monthly organ of the Central Union of Ukrainian Students, was published in Prague. The Ukrainian Academic Hromada in Prague published the journal Ukraïns'kyi student (1920–5). Students at the Ukrainian Higher Pedagogical Institute in Prague published a student hromada bulletin and the journal Spudei (1925–6, ed B. Homzyn). The Democratic Alliance of Students there issued Ob'iednannia; socialist students published the irregular *Zhyttia (1924–5) and Vartovyi (1926–9). Soviet citizens studying in Prague published Vpered. Students at the Ukrainian Husbandry Academy in Poděbrady published the annual Zapysky Ukraïns'koï akademichnoï hromady (1923–5), the semimonthly Nasha hromada (1923–35), the humor magazine Podiebradka (1923–4), and the bibliographic journal Ukraïns'ke knyhoznavstvo (4 issues, 1922–?). The nationalist Group of Ukrainian National Youth, a student organization, issued the monthly *Natsional'na dumka (1924–7) in Prague. In Brno the Ukrainian Student Association published Hurtom (1925–6).

In Berlin students published four issues of *Spartak (1926–8), the organ of the youth wing of the Communist Party of Western Ukraine, which was smuggled into Western Ukraine. Ukrainian student journals in Vienna included the monthly Molode zhyttia (1921), the pro-communist Nash stiah (1921–3?, ed R. Rozdolsky) and Novyi shliakh (1924–6), and the satirical Ieretykon (1924–5). Dumka (1924–?) appeared briefly in Graz, and the humorous Smikholet (1924) was published by students at the Danzig Polytechnic. In Warsaw the Ukrainian Student Hromada published Na chuzhyni (1924–5), *Students'kyi holos (1927–31), and the irregular Chornomore (1928–33). Transcarpathian students in Prague published four short-lived Russophile journals in the 1920s and the nationalist *Proboiem (1933–44). In Bukovyna repression by the Rumanian authorities retarded the development of a Ukrainian student press. Ukrainian students were, however, involved in the publication of the literary monthly *Promin' (1921–3). Later the Union of Ukrainian Student Organizations in Rumania published Students'ki visty (1935–7) as a supplement to the paper Chas and then the journal Samostiinist'. In Canada students living at the Mohyla Ukrainian Institute in Saskatoon issued the bimonthly journal Kameniari (1918–19).

The Ukrainian student movement, and with it the student press, declined in Central and Western Europe in the 1930s, owing to the Depression and the consequent lack of a stable community of university students. As a result Lviv re-emerged as the center of the student press. Published there were *Students'kyi shliakh (1931–4), the monthly organ of the Union of Ukrainian Student Organizations under Poland and then of the Central Union of Ukrainian Students, and its successor, *Students'kyi vistnyk* (1935–9); they were closely allied with the OUN. Both were banned after the 1939 Soviet occupation of Galicia. During the Second World War, under the German occupation *Students'kyi prapor* (1943–4) was published in Lviv as the monthly organ of the Labor Alliance of Ukrainian Students, and the Nationalist Organization of Ukrainian Students published *Biuleten' NOUS-u* (1942–3, ed V. Rudko) for students in Germany.

After the war, over 20 student periodicals were established by Ukrainian refugees studying in Germany and Austria; most were published in Munich. They included *Students'kyi shliakh* (1945–7), *Stezhi* (1946–7), *Students'kyi visnyk* (1947–8), *Visti TseSUSu* (1948–55), and *Visnyk TseSUSu* (1946–7), all of them organs of the Central Union of Ukrainian Students; *Students'kyi informator* (1945), *Student* (1945–6), *Students'ki visti* (1946–7), *Students'ki obrii* (1946–7), and *Students'ke zhyttia* (1949–50); *Students'ka dumka* (1946–7) in Augsburg; *Students'ka dumka* (1946–8) in Regensburg; *Students'kyi shliakh* (1945–7) in Innsbruck; *Students'kyi prapor* in Graz; the journal *Bohoslov* (1948–9) of the Student Society at the Theological Academy of the Ukrainian Autocephalous Orthodox church; *Biuleten'* (1949–56) of the Ukrainian Student Society of Mikhnovsky; the Catholic journal *Obnova* (1947–9); *Seminariini visti* (1946) at the Greek Catholic Seminary in Hirschberg; the Zarevo Ukrainian Student Organization's monthly journal *Zarevo* (1949–50); *Iunats'ka borot'ba* (1947–8), the student organ of the Ukrainian Revolutionary Democratic party; and the satirical wall gazette *Elita* (1947–51) at the Ukrainian Student Center in Louvain, Belgium.

After the mass resettlement of the refugees in other Western countries, student periodicals were established there. *Feniks* (1951–74) was published by the pro-OUN (Bandera faction) Ukrainian Student Organization of Mikhnovsky, and the pro-OUN (Melnyk faction) *Smoloskyp* organization and *Zarevo issued *Smoloskyp* (1950–68) and *Rozbudova derzhavy* (1949–57) respectively; all three were begun in Europe and moved to the United States. The Federation of Ukrainian Student Organizations of America published a regular page in the newspaper *Svoboda* (130 issues in 1954–72), the annual *Horizons* (1956–68), and irregular newsletters. The bilingual (Ukrainian and English) and often provocative *Student* (est 1968) was the longest-running Ukrainian student organ, although it did not always appear regularly. In the early 1990s a new student paper, *Studenets'*, edited by S. Bandera, Jr, surfaced in Toronto. The Union of Ukrainian Student Societies in Europe has published an irregular bulletin. In Argentina the Union of Ukrainian Students published *Students'ke zhyttia* (20 issues, 1959–61). In Australia the Ukrainian Student Hromada in Victoria published *Students'ke oko* (25 issues, 1969–73). In Brazil students at the Basilian seminary in Curitiba have published the irregular magazine *Tsvirkun* since 1945. Local student groups have issued various ephemeral periodicals. Notable among them was *New Directions* (1969–74) in New York and *Vitrazh* (1977–80?) in London. (See also *Press.)

BIBLIOGRAPHY
Ianiv, V. 'Ukraïns'ka students'ka presa (Istorychno-biblio-
hrafichnyi narys),' in *Studiï ta materiialy do novishoï ukraïns'koï istoriï*, vol 2 (Munich 1983)

V. Yaniv

***Student revoliutsiï*** (Student of the Revolution). A student journal published in Kharkiv in 1922 in Russian and in 1924–33 in Russian and Ukrainian as the organ of the Central Bureau of Proletarian Students. It appeared six to eight times a year until 1929, semimonthly in 1930, and then three times a month until March 1933. Edited by E. Rabkin, it published articles on political and academic affairs, prose, and poetry.

## Students, postsecondary.

From the mid-14th century on, before there were universities in Ukraine, Ukrainians studied at European universities, particularly at Cracow (800 were educated there in the 15th and 16th centuries) and Prague (there was a special residence for Lithuanian and 'Ruthenian' students there). They also studied at the universities of Heidelberg, Leipzig, Königsberg, Göttingen, Köln, Wittenberg, Halle, Kiel, Vienna, Paris, Strasbourg, Basel, Leiden, Oxford, Rome (theology students), Padua, and Bologna and at Polish Jesuit academies and colleges in Poland, Ukraine, Belarus, and Lithuania.

The first postsecondary school in Ukraine was the Orthodox *Kievan Mohyla Academy (1632–1817). Its students – the sons not only of nobles, the Cossack *starshyna*, and clerics but also of rank-and-file Cossacks, burghers, and peasants – had few liberties or prerogatives and were subjected to strict supervision and discipline, including beatings and various humiliations. Such treatment did not, however, deter them from engaging in petty theft, drinking, brawling, and even terrorizing and robbing townsfolk. In the 17th century the academy rarely had more than 200 students. By 1710 their number had grown to over 2,000, but then it declined to 1,100 in 1715, not more than 800 in the 1720s and 1730s, and approx 1,100 from 1744 to the 1770s. Most of the students were from outside Kiev. In the second half of the 18th century they hailed primarily from within the Hetman state. Only those from rich families could afford private quarters, and they were treated with deference by the administration. Many (200 in the early 18th century, nearly 400 in 1765) were poor and received room and board in the academy's *bursa, and others resided with parish priests and elsewhere in Kiev. Their meager incomes derived from begging door to door, appearing in public choral and theatrical performances, and serving as precentors, Sunday school teachers, and servants and tutors to the rich. Those who belonged to the academy's Young Brotherhood and, later, two sodalities were instilled with an Orthodox zeal, and aided their needy peers. From 1701 on, Orthodox Ukrainians from Polish-ruled territories, Russians, Serbs, Bulgarians, and even Moldavians, Wallachians, and Greeks were allowed to study at the academy. In the second half of the 18th century the largest group of students were the sons of clerics.

**Ukraine under Russian rule, 1805–1917.** Increasingly more students received higher education in Ukraine after the opening of Kharkiv University (1805), the Kiev Theological Academy (1819), the Nizhen Lyceum (1820), Kiev University (1834), the Richelieu Lyceum in Odessa (a postsecondary school from 1837), and Odessa University (1865). Many postsecondary professional and technical schools were opened in the second half of the 19th century, and many postsecondary schools for the *education of women arose after the Revolution of 1905. In 1914–16 there were 26,700 students in Ukraine: approx 10,000 at universities, 13,000 at professional and technical schools, and 4,000 in higher courses for women.

The rights and obligations of students in the Russian Empire were defined by a general statute on universities. The 1804 statute formally guaranteed self-government to universities and academic freedom to students. The 1835 statute that replaced it put universities under the supervision of trustees and the political conduct of students under the control of university inspectors. In 1845, to restrict the non-gentry's access to higher education, the state raised tuition fees. In 1847 the right of unregistered persons to audit lectures was withdrawn. In 1863 university autonomy was reinstated, but students came under the jurisdiction of university tribunals. In 1872 the Ministry of Education responded to widespread student unrest in the empire by introducing stricter disciplinary rules, but they were not confirmed by the various university professorial councils. Subsequent student unrest, which began with a demonstration at Kiev University on 14 March 1878 and the expulsion of some 100 students there, and then spread to other universities, resulted in the introduction of harsher governmental restrictions. An 1884 law again rescinded university autonomy, and in 1887 tuition fees were raised fivefold. In 1899 the state introduced punitive measures subjecting participants in student unrest to military conscription. The students responded with further walkouts, boycotts of classes, and demonstrations, and in 1901 the minister of education, N. Bogolepov, was assassinated.

Members of the Kharkiv Student Hromada and guests (1899). Top row, from left: Dmytro Antonovych, L. Kuliabko-Koretsky, Dmytro Poznansky, Yevlampii Tyshchenko, Oleksander Kovalenko, Bonifatii Kaminsky, Yurii Kollard, K. Rumnytsky; middle row: Dmytro Drobiazko, Oleksandra Matsiievych, K. Matsiievych, K. Kotliarova, Mykola Levytsky (guest), Mykola Mikhnovsky; bottom row: Mykhailo Rusov, Lev Matsiievych, Severyn Pankivsky (guest), Oleksander Stepanenko

In 1855 universal access to higher education was introduced. Consequently the number of students in Russian-ruled Ukraine grew from 3,141 in 1855 to 38,853 in 1916, and the proportion of students whose parents were nobles or civil servants fell from 65 percent in 1855 to 36 percent

in 1914. In 1894, of the 4,016 students at Kharkiv, Kiev, and Odessa universities, 59.7 percent were Orthodox (of whom half, approx 1,200, were Ukrainians), 25.3 percent were Jewish, 12.8 percent were Roman Catholic Poles (mostly at Kiev University), and 2 percent were Protestants. Students' living conditions were poor. In the 1880s and 1890s fewer than 15 percent of them were exempted from paying tuition, and few received state stipends. They were all obliged to wear prescribed uniforms.

Ukrainians also studied at imperial universities outside Ukraine, mostly in Moscow (20.4 percent of students at Moscow University in 1891 were from Ukraine), St Petersburg, and, from 1896, when the Ministry of Education allowed the graduates of theological seminaries to enter university, Warsaw, Tartu, and Tomsk.

For many years ethnic Ukrainian student organizations did not exist. Instead students were active in various Russian and Ukrainian underground and semilegal organizations (eg, the *Cyril and Methodius Brotherhood), in local *hromadas (especially the Hromada of Kiev), in various revolutionary populist organizations, and in the *Brotherhood of Taras. From the late 19th century they belonged to general Russian student organizations, which championed academic freedom, autonomy, and corporate rights (ie, the right to have meetings, assemblies, student tribunals, and mutual aid savings banks). At the 'all-Russian' student congresses 23 of 98 delegates were Ukrainians.

The first Ukrainian student organizations date from the second half of the 19th century, when semilegal *zemliatstva*, which united students from the same region studying in a particular city, were founded. Those groups chose delegates to student executives at universities and institutes. Later, clandestine Ukrainian student hromadas were created in Kiev (1893), Kharkiv (1897), Moscow (1898), St Petersburg (the *Ukrainian Student Hromada in St Petersburg, 1898), Tartu (1898), Warsaw (1901), and Odessa (1902). The involvement of many of their members in various Russian and Ukrainian revolutionary *parties brought about expulsion, police persecution, imprisonment, and even exile to Siberia. After the Revolution of 1905 the student hromadas tried to operate independently of the parties and concentrated on professional and academic activities. Consequently they were legalized, and their combined membership grew from approx 260 at the beginning of the century to approx 1,000 in 1908. Hromada membership grew from 22 to 250 in Moscow, from 50 to 150 in Kharkiv, from 68 to 130 in Kiev, from 20 to 98 in Tartu, from 30 to 64 in Odessa, to approx 120 in Warsaw, to approx 100 in St Petersburg, and to 40 each in Tomsk and at the Kiev Higher Courses for Women.

The work of the student hromadas was co-ordinated by secret congresses of delegates, which were convened in Kiev in 1898, 1899, and 1908, in Poltava in 1901, and in St Petersburg in 1904. In 1913 a Supreme Council of Ukrainian Students was created (it published irregularly the miscellany *Ukraïns'kyi student* in 1913–14). From the 1890s on, the hromadas had contacts with Western Ukrainian student organizations. Delegates from the Sich student society of Vienna and the Academic Hromada of Lviv took part in the 1898 congress in Kiev; hromada representatives visited Galicia and Bukovyna; students from Russian-ruled Ukraine attended summer courses in Lviv and Chernivtsi; and student excursions were jointly organized.

**Western Ukraine under Austrian rule, 1772–1918.**
Western Ukrainian students attended the Barbareum Greek Catholic seminary in Vienna (1774–84) and Lviv University (est 1784) and its theological Studium Ruthenum (1787–1809), the Polytechnic (est 1814), Agricultural School (est 1855), and Veterinary Academy (est 1881) in Lviv, and Chernivtsi University (est 1875). In those institutions they made up 10–25 percent of the total number of students. Small numbers of Western Ukrainian students also studied at the universities of Vienna, Budapest, and Cracow and elsewhere in the Austrian Empire. All postsecondary schools in the empire, as elsewhere in Western and Central Europe, were self-governing. The students' 'academic freedoms,' however, were subject to local government control during the period of absolutism (until 1860). Theology students were also subject to ecclesiastical sanctions.

The first Western Ukrainian student organizations and the largest number of them were founded in Lviv: the populist Sich (1861–3), Akademichna Besida (1870–1), Druzhnyi Lykhvar (1871–82), and Vatra (1892–6) societies; the Russophile *Academic Circle (est 1870); the Ukrainophile socialist *Academic Brotherhood (1882–96); the *Academic Hromada (1896–1921), which arose from the amalgamation of the Vatra society and the Academic Brotherhood; and the *Osnova society (1897–1939) at the Lviv Polytechnic. In Chernivtsi the initially Russophile but from 1879 Ukrainophile-dominated *Soiuz society (1875–1902, 1904–22), the Russophile Bukovyna (1888–94) and Karpat (est 1894) societies, the Moloda Ukraina (1900–2) and Sich (1902–23) student societies, and the *Orthodox Academy's theology students' society (1907–23) were established. Elsewhere in the Austrian Empire, Ukrainian students founded the Society of SS Cyril and Methodius (est 1864) and the *Sich student society (1868–1947) in Vienna, the Academic Hromada (1887–95) in Cracow; the Rus' mutual aid association (1895–1910) and Sich student society (1902 to ca 1947) in Graz, and the Ukrainian Hromada (1902–14) in Prague.

To co-ordinate their activities the existing organizations convened congresses in Kolomyia in 1881 and 1884. In 1889 the students first lent their support to the public campaign for the creation of a Ukrainian university in Lviv. Later they organized secret political cells and advocated Ukrainian independence in their journal *Moloda Ukraïna (1900–3, 1905). An influential factor in the students' political development was their contact with their peers in Russian-ruled Ukraine, particularly those belonging to the *Revolutionary Ukrainian party. The failure of the campaign for a Ukrainian university resulted in the *secession of Ukrainian students from Lviv University in 1901–2. After their return the militant struggle between Ukrainian and Polish students in Lviv became even more acute (it resulted in the murder of A. *Kotsko in 1910), and the clandestine Committee of Ukrainian Youth (KUM) was created to spearhead it. The first 'all-student' congress took place in Lviv in 1909 with the participation of delegates from Russian-ruled Ukraine. At the second congress in 1913, an umbrella organization, the Ukrainian Student Union, was created. Headed by Mykola Zalizniak, in 1913–14 it had in Galicia 1,786 members in 38 chapters, which conducted cultural-educational work among the peasantry and published the journal *Shliakhy.

The first Ukrainian *student fraternities modeled on the German *Burschenschaften*, *Zaporozhe (est 1906) and *Chornomore (est 1913), were founded at Chernivtsi University. Later chapters were created in Lviv, Warsaw, Prague, Vienna, Cracow, and Gdańsk (Danzig), where they survived until 1940. Another fraternity, Roksoliianiia, was created in Lviv.

The students of Western Ukraine had various class origins (in the 1880s, 40 percent of them were sons of priests). Because many of those from the peasantry and working class were poor, charities, such as Lykhvar, were established to support them, and a publicly funded residence, the Academic Home, was founded in Lviv in 1907 with the substantial financial support of Ye. *Chykalenko.

In 1912–13 there were 1,868 Ukrainian postsecondary students in the Austrian Empire: 1,287 studied in Lviv (constituting approx 17 percent of all students there), 187 in Chernivtsi (16 percent; in 1914, 300, or 25 percent), 166 in Vienna, 55 in Cracow, 97 in Stanyslaviv (theology students), 28 in Peremyshl (theology students), and 48 elsewhere. Of the total number, 843 were studying law; 430, theology; 271, humanities; 129, medicine and pharmacology; 85, technical sciences; 45, agronomy; 32, veterinary medicine; 17, commerce; and 5, art.

*1914–17.* After the outbreak of the First World War most students were conscripted. Many Galician and Bukovynian students served in the *Ukrainian Sich Riflemen and *Ukrainian Galician Army. After the February Revolution of 1917, students took part in the creation of the Central Rada in Kiev (student representatives in the Rada included V. Boiko, M. Samoilovych, A. Zhuravel, Yu. Okhrymovych, O. Sevriuk, M. Saltan, M. Chechel, and M. Yeremiiv). They became active in various political parties, particularly the Ukrainian Party of Socialist Revolutionaries, whose leadership was overwhelmingly student-based, and were involved in the UNR diplomatic corps (eg, at negotiations of the Peace Treaty of Brest-Litovsk), military, and civil service. In March 1917 a Supreme Ukrainian Student Council was formed in Kiev. It organized three all-Ukrainian student conferences and published a journal, *Sterno* (1917). Students at Kiev University formed the *Student Battalion that was decimated by the Red Army in the Battle of *Kruty in January 1918.

**Western Ukrainian and émigré students, 1920–45.** The greatest Ukrainian student achievement in the interwar period was the establishment of the *Central Union of Ukrainian Students (TseSUS) in Prague in 1922. By 1924 TseSUS had 22 constituent organizations in nine countries outside Soviet Ukraine: 1,324 members were in Galicia and elsewhere in Poland; 1,442, in Czechoslovakia; 160, in Rumania; 237, in Germany; and 201, in Austria. In 1924 pro-communist and Sovietophile students in Galicia quit TseSUS and created their own umbrella, the *Working Alliance of Progressive Students, which was affiliated with the Central Bureau of Proletarian Students in Kharkiv, and survived until the late 1920s.

In Polish-occupied Western Ukraine native Ukrainian émigrés from Soviet-occupied Ukraine encountered obstructions from the new Polish government, which allowed only Polish army veterans (thereby excluding veterans of the UNR and Ukrainian Galician armies) to enroll at Lviv University and other postsecondary schools in Poland from November 1919, abolished the Ukrainian chairs at Lviv University, and outlawed the Academic Hromada in 1921. The Ukrainians tried to overcome the impediments by attending the *Lviv (Underground) Ukrainian University (over 1,500 students) and *Lviv (Underground) Ukrainian Higher Polytechnical School (64 students) in 1921–5 and the *Greek Catholic Theological Seminary in Lviv, and by studying abroad, especially in Czechoslovakia. They established the underground Ukrainian Provincial Student Organization, renamed the Professional Organization of Ukrainian Students (PROFORUS, 1921–5). Headed by P. Gan (also the first president of TseSUS) and a council in Lviv, it had 10 district and 50 county branches, totaling 1,252 members in 1924. PROFORUS sponsored the Third Congress of Ukrainian Students in Western Ukraine in 1925. Students were also active in 34 student sections of local Prosvita societies.

Emigrés from Soviet-occupied Ukraine in Warsaw, Cracow, and Polish *internment camps established Ukrainian student hromadas in Warsaw (1921–39) and Cracow (1924–39; 300 members in 1928, 271 in 1933, and 83 in 1938) and the Union of Ukrainian Student Emigrés in Poland in 1923 (five affiliates with 157 members in 1923 and 68 in 1924).

From the second half of the 1920s, after Ukrainians returned to Polish schools, student life centered around the Academic Home and the newly created Student Hromada in Lviv. The Ukrainian students in Lviv (1,506 in 1929–30) and elsewhere were divided into mutually hostile nationalist and pro-communist camps (the latter lost much of its support in 1926–7). Ukrainians also studied at Polish universities and other schools in Cracow (389 students in 1929–30), Warsaw (approx 200 students), Poznań, Vilnius, and Lublin, where they did not encounter administrative hindrances, and established student clubs. According to official statistics on religious affiliation, under Polish rule there were 3,000 Ukrainian students in 1927–8, 2,800 in 1933–4, and 2,500 in 1937–8, not counting Greek Catholic theology students in Lviv, Peremyshl, and Stanyslaviv. Organized activity was revitalized after the creation of the semilegal, pro-OUN *Union of Ukrainian Student Organizations under Poland (1931–9), which united 2,500 students at five universities and 27 societies (18 in Lviv, 5 in Cracow, 2 in Poznań, 1 in Vilnius, 1 in Warsaw) with 65 county affiliates. The students' revolutionary activities resulted in the imprisonment of many of them during the 1920s and 1930s.

Participants at the Second Student Congress (Lviv, 1931)

In Rumanian-occupied Bukovyna the Soiuz, the Sich, and the Orthodox Academy student societies were banned after 1922–3. Only the fraternities Zaporozhe (it was also banned in 1926–8) and Chornomore and their Fraternal Union (est 1929) were allowed to function. Their activity was co-ordinated by the clandestine Committee of Ukrainian Students of Bukovyna (1921–5), linked to TseSUS. Small groups of Ukrainians studying elsewhere in Rumania established new societies: Zoria (1921–6) and Bukovyna (1926–44) in Bucharest and Hromada (ca 1928 to ca 1936) in Iaşi. From 1929 to 1937 the activity of all existing societies (totaling 160 members in 1929) was co-ordinated by the *Union of Ukrainian Student Organizations in Rumania. Rumanian oppression, like Polish oppression in Galicia, politicized the students, who became active in clandestine nationalist and left-wing organizations, and the overtly pro-OUN *Zalizniak society (1934–7) was created by former members of Chornomore and Zaporozhe. Because of discrimination many Ukrainians were forced to study abroad. Whereas in 1920 there had been 239 Ukrainian students at Chernivtsi University alone (14 percent of the student body), in 1939 there were only 80 Ukrainian students in all of Rumania.

Because there were no postsecondary schools in Czechoslovak-ruled Transcarpathia, Transcarpathian students (350 by the late 1930s) studied in state schools in Prague, Brno, and Bratislava, at the *Ukrainian Free University (UVU) and *Ukrainian Higher Pedagogical Institute in Prague, and at the *Ukrainian Husbandry Academy (UHA) and its successor, the *Ukrainian Technical and Husbandry Institute (UTHI), in Poděbrady. From 1921 those with a populist orientation belonged to the *Union of Subcarpathian Ukrainian Students (164 members in 1931). Russophile students belonged to the Vozrozhdenie society (est 1920), which published the monthly *Molodaia Rus'* (1930–1), and the Central Union of Carpatho-Russian Students (est 1927). In 1939–40 there were about 600 students from Transcarpathia studying in Czechoslovakia, most of them in Prague.

In the 1920s and 1930s many émigré veterans of the UNR and Ukrainian Galician armies and Western Ukrainians studied abroad. Their largest concentration was in Czechoslovakia, where from 1921 to 1931 the state provided them with stipends, clothing, medicine, textbooks, and instruments (distributed by a Czech-Ukrainian Committee) and subsidized the UVU and UHA. The students also received aid from the European Student Relief Fund. In 1924 there were 1,896 Ukrainian émigré students in Czechoslovakia: 1,255 in Prague, 382 in Poděbrady, 170 in Brno, 83 in Příbram, and 6 in Bratislava. The largest Ukrainian student organization in Czechoslovakia was the *Ukrainian Academic Hromada in Prague, which had 1,258 members in 1922 but declined to 321 members in 1923, after ideological splits resulted in the creation of the 249-member Hromada of Students from Great Ukraine (ie, Soviet-ruled Ukraine), the 222-member socialist Hromada Student Society, the 55-member Union of Student Emigrés from the Northwestern Lands of Ukraine (ie, Polish-ruled Volhynia, the Kholm region, Podlachia, and Polisia), and other nationalist, socialist, and communist groups. Dozens of other associations based mostly on fields of study were also formed.

In the early 1920s a sizable group of Ukrainians studied briefly in Austria, particularly in Vienna (there the Sich society fell from 327 members in 1922 to 46 in 1931), Graz (about 50 students), and Leoben (about 25 students). Most of them completed their studies at the UVU and UHA.

In interwar Germany about 200 Ukrainians studied in Berlin, where in 1921 they formed the *Ukrainian Student Association in Germany and the small Academic Hromada and Osnova society. Over 200 others studied at the Gdańsk (Danzig) Polytechnic, where they founded the *Osnova Union of Ukrainian Students (1922–45), a student co-operative in 1925, the fraternities Chornomore, Halych, and Zarevo in 1924–5, the socialist Ivan Franko Society, and the Sovietophile Drahomanov Hromada. The students in Gdańsk hosted the first TseSUS congress (1923) and published the irregular humorous bulletin *Smikhomet* (1923–38). Upon graduation they played key roles in the Galician co-operative movement and industry. Smaller numbers of students studied in Königsberg, Kiel, Göttingen, and Wrocław (Breslau) and elsewhere. Organizational activities were co-ordinated by the *Union of Ukrainian Student Organizations in Germany and Danzig (SUSOND, 1924–41), which was reconstituted as the *Nationalist Organization of Ukrainian Students in Germany (NOUS, 1941–7).

Elsewhere in Europe, small numbers of Ukrainians studied in Zagreb, Ljubljana, Paris, Leuven, Liège, Sofia, Geneva, Rome, Budapest, and other cities, where they founded student societies. Societies were also founded in the United States: the Ukrainian Academic Hromada in Philadelphia (est 1923), the Society of Ukrainian Youth in New York City (est 1924), the Ukrainian Student Hromada in Chicago, and, in the 1930s, student clubs in Detroit, Pittsburgh, Scranton, Cleveland, and other cities. An estimated 700 Ukrainians had received master's degrees and doctorates in the United States by 1936. In Canada Ukrainian students founded the Kameniari club in Saskatoon in 1917 (135 members in 1926), other clubs in Winnipeg, Yorkton, Brandon, Edmonton, Regina, and Toronto, and a student federation with over 400 members in 1929.

*1939–45.* During the Soviet occupation of Western Ukraine in 1939–41, all existing student organizations were abolished. In the Nazi-occupied countries the activity of TseSUS was restricted, and the German-supervised SUSOND and NOUS co-ordinated the activities of 600 students belonging to the Sich societies in Vienna (200 members in 1942–3) and Graz (50 members), the Ukrainian Academic Hromada in Prague (164 members), the Mazepynets society in Berlin (91 members), the Chornomore society in Wrocław (Breslau, 27 members), the Osnova union in Gdańsk (Danzig, 20 members), the Baturyn society in Munich (10 members), and other student groups in Dresden, Leipzig, Freiburg, Göttingen, and Innsbruck.

The German authorities hindered the reactivation of student life in Nazi-occupied Galicia in the fall of 1941. Nonetheless, the teaching of postsecondary professional courses was allowed in Lviv in 1942, and the Ukrainian Central Committee (UTsK) created the *Labor Alliance of Ukrainian Students, which united 1,355 medicine, 441 technical science, 192 veterinary science, 184 forestry, 182 pharmacology, 121 agronomy, and 93 theology students. Student aid was provided by the *Ukrainian Students' Aid Commission (KoDUS) of the UTsK in Cracow; in 1943–4 it granted 530 scholarships to students in Galicia and 213 to Ukrainians studying elsewhere in the Third Reich and Bohemia. Additional support came from the Humboldt Foundation.

After Germany invaded the USSR in 1941, in the Reichskommissariat Ukraine the Nazis closed down all postsecondary schools and deported most students as *Ostarbeiter* to the Third Reich. In Bukovyna the Rumanian regime expelled all Ukrainian students from Chernivtsi University, and in Transnistria it Rumanianized Odessa University. Only in Hungarian-occupied territories were some 300 Transcarpathian students allowed to attend postsecondary schools (mostly in Budapest and Debrecen, where the Society of Ruthenian Students of Transcarpathia was allowed to function).

**Soviet Ukraine.** After the consolidation of Soviet rule in Ukraine a new educational system was introduced. Existing postsecondary schools were reorganized into institutes and *tekhnikums (transformed in the 1930s into secondary special schools), and their autonomy, student councils, and academic freedom were abolished. Access to higher education was denied persons with 'non-working-class origins,' and in order to register, all aspiring students had to get recommendations from Party, Komsomol, or trade-union committees. In the 1920s Soviet Ukraine's student body was repeatedly purged of those who had concealed their social origins or lacked 'work service,' that is, whose relatives had been repressed as political opponents of the regime, *kulaks, or clerics. As a result a dramatic decline in the number of students occurred (see table 1).

To increase the proportion of students with proletarian and poor-peasant backgrounds, from 1921 to 1940 so-called *workers' faculties (10 in 1921, 30 in 1925, 78 in 1929) provided workers and peasants with two years of preparatory courses. Consequently the social composition of Ukraine's students changed dramatically, from 22.5 percent working class and 20.5 percent peasant in 1924–5 to 28.5 percent and 42 percent respectively in 1926–7. By 1936, persons with working-class origins constituted 44.4 percent of all postsecondary students and 39.7 percent of all university students; those with professional-class origins, 9.5 percent and 16.3 percent; those with civil service origins, 24 percent and 28 percent; those with collective farmer origins, 19.6 percent and 12.9 percent; those with private farmer origins, 2.8 percent and 2.3 percent; and those with other origins, 0.7 and 0.8 percent.

In the early 1930s all postsecondary schools were reorganized, and traditional forms of education were partly reintroduced. From 1936 less attention was paid to students' social backgrounds, and many more students received stipends. Thenceforth *ten-year-school graduates had the right to pursue a postsecondary education, although the ability to pay newly introduced tuition fees limited the admission of many children of peasants and

TABLE 1
Students at Soviet Ukraine's postsecondary institutes and tekhnikums, 1921–9

|      | Institutes | Tekhnikums |
|------|-----------|-----------|
| 1921 | 56,915 | 20,215 |
| 1922 | 48,233 | 42,100 |
| 1923 | 37,538 | 30,688 |
| 1924 | 29,474 | 29,967 |
| 1925 | 27,205 | 25,631 |
| 1926 | 27,909 | 24,122 |
| 1927 | 28,207 | 29,319 |
| 1928 | 33,406 | 26,896 |
| 1929 | 40,890 | 26,778 |

workers. Consequently, by the 1950s the children of functionaries, professionals, and Party bureaucrats constituted 42 percent of all students.

In the post-Stalin period, particularly after the introduction of the 1958 law 'On the Strengthening of the Link between the School and Life and on the Further Development of Public Education in the USSR,' the usual prerequisite for admission to postsecondary schools was two years of 'productive' employment, and higher education was subordinated to the needs of the economic sector. The years 1959–65 saw the greatest growth in the number of such full-time employees studying part-time. Whereas in 1940–1 they had constituted 31 percent of all students and in 1960, 52.4 percent, in 1965–6 they constituted 61 percent (15 percent in evening programs, 46 percent in correspondence programs). From 1964 less emphasis was placed on the employment prerequisite (in 1988, only 19 percent of full-time students had worked at least two years), and the proportion of full-time students increased. In 1987–8 they constituted 53.3 percent, whereas evening students constituted 10.4 percent and correspondence students, 36.3 percent. Concurrently, the disadvantage experienced by rural youths grew markedly. In 1969, for example, only 16 percent of all USSR students were from collective farms, whereas 39 percent were from the urban working class. Because in Ukraine almost half of all Ukrainians live in rural areas, that disadvantage could also be viewed as ethnic discrimination. It was reflected statistically: whereas in Soviet Ukraine for every 10,000 inhabitants there were 47 students in 1940, 54 in 1950, 97 in 1960, 170 in 1970, and 166 in 1988, the corresponding numbers in the RSFSR were 43, 77, 124, 204, and 190. Discrimination could also be seen in the way stipends were distributed in favor of the privileged social strata. Of all students in Soviet Ukraine, 48 percent in 1928, 78.6 percent in 1936, 80.5 percent in 1958–9, and 79 percent in 1988–9 received stipends. Of the total number of stipends granted in the USSR in 1988–9, 17.3 percent were allotted to students in Ukraine, but 56 percent to students in the RSFSR. A large proportion of Ukraine's students (33.4 percent in 1988–9) lived in near poverty in student residences.

In the Soviet period the number of postsecondary students in Ukraine grew considerably. The growth was not a balanced one, however. The first significant increase, from 57,526 students in 1927 to 97,500 students in 1933, occurred because fulfillment of the First Five-Year Plan required a considerably larger number of educated cadres. Further growth was constant (with the exception of the wartime years 1941–4 and those immediately following), but it took place at the expense of the development of correspondence and evening studies. The number of students in Ukraine more than doubled between 1960 and 1980, but from 1980 it declined (see tables 2 and 3). The percentage of female students increased from 10 percent before the Revolution of 1917 to 29.9 percent in 1925, 38.1 percent in 1936, 41.7 percent in 1960, and 55.2 percent in 1987.

The ethnic composition of Ukraine's students did not correspond to that of Ukraine as a whole. Jews (in the 1920s and 1930s) and Russians (in the postwar period) constituted disproportionately large percentages of the total number of students in relation to their weight in the total population (see table 4). That the USSR Ministry of Higher and Secondary Special Education discriminated against ethnic Ukrainians in regard to admission to post-

TABLE 2
Number of postsecondary schools and students in Ukraine, 1914 to 1990–1

|  | Schools | Students |
|---|---|---|
| 1914 | 27 | 35,200 |
| 1917 | 41 | 36,500 |
| 1921 | 197[a] | 77,130 |
| 1928 | 164[b] | 60,300 |
| 1940–1 | 173 | 196,800 |
| 1945–6 | 154 | 137,000 |
| 1950–1 | 160 | 201,600 |
| 1955–6 | 134 | 325,900 |
| 1960–1 | 135 | 417,700 |
| 1965–6 | 132 | 690,000 |
| 1970–1 | 138 | 806,600 |
| 1975–6 | 142 | 831,300 |
| 1980–1 | 147 | 880,400 |
| 1985–6 | 146 | 853,100 |
| 1990–1 | 149 | 881,300 |

[a]42 institutes and 155 tekhnikums
[b]38 institutes and 126 tekhnikums

TABLE 3
Postsecondary students in Ukraine by specialization, 1960–1 to 1987–8 (thousands)

|  | 1960–1 | 1970–1 | 1980–1 | 1987–8 |
|---|---|---|---|---|
| Geology & mineral-resource exploration | 2.3 | 5.0 | 5.3 | 4.5 |
| Mining | 8.4 | 14.8 | 11.7 | 12.4 |
| Energy development | 14.0 | 16.9 | 20.4 | 17.0 |
| Metallurgy | 8.1 | 13.4 | 12.9 | 11.9 |
| Machine & instrument building | 51.4 | 114.2 | 111.8 | 95.2 |
| Electronics & automation | 14.8 | 64.1 | 66.5 | 65.3 |
| Radio technology & communications | 11.5 | 30.4 | 29.2 | 25.9 |
| Chemical technology | 9.3 | 21.8 | 16.0 | 14.2 |
| Food technology | 6.5 | 16.4 | 18.9 | 16.6 |
| Consumer-goods technology | 5.1 | 8.6 | 10.8 | 10.1 |
| Construction | 31.4 | 53.7 | 72.0 | 57.2 |
| Geodesy & cartography | 0.9 | 1.8 | 2.8 | 2.4 |
| Hydrology & meteorology | 1.5 | 2.1 | 2.3 | 2.1 |
| Agriculture & forestry | 39.1 | 58.8 | 72.9 | 73.8 |
| Transportation | 14.1 | 30.8 | 33.9 | 32.8 |
| Economics | 34.9 | 97.2 | 115.5 | 112.0 |
| Law | 6.3 | 10.6 | 12.7 | 12.7 |
| Public health & physical education | 37.6 | 54.6 | 60.7 | 56.9 |
| University specialties | 42.2 | 71.7 | 69.2 | 66.8 |
| Pedagogical & cultural specialties | 73.0 | 110.4 | 123.0 | 152.7 |
| Art | 3.4 | 5.5 | 7.2 | 6.6 |
| Forest engineering & pulp-and-paper technology | 1.9 | 3.8 | 4.7 | 3.2 |
| Total | 417.7 | 806.6 | 880.4 | 852.3 |

secondary schools can be shown statistically. In 1965, for example, for every 10,000 inhabitants in the USSR there were 127 Ukrainian students and 174 Russian students. In Ukraine there were two graduate students for every 10,000 inhabitants, whereas in the RSFSR there were four. Until recently Ukrainian students were also subjected to *Russification pressures. Outside Ukraine and, in most cases, within Ukraine students could write entrance

TABLE 4
Ethnic composition of Ukraine's postsecondary students,
1926–60 (percentages)

|  | 1926 | | 1935 | 1960 | |
|---|---|---|---|---|---|
| Ukrainians | 45.1 | (80.8*) | 53.1 | 62.5 | (76.8*) |
| Russians | 20.3 | (8.4*) | 16.0 | 30.0 | (16.9*) |
| Jews | 33.4 | (5.6*) | 26.0 | 4.5 | (2.0*) |

* Weight of ethnic group in Ukraine's population in 1926 and
  1959 censuses

examinations only in Russian, and most teaching in Ukraine's postsecondary schools was conducted solely in Russian. After graduating, many Ukrainians were sent to work in other republics, and graduates from other republics were sent to Ukraine.

In 1984–5, 576,300 students in Ukraine, or 66 percent of all students there, were ethnic Ukrainians. An additional 134,400 ethnic Ukrainian students (20 percent of all ethnic Ukrainian students in the USSR) were studying in other republics, primarily in the RSFSR. In 1971–2 there were 6,084 foreign students in Ukraine: 3,451 from communist countries (1,423 from North Vietnam, 933 from East Germany, 337 from Bulgaria, 260 from Hungary, 163 from Cuba, and 156 from Mongolia); 1,253 from Africa; 1,203 from Asia; 95 from South America; and 82 from noncommunist European countries.

Soviet student organizations underwent change. In the 1920s and early 1930s the Central Bureau of Proletarian Students in Kharkiv, attached to the All-Ukrainian Council of Trade Unions, organized congresses and published the monthly *Student revoliutsiï. In the 1930s the bureau was abolished, and all student councils came under the direct control of the Party and Komsomol, through such agencies as the Student Division of the Antifascist Committee of Soviet Youth (1941–55) and the USSR Student Council (since 1955). Student membership in the Komsomol increased from 18.2 percent in 1928 to 32.6 percent in 1935 and 95 percent in 1974. Students in the USSR had no independent organization or periodicals, with the exception of the Moscow journal *Studencheskii meridian*. As under tsarism, Soviet students, particularly those at special institutes, wore uniforms, until the late 1960s. From the late 1950s they were assigned additional tasks, such as working during summer vacations in 'voluntary' student brigades, especially in Soviet Asia (eg, building the Baikal-Amur Trunk Railway and working Kazakhstan's 'virgin lands'). The voluntary scholarly, sports, and other mass associations that students took part in were closely monitored by Party, trade-union, and Komsomol organizations and the administrations of individual schools. Student clubs at individual schools (eg, Kiev's Hlobus club) co-ordinated the activity of various sports, travel, art, drama, music, and atheism circles and sections. Over 25 percent of all students belonged to different student research societies, worked in design offices, and took part in republican and Union competitions. In 1957 the all-Union Burevestnik voluntary student sports society was created. In 1984 it claimed to have 560,000 members in Ukraine (see *Burevisnyk).

Many, if not most, students were dissatisfied with the sanctioned forms of student activity and spoke out against being sent to do 'voluntary' summer work. From the 1960s those who studied in Kiev and were involved in the *dissident movement organized annual gatherings in May at the Shevchenko monument in Kiev. In the 1970s they published the samvydav journals *Postup* (ed Z. Popadiuk) and *Koryto*. Those who became involved in the dissident movement and 'clubs of creative youth' suffered expulsion, persecution, and even imprisonment. Students at Lviv University, in particular, were victimized in 1973. That year a secret directive instructed schools in the western oblasts not to accept more than 25 percent of its students from among the local population.

Beginning in 1988, Ukrainian students founded independent, noncommunist organizations (eg, the Association of Independent Ukrainian Youth in Lviv, Kiev, and Bukovyna, the Association of Ukrainian Youth in Kharkiv, the Hromada society at Kiev University, and the Student Brotherhood at Lviv University), initiated the revival of the Plast scouting organization, and joined en masse the Ukrainian Language Society, the Popular Movement of Ukraine (Rukh), the Zelenyi Svit Ukrainian Ecological Association, the *Lev Society, and other *neformaly and new political parties that promoted Ukrainian as an official language, de-Russification, democratic and national rights, Ukrainian independence, and cultural and environmental protection. Many students were allowed to study in the West. Ukraine's student cohort became a political force to be reckoned with. From 2 to 17 October 1990, for example, a large group of students held a 'camp-in' and hunger strike in the center of Kiev. Two weeks into the strike, 120,000 students in Kiev walked out of their classes to show sympathy with the strikers. The strike ended only after the Communist majority in the Supreme Council agreed to discuss the students' demands. Those included removing V. Masol as chairman of the Supreme Soviet, not signing the new, Kremlin-sponsored Union treaty, transferring all CPSU and Komsomol property in Ukraine to organs of local government, allowing military service outside Ukraine only on a voluntary basis, and holding a referendum on new elections to the Supreme Soviet. Soon after a Union of Ukrainian Students was formed. In October 1992, the union organized another hunger strike in Kiev, but failed to achieve its goal of convincing the Ukrainian government to leave the Commonwealth of Independent States and to call new national elections.

**Ukrainian students in the postwar West**. In the years 1945–51 around 2,000 Ukrainian displaced persons in Germany, 500 in Austria, and 200 in other Western European countries pursued higher educations. The main center of émigré activity, Munich, where the UVU and UTHI were re-established and the United Nations Relief and Rehabilitation Administration (UNRRA) University was founded, had 800 Ukrainian students. Innsbruck had 250, Graz 200, Erlangen 170, and Regensburg 120. Many students took part in the political conflicts and rivalry between the OUN Bandera and Melnyk factions, and only in 1947 did TseSUS manage to reunite the 31 social, political, and religious student organizations existing after the war. Organizations founded or revived in that period include the Melnyk-faction *Zarevo Ukrainian Student Association, the Bandera-faction *Ukrainian Student Organization of Mikhnovsky, the *Obnova Society of Ukrainian Catholic Students (est 1930 in Lviv), the Alliance of Orthodox Students, the National Union of Ukrainian Students in Belgium, the Representation of Ukrainian Student Societies in Austria (PUSTA), and the Association of Ukrainian Students in Paris. New student clubs were founded in Heidelberg, Hirschberg, Frankfurt am Main, Aachen, Stuttgart, Augsburg, Freiburg, Salzburg, Innsbruck, Leuven, Madrid, Rome, Switzerland, and England, and the number of periodicals in the Ukrainian *student press increased. Most students lived in the poor conditions of the UNRRA and International Refugee Organization camps and the Ukrainian student residence in Munich, and received financial support from KoDUS. Most Ukrainian refugees completed their studies and emigrated to North America and Australia in the late 1940s. By 1950 there were only 660 Ukrainian students at West German universities.

A new period in émigré student life began in the 1950s. Postwar Ukrainian refugees in the Americas and Australia pursued and completed postsecondary degrees, as did Ukrainians already born on those continents, and founded branches of existing émigré student societies and new university clubs. With the creation of five umbrella organizations – the *Federation of Ukrainian Student Organizations of America and the *Ukrainian Canadian Students' Union in 1953, a central federation of Ukrainian student societies in Australia (active from 1959 until approx 1968), and the *Union of Ukrainian Student Societies in Europe and Union of Argentinian-Ukrainian Students in 1963 – the co-ordinating function of TseSUS was by and large eclipsed.

Since the 1960s, Ukrainian student organizations in the West have consisted overwhelmingly of people born and educated there, for whom local and national issues are much more relevant than ideological differences. Since the 1970s the defense of Soviet political prisoners and national and democratic rights in Ukraine, and the preservation and development of the Ukrainian identity, language, and culture in both Ukraine and the host countries, have been key issues for the more politicized and radicalized members of student organizations, particularly in Canada and the United States. Certain student periodicals – particularly *Student* in Canada (1968 to late 1980s), *New Directions* in New York (1970–4), *Vitrazh* in London (1977 to early 1980s), and *Apprendre ou à laisser* in Paris (1977–80) – have offered alternative views and criticized the émigré status quo and nationalist politics.

**Ukrainian students in postwar Eastern Europe.** In Czechoslovakia, Rumania, and Yugoslavia indigenous Ukrainian students did not have their own organizations. They were, however, active in national student and Ukrainian umbrella organizations there and organized unauthorized gatherings and events. Such was the case also in Poland until 1981, when, in the wake of the Solidarity movement, Ukrainian students tried but failed to gain official recognition for an independent, self-governing organization, the Association of Ukrainian Students in Poland (SUSP). They succeeded, however, in getting the Ukrainian Cultural Section officially registered as part of the Socialist Union of Polish Students in Olsztyn voivodeship. Since that time Ukrainian students in Poland have championed Ukrainian cultural and minority rights and organized youth fairs, hiking camps in the Lemko region, folk-music festivals, and the restoration of Ukrainian churches and cemeteries. In 1984 they initiated the creation of the General Polish Cultural Council of National Minority Students within the Union of Polish Students and began publishing the council's organ, *Zustrichi*, in Warsaw. In October 1989, students in Gdańsk initiated the creation of the Union of Ukrainian Independent Youth, linked up with new fraternal organizations in Ukraine. In 1990, after the 'velvet revolution,' Ukrainian students in Prague organized themselves into the Ukrainian Studies Student Society (SUT). The society's primary aim is to enrich and further Ukrainian studies; its activities have consisted mostly of organizing lectures, especially by scholars from outside Czechoslovakia.

(See also *Education and *Higher education.)

BIBLIOGRAPHY
Levitskii, O. 'Kievskie studenty,' *KS*, 1901, no. 12
*Sich: Al'manakh v pamiat' 40-ykh rokovyn osnovannia t-va Sich u Vidni (1868–1908)* (Lviv 1908)
Kohut, O. 'Statystyka ukraïns'koho studentstva v Avstrii,' *Shliakhy* (Lviv), 1913, nos 8–9
Orelets'kyi, V. 'Pochatky i rozvii ukraïns'kykh students'kykh orhanizatsii,' *Kalendar Chornomore* (Warsaw 1933)
Oljančyn, D. 'Aus dem Kultur- und Geistesleben der Ukraine; II. Schule und Bildung; Anhang: Russisch-ukrainische Studenten im Abendlande (Verzeichnisse aus dem 16. bis 18. Jahrhundert),' *Kyrios*, 7 (1937)
*Ukraïns'kyi students'kyi rukh u rosiis'kii shkoli.* Vol 2 of *Z mynuloho*, ed R. Smal'-Stots'kyi (Warsaw 1939)
Lisovyi, R. *Trydsiati roky students'koho L'vova (Do geneal'ogiï nashykh dniv)* (Prague 1941)
Zhukovs'kyi, A. 'Ukraïns'ke studentstvo,' in *Bukovyna: Ïi mynule i suchasne*, ed D. Kvitkovs'kyi, T. Bryndzan, and A. Zhukovs'kyi (Paris, Philadelphia, and Detroit 1956)
Zinkevych, O.; Prybyla, W.; Kupchyk, L. (eds). *Ukraïns'ke studentstvo v Amerytsi: Propam'iatna knyha SUSTA z nahody desiatylitn'oï diial'nosty* (Baltimore and New York 1963)
Łukawski, Z. 'Organizacje ukraińskie na Uniwersytecie Jagiellońskim w okresie międzywojennym (1919–1939),' in *Studia z dziejów młodzieży Uniwersytetu Krakowskiego od Oświecenia do połowy XX wieku*, 1, ed C. Bobińska (Cracow 1964)
Serczyk, W. '"Akademiczna Hromada" w Krakowie (1887–1895),' ibid
Ianiv, V. 'Prychynky do pytannia pro uchast' ukraïns'koho studentstva v kul'turno-osvitnim zhytti,' in his *Studiï ta materiialy do novishoï ukraïns'koï istoriï* (Munich 1970)
Shyprykevych, V. (ed). *Propam'iatna knyha dantsigeriv: Istorychni narysy ta spomyny kolyshnikh studentiv Politekhniky Vil'noho Mista Dantsigu, 1921–1945* (Philadelphia, Toronto, and New York 1979)
Blažejovskyj, D. *Byzantine Kyivan Rite Students in Pontifical Colleges, and in Seminaries, Universities, and Institutes of Central and Western Europe (1576–1983).* Vol 43 of AOBM, series 2, sec 1 (Rome 1984)
Shchetinina, G. *Studenchestvo i revoliutsionnoe dvizhenie v Rossii: Posledniaia chetvert' XIX v.* (Moscow 1987)
Kassow, S. *Students, Professors, and the State in Tsarist Russia* (Berkeley, Los Angeles, and London 1989)
Oliven, E.J. 'Student Activism in the Ukrainian Independence Movement,' *Michigan Journal of Political Science*, 14 (Winter 1991–2)

                                          R. Senkus, A. Zhukovsky

**Students'kyi holos** (Student Voice). A monthly organ of the Ukrainian Student Hromada in Warsaw, published in 1927–31 and edited by E. Chekhovych.

**Students'kyi prapor** (Student Flag). A monthly organ of the Labor Alliance of Ukrainian Students, published in Lviv from July 1943 to June 1944 (a total of 12 issues). The chief editor was B. Lonchyna.

**Students'kyi shliakh** (Student Path). A monthly journal of the *Union of Ukrainian Student Organizations under Poland and, from 1933, the *Central Union of Ukrainian

*Students'kyi shliakh*

Students, published in Lviv from March 1931 to October 1934 (a total of 42 issues). It was edited by M. Duzhy, V. Yaniv (1932–4), and O. Matla (1934). The journal promoted OUN ideology among Ukrainian students, popularized Ukrainian nationalist heroes, and published works by the *Lystopad writers' group. It was closed down by the Polish authorities and was succeeded by the semilegal *Students'kyi vistnyk* (8 issues, 1935–9), edited by V. Rudko and M. Prokop.

**Students'kyi visnyk** (Student Herald). A monthly (from 1929 irregular) organ of the *Central Union of Ukrainian Students (TseSUS), published in Prague in 1923–31. It was edited by an editorial board until 1929, when TseSUS president V. Oreletsky became the official editor and publisher. Until 1924 the journal was lithographed, and dealt almost exclusively with student issues. Later it was printed as a general journal of literature, culture, scholarship, and politics. It had a wide range of contributors, among them scholars, writers, publicists, and political activists in Prague and elsewhere. *Students'kyi visnyk* generally remained nonpartisan and published articles reflecting the opinions of a broad spectrum of Ukrainians, primarily of the younger generation.

**Students'kyi vistnyk**. See *Students'kyi shliakh*.

**Studenytsia River** [Studenycja]. A left-bank tributary of the Dniester River that flows southward for 85 km through southern Khmelnytskyi oblast and drains a basin area of 477 sq km. The river is 5–10 m in width.

**Studio of the Oral Arts.** See Krushelnytska, Lidiia.

**Studite Fathers** (*studyty*). An Eastern Christian monastic order founded in Constantinople in 463. Its adherents followed an entirely contemplative life, living by the Gospels and singing daily all the offices. The eminent theologian St Theodore Studite (759–826) compiled the *Typikon* or basic monastic book of rules. The Studite *Typikon* was later adopted by monasteries on Mount Athos and in the Slavic East. St Theodosius of the Caves introduced the Studite *Typikon* at the Kievan Cave Monastery in 1070, and from there its use spread to most monasteries in Kievan Rus'. In addition to prayer, the monks practiced charity, painted icons, copied books, and wrote chronicles.

In the early 20th century Metropolitan A. *Sheptytsky wrote a new *Typikon* and renewed the Studite order in Western Ukraine, and also became archimandrite of the order. In 1901 he transferred the first group of novices from Olesko to the village of Vulka, near Lviv, and in 1904 to Sknyliv. Their monastery there, which housed 30 monks, a fine library, and a school for precentors, was destroyed during the First World War. In 1919 the Studites were re-established at Sheptytsky's summer residence in Univ. The order grew: monasteries were founded in Zarvanytsia (1921), Lviv, Luzhky, and elsewhere, and missions in Podlachia, Polisia, and even the Ukrainian settlement at Kamenica, Bosnia (1908–24). From 1917 K. *Sheptytsky assisted his brother in administering the order; he eventually succeeded him as archimandrite. They worked on the Studite *Typikon* together, and completed a major revision in 1936.

Studite monks farmed; ran workshops, orphanages, and boarding schools; engaged in icon painting and book-binding (in Univ); and administered the Studion library in Lviv. In 1935 they began to publish the monthly *Iasna put'* for Studites and *Prominchyk sontsia liubovy* for a popular readership. By 1939 there were 8 Studite monasteries, 3 missions, and 225 monks.

The Studite monastery in Castel Gandolfo (painting by Mykhailo Moroz)

After the Soviet occupation of Western Ukraine the Studite order was suppressed. Some monks who had managed to flee founded monasteries in Buche and Krefeld-Traar (West Germany) and in Woodstock, Ontario (1951); for a time (1974–84) there was also a Studite monastery in Paraguay. In 1965 Cardinal Y. Slipy founded a Studite monastery, the Studion, in Castel Gandolfo, near Rome. Today, Studite Fathers work as icon painters, scholars, and printers. A contemporary Studite iconographer, Yu. Mokrytsky, painted the iconostasis of the St Sophia Cathedral in Rome. In 1978 the hieromonk L. *Huzar was consecrated by Cardinal Slipy as archimandrite for Studites outside Ukraine.

BIBLIOGRAPHY

Sheptytsky, A. *Typikon studitskoj Lavry sviatoho Antoniia pecherskoho v Sknilovi pod Lvovom* (Zhovkva 1910)
Amman, A.; Iieromonakh Marko. *Chentsi Studyts'koho ustava* (Edmonton 1955)
Wolinski, E.; McCully, W. *Studyty idut' vpered: Studite Monks Move Onward* (Toronto 1985)

I. Khoma

**Studite Sisters** (*studytky*). An order of nuns who follow the Studite rules. Originally centered in Yaktoriv, Peremyshliany county, Galicia, the sisters maintained residences near Lviv and Ternopil as well as in Pidhaitsi. They ran child-care facilities and orphanages in addition to farming, sewing, and making church goods. Before the Second World War a total of 72 sisters belonged to the order. All of them remained in Ukraine following the Soviet occupation of Galicia, but the order was dissolved, and their superior, Sister Yosyfa, was sentenced to 30 years in a forced labor camp. Today the Studite Sisters maintain small communities in Krefeld-Traar and Altenbeken, Germany, and Dundalk, Ontario.

**Studium Ruthenum.** A Greek Catholic seminary founded by Emperor Joseph II in Lviv in 1787 for the education of candidates to the priesthood who did not speak Latin. The language of instruction at the Studium Ruthenum was *\*yazychiie*. The Studium was affiliated with \*Lviv University, and its professors were adjunct professors of the university. The program of study duplicated that of the parallel Latin-language Studium Latinum: two years of philosophy followed by four or five years of theology. Students of both institutes were housed in the \*Greek Catholic Theological Seminary in Lviv. The faculty at the Studium Ruthenum included I. Zemanchyk and P. Lodii in the philosophy department and M. Harasevych, I. Lavrivsky, M. Levytsky, I. Mokhnatsky, and I. Yavorsky in the theology department. The Studium was always considered to be an interim institution created to provide access to education for Ukrainians until enough Ukrainian students were able to be integrated into mainstream Latin, German, and Polish institutions. By the beginning of the 19th century the Studium had outlived its usefulness, and between 1803 and 1809 it was gradually phased out. A total of 470 students were educated at the Studium.

Kyrylo Studynsky    Yurii Studynsky

**Studynsky, Kyrylo** [Studyns'kyj], b 4 October 1868 in Kypiachka, Ternopil county, Galicia, d 1941. Literary scholar and community activist; member of the Shevchenko Scientific Society (NTSh) from 1899; full member of the VUAN from 1929. He was dismissed from the VUAN in 1934 for 'counterrevolutionary activities,' but was readmitted to the AN URSR (now ANU) in 1939. He studied at Lviv and

Vienna universities, where he focused on V. Jagić. After completing his studies he worked as a researcher at Berlin University, under the guidance of A. Brückner. From 1897 to 1899 he was a docent at Cracow University, and then he became a professor at Lviv University (1900–18, 1939–41), where he also served as vice-rector (1939–41). Studynsky was one of the leading members of the Christian Social party in Galicia and coedited its organ *Ruslan*. He was head of the Teachers' Hromada (1916–20) and of the Ukrainian National Council (1921–2). He was head of the NTSh (1925–31) and was instrumental in establishing close relations between the NTSh and the VUAN in Kiev. During the first Soviet occupation of Western Ukraine in 1939, he headed the People's Assembly of Western Ukraine; then, in 1940, he was a deputy to the Supreme Soviet of the Ukrainian SSR. His influential positions enabled him to intervene and save many Ukrainians from Soviet repressions. During the evacuation of the Red Army from Lviv in June 1941, he was deported. The circumstances of his death are unclear.

Studynsky is the author of over 500 works, mainly scholarly works on literature, in which he generally employed sociological and comparative methods. He published writings on polemical literature, such as *Perestoroha* (Warning, 1895), *Pam'iatky polemichnoho pys'menstva kintsia XVI i pochatku XVII viku* (Monuments of Polemical Literature of the Late 16th and Early 17th Centuries, 1900), *Pierwszy występ literacki Pocieja* ([I.] Potii's Literary Debut, 1902), *Antigrafe, polemichnyi tvir M. Smotryts'koho* (Antigraph, a Polemical Work of M. Smotrytsky, 1925); works on the cultural and literary movement in Galicia, such as *Geneza poetycznych utworów Markiana Szaszkiewicza* (The Genesis of Markian Shashkevych's Poetry, 1896; Ukrainian trans 1910), *Korespondentsiia Ia. Holovats'koho* (The Correspondence of Ya. Holovatsky, 2 vols, 1905, 1909), *Kopitar i Zubryts'kyi* (1918), and *Materiialy do istoriï kul'turnoho zhyttia v Halychyni v 1795–1857 rr.* (Materials on the History of Cultural Life in Galicia, 1795–1857, 1920); works on folklore, such as *Lirnyky* (Lirnyks, 1894); works on relations between Galicia and Russian-ruled Ukraine, such as *Do istoriï vzaiemyn Halychyny z Ukraïnoiu* (On the History of Relations between Galicia and Ukraine, 1906) and *Z lystiv P. Kulisha do Om. Partyts'koho* (From the Letters of P. Kulish to O. Partytsky, 1908); works on 19th-century Ukrainian literature, such as *Kotliarevs'kyi i Artemovs'kyi* (1901), *Literaturni zamitky* (Literary Notes, 1901), and *V piat'desiatylitie smerty T. Shevchenka* (On the 50th Anniversary of T. Shevchenko's Death, 1911); and works on Ukrainian-Polish relations, such as *Pol'ska konspiratsiia sered rus'kykh pytomtsiv i dukhovenstva v Halychyni v rokakh 1831–1848* (The Polish Conspiracy among Ruthenian Seminarians and Clergy in Galicia in 1831–48, 1908) and *Lysty ministra Fl'oriiana Ziemialkovs'koho do iepyskopa Ivana Stupnyts'koho* (Letters of Minister Florian Ziemiałkowski to Bishop Ivan Stupnytsky, 1908). Studynsky also wrote poetry and short stories, which he published in the Ukrainian press under the pseudonyms K. Viktoryn, I. Lavryn, K. Zorian, and others.

D. Shtohryn

**Studynsky, Yurii** [Studyns'kyj, Jurij], b 9 December 1903 in Lviv, d 24 February 1965 in Munich. Economist and publicist; son of K. \*Studynsky. After graduating from the universities of Graz (JD, 1926) and Paris (JD, 1930) he worked as the Paris correspondent for the Lviv newspapers *Novyi chas* and *Dilo*. After the Second World War he taught economics, political science, and history at the Ukrainian Free University in Munich and served as dean of the Faculty of Law and Social Sciences. He was president of the *Central Representation of the Ukrainian Emigration in Germany (1950–1, 1957–61). Besides articles he wrote *Le problème agraire en Ukraine* (1930), based on his doctoral dissertation, and translated three books on co-operation by C. Gide and G. Fauquet, which were published by the Audit Union of Ukrainian Co-operatives.

**Stukovenkov, Mikhail,** b 17 September 1842 in St Petersburg, d 14 March 1897 in Kiev. Dermatologist and venereologist. A graduate of the Medico-Surgical Academy in St Petersburg (1866), during the Russo-Turkish War (1877–8) he was in charge of sanitation in Plevna, Bulgaria. From 1883 he lectured on dermatology and syphilis at Kiev University (professor from 1887). His publications dealt with the treatment of various skin diseases. He introduced a new method of treating syphilis with mercury. Stukovenkov was the founding president of the Kiev Physico-Medical Society.

**Stundists.** Adherents of a religious revival movement in Southern Ukraine in the latter half of the 19th century that gave impetus to the formation of a variety of Protestant-oriented religious denominations. Stundism never constituted a formal religious body. It started in the early 1860s as a movement of Ukrainian peasants in Kherson gubernia who gathered for communal readings of the Scriptures and hymn-singing, in the manner of the German colonists in the region; the name 'Stundist' was derived from the German *Stunde* 'hour,' and was a reference to their participation in fellowship hours of readings and hymn-singing.

The movement first appeared in the village of Osnova, northeast of Odessa (in present-day Berezivka raion, Odessa oblast), and soon spread to surrounding settlements. As it grew, it came under investigation by civil and ecclesiastical authorities, and the Stundists were harassed with fines, confiscation of religious books, and imprisonment. Rather than deterring the movement, the harassment strengthened the resolve of its adherents, who found it increasingly difficult to reconcile themselves to the sacerdotal nature of the Russian Orthodox church and by 1870 openly broke with it. In the 1870s the movement spread into Kiev, Katerynoslav, and Tavriia gubernias, and by the end of the decade there were approx 3,000 Stundists in Kherson gubernia and 2,000 in Kiev gubernia. By the end of the 1880s these figures had doubled, and the official estimate of the number of Stundists stood at 20,000. The catalyst for the growth of the Stundists was the presence of German and Mennonite colonists in southern Ukraine who had prospered as farmers and were known for their social decorum. Many neophyte Stundists adopted the tenets of thrift, hard work, and sobriety underlying Protestant beliefs and subsequently improved their economic well-being. But they were not overtly political, posed no challenge to the secular authorities, and tended to be prosperous farmers and regular taxpayers. For these reasons the civil authorities initially refrained from any concerted actions against the 'sectarians.' Stundists were granted some rights in 1883, along with other sectarian

groups, but their most vehement opponent was the director general of the Russian *Holy Synod, K. *Pobedonostsev. Along with other Russian Orthodox hierarchs, he saw the Stundists as heretics, and he had them declared an especially dangerous sect and brought the forces of the Ministry of the Interior against them. A sustained campaign of persecution followed, as the rights of 1883 were revoked, and meetings in prayer houses prohibited; Stundist schools were closed, adherents were denied internal passports, and the law was used to harass them in every conceivable manner.

The campaign against the Stundists continued until 1905, when new legislation was passed guaranteeing certain religious freedoms. A number of Stundists had emigrated to the United States, particularly North Dakota, and Canada, where in 1921 they formed separate Ukrainian congregations under P. Kindrat. By that time, however, most Stundists had affiliated themselves with one of a number of growing Protestant religious denominations, including *Baptists, *Evangelical Christians, *Adventists, and Pentecostals.

BIBLIOGRAPHY
Brandenburg, Hans. *The Meek and the Mighty* (New York 1977)
A. Makuch

Bohdan Stupka

**Stupka, Bohdan,** b 27 August 1941 in Kulykiv, Nesterov raion, Lviv oblast. Stage and film actor. His repertoire includes roles from farce, satirical comedy, contemporary Soviet and other plays, and tragedy (including such roles as W. Shakespeare's Richard III and Edmund in *King Lear*). He completed study in the drama studio at the Lviv Ukrainian Drama Theater (1961–7) and worked there as a lead actor (until 1967 and in 1973–7). In 1968–73 he was a student in the Faculty of Theater Studies at the Kiev Institute of Theater Arts, and in 1978 he joined the Kiev Ukrainian Drama Theater. He acted in the films *Bilyi ptakh z chornoiu oznakoiu* (A White Bird with a Black Mark, 1972), *Dudaryky* (The Pipers, 1980), and *Chervoni dzvony* (The Red Bells, 1982).

**Stupnytsky, Ivan** [Stupnyc'kyj], b 1816, d 1890. Ukrainian Catholic bishop of Peremyshl in 1872–90. He warded off attacks made by Polish authorities against the Ukrainian Catholic church for which the pretext was a Russophile orientation in the church. He also used his position in the Galician Diet to obtain a Ukrainian-language class in the Polish gymnasium in Peremyshl in 1888, the first step toward the state-supported Ukrainian-language gymnasium that was created in that city in 1895.

**Stupnytsky, Ivan** [Stupnyc'kyj], b 7 July 1928 in Balabanivka, Uman okruha. Economist. A graduate of Kiev University (PH D, 1965), he has taught there as a docent (from 1956), dean of the economics faculty (since 1967), and chairman of the political economy department (since 1971). His publications, which focus on the political economy of socialism and the technological base of communism, include the monographs *Produktyvnist' pratsi ta shliakhy ïï zrostannia u promyslovosti* (Labor Productivity and Ways to Its Growth in Industry, 1958) and *Rozvytok material'noho vyrobnytstva u protsesi rozshyrenoho sotsialistychnoho vidtvorennia* (The Development of Material Production in the Process of the Expanded Socialist Re-Creation, 1965).

**Stupnytsky, Leonid** [Stupnyc'kyj] (nom de guerre: Honcharenko), b 1891? in Volhynia, d 30 July 1944 near Ostrih, Rivne oblast. Senior UPA officer. As a lieutenant colonel in the UNR Army, he commanded a cavalry brigade in the Second Winter Campaign (November 1921). In the interwar period he was a community leader in Volhynia and then was imprisoned by the NKVD (1939–41). Under the German occupation he organized and commanded a militia regiment in Rivne and then directed a school for paramilitary guards. In April 1943 he joined the UPA as an instructor, and in August he was appointed chief of staff of the UPA-North. He was killed in combat with NKVD units and posthumously promoted to brigadier general.

**Stupnytsky, Vasyl** [Stupnyc'kyj, Vasyl'], b 2 January 1879 in Mykhailivka, Kharkiv gubernia, d 1945? Composer, folk song collector, conductor, and teacher. A graduate of Kharkiv University, he conducted the DUKH kapelle, organized traveling concerts, and undertook pioneering research into the music ethnography of the Kharkiv area. He emigrated to the West in 1944 and disappeared in Berlin the following year. His compositions include choral works to texts by T. Shevchenko, church music, and folk song arrangements: *Pisni Slobidskoï Ukraïny* (Songs of Slobidska Ukraine, 1929) and the posthumously published *Slobozhanski narodni pisni* (Folk Songs of Slobidska Ukraine, 1962) and *Muzyka dlia ditei* (Music for Children, 1978).

**Sturgeon** (Ukrainian: *oseter*). Any of the sharklike fishes of the family Acipenseridae, most belonging to the genus *Acipenser*. They are valuable for their flesh, roe (for caviar), and swim bladder (for isinglass). In some areas fishing for sturgeons is restricted. A number of species live in the Black Sea and the Sea of Azov – common sturgeon (*A. sturio*), sterlet (*A. ruthenus*; see *Sterlet), beluga (*Huso huso* or *A. huso*), and *A. stellatus*. These species migrate up rivers to spawn. There are also some nonmigratory, freshwater sturgeons living in lakes. Pollution, the construction of electric-power plants, and overfishing have resulted in a drastic decrease in the number of migratory sturgeons in recent years.

**Stus, Vasyl,** b 8 January 1938 in Rakhnivka, Haisyn raion, Vinnytsia oblast, d 4 September 1985 in Soviet

Vasyl Stus

strict-regime concentration camp no. 389/36-1, Perm oblast, RSFSR. Dissident poet. Stus studied at the pedagogical institute in Donetske and began his graduate work at the Institute of Literature of the AN URSR (now ANU) in 1964. A year later, because of his protests against the secret arrests and closed trials which were becoming prevalent, he was expelled from the institute, and in 1972 he was arrested. He was sentenced to five years of strict-regime labor camp followed by three years of exile. While in exile he joined the *Ukrainian Helsinki Group, and for that he was rearrested in 1980 and sentenced to 10 years of strict-labor camp and 5 years of exile. A man of uncompromising principles, Stus refused to kowtow to the regime and was subjected to constant persecutions, which finally were responsible for his death. After facing repeated refusals and bureaucratic impediments, family and friends received permission to transfer his body to Ukraine. On 19 November 1989 a procession of over 30,000 mourners attended the interment of Stus and two other dissidents (O. Tykhy and Yu. Lytvyn) at the Baikove Cemetery in Kiev. The event became a manifestation of national solidarity and censure of the repressive regime.

Stus began writing poetry as a student, and some of his poems appeared in the journals *Dnipro* and *Zmina* in 1963–5. Because of his activities in the dissident movement, his first collection of poems was not printed. Although he continued to write while he was incarcerated, the KGB systematically confiscated and destroyed his work. Up to 600 poems and translations from J.W. von Goethe, R.M. Rilke, R. Kipling, and C. Baudelaire were destroyed in 1976. Some poems miraculously survived and were smuggled out to the West, where Stus's poetry appeared in several collections. The first collection, *Zymovi dereva* (Winter Trees, 1970), was followed by *Svicha v svichadi* (A Candle in a Mirror, 1977) and the posthumous *Palimpsesty: Virshi 1971–1979 rokiv* (Palimpsests: Poems of 1971–9, 1986). The first collection to appear in Ukraine was an underground samvydav collection, *Povernennia* (The Return), which appeared in Ivano-Frankivske in 1990. Final 'acceptance' came also in 1990, with the publication of the first official edition of his poetry, *Doroha boliu* (The Road of Pain). In 1992 two collections were published in Ukraine: *Vikna v pozaprostir* (Windows into Beyond-Space), containing his poetry, articles, letters, and diary excerpts, and *Zolotokosa krasunia* (The Golden-Braided Beauty), containing Stus's poetry found in the KGB archives.

Traditional in form, Stus's poetry began as 'lyricism of actuality,' in the manner in which the poets of the 1970s responded to the realities of the day. Content prevailed over form, message over myth, and the satire found in the poetry of the 1960s often turned to scorn, anger, and abuse. The poetry written behind bars, however, is more serene; it expresses a longing, philosophical contemplation of life, nature, man the prisoner, and man the jailer, and reveals Stus's attempt to come to some synthesis with respect to the contradictions of the human experience.

D.H. Struk

**Stvyha River.** A right-bank tributary of the Prypiat River that flows for 178 km through eastern Rivne oblast as well as southern Brest and Homel oblasts (Belarus) and drains a basin area of 5,440 sq km. The river is 2–4 m wide near its source and 30–50 m wide in its lower course. Over 40 percent of its basin area is wetland. It provides a channel for a drainage system developed in the region and is also used for log rafting.

**Stylistics.** The study of the expressive devices of language and of various elements of literary style. Stylistics developed in the 19th and 20th centuries out of the study of *rhetoric. In Ukraine, Latin and Polish baroque versions of the theory of Greek and Roman rhetoric and *poetics were taught at Orthodox brotherhood schools and the Kievan Mohyla Academy. The traditional rhetorical concepts of euphony, rhythmics, rhyme, figures, and tropes, which form the core of stylistics, had already been discussed in M. Smotrytsky's Slavonic grammar (1619). Combined with the rules of poetics and *versification (eg, A. Baibakov's book of poetic rules [1774]), they became part of the secondary-school curriculum in the 19th century. The first textbooks of Ukrainian stylistics and rhetoric were published by the Galician gymnasium teacher V. Dombrovsky in the early 1920s.

Modern Ukrainian stylistics was developed in the 1920s in Soviet Ukraine by proponents of *purism, such as O. Kurylo, O. Syniavsky, M. Hladky, M. Sulyma, A. Nikovsky, S. Smerechynsky, B. Tkachenko, T. Sikirynsky, H. Maifet, M. Osypiv, and Z. Veselovska, and in Warsaw, Prague, and Lviv by I. Ohiienko, V. Simovych, and O. Paneiko. Accepting the folk vernacular as the basis of *Standard Ukrainian and rejecting Church Slavonic, Russian, Polish, and German calques, they produced studies of the stylistics of Ukrainian folklore, 19th-century writers who wrote in the vernacular, and non-belletristic, non-vernacular genres.

Ukrainian stylistics has grown considerably since the Second World War. In the 1950s statistical methods began to be used by V. Perebyinis and others. Textbooks of Ukrainian normative stylistics ideas have been written by V. Vashchenko, A. Koval, and I. Cherednychenko. The course on contemporary Ukrainian edited by I. Bilodid includes a volume on stylistics (1973). Books have been published on the style of the Ukrainian press (by M. Zhovtobriukh, 1963, 1970), the style of dialogue and monologue (D. Barannyk, 1961, 1969, and P. Dudyk, 1972), scientific style (A. Koval, 1970), phonostylistics (V. Shyprykevych, 1972), the style of 14th-century official documents (M. Peshchak, 1979), and the stylistic functions of grammatical parallel forms (V. Vashchenko, 1956).

Research in literary stylistics has been limited to the works of officially sanctioned writers. Studies on the style of premodern Ukrainian authors (by Z. Veselovska, I.

Svientsitsky, A. Hensorsky, A. Nizhenets, L. Batiuk, Ye. Markovsky, V. Krekoten, V. Sych, V. Mykytas, V. Kolosova, P. Yaremenko) have been few. In modern Ukrainian literature, studies have been produced on the language of I. Kotliarevsky, Ye. Hrebinka, H. Kvitka-Osnovianenko, M. Vovchok, T. Shevchenko, A. Svydnytsky, I. Tobilevych, P. Myrny, I. Nechui-Levytsky, P. Hrabovsky, I. Franko, L. Hlibov, Lesia Ukrainka, O. Kobylianska, M. Kotsiubynsky, V. Stefanyk, A. Teslenko, M. Cheremshyna, L. Martovych, P. Tychyna, M. Rylsky, V. Sosiura, P. Panch, I. Mykytenko, O. Vyshnia, M. Yohansen, A. Holovko, Yu. Yanovsky, M. Bazhan, I. Kyrylenko, O. Korniichuk, I. Kocherha, O. Dovzhenko, L. Pervomaisky, A. Malyshko, O. Honchar, H. Tiutiunnyk, N. Rybak, and M. Stelmakh.

Articles are published in the journals *Movoznavstvo* and *Ukraïns'ka mova i literatura v shkoli* and in the annual *Kul'tura slova*. Emigré scholars who have contributed to the study of stylistics include D. Chyzhevsky, G.Y. Shevelov, I. Bezpechny, and D. Nytchenko.

BIBLIOGRAPHY
Kurylo, O. *Paralel'ni formy v ukraïns'kii movi, ïkh znachennia dlia styliu* (Kiev 1923)
Ohiienko, I. *Ukraïns'kyi stylistychnyi slovnyk* (Zhovkva 1924)
Kurylo, O. *Uvahy do suchasnoï ukraïns'koï literaturnoï movy*, 3rd edn (Kiev 1925; repr, Toronto 1960)
Tkachenko, B. *Narys ukraïns'koï stylistyky*, 5 fasc (Kiev nd [ca 1930])
Syniavs'kyi, O. (ed). *Kul'tura ukraïns'koho slova* (Kharkiv–Kiev 1931)
Matviienko, O. *Stylistychni paraleli: Proty puryzmu* (Kharkiv 1932)
Skrypnyk, L. *Osoblyvosti movy i styliu ukraïns'koï radians'koï khudozhn'o-istorychnoï prozy* (Kiev 1958)
Vashchenko, V. *Stylistychni iavyshcha v ukraïns'kii movi* (Kharkiv 1958)
Cherednychenko, I. *Narysy z zahal'noï stylistyky suchasnoï ukraïns'koï movy* (Kiev 1962)
Butryn, M. *Mova i styl' ukraïns'kykh pys'mennykiv: Bibliohrafichnyi pokazhchyk literatury za 1953–64 rr.* (Lviv 1966)
*Statystychni ta strukturni linhvistychni modeli* (Kiev 1966)
Koval', A. *Praktychna stylistyka suchasnoï ukraïns'koï movy* (Kiev 1967; 2nd rev edn, Kiev 1978)
Perebyinis, V. (ed). *Statystychni parametry styliv* (Kiev 1967)
Koval', A. *Naukovyi styl' suchasnoï ukraïns'koï literaturnoï movy: Struktura naukovoho tekstu* (Kiev 1970)
Zhovtobriukh, M. *Mova ukraïns'koï periodychnoï presy (kinets' XIX–pochatok XX st.)* (Kiev 1970)
Īzhakevych, H. (ed). *Teoretychni problemy linhvistychnoï stylistyky* (Kiev 1972)
Koval', A. *Kul'tura dilovoho movlennia: Pysemne ta usne dilove spilkuvannia* (Kiev 1974)
Nytchenko, D. *Elementy teoriï literatury i stylistyky* (Melbourne 1975)
Pylyns'kyi, M. *Movna norma i styl'* (Kiev 1976)
Rusanivs'kyi, V. (ed). *Mova i chas: Rozvytok funktsional'nykh styliv suchasnoï ukraïns'koï movy* (Kiev 1977)
Iermolenko, S. *Syntaksys i stylistychna semantyka* (Kiev 1982)
Pylyns'kyi, M. (ed). *Vzaiemodiia usnykh i pysemnykh styliv movy* (Kiev 1982)
Bezpechnyi, I. *Teoriia literatury* (Toronto 1984)
Kukhar-Onyshko, O. *Indyvidual'nyi styl' pys'mennyka: Henezys, struktura, typolohiia* (Kiev 1985)

O. Horbach

**Styr River.** A right-bank tributary of the Prypiat River that flows for 483 km through Lviv, Rivne, and Volhynia oblasts as well as Brest oblast (Belarus) and drains a basin area of 13,100 sq km. The banks of its lower reaches are particularly muddy. The river is used for industrial and water-supply purposes and as an output channel for a regional drainage system. In addition a water reservoir and hydroelectric station have been built on it. The largest center on the river is Lutske, from which point it is navigable on its lower course.

**Styranka, Mariia** (née Fitsalovych), b 1 March 1922 in Lypytsia, Rohatyn county, Galicia. Painter. A postwar émigré, she has lived in Canada since 1955. In 1965 she graduated from the Ontario College of Art. She paints mostly watercolor still lifes and landscapes. Solo exhibitions of her works have been held in Toronto (six times, 1967–80), Paris (1976), Brussels (1977), New York (1978), and Edmonton (1982).

**Styranka, Myroslav** (pseuds: O. Zelenetsky, M. Petrovych), b 27 October 1910 in Hovyliv Malyi, Kopychyntsi county, Galicia. Journalist. From the mid-1930s he contributed to various nationalist periodicals in Galicia. As a postwar émigré he was a member of the CC of the Ukrainian Revolutionary Democratic party, published the newspaper *Ukraïns'ki visti* in Neu-Ulm, and worked as an editor for the Ukrainian Press Service (1946–9) and the newspaper *Ukraïns'ka trybuna* in Munich. Later he worked for Radio Liberty (1954–64) and coedited the weekly *Shliakh peremohy* (1965–8) in Munich before becoming coeditor of the Paris-based *Ukraïns'ke slovo* in 1969. He was chief editor of that paper from 1977 to 1992. He has also contributed regularly to the newspaper *Novyi shliakh* in Toronto.

**SUB.** See Association of Ukrainians in Great Britain.

Serafim Subbotin

**Subbotin, Serafim,** b 3 May 1906 in Kazan, Russia, d 16 January 1976 in Kiev. Geophysicist; AN URSR (now ANU) full member from 1961. A graduate of Kazan University (1931), he worked for the Ukrainian Geological Administration (1931–40), and as a researcher at the ANU Institute of Geological Sciences in Kiev (1944–5) and Lviv (1945–50) and at the Institute of Geology of Useful Minerals (1951–60) in Lviv. From 1960 until his death he directed the ANU Institute of Geophysics in Kiev. He also taught at the Dnipropetrovske Mining Institute, Lviv University, and the Lviv Polytechnical Institute. His research included studies of the forces responsible for tectonic movements, gravimetry, and the structure of the earth's core and its outer

mantle. He developed a new theory of tectogenesis and made key contributions to the geophysical knowledge of Ukraine. The ANU Institute of Geophysics is now named in his honor.

**Subbotin, Viktor,** b 13 March 1844 in Pryluka, Poltava gubernia, d 29 September 1898 in Kiev. Hygienist. A graduate of Kiev University (1867), he completed a doctoral dissertation (1869) and specialized abroad. From 1872 he was a professor in the departments of hygiene, forensic medicine, medical geography, and statistics at Kiev University, and from 1884 he was dean of the medical faculty. He was an active member of the Society of Kiev Physicians and a founder of the Russian Society of Public Health (1887). He took part in efforts to control cholera and typhus epidemics in Kiev. His publications, written mostly in German, dealt with food hygiene, community hygiene, epidemiology, questions of physiology, and the organization of health care. His textbook on hygiene was printed in 1882.

**Subcarpathia** (Pidkarpattia). A physical-geographic region located between the Carpathian Mountains to the southwest, the Pokutian-Bessarabian Upland to the east, the Podolian Upland with its subregion, Opilia, to the northeast, and the Roztochia plateau to the north. To the northwest Subcarpathia passes into the Sian Lowland. The length of Subcarpathia (excluding the Sian Lowland) is 250 km; the width varies from 30 km in the southeast to 60 km in the northwest, for an approximate area of 10,000 sq km. Subcarpathia occupies approx one-fifth of the historical regions of Galicia and Bukovyna and has a population of about 1.4 million.

**Physical geography.** From a geological-tectonic standpoint Subcarpathia represents a portion of a large foredeep that formed during the Miocene epoch in front of the folding Carpathian Mountains. The outer zone of the foredeep has as its foundation the Podolian Platform; the inner zone consists of severely dislocated flysch deposits. The foredeep itself is filled with thick Miocene deposits of clays, argillites, calcareous clays, and sandstones covered by diluvial and alluvial deposits. At the end of the Pliocene epoch Subcarpathia was an accumulative-denudational peneplain covered by fluvial deposits of sand, silt, and clay originating from the Carpathians. As a result of an uplift at the end of the Pliocene and the beginning of the Pleistocene epoch the rivers intensified their erosion and sculpted into the surface a number of wide valleys, lowlands, and intervening ridges. The uplift of Subcarpathia was not uniform, however, and the relief features are partly of tectonic origin. In the Dnieper glacial phase the northeastern part of Subcarpathia was occupied by a lobe of the European continental glacier, and the meltwaters temporarily ponded. By the end of the Pleistocene epoch Subcarpathia was covered by deposits of loess. At present the rivers from the Carpathian Mountains, most notably the Stryi, carry silt and sand on to Subcarpathia and deposit them in their floodplains.

Intervalley ridges, with elevations of 300–500 m above sea level (asl), rise 80–120 m or more above the general surface of the lowland. The highest, Mt Tsetsyna, near Chernivtsi, attains 537 m asl. Some are relatively smooth; others are dissected, with a number (up to eight) of terraces of various ages along their sides. The major intervalley ridges are the Drohobych Ridge (300–400 m asl, dissected relief), the Middle Subcarpathian Ridge (between the Stryi and the Bystrytsia rivers, with elevations of 350–450 m asl or more and slopes dissected by a network of gullies and ravines), the Southern Pokutian Ridge (300–500 m asl, with buttes near Sloboda-Rungurska consisting of Miocene deposits rising to 780 m asl), the Seret-Prut Ridge (a deeply dissected chain of hills with elevations of up to 550 m asl), and the Bukovyna Ridge. Of the lowlands, the Sian Lowland and the adjacent northwestern part of the Upper Dniester Basin were covered by the glacier, and thus acquired distinct landscape attributes of the moraine-fluvioglacial lowlands; the rest of the Upper Dniester Basin is an alluvial-outwash plain. The remaining lowlands include the Halych-Bukachivtsi Basin, the Kalush Basin, the Stanyslaviv Depression (with an accumulative relief), the Kolomyia-Chernivtsi Basin along the Prut River (an alluvial-terraced valley), and the Seret Basin.

The soils of Subcarpathia are related to the relief and the recent geological past. The interbasin ridges and slopes are dominated by the gray-brown luvisols; in the valley bottoms are alluvial soils (gleysols). On the loess loams of both western and eastern parts of Subcarpathia are the gray forest and podzolized chernozem soils.

The climate of Subcarpathia is temperate continental, with increasing continentality from the northwest to the southeast. The mean annual temperatures range from 7°C to 8°C, the mean January temperatures, from –4°C in the west to –5°C in the east, and the mean July temperatures, from 18°C to 19.5°C. The number of days with temperatures above 15°C increases toward the southeast (95 at Sambir, 117 at Chernivtsi). The mean annual precipitation increases from 600 mm in the east to 800 mm at the higher elevations to the southwest. Three-quarters of the annual precipitation occurs from April to October, with 45 percent concentrated in June, July, and August. Locally the climate varies from the relatively cooler and more humid uplands to the warmer (notably in the summer) and drier basins.

The rivers of the region are right-bank tributaries of the Dniester. With their sources in the Carpathian Mountains, they form a well-developed network. They include the *Stryvihor (Strviazh), the Tysmenytsia, the *Stryi, the *Svicha, the *Limnytsia, and the *Bystrytsia Solotvynska and the *Bystrytsia Nadvirnianska (which combine into one before joining the Dniester). In southeastern Subcarpathia the main rivers are the *Prut, the *Cheremosh, and the *Seret. The rivers of Subcarpathia flow swiftly over their stony river beds but freeze during the winter for two to two-and-one-half months. Rainfall and melting snow feed the rivers, which flood in the spring when the thaw combines with rainfall, or in the summer following downpours in the mountains.

The vegetation of Subcarpathia belongs to the Central European broad-leaved forest zone. In the uplands two basic types of forest are found, the oak forest (with an admixture of hornbeam, ash, elm, and sometimes aspen, birch, linden, and other trees) and the beech forest (with an admixture of hornbeam, maple, oak, and, at higher elevations, fir and spruce). The thickets are represented by the hazel, maple, honeysuckle, buckthorn, wild rose, and other shrubbery. Large areas in the uplands have been deforested and are now occupied by meadows (where the prominent grasses are meadow fescue, bent grass, mat grass, and many others) with intrusions of scrub. In the Upper Dniester Basin pine forests occur. Lowland vegeta-

tion is represented by riverbank groves (consisting mainly of alder, with an undergrowth of currants, osier, and other shrubbery) and sedge meadows. In the warmer reaches of southeastern Subcarpathia some steppe plants characteristic of the forest-steppe occur. Natural vegetation has been altered by human activity. Forests now constitute 25 percent of the area (ranging from 20 to 40 percent in the uplands and from 5 to 20 percent in the lowland basins); hayfields, meadows, and pastures cover 30 percent; and plowland (mostly in the basins) occupies 40 percent.

**Population.** Subcarpathia is one of the most densely populated areas of Ukraine. It supports 220 persons (including 80 rural residents) per sq km. For every rural resident there is about 0.5 ha of plowland and less than 0.8 ha of all agricultural land. Moreover, the distribution of population is uneven. The interbasin uplands and the Upper Dniester Basin are less densely settled, with 75 persons per sq km, whereas the basins and valleys, notably the Stryi Basin, the Stanyslaviv Basin, the Prut Basin (over 200 persons per sq km), and especially the Drohobych-Boryslav Industrial Region (where the local concentration exceeds 300 persons per sq km), are densely settled. Urban population made up almost 25 percent of the population in the 1930s; it has grown to 43 percent (1987). The cities are located along major land routes (along the foothills and in the basins) parallel to the Carpathian Mountains at points of intersection with major routes crossing the Carpathians into Transcarpathia. The towns in the Carpathian foothills are generally small: Dobromyl (5,300), Khyriv (4,000), Staryi Sambir (3,800), Boryslav (41,800), Bolekhiv (10,700), Dolyna (21,200), Nadvirna (11,900), Deliatyn (7,900), Kosiv (7,100), Kuty (4,800), Vyzhnytsia (4,300), and Storozhynets (14,000). The larger cities are located at some distance from the Carpathians: Sambir (27,000), Drohobych (76,000), Stryi (63,000), Kalush (67,000), Ivano-Frankivske (225,000), Kolomyia (63,000), Sniatyn (6,400), and Chernivtsi (254,000). All the larger cities have possessed administrative, trade, and industrial functions for a long time. The historical influence of some of the cities as Ukrainian cultural-educational centers extended well beyond their immediate areas, notably in the case of Sambir, Stryi, Ivano-Frankivske, Kolomyia, and, especially, Chernivtsi, the main city of Bukovyna. Drohobych and Boryslav were industrial centers. Today all the larger cities are also centers of industry.

At the end of the 18th century Ukrainians made up 90 percent of the population of Subcarpathia. As a result of the influx of Poles, Jews, and Germans, mainly into the cities and the Drohobych-Boryslav Industrial Region, the proportion of Ukrainians declined. By 1939 they constituted 70 percent of the population (81 percent of the rural population, but only 27 percent of the urban population). Poles, the dominant minority, represented 13 percent of the population, and the associated *latynnyky* (Ukrainian-speaking Roman Catholics), 3 percent. Jews formed 11 percent, Germans 2 percent, and others (mostly Rumanians in Bukovyna) 1 percent. The largest Polish concentrations were in Sambir and its vicinity, the Drohobych-Boryslav Industrial Region, Stanyslaviv (now Ivano-Frankivske), Kolomyia, and Stryi. The Germans were concentrated in Chernivtsi (the administrative center of Bukovyna) and rural colonies in the vicinity of Stryi and Drohobych. The Jews constituted a relative majority in almost every city.

The events of the Second World War and the subsequent resettlement of population changed Subcarpathia's population and its ethnic composition. Census figures from 1959 show that Ukrainians made up about 89 percent of the population (96 percent of the rural and 73 percent of the urban population); Russians, now the dominant minority, represented 5 percent; Jews had declined to 3 percent; Poles were down to 1 percent; and Rumanians remained at about 1 percent. The largest concentrations of minorities were recorded in Chernivtsi (58 percent), Ivano-Frankivske (33 percent), and Stryi and Drohobych (30 percent each). For the 1979 census year the approximate composition was as follows: Ukrainians, 87 percent; Russians, 6 percent; Jews, 2 percent; Poles, 1 percent; Rumanians, 3 percent; and others, 1 percent.

**Economy.** Most of the Subcarpathian population is employed in agriculture in spite of the fact that the region, with its acidic soils and surplus moisture, does not have the best natural conditions for crop growing. At the beginning of the 1960s nearly one-half of the sown area was occupied by grains: wheat (nearly 20 percent), rye (nearly 15 percent), corn for grain (mostly in the southeast), oats, leguminous grains, and barley. Potatoes occupied 20 percent, feed crops approximately 25 percent, and industrial crops (sugar beets, flax, and hemp) almost 10 percent, of the sown area. By the late 1980s the share of the grains had declined to about 40 percent (especially rye and oats), potatoes and vegetables had declined to about 11 percent, technical crops remained at approximately 10 percent, and feed crops had increased to about 39 percent, of the sown area. Animal husbandry, in fact, has become more important than crop production. Specializing in meat and milk production, it is supported by a strong feed base consisting of natural pastures and hayfields as well as feed crops.

The raw materials for industry consist not only of agricultural products and the Carpathian forests but also of the numerous mineral deposits found in the Subcarpathian foredeep. They include oil (near Boryslav and Dolyna), natural gas (deposits at Rudky, Opary, Uherske, Dashava, Kosiv, and elsewhere), ozocerite (at Boryslav), common salt (Stebnyk, Truskavets, Dobromyl, Deliatyn), potash (Stebnyk, Kalush), native sulfur (Tovmach), and lignite (near Kolomyia). Despite the base of raw materials, industries were poorly developed in Subcarpathia, and simple extraction was emphasized. Hydroelectric energy resources likewise were scarcely tapped. Industrial development has increased since the 1960s. Today the main industrial branches of Subcarpathia are petroleum extraction and/or refining (Boryslav, Drohobych, Dolyna, Nadvirna, and Chernivtsi), the chemical processing of potash and natural gas, at Stebnyk (fertilizers) and Kalush (fertilizers and vinyl chloride), paints and enamels (Boryslav and Chernivtsi), woodworking (Chernivtsi, Ivano-Frankivske, Kolomyia, Dolyna, Bolekhiv, Rozhniativ, Nadvirna, Dobromyl, Vyzhnytsia, Berhomit, Storozhynets, and other places), food processing (Chernivtsi, Kolomyia, Ivano-Frankivske, Stryi, Drohobych, Sambir, and other places), light industries (Chernivtsi, Kolomyia, Ivano-Frankivske, Bolekhiv, Stryi, Drohobych, and other places), construction materials (Chernivtsi, Stryi, Kalush, and other places), and machine building (Chernivtsi, Kolomyia, Ivano-Frankivske, Stryi, Drohobych, and Sambir).

BIBLIOGRAPHY
Bondarchuk, V. *Radians'ki Karpaty* (Kiev 1957)

Voropai, L.; Kunytsia, M. *Ukraïns'ki Karpaty: Fizyko-heohrafichnyi narys* (Kiev 1966)
Herenchuk, K. (ed). *Pryroda Ukraïns'kykh Karpat* (Lviv 1968)
Buchyns'kyi, I.; Volevakha, M.; Korzhov, V. *Klimat Ukraïnskykh Karpat* (Kiev 1971)
Kopchak, S. *Naselennia Ukraïns'koho Prykarpattia: Istoryko-demohrafichnyi narys: Dokapitalistychnyi period* (Lviv 1974)
Hoshko, Iu. *Naselennia Ukraïns'kykh Karpat XV–XVIII st: Zaselennia. Mihratsii: Pobut* (Kiev 1976)
*Geodinamika Karpat* (Kiev 1985)
*Ukrainskie Karpaty*, 4 vols (Kiev 1988–9)

V. Kubijovyč, I. Stebelsky

**Subcarpathian Lignite Region.** A region of lignite deposits in the Carpathian foothills of Chernivtsi and Ivano-Frankivske oblasts. Although the lignite is of a high quality with a capacity of 5,000–8,000 kcal/kg, the limited reserves (1970 estimate: 9.3 million t), the small size of the coal lignite veins, and other factors make intensive mining uneconomical. Lignite was discovered in the area in the mid-19th century, and some mining was conducted irregularly until the Second World War. Immediately after the war three mines were sunk in the largest deposit; the last of them closed in 1968.

**Subcarpathian Petroleum and Natural Gas Region.** A major oil and gas region covering some 14,800 sq km in Lviv, Ivano-Frankivske, and Chernivtsi oblasts. The oil is concentrated in Paleocenic sand, and the gas is usually found in Jurassic limestone and Upper Cretaceous and Miocenic sands. The major oil deposits are found at depths of 1,000–4,500 m, and the gas, at depths of 800–1,800 m. The oil in the region is low in sulfur; the gas is high in methane (95–99 percent). Oil has been extracted in the area since 1881, and gas since 1920. Extensive geological research after the Second World War has identified 26 oil, 7 oil-gas, and 27 gas deposits, including the *Dolyna oil field and the *Rudky natural gas field.

**Subcarpathian Ruthenia** (Pidkarpatska Rus'). The historical-geographic name used in the 19th and early 20th centuries to designate the territory of Transcarpathian Ukraine; also called Hungarian Ruthenia. Later it became the official name of the eastern and central parts of *Transcarpathia, which was a separate province of Czechoslovakia (CSR) in 1920–38. The Treaty of *Saint-Germain (1919), which joined Transcarpathia to the CSR, described 'the Ruthenian territory south of the Carpathians' as Subcarpathian Ruthenia, and that was the name used in the CSR constitution at the end of 1919. From 1920 individual laws and administrative orders used the name Subcarpathian Ruthenia, and from 1928 the name Subcarpathian-Ruthenian Land (Podkarpatoruská Zem) was also in use. Although Subcarpathian Ruthenia was officially supposed to be autonomous, the promised territorial and national autonomy was realized only in 1938, when the new autonomous government of the land changed the name to *Carpatho-Ukraine. Subcarpathian Ruthenia did not include western Transcarpathia (Ukrainian parts of eastern Slovakia, ie, the Prešov region) or the narrow Ukrainian ethnographic territory near the border in the Rumanian Maramureş region.

V. Markus

**Subcarpathian Scientific Society** (Russian: Podkarpatskoe obshchestvo nauk; Hungarian: Kárpátaljai Tudományos Társásag). A scholarly institution in Uzhhorod, created and supported by the Hungarian occupational regime in the years 1941–4. Its goal was to counter the influence of the Transcarpathian Russophiles by fostering an independent, pro-Hungarian 'Ruthenian' national identity, culture, and language. The society had 35 scholarly members (some of them Hungarians nominated by the regime) in three sections, science, literature and linguistics, and art and ethnography. Its presidents were A. Hodinka (in Budapest) and Rev O. Ilnytsky, and the de facto director and editor in chief was I. Haraida. Using *etymological spelling the society published the semimonthly *Lyteraturna nedilia* (1941–4), the monthly *Rus'ka molodezh* (1942–4), I. Haraida's officially sanctioned Ruthenian school grammar (1940), 29 books of short stories, 8 children's books, 2 agricultural almanacs, a bibliography of Transcarpathia (1944), a few collections of folktales and folk songs, and popular educational books and translations of world classics by Transcarpathian writers (eg, of W. Shakespeare's *Richard III* [1942]). Using the local Transcarpathian dialect and Hungarian it also published the bilingual scholarly quarterly *Zoria-Hajnal* (1941–3). To acquaint the Hungarian public with Ruthenian culture, it also published a few monographs and an anthology of Transcarpathian short stories (1943) in Hungarian translation.

**Subcarpathian Sulfur Basin.** One of the largest concentrations of sulfur in the world, located in parts of Lviv, Ivano-Frankivske, and Chernivtsi oblasts and extending into Rumania and Poland. In Ukraine it covers an area approx 300 km long and 10–30 km wide and extends from the northwest to the southeast in the Dniester and Prut river basins. The sulfur is found primarily in limestone deposits of the Miocene epoch. The veins of sulfur ore are up to 30 m wide and located at depths of 3–500 m. The sulfur content of the ore is up to 25 percent. The sulfur deposits were discovered in 1950 and have been exploited by open-pit mining since 1958. Some 20 separate deposits have been identified, in Rozdol, Nemyriv, Yavoriv, Liubyni, Yaziv, Soroky, Humenets, Zhydachiv, and Podorozhnie, in Lviv oblast, and Tovmach, in Ivano-Frankivske oblast. The sulfur from the basin is processed at the *Rozdol Sirka Manufacturing Consortium and another facility in Shklo.

**Subcaucasia** (Peredkavkazzia). The northern section of Caucasia, situated between the Great Caucasus Range in the south and the Kuma-Manych Depression in the north. Subcaucasia is divided into three parts: the *Kuban Lowland and the Taman Peninsula in the west, the *Stavropol Upland (with its outlier elevations near Mineralnye Vody) in the central reaches, and the Terek-Sunzha Upland and the Terek-Kuma Lowland to the east. The western and central areas of Subcaucasia represent a geographical extension of the lowland formations of Southern Ukraine. Its eastern reaches are part of the Caspian Lowland. Western Subcaucasia is situated largely in Ukrainian ethnic territory; the central and eastern regions fall in a mixed settlement area. Subcaucasia encompasses a large section of the *Kuban, the *Stavropol region, and the *Terek region.

Most of northwestern and central Subcaucasia sits on the Scythian Platform, which has a Hercynian foundation and Cretaceous (Chalk), Paleogene, Neogene, and Quaternary layers covered with loess, loam, and clay. The region's relief consists of low-lying (up to 150 m) plateaus in

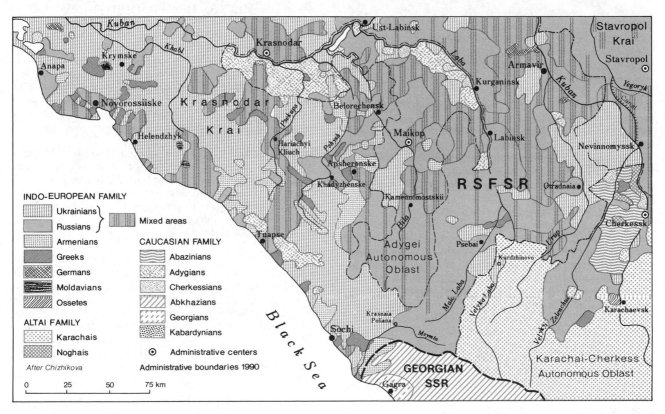

NATIONALITIES IN SOUTHERN SUBCAUCASIA

the west and east and the wavelike Stavropol Upland (elevations up to 600–800 m). The most varied relief can be found in the foothill regions near the Great Caucasus Range. The region has a mild continental climate in the west and a continental climate in the east. The average annual temperature is 8–12°C, with a January average of –2°C in the west and –7°C in the east and a July average of 22°C in the west and 25°C in the east. The greatest precipitation (600–800 mm) is found in the higher reaches of the Stavropol Upland foothills; the western part of Subcaucasia generally receives 400–600 mm and the east about 200–300 mm of precipitation. The soils consist of arable chornozem in the west and dark and light chestnut types in the east. At one time virtually all of Subcaucasia was open steppe. Today most of it is under cultivation, with the exception of the more arid reaches of the east and a forest-steppe belt in the south.

V. Kubijovyč

**Subotin, Stojan,** b 1 March 1921 in Jakovo, Srem, Serbia, d 9 August 1977 in Belgrade. Yugoslav Slavist. He received his PH D from Belgrade University and taught there from 1959. Among his works are a book on Polish-Yugoslav literary relations (1969) and articles about T. Shevchenko and Ukrainian literature in Yugoslav journals. His Slovenian translation of Yu. Yanovsky's *Vershnyky* (The Horsemen) was published in 1965.

St Elijah's Church (1653) in Subotiv

**Subotiv.** IV-13. A village (1972 pop 1,700) on the Tiasmyn River in Chyhyryn raion, Cherkasy oblast. At the beginning of the 17th century Subotiv was a *khutir* belonging to M. *Khmelnytsky, and after 1622, to his son Bohdan. After coming to power in 1648, B. Khmelnytsky built a fortified palace there and established Subotiv as the hetman's residence. The town was destroyed by the Poles in 1664 and was annexed by Poland three years later under the Treaty of Andrusovo. In 1793 the village was ceded to Russia, and became a part of Bratslav vicegerency and, from 1797, Kiev gubernia. B. Khmelnytsky and his son, Tymish, were buried in St Elijah's Church (built in 1653) in Subotiv. A fortified settlement from the 9th century BC has been excavated nearby.

**Subotiv fortified settlement.** A multi-occupational Bronze to early Iron Age fortified settlement located near Subotiv, Cherkasy oblast. Founded in the 9th century BC as a *Chornyi Lis culture center, Subotiv consisted of a 0.5 ha fortress and 1.5 ha settlement area. Excavations in 1951 and 1955 revealed both pit and semi-pit dwellings. The site is best known for producing the first iron objects in the region.

Orest Subtelny

**Subtelny, Orest** [Subtel'nyj], b 17 May 1943 in Cracow. Ukrainian historian; member of the Shevchenko Scientific Society and foreign member of the ANU since 1992. Together with his parents he emigrated to the United States after the Second World War, where he graduated from the University of North Carolina (1967) and Harvard University (PH D, 1972). He taught at Hamilton College in Clinton, New York (1975–82), and has been a professor of Ukrainian history at York University in Toronto since 1982. He has written *The Mazepists: Ukrainian Separatism in the 18th Century* (1981), *Domination of Eastern Europe: Native Nobilities and Foreign Absolutism, 1500–1715* (1986), *Ukraine: A History* (1988; Ukrainian trans 1991), and *Ukrainians in North America: An Illustrated History* (1991). An expanded version of Subtelny and A. Zhukovsky's article on the *history of Ukraine in *Encyclopedia of Ukraine* (vol 2, 1988) was published in Ukrainian translation in Lviv as *Narys istoriï Ukraïny* (1991).

**Subutai** or **Subodai,** b and d ? A 13th-century Mongol military figure. One of Genghis Khan's ablest generals, in 1223 he commanded (together with Jebe) a large expeditionary force against the Kipchaks, which defeated a Rus'-Cuman alliance at the Kalka River. Subutai also led Batu Khan's campaigns in eastern Europe from 1236, including the sack of Kiev in 1240.

**Suceava.** VI-7. A city (1975 pop 54,000) on the Suceava River and a county center in Rumania. The city is mentioned in 12th-century chronicles and in a charter of 1388 as a trade center on the Lviv–Galaţi route. During 1375–1564 it was the capital of the Moldavian principality. In 1653 T. *Khmelnytsky died during the Battle of Suceava. Under Austrian rule Ukrainians settled in the region. Today there are about 35 Ukrainian villages and nearly 40,000 Ukrainians in the northern part of the Suceava region.

**Suceava, Battle of.** An engagement of the armies of T. *Khmelnytsky and some detachments of the Moldavian army against the Polish Wallachian leader M. Basarab, the Transylvanian György II Rákóczi, and the Moldavian army of Gheorghe Ştefan. The latter group, fearing a Ukrainian-Moldavian alliance, attacked the area controlled by the Moldavian hospodar V. *Lupu, captured Iaşi (the capital), and besieged Suceava. Upon Lupu's call for assistance B. Khmelnytsky sent a 12,000-man force under T. Khmelnytsky. In 1653 they broke through the encirclement, and for the ensuing three weeks they staged a staunch defense of the city against an attacking force of 20,000 men. T. Khmelnytsky was mortally wounded on 12 September 1653, and died four days later. After his death the leadership of the Cossack contingent was taken over by I. Fedorenko, who saw no reason to continue fighting for Lupu's interests. Having secured a right of safe passage from Suceava, the Cossack force returned to Ukraine with T. Khmelnytsky's body.

**Suceava River** [Sučava] (also Suchava). A right-bank tributary of the Seret River. It is 160 km long and drains a basin area of 3,800 sq km. The river has its source in the Bukovynian Carpathians, although most of its course is in Rumania. Its upper reaches flow along the Ukrainian-Rumanian borderland region. The river is used for log rafting.

***Suchasna Ukraïna*** (Contemporary Ukraine). A semimonthly paper published in Munich in 1951–60, until 1956 by the External Representation of the *Ukrainian Supreme Liberation Council (UHVR) and then by the Ukrainian Society for Foreign Studies. It contained articles on political and cultural developments in Soviet Ukraine, on the Ukrainian struggle for independence, and on international politics. The editor was V. Stakhiv. Until 1955 it published a monthly supplement, edited by Yu. Lavrinenko and I. Koshelivets, devoted to literature, culture, and the arts; in 1956 this supplement became the separate *Ukraïns'ka literaturna hazeta*. From 1955 the paper included another supplement devoted to economics and social issues, edited by K. Kononenko. Contributors to *Suchasna Ukraïna* included members and supporters of the UHVR (eg, D. and L. Rebet, L. Ortynsky, B. Kordiuk, B. Halaichuk, Ye. Shtendera, and M. Martynets) as well as émigré academics and publicists (eg, B. Wynar, V. Holubnychy, Ye. Glovinsky, Ya. Levytsky, Ya. Pelensky, and S. Protsiuk). The paper's publishing house also issued a series of books and pamphlets on political topics and one of literary works. In 1961 the paper merged with *Ukraïns'ka literaturna hazeta* to form the monthly *Suchasnist'*.

***Suchasnist'*** (Contemporaneity). A monthly journal of literature, translation, the arts, history, and political, social, and economic affairs, published from 1961 to 1990 in Munich, in 1990–1 in Newark, New Jersey, and since 1992 in Kiev. It was formed through the merger of *Suchasna Ukraïna* and *Ukraïns'ka literaturna hazeta*. The chief editors of the journal have been I. Koshelivets (1961–6, 1976–7, 1983–4), W. Burghardt (1967–70), B. Kravtsiv (1970–5), G.Y. Shevelov (1978–81), M. Skorupska (1978, 1981–3), and T. Hunczak (since 1984) and I. Dziuba (coeditor since 1992).

Although it has been closely associated with the For-

*Suchasnist'*

eign Representation of the *Ukrainian Supreme Liberation Council, *Suchasnist'* has reflected a wide spectrum of émigré and Western opinion. Among its contributors have been many of the most prominent émigré writers, scholars, critics, and cultural and political figures. *Suchasnist'* has been a major forum for émigré poets and prose writers, and has devoted much attention to political developments in Ukraine, especially the *dissident movement and, since the late 1980s, the democratic movement there; it has published samvydav literary works and documents, prose and poetry by the *shestydesiatnyky, banned literary works, criticisms of Russification and national discrimination in the USSR, and news and analyses of political and social developments there. It has also published articles on international politics, culture, and intellectual life.

The Suchasnist publishing house has issued separately approx 80 poetry collections, novels, translations, monographs, memoirs, and anthologies since 1968. It has also reprinted Soviet works that were unavailable or banned in the USSR (eg, the writings of M. Skrypnyk, the collected prose of V. Domontovych [Petrov], and poetry by M. Bazhan, V. Svidzinsky, and V. Symonenko) and published samvydav works by Soviet Ukrainian dissidents and books of foreign literature translated into Ukrainian.

***Sud i rozprava*** (Court and Trial). An important 18th-century legal monument written by the Cossack jurist F. *Chuikevych on the basis of his private compilation in 1750–8 of the laws of the Hetman state. The collection is concerned primarily with civil procedure and the court system, as well as with some family and land law. It is also an important source of legal thought in the Hetman state. Responding to the major political and social developments arising from B. Khmelnytsky's uprising (1648–57), the author tried to justify changes in the court system that was established after 1648 and to promote a return to the old system based on the Lithuanian Statute. He proposed renewing the so-called statute courts, and thus separating the judiciary from the administration, and defended the independence of the Hetman courts from the interference of Russian authorities by arguing that there should be no appeal from the decisions of the General Military Court.

The collection was dedicated to Hetman K. *Rozumovsky and was influential in the judicial reform carried out under him in 1760–3. The structure of the General Military Court, for example, was changed (1760) to resemble that of the Tribunal of the Great Duchy of Lithuania, and statute laws were introduced (1763). Although it was an unofficial code, *Sud i rozprava* was extensively used by the courts of the Hetmanate, and some court decisions contain references to it. Its obvious patriotism and its literary style add to its importance beyond the legal sphere.

*Sud i rozprava* is divided into sections dealing with evidence, sentences, procedure, appeals, the execution of judicial decisions, and dowries. These sections were compiled between 1750 and 1752. Later additions include sections on appeals according to the Lithuanian Statute (1754), prescriptive land rights (1755), and land courts (1758). A copy of the text from the late 18th or early 19th century was published by M. Vasylenko in *Materiialy do istorii ukraïns'koho prava* (Materials toward the History of Ukrainian Law, vol 1, 1929). A 1791 transcription is found in the Saltykov-Shchedrin Library in St Petersburg.

BIBLIOGRAPHY
Vasylenko, M. 'Pam'iatnyk ukraïns'koï pravnychoï literatury XVIII viku,' *ZNTSh*, 138–40 (1925)
Tkach, A. *Istoriia kodyfikatsiï dorevoliutsiinoho prava Ukraïny* (Kiev 1968)

Ya. Padokh

The Genoese fortress in Sudak

**Sudak.** IX-15. A city (1989 pop 13,900) on the Black Sea and a raion center in the Autonomous Republic of Crimea. A fortress called Sugdei was built there in 212. At the end of the 8th century it became an important seaport, which maintained economic ties with Byzantium. In documents of Rus' principality it is called Surozh. In the 13th century it became part of the Crimean Khanate, and in 1365, a Genoese trading colony called Soldaia. The Genoese built a fortress with 16 turrets and a church, remnants of which have been preserved. In 1475 Sudak was annexed by Tur-

key, and in 1783, by Russia. Sudak was granted city status in 1982. Most of the inhabitants are employed in the city's health resorts.

**Sudan grass** (*Sorghum sudanese*; Ukrainian: *sudanska trava*). An annual herbaceous plant of the family Gramineae, a leafy bush 50–300 cm in height. Highly drought resistant, it was introduced in Ukraine in 1912 and is now cultivated in steppe and forest-steppe regions for green fodder, hay, silage, and grazing. The popular brands in Ukraine include Odessa 25, Myronivka 10, Black Sea, and Dnipropetrovske 876. Sudan grass is planted as an after crop in mixed planting with soybean, sunflower, etc (see *Sorghum).

John Stefura's sculpture commemorating Ukrainian-Canadian pioneers in front of St Mary's Ukrainian Catholic Church in Sudbury

**Sudbury.** A city (1981 pop 91,800; metropolitan pop 149,900) in northern Ontario, and the world's largest nickel producer and Canada's largest copper producer. Immigrants from Western Ukraine began to work in the mines as early as 1904. In 1914 the Ukrainian Catholics built a small frame church, which was replaced in 1928 with St Mary's Church. The local branch of the Ukrainian National Federation (est 1933) maintained a Ukrainian school, the Dnipro Choir, an orchestra, a folk dance group, and, after the war, the Tryzub sports club. In 1935 the Buduchnist food co-operative, which is still the only Ukrainian food co-operative in Ontario, was organized. Sudbury's first Ukrainian credit union opened in 1944. Of organizations established after the Second World War, the branches of the Ukrainian Youth Association and the Canadian League for Ukraine's Liberation have been most active. In 1981 approx 5,300 of the residents of the Sudbury metropolitan area were of Ukrainian origin. In 1991, 1,205 inhabitants declared Ukrainian as their mother tongue.

**Sudebnik.** A collection of legal norms in the Grand Duchy of Lithuania and Muscovy. Such collections were used in the courts as law manuals and particularly as manuals of criminal and procedural law. The *sudebnik* of 1468 of the Grand Duchy of Lithuania was codified under Grand Duke Casimir IV Jagiellończyk and made public at the Vilnius Diet. It was the first general, though incomplete, legal code for Lithuania, and a precursor of the *Lithuanian Statute. Focused on criminal and procedural law, it was based primarily on *Ruskaia Pravda*, customary law, and articles of later legislative acts. Some influences of Western law are also evident, such as the introduction of capital punishment, which is not found in *Ruskaia Pravda*. In Muscovy the first general legal code was the *sudebnik* of 1497, which marks the beginning of the legal enserfment of the peasantry by limiting their mobility. It was based also on *Ruskaia Pravda*, as well as on various princely decrees and customary law. It was succeeded by the *sudebnik* of 1550, which set the legal groundwork of an estate monarchy and remained in force until the major legal reform of 1649.

**Sudets, Volodymyr** [Sudec'], b 23 October 1904 in Nyzhno-Dniprovske, now part of Dnipropetrovske, d 6 May 1981 in Moscow. Soviet aviation marshal. During the Second World War he commanded an aviation corps and the 17th Aviation Army (1943–5). After the war he graduated from the General Staff Academy (1950) and was promoted to marshal of aviation (1955). He served in various positions, including commander of air defense forces and deputy defense minister of the USSR (1962–6). After retiring in 1966, he became an inspector-consultant to the defense ministry.

**Sudiienko** [Sudijenko]. A Cossack *starshyna* family from the Novhorod-Siverskyi region. Its founder was Ivan, who lived in the mid-17th century. His son, Andrii (d 1688), served as judge of Starodub regiment (1670–4) and *horodovyi* otaman of Novhorod-Siverskyi (1672–7). Andrii's son, Ivan (d 1729), was *horodovyi* otaman of Novhorod-Siverskyi (1709–25) and took part in the Chyhyryn, Perekop, and Poltava campaigns. Ivan's son, Stepan (ca 1689–1763), was *horodovyi* otaman (1727–39) and captain (1739–63) of Novhorod-Siverskyi. His son, Osyp (ca 1743–4 December 1811), was appointed to the General Postal Authority of the Russian Empire in 1784 and promoted to the rank of secret counselor in 1800. He was a friend of Prince O. *Bezborodko, who rewarded him with estates in the Novhorod-Siverskyi region. Osyp's son, M. *Sudiienko, was a historian and civic leader. Of his two sons, Yosyf (27 July 1830–5 December 1892) served as deputy governor of Chernihiv gubernia (1870) and governor of Vladimir gubernia, and Oleksander (28 July 1832–12 April 1882) was local marshal of the nobility in Novhorod-Siverskyi. Oleksander's son, Yevhen (25 May 1870–1918), was a marshal of the nobility and in 1913 was elected to the State Duma.

BIBLIOGRAPHY
Modzalevskii, V. *Malorossiiskii rodoslovnik*, vol 4 (Kiev 1914)
A. Zhukovsky

**Sudiienko, Mykhailo** [Sudijenko, Myxajlo], b 1802 in Novhorod-Siverskyi county, Chernihiv gubernia, d 8 September 1874 in Novhorod-Siverskyi (buried in the Cathedral of the Transfiguration in Chernihiv). Benefactor, historian, and archeographer; son of O. Sudiienko. He was a marshal of the nobility for Novhorod-Siverskyi in 1835–41; a patron of the gymnasiums in Novhorod-Siverskyi, Chernihiv (to which he donated 30,000 rubles), and Bila Tserkva; and head of the Kiev Archeographic Commis-

sion (1848–57) and the Chernihiv Gubernial Committee for the Improvement of the Lot of the Local Peasantry (1857–8). On his estate in Ochkynia he had a large library and a valuable collection of archival material pertaining to the 17th- and 18th-century Hetman state, which was bequeathed to Kiev University by his heirs (later housed in the Manuscript Division of the Central Scientific Library of the AN URSR [now ANU]). Sudiienko published *Materialy dlia otechestvennoi istorii* (Materials for the History of the Fatherland, 2 vols, 1853, 1855) and O. Shafonsky's *Chernigovskogo namestnichestva topograficheskoe opisanie* (A Topographical Description of Chernihiv Vicegerency, 1851) and contributed to the publication of the Chronicle of S. *Velychko (1848–55). A sympathizer of the Decembrists, he was the brother-in-law of O. *Myklashevsky and a friend of A. Pushkin (whose letters to Sudiienko were published in *Russkii arkhiv*, 1895).

A. Zhukovsky

**Sudkovsky, Rufin** [Sudkovs'kyj], b 7 April 1850 in Ochakiv, Odessa county, Kherson gubernia, d 4 February 1885. Seascape painter. He studied at the Odessa Drawing School and the St Petersburg Academy of Arts (1868–73), of which he was elected a member in 1882. His works include *Ochakiv Harbor* (1881), *Calm Sea* (1883), *The Calm* (1884), *Clear Water* (1879–84), *Storm on the Sea*, *On the Bank of the Dnieper*, *View of Ochakiv*, and *Before a Storm near Odessa*.

A book-cover design by Okhrim Sudomora (early 20th century)

**Sudomora, Okhrim,** b 19 March 1889 in Boryspil, Pereiaslav county, Poltava gubernia, d 13 October 1968 in Kiev. Graphic artist. After studying at the Kievan Cave Monastery Icon Painting Studio (1904–7) under I. Izhakevych and at the Kiev Art School (1907–13) he worked as a book illustrator and designer for publishing houses, such as Chas, Dniprosoiuz, Dzvin, and Vernyhora. He designed the journal *Siaivo* (1913–14) and numerous stories for children. In the 1920s he worked for Kiev and Kharkiv publishing houses, where he designed books, such as B. Hrinchenko's *Sam sobi pan* (One's Own Master, 1924), T. Shevchenko's *Kobzar* (1927), and O. Vyshnia's *Siisia, rodysia, zhyto, pshenytsia* (Sow and Grow, Rye and Wheat, 1929), and journals such as *Radians'ka shkola*, *Zhovten'*, and *Pioneriia*. In 1943 he moved to Lviv, where he illustrated the children's magazine *Mali druzi* and children's books for Ukrainske Vydavnytstvo publishers. After the Second World War he worked for publishing houses in Kharkiv and Kiev. He was accused by Soviet critics of formalistic deviations.

**Sudost River** [Sudost']. A right-bank tributary of the Desna River. It is 208 km long and drains a basin area of 5,805 sq km. Most of the river runs through Briansk oblast (RF), but its last section cuts through the northeastern corner of Chernihiv oblast. The city of Pochep is situated along the river.

**Sudova Vyshnia** [Sudova Vyšnja]. IV-4. A city (1989 pop 6,300) on the Vyshnia River in Mostyska raion, Lviv oblast. It was first mentioned in historical documents, as Vyshnia, in 1230. From 1349 it was under Polish rule, and in 1368 it was granted the rights of *Magdeburg law. From 1443 it was the site of dietines for nobles from Rus' voivodeship – hence the name Sudova (from *sud* 'court'), which was added to Vyshnia in 1545. From 1772 to 1918 it belonged to Austria, and in the interwar period it was under Polish rule. Today Sudova Vyshnia has a mixed-feed plant and a haberdashery factory. The remains of a fortified settlement of the 9th to 11th centuries have been preserved, and a statue to its famous son I. *Vyshensky (by D. Krvavych) was erected in 1979.

**Sudovshchykova, Oleksandra.** See Hryhorenko, Hrytsko.

**Sudyslav,** b and d ? A 13th-century Galician boyar. An opponent of Prince Danylo Romanovych, he assisted Hungarian forces several times in their attempts to take over Halych. When they were routed in 1230, he retreated with them to Hungary and organized two more campaigns (1232 and 1233), which were unsuccessful.

**Sudzha** [Sudža]. II-16. A town (1962 pop 4,700) on the Sudzha River and a raion center in Kursk oblast, RF. It was founded in 1664 and was a company center in Slobidskyi regiment and then a county center in Kursk vicegerency (1779–97) and Kursk gubernia. According to the census of 1926, Ukrainians accounted for 30.8 percent of the town's population and 61.2 percent of the *volost*'s population.

**Sugar beet** (*Beta vulgaris saccharifera*; Ukrainian: *tsukrovyi buriak*). The most important industrial crop in Ukraine and the raw material base for the Ukrainian sugar industry. Its white taproot, weighing an average of 400–500 g, yields a sugar content of 16–20 percent. The by-product treacle (or sugarhouse molasses) is used for making spirit yeast, glycerin, and other products. Beet tops are used as fodder.

Sugar beets began to be cultivated in Ukraine in the 1820s. By the 1840s Ukraine was the main sugar-producing region in the Russian Empire. The area sown to sugar beets increased, from about 323,000 ha in 1880–90 to 378,000 ha in 1908–9 and 574,000 ha in 1911–12. In 1913 the 558,000 ha of sugar beets in the nine Ukrainian gubernias accounted for 82 percent of the sugar-beet area in the Russian Empire (excluding Poland). Sugar beets were grown predominantly in the forest-steppe belt – in Kiev and Podilia gubernias and in the Sumy region. The largest fields belonged to large landowners, and the next largest, to sugar-beet mills. Only 20 percent of the sugar-beet area belonged to peasants. Yields in 1913 averaged about 170 centners per ha, and harvests amounted to about 10 million t.

After the revolution the sown sugar-beet area returned to its prewar levels (630,000 ha by 1928). The sown area increased steadily until 1965, then stabilized, and then even receded slightly (see the table). By the late 1980s the Ukrainian SSR accounted for 49 percent of the sugar-beet area in the USSR. In the postwar period the sown area of sugar beets increased also in Western Ukraine, from 116,000 ha in 1940 to 396,000 ha in 1960. Sugar-beet farming was extended into the steppe (Odessa, Mykolaiv, Kherson, Dnipropetrovske, and Luhanske oblasts), where the sown area increased from 18,000 ha in 1940 to 120,000 ha in 1960. Today 77 percent of the sugar-beet fields are in the forest-steppe, 15 percent in the steppe (mostly the northern and central parts of the belt), and 7 percent in the forest belt, particularly in Subcarpathia. Over 95 percent of the sugar-beet area belongs to collective farms; the remainder belongs to state farms.

Harvests of sugar beets grew even more rapidly than the sown areas and continued to grow when the sown

Sugar beets: sown areas, yields, and harvests, 1940–87

| Year or annual average for five-year period | 1940 | 1950 | 1960 | 1961–5 | 1966–70 | 1971–5 | 1976–80 | 1981–5 | 1987 |
|---|---|---|---|---|---|---|---|---|---|
| *Sown area* (1,000 ha) | | | | | | | | | |
| Ukraine | 820 | 828 | 1,457 | 1,708 | 1,757 | 1,716 | 1,791 | 1,696 | 1,667 |
| USSR | 1,226 | 1,308 | 3,043 | 3,604 | 3,582 | 3,527 | 3,745 | 3,506 | 3,404 |
| *Yield* (centners/ha) | | | | | | | | | |
| Ukraine | 159 | 177 | 218 | 198 | 267 | 268 | 300 | 259 | 298 |
| USSR | 146 | 159 | 191 | 165 | 228 | 217 | 237 | 218 | 266 |
| *Harvest* (million t) | | | | | | | | | |
| Ukraine | 13.1 | 14.6 | 31.8 | 34.1 | 46.7 | 46.0 | 53.9 | 43.9 | 49.7 |
| USSR | 18.0 | 20.8 | 57.7 | 59.2 | 81.0 | 76.0 | 88.7 | 76.4 | 90.4 |
| *Ukraine's share of USSR* (%) | | | | | | | | | |
| Sown area | 66.9 | 63.3 | 47.9 | 47.4 | 49.1 | 48.7 | 47.8 | 48.4 | 49.0 |
| Yields | 108.9 | 111.3 | 114.1 | 120.0 | 117.1 | 123.5 | 126.6 | 118.8 | 112.0 |
| Harvest | 72.4 | 70.2 | 55.0 | 57.7 | 57.6 | 60.5 | 60.7 | 57.5 | 55.0 |

area stabilized (see the table). Since yields in Ukraine were higher than in most regions of the Soviet Union, Ukraine's share of the Soviet sugar-beet harvest came close to 55 percent. With an annual output of about 50 million t (1987) Ukraine is the largest producer of sugar beets in the world.

Yield increases have been achieved by the development and use of high-quality seeds, generous quantities of fertilizer, and irrigation in dry areas and the full mechanization of seeding, cultivating, harvesting, and processing. Problems of sugar-beet farming are studied at the Scientific Research Institute of Sugar Beets in Kiev and a network of research stations. The latter have developed many sugar-beet cultivars for different regions of Ukraine, which are named after the respective research stations: the Verkhnia 031, 038, and 072, the Ivanivka 1745 (improved), the Yaltushkiv (single-seed), the Yaltushkiv (hybrid), and the Bila Tserkva 1 and 2 (polyhybrid).

BIBLIOGRAPHY

Voblyi, K. Narysy z istoriï rosiis'ko-ukraïns'koï tsukroburiakovoï promyslovosty, 3 vols (Kiev 1928–30)

Sveklovodstvo, 3 vols (Kiev 1940, 1951, 1959)

Palamarchuk, M. Sveklosakharnoe proizvodstvo Ukrainskoi SSR (Kiev 1964)

Sveklovodstvo na Levoberezhnoi Ukraine (Kharkiv 1970)

Sakharnaia svekla (Kiev 1972)

Sveklosakharnyi agrarno-promyshlennyi kompleks i effektivnost' ego funktsionirovaniia (Kiev 1978)

I. Stebelsky

**Sugar industry.** A branch of the *food industry that makes granular and refined sugar. It is one of the oldest and most important food industries in Ukraine. Until 1914 sugar was one of the country's major exports. Sugar in Ukraine is made primarily from *sugar beets; since the 1950s, however, a growing proportion (in 1980s over one-third) has been made from imported Cuban sugar cane. Over one-half of all sugar is consumed directly by the population; some portion is also used as a raw material in other food industries.

**Before 1915.** Sugar making from sugar beets began in Western Europe in the mid-18th century. In the Russian Empire the first sugar factories were established in the early 19th century. They used imported sugar cane. The first sugar factories in Ukraine were built in 1824 in the village of Troshchyn, near Kaniv, Kiev gubernia, and in Makoshyne, Chernihiv gubernia. By 1830 there were six sugar factories in Russian-ruled Ukraine. The industry expanded very quickly in the 1840s, from 52 factories in 1842 to 192 in 1848 (almost two-thirds of all the sugar factories in the empire). Initially sugar processing was limited almost entirely to nobles' estates. It expanded as commercial farming spread and as the land under commercial crops increased.

The sugar industry was most developed in Right-Bank Ukraine, specifically in the Kiev region and Podilia, which in 1848–9 accounted for over 74 percent of all Ukrainian sugar production. Chernihiv gubernia, in Left-Bank Ukraine, accounted for another 10 percent. Ukrainian sugar factories were usually quite small, with limited capacities. Until the abolition of serfdom in 1861 they relied primarily on serf labor, and production was highly labor-intensive. The sugar beets were harvested, washed, and pressed to produce juice, which was filtered, concentrated

by boiling, and centrifuged to produce crystallized sugar. Most factories operated for only 3 to 4 months in the late fall and early winter, on two 12-hour shifts. In 1848–9, of the 29,250 people employed in the industry in Ukraine, only 3,300 worked year round. In Kiev gubernia 1,990 of 15,250 workers worked year round; in Podilia gubernia, 480 of 3,970; in Chernihiv gubernia, 235 of 3,500; in Kharkiv gubernia, 350 of 3,300; in Poltava gubernia, 170 of 1,900; in Volhynia, 72 of 1,100; and in Kherson gubernia, 12 of 130. Most of the factories were located on the large estates of the Polish magnates, such as the Potockis, Branickis, and Poniatowskis.

From the 1850s the sugar industry began to modernize and grow quickly. New machinery and techniques were introduced, and production was concentrated in larger plants. Some Jews (eg, the Brodsky family) and Ukrainians became involved in the industry. The *Yakhnenko and the *Symyrenko families established a sugar refinery in the 1840s that soon grew into one of the largest sugar companies in the Russian Empire, and the *Tereshchenko family developed a major sugar enterprise after 1860. After the emancipation of the serfs in 1861, the nobility were quickly displaced by capitalists as the leading sugar refiners, although most of the sugar beets were still grown on the large estates. Total production of sugar in Ukraine increased from 200,900 t in 1881–2 to 1.1 million t in 1913–14. At that time Ukraine's output accounted for 80–85 percent of the crystal sugar and almost 75 percent of the refined sugar output of the Russian Empire. Ukraine was second only to Germany in sugar production from beets. In 1914, of the 214 sugar factories in the Russian Empire, 203 were located in Ukraine. Sugar was exported from Ukraine to the rest of the empire and abroad. In 1887 the *Syndicate of Sugar Manufacturers was established to regulate the sugar industry in the Russian Empire. It ensured high profits for the sugar manufacturers by maintaining high prices on the domestic market and low prices on the foreign market.

The sugar industry began in Galicia in the first half of the 19th century, but the factories were closed following the emergence of a single syndicate for the entire Austro-Hungarian Empire. One new factory was established in Khodoriv in 1913.

**1915–40.** The sugar industry declined during the First World War and was almost destroyed during the revolution and the struggle for Ukrainian independence. In 1921–2, production was only approx 4 percent of the 1913 level. The industry was rebuilt quickly, and by 1927–8 production had reached prewar levels (1.1 million t). In the first years of collectivization the area devoted to sugar beets fell sharply, and sugar output declined to 550,000 t in 1932. It rebounded again in the mid-1930s and reached 1.5 million t in 1940. Many of the older factories were reconstructed, and four especially large ones were built, including the *Lokhvytsia Sugar Refining Complex in Poltava oblast, the largest sugar complex in the USSR. Those factories were larger and more mechanized than the older factories, some of which were closed. Whereas in 1913 the average factory processed 70,000 centners of sugar beets, in 1940 the figure was 103,000 centners. In 1940, of all sugar factories in the USSR, 74.5 percent were located in Ukraine, and Ukraine's output accounted for 73 percent of the Soviet output. In the 1930s a sugar industry was established in the Kuban; in Galicia there were two factories, and in Bukovyna, three.

**Since 1941.** Sugar manufacturing was largely interrupted in Ukraine during the Second World War, and many factories were completely destroyed. In 1945 only 329,000 t of sugar were produced, and pre–Second World War levels were achieved only in 1954. After that, however, the industry grew quickly. Between 1955 and 1970, 38 new, highly mechanized factories were built, and many older ones were modernized. The average daily capacity of Ukrainian sugar factories increased from 860 centners in 1950 to 1,700 centners in 1970. In that period the production of sugar from sugar beets increased, from 2.2 million t in 1955 to 3.8 million t in 1960 and 5.9 million t in 1970. After stagnating somewhat in the 1970s, the industry began to grow again, and annual production reached 6.2 million t in 1985 and 7.5 million t in 1987. Since 1960 an increasing percentage of Ukrainian sugar has been produced from imported sugar cane (537,000 t in 1960, 912,000 t in 1970, 1.8 million t in 1985, and 2.2 million t in 1987). Some 60 percent of all Ukrainian sugar was exported to other parts of the USSR, but the overall importance of sugar exports in the Ukrainian economy has fallen.

In 1982 there were 191 sugar factories in Ukraine. The major centers of the industry are the Right-Bank forest-steppe region (Vinnytsia, Cherkasy, Khmelnytskyi, and Kiev oblasts), the Left-Bank oblasts of Sumy, Poltava, and Kharkiv, and the southern oblasts of Kirovohrad and Odessa. Since 1980 there has also been a rapid increase in sugar production in Lviv oblast. The development of the industry in the south is due to the increasing use of imported sugar cane, which is brought into the port of Odessa. The largest factory is the one in Lokhvytsia. Granulated sugar is refined in 15 factories (the largest are in Sumy and Odessa), but overall demand for refined sugar has declined since the 1960s. Problems of the sugar industry in Ukraine are studied at the *Scientific Research Institute of Sugar Beets in Kiev (an All-Union institute until December 1991).

BIBLIOGRAPHY

Plevako, O. 'Z materiialiv do istoriï tsukro-buriakovoï promyslovosty na Ukraïni,' *Pratsi Seminaru dlia vyuchuvannia narodn'oho hospodarstva Ukraïny*, 2 (1927)

Voblyi, K. *Narysy z istoriï rosiis'ko-ukraïns'koï tsukroburiakovoï promyslovosty*, 3 vols (Kiev 1928–30)

Timoshenko, V. *The Soviet Sugar Industry and Its Postwar Restoration* (Stanford 1951)

Lips'kyi, V. *Rozvytok i rozmishchennia tsukrovoho yrobnytstva Ukraïns'koï RSR* (Kiev 1962)

Palamarchuk, M. *Sveklosakharnoe proizvodstvo Ukrainskoi SSR* (Moscow 1964)

Korchinskii, A. *Tekhniko-ekonimicheskii uroven' ispol'zovaniia osnovnykh sredstv i proizvodstvennykh moshchnostei v sveklosakharnoi promyshlennosti USSR* (Kiev 1965)

*Territorial'nye osobennosti razvedeniia pishchevoi promyshlennosti USSR* (Kiev 1982)

V. Kubijovyč, B. Wynar

**Sugdei.** See Sudak.

**Suite.** A composite musical form of related pieces or movements. Before the mid-18th century the genre usually consisted of a set of dances. Ukrainian lutenists and torban players of this period often composed and performed their own dance suites at the courts of Polish and Ukrainian nobles. In the late 19th century the word 'suite' was revived to describe a combination of instrumental movements forming a unified whole. One of the first Ukrainian composers to explore this genre was M. *Lysenko, whose *Ukrainian Suite* (1869) for piano used Ukrainian folk songs within the framework of baroque dance forms. The genre continued to develop in the works of V. Barvinsky and N. Nyzhankivsky. In the 20th century the programmatic orchestral suite became a favorite vehicle of Ukrainian symphonists. Notable examples are A. *Shtoharenko's *In Memory of Lesia Ukrainka* (1951), H. *Maiboroda's *King Lear* (1959), and S. *Liudkevych's *Carpathian Voices* (1962), as well as works by M. Kolessa and R. Simovych. Excerpts from ballets, musicals, and film scores in Ukraine were often arranged as suites in order to popularize the music. One of the best-known examples of this practice is B. *Liatoshynksy's orchestral suite *Taras Shevchenko* (1952), derived from the same composer's film score.

**Sujkowski, Antoni,** b 21 May 1867 in Zakroczym, Poland, d 12 December 1941 in Warsaw. Polish geographer. He served as a professor of geography in Warsaw and president of the Polish Geographic Society (1932–41). His works, particularly *Geografia ziem dawnej Polski* (A Geography of the Lands of Ancient Poland, 1918), contain information about Ukraine. Sujkowski also served as a Polish delegate to the Paris Peace Conference.

**Suk, Vojéch,** b 18 September 1879 in Prague, d 8 March 1967 in Brno. Czech anthropologist and ethnographer. After graduating from Zurich University (PH D, 1917), he lectured in anthropology and ethnography at Prague (1922–3) and Brno universities. Many of his works deal with the Ukrainian inhabitants of Transcarpathia – for example, his articles on the anthropology of the Hutsuls (1922, 1923), on cabbage and goiter in Carpathian Ruthenia (1931), on the anthropology of Carpathian Ruthenia (1932), and on Subcarpathian Ruthenians at the beginning of the 19th century (1936).

**Sukachov, Leonyd** [Sukačov] (pseuds: Yurii Vitrenko, Omelko Bliudenko, Leonyd Hadiatsky, El Cho), b 1912 in Poltava, d 1937. Writer and literary scholar. In the 1920s he contributed stories to the children's monthly *Pioneriia*. From 1935 he was a senior associate of the Taras Shevchenko Scientific Research Institute in Kharkiv. He wrote several articles about T. Shevchenko and annotated the 1936 edition of Shevchenko's journal. A victim of the Stalinist terror, he was posthumously rehabilitated in 1955.

**Sukha, Liubov** [Suxa, Ljubov], b 27 July 1910 in Liubelia, Zhovkva county, Galicia, d 16 May 1988 in Lviv. Art scholar. She graduated from Lviv University in 1937 and obtained a candidate's degree in 1956. She is the author of articles on Ukrainian folk and decorative art and the monograph *Khudozhni metalevi vyroby ukraïntsiv Skhidnykh Karpat druhoï polovyny XIX–XX st.* (Metal Handicrafts of Ukrainians of the Eastern Carpathians in the Second Half of the 19th and the 20th Century, 1959).

**Sukhodilske** [Suxodol's'ke]. A city (1989 pop 27,800) under the city council of Krasnodon (V-20, DB III-7) in Luhanske oblast. It originated as a mining settlement around the village of Verkhnoduvanne in the 1950s, and it was promoted to city status in 1972. There are two coal mines and two coal enrichment plants in the city.

**Sukhodolov, Mykola** [Suxodolov], b 4 May 1920 in Nagutskoe, Stavropol gubernia, Kuban. Sculptor. A graduate of the Kiev State Art Institute (1951), he created the monument to M. Shchors in Kiev (1954, with M. Lysenko and V. Borodai) and several monuments to V. Lenin, including those in Zaporizhia (1964, with M. Lysenko), Ovruch (1972), Novomoskovske (1975), and Popasna (1979). He has also sculpted a marble portrait of N. Gogol (1958) and the wood composition *Female Banduryst* (1960).

Oleksii Sukhodolsky  Volodymyr Sukhodolsky

**Sukhodolsky, Oleksii** [Suxodol's'kyj, Oleksij], b 28 March 1863 in Kiev, d 15 April 1936 in Moscow. Stage actor, director, and playwright. He began his theatrical career as a makeup man in the Kiev Russian Drama Theater (1879) and then acted in the Ukrainian troupes of O. Vasylenko, M. Kropyvnytsky, and H. Derkach (1891–4); led a Ukrainian troupe with O. Suslov (1894–8) and his own troupe (1898–1918; in 1911 it performed in Sofia, Bulgaria); and directed in a Ukrainian troupe in Yugoslavia and at the Belgrade Opera Theater (1920–8). He returned to Soviet Ukraine in 1929, where he directed in the Hart Ukrainian touring theater (1930–2), and he acted in the Moscow Ukrainian Theater of the RSFSR (1932–3). He wrote the plays *Khmara* (A Cloud) and *Pomsta, abo Zahublena dolia* (The Revenge, or Lost Fate).

**Sukhodolsky, Volodymyr** [Suxodol's'kyj], b 16 June 1889 in Romen, Poltava gubernia, d 13 November 1962 in Kiev. Writer and playwright. He graduated from the St Petersburg Polytechnical Institute (1917) and worked in Leningrad and then in Ukraine as a hydroelectrical engineer. He began to publish his work in 1930. Published separately were the plays *Ustym Karmaliuk* (1937), *Tarasova iunist'* (Taras's Youth, 1938), *Dal'nia Olena* (Distant Olena, 1947), *Arsenal* (1957), the plays about collectivization *Na poriadku dennomu* (On the Daily Agenda, 1930) and *Step chekaie* (The Steppe Awaits, 1930), and many others. He published a collection of one-act plays for amateur groups, *Dvi viiny* (Two Wars, 1943), and the collected editions *P'iesy* (Plays, 1960, 1980). He also wrote a biography

of M. Zankovetska, *Narodna artystka* (People's Artist, 1961), and adapted N. Gogol's *Sorochinskaia iarmarka* (The Fair at Sorochyntsi, 1933) for the stage.

Heorhii Sukhomel  Vasyl Sukhomlynsky

**Sukhomel, Heorhii** [Suxomel, Heorhij], b 11 September 1888 in Mykolaivka, Berdychiv county, Kiev gubernia, d 18 July 1966 in Kiev. Hydraulics and hydromechanics scientist; full member of the AN URSR (now ANU) from 1951. He studied and taught at the Kiev Polytechnical Institute and served as director of the ANU Institute of Hydrology. He developed a mathematical model for calculating the flow of water with a free surface; specifically, he discovered and proved experimentally the possibility of there being two types of flow in open channels. He worked out practical engineering guidelines for designing hydraulic structures and wrote four major textbooks on hydraulics.

**Sukhomlyn, Kyrylo** [Suxomlyn], b 23 May 1886 in Krasnopillia, Krolevets county, Chernihiv gubernia, d 26 August 1938. Communist party and Soviet government leader. After the Ukrainian-Soviet War he served in Ukraine as head of the Southern Bureau of the Railwaymen's Union (1921–3), member of the Presidium of the CP(B)U Central Control Commission (CCC, 1923–5) and the CC CP(B)U (1925–38), people's commissar of labor (1925–7), CC CP(B)U Politburo candidate (1926–30) and member (1930–7), chairman of the Supreme Council of the National Economy (1927–32), deputy premier of the Council of People's Commissars (1932–3, 1935–8) and chairman of the All-Ukrainian Council of Trade Unions (1932–3), CCC chairman and people's commissar of worker-peasant inspection (1933–4), people's commissar of local industry (1935), and chairman of the State Planning Commission (1935–8). He was elected a number of times to the All-Ukrainian Central Executive Committee and its Presidium. Despite his leading role in the Stalinist industrialization drive in Ukraine, he was arrested and executed during the Yezhov terror.

**Sukhomlynsky, Vasyl** [Sukhomlyns'kyj, Vasyl'], b 28 November 1918 in Vasylivka, Onufriivka raion, now in Kirovohrad oblast, d 2 November 1970 in Pavlysh, Onufriivka raion. Pedagogue. He graduated from the Poltava Pedagogical Institute in 1939. In 1947–70 he was director of the Pavlysh secondary school. In 1957 he became a corresponding member of the RSFSR Academy of Pedagogical

Sciences, and in 1968 a corresponding member of the USSR Academy of Pedagogical Sciences. He wrote books and numerous articles (in both Ukrainian and Russian) devoted to questions of the education of young people, parental involvement in the educational process, and the methodology of literature and language instruction in secondary schools. He is representative of the more humanist current of Soviet pedagogical thought. Although he did not reject the collective, he emphasized the need to foster the individual development of young people. He also opposed the trend toward the vocationalization of secondary education under N. Khrushchev. Five volumes of his selected works were published in 1976–7. His best-known work is *Sertse viddaiu ditiam* (I Give My Heart to Children, 1969).

**Sukhorsky, Andrii** [Suxors'kyj, Andrij], b 21 August 1932 in Vilka, Sianik county, Galicia. Wood carver. He learned his trade from his father, Petro, and M. Orysyk. Since 1948 he has worked at the Lviv Arts and Crafts Complex as a carver of small figures. His works include *Poor Peasant behind the Plow* (1949), *Return from War* (1949), *The Dogs Attacked* (1949), *I Was Turning Fourteen ...* (1951), *Kobzar with Guide* (1964), *Shepherd* (1966), and *Master of the Highland* (1969).

**Sukhoversky, Ihor** [Suxovers'kyj] (Suchoversky), b 27 July 1927 in Chernivtsi. Engineer and executive. In 1992 he was inducted into the Academy of Engineering Sciences of Ukraine. Sukhoversky studied at the UNRRA University in Munich (1945–7), at Leuven (1947–9), and at the Federal Institute of Technology in Zurich as a specialist in mechanical and aeronautical engineering (Eng, M SC, 1951). He emigrated to Canada in 1953 and began working for Alcan Aluminum, with which company he rose to the position of president of Alcan Europe (1975–82) and then president of Alcan International (1982–9) responsible for research and development. A longtime member of the Plast Ukrainian Youth Association and an avid glider pilot, Sukhoversky was one of the first two Ukrainians to climb Mont Blanc (1947; see *Mountaineering).

**Sukhoversky, Tselestyn** [Suxovers'kyj, Celestyn] (Suchowersky, Celestin), b 8 May 1913 in Chernivtsi, Bukovyna. Community and political activist. While studying law and political science at Chernivtsi University (PH D, 1939) he was active in student and sports organizations, such as the Zaporozhe academic society. He joined the nationalist movement and rose in the OUN Leadership to the position of general judge. As an émigré in Germany in 1945, he helped found the *Central Representation of the Ukrainian Emigration in Germany and helped reorganize the State Center of the UNR. After settling in Canada in 1949, he worked as a librarian of Slavic and East European studies (1960–7) and lecturer at the University of Alberta. He also served on the executives of the Ukrainian National Federation, the Ukrainian War Veterans' Association of Canada, and the Ukrainian Canadian Congress and was president of the court of the Ukrainian National Council.

**Sukhovii, Petro** [Suxovij] (Sukhoviienko), b 1645 in Poltava, d ? Cossack leader. He served in Poltava regiment and then became chancellor of the Zaporozhian Sich. In November 1668, at the height of Hetman P. *Doroshenko's power, he proclaimed himself hetman of Right-Bank Ukraine with the support of the Zaporozhian Cossacks.

To win the support of the Crimean Tatars he accepted the suzerainty of the Crimean khan. Sukhovii's intrigues and a Polish offensive in Right-Bank Ukraine forced Doroshenko to abandon Left-Bank Ukraine. At the end of 1668 Sukhovii and the Tatars attacked Doroshenko's domain in Right-Bank Ukraine but were defeated at Olkhivets by Doroshenko's troops and I. Sirko's Zaporozhian Cossacks. In the summer of 1669 Sukhovii, with Tatar reinforcements, attacked Doroshenko again, but Turkey ordered the Crimean khan to withdraw his support of Sukhovii. In June 1669 Sukhovii was deposed, and in July M. Khanenko, who was supported by Poland, was proclaimed hetman. After Doroshenko's victory over Khanenko at Stebliv on 29 October 1669, Sukhovii escaped to the Crimea.

*Sukhovii.* A dry, hot flow of air that occurs when the air temperature rises to 25°C or more with a simultaneous drop of relative humidity to less than 30 percent and a wind of 5 m/sec or more. It can cause the wilting of vegetation in a matter of hours. In the spring, when the annual plant roots are not well developed, temperatures as high as 25–28°C with a relative humidity of 19–22 percent and winds of 7–8 m/sec are sufficient to yellow the leaves of grain in 4 to 10 hours. In the summer faster increases in temperatures (2–4°C per hour), higher temperatures (35–40°C), and lower relative humidity (10–17 percent) produce conditions during which a weak wind (3 m/sec) can yellow the leaves in two hours or less. In Ukraine the *sukhovii* is most hazardous in June, before grain crops have ripened. The *sukhovii* is common in the steppe, with increasing incidence to the east and in Subcaucasia. Those areas have, on average, 15 to 30 days with the *sukhovii*, but in some years it may be present on as many as 50 or 60 days.

Dust storms are sometimes associated with the *sukhovii*. Generated by strong winds in the spring, they can blow away much dry topsoil. Powerful storms, which carried dust all the way into Poland and to the Baltic Sea, occurred in Ukraine in April and May 1892, April 1928, and March and April 1960. Excessive cultivation makes the soil particularly susceptible to such wind erosion. Methods of combating the *sukhovii* include using drought-resistant crop varieties and planting strips of crop perpendicular to the prevailing direction of the wind. Irrigation is particularly effective, in providing the plants with water and adding moisture to the atmosphere (the moisture, through evaporation, helps to cool the atmosphere). The planting of shelterbelts is most common where trees can be grown. Shelterbelts reduce the velocity of winds over the fields up to 600 m and provide for snow accumulation in winter that provides more soil moisture in the spring.

I. Stebelsky

**Sukhyi Torets River** [Suxyj Torec']. A left-bank tributary of the Kazennyi Torets River that flows eastward for 101 km through Kharkiv and Donetske oblasts and drains a basin area of 1,610 km. It is generally level, with a width of 10 m and a valley of 3–4 km. Its waters are used mainly for irrigation and domestic consumption. The major centers along the river include Barvinkove and Sloviianske.

**Sukhyniv, Ivan** [Suxyniv] (Sukhinov), b ca 1794–5 in Krasnokamianka (now Chervona Kamianka), Oleksandriia county, Kherson gubernia, d 13 November 1828 in Nerchinsk county, Siberia. A Decembrist, descended from Cossack officers. He took part in the War of 1812 and the western campaigns of the Russian army in 1813–14, and served in the Chernihiv Regiment (from 1819) and as lieutenant of the Oleksandriia Hussar Regiment (from 1825). He was a member of the Society of United Slavs and the Southern Society of the *Decembrist movement, and one of the organizers and leaders of the Chernihiv regimental uprising in early 1826. He was captured, and his death sentence was commuted to lifelong hard labor. At the Zerentui mines in Siberia he planned a revolt to free Decembrist prisoners, but the scheme was discovered, and he was again sentenced to death. He hanged himself on the eve of his scheduled execution.

**Sukhyno-Khomenko, Volodymyr** [Suxyno-Xomenko], b 28 July 1900 in Kakhivka, Oleshky county, Tavriia gubernia, d 1966. Publicist, historian, and literary critic. In the 1920s and early 1930s he worked at the Ukrainian Institute of Marxism-Leninism, taught at the Communist University and Institute of Journalism in Kharkiv, and contributed to *Litopys revoliutsiï* (LR), *Chervonyi shliakh*, and other periodicals. He was a close associate of M. Skrypnyk in researching Marxist theory in Ukraine. His teacher, M. Yavorsky, emphasized the separate historical development and the unique nature of the revolution in Ukraine. Sukhyno-Khomenko's article supporting Yavorsky's ideas, 'Z pryvodu osoblyvostei proletars'koï revoliutsiï na Ukraïni' (Concerning the Peculiarities of the Proletarian Revolution in Ukraine, LR, 1928, no. 4), was severely criticized by P. Horyn in the article 'Iak ne treba pysaty istoriï' ('How Not to Write History,' LR, 1928, no. 6). Although he recanted and criticized his mentor's work in *Odminy i bankrutstvo ukraïns'koho natsionalizmu: Istorychno-politychni narysy* (The Mutations and Bankruptcy of Ukrainian Nationalism: Historical and Political Overviews, 1929), Sukhyno-Khomenko was arrested and imprisoned in 1933. After the Second World War he was rehabilitated.

Andrew Suknaski

**Suknaski, Andrew,** b 30 July 1942 near Wood Mountain, Saskatchewan. Poet. The son of Ukrainian-Polish immigrants, Suknaski received a diploma in fine arts from the Kootenay School of Arts (1967). In 1978 he was writer-in-residence at St John's College, University of Manitoba. Among his poetry collections are *Wood Mountain Poems*

(1972) and *In the Name of Narid* (1981). His work has also appeared in the anthologies *Canadian Literature in the 70s* (1980) and *The Oxford Book of Canadian Verse in English* (1972).

**Sukovkin, Mikhail,** b and d ? Civic and political leader. Prior to 1917 he was president of the Kiev gubernia zemstvo, and for several months after the February Revolution he was the Russian Provisional Government's commissioner of Kiev gubernia. He main-tained friendly relations with Ukrainian political circles, and the Hetman government appointed him head of the Ukrainian mission to Turkey. He proceeded to Russify the mission. After being dismissed by the Directory of the UNR at the beginning of 1919, he made every effort to discredit the Ukrainian government in the eyes of foreign powers.

**Sula region** (Posullia). A historical-geographic region above the Sula River that once formed part of the *Pereiaslav principality. The towns of the Sula's upper reaches were fortified, and the area around them colonized, by Volodymyr the Great as a first line of defense against nomadic onslaughts. Those efforts were continued by Yaroslav the Wise, albeit with mixed success. By the end of the 11th century the region had been devastated by Cuman attacks. It was a century after the nomads had been routed by a combined force of Kievan princes organized by Volodymyr Monomakh in the early 12th century before the Sula region could again be settled. The colonization effort was wiped out by the Mongol invasion in the mid-13th century, and the region was revived again only in the 16th and 17th centuries.

**Sula River.** A left-bank tributary of the Dnieper River that flows for 310 km through Sumy and Poltava oblasts and drains a basin area of 18,100 sq km. The river is 10–75 m in width, and its valley is 1.5 to 8 km wide (15 km at its widest point). It originates on the southwestern slope of the Central Upland and empties into the Kremenchuk Reservoir. It freezes over from December to late March. The river is used for water supply, irrigation, and fishing as well as navigation (along its lower course). The cities of Romen and Lubni are situated on it.

**Süleyman I Kanuni** (Suleiman the Magnificent), b 27 April 1495 (other sources cite November 1494), d 6 September 1566 near Szigetvár, Hungary. Sultan of the Ottoman Empire (1520–66). He ruled during the apogee of the Ottoman Empire, marked by military campaigns and territorial aggrandizement (including forays into Persia and central and eastern Europe), as well as significant cultural achievements (notably in the field of law, for which he was named Kanuni, meaning Lawgiver). He took as his wife a Ukrainian captive, *Roksoliana, who came to have a considerable influence in the affairs of state. Their eldest son, Selim, succeeded Suleyman, who died during a campaign in Hungary.

**Sulfur.** A nonmetallic, highly reactive chemical element. It occurs naturally in volcanic and sedimentary deposits, in ores such as pyrite, galena, and cinnabar, and in petroleum, coal, and natural gas. Sulfur has many commercial and industrial uses, in the manufacture of gunpowder, fertilizers, insecticides, matches, paper pulp, fungicides, and sulfuric acid, and in the vulcanization of rubber.

In Ukraine large sulfur deposits were discovered in 1887 on the Kerch Peninsula. Mining began in 1928, and in the 1930s the average annual production was 600–700 t. By 1941 the reserves were exhausted. The largest concentration of sulfur in the former USSR, and one of the largest in the world, is found in the *Subcarpathian Sulfur Basin. The sulfur is processed by the *Rozdol Sirka Manufacturing Consortium and the Yavoriv Mining and Chemical Complex in Shklo. Ukraine's production of sulfur supplies its own needs, and some 70 percent of the mined sulfur was exported to other parts of the USSR (especially the RSFSR and the Baltic republics) and to Eastern and Central Europe. (See also *Chemical industry.)

**Sulfuric acid industry.** See Chemical industry.

**Suliatytsky, Pavlo** [Suljatyc'kyj], b 1884 in Velyki Sorochyntsi, Myrhorod county, Poltava gubernia, d 1932 in Warsaw. Lawyer and civic and political leader. A member of the Revolutionary Ukrainian party in his youth, he served as a civil court judge in Mariiupil (1914–16) and then in Katerynodar. After the February Revolution he played an important role in the political developments in the Kuban and served as minister of justice of the Kuban People's Republic. He later emigrated to Prague and then Warsaw. He wrote *Narysy z istoriï revoliutsiï na Kubani* (Sketches from the History of the Revolution in the Kuban, 1926), a survey book of the Kuban in Polish (1930), and articles for *Kubans'kyi krai*.

Bishop Stephen Sulyk          Hetman Ivan Sulyma

**Sulyk, Stephen,** b 2 October 1924 in Balnytsia, Lisko county, Galicia. Ukrainian Catholic bishop. His studies in Sambir were interrupted by the Second World War, and he moved to the United States in 1948 and completed his training at St Josephat's Seminary and the Catholic University in Washington. He was ordained in 1952, served as a parish priest in a variety of locations, including Perth Amboy, New Jersey (1962–81), and held a number of church administrative offices before being consecrated metropolitan of Philadelphia in 1981.

**Sulyma.** A line of Cossack starshyna in Left-Bank Ukraine. The family name was established by Mykhailo, who lived in the 16th century. His son was Hetman Ivan *Sulyma (d 1635). The hetman's sons included Stepan (d

1659), a captain of Boryspil company, and Fedir (d 1691), a colonel of Pereiaslav regiment. Fedir's son, Ivan (d 1721), was a captain of Voronkiv company (1687) and general flag-bearer under I. Mazepa and I. Skoropadsky (1708–21). Ivan's son, Semen (d 27 May 1766), was colonel of Pereiaslav regiment (1739–66). Semen's sons included Yakym (1737–1818), a general judge in Chernihiv (1797–1818), and Khrystofor (d 18 May 1813 in the Transfiguration Monastery in Kharkiv), the bishop of Teodosiia and Mariiupil (1791–9) and then of Kharkiv (1799–1813). Their nephew, Mykola (b 12 December 1777, d 21 October 1840), was colonel of the Izmail Regiment (1803), a major general (1812–16), governor-general of eastern, then western, Siberia (1834–6), and a member of the Military Council (1836). The Russian revolutionary and anarchist theoretician P. Kropotkin (1842–1921) was related to the family through the female line. The family archive was published in part by O. Lazarevsky in *Sulimovskii arkhiv: Famil'nye bumagi Sulim, Skorup, i Voitsekhovichei XVII–XVIII vv.* (The Sulyma Archive: The Family Papers of the Sulymas, Skorupas, and Voichekhovyches in the 17th–18th centuries, 1884).

A. Zhukovsky

**Sulyma, Ivan,** b ? in Rohoshchi, Chernihiv region, d 12 December 1635 in Warsaw. Hetman of the Zaporozhian Cossack host in 1628–9 and 1630–5. A member of the petty gentry, he served as an estate manager for the Polish magnate S. Żółkiewski and his heirs, the Daniłowicz family, in the Pereiaslav region. For that service the villages of Sulymivka, Kuchakiv, and Lebedyn were placed under his control in 1620. He later left for the Zaporozhian Sich, where he was first elected hetman in 1628. He took part in several campaigns against the Crimea and Turkey and received a golden portrait medal from Pope Paul V in recognition of his efforts. While returning with an army of nonregistered Cossacks from a campaign against Turkey in August 1635, he laid waste the Polish fortress of Kodak, which had recently been built on the Dnieper River to contain the Cossacks, and killed all of its German mercenaries and its commander. A group of registered Cossacks, wishing to curry favor with Commonwealth officials, subsequently handed over Sulyma, along with other members of the Zaporozhian leadership, to the Poles. The hetman was executed in Warsaw.

**Sulyma, Mykola,** b 27 August 1892 in Huliai-Pole, Zmiiv county, Kharkiv gubernia, d ? Linguist. A professor at the Kharkiv Institute of People's Education in the 1920s and early 1930s, he played a role in the establishment of Standard Ukrainian syntactic norms. He wrote a survey history of Ukrainian literature (1923), a brochure (1927) and lectures (1928) on the history of the Ukrainian language, a book on Ukrainian phrases (1928), and articles on Ukrainian syntax, word formation, phraseology, and vocabulary and on the language of T. Shevchenko, Lesia Ukrainka, A. Teslenko, and M. Khvylovy. Accused in 1934 of propagating 'Ukrainian bourgeois nationalism in syntax,' he was arrested and either shot or sent to a concentration camp, where he perished.

**Sulyma, Tetiana** (Bichikhina), b ca 1863 in Novopavlivka, Pavlohrad county, Katerynoslav gubernia, d ? Writer and actor. While studying in Kharkiv she began writing in Russian (her first story appeared in *Iuzhnyi krai* in 1884) but switched to Ukrainian under the influence of her mentors, Ya. Shchoholiv, Kh. Alchevska, and A. Yefymenko. Sulyma's play *Diachykha* (The Precentor's Wife) was first staged in Katerynoslav in 1888; it proved popular and was also performed in Kharkiv, Poltava, towns and villages in Katerynoslav, Poltava, and Chernihiv gubernias, New York City, and several Russian towns. After the Revolution of 1905 her stories appeared in *Ridnyi krai*, *Svitova zirnytsia*, and *Selo*. Published separately were *Diachykha* (1908), the ethnographic comedy *Na imenynakh* (At the Name Day Celebration, 1909), and a collection of six stories, *Narodni opovidannia* (Folk Tales, 1911).

**Sulymenko, Petro,** b 29 July 1914 in Katerynodar (now Krasnodar), Kuban. Painter. In 1947 he graduated from the Kiev State Art Institute, where he studied under O. Shovkunenko. Many of his paintings deal with the Second World War and the Black Sea. They include *Flag of Victory* (1949), *Black Sea* (1953), *Sevastopil Is Ours!* (1960), *Sailors of October* (1963), *Immortality* (1975), the diptych *War and Peace* (1981), *Dockers at Rest: Rangoon,* and *Pearl Divers.*

**SUM.** See Ukrainian Youth Association.

**Sumac** (*Rhus*; Ukrainian: *sumakh*). Shrubs and small trees of the cashew family Anacardiaceae, native to subtropical and warm temperature regions. In Ukraine one species grows in the wild, on rocky slopes in the Crimea and Caucasia – tanning sumac (*R. coriaria*). It is a valuable plant in that it yields tanning and medicinal reagents as well as some dyes. Staghorn sumac (*R. typhina*; Ukrainian: *otstove derevo*), smoke tree (*R. cotinus*; Ukrainian: *skumpiia, raiderevo*), and *R. javanica* are cultivated as ornamental trees.

**SUMK.** See Canadian Ukrainian Youth Association.

**Sumny, Semen** [Sumnyj], b 2 August 1897 in Letychiv, Podilia gubernia, d 9 March 1960. Writer. He graduated from the Kherson Institute of People's Education (1924). He published collections of prose, short stories, and novelettes, such as *Shliakhom novitnim* (Path of the New Age, 1927), *Vohni Donbasu* (Donbas Fires, 1929), *Pershyi ispyt* (The First Examination, 1931), *Peremozhena zemlia* (The Conquered Earth, 1931), *Nad Dniprom* (By the Dnieper, 1938), *Molodist' Teslenka* (The Youth of Teslenko, 1940), and *V Karpatakh* (In the Carpathians, 1945).

**Sumtsov, Mykola** [Sumcov], b 18 April 1854 in St Petersburg, d 12 September 1922 in Kharkiv. Folklorist, ethnographer, literary scholar, and civic figure; full member of the Shevchenko Scientific Society from 1908 and the All-Ukrainian Academy of Sciences from 1919, and corresponding member of the Russian Academy of Sciences from 1905. After graduating from Kharkiv University (1875) he studied in Germany and from 1878 lectured on Russian literature at Kharkiv University. For many years he was secretary (1880–96) and president (1897–1919) of the *Kharkiv Historical-Philological Society and director of the university's ethnography museum (1904–18).

Sumtsov's major area of interest was ethnography, particularly folklore. An adherent of the mythological school, he moved, gradually at first, toward a comparative method which drew heavily upon philology. His major ethnographic works include *Khleb v obriadakh i pesniakh* (Bread in [Folk] Rituals and Songs, 1885); articles in *Kiev-*

Mykola Sumtsov

*skaia starina* on carols (1886), cultural experiences (1889–90), Easter eggs (1891), and contemporary 'Little Russian' ethnography (1892, 1896); *Razyskaniia v oblasti anekdoticheskoi literatury* (Research in the Field of Anecdotal Literature, 1898); *Ocherki narodnogo byta* (Sketches of Folk Life, 1902); and *Slobozhane: Istorychno-etnohrafichna rozvidka* (The Slobidska Ukrainians: A Historico-Ethnographic Study, 1918).

He regarded his articles on I. Vyshensky, L. Baranovych, I. Galiatovsky, and I. Gizel (in *Kievskaia starina*, 1884–5) as contributions to a systematic history of Ukrainian literature. Later he wrote articles on T. Shevchenko (1898, 1902, 1906, 1913, 1918), I. Kotliarevsky (1897, 1905), P. Kulish (1919), M. Starytsky (1908), I. Manzhura (1893), I. Franko (1906), B. Hrinchenko (1906), O. Oles (1906, 1909), and O. Potebnia (1887, 1892, 1922). Sumtsov is known for popularizing Ukrainian culture through works such as his anthology of Ukrainian literature (1922). Following the 1905 Revolution he was the first professor at Kharkiv University to lecture in Ukrainian. He was a founder of the Kharkiv Public Library and a supporter of literature for the people.

P. Odarchenko

A view of Sumy, with the Transfiguration Cathedral (1788) in the center

**Sumy.** III-15. A city (1990 pop 296,000) at the confluence of the Psol and the Sumka rivers and an oblast center. It was founded in 1652 by peasants and Cossacks from Bila Tserkva regiment in Right-Bank Ukraine led by H. Kondratiev. The new settlement was soon fortified by the Muscovite voivode K. Arsenev (1656–8) to protect the territory from the Tatars. Located on the Putyvl–Moscow trade route, the town prospered. In 1660–1732 its population grew from 2,700 to 7,700. It was the center of Sumy regiment (1658–1765) and the seat of administration for all the regiments of Slobidska Ukraine (1732–43). Then it became the center of Sumy province of Slobidska Ukraine gubernia (1765–80) and a county center in Kharkiv vicegerency (1780–96), Slobidska Ukraine gubernia (1796–1835), and Kharkiv gubernia (1835–1923). By the mid-19th century Sumy was a well-established industrial and trading town: it had a glass factory (est 1710), three tanneries, a coach works, four brick factories, four candle works, a soap factory, and four major fairs a year. In 1732 it had five schools. A state-funded school opened in 1790 was reorganized as a county school in 1806 and provided with a library in 1834. The first theater was established in 1806. In the second half of the 19th century the town's industrial base grew rapidly. In 1869 a sugar refinery was built, and Sumy became a major center of the sugar industry. The construction of the Vorozhba–Merefa railway line stimulated the development of the machine-building and metalworking industries. In 1891 a machine-building plant and in 1896 a sugar machinery plant were built. The trade in food products and metal goods expanded greatly. The town's population increased from 10,300 in 1850 to 27,600 in 1897 and 50,400 in 1913.

In the Soviet period Sumy was an okruha center (1923–30), a raion center of Kharkiv oblast, and then an oblast center (from 1939). In 1926 its population was only 44,000 (80.7 percent of it Ukrainian, 11.8 percent Russian, and 5.5 percent Jewish). By 1939 the population had reached 63,900. In the 1930s the existing plants were expanded, and an electric machinery plant was set up. A pedagogical institute and several tekhnikums were opened. Rapid industrial expansion began in the 1950s: a furniture factory, a superphosphate plant, two reinforced-concrete plants, and an electron microscope plant were brought into operation. The population had reached 98,000 by 1959 and 159,000 by 1970. Today Sumy is one of the chief industrial and cultural centers in northern Ukraine. Its main industries are machine building (to which belong the Machine-Building Manufacturing Consortium and the Electron Microscope Plant), the chemical industry (the Khimprom Manufacturing Consortium and a resins plant), the food industry (a distillery, a sugar refinery, and meat- and fish-processing plants), light industry (footwear, woolen-cloth, and clothing factories), and the construction-materials industry. The city has 12 vocational schools and 9 specialized high schools, a pedagogical institute, a branch of the Kharkiv Polytechnical Institute, and a branch of the Kharkiv Agricultural Institute. It is the home of two research and design institutes, one specializing in compression machinery and the other in pumps for nuclear and thermal power stations. Its cultural facilities include an art museum, a museum of decorative and applied art, a regional museum, a theater of drama and musical comedy, and a young spectator's theater. The main architectural monuments are the guildhall (17th century), the Church of the Resurrection (1702), the Cathedral of the Transfiguration (1776–88), and St Elijah's Church (1836–51).

V. Kubijovyč

**Sumy Art Museum** (Sumskyi khudozhnii muzei). A museum established in 1920 in Sumy on the basis of nationalized private art collections. The first director was N.

*Onatsky. Until 1939 it was called the Sumy Art and History Museum. The museum was moved to a new building in 1978. It contains over 11,000 objects, divided among its departments of Ukrainian and Russian prerevolutionary art, Western European art, Soviet art, and, in the former Church of the Resurrection, decorative and applied art. Its collection contains works by painters such as V. Borovykovsky, I. Aivazovsky, T. Shevchenko, I. Sokolov, D. Bezperchy, M. Pymonenko, P. Levchenko, S. Vasylkivsky, N. Onatsky, S. Svitoslavsky, I. Repin, A. Kuindzhi, F. Krychevsky, M. Samokysh, I. Trush, K. Trokhymenko, O. Shovkunenko, O. Bohomazov, P. Volokydin, M. Burachek, I. Hrabar, H. Svitlytsky, T. Yablonska, P. Sulymenko, H. Melikhov, M. Manizer, and M. Hlushchenko. The collection of decorative and applied art includes sets of Mezhyhiria porcelain and wares from A. Myklashevsky's factory in Volokytyna. A branch of the museum is located in Lebedyn. The I. Kavaleridze Sculpture Gallery was established recently as a department of the museum. Albums of works in the museum were published in Kiev in 1981 and 1988.

**Sumy Electron Microscope Plant** (Sumskyi zavod elektronnykh mikroskopiv). A factory of the equipment-building industry, established in Sumy in 1959. It produces a wide range of microscopes used in scientific research and in automated manufacturing, including microscope controls for welders and lathes. The plant also produces mass spectrometers.

**Sumy Khimprom Manufacturing Consortium** (Sumske vyrobnyche obiednannia Khimprom). A chemical enterprise located in Sumy. It was founded in 1975 on the basis of a chemical plant that had been established in 1954 to produce superphosphates. It now produces over 40 items, including sulfuric acid, phosphate fertilizers, feed supplements, paints, and pigments. In 1971 the plant employed over 1,500 workers.

**Sumy Machine-Building Manufacturing Consortium** (Sumske mashynobudivne vyrobnyche obiednannia). A chemical machine-building enterprise founded in 1976 in Sumy. It is based on a plant originally built in 1896 to produce equipment and machinery for the sugar-beet, distilling, mining, railroad, and other industries. In 1926 the factory was rebuilt, and in 1930 it became the first factory in the USSR to produce equipment for the chemical industry. Previously that kind of equipment had been imported. In 1933 it built the first high-pressure compressor. After the Second World War it became one of the largest chemical machine-building plants in the USSR. Now it builds processing lines for the manufacture of chemical fertilizers, machines for extracting ethylene and propylene from petroleum and coal gas and helium from natural gas, centrifuges, various pumps and compressors, and other machines and equipment. In the 1970s the factory employed over 3,500 workers.

**Sumy oblast.** An administrative territory (1989 pop 1,433,000) in northeastern Ukraine, formed on 10 January 1939. It covers an area of 23,800 sq km and is divided into 18 raions, 15 cities, 355 rural councils, and 21 towns (smt). The capital is *Sumy.

**Physical geography.** Most of the oblast lies in the Dnieper Lowland; only the northern part is in eastern

Polisia. A spur of the Central Upland runs along its eastern and northeastern boundaries. The landscape is a rolling plain, dissected by valleys, ravines, and gorges. The southern part of the oblast lies in the forest-steppe zone and is covered by chernozems with a low humus and a moderate loam content. The forested northern part has soddy podzolized soils characteristic of Polisia. The oblast's climate is temperate continental: the average January temperature in the north is –8°C and in the south – 7.3°C, and the average July temperature is 18.6°C and 20°C, respectively. The growing season is 188 to 196 days. In the north the annual precipitation is 530–600 mm, and in the south, 460–520 mm. The main rivers include the Desna, the Seim, the Psol, and the Vorskla. The natural steppe vegetation has been displaced almost everywhere by cultivated crops. Forests (mainly pine, birch, and oak in the north and linden, maple, ash, and oak in the central and southern reaches) constitute 17 percent of the oblast's territory. The oblast supports about 150 nature reserves of different kinds and sizes, including the Mykhailivka Virgin Soil Preserve and the Trostianets Dendrological Park. It is rich in natural resources, such as oil, gas, peat, and coal.

**History.** The territory of the present-day oblast was settled as early as the Paleolithic period. In the 9th to 11th centuries it belonged to Kievan Rus', and in the 11th to 13th centuries, to Chernihiv and Siversk principalities. It was under Tatar control until the mid-14th century, when the Grand Duchy of Lithuania expanded into the region. In the 16th century the southern and western parts of the oblast came under Polish control, and the northern parts (notably Putyvl) fell under Russian control. After B. Khmelnytsky's uprising the northern and western reaches of the Sumy region became part of the Hetman state (Nizhen and Lubni regiments), and the southern and eastern areas became part of Slobidska Ukraine (Sumy and Okhtyrka regiments). In 1802 the region was divided among Chernihiv, Poltava, and Slobidska Ukraine (from 1835 Kharkiv) gubernias. When the gubernias were abolished in 1925, the territory of the present-day oblast was divided among Sumy, Kharkiv, and Romen okruhas.

**Population.** According to the 1989 census, Ukrainians account for 85.5 percent of the oblast's population, and Russians, for 13.3 percent. A decade earlier the respective figures were 87.2 and 11.7 percent. About 62 percent of the population is urban. The population density in the central and southeastern areas is higher than in the swampy north. The largest cities are Sumy, *Konotip, *Shostka, *Romen, and *Okhtyrka.

**Industry.** The oblast's main industries are food processing (31.2 percent in 1989), machine building and metalworking (25 percent), petroleum and chemicals manufacturing (22.4 percent), and light industry (9 percent). The largest branches of the food industry are sugar refining (in Sumy, Druzhba, Chupakhivka, Mezenivka), meat packing (Sumy, Shostka, Okhtyrka, Vorozhba, Lebedyn, Hlukhiv), and flour milling (Sumy, Konotip, Shostka, and Okhtyrka). The chief plants of the machine-building and metalworking industries are in Sumy (equipment for the chemical industry, electron microscopes, pumps, heavy compressors), Konotip (fittings and automated equipment for the mining industry, pistons, and locomotive repair), Romen (printing machinery), Hlukhiv (electrical machinery), and Svesa (pumps). The largest chemical enterprises are in Shostka (film and mag-

netic tape, chemical reagents) and Sumy (fertilizers, sulfuric acid, petrochemicals). Enterprises of light industry include textile factories in Sumy and Hlukhiv, clothing factories in Sumy, Okhtyrka, Lebedyn, Romen, and Konotip, and footwear plants in Sumy, Okhtyrka, and Romen. The chief centers of the lumber and woodworking industries are Sumy, Shostka, Trostianets, Romen, and Okhtyrka. The building-materials industry is based on local deposits of kaolin, chalk, and clay.

**Agriculture.** The value of the oblast's agricultural output in 1990 was estimated at 1,908 million rubles (in 1983 prices, or 3.9 percent of that of Ukraine). In 1985, 320 collective farms and 71 state farms controlled 1,734,000 ha of land. Of that area 81.6 percent was cultivated, 9.4 percent was hayfield, and 8 percent was pasture. A total of 25,400 ha were irrigated, and 88,700 ha were drained. The main crops were grains (winter wheat, barley, rye, buckwheat), industrial crops (sugar beets and sunflowers), potatoes, hemp, flax, vegetables, and feed. Animal husbandry consists largely of dairy- and beef-cattle raising and pig farming. In 1990 the oblast produced 160,000 t of meat.

**Transportation.** In 1989 there were 823 km of railroads in the oblast. The main lines are Kiev–Moscow, Kiev–Kharkiv, Minsk–Kharkiv, Riga–Kharkiv, and Vorozhba–Kursk and the major junctions are Konotip, Vorozhba, and Khutir Mykhailivskyi. There were 6,800 km of highway, 4,900 of which were paved. The main highways crossing the oblast are Kiev–Orel–Moscow, Kiev–Sumy–Kursk, and Sumy–Kharkiv. There is an airport in Sumy. The Urengoi–Uzhhorod gas pipeline runs through the oblast.

BIBLIOGRAPHY
*Znakom'tes': Sumshchyna* (Kharkiv 1966)
*Istoriia mist i sil URSR: Sums'ka oblast'* (Kiev 1973; Russian edn 1980)

**Sumy Pedagogical Institute** (Sumskyi pedahohichnyi instytut im. A. Makarenka). An institution of higher learning, under the jurisdiction of the Ministry of Education. Founded in 1924 as an institution offering higher pedagogical courses, it became a *pedagogical tekhnikum in 1925 with the rights of a higher pedagogical institution. In 1930 it was transformed into one of the *institutes of social education, and in 1933 it became a pedagogical institute. It was named after A. Makarenko in 1955. The institute has seven faculties: philology, physics-mathematics, musical education, English and German language, history, natural sciences, and physical education. The student enrollment in 1988–9 was over 7,000. The institute has a research library of over 250,000 volumes.

**Sumy regiment.** An administrative territory and military formation in Slobidska Ukraine, settled by peasants and Cossacks from Right-Bank Ukraine. It was formed by the Russian authorities in 1658 to protect Russia's southern flank from attacks by Crimean and Nogay Tatars. By 1732 the regiment had a population of 86,000, including 3,700 elect Cossacks and 13,900 Cossack helpers, and was divided into 20 companies. The regiment took part in the Chyhyryn (1677, 1678), Crimea (1687, 1689), and Azov (1695–6) campaigns against the Tatars, the Northern War, and the Seven Years' War. It was abolished in 1765, and its territory was incorporated into Slobidska Ukraine gubernia.

The Sumy Regional Studies Museum

The Women's Sunday School in Kharkiv. The teacher is Khrystyna Alchevska.

**Sumy Regional Studies Museum** (Sumskyi kraieznavchyi muzei). A museum founded in 1920 as the Sumy Art and History Museum. In 1939 it and the *Sumy Art Museum became independent institutions. In 1971 the museum's three exhibit sections – natural science (geology, flora, fauna), pre-Soviet history (including archeology, ethnography, and numismatics), and Soviet society – contained over 10,000 artifacts from the Sumy region, and its library contained over 12,000 volumes. The Okhtyrka and Putyvl regional museums, the Anton Chekhov Building and Memorial Museum in Sumy, and the Museum of Partisan Glory in the Spadshchanskyi Forest are branches of the museum. A guide to the museum was published in 1976.

**Sumy Theater of Drama and Musical Comedy** (Sumskyi teatr dramy i muzychnoi komedii). A theater established in Lubni in 1933 on the basis of the Kharkiv Workers' and Collective-Farm Theater. In 1939 it was moved to Sumy and renamed the Sumy Ukrainian Music and Drama Theater; it acquired its present name in 1980. During the war it worked in Central Asia, and in 1944 it returned to Sumy. Its repertoire has included Ukrainian and world classics by dramatists such as M. Kropyvnytsky, M. Starytsky, O. Korniichuk, Euripides, and W. Shakespeare. In 1984 its artistic director was I. Ravytsky.

**Sunday schools** (*nedilni shkoly*). Private educational institutions for minors and adults who, because of work, could not attend regular schools. In Ukraine the first Sunday school opened in Poltava in 1858, and another in Kiev in October 1859. Eventually there were 5 in each of Kiev, Poltava, and Odessa, and schools in Kharkiv, Chernihiv, Nizhen, Yelysavethrad (Kirovohrad), and some larger villages; in 1859–60 there were 68 altogether. Eventually some 111 Sunday schools operated in Ukraine. Members of the intelligentsia acted as instructors in the schools. The language of instruction was Ukrainian, a measure agreed to in Kiev by the warden of the Kiev school district, N. Pirogov, although in some schools, because of the lack of proper instructional materials, both Ukrainian and Russian were used. Teaching material included T. Shevchenko's primer *Bukvar' iuzhnorusskii* (South Russian [Ukrainian] Primer, 1861) and P. Kulish's *Hramatka* (Grammar, 1857). Several well-known personalities took an active part in the school movement – Khrystyna *Alchevska, V. *Antonovych, M. *Drahomanov, O. *Konysky, V. *Loboda, Ye. *Myloradovych, D. *Pylchykov, A. *Svydnytsky, and P. *Chubynsky, all of whom taught in the schools. M. Kostomarov and P. Pavlov were also active participants, although they did not teach. Classes lasted from one to three hours every Sunday, and the instructors usually divided their time between those with some education and those without. The subjects of study, according to the 1861 laws, were religion, reading and writing, arithmetic, and drawing. In 1862 the tsarist authorities closed the schools. They were reopened in 1864, but with heavy restrictions. Sunday school activists in Poltava experienced repression and even exile over their participation in the schools. Among the exiled were Konysky, Loboda, V. Shevych, and O. Stronin. Sunday schools were founded for a second time in the 1870s, but these schools were supported by the local *zemstvos and by the church, which in 1891 gained complete control over all Sunday schools.

O. Skrypnyk

**Sundew** (Ukrainian: *rosychka, rosianka*). Insectivorous, flowering plants of the family Droseraceae, usually of the genus *Drosera*. Their leaves are covered with sticky glandular hairs that entrap insects and decompose them. Of the 100 species of sundew, 3 grow in Ukraine, mostly in boggy soil – *D. rotundifolia, D. anglica,* and *D. intermedia*. Sundew extracts have been used in folk medicine to treat whooping cough, chronic bronchitis, asthma, and arteriosclerosis. The Venus's-flytrap is the most famous sundew.

**Sunflower** (*Helianthus annuus*; Ukrainian: *soniashnyk*). A plant of the family Asteraceae, native to the Americas, and brought to Europe by the Spaniards in the early 17th century. By the mid-18th century it had been introduced in Ukraine. Today sunflower represents the principal *oil plant in the Ukrainian economy and Ukrainian agriculture. Of arable land designated for *industrial crops, 42 percent is devoted to sunflower (the second industrial crop after sugar beets); this land makes up 93 percent of the land surface devoted to the *vegetable-oil industry.

Ukraine produces approx 37 percent of the former USSR's and 19 percent of the world's sunflower. The average yield amounts to 1.2 to 1.5 t of seeds per ha and 80 to 100 t of greens. Sunflower seeds yield 47 to 67 percent oil. In addition to oil and seeds for direct food consumption (the seeds are the most popular chewing snack food in Ukraine), sunflower yields oil cakes and seed meal (high in protein) and so provides valuable fodder for farm animals. Potash is obtained from the ashes of burned greens.

There are four principal varieties of sunflower in Ukraine: fine-seed sunflower for oil production, large-seed sunflower for direct consumption, giant-fodder sunflower, and American long-seed sunflower. They are planted in crop rotation after cereal, corn, or other plants which do not use water from deep soil layers, since the sunflower's root system extends 2–3 m deep into the ground. The following brands are favored: VNYY MK 1646, 6540, and 8931; Armavir 3497; Zelenka 368; Peredovyk; and Maiak. In addition to the commercial variety, the ornamental sunflower, a good nectar bearer, is planted widely. The ubiquitous presence of the sunflower in the villages and countryside of Ukraine has made it an unofficial national symbol. It appears as such (woodcut by J. Hnizdovsky) on the cover of the *Encyclopedia of Ukraine*.

BIBLIOGRAPHY
Hordiienko, H. *Istoriia kul'turnykh roslyn* (Munich 1970)
I. Masnyk

**Supii River** [Supij]. A left-bank tributary of the Dnieper River that flows for 144 km through Chernihiv, Kiev, and Cherkasy oblasts before emptying into the Kremenchuk Reservoir. It drains a basin area of 2,160 sq km. It is 2–8 m wide in its upper reaches (up to 20 m in its lower course) and has a valley 1.3–3 km wide. Fed mainly by meltwaters, the river is used for industry, water supply, and irrigation. It is also fished, and forms a key part of the Supii drainage system. The city of Yahotyn is situated on it.

**Suprasl Chronicle** (Supraslskyi litopys). A collection of texts assembled in the late 15th or early 16th century in Belarus, found in the Suprasl monastery near Białystok (now in Poland). It describes events from the 9th century to 1515. It includes the Short Novgorod Chronicle (which deals with events from ancient times to 1382) and the Short Kievan Chronicle (which covers the period 862–1515). The first section is a compilation of histories of Rus' before 1500, and the second, written by an unknown contemporary author, provides a detailed account of events in 1480–1512 (including the Tatar destruction of Kiev in 1482, Tatar attacks on Volhynia in 1491 and 1496, and Mykhailo Olelkovych's plot against Lithuania in 1481), a lengthy description of the Battle of Orsha (1514), and a panegyric to Prince K. Ostrozky, who defeated the great prince of Muscovy, Vasili III, in that battle. It concludes with a statement dated 1543. The chronicle was first published by M. Obolensky as *Suprasl'skaia rukopis' soderzhashchaia Novgorodskuiu i Kievskuiu sokrashchenye letopisi*

(The Suprasl Manuscript Containing the Novgorod and Kievan Abreviated Chronicles, 1836).

**Suprasl Lexicon.** A 4,000-word Church Slavonic–Polish dictionary titled *Leksykon syrech slovesnyk slavenskii* (Lexicon or Slavonic Glossary) that was printed in 1722 at the Basilian monastery in Suprasl near Białystok, Poland. It was intended for use by the clergy. Its Church Slavonic content was based almost entirely on P. *Berynda's lexicon. Its Serbian-Bulgarian orthography was modernized, however, stresses were changed, and Volhynian-Polisian pronunciation was introduced (eg, the confusion of *rĕ/ry/ri/rы, rja/ra, ы* with *y/i*, and *ĕ* with *y*). As a result, erroneous Polish versions of Berynda's Ukrainian definitions of words occurred. The lexicon was reprinted with few changes as an appendix in a book on moral theology in Pochaiv in 1751 and 1756, and separately in 1804. It was used by Y. *Levytsky in the compilation of his Slavonic-Polish dictionary (1813).

**Suprematism.** The first modern purely geometric and nonfigurative style of painting, launched by K. *Malevich in 1915. At first it was a one-man style: Malevich attracted new proponents only in 1919, from among his students at the Vitsebsk Institute of Fine and Applied Art in Belarus. They included I. Chasnik, E. Lissitsky, and N. Suetin. Suprematism began waning in the mid-1920s as Malevich and his disciples shifted to *constructivism. In the late 1920s, under state pressure, Malevich and other painters abandoned suprematism altogether and returned to a figurative style. In its purest form suprematism had little direct influence on Ukrainian avant-garde art. Applied suprematist design and topographic ideas, however, influenced the development of the constructivist styles of artists such as V. Yermilov.

**Supreme Attestation Commission** (Vyshcha atestatsiina komisiia). An all-Union organ of the Council of Ministers of the USSR which conferred all advanced education degrees and academic appointments in all branches of scholarship. Established in 1932, it began its functions in 1934 as a unit of the USSR Ministry of Higher and Secondary Special Education, and in 1975 was transferred directly to the Council of Ministers. The commission gave the Moscow center control over higher education in Ukraine and other republics. It granted permission to higher educational establishments and research institutes to engage in advanced training and to conduct public defense of dissertations for an advanced degree. It reviewed the decisions of these establishments as to the awarding of candidate's degrees and itself decided the awarding of doctoral degrees as well as appointments to advanced academic rank. It designated the fields in which each institution could conduct advanced degree training and accept dissertations. It could also revoke an advanced degree or advanced rank certification. In addition the commission was a central office where personnel files on all recipients of advanced degrees and all advanced academic teaching and research personnel were kept and processed for appointment, transfer, or reappointment purposes. In Ukraine the commission was seen as a major agency of censorship, political control over higher education, and *Russification. (At its insistence, for example, doctoral dissertations had to be written in Russian.) With the assertion of the sovereignty of non-Russian republics in recent years, the commission's authority has been challenged. The Baltic republics, for example, no longer recognize the commission's jurisdiction over higher education. The *Popular Movement of Ukraine advanced a similar demand in its program adopted in 1989. In February 1992 the Ukrainian government created the Ukrainian Supreme Attestation Commission. I. *Dziuba was appointed its chairman.

**Supreme Council of the National Economy** (Vyshcha rada narodnoho hospodarstva, or VRNH). The leading republican agency which planned and guided the economy of Soviet Ukraine. In early 1918, during the first attempt to establish a Bolshevik regime in Ukraine, a Southern Council of the National Economy was formed. In January 1919 a Ukrainian Council of the National Economy was created and modeled after the Russian Supreme Council of the National Economy (Vesenkha). Its chairmen were E. Kviring and the Borotbist M. Poloz. Under the leadership of V. *Chubar a stable institution was formed in January 1920, named the Organizing Bureau for the Reconstruction of Industry (Prombiuro). On 31 December 1920 it was renamed the Supreme Council of the National Economy, and began to play an assertive and independent role in the administration of the economy. Its independence from the all-Union Vesenkha was formalized when the USSR was formed in 1922. In August 1926, central administrations for various branches of industry were established in the Vesenkha, and investment decisions for those branches were centralized. Under the new arrangement the VRNH ceased to participate in the preparation of control figures for Union enterprises in Ukraine. In 1932 another step in centralizing economic control was taken: the Vesenkha and the VRNH were abolished and replaced by people's commissariats of heavy and light industry. Heavy industry became the exclusive responsibility of the All-Union Commissariat of Heavy Industry. The VRNH was therefore succeeded only by the People's Commissariat of Light Industry of the Ukrainian SSR.

*Regional economic councils (*sovnarkhozy*) were created in 1957 as part of N. Khrushchev's attempt to decentralize the economy. Ukraine had 11, and later 14, such councils, which were subordinated to a republican Council of the National Economy in 1960. During that period 97 percent of gross industrial production was under the operational control of republican authorities, as opposed to only 36 percent in 1953. Ukrainian economists considered the period to be one of balanced growth with lower transportation costs, greater interbranch co-ordination, and higher spending on social and cultural projects. The central authorities, however, were dissatisfied with the council's tendency to favor republican over Union orders for supplies. In 1963 the *sovnarkhozy* were turned into Union-republican organs subject to increasing interference from the all-Union State Planning Committee and the Central Administration of Material and Technical Supplies. They were abolished in 1965 and replaced by a sectoral system of economic management.

B. Somchynsky

**Supreme Court of the Ukrainian SSR** (Verkhovnyi sud Ukrainskoi RSR). The highest court in Ukraine, established on 16 December 1922. It consisted of the chief justice, the deputies of the chief justice, several members, and *people's assessors, who were elected to a five-year term by the Supreme Soviet of the Ukrainian SSR (in fact by its presidium). The court dealt with exceptionally grave criminal cases, administrative crimes of senior officials, and civil suits between state institutions of republican stature; reviewed the decisions of lower courts; and oversaw the operation of the court system. It was divided into two collegia, the criminal and the civil, whose decisions were reviewed by the court's presidium. Decisions of the Ukrainian Supreme Court could be appealed to the Supreme Court of the USSR.

**Supreme Criminal Appeal Court of the Ukrainian SSR** (Verkhovnyi kasatsiinyi sud URSR). A Soviet judicial body established 16 April 1919 to review appeals against sentences passed by revolutionary tribunals. The appeal court was under the jurisdiction of the People's Commissariat of Justice and consisted of the chief judge and four members. It could annul the decisions of the tribunals and order retrials, or retry cases itself. In 1921 it was transformed into the Supreme Appeal Tribunal of the All-Ukrainian Central Executive Committee and shortly thereafter merged with the *Supreme Revolutionary Tribunal of the All-Ukrainian Central Executive Committee to form the Unified Supreme Tribunal of the Ukrainian SSR, which at the end of 1922 was abolished and replaced by the Supreme Court of the Ukrainian SSR.

**Supreme Emigration Council** (Holovna emigratsiina rada; or Ukrainska holovna emigratsiina rada). A federation of Ukrainian émigré organizations in Europe, established in Prague in 1929 for the purpose of representing Ukrainian interests at international forums (particularly the League of Nations) and for co-ordinating the political activities of émigré circles. Its membership consisted of 11 organizations: the Ukrainian hromadas in Belgium, Bulgaria, Luxembourg, Turkey, and Yugoslavia; the Ukrainian Central Committee in Poland; the Ukrainian Relief Committee in Rumania; the Ukrainian Alliance and the Ukrainian Republican-Democratic Club in Czechoslovakia; and the Union of Ukrainian Emigré Organizations and the Society of Former Combatants of the Ukrainian Republican Democratic Army in France. The council's head office was in Paris. Its presidents were O. Lototsky (1929–32) and O. Shulhyn. Other prominent figures included M. Slavinsky, Gen O. Udovychenko, I. Kosenko, and M. Kovalsky. The council was influenced strongly by the UNR government-in-exile.

**Supreme otaman** (*holovnyi otaman*). The title of the commander in chief of all Ukrainian armed forces adopted by the Directory of the UNR. On 13 November 1918 S. *Petliura was elected to the office. The Ministry of Defense, which was set up at that time and headed by Gen O. Hrekov, was placed under the jurisdiction of the supreme otaman. During the uprising against the Hetman government the insurgent army was commanded by Gen O. Osetsky as *acting otaman. On 11 August 1919, after the Army of the UNR united with the Ukrainian Galician Army, command of the joint forces was given to the Staff of the Supreme Otaman, headed by Gen M. Yunakiv. Petliura remained supreme otaman until his death.

**Supreme Revolutionary Tribunal of the All-Ukrainian Central Executive Committee** (Verkhovnyi revoliutsiinyi trybunal pry VUTsK). A Soviet judicial body established 15 April 1919 to deal with the gravest cases of counterrevolutionary activity referred to it by the Central Executive Committee, the Council of People's Commissars, and the People's Commissariat of Justice. Its decisions were final. From April 1921 the tribunal helped the newly formed Supreme Appeal Tribunal direct and oversee the work of all the revolutionary tribunals in Ukraine. In June 1921 the two tribunals were merged to form the Unified Supreme Tribunal of the Ukrainian SSR, which in 1922 was replaced by the Supreme Court of the Ukrainian SSR.

**Supreme Ruthenian Council** (Holovna ruska rada, or HRR). The first legal Ukrainian political organization in modern times, founded in May 1848 in Lviv. The HRR was established in direct response to the *Revolution of 1848–9 in the Habsburg monarchy, in particular to the formation in Galicia of the Polish People's Council (the Rada Narodowa), which declared itself the representative political body for the province. The emergence of the HRR in turn prompted the creation of yet another council, the pro-Polish *Ruthenian Congress (Sobor Ruskyi).

Encouraged by the Austrian governor of Galicia, Count F. *Stadion, over 300 Ukrainians representing various social groups (except the peasantry) met on 2 May at the chancery of St George's Cathedral under the leadership of the Greek Catholic clergy headed by Canon M. Kuzemsky. They organized a council of 30 members (eventually increased to 66) and nominated Bishop H. Yakhymovych as chairman. Membership in the HRR was restricted to Greek Catholics (almost exclusively Ukrainians) born in Galicia. Its social composition was dominated by the urban clerical and secular intelligentsia, nearly one-third of its members being Greek Catholic priests, one-third civil servants, and the remainder students, teachers, lawyers, and townsmen.

The purpose of the HRR was to strengthen the Ukrainian people in Austria by encouraging publications in Ukrainian, introducing the Ukrainian language in schools and the local administration, and defending the constitutional rights of Ukrainians. At the same time it served the parallel function of upholding the interests of the Greek Catholic clergy. From the outset the HRR was loyal to the Habsburg emperor and Austrian government and maintained close ties with Galicia's governor, Stadion. To promote its views the HRR founded on 15 May the newspaper *Zoria halytska. The first issue contained a clear statement of the national orientation of the HRR: Galicia's Ukrainians were a nationality distinct from both Poles and Russians, and they belonged to 'the great Ruthenian nation' living across the border in the southwestern part of the Russian Empire. The sense of national unity with Ukrainians in the east was complemented by an awareness of a common historical past with its once-independent state and 'perfected language.'

The HRR encouraged Ukrainians to form smaller councils throughout Galicia. They came into being in the spring and summer of 1848, and before the end of the year there were 50 local councils as well as 13 district councils. The size of the local councils ranged from a dozen members to as many as 540. Unlike the HRR, the local councils were made up primarily of peasants, and some included Polish and Jewish members as well as Ukrainians. Although the local and district councils had independent statutes, they maintained close ties with the HRR, whose representatives frequently participated in their meetings to present the political views of the central organization. The local councils were also a valuable transmission belt through which the HRR was able to learn the views and demands of the Ukrainian rural masses.

The HRR advised the local and district councils how to select candidates for elections to Austria's new national parliament in May 1848. Nonetheless, of the 25 Ukrainian deputies elected, not one was a candidate favored by the HRR. In late 1848 through 1849 the HRR issued several memorandums to the Austrian government on behalf of peasant demands for a favorable resolution of the rural and manorial land question.

Another primary concern of the HRR was the partition of Galicia into separate Ukrainian and Polish provinces. The council issued its first memorandum to the emperor on that matter in June 1848, and it continued to call for partition until its last statement on the issue in March 1849. The HRR was more successful in its request to establish a Ukrainian national guard in Galicia. The group was especially opposed to the revolution in Hungary, and in early 1849 it called on the people in Galicia's borderland districts to arm themselves and to join the newly established *Ruthenian Battalion of Mountain Riflemen.

The HRR also interacted with fellow Slavs. It sent three delegates, including its vice-chairman, I. Borysykevych, to participate in the Slavic Congress in Prague in June 1848. Although the HRR delegates disagreed with the protocol of the congress, which did not favor the partition of Galicia, their presence made the rest of the Slavic world aware of Galicia's Ukrainians.

The HRR played an active but indirect role in cultural matters. It encouraged the development of the Ukrainian vernacular through its official organ, *Zoria halytska*, by calling for its standardized use in publications, its use as a language of instruction in schools, and its use in Galicia's civil and Greek Catholic church administrations. To further cultural goals a new organization, the *Halytsko-Ruska Matytsia, came into being in October 1848. The HRR also supported the initiative of the Austrian government to create a chair of Ruthenian (Ukrainian) language and literature at the University of Lviv (September 1848).

From its inception the HRR combined work on behalf of the Ukrainians of Galicia with unswerving loyalty to the Austrian government. Such loyalty, however, proved insufficient protection in changing political circumstances. With the end of the revolutionary era in 1849 and the onset of Austrian neoabsolutism, the HRR again followed the wishes of the state authorities and dissolved itself in 1851. Nonetheless, throughout its four years of existence it had initiated a national revival among Ukrainians in Galicia which was to guarantee their political and cultural survival.

BIBLIOGRAPHY

Levyts'kyi, K. *Istoriia politychnoï dumky halyts'kykh ukraïntsiv, 1848–1918*, vol 1 (Lviv 1926)

Bohachevsky-Chomiak, M. *The Spring of a Nation: The Ukrainians in Eastern Galicia in 1848* (Philadelphia 1967)

Kozik, J. *The Ukrainian National Movement in Galicia, 1815–1849* (Edmonton 1986)

P.R. Magocsi

**Supreme Socialist Inspection of Ukraine** (Verkhovna sotsialistychna inspektsiia Ukrainy, or VSIU). A higher administrative body set up in January 1919 by the Provisional Workers' and Peasants' Government of Ukraine. The VSIU collaborated with the People's Commissariat of State Control (NKDK); both were headed by M. Skrypnyk. On 5 May 1919 it was reorganized into an independent agency, the People's Commissariat of Socialist Soviet Inspection of Ukraine, and placed under the supervision of Commissar A. Yoffe and his deputy, V. Menzhinsky. The Higher Administrative and Political Inspection, the Higher Military Inspection, the Higher National Economy Inspection, and the Higher Highways and Communications Inspection were all placed under the VSIU. Whereas the NKDK dealt primarily with economic affairs, the VSIU ensured that the general policies of the Party were adhered to by all government institutions. In 1920 the two agencies were superseded by a single body, the People's Commissariat of Workers' and Peasants' Inspection.

The building of the Supreme Council of Ukraine (formerly Supreme Soviet of the Ukrainian SSR)

**Supreme Soviet of the Ukrainian SSR** (Verkhovna Rada Ukrainskoi RSR). The highest governing and legislative body in Soviet Ukraine. It was created according to the Constitution of 1937 in place of the *All-Ukrainian Congress of Soviets on the model of the Supreme Soviet of the USSR. The Supreme Soviet had the authority to change the constitution of the Ukrainian SSR, to approve state plans for the economic and political development of the country, to enact legislation, to change administrative territorial borders, and to establish the budget. It also elected the *Council of Ministers and accepted its reports, and appointed judges to the *Supreme Court. The Supreme Soviet initially met only a few weeks a year; it elected a Presidium, consisting of a chairman, 3 deputy chairmen, a secretary, and some 20 members, to act in its place between sessions. The Presidium was delegated almost complete authority by the Supreme Soviet, although some decisions had to be ratified later by the entire Soviet. The chairman of the Presidium (and of the Supreme Soviet) was legally the head of state.

Deputies were elected on the basis of universal suffrage by all citizens of Ukraine over the age of 18 (earlier, 21) through direct, secret balloting. The number of deputies increased from 435 (in 1955) to 650 (in 1977) but subsequently decreased to 450 (in 1990). Deputies were elected from electoral districts, each with approx 110,000 inhabitants. The Communist party exercised total control over the Supreme Soviet. Only the Party or organizations it controlled could nominate deputies for elections, which were not contested, and the Party faction in the Soviet dominated the proceedings. In response to the reforms initiated by M. Gorbachev, however, a new electoral law was passed by the Ukrainian Supreme Soviet in November 1989. It liberalized somewhat the nominating procedure (although Party-dominated local electoral commissions retained inordinate power) and permitted multiple candidates to stand for elections. Despite many irregularities and official interference, over 120 supporters of the Democratic Bloc, a loose coalition of some 40 groups opposed to the Communist party, were elected in March 1990. By 1991 the Supreme Soviet had emerged as the most important forum of the struggle for democratic change in Ukraine. After the collapse of Soviet rule in 1991, the Supreme Soviet was renamed the Supreme Council of Ukraine.

B. Balan

**Supreme Ukrainian Council** (Holovna ukrainska rada). A body established at the outbreak of the First World War, on 1 August 1914, in Lviv by the three main Galician parties, National Democratic, Ukrainian Radical, and Ukrainian Social Democratic. It was headed by K. Levytsky, and its purpose was to decide on the general direction of Ukrainian politics in the war period and to organize the Ukrainian Sich Riflemen. The council was active until 1915, when it was reorganized into the *General Ukrainian Council in Vienna.

*Supriaha.* A form of peasant co-operation in Ukraine, under which two or three peasant households shared their oxen or draft animals and plows. It was especially common in those parts of Ukraine where the soil was hard, and two or three pairs of animals were needed to pull a plow. Several peasant households contributed a pair of draft animals each and then assisted in the plowing. The practice declined with the introduction of tractors.

**SUPROM.** See Union of Ukrainian Professional Musicians.

**SUPRUHA.** See Union of Ukrainian Private Office Employees.

**Suprun, Oksana,** b 14 October 1924 in Uman, d 1 May 1990 in Kiev. Sculptor; daughter of H. *Petrashevych. In 1951 she graduated from the Kiev State Art Institute, where she studied under her mother and M. Helman. Working in bronze, wood, marble, and plaster, she sculpted works such as *Partisan Woman* (1951), *Friendship* (1954), *The Future* (1960), *Reflections* (1964), *The Field Princess* (1966–7), *Farmer* (1969), and *Summer* (1976). With A. Bilostosky she created the composition *Before the Battle* (1954), depicting B. Khmelnytsky, I. Bohun, and M. Kryvonis on horses. She also sculpted (with A. Bilostotsky) the monuments to I. Franko in Kiev (1956) and T. Shevchenko in Odessa (1966).

Oksana Suprun: *Partisan Woman* (marble, 1951)

**Suprunenko, Mykola,** b 17 February 1900 in Poltava, d 11 September 1984 in Kiev. Historian; member of the AN URSR (now ANU) from 1972. After graduating from the Institute of Red Professors (1937) he worked at the ANU Institute of History (as professor from 1955 and as director of the Department of the Great October Revolution and Civil War from 1960). His works include *Ukraïna v period inozemnoï voiennoï interventsiï i hromadians'koï viiny (1918–1920 rr.)* (Ukraine in the Period of Foreign Armed Intervention and Civil War [1918–20], 1951), *Ukraina v Velikoi Otechestvennoi voine Sovetskogo Soiuza (1941–1945 gg.)* (Ukraine in the Great Patriotic War of the Soviet Union [1941–5], 1956), and *Pobeda Sovetskoi vlasti na Ukraine* (The Triumph of Soviet Power in Ukraine, 1967 [coauthor]).

**Suprunenko, Petro,** b 30 June 1893 in Kremenchuk, Poltava gubernia, d 17 November 1945. Mechanics scientist; full member of the AN URSR (now ANU) from 1934. He studied and taught at the Kiev Polytechnical Institute and worked in the weighing service of the Southwestern Railway (1919–27). He served as director of the ANU Commission of Transportation Mechanics (1929–38) and held a chair at the Kiev Institute of Railroad Transport. He studied theoretical questions connected with railroad transportation and developed a method of integrating differential equations describing the movements of rail stock. He was arrested during the Soviet terror of the late 1930s.

**Sura River.** See Mokra Sura River.

**Surgery.** A branch of medicine that deals with the treatment of illness, injuries, malformations, and other disorders by manual and instrumental means. In Kievan Rus' folk medicine included operations performed by *kostopravy* (bonesetters), *rizalnyky* (cutters), and *zubovoloky* (tooth-pullers). In the late Middle Ages, in some areas up to and including the 19th century, the *tsyrulnyk* (barber-surgeon) treated people by administering ointments, bloodletting, pulling teeth, and setting broken bones, dislocations, and sprains. Guilds for *tsyrulnyky* were formed in Kiev (15th century) and Lviv (1715), the members of which had to pass a practical examination after their training. Some *tsyrulnyky* also removed urinary bladder stones, performed amputations, and did hernia repair.

The first medical-surgical schools were established in Ukraine at the time of Peter I in conjunction with the mili-

tary needs of the Russian Empire. By the end of the 19th century a noticeable development in surgery resulted when problems of anesthesia, antisepsis, and aseptics were resolved. General surgery was subdivided into many specialized branches: ophthalmology, gynecology, otolaryngology, urology, thoracic surgery, *neurosurgery, and heart surgery and organ transplants.

The early contributions made by N. *Pirogov were followed by the work of V. *Karavaiv, Yu. Shimanovsky, and O. *Yatsenko, and later of N. *Sklifosovsky, M. *Volkovych, O. *Krymov, I. *Ishchenko, O. Avilov, A. *Arutiunov, M. *Amosov, A. Romodanov, and O. *Shalimov.

Research is conducted at the Kiev Scientific Research Institute of Clinical and Experimental Surgery and the Kharkiv Scientific Research Institute of General and Emergency Surgery, as well as at departments of surgery at medical education institutes, institutes for the upgrading of physicians, and scientific societies of surgeons. The journal *Klinicheskaia khirurgiia* is published in Russian in Kiev.

(See also *Medicine and *Veterinary science.)

BIBLIOGRAPHY

Deineka, I.; Mar'ienko, F. *Korotki narysy istoriï khirurhiï v Ukraïns'kii RSR* (Kiev 1968)
Shalimov, O.; Khokholia, V. *Pro khirurhiv i khirurhiiu* (Kiev 1979)
P. Dzul

**Surma** (shawm). A wind instrument made of wood. Generally conical with a flaring bell, double-reed mouthpiece, and five to seven finger holes, this oboe-type instrument has a long history, stretching back to Sumer and ancient Egypt. The *surma* in Ukraine is known from the Princely period of the Kievan state. It is depicted on an 11th-century fresco in Kiev's St Sophia Cathedral. The Cossacks used it primarily as a military instrument; eventually its musical function was supplanted by the trumpet. Today the *surma* has been revived and is often featured in folk instrumental ensembles. Prominent *surma* players include H. Fedkin and V. Zuliak.

*Surma*

**Surma** (Clarion). An underground monthly organ of the Ukrainian Military Organization and, from 1929, the OUN. It was printed secretly in Berlin (1927–8) and then Kaunas, Lithuania (1928–34), from which copies were smuggled and mailed into Western Ukraine and distributed free of charge. Initially the journal was edited by I. Gyzha (no. 1) and O. Senyk (nos 2–3); from the fourth issue the chief editor was V. Martynets. At first *Surma* published political and ideological articles by nationalist leaders such as Martynets, Ye. Konovalets, R. Jary, O. Senyk, and S. Chuchman. After the formation of the OUN in 1929, it devoted most attention to military topics, and featured articles on military tactics and theory by R. Sushko, V. Kolosovsky, V. Kurmanovych, M. Kapustiansky, and others.

*Surma* (Clarion). A monthly organ of the External Units of the OUN (Bandera faction), published in Munich in 1949–54. Edited by S. Lenkavsky, it published political analyses, ideological articles, and news and documents of the OUN underground still operating in Ukraine.

Myron Surmach

**Surmach, Myron** [Surmač], b 8 January 1893 in Zheldets, Zhovkva county, Galicia, d 12 May 1991 in New York. Book dealer, publisher, and community figure. He emigrated to the United States in 1910 and opened his first bookstore in New York City in 1916. In 1927 he opened the Surma Book and Music Company there, the oldest existing Ukrainian bookstore in the United States. Surmach published the humorous biweekly *Lys Mykyta* (1921–2), the monthly *Bazar* (1922–3), several books, and music collections. He also produced several Ukrainian records; began and ran the first Ukrainian radio program in the United States (est 1928); and sponsored numerous Ukrainian concerts, dance performances, and balls. A volume of his memoirs was published in 1982.

*Surmach* (Bugler). A journal published in London by the *Ukrainian Former Combatants in Great Britain. At first (1955) it was a monthly, then a quarterly, and in the late 1960s, an annual. Its editor was S. Fostun.

**Surmach-Mills, Yaroslava** [Surmač-Mills, Jaroslava], b 11 July 1925 in New York City. Painter, illustrator, and educator; daughter of M. *Surmach. A graduate of the Cooper Union art school (1950), she has taught art at Manhattanville College (1950–5) and Rockland Community College (from 1970) and was art director of the children's magazine *Humpty Dumpty* (1959–69). She has illustrated many children's books with Ukrainian themes (eg, *The Mitten, Stocking for a Kitten, An Egg Is for Wishing, Ivanko,* and *How a Shirt Grew in the Field*); has written and illustrated *Tusya and the Pot of Gold* (1971); has written the popular booklet *Ukrainian Easter Eggs* (1957); has popularized Ukrainian Easter egg painting in the United States; and has revived the art of reverse glass painting. Her popular Christmas, Easter, and other greeting cards depicting Ukrainian genre scenes and folk traditions are reproduced from her glass paintings. She created the stained-glass windows of the St Demetrius Ukrainian Catholic Church

Yaroslava Surmach-Mills with one of her icons and one of her paintings on glass

in Toronto (1982) and the etched-glass entrance doors of the New York Senate Building in Albany. Over 20 solo exhibitions of her glass paintings have been held since 1974.

Nadiia Surovtsova

**Surovtsova, Nadiia** [Surovcova, Nadija], b 18 March 1896 in Uman, Kiev gubernia, d 13 April 1985 in Uman, Cherkasy oblast. Historian, translator, and civic activist. With the outbreak of the February Revolution she returned from St Petersburg University to Ukraine to take part in the movement for national independence: she worked in the zemstvo and Peasant Association branch in the Uman region, contributed to *Trybuna* and other newspapers, and headed a department in the UNR Ministry of Foreign Affairs. In 1919 she emigrated from Ukraine and settled in Vienna, where she completed a PH D in history and worked in Ukrainian publishing houses, women's organizations, and the pacifist movement. In 1925 she returned to Ukraine, where she worked at the Radio-Telegraph Agency, the All-Ukrainian Photo-Cinema Administration, and the People's Commissariat of Foreign Affairs. For refusing to collaborate with the Soviet secret police, she was arrested in 1927, charged with spying for Austria, and sent to the Gulag, from which she emerged only in 1954. She then returned to Uman, where she devoted her energies to volunteer work at the regional museum and to writing her memoirs. In the 1970s the authorities placed her under close surveillance and confiscated her memoirs. They were published posthumously in *Nauka i kul'tura: Ukraïna*, vols 24–5 (1990–1).

**Surozh.** See Sudak.

**Surozh Sea** (Surozke more). The ancient name for the Sea of Azov, used also for the Black Sea. It was derived from the name of the Crimean coastal settlement of Surozh (present-day Sudak). The sea was alternately called the Sea of Sudak.

**Surplus appropriation system** (Russian: *prodrazverstka*). A policy of compulsory food deliveries to the state, imposed by the Soviet regime during the period of *War Communism. It was decreed by the RSFSR Council of People's Commissars on 11 January 1919 and was introduced in the part of Ukraine under Bolshevik control in March 1919. In March 1921 the surplus appropriation system was replaced by the *tax in kind under the *New Economic Policy.

In Russia the *prodrazverstka* was adopted in response to the disruption of normal economic exchange between the city and the countryside, caused by the revolution and the civil war. The government's failure to procure enough food, especially grain, for the cities at official prices led the Bolsheviks to introduce forcible requisitioning of food supplies. In Ukraine the appropriation system was implemented by the Provisional Workers' and Peasants' Government of Ukraine (November 1918 to June 1919) and its successor (est December 1919), both of which were ordered by Moscow to expropriate as much food as possible for the Red Army and the Russian cities.

The system consisted of a state monopoly on trade. Each peasant household was ordered to deliver its surplus to the state at fixed prices. The measure amounted to outright confiscation, for the prices were very low, and practically nothing could be bought with the money. The state demanded all the food except an ill-defined minimum for the peasant family's own use. The peasants resisted by either hiding their grain or selling it on the black market or through illegal barter. Moreover, having lost any interest in producing farm surpluses, the peasants reduced their sowings: in 1920 the total sown area in Ukraine was 30 percent below that of 1913, and grain yields dropped to 452 kg per ha from 721 kg per ha. The policy was enforced by armed brigades sent into the villages to search the farms, seize grain, and punish the hoarders. Repressions were widespread and provoked peasant revolts throughout Ukraine. The Soviet regime also used the *Committees of Poor Peasants to requisition food: their members became tax farmers, who kept 10–25 percent of all collected foodstuffs for their own consumption.

Throughout 1919 the *prodrazverstka* was applied only to grain, because of widespread peasant resistance and the weakness of the Soviet regime. In March 1920 it was extended to cattle and a wide range of agricultural produce. The policy applied to all regions of Ukraine under Bolshevik control, including eastern Galicia, for a part of 1920. During 1919, 172 million kg of grain were collected under the *prodrazverstka* in Ukraine. That amount represented a mere 7.6 percent of the planned quota. In 1920, 391 million kg were requisitioned (14.8 percent of the quota), and in 1921, 1171 million kg (68.1 percent of the quota). Although formally abandoned in March 1921, the *prodrazverstka* continued in a number of gubernias, especially in central and southern Ukraine, until July 1921. It was an important factor in bringing about the 1921–2 man-made *famine in Ukraine, and it widened the breach between the Ukrainian peasantry and the Soviet regime.

BIBLIOGRAPHY
Nove, A. *An Economic History of the USSR* (London 1970)
B. Krawchenko

**Surrealism.** A movement in art and literature that originated in interwar France. It became popular with the publication of the *Surrealist Manifesto* (1924) by the French poet A. Breton. As stated by Breton, surrealism's purpose was to unite the previously contradictory conditions of dream/fantasy and reality in 'an absolute reality, a surreality.' Surrealism was introduced in Ukraine in Lviv in the late 1920s by R. *Selsky and other members of the Artes left-wing artists' group. Renewed interest in surrealism can be seen in the early 1960s in the paintings of L. *Medvid, I. *Zavadovsky, P. *Markovych, and B. Soika; in the 1970s in the paintings of nonconformist artists, such as V. *Makarenko, I. *Marchuk, and P. Hulyn; and in the late 1980s in the paintings of O. *Tkachenko, S. *Yushkov, S. Baroiants, A. Haidamaka, N. Herasymenko, and V. Pasyvenko. Surreal elements can also be found in the works of contemporary North American artists of Ukrainian origin, such as S. *Lada, A. *Lysak, V. *Yurchuk, N. *Husar, and I. Kordiuk. In Ukrainian literature the influence of surrealism is evident in the works of the émigré writers E. *Andiievska and G. *Tarnawsky.

**Surskyi-Dnieper culture.** A Neolithic culture of the mid-7th to late 5th millennium BC that existed along the Dnieper River south of Dnipropetrovske. It was named after a site excavated in 1946. The people of this culture lived on islands of the Dnieper in semi-pit dwellings and engaged in animal husbandry, fishing, and hunting. Excavations revealed that their microlithic flint technology was well developed. Their pottery tended to have a sharply curved base and occasional linear-spiral meandering ornamentation. The culture was assimilated by new tribes settling in the region and played a role in forming the *Pit-Grave culture.

**Surzha, Yurii** [Surža, Jurij], b 3 September 1937 in Sabivka (now in Slovianoserbske raion, Luhanske oblast). Stage actor. After completing the studio course at the Kiev Ukrainian Drama Theater (1961) he worked in the Donetske (1961–5), Cherkasy (1965–75), and Ivano-Frankivske Ukrainian Music and Drama Theaters. He has portrayed V. Lenin in contemporary Soviet plays and was acclaimed for his portrayal of the title role in O. Kolomiiets's *Dykyi anhel* (The Wild Angel).

**SUS.** See Ukrainian Self-Reliance League.

**Susha, Yakiv** [Suša, Jakiv], b 1610 in Minsk, Belarus, d 1687. Uniate bishop of Kholm. He joined the Basilian order in 1626 and then studied in Prussia (1626–32) and Olomouc, Moravia (1632–6). After several postings he was brought to Kholm as a lecturer at the gymnasium and assistant to Bishop M. Terletsky. When the bishop died in 1649, he became administrator and then bishop (1651) of

Bishop Yakiv Susha          Kornylo Sushkevych

the eparchy. In the wake of the Khmelnytsky uprising, Susha proved to be an exceptional diplomat. He negotiated with Cossack leaders, and in 1664–6 he lived in Rome as delegate of the Uniate church to the papacy. There he persuaded the pope to name a new Uniate metropolitan of Kiev, healed a serious rift in the Basilian order, and obtained an agreement prohibiting Catholics from changing their rite. He also led the drive to beatify Y. *Kuntsevych. Susha's writings included biographies of Kuntsevych and M. Smotrytsky. A collection of his extensive correspondence was published in Rome in 1973–4 in *Litterae Episcoporum*, vols 2–3. I. Nazarko published Susha's biography in *Zapysky Chyna sv. Vasyliia Velykoho* (1971).

**Sushkevych, Anton** [Suškevyč], b 22 January 1889 in Borisoglebsk, Voronezh gubernia, Russia, d 30 August 1961 in Kharkiv. Mathematician. After completing his studies at St Petersburg University (1913) he taught at various institutions of higher learning in Kharkiv (1916–21) and at Voronezh University (1921–9). From 1929 he worked as a mathematical researcher in Kharkiv, and from 1933 he was a professor at Kharkiv University. His contributions are in the fields of number theory, algebra, and, particularly, group and semigroup theories. His major work on the theory of generalized groups was published in 1937. He also wrote textbooks on higher algebra and number theory and essays on the history of mathematics.

**Sushkevych, Kornylo** [Suškevyč], b 1840 in Lviv, d 8 June 1885 in Lviv. Civic and cultural leader. A lawyer by vocation, he was a leading populist in Galicia. He helped found the Prosvita society and served as its vice-president. He was the first president (1873–85) of the Shevchenko Society in Lviv, which he helped establish, as well as one of the founders of the Ruthenian Pedagogical Society (1881). The two-volume 1867 edition of T. Shevchenko's poetry was financed by him.

**Sushkevych, Petro** [Suškevyč], b 1844 in Lviv, d 5 December 1913 in Lviv. Physician, civic activist, and philanthropist. He was one of the founders of the Ukrainian Medical Society in Lviv and deputy director of the Lysenko Higher Institute of Music. He bequeathed most of his fortune (200,000 kronen) to the Prosvita society for scholarships for young tradesmen and relief for indigent old writers.

**Sushkivka settlement.** A Trypilian settlement located near Sushkivka, Uman raion, Cherkasy oblast. Excavations in 1916 and 1926 uncovered several surface dwellings with clay floors, ovens, and religious structures. Among the artifacts recovered were various types of pottery, earthenware figurines of humans and animals, and a unique clay model of the interior of a *Trypilian culture dwelling.

**Sushko, Mykola,** b 1909 in Vienna. Student and political activist. A lawyer by profession, he finished law school in Vienna. In 1931–2 he headed the *Sich student society in Vienna, and in 1933 he was a delegate of the Central Union of Ukrainian Students at the international student congresses. In 1938–45 he headed the *Ukrainian Institute of Trust in Berlin. After the war he settled in Salzburg and became a publisher.

**Sushko, Oleksander** [Suško], b 1880 in Galicia, d 1966 in Chicago. Journalist, civic figure, and teacher. He studied history in Lviv and Vienna, published articles on the 16th-century history of the Ukrainian church, and taught at the Academic Gymnasium in Lviv. He emigrated to Canada in 1913 and became an adviser to Bishop N. Budka and editor of the Ukrainian Catholic newspaper *Kanadiis'kyi rusyn* (1914–16) in Winnipeg. His writings were particularly noted for their Austrophilism. Sushko organized the first conference of Ukrainian Canadians (1915) and then worked for the Protestant monthly *Ranok* (1916) and the journal *Ukraïna* (2 issues, 1918–19). After moving to the United States he lectured at the University of Chicago and Columbia University in New York and was the founding president (early 1930s) of an organization called the Ukrainian Academy of Sciences of America (in Detroit, later in Chicago).

Roman Sushko          Onysym Suslov

**Sushko, Roman** [Suško], b 1894 in Remeniv, Lviv county, Galicia, d 12 January 1944 in Lviv. Senior military UNR officer and OUN leader. Commanding a company of Ukrainian Sich Riflemen during the First World War, he was captured and interned by the Russians in 1916. He helped organize the *Sich Riflemen in Kiev, and as the force grew, he steadily rose from company, to battalion, regiment, and division (1919), commander and finally was promoted to colonel of the UNR Army. In 1920 he commanded a brigade of the Sich Riflemen Division, and in 1921 he led a brigade in the Second Winter Campaign. He was a cofounder of the *Ukrainian Military Organization and its home commander during 1927–31. He took part in setting up the *Organization of Ukrainian Nationalists (OUN) and was active in its military department. He was military editor of *Surma*. In 1939 he helped organize and commanded the *Legion of Ukrainian Nationalists. He lived in Cracow in 1939–41, where he was OUN leader in the Generalgouvernement. When the internal split occurred within the OUN, he remained loyal to Col A. *Melnyk. From 1941 he was active in the OUN underground in Lviv, where he was killed by an unknown assassin.

**Sushytsky, Teoktyst** [Sušyc'kyj], b 1883, d 1920. Literary scholar and civic figure. A privatdocent at Kiev University, in March 1917 he was appointed director of the new Second Ukrainian State Gymnasium in Kiev. In April he chaired the Ukrainian Pedagogical Congress. He was appointed secretary of the Kiev Ukrainian People's University in October and a lecturer at the Ukrainian Pedagogical Academy in November. In October 1918 the Hetman government appointed him professor of Ukrainian literature and rector of the Kiev Ukrainian State University. He also directed a department of the Hetman government's Ministry of Education. His major work, a study of Western Rus' chronicles as literary monuments (2 vols, 1921, 1929), was published after his death by the VUAN.

**Suslov, Onysym** (real surname: Reznikov), b 1857 in Yelysavethrad (now Kirovohrad), Kherson gubernia, d 2 December 1929 in Odessa. Stage and film actor and director. He acted in the troupes of M. Kropyvnytsky (1888–92), P. Saksahansky (1892–3), H. Derkach (1893–4), D. Haidamaka (1909–10), and S. Hlazunenko (1910–12) and led his own troupes in 1894–1909 (1894–8 with O. Sukhodolsky) and 1913–14. In 1918–29 he led several workers' and peasants' theaters and taught in the studio at the Odessa Ukrainian Drama Theater. He acted in the films *Sumka dypkur'iera* (The Diplomatic Pouch, 1927) and *Prodanyi apetyt* (Sold Appetite, 1928).

**Sutkivtsi** [Sutkivci]. IV-7. A village (1972 pop 2,100) in Yarmolyntsi raion, Khmelnytskyi oblast. The remnants of a castle (16th century) and the fortified Church of the Holy Protectress, built in 1476 by the Sutkowski family, are located there. The church-stronghold is a two-story, cruciform structure with a square center and four apses that form semicircular towers. Each corner of the center is topped by a small turret. Incompetent restoration at the beginning of the 20th century changed the original appearance of the church. The interior frescoes have been covered over with plaster.

**Suuksu.** A burial ground of the 6th to 10th century located near Hurzuf, Crimea. Excavations in 1903–7 uncovered approx 200 graves, the majority in ossuaries. The question of whether the deceased were Crimean Goths or Hellenized Sarmato-Alans has been debated by scholars.

**Suvorov, Heorhii** (Georgii), b 19 May 1919 in Saratov, Russia, d 12 October 1984 in Donetske. Mathematician;

The Church of the Holy Protectress in Sutkivtsi

corresponding member of the AN URSR (now ANU) from 1965. He completed his studies at Tomsk University in 1941 and worked there in 1946–65. From 1965 he headed a department of the Institute of Applied Mathematics and Mechanics of the ANU in Donetske. He made significant contributions to the theory of functions, particularly to the theory of topological and metric mappings on two-dimensional domains, and obtained important results in the theory of conformal and quasi-conformal mappings. Suvorov introduced a new method for the study of metric properties of mappings with bounded Dirichlet integral.

**Suvorov army cadet schools** (*suvorovski viiskovi uchylyshcha*). Specialized secondary military-educational institutions in what was the USSR, named after the Russian field marshal A. Suvorov, which prepared youths for entry into higher military schools and eventually into the armed forces of the Soviet Union. They were formed in August 1943 for children orphaned by the Second World War. From 1956 the sons of retired soldiers as well as members of the general public were admitted. From 1969 the program of study was two years (the ninth and tenth years of secondary education). In 1980 there were eight Suvorov schools in the USSR, one of which was in Kiev.

**SUZhERO.** See Ukrainian Association of Victims of Russian Communist Terror.

*Suzir'ia* (Constellation). An illustrated serial published annually (1967–81) and semiannually (from 1982) in Kiev by the Dnipro publishing house. It printed translations of contemporary prose, poetry, plays, and criticism by writers from the other Soviet republics. *Suzir'ia* stressed the 'fraternity' of the nations of the USSR and the ideals of Soviet patriotism.

St Nicholas's Church (18th century) in Svaliava

**Svaliava** [Svaljava]. V-3. A city (1989 pop 17,300) on the Liatorytsia River and a raion center in Transcarpathia oblast. The village was first mentioned in a historical document of 1263. In the 13th century it belonged to the Principality of Galicia-Volhynia. Then for many centuries it was under Hungarian rule. In the 16th to 18th centuries it was part of the Mukachiv-Chynadiieve dominion. By the end of the 18th century Svaliava was an important economic center with a distillery, a fair, a lumber mill, and a potash and brick factories. On 8 December 1918 the Ruthenian People's Council met in Svaliava and voted to join Transcarpathia with Ukraine. The town was annexed by Czechoslovakia in 1919, recaptured by Hungary in 1939, and incorporated into the Ukrainian SSR in 1945. It attained city status in 1957. Today Svaliava is an industrial center with a lumber-manufacturing complex, a wood-chemistry complex, and a handicrafts factory. There are health resorts just outside the city. The most interesting architectural monuments are the wooden churches of St Michael (1588) and St Nicholas (1759).

**Svaliava Forest Products Complex** (Svaliavskyi lisokombinat). A wood-processing and woodworking plant located in Svaliava, Transcarpathia oblast. It was organized in 1950 out of several enterprises in Svaliava: a lumber factory (est 1928), a woodworking complex (est 1931), and a forest farm (est 1900). In 1970 the Svaliava Furniture Factory (est 1963) was added to the complex. The main products of the complex are lumber, flooring, furniture, and consumer goods.

**Svarich, Peter.** See Zvarych, Petro.

**Svarnyk, Ivan,** b 1 June 1921 in Lysohirka, Tahanrih county, Don Cossack province, d 13 February 1989 in Lviv. Writer, humorist, and pedagogue. He graduated from Lviv University in 1951 and then worked as a teacher. From 1957 he was an editor in the publishing house Kameniar and for the journal *Zhovten'*. Svarnyk is the author of collections of tales and humorous stories, among them *Na chystu vodu* (Into the Calm Water, 1962), *Personal'nyi barlih* (A Personal Lair, 1966), *Baiky* (Tales, 1971), and *Zaiacha nauka* (The Rabbit's Education, 1977).

**Svaroh.** A major pagan deity of the Eastern and Baltic Slavs. He was the god of the sky (from the Sanskrit *swarga* 'sky'), the sun, and heavenly fire (thunder); the precursor of *Perun; and the father of *Dazhboh and *Svarozhych. According to an ancient myth 'men began to forge arms' when Svaroh threw down a pair of pliers from heaven. It can be inferred from this detail that the cult emerged at the beginning of the 1st millennium BC, at the end of the Bronze and the start of the Iron Age. The god is first mentioned by Procopius of Caesarea in the 6th century AD. The German chronicler Thietmar of Merseburg (d 1018) claimed that Svaroh (Zwarazici) was the principal deity of the Baltic Slavs. Svaroh is mentioned in the Kievan Chronicle under the year 1114. The Byzantine chronicler John Malalas identifies Hephaestos with Svaroh and Hephaestos' son Helios with Svaroh's son Dazhboh. In the 14th century Christian churchmen censured the common people for 'praying to fire, calling it Svarozhyche' (Hypatian Chronicle). In Ukrainian the archaic nouns *svara* and *svarka*, which are related etymologically to the name of the god, mean 'conflict,' 'sharp dispute,' and even 'battle' and 'war.' It seems reasonable to assume, therefore, that Svaroh was also the god of war. M. Hrushevsky considered Svaroh to be the sole god in Slavic mythology, the god of the creative power of nature. Later Svaroh's various functions were assigned to other deities, and his cult declined. He is not mentioned in the pagan pantheon of Volodymyr the Great.

BIBLIOGRAPHY
Hrushevs'kyi, M. *Istoriia Ukraïny-Rusy*, vol 1 (Lviv 1898; New York 1954)
Rybakov, B. *Iazychestvo drevnikh slavian* (Moscow 1981)
                                                              M. Mushynka

**Svarozhych.** A god of earthly fire and war in Western and Eastern Slavic mythology. In the Chronicle of John Malalas, Svarozhych is described as the second son of *Svaroh. He was probably a member of the early Slavic trinity: Svaroh (god of the heavens and thunder), Dazhboh (god of the sun), and Svarozhych (god of fire).

**Svashenko, Semen** [Svašenko], b 1 September 1904 in Derkachi (now in Lebedyn raion, Sumy oblast), d 23 November 1969 in Moscow. Stage and film actor. He studied in the Lysenko Music and Drama Institute (1922–5) and worked in Berezil (1922–8). In the Odessa Artistic Film Studio he acted in O. Dovzhenko's films *Zvenyhora* (1928), *Arsenal* (1929), and *Zemlia* (The Earth, 1930), B. Tiahno's *Fata morgana* (1931), and H. Chukhrai's *Balada pro soldata* (A Ballad of a Soldier, 1959).

**Svatove.** IV-19. A city (1989 pop 22,600) on the Krasna River and a raion center in Luhanske oblast. It originated in the 1660s and was called Svatova Luchka. In 1825 the village was turned into a military settlement and became

Semen Svashenko

Yevhen Sverstiuk

known as Novokaterynoslav. When military settlements were abolished in 1857, the old name was restored. The construction of the Kupianka–Lysychanske railway line in 1895 gave the village easy access to grain markets and stimulated development. In 1923 the village was renamed Svatove and made a raion center of Kharkiv gubernia. In 1938 it was promoted to city status. Today Svatove is an industrial center with several food-processing enterprises, a machine repair plant, and a sewing factory.

**Svechnikov, Serge** [Svečnikov, Serhii], b 21 July 1926 in Dnipropetrovske. Solid-state physicist; AN URSR (now ANU) corresponding member since 1973 and full member since 1988. After graduating from the Kiev Polytechnical Institute in 1948, he worked there until 1961 and then joined the newly established ANU Institute of Semiconductors in Kiev. He has contributed to the understanding of the fundamental optoelectric processes of charge-carrier generation and recombination resulting from the interaction of ionizing radiation with semiconductor lattices.

**Svechnikov, Vasilii** [Svečnikov, Vasilij], b 6 January 1891 in Kozmodemianske (now Babino), Viatka gubernia, Russia, d 20 August 1981 in Kiev. Metallurgist; full member of the AN URSR (now ANU) from 1939. He studied in St Petersburg, worked at the ANU Institutes of Ferrous Metallurgy (1940–53) and Metal Physics (1953–75, as department head), and taught at the Kiev Polytechnical Institute (1944–66). In the field of ferrous metallurgy he studied nitrogen compounds in steel, phase transitions, and phase diagrams of various steels. He developed and established a whole new branch of metallurgy, the physicochemical analysis of refractory and rare metal alloys.

**Svekla, Oleksandra,** b 9 April 1902 in Valehotsulove (now Dolynske), Ananiv county, Kherson gubernia, d 1966 in Pryluka, Chernihiv oblast. Writer of Moldavian descent. She began publishing in 1924. A member of the peasant writers' group Pluh from 1925, she wrote the story collections *Nad Dnistrom* (At the Dniester, 1926) and *Podarunok i podiaka* (The Gift and the Expression of Gratitude, 1927) and the novels *Nadlomleni sertsem* (Broken by the Heart, 1930) and *Petria Slymak* (1930). She was persecuted during the Stalinist terror, and her works ceased to be published.

**Sverdlovske** or **Sverdlovsk** [Sverdlovs'ke or Sverdlovs'k]. V-20, DB III-7. A city (1989 pop 84,900) and raion

center in Luhanske oblast. It originated as the settlement Dovzhykove-Orlovske at the end of the 18th century and was renamed Sharapkyne later. The first coal mines were developed in the area in the 1870s. In 1938 several mining settlements were amalgamated to form the city of Sverdlovske. Today the city is an industrial center with 12 mines, 4 coal enrichment plants, a machine-building and metalworking industry, mining-equipment repair shops, and a clothes-sewing complex. It has a regional and a history museum.

**Sverstiuk, Yevhen** [Sverstjuk, Jevhen], b 13 December 1928 in Siltse, Volodymyr-Volynskyi county, Volhynia. Literary and social critic, publicist, and political prisoner. He did graduate work at the Institute of Psychology in Kiev and Odessa University (candidate's degree, 1965) and worked as a teacher in Ternopil oblast and the Poltava Pedagogical Institute. From 1959 he published articles and reviews in Soviet literary periodicals. Because of his criticism of Russification and other injustices, in 1965 he was blacklisted and dismissed from his job at the Ukrainian SSR Pedagogical Institute in Kiev. Thenceforth his essays were circulated in Ukrainian samvydav and published in émigré periodicals. He was fired from his job at *Ukraïns'kyi botanichnyi zhurnal* in December 1970 for his eulogy at A. Horska's funeral, and arrested in January 1972 and sentenced in March 1973, along with I. Svitlychny, for his involvement in the dissident movement and his defense of political prisoners, to seven years in strict-regime labor camps in Perm oblast and five years' exile in the Buriat ASSR, in Siberia. In the camps he participated in hunger strikes and other political protests. In April 1979 he was elected an honorary member of the International Association of Poets, Playwrights, Editors, Essayists, and Novelists (PEN). Since his release he has lived in Kiev. In the late 1980s his articles reappeared in the Soviet and émigré press. Editions of Sverstiuk's writings have been published in the United States in Ukrainian (1970, 1979, 1980) and in English translation (*Clandestine Essays*, 1976).

**Svesa** or **Svisa.** II-14. A town smt (1986 pop 8,800) on the Svisa River in Yampil raion, Sumy oblast. It originated in the 17th century as a *khutir* in Nizhen regiment. In the 19th century it was a village in Chernihiv gubernia. It acquired a distillery, sugar refinery, lime factory, and railway station in the second half of the century. Today it has a pump-manufacturing plant and Ukraine's only tannic-extracts plant.

**Sviati Hory Dormition Monastery** (Sviatohirskyi uspenskyi manastyr). An Orthodox monastery situated in present-day Slovianohirske, Donetske oblast. Although it is believed to have been founded as early as the 13th century, the first written record of it dates from 1624. In the 15th century monks began living in caves on a hill overlooking the Siverskyi Donets River and worshiping in a grotto church. Their settlement developed both as a religious community centered around the 17th-century St Nicholas's Church and as a fortified outpost on the frontier with the Crimean Tatars. Although protected by defensive walls and artillery, it was sacked by the Tatars in 1679; it was later rebuilt. Its properties were secularized in 1783.

The monastery expanded quickly in the second half of the 19th century along a terrace lower down the hill. At

The Sviati Hory Dormition Monastery (drawing by F. Dzhunkovsky, 1845)

that time the complex came to include the Dormition Cathedral, with three naves and five cupolas (1859–60), a hospice (1877), monks' cells (1887), the supervisor's residence (1900), and an elaborate pavilion for pilgrims, in addition to several smaller chapels and buildings. By 1908 the entire complex housed 280 monks and novices and 340 retirees. Closed down by the Soviet authorities in the antireligious terror after the revolution, in 1922 the monastery was turned into a sanatorium. The complex was severely damaged during the Second World War but was restored in 1969–80 and declared a historical preserve.

BIBLIOGRAPHY
Kluzhinskii, G. *Sviatgorskaia uspenskaia obshchezhitel'naia pustyn' v Kharkovskoi eparkhii* (Odessa 1898)

**Sviatopolk I** [Svjatopolk] (appellation: Okaiannyi [the Damned or the Accursed]), b 978, d 24 July 1019. Rus' prince; son of *Volodymyr the Great. In actuality Sviatopolk was probably the son of Volodymyr's brother, *Yaropolk I Sviatoslavych, whose widow, Predslava, Sviatopolk's Greek mother, Volodymyr took as his third wife; thus Sviatopolk is counted among Volodymyr's sons. He was the son-in-law of the Polish prince *Bolesław I the Brave and prince of Turiv, from which position he was ousted in 1012 because of a conspiracy against Volodymyr. Sviatopolk captured Kiev on 15 July 1015, after Volodymyr's death. According to the Primary Chronicle he ordered the death of his brothers, Borys (see *Saints Borys and Hlib), Hlib (see *Hlib Volodymyrovych), and Sviatoslav, for which the chronicler dubbed him 'Okaiannyi.' Sviatopolk planned to unite the lands inherited from his father, but his stepbrother, *Yaroslav the Wise, then prince of Novgorod, opposed him. Sviatopolk allied with the Pechenegs, but he was defeated by Yaroslav's armies at the Battle of Liubech at the end of 1016, and fled to Poland. With assistance from the Polish army Sviatopolk regained the Kievan throne on 14 August 1018; that same year, however, Yaroslav returned and banished him. Sviatopolk again enlisted the help of the Pechenegs, but he was defeated at the Alta River on 24 July 1019, and died while fleeing westward to the wilderness between Czech and Polish lands. During his reign in Kiev Sviatopolk minted a silver coin, ornamented after the style of Volodymyr's silver coins, with the inscription 'Sviatopolk na stole a se eho srebro' (Sviatopolk Is on the Throne and This Is His Silver).

A. Zhukovsky

**Sviatopolk II Iziaslavych** [Svjatopolk Izjaslavyč], b 8 November 1050, d 16 April 1113 near Vyshhorod, north of Kiev. Rus' prince of Polatsk (1069–71), Novgorod (1078–88), and Turiv (1088–93) and grand prince of Kiev (1093–1113); grandson of Yaroslav the Wise. His reign was marked by feuding with the Sviatoslavych dynasty of Chernihiv princes (allied with Khan *Boniak) and by devastating attacks by Polovtsians (which he tried to allay, to no avail, by marrying Khan Tugorkan's daughter in 1094), particularly in 1093 and 1096, when they reached the outskirts of Kiev. Sviatopolk participated in the *Liubech congress of princes in 1097, after which he and Davyd Ihorevych of Volhynia captured Vasylko Rostyslavych of Terebovlia and blinded him. Sviatopolk was then pressured into leading a punitive campaign against Davyd, who was expelled from his principality in 1099. After the *Vytychiv congress of princes in 1100, Sviatopolk accompanied Volodymyr Monomakh on a series of successful campaigns against the Polovtsians (1103, 1107, and 1111). He was a benefactor of the Kievan Cave Monastery and commissioned the construction of a church dedicated to his patron, the Archangel Michael (see *Saint Michael's Golden-Domed Monastery). His oppressive administrative policies, however, sparked the *Kiev Uprising of 1113 after his death.

**Sviatopolk-Chetvertynsky** [Svjatopolk-Četvertyns'kyj] (often just Chetvertynsky). A Ukrainian princely family, descended from the Turiv-Pynske or Volhynia appanage princes of the Riurykide dynasty, known from the late 14th century. The village of Chetvertnia on the Styr River in Lutske county, Volhynia, was the ancestral estate of the Chetvertynsky princes. Prince Oleksander Chetvertynsky was first mentioned in documents dated 1388. Prince Fedir Mykhailovych Chetvertynsky was ambassador of the Lithuanian-Ruthenian state to Wallachia in 1492. In the 15th and 16th centuries two branches of the Sviatopolk-Chetvertynsky family developed; one settled in Stara Chetvertnia, and the other in Nova Chetvertnia. In the 16th century the Sviatopolk-Chetvertynsky family ruled over large estates in Ukraine (Volhynia, Bratslav voivodeship) and Belarus. Certain members of the family later became Catholicized, but most remained fervent Orthodox believers, and some became high church dignitaries. They founded men's and women's monasteries in Stara Chetvertnia (Prince Hryhorii Chetvertynsky founded a printery at the Transfiguration Monastery there in 1624) and a monastery in Nova Chetvertnia.

Among the members of the Stara Chetvertnia branch of the family were Prince Hryhorii Ostapovych Sviatoslav-Chetvertynsky (d 1651), the chamberlain of Lutske (1647), who participated in church affairs, particularly in the nomination of Metropolitan P. Mohyla (1632) and of S. Kosiv (1647). Hryhorii's son, Zakhar Sviatopolk-Chetvertynsky, served as an assistant judge in Lutske (1647) and company commander (1649) and was a member of A. Kysil's delegation to B. Khmelnytsky in Pereiaslav (late 1648 to early 1649). Zakhar's son, Hedeon (Hryhorii) *Sviatopolk-Chetvertynsky, was bishop of Lutske and metropolitan of Kiev. Hedeon's first cousin, Serhii Sviatopolk-Chetvertynsky (religious name: Sylvestr), was bishop of Mahiliou and of Belarus (1705–27). Hedeon's brother, Andrii Sviatopolk-Chetvertynsky, was a company commander of the Cossack standard in the Great Ruthenian principality (1660).

Andrii's sons, Yurii and Yanush Sviatopolk-Chetvertynsky, lived during the time of the Hetman state. Yurii Sviatopolk-Chetvertynsky (d ca 1717–22), the son-in-law of the former hetman I. Samoilovych, was a high-ranking administrative officer in Moscow and an opponent of I. Mazepa (although he had received estates in Galicia from him). Through the marriages of his daughters he became related to the Myklashevsky, Skoropadsky, and Kondratev families. His brother, Yanush Sviatopolk-Chetvertynsky (d 1728), a colonel in service to the Russians, married Anna Vasylivna Kochubei, daughter of the general judge (she had been married to I. Obydovsky, colonel of Nizhen regiment and Mazepa's nephew). Another member of the Stara Chetvertnia branch of the family was Antin-Stanyslav Sviatopolk-Chetvertynsky, the castellan of Peremyshl (1790), an adviser to the Torhovytsia Confederacy; he was killed by Polish insurgents in Warsaw in 1794. From him is descended the line of 19th-century Sviatopolk-Chetvertynsky nobles that governed estates in Belarus and Ukraine (Kharkiv gubernia).

Among the members of the Nova Chetvertnia branch of the family were Prince Stepan Sviatopolk-Chetvertynsky (b ca 1575, d 1659), the chamberlain of Bratslav, who participated in the renewal of the Orthodox hierarchy (under Theophanes III) in 1620 and is mentioned in Mohyla's testament (1646). He was a leading member of that group of the Ukrainian Orthodox nobility that recognized the authority of the Zaporozhian Army. His son, Prince Illia Sviatopolk-Chetvertynsky (d 1641), however, a company commander, fought in the 1620s and 1630s against Cossack insurgents. A. Kalnofoisky dedicated his *Teraturgima* (1638) to him, and the rector of the Kievan Mohyla College, I. Oksenovych-Starushych, read a grave-side sermon during his funeral. Stepan's second son, Mykola Sviatopolk-Chetvertynsky (d 1659), was the castellan of Minsk and a relative of Hetman I. Vyhovsky. During the 18th century the Sviatopolk-Chetvertynsky princes of that branch served as castellans and chamberlains in Ukraine and Belarus; Oleksander Sviatopolk-Chetvertynsky (d 1769), the chamberlain of Bratslav, was an activist in the Confederation of Bar. That branch of the Sviatopolk-Chetvertynsky family became Catholicized in the late 17th and early 18th centuries; it ruled over large estates in Volhynia and Podilia until the 20th century.

O. Ohloblyn

**Sviatopolk-Chetvertynsky, Hedeon** [Svjatopolk-Četvertyns'kyj] (secular name: Hryhorii), b ?, d 1690. Orthodox metropolitan. A descendant of the Riurykide dynasty, ca 1661 he was consecrated bishop of Lutske and Ostrih. He defended the rights of the Orthodox in the Polish-Lithuanian Commonwealth. When his relations with King Jan III Sobieski, the Catholic church, and Y. Shumliansky, the Orthodox bishop of Lviv, deteriorated, however, he moved to the Baturyn Monastery in the Hetmanate. In June 1685 a church sobor elected Sviatopolk-Chetvertynsky metropolitan of Kiev, and in October 1685 he went to Moscow to be installed formally by Patriarch Y. Savelov. His election and his decision to accept his installation from the patriarch of Moscow, which undermined the independence of the church and cut its historical link to the patriarch of Constantinople, were opposed by many church leaders in Ukraine. When Hetman I. Samoilovych, his main supporter, who also favored a pro-Muscovite orientation for the Ukrainian church, was replaced by I.

Metropolitan Hedeon
Sviatopolk-Chetvertynsky

Mazepa, his authority began to fall. By 1688 Mazepa had forbidden his use of the title 'Metropolitan of All Rus'.'

**Sviatoshyne** or **Sviatoshyno** [Svjatošyne]. A suburb of Kiev, 10 km west of the city center. The area was first mentioned in a charter of the Polish king Sigismund III Vasa in 1619. In the second half of the 19th century the district, with its fine pine forests, was developed into a resort area. By the end of the century it was connected to the city by a horse and then a steam tram. Today it is the home of some research institutes, sanatoriums, and rest homes.

**Sviatoslav (Sviatosha)** [Svjatoslav (Svjatoša)] (Pankratii), b 1080, d 14 October 1142 in Kiev. Prince of Lutske; son of *Davyd Sviatoslavych. He was ousted from Lutske in 1099 by Davyd Ihorevych, and fled to his father in Chernihiv principality. On 17 February 1106 he entered the *Kievan Cave Monastery, where he adopted Nikolai (Mykola) as his monastic name. During his 36 years as a monk and ascetic he built the Trinity Church above the main gate of the monastery, as well as a hospital with the St Nicholas's Church. He also collected many manuscripts, which he donated to the Kievan Cave Monastery, thereby initiating the large library collection there. In 1142 he negotiated for peace among his warring brothers. Sviatoslav was recognized as a saint, and his achievements were described in the *Kievan Cave Patericon. His remains were preserved in St Anthony's Cave at the Kievan Cave Monastery.

**Sviatoslav I Ihorevych** [Svjatoslav Ihorevyč] (appellation: Khorobryi [the Brave]), b 942?, d 972. Grand prince of Kiev (de jure from 945, de facto from 964) and noted military commander; son of *Ihor and *Olha. While he was a minor, Sviatoslav's mother was regent of the Kievan state, and he was raised by a steward, Asmud. During his reign the territory of *Kievan Rus' was greatly expanded. In his campaigns to the east (964–6) he defeated the Khazars near Itil and captured the White Tower fortress in Sarkil. He later conquered the Volga Bulgars and forced the Yasians and the Kasogians in northern Caucasia to pay tribute, thereby opening the way for Rus' merchants to the Caspian Sea coast. In 966 he subjugated the Viatichians and exacted tribute from them. The emperor of Byzantium, Nicephorus II Phocas (through the offices of the patrician Kalokir of Chersonesus), convinced Sviatoslav to attack the Balkan Bulgars; he did so in 967 (some historians say 968). He captured many cities (80, according to the chronicles), including Dorostol and *Pereiaslavets on the

Danube, an important trading center, where he planned to transfer his capital.

Threatened by his Balkan expansionism, Byzantium convinced the *Pechenegs to attack Kiev. Sviatoslav reluctantly returned and drove the Pechenegs, who already had been repelled from the city, back to the steppe. After Olha's death he consolidated his control of Rus' and appointed his sons as viceregents: *Yaropolk I Sviatoslavych in Kiev, *Oleh Sviatoslavych in the Derevlianian land, and *Volodymyr the Great in Novgorod. In July 969 Sviatoslav embarked on a second campaign in the Balkans in order to strengthen the conquered cities and to punish Byzantium for provoking the Pecheneg attack on Kiev. That time, however, he was met by stronger opposition from a combined Bulgarian and Byzantine force. The relatively small size of his army and the lack of assistance from Kiev were responsible for his defeat near Dorostol (now Silistra). He was besieged by the Byzantine army (23 April to 22 July 971) and forced to sign a peace treaty (23 July), under which he ceded his territories in the Danube region. On the way back to Kiev he was ambushed by Pechenegs (once again at the behest of Byzantium). His army was destroyed, and he was slain.

The Primary Chronicle praises Sviatoslav as a heroic figure and describes his cordial relations with his wife. It also remarks on his practice of warning the enemies he was about to attack, with the message 'Idu na vas' (I am coming at you). He is the subject of Yu. Opilsky's novel *Idu na vas* (1918) and S. Skliarenko's novel *Sviatoslav* (1959).

BIBLIOGRAPHY
Zavitnevich, V. 'Velikii kniaz' kievskii Sviatoslav Igorevich,' *Trudy Kievskoi dukhovnoi akademii*, 3 (1888)
Grégoire, H. 'La dernière campagne de Jean Tzimisces contre les Russes,' *Byzantion*, 12 (1937)
Karishkovskii, R. 'K khronologii russko-vizantiiskoi voiny pri Sviatoslave,' *Vizantiiskii vremennik*, no. 5 (1952)
Stokes, A. 'The Balkan Campaign of Svyatoslav Igorevich,' SEER, June 1962
Karyshkovs'kyi, R. 'Povist' vremennykh lit pro balkans'ki pokhody Rusi pry kniazi Sviatoslavi,' *Pratsi Odes'koho derzhavnoho universytetu*, 152 (1962)
Ševčenko, I. 'Sviatoslav in Byzantine and Slavic Miniatures,' SR, 24, no. 4 (1965)
Sakharov, A. 'Rus'ko-vizantiis'kyi dohovir 971 r.,' UIZh, 1982, no. 10

A. Zhdan, A. Zhukovsky

**Sviatoslav II Yaroslavych** [Svjatoslav Jaroslavyč], b 1027, d 27 December 1076 in Kiev. Rus' prince; son of *Yaroslav the Wise. Sviatoslav ruled in Volodymyr-Volynskyi while his father was alive and then became prince of Chernihiv (from 1054). At first the three oldest sons of Yaroslav ruled in harmony; together with *Vsevolod Yaroslavych, the prince of Pereiaslav, and *Iziaslav Yaroslavych, the grand prince of Kiev, Sviatoslav defeated the Torks in 1060 and Vseslav Briachislavych, the prince of Polatsk, in 1067. In 1068 he and his brothers took some losses from the Polovtsians on the Alta River near Pereiaslav, but later that year he himself won a significant victory over the Polovtsian forces on the Snov River in Chernihiv principality. With Vsevolod's help Sviatoslav deposed Iziaslav on 22 March 1073 and took over as grand prince of Kiev. During his rule the territory of Kievan Rus'

was greatly increased. He was a patron of education, and he sponsored the compilation of the *Izbornik* of Sviatoslav (both 1073 and 1076), which had a great influence on the further development of educational literature in Kievan Rus'. Sviatoslav also contributed to *Ruskaia Pravda*, notably a chapter called 'Pravda Iaroslavychiv' (The Law of the Yaroslavych Dynasty). He was buried in the Cathedral of the Transfiguration in Chernihiv.

**Sviatoslav III Vsevolodovych** [Svjatoslav Vsevolodovyč], b 1126 in Chernihiv, d 27 July 1194 in Kiev. Rus' prince; son of Vsevolod Olhovych. He reigned in the principalities of Volhynia, Turiv-Pynske, Novhorod-Siverskyi, and Chernihiv and then became grand prince of Kiev in 1181. He established a coalition among Rus' princes to fight marauding Polovtsians (Khans Boniak and Konchak) and achieved a major victory against them in 1184 at the Orel River. The effectiveness of that effort subsequently declined as the princes set off against the nomads in an uncoordinated manner (eg, the famous campaign of Ihor Sviatoslavych in 1185). Sviatoslav's later efforts to stem the Polovtsians were somewhat more successful. He was buried in St Cyril's Church.

**Sviatovyt** (aka Sventovit, Svantevit). A principal pagan deity of the Western Slavs in the medieval period; the god of the sun and war and the protector of crops. At the end of the harvest season each year, sacrifices were brought to him, and festivals were held in his honor. His shrine was in Arkon, on Rigen Island. Inside stood a four-faced wooden idol in the form of a warrior with an aurochs horn in one hand and a sword in the other. During a ceremony the horn was filled with wine. Some scholars consider this idol to be a version of the *Zbruch idol. According to recent studies the Zbruch idol belongs to the mythology of the Eastern Slavs and does not represent Sviatovyt.

**Svicha River** [Sviča]. A right-bank tributary of the Dniester River that flows for 106 km through Ivano-Frankivske and Lviv oblasts and drains a basin area of 1,490 sq km. The river originates in the Gorgany Mountains and initially has a mountainous character; it then develops a wider valley (5–6 km) along its lower course. It is used for water supply and irrigation.

Leontii Svichka

**Svichka, Leontii** [Svička, Leontij] (Nazarenko, Levko), b ?, d 1699. Cossack officer during the Hetmanate. He held various posts in Lubni regiment, including those of osaul (intermittently in 1655–88), chancellor (1671), judge (1672), and colonel (1688–99). He was also the Pyriatyn town otaman in 1677 and a participant in the Muscovite Crimean (1687 and 1689) and Azov (1696) campaigns.

**Svidersky, Mykola** [Sviders'kyj], b 17 October 1920 in Pochaiv, Kremianets county, Volhynia gubernia, d 22 January 1987 in Sydney, Australia. Civic leader. After arriving in Australia in April 1949, he became a founding member of the Ukrainian Association in Sydney, the weekly *Vil'na dumka*, the Ukrainian Artistic Society in Sydney, the Ukrainian Dramatic Society in Australia (also a leading actor), the Ukrainian Studies Foundation in Australia, the Ethnic Communities Council in New South Wales, and the Plast Ukrainian Youth Association in Australia. He served as a state and national commissioner for Plast (1952–60), the vice-president of Plast in the West (1960–2), the organizer and choreographer of the first Ukrainian dance ensemble in Sydney (1949–60), the co-ordinator and a broadcaster of the Ukrainian-language radio program in Sydney (1976–87), a founder of the Ukrainian Senior Citizens' Club in Sydney, and a playwright for the Ukrainian Children's Theater. He also taught in Ukrainian Saturday schools for 22 years, lectured at the Ukrainian Teachers' College in Lidcombe, served on the Ukrainian Council in New South Wales for 18 years (president for 4 years), and was president of the Federation of Ukrainian Organizations in Australia (1977–9).

**Svidersky, Venedykt** [Sviders'kyj], b and d ? Painter. A precursor of romanticism, in the 1760s he lived and worked in Kharkiv. His works include many paintings of the Madonna, an icon of the Holy Protectress in the Church of the Holy Protectress in Romen, and the altar icon *Jacob's Dream* and the Passion cycle in the church in Mezhyrichia, near Sumy. He presented biblical themes in a manner close to that of genre painting.

**Svidnik.** See Svydnyk.

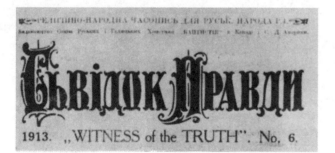

*S'vidok pravdy*

***S'vidok pravdy*** (Witness of the Truth). A Baptist journal published monthly (with interruptions) from 1909 to 1925 in Toronto; the first Ukrainian-language periodical in eastern Canada. It was the organ of the Alliance of Ruthenian and Galician Baptists in Canada and the United States and was edited by I. Koliesnykov (to 1918) and M. Androv.

***Svidoma syla.*** See *Robitnyche slovo*.

Volodymyr Svidzinsky          Vira Svientsitska

**Svidzinsky, Volodymyr** [Svidzins'kyj] (Svidzynsky), b 9 October 1885 in Maianiv, Vinnytsia county, Podilia gubernia, d 18 October 1941. Poet and translator. His first collection, *Lirychni poeziï* (Lyrical Poetry), was published in 1922; it was followed by *Veresen'* (September 1927) and *Poeziï* (Poems, ed Yu. Yanovsky, 1940). His poems, written in 1927–36 and printed in Ukraine in the years 1937–40, were collected by O. Veretenchenko and published in Munich in 1975 in the collection *Medobir* (Honey Wood). *Poeziï* (Poems, 1986) is one of the more recent editions of his work published in Ukraine. In his early collections Svidzynsky leaned toward symbolism, but in the two last collections there are elements of surrealism combined with classical forms. An important part of Svidzinsky's work is stories with folk or exotic motifs; there are also translations from the classics (Hesiod, Aesop, Ovid, Aristophanes) and from French, German, Polish, and Russian poetry. Svidzinsky died while under arrest, during the evacuation of Kharkiv in the fall of 1941. (According to eyewitness accounts, he was burned alive together with other prisoners in Saltiv, near Kharkiv. According to Soviet records, he was killed by a German bomb.)

B. Kravtsiv

**Sviechnykov, Anatolii** [Svječnykov, Anatolij], b 15 June 1908 in Kiev, d 12 March 1962 in Kiev. Composer and pedagogue. After graduating from the Lysenko Music and Drama Institute (1932) in the composition class of L. Revutsky and V. Zolotarev, he became the musical director of drama broadcasts on Ukrainian State Radio (1936–51) and a teacher of composition at the Kiev Conservatory (1945–61). His works include the ballets *Marusia Bohuslavka* (1951) and *The Night before Christmas* (1959), the symphonic poems *Karmeliuk* (1945) and *Shchors* (1949), choruses, pieces for piano, arrangements of Ukrainian folk songs, incidental music, and film scores.

**Svientsitska, Vira** [Svjencic'ka], b 28 August 1913 in Lviv, d 21 May 1991 in Lviv. Art scholar; daughter of I. *Svientsitsky. After graduating from Lviv University in 1938, she worked at the National Museum in Lviv. In 1947 she was arrested for co-operating with the Ukrainian underground resistance and imprisoned in a labor camp. After being released in 1956, she returned to Lviv, obtained a candidate's degee (1966), and was placed in charge of the Department of Medieval Painting at the Lviv Museum of Ukrainian Art. She wrote many articles on Ukrainian painting and wood carving; books on 17th- to 20th-century carved hand crosses (1939), I. Rutkovych and 17th-century Ukrainian painting (1966), medieval Ukrainian painting (1976, with H. Lohvyn and L. Miliaieva), and 14th- to 18-century Ukrainian painting in Lviv's museum collections (1900, with O. Sydor); and the chapter on 14th- to 16th-century painting in vol 2 of the AN URSR (now ANU) history of Ukrainian art (1967). She also compiled a dictionary of Zhovkva master painters and carvers, published in *Ukraïns'ke mystetstvoznavstvo* (vol 1, 1967), and coauthored a book on 13th- to 20th-century Ukrainian folk painting (1991).

Ilarion Svientsitsky          Pavlyn Svientsitsky

**Svientsitsky, Ilarion** [Svjencic'kyj] (Sventitsky, Sviatytsky), b 7 April 1876 in Buzk, Kaminka-Strumylova county, Galicia, d 18 September 1956 in Lviv. Philologist, paleographer, museologist, art historian, and bibliographer; full member of the Shevchenko Scientific Society from 1914 and the Ukrainian Theological Scholarly Society. He graduated from Lviv University (1899) and studied at the universities of St Petersburg (1900) and Vienna (PH D, 1902). He was editor of the Lviv Russophile journal *Zhivaia mysl'* (1902–5). He was director of the *National Museum in Lviv (1905–39, later the Lviv Museum of Ukrainian Art, 1939–41, 1944–52). He was a docent at Lviv University (1914, 1934–9) and was appointed deputy director of the scholarly section of the Kiev Municipal Museum. He was a lecturer at Kiev University (1917–18), a professor at the *Lviv (Underground) Ukrainian University (1922–5), and president of the *Mohyla Scholarly Lectures Society. In 1927 he took part in the All-Ukrainian Orthographic Conference in Kharkiv. After the Soviet takeover of Western Ukraine he headed the Slavic philology department at Lviv University (1939–41, 1944–50) and the Division of Linguistics at the AN URSR (now ANU) Institute of Social Sciences in Lviv (1944–50).

Svientsitsky studied the language of medieval East and South Slavic literary monuments. He wrote a book of essays on the history of the 11th- to 18th-century Ukrainian language (1920) and articles about the 13th-century Buchach Gospel (1912), the testaments of Yaroslav the Wise and Volodymyr Monomakh (1902), the 14th-century Lavryshevo Gospel (1913) and Novi Sad *Apostol* (1918),

the Galician-Volhynian Chronicle, 14th- and 15th-century Western Ukrainian charters, the treaties of Kievan Rus' with Byzantium, the 1229 Smolensk Charter, and Old and Middle Ukrainian literary monuments (1901). He also published two volumes of historical materials about the national revival in 19th-century Transcarpathia (1906, 1909). Among his other works are a short book on T. Shevchenko in criticism and reality (1922); a Ukrainian grammar in Polish (1922) and Russian grammars in Ukrainian (1902) and Polish (1915, 1931); a Ukrainian-Polish/Polish-Ukrainian dictionary (1920); booklets on the rebirth of Belarusian literature (1908, 1914), on the foundations of scholarship concerning the Ukrainian language (1917), on V. Vynnychenko as a writer (1920), and on M. Drahomanov and the Galicians (1922; repr 1975); and articles on various subjects. A book of his essays on the history of Bulgarian literature was published posthumously in 1957. As an ethnographer he was particularly interested in funeral *laments, and published a long article on the subject in *Etnohrafichnyi zbirnyk* (1912).

Under Svientsitsky's direction the National Museum and its library became major repositories of Ukrainian artifacts and Church Slavonic and Old Ukrainian books and manuscripts, and centers of scholarly research. He published an illustrated guide to the museum in 1913. He prepared important descriptions of the manuscript holdings of the People's Home library in Lviv (1904–5) and its A. Petrushevych collection (3 vols, 1906–11), the 12th- to 15th-century Cyrillic manuscript holdings at the National Museum (1933), and the manuscripts at the Stauropegion Institute (1908), and a catalog of Church Slavonic printed books (1908). As an art historian he produced books on the ornamentation of 16th-century Galician Ukrainian manuscripts (3 fasc, 1922–3), the beginnings of printing in Ukraine (1924), church painting in 15th-and 16th-century Galicia (1914), and the development of Ukrainian art in Western Ukraine (1944). His book on 15th- and 16th-century Galician icons (1929) remains an important illustrated source on the subject. Svientsitsky was also an enthusiastic amateur of modern Ukrainian art, and in 1931 he established a gallery for such art at the National Museum.

A bibliography of Svientsitsky's works, compiled by O. Kizlyk and R. Lutsyk, was published in Lviv in 1956.

O. Horbach, S. Hordynsky, R. Senkus

**Svientsitsky, Pavlyn** [Svjencic'kyj] (Polish: Święcicki, Paulin; pseuds: Pavlo Svii, Danylo Lozovsky, Pavlyn Stakhursky, S. Holod, Pevny, Liakh z Ukrainy), b 1841 in Varshytsia (now Kalynivka), Vinnytsia county, Podilia gubernia, d 12 September 1876 in Lviv. Ukrainian writer of Polish descent. He studied at Kiev University. During the Polish Insurrection of 1863, which he supported, he emigrated to Austrian-ruled Lviv. There he worked as an actor with the Ruska Besida Theater, collected folklore, and contributed to *Nyva*, *Meta*, and *Lastivka*. He also published the Polish-Ukrainian miscellany *Sioło (1866–7) and edited the weekly *Nowiny* (1867–9). From 1869 he taught Ukrainian at the Academic Gymnasium of Lviv. In Ukrainian Svientsitsky wrote articles, stories, the novel *Kolys' bulo* (Once upon a Time; in Polish as *Przed laty*, 1865), the plays *Halia* (1866), *Mishchanka* (The Bourgeoise, 1866), and *Kateryna* (1866, based on T. Shevchenko's poem), some poems, and the fable collections *Baiky: Darunok malym* *ditiam* (Fables: A Gift for Small Children, 1864) and *Baiky v nauku molodym i starym* (Fables as a Lesson for Young and Old, 1874, 1891). A book of his Polish stories based on Ukrainian history and folklore, *Opowieści stepowe* (Steppe Tales), was published in Lviv in 1871. He translated Shevchenko's and Yu. Fedkovych's poems and M. Vovchok's stories into Polish, and W. Shakespeare's *Hamlet*, Molière's *George Dandin*, and A. Mickiewicz's sonnets into Ukrainian. He also prepared a Ukrainian grammar (unpublished) and wrote a brochure on 19th-century Ukrainian literature (1871). V. Radzykevych's 119-page article about him was published in *Zapysky NTSh* in 1911, and many of his fables were reprinted in the 1971 Soviet Ukrainian anthology *Ukraïns'koiu muzoiu natkhnenni* (Inspired by the Ukrainian Muse).

R. Senkus

**Sviezhynsky, Petro** [Svježyns'kyj], b 5 October 1911 in Usa, near Ushachy, Vitsebsk gubernia (now Belarus). Historian. A graduate of Odessa University (1939), he was a lecturer (from 1962) and head (from 1970) of the Department of the History and Theory of Co-operatives at the Lviv Trade and Economics Institute. A specialist in Western Ukrainian socioeconomic history, he published numerous works, including *Ahrarni vidnosyny na Zakhidnii Ukraïni v kintsi XIX–na pochatchku XX st.* (Agrarian Relations in Western Ukraine in the Late 19th and Early 20th Centuries, 1966).

**Svii, Pavlo.** See Svientsitsky, Pavlin.

**Svineld** (Sveneld, Svindil), b and d ? 10th-century Rus' noble. He was a close associate of and vassal to the Kievan Rus' leaders Ihor, Olha, and Sviatoslav Ihorevych. He fought with the Ulychians (938–40), ruled over Ulychian and Derevlianian lands granted him by Ihor, helped Olha to suppress the Derevlianian revolt of 945 after Ihor was killed, and took part in Sviatoslav's Balkan campaigns. After Sviatoslav's death in 972, he became embroiled in the internecine Rus' struggle for power. According to some scholars Svineld was the model for the legendary folk character 'black raven Santal.'

**Svistel, Frants** [Svistel', Franc], b 17 July 1887 in Buchach, Galicia, d 4 July 1966 in Syracuse, New York. Lawyer and civic and political leader. After graduating in law from Lviv University (1912) he joined the Legion of Ukrainian Sich Riflemen and served as its quartermaster during the war. In 1922 he opened his own law office in Peremyshliany and became active in local political, civic, and co-operative's affairs. In 1935 he moved to Lviv, where he became director of the head office of the Ukrainian National Democratic Alliance. During the Second World War he was arrested by the Gestapo and was imprisoned for four years at Auschwitz. After emigrating to the United States from Germany in 1950, he was active in local Ukrainian organizations in Syracuse.

**Svit, Ivan** (Sweet, John), b 27 April 1897 in Kharkiv gubernia, d 8 March 1989 in Seattle. Journalist and community leader; member of the Shevchenko Scientific Society from 1984. In 1918 he made his way to the *Far East (Zelenyi Klyn). From there he fled from Soviet rule to *Harbin, Manchuria, where he was assistant editor of the Russian

Ivan Svit

newspaper *Kommercheskii telegraf* (1925–9), published and edited the Ukrainian *Man'dzhurs'kyi vistnyk* (1932–7), and contributed articles on Ukrainian life in the Far East to *Dilo* in Lviv and other papers. In 1942 he edited *The Call of the Ukraine* in Shanghai. As a postwar refugee in the United States from 1951, he contributed to *Svoboda* and other Ukrainian periodicals. Svit wrote several works in Russian, Ukrainian, and Japanese on Ukrainian life in China and the Far East, including *Ukrainskii dal'nii vostok* (The Ukrainian Far East, 1934), *Zelena Ukraïna* (Green Ukraine, 1949), and *Ukraïns'ko-iapons'ki vzaiemyny, 1903–1945* (Ukrainian-Japanese Relations, 1903–45, 1973).

*Svit* (World). The first Ukrainian newspaper published in Transcarpathia; the weekly organ of the Russophile *Society of St Basil the Great, published in *yazychiie in Uzhhorod in 1867–71. Edited by three teachers at the Uzhhorod gymnasium, Yu. Ihnatko, K. Sabov, and V. Kymak, it contained articles on Transcarpathian folklore, ethnography, religious and church affairs, history, economic affairs, and farming, as well as literary works. Following a split in the society and its takeover by the Magyarone faction, the newspaper was replaced by *Novyi svit* (1871–2). Edited by Rev A. Gebei, it forsook *yazychiie* and promoted the use of the vernacular.

*S'vit*

*S'vit* (World). A socialist literary, political, and scholarly monthly published in Lviv from January 1881 to September 1882. It was envisaged as a pan-Ukrainian progressive forum. I. *Belei figured as its publisher and editor, but its de facto editor and main contributor was I. *Franko. In it Franko serialized his novel *Boryslav smiietsia* (Boryslav Is

Laughing) and published several poems, a story, and many political, literary, and ethnographic articles. The magazine's polemical and satirical articles criticized the Galician populists and denounced the Russophiles. Because of its then unpopular radical politics and use of the phonetic orthography, *S'vit* attracted only about 150 subscribers. Issues 4 and 13 were held up by the Austrian authorities, and the magazine folded after 21 issues. P. Babiak's index to *S'vit* was published in Lviv in 1970.

**S'vit** (World). A literary and scholarly semimonthly magazine published in Lviv in 1906 (20 issues) and 1907 (17 issues; the last issue for 1907 appeared in 1908). Until October 1906 it was the organ of the Galician modernist group *Moloda Muza. In 1907 it was subtitled 'An Illustrated Periodical for Ruthenian Families' and had ties with moderate circles in the Ukrainian Radical party. *S'vit* was initially published and edited by V. Birchak with the aid of P. Karmansky, O. Lutsky, and M. Yatskiv. B. Lepky, V. Shchurat, and V. Pachovsky were artistic advisers. Later V. Budzynovsky (nos 14–20) and M. Yatskiv (in 1907) were the editors and publishers. All of the aforementioned contributed prose, poetry, articles on literature and art, and/or reviews. Besides translations from European and American authors (eg, M. Maeterlinck, G. de Maupassant, E.A. Poe, O. Wilde, F. Nietzsche), *S'vit* was the first to publish Kobylianska's novel *Nioba*, I. Karpenko-Kary's drama *Sava Chalyi*, and M. Starytsky and L. Starytska's novel *Pered bureiu* (Before the Storm). Its 'art for art's sake' orientation was criticized by I. Franko. Like its antecedent *Ruska khata*, it folded because of a lack of subscribers.

**Svit** (World). A semimonthly and, in 1929, monthly journal of politics and culture, published in Lviv in 1925–9. It was the organ of the right faction of the Ukrainian Social Democratic party and was edited by I. Kvasnytsia.

*Svit dytyny*

**Svit dytyny** (Child's World). An illustrated semimonthly and, from 1925, monthly children's magazine, published in Lviv in 1919–39. In 1923–5 it was a supplement to *Moloda Ukraïna*. It was published and edited by M. *Taranko, and its contributors included some of the best writers of children's literature and teachers in Western Ukraine. It was very popular there and among Ukrainian immigrants in North America. From 1920 the Svit Dytyny publishing house (est November 1919) also issued a series of some 230 illustrated children's books by foreign authors in translation and by Ukrainian writers, such as O. Wilde, J. Swift, A. Chekhov, N. Gogol, J. Verne, A. Lototsky (pseuds: Ya. Vilshenko, O. Bilousenko), V. Khronovych, O. Makovei, V. Levytsky-Sofroniv, M. Pidhirianka, F. Kokovsky, and B. Lepky.

**Svit molodi** (World of Youth). A monthly organ of the Youth Section of the pro-Communist *Ukrainian Labour-Farmer Temple Association, published in Winnipeg from March 1927 to July 1932. It was edited by M. Irchan (1927–9), M. Lenartovych (1929–30), and J. Boyd (1930–2) and was renamed *Boiova molod'* (Militant Youth) in June 1930. It contained articles on socialism, organizational news, prose, poetry, and plays. It published harsh criticisms of capitalism, fascism, and Ukrainian nationalism, and consistently defended the USSR. In 1929 it had a circulation of approx 3,700.

**Svit molodi** (World of Youth). A monthly cultural and educational journal for teenage girls, published in Kolomyia in 1934–9. In 1934–5 it appeared as a supplement to *Zhinocha dolia. The editor was I. Vilde, and contributors included U. Kravchenko, D. Vikonska, S. Yablonska, V. Simenovych, and I. Zubenko.

Mykola Svitalsky

**Svitalsky, Mykola** [Svital's'kyj], b 12 December 1884 in Rohizne, Sumy county, Kharkiv gubernia, d 15 September 1937. Geologist; full member the AN URSR (now ANU) from 1930. He graduated from the St Petersburg Mining Institute in 1911. He conducted geological research in eastern Siberia and worked in St Petersburg before moving to Ukraine in 1921. There he studied the Kryvyi Rih Iron-ore Basin and other geologically significant areas, and assessed their ore and oil potential. He became an associate director of the Ukrainian Geological Committee (1926), director of the ANU Institute of Geological Sciences (1934), and vice-president of the ANU (1935). His main scholarly work dealt with the structures and origins of ore deposits as well as the petrography of mountain rocks. Svitalsky died during the Stalinist terror.

**Svitlo** (Light). The first and only Ukrainian-language pedagogical journal in Russian-ruled Ukraine before the 1917 Revolution. It was published nine times a year by the Ukrainskyi Uchytel society in Kiev, from September 1910 to August 1914 (a total of 36 issues). The founder and first editor was H. Sherstiuk; he was succeeded after his death in 1911 by his wife, L. Sherstiuk. *Svitlo* contained articles on educational theory and preschool, elementary, secondary, and extracurricular education; prose; poetry; news; criticism; and book reviews. It advocated teaching in Ukrainian in elementary schools and worked to organize Ukrainian teachers and cultural workers. Among the contributors were prominent pedagogues, cultural figures, and writers. The journal was frequently confiscated by the tsarist authorities. It was closed down after Russia entered the First World War.

*Svitlo* (Light). A monthly children's journal published in Uzhhorod in 1913–14 and 1916. It was edited by Rev T. Skyba.

*Svitlo* (Light). An unofficial weekly organ of the Communist Party of Western Ukraine, published in Lviv in 1925–8 (a total of 139 issues). It was edited by V. *Bobynsky to April 1927. For a short time in 1927–8 it was under the influence of a faction of the more independent Ukrainian Social Democratic party, led by I. Kvasnytsia. When pro-Soviet forces re-established their control over the paper, it was closed by the Polish authorities. *Svitlo* generally supported the Soviet Union and harshly criticized Ukrainian nationalists in Western Ukraine.

*Svitlo* (Light). A popular journal published monthly (with interruptions) by the Prosvita society in Mukachiv in 1933–8. Edited by P. Petrychko, L. Romaniuk, and V. Kurylenko, it provided practical advice on agricultural and economic affairs.

*Svitlo* (Light). A Sovietophile newspaper published by the Union of Ukrainian and Belarusian Workers' Organizations in Buenos Aires semimonthly from 1935 and semiweekly in 1942–3. The first editor was S. Valchuk. *Svitlo* contained articles on cultural and economic topics and political commentary, and strongly criticized the Ukrainian nationalist community in Argentina. It was closed down by the Argentinian government in 1943. It was revived in 1946 and succeeded by the weekly *Znannia* in 1949.

*Svitlo* (Light). A popular religious monthly magazine published semimonthly (1938–55) and then monthly by the Basilian order in Canada. It appeared in Mundare, Alberta, to 1949 and since then has been published in Toronto. Its editors have been Revs M. Romanovych (1938–43), A. Trukh (1943–6), I. Nazarko (1946–8), V. Dribnenky (1948–56), M. Solovii (1957–64), O. Kupranets (1964–88), and N. Svirsky (since 1988). The magazine publishes church news and articles on religious, cultural, and historical topics. Since 1940 it has also published an annual almanac.

*Svitlo i tin'* (Light and Shade). An organ of the Ukrainian Photographic Society, published monthly in Lviv in 1933–9. The journal's editors and contributors included Yu. Dorosh, S. Shchurat, O. Mokh, D. Figol, and Ya. Savka.

**Svitlovodske** or **Svitlovodsk** [Svitlovods'ke or Svitlovods'k]. IV-14. A city (1990 pop 57,000) on the Kremenchuk Reservoir and a raion center in Kirovohrad oblast. It

*Svitlo i tin'*

arose in 1961, when the inhabitants of Novoheorhiivske (est 1680s), Taburyshche (est 17th century), and Kryliv (est 12th century) were resettled in the workers' settlement of Kremenchukhesbud (est 1954) to make way for the flooding of the reservoir. In 1962 the city was renamed Kremhes, and in 1969, Svitlovodske. It is a river port and an industrial center with a hydroelectric station, several nonferrous metallurgical plants, and a furniture, a ceramics, and a plastics factory.

**Svitlychna, Hanna** [Svitlyčna], b 20 April 1939 in Pavlohrad, Dnipropetrovske oblast. Poet of the *shestydesiatnyky. She is the author of the collections *Stezhky nekhodzheni vesniani* (Untrodden Spring Paths, 1961), *Zolote pereveslo* (The Golden Sheaf Band, 1963), *Soniachni prychaly* (Sunny Docks, 1966), *Dozrivannia* (Maturation, 1969), *Kol'ory* (Colors, 1970), *Dobroho ranku* (Good Morning, 1972), *Litozbir* (The Summer Harvest, 1973), *Kordony sertsia* (Borders of the Heart, 1974), *S'ohodni i zavzhdy* (Today and Forever, 1978), *Zorom sertsia* (With the Vision of the Heart, 1980), *V siaivi kryla* (In the Wing's Glow, 1982), and *Ternovyi svit* (The Thorny World, 1985).

Nadiia Svitlychna

**Svitlychna, Nadiia** [Svitlyčna, Nadija], b 8 November 1936 in Polovynkyne, Starobilske raion, Luhanske oblast. Dissident and political prisoner; sister of I. Svitlychny. She was arrested in April 1972 and sentenced in March 1973 to four years in a labor camp for women in the Mordovian ASSR, for her involvement in the Ukrainian dissident movement, her defense of political prisoners, and her dissemination of samvydav literature. After her release in May 1976, she returned to Kiev, where she was further persecuted. In October 1978 she was allowed to emigrate to the United States with her two sons. She has been active in the *Ukrainian Helsinki Group's External Representation, published the *Herald of Repression in Ukraine* (1980–5), and edited a pamphlet on Yu. Lytvyn (1980) and an edition of V. Stus's poetry (1986).

Ivan Svitlychny

Hryhorii Svitlytsky (self-portrait, pastel and pencil, 1925)

**Svitlychny, Ivan** [Svitlyčnyj], b 20 September 1929 in Polovynkyne, Luhanske okruha, d 25 October 1992 in Kiev. Poet, literary critic, human rights activist, and dissident. After graduating in philology from Kharkiv University in 1952, he worked as an editor of *Radians'ke literaturoznavstvo*, a research associate of the AN URSR (now ANU) Institute of Literature, and a researcher in the dictionary department of the ANU Institute of Linguistics. In 1965 he was fired from his job and arrested for his 'nationalistic' activities, namely, smuggling abroad V. Symonenko's works. After eight months in prison he was released. In 13 January 1972 he was arrested for contributing to and distributing samvydav literature and was sentenced to seven years' hard labor and five years' internal exile. He was seriously ill in labor camp and suffered two strokes during exile. Upon his release in 1984 he returned to Kiev permanently crippled.

Svitlychny's critical articles began to appear in such journals as *Vitchyzna*, *Radians'ke literaturoznavstvo*, and *Dnipro* while he was a student. In his early works on literary theory he rejected the application of philosophical concepts to the study of esthetics and literature. He was closely identified with the *shestydesiatnyky* in the 1960s, and devoted much attention to their work. He translated Czech (V. Nezval, F. Halas, J. Mahen, J. Hanzlik), Slovak (M. Rufus), and French (J. de La Fontaine, P.-J. de Béranger, C. Baudelaire) works and *Slovo o polku Ihorevi* (The Tale of Ihor's Campaign) into Ukrainian. During imprisonment and exile he wrote poetry, some of which has appeared in the West. In the late 1980s under Perestroika some of his works and some articles about him began to appear again in the Soviet press. A collection of his poetry,

*Sertse dlia kul' i dlia rym* (A Heart for Bullets and Rhymes), appeared in 1991.

B. Balan

**Svitlychny, Kostiantyn** [Svitlyčnyj, Kostjantyn], b 5 March 1922 on the Hruzkyi state farm, now in Makiivka raion, Donetske oblast. Humorist and satirist. A former teacher and an editor of the journal *Donbas*, he began publishing in 1948 and has written the storybooks *Rep'iakhy* (Burrs, 1957), *Z vysoty suputnyka* (From a Sputnik's Height, 1958), *Ia i Kamila* (I and Kamila, 1961), *Sterezhys' avtomobilia* (Beware of the Automobile, 1962), *Nerentabel'na liubov* (Inexpedient Love, 1965), *Serenada pid terykonamy* (Serenade below the Slag Heaps, 1970), *Humorystychni opovidannia* (Humorous Stories, 1973), and *Ne bez usmishky* (Not without a Smile, 1982), and the novelettes *Chyie ty, nebo?* (Whose Are You, Sky?, 1960), *Mizh solov'iamy* (Among Nightingales, 1963), *Lehendy Chernechoho ozera* (Legends of Cherneche Lake, 1973), *Holubooka Serhiïvka* (Blue-eyed Serhiivka, 1977), and *Vit'ko Kushch – peteushnyk* (Vitko Kushch the PTU-man [vocational-technical school student], 1985).

**Svitlychny, Yefrem** [Svitlyčnyj, Jefrem], b 10 February 1901 in Zhykhar, Kharkiv county, d ? Socialist-realist painter and graphic artist. He studied (1922–9) and taught (1941–63) at the Kharkiv Art Institute. Most of his paintings depict Soviet Ukrainian genre scenes; they include *Tractor Column in the Field* (1933), *Hay Gathering* (1934), *On Collective-Farm Fields* (1947), and *Evening in the Field* (1960). He also designed propaganda posters and prints.

**Svitlychny, Yevhen** [Svitlyčnyj, Jevhen], b 24 August 1948 in Kaunas, Lithuania. Theater set designer and painter. Svitlychny was born into a Ukrainian family of artists from Kharkiv and has lived in Kharkiv since 1955. Since graduating in 1974, he has worked as an artist at the Kharkiv Theater of Opera and Ballet. His work there has inspired paintings such as *Carmen* (1983) and *Torero* (1984). More recently Svitlychny has embraced Ukrainian and Christian subject matter. His first solo exhibition was held in Kiev in 1986. He is a founding member of Panorama, an informal artists' society created in 1986 in Kharkiv. His work was published for the first time in 1989, in the journal *Kafedra* (no. 9).

**Svitlytsky, Hryhorii** [Svitlyc'kyj, Hryhorij], b 27 September 1872 in Kiev, d 28 July 1948 in Kiev. Realist painter and graphic artist. He studied at the Kiev Drawing School (1889–93) and under I. Repin, M. Kuznetsov, and A. Kuindzhi at the St Petersburg Academy of Arts (1893–1900). From 1918 he took part in the exhibitions of the *Peredvizhniki society, was a member of the Association of Artists of Red Ukraine (1926–9) in Kiev, and taught at the Kiev State Art Institute (1946–8). His early works are mostly portraits, genre paintings, and nocturnal landscapes, often on a musical theme, such as *Melody* (1900), *To the City* (1907), *Musicians* (1912), and *Nocturne* (1914). In 1918–20 he worked as a book illustrator and poster designer. In the Soviet period he painted portraits; genre paintings, such as *Village Council* (1918), *Flourishing Collective Farm in Bloom* (1935), and *Motherland* (1945); and lyrical landscapes, such as *Podil* [*District*] *in Kiev* (1924) and *On the Dnieper* (1939). By applying different colors with tiny brush strokes, he achieved an effect similar to that of pointillism. B. Butnyk-Siversky's book about him was published in Kiev in 1958.

Serhii Svitoslavsky: *The Dnieper Rapids* (oil, 1885)

**Svitoslavsky, Serhii** [Svitoslavs'kyj, Serhij], b 6 October 1857 in Kiev, d 19 September 1931 in Kiev. Landscape painter. After studying at the Moscow School of Painting, Sculpture, and Architecture (1875–83) he returned to Kiev. From 1884 he took part in the exhibitions of the *Peredvizhniki society, and in 1891 he became a member of the society. During the 1905 Revolution he contributed to the satirical magazine *Shershen'* and helped students expelled from the Kiev Art School. His landscapes are noted for their colors. Some of his best-known works are *Dnieper Rapids* (1885), *Oxen in the Field* (1891), *Street in a County Town* (1895), *Myrhorod* (1905), *Winter* (1905), *On a River* (1909), *Ferry on the Dnieper* (1913), *Vicinity of Kiev: Winter, Vicinity of Kiev: Summer*, and *The Dnieper at Dusk*. His travels in Central Asia in the late 1890s gave rise to a group of landscapes, including *Steppe, Goat Herd in the Mountains*, and *Ships of the Desert* (1900). After his eyesight deteriorated in the early 1920s, Svitoslavsky gave up painting. Albums of his works were published in Kiev in 1955 and 1989.

*Svitova zirnytsia* (Morning Star). A newspaper for peasants published by the Polish magnate J. *Wołoszynowski weekly (with interruptions) in 1906–12, semimonthly in 1913, and irregularly in 1917 and 1920. It appeared in Mohyliv-Podilskyi (1906–8), the village of Penkivka, in Podilia gubernia (1909–11), Kiev (1911–13, 1917), and Kamianets-Podilskyi (1920). The paper provided practical advice on farming, beekeeping, orcharding, and the co-operative movement in Ukraine. It also published literary works by P. Hrabovsky, B. Hrinchenko, O. Kovalenko, L. Hlibov, S. Rudansky, I. Nechui-Levytsky, O. Kobylianska, and other writers, as well as translations of H.C. Andersen and G. de Maupassant. In 1906 the newspaper was printed in the *yaryzhka* alphabet, but it soon switched to Standard Ukrainian. In 1906–7 it published the children's supplement *Chytaite, dity!*

*Svito-vyd* (World Look). A literary and art journal published semiannually since 1990 as the organ of the *New York Group and the Kiev branch of the Writers' Union of Ukraine. The aim of the journal is to manifest the unity of Ukrainian creative forces by providing a forum for writers and artists regardless of their habitat or political orientation. The editor in chief is B. *Boychuk, and the editor from Ukraine is I. *Rymaruk. *Svito-vyd* was the first Ukrai-

*Svito-vyd*

nian literary journal to have an editorial board composed of authors from Soviet Ukraine and from the diaspora. The journal solicits contributions of poetry, short prose, criticism, and translations from contemporary Ukrainian authors from all parts of the world. The publication is financed by M. Kots, an émigré benefactor, and is sold both in Ukraine and abroad.

**Švitrigaila** (Orthodox names: Oleksander and Lev; Catholic name: Boleslav), b ca 1370, d 10 February 1452 in Lutske, Volhynia. Grand duke of Lithuania (1430–2); son of Algirdas and brother of Władysław II *Jagiełło. He ruled the Vitsebsk appanage (from which he was expelled by *Vytautas in 1393) and the Polish fiefdom of Podilia (1400–2). Later, supported by the Teutonic Knights, Muscovy, and Moldavia, he fought against Vytautas and Jagiełło. In 1420 he made peace with Vytautas and received the Novhorod-Siverskyi and Briansk appanages. After Vytautas's death Švitrigaila was backed by Ukrainian and Belarusian magnates (who were promised high offices in the Grand Duchy of Lithuania) and by Lithuanian magnates (who wanted independence from Poland) in his appointment as grand duke of Lithuania (1430). In 1432 he fought against Poland for the control of Podilia. Jagiełło's supporters instigated a rebellion against Švitrigaila in Lithuania, as a result of which he was defeated and replaced by *Žygimantas. To neutralize Švitrigaila's popularity with Ukrainian and Belarusian subjects Jagiełło and Žygimantas granted the Orthodox equality with the Catholics (1432). Švitrigaila continued to fight for the throne, but he suffered a major defeat in Lithuania on 1 September 1435. For a while he preserved his control over the Ukrainian territories of the Grand Duchy of Lithuania, but after 1438 he ruled only Volhynia and eastern Podilia. He was buried in the Vilnius cathedral.

BIBLIOGRAPHY
Lewicki, A. *Powstanie Świdrygiełły* (Cracow 1892)
Matusas, J. *Švitrigaila* (Kaunas 1938)

A. Zhukovsky

**Svoboda, Yosyf,** b ?, d ca 1885. Painter and graphic artist of Czech origin. From 1838 he worked as a lithographer in Lviv, where he made portraits, landscapes, and historical prints, sometimes on Ukrainian themes (eg, *Cossacks from Chyhyryn in Istanbul, Sava Chaly*, and *Nastia Lisovska, Wife of Süleyman II*). He also illustrated books and magazines.

*Svoboda*

**Svoboda** (Liberty). The oldest existing Ukrainian newspaper and the most widely read in the Western world. Founded by members of the *American Circle as a semimonthly in September 1893, it appeared weekly from March 1894 and three times a week from August 1914. Since January 1921 it has appeared five days a week. The paper was from the beginning the official organ of the *Ukrainian National Association (UNA) and has been owned by it since 1908. Until June 1895 it was published in Jersey City, New Jersey, and then in Shamokin (1895–6), Mt Carmel (1896–1900), Olyphant (1900–3), and Scranton (1903–6), Pennsylvania. Until 1903 the paper used *etymological spelling. In December 1906 it moved to New York, and since April 1911 it has again been published in Jersey City. The chief editors have been Revs H. Hrushka, N. Dmytriv, and I. Konstankevych (1895–7), S. Makar (1897–1900), and I. Ardan (1900–7), who were also the publishers; A. Tsurkovsky (1907–9, 1911–12); O. Stetkevych (1910–11, 1912–19); V. Lototsky (1919–26); O. Reviuk (1926–33); L. Myshuha (1933–55); A. Drahan (1955–78); V. Tershakivets (1979–80); and Z. Snylyk (1980–). In the interwar period the associate editors were V. Kedrovsky, E. Liakhovych, and S. Demydchuk; since the Second World War they have been I. Korovytsky, L. Lutsiv, I. Kedryn, V. Davydenko, B. Kravtsiv, and M. Sosnovsky. Many prominent Western Ukrainian and émigré journalists have been regular contributors to *Svoboda*, including, in its first decades, V. Budzynovsky, I. Franko, M. Pavlyk, K. Genik, V. Hnatiuk, M. Lozynsky, B. Lepky, O. Oleksiv, and M. Pavlyk.

From the outset, in addition to providing news, information, and analyses to a Ukrainian-speaking audience, *Svoboda* has served as an important vehicle for the Ukrainian national movement in the United States. Initially it spearheaded the fight against the Russophiles among Ukrainian immigrants and successfully discredited tsarist propaganda. It was instrumental in raising support for creation of the *American Ruthenian National Council in 1914 and the *Ukrainian Congress Committee of America in 1940. The paper covered the Ukrainian struggle for independence following the February Revolution of 1917, and expressed its support for the Central Rada, the UNR, and the Western Ukrainian National Republic. In the interwar period it raised awareness of Polish oppression and atrocities in Western Ukraine, the man-made famine of 1932–3 in Soviet Ukraine, and the Stalinist terror in the USSR. At that time it maintained close relations with several Ukrainian newspapers in Galicia. After the Second World War it led the action to bring Ukrainian displaced persons to the United States. *Svoboda* has always reported extensively on Ukrainian life in the United States and elsewhere, and also served as the main source of information for Ukrainians in Canada and Brazil before the emergence of Ukrainian newspapers there. It has contained supplements for various Ukrainian youth, community, and cultural organizations in the United States. The paper's

circulation has remained steady in recent years at approx 18,000, the largest among Ukrainian papers in the West.

At various times the Svoboda Press has published several series of informational and educational booklets and brochures on a variety of topics. Since 1896, together with the UNA, it has issued approx 300 Ukrainian-language books (memoirs, collections, monographs, and literary works) and over a dozen English-language works on Ukrainian history and literature (by authors such as M. Hrushevsky, D. Doroshenko, D. Dontsov [Snowyd], G. Vernadsky, S. Shumeyko, C. Manning, W. Chamberlain, L. Myshuha, J. Panchuk, and A. Drahan); was involved in the preparation and publication of the two-volume *Ukraine: A Concise Encyclopaedia* (1963, 1971); has printed the English-language quarterly *Ukrainian Juvenile Magazine* (1927–33), the *Ukrainian Weekly* (since 1933), and the children's magazines *T'svitka* (1914–17) and *Veselka* (since 1954); and published in 1897, 1901–36, 1940, 1944, 1949, and since 1951 annual calendar-almanacs containing literary works, articles on historical and cultural topics, and information about the history of the newspaper and the UNA (especially in the anniversary issues of 1936, 1944, 1953, 1963, 1973, 1978, and 1983). An index of Ukrainian-Canadian content in *Svoboda* to 1904 was prepared by F. Swyripa and A. Makuch and published in 1985. Since 1983 a selective index to *Svoboda* has been compiled by the Immigration History Research Center at the University of Minnesota; vol 1 (1893–99) was published in 1990.

B. Balan, B. Kravtsiv

**Svoboda** (Freedom). A newspaper of political and economic affairs, published in 1897–1919 and 1922–39; after *Dilo* one of the longest-running Ukrainian newspapers in Galicia. The organ of the *National Democratic party and, from 1925, the *Ukrainian National Democratic Alliance, it was published in Lviv except during the Russian occupation of 1915, when it appeared in Vienna, and in 1919, when it was published in Stanyslaviv (now Ivano-Frankivske). Its periodicity varied, but for most of its existence it appeared weekly. In its early years *Svoboda* devoted particular attention to rural issues and published practical advice on farming and the prices of agricultural products. It featured regular reports from correspondents throughout the countryside and reports on the activities of the Prosvita society and various co-operatives. Later it devoted more attention to international political affairs. The editors of *Svoboda* included prominent political figures, such as K. Levytsky, V. Okhrymovych, V. Budzynovsky, L. Tsehelsky, V. Bachynsky, M. Zaiachkivsky, S. Baran, M. Strutynsky, O. Kuzma, and V. Tselevych. The paper had a pressrun of 1,850 in 1897, 6,500 in 1912, 9,500 in 1913, 8,500 in 1917, and 2,350 in 1930.

**Svoboda** (Freedom). A weekly Ukrainophile newspaper published in Uzhhorod in 1922–38 as the continuation of *Nauka*. The editor and publisher was A. Voloshyn; V. Zheltvai and Yu. Sopko were the managing editors. The organ of the *Christian People's party in Transcarpathia from 1925, *Svoboda* was published in the Transcarpathian dialect until 1930, but afterward it appeared in Standard Ukrainian. It was succeeded by *Nova svoboda*.

**SVU.** See Union for the Liberation of Ukraine.

Vasyl Svyda: *To the Mountain Pasture* (wood, 1954)

Festival time in Svydnyk

**Svyda, Vasyl,** b 22 October 1913 in Patskanove, Transcarpathia, d 19 April 1989 in Uzhhorod. Sculptor. After graduating from a handicrafts school in Yasynia (1934) he wandered about Czechoslovakia before finding work in a church art workshop in Brno. After the Second World War he taught for many years at the Uzhhorod School of Applied Art. He worked in plaster, clay, and, particularly, wood. His works include the bas-relief series 'Seasons of the Year' (1947) and 'To School' (1949); many-figured compositions, such as *To the Mountain Pasture* (1954) and *Wedding* (1965); high reliefs, such as *Opryshoks* (1954) and *Transcarpathia* (1959–61); and majolica or terra-cotta figurines.

**Svydivets** [Svydivec'] (also Svydovets). The largest mountain group in the Polonynian Beskyds of the Carpathians, situated between the Teresva and the Chorna Tysa rivers in Transcarpathia oblast. The main portion of the ridge has elevations ranging from 1,400 to 1,880 m (Mt Blyznytsia). A short spur juts from its northern end, and a longer one along its southern edge. Deep, narrow valleys cut sharply into the wide, smooth mountains. Postglacial cirques, some of them now filled with lakes, can be found along the ridge's northern slopes. Fir forests up to an elevation of 1,400 m are also located there. The southern slopes of the formation are covered with beech forests up to an elevation of 1,300 m. In the higher reaches of the mountains pastures can be found as well as the seasonal dwellings of shepherds. Permanent settlement in the region is found in the river valleys, most notably at Rakhiv and Ust-Chorna.

**Svydnyk** (Slovak: Svidník). An administrative center (1980 pop 7,500) of the Dukla krai, in the Prešov region of Slovakia. The town arose through the merger of Vyshnii and Nyzhnii Svydnyk in 1943. It is mentioned in historical documents as early as 1330. Today Svydnyk has a gymnasium and a sewing, farming, and building tekhnikum. It has two museums, the Museum of the Dukla Battles and the *Svydnyk Museum of Ukrainian Culture. The Festival of Ukrainian Song and Dance, renamed in 1977 the *Ukrainian Cultural Festival in Czechoslovakia, has been held in Svydnyk since 1956. Writers and scholars, such as Ye. Biss, O. Pavlovych, and J. Polívka, lived and worked

there. O. Zilynsky is buried in the local cemetery. The surrounding district includes 105 villages, 93 of which are Ukrainian (1980, 27,312 residents). Some of them (Bodružal, Dobroslava, Hunkovce, Korejovce, Krajné Čierno, Ladomirová, Myrol'a, and Nyžný Komárnik) have wooden churches which have been declared monuments of national culture by the Czech government.

A book by Myroslav Sopolyha (1990) documenting the first 35 years of the Svydnyk Museum of Ukrainian Culture

**Svydnyk Museum of Ukrainian Culture** (Muzei ukrainskoi kultury u Svydnyku). A state-funded museum in Slovakia, specializing in the culture, history, and contemporary life of the Ukrainian population of the *Prešov region. The museum was formerly located in Medzilaborce (1956–7), Prešov (1957–60, as part of the Prešov Regional Museum), and Krasný Brod (1960–4); in 1964 it was moved into its own building in Svydnyk. A library (24,500 vols in 1981) and manuscript, tape, photo, film, and phonorecord archives are located at the museum. The Dezyderii Myly Art Gallery was established there in 1983, and an outdoor museum of folk architecture on the grounds of the Svydnyk open-air theater was created as part of the museum in the early 1980s. One-room museums in the villages of Čertižné and Habura and the small Oleksander Dukhnovych Museum in the village of Topol'a were branches of the museum. The museum published exhibition catalogs and 11 large volumes (1965–7, 1969–72, 1976–7, 1979–80, 1982–3) of its serial *Naukovyi zbirnyk*, containing valuable studies on the Prešov region by I. Chabyniak, M. Rusynko, S. Hostyniak, V. Lakata, M. Shmaida, M. Sopolyha, I. Chyzhmar, and other Ukrainian scholars in Czechoslovakia. An anniversary guide to the museum was published in 1981. The museum's directors have been O. Hrytsak, Chabyniak, and, since the mid-1970s, Rusynko. In 1991 the museum was renamed the Dukhnovych Museum.

R. Senkus

Anatolii Svydnytsky          Pavlo Svyrydenko

**Svydnytsky, Anatolii** [Svydnyc'kyj, Anatolij], b 13 September 1834 in Mankivtsi, Lityn county, Podilia gubernia, d 18 July 1871 in Kiev. Writer, community activist, and folklorist. He began his activities as a member of the clandestine *Kharkiv-Kiev Secret Society, which set itself the task of struggling with the tsarist regime, disseminating forbidden literature, and establishing Sunday schools. During that period he wrote a number of lyric poems against arbitrary rule and national oppression, of which only 'Horlytsia' (Turtledove, 1860) was published during his lifetime. 'Koly khochesh nam dobra' (If You Wish Us Well), 'V poli dolia stoiala' (Fate Stood in the Field), and part of 'Vzhe bil'sh lit dvisti' (For More Than Two Hundred Years Now) were published in *Literaturno-naukovyi vistnyk* by I. Franko in 1901. In 'Vzhe bil'sh' Svydnytsky decries B. Khmelnytsky's signing of the Pereiaslav Treaty of 1654.

Only 'Velykden' u podolian' (Easter among the Podilians) and 'Iz Mirgoroda' (From Myrhorod) were published in *Osnova* in 1861, out of the many articles on ethnography and against tsarist absolutism which Svydnytsky wrote in 1860–2. After the tsarist ban on all Ukrainian publications he published a number of articles and stories in Russian in the newspaper *Kievlianin*.

*Liuboratski* is considered to be Svydnytsky's major work. It is a chronicle, to a large extent autobiographical, of the downfall of the Liuboratsky family of clergymen over the course of three generations. It is set in the Podilia region, which was dominated by the Polish aristocracy, tsarist oppression, and the inimical official Orthodox clergy. Its far-reaching range of subject matter prompted I. Franko to designate the work as the first realist novel in Ukrainian literature. In both form and content *Liuboratski* serves as a transition between the prose of H. *Kvitka-Osnovianenko and M. Vovchok and the later epic realism of I. Nechui-Levytsky and P. Myrny. The novel had no immediate influence on contemporary writers, however, because it was published for the first time, in *Zoria* (1886), 15 years after the author's death. It has appeared in many editions since then. A collection of Svydnytsky's writing (*Tvory* [Works]) appeared in 1958.

I. Koshelivets

**Svyrenko, Dmytro,** b 5 November 1888 in Merchyk, Valky county, Kharkiv gubernia, d 26 October 1944 in Orenburg, Russia. Botanist and hydrobiologist; corresponding member of the AN URSR (now ANU) from 1934. A graduate of Kharkiv University (1912), he taught at Dnipropetrovske (1920–3 and 1927–41) and Odessa (1923–7) universities and at the Orenburg Pedagogical and Agricultural institutes in the Urals (1941–4). He also initiated the creation of the Dnipropetrovske Scientific Research Station of Hydrobiology (est 1927).

**Svyrydenko, Pavlo,** b 20 March 1893 in Putyvl, Kursk gubernia, d 25 December 1971 in Kiev. Zoologist; full member of the AN URSR (now ANU) from 1948. A graduate of Moscow University (1915), he was director of the Northern Caucasian Plant Conservation Station in Rostov-na-Donu, lecturer at Moscow University (1932–41), and director of the entomology laboratory of the All-Union Scientific Research Institute of the Sugar Industry (from 1941), and the ecology department of the ANU Institute of Zoology (1947–54). His major work was on the control of agricultural pests (vermin and insects) and the conservation of mammals and birds. He was one of the initiators of aerial spraying in Ukraine.

**Svystun, Mykola** (nom de guerre: Yasen, Voron), b 1912 in Odriv, Radekhiv county, Galicia, d 8 December 1944 in Rivne oblast. Senior UPA officer. He joined the Ukrainian Military Organization (1928) and the OUN, and as their leading activist in Radekhiv county, he was twice arrested by Polish authorities. During 1942–3 he organized and commanded UPA units in Volhynia. In 1944 he commanded a brigade in the UPA-South and was the top UPA commander at the Battle of *Hurby. He was killed in action while performing the duties of chief of staff of the UPA-South.

**Svystun, Pylyp,** b 15 November 1844 in Toboliv, Zolochiv circle, Galicia, d 21 July 1916 in Rostov-na-Donu. Historian, educator, and Russophile leader in Galicia. After teaching at a gymnasium in Rzeszów he served as director of the library of the People's Home in Lviv (1904–12) and editor of its organ *Vistnyk Narodnoho doma*. He was an executive member of the Stauropegion Institute and president of the *Kachkovsky Society and editor of its publications. He wrote many articles and several books on the history of Galicia, including the study of T. Shevchenko *Chem est' dlia nas'' Shevchenko* (What Shevchenko Is for Us, 1885) and *Prikarpatskaia Rus' pod'' vladeniem Avstrii*

(Subcarpathian Ruthenia under the Rule of Austria, 2 vols, 1896–7; repr 1970), which criticized both the Austrian and the Polish authorities for restricting contacts with the Russian Empire as well as aiding Ukrainian 'separatism.'

**Svystun, Vasyl.** See Swystun, Wasyl.

**Svytiaz Lake** [Svytjaz'ke ozero]. II-4. A lake situated in the northwestern part of Volhynia oblast between the Buh River and the headwaters of the Prypiat River near the town of Svytiaz. The lake is 7.5 km long and approx 4 km wide, with a total area of 24.2 sq km. It is generally about 7 m deep, albeit with a maximum depth of 58.4 m. Its shores are mainly low-lying, and it has a large supply of fish. The lake is fed by artesian sources, and its water is clean and clear. Svytiaz is a popular resort area and a focal point of the recently established (1983) Shatsk National Park.

**Swallow** (Ukrainian: *lastivka*). A small, long-winged bird with a deeply forked tail, belonging to the family Hirudinidae. In Ukraine swallows are migrating birds with a strong homing instinct. Three species are common, the barn swallow (*Hirunda rustica*), the urban swallow or house martin (*Delichon urbica*), and the bank swallow or sand martin (*Riparia riparia*). The barn and urban swallows nest in human settlements in cup-shaped clay nests fastened beneath eaves. The bank swallows settle in colonies along steep banks of water bodies, where they build their nests in burrows. Owing to their close contact with humans, swallows figure prominently in Ukrainian folklore, folk songs, and poetry, as symbols of beauty and family unity. Their graceful flight pattern (in search of insects) was used to predict coming rains. Swallows are beneficial birds since they protect crops and forests by destroying flying insects.

**Swamps.** See Wetlands.

**Swan** (*Cygnus*; Ukrainian: *lebid*). The largest of the waterfowl in the subfamily Anserinae, family Anatidae, measuring up to 180 cm in length and 13 kg in weight. These graceful, long-necked birds glide majestically on water, although they cannot dive, and fly with slow wing-beats. Swans are often kept in park ponds. In Ukraine only the mute swan (*C. olor*) is found, in the Danube and Dniester deltas; the trumpeter swan (*C. cygnus*) and occasionally the Bewick's swan winter during their overflights on the Black Sea shores. The swan has been listed as an endangered species in Ukraine.

**Sweden.** A country on the eastern side of the Scandinavian Peninsula (1990 pop 8,529,000), with an area of 449,960 sq km. The majority of its inhabitants (90.8 percent) are Swedish, and there is a notable (3.1 percent) Finnish presence. There are about 2,000 Ukrainians in Sweden.

Although Sweden does not share borders with Ukraine, it has played an important role in Ukraine's history (particularly in the Princely and Cossack periods). The initial contacts between the two countries resulted from trade along the *Varangian route in the 9th century. The influence of the *Varangians contributed to the economic, cultural, and political development of Kievan Rus'. Even-

tually, dynastic ties were formed: Yaroslav the Wise married Olof Skötkonung's daughter Ingigerth, and Mstyslav (Harald) Volodymyrovych, who became grand prince in 1125, married Christina, the daughter of the Swedish king Ingi Stenkil.

Swedish-Ukrainian contacts were re-established after a long interruption at the beginning of the 17th century with the rise of the Cossacks as a power. Gustavus II Adolphus (1611–32), one of the Protestant leaders in the Thirty Years' War, solicited Cossack help against the Poles, and eventually (in 1631) sent his envoys directly to offer them a Swedish protectorate and an alliance against Poland. These overtures were rejected by Hetman I. Petrazhytsky-Kulaha and the Cossack council.

Between 1650 and 1653 Hetman B. Khmelnytsky sought an alliance with Sweden against Poland, but Queen Christina (1632–54) did not wish to embark on a war with Poland. Her successor, *Charles X Gustav (1654–60), however, helped set up a broader anti-Polish coalition consisting of Ukraine, Sweden, Transylvania, Brandenburg, Moldavia, and Wallachia. A Ukrainian delegation headed by Hegumen Daniel Oliveberg de Graecani Atheniensis was sent to Stockholm in 1654 for detailed discussion. The following year Charles attacked Poland and quickly took Warsaw and Cracow. Feeling threatened by Sweden's victory, Muscovy signed a peace agreement with Poland in Vilnius in November 1656, which led to war with Sweden. Khmelnytsky then tried to extend the anti-Polish coalition. That prospect fell apart in the summer of 1657, however, when Charles was forced to transfer his forces and his attention from the Polish to the Danish front after Denmark declared war on Sweden, and Austria came to the aid of Poland.

Hetman I. Vyhovsky revived and strengthened ties with Sweden. In October 1657 a Ukrainian-Swedish alliance was concluded in Korsun, according to which the independent Ukrainian Cossack state was to extend to the Vistula River and include the Lithuanian voivodeships of Brest and Smolensk. But this treaty had no practical effect, because Sweden was tied down with the Danish war, and Vyhovsky's own position was precarious. The hetman soon severed his Swedish connections and tried to come to terms with Poland in the Treaty of Hadiache.

During the Northern War (1700–21) Russia, allied with Denmark and Poland against Sweden, compelled the Cossacks of the Hetman state to take part in the Baltic campaigns. This development set in motion secret negotiations by Hetman I. *Mazepa with *Charles XII of Sweden in 1705 and led to the creation of an anti-Russian coalition in 1708. By October 1708 the Swedish army had entered Ukraine. Otaman K. Hordiienko brought the Zaporozhian Host into the coalition as well by signing a treaty with Charles XII on 28 March 1709. On 8 July 1709 the joint Swedish-Ukrainian force was defeated at the Battle of *Poltava. About 10,000 Swedes were killed and 3,000 captured in the battle. The Swedes retreated and finally capitulated at Perevolochna, while Charles and Mazepa fled to Bendery on Turkish territory with the remnants of their troops. After Mazepa's death (22 September 1709) Charles concluded a treaty with his successor, Hetman P. Orlyk, promising to help Ukraine in the struggle against Russia. After an unsuccessful attempt to gain control of Right-Bank Ukraine, Orlyk and 24 of his supporters emigrated to Sweden (1715–20). The wife of A. Voinarovsky, Anna, lived in Tynnelsö near Stockholm at this time.

In the second half of the 19th and in the early 20th century a number of women and girls from Galicia (Galicierna) worked in Sweden as farm laborers. Some of them stayed there and were assimilated. During the same period academic ties were established. The Kiev Archeographic Commission sent N. Molchanovsky to Sweden in 1898 to collect documents (published in 1908 in *Arkhiv Iugo-Zapadnoi Rossii*) in state archives pertaining to Ukrainian history. The Swedish archeologist and honorary member of the Archeological Committee of the All-Ukrainian Academy of Sciences T. Arne wrote about La Tenne culture relics, Roman and Arab coins, Gothic fibulae, and Vikings in Ukraine in *La Suède et l'Orient* (1914). The Swedish Slavist and writer A. Jensen visited Ukraine in 1909 and met M. Kotsiubynsky, I. Franko, O. Makovei, and V. Hnatiuk; translated works by I. Kotliarevsky, T. Shevchenko, and M. Kotsiubynsky into Swedish and German; and wrote articles and a monograph (1916) on Shevchenko. The Finnish writer J. Hemmer translated Shevchenko's poetry into Swedish (1919). V. von Heidenstam dealt with Ukraine in the late 17th century in his *Karolinerna* and *Mazepa och hans ambassadör*.

During the First World War a representation of the Union for the Liberation of Ukraine (SVU) was set up in neutral Sweden. It cultivated Swedish public opinion and published L. Tsehelsky's *Ukraïna kolyshnia shveds'ka soiuznytsia* (Ukraine, the Former Swedish Ally) in 1915. The Ukrainian Information Bureau, directed by V. Stepankivsky and M. Zalizniak, was opened in Stockholm in 1916. Although Sweden did not recognize the UNR, a Ukrainian diplomatic mission for Sweden and Norway was established in Stockholm in 1918. It was headed by B. Bazhenov and, in 1919, by K. Losky. Through Losky's efforts a book on Ukrainian history, geography, literature, and culture, *Ukrainarna* (Stockholm 1921), came out in Swedish under the editorship of A. Jensen and M. Erenpreis. The Swedish economist and sociologist G. Steffen supported Ukrainian independence and wrote a brochure in Swedish and English on Ukraine's relations with Russia and Poland.

In the interwar period the Finnish historian H. Gummerus wrote articles about Ukraine in Swedish and a book of recollections about Kiev, *Orostider i Ukraina* (1931). As well, the Ukrainian singer M. *Menzinsky (who had performed in the Swedish opera in 1904–8) moved to Stockholm in 1925, where he sang in the state opera and opened his own school of singing.

During the Second World War the Ukrainian Information Bureau for Finland and Scandinavia (UIFS) was set up in Helsinki by B. *Kentrzhynsky. It published a bulletin in Finnish, Swedish, and German and supplied aid to Ukrainian POWs from the Red Army. In 1944 the bureau was moved to Stockholm. Kentrzhynsky later directed the Ukrainian Press Bureau in Stockholm (1949–55); Yu. Borys and B. Zaluha were on the staff. Kentrzhynsky was an associate of the historical association Karolinska Förbundet, which published his works on Swedish-Ukrainian relations and, particularly, on Charles X Gustav (1956), Charles XII (1959), and I. Mazepa (1962). Works by well-known Swedish writers, such as A. Strindberg, S. Lagerlöf, and E. Lindgren, have been translated into Ukrainian.

Most of the Ukrainian newcomers to Sweden during the interwar period were refugees from the USSR who had managed to flee via Finland. Some Ukrainians who had been deported to Karelia during the collectivization drive

Members of the executive of the Ukrainian Hromada in Sweden in 1949. From left: Hryhor Pukalo, Yurii Borys, Vasyl Stasiuk, Bohdan Skobovych-Okolot, Valerian Fedorchuk, Roman Rudnyk, Kyrylo Harbar, Bohdan Kentrzhynsky

of 1932–5 escaped across the border in 1944. After the war the Swedish Red Cross sponsored a group of Ukrainian inmates of German concentration camps and Ukrainian workers in Germany and Austria. Some refugees from Poland, Karelia, and Bačka ended up in Sweden. In the years immediately following the war there were approx 2,000 to 2,500 Ukrainians in Sweden. A number of them subsequently emigrated to Canada or the United States. Today most Swedish Ukrainians live in the southern or central cities of Stockholm, Malmö, Göteborg, and Örebro. At one time Lund and Borås were also significant centers. Most Ukrainians worked as laborers, although there were a number of physicians, engineers, and teachers among them. The Orthodox community was served by Rev H. Matviienko from Hamburg and occasionally by Archbishop A. Dubliansky. Catholics were tended by Bishop I. Buchko and Rev M. van de Maele, and later by Bishop P. Kornyliak.

In 1947 the Ukrainian Hromada in Sweden (Ukrainska Sällskapet, or UHSh) was founded in Stockholm. Its presidents have been V. Fedorchuk (1947–51), V. Butko (1952), K. Harbar (1953–78), and B. Zaluha (1979–). Since 1954 it has published a quarterly bulletin, *Skandynavs'ki visti*. UHSh has three local affiliates: the Ukrainian-Swedish Hromada in Örebro (est 1975; president, H. Budiak), the Ukrainian-Swedish Cultural Association in Malmö (president, H. Horyn), and the Ukrainian-Swedish Cultural Alliance in Stockholm (president, B. Zaluha). The Orlyk Ukrainian Hromada functioned independently in Stockholm under the leadership of V. Dekhtiar in 1948–61. In the 1950s and 1960s the Ukrainian Academic Club, headed by Yu. Borys and B. Zaluha, was also active in the capital. B. Kentrzhynsky, who for a time published *Stokhol'ms'kyi visnyk*, was a representative of the Ukrainian National Rada for Scandinavia.

BIBLIOGRAPHY
Elmén, C. *Några underrätteise om Kossakerna* (Stockholm 1810)
Patritskii, O. *Skandinavshchina v davnoi Rusi* (St Petersburg 1887)
*Akty Shvedskogo gosudarstvennogo arkhiva otnosiashchiesia k istorii Malorossii (1649–1660 gg.)* Vol 6 of *Arkhiv Iugo-Zapadnoi Rossii*. (Kiev 1908)

Cehelskyj, L. *Ukraina sveriges bortglömda bundsförvant* (Stockholm 1915)

Jensen, A. *Ukrainarna* (Stockholm 1921)

Kentrschynskyj, [Kentrzhyns'kyj], B. *Sanningen om Ukraina* (Helsinki 1943)

– 'Na skandynavs'komu sektori OUN v druhii svitovii viini,' in *OUN, 1929–1954* (Paris 1955)

– *Karl X Gustav inför Krisen i Öster, 1654–1655* (Stockholm 1956)

– *Propagandakriget i Ukraina, 1708–1709* (Stockholm 1958)

Nordmann, C. *Charles XII et l'Ukraine de Mazepa* (Paris 1958)

A. Zhukovsky

**Sweet flag** (*Acorus calamus*; Ukrainian: *lepekha, air,* or *tatarske zillia*). A tall, herbaceous perennial plant (60–120 cm in height) of the family Araceae, also known as calamus root. In Ukraine sweet flag grows in Polisia and the forest-steppe territory on riverbanks, on lakeshores, and in marshy meadows. Volatile oil is extracted from the sweet flag rhizome to be used in perfumery, flavoring, and confectionery, and in medicine to stimulate the appetite and improve digestion and as a tonic against depression of the central nervous system.

**Sweet sultan** (Ukrainian: *hirchak*). A perennial herbaceous plant of the family Compositae, genera *Centaurea* and *Picris* (also called *Acroptilon*), with lanceolate leaves and pink, tubular flowers. It is toxic to horses and sheep and contaminates young crops. In Ukraine the most predominant is the creeping or common sweet sultan (*C. moschata*), which infests fields in Kharkiv, Zaporizhia, and Crimea oblasts. Control measures include quarantine, deep plowing, and herbicides.

**Sweet vernal grass** (*Anthoxantum odoratum*; Ukrainian: *pakhucha trava*). A fragrant annual and perennial grass of the family Poaceae, the only one of four species that grows in Ukraine. It has thin, flat leaves and narrow flower clusters; its sweet scent of freshly mown hay is derived from the coumarin present in the leaves. Sweet vernal is used as a component of hay in feeding domestic animals.

**Sweetbrier** (*Rosa eglanteria* or *R. rubiginosa*; Ukrainian: *shypshyna, dyka rozha*). A small, prickly, wild rosebush with fragrant foliage, often planted as a roadside or screening shrub; it is also known as eglantine. Its pink flowers ripen into red hips that are rich in vitamin C (4,500 mg per 100 g) as well as sugars, organic acids, carotene, and pectin. The brown sweetbrier (*R. cinnamomea*) has the greatest concentration of vitamin C. The rose hips are used for the production of vitamin concentrates to treat vitamin deficiency or arteriosclerosis, to increase the resistance to local and general infections, in folk medicine to treat liver ailments, and to make syrups, liqueurs, and herbal teas.

**Sweetgrass** (*Hierochloe*; Ukrainian: *chapoloch*). A creeping perennial grass of the family Gramineae. In Ukraine aromatic (*H. odorata*), steppe, and southern sweetgrasses often grow as weeds in meadows, in fields, and among bushes. It is the favorite food of the bisons of the Bilovezha Forest. Sweetgrass contains the odorous compound coumarin; soaked in grain alcohol, dried sweetgrass yields the alcoholic beverage Zubrivka.

**Swiderian culture**. A late Paleolithic to early Mesolithic culture of the 9th to 8th century BC that existed in the Baltic Basin, in Ukraine along the Desna River, and in the Crimea. It was named after a site near Warsaw. The people of this culture engaged in hunting, gathering, and fishing. They were quite mobile and usually established temporary shelters along river banks or on high dunes. Their flint technology was well developed and they employed a distinctive type of arrowhead. The best-known Swiderian site in Ukraine is located at *Smiach.

**Święcicki, Paulin.** See Svientsitsky, Pavlyn.

**Święty Krzyż.** A strict-regime Polish prison located at Łysa Góra, Kielce voivodeship. Formerly a Benedictine monastery, it was converted into a prison in 1825. During the interwar period (1919–39) some political prisoners were kept there, including the OUN members (S. Bandera, M. Lebed, M. Klymyshyn, Ya. Karpynets, and Ye. Kachmarsky) who were sentenced at the Warsaw Trial in 1935.

**Swimming** (*plavannia*). The first swimming clubs in Ukraine were established in Odessa and Mykolaiv in the early 1900s. In 1913 an all-Russian swim meet was held in Kiev. In the 1920s swimming became a part of the Soviet physical education and sports competition programs, and in Polish-ruled interwar Western Ukraine, the *Ukrainian Sports Union promoted the sport. In 1947, Soviet Ukrainian swimmers began competing in some international competitions as members of USSR teams; from 1952 they competed in the Olympic Games. The Ukrainian M. Havrysh placed sixth in the women's 200-m backstroke event in the 1952 games. In the 1964 games G. *Prozumenshchikova of Sevastopil won a gold medal (women's 200-m breaststroke OR, 2:46.4). In the 1980 games gold medals were won by S. Fesenko (men's 200-m butterfly, 1:59.76) and O. Sydorenko (men's 400-m individual medley OR, 4:22.09); both gold medalists were trained by the Ukrainian V. Smelova-Polishchuk. In the Olympic Games since 1952, Ukrainian swimmers have captured three gold, five silver, and five bronze medals in individual events. Other Ukrainian swimmers who have done well in international competitions are T. Deviatova (1964 Olympic bronze medal, women's 4 × 100-m medley relay), V. Dolhov (1980 Olympic bronze medal, men's 100-m backstroke), L. Hrebets (1968 Olympic bronze medal, women's 4 × 100-m medley relay), Yu. Hromak (1968 Olympic bronze medal, men's 4 × 100-m medley relay), V. Nemshilov (1968 Olympic bronze medal, men's 4 × 100-m medley relay), H. Prokopenko (1964 Olympic silver medal, men's 200-m breaststroke), V. Raskatov (1976 Olympic bronze medal, men's 400-m freestyle), V. Tkachenko (1988 Olympic silver medal, men's 4 100-m freestyle relay), V. Yaroshchuk (1988 Olympic bronze medals, men's 200-m individual medley and 4 100-m medley relay), M. Yurchenia (1976 Olympic silver medal, women's 200-m breaststroke), Yu. Bocharova, S. Kopchykova, V. Lozyk, Ye. Mykhailov, N. Shibaeva, N. Stavko, I. Ustymenko, and I. Zasieda. In 1987 there were 966 swimming coaches and 419 swimming pools in Ukraine.

O. Zinkevych

**Swine** (*Sus scrofa domestica*; Ukrainian: *svynia*). A mammal of the Suidae family, a stout-bodied, thick-skinned, short-legged omnivorous animal domesticated since the Neolithic period. Among farm animals it is the earliest to

A Ukrainian Spotted Steppe swine

mature and the most fertile. Most modern breeds produce 10 to 12 young per furrow, twice a year (even five times in two consecutive years). Swine are raised principally for meat and lard. Pork is the most popular meat in Ukrainian traditional *foods. The skin and bristles are also valuable, and in fact almost the entire animal is used effectively: the blood yields albumin, sausages, and feed meal; the bones provide bonemeal; and the guts are used as casing for sausages.

Commercial swine breeding in Ukraine developed toward the end of the 19th century. The most popular breeds of swine are the following: (1) Ukrainian White Steppe swine, of universal use, developed in Askaniia-Nova by M. Ivanov by crossing late-maturing local sows with Large White boars. The breed, well adapted to the arid steppe climate, was confirmed in 1934. (2) Ukrainian Spotted Steppe swine, bred for universal use in Askaniia-Nova during the period 1938–61 (confirmed in 1961) by crossing black spotted swine (which appeared as a mutant during the development of the White Steppe breed) with Berkshire, Mangalitsa, and Landrace breeds. (3) Medium White swine, developed in the 19th century in Britain and crossed with Transcarpathian long-eared swine, well adapted to local conditions. They were used in breeding Myrhorod (Mirgorod) swine. (4) Myrhorod swine, developed for meat and bacon in 1940 in Poltava oblast by crossing domestic sows with Berkshire, Medium White, Large White, and Large Black boars. These are well-proportioned, strong-bodied animals. Other specifically Ukrainian regional breeds include the Transcarpathian, the Subcarpathian, and the long-eared and the black-spotted swine of the Dnieper, Chernihiv, and Podilia regions. (See also *Hog raising.)

BIBLIOGRAPHY
Ocheretko, F. *Porody svynei* (Kiev 1954)
*Svynarstvo* (Kiev 1956)
Volkopialov, B. *Svinovodstvo*, 4th edn (Leningrad 1968)
                                              I. Masnyk

**Switło** (Light). A semimonthly newspaper for peasants, published in Kolomyia in 1881–2 in the Polish alphabet. The editor and publisher was M. Korenevych.

**Switzerland.** A country (1990 pop 6,756,000) in the Alpine region of central Europe, covering an area of 41,290 sq km. The major languages of the country are German (mother tongue of 65 percent), French (18 percent), and Italian (10 percent). About 48 percent of the population is Roman Catholic, and 44 percent is Protestant. Switzerland's liberal government and neutrality in the world wars made it a refuge for political émigrés, including Ukrainians. Although their number was never large, Ukrainians in Switzerland have played an important role in Ukrainian cultural and political history.

**Before the 1870s.** The earliest contacts between Ukraine and Switzerland were sporadic. The first Swiss visitors to Ukraine were *Socinians in the 16th century. The archives of the Reformation Library in Geneva contain the works of S. Budny and other Socinians from Ukraine. The architect Petrus Italus of Lugano built the Dormition Church (1547), a Roman Catholic church, and a number of other buildings in Lviv. Starting in the 16th century Ukrainians (registered as Rutheni, Lituani, or Poloni) studied at Basel University.

Before 1708 I. Skoropadsky, colonel of the Starodub regiment, visited Switzerland several times and corresponded with Swiss acquaintances. One of his descendants, I. Skoropadsky, built a dendrological park in Trostianets in the mid-19th century and named a section of it Switzerland. After abdicating his hetmancy K. Rozumovsky lived in Switzerland, in 1765–7. His son Hryhorii worked on an estate near Lausanne in 1783–93 and founded the Society of Physical Science there. During the first half of the 19th century N. Gogol (1837) and Prince N. Repnin, with his wife and daughter Varvara, stayed briefly (1836–9) in Switzerland. Varvara's correspondence with Swiss public figures has been preserved in libraries in Geneva and Lausanne.

In 1820–46 the Russian government supported the immigration of French-speaking Swiss from Vaud canton into southern Bessarabia. Under the leadership of L.V. Tardan from Vevey, they established the Shabo (Shaba) colony on the Dniester Estuary near Akkerman. The settlers helped develop viniculture, wine making, and fruit growing there. In the 1850s there were 300 Swiss living in Shabo. In the 1860s and 1870s they were joined by newcomers from German cantons. The colonists imported valuable varieties of grape – Cabernet, Sauvignon, Riesling, and Muscat. The Rumanian census of 1930 recorded 300 German and 250 French Swiss in Shabo. When the Soviets occupied the region in 1940, most of the Swiss colonists returned to Switzerland. The few that stayed assimilated with the Ukrainian population.

**1870s–1905.** Ukrainian immigrants and students began to arrive in Switzerland in the second half of the 19th century. The first important center of Ukrainian and Russian immigration was Zürich, where Ukrainian students studied at the university and the polytechnic. In 1872 a student reading hall was established, with approx 100 Ukrainian and 100 Russian members. The Ukrainian colony included S. Podolynsky, I. Chernyshov, S. Slyvynsky, and V. Nahirny (who stayed in Switzerland to work as an architect until 1882). M. *Drahomanov lived in Zürich for a few months and participated with S. Podolynsky and M. Ziber in a Ukrainian-Russian socialist conference in 1873.

After leaving Ukraine in 1876, Drahomanov settled in Geneva and devoted himself to political work and publishing until 1889. He established a socialist circle, which included S. Podolynsky, M. Pavlyk (1878–82), F. Vovk (1879–87), M. Ziber, and Ya. Shulhyn. In Geneva Drahomanov published the collection *Hromada* (5 vols, 1878–82) and (together with M. Pavlyk and S. Podolynsky) *Hromada – ukraïns'ka chasopys'* (2 issues, 1881). As well, he published a large number of brochures on the Ukrainian question in Ukrainian, Russian, and the west European languages. In 1876 he established the \*Ukrainian Press, which was run by A. Liakhotsky (Kuzma) from 1878 to 1917.

Various Russian anarchist and revolutionary groups had branches in Switzerland, in which Ukrainians such as M. Zhukovsky, S. Stepniak, M. Kybalchych, and Ya. Stefanovych were active. Among the Ukrainians who lived in Switzerland during this period were Y. Polinkovsky (d 1935), a lecturer at the Commercial Higher School in Sankt Gallen and an opponent of M. Drahomanov, and the physician K. Yuriiv (1846–1927), a resident of Lausanne for the last 25 years of his life. Before the First World War V. Antonovych, A. Honcharenko, M. Sudzylovsky, P. Chyzhevsky, and O. Kovalenko stayed briefly in Switzerland.

**1906–20.** Other than M. Drahomanov's circle Ukrainian organizations in Switzerland arose late and were usually short-lived. In 1906–7 the Ukrainian Hromada, headed by A. Liakhotsky, was active in Geneva. Before the war T. Halushchynsky, H. Kostelnyk, and V. Laba studied at Fribourg University. With the outbreak of the First World War Ukrainians in Switzerland became more active, not only in social and cultural but also in political activities. There were about 50 Ukrainians known to be there: 20 in Geneva, 15 in Lausanne, and the rest in Zürich, Bern, and Basel. In 1915 another Ukrainian hromada, the Société Ukrainienne Gromada, was set up under the presidency of A. Liakhotsky. Unable to reconcile himself to the political engagement and independentist posture introduced by the recently arrived V. Levynsky and E. Batchinsky, Liakhotsky soon resigned from the hromada. On 15 May 1915 the hromada appealed to European public opinion to protest Russian policy in occupied Galicia and to defend the persecuted Greek Catholic churches.

During the war (1914–18) the Ukrainians in Lausanne informed the general public about Ukrainian issues. The French-language organ of the Union for the Liberation of Ukraine, *La \*Revue ukranienne*, was published there. E. \*Batchinsky organized a Ukrainian library and bookstore, which distributed Ukrainian publications not only in Switzerland but in all European countries. The semimonthly *L'Ukraine* (1915–20), published by V. Stepankivsky with the collaboration of M. Tyshkevych, also came out in Lausanne. In 1918–19 its chief editor was the Swiss journalist E. Privat; his assistant was E. Batchinsky. In 1917 V. Stepankivsky organized the Ukrainian Bureau, a special representative office with information and political tasks. It had 20 employees, only 8 of them Ukrainians (including M. Tyshkevych, E. Batchinsky, O. Kovalenko, D. Manuilsky, and V. Polisadiv). The office manager was the pastor G. Neymark, and the chief secretary was J. Fortey, who later worked in the Secretariat of the League of Nations. The bureau closed down in 1921.

Because the hromada in Geneva became inactive, an émigré group of the Ukrainian Social Democratic Workers' party began mobilizing and published the journal *Borot'ba* (1915–16) under the editorship of L. Yurkevych. Yurkevych published the brochure *L'Ukraine et la Guerre* in 1916, in Geneva, as well as an essay criticizing Lenin's nationalities policy in 1917. In 1916–17 D. Dontsov headed the Bureau of the Nationalities of Russia in Bern and pub-

lished its bulletins (65 issues), with the assistance of F. Koroliv. In 1917 the Ukrainian General Union, which included not only Ukrainians from Galicia and central Ukraine but also Jews from Ukraine, was active for a short time in Zürich.

At the end of 1918 a Ukrainian diplomatic mission, headed by Ye. Lukasevych and then M. Vasylko, was sent to Switzerland by the Hetman government and was kept there by the Directory. A semiofficial Ukrainian consulate was opened in Lausanne and then in Bern. It was directed by E. Batchinsky and Ye. Sokovych. There was also a Ukrainian consulate in Zürich, where S. Kuoni served as honorary consul. Under the Hetman regime there was a Swiss consulate in Kiev. P. \*Chyzhevsky headed a Ukrainian trade delegation that arrived in Switzerland in 1918 and then initiated the Ukrainian-Swiss Chamber of Commerce, which supplied all of Europe with information on trade with Ukraine as well as information about Ukraine's political aspirations. The Swiss diplomat Ch. Nicole was president of the chamber. With the help of S. Perepelytsia, F. Koroliv, and Ye. Tymchenko, P. Chyzhevsky founded the Ukrainian Committee in Geneva in 1919. It published a number of brochures in French and English arguing for Ukraine's independence. At the end of 1919 the Ukrainian Club, headed by P. Chyzhevsky and then by E. Batchinsky, was set up in Geneva. It collaborated with the UNR mission in Berlin, and in 1934 it was renamed the Ukainian-Swiss Club.

In 1917–20 many Swiss visited Ukraine, and many supported Ukraine's independence or in some way helped the envoys of the Ukrainian government to Switzerland. Col Du Bois was a member of a mission sent by the political department of the Swiss government to Ukraine in the summer of 1918. In his articles in *Der Bund* and *Neue Züricher Zeitung* Du Bois spoke out for Ukraine's independence. The editor of *Journal de Genève*, P. Du Bochet, visited S. Petliura in Vinnytsia in February 1919 and published articles favorable to Ukraine in *Tribune de Genève*. J.E. David, the editor of *Gazette de Lausanne* (1913), and Col E. Lederrey, whose reports appeared in *Tribune de Genève* and *Journal de Genève*, visited Ukraine in 1919. E. Kuhne, the editor of *Tribune de Genève*, supported Ukraine's renaissance in his numerous articles in 1917–21. The editor of *Exprès de Neuchâtel*, J. Patrie, collaborated with the UNR diplomatic mission in Bern and included articles on Ukrainian affairs in the publication. Among Swiss politicians who co-operated with the UNR mission were E. Oesch, the author of the brochure *Ukraine und Schweiz* (1918), and R. Claparède.

**1920–40.** In the interwar period Switzerland continued to be a haven for Ukrainian political leaders. \*Geneva, which was the seat of the League of Nations and a major center for foreign diplomats, politicians, and journalists, became particularly important. The question of minority rights in Poland (and, to a lesser degree, Rumania and Czechoslovakia) was raised at the league, and the Ukrainian position was presented by Ukrainian parliamentarians from Western Ukraine – M. Rudnytska, V. Mudry, S. Baran, D. Levytsky, Z. Pelensky, V. Zalozetsky, and I. Kurtiak; the Canadian MP M. Luchkovich; and the unofficial representative of the UNR government-in-exile, O. Shulhyn. The plenipotentiary of the UNR government-in-exile for Switzerland was H. \*Chykalenko-Keller. Political activists, such as Ye. Konovalets (1930–6), M. Kushnir, O.

Boikiv, and V. Paneiko, stayed in Switzerland. The 1933 man-made famine in Ukraine was extensively covered by *Le Journal de Genève, Gazette de Lausanne,* and *La Suisse libérale* in Neuchâtel, *La Liberté* in Fribourg, and *Neue Züricher Zeitung.* G. Motta, a long-term member and head of the Swiss government, was particularly well disposed to Ukrainians.

From 1922 E. Batchinsky was the official representative of the Ukrainian Autocephalous Orthodox church in Western Europe and the liaison of the Ukrainian Red Cross to its parent International Committee in Geneva. The press agency Ofinor (Office of Eastern Information) was headed by M. *Yeremiiv in Geneva (1928–44). M. Trotsky ran the Ukrainian Information Bureau in Geneva from 1932. The Ukrainian student association Ukraina, which had several dozen members, was active in Geneva in 1929–35.

**1940–5.** During the Second World War only charitable and cultural organizational activities were permitted by the Swiss authorities. The country's Ukrainian population was increased by POWs from the Polish army (1940) and then from the Soviet army as well as by escapees from forced labor in Germany. They were interned in camps until 1945, when most of them were deported to Ukraine on the demand of the Soviet repatriation committee.

Members of the Ukrainian Hromada in Switzerland

**Post–1945.** After the war new Ukrainian immigrants began to arrive in Switzerland from Germany, Austria, and Italy. By the beginning of the 1950s there were almost 70 Ukrainians in Switzerland. In 1945 the Sokil Student Society (later the Academic Hromada) was organized in Bern. It was headed by M. Vus and R. Prokop. Now the Ukrainian Committee in Switzerland has its head office in Bern.

The Ukrainian Relief Committee, led by M. *Rudnytska, was active in Geneva (1946–50). The Ukrainian Relief Alliance was founded in Zürich in 1950 and was headed by V. Lytvyn and then V. Stykhar. For a while it published *Tryzub.* The Ukrainian community in Zürich included the singer I. Malaniuk, the ballet master V. Libovicki, the writer L. Semaka, and the K.G. Jung Institute lecturer P. Polishchuk.

In 1951 the Alliance of Ukrainians in Switzerland (OUSh) was formed as a central representative body. Its presidents have been A. Chernetsky, I. Porodko, I. Luchyshyn, M. Havryliuk, A. Huchkivsky, and R. Prokop. The OUSh has a membership of about 70 families or 100 individuals. In 1974 it changed its name to the Ukrainian Society in Switzerland. In 1981 the Ukrainian Women's Society in Switzerland was formed.

A number of artists and musicians worked in Switzer-

land: the pianist and composer Omelian Nyzhankivsky, the Geneva Opera singer Oleh Nyzhankivsky, the painter Z. Lisovska, the graphic artist L. Vynnyk, and the painter I. Kurakh. Other notable Swiss Ukrainians include A. Chernetsky, I. Luchyshyn, Ye. Vretsona, M. Kachaluba, S. Shutko, B. Hawrylyshyn, I. Sukhoversky, and B. Lototsky. In the 1970s and 1980s the Berlin correspondent of *Neue Züricher Zeitung,* B. Osadchuk, informed the Swiss public about Ukrainian affairs.

Revs P. Holynsky, M. Liubachivsky, Ya. Peridon, D. Dzvonyk, O. Sydoriv, and P. Kostiuk and Bishops I. Buchko, M. Marusyn, and M. Hrynchyshyn have served the Ukrainian Catholic community in Switzerland; Revs H. Metiuk, V. Vyshnivsky, and V. Husiv have served the Orthodox. In 1955–78 E. Batchinsky was bishop of the Ukrainian Autocephalous Orthodox Church (Conciliar) in Switzerland.

The pedagogical works of J. Pestalozzi (1938) and some literary works of G. Keller (1900, 1906) and C. Meyer (1913) have been translated into Ukrainian. Of contemporary literature, some works by F. Dürrenmatt and M. Frisch have appeared in Ukrainian.

BIBLIOGRAPHY
Oesch, E. (ed). *Ukraine und Schweiz* (Zürich 1918)
Hrushevs'kyi, M. (ed). *Zpochatkiv ukraïns'koho sotsiialistychnoho rukhu: M. Drahomanov i zhenevs'kyi sotsiialistychnyi hurtok* (Vienna 1922)
Bachyns'kyi, Ie. 'Ukraïns'ka Drukarnia v Zhenevi,' *Naukovyi zbirnyk UVAN,* 2 (New York 1953)
Makovets'kyi, Ia. 'Ievhen Konovalets' u Shvaitsarii,' in *Ievhen Konovalets' ta ioho doba* (Munich 1984)

A. Zhukovsky

**Swoboda, Victor** [Svoboda, Viktor] (pseuds: M. Davies, Michael Browne), b 20 February 1925 in Kompaniivka, now in Kirovohrad oblast, d 1 July 1992 in London. Writer and teacher. Displaced by the Second World War, Swoboda settled in England in 1948. He studied at the School of Slavonic and East European Studies at London University (1950–3) and was an assistant (1955–9), lecturer (1959–73), and senior lecturer (1973–83) in Russian and Ukrainian there. Swoboda is the author of articles on early Ukrainian lexicography, Ukrainian-Belarusian and Ukrainian-Yiddish linguistic relations, and T. Shevchenko. Under the pseudonym M. Davies he translated and published I. *Dziuba's *Internatsionalizm chy rusyfikatsiia?* as *Internationalism or Russification?: A Study in the Soviet Nationalities Problem* (1968). In the 1970s he contributed reports on political persecution in Ukraine to *Index on Censorship* and edited, under the pseudonym Michael Browne, *Ferment in Ukraine: Documents by V. Chornovil, I. Kandyba, L. Lukyanenko, V. Moroz, and Others* (1971). He contributed articles on Ukrainian literature and writers to *The Penguin Companion to European Literature* (1969) and *Cassell's Encyclopaedia of World Literature* (1973) and was the coauthor (with B. Nahaylo) of *Soviet Disunion: A History of the Nationalities Problem in the USSR* (1990).

**Swyrydenko, Walter** [Svyrydenko, Volodymyr], b 12 October 1942 in Slovianske, Staline [now Donetske] oblast. Painter. A postwar refugee in the United States, he studied art at Kent State University and in Paris. He is an art professor and the gallery director at Lakehead Community College in Mentor, Ohio. In his oils and acrylics he attempts to depict humankind's perpetual striving for perfection. He describes his style as figurative expressionism. Over 30 solo exhibitions of his works have been held.

Wasyl Swystun

**Swystun, Wasyl** [Svystun, Vasyl'], b 13 January 1893 in Sorotsko, Terebovlia county, Galicia, d 25 December 1964 in Winnipeg. Community leader. After emigrating to Canada in 1913, Swystun graduated from the University of Saskatchewan (1918) and the University of Manitoba (LLB, 1930). In 1916 he helped found and was first rector (1917–21) of the *Mohyla Ukrainian Institute in Saskatoon, where his activities brought him into conflict with Bishop N. Budka of the Ukrainian Catholic church and led to the formation of the *Ukrainian Orthodox Church of Canada in 1918. He helped found the *Ukrainian Self-Reliance League (SUS) in 1927 and was its first president.

In 1935 Swystun precipitated a crisis in the Orthodox church when he openly raised questions regarding its administrative procedures and canonical status. He also turned his energies to the Ukrainian National Federation (UNF) from 1938 and emerged as a major spokesperson for it; he played a leading role on its behalf in the creation of the Ukrainian Canadian Committee (now Congress, or UCC) in 1940. Swystun abruptly resigned from his UNF vice-presidency and his UCC involvements in 1943 and withdrew temporarily from public life. He re-emerged in 1945 as an advocate of reconciliation with the existing regime in the Ukrainian SSR and in 1946 became head of the Society for Cultural Relations with Ukraine.

M. Lupul

**Sycamore maple.** See Maple.

**Sychevsky, Vasyl** [Syčevs'kyj, Vasyl'], b 31 December 1923 in Khvastiv, Kiev gubernia. Writer. He graduated from the Kiev Institute of Theater Arts (1948) and has worked as deputy chief editor of *Radians'ka kul'tura*, a play director, director of the Ukrainian Studio of Chronicle Documentary Films, chief editor of *Novyny kinoekranu*, and head of the Scenario Workshop at the Kiev Artistic Film Studio. Since 1955 he has written articles, feuilletons, humorous stories, plays, television film scripts, and the novels *Chaklunka Syn'oho vyru* (The Sorceress of the Blue Vortex, 1962), *Chornyi labirynt* (The Black Labyrinth, 1963), *Vernys', Ruzheno* (Come Back, Ruzhena, 1965), and *Karpats'ki povisti* (Carpathian Tales, 1975). A Russian edition of his plays and film scripts appeared in 1984.

**Sydiak, Viktor** [Sydjak], b 24 November 1943 in Anzhera-Sudzhensk, Kemerovo oblast, RSFSR. Champion fencer. While living in Lviv he became one of Ukraine's best fencers. Since 1969 he has lived in Minsk, Belarus. He was a member of the USSR teams that won the 1968 and 1976 Olympic gold medals; the 1972 silver medal; the 1976 bronze medal; and the 1969–71, 1974, and 1975 world championships in fencing. He himself won the 1972 Olympic silver and 1976 bronze medal in the saber. He has been a Ukrainian, Belarusian, and USSR champion many times.

St Andrew's Ukrainian Catholic Church in Sydney (Lidcombe)

**Sydney.** The capital (1988 pop 3,596,000) of New South Wales, Australia, and one of the major ports of the South Pacific. Its Ukrainian community, numbering approx 10,000, is the largest in Australia. The first Ukrainian immigrants began to arrive in Sydney in 1947 under the International Refugee Organization resettlement program. By 1949 they had organized the Ukrainian Hromada of New South Wales, and in 1952 they acquired a Ukrainian Home in Redfern and in 1958 another in Lidcombe. Ukrainian life in Sydney consists of the Boian singing society (est 1951), with both a male and mixed choirs; a drama group established in 1950 by the Ukrainian Hromada and reorganized two years later into the Ukrainian Artistic Society; the Dnipro Ukrainian Folk Ballet (est 1957); and its successor, the Ukrainian Dance Ensemble (est 1967). Religious life centers around the Ukrainian Catholic parish of St Andrew (built in 1958) and three parishes of the Ukrainian Autocephalous Orthodox church: St Mary's (since 1949), St Athanasius's (1950), and the Church of the Transfiguration (1953). The weekly newspaper *Vil'na dumka* has been published since 1949. In 1984 the *Ukrainian Studies Center at Macquarie University was established through the efforts of the Ukrainian community.

**Sydor, Vasyl** (pseuds: Shelest, Vyshyty, Konrad, Zov), b 24 February 1910 in Spasiv, Sokal county, Galicia, d 17 April 1949 in Perehinske raion, Ivano-Frankivske oblast.

Col Vasyl Sydor          Hryhorii Sydorenko

Senior UPA officer. In February 1935 he was sentenced to four years' imprisonment for his OUN activities. After he was paroled in 1936, he became a member of the OUN Home Leadership and organized the OUN network in Volhynia and the Kholm region. He was imprisoned again in August 1937 and was elected spokesman of Ukrainian political prisoners in the Brygidky prison in Lviv. During the 1939–41 Soviet occupation of Galicia he was in charge of military affairs in the OUN Home Leadership. A member of the OUN Supreme Military Staff in 1941, he served in the *Legion of Ukrainian Nationalists (1941–3) until his arrest by the Gestapo on 8 January 1943. After his release he joined UPA in Volhynia and became its second chief of staff. In 1943 he was elected to the OUN Supreme Council by the OUN Third Extraordinary Grand Assembly and in January 1944, with the rank of major, assumed command of the UPA-West. He was promoted to colonel (1946) and OUN general judge (1947) and appointed OUN chief for the Carpathian region. He was killed in combat with Soviet troops in the Limnytsia Valley.

**Sydor-Chartoryisky, Mykola** [Sydor-Čartoryjs'kyj], b 1 July 1913 in Kamiane, Bibrka county, Galicia. Journalist and publisher. In the 1930s he studied at the Ukrainian Free University and Charles University in Prague and contributed to the Ukrainian nationalist press in Paris, Bucharest, Canada, and Transcarpathia. A postwar refugee in the United States since 1947, he edited the weekly *Narodne slovo* (1949–52), and founded the Hoverlia publishing house and bookstore in New York City in 1951. It published or reprinted 500 books and issued the bibliographic magazine *Biblos* (1955–79). Sydor-Chartoryisky has written a book on the Union of Horodlo (1951), several volumes of memoirs, the poetry collection *Inter Arma* (1949), stories for children, several booklets on children's education, and a book on the Karlsfeld and Mittenwald DP camps (1983), and translated D. Defoe's *Robinson Crusoe* into Ukrainian (1953).

**Sydorenko, Hryhorii,** b 1874 in the Kherson region, d 6 February 1924 in Prague. Engineer, political activist, and diplomat. A graduate in engineering (1889), he became a director of the Siberian Trunk Railway and headed the Ukrainian Hromada in Tomsk. He became a member of the Central Rada, although not affiliated with a specific party (he considered himself a nonpartisan social democrat). He was an assistant to the deputy secretary of rail-

ways and then was minister of postal and telegraph services in the UNR government led by V. Holubovych (February–April 1918). In the Hetman government he was a member of the presidium of the All-Ukrainian Union of Zemstvos and then a delegate (together with D. Antonovych) of the Ukrainian National Union in negotiations with representatives of the Entente powers in Iaşi (November 1918). He was leader of the UNR delegation at the Paris Peace Conference (January–August 1919) and UNR ambassador in Vienna (succeeding V. Lypynsky) in 1919–22. In 1923 he became an instructor and library director at the Ukrainian Husbandry Academy in Poděbrady, Czechoslovakia. He wrote a number of works on railway construction.

**Sydorenko, Mykhailo,** b 4 November 1859 in Odessa, d 28 March 1927 in Odessa. Geologist. After being sent to Siberia in 1879 for two years because of his political involvements, he returned to Odessa and completed a degree at the university there (1886). He then worked in Volhynia until 1890 and became a lecturer at Odessa University (professor in 1906). His major works concerned the lithology and mineralogy of rock formations, particularly in the Odessa region. He wrote textbooks on mineralogy and petrography and assisted with M. Komarov's Ukrainian-Russian dictionary.

**Sydorenko, Oleksander,** b 14 June 1907 in Osnova (now part of Kharkiv). Architect. After graduating from the Kharkiv Art Institute (1930) he designed club buildings, a flying school, airport, and clinic in Kharkiv (1930–2), and rest homes in Sviatohirske, Slovianske, and Staline (now Donetske, 1933–4), and taught at the Kharkiv Institute of Engineers of Communal Economy (1934–41). After the Second World War he was involved in planning the reconstruction of Ternopil, Krasnodon, and Mykolaiv and taught at the Kiev Civil-Engineering Institute.

Oleksander Sydorenko          Lev Sylenko

**Sydorenko, Oleksander,** b 19 October 1917 in Novomykilske, Kupianka county, Kharkiv gubernia, d 23 March 1982 in Moscow. Geologist and administrator; full member from 1966 and vice-president from 1975 of the USSR Academy of Sciences (AN SSSR). He graduated from Voronezh University (1940) and then worked (1943–50) as a research associate at the Turkmen branch of the AN SSSR. He held a number of administrative and political positions, including those of chairman of the presidium of the

Kola (Murmansk oblast) branch of the AN SSSR (1952–61), USSR minister of geology and the conservation of natural resources (1962–3, 1965–76), and chairman of the USSR State Geological Committee (1963–5). His main works deal with the geology and geomorphology of deserts, the process of mineral formation in the weathering mantle, mineral evaluation, and environmental protection. He developed the lithology of metamorphosed sedimentary Precambrian strata as a field of study.

**Sydorenko, Oleksandr,** b 27 May 1960 in Mariiupil. Swimmer. He won the 1980 Olympic gold medal in the 400-m medley (new Olympic record), was the 1981 European and 1982 world champion, and won the 1982 European Cup and several USSR championships (1978–82).

**Sydorenko, Petro,** b 16 May 1926 in Ternovatka, Kryvyi Rih okruha. Painter, illustrator, and teacher. A postwar émigré in Canada, he graduated from the Ontario College of Art (1955) and ran his own art school in Toronto (1959–84). He has painted portraits, landscapes, and depictions of the history of the Ukrainian pioneers in Canada, and illustrated Ukrainian books.

**Sydorenko, Wasyl** (Vasyl), b 15 March 1960 in Toronto. Musicologist and composer. A graduate of the Royal Conservatory of Music and the University of Toronto, he studied composition under W. Buczynski. His works include *Chystyi Chetver* (Easter Thursday, 1991) for choir, *Musical Abstract* (1986) and *Reverie* (1992) for piano, the children's operetta *The Monkey King* (1974), chamber music, and songs to words by H. Chuprynka, M. Rylsky, and L. Poltava. He has contributed to the *Encyclopedia of Ukraine* and publications of the ANU.

**Sydorenko, Yevheniia,** b 26 December 1886 in Ivanovskoe, Kursk gubernia, Russia, d 21 February 1981 in Kiev. Stage actress. She completed study at the Moscow Drama School (1909, pupil of V. Kachalov and L. Leonodov) and then acted in the State Drama Theater in Kiev (1918–19), the Shevchenko First Theater of the Ukrainian Soviet Republic (1919–23), the Franko New Drama Theater in Kharkiv (1923–6), the Dnipropetrovske Drama Theater (1927–9), the Leningrad Zhovten Theater (1930–1), and various Ukrainian theaters in Kharkiv, Odessa, and Kiev (1932–41).

**Sydorenko-Maliukova, Tamara** [Sydorenko-Maljukova], b 15 February 1919 in Krasne, Dnipro county, Tavriia gubernia. Composer and administrator. She graduated from the Odessa Conservatory (1946) in the composition class of S. Orfeev, and then taught music theory there from 1946 (as head of its theory and composition department from 1966). Her works include two symphonies (1950, 1971), the ballet *Charivni cherevychky* (Magical Shoes, 1982), cantatas, chamber music, pieces for piano, choruses, art songs, arrangements of Ukrainian folk songs, incidental music, and film scores.

**Sydoriak, Mykola** [Sydorjak], b 24 December 1922 in Velykyi Bychkiv, Transcarpathia. Writer and critic. He has worked as a journalist in Uzhhorod, an editor of *Literaturna Ukraïna*, chief editor of criticism at the Radianskyi Pysmennyk publishing house, and deputy chief editor of

*Vitchyzna*. Since 1946 he has written publicistic articles, literary criticism, film scripts, and the novels *Zalizna trava* (Iron Grass, 1968), *Iosyf prekrasnyi* (Joseph the Beautiful, 1969), *Trukhaniv ostriv* (Trukhaniv Island, 1972), and a trilogy, *Dovirnyky* (The Trustees, 1979).

**Sydorovych, Savyna** [Sydorovyč], b 1895, d 1972. Pedagogue and ethnographer; member of the Sich and Plast organizations. Prior to 1940 she taught crafts in Lviv secondary schools. After the Second World War she was a researcher at the *Ukrainian State Museum of Ethnography and Crafts of the AN URSR (now ANU) in Lviv. She published articles in the museum's periodical on the development of peasant weaving in Ukraine, focusing on Western Ukraine (in *Materialy z etnohrafiï ta mystetstvoznavstva*, vols 3–8, 1957–63). She also published *Vkazivky dlia vedennia ruchnoi pratsi na pershomu rotsi navchannia* (Instructions for Teaching Crafts to First-Year Students, 1924) and coedited, among other works, *Ukraïnski vybiiky* (Ukrainian Printed Linens, 1959) and *Tkanyny i vyshyvky* (Weaves and Embroideries, 1960).

**Syhit Marmaroskyi.** See Sighetul Marmaţiei.

**Syla** (Strength). An association of domestic and unskilled workers in Lviv, founded in 1907 by V. *Nahirny. By 1914 it had almost 1,000 members. Although it declined during the First World War, it revived in 1918 and operated until 1939, when it was dissolved by the Soviet authorities. Its presidents were Nahirny, Ye. Husar, and A. Kashtaniuk (from 1918).

*Syla* (Strength). An unofficial organ of the Communist Party of Western Ukraine, published weekly in Lviv from January 1930 to September 1932 (a total of 153 issues). It was edited by R. Skazynsky and P. Kozlaniuk. Several supplements to the newspaper were published, including the monthly *Masovyi teatr* (1930–2) and the irregular *Iliustrovani visti* (1931). In 1930 *Syla* had a pressrun of 3,000 copies. It was frequently confiscated and finally closed down by the Polish authorities.

**Sylenko, Lev** (pseud: Lev T. Orlyhora), b 27 September 1927 in Bohoiavlenske (now Oleksandrivka), Kherson gubernia. Emigré writer, filmmaker, and religious leader. In postwar Germany he published publicistic pamphlets condemning the Soviet regime. In 1953 he moved to Canada, where he wrote the political novel *Budni nashoï epokhy* (The Ordinary Days of Our Epoch, 2 vols, 1953), the story collection *Heroï nashoho chasu* (Heroes of Our Time, 1959), and poetry, and made several little-known, though well-received, documentary and docudrama films in Ukrainian. In 1964 he founded the *Ukrainian Native Faith (RUNVira) church. He wrote its *Maha vira* (Great Faith, 1979) and other scriptures and has edited its monthly *Samobutnia Ukraïna* (1966 ). He has traveled widely to compile a Sanskrit-Ukrainian-English dictionary and to research the links between Vedic India and ancient Ukraine, an interest stemming from his research into Ukrainian pre-Christian religious beliefs.

**Sylvansky, Mykola** [Syl'vans'kyj], b 1806, d 1879. Orthodox priest and beekeeper. While serving as a parish priest in Slobidska Ukraine he wrote popular articles and pamphlets on beekeeping, such as *Nastavlenie po chasti du-plianochnogo pchelovodstva* (Directions for Hollow-Log Bee-keeping). Using the pseudonym Lisovyk he contributed articles to P. Kulish's *Zapiski o Iuzhnoi Rusi.* He also col-lected folk songs.

**Sylvestr** [Syl'vestr], b ?, d 12 April 1123. Chronicler and bishop. He was hegumen of the St Michael's Vydubychi Monastery in Kiev and then bishop of Pereislav (from 1118). He was close to Prince Volodymyr Monomakh and advised him on church and political affairs. Sylvestr is be-lieved to have copied and updated the *Laurentian Chronicle, the second redaction of *Povist' vremennykh lit* prepared after the death of Nestor the Chronicler, which includes an account of the years 1113–16.

**Sylvestr.** See Liutkovych-Telytsia, Pavlo.

Rostyslav Sylvestrov: *Portrait of a Girl* (tempera, 1966)

**Sylvestrov, Rostyslav** [Syl'vestrov], b 17 October 1917 in Vinnytsia. Painter. He graduated from the Kiev State Art Institute (1949), where he studied under O. Shovkunenko. He taught at the Lviv Institute of Applied and Decorative Arts (1949–59) and the Lviv Printing Insti-tute (1961–5). His works include *Winter Landscape* (1947), *Chemical Complex in Rozdil* (1965), *Children Asleep* (1966–7), *Jockeys* (1969), and *Rain* (1970).

Valentyn Sylvestrov

**Sylvestrov, Valentyn** [Syl'vestrov] (Silvestrov), b 30 September 1937 in Kiev. Composer. He studied composi-tion under B. *Liatoshynsky at the Kiev Conservatory (1958–64). Working in a modernist idiom, he quickly es-tablished a reputation as one of several innovative musi-cians in the 'Kiev Avant-Garde.' In many of his works he adopted the newest techniques, at the same time retaining a characteristically lyrical expression. He used a ramified tonal system, including polytonal counterpoint, also in-troducing 12-tone serialism. Starting in the 1970s he em-ployed polystylistic methods in which tonality, atonality, modality, texture, and audiovisual elements all enter into dialogue with each other, forming broadly based dramatic compositions. Sylvestrov's works were criticized in the Soviet press, but he was not forced to alter his style or sus-pend composing. He soon started developing an interna-tional reputation, winning the International Koussevitsky Prize (USA, 1967) and the International Young Composers' Competition Gaudeamus (Holland, 1970). Some of his compositions had their world premieres at European fes-tivals of modern music or at performances by the Las Ve-gas Symphony, V. Baley conducting.

Sylvestrov's works include five symphonies (1963, 1965, 1966, 1976, 1980–2); the symphonic works *Classic Overture* (1964), *Hymn* (1967), and *Poem* (in memory of B. Liatoshynsky, 1968); *Spectrum* (1965) and *Intermezzo* (1983) for chamber orchestra; *Serenade* for string orchestra (1978); *Postludium,* a symphonic poem for piano and orchestra (1984); *Meditation* for cello and chamber orchestra (1972); *Mysteries* for alto flute and percussion (1964); *Projections* for harpsichord, vibraphone, and bells (1965); *Sonata* for violin and piano (1970); *Postludium* for cello and piano (1982); *Drama* for violin, cello, and piano (1971); *Children's Music* (1973); and cantatas to texts by T. Shevchenko, A. Pushkin, M. Lermontov, J. Keats, and others. He has also scored film music.

BIBLIOGRAPHY
Schwarz, B. *Music and Musical Life in Soviet Russia 1917–1970* (London 1972)
Pavlyshyn, S. *V. Syl'vestrov* (Kiev 1988)

R. Savytsky

**Sylych, Onykii** [Sylyč, Onykij], b ?, d 1663. Cossack of-ficer. A fellow (1654–6) and colonel (1657–63) of Chernihiv regiment, he was opposed to the pro-Polish orientation of Hetman Yu. Khmelnytsky and the 1660 Treaty of Slobodyshche, and supported Ya. Somko and V. Zolotarenko in renouncing Khmelnytsky's initiative. He was killed in Borzna during Hetman I. Briukhovetsky's purge of opponents.

**Symakovych, Vadym** [Symakovyč], b 18 April 1903 in Bakhtyn, Ushytsia county, Podilia gubernia, d 12 February 1969. Writer. From 1926 to 1963 he worked as a journalist. He wrote the poetry collection *Shchodennyi rytm* (The Daily Rhythm, 1932), the novels *Maiaky* (Lighthouses, 1955), *Kresy v ohni* (The Borderlands on Fire, 1960), and *Ostannia iavka* (The Last Appearance, 1968), and several plays.

**Symashkevych, Mylitsa** [Symaškevyč, Mylica], b 22 July 1900 in Kamianets-Podilskyi, Podilia gubernia, d 11 December 1976. Theatrical and cinema designer. She studied in the Kiev State Arts Institute (1920–6, pupil of V. Meller and F. Krychevsky) and then worked in Berezil (1924–8), the Odessa (1929–35) and Kiev (1935–41) Artistic Film studios, and the Ivano-Frankivske Ukrainian Music and Drama Theater (1945–65); she created designs for over 30 films and over 20 theatrical productions. Her designs were exhibited in Lviv (1970) and Kiev (1975).

**Symashkevych, Mytrofan** [Symaškevyč], b 23 November 1845 in Podilia, d ? Regional historian and Orthodox hierarch. He studied at the St Petersburg Theological Seminary and taught at the Podilia Theological Seminary. His historical, geographical, and archeological studies about Podilia were published separately and in the periodical *Podol'skie eparkhial'nye vedomosti*. After 1905 he was bishop of Cheboksary and Penza (from 1907) and rector of the Don Theological Seminary.

**Symbolism.** A poetic movement of the second half of the 19th century that originated in France, where it attained its greatest flowering between 1885 and 1895, and exerted strong influence throughout Europe. French symbolism represented a reaction against naturalism and realism in favor of subjective and esthetic experience. Seeking analogies in music, armed with a sense of the magical power of the word, predisposed toward esoteric symbols, metaphors, and synesthesia, symbolist poets created a highly evocative, personal, and transcendental poetry.

Symbolism in Ukraine was influenced by both the French and the Russian movements (in Galicia, Polish influence was also pronounced), but it never attained the stature it did in France or Russia. Symbolist trends rather than a self-conscious organized movement existed in Ukraine, although there were periods during which symbolist or quasi-symbolist groupings were active.

The first symbolist tendencies manifested themselves during the late 1890s in a noticeable de-emphasis on civic themes, the abandonment of realist poetics, the rejection of 'utilitarian' literature, and the revival of poetry (including prose poems). In 1901 I. Franko noted that young writers were placing emphasis on psychology and mood. Pursuit of the beautiful and defense of the autonomy of poetry ('art for art's sake') became prominent leitmotivs in the literary community. Writers betraying any of those inclinations were variously referred to as symbolists, decadents, or modernists. Alarmed reactions to the new literary vogue on the part of populist and realist figures (I.

Nechui-Levytsky, S. Yefremov, Franko), a conservative reading public, and the unenviable political status of Ukraine no doubt restrained poets from moving away more decisively from their social obligations into private and personal spheres.

M. *Vorony was the first major exponent of modernist sentiments in Ukraine. The guidelines he set for contributors to the almanac *Z nad khmar i dolyn* (From Above the Clouds and Valleys, 1903) testify to a distinct symbolist orientation, and in his correspondence with Ukrainian writers he speaks explicitly of 'taking from symbolism' its best virtues. Vorony spoke out in defense of 'pure art,' a refined estheticism, and urged writers to embrace a philosophical attitude (whether pantheistic, metaphysical, or mystical) that would depict the ideal, the beautiful, and the mysterious. His own poetry fulfilled those requisites with considerable formal merit, although like a majority of his generation he never completely rejected engagé verse. Vorony's symbolist poetry was not designed to supplant the poet's civic responsibility; it was designed to serve as its complement, which would reinvigorate the poet for the challenges of the 'real' world.

Ukrainian criticism of the 1900s and 1910s linked (not always appropriately) a number of names to the symbolist or decadent trend. Among them were O. Kobylianska, N. Kobrynska, O. Pliushch, H. Khotkevych, and A. Krymsky. It is a testament to the uncrystallized nature of early Ukrainian modernism that many writers expressed indignation at those labels and renounced them.

A far more self-conscious modernist attitude, with definite symbolist overtones, was evinced by the group *Moloda Muza, founded in Lviv in 1906. Its theoretical positions (as expressed by O. Lutsky) were nearly identical to those promoted by Vorony, but the actual extent of the symbolist or decadent presence in the members' works varied considerably from author to author (V. *Pachovsky, P. *Karmansky, M. *Yatskiv, B. *Lepky, S. *Charnetsky, S. *Tverdokhlib, V. *Birchak). Those Western Ukrainian writers found kindred spirits in the celebrated poets O. *Oles and M. *Filiansky, whose works reached them from Kiev, where *Ukrains'ka khata promoted modernist tendencies (most notably through the critical writings of M. *Yevshan and the poetry of H. *Chuprynka), although the journal's shift away from 'estheticism' and 'pure art' in the direction of ideological and political commitment is noticeable.

'Symbolism' acquired wide currency in Kiev during 1918–19, when a loosely organized but coherent group of poets became associated with the name. Their identity was derived less from explicit self-definition than from opposition to the futurists and the older generation of realist writers. In their circle P. *Tychyna was the outstanding poet; others included Ya. *Savchenko, O. *Slisarenko, D. *Zahul, V. Yaroshenko, V. Kobyliansky, and K. Polishchuk. In 1918 those writers created an ephemeral association, Bila Studiia, and collaborated on *Literaturnokrytychnyi al'manakh*. In May 1919 (with the participation of M. *Zhuk, P. *Fylypovych, H. Zhurba, and others) they published *Muzahet, which, however, officially declared itself a nonpartisan publication. As an organized literary coterie the poets remained elusive; their literary credo was poorly articulated, yet their collections and periodic publications gave them a distinctive presence in the literary world. Symbolist influence extended beyond that identifiable group, to touch such diverse writers as M. *Rylsky and H. Mykhailychenko (his *Blakytnyi roman* [The Blue Novel, 1921]). The consolidation of Soviet power in Ukraine undermined the ideological and material foundations of the movement, and it quickly declined. Some poets, such as O. Slisarenko and Savchenko, became active later in futurist organizations. For all its limitations and vagaries, symbolism played an important revitalizing role in Ukrainian literature during the first two decades of the 20th century.

O. Ilnytzkyj

**Symeon.** Metropolitan of Kiev (1480–8). A bishop of Polatsk, he assumed the post of metropolitan and was confirmed in his position by the patriarch of Constantinople in 1481. His tenure was hampered by the anti-Orthodox sentiments of the Polish king Casimir IV Jagiellończyk, as well as by the damage caused by the plundering of the St Sophia Cathedral and the Kievan Cave Monastery during a raid on Kiev by the Crimean khan Mengli-Girei in 1482.

**Symferopil** [Symferopil'] (Simferopol). IX-15. A city (1990 pop 346,000) on the Salhyr River and the capital of the Crimea. The vicinity has been inhabited since the Paleolithic period. The Scythian capital of *Neapolis occupied the southeastern part of present-day Symferopil. By the early 16th century the Tatar stronghold of Kermenchyk and settlement of Ak-Mechet had been established at the site. After annexing the Crimea Catherine II set up the fortified town of Symferopil as the capital of Tavriia oblast (from 1802, gubernia). The town developed slowly as a trading and manufacturing center. In the early 19th century it held two annual fairs. Its tobacco, brick, and lime factories and flour mills supplied the local demand. Its population increased from 7,000 in 1836 to 17,000 in 1864. The first school was opened in 1793, and a secondary school, by 1812. An amateur theater was formed in the 1820s, a printing press was set up in 1830, and the gubernia newspaper began to come out in 1838. The opening of the Kharkiv–Sevastopil railway line in 1874 ushered in rapid industrial growth. The city's population had increased to 38,000 by 1887, 49,000 by 1897, and 91,000 by 1914. New fruit- and vegetable-canning factories, a confectionery factory, two tobacco-processing factories, several steam flour mills, and a farming-implements foundry were opened. The city expanded to the other bank of the river, where a fine residential district was developed. In the absence of a safe water supply and sewage system epidemics were frequent. A number of learned societies were established: a gubernia archival commission (1887) with a museum of antiquities and a library, and a natural history museum set up by the gubernia's zemstvo (1889).

During the revolutionary period Symferopil was occupied by various armies. On 24 April 1918 the Crimean Group of the UNR Army took the city. In 1921 it became the capital of the Crimean ASSR. In 1926 its population reached 88,000, 45.6 percent of whom were Russian, 23.5 percent, Jewish, 12.6 percent, Tatar, and 8.3 percent, Ukrainian. After the Second World War Symferopil was the capital of Crimea oblast, which in 1954 was transferred from the RSFSR to the Ukrainian SSR. In 1959 the city's population was 186,000, about 70 percent of whom were Russian, and 20 percent, Ukrainian.

Today Symferopil is a transportation and industrial center. Its food industry includes two canning plants, an

The Symferopil train station

oil-manufacturing consortium, and a tobacco-curing complex. Its light industry manufactures leather goods, footwear, clothing, and knitwear. Its machine-building plants produce food-processing equipment, television sets, and farm-machine parts. The chemical industry produces plastic products and household chemicals. The power to run the industries is supplied by a thermoelectric station.

The city supports 13 vocational schools and 12 specialized high schools. Higher education is provided by a university, a medical and an agricultural institute, and a branch of the Dnipropetrovske Institute of Civil Engineering. There are a number of research institutions, including a branch of the Institute of Archeology and a seismic station. Among the city's cultural facilities are the theaters of Ukrainian music and drama and Russian drama, a puppet theater, a circus, a philharmonic orchestra, an art museum, and a regional museum. The most interesting architectural monuments are the Taranov-Belozerov residence (1822–6) and the Vorontsov palace (1827). Some of the old Tatar quarter, with its winding, narrow streets and Oriental buildings, has been preserved.

**Symferopil Art Museum** (Symferopilskyi khudozhnii muzei). A museum in Symferopil, established in 1920 as the cultural-historical department of the Central Museum of Crimean Studies. In 1937 it became an independent museum. Its departments of Ukrainian and Russian prerevolutionary art and Soviet art contain over 5,000 objects, including works by D. Levytsky, I. Aivazovsky, V. Tropinin, M. Yaroshenko, A. Kuindzhi, S. Svitoslavsky, V. Yanovsky, M. Murashko, S. Vasylkivsky, K. Trutovsky, M. Samokysh, I. Trush, I. Hrabar, M. Voloshin, T. Yablonska, M. Bozhii, M. Derehus, and M. Manizer.

**Symferopil University** (Symferopilskyi universitet). An institution of higher learning under the jurisdiction of the Ministry of Higher and Specialized Secondary Education; the first institution of higher learning in the Crimea, founded in 1918 as Tavriia University. At the university's founding, the members of the faculty included the scholars M. Andrusiv, V. Vernadsky, B. Grekov, V. Luchytsky, and O. Palladin. The physical-mathematical department in particular has thrived remarkably during its relatively brief but high-powered existence. Its physics staff has included such world-renowned scholars as Ye. Frenkel, M.(N.) Krylov, A. Yoffe, and I. Tamm (Nobel Prize, 1958). Among the 1923 physics graduates of the Crimean University were I. Kurchatov, the pioneer of nuclear energy in the USSR (a nuclear research institute in Moscow is named after him), and K. Synelnykov, the Ukrainian designer of charged-particle accelerators and long-term (1944–65) director of the Physical-Technical Institute of the AN URSR (now ANU) in Kharkiv. In 1921 the institution was renamed Crimean University and named in honor of M. Frunze. In 1925 it was reorganized as the Crimean Pedagogical Institute. In 1972 it was renamed Symferopil University. Since 1981–2 the university has had eight faculties: history, philology, Romance and Germanic languages, sciences, geography, physics, mathematics, and physical education. The student enrollment in 1988 was 6,300. The library has over 900,000 volumes in its collection.

**Symko, Stepan,** b 27 July 1911 in Dakhniv, Liubachiv county, Galicia. Plant selection scientist. He studied and worked in Belgium and was an agricultural director in the Drohobych region in 1941–4. After the Second World War he worked briefly in Belgium and then emigrated to Canada, where he worked from 1949 in Ottawa for the Central Research Station of the Department of Agriculture. He developed a breed of barley that is resistant to frost.

**Symonenko, Demian,** b 1871 in Stolne, Sosnytsia county, Chernihiv gubernia, d 30 April 1948 in Stolne. Kobzar. He was blinded in childhood and learned to play the kobza much later under T. Parkhomenko. His repertoire included dumas, historical and comic songs, and psalms.

**Symonenko, Rem,** b 28 June 1928 in Kiev. Soviet historian. He studied international relations at Kiev University (1950; PH D, 1968). He began working at the AN URSR (now ANU) Institute of History in 1953 and became director of the Department of Foreign Historiography there in 1969. His publications include *Imperialistychna polityka Antanty i SShA shchodo Ukraïny v 1919 r.* (Imperialist Policies of the Entente and the United States vis-à-vis Ukraine in 1919, 1962), *Ukraïna i kapitalistychnyi svit v period Zhovtnevoï revoliutsiï i hromadians'koï viiny, 1917–1920 rr.* (Ukraine and the Capitalist World during the Time of the October Revolution and Civil War, 1917–20, 1970), and *Brest: Dvobii viiny i myru* (Brest: A Duel between War and Peace, 1970). He contradicted the historiographical work of M. Hrushevsky in *Pravda istoriï – virnist' istoriï* (The Truth of History Is the Faithfulness to History, 1988). Symonenko was a representative of the official Soviet line in Ukrainian historiography and one of the most active supporters of Communist rule in Ukraine and of the opponents of Ukraine's national revival in the late 1980s.

**Symonenko, Vasyl,** b 8 January 1935 in Biivtsi, Lubni raion, Poltava oblast, d 13 December 1963 in Cherkasy. Poet, journalist, and dissident. He graduated with a degree in journalism from Kiev University in 1957. He worked for the regional newspapers *Cherkas'ka pravda* and *Molod' Cherkashchyny* and then became a regional correspondent of *Robitnycha hazeta*. Symonenko began writing poetry while a student, but because of the harsh environment of Soviet censorship he published little. Only one collection of his poetry appeared during his lifetime, *Tysha i hrim* (Silence and Thunder, 1962). His poetry, howev-

Vasyl Symonenko

er, was popular and was widely circulated in samvydav, and it largely marks the beginning of the Ukrainian opposition movement of the 1960s and 1970s. Thematically, his verse consists of satires on the Soviet regime, such as 'Nekroloh kukurudzianomu kachanovi' (Obituary for a Corncob), 'Zlodii' (The Thief), and 'Sud' (The Trial); descriptions of the difficult life of the peasantry, such as 'Duma pro shchastia' (Duma about Happiness); condemnations of Soviet despotism, such as 'Brama' (The Gate) and 'Granitni obelisky, iak meduzy' (Granite Obelisks, Like Jellyfish); and protestations against Russian chauvinism, such as 'Kurds'komu bratovi' (For My Kurdish Brother). Of particular importance is a cycle of poems in which the poet speaks of his love for Ukraine. Selections from Symonenko's diary, *Okraitsi dumok* (The Crusts of Thoughts), were published in the journal *Suchasnist'* (1965, no. 1). Collections of his poetry appeared in the West as *Bereh chekan'* (The Shore of Waiting, 1965, 1973). His story 'Podorozh v kraïnu Navpaky' (A Journey to the Country of Backwards) was published posthumously in Ukraine in 1964, as was the collection of poetry *Zemne tiazhinnia* (Earth's Gravity). The collection of short stories *Vyno z troiand* (The Wine from Roses) appeared in 1965, and a selection of works, *Poeziï* (Poems), appeared in 1966. The poems and novellas in the last-named selection were included in the second edition of *Bereh chekan'*, which appeared in 1973. The collection *Narod mii zavzhdy bude: virshi ta kazky* (My People Will Always Exist: Poems and Stories) appeared in 1990.

In the first decade following Symonenko's death Soviet criticism attempted to paralyze the influence of his samvydav poetry, by suppressing it and simultaneously praising it as 'irreproachably devoted to the Party line.' Later the suppression of his works became total, and they were deemed by M. *Shamota 'incompatible' with the Party line. A book about Symonenko, by A. Tkachenko, was published in Kiev in 1990.

I. Koshelivets

**Symoniv, Dmytro,** b ?, d 1919. Civic figure and state administrator. A leading member of the Ukrainian Party of Socialists-Independentists, he was a director of the state auditing commission in the Hetman government (1918) and the state comptroller in the UNR Directory under V. Chekhivsky and S. Ostapenko (December 1918 to April 1919).

**Symoniv, Matvii.** See Nomys, Matvii.

**Symonov, Oleksander,** b 1875 in Hadiache county, Poltava gubernia, d 12 July 1957 in Gagra, Abkhazian ASSR. Painter. A graduate of the Moscow School of Painting, Sculpture, and Architecture (1901), he studied in Paris in 1907. From 1922 to 1934 he taught at the Kharkiv Art Institute. From 1948 he lived in Gagra, where a permanent exhibition of his works has been established. He painted landscapes of the Poltava region, Kharkiv, the Donbas, and Georgia, such as *The Last Shepherd* (1927), *Environs of Kharkiv* (1936), *Mine Shafts*, and *Morning in the Donbas*. An album of his works was published in Tbilisi in 1959.

**Symonova, Nadiia.** See Kybalchych-Kozlovska, Nadiia.

**Symonovsky, Petro** [Symonovs'kyj], b 1717, d 30 June 1809 in Kiev. Historian, jurist, and government official. After being educated at the Kievan Mohyla Academy (1746–7) and the universities of Halle, Wittenberg, and Königsberg (1748–51) he served as translator at the General Military Chancellery (1753), captain in Kiev regiment (1757–64), land judge of Oster county (1764), member of the General Court (1767–81), and chairman of the First Department of the Kiev Supreme Land Court (1782–97). One of the most educated figures of his day in Left-Bank Ukraine, he wrote *Kratkoe opisanie o kozatskom malorossiiskom narode i o voennykh ego delakh* (A Short Description of the Cossack Little Russian People and Their Military Feats, 1765), which outlines the history of the Hetman period to 1750 with respect to Ukrainian statehood. It was first published by O. Bodiansky in 1847. Symonovsky took part in the topographic-economic survey of Left-Bank Ukraine (1770s and 1780s) and was the editor, and perhaps the author, of *Topograficheskoe opisanie Kievskogo namestnichestva* (A Topographic Description of Kiev Vicegerency, 1786), which was published by the Archeographic Commission of the ANU in 1991.

**Symphonic music.** The most developed form of instrumental music for an orchestra. The first symphonic works by a Ukrainian composer were the *Sinfonia Concertante* and *Symphony in B-Flat Major* written by D. *Bortiansky in the late 18th century. The 19th century produced symphonic overtures by M. Verbytsky, a symphony and a fantasia by M. *Lysenko, the *Ukrainian Symphony* by M. Kolachevsky, and a symphony by P. Sokalsky. Ukrainian symphonic music reached its highest level of development in the 20th century, with works by such composers as S. *Liudkevych, P. Senytsia, L. *Revutsky, B. *Liatoshynsky, M. Verykivsky, P. Pecheniha-Uhlytsky, M. Kolessa, R. Simovych, A. Rudnytsky, M. Fomenko, K. Dankevych, H. Maiboroda, L. Kolodub, G. Fiala, L. Hrabovsky, and V. *Sylvestrov. (See also *Orchestra.)

BIBLIOGRAPHY
Hordiichuk, M. *Ukraïns'ka radians'ka symfonichna muzyka* (Kiev 1969)

**Symphony Orchestra of Ukraine.** Established in 1937 on the basis of an orchestra that performed for Ukrainian Radio Committee broadcasts, the ensemble numbers over 100 members. It has premiered important works by Ukrainian composers and frequently records for the Melodiya label. Its main conductors have included N. Rakhlin and K. Simeonov (1937–63), S. Turchak (1963–7), V. Kozhukhar (1967–77), and F. Hlushchenko (since 1977). The orchestra, based in Kiev, has an extensive repertoire including world classics, 20th-century Ukrainian symphonic music, and works by early Ukrainian composers.

**Symyrenko** (Semyrenko, Simirenko). A family line of manufacturers, sugar refiners, pioneers of shipping traffic on the Dnieper River, *orcharding experts, and patrons of Ukrainian culture. The first reliable information about the Symyrenko line concerns Stepan Symyrenko, who lived in the later 18th century. He was a Sich Cossack for over 20 years and then became a *chumak. His son, Fedir *Symyrenko, was classified a serf, reputedly for refusing to pledge allegiance to Catherine II. He purchased his freedom and became one of the first Ukrainian sugar manufacturers (1840s). Fedir's sons, Platon *Symyrenko and Vasyl *Symyrenko, were noted technologists and manufacturers and also patrons of Ukrainian culture; Platon assisted T. *Shevchenko in publishing *Kobzar* (1840). Platon's son, Lev *Symyrenko, and Lev's son, Volodymyr *Symyrenko, were noted pomologists and founders of rational orchard-growing in the Russian Empire. Volodymyr's son, Alex *Simirenko, was a sociologist in the United States.

**Symyrenko, Fedir,** b 1791 in Horodyshche, Cherkasy county, Kiev gubernia, d 1867. Entrepreneur; father of P. and V. Symyrenko. Descended from an enserfed Cossack family, he became one of the first industrialists in Ukraine. In the 1820s and 1830s he leased a sugar mill with his father-in-law, K. Yakhnenko, and traded in grain, livestock, and leather goods. Eventually he bought his freedom and together with the *Yakhnenko family established a sugar-manufacturing company. In 1843 in the village of Tashlyk, near Smila in Kiev gubernia, they built the first mechanized steam sugar refinery in the Russian Empire. In 1846 they set up a machine-building factory in Mliiv, which built sugar-refining equipment, and in 1848 a second sugar refinery near Mliiv. The Mliiv factory produced the first steamships used on the Dnieper.

**Symyrenko, Lev,** b 18 February 1855 in Mliiv, Cherkasy county, Kiev gubernia, d 6 January 1920 in Mliiv. Pomol-

Lev Symyrenko                    Platon Symyrenko

ogist; son of P. *Symyrenko. A graduate of Odessa University (1879), he was arrested for political activity and sentenced to eight years of exile in eastern Siberia. During the period 1879–87 he organized greenhouses, planted decorative and fruit-bearing trees, and established a civic park in Krasnoiarsk. After returning to Mliiv in 1887, he developed one of the largest collections of fruit trees in all of Europe on his property. The orchard included apples (900 varieties), pears (889), cherries (350), gooseberries (165), plums (84), walnuts (54), apricots (36), and peaches (15). He used the varieties for *selection purposes and established an orcharding school. His major work was *Pomolohiia* (Pomology), which was not printed until 1961–3 (3 vols). Symyrenko was assassinated during the revolution, and his property was nationalized and turned into the *Mliiv Orcharding Research Station. He was rehabilitated in the late 1950s.

**Symyrenko, Platon,** b 2 January 1821 in Smila, Cherkasy county, Kiev gubernia, d 26 January 1863. Industrialist and philanthropist; son of F. *Symyrenko. He studied manufacturing and sugar refining in Paris in the early 1840s. When he returned to Ukraine, he helped direct his family's sugar refining and other business activities. In 1856 he established an orchard near Mliiv, in Kiev gubernia. There he developed new strains of fruit trees, especially apple trees, some of which gained great popularity throughout Ukraine; his son, L. *Symyrenko, developed the orchard into one of the most important nurseries in the Russian Empire. Symyrenko was a friend of T. Shevchenko and helped fund the publication of his *Kobzar*. He was a generous donor to various Ukrainian cultural projects.

Vasyl Symyrenko          Volodymyr Symyrenko

**Symyrenko, Vasyl,** b 7 March 1835, d 17 December 1915 in Kiev. Industrialist, inventor, and philanthropist; son of F. *Symyrenko. He managed his family's sugar-refining company. In the 1860s he built a sugar refinery in Sydorivka, near Kaniv, in Kiev gubernia, which was equipped with ultramodern machinery, some of it of Symyrenko's own design. It was the most productive plant of its kind in the Russian Empire. For some 40 years Symyrenko provided substantial financial support for Ukrainian cultural work. He covered the deficits of the journals *Kievskaia starina, Literaturno-naukovyi vistnyk,* and *Ukraïna,* and the newspapers *Hromads'ka dumka, Rada,* and *Ukrainische*

*Rundschau.* He also funded the work of the Vik publishing house and supported such scholars and writers as M. Drahomanov and M. Kotsiubynsky. In 1912 he donated 100,000 rubles to purchase a new building for the Shevchenko Scientific Society in Lviv. In Sydorivka he founded and maintained one of the finest Ukrainian national theater troupes of the time. Symyrenko left his entire estate (some 10 million rubles) to Ukrainian cultural causes, but because of the First World War and the revolution his will could not be executed, and the money was lost. He was largely ignored by Soviet Ukrainian scholarship, despite his importance in Ukrainian economic and cultural history.

**Symyrenko, Volodymyr,** b 29 December 1891 in Mliiv, Cherkasy county, Kiev gubernia, d 15 November 1943? Pomologist and selection scientist; son of L. Symyrenko. A graduate of the agricultural faculty of the Kiev Polytechnical Institute (1915), he founded and directed the *Mliiv Orcharding Research Station (1921–30) and chaired the orcharding section of the Agricultural Scientific Committee of Ukraine. He was a key figure in the interwar reconstruction of orchards in Ukraine; in 1928 his nurseries contained 40,000 hybrids of fruit trees and berry bushes. He worked for the Ukrainian Scientific Research Institute of Orcharding (1930–3) and taught at the Uman Agricultural Institute (1932–3). His views on orchard development and heredity were in conflict with Soviet views and with those of the geneticist I. Michurin. Early in 1933 Symyrenko was arrested and given a 10-year term in prison near Kherson. He was released in 1937 but was arrested a second time, in 1938, and his subsequent fate is unknown. He was posthumously rehabilitated. Symyrenko prepared many scholarly and popular works in his field, including *Sadovyi rozsadnyk* (The Orchard Nursery, 1929) and *Plodovi sortymenty Ukraïny* (Fruit Varieties of Ukraine, 1930). A biography, by I. Rozhin, was published in Winnipeg (1960).

*Syn Ukraïny* (Son of Ukraine). A weekly newspaper published in Warsaw in 1920–1. Initially the organ of the UNR military mission, it later became a more general journal of political affairs, although it continued to support the UNR government-in-exile and serve as a forum for veterans of the UNR Army. *Syn Ukraïny* was edited by M. Vorony with the assistance of A. Korshnivsky and M. Bukshovany.

**Syndicate of Sugar Manufacturers** (Russian: Sindikat sakharozavodchikov). The first manufacturing syndicate established in Ukraine. It was founded on 28 April 1887 at a conference of sugar producers in Kiev with the assistance of the Russian government and was led by Polish, Russian, Jewish, and Ukrainian businessmen. The syndicate was based on a series of long-term agreements among sugar producers. It maintained a permanent office in Kiev and a branch in Warsaw, and charged a nominal membership fee, but did not issue shares or keep a common capital base. Hence, it was something between a pool and a cartel in form. At the height of its power in the early 1890s, its members owned over 90 percent of all the sugar factories in the Russian Empire.

The main goal of the syndicate was to prevent a fall in sugar prices on the domestic Russian market. That goal was supported by the government, which collected an excise tax on sugar. Although the poverty of the Ukrainian and Russian consumers kept demand low, continual modernization and growth in the sugar industry resulted in large sugar surpluses. In order to maintain high prices, the syndicate agreed to export up to 25 percent of its production. The sugar was dumped on the international market at lower than domestic prices. The measure was also supported by the government, which waived its excise tax on exported sugar. The members of the syndicate agreed to control prices for sugar but did not divide the market or set quotas for each producer, which tactic resulted in strong competition for sales among the producers. During the history of the syndicate domestic sugar prices ranged from 4.18 to 4.50 rubles per 16.38 kg (the excise tax increased from 0.85 to 1.75 rubles), and export prices ranged from 2.50 to 3 rubles. In 1895, after syndicate members had begun to quarrel over pricing, the government passed legislation to limit sugar production and assigned production quotas to individual producers. Companies that ignored the quotas were fined. The syndicate was transformed into a committee of sugar refiners, which held periodic congresses and acted as a liaison body between the government and the industry until 1917.

V. Holubnychy

**Synelnikov, Ivan** [Synel'nikov], b ? in Voronezh province, d 1789 in Ochakiv. Russian imperial military functionary, descended from Cossack officers of Ostrohozke regiment. He was a voivode of Poltava, Slovianske, and Kherson provinces, and he assisted A. Suvorov in resettling peasants from the Crimea in the area beyond the Sea of Azov. Suvorov recommended Synelnikov to Prince G. Potemkin, who appointed him the builder and first governor of Katerynoslav (1783–8). He received large estates in Southern Ukraine and was a friend of V. Kapnist. His descendants established ties with the Seletsky and Vyshnevsky *starshyna* families.

Kyrylo Synelnykov (Kirill Sinelnikov)

**Synelnykov, Kyrylo** [Synel'nykov] (Sinelnikov, Kirill), b 29 May 1901 in Pavlohrad, Katerynoslav gubernia, d 16 October 1966 in Kharkiv. Experimental physicist; full AN URSR (now ANU) member from 1948. A graduate (1923) of Crimean University in Symferopil, where he was a student of A. *Yoffe, he worked under Yoffe in the Leningrad Physical-Technical Institute (1924–8) and under Sir E. Rutherford in Cambridge, England (1928–30). In 1930 he joined the Ukrainian Physical-Technical Institute (from

1938 the ANU Physical-Technical Institute [PTI]) in Kharkiv and rapidly became one of its moving forces, particularly in the development and construction of nuclear-particle accelerators. In 1932, using accelerated protons, Synelnykov, G. *Latyshev, A. *Leipunsky, and A. *Walter became the first in the USSR to accomplish the transmutation of one stable nucleus (lithium) into another (helium), only a few months after the first-ever artificial nuclear transmutation was achieved by J. Cockcroft and E. Walton in Cambridge. Synelnykov rapidly became an unrivaled specialist in accelerator design and in associated vacuum technology. In 1937 he and A. Walter built a 2.5-MeV electrostatic particle accelerator; at the time it was the most powerful in Europe. Subsequently he was instrumental in the development and construction of a number of other linear accelerators.

In 1944 he became director of the PTI, but he continued his active involvement in nuclear and materials research and made major contributions to the application of vacuum technology in the creation of new materials and to the purification of metals by vacuum distillation (vacuum metallurgy). Under his leadership the PTI became heavily involved in controlled thermonuclear-fusion research and rapidly grew into a leading research center in plasma confinement and heating. One of its plasma confinement devices is called the Synelnykov trap. Since 1974 the ANU has awarded the Synelnykov Prize for exceptional accomplishments in physics research.

O. Bilaniuk

**Synelnykove** [Synel'nykove]. V-16. A city (1989 pop 36,600) and raion center in Dnipropetrovske oblast. It sprang up as a railway construction settlement in 1869 and developed into a transport junction. In 1938 it attained city status. Today it is a transportation and industrial center, with machine-building and metalworking factories serving the railway industry, a porcelain plant, a footwear factory, and several food-processing enterprises.

**Synenka-Ivanytska, Ivanna** [Synen'ka-Ivanyc'ka], b 24 July 1897 in Chornokintsi, Husiatyn county, Galicia, d 28 August 1988 in Munich. Opera and concert singer (soprano). She graduated from the Prague State Conservatory (1927) and furthered her voice training in Milan (1931–2). She toured as a soloist throughout Galicia and Bukovyna, as well as to Prague, Vienna, and Berlin, and appeared on radio in Rumania, Czechoslovakia, Germany, Austria, and Italy. Her main roles included Mařenka in B. Smetana's *The Bartered Bride*, Nedda in R. Leoncavallo's *I Pagliacci*, Micaëla in G. Bizet's *Carmen*, Violetta in G. Verdi's *La Traviata*, Madame Butterfly in G. Puccini's opera, Odarka and Oksana in S. Hulak-Artemovsky's *Zaporozhian Cossack beyond the Danube*, Natalka in M. Lysenko's *Natalka from Poltava*, and Kateryna in M. Arkas's opera. Her recording legacy includes art songs and settings of Ukrainian folk songs by M. Lysenko, K. Stetsenko, D. Sichynsky, and others.

**Synevyr Lake** [Syn'ovyrs'ke ozero] (aka Synevir). V–4. A lake situated in the southern part of the Gorgany Mountains in Transcarpathia oblast. It is up to 24 m deep, has an area of approx 0.07 sq km, sits at an elevation of 989 m, and flows into the Tereblia River. It was formed when the

Synevyr Lake

Antin Syniavsky

river was dammed by a landslide. Synevyr is a popular tourist site.

**Synhaivsky, Mykola** [Synhajivs'kyj], b 12 November 1936 in Shatryshche, Korosten raion, Zhytomyr oblast. Poet of the *shestydesiatnyky. He graduated from Lviv University (1961) and worked as a journalist and chief editor of *Pioneriia* (1974–81). Since 1958 he has published numerous poetry collections, including many for children. He has also translated modern Greek, Russian, and Polish literary works into Ukrainian. An edition of his selected works was published in 1986.

**Synhalevych-Mazepa, Nataliia** [Synhalevyč-Mazepa, Natalija], b 1882 in Kamianets-Podilskyi, Podilia gubernia, d 1945. Physician and civic leader; wife of Isaak *Mazepa. As a student at St Petersburg University she belonged to the local branch of the Revolutionary Ukrainian party and the Ukrainian Social Democratic Workers' party. She worked as a bacteriologist in Katerynoslav and Volhynia. In 1923 she settled in Prague, where she did bacteriological research and contributed articles to Czech scientific journals. She also wrote a Ukrainian textbook on social hygiene.

**Syniak** [Synjak]. A health resort located approx 20 km from Mukachiv outside the town of Chynadiieve. Scenically situated on a hill at an elevation of 450 m, Syniak is known for its sulfur mineral baths and health resort facilities.

**Syniavsky, Antin** [Synjavs'kyj], b 24 June 1866 in Bila Tserkva, Kiev gubernia, d 1951 in Symferopil. Historian and economist, teacher, and civic figure. After graduating from Kiev University he worked under V. Antonovych and continued his studies (now in law) at Odessa University and in Germany. A member of the Odessa *Hromada, he had contacts in Galicia (particularly with I. Franko) and published articles in Galician periodicals of the late 1890s (such as *Narod* and *Zoria*) under various pseudonyms (A. Katran, Kh. Skrahliuk, and others). From the beginning of the 1900s Syniavsky was director of the commerce school in Katerynoslav and deputy head of the Katerynoslav Archival Commission as well as editor of its publication *Letopis'* (1904–15), in which he printed his own papers on the history and archeology of Southern Ukraine. He helped cofound a local Prosvita society (1906) and was a supporter of the Society of Ukrainian Progressives. In 1918–19 Syniavsky was director of the Department of Secondary Schools of the Ministry of People's Education in Ukraine. During the 1920s he was a professor (lecturing on economic geography, statistics, and other subjects) at several institutes of higher learning in Kiev, including the Institute of People's Education and the Institute of the National Economy. He was also a research associate of the All-Ukrainian Academy of Sciences (working in the historical section, the Oriental commission, and other areas and heading the Dniprelstan commission). In 1931 Syniavsky was sent by the VUAN to teach among the Ukrainian population in the Soviet Far East. Within a year his position was canceled. He then moved among appointments in the Far East (until 1934), Stalingrad, the Crimea, and Caucasia before settling down in Symferopil. Syniavsky's works include research and memoirs about Antonovych, P. Tutkivsky, L. Dobrovolsky, D. Syharevych, and others as well as articles and critical reviews in a variety of Ukrainian, Russian, and other journals.

A. Zhukovsky

**Syniavsky, Oleksa** [Synjavs'kyj], b 17 October 1887 in Andriivka, Berdianske county, Tavriia gubernia, d 24 October 1937. Linguist. A graduate of Kharkiv University, he was a professor of the Ukrainian language at the Kharkiv Institute of People's Education (1920–8), head of the VUAN Dialectological Commission (1928–34) and the Department of Dialectology at the VUAN Institute of Linguistics (1930–4), and lecturer on Ukrainian at Kiev University and the Kiev Pedagogical Institute (1932–7). Syniavsky played a key role in the normalization of *Standard Ukrainian and was editor of the final text of the Ukrainian *orthography adopted as the standard in 1927. In dialectology he supported the phonological principle and criticized the subjectivism of neogrammarians. He wrote a Ukrainian grammar for adults (5 edns, 1918); a survey of the Ukrainian language (1918); reference books on how to write (1918, 1923) and on the Ukrainian language (1922); a program for collecting materials on the Left-Bank Ukrainian dialects (1924); a Russian textbook of Ukrainian (5 edns, 1923–6); a textbook of Ukrainian for schools of social education (4 edns, 1924–8); a booklet on the main rules of Ukrainian (4 edns, 1929–31); and articles on the phonic traits of literary Ukrainian (1929), the phonetic principle in Ukrainian dialectology (1929), the history of Ukrainian orthography (1931), the language of Liubech in the Chernihiv region (1934), and the language of H. Skovoroda (1924), I. Kotliarevsky (1928), and T. Shevchenko (including fundamental works based on Shevchenko's manuscripts, 1925, 1931). The results of his research were synthesized in his authoritative *Normy ukraïns'koï literaturnoï movy* (The Norms of Literary Ukrainian, 1931). Syniavsky was arrested during the Stalinist terror in 1934, and perished in a concentration camp.

R. Senkus

**Syniavsky, Volodymyr** [Synjavs'kyj], b 18 February 1932 in Vilshana, Derkachi raion, Kharkiv oblast. Freestyle lightweight wrestler. A graduate of the Kiev Institute of Physical Culture (1962), from 1955 he won five Ukrainian and four USSR freestyle wrestling championships, the 1958 World Cup, the 1959 world championship, and the 1960 Olympic silver medal.

**Syniuk, Ivan** [Synjuk] (pseud: I. Berezovsky), b 1 May 1866 in Kamenka, Seret county, Bukovyna, d 1953 in Rohizna (now part of Chernivtsi). Writer and teacher. He studied in Chernivtsi and organized several pedagogical publications there. He also published articles on Ukrainian life and educational matters in German-language periodicals. From 1896 to 1909 he contributed realistic and satirical stories, sketches, and fairy tales to *Bukovyna*. The prose collections *Obrazky z pryrody* (Pictures from Nature, 1897), *Obrazky z zhyttia i pryrody* (Pictures from Life and Nature, 1899), and *Feiletony* (Feuilletons, 1935) appeared separately. Syniuk also published works about and for children in *Dzvinok* and *Lastivka* and the plays *Muzhyky* (Peasants, 1901) and *Chesna Veronia* (Honorable Veronia, 1933). His works depict Hutsul life and nature in the Carpathians.

**Syniukha River** [Synjuxa]. A left-bank tributary of the Boh River, which it joins at Pervomaiske, that flows southward for 111 km through Kirovohrad and Mykolaiv oblasts and drains a basin area of 16,725 sq km. Formed by the confluence of the Hirskyi Tikych and the Velykyi Vys rivers, the Syniukha is 40–50 m wide in its upper reaches and up to 90 m wide in its lower course. The Syniukha has several areas of rapids, and a number of small hydroelectric stations are located along it. The river is used for industry, water supply, and irrigation. Its main tributaries include the Yatran, the Sukhyi Tashlyk, and the Chornyi Tashlyk.

**Synkevych, Yulii** [Syn'kevyč, Julij], b 8 April 1938 in Kiev. Sculptor. A graduate of the Kiev State Art Institute (1962), where he studied under M. Lysenko, he has sculpted compositions, such as *Toward Freedom* (1966) and *Bird* (1970); portraits, such as *Valia* (1969) and *Irena* (1971); and, with M. Hrytsiuk and A. Fazhenko, the monument to T. Shevchenko in Moscow (1964), the monument to victims of the Nazis in Kiev's Shevchenkivskyi raion (1966–9), and the memorial complex in Melitopil to Soviet soldiers who died fighting the Nazis (1965–7).

The 1992 synod of Ukrainian Catholic bishops in Lviv's St George's Cathedral

**Synod.** An upper-level church administrative and decision-making body under the direction of the ecclesiastical hierarchy or a council of the Ukrainian Catholic church (UCC), comparable to a *sobor. Until the establishment of the Uniate church, all Ukrainian church gatherings were known as sobors. The UCC then increasingly used the term 'synod' to describe their ecclesiastic assemblies at various levels (eparchial, metropolitan, etc), except for general councils (ecumenical sobors). Synods are attended by the hierarchy and senior priests of the jurisdiction. The election of bishops is performed by special electoral synods.

The most significant synods of the UCC were those held at *Zamostia (or Zamość, 1720) and *Lviv (1891). A permanent Synod of the Major Archbishop was established in Rome in 1972 as the standing administrative body of the UCC. It consists of the head of the church together with four bishops – the two most senior bishops, one elected by all bishops of the church, and one designated by the head of the church or the major archbishop. It serves an administrative function in all major matters. In 1979 the pope granted the major archbishop of the UCC the right to call synods of the church outside Ukraine, with the prior approval of the pope. The first such gathering was held in Rome in 1980. Inside Ukraine, on the traditional Ukrainian ecclesiastical territory, no approval of the pope is needed to call a synod.

The Ukrainian Orthodox church did not have a standing synod of its own. It was subjugated to the Moscow-based *Holy Synod, which functioned as the executive arm of the Russian Orthodox church in 1721–1917. Attempts were made to establish a synod for the Orthodox church in interwar Poland, in Ukraine during the Second World War, and in the diaspora after the war. At present the Ukrainian Autocephalous Orthodox church is headed by a Higher Church Administration or a Church Council. In 1990 the Ukrainian Orthodox church (under the Moscow patriarchate) obtained a certain degree of autonomy, including its own synod.

BIBLIOGRAPHY
Blažejowskyj, D. *Hierarchy of the Kyivan Church (861–1990)* (Rome 1990)
Fedoriv, Iu. *Orhanizatsiina struktura Ukraïns'koï Tserkvy* (Toronto 1990)

I. Patrylo

**Synodal church.** See Living church.

**Synonima slavenorosskaia** (Slavonic-Ruthenian Synonyms). A manuscript dictionary of the so-called *Slavonic-Ruthenian language, compiled in the second half of the 17th century by an anonymous author. It contained approx 5,000 words (including many Church Slavonicisms, Polonisms, and Latinisms) used in Ukrainian and Belarusian scholarly, polemical, and literary works. The author, who was probably from northeastern Ukraine, based his work on P. *Berynda's Slavonic-Ruthenian lexicon of 1627, excluding its southwestern dialectal lexemes, and on the Slavonic-Latin lexicon of A. *Koretsky-Satanovsky and Ye. *Slavynetsky. A copy of the *Synonima* made from the original and containing errors was bound with M. Smotrytsky's grammar of 1619; it is now preserved at the ANU Central Scientific Library in Kiev. *Synonima* was published as an appendix to P. Zhytetsky's survey of 17th-century Ukrainian (1889; Ukrainian trans 1941) and together with a facsimile edition of L. Zyzanii's lexicon (1964). Its language has been studied by the linguists J. Janów and V. Nimchuk.

**Synozhupannyky.** See Bluecoats.

**Syntax.** The part of *grammar dealing with the way words are put together to form phrases, clauses, and sentences and with the study of the structure, types, and functions of sentences and their component parts. Scholars of the Middle Ages and the Enlightenment discussed syntax in the context of logic and philosophy. Based on contemporary Greek and Latin grammars, M. Smotrytsky's Slavonic grammar (1619) approaches syntax in this way too. Early 19th-century Galician grammarians followed the example of Polish and German grammars and of N. Grech's (1829) and A. Vostokov's (1831) Russian grammars modeled on them. A positivist approach, based on data from existing languages and partly influenced by Romanticism, was introduced by the Slovenian linguist F. Miklosich in his comparative Slavic grammar (4 vols, 1852–75). The grammars of Miklosich's Western Ukrainian disciples M. Osadtsa (1862), O. Ohonovsky (1889), and S. Smal-Stotsky (1893, 1913) were not free of the influence of logical syntax (particularly that of the Russian F. Buslaev).

New approaches to syntax were introduced by O. Potebnia in his studies of Russian grammar (4 vols, 1874, 1888, 1899, 1941; repr 1958, 1968, 1978). Combining the romantic ideas of W. Humboldt with a rigorous positivist method, he incorporated a great deal of Ukrainian data in his writings on the parts of speech, gerund, predicate phrase, and 'other inflections' in the sentence, and laid the foundations for the historical syntax of the Slavic languages. Romantic views could still be found in I. Ohiienko's book on Ukrainian syntax (1936) and other studies. Description was combined with linguistic normalization in O. Kurylo's book on modern literary Ukrainian (1925), M. Sulyma's book on the Ukrainian phrase (1928), M. Hladky's study of the language of the press (1928), and S. Smerechynsky's book of studies on Ukrainian syntax (1932). Rejecting the mechanical acceptance of traditional, Russian, and Polish constructions based on Church Slavonic, Latin, German, and French patterns, they advocated the introduction of equivalent construc-

tions from the folk vernacular. A compromise position was expressed in O. Syniavsky's seminal book on the norms of literary Ukrainian (1931). K. Vossler's methodology, the structuralist linguistics of F. de Saussure and K. Bühler, and the psychological approaches of W. Wundt and A. Shakhmatov influenced certain followers of L. Bulakhovsky, such as M. Perehinets (coathor of an advanced textbook of Ukrainian [1930]).

Most Ukrainian linguists perished during the Stalinist terror of the 1930s. Since that time, views about Ukrainian syntax that have been normative in the postwar period were initially developed by L. Bulakhovsky in the spirit of the teachings of the Russian linguists A. Shakhmatov and A. Peshkovsky. Bulakhovsky's influence is reflected in the university textbooks of Ukrainian syntax by O. Parkhomenko (1957; 3rd edn 1967), A. Medushevsky (1959), and B. Kulyk (1961; 2nd edn 1965); in the university textbooks of modern Ukrainian by M. Ivchenko (1960; repr 1962, 1965) and M. Zhovtobriukh and B. Kulyk (1959, 2nd edn 1961; 3rd edn 1965; 4th edn 1972); in B. Kulyk's book on the syntax of the complex sentence (1963); and in other textbooks. In 1972 an authoritative AN URSR (now ANU) multiauthor monograph on Ukrainian syntax edited by I. Bilodid and O. Melnychuk was published. It is also based on Russified linguistic norms, but relies even more on the approach of Russian linguists, such as A. Peshkovsky, L. Shcherba, and, in particular, V. Vinogradov.

Despite ideological constraints, important work has been done. Ukrainian historical syntax has been covered in university textbooks by O. Bezpalko et al (1957; 2nd rev edn 1962), I. Slynko (1973), and M. Zhovtobriukh et al (1980); in monographs by O. Bezpalko (1960), U. Yedlinska (1961), and I. Slynko (1968); and in the multiauthor ANU monograph on Ukrainian historical syntax edited by A. Hryshchenko (1983). Monographs have been written on Ukrainian comparative constructions (I. Kucherenko, 1959), the hypotactic complex sentence (I. Cherednychenko, 1959), adverbs (I. Chaplia, 1960), prepositions (A. Kolodiazhny, 1960; I. Vykhovanets, 1980; Z. Ivanenko, 1981), conjunctions (F. Medvediev, 1962), gerunds (L. Kots, 1964), word groups (H. Udovychenko, 1968), the syntax of poetic language (S. Yermolenko, 1969), the paratactic complex sentence (A. Hryshchenko, 1969), verbal structure (V. Rusanivsky, 1971), the syntax of the accusative case (I. Vykhovanets, 1971), the syntax of colloquial speech (P. Dudyk, 1973), the syntax of word groups and simple sentences (ed M. Zhovtobriukh, 1975), the systemic-semantic relations of Ukrainian and Russian syntax (V. Kononenko, 1976), complex asyndetic constructions (S. Doroshenko, 1980), the comparison of Russian and Ukrainian syntactic synonyms (V. Britsyn, 1980), the structural-semantic construction of sentences (H. Arpolenko, 1982), syntax and stylistic semantics (S. Yermolenko, 1982), the syntax of the simple sentence (L. Kadomtseva, 1985), complex sentences (K. Shulzhuk, 1986), and the comparison of the typology of Czech and Ukrainian simple verbal sentences (1987).

Postwar émigré scholars who have contributed to the study of Ukrainian syntax include G.Y. Shevelov (*The Syntax of Modern Literary Ukrainian: The Simple Sentence*, 1963), S. Chorny (textbook of Ukrainian syntax in Ukrainian, 1969), and P. Kovaliv (grammar [1946], and phrase construction [1946]).

O. Horbach

**Synthetic-materials industry.** See Chemical industry.

Dmytro Syntsov (Dmitrii Sintsov)

Ivan Syrnyk

**Syntsov, Dmytro** [Syncov] (Sintsov, Dmitrii), b 21 November 1867 in Viatka, Russia, d 28 January 1946 in Kharkiv. Mathematician; full member of the AN URSR (now ANU) from 1939. After graduating from Kazan University (1890) he taught there (1894–9), at the Odessa Higher Mining School, and at Kharkiv University (1903–46). His main studies are in the theory of conics and its application to the solvability of differential equations and in the theory of nonholonomic differential geometry. In the geometry of Monge equations he introduced the notion of asymptotic line curvatures of the first and second kind. This and other geometrical contributions laid the foundation of the Kharkiv school of geometry. For many years he was the president of the *Kharkiv Mathematics Society.

**Synytsky, Maksym** [Synyc'kyj], b 1882, d 2 May 1922 in Kiev. Lawyer and civic and cultural organizer. He was a founder and president of the Ukrainian Club and the Prosvita society (1905–6) in Kiev. He worked as business manager of and was a contributor to the paper *Rada*. Together with V. Koroliv-Stary and Modest Levytsky he founded the *Chas publishing house in Kiev. He died from typhus.

**Synytsky, Volodymyr** [Synyc'kyj], b 25 August 1896 in Pokrovka, Odessa county, d 2 December 1986 in Odessa. Painter. He graduated from the Odessa Art School (1919), where he studied under K. Kostandi, and from the Odessa Art Institute (1928). His works include *At the Window: Portrait of My Wife* (1926), *Sorting Tomatoes* (1934), *Odessa: City Park* (1947), *Native Shores: Odessa's Environs* (1956), *Winter* (1962), *Near Odessa's Shore: Spring* (1964), *In the Park* (1968), and *Landscape* (1971). An album of his works was published in 1977.

**Syphilis.** An infectious systemic disease caused by the spirochete *Treponema pallidum*, usually transmitted through sexual contact and less frequently occurring congenitally. Advice on how to treat syphilis appears in Ukraine in 16th- and 17th-century *zelnyky* (herbaria). In 1776 S. Venechansky wrote one of the first textbooks about the prophylaxis and treatment of syphilis. In 1857 P. *Zablotsky-Desiatovsky wrote the manual *Rukovodstvo k izucheniiu i lecheniiu sifiliticheskoi bolezni* (Guide to the Study and Treatment of the Syphilitic Malady). Independently of the two German scientists F. Schaudin and E. Hoffmann, D. *Zabolotny studied the pathogen of syphilis in 1903. The journal *Russkii zhurnal kozhnykh i venericheskikh boleznei* was published in Kharkiv by I. *Zeleniv (1901–18).

In Ukraine before 1914, syphilis was recorded at 40–150 per 10,000 population, with the most frequent occurrence in seaports and the Hutsul region. During and after both world wars it reached a rate of 300 in some cities. A venereological expedition to the Hutsul region in 1938 recorded a 20 percent infection rate in some villages. Drastic measures to contain the rapid spread of syphilis were employed in the Ukrainian SSR. The infected were forced to get treatment in hospitals, polyclinics, and venereal and skin disease dispensaries. Disclosure of the source of infection was mandatory, and a checkup with a follow-up of the health of the infected person's family was observed. Punishment under the criminal code by confinement in jail was enforced if the infected knowingly spread the disease. With the introduction of penicillin the treatment of syphilis has become simple and effective. The number of new diagnoses of all forms of syphilis in Ukraine per 100,000 population was 15.0 (19.7 in the USSR) in 1980, 7.8 (9.7) in 1985, and 5.7 (5.6) in 1987. At the end of 1987 the total recorded number of syphilis patients (ie, in treatment) in the USSR stood at 152,000, a rate of 54 per 100,000 population.

P. Dzul

**Syracuse.** A city (1980 pop 170,000, metropolitan area 642,000) in central New York State, and a manufacturing center for chemicals, machinery, and electronics. An estimated 7,400 Ukrainians live in the city. The first arrived from Galicia and the Lemko region at the end of the 1880s. A branch of the Ruthenian (now Ukrainian) National Association was set up in 1900, a Ukrainian Catholic parish was established in 1903, and a Ukrainian People's Home was built in 1929. In addition, branches of major Ukrainian organizations in the United States were founded there. A Ukrainian Orthodox parish arose in 1950. Ukrainian extracurricular classes have been offered by the Ukrainian churches, and the Ukrainian Catholic parish has maintained a day school.

**Syrkin, Mykhailo,** b 9 June 1922 in Kharkiv. Architect. A graduate of the Kiev Civil-Engineering Institute (1949), he has worked as an architect in Kiev. He collaborated on the design of the Technology Building (1950–3) and Administrative Building (1957) in Luhanske, and on the Computing Center and the Economics Institute of the State Planning Committee of the Ukrainian SSR (1968), the buildings of the AN URSR (now ANU) Institute of Superhard Materials (1969), and the Universytet (1960), Politekhnichnyi instytut (1963), and Sviatoshyne (1971) metro stations in Kiev.

**Syrnyk, Ivan** (Syrnick, John), b 4 May 1904 in Ethelbert, Manitoba, d 21 May 1972 in Winnipeg. Editor and community leader. A school teacher in interwar rural Manitoba, Syrnyk became rector of the Mohyla Ukrainian Institute in Saskatoon in 1943–7 and was a longtime editor of *Ukraïns'kyi holos* in Winnipeg (1947–70). He was active in the Ukrainian Self-Reliance League (SUS), the consistory of the Ukrainian Greek Orthodox Church of Canada, the Ukrainian Canadian Committee (now Congress), the Pan-American Ukrainian Conference, and the World Congress of Free Ukrainians.

**Syrokomla, Władysław** (pseud of Ludwik Kondratowicz), b 29 November 1823 in Smolhava, near Liuban, Belarus, d 15 November 1862 in Vilnius. Polish poet, dramatist, and translator. His Polish translation of T. Shevchenko's 1860 *Kobzar* (except 'Haidamaky' [The Haidamakas]) was published in Vilnius in 1863. Although it is considered an artistic failure, it served to popularize Shevchenko's works in Poland.

**Syrotenko, Hryhorii,** b 1884, d 1925. Lawyer and political activist. He was a member of the Ukrainian Social Democratic Workers' party. In 1914–17, as a representative of the Union for the Liberation of Ukraine, he organized cultural and educational programs for the internees of the Rastatt internment camp. At the beginning of 1919, under the Directory of the UNR, he served as deputy minister for military affairs in V. Chekhivsky's and S. Ostapenko's cabinets. He served as military specialist on the Committee for the Defense of the Republic in Kamianets-Podilskyi (March 1919) and then as defense minister in B. Martos's cabinet (April to 9 July 1919). In 1920 he emigrated to Poland and then Czechoslovakia.

Oleksander Syrotenko: *Rest* (1927)

**Syrotenko, Oleksander,** b 22 June 1897 in Vorozhba, Sumy county, Kharkiv gubernia, d 16 October 1975 in Kiev. Painter. He studied at the Kiev Art School under F. Krychevsky (1913–18), at the Ukrainian State Academy of Arts, and at the Kiev State Art Institute (1921–7). A member of the Association of Artists of Red Ukraine (1928–9) and Ukrainian Artistic Alliance (1929–31), he taught at the Kharkiv Art Institute (1931–4) and Kiev State Art Institute (1934–69). His work consists of landscapes, portraits, and genre and historical paintings, such as *Rest* (1927), *A Worker's Family* (1929), *Motherhood, Female Bathers* (1937), *Ustym Karmaliuk* (1937), *Chaikhan* (1947), *Field* (1949), *At T. Shevchenko's Grave* (1948), and *Above the Dnieper* (1970).

**Syrotenko, Volodymyr** (pseuds: Did Danylo, S. Dolov, Zub), b 1892 in Chernihiv gubernia, d 1941. Early Ukrainian-American poet and artist. He emigrated to the United

States before the First World War. His poems about the plight of Ukrainian immigrants and his caricatures appeared in New York City's satirical semimonthly *Molot* (1919–23) and the daily *Ukraïns'ki shchodenni visty* (from 1920 on). Published separately were his play *Zhertvy tsaryzmu* (The Victims of Tsarism, 1917) and the poetry collection *Zmahannia* (The Struggle, 1924).

**Syrotiuk, Mykola** [Syrotjuk], b 9 July 1915 in Teklivka, Olhopil county, Podilia gubernia, d 29 October 1984 in Kiev. Literary scholar and writer. After finishing graduate studies at the Odessa Pedagogical Institute (1953) he taught there and was a senior research fellow at the Institute of Literature of the AN URSR (now ANU). In 1966 he became a department head at the Kiev Institute of Theater Arts, and later, a professor at Kiev University. Among his scholarly works are monographs on M. Trublaini (1956), Ukrainian historical prose (1958), I. Mykytenko (1959), the Soviet Ukrainian historical novel (1962, 1981), and Z. Tulub (1968). His literary works include the story collection *Na dorohakh ternystykh* (On Thorny Roads, 1961) and the historical novels *Sestra* (Sister, 1960), *Pobratavsia sokil* (The Falcon Took a Brother, 1964), *Zabilily snihy* (The Snows Whitened, 1970), *Sertse klykalo* (The Heart Called, 1971), *Na krutozlami* (At the Acute Break, 1980), *Velykyi blahovist* (The Great Herald, 1983), and *Turbaïvtsi* (1985, together with the novel 'Ostrohoz'kyi polkovnyk' [The Colonel of Ostrohozke]).

**Syrotynin, Mykola** (Syrotinin, Nikolai), b 26 November 1896 in Saratov, Russia, d 4 April 1977 in Kiev. Pathophysiologist; corresponding member of the AN URSR (now ANU) from 1939 and full member of the USSR Academy of Medical Sciences (AMN SSSR) from 1957. A graduate of Saratov University (1924), he worked in Kiev from 1934. He headed a department in the Ukrainian SSR Ministry of Health Institute of Experimental Biology and Pathology (1934–53), the ANU Institute of Clinical Physiology (1946–53), the AMN SSSR Institute of Infectious Diseases (1950–6), the ANU Institute of Physiology (from 1956), and the Kiev Medical In- stitute (1955–61). He wrote works on immunology, hypoxia, comparative pathology, and medical history and methodology.

**Sysak-Cavazzi, Juliette.** See Juliette.

**Sysyn, Frank,** b 27 December 1946 in Passaic, New Jersey. Historian. He graduated from the universities of Princeton (1968), London (1969), and Harvard (PH D,

Frank Sysyn

1976), taught at Harvard (1976–85), and was an associate director of the Harvard Ukrainian Research Institute (1985–8). In 1989 he was appointed the first director of the Peter Jacyk Centre for Ukrainian Historical Research at the University of Alberta, and has been acting director of the Canadian Institute of Ukrainian Studies since 1991. A specialist on 17th-century Ukraine, he has published *Between Poland and the Ukraine: The Dilemma of Adam Kysil, 1600–1653* (1985) and many articles.

Mykhailo Sytenko                    Oleksii Sytenko

**Sytenko, Mykhailo,** b 12 November 1885 in Riabushky, Lebedyn county, Kharkiv gubernia, d 13 January 1940 in Kharkiv. Orthopedist; corresponding member of the AN URSR (now ANU) from 1935. A graduate of Kharkiv University (1910), he worked in the Kharkiv Women's Medical Institute (1911–14), and was chief doctor at the Kharkiv Medico-Mechanical Institute (from 1921), director of the Scientific Research Institute of Orthopedics and Traumatology (from 1926), and head of the orthopedics department at the Kharkiv Institute for the Upgrading of Physicans. He founded and edited the journal *Ortopediia i travmatologiia* (from 1927) and introduced new orthopedic instruments and operations. His publications dealt with field surgery, plastic bone surgery, and inherited deformities.

**Sytenko, Oleksii** (Sitenko, Aleksei), b 12 February 1927 in Novi Mlyny, now in Baturyn raion, Chernihiv oblast. Theoretical physicist; AN URSR (now ANU) corresponding member since 1967 and full member since 1982. A graduate of Kharkiv University (1949; candidate's degree, 1952), he taught theoretical nuclear physics there (1949–59) and did research at the ANU Physical-Technical Institute in Kharkiv (1955–9). Since receiving his doctorate (1959) he has been a professor at Kharkiv University (1960–1) and Kiev University (since 1963), headed the Department of Theoretical Nuclear Physics at the ANU Institute of Physics in Kiev (1961–8), organized the department of theoretical nuclear physics at Kiev University (1965) and directed it for several years, headed the Department of Nuclear Theory and Nuclear Reactions at the ANU Institute of Theoretical Physics (since 1968), and served as the institute's director (since 1988). His major contributions have been in the fields of scattering theory (he developed the Sitenko-Glauber multiple-scattering theory), nuclear-reaction theory, nuclear few-body problems, and plasma physics. He

has written or cowritten approx 300 papers and 8 monographs. His monographs *Electromagnetic Fluctuations in Plasma* (1967), *Lectures in Scattering Theory* (1971), *Lectures on the Theory of the Nucleus* (with V. Tartakovsky, 1975), *Fluctuations and Non-Linear Wave Interactions in Plasmas* (1982), and *Theory of Nuclear Reactions* (1990) have been translated and published in English.

O. Bilaniuk

Kostiantyn Sytnyk                    Yevheniia Sytnyk

**Sytnyk, Kostiantyn,** b 3 June 1926 in Luhanske. Botanist and plant physiologist; full member of the AN URSR (now ANU) since 1973 and its vice-president since 1974. A graduate of the Voroshylovhrad Pedagogical Institute (1949), he has worked for the ANU Institute of Botany as an associate (from 1950), department head (1960–79), and director (since 1970). His major research interests include the physiology of plant growth and development, plant ecology, and phytobiology. He coedited *Biolohichnyi slovnyk* (The Biology Dictionary, 2nd edn, 1986).

**Sytnyk, Mykhailo,** b 6 June 1919 in Vasylkiv, Kiev gubernia, d 21 August 1959 in Chicago. Lyric poet. He began publishing in Kiev and Kharkiv journals in 1937. He was an editor of *Litavry* in Kiev in 1941, and he published two poetry collections, *Vid sertsia* (From the Heart) and *Novi obrii* (New Horizons), in Vasylkiv in 1942. As a postwar refugee in Germany he published the well-received collection *Vidlitaiut' ptytsi* (The Birds Fly Away, 1946) and a narrative poem about wartime Ukraine, *Zaliznychyi storozh* (The Railway Guard, 1947). He emigrated to the United States in the early 1950s. Unable to cope with displacement, he led a transient's life before being murdered in Chicago. Over 160 of his poems and a few feuilletons and humorous sketches appeared in émigré periodicals. A posthumous edition of his poems, *Tsvit paporoti* (Flower of the Fern, 1975), has a bibliography of his works.

**Sytnyk, Oleksander,** b 24 January 1920 in Baturyn, Konotip county, Chernihiv gubernia. Sculptor. A graduate of the Institute of Painting, Sculpture, and Architecture in Leningrad (1950), he has created sculptures such as *Smolnyi* (1950), *Defenders of the Brest Fortress* (1958), *The Only Son* (1960), *Life Calls* (1961), and *Heretic* (1964) and the monuments to students who died in the Second World War (1967, with K. Chekanov and V. Shchedrova) and M. Lomonosov (1970) in Dnipropetrovske.

**Sytnyk, Yevheniia** (née Onuferko), b 1 May 1900 near Ternopil, Galicia, d 6 February 1975 in Winnipeg. Educator and civic leader. After emigrating to Canada in 1927, she taught Ukrainian school and was active in the Ukrainian People's Home in Winnipeg. With A. Yonker she was active in the Canadian Ukrainian Women's Society and then founded the women's section of the local Ukrainian War Veterans' Association (1930). For 15 years she served on the national executive of the Ukrainian Women's Organization of Canada. In 1944 she helped found the women's section of the Ukrainian Canadian Committee (now Congress). She was one of the founders and vice-presidents of the World Federation of Ukrainian Women's Organizations. For three years she edited the women's page in *Novyi shliakh*, and she contributed many articles to the Ukrainian press.

**Sytsianko, Yosyp** [Sycjanko, Josyp], b ? d 1886 in Kharkiv. Physician. A graduate of Moscow University (1851), he wrote a doctoral dissertation on the treatment of relapsing fever (1856). In 1864 he was appointed docent in electrotherapy at Kharkiv University. His publications deal with the therapeutic uses of electric current. He also wrote a popular manual of daily exercises (1880).

Mykola Syvachenko          Hryhorii Syvokin

**Syvachenko, Mykola** [Syvačenko], b 22 November 1920 in Yampil, Zvenyhorodka county, Kiev gubernia, d 7 October 1988 in Kiev. Literary scholar; corresponding member of the AN URSR (now ANU) from 1948. He graduated from Kiev University (1947) and was a senior and later the chief associate of the Institute of Literature of the ANU (1947–64, 1973–88) and the director of the Institute of Fine Arts, Folklore, and Ethnography. He also headed the *Znannia Society. A leading authority on 19th-century Ukrainian literature, he wrote numerous works, including chapters in Soviet histories of Ukrainian literature and books on P. Myrny and I. Bilyk's *Khiba revut' voly iak iasla povni?* (Do the Oxen Bellow, When Their Mangers Are Full?, 1957), A. Svydnytsky and the origin of the Ukrainian social novel (1962), Myrny (1967), L. Hlibov (1969), S. Rudansky's humorous stories (1979), and the texts of P. Hrabovsky's poetic works (1988). Syvachenko was also chief editor of Myrny's works (7 vols, 1968–71), copublished a book of literary and folkoristic studies (1974), and published a book of essays on texts of Ukrainian writers (1985). He was awarded the I. Franko Prize for his comparative and textual studies.

**Syvash Lake** (Syvashs'ka zatoka). VII–14. A shallow closed-off bay connected to the western part of the Sea of Azov. Known also as the 'Putrid Sea' (Hnyle more), the lake is situated between Kherson oblast and the Crimea and is linked indirectly to the Sea of Azov by Lake Henicheske (itself connected to the Azov through a small opening off the end of the Arabat Spit). It might best be described as a loosely connected string of 11 bays, the western reaches of which run along an east–west axis and the eastern reaches along a northwest–southeast axis. Syvash has a total length of approx 200 km, a width of 2–35 km, and a maximum depth of 3.2 m. Its area (including the 100 sq km of space occupied by islands in the lake) fluctuates between 2,500 and 2,700 sq km as sections of the lake dry up during the year. The lake bottom is covered with a layer of gray and gray-green mud, 8–10 m thick in the west and up to 15 m thick in the east. Its banks are generally low-lying and covered with a layer of salt in the summer. The estimated salt reserves of the lake total approx 200 million t. They are replenished constantly by an estimated 12 million t brought in annually as the Sea of Azov feeds the lake. The lake also contains other chloride compounds, including magnesium chloride, magnesium sulfate, and traces of magnesium bromide. The compounds are processed at Perekop. Part of the lake is included in the Azov-Syvash Game Preserve.

**Syvokin, Hryhorii** [Syvokin', Hryhorij], b 19 August 1931 in Artemivka, Chutove raion, Poltava oblast. Literary scholar and critic. He graduated from Kharkiv University (1955) and did postgraduate work there in Old Ukrainian literature. A senior associate of the Institute of Literature of the AN URSR (now ANU), he has written many critical and theoretical articles; books on old Ukrainian poetics (1960), creative literature and the reader (1971), the artistic development of contemporary Soviet literature (1980), and Ukrainian literature and the reader (1984); and books of literary criticism (1965, 1972, 1978).

**Syvulia** [Syvulja]. V–5. The highest peak (elevation 1,836 m) in the Gorgany Mountains. Situated in Ivano-Frankivske oblast between the sources of the Limnytsia and the Bystrytsia Solotvynska rivers, the mountain consists largely of sandstones and shales and is marked by numerous rock deposits. Its slopes are forested to approx 1,500 m, with a ring of pines and alders above that.

**Syzonenko, Oleksandr,** b 20 September 1923 in Novooleksandrivka, Kherson okruha. Writer. He graduated from the Mykolaiv Pedagogical Institute (1955), and worked at the Mykolaiv Shipyard and as a scenarist at the Kiev Artistic Film Studio (1961–9). He wrote several prose collections, with the Second World War as their main theme, the first being *Ridni vohni* (Native Fires, 1951) and the most recent, *Khlib z ridnoho polia* (Grain from One's Own Field, 1978). He has also written numerous novels, such as *Bili khmary* (White Clouds, 1965), *Khto tvii druh* (Who Your Friend Is, 1972), *Step* (Steppe, 1976), *Bula osin'* (It Was Autumn, 1980), and *Meta* (The Aim, 1983). For the trilogy *Step* he was awarded the T. Shevchenko Prize in 1984. A book of his literary portraits and essays was published in 1986.

Oleksandr Syzonenko        Roman Szporluk

**Szczecin** (German: Stettin). A city in Poland (1989 pop 412,000), and a Baltic Sea port. First mentioned in records of the 9th century, it became the center of a voivodeship. In 1945 it was ceded to Poland by Germany, and it is now the country's most active transit port. About 10,000 Ukrainians reside in Szczecin voivodeship, most of whom were deported there during *Operation Wisła in 1947 from the Rzeszow and Lublin regions. They live mainly near the cities of Stargard, Gryfice, and Łobez. Since 1956 one of the best-organized Ukrainian Social and Cultural Society groups has been active in Szczecin, with a membership of 250, a contemporary music ensemble named 'Chumaky,' a children's section, and regular literary evenings. The local Ukrainian Catholic center is also active. In 1957–63 the local teachers' college trained about 100 teachers in Ukrainian philology. In 1956–66 a local theater group staged about 70 productions, and a banduryst kapelle was also active. Radio Szczecin carries a monthly Polish-language broadcast about Ukrainian affairs.

**Szczepiórno.** A town in Poznań voivodeship, Poland, that in 1921–3 was the site of an internment camp for UNR Army soldiers. The internees were transferred there from a camp in Aleksandrów Kujawski in December 1921. They continued the cultural and educational programs organized in the first camp and set up some new organizations. At the beginning of 1922 the Chief Military Council of the Brotherhoods of the Holy Protectress was set up to co-ordinate the work of the numerous brotherhoods that sprang up in various army units. The Do Svitla publishing company (est March 1922) published several books, including V. Ern's book on H. Skovoroda. The printing press of the Fourth Kiev Division printed *Religiino-naukovyi vistnyk* in the camp. A secondary school and a Ukrainian scouts school were supported by the YMCA. The Sadovsky Drama Society was organized in 1922. The Mystetstvo literary and artistic society (est 1922) organized research, publications, and lectures, and the Philosophical Circle (est 1923) held weekly meetings with discussions. The cultural and educational work at the camp was closely co-ordinated with the program of the *Kalisz camp, which was only a few kilometers away.

**Szeliga, Jan,** b ?, d 1637 in Lviv. Polish printer. He operated an itinerant press in Cracow (1605–9) and the Galician towns of Dobromyl (1611–17), Yavoriv (1618–19), Jarosław (1621–6), and Lviv (1618, 1621–36), at which he printed literary works in Latin and Polish, a collection of poems by J. Herburt (1612) that included a Ukrainian song, and J. Gawatowicz's Polish drama about the death of John the Baptist (1619), which contained the first two *intermedes published in Ukraine. After Szeliga's death his press was acquired by M. Slozka.

*Szlachta.* See Nobility.

**Szporluk, Roman** [Šporljuk], b 8 September 1933 in Hrymaliv, Skalat county, Galicia. Historian; member of the Shevchenko Scientific Society and the Ukrainian Academy of Arts and Sciences. He studied law at the University of Lublin, social sciences at Oxford University, and history at Stanford University (PH D, 1965). He taught Eastern European history at the University of Michigan in Ann Arbor (as full professor since 1975). In 1991 he was appointed to the Mykhailo Hrushevsky Chair of Ukrainian History at Harvard University. He has published essays dealing with Ukrainian political thought and the nationalities question in the USSR, the handbook *Ukraine: A Brief History* (1979; 2nd edn 1982), and monograph *The Political Thought of Thomas Masaryk* (1981). He has also compiled and edited *Russia in World History: Selected Essays by M.N. Pokrovskii* (1970) and *The Influence of East Europe and the Soviet West on the USSR* (1975 and 1976).

**Szreter, Tymoteusz,** b 1901 in Volhynia, d 20 May 1962 in Warsaw. Metropolitan of the *Polish Autocephalous Orthodox church. The descendant of German colonists, he studied in the department of Orthodox theology at Warsaw University and then served as a military chaplain in the Lublin region. In 1938 he became bishop of Lublin. In October 1940, together with Metropolitan D. Valedinsky and the archbishop of Prague, he consecrated I. Ohiienko as bishop of Kholm and Podlachia. During the Second World War, Szreter withdrew from office and served as hegumen of the Yablochyn St Onuphrius's Monastery. He was elevated to the office of archbishop of Białystok in 1948, and to that of metropolitan of Warsaw and all Poland in 1959.

# T

**Tabinsky, Petro** [Tabins'kyj], b 1888 in Berestechko, Dubno county, Volhynia gubernia, d 1948? Church activist. He studied at theological seminaries in Zhytomyr and St Petersburg, was ordained in 1913, and then taught at the St Petersburg Theological Academy (1913–17) and the Kamianets-Podilskyi Ukrainian State University (1918–20). He was suspended from his priestly duties by the Moscow patriarch Pimen at this time for celebrating the Liturgy and other religious services in the Ukrainian language. When the Bolsheviks occupied Ukraine, he fled to Poland, where he was interned by the authorities in 1920–2. He became a priest in Volodymyr-Volynskyi (1922–4) and rector of the theological seminary in Kremianets (1924–30). During this time he was an associate of the religious publication *Na varti* and a vocal critic of the Russian and Russified Orthodox church hierarchy in Volhynia. His conflicts with the latter led ultimately to his dismissal from the Kremianets seminary. Tabinsky then joined the Ukrainian Catholic church and moved to Lviv in 1931–2 to teach at the Greek Catholic Theological Academy. He was arrested in 1944 by the Soviet authorites and sent to a labor camp in Siberia, where he died.

*Tabor* (Camp). A military journal founded on the initiative of S. Petliura in the Kalisz internment camp in 1923. It appeared in 1923–4 and 1927–39 (a total of 37 issues). In 1930 its office was moved permanently to Warsaw. It contained articles on different periods of Ukrainian military history, but mostly on the recent period and on contemporary developments in military theory, weaponry, and organization. The editor was V. Kushch.

**Tabouis, Georges,** b 17 January 1867 in Paris, d 7 November 1958 in Bayeux, Calvados province, France. French general. In February 1917 he was assigned to the Russian general staff at the southwestern front (headed by Gen A. Brusilov) in Kamianets-Podilskyi. In December 1917 he moved to Kiev to work as a liaison officer for Gen H. Berthelot, the head of the French mission in Rumania. On 19 December France initiated diplomatic ties with the UNR, and on 28 December Tabouis became commissioner of the French republic to the UNR government. On 3 January 1918 France officially recognized the UNR, and the next day Tabouis had an audience with the head of the General Secretariat, V. Vynnychenko. He remained in Ukraine until 23 February 1918. His memoirs, 'Comment je devins Commissaire de la République Française en Ukraine,' were published in the *Pratsi* of the Ukrainian Scientific Institute in Warsaw (vol 8 [1932]).

**Tadzhikistan.** A republic (1989 pop 5,109,000) in Central Asia, bordering on the People's Republic of China in the east, Afghanistan in the south, Kirgizia in the north, and Uzbekistan in the west and known as the Tadzhik SSR until the end of 1991. It covers an area of 143,100 sq km, and its capital is Dushanbe. From the 16th century it belonged to the Bukhara khanate. In the 1860s and 1870s it was annexed by the Russian Empire. In 1917–23 its inhabitants resisted the Red Army, but they were eventually conquered and forced to join the USSR. In 1924 Tadzhikistan was declared the Tadzhik ASSR, part of the Uzbek SSR, and in 1929 it was given the status of a separate republic in the USSR. In 1959 there were 31,700 Ukrainians in Tadzhikistan, in 1979, 36,000, and in 1989, 41,000. Over 90 percent of them lived in Dushanbe.

**Tadzhiks.** A people of Indo-European descent who call themselves Todzhik, and whose language is related to Persian. They number approx 7,651,000 (1991), of which 4,215,400 live in the territories of the former USSR (according to the 1989 census): 3,173,000 in *Tadzhikistan, 931,070 in Uzbekistan, 23,000 in Kirghizia, and 4,500 in Ukraine. They also live in northern Afghanistan and Iran. Cultural ties between Ukrainians and Tadzhiks have been manifested almost exclusively in the translation of works of literature. The first Ukrainian translator and researcher of Tadzhik literature was A. *Krymsky. Authors writing about Tadzhiks included L. Pervomaisky, V. Mysyk, and I. Kaliannyk. After the Second World War, translations of Tadzhik and Persian literature were published, including works by the 10th-century writers Rūdakī and Ferdowsī, the 14th-century poet Ḥāfez, and contemporary writers, such as S. Aini and A. Lāhūti. In 1962 a Tadzhik Literature Week was held in Ukraine. There are comparatively few translations from Ukrainian to Tadzhik; among them are the works of T. Shevchenko, I. Franko, Lesia Ukrainka, M. Kotsiubynsky, P. Tychyna, and M. Rylsky. A Ukrainian Literature Week was held in Tashkent in 1961.

A. Zhukovsky

**Tahaiv, Anna** [Tahajiv] (née Maliieva), b 4 November 1895 in Kharkiv, d 21 December 1976 in Toronto. Stage actress and singer; wife of M. *Tahaiv. She began her theatrical career in 1918 in L. Sabinin's troupe and then worked in the Podolian Ukrainian Drama Theater (1925–7), in the People's Musical Comedy and Chervonozavodskyi Ukrainian Drama theaters in Kharkiv (1923–33), and in the Kharkiv Young Spectator's Theater (1934–41). After 1945 she and her husband, Mykhailo, were active in theaters in German DP camps. In 1951 they emigrated to Canada.

**Tahaiv, Mykhailo** [Tahajiv, Myxailo], b 24 January 1885 in Kharkiv, d 13 May 1972 in Toronto. Stage actor and singer (tenor). He began his theatrical career, playing mostly character and comic roles, in M. Kropyvnytsky's troupe (1905) and then worked in D. Haidamaka's troupe (1906–23), the Podolian Ukrainian Drama Theater (1925–7), the Kharkiv People's and Chervonozavodskyi Ukraini-

Mykhailo Tahaiv          Bishop Vasyl Takach

an Drama theaters (1923–33), and the Kharkiv Young Spectator's Theater (1934–41). After the Second World War he performed in Ukrainian DP camps in Germany with his wife, Anna. They emigrated to Canada in 1951.

**Tahanrih** (Russian: Taganrog). VI-19. A city (1989 pop 291,000) on Tahanrih Bay in the Sea of Azov in Rostov oblast, RF. It was founded in 1698 as a Russian naval base and was destroyed and annexed by Turkey in 1712. It was reclaimed by the Russian Empire in 1774. Tahanrih lost its military significance when Sevastopil was founded, but it developed as a commercial port. In the 19th century it exported grain. At the end of that century it began to develop a large metallurgical and machine-building industry. In 1887–1920 it was an administrative center of an okruha in the Don Cossack province. From 1920 to 1924 Tahanrih and its okruha were part of the territory of Soviet Ukraine. According to the census of 1926, Ukrainians accounted for 34.6 percent of the city's population and 71.5 percent of the okruha's population. Today Tahanrih is an important industrial center with metallurgical, boiler-manufacturing, and combine-building plants, ship repair yards, and metalworking factories. It has an art museum, a regional museum, and a memorial museum dedicated to A. Chekhov, who was born in Tahanrih.

**Tahanrih Bay** [Tahanriz'ka zatoka]. VII–18. The largest bay in the Sea of Azov. Situated in the sea's northeast corner with an entrance marked by Dovhyi Island and the Bilosarai Spit, the bay is approx 150 km long, 31 km wide (at its entrance), and 5 m deep. Its shore is generally quite high and is marked by a number of spits (such as Kryva and Yeia), shallow inlets, and coastal islands. The Don, the Kalmiius, the Miius, and the Yeia rivers empty into the bay and add several estuaries to its geographical features. The bay freezes from December to March. The largest ports on it include Tahanrih, Mariiupil, and Yeiske.

**Tahanrih Bolshevik Conference.** On 19–20 April 1918, during the Bolsheviks' retreat from Ukraine, 71 delegates of Bolshevik and pro-Bolshevik organizations in Ukraine (excluding those of the Donets–Kryvyi Rih Soviet Republic) met secretly in Tahanrih to discuss matters of organization, program, and tactics. There the proponents of two divergent views clashed. The Poltava delegates, headed by V. *Shakhrai and Yu. *Lapchynsky, pushed for

the creation of an independent 'Ukrainian Communist party,' while the Katerynoslav delegates, headed by E. Kviring, advocated the creation of an autonomous 'Russian Communist party (of Bolsheviks) (RCP[B]) in Ukraine,' subordinated to Moscow. In the end the compromise suggested by M. *Skrypnyk – to create a Communist Party (of Bolsheviks) of Ukraine linked to the RCP(B) through the Comintern – was adopted by a vote of 35 to 21; it was supported by G. Piatakov and other left Bolsheviks who, unlike their Moscow comrades, wanted to continue fighting the Central Powers and therefore supported for tactical reasons the notion of a party independent of Moscow. The Central Executive Committee and *People's Secretariat were abolished and replaced by the 'Insurgent Nine' (four Bolsheviks, four left Socialist Revolutionaries, and one left Social Democrat) to direct the partisan struggle in Ukraine, and an Organizational Bureau (Piatakov, Skrypnyk, S. Kosior, V. Zatonsky, Ya. Hamarnyk, A. Bubnov, I. Kreisberg) was elected to prepare the First CP(B)U Congress, to be held in July in Moscow. At the congress the independence of the CP(B)U was abolished, and it was transformed into a regional organization of the Moscow-controlled RCP(B).

R. Senkus

**Taiakina, Tetiana** [Tajakina, Tetjana], b 12 January 1951 in Kiev. Ballet dancer. In 1969 she completed study at the Kiev Choreography School. She then became the leading ballerina in the Kiev Theater of Opera and Ballet, notably in the ballets of P. Tchaikovsky, L. Minkus, and A. Adam and in H. Lovenskjold's version of *La Sylphide*.

**Taiber, Pavlo** [Tajber], b 16 February 1940 in Kharkiv. Jewish-Ukrainian painter-muralist. A graduate of the Kharkiv Industrial Design Institute (1971), in 1972 he was accused of Ukrainian nationalism for his triptych *Sedniv Motifs*, which was painted in the manner of folk art. Taiber's work is representational and employs a thick application of pigment, usually in earthy brown and ocher tones. Recurring subjects in his work include children (eg, *With a White Goat*, 1988) and the staging of puppet theaters by youngsters (eg, *A Play*, 1978; *Evening*, 1984).

**Tairov, Vasilii,** b 1 November 1859 in Karaklis, Yerevan gubernia, Armenia, d 23 April 1938 in Odessa. Specialist in viticulture and wine making. Upon graduating from the Petrovskoe Agricultural Academy near Moscow (1884) he spent three years studying wine growing and wine making in all the major wine-producing countries of Europe. After he returned to Ukraine he founded the journal *Vestnik vinodeliia* and served as its editor (1892–1918, 1927–32). In 1899 he set up a research bureau for vine diseases. He also devoted much attention to the problem of wine adulteration and helped organize a scientific committee that worked out quality standards for wine and other foods. From 1905 to 1927 he presided over the Central Wine-Making Research Station near Odessa, which he founded, the first research institution of its kind in Ukraine. Tairov published many articles on wine growing and wine making in Russian and foreign journals, as well as a number of monographs.

**Takach, Vasyl** [Takač, Vasyl'] (Basil), b 27 October 1879 in Vuchkove, Maramureş region, Transcarpathia, d 13

May 1948 in Pittsburgh. Greek Catholic bishop. He studied theology in Uzhhorod and was ordained in 1902. From 1911 he was administrator of the eparchial endowment fund and director of the Uniia publishing company in Uzhhorod, and from 1919 he was chaplain to the eparchial seminary. In 1924 Takach was consecrated as bishop in Rome and appointed head of the exarchate created for Transcarpathian emigrants and their descendants in the United States. This creation marked the formal division of the Greek Catholic church into two separate jurisdictions, and the exarchate later became *Pittsburgh metropoly. Under the influence of the Vatican, Takach introduced celibacy for the clergy of his exarchate, thereby causing several parishes to leave the church and form the independent American Carpatho-Russian Orthodox Greek Catholic church. Owing to Takach's illness, his assistant, Bishop D. Ivancho, administered the eparchy from 1946.

**Talalai, Leonid** [Talalaj], b 11 November 1941 in Savyntsi, Balakliia raion, Kharkiv oblast. Poet. He began publishing in 1956. He has written the poetry collections *Zhuravlynyi lemish* (The Crane's Plowshare, 1967), *Vitryla tryvoh* (The Sails of Anxieties, 1969), *Osinni hnizda* (Autumn Nests, 1971), *Ne zupyniaisia, myt'!* (Don't Stop, Moment!, 1974), *Dopoky tvii chas* (As Long As It's Your Time, 1979), *Vysoke bahattia* (The High Pyre, 1981), *Hlybokyi sad* (The Deep Orchard, 1983), and *Vist'* (A Tiding, 1987). A lyrical, meditative poet, he gained prominence in the 1980s.

**Talalaivka** [Talalajivka]. III-14. A town smt (1986 pop 5,200) on the Olava River and a raion center in Chernihiv oblast. It was founded in 1877 as a settlement near a new railway station, and belonged to Romen county of Poltava gubernia. It attained smt status in 1958. The town has a dairy and brick and asphalt factories.

**Tale of Borys and Hlib.** See *Skazaniie i strast' i pokhvala sviatuiu muchenyku Borysa i Hliba.*

**Tale of Ihor's Campaign.** See *Slovo o polku Ihorevi.*

**Taler** or **thaler** (*taliar*). The name of numerous 28- to 30-g silver coins issued by various European states from the 16th to 19th centuries. First minted in 1484 in the Tirol as *Güldengroschen*, the taler was issued systematically from the 1520s, beginning in Joachimsthal (whence its name), Bohemia. It was minted in the Polish Commonwealth from 1564. In the Russian Empire it was called *efimok* (from 'Joachim'). In the 17th century 1 taler equaled the value and weight of 3 Polish *zlotys or 60 Russian kopecks. Because of their intrinsic value talers (mostly from Spain, the Netherlands, and the German states) and their smaller denominations (called *lev* and *orlianka* in Ukraine) circulated as hard currency in much of Europe until the adoption of the gold standard.

**Talerhof.** See Thalerhof.

**Taliarevsky, Yakiv** [Taljarevs'kyj, Jakiv] (monastic name: Iliodor), b and d ? Wood engraver. He engraved illustrations for books of the Chernihiv printing press, such as the Anthologion of 1753, the Liturgicons of 1754 and 1763, the Sacramentarion of 1754, the Psalters of 1755, 1763, 1764, 1766, and 1769, the Octoechos of 1757, and the New Testament of 1759.

**Talko-Hryncewicz, Julian,** b 18 August 1850 in Rukša, Lithuania, d 1936 in Cracow. Polish anthropologist and ethnographer; full member of the Polish Academy of Learning. After graduating from Kiev University (1876) he practiced medicine in Zvenyhorod (1878–91) and in eastern Siberia (1891–1908) and then served as a professor of anthropology at Cracow University. He published approx 300 works in Russian or Polish on the anthropology, archeology, and ethnography of Ukraine and eastern Siberia, including *Zarysy lecznictwa ludowogo na Rusi południowej* (An Outline of Folk Medicine in Southern Rus', 1893) and *Szlachta ukraińska: Studyum antropologiczne* (The Ukrainian Gentry: An Anthropological Study, 1897).

**Talne** [Tal'ne]. V-11. A city (1989 pop 18,000) on the Hirskyi Tikych River and a raion center in Cherkasy oblast. It was founded at the beginning of the 17th century. After B. Khmelnytsky's uprising in 1648, it was part of Romanivka company in Uman regiment but was soon reclaimed by Poland. Its inhabitants took part in the haidamaka rebellions of 1738, 1750, and 1768. After the partition of Poland in 1793, the town was annexed by Russia, and from 1797 it belonged to Uman county of Kiev gubernia. By the mid-19th century it had a paper factory and sugar refinery. In 1938 Talne attained city status. Today it has a canning factory, mineral-water bottling plant, sugar refinery, and gravel quarry.

**Talvi** (pseud of Theresa von Jacob; married name: Robinson), b 26 January 1797 in Halle, d 13 April 1870 in Hamburg. German Slavist. While growing up in Kharkiv, where her father, L. von Jacob, taught philosophy (1806–9), she learned Ukrainian and Russian and became fond of Ukrainian folk songs and legends. She studied Slavic folklore and literatures and translated Serbian songs. After settling in the United States (1830) she wrote a *Historical View of the Languages and Literatures of the Slavic Nations with a Sketch of Their Popular Poetry* (1850), which included a brief history of Ukrainian literature, a description of Ukrainian folklore, and a translation of six Ukrainian folk songs.

**Taman** [Taman']. VIII-17. A stanytsia and port on Taman Bay in Temriuk raion, Krasnodar krai, RF. The earliest settlement at the site was the Greek colony of *Hermonassa (6th century BC). In the 8th and 9th centuries AD the territory was ruled by the Khazars. At the end of the 10th century it was annexed by Kievan Rus', and formed *Tmutorokan principality. From the 12th century the site was occupied by a Genoese trading post. At the end of the 15th century it fell under Turkish rule, and in 1774, under Russian rule. The Black Sea Cossacks established a stanytsia there in 1792.

**Taman Peninsula** [Tamans'kyj pivostriv]. VIII–17. A peninsula in the western part of Krasnodar krai, situated between the Black Sea and the Sea of Azov across from the Kerch Peninsula. Covering an area of approx 2,000 sq km, the peninsula has a low shoreline indented by many bays. It consisted of a series of islands until the 5th century AD, when they were joined together by alluvial deposits. The former islands now form domelike ridges up to 164 m high on which 25 mud volcanoes, some still active, are located. A number of saltwater lakes lie between the ridges. The peninsula has a steppe vegetation cover and has been sown with wheat and corn. Viticulture and fruit growing constitute other agricultural pursuits. Iron-ore and mineral deposits are also found there.

**Tamarisk** (*Tamarix*; Ukrainian: *tamarysk*). A shrub or low tree of the family Tamaricaceae, with long, slender branches and numerous scalelike leaves. Clusters of small pink, white, and violet flowers hanging at the ends of branches create a feathery appearance. Tamarisks grow in the southern Ukrainian steppe, in the Crimean peninsula, and on the seashore sands and are planted to prevent erosion. They contain tanning and dyeing reagents and are good nectar bearers; their wood is used for fuel. The most popular species in the Ukrainian steppe, *T. ramosissima*, is also cultivated as an ornamental plant.

**Tamarsky, Yurii** [Tamars'kyj, Jurij], b 30 March 1903 in Podilia gubernia, d 23 January 1987 in Jersey City, New Jersey. Film director and producer. He was a member of the Free Cossacks and the Separate Cavalry Division of the UNR Army. After graduating from the Odessa Cinematography Institute (1927) he worked under O. Dovzhenko and A. Kordium at the Kiev Film Factory (now the Kiev Artistic Film Studio). During the German occupation of Ukraine he made several documentary movies. After the war he emigrated to Germany and, in 1947, to Brazil, where he set up a color film laboratory and made the first color film there (1952) and a number of documentary films on Brazil. After moving to the United States in the early 1960s, he made *Shevchenko v Vashingtoni* (Shevchenko in Washington, 1964) and *Shchob dzvony dzvonyly* (May the Bells Ring, 1972), both with S. *Nowytski. He wrote *Pryhody fil'mara* (Adventures of a Filmmaker, 1986).

**Tana.** A medieval town and trading center on the left bank of the Don River near present-day Azov. It is first mentioned in historical sources in the late 12th century. Tana came under Venetian control in 1313 and then under Genoese. The Italian merchants used it as a transit port, where the merchandise brought by caravan from China was transferred to ships. Tana was sacked in 1395–6 during Tamerlane's campaign against the Golden Horde, and never recovered its commercial importance. In 1475 it was captured by the Turks, and it soon died out.

**Tanais.** An ancient city near the mouth of the Tanais (later Don) River. It was established by the Greeks of the Bosporan Kingdom at the beginning of the 3rd century BC as a trade center between the steppe nomads and the Greeks. It quickly grew into a prosperous city with a mixed population of Greeks, Sarmatians, and Maeotians. In the mid-3rd century AD Tanais was destroyed by the Goths. Although it was rebuilt, it never regained its prominence. After some nomad raids it died out in the early 5th century. Archeological research at the site started in 1853 and has been conducted systematically since 1955.

**Tanais River.** The ancient Greek name of the Don River. It served as a major trade link between the Greeks and the

A votive relief from Tanais

Scythians. According to Plutarch the river's earlier name was the Amazon.

**Tanatar, Sevastian,** b 19 October 1849 in Odessa, d 13 December 1917 in Odessa. Chemist. A graduate of the university in Odessa (1872), he taught there from 1874 and became a professor in 1896. He demonstrated in 1880 that fumaric and maleic acids produce two isomeric oxyacids upon oxidation; achieved in 1895 the thermal rearrangement of cyclopropane to propylene; and discovered several peroxy species, such as percarbonate (1899) and persulfate (1901).

Stepan Tanchakovsky          Gavriil Tanfilev

**Tanchakovsky, Stepan** [Tančakovs'kyj], b 1854 in Verbovets, Terebovlia county, Galicia, d 29 August 1928 in Potik Zolotyi, Buchach county, Galicia. Civic and educational leader. After graduating from Lviv University he rose through the court system to become a judge. In 1896 he resigned his judgeship and became a notary public. He organized 17 Prosvita reading rooms in the Potik Zolotyi region and provided them with their own buildings. He also set up a fund for building People's Homes. For his work and financial support he was elected honorary member of the Prosvita society. As a member of the National Democratic party he took part in election campaigns, and in 1907 he was appointed assistant to Ye. Levytsky, who had won a seat in the Austrian parliament.

**Tancher, Volodymyr** [Tančer], b 20 April 1915 in Bakhmach, Konotip county, Chernihiv gubernia. Philosopher. After graduating from Kiev Pedagogical Institute (1948) and Kiev University (1949) he taught philosophy and scientific atheism at Kiev University. There he served as deputy dean of philosophy (1953–5), dean of the history and philosophy faculty (1955–7), and chairman of the department of the history and theory of atheism (from 1959). He has written over 160 works on religion and sociology; most important are his books on religious morality (1959), dialectical materialism and religion (1966), and historical materialism and religion (1967).

**Tanew River** (also Tanev or Tanva). A right-bank tributary of the Sian River that flows for 93 km through the Kholm region and drains a basin area of 2,300 km. Its upper reaches are in the Roztochia region; it then passes through the Sian Lowland.

**Tanfilev, Gavriil,** b 6 March 1857 in Revel (now Tallinn, Estonia), Estland gubernia, d 4 September 1928 in Odessa. Geographer, botanist, and soil scientist. He graduated from St Petersburg University in 1883. In 1905 he was appointed a professor at Odessa University, where he organized a geography department and later helped create an agricultural institute. He presided over the New Russia Society of Naturalists from 1911 and headed the natural history department of the Odessa Gubernia Agricultural Station (1918–26). Tanfilev continued the work of his teacher, V. Dokuchaev. He studied the geography of marshes (notably in the Polisia region) and the relationship between soil and vegetation. He attributed the treelessness of the steppe to the salinity of the soil and subsoil caused by the dry climate. He developed one of the first physicogeographic regionalization schemes for European Russia (1897) and the entire Russian Empire (1903) and wrote the four-volume *Geografiia Rossii* (Geography of Russia, 1916–26).

**Taniachkevych, Danylo** [Tanjačkevyč], b 18 November 1842 in Didyliv, Kaminka-Strumylova county, Galicia,

Rev Danylo Taniachkevych

Les Taniuk

d 1906 in Zakomaria, Zolochiv county, Galicia. Greek Catholic priest, publicist, and civic and political leader; honorary member of the Prosvita society. After completing his theological studies in Lviv (1867) he was appointed pastor of Zakomaria parish. He was one of the leading early populist leaders in Galicia: he organized clandestine student circles in gymnasiums, wrote numerous political pamphlets, and contributed to populist papers, such as *Vechernytsi, Meta, Nyva,* and *Pravda.* His protest letter from Ruthenian populists to the editor of *Rus'* (1867) was the first manifesto of the Galician populist movement. His work in establishing Ukrainian economic institutions was pioneering: he set up Pravda credit unions in Zolochiv and Brody counties as well as the first \*Silskyi Hospodar society in Zolochiv. In 1897–1900 he served as deputy to the Austrian parliament.

**Taniuk, Les** [Tanjuk, Les'], b 8 August 1938 in Zhukove, Kiev oblast. Theater director, writer, and political activist. A pupil of M. Krushelnytsky and a proponent of L. Kurbas's method, he completed study at the Kiev Institute of Theater Arts (1963). In 1959–63 he was president of the Club of Creative Youth in Kiev and organizer of the New Kiev Theater. He also worked in theaters in Odessa and Kharkiv, where he staged M. Kulish's plays. After being heavily censored and accused by officials of abstract art and formalism in his productions, Taniuk left the Ukrainian SSR, in 1965. He directed over 50 productions in Moscow (Maiakovsky and Stanislavsky theaters), Leningrad, and Smolensk, worked for Moscow television, wrote a monograph about Krushelnytsky (1974), and translated G. Craig's *On the Art of the Theater* (1974). In 1986 he was invited to lead the Kiev Youth Theater, where he translated (with I. Drach) and premiered a controversial production of M. Shatrov's *Dyktatura sovisti* (The Dictatorship of the Conscience) and staged the works of Kurbas, W. Shakespeare, I. Franko, A. Pushkin, and V. Stus. Prior to his intended production of Kulish's *Myna Mazailo* (to have been staged in Lviv), Taniuk was removed from the Youth Theater for 'professional ineligibility' and replaced by V. Ohloblyn (1988). He became involved in the \*Memorial society and the \*Popular Movement of Ukraine. In 1990 he was elected to the Supreme Council of Ukraine, where he heads the parliamentary commission on culture and spiritual rebirth.

**Taniuk, Nelli** [Tanjuk] (family and author name: Korniienko), b 7 April 1939 in Khabarovsk, RSFSR. Theater scholar and sociologist. She graduated from Kiev University (1961) and was a member of the Club of Creative Youth (1961–3). She completed a candidate's thesis on L. Kurbas and M. Kulish at the Moscow State Art Institute (1970); coedited a translation by her husband, L. \*Taniuk, of G. Craig's *On the Art of the Theater* (1974); edited a Russian-language collection of Kulish's plays (1980); and wrote *Teatr sogodnia, teatr zavtra* (Theater Today, Theater Tomorrow, 1986), a chapter in the book *Les' Kurbas* (1987), and articles on the contemporary art of national minorities in the Soviet Union. She was an editor of Soviet materials for UNESCO publications (1982–1991).

**Tank.** A literary group of Ukrainian writers and artists of nationalist outlook, established in Warsaw in 1929. Its membership included Yu. \*Lypa (its ideologist), Ye. \*Malaniuk, A. \*Kolomyiets, Yu. \*Kosach, P. \*Zaitsev, A.

Kryzhanivsky, N. *Livytska-Kholodna, P. *Kholodny, Jr, O. *Babii, O. *Teliha, and A. Kara. In 1933 the group reorganized itself into the Variah publishers.

**Tansky, Antin** [Tans'kyj], b ?, d ca 1734–7. Cossack officer, descended from Serbian nobility; son-in-law of S. Palii. He moved to Ukraine in the 1670s and joined the Zaporozhian army. He took part in numerous Right-Bank campaigns until after the Palii rebellion in 1704. He then recognized I. Mazepa's authority and was granted lands in the Korsun region. In 1706–10 Tansky was colonel of a mercenary regiment, and in 1708 he switched his support to I. Skoropadsky. Later he was colonel of Bila Tserkva (1710–12) and Kiev (1712–34) regiments.

**Tansky, Vasyl** [Tans'kyj, Vasyl'], b ?, d 1763. Cossack officer; younger brother of A. Tansky. A squadron commander in the so-called Wallachian company (1708–9), he became a notable military fellow and received huge tracts of land from the Hetmanate and the Russian government (1715). He was a fellow of the standard (1725) and colonel of Pereiaslav regiment (from 1726). He was investigated for corruption in Hlukhiv (1728) and Moscow (1731), tried in 1734, and sent to Siberia (1735). He received an amnesty in 1741 and returned to Ukraine, where he was granted land in Pereiaslav regiment (including Yahotyn) and Slobidska Ukraine (Merefa).

**Tansy, common** (*Tanacetum vulgare* or *Chrysanthemum vulgare*; Ukrainian: *pyzhmo zvychaine* or *dyka horobynka*). A perennial, strong-smelling, herbaceous plant of the family Compositae, sometimes known as golden-buttons. Its leaves and heads contain volatile oils, flavonoids, tannins, and alkaloids. In Ukraine tansy grows in dry meadows, on river banks, in forest glades, and as a weed. In folk medicine tansy was used in the treatment of a variety of conditions, including bruises, sprains, cholecystitis, hepatitis, and rheumatism, and as an anthelmintic reagent. Powdered tansy is an effective insecticide. Another species of tansy, *T. balsamita*, is cultivated in Ukraine because of its painkilling properties.

**Tantsiura, Hnat** [Tancjura], b 10 June 1901 in Ziatkivtsi, Haisyn county, Podilia gubernia, d 12 November 1962 in Haisyn, Vinnytsia oblast. Folklore collector. While working as a teacher in his native region, he collected over 2,500 songs and melodies, about 300 tales, over 1,500 proverbs, and 600 riddles and wrote detailed accounts of the folk ways and customs of his village. Some of these materials were published in his collections *Zhinocha dolia v narodnykh pisniakh* (Woman's Fate in Folk Songs, 1930), *Tsvite kalynon'ka* (The Viburnum Is Flowering, 1965), and *Pisni Iavdokhy Zuïkhy* (The Songs of Yavdokha Zuikha, 1965). The archives of the ANU Institute of Fine Arts, Folklore, and Ethnography contain his manuscripts on the history of Ziatkivtsi village (2 vols) and his unpublished collections of historical, lyrical, recruits', chumak, wedding, satirical, and Kupalo festival songs, and *vesnianky* and carols. Some of them have been included in the institute's series of folk song collections. His autobiography came out under the title *Zapysky zbyracha fol'kloru* (Notes of a Folklore Collector, 1958).

**Tapestry.** See Weaving.

**Tarabarynov, Leonyd,** b 8 November 1928 in Shalyhyne (now in Hlukhiv raion, Sumy oblast). Stage and film actor and pedagogue. He completed study at the Kharkiv Theater Institute (1955, pupil of D. Antonovych) and joined the Kharkiv Ukrainian Drama Theater. He acted in O. Dovzhenko's film *Poema pro more* (A Poem about the Sea, 1953) and has taught in the Kharkiv Institute of Arts since 1968.

**Tarakanov, Mykola,** b 19 December 1898 in Yelysavethrad (Kirovohrad), d 21 September 1976 in Kiev. Chorus conductor. After graduating from the Lysenko Music and Drama Institute (1926) he served as choirmaster or conductor in a succession of appointments. These included the Kiev Ukrainian Opera (1926–8), the DUMKA Chorus (1928–9), the Right-Bank Ukrainian Opera in Vinnytsia (1929–32), and the theaters of opera and ballet in Kharkiv (1932–4), Kiev (1934–41), Donetske (1954–63), and Odessa (1964–6). His conducting style is remembered for its effective interpretation of dramatic action and close attention to detail. He was involved with the premieres of many operas, including *Taras Bulba* (Lysenko-Liatoshynsky, 1937), *Perekop* (Meitus-Tits-Rybalchenko, 1939), and *Vulkan* (Yutsevych, 1963).

**Taran, Anatolii,** b 5 July 1940 in Myropillia, Krasnopillia raion, Sumy oblast. Writer. He graduated from the Soviet Higher Military Political School (1964) and has worked for military newspapers. He wrote the poetry collections *Ia – mil'iarder* (I'm a Billionaire, 1963), *Real'nist'* (Reality, 1966), *Rankova shybka* (The Morning Windowpane, 1969), *Aerodrom* (Aerodrome, 1976), *Kvity vohniu* (Flowers of Fire, 1978), *Nevtrachena myt'* (The Moment Not Lost, 1981), and *Soldats'ke pole* (The Soldiers' Field, 1982); a documentary novel (coauthor, 1978); and a book of documentary tales about Soviet soldiers (1988).

Andrii Taran: *At the Quarry* (1938)

**Taran, Andrii,** b 31 August 1886 in Nykopil, Katerynoslav county, Katerynoslav gubernia, d 5 March 1967 in Leningrad. Painter. He studied painting in Penza (1901–5), St Petersburg (1906–9), and Paris (1909–12). In 1923 he returned to Ukraine to teach at the Kiev State Art Institute, where he organized a mosaic workshop in 1937. A member of the *Association of Revolutionary Art of Ukraine (1925–7) and *Union of Contemporary Artists of Ukraine (1927–32), he painted large industrial landscapes, such as *The Blast Furnace Begins to Smoke* (1927), *At the Dnieper Hydroelectric Station* (1929), *Kryvyi Rih Etudes* (1937), and *At the Quarry* (1938), and still lifes done in a postimpressionist style.

**Taran, Liudmyla,** b 2 March 1954 in Hrebinky, Vasylkiv raion, Kiev oblast. Poet. Taran completed her studies in literature at Kiev University in 1976 and has been employed as a senior researcher at the Maksym Rylsky Museum in Kiev. She is the author of several collections of intimate lyrical poetry, sensuous but with a predilection for philosophical contemplation: *Hlyboke lystia* (Deep Leaves, 1982), *Oforty* (Etchings, 1985), and *Krokvy* (Rafters, 1990). She has also written a book of literary criticism, *Enerhiia poshuku* (The Energy of the Search, 1988).

**Taran, Teodosii** (pseud of Honcharenko), b 1896 in Lokhvytsia county, Poltava gubernia, d 1938. Soviet Ukrainian journalist. A member of the Ukrainian Social Democratic Workers' party (Independentists), in 1919 he joined the *Borotbists and led one of their partisan detachments in the Kremenchuk region. He was one of P. *Liubchenko's closest associates, and in the 1920s he joined the CP(B)U and became associate editor of the central Soviet Ukrainian government newspaper, *Visti VUTsVK*. In its literary supplement, *Kul'tura i pobut*, he serialized M. *Khvylovy's polemical pamphlets. When the CP(B)U paper *Komunist* was Ukrainized in 1926, he served as its associate editor and later as its de facto chief editor. After the Party's condemnation of Khvylovyism he published Stalinist articles in *Komunist* denouncing Khvylovy, the writers' group Vaplite, L. Kurbas, and the Berezil theater and criticizing cultural trends in Soviet Ukraine. In 1933 he became chief editor of *Visti VUTsVK*. Shortly after being elected to the CC CP(B)U he was arrested together with the other CC members and executed.

**Taran** (*Rutilus rutilus heckeli*; Ukrainian: *tarania*). A semimigratory fish of the carp family Cyprinidae that inhabits the estuary regions of the Black Sea and the Sea of Azov and enters the lower reaches of the Dnieper, Don, and Kuban rivers to spawn. It reaches a length of up to 40 cm and weight of up to 1.5 kg. It is a valuable commercial fish, but its stocks are continuously being depleted.

**Taranenko, Kornii,** b ca 1895 in Kremenchuk county, Poltava gubernia, d ca 1935. Borotbist revolutionary. In 1919 he led the Borotbist faction at the UNR Labor Congress and then served as deputy chairman and chairman of the Supreme Council of the National Economy in Kh. Rakovsky's Bolshevik-Borotbist coalition government. After joining the CP(B)U in 1920, Taranenko was sent to Moscow to direct the All-Union Sugar Trust. He was arrested there during the Stalinist terror and most likely executed.

**Taranets, Tymofii** [Taranec', Tymofij], b 1896 in Opryshky, Kremenchuk county, Poltava gubernia, d 1941 in Staryi Saltiv, Kharkiv oblast. Soil scientist. He was a professor at the Poltava Agricultural Institute and specialized in the soils of southern Ukraine, particularly saline soils.

He was arrested by the NKVD during the Soviet retreat in 1941 and burned alive in prison.

**Taranko, Mykhailo** [Taran'ko, Myxajlo], b 1887 in Galicia, d 1956 in Canada. Publisher and teacher. In Lviv he founded the Svit Dytyny publishing house, which issued, under his editorship, the children's magazines *Svit dytyny* (1929–39) and *Moloda Ukraïna* (1923–6), and the Ditocha biblioteka (Children's Library) and Populiarna biblioteka (Popular Library) book series, in which over 230 titles had appeared by 1939. In the 1930s Taranko served as executive secretary of the Prosvita society in Lviv.

Hlib Taranov

**Taranov, Hlib,** b 15 June 1904 in Kiev, d 25 January 1989 in Kiev. Composer, conductor, and pedagogue. A graduate of the Lysenko Music and Drama Institute (1925), he studied composition with R. Glière and B. Liatoshynsky and conducting with M. Malko. He began teaching music theory and orchestration at the institute in 1925 and wrote the handbook *Kurs chteniia partitur* (A Course in Reading Music Scores, 1939). In 1945–74 he headed the Faculty of Orchestration at the Kiev Conservatory. He also taught orchestration at the Leningrad Conservatory (1941–50) and served as vice-chairman of the Union of Composers of Ukraine (1956–68). His works include the opera *The Battlefield of Ice* (1943), nine symphonies, chamber music, pieces for piano, and choruses, as well as a reorchestration and re-edition of the M. Arkas opera *Kateryna* (1956).

**Taranovsky, Fedir** [Taranovs'kyj], b 24 May 1875 in Płońsk, Poland, d 23 January 1936 in Belgrade. Legal historian, member of the Serbian Academy of Sciences, and corresponding member of the Bulgarian Academy of Sciences. After graduating from Warsaw and St Petersburg universities he taught at the universities of Warsaw (1899–1907), Dorpat (1908–17), and Petrograd (1919). In 1918 he became a member of the newly formed Ukrainian Academy of Sciences, where he chaired the department of comparative legal history. After emigrating to Yugoslavia in 1919, he taught at Belgrade University (1920–36). Taranovsky wrote a survey of the monuments of Magdeburg law in Ukrainian cities of the Grand Duchy of Lithuania (1897), a critical outline of feudalism in Russia (1902), a book on the Normanist theory in the history of Russian law (1909), and a book on state law in France (1911). In 1926–7 he contributed several articles on the legal history of the Polish-Lithuanian Commonwealth to *Zapysky Sotsial'no-ekonomichnoho viddilu VUAN*. In the 1920s and 1930s he published several works on the legal history of the Slavs and Russians.

**Taranovsky, Semen** [Taranovs'kyj], b and d ? Kievan goldsmith of the 18th century. His extant works include a silver tabernacle (preserved at the Kiev Historical Museum) and the copper model of the silver Royal Gates in the St Sophia Cathedral in Kiev.

Stefan Taranushenko

**Taranushenko, Stefan** [Taranušenko], b 21 December 1889 in Lebedyn, Kharkiv gubernia, d 13 October 1976 in Kiev. Art scholar and museologist. A graduate of Kharkiv University (1916), he lectured at the Poltava Historical-Philological Faculty (from 1918) and the Poltava Ukrainian Institute of Social Sciences (from 1920), organized and directed the Kharkiv Museum of Ukrainian Art (1920–33), and was a professor at the Kharkiv Art Institute (1924–9), a sector head at the Department of the History of Ukrainian Culture in Kharkiv (1924–33), secretary of the subsection of Ukrainian art at the Kharkiv section of the Department of Art Studies in Kiev (1926–33), and inspector of the All-Ukrainian Committee for the Protection of Artistic Monuments for all of Left-Bank Ukraine (1926–30). He was arrested in October 1933 and imprisoned in a Siberian labor camp (1934–6). After his release he taught in Perm (1937) and worked at the Kursk (1939–50) and Astrakhan (1950–3) art galleries. After returning to Ukraine in 1953, he worked at the Institute of the History, Theory, and Developmental Problems of Soviet Architecture. He wrote monographs, based on the many research expeditions he undertook, on the old peasant houses of Kharkiv (1922), the artistic monuments of 17th-and 18th-century Slobidska Ukraine (1922), the Cathedral of the Holy Protectress in Kharkiv (1923), the 17th- and 18th-century art of Slobidska Ukraine (1928), and the Lyzohub Residence in Sedniv (1932), and his magnum opus on the wooden church architecture of Left-Bank Ukraine (1976). He also wrote booklets on the artists P. Martynovych (1958) and T. Shevchenko (1961) and articles on Shevchenko, V. Krychevsky, H. Narbut, O. Kulchytska, S. Gebus-Baranetska, book graphics, Easter eggs, folk architecture, interior painting, handicrafts, furniture, and kilims.

**Taran-Zhovnir, Yurii** [Taran-Žovnir, Jurij], b 26 June 1927 in Novomoskovske, Dnipropetrovske okruha. Metallurgist; corresponding member of the AN URSR (now ANU) since 1972. He studied and taught in Dnipropetrov-

ske, headed a department at the ANU Institute of Ferrous Metallurgy (1963–73), and has served as rector of the Dnipropetrovske Institute of Metallurgy since 1974. His main scientific contributions are in the fields of crystal formation in alloys during solidification and the metallography of cast iron. He has developed a theory of multiphase crystallization processes in eutectic alloys.

Staff members and students of the Taras Shevchenko Scientific Research Institute in 1929–30. Sitting, from left: Mykhailo Novytsky, Oleksander Doroshkevych, Serhii Pylypenko, Oleksander Bahrii, Volodymyr Miiakovsky, Borys Navrotsky; standing: Ananii Lebid, Yevhen Kyryliuk, Volodymyr Pokalchuk

**Taras Shevchenko Scientific Research Institute** (Naukovo-doslidnyi instytut Tarasa Shevchenka). A scholarly institute under the jurisdiction of the People's Commissariat of Education, established in Kharkiv in 1926 as the central repository and research institution of all published, archival, and artistic materials pertaining to T. *Shevchenko in particular and to modern Ukrainian literature in general. Until 1932 the director was D. *Bahalii. S. *Pylypenko was Bahalii's deputy and the institute's managing director, and Ya. *Aizenshtok was the scholarly secretary. A branch of the institute was founded in Kiev; O. *Doroshkevych was its director, and B. *Navrotsky was its secretary. Many other prominent scholars (eg, O. Bahrii, O. Biletsky, V. Boiko, V. Derzhavyn, P. Fylypovych, V. Koriak, Ye. Kyryliuk, A. Loboda, V. Miiakovsky, M. and O. Novytsky, V. Petrov, M. Plevako, D. Revutsky, A. Richytsky, P. Rulin, A. Shamrai, H. Sinko, B. Yakubsky, M. Yashek, S. Yefremov) taught at the institute and/or took part in its projects and publications.

Research work was divided among seven cabinets. The cabinets of pre-Shevchenko literature, Shevchenko's works, Soviet Ukrainian literature, bibliography, and history (added in the early 1930s) were in Kharkiv. The cabinets of Shevchenko's biography and post-Shevchenko literature, and sections for the study of Shevchenko's poetics and the links between Shevchenko's works and post-Shevchenko literature, were in Kiev. Work was also done by several commissions: the commission of Shevchenko's period and milieu, the commission for the study of Shevchenko's art, the commission to study the Soviet Ukrainian reading public, an archival commission, the commission for contemporary oral literature (the living word), and, in Kiev, the commission for the preparation of a dictionary of Shevchenko's language. The institute's library had a collection of manuscripts by Shevchenko, P.

Kulish, Ya. Shchoholiv, V. Samiilenko, I. Nechui-Levytsky, H. Barvinok, and A. Teslenko; the archives of O. Potebnia and the Soviet Ukrainian writers' organizations Pluh and Hart; and a collection of journals, including *Chervonyi shliakh*. In 1932 the Shevchenko Literary Museum was founded at the institute; a large part of its collection of 700 of Shevchenko's paintings, drawings, and engravings was transferred to the *Shevchenko Gallery in Kharkiv in 1933.

The institute published two collections of articles titled *Shevchenko* (1928, 1930), the bimonthly journal *Literaturnyi arkhiv* (1930–1), Shevchenko's journal and correspondence (2 annotated vols), four monographs and collections of articles on Shevchenko by single authors (Navrotsky, Bahrii, Doroshkevych), four collections of articles on Shevchenko by various authors, and several popular editions of Shevchenko's individual works with commentaries. It prepared a series of memoirs about Shevchenko (eg, by P. Kulish), trained graduate students (including scholars such as H. Kostiuk, Yu. Lavrinenko, and D. Kopytsia), and organized art exhibitions, seminars, and lectures. Its holdings and research facilitated the preparation of scholarly editions and textological studies of works by Shevchenko, M. Vovchok, and other Ukrainian writers. Most of the institute's personnel fell victim to the Stalinist terror between 1930 and 1933. Under Bahalii's successor, Ye. *Shabliovsky (1933–5), the institute was basically inactive. In 1936 jurisdiction over the institute was transferred to the AN URSR (now ANU) and it was renamed the Institute of Ukrainian Literature; that name was changed to the *Institute of Literature in 1952.

R. Senkus

**Tarasenko, Ivan,** b ? in Voronizh, Hlukhiv county, Chernihiv gubernia, d 28 August 1922 in Kiev. Civic and church activist. The descendant of an old Cossack family, he was a village scribe in Voronizh and a delegate from Chernihiv gubernia to the First Russian State Duma (1906). He served on the executive of the Ukrainian caucus in the First Duma and as an adviser to the caucus in the Second Duma. He also contributed articles to *Hromads'ka dumka*. With the outbreak of the revolution in 1917, he became an active promoter of the Ukrainian Autocephalous Orthodox church and served as a secretary for the First All-Ukrainian Orthodox Sobor (1921) and the First All-Ukrainian Orthodox Council. He was executed by Soviet authorities in 1922, after being arrested, together with his daughter and son, and accused of planning an anti-Bolshevik uprising.

**Tarasenko, Ivan.** See Savych, Oleksander.

**Tarasenko, Oleksii,** b 30 September 1909 in Domakha, Kharkiv gubernia, d 27 February 1991 in Sumy. Stage actor and director. He was an actor and stage director in the Kharkiv First Workers' and Collective-Farm Theater (from 1929), and from 1939 he worked in the Sumy Ukrainian Music and Drama Theater, where he played heroic and character roles, including the title role in W. Shakespeare's *Othello*.

**Tarasenko, Vasyl,** b 19 March 1859 in Odessa, d 25 July 1926. Geologist. He graduated from Kiev University in 1884 and then taught there and at Yurev (now Tartu) and Voronezh universities (1904–18). He took part in the geo-

logical mapping of the Kryvyi Rih Iron-ore Basin. His research dealt with crystalline rocks in Ukraine. Tarasenko was the first geologist in Ukraine to apply the method of microscopic study and detailed chemical analysis of rocks.

Leontii Tarasevych: *Blessing of the Dormition Cathedral at the Kievan Cave Monastery* (copper engraving, 1702)

**Tarasevych, Leontii** [Tarasevyč, Leontij], b ca 1650, probably in Carpathian Ukraine, d 1710 in Kiev. Master engraver. He and his brother, O. *Tarasevych, learned engraving in Augsburg at the workshop of B. and P. Kilian. In 1680–8 he worked in Vilnius, where he engraved illustrations for the Basilian, Franciscan, and Jesuit presses there. From 1688 he worked in Ukraine, first in Chernihiv and then in Kiev under the patronage of Metropolitan V. Yasynsky. Tarasevych engraved portraits of prominent Ukrainians, Poles, and Russians, including Hetman I. Mazepa; portrayals of the Catholic and Orthodox saints; heraldic and corporation crests; theses of scholarly disputes at the Vilnius and Kievan Mohyla academies, decorated with many symbols, allegories, and saints; and book illustrations, notably 45 engravings for the Kievan Cave Patericon printed by the Kievan Cave Monastery Press in 1702. Tarasevych helped establish the art of copper engraving in Ukraine and created some of the best works in Ukrainian baroque art. A book about him by D. Stepovyk was published in Kiev in 1986.

**Tarasevych, Lev** [Tarasevyč], b 14 February 1868 in Tyraspil, Kherson gubernia, d 12 June 1927 near Dresden (buried in Moscow). Microbiologist and pathologist; full

Lev Tarasevych

Oleksander Tarasevych: *St Cletus* (copper engraving, 1685)

member of the VUAN from 1926. After graduating from the medical faculty of Odessa University (1891), he continued his studies at the Medico-Surgical Academy in St Petersburg (1891–6), in Paris (1897), at Kiev University (1898–1900), and at the Pasteur Institute in Paris (1900–2). He served as a professor at Odessa (1902–7) and Moscow (1907–11) universities. He taught at the Bestuzhev Higher Courses for Women (1908–18), founded and edited *Meditsinskaia mikrobiologiia* (3 vols, 1912–15) and the influential Moscow monthly *Priroda* (1912–27), and worked with the Moscow Scientific Institute Society (1913–18). During the First World War he was active in preparing vaccines against cholera, typhus, and tuberculosis, and in 1918 he founded a bacteriological station. After the revolution he presided over the scientific medical council in the Commissariat of Public Health (1918–27), founded and directed the State Pasteur Institute for Public Health Care (1918–27), and returned to the Moscow University Medical School as a professor (1918–24).

**Tarasevych, Oleksander** [Tarasevyč] (Tarasovych; monastic name: Antonii), b ca 1640, probably in Transcarpathia, d ca 1727 in Kiev. Engraver and church figure; founder of the Ukrainian school of metal engraving. He and his brother, L. *Tarasevych, learned engraving in Augsburg at the workshop of B. and P. Kilian until ca 1672. He lived and worked in Hlusk, Belarus (ca 1672–9), and in Vilnius before returning to Ukraine in 1688 to take monastic vows at the Kievan Cave Monastery and direct the engraving workshop at its press. Later he served as acting archimandrite of the Svensk Monastery, near Briansk (1705–10), and the Kievan Cave Monastery (ca 1718–27). His patrons included Marshal A. Połubiński of the Grand Duchy of Lithuania, Metropolitans K. Zhokhovsky and V. Yasynsky, Hetman I. Mazepa, and rectors of the Kiev Mohyla Academy. Tarasevych masterfully executed copper engravings depicting scenes from the New Testament, heraldic compositions, and portraits of Catholic and Orthodox saints and contemporary Ukrainian and Belarusian hierarchs, Cossack colonels, and Polish and Lithuanian monarchs and nobles. The best of his works illustrate books, such as the *Rosarium* dedicated to

Połubiński (1678), *Thesaurus* (1682), *Żywoty świątych* (Lives of the Saints, 1693), and *Bozhyeiu mylostyiu* (By God's Mercy, 1688). Tarasevych engraved the title pages of theses on theological and philosophical scholarly disputes. In Vilnius and Kiev he trained many professional engravers. Books and albums from his personal library were used as instructional materials in the workshops of the Cave Monastery in the 18th and 19th centuries. A book about Tarasevych by D. Stepovyk was published in Kiev in 1975.

D. Stepovyk

**Tarasevych, Yurii** [Tarasevyč, Jurij], b 19 March 1937 in Shostka, now in Sumy oblast. Colloid chemist. A graduate of the Kiev Polytechnical Institute (1959), he has worked at the AN URSR (now ANU) institutes of General and Inorganic Chemistry (1961–8) and Colloid Chemistry and Hydrochemistry (since 1968). His research has dealt mainly with the colloid chemistry of natural dispersed materials, the chemistry of their surfaces, and adsorption phenomena. He has optimized ways of using these materials in industry.

**Tarashcha** [Tarašča]. IV-11. A city (1989 pop 13,500) on the Kotlui River and a raion center in Kiev oblast. It was founded on territory belonging to Poland in 1709 and was granted the rights of *Magdeburg law in 1791. After the partition of Poland in 1793, it was annexed by Russia, and in 1800 it became a county center in Kiev gubernia. In 1957 the town was granted city status. Today Tarashcha is an agricultural town with a cheese factory, fruit-canning factory, fish farm, and mixed-feed plant. It is the home of a research station of the Ukrainian Scientific Research Institute of the Economics and Organization of Agriculture.

**Tarashcha Division** (Tarashchanska dyviziia). A Bolshevik military unit formed in September 1918 near Sumy as the First Soviet Ukrainian Division. Its strength was about 3,000 men, of whom only 27 percent were Ukrainians. It participated in the capture of Kiev on 5 February 1919 and then operated on the Ukrainian front in Volhynia and central Ukraine. In June 1919 it was transferred to the 12th Soviet Army and redesignated the 44th Tarashcha Rifle Division. It was commanded at the time by M. Shchors and operated mainly against the UNR Army. In 1920–2 the division was renamed the 44th Kiev Rifle Division, and fought Ukrainian partisans in central Ukraine.

**Tarashcha uprising.** One of several insurrections against the German occupation and the Hetman government in Ukraine. The uprising broke out on 8 June 1918, when the peasants of 24 villages of Kryvets and Stryzhavka volosts took up arms. It spread quickly to the southern part of Tarashcha county. After routing the Hetman detachments at Yanyshivka (10 June) some 4,000 rebels took Tarashcha itself (12 June) and then almost the whole county. The Germans sent two infantry and one cavalry division to crush the uprising as well as a similar outbreak in the neighboring Zvenyhorodka region. On 20 June they captured Tarashcha, but the fighting continued until the end of July. The rebels were commanded by the soldiers V. Balias and F. Hrebenko and the sailor P. Hryhorenko. Besides Bolsheviks the leadership included left Ukrainian Social Revolutionaries (later Borotbists) led by M. Shynkar. The rebels demanded revolutionary rights and privileges, the restoration of the Central Rada, and the convening of a constituent assembly for Ukraine. The Zvenyhorodka uprising, begun by peasants, was supported by a kish of Free Cossacks led by L. Shevchenko.

**Tarasiuk, Andrey** [Tarasjuk, Andrij], b 6 December 1951 in Winnipeg. Theater, festival, and live entertainment producer. He studied at the University of Manitoba and at the Royal Winnipeg Ballet School and graduated from the National Theatre School of Canada (1976). He was the producer of the first annual *Dream in High Park* outdoor Shakespeare production in Toronto (1982) and the National Celebrations Program for the millennium of Ukrainian Christianity in Ottawa (1988), and artistic director of the Canadian Heritage Festival (1989–90). He is the artistic producer of Theatre Direct in Toronto and leads his own company, Chysta Productions.

*Tarasivtsi*. See Brotherhood of Taras.

**Tarasovych, Vasyl** [Tarasovyč, Vasyl'], b ?, d 1651. Bishop of Mukachiv. Originally from Galicia, he came to Transcarpathia in the 1620s as an assistant to Bishop I. Hryhorovych. He succeeded Hryhorovych in 1633 and started planning for a union of the traditionally Orthodox eparchy with Rome. This plan brought him into direct conflict with the secular ruler of the region, Prince G. Rákóczi, who suspected that a Catholic presence in his domain would weaken his control over the church. Accordingly, Tarasovych was arrested in 1640 and banished from the region in 1642. Tarasovych then formally adopted the Catholic faith and established himself in the western region of his eparchy. He was returned to his traditional see in Mukachiv in 1644 as part of a diplomatic settlement following a military setback for Rákóczi, but he subsequently renounced his Catholicism, returned to Orthodoxy, and refrained from taking part in the 1646 Union of *Uzhhorod, which established a formal Catholic presence in the eparchy.

**Tardenoisian culture.** A Mesolithic archeological culture of the 7th to 4th millennium BC that existed in Europe from France to Transcaucasia, with settlements in the Crimea and in Ukraine mainly along the Donets and Vorskla rivers. It was named after the Fère-en-Tardenois site in France. An increasingly well-developed microlithic flint technology characterized this culture. This was reflected in the numbers of small, almost standardized flint pieces found at sites. The Tardenoisians lived by gathering, fishing, and hunting (employing bows for the latter activity), and were quite mobile. They maintained a matriarchal clan order and collectively buried their dead in a flexed position. (See also *Mesolithic Period.)

**Tariffs.** Duties on goods that are carried across borders, or fees for the use of roads, bridges, ports, or market facilities. In the past duties were primarily a source of government income, but in recent times they have become an instrument for protecting industry from foreign competition. Duties in Ukraine are first mentioned in the 9th century. They were negotiated in treaties between Ukraine-Rus' and Byzantium in the 10th century. The Lithuanian-Polish Commonwealth had quite a complex system of tariffs. Duties (*myto*) included various trade fees exacted by the state, community, church, or private individuals (whether legally or not). Tariffs collected at borders from foreign traders were called customs (*tslo*). They were collected by special customs houses, which first appeared in the 13th century. Besides customs there were internal duties collected at the boundaries of localities, cities, and marketplaces.

The Hetman state of the 18th century had a more organized system of tariffs than did the princely era. Beginning with B. Khmelnytsky's rule the state treasury collected customs duties at the borders through the military exactor or tax farmers. There were two kinds of duties, import duties (*inducta*) and export duties (*evecta*). Khmelnytsky's universal of 28 April 1654 imposed a state duty on foreign goods and appointed a special collector. But the government exempted local traders – Ukrainians and foreigners, particularly Greeks – and even foreign merchants from those duties. Khmelnytsky also tried to free Ukrainian trade abroad from the tariffs of other governments (eg, in the treaty with Turkey at the beginning of the 1650s). Internal duties were levied by the government or by various communities – towns or monasteries – which were granted the right to levy by the government. Private duties were rather rare in the Hetman state. With some modifications the system persisted to the middle of the 18th century. Beginning with Peter I the Russian government used duties to further its imperial policies in Ukraine. A series of important changes in the Hetmanate system of duties was introduced. In 1754 the tariff border between Russia and Ukraine was abolished, and Ukraine lost its tariff autonomy.

The Russian customs law of 1767 prohibited the importation from abroad of the kind of products that were manufactured within the Russian Empire, including Ukraine, and imposed heavy duties on other imported goods. In 1850 and 1877 the customs duties were greatly lowered, and various products were imported from Europe into Ukraine. At the same time foreign competitors, especially German, undermined the development of industrial enterprises in Ukraine. In 1877 the Russian government returned to protectionist policies. From then until the revolution customs duties increased; they reached 33–100 percent of the value of the goods imported. To some extent such policies promoted the rapid growth of industry in Ukraine during the period.

In 1918 the Hetman government re-established the tariff border between Ukraine and Russia. In the first half of 1919 the government of the Ukrainian SSR officially recognized the tariff border between Ukraine and the Russian SFSR. Later the border was abolished again.

The customs duties between the Ukrainian SSR and countries not belonging to the USSR were determined by the USSR Ministry of Foreign Trade on the basis of the customs code adopted on 5 May 1964 (until then the 1928 code was in force). The duties were collected by the Main Customs Administration (Holovne myrne upravlinnia), which was in charge of the customs offices in Odessa, Lviv, Chernivtsi, Uzhhorod, Kiev, and Brest, with their departments at the border control stations.

V. Holubnychy, O. Ohloblyn

**Tarkhankut Peninsula** [Tarxankuts'kyj pivostriv]. VIII–13. A western extension of the Crimean Peninsula, situated between Karkinitska Bay and the Black Sea, covering an area of 1,550 sq km. It consists largely of rolling lime-stone elevations (of up to 179 m) dissected by ravines and gullies. It has a number of saltwater lakes (Donuzlav and others) and deposits of natural gas. The peninsula has a steppe vegetation cover, with brush found in its valleys.

Bishop Hryhorii Tarkovych          Marta Tarnavska

### Tarkovych, Hryhorii [Tarkovyč, Hryhorij], b 8 November 1754 in Pasika, Transcarpathia, d 16 January 1841 in Prešov. Uniate bishop. Upon completing theological studies at the Barbareum in Vienna (1778), he became a professor at the Mukachiv theology school and then a parish priest in that region (1793–1803). In 1803–13 he worked as a censor of Slavic books in Budapest and represented Mukachiv eparchy in the Hungarian Diet. He was promoted to the office of vicar-general for the Prešov region in 1813. After that jurisdiction was made into a separate eparchy, he was named (1818) as its first bishop, although he was not formally installed until 1821. As bishop, Tarkovych sought to maintain traditional church rites and established the I. Kovach Eparchial Library in 1826.

### Tarnavska, Marta [Tarnavs'ka] (Tarnawsky; née Senkovska), b 15 November 1930 in Lviv. Writer and bibliographer; wife of O. *Tarnavsky. She has lived in Philadelphia since the 1950s. A librarian at the University of Pennsylvania since 1967, she has compiled several bibliographies, including one on the subject of the Ukrainian national revolution in Ukrainian poetry (1969) and one on Ukrainian literature in English (in *Journal of Ukrainian Studies* and separately as *Ukrainian Literature in English Books and Pamphlets*, 1988). Her literary articles, poems, stories, and book reviews have appeared in *Nashe zhyttia*, *Kyïv*, *Suchasnist'*, and *Ukrainian Quarterly*. She is the author of the poetry collections *Khvaliu iliuziiu* (I Praise Illusion, 1972) and *Zemletrus* (Earthquake, 1981); the latter collection contains her translations of poems by Russian, German, Polish, and American women poets.

### Tarnavsky, Ilarion [Tarnavs'kyj], b 1890 in Sambir county, Galicia, d ? Civic and political activist. He was deputy to the Polish Sejm in 1938–9. He was arrested by the Soviet authorities after the occupation of Western Ukraine in 1939; his subsequent fate is unknown.

### Tarnavsky, Myron [Tarnavs'kyj], b 29 August 1869 in Baryliv, Kaminka-Strumylova county, Galicia, d 29 June 1938 in Lviv. Commander of the *Ukrainian Galician

Gen Myron Tarnavsky          Ostap Tarnavsky

Army (UHA). After attaining the rank of major (1916) in the Austrian army, he was given command of the Legion of *Ukrainian Sich Riflemen. He was promoted to lieutenant colonel (1918), and commanded the 16th Infantry Regiment in central Ukraine. In February 1919 he joined the UHA, and soon he became commander of the Second Corps and a full colonel. In July 1919 Tarnavsky was appointed supreme commander of the UHA and was promoted to brigadier general. He oversaw UHA operations in central Ukraine, its Kiev offensive, and its tragic demise in the so-called Quadrangle of Death. On 7 November 1919 he was relieved of duty and courtmartialed for arranging a politically unauthorized armistice with A. Denikin. After his acquittal he served briefly as acting supreme commander of the UHA.

### Tarnavsky, Omelian [Tarnavs'kyj, Omeljan], b 27 May 1910 in Stanyslaviv, Galicia. Economist, journalist, and civic activist. He studied law at Lviv University and economics at the Higher School of Economics in Berlin. During the Second World War he was director of the Ukrainske Vydavnytstvo publishing house in Cracow (1942–4) and financial manager of the *Ukrainian Central Committee. In 1949, after several years in Germany, he emigrated to Canada. There he served as president (1951–3) and national executive member of the *Plast Ukrainian Youth Association (1949–74) and edited Plast journals, such as *Plastovyi shliakh*.

### Tarnavsky, Ostap [Tarnavs'kyj], b 3 May 1917 in Lviv, d 19 September 1992 in Philadelphia. Writer and community figure; husband of M. *Tarnavska. As a postwar refugee he lived in Austria and Philadelphia and served as executive director of the *United Ukrainian American Relief Committee (ZUADK) and secretary (1960s–1975) and head (since 1975) of the *Slovo Association of Ukrainian Writers in Exile. His first poems appeared in Lviv journals in 1935. He wrote the poetry collections *Slova i mriï* (Words and Dreams, 1948), *Zhyttia* (Life, 1952), *Mosty* (Bridges, 1956), *Samotnie derevo* (The Solitary Tree, 1960), and *Sotnia sonetiv* (A Hundred Sonnets, 1984), the literary essay collection *Podorozh poza vidome* (Voyage beyond the Known, 1965), the essay *Tuha za mitom* (Longing for Myth, 1966), a history of the ZUADK (1971), and the prose collection *Kaminni stupeni* (Stone Levels, 1979). His poems, literary articles, criticism, translations of Western poetry, and

reminiscences have appeared in *Svoboda, Suchasnist', Lysty do pryiateliv, Kyïv, Ukrainian Quarterly,* and *Books Abroad.* A volume of collected works, *Virshi* (Poems), was published in 1992.

**Tarnavsky, Yurii.** See Tarnawsky, George.

Zenon Tarnavsky

George Tarnawsky

**Tarnavsky, Zenon** [Tarnavs'kyj] (pseud: Zhan Zhak Burvil), b 9 September 1912 in Sambir, Galicia, d 8 August 1962 in Detroit. Theater figure, writer, translator, and journalist. His first story appeared in *Novyi chas* in 1930. During the 1930s he worked as a journalist for the Lviv papers *Ukraïns'ki visty* and *Bat'kivshchyna,* translated French plays into Ukrainian and adapted novels for the Zahrava and Tobilevych theaters, and wrote the play *Taras Shevchenko* (1938). During the Second World War he worked as a radio journalist, was the founder and artistic director of the \*Veselyi Lviv theater (1942–4), and was director of Lviv's Literary-Artistic Club. As a postwar refugee Tarnavsky was a coeditor of *Arka* and the first editor of \**Ukraïns'ka trybuna* in Munich. After emigrating to the United States in 1949, he worked as an industrial artist in Detroit and was active in Ukrainian community organizations there. He translated into Ukrainian the morality play *Everyman* (and directed its premiere in Detroit in 1961), T.S. Eliot's *Murder in the Cathedral* (pub 1963), and T. Wilder's *Our Town,* and wrote or cowrote several unpublished plays (eg, 'Chai u pana prem'iera' [Tea at the Premier's], with B. Nyzhankivsky). His articles and stories appeared in the émigré periodicals *Arka, Ukraïns'ka trybuna, Teatr, Shliakh peremohy,* and *Kyïv.* A posthumous edition of his selected prose and journalistic writings was published in 1964, and no. 8 of \**Terem* (1982) was devoted to him.

R. Senkus

**Tarnawsky, George** [Tarnavs'kyj, Jurij] (pseuds: Romulius, Yu. T.), b 3 February 1934 in Turka, Sambir county, Galicia. Linguist, poet, novelist, and translator. Tarnawsky was displaced by the Second World War, and grew up in a DP camp in Germany. He emigrated to the United States in 1952 and completed a degree in electrical engineering at the Newark College of Engineering in New Jersey (1956) and then turned to linguistics, in which discipline he was awarded a PH D from New York University in 1982. He has worked at IBM on automated language-translation projects and artificial intelligence and has pub-

lished a number of scientific papers on those subjects. He has also worked on developing a natural-language interface for the computer programming language PROLOG. Tarnawsky's linguistic studies have had a profound influence on him as a writer. In his poetry as well as in his prose he has eschewed the more usual embellished language and has sought the utmost semantic and syntactic directness, as if his creations were to enter into a one-to-one computerized relationship between word and meaning. Tarnawsky is unique in his expression, and his poems reflect well the mechanized and dehumanized contemporary world. He began writing in the early 1950s and has published several collections of verse: *Zhyttia v misti* (Life in the City, 1956), *Popoludni v Pokipsi* (Afternoons in Poughkeepsie, 1960), *Idealizovana biohrafiia* (Idealized Biography, 1964), *Spomyny* (Memories, 1964), and *Bez Espaniï* (Without Spain, 1969); a collection encompassing all of the aforementioned and some new cycles, *Poeziï pro nishcho i inshi poeziï na tsiu samu temu* (Poems about Nothing and Other Poems on the Same Subject, 1970); and a bilingual English-Ukrainian collection, *Os', iak ia vyduzhuiu* (This Is How I Get Well, 1976). A collection of his poetry, *Bez nichoho: Poeziï* (Without Anything: Poems), appeared in Ukraine in 1991. He has two novels to his credit, the Ukrainian *Shliakhy* (Roads, 1961) and the English *Meningitis* (1978). Tarnawsky was one of the founding members of the \*New York Group of poets and the cofounder and editor of their periodic publication \**Novi poeziï* (1959–71). He has translated from Spanish and English into Ukrainian (F. García Lorca and S. Beckett) as well as from Ukrainian into English (*Ukrainian Dumy,* together with P. Kylyna [P. \*Warren] in 1979). His literary criticism, published in various journals, concerns modern poetry, particularly poetic translations and bilingualism.

D.H. Struk

**Tarnawsky, Marta.** See Tarnavska, Marta.

Walter S. Tarnopolsky

**Tarnopolsky, Walter Surma** [Tarnopol's'kyj], b 1 August 1932 in Gronlid, Saskatchewan. Scholar and jurist. Tarnopolsky was educated at the University of Saskatchewan (1957), Columbia University (1955), and the University of London (LLM, 1962). He was a professor of law at several Canadian universities before his appointment to the Supreme Court of Ontario (Appeals Division) in 1983. He was also president of the Federation of Canadian University Students (1957–8), a member of the United Nations Human Rights Committee (1977–83), president of the Canadian Civil Liberties Association (1977–81), vice-president of the board of directors of the Mohyla Ukrainian Institute in Saskatoon (1964–6), and president of the Canadian Foundation for Ukrainian Studies (1976–7). The recipient of honorary doctorates from St Thomas University (1982) and the University of Alberta (1986), he is the author of *The Canadian Bill of Rights* (1966, 1975) and *Discrimination and the Law in Canada* (1982) and coeditor of *The Canadian Charter of Rights: Commentary* (1982).

**Tarnovska, Mariia** [Tarnovs'ka, Marija] (pseud: M. Virliana), b 8 December 1892 in Kotsiubyntsi, Husiatyn county, Galicia, d 17 May 1975 in Detroit. Ukrainian-American writer; sister of M. *Tarnovsky. She emigrated to the United States in 1909. She began publishing in 1919, and in the 1920s she belonged to the 'transoceanic' branch of the Soviet Ukrainian proletarian writers' organization Hart. Her socialist poems and stories about the plight of Ukrainian immigrant women appeared in communist periodicals such as *Robitnytsia* (Winnipeg) and *Ukraïns'ki shchodenni visty* (New York City).

**Tarnovsky** [Tarnovs'kyj] (Tarnavsky). A family line of Cossack officers from Right-Bank Ukraine, dating from the late 17th century, when their surname was Liashko. Ivan Liashko was a military fellow of Pryluka regiment (1661), and his son, Fedir Liashko-Tarnovsky, was captain of Varva regiment (1689–93). Fedir and his older brother, Vasyl, were the originators of two lines of the Tarnovsky family, the senior, Chernihiv line and the junior, Poltava line. A number of captains of Varva regiment during the period 1689–1769 were from the junior line, including Ivan Tarnovsky (1760–9), who was also colonel of Hadiache regiment (1772–9). Members of the senior line were more prominent in Ukrainian history. Vasyl's son, Stepan Tarnovsky (stepson of D. Nesterenko, d ca 1730), was captain of Baturyn (and its defender during the sacking of 1708), a fellow of the standard, and codirector (with S. Chuikevych) of the General Military Chancellery in 1728. Stepan's son, Yakiv Tarnovsky, was a general standard-bearer (1761–79). Yakiv's sons were Vasyl Tarnovsky, a graduate of Königsberg University and the marshal of Chernihiv gubernia (1790–4), and Stepan Tarnovsky, the marshal of Kiev gubernia (1791–2). Vasyl's son, Volodymyr Tarnovsky, was a member of the Poltava general court (1818–26) and the Love of Truth Masonic lodge. Stepan's son, Hryhorii Tarnovsky (1788–1853), an art scholar and patron, owned the Kachanivka estate in Borzna county and was a friend of T. Shevchenko. Vasyl's grandson, Vasyl *Tarnovsky (1810–1866), was a leader of the peasant reform movement and also a friend of Shevchenko. The great-grandson, Vasyl *Tarnovsky (1837–1899), founded a museum dedicated to Cossack history in Chernihiv (opened in 1901). Their relative, Mykola Tarnovsky (1858–1898), a magnate in Kaniv county, was an amateur archeologist and collector of Kiev antiquities. He published a catalog of his collection of Ukrainian artifacts (1898, with an introduction by V. Antonovych). Serhii Tarnovsky (1883–?), a pianist and a professor at the Kiev Conservatory in the 1920s, was also a member of the family. It is unknown whether the colonel Ivan Tarnovsky, who commanded Cossack garrisons in Volhynia in 1657–8, belonged to the line.

O. Ohloblyn

**Tarnovsky, Mykola** [Tarnovs'kyj] (pseuds: Ostap Ochko, M. Haliada, Yurko Slyvka, Emmanuil, M. Shcherbak, M. Naraivsky, M. Dumka, and Mykola Mykolaiovych), b 1 January 1895 in Kotsiubyntsi, Husiatyn county, Galicia, d 20 June 1984 in Kiev. Ukrainian-American and Soviet writer. He emigrated to New York City in 1910. He was active in the Ukrainian Federation of the American Socialist party, the American Communist party (from 1919), and the League of Ukrainian Americans (secretary, 1952–5, and president, 1955–8). In 1958 he returned to Ukraine and became deputy head of the *Ukraina Society. Tarnovsky began publishing poetry in the Ukrainian-American press in 1915 and was an editor of such periodicals as *Robitnyk* (Detroit), *Molot, Smikh i pravda,* and *Ukraïns'ki shchodenni visty.* In the 1920s he belonged to the 'transoceanic' branch of the Soviet Ukrainian proletarian writers' group Hart and to Zakhidnia Ukraina. Most of his works depict the hardships of Ukrainian immigrant life. Others attack the 'bourgeois nationalists' or glorify life in the USSR. They include the poetry collections *Patrioty* (Patriots, 1918), *Shliakhom zhyttia* (Along the Road of Life, 1921), and *Velyke misto* (The Big City, 1926), the novel in verse *Emihranty* (Emigrants, 1958), and the prose collection *V zaokeans'kii hushchi* (In the Transoceanic Thicket, 1964). Several large editions of Tarnovsky's selected poems have been published in both New York City (1951) and Kiev. B. Burkatov published a book about him in 1964, and a book of his memoirs was published in 1979.

R. Senkus

**Tarnovsky, Mykola** [Tarnovs'kyj], b 2 May 1919 in Oleksandrivka, Bratslav county, Podilia gubernia. Writer. He graduated from the Gorky Literary Institute (1957) and has worked as a newspaper editor in Vinnytsia and Uzhhorod and as an editor of *Zhovten'.* He has written two story collections and over 20 novels, among them *Shliakhamy brativ* (Along the Brothers' Paths, 1950), *Krutohora* (1957), *Den' pochynaiet'sia nespokiino* (The Day Begins Restlessly, 1963), *Vyrok* (The Sentence, 1965), *Kvity na morozi* (Flowers in the Frost, 1966), *Za ridnym porohom* (Beyond the Native Threshold, 1967), *Dev'iatyi val* (The Ninth Wave, 1970), *Vzaiemnist'* (Reciprocity, 1972), *Zoloti verby* (Golden Willows, 1979), *Horinnia* (Burning, 1983), and *Spynysia, khvylyno!* (Stop, Minute!, 1984).

**Tarnovsky, Vasyl** [Tarnovs'kyj, Vasyl'], b 26 June 1810 in Kachanivka, Borzna county, Chernihiv gubernia, d 16 December 1866. Jurist and civic figure. After graduating in law from Moscow University he taught at Zhytomyr gymnasium and then managed the family estate. He studied the economic condition of the peasantry in Kiev gubernia and wrote an article on legal practice in Russian-ruled Ukraine (1842). As an opponent of serfdom he was active in preparing the emancipation reforms: he sat on the Chernihiv Gubernia Committee for Improving the Lot of Landlords' Peasants (1858–9) and on the editing committees for the reform legislation in St Petersburg. After inheriting his uncle's estate he underwrote the publication of P. *Kulish's *Zapiski o Iuzhnoi Rusi* (Notes on Southern Rus') and *Chorna rada* (The Black Council) and supported other cultural projects.

**Tarnovsky, Vasyl** [Tarnovs'kyj, Vasyl'], b 1 April 1837 in Antonivka, Pyriatyn county, Poltava gubernia, d 25

Vasyl Tarnovsky, Jr (portrait by Andrii Horonovych, 1870s)

Yuliian Tarnovych

June 1899 in Kiev. Civic and cultural activist; son of V. *Tarnovsky. A graduate of Kiev University, he served as marshal of Nizhen county (1875–87). Recognizing T. Shevchenko's genius he extended his friendship and help to him. He supported various Ukrainian cultural developments, particularly the publication of *Kievskaia starina* in the 1890s, the founding of the Kiev Historical Museum, and the upkeep of Shevchenko's grave in Kaniv. He amassed a large collection of articles and documents from the Cossack era and a unique collection of Shevchenko memorabilia. A number of important books were published by Tarnovsky: a catalog of his historical collections, a photograph album of Shevchenko's etchings, and V. Antonovych and V. Bets's album of hetmans, *Istoricheskie deiateli Iugo-Zapadnoi Rossii* (Historical Figures of Southwestern Russia, 1883). In 1897 he bequeathed the Museum of Ukrainian Antiquities in Chernihiv, which he had financed, to the Chernihiv zemstvo. Leading Ukrainian writers and scholars, such as M. Kostomarov, P. Kulish, M. Vovchok, O. Lazarevsky, and V. Horlenko, met at his estate in Kachanivka, in Borzna county. Among his friends Tarnovsky was called 'Hetman.'

**Tarnovych, Yuliian** [Tarnovyč, Julijan] (pseuds: Yu. Beskyd, Yu. Zemlian, O. Zubryd), b 1 January 1903 in Rostaine, Jasło county, Galicia, d 28 September 1977 in Toronto. Journalist and writer. In Lviv he edited the Biblioteka Lemkivshchyny (Library of the Lemko Region) book series (1936–9) and *Nash lemko* (1934–9), a Ukrainian patriotic paper distributed in the Lemko region. During the Second World War he edited the special weekly edition of *Krakivs'ki visti* in Cracow and then the weekly *Ridna zemlia* (1941–4) in Lviv. A postwar refugee, he worked for the paper *Ukraïns'ke slovo* in Regensburg, Germany, before emigrating to Canada in 1948. In Toronto he edited the newspapers *Lemkivshchyna-Zakerzonnia* (1949–53), *Ukraïns'kyi robitnyk* (1950–5), and *Lemkivs'ki visti* (1964–70) and the annual *Lemkivs'kyi kalendar* (to 1969), and coedited the Catholic weekly *Nasha meta*. Tarnovych wrote many articles and stories and over 25 separate works, many of them on Lemko subjects. They include an illustrated history of the Lemko region (1936; repr 1964); a book on historical monuments there (1937); the first Lemko primer in Ukrainian (ca 1937); a book on the region's material culture (1940; repr 1941, 1972); a hiker's guide to the region's

physical and cultural geography (1940); a book on 20 years of Polish oppression of the Lemkos (1940); a booklet about the town of Sianik (1941); the prose collections *Mova stolit' (Lemkivshchyna v perekazakh)* (The Language of Centuries [The Lemko Region in (Folk) Legends], 1938), *Teofanova dochka* (Teofan's Daughter, 1946), and *Za rodyme pravo: Opovidannia z chasiv vyzvol'nykh zmahan' Lemkivshchyny za svoie natsional'ne zhyttia* (For the Inherent Right: Stories from the Times of the Liberation Struggle of the Lemko Region for Its National Life, 1948); the plays *Pisnia Beskydu* (Song of the Beskyd, 1938) and *Rvut'sia kaidany* (The Shackles Are Breaking, 1941); the novelette *Na rikakh vavylons'kykh* (On Babylonian Rivers, 1952); and the memoirs *Na zharyshchakh Zakerzonnia* (In the Razed Region beyond the Curzon Line, nd).

**Tarnów.** A city (1981 pop 107,000) on the Dunajec River and a voivodeship center in southern Poland. In 1920–3 Tarnów was the seat of a section of the UNR government-in-exile and the residence of S. Petliura. In February 1921 the *Council of the Republic was convened there. The UNR government-in-exile moved to Warsaw in 1923. Not far from Tarnów was the Wadowice internment camp for soldiers of the UNR Army. In the early 1920s the Ukrainska Avtokefalna Tserkva publishing house, directed by I. Ohiienko, published some religious pamphlets in Tarnów.

**Taromske** [Taroms'ke]. V-15. A town smt (1986 pop 15,700) under jurisdiction of a city raion council of Dnipropetrovske. The village was founded in the late 18th century, and became known for its ceramics. In 1938 it attained smt status. Today it has a fish farm and two granite quarries. It is the home of the Dnipropetrovske branch of the Ukrainian Scientific Research Institute of Cattle Breeding and Artificial Insemination.

**Tartakovsky, Isaak** [Tartakovs'kyj], b 25 April 1912 in Volochyske, Starokostiantyniv county, Volhynia gubernia. Painter. In 1951 he graduated from the Kiev State Art Institute, where he studied under O. Shovkunenko and V. Kostetsky. He has painted socialist-realist historical and genre paintings, portraits of L. Revutsky (1950), P. Tychyna (1964), and A. Shtoharenko (1979), and the portrait *Natalka* (1966).

**Tartu.** A city (1986 pop 111,000) in Estonia, known formerly as Dorpat in German and Yurev in Russian. Its university, founded in 1632, was closed in 1710 and reopened in 1802. In the 19th century numerous Ukrainians studied at the university, and in the 1880s a Ukrainian student hromada was founded there. At its peak the hromada had up to 200 members. It was active until 1917, when its membership hovered between 80 and 100. Its presidents included M. Vasylenko and F. Matushevsky. At the end of the 19th century a number of Ukrainian professors lectured at the university: O. Ostrohradsky (financial law), O. Myklashevsky (political economy), A. Tsarevsky (theology), and F. Yevetsky (medicine).

**Tarutyne.** VII-10. A town smt (1986 pop 6,000) and raion center in Odessa oblast. It was founded in 1814 as a German colony. After the Crimean War the region belonged to Moldavia principality until 1878, when it was retaken by Russia. Until 1940 Tarutyne was a cultural and economic center of the German minority in Akkerman county. In 1958 it attained smt status. Today most of the town's inhabitants are employed in the food industry.

Dmytro Tas    Heorhii Tasin

**Tas, Dmytro** [Tas'] (pen name of Dmytro Mohyliansky), b 10 February 1901 in Chernihiv, d 20 September 1942. Writer; son of M. *Mohyliansky and brother of L. Mohylianska. He began publishing poems in the Chernihiv press in 1918 and was active in Ukrainian literary life in Kiev (from 1925) and Kharkiv (from 1930). His impressionistic stories and lyrical, expressionistic poems (many on urban themes) appeared in journals, such as *Chervonyi shliakh, Zhyttia i revoliutsiia, Hlobus, Kino,* and *Vsesvit.* Published separately were the story collections *Vedmedi tansiuiut'* (The Bears Are Dancing, 1927) and *Sad* (The Orchard, 1930). He was arrested in 1930, and perished in a Soviet labor camp. A selection of his poems was republished in *Poeziï* (1986, no. 1).

**Tashkent.** The capital (1989 pop 2,073,000) of Uzbekistan. It was one of the largest economic and cultural centers of the former USSR. It has one of the largest Ukrainian communities in Asia, and one of the largest outside Ukraine: in 1970 there were 40,700 Ukrainians in the city (2.9 percent of its population). The other major nationalities were the Russians (41 percent), Uzbeks (37 percent), Tatars (7 percent), and Jews (4 percent). In 1867–1917 Tashkent was the capital of Turkestan general gubernia. Ukrainians began to settle there at the end of the 19th century. During the revolutionary period Tashkent became the center of Ukrainian political activity in Turkestan: the Ukrainian Hromada (est April 1917) was reconstituted as the Ukrainian Central Hromada of Turkestan, and in 1918 the Ukrainian National Council of Turkestan (complete with an executive branch) was set up. The Prosvita society was active, and the weekly *Turkestans'ka rada* was published. When the Soviet regime consolidated its power in Tashkent (1920), the Ukrainian movement died out. In the 1930s Ukrainian was still taught in a few schools, and the Pedagogical Institute maintained a Ukrainian department. During the Second World War many Ukrainians were evacuated to Tashkent, and Tashkent Radio had a Ukrainian program. A branch of the Kiev Institute of Civil Aviation Engineers was located in Tashkent.

**Tasin, Heorhii** (real name: Georgii Rozov), b 22 March 1895 in Shumiachi, near Roslavl, Smolensk gubernia, d 6 May 1956 in Kiev. Film director. He graduated from the Petrograd Psychoneuropathological Institute and then became a screenwriter (1920). He was administrative director of the Odessa and Yalta Artistic Film studios (1922–3) and then a film director at the Odessa studio (from 1926) and the Kiev Studio of Chronicle-Documentary Films (1944). Among his films are *Alim* (1926), *Jimmie Higgins* (1928), *Nichnyi viznyk* (The Night Coachman, 1929), *Karmeliuk* (1939), and the propagandistic *Radians'ka Ukraïna* (Soviet Ukraine, 1947, with M. Slutsky) and *Pisnia pro Ukraïnu* (A Song about Ukraine, 1955).

**Tatarbunary.** VIII-10. A city (1989 pop 11,400) on Lake Sasyk and a raion center in Odessa oblast. It was founded in the 16th century, when the territory was under Turkish rule. During the Russian-Turkish wars in 1768–74 and 1787–91 the settlement was occupied by Russia, and some Danubian Cossacks moved there. In 1812 it was annexed by the Russian Empire. During the 19th century Bulgarian colonists and Ukrainian and Russian serfs found refuge there. From 1918 to 1940 Tatarbunary belonged to Rumania. In 1924 the town was the site of the *Tatarbunary uprising against the Rumanian occupation. In 1978 it attained city status. Today it has a woolen-cloth factory and a winery.

Participants in the Tatarbunary uprising (photographed in the Kishinev prison)

**Tatarbunary uprising of 1924.** A peasant uprising against the Rumanian occupation and for unification with the Ukrainian SSR which took place in *Tatarbunary and in the neighboring towns of Bessarabia. It was the result of widespread dissatisfaction with the Rumanian agrarian reforms of 1921. A famine, a drought in 1924, and social and national discrimination against the Bessarabian population were also contributing factors. Nearly 4,000 peasants (Soviet sources claim 6,000) participated. The uprising was centered in Tatarbunary and was joined by residents of Akkerman, Bendery, Izmail, and Cahul counties. It began on 16 September 1924, led by a pro-Soviet revolutionary committee. After a three-day battle with Rumanian troops, artillery, and naval forces (on Lake Sasyk, near the Black Sea) the uprising was suppressed. Many of the rebels perished, and nearly 500 were arrested.

The subsequent trial in Kishinev (1925) lasted 103 days, during which 386 of the accused were tried, of whom 86 were sentenced to prison terms ranging from 1 to 15 years. The trial drew international attention to Bessarabia and its colonial status. L. Aragon, H. Barbusse, T. Dreiser, A. Einstein, P. Éluard, R. Rolland, M. Sadoveanu and G.B. Shaw spoke out in defense of the Tatarbunary rebels.

BIBLIOGRAPHY
Badulesku, A. Vosstanie v Tatarbunarakh (Moscow 1925)
Salomon, R. 'Le procès monstre de Kichinev: L'affaire de Tatar-Bunar,' La Bessarabie et la Paix Européenne (Paris 1927)
Smishko, P. Tatarbunars'ke povstannia 1924 r. (Kiev 1956)
                                              A. Zhukovsky

**Tatars** (tatary). The name given to various Turkic and Mongol peoples and tribes of the 13th- to 14th-century Mongol Empire. In 1223 they invaded Rus' under the leadership of Subedei Bahadur and defeated the armies of the southern Rus' princes and their *Cuman allies at the Kalka River (see *Mstyslav Mstyslavych and *Mstyslav Romanovych). Having plundered Left-Bank Ukraine they returned to the steppes of Central Asia. After the reign of *Genghis Khan the western part of the Mongol Empire was ruled by his grandson, *Batu Khan, who expanded his realm into eastern and central Europe in 1236–43. Batu subdued the *Volga Bulgars in 1237–8 and then took the northern Rus' towns of Riazan, Kolomna, Moscow, Vladimir, Rostov, Torzhok, and Kozelsk and slaughtered the northern Rus' army at the Sit River before turning south and conquering the Cumans along the lower Don.

Batu then invaded southern Rus' and sacked Pereiaslav (3 March 1239) and Chernihiv (18 October 1239), thereby laying the path clear to Kiev. Kiev's defense was directed, in Prince *Danylo Romanovych's name, by the voivode Dmytro. Batu directed the Tatar siege himself. After taking Kiev he massacred its residents on 6 December 1240 and laid waste the city. His forces then proceeded westward and took Kolodiazhyn (by surprise), Kamianets, Iziaslav, Volodymyr-Volynskyi, Halych, and many other Ukrainian towns. In Volhynia the Tatars split into three armies. One attacked Poland, where on 9 April 1241, near Legnica, it defeated Polish, Czech, and Teutonic Knights; the second invaded Wallachia and Transylvania; and the third and largest army, headed by Batu himself, destroyed Halych before crossing the Carpathians into Hungary. There, on 12 April 1241, it annihilated the Hungarian army at the Sajó River. In the spring of 1242 the Tatars ravaged Serbia, Bulgaria, and the Black Sea littoral before returning to the Volga Basin, the center of Batu's state, known as the *Golden Horde.

The Tatars were successful in controlling their large empire because of their administrative method. It included census-taking to determine the amount of tribute; a system of enumerators, scribes, and tax collectors; the division of conquered lands into districts; and the establishment of local administrators to enforce obedience and the payment of tribute. Military service and a type of tax farming were imposed on the people. To maintain full control the Tatars resorted to almost systematic extortion, hostage-taking, and granting of patronage to local princes for faithful service. Periodic bloody raids helped to maintain fear and obedience.

The Tatars were sophisticated warriors. Accustomed to riding and archery from childhood, they were particularly skilled at feigning retreats and luring opponents into ambushes. Such maneuvers brought them victory at the Kalka, Legnica, and the Sajó. Their success in capturing fortified towns was based on their adaptation of Chinese military technology.

The Tatars were shamanists but were tolerant of other religions. In 1261 they allowed an Orthodox bishopric to be established at Sarai, the capital of the Golden Horde, and the Rus' clergy were exempted from paying taxes. Batu's sons and successors, Sartak (1256–7) and Berke (1257–66), were themselves Christian and Muslim respectively. In the early 14th century Khan Uzbek adopted Islam as the official religion of the Golden Horde.

The Tatars were primarily nomadic herders. Merchants were highly valued by the government, and foreign traders received special privileges. The Tatars' Slavic subjects were mostly peasants and artisans. The Golden Horde's principal trading partners were the Italian colonies along the Black Sea littoral and Egypt. Its chief exports were slaves and grain.

The Tatars did not impose uniform demands on all the peoples under their yoke, but modified them according to local conditions. Of all the Ukrainian territories the Principality of Galicia-Volhynia had the shortest and least onerous experience with Tatar suzerainty. After the Tatars returned to the Volga, Prince Danylo Romanovych attempted to organize a European coalition against them and sent Metropolitan P. *Akerovych to the Church Council of Lyons in 1245 to warn of the Tatar menace. When aid from the Catholic West was not forthcoming, Danylo was forced to travel to Sarai, the capital of the Golden Horde, in 1246 to accept the khan's suzerainty. In 1253, however, he recognized the authority of the pope and was crowned a king. He fought the neighboring *Bolokhovians and other *Tatar people who had voluntarily submitted to the Tatars, and in 1252–7 he waged war against Kuremsa, the overlord of the westernmost reaches of the Golden Horde. In 1259 *Burundai, Kuremsa's successor, launched a successful campaign against Galicia-Volhynia. Even then, however, the Principality of Galicia-Volhynia did not become entirely subservient to the Tatars until the reign of *Lev Danylovych, who was forced to accept the suzerainty of Nogai, the ruler of the Black Sea littoral, in the early 1270s. Living in harmony with the Tatars enabled Lev to annex Polish and Hungarian borderlands, and he participated in Khan Teleboh's campaign against Poland in 1286–7. His son, *Yurii Lvovych, and grandsons, *Lev and *Andrii Yuriiovych, were actually independent rulers, and the latter two gained recognition in Europe as 'invincible shields against the Tatars.' The annexation of Galicia by Poland and of Volhynia by Lithuania spelled the end of the Golden Horde's influence in the western Ukrainian territories.

Other Ukrainian territories were dominated much longer and more harshly by the Golden Horde. *Ponyzia, southern Podilia, and southern Pereiaslav principality were under its direct control, and Kiev and Chernihiv principalities were administered by vassals from among the Riurykide dynasty. The long duration of the Tatar yoke was catastrophic for the Ukrainian territories. They lost political independence, priceless manuscripts and art treasures perished during the sacking of cities, the decimated population was impoverished by heavy taxation, and cultural stagnation ensued. Tribute, which had earlier been used by Rus' princes for internal development, was now taken out of Ukraine for the enrichment of the Golden Horde.

The Lithuanian grand duke *Algirdas was the first to wrest Ukrainian lands from the Golden Horde, by taking advantage of the chaos that prevailed within it in 1360–80. In 1363 he routed a Tatar army in Podilia near Syni Vody, deposed the Tatar vassal Prince Fedir in Kiev, and replaced him with his own son, Volodymyr. He also occupied the lands of Chernihiv and Novhorod-Siverskyi. Algirdas's successor, *Vytautas, resolved to make the Golden Horde his dependent. He assisted Khan Tokhtamysh in the khan's struggle for control of the Golden Horde. In return Vytautas received the Tatar title to all of Ukraine. Vytautas's military campaign in support of Tokhtamysh ended in the defeat of his Lithuanian-Ruthenian army at the Vorsklo River in 1399. He managed, however, to extend his borders to the Vorsklo and lower Dnieper rivers, thereby incorporating most of Ukraine in the Grand Duchy of Lithuania.

In the early 15th century the Golden Horde weakened and then disintegrated, and independent khanates, such as the Crimean, Kazan, and Astrakhan, emerged on its peripheries. The Great Horde (the nucleus of the former Golden Horde) proved to be the most detrimental to Ukraine: it repeatedly invaded the Kiev region, Podilia, Volhynia, and even Galicia, in 1444, 1447, 1450, and 1457. In 1482 it sacked Kiev. The eventual fall of the Great Horde came after the death of its last leader, Khan Shah-Ahmet, in 1505.

In the mid-16th century the *Nogay Tatars penetrated into Ukraine from the Volga, Ural, and Caspian steppes and established there the *Bilhorod, Yedisan, Yedichkul, and Dzhambulak hordes as vassals of the Crimean Khanate and Ottoman Turkey. In the 1770s the lands of the Nogays were annexed by the Russian Empire, and the hordes were resettled in the Kuban. In 1790 they were allowed to return to the Azov littoral, and after the Crimean War of 1853–6 they emigrated to Turkey.

The *Crimean Khanate existed as an independent state from 1449 to 1478, when it recognized the supremacy of the Ottoman Empire. Ruled by the *Girei dynasty, the Crimean Tatars behaved not unlike the Golden and Great Hordes toward Ukraine. By 1556 they had mounted more than 80 invasions of Podilia, Volhynia, Galicia, and the Kiev and Novhorod-Siverskyi regions, where they destroyed towns and villages and took slaves (more than 35,000 in 1575 alone) to sell at markets in the Crimea. The Ukrainian Cossacks, and after 1648 the Cossack Hetman state, alternated between war and alliance with the khanate (see *Crimea). In 1783 the Crimean Khanate with its population of approx 140,000 was annexed by the Russian Empire. Tsarist national, social, and religious oppression of the *Crimean Tatars continued through the 19th century, and thousands of them fled to Turkey. Over 141,000 left after the Crimean War; only 103,000 remained in the Crimea. Colonization of the Crimea by Russians, Ukrainians, Germans, Greeks, and others transformed the Tatars into a minority. A Tatar national revival was initiated in the 1880s by I. Bey Gaspirali, the mayor of Bakhchesarai in 1877–81. It promoted the use of one Turkic language for all Turkic and Tatar peoples in the Russian Empire, educational reforms, modifications in Muslim society, and the emancipation of women. From 1883 to 1914 Gaspirali's journal *Tercuman-Perevodchik* was published in Bakhchesarai for the Turkic and Tatar intelligentsia in the empire; it propagated pan-Islamic and pan-Turkic ideas. In the early 20th century a nationalist movement of 'Young Tatars,' led by A. Mehdi, engaged in revolutionary activity in the Crimea akin to that of the Russian Socialist Revolutionaries. Mehdi and the Young Tatars played an active part in the Russian State Duma of 1907 and co-operated with Ukrainian delegates in the *Autonomists' Union. In 1909 N. Çelebi Cihan, C. Seidahmet, and other Crimean students at Istanbul University founded a secret organization for Crimean independence, Vatan (Homeland), which became the basis for the Crimean political rebirth after the February Revolution of 1917.

From 1917 to 1920 the Crimean Tatars struggled for their own independence and took varying stances with regard to the Russian White and Bolshevik regimes and Ukrainian claims to the Crimea. After three years of civil war, terror, and slaughter, in November 1920 Bolshevik forces captured the Crimea, and on 18 October 1921 the Crimean ASSR was established as part of the RSFSR.

Under Soviet rule the Crimean Tatars continued to suffer national discrimination. In 1928, after a brief period of national-communist 'Tatarization' the chairman of the Crimean Central Executive Committee, V. Ibrahimov, and 3,500 of his Party supporters were purged as bourgeois nationalists. Some were executed, and many were imprisoned in Soviet concentration camps. In 1928–9, 35,000 to 40,000 Tatar *kulaks were arrested and deported to Siberia and Soviet Central Asia. As in Ukraine, Tatar peasants opposed collectivization, and many of them perished in the man-made *famine of 1932–3. In 1936 a campaign to Russify the remaining Tatars was begun in tandem with further terror, arrests, and purges. The number of periodicals in Tatar was reduced from 23 in 1935 to 9 in 1938. In 1938 the Latin alphabet, which had been used instead of the Arabic alphabet in Tatar education and publications since 1929, was replaced by the Russian Cyrillic alphabet, and many Arabic, Persian, and Turkish words were excised from the language and replaced by Russian words.

Between 1917 and 1933 approx 150,000 Crimean Tatars – half of their population – had been killed, imprisoned, deported to Soviet Asia, or forced to emigrate. Those who had emigrated to Turkey (eg, E. Kirimal) and Rumania remained politically and culturally active. The Tatar émigré cause was supported by the interwar Polish government through the state-funded Oriental Institute in Warsaw. Tatar émigrés collaborated with their Ukrainian counterparts in the *Promethean movement in Warsaw and Paris.

During the Second World War, from 1941 to 1944, the Crimea was occupied by the German army and ruled by a Nazi military government. Because some Tatars had fought against the Soviet partisans in the Crimea, the Soviet government accused the Tatars collectively of collaboration with the Germans, and in 1944 they were brutally deported to Siberia, Kazakhstan, and Uzbekistan. The largest Tatar center became Tashkent. Although a Soviet decree of 5 September 1967 absolved the Tatar nation of collective collaboration, they were not permitted to return to the Crimea until the late 1980s. Ukrainian dissidents spoke out in support of the Tatar community's campaign for the right to return there (eg, P. Grigorenko, S. Karavansky, and V. Chornovil).

The movement to return to the Crimea attracted international attention in the mid-1980s and resulted in the creation of the Soviet State Commission for the Review of the National Demands of the Crimean Tatars in 1987, headed by President A. Gromyko. The commission, however, rejected the Tatars' demands for the right to return and for the re-establishment of the Crimean ASSR. The Ukrainian Helsinki Association spoke out in defense of the Tatars, and in its Fundamental Principles of 7 July 1988 it demanded 'the immediate restoration of the Crimean Autonomous SSR as a part of the Ukrainian SSR, and an organized resettlement of the autonomous republic's population repressed by Stalin to places of their former residence.'

Ukrainian–Crimean Tatar relations have been studied by Ukrainian historians, such as M. Kostomarov, M. Hrushevsky, T. Sushytsky, O. Ohloblyn, D. Doroshenko, D. Olianchyn, V. Dubrovsky, M. Tyshchenko, O. Subtelny, and V. Ostapchuk. Tatar motifs have appeared in the works of Ukrainian writers, including those of M. Kostomarov, S. Rudansky, M. Kotsiubynsky, and Lesia Ukrainka. A. Krymsky wrote surveys of Crimean Tatar history and literature, and materials about the Crimean Tatars were published in the journal *Skhidnii svit* (1927–31).

After the Second World War Soviet scholars paid attention only to the Tatar ASSR (Tataria), that is, to the Tatars of the Volga Basin and the Urals, descended from the Volga Bulgars, the Golden Horde, and the Kazan Khanate.

According to the 1989 Soviet census there were 271,715 Crimean Tatars in the USSR, of whom 251,537 stated that Tatar was their native language. Of the total number only 46,807 lived in Ukraine, 43,334 of whom stated that Tatar was their native language. In 1989, 86,875 other (non-Crimean) Tatars also lived in Ukraine; only 42,489 gave Tatar as their native language, and 42,601 gave Russian.

BIBLIOGRAPHY

Smirnov, V. *Krymskoe khanstvo pod verkhovenstvom Ottomanskoi Porty do nachala XVIII veka* (St Petersburg 1887)
– *Krymskoe khanstvo pod verkhovenstvom Ottomanskoi Porty v XVIII stoletii* (Odessa 1889)
Curtin, J. *The Mongols: A History* (Boston 1908)
Seidamet, D. *La Crimée: Passé-présent, revendications des Tatars de Crimée* (Lausanne 1921)
Kryms'kyi, A. (ed). *Studiï z Krymu* (Kiev 1930)
Doroshenko, D.; Rypka, J. *Polsko, Ukraina, Krym a Vysoká Porta v první pol. XVII stol.* (Prague 1936)
Nasonov, A. *Mongoly i Rus': Istoriia tatarskoi politiki na Rusi* (Moscow and Leningrad 1940)
Kirimal, E. *Der nationale Kampf der Krimtürken* (Emsdetten 1952)
Zhdan, M. 'The Dependence of Halych-Volyn' Rus' on the Golden Horde,' *SEER*, 25 (1956–7)
Horn, M. *Skutki ekonomiczne najazdów tatarskich z lat 1605–1633 na Ruś Czerwoną* (Wrocław 1964)
Zhdan, M. 'Ukraïna pid panuvanniam Zolotoï Ordy,' *UI*, 7–8 (1970–1)
Spuler, B. *The Mongols in History* (New York, Washington, and London 1971)
Grekov, I. *Vostochnaia Evropa i upadok Zolotoi Ordy (na rubezhe XIV–XV vv.)* (Moscow 1975)
Fisher, A. *The Crimean Tatars* (Stanford 1978)
Allsen, T. 'Mongol Census Taking in Rus', 1245–1275,' *HUS*, 5, no. 1 (March 1981)
Egorov, V. *Istoricheskaia geografiia Zolotoi Ordy v XIII–XIV vv.* (Moscow 1985)
Halperin, C. *Russia and the Golden Horde* (Bloomington 1985)
Sanin, G. *Otnosheniia Rossii i Ukrainy s Krymskim khanstvom v seredine XVII veka* (Moscow 1987)
Chambers, J. *The Devil's Horsemen: The Mongol Invasion of Europe*, 2nd rev edn (London 1988)
Tyszkiewicz, J. *Tatarzy na Litwie i w Polsce: Studia z dziejów XIII–XVIII w.* (Warsaw 1989)

M. Zhdan, A. Zhukovsky

**Tatars' people** (*tatarski liudy*). The inhabitants of a 13th-century settlement in eastern Podilia and northeastern Volhynia near the confluence of the Sluch, the Teteriv, and the Boh rivers. Along with the *Bolokhovians they submitted to the Tatars during Batu Khan's advance on central Europe (1240–1). Danylo Romanovych waged successful campaigns against them in 1241 and 1254–5 despite the Tatar garrisons in place to protect them. The term 'tatars' people' is used in current publicistic literature to designate the collaborators with occupying powers.

**Tatarynov, Yevhen,** b 2 March 1892 in Saratov, Russia, d 10 May 1950 in Kiev. Pathophysiologist; corresponding member of the AN URSR (now ANU) from 1939. A graduate of Saratov University (1916), in 1931 he was appointed head of the pathophysiology department at the Kiev Medical Institute and department chairman at the Institute of Experimental Biology and Pathology of the Ministry of Health of the Ukrainian SSR. From 1934 he worked in the ANU Institute of Clinical Physiology. His publications dealt with the mechanisms of immunity and how the reactivity of an organism is affected by blood disorders, blood loss, and cancer.

**Tatlin, Vladimir,** b 28 December 1885 in Moscow, d 31 May 1953 in Moscow. Painter, designer, and cofounder of *constructivism. He grew up in Kharkiv and worked as a

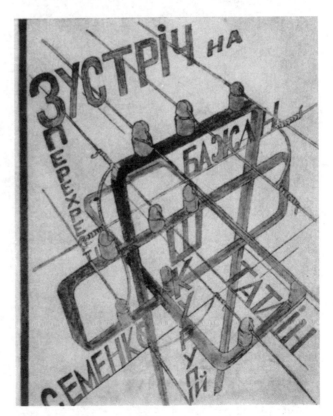

Vladimir Tatlin's book-cover design for the poetry collection *Zustrich na perekhresti* (1927)

merchant marine. He studied art in Penza (1905–10) and at the Moscow School of Painting, Sculpture, and Architecture (1909–10) and private studios in Moscow. There he took part in avant-garde exhibitions (eg, the Donkey's Tail, Knave of Diamonds, and Union of Youth). Around 1914 he shared his studio with O. Hryshchenko and began working on painterly reliefs and 'counterreliefs' inspired at first by P. Picasso's relief sculptures. His constructions were entirely abstract combinations of materials (wood, metals, and glass). While heading the Moscow branch of the Division of Visual Arts of the Commissariat of Education (1918–19) and chairing the Department of Material Culture at the Moscow Higher State Artistic and Technical Workshops (1919–29) he worked on his famous model of the Monument to the Third International. He then chaired the Department of Material Culture at the Academy of Arts (1920–2) and the Museum of Artistic Culture (1922–5) in Petrograd. In 1925–7 he chaired the theater, film, and photography department of the Kiev State Art Institute. While in Kiev he designed the cover for M. Semenko, G. Shkurupii, and M. Bazhan's poetry collection *Zustrich na perekhresti* (Meeting at the Crossroad, 1927) and established ties with the *Nova Generatsia futurist group in Kharkiv, and these ties he maintained after his return to Moscow. He was a major exponent of avant-garde art and design of the 1910s and 1920s. His intuitive constructivism is similar to that of V. *Yermilov and of the set designs of A. *Petrytsky and V. *Meller.

BIBLIOGRAPHY
Milner, J. *Vladimir Tatlin and the Russian Avant-Garde* (New Haven and London 1983)
Zhadova, L. (ed). *Tatlin* (New York 1988)

N. Mykytyn

**Tatomyr, Kostiantyn,** b 16 March 1900 in Yelysavethrad (now Kirovohrad), Kherson gubernia, d 4 March 1979 in Kiev. Mining engineer and scientist; corresponding member of the AN URSR (now ANU) from 1939. He studied in Dnipropetrovske and worked there in the mining concern Shakhtobud and at the ANU Institute of Mining (1938–63). He taught at the Dnipropetrovske Mining Institute (1929–41, 1945–50). He headed departments at the Donetske Coal Scientific Research Institute (1963–5) and the ANU Institute of the Economics of Industry (1965–79). He developed a basic theory for complex calculations of optimal cross sections of mining tunnels, which led to the theory of the optimal planning of mines.

**Tatomyr, Volodymyr,** b 1902 in Stryi county, Galicia, d 1962 in Philadelphia. Engineer and youth and education activist. He was an inspector for the *Prosvita society in Lviv and an organizer of Young Prosvita societies. In 1941–3 he headed the youth section of the Cracow-based Ukrainian Central Committee. He emigrated to the United States after the Second World War. He wrote *Iunatstvo v oboroni ridnoï zemli* (Youth in Defense of Their Native Land, 1960).

**Tatomyr, Yuliian,** b 3 January 1883 in Sprynia, Sambir county, Galicia, d 26 March 1946 in Salzburg. Civic and political activist and Ukrainian Catholic priest. After completing his studies in Peremyshl in 1908, he became a priest in Sambir. There he worked with the Prosvita society, set up a credit union, and served as director of the

Rev Yuliian Tatomyr

Ryznytsia church-goods store. In 1918 he organized an action to take control of the region for Ukrainians, and through the 1920s he set up co-operatives, cultural groups, and People's Homes in the district. In 1928 he was elected to the Polish Senate from the Ukrainian National Democratic Alliance, and in 1939–41 he headed the Ukrainian Aid Society in Peremyshl. From 1944 he was a refugee in Austria.

**Tatsii, Oleksii** [Tacij, Oleksij], b 1903 in Poltava, d 12 March 1967 in Kiev. Architect. In 1930 he graduated from the Kharkiv Technological Institute. He designed the Exhibition Pavilion (1932) and Red Army Building (1932–3) in Kharkiv; residential buildings in Kiev (1930s), the Donbas (1929–35), and Poltava (1932); the building of the Kryvyi Rih City Council (1933–4); the Ukrainian Pavilion at the All-Union Agricultural Exhibition in Moscow (1939, with M. Ivanchenko); and the Kyiv Cinema in Kiev (1952, codesigner).

**Taurians** (*tavry*). An ancient tribe of unknown origin that inhabited the mountainous regions of the Crimea in the 1st millennium BC. They engaged primarily in animal husbandry, some agriculture in the river valleys, and fishing along the coast. Although technologically less advanced than their neighbors, they defended themselves from encroachment by Chersonesus and the Bosporan Kingdom. At the end of the 3rd century BC the Scythians retreated south from the Sarmatians and intermixed with the Taurians; references to Tauroscythians and Scythotaurians thereupon appeared in the ancient Greek writers. In the late 2nd century BC the Taurians came under the Pontic Kingdom, and in the 1st century AD they were Romanized. Eventually they were assimilated by the Alans, the Goths, and other invaders. The last historical references to them date from the 4th century.

**Tavriia.** The ancient Greek name for the territory inhabited by the Taurians was Taurica. From the 16th century the term Tavriia, a Slavic derivative of the Greek name, was widely used for the Crimean Peninsula. From the beginning of the 19th century the term was used to refer to the Crimea and the adjacent steppes north of it, which area constituted *Tavriia gubernia until the 1920s.

**Tavriia gubernia.** An administrative territory of the Russian Empire set up in 1802. It included the entire Crimean

Peninsula, Dnipro (Oleshky) and Melitopil counties, which had previously belonged to New Russia gubernia, and Tmutorokan county, which was separated from the gubernia in 1820. Its administrative center was Symferopil. In its Crimean counties (Symferopil, Teodosiia, Perekop, Yevpatoriia, and Yalta), which had a population of 740,000 in 1914, Ukrainians were in a minority, but in the steppe counties (Dnipro, Melitopil, and Berdianske), with a population of 1,760,000, Ukrainians formed a majority. In the 1920s the steppe counties were incorporated into the Ukrainian SSR, and the Crimea was set up as the Crimean ASSR under the RSFSR.

**Tavriia Learned Archival Commission** (Tavriiska uchena [naukova] arkhivna komisiia). A gubernial commission established in 1887 in Symferopil to collect, study, and preserve historical and archeographic documentary materials and to protect monuments of antiquity in Tavriia gubernia. The commission's permanent chairman was A. Markevich. Among its approx 300 members were prominent scholars, such as V. Gorodtsov, A. Krymsky, Yu. Kulakovsky, and N. Veselovsky. The commission conducted archeological excavations in the Crimea and the Black Sea littoral region, established the Symferopil Museum of Antiquities (1887), and published 57 volumes (1887–1920) of its Russian-language serial *Izvestiia*, which contained the texts of almost all the 419 lectures delivered at its 260 meetings. In 1920 the commission's valuable historical archive (10,000 items) was transferred to the Crimean Central Archive (later the Crimea Oblast State Archive). In 1921 its museum holdings became part of the Tavrida Central Museum (now the Crimean Regional Museum) in Symferopil, and the Commissariat of Education took over its functions regarding the protection of monuments. In 1923 the commission was transformed into the Tavriia Historical, Archeological, and Ethnographic Society, under which name it published three additional volumes of *Izvestiia* (1927–9). In 1929 the society ceased to exist. P. Nikolsky's detailed description of the senate files in its archive was published in 1917.

**Tavrika Library.** A historical and regional studies library in Symferopil, established in 1881 by A. Steven (son of the founder of the Nikita Botanical Garden), consisting of the library holdings of the Tavriia gubernia zemstvo, the Tavriia Learned Archival Commission, and several personal libraries and archives. In 1891 it had 734 volumes of books, maps, and other materials pertaining to Tavriia gubernia and southern Ukraine. In the late 19th century the papers of P. *Köppen and his family were deposited there. In 1922 the library (3,500 vols) became part of the Tavrida Central Museum (later the Crimean Regional Museum). In 1971 the library had over 30,000 volumes pertaining to the Crimea, including some rare 16th- to 19th-century publications. A catalog of the library (1903) and supplements (1911–12) were published in Symferopil

**Tax farming** (*orendarstvo, vidkup*). Private leasing of the right to collect taxes and other state revenues. The practice was introduced in Ukraine after the Union of Lublin in 1569. The state also leased its exclusive rights to sell liquor, tobacco, and salt. To maximize their profits the private leaseholders imposed exorbitant rates and applied various pressures, including force. Their conduct aroused popular indignation and stirred unrest. Nevertheless rulers often resorted to tax farming as a quick and easy way of obtaining revenues. In the first half of the 18th century half the budget of the Hetman state was derived from its leasing of its liquor monopoly. In 1754 the Russian government began to replace tax farming by excise taxes, but the leasing of the right to sell liquor was not discontinued until a century later. (See *Propination.)

**Tax in kind** (*prodpodatok*). A system of agricultural taxation adopted at the 10th Congress of the Communist Party of the USSR in March 1921 in place of the *surplus appropriation system. Although taxes were collected in produce, as under the previous system, the rates were much lower than before, and more food was left for domestic consumption and private sale. The tax in kind was a major step in re-establishing a market economy in the USSR (see *New Economic Policy). It was necessitated to some extent by the weakness of the monetary system at the time. It led to a great improvement in the rural economy. The tax in kind was replaced in 1924 by a monetary agricultural tax, which remained in force until the collectivization of agriculture began in 1929.

**Taxation.** The imposition of compulsory levies by governments to obtain revenues for their expenditures. Today taxes also have other purposes, economic (promoting employment, growth, stability) or social (income redistribution). Taxes are either direct or indirect: the first are levied on individuals, their income, or property, and the second on goods and are passed on to the consumer.

The medieval system of feudal taxation operated in Ukraine until the mid-17th century, and some elements of it survived until the 19th century. A great number of different taxes were levied by different authorities. The sums were arbitrary and were not collected regularly. Often the duties were discriminatory against certain religious, social, or national groups and bore no relation to ability to pay. Tax collectors had a direct interest in the sum collected, and no distinction was made between the state treasury and a ruler's personal income. The oldest form of direct taxation was the *tribute, which was collected by the prince or his special appointees for the upkeep of his court and retinue. The tribute took various forms in Kievan Rus': besides gifts in goods or money, such as the *poklon* (bow), *pochest* (salute), and *stan* (estate), services, such as transport (*povoz*) and labor on fortifications and road construction, were required. The obligations were imposed on the *dvoryshche or *hromada, and the community was often responsible for dividing and collecting the tax from each house (*podymne*) or plow (*pososhne* or *popluzhne*). In the late 13th and early 14th centuries the Tatars set up their own taxation system in some parts of Ukraine and conducted periodic censuses of the population and property. They divided their territories into districts of about 10,000 taxpayers each. The payments were made in goods, money, services, or human beings (young boys, recruits, concubines, or slaves). The old tax system of Kievan Rus' was preserved in Western Ukraine under Polish rule until the mid-15th century and in central and eastern Ukraine under Lithuanian rule until the second half of the 16th century. The system became more decentralized and complex as special categories of military, administrative, labor, and cash taxes were introduced.

Monetary payments became the practice in the towns.

In the mid-16th century the Polish system of taxation was introduced in Ukrainian territories. The gentry (from 1374) and the Roman Catholic church (from 1381) were exempted from taxes. The Polish kings renounced the rights to tax and limited their treasury to duties from the rural and urban population, income from royal estates, and contributions from self-governing cities under Magdeburg law. The peasants and some town residents had to perform corvée labor and pay various fees to their lords.

General levies could be approved only by gentry diets to meet special military expenditures. They were imposed on certain estates for a limited term and a specific purpose. Their character and base was specified: a poll, field, and house tax; an urban income tax, or *shos*; a beer, mead, and liquor tax, or *chopove* (spigot); and a *hiberna* tax for the winter support of troops. In the second half of the 16th century special diets approved levies of over 600,000 zlotys. The field tax was usually collected from the peasants', not the lord's, land. The *shos* was initially an income tax and then a real-estate tax (usually 4.16 percent of assessed value). Besides a poll tax the Jews paid a double *shos*: their *kahal divided the tax among the families and collected it. Apart from the *shos* and emergency taxes imposed by the diets, the townsfolk paid duties on different types of income and for various services to the town treasury: a window tax, visiting tax, weights-and-measures tax, warehouse tax, city security tax, fortification tax, road and bridge tax, and sanitation tax.

A religious and national bias in the division of the tax burden and abuses in its collection often resulted in social and national conflicts in the towns. The Orthodox, for example, were taxed to support the Roman Catholic clergy. The patricians in cities often tried to transfer the tax burden from themselves to the common people. Efforts to reform the tax system did not succeed. The practice of leasing out tax-collecting only increased the inequities and abuses in the system (see *Tax farming).

After the Cossack uprising of 1648 the former royal and other large estates and income from them were transferred to the Cossack military treasury. A large part of the royal estates was distributed among the Cossack *starshyna*. The Cossacks and their officers claimed exemption from taxes on the basis of their military service. Economic competition from the Cossacks impeded the growth of the burgher estate. The number of free peasant households declined steadily. The Cossack treasury derived little revenue from direct taxation. Its principal source of income was import and export tariffs and indirect taxes on mills, foundries, mines, tobacco, tar, and saltpeter. Those taxes were inherent in a form of state monopoly: the owners of such enterprises could not sell their products retail but had to deliver them at fixed prices to leaseholders, who paid the government fixed tax. Conflicts often arose between the municipal authorities and the Cossack administration over local taxes from tradesmen, hostels, bathhouses, and market fees.

After the Pereiaslav Treaty of 1654 the tsar's envoys in Ukraine interfered in the financial affairs of the Hetman state. Hetman I. Briukhovetsky consented to transfer all the direct taxes from the common people and townsfolk to the tsar's treasury. After I. Mazepa's defeat at Poltava in 1709, the Little Russian Collegium (est 1722) introduced more and more taxes in Ukraine. The Russian government

and its military representatives in the Hetman state exacted taxes (known as *portsii*) to support the Russian garrisons in Ukraine, requisitioned grain, livestock, and horses, and conscripted labor for constructing defense lines and canals. Hetmans P. Polubotok and D. Apostol protested against those measures.

**Under Russian rule.** In 1765–9, following the abolition of the Hetmanate in 1764, the *Rumiantsev census was conducted to bring Left-Bank Ukraine into the imperial taxation system. Taxes in kind were eliminated in favor of a monetary household tax (*podvirnyi*). In 1783 that tax was replaced by the *poll tax, which was extended to Right-Bank Ukraine in 1795. At first the tax was distributed evenly, but eventually, regional disparities arose; in Ukraine the tax was 40–50 percent higher than in Russia. At first the poll tax accounted for 50 percent of the Russian imperial revenues. When it was abolished in 1887, it constituted only 10 percent of the revenues.

Prior to the emancipation of 1861 the drinking duty from the liquor trade was a leading source of revenue in the imperial budget. In 1819–27 the trade was a government monopoly, and later, trading licenses were sold. The price of liquor was 5 to 10 times the cost of production, and the licensees, most of whom were Russian, made enormous profits. In 1863 the system was replaced with a regular excise tax on liquor. By 1913 the tax accounted for 88 percent of the price of liquor. In 1848–52 an excise tax on sugar was introduced, and then a tax on salt, gas, matches, tobacco, and cigarette paper. The excise tax was paid by the producer or wholesaler. Since sugar, tobacco, and liquor were produced mainly in Ukraine, 30–40 percent of the excise revenues were raised in Ukraine. The burden of the tax, however, fell ultimately on the consumers, that is, the peasants. The excise tax became the principal source of government revenue.

Direct taxes did not play an important role in the imperial budget. In 1875 a land tax was introduced. Its rates on peasant holdings were substantially higher than on landowners' estates. In 1899 the average rate paid by peasants in Left-Bank Ukraine was 1.80 rubles per desiatin, and by landowners, 0.70 ruble. In Right-Bank Ukraine the average rates were 1.06 and 0.18 respectively; in Southern Ukraine, 1.70 and 0.29 respectively. In addition peasants had to pay zemstvo contributions and various local taxes and had to buy compulsory fire insurance. Direct taxes accounted for 40 percent of a peasant's net income. The tax burden on small landholders exceeded their ability to pay.

From 1863, urban residents paid a property tax. Merchants paid 10 percent of their declared capital. New taxes were introduced: in 1885 a capital income tax of 5 percent of the income from investment capital and securities, in 1894 a tax on housing, and in 1899 an industrial tax. Joint-stock companies paid an equity tax of 0.15 percent, and enterprises with profits above 3 percent paid a slight gains tax. Despite this array of taxes, the middle class was not overburdened. After numerous attempts an income tax was introduced in 1917.

Using the tax system, the tsarist government exploited Ukraine: it took in much more than it spent in the Ukrainian gubernias. According to M. Yasnopolsky's estimate based on budget balance sheets, in 13 years (1868–81) taxes in Ukraine brought in 2,899.2 million rubles, whereas state expenditures in Ukraine were 1,749 million rubles. M. Porsh's estimate of revenues and expenditures in

Ukraine for 1895–1910 was 3,289.6 million rubles and 2,605.2 million rubles respectively. The tsarist treasury in this way stripped the Ukrainian gubernias of their trade surplus and artificially lowered Ukraine's standard of living, which had been higher than Russia's. Tax revenues were spent outside of Ukraine, mostly on wars in the East, on interest payments for state loans, and for financing industrial development.

**Under Austrian rule.** After Austria's annexation of Western Ukraine in 1772, the government gradually extended its tax system to the new provinces. To strengthen the peasant tax base, the regime reduced the corvée obligations and separated peasants' and landlords' landholdings. The land tax on landowners' estates was almost 6 percent of their net income; peasant lands were taxed at a somewhat lower rate. In 1785 the land tax in Galicia generated 1.3 million zlotys. The state had a huge income from its monopolies on salt, tobacco, and the lottery. After the agrarian reforms of 1848 the largest part of the tax paid by the peasantry consisted of the redemption payment to the landowners. The cost of compensating the landowners for their loss of the alcohol monopoly in 1898 was recovered through taxes.

In 1910 Galicia paid 34.3 million crowns, or 58.5 percent of its tax contribution, in direct taxes. That sum accounted for 8.85 percent of Austria's direct taxes, whereas Galicia's population accounted for 28.1 percent of the empire's. The land tax yielded the largest part: 8.9 million crowns, or 14.3 percent of Austria's land tax revenues. Next in importance was the residence tax: together the two taxes accounted for 58.8 percent of the revenues from Galicia. In 1911 Galicians paid another 21.9 million crowns above the direct taxes: consumption taxes accounted for 33.7 percent of the Galician provincial budget. Additional levies were imposed to cover country and communal needs. In 1913 Galicia contributed 195.9 million crowns to the Austrian budget. According to estimates by Galician economists, 16 to 20 million crowns of its annual contribution never returned to Galicia.

In the interwar period Western Ukrainian territories were divided among Poland, Rumania, and Czechoslovakia and came under their tax systems. For Ukrainians the greatest burden was the land tax, and then the various indirect taxes. Under the Polish regime the state had a monopoly on salt, alcohol, tobacco, and matches and taxed some food products, such as sugar, yeast, tea, and coffee. Poland and Rumania treated their Ukrainian territories as second-class provinces and spent virtually nothing on their economic development. Most of the government expenditures in those regions were on administration. The situation in Transcarpathia was different: the Czechoslovak treasury supported local cultural and economic development.

The period of Ukrainian statehood (1917–20) was too brief for a regular tax system to be developed. The main source of revenue, while supplies lasted, was the sugar excise tax. There was also a tax on flour milling. Budget deficits were handled by the printing of more money. The governments of the UNR and the Western Ukrainian National Republic planned to introduce a graduated income tax.

**Soviet Ukraine.** At their Sixth Party Congress in the summer of 1917 the Bolsheviks proposed a tax policy based on a direct property tax, an indirect luxury tax, and a progressive income tax. During their first years in power, however, they resorted to special taxes on the 'exploiting classes.' Instead of monetary taxes a *surplus appropriation system was introduced in 1919 and was replaced by a *tax in kind in 1921. In 1923 the latter was replaced by a uniform farm tax, which set high rates for the kulaks and exempted the poor peasants. Contrary to the recommendations of the 11th Congress of the Russian Communist Party (Bolshevik) in 1922, indirect taxes remained the main source of state revenues. In Ukraine the percentage of tax revenues raised indirectly even increased, from 63 in 1913 to 68 in 1940 and 73 in 1950, and then declined, to 63 in 1956 and 50 in 1967 (compared to 17 in the United States). In 1930 all excise taxes were consolidated in a single general indirect tax known as the turnover tax. J. Stalin used the tax to form the capital needed for the rapid expansion of heavy industry and the military buildup. In 1932 a uniform tax rate was replaced by a differentiated one. The tax base consisted mostly of goods produced by light industry and the food industry, although for a time even some means of production were subject to the tax. The effect on consumers, who had to pay the tax with every article purchased, was to undercut their buying power and lower their living standard.

The turnover tax was a universal excise tax that did not exist in other countries. In the Soviet economy it was used as the chief means of capital formation at the consumer's expense. The tax was collected for the state not by the retailer but by the producer of manufactured goods and the wholesaler. Although after Stalin's death the tax was reduced somewhat so that the standard of living would improve, it continued to function as the main brake on the expansion of consumer production. The share of output appropriated by the state by means of the turnover tax is given in table 1.

TABLE 1
Share of the turnover collected through the turnover tax in 1961 prices, 1940–65 (in million rubles)

| Year | Turnover | Revenues from turnover tax | % of tax to turnover |
|------|----------|----------------------------|----------------------|
| 1940 | 3,202.8 | 2,120.1 | 66.2 |
| 1950 | 5,731.2 | 3,407.7 | 59.5 |
| 1960 | 13,346.8 | 5,441.7 | 40.8 |
| 1965 | 18,503.7 | 6,789.4 | 36.6 |

In the 1960s the tax share in the retail prices of consumer goods was as follows: beer and liquor, cigarettes, and cosmetics, 95–99 percent; salt and wine, 85–90 percent; sunflower oil, leather footwear, cloth, bicycles, automobiles, gasoline, and records, 50–75 percent; flour, sugar, matches, electricity, and gas, 50–65 percent; cutlery, bowls, nails, sewing machines, televisions, radios, and writing paper, 33–65 percent; lard, butter, eggs, tea, and peas, 20–40 percent.

Light industry and the food industry generated 70–75 percent of tax revenues; agricultural procurements, 10–11 percent (compared to 30–40 percent in the 1930s and 1940s); and heavy industry, 10 percent. The rest came from co-operatives, restaurants, cafeterias, and the like. No less than 90 percent of the tax burden, therefore, was carried by consumers.

The turnover tax was applied in a discriminatory way. The 'closed' stores, restaurants, and other enterprises of the defense ministry, the KGB, the militia, the writers' union, and academic and cultural institutions were exempted from the tax. The tax did not apply to export goods, to goods transferred to state reserves, or to fuel and construction materials for state farms. From 1959 the central Ministry of Finance set the tax targets for each republic, and from 1964 for individual enterprises.

The second-largest source of state revenues in the USSR was the direct tax on the net profits of enterprises, which until 1966 was known as the 'deduction from profits.' Introduced in 1931, it was applied annually to each state enterprise at an individual rate of 10–99 percent of the enterprise's net profits and was added to the production plan as a compulsory indicator. Sixty-four percent of all profits produced in Ukraine were appropriated in this way by the central USSR budget in 1958, 71 percent in 1967 (in the United States the maximum tax on corporate profit was 52 percent). Co-operatives paid 35 percent of their profits in taxes, and public organizations, trade unions, and sports clubs paid 25 percent. But no enterprises belonging to the Party or the Komsomol were taxed.

In the tax law of 5 July 1991 taxes on profits from various enterprises were raised to 35 percent; co-operatives engaged in the role of 'middleman' were to be taxed at 65 percent, and those engaged in the growing of food products, only 1.5 percent. Still other enterprises, such as research institutes, were to pay only 10 percent on profits. Student groups and artistic collectives, as well as enterprises located in the radioactive zone, were exempt from taxation.

Beginning in 1987, enterprises were formed in Ukraine in which part of the capital came from outside Ukraine. In 1990 there were about 113 such 'joint ventures.' The enterprises were to be taxed like all others unless the foreign capital exceeded 30 percent. If the enterprise was more than 30 percent foreign-owned, however, there were no taxes for the first two years after the first profit was generated, and a rate of 30 percent thereafter. The dividends of such joint ventures were also taxable (at 15 percent if they were to be paid out outside Ukraine).

The third major source of revenue was the personal income tax, which in 1989 brought in 3,224 million rubles, or 92.4 percent of the revenues from personal taxes in Ukraine. In developed countries the income tax has been an instrument for equalizing incomes; in the USSR the income tax was not progressive, and favored the bureaucracy. In 1970 a monthly wage of 100 rubles was taxed at 8.2 percent, and any sum over 100 rubles, regardless of the size, at 13.6 percent. Wage earners of under 60 rubles a month and members of the armed forces or the KGB were exempted, but some classes were taxed differently from others: in 1970, for example, wage and salary workers, writers, and artists earning up to 1,500 rubles per year were taxed at 9.16 percent; artisans, doctors, and lawyers with a private practice, at 21.46 percent; and priests and home owners who rented rooms, at 28.44 percent. Inventors, prospectors, and families with many children were taxed at lower rates. Interest on savings or government bonds, prizes, pensions, and lottery winnings were not taxed. Prior to 1934 the income tax was more differentiated and progressive. In 1931–41, besides income tax, everyone had to pay a levy of about 7 percent of personal income for the construction of residential and public buildings. A special direct tax on unmarried and childless people was introduced in 1944. Its rate was 0.4–0.6 percent of personal income. Inheritances were taxed at 5 percent for the first 1,000 rubles and 10 percent for the rest.

The tax laws of 1991 also affected personal income. In an attempt to make the tax system more progressive the rate of taxation was varied according to income (eg, no tax on income of up to 161 rubles per month, 12 percent on income of between 161 and 1,000 rubles per month). A progressive three-tier scale was to be applied to income above 1,000 rubles per month, up to a maximum of 30 percent. According to the new tax laws all income for tax purposes is considered equal, but some categories of taxpayers are to be exempt from tax (invalids, veterans, etc).

Another direct tax was the income tax on collective farms and their workers, which came to 1–2 percent of the USSR's budget in the 1960s and more in Stalin's time. A tax of 12 percent was levied on a farm's net income plus 8 percent of its workers' wages. Collective farms whose profit margin was less than 15 percent, and whose workers earned less than 60 rubles per month, were exempt. A compulsory insurance on the livestock, crops, and buildings against fire and natural disasters (from which state farms were exempt) was a form of direct taxation. Agricultural procurements were another form of direct taxation. An agricultural tax was also levied on the *private plots of collective-farm workers: 0.50–1.20 rubles per 0.01 ha in eastern Ukraine, and 0.20–0.60 in western Ukraine. If worker's did not meet their quota of *workdays, their tax was doubled. Furthermore, from 1933, holders of private plots had to deliver high quotas of meat, milk, eggs, potatoes, and wool to the state. In 1951 the quota per household was 45 kg of meat, 160 L of milk, 130 eggs, and 1 kg of wool. In 1958 those deliveries were formally abolished, but compulsory 'purchases' of any private-plot 'surpluses' by the state continued.

Taxes increased steadily in the Soviet period. In 1913 each inhabitant of Ukraine's present territory paid an average tax of 3.74 gold rubles, or about 3 percent above the average in the rest of the empire. In 1924–5 the amount was 7.03 gold rubles, or 28.4 percent above the average in the rest of the USSR. Agricultural taxes per capita were 70 percent higher in Ukraine than in the rest of the USSR. Ukrainian economists pointed out that the Ukrainian peasant was being exploited. After collectivization the tax burden became much greater. At 1961 prices the tax per capita in Ukraine rose to 43 rubles in 1940, 107 rubles in 1950, 144 rubles in 1960, and 193 rubles in 1965. Most of the taxes were paid by the urban population: its wages had increased, but so did the income tax in the 1930s and 1940s. As prices on consumer goods fell in the 1950s, the turnover tax decreased, and the tax burden shifted from the city to the countryside. In 1970, according to some estimates, the average Ukrainian worker worked the tax equivalent of 3 to 3.5 months per year (2 months in the United States). In the RSFSR taxes per capita were 10–15 percent higher, but incomes were higher as well.

The growth of the tax burden is evident when one compares the tax revenues with the national income, as in table 2. The government's appropriation of a huge share of the national income has stunted economic growth.

The central government in Moscow, like its imperial predecessor, used the tax system to exploit Ukraine financially. It extracted much more revenue from the republic than it spent there. It has been estimated on the basis of

TABLE 2
Share of tax revenues in the national income of Ukraine,
1924–5 to 1965

| Year | National income (billions of rubles) | Total taxes (billions of rubles) | % of tax in national income |
|---|---|---|---|
| 1924–5 | 3.1 | 0.2 | 6.4 |
| 1940 | 9.7 | 2.3 | 23.8 |
| 1954 | 19.7 | 6.2 | 31.7 |
| 1960 | 27.0 | 10.6 | 39.2 |
| 1965 | 37.9 | 16.8 | 44.3 |

Ukraine's budgets that in the four fiscal years 1923–4 to 1926–7 the state treasury in Moscow received 2,378.8 million rubles from Ukraine and spent only 1,906.8 million rubles in Ukraine. The respective figures for 1928–9 to 1932 (the First Five-Year Plan) were 16,789 million and 11,790 million, and for 1959 to 1961, 15,015 million and 3,287 million. Such tax discrimination wiped out Ukraine's favorable trade balance with the other Union republics and depressed its standard of living below Russia's by the mid-1950s.

Although the USSR was considered to be a federated state, Moscow had the exclusive power to levy and allocate taxes. The budget of the Ukrainian SSR was assigned a certain percentage of the taxes collected in its territory (eg, 29.5 percent of its turnover tax). Only some taxes with insignificant returns, such as the income tax on collective farms and co-operatives, were handed over to the republican budget by Moscow.

Municipal and rural governments derived their revenues from local taxes, which were levied on private buildings (0.5–1.0 percent of the assessed value), cars and motorcycles, and commercial space at markets. Those revenues were usually inadequate for maintaining buildings, roads, and public baths. Only villages had a strictly circumscribed power to levy taxes for the construction of schools, roads, bridges, and wells. The share of tax revenues in the state budget of Ukraine for 1960–90 is given in table 3.

Although new tax laws were adopted from the time of the proclamation of sovereignty on 16 July 1990, it was the declaration of Ukraine's independence on 24 August 1991 that set the legal foundation for a new and independent tax system.

TABLE 3
Share of different tax revenues in the budget of Ukraine, 1960–90
(in million rubles; percentages in parentheses)

| | 1960 | 1970 | 1980 | 1985 | 1990 |
|---|---|---|---|---|---|
| 1. Total revenues | 7,545 | 13,550 | 24,674 | 31,978 | 45,120 |
| 2. Turnover tax | 1,509 | 2,524 | 8,061 | 12,257 | 12,686 |
| | (20.0) | (18.6) | (32.7) | (38.3) | (28.1) |
| 3. Income tax from enterprises and organizations | | | | | |
| | 2,695 | 26,468 | 9,083 | 12,257 | 12,686 |
| | (35.7) | (47.7) | (36.8) | (35.8) | (24.2) |
| 4. Income tax from collective farms and co-operative and public enterprises and organizations | | | | | |
| | 453 | 292 | 344 | 498 | 747 |
| 5. Personal taxes | 591 | 1,174 | 2,069 | 2,462 | 4,045 |
| | (7.8) | (8.7) | (8.4) | (7.7) | (9.0) |

BIBLIOGRAPHY
Alekseenko, M. *O podushnoi podati v Rossii* (Kharkiv 1870)
Iasnopol'skii, N. *O geograficheskom raspredelenii gosudarstvennykh dokhodov i raskhodov Rossii*, 2 vols (Kiev 1891, 1897)
Bogolepov, R. *Gosudarstvennye i mestnye nalogi* (Kharkiv 1902)
Mal'tsiv, P. *Ukraïna u derzhavnomu biudzheti Rosiï* (Lubny 1917)
Slabchenko, M. *Organizatsiia khoziaistva Ukrainy ot Khmel'nitskogo do mirovoi voiny* (Odessa 1922)
Gurevich, M. *Priamoe oblozhenie sel'skogo khoziaistva Ukrainy* (Kharkiv 1923)
*Materialy dlia opredeleniia roli Ukrainy v obshchegosudarstvennom biudzhete SSSR* (Kharkiv 1925)
*Sbornik postanovlenii, prikazov, i instruktsii po finansovo-khoziaistvennym voprosam* (Moscow 1940–62)
Pogrebinskii, A. *Ocherki istorii finansov dorevoliutsionnoi Rossii* (Moscow 1954)
Holzman, F. *Soviet Taxation* (Cambridge, Mass 1955)
Suchkov, A. *Gosudarstvennye dokhody SSSR* (Moscow 1955)
Rozdolski, R. *Die grosse Steuer- und Agrarreform Josefs II* (Vienna 1961)
*Natsional'nyi dokhod Ukraïns'koï RSR* (Kiev 1963)
Mar'iakhin, G. *Ocherki istorii nalogov s naseleniia v SSSR* (Moscow 1964)
Melnyk, Z. *Soviet Capital Formation: Ukraine, 1928–1932* (Munich 1965)
Tur, V. (ed). *Spravochnik po nalogam naseleniia* (Moscow 1984)
Newcity, M. *Taxation in the Soviet Union* (New York 1986)
        V. Holubnychy, A. Revenko, O. Rohach, I. Vytanovych

**Tbilisi.** The capital (1989 pop 1,260,000) of Georgia, known from the Russian transcription as Tiflis until 1936. The city was founded in the 5th century AD and was subject to Russian rule from 1801 to 1917. From the mid-19th century a small Ukrainian colony existed in Tbilisi, and the city often hosted Ukrainian theater troupes, beginning with M. Starytsky's troupe in 1889. In 1917 the Ukrainian Military Congress of Transcaucasia took place in Tbilisi and set up the Transcaucasian Ukrainian Council. The council published its *Visty* and then *Ukraïns'ki visty Zakavkazzia*. In 1918 a general consulate of the UNR was established in Tbilisi, and then a Ukrainian legation headed by I. *Krasovsky. According to census figures, there were 10,600 Ukrainians in Tbilisi in 1970.

**Tchaikovsky, Peter** [Čajkovskij, Petr], b 7 May 1840 in Votkinsk, Viatka gubernia, Russia, d 6 November 1893 in St Petersburg. Composer and conductor. A descendant (on his father's side) of an old Cossack family (Chaika), Tchaikovsky first visited Ukraine in 1864 and thereafter often spent his summers there in Kamianka (Chyhyryn county) at the home of his sister and in Nyzy (Sumy county), where he lived during 1876–9. He is commonly regarded as one of the greatest 19th-century Russian composers, but at least 30 of his works have Ukrainian subjects or incorporate Ukrainian folk melodies. Among these are the operas *Mazepa* (based on A. Pushkin's poem), *Little Shoes*, and *Night before Christmas* (or *Vakula the Smith*, based on N. Gogol's story); symphonies no. 2 (*Little Russian*), no. 4, and no. 7 (finished and edited by S. Bogatyrev); the *Concerto for Piano and Orchestra no. 1 in B-flat Minor*; the *1812 Overture*, the opening of which is based on the first mode of the *Kievan chant; the transcription for piano solo of A. Dargomyzhsky's orchestral fantasy *Kozachok*; and songs to Russian translations of T. Shevchenko, such as 'Sadok vyshnevyi' (Cherry Orchard). Tchaikovsky also edited 10 volumes of D. Bortniansky's sacred choral works, which were published in Moscow in 1882.

Studies of Tchaikovsky's Ukrainian connections have been published in Kiev, edited by A. Olkhovsky (1940), H. Tiumenieva (1955), and N. Semenenko (1989).

**Tcherikower, Elias,** b 1881 in Poltava, d 1943. Jewish historian. He published numerous works about Ukrainian Jewry and became one of the founding members of the YIVO Institute for Jewish Research. His archives were evacuated from Vilnius to New York at the start of the Second World War. The Elias Tcherikower Archives of the YIVO Institute constitute one of the most important sources of information in the world on the history of Ukrainian Jewry.

**Tchoubar, Bianca** [Čubar], b 22 October 1910 in Kharkiv, d 24 April 1990 in Paris. Organic chemist. She studied at the Sorbonne (doctorate, 1946). In 1946 she joined the Centre National de Recherche Scientifique, where in 1955 she attained the rank of director of research. She retired in 1978 but continued to be active in research and publishing until 1988. Tchoubar was a pioneer in the study of organic reaction mechanisms and made major contributions to the understanding of rearrangement reactions. In the 1960s she collaborated with E. *Shilov of the Institute of Organic Chemistry of the Academy of Sciences of Ukraine. Among the most important of her publications are *Reaction Mechanisms in Organic Chemistry* (1960) and *Salt Effects in Organic and Organometallic Chemistry* (1988).

The chief executive of the Teachers' Hromada in 1924–5. Standing, from left: Ivan Rybchyn, Mykola Panchuk, Hryhorii Myketei, Volodymyr Kycher; sitting: Ivan Sitnytsky, Ivan Bryk, Sydir Hromnytsky, Ivan Rakovsky

**Teachers' Hromada** (Uchytelska hromada). A Lviv-based professional organization for teachers of Ukrainian secondary and postsecondary schools, active in Western Ukraine in 1908–39. Formed through the initiative of Yu. Stefanovych in 1908, the group established branches in the major eastern Galician cities and towns with Ukrainian institutions of secondary education (a total of 11 by 1914). It sought the establishment of new Ukrainian state gymnasiums in the larger centers of Galicia, the Ukrainization of bilingual (Polish-Ukrainian) gymnasiums, and an upgrading of the status of Realschule education to gymnasium level. The group also lobbied for a supervisor of Ukrainian schools under the education ministry and pro-

tested against the Polonization of Lviv University. The failure of these efforts, however, led to the group's involvement with private educational undertakings, including the organization of private secondary schools and gymnasium preparatory courses.

The Teachers' Hromada remained active after the First World War, albeit at a significantly reduced level. It continued in its efforts to Ukrainize education in Galicia, by fighting against the Polonization of Ukrainian gymnasiums; working toward the development of a Ukrainian-language curriculum in fields such as Ukrainian language (co-ordinated by Ya. Bilenky), history (O. Terletsky), and geography (O. Dashkevych); and publishing organizational journals – *Nasha shkola* (1909–14), *Svitlo* (1921–2), and *Ukraïns'ka shkola* (1925–39). As well, the group engaged in several mutual-aid ventures, such as the establishing of a relief fund for the families of war victims, the unemployed, and the widows or orphans of teachers, and the building of vacation centers and retreats for teachers. In its organizational activity the group worked in conjunction with the *Ridna Shkola and *Prosvita societies. By 1939 the Teachers' Hromada had 12 branches, with nearly 500 members; the group was disbanded that year, following the Soviet occupation of Western Ukraine.

Some of the outstanding figures involved with the Teachers' Hromada were K. Studynsky, S. Hromnytsky, S. Karkhut, V. Radzykevych, L. Salo, S. Nedilsky, K. Kysilevsky, I. Rybchyn, and S. Levytsky.

BIBLIOGRAPHY
*Dvadtsiat'piat'littia tovarystva 'Uchytel's'ka hromada': Iuvileinyi naukovyi zbirnyk* (Lviv 1935)

A. Makuch

**Teachers' Hromada of Subcarpathian Ruthenia** (Uchytelska hromada Pidkarpatskoi Rusy). A teachers' society founded in 1929, with its headquarters in Uzhhorod. Its membership consisted of disaffected members of the Russophile Teachers' Society of Subcarpathian Ruthenia. The Hromada campaigned for the Ukrainization of Transcarpathian Ruthenian schools and was active in many facets of Ukrainian cultural and educational life. It published the monthly *Uchytel's'kyi holos* and advocated the use of Ukrainian-language books in schools. The leading members of the organization were A. Voloshyn, Yu. Revai, and A. Shtefan. The Hromada was soon supported by the overwhelming majority of Ukrainian teachers in Transcarpathia, and claimed a membership of 1,650 in 1938. It was dissolved following the Hungarian occupation of Transcarpathia in 1939.

**Teachers' institutes** (*uchytelski instytuty*). In Ukraine, pedagogical institutions which prepared teachers for the middle grades of general secondary-education schools. These institutes were first established in the Russian Empire in 1817 for the training of teachers for *county and *parochial schools, and from 1912 they undertook the training of teachers for urban and higher-elementary schools. The first teachers' institute in Ukraine was founded in Hlukhiv in 1874. In 1917 there were 11 such institutes in Russian-ruled Ukraine (there were 47 in the entire Russian Empire). They were abolished in the early period of Soviet rule in Ukraine and re-established in 1934 in conjunction with the introduction of the *seven-year school. Teacher's institutes were affiliated with *pedagogical institutes. Graduates of teachers' institutes were considered to have incomplete pedagogical education and were assigned to teach grades five to seven of the seven-year schools. In 1955 there were 33 teachers' institutes in Ukraine. In the 1950s, as a result of the growth and development of the secondary-school system and the ensuing increase in the training required of teachers, teachers' institutes were reorganized into pedagogical institutes or *pedagogical schools.

**Teachers' seminaries** (*uchytelski seminarii*). Pedagogical institutions which prepared teachers of elementary schools. They first appeared in the Russian Empire in 1779; the first teachers' seminary in Ukraine was established in Kiev in 1869 (and moved in 1873 to Korostyshiv, now in Zhytomyr oblast). In the 1870s teachers' seminaries were founded in Kherson, Pereiaslav, Vovchanske, and Ostrih. A zemstvo teachers' seminary in Chernihiv was also founded at that time. Graduates of 'two-class' (five-year) elementary school's could enrol in the teachers' seminaries, where the program of study was three to four years. In 1917 there were 26 teachers' seminaries in Ukraine (171 in the Russian Empire).

In Western Ukraine under Austrian rule, teachers' seminaries were established in the wake of the educational reform of 1869. They had a four-year program of instruction and were the only institutions preparing teachers for elementary schools. In Galicia there were 10 state teachers' seminaries, with Ukrainian and Polish as languages of instruction (7 for men and 3 for women). In addition there were three private Ukrainian-language teachers' seminaries. Bukovyna had three state teachers' seminaries (one Ukrainian), and Transcarpathia three, albeit with Hungarian as the language of instruction. In Galicia under Polish rule, teachers' seminaries were reorganized into pedagogical lyceums with a three-year program of study. In Transcarpathia in 1938, there were five teachers' seminaries (of which four were Ukrainian-language institutions). During the Second World War, in the Ukrainian parts of the *Generalgouvernement there were nine teachers' seminaries.

B. Krawchenko

**Teachers' Society of Subcarpathian Ruthenia** (Uchytelskoe tovaryshchestvo Podkarpatskoi Rusy). A teachers' organization founded in Uzhhorod in 1920. It soon developed a Russophile orientation, which caused a split in the society in 1929 and the formation of the Ukrainophile *Teachers' Hromada of Subcarpathian Ruthenia. The society campaigned for the introduction of Russian as the language of instruction in the schools of Subcarpathian Ruthenia and attempted to organize a broad cultural program and support for students and teachers. It published the monthly *Narodnaia shkola (1921–38). Among the leading activists in the society were V. Shpenik (the first head), M. Vasylenkov, and P. Fedor. After 1929 the society declined, together with the entire Russophile movement in Transcarpathia, and most teachers joined the Teachers' Hromada; unlike the Hromada, however, it was not closed down following the Hungarian occupation of Transcarpathia, and it continued its activities until the end of the Second World War.

**Teaching gospels.** See Didactic gospels.

*Teatr* (Theater). An illustrated journal of the arts administration at the Council of People's Commissars of the Ukrainian SSR, published bimonthly (1936–40, ed A. Borshchahivsky) and then monthly (1940–1, ed I. Kocherha) in Kiev (a total of 41 issues). It commented on the activities of professional and amateur theaters and featured memoirs and letters from the history of Ukrainian theater. Its successor was *Ukraïns'kyi teatr.

**Teatr u Piatnytsiu.** See Ukrainian Theater in Philadelphia.

*Teatral'ne mystetstvo* (Theatrical Art). A monthly journal published by H. Hanuliak in Lviv in 1922–5 (a total of 35 issues) with the literary supplement *Teatral'na biblioteka* (edited by F. Dudko). It contained information on the history of Ukrainian theater in Galicia, biographies of theatrical workers, criticism, texts of original Ukrainian and translated dramas, and instructions for amateur groups.

*Teatral'ni visty* (Theatrical News). A weekly journal of the Theatrical Committee under the auspices of the UNR government, published in Kiev from April to October 1917. Edited by L. Kurbas, it contained articles on the development of Ukrainian professional and amateur theater, parts of Kurbas's translation of G. Lessing's *Hamburgische Dramaturgie*, and O. Wilde's theatrical aphorisms.

**Technical journals.** The earliest technical journals published in Ukraine were financed by branches of the Imperial Russian Technical Society (IRTO, est 1866 in St Petersburg). The Kiev branch published *Zapiski Kievskogo otdeleniia Imperskogo russkogo tekhnicheskogo obshchestva po sveklosakharnoi promyshlennosti* (1871–1916), *Tekhnicheskii listok* (1878–81), and *Inzhener* (1882–1916). Similar *Zapiski* were published by the Kharkiv (1881–1908), Odessa (1885–1916), Mykolaiv (1904–5, 1914, 1916), and Katerynoslav (1902–16) IRTO branches. The journals dealt with scientific and technical problems in various branches of industry. The first specialized technical journals were devoted to mining: *Iuzhno-russkii gornyi listok* (1880–7, 1888–1909), which was continued as *Gornozavodskoe delo* (1910–16), and *Novosti tekhniki i promyshlennosti* (1908–13), which was continued as *Iuzhnyi inzhener* (1914–16). Journals such as *Vestnik iugozapadnykh zheleznykh dorog* (1903–16) and *Vestnik Ekaterininskoi zheleznoi dorogi* (1907–16) dealt with railway construction; *Listok inzhenernogo kruzhka* (1901–12) dealt with civil engineering.

Ukrainian-language technical journals appeared under the Soviet regime in the 1920s. The most important was the monthly *Naukovo-tekhnichnyi visnyk* (1926–36), published by the *Kharkiv Scientific Society. Its specialized supplements eventually became separate journals: *Problemy teplotekhniky* (1927–31), *Sil's'kohospodars'ka mashyna* (1928–38), *Ukraïns'ki sylikaty* (1929–32), *Budivnytstvo* (1929–35), and *Kharchova ta sil's'kohospodars'ka promyslovist'* (1930–4). In the late 1920s a number of technical research institutions, such as the Kiev Polytechnical Institute, the Institute of Technical Mechanics, and the Kharkiv Technological Institute, published their own transactions, and collections of papers were issued at irregular intervals by the Institute of Welding (40 vols in 1932–9), the Institute of Chemical Technology (13 vols in 1929–39), and the Institute of Chemistry (9 vols in 1934–48). With the suppression of Ukrainian culture, Ukrainian journals were discontinued gradually in the 1930s, and Russian technical journals, such as *Energetika* (1930–7), *Novyi gorniak* (1929–41), *Stal'* (1931–40), and *Koks i khimiia* (1931–41), were started. A few popular magazines were published in Ukrainian (*Tekhnika masam*, 1929–37, and *Radio*, 1930–41) or Russian (*Rabochii metallurg*, 1931–5). During the 1930s, besides journals and collections, a number of technical books came out in Ukrainian. Whereas Ukrainian publishers in the social sciences were completely dismantled in 1934–9, those in technical fields and some in mathematics and the natural sciences were left untouched until 1948. During the Zhdanov period practically all technical publications in Ukraine were converted to Russian.

Ukrainian-language technical journals began to come out again only in the 1950s. The AN URSR (now ANU) published *Avtomatyka*, *Prykladna mekhanika*, and *Narysy z istoriï tekhniky*. Many irregular collections by technical institutes appeared, mostly in Ukrainian. In the mid-1960s, interdepartmental republican collections began to appear regularly, of which about 50 series were devoted to technology. Only a few of them came out in Ukrainian: *Detali mashyn*, *Mekhanika tverdoho tila*, *Pidiomno-transportne ustatkuvannia*, and *Hihiiena naselenykh mists'*. In the 1970s there were *Avtomobil'ni shliakhy i shliakhove budivnytstvo*, *Nauka i tekhnika v mis'komu hospodarstvi*, *Polihrafiia i vydavnycha sprava*, and certain series of the *Visnyk* of the Lviv and Kiev polytechnical institutes (up to eight issues annually). By the end of 1977 the only Ukrainian-language technical journal in Ukraine was *Avtomatyka*.

After 1978 only the bimonthly *Narysy z istoriï pryrodoznavsta i tekhniky* has appeared in Ukrainian. About 30 technical journals published in Ukraine have come out in Russian, including *Tekhnologiia i organizatsiia proizvodstva*, *Energetika i elektrifikatsiia*, *Mekhanizatsiia i avtomatizatsiia upravleniia*, *Ugol' Ukrainy*, *Iskusstvennye almazy*, *Kibernetika*, *Radioelektronika*, *Problemy prochnosti*, *Upravliaiushchie sistemy i mashiny*, *Prikladnaia mekhanika*, *Poroshkovaia metallurgiia*, *Stroitel'stvo i arkhitektura*, and *Fiziko-khimicheskaia mekhanika materialov*. The scientific level of the technical journals published in Ukraine is high, and some of the thematic collections of the 1970s are unequaled, among them *Mekhanika tverdogo tela* (on the mechanics of solids), *Tochnost' i nadezhnost' kiberneticheskikh sistem* (on cybernetics systems), *Problemy mashinostroeniia* (on machine building), *Teoriia sluchainykh protsessov*, *Kibernetika na morskom transporte* (on naval cybernetics), *Ergaticheskie dinamicheskie sistemy upravleniia*, and *Narysy z istoriï pryrodoznavstva i tekhniky* (on natural and technological history).

Outside of the Ukrainian SSR the most important Ukrainian technical journal was *\*Tekhnichni visty*, published in Lviv in the interwar period. In Czechoslovakia the *\*Ukrainian Technical and Husbandry Institute published *Visty UTHI*, and after the war the institute published *Visti* and *Biuleten'*. In the United States the *\*Ukrainian Engineers' Society has published *Visti ukraïns'kyh inzheneriv* since 1950.

S. Protsiuk

**Technical schools** (*tekhnichni uchylyshcha*). Educational establishments founded in 1954 in the USSR and the Ukrainian SSR. Only students with a complete secondary education were eligible for admission to the schools. The mandate of the technical schools was to train skilled workers in some 600 professions, from all branches of the economy. In 1959–64 they existed within the network of urban and rural *\*vocational-technical schools. In 1966 technical schools were established in large industrial and construction enterprises, state farms, and other organizations. Technical schools had a program of study that varied from one to three years. In 1984 there were 242 technical schools in Ukraine, with an enrollment of 146,000.

**Techno-Artistic Group A** (Tekhnomystetska hrupa A). A writers' group in Kharkiv, founded by M. *\*Yohansen in 1928. Like the Russian constructivists, Yohansen and the group's other members, among them Yu. Smolych, L. Kovaliv, O. Dovzhenko, and O. Slisarenko, sought to combine art and literature with the achievements of technology and industrialization. The group ceased functioning ca 1930 and had little impact.

**Technological sciences.** A group of disciplines including the traditional branches of engineering and agricultural sciences and the modern fields of space, computers, and automation. The technological sciences are related closely to the natural sciences of physics, chemistry, geology, and biology, as well as to mathematics and practical engineering. They draw upon scientific knowledge to solve technological problems.

In Ukraine technological research for scientific purposes began at the end of the 18th century. During the 19th and the early 20th centuries researchers focused on improving the technology of metals production, machine building, and mining. Until the First World War the technological sciences developed mostly in higher schools, such as Kiev and Kharkiv universities, the Kharkiv Technological and the Kiev and Lviv polytechnical institutes, and the Katerynoslav (later Dnipropetrovske) Mining Institute. After the imposition of Soviet rule progress in the technological sciences became a priority. From the mid-1930s the Soviet government's science policy favored the technological sector.

Research institutes in the technological sciences were frequently reorganized. They were consolidated or separated and transferred from the control of the people's commissariats to the Academy of Sciences and back. In the 1920s and 1930s most of them came under the jurisdiction of Ukrainian republican centers. Ukrainian scientists achieved significant success in their research, and Ukraine's contribution in technological sciences won increasing recognition around the world. The technological sciences in Ukraine suffered irredeemable setbacks with the Stalinist terror, the increasing bureaucratization and centralization of the Soviet system, and the Second World War. Postwar reconstruction required more time than expected; it lasted in some respects until the mid-1950s.

New institutes were set up in the 1960s and 1970s. Besides traditional branches of the technical sciences, new ones were instituted, in cybernetics, nuclear and power engineering, radio communications, space engineering, aeronautical engineering, high-temperature (plasma) and low-temperature (cryogenics) technologies, materials science, and the chemistry of giant molecules. At the end of 1973 approx 200 of 348 scientific research institutes in Ukraine belonged to different branches of industry. Almost all technological institutes were tied to industries, and 62 belonged to the institutional system of the AN URSR (now ANU). In 1977 approx 105,000 of 178,000 scientific personnel in Ukraine worked in the technological sciences. Owing to the policy of Russification nearly all the *technical journals were published in Russian. (See also *Agricultural machine building, *Agricultural technology, *Construction industry, *Cybernetics, *Electric power, *Hydrology, *Machine science, *Materials science, *Mechanics, *Metallurgy, *Mining science, *Radio technology, *Rocket, *Space travel, *Structural mechanics, and *Welding.)

S. Protsiuk, A. Zhukovsky

**Teisseyre, Wawrzyniec**, b 10 August 1860 in Cracow, d 2 April 1939 in Lviv. Geologist. From 1925 he served as a professor at the Lviv Polytechnical Institute and conducted oil explorations in Galicia and Rumania. His works deal with the tectonic formations of the Carpathian Mountains, Subcarpathia, and Podilia. They include a geological atlas of Galicia (1900).

*Tekhnichni visty* (Technical News). A journal of the *Ukrainian Technical Society in Lviv, published from 1925 to 1939. It came out monthly (1925–6, 1937–9), quarterly (1927–30, 1935–6), and bimonthly (1931–4). Its editors were Ya. Stefanovych (1925–30), I. Kondiak (1930–2), S. Pasternak (1932–8), and A. Figol (1938–9). The journal was distributed to the society's members throughout Western Ukraine and the diaspora; it was discontinued with the Soviet occupation.

**Tekhnikum.** The name given to educational institutions in the USSR, in the Ukrainian SSR, and now in Ukraine which train personnel for industry, agriculture, construction, transport, and communication by offering a program of *secondary special education. The first institutions called tekhnikums appeared in Russian-ruled Ukraine at the beginning of the 20th century. Their equivalent in Western Ukraine could be considered to be the technical *lyceums. In 1922–30 in Soviet Ukraine, unlike in Russia, tekhnikums had the status of institutions of higher education and trained specialists in various narrow technical fields.

During the 1920s tekhnikums were Ukrainized. Whereas in 1922 only 16 percent of the students in these institutions were Ukrainians, by 1928 the figure had risen to 62 percent. In 1928 there were 145 tekhnikums in Ukraine, 80 of which offered Ukrainian-language instruction. In 1931 tekhnikums in Ukraine were reorganized along Russian lines into secondary schools offering vocational education, and the Ukrainization was reversed, in favor of Russian-language instruction. With industrialization the network of tekhnikums expanded, from 165 schools and 89,000 students in 1932 to 693 schools and 196,200 students in 1940. Tekhnikums were under the jurisdiction of various industrial commissariats. Today the program of study can last up to three years for those with complete secondary education, and up to four for those entering with eight years of schooling. Students gain practical work experience and can enroll for full or part time study. In 1990–1 there were 742 tekhnikums in Ukraine, with 757,000 students.

B. Krawchenko

**Telegraph communications.** The transmission of encoded messages by electric impulses. The first telegraph line in Ukraine was built in 1838; it linked St Petersburg and Warsaw through Kiev. In the 1840s a telegraph line between Lviv and Vienna was established. In 1854 the Kiev-Moscow line was opened. In the 20th century the telegraph network in Ukraine developed rapidly. In 1913 some 9.2 million telegrams were sent (within the present boundaries of Ukraine). In 1928 the figure was 4.5 million; in 1932, 15.6 million; in 1940, 23.3 million; and in 1970, 58.0 million. Reliance on the telegraph declined as telephones became more available: the number of telegrams decreased from 84 million in 1980 to 70 million in 1987. But the number remains higher in Ukraine than in the developed Western countries, where telephone and facsimile transmission have all but supplanted telegraph communications.

**Telephone communications.** The transmission of speech by electrical impulses. In 1880 G. Ignatev successfully tested a system of simultaneous telegraph and telephone transmission in Kiev. The first telephone lines in Ukraine were laid in Odessa (1882), Lviv (1884), Kiev (1886), and Kharkiv (1888). The first intercity communications were established between Odessa and Mykolaiv and between Kharkiv and Katerynoslav (1910–12). The first rural line was built in Lebedyn county, Kharkiv gubernia. In the 1920s direct lines were laid between Kharkiv and Petrograd, Moscow and Katerynoslav, and Kharkiv and Kiev.

The number of intercity telephone calls in the Ukrainian SSR increased from 3.7 million in 1928 to 19.1 million in 1940 and 567 million in 1988. Telephone ownership expanded from 187,000 in 1940 to 6 million in 1987. Most telephones (85 percent in 1988) are located in urban centers; the rural areas have inadequate service. Only 4.1 million telephones are in private homes. Ukraine, like other former Soviet republics, lags far behind Western countries in per capita telephone ownership; in the United States, for example, there were 90 telephones per 100 people, compared to 10 in the former USSR (1988). The quality of telephone service in Ukraine is poor, and the equipment is outdated. The lack of a modern telephone network has prevented the society from entering the information age and hampered the development of the economy.

D. Goshko, B. Krawchenko

**Teleshek, Kyrylo** [Telešek], b 31 March 1894 in Kozelshchyna, Kremenchuk county, Poltava gubernia, d 7 August 1974 in Kharkiv. Economist. A graduate of the Kharkiv Institute of the National Economy (1928), he taught in various higher educational institutions. He was assistant director of the Kharkiv Zootechnical Institute and from 1945 chaired the Department of Economics and Agricultural Administration at the Kharkiv Agricultural Institute. His works on Ukrainian agriculture include *Problema sil's'ko-hospodars'koho osvoiennia Nyzhn'odniprovs'kykh piskiv* (The Problem of Agricultural Reclamation of the Lower Dnieper Sands, 1948).

**Television.** In the 1920s P. *Hrabovsky's son, Borys, experimented with electronic transmission of images over space, and in 1928 he demonstrated a crude transmission in Tashkent. The unsophisticated state of the Soviet electronic industry at the time left Hrabovsky's invention unutilized. The first television broadcast in Ukraine was a short telecast in Kiev in 1939, which was based on the so-called mechanical system. The transmission lasted 40 minutes and consisted of televised portraits and signs. The first television center was built in Kiev only in 1949. The first telecasts made with high-clarity pictures appeared in Kiev in 1951 and in Kharkiv in 1955. The television network spread to the Donetske and Odessa oblasts (1956), Lviv (1957), Dnipropetrovske and Luhanske (1958), Symferopil, Kherson, Zaporizhia, and Mykolaiv (1959), and, later, Sumy, Chernivtsi, and Uzhhorod. Since 1962 television programs have been retransmitted from Kiev to Chernihiv, Zhytomyr, Bila Tserkva, Pryluka, Vinnytsia, and other cities in Ukraine. In 1962 a second channel was added, from Moscow. A unified 'Ukrainian' program began to be telecast in 1965 and was limited to 200 broadcast hours weekly. In 1968 telecenters in Ukraine began to receive color telecasts from other centers, and in 1969 the Kiev telecenter began its own color broadcasts (Lviv in 1976). All telecasting is done through a comprehensive common-carrier network consisting of centers, studios, and retransmission stations using relay systems (eg, Kiev with Kishinev) or cable (eg, Kiev and Lviv). In 1975 a powerful telecommunications terminal outside Lviv became a port of the international telesystem Intelcat.

More than 90 percent of the population can receive two-channel programming. Kiev has had four channels since 1982, with 60 hours of broadcasting per day. In 1991 there were more than 15 million television sets, of which more than half were color sets. Only some programs on oblast and republic levels were in Ukrainian; most were in Russian, and many of them were broadcast directly from Moscow (or prepared in Ukraine but approved by the State Committee), the role of Ukrainian television having been quite insignificant. Republic and oblast broadcasts included local informative reports and propaganda but mostly consisted of entertainment of different genres: musical films, film concerts, teledrama, and tele-almanacs, including performances of the Kiev Ukrainian Drama Theater, the Lviv Ukrainian Drama Theater, and the Kiev Young Spectator's Theater. The majority were produced by Ukrtelefilm, the Kiev Artistic Film Studio, and the Odessa Studio of Chronicle-Documentary Films.

Television sets are manufactured by plants in Kiev, Lviv, Symferopil, Dnipropetrovske, and Kharkiv and distributed throughout the former USSR and abroad. In 1988 there were 350 television stations in Ukraine, and 306 television sets for every 1,000 inhabitants.

BIBLIOGRAPHY
Dombruhov, P. Rospovidi pro telebachennia (Kiev 1971)
Veryha, W. Communication Media and Soviet Nationality Policy: Status of National Languages in Soviet T.V. Broadcasting (New York 1972)
Mickiewicz, E. Split Signals: Television and Politics in the Soviet Union (New York 1988)
Mashchenko, I. 'Telebachennia Ukraïny,' Suchasnist', 1991, nos 7–8

V. Revutsky, D.H. Struk

**Teliha, Mykhailo,** b 1900 in Okhtyrskyi, Kuban oblast, d February 1942 in Kiev. Civic activist and banduryst; husband of O. *Teliha. He took part in the struggle for Ukrainian independence in 1917–20 and then emigrated to Czechoslovakia. In 1929 he moved to Warsaw. A forester by profession, he was active in the Union of Ukrainian Emigrant Engineers and Technicians in Poland. Toward the end of 1941 he accompanied his wife, a member of an OUN expeditionary group, to Kiev, and he was arrested with her by the Gestapo on 9 February 1942. He was executed a few days later in prison.

Mykhailo Teliha                    Olena Teliha

**Teliha, Olena** b 21 July 1907 in St Petersburg, Russia, d 21 February 1942 in Kiev. Poet, publicist, and nationalist leader; daughter of I. *Shovheniv. Teliha emigrated with her parents to Czechoslovakia in 1922, where she studied at the Ukrainian Higher Pedagogical Institute in Prague. The intellectual milieu of the Ukrainian émigrés after the failure of the struggle for Ukraine's independence and especially the Ukrainian student life in Prague in the 1930s had a profound influence on Teliha's development. She married M. *Teliha and moved to Warsaw (1929–39), where she taught at a Ukrainian school and was active in the Ukrainian community. From 1933 she contributed to the nationalist journal *Vistnyk (Lviv). In Cracow from 1939 to 1941, she headed the literary-artistic society Zarevo and together with O. *Olzhych worked in the cultural sector of the Leadership of Ukrainian Nationalists (see *Organization of Ukrainian Nationalists). With the outbreak of the war between Nazi Germany and the Soviet Union she moved to Lviv and then left with the *OUN expeditionary groups for Kiev in 1941. There she became head of the Writers' Union and editor of the literary weekly *Litavry. When the Nazi regime closed down Litavry's parent newspaper, Ukraïns'ke slovo, and replaced it with the pro-regime Nove ukraïns'ke slovo, Teliha refused to cooperate. She was arrested by the Gestapo and shot, together with other Ukrainian nationalists.

Teliha's poems were published mainly in the nationalist Vistnyk and were collected posthumously in Dusha na storozhi (The Soul on Guard, 1946). That collection was augmented by her prose and republished as Prapory dukha (The Banners of the Spirit, 1947), and then Olena Teliha: Zbirnyk (Olena Teliha: Collection, 1977). Her poems also appeared in English, translated and edited by O. Prokopiv, as Boundaries of Flame (1977). Firmly rooted in the nationalistic poetry of the interwar period, her lyrical poetry draws strength more from sincerity than from formal sophistication and reflects the oxymoron of 'soft firmness' that Teliha espoused for the contemporary Ukrainian woman, whom she saw as integral to and an equal partner in the struggle for Ukraine's independence. In February 1992 a cross was erected to her memory in *Babyn Yar in Kiev.

O. Shtul, D.H. Struk

**Telishevsky, Kostiantyn** [Teliševs'kyj, Kostjantyn], b 1851, d 1913. Civic and political activist in Galicia. A notary public in Turka, he served as a deputy in the Galician Diet (1889–95) and the Austrian parliament (1891–7). He was one of the advocates of the *New Era policy.

**Telizhyn, Daria** [Teližyn, Darija], b 31 March 1960 in Toronto. Pianist and educator; daughter of O. Telizhyn. A graduate of the University of Western Ontario and the Peabody Conservatory of Music, she has appeared in recital in Toronto, London, Paris, Brussels, Amsterdam, Frankfurt, and Washington. The British recording company Claudio Records has released CDs of her renditions of works by F. Liszt and P. Tchaikovsky. She is on faculty at the Levine School of Music, Washington.

**Telizhyn, Omelian** [Teližyn, Omeljan] (Telizyn, Emil), b 18 January 1930 in Rakiv, Dolyna county, Galicia. Painter, sculptor, and scenery designer. A postwar refugee, he studied at the Ukrainian Art Studio in Aschaffenburg, Germany (1947–9), and at the Ontario College of Art in Toronto. From 1965 to 1987 he worked for the CFTO and CBC television stations in Toronto as a designer. A member of the amateur Zahrava Theater troupe in Toronto since 1953, in 1987 he established his own design company. As a commercial artist he has produced many enamels, bronzes, and paintings.

Stanislav Telniuk

**Telniuk, Stanislav** [Tel'njuk], b 26 April 1935 in Iskrivka, Yakymivka raion, Zaporizhia oblast, d 2 September 1990. Writer, literary critic, book editor, and translator. He graduated from Kiev University in 1959. He worked as an editor of *Literaturna Ukraïna* (1962–6) and as secretary of the Literary Criticism and Theory Commission of the Writers' Union of Ukraine. He wrote the poetry collections *Lehenda pro budni* (Legend of Workadays, 1963), *Zalizniaky* (The Zalizniaks, 1966), *Opivnichne* (Around Midnight, 1972), *Lehenda pro tr'okh sester* (Legend of Three Sisters, 1972), *Robota* (Work, 1976), *Doloni svitu* (Palms of the World, 1983), *Myt'* (Moment, 1985), and *Suzir'ia liubovi* (Constellation of Love, 1987); the novelettes *Tudy, de sontse skhodyt'* (There, Where the Sun Rises, 1967) and *Pavlo z Mukunhy* (Paul from Mukunga, 1981); and the prose collection *Bilyi kamin'* (White Rock, 1984). The second part of his best-selling novel set in Cossack times, *Hraie synie more* (The Blue Sea Roars, 1971), was unpublished, for political reasons, until 1985, when it appeared under the title *Strily*

*nad stepom* (Arrows above the Steppe). Telniuk published three books (1968, 1974, 1989) and a biographical novel (1979) about P. Tychyna and translated into Ukrainian the novel *Taras na Arali* (Taras [Shevchenko in Exile] near Lake Aral, 1975) by the Karakalpak author U. Bekbaulov. Together with L. Horlach he wrote in Russian three documentary books about Siberia and the Far East. In the 1960s his satirical poems about Russification were circulated in samvydav. His poems and stories have been translated into 14 languages.

R. Senkus

*Tema* (Theme). An official publication of the Saskatchewan Teachers of Ukrainian (a special subject council of the Saskatchewan Teachers' Federation), published quarterly since 1968. *Tema* includes articles of professional interest about Ukrainian language education and multicultural issues; reviews of multimedia resource materials, teaching strategies, and classroom activities; and items of general interest to teachers of Ukrainian. The journal's editors have included C. Kachkowski, G. Zerebecky, S. (Cipywnyk) Morris, N. Labiuk, R. Franko, V. Labach, and N. Prokopchuk.

Ludmilla Temertey: monument in Edmonton to the victims of the 1932–3 famine in Soviet Ukraine

**Temertey, Ludmilla** [Temertej, Ljudmyla], b 21 August 1944 in Košice, Slovakia. Ukrainian-Canadian painter. From 1962 to 1969 she studied at Sir George Williams School of Fine Arts and the School of Fine Arts in Montreal, and the Royal Academy of Fine Arts in Brussels. She has worked as an illustrator for Canadian magazines and as associate art director of *Chatelaine* magazine. Solo exhibitions of her work have been held in Montreal (1974, 1978) Toronto (1975, 1982) Detroit (1976), Ottawa (1977), Edmonton (1977), the Ukrainian Cultural Heritage Village in Alberta (1981), and Philadelphia (1983). Commissioned portraits constitute a major part of her work. Her paintings can be found at the Museum of Civilization in Ottawa and the Kiev Museum of Ukrainian Art. Temertey designed the monument to the 1933 famine in Ukraine erected in front of Edmonton's city hall in 1983. She has also done colored-pencil drawings, temperas, and pastels noted for their delicate lines and shading. Many depict a beautiful female figure dressed in an embroidered Ukrainian costume.

**Temnytsky, Omelian** (Milon) [Temnyc'kyj, Omeljan], b 1882 in Husiatyn county, Galicia, d 14 August 1918 in Odessa. Civic and political figure; brother of V. *Temnytsky. He was a Galician political activist involved with the Ukrainian Social Democratic party and a contributor to several newspapers (*Volia*, *Zemlia i volia*, *Vpered*, and *Naprzód*) until he was arrested and sent to Siberia by invading Russian forces in 1915. With the outbreak of the revolution he escaped to Odessa, where he was editor of the daily newspaper *Vistnyk Odesy*, a financial commissioner and fellow of the city council, and head of the local Ukrainian Social Democratic Workers' party.

Volodymyr Temnytsky

**Temnytsky, Volodymyr** [Temnyc'kyj], b 1879 in Shydlivtsi, Husiatyn county, Galicia, d 26 January 1938 in Lviv. Lawyer, journalist, and civic and political leader. He studied law at Lviv University and, after the secession of Ukrainian students in 1902, at Cracow and Vienna universities. He was one of the organizers of the 1902 peasant strike in Galicia. A lifelong member of the *Ukrainian Social Democratic party (USDP), he served as its leader in 1914–21. During the First World War he was a member of the Combat Board of the Ukrainian Sich Riflemen and of the Supreme Ukrainian Council in Vienna and collaborated with the Union for the Liberation of Ukraine. He was appointed deputy minister of foreign affairs in the UNR Council of National Ministers in December 1918 and minister of foreign affairs in April 1919. From May 1919 he coordinated the efforts of UNR diplomatic missions in Europe to gain recognition and military support for the UNR. After returning to Galicia in 1922, he resumed his political activities. Together with L. Hankevych he attempted to revive the USDP in the 1930s. He also contributed political articles to various Galician papers and was a member of the Lviv City Council.

**Temperance movement.** An organized effort to secure complete abstention from alcoholic beverages or to ensure moderation in their use. The late 18th and early 19th centuries witnessed an increasing interest in North America and Europe in problems connected with the abuse of alcohol. Moves to promote temperance spread from the United States to Ireland, where the earliest temperance organization in Europe was founded in 1818. It and other temperance societies provided models for subsequent Ukrainian activities. Their characteristic features included the identification of distilled spirits as a prime enemy and the voluntary pledging of temperance or abstinence by members. Leadership was usually provided by the clergy.

**Western Ukraine.** The earliest Ukrainian temperance movement was begun in Galicia in the 1840s. Modeled on Irish temperance missions and societies, it was part of a wider sobriety campaign supported by the Catholic church in many parts of Europe. The sobriety movement of the 1840s was under the patronage of the governor of Galicia and had the full support of Metropolitan M. Levytsky. Many village and town sobriety brotherhoods were formed at that time, their purpose more to foster moderation than to bring about abstinence. By the 1850s, however, the movement had faltered.

The impetus for the movement's revival was provided by the publication in 1869 of Rev S. *Kachala's pamphlet *Shcho nas hubyt' i shcho nam pomochy mozhe* (What Is Destroying Us and What Can Help Us) and by two pastoral letters from Metropolitan Y. Sembratovych in 1874 on the harmful effects of alcohol and the need for sobriety missions. Priests began to encourage temperance from their pulpits, and the best orators from among the clergy went among the general population and proclaimed the sobriety message. Their activity gave rise to an upsurge in missions, the goal of which was the establishment of sobriety brotherhoods. Those largely religious events tended to follow a definite pattern. They lasted several days and included religious services, special homilies rich in appropriate imagery, and prayers led by the most talented missionary priests. The focal moment was the taking of the vow to abstain from alcohol or from the use of distilled spirits. Total abstinence was usually the goal in the 1870s and 1880s. People who took the vow solemnly signed their names (or made their marks) in a 'golden book.' The statute of the brotherhood was then read. Typically that document would give the name of the brotherhood and of the parish with which it was connected, and stipulate the need for a monthly brotherhood service and a festive but nonalcoholic brotherhood celebration every six months. Between the monthly services each member was to observe the behavior of the others and to encourage them to keep to their oaths. A prayer for the brotherhood ended the mission. Special crosses were often erected afterward to commemorate sobriety missions. The *Prosvita and *Kachkovsky societies contributed further to the spread of sobriety through the provision of temperance literature and the engagement of occasional speakers on the topic.

The Greek Catholic church wished to retain control over the temperance movement in eastern Galicia. In 1886 the consistory systematized the operations of church sobriety brotherhoods, which were required to send periodic reports to a special consistory commission. In 1895 a pastoral letter of Metropolitan S. Sembratovych reformulated the regulations for the brotherhoods: the priest was the true head of each brotherhood, and only he had the right to accept new members into it; vows were to be binding either for life or for a specified period; breaking a vow was a venial, not a mortal, sin and could be cause for expulsion from the brotherhood; except for those on military service, release from vows could be obtained only from the ordinariate; drinking distilled spirits for medicinal purposes was permitted; and there were to be special certificates and prayers for members of such 'canonical' brotherhoods.

There are many indications that the temperance movement of the 1870s and 1880s was effective. The fact that women were permitted to join the sobriety brotherhoods may well have boosted their prospects. By 1888 three-quarters of all Greek Catholic parishes in Galicia had temperance brotherhoods. In some instances membership was very large, and even encompassed all the adults in a community. The Terebovlia deanery alone had 13,353 members. The number of taverns decreased. Some brotherhoods forswore alcohol altogether; in others the vow specified distilled spirits, and the people drank beer, mead, and homemade fruit wines, or tea with rum, instead of vodka. In 1894 Prof N. Cybulski of Cracow University concluded that there had been a definite decline in the consumption of vodka, and that in some counties of eastern Galicia one-third or even one-half of the people did not drink vodka at all.

The number of church-related sobriety brotherhoods remained fairly constant into the 20th century. Not until after Galicia fell under the rule of the new Polish state were the ties with the church markedly weakened. New secular temperance associations emerged in the 1920s. The most prominent was the *Vidrodzhennia (Rebirth) society, headed by the physician and writer S. Parfanovych in the later 1920s. Intellectual leaders and students contributed significantly to the interwar temperance campaigns by encouraging thrift and highlighting the amounts of money spent on alcohol as well as promoting the playing of sports as a substitute for drinking. For reasons that are not entirely clear the campaigns were not as effective as those prior to the First World War.

**Central and eastern Ukraine.** A widespread temperance movement never developed in Russian-ruled Ukraine, and those efforts that existed were usually either localized or part of a broader campaign in the Russian Empire or the Soviet Union. In the mid-19th century the Europe-wide temperance movement began to have a minor influence in Ukraine, where it resulted in the establishment of some private, church-supported sobriety brotherhoods. Particularly from the 1870s on, the drinking of tea instead of vodka was encouraged by concerned private citizens. Not until excessive drinking by the working population of the empire had started to become an obvious impediment to industrial development did the imperial government begin to concern itself with temperance, in the 1890s. A state monopoly on liquor production and sale was proclaimed in 1894; by 1901 it was in force throughout the empire, including Ukrainian lands. The government also gave financial support to temperance societies called Wardens of Public Sobriety. Those efforts, however, failed to produce a decline in the per capita consumption of alcohol.

In 1897 a group of medical and social scientists in St Petersburg, concerned with problems stemming from the overconsumption of alcohol, founded the Russian Society for the Protection of Public Health. The society provided a focal point for the establishment of the special Commission on the Question of Alcoholism, the printing of the periodical *Trezvost' i berezhlivost'*, and petitions to the government for socioeconomic reforms to combat drunkenness. In turn, the government established a department in the Ministry of Finance popularly known as the Guardianship of Public Sobriety, which was largely ineffectual and was regarded as suspect by the general public. An Anti-Alcohol Commission was established by the First State Duma. Partly because of differences in approach between scientists and politicians no effective temperance legislation was enacted. The scientists convened a national congress in St Petersburg in December 1909, to which

reform-minded persons (but no government representatives) were invited. Although the congress drew attention to much-needed reforms in housing, education, and labor conditions, the government in 1912 proceeded with restrictive legislation that aimed to reduce production and increase the price of alcohol. From 1911 on, however, the tsarist authorities provided some financial assistance to certain temperance activities, especially those supported by the Holy Synod and the Ministry of Public Education. Existing church temperance societies were reorganized and expanded. With the outbreak of war in 1914, total prohibition was introduced, initially for the period of mobilization, but soon it was extended for the duration of the war. In theory the measure brought compulsory temperance to all lands in the Russian Empire, but it is clear that from 1915 on there was much illicit drinking.

**The Soviet period.** In 1918 the Bolshevik regime established a ban on the manufacture and sale of alcoholic beverages. The prohibition was difficult to enforce. New measures in 1925 reintroduced a state monopoly on the production and sale of alcohol. The All-Union Council of Anti-Alcohol Societies co-ordinated temperance activities in the Soviet Union until it was disbanded in 1930. Women's groups also organized lectures on the harmful effects of alcohol during the 1920s. From 1930 until 1971 state and party bodies, and state medical personnel, were responsible for anti-alcohol propaganda. Cultural-educational measures were undertaken, without any obvious central co-ordination, by workers' clubs, reading halls, women's groups, the Communist Youth League, and the media.

Alcohol consumption increased after 1945, and there was an attendant rise in alcohol-related illness, birth defects, deaths, and crime and a lowering of labor productivity, all of which drew attention again to the need for enhanced temperance activities. A decree of the Supreme Soviet in 1972 to combat drunkenness produced little change. By 1980 it was estimated that each person over the age of 15 in the Soviet Union consumed, on average, 16–17 L of pure alcohol annually. Two CPSU general secretaries, Yu. Andropov and M. Gorbachev, demonstrated considerable concern about alcohol abuse. Gorbachev's efforts had their counterpart in the Ukrainian SSR with the 1985 decree 'On Measures to Step Up the Struggle against Drunkenness and Alcoholism and to Eradicate Home Brewing.' It was a serious anti-alcohol campaign, in which leading roles in promoting temperance and abstention were to be played by Communist party and Communist Youth League members, who were also to serve as examples to others. An All-Union Voluntary Temperance society was created; it had its own press organ, *Trezvost' i kul'tura* (Sobriety and Culture), the first issue of which appeared in January 1986. Reduced production of alcohol, restrictions on its sale, and educational and preventative programs were other aspects of the government-initiated temperance campaign. From the state's point of view the results were disappointing, for there was widespread resentment, passive resistance, and a significant increase in home distilling. In 1989 the campaign was quietly and unofficially brought to an end.

BIBLIOGRAPHY
Bryk, I.; Kotsiuba, M. (eds). *Pershyi ukraïns'kyi pros'vitno-ekonomichnyi kongres* (Lviv 1910)
Reid, C.V. *Soviet Social Reform in the 1980s: The Anti-Alcohol Campaign as Antidote for a Flagging Economy* (Ottawa 1986)
S. Hryniuk

**Temriuk** [Temrjuk]. VIII-18. A city (1979 pop 31,900) on the Kuban River near the Sea of Azov and a raion center in Krasnodar krai, RF. It was founded in the mid-19th century. Today it has a seaport 4 km away and a food industry. According to the census of 1926, Ukrainians accounted for 26.2 percent of the city's population and 71.9 percent of the raion's population.

**Temriuk Bay** [Temrjuc'ka zatoka]. VIII-18. A bay situated in the southeastern part of the Sea of Azov near the mouth of the Kuban River. The bay is 60 km wide at its entrance, 27 km long, and nearly 10 m deep. Near the shore the water is quite shallow and overgrown with reeds. The bay is connected to the Kurchanskyi and the Akhtanyzovskyi estuaries. It freezes over from mid-January to March. The city of Temriuk is located by the bay.

Borys Ten                Borys Teneta

**Ten, Borys** (pseud of Mykola Khomychevsky), b 9 December 1897 in Derman, now Ustenske Druhe, Zdolbuniv raion, Rivne oblast, d 13 March 1983 in Zhytomyr. Poet and translator. His first published work appeared in 1923. He wrote a collection of sonnets, *Zoriani sady* (Starry Orchards, 1970), but he is known primarily for his translations of classical texts, such as Homer's *Iliad* and *Odyssey* and the works of Aeschylus, Aristophanes, and Aristotle. He also translated works by W. Shakespeare, F. Schiller, A. Mickiewicz, A. Pushkin, and L. Tolstoy. He was one of the leading translators of the middle and late 20th century, and he contributed greatly to the enrichment of Ukrainian cultural expression and the Ukrainian lexicon.

**Tendiuk, Leonid** [Tendjuk], b 3 March 1931 in Volodymyrivka, Kirovohrad raion. Writer. He graduated from Kiev University (1956) and has traveled widely in the Pacific and Indian oceans as a Soviet sailor. He began publishing in 1950 and has written several poetry collections, the first being *Pole moie, polechko* (O My Field, Little Field, 1961), and the most recent, *Holos moria i stepu* (The Voice of the Sea and the Steppe, 1981); travel-sketch books based on his experiences at sea (1964, 1965, 1968); novels, including *Zemlia, de pochynaiut'sia dorohy* (The Land Where Roads Begin, 1972) and *Holova Drakona* (Draco's Head, 1985); and the prose collections *Vohnyky v okeani* (Fires in the Ocean, 1974), *Dyvovyzhna ryba murena* (Moray the Odd Fish, 1977), and *Na koralovykh atolakh* (On the Coral Atolls, 1977).

**Tendriv Bay.** VII-12, 13. A Black Sea bay situated off the southwestern corner of Kherson oblast. This shallow bay is nearly 45 km long, 7 km wide, and up to 6 m deep. It is set off from the Black Sea by the long Tendriv Spit and contains a number of islands. It freezes over in the winter. A section of the bay is situated within the Black Sea Nature Reserve, which is responsible for its overall maintenance.

**Tendriv Spit.** VII-12. A long, narrow strip of land situated off the southwestern corner of Kherson oblast in the Black Sea. The spit is nearly 65 km long and up to 1.8 km wide. It consists mainly of sand deposits and provides a sanctuary and wintering ground for birds. It also separates Tendriv Bay from the Black Sea.

**Teneta, Borys** (pseud of Borys Hurii), b 1903 in the Donbas, d 6 February 1935. Writer. His poetry was first published in 1924 in the journal *Chervonyi shliakh*. He contributed to the periodicals *Zoria*, *Nova hromada*, *Zhyttia i revoliutsiia*, and *Hlobus*. He was a member of the literary organization MARS and is best known for his prose, such as the collections of short stories *Lysty z Krymu* (Letters from the Crimea, 1927), *Harmoniia i svynushnyk* (Harmony and the Pigsty, 1928), *Desiata sekunda* (The Tenth Second, 1929), *Budni* (Ordinary Days, 1930), *Nenavyst'* (Hatred, 1930), and *P'ianytsi* (Drunkards, 1930). He was arrested in 1935, and committed suicide in prison.

**Tenianko, Petro** [Tenjanko], b 27 June 1884 in Sorochyntsi, Myrhorod county, Poltava gubernia, d 7 March 1957 in Winnipeg. Poet, teacher, and journalist. While teaching in Pyriatyn county he published his first poems in the almanac *Persha lastivka* (The First Swallow, 1905), in *Literaturno-naukovyi vistnyk*, and in other almanacs. His collection *Do raiu zlotosiainoho* (Toward Glittering Paradise) appeared in 1917. An interwar émigré in Poland and Czechoslovakia, he was a teaching assistant at the Ukrainian Higher Pedagogical Institute in Prague, where he received his doctorate; later he became a professor at the Ukrainian Gymnasium in Czechoslovakia. After the Second World War he emigrated to Winnipeg, where he taught theology at St Andrew's College and contributed to *Ukraïns'kyi holos*.

**Tenner, Hryhorii,** b 13 October 1889 in Akkerman (now Bilhorod-Dnistrovskyi), Bessarabia gubernia, d 31 October 1943 in Ufa, Bashkir ASSR. Sculptor. He studied at the St Petersburg and Munich (1914) academies of arts. From 1932 he taught at the Odessa Art Institute. A member of the Association of Revolutionary Art of Ukraine (1925–32), he sculpted the bas-reliefs on the 40-m obelisk in memory of those who died during the revolution in Katerynoslav (1919), designed the monuments to T. Shevchenko in Katerynoslav (1921) and Kharkiv (1925), created the monument to V. Lenin in Dnipropetrovske (1925), and sculpted busts of A. Herzen (1927), G. Plekhanov (1930), O. Shovkunenko (1933), and M. Skrypnyk and compositions depicting Lenin (1930), A. Pushkin (1935), and K. Marx (1935–6).

**Tennis** (*tenis*, *sytkivka*). Lawn tennis was introduced in Ukraine by British merchants, who founded tennis clubs in Odessa and Tahanrih in 1890. In 1913, all-Russian championships were held in Kiev. In the 1920s the sport was revived in Soviet Ukraine, and exhibition games were held in Odessa. In 1930, competitions for the championship of Soviet Ukraine were introduced. The USSR Tennis Section (est 1923) was reorganized into the USSR Tennis Federation in 1956, and that year it became a member of the International Tennis Federation. Ukrainian women players have won the amateur European tennis championship: M. Kroshyna (1972, 1977), O. Yelyseienko (1980, 1981), and L. Savchenko (1983). N. Medvedeva won the 1987 women's Satellite Tournament in Great Britain. Savchenko captured first place in women's doubles at Wimbledon in 1991.

Tennis was introduced in Galicia under Austrian rule, and the first clubs appeared in the 1890s. The sport was promoted by the *Sokil societies and student sports clubs. I. *Bobersky wrote the first tennis manual (1911) and the Ukraina sports society in Lviv organized the first competition in 1911. In 1924 the Lviv Tennis Club was founded; until 1939 it owned its own courts and held competitions for the championship of Western Ukraine. In the postwar United States and Canada the sport has been promoted by the Ukrainian Sports Federation of the USA and Canada, which has held annual competitions since 1955.

E. Zharsky

**Ten-year school** (*desiatyrichka*). The popular name given to the 10-year *secondary general-education school, established in the Ukrainian SSR in 1934. Graduation from the 10-year schools gives pupils complete secondary education and makes them eligible for entry into institutions of *higher education. As of 1986, 10-year schools are gradually being transformed into 11-year schools in connection with the extension of complete secondary education by one year.

**Teodor, A.** b and d ? Kievan wood engraver. From the early 1690s he engraved illustrations for the Kievan Cave Monastery Press, which were printed in the press's *Apostol* (1695), Octoechos (1699), and Gospel of Christ's Passion (1704).

**Teodoro.** A medieval fortified town in the Bakhchesarai region of the Crimea. The fortress was built in the 6th century, and it is possible that the town was the capital of the Gothic state or the seat of the Gothic bishops. In the 13th century, when the Tatars invaded the Crimea, Teodoro was the capital of the Gothic principality of Mangup. For two centuries it resisted Genoese and Tatar attacks. The principality remained independent until 1475, when it was destroyed by the Turks. The town of Teodoro burned down in 1592, but the fortress continued to be used as a refuge by the Tatar khans. Today only the ruins of the fortress and palace are left.

**Teodorovych, Ananii** [Teodorovyč, Ananij], b 16 December 1900 in Bilyn, Kovel county, Volhynia gubernia, d 3 November 1971 in Jamaica, New York. Orthodox church leader. After completing theological studies in Zhytomyr and Kamianets, he served as a parish priest in the Rivne area. A postwar refugee in Germany, he emigrated to Australia in 1948. There he helped organize the Ukrainian Autocephalous Orthodox church and served as head of the church's consistory and administrator. He died while taking part in a sobor in the United States and was buried in Sydney.

Metropolitan Ioan
Teodorovych

**Teodorovych, Ioan** [Teodorovyč, Joan], b 6 October 1887 in Krupets, Dubno county, Volhynia gubernia, d 3 May 1971 in Philadelphia. Orthodox metropolitan. He was ordained in 1915, during the First World War, and worked for the Red Cross on the southwestern front. In 1918 he served as divisional chaplain for the Graycoats and other units of the Army of the UNR in Kholm, Kiev, and Podilia regions. In 1920 he joined the newly formed *Ukrainian Autocephalous Orthodox church (UAOC), and in 1921 was consecrated bishop of Podilia and metropolitan by V. Lypkivsky. At the request of Orthodox Ukrainians in North America and at the behest of the All-Ukrainian Orthodox Church Council, he was sent in 1924 to the United States. In June 1924 he was elected bishop of the *Ukrainian Orthodox Church in the USA (UOC-USA), and in July 1924 he was elected bishop of the *Ukrainian Orthodox Church of Canada (UOCC; most of that church's affairs were administered by its consistory, because Teodorovych had settled in Philadelphia). In the 1930s and 1940s Teodorovych worked to unite the two major Ukrainian Orthodox jurisdictions in the United States, the UOC-USA and the *Ukrainian Orthodox Church of America (UOCA). He faced opposition from leaders of the UOCA, who questioned the canonicity of his episcopal consecration in the UAOC. In 1949 he was reconsecrated by the exarch of the patriarch of Alexandria in the United States, and the next year most parishes of the UOCA accepted his leadership. His negotiations with the UOCA jurisdictions were opposed by the leadership of the UOCC, however, and in 1947 he was forced to resign as bishop of that church. *U velyke nevidome* (Into the Great Unknown, 3 vols), a collection of Teodorovych's sermons, popular theological works, meditations, and fiction, was published in 1968–70.

A. Zhukovsky

**Teodorovych, Mykola** [Teodorovyč], b 1755 in Dubrynych, Transcarpathia, d ca 1820 in Korytniany, Transcarpathia. Greek Catholic priest, cultural and educational leader, and writer. After completing his theological studies in Vienna, he served as an administrator in Mykhailivtsi and then as parish priest in Korytniany. He wrote a handbook on home management and etiquette (1791; published 1919) and translated a Hungarian handbook on home medical care (unpublished). His account of the Korytniany parish (written in Latin) contains source material on the cultural and educational movement in Transcarpathia at the beginning of the 19th century, as does his short autobiography, which was published in *Podkarpats'ka Rus'* in 1934.

**Teodorovych, Mykola** [Teodorovyč], b 1856 or 1859, d ? Historian. After graduating from the St Petersburg Theological Academy he served as a school inspector in Siedlce, Podlachia. He compiled many studies of Volhynia, particularly of its church history, and published a description of Volhynia's cities, towns, and villages (5 vols, 1840), an essay on the Orthodox and Protestant doctrines of original sin (1886), a historical and statistical description of the churches and parishes of Volhynia eparchy (5 vols [incomplete], 1888–99), an analysis of Volodymyr-Volynskyi in relation to the history of the Volhynian hierarchy (1893), and a history of the Volhynian Theological Seminary (1901).

**Teodorovych, Petro** [Teodorovyč] (monastic name: Pavlo), b 23 April 1894, d 1946. Basilian priest; brother of Ye. Teodorovych. After completing studies in Rome (1923) he became a professor of philosophy at the Greek Catholic Theological Seminary in Lviv (1924–5) and then head of the novitiate (1928–39) at the Krekhiv monastery and, later, hegumen of the Buchach monastery. He was arrested in 1945 after the Soviet occupation of Galicia and died the following year in a labor camp.

Rev Yepifan Teodorovych

**Teodorovych, Yepifan** [Teodorovyč, Jepifan] (Theodorowych, Epiphanius), b 12 May 1881 in Ivanykivka, Stanyslaviv county, Galicia, d 3 February 1958 in Glencove, New York. Basilian priest; brother of P. Teodorovych. He edited the journal *Misionar* in Zhovkva (1908–12) and compiled a Lives of the Saints (1912) before being sent to Canada as a missionary in 1921 and then to the United States in 1927. A strong supporter of Bishop K. Bohachevsky, he edited the newspaper *Katolyts'kyi provid* (1927–32) in Chicago and later served as a parish priest there and elsewhere. Teodorovych published a collection of sermons titled *Katolyts'ke zhyttia* (Catholic Life, 2 vols, 1946, 1948).

**Teodosii Pecherskyi.** See Saint Theodosius of the Caves.

**Teodosiia** [Teodosija] (aka Feodosiia). VIII-16. A city (1990 pop 85,000) on the coast of the Black Sea in southeastern Crimea. It originated in the 6th century BC as a colony of the Greek city-state of Miletus and developed into

The Mufti-Jami Mosque (1623) in Teodosiia

an important trading center. From 355 BC it was part of the *Bosporan Kingdom. In the 4th century AD Teodosiia was sacked by the Huns, and at the end of the 6th century it was captured by the Khazars. During the second half of the 1st millennium the city had close ties with Byzantium. The Genoese established a trading post called Kaffa on Tatar-held territory in the 13th century. In 1475 it was captured by the Turks, who developed it into the largest slave market in the Crimea. The Zaporozhian Cossacks sacked Kaffa and freed the slaves in 1616, 1628, and 1675. During the Russian-Turkish War the town was captured by the Russian army, in 1771, and annexed by the Russian Empire in 1783. It reassumed its ancient name of Teodosiia, and it became a county center of Tavriia gubernia in 1802. The completion of a railway line (1892) and new port facilities (1895) stimulated economic development: the number of factories in the town increased from 13 in 1891 to 30 in 1894. By 1904 the population had reached 30,600. The main exports were grain and tobacco. Under Soviet rule Teodosiia was part of the Crimean ASSR from 1921. Its population declined from 35,400 in 1921 to 28,700 in 1926. Under the five-year plans Teodosiia developed into a manufacturing and health resort center. Most of its inhabitants are occupied in the sanatoriums, mud baths, rest homes, and children's resorts. Its industrial base consists of a tobacco factory (est 1861), a machine plant, a building-materials manufacturing complex, a furniture factory, and several food-processing plants. It has the Aivazovsky Art Gallery (est 1880) and a regional museum. Its main architectural monuments are the remaining walls and turrets of the Genoese fortress (14th–15th century), a 13th- to 15th-century church, and a 17th-century mosque.

**Teofipil** or **Teofipol** [Teofipil' or Teofipol']. IV-7. A town smt (1986 pop 6,200) on the Polkva River and a raion center in Khmelnytskyi oblast. It was first mentioned in historical documents in 1420, as the Lithuanian fortress of Kamin. Later the town was called Chovhanskyi Kamin and Chovhan and was owned by Polish magnates. It was destroyed by the Tatars in 1593, 1618, and 1649. Its inhabitants supported B. Khmelnytsky's uprising in 1648 but were soon subjugated by the Poles. In 1740 the town was renamed after its new owner, Princess Teofilia Jabłonska. After the Second Partition of Poland in 1793, Teofipil was annexed by the Russian Empire, and became a volost center in Starokostiantyniv county, Volhynia gubernia. In the second half of the 19th century the town acquired a brewery, a potash and soap factory, and a printing press, and its trade expanded. By the end of the century its population had reached 5,000. After the First World War Teofipil became a border town in Soviet Ukraine. Today it is an agricultural center with a sugar refinery, cheese factory, farm-machinery repair shop, and brick factory and its own airport.

**Teplohirske** [Teplohirs'ke]. A city (1989 pop 18,900) under the jurisdiction of the Stakhanov city council in Luhanske oblast. A mining settlement, it was granted city status in 1977. It has a coal mine, a coal-enrichment plant, and a mining-equipment manufacturing plant.

**Teplov, Grigorii,** b 20 November 1717 in Pskov, d 30 March 1779 in St Petersburg. Russian state and cultural figure; honorary member of the Russian Academy of Sciences. He was a personal aide to and manager for K. Rozumovsky before becoming an adviser to Catherine II after she assumed power in 1762. He prepared a memorandum (ca 1763) about the 'disorders in Little Russia' which criticized political, economic, and (particularly) legal practices in the Hetmanate. He asserted that Ukraine was actually an ancient Russian area that had developed distinctive institutions and ways only because of its long period of Polish rule. His recommendation for more direct Russian rule influenced Catherine's decision to abolish the Hetmanate.

**Teplyk.** V-10. A town smt (1986 pop 6,100) at the junction of the Teplychka and the Svynarka rivers and a raion center in Vinnytsia oblast. It originated in the 15th century as a fortified border settlement of the Grand Duchy of Lithuania. In 1569 it became part of the Polish Commonwealth. By the 18th century it was a small manufacturing and trading town owned by the Potocki family. Its inhabitants took part in the haidamaka uprisings of 1750 and 1768. The town was annexed by Russia in 1793 and assigned to Haisyn county in Podilia gubernia. Under the Soviet regime it became a raion center in 1923 and obtained smt status in 1956. It is an agricultural town with a powdered-skim-milk factory and a mixed-feed factory.

**Teplytsky, Vasyl** [Teplyc'kyj, Vasyl'], b 14 January 1902 in Avramivka, Yelysavethrad county, Kherson gubernia. Economic historian. After graduating from the Institute of Red Professors in 1936, he worked at the AN URSR (now ANU) Institute of Economics. He edited several collected works on Ukrainian economic history and wrote many articles and the monograph *Reforma 1861 roku i ahrarni vidnosyny na Ukraïni (60–90-ti roky XIX st.)* (The Reform of 1861 and Agrarian Relations in Ukraine [1860s to 1890s], 1959).

**Tereblia River** [Tereblja]. A right-bank tributary of the Tysa River that flows for 91 km through Transcarpathia oblast and drains a basin area of 750 sq km. With its source at Lake Synevyr, the river is fed by streams from the southern slopes of the Gorgany Mountains. It is notable for its deep valley (up to 350 m). A section of the river is dammed and some of its water diverted, by means of a 3.6-km tunnel (built in 1949), into the adjacent Rika River through the Tereblia-Rika Hydroelectric Station.

Terebovlia

**Terebovlia** [Terebovlja]. IV-6. A town (1989 pop 14,700) on the Hnizna River and a raion center in Ternopil oblast. It was first mentioned in the Hypatian Chronicle under the year 1097, when it was the center of a separate principality. Then it became part of Halych and Galicia-Volhynia principalities. The town was annexed by Poland in 1349, fortified with a new castle in 1366, and granted the rights of *Magdeburg law in 1389. As a frontier town Terebovlia was subject to frequent attack and destruction by the Tatars (1453, 1498, 1508, 1516) and Turks (1675, 1688). In 1772 it was annexed by Austria. At that time its population was only 2,100. It grew slowly as a manufacturing and trading center. In 1918–19 it was briefly part of the Western Ukrainian National Republic, and then it came under Polish rule. From 1939 it was part of Soviet Ukraine. Today its industry consists of footwear, canning, and powdered-milk factories. The town's architectural monuments include the remains of the fortress, which was destroyed and rebuilt several times between the 14th and 17th centuries, the 16th-century St Nicholas's Church, and the Carmelite monastery and church (1635).

BIBLIOGRAPHY
Vynnyts'kyi, I. (ed). *Terebovel's'ka zemlia: Istorychno-memuarnyi zbirnyk* (New York–Paris–Sidney–Toronto 1968)

**Terebovlia principality.** A southeastern appanage principality of Kievan Rus', the capital of which was *Terebovlia. Its territories included parts of southeastern Galicia, Bukovyna, and western Podilia. It bordered on Kiev principality to the east, Zvenyhorod (later Galician) principality to the west, and parts of Volodymyr-Volynskyi, Lutske, and Peresopnytsia principalities to the north.

It was established as an appanage principality ca 1084 and was given to *Vasylko Rostyslavych (his brothers, Volodar and Riuryk, ruled Zvenyhorod and Peremyshl respectively). Vasylko extensively colonized the territories southeast of Terebovlia by employing Turkic peoples (Berendeys, Torks, and Pechenegs), and he annexed Ponyzia, thereby securing it against nomadic raiders. Halych gained importance as a political and economic center; other important cities and fortresses included Terebovlia, Mykulyn (now Mykulyntsi), Chern (now Chernivtsi), Vasyliv, Onut, Kuchelemyn, Bakota, Ushytsia, and Kalius. After Vasylko's death in 1124, Halych principality seceded, and by 1141 Terebovlia principality had become a part of the Principality of *Galicia-Volhynia. After the Rostyslavych dynasty died out, it was briefly an appanage principality under Iziaslav Volodymyrovych.

**Terek region** (Tershchyna). A historical-geographic land located in eastern Subcaucasia, between the Kuban to the west, the Stavropol region to the northwest, Dagestan to the east, and the Caucasus Mountains to the south. In a specific sense the Terek region (about 30,000 sq km) was the land of the Terek Cossack Army, which was settled mostly by Russians and Ukrainians and constitutes one of the furthest reaches of the mixed Russian-Ukrainian ethnographic territory. In a broader sense the term refers to the entire former Terek oblast (72,900 sq km).

The southern part of the Terek region is occupied by the Caucasus Mountains. North of the mountains is a belt of steppe foothills, now almost completely plowed for crops. Beyond it is the semidesert Terek-Kuma Lowland. The mountains and a narrow portion of the adjoining foothills are settled by the Caucasian mountain peoples (the Chechens, the Ingushes, the Kabardians, and the Ossetes). The remaining part of the foothills and much of the Terek-Kuma Lowland are settled by Russians and Ukrainians. Some of the eastern parts of the Terek-Kuma Lowland are settled by the peoples of Dagestan (the Avars, the Dargins, the Nogays, and the Kumyks).

The colonization of the sparsely settled steppe portions of the Terek region by Slavs began at the end of the 15th century, when runaway serfs and frontier Cossacks from Riazan (Upper Don) established themselves along the Terek River and formed the Grebensk Cossacks. The Cossacks, however, were unable to deal decisively with the local populations, and the region remained a battleground for hundreds of years. The ongoing struggle against the mountain peoples finally ended in the 1860s with their subjugation. At the same time the emancipation of the serfs in the Russian Empire (1861) brought with it a flood of Slavic settlers to the sparsely settled region, most notably from Ukraine.

According to the census of 1897 Terek oblast had a population of 934,000. Its ethnic composition was as follows: 271,000 (29 percent) Russians, 42,000 (4.5 percent) Ukrainians, 375,000 (40.2 percent) Caucasian mountain peoples, 97,000 (10.4 percent) Ossetes, 98,000 (10.5 percent) Nogays (Tatars), 12,000 (1.3 percent) Armenians, 9,000 (1 percent) Germans, and 30,000 (3.2 percent) others. Of the townships of Terek oblast Piatigorsk had the largest number of Ukrainians (25,000, or 13.8 percent). The assumption is that the census understated the number of Ukrainians because the Cossacks, who numbered 170,000 and made up 18.2 percent of the total population or 53 percent of all the 'Russians' in 1897, in fact included large numbers of

Ukrainians. The population of the Terek region grew continuously and by 1916 had reached 1,360,000 (an increase of 46 percent over 1897), among whom there were 255,000 Cossacks (18.8 percent of the population).

The history of the Terek region in 1917–20 resembles that of the Don and Kuban regions. Like the other two regions, the Terek expressed its desire for autonomy within a federated Russian republic and for close co-operation with the two other Cossack armies. Late in 1917, following the October Revolution, the newly established governments of the Terek army and the Union of the United Caucasian Mountain Peoples established a Terek-Dagestan government, with its seat in Vladikavkaz. As an opposing measure the Terek Soviet Republic within the RSFSR was established in March 1918. Ukrainians in the Terek region did not undertake any pro-Ukrainian political activity during the struggle for independence in Ukraine (1918–20).

The Soviet government split the Terek region into the predominantly Slavic Terek gubernia and the Mountain Peoples' ASSR (which was subsequently subdivided into a number of autonomous oblasts and ASSRs). During the period 1924–9 Terek gubernia was divided into Terek and Sunzha okrugs, which formed part of a much larger administrative unit known as North Caucasian krai. Terek as an administrative-territorial unit thereupon ceased to exist. The former Terek oblast now occupies the southern part of Stavropol krai and the following ARs: Kabardino-Balkaria, North Ossetia, Checheno-Ingushetia, and the northern part of Daghestan.

The Soviet administrative structure precluded the calculation of precise numbers of Ukrainians in the Terek region as given by the post–Second World War censuses. An approximation by I. Stebelsky indicates 41,300 in 1970 and 43,100 in 1979 in the ARs – about the same number as recorded for that part of the Terek region in 1926. Most of the Ukrainians now living in those areas, however, are urban and probably represent a subsequent immigration to assume administrative and industrial positions in the cities (rather than being the descendants of the earlier Ukrainian settlers). Of the 56,600 Ukrainians indicated by the 1979 census as living in Stavropol krai (53,500 in 1970), perhaps one-third (some 20,000) are concentrated in the Piatigorsk area, which was part of Terek oblast before 1920 and hence also part of the Terek region. Altogether some 60,000 Ukrainians, mostly newcomers, have been identified by the 1970 and 1979 censuses in the Terek region, only one-half the number counted in 1926.

BIBLIOGRAPHY

Fadeev, A. *Ocherki ekonomicheskogo razvitiia stepnogo Peredkavkaz'ia v doreformennyi period* (Moscow 1957)
*Severnyi Kavkaz* (Moscow 1957)
*Don i stepnoe Predkavkaz'e: XVIII–pervaia polovina XIX v.*, 2 vols (Rostov-na-Donu 1977)

V. Kubijovyč, I. Stebelsky

**Terekh, Oleksandr** [Terex], b 8 December 1928 in Kiev. Translator. He graduated from Kiev University (1952) and has worked in Kiev as a book editor, English teacher, and section editor of *Vsesvit*. He has translated into Ukrainian R. Bradbury's *Martian Chronicles* (1962), R.M. Ballantyne's *Coral Island* (1966), J. Galsworthy's *The Forsyte Saga* (1975), J.F. Cooper's *The Deerslayer*, and other English and American works (eg, by J. Joyce, J.D. Salinger, and K. Amis).

Yosyp Terelia

*Terem* (cover design by Jacques Hnizdovsky)

**Terelia, Yosyp** [Terelja, Josyp], b 27 October 1943 in Transcarpathia. Dissident and political prisoner. He was first sentenced to four years in Uzhhorod prison in 1962. For repeated escapes or attempts at escape, in 1963, 1965, 1967, and 1969, he was sentenced to additional terms of five, seven, eight, and three years, respectively, in labor camps in the Mordovian ASSR and in the Vladimir prison near Moscow. He was 'diagnosed' as mentally ill in 1972 and incarcerated in psychiatric prisons in Berehove, Sychevka, Cheliabinsk, Vinnytsia, and Dnipropetrovske. In the camps and prisons he was brutally abused. In 1976 he wrote an open letter protesting his and other inmates' treatment to the KGB chief, Yu. Andropov, which was published as *Notes from a Madhouse* (1977) in the United States. After being released in 1980, he returned to Transcarpathia and became active in the clandestine Ukrainian Catholic church. In September 1982 he founded and headed the Initiative Group in the Defense of the Rights of the Faithful and the Church in Ukraine, for which he was sentenced to a year in prison. In 1984 he renounced his Soviet citizenship and began publishing *\*Khronika Katolyts'koï tserkvy na Ukraïni*. He was rearrested in February 1985, and sentenced in August to seven years in labor camps in Perm oblast and five years' exile. In the spring of 1987, however, he was released, and in September allowed to emigrate to Canada with his family. In Canada he has published the journal *Khrest*.

O. Zinkevych

**Terem** (Tower). An irregular illustrated cultural serial published from 1962 to 1975 in Detroit by the Institute of Ukrainian Culture, and since 1979 in Warren, Michigan, by the Association for the Advancement of Ukrainian Culture. By 1990, 10 issues had appeared. The chief editor has been Yu. \*Tys. Each issue of *Terem* has been devoted to a specific subject: the archeologist Ya. Pasternak (1962); postwar modernist literature (1966); the artists M. Dmytrenko (1968), J. Hnizdovsky (1975), and L. Hutsaliuk (1981); the writers B. Nyzhankivsky (1971), V. Barka (1979), Z. Tarnavsky (1982), and H. Luzhnytsky (1984); and the artist and writer S. Hordynsky (1990).

**Teren, Teodor.** See Yuskiv-Teren, Teodor.

**Terenozhkin, Aleksei** [Terenožkin, Aleksej], b 26 November 1907 in Nikolaevsk (now Pugachev), Saratov oblast, Russia, d 19 May 1981 in Kiev. Russian archeologist. A graduate of Moscow University (1930), from 1949 he headed a department of the AN URSR (now ANU) Institute of Archeology. He established a workable chronology of development in the Scythian and pre-Scythian eras. His major works include *Predskifskii period na dneprovskom Pravoberezh'e* (The Pre-Scythian Period on the Dnieper's Right Bank, 1961) and *Kimmeriitsy* (The Cimmerians, 1976); he was also an editor and coauthor of *Akheolohiia Ukraïns'koï RSR* (Archeology of the Ukrainian SSR, 3 vols, 1971–5).

**Tereshchenko** [Tereščenko]. A Cossack-burgher family in the Hlukhiv region that became ennobled in 1870. The founder of the line was Artem Tereshchenko (d 1873), who made a fortune during the Crimean War by supplying the army with bread and boat timber and then turned to sugar refining and other manufacturing industries. After the agrarian reform of 1861 he and his sons, Mykola, Fedir, and Semen, accumulated estates in Ukraine and Russia. By the turn of the century they owned 140,000 desiatins (approx 153,000 ha) and were among the largest landowners in the Russian Empire. In 1911–12 they also owned 10 large sugar refineries. Mykola Tereshchenko (1820–1903) and his sons, Ivan and Oleksander \*Tereshchenko, were well-known patrons of the arts; Mykola was a financial supporter of the Kiev and Hlukhiv art museums, and Ivan supported the Kiev Drawing School. Mykola's collections later formed the basis of the Ukrainian and Russian art museums in Kiev. His daughter, Varvara, and her husband, B. \*Khanenko, financed the Museum of Western European Art in Kiev. She also promoted artisanship and organized embroidery workshops in the Kiev region. Mykola's grandson, Mykhailo Tereshchenko (1888–1956), was a prominent figure in Russian politics. He was a member of the Fourth State Duma, chairman of the War Industry Committee in Kiev (1915–17), minister of finance (March–May 1917) and of foreign affairs (May–October 1917) in the Provisional Government, and a participant in negotiations with the Central Rada. After the October Revolution of 1917 he emigrated to Monaco.

A. Zhukovsky

**Tereshchenko, Kalenyk** [Tereščenko], b 11 August 1879 in Popivka, Zvenyhorodka county, Kiev gubernia, d 3 June 1969 in Zvenyhorodka, Cherkasy oblast. Sculptor. After graduating from the Shtiglits School of Technical Drawing in St Petersburg (1908) he worked in V. Beklemishev's studio (1908–14) and took part in decorating the tsar's palaces in Peterhof and Tsarskoe Selo. He designed busts for the monuments to T. Shevchenko at Shevchenko's grave in Kaniv (1923), and in Shpola (1926), Moryntsi (1927), and Kyrylivka (now Shevchenkove, 1930).

**Tereshchenko, Marko** [Tereščenko], b 19 January 1894 in Kovalykha, near Smila, Cherkasy county, Kiev gubernia, d 18 August 1982 in Kharkiv. Stage and film director and actor. He completed study at the Lysenko Music and Drama School (1914) and then worked as an actor in Molodyi Teatr (1916–19), founded and led Tsentrostudiia (later the \*Mykhailychenko Theater, 1921–5), and was artistic director of the Odessa Ukrainian Drama Theater (1925–7, 1929–31), the Kharkiv Theater of the Revolution

Marko Tereshchenko          Bishop Kyrylo Terletsky

(1931–5), and the Ternopil Franko Ukrainian Drama Theater (1940–1). He also worked as guest director in Kiev, Chernihiv, Poltava, and Okhtyrka theaters (1935–40). In 1927 he directed the films *Mykola Dzheria* and *Navzdohin za doleiu* (Pursuing Fate). He wrote *Mystetstvo diistva* (The Art of the Performance, 1921) and *Kriz' let chasu* (Through the Flight of Time, 1976) and taught in the Kharkiv Institute of Culture (1945–76).

**Tereshchenko, Mykola** [Tereščenko], b 13 September 1898 in Shcherbynivka, Zolotonosha county, Poltava gubernia, d 30 May 1966 in Kiev. Poet and translator. His first published work appeared in 1918. He belonged to Komunkult and the All-Ukrainian Association of Proletarian Writers and edited the journal *Zhyttia i revoliutsiia*. His collections of poetry include *Laboratoriia* (The Laboratory, 1924), *Kraïna roboty* (The Land of Work, 1928), *Ryshtuvannia* (Scaffolding, 1930), *Poryv* (Impulse, 1932), *Poemy* (Poems, 1935), *Divchyna z Ukraïny* (A Girl from Ukraine, 1942), *Verba riasna* (The Fulsome Willow, 1943), *Uzhynok* (Reaped Grain, 1946) and *Sertse liuds'ke* (The Human Heart, 1962). He translated verse, particularly from French (J.-P. Béranger, V. Hugo, E. Poitier, L. Aragon, and others) and published the anthology *Suzir'ia frantsuz'koï poeziï* (A Constellation of French Poetry, 2 vols, 1971). He also translated the works of A. Mickiewicz and of Russian and Belarusian poets.

**Tereshchenko, Oleksander** [Tereščenko], b 1806 in Zinkiv, Poltava gubernia, d 1865. Ethnographer and archeologist. He was an associate of the Russian Imperial Archeological Commission and a collector of ethnographic materials. His chief works, *Byt russkogo naroda* (The Folkways of the Russian People, 1848) and *Ocherki Novorossiiskogo kraia* (Sketches of New Russia, 1854), contain much information about Ukrainians. He wrote one of the first biographies of I. *Kotliarevsky (published in *Osnova*, 2 [1861]). His study of the burial mounds and stone *baby* in Katerynoslav and Kherson gubernias was published posthumously by the Society of History and Antiquity Lovers.

**Tereverko, Yurii** (Heorhii), b 5 May 1888 in Vilshana Slobidka, Uman county, Kiev gubernia, d 3 February 1912 in Tbilisi, Georgia. Pilot. A pioneer in gliding (see *Soaring or gliding) in the Russian Empire, in the years 1910–12 he made numerous flights in gliders he built himself, set a flight record (1 min, 33 sec), and was the first to fly with a passenger. He died from injuries sustained in a crash.

**Terletsky, Ipolit Volodymyr** [Terlec'kyj] (Terlecki, Hipolit Vladimir), b 1808 in Starokostiantyniv county, Volhynia gubernia, d 17 January 1888 in Odessa. Religious and Pan-Slavist figure. A scion of a Polonized noble family in Volhynia, he studied at the Kremianets Lyceum and Vilnius University (1825–30). After being expelled with other émigrés in 1836, he settled in Montpellier, France, and became part of Prince A. Czartoryski's Hôtel Lambert circle in Paris. In 1839 Terletsky moved to Rome, where he joined the Polish Resurrectionist Order, was ordained a priest in 1842, and obtained a doctorate in theology in 1843. In 1846 and 1848 he submitted memorandums to Pope Pius IX elaborating a program for unification of the Catholic and Orthodox churches, which included a proposal for the creation of a Ukrainian patriarchate. To that end and with Pius's permission Terletsky became a Byzantine rite priest and initiated the creation of the Oriental Society for the Union of Churches (1847).

Terletsky published his anonymous historical and militant Catholic treatise *Słowo Rusina ku wszej braci szczepu słowiańskiego o rzeczach słowiańskich* (A Word of a Ruthenian to All the Brothers of the Slavic Branch about Matters Slavic, 1849). In it he developed the idea of a Slavic federation based on Christian-democratic principles, in which the Ukrainian nation would be an equal partner. In 1850 he became rector of SS Cyril and Methodius church, the first Byzantine rite church in Paris. With the support and participation of the archbishop of Paris he established the Oriental Society for the Union of All Christians of the East and an institute for the education of missionary priests. Having fallen out of favor with the Polish émigrés and the Vatican bureaucracy, in 1855 he closed down the institute and donated its books, archives, and possessions to the People's Home in Lviv.

In 1857 Terletsky moved to Lviv, but he was forced to leave by Gov A. Gołuchowski, and settled in Transcarpathia. There he entered the Basilian order, contributed occasionally to the Lviv newspaper *Slovo*, became a close friend of O. Dukhnovych, and served as hegumen of the Basilian monasteries in Malyi Bereznyi and Krasný Brod. In the 1860s he inspired a clerical movement to purge the Greek Catholic liturgy and rituals of Latin accretions, translated into Ukrainian a book of B. Zaleski's poems (1861) and T. à Kempis's *Imitation of Christ* (1862), and wrote in Ukrainian an account of his travels in the Near East (1861) and a collection of sermons (1862). He was arrested for his Pan-Slavist activities by the Hungarian authorities (1871) and, having been accused of spying for Russia, he was expelled in 1872. After being allowed to return to the Russian Empire he converted to Russian Orthodoxy, lived in St Michael's Golden-Domed Monastery in Kiev, and wrote in Russian a book about the rebirth of Ruthenian national consciousness in Hungarian-ruled Transcarpathia (1874). He then served as the private chaplain at Prince P. Demidov's estate near Florence (1874–9), and he lived from 1881 in Odessa as an archimandrite. His reminiscences were published posthumously in *Russkaia starina* (vols 63 [1889], 70–1 [1891]).

I.L. Rudnytsky

**Terletsky, Kyrylo** [Terlec'kyj], b ?, d 1607. Bishop. He was born into a Ukrainian gentry family and became Orthodox bishop of Pynske-Turiv (1572–85) and then Lutske-Ostrih (from 1585). He was a leading proponent of union with the Catholic church, and in 1595 he traveled to

Rome with I. Potii to negotiate the terms of a union agreement and to set forth the confession of faith. The following year Terletsky took part in the sobor that led to the proclamation of the Church Union of *Berestia, which formally established the Uniate church.

**Terletsky, Liubomyr** [Terlec'kyj, Ljubomyr], b 16 May 1922 in Skoviatyn, Borshchiv county, Galicia. Sculptor and medallionist. After serving a 10-year sentence in the Soviet Gulag for 'Ukrainian nationalism,' he returned to Lviv in 1957 and graduated from the Lviv Institute of Applied and Decorative Arts in 1966. Terletsky's sculptures and medallions are marked by vivid individual specificity, and combine classical tradition with elements of schematization and improvisation. In the 1960s, by choosing the chief designer of the Soviet space effort, S. *Korolov, as a subject of his sculptures and representing him and his rockets as distinctly Ukrainian Kievan warriors waiting to be launched, Terletsky ran afoul of his Soviet art mentors, and his work was removed from the Lviv Museum of Ukrainian Art. Only after executing 'patriotic' sculptures and medallions ('Soldier with Child,' 'The Great War for the Fatherland') was Terletsky again permitted to accept commissions for his sculptures. In the mid-1980s he became incapacitated by a serious chronic illness. His sculptures were readmitted to the Lviv Museum of Ukrainian Art only after the collapse of the USSR.

Markiian Terletsky          Omelian Terletsky

**Terletsky, Markiian** [Terlec'kyj, Markijan], b 1 November 1885 in Polniatychi, Jarosław county, Galicia, d 2 May 1963 in Bayside, New York. Pedagogue, community activist, and historian; brother of Omelian Terletsky. He taught in a gymnasium in Peremyshl in 1908–18. In 1923–6 he was a professor of ancient history at the Ukrainian Higher Pedagogical Institute in Prague, where he also served as vice-dean of the Faculty of History. After his return to Galicia he served as director of the *Ridna Shkola gymnasiums in Yavoriv and Stanyslaviv. In 1934–9 he was inspector of Ridna Shkola secondary schools. He was editor of the biweekly *Ridna shkola (1936–9). In 1940 he became director of the Ukrainian gymnasium in Jarosław, a post he held until 1944. He lived in the United States from 1952. Terletsky wrote a popular short history of Ukraine and various historical essays.

**Terletsky, Metodii** [Terlec'kyj, Metodij], b ? in Terlo, near Sambir, Galicia, d 1649. Uniate bishop. A Basilian hi-

eromonk in Kholm (to 1626), he completed a doctorate of divinity in Vienna and undertook missionary work in Transcarpathia and Croatia. As bishop of Kholm (1630–49) he sought to improve the educational standards of the clergy and established a seminary in Kholm. He was a fervent believer in the Church Union of *Berestia and devoted his energies to incorporating the remaining Orthodox Ukrainians into the union. In the 1640s he acted as an intermediary in discussions between the Orthodox metropolitan P. Mohyla and A. Kysil concerning the creation of a Kiev patriarchate in union with Rome.

**Terletsky, Omelian** [Terlec'kyj, Omeljan], b 2 December 1873 in Kramarivka, Jarosław county, Galicia, d 13 February 1958 in Lviv. Pedagogue and historian; full member of the Shevchenko Scientific Society from 1921; brother of M. Terletsky. He taught in gymnasiums in Ternopil and Chortkiv and at the Academic Gymnasium in Lviv. In conjunction with the *Union for the Liberation of Ukraine he worked among Ukrainians who had been captured by the Central Powers and were being held in Germany. He was a long-standing member of the executive of the *Ridna Shkola society (twice its head, 1923–4 and 1926–8), a member of the Lviv branch of the Prosvita society, and a member of the Teachers' Hromada in Lviv (acting head in 1923–4 and 1926–8). After the Second World War Terletsky worked at the Lviv branch of the Institute of Ukrainian History of the Academy of Sciences of the Ukrainian SSR and at Lviv University. He wrote works which were published in ZNTSh and various monographs, including *Politychni podiï na Halyts'kii Rusi v 1340* (Political Events of 1340 in Galician Rus', 1896), *Kozaky na Bilii Rusi 1654–56* (The Cossacks in Belarus, 1654–56, 1897), *Istoriia Ukraïns'koï hromady v Rashtati 1915–18* (History of the Ukrainian Community in Rastatt, 1915–18, 1919), *Istoriia Ukraïns'koï derzhavnosty* (History of Ukrainian Statehood, 2 vols, 1923–4), *Ukraïna zaborolom kul'tury i tsyvilizatsiï pered stepovykamy* (Ukraine as the Bastion of Culture and Civilization against the Peoples of the Steppe, 1930), and *Het'mans'ka Ukraïna i Zaporizhs'ka Sich* (The Hetman [State of] Ukraine and the Zaporozhian Sich, 1935).

**Terletsky, Ostap** [Terlec'kyj] (pseuds: V. Kistka, I. Zanevych, R. Mak), b 5 February 1850 in Nazirna, Kolomyia county, Galicia, d 22 July 1902 in Lviv. Civic and political leader, and literary scholar. A graduate of the humanities faculty at Lviv University (1872) and the law faculty at Vienna University (1883), he played a key role in the development of a populist socialist movement among Galician Ukrainians. In Vienna he served as president of the *Sich student society (1874–7) and was strongly influenced by the political ideals of M. Drahomanov and S. *Podolynsky, whom he helped to publish four influential socialist pamphlets in Ukrainian. He also wrote economic and political articles for the Ukrainian press, including a blistering attack on old-line Galician populists in *Pravda* (1874). He was arrested in 1877 along with I. Franko, M. Pavlyk, and others and convicted of membership in a secret society. Subsequently he devoted much of his energy to his law career and his literary research. He published several short surveys of 19th-century Galician Ukrainian literature and wrote economic and political articles. He aided a radical circle in Stanyslaviv in the mid-1880s and

Ostap Terletsky          Stefan Terlezki

became a founding member of the Ruthenian-Ukrainian Radical party in 1890.

**Terletsky, Sydir** [Terlec'kyj], b 7 June 1892 in Chernivtsi, Bukovyna, d 8 February 1953 in Bad Salzufleu, West Germany. Actor and stage director. He worked as an actor in the Ruska Besida Theater and the Lviv Ukrainian People's Theater under Y. Stadnyk (1911–14) and then led the Ukrainian Drama Theater at the People's House in Chernivtsi (1918–28) and acted in amateur theaters in Bukovyna (1928–39) and the Chernivtsi Oblast Ukrainian Music and Drama Theater (1940–1). He was arrested in August 1943 and sent to Nazi concentration camps in Auschwitz and Buchenwald. He was released in 1945.

**Terletsky, Teofil** [Terlec'kyj, Teofil'], b 1870 in Lviv, d 14 March 1902 in Munich. Graphic artist. After studying at the Cracow School of Fine Arts (1890–3) he moved to Munich. From there he contributed caricatures to Ukrainian, Polish, and German papers, such as *Zoria, Tygodnik ilustrowany, Jugend,* and *Fliegende Blätter.* His translations of I. Turgenev's prose poems were published in *Zoria.* He also did portrait studies (eg, a grandmother and a youth with a guitar) and the ink drawing *Burial of a Soldier* (1894). He died destitute, from tuberculosis.

**Terlezki, Stefan** [Terlec'kyj], b 29 October 1927 in Antonivka, Tovmach county, Galicia. Businessman and politician. Having emigrated to England after the Second World War, he graduated from the Cardiff College of Food Technology and Commerce (1952) and then became active in public affairs. He was a member of the Hotel and Catering Institute (1965–80) and the Welsh Tourist Council (1965–80) and press officer of the Cardiff Chamber of Commerce (1970–83). In 1973 he was chairman of the Keep Britain in Europe campaign. He was the Conservative representative of Cardiff West in the House of Commons (1983–7), the first British MP of Ukrainian origin. In 1992 he was appointed Commander of the Order of the British Empire for his political and public service.

**Terminology.** The set of words or expressions that have specific meanings in science, arts, or the professions. They differ from common words by their semantic precision. A special term is created in a language by (1) changing the meaning of a common word, (2) coining a neologism, or (3) borrowing a term from another language.

**To the 19th century.** The earliest extant source of Ukrainian terminology is the *Izbornik* of Sviatoslav (1073). It contained Church Slavonic glosses of little-understood words (mainly calques from the Greek) and 27 literary figures and tropes found in the Scriptures and Georgios Choiroboschos' article on images. *Ruskaia Pravda* shows that legal terminology was highly developed in 11th- to 12th-century Rus'. *Adelphotes* (1591) systematically used Greek calques in the Ukrainian redaction of Church Slavonic for Greek grammatical and literary-stylistic terms. Its terminology set the standard for the terminology used in the Slavonic grammars of L. *Zyzanii* (1596) and M. *Smotrytsky* (1619). The earliest examples of Ukrainian medical terms are found in a preserved fragment from a late 16th-century pharmacotherapeutic tract, and scientific terms can be found in a textbook translated from the German, *Lutsidarii* (1636). I. Velychkovsky was the first to explain terms of figurative versification in his collection *Mleko* (Milk, 1691).

**1850–1914.** Ukraine's national rebirth in the 19th century and the concurrent growth of science and technology made Ukrainians aware of the need for Ukrainian terminology. Under Polish, Russian, Austrian, and Hungarian rule the scientific and technical educational institutions in Ukraine used either Polish, Russian, or German. In the Austrian Empire, where there were fewer restrictions on the Ukrainian language, the Ukrainian members (Ya. Holovatsky, H. Shashkevych, Yu. Vyslobotsky) of a government commission for the compilation of Slavic legal terminology published *Juridisch-politische Terminologie für die slavischen Sprachen Österreichs ... Deutsch-ruthenische Separatausgabe* (17,000 words, 1851). I. Verkhratsky collected popular Ukrainian natural-science nomenclature and published it with equivalent Latin and German terms in seven fascicles (Lviv, 1864, 1869, 1872, 1879, 1908). He also prepared a list of Ukrainian botanical terms (1892). A new German-Ukrainian legal and administrative dictionary was compiled by K. Levytsky (1893; 2nd edn 1920). It contained terms based on the folk vernacular, neologisms, and borrowings from other Slavic languages. In 1894 the Shevchenko Scientific Society (NTSh) appealed to the reading public to collect popular terms in 'the trades, the cottage industry, agriculture, commerce, and folk medicine' because 'scholars ... frequently are forced to borrow them from other Slavic languages or to create them sometimes ... very unsuccessfully and counter to the spirit of our language.' Beginning in the mid-1890s, materials on Ukrainian terms in mathematics, physics, and chemistry (by V. Levytsky, 1895–6, 1903), geography (S. Rudnytsky, 1908, 1913), mineralogy (I. Verkhratsky, 1909), and botany (M. Melnyk, 1922) were published in NTSh serials. I. Zatserkovny published a list of legal terms in *Chasopys' pravnycha i ekonomichna* (1902, nos 4–5).

In the Russian Empire, M. Levchenko, the author of the first Russian-Ukrainian dictionary (1874), first wrote of the need to develop Ukrainian terminology on the basis of the folk vernacular and provided a glossary of his translations of several dozen internationally used terms (*Osnova,* no. 7 [1861]). In reply, P. Yefymenko added a number of new terms (*Osnova,* no. 8 [1862]). Because of tsarist restrictions on the use of the Ukrainian language (see *Ems Ukase* and P. *Valuev*), only a few contributions to Ukrainian terminology were published: a glossary of vernacular plant names by O. Rohovych and a Latin-Ukrainian list of 1,000 plant names by F. Vovk in *Zapiski Iugo-zapadnago otdela Russkago geograficheskago obshchestva* (1873); a list of agricultural terms by S. Vengrzhynovsky in *Kievskaia starina* (1898, nos 7–8); and V. Vasylenko's dictionary of technical (handicrafts and agriculture) terms from Poltava gubernia (Kharkiv 1902). After the Revolution of 1905, conditions improved with the lifting of restrictions. *Zapysky Ukraïns'koho naukovoho tovarystva u Kyievi* (18 vols, 1908–18) provided terminological indexes to every study published therein. Ukrainian student circles or commissions at the Kiev Polytechnical Institute, the Moscow Agricultural Institute, and the Kvitka-Osnovianenko Society in Kharkiv began compiling terminological materials from literary and folk sources. In 1913 the Ukrainian Scientific Society in Kiev (UNTK) assumed the task of co-ordinating this work and received the materials – several thousand cards of agricultural, natural-science, and technical terms – collected by the circles and commissions.

**1917–20.** The First World War interrupted the research on terminology. In January 1917 O. Yanata, predicting the imminent opening of Ukrainian schools, called upon linguists to devise a terminology based on the popular vernacular and literary materials before technical language became polluted with artificial terms. In March 1917 M. Hrushevsky spoke out against extreme 'ethnographism' and urged that previous work in the field be used in preparing new educational and popular scientific literature. That task was taken up jointly by the newly created Society for School Education and the UNTK, and in 1917 the first short drafts of geographic, grammatical, arithmetical, geometric, and algebraic dictionaries were published. At the time at least 12 terminological dictionaries were published by various institutions and societies in Kiev, Poltava, Kobeliaky, Mohyliv-Podilskyi, Hadiache, Vinnytsia, and Kamianets-Podilskyi. The most important ones were I. Zhyhadlo's short Russian-Ukrainian legal dictionary (3 edns, 1917–19), L. Padalka's Russian-Ukrainian administrative dictionary (2 edns, 1917–18), and V. Leontovych and O. Yefymov's Russian-Ukrainian legal dictionary (2 edns, 1917, 1919).

In the autumn of 1917 the UNR General Secretariat of Education and Ministry of Justice asked O. *Kurylo of the UNTK Terminological Commission to prepare terminological glossaries for schools and the courts. In 1918 Kurylo published a brief dictionary of Ukrainian medical terms in *Ukraïns'ki medychni visty* and, together with H. Kholodny, a draft dictionary of Ukrainian physics terms. The VUAN Russian-Ukrainian legal dictionary edited by A. Krymsky (1926) was based on Kurylo's materials. In August 1918 the Terminological Commission of the UNTK and in 1919 the VUAN Orthographic and Terminological Commission were established. By the end of 1920 the UNTK commission had collected over 200,000 cards of materials from published sources. In 1917–19 many small dictionaries of mathematical, physics, chemical, medical, natural-science, zoological, geographic, and meteorological terms appeared, but most of them were inadequately and amateurishly prepared.

**Soviet Ukraine.** In the first three years of Soviet rule only three terminological dictionaries were published, the most important of which was M. Halyn's Russian-Ukrainian medical dictionary (1920). From 1921 the VUAN *Insti-

tute of the Ukrainian Scientific Language (IUNM) under the direction of A. *Krymsky and, later, H. *Kholodny co-ordinated all terminological work in Soviet Ukraine with the aim of developing a national terminology based on the vernacular and neologisms. In 1923–30 the IUNM published 20 of the planned 34 Ukrainian-Russian terminological dictionaries (with German and French or Latin equivalents), many of them in association with the NTSh. The most important of them were in the fields of chemistry (O. Kurylo, 1923), geology (P. Tutkovsky, 1923), anatomy (Latin-Ukrainian, ed F. Tseshkivsky and O. Cherniakhivsky, 1925), mechanics (T. Sekunda, 1925), mathematics (F. Kalynovych, 1925), ornithology (M. Sharleman, 1925), pathology (Latin-Ukrainian, O. Korchak-Chepurkivsky, 1926), theoretical mechanics (F. Kalynovych, 1926), technical sciences (M. and L. Darmoros, 1926; I. Sheludko and T. Sadovsky, 1928), vertebrate zoology (M. Sharleman and K. Tatarko, 1927), manufacturing (F. Lokhanko, 1928), natural science (Kh. Polonsky, 1928), botany (Latin-Ukrainian, O. Yanata and N. Osadtsa, 1928), public services (K. Turkalo and V. Favorsky, 1928), electrical engineering (I. Sheludko, 1928), invertebrate zoology (I. Shchoholiv and S. Panochini, 1928), mechanics (ed V. Favorsky, 1929), administration (M. Doroshenko et al, 1930), construction (S. Bulda, 1930), music (1930), and surveying (Yu. Trykhvyliv and I. Zubkov, 1930).

In 1930 the leading figures at the IUNM were implicated in the Stalinist show trial of the *Union for the Liberation of Ukraine, and the IUNM was dissolved. Its surviving associates were transferred to the Division (later Sector) of Terminology and Nomenclature at the newly created VUAN Institute of Linguistics, where by 1933 they managed to publish 10 terminological dictionaries in fields such as mining (P. Vasylenko and I. Sheludko, 1931), economics (H. Kryvchenko and V. Ihnatovych, 1931), human geography (A. Nosov, 1931), astronomy (F. Kalynovych and H. Kholodny, 1931), transportation and communications (I. Sheludko, 1932), physics (ed V. Favorsky, 1932), botany (V. Vovchanetsky and Ya. Lepchenko, 1932), and agriculture (1933).

During the early Soviet period about 70 terminological dictionaries came out in Ukraine, including medical (V. Kysilov, 1928; V. Kramarevsky et al, 1931), financial (1924), legal (S. Veretka and M. Matviievsky, 1926; ed A. Krymsky et al, over 67,000 words, 1926), accounting and statistical (A. Girzhel and D. Rin, 1926), transportation (V. Zhurkovsky, 1926), administration (Ye. Linkevych et al, 1926), pedagogical, psychological, and school administration (P. Horetsky, 1928), military (S. and O. Yakubsky, 1928), agricultural (P. Sabaldyr, 1931), manufacturing (I. Sheludko, 1931), and biological (S. Panochini, 1931) dictionaries. After P. *Postyshev's arrival in Ukraine in the spring of 1933, the Institute of Linguistics was purged. The surviving linguists were ordered to eliminate the puristic elements (see *Purism) from already-published dictionaries and to replace them with words common to both Ukrainian and Russian. Thus, five terminological bulletins (1934–5) with corrections were issued. Also, 21 Russian-Ukrainian terminological dictionaries that were being prepared or printed at the time had to be vetted. Only I. Kyrychenko's medical dictionary (1936) was published by the institute. With the terror of 1936–7, terminological work at the institute ceased for two decades. From late 1933 to 1935 ten Russified terminological dictionaries for elementary and secondary schools and in 1948 M. Knipovych's Ukrainian-Russian medical dictionary were published outside the institute.

Terminological research was resumed only in 1957 with the creation of a Dictionary Commission at the AN URSR (now ANU) Institute of Linguistics. Since then over 20 specialized Russian-Ukrainian dictionaries have been published, mostly by the academy, in fields such as geology (S. Holovashchuk and I. Sokolovsky, 1959), machine science and machine building (V. Khilchevsky and V. Shashlov, 1959), physics (V. Heichenko et al, 1959), mining (O. Kovshulia et al, 1959), chemistry (Ye. Nekriach et al, 1959), hydraulics (H. Shvets et al, 1960), mathematics (F. Hudymenko et al, 1960), medicine (Latin-Ukrainian-Russian, H. Kazier et al, 1960), engineering (M. Matiiko et al, 1961), electrical engineering (Yu. Velychko et al, 1961), botany (D. Afanasiev et al, 1962), thermal and gas engineering (I. Sheludko et al, 1962), agriculture (A. Biloshtan et al, 1963), physiology (B. Yesypenko and M. Kondratovych, 1963), veterinary science (Ya. Yarema et al, 1964), welding (A. Potapievsky, 1964), social sciences and economics (S. Vorobiova and T. Molodid, 1966; rev edn 1976), metallurgy (V. Chekhranov and V. Meleshko, 1970), anatomy (M. Netliukh, 1972), sports (N. Firsel and V. Kaliuzhnaia, 1973), mineralogy (Ukrainian-Russian-English, Ye. Lazarenko and O. Vynar, 1975), and law (ed B. Babii, 1985). The puristic approach of the 1920s had been abandoned, and the dictionaries were based on the Russian language. Only in exceptional cases were all synonyms for a term provided, and then one of them – the one identical or similar to the Russian – recommended.

**Outside Soviet Ukraine.** In interwar Galicia, only one terminological dictionary – of musical terms, by Z. Lysko (1933) – was produced. In Cracow the Polish scholar S. Makowiecki published a major Latin-Ukrainian botanical dictionary (1936). In the interwar period émigré scholars affiliated with the *Ukrainian Husbandry Academy in Poděbrady, Bohemia, and the *Ukrainian Scientific institutes in Warsaw and Berlin prepared and published several specialized dictionaries in fields such as the strength of materials (S. Ryndyk, Prague 1924), mathematics (Ukrainian-Russian-German, M. Chaikovsky, Berlin 1924), medicine (Latin-Ukrainian, M. Halyn, Prague 1926; German-Ukrainian, P. Oesterle with Z. Kuzelia, Berlin 1944), anatomy (Ye. Lukasevych, Warsaw 1926), agriculture (Russian-Ukrainian, ed Ye. Chykalenko, Poděbrady 1927), forestry (German-Ukrainian, ed Ye. Chykalenko, Poděbrady 1931), aeronautics (German-Ukrainian, I. Ilnytsky-Zankovych, Berlin 1939), and military science (German-Ukrainian, I. Ilnytsky-Zankovych, 20,000 words, Berlin 1939). Their work has been continued since the war in the United States by the *Research Society for Ukrainian Terminology and the *Ukrainian Terminological Center of America, and in Europe by the *Ukrainian Technical and Husbandry Institute. The work of these institutions resulted in such publications as an *American-Ukrainian Nautical Dictionary* (W. Stepankowsky, 1953); *A Selective English-Ukrainian Dictionary of Science, Technology, and Modern Living* (A. Wowk, 1982); the *English-Ukrainian Dictionary of Color Names and Color Science* (A. Wowk, ed B. Struminsky, 1986); a German-Ukrainian electrotechnical dictionary (M. Savchuk, 1981); and the reprints of M. Halyn's medical dictionary (1969), A. Krymsky's legal dictionary of 1926 (1984), M. Knipovych's medical dictionary (1985),

and P. Oesterle's German-Ukrainian medical dictionary (1986).

(See also *Lexicography.)

BIBLIOGRAPHY

Kholodnyi, H. 'Do istoriï orhanizatsiï terminolohichnoï spravy na Ukraïni,' *Visnyk Instytutu ukraïns'koï naukovoï movy*, no. 1 (1928)

Kalynovych, F. 'Pryrodnychyi viddil IUNM: Korotkyi ohliad ioho roboty za chas ioho isnuvannia,' ibid, no. 2 (1930)

Pezhans'kyi, M. 'Vklad inzheneriv Zakhidn'oï Ukraïny v ukraïns'ku terminolohiiu ta ohliad suchasnoho ïi stanu,' in *Ukraïns'kyi inzhener* (New York 1969)

Smal'-Stots'kyi, R. *Ukraïns'ka mova v Soviets'kii Ukraïni*, 2nd edn (New York–Toronto–Sydney–Paris 1969)

Kryzhanivs'ka, A. (ed). *Sklad i struktura terminolohichnoï leksyky ukraïns'koï movy* (Kiev 1984)

Kryzhanovskaia [Kryzhanivs'ka], A. *Sopostavitel'noe issledovanie terminologii sovremennykh russkogo i ukrainskogo iazykov: Problemy unifikatsii i integratsii* (Kiev 1985)

Musaev, K. (ed). *Razvitie terminologii na iazykakh soiuznykh respublik SSSR: Obshchaia problematika. Terminologiia na russkom, ukrainskom i belorusskom iazykakh* (Moscow 1986)

R. Senkus, V. Swoboda

**Ternivka.** V-17. A city (1969 pop 13,200) on the Ternivka River in Pavlohrad raion, Dnipropetrovske oblast. A village was founded at the site in 1775. The first mine was opened there in 1964. In 1976 the village was granted city status. Today it has four coal mines and a coal-enrichment factory.

**Ternivka.** VI-13. A town smt (1986 pop 9,300) on the Inhul River in Mykolaiv oblast, 9 km from Mykolaiv, under the administration of its city council. The first houses at the site were built in 1791–2 by the Russian navy for its shipbuilding workers. In 1801 some Bulgarian refugees settled there and developed grain and fruit farming. In 1949 the village attained smt status. Today most of its residents work in Mykolaiv.

Ternopil

**Ternopil** [Ternopil']. IV-6. A city (1990 pop 212,000) on the left bank of the Seret River and a raion center and the capital of Ternopil oblast. In 1540 the Polish magnate J. Tarnowski built a fortress there against Tatar attacks, and in 1548 the town was granted the rights of *Magdeburg law. In 1570 it became the property of Prince K. Ostrozky, who set up a hospital foundation and a church brotherhood. Subsequently it was owned by other magnates. In spite of frequent Tatar attacks (1544, 1575, 1589, 1618, 1672, 1694) Ternopil developed as a manufacturing and trading center. In 1648 and 1655 it was captured by B. Khmelnytsky's army. In 1675 the Turks dismantled its fortifications. By 1672 Ternopil had a population of 2,400, composed of Ukrainians, Jews, and Poles (mostly soldiers of the garrison). The Jews increased in number steadily and gained control of the trade; they pushed the Ukrainian burghers into the suburbs and *khutory* outside the town. In the 17th century there were three Orthodox churches, a Catholic church, and several synagogues in Ternopil. In the 18th century, although the Tatar and Turkish attacks had ceased and there was relative calm, the town's, and Podilia's, economy declined. The Confederation of *Bar inflicted widespread suffering, and a cholera epidemic in 1770 took a heavy toll (40 percent of the population).

In 1772 Ternopil was annexed by Austria and was chosen as an administrative center of a circle. In 1809–15 it was held by Russia. By the mid-19th century it had become the largest city of Galician Podilia, mainly because of its trade in farm products and the transit trade between the Russian Empire and Europe. The construction of a railway line to Pidvolochyske in 1870 strengthened Ternopil's position as a commercial center. Its population grew steadily, from 10,200 in 1817 to 20,100 in 1869, 30,415 in 1900, and 35,200 in 1914. It was one of the wealthier and cleaner cities in Galicia.

At the beginning of the 20th century there were five secondary schools in Ternopil, including a state gymnasium (est 1898) in which Ukrainian was the language of instruction (principals, O. Kalytovsky and O. Savytsky). It was the only major Galician city in which Ukrainians outnumbered the Poles and Ukrainian burghers had attained substantial wealth and influence. In 1900, 28.3 percent of Ternopil's residents were Ukrainian, 27.1 percent were Polish, and 44.3 percent were Jewish. In the 1860s the Ukrainian national movement began there under the leadership of O. *Barvinsky and V. *Luchakovsky. The newspapers *Podil's'ke slovo* (1909–12) and *Podil's'kyi holos* (1904–8) were published there. Under the Russian occupation of Ternopil (August 1914 to July 1917) all Ukrainian public life was suspended. Only in 1916 did the Russian authorities permit the Ternopilski Teatralni Vechory theater to open. Then they allowed Ukrainian to be introduced in the schools. After the February Revolution of 1917 Ukrainian cultural and political life in Ternopil revived quickly. Association with Galician Ukrainians re-

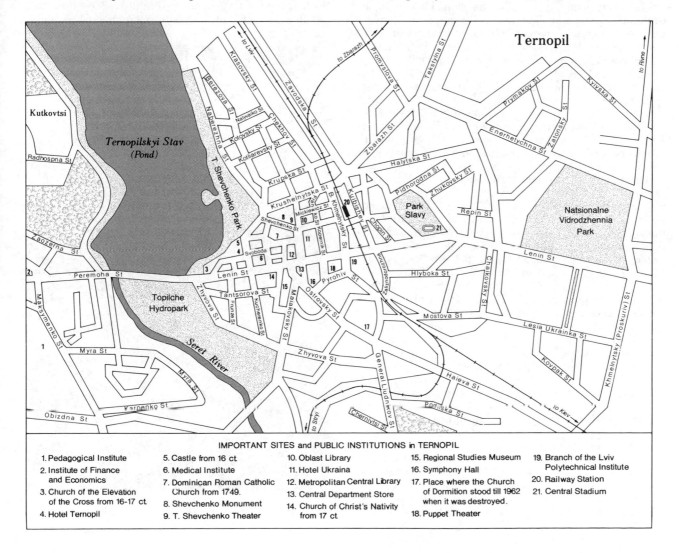

**IMPORTANT SITES and PUBLIC INSTITUTIONS in TERNOPIL**

1. Pedagogical Institute
2. Institute of Finance and Economics
3. Church of the Elevation of the Cross from 16-17 ct.
4. Hotel Ternopil
5. Castle from 16 ct.
6. Medical Institute
7. Dominican Roman Catholic Church from 1749.
8. Shevchenko Monument
9. T. Shevchenko Theater
10. Oblast Library
11. Hotel Ukraina
12. Metropolitan Central Library
13. Central Department Store
14. Church of Christ's Nativity from 17 ct.
15. Regional Studies Museum
16. Symphony Hall
17. Place where the Church of Dormition stood till 1962 when it was destroyed.
18. Puppet Theater
19. Branch of the Lviv Polytechnical Institute
20. Railway Station
21. Central Stadium

sulted in a national awakening among the Ukrainian officers of the Russian army stationed in the area.

From 1 November 1918 until July 1919 Ternopil was part of the Western Ukrainian National Republic, and from 21 November 1918 to 2 January 1919 it served as the republic's provisional capital. In June 1919 the Ukrainian and Polish armies fought for control of the city. Except for an interval (26 July to 20 September 1920) when it was held by Soviet forces and served as the base of the Galician Revolutionary Committee, Ternopil remained under Polish control until September 1939. The sealing of the eastern border reduced trade and hurt the city's economy, although Ternopil became the administrative center of a voivodeship. Its population grew slowly, from 30,900 in 1921 to 34,000 in 1931. As a Polish administrative center the city served as the base of a concerted Polonization campaign, which included measures such as the introduction of Polish colonies in Podilia, inducements to religious conversion, the closing of Ukrainian schools (Ternopil gymnasium in 1930), and organized violence (see *Pacification). The campaign resulted in greater changes in Ternopil's national profile than in that of other Galician towns: by 1939, 39.7 percent of the city's 37,500 residents were Poles, 39.3 percent were Jews, and only 19.2 percent were Ukrainians. Nevertheless, Ternopil remained the largest Ukrainian center in Podilia. It had a Ukrainian Catholic parish, four churches, a Redemptorist monastery, two Ukrainian gymnasiums, and a branch (est 1925) of the Lysenko Music Society of Lviv. Its main Ukrainian cultural organizations were the Burgher Brotherhood, the Boian musical society, a branch of the Prosvita society, and the Ostrozky Foundation. It was the base of a number of Ukrainian economic institutions, such as the Podilia Union of Co-operatives and the Kalyna guild. Several local factories were owned by Ukrainians. The newspaper *Podil's'kyi holos* resumed publication in 1928–30. In the interwar period the leading political and civic activists in Ternopil were S. Baran, I. and S. Brykovych, S. Chumak, N. Hirniak, Ya. Mykolaievych, R. Tsehelsky, V. Vitoshynsky, and Ya. Yarema.

During the Second World War Ternopil was occupied by the Soviets (September 1939 to July 1941) and the Germans (to May 1944). The Soviet authorities arrested and deported many Ukrainian activists and murdered 640 prisoners just before abandoning the city in 1941. In March and April 1944 over half of the city was destroyed before it was recaptured by the Soviet army. By 1946 there were only 12,000 inhabitants. The city was rebuilt according to a general plan adopted by the government in August 1945. As industrial development progressed, the population increased, from 26,000 in 1950 to 52,000 in 1959, 85,000 in 1970, and 139,000 in 1978. In Western Ukraine Sovietization meant a profound change in all areas of life – economic, cultural, civic, and private. There was also a marked shift in Ternopil's ethnic composition. In 1959, 78 percent of the population was Ukrainian, 15 percent Russian, and 5 percent Polish; in 1989, 91.2 percent of the population was Ukrainian, 7.2 was Russian, and 0.6 percent was Polish.

At the end of the 1980s the city became one of the leading centers of the national revival in Ukraine. Democrats were voted into power in the municipal and oblast councils, and a strong branch of the Popular Movement of Ukraine was set up. The city's publications now include the journal *Ternopil'* and the newspapers *Zakhidna Ukraïna*, *Vil'ne zhyttia* (Oblast Council), *Ternystyi shliakh* (Ukrainian Republican party), and *Ternopil' vechirnii* (City Council).

Today Ternopil is one of the major industrial centers of western Ukraine. The major branches of industry are food processing, including a sugar-refining complex (built in 1937, reconstructed in 1954–8), a meat-packing plant, a dairy, and a brewery; light industry, including one of the largest cotton-cloth manufacturing complexes in Ukraine and a synthetic leather and sewing factory; the building-materials industry, including a reinforced-concrete plant and the Budindustriia complex; and the machine-building industry, which produces electric armatures and farm machinery. There are six vocational schools and four specialized secondary schools in the city. Higher education is provided by the city's medical, pedagogical, and financial-economic institutes. There are also several local branches of large educational institutes, such as the Lviv Polytechnical Institute. The chief cultural institutions are the theater of Ukrainian music and drama, the puppet theater, the oblast philharmonic orchestra, the regional studies museum, and the picture gallery.

The chief architectural monuments of the city are the castle (built in 1540–8, destroyed in 1675 and restored in the Renaissance style, renovated in the 19th century, and rebuilt after each world war), the Church of Christ's Na-

The Church of Christ's Nativity (1602–8) in Ternopil

tivity, with a defense tower (1596–8), the Church of the Elevation of the Cross (1540), the SS Peter and Paul Church of the Dominican monks, built in the baroque style (1749), and the Dormition Church (1632, destroyed by the Soviet authorities in 1962). The section of the municipal cemetery reserved for the Ukrainian Sich Riflemen was destroyed by the Soviets in 1976.

The city's layout was completely changed during postwar reconstruction. Some of the streets were designed differently and widened. The buildings were enlarged to three or four stories. A series of new public buildings and squares was designed. Whole new residential districts were put up in the eastern section and west of the Seret River. The Zahrobelia suburb was expanded. The central core of the city lies outside the old quarter, as it did before the war.

BIBLIOGRAPHY
*Rocznik Kółka Naukowego Tarnopolskiego* (Ternopil 1892–5)
Bilyns'kyi, P. *Misto Ternopil' i ioho okolytsia*, 2 vols (Ternopil 1894–5)
*Shliakhamy zolotoho Podillia: Regional'nyi zbirnyk Ternopil'shchyny*, 3 vols (Philadelphia 1960, 1970, 1983)
V. Kubijovyč, R. Mykolaievych

A hydroelectric station in Borshchiv raion, Ternopil oblast

**Ternopil oblast.** An administrative territory (1990 pop 1,171,500) in Western Ukraine, formed on 4 December 1939. Its area is 13,800 sq km, divided among 16 raions, 16 cities, 21 towns (smt), and 458 rural councils. The capital is *Ternopil.

**Physical geography.** The oblast occupies the western part of the Podolian Upland. It consists largely of a plateau with an elevation of 300–400 m sloping southward to the Dniester River. The Kremianets Mountains cut through the northern part of the oblast; the Opilia Upland runs along its southwestern border. The main rivers in the oblast are left-bank tributaries of the Dniester – the Zolota Lypa, the Koropets, the Strypa, the Seret, and the Zbruch, which marks its eastern border. The oblast has a temperate continental climate: the average January temperature is –5.5°C in the north and –4.5°C in the south, and the average July temperature is 18°C and 19°C respectively. The annual precipitation ranges from 520 mm in the southeast to 700 mm in the northwest. The soils are mostly chernozems and gray forest soils. The oblast's vegetation belongs to the forest-steppe belt. Almost 13 percent of the

Cossack graves near Kremianets, Ternopil oblast

oblast's surface is forested; the prevalent forests are hornbeam, hornbeam and oak, beech, and pine.

**History.** The territory of the oblast has been inhabited since the Paleolithic period. In the 9th to 12th centuries it was part of Kievan Rus', and in the 13th and 14th centuries, of Galicia-Volhynia principality. Except for a brief interval during the B. Khmelnytsky period, the territory was dominated by Poland from the mid-14th century until the First Partition of Poland. In 1772 most of the territory was annexed by the Austrian Empire. The northern part, including Kremianets and Zbarazh, was taken by Russia in 1793. Austria ceded the so-called Ternopil krai to the Russian Empire in 1809, but got it back at the Congress of Vienna in 1815. For more than a century the Zbruch River defined the border between Austrian- and Russian-ruled Ukrainian territories. In 1918 the Ternopil region became part of the Western Ukrainian National Republic, but soon thereafter it was occupied by Poland. In September 1939 it was occupied along with the rest of Galicia by Soviet troops, who were driven out by the Germans in June 1941, and returned in July 1944. Since 1944 the territory has been part of Ukraine.

**Population.** The overwhelming majority of the oblast's population is Ukrainian: according to the 1989 census, 96.8 percent is Ukrainian, 2.3 percent is Russian, and under 1 percent is Polish. The figures represent a radical departure from the national composition of the area before the Second World War. For centuries substantial Jewish and Polish minorities lived in the region, and even predominated in the towns. In 1989, 41 percent of the population was urban. The major cities in the oblast are Ternopil, *Chortkiv, *Kremianets, *Berezhany, *Buchach, *Terebovlia, *Zbarazh, and *Borshchiv.

**Industry.** The oblast's main industries are food processing (40.2 percent of the output in 1983), light industry (26.9 percent), machine building and metalworking (17.7 per cent), and building-materials manufacturing (4.2 percent). The food industry is distributed throughout the oblast: the chief sugar refineries are in Borshchiv, Buchach, Zbarazh, Kozova, Khorostkiv, Kremianets, Lanivtsi, Chortkiv, and Ternopil; the largest meat-packing plants are in Ternopil and Chortkiv; the major fruit-canning factories are in Zalishchyky and Berezhany; the main distilleries are in Kremianets, Borshchiv, Khorostkiv, and

Monastyryska; and the creameries and dairies are in Borshchiv, Kremianets, Berezhany, Zalishchyky, and Ternopil. Light industry manufactures textiles in Ternopil (cotton) and Zalishchyky, clothing in Ternopil and Chortkiv, footwear in Ternopil and Terebovlia, and leather goods in Ternopil and Vyshnivets. Machine-building enterprises producing farm machinery are concentrated in Ternopil and Zbarazh. Buchach is known for its metal products. Building-materials plants are based on local resources and are located mainly in Ternopil, Berezhany, Skala-Podilska, and Monastyryska. Woodworking plants, mostly furniture factories, are found in Ternopil, Berezhany, Kremianets, and Mykulyntsi.

**Agriculture.** In 1989 there were 339 collective farms and 20 state farms in the oblast. Of 1,059,000 ha of farmland, 90.4 percent was cultivated, 5.5 percent was hayfield, and 2.6 percent was pasture. Drained land accounted for 126,200 ha. The major crops are the grains (winter wheat, spring barley, legumes, and corn), industrial crops (sugar beets, flax, and tobacco), potatoes, vegetables, and fodder crops. Fruit growing is extensively practiced in the Dniester region. Animal husbandry consists mostly of dairy- and beef-cattle raising, hog farming, and sheep breeding. It accounts for almost half of the agricultural output. Poultry farming, beekeeping, and fish farming are supplementary enterprises.

**Transportation.** In 1989 there were 574 km of railroads. The trunk lines that cross the oblast are the Kiev–Zhmerynka–Ternopil–Lviv–Chop, Kiev–Shepetivka–Ternopil–Chernivtsi, and Yarmolyntsi–Ternopil–Khodoriv lines. The main railway junctions are Ternopil and Chortkiv. There are 5,500 km of highways, of which 4,700 are paved. The main highways crossing the oblast are Vinnytsia–Lviv–Krakovets, Kamianets-Podilskyi–Chortkiv–Ivano-Frankivske, Brest–Lutske–Ternopil–Chernivtsi, and Ternopil–Stryi. An airport is located in Ternopil. The Dniester is navigable, and Zalishchyky serves as the oblast's major river port. The Soiuz gas pipeline passes through the oblast.

BIBLIOGRAPHY

Shliakhamy zolotoho Podillia: Regional'nyi zbirnyk Ternopil'shchyny, 3 vols (Philadelphia 1960, 1970, 1983)

Istoriia mist i sil URSR: Ternopil's'ka oblast' (Kiev 1973)

**Ternopil Ukrainian Music and Drama Theater** (Ternopilskyi ukrainskyi muzychno-dramatychnyi teatr im. T. Shevchenka). A theater established in 1939 as the Ternopil Franko Ukrainian Drama Theater on the basis of O. Karabinevych's *Sadovsky Ukrainian Drama Theater, M. Komarovsky's Promin Theater, and a touring operetta troupe. In 1940–1 its director was M. *Tereshchenko. In 1945 it merged with the Okhtyrka Shevchenko Ukrainian Workers' and Collective-Farm Touring Theater (est 1930) and acquired its present name. Its repertoire has included works by M. Kropyvnytsky, M. Starytsky, I. Mykytenko, O. Dovzhenko, M. Gorky, and B. Brecht. In 1984 its artistic director was P. Zahrebelny.

**Ternopilski Teatralni Vechory** (Ternopil Theatrical Evenings). The first Western Ukrainian stationary theater, organized in Ternopil by L. *Kurbas in September 1915. In March 1916 Kurbas departed for *Sadovsky's Theater in Kiev, and M. *Bentsal took over the directorship of Teatralni Vechory. Its repertoire consisted mostly of populist-

The Ternopil Ukrainian Music and Drama Theater

ethnographic plays, some works by S. Vasylchenko and S. Cherkasenko, and Ukrainian musicals. Among its actors were H. Yurchakova, F. Lopatynska, Ya. Bortnyk, F. Lopatynsky, M. Krushelnytsky, I. Rubchak, and A. Osypovycheva. Teatralni Vechory performed for Ukrainian soldiers in the Russian army, and was active until June 1917.

**Ternovsky, Pylyp** [Ternovs'kyj], b 1838 in Moscow, d 23 May 1884 in Kiev. Church historian. He graduated from the Moscow Theological Seminary (1862) and then taught the history of 'Rus'' at the Kiev Theological Academy and general church history at Kiev University (from 1869), and contributed to *Kievskaia starina, Trudy Kievskoi dukhovnoi akademii*, and *Novoe vremia*. He was dismissed in 1883 for 'not moving in accordance with the spirit of Orthodoxy' and for having 'a tendency towards the opinions of Protestant historians.' A specialist in Byzantine and Ukrainian church history, he wrote monographs on sermonizing in 'South Russia' in the 16th and 17th centuries (1869) and on the history of Kiev eparchy in the 18th century (1879), as well as articles on Metropolitan S. Yavorsky and his writings, the participation of ancient Russian archpriests in social issues, the archpriest of Kiev's St Sophia Cathedral, I. Levanda (with S. Golubev), Metropolitan P. Mohyla, the lifestyle of Little Russian monks in the late 18th century, and Serapion.

**Ternovsky, Serhii** [Ternovs'kyj, Serhij], b 1848 in Moscow, d ? Church historian; brother of P. *Ternovsky. He graduated from the Kiev Theological Academy and then taught Hebrew and biblical archeology at the Kazan Theological Academy and worked for the Kiev Archeographic Commission. His monograph 'Issledovanie o podchinenii Kievskoi mitropolii Moskovskomu patriarkhatu' (Research on the Subordination of Kiev Metropoly to Moscow Patriarchate) appeared as an introductory essay to a collection of archival documents, edited by him, which was published in *Arkhiv Iugo-Zapadnoi Rossii* (Archives of Southwestern Russia, pt 1, vol 5 [1872]), for which he received a master's degree in theology. He also wrote an outline of biblical archeology (2 vols, 1891, 1895; repub as *Bibleiskaia starina* [Biblical Antiquity], 1900), a history of the Greek-Eastern church during the period of the ecumenical councils (1883), and a study of the first three centuries of Christianity (1878).

**Ternovy, Kostiantyn** [Ternovyj, Kostjantyn], b 16 April 1924 in Odessa. Orthopedist and traumatologist; full member of the AN URSR (now ANU) since 1982. A graduate of the Odessa Medical Institute (1949), he worked at the Odessa Oblast Hospital and the Odessa Medical Institute (1953–70) and in 1970 was appointed deputy minister of health and head of the clinical division of the Kiev Scientific Research Institute of Orthopedics. His publications deal with the interrelationships of transplantation and regeneration of bone tissue, growth disorders, the chemical composition of bones, inflammatory diseases of the skeletal system, and bone-joint tuberculosis.

Arystarkh Ternychenko

**Ternychenko, Arystarkh** [Ternyčenko, Arystarx], b 15 April 1882 in Okhtyrka, Kharkiv gubernia, d 1 February 1927 in Kiev. Agronomist and publisher. Before graduating from the Kiev Polytechnical Institute (1914) he edited and published the first popular Ukrainian-language agricultural periodical, *Rillia (1910–14), for which he also wrote most of the material, and contributed to the weekly *Selo (1909–11). His brochures, posters, and farmers' almanacs (1912–14), which came out as supplements to *Rillia*, were popular among Ukrainian peasants. He was president of the Ukrainskyi Ahronom society (est 1913) and became the publisher of *Rillia*. He served as agriculture minister in the Council of National Ministers of the UNR (February–April 1918) and then headed the Kiev branch of the *Agricultural Scientific Committee of Ukraine and edited its journal *Ahronom* (1923–6) as well as the journals *Trudove hospodarstvo* (1920) and *Selo* (1922). In 1922 he was appointed a lecturer and then a professor at the Veterinary-Zootechnical and Agricultural institutes in Kiev. He wrote a number of textbooks, on animal husbandry

(1918), land cultivation (3 pts, 1918–22), and hayfield improvement (1923).

**Teron, William,** b 15 November 1932 in Gardenton, Manitoba. Business executive and developer of Ukrainian origin. The owner of a land and housing development company, Teron won the National Award for Community Design for the Ottawa suburb of Kanata. As president and chairman of the Canada Mortgage and Housing Corporation (1973–9) he was the first Canadian of Ukrainian descent to head a crown corporation in Canada. He served as secretary to the federal minister of state for urban affairs (1976–9) and became an officer of the Order of Canada in 1982.

**Ter-Ovanesian, Ihor,** b 19 May 1938 in Kiev. Long jumper of Armenian origin. He was the European champion in 1958, 1962, and 1969 and the Olympic bronze medalist in 1960 and 1964. He set world records in the long jump in 1962 and 1967 and was a Ukrainian and USSR champion many times. As a track-and-field coach in Moscow, he launched a campaign against drug-taking in Soviet sports after the 1988 Olympic Games.

**Terpylo, Danylo.** See Zeleny, Danylo.

**Territory, national and ethnic.** Ethnic territory is the territory inhabited compactly by a given people or nation, such as by Ukrainians; national territory is the territory held by a given nation-state. The dimensions of the Ukrainian national and ethnic territory have undergone many changes in the past millennium. Whereas in the north, west, and southwest the changes were relatively small, in the south and southeast, along the steppe frontier and the Black Sea coast, the fluctuations were dramatic. At the beginning of the 13th century the Cumans pushed back from the Black Sea the Ukrainian tribes of the Ulychians and Tivertsians, who lived between the Dniester and the Dnieper rivers, and thereby reduced the Ukrainian ethnic territory to about 400,000 sq km. The Tatar invasion (1239) reduced the Ukrainian ethnic territory in the steppe and most of the forest-steppe, and left a little over 250,000 sq km, mostly in the forest belt, under the control of Ukrainian princes. Under Lithuanian rule the Ukrainian ethnic territory had nearly doubled by the end of the 14th century, but it contracted again, to some 280,000 sq km, at the end of the 15th century, when the Tatars resumed their attacks. Intensive Ukrainian colonization, which began at the end of the 16th century in the forest-steppe on the right bank of the Dnieper, soon expanded eastward to *Left-Bank Ukraine, *Slobidska Ukraine, and the *Zaporizhia. As a result the Ukrainian ethnic territory had increased to about 450,000 sq km by the mid-18th century. In the 19th century, after the steppe, the Black Sea littoral, and the Kuban Lowland had been settled by Ukrainians, the Ukrainian ethnic territory reached nearly 700,000 sq km. The eastern *Kuban, *Terek, and *Stavropol regions were settled by Ukrainians and Russians. Thus a large mixed Ukrainian-Russian ethnic territory arose to the southeast of the Ukrainian ethnic territory. Although it expanded to the south and east, the Ukrainian ethnic territory lost small areas in the west to encroaching Polish, Slovak, and Hungarian settlements.

The first accurate estimates of the size of the Ukrainian

## UKRAINE'S NATIONAL AND ETHNIC TERRITORY

ethnic territory were made at the beginning of the 20th century, following the publication of the results of the first Russian population census of 1897. By counting all the counties with a rural population over 50 percent Ukraini-

### Constituents of the Ukrainian ethnic territory (1,000 sq km)

| | |
|---|---|
| *Ukraine* | 603.7 |
| Compact Ukrainian ethnic territory | 574.3 |
| Mixed Ukrainian ethnic territory (Crimea) | 27.0 |
| Territory with non-Ukrainian majorities | 2.4 |
|    Hungarian | 1.4 |
|    Rumanian | 1.0 |
| | |
| *Russian Federation* | |
| Compact Ukrainian ethnic territory | 114.3 |
|    Southern parts of Belgorod, Kursk, & Voronezh oblasts | 43.9 |
|    Western parts of Rostov oblast | 23.8 |
|    Kuban | 46.6 |
| Ethnically mixed Ukrainian ethnic territories | 177.6 |
|    Northern Chernihiv region | 14.2 |
|    Eastern Subcaucasia | 163.4 |
| | |
| *Belarus* | |
| Compact Ukrainian ethnic territory | 27.0 |
| | |
| *Poland* | |
| Formerly compact, now mostly ethnically mixed | |
|    Ukrainian ethnic territory | 19.5 |
| | |
| *Czechoslovakia* | |
| Compact Ukrainian ethnic territory | 3.5 |
| | |
| *Rumania* | |
| Compact Ukrainian ethnic territory | 1.7 |
| | |
| Total, compact Ukrainian ethnic territory | 720.8 |
| Total, compact and mixed Ukrainian ethnic territory | 944.9 |

an, O. Rusov computed the size of the Ukrainian ethnic territory within the Russian Empire to be 576,600 sq km. At the same time V. Okhrymovych (for Galicia and Bukovyna) and S. Tomashivsky (for Transcarpathia) calculated the Ukrainian ethnic territory within Austria-Hungary to be 74,000 sq km. In 1918 M. Korduba delineated the Ukrainian ethnic territory even more precisely: the part within the former Russian Empire was 664,600 sq km, and the part within Austria-Hungary, 74,500 sq km. S. Rudnytsky estimated the Ukrainian national territory at two levels: its minimal area was 905,000 sq km, and its maximal area (which included the mixed and sparsely settled territories to the southeast), 1,056,000 sq km.

On the basis of the first Soviet census in 1926 and other data, V. Kubijovyč estimated the Ukrainian ethnic territory at 930,500 sq km, including the predominantly Ukrainian part of 718,300 sq km, and the mixed part of 212,200 sq km (eastern Subcaucasia, the Crimea, and the northern Chernihiv, Kholm, and Podlachia regions).

After the Second World War the compact Ukrainian ethnic territory diminished in the west as a result of the forced resettlement of Ukrainians from lands assigned to Poland (about 19,500 sq km). The dispersion of Ukrainians throughout the USSR and their Russification outside the Ukrainian SSR also contributed to the diminishment of the Ukrainian ethnic territory. Even within the Ukrainian SSR, the Donets Basin has evolved into a mixed territory, because of the influx of Russians in the cities. The present constituents of the Ukrainian ethnic territory are listed in the table.

BIBLIOGRAPHY

Rusov, A. 'Karta rasseleniia ukrainskogo naroda,' *Ukrainskii vestnik*, 1906

Tomashivs'kyi, S. 'Etnohrafichna karta Uhors'koï Rusy,' *Stat'i po slavianovedeniiu*, vol 3 (St Petersburg 1910)

Korduba, M. *Terytoriia i naseleniie Ukraïny* (Vienna 1918)
Rudnyts'kyi, S. *Ukraine: The Land and Its People* (New York 1918)
– *Ohliad natsional'noï terytoriï Ukraïny* (Berlin 1923)
Kubiiovych, V. *Terytoriia i liudnist' ukraïns'kykh zemel'* (Lviv 1935)
– *Heohrafiia ukraïns'kykh i sumezhnykh zemel'* (Cracow–Lviv 1943)
I. Stebelsky

**Terror.** An instrument of political rule that consists in inducing fear and helplessness in subjects of the state through arbitrary violence. In the 20th century, state terror has played a key role in thwarting Ukraine's aspirations to independence and subjugating the Ukrainian people to Russian domination under the Soviet regime. This fact accounts for the caution and ethnic tolerance with which Ukrainians approached national independence during the disintegration of the Communist regime in the late 1980s and early 1990s.

Nowhere have the techniques of terror been developed to a higher degree and applied on a wider scale than in the USSR. The repertoire consisted of secrecy, ruthless violence, unpredictable targeting, and irrational destructiveness. It was implemented by a vast network of secret agents and informers, which seemed to be omnipresent, omniscient, and omnipotent. No person could be certain that even his or her most intimate thoughts expressed to closest friends or relatives were not monitored and analyzed for political loyalty by the police. Arrests were carried out, usually in the dead of night, without forewarning or explanation. People simply disappeared from their homes, and their families were not informed where and how long they would be held. No one could know who would be arrested next. Even whole villages or categories of the population were uprooted and deported to distant, unannounced regions. Besides beatings, weeklong deprivation of sleep, and other forms of physical torture, threats, blackmail, and promises were used to extract false confessions of treason and to implicate others. Elaborate show trials of noted political leaders deflected attention from the real causes of society's failures and sowed universal suspicion and fear. Most of the detainees were condemned without trial to be shot or to die slowly in remote labor camps. Very few inmates survived and returned home. Those who did were forced to remain silent about their imprisonment. Compulsory participation in elections and mass demonstrations of support gave the government an aura of invincibility and implicated everybody in its crimes. The end result was the disintegration of civil society: universal mistrust, corruption, guilt, and dehumanization.

Beginning with V. Lenin's Red Terror, terror was a permanent instrument of the Soviet state, but its intensity and scale varied. In the decade 1929–39 Ukraine was subjected to three particularly horrendous waves of terror: the *collectivization and dekulakization campaign (1929–32), the terror-*famine of 1932–3, and the Great Terror of 1936–8. The collectivization drive, with the deportation of over a million of the most productive 'kulak' peasants, and the state-made famine, with the loss of 6 to 10 million lives, destroyed the Ukrainian peasantry as the base of aspirations to national independence and resistance to the central government. The recurrent *purges of Ukrainian Communist party and government cadres as well as of Ukraine's intellectual and cultural elite left the nation leaderless and totally under Moscow's control.

In Western Ukraine, which was annexed by J. Stalin in 1939 as a result of the *Molotov-Ribbentrop Pact, Soviet rule was introduced deliberately by means of terror. A manipulated election gave overwhelming support to the region's incorporation into Soviet Ukraine. Hundreds of thousands of Ukrainians and Poles were deported from the territory to Siberia. When the Germans launched their offensive against the USSR in mid-1941, thousands of political prisoners in Western Ukraine were force-marched eastward or slaughtered in their jail cells.

The survivors of Nazi rule in Soviet territories that had been captured by the Germans were suspected of wholesale collaboration with the enemy. In the 1940s eight ethnic minorities, including the Crimean Tatars, were deported en masse, with heavy losses, from their traditional homelands. According to N. Khrushchev, had there been enough railway cars, Stalin would have deported the Ukrainian people too. Ruthless terror was used against the Ukrainian population in Western Ukraine to overcome the resistance put up by the *Ukrainian Insurgent Army.

After Stalin's death Khrushchev partially renounced terror as an instrument of rule. Although Soviet leaders tried to distance themselves from the Stalinist heritage of terror, the basic doubt about the legitimacy of Communist rule that was raised by the use of terror in the past was not resolved. The Party's attempt to place all blame on Stalin, and its 'rehabilitation' of victims of the terror, were grossly inadequate responses to the problem.

Hryn Tershakovets

**Tershakovets, Hryn** [Teršakovec', Hryn'], b 15 February 1877 in Yakymchytsi, Rudky county, Galicia, d 28 July 1959 in Lviv. Civic and political leader. A farmer by vocation, he set up various Ukrainian organizations in his home village and in Rudky county – a Prosvita reading room, Raiffeisen credit unions, dairy co-operatives, a branch of Silskyi Hospodar, and a Sokil society. He was active among the peasants in election campaigns and in 1913, as a candidate of the National Democratic party, won a seat in the Galician Diet. During the First World War he was captured by the Russians and deported to Central Asia. After returning to Lviv in 1918, he became a member of the Ukrainian National Rada and attended the Labor Congress in Kiev in 1919. After the war he was one of the founders of the Ukrainian National Democratic Alliance and a member of its Central Committee. He was repeatedly elected to the Polish Sejm (1928, 1930, 1935). The Silskyi Hospodar and Prosvita societies elected him as an honorary member. In September 1939 he was arrested by the NKVD and sentenced to hard labor. He was released in 1947 but arrested again in November 1948 and imprisoned until 1956.

Mykhailo Tershakovets

Zinovii Tershakovets

**Tershakovets, Mykhailo** [Teršakovec', Myxajlo], b 11 June 1883 in Klitsko, Rudky county, Galicia, d 6 February 1978 in Philadelphia. Slavist and pedagogue; member (from 1914) and honorary member (from 1974) of the Shevchenko Scientific Society (NTSh). He studied at the Academic Gymnasium of Lviv (1894–1902) and at the universities of Lviv (1902–5, 1906–7) and Vienna (1905–6). He then taught Ukrainian and classical philology for many years (1906–12, 1913–39, 1941–4) at the Academic Gymnasium and briefly (1940–1) at Lviv University. As a postwar refugee he taught Ukrainian at Vienna University (1945–7), where he received his PH D in Slavic philology in 1948. In 1949 he emigrated to Philadelphia.

Tershakovets's first scholarly article, a study of M. Shashkevych which was published in *Zapysky NTSh* in 1904 and was based on pioneering archival research at the library of the People's Home in Lviv, resulted in his election to the NTSh while he was still a student. In Vienna's archives he discovered many valuable documents illuminating the Western Ukrainian national revival of the 1830s and 1840s, which he published as a book in 1907. In 1908 he published a separate monograph on the revival. He also published articles, in *Zapysky NTSh* and elsewhere, on M. Shashkevych's biography and his translation of the Králové Dvůr manuscript, Ukrainian and South Slavic folk songs, V. Kopitar, the censorship of Slavic publications under Austrian rule, *Rusalka Dnistrovaia* (The Dniester Nymph), D. Zubrytsky, K. Studynsky, the legend of Kyi, Shchek, Khoryv, and their sister Lybed, Metropolitan Ilarion, Prince Volodymyr Vasylkovych, T. Shevchenko, and V. Ilnytsky. His postwar monograph on Shashkevych has not been published.

R. Senkus

**Tershakovets, Zinovii** [Teršakovec', Zinovij] (nom de guerre: Fedir), b 19 August 1913 in Yakymchytsi, Rudky county, Galicia, d 4 November 1948 in Lviv oblast. Senior OUN leader. An attorney by profession, he was one of the principal leaders of the anti-Soviet underground: leader of the OUN (Bandera faction) in Drohobych oblast (1944–5), deputy leader of the OUN in the Carpathian region (1945–6), and OUN leader for the Lviv region (1946–8). He was killed in battle with MVD troops.

**Tesla, Ivan.** See Teslia, Ivan.

Arkhyp Teslenko

Ivan Teslia

**Teslenko, Arkhyp,** b 2 March 1882 in Kharkivtsi, Lokhvytsia county, Poltava gubernia, d 28 June 1911 in Kharkivtsi. Writer. He studied in the church school for teachers in Kharkivtsi, from which he was expelled for 'freethinking.' In 1905 Teslenko was arrested for taking part in peasant riots, and in 1906 he was arrested a second time and exiled to Russia, at first to Vologda gubernia and then to Viatka gubernia. He returned from exile to his native village in 1910. He began to write poetry in Russian in 1902, and then in Ukrainian. His first short stories, written in 1904, were printed in 1906 in the journal *Nova hromada* and the newspapers *Hromads'ka dumka* and *Rada*. Later Teslenko published his short stories and other writings about peasant life in the newspaper *Selo* and the periodical *Svitlo*. Many of his short stories are on the subject of the poverty of Ukrainian peasants and their lack of rights under tsarist rule. His autobiographical short stories cover similar concerns; among them are 'Nemaie matusi' (Mother Is Gone, 1910) and 'Pohaniai do iamy!' (Drive into the Ditch!, 1910). He wrote of his prison experiences in 'Na chuzhyni' (In Foreign Lands, 1910) and 'V tiurmi' (In Prison, 1910). One of Teslenko's best works is the novel *Strachene zhyttia* (A Wasted Life, 1910). The critics of the time commented on Teslenko's talent and his animated narrative style, in which there are discernible Ukrainian literary influences (M. Vovchok in particular) and elements of impressionism. His prison stories and other tales are similar to V. Vynnychenko's early short stories in language and narrative style. The works of Teslenko have been published many times; the more complete editions are *Z knyhy zhyttia* (From the Book of Life, 1912, 1918, 1925), *Povne zibrannia tvoriv* (Complete Works, 1928 and 1967), and *Tvory* (Works, 1956 and 1977). A Teslenko literary memorial museum has been created in Kharkivtsi.

BIBLIOGRAPHY
Pivtoradni, V. *Arkhyp Teslenko* (Kiev 1951, 1956, 1982)
Smilians'ka, V. *Arkhyp Teslenko* (Kiev 1971)

I. Koshelivets

**Teslenko, Oleksandr,** b 1 January 1949 in Donetske, d 1990. Science fiction writer and anesthesiologist. He graduated from the Kiev Medical Institute (1975) and was senior prose editor for the journal *Dnipro*. Editions of his works have been published under the titles *Dozvol'te na-*

*rodytysia* (Let Me Be Born, 1979), *Kut paralel'nosti* (Angle of Parallelism, 1982), *Koryda* (Corrida, 1983), *Vykryvlenyi prostir* (Curved Space, 1985), and *Kam'iane iaitse* (Stone Egg, 1988). He died prematurely after working voluntarily in a hospital in the zone contaminated by the Chornobyl nuclear disaster.

**Teslia, Ivan** [Teslja] (Tesla), b 19 August 1902 in Nastasiv, Ternopil county, Galicia. Demographer and scholar; full member of the Shevchenko Scientific Society since 1949. Teslia was educated at Lviv University (PH D, 1939), where he served as a research associate in the Institute of Geophysics and Meteorology (1932–9). During the Second World War he headed the school section of the *Ukrainian Central Committee in Cracow. A lecturer at the Ukrainian Free University on climatology and meteorology, he emigrated to Canada in 1948, where he helped to organize the Shevchenko Scientific Society and became a specialist in the demography of the Ukrainian population in Canada. He is the author of *Heohrafiia Ukraïny* (Geography of Ukraine, 1938), *Nasha bat'kivshchyna* (Our Fatherland, 1942), *Ukraïns'ke naselennia Kanady* (The Ukrainian Population of Canada, 1968), and *The Ukrainian Canadians in 1971* (1976), as well as a coauthor of *Istorychnyi atlas Ukraïny* (A Historical Atlas of Ukraine, 1980).

Mykhailo Tesliuk          Hetman Pavlo Teteria

**Tesliuk, Mykhailo** [Tesljuk, Myxajlo] (pseuds: Ernest, Horyn, Led, Masalsky), b 12 November 1899 in Kaminka-Strumylova, Galicia, d 19 February 1985 in Lviv. Galician Communist figure. A founding member of the *Communist Party of Western Ukraine (KPZU) in 1919, he organized Party cells in Kaminka-Strumylova, Radekhiv, and Buzke and from 1921 served as the secretary of its committees for Kaminka-Strumylova and the Drohobych, Stryi, and Lviv districts. For his activities Tesliuk spent time in Polish prisons (1919, November 1921 to February 1923, October 1923 to June 1924). As a KPZU CC secretary (1924–8) and a candidate (1925–6) and member (1926–8) of its Politburo, he was in charge of the party's trade-union, rural, and Jewish work. A member of the Vasylkiv faction, which supported O. Shumsky in his Ukrainian policies, he was removed from the CC in 1928 but remained active in the Lviv organization. In 1932 he was called to Soviet Ukraine, where he worked as a lecturer in Kharkiv and was arrested in 1933 along with many other national-communists. In 1949 he was released from the concentration camps in the far north and sent to cultivate the virgin lands in Central Asia. After being amnestied and rehabilitated in 1956, he returned to Lviv and worked as a researcher at the Lviv Oblast Archive. His memoirs appeared in 1979 and were republished in 1988.

**Tetelbaum, Semen,** b 7 July 1910 in Kiev, d 24 November 1958 in Kiev. Radio engineer and scientist; corresponding member of the AN URSR (now ANU) from 1948. He studied and taught at the Kiev Polytechnical Institute. He worked at the ANU Institute of Electrodynamics (from 1945) and held the chair of radio-transmitting electronics at the Kiev Polytechnical Institute. He made contributions to the development of television and radio networks, ultra-high-frequency generators, efficient methods of modulation, and wireless power transmission methods over long distances. He wrote numerous technical papers.

**Teteria, Pavlo** [Teterja] (Morzhkovsky), b ? in Pereiaslav, d ca 1670 in Adrianopolis, Turkey. Hetman of Right-Bank Ukraine. He studied at the Kievan Mohyla College and was a member of the Lviv Dormition Brotherhood. He married Kateryna (Olena), the daughter of B. Khmelnytsky, in 1660. Until 1648 he was city-court secretary of Volodymyr-Volynskyi, and in 1649 he was appointed chancellor of Pereiaslav regiment. In 1653 he became colonel of the regiment, and in March 1654 he was a member of the Ukrainian mission to Moscow to negotiate the Pereiaslav Treaty. In 1657–9 he was general chancellor to Hetman I. *Vyhovsky, and in 1658 he participated (with Yu. Nemyrych) in the negotiations aimed at uniting Ukraine with the Polish-Lithuanian Commonwealth. He then became openly pro-Polish and (with S. Bieniewski) attempted to have the fundamental concept of the Grand Principality of Rus' stricken from the Treaty of Hadiache. Teteria eventually opposed Vyhovsky and was instrumental in the execution of Vyhovsky and I. Bohun by the Poles. He is suspected by some historians (M. Kostomarov) of having accused Metropolitan Y. Neliubovych-Tukalsky and his brother-in-law, Yu. Khmelnytsky, of treason, which accusation resulted in their imprisonment in the Marienburg Fortress (1664).

Teteria was the hetman of Right-Bank Ukraine in 1663–5. In late 1663 and early 1664 he participated in Jan II Casimir Vasa's campaign in Left-Bank Ukraine. He assisted S. Czarniecki's Polish and Tatar forces in fighting against Cossack-led peasant uprisings in Right-Bank Ukraine. In 1665 the leader of the rebellion, B. Drozdenko, destroyed Teteria's army near Bratslav and forced him to resign the hetmancy. Teteria seized the military war chest, the state archive, and the state insignia and fled to Poland, where he converted to Catholicism and was given high administrative posts in Polatsk and the counties of Bratslav, Nizhen, and Chyhyryn. Soon thereafter he became embroiled in disputes with Polish magnates and fell upon misfortune. Unable to obtain support from the Polish government, he left for Turkey (via Iaşi, in Moldavia) and began plans for an attack on Poland, which was pre-empted by his death.

A. Zhukovsky

**Teteriv River.** A right bank tributary of the Dnieper River which empties into the Kiev Reservoir after flowing northeast for 385 km through Zhytomyr and Kiev oblasts and draining a basin area of 15,300 sq km. In its upper

The Teteriv River

reaches the river and its valley are narrow and winding. It becomes 40–90 m wide with a valley of 4 km in its navigable lower course in Polisia. The river is used for industrial water supply, fishing, and irrigation. Granite and marble deposits occur in the river's basin. The major centers along the Teteriv include Zhytomyr, Korostyshiv, and Radomyshl. The ancient Rus' town of Horodske was also on the river.

**Tetiana.** A lively and humorous folk dance related to the *hopak*. Performed in 2/4 time, it enacts the story of an attractive, vivacious woman who is courted by many. The words of the song accompanying the dance vary from region to region.

**Tetiiv** [Tetijiv]. IV-10. A town (1989 pop 15,200) on the Roska River and a raion center in Kiev oblast. It was founded in the 12th century and razed by the Mongols. It is mentioned in a document in 1514 as the property of Lithuanian nobles. In 1569 it became part of Bratslav voivodeship, and in 1596 it was acquired by Prince K. Ostrozky, who moved the village to the other side of the river and fortified it. In 1601 it received the rights of *Magdeburg law. After being taken by the Cossacks in 1648, Tetiiv was recaptured by Poland in 1667. In 1793 it was annexed by Russia and became a volost center of Tarashcha county, Kiev gubernia. Today Tetiiv is an agricultural town with several food-processing enterprises, a brick factory, and a branch of the Bila Tserkva Haberdashery Sewing Consortium.

**Teutonic Knights** (*khrestonostsi*; German: Kreuzritter). A German order of knights established in 1198, during the Third Crusade, with the aim of liberating the Holy Land from Turkish rule. When the Turks regained control of Palestine, the knights stayed in Transylvania (1211–25) on the invitation of the Hungarian king, Andrew II. After a proposition by the Polish prince, Konrad of Mazovia, they resettled in the Baltic territories in order to defend Mazovia from attack by the pagan Prussians. The Teutonic Knights soon conquered Prussia and grew increasingly more powerful. The Galician prince Danylo Romanovych maintained good relations with them and participated in a joint campaign with them against the Yatvingians. The last Galician-Volhynian princes, Andrii and Lev II (1316), and Yurii II Boleslav entered into anti-Tatar alliances with them. Commercial relations between the Teutonic Knights and the Galician-Volhynian state were brisk; the Toruń–Lviv trade route originated in their territory and passed through the border town of Dorohychyn (a large number of lead seals usually affixed by state customs officers on imported German goods have been found there).

After the annexation of Ukrainian territories by Lithuania and Poland Ukraine's history continued to be linked with that of the Teutonic Knights. In a battle at the Vorsklo River (1399) a company of Teutonic Knights assisted a Ukrainian-Lithuanian force in fighting the Tatars. Later, in 1410, a combined Lithuanian, Polish, Belarusian, and Ukrainian force defeated the Teutonic Knights at the Battle of Tannenberg (Grunwald). After that defeat the order declined, and in 1466 it became a vassalage of Poland. In 1525 the Teutonic Knights converted to Protestantism, became secularized, and established an aristocratic Prussian duchy headed by the Hohenzollern dynasty.

BIBLIOGRAPHY
Rhode, G. *Die Ostgrenze Polens*, vol 1 (Köln 1955)
Tumler, M. *Der Deutsche Orden im Werden, Wachsen und Wirken bis 1400* (Vienna 1955)
Shaskol'skii, I. *Bor'ba Rusi protiv krestonosnoi agressii na beregakh Baltiki v XII–XIII vv.* (Leningrad 1978)
M. Zhdan

**Textile industry.** A branch of *light industry that processes plant (cotton, flax, hemp, jute, kenaf, ramie), animal (wool, silk), and synthetic fibers into thread, woven and nonwoven fabrics, sack, rope, and other products. The textile industry in Ukraine includes the *wool, *cotton, *silk, *jute-hemp, *linen, and *knitwear industries.

As a cottage industry, weaving has been practiced in Ukraine since the Neolithic period. During the medieval period cloth was produced not only by peasants for their own use but also by craftsmen for the market. Kiev became an important center of textile manufacture and trade of textiles: silk and brocade were imported from Byzantium and Persia, and woolen cloth from Western Europe. During the Tatar period, as Kiev declined, the center of the textile industry moved west to Volhynia and Galicia. In the 16th and 17th centuries Lviv, Lutske, Kremianets, and Volodymyr-Volynskyi became the main centers of the industry. In the mid-17th century the industry spread to Left-Bank Ukraine. As trade guilds arose, the technology improved and the industry expanded. The Hetman state encouraged its development by means of protective tariffs. When Ukraine lost its autonomy in the

18th century, the industry declined. The mercantile policies of the Russian government favored the textile industry in central Russia and emphasized production for military purposes. The Ukrainian textile industry was cut off from foreign markets by the ban on the export of linen and hemp products (1714) and wool and yarn (1720) and the import of woven cloth, silk, and hosiery (1721). Moreover, Russian companies bought up the Ukrainian products at low prices and sold them in Moscow or abroad at high prices. In 1757, tariffs between Ukraine and Russian were abolished. A new tariff introduced in 1822 gave Russian textiles a monopoly in Ukraine. A special duty (1830) restricted the import of Polish woolen products into Ukraine.

At the end of the 17th century two chief forms of textile manufacturing were established in Ukraine: landowner or estate manufacturing based on the unpaid labor of serfs, and merchant or capitalist manufacturing based on hired labor. The owners of textile enterprises were the Cossack *starshyna*, Russian and Polish landowners, merchants (mostly Russians), and the imperial government. Almost all of the enterprises produced woolen cloth. They varied in size from shops with 15 workers to manufactories with 1,000.

The first large textile enterprises in Ukraine included the manufactories in Hlushytsia, near Putyvl (est 1719), and in Riashky, near Pryluka (est 1722). Both were owned by landlords. The first was one of the largest woolen-cloth factories in the Russian Empire: in 1797 it produced 145,400 m of cloth and employed 9,478 workers. By the end of the 18th century there were 12 cloth manufactories in Ukraine, producing 216,600 m of woolen cloth per year, or 14 percent of the empire's output. Almost all the cloth produced in landowners' manufactories was purchased by the state; merchant shops sold their output on the free market. The wool industry was closely tied to *sheep farming. Only a small part of the wool produced in Ukraine was processed there: most of it, particularly that from Southern Ukraine, was exported to Russia. By 1859 there were 160 textile enterprises in Ukraine, with an output of 1,256,000 m of woolen cloth and a work force of 15,370. Their total production was worth 3.1 million rubles. Although Ukraine's textile industry grew, its share in the imperial output fell to 12 percent, and in the textile work force, to 20 percent (1859). Its geographical distribution changed somewhat during that period. In the first half of the 19th century many small enterprises appeared in Right-Bank Ukraine, particularly in Volhynia. By mid-century 69 percent of all woolen-cloth manufactories were located in Podilia and Volhynia, but their output was only 26 percent of Ukraine's total. The industry elsewhere was

on a larger scale: in Chernihiv gubernia only 9.6 of Ukraine's enterprises produced 25.8 percent of the total output, and in Kiev gubernia 5 percent of the enterprises produced 17.8 percent of the output. The gradual but irreversible mechanization of the industry, which began in the 1830s, resulted in its being concentrated in fewer and larger factories. The largest of them was in Klyntsi, in northern Chernihiv gubernia. In 1860 it manufactured 47.5 percent of the woolen cloth produced in Ukraine and accounted for 92 percent of the merchant-enterprise output.

Other branches of the textile industry, such as the linen and silk industries, were of secondary importance. The cotton industry, which held first place in the Russian textile industry, did not exist in Ukraine.

The emancipation of the serfs put an end to estate manufacturing, which in 1860 accounted for 47 percent of the textile production in Ukraine. Large capitalist enterprises did not replace the landowners' factories, and the textile industry declined in the second half of the century: by 1900 it consisted of only 51 enterprises, employing 4,469 workers. The decline cannot be attributed to natural factors: Ukraine possessed a supply of wool, flax, and hemp and could easily import other raw materials (cotton and jute), and it had a large labor base and a sizable home market. The decline was the result of the government's colonial policy, which treated Ukraine as a source of raw materials and a market for Russian manufactured goods. Of the various branches of the textile industry cotton and silk manufacturing hardly existed, and the linen and hemp industries were poorly developed, in Ukraine. The wool-processing industry accounted for 3.4 percent of the empire's wool output. The woolen-cloth industry consisted of small enterprises in the Dunaivtsi region of Podilia gubernia and the large factories in Klyntsi, on the edge of Ukrainian territory. The jute-hemp industry in Ukraine fared better: at the end of the century it accounted for 20 percent of the empire's output. In 1914 there were only six large textile factories in Ukraine: two wool-washing and a sack-weaving factory in Kharkiv, a sack-and-rope and a jute factory in Odessa, and the Luhanske felt factory. They accounted for only 0.6 percent of the total industrial output of Ukraine and employed only 14,800 workers (4 percent of the industrial work force). Ukraine's textile production accounted for only 1 percent of the empire's output, and Ukraine had to import textiles: in 1910–13 Ukraine spent 188.6 million rubles per year (40.4 percent of the total value of imports) on cotton and linen products from Russia and on woolen products from Poland.

During the First World War a number of small textile enterprises moved from Russia and Poland to Ukraine.

Output of the main branches of Ukraine's textile industry, 1940–88 (in million sq m; percentage of USSR output in parentheses)

|  | Knitwear* | Cotton | Woolen | Linen | Silk |
|---|---|---|---|---|---|
| 1940 | 42.3 (22.7) | 13.8 (0.3) | 12.0 (10.0) | 2.1 (0.7) | – (0.0) |
| 1960 | 128.6 (22.1) | 94.9 (1.5) | 19.1 (5.6) | 27.0 (5.2) | 40 (4.0) |
| 1970 | 217.9 (17.7) | 238.0 (3.9) | 66.0 (10.3) | 61.0 (8.6) | 88 (7.7) |
| 1980 | 293.7 (18.1) | 481.0 (6.8) | 75.0 (9.8) | 82.0 (11.9) | 258 (14.5) |
| 1985 | 319.6 (18.5) | 534.0 (7.0) | 67.0 (10.0) | 96.0 (12.0) | 283 (14.6) |
| 1988 | 346.5 (18.3) | 558.0 (6.9) | 71.0 (10.0) | 103.0 (10.7) | 299 (14.1) |

* In million items

After 1917 the textile industry collapsed: in 1920 its output was only 28.9 percent of the 1915 output, and even then most of it was designated for military use. The civilian population turned to homemade products. The New Economic Policy improved the economic situation: 65 percent of the small factories were leased by private business. Under the first two five-year plans several new branches sprang up: a knitwear industry in Odessa, Kharkiv, and Kiev and plant-fiber-processing industry in Odessa, Mykolaiv, and Dnipropetrovske oblasts. The other branches of the industry were restructured and expanded, particularly the wool industry. The value of Ukraine's textile production rose from 34.6 million in 1913 to 69.2 million rubles in 1927–8 (at fixed 1926–7 prices). Nevertheless, Ukraine's textile industry remained underdeveloped compared to the rest of the USSR. Ukraine continued to export materials in exchange for finished textile products from Russia. Ukraine accounted for only 1.3 percent of the Union textile production and employed 1.6 percent of the industry's labor force. In the First Five-Year Plan the Ukrainian industry was to receive only 2.3 percent of the USSR capital investment in the textile industry.

By 1940 Ukraine's textile output was valued at 797.4 million rubles. The knitwear industry by then was the most productive branch: it accounted for nearly 39 percent of the value of all textile production. Next came the jute-hemp industry (11 percent), and then the wool industry. Other branches, such as the linen and cotton industries, were less developed. With the exception of knitwear products, Ukraine continued to import finished textile goods from Russia.

The Second World War destroyed the textile industry in Ukraine, and its reconstruction was not completed until the mid-1950s. In the 1960s and 1970s new plants, such as the large *Kherson Cotton Textile Manufacturing Complex and smaller cotton factories in Ternopil, Chernivtsi, Lviv, Kiev, and Novovolynske, were built. The wool industry was expanded, with new factories in Stryi, Donetske, and Chernihiv. Silk factories were built in Kiev, Darnytsia (Kiev), and Cherkasy. New synthetic-fiber plants in Chernihiv, Cherkasy, and Kiev reduced the industry's dependence on natural fibers. During the 1980s Ukraine's textile industry continued to grow, although at a somewhat slower pace than other industries, such as machine building, chemicals, and food processing. Within the textile industry itself, knitted fabrics continued to be the fastest-growing branch. Cotton, linen, and silk manufacturing expanded at moderate rates; the woolen industry declined. The Ukrainian textile industry is still underdeveloped in the manufacture of consumer goods and cannot meet the demand for certain types of clothing.

B. Somchynsky, B. Wynar

**Thalerhof.** A village near Graz, Austria, where an internment camp was located during the First World War. Austria-Hungary's initial military failures and the Russian offensive on the eastern front in August and September 1914 resulted in widespread panic and paranoia in the Austro-Hungarian Empire. Thenceforth hundreds of Galician and Bukovynian *Russophiles suspected of being Russian sympathizers and fifth columnists were denounced by neighbors and savagely beaten by local mobs and soldiers (especially Hungarian troops). Many were murdered, and many others were court-martialed as trai-

The entrance to the Thalerhof internment camp

tors and summarily hanged or shot. Thousands of others were arrested and imprisoned or deported to several camps in Austria and Hungary. The arrests were abetted by the Polish-dominated civil service in Galicia, which exploited Austrian fears to undermine the organized Western Ukrainian community. Consequently not only Russophiles but also many nationally conscious Ukrainians were interned. The first 2,000 prisoners at Thalerhof, the largest camp, arrived on 4 September 1914, and by late 1914 the camp held 8,000 prisoners, 5,700 of them Ukrainians. In November 1916 it had 2,717 prisoners; 85 percent were Ukrainian, 76 percent were peasants, and 7 percent were Greek Catholic priests. Between 1914 and 1916, 14,000 internees passed through the camp. Its strict regime, the authorities' arbitrary actions, the starvation rations, the extremely unsanitary conditions, and various outbreaks of typhus and other diseases resulted in a high mortality rate among the prisoners. Although 1,767 deaths were registered, it can be assumed that there were many more; between 17 January and 31 March 1915 alone, 524 people died. The camp was closed down in May 1917. In the interwar years Galicia's Russophiles propagated the cult of 'Thalerhof martyrs.' The Thalerhof Committee in Lviv organized two reunions (1928, 1934) and published four volumes (1924–5, 1930, 1932; repr, Trumbull, Conn 1964) of eyewitness accounts of the repressions, deportations, and life in the camp. A Ukrainophile perspective is found in V. Makovsky's 1934 book of memoirs and documents about Thalerhof.

R. Senkus

**Theater.** Elements of theatricality can be traced in Ukrainian *folk customs and rites, *games, *folk oral literature, and *folk dances back to pre-Christian *pagan traditions and rituals. They are especially evident, even today, in the spring *vesnianky-hahilky, the summer *Kupalo festival, and the winter *carols and above all in the ceremony of the Ukrainian *wedding. Theatrical entertainment and participation in many rituals was provided by *skomorokhy. With the acceptance of Christianity in Ukraine, the Divine Liturgy took on elements of theatricality, and the church adopted or converted many pagan rituals for its own purposes. The recorded history of nonritual Ukrainian theater begins in 1619 with two *intermedes staged between the acts of a religious drama. The further development of Ukrainian theater was influenced by European medieval theater, the Renaissance, and classicism in the court (see

*Rozumovsky's Theater) and in *school drama, particularly at the Kievan Mohyla Academy. The prohibition of school performances at the academy by Metropolitan S. Myslavsky in 1765 resulted in many of its students contributing to the development and popularization of *vertep* puppet theater, which was portable so that those involved were less likely to be prosecuted. *Vertep* performances consisted of two parts, religious and secular, and were the prevailing form of theatrical entertainment in rural areas. Also common was a folk drama consisting of a one-act play based on a local event – for example, *Koza* (The Goat), *Mlyn* (The Mill), *Did i baba* (Old Man and Old Woman), and *Pip i smert'* (The Priest and Death). Eventually more historical portrayals evolved – *Tsar Maksymillian*, *Tsar Herod*, and *Lodka* (The Boat); these were the archetype of 19th-century ethnographic theater.

Ukrainian secular theater became popular during the 19th century, beginning with the staging of the first Ukrainian-language plays of I. Kotliarevsky and H. Kvitka-Osnovianenko by the *Poltava Free Theater in 1819. From the end of the 18th century, Ukrainian landlords organized *serf theaters at their estates, where Ukrainian plays were sporadically performed. Ukrainian performances were also staged by Russian-Polish troupes. The pioneering Ukrainian actors were K. Solenyk, M. Shchepkin, and L. Mlotkovska. In Western Ukraine, Ukrainian performances (particularly by H. Yakhymovych in Lviv), such as the dramatization of a Ukrainian wedding in 1835, first occurred in theological seminaries. Amateur secular performances began at the end of the 1840s in Kolomyia, Peremyshl, and Ternopil with adaptations of Kotliarevsky's dramas and with plays by European dramatists, such as J. Korzeniowski, A. Kotzebue, and Molière.

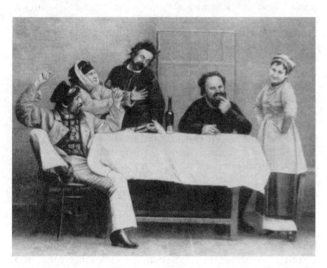

A scene from Marko Kropyvnytsky's *Po reviziï* (After the Audit) staged by Kropyvnytsky's troupe in the 1880s. From left: Mykola Sadovsky, Hanna Zatyrkevych-Karpynska, Panas Saksahansky, Kropyvnytsky, and Mariia Zankovetska

In Russian-ruled Ukraine many amateur and *touring theater groups were active by the end of the 1850s. In Kiev the leader in setting up amateur troupes was M. *Starytsky, and in rural areas, I. *Karpenko-Kary. Although the 1863 tsarist government circular prohibited the use of the Ukrainian language on stage, the development of Ukrainian amateur theater continued. It reached its apex in the performance in 1873 of M. Lysenko's opera *Rizdviana nich* (Christmas Eve, based on N. Gogol's story), directed by Starytsky in a populist-ethnographic style.

The first professional Ukrainian theater was a touring troupe in Austrian-ruled Galicia and Bukovyna under the auspices of the Ruska Besida Society (see *Ukrainska Besida Theater). Founded in 1864, it is an important landmark in the evolution of modern Ukrainian theater, and notable for its productions, in Ukrainian only, directed by O. Bachynsky. The Ruska Besida Theater reached the height of its popularity under I. Hrynevetsky and was active until 1914.

In contrast to the more liberal circumstances in Western Ukraine, the 1876 *Ems Ukase completely prohibited Ukrainian performances in Russian-ruled Ukraine, thereby paralyzing Ukrainian theatrical life there until 1881, when the first touring theater in eastern Ukraine was founded, under M. *Kropyvnytsky. Touring theaters led by Starytsky (1885) and M. *Sadovsky (1888) and *Saksahansky's Troupe (1890) followed. Their repertoire consisted mostly of populist-romantic and realistic plays by Kropyvnytsky, Starytsky, and Karpenko-Kary. Censorship did not permit performances of plays with historical and social themes and completely prohibited the staging of plays translated from other languages. Each performance had to include at least one Russian play, and the territory of the touring theaters was limited to Russian-ruled Ukraine. In 1897 Starytsky, Sadovsky, M. *Zankovetska, and P. Saksahansky attended the First All-Russian Conference of Stage Workers in Moscow, presented Karpenko-Kary's *Zapyska* (Memorandum), and spoke out against the restrictive conditions imposed on Ukrainian theater.

In 1905 censorship eased, and Sadovsky was able to organize the first resident Ukrainian theater in Kiev in 1907 (see *Sadovsky's Theater). He successfully produced Ukrainian operas as well as melodramas and comedies of manners in translation. His staging of the new Ukrainian repertoire, including psychological dramas by V. Vynnychenko and Lesia Ukrainka and impressionistic études by O. Oles, was less successful. Populist-ethnographic theater gave way to the realistic-psychological style of acting of I. *Marianenko and the *Society of Ukrainian Actors (1916), the *State Drama Theater (1918), and the *People's Theater (1918, under Saksahansky).

In March 1917 the fledgling Central Rada endorsed the creation of a Theatrical Committee. The committee began publishing *Teatral'ni visty* and organized the *Ukrainian National Theater, under I. Marianenko, M. Hrushevska, M. Vorony, and O. Koshyts, which was active until July 1918 and performed in a realistic style.

Undoubtedly, the boldest innovations in the modernization of Ukrainian theater were initiated by L. *Kurbas, whose early work developed at *Ternopilski Teatralni Vechory (1915) and *Molodyi Teatr (1917–19). At Molodyi Teatr Kurbas experimented with a varied repertoire, including psychological-realistic performances of Vynnychenko's plays, a stylized *vertep*, and a nascent expressionism in Sophocles' *Oedipus Rex* and in stagings of T. Shevchenko's poetry, particularly 'Ivan Hus (Jan Hus).' In 1920 Kurbas produced an adaptation of Shevchenko's poem *Haidamaky* (Haidamakas) for the *Shevchenko First

Theater of the Ukrainian Soviet Republic, M. *Tereshchenko founded the leftist Tsentrostudiia (see *Mykhailychenko Theater), and H. *Yura founded the Franko New Drama Theater (see *Kiev Ukrainian Drama Theater). The leading new Ukrainian theaters after 1917 also included the Zankovetska Theater in Kiev (see *Lviv Ukrainian Drama Theater) and the Odessa Derzhdrama (see *Odessa Ukrainian Music and Drama Theater). The core of Molodyi Teatr formed the nucleus of Kurbas's *Kyidramte (1920) and *Berezil (1922).

The Berezil Artistic Association (1922–33) was an avant-garde theater of European significance. Here Kurbas developed his method of 'transformed gestures' and trained a whole generation of theater artists. Berezil was composed of six studios and had a staff of directors and many committees. It was first located in Kiev (1922–6), and there Kurbas staged European expressionistic plays, adaptations, and new interpretations of world classics. Later it moved to Kharkiv (1926–33), where Kurbas's most important productions were of new Ukrainian plays by M. *Kulish – *Narodnii Malakhii* (The People's Malakhii), *Myna Mazailo*, and *Maklena Grassa*. For contravening the principles of *socialist realism Kurbas was removed from Berezil in October 1933 and was later arrested.

A scene from W. Shakespeare's *Hamlet* performed at the Lviv Theater in 1943 (director: Yosyp Hirniak). In front, from left: Bohdan Pazdrii (King Claudius), I. Lisnenko, Voldodymyr Zmii, V. Melnyk, Volodymyr Blavatsky (Hamlet), S. Kryzhanivsky, S. Dubrovsky (Laertes); in the rear, Bezkorovaina, Vira Levytska (Queen Gertrude), T. Nahirniak, V. Kalyn

In Western Ukraine in 1919, some Ukrainian theaters were attached to the Galician military units (see *Theater of the Legion of Ukrainian Sich Riflemen, *Lviv Ukrainian Independent Theater, and *New Lviv Theater). The Theater of the Western Ukrainian National Republic was led by K. *Rubchak. In Lviv in 1922 the *Ukrainian Drama School was founded, and the journal *Teatral'ne mystetstvo* appeared. Many touring theaters – notably those under Y. *Stadnyk, I. Kohutiak, O. Karabinevych, and S. Terletsky as well as *Nova Stsena and the *Ruthenian Theater of the Prosvita society – were active in Galicia, Volhynia, Bukovyna, and Transcarpathia. Berezil's ideas were adopted by the experimental *Zahrava Theater (1933–8), led by V. Blavatsky, and by the moderate *Tobilevych Theater, led by M. Bentsal. In 1939 both were forcibly united to form the first Soviet theater in Western Ukraine, the *Lesia Ukrainka Theater, and, under the Nazi occupation (1941–

4), the drama section of the Lviv Opera Theater. By the Second World War there was also noticeable theatrical activity in Bukovyna and Transcarpathia – the *Ruthenian Theater of the Prosvita Society in Uzhhorod, for example. In 1934 the musical-drama theater Nova Stsena was founded.

After the institution of Soviet rule all Ukrainian theaters fell under state control. In 1919 the All-Ukrainian Theater Committee set out to 'implement reforms': it nationalized theaters, sponsored competitions for revolutionary plays, organized touring theaters for the Soviet army (eg, the Poltava Ukrainian Drama Society), founded workers' and peasants' theaters (see *Workers' and collective-farm theaters), and forced many theatrical workers to participate in *agitprop theaters.

In 1934 socialist-realism, the 'most progressive method of portraying reality,' was applied to Ukrainian theater. It affected every aspect – *theater arts education, *scenery design, *drama, *theater studies, and even *film and *television. The insistence upon socialist realism resulted in the dominance of contemporary Soviet drama and an almost complete absence of new contemporary European repertoire (approved repertoire was published in *Masovyi teatr*), the subjugation of all theaters to the Stanislavsky method of acting and directing, a negation of all stylistic variation in performances, and the suppression of any experimentation whatsoever. Its major effects have been a dearth of contemporary Ukrainian dramaturgy, a drastic reduction in the number of spectators, and a sense of frustration among Ukrainian theater workers, not unlike that of a century ago. The partial rehabilitation of Kurbas and his followers in 1961 brought about no significant improvements, and neither did the introduction of perestroika in 1986. In recent years, however, new Ukrainian theaters – among them the Kiev Experimental Theater-Studio, the Kiev Youth Theater (est 1979) led by L. *Taniuk, the political cabaret-style Ne Zhurys Theater in Lviv, and the *Lviv Ukrainian Youth Theater-Studio – have attained remarkable theatrical success.

The Soviet regime, assisted by Party-backed organizations such as the *Ukrainian Theatrical Society (which publishes *Ukraïns'kyi teatr*) and the Union of Theatrical Workers of Ukraine (est 1987), closely monitored and regulated the activity of Ukrainian theaters. They were classified according to status – municipal, oblast, state, *puppet, amateur, or *young spectator's – and profile – Ukrainian, Russian, drama, musical-drama, *opera, comedy, small forms, and so on. The number of theaters in Ukraine was reduced from 81 in 1950 to 60 in 1964 – 42 drama (many have become musical-drama), 5 opera, and 13 young spectator's (8 in 1987). In 1988 there were 38 Ukrainian, 51 Russian, and 24 bilingual theaters in Ukraine. Only half the theaters in Kiev are Ukrainian; two are Jewish. The Kiev Museum of Theater, Music, and Cinema Arts and the Museum of Literature of Ukraine have outstanding theatrical exhibits.

In the West after the Second World War, the *Ukrainian Theater Artists Association was formed to co-ordinate theaters in the DP camps. Among these were the Ensemble of Ukrainian Actors (see *Ukrainian Theater in Philadelphia) and the *Theater-Studio of Y. Hirniak and O. Dobrovolska.

In the diaspora, Ukrainian communities have not been sufficiently concentrated to support professional theater.

Olimpiia Dobrovolska and Yosyp Hirniak in 'Maty i ia' (Mother and I; script by Yurii Lavrinenko and Ivan Koshelivets based on Mykola Khvylovy's stories) staged by their Theater-Studio in New York on 9 October 1949

Nevertheless, amateur theaters have sporadically performed in most cities where Ukrainians have settled, and Ukrainian church, school, and youth organizations, such as Plast, have staged theatrical performances. In Toronto the Zahrava Theater has been active since 1953, and the Avant-Garde Ukrainian Theater (est 1983) was notable for its staging of contemporary dramas by S. Mrożek, S. Beckett, and I. Kostetsky as well as a production of a *zhyvyi vertep*. Since the 1970s, theatrical and film activists, such as J. Karasevich, H. Kuchmij, L. Mykytiuk, T. Shipowick, and S. Wodoslawsky, have brought productions on Ukrainian themes into the mainstream of Canadian culture. In Australia there are Ukrainian theaters in Sydney and Melbourne. In Detroit the Ukrainian Theatrical Society was founded in 1960. In New York L. Krushelnytska has headed the Ukrainian Theater Ensemble since 1965. Also in New York the Yara Arts Group, led by V. Tkacz, has created theater pieces (in English) based on Ukrainian drama, poetry, and documentary material since the late 1980s.

BIBLIOGRAPHY

Antonovych, D. *Trysta rokiv ukraïns'koho teatru, 1619–1919* (Prague 1925)

Kysil', O. *Ukraïns'kyi teatr* (Kiev 1925)

Charnets'kyi, S. *Narys istoriï ukraïns'koho teatru v Halychyni* (Lviv 1934)

*Ukraïns'kyi dramatychnyi teatr*, 2 vols (Kiev 1959, 1967)

Rulin, P. *Na shliakhakh revoliutsiinoho teatru* (Kiev 1973)

Luzhnytsky, H.; et al (eds). *Nash teatr: Knyha diiachiv ukraïns'koho teatral'noho mystetstva*, vol 1 (New York 1975)

Chornii, S. *Ukraïns'kyi teatr i dramaturhiia* (Munich–New York 1980)

Voronyi, M. *Teatr i drama*, ed O. Babyshkin (Kiev 1989)

V. Revutsky

**Theater, amateur.** In the 1920s the number of amateur theaters in Soviet Ukraine performing works by local authors and professional playwrights for millions of spectators was estimated at 7,000. Some of their repertoire was taken from the journal *Sil's'kyi teatr* (later *Masovyi teatr*). From 1930 amateur theaters were regulated by central registration and instruction facilities. During periodic performing competitions held by the Ukrainian Ministry of Culture and republican trade-union councils, a few amateur theatrical circles (eg, 58 from approx 10,000 in 1964) were granted the higher designation Amateur People's Theater, with a drama, opera, ballet, or musical comedy profile. These theaters were also responsible for preparing cultural-educational programs for tekhnikums. Because of their controlled activity and restricted repertoire and the dominance of Russian-language performances, amateur theaters did not have a positive impact in Ukraine.

**Theater arts education.** Early theatrical training in Ukraine took place from the late 18th century in schools attached to the *serf theaters on estates. In the 19th century private theatrical schools became popular. During this time M. *Shchepkin, who lectured in theaters in Kharkiv and Poltava, helped develop a more realistic style of acting. His methods were developed by the noted Ukrainian directors M. Kropyvnytsky, M. Starytsky, M. Sadovsky, and P. Saksahansky.

Professional theater arts education in Kiev began in 1904 with the opening of a drama department at the *Lysenko Music and Drama School in Kiev, under the directorship of M. *Starytska. The curriculum included drama, dance, fencing, makeup, history and theory of drama, and history of costumes. The main goal of the department was to train young actors for work in a contemporary Ukrainian theater. In 1918 the school was reorganized as the Lysenko Music and Drama Institute; it existed until 1934. Its director, L. *Kurbas (assisted by H. Ihnatovych), trained the students in his method of 'transformed gestures.' In 1934 the Lysenko Institute was abolished, and the *Kiev Institute of Theater Arts was formed in its place, with training based on K. Stanislavsky's method. The Berezil theater (1922–33), at first in Kiev and then in Kharkiv, also held educational workshops and lectures. In Kharkiv the Music and Drama Institute was formed in 1923, and until 1934 the training was based on Kurbas's method. In 1939 it became the *Kharkiv Theater Institute (since 1963 the *Kharkiv Institute of Arts). Its theater program includes stage acting, directing, puppetry, and *theater studies. In Lviv there was a theatrical school in 1922–44 led by the former Berezil actors Y. *Hirniak and O. *Dobrovolska. In Odessa the Theater Arts and Technology Institute (est 1945) teaches stage and scenery design, makeup, lighting, and costume and prop making. The Dnipropetrovske Theater Academy teaches drama and puppetry. Theatrical *scenery education is offered by the Kiev State Art Institute and the Kharkiv Industrial Design Institute. Theater administration is taught at the institutes of culture in Kiev, Kharkiv, and Rivne and in other cultural education schools. (See also *Music education.)

V. Revutsky

**Theater of the Legion of Ukrainian Sich Riflemen** (Striletskyi teatr). A touring theater (est 1916) under the artistic directorship of K. *Rubchak, consisting mostly of female actors from the *Ukrainska Besida Theater, that enjoyed the protection of senior Ukrainian officers in the Austrian army and employed actor soldiers for the male roles in its productions. For official purposes it used the name Ukrainska Besida Theater. Ye. Kokhanenko and M. Bentsal were stage directors; among the male actors were

Y. Hirniak, V. Kossak, P. Soroka, A. Nyzhankivsky, and I. Rubchak; among the female actors, besides Rubchak, were K. Pylypenko, A. Osypovycheva, and N. Levytska; Ya. Barnych was composer and conductor. The theater's productions – Ukrainian ethnographical plays, Western classical operettas, and the operas *Halka* by S. Moniuszko and *Kateryna* by M. Arkas – were staged throughout Galicia and along the front until November 1918.

**Theater of the Supreme Command of the Ukrainian Galician Army.** See Lviv Ukrainian Independent Theater and New Lviv Theater.

**Theater studies.** A field of study established in Ukraine in the 20th century. From the 1860s, individual articles on Ukrainian theater appeared in Ukrainian, Russian, and Polish periodicals. In his historical survey *Rus'ko-ukraïns'kyi teatr* (Ruthenian-Ukrainian Theater, 1894) I. Franko was the first to separate theater studies from literature studies. A substantial review of the previous 25 years of Ukrainian theater was made by L. Starytska-Cherniakhivska in *Ukraïna* (nos. 10–12, 1907), and M. Vorony published *Teatr i drama* (Theater and Drama, 1913). From 1917 research on Ukrainian theater was concentrated in Kiev, at the *Lysenko Music and Drama Institute, the theater history department of the AN URSR (now ANU), and the Theater Museum. With the crackdown on Ukrainian culture during the 1930s, this research was drastically reduced. Important histories were published, however, including those by O. Biletsky (1923), O. Kysil (1918, 1920, 1925), K. Solenyk (1928), P. Rulin (1927, 1929), Ye. Markovsky (1929), D. Antonovych (1925), H. Khotkevych (1924), S. Charnetsky (1934), and O. Biletsky and Ya. Mamontov (1941); M. Sadovsky's (1933, 1956) and P. Saksahansky's (1935) memoirs; and A. Borshchahivsky and M. Yosypenko's *Shevchenko i teatr* (Shevchenko and Theater, 1941). Among theatrical critics of that period were H. Aleksandrovsky, K. Burevii, V. Chahovets, D. Hrudyna, V. Khmury, Yu. Mezhenko, Ya. Savchenko, Y. Shevchenko, Yu. Smolych, and, in Western Ukraine, V. Levytsky, H. Luzhnytsky, I. Nimchuk, M. Rudnytsky, and O. Tarnavsky.

After the Second World War the center of theatrical studies became the Department of Theater (until 1963 the Department of Music and Theater) at the AN URSR (now ANU) Institute of the History of Arts, Folklore, and Ethnography and the *Kiev Institute of Theater Arts, but little was published until the 1950s. The first important postwar history was I. Marianenko's *Mynule ukraïns'koho teatru* (The Past of Ukrainian Theater, 1953). Tendentious descriptions of the activities of Berezil, Zahrava, and other experimental theaters were given in I. Piskun's *Ukraïns'kyi radians'kyi teatr* (Ukrainian Soviet Theater, 1957) and *Ukraïns'kyi dramatychnyi teatr* (Ukrainian Drama Theater, vol 2, 1959). Biographies and memoirs written by or about M. Zankovetska (1955), S. Tobilevych (1957), V. Chahovets (1956), L. Linytska (1957), P. Saksahansky (1958), F. Levytsky (1958), P. Kovalenko (1962), L. Bilotserkovsky (1962), M. Rudnytsky (1963), H. Yura (1965), H. Zatyrkevych-Karpynska (1966), I. Marianenko (1968), and O. Zaharov (1969) were published, as were monographs about theaters – Sadovsky's Theater (1962), the Ruthenian People's Theater (1960), and the Kharkiv Ukrainian Drama Theater (1979). Works were published also on *ballet,

on *opera, on the stage directorship of Marian Krushelnytsky (1969), V. Vasylko (1980), and L. Kurbas (1987, 1988, 1989), and on *scenery design. Periodical literature includes the annual *Teatral'na kul'tura* and the bimonthly *Ukraïns'kyi teatr*. Works on Ukrainian theater in the West have been written by Y. Hirniak (1954, 1982), the Ukrainian Theater Artists' Association (OMUS, 1975), B. Boychuk (1975), and M. Radysh (1966). Theatrical critics in the diaspora include V. Haievsky, I. Kostetsky, H. Luzhnytsky, I. Nimchuk, Yu. Sherekh, O. Tarnavsky, and L. Onyshkevych. R. Bahry and V. Tkacz have written in English on the work of L. Kurbas.

V. Revutsky

**Theater-Studio of Y. Hirniak and O. Dobrovolska.** An actors' studio established by Y. *Hirniak and O. *Dobrovolska in 1946 in Landeck, Austria. It was based in Mittenwald, Germany, and staged over 250 performances throughout West Germany until 1949. It resumed its activities that year in New York and was dissolved in 1951; its successor was the *Ukrainian Theater in America. The Theater-Studio synthesized modern elements and traditional Nativity plays in I. Cholhan's satirical revues, such as *Zamotelychene telia* (The Confused Calf), *Blakytna avantura* (The Blue Adventure), and *Son ukraïns'koï nochi* (A Dream of a Ukrainian Night); adapted the old ethnographical repertoire, such as M. Kropyvnytsky's *Poshylys' u durni* (They Made Fools of Themselves); introduced modernist Ukrainian plays, such as Lesia Ukrainka's *Orhiia* (The Orgy); adapted for the stage M. Khvylovy's *Maty i ia* (Mother and I) and *Zaivi liude* (Superfluous People); and staged Western European classics such as C. Goldoni's *The Servant of Two Masters* and H. Ibsen's *Ghosts*. Among the actors were V. Zmii, S. Zalesky, B. Khabursky, T. Pozniakivna, A. Kryvetsky, L. Krushelnytska, V. Lysniak, and M. Cholhan.

BIBLIOGRAPHY
Boichuk, B. *Teatr-studiia Iosypa Hirniaka Olimpiï Dobrovol's'koï* (New York 1975)

**Theoctistos,** b ?, d 6 August 1123 in Chernihiv. Bishop. He was the sixth hegumen (from 1103) of the Kievan Cave Monastery, where he lived from the 1070s. During his period in office, construction of the refectory was concluded (1108). In 1108 he led the movement for the canonization of *St Theodosius of the Caves. In January 1112 he was consecrated bishop of Chernihiv. He is believed to have been buried in the Kievan Cave Monastery.

**Theodosius of the Caves.** See Saint Theodosius of the Caves.

**Theodosius the Greek** (Teodosii Hrek). Hegumen of the Kievan Cave Monastery (1142–56). A Byzantine monk, he arrived in Kiev in the first quarter of the 12th century and became a close friend of the princely monk *Sviatoslav (Sviatosha) and an emissary of Grand Prince *Iziaslav Mstyslavych. For Sviatoslav he translated into Church Slavonic the famous *Dogmatic Letter* of Pope St Leo I to Patriarch St Flavian and wrote an epilogue and prologue to it.

**Theognostos,** b ?, d 1353 in Kiev. A Greek who was ordained as metropolitan of Kiev in 1328 in Constantinople by Patriarch Isaiah, and served until 1353. He resided in Moscow and attempted to suppress the rival Halych and Lithuanian metropolitans, who also claimed jurisdiction over eparchies of Kiev metropoly. In 1342 he was interned by the Tatars, but later the church's privileges were restored. He was canonized by the church.

**Theologica Societas Scientifica Ukrainorum.** See Ukrainian Theological Scholarly Society.

**Theological Academy of the Ukrainian Autocephalous Orthodox Church** (Bohoslovska akademiia Ukrainskoi Avtokefalnoi Pravoslavnoi Tserkvy). A theological academy founded in 1946 in Munich to provide Orthodox priests and hierarchs in the diaspora with higher education, and to develop Ukrainian theological studies and church historiography. In addition to its faculty of theology, until 1947 it included a pedagogical faculty (called the Theological-Pedagogical Academy) that was to train teachers and scholars. Archbishop M. Khoroshy (1946–9) and Bishop B. Malets (from 1949) were the trustees of the academy, and P. Kovaliv (1946–9) and H. Vashchenko (1950–2) served as rectors. The professors included P. Kalynovych (dean of the theology faculty), V. Petrov, P. Kurinny, O. Ohloblyn, N. Polonska-Vasylenko, V. Derzhavyn, Ya. Moralevych, M. Markevych, I. Vlasovsky, and P. Dubytsky. The academy published a bulletin (6 issues, 1946–9) edited by V. Ivashchuk, and its students' association published its own organ, *Bohoslov* (Theologian), as well as texts of lectures read at the school. The academy offered regular courses until late 1950, by which time most Ukrainian refugees had settled in North America. It then offered correspondence courses until it closed in 1952.

**Theological education.** See Theological seminaries.

**Theological Scholarly Society.** See Ukrainian Theological Scholarly Society.

**Theological seminaries.** Educational institutions for spiritual formation and instruction on religious doctrine and rite, largely or exclusively for future clergymen. Seminaries were first established in Ukraine in the 18th century. Before that, prospective clergymen obtained their theological education in a variety of formal and informal settings, mostly through schools affiliated with a church or monastery run by clerics. From Rus' times to about the 17th century, religious instruction was the major part of any general education. Candidates for the priesthood usually supplemented their formal studies with a period of apprenticeship to a senior priest. Religious training could also be acquired through private studies or study abroad; following such a study a person who could demonstrate to a bishop or his designate that he was literate and qualified could be admitted to the priesthood. The growth of new educational institutions in Ukraine in the 16th and 17th centuries, such as the brotherhood schools, the Ostrih Academy, the Zamostia Academy, and the Kievan Mohyla Academy, increased the options available to prospective clerics for gaining a general education and rudimentary theological training.

The first seminaries in Ukraine were established on the basis of Orthodox colleges and cathedral theology schools. *Chernihiv College, established in 1700, was reorganized as a theological seminary in 1776. *Pereiaslav College, established in 1738, soon became a seminary. Sometimes referred to as the 'Little Russian seminary,' it was active until 1862. A theological seminary existed in Novhorod-Siverskyi from 1785 until 1797, when it was transferred to Poltava. It closed down in 1819 and was not reopened until 1862. *Kharkiv College was initially (1722–34) an eparchial seminary before growing into a more general college; it reverted to its original role in 1817. Other seminaries were created in the late 18th and early 19th centuries in Zhytomyr, Sharhorod (1797, moved to Kamianets-Podilskyi in 1806), and Kiev (1817).

Through the 19th and early 20th centuries a full system of Orthodox theological seminaries under the control of the Russian *Holy Synod was established in Ukraine as part of a general overhaul of theological training in the Russian Empire. Each eparchy set up a seminary to train candidates for the priesthood. The course of studies consisted of four years of general studies followed by two years of theological studies, with the language of instruction being Russian. If a seminarian wished to continue his studies, he could enter a theological academy; other options were available after 1896, when the universities of Warsaw, Dorpat, and Tomsk were opened to seminarians. Theological academies (eg, the *Kiev Theological Academy) also trained professors for the seminaries. The eparchial seminaries were also charged with overseeing lower-ranking theological schools at the county level which prepared candidates for seminaries. By 1911 the seminary system was fully in place, and institutions could be found in Kiev, Kamianets-Podilskyi, Zhytomyr, Kharkiv, Odessa, Katerynoslav, Symferopil, Yelysavethrad (now Kirovohrad), Poltava, Chernihiv, and Kholm. In the early 1920s the Soviet regime liquidated the theological seminaries. Only after the Second World War were seminaries reopened in Ukraine, in Kiev, Odessa, and Lutske.

In the interwar period some Ukrainian priests were trained at the seminary of the Polish Autocephalous Orthodox church in Kremianets. There was a department of Orthodox theology, with such prominent Ukrainians as O. Lototsky and V. Bidnov on the staff, at the University of Warsaw. In Bukovyna limited training was provided for Ukrainian priests at the residence of the metropolitan of Bukovyna in Chernivtsi. In Canada, Ukrainian Orthodox theological training has been centered at *St Andrew's College in Winnipeg; in the United States the St Sophia Seminary was established at South Bound Brook, New Jersey, in 1975.

A systematic approach to theological education for Catholic Ukrainians was not developed until the late 18th century. A good number of prospective clergymen were schooled in Catholic cathedral schools or Jesuit-run colleges with a Latin rite orientation. In the 18th century a network of approx 50 schools modeled on Jesuit counterparts and run largely by Basilian monks was established in Right-Bank Ukraine. The majority of their pupils were Polish or Polonized gentry, although the schools provided a basic education for future Uniate clerics as well. Some efforts were made to establish Uniate theological seminaries during the 17th century, but these institutions, such as those found in Zhytomyr, Radomyshl, and Kamianets-Podilskyi, were usually short-lived. A number of private seminaries also sought to meet the demand for qualified Uniate clergymen. Nevertheless, the majority of Uniate clergymen ultimately received their education in Roman Catholic institutions. Many of them, particularly future hierarchs, even studied outside of Poland, at schools in Rome, Vienna, Prague, or elsewhere.

Following the incorporation of Galicia into Austria, demands were made by both secular and ecclesiastical authorities for an improvement in the qualifications of the Uniate clergy. Subsequently a Greek Catholic seminary called the *Barbareum was formed in Vienna, in 1774. It was succeeded by the *Greek Catholic Theological Seminary in Lviv in 1783, which provided theological training for future clergymen until 1944. The program was supplemented by courses, some of them taught in Ukrainian, offered by the theology department of Lviv University. During the interwar period difficulties emerged in maintaining the Ukrainian presence in the theology department because of hindrance from Polish authorities. A theology faculty was thereupon added to the seminary, and in 1928 it was expanded into the separate *Greek Catholic Theological Academy. A higher education in theological studies could also be obtained by prospective Uniate clergymen at Lviv University or at a number of other Catholic religious study centers, particularly in Rome, Vienna, Innsbruck, Budapest, and Warsaw. For a period after the establishment of the Lviv seminary, the *Studium Ruthenum (1787–1809) offered a remedial means of providing upper-level theological training for Ukrainian seminarians not fluent in Latin.

Other eparchies in Western Ukraine also established Ukrainian Catholic theological seminaries. A seminary existed in Peremyshl in 1780–3. In 1845 it was revived, but offered only a fourth and final year of study. It became a full seminary in 1912. Stanyslaviv eparchy opened its own seminary in 1907. Two seminaries were established in Transcarpathia, one in Uzhhorod (1778) and the other in Prešov (1880). As well, a Jesuit-supported Catholic seminary was opened in Dubno, Volhynia, in 1931 in order to shore up the *Neounion church movement. All these institutions were liquidated by the Soviet authorities, starting in 1939, with the first occupation of Western Ukraine, and continuing after 1945, with the annexation of the region into the Ukrainian SSR. With the renewed religious tolerance in the last years of the USSR seminaries were opened in 1990 in Lviv, Uzhhorod, and Ivano-Frankivske.

Ukrainian Catholic seminaries have also been established outside of Ukrainian territories. *Križevci eparchy operates a small seminary in Zagreb. In the United States St Josaphat Seminary was founded by the Philadelphia exarchate in 1942; it was moved to Washington in 1950. A second seminary (Cyril and Methodius) for Transcarpathian Ukrainians was established in 1951 in a suburb of Pittsburgh. A seminary was founded in Hirschberg, Bavaria, in 1946 and moved in 1949 to Culemborg, Holland, where it functioned until 1951. The Holy Spirit Intereparchial Seminary was opened in Ottawa in 1981. The oldest Ukrainian Catholic seminary in the West remains *St Josaphat's Ukrainian Pontifical College in Rome, which was established in 1897. Its program of theological studies was augmented and completed by the formation of the Ukrainian Catholic University of St Clement the Pope, in Rome in 1963.

Candidates for the priesthood commonly receive part of their training in other institutions, such as theological institutes, the theology faculties of universities, or colleges. Particularly significant are the *minor seminaries established by the Ukrainian Catholic church in Galicia during the interwar era and in the West. Basilian monasteries also have trained many people for the priesthood in their novitiates.

BIBLIOGRAPHY

Znamenskii, P. *Dukhovnye shkoly v Rossii do reformy 1808 g.* (Kazan 1881)

Dianin, A. 'Malorossiiskoe dukhovenstvo vo vtoroi polovine XVIII v,' *Trudy Kievskoi dukhovnoi akademii*, 1904, nos 8–9

Titlinov, B. *Dukhovnaia shkola v Rossii v XIX v*, 2 vols (Vilnius 1908–9)

Okenfuss, M. 'Education in Russia in the First Half of the Eighteenth Century,' PH D diss, Harvard University, 1970

**Theology** (*teolohiia, bohosloviie,* or *bohosloviia*). The study of religious, especially Christian, faith, practice, and experience, including subjects such as God, his relation to humankind and the world, and eschatology.

The origins of Christian theology in Ukraine date from the period of Kievan Rus'. From the reign of Yaroslav the Wise on, many Byzantine scriptures and homiletic collections were transcribed and translated: eg, the *Shestodnev* (Hexaemeron) of St Basil the Great, the *Zlatostrui* (Golden Ray) of St John Chrysostom, *Zlatoust* (Chrysostom), *Zlataia tsip* (Golden Chain), *Izmarahd* (Emerald), and *Pchela* (Bee). The first Old Ukrainian theological homilies and epistles were written in the 11th and 12th centuries by the Kievan metropolitans Ilarion, Nicephorus I, and Klym Smoliatych; by St Theodosius of the Caves; and by Bishop Cyril of Turiv. Klym Smoliatych advocated the use of ancient texts in philosophical education and the symbolic method of explicating the Bible. A certain revival in scholarly theology occurred after the 1439 Church Union of *Florence, as reflected in the 1476 epistle of Metropolitan M. Pstruch of Kiev to Pope Sixtus IV.

In the 16th century, conflict developed between the Ukrainian supporters of the Christian West and the Orthodox; it culminated in bitter polemics around the 1596 Church Union of *Berestia between P. Skarga and I. Potii on the Catholic side and S. Zyzanii, Kh. Filalet, Ostrozkyi Kliryk, H. Smotrytsky, Yu. Rohatynets, and I. Vyshensky on the Orthodox side. In his treatment of a number of general religious and religious-social problems, Vyshensky voiced his opposition to contemporary philosophical and theological teaching methods. The second half of the 16th century saw the rise of a group of translators of and commentators on the Bible (eg, Hegumen Hryhorii of the Peresopnytsia Monastery, V. Nehalevsky, V. Tsiapinsky), the writing of many *didactic gospels, and the gathering of a group of theologians in Ostrih (eg, H. Smotrytsky, V. Surazky, M. Broniewski, Ostrozkyi Kliryk, M. Smotrytsky). The supporters of Western Christianity based their views in dogmatics on the Greeks, but used the methodology and certain theological theses of the Roman church.

In the first half of the 17th century, religious polemics became more sophisticated and theological. The leading exponents were Z. Kopystensky, M. Smotrytsky (to 1627), L. Karpovych, K. Stavrovetsky (to 1626), A. Muzhylovsky, and, later, P. Mohyla, I. Gizel, I. Galiatovsky, and L. Baranovych on the Orthodox side, and I. Potii, P. Arkudii, Y. Rutsky, M. Smotrytsky (from 1627), L. Krevza, I. Dubovych, and A. Seliava among the Uniates. Despite confessional differences, both sides together constituted what could be called a 'Kievan theological school.' In the second half of the 17th century, the 'school's' teachings were introduced by Ye. Slavynetsky and S. Polotsky in Muscovy; the influence they exerted there evoked a strong negative reaction. In his attempts to reform the Russian church, Tsar Peter I turned to the writings of Ukrainian theologians serving in Russia, such as T. *Prokopovych, who was sympathetic to Protestant ideas; S. *Yavorsky, whose works were rife with Catholic principles and the methodology of scholasticism; and D. *Tuptalo.

In the first half of the 18th century, systematic courses in theology were taught at the *Kievan Mohyla Academy by Y. Krokovsky, I. Popovsky, Kh. Charnutsky, Y. Volchansky, I. Levytsky, S. Kuliabka, V. Liashchevsky, S. Liaskoronsky, and T. Lopatynsky. Lopatynsky later introduced similar courses at the Moscow Theological Academy and wrote a book on theology (1706–10). In the second half of the 18th century, theology in Kiev was guided primarily by Prokopovych's Protestant-influenced theological system and teachings, the followers of which included S. Myslavsky and I. Falkovsky. Over time, elements of the Latin church and scholasticism propagated by the 'Kievan school' became obsolete, as the Ukrainian church was Russified. Theological works produced in Polish-ruled Ukraine in the 18th century included *Bohosloviia nravouchytel'naia* ... (Moral Theology ..., 1751) and *Narodovishchanie* ... (Public Tidings ..., 1756), both published at the Basilian Pochaiv Monastery Press; A. Zavadovsky's work on the Holy Eucharist; T. Basarabsky's book of theological writings (1771); and Yu. Dobrylovsky's book of parish teachings for Sundays and holy days (1792).

Throughout the 19th century and until 1917, Russian 'synodal' theology held sway in Russian-ruled Ukraine. It was directed against the earlier Ukrainian teachings and system at the same time that theology in general was being destroyed by means of various Russian ecclesiastical and administrative sanctions. Ukrainians who contributed to the development of 'synodal' theology included S. Malevansky in dogmatics, M. Olesnytsky and M. Stelletsky in moral theology, and V. Pevnytsky in homiletics. The main center of theological thought from 1819 to 1917 was the *Kiev Theological Academy, which published many theological writings in its *Trudy Kievskoi dukhovnoi akademii* (1860–1917). A major philosophical-theological thinker outside those strictures was P. *Yurkevych. During the 1920s the Ukrainian Authocephalous Orthodox church (UAOC), led by Metropolitan V. Lypkivsky, developed its own theological thought, but the suppression of the UAOC in 1930 cut the development short.

In Austrian-ruled Western Ukraine the major centers of Greek Catholic (Uniate) theology were the Greek Catholic Theological Seminary in Lviv (est 1783); Lviv University; and the seminaries in Uzhhorod (est 1778), Peremyshl (est 1845), and Stanyslaviv (est 1907). Ukrainian Catholic theology was also cultivated at the Barbareum in Vienna (1774–84) and at the Greek-Ruthenian (est 1845) and St Josephat's Ukrainian Pontifical (est 1897) colleges in Rome. Prominent Western Ukrainian theologians included O. Bachynsky, I. Bartoshevsky, I. Dolnytsky, M. Harasevych, M. Malynovsky, Y. Milnytsky, Yu. Pelesh, A. Petrushevych, K. Sarnytsky, S. Sembratovych, I. Snihursky, and H. Yakhymovych.

In the interwar period the main center of Ukrainian

Catholic theology was Lviv, especially after the *Ukrainian Theological Scholarly Society (est 1923) and *Greek Catholic Theological Academy (est 1928) were created. Active in those institutions were theologians such as Metropolitan A. Sheptytsky; Bishop Y. Botsian; Rev Professors Y. Slipy, I. Buchko, I. Chorniak, D. Dorozhynsky, Yu. Dzerovych, I. and V. Figol, A. Ishchak, S. Karkhut, T. Halushchynsky, L. Hlynka, V. Laba, Ya. Levytsky, L. Luzhnytsky, B. Lypsky, T. Myshkovsky, S. Rud, S. Sampara, P. Tabinsky, and I. Tsehelsky; and Prof M. Chubaty. The center of Orthodox theology was Warsaw University, where a department of Orthodox theology was created. Ukrainians affiliated with the faculty were Rev (later Metropolitan) N. Abramovych, V. Bidnov, O. Lototsky, I. Ohiienko, and I. Vlasovsky.

In the postwar West the *Ukrainian Catholic University (est 1963) in Rome has been the main center of Ukrainian Catholic theology; Revs Yu. Fedoriv, I. Khoma, M. Liubachivsky, I. Muzychka, and P. Pavlyk, and the lay scholars B. Kazymyra and W. Lencyk, have taught theology there. The Theological Academy of the Ukrainian Autocephalous Orthodox church functioned for several years in Munich after the war. Since then the main centers of Ukrainian Orthodox theology have been *St Andrew's College in Winnipeg (theology has been taught there by Metropolitan I. Ohiienko and Revs O. Krawchenko, A. Teterenko, S. Yarmus, R. Yereniuk, and M. Yurkiwsky) and the seminary of the Ukrainian Orthodox Church in the USA. With the revival of the Russian Orthodox church in the USSR after the Second World War, its theological academies in Zagorsk, Leningrad, and Odessa dominated theological thought in Ukraine. With the revival of the Ukrainian churches in Ukraine after 1989, new Ukrainian Catholic and UAOC seminaries have been established. (See also *Theological seminaries.)

BIBLIOGRAPHY
Palmieri, A. *Theologica dogmatica orthodoxa* (Florence 1911)
Jugie, M. *Theologia dogmatica christianorum orientalium ab Ecclesia catholica dissidentium*, 5 vols (Paris 1926–35)
Ishchak, A. *Dogmatyka neziedynenoho Skhodu* (Lviv 1936)
Gordillo, M. *Compendium theologiae orientalis* (Rome 1950)
Florovsky, G. *Ways of Russian Theology*, pt 1 (Belmont, Mass 1979)
Podskalsky, G. *Christentum und theologische Literatur in der Kiever Rus' (988–1237)* (Munich 1982)
Bilaniuk, P. *The Apostolic Origin of the Ukrainian Church* (Parma, Ohio 1988)

I. Khoma, S. Tyshkevych, A. Velyky

**Theophanes III.** Patriarch of Jerusalem in 1608–44. In 1618, during a journey to Moscow, he stopped in Ukraine and stayed in a Polish-Cossack military camp. In 1620–1, on his return, he spent several months in Ukraine. He had been empowered by the patriarch of Constantinople to decide all religious affairs in eparchies belonging to the jurisdiction of the patriarch of Constantinople in Poland. In Kiev he consecrated a new hierarchy for the Orthodox church in Ukraine, which had been left with only one bishop following the conversion of most bishops to the Uniate church. The new hierarchy consisted of Metropolitan Y. Boretsky and Bishops I. Kopynsky, M. Smotrytsky, I. Boryskovych, Ye. Kurtsevych, and P. Ipolytovych. He also granted stauropegion to the *Kiev Epiphany Brotherhood. Later he organized a congress of church dignitaries and priests to proclaim formally the re-establishment of the hierarchy. He stayed at the Trakhtemyriv Monastery until January 1621, when he left for Busha (Podilia) escorted by 3,000 Cossacks led by P. Sahaidachny. There he participated in a local sobor and called on the Cossacks to fight against the Turks and to live in peace with other Orthodox peoples. He then traveled to Moldavia. His person and activities were the subject of controversy in the polemical literature of the period.

BIBLIOGRAPHY
Hering, G. Ökumenische Patriarchat und europäische Politik 1620–1638 (Wiesbaden 1968)

**Theotokis, Nicephorous**, b 1731, d 1800. Orthodox bishop of Greek origin. He came to Ukraine in 1776 (probably from Corfu) and served as bishop of Kherson and Slovianske, with his see in Poltava, in 1779–86. He established a seminary in Poltava, which was moved to Katerynoslav in 1786. He left several writings in Greek and Russian, most notably an epistle to the Old Believers in his eparchy.

**Thietmar of Merseburg** (Dietmar, Dithmar), b 25 July 975 in Hildesheim, Germany, d 1 December 1018 in Merseburg, Germany. Chronicler and bishop of Merseburg (from 1002). In 1012–18 he wrote an eight-part chronicle based on German annals dating from 908 to 1018, and was the first to use the term Teuton to distinguish Germans within the Holy Roman Empire. He accompanied Henry II on military campaigns in eastern Europe and noted events from that region in his writings, including the attack of *Sviatopolk I and the Polish king Bolesław on Kiev. Thietmar's chronicle was published in Polish as *Kronika Thietmara* (1953).

**Third (Berezhany) Brigade of the Ukrainian Galician Army** (Berezhanska [3] brygada UHA). A military unit formed in January 1919 out of the Navariia Group. As part of the Second Corps of the UHA it besieged Lviv from the south during the Volukhiv Operation in February–March 1919. The brigade participated in the Chortkiv offensive in June 1919 and together with the Seventh Brigade broke through the Polish front at Chortkiv. Subsequently it fought against Soviet troops in Proskuriv, Starokostiantyniv, and Korosten. Its remnants were reorganized into the Third Infantry Regiment of the First Brigade of the Red Ukrainian Galician Army. On 10 May 1920 the regiment surrendered to the Poles. The commanders of the brigade were Lt Col A. Wolf, Maj O. Lesniak, and Capt P. Bakovych.

**Third Iron Rifle Division of the Army of the Ukrainian National Republic** (Tretia zalizna striletska dyviziia Armii UNR). A division formed in June 1919 out of the infantry unit led by Col M. Shapoval, the battalions under Col V. Olshevsky and Col P. Shandruk, and the Bukovynian Battalion under Capt O. Kantemyr. The division consisted of three infantry regiments (7, 8, and 9), a cavalry regiment, a light artillery regiment of Sich Riflemen, a technical unit, and reserves. Its commander was Col O. *Udovychenko, and his deputy was Col V. Olshevsky. At its peak in August 1919, the division had 2,200 infantry and 150 cavalry. For its bravery and endurance in combat against the 14th Soviet Army in August 1919, the division officially received the name Iron. During the autumn of 1919 it sustained heavy casualties in battles with

A. Denikin's forces. Commanded by Col V. Trutenko in the First Winter Campaign, it was decimated by typhus, and crushed by the Whites on 25 December.

In March 1920 Col O. Udovychenko revived the division in Mohyliv and renamed it the Second Rifle Division. Together with the Sixth Polish Army it fought against the Red Army. After the reorganization of the UNR Army the division's old name was restored (9 June 1920). It continued to fight the Red Army until it was forced to retreat across the Zbruch River on 21 November and was disarmed by the Poles.

**Third Rome.** A Russian ideological concept created in the 16th century during the consolidation of Muscovy as a major power in eastern Europe and the early phases of its development into an empire. It was based on the doctrine that Muscovy was the spiritual successor to the legacy of ancient Rome and Byzantium (the Second Roman Empire). Religion played an important role in the formula, and the decline of the Byzantine Empire (with respect to both its perceived fall from grace by the Church Union of *Florence and the capture of Constantinople by the Ottoman Turks in 1453) helped to shape the notion that Muscovy remained the only true bastion of Orthodox Christianity.

The earliest articulation of the concept of the Third Rome is attributed to Filofei, a hegumen of the Eleazar Monastery, who sent a series of missives to the grand princes of Moscow in the early 16th century (the exact dates are a subject of debate, although they likely fall between 1510 and 1530) and established the classic formulation of the doctrine: 'Two Romes have fallen, the third one stands, and a fourth will never be.' The concept was not without precedent. The second Bulgarian Kingdom, under Simeon (925–7), had pretensions to having assumed the legacy of Byzantium. The notion was carried by priests and monks of Balkan origin through Ukraine to Novgorod and Pskov (where it was regarded favorably) and finally to Moscow. The doctrine of Moscow as the Third Rome was further developed in writings such as *The Tale of the White Cowl* (later 16th century) and *The Tale of the Origin of Moscow* (early 17th century).

The idea of the Third Rome had been embraced by both the secular and the ecclesiastical authorities in Muscovy by the mid-16th century (by the time of the coronation of Ivan IV in 1547). It received further sanction from Metropolitan Makarii and was mentioned in the articles establishing the Moscow patriarchate (*Ulozhennaia gramota*, 1589). Although the doctrine was not adopted as an official state policy, it proved an influential guiding principle; it also complemented the claim to the historical legacy of the Kievan Rus' state that Muscovy was developing. The concept was particularly well suited to the needs of an autocratic and expansionist power: it buttressed the position of the grand prince (now tsar) by making him not only the personification of the state but also the defender of the Orthodox faith and a figure who could invoke a lineage stretching (albeit indirectly) to ancient Rome; it elevated Muscovy relative to the states surrounding it; and it provided an ideological justification for Muscovy's quest to acquire the lands of the former Rus' state from Poland-Lithuania (the 'reunification' of an Orthodox realm).

The doctrine of Moscow as the Third Rome had broad circulation until the fall of the Russian Empire in the early

20th century. It also carried with it the notion that the Muscovite realm was a unique entity with a special destiny, which was largely transmuted into the broader notion of Holy Russia. Echoes of those ideas can be noted in Russian literature, publicistic writings, and politics of the 17th to 20th centuries (eg, the writings of F. Dostoevsky or the ideas of the *Slavophiles). In the 20th century the idea of Holy Russia has been retained by Russian conservative thinkers, such as A. Solzhenitsyn. Some observers have claimed that the idea of Moscow as a Third Rome was reflected in the messianic zeal of the Bolshevik regime that succeeded the Russian Empire.

BIBLIOGRAPHY
Malinin, V. *Starets Eleazarova monastyria Filofei i ego poslaniia* (Kiev 1901)
Schaeder, H. 'Moskau, das Dritte Rom,' *Osteuropäische Studien*, vol 1 (Hamburg 1929; 2nd edn, Darmstadt 1957)
Ohloblyn, O. *Moskovs'ka teoriia III Rymu v XVI–XVII st.* (Munich 1951)
Polons'ka-Vasylenko, N. *Teoriia III Rymu v Rosiï protiahom XVIII ta XIX storich* (Munich 1952)
Hryshko, V. *Istorychno-pravne pidhruntia teoriï III Rymu* (Munich 1953)
Koch, H. *Teoriia III Rymu v istoriï vidnovlenoho Moskovs'koho Patriiarkhatu (1917–1952)* (Munich 1953)
Krupnyts'kyi, B. *Teoriia III Rymu i shliakhy rosiis'koï istoriohrafiï* (Munich 1953)
Mirchuk, I. *Istorychni-ideolohichni osnovy teoriï III Rymu* (Munich 1954)
Poliakov, L. *Moscou, Troisième Rome: Les intermittences de la mémoire historique* (Paris 1989)
　　　　　　　　　　　　　　　　A. Zhukovsky

**Third Section** (Russian: Trete otdelenie sobstvennoi ego imperatorskogo velichestva kanstseliarii). The organ of political intelligence-gathering and investigation in the Russian Empire, established under Nicholas I in 1826 with the aim of combating revolutionary movements, opposition movements and organizations, and national movements. Its executive branch was a corps of gendarmes (est 1827). The Third Section oversaw the hearings of political cases and supervised political prisons, and until 1865 it also controlled censorship. It conducted the arrests and investigations of the *Cyril and Methodius Brotherhood (1847) and, specifically, T. *Shevchenko (1847 and 1850). The Third Section was liquidated in 1880, and its functions were taken over by the newly created police department of the Ministry of Internal Affairs. Its activities were chronicled by S. Monas in *The Third Section: Police and Society in Russia under Nicholas I* (1961).

**Thirty Years' War.** An extended European conflict (1618–48) between two shifting coalitions, the Catholic Habsburg bloc and the largely Protestant anti-Austrian bloc. The Zaporozhian Cossacks took part as mercenaries in all four phases of the war, sometimes against the orders of the Polish crown. At the outbreak of the Bohemian rebellion Emperor Ferdinand II sent recruiting agents to the Cossacks. In 1619, Cossack detachments fought in northern Hungary. In the following year six expeditionary forces numbering 12,000 to 14,000 light Cossack cavalry fought on the Habsburg side in Moravia, Silesia, and Lower Austria. In 1622 they campaigned under Archduke Leopold in Germany, and in 1623 they helped defend Moravia from a joint Hungarian, Turkish, and Tatar inva-

sion. In the Danish phase of the war (1625–8) 5,000 Cossack mercenaries fought under Col G. Pappenheim in northern Italy, where they laid siege to Genoa and repelled the French army. In the following year 4,000 Cossacks were hired to pacify Silesia. About half of the force joined the regular imperial cavalry and stayed in the West. In the Swedish phase (1630–8) 6,000 Cossacks led by Cols Herbertstein and W. Butler helped capture Frankfurt-on-the-Oder and then fought the Swedes in Saxony. In 1633 about 500 Cossacks died at Strehlen. In 1635 Capt P. Noskowski raised an expeditionary force of 6,000, which he led across Europe to northern France. With their swift raids behind the front, the Cossacks paralyzed the French army. In the following year they scored several victories in Hesse. Another Cossack force invaded Picardy with Gen J. Werth's army. The French realized the value of the Cossack cavalry and after several failed attempts commissioned B. Khmelnytsky to recruit an expeditionary force for them. In August 1646, 2,000 to 2,500 men under the command of Cols I. Sirko and Soltenko sailed from Danzig to Calais. They arrived in time to take part in the siege of Dunkirk. After campaigning in Lorraine some of them switched to the Spanish side, and others enlisted in the French cavalry. Their experience in the West had a profound influence on the Cossacks. They restructured their army from a defensive, predominantly infantry, force into an offensive cavalry. But most important, having won recognition as an independent military power from the Western states, the Cossacks began to aspire to full independence and to a state of their own.

BIBLIOGRAPHY
Gajecky, G.; Baran, A. *The Cossacks in the Thirty Years War.* Vols 24 and 42 of *AOBM* (Rome 1969, 1983)
　　　　　　　　　　　　　　　　A. Makuch

**Thistle** (Ukrainian: *osot*). A prickly leaved weedy plant of the family Astevaceae (Compositae), especially the genera *Cirsium* and *Carduua*. Of its 150 species Ukraine has 20, of which the most common is the creeping or Canada thistle (*Cirsium arvense*; Ukrainian: *polovyi* or *rozhevyi osot*), a perennial, soboliferous weed found in the Right-Bank forest-steppe, Polisia, and the Carpathian Mountains. Thistles choke out crops and reduce harvests; they are difficult to eradicate. To control them, crop rotation is practiced, along with early and deep autumn plowing, tilling, the use of herbicides, and proper fertilization.

**Thracian Hallstatt culture.** An early Iron Age culture of the late 2nd to early 1st millennium BC that existed in the Carpathian-Danube region. It has been studied intermittently since the late 19th century. Scholars regard the people of this culture as a proto-Thracian tribe. They engaged primarily in agriculture and animal husbandry; their metal-working was well developed. Approximately 30 sites of this culture have been found in Ukraine, including Holihrady, *Mahala, Zalishchyky, and the *Mykhalkiv hoard.

**Three Saints, Church of the** (Trokhsviatytelska tserkva). A church, originally called St Basil's, built near the wall of the upper city of Kiev during the reign of Grand Prince Sviatoslav III Vsevolodovych, in 1183. The small Romanesque structure had three naves, a façade divided by pilasters, and a dome supported by four columns. It was typical of the architecture of the late 12th century. In the 17th century Metropolitan P. Mohyla placed the church under the jurisdiction of the Kiev Epiphany Brotherhood Monastery, and it was restored and rededicated to SS Basil the Great, Gregory the Theologian, and John Chrysostom. The church was heavily damaged by Muscovite shells in 1658–60. Its reconstruction, in the baroque style, was begun under Metropolitan V. Yasynsky in the 1690s and completed by General Judge V. Kochubei in 1707. Two of its original pillars were removed, and a hexagonal narthex was added. In the mid-18th century the Zaporozhian Host added a small chapel to the southern wall and installed a new rococo iconostasis. The church was dismantled by the Soviet authorities in 1935 to make room for a large government building.

**Thrush** (Ukrainian: *drizd*). A songbird of the family Turdidae, which includes approx 300 species in 45 genera. Thrushes are up to 30 cm in body length. They live in pairs or colonies in deciduous or mixed forests, parks, and orchards. The songs of the males are beautiful, rich and varied. In Ukraine thrushes are found in Polisia, in the forest-steppe, and in the Carpathian and Crimean mountains. The most common is the European blackbird (*Turdus merula*; Ukrainian: *kis*).

**Thunder Bay.** A city (1986 metropolitan area pop 122,000) on the western shore of Lake Superior in northern Ontario, created in 1970 by the amalgamation of Port Arthur and Fort William. Its main industries are forest products, transportation, and tourism. In 1981 its total Ukrainian population was 14,015. Ukrainians began to settle in the area in the early 1900s. In 1911 approx 60 percent of Ontario Ukrainians (1,856 of 3,078) lived there. This ratio dropped over time, although the city's Ukrainian population increased to 2,394 in 1921, 5,156 in 1931, 8,235 in 1941, and 11,004 in 1951. In 1989, 2,225 inhabitants claimed Ukrainian as their mother tongue.

The first Ukrainian organization, a branch of the Prosvita society in Fort William (est 1906), is still active. Two other Prosvita branches were organized in 1909, one in Port Arthur and the other in West Fort William. A branch of the Ukrainian National Federation arose in Fort William in 1938, and by 1947 it had built its own hall. A Ukrainian Catholic parish was established in Fort William in 1909, and by 1918 it had built the Church of the Transfiguration. A second Catholic parish, dedicated to the Ascension of Our Lord, arose in 1911, and in 1968 a third parish, of the Elevation of the Holy Cross, was created. The Church of the Holy Protectress was built in Port Arthur in 1966. The first Ukrainian Orthodox parish, of the Ascension of the Holy Virgin, was founded in Fort William in 1924, and another, St Volodymyr's parish, was formed in 1935 by 200 former members of the Catholic parish of the Ascension. The Ukrainian Credit Union (est 1949) had over 1,100 members and assets of 3,683,000 dollars by 1985. The local branch of the Canadian League for Ukraine's Liberation (est 1950), along with the fraternal organizations, bought its own building in 1961.

**Thuya** (*Thuja*; Ukrainian: *tuia*). Aromatic, evergreen trees and bushes of the family Cupressaceae. These beautiful trees grow to up to 20 m in height and live up to 100 years or more. Their pyramidal crown is easily trimmed, so they are popular ornamental trees in parks and gardens. Most widespread in Ukraine is the American arborvitae (*T. occidentalis*), cultivated since the 19th century throughout Ukrainian territory. It has a light wood suitable for the construction of boats; the trunks are also used as power and telegraph poles. Extracts from the thuya were used as folk remedies to treat warts and tapeworm.

**Tiachiv** [Tjačiv]. VI-4. A city (1989 pop 9,800) on the Tysa River and a raion center in Transcarpathia oblast. It was founded in the mid-13th century and granted the status of a crown city by the Hungarian king in 1329. For centuries the town was under Austro-Hungarian rule. In the interwar period it belonged to Czechoslovakia. In 1939 it was seized by Hungary, and in October 1944 it was captured by the Red Army. In 1961 Tiachiv was promoted to city status. Since the 1870s the region has been known for its apple orchards. The city has canning, brick, and handicrafts factories. Its chief architectural monument is a Roman Catholic church built in the Gothic style in the 15th and 16th centuries.

**Tiahnii, Sofiia** [Tjahnij, Sofija], b 10 April 1927 in Kiev. Handgun markswoman. She was the 1964 women's world champion in paper-target shooting, the USSR champion five times (1962, 1964–5), and the Ukrainian champion many times. Since the late 1970s she has coached the Kiev Dynamo shooting team.

Borys Tiahno

František Tichý

**Tiahno, Borys** [Tjahno], b 23 August 1904 in Kharkiv, d 18 January 1964 in Lviv. Stage and film director and pedagogue. He completed study at the Lysenko Music and Drama Institute (1923) and worked in *Berezil (1923–9), where he first directed *Sekretar profspilky* (The Secretary of the Trade Union, 1924). He worked in the Odessa and Kiev Artistic Film studios (1929–32) and then was artistic director of the Kharkiv Theater of Working Youth (1932–7), the Dnipropetrovske Ukrainian Drama Theater (1938–40), the Dniprodzerzhynske Russian Drama Theater (1940–4; from 1941 in Kazakhstan), the Odessa Ukrainian Drama Theater (1944–7), and the Lviv Ukrainian Drama Theater (1948–62). He taught in the drama studios of Berezil (1926–9) and the Lviv Ukrainian Drama Theater (1948–62). Among his films are *Okhoronets' muzeiu* (The Guardian of the Museum, 1930) and *Fata morgana* (1931).

**Tiahnyhore, Dmytro** (real name: Sidletsky), b ?, d 1945 in Iracema, Brazil. Ukrainian Orthodox priest and church organizer in Brazil. A former officer of the UNR Army, he emigrated to Poland, Cuba, and then the United States (1924–30). In 1931 Archbishop I. Teodorovych appointed him to head a Ukrainian Orthodox mission to Brazil. His work proved fruitful, and he had helped to establish approx 20 parishes and outposts by the end of the 1930s. Tiahnyhore also actively promoted the Molode Kozatstvo society.

**Tiasmyn fortified settlement.** A Chornyi Lis culture settlement of the 8th to early 7th century BC near Velyka Andrusivka, Svitlovodske raion, Kirovohrad oblast. Excavations in 1956–7 uncovered the remains of a round fortress, approx 60 m in diameter, with defensive walls built on wooden foundations which were flanked by ditches. The remains of deep rectangular pit dwellings with posts and wooden walls, pottery, and items of daily use were found in the settlement area.

**Tiasmyn River** [Tjasmyn]. A right-bank tributary of the Dnieper River that flows for 161 km through Kirovohrad and Cherkasy oblasts before emptying into the Kremenchuk Reservoir. It drains a basin area of 4,540 sq km. It is 5–20 m in width and has a valley of 1–4 km. Fed mainly by meltwater, the river is used for industry, domestic water consumption, and irrigation. Several reservoirs are located on it, as well as the cities of Kamianka, Smila, and Chyhyryn.

**Tichý, František,** b 21 May 1886 in Chyňava, near Beroun, Bohemia, d 31 April 1968 in Chyňava. Czech philologist, writer, translator, and pedagogue. He graduated from Prague and Leipzig universities and taught in Bohemia until 1922, when he became the director of a gymnasium in Prešov. That year he published the first book of O. Dukhnovych's poetry. In 1923 he became chief editor of the newpaper *Rusyn* in Uzhhorod. In 1934 he settled in Prague, where he published in Czech a book on the development of the literary language of Transcarpathia (1938) and a Ukrainian-language textbook (1939). In the early 1950s he was forced to live in Beroun. From the 1920s on he published articles and Czech encyclopedia entries on Transcarpathian literary figures and monuments, folk songs, theater, history, and education, on the folklore and dialect of the Bačka Ruthenians, on Ukrainian language and literature, and on Ukrainian-Czechoslovak relations. He also translated into Czech T. Shevchenko's *Jan Hus* (1918), a comedy by I. Korytniansky (1922), a book of tales from Transcarpathia (1930), a booklet of poems dedicated to T. Masaryk by various Ukrainian poets (1936), and poems by Lesia Ukrainka, I. Franko, O. Oles, Dukhnovych, and other Ukrainians. His manuscript on 500 years of Transcarpathian literature (1404–1904) and correspondence with I. Pankevych are preserved at the Svydnyk Museum of Ukrainian Culture.

R. Senkus

**Timber-Grave culture**. A Bronze Age culture of the late 2nd to early 1st millennium BC that existed in Ukraine along the Dnieper River and in the Black Sea and upper Donets River regions. It was first identified by V. *Gorodtsov in the early 20th century. The culture had similar-

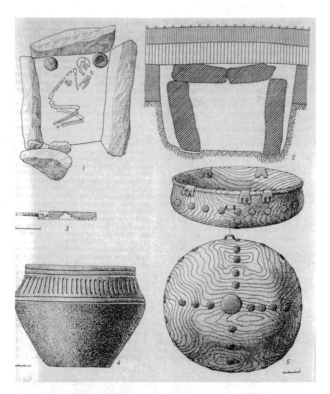

A burial of the Timber-Grave culture excavated in a kurhan in Orikhiv (1), a vertical view of the burial chamber (2), and bronze-and-wood articles (3, 5) and pottery (4) found therein

ities with tribal groupings from the Dniester River in the west to the Caspian Sea in the east, leading to a scholarly debate as to whether a single or several cultures existed in this area. The defining characteristic of the Timber-Grave culture was its use of wooden vaults in graves. Bodies were commonly placed into these in a flexed position. Settlements in which the inhabitants lived in semi-pit or surface dwellings and engaged in agriculture, animal husbandry, and metal-working were located in raised areas near major waterways. Excavations there revealed large numbers of bronze items (particularly implements and weapons), pottery decorated with geometric designs and a rounded lip under the crown, bone implements, and molds and remains from metal workshops. Scholars have divided the Timber-Grave culture into an early (14th–12th century BC) *Sabatynivka culture phase and a later (11th–9th century BC) Bilozerka culture phase. Its people eventually assimilated into the Scythian tribal structures of the latter 1st millennium BC.

**Timofeev, Boris,** b 18 October 1915 in Petrograd. Mathematician specializing in systems analysis; full member of the AN URSR (now ANU) since 1978. A graduate of the Georgian Industrial Institute (1937), he worked at the Tbilisi Hydroenergetics Institute (1937–9, 1944–59) and the ANU Computing Center and Institute of Cybernetics (1960–4, deputy director in 1962–4). Since 1964 he has been director of the USSR Automation Institute in Kiev. His work deals with surface effects of ferromagnets, automation-systems, and information theory and technology.

**Timofeevsky, Aleksandr** [Timofeevskij], b 20 February 1887 in Moscow, d 15 September 1985 in Moscow. Russian pathophysiologist and oncologist; corresponding member of the AN URSR (now ANU) from 1939 and full member of the USSR Academy of Medical Sciences (AMN SSSR) from 1945. A graduate of Tomsk University (1912), he directed a department of the Kharkiv Roentgeno-Oncological Institute (1934–41), laboratories of the ANU Institute of Clinical Physiology (1941–53) and Institute of Physiology (1953–5), and a department of the AMN SSSR Institute of Experimental Clinical Oncology in Moscow (1956–63). He wrote numerous works in experimental hematology and oncology. In 1912 he was one of the first scientists in Russia to use a new method of cultivating cells and tissues. He described the malignancy of tissues affected by carcinogenic substances and tumorigenic viruses.

Stephen Timoshenko          Vladimir Timoshenko

**Timoshenko, Stephen** [Tymošenko, Stepan], b 23 December 1878 in Shpotivka, Konotip county, Chernihiv gubernia, d 29 May 1972 in Wuppertal, West Germany. Mechanical engineer and scientist; founder of the field of the strength of materials; full member (and cofounder) of the Ukrainian Academy of Sciences (UAN, now ANU) from 1918, the USSR Academy of Sciences from 1929, the Ukrainian Academy of Arts and Sciences in the US, the Shevchenko Scientific Society, and many international academies of science, including the Royal Society of London. He graduated from the St Petersburg Institute of Civil Engineers (1901) and taught at the Kiev Polytechnical Institute (1907–20, with interruptions in 1911–17, because of his political activity). He served as director of the UAN Institute of Mechanics (1919–20). He emigrated via Yugoslavia (1920) to the United States (1922) and worked at the Westinghouse Co. In 1927–36 he taught at the University of Michigan, and in 1936–60 at Stanford University. In 1960 he retired and moved to West Germany. Timoshenko's main contributions were in the area of the mechanics of solids and structures. He developed the mathematical basis for the discipline the strength of materials; formulated equations for calculating bending, twisting, deformation, vibrations, and collisions of solid deformable bodies, beams, membranes, trusses, and so forth; solved problems of stress concentrations around corners and apertures; and provided methods for calculating the load strengths of bridges, retaining walls, rails, gears, and so forth. His equations form the basis of all modern designs in mechanical and civil engineering. Timoshenko wrote numerous monographs in English, including *Strength of Materials* (1930; 6th edn 1965), *Theory of Structures* (1945; 2nd edn 1965), *Theory of Elasticity* (1934; 3rd edn 1970), *Mechanics of Materials* (1972), and *Vibration Problems in Engineering* (1937; 5th edn 1990). His *Collected Papers* were published in 1953. His textbooks are widely used in universities around the world, and his handbooks are considered standard in the field. In 1957 the Society of American Mechanical Engineers inaugurated the Timoshenko Medal, awarded for major accomplishments in applied technological sciences.

L. Onyshkevych

**Timoshenko, Vladimir** (Tymošenko, Volodymyr), b 25 April 1885 in Bazylivka, Konotip county, Chernihiv gubernia, d 15 August 1965 in Menlo Park, California. Economist and economic historian; member of the American Economic Association, the Royal Economic Society, the Shevchenko Scientific Society, and the Ukrainian Academy of Arts and Sciences in the US; brother of S. *Tymoshenko. After graduating from the St Petersburg Polytechnical Institute (1911) he worked in the economics department of the imperial ministries of Railroads, Agriculture, and Commerce and Industry. In December 1917 he returned to Ukraine and became a consultant to the Ukrainian Ministry of Finance and director of the UAN Institute of Economic Conjuncture. In 1919 he was appointed economic adviser to the Ukrainian delegation to the Paris Peace Conference. In that capacity he prepared several memorandums on the Ukrainian economy and Ukrainian economic relations with Russia and France, which were published in French and English.

After the fall of the UNR he remained in the West. He taught economic geography at the Ukrainian Free University and the Ukrainian Husbandry Academy in Poděbrady and published the textbooks *Vstup do vchennia pro svitovyi rynok* (An Introduction to the Study on the World Market, 1923) and *Vchennia pro svitove hospodarstvo* (Study on the World Economy, 1923). In 1925 he won a Rockefeller Fellowship to continue his studies in the United States. After completing his PH D at Cornell University in 1927, he taught economics there and at the University of Michigan (1928–34). He was the senior agricultural economist at the US Department of Agriculture in Washington in 1934–6 and then a professor at Stanford University (1936–50).

Most of Timoshenko's published works dealt with agricultural economics, international trade, Soviet agriculture, and the theory and function of markets. His English-language monographs include *The Role of Agricultural Fluctuations in the Business Cycle* (1930), *Agricultural Russia and the Wheat Problem* (1932; repr 1972), *The Soviet Sugar Industry and Its Postwar Restoration* (1951), and *The World's Sugar: Progress and Policy* (1957, with B. Swerling). He also published some articles on subjects such as the Ukrainian economy and on the theories of M. Tuhan-Baranovsky.

B. Wynar

**Timothy** (*Phleum*; Ukrainian: *tymofiivka*). An annual or perennial grass of the Poaceae family that provides excellent forage. There are 15 species, 9 of which are found in Ukraine. One of the best perennial hay and forage grasses is *P. pratense*, which is widely distributed outside the chernozem belt. Other common species are *P. alpinum*, which grows in the Carpathians, *P. montanum* C. Koch, which grows in the Carpathians and in the Caucasus, and *P. phleoides* L. Karsten, which grows in the steppes and in dry meadows.

**Tiraspol.** See Tyraspil.

**Tiritaka.** An ancient Greek city of the Bosporan Kingdom, located immediately south of Panticapaeum. The town was founded in the 6th century BC at the site of a former Cimmerian settlement. It developed into a small trading center. In the 4th century AD it was destroyed by the invading Huns. Archeological excavations conducted intermittently in 1932–52 by V. Haidukevych have uncovered the remains of fortifications, homes, and a temple to Demeter, hoards of coins, and various tools and farm implements.

Cardinal Eugène Tisserant

**Tisserant, Eugène,** b 24 March 1884 in Nancy, France, d 21 February 1972 in Albano, Italy. Cardinal and Orientalist. After being ordained in 1907, he studied at the Sorbonne and in Jerusalem and then taught in Rome and worked in the Vatican Library. He was made a cardinal in 1936 and dean of the College of Cardinals in 1951. As prefect of the *Congregation for Eastern Churches (1936–59) he visited Ukrainian Catholic communities in North America in 1947 and 1950, and supported the creation of Ukrainian Catholic metropolies in Canada and the United States, and exarchates or vicariates in Australia, Western Europe, and South America. He also founded the St Josaphat's Ukrainian Pontifical Seminary in Lourdes. Tisserant defended the right of churches to maintain the Eastern rite, and warned against universal Latinization. In later years, however, he was seen as an opponent of the patriarchate movement and a supporter of the Vatican's *Ostpolitik*. He also supported various Ukrainian community institutions, including the Shevchenko Scientific Society in Sarcelles and the Ukrainian Free University.

**Tisza culture**. A Neolithic culture of the late 5th to early 4th millennium BC that existed along the Tysa River basin in Transcarpathia and in the adjacent Hungarian and Slovak borderlands. It was studied initially in the late 19th century and then in the interwar period. The people of this culture engaged in agriculture, animal husbandry, fishing, and hunting. They lived in permanent surface houses (sometimes in temporary semi-pit dwellings) and buried their dead on their sides in a flexed position in shallow graves. Excavations at culture sites revealed pottery, earthenware figurines of humans, and large flint and stone inventories, including scrapers, axes, and arrowheads.

**Titanium ores.** Titanium is a metal of great economic and technological value. Because of its strength and resistance to corrosion, it is used extensively in the building of airplanes, rockets, and equipment for the chemical and nuclear power industries.

Ukraine is rich in titanium. The first deposits were discovered in the early 1950s. Titanium ores are found throughout the Ukrainian Crystalline Shield, especially in eastern Volhynia (the Irshanske deposit) and the Dnieper Basin (the Samotkan deposit – the largest in Ukraine). The ores in Ukraine are mostly ilmenite or rutile. Exploitation of the titanium deposits in Ukraine began soon after their discovery. In 1956 the first titanium-processing plant was opened in Zaporizhia. It refines ilmenite from the Irshanske Mineral Enrichment Complex in Zhytomyr oblast and elsewhere. Another major facility for the processing of titanium ore is the *Verkhnodniprovske Mining and Metallurgical Complex. Ukraine produces much titanium sponge, an intermediary product from which titanium ingots are made, some of which is exported. Some titanium alloys are produced at the Dnieper Hard Alloys Factory in Svitlovodske, Kirovohrad oblast. Problems of the industry are studied at the (until 1992 all-Union) Scientific Research and Planning Institute of Titanium in Zaporizhia. The titanium refining process is dangerous and produces toxic by-products. Besides being used in alloys titanium is used in paint, pigments, lacquers, and other products.

BIBLIOGRAPHY
Tsymbal, S.; Polkanov, Iu. *Mineralogiia titano-tsirkonievykh rossypei Ukrainy* (Kiev 1975)

S. Protsiuk

**Tithe** (*desiatyna*). A type of church tax in medieval Ukraine. Originally the tithe was a donation granted by a prince to a bishop, amounting to one-tenth of the prince's annual income. Volodymyr the Great donated one-tenth of his income toward the building and maintenance of the Church of the *Tithes in Kiev. Later this tax was collected from the whole populace and used to support the parish clergy. In the Lithuanian-Ruthenian state the tithe ceased to be a regular source of income for the Ukrainian clergy. In the 17th and 18th centuries the tithe disappeared, but periodic donations to the clergy continued to be made by the community or parishioners. In Transcarpathia monetary fees or payments in kind to the clergy were called tithes until the First World War.

**Tithes, Church of the** (Desiatynna tserkva). The first and largest stone church in Kiev and the burial place of the Kievan princes. Dedicated to the Dormition, it was built by Byzantine and Rus' artisans between 989 and 996 amid the palaces of Grand Prince Volodymyr the Great, who set aside a tithe of his income for its construction and maintenance (hence the name). The church was besieged and ruined in 1240 by Batu Khan's Mongol horde. In the early 17th century, under Metropolitan P. Mohyla, the smaller, wooden St Nicholas's Church was built on a portion of the site. Between 1828 and 1842 the Russian administration leveled the remaining ruins and erected a new stone church that occupied half the original area. Its Russian style had nothing in common with that of the original structure. In 1928 Soviet authorities dismantled the 19th-century church.

The church built on the site of the Church of the Tithes during the time of Metropolitan Petro Mohyla

The church on the site of the Church of the Tithes in the 19th century

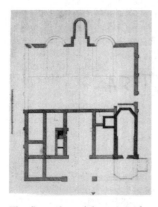

The floor plan of the original Church of the Tithes

A sarcophagus excavated at the site of the Church of the Tithes

Excavations of the foundations of the original church indicate that it was a three-nave structure with six pillars and wide, covered galleries on the sides. It occupied an area of approx 1,700 sq m. Its numerous cupolas in cruciform arrangement – a feature recorded in a 14th-century source – distinguished it from Byzantine prototypes and made it a model in the further development of Ukrainian architecture. The plan and surviving fragments of the mosaic floor, marble column, capitals, ceramic tiles, ornamental slate, frescoes, and sarcophagi (eg, of Volodymyr the Great and his grandmother, Olha) testify to the artistry of the early period of Ukrainian architecture. The artifacts collected on the site of the church are preserved in the St Sophia Museum in Kiev.

**Titmouse.** One of the small, active, woodland and garden birds of the family Paridae, divided into the subfamilies Parinae and Remizinae, and widely distributed throughout Ukraine. The *Parus* genus (*synytsia*) has seven species in Ukraine, including the great tit (*P. major*), the blue tit (*P. caeruleus*; Ukrainian: *lazurivka*), the crested tit (*P. cristatus*), and the marsh tit (*P. palustris*). The penduline or Old World titmice (*Remiz*; Ukrainian: *remez*) have yellow, reddish, or brown plumage and a long, sharp beak. The common penduline titmouse (*R. pendulinus*) nests close to water; it suspends its nest on fine branches often just above it. In folklore titmouse nests were believed to possess miraculous healing power. Because they feed primarily on insects, titmice are beneficial and desirable birds.

**Titov, Teodor** (Khvedir, Fedor), b 1864 in Kursk gubernia, d 1922 in Hrehetek monastery in Srem, Yugoslavia. Church historian, theologian, and archpriest. After graduating from the Kiev Theological Academy in 1890, he lectured there and in 1905 became professor of Russian church history. He was editor of *Kievskie eparkhial'nye vedomosti* and a contributor to *Trudy Kievskoi dukhovnoi akademii* (*TKDA*). During the First World War he served as assistant chaplain in the Russian army at the southwestern front. At the All-Ukrainian Church Sobor in 1918 he was elected to the All-Ukrainian Higher Holy Council. When the Bolsheviks occupied Kiev in 1919, Titov emigrated to Yugoslavia.

Titov was one of the more productive scholars of the Kiev Theological Academy; his main interest was the history of the Kievan Mohyla Academy. He compiled and edited the third section of *Akty i dokumenty, otnosiashchiesia k istorii Kievskoi akademii, 1796–1869* (Acts and Documents Pertaining to the History of the Kiev Academy, 1796–1869, 5 vols, 1910–15), wrote a monograph on the academy, which came out under the title *Stara vyshcha osvita v Kyïvs'kii Ukraïni: XVI–pochatok XIX v.* (Old Higher Education in Kievan Ukraine: The 16th to the Beginning of the 19th Century, 1924) in the collection series of the VUAN Historical-Philological Division, and published a string of articles on the academy and its graduates in *TKDA*: an outline of its history (1898), its role in the Russian church and culture in the 17th and 18th centuries (1906), D. Tuptalo as a student of the academy (1909), the academy's graduates at the Kievan Cave Monastery (1911–12), the relation of the Romanov dynasty to the Kiev Theological Academy (1913), the Kiev Theological Academy in the reform period (1910–15), and the memory of Prince Volodymyr at the Kiev Theological Academy (1916). He was also the author of the three-volume work *Russkaia Pravoslavnaia Tserkov' v Pol'sko-Litovskom gosudarstve v XVII–XVIII vv.* (The Russian Orthodox Church in the Polish-Lithuanian State in the 17th–18th Centuries, 1905) and the editor of the collection

*Materiialy dlia istoriï knyzhnoï spravy na Vkraïni v XVI–XVIII vv.* (Materials on the History of Book Publishing in Ukraine in the 16th–18th Centuries, 1924; repr, Köln–Vienna 1982).

A. Zhukovsky

**Tits, Mykhailo** [Tic, Myxajlo], b 8 March 1898 in St Petersburg, d 12 October 1978 in Kharkiv. Composer, pianist, and pedagogue. A student of S. Bohatyrov (composition) and P. Lutsenko (piano), he graduated (1924) from the Kharkiv Music and Drama Institute (later Conservatory) and then taught music theory and composition there. In 1943–71 he headed the Faculty of Music Theory and Composition at the conservatory. Among his students were P. Haidamaka, L. Kolodub, V. Siechkin, and O. Zhuk. His works include the operas *Perekop* (1939) and *The Haidamakas* (1941; based on the poem by T. Shevchenko), both authored with Yu. Meitus and V. Rybalchenko; symphonic and chamber music; and works for piano, choruses, songs, and incidental music. He also wrote *Pro suchasni problemy teorii muzyky* (Regarding Current Problems in Music Theory, 1976).

**Tiuleniev, Mykola** [Tjulenjev], b 17 April 1889 in Hannivka, Tyraspil county, Kherson gubernia, d 2 December 1969 in Kiev. Soil scientist; corresponding member of the AN URSR (now ANU) from 1948. A graduate of the Kiev Polytechnical Institute (1914), he worked at the Rudnia-Radovelska marsh research station in the Zhytomyr region (1923–32), the Ukrainian Scientific Research Institute of Hydro-Technology and Melioration (1932–41 and 1956–69), and the ANU Institute of Plant Physiology and Agrochemistry (1949–55). His works deal with soil drainage and the reclamation of peat bogs for agricultural purposes.

**Tiumenieva, Halyna** [Tjumenjeva], b 7 January 1908 in Poltava. Musicologist. She graduated (1936) in music history and theory from the Kharkiv Conservatory and then taught there (assistant professor from 1947, full professor from 1979). Her main works include *Chaikovs'kyi i Ukraïna* (Tchaikovsky and Ukraine, 1955) and *Gogol' i muzyka* (Gogol and Music, 1966). She has also written articles in books and collections, edited two collections of works by M. Koliada (1964), and contributed to encyclopedias.

**Tiutiunnyk, Hryhir** [Tjutjunnyk], b 5 December 1931 in Shylivka, Zinkiv raion, Poltava oblast, d 7 March 1980 in Kiev. Writer; brother of Hryhorii *Tiutiunnyk. He graduated from Kharkiv University in 1962 and then worked on the editorial board of *Literaturna Ukraïna* and *Molod'* and as a screenwriter for the Kiev Artistic Film Studio. He was first published in 1961. His works include the collections of short stories *Zav'iaz'* (The Bud, 1966), *Derevii* (Yarrow, 1969), *Bat'kivs'ki porohy* (Parents' Thresholds, 1972), *Krai-nebo* (Horizon, 1975), and a number of stories, 'Obloha' (The Siege), 'Den' mii subotnii' (My Day of Rest), and 'Zhytiie Artema Bezvikonnoho' (The Life of Artem Bezvikonny [Windowless]), which were published posthumously. Tiutiunnyk did not conform to the dictates of *socialist realism and left a gallery of portraits of his contemporaries that shed light on both their negative and their positive qualities. His vivid renderings of psycholog-

Hryhir Tiutiunnyk              Hryhorii Tiutiunnyk

ical types, frequently punctuated by a wry humor that reached into biting satire, made his works stand out amid the mediocre efforts of his contemporaries. In general, Soviet critics were ill-disposed to his works because of their divergence from the official style. In response to the hostility of the critics, Tiutiunnyk committed suicide. The value of his work was recognized only posthumously, during the period of democratization of the 1980s, when an edition of his *Tvory* (Works, 2 vols, 1985) was published. A selection of his stories, *Cool Mint*, was published in English translation in 1986, and a book about him, by L. Moroz, appeared in 1984.

I. Koshelivets

**Tiutiunnyk, Hryhorii** [Tjutjunnyk, Hryhorij], b 6 May 1920 in Shylivka, Zinkiv county, Poltava gubernia, d 29 August 1961 in Lviv. Writer and pedagogue; brother of Hryhir Tiutiunnyk. He graduated from Kharkiv University in 1946 and worked as a teacher in Galicia. From 1956 he contributed to the journal *Zhovten'*. He began writing verse in his student days and then switched to prose. A collection of his short stories, *Zorani mezhi* (Plowed Boundaries, 1951), and a novel, *Khmarka sontsia ne zastupyt'* (A Small Cloud Won't Blot Out the Sun, 1956), have been published. His major work, one of the most outstanding contributions to Soviet Ukrainian postwar prose, was his novel *Vyr* (The Vortex, 1960–2), in which a collective farm and the events of the Second World War are realistically portrayed. A collection of his poetry, *Zhuravlyni kliuchi* (Skeins of Cranes, 1963), was published posthumously. Books about Tiutiunnyk have been written by L. Volovets (1967) and I. Semenchuk (1971), and an edition of his works (2 vols) appeared in 1970.

**Tiutiunnyk, Vasyl** [Tjutjunnyk, Vasyl'], b 1882 in Yenky, Khorol county, Poltava gubernia, d 20 December 1919 in Rivne, Volhynia gubernia. Senior UNR Army officer. He joined the Army of the UNR in 1917 as a colonel of the General Staff. During 1917–18 he served at the General Staff as chief of the operations department. In 1919 he was deputy chief of staff of the UNR Army, its supreme commander, and then its chief of staff. He died of typhoid.

Gen Vasyl Tiutiunnyk

Gen Yurii Tiutiunnyk

**Tiutiunnyk, Yurii** [Tjutjunnyk, Jurij], b 20 April 1891 in Budyshcha, Hlukhiv county, Chernihiv gubernia, d 1929 in Moscow. Senior UNR Army officer. In 1917 he organized Ukrainian military units in Symferopil and Zvenyhorodka. He was a member of the Central Rada and chairman of the Kiev Revolutionary Committee, which prepared the anti-Hetman uprising. From February 1919 he was chief of staff of N. *Hryhoriiv's partisan force in southern Ukraine. Having broken through the Bolshevik front, he rejoined the Army of the UNR, and was appointed commander of the Kiev Group in the Kiev offensive in August 1919. During the First *Winter Campaign (1919–20) he was commander of the *Kiev Division and deputy commander of the UNR Army. He was promoted to brigadier general. In 1921 he organized and led the Second Winter Campaign. In 1923 he returned to Soviet Ukraine, where he taught at the Kharkiv Red Officer School and wrote film scripts for the All-Ukrainian Photo-Cinema Administration until he was arrested and executed by the GPU. His memoirs appeared in *Literaturno-naukovyi vistnyk* and *Zahrava*, and his political and military essays were published in the collections *Zymovyi pokhid 1919–1920* (The Winter Campaign, 1919–20, 1923), *Z poliakamy proty Vkraïny* (With the Poles against Ukraine, 1924), and *Revoliutsiina stykhiia* (The Revolutionary Force, 1937).

**Tivertsians** (*tivertsi*). An East Slavic tribe that lived between the Dniester, the Prut, and the Danube rivers and southeast from there to the Black Sea, and whose primary activity was agriculture. They are first mentioned in the Primary Chronicle in the 9th century as one of the *tribes that 'lived on the Dniester, in close proximity to the Danube.' They participated as allies of the Kievan Rus' princes Oleh (907) and Ihor (944) in their campaigns against Byzantium. In the mid-10th century they became part of *Kievan Rus'. Under pressure from the Pechenegs and Polovtsians in the 10th to 12th centuries, they moved northward and mixed with neighboring Ukrainian tribes. During the 12th and 13th centuries their territories belonged to the Halych principality. Their descendants became *Ukrainians, and some were Rumanianized. Historical information on the Tivertsians has been gleaned from the chronicles and from archeological artifacts of their settlements and town sites between the Dniester and the Prut rivers. Excavations of the sites, including the Alchedar settlement and the ancient town of Ekimautsy in the Rezina region of Moldavia, began in 1950.

**Tkach, Dmytro** [Tkač], b 24 September 1912 in Orlyk, Kobeliaky county, Poltava gubernia. Socialist-realist children's writer. He worked for newspapers in Kryvyi Rih and Dnipropetrovske, was deputy chief editor of *Dnipro*, chief editor of Molod publishers, and director of Veselka publishers. He began publishing in 1932. Among his works (many of them on Soviet naval themes) are the prose collections *Moriaky* (Sailors, 1948), *Zhdy, liuba divchyno* (Wait, Beloved Girl, 1959), *Malen'ki mriinyky* (Little Dreamers, 1972), *Sadivnyk* (The Orchardist, 1978), and *Pomsta Sapun-hory* (The Revenge of Sapun Mountain, 1987), and the novels *Kruta khvylia* (The Steep Wave, 1954), *Plem'ia duzhykh* (The Tribe of the Powerful, 1957), *Arena* (Arena, 1960), *Shtorm i shtyl'* (The Storm and the Calm, 1978), and *Doroha v Iasne* (The Road to Yasne, 1980). He was awarded the 1981 Lesia Ukrainka Prize for *Shtorm i shtyl'*. A two-volume edition of six other previously published novelettes appeared in 1982.

**Tkach, Mykhailo** [Tkač, Myxajlo], b 26 November 1932 in Lukachany, Bukovyna. Writer. He graduated from the Chernivtsi Medical Institute (1957) and the Gorky Literary Institute (1961) and has worked for the Cinematography Committee of the Ukrainian SSR Council of Ministers. He has written several poetry collections, the first being *Idemo na verkhovyny* (We're Going to the Highlands, 1982), and the most recent, *Krok za obrii* (A Step across the Horizon, 1982) and *Nebo tvoïkh ochei* (The Sky of Your Eyes, 1982); the prose collection *Soniachnyi poluden'* (A Sunny Midday, 1979); the novel *Khlib z dobrykh ruk* (Bread from Good Hands, 1981); song lyrics; and film scripts for Soviet Ukrainian feature and documentary films. He received the 1973 T. Shevchenko Prize for his script for the documentary film *Soviet Ukraine*.

**Tkach, Yurii** [Tkač, Jurij], b 17 February 1954 in Melbourne, Australia. Ukrainian-Australian publisher and translator. An engineer by training, he has been a full-time translator and publisher since 1979 for his own company, Bayda Books in Melbourne. His translations include *Before the Storm: Soviet Ukrainian Fiction of the 1920s*, A. Dimarov's *Across the Bridge*, D. Chub's *So This Is Australia*, O. Honchar's *The Cathedral*, I. Kachurovsky's *Because Deserters Are Immortal*, and *On the Fence: Ukrainian Prose in Australia*.

**Tkachenko, Borys** [Tkačenko], b 1899, d? Linguist and translator. A student of L. Bulakhovsky and O. Syniavsky, in the 1920s and 1930s he lectured at the Kharkiv Institute of People's Education and was a member of the VUAN Dialectological Commission. In 1925–7 he was a member of the special state commission that regulated Ukrainian orthography. He wrote a study of Ukrainian stylistics (5 fasc, late 1920s–early 1930s) and a few articles on Ukrainian lexicology and dialectal morphology, and was the coauthor of a Russian-Ukrainian dictionary (with M. Yohansen, K. Nimchynov, and M. Nakonechny, 1926) and a book of five lectures on the Ukrainian language for teachers (with M. Yohansen, 1928). He also translated foreign literature into Ukrainian. In 1937 he was imprisoned in a

Soviet labor camp, where he perished (in 1940, according to unconfirmed Soviet sources).

**Tkachenko, Ivan** [Tkačenko], b 10 June 1892 in Semenivka, Izium county, Kharkiv gubernia, d ? Literary scholar. In the 1920s he taught the history of Ukrainian literature at the Kharkiv Institute of People's Education and was an associate of the Taras Shevchenko Scientific Research Institute. He compiled a bibliography of Slobidska Ukrainian writers and researched the life of M. Drahomanov and the works of P. Myrny. He published articles on Myrny in *Chervonyi shliakh* and *Literaturnyi arkhiv*, on I. Franko in *Chervonyi shliakh*, and on P. Kulish's poetry in *Zapysky Istorychno-filolohichnoho viddilu VUAN*. Tkachenko also edited, with an introduction, the 1928 and 1929 editions of Myrny's works (vols 1–2, 5) and wrote biographical booklets about Franko (1926) and Kulish. He was arrested during the Stalinist terror, and most likely died or was killed in a labor camp.

Mykhailo Tkachenko: *Spring* (oil, 1907)

**Tkachenko, Mykhailo** [Tkačenko, Myxajlo], b 1860 in Kharkiv, d 1916 near Slovianske, Bakhmut county, Katerynoslav gubernia. Painter. He studied at the St Petersburg Academy of Arts and then under F. Cormon at the Académie des beaux arts in Paris (1888–92). He remained in Paris until 1914 and from there visited Ukraine each year. A specialist in landscapes and seascapes, he created canvases such as *Landscape in Kharkiv Gubernia*, *Donets River*, *By the Road*, *Village Cemetery* (1887), *Sunset on the Sea* (1901), *Incoming Waves* (1902–6), and *Spring* (1907). His works, many of which depict Ukraine, were exhibited in Paris (solo exhibition in 1909) and have been preserved in museums in Kharkiv, Lviv, Paris, Liège, and Toulon. He also painted a landscape mural for the library of the Poltava Zemstvo Building and other canvases there (1903–8). A monograph about him was published in 1963.

**Tkachenko, Mykhailo** [Tkačenko, Myxajlo] (pseud: Khvylia), b 1879 in Starodub county, Chernihiv gubernia, d 1920 in Moscow. Civic and political activist; husband of N. *Romanovych-Tkachenko. A lawyer by profession, he was a member of the Revolutionary Ukrainian party

Mykhailo Tkachenko
(1879–1920)

(1902–4) and then of Spilka and the *Ukrainian Social Democratic Worker's party (USDRP). He became one of the leading ideologues of the USDRP, as well as its representative to the Central Rada. He was the Rada's secretary general (1917), and in the UNR he served as minister of justice (November 1917 to March 1918) and the interior (to April 1918). From January 1919 he led the left, Independentist faction of the USDRP, which in 1920 established the *Ukrainian Communist party (UCP). He died during negotiations for the legalization of the UCP.

**Tkachenko, Mykola** [Tkačenko], b 4 January 1893 in Talne, Cherkasy county, Kiev gubernia, d 7 November 1965 in Kiev. Historian and literary scholar. A graduate of Kiev University (1916), he worked at the VUAN (from 1919) on the Historical-Geographical Commission and as head of the Archeographic Commission. He also worked at the AN URSR (now ANU) institutes of History and Literature and studied the socioeconomic history of 17th- and 18th-century Ukraine. He wrote *Istoriia revoliutsiinoï borot'by u Kyievi v XIX ta na pochatku XX st.* (A History of the Revolutionary Struggle in Kiev in the 19th and Early 20th Centuries, 1930), *Narysy z istoriï selian na Livoberezhnii Ukraïni v XVII–XVIII st.* (Essays in the History of the Peasantry in Left-Bank Ukraine during the 17th–18th Centuries, 1931), and *Litopys zhyttia i tvorchosti T.H. Shevchenka* (A Chronicle of the Life and Works of T. Shevchenko, 1961); coauthored the collective work *Istoriia Kyieva* (History of Kiev, 1959–60); and coedited the complete collection of Shevchenko's works (6 vols, 1963–4).

**Tkachenko, Nadiia** [Tkačenko, Nadija], b 9 September 1948 in Kremenchuk, Poltava oblast. Pentathlete. The 1973–5 and 1978 USSR and 1974 European champion and the 1977 European Cup winner, she set a world record in 1977. In 1980 she won the Olympic gold medal and set another world record.

**Tkachenko, Ninel** [Tkačenko, Ninel'], b 21 November 1928 in Kharkiv. Opera singer (lyric-dramatic soprano). In 1958 she completed study at the Kharkiv Conservatory. She then appeared as a soloist in Lviv and Minsk before joining the Odessa Theater of Opera and Ballet in 1968. Her main roles were Lisa in P. Tchaikovsky's *The Queen of Spades*, Mavka in V. Kyreiko's *The Forest Song*, and the name-part in G. Verdi's *Aida*.

Oleksandr Tkachenko: *Flowering Cactus* (mixed media, 1988)

**Tkachenko, Oleksandr** [Tkačenko], b 15 May 1952 in Kryvyi Rih. Painter. A graduate of the Dnipropetrovske Art School (1971), he has made a living as a commercial artist. His mixed-media paintings on an etched surface consist of watercolors and pen-and-ink line drawings. They are surrealistic, dreamlike visions of the fantastic intertwined with reality. Tkachenko's first solo exhibitions were held in Dnipropetrovske in 1989 and in Warsaw and Toronto in 1990.

**Tkachenko, Orest** [Tkačenko], b 10 December 1925 in Kharkiv. Linguist; son of B. *Tkachenko. He studied at Kharkiv (1945–7) and Kiev (1947–50) universities and completed his graduate work in Slavic linguistics under L. Bulakhovsky at the AN URSR (now ANU) Institute of Linguistics (1950–3, doctorate in 1982). After joining the institute as a researcher, he chaired the Terminological Commission of the Ukrainian Committee of Slavists (1965–8) and helped compile the dictionary of Slavic linguistic terminology. Tkachenko has written articles in the fields of Slavic, Finno-Ugric, Romance, and Indo-European linguistics, sociolinguistics, and interlinguistics (Esperanto); on Ukrainian language stability; and on Oriental studies in Ukraine. His monographs (in Russian) deal with the comparative-historical phraseology of the Slavic and Finno-Ugric languages (1979), the Meri language (1985), and the theory of the linguistic substratum (1989). He is also the coauthor of a book in Ukrainian on the comparative-historical study of the Slavic languages (1966) and a coeditor and coauthor of the ANU Ukrainian etymological dictionary (7 vols, 1982–).

**Tkachenko, Valentyna** [Tkačenko], b 6 March 1920 in Koriukivka, Chernihiv gubernia, d 19 December 1970 in Kiev. Lyric poet. After the Second World War she worked as an editor at the republican radio committee and for the publishing house Molod. She published 16 poetry collections, including *Zelena storona* (The Green Side, 1940), *Vesniani vitry* (Spring Winds, 1950), *Liryka* (Lyricism, 1956), *Zhyttia iednaie ruky* (Life Joins Hands, 1960), *Zemlia radiie sontsiu* (The Earth Is Glad of the Sun, 1962), *Skoro bude vesna* (Soon It Will Be Spring, 1963), *Ne mynaie molodist'* (Youth Doesn't Pass, 1966), and *Zelene peredzym'ia* (The Green Prewinter, 1970). She also wrote two books of articles, both titled *Rozmova pro liubov* (A Talk about Love, 1960, 1964), and four books of poetry for children.

**Tkachenko, Yuliia** [Tkačenko, Julija], b 25 July 1928 in Kiev. Stage actress. She completed study at the Kiev Institute of Theater Arts (1950) and was a leading actress in the Kiev Ukrainian Drama Theater, acclaimed for playing the title role in Lesia Ukrainka's *Kassandra* and Inhiherda (Ingigerth) in I. Kocherha's *Iaroslav Mudryi* (Yaroslav the Wise).

**Tkachenko-Halashko, Petro** [Tkačenko-Halaško], b 2 January 1879 in Syniavka, Sosnytsia county, Chernihiv gubernia, d 3 January 1919 in Syniavka. Kobzar. He was blinded at a young age and learned to play the kobza from T. Parkhomenko. His repertoire included the dumas about a brother and sister, the widow, and the captives' lament, as well as historical songs and musical adaptations of T. Shevchenko's verses. He wandered through much of Ukraine and the Kuban region.

Archimandrite Dionysii    Ivan Tkachuk
Dmytro Tkachuk

**Tkachuk, Dionysii Dmytro** [Tkačuk, Dionysij Dmytro], b 9 November 1867 in Kniahynyn, Stanyslaviv county, Galicia, d 24 January 1944 in Rome. Basilian priest. He instructed novices and headed the Basilian monasteries in Buchach, Lavriv, Dobromyl, and Krekhiv. In 1931 he was appointed the first superior general of the Basilian order following the reforms of 1882. From then he lived in Rome and directed the order's activites.

**Tkachuk, Ivan** [Tkačuk] (pseud: Ivan Chornobyl), b 25 September 1891 in Piadyky, Kolomyia county, Galicia, d 9 October 1948 in Lviv. Writer and journalist. After being released from a Russian POW camp following the February Revolution of 1917, he joined the Bolshevik party and remained in Soviet Ukraine. He edited the newspapers *Chervona pravda* (Kiev, 1920), *Selians'ka pravda* (Katerynoslav, 1921–3), *Zirka* (Katerynoslav, 1923–4), and *Radians'kyi step* (Melitopil, 1924), and the journal *\*Zoria* (Dnipropetrovske, 1925–9). From 1925 to 1933 he belonged to the writers' group Zakhidnia Ukraina. His stories and articles on political, literary, and cultural topics appeared in Soviet Ukrainian and Ukrainian communist periodicals in Lviv, the United States, and Canada. Published separately were his prose collections *Pomsta* (Revenge, 1927), *Smerekovi shumy* (The Spruces' Murmurings, 1929), *Nezakinchenyi lyst* (An Unfinished Letter, 1930), *Na vkradenii zemli* (On the Stolen Land, 1930; 2nd edn 1933), *Prostrilenyi dekret* (The Plugged Decree, 1930), *Ukraïntsi za okeanom* (Ukrainians across the Ocean, 1930), *Straik* (Strike, 1931), and *Za Kavkaz'kymy khrebtamy* (Beyond the Caucasian Ranges, 1932). He also coauthored (with M. Skrypnyk and Ye. Cherniak) a book of essays on contemporary Western Ukrainian literature (1930) and wrote a short book about revolutionary proletarian literature in Western Ukraine (1932). He was arrested in 1933, and was imprisoned in a Soviet labor camp. When he was released and settled in Lviv after the Second World War he was a very sick man. Posthumous editions of his works were published in 1955, 1962, and 1968.

R. Senkus

Lukian Tkachuk   Virlana Tkacz

**Tkachuk, Lukian** [Tkačuk, Lukjan], b 28 October 1902 in Nemyryntsi, Berdychiv county, Kiev gubernia, d 20 June 1981 in Kiev. Geologist; full member of the AN URSR (now ANU) from 1972. He graduated in 1926 from the Kiev Institute of People's Education and then taught at institutes of higher education in Kiev. He was director of the petrography laboratory at the ANU Institute of the Geology and Geochemistry of Fossil Fuels in Lviv (1945–61) and at the same time chaired the mineralogy and petrography department at the Lviv Polytechnical Institute. He moved to Kiev in 1961, where he became head of the lithology department at the ANU Institute of Geologi-

cal Sciences and then of the Department of the Geology and Geochemistry of Lithogenesis at the Institute of the Geochemistry and Physics of Minerals. His research centered on the lithology of sedimentary and sedimentary-vulcanogenic formations in the Ukrainian part of the Carpathian Mountains and the southwestern part of the East European plate, as well as on the petrography of magmatic and metamorphic rocks of the Ukrainian Crystalline Shield.

**Tkachuk, Olha** [Tkačuk, Ol'ha], b 6 January 1913 in Zhubrovychi, Ovruch county, Volhynia gubernia, d 9 June 1983. Writer and teacher. She graduated from Warsaw University and then worked as a teacher. From 1954 on she contributed articles, sketches, stories, and novels to Soviet periodicals. Published separately were her novels *Nazustrich voli* (Meeting Freedom, 1955) and *Pereorani mezhi* (Plowed-over Boundaries, 1973) and the prose collections *Maty* (Mother, 1960) and *Stezhky zhyttia* (Life's Paths, 1967).

**Tkachuk, Stepan** [Tkačuk], b 13 January 1936 in Dănila, Suceava county, Bukovyna. Ukrainian writer in postwar Rumania. An engineer in Bucharest, since 1954 he has contributed poems, translations of Rumanian poetry, and articles to the Bucharest Ukrainian paper *Novyi vik*. Published separately have been numerous poetry collections, the first being *Rozkolote nebo* (The Cloven Sky, 1971), and the most recent, *Smikh i plach sliv* (The Laughter and Crying of Words, 1986); the story collections *Suzir'ia predkiv* (Constellation of the Ancestors, 1974) and *Kaleidoskop* (Kaleidoscope, 1985); and the novel *Nichyia pora* (Nobody's Time, 1979). Tkachuk has also written two poetry collections in Rumanian. Since 1979 his poems, stories, and literary profiles have appeared in the Bucharest almanac *Obriï* (Horizons). He has also translated into Rumanian poetry collections by L. Kostenko, I. Drach, D. Pavlychko, and B. Oliinyk and an anthology of contemporary Soviet Ukrainian poetry. In 1990 Tkachuk was elected the first head of the Union of Ukrainians of Rumania.

**Tkachuk, Vasyl** [Tkačuk, Vasyl'], b 13 January 1916 in Ilyntsi, Sniatyn county, Galicia, d ? Writer. A self-educated peasant, he wrote novellas in the manner of V. \*Stefanyk. They appeared in Galician periodicals of the 1930s, such as *Zhinocha dolia*, *Narodnia sprava*, *Nedilia*, *Nash prapor*, *Novyi chas*, *Dilo*, *Nazustrich*, and *Duzhboh*. Published separately were the collections *Syni chichky* (Blue Florets, 1935), *Zoloti dzvinky* (Golden Bells, 1936), and *Zymova melodiia* (A Winter Melody, 1938). Tkachuk disappeared in 1944 without a trace.

**Tkacz, Virlana** [Tkač], b 23 June 1952 in Newark, New Jersey. Theater director. Tkacz received degrees in literature and drama from Bennington College in Vermont (1974) and theater directing from Columbia University (1983). Based at the La Mama theater in New York since 1985, she has directed *Three Moons* (1984) and *An Altar to Himself* (1989). In 1990 she founded the Yara Arts Group, for which she created and directed 'A Light from the East,' based on L. \*Kurbas's diary and P. \*Tychyna's poetry (translated by Tkacz and the African–American poet W. Phipps). Tkacz toured Ukraine with the group (1991), developed a bilingual version of the show, and conducted theater workshops in Kiev, Lviv, and Kharkiv. She has written articles in English on L. Kurbas, and together with L. and N. Taniuk and R. Bahry she founded the International Kurbas Society (1989).

**Tlumach.** See Tovmach.

An 11th-century stone icon of St Hlib from Tmutorokan

Sofiia Tobilevych

**Tmutorokan** [Tmutorokan']. A city of Kievan Rus', at the site of the ancient Greek colony of *Hermonassa (now Taman village, Krasnodar krai) in the Taman Peninsula. From the 6th century the territory was under Byzantine rule. The earliest reference to Tmutorokan (Tamantarcha in Greek) appears in an early 8th-century list of the eparchies of the Byzantine patriarchate. The eparchy came under Dorus metropoly in the Crimea. In the 10th century it was elevated to the status of an archeparchy under the jurisdiction of the patriarch of Constantinople. In the 8th and 9th centuries the whole Taman Peninsula belonged to the Khazar kaganate. After Sviatoslav the Conqueror's decisive defeat of the Khazars in 965, Tmutorokan emerged as the center of an appanage principality of the Kievan state. Through Tmutorokan Kiev maintained political and economic contacts with the Byzantine Empire and northern Caucasia. The remote principality also provided refuge for princes who had been defeated in the power struggles at the center. When the Cumans gained control of the steppes, Tmutorokan became cut off from the rest of Rus', but it preserved its independence until the late 11th century. Thereafter it was dominated by the nomads, the Byzantine emperors, the Genoese merchants (13th century), and the Golden Horde. In the 15th century it was recovered by Genoa, and at the end of the century it was razed by the Turks and Tatars.

Major excavations of the site in 1824–45 (led by A. Tarasenko), 1930–1 (O. Miller), and 1952–5 (B. Rybakov) showed that the city had been encircled with a brick wall, its streets had been paved with stone, and the houses had been built of brick and covered with tiled roofs. The foundations of the Church of the Theotokos, built in 1023 by Mstyslav Volodymyrovych in gratitude for his victory over Rededia, and of the monastery founded by *Nykon in 1061 have been unearthed. The *Tmutorokan plate was discovered in the vicinity.

BIBLIOGRAPHY
Rybakov, B. *Keramika i steklo drevnei Tmutarakani* (Moscow 1963)
Korovina, A. *Raskopki Tmutarakanskogo gorodishcha: Arkheologicheskie otkrytiia* (Moscow 1973)

A. Zhukovsky

**Tmutorokan plate.** A marble plate with the Slavonic inscription 'In the Year 6576 [ie, 1068] Prince Hlib Measured the Sea by Ice from Tmutorokan to Korch [Kerch] at 14,000 *sazhni* [approx 28 km].' It was discovered in 1792 on the eastern shore of Kerch Strait and has been preserved at the Hermitage in St Petersburg since 1851.

**Tmutorokan principality.** An appanage principality of Kievan Rus' in the 10th and 11th centuries. It encompassed the Taman and Kerch peninsulas, and its capital was *Tmutorokan. The principality arose and became part of the Rus' state in the mid-10th century, after Sviatoslav the Conqueror's defeat of the Khazars. It is first mentioned in the chronicles under the year 988, when Volodymyr the Great granted the principality to his son, Mstyslav (988–1036), who added Chernihiv principality to his possessions in 1024 after defeating his brother, Yaroslav. For Rus' Tmutorokan served not only as a strategic stronghold but also as a trading center and access point to the Near East. At Mstyslav's death in 1036, the principality became part of the unified state ruled by Yaroslav the Wise. At his death (1054) it was inherited by his son, Sviatoslav, the prince of Chernihiv, who placed his son, Hlib, on the Tmutorokan throne. But Hlib was deposed immediately by his cousin, Rostyslav Volodymyrovych, who had been expelled from Halych. When Rostyslav was poisoned in 1067 by the Byzantine authorities, Hlib Sviatoslavych returned to Tmutorokan. Then the brothers Roman and Oleh Sviatoslavych, from Chernihiv, contested Tmutorokan with Vsevolod and Iziaslav Yaroslavych. The Cumans, Khazars, and Greeks became involved in the struggle. In 1079 Roman was killed by the Cumans, and Oleh was captured by the Khazars and handed over to the Greeks. With Greek military support Oleh captured the principality in 1083. Ten years later he won control of Chernihiv principality and left Tmutorokan for good. After 1094 the chronicles are silent about Tmutorokan, which was cut off from Rus'. Some historians believe that the principality continued to exist under the domination of the Cumans and Byzantium until it was destroyed by the Mongols in the 13th century.

M. Zhdan

**Toad** (*Bufo*; Ukrainian: *ropukha*). A squat, rough-skinned, tailless amphibian of the family Bufonidae. Its stout body and short legs give it a characteristic hopping gait. Toads possess poison-secreting glands on the back and behind the eyes. Of the more than 150 species of true toads (*Bufo*) there are 3 in Ukraine, the European toad (*B. bufo*; Ukrainian: *ropukha sira*), the green toad (*B. viridis*), which inhabits mostly the Crimean Peninsula, and the natterjack toad (*B. calamita*; Ukrainian: *ropukha ocheretiana*), a protected species living in western Ukraine. As consumers of agricultural pests they are considered beneficial animals.

**Toad, European spadefoot** (*Pelobates fuscus*; Ukrainian: *chasnychnytsia*). A relatively smooth-skinned, tailless Old World amphibian of the family Pelobatidae. It is a nocturnal animal. Its body is gray to yellowish gray on top and white on the bottom, and it has a broad projection from the inside of each hind foot adaptable for burrowing. In the spring the spadefoot emanates a garlicky smell – hence the Ukrainian name, 'garlic toad.'

**Tobacco** (*Nicotiana*; Ukrainian: *tiutiun*). An annual or perennial leafy herb of the family Solanaceae, including true tobacco (*N. tabacum*) and Indian tobacco (*N. rustica*; Ukrainian: *makhorka*). Tobacco is a widely cultivated narcotic that is no longer found in the wild state. It was introduced into Cossack Ukraine through Turkey during the 17th century. The Pereiaslav regiment was authorized by King Władysław to distribute tobacco throughout Poland, but export to Muscovy was forbidden by a provision of the *Hlukhiv Articles of 1687. Peter I introduced tobacco into Muscovy in the early 18th century, and the first tobacco factory in the Russian Empire was established (1718) in Okhtyrka, a regimental center in Slobidska Ukraine. The crop was suited to large estates with an enserfed population. Chernihiv and Poltava gubernias emerged as major centers of tobacco production; they accounted for approx 60 percent of the empire's tobacco in the 1860s and 1870s outside Caucasia. Tobacco products are smoked, snuffed, chewed, and extracted to produce nicotine. Ukraine produces large-leaf tobacco and *makhorka* (shag) for cigars and cigarettes; the yield is 4–6 t of leaves per ha. The following types are popular: Hostrolyst B2474, Soboltskyi, Amerykan 572, Diubek 44, and Peremozhets 83. Tobacco is also used to produce citric acid and pesticides.

**Tobacco industry.** A branch of industry that manufactures tobacco goods, such as cigarettes, cigars, and pipe tobacco. The first tobacco factory in the Russian Empire was a state-owned enterprise established on the orders of Peter I in Okhtyrka, Slobidska Ukraine, in 1718. Until the 1860s the tobacco grown in the Ukrainian gubernias was either processed on the plantations where it was grown, or exported to Russia or Holland for processing. After the abolition of serfdom the number of small tobacco factories in Ukraine increased rapidly. At the beginning of the 20th century a number of joint-stock tobacco companies arose in Russian-ruled Ukraine. In 1913 a monopolistic tobacco consortium achieved control of 75 percent of the cigarette market. There were 109 tobacco factories in the Ukrainian gubernias at that time. They employed about 6,000 workers and produced 3.1 billion cigarettes (12 percent of the empire's output). In 1911 1,883 t of *makhorka* (shag) and 194 t of tobacco were produced in Ukraine. The lower-grade *makhorka* was usually processed by small enterprises located close to the source of the raw material, and the higher-grade tobacco was shipped to the larger manufacturing centers in Ukraine, such as Odessa, Kiev, Kremenchuk, and Teodosiia. The large factories used not only Ukrainian-grown but also imported tobacco, and their products were shipped to other parts of the empire and abroad.

In Galicia the Austrian government established a state monopoly on tobacco and tobacco products in 1778. By the end of the 18th century large tobacco factories had been built in Vynnyky, near Lviv, and Manastyryska, and by the end of the 19th century, in Yaholnytsia, Zabolotiv, and Borshchiv. The factories used domestic and imported tobacco. The profits on tobacco sales rose steadily, from approx 34 million kronen in 1848 to 340 million kronen in

1913. On the eve of the First World War the tobacco industry in Galicia employed nearly 4,000 people (over 1,500 in Vynnyky alone). Most of the prewar tobacco factories continued to operate in the interwar period.

Under the Soviet regime tobacco factories were nationalized, and the industry was concentrated in the larger cities. By 1940 there were only 15 enterprises in Ukraine. Their output consisted mostly of cigarettes, the production of which in 1940 totaled 22.3 billion. After the Second World War the industry was modernized. Today there are 10 tobacco factories in Ukraine. The largest ones are in Lviv, Kiev, Cherkasy, Pryluka, and Kharkiv. There is a similar number of tobacco fermentation plants, the largest of which are in Zhmerynka, Symferopil, Berehove, and Borshchiv. In 1982 the Ukrainian SSR produced 77.9 billion cigarettes.

After Ukraine's declaration of independence in 1991 R.J. Reynold's Tobacco International purchased 70-percent ownership in two of the largest tobacco factories in Ukraine (in Lviv and Kremenchuk), which produce a quarter of the 80 billion cigarettes consumed by Ukrainians annually.

**Tobilevych** [Tobilevyč]. A family of distinguished theater activists of the late 19th and early 20th centuries that greatly influenced the development of Ukrainian theater and drama. The brothers were known by their pseudonyms – the actor and playwright Ivan *Karpenko-Kary and the actors and troupe directors Mykola *Sadovsky and Panas *Saksahansky. Their sister, M. *Sadovska-Barilotti, was an actress and singer. Karpenko-Kary's wife, Sofiia *Tobilevych, was an actress, translator, and author of memoirs.

**Tobilevych, Ivan.** See Karpenko-Kary, Ivan.

**Tobilevych, Sofiia** [Tobilevyč, Sofija] (née Ditkovska), b 15 October 1860 in Novoselytsia, Lityn county, Podilia gubernia, d 7 October 1953 in Kiev. Character actress, writer, and ethnographer; wife of I. Karpenko-Kary. She sang in M. Lysenko's choir (1880–3) and in the choir in M. Starytsky's troupe (1883–4) and then acted in the troupes of P. Saksahansky (1890–1907) and M. Sadovsky (1888–90) and in Sadovsky's Theater (1908–16), the Franko New Drama Theater (1920–2), and the Shevchenko First Theater of the Ukrainian Socialist Republic (1924). She toured with Saksahansky and Sadovsky (1926–30). In 1935 she appeared on stage for the last time, as Natalka's mother in I. Kotliarevsky's *Natalka Poltavka* (Natalka from Poltava). Tobilevych translated many plays into Ukrainian (mostly from French and Polish) and wrote *Zhyttia Ivana Tobilevycha* (The Life of Ivan Tobilevych, 1945) and her memoirs, *Moï stezhky i zustrichi* (My Paths and Meetings, 1957).

**Tobilevych Theater** (Teatr im. I. Tobilevycha). One of the foremost theaters in Western Ukraine, established in 1928 as a stationary theater in Stanyslaviv, with a cast from a drama circle (active in 1919–28) and a predominantly musical repertoire. In 1929–30 it became a touring theater under M. *Bentsal and V. *Blavatsky. Bentsal was a director of the realistic school, and Blavatsky was a proponent of the *Berezil experimental style. Besides Ukrainian classics of the 19th century, contemporary European dramas, and operettas the Tobilevych Theater successfully staged new heroic-romantic plays, including *Mazepa* (an adaptation of B. Lepky's trilogy), *Hory hovoriat* (The Mountains Speak, based on U. Samchuk's novel), and Yu. Horlis-Horsky's *Kholodnyi iar*. Blavatsky departed with part of the cast in 1932 to form the *Zahrava Theater, and the Tobilevych Theater continued under Bentsal and Y. Stadnyk (1933–5) until 1938, when it and Zahrava combined to form the Kotliarevsky Theater (later the *Lesia Ukrainka Theater).

**Tochylo, Mykola.** See Koliankivsky, Mykola.

*Tochylo* (Grindstone). A monthly humor magazine published in Winnipeg from January 1930 to December 1947. It satirized Ukrainian political, religious, and community life in Canada. *Tochylo* was published and edited by S. Doroshchuk and then I. Andrusiak.

**Todorov, Mykhailo,** b 6 June 1915 in Odessa. Artist. He studied at the Institute of Painting, Sculpture, and Architecture in Leningrad (1939–41, 1945–9) and taught at the Odessa Art School (1951–7). He has painted landscapes, portraits, still lifes, and canvases on athletic and sports themes. They include *Bilhorod-Dnistrovskyi Fortress* (1958), *Swallow* (1960), *Near Odessa's Shores* (1960, 1964), *Midday* (1964), *Shevchenko Park in Odessa* (1964), *White Cloud* (1964), *Kabuki Theater in Tokyo* (1964), *A Partisan Land: Kodyma Forests* (1964), *Young Sportsman* (1964), *Crimea: Sudak* (1965), *Red Trees* (1965), *Above the Precipice* (1966), *Morning: Odessa* (1965–7), *Olympic Fire* (1966–7), *Youths* (1970–1), and portraits of the Olympic athletes M. Avilov (1975) and Yu. Riabchynska (1977).

**Tohobichny, Ivan.** See Shchoholiv, Ivan.

**Tokarevsky, Makarii** [Tokarevs'kyj, Makarij], b ? in Ovruch, Volhynia, d 13 September 1678 in Kaniv. Orthodox monk. He was forced out of his position as archimandrite of the Ovruch Monastery when the Uniates gained control of the monastery, and he became hegumen of the Dormition Monastery in Kaniv in 1671. He was tortured and killed by the Turks during a raid on the city and came to be regarded as a martyr for his faith. His remains were at a later time moved to Pereiaslav, where they eventually came to rest at the Ascension Monastery. The Ukrainian Orthodox church considers him a saint; his feast day is 20 September (7 September OS).

**Tokarevsky, Mykhailo** [Tokarevs'kyj, Myxajlo], b 19 November 1884 in Mashivka, Kostiantynohrad county, Poltava gubernia, d ? Co-operative and civic activist in the Poltava region. He studied at the Moscow Commercial Institute and was a member of the Ukrainian Social Democratic Workers' party until his arrest in 1911. His three-year term of exile was served in Ostrohozke. He was an executive member of the Poltava Association of Consumer Co-operatives, and in 1917–18 he was president of the executive of the Poltava gubernia zemstvo. In the Soviet period he worked for the All-Ukrainian Association of Consumer Co-operative Organizations as deputy director of its Co-operative Institute in Kiev and then head of its Co-operative Museum. Twice arrested (1929 and 1936) and twice released, he led a precarious existence in Kharkiv through the 1930s. He disappeared completely

Mykhailo Tokarevsky        Jan Tokarzewski-Karaszewicz

after his arrest in 1943 for active involvement in the co-operative movement (considered as collaboration) that revived in the region following the Soviet retreat in 1941.

**Tokarzewski-Karaszewicz, Jan** (Tokarzhevsky-Karashevych), b 24 June 1885 in Chabanivka, Ushytsia county, Podilia gubernia, d 18 November 1954 in London (buried in Bound Brook, New Jersey). Ukrainian diplomat and heraldist, descended from Polish nobility (the Janiszewski family). He obtained a doctorate at Fribourg University in Switzerland. In 1911–18 he worked in the Poltava gubernial and zemstvo administrations and was general comptroller of the zemstvo Red Cross Committee. He served as an adviser to the UNR missions in Vienna (June 1918 to June 1919) and Istanbul (August 1919 to March 1920) and as consul general in Istanbul (to December 1921). In January 1922 he became director of the Ministry of External Affairs for the UNR government-in-exile. In Paris (from 1924) he headed the International Heraldic Institute and supported the Promethean movement; in Rome (from 1936) he worked in the archives of the Vatican; and in London (from 1948) he was a leading member of the Anti-Bolshevik Bloc of Nations. His writings included numerous articles in Polish, French, Italian, German, and English on Ukrainian history, literature, and heraldry, as well as the unpublished monograph 'Istoriia ukraïns'koï dyplomatiï' (A History of Ukrainian Diplomacy).

**Tokmak.** VI-16. A city (1989 pop 45,800) on the Molochna River and a raion center in Zaporizhia oblast. It originated in 1784 as a settlement of state peasants from Poltava gubernia. The village prospered: by 1861 it had 8,000 inhabitants, and that year it was renamed Velykyi Tokmak. In 1882 a farm-machinery shop was set up. The construction of the Velykyi Tokmak–Fedorivka railway line (1910) stimulated industrial development. In 1938 the town was given city status, and in 1962 its original name was restored. Today Tokmak is an industrial center that produces sheet metal, diesel engines, agricultural machinery, canned and baked goods, granite, and furniture.

**Tolba, Veniamin** [Tol'ba, Venjamin], b 12 November 1909 in Kharkiv. Conductor and pedagogue. A graduate of the Kharkiv Institute of Music and Drama (1932), he studied score reading with D. Shostakovich and conducting with Y. Rosenstein. In 1931–44 he conducted the Kharkiv Opera and lectured at the Kharkiv Conservatory.

He then went on to the Kiev Opera (1944–59) and Kiev Conservatory (1946–73), where he lectured and conducted its opera studio. He premiered a number of works, including M. Verykivsky's opera *The Servant-Girl* (1943), H. Maiboroda's opera *Arsenal* (1960), and H. Zhukovsky's ballet *Rostyslava* (1955). He also orchestrated M. Lysenko's opera *Nocturne* and edited L. Revutsky's *Second Symphony*.

A mural by Zinovii Tolkachov in the Komsomol Club in Kiev (1921)

**Tolkachov, Zinovii** [Tolkačov, Zinovij], b 25 February 1903 in Shchadryn, Rahachou county, Mahiliou gubernia, Belarus, d 30 August 1977 in Kiev. Painter and graphic artist. He studied at the Moscow Higher Artistic and Technical Workshop (1919–20) and the Kiev State Art Institute (1928–9). He painted murals in Communist Youth League clubs in Kiev (1921–2); created the lithograph series 'Lenin – the Masses' (1924–8), 'The Trypilia Tragedy' (1937), 'Occupiers' (1941–3), 'Majdanek' (1944–5), and 'Auschwitz' (1945); painted portraits of political and literary figures (eg, Artem, V. Blakytny, V. Chumak); illustrated editions of works by O. Korniichuk (1939) and M. Vovchok (1950); designed posters; and drew caricatures for *Perets'*. A book about him was published in 1933, and an album of his 'Auschwitz' series came out in 1965.

*Tolkovaia paleia* (Explanatory Old Testament). An Old Church Slavonic literary monument of the 10th to 13th centuries. It contains stories from the Old Testament with commentaries, most of which are used to illustrate the faults of Judaism; apocrypha; and parts of the *Hexaemeron* of Basil the Great as translated and revised by the Bulgarian John the Exarch. Fifteen copies of the manuscript have survived, in several redactions. The *Tolkovaia paleia* had a great influence on the original literature of Kievan Rus' and was one of the sources used in the compilation of the Primary Chronicle.

**Tolochko, Petro** [Toločko], b 21 February 1938 in Prystromy, Pereiaslav-Khmelnytskyi raion, Kiev oblast. Archeologist; full member of the AN URSR (now ANU) since 1990 and vice-president of ANU since 1993. A graduate of

Petro Tolochko

Kiev University (1960), he has worked at the ANU Institute of Archeology since 1961, as director since 1988. He has played a prominent role in recent archeological excavations in Kiev that have revealed a clear picture of the city's growth. Tolochko is a strong proponent of the theory that the state of Rus' was formed at the same time that Kiev was founded in the late fifth century. He has written or edited many works, including *Istorychna topohrafiia starodavn'oho Kyieva* (The Historical Topography of Ancient Kiev, 1970), *Starodavnii Kyïv* (Ancient Kiev, 1975), *Arkheolohichni doslidzhennia storodavn'oho Kyïva* (Archeological Research on Ancient Kiev, 1976), *Kiev i Kievskaia zemlia v epokhu feodal'noi razdroblennosti XII–XIII vv.* (Kiev and the Kievan Land during the Period of Feudal Fragmentation in the 12th and 13th Centuries, 1980), and *Drevniaia Rus': Ocherki sotsial'no-politicheskoi istorii* (Ancient Rus': Surveys of Social-Political History, 1987).

Viktor Tolochko: *In the Feather-Grass Steppe* (oil, 1982)

**Tolochko, Viktor** [Toločko], b 22 October 1922 in Melitopil, Tavriia gubernia. Painter. He graduated from the Kharkiv Art Institute (1957), where he studied under O. Kokel and O. Liubymsky. A resident of Donetske, he has painted landscapes, still lifes, and depictions of the Second World War. They include *Moonlit Night in Crimea* (1960), *Lilac and Tulips* (1964), *Old Dock* (1969), *Azure Landscape* (1971), *In the Artist's Studio* (1975), *Still Life with Cacti* (1977), *Fishermen's Nets* (1978), *Sevastopil* (1980), *The Almond Blooms* (1981), *In the Feather-Grass Steppe* (1982), *Par-*

*tisans* (1982), *Cliffs by the Sea* (1982), *Rains* (1982), *In Memory of the Soldier* (1983), and *The Storm Passed* (1985). An album of his works was published in 1987.

**Tolochynov, Mykola** [Toločynov], b 8 March 1838 in Starodub, Chernihiv gubernia, d 23 May 1908 in Kharkiv. Obstetrician and gynecologist. A graduate of the St Petersburg Medico-Surgical Academy (1864), he completed a doctoral dissertation in 1867 and specialized in Vienna. He lectured at Kiev (1870–85) and Kharkiv (1885–1902) universities and in 1902 became director of the zemstvo childbirth center in Kharkiv. His publications dealt with asepsis and antisepsis in obstetric practice, the mechanisms of birth, extrauterine pregnancy, and the history of obstetrics and pediatrics.

**Tolok, Volodymyr,** b 25 December 1926 in Uman, now in Cherkasy oblast. Experimental physicist; AN URSR (now ANU) corresponding member since 1972. A graduate of Kharkiv University (1951), since 1952 he has worked at the ANU Physical-Technical Institute in Kharkiv. Considered to be one of the top experts on the high-frequency heating of thermonuclear plasma for controlled fusion, he has made significant contributions to the design and construction of particle accelerators and experimental controlled thermonuclear devices.

**Tolopko, Leon** (pseud: M. Pilny), b 11 August 1902 in New York, d 20 January 1991 in New York. Ukrainian-American journalist and community leader. In 1908 he moved with his parents to Galicia, where he completed study at the Lviv Teachers' Seminary. Afterward he worked as a teacher in Poland. He returned to the United States in 1927, and from the 1930s he was active in the Communist party there. From 1956 to the mid-1980s he edited the pro-Soviet newspaper *Ukraïns'ki visti*, and in 1980 he became president of the League of American Ukrainians. Tolopko wrote several propagandistic plays about Ukrainian life in the United States and about the USSR, which were staged by amateur Ukrainian theater groups in North America, and a history of Ukrainians in the United States (2 vols, 1984, 1991).

**Tolpyho, Kyrylo** (Tolpigo, Kirill), b 3 May 1916 in Kiev. Theoretical physicist; AN URSR (now ANU) corresponding member since 1965. A graduate of Kiev University (1939), he worked at the ANU Institute of Physics (1945–59), chaired the department of theoretical physics at Kiev University (1960–6), headed a department at the ANU Physical-Technical Institute in Donetske (from 1966), and chaired the department of theoretical physics at Donetske University (1967–70). His major contributions are in solid-state theory, where he developed a quasimolecular model of covalent crystals. He has written over 120 works, including a monograph on thermodynamics and statistical physics (1966).

**Tolstoi, Dmitrii** [Tolstoj, Dmitrij], b 13 March 1823 in Moscow, d 7 May 1889 in St Petersburg. Russian imperial official; president of the Imperial Russian Academy of Sciences from 1882. He was procurator of the Holy Synod (1865–80) and minister of public education (1866–80). A reactionary, he opposed the development of any form of Ukrainian national consciousness. With A. Pazukhin he

prepared the draft of the *Ems Ukase (1876), and in 1884 he placed further restrictions on Ukrainian theater troupes and known Ukrainophiles.

Fedor Tolstoi (etching by Taras Shevchenko, 1860)     Vsevolod Tolubynsky

**Tolstoi, Fedor** [Tolstoj], b 21 February 1783 in St Petersburg, d 25 April 1873 in St Petersburg. Russian sculptor and graphic artist. He attended the St Petersburg Academy of Arts, was elected an honorary member (1809), and served as its vice-president (1828–59). In 1835 he met T. Shevchenko, and from 1855 he worked for his release. The Tolstois were the first family Shevchenko visited when he returned to St Petersburg in 1858. In 1860 Shevchenko did an etching of Tolstoi.

**Tolstoy, Leo** [Tolstoj, Lev], b 28 August 1828 at Yasnaia Poliana, Russia, d 7 November 1910 at Astapovo railway station. Russian novelist and thinker, author of *War and Peace* (1863–9), *Anna Karenina* (1873–7), *The Death of Ivan Illich* (1886), *Resurrection* (1899), and numerous religio-philosophical essays and treatises. His ethical precepts entailed a belief in the passive resistance to evil, the rejection of private property, the abolition of government and church authority, a personal God, and the supremacy of love in all spheres of life. His writings influenced many authors and intellectuals in Russia and abroad, including major figures such as G.B. Shaw, Gandhi, R. Rolland, and G. de Maupassant.

Tolstoy exerted a significant influence on several Ukrainian authors. The majority of them assimilated his literary techniques and devices but rejected Tolstoy's weltanschauung. In 'Autobiography,' I. Franko acknowledged Tolstoy's influence on his prose of the 1870s. O. Kobylianska also stated that under the influence of Tolstoy she wrote a number of stories and the novels *Zemlia* (Land, 1901) and *Cherez kladku* (Over the Footbridge, 1911). Quite prominent was Tolstoy's influence on Ukrainian historical novels written in the 20th century. They include *Nalyvaiko* (1940) and *Khmel'nyts'kyi* (1957) by I. Le, *Semen Palii* (1954) by Yu. Mushketyk, *Homonila Ukraïna* (Ukraine Was Astir, 1954) by P. Panch, and *Pereiaslavs'ka rada* (The Pereiaslav Council, 1948) by N. Rybak. Tolstoyan influences can also be discerned in some novels presenting recent or contemporary events: *Myr khatam – viina palatsam* (Peace to Houses, War on Palaces, 1958) and *Reve ta stohne Dnipr shyrokyi* (The Broad Dnieper Roars and Groans, 1960) by

Yu. Smolych, and *Praporonostsi* (The Standard-Bearers, 2 vols, 1947–8), *Liudyna i zbroia* (Man and Arms, 1960), and *Tronka* (The Sheep's Bell, 1963) by O. Honchar.

The first translation of Tolstoy into Ukrainian was of his trilogy *Childhood, Boyhood, and Youth*, which appeared in 1894 in Lviv. Owing to Franko's efforts the following works of Tolstoy were published in Ukrainian: *Resurrection* (1901), *The Kreuzer Sonata* (1902), *The Death of Ivan Illich* (1903), *The Cossacks* (1906), and a host of essays and short stories. Under the Soviet regime Ukrainian translations of Tolstoy's works were published frequently, but they consisted mostly of reprints or writings for children. Translations of Tolstoy's major novels were issued with great delays. A translation of *Anna Karenina* appeared only in 1935, and a complete edition of *War and Peace* was not available until 1953. A 12-volume Ukrainian edition of Tolstoy's complete works was first published in 1960. The most accomplished translations of Tolstoy into Ukrainian were by O. Kundzich.

Of the abundant studies of Tolstoy's influence on Ukrainian literature, the majority are articles dealing with his influence on individual authors, his translations into Ukrainian, or certain literary processes; they offer no detailed examination of his influence on Ukrainian literature. Much more comprehensive, although not exhaustive, are the monographs, including N. Krutikova's study of Tolstoy and Ukrainian literature (1958), which is confined to the Ukrainian reception of Tolstoy in the 19th century, and A. Sakhaltuev's *L.M. Tolstoi i ukraïns'ka literatura* (L.M. Tolstoy and Ukrainian Literature, 1963), which outlines Tolstoy's influence on the writers of the 19th and 20th centuries and provides a brief outline of Ukrainian translations of his works.

W. Smyrniw

**Tolubynsky, Vsevolod** [Tolubyns'kyj], b 27 March 1904 in Tartak, Olhopil county, Podilia gubernia. Thermodynamics and thermal energy specialist; full member of the ANU (formerly AN URSR) since 1964. He studied and taught at the Kiev Polytechnical Institute, where he held a chair in 1938–64. From 1939 he also worked at the ANU Institute of Technical Thermodynamics, where he served as director. He contributed to research on thermal exchange, particularly in two-phase systems. He developed practical methods of designing steam turbines, heat exchangers, and evaporators and analyzed heat exchange in nuclear reactors. He wrote handbooks and numerous technical papers.

**Tołwiński, Konstanty,** b 7 January 1877 near Vitsebsk, Belarus, d 15 May 1961 in Cracow, Poland. Geologist; full member of the Polish Academy of Sciences (from 1938). After spending several years in exile in Siberia for his political activities, he studied at Zurich University. He later became a specialist in the geology of the Carpathians and director (1919–39) of the Carpathian Institute of Petroleum Geology in Boryslav. After the Second World War he lived and worked in Poland. Among his major works is *Geologia polskich Karpat Wschodnich od Borysławia do Prutu* (The Geology of the Polish Eastern Carpathians from Boryslav to the Prut, 1927).

**Tołwiński, Mikołaj,** b 1857, d 7 December 1924 in Warsaw. Architect. He designed many buildings in Odessa, including the university library, the anatomy building, the laboratory and clinic of the medical faculty, the magnetic and meteorological observatory, schools, and the Kuialnyk baths. In 1917 he was appointed professor of the Polytechnical Institute in Warsaw.

**Tomakivka.** VI-15. A town smt (1986 pop 7,400) on the Tomakivka River and a raion center in Dnipropetrovske oblast. It was settled in 1740 by the families of Khortytsia dockworkers. An influx of colonists and refugee serfs brought its population to 6,200 in the mid-19th century. In 1956 the village was granted smt status. The town's main industry is food processing.

**Tomakivka Sich.** A Zaporozhian Cossack fortification on Tomakivka Island, in the Dnieper River near Marhanets, 60 km south of Khortytsia Island. It was a *kish* of the Zaporozhian Sich; reportedly it stood from 1540 to 1593, when it was destroyed by the Tatars. After 1593 the Zaporozhians built the *Chortomlyk Sich. Later the site of the Tomakivka Sich served as a rendezvous point and refuge for Hetman B. Khmelnytsky and assorted Cossack-peasant rebel groups during the Cossack-Polish War (1648–57). Even in the 18th century it was used by imperial Russian army divisions and Cossack companies during their campaigns in Southern Ukraine. Tomakivka Island now lies under the waters of the Kakhivka reservoir (flooded in 1955).

**Tomara.** A family line of Cossack officers that originated in Greece in the 17th century. Ivan (Jan) Tomara was a wealthy merchant in Pereiaslav who served as a military inductor in the 1660s. During the tenure of Hetman P. Doroshenko he moved to Kaniv. His sons served in the court of Hetman I. Samoilovych: Stepan Tomara (d 1715) was a captain of Domontov company (1689) and colonel of Pereiaslav regiment (1706–15), who initially supported I. Mazepa but later went over to I. Skoropadsky; and Vasyl Tomara (d 1726) was a captain of Vybli company (1704–15) and the judge of Chernihiv regiment (1715–26). Stepan's son, Vasyl Tomara, studied in Germany and served as colonel of Pereiaslav regiment (1735–9). Stepan's grandson, Vasyl Tomara (1746–1819), was a student of H. Skovoroda in 1753–9 (some items of their correspondence from 1772 and 1788 have been preserved); he later served as a Russian diplomat (imperial representative to Constantinople in 1802–9) and as a senator. He was also a friend of V. Kapnist and a notable Mason. In the 18th and 19th centuries the Tomara family controlled massive estates in Poltava and Katerynoslav gubernias and held high administrative positions in Ukraine and Russia. Lev Tomara (b 1839) was governor of Kiev gubernia and later a senator.

**Tomasevych, Stepan** [Tomasevyč], b 1859 in Mykulyntsi, Sniatyn county, Galicia, d 1932. Painter and graphic artist. He learned to paint from a church painter in Zbarazh and studied at the Cracow School of Fine Arts (1886–7). He painted portraits, such as *Man with a Beard* (1892) and *Portrait of Dukevych* (1896); genre paintings, such as *Don't Go to Parties, Hryts; Hahilky*; and *Village Lesson*; historical canvases, such as *Tatars Attacking a Church*; and landscapes. In the 1890s he painted the murals in the church in Butyny, near Zhovkva, with K. Ustyianovych.

He also designed scenery for the Ruska Besida Theater in Lviv and contributed illustrations and caricatures to *Strakhopud* in Lviv.

**Tomashevsky, Serhii** [Tomaševs'kyj, Serhij], b 18 October 1854 in Krolevets, Chernihiv gubernia, d 21 March 1916 in Kiev. Dermatologist and venereologist. A graduate of the Medico-Surgical Academy in St Petersburg (1876), from 1897 he was professor of syphilology at Kiev University. He organized and directed (1906–16) the medical division of the Higher Courses for Women in Kiev and was the founding director of the Kiev Society of Dermatologists and Venereologists (1900–16).

Toma Tomashevsky        Stepan Tomashivsky

**Tomashevsky, Toma** [Tomaševs'kyj], b 15 May 1884 in Stetseva, Sniatyn county, Galicia, d 4 February 1969 in Edmonton. Ukrainian-Canadian journalist and publisher. After emigrating to western Canada in 1900, he was active in Ukrainian socialist and community organizations there and coedited the weekly *Nova hromada* (1911) in Edmonton. Later he adopted an anticommunist, social-democratic position and supported the United Farmers of Alberta and, eventually, the Commonwealth Co-operative Federation (CCF). His leanings were clearly reflected in the weekly newspapers he edited: *Postup* (1915–17) in Mundare, Alberta; *Pravda i volia* (1920) in Vancouver; and *Nash postup* (1922–9) and *Farmers'kyi holos* (1932-3) in Edmonton. In Edmonton he also published a temperance journal, *Vidrodzhennia* (1930), and coedited the satirical journal *Harapnyk* (1921–35). Later, to preserve the legacy of Ukrainian pioneers in Canada, he published and edited the quarterly *Ukraïns'kyi pionir* (1955–60) and cofounded the Ukrainian Pioneers' Association of Alberta.

**Tomashivsky, Stepan** [Tomašivs'kyj], b 9 January 1875 in Kupnovychi, Rudky county, Galicia, d 21 December 1930 in Cracow. Historian, publicist, and politician; member of the Shevchenko Scientific Society (NTSh) from 1899 and an active member of the National Democratic party and the Prosvita society. After receiving a PH D from Lviv University he worked in 1900–10 as a gymnasium teacher in Berezhany and Lviv and in 1910–14 as a docent of Austrian history at Lviv University. A founding member of the *Teachers' Hromada, he edited its journal *Nasha shkola* in 1913. During the First World War he was a member of the Combat Board in charge of charity work, propaganda, and publishing for the Ukrainian Sich Riflemen. In 1919 he

was an adviser to the UNR and Western Ukrainian National Republic (ZUNR) delegations at the Paris Peace Conference, and in 1920 he headed the ZUNR mission in London. From 1921 to 1925 he lived in Berlin and worked for the conservative Berlin papers *Ukraïns'ke slovo* and *Litopys polityky, pys'menstva i mystetstva* (1924). After returning to Lviv he edited *Polityka* (1925–6) and coedited *Literaturno-naukovyi vistnyk* and *Nova zoria*. From 1928 until his death he was a docent of Ukrainian history at Cracow University. He was a prolific conservative Catholic publicist throughout the 1920s; some of his articles and lectures were reprinted as the collections *Pid kolesamy istoriï* (Under the Wheels of History, 1922; 2nd edn 1962), *Pro ideï, heroïv i polityku* (On Ideas, Heroes, and Politics, 1929), and *Desiat' lit ukraïns'koho pytannia v Pol'shchi* (Ten Years of the Ukrainian Question in Poland, 1929).

Tomashivsky published most of his studies in NTSh serials; edited vols 116–24 of its *Zapysky NTSh*, vols 4–6 of its *Zherela do istoriï Ukraïny-Rusy* (1898, 1902, 1913), and vol 4 of its *Ukraïns'ko-rus'kyi arkhiv* (1909); and served as its vice-president and acting president (1913–18). He published official documents about popular rebellions and the Ruthenian dietines in Galicia in 1648–51 (in vols 4–6 of *Zherela*); the reports of papal nuncios about Ukraine in 1648–57 (vol 16 of *Zherela*); and Polish and Austrian archival materials on the history of the period of Hetman I. Mazepa (in *ZNTSh*).

In his later scholarly investigations, particularly on the period of Hetman Mazepa, Tomashivsky became concerned with the problem of state-building in Ukrainian history. That concern is reflected in his articles (1906–9) and in his book on the history of the Mazepa period (1910). The influence of such ideas can also be found in his later articles (1913, 1927) on the Khmelnytsky period. In his 1919 book (repr 1948) on the history of ancient and medieval Ukraine he provided a synthetic survey of Ukraine under the Rus' princes and the Lithuanian-Ruthenian state. He singled out the role of the Western Ukrainian lands and discussed the Principality of Galicia-Volhynia as the first Ukrainian nation-state. The evolution of Tomashivsky's views from populism to statism deepened the philosophical, political, and personal differences between him and M. Hrushevsky but also assured him a prominent place, alongside V. Lypynsky, in the 'statist' school of Ukrainian *historiography.

Tomashivsky's research into the history of Ukrainian statehood was closely linked to his studies of Ukrainian church history. He published a pamphlet on the religious aspect of the Ukrainian question (1916), various articles, and longer studies on P. Akerovych, the metropolitan of Rus' in 1241–5 (1927), and on the history of the church in Ukraine to 1169 (1932) in *Zapysky Chyna sv. Vasyliia Velykoho*. Tomashivsky also made important contributions to the study of Transcarpathia. His analysis of the Hungarian census of 1900 and calculation of the number of Ukrainians in Transcarpathia, published together with a detailed ethnographic map of Transcarpathia by the Russian Academy of Sciences in 1910, was the first scholarly exposition of ethnographic relations in Transcarpathia. In 1915 the Union for the Liberation of Ukraine published his political-historical outline of Galicia (German trans: *Die weltpolitische Bedeutung Galiziens*). A bibliography of his works is found in *ZNTSh* (vol 151 [1931]), and a booklet about him was written by I. Krypiakevych (1932).

A. Zhukovsky

**Tomashpil** [Tomašpil']. V-9. A town smt (1986 pop 6,300) on the Tomashpil River and a raion center in Vinnytsia oblast. It was first mentioned in historical documents in 1616, when it was part of the Polish Commonwealth. During the Cossack-Polish War the village belonged to Yampil company in Bratslav regiment. Tomashpil was returned to Poland in 1667 and destroyed by the Turks in 1672. In 1793 it was annexed by Russia, and became part of Yampil county in Podilia gubernia. Toward the end of the 19th century a winery, a brick and a soap factory, and a steam flour mill were built there. By 1908 the town had a population of 8,000. Today Tomashpil has a sugar refinery, a bakery, and a furniture factory.

**Tomaszów Lubelski** (Ukrainian: Tomashiv). III-4. A town (1989 pop 19,800) on the Solokiia River in the southern Kholm region and a county town in Zamość voivodeship, Poland. It is on the border of Ukrainian ethnic territory. In 1931 Ukrainians represented 6.3 percent of the town's population, Jews, 54.3 percent, and Poles, 38.1 percent. But in Tomaszów county Ukrainians accounted for 43.6 percent of the population in 1905, 23.8 percent in 1921, and 26.8 percent in 1931. In 1946–7 the remaining Ukrainian inhabitants of the county were forcibly resettled.

**Tomato** (*Lycopersicon*; Ukrainian: *pomidor*, also *tomat, baklazhan chervonyi*). A cultivated fruit plant of the family Solanaceae, closely related to the potato and the eggplant, native to South America. It was introduced in the Crimea from Turkey toward the end of the 18th century and spread rapidly. Tomato fruit is roundish, soft, and succulent, red or yellow in color, and rich in vitamins, provitamin A, carbohydrates, mineral salts, and organic acids. Tomatoes are consumed fresh, canned, cooked, marinated, in sauces, pastes, purees, and so on. Several Ukrainian varieties (Slyvovydnyi maiak 12/20–4, Donets 312–1, Pervenets 190, Kiev 139, and Brekodli) have been developed and popularized.

Mykhailo Tomchanii

**Tomchanii, Mykhailo** [Tomčanij, Myxajlo], b 16 July 1914 in Horiany (now part of Uzhhorod), Transcarpathia, d 19 January 1975 in Uzhhorod. Writer. He began publishing stories in Transcarpathian periodicals in 1934. Beginning in 1950 he wrote several prose collections and the novels *Nasha sim'ia* (Our Family, 1953), *Terezka* (1957), *Vitchym* (The Stepfather, 1962), *Skrypka – ioho molodist'* (The Violin Is His Youth, 1968), *Zhmeniaky* (The Zhmeniaks,

1964), *Tykhe mistechko* (The Quiet Town, 1969), and *Braty* (Brothers, 1972). In his works he introduced Transcarpathian rural and urban themes into Soviet Ukrainian literature. He also translated Hungarian and Czech literary works into Ukrainian.

Hryhorii Tomenko: *Guests from Transcarpathia* (oil, 1960)

**Tomenko, Hryhorii,** b 16 November 1915 in Velyka Rohozianka, Kharkiv county, Kharkiv gubernia. Painter and graphic artist. He graduated from the Kharkiv Art Tekhnikum (1938) and the Kharkiv Art Institute (1942) and taught at the Kharkiv Commercial Arts and Design Institute (1947–53). He has painted landscapes and genre and historical paintings, such as *Future Farmers* (1960), *Above the Dnieper* (1964), *Favorite Verses* (1965), *May Morning* (1969), *Wide Field* (1974), and *Rainbow in the Field* (1975). He also created propaganda posters and etchings. An album of his works was published in 1975.

**Tomilin, Serhii,** b 19 October 1877 in Suwałki, in Poland, d 19 July 1952 in Kiev. Hygienist, sanitation statistician, and medical historian. A graduate of Moscow University (1901), he headed the statistical department of the People's Commissariat of Public Health of the Ukrainian SSR (1919–30), chaired the Department of Community Hygiene at the Kharkiv Medical Institute (1924–34), and worked at the AN URSR (now ANU) Institute of Demography and Sanitation Statistics (1934–8) and the Ukrainian Scientific Research Bureau of Sanitation Statistics (1932–52). He wrote numerous works on sanitation in Ukraine, the spread of venereal diseases, infant mortality, and the use of medicinal plants.

**Tomsk.** An oblast and raion center (1989 pop 502,000) of Russia, located on the right bank of the Tom River in western Siberia. Founded in 1604, it was a gubernia capital in 1804–1924. With a university (est 1888) and technological institute (1900), it has been a major cultural center of Siberia. A small Ukrainian colony, including a student hromada (40 members in 1908), formed in Tomsk before the 1917 Revolution. The city subsequently became one of the centers of Ukrainian life in Siberia: the Ukrainian District Council and a Ukrainian military formation were organized there, and the weekly *Ukraïns'ke slovo* was published. In 1926, 1,200 of its residents were Ukrainian, and in 1970, 9,000.

**Tomson, Aleksandr** (Thomson), b 3 June 1860 near Dorpat (now Tartu), Estonia or in Pskov, Russia, d 27 November 1935 in Odessa. Russian and Ukrainian linguist; corresponding member of the Russian (later USSR) Academy of Sciences from 1910. A graduate of the universities of St Petersburg (1882) and Moscow (PH D, 1892), he was a professor of comparative Indo-European grammar and Sanskrit at Odessa University (1897–1920) and the Odessa Institute of People's Education (1920–30). At the university he set up the first laboratory of experimental phonetics in Ukraine. In the Soviet period he was a member of the All-Ukrainian Learned Association of Oriental Studies. He wrote books on Russian syntax and semasiology (1903) and general linguistics (1906; rev edn 1910) and studies on the Sanskrit, Armenian, and Slavic languages, including articles on Ukrainian phonetics.

William Tomyn              Oleksander Topachevsky

**Tomyn, William** (Vasyl), b 4 September 1905 in Warwick, Alberta, d 5 October 1972 in Edmonton. Politician and community activist. After graduating from teachers' college in Calgary, he worked as a teacher and principal for two decades. A member of the Social Credit party, he served 29 years in the Alberta legislature, representing the electoral districts of Whitford (1935–40), Willingdon (1940–52), and Edmonton Norwood (1959–71). He was active in the Ukrainian Canadian Committee (now Congress) and the Ukrainian People's Home in Edmonton. He supported the introduction of Ukrainian as a subject in Alberta public schools and defended the rights of new immigrants to Canada after the Second World War.

**Tongue twister** (*skoromovka, skorohovorka, spotykanka*). A genre of children's folklore, its examples consisting of words and word combinations that are difficult to pronounce. Such phrases, which lack any deeper meaning, figure in word games by means of which children learn to articulate the sounds of their language: *Sydyt' Prokop, kypyt' okrop, | Pishov Prokop, kypyt' okrop. | Iak pry Prokopovi kypiv okrop, | tak i bez Prokopa kypyt' okrop.* 'Prokop sits, water boils / Prokop leaves, water boils. / As it boiled when Prokop was there / So it boils when Prokop's not.' Others are like proverbs: *Sune sova svoï slova. | Iaka sova, taki i slova* 'An owl speaks her words. As is the owl, so are the words.'

**Toniuk** [Tonjuk]. A family of master wood carvers of the Hutsul region. Yakiv (b 1903 in Richka, Kosiv county,

Galicia, d 1958 in Richka) carved household articles, caskets, trays, powder boxes, and drinking vessels, which he decorated with flat carved ornaments and inlays. His products were exhibited outside Galicia, and some have been preserved in Ukrainian museums. His son, Vasyl (b 7 August 1928 in Richka), learned his craft from Yakiv. Both Yakiv and Vasyl taught their relative, Dmytro (b 29 July 1924 in Richka, d 17 January 1977 in Kosiv), who combined geometric Hutsul ornamentation with thematic pictures. His works can be found in museums in Kiev, Ivano-Frankivske, and Kolomyia.

**Topachevsky, Oleksander** [Topačevs'kyj], b 13 March 1897 in Bobrivka *khutir*, Tarashcha county, Kiev gubernia, d 1 December 1975 in Kiev. Botanist and hydrobiologist; full member of the AN URSR (now ANU) from 1972. A graduate of the Kiev Institute of People's Education (1930), he worked at Kiev University (1935–59) and the ANU Institute of Botany (1932–52), directed the ANU Institute of Hydrobiology (from 1959), and headed the Ukrainian Hydrobiology Society (from 1964). His research interests included the morphology, systematics, and phylogeny of algae, as well as problems in sanitary and technical hydrobiology.

**Topachevsky, Vadym** [Topačevs'kyj], b 16 July 1930 in Cherkasy. Zoologist; corresponding member of the AN URSR (now ANU) since 1978; son of O. *Topachevsky. A graduate of Kiev University (1953), he has worked since 1956 at the ANU Institute of Zoology, from 1973 as its director. His work centers on the systematics, phylogeny, ecological morphology, and zoogeography of fossil and living mammals. He is one of the founders of micropaleontology theory in Ukraine.

**Toplia River** [Toplja] (Slovak: Tepla). A right-bank tributary of the Ondava River that flows for 130 km through eastern Slovakia and drains a basin area of 1,500 km. Its source is in ethnic Ukrainian territory.

**Topography.** The science which studies the earth's surface, plots and measures its features in their geometric relationship to one another, and devises methods of their representation on maps.

The first maps of Ukrainian territories based on topographical surveying were commissioned by the Polish Commonwealth, which controlled Ukraine in the early 17th century. Both the map of Lithuania (published by H. Gerritsz in Amsterdam in 1613 on four sheets at a scale of 1:1,300,000) and the map of the Dnieper (1:1,300,000) were prepared by T. Makowski. Makowski's map of Lithuania covered the Ukrainian territories only slightly east of the Dnieper and did not extend south of the line Sniatyn–Kamianets-Podilskyi–Bratslav–Cherkasy. The French cartographer G. de *Beauplan, commissioned by the Polish government, surveyed Ukraine from 1630 to 1647.

Topographical maps were often supplemented with topographical drawings or paintings. Those were detailed panoramas of cities, towns, or other sites of interest. An early example is a view of Lviv (in H. Braun's *Villes du monde*, 1618) engraved by A. Hohenberg on the basis of a painting by A. Pasarotti, an Italian engineer who designed fortifications for the Lviv suburbs. In 1651, topographic drawings of Kiev were made by the Dutchman A. Westerfeld, court painter to the Lithuanian duke, who was in

Kiev for one month during the Cossack-Polish War. The Dutch topographer J. Bruce prepared a map of western and southern Russia, published in Amsterdam in 1679, which showed not only Left-Bank Ukraine but also the Kiev and Bratslav regions of Right-Bank Ukraine. Shortly thereafter a series of maps titled Sketch (*Chertezh*) of Ukrainian and *\*cherkasy* towns from Moscow to the Crimea was prepared, probably in conjunction with the 1687 campaign against the Khanate of Crimea. Hetman I. Mazepa commissioned topographical surveys of individual Cossack regiments.

With the abolition of the Hetmanate, detailed surveys were commissioned to describe Ukrainian lands textually, cartographically, and statistically for the purpose of facilitating the administrative reorganization (1775) of Left-Bank Ukraine from Ukrainian Cossack regiments into standard Russian provinces (vicegerencies, later gubernias). Written reports described the history, the way of life, and the economic development of each province. By 1784 the General Staff had compiled a set of atlases for the vice-regencies with maps showing rivers, lakes, roads, settlements, fortifications, factories, foundries, and wooded areas, and two tables, one of distances between settlements and the other of population data.

The Ukrainian territories annexed by Austria in the 1770s were surveyed and mapped toward the end of the 18th century in unprecedented detail. In 1779–83 Mieg prepared a manuscript map in 413 sheets at a scale of 1:28,000. It was later used by the Military Geographic Institute of the Austro-Hungarian Empire as a source for their topographic map series at a scale of 1:75,000 (1873–89) and 1:25,000 (1867–88). By that time modern survey methods were also being employed in Russia to produce increasingly more accurate and detailed topographic maps. On the basis of those surveys and previous maps the Russian Military Topography Corps published maps of European Russia (1:420,000) in 60 sheets (1832–44), Eastern Europe (1:420,000) in 158 sheets (1864–71), western Russia (1:126,000) in 435 sheets (1845–63), and, again, the area west of the Kiev–Odessa line at a scale of 1:84,000 (1845–82 and 1907–17). The most accurate maps were produced on the basis of new surveys of the Crimea, the Taman Peninsula, the Donbas, and the territories west of Kiev (1:42,000) in 84 sheets (1855) and, especially, of the western borderlands (western Volhynia, the Kholm region, and Podlachia) and the Crimea at a scale of 1:21,000.

Despite increasingly precise surveying and comprehensive topographic mapping, topographic painting of settlements became popular in the 18th century and continued into the 19th. Also common were detailed plans of cities and towns, drawn to various large scales, identifying main topographical features, street patterns, and main buildings and their names. As well the General Staff put together a compendium titled *Materialy dlia geografii i statistiki Rossii* (Materials on the Geography and Statistics of Russia), which provided brief histories, geographical descriptions, and statistical data for each gubernia together with maps, charts, or drawings.

During the First World War the Germans reproduced the Russian topographical maps (1:84,000 and 1:126,000 series) and reissued them at a scale of 1:100,000. They also published the first aviation map of Kiev (1:26,600), in 1916. With the establishment of the Ukrainian state, the Chief Geodesic Administration in Kiev revised and issued the Russian general topographic maps for Ukraine (54 sheets at a scale of 1:420,000) and two versions of a map of Kiev (6 sheets at 1:21,000) in 1918. It also produced two maps of Ukraine (4 sheets at 1:1,050,000) and a wall map at 1:1,680,000 by the Ukrainian geographer P. Tutkovsky).

In the Soviet period work began in 1924 on a new set of topographical maps based on conic projections and metric units. Revisions were made with the help of air photography. Fundamental to the topographic maps was the series at the scale of 1:100,000, with coverage extending eastward to the Volga River until 1941. With that as a base, more detailed maps were prepared at scales of 1:50,000, 1:25,000, and even 1:10,000, and more general aviation charts at a scale of 1:1,000,000. Meanwhile the Military Geographic Institute in Warsaw prepared topographic maps at scales of 1:25,000, 1:100,000, and 1:300,000, and aviation charts at scales of 1:500,000 and 1:1,000,000 that included Ukrainian territories in Poland. The government of Czechoslovakia produced topographic map series at scales of 1:25,000, 1:75,000, 1:200,000, and 1:750,000 that included Transcarpathia. The Rumanian government also prepared topographical maps at scales of 1:100,000 (1926–39), 1:200,000, 1:300,000, and 1:500,000 that included the Ukrainian-settled Bukovyna, Bessarabia, and Maramureş region.

During the Second World War the Germans quickly revised Polish topographical maps (using air photography) and added German nomenclature. In addition the Luftwaffe produced detailed maps of Ukrainian cities based on air photography. After the war the Soviet Union issued a new set of topographical maps (at scales of 1:25,000, 1:50,000, 1:100,000, 1:200,000, 1:300,000, 1:500,000, and 1:1,000,000) based on Krasovsky's ellipsoidal and the Gauss projection. Again, air photography was used to revise details. Meanwhile the United States Army Map Service issued its 1:250,000 topographical map series, based on captured German topographical maps, and updated details with data collected from air photographs (gathered on U-2 flights) and satellite imagery.

Geographic nomenclature on the territory of Ukraine was determined by the Chief Administration of Geodesy and Cartography and by the government in Moscow. It has ignored traditional Ukrainian toponymy. Topographic maps produced elsewhere (as in the United States) that cover the territory of Ukraine observe the official nomenclature used on the topographical maps of those countries (ie, USSR, Poland, Czechoslovakia, and Rumania). As a result traditional Ukrainian toponymy has been absent from modern topographical maps. (See also *Cartography.)

BIBLIOGRAPHY
Gospodinov, G.; Sorokin, V. *Topografiia* (Moscow 1974)

I. Stebelsky

**Topolnisky, George** [Topol'nyc'kyj], b 13 August 1929 in Pakan, Alberta. Politician and high-school teacher. Educated at the University of Alberta (B ED), Topolnisky was mayor of Andrew, Alberta, before his election to the legislature of Alberta in 1971 as the Progressive Conservative member for the constituency of Redwater-Andrew. He was the minister responsible for rural development in 1971–5. He was re-elected in 1975, 1979, and 1982 but did not run in the 1986 election.

Vasyl Topolnytsky

**Topolnytsky, Vasyl** [Topol'nyc'kyj, Vasyl'], b 3 April 1893 in Serafyntsi, Horodenka county, Galicia, d 7 November 1978 in Winnipeg. Civic leader and co-operative organizer in Canada. A veteran of both the Austrian army and the Ukrainian Galician Army, he graduated from Prague's Higher Commercial School in 1926. The following year he emigrated to Canada and settled in Winnipeg, where he organized the head office of the *Ukrainian War Veterans' Association (1930), and its *Kalyna consumer co-operative (1930). He went on to set up the first Ukrainian credit union in Canada in 1939 (Nova Hromada or New Community in Saskatoon) and then the Carpathia (1940), Dnipro, and Steppe credit unions in Winnipeg. He served on the board of directors of the Association of Credit Unions in Manitoba and as coeditor of *Novyi shliakh* (1946–8). He taught courses and wrote some brochures on co-operation, including *De pomich dlia nas* (Where Is There Help for Us, 1944).

**Toponymy.** The study of place-names or toponyms, sometimes called toponomastics. Crossed by many migratory peoples in the 1st millennium AD, Ukraine is an important region for the study of hydronyms – names of rivers and other bodies of water. Hydronyms change much less than other toponyms and therefore better reflect ethnohistorical changes. The data for Ukrainian hydronymy are found in P. Mashtakov's Russian registers of rivers in the Dnieper Basin (1913), the Dniester and Boh basins (1917), and Don Basin (1934); in H. Shvets, N. Drozd, and S. Levchenko's catalog of Ukraine's rivers (1957), which is unfortunately very Russified; and in *Wörterbuch der russischen Gewässernamen* (1960–73), edited by M. Vasmer.

The linguistic study of Ukraine's hydronyms began only after the Second World War. The AN URSR (now ANU) Institute of Linguistics began work on a hydronymic atlas in 1960, and in 1979 it published a dictionary of over 20,000 of Ukraine's hydronyms (with 24,000 variants) edited by A. Nepokupny, O. Stryzhak, and K. Tsiluiko. Monographs have been written by J. Rozwadowski (on Slavic hydronyms [1948]), O. Stryzhak (river names of Poltava oblast [1963] and of Zaporizhia and Kherson oblasts on the lower Dnieper's Left Bank [1967]), I. Muromtsev (word-forming types of hydronyms in the Donets River Basin [1966]), O. Trubachev (river names of Right-Bank Ukraine [1968] and, with V. Toporov, a linguistic analysis of hydronyms of the upper Dnieper Basin [1962]), A. Korepanova (word-forming types of hydro-

nyms in the lower Desna Basin [1969], J. Rieger (hydronyms of the Sian Basin [1969]), V. Loboda (toponyms of the Dnieper-Boh basins [1976]), Ye. Otin (hydronyms of eastern Ukraine [1977]), Z. Franko (the grammatical structure of Ukrainian hydronyms [1979]), and L. Masenko (hydronyms of western Podilia [1979]). Yu. Karpenko edited a book on the hydronyms of the lower Dniester Basin (1981), and O. Stryzhak edited a book on the interlingual and interdialectal aspects of Ukrainian hydronyms (1981).

Hydronyms have been less subject to political manipulation and cultural fashion than names of mountains (oronyms) and inhabited places. In Russian-ruled Ukraine, the latter were Russified from the 18th century on. The ancient settlement Polovytsia, for example, became the city of Katerynoslav (Ekaterinoslav), named in honor of Catherine II, and in the Soviet period it was renamed Dnipropetrovsk(e) in honor of the Bolshevik leader H. Petrovsky. Russian lexical forms, such as the suffix *-sk*, were imposed on many places. In Southern Ukraine, the late 18th-century Russian classicist vogue for things Hellenic resulted in such city names as Yevpatoriia (former Tatar, G'ozlev, Ukrainian Kozliv) and Kherson.

Monographs dealing wholly or partly with Ukrainian toponymy have been written by V. Chubenko (toponyms on the territory of the Donets Ridge [1939]), J. Rudnyckyj (toponyms of the Boiko region [1939; repr 1962]), S. Hrabec (toponyms of the Hutsul region [1950]), S. Rospond (a structural-grammatical classification of Slavic geographic names [1957], a work on Slavic place-names with the suffix *-s'k* [1969], and a stratigraphy of Slavic toponyms [1974]), A. de Vincenz (*La toponymie des Carpates du Nord* [1959]), Yu. Karpenko (toponyms of the mountain, central, and eastern raions of Chernivtsi oblast [1964–5] and toponyms of Bukovyna [1973]), V. Šmilauer (a handbook of Slavic toponomastics [1970]), V. Loboda (the interaction of the East Slavic languages in Ukrainian toponymy [1976]), Yu. Kruhliak (the origins of the names of Ukraine's cities and towns [1978]), and O. Kupchynsky (the oldest Slavic toponyms of Ukraine as a source of historical and geographic research [1981]). Yu. Karpenko edited a book on toponyms in northeastern Odessa oblast (1975). Ukrainian toponyms outside Ukraine's political borders are treated in books by Z. Stieber (toponyms of the Lemko region [2 vols, 1948–9]), A. Yashchenko (toponyms in Kursk oblast [1958]), S. Warchoł (town names in the Lublin region [1964]), E. Pawłowski (place-names in the Nowy Sącz region [2 vols, 1971, 1975]), A. Yeremiia (Moldavian place-names [1970]), V. Prokhorov (a historical-toponymic dictionary of Voronezh oblast [1953]), and M. Kondratiuk (place-names in the southeastern Białystok region [1974] and Baltic elements in the toponyms and microtoponyms [names of uninhabited places] of the Białystok region [1985]). Books on microtoponyms have been written by A. Petrov (mid-19th to early 20th-century Transcarpathia [1929]), M. Lesiv (the Lublin region [1972]), E. Pawłowski (the Nowy Sącz region [1984]), and E. Cherepanova (Chernihiv-Sumy Polisia [1984]). M. Vasmer's *Iranische Ortsnamen in Südrussland: Untersuchen über die ältesten Wohnsitze der Slaven* (1923) is a valuable contribution on the linguistic substratum of Ukrainian toponymy. Toponyms of Kievan Rus' is the subject of E. Barsov's geographic dictionary of 9th- to 14th-century Rus' (1865) and of his book on the geography of the Primary Chronicle (1874; 2nd edn 1885), as also of V. Nerozniak's recent book on the names of the ancient Rus' cities (1983), and of the Ukrainian etymological dictionary of place-names in Southern Rus' found in the Rus' chronicles (1985), edited by O. Stryzhak. In the United States, A. Vlasenko-Bojcun wrote a study of Ukrainian place-names in the United States (1977; English trans 1984), and S. Holutiak-Hallick Jr produced a Ukrainian toponymic atlas of the United States (1982).

Data on Ukrainian toponyms can be found in Ya. Holovatsky's geographic dictionary (1884); the geographic dictionary of the Polish Kingdom and other Slavic countries (15 vols, 1880–1904) edited by F. Sulimierski, W. Walewski, and B. Chlebowski; M. Yanko's toponymic dictionary and handbook of Soviet Ukraine (1973); the Russian geographic dictionary (11 vols, 1964–88) edited by M. Vasmer and H. Bräuer; and M. Bodnarsky's Ukrainian dictionary of geographic names (1955; rev edn 1959 adapted from the Russian). Lists of place-names in Ukraine by oblast and raion are found in reference books of the administrative-territorial division of Soviet Ukraine (most recently published in 1973). Ukrainian textbooks on toponymy have been written by B. Bezvenglinsky (1938) and S. Babyshyn (1962). Interlingual toponymic concordances can be found in J. Rudnyckyj's Ukrainian-German/German-Ukrainian dictionary of place-names (1943), A. Kara-Mosko and M. Tokarsky's Russian-Ukrainian dictionary of geographic names (1953), H. Batowski's dictionary of Central and East European place-name changes (1964), V. Nezhnypapa's Ukrainian-Russian dictionary of geographic names in Soviet Ukraine (1964; rev edn 1971), and L. Dezső's monograph on the history of the Transcarpathian dialects (1967).

R. Senkus, B. Struminsky

**Torban.** A music society founded in Lviv in 1869 by A. *Vakhnianyn. The group was dedicated to the advancement of musical education and sensibility among the general population. It established a school of music in Lviv and sponsored concerts throughout Galicia. Prominent members included the singers O. Myshuha and Yu. Zakrevsky. Lacking finances and a facility of its own, the society dissolved in 1871.

**Torban.** A music publishing house in Lviv. Established in 1905 by Ya. Yaroslavenko, who directed the company with (initially) D. Sichynsky and Ya. Lopatynsky, Torban had published almost 350 scores and songbooks by 1939. It issued mostly works by Western Ukrainian composers, including K. Stetsenko, Ya. Stepovy, M. Verbytsky, A. Vakhnianyn, V. Matiuk, O. Nyzhankivsky, and Rev D. Rozdolsky, as well as by conductors and prominent composers from Russian-ruled Ukraine, such as M. Lysenko.

**Torban.** A musical string instrument that is plucked. The Ukrainian *torban* is closely related to the shorter-necked Paduan theorbo as described by M. Praetorius (*Syntagma musicum*, 1618), but differs from the Western European instrument in that it has three sets of courses instead of two. In addition to the diapason and stopped strings, the *torban* has high-pitched *prystrunky* (accompaniment strings) which run along the deck of the instrument. In total the *torban* has 25 to 60 strings. During the 17th century the *torban* was the instrument of the Ukrainian nobility. It spread into Poland and Russia but remained in use until the end

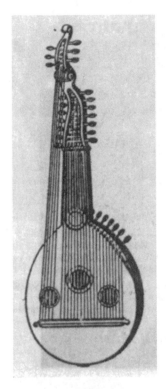

A *torban*

of the 19th century only in Ukraine. Well-known torbanists included I. Koshovy, I. Oleksandrov, and members of the Vidort family.

**Torez.** V-19; III-5. A city (1989 pop 87,900) in Donetske oblast. It originated in the 1770s as a settlement of runaway serfs and was first called Oleksiivka. In 1840 it was renamed Oleksiieve-Leonove, and in 1867, Chystiakove. Since the discovery of anthracite deposits in the 1860s, a large mining industry has developed in the region. By 1907 the settlement had been linked by railway to Debaltseve. In 1932 Chystiakove was granted city status, and in 1964 it was renamed Torez in memory of M. Thorez (1900–64), the leader of the French Communist party. Today the city has 10 mines and 4 coal enrichment factories, an electric-machine plant, a hard-alloys foundry, a concrete shaft-reinforcing parts plant, and a food industry.

*Torhovlia i promysl* (Trade and Manufacturing). A semimonthly organ of the *Union of Ukrainian Merchants and Entrepreneurs, published in Lviv from November 1934 to August 1939 (a total of 118 issues). It published business and political news and reports on the activities of the union. A separate page in the paper was devoted to Volhynia, and another to the skilled trades. The chief editor was V. *Nesterovych, and contributors included S. Baran, S. Biliak, T. Hlynsky, M. Derevianko, V. Ostrovsky, D. Koniukh, Yu. Krokhmaliuk, A. Milianych, and Ya. Skopliak.

**Torhovytsia Confederacy.** An alliance of Polish magnates, led by K. Brancicki, S. Potocki, and S. Rzewuski (all of Right-Bank Ukraine), against the liberal reforms of the Four-Year Sejm and the 3 May Constitution of the Polish state. With the support of Catherine II and the participa-

*Torhovlia i promysl*

tion of the Russian government they conspired to have Russian armies occupy Poland in mid-1791. The confederacy was proclaimed on 14 May 1792 in Torhovytsia, a border town (now a village in Kirovohrad oblast). Russian armies then moved into Poland, and their occupation touched off a Russo-Polish war. After the alliance managed to attract the Polish king, Stanisław Poniatowski, to its cause, the movement spread throughout Poland. Eventually its actions resulted in the second partition of Poland in 1793.

**Torks** (*torky*). The name given in chronicles to the Turkic tribes of *Oghuz. In the late 9th and early 10th centuries they lived as nomads in the northern steppes between the Aral and Caspian seas, ranging all the way to the Volga Delta. In the late 10th century they migrated closer to the Sea of Azov. In one chronicle Torks are said to have participated in Volodymyr the Great's campaign of 985 against the Bulgars. In the 11th century, when they were pressed by the Polovtsians (see *Cumans) from the east, larger waves of Torks swept over the Black Sea steppes and sent the Pechenegs westward. In 1054 Torks attacked the Pereiaslav region but were defeated by the army of the prince of Pereiaslav, Vsevolod Yaroslavych. They continued to invade Rus', however, and only in 1060 were they decisively defeated by a coalition of Iziaslav III (the son of Davyd Sviatoslavych) of Kiev, Vsevolod of Pereiaslav, Sviatoslav of Chernihiv, and Vseslav II (the son of Vasylko Sviatoslavych) of Polatsk. In 1116 an army of Torks and Pechenegs was annihilated by the Polovtsians, and the defeat caused some Torks to resettle in the Balkans. Others obtained the permission of Ukrainian princes to settle on the right bank of the Dnieper, in the Ros and the Rosava basins, and in southern Pereiaslav principality along the Sula River. There they mixed with the remaining Pechenegs and Berendeys and became known as the *Chorni Klobuky. The duties imposed on them by the Ukrainian princes included defending the southern borders of Rus' against Polovtsian attack and participating in offensive military campaigns, in which they proved to be loyal allies. During the raids of Batu Khan in 1240, particularly during the siege of Kiev, many Torks were killed, and the Tatars resettled many others in the Volga region. The rest assimilated completely with the local inhabitants. Torks introduced a Turkic element into the anthropological features of the population along the banks of the Dnieper.

They also contributed to the toponymy of Ukraine, in the names of the rivers Torets and Torch, the Torskyi route along the Tetliha River, and the towns Torets, Torky, Torkiv, Toretske, and Torchyn.

M. Zhdan

**Toronsky, Oleksii** [Torons'kyj, Oleksij], b 1838, d 1899. Galician pedagogue and Greek Catholic priest. He taught religion at various gymnasiums and wrote textbooks on literature and religion for secondary schools. He coedited *Ruskii Sion* (1874–9, 1883) and wrote the novel *Hantsia* (1862), which dealt with the daily life of the inhabitants of the Lemko region. He also translated works from Polish and German into Ukrainian and wrote articles for various periodicals.

**Toronto.** The capital (1986 metropolitan pop 2,976,000) of Ontario, and the largest industrial, trade, and financial center in Canada. With 71,730 residents of Ukrainian origin in 1981, it has one of the largest Ukrainian communities in Canada, and one of the most important Ukrainian communities outside Ukraine. In 1989, 24,605 inhabitants claimed Ukrainian as their mother tongue.

Ukrainian immigrants began to settle in Toronto early in the 20th century. The social structure of the Ukrainian community has changed considerably over the years. The first immigrants were mostly unskilled, low-paid laborers, single men and women from Western Ukraine attracted by jobs on the railways, in factories and construction, and in domestic service. During the First World War a stratum of skilled workers, tradesmen, and small businessmen emerged. After the Second World War a significant number of Ukrainian veterans, many of them with a professional education, settled in Toronto. By 1971 the social profile of the Ukrainian community almost matched that of the general community. About 30 percent were employed in the manufacturing industries, 25 percent in the service industries, 14 percent in trade, 7 percent in transportation, 6 percent in administration, and 4 percent in construction. The professional group grew rapidly after the Second World War: by 1978 there were over 200 lawyers, 100 physicians, 50 dentists, 200 engineers, and a few hundred teachers and librarians of Ukrainian origin. Relatively few Ukrainians are found among university professors, top financiers, and civil servants.

Ukrainians have developed strong economic institutions in Toronto. They have organized 16 credit unions, the oldest and largest of which is the *Ukrainian Credit Union (est 1944), and the Community Trust Co. They own large development firms (such as Prombank Investments) and trade companies (such as the UBA Trading Company), real estate and insurance companies, dozens of hotels, and hundreds of stores. The Ukrainian Professional and Business Club of Toronto (est 1935) has over 500 members and plays a leading role in Ukrainian economic and cultural affairs.

The first Ukrainian institutions to be established in the city were churches and schools. A Greek Catholic parish was founded in 1906 in the west end, and St Josaphat's Church was built in 1913–14. In the interwar period two more parishes were formed. Today there are eight parishes in the city. In 1948 the eparchy of Toronto, covering Eastern Canada, was set up. Its weekly paper, *Nasha meta*, is published in Toronto. The Basilian order runs a parish in the city and in nearby Mississauga and publishes the monthlies *Svitlo* and *Beacon* at its own publishing house. Another parish is run by the Redemptorist Fathers.

The first Ukrainian Orthodox parish was organized in 1931, and in 1948 St Volodymyr's Cathedral was consecrated. Two more parishes were founded, one in 1940 and another in 1950. Since 1953 Toronto has been the seat of the Orthodox eparchy of Eastern Canada. St Vladimir Institute, organized by the Orthodox community, maintains a student residence, library, and museum. The main Orthodox lay associations are the Ukrainian Self-Reliance League, the Ukrainian Women's Association of Canada, and the Canadian Ukrainian Youth Association. There are five Ukrainian Protestant churches and three Protestant periodicals (*Ievanhel's'kyi ranok*, *Ievanhel's'ka pravda*, and *Ievanhelyst*) in Toronto.

The first secular associations in the city were the St Nicholas Mutual Benefit Society (est 1906), renamed the

Holy Eucharist Ukrainian Catholic Church (architect: Radoslav Zuk) in Toronto

Ruthenian National Benefit Society (est 1910), and the Shevchenko Prosvita Reading Room (est 1914), which in 1928 was reorganized into the Ukrainian People's Home. In 1924 supporters of the hetmanite movement founded the United Hetman Organization. Former soldiers of the Ukrainian armies (1918–20) formed the Ukrainian War Veterans' Association of Canada in 1928, which became the nucleus for the Ukrainian National Federation, the Ukrainian Women's Organization of Canada, and the Ukrainian National Youth Federation of Canada. The postwar immigration reinforced the existing Ukrainian organizations or set up new organizations, such as the Canadian League for Ukraine's Liberation, the Plast Ukrainian Youth Association, the Ukrainian Democratic Youth Association, the Ukraina and Trident sports associations, a number of veterans' associations, and several professional associations (engineers, teachers, lawyers). The head offices of practically all recently formed national organizations are in Toronto. The office of the *World Congress of Free Ukrainians is also found there. A strong branch of the pro-Communist Ukrainian Labour-Farmer Temple Association was active in Toronto between the wars. Reconstituted as the *Association of United Ukrainian Canadians, the group moved its head office to Toronto after the Second World War.

The statue of Lesia Ukrainka (sculptor: Mykhailo Chereshnovsky) in Toronto's High Park

The Future Bakery and café in Toronto

The larger civic organizations run elementary and secondary Ukrainian classes on Saturdays, and four Catholic schools have a heritage language program in Ukrainian. The independent I I. Skovoroda courses on the secondary-school level, directed by O. Kopach (1951–78), made a major contribution to education. The Tsiopa Paliiv co-operative Saturday school (est 1972) offers a 12-year program, and an accredited language course is available at Humberside Collegiate. The University of Toronto and York University provide courses in Ukrainian language, literature, and history. The Chair of Ukrainian Studies at the University of Toronto (est 1980) is devoted to history. A *Ukrainian Canadian Research and Documentation Centre was established in 1982. Besides the university libraries, the richest collections of Ukrainian books and journals are found at the library of the former Ukrainian People's Home, the Ukrainian National Federation, the Ukrainian Youth Association, and St Vladimir Institute. Since 1950 the Patronage of the Shevchenko Scientific Society has raised funds for *Entsyklopediia ukraïnoznavstva* (Encyclopedia of Ukrainian Studies), and since 1975 the Toronto publications office of the Canadian Institute of Ukrainian Studies has been preparing the *Encyclopedia of Ukraine* at the University of Toronto.

Toronto is the most important Ukrainian publishing center in Canada. The Ukrainian press published in Toronto includes the weekly papers *Nasha meta, *Homin Ukraïny, *Novyi shliakh, *Zhyttia i slovo*, and *Ukraïna i svit*; the biweekly *Bat'kivshchyna*; the monthly magazines *Novi dni, *Ukrainian Canadian, *Svitlo*, and *Zhinochyi svit*; the bimonthly *Visti kombatanta*; and the quarterly *Plastovyi shliakh*. There are two daily radio programs and two weekly Ukrainian TV shows.

A number of musical institutions are active in Toronto: the Lysenko Music Institute, the Canadian Ukrainian Opera Association (est 1978), and the Ukraine Millennium Foundation (est 1983). Besides numerous church choirs, there are several concert choirs: the male Prometheus and Burlaka choirs, the female Dibrova and *Vesnivka choirs, the chamber choir of *Musicus Bortnianskii, and the *Lysenko Chorus. Of the various drama groups that were active after the war the *Toronto Zahrava Theater continues to perform, and the Avant-Garde Ukrainian Theater has staged experimental plays since 1984. A number of well-known Ukrainian artists work in Toronto. The Focus Gallery, St Vladimir Institute, and the *Ukrainian Canadian Art Foundation exhibit the works of Ukrainian artists from around the world.

**Toronto Zahrava Theater.** An amateur troupe established in 1953 by Yu. Belsky, V. Dovhaniuk, and A. Ilkiv. Its repertoire has consisted of world and Ukrainian classical and contemporary plays, including Canadian plays. Zahrava has participated in the festivals of the Canadian Multicultural Theatrical Society, toured Canada and the United States, and performed in Ukraine (in 1990). Among its leading members have been Z. Turzhansky, M. Levytska, O. Telizhyn, M. Levytsky, N. Mykolenko, N. Tarnovetska, and M. Lialka.

**Torysyn.** See Zubrytsky, Dionisii.

**Torzecki, Ryszard,** b 20 March 1925 in Łódź, Poland. Polish historian. A graduate of Warsaw University (PH D, 1970), since 1971 he has worked at the Institute of History of the Polish Academy of Sciences. He has written on the Ukrainian problem in the policies of the Third Reich in 1939–45 (PH D diss; pub 1972) and the Ukrainian question

in Poland in 1923–9 (habilitation diss, 1983; pub 1989), as well as on the history of Western Ukraine and Ukrainian-Polish relations in the years 1918–45.

**Totska, Nina** [Toc'ka], b 12 May 1923 in Ozerna, Bila Tserkva district, Kiev oblast. Linguist. A graduate of Kiev University (1947), she taught Ukrainian language there (1950–87) and oversaw an experimental phonetics laboratory (1964–84). In 1987 she joined the Ukrainian language department at the Vinnytsia Pedagogical Institute. She has published works on experimental research in Ukrainian phonetics, such as on the articulatory and acoustic characteristics of vowels, sound reduction, the acoustical properties of stress, accentual and rhythmic structure of words, and interlinguistic interference. She has also published texts and manuals for secondary and postsecondary schools for foreign students.

**Totsky, Ivan** [Toc'kyj], b 24 April 1896 in Buianychi, Mahiliou county, Belarus, d 16 December 1957 in Odessa. Opera singer (bass) and actor. A graduate of the Kiev Conservatory (1925), he was a soloist of the Kharkiv (1925–7), Odessa (1924–41, 1946–51), and Leningrad (1943–5) opera theaters.

**Touring theaters** (*peresuvni teatry*). Touring theaters in Ukraine evolved in the 18th century from *serf and amateur theaters and (except for *Sadovsky's Theater in Kiev) were the only form of Ukrainian theater until 1917. At the beginning of the 19th century there existed mixed Ukrainian-Russian-Polish troupes, such as those under I. Shtein, L. Mlotkovska, A. Zmiievsky, P. Rekanovsky, O. Bachynsky, and H. Kvitka-Osnovianenko. The first professional Ukrainian theater was the touring Ruska Besida Theater (see *Ukrainska Besida Theater), established in 1864 under O. Bachynsky.

After the ban on theater performances was lifted in Russian-ruled Ukraine, in 1881, leading troupes led by M. Kropyvnytsky, M. Starytsky, and M. Sadovsky, *Saksahansky's Troupe, and others also became touring theaters. Some toured outside Eastern Europe; H. Derkach's troupe, for example, toured France in 1893–4. Because of severe censorship their repertoire consisted mainly of populist-ethnographical plays, and only after 1905 were translated dramas occasionally performed. By this time there were approx 300 touring theaters in Ukraine. In the face of censorship and the tsarist ban on resident Ukrainian theaters they were the vanguard of the Ukrainian theater movement, and they developed an impressive number of outstanding performers, including M. Zankovetska, H. Borysohlibska, I. Marianenko, D. Haidamaka, K. Luchytska, O. Petliash, H. Yura, and I. Zamychkovsky. They also spawned an antipodal genre, the fringe-grotesque *Lubok theaters.

In 1916–18 the *Theater of the Legion of Ukrainian Sich Riflemen toured throughout Galicia and along the front. The *New Lviv Theater toured under the auspices of the Ukrainian Galician Army in 1919–20. In Vinnytsia the touring Franko Ukrainian Drama Theater was founded by H. Yura in 1920. During 1920–39 touring theaters were active in Western Ukraine in Galicia (the *Zahrava Young Ukrainian Theater, the *Tobilevych Ukrainian People's Theater, Y. Stadnyk's Union of Ukrainian Actors, the Ukrainskyi Teatr Co-operative, Stadnyk's Artistic Tour, I.

Kohutiak's Ukrainian Touring Theater, and O. Karabinevych's *Sadovsky Ukrainian Drama Theater), in Volhynia (N. Boyko and O. Mitkevych's troupes), in Bukovyna (a drama section in the Bukovynian Kobzar Association and S. *Terletsky's troupe), and in Transcarpathia (the *Ruthenian Theater of the Prosvita Society and, later, *Nova Stsena Theater). A Western Galician touring theater, Melpomena, headed by M. Aidariv, successfully toured throughout Poland in 1933–7, including Cracow, Kielce, Łódź, and Warsaw voivodeships in its tour. In eastern Ukraine, for the first few years after 1917, agitprop theater existed as a form of touring theater, whose activities consisted mostly of concert-meetings under the auspices of the Soviet army. In the 1920s there appeared workers' and peasants' touring theaters (since 1929 *workers' and collective-farm theaters), which also sponsored touring displays on housekeeping, educational, and sanitary topics and were subordinated to the larger resident theaters. There were also touring theaters of small forms, such as Veselyi Proletar in Kharkiv, the *Poltava Chervonyi Perets Theater, touring contemporary variety theaters, and the Siiach touring theater from Poltava (1923–7). Since 1961 oblast-level theaters have been responsible for touring to towns, workers' settlements, and collective farms.

V. Revutsky

**Tourism.** Recreational travel and tourism developed fairly recently in Ukraine. Tourism includes sight-seeing and various forms of leisure activity (such as hiking and skiing). Initially tourism in Ukraine, as in other countries, was limited to the wealthy and privileged classes. Only in the 20th century, with the general rise in the standard of living and the development of modern forms of communication and travel, has tourism become a major industry.

In the Ukrainian SSR organized tourism went through several stages of development. In the 1920s the Soviet Tourist Society was organized under the Council of People's Commissars of the Russian republic. Its Ukrainian branch was know as Ukrtura. The Society for Proletarian Tourism was founded in 1928 and merged with the All-Union Voluntary Society of Proletarian Tourism and Excursions in 1930. In 1936 this body was dissolved and the task of promoting tourism, hiking, and mountain climbing was left to various trade-union and physical education organizations. At the same time a tourism and expeditions administration was formed at the All-Union Central Council of Trade-Union Organizations. It controlled 150 tourist buildings and complexes. There were not enough tourist facilities in Ukraine to satisfy local demand. All these tourist organizations handled tourism only within the USSR and only for Soviet citizens. In the interwar period most tourists were groups of workers visiting resorts or sanatoriums run by various government ministries or trade unions. Popular destinations included the Black Sea coast, Crimea, and Kuban. Building hotels and other facilities for tourism was not a priority, and little was done to encourage or even permit tourism other than for workers. Trips to resorts were used by the authorities to reward loyal workers and build allegiance to the Party. Under the system of totalitarian control there was little individual travel even within the USSR and virtually none outside the Union.

That situation prevailed throughout the postwar Stalinist period. Only in 1962 was a Central Council for Tourism with republican branches formed, under the trade-union movement. The regime came to realize the value of tourism and travel for building Soviet patriotism and improving the health and morale of the population. The council, which was renamed the Central Council for Tourism and Excursions in 1969, organized individual and especially group tours, trained guides and excursion leaders, and administered recreational facilities and events. In 1963 there were 43 tourist bases or resorts and over 320 other facilities (camping grounds, hotels) that offered accommodation for tourists in Ukraine. By the mid-1970s over 2,000 separate excursions (usually bus tours) had been developed by the council, which at that time employed 1,700 full- and 3,000 part-time guides. Many of the excursions were designed to strengthen Party loyalty or build patriotism: tourists were taken to historical sites highlighting Soviet achievements, model factories and state farms, and so forth. Trains and buses for overnight trips to points of interest were organized. The most popular destinations were large cities and cultural centers, such as Kiev, Kharkiv, Odessa, and Lviv. T. Shevchenko's grave in Kaniv drew many tourists. Since 1965, boat tours on the Dnieper River and the Black Sea have been available. Skiing is popular in the Carpathian Mountains, and the Ukrainian Association of Hunters and Fishermen maintains camps for hunting and fishing.

The system of *health resorts and sanatoriums in Ukraine is an important component of the tourist industry. Besides providing recuperative mud baths and mineral waters they offer recreational activities and simple relaxation. The most popular resort areas in Ukraine are the Crimea (over 8 million visitors annually), the Black Sea coast near Odessa, the northern and eastern coasts of the Azov Sea, and the Carpathian Mountains. Those areas drew visitors from the whole USSR. Many resorts are affiliated with specific enterprises, institutes, or ministries and are reserved for workers from those institutions. The writers', composers', and artists' unions maintain their own facilities.

Foreign touring groups and individual tourists visiting Ukraine were administered by the all-Union organization, *Intourist, which had branches in Ukraine.

Special programs for student-tourists were organized by the Ukrainian branch of the Sputnik International Youth Travel Agency, established in 1958 with headquarters in Moscow. It ran exchanges with student travel groups throughout the Soviet bloc, and with pro-Soviet student organizations in foreign coutries. In 1987 it had 54 offices in Ukraine. During vacation periods the organization was allocated hotel rooms and student residences along with food services, transportation, and other services. In the 1980s, Sputnik in Ukraine handled approx 1.3 million students, including 130,000 foreigners, and arranged over 50 specialized excursions. The Pioneer Organization of Ukraine maintained its own system of campgrounds and organized excursions for its members.

In general the tourist industry in Ukraine is underdeveloped. There are too few hotels and other facilities to satisfy demand, and the general quality of accommodations and services, compared to those in the West, is poor. The most popular destinations on the Black Sea face a serious shortage of fresh water, which restricts their future development. Foreign tourists had been discouraged from visiting Soviet Ukraine by strict visa requirements, restrictions on their travel in Ukraine to designated cities and resorts, and exploitive fiscal policies. Nonetheless, large numbers of tourists, especially of Ukrainian descent, have traveled each year to Ukraine. Many of them have done so to see relatives. Today the major problems are shortage of hotel space, inadequate transportation, and inferior service.

BIBLIOGRAPHY
Pohrebets'kyi, M. *Turyzm ta podorozhi* (Kiev–Lviv 1948)
*Turistskie marshruty po Ukraine* (Kiev 1957)
Khvostenko, S. *Turyzm na Ukraïni* (Kiev 1976)
Kameneva, Z. *Finansy turistskikh organizatsii* (Moscow 1982)
Preobrazhensky, V.; Krivosheyev, V. (eds). *Recreational Geography of the USSR* (Moscow 1982)

B. Balan, E. Zharsky

Kostiantyn Tovkach

**Tovkach, Kostiantyn** [Tovkač, Kostjantyn], b 1883 in Poltava gubernia, d after 1930 in Yaroslavl, Russia. Ukrainian Orthodox church figure. A graduate of the Poltava Theological Seminary and the law faculty of Kharkiv University, he worked as a judge and was a member of the Society of Ukrainian Progressives and the Ukrainian Party of Socialists-Federalists. From 1920 he was active in the rebirth of the Ukrainian Autocephalous Orthodox church, and he became head of its Poltava regional council. He was arrested in 1929 and sentenced in the show trial of the *Union for the Liberation of Ukraine in 1930 to a five-year term in extreme isolation. He died in the Yaroslavl solitary confinement prison for political prisoners.

**Tovmach** [Tovmač] (aka Tlumach, from the Polish variant). v-5. A town (1989 pop 7,500) on the Tlumachyk River and a raion center in Ivano-Frankivske oblast. It was founded in the 12th century and named after the translators (*tovmachi*) who served at Prince Yaroslav Osmomysl's customs post. It is mentioned in the Hypatian Chronicle under the year 1213. From the 14th century the town belonged to Poland. In 1448 it was granted the rights of *Magdeburg law. It was destroyed by the Tatars in 1594 and 1678 and then fortified with earthworks and stockades. Tovmach changed hands several times during the Cossack-Polish War and suffered heavy losses. After the partition of Poland in 1772, the town was annexed by Austria. It was linked by rail to the larger cities of the Austrian Empire in 1886 and subsequently became an exporter of farm products and livestock. In the interwar period Tovmach was a county center in Polish-ruled Galicia. In 1939 it was incorporated into the Ukrainian SSR. Today

the town has a food-processing industry and a folk-art museum.

**Tovmachiv, Hryhorii.** See Piddubny, Hryhorii.

**Tovsta Mohyla.** See Krasnokutskyi kurhan.

**Tovstiuk, Kornii** [Tovstjuk, Kornij], b 22 March 1922 in Mamaivtsi, Bukovyna. Specialist in the field of semiconductors and semiconductor materials, corresponding member of the ANU (formerly AN URSR) since 1978. He studied and taught at Chernivtsi University, where he held a chair from 1956 to 1967. In 1968–9 he held a chair at Lviv University. He served as assistant director of the ANU Institute of Semiconductors (1969–77) and headed its Chernivtsi branch, and he was appointed to the position of assistant director of the ANU Institute for Applied Problems of Mechanics and Mathematics (1977–81). Since 1981 he has been assistant director of and department head at the ANU Institute for Problems of Materials Science. He has researched the properties of anisotropic and layered semiconductors, magnetic and physical phenomena in semiconductors, the physics of semiconductor materials, and other topics.

**Tovstolis, Dmytro,** b 20 September 1877 in Chernihiv, d 28 July 1939 in Kiev. Forester. He graduated from the St Petersburg Forestry Institute (1902) and from 1912 taught at the Higher Agricultural Courses for Women in St Petersburg. He was appointed to the positions of professor at the Belarusian Agricultural Institute (1923–5) and chairman of the Department of Forest Appraisal at the Kiev Agricultural Institute and the Kiev Institute of Forest Management (from 1925). Among his publications are a number of monographs, such as *Opyt izucheniia sistem lesnogo khoziaistva* (An Attempted Study of the Systems of Forest Management, 1929).

**Tovstolis, Mykola,** b 21 March 1872 in Andronyky, Sosnytsia county, Chernihiv gubernia, d ? Lawyer and political figure; member of the Imperial Senate before 1917 and of the Hetman State Senate (1918). In the 1920s he was a professor at the Kiev Institute of the National Economy and a research associate of the VUAN Commission for the Study of Ukraine's Customary Law. A number of his works were published in the commission's *Pratsi*, including articles on discovery under Lithuanian-Ruthenian law (1926) and on the history of cus-tomary law (1928). He was arrested in 1933, and disappeared in Stalin's concentration camps.

**Tovstonos, Vitalii** (pseuds: V. Vital, V. Zabhai-Tovstonis, V. Tal), b 5 April 1883 in Znamianka, Oleksandriia county, Kherson gubernia, d 11 February 1936 in Hadiache, Poltava oblast. Writer. From 1908 on he published stories in *Rada, Ridnyi krai, Selo,* and, in the Soviet period, *Pluh,* and other periodicals. In the years 1917–27 he published 13 plays; he also wrote three novels, *Liubi brodiahy* (Beloved Tramps, 1927), *Nezvychaini pryhody bursakiv* (The Unusual Adventures of the Boarding-School Students, 1929), and *U svit* (Out into the World, 1930). He belonged to the peasant writers' group Pluh from 1925 to 1932.

**Tovt, Aleksei** (Toth, Alexis), b 18 March 1854 in Gelnica, Slovakia, d 7 May 1909 in Wilkes-Barre, Pennsylvania.

Russian Orthodox church figure in the United States. A Greek Catholic clergyman and professor of canon law at the Prešov seminary, he was sent to North America in 1889 as a missionary priest for the St Mary's parish in Minneapolis. He converted to Russian Orthodoxy (together with 365 of his charges) in 1891 after an acrimonious confrontation with the Roman Catholic bishop of St Paul, J. Ireland. He became a leading figure in establishing Russian Orthodox parishes in the United States and brought approx 20,000 converts into the church's fold, many of them immigrant Ukrainians. He also organized the Russian Orthodox Mutual Aid Society in Wilkes-Barre in 1895. For his tireless devotion and proselytizing Tovt was labeled the father of American Russia.

**Tovt, Nykolai,** b 10 August 1833 in Mukachiv, d 21 May 1882 in Prešov, Slovakia. Transcarpathian church figure. He studied theology at the Budapest Central Seminary and in Vienna. He was ordained in 1857, and after receiving a D TH in 1860, he was a professor at the Uzhhorod Theological Seminary and at Budapest University (1870–5). He was appointed a canon and rector of the seminary in Uzhhorod in 1873 and bishop of the Greek Catholic Prešov eparchy in 1876. He founded the Prešov Theological Seminary in 1881 and introduced Ukrainian (the Prešov dialect) as the language of instruction in the eparchy's parochial schools.

**Tovtry** (also Medobory Mountains). A belt of limestone ridges extending northwest–southeast across the Podolian Upland for nearly 250 km from Brody in the north to Stelanivtsi, on the Prut River in Moldova, in the south. Originally formed as barrier reefs and atolls in a Neogene sea the Tovtry are marked by karst features. They provide a picturesque, albeit harsh, landscape of blue-gray and white cliffs and gullies. They reach a height of roughly 350–400 m (430 m at the tallest point) and stand 50–100 m above the surrounding plateau. The Tovtry slopes and tops are covered with forests of oak, beech, hornbeam, hazel, and other trees, in sharp contrast to their surrounding farmland areas. The western slopes of the elevations tend to be much steeper than the eastern ones. A number of notable caves (including Dovbush, Perlyn, Tatar, and Karmaliuk) are situated in the mountains.

**Town Cossacks** (*horodovi kozaky*). Cossack garrisons in fortresses in the steppes along the Dnieper River (especially in Kaniv, Vinnytsia, Cherkasy, Khmilnyk, Bratslav, and Bar), set up in the 16th and 17th centuries by the Lithuanian and, later, Polish authorities to defend the southern borders of the Commonwealth against Tatar raids. The town Cossack units were organized by local starostas, and the Polish government introduced a register in the second half of the 16th century to control their number and activities (see *Registered Cossacks).

Some historians also use the term 'town Cossacks' to refer to the Cossacks of the *Hetman state in Left-Bank Ukraine from the second half of the 17th century until the early 1780s. They were organized into *regiments, which were named after their chief towns, and formed the bulk of the Hetmanate's military force. The regiments differed in size of territory and population and number of Cossacks. At the beginning of the 18th century there were 40,000 to 50,000 town Cossacks altogether, divided into companies, with 8 to 20 companies per regiment. Each

*company was to consist nominally of 200 to 250 Cossacks, but actually numbered 700 to 750. The companies were further divided into *kurins.

Town Cossacks were exempted from taxes and labor services but were obliged to do military duty without pay. Each man had to equip himself with a horse, arms, uniform, and supplies. Between campaigns the town Cossacks lived at home. According to an ukase of 1735 of the Governing Council of the Hetman Office, which was approved by the Senate in Moscow, a new list of Left-Bank regiments was drawn up. It included 30,000 wealthy Cossacks, who became known as *elect Cossacks; most of the rank-and-file Cossacks were stripped of their privileges and turned into *Cossack helpers, who were required to supply the Cossack army with forage and provisions and to defend the estates of the elect Cossacks during campaigns. In 1789 all Cossack privileges were abolished by imperial decree, the status of the Cossacks was degraded to that of state peasants, and they became known as Little Russian Cossacks. Some of them were conscripted into *lancer regiments.

A. Zhukovsky

**Towns.** See Cities and towns.

**Townspeople.** See Burghers, Cities and towns, and Urbanization.

**Toxic plants and animals.** Organisms containing natural products which upon contact with humans or animals cause allergic or toxic reactions, in extreme cases death. Their toxicity is a chemical rather than physical means of natural defense.

Toxic plant substances common in Ukraine can be categorized according to the organic processes they affect: the central nervous system (ben-bane, Indian poke, greater celandine, colchicum), the respiratory and digestive system (*nasturtium and yellow *rhododendron), the gastrointestinal system (milkwort, water dropwort, cockle, *nightshade, spurge flax, and some *mushrooms), the cardiovascular system (digitalis, foxglove, and lily of the valley), the liver (ragweed and heliotrope), and cellular respiratory processes (flax, almonds, and various sensitizers, including buckwheat and St-John's-wort). Some naturally toxic plants serve as sources for medicinal preparations (see *Medicinal plants). Many modern drugs were first discovered through *folk medicine therapies based on various herbs.

There are few life-threatening toxic animals in Ukraine; only some snakes and some Black Sea fish (eg, ruff) are truly toxic. The bites of other animals – scorpions, tarantulas, *Scolopendra* centipedes, *bees, wasps, hornets – may be very painful and may cause excessive swelling but rarely result in death. The venom of some animals has medicinal value.

I. Maonyk

**Track-and-field sports** (*lehka atletyka*). Competitive athletic events performed on a running-track or on an adjacent field. Twenty-four such events for males and 18 for females constitute a large part of the *Olympic Games and other international, continental, national, and regional championships. Track-and-field sports are also a basic part of *physical education.

In Ukraine the first documented track-and-field meet

TABLE 1
World records in track-and-field sports set by Ukrainian athletes

| Athlete | Event | Record | Place and year |
|---------|-------|--------|----------------|
| Synytska, Zoia | women's discus throw | 74.23 m | Kiev 1937 |
| Pletneva, Nina | women's 800-m run | 2:12.0 | Minsk 1951 |
|  |  | 2:08.5 | Kiev 1952 |
|  |  | 2:07.3 | Moscow 1953 |
| Kuts, Volodymyr | 5,000-m run | 13:56.6 | Berne 1954 |
|  |  | 13:51.2 | Prague 1954 |
|  |  | 13:46.8 | Belgrade 1955 |
|  |  | 13:35.0 | Rome 1957 |
|  | 10,000-m | 28:30.4 | ? 1956 |
| Koniaieva, Nadiia | women's javelin throw | 53.56 m | Leningrad 1954 |
|  |  | 55.11 m | Kiev 1954 |
|  |  | 55.48 | Kiev 1954 |
| Holubnychy, Volodymyr | 20,000-m walk | 1:30:02.8 | Kiev 1955 |
|  |  | 1:27:05.0 | Symferopil 1958 |
|  |  | 1:26:13.2 | Odessa 1959 |
| Krepkina, Vira | women's 100-m dash | 11.3 | Kiev 1958 |
| Lysenko, Liudmyla | women's 800-m run | 2:04.3 | Moscow 1958? |
|  |  | 2:04.3 | Rome 1960 |
| Taran, Hryhorii | 3,000-m steeplechase | 8:31.2 | Kiev 1961 |
| Brumel, Valerii | men's high jump | 2.23–2.28 m, 4 WR | 1961–3 |
| Press, Iryna | pentathlon | 5,246 points | Tokyo 1964 |
| Bondarchuk, Anatolii | hammer throw | 74.68 m | Athens 1969 |
|  |  | 75.48 m | Rivne 1969 |
| Avilov, Mykola | decathlon | 8,454 points | Munich 1972 |
| Solomin, Anatolii | 20,000-m walk | 1:23:29.86 | Edinburgh 1977 |
| Tkachenko, Nadiia | pentathlon | 4,604 points | Mykolaiv 1977 |
|  |  | 4,839 points | Lille 1977 |
|  |  | 5,083 points | Moscow 1980 |
| Yashchenko, Volodymyr | men's high jump | 2.31 m | Richmond, VA 1977 |
|  |  | 2.33 m | Richmond, VA 1977 |
|  |  | 2.34 m | Tbilisi 1978 |
| Olizarenko, Nadiia | women's 800-m run | 1:53.50 | Moscow 1980 |
| Sedykh, Yurii | hammer throw | 80.38 m | 1980 |
|  |  | 86.74 m, 6th WR | Stuttgart 1986 |
| Bubka, Serhii | pole vault | 5.81 m | Bratislava 1984 |
|  |  | 6.06 m | Nice 1988 |
|  |  | 6.08 m, 11th outdoor WR | Moscow 1991 |
|  |  | 6.12 m, 15th indoor WR | Grenoble 1991 |
| Bryzhina, Olha | women's 4 × 400-m relay | 3:15.18 | Seoul 1988 |
| Pinihina, Mariia | women's 4 × 400-m relay | 3:15.18 | Seoul 1988 |

took place in June 1858 in Mykolaiv, where 52 sailors and soldiers took part in races. The first amateur athletics club in Ukraine was established in 1905 in Katerynoslav (now Dnipropetrovske), and others were soon founded in Chernihiv, Kiev, Kharkiv, Melitopil, Mykolaiv, Odessa, and Zhytomyr. In Austrian-ruled Galicia, track-and-field sports were among the activities of the *Sokil and *Plast associations, and constituted an important part of their jamborees in the years preceding the First World War. At the Russian Imperial Games held in October 1912, the Kiev athlete K. Veshke won the 100-m run with a time of 12.0 seconds and the broad jump with a distance of 6.19 m. In September 1912 the first athletic meet on Ukrainian territory in this century took place in Kharkiv. In September 1913 the first All-Russian Olympiad took place in Kiev. Ukrainians took 7 gold, 12 silver, and 13 bronze medals in 25 events and set 11 All-Russian records (7 of them by Kiev athletes). On the eve of the First World War, in June

1914, a Kiev-Moscow intercity competition took place; Kiev athletes won most of the events. Other track-and-field clubs were founded at the time, such as Feniks in Kharkiv and Sporting-kliub, Sokol, and Makkabi in Odessa. At the second All-Russian Olympiad in July 1914 in Riga, the Kiev athletes M. Orlov, M. Sokolov, and K. Veshke won various events.

After the First World War, track-and-field sports gained mass popularity in the Ukrainian SSR, Polish-ruled Galicia, and émigré communities. In August 1921 the first Soviet All-Ukrainian Olympiad was held in Kharkiv. In 1923 sports clubs in Soviet Ukraine were incorporated into the Spartak association, and annual all-Ukrainian competitions were thenceforth called Spartakiads. That year the Higher Council for Physical Education at the Presidium of the All-Ukrainian Central Executive Committee was established. In 1928 the Ukrainian Spartakiad was replaced by an all-Union Spartakiad. At it the Ukrainian runners M.

TABLE 2
European records in track-and-field sports set by Ukrainian athletes

| Athlete | Event | Record | Place and year |
|---|---|---|---|
| Denysenko, Petro | pole vault | 4.42 m | Kiev 1952 |
| | | 4.44 m | Moscow 1953 |
| | | 4.46 m | Kiev 1954 |
| Ter-Ovanesian, Ihor | men's broad jump | 8.01 m | Moscow 1959 |
| | | 8.04 m | Rome 1960 |
| Brumel, Valerii | men's high jump | 2.17 m | Moscow 1960 |
| | | 2.18 m | Odessa 1960 |
| Kutenko, Yurii | decathlon | 7,968 points | Kiev 1961 |
| Borzov, Valerii | men's 100-m | 10.0 | Kiev 1969 |

Pidhaietsky and V. Spiridonova set new records. In all-Soviet competitions of the 1930s and 1940s, Ukrainian athletes, such as I. Anysymov (hurdles), O. Bezrukov (hurdles), Z. Borysova (discus throw and shot put), Yu. Bulanchyk (hurdles), N. Dumbadze (discus throw), O. Kanaki (shot put, decathlon, and hurdles), V. Pizhurina (running), H. Raievsky (pole vault and decathlon), P. Savelev (running), V. Sydorko (high jump), Z. Synytska (discus throw, ball throw, shot put, triathlon), and K. Shylo (running), placed first and set new records.

From the end of the Second World War, all sports competitions in Ukraine were conducted in accordance with centralized regulations issued from Moscow. From 1949, Ukrainians were part of USSR teams in international competitions. In August 1951, N. Pletneva from the Donbas became the first Soviet Ukrainian athlete to set a postwar world record in a track-and-field event (women's 800-m run, 2:12). In 1952, 25 athletes from the Ukrainian SSR were part of the first USSR Olympic team sent to the Olympic Games in Helsinki. Of the 11 who competed in track-and-field events, three secured 4th place, one 5th place, and one 6th place. At the 1956 Olympic Games in Melbourne, V. Kuts became the first Ukrainian athlete to win a gold medal in a track-and-field event. At the 1960 Olympic Games in Rome, four track-and-field athletes from Ukraine won gold medals, V. Holubnychy, V. Krepkina, L. Lysenko, and V. Tsybulenko; in 1964, V. Brumel and I. and T. Press; in 1968, V. Holubnychy; in 1972, M. Avilov, V. Borzov, A. Bodnarchuk, and F. Melnyk; in 1976, Yu. Sedykh; in 1980, V. Kyselov, N. Olizarenko, Yu. Sedykh, N. Tkachenko, T. Prorochenko, and N. Ziuskova; and in 1988, H. Avdiienko, S. Bubka, O. Bryzhina, T. Samolenko, V. Bryzhin, and M. Pinihina. After Ukraine regained its independence in 1991, Ukraine's athletes participated in the 1992 Summer Olympic Games as members of the 'Unified Team' of the former Soviet Republics. T. Dorovsykh (women's 3,000-m run) and I. Kravets (women's long-jump) won silver medals for Ukraine and the gold in world championships in Toronto in 1993. S. Bubka (pole vault) did not qualify at the Summer Games but subsequently set his 32nd world record by jumping 6.13 m (Tokyo, 1992).

BIBLIOGRAPHY
Al'manakh Rady fizychnoï kul'tury (Munich 1951)
Dmytryk, V. Sport na Ukraïni (Kiev 1976)
Bielykh, M.; Bohachuk, P.; Synyts'kyi, Z. Lehkoatlety Ukraïny, 2nd rev edn (Kiev 1979)

O. Zinkevych

Serhii Bubka, the Olympic gold medalist and world-record holder in the pole vault

**Tractor industry.** A branch of the machine-building industry that produces various types of tractors, tractor and combine motors, parts, and equipment. Tractors are used in agriculture, heavy industry, construction, forest management, and other sectors of the economy. They have replaced much human and animal labor and have raised productivity in many branches of the economy.

Before the Revolution of 1917 there were no tractor factories in Ukraine. Only in the late 1920s did mass production of tractors begin in the USSR. Until then draft animals and a very small number of imported tractors were used. Some small tractors were built in Tokmak, in Zaporizhia oblast, from 1923. The first specialized tractor plant in Ukraine, the *Kharkiv Tractor Plant, opened in 1931. Initially it produced the SKhTZ tractor, which was an effective machine but somewhat underpowered. Tractor building became an important priority for the regime following the collectivization of agriculture, when many draft animals died or were slaughtered, and the introduction of *machine-tractor stations, which were to promote the mechanization of agriculture and Party control over the peasantry. Total output of the industry in Soviet Ukraine increased from 2,000 tractors in 1928 (15 percent of total Soviet production) to almost 41,000 in 1934 (26 percent of Soviet production). In 1937 output dropped to 10,600, but the tractors then built were much larger and more powerful. Ukraine accounted for 21 percent of the

Soviet output. In 1940 some 10,400 tractors, or one-third of the Soviet total, were built in Ukraine.

At the outset of the Second World War many of the industry's plants were converted to military production and then evacuated to the east. The industry was reconstructed after the war, and since then much has been done to improve the quality of Ukrainian tractors. Ukraine's output of tractors steadily increased from 22,600 tractors (19 percent of total USSR production) in 1950 to 147,500 (32 percent) in 1970; production leveled off during the 1980s, 135,600 were built in 1980, 140,000 (25 percent) in 1986, and 130,900 in 1987. Several specialized tractors have been developed, including small garden tractors and both wheel-driven and caterpillar machines. Today the most popular tractors built in Ukraine are the T-150, a 150-hp tractor available in both wheel-driven and caterpillar versions and introduced in 1971; the T-25, a small garden tractor; the T-16, for hauling; and the all-purpose T-74. In 1982 there were 25 tractor factories in Ukraine. Almost all of the finished tractors were still being produced at the Kharkiv Tractor Plant; the other enterprises, located mostly in the Donets Basin, provided parts, equipment, engines, or semifinished machines. In the last years of the USSR, the tractor industry in Ukraine stagnated, although the total Soviet output continued to grow. The most powerful new models (eg, the K-700) are being built in the RF.

**Trade.** The branch of the national economy that deals with the flow of goods from the producer to the consumer. In the narrow sense trade consists of the wholesale and retail distribution of consumer goods (including prepared food). In Ukraine prior to 1992 trade included two more branches of the Soviet economy, material and technical supply (known in the West as the wholesale trade in the means of production) and state procurement of farm products. Besides internal trade there was also external or foreign trade and economic relations with other republics of the USSR. Statistics on those two forms of exchange began to be collected only at the end of the 1980s.

The weight of internal trade in Ukraine's national economy is indicated in table 1. Ukraine's income from external trade in 1989 was 6.4 billion rubles, or 5.85 percent of the national income produced (NIP).

TABLE 1
The share of the different branches of trade in Ukraine's national income and in the work force in 1989 (percentages)

|  | National income produced (in real prices) | Number of wage & salary workers |
| --- | --- | --- |
| All branches | 6.93 | 8.80 |
| Retail trade & food services | 5.34 | 7.58 |
| Material & technical supply | 0.88 | 0.73 |
| State procurement of farm products | 0.71 | 0.49 |

Every branch of trade in Ukraine has been poorly developed, a state of affairs that hampered the other branches of the economy and caused social tension. Demand for almost every commodity in wholesale and retail trade greatly exceeded the country's capacity to produce or import such commodities. The network of trade enterprises, particularly modern ones such as department stores, was inadequate. Stores and businesses were poorly equipped with modern cash registers, computers, and communications machines. The assortment of goods, particularly since 1990, has been limited. Food-services enterprises for the general public and commercial space have been in short supply. Most of the workers in the various branches of trade have been poorly trained and motivated, and customer service has therefore been low. Because of poor organization customers have had to put up with long queues.

In the last few years new trade enterprises – co-operatives and joint ventures – have appeared alongside the established organizations. In 1991 the first stock exchanges were set up. Collective-farm markets, which sell farm produce, and flea markets, which sell manufactured and mostly imported goods, have been opened in almost all cities and towns. The prices there are unregulated and much higher than state prices. In 1989, 5.1 percent of consumer goods were bought at these markets.

**Material and technical supply and sale.** Organizationally distinct, this branch of trade supplies raw materials and fuel to various branches of the economy and markets the industrial output, except for consumer goods. In 1990 there were 2,170 independent enterprises of this branch in Ukraine; their annual turnover was 63.34 billion rubles. The largest share of the output in this branch – 20.765 billion rubles' worth, or 32.8 percent of the total – was produced by the organizations that had previously come under the State Committee for Material and Technical Supply. The second-largest output came from the organizations under the State Committee of the Coal Industry: 14.89 billion rubles' worth, or 23.5 percent of the total. The former State Agroindustrial Committee oversaw a large network of supply organizations with an output of 9.74 billion rubles, or 15.4 percent of the total, and the state Committee for Petroleum Products had a network with an output of 7 billion rubles, or 11.1 percent of the total. For many years the material and technical supply system was used not for conducting wholesale trade but for distributing production according to fixed and usually low prices set by the state. When many kinds of products were in short supply, priority was given to the needs of the defense industry and heavy industry. The system was too large and centralized to ensure an efficient use of resources. In 1987 the first steps were taken to change gradually from a centralized division of material resources to their wholesale marketing and to direct long-term ties between producers and consumers. But under the existing conditions the plan could not be carried out. In 1990–1 the supply of resources declined seriously. At the same time the first commodity exchanges with free-market prices appeared.

**Agricultural procurement.** The state purchased farm products for further processing and consumption by the population. In 1989 the government bought 31.94 billion rubles' worth of farm products, or 58.6 percent of Ukraine's gross agricultural output (including seed and feed). Ninety-six percent of the procurements came from collective and state farms and other agricultural enterprises, and 4 percent from private plots. The breakdown by product is given in table 2.

In the last few years of the Soviet Union, in spite of higher procurement prices, the collective and state farms turned away from procurement organizations to sell their

TABLE 2
Agricultural procurement in Ukraine in 1990 (at 1989 prices)

| Product | 1,000 tonnes | Million rubles | % of total |
|---|---|---|---|
| *Total procurement* | – | 30,475 | 100 |
| | | | |
| *From farms & enterprises* | – | 29,277 | 96.1 |
| Grains | 14,288 | 2,768 | 9.1 |
| Wheat | 10,712 | 1,800 | 5.9 |
| Sunflower | 1,991 | 960 | 3.2 |
| Flax fiber | 106 | 206 | 0.7 |
| Sugar beets | 43,283 | 2,078 | 6.8 |
| Vegetables & melons | 4,360 | 899 | 2.9 |
| Potatoes | 2,201 | 370 | 1.2 |
| Fruits, berries, grapes | 1,891 | 826 | 2.7 |
| Livestock & poultry (live weight) | 4,587 | 11,332 | 37.2 |
| Cattle | 2,806 | 7,445 | 24.4 |
| Hogs | 1,058 | 2,383 | 7.8 |
| Poultry | 440 | 971 | 3.2 |
| Milk & dairy products | 17,965 | 7,653 | 25.1 |
| Eggs (in millions) | 8,598 | 714 | 2.3 |
| Wool | 30 | 252 | 0.8 |
| Furs | – | 119 | 0.4 |
| | | | |
| *From private plots* | – | 1,198 | 3.9 |
| Meat (carcass weight) | 95 | 311 | 1.0 |
| Vegetables & melons | 374 | 211 | 0.7 |
| Fruits, berries, grapes | 203 | 208 | 0.7 |

products to other purchasers at better prices or to barter their products for farm machinery, trucks, or building materials. The difficulty in obtaining deliveries at state prices was largely due to unbalanced price reforms, which raised industrial prices at a greater rate than farm prices. (See also *Agricultural procurement and *Grain procurement.)

**Retail trade and food services.** These branches sold goods directly to the consumer and represented the final stage of commodity turnover. In 1989, 79.8 percent of personal consumption was handled by these two branches. The basic statistics on them are given in table 4.

Since 1980 the growth rate of food sales in the retail trade, including the food services industry, has fallen behind that of nonfood sales, and the increase in the food services turnover has lagged behind the growth rate of the total turnover (see table 3). The division of retail sales between state and co-operative trade (including food services) shifted slightly in favor of the first, from 70.1 percent in 1980 to 71.7 percent in 1989.

In 1989 the Ukrainian Ministry of Trade controlled 45.2 percent of the total turnover, the consumer co-operatives 28.4 percent, the organizations of the State Agroindustrial Committee 2.7 percent, and various Union and republican ministries the rest. In the few years before that the network of state consignment stores had grown; in 1989 their turnover was 1,873 million rubles, or 2.7 percent of the total turnover. They resold used cars (60.5 percent of their turnover) and imported goods, such as clothes and underwear (10.6 percent) and radios (4.3 percent). Co-operative stores began to be organized in 1988. In 1989 they accounted for only 0.46 percent of the turnover.

Until 1990 the official state and co-operative retail price indexes did not reflect real price changes, particularly on nonfood products. In 1989 the official price index for all

TABLE 3
Product structure of state and co-operative retail trade
(including food services) in Ukraine, 1960–89
(in million rubles)

| | 1960 | 1970 | 1980 | 1985 | 1989 |
|---|---|---|---|---|---|
| *All goods* | 13,347 | 27,548 | 46,742 | 55,427 | 68,341 |
| | | | | | |
| *Food products* | 6,808 | 14,484 | 22,471 | 25,752 | 30,470 |
| Meat & meat products | 801 | 2,081 | 3,519 | 4,231 | 5,319 |
| Fish & fish products | 311 | 566 | 835 | 910 | 1,042 |
| Canned vegetables, fruits, berries | 61 | 264 | 418 | 509 | 654 |
| Fats | 467 | 902 | 1,341 | 1,518 | 1,631 |
| Butter | 254 | 544 | 796 | 914 | 1,018 |
| Oil | 120 | 186 | 265 | 314 | 335 |
| Milk & dairy products | 308 | 916 | 1,217 | 1,407 | 1,603 |
| Cheese | 38 | 127 | 208 | 275 | 312 |
| Eggs | 34 | 193 | 527 | 658 | 612 |
| Sugar | 652 | 1,059 | 1,401 | 1,249 | 1,217 |
| Confectionery products | 457 | 1,007 | 1,517 | 1,955 | 2,399 |
| Preserves, jam, honey | – | 58 | 82 | 105 | 165 |
| Bread & buns | 786 | 1,315 | 1,675 | 1,785 | 2,083 |
| Flour, grits, pasta | 462 | 631 | 876 | 874 | 1,044 |
| Potatoes | 83 | 138 | 165 | 234 | 280 |
| Vegetables | 136 | 366 | 691 | 847 | 1,021 |
| Fruits, berries, melons | 136 | 311 | 440 | 625 | 810 |
| Alcoholic beverages | 1,560 | 3,462 | 5,860 | 6,524 | 7,357 |
| Non-alcoholic beverages | 134 | 246 | 327 | 397 | 666 |
| Ice cream | incl above | 123 | 177 | 225 | 285 |
| | | | | | |
| Added value in food services | 164 | 416 | 735 | 755 | 871 |
| | | | | | |
| *Non-food products* | 6,539 | 13,064 | 24,271 | 29,675 | 37,871 |
| Woven cloth | 1,074 | 826 | 1,237 | 1,188 | 1,316 |
| Clothes, underwear, headgear, furs | 1,327 | 2,875 | 4,716 | 5,625 | 5,970 |
| Knitwear | 306 | 1,161 | 2,019 | 2,371 | 2,753 |
| Hosiery | 127 | 315 | 475 | 535 | 794 |
| Footwear | 689 | 1,474 | 2,313 | 2,639 | 2,857 |
| Industrial soap, cleaning substances | 68 | 131 | 226 | 229 | 386 |
| Toilet soap, perfumes | 98 | 210 | 531 | 698 | 1,149 |
| Haberdashery, thread | 331 | 701 | 1,358 | 1,576 | 2,044 |
| Tobacco products | 276 | 513 | 764 | 1,052 | 1,234 |
| Domestic goods | 1,240 | 3,301 | 6,938 | 8,381 | 10,938 |
| Watches | 85 | 98 | 227 | 230 | 317 |
| Radios | 125 | 582 | 900 | 1,264 | 1,821 |
| Sports goods | 33 | 85 | 138 | 167 | 235 |
| Toys, tree decorations | 46 | 125 | 261 | 331 | 459 |
| Paper, notebooks, office supplies | 79 | 194 | 300 | 347 | 424 |
| Printed matter | 159 | 343 | 583 | 865 | 1,089 |
| Electrical products | 68 | 361 | 596 | 711 | 1,053 |
| Furniture | 283 | 633 | 1,199 | 1,482 | 1,846 |
| Kilims, rugs | – | 128 | 634 | 853 | 775 |
| Tableware | 184 | 334 | 722 | 880 | 1,037 |
| Building materials, glass | 396 | 436 | 543 | 998 | 1,782 |
| Consumer chemical products | 67 | 132 | 175 | 262 | |
| Jewelry | – | 87 | 801 | 569 | 1,078 |
| Cars | – | – | 1,519 | 2,158 | 2,605 |
| Petroleum, oil | – | – | 130 | 380 | 777 |
| | | | | | |
| Co-operative turnover | – | – | – | – | 308 |

TABLE 4
Basic growth indicators of Ukraine's retail trade, 1960–89

| | 1960 | 1970 | 1980 | 1985 | 1989 |
|---|---|---|---|---|---|
| Total retail trade, state & co-operative, in real prices (in million rubles) | 13,347 | 27,548 | 46,742 | 55,427 | 68,649 |
| Food services | 1,360 | 2,966 | 4,426 | 5,081 | 5,832 |
| Goods reserves at year's end in real prices (in million rubles) | 3,111 | 6,554 | 8,847 | 11,939 | 10,021 |
| Average annual work force in retail trade (in 1,000s) | 399 | 716 | 871 | 894 | 936 |
| in food services (in 1,000s) | 18 | 384 | 478 | 488 | 481 |
| Number of enterprises in retail trade (in 1,000s) | 121.8 | 148.2 | 143.7 | 142.0 | 145.9 |
| Commercial space in stores (in 1,000 sq m) | – | – | 9,134 | 10,195 | 11,129 |
| Number of food-service enterprises (in 1,000s) | 26.1 | 47.7 | 56.0 | 59.4 | 62.3 |
| Seating places in food-service enterprises (in 1,000s) | – | 2,042 | 3,458 | 4,054 | 4,436 |

goods amounted to 109 percent of the 1980 figure: food prices were 117 percent higher than in 1980, alcohol prices 209 percent higher, and nonfood prices only 104 percent higher.

At the end of 1990 special coupons were introduced to stem the outflow of goods from Ukraine to the other Soviet republics. Ukrainian residents received coupons corresponding to 70 percent of their personal income and used them to purchase most kinds of consumer goods.

At the beginning of April 1991 retail prices on almost all consumer goods, except alcoholic beverages and petroleum, were raised. Prices in the second quarter of 1991 were 1.93 times higher than a year earlier: food prices went up by a factor of 1.84, clothes prices more than

doubled, and durable goods prices went up by a factor of 1.9.

**Interrepublican and foreign trade.** In 1913 Ukraine exported 789 million rubles' worth of goods to other countries and parts of the Russian Empire and imported only 261 million rubles' worth. Some data on Ukraine's *foreign trade were collected when the economy was under territorial control, and the councils for the national economy were active. It was only in 1987 that the foreign ties of some branches of the national economy began to be monitored. The basic data about Ukraine's foreign trade in 1989 are summarized in table 5. The most important commodities that Ukraine must import are petroleum (under 10 percent of the demand can be met by domestic produc-

TABLE 5
Ukraine's imports and exports according to branches of the economy in 1989 at internal prices (in million rubles)

| Branch | Imports | | Exports | |
|---|---|---|---|---|
| | from Soviet republics | from foreign countries | to Soviet republics | to foreign countries |
| Total | 39,969 | 14,569 | 40,464 | 7,596 |
| Industry | 38,952 | 13,433 | 38,687 | 7,343 |
| Electric power | 178 | – | 160 | 499 |
| Petroleum, gas | 4,320 | 61 | 368 | 495 |
| Coal | 293 | 79 | 276 | 582 |
| Ferrous metallurgy | 2,512 | 381 | 6,258 | 1,830 |
| Nonferrous metallurgy | 2,008 | 180 | 918 | 47 |
| Chemicals, petrochemicals | 4,476 | 1,407 | 3,132 | 812 |
| Machine building, metalworking | 14,200 | 3,846 | 15,913 | 2,251 |
| Lumber, woodworking, paper | 1,529 | 404 | 379 | 67 |
| Building materials, porcelain | 424 | 84 | 678 | 31 |
| Light | 5,601 | 4,093 | 2,501 | 173 |
| Food | 2,342 | 2,716 | 7,315 | 475 |
| Other branches | 1,069 | 182 | 789 | 81 |
| Agriculture | 291 | 1,119 | 1,430 | 64 |
| Other forms of material production | 726 | 17 | 347 | 189 |

tion), natural gas (20–25 percent), lumber, and cotton. Ukraine produces a surplus of ferrous metals and certain foodstuffs. In 1987–9 the average annual imports came to 17.7 percent of Ukraine's gross social product (in real internal prices). Of that, 12.9 percent was imported from other Soviet republics, and 4.8 percent from abroad. At the same time Ukraine consumed 83.8 percent of its output and exported 13.8 percent of it to other Soviet republics and only 2.4 abroad. In 1990, 78 percent of Ukraine's exports abroad consisted of raw materials and consumer goods; 16 percent, of machines and equipment; and 6 percent, of equipment and materials for construction projects supported by the USSR. About two-thirds of the interrepublican trade was with the RSFSR, and a similar proportion of the foreign trade was with former Comecon members.

For many years Ukraine had a favorable trade balance with the other Soviet republics. With the dissolution of the USSR and the introduction of world prices the situation changed, because of the high cost of petroleum and natural gas. In regard to foreign trade, Ukraine's imports have always outweighed its exports, in 1987 by almost 7 billion rubles.

A. Revenko

**Trade and Industry Chamber of the Ukrainian SSR** (Torhovelno-promyslova palata URSR). A republican commercial institution formed in 1973 out of the Ukrainian branches of the USSR Trade and Industry Chamber in Kiev, Odessa, and Kharkiv. It represented Ukrainian state, cooperative, and communal enterprises and promoted international trade by exchanging commercial information, arranging exhibitions, and testing the quality of industrial products. It informed foreign companies about products made in Ukraine and Ukrainian enterprises about foreign products, translated technical instructions, and prepared advertisements. The chamber had 9 interoblast departments, 16 oblast branches, and 24 municipal product-testing offices.

**Trade unions** (*profsoiuzy* or *profspilky*). Mass voluntary organizations of workers according to occupation. In the Ukrainian SSR trade unions (TU), according to their statutes, accepted the authority of the CPSU. They were formed and developed within the framework of the all-Russian trade-union movement. Under the Soviet regime Ukrainian TU functioned as organizationally subordinate parts of all-Soviet TU.

**To 1917.** Associations of workers and tradesmen began to appear in Western Europe with the beginning of industrialization in the late 18th century. They were opposed by employers and government. Great Britain was the first country to grant at first partial (1824) and then full (1871) legal status to TU. Next TU were legalized in France, and then in other Western European countries. In the Russian Empire they were legalized only after the Revolution of 1905.

In Russian-ruled Ukraine the demand for workers' organizations and unions began to grow after the emancipation of the serfs in 1861 and the rapid growth of industry in the Donets Basin and some other parts of the country. Working conditions in the mines and factories of the Donbas Basin were especially difficult and gave rise to worker opposition, initially in the form of spontaneous work

stoppages and then in the form of organized strikes. The number of strikes increased quickly, from 52 in 1860–79 to 71 in 1885–94 and 212 in 1895–9. They were led by illegal strike committees, which later became the nuclei of the developing trade unions. From the 1880s some legally recognized workers' benevolent societies were formed to represent and aid workers.

The first formal workers' organization in Ukraine was the illegal South Russian Union of Workers, founded in Odessa in 1875 and headed by E. Zaslavsky. It consisted of nine groups of 15 to 20 workers each. Although the union was soon disbanded by the authorities, it had a great influence on the workers' movement throughout the empire. In 1901–5 the tsarist authorities attempted to organize proregime TU under the control of the police. The movement was initiated by the head of the Moscow secret police, S. Zubatov (hence, the movement was often referred to as *zubatovshchina*). It had only limited success in Russia and even less success in Ukraine, where a few small unions were established for a short time in Kiev and Odessa. Illegal TU sprang up in Ukraine toward the end of the 19th century. They grew quickly in number and size during the Revolution of 1905, and attracted particularly workers in small factories and shops, printers, bakers, tailors, and clerks. TU were officially recognized by the Temporary Regulations on Trade Unions in 1906, which were intended also to limit union activities and impede the proliferation of unions by permitting the authorities to refuse registration to any union they chose. Nonetheless, by 1907 there were 281 TU in Ukraine, or 40 percent of the total in the Russian Empire. They were small local unions that did not represent all the workers of either a region or a specific occupation. The political reaction and economic crisis that began in 1907 resulted in a rapid decline in TU: by 1909 the number of TU in Odessa had declined from 55 to 2, in Katerynoslav (Dnipropetrovske), from 30 to 6, and in Kharkiv, from 16 to 5. Illegal political parties (Ukrainian, Russian, and Jewish) attempted to find support among the TU and to politicize them. Most TU, however, refrained from political action and limited themselves to economic issues and the defense of individual workers. The Mensheviks advocated such a role for the TU and enjoyed the greatest influence on them.

The TU movement in Western Ukraine was concentrated in eastern Galicia. Workers' organizations and benevolent societies began to appear there in 1869. Initially they represented mostly Polish artisans in Lviv. Ukrainians were most active in the unions of tobacco and railway workers. A Ukrainian branch of the Austro-Hungarian union of railway workers was set up, and a separate Ukrainian workers' paper was published. That organization also attracted members in Bukovyna, where the *Ukrainian Teachers' Mutual Aid Society and *Union of Ukrainian Private Office Employees were active, as also in Galicia. In Galicia some local Ukrainian unions were under the influence of Ukrainian socialists, such as M. Pavlyk and O. Terletsky.

**1917–45.** The February Revolution of 1917 opened the way for the spontaneous growth of mass TU, in Russian-ruled Ukraine. By May 1917 in Kiev there were 30 TU, with almost 40,000 adherents; in Odessa, 40, with 35,000 members; in Kharkiv, 35, with 45,000 members; and in the Donbas, 45, representing almost half of all the workers in the region. At the same time several central TU associations and co-ordinating councils were formed. The unions attracted workers of all nationalities. Ukrainians were particularly active in the railway union, which published a Ukrainian-language organ and maintained close ties with Ukrainian railway workers in Western Ukraine (see *All-Ukrainian railway workers' congresses). The *Peasant Association (est 1917) defended the interests of farmers and farm workers.

Many Ukrainian workers and TU supported the Ukrainian national cause and opposed the Bolsheviks. The First *All-Ukrainian Workers' Congress, which was dominated by the Ukrainian Social Democratic Workers' party, recognized the authority of the Central Rada. The mood of the First All-Ukrainian Congress of Trade Unions, which was held in Kiev in May 1918, and elected the All-Ukrainian Central Council of Trade Unions (Utsentrprof), was also anti-Bolshevik. It passed resolutions condemning political interference in TU activities. The Second All-Ukrainian Workers' Congress, held in Kiev in July 1917, attracted mostly Russian and Jewish workers. Yet it too supported Ukrainian independence and the principles of the Central Rada and condemned the Hetman government. Russian-dominated Menshevik TU along with Ukrainian railway workers organized mass strikes to stop the export of foodstuffs to Germany and thus contributed to undermining the Peace Treaty of Brest-Litovsk. In that period Bolsheviks had little influence over TU in Ukraine. They gained control over the unions only after they had consolidated political power in the country.

TU had considerable influence in the Western Ukrainian National Republic (ZUNR). Their representatives (A. *Chernetsky, O. Pisetsky, and M. Parfanovych) sat on the Ukrainian National Rada and State Secretariat. As in the UNR, the railway workers in Galicia were particularly active and well organized; they even created their own battalion under the command of I. *Siiak.

In April 1919 a Bolshevik-sponsored all-Ukrainian congress of TU was held in Kharkiv. It rejected the Utsentrprof and began to bring the TU movement in Ukraine under Moscow-based central TU organizations. In 1920 a Bureau for the South of Russia, consisting of A. Andreev, D. Shvartsman, and V. Storozhenko, was established by the Bolsheviks; it reinforced the subordinate status of Ukrainian TU. Although the body was soon renamed the Ukrainian Bureau of the All-Union Central Council of Trade Unions, it remained ineffective, because most local TU remained under Menshevik control. The Bolshevik policy of War Communism was designed to bring TU under complete state control and even to reorganize them into *labor armies with strict military discipline and centralized control by Communist functionaries. The workers opposed that tendency.

In the first few years of Soviet rule a major debate took place in government and Party circles on the role of TU in the Soviet system. The so-called Workers' Opposition, headed by A. Kollontai and A. Shliapnikov and supported widely by workers and TU functionaries, argued that TU and the workers should have control over much of the economy and production and should be free of Party intervention. The other faction, led by L. Trotsky and N. Bukharin, viewed the TU as a means of increasing productivity and enforcing worker discipline and demanded their complete subordination to the Party. A compromise position advocated by V. Lenin that TU should both de-

fend workers' interests and serve the goals of the state was adopted at the 10th Congress of the Russian Communist Party (Bolshevik) (RCP[B]) in March 1921. In Ukraine the Workers' Opposition was led by I. Perepichka and M. Lobanov; prominent figures such as Kh. Rakovsky and G. Piatakov were associated with the Trotskyist position. Initially the followers of Lenin were a minority in Kharkiv and the Donbas. In Odessa, Luhanske, and other cities there were workers' demonstrations against the Party. After the Party consolidated its power over TU in Ukraine, it conducted a major purge directed primarily at Mensheviks, Socialist Revolutionaries, and 'nationalists' in the TU. Total TU membership in Ukraine had dropped from 1,370,500 to just 794,300 by October 1922. The members of some of the higher TU bodies were dismissed and replaced by functionaries appointed from Moscow. In 1922 the 11th RCP(B) Congress passed a resolution stating that all leading posts in TU had to be held by Party members. Lenin himself argued that TU should be seen as 'transmission belts' from the Party to the masses and should be used to ensure workers' compliance with Party dictates. TU leaders increasingly saw themselves as representatives of the Party or state, not of the workers. The *All-Ukrainian Council of Trade Unions (VURPS) was established only in 1924 and was treated as a branch of the All-Union Central Council of Trade Unions (VTsSPS) in Moscow. Mass purges of TU activists were carried out in 1929–30 and 1937–8.

In the 1930s the rights and responsibilities of TU were reduced gradually. In 1929 the Party declared strikes to be unproductive and antiproletarian. Since then TU have not organized any major work stoppages. To settle disputes enterprise-level commissions composed of union and management representatives were established, but they sided with management rather than with the workers. In the mid-1930s, provisions for collective bargaining were abolished in the USSR. The regime's uncompromising commitment to rapid industrialization overrode the unions' traditional concern for safe working conditions. The TU were used increasingly to exploit and control the workers. *Production conferences and *socialist competition were used to mobilize workers. All leading positions in the unions were reserved for Party members. From 1932 to 1948 no TU congresses were held in Ukraine. In 1937 the VURPS and all republican TU bureaus were disbanded in an attempt to ensure the total subordination of Ukrainian TU to Moscow.

In the interwar period most independent Ukrainian TU in Polish-ruled Ukraine were disbanded by the regime or absorbed into Polish unions. Ukrainian participation in the international TU movement was restricted. Only the Union of Ukrainian Private Office Employees and some teachers' associations were allowed to operate. The *Union of Peasant Associations, which was controlled by the Ukrainian Radical party, represented the interests of the Ukrainian small farmer. The Ukrainian Social Democratic party published *Profesional'nyi vistnyk* (1920–1) to stimulate the Ukrainian TU movement, and the Communist Party of Western Ukraine published *Profesiini visty* (1926–8). A repressive labor law adopted in 1929 put an end to trade-union activities in Poland. No independent Ukrainian unions were allowed to exist in either Transcarpathia or Bukovyna in the interwar period.

**After 1945.** The first TU congress in Ukraine after the

Second World War, and the first since 1932, was held in 1948. It set up the *Ukrainian Republican Council of Trade Unions (URRPS). The four congresses held up to 1956 were called conferences, a term that underscored their limited importance. Since 1958 there have been nine congresses. The structure of Soviet TU was determined by their statute, which was ratified at TU congresses held every five years. Their organization was based on three principles: the production principle, according to which all workers and managers in a given branch of the economy must belong to a single union; the principle of democratic centralism, which ensured the strict subjugation of lower bodies to higher ones; and the principle of subordination, which placed the unions under the direction of the Communist party. Soviet TU had to adhere to communist ideology and accept instructions from the Party. Any decision of the VTsSPS could be overruled by the CC CPSU. In the mid-1980s there were 20 TU in Ukraine organized by sectors: aviation, highways and automotive transport, construction and construction materials, coal industry, geological research, state trade and consumer co-operation, civil service, electrical services, transportation, municipal services and housing, cultural services, forestry and paper products, health care, metallurgy, oil and gas, education and academics, agriculture, textiles and light industry, food services, and chemicals and petrochemicals. There were trade-union councils in every oblast and in the city of Kiev. Although formally membership was voluntary, in fact almost all workers and collective and state farmers belonged to a union. Every union had its own elected leadership. At the lowest level the system consisted of enterprise committees, elected for one year. Above them rose the raion- or city-level committees, then the oblast committees, the republican committees, the central Union committees in Moscow, and finally the VTsSPS. According to that structure, TU in Ukraine were subordinated in theory both to their central committees in Moscow and to the URRPS, but in reality the latter had little authority.

According to their statutes the basic goals of TU were to inculcate communist ideology, to ensure fulfillment and overfulfillment of plans, to raise labor discipline, efficiency, and quality of work, to monitor work safety, to administer social security programs, to monitor compliance with labor laws, and to defend the interests of the workers before plant administrators. They also had a supervisory role in the fields of housing construction, trade, and consumer services. TU organized recreational, cultural, and educational activities for the workers and ran their own press organs, theaters, cinemas, clubs, libraries, sports facilities, tourist bases, rest homes, and sanatoriums. Unions also sponsored large sports associations that provided not only physical-education programs for union members but also training for top-ranking athletes and professional teams. There were 15 republican (the largest was *Avanhard) and 2 all-Union (Lokomotyv, associated with the railway union, and Vodnyk, associated with the river and sea transport union) sports associations in Ukraine.

Leading union functionaries were trained at two higher schools, located in Moscow and Leningrad. Since the Second World War there have also been two schools for training lower-level union workers in Lviv and Kharkiv. In recent years almost all the central organs as well as the particular unions have been headed by people with a higher specialized education.

Union membership in Ukraine has increased steadily. In 1950 it was 5.02 million, or about 92.1 percent of the total work force. In 1960 it was 10.31, or 95.5 percent; in 1972, 18.43, or almost 100 percent; and in 1987, over 26, 100 percent. TU activities were funded by membership dues (which came to 1 percent of a worker's wages), income from cultural-social and sporting events, and contributions from enterprises and factories.

The TU of Ukraine participated in international labor organizations, primarily Soviet-bloc ones, only through their all-Union offices. Their international activities included exchanges of labor delegations and cultural and sports groups.

**Ukrainian unions outside Ukraine.** Ukrainians in the United States and Canada did not form separate TU. Immediately after the Second World War Ukrainian sections were formed in some British TU to serve the needs of Ukrainian workers. The Union of Ukrainian Workers in Belgium was short-lived, but the *Union of Ukrainian Workers in France was active for 25 years.

BIBLIOGRAPHY
Sadovs'kyi, V. *Pratsia v USSR* (Warsaw 1932)
Stadnyk, A.; Prokhorenko, M. *Profsoiuzy Ukrainy do Velikoi Oktiabr'skoi sotsialisticheskoi revoliutsii* (Moscow 1959)
Slutskii, A.; Sidorenko, V. *Profsoiuzy Ukrainy posle pobedy Velikogo Oktiabria* (Moscow 1961)
*Dovidnyk profspilkovoho aktyvu Ukraïny* (Kiev 1964)
Hayenko, F. *Trade Unions and Labor in the Soviet Union* (Munich 1965)
Skliarenko, Ie. *Narysy istoriï profspilkovoho rukhu na Ukraïni, 1917–1920* (Kiev 1974)
*Istoriia profsoiuzov SSSR*, 2 vols (Moscow 1977, 1979)
Ruble, B. *Soviet Trade Unions: Their Development in the 1970s* (New York 1981)
Himka, J.-P. *Socialism in Galicia: The Emergence of Polish Social Democracy and Ukrainian Radicalism (1860–1890)* (Cambridge, Mass 1983)
F. Haienko

**Trajan's Walls.** A series of defensive walls in southwestern Ukraine built by the Roman emperor Trajan in the late 1st to early 2nd century AD in order to prevent steppe nomads from descending on the recently conquered (and colonized) province of Dacia. Slavic tribes (particularly the Antes) used the walls in the 3rd to 4th centuries as a defense against incursions into their lands. For this purpose they filled in the ditches along the northern elevations of the walls and dug out ditches along their southern portions. Remains of the walls can be found today in Vinnytsia, Khmelnytskyi, and Ternopil oblasts. Similar walls of uncertain origin, known as *Zmiiovi Valy, were built in the Dnieper region.

**Trakhtemyriv fortified settlement.** A fortified settlement of the 6th century BC near Trakhtemyriv, Pereiaslav-Khmelnytskyi raion, Kiev oblast. Excavations in 1964–8 revealed 44 dwellings, including one that housed a sacrificial altar. Iron and bronze implements, articles of adornment, and local and imported pottery (the latter from northern Black Sea trading centers) were also found at the site. The inhabitants practiced agriculture, animal husbandry, and various crafts (including bronze casting).

**Trakhtemyriv Monastery.** An Orthodox monastery that was located near the town of Trakhtemyriv and the village of Zarubyntsi (hence, it is also known as the Zarubyntsi Monastery) on the right bank of the Dnieper River near Kaniv (now Pereiaslav-Khmelnytskyi raion, Kiev oblast). Little is known of its early history. In 1578 the Polish king Stephen Báthory gave the monastery to the Registered Cossacks for use as a hospital; wounded and ill Cossacks were treated by the monks, and often retired to live in the area. It was also used as a staging area for Cossack military campaigns, and the town served almost as a capital for the Zaporozhian Host. Ruined by a Polish army following the rebellion led by P. Pavliuk in 1637, it was rebuilt under B. Khmelnytsky, who granted it land and villages on the condition that it continue to aid Cossacks. It was destroyed by a Turkish attack in 1678, and most of the people in the surrounding villages fled the area. The Trakhtemyriv hospital remained an important symbol of Cossack autonomy, and as late as 1710 (in the *Bendery Constitution) the Cossacks were demanding that it be returned to them.

**Tranquillon, Kyrylo.** See Stavrovetsky-Tranquillon, Kyrylo.

**Transbuh region** (Zabuzhzhia; also Zabuzka Rus'). A historical-geographic region on the left bank of the Buh River that includes the Kholm region and Podlachia.

**Transcarpathia** or **Transcarpathian Ukraine** (Zakarpattia). A historical-geographic region in southwestern Ukraine, incorporating the southern slopes of the Carpathian Mountains and a portion of the adjoining Tysa Lowland.

**Territory.** Transcarpathia is the only part of Ukraine located beyond the Carpathian Mountains that makes up part of the Pannonian Basin. Accessible to the main territory of Ukraine through numerous mountain passes, it joins Ukraine with that part of East-Central Europe. Moreover, along the southern rim of the Carpathians and the upper Tysa (the Maramureş Basin) a route connects Transcarpathia with Czechoslovakia to the west and with Transylvania and Moldova (within Rumania) to the east. As a small region located off major routes Transcarpathia constituted a marginal province of Hungary for many centuries. Moreover, it was subdivided into a number of counties (Hungarian names: Máramaros, Ugocsa, Bereg, Ung, Zemplén, Sáros, Szepes) that incorporated parts of Hungarian, Slovak, and Rumanian ethnographic territories.

Until 1919 Transcarpathia denoted that part of *Hungary where Ukrainians lived, and the synonymous terms Hungarian Ruthenia (Uhorska Rus') and Hungarian Ukraine (Uhorska Ukraina) were widely used. Bounded by the ethnographic boundary with Rumanians and Hungarians in the south and Slovaks in the west, the region encompassed 15,600 sq km.

After the First World War Transcarpathia was separated from Hungary, and the bulk of its territory was formed into an autonomous region within Czechoslovakia called Subcarpathian Ruthenia (Pidkarpatska Rus') or Carpatho-Ukraine. A small part of Transcarpathia, located south of the Tysa River within the drainage basin of the Vyshava River (Vişeu in Rumanian), became part of Rumania (see *Maramureş region); in Transcarpathia's western reaches, the Prešov region was allocated to Slovakia. A narrow strip of Hungarian ethnographic territory was added to Carpatho-Ukraine with the intent of securing an east–west railroad link (Košice–Chop–Khust–Rakhiv) for direct communication with the rest of Czechoslovakia and a connection, via a branch line, to Rumania. Transcarpathia's status for the 1918–38 period with respect to area and population is summarized in table 1.

TABLE 1
Territories and population of Transcarpathia, 1930
(area in sq km; population in thousands)

| Territory | Area | Population |
|---|---|---|
| Carpathian Ukraine within ethnographic limits | 11,400 | 616 |
| Prešov region | 3,500 | 118 |
| Transcarpathia in Rumania | 700 | 26 |
| Total ethnographic Transcarpathia | 15,600 | 760 |
| Carpathian Ukraine within its administrative borders | 12,600 | 725 |

Within Czechoslovakia Transcarpathia played an important geopolitical role as the bridge linking Czechoslovakia with Rumania (the territorial axis of the Little Entente). At the same time it separated Hungary from its traditional ally, Poland. Later, Transcarpathia provided the USSR with a foothold in the Pannonian Plain.

Beginning in 1938 the borders of Carpatho-Ukraine underwent a number of changes. After the *Vienna Arbitration, Carpatho-Ukraine was transferred as a dependency to Hungary, with a compensation (1,050 sq km, 41,000 people) made in the west at the expense of Slovakia. Consequently, the administrative territory of Transcarpathia within Hungary in 1939–44, according to 1941 data, encompassed 12,060 sq km and contained 622,000 residents. Within the borders of Ukraine Transcarpathia occupies almost the same territory as it did within prewar Czechoslovakia, with a slight increase in the southwest around Chop. It constitutes a separate administrative unit, Transcarpathia oblast, with a territory of 12,800 sq km and a population of 1,252,000 (1989).

**Physical geography.** Transcarpathia encompasses two different natural regions, the *Tysa Lowland (now also

Hikers in the mountains of Transcarpathia

called the Transcarpathian Lowland) and the southern watershed of the Ukrainian Carpathians. The Carpathians in Transcarpathia have a banded structure common to the rest of the Eastern Carpathians, consisting of alternating parallel ridges and valleys. The parallel ridges are cut occasionally by the tributaries of the Tysa, which join the entire region into a unified whole. The western part of Transcarpathia (the Prešov region) in Czechoslovakia lies mainly in the *Low Beskyd and the West Beskyd.

The Carpathian Nature Preserve in Transcarpathia

The climate of Transcarpathia is temperate continental. Sheltered by the Carpathians from cold, northern winds, it is warmer than other parts of Ukraine at similar latitudes. In the Tysa Lowland and the foothills the climate is conducive to the cultivation of orchards, vineyards, and even some subtropical plants. Uzhhorod, at an elevation of 115 m, has a mean January temperature of −3.1°C and July temperature of 20.5°C. Its mean annual precipitation is 800 mm. At higher elevations in the mountains the climate gets colder and damper. In Yasinia, at an elevation of 645 m, the mean January temperature is −5.9°C and the mean July temperature 16.0°C, and the mean annual precipitation is 955 mm. Even more noticeable is the influence of elevation on vegetation zones, which progress from the forest-steppe in the lowland (105–200 m), where the forest groves consist of English oak (*Quercus robur*) with hornbeam and, less frequently, ash, through the broad-leaved forests in the foothills (200–600 m), where Durmast oak (*Quercus petraea*) with hornbeam and, occasionally, beech is common, to the mountain slopes, which range from beech forests (800–1,000 m) to mixed beech-spruce forests (1,000–1,300 m, with admixtures of ash, maple, and elm), coniferous forests (1,200–1,600 m, spruce, with occasional beech and maple), and stunted forest (up to 2,000 m, consisting of maple, beech, alder, spruce, juniper, and mountain pine). Alpine meadows prevail on exposed slopes and at higher elevations.

**Prehistory and early history.** The oldest remains of human activity in Transcarpathia indicate the presence of the Acheulean culture (300,000 years ago) of the Lower Paleolithic period. From that time people (including the Mousterian culture of the Lower Paleolithic) have inhabited Transcarpathia. During the Neolithic there was trade involving the export of obsidian artifacts from Transcarpathia across the Carpathian Mountains to the Dniester Valley. In the Bronze Age (ca 1800 BC) Transcarpathia maintained continuity in its painted pottery style of the Stanove culture but gained metalworking skills (swords, knives, sickles, axes) as a result of the arrival of Thracian tribes from Transylvania. Subsequently Transcarpathia came under the control of the Celts, who arrived from the west and brought with them iron-smelting (ca 400–200 BC); the first local coins were minted in the 3rd century BC. Of the eastern nomadic peoples the earliest to influence Transcarpathia were the Iranian-speaking Scythians (expressed locally from the 6th century BC in the *Kushtanovytsi culture) and then the Iazyges, a Sarmatian tribe confronting the Romans in Dacia (50 AD); their influence was followed by the invasions of the Turkic-speaking Huns (380 AD), the Avars (558 AD), and, finally, the Ugro-Finnic Magyars (896 AD). In the 2nd century AD neighboring Dacia (Transylvania) became a Roman province, and Roman merchants visited Transcarpathia. In the early Middle Ages Transcarpathia was traversed by Germanic tribes. Remnants of the Ostrogoths (the Gepidae) remained in neighboring Transylvania until the 10th century.

The Slavic colonization of Transcarpathia began in the 2nd century, with migration from the north across the mountain passes. By the 8th and 9th centuries the lowlands of Transcarpathia were fairly densely peopled by *White Croatians (at the time inhabiting both the north and the south side of the Carpathians). The Slavs in the upper Tysa and in Transylvania were subject to the Avars (6th–8th centuries) and later to the Bulgarian kingdom (9th–10th centuries). With the collapse of Bulgaria in the second half of the 10th century, Transcarpathia came under the sphere of influence of Kievan Rus'. The Kievan chroniclers noted the participation of the White Croatians in the campaigns on Byzantium. Following the incorporation of the White Croatians by Prince Volodymyr the Great into his realm, the name Rus' or Ruthenia became entrenched in Transcarpathia.

**11th to 15th centuries.** King Stephen I joined Transcarpathia to Hungary while his son, Imre (Emeric), was titled Prince of the Ruthenians. From that time until the beginning of the 20th century Transcarpathia remained within the Hungarian state as its border province in the northeast. Through Transcarpathia passed a fortified defense line consisting of stockades and wooden forts manned by the local Slovak and Ruthenian population (the Ruthenian March). It was completely destroyed during the Tatar campaign against Hungary (1241), when the invaders made their way through the mountain passes. In the 13th and 14th centuries stone castles capable of withstanding a long siege were built in place of wooden stockades. Feudalism developed as well, and royal domains were transformed into gentry latifundia, which in part survived into the 20th century. Simultaneously Transcarpathia was subdivided according to a new *komitat, or territorial-administrative structure.

Ukrainians constituted a minority element among the feudal aristocracy in Transcarpathia. Initially the Mukachiv dominion was granted in succession to two Rus' sons-in-law of the Hungarian king Béla IV (1235–70), Prince Rostyslav Mykhailovych of Chernihiv and Prince Lev Danylovych of Galicia (Halych). In the period from 1315 to the 1320s a group of nobles from northern Hunga-

The small town of Yasinia on the Chorna Tysa River in Transcarpathia

ry, hostile to the Anjou dynasty, even attempted to invite to the Hungarian throne one of the Yuriiovych brothers, Andrii or Lev II. In 1393–1414 the lord of the Mukachiv dominion was Prince Fedir Koriiatovych, a Ukrainianized Lithuanian who was instrumental in the Ukrainian colonization of Transcarpathia. By the first half of the 15th century, however, the Mukachiv dominion was being ruled by the Serbian 'despot' princes, S. Lazarević and D. Branković. After that the Slavic and Orthodox element completely disappeared from the aristocracy of Transcarpathia. The indigenous Ukrainian population was reduced to serfdom, and only occasionally did one of its members achieve the status of petty gentry or clergy.

From the middle of the 13th century until the end of the 15th century, Transcarpathia was affected by two colonizing movements, the Wallachian movement from the east and the German-Slovak movement from the west. The Wallachians in Transcarpathia were not exclusively Rumanians but consisted of Rumanian and Ukrainian pastoralists who had transplanted themselves first to Transylvania and then to the valleys of both sides of the Carpathians. German colonization came on the heels of the Tatars and built up the area with a number of towns with German (Magdeburg) law – Prešov, Bardejov, Berehove, Sevliush, Khust, and others.

Deprived of a political structure and social elite the Transcarpathian Ukrainians preserved their ethnic identity principally through their religious distinction. Eastern rite Christianity began to spread in Transcarpathia probably in the 9th and 10th centuries, when the region was part of Bulgaria. Factual accounts about church life did not appear until later. By the 14th century several monasteries had been established in Transcarpathia, among them two of outstanding importance, the St Nicholas Monastery near Mukachiv and St Michael's Monastery at Hrushiv, in the Maramureş (Marmarosh) area. The latter obtained the right of stauropegion in 1391. Mukachiv was the seat of an Orthodox eparchy (first mentioned in 1491), the religion of which was merely tolerated in Hungary, and the clergy and monasteries of which were dependent on the goodwill of the local gentry.

**16th and 17th centuries.** In the early 16th century the Transcarpathian population participated in the uprising led by G. Dózsa (1514) of Transylvania, which was brutally repressed. It also suffered as a result of its opposition to Austrian hegemony. The enserfment of the peasantry was ultimately formalized through I. Verböczy's codex, which remained the basis of Hungarian law until 1848.

After the defeat of Hungary by Turkey at the Battle of Mohács (1526) and its partition among the Ottoman Empire, Austria, and Transylvania, the history of Transcarpathia was marked by a constant threat from the Turks and by an ongoing rivalry between Austria and Transylvania. The lowland parts of Transcarpathia frequently suffered from Turkish raids, and the population of western Transcarpathia, under the jurisdiction of the Habsburgs (Prešov, Uzhhorod regions), was commonly called upon for organized defense. Eastern Transcarpathia, under Transylvanian control, became a battlefield in the 17th century between the native Hungarian aristocracy (headed by Transylvania) and pro-Austrian forces (with Hungarian adherents). Transcarpathian Ukrainians took a particularly active part in the insurrection of Ferenc II Rákóczi, which in its incipient stages resembled a social revolution. They formed a personal guard for the prince and thus earned from him the title 'most trusted people' (*gens fidelissima*). As a result of the constant wars in Transcarpathia the region was economically devastated, and the German cities declined. Serfdom, too, weakened its hold, and in the mountains it was never introduced. As a consequence there was an influx of new settlers from the Galician side, where the effects of serfdom were more strongly felt.

From the mid-17th century a struggle began in Transcarpathia between the Orthodox and the Uniates. It had not only a religious but also a political basis stemming from a dynastic struggle between Catholic and Protestant factions in Hungary. The Orthodox church of Transcarpathia was in a state of decline. The clergy lacked proper education and like their congregations were enserfed; the bishops of Mukachiv were dependent on the Hungarian Calvinist lords, who tried to bring about Reformationist changes in the Orthodox parishes. At the same time the Counter-Reformation movement that began in Hungary supported Uniate conversions among the Orthodox. The first (unsuccessful) attempt to establish the Uniate church was made in 1612 by the bishop of Peremyshl, A. Krupetsky, in western Transcarpathia, the domain of the Catholic, royalist Drugeth family. The Uniate effort then gained support from V. Tarasovych, the renegade Orthodox bishop of Mukachiv (who became a Uniate and fled to Uzhhorod), and P. Partenii. The outcome of their efforts was the *Uzhhorod Union of 1646. Much effort into strengthening the Uniate Church was expended by the Greek-born bishop J. de Camillis. Under the protection of the Rákóczis, however, the Orthodox continued their activity. Until the end of the 18th century the bastion of Orthodoxy in Transcarpathia remained the Maramureş area, which belonged to Transylvania until 1720. After the death (ca 1728) of the last Orthodox bishop, Dosytei, the Uniate Church prevailed throughout Transcarpathia.

Despite its political separation the spiritual contacts of Transcarpathia with other Ukrainian lands were close. Liturgical and theological books published in Kiev and Lviv were used widely in Transcarpathia and in the 17th and 18th centuries a local religious literature developed there, resembling in character Ukrainian baroque literature,

A boulevard in Uzhhorod, Transcarpathia

St Parasceve's Church (1643) in Oleksandrivka, Khust raion, Transcarpathia oblast

with minor Hungarian and Slovak influences. The common forms included bibles for teaching purposes, legends and apocrypha, collections of sermons, polemical writings and apologia (including those of the most interesting religious polemicist of the end of the 17th century, M. *Andrella), chronicles (such as the Huklyvyi Chronicle), tales of the Middle Ages, and poetry. Transcarpathian literature of the 17th and 18th centuries used the vernacular. Most writings were disseminated in manuscript form; the first printed books for Transcarpathia within the Austrian Empire were produced in Trnava, Slovakia. Like education, which was provided by monastery-run schools, popular literature was permeated with a religious character.

**18th to mid-19th century.** The rule of Maria Theresa and Joseph II, representatives of enlightened absolutism in Austria and Hungary, was marked by concessions to the peasantry and a number of other reforms. After abolishing personal servitude in Hungary in 1785, Joseph II wanted to go even further. But his death made possible the return of old gentry privileges, and serfdom continued until 1848. The Hungarian gentry strongly opposed the liberal measures of Vienna. The revived serfdom at the end of the 18th century brought about a rebellious movement of *opryshoks in Transcarpathia, which was comparable to the haidamaka uprisings in Right-Bank Ukraine.

The Uzhhorod Union did not bring about improvement in church relations. The bishops of Mukachiv were reduced to the role of vicars for the Roman Catholic archbishops of Hungary. The situation improved after Maria Theresa intervened on behalf of the Greek Catholic church, and in 1771 the Mukachiv eparchy was freed from its subordination to the Hungarian Roman Catholic archbishops. The second half of the 18th century was marked by the achievements of the bishops M. Olshavsky, I. Bra-

dach, and, especially, A. Bachynsky in both ecclesiastical and cultural areas as well as in the improved well-being and education of the priests. The seat of the eparchy was moved to Uzhhorod (1780), a seminary was established there, and a new Prešov eparchy was formed (1816).

During the late 18th and early 19th centuries a number of Transcarpathian intellectuals who had graduated from foreign universities but could not employ their skills in their homeland went to work in Galicia or the Russian Empire. P. Lodii and I. Zemanchyk, for example, were professors at the Lviv Studium Ruthenum; M. Baluhiansky (Baludiansky), I. Orlai, Yu. (Hutsa) Venelin, K. Pavlovych, M. Bilevych, and others gained high civil service or academic positions in Ukraine and Russia. The nature of Transcarpathian literature also changed, in that it began to reflect its authors' greater degree of schooling. Writing now diverged from the folk language, in making use of the fashionable Latin and Old Church Slavonic. Among the literati of the period were the author of a Ukrainian grammar, A. *Kotsak; the first historian, Y. *Bazylovych; the linguist I. Fogarashii; the poet and philosopher V. Dovhovych; and, above all, the linguist, historian, and church activist M. *Luchkai (1789–1843).

**1848–1918.** The *Revolution of 1848–9 in the Habsburg monarchy partially touched Transcarpathia. The chauvinist nature of the Hungarian movement, however, repelled the Slavic peoples and caused them to side with Vienna. Among the Ukrainians who opposed the Hungarian revolution were two of the most outstanding persons of Transcarpathia in the 19th century, the writer and educator Rev O. *Dukhnovych (1803–65) and the energetic politician and publicist A. *Dobriansky (1817–1901). Under the influence of Dobriansky the *Slavic Congress of 1848 in Prague proposed the creation of an autonomous Slovak-Ukrainian province within Hungary. In April 1849 Dobriansky proposed to the Supreme Ruthenian Council in Lviv a program of unifying Galicia with Transcarpathia in a separate autonomous crownland within the Austrian Empire. Then he headed a delegation from the Transcarpathian Ukrainians to the Emperor Francis Joseph I requesting the creation of a Ruthenian province with national-territorial and cultural autonomy within the borders of Hungary. The project was never realized, and the only specific action toward it was the appointment of Dukhnovych and other Transcarpathian activists to administrative posts in their region.

With the strengthening of absolutism in Austria and the growth of Hungarian nationalism, the Transcarpathian intelligentsia began to gravitate toward external forces: some succumbed to Magyarization, and the rest began to share *Russophile sympathies. The orientation to Moscow was fanatically propagated by Rev I. Rakovsky, editor of the government-published *Tserkovnaia gazeta* (1856–8). The development of the pro-Moscow orientation was assisted by the traditional views among the clergy of Transcarpathia about the need for an all-Slavic written language: the role of Old Church Slavonic was now being supplanted by Russian or a macaronic *yazychiie*. Moreover, the Russian troops, invited by Austria to put down the Hungarian revolution in 1849, also left a deep impression. As exemplified by Dobriansky, Russophilism in Transcarpathia did not negate loyalty to the Habsburgs, but in time it turned even more toward Russia. The Russophile tendency in Transcarpathia, unlike that in Galicia, was not counterbalanced by a populist Ukrainophile movement and thus became prevalent. At the same time the Russophile orientation led to a cleavage between the intelligentsia and the peasantry and failed to provide the latter group with an effective countermeasure to Hungarian influences.

The political compromise between Austria and Hungary in 1867 that formed the Austro-Hungarian dual monarchy left the national minorities at the mercy of a now-dominant Hungarian oligarchy. The Hungarian government gained the right to name the Transcarpathian bishops. Ukrainian parish schools ceased to exist; newspapers (*Svit*, 1867–71; *Novyi svit*, 1871–2; *Karpat"*, 1873–86; and *Listok*, 1885–1903) led a precarious existence; and the activity of the educational *Society of St Basil the Great declined. Transcarpathia became more and more isolated from Galicia. Transcarpathian authors of the second half of the 19th century (O. Pavlovych, A. Kralytsky, I. Silvai, Ye. Fentsyk, O. Mytrak, Yu. Stavrovsky-Popradov, and others) continued to write in the *yazychiie*. Moreover, their works were commonly far removed from the vital social, economic, and cultural interests of the local population.

The later 19th century was marked also by the growth of new social and economic problems. As a result of population growth and subdivision of properties with slow urbanization and industrialization, land hunger soon be-

came evident. Alcoholism, usury, and poor harvests in the 1890s exacerbated the situation. The chronic difficulties provided an impulse for emigration to the United States, and beginning in the 1880s such emigration became massive. Movement was most intense from western Transcarpathia, where there was a long tradition of seasonal labor migration. In the western provinces of Sáros, Zemplén, and Ung emigration canceled the entire natural increase of the population, and in 1905–7 it was twice the size of the natural increase.

The period 1900–14 was marked by three important processes: increased Hungarian pressure for assimilation, a new wave of Russophile propaganda, and the emergence of a populist Ukrainophile movement. The Apponyi Laws of 1902 and 1907 introduced the Hungarian language into the remaining Greek Catholic church schools, thereby Magyarizing all the schools. With regard to church matters, a number of parishes from the Mukachiv and Prešov eparchies were combined in 1912 to form the new *Hajdúdorog eparchy, where Hungarian was introduced as the language of liturgy. The bishop of Prešov, I. Novak, introduced the Gregorian calendar (to correspond with that used by the Roman Catholic Church) and the Ministry of Education in 1916 adopted the use of the Hungarian alphabet for Ukrainian publications. From 1900 the fate of Transcarpathia began to interest the Russian Pan-Slavists in St Petersburg and the Russophiles in Galicia. With the support of Count V. Bobrinsky in St Petersburg, a campaign was started to demand the return of Orthodoxy in Transcarpathia. It found fertile ground among victims of the Hungarian denationalization policies, but it was quickly stifled by the Hungarian authorities at a show trial in Sighetul Maramaţiei (December 1913 to March 1914).

The worsening conditions of Transcarpathia, on the one hand, and the example of Galician Ukrainian populism, on the other, prompted a call to action by a group of young secular and clerical intelligentsia. The first representative of modern Ukrainianism, M. Drahomanov, was much concerned about the fate of Transcarpathia and visited it twice in 1875–6. Beginning in the 1890s a number of Galician-Ukrainian scholars became interested in Trans-

Transcarpathian shepherds

Girls in traditional Transcarpathian dress

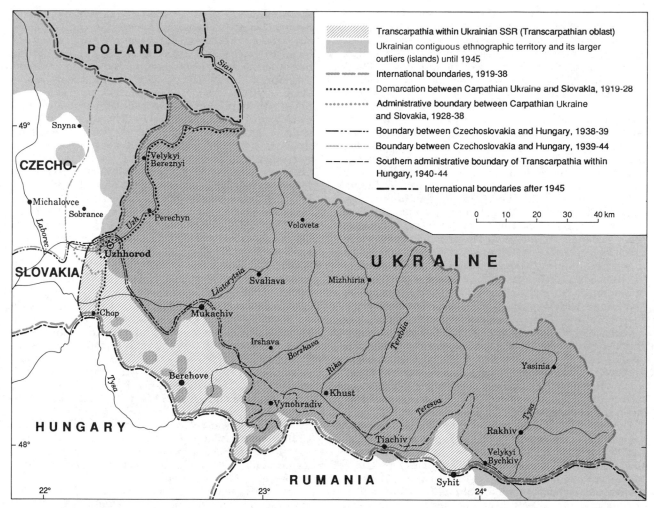

TRANSCARPATHIA IN 1919–45

carpathian topics, among them I. Franko (historical literature), V. Hnatiuk (ethnography), I. Verkhratsky (dialectology), and S. Tomashivsky (history and statistics). Under their influence local scholars, such as Yu. Zhatkovych (history) and H. Strypsky (literature), began to collaborate in the publications of the Shevchenko Scientific Society. In the area of language and literature the populist movement was started by L. *Csopey, who wrote Ukrainian-Hungarian primers and a dictionary based on the vernacular of Transcarpathia. A notable educator of the first half of the 20th century was Rev A. *Voloshyn. His grammar of the Ukrainian language (in Hungarian, 1907) became the standard. He published the newspaper *Nauka* and compiled a number of popular handbooks, calendars, and educational books. Although not massive, the populist movement became deeply rooted before the First World War. With the fall of the Habsburg monarch in 1918, it assumed an overtly political role.

**Since 1918.** The independentist efforts of Galician Ukrainians influenced Transcarpathians to embark on a similar path. Town and village councils were convened, and on 8 November 1918 a *Ruthenian People's Council was held in Stará L'ubovňa. It was the first of several gatherings (notably in Svaliava on 8 December 1918 and Sighetul Maramaţiei on 18 December 1918) that attempted to come to grips with the region's political future. A grand congress of 'all Ukrainians living in Hungary' involving 400 delegates was convened in Khust on 21 January 1919. Chaired by the brothers M. and Yu. Brashchaiko, the gathering expressed its will to join the Ukrainian National Republic. A different council met in Uzhhorod on 8 May 1919, established the *Central Ruthenian People's Council, and chose to seek regional autonomy within the newly created state of Czechoslovakia. That council was influenced and supported by the activity of Transcarpathian émigrés in the United States, whose representatives were negotiating with Czechoslovak politicians to include Transcarpathia in the future republic on a federative basis. A plebiscite carried out among the Transcarpathian communities in the United States yielded a two-thirds majority vote in favour of the union. As a result of those acts of the popular expression of political will and of diplomatic measures of the Czechoslovak politicians, the Paris Peace Conference sanctioned (through the Treaty of *Saint-Germain) the transfer of Transcarpathia and guaranteed its autonomous status within Czechoslovakia.

Czech rule in Transcarpathia was distinguished by a number of reforms, most of which had positive results. Nevertheless a number of measures were taken which contradicted the desires of the Transcarpathian Ukrainians for self-administration. The administrative-political organization of the region was defined by the statutes of the Prague government (1919, 1920), which contravened the Treaty of St-Germain and the Czechoslovak constitution concerning autonomy. Transcarpathia was established as a separate administrative region, Subcarpathian Ruthenia. But the western boundary was so defined that approx 100,000 Ukrainians, living mostly in the Prešov region, were placed within Slovakia. The boundary issue and questions about the degree of Subcarpathian Ruthenia's antonomy led the appointed governor of the province, H. *Zhatkovych, to resign in protest after 1921. The second governor, A. *Beskyd (1923–33), had only nominal powers; the actual executive power was wielded by a Czech vice-governor (A. Rozsypal), who presided over an administration composed mostly of Czechs. Administrative reorganization in 1925 and 1927 involved greater centralization: Subcarpathian Ruthenia as a whole was given equal status with four other provinces of Czechoslovakia, the subdivision of the region into *zhupas* (komitats) was abandoned, and the self-administration of the rural communities (hromadas) was limited. Only in 1937, with the creation of the governor's council during the governorship of K. Hrabar (1935–8), was a first step toward actual autonomy taken. The council was substantially broadened in the autumn of 1938 during the reorganization of the Czechoslovak Republic.

The political life of the region centered initially around the activity of two people's councils, one pro-Ukrainian and the other Russophile. In time 10 political parties emerged in Transcarpathia, mostly branches of Czech parties. Although the emergence of the parties promoted broader political participation, it also diffused the local efforts for regional development. The elections of 1924 and 1925 gave a majority in Transcarpathia to the Communists; only in 1928 and 1935 were majorities of noncommunist members of parliament and senators elected. Even then Ukrainians constituted a minority of the elected politicians. The greater social and political freedom afforded Transcarpathia under Czechoslovak than under Hungarian rule provided an impetus for increased civic life. At the same time, however, it brought forward problems related to the national self-identification of the people in the region. Three orientations were articulated in the interwar era, Ukrainophile, Russophile, and Rusynophile. The Ukrainophiles continued to take their cues from their counterpart movement in Galicia. Centered around institutions such as the *Prosvita (which had grown to include 14 branches with 232 reading rooms by 1936), the Teachers' Hromada, the national theater and choir in Uzhhorod, the Plast Ukrainian Youth Association, and the newspaper *Nauka* and then *Svoboda*, the movement included figures such as A. Voloshyn, A. *Shtefan, M. and Yu. *Brashchaiko, Yu. and F. *Revai, S. Klochurak, and Rev V. Hadzhega.

The pro-Russian activists belonged to the Dukhnovych Society and the Orthodox church, organized by Russian émigrés and supported by the Czech government to counterbalance the Greek Catholic church (which included a significant number of Magyarone clergymen). In 1936–7 the pro-Russian activists tried to gain control of schooling by organizing so-called school plebiscites concerning the language of instruction. The Rusynophile orientation, adhered to by some individuals, developed a specific institutional form only with the creation of the *Subcarpathian Scientific Society in 1941. Viewing themselves as *Ruthenians, a people distinct from Ukrainians, the Rusynophiles promoted a local patriotism that invoked the spirit of Dobriansky and Dukhnovych. The Rusynophiles remained the least developed of the three orientations throughout the interwar period. Yet a strong current of Rusynophilism developed among the region's Greek Catholic clergy during the 1930s as it purged itself of the Magyaronism that had entrenched itself deeply during the many decades of Hungarian rule. The Russophiles remained quite active in the 1920s but faltered in the 1930s. The Ukrainophile orientation enjoyed official support in the 1920s and had developed a dynamic institutional network by the mid-1930s.

During two decades of Czech government in Transcarpathia, considerable progress was made in improving the infrastructure and social organization of the region (such as in the building of new roads, the modernizing of the cities, the construction of community buildings, hospitals, and clinics, and the founding of assistance schemes for poor highlanders). But the chronic unemployment of the Transcarpathian poor increased as a number of local industrial enterprises closed, unable to compete with Czech industry. Migration for seasonal labor, emigration, and government financing of public works only partly alleviated the difficult conditions of the mountain folk. The depression in the early 1930s caused hunger in Transcarpathia, and massive unemployment gave rise to worker unrest. Communists proclaiming pro-Soviet slogans in favour of the USSR and the Ukrainian SSR attained considerable support in the region.

Anti-Czech sentiments began to grow in the 1930s as a response to the increasingly centralist policies of Prague and the presence of a large number of Czechs in Transcarpathia (30,000 in 1930), 70–80 percent of whom were part of the administrative apparatus. The sentiments added impetus to the calls for an autonomous government in Transcarpathia. *Carpatho-Ukraine was established on 11 October 1938 in the wake of the restructuring of Czechoslovakia brought on by the *Munich Agreement. A. *Brodii served as the first premier. After being discredited as an agent of Hungary and arrested for treason he was replaced (26 October 1938) by Voloshyn.

The new political-legal status of Transcarpathia was defined by a constitutional law dated 22 November 1938, which stipulated a separate autonomous government with its own legislature consisting of an elected Carpatho-Ukrainian Diet. After the Vienna Arbitration, which allocated to Hungary the southern part of Transcarpathia, along with the cities of Uzhhorod, Mukachiv, and Berehove, the capital was transferred to Khust. On 12 February 1939, elections to the first parliament of Carpatho-Ukraine took place. The *Ukrainian National Alliance party won a resounding victory.

International events interfered with the normal development of Carpatho-Ukraine. Hungary and Poland agitated for a common border at the expense of Transcarpathia and sent groups of agents to raise turmoil and disorder. Tension between the Czechs and the Ukrainians also increased with the appointment of a Czech minister to Khust, General L. Prchala. Simultaneously with the Nazi German occupation of Bohemia and Moravia on 14 March 1939, Hitler entrusted Hungary with the occupation of Transcarpathia. On 15 March 1939, before the Hungarians had overrun Transcarpathia, the Carpatho-Ukrainian Diet in a symbolic gesture declared independence, approved a constitution, and elected Voloshyn president. Subsequently the government of Carpatho-Ukraine and many activists fled abroad to escape Hungarian repressions.

The Hungarian occupation of Transcarpathia was connected with terror and repressions directed against Ukrainian activists. Instead of the autonomy initially promised, the Hungarians allowed for a narrow-based self-rule while conducting a policy of Magyarization in cultural life and administration. Budapest promoted the development of a Ruthenian language and culture and tolerated the activities of the Russophiles but prosecuted Ukrainophile activism. The Subcarpathian Scientific Society and Rusynophile publications were supported by the government. Political organizations were forbidden. The reaction to the pressure was a massive escape on the part of Transcarpathian youths across the mountains to the Ukrainian SSR in 1940–1 and growing activity on the part of the Ukrainian nationalist underground. The Hungarians failed to gain support from the local population during their administration in 1939–44.

The arrival of the Soviet armed forces in Transcarpathia in the autumn of 1944 was regarded by most of the population as liberation. Transcarpathia was quickly brought under Soviet control. On 26 November 1944 the Communist party organized a congress of people's committees of Transcarpathian Ukraine in Mukachiv which expressed its desire for the unification of Transcarpathia with the Ukrainian SSR. The Communist-dominated *People's Council of Transcarpathian Ukraine led the local effort toward that goal. An agreement between Czechoslovakia and the USSR sanctioning the transfer of Transcarpathia from Czechoslovakia to the Ukrainian SSR was concluded on 29 June 1945. By January 1946 the Transcarpathian oblast organs of Ukraine had been established. *Transcarpathia oblast, corresponding in territory to the Subcarpathian Ruthenia of 1919–38, underwent a social, economic, and cultural development in the post–Second World War period similar to that of the rest of the Ukrainian lands within the Ukrainian SSR. The *Prešov region remained in Slovakia.

In its first years of power the new regime nationalized all enterprises, and in 1949–50 it collectivized agriculture. The Soviet education system was introduced, and in 1946 Uzhhorod University was established. The Greek Catholic church was persecuted, and Bishop T. Romzha was assassinated (1947); in 1949 the church was formally liquidated.

The new administration also pursued a definite cultural policy of Sovietization and Ukrainization, which ultimately integrated the Transcarpathian region into the mainstream of Ukrainian civic life. That integration was reflected in the December 1991 referendum on Ukrainian independence, in which the residents of the oblast, notwithstanding their unique history, voted 92.5 percent in favor of independence (with a voter turnout of 82.9 percent). Rusynophile sentiment, already eroding by the 1930s, continued to decline in the postwar period. A Rusynophile consciousness, however, developed to a greater extent among Transcarpathian émigrés (or their descendants) in the United States, who established an institutional base around a separate eparchy of the Greek Catholic church and a variety of civic organizations and became endowed with a scheme of history through the writings of the historian P. *Magocsi.

**Population.** The population of Transcarpathia is distributed according to the topography and is therefore uneven. The mean population density of Transcarpathia is 98 persons/sq km (1989). The most densely and completely settled areas are the Tysa Lowland along with the foothills of the Volcanic Carpathians (120–145 persons/sq km) and the Maramureş Basin (75–95 persons/sq km). In the mountains (with densities of 35–45 persons/sq km) the population is concentrated in the two bands of lower elevations and, to some extent, in the perpendicular valleys. The high mountainous areas are almost devoid of permanent settlement, although in the summer their alpine meadows support a considerable number of shepherds tending their flocks.

Urbanization in Transcarpathia is relatively low. In 1989 some 41 percent of the population was urban (tied with Ternopil oblast for the lowest in Ukraine). That percentage represents an increase, from 23 percent in 1956 and 20 percent in 1930. Transcarpathia (1987) has 2 major cities, Uzhhorod (1989 pop 117,000) and Mukachiv (85,000), as well as 8 larger towns (Berehove, Khust, Vynohradiv, Rakhiv, Svaliava, Tiachiv, Irshava, and Chop) and 28 town smts. For a long time the region's cities had an exclusively commercial-administrative profile; more recently they have also acquired an industrial aspect. They emerged on the crossroads of routes parallel and perpendicular to the mountains, the largest ones being located on the border between the mountains and the Tysa Lowland.

The population of Transcarpathia has grown rapidly since the last quarter of the 19th century, despite a relatively large transoceanic emigration, because of a high natural increase and relatively small population losses during both world wars. In the Prešov region the natural increase was the same as in Transcarpathia, but the actual population growth was lower because of sizable emigration.

About 100,000 Ukrainians from Transcarpathia (together with the Slovak-speaking Greek Catholics from the Prešov region) emigrated, almost exclusively to the United States, before 1914. In the 1920–38 period the number of emigrants fell to approx 40,000. That emigration rate (per thousand residents) was higher than in any other region of Ukraine. Accordingly, in 1988 in the United States there were an estimated 450,000 persons of Transcarpathian origin, who make up about 30 percent of all Transcarpathian Ukrainians (or 45 percent of all western Transcarpathian Ukrainians).

The ethnic composition of Transcarpathia's population in 1930, within the Ukrainian ethnographic limits and, separately, within the administrative limits of Subcarpathian Ruthenia and Transcarpathia oblast, is summarized in table 2. The largest minority was and continues to be the Hungarian, which constituted a majority in a narrow southern strip of the administrative unit and was also concentrated in the larger cities. Within Ukrainian ethnographic territory the Jews were the largest minority, not

TABLE 2
Ethnic composition of Transcarpathia within Ukrainian ethnic territory, 1930
(in thousands; percentage in parentheses)

| Ethnic group | Subcarpathian Ruthenia | | Prešov region | | Maramureş region in Rumania | | Total | |
|---|---|---|---|---|---|---|---|---|
| Ukrainians | 438 | (71.1) | 87 | (73.8) | 17 | (65.4) | 542 | (71.4) |
| Jews | 85 | (13.8) | 11 | (9.3) | 6 | (23.1) | 102 | (13.4) |
| Hungarians | 40 | (6.5) | 1 | (0.8) | 1 | (3.8) | 42 | (5.5) |
| Czechs & Slovaks | 29 | (4.7) | 16 | (13.6) | 0 | | 45 | (5.9) |
| Rumanians | 13 | (2.1) | 0 | | 2 | (7.7) | 15 | (2.0) |
| Russians | 0 | | 0 | | 0 | | 0 | |
| Other | 11 | (1.8) | 3 | (2.5) | 0 | | 14 | (1.8) |
| Total | 616 | (100.0) | 118 | (100.0) | 26 | (100.0) | 760 | (100.0) |

TABLE 3
Ethnic composition of Transcarpathia within administrative units, 1931–1979
(in thousands; percentage in parentheses)

| Ethnic group | Subcarpathian Ruthenia 1931 | | Transcarpathia oblast 1959 | | 1970 | | 1979 | |
|---|---|---|---|---|---|---|---|---|
| Ukrainians | 450 | (62.1) | 687 | (74.6) | 808 | (76.5) | 899 | (77.8) |
| Jews | 102 | (14.1) | 12 | (1.3) | 11 | (1.0) | 8 | (0.7) |
| Hungarians | 113 | (15.6) | 146 | (15.9) | 152 | (14.4) | 158 | (13.7) |
| Czechs & Slovaks | 33 | (4.5) | 12 | (1.3) | 10 | (0.9) | 6 | (0.5) |
| Rumanians | 13 | (1.8) | 18 | (2.0) | 23 | (2.2) | 27 | (2.3) |
| Russians | 0 | | 30 | (3.3) | 35 | (3.3) | 42 | (3.6) |
| Other | 14 | (1.9) | 15 | (1.6) | 18 | (1.7) | 16 | (1.4) |
| Total | 725 | (100.0) | 920 | (100.0) | 1,057 | (100.0) | 1,156 | (100.0) |

only in the cities (26 percent in 1930) but also in the villages (11 percent). The Germans had seven small colonies in the mountains, and the Rumanians were concentrated in four large villages to the north of Sighetul Maramaţiei. Itinerant Gypsies were not uncommon. After the Second World War the proportion of minorities declined, especially the Jews, Germans, and Czechs (the last group being replaced by Russians). Consequently the share of the Ukrainian population increased to more than 75 percent.

**Economy.** The development of the Transcarpathian economy reflected the region's natural resources and the policies of the countries to which it belonged. The mountainous part of Transcarpathia, occupying 80 percent of the region, was dominated by forestry and animal husbandry, whereas the lowlands and foothills were the domain of field crops, orchards, and vineyards. Extractable minerals included salt, lignite, building materials, and some metal ores, and there were numerous sources of mineral water.

Those natural resources were little developed during the long Hungarian rule. Agricultural development was impeded by the minute size of peasants' plots, and industrial development was inhibited by competition from the Hungarian heartland. Capital was in non-Ukrainian hands (mainly Jews and Hungarians), and the Ukrainian peasantry could not improve its own well-being because of lack of schools and administrative controls. Of the various branches of the economy the most developed was forestry. Hungary, generally devoid of trees, had a need for lumber and firewood. The Ukrainian peasantry supplemented its household budgets with earnings from for-

estry and seasonal (harvest) work on distant Hungarian estates.

The incorporation of Transcarpathia into Czechoslovakia raised the economic level of the region. An agrarian reform was implemented, the yields improved significantly (on average by 50 percent), a road network was constructed, a school system was developed (including trade schools), co-operatives began to flourish, and a middle class began to emerge. The Czech government, however, did not favor the industrialization of Transcarpathia, but preferred that it serve as a market for Czech industry. The economy was also hindered by the distance to the Czech heartland and the border that separated Transcarpathia from the Pannonian Plain, which complicated the marketing of lumber and wood products. Land shortage among the peasantry continued (45 percent of the households did not have even 2 ha of land, 30 percent had 2–5 ha) while earnings from forestry declined, seasonal harvest work in Hungary was curtailed, and emigration to North America slowed down during the depression. All that contributed to the increased pauperization of the Ukrainian peasantry, particularly in the mountains.

Under Soviet rule Transcarpathia became an integral part of the economy of the Ukrainian SSR and the USSR as a whole. Existing industries were developed (forestry, food processing, salt mining), and new ones were started (lignite mining, light industry, and, most recently, machine building and metallurgy). Agriculture was collectivized, and more intensive branches (grapevine cultivation, orcharding, tobacco growing, and livestock raising) were developed.

Agriculture, until recently the main economic sector, employed (1987) approx one-third of the labor force. Agricultural lands, however, occupy only 35.8 percent of the total land area, with 17.9 percent in hayfields and pastures, 15.1 percent in cultivated land, and 2.8 percent in vineyards, orchards, and other planting; another 3.8 percent is in household gardens. About 52 percent of the land is forested. The total sown area in 1987 was 197,000 ha (down from 211,000 in 1956); grains accounted for 64,000 ha (98,700 ha in 1956), or 32.5 percent of all the crops sown. The leading grain in 1974 was winter wheat (41,000 ha, or 57 percent of all grains); it was followed by corn for grain (13,000 ha, or 18 percent). Oats, barley, buckwheat, and other grains were of less importance. Fodder crops in 1987 occupied 96,000 ha (49 percent of the sown area), potatoes and vegetables, 30,500 ha (16 percent), and technical crops, mainly tobacco and sunflower, less than 6,000 ha (3 percent). The lowlands and foothills remain the domain of wheat and corn; in the mountains the prevalent crops are oats, rye, and potatoes. The total sown area has declined from what it was in the pre–Second World War period by about 16 percent, and the grain area by 58 percent; the feed crop area has increased fourfold. Vineyards, which are of considerable significance, produce for export (mainly in Berehove, Uzhhorod, Mukachiv, Serednie, and Vynohradiv) both table grapes and white wine. The vineyard area increased from 2,900 ha in 1936 to 6,700 ha in 1956 and reached 12,300 ha in the 1970–5 period. The area of orchards and berry plantings increased from 4,000 ha in 1936 to 18,500 ha in 1956 and 56,100 ha in 1966, and declined to 41,200 ha in 1975. Among industrial crops the most important is tobacco (3,000 ha in 1956). All productive livestock except horses increased in number from the pre–Second World War period (1937): horses declined from 41,300 to 32,000 in 1956, but cattle increased from 219,500 to 244,000 in 1956 and 354,000 in 1987; hogs, from 82,000 to 196,000 in 1956 and 302,000 in 1987, with fluctuations down to 188,700 in 1976; and sheep and goats, from 132,000 to 309,000 in 1956 and 1966, with a slow downward adjustment to 304,400 in 1987. Livestock husbandry was intensified with the introduction of more productive breeds. In the lowlands and foothills animal husbandry is closely related to crop production; in the mountains the livestock feed base consists of mountain meadows and natural hayfields.

Transcarpathia's greatest source of wealth is the forest, which occupies about 628,000 ha, or 49 percent of the land area. The main tree species are beech (58 percent of the forest area), fir (29 percent), oak (7 percent), and spruce (4 percent). In 1956, the *lumber industry and woodworking, the basic industries of Transcarpathia, provided 53 percent of the industrial output in the region and employed 29,000 persons, or 57 percent of the industrial labor force. At that time the lumber industry produced 2.6 million cu m of wood and 0.7 million cu m of sawn timber. Since then the industry has been modernized, and its capacity increased, but its share of the total industrial output had declined to 20 percent by 1985. Almost all the timber is processed locally in numerous woodworking establishments, scattered throughout Transcarpathia. The largest ones are located in Svaliava (logging, milling, furniture, and wood chemicals), Teresva (logging and milling), Rakhiv (logging and cellulose-paper and cardboard manufacturing), Velykyi Bychkiv (logging and wood chemicals), Muka-

chiv (logging, milling, and furniture), Uzhhorod (logging, milling, furniture, and other wood-based industries), Perechyn (logging and wood chemicals), Velykyi Bereznyi (logging, milling, and furniture), Khust (logging and furniture), and Berehove (milling and furniture). Beech is the principal raw material for furniture.

The hydroelectric power potential of the mountain region is only partially developed. Two small hydroelectric power stations on the Uzh River were in operation before the Second World War. During the Soviet period the Tereblia-Rika system, brought into production in 1956, together with a large thermoelectric power station between Uzhhorod and Mukachiv, became the major regional source of electricity. The mining of lignite was begun after the Second World War; it had reached considerable production (460,000 t) by 1955 but it subsequently declined to about 150,000 t per year (1985). Two gas deposits of commercial volume have been tested, and there is potential for more. The *Solotvyna rock-salt deposits have been mined for a long time. During the Czech regime the mine was modernized, and production was raised to 170,000 t per year (it was the main source of salt within Czechoslovakia). Subsequently the output was raised even more (to 332,000 t by 1956 and 837,800 t by 1980). There is a broad diversity of metal ores (iron, manganese, lead, zinc, mercury, gold, silver, alunite, and bauxite) and barites (for white pigments), but the deposits are usually small. Of considerable importance is the building-materials industry, including the mining of andesite, tufa, and marble, the extraction of chalk and clay for cement, and the making of brick and tiles in larger cities.

The food-processing industry, second in the share of value of production (28 percent of all industry in 1956, 22 percent in 1985), is concentrated mostly in the larger cities. Meat packing is located in Uzhhorod and Mukachiv; dairy, flour milling, confectionery, and macaroni-making, in Mukachiv; wine-making, in Vynohradiv; fruit preserving, in Solotvyna; and tobacco-packing, in Mukachiv. Light industry, developed mostly after the Second World War, continued to increase its share of the industrial output, from 12 percent in 1956 to 18 percent in 1970, where it remained until 1985. The cottage industry of folk arts, notably embroidery and wood carving, is important even today, especially in the eastern, Hutsul, part of the region. Modern industries, specifically machine building and chemicals, have grown most rapidly in the postwar period (from 2.3 percent in 1956 to 33 percent in 1985). They are concentrated almost exclusively in the two major cities of Transcarpathia (equipment and machine building in Uzhhorod and Mukachiv and chemicals in Uzhhorod), and so give rise to even greater differentiation in the level of economic development between the lowland urban centres and the backwoods mountain areas. The major industrial centres are Uzhhorod, Mukachiv, Berehove, and Khust.

Transcarpathia has 652 km of standard-gauge railway (excluding narrow gauge) and 3,400 km of hard-surface roads (1987), both of which provide a higher-density network than has Ukraine as a whole. The railway lines with most significance today are those connecting Transcarpathia with the rest of Ukraine across the Carpathians: the Uzhhorod–Lviv line via the Uzhok Pass, the Mukachiv–Lviv line via the Volovets Pass, and the Rakhiv–Diliatyn line via the Tatar Pass. The line traversing the length of Transcarpathia from Prešov (now in Slovakia) through

Chop and Khust (with a short stretch in Rumania) to Rakhiv has diminished in importance: in 1920–45 the main line of Transcarpathia, it is now a connector of regional importance. Automobile transport has grown rapidly and is particularly significant in Transcarpathia, where it supplements the railway, notably in the mountain valleys. The most important segments of the road network include the major highway from Uzhhorod through Mukachiv and then past Svaliava to Lviv, the Mukachiv–Khust–Tiachiv–Rakhiv–Yasinia highway, the Chop–Uzhhorod–Perechyn–Velykyi Bereznyi route to Sambir and Lviv, and the Chop–Berehove–Vynohradiv–Khust–Mizhhiria route to Kalush and Ivano-Frankivske.

As an economic region Transcarpathia generates a surplus of lumber and forest products, wine, fruit and vegetables, and tobacco. The mineral springs and picturesque landscapes still represent a largely undeveloped potential that is rapidly gaining popularity as an area for resorts and tourism.

BIBLIOGRAPHY
Bidermann, H.J. Die ungarischen Ruthenen, ihr Wohngebiet, ihr Erwerb, und ihre Geschichte, 2 vols (Innsbruck 1862)
Sventsitskii, I. Materialy po istorii vozrozhdeniia Karpatskoi Rusi, 2 vols (Lviv 1906)
Pachovs'kyi, V. Istoriia Pidkarpats'koï Rusy, 2 vols (Uzhhorod 1920, 1922)
Birchak, V. Literaturne stremlinnia Pidkarpats'koï Rusy (Uzhhorod 1921; 2nd edn 1937)
Král, J. Podkarpatská Rus (Prague 1924)
Kondratovych, I. Istoriia Pidkarpats'koï Rusy (Uzhhorod 1930)
Martel, R. La Ruthénie subcarpathique (Paris 1935)
Kubijovyč, V. Pastyřsky život v Podkarpatské Rusi, 2 vols (Bratislava 1935, 1937)
Mytsiuk, O. Narysy z sotsial'no-hospodarchoi istoriï Pidkarpats'koï Rusy, 2 vols (Prague 1936, 1938)
Borshchak, I. Karpats'ka Ukraïna v mizhnarodnii hri (Lviv 1938)
Mousset, J. Les villes de la Russie subcarpathique, 1919–1938 (Paris 1938)
Karpats'ka Ukraïna: Zbirnyk Ukraïns'koho vydavnychoho instytutu (Lviv 1939)
Karpats'ka Ukraïnia v borot'bi: Zbirnyk (Vienna 1939)
Dami, A. La Ruthénie subcarpathique (Geneva 1944)
Shtephan, A. From Carpatho-Ruthenia to Carpatho-Ukraine (New York 1954)
Markus, V. L'incorporation de l'Ukraine subcarpathique à l'Ukraine soviétique, 1944–1945 (Leuven 1956)
Kolomiets, I. Ocherki po istorii Zakarpat'ia, pt 2 (Tomsk 1959)
Bidzilia, V. Istoriia kul'tury Zakarpattia na rubezhi nashoï ery (Kiev 1971)
Stercho, P. Diplomacy of Double Morality: Europe's Crossroads in Carpatho-Ukraine, 1919–1939 (New York 1971)
Magocsi, P. The Shaping of a National Identity: Subcarpathian Rus', 1848–1948 (Cambridge, Mass 1978)
Pap, S. Pochatky Khrystyianstva na Zakarpatti (Philadelphia 1983)
Pryrodni bahatstva Zakarpattia (Uzhhorod 1987)
Rudnytsky, I.L. 'Carpatho-Ukraine: A People in Search of Their Identity,' in Essays in Modern Ukrainian History, ed P.L. Rudnytsky (Edmonton 1987)
            V. Kubijovyč, V. Markus, I.L. Rudnytsky, I. Stebelsky

**Transcarpathia oblast.** An administrative territory (1989 pop 1,252,000) in the southwest corner of Ukraine, formed on 22 January 1946. It covers an area of 12,800 sq km and is divided into 13 raions, 10 cities, 28 towns (smt), and 269 rural councils. It encompasses most of the territory of the historic region of *Transcarpathia. The oblast capital is *Uzhhorod.

**Physical geography.** The oblast encompasses the southwestern slopes of the Ukrainian Carpathian Mountains. Several mountain ridges, running through the oblast from the northwest to the southeast, cover approx 80 per cent of its area. Their highest elevation is 2,061 m. The ridges are separated by longitudinal valleys. The southwestern corner of the oblast consists of the Transcarpathian Lowland, which has an elevation of 105–120 m and is part of the Middle-Danubian Lowland. Protected by the mountains from the cold northern winds, the oblast has a temperate continental climate. The average January temperature ranges from –2°C in low areas to –7°C in the mountains, and the average July temperature, from 20°C to 8°C. The annual precipitation varies from 600 mm in low areas to 1,400 mm in the mountains. The growing season ranges from 230 days in the valleys to 90 days in the highlands. The main rivers are all tributaries of the Tysa: the Teresva, the Tereblia, the Rika, the Borzhava, the Liatorytsia, and the Uzh. The soils in the lowlands are peat, podzolized, and clayey; in the foothills, podzolized brown soils; and in the mountains, brown forest, podzolized mountain, and mountain meadow soils. Almost 50 percent of the oblast is forested, mostly with oak-hornbeam forests in the lowlands, oak and oak-beech forests in the foothills, and coniferous (fir or pine) forests in the mountains, up to 1,500 m. Higher up, the slopes are covered with subalpine meadow vegetation.

**History.** The territory of the oblast has been inhabited since the Paleolithic period. In the 9th and 10th centuries it was under the control of the Bulgar Kingdom, and in the 10th and 11th centuries, under Kievan Rus'. King Stephen I annexed Transcarpathia in the 11th century, and it remained under Hungarian rule until the 17th century. Even under the Austrian regime the Hungarian influence in the territory remained strong, particularly after the reorganization of the empire in 1867. After the First World War much of the oblast was incorporated into the newly formed Czechoslovakian state. After a brief interval of autonomy in 1938–9, the territory was occupied by Hungary until 1944 and incorporated into the Ukrainian SSR in 1946.

**Population.** According to the 1989 census, the national composition of the oblast is 78.4 percent Ukrainian, 12.5 percent Hungarian, 4 percent Russian, under 2 percent Rumanian, and under 1 percent Jewish. The average population density in 1984 was 93.5 persons per sq km. In 1989, 41 percent of the population was urban. The major cities are Uzhhorod and *Mukachiv.

**Industry.** The main industries in the oblast are machine building and metalworking (28.9 percent of the industrial output in 1983), food processing (21.5 percent), forest products, woodworking, and paper manufacturing (19.2 percent), and light industry (16.7 percent). The machine-building and metalworking enterprises are concentrated in Uzhhorod, Mukachiv, and Irshava, and produce machine tools, stripping, planing, and sanding machines, lathes, and hydraulic presses. The main branches of the food industry are wine-making (Irshava), fruit canning (Tiachiv, Teresva Vynohradiv, Mukachiv), meat packing (Mukachiv, Uzhhorod), and dairying (Uzhhorod, Mukachiv, Rakhiv, Berehove, Khust). The largest forest products manufacturing complexes are in Svaliava and Ust-Chorna, and the largest woodworking complex is in Teresva. Cardboard is manufactured in Rakhiv, and furniture in Uzhhorod, Svaliava, Mukachiv, Berehove,

The Ust-Chorna Forest-Products Manufacturing Complex in Transcarpathia oblast

Teresva, Khust, and Irshava. Various wood chemicals are extracted in Svaliava, Perechyn, and Velykyi Bychkiv. The main branches of light industry are footwear manufacturing (Uzhhorod, Khust, Vynohradiv, Vylok), clothing (Uzhhorod, Mukachiv, Vynohradiv, Berehove), and knitwear (Mukachiv). The oblast is rich in mineral resources, such as coal, marble, and rock salt.

A vineyard in Vynohradiv raion, Transcarpathia oblast

**Agriculture.** In 1989 there were 106 collective farms and 52 state farms in the oblast. Of 458,000 ha of farmland 41.6 percent was cultivated, 28.2 percent was pasture, and 20.7 percent was hayfield. Of the farmland 173,400 ha were drained, and 14,600 ha were irrigated. The tilled land was devoted to grain crops, such as winter wheat and corn (37 percent), fodder (42), tobacco and other industrial crops (4), and potatoes, grapes, and fruits (17). Animal husbandry represented 59.2 percent of the agricultural output. The most productive branches are beef- and dairy-cattle raising, hog farming, and sheep and goat raising. Grain farming and animal husbandry are concentrated in the lowland areas and viticulture and fruit growing in the foothills region. Sheep graze in the highlands.

**Transportation.** There were 617 km of rail track in the oblast in 1989. The trunk lines running through the oblast include Chop–Uzhhorod–Uzhok–Lviv, Chop–Mukachiv–Lavochne–Lviv, and Chop–Solotvyna. There were 3,400 km of highway, of which 3,300 were paved. The major highways running through the oblast are Uzhhorod–Mukachiv–Khust–Ivano-Frankivske, Mukachiv–Svaliava–Stryi, and Uzhhorod–Perechyn–Uzhok–Lviv. Uzhhorod has an airport.

BIBLIOGRAPHY
*Istoriia mist i sil URSR: Zakarpats'ka oblast'* (Kiev 1969)

**Transcarpathian Art Museum** (Zakarpatskyi khudozhnii muzei). A museum established in 1947 as a branch of the *Transcarpathian Regional Studies Museum. It is housed in the castle in Uzhhorod and has permanent exhibitions of Western European, prerevolutionary Ukrainian and Russian, and Soviet art. It contains a fine collection of works by Transcarpathian artists, such as Y. Bokshai, A. Erdeli, F. Manailo, Z. Sholtes, A. Kotska, A. Kashshai, V. Svyda, E. Kontrtovych, and H. Hliuk.

**Transcarpathian dialects.** Archaic variants of the *Boiko dialect spoken in Transcarpathia. The dialects are divided into four groups: Uzh, Borzhava, Maramureş, and Highland (*verkhovyna*). The Highland subdialects, which are spoken as far south as the line Velykyi Bereznyi–Mizhhiria–Synevyr, are transitional to the Boiko dialect. In the west, along the Laborets River, the dialects border on the southern *Lemko dialects, whose southeasterly expansion in the 16th to 18th centuries created transitional belts along the Tsirokha and Uzh rivers. In the east, along the Shopurka River, they border on the *Hutsul dialect, whose 17th- to 18th-century expansion resulted in mixed dialects along the Ruskova River and Hutsul features as far west as the Teresva River. West of Uzhhorod, as a result of Slovak expansion, mixed 'Sotak' dialects (named after the pronunciation of *shcho* 'what, who' as *so*), which are transitional to the East Slovak dialects, evolved.

The features of the Transcarpathian dialects are: (1) retention of *dž* < *dj* (eg, *molódžyj* [Standard Ukrainian (SU) *molódšyj*] 'younger'); (2) retention of soft *r'* before a consonant and at the end of a word (eg, *ver'x, písar'* [SU *verx, písar*] 'top, scribe'); (3) retention of the difference between *ы* and *y* (eg, *rыba, nytkы́* [SU *rýba, nytký*] 'fish, threads'); (4) hardened *š, ž*; (5) softened *dž'* west of the Liatorytsia River and softened *č'* west of the Borzhava River, accompanied by the mixing of the groups *č'k* and *šk* (eg, *káš'ka, dóč'ká, č'kóda* [SU *káčka, dóška, škóda*] 'duck, board, harm'); (6) appearance of the tense-positional variants *ô, ê* of the phonemes *o, je* before a palatal consonant and before *i, u, ü, ô, ê* (eg, *cêr'kôu, na dôrô'zi, dên'* [SU *cérkva, na dorózi, den'*] 'church, on the road, day', in which *ê* can change to *y*); (7) in newly closed syllables the change of *ō, ē* into *û, 'ú/jú* between the Laborets and Liatorytsia and between the Rika and Shopurka rivers (eg, *kûn, n'ûs, vjûx* [SU *kin', nis, viv*] 'horse, nose, he led', in which *-x* < *-f/-v*), or into *ü, 'ü/jü* between the Liatorytsia and Rika (eg, *kün', n'üs, vjüx*), or into *i, 'i* in the Highland dialects (eg, *kin', n'is, viv/viü*); (8) forms of the type *yrstýty, kýrve, jáblyko, žы́t'a, z'íl'a, tôũ dôbrôũ rukôũ, má(v)u* [SU *xrystýty, króvy, jábluko, žyttjá, zíllja, tóju dóbroju rukóju, máju*] 'to christen, of the blood, apple, life, herbs, with that good hand, I have'); (9) stress peculiarities, ie, frequent stress on the prefix (eg, *názad, zácvyte, nájstaršyj, né znaje* [SU *nazád, zacvité, najstáršyj, ne znáje*] 'back [adv], will bloom, oldest, does not know'), but also stresses such as *veselýj, pêr'šá, idó mni* (SU *vesélyj, pérša, do méne*) 'happy, the first, to me'; (10) frequent archaic endings in nouns (eg *brýtôŭ, z cêr'kve, u cêr'kvy, na zemlý, vôŭcy, dvóme majstróve, vôlum/-lým/lыm, z týma malýma psóma, v l'isóx, na kôn'ox, dva séla* [west of the Uzh], *dvi séla* [east of the Uzh], *trijé/četыré brát'a* [SU *brýtva, z cérkvy, u cérkvi, na zemlí, vovký, dva májstry, volám, z týmy malýmy psámy, v lisáx, na kónjax, dva selá, try/čotýry bráty*] 'razor, from church, in church, on land, wolves, two masters, oxen (dat), with those little dogs, in forests, on horses, two villages, three/four brothers'); (11) influence of hard-declension endings on the soft (eg, *kôn'óvy, kôn'óm, pôl'om, vôlós'om, zêml'ôŭ, cér'kôŭl'ôŭ, môjéŭ* [SU *konévi, koném, pólem, volossjam, zemléju, cerkvoju, mojeju*] 'horse (dat and instr), field, hair, land, church, my (instr); (12) adjectival endings such as *nыn'išn'yj, nášoje, dóbroje, dóbroj* (in the west), *tótы* (SU *nýnišnij, náše, dóbre, dóbryj, ti*) 'today's, our, good (neut), good (masc), those'; (13) enclitic pronominal forms, eg, *(m)n'a, t'a, s'a, ho, ju/ji, mn'i, ty/t'i, sy, mu, jûj/jüj, na n'um/n'üm, oná, n'ôŭ/nêŭ, na n'ûŭ/n'ýŭ* (SU *mené, tebé, sebé, johó, jijí, mení, tobí, sobí, jomú, jij, na n'omú, voná, néju, na níj*) 'me, you, oneself, him, her (acc), me, you, oneself, him, her (dat), on him, she, with her, on her'; (14) numeral forms such as *dvásto, šíst'sto, samodrúhыj, piŭdrúha* (SU *dvístá, šistsót, vdvox, pivtorá*) 'two hundred, six hundred, two (both), one and a half'; (15) verb forms such as *močý, veréčy, môhú, môhut', čýtam, -aš, -at('), -ame, -ate, -ávut('), kupíju/-ýju'-ыju, nós'u, xodýŭjem, -jês', xodýlys'me, -s'te, ož jem ukráŭ, pl'ûx, vjûx, mjûux, mu čytaty, ja bыx maŭ, id', id'ím(e)* (SU *mohtý, kýnuty, móžu, móžut', čytáju, -ješ, -je, -jemo, -jete, -jut', kupúju, nošú, ja xodýv, ty xodýv, my xodýly, vy xodýly, ščo ja vkrav, pliv, viv, miv, búdu čytáty, ja mav by, idý, idímo*) 'to be able to throw, I can, they can, I read, you (sing) read, he reads, we read, you (pl) read, they read, I buy, I carry, I went, you (sing) went, we went, you (pl) went, what I stole, I wove, I led, I could, I will read, I should have, go (2nd sing imp), let us go'; (16) word forms such as *môrkôŭ, jablýnča* [SU *mórkva, jáblunja*] 'carrot, apple tree'; (17) many lexical archaisms and Hungarian, Rumanian, German, and Slovak loanwords.

The dialects have been studied by S. Bonkáló, O. Broch, N. Durnovo, G. Gerovsky, V. Hnatiuk, P. Lyzanets, I. Pankevych, I. Verkhratsky, Y. Dzendzelivsky, and others.

BIBLIOGRAPHY
Pan'kevych, I. *Ukraïns'ki hovory Pidkarpats'koï Rusy i sumezhnykh oblastei z prylozhenniam 5 diialektolohichnykh map*, pt I, *Zvuchnia i morfolohiia* (Prague 1938)
Dzendzelivs'kyi, I. *Linhvistychnyi atlas ukraïns'kykh narodnykh hovoriv Zakarpats'koï oblasti URSR (leksyka)*, 2 vols (Uzhhorod 1958, 1960)
Pan'kevych, I. 'Narys istoriï ukraïns'kykh zakarpats'kykh hovoriv, Chastyna I: Fonetyka,' *Acta Universitatis Carolinae: Philologica*, 1 (1958)
Dezhe [Dezső], L. *Ocherki po istorii zakarpatskikh govorov* (Budapest 1967)
Pan'kevych, I. *Materialy do istoriï movy pivdennokarpats'kykh ukraïntsiv*, vol 4, bk 2 of *Naukovyi zbirnyk Muzeiu ukraïns'koï kul'tury v Svydnyku* (Svydnyk 1970)
Lizanets [Lyzanets'], P. *Vengerskie zaimstvovaniia v ukrainskikh govorakh Zakarpat'ia: Vengersko-ukrainskie mezh"iazykovye sviazi* (Budapest 1976)

O. Horbach

**Transcarpathian Folk Chorus** (Zakarpatskyi narodnyi khor). A professional performing troupe founded in Uzhhorod in 1945. The group consists of a mixed chorus, an instrumental section, and a dance ensemble. Its repertoire includes the folk songs and dances of the Transcarpathian region, contemporary works, classical music, and modern choreography, in addition to requisite state pieces. Its artistic and musical directors have been P. Myloslavsky (1945–54), M. Krechko (1954–69), and M. Popenko (since 1969). The chorus has performed in Czechoslovakia, Hungary, Poland, and Rumania, as well as throughout the former USSR.

**Transcarpathian Lowland.** See Tysa Lowland.

**Transcarpathian Museum of Folk Architecture and Folkways.** See Museums of folk architecture and folkways.

**Transcarpathian Regional Studies Museum** (Zakarpatskyi kraieznavchyi muzei). A museum founded in Uzhhorod in 1945 on the basis of the holdings of the Tivadar Lehoczky (T. *Lehotsky) Regional Museum (est 1911) and the Uzhhorod Ethnographic Museum (est 1933). In 1950 the holdings of the Mukachiv Historical Museum were also deposited there. The museum is housed in the 14th- to 17th-century Uzhhorod Castle. In 1979 its three exhibit sections (natural science, pre-Soviet history, and Soviet history) contained over 60,000 items. The museum's manuscript collection contained some of the former holdings of the Uzhhorod Prosvita society's museum and library, the Uzhhorod Greek Catholic Eparchial Library, and the Chernecha Hora Basilian monastery in Mukachiv, and historical documents and photographs pertaining to Transcarpathia. Branches of the museum are the *Transcarpathian Art Museum and historical museums in Mukachiv, Vynohradiv, and Svaliava. V. Mykytas's description and catalog of old books in the museum was published in 1964, and guides to the museum were published in 1969 and 1972.

**Transcarpathian Ukraine.** See Transcarpathia.

**Transcarpathian Ukrainian Music and Drama Theater** (Zakarpatskyi ukrainskyi muzychno-dramatychnyi teatr). A theater established in 1946 in Uzhhorod under the artistic direction of H. *Ihnatovych. Its repertoire has consisted of Ukrainian and Russian classics and contemporary plays, such as O. Dovzhenko's *Nezabutnie* (The Unforgettable), as well as some Western classics. The theater toured Czechoslovakia in 1958. In 1974–85 its artistic director was Ya. Helias.

**Transcaucasia.** See Caucasia.

**Transdnieper region** (Zadniprovia). A term used mostly in the 16th and early 17th centuries to designate Ukrainian lands on the left bank of the Dnieper River. At that time those territories were sparsely settled and came under the control of Lithuania (from 1569, Poland) and Muscovy. (See also *Left-Bank Ukraine and *Slobidska Ukraine.)

**Transfiguration** (*Preobrazhennia Hospodnie* or *Spas*). A church and ritual holiday observed on 19 August (6 August OS). This feast, which commemorates a demonstration by Jesus Christ of his divinity before three apostles on the top of Mt Tabor, was in practice a celebration of the transition from summer to fall. The most obvious folk tradition relating to the day consisted of the blessing of fruits (particularly apples and pears), wreaths of wheat or rye (by women), a variety of grains, and herbs. A social proscription existed against eating fruits before the feast day, when they could be properly blessed. The wreaths were used in conjunction with practices related to *harvest rituals. The grains were believed to possess magical qualities and were kept in homes to guard the inhabitants from bad weather and ill health. The herbs were commonly placed in the coffin of deceased family members, usually under the head. The importance of the Transfiguration as a feast day was underlined by its frequent use in colloquial conversation as a standard for measuring time.

The Cathedral of the Transfiguration in Chernihiv

**Transfiguration, Cathedral of the** (Spaso-Preobrazhenskyi sobor). One of the oldest stone buildings in Ukraine and the finest extant monument of the medieval Chernihiv principality. Its construction was begun in 1036, during the reign of Prince Mstyslav I Volodymyrovych the Great, and completed about 30 years later, during the reign of Sviatoslav II Yaroslavych. The cathedral stood at the center of the palace buildings in Chernihiv and served as the mausoleum of the Chernihiv princely dynasty. It was a rectangular three-nave, three-apse structure with a narthex, five domes, burial chapels against the side walls, a three-apse one-story baptistery on the southern side, and a circular tower on the northern side. In 1791–9 and later the church was thoroughly reconstructed: the chapels were replaced with tambours with decorative baroque fronts, the original tower was extended, the baptistery was replaced by a second tower, and both towers were topped by spires. A new iconostasis, designed by I. Yasnyshyn, was carved and installed in 1793–8; it con-

tains 62 icons painted by T. Myzko and O. Murashko. Some parts of the original building have been preserved: the carved slate parapets in the choir balconies, fragments of 11th-century frescoes and oil paintings, impost capitals and the base of marble columns, and inlaid slate floor plates. Some of the rich gold and silver church vessels have been preserved in the Chernihiv State Historical Museum. In 1967 the cathedral became part of the Chernihiv Architectural and Historical Preserve.

S. Hordynsky

**Transfiguration Church** (Preobrazhenska tserkva). A monument of baroque architecture in Velyki Sorochyntsi (now in Poltava oblast), built in 1732. Its construction and decoration were funded by Hetman D. Apostol. Built on a cruciform plan, the original church had nine domes. After a fire in 1811 the four corner domes were dismantled. The central dome rests on a 12-sided cylinder surrounded by four octagonal and four square chambers. The pilasters, cornices, and fronts are decorated with carved classical and folk designs. Apostol's coat of arms is painted on the vestibule wall. The carved wooden iconostasis contains over 100 icons, which are rich in genre elements.

The Transfiguration Church in Berestove

**Transfiguration Church in Berestove** (Tserkva Spasa na Berestovi). A medieval architectural monument built probably in the early 12th century during the reign of Prince Volodymyr Monomakh in the village of Berestove (now part of Kiev). It was a typical three-nave, three-apse church with a single dome resting on six pillars. First mentioned in the Rus' chronicles under the year 1072, it served as the mausoleum of the Monomakh dynasty (including Grand Prince Yurii Dolgorukii). The church was destroyed by Khan Mengli-Girei in 1482. A new church was built on its ruins under Metropolitan P. Mohyla in the Cossack baroque style in 1640–2 and decorated in 1644. The interior (including a portrait of Mohyla) was painted by Greek masters, the ground plan was changed to form a cross, and four domes were added. The church was renovated in 1751–2 and again in 1813–14, when F. Korobka carved an elaborate altar, and A. Melensky designed a campanile in the classicist style. Of the original structure only the western part, with the narthex and choir, has been preserved. In the early 1970s a 12th-century fresco was uncovered in the church. The church is part of the Kievan Cave Historical-Cultural Preserve.

**Transhoryn region** (Zahorynnia). The colloquial name for the marshiest reaches of Polisia. The region is situated to the east of the Horyn River in the northern corners of Rivne and Zhytomyr oblasts and southern Belarus. It includes the lands on both sides of the Lva, the Stvyha, and the Ubort rivers.

**Translated literature.** As distinct from Ukrainian *literature in translation, translated literature is literature translated into Ukrainian from other languages. The introduction of Christianity into Kievan Rus' (988) and the decision to forgo Greek in favor of Slavonic gave rise to translations of the Gospels and various texts necessary for religious celebration (the Epistles, Psalter, etc). Parallel and analogous to those translations were numerous collections of saints' lives (prologues, Patericons) and collections of the works of the Fathers of the Church. Especially popular were the sermons of St John Chrysostom (*Zlatostrui, *Zlatoust) and other excerpts and aphorisms from the Bible, apocrypha, tales, and the like, collected in miscellanies, such as Pchela, in the two Izborniki of Sviatoslav (1073 and 1076), and in compendiums of the more wondrous and 'scholarly' nature, such as the chronicles of John Malalas, Georgios Hamartolos, and Georgios Synkellos. Also popular were translations of secular tales, such as *Varlaam i Ioasaf, *Aleksandriia, the Story of Troy, the Story of the Kingdom of India, and various historical compilations (eg, History of the Jewish Wars by Josephus Flavius). Such translated literature was typical of the 10th to 14th centuries and reached its high point during the reign of Yaroslav the Wise in the 11th century.

In the second half of the 14th century similar translations were common, but often they were no longer translations of the primary source but of Bulgarian or Serbian adaptations (eg, Zlataia tsip [Golden Chain] and Izmarahd [Emerald]). At that time translations of Latin tales appeared (via Poland and Bohemia), such as the stories of the Three Kings (the Magi) and new versions of the tales of St Alexis of the Aleksandriia, and of the Trojan War. In the 16th and 17th centuries attempts were made at translations of the New Testament into Ukrainian and Belarusian (the Peresopnytsia Gospel, the Gospels of V. Tsiapinsky, V. Nahalevsky, and others). The Ostrih Bible appeared in Church Slavonic. In the 17th and 18th centuries tales of chivalry circulated either indirectly through Polish or Czech translations or directly from Italian (Tristan and Isolde, Prince Bova, the Seven Wise Men, Attila, Emperor Otto, and the like). All of those were reworkings far removed from the original and often adapted to specific Ukrainian customs. Simultaneously G. Boccac-

cio's Decameron became known in Ukraine, as well as T. Tasso's Jerusalem Delivered (an adaptation from a Polish translation). Other translations of tales, anecdotes, and fables abounded. The translations were loose at best, most often transformations and adaptations. That type of adaptive translation finally led to I. Kotliarevsky's travesty 'translation' of Virgil's Aeneid.

In the first half of the 19th century translated literature in Ukraine followed Kotliarevsky's success. Travesties of classical works were attempted by P. Hulak-Artemovsky, Ye. Hrebinka, K. Dumytrashko, and P. Biletsky-Nosenko. Even in the second half of the 19th century translation as 'rendering in Ukrainian' with elements of travesty continued in S. Rudansky's Iliad (1872–7), in P. Nishchynsky's (P. Baida) Odyssey (1890), Iliad (1902–3), and Antigone (1883), and in the numerous translations by O. Navrotsky. No longer travesties but far from real translations were the Ukrainianized versions done by the Romantics L. Borovykovsky (poems of A. Pushkin, A. Mickiewicz, V. Zhukovsky), A. Metlynsky (German poems), M. Shashkevych (Serbian and Polish poems), and M. Kostomarov (G. Byron and W. Shakespeare). The artistic height reached in such transformational translation can be seen in T. Shevchenko's 'Psalms of David.'

The pioneer of proper translations was Shevchenko's friend and contemporary P. *Kulish. Translation became a prime activity of his mature life, as in his arduous translation of the Bible, which he began in 1868 with renderings of the 'Psalms of David' and completed only just before his death. The final edition of his translation of the Bible came out in 1903, with I. Puliui and I. Nechui-Levytsky as cotranslators. Kulish's Shekspirovi tvory: Z movy brytans'koï movoiu ukraïns'koiu perekladov P. Kulish, T. I, Otello; Troïl ta Kressyda; Komediia pomylok (Shakespeare's Works: From the British Language Translated into the Ukrainian Language by P. Kulish, vol 1, Othello; Troilus and Cressida; The Comedy of Errors) published by the Shevchenko Scientific Society in Lviv in 1882 was followed by translations of G. Byron's Don Juan (1890–91), excerpts from J.W. von Goethe, H. Heine, and F. von Schiller (1885–6), and posthumous publications of other Shakespearean plays: Hamlet (1899), The Taming of the Shrew (1900), Macbeth (1900), Coriolanus (1900), Julius Caesar (1901), Romeo and Juliet (1901), Much Ado about Nothing (1901), Antony and Cleopatra (1901), Measure for Measure (1902), and King Lear (1902). All the posthumously published translations of Shakespeare's plays were edited and introduced by I. *Franko, who also contributed to the store of translated literature by translating over 60 authors (Sappho, Sophocles, Horace, Ovid, M. de Cervantes, Dante, E. Zola, G. Flaubert, V. Hugo, P. Verlaine, J.W. von Goethe, H. Heine, W. Shakespeare, G. Byron, R. Burns, Mark Twain, N. Gogol, V. Solovev, A. Mickiewicz, J. Neruda, K. Havlíček-Borovský, H. Ibsen, A. Strindberg, and many others).

Others who worked in the field of translation at the beginning of the 20th century were V. *Samiilenko (one song of the Iliad [1887], the 'Inferno' from Dante's Divine Comedy [1892–1902], some Molière, B. Hart, Byron, P.-J. de Béranger, and other authors), and Lesia *Ukrainka (H. Heine's Buch der Lieder [1892], translated with M. Stavynsky], some of N. Gogol, I. Turgenev, V. Hugo, G. Hauptmann, and M. Maeterlinck). Quite prolific as translators were P. Hrabovsky (Byron's Childe Harold's Pilgrimage [1895], E.A. Poe's 'Raven' [1897], some poems by A. Lord

Tennyson, and about 270 poems by other poets) and M. Starytsky (Tales of H.C. Andersen [1873], I. Krylov's *Fables* [1874], Serbian epic songs [1876], and poems by A. Pushkin, G. Byron, H. Heine, A. Mickiewicz, and others). V. *Shchurat's translation of the 11th-century French epic *Chanson de Roland* (1895) has yet to be surpassed and has been republished (1957, 1962). Shchurat also adapted into contemporary Ukrainian the Old Ukrainian epic *Slovo o polku Ihorevi* (The Tale of Ihor's Campaign, 1907) and translated works by many authors, such as S. Petőfi, K. Tetmajer, J. Słowacki, N. Nekrasov, N. Aksakov, A. Pushkin, E.A. Poe, and V. Hugo. A. *Krymsky translated from Persian, Turkish, Arabic, Russian, and German. Translation into Ukrainian was also part of the program of the literary group *Pleiada. In Ukraine under Russian rule translating activity was greatly hindered by the *Ems Ukase (1876), which prohibited the printing and distribution of all Ukrainian-language original and translated works. As a result translated works could be published only in Galicia or Bukovyna.

In Western Ukraine in the first decades of the 20th century, translated literature was much in vogue in such publications as *S'vit*, the magazine of the modernists *Moloda Muza, and in the series Biblioteka naiznamenytshykh povistei (The Library of the Best Novelettes, 74 vols), published by the newspaper *Dilo*. The quality of the translations in that series was poor because works were often translated from Polish, Russian, or German translations of the original text. Much more precise were the translations published by the Ukrainian-Ruthenian Publishing Company under the editorship of I. Franko, V. Hnatiuk, and M. Hrushevsky. Through the efforts of the editors as well as other contributors (eg, P. Karmansky, Ye. Tymchenko, O. Cherniakhivska, I. Krevetsky) many works from various literatures appeared in Ukrainian translation. In addition to the Finnish epic *Kalevala* (translated by Ye. Tymchenko, 1901) and the Shakespearean plays (translated by P. Kulish) the company published translations of the works of G. de Maupassant, K. Hamsun, H. Pontoppidan, G. Hauptmann, V. Korolenko, K. Gutzkow, W. Orkan, K. Havlíček-Borovský, H. Heine, N. Gorky, A. Chekhov, E. Zola, G. Byron, L. Tolstoy, U. Sinclair, and others. A similar contribution to translated literature came from *Literaturno-naukovyi vistnyk*, which systematically published good translations of world classics and contemporary works. The Novitnia biblioteka (New Library) book series, published in Lviv 1912–23 and edited by F. Fedortsiv, included many of the aforementioned authors and also the works of L. Andreev, S. Żeromski, E.A. Poe, A. France, and E.T.A. Hoffmann. Ukrainska Nakladnia (a publishing house established as Halytska Nakladnia in 1903 by Ya. Orenshtain) published the works of Aesop, J. de La Fontaine, F. Nietzsche, R. Kipling, B. Bjørnson, H. Ibsen, and others in the Zahalna biblioteka (General Library) book series. The publishing house Vsesvitnia Biblioteka, founded by I. Kalynovych in 1913–14 in Lviv, published the works of F. von Schiller, J.W. von Goethe, and A. Pushkin, which were translated and edited, for the most part, by I. Franko.

Translating activity increased after the hiatus created by the First World War, although neither was the activity planned nor was the translation always from original languages directly into Ukrainian. Some translations done by the better translators from the prewar years were the ex-

ception. Most notable were V. Samiilenko's translation of Molière's *Tartuffe* (1917) and stories by V. Blasco Ibáñez (1926) and Khrystia Alchevska's translations of V. Hugo. Although many authors engaged in sporadic translation, there were several who excelled, and whose activity greatly contributed to the store of translated literature. The *Neoclassicist group of poets were all engaged in translation. P. Fylypovych translated mainly from Russian poets (eg, A. Pushkin, V. Briusov, and E. Baratynsky). M. Drai-Khmara, in addition to translating Russian (eg, Pushkin, M. Lermontov) and Czech (J. Machar, J. Hora) poets, translated the Belarusian poet M. Bahdanovich (*Vinok* [Wreath, 1929]). His work on the *Kalevala* and the *Divine Comedy* was interrupted by his arrest. Yu. Klen (then still O. Burghardt) translated primarily German but also French and English poetry (eg, *Zalizni sonety* [Iron Sonnets, 1926]). M. Zerov translated the sonnets of the French poets J.-M. de Heredia and C.-M.-R. Leconte de Lisle, and J. Słowacki's *Mazepa* (staged in 1922). He collaborated with P. Fylypovych and M. Rylsky on the translations of A. Pushkin (his translation of *Boris Godunov* appeared in 1937 under the name of B. Petrushevsky) but concentrated mainly on Latin poets (*Antolohiia ryms'koï poeziï* [Anthology of Roman Poetry, 1920]). M. Rylsky was the most prolific of the Neoclassicist translators. He translated throughout his life and is credited with rendering works from more than 20 literatures into Ukrainian, among them Belgian (C. Van Lerberghe's *Pan* [1918], M. Maeterlinck), French (T. Gautier, J.-M. de Hérédia, P. Verlaine, S. Mallarmé, F. Jammes, H. de Régnier, J. Bédier's *Le Roman de Tristan et Iseult* [1928; 3rd edn 1972], G. de Maupassant, G. Flaubert's *Salammbô*, P. Corneille's *Le Cid* [1931], Molière's *Le misanthrope* [1931], J. Racine's *Phèdre* [1931], N. Boileau's *L'art poétique* [1931], Voltaire's *La pucelle d'Orléans* [1934], E. Rostand's *Cyrano de Bergerac* [1947]), English (W. Shakespeare's *King Lear* and *Twelfth Night* [1958]), Armenian (Sayat-Nova, A. Isaakaian), Georgian (H. Tabidze), Belarusian (Ya. Kupala, Ya. Kolas), Russian (M. Lermontov, F. Tiutchev, A. Fet, A. Blok, and most of A. Pushkin), Polish (primarily A. Mickiewicz but also J. Słowacki, K. Tetmajer, J. Tuwim, C. Norwid). Rylsky's translation of A. Mickiewicz's *Pan Tadeusz* (first version published in 1927, but reworked several times during Rylsky's life) was awarded the prize of the Polish PEN club for the mastery of the translation in 1949.

Other important translations were D. Zahul's from German literature (H. Heine [1918–19], J.W. von Goethe's *Faust* [1925], F. Schiller's ballads [1927], German ballads [1929]), I. Kulyk's *Antolohiia amerykans'koï poeziï* (Anthology of American Poetry, 1928), V. Svidzinsky's comedies of Aristophanes (1939), and M. Bazhan's translations from Armenian and Georgian, most notably of S. Rustaveli's *The Knight in the Tiger Skin* (1937). V. Pidmohylny concentrated on translating French prose (eg, A. France's stories [1925], *Thaïs* [1927], *La rôtisserie de la Reine Pédauque* [1929] – he also edited the first 8 vols of a 24-vol collection of France's works [1930] – Voltaire's *Candide* [1927], P. Mérimée's *Colomba* [1927], H. de Balzac's *Le Père Goriot* [1927], *Les parents pauvres* [1929], G. de Maupassant's *Fort comme la mort*, *Bel-Ami*, and *Mont-Oriol* [published separately and as part of the 10-vol works, 1928–30], and D. Diderot [2 vols, 1933]). M. *Tereshchenko's lifelong interest in translating French poetry began with his volume of E. Verhaeren's verse (1927) and culminated in the posthumous publication of the anthology of French verse *Suzir'ia frantsuz'koï poeziï* (The Constellation of French Poetry, 2 vols, 1971).

Devoted specifically to literary translation were translators such as M. Ivanov (Cervantes's *Don Quixote* [1927], some C. Dickens, R. Kipling, Mark Twain, A. Conan Doyle [2 vols in 1928], and other works), H. Kasianenko (some J. Conrad, A. Conan Doyle, J. Dos Passos, and J. London), and K. Lubensky (Aristophanes' *Lysistrata* [1928]). The flurry of translation activity included the founding of *Vsesvit* in 1925, a journal dedicated to opening worldwide literary horizons. During the 1930s the wholesale destruction of Ukrainian cultural life under Stalinism also brought an end to most of the translation activity. Only a trickle continued. The most notable translations were an anthology of world literature (of which only the third volume was published, 1931) and an anthology of ancient literature (1938), both edited by O. Biletsky, in which, indicative of the times, the names of repressed translators (eg, M. Zerov, V. Pidmohylny, I. Steshenko, and D. Zahul) were intentionally left out. The increased interest in Spain resulting from the civil war there justified some translation of Spanish poetry, but on the whole only pro-Soviet authors were translated. The only regular translation activity before the Second World War consisted of translation from the literature of the various nationalities in the Soviet Union, from Russian in particular.

In Western Ukraine and among émigrés, however, translation activity continued between the two world wars. Translations, mainly from classical, Old Ukrainian, French, Scandinavian, Italian, and English literature, were done by authors such as O. Babii, S. Hordynsky, P. Karmansky, M. Rudnytsky, V. Sofroniv-Levytsky, and V. Shchurat. Of special note were the editions from Ya. Orenshtain in Berlin in the Zahalna biblioteka book series and in separate volumes of translations of G.B. Shaw, A. Schnitzler, Plato, F. Mistral, A. France, R. Rolland, and V. Korolenko. From 1921 to 1924 the Chaika publishing house in Vienna, under the editorship of O. Hrytsai, published 13 volumes of translations done by V. O'Connor-Vilinska, M. Shrah, N. Surovtsova, B. Chorny, M. Trotsky, and S. Pashchenko of V. Hugo, T. Gautier, C. Dickens, A. Daudet, G. Ebers, G. de Maupassant, A. de Musset, Stendhal, L. Tolstoy, and G. Flaubert.

The end of the 1950s, after the 20th Congress and N. Khrushchev's 'thaw,' brought about the revival of *Vsesvit*, in 1958, with a mandate to introduce its readers within the Soviet Union to foreign literature. Foremost translators who had made their debuts in the 1930s and had managed to survive the Stalinist terror now came forth with excellent translations. B. *Ten, who published his translation of Aeschylus' *Prometheus Bound* in 1949 and the comedies of Aristophanes in 1956, made his greatest contribution in his translations of Homer's *Odyssey* (1963) and *Iliad* (1978). I. *Steshenko concentrated on drama and translated comedies by Molière and C. Goldoni, several plays by W. Shakespeare (in the 3-vol edn of 1964), J.W. von Goethe's *Egmont*, F. von Schiller's *Don Carlos*, F. Crommelynck's *Tripes d'or*, and A. Berg's *Wozzeck*. V. Mysyk became a leading translator of English, American, German, and Persian literature, in particular of the poetry of R. Burns (1932), Rūdakī (1962), Omar Khayyám (1965), J. Keats (1968), Ḥāfez (1971), and Firdousi (1975). Ye. *Drobiazko translated from Russian, French (particularly H. de Balzac and Molière), German (eg, H. Heine, J.W. von Goethe, F.

Some recent Ukrainian editions of translated literature

von Schiller), and Polish (J. Słowacki and J. Tuwim). His greatest achievement was a full translation of Dante's *Divine Comedy* in 1976.

The 1960s in Ukraine saw an outburst of literary activity (see *Shestydesiatnyky*) including a renewed interest in translations. New translators appeared, such as O. Terekh, R. Dotsenko, A. Perepadia, Ye. Popovych, O. Seniuk, M. Pinchevsky, V. Mytrofanov, and Yu. Lisniak. They gathered around *Vsesvit*, where the first translations of F. Kafka, W. Golding, E. Hemingway, W. Faulkner, and other modern authors appeared. The decade also marked the first of the translations of two master translators, M. *Lukash and H. *Kochur. The two collaborated on a translation of P. Verlaine's poetry in 1968. The appearance of Boccaccio's *Decameron* in 1964 (repr 1969 and 1985), translated by Lukash with proper rendition in Ukrainian of the nuances of Boccaccio's language, was a cultural landmark in the struggle for the development of the Ukrainian language under the constant pressure of Russification. At that time the works of J. London appeared in 12 volumes, including translations done in the 1920s by repressed translators. The eight volumes of G. de Maupassant (1969–72) also included translations done by V. Pidmohylny. Translations of literature for children, outside of the normal fairy tales, legends, and myths, were published by the Veselka publishing house; *Braty Maugli* (1967), a translation of R. Kipling's *The Jungle Book*, is an example.

In the 1970s, however, new waves of repression began against Ukrainian culture, including literature and translation. The use of dialectal words, especially from Western Ukraine, was deemed a subversive act by which the translator was attempting to keep the Ukrainian language from a 'merger with the brotherly Russian tongue.' M. Lukash and H. Kochur were expelled from the *Writers' Union of Ukraine. R. Dotsenko and A. Perepadia were especially persecuted for the use of dialectal words and were prevented from working. The editor of *Vsesvit*, D. *Pavlychko, was removed in 1978, and the journal itself was severely criticized. Yet some translations continued to appear, of F. Villon (1973) by L. Pervomaisky and of R.M. Rilke (1974) by M. *Bazhan. Only Bazhan's personal authority prevented complete censorship of his translation, which was severely criticized. Other noteworthy translations that appeared at that time were volumes of works by A. France (4 vols, 1976–7), B. Prus (5 vols, 1978–9), and É.

Hemingway (4 vols, 1979–81), H. Hesse's *Das Glasperlenspiel* (translated by Ye. Popovych and L. Kostenko, 1978 and 1983), J. Galsworthy's *The Forsyte Saga* (translated by O. Terekh, 1976; repub 1982, 1988), D. Defoe's *Robinson Crusoe* (1965; repub 1976, 1978, and 1985), L. Carroll's *Alice's Adventures in Wonderland* (translated by H. Bushyn, 1976), J. Swift's *Gulliver's Travels* (translated by Yu. Lisniak, 1976; repub 1983), K. Vonnegut's *Slaughterhouse Five* (translated by P. Sokolovsky, 1976), H.G. Wells's *War of the Worlds* and other novels (translated by D. Palamarchuk and M. Ivanov, 1977), T. Capote's collection (translated by V. Mytrofanov, 1977), J. Baldwin's *If Beale Street Could Talk* (translated by L. Honchar, 1978), works by W. Faulkner (translated by R. Dotsenko, 1978) and E. Waugh (1979), J. Carol Oates's collection of stories (1979), Aristophanes' comedies (a reissue of the translations by B. Ten and V. Svidzinsky, and new ones by A. Sodomora, 1980), and C. Brontë's *Jane Eyre* (translated by P. Sokolovsky, 1971; repub 1983 and 1987). Yet G. Apollinaire's poetry as translated by M. Lukash in the 1970s had to wait untill 1984 to be published. With the fall of L. Brezhnev, the situation began to improve. Lukash's unique talents as a master translator were recognized with the establishment of a translation prize in his name in 1989 for the best translation in a given year to appear in *Vsesvit* (the first recipient was V. Shovkun, for his translation of G. Vidal's *Creation*). Lukash died before finishing his translation of Cervantes's *Don Quixote*, which was being finished by A. Perepadia.

Interest in South American literature produced translations of the works of G. Amado, J. Cortázar, M. Vargas Llosa, G. García Marquez, J.L. Borges, A. Carpentier, and others. Of special significance was a six-volume edition of W. Shakespeare (1983–6), in which the best of both previous and new translations were collected. The 1980s produced some notable translations, among which the following stand out: an anthology of Greek tragedies (translated by B. Ten, 1981), the tragedies of Sophocles (by B. Ten and A. Sodomora, 1989), two volumes of G. Flaubert (1987), Ovid's *Metamorphoses* (by A. Sodomora, 1985), E.T.A. Hoffmann's stories (by Ye. Popovych, 1987), P. Lagerkvist's *Mariamna* (by O. Seniuk, 1988), L. de Camões's *Os Lusíadas* (by M. Lytvynets, 1987), F.S. Fitzgerald's *The Great Gatsby* (by M. Pinchevsky, 1982), W. Thackeray's *Vanity Fair* (by O. Seniuk, 1983), H. Melville's *Moby Dick* (by Yu. Lisniak, 1984), G. Byron's *Don Juan* (by S. Holovanivsky, 1985), J. Conrad's *Lord Jim* (by L. Honchar, 1985), and J.R.R. Tolkien's *The Hobbit* (by O. Mokrovolsky, 1985). Of interest is the newly established series *Svitova proza 20 st.* (World Prose of the 20th century), established in 1988, in which works such as J. Heller's *Catch 22* (1988), J. Updike's *The Centaur of the Farm* (1988), and W. Somerset Maugham's *The Moon and Sixpence* and *The Razor's Edge* (1989) have appeared. In 1990 an edition of Aeschylus' *Tragedies* was published (cotranslated by A. Sodomora and B. Ten).

The numerous professional translators in Ukraine form a school of literary translation; at the present time the most important translator is H. Kochur. But translation also continues to be done by literary scholars specializing in various foreign literatures, such as D. Zatonsky, T. Denysova, K. Shakhova, Yu. Pokalchuk, O. Pakhlovska, S. Pavlychko, and V. Kukhalashvili. There is a special commission at the Writers' Union of Ukraine for translations of literature. Most translated works are published by the Dnipro publishing house, where several book series have been established, such as Biblioteka svitovoi klasyky (World Classics Library, since 1967), Perlyny svitovoi liryky (Pearls of World Lyric Poetry, since 1965), and Svitova proza 20 st. (World Prose of the 20th Century, since 1988). Most recently Dnipro published an edition of selected poems by T.S. Eliot (several translators; edited by S. Pavlychko, 1990). Important work in the theory of literary translation has been done by M. Rylsky, O. Kundzich, Y. Bahmut, B. Ten, Z. Bilenko, S. Kovhaniuk, and H. Kochur. Since 1972 a yearly bibliographic survey of translations into Ukrainian has been provided by the journal *Vsesvit*.

Translation has also continued in the emigration since 1945, mainly in drama and poetry. Translations were done mostly by authors who augmented their own literary output with translations. Most prolific was M. *Orest, who translated S. George (1952), M. Dauthenday (1953), R.M. Rilke, H. Hofmannsthal, and C.-M.-R. Leconte de Lisle (1956), and prepared anthologies of German (1954), French (1954), and European poetry (including Italian, English, Spanish, Portuguese, Russian, and Polish, 1959) and a collection of German novellas (1962). V. Vovk prepared an anthology of Portuguese and Brazilian poetry, *Zelene vyno* (Green Wine, 1964), S. Hordynsky compiled *Poety zakhodu* (Poets of the West, 1961), and W. Burghardt edited *Poeziia Kvebeku* (Poetry of Quebec, 1972). V. Vovk and W. Burghardt collaborated on *Four Plays of F. Garcia Lorca* (1974). I. *Kostetsky did much to expand the store of translations into Ukrainian and his publishing house, Na Hori, published some of the finest translations in the postwar emigration: selected poems of F.G. Lorca (edited by I. Kostetsky and translated by members of the *New York Group, 1958); T.S. Eliot's *Murder in the Cathedral* (translated by Z. Tarnavsky, 1963); S. George's two volumes, rendered into Ukrainian and other Slavic languages by I. Kostetsky and O. Zuievsky (1968–71); P. Claudel's *L'annonce faite à Marie* (translated by M. Kalytovska, 1962); selections of E. Pound (by I. Kostetsky, 1960), and W. Shakespeare's *Macbeth, Henry IV* (by T. Osmachka, 1961), and *King Lear* (by V. Barka, 1969). I. Koshelivets translated D. Diderot's *Jacques le fataliste et son maître* (1970) and F. Kafka's stories (1989). Selected poems of J. Keats were translated by Ya. Slavutych (1958), some Japanese haiku by I. Shankovsky (1966), and S. Beckett's *Waiting for Godot* and *Krapp's Last Tape* by B. Boychuk (1972). An interesting collaboration between émigré poets and poets from Ukraine is the translation of S. Kunitz's *This Garland, Danger* (1977), in which B. Boychuk, V. Burghardt, I. Drach, V. Lesych, and G. Tarnawsky collaborated.

BIBLIOGRAPHY

Mezhenko, I.; Iashek, M. 'Chuzhomovne pys'menstvo v ukraïns'kykh perekladakh,' *ZhR*, 1929, nos 4–8
Rodzevych, S. 'Novyny perekladnoï literatury,' *ZhR*, 1928, nos 9, 11; 1929, nos 1, 3–5, 11; 1930, no. 4; 1931, no. 7
Derkach, B. *Perekladna ukraïns'ka povist' XVII–XVIII stolit'* (Kiev 1960)
'Zarubizhna literatura na Ukraïni,' *Vsesvit*, 1960, no. 10
Kravtsiv, B. 'Poeziia Zakhodu v ukraïns'kykh perekladakh,' *Suchasnist'*, 1962, no. 4
Kushch, O. *Rosiis'ka literatura v ukraïns'kykh perekladakh i krytytsi: Halychyna i Bukovyna XIX st.–1939* (Kiev 1963)
Kochur, H. 'Na perekladnyts'ki temy,' *Dnipro*, 1965, no. 6
– 'Maistry perekladu,' *Vsesvit*, 1966, no. 4
– 'Zdobutky i perespektyvy,' *Vsesvit*, 1968, no. 1
Zarubizhna literatura na Ukraïni,' *Vsesvit*, 1972, no.1; 1973, no.1; 1974, no. 1; 1975, no. 1; 1976, no. 1; 1977, no. 4; 1978, no. 5; 1979,

no. 7; 1980, no. 6; 1981, no. 6; 1982, no.6; 1983, no. 6; 1984, no. 6; 1985, no. 6; 1986, no. 10; 1987, no. 6; 1988, no. 7
Kachurovs'kyi, I. 'Perekladachi ukraïns'koï diaspory,' *Vsesvit*, 1991, no. 11

B. Kravtsiv, Yu. Pokalchuk, D.H. Struk

**Transliteration.** The representation of the letters of one alphabet by those of another. Phonetically, the most accurate form of transliteration is the International Linguistic (IL) system used by linguists. The one most commonly used by library catalogers and non-linguistic scholars in the English-speaking world is the Library of Congress (LC) system. Both systems, as well as a modified LC system, are used in this encyclopedia (see vol 1, pp xi–xii). There is no universally accepted transliteration system of Cyrillic. Consequently, when the Ukrainian Cyrillic alphabet is transliterated to the various European languages whose orthography is based on the Latin alphabet, phonetic ambiguities for speakers unfamiliar with other languages sometimes arise. The surname 'Ševčenko' (IL)/'Shevchenko' (LC), for example, is spelled 'Chevtchenko' in the French alphabet, 'Schewtschenko' in the German alphabet, and 'Szewczenko' in the Polish alphabet.

A universally acceptable system for transliterating foreign languages to the Ukrainian Cyrillic alphabet also does not exist. The official orthographic rules of 1928–9, 1933–46, and 1960 regulated only the phonetic assimilation of foreign words by the Ukrainian language, not transliteration. In the Russified system of Soviet Ukrainian orthography, the use of the grapheme 'g' had been banned until 1990, and the spelling of foreign names is determined by their spelling in Russian, which lacks the phoneme (and grapheme) 'h'. Consequently, certain foreign names are distorted; eg, the name 'Hemingway', which would have been spelled 'Hemingvej' (IL) according to the 1928–9 orthography, is instead spelled 'Xeminhvej' under the impact of the Russian spelling 'Xemingvej'.

R. Senkus

**Transnistria.** An artificial name, meaning 'beyond the Dniester,' for southwestern Ukraine that was introduced at the beginning of the 20th century by Rumanian historians to bolster Rumanian claims to the territory. In 1924 a part of Transnistria was assigned to the Moldavian ASSR. During the Second World War Transnistria was an administrative territory that the Germans had placed temporarily under Rumanian civil authority on 30 August 1941. It covered an area of 40,000 sq km between the Dniester and the Boh rivers as far north as the Liadova and the Riv rivers. It was divided into 13 counties (Mohyliv, Tulchyn, Yampil, Rybnytsia, Balta, Dubosari, Ananiv, Kryve Ozero, Tyraspil, Ovidiopil, Berezivka, Odessa, and Ochakiv) and 65 volosts. Its population was 2.25 million. The governor of Transnistria was G. Alecsianu (1941–4); his capital was Tyraspil and then Odessa. He was subject to the Military-Civilian Cabinet for the Administration of Bessarabia, Bukovyna, and Transnistria, which came under the Rumanian Council of Ministers. The administration of Transnistria was staffed with newcomers from Rumania. Special Rumanianization commissions, known as Directoratul de Romanizare, substituted Rumanian place-names for the existing Ukrainian ones. The official languages were Rumanian, German, and Russian. The Rumanians treated Transnistria like a colony for economic exploitation. In late 1941 about 101,400 Jews from Bessara-

| ——— Boundary of Rumania 1941 - 1944 | ——— County boundary |
| – – – Western boundary of Transnistria | ⊙ County center |
| 0   50   100   150 km | Note: Counties are named after their centers |

## TRANSNISTRIA

bia and Bukovyna were transported to Transnistria, where many of them perished. In April 1943, 3,000 Ukrainians were deported from Rybnytsia to Ochakiv county, and the villages were repopulated with Rumanian colonists. In July 1943 the Rumanian government deported 23,300 Gypsies from Rumania to Transnistria, where almost half of them died.

In the schools (1,300 four-grade schools, 700 seven-grade, and a few secondary schools in 1943) the languages of instruction were Ukrainian, Rumanian (10 percent), Russian, and German. In Odessa there were 12 Russian but only 1 Ukrainian lyceum. At the postsecondary (university) level the language of instruction was Russian. Ukrainian cultural activity was banned. At first the state and collective farms were left intact. In March 1942 they were reorganized into labor communes, which were divided into brigades of 20 to 30 families and were assigned 200–400 ha of land. Industrial or commercial concerns were handed over to officials or to Rumanian state co-operatives. The Orthodox population was placed under the authority of the Rumanian patriarchate in Bucharest, which set up the Rumanian Orthodox Mission in Transnistria. It was headed by Archimandrite J. Scriban, Metropolitan V. Puiu (1942), and Bishop A. Nica (1943). Local priests of the Ukrainian Autocephalous Orthodox church and the Tikhonites and Renovationists of the Russian Orthodox church continued to be active. In all there were 12 monasteries and 300 to 400 churches, with 600 priests.

When the eastern front approached in early 1944, the administration of Transnistria was turned over to the Rumanian military (Gen Potopianu) and then to the German military authorities. In March 1944 Transnistria was occupied by Soviet forces.

BIBLIOGRAPHY
Hillgruber, A. *Hitler, König Carol, und Marschall Antonescu: Die deutsch-rumänischen Beziehungen, 1938–44* (Wiesbaden 1954)

Zhukovs'kyi, A. 'Ukraïns'ki zemli pid rumuns'koiu okupatsiieiu v chasi Druhoï svitovoï viiny: Pivnichna Bukovyna, chastyna Basarabiï, i Transnistriia, 1941–1944,' *UI*, nos 93–6 (1987)
A. Zhukovsky

**Transportation.** Transportation plays a vital role in the production process of any society. It serves as an intermediary, transferring materials and products from one branch of the economy to another and people from one location to another. By linking regions and countries into one market transportation stimulates economic activity and raises the people's standard of living. Ukraine's transportation system was a part of the larger Union system. It was not a competitive but a complementary service, centrally planned and state owned. The Soviet transportation system consisted of universal modes, such as *railroad, *motor vehicle, *sea, *river, *air, and *urban transit, and specific modes, such as electronic, *pipeline, and high-voltage transportation. All of them are well established in Ukraine and have different degrees of efficiency. The size of the basic transportation networks is given in table 1.

The most basic mode remains the railroad. Although its share of the total transportation output has been declining gradually, it is still the most reliable mode of long-distance freight transportation. Between 1940 and 1986 the growth of railroads was low, and quite inadequate for the country's needs. River and sea transportation recovered slowly after the Second World War. To meet the rapidly growing demand for transportation large investments were made in the motor vehicle transport system. The

TABLE 1

Length of surface transportation networks, 1940–86
(in 1,000 km)

| Network | 1940 | 1970 | 1980 | 1986 |
|---|---|---|---|---|
| Railroads (general use) | 20.1 | 22.1 | 22.6 | 22.7 |
| Railroads (restricted use) | nd | 20.5 | 24.8 | 26.3 |
| Paved highways (general use) | 29.3 | 90.8 | 133.7 | 149.5 |
| Paved highways (general and special use) | – | – | 165.7 | 209.2 |
| Soft-surface improved highways | 241.4 | 132.7 | 29.5 | 13.7 |
| Navigable rivers | 3.2 | 4.8 | 4.9 | 5.0 |
| Canals | 0.1 | 1.2 | 2.2 | 2.4 |

TABLE 2

Share of freight output in total output, 1970 and 1985
(percentages; 1985 as percentage of 1970 in parentheses)

| Mode | Ukraine 1970 | 1985 | | USSR 1970 | 1985 | |
|---|---|---|---|---|---|---|
| Rail | 62.1 | 56.1 | (90.4) | 65.4 | 49.7 | (76.0) |
| Motor vehicle | 6.8 | 8.1 | (119.1) | 1.6 | 1.8 | (112.5) |
| River | 1.0 | 1.4 | (140.0) | 4.5 | 3.4 | (75.6) |
| Sea | 28.2 | 28.3 | (100.4) | 17.2 | 12.0 | (69.8) |
| Air | 0.1 | 0.1 | (100.0) | 0.5 | 0.5 | (100.0) |
| Pipeline (oil only) | 1.8 | 6.0 | (333.3) | 10.8 | 32.6 | (301.9) |

TABLE 3

Share of freight volume in total volume, 1970 and 1986
(percentages; 1986 as percentage of 1970 in parentheses)

| Mode | Ukraine 1970 | 1986 | | USSR 1970 | 1986 | |
|---|---|---|---|---|---|---|
| Rail | 20.2 | 17.0 | (84.2) | 37.5 | 31.8 | (84.8) |
| Motor vehicle | 77.5 | 79.0 | (101.9) | 49.4 | 51.9 | (105.1) |
| River | 0.7 | 1.0 | (142.9) | 4.6 | 5.0 | (108.7) |
| Sea | 1.0 | 1.0 | (100.0) | 2.1 | 1.9 | (90.5) |
| Air | – | – | – | 0.2 | 0.3 | (150.0) |
| Pipeline | 0.6 | 2.0 | (333.3) | 6.2 | 9.1 | (146.8) |

TABLE 4

Passenger output for different modes of transportation, 1940–86 (in billion Pkm*; percentage of USSR output in parentheses)

| Mode | 1940 | | 1970 | | 1980 | | 1986 | |
|---|---|---|---|---|---|---|---|---|
| Rail | 16.4 | (16.3) | 42.1 | (15.4) | 60.1 | (17.5) | 68.3 | (17.5) |
| Motor vehicle | 0.3 | (8.3) | 46.6 | (23.0) | 81.7 | (21.0) | 88.5 | (19.1) |
| River | 0.4 | (10.5) | 0.5 | (9.3) | 0.6 | (9.8) | 0.5 | (8.3) |
| Sea | – | – | 0.8 | (50.0) | 1.3 | (52.0) | 1.4 | (56.0) |
| Air | – | – | 6.1 | (7.8) | 10.9 | (6.8) | 13.2 | (6.7) |
| Total | 17.1 | | 96.1 | | 154.6 | | 171.9 | |

*Pkm = passengers per kilometer

TABLE 5

Share of passenger output in total output, 1970 and 1986
(percentages; 1986 as percentage of 1970 in parentheses)

| Mode | Ukraine 1970 | 1986 | | USSR 1970 | 1986 | |
|---|---|---|---|---|---|---|
| Rail | 43.8 | 39.7 | (90.6) | 48.7 | 36.9 | (75.8) |
| Motor vehicle | 48.5 | 51.5 | (106.2) | 36.1 | 43.8 | (121.3) |
| River | 0.5 | 0.3 | (60.0) | 1.0 | 0.6 | (60.0) |
| Sea | 0.8 | 0.8 | (100.0) | 0.3 | 0.2 | (66.7) |
| Air | 6.4 | 7.7 | (120.3) | 13.9 | 18.5 | (133.1) |

highway network expanded fivefold in 1940–86, and the freight and passenger output increased by 44 and 111 times respectively. Starting in the mid-1960s the share of other forms of transportation increased. The railroad output continued to decline in relative terms, and the motor vehicle output grew at a slower rate than before. The slowdown in motor vehicle transport is related to the growth in the number of personal cars (in 1987, 105 cars per 1,000 people), a lower level of employment search, and lower mobility.

The significant differences between Ukraine's share of the former USSR's freight output (see table 6) and of the USSR freight volume (see table 7) in all modes of transportation (except sea transportation) are attributable to the difference in the average haul distance. The hauls become longer as one moves eastward through the former USSR. Ukrainian territory is better suited to intensive surface traffic than many regions in Siberia. Population density together with the intensity of economic activity is responsible for the relatively higher growth rate of motor vehicle

TABLE 6
Freight output of different modes of transportation, 1940–86 (in billion Tkm*; percentage of USSR output in parentheses)

| Mode | 1940 | 1970 | 1980 | 1986 |
|---|---|---|---|---|
| Rail | 71.9 (17.1) | 380.2 (15.2) | 469.6 (13.7) | 506.2 (13.2) |
| Motor vehicle | 1.7 (18.8) | 41.6 (18.9) | 70.1 (16.2) | 73.3 (14.8) |
| River | 1.1 (3.1) | 6.1 (3.5) | 10.7 (4.4) | 12.7 (4.8) |
| Sea | 4.3 (17.3) | 172.3 (26.3) | 168.8 (19.9) | 283.5 (29.2) |
| Air | – – | 0.2 (1.1) | 0.2 (0.6) | 0.2 (0.6) |
| Pipeline (oil only) | – – | 11.2 (4.0) | 54.6 (4.5) | 56.5 (3.9) |
| Total | 79.0 | 611.6 | 774.0 | 932.4 |

*Tkm = tonnes per kilometer.

TABLE 7
Freight volume of different modes of transportation, 1940–86 (in million tonnes; percentage of USSR volume in parentheses)

| Mode | 1940 | 1970 | 1980 | 1986 |
|---|---|---|---|---|
| Rail | 200.0 (33.1) | 794.7 (27.4) | 981.1 (26.3) | 1,042.9 (26.4) |
| Motor vehicle | 187.2 (21.8) | 3,058.1 (20.9) | 4,391.5 (18.2) | 4,832.0 (18.7) |
| River | 4.6 (6.2) | 27.3 (7.6) | 51.3 (9.0) | 58.5 (9.3) |
| Sea | 5.4 (16.4) | 38.2 (23.6) | 47.1 (20.6) | 59.8 (24.9) |
| Air | – – | 0.2 (11.1) | 0.3 (10.0) | 0.3 (9.4) |
| Pipeline (oil only) | – – | 22.1 (6.6) | 101.6 (10.7) | 124.2 (11.2) |
| Total | 397.2 | 3,940.6 | 5,572.9 | 6,117.7 |

TABLE 8
Passenger volume for different modes of transportation, 1940–86 (in million passengers; percentage of USSR volume in parentheses)

| Mode | 1940 | 1970 | 1980 | 1986 |
|---|---|---|---|---|
| Rail | 242.6 (17.6) | 506.4 (15.1) | 648.9 (16.0) | 635.5 (14.6) |
| Motor vehicle | 29.4 (5.0) | 5,060.9 (18.5) | 7,801.1 (18.5) | 8,228.2 (16.9) |
| River | 6.8 (9.3) | 21.4 (14.8) | 24.8 (18.0) | 21.0 (15.4) |
| Sea | 13.7 – | 19.8 (50.8) | 28.5 (54.8) | 28.7 (56.3) |
| Air | – – | 9.7 (13.7) | 12.5 (12.0) | 12.8 (11.0) |
| Total | 292.5 | 5,618.2 | 8,515.8 | 8,926.2 |

output in Ukraine (see table 2). The slow but constant drop in rail traffic relative to other modes may indicate that rail cargo has been rerouted to trucks or that the density of the railway network has not kept up with increases in economic activity (see table 3)

After the war passenger traffic in Ukraine grew rapidly but at a slower rate than in the Baltic republics. In the mo-

tor vehicle sector the growth in passenger output and volume was sharp between 1940 and 1970, and rose to 180 and 160 percent respectively between 1970 and 1986 (see tables 4 and 8). Passenger traffic would be much higher today had both railroads and highways grown at faster rates, and had significant improvements been made in the frequency of services. The dynamics of passenger traffic is shown in tables 5 and 9.

The performance of Ukrainian transportation is less

TABLE 9
Share of passenger volume in total volume, 1970 and 1986 (percentages; 1986 as percentage of 1970 in parentheses)

| Mode | Ukraine | | USSR | |
|---|---|---|---|---|
| | 1970 | 1986 | 1970 | 1986 |
| Rail | 9.0 | 7.1 (78.9) | 10.9 | 8.1 (74.3) |
| Motor vehicle | 90.0 | 92.2 (102.4) | 88.3 | 91.3 (103.4) |
| River | 0.4 | 0.3 (75.0) | 0.5 | 0.3 (60.0) |
| Sea | 0.4 | 0.3 (75.0) | 0.1 | 0.1 (100.0) |
| Air | 0.2 | 0.1 (50.0) | 0.2 | 0.2 (100.0) |

TABLE 10
Transportation and communications: fixed capital, 1971–85 (in billion rubles)

| Five-year plan | USSR | Ukraine | Ukraine's share (%) |
|---|---|---|---|
| 10th (1971–75) | 52.9 | 8.9 | 16.8 |
| 11th (1976–80) | 73.2 | 10.73 | 14.7 |
| 12th (1981–85) | 95.0 | 11.97 | 12.6 |

TABLE 11
Transportation and communications: capital investments, 1971–85 (in billion rubles)

| Five-year plan | USSR | Ukraine | Ukraine's share (%) |
|---|---|---|---|
| 10th (1971–75) | 60.2 | 9.84 | 16.3 |
| 11th (1976–80) | 85.0 | 11.96 | 14.1 |
| 12th (1981–85) | 104.3 | 12.64 | 12.1 |

TABLE 12
Share of fixed capital for various modes of transportation in Ukraine (percentages)

| Mode | 1960 | 1970 | 1980 |
|---|---|---|---|
| Rail | 63.7 | 44.8 | 38.2 |
| Motor vehicle, highway | 18.8 | 29.9 | 40.1 |
| River | 2.2 | 1.7 | 1.6 |
| Sea | 10.8 | 16.7 | 10.9 |
| Pipeline (gas and oil) | 2.5 | 4.5 | 6.3 |
| Other modes (ie, urban transportation) | 2.0 | 2.4 | 2.9 |

than desirable for a country with a large industrial base. Under the last three five-year plans Ukraine's share of the USSR fixed capital and capital investments in transportation fell below its share in the USSR industrial output. Its share of fixed capital and investment declined with time (see tables 10 and 11). The distribution of fixed capital among various branches of Ukraine's transportation system was discriminatory against the railways, where larger investments were crucial for industrial growth (see table 12).

E. Bej

**Transylvania** (Rumanian: Transilvania, Ardeal; Hungarian: Erdély; Ukrainian: Semyhorod, Transylvaniia, Zalissia). A historical land, until 1918 mainly within the borders of Hungary. Since 1918 it has been part of *Rumania. Transylvania has an area of approx 99,600 sq km. The *Maramureş and *Banat regions have usually been considered part of Transylvania. In ancient times Transylvania was settled by the Dacians. From 106 to 271 it was a Roman province, and its population was partly Romanized. Later it was conquered by the Goths, Getae, Avars, and Bulgarians. Slavs began settling in Transylvania in the 6th century, and from the 9th century *Vlachs settled there. In the 10th century Magyar colonization by freemen known as Szeklers began, and in the 12th century Saxon and other German colonists arrived, who gave the land the name Siebenbürgen (hence, the Ukrainian name Semyhorod).

From the late 9th century Transylvania was under Hungarian rule. In the early 11th century it became part of the Hungarian kingdom but continued to enjoy a high degree of autonomy. After the fall of Hungary and the Battle of Mohács (1526) an independent Transylvanian principality arose. From 1541 to 1687 it was an Ottoman vassal-state. In the 17th century Transylvania was the object of Ottoman-Habsburg contention. In 1699 it became an Austrian crownland. From 1867 until it became part of Rumania it was ruled by the autonomous Hungarian kingdom. In 1940 northern Transylvania was occupied by Hungary, but in October 1944 Rumania regained that area. Rumania's claim was confirmed in the 1947 Treaty of Paris.

Medieval Ukrainian colonization of Transylvania is evidenced by place-names in the region (eg, Rusz, Reusdorfel, Russdorf, Ruseşti). The earliest extant documentation of such settlement is a 1220 charter, which refers to the mountain Ruscia and the town Forum Ruthenorum. In the 15th century there were sizable Ukrainian colonies in Transylvania, but they were later assimilated by the Magyars or Vlachs. The 1930 Rumanian census identified only 2,100 Ukrainians in Transylvania outside the Maramureş and Banat regions, most of them in Oradea county.

Ukrainian-Transylvanian cultural and political relations began during the Cossack era. Cossacks serving in the Wallachian army helped Prince Michael the Brave to unite Transylvania with Wallachia and Moldavia (1593–1601). In 1628 Prince Gábor Bethlen supported the idea of Ukraine's secession from Poland as a separate state. Hetman B. Khmelnytsky maintained diplomatic relations with the princes György *Rákóczi I (1630–48) and György *Rákóczi II (1648–60), and he signed an anti-Polish military pact with the latter prince in 1656. In the early 18th century the hetman-in-exile P. *Orlyk maintained relations with Prince Ferenc Rákóczi II. In 1699 some of I. *Galiatovsky's homilies were translated into Rumanian and published in Alba Iulia. In 1757 the Transylvanian D. Braşoveanul modeled the first Rumanian grammar, *Gramatica românească*, on M. *Smotrytsky's grammar; he also translated into Rumanian several Slavonic (ie, Ukrainian) books, which were printed in 1792 in Sibiu. Since the Second World War Ukrainian migrants have lived in Cluj, Braşov, and Oradea, and a Ukrainian Orthodox vicariate of the Rumanian metropoly of Transylvania has ministered to parishes where liturgies are celebrated in Church Slavonic.

A. Zhukovsky

**Tratsevsky, Mykhailo** [Tracevs'kyj, Myxajlo], b 3 January 1897 in Liubinichy, Babruisk county, Minsk gubernia, d 1979. Demographer and statistician. After graduating from the Kiev Institute of the National Economy (1924) he worked at the VUAN Demographic Institute. He wrote a historical study of the populations of Ukrainian towns from 1825 to 1926 (unpublished) and published an analysis of Kiev's population (1929) and infant mortality in Ukraine (1936). In 1937 he was arrested with his colleagues and sent to Siberia.

**Travesty.** A form of humorous poetry in which a work of serious or heroic content is made comic. The classic example of travesty in Ukrainian literature is I. *Kotliarevsky's *Eneïda*, based on Virgil's *Aeneid*, in which the characters (gods and heroes) were dressed in traditional Ukrainian folk garb and amusingly portrayed against the background of daily Ukrainian life. Kotliarevsky's epigones (K. Dumytrashko and others) also wrote in the genre, which came to be known as *kotliarevshchyna*. Travesties also played an important role in the Ukrainian renaissance of the late 18th and early 19th centuries, when literature sought to get closer to the daily language of the people.

**Treasurer** (*pidskarbii*). A senior court functionary in the Grand Duchy of Lithuania and the Polish Kingdom (15th–18th centuries), who managed the state treasury. The officeholder was also known as the great, crown, or land treasurer, and from 1590 there was also a court treasurer to oversee the personal finances of the king. Until the 18th century the treasurer was not remunerated, a state of affairs which led to persistent corruption. In Lithuania the income of the grand duke was managed by court treasurers until 1569, when the treasurer's position was transferred to the Polish Senate. The Hetman state had a *general treasurer, who was a member of the General Officer Staff (mid-17th to late 18th centuries).

**Treaties.** Bilateral or multilateral agreements between states or other subjects of international law that set forth the rights and obligations of the signing parties. They are the standard method for establishing international relations and the main source of international law. The parties to treaties are sovereign states, sometimes partly sovereign entities, and international organizations. In the course of its history Ukraine has concluded many treaties. It has often been the object of treaties drawn up by other states.

**The Princely era.** Kievan Rus' concluded treaties with many states. The texts of Oleh's (911), Ihor's (945), and Sviatoslav I Ihorevych's (971) treaties with Byzantium have been preserved. Those treaties put an end to hostilities and set the conditions for political and economic relations between the states. They also included articles on the legal status and the criminal liability of a state's subjects on the other signatory's territory. In the chronicles there are frequent references to treaties with other states, such as Poland, Bohemia, Hungary, and Bulgaria, but their texts have been lost. There is some information about a defensive alliance against Poland, Lithuania, and the Tatars concluded by the Principality of Galicia-Volhynia and the Teutonic Knights between 1308 and 1316. To some extent the agreements among the princes of the Kievan and Galician-Volhynian states can be regarded as treaties, since the constituent principalities were somewhat autonomous.

In the 14th and 15th centuries the northern and western Ukrainian territories were often the subject of treaties among neighboring states. In 1339 Hungary and Poland reached a compromise on their control of Galicia, and in 1352 and 1366 Poland and Lithuania divided western Ukraine between them. In the Grand Duchy of Lithuania, as in Kievan Rus', both the grand prince and the appanage princes had the power to make treaties. But the appanage princes could sign agreements affecting only their own lands, and under the supervision of the grand prince. Political treaties affecting the whole state were entered into by the grand prince in consultation with the Council of Lords; trade agreements could be concluded by the prince alone. The most important Lithuanian-Polish treaties affecting Ukrainian territories were the unions of *Krevo (1385), *Horodlo (1413), and *Lublin (1569). In the 15th to 17th centuries there were also some agreements between Muscovy on the one side and Lithuania and Poland on the other that dealt with Ukrainian territories.

**The Cossack period.** From the mid-16th century, when the Zaporizhia became a separate military-political entity, its leaders concluded military agreements with the rulers of Poland, Lithuania, the Austrian Empire, Muscovy, Moldavia, the Don Cossacks, and the Crimean Khanate. Issues such as the Cossack register, Cossack privileges, and the political and religious rights of the Ukrainian people were settled by negotiation between the *starshyna* of the town Cossacks and the Polish crown. Agreements such as the *Kurukove (1625) and *Pereiaslav (1630) treaties were somewhat less than full-fledged international treaties.

Upon setting up an independent Cossack state Hetman B. Khmelnytsky established a wide range of diplomatic contacts. He entered into a number of military-political alliances with the Crimean Khanate (1648), Turkey (1648 and 1651), Poland (the *Zboriv and *Bila Tserkva treaties), Moldavia (1653), Muscovy (the *Pereiaslav Treaty of 1654), Sweden (the military convention of 1655), and Transylvania (1656). The further development of Ukraine's relations with those countries was marked by new treaties. The more important treaties with Poland were those of *Hadiache (1658) and *Slobodyshche (1660) and I. Mazepa's secret alliance with Stanislaus I Leszczyński (1708). Ukraine's gradual subjugation by Muscovy is reflected in the so-called Hetman articles, consisting of the *Pereiaslav (1659 and 1674), *Moscow (1665), *Hlukhiv (1669), *Konotip (1672), and *Kolomak (1687) articles. Hetmans I. Vyhovsky (1657) and I. Mazepa (1708, 1709) entered into military alliances with Sweden. P. Doroshenko (1668), Yu. Khmelnytsky (1677), and P. Orlyk (1712) signed treaties with Turkey, and P. Ivanenko (1692) and P. Orlyk (1711) made agreements with the Crimean Tatars.

Ukraine's neighbors fought among themselves for control over Ukrainian territories and divided the spoils in a number of treaties. The more important ones were the Treaty of *Andrusovo (1667) and the *Eternal Peace of 1686 dividing Ukraine along the Dnieper River between Poland and Muscovy, the *Buchach Peace Treaty of 1672 between Poland and Turkey recognizing Turkey's protectorate over Doroshenko's state, and the peace treaties of *Küçük Kaynarca (1774), Iaşi (1791), and *Bucharest (1812), by which Turkey surrendered control of the northern coast of the Black Sea to Russia. In the three partitions of Poland, Prussia, Austria, and Russia agreed to hand Galicia (1772) and the Kholm region with southern Podlachia (1795) to Austria and Right-Bank Ukraine (1793) and Volhynia (1795) to Russia. By a separate agreement between Austria and Turkey in 1775, Bukovyna was acquired by Austria. In the Paris Peace Treaty (1856) ending the *Crimean War Russia surrendered the Danube Estuary and its right to keep a navy on the Black Sea.

**Ukrainian statehood, 1917–20.** On 9 February 1918 the UNR signed the Peace Treaty of *Brest-Litovsk with the Central Powers. It was followed by a series of international treaties with the Central Powers and other neighboring countries. Economic agreements were reached with Germany, Austria-Hungary, and Rumania, and trade and communications conventions with the Don krai, the Kuban, and Georgia. The preliminary peace treaty (12 June 1918) and the agreement on communications with Russia did not, however, culminate in a final peace treaty. On 21 April 1920, after long negotiations, the UNR signed the Treaty of *Warsaw with Poland.

In a formal sense the agreement on the unification of the UNR and the Western Ukrainian National Republic, concluded on 1 December 1918 at Khvastiv and ratified by the Directory of the UNR on 4 January and the Labor Congress on 22 January 1919, was an international treaty, since the signatories were separate states.

**Soviet Ukraine.** The Soviet government of Ukraine signed a number of fundamental treaties regulating its relations with Soviet Russia: the economic and military union among Soviet republics of 1 June 1919 (in the form of a resolution of the All-Russian Central Executive Committee), the so-called workers' and peasants' union treaty of 28 December 1920 between Ukraine and Russia, and the founding treaty of the USSR on 30 December 1922, signed by the RSFSR, the Ukrainian SSR (URSR), the Belorussian SSR (BSSR), and the Transcaucasian SFSR.

In 1919–23 the URSR exercised its power to conduct foreign relations and signed, alone or together with other Soviet republics, over 50 international treaties with non-Soviet states. The most important of them was the Peace Treaty of *Riga, signed on 18 March 1921 by Poland, the RSFSR, and the URSR. The other international treaties fall into four groups. Political treaties granting formal recognition, providing for diplomatic and consular exchanges, and rejecting interference in internal affairs were signed with Poland, Estonia, Latvia, Lithuania, Austria, Czechoslovakia, Germany (an extension of the Rapallo Treaty), and Turkey (21 January 1922). Special agreements on legal issues, such as option procedure, resettlement, citizen status on foreign soil, the resolution of jurisdictional conflicts, and border arrangements, were concluded with the Baltic countries and Poland. Ukraine entered into some social and humanitarian treaties (agreements on exchange of war prisoners, internees, and refugees and on sanitation) with Germany, Austria, Hungary, Italy, Turkey, Poland, and the Baltic states and a special agreement with the Epidemiological Commission of the League of Nations. Special communications agreements on rail transportation and postal services were made with Poland and the Baltic countries. Economic issues were mentioned in the peace treaty with Poland, the Rapallo Treaty, and the provisional agreements on diplomatic relations with Austria and Czechoslovakia. There are also many treaties to which the URSR was a partner with the RSFSR or other Soviet countries. Some of them were signed by the Russian government on Ukraine's behalf under the pretext of the so-called diplomatic union of Soviet republics. Some of the international treaties of the URSR were ratified by its constitutional organs; others came into effect without ratification. With the creation of the USSR Ukraine's treaty obligations were assumed by the Union institutions according to diplomatic notes from the URSR government (16 June 1923) and the USSR People's Commissariat of External Affairs (21 July 1923) to foreign governments.

From 1923 to 1944 the URSR did not have the power to conduct its own foreign policy and to conclude treaties. The constitutional changes of 1 February 1944 restored its right 'to have direct relations with other countries, enter into treaties with them, and exchange diplomatic and consular representations' (Art 15b, URSR Constitution). But that was not an exclusive or indivisible right, for the USSR reserved for itself the same right. The republics exercised the right only under the supervision of the Union organs. The only bilateral treaties signed by the URSR after 1944 were the resettlement agreement with the Polish Committee of National Liberation (9 September 1944) and the cooperation and relief agreement with the United Nations Relief and Rehabilitation Administration (18 December 1945). All other treaties affecting Ukraine's territory and economic and cultural relations with other countries were concluded by the USSR, not by the URSR – Czechoslovakia's surrender of Transcarpathia (26 June 1945), for example, and the settlement of the Ukrainian-Polish border (18 August 1945). The URSR was a separate participant with its own delegation in many multilateral treaties, however. It was a signatory of the *Paris Peace Treaties of 1947 with Bulgaria, Italy, Rumania, Hungary, and Finland. On 18 August 1948 it signed the Belgrade Convention on the use of the Danube River, but it turned down a seat on the Danube Commission.

The URSR signed and ratified the statutes of various *international organizations, such as the United Nations and its special bodies. As a member of those organizations the URSR signed many multilateral conventions. In 1953 it joined the convention on UN privileges and immunities, in 1958, the convention on slavery, and in 1948, the convention of the World Meteorological Organization. By 1956 the URSR had ratified 18 conventions (out of 110) of the International Labor Organization dealing with labor and social security. By the end of 1983 it had adopted 43 such conventions. The representatives of the URSR participated in the conferences of the World Health Organization and signed several treaties and protocols on health (1946). By signing the respective conventions the URSR became a member of the Universal Postal Union (1947) and the International Telecommunication Union (1947). In the 1950s the URSR joined several conventions on social questions: the Convention on the Political Rights of Women (1953), the Convention on the Prevention and the Punishment of the Crime of Genocide (1948, ratified by the URSR in 1955), the Supplementary Convention on the Abolition of Slavery, the Slave Trade, and Institutions and Practices Similar to Slavery (1956), and the Convention on the Nationality of Married Women (1957). The URSR was party to two important human rights treaties adopted in 1966 and put into effect in 1976: the International Covenant on Civil and Political Rights and the International Covenant on Economic, Social, and Cultural Rights. In that field Ukraine also signed the International Convention on the Elimination of All Forms of Racial Discrimination (1965) and a convention against apartheid (1974). Having become a member of UNESCO in 1954, the URSR participated in the preparation of its Convention on the Preservation of Cultural Property in the Event of Armed Conflict and adopted the convention along with the supplements. In the 1970s the URSR signed three conventions drafted by UNESCO as well as several technical conventions prepared by the Universal Postal Union and the International Telecommunication Union. In 1970 and 1971 the URSR ratified two conventions on the prevention of airplane hijacking, which were prepared by the International Civil Aviation Organization. The URSR was also party to three conventions proposed by the International Maritime Organization dealing with the improvement of maritime shipping (1965), the prevention of marine pollution by dumping waste and other matter (1972), and the safety of life at sea (1974). The URSR participated in the Red Cross conference in Stockholm that drafted a number of conventions dealing with the relief of the wounded and sick in armies of the field, the treatment of prisoners of war, the adapting of the principles of the Geneva convention of 1906 to maritime warfare, and the protection of civilians in wartime. Those conventions were ratified by the URSR in 1954. As a participant in the UN Conference on the Law of the Sea in

1958, the URSR helped codify and adopted three laws: on territorial sea and the contiguous zone, on the high seas, and on the continental shelf. In 1982 also it was a party to the UN Convention on the Law of the Sea. It participated in the codification of other branches of international law, such as the Vienna Convention on Diplomatic Relations (1961) and the Vienna Convention on Consular Relations (1963). The URSR was a signatory of several arms-limitation treaties: the Moscow treaty banning all but underground nuclear testing (August 1963), the treaty dealing with the principles of the activity of states in the exploration and use of outer space, the moon, and other celestial bodies (1967), the treaty prohibiting the emplacement of nuclear weapons and other weapons of mass destruction on the seabed and ocean floor (1971), and the convention against developing, producing, and stockpiling bacteriological and chemical weapons (1972).

The URSR Constitution did not stipulate who had the power to ratify or annul international treaties. Following the practice of the USSR government the Presidium of the Supreme Soviet of the URSR made those decisions. The peace treaties of 1947 were ratified only by the Presidium of the Supreme Soviet of the USSR, which noted that 'the ratification extends also to the URSR and the BSSR.' Ukraine's power to negotiate and ratify international treaties was exercised in fact by the USSR government, which decided when and how the URSR could pose as a separate entity in foreign affairs. It used the fiction of Ukraine's sovereignty to bolster Soviet influence in international diplomacy.

**Independent Ukraine.** After the referendum of 1 December 1991 confirming Ukraine's independence Ukraine won quick recognition from other countries and began to establish diplomatic relations with them. The United States exchanged notes with Ukraine on full diplomatic relations on 23 January 1992; it was followed by Canada on 27 January. By February 102 countries had recognized Ukraine, and 41 of them had exchanged notes on diplomatic relations. In the next three months Ukraine signed a treaty of friendship and co-operation with Turkey, agreements on economic and political co-operation with Iran, and agreements on unrestricted diplomatic travel, economic co-operation, and co-operation on environmental protection with the United States (see also *International legal status of Ukraine).

BIBLIOGRAPHY

Iakovliv, A. *Ukraïns'ko-moskovs'ki dohovory v XVII–XVIII st.* (Warsaw 1934)

Horak, S. *Ukraine in der internationalen Politik, 1917–1953* (Munich 1957)

Markus, V. *L' Ukraine Soviétique dans les relations internationales et son statut en Droit International, 1918–1923* (Paris 1959)

*Ukraïns'ka RSR u mizhnarodnykh vidnosynakh: Mizhnarodni dohovory, konventsiï, uhody ta inshi dokumenty* (Kiev 1959)

*Ukraïns'ka RSR na mizhnarodnii areni: Zbirnyk dokumentiv i materialiv 1944–1961 rr.* (Kiev 1963)

*Ukraïns'ka RSR na mizhnarodnii areni: Zbirnyk dokumentiv 1917–1923 rr.* (Kiev 1966)

*Ukraïns'ka RSR na mizhnarodnii areni: Zbirnyk dokumentiv i materialiv 1962–1970 rr.* (Kiev 1977)

*Ukraïns'ka RSR na mizhnarodnii areni: Zbirnyk dokumentiv i materialiv 1971–1975 rr.* (Kiev 1981)

*Ukraïns'ka RSR na mizhnarodnii areni: Zbirnyk dokumentiv i materialiv 1976–1980 rr.* (Kiev 1984)

*Ukraïns'ka RSR u mizhnarodno-dohovirnykh vidnosynakh: Zbirnyk dokumentiv 1966–1975 rr.* (Kiev 1985)

V. Markus

Pages from the *Trebnyk* of Metropolitan P. Mohyla (1646)

**Trebnyk.** A liturgical book that contains the services and prayers used for all the sacraments except Holy Orders and the Holy Eucharist. Called a Book of Needs or Sacramentarion, it is one of the most essential *liturgical books. The first translations into Church Slavonic were made in the 9th century. The most complete edition of the *trebnyk* includes the ritual for the blessing of a church, its furnishings, and appointments; the ritual for the blessing of holy objects; and blessings and prayers for specific needs. The shorter version contains the rituals for the administering of sacraments (baptism, marriage, anointing with oil, penance), the offices for the dead, and certain blessings used during the year.

The definitive version of the *trebnyk* used in the Ukrainian Orthodox Church was prepared by P. *Mohyla and published in 1646 (republ in Paris in 1988). This edition contains some 20 rituals not performed in other Eastern churches – eg, services for the uncovering of holy relics and for the blessing of monasteries – that were of local origin.

**Tree of heaven** (*Ailanthus altissima*; Ukrainian: *ailant vysokyi* or *kytaiskyi yasen*). A rapid-growing tree of the family Simaroubaceae, also known as the copal tree or the varnish tree. In Ukraine it is found in the southern and southwestern territory as a decorative tree in parks and as a protector against erosion for steep banks, ravines, and gullies.

**Treecreeper** (*Certhia*; Ukrainian: *pidkoryshnyk*). Small, slender, valuable birds of the family Certhidae or Climacteridae, with downcurved bills. Some treecreepers migrate in the winter, depending on the latitude. The birds nest behind loose tree bark or in tree cracks and feed on insects and spiders found in the trees. In Ukraine the common treecreeper (*C. familiaris*) inhabits the territory of Polisia, the forest-steppe, and the Carpathian and Crimean mountains; the short-toed creeper (*C. brachydactyla*) is found in Transcarpathia.

**Trefilov, Viktor,** b 6 August 1930 in Baku, Azerbaidzhan. Physicist and metallurgist; AN URSR (now ANU) corresponding member since 1973. A graduate of the Kiev

Viktor Trefilov

Polytechnical Institute (1952), he worked at the ANU Institute of Metal Physics (1955–73). Since 1973 he has directed the ANU Institute for Problems of Materials Science, and in 1974 he was elected a vice-president of the ANU. Trefilov has contributed to the physics of metals, materials science, the theory of the strength of materials, the theory of the plasticity of materials, and powder metallurgy. As a member of the CC CP(B)U in 1976–86, he influenced science policies and strove to impose the Russian language in all scientific communications in Ukraine.

**Trehubov, Yelysei,** b 1848 in Poltava, d 4 December 1921. Teacher and journalist. A graduate (1872) of Kiev University, he taught in Hlukhiv, Kursk, and Sumy before settling in Kiev in 1876. There he taught at the Galagan College, was involved with the Old Hromada, and worked closely with V. Naumenko in the publishing of *Kievskaia starina*. In 1918 he became involved in the early work of the Ukrainian Academy of Sciences.

**Trehubova, Valentyna,** b 15 May 1926 in Brovary, Kiev okruha. Porcelain artist. A graduate of the Lviv Institute of Applied and Decorative Arts (1954), she has worked at the Korosten Porcelain Factory as a sculptor of porcelain figurines. Many have folk themes, such as *Ukrainian Wedding* (1960), *Where Are You Going, Yavtush?* (1965), *Natalka from Poltava* (1966), and *Marusia Churai* (1978).

**Trembita.** A publishing house in Kolomyia, owned and directed by Z. Kurylovych (pseud: Bohdan Hryhorenko). From 1922 to 1929 it published popular literature, children's books, plays, and an annual almanac. Among the works published were Yu. Tiutiunnyk's memoirs of the 1919–20 Winter campaigns, A. Chaikivsky's novel *Oleksii Korniienko*, K. Polishchuk's novel *Otaman Zelenyi*, K. Kobersky's booklet on Ukrainian populism, O. Kuzma's Esperanto textbook, K. Verbytsky's Ukrainian-Esperanto dictionary, T. Shevchenko's *Kobzar*, B. Hrinchenko's brief history of Ukraine, and Ye. Yavorivsky's book on Greek and Roman mythology.

**Trembita.** A professional mixed chorus founded in Lviv in 1940. The group's first artistic director and conductor was D. Kotko, who was followed by P. Honcharov, O. Soroka, M. Kolessa, P. Muravsky, V. Vasylevych, Y. Vakhniak, V. Pekar, and (since 1978) I. Zhuk. The ensemble's repertoire includes the folk songs of Ukraine, contempo-

rary choral works, and classical music. The chorus has performed throughout the former USSR and has recorded on the Melodiya label.

*Trembita* players and other members of a Transcarpathian folk-instrument orchestra

**Trembita** (alpine horn). A wind instrument made from hollowed halves of spruce wood and bound with birch bark. Generally conical, with a metal or horn mouthpiece at the narrow end, 1 to 3 meters in length, it has a musical range of over two octaves. The sound is strong and can carry over 10 kilometers. The *trembita* is found mainly in the Carpathian region of Ukraine. It has served as a means of communication for people and herdsmen in isolated mountain areas, who would use a series of predetermined signals, especially to give notice of a death, a funeral, or a wedding. Occasionally the *trembita* is included in modern symphony orchestras as an exotic instrument.

**Trembovetsky, Apollon** [Trembovec'kyj] (pseud: Petro Pavlovych), b 27 February 1913 in Pidzamche, Kamianets-Podilskyi county, Podilia gubernia, d 1 March 1968 in Ortanna, Pennsylvania. Journalist and civic activist. A teacher by vocation, he witnessed the *Vinnytsia Massacre during the Second World War and wrote many books and articles about it, including *Zlochyn u Vinnytsi* (A Crime in Vinnytsia, 1973). After emigrating to the United States following the Second World War, he served for many years as president of the Democratic Alliance of Formerly Repressed Ukrainians from the Soviet Union and as vice-president of the Ukrainian Congress Committee of America. He also contributed articles to *Svoboda* and wrote a number of booklets about T. Shevchenko and M. Kotsiubynsky.

**Trembytsky, Isydor** [Trembyc'kyj], b 1847 in Stanyslaviv, Galicia, d 23 July 1922 in Rava Ruska, Galicia. Stage actor, director, and writer. He played in the Ruska Besida Theater in the 1870s, wrote the dramas *Obloha Plevny* (The Siege of Plevna, 1878) and *Na sviatoho Andriia* (On St Andrew's Day, 1880), and founded the H. Kvitka-Osnovianenko Literary-Dramatic Society in Kolomyia (1879).

**Trenton.** The capital (1980 pop 92,000, metropolitan area 308,000) of New Jersey, and an industrial center on the Delaware River. In 1980 there were about 2,000 Ukrainians in the area. Immigrants from Transcarpathia began to arrive in Trenton in the 1890s. By 1900 they had established a Greek Catholic parish, and by 1919 an Orthodox parish. In 1903 a branch of the Ruthenian (now Ukrainian) National Association was set up. St Josaphat's Catholic parish was founded in 1949. A large Ukrainian-American cultural center is situated on the south side of the city.

**Treshchakivsky, Lev** [Treščakivs'kyj], b 1810, d 1874. Greek Catholic priest and Galician civic leader. He was a member of the Supreme Ruthenian Council and the Halytsko-Ruska Matytsia society. In 1861–6 he served as deputy to the Galician Diet. His articles appeared in *Zoria halytska* and other papers. He also wrote the first Ukrainian handbook on beekeeping (1855).

**Tretiak, Józef,** b 28 September 1841 in Mali Biskupychi (now Novovolynske), Volodymyr-Volynskyi county, Volhynia gubernia, d 18 March 1923 in Cracow. Polish literary scholar and historian of Ukrainian origin; member of the Polish Academy of Sciences from 1888. During the Polish Insurrection of 1863–4 he was the rebel commander of Kiev. From 1867 to 1886 he lived in Lviv, where he worked as a Polish theater critic and teacher. He received a PH D from Lviv University. From 1894 to 1911 he was a professor of Ukrainian literature and language at Cracow University. His works with Ukrainian content include a study, in Ukrainian, of A. Mickiewicz's influence on T. Shevchenko (1892); monographs, in Polish, on J. Słowacki (2 vols, 1904), B. Zaleski (3 vols, 1911–14), and P. Skarga and the Church Union of Berestia (1912); a survey of Old Ruthenian poetry (1918); and a history of the Battle and Peace Treaty of Khotyn (1921).

**Tretiak, Oleh** [Tretjak], b 18 January 1939 in Pidkamin, Brody county, Galicia. Computer scientist, specialist in computer image processing. He studied at the Cooper Union (New York) and at the Massachusetts Institute of Technology (ScD, 1963). Since 1973 he has been on the faculty (professor, 1984) of the Department of Electrical and Computer Engineering at Drexel University in Philadelphia. He is currently director of the Drexel University Imaging and Computer Center. Tretiak has served as managing editor of *Information and Control* and as associate editor of IEEE *Transactions on Medical Imaging*. He has made major contributions to computed tomography, biomedical image processing, and quantitative autoradiography.

**Tretiak, Vasyl** [Tretjak, Vasyl'], b 6 December 1926 in Komarivka (now in Kursk oblast RF), d 16 April 1989. Opera singer (dramatic tenor). He graduated from the Kharkiv State Conservatory in 1958, and from 1962 was a soloist of the Kiev Theater of Opera and Ballet.

**Tretiak, Vladislav** [Tretjak], b 25 April 1952 in Orudevo, Moscow oblast, Russian SFSR. Soviet hockey goalkeeper of Ukrainian descent. Since 1971 he has played lead goalkeeper on Soviet hockey teams in international competitions; he won gold medals at the 1972 and 1976 Olympic Games and has won the world championship 10 times.

**Tretiakov, Dmytro** [Tret'iakov], b 5 November 1878 in Shumorovo, Mologa county, Yaroslavl gubernia, Russia, d 26 September 1950 in Kiev. Zoologist and morphologist; full member of the AN URSR (now ANU) from 1929. A graduate of St Petersburg University (1900), he was a professor at Odessa University (1912–41) and founder and director of its Scientific Research Institute of Zoology (1930–41). He worked at the ANU Institute of Zoology in Ufa (1941–4) and was its director (1944–8), and taught at Kiev University (1944–8). His research was in the fields of histology, comparative anatomy, and phylogeny.

**Tretiakov, Robert** [Tretjakov], b 26 February 1936 in Perm, Russia. Ukrainian poet of Russian origin. He graduated with a degree in journalism from Kiev University in 1985 and worked on the editorial boards of various newspapers in Kharkiv and the journal *Prapor* (now *Berezil*). His first published work appeared in 1955. His collections of verse include *Zorianist'* (Starriness, 1961), *Palitra* (Palette, 1965), *Portrety* (Portraits, 1967), *Poeziï* (Poems, 1971), *Osinnie skresalo* (Autumnal Thaw, 1980), and *Poeziï* (Poems, 1986).

**Trial by jury.** A court proceeding in which, besides a judge, a body of ordinary citizens known as the jury takes part. Trial by jury originated in England and spread from there to the United States. In the 19th century it became widely accepted in Europe. The jury does not play an active role in the trial; it follows the proceedings and, at the end, makes a judgment on the guilt or innocence of the defendant. Depending on the verdict, the judge or judges determine the punishment. Jurors do not serve continuously but only for limited terms.

Trial by jury was introduced in Russian-ruled Ukraine with the judicial reform of 1864. It was compulsory for serious criminal offenses punishable by over 10 years' imprisonment or by death, and for political and religious crimes. In the early 20th century, doubts about the institution's usefulness arose, and the powers of the jury were gradually reduced. Efforts were made to exclude the jury from political trials. One of the strongest defenders of the institution in Ukraine was O. *Kistiakovsky.

In Austrian-ruled Ukraine, trial by jury was introduced in 1873 for political crimes, illegal publications, and other crimes punishable by over 10 years' imprisonment or by death.

In Ukrainian territories under Polish rule, trial by jury was grounded in the Polish Constitution of 1921 and the Austrian criminal law that continued to be binding in Galicia. The Polish Criminal Code of 1928 also provided for jury trials, but they were abolished a few years later, and the new constitution did not mention them.

In Rumanian-ruled Ukrainian territories, trial by jury was practiced until 1936. In Czechoslovakia, juries were also abolished in the 1930s. The abolition of trial by jury reflected the theoretical argument that jurors who are unfamiliar with the law cannot render a fair verdict.

In the USSR, trial by jury was considered to be 'bourgeois.' Citizen participation in the court system was limited to so-called *people's assessors, who sat with the professional judges on all courts of first instance. Although assessors had the same rights as judges, they were in practice dependent on them.

A. Bilynsky

**Trial by ordeal.** A primitive way of determining the truth of a claim or accusation, based on the belief that the outcome reflects the judgment of some divine power. Usually known in Ukrainian as *sud Bozhyi* (divine trial), such trials were first mentioned in *Ruskaia Pravda*. The ordeal can take several forms. In Ukraine the most common form was casting lots, submersion in cold water, or burning by hot iron. From the 13th century the *duel was accepted as a form of trial by ordeal. Swearing an oath on the Bible or kissing a cross could also be considered a form of trial by ordeal. Ordeals were used only when it was difficult to establish a person's guilt or innocence. They were practiced in Ukraine as late as the 17th century.

**Trial of the 59** (aka Trial of the Second OUN Executive in the Western Oblasts of Ukraine). The trial of a group consisting of university students (the majority of the defendants), Rev R. Berest, and several leading OUN members (A. Berezovsky, D. Kliachkivsky, M. Kovaliuk, B. Kunytsky, I. Maksymiv, M. Matiichuk, and S. Nyrka), held in Lviv at the NKVD headquarters on 17–19 January 1941. The charges included treason and preparation for an uprising. The defendants, most of whom were active in the OUN resistance to the Soviets, had been arrested during September 1940. Their defense counsel included R. Kryshtalsky, V. Zhovnir, and I. Skybinsky. The court sentenced 42 of the defendants, including 11 women, to death and the others to 10 years of hard labor. In February the Supreme Court of the Ukrainian SSR confirmed the death sentences, but in March the Supreme Soviet of the USSR commuted the death sentences of 10 women and 11 men to 25 and 15 years of hard labor. The rest were executed. Those sentenced to labor camp were deported to Omsk in March. On 20–21 June 1941 the remaining prisoners, except for four sick women, were taken to Berdychiv. When German troops approached the town the guards set the prison on fire. The inmates broke down the doors and tried to escape but were forced back by gunfire. Two were killed; the survivors emerged from the prison after the guards had fled.

**Trial of the Union for the Liberation of Ukraine.** See Union for the Liberation of Ukraine.

**Trianon, Treaty of.** A treaty concluded on 4 June 1920 at the Grand Trianon Palace in Versailles between Hungary and the Allies. Under the terms of the treaty Hungary was compelled to cede Transcarpathia and Slovakia, which would form part of the republic of Czechoslovakia. In addition Hungary surrendered territory to Rumania, Yugoslavia, and Austria. The Treaty of Trianon became effective on 26 July 1921. After the Second World War the territorial delimitations of the Trianon Treaty were confirmed by the Paris Peace Treaty of 1947.

**Triasylo, Taras.** See Fedorovych, Taras.

**Tribe.** A group of people with a common language, culture, and way of life and a tradition of common descent. Larger societies that are unified by a state and have lost the sense of kinship are not called tribes. For many millennia before the rise of Kievan Rus', Ukraine was inhabited by various tribes. They engaged mostly in agriculture and animal husbandry and held an animistic view of the world. By the 6th century AD a number of proto-Ukrainian tribes had emerged, including the *Polianians, *Siverianians, *Derevlianians, *Dulibians (later known as Buzhanians and Volhynians), *White Croatians, *Ulychians, and *Tivertsians. They traded among themselves and with their neighbors. The tribes generally were ruled by an assembly (*viche*) of all the free men and the elders elected by it. They themselves did not establish a common state. It was the foreign *Varangians who, in the mid-9th century, laid the foundation of the Rus' state by bringing the tribes under their rule. Eventually dynastic ties and a sense of national identity superseded tribal loyalties.

**Tributary peasants** (*seliany-dannyky*). The largest group of *pokhozhi peasants in the Lithuanian-Ruthenian state, Volhynia, and the Kiev region during the 15th and 16th centuries. They lived on state or private lands that were mostly forested, and their primary activities were hunting, fishing, and beekeeping. They also mined ores, coal, and salt. Besides a *tribute (*danyna*) in kind (eg, furs, honey) they paid a monetary tribute (*serebshchyna*) for the use of cultivated land and performed various services for the landowner, including harvesting and tilling. In 1588 the status of tributary peasants was changed to that of state or landowner's serfs (see *Serfdom).

**Tribute** (*danyna*). A direct tax paid by subjects (*piddani*) to the state. In ancient times Slavic tribes paid a tribute to their conquerors. Later the tribute became a permanent ongoing duty to the state. In Kievan Rus' the units of *taxation were the household (*dym*) and the farming family (*ralo*). In the 13th century a head tribute was introduced by the Tatars, who conducted a census. Persons obliged to pay the tribute were known as *danski liudy* (tribute people) or *dannyky* (tributors); they were registered in tribute books by the volost in which they lived. The tribute was paid with money or in kind (eg, bread, honey, furs, livestock). During the period of the Lithuanian-Ruthenian state the tribute was paid to the princes and the grand dukes, who collected it by traveling around their realms (*poliuddia*). Beginning in the 15th century the tribute was exacted by landowners, and labor was added to the possible forms of tribute; peasants provided the labor, for example, for road building and maintenance. Under the Hetman state the peasants and burghers paid tribute, which was spent on the administration of the Hetmanate and local governments and was also sent to the tsar in Moscow. (See also *Land tenure system and *Quitrent.)

**Trident** (*tryzub*). The official coat of arms of Ukraine is a gold trident on an azure background. As a state emblem the trident dates back to Kievan Rus', when it was the coat of arms of the Riuryk dynasty. There are various theories about its origins and meaning. A trident was the symbol of Poseidon, the sea god of Greek mythology. It has been found in different societies, such as the Bosporan and Pontic kingdoms, the Greek colonies on the Black Sea, Byzantium, Scandinavia, and Sarmatia, and has been used in various ways: as a religious and military emblem, a heraldic symbol, a state emblem, a monogram, and simply a decorative design. The oldest examples of the trident discovered by archeologists on Ukrainian territory date back to the 1st century AD. At that time the trident probably served as a symbol of power in one of the tribes that later became part of the Ukrainian people. The trident was

Depiction of a trident on a tile unearthed at the site of the Church of the Tithes in Kiev

The tridents of the great and small coats of arms and great seal of the UNR

stamped on the gold and silver coins issued by Prince Volodymyr the Great (980–1015), who perhaps inherited the symbol from his ancestors as a dynastic coat of arms and passed it on to his sons, Sviatopolk I (1015–19) and Yaroslav the Wise (1019–54). Iziaslav Yaroslavych (1054–78), Sviatopolk II Iziaslavych (1093–1113), and Lev Danylovych (1264–1301) used the bident as their coat of arms. Although the trident continued to be used by some ruling families as a dynastic coat of arms until the 15th century, it was replaced as a state emblem in the 12th century with the Archangel Michael. The trident was also used as a religious symbol in Ukrainian folklore and church heraldry.

arms of the UNR. By that act the UNR leaders linked the modern Ukrainian state with the medieval state of Kievan Rus'. The Great and Minor state emblems of the UNR were designed by V. Krychevsky. The trident also appeared on the UNR bank notes, which were designed by H. Narbut, O. Krasovsky, V. Modzalevsky, Krychevsky, and others. It was retained as the official coat of arms by the Hetman government and the Directory. The trident with a crossed middle arm was confirmed on 18 July 1918 as the emblem of the Black Sea Fleet. On 15 March 1939 the Diet of Carpatho-Ukraine adopted the trident with a cross as its official coat of arms. On 19 February 1992, after the restoration of Ukraine's independence in 1991, the Supreme Council accepted the trident as the chief element in the state coat of arms.

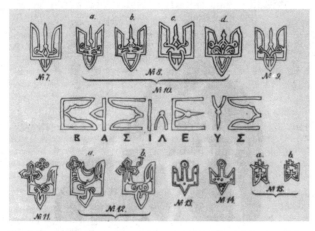

The tridents on the various coins minted in Kievan Rus' and, in the middle, trident shapes and letters laid out to spell 'Basileus,' the Greek title used by all eastern rulers

The gold trident on a blue shield adopted as Ukraine's small coat of arms by the Supreme Council of Ukraine on 19 February 1992

The trident appeared not only on coins but also on the bricks of the Church of the Tithes in Kiev (986–96), the tiles of the Dormition Cathedral in Volodymyr-Volynskyi (1160), and the stones of other churches, castles, and palaces. It was also used as a decorative element on ceramics, weapons, rings, medallions, seals, and manuscripts. Because of its wide use in Rus' the trident evolved in many directions without losing its basic structure. Some of the variations include the bident, the trident with a cross on one of the arms or at the side, and the trident with a halfmoon. Almost 200 medieval variations on the trident have been discovered.

At M. Hrushevsky's recommendation Prince Volodymyr's trident was adopted by the Little Rada (12 February 1918) and the Central Rada (22 March 1918) as the coat of

Various versions of the trident are used by Ukrainian organizations: supporters of the Hetman regime and certain affiliates of the Ukrainian Catholic church use a trident with a cross, nationalist organizations use a trident with a sword in the middle (designed by R. Lisovsky), and the Ukrainian Native Faith church has incorporated the trident into its blazing sun emblem.

BIBLIOGRAPHY

Pasternak, O. *Poiasnennia tryzuba, herba Velykoho Kyïvs'koho Kniazia Volodymyra Sviatoho* (Uzhhorod 1934; repr, Kiev 1991)
Skotyns'kyi, T. *Ukraïns'kyi herb ta prapor* (Lviv 1935)
Andrusiak, M. *Tryzub* (Munich 1947)
Sichyns'kyi, V. *Ukraïns'kyi tryzub i prapor* (Winnipeg 1953)
Lebedynsky, Ya. *L'origine et l'histoire du trident ukrainien* (Paris 1982)

A. Zhukovsky

**Trident Press** (Vydavnycha spilka Tryzub). One of the major Ukrainian publishing houses in Canada. Originally called the Ukrainian Publishing Company of Canada, the Trident Press was established in Winnipeg in 1909 by Ukrainian bilingual teachers to publish the newspaper *Ukraïns'kyi holos*. By 1918 the newspaper and the press were identified with the nascent Ukrainian Orthodox Church of Canada. Other Trident Press publications include *Visnyk* (organ of the Ukrainian Orthodox church), *Promin'* (organ of the Ukrainian Women's Association of Canada), and books in Ukrainian and English, including many works on Ukrainian-Canadian themes. In 1973 Trident Press bought out the rival *Kanadiis'kyi farmer*.

**Trier Psalter** (Trirskyi psaltyr). A medieval Latin literary and artistic monument written and illuminated in the late 10th century for Archbishop Egbert of Trier. The psalter was later brought to Rus' by Gertrude, the daughter of King Bolesław II of Poland and the wife of Grand Prince Iziaslav Yaroslavych of Kiev. In 1078–87 five illuminated miniatures were added to the book: a portrayal of Iziaslav's son Yaropolk and Yaropolk's wife, Kunigunde, praying to St Peter, by one artist; depictions of Christ's Nativity, the Crucifixion, and Christ crowning (marrying) Yaropolk and Kunigunde, by another artist; and a miniature of the Theotokos, by a third artist. The miniatures were done in either Lutske, Volodymyr-Volynskyi, or, most likely, St James's Monastery on the Danube. They are similar in style and motifs to those in the *Izbornik* of Sviatoslav (1073) in their combination of folk ornamentation with the features of Byzantine-Rus' and Romanesque illumination. The psalter is now in Italy.

**Trinity Cathedral** (Troitskyi sobor). A monument of Ukrainian wooden architecture in Novomoskovske (formerly Novoselytsia), Dnipropetrovske oblast. It was built in 1775–80 by Ya. Pohrebniak and financed by leaders of the Zaporozhian Sich (Otaman I. Chepiha, A. Holovaty), other Cossacks, and the cathedral elders. The 27 × 27 m structure is the only wooden church in Ukraine consisting of nine sections, each topped with a three-tier dome. Its central dome is the highest (approx 65 m). It is surrounded by four slightly lower domes separated from each other by still lower domes. The church was repaired in 1830 and renovated in 1888 with some basic changes: the interior walls no longer sloped toward the center, the form of the domes and arches was simplified, and the rotten vertical planking was replaced by horizontal planking.

**Trinity Church in Pakul** (Troitska tserkva). A masterpiece of the Chernihiv school of wooden architecture, built by an unidentified master builder in 1710 in the village of Pakul, now in Chernihiv raion, Chernihiv oblast. The church no longer exists. Its five pine-log frames, standing on a cruciform ground plan (21.5 × 17.5 m), had two tiers and were connected internally by carved arches 10 m high. The church's height (including the crosses at the top) reached 31 m. To create the illusion of greater height the builder had sloped the interior walls inward at an incline of 5–6 cm per m of height. The door frames, cornices, and parapets of the choir balcony were decorated with carvings. The technical and artistic design of the church's inner space had no parallel among the world masterpieces of wooden architecture.

The Trinity Church in Pakul

**Trinity–Saint Elijah's Monastery** (Troitsko-Illinskyi manastyr). An Orthodox monastery situated in Chernihiv. It is believed to have been founded in 1069 by St Anthony of the Caves and situated beside the late 12th-century St Elijah's Church. It was sacked by the Tatars in 1239 and not rebuilt until the mid-17th century. Reconstruction of St Elijah's Church started in 1646 under the patronage of the colonel of Chernihiv, S. Pobodailo. Buildings added later included the baroque-style Trinity Cathedral in 1679–95 (funded by the Chernihiv colonel V. Dunyn-Borkovsky and Hetman I. Mazepa), refectories, the Church of the Presentation (1677), monks' cells (1670s–1680s and 1750s–1780s), a baroque bell tower (1775), and a surrounding wall (early 18th century). From 1679 the monastery housed the *Chernihiv printing press. The monastery was closed down in 1799 and converted into the residence of the bishop of Chernihiv. It served that function until it was closed by the Soviet regime in the 1920s.

**Trinkler, Mykola,** b 19 November 1859 in St Petersburg, d 10 August 1925 in Kharkiv. Surgeon. A graduate of Kharkiv University (1883), he taught there (as professor from 1905) and at the Kharkiv Medical Institute (from 1921). He researched aseptic methods in surgery, traumatology, neurosurgery, and oncology. His publications include a handbook on treating syphilitic wounds of the internal organs (1926).

Title page of the Triodion printed by the Kievan Cave Monastery Press in 1640

**Triodion** (Ukrainian: *triod*), from the Greek word for 'three odes.' A liturgical book used in the Orthodox and Eastern Catholic churches on the 10 Sundays before Easter and on all the other days of Lent and the Easter period. It contains canons having usually only three odes instead of the regular nine – hence its name. In the Ukrainian church two triodia are used. The *triod pisna* (lenten triodion) contains religious songs, mostly of a penitential nature, that are sung during Lent. The *triod' tsvitna* (floral triodion or Pentekostarion) contains liturgical services performed from Palm Sunday to Easter Sunday, on Pentecost, and on All Saints' Sunday. Some of the oldest Slavic incunabula were triodia (eg, those printed by S. Fiol in Cracow ca 1491). They were frequently printed in Ukraine (eg, in Kiev in 1627, 1631, and 1640 and in Lviv in 1642 and after). In the 17th and 18th centuries the text of the Ukrainian triodion differed from that of the Russian.

*Trisetum* (Ukrainian: *tryshchetynnyk*). A widely distributed genus of perennial tufted forage grasses in the family Gramineae that grows in meadows, in glades, and on rocky slopes. Some species are valuable hay and pasture plants. In Ukraine *T. sibiricum* and *T. flavescens* are found, predominantly in the Carpathian Mountains.

**Trofimenko, Swiatoslaw** [Trofymenko, Svjatoslav], b 15 December 1931 in Lviv. Ukrainian-American organic and inorganic chemist. A graduate of Wesleyan (1955) and Northwestern (PH D, 1958) universities, he has held various positions at the Du Pont Co since 1959. He is a member of the Shevchenko Scientific Society and the Ukrainian Academy of Arts and Sciences in the US and chemistry editor of the *Encyclopedia of Ukraine*. His research areas include cyanocarbons, heterocycles, boron chemistry, cyclometallation (a term he coined), catalysis, and co-ordination chemistry. The author of 90 publications and 30 patents, he discovered new heterocycles (pyrazaboles) and is best known for the discovery and development of the polypyrazolylborate ligand system, which has been used worldwide.

**Trofymovych, Teofan** [Trofymovyč], b ?, d ca 1736. Writer. After graduating from the Kievan Mohyla Academy (1725) he taught poetics there. In 1736 he became archimandrite of Moscow's Zaikonospasskii Monastery and rector of its Slavonic-Greek-Latin Academy. It has been conjectured that he, instead of T. Prokopovych or I. Nerunovych, is the author of *Mylost' Bozhiia Ukrainy ... svobodyvshaia*.

**Troian.** A deity of the ancient Slavs who was worshiped in Kievan Rus'. He is mentioned alongside Khors, Perun, and Veles in old Ukrainian literature. His place in mythology has never been adequately explained. Some scholars believe that he was the god of the moon, night, and building (S. Plachynda), of the sun (Ya. Borovsky), and of war (M. Andrusiak). B. Kravtsiv claimed he was the highest deity in ancient Ukraine. Other scholars deny the existence of such a deity and hold that the name belongs to the Roman emperor Trajan (Ya. Hamza) or to the triumvirate of Rus' princes – Iziaslav, Vsevolod, and Sviatoslav (S. Pushyk).

Kornylo Troian

**Troian, Kornylo** [Trojan], b 26 August 1885 in Sydoriv, Husiatyn county, Galicia, d 5 March 1959 in New York. Lawyer and civic and political leader. A veteran of the Austrian army in the First World War, he completed his law studies in 1921 and opened his own law office in Khodoriv (Bibrka county) in 1924. There he also set up a branch of the Prosvita society, a county co-operative union, and a Ridna Shkola circle. As a candidate of the Ukrainian National Democratic Alliance and a member of its presidium (1925–6) he won election to the Polish Senate in 1928 and to the Polish Sejm in 1935. After the Second World War he worked as a refugee in the law department of the Central Representation of the Ukrainian Emigration in Germany. He moved to the United States in 1952.

*Troisti muzyky* (trio musicians). A trio ensemble of folk instruments consisting of violin, basolia (folk violoncello), and frame drum. In Western Ukraine the *tsymbaly* (cimbalom) was commonly used instead of the basolia. On occasion the *sopilka* (fipple flute) replaced the violin as the leading instrument. The trio ensemble arose after the violin was introduced into Ukraine early in the 1600s, and became widespread by the end of the 17th century. Until the beginning of the 20th century *troisti muzyky* provided most of the musical entertainment on feast days, and at weddings, birthdays, social gatherings, and fairs. Their repertoire consisted of dance music and folk songs. Today the tradition is maintained by musicians in such ensembles as the Kiev Orchestra of Folk Instruments.

*Troisti muzyky*

Karpo Trokhymenko: *Above the Great Route* (oil, 1926)

**Troitske** [Trojic'ke]. IV-19. A town smt (1986 pop 7,600) and raion center in Luhanske oblast. It originated in the 1740s as a small herding settlement called Kalnivka or Kalynivka. From 1815 it was known as the *sloboda* Novotroitska, and from the 1870s, as Troitske village. In 1957 it was promoted to smt status, and in 1961 it was amalgamated with Tsyhanivka village. Troitske has an oil-pressing mill, a canning factory, and a dairy.

**Troitsky, Ivan** [Trojic'kyj], b 22 October 1854 in Chernihiv gubernia, d 17 March 1923 in Katerynoslav. Pediatrician. A graduate of Kiev University (1878), he was a professor at Kharkiv University (1903–19), head of the pediatrics department of the Katerynoslav Medical Institute (1920–3), and the founding president of the Kiev (1900–2) and Kharkiv (1912) societies of pediatricians. He helped organize the first International Conference of Pediatricians (1912) and wrote *Kurs lektsii o bolezniakh detskogo vozrasta* (A Course of Lectures on Childhood Diseases, 1887, 1888–9) and *Gigiena detskogo vozrasta* (Childhood Hygiene, 1912).

**Trokhymenko, Karpo** [Troxymenko], b 25 October 1885 in Sushchany, Vasylkiv county, Kiev gubernia, d 1 October 1979 in Kiev. Painter. He studied at the Kiev Art School (1902–10), the Moscow School of Painting, Sculpture, and Architecture (1906–7), and under M. Samokysh at the St Petersburg Academy of Arts (1910–16). He worked in Kiev as an instructor for the Commission for the Protection of Historical and Artistic Monuments (1918–20) and taught at the Kiev Art School (1918–19), the Kiev Artistic-Industrial Professional School and Kiev Art Tekhnikum (1926–33), and the Kiev State Art Institute (1933–74). He belonged to the Association of Artists of Red Ukraine (1926–32) and became vice-chairman of the Arts Council of the Ministry of Education. Trokhymenko worked in watercolors, oils, and pencil. He painted mu-

rals in the church at the Swedish Grave in Poltava; realistic historical scenes, such as *Cossacks' Supper at Their Battle Posts* (1917); and landscapes such as *The Dnieper from Ivanova Mountain* (1926), *The Dnieper and the Museum from Chernecha Mountain* (1953), and *Barley in Bloom* (1965). He also created Soviet genre paintings. T. Shevchenko and his works inspired his canvases *Shevchenko and Engelhardt* (1939), *Kateryna* (1954), and *Shevchenko on Chernecha Mountain* (1954). Books about Trokhymenko have been written by P. Musiienko (1946) and I. Vrona (1957), and an album of his works was published in 1969.

**Trokhymenko, Klym** [Troxymenko], b 5 February 1898 in Pekarshchyna, Zhytomyr county, Volhynia gubernia, d 12 May 1979 in Philadelphia. Primitivist painter. After the First World War he was a businessman and art collector in Lviv. A postwar émigré, he settled in the United States in 1950. He began painting at the age of 45. His works have simplified, often nonrealistic forms and strong, clashing colors. They have been exhibited in solo and group exhibitions in Detroit (1960), Munich (1971), New York, and Toronto (1972).

**Trokhymovsky, Mykhailo** [Troxymovs'kyj, Myxajlo], b 1739 in Bezuhlivka, near Nizhen, d 3 October 1813 in Velyki Sorochyntsi, Myrhorod county, Poltava gubernia. Physician; corresponding member of the St Petersburg Medico-Surgical Academy. After being educated at the Kievan Mohyla Academy (1752–61) and the Medical School of the St Petersburg Army Hospital (1761–3), he served as an army doctor in Ukraine and took part in the Russo-Turkish War (1768–74). In 1772 he was appointed physician for Myrhorod county. He maintained a hospital at his own expense. He wrote on hydrotherapy, female infertility, and Crimean flora.

**Trolleybus transport.** See Urban transit.

**Tronko, Petro** [Tron'ko], b 12 July 1915 in Zabrody, Bohodukhiv county, Kharkiv gubernia. Communist party and Soviet government leader, and historian; AN URSR (now ANU) full member since 1978. A graduate of Kiev University (1948) and the Party Academy of Social Sci-

Petro Tronko

ences in Moscow (1951), he worked as an educator (1932–7) and Komsomol leader (1937–47) and then rose in the Party to the positions of secretary in charge of propaganda and agitation in the CC CPU (1960–1) and CC member (1961–78). He has been deputy chairman of the Ukrainian Council of Ministers, head of the Soviet Ukrainian delegation at the UN General Assembly (1965), and chairman of the Ukrainian Society for the Protection of Historical and Cultural Monuments (since 1967). At the ANU he has served as vice-president (1978–9), head of the regional history department in the Institute of History, and chairman of the regional studies council (since 1982). Tronko has written books on the Ukrainian Komsomol during the Second World War (1957, 1960, 1968), on culture (1977), and on 'socialist' Kiev (1982) and over 300 articles. He was a coauthor of histories of the Ukrainian Komsomol (1967; 4th edn 1978) and of Ukraine during the Second World War (1967, 1977). He has edited collections of documents and materials on the Kiev region in 1917–20 (1957, 1962) and during the Second World War (1963), and books on the 1768 Koliivshchyna rebellion (1970) and Kiev's Arsenal plant (1986). He was chief editor of the monumental history of Ukraine's cities and villages (26 vols, 1967–74) and its Russian translation, of the journal *Pam'iatky Ukraïny* (1985–8), and of a detailed reference guide to Ukraine's historical and cultural monuments (1987).

**Troparion** (*tropar*), from the Greek *tropos*. A short liturgical hymn that traditionally has been sung or chanted, and now is usally recited, in the Orthodox and Eastern Catholic churches. Stanzas of the kontakion (Ukrainian: *kondak*) and canon, other types of liturgical hymns sung since the 8th century, are also called troparia. Troparia vary in length from one or two verses to long poems. Many troparia glorifying native saints (eg, St Olha, St Volodymyr) were composed in Ukraine.

**Tropinin, Vasilii,** b 30 March 1776 or 1780 in Karpovo, Novgorod gubernia, Russia, d 15 May 1857 in Moscow. Russian painter. He was born a serf and was sent to study at the St Petersburg Academy of Arts (1798–1804). He then lived on his owner's estate in Kukavka, Mohyliv county, Podilia gubernia (1804–12, 1818–21), where he painted icons and portraits of Ukrainian peasants, such as *A Girl from Podilia, Peasant Woman, Ustym Karmeliuk, Wedding in Kukavka*, and *Young Ukrainian Peasant*. In 1823 he was given his freedom, and in 1824 he moved to Moscow and was elected a member of the Academy of Arts.

Vasilii Tropinin: *Portrait of Ustym Karmeliuk* (oil, early 19th century)

**Tropotianka** (aka *tropak*). A lively folk dance in 2/4 time performed by eight or more couples. It is popular in Transcarpathia.

**Troshchanovsky, Arkadii** [Troščanovs'kyj, Arkadij], b 21 January 1914 in Simianivka, Konotip county, Chernihiv gubernia, d 10 May 1986 in Zaporizhia. Heroic and character stage and film actor and director. He completed study in the drama studio at the Moscow Ukrainian Theater of the RSFSR (1934) and then worked in theaters in Rivne and Kharkiv (1935–41) and directed in the Zaporizhian Ukrainian Music and Drama Theater (1942–77). He acted in the film *Rodyna Kotsiubyns'kykh* (The Kotsiubynsky Family, 1970).

**Troshchenko, Valerii** [Troščenko, Valerij], b 15 May 1929 in Sreplevo, near Smolensk, Russia. Scientist in the field of mechanics; full member of the ANU (formerly AN URSR) since 1979. He studied at the Kiev Polytechnical Institute and worked in 1955–66 at the ANU Institute of Metal Ceramics and Special Alloys (now the Institute for Problems of Materials Science). Since 1966 he has been assistant director and department head at the ANU Institute for Problems of the Strength of Materials. His main contributions are in the areas of the strength of materials at high temperatures, the fatigue phenomena of materials and structures, and the reliability of machines and structures.

**Troshchynsky** [Troščyns'kyj]. A family line of Cossack officers and noblemen, originally from the Bila Tserkva region. At the behest of Hetman I. Mazepa they resettled in

Left-Bank Ukraine in the late 17th century. Vasyl Troshchynsky (Trushchynsky) was one of a group of noblemen from Bila Tserkva county who stayed and swore allegiance to the tsar of Muscovy in 1654. His descendant (son or grandson) Stepan *Troshchynsky was colonel of Hadiache regiment. Stepan's son, Andrii Troshchynsky, was head of the General Military Chancellery in 1716–25 and a fellow of the standard in 1725–40. Stepan's great-grandson was Dmytro *Troshchynsky. Dmytro's nephew, Andrii (b 1774, d 1852), was a general in the imperial army and a relative of N. Gogol. The Troshchynsky family line declined in the late 19th century.

**Troshchynsky, Dmytro** [Troščyns'kyj], b 1749 in Hlukhiv, Nizhen regiment, d 1829 in Kybyntsi, Myrhorod county, Poltava gubernia. Official of the Russian imperial government and patron of Ukrainian culture. After graduating from the Kievan Mohyla Academy he worked in the Little Russian Collegium (1766), fought in the Russo-Turkish War of 1768–74, and served on Prince N. Repnin's staff. Upon moving to St Petersburg he rose from director of Count O. Bezborodko's office (1784) to state secretary (1793) and senator. He was rewarded by Alexander I for his part in the plot against Paul I with an appointment to the State Council and the directorship of the imperial postal board. After serving as minister of appanages (1802–6) he returned to his estate and was elected marshal of the nobility in Poltava gubernia (1812–14). During Napoleon's invasion he helped raise troops and then was minister of justice (1814–17). After retiring to his Kybyntsi estate Troshchynsky turned it into a Ukrainian cultural and political center, called the Ukrainian Athens by his contemporaries. He shared the autonomist aspirations of his colleagues V. Kapnist, P. Koropchevsky, and M. Myklashevsky and supported or encouraged Ukrainian scholars such as Ya. Markovych and V. Lomykovsky, writers such as Kapnist, V. Hohol-Yanovsky, and A. Rodzianko, painters such as V. Borovykovsky, and composers such as A. Vedel. He acted through his friend O. Kamenetsky to get I. Kotliarevsky's *Eneïda* (The Aeneid, 1798) published. At his estate he set up a large library of over 4,000 titles and a private theater run (from 1812) by Hohol-Yanovsky, assisted by Kapnist. According to recent research Troshchynsky headed a clandestine circle of Ukrainian autonomists in the late 18th and early 19th centuries and maintained contacts with opposition circles in the military through his relative Gen P. Bilukha-Kokhanovsky, the brothers F. and V. Lukashevych, and other participants in the Smolensk conspiracy of 1798. He assigned great importance to the organization of Ukrainian military units; hence, he supported Kapnist's project for a Cossack regiment in 1788 and the Cossack mobilization in Left-Bank Ukraine in 1812.

BIBLIOGRAPHY
Ohloblyn, O. *Liudy Staroï Ukraïny* (Munich 1959)
Saunders, D. *The Ukrainian Impact on Russian Culture, 1750–1850* (Edmonton 1985)

A. Zhukovsky

**Troshchynsky, Stepan** [Troščyns'kyj], b ?, d 1709 in Kiev. Cossack officer. A relative of I. Mazepa, he was a military fellow (from 1693), an official of the Hetmanate court and keeper of the Hadiache jail (1690–7), and quartermaster (1697–1704) and colonel (1704–8) of Hadiache regiment. He undertook a number of diplomatic representations for Mazepa, including a mission to the Sich in 1693. His regiment was in Right-Bank Ukraine in 1708 and was unable to join Mazepa's forces at the start of hostilities against Russia. Troshchynsky was arrested by the Russian authorities, and died in prison.

**Trostianets** [Trostjanec']. III-15. A city (1989 pop 25,400) on the Boromlia River and a raion center in Sumy oblast. It was founded in the early 17th century by Cossacks from Right-Bank Ukraine. From 1780 the village belonged to Okhtyrka county of Kharkiv vicegerency, which was reorganized into Slobidska Ukraine gubernia in 1797 and into Kharkiv gubernia in 1835. From 1877 a railway line connected Trostianets with Kharkiv and Sumy and stimulated its industrial growth. In 1940 it was granted city status. Today it has an electric-appliance factory, a sugar refinery, a chocolate factory, and a lumber and woodworking plant. It is the home of a forestry research station of the Ukrainian Scientific Research Institute of Forest Management and Agroforest Amelioration.

**Trostianets** [Trostjanec]. V-10. A town smt (1986 pop 7,900) on the Trostianets River and a raion center in Vinnytsia oblast. It was first mentioned in historical documents in 1598, when it belonged to the Polish Commonwealth. In 1793 it was annexed by Russia, and became part of Bratslav county in Podilia gubernia. In 1957 the village was granted smt status. It has a distillery, a mixed-feed factory, a dairy, and a meat-packing complex.

**Trostianets Dendrological Park** [Trostjanec']. A dendrological park in Trostianets, Ichnia raion, Chernihiv oblast, 205 ha in size and administered by the ANU. The park was constructed starting in 1834 by the estate owner I. Skoropadsky (1805–87), who made its development a lifelong undertaking (he was even buried there). The original site consisted of a flat, treeless stretch of steppe valley. Local varieties of trees, pines, firs, birches, oaks, poplars, and the like, were introduced first, and from 1840, various imported trees were brought onto the site. Several theme areas were developed, including Monomakh's Hat, The Pine Bouquet, and The Crown. Work began on an area of man-made hills 20–30 m in size (called Shvaitsariia 'Switzerland') in 1858. Artificial lakes and ponds were added. No large structures were erected on the site, so that its natural features would remain prominent. Footbridges, columns, and *stone baby*, however, were placed there.

By 1890 all work on the park had been completed. In 1920 the park came under the control of the local authorities, and in 1940, after being declared a nature preserve, it came under the jurisdiction of the Ukrainian SSR Council of Ministers. The ANU was placed in charge of the park in 1951. Today approx 520 types of trees and plants grow there. The park is also used as a research center.

**Trostianetsky, Aron** [Trostjanec'kyj], b 17 July 1914 in Zlatopil (now part of Novomyrhorod), Chyhyryn county, Kiev gubernia, d 7 November 1986. Literary scholar and critic of Jewish origin. He graduated from the Kiev Pedagogical Institute (1939) and worked as a department head for the journal *Literaturna krytyka*, secretary of the newspaper *Literatura i mystetstvo*, and, from 1947, senior associate

A Cuman stone *baba* in the Trostianets Dendrological Park

of the Institute of Literature of the AN URSR (now ANU). He began publishing articles in 1934. He wrote several booklets on V. Maiakovsky and Soviet Ukrainian poetry, critical biographies of Yu. Yanovsky (1959 in Russian, 1962 in Ukrainian), and a monograph on the consolidation of literary forces in Soviet Ukraine in the years 1917–32 (1968). He also contributed chapters to several postwar multiauthor histories of Soviet Ukrainian literature and monographs. An edition of his literary criticism was published in 1985.

**Trotsenko, Viktor** [Trocenko], b 13 May 1888 in Nyzhnia Syrovatka, Sumy county, Kharkiv gubernia, d 4 June 1978 in Kharkiv. Architect. He acquired his knowledge of architecture as a member of the Ukrainian architecture and art department of the Kharkiv Literary and Artistic Circle organized by S. Vasylkivsky. He designed apartment buildings, schools, clubs, and hospitals in the Kryvyi Rih and Donbas regions, the Ukraine pavilion at the First All-Union Agricultural Exhibition in Moscow (1923), the workers' residences of the Kharkiv Steam Engine Plant (1923), and the Kharkiv Chervonozavodskyi Ukrainian Drama Theater (1931–8, codesigner). He researched Ukrainian folk architecture and copublished S. Taranu-

shenko's booklets about a traditional peasant house on Yelysavetynskyi Lane in Kharkiv (1921) and old houses in Kharkiv (1922). His articles were published in *Arkhitektura Radians'koï Ukraïny*.

**Trotsky, Leon** [Trockij, Lev] (pseud of Lev Bronshtein), b 7 November 1879 in Yanivka, Yelysavethrad county, Kherson gubernia, d 20 August 1940 in Coyoacán, near Mexico City. Russian revolutionary, Soviet political leader, and publicist. In March 1918 he was appointed people's commissar for war and chairman of the Supreme War Council and played the leading role in organizing the Red Army into a regular, professional force. A member of the Bolshevik government, he opposed the UNR. As a theoretician Trotsky is best known for his theory of permanent revolution and his criticism of J. Stalin's theory of socialism. His *Revolution Betrayed* (1937) is one of the first Marxist analyses of the nature of Stalinism.

Trotsky was unpopular in Ukraine because in 1917–20 he had commanded the alien Red Army and had organized the Red Terror. His calls for the militarization of labor in 1920–1 and for higher taxation of the peasantry to finance industrialization diminished his popularity even further. In the 1920s and 1930s Stalin unleashed a campaign against Trotsky and his *Left Opposition within the Party. Trotsky was expelled from the party in November 1927, then exiled to Alma Ata, and finally deported from the USSR in 1929. After the Molotov-Ribbentrop Pact of 1939 Trotsky called for the formation of an independent soviet socialist Ukraine. Tens of thousands of people accused of Trotskyism were executed or sent to the labor camps.

Outside the Ukrainian SSR Trotsky's Ukrainian following was limited to a small number of revolutionary socialist intellectuals in Galicia and to a small faction of Ukrainian-Canadian Communists, who published the newspaper *Robitnychi visty* (1933–8) and Ukrainian translations of several of Trotsky's works. In the 1970s some Ukrainian students in the West, particularly in Canada, were attracted to the ideas of the Left Opposition and contributed articles about Ukraine to various Trotskyist publications. An Italian Trotskyist publishing house translated I. Dziuba's *Internationalism or Russification?*

BIBLIOGRAPHY
Trotsky, L. *For a Free Independent Soviet Ukraine* (Toronto nd)
Trots'kyi, L. *SRSR i IV internatsional: Kliasova pryroda radians'koï derzhavy* (Toronto 1934)

H. Kasianov, B. Krawchenko

**Trotsky, Mykola** [Troc'kyj] (pseuds: M. Danko, Mykola Druhy, M. Slavhorodsky, M. Bradovych), b 1883 in Lutske, Volhynia gubernia, d 6 November 1971 in Geneva. Journalist, writer, and political figure. To avoid imprisonment by the tsarist authorities for political activity, he fled abroad in 1909. He was the Vienna correspondent of the Kiev paper *Rada* from 1910, and he contributed to periodicals in other cities, such as *Ukrainische Rundschau, Dilo, Nash holos, Moloda Ukraïna, Ukrainskaia zhizn', Maiak*, and *Literaturno-naukovyi vistnyk*. A leading member of the *Union for the Liberation of Ukraine, he coedited its *Vistnyk Soiuza vyzvolennia Ukraïny* and *Ukrainische Nachrichten* and wrote its brochures. He served as secretary of the UNR mission in Vienna (1918–22), published the anti-Soviet monthly *Die Völkerbrücke* (1931), and from 1932 ran the

Mykola Trotsky          Ivan Truba

Ukrainian Information Bureau in Geneva. After the war he contributed to the émigré press and published the novelettes *Chuzhynoiu* (In a Foreign Land, 1947), *Na Moskvu* (Against Moscow, 1951), and *Ideia i chyn* (The Idea and the Deed, 1952) and the publicistic works *Odna natsiia – odna tserkva* (One Nation – One Church, 1950) and *Derzhava bez natsiï* (A State without a Nation, 1952).

**Trout** (*Salmo*; Ukrainian: *pstruh, forel*). The name commonly given to several types of prized freshwater commercial fish of the Salmonidae family, and also, inaccurately, to char. The trout in Ukraine are the brown trout (*S. trutta*; Ukrainian: *strumkovyi pstruh*), found in the lakes and streams of the Carpathian and Crimean mountains, and the rainbow trout (*S. gairdneri*). The trout is used in fish-farming research for the *fishing industry.

**Truba, Ivan,** b 28 September 1878 in Homel, Mahiliou gubernia, Belarus, d 27 August 1950 in Plzeň, Czechoslovakia. Engineer and civic activist. As a student at the St Petersburg Technological Institute he was active in the Ukrainian Student Hromada there, and in 1902 he was exiled to Irkutsk for his role in student demonstrations. In 1905 he was imprisoned again for revolutionary activity. From 1909 he worked as an engineer in Katerynoslav and took part in the Ukrainian national movement. Appointed gubernial commissioner for education in 1917, he Ukrainized the school system, compiled anthologies for students, and organized Prosvita reading rooms. Later he emigrated to Czechoslovakia, where he lectured on mechanical engineering at the Ukrainian Husbandry Academy.

**Trubachev, Oleg** [Trubačev], b 23 October 1930 in Stalingrad (now Volgograd), Russia. Russian etymologist; corresponding member of the USSR Academy of Sciences since 1972. A graduate of Dnipropetrovske University (1952), he has worked at the academy's Russian Language Institute since 1961 and is head of its Sector of Etymology and Onomastics. He has written many articles on the etymology of Slavic (including Ukrainian) words and names and on the ancient Slavs' linguistic contacts with other Indo-Europeans, particularly on the Black Sea and Sea of Azov littorals. He is the author of books on the history of Slavic kinship terms (1959), the origin of Slavic names for domestic animals (1960), the hydronyms of the upper Dnieper Basin (1962), the Slavic terms in the crafts (1966), and the names of rivers in Right-Bank Ukraine (1968). He

is editor of the academy's multivolume Slavic etymological dictionary (1974–) and of annual collections of articles on etymology.

**Trubetskoi, Nikolai** [Trubeckoj] (Trubetzkoy), b 28 April 1890 in Moscow, d 25 June 1938 in Vienna. Russian philologist. He taught at Moscow (1915–17), Rostov (1918–19), and Sofia (1920–2) universities. From 1923 he was the professor of Slavic philology at Vienna University. A cofounder of the Prague Linguistic Circle and an ideologist of *Eurasianism, he wrote the linguistic classic *Grundzüge der Phonologie* (1939; English trans: *Principles of Phonology*, 1969, with his autobiographical notes and bibliography), in which he included many Ukrainian examples. A proponent of a 'common Russian' literary language (eg, in his book on the problem of Russian self-awareness, 1929; repr 1977), he nonetheless studied modern Ukrainian phonology as an independent phenomenon. In his lectures on Old Russian literature (1925–8; repr 1973) he confused Old Ukrainian and Middle Russian literature.

**Trubizh Drainage and Irrigation System.** A melioration system encompassing the floodplains of the Trubizh River and its main tributaries, the Karan and the Nedra rivers. The floodplains began to be drained in 1909, and the system was completed in 1954–63. It covers an area of 32,000 ha and serves 49 farms in Kiev and Chernihiv oblasts.

**Trubizh River** [Trubiž] (also Trubailo). A left-bank tributary of the Dnieper River that flows southward for 125 km through Chernihiv and Kiev oblasts before emptying into the Kaniv Reservoir. It drains a basin area of 4,700 sq km. It is fed by rain and groundwater and is a central feature of the Trubizh Drainage and Irrigation System. The river is also used for industry. The city of Pereiaslav-Khmelnytskyi is situated near the mouth of the river.

**Trublaini, Mykola** [Trublajini] (pseud of M. Trublaievsky), b 25 April 1907 in Vilshanka, Olhopil county, Podilia gubernia, d 4 October 1941. Writer. He belonged to the literary organization Molodniak and was first published in 1924. He wrote travelogues and stories, mainly for children. Among them are *Do Arktyky cherez tropiky* (To the Arctic through the Tropics, 1931), *Liudyna pospishaie na pivnich* (One Hurries to the North, 1931), *Tepla osin' 1930-oho* (The Warm Autumn of 1930, 1931), *Bii za perepravu* (The Battle for the Crossing, 1932), and *Opovidannia pro khorobrist'* (Stories about Courage, 1941). His novels include *Lakhtak* (1935), *Shkhuna Kolumb* (Schooner Columbus, 1937), and *Hlybynnyi shliakh* (The Deep Route, 1948). Posthumous collections of his work appeared as *Tvory* (3 vols, 1949–50; 4 vols, 1955–6).

**Trucks.** See Automotive industry.

**Trud** (Labor). A women's manufacturing co-operative founded in 1901 in Lviv by the Club of Ruthenian Women. Until 1914 it was known as the Women's Manufacturing Association. Trud owned a building and maintained a student residence and workshops for making dresses and undergarments. It organized sewing courses for girls over 13 years of age, which in 1929 were replaced with a three-year trade school, directed by O. *Zalizniak. Similar women's co-operatives existed in 11 other cities in Galicia. In 1927 they held a congress in Lviv. The board of directors of Trud was headed by H. Shukhevych and Ye. Makarushka. The co-operative ceased operations during the Soviet occupation in 1939–41 and was dissolved by the Soviet authorities in 1944.

**Trudosoiuz** (full name: Vseukrainskyi soiuz vyrobnychykh kooperatyv, or All-Ukrainian Union of Manufacturing Co-operatives). The central organization for manufacturing co-operatives in Ukraine, established in Odessa in 1919 by S. Borodaievsky. Its goal was to organize manufacturing co-operatives throughout Ukraine. The union was dissolved following the Bolshevik seizure of power in Ukraine in 1919.

*Trudova Ukraïna* (Toiling Ukraine). An irregular organ of the Central Committee of the Ukrainian Party of Socialist Revolutionaries, published in Prague in 1932–9 as the continuation of *Vistnyk UPSR*. It was edited by P. Bohatsky and N. Hryhoriiv.

*Trudy Etnografichesko-statisticheskoi ekspeditsii v Zapadno-russkii krai* (Works of the Ethnographic-Statistical Expedition to the West Russian Land). A seven-volume collection of materials on Ukrainian folklore and ethnography, published in 1872–9. It contains folk songs and anecdotes, proverbs, carols, riddles, spells, folk beliefs and superstitions, and the folk calendar, as well as wedding, baptism, funeral, and birth rites and statistical data on the minorities of Ukraine which were collected in 1869–70 by the members of an expedition in Russian-ruled Ukraine, Moldavia, and Belarus. The head of the expedition and the editor of the collection was P. *Chubynsky.

*Trudy Kievskoi dukhovnoi akademii* (Works of the Kiev Theological Academy). A Russian-language scholarly journal of the *Kiev Theological Academy published monthly in Kiev in 1860–1917 (a total of over 600 issues). It published articles on theology (dogma, general theology, moral theology, comparative theology), philosophy, church history (particularly in Ukraine), general history, pastoral theology, homiletics, liturgics, church law, and the history of Ukrainian ('Ruthenian') literature. It also contained a chronicle of activities at the academy, its library, its museum of church archeology, and the Kiev Epiphany Brotherhood. Contributors included many prominent scholars, among them M. Maksymovych, S. Golubev, M. Petrov, F. Titov, F. Rozhdestvensky, P. Orlovsky, I. Malyshevsky, V. Zavitnevych, P. Ternovsky, P. Viktorovsky, and N. Semeikin (church history); P. Yurkevych, P. Linytsky, D. Znamensky, and P. Kudriavtsev (philosophy); M. Petrov (literature); I. Balytsky (Slavic philology); Ya. Olesnytsky, K. Skvortsov, A. Khoinatsky, S. Malevansky, M. Yastrebov, M. Olesnytsky, D. Bohdashevsky, and V. Pevnytsky (theological studies); and V. Zavitnevych and P. Lashkarev (church law). The editors were F. Filaretov (1860–77); A. Olesnytsky, V. Pevnytsky, and V. Rubynsky (1906–10); and D. Bohdashevsky and N. Grossu (1915–17).

BIBLIOGRAPHY
Zhukovs'kyi, A. 'Vklad kyïvs'koï dukhovnoï Akademiï i ïï 'Trudiv' na kul'turnomu i bohoslovs'komu vidtynkakh,' *UI*, 1988, nos 1–4; 1989, nos 1–3

A. Zhukovsky

Rev Hryhorii Trukh   Ivan Trush (self-portrait, oil)

**Trukh, Hryhorii Andrii** [Trux, Hryhorij Andrij], b 18 February 1894 in Stryi, Galicia, d 9 May 1959 in Grimsby, Ontario. Basilian priest and writer. After interrupting his theological studies in Lviv to enter the ranks of the Sich Riflemen during the First World War, he joined the Basilian order in 1920 and was ordained in 1926. He had a Kholm region posting until 1932, when he was sent to Canada. There he edited the newspaper *Svitlo* (1943–6) and wrote several popular religious books and pamphlets, including *Zhyttia sviatykh* (The Lives of the Saints, 4 vols, 1958), and a Ukrainian grammar (1947).

**Trukhaniv Island** [Truxaniv ostriv]. An island (area approx 450 ha) situated in Kiev on the Dnieper River. The first structures on the island were built in the 19th century, and from the 1880s it was a working-class residential area. The island started to become a popular recreational area after its beaches were developed in 1918 during the German occupation of Ukraine. After much of the island was leveled during the Second World War, it was turned into an exclusively recreational area with facilities for swimming and water sports. It is connected to the city by a pedestrian bridge constructed in 1956–7.

**Trush, Ivan** [Truš], b 17 January 1869 in Vysotske, Brody county, Galicia, d 22 March 1941 in Lviv. Painter, community figure, and art and literary critic; son-in-law of M. *Drahomanov. After studying at the Cracow Academy of Fine Arts (1891–7) under L. Wyczółkowski and J. Stanisławski he lived in Lviv, where he was active in Ukrainian artistic circles and community life. A friend of I. Franko, he organized the *Society for the Advancement of Ruthenian Art and the *Society of Friends of Ukrainian Scholarship, Literature, and Art and their exhibitions; co-published the first Ukrainian art magazine, *Artystychnyi vistnyk*; painted many portraits for the Shevchenko Scientific Society; lectured on art and literature; and contributed articles to *Buduchnist'*, *Literaturno-naukovyi vistnyk*, *Moloda Ukraïna*, *Artystychnyi vistnyk*, *Dilo*, and *Ukrainische Rundschau*. He traveled widely: he visited Kiev several times (he taught briefly at M. Murashko's drawing school in 1901), Crimea (1901–4), Italy (1902, 1908), and Egypt and Palestine (1912).

Trush was an outstanding Ukrainian impressionist, noted for his original use of color. A major part of his large legacy (over 6,000 paintings) consists of landscapes. They include masterpieces, such as *Sunset in the Forest* (1904),

ART 1) V. Strelnikov: *Autumnal* (oil, 1977; private collection). 2) V. Tatlin: *Assemblage* (wood, iron, various materials, 1915–16; Tretiakov Gallery, Moscow). 3) V. Yermilov: *Harlequin* (relief, oil and wood, 1923–4; collection of I. Dychenko; photo courtesy of Winnipeg Art Gallery). 4) T. Yablonska: *Youth* (oil, 1969; Kiev Museum of Ukrainian Art). 5) I. Trush: *Hutsul Women by a Church* (oil, 1920s; National Museum, Lviv). 6) O. Zalyvakha: *Kalyna* (oil, 1989).

*Solitary Pine* (1919), *Grain Stacks near the Woods* (1919), *Haystacks*, and *Moonlit Night by the Sea* (1925); the cycles 'The Solitary Pine' and 'The Jewish Cemetery' (1929); *St Michael's Cathedral*, and *St Andrew's Church* [in Kiev] and *T. Shevchenko's Grave in Kaniv* (1900); and landscapes of Crimea, Rome, Venice, Egypt, and Palestine. His many genre paintings are noted for their simplicity of composition; they include *Hahilky* (1905), *Hutsul Woman with Child* (1912), *Trembita Players*, *Washerwomen*, *Hutsul Women near a Church*, *Arabs on the Road*, and *Arab Women*. His gallery of 350 portraits includes ones of his wife, Ariiadna, Cardinal A. Sembratovych, I. Franko, V. Stefanyk, Lesia Ukrainka, O. Konysky, I. Nechui-Levytsky, V. Antonovych, B. Hrinchenko, M. Drahomanov, M. Hrushevsky, and M. Lysenko. The first solo show of Trush's works took place in Lviv in 1899, and a large retrospective exhibition was held posthumously there in 1941. Major collections of his work are at the National Museum and the memorial museum in his former residence in Lviv. A selection of his essays on art and literature appeared posthumously in 1959.

BIBLIOGRAPHY
Khmuryi, V. *Ivan Trush* (Kharkiv 1931)
*Ivan Ivanovych Trush, 1869–1941: Kataloh posmertnoï vystavky* (Lviv 1941)
Ostrovs'kyi, H. *I.I. Trush: Narys pro zhyttia i tvorchist'* (Kiev 1955)
Nanovs'kyi, Ia. *Ivan Trush* (Kiev 1967)
Kostiuk, S. *Ivan Ivanovych Trush: Bibliohrafichnyi pokazhchyk* (Lviv 1969)

S. Hordynsky

**Trushch, Volodymyr** [Trušč], b 21 April 1869 in Zolochiv, Galicia, d 6 June 1931 in Stanyslaviv. Russophile activist. A secretary of the Academic Circle while studying at Lviv University in the 1890s, he lived from 1899 in Stanyslaviv, where he was director of a Russophile student residence and head of the local People's Home. During the First World War he was imprisoned in Thalerhof. In the early 1920s he was instrumental in regrouping Galician Russophiles into the Russian People's Organization and served as its first president.

A sanatorium in Truskavets

**Truskavets** [Truskavec']. IV-4. A city (1989 pop 31,400) under oblast jurisdiction in the Carpathian foothills of Lviv oblast. The village has been a source of salt since the 11th century. It was first mentioned in historical documents in 1462. It belonged to the crown estates of the Polish kings until the First Partition of Poland (1772), when it was transferred to Austria. It was under Polish rule in the interwar period, was annexed by the USSR in 1939, and was incorporated into the Ukrainian SSR in 1944. The first health resorts in Truskavets were opened in 1827, and today the city is the most famous health resort center in Ukraine. Its 17 sanatoriums and 20 hotels accommodate 60,000 patients and 300,000 tourists annually. Its mineral water, known as Naftusia, is used to treat liver, gall bladder, urological, and metabolic disorders. Ozokerite began to be used in balneotherapy there in 1947 and was found to be more effective than clay or peat. The town was granted city status in 1948. It has a mineral-water bottling plant and a branch of the Scientific Research Institute of Health Resorts. Petroleum, ozokerite, salt, and other minerals are mined in the vicinity.

**Trust** (*trest*). The most integrated form of economic association among a number of companies. Members of a trust surrender their autonomy in production and marketing and accept a single administration. Trusts arose in Western Europe and North America in the 19th century. Eventually they came under government regulations on competition and monopoly. In comparison with other forms of *monopoly that emerged in Ukraine in the last quarter of the 19th century, such as *cartels and syndicates, trusts were relatively unimportant and underdeveloped.

Trusts were also a common form of economic organization in the USSR. Many were formed during the NEP period in an attempt to rationalize production, reduce costs, and eliminate duplication. They were usually a combination of enterprises in a single territory. The process of defining the legal status of the trusts was not systematic, and culminated in a law on trusts passed by the USSR Central Executive Committee and the Council of People's Commissars on 10 April 1923. In Ukraine trusts developed more rapidly than in other republics. The Pivdenstal trust was established in October 1921. It consisted of 3 large steel plants, in Makiivka, Yuzivka, and Petrivske, 19 smaller plants, several coal mines, and some coking plants. The other large trusts in Soviet Ukraine were Donbasvuhillia, in the coal industry; Pivdennorudnyi, in iron-ore mining; the Southern Machine-Building Trust; and Pivdennyi Silmashtrest, based in Zaporizhia, and Ukrtrestsilmash, based in Kharkiv, both in agricultural-machine building. Specialized trusts were also formed in the chemical, paper, leather, ceramics, dairy products, tobacco, sugar, electrical, textile, alcohol, glass, and flour-milling industries. Under the NEP there were, altogether, 36 regional and 24 republican trusts in Ukraine. Nominally the trusts were regulated by the Supreme Council for the National Economy (VRNH), but from 1925 some of its responsibilites were transferred to the State Planning Committee. The struggle for control of the trusts among the VRNH, the republic's Planning Committee, and the USSR people's commissariats resulted in the gradual dismantling of most trusts in 1929–30. Some were abolished outright in 1932, along with the VRNH, and enterprises were placed under the direct control of the commissariats.

Under N. Khrushchev's reforms in the early 1960s, which introduced regional economic councils throughout Ukraine and the USSR, trusts were revived. But they were no more than associations that served as a link between the ministries and the individual enterprises and helped co-ordinate production plans. Trusts such as the coal-mining trusts Antratsyt and Chervonohradvuhillia, the manganese-mining trusts Nykopilmarhanets, the construction trusts Holovkharkivbud and Poltavaspetsbud, and the lumbering trust Lvivderevprom operated until the mid-1970s. Then they were abolished and replaced by *manufacturing consortia.

**Trutenko, Valentyn,** b 12 March 1881 in Zvenyhorodka, Kiev gubernia, d 30 January 1953 in Santiago, Chile. Military figure. A lieutenant colonel commanding the 175th Baturyn Regiment of the Russian army during the First World War, after the February Revolution he Ukrainianized his unit and brought it from Riga to Kiev, where it became part of the UNR Army. Under the Hetman government of 1918 he was in charge of the waterway between Sicheslav (now Dnipropetrovske) and Cherkasy. Under the UNR Directory he became director of the officer school in Mohyliv-Podilskyi. He took part in the First Winter Campaign (1919–20) and then was interned with other UNR Army personnel in Poland. After emigrating to Bohemia in 1924, he headed the Ukrainian Military Council, the United Hetman Organization, the Ukrainian-Belarusian Society, and the Ukrainian Orthodox Parish Council in Prague. After the Second World War he lived in Germany, where he was a member of the Supreme Leadership of the Hetmanite Movement, a deputy otaman of the Ukrainian Free Cossacks, and a member of the Hetmanite Council. He emigrated to Chile in the late 1940s.

Kostiantyn Trutovsky: *Bleaching Cloth* (oil, 1874)

**Trutovsky, Kostiantyn** [Trutovs'kyj, Kostjantyn], b 9 February 1826 in Kursk, Russia, d 29 March 1893 in Yakovlevka, Kursk gubernia. Ukrainian painter and graphic artist. He was raised on his family's estate in Popivka, Okhtyrka county, Kharkiv gubernia. He audited classes at the St Petersburg Academy of Arts (1845–9) and in 1860 was elected a member of the academy. Having adopted the prevailing realist academic style, he specialized in genre paintings depicting life in Kursk gubernia and Ukraine. They include *Woman with Homespun Cloth* (1850s), *Carolers in Ukraine* (1864), *Kobzar on the Dnieper* (1875), *On a Moonlit Night* (1881), and *The Sick One* (1883). Trutovsky also did hundreds of pencil drawings and illustrations. *Russkii khudozhestvennyi listok* printed his illustrations to M. Vovchok's stories in 1860. Other illustrations were published in *Zhivopisnaia Ukraina* (1861–2) and an album of lithographs illustrating N. Gogol's *Vechera na khutore bliz Dikanki* (Evenings on a Farm near Dykanka, 1874–6). He also did illustrations to Vovchok's stories 'Sestra' (Sister) and 'Chumak' (1860), T. Shevchenko's poems 'Haidamaky' (1886), 'Naimychka' (The Hired Girl), and 'Nevol'nyk' (The Captive, 1887), N. Gogol's stories 'Sorochinskaia iarmarka' (Sorochyntsi Fair) and 'Vecher nakanune Ivana Kupala' (St John's Eve, 1876), and I. Krylov's fables. Most of his works were within the framework of the ethnographic sentimental style fashionable at the time; some, however, touched on painful social problems. Trutovsky influenced younger painters, such as S. Vasylkivsky, I. Izhakevych, M. Pymonenko, and O. Slastion. Books about him by A. Artiukhova (1931), L. Miliaieva (1955), A. Vereshchagina (1955), and Z. Lashkul (1974) have appeared.

S. Hordynsky

**Trutovsky, Vasyl** [Trutovs'kyj, Vasyl'], b ca 1740 in Ivaniv *sloboda*, Belgorod region, Russia, d ca 1810 in St Petersburg. Singer, musician, and musicologist. After training at the Hlukhiv Singing School he became (1761) a singer and *husli* player at the imperial court and later (1766) a chamber musician there. His outstanding contribution to music was the compilation of *Sobraniie russkikh prostykh pesen s notami* (A Collection of Russian Common Songs with Notes) in four parts (1776, 1778, 1779, and 1795; repub 1953). This ground-breaking work, which included Ukrainian songs, represented the first systematic collection of 'Russian' folk music. Trutovsky also scored variations on folk songs for piano as well as choral works.

**Truvor,** b ?, d 864. Semilegendary Rus' prince. According to the chronicle *Povist' vremennykh lit*, Truvor and his brothers, *Riuryk and Syneus, were *Varangians. Truvor ruled the city of Izborsk, in the Novgorod region, from 862 until his death, and then Riuryk assumed control of the city.

**Trybratni mohyly.** Three (hence the name 'trybratni' or 'three brothers') 4th-century BC burial mounds of *Bosporan Kingdom nobility located south of Kerch, Crimea. Also known as Ych Oba, the mounds were excavated in 1966–7. Although some of the graves at the site had been looted in the past, a stone vault containing the remains of two women and numerous gold and silver adornments, Greek tableware, and amphoras was found intact. Another kurhan revealed the remains of a man and woman in a wooden sarcophagus which contained (among other items) pieces of a wooden bow.

*Trybuna* (Tribune). A daily nonpartisan, pro-UNR newspaper published in Kiev from December 1918 to February 1919 by Z. Bisky. It was edited by O. Salikovsky, and among its more prominent contributors were S. Petliura, V. Sadovsky, S. Yefremov, O. Kovalevsky, L. Starytska-Cherniakhivska, P. Stebnytsky, M. Kushnir, and N. Surovtsova. The newspaper had a well-organized group of regular reporters and was one of the best and most popular papers of the time; it appeared in a pressrun of 7,000 to 15,000 copies. For some time a separate Russian-language edition, *Stolichnyi golos*, was also published.

A 4th-century-BC gold and enamel earring excavated at Trybratni mohyly

**Trybuna Ukraïny** (Tribune of Ukraine). An irregular publication of the Ukrainian Central Committee in Warsaw in 1923. The unofficial organ of the Government-in-exile of the UNR, it succeeded *Ukraïns'ka trybuna* and was edited by O. Salikovsky.

**Tryhub, Mykola** (Trehub), b 20 March 1943 in Mykhailivka, Bila Tserkva raion, Kiev oblast, d 23 March 1984 in Kiev. Painter and graphic artist. He received his train-ing at a technical and art high school in Kiev and worked as a handyman at the Kiev Artistic Film Studio (until 1974) and as an artist for the AN URSR (now ANU) Institute of Archeology. Ukrainian subject matter predominated in his modernist paintings and collages (landscapes of Kiev, churches, historical subjects, and portraits of Ukrainian poets). He created over 1,000 works but was able to exhibit publicly only once during his lifetime. Most of his works are in private collections. In 1989, five years after his suicide, his friends organized exhibitions of his work in Kiev. Two hundred of his works are preserved at the Pereislav-Khmelnytskyi Museum of Folk Architecture and Folkways.

**Trylisky, Oleksa** [Trylis'kyj], b ca 1895, d ca 1936–7. Soviet Ukrainian official and agronomist. A former *Borotbist, he joined the CP(B)U in 1920. In the late 1920s he was chairman of the Odessa Okruha Executive Committee. Later he served as deputy people's commissar of agriculture and chairman of the Vinnytsia Oblast Executive Committee. He was arrested and executed during the Stalinist terror.

Kyrylo Trylovsky

**Trylovsky, Kyrylo** [Tryl'ovs'kyj], b 6 May 1864 in Bohutyn, Zolochiv county, Galicia, d 19 October 1941 in Kolomyia, Galicia. Civic and political leader, lawyer, journalist, and publisher. After graduating from Lviv University he practiced law in Kolomyia. In Zavallia, Sniatyn county, he founded the *Sich society (1900) and then oversaw its spread to other localities. From 1908 he was president of the Supreme Sich Committee, and from 1912, general otaman of the Ukrainian Sich Committee, which headed the alliance of Sich societies. Commonly known as the 'Sich father,' he had a great impact on the growth of national consciousness in Galicia, particularly in the Pokutia region. In 1913 he established the paramilitary *Ukrainian Sich Riflemen (USS). A founder and one of the key members of the *Ukrainian Radical party, he was elected to the Austrian parliament in 1907 and 1911 and to the Galician Diet in 1913. In parliament he made almost 1,000 motions and, during a Ukrainian filibuster, a 10-hour speech. At the outbreak of the First World War he became chairman of the Combat Board of the USS and a member of the General Ukrainian Council. In 1918 he was a member of the Ukrainian National Rada. After setting up a Sich committee in Vinnytsia (1919) he organized several Sich societies in Transcarpathia and, eventually, Vienna. As an émigré in Vienna he served on the codification

Mykola Tryhub and his *Azure Girl* (ink and oil, 1972)

commission of the Government-in-exile of the Western Ukrainian National Republic. He returned to Galicia in 1927. Occasionally using the pen name Klym Obukh he wrote many articles and Sich songs and published a series of brochures and Sich songbooks. For many years he was a correspondent for *Svoboda* and *Narodne slovo* in the United States. He edited the monthly *Zoria* and the semi-monthly *Khlops'ka pravda*, as well as almanacs such as *Zaporozhets'* and *Otaman*. An extended excerpt from Trylovsky's memoirs was published in *Hei, tam na hori 'Sich' ide* (Hey, the Sich Is Marching on the Hill, 1965).

**Trynchy, Peter** [Trynčij], b 22 August 1931 in Rochfort Bridge, Alberta. Politician. A farmer and businessman, Trynchy was first elected to the Alberta provincial legislature as the Progressive Conservative member for Whitecourt constituency in 1971. He was re-elected in 1975, 1979, 1982, and 1986. He served in the cabinet as minister of recreation and parks (1979–86).

**Tryndyk, Fed.** See Hirny, Vasyl.

**Trypilian culture.** A Neolithic–Bronze Age culture that existed in Right-Bank Ukraine ca 4500 to 2000 BC. It is named after a site in the Kiev region uncovered by V. *Khvoika in 1898. The Trypilians were primitive agricultural and cattle-raising tribes that migrated to Ukraine from the Near East and from the Balkans and Danubian

Artifacts of the Trypilian culture: 1) stone ax-hammer head; 2) stone hammer head; 3) flint ax head; 4) clay spindle weight; 5) copper dagger blade; 6) and 7) copper ax heads; 8) elk-bone hoe blade; 9) elk-bone sickle with flint inlays; 10) and 11) stone cult figures; 12) and 13) painted clay pottery

regions in the east. Scholars have identified three periods in the development of this culture – early (4500–3500 BC), middle (3500–2750 BC), and late (2750–2250 BC). The differentiation of periods is characterized by an increase in population and the geographic spread of the culture: initially concentrated in the upper and middle Prut and Seret and the middle Dniester and Boh river basins, the culture spread in the middle period to include the right bank of the Dnieper, and in the late period to the left bank of the Dnieper, the southwest steppe region, and the Sluch,

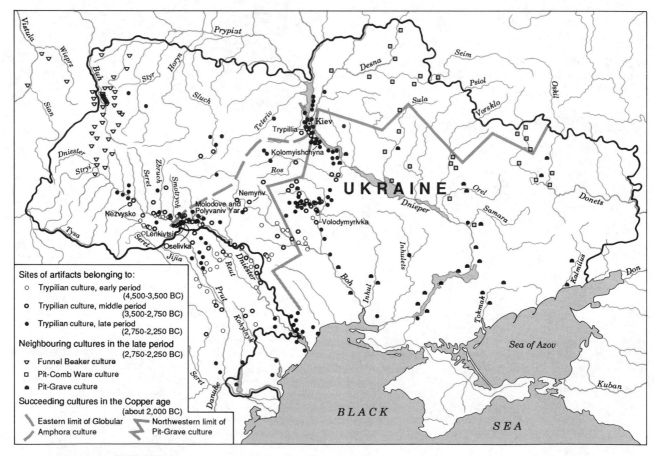

Sites of artifacts belonging to:

○    Trypilian culture, early period
      (4,500-3,500 BC)

◉    Trypilian culture, middle period
      (3,500-2,750 BC)

●    Trypilian culture, late period
      (2,750-2,250 BC)

Neighbouring cultures in the late period
      (2,750-2,250 BC)

▽    Funnel Beaker culture

□    Pit-Comb Ware culture

▪    Pit-Grave culture

Succeeding cultures in the Copper age
      (about 2,000 BC)

      Eastern limit of Globular          Northwestern limit of
      Amphora culture                     Pit-Grave culture

TRYPILIAN CULTURE

Horyn, and Styr river basins. As it spread, the Trypilian culture assimilated the cultures of existing tribes. The periods are also differentiated by changes in settlement patterns, the economy, and the spiritual life of the people.

During the 4th millennium BC, Trypilian tribes began settling in low-lying riverbank areas and on plateaus in the Dnieper and Boh river basins. They built pit and semi-pit dwellings with clay floors and hearths or ovens, and walls of wattle and dab. Rectangular surface dwellings, constructed with similar materials but on a raised log platform covered with clay and (probably) with a thatched roof, also began to appear at this time. Clay altars, usually either round or cross-shaped, were also commonly constructed in dwellings (Kolomyishchyna, Volodymyrivka). Settlements were established by clans and contained 15 to 30 dwellings. Initially, extended families usually shared a single dwelling and houses were simply enlarged to accommodate new members, but from the middle period nuclear families generally occupied their own dwellings. In the later periods of the culture, settlements were usually established on high plateaus that were drier and more defensible, sometimes by moats and walls. These settlements were generally larger than earlier ones (eg, *Volodymyrivka contained almost 200 dwellings). In later settlements houses often had a rounded floor plan, and they were arranged in a circle for defensive purposes and to pen livestock in a central enclosure.

The major economic activities of the early Trypilians were primitive agriculture and animal husbandry, supplemented by extensive hunting, fishing, and food gathering. Wheat, millet, and barley were sown on land tilled with mattocks made from antlers or with digging sticks with sharpened points. Crops were harvested using bone sickles with flint blades and the grain was ground by stone querns. Horned cattle, together with pigs, sheep, and goats, were the most-domesticated animals; deer, wild boar, and roebucks were the animals most commonly hunted. Animal husbandry emerged as the most important economic activity in the middle and late periods. This not only influenced the arrangement of dwellings in the settlement to protect livestock, but also led to the development of a pastoral lifestyle; the remains of many temporary settlements by floodplains and other grazing areas have been uncovered. The late period was also marked by the introduction of the domesticated horse. Although greater areas were brought under cultivation, agricultural techniques changed little.

The basic tools of the Trypilian culture were made of stone, bone, and flint. Some small bronze items, especially fishhooks, bracelets, and rings, have been found at Trypilian excavations. The tribes of the culture traded with peoples in the Balkans or Transylvania (the source of copper found at *Luka-Vrublivetska) and on the Aegean (this was especially true of tribes located in southern Ukraine). Weaving also developed, although the looms remained rather primitive.

The Trypilian culture is especially known for its ceramic pottery. In the early period, handbuilt large pear-shaped vessels for storing grains and various types of pots, plates, spoons, colanders, and the like were all common. Earthenware was also used to make figurines of women, scale models of homes, jewelry, and amulets. The exterior of the pottery was decorated with inscribed ornamentation in the form of spiralling bands of parallel dou-

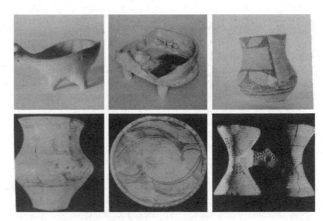

Pottery of the Trypilian culture

ble lines. Most figurines were decorated with the same type of ornamentation. The figurines, house models, and amulets had ritual significance linked to an agrarian cult of fertility and prosperity. This cult, in turn, was linked to burials in homes. White, red, and black polychromatic spiral ornamentation was found on pottery unearthed at several early Trypillian sites (Kadiivtsi, Bavky, Kudryntsi, Nezvysko, and Frydrivtsi). Pottery-making reached an especially high level of development in the middle and late periods of the culture.

The Trypilians initially had a matriarchal-clan order in which women engaged in agricultural work, headed households, manufactured pottery, textiles, and clothing, and played a leading role in societal affairs, while men hunted, tended to cattle, and prepared tools out of flint, stone, and bone. Later, with the increase in importance of animal husbandry, a patriarchal order developed.

As a result of incursions by other cultures (particularly the *Pit-Grave culture) into Ukrainian territory in the mid-3rd to early 2nd millennium BC, many characteristic Trypilian traits changed or disappeared altogether. The technique of house construction was altered and the spiraling motif common to Trypilian pottery was replaced by corded designs. Anthropomorphic designs became schematized and older forms of pottery disappeared. Burial practices showed the influence of the Pit-Grave culture with its characteristic graves, tumuli, and patriarchal burial rites. The *Usatove tribe of the western Black Sea steppe region was assimilated by the Pit-Grave culture. The historical fate of other Trypilian tribes was varied, as evidenced by the transition of tribes of the middle and upper Dniester regions into the *Globular Amphora culture during the middle Bronze Age.

The Trypilian culture is perhaps the most investigated archeological culture in Ukraine (see *archeology). Hundreds of Trypilian sites have been excavated and studied, including major ones at *Lenkivtsi, *Nezvysko, *Oselivka, *Polyvaniv Yar, *Molodove, and *Nemyriv.

BIBLIOGRAPHY

Passek, T. Trypil's'ka kul'tura: Naukovo-populiarnyi narys (Kiev 1941)
– Periodizatsiia tripol'skikh poselenii (Moscow–Leningrad 1949)
Chernysh, K. Rann'otrypil's'ke poselennia Lenkivtsi na seredn'omu Dnistri (Kiev 1959)
Sulimirski, T. Prehistoric Russia: An Outline (London 1970)
Arkheolohiia Ukraïns'koï RSR, vol 1 (Kiev 1971)

Dergachev, V. *Pamiatniki pozdnego Tripol'ia* (Kishinev 1980)
*Arkheologiia Ukrainskoi SSR v trekh tomakh*, vol 1 (Kiev 1985)

**Trypilska, Yelyzaveta** [Trypil's'ka, Jelyzaveta], b 31 November 1881 in Poltava, d 6 November 1958 in Baku, Azerbaidzhan. Sculptor. She studied in the studios of R. Bakh, V. Beklemishev, and L. Shervud in St Petersburg and N. Aronson in Paris. From 1922 she lived in Baku. Her works on Ukrainian themes include *Peasant*, *Water Spirit* (1904–9), *Chatterbox* (1910), *Ashamed* (1911), *Uncle Kryvonis* (1911), *Priest's Wife* (1911), and *Joking* (1916–17).

**Tryzna, Yosyf** [Tryzna, Josyf], b ?, d 1655 or 1656. Orthodox churchman. He graduated from the Kievan Mohyla Academy. In 1640–7 he was hegumen of the Vilnius Holy Ghost Monastery, and in 1647 he succeeded P. Mohyla as archimandrite of the Kievan Cave Monastery. He opposed the *Pereiaslav Treaty of 1654. A manuscript of the Kievan Cave Patericon known as the Yosyf Tryzna redaction was completed during his tenure as archimandrite, possibly by Tryzna himself. He also wrote a foreword to the *Sluzhebnyk* (Liturgicon) of 1653.

*Tryzub* (Trident). A weekly journal of politics, civic affairs, history, and culture, published in Paris from 15 October 1925 to 1940 (705 issues); the unofficial organ of the *Government-in-exile of the UNR. Founded on the initiative of S. Petliura, it was edited by V. Prokopovych and, in 1940, by O. Shulhyn. In 1926–7 it issued 10 extra editions covering the trial of S. Schwartzbard, Petliura's assassin. In 1938–9 it published regular supplements for women (ed Z. Mirna), young people (ed B. Olkhivsky), the Plast scouting organization (ed S. Nechai), and children (ed S. Siropolko). *Tryzub* devoted considerable attention to political and cultural developments in Soviet Ukraine (it remains an important source of information for that period) and reported on efforts by Ukrainian émigrés to promote the Ukrainian question in the West. It published regular accounts of activities in the centers of Ukrainian émigré life (Paris, Prague, Warsaw, Vienna) and several memoirs of the period of Ukrainian statehood.

*Tryzub* (Trident). An organ of the émigré *Ukrainian National State Union (UNDS), published in New York City bimonthly from January 1961 to December 1970 and then quarterly to 1975 (a total of 78 issues). It was preceded by the bimonthly *Biuleten' UNDS* (1955[?]–60). Both periodicals contained organizational news and documents, articles and memoirs about events and figures of the 1917–20 struggle for Ukrainian independence, critiques of Soviet communism, and information and commentaries about émigré political life. The chief editors were A. Zubenko and Z. Ivasyshyn.

**Trzciniec culture.** A Bronze Age culture of the 16th to 12th centuries BC which existed in north central and northwestern Ukraine and parts of eastern Poland. It was named after an archeological site in Poland. Although excavations of this culture had been made as early as the 1870s and 1880s, it was regarded as a part of the *Komariv culture and not recognized as a distinctive grouping until the 1960s. The people of the Trzciniec culture lived in semi-pit and surface dwellings and had outbuildings built on pilings for storing grain. Their funeral practices included both full body burials and cremations. They engaged in agriculture, animal husbandry, hunting, and fishing. In addition to flint and stone implements, a wide variety of pottery, bronze adornments, and evidence of several flint workshops have been uncovered at culture sites.

**Tsalai-Yakymenko, Oleksandra** [Calaj-Jakymenko], b 27 March 1932 in Lubni, Dnipropetrovske (now Poltava) oblast. Musicologist. She graduated from the Lviv State Conservatory (1958) in the class of L. Umanska and S. Liudkevych, and finished postgraduate studies at the Kiev State Conservatory (1962) in the class of H. Taranov. Since 1963 she has taught at the Lviv State Conservatory. She has written numerous articles on Ukrainian musical culture of the 16th to 18th centuries for *Ukraïns'ke muzykoznavstvo* and other scholarly journals, as well as reviews of the works of Lviv composers for radio, television, and the press.

**Tsamblak, Gregory** [Camblak, Hryhorij], b 1364 in Trnovo, Bulgaria, d ca 1419. Churchman and writer. He was probably educated in Trnovo and Constantinople. In 1401 he was sent to Suceava by the Byzantine patriarchate to improve relations with the Moldavian church. He was consecrated (on the initiative of the Lithuanian grand duke Vytautas) by several bishops from Belarus and Ukraine in Navahrudak in November 1415 and installed as metropolitan of the renewed *Lithuanian metropoly. His installation was against the wishes of Euphemius II, the patriarch of Constantinople, who opposed a division of Kiev metropoly and supported Photios, the metropolitan in Moscow. In February 1418 Tsamblak attended the ecumenical council in Constance. Subsequently he was accused of Uniate tendencies by the Muscovite church. In order to avoid persecution he abdicated, and probably died soon afterward.

Tsamblak wrote a number of sermons and panegyrics in the rhetorical style of the Trnovo school. His sermons for Palm Sunday, the Ascension, the Transfiguration, the Assumption, the Elevation of the Cross, the festival of St Demetrius, and the Confession of Faith (read on the occasion of his consecration), his panegyrics on Metropolitan Cyprian (1409) and Patriarch Euphemius, and other works are all from his Ukrainian period; a selection of his writings, edited by A. Yatsimirsky, appeared in 1904.

BIBLIOGRAPHY
Iatsimirskii, A. *Grigorii Tsamblak: Ocherk ego zhizni, administrativnoi i knizhnoi deiatel'nosti* (St Petersburg 1904)
Heppell, M. *The Ecclesiastical Career of Grigorij Camblak* (London 1979)

A. Zhukovsky

**Tsapenko, Mykhailo** [Capenko, Myxajlo], b 6 November 1907 in Biliaky, Khorol county, Poltava gubernia. Architect and art scholar. After graduating from the Moscow Architectural Institute (1935) he worked as an architect in Caucasia and Moscow. After the Second World War he moved to Kiev, where he headed the AN URSR (now ANU) Institute of the Theory and History of Architecture (1951–9) and edited *Budivnytstvo i arkhitektura* (1953–8). He wrote books in Russian on Soviet architecture (1952, 1955, 1967), Bulgarian architecture (1953), and the architecture of 17th- and 18th-century Left-Bank Ukraine (1967) and a chapter on stone architecture in 17th- and 18th-century Ukraine in vol 3 of the ANU history of Ukrainian art (1968).

Heorhii Tsapok          Olena Tsehelska

Lonhyn Tsehelsky        Rev Mykhail Tsehelsky

**Tsapok, Heorhii** [Capok, Heorhij], b 1 May 1896 in Kharkiv, d 21 June 1971 in Kharkiv. Scenery designer and graphic artist. He studied at the Kharkiv Art School (1914–18). In the interwar years he designed scenery for the Kharkiv Operetta Theater, the Kharkiv First Theater for Children, the Kharkiv Theater of the Revolution, the Kiev Ukrainian Drama Theater, and the Kharkiv Russian Drama Theater. His sets of the 1920s were interesting examples of constructivist design. He also designed book covers and posters.

**Tsarskyi kurhan.** A 4th-century BC Bosporan burial mound located southwest of Kerch, Crimea. The tomb is an elaborate structure built of finished blocks of stone. It contains a corridor (7 m high and 36 m long) leading to a chamber, in which a king was probably buried. The corridor is vaulted in a striking manner, while the main burial chamber is a rectangular room in which the walls gradually close in overhead to form a cupola. A layer of stones and 17 m of earth were placed over the structure. Excavations in 1837 found the structure had been thoroughly looted.

**Tsarychanka** [Caryčanka]. V-15. A town smt (1986 pop 7,800) on the Orel River and a raion center in Dnipropetrovske oblast. It originated in 1604 as a Cossack *khutir* and was settled by Uman Cossacks in 1673. A few years later it became a company center of Poltava regiment. It was destroyed by the Tatars in 1696, but it revived and in 1765 became part of New Russia gubernia. From 1802 to 1923 it belonged to Poltava gubernia. Today it is an agricultural town with a dairy, canning factory, mineral-water bottling plant, and folk-crafts factory.

**Tschyzewskyj, Dmitrij.** See Chyzhevsky, Dmytro.

**Tsehelska, Olena** [Cehel's'ka] (née Kyzyma), b 1887 in Hora, Sokal county, Galicia, d 16 September 1971 in Philadelphia. Pedagogue and writer of books for children. A teacher in a village near Zolochiv until 1939, she fled in 1940 to Germany and later emigrated to the United States. She made her debut in 1910 with a short story in the newspaper *Dilo*. Subsequently she contributed to and was on the staff of various children's journals, such as *Dzvinok*, *Svit dytyny*, *Mali druzi*, and (later) *Veselka*. Her notable works include *Hanusia ide do mista* (Hanusia Goes to Town, 1930) and *Petruseva povist* (Peter's Story, 1950).

**Tsehelsky, Lonhyn** [Cehel's'kyj, L'onhyn], b 1875 in Kaminka-Strumylova, Galicia, d 13 December 1950 in Philadelphia. Lawyer, journalist, and political leader; son of Rev M. *Tsehelsky. While studying law at Lviv University he was a founder of the *Academic Hromada, co-editor of the journal *Moloda Ukraïna* (1900–2), and the author of the pamphlet *Rus'-Ukraïna i Moskovshchyna-Rosiia* (Rus'-Ukraine and Muscovy-Russia, 1901), which had a great influence in the development of national consciousness among the people in Galicia and Russian-ruled Ukraine. He maintained ties with the Revolutionary Ukrainian party, particularly with M. *Mikhnovsky, whose *Samostiina Ukraïna* (Independent Ukraine, 1900) he published in Lviv. He was an organizer of the agrarian strike of 1902 in Galicia. While editing *Dilo* (1908), *Svoboda* (1907–8), and *Ukraïns'ke slovo* (1915–18) he was active in politics, and he was elected to the Austrian parliament in 1907 and 1911 and the Galician Diet in 1913. With the outbreak of the First World War he joined the Supreme Ukrainian Council, the Combat Board of the Ukrainian Sich Riflemen, and the General Ukrainian Council. He was active in the *Union for the Liberation of Ukraine and wrote its political pamphlets (published in several languages) and articles. In 1918 he became a member of the Ukrainian National Rada and state secretary of internal affairs for the Western Ukrainian National Republic (ZUNR). On 1 December 1918 he and D. Levytsky signed the initial agreement with the UNR Directory on the union of the UNR and the ZUNR. In January 1919 he was appointed director of the Secretariat of Foreign Affairs for the Western Province of the UNR and deputy foreign minister of the UNR. Having been sent to the United States in 1920 by Ye. Petrushevych as a representative of the ZUNR government he settled in Philadelphia and worked on the staff of *Ameryka, of which he became editor in 1943. He was one of the founders and vice-presidents of the Ukrainian Congress Committee of America and vice-president of the Pan-American Ukrainian Conference. His memoirs were serialized in *Ameryka* and then published as *Vid legendy do pravdy* (From Legend to Truth) in 1960.

**Tsehelsky, Mykhail** [Cehel's'kyj, Myxajil], b 1848 in Vysotske, Brody county, Galicia, d 1944. Ukrainian Catholic priest and civic activist. A parish priest in Kaminka-Strumylova from 1875 until the end of his life, he established and led local and regional branches of several Ukrainian community organizations, including Prosvita, the Ruthenian Pedagogical Society, and the Ukrainian National Democratic party. He was taken as a hostage to Russia by the tsarist army in 1915–17. He was Metropolitan A. Sheptytsky's vicar-general for central Ukraine in 1917–18, a member of the Ukrainian National Rada in Stanyslaviv in 1919, and papal chamberlain for the region.

Roman Tsehelsky                Hryhorii Tsehlynsky

**Tsehelsky, Roman** [Cehel's'kyj], b 12 July 1882 in Kaminka-Strumylova, Galicia, d 3 October 1956 in Lviv. Experimental physicist; full member and secretary (1926–36) of the Shevchenko Scientific Society; son of M. Tsehelsky. He studied at the universities of Lviv, Prague, and Chernivtsi (PH D, 1911), and he taught at secondary schools in Ternopil (1904–5), Chernivtsi (1905–14), and Lviv; at the Lviv (Underground) Ukrainian University; at the Lviv Pedagogical Institute (1937–9); and at Lviv University (1939–40). In 1940 he was exiled to Tomsk, in Siberia, where he continued teaching. After Stalin's death he was rehabilitated, and returned to Lviv. He is the author of Ukrainian textbooks on chemistry (1911) and arithmetic.

**Tsehelsky, Yevhen** [Cehel's'kyj, Jevhen], b 5 May 1912 in Chernivtsi, d 9 October 1980 in Rochester, New York. Violinist, musicologist, and teacher. He studied at the Prague State Conservatory (violin major, 1937) and Charles University in Prague (PH D in musicology) and then directed the Peremyshl school of the Lysenko Higher Institute of Music (1937–9). He toured Ukraine as a solo violinist, and he was the main organizer and artistic director of the 1942 Regional Choral Competition in Lviv. He emigrated to the United States in 1949, where he taught violin and was a member of the Rochester Community Symphony Orchestra. Among his musicological works are the monograph *Chekhy i halyts'ko-ukraïns'ka svits'ka muzyka v 19 stolitti* (The Czechs and Galician-Ukrainian Secular Music of the 19th Century, 1943) and several articles and reviews.

**Tsehliar, Yakiv** [Cehljar, Jakiv] (Ziegler), b 29 February 1912 in Kiev. Composer. After graduating from the Kiev Music School (1939) and the Tbilisi Conservatory (1946) he became the music editor of the Kiev Studio of Popular Science Films (1953–73). His works include the operettas *Hist' z Vidnia* (The Guest from Vienna, 1960) and *Divchyna i more* (The Girl and the Sea, 1965), the cantata *Bezsmertnomu Kobzariu* (To the Immortal Bard, 1963), and chamber music, choruses, Ukrainian folk song arrangements, and film scores.

**Tsehlynsky, Hryhorii** [Cehlyns'kyj, Hryhorij] (pseud: Hryhorii Hryhoriievych), b 9 March 1853 in Kalush, Galicia, d 23 October 1912 in Vienna. Writer, teacher, and civic figure. As a student at Vienna University (1874–9) he was active in the Sich student society. After graduating he was a teacher at the Academic Gymnasium of Lviv (1880–8), the person in charge of the Ruska Besida Theater's repertoire (1882–8), editor of the Lviv biweekly *Zoria* (1887–8), and director of the *Peremyshl State Gymnasium's Ukrainian classes (1888–95) and its principal (1895–1910). In Peremyshl he helped to found the St Nicholas Bursa society, the Ukrainian Girls' Institute, the Vira and Ukrainska Shchadnytsia credit co-operatives, and the People's Home, and he prepared textbooks for use in Galicia's Ukrainian gymnasiums. In 1907 he was elected to the Austrian parliament, and became a member of the presidium of the Ukrainian Parliamentary Club in Vienna. He was buried in Peremyshl. Tsehlynsky's poems, stories, reviews, political articles, and literary criticism appeared in *Dilo* and *Zoria* in the 1880s and 1890s. In the years 1883–5 he wrote a column called 'Z teky Padury' (From Padura's Portfolio) in *Zerkalo*. For the Ruska Besida Theater he wrote the first (albeit commonplace and superficial) Ukrainian comedies about the contemporary Galician bourgeoisie, nobility, and intelligentsia: *Na dobrodiini tsily* (For Good Causes, 1884), *Sokolyky* (The Falconets, 1885), *Tato na zaruchynakh* (Father at the Betrothal, 1885), *Lykhyi den'* (A Terrible Day, 1886), *Shliakhta khodachkova* (The Petty Nobility, 1886), *Torhovlia zhemchuhamy* (Trade in Pearls, 1895), and *Argonavty* (Argonauts, 1898). He also wrote the didactic dramas *Vorozhbyt* (The Soothsayer, 1902) and *Kara sovisty* (Punishment of the Conscience, 1903). He was the most popular playwright in Galicia in the years 1883–95.

R. Senkus

Mykola Tsehlynsky            Volodymyr Tselevych

**Tsehlynsky, Mykola** [Cehlyns'kyj] (Ceglinsky, Nicholas), b 1883 in Lviv, d March 1956 in New York. Journalist and community figure. He was educated in Switzerland, and emigrated to the United States around 1916. He became involved with the Federation of Ukrainian Socialist Parties in the United States (FUSP) and established a close working relationship with M. *Sichynsky. He was forced out of his position as editor of the federation's newspaper *Robitnyk* when the group began to move ideologically toward bolshevism. He edited the Ukrainian Fraternal Association's newspaper *Narodna volia* in 1922–3, 1942–3, and 1946–7. He was one of the initiators of (1922) and leading figures in the *Oborona Ukrainy society, but broke with that group in 1936 and established a Ukrainian Workers' Hromada that briefly published *Robitnycha hromada* in Newark, New Jersey.

**Tsekhanovetsky, Hryhorii** [Cexanovec'kyj, Hryhorij], b 1833 in the Chernihiv region, d 1898 in Kharkiv. Economist and statistician. A graduate of Kiev University (PH D, 1869), he taught economics there (1859–72) and then at Kharkiv University (1873–98), where he also served as rector (1881–4). He wrote *Znachenie Adama Smita v istorii politiko-ekonomicheskikh sistem* (The Importance of Adam Smith in the History of Political-Economic Systems, 1859), in which he criticized some aspects of Smith's theories and advocated a historical approach to the study of economics; *Zheleznyia dorogi i gosudarstvo* (Railroads and the State, 1869), based on his dissertation; and articles on political economy and other topics. He favored state intervention in some sectors of the economy, including railroad construction.

**Tsekhnovitser, Marko** [Cexnovicer], b 1890 in Staryi Oskol, Kursk gubernia, Russia, d 13 May 1945 in Moscow. Microbiologist; full member of the USSR Academy of Medical Sciences (AMN SSSR) from 1944. A graduate of Kharkiv University (1915), he worked for the Kharkiv Bacteriological Institute (from 1925 as department head, from 1932 as director), taught at Kharkiv University (from 1930), and headed the microbiology departments at the Kharkiv Institute for the Upgrading of Physicians (1930–5) and the Kharkiv Medical Institute (from 1935). In 1944 he joined the Bureau of Hygiene, Microbiology, and Epidemiology of the AMN SSSR. He researched the microbiology and immunology of tuberculosis, children's diseases, rickets, typhus, malaria, and rabies.

**Tselevych, Volodymyr** [Celevyč], b 1891, d ca 1944. Political leader in Galicia. A graduate in law from Lviv University, he was one of the leading Ukrainian politicians in Galicia in the interwar period. In 1919–22 he was secretary of the Ukrainian Citizens' Committee in Lviv and then general secretary of the Ukrainian National Democratic Alliance (1925–8 and 1932–7). In 1928 and 1935 he was elected to the Polish Sejm, where he served as vice-president of the Ukrainian Club. In 1930 he was imprisoned in Brest, and in 1935 he conceived the so-called Normalization policy with V. Mudry. He was chief editor of the weekly *Svoboda* from 1932 to 1935. His political articles, which appeared in *Svoboda* and *Dilo*, included items on electoral law, self-government, and municipal law. He also wrote political pamphlets, such as *Narid, natsiia, derzhava* (A People, Nation, and State, 1934). In 1939 he was arrested by the Soviets, and disappeared in a Moscow prison.

**Tselevych, Yuliian** [Celevyč, Julijan], b 23 March 1843 in Pavelche, Stanyslaviv circle, Galicia, d 24 December 1892 in Lviv. Teacher and historian. After studying at the universities of Lviv (1862–5) and Vienna (1865–8; PH D,

Yuliian Tselevych          Mykola Tsenko

1878), where he was involved in the Sich student society, he taught in Stanyslaviv and Lviv (from 1875 at the Academic Gymnasium) and wrote works on Galician history, including *Istoriia Skytu Maniavs'koho* (History of the Maniava Hermitage, 1886) and some of the first studies of the opryshoks. In 1892 he became the first head of the reorganized Shevchenko Scientific Society.

**Tselevych-Stetsiuk, Uliana** [Celevyč-Stecjuk, Uljana] (née Dyda), b 28 April 1915 in Chicago, d 18 August 1981 in Chicago. Political activist. In the 1920s she returned with her parents to Ukraine, where she completed her education and became active in the OUN (1933) and the co-operative movement. During the war she joined the OUN expeditionary groups. After returning to Chicago in 1948, she became active in the Anti-Bolshevik Bloc of Nations (ABN) and served for many years as vice-president of the *Ukrainian Liberation Front and the World Federation of Ukrainian Women's Organizations. She was one of the founders and a president (1967–81) of the Women's Alliance of the *Organization for the Defense of Four Freedoms for Ukraine.

**Tseltner, Volodymyr** [Cel'tner] (Popov), b 26 April 1926 in Kiev. Art scholar. A graduate of the Kiev Institute of Theater Arts (1950), he has written books on Soviet Ukrainian art of the 1920s and 1930s (1966, with L. Popova) and on K. Ahnit-Sledzevsky (1968), T. Yablonska (1968, with L. Popova), F. Manailo (1970), and V. Lytvynenko (1971).

**Tsemeska Bay** [Cemes'ka zatoka]. IX–18. The largest bay along the east-central Black Sea coast. Located southeast of Kerch Strait, it is 9 km wide at its entrance, 15 km long, and 21–27 m deep. It does not freeze over in the winter. The city of Novorossiisk is situated at its sheltered northern corner.

**Tsenko, Mykola** [Cenko], b 5 May 1910 in Synevidsko Nyzhnie, Stryi county, Galicia. Civic activist. After graduating from Lviv University (1933) he practiced law and served as president of the *Vidrodzhennia society in Lviv (1936–9). During the Second World War he headed the organizational department of the *Ukrainian Central Committee in Cracow and Lviv (1940–4) and obtained a doctorate of law from the Ukrainian Free University in

Prague (1943). In 1949 he emigrated to the United States, where he developed a successful real estate business and was active in several Ukrainian organizations. He is a patron of Ukrainian scholarship and the benefactor of the Cenko Prize for bibliography.

**Tsentral** (full name: Tsentralnyi ukrainskyi silsko-hospo-darskyi kooperatyvnyi soiuz [Central Ukrainian Agricultural Co-operative Union]). A co-operative association established in Kiev in January 1918 to represent agricultural organizations and co-operatives throughout Ukraine, supply them with farm machinery, equipment, and fertilizers, organize a distribution system for agricultural produce, and promote associations for the joint cultivation of land. The Kiev Central Agricultural Society (est 1915), which had been run by P. Pozharsky as president, V. Koval as vice-president, and Rev T. Dobriansky as a member of the executive, was the predecessor of Tsentral. The Tsentral congress at the end of August 1918 elected an executive of Koval (president), K. Shemetiv, N. Filipovsky, M. Shapoval, O. Mytsiuk, and V. Domanytsky (secretary) and a board of directors headed by K. Matsiievych. By July 1919 the union represented 41 co-operative associations and 728 individual co-operatives. Its assets increased from 5,400,000 *karbovantsi* in January 1918 to 21,148,000 *karbovantsi* in January 1919 and 147,707,000 *karbovantsi* in October 1920. It maintained offices in Odessa, Kharkiv, Poltava, Katerynoslav, and Vinnytsia. In the summer of 1918 it acquired a large plow factory in Odessa and owned several sawmills. Tsentral's organ was the semimonthly *Sil's'kyi hospodar*, published in Kiev in 1918–19.

In 1920 the Soviet authorities abolished all independent co-operatives in Ukraine, including Tsentral. In 1922 they set up the government-controlled *Silskyi Hospodar association of farm co-operatives in its place.

**Tsentrobank** (full name: Tsentralnyi kooperatyvnyi bank [Central Co-operative Bank]). The main financial institution and organizational center for all Ukrainian co-operatives in Galicia. It was established in Lviv in 1898 by K. *Levytsky, S. *Fedak, and Ya. *Kulachkovsky. It was known at first as the Provincial Credit Union; its purpose was to organize credit and other co-operatives, accept deposits from and grant credit to the individual co-operatives, and oversee the development of the entire co-operative movement in Galicia. The first director, Levytsky, was succeeded by K. Pankivsky, H. Vretsona, and O. Saievych. The board of directors was chaired by H. Kuzma. Initially the union represented 17 credit and 2 trade co-operatives. By 1913 it had 906 members, including 427 co-operatives. Its assets reached 1.1 million kronen, its outstanding loans 4.3 million kronen, and its turnover 106 million kronen. In 1904 its organizational responsibilities for the co-operative movement in Galicia were transferred to the newly created *Audit Union of Ukrainian Co-operatives.

After the First World War the union was revived and reorganized. Its name was changed to Tsentrobank in 1924. The bank continued to function as the overall co-ordinating body for the rural *Raiffeisen credit co-operatives and the urban *Ukrainbank credit unions. Initially growth was slow because of the economic depression. In 1928 the membership was 565. By March 1939 the union had 1,889 members, of which 1,732 were co-operatives (in-cluding 113 Ukrainbank branches). Tsentrobank shares were worth over 323,000 zlotys. Its reserve funds were 320,000 zlotys, its deposits 2.2 million, its outstanding loans 2.7 million, and its turnover more that 70 million zlotys. From 1924 the managing director of Tsentrobank was Levytsky; his assistants were Saievych, S. Kuzyk; and I. Olkhovy. V. Okhrymovych, L. Kulchytsky, M. Voloshyn, and then A. Mudryk served as chairmen of the board of directors. Tsentrobank ceased to function in 1939, following the first Soviet occupation of Western Ukraine. Under German occupation (1941–4) it was revived partially: it had 71 Ukrainbank branches, but its activities were limited. The second Soviet occupation put an end to its activities.

A Tsentrosoiuz store in Lviv

**Tsentrosoiuz** (full name: Soiuz kooperatyvnykh soiuziv [Union of Co-operative Unions]). A central association of Ukrainian agricultural co-operatives in Galicia for marketing their farm products and purchasing various commodities for them. It was established on the initiative of T. Kormosh in Peremyshl in 1899 as the Farming and Trading Association and had 40 members. In 1911 it transferred its headquarters to Lviv and affiliated itself with the *Silskyi Hospodar society, forming the Provincial Union of Agricultural Associations, a trade syndicate of the Silskyi Hospodar. By the outbreak of the First World War the union had 16 branches in the major towns and 481 members, including 66 co-operatives. Its turnover in 1912 totaled almost 11 million Austrian kronen, and its operations extended to Bukovyna, Transcarpathia, Bosnia, and the Ukrainian communities in Canada and the United States. Before the war the directors of the union included D. Korenets, Kormosh, I. Lypetsky, and S. *Herasymovych; Ye. Olesnytsky served as chairman of the board of directors. During the war the union dissolved.

In 1921–2 co-operative associations on a regional or county level arose throughout Galicia, and the Union of Agricultural Associations was established to co-ordinate their activities. In 1924 the union adopted a new statute and changed its name to the Union of Co-operative Unions, or Tsentrosoiuz. At the time it represented 5 central co-operative organizations, 25 county or regional associations, and 1,491 primary co-operatives. Its turnover was 1.7 million zlotys. It supplied Ukrainian rural co-

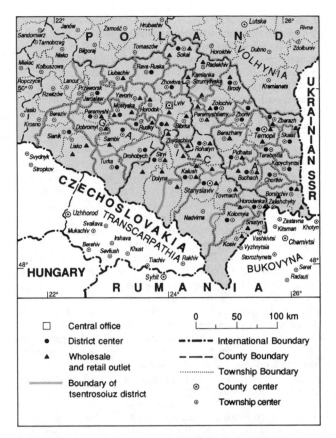

## BOUNDARIES OF TSENTROSOIUZ

operatives with consumer and dry goods, agricultural machinery and equipment, building materials, fuel, artificial fertilizers, and seed. Tsentrosoiuz owned and operated factories manufacturing soap, thread, and batteries and processing meat. It marketed Ukrainian agricultural produce (meat, eggs, etc) throughout Poland and even in Central and Western Europe. The farm co-operative movement grew quickly in the late 1920s before the onset of the Great Depression and then revived in the mid-1930s. By the end of 1938 Tsentrosoiuz represented 4 central co-operative organizations, 26 county or regional associations, and 143 other co-operatives. Its turnover increased from 10.6 million zlotys in 1933 to 37.5 million in 1937. Its top executives in the interwar period were Herasymovych, Yu. *Sheparovych, V. Medvetsky, M. Tvorydlo, I. *Martiuk, and O. Radlovsky; the chairman of the board of directors was Korenets and then O. Lutsky. During the Second World War the organization was directed by I. Semianchuk. When Soviet power was established in Western Ukraine, Tsentrosoiuz was dissolved.

A. Kachor

**Tsentrostudiia.** See Mykhailychenko Theater.

**Tsependa, Kyrylo** [Cependa], b 24 December 1914 in Dzhuryn, Chortkiv county, Galicia. Conductor. In 1938–9 he studied at the Lysenko Higher Institute of Music in Lviv in the choral conducting class of M. Kolessa and theory classes of S. Liudkevych, B. Kudryk, Z. Lysko, and W. Wytwycky. He conducted the St Barbara Church choir in

Vienna (1941–2) and the Vienna Sich student chorus (1942–5). In 1946–9 he led the male chorus Trembita in Berchtesgaden, Germany. Since 1949 he has lived in the United States, where from 1955 he conducted the mixed chorus Trembita in Detroit. His conducting skill is preserved on numerous recordings.

**Tsepko, Ivan** [Cepko], b 11 November 1899 in Korshyliv, Zolochiv county, Galicia, d 28 October 1922. Political activist and insurgent. After serving in the Austrian and the Ukrainian Galician armies he joined the Communist party in 1920 and fought with the Red Army against Polish forces. He was a delegate to a conference of Galician and Bukovynian Communists in Kiev. In 1922, with S. Melnychuk and M. Sheremeta, he led an insurgent Communist partisan group which was active in the Ternopil region. He died in action against Polish gendarmes.

**Tserkevych, Konstantyn** [Cerkevyč], b 25 May 1911 in Lidavo, Ostrih county, Volhynia gubernia, d 22 October 1987 in Staten Island, New York. Aeronautical engineer, economist, lexicographer, and community figure. Displaced during the Second World War, he emigrated to the United States in 1951, where he headed the New York branch of the Ukrainian Engineers' Society of America (1952–73). From 1971 he was the president of the *Research Society for Ukrainian Terminology and coeditor of its dictionary of Ukrainian synonyms (1975), orthographic dictionary (1975), handbook in Ukrainian (1982), and Russian-Ukrainian legal dictionary (1984).

**Tserkovnaia gazeta** (Church Newspaper). A newspaper published weekly from March 1856 to June 1858 (a total of 106 issues) in Budapest by the Roman Catholic St Stephen Society. It contained sermons, literary works, many letters and obituaries, and articles on theological issues, church rites, and historical themes. The paper was published in the *yazychiie and edited by Rev I. Rakovsky. It was succeeded by Tserkovnyi viestnik dlia rusynov avstriiskoi derzhavy, which appeared for 10 issues. Owing to their extreme conservatism, archaic language, and Russophile tendencies, neither paper had much support among the Transcarpathian population.

**Tserkovnyi visnyk** (Church Herald). A semimonthly Catholic newspaper published by the SS Volodymyr and Olga parish in Chicago since 1968. Until 1970 it was called Visnyk. In addition to local church news and articles on religious topics, it includes articles on the Ukrainian Catholic church in the USSR and elsewhere and on historical and cultural topics. The editors of Tserkovnyi visnyk have been V. Markus and (since 1971) M. Butrynsky.

**Tserkva i narid** (Church and Nation). The semimonthly organ of the Volhynian eparchial council of the Polish Autocephalous Orthodox church published from March 1935 to December 1938 in Kremianets. Edited by I. *Vlasovsky, the journal supported the autocephaly and Ukrainianization of the church. Ninety-one issues appeared before the journal was forced to close by the Polish authorities. The journal's press also published some 30 books and pamphlets.

*Tserkva i narid* (Church and Nation). An illustrated Orthodox religious monthly published in Winnipeg and Grimsby, Ontario, in 1949–51. The journal was initiated by Archbishop M. *Skrypnyk and edited by I. *Vlasovsky. It contained news of the Ukrainian Orthodox church in Canada and the United States, information on the contemporary religious situation in Ukraine, and essays on historical and political topics. It ceased publication after Skrypnyk moved to the United States.

*Tserkva i zhyttia*

*Tserkva i zhyttia* (Church and Life). The organ of the Ukrainian Autocephalous Orthodox church (UAOC), published by the All-Ukrainian Orthodox Church Council and its commission at the Kharkiv District Church Council. Published in Kharkiv in 1927–8, it was edited first by Metropolitan V. Lypkivsky and then by Archbishop I. Pavlovsky. The journal reported on the activities of the UAOC and published the minutes of meetings of the church council and documents in the history of the UAOC. It also contained articles on religious and theological topics. Among the main contributors were V. Chekhivsky, V. Yukhymovych, and Bishops K. Maliushkevych, K. Krotevych, and M. Pyvovariv. Only seven issues of the journal appeared before it was closed owing to a lack of funds and the opposition of the Soviet authorities.

*Tserkva i zhyttia* (Church and Life). The bimonthly organ of the Metropolitan Lypkivsky Ukrainian Orthodox Brotherhood and the unofficial organ of the *Ukrainian Autocephalous Orthodox Church (UAOC) (Conciliar), published from 1957 to 1977 in Chicago (until 1971 it was printed in Neu-Ulm, Germany). The journal contained many documents on the history of the UAOC and on Metropolitan V. *Lypkivsky (including many of his writings and sermons), and articles on the activities of the UAOC (Conciliar) and religious and political topics. The editors were M. Yavdas and A. Yaremenko, and the contributors included P. Maievsky, O. Bykovets, S. Kindzeriavy-Pastukhiv, I. Hrushetsky, S. Hardansky, and V. Dubrovsky. A total of 116 issues of the journal appeared. The Tserkva i Zhyttia publishing house issued Lypkivsky's *Propovidi na nedili i sviata* (Sermons for Sundays and Feast Days, 1969) and several other books.

*Tserkva i zhyttia* (Church and Life). The organ of the Ukrainian Catholic apostolic exarchate (later eparchy) of Australia, New Zealand, and Oceania. It began to appear in 1960 as a quarterly, published in Lindholme and then, from 1962, in Melbourne. In 1967 it became a biweekly newspaper and in 1973 a weekly. The publication deals mainly with religious topics and church affairs, but also provides information about matters of general interest and the religious situation in Ukraine. Its editors have included Rev I. Shevtsiv, Ye. Zavalynsky, and Yu. Venhlovsky.

**Tsertelev, Nikolai** [Certeljev, Nikolaj] (Tsereteli), b 1790 in Khorol, Kiev vicegerency, d 20 September 1869 in Morshansk, Tambov gubernia, Russia. Ethnographer and educator; prince of Georgian descent. After graduating from Moscow University (1814) he collected and studied Ukrainian folklore. In the 1820s he worked in the schools of the Tambov and Poltava gubernias and belonged to the Free Society of Lovers of Russian Literature, which was connected with the Decembrists. His *Opyt sobraniia starinnykh malorossiiskikh pesnei* (An Attempt at Collecting Ancient Little Russian Songs, 1819) was one of the first collections of Ukrainian dumas and songs. It had an important impact on Ukrainian writers and scholars such as M. Maksymovych, H. Kvitka-Osnovianenko, I. Sreznevsky, A. Metlynsky, and M. Kostomarov. He also wrote articles on Ukrainian folk poetry (1825, 1827) and old Russian tales and songs (1820).

**Tsesevych, Platon** [Cesevyč], b 7 December 1879 in Niahnevichy, Minsk gubernia, Belarus, d 30 November 1958 in Moscow. Opera singer (bass). He worked in the theater troupes of D. Haidamaka and O. Suslov and studied singing under Y. Liubin in St Petersburg (1902–4), before his debut at the Kharkiv Opera (1904). He sang with the opera theaters of Kharkiv, Kiev, and Odessa; at the Bolshoi and the Zymin operas in Moscow; and in France and Italy (1925–6 and 1932). In 1933–48 he concertized throughout the USSR. His operatic roles included the name-parts in M. Lysenko's *Taras Bulba* and M. Mussorgsky's *Boris Godunov*, Mephistopheles in C. Gounod's *Faust*, and Basilio in G. Rossini's *Il Barbiere di Siviglia*. I. Kozlovsky was his pupil.

**Tsesevych, Volodymyr** [Cesevyč] (Tsesevich, Vladimir), b 11 October 1907 in Kiev, d 28 October 1983 in Odessa. Astronomer; AN URSR (now ANU) corresponding member from 1948. A graduate of Leningrad University (1929), he worked at astronomical observatories in Dushanbe and Leningrad. From 1944 he directed the Odessa Astronomical Observatory; in 1948–50 he simultaneously directed the ANU Main Astronomical Observatory. His main field of research was variable stars (the variation in their brightness, the theory of their occultation, and the behavior of binary stars). He also studied the rotation of man-made satellites and asteroids, and worked out and published extensive tables of binaries.

**Tsiluiko, Kyrylo** [Cilujko], b 1908 in Pokrovske, Oleksandrivske county, Katerynoslav gubernia, d 12 October 1981 in Kiev. Linguist. After graduating from the Dnipropetrovske Pedagogical Institute (1935) he taught in Moscow and Leningrad. From 1946 he lectured at Kiev

Volodymyr Tsesevych          Olha Tsipanovska

University and worked at the AN URSR (now ANU) Institute of Linguistics. As the institute's learned secretary and deputy director, he co-ordinated onomastic research in Ukraine, oversaw work on a hydronymic atlas of Ukraine, and established a massive toponymic reference file. In 1960 he organized and thenceforth headed the *Ukrainian Onomastic Commission, and edited its *Povidomlennia* (Reports, 1966–76). Tsiluiko wrote programs for compiling and studying Ukraine's toponyms (1950, 1954, 1962) and articles on Ukrainian toponymy, orthography, and linguistics, toponyms in Dnipropetrovske and Poltava oblasts, and hydronyms of the Samara Basin. He was the editor responsible for toponymy of the ANU series *Istoriia mist i sil* URSR (History of the Cities and Villages of the Ukrainian SSR, 24 vols, 1967–74) and chief editor of the ANU dictionary of Ukraine's hydronyms (1979).

**Tsipanovska, Olha** [Cipanovs'ka, Ol'ha], b 18 December 1866 in Kozova, Dolyna county, Galicia, d 10 December 1941 in Lviv. Civic activist, pianist, and educator. After graduating from a teachers' seminary in Peremyshl she taught at a girls' school (1880–92) and at the women teachers' seminary in Peremyshl (1892–1925). She founded a Ukrainian teachers' seminary at the Girls' Institute (1920), a seamstress school, and a domestic school (1932) in Peremyshl. She gave piano recitals in Peremyshl, Lviv, Yaroslav, and Vienna and was renowned for her rendition of M. Lysenko's music. She was a founder and the first conductor of the Boian chorus in Peremyshl (1904–5) and the founder of the local branch of the *Lysenko Higher Institute of Music, which she also directed (1925–32). She taught piano, solo and choir singing, and conducting. She was also known for her charitable work. She died of typhus, which she contracted while caring for former inmates of German POW camps.

**Tsipyvnyk, Dmytro** [Cipyvnyk] (Cipywnyk), b 15 April 1927 in Brooksby, Saskatchewan. Psychiatrist and community leader. After graduating in medicine from the University of Saskatchewan (1963) he set up a private practice and lectured at the university. He is a member of several medical associations, including the Ukrainian Medical Association of North America, and served as regional director of the Canadian Addiction Foundation (1977–81). He sat on the senate of the University of Saskat-

chewan (1983–6). He has been active in the Ukrainian Orthodox Church of Canada, the Ukrainian Professional and Business Club, and, most notably, the Ukrainian Canadian Committee (now Congress; Saskatchewan president, 1982–6; national president, 1986–92). He has written over 20 articles on suicide and addiction.

**Tsisyk, Volodymyr** [Cisyk], b 20 September 1913 in Lisky, Kolomyia county, Galicia, d 7 February 1971 in New York. Violinist, teacher, and conductor. He studied at the Prague State Conservatory and the Lviv Conservatory (graduated 1936) and in Munich and was a concertmaster (from 1935) with the Lviv symphony and opera orchestras. Emigrating to the United States after the Second World War, he led his own violin studio in New York (1950–2), organized a string quartet and conducted a string orchestra, and cofounded (1952) and taught at the Ukrainian Music Institute of America.

***Tsitologiia i genetika*** (Cytology and Genetics). A bimonthly scientific journal published in Kiev by the *Institute of Molecular Biology and Genetics of the AN URSR (now ANU) since 1967. It contains articles on the structure and function of cells, cellular reproduction, general and molecular *genetics, the genetic principles of *selection, medical genetics, and genetic engineering. In 1988 I. Shevtsov was replaced by A. Sozinov as editor. The periodical is published in Russian and is translated into English in the United States.

**Tsiupa, Ivan** [Cjupa], b 29 October 1911 in Birky, Zinkiv county, Poltava gubernia. Writer. He worked as a journalist from 1933 on and was deputy chief editor of *Kolhospnyk Ukraïny* and *Vitchyzna* (1950–2) and chief editor of *Ukraïna* (1952–5). Since 1946 he has published numerous prose collections, a popular book on Soviet Ukraine (1960), several propagandistic pamphlets, and the novels *Braty* (Brothers, 1950), *Nazustrich doli* (To a Meeting with Fate, 2nd edn, 1958), *Hrozy i raiduhy* (Storms and Rainbows, 1961), *Vichnyi vohon'* (Eternal Fire, 1962), *Cherez terny do zirok* (Through the Thorns to the Stars, 1966, about Yu. Kotsiubynsky), *Kraiany* (Countrymen, 1971), *Muzhnii vershnyk* (The Brave Rider, 1974), *Homin Dniprovs'koho kosohoru* (The Echo of the Dnieper's Slope, 1977), *Dzvony iantarnoho lita* (Bells of an Amber Summer, 1981), *U sertsi dzvoniat' holosy* (In the Heart Voices Ring, 1984), and *Rokit syn'oho moria* (The Roar of the Blue Sea, 1986). For the novel *U sertsi dzvoniat' holosy* he was awarded the Shevchenko Prize in 1985.

**Tsiupko, Volodymyr** [Cjupko], b 24 September 1936 in Yosypivka, Kirovohrad oblast. Painter and muralist. A graduate of the Leningrad Institute of Applied Art (1970), he took part in exhibitions in private apartments in Odessa and in the Second Exhibition of Ukrainian Nonconformist Artists (1976), held in a Moscow flat. His compositions appear abstract but in fact are often inspired by the surrounding landscape (eg, *Boats*, 1977). Tsiupko works with patches of color, which he applies with a palette knife (eg, *White Composition*, 1987). He painted the murals inside the Odessa Literary Museum, the Odessa Student Palace, and the Museum of the Tatarbunary Uprising.

**Tsiurupynske** [Cjurupyns'ke]. VII-13. A city (1989 pop 25,200) and port on the Konka River and a raion center in Kherson oblast. In the 10th to 13th centuries the trade and defense outpost of Oleshia stood in the vicinity of today's city. From the 15th to 18th centuries the territory was under the control of the Crimean Khanate, which permitted the Zaporozhian Cossacks to establish the Oleshky Sich there (1711–28). In 1784 the site of the Cossack fortress was settled by state peasants, and the village was named Oleshky. When Tavriia gubernia was set up in 1802, Oleshky became the center of Dnieper county. Its name was changed to the current one in 1928. Today the city is an agricultural and health resort center. It has a cellulose and paper plant, a fish-processing complex, a juice factory, and a winery. It is the home of the Lower Dnieper Scientific Research Station for Sands Afforestation and Viticulture.

**Tsiutsiura, Bohdan.** See Ciuciura, Theodore.

**Tsiutsiura, Tymish** [Cjucjura, Tymiš] (Tsytsiura, Tsetsiura), b and d ? Cossack statesman, originally from the Pereiaslav region, active during the period of the *Ruin. He was a captain in Boryspil regiment (1656–8) and the colonel of Pereiaslav regiment (1658–60). At first a follower of Hetman I. Vyhovsky, Tsiutsiura helped him to defeat the Muscovite army at Konotip in 1659. Later he planned the mutiny against Vyhovsky and maintained a pro-Muscovite policy with an eye to obtaining the hetman's post for himself. Tsiutsiura's conduct enabled Moscow to initiate proceedings against Hetman Yu. Khmelnytsky during the drawing up of the Pereiaslav Articles of 1659. In 1660 Tsiutsiura went to Moscow with his petition, and that year he participated in the Muscovite voivode V. Sheremetev's campaign against Poland as acting hetman in charge of the Left-Bank regiments (20,000 Cossacks). After the defeat of Sheremetev near Chudniv in 1660, Tsiutsiura abdicated and joined Khmelnytsky and the Poles, but he was imprisoned in Cracow nonetheless (1660–2). After his release Tsiutsiura returned to Pereiaslav, whence he was sent to Moscow and exiled to Tomsk, Siberia (1667).

**Tsmokalenko, Dmytro** [Cmokalenko], b 25 September 1922 in Betiahy, Kremenchuk county, Poltava gubernia. Writer and government figure. In the 1950s he worked for the journal *Zhovten'*. He has been chief editor of *Literaturna Ukraïna* (1963–6), deputy director of the CC CPU Department of Culture (1966–72), and deputy head of the Ukrainian State Committee for Publishing, Printing, and the Book Trade (1972–84). He has written the prose collections *Zirnytsi nad Dniprom* (Auroras over the Dnieper, 1952), *Shakhtars'ka storona* (A Miner's Side, 1954), and *Pravo na druzhbu* (The Right to Friendship, 1956), the novel *Suvore povnolittia* (Severe Adulthood, 1959), and four pamphlets attacking 'Ukrainian bourgeois nationalists.'

**Tsokan, Illia** [C'okan', Illja], b 1887 in Storonybaby, Zolochiv county, Galicia, d 1940 in Semipalatinsk, Siberia. Senior military officer. During the First World War he was an officer in the Legion of Ukrainian Sich Riflemen. As a member of the Ukrainian Military Committee, he helped organize the *November Uprising in Lviv. In the Ukraini-

Illia Tsokan

an Galician Army (UHA) he was given command of the Zolochiv Military District and was one of the first officers to be promoted to captain. In June 1919 he was appointed commander of the Ternopil Military District, where he organized and then commanded the Ternopil Brigade of the UHA. In August he became chief logistics officer of the UHA. In the interwar period he settled in Transcarpathia and then emigrated to Soviet Ukraine. He was arrested in the 1930s and sent to a Siberian labor camp.

**Tson, Vasyl** [C'on', Vasyl'], b 20 February 1884 in Yasenivtsi, Zolochiv county, Galicia, d 17 August 1959. Kilim designer. He graduated from the weaving school in Hlyniany (1903) and from the industrial school in Lviv (1905) and designed kilims in Lviv, using Ukrainian folk designs. He taught kilim weaving and dyeing at the Lviv Technical School (1920–38) and the Lviv School of Applied Art and Lviv Institute of Applied and Decorative Arts (1939–56).

**Tsukanova, Mariia** [Cukanova, Marija], 1905–? Writer. In 1944 she published the novel *Ïkh taiemnytsia* (Their Secret) in Lviv, and her play *Prolisky* (Anemones) was staged in several Galician towns. As a postwar refugee in Germany (from 1945) and Argentina (from 1950) she contributed prose to *Litavry* and *Porohy*. In 1970 she moved to the United States. Published separately were her collection of five stories, *Buzkovyi tsvit* (Lilac Blossoms, 1951), and book of selected works, *Na hrani dvokh svitiv* (On the Edge of Two Worlds, 1968).

**Tsuman** [Cuman']. III-6. A town smt (1986 pop 5,100) on the Putylivka River in Kyvertsi raion, Volhynia oblast. It was first mentioned in historical documents in 1557. In 1943 the Ukrainian Insurgent Army fought the Germans and the Soviet partisans in the forests around Tsuman. In reprisal the Germans executed approx 300 inhabitants and burned the village in November 1943. Today the main industries in Tsuman are forestry and fishing.

**Tsurkovsky, Antin** [Curkovs'kyj] (Curkowsky, Anthony), b 24 February 1882 in Zolochiv, Galicia, d 31 July 1955 in Camden, New Jersey. Journalist and civic figure; member of the Shevchenko Scientific Society. After being educated in Berezhany he emigrated to the United States, where he edited *Svoboda (1907–9, 1911) and *Ameryka (1914–26). Subsequently he served as recording secretary of the Providence Association of Ukrainian Catholics in America (1926–55). He translated some English literature into Ukrainian and wrote popular articles.

**Tsurkovsky, Yaroslav** [Curkovs'kyj, Jaroslav], b 1 January 1905 in Ternopil. Poet and psychologist. He graduated from Lviv (1927) and Prague (1927) universities and wrote the poetry collections *Prozolot' svitanku* (The Gilding of the Dawn, 1925), *Vohni* (Fires, 1926), *Smoloskypy* (Torches, 1926), and *Momenty i vichnist'* (Moments and Eternity, 1927); the narrative poems 'Zbentezhenyi litak' (The Confused Airplane, *Sluzhbovyk*, 1928, nos 4–6) and 'Boianovyi homin' (Boian's Echo); the novel *Bohach ta nuzhdar* (The Rich Man and the Indigent); and the drama *Teklia Moroz*. In the years 1932–9 he was director of Lviv's Institute of Psychological Research by the Integral Method. During the 1939–41 Soviet occupation of Galicia he headed the Writers' Union of Ukraine's organizing committee in Lviv and was secretary of *Literatura i mystetstvo*. After the war he organized the first Soviet Ukrainian experimental laboratory of the psychology and physiology of labor at the Lviv Forklift Plant; in 1966 it became the Central Branch Laboratory of Psychology, Physiology, and Working Conditions of the USSR Ministry of the Automobile Industry. The author of works in psychology and human engineering and the originator of the theory of psychological controllability, he invented a 'controlograph' for use in psychological diagnoses.

**Tsvetkov, Viktor** [Cvetkov], b 23 March 1923 in Kamenka, Kolomna raion, Moscow oblast. Russian jurist; corresponding member of the AN URSR (now ANU) since 1972. A graduate of the law faculty of Kiev University (1950) and the Academy of Social Sciences of the CC CPSU (1954), he worked in the apparat of the CC CPU (1954–8, 1968–72) and taught law at Kiev University (1958–68). Since 1973 he has chaired the department of the legal problems of administration at the Institute of State and Law of the ANU. He has written books on Soviet state law (1969), the science of administration and local soviets (1970), social and state-legal aspects of administration in the USSR (1978), and the improvement of state administration (1982).

**Tsvietkov, Hlib** [Cvjetkov], b 27 June 1922 in Tyraspil, Kherson gubernia (now in Moldavia). Soviet Ukrainian historian. A graduate of Kiev University (1952), he worked there as a lecturer (from 1955, professor from 1973), prorector (1962–73), and department head (from 1969). His specialization is Soviet-American relations. He was a delegate of the USSR to sessions of the UNESCO General Conference (1968, 1980, 1982) and a member of its Executive Council (from 1981). His writings include *Shestnadsat' let nepriznaniia* (Sixteen Years of Nonrecognition, 1971) and *Politika SShA v otnoshenii SSSR nakanune vtoroi mirovoi voiny* (The Policies of the United States Regarding the USSR on the Eve of the Second World War, 1973).

**Tsviklivtsi settlement.** A late Trypilian settlement (mid-3rd to early 2nd millennium BC) near Tsviklivtsi, Kamianets-Podilskyi raion, Khmelnytskyi oblast. Excavations in 1960–1 revealed semi-pit dwellings, flint and bone tools, adornments (including copper bracelets), and pear-shaped pottery with anthropomorphic handles.

**Tsvilyk, Pavlyna** [Cvilyk] (née Sovizdraniuk), b 22 April 1891 in Kosiv, Galicia, d 31 March 1964 in Kosiv. Folk ceramist. Tsvilyk learned her craft from her father, and for many years she collaborated with her husband, Hryhorii. Her earthenware vases, plates, pots, cups, candlesticks, and figurines were usually decorated with Hutsul floral and faunal motifs and scenes of hunters, musicians, and dancers, painted in green, yellow, and brown on a white surface. Examples of her work are found in museums throughout Ukraine and in other republics of the former USSR.

*Tsvirkun* (The Cricket). An irregular magazine published by the students at the Basilian seminary in Curitiba, Brazil, since 1945. It contains information about student activities, stories and poems, games, and educational articles. By 1978, 164 issues had appeared.

*Ts'vitka* (Floweret). An illustrated children's monthly and, from July 1915, bimonthly magazine, published in 1914 by the Board of Education of the Little Russian National Union of America, and from 1915 to 1917 by the Ukrainian National Association in Jersey City, New Jersey. Edited by D. Andreiko and printed by the Svoboda Press, it contained poetry and stories by Ukrainian authors; folktales; songs; translations of English and American children's literature; materials on Ukrainian history, literature, geography, and folklore; and stories about American history. *Ts'vitka* did much to inculcate Ukrainian national consciousness in its readers.

**Tsybenko, Pavlo** [Cybenko], b 21 August 1909 in Borovytsia, Chyhyryn county, Kiev gubernia. Art historian. He graduated from the Kiev Cinematography Institute (1934) and received a doctorate in 1949. He wrote a monograph on A. Petrytsky (1951), prepared a catalog of Yu. Stefanchuk's works (1965), and wrote the chapters on theatrical scenery design in vols 4 and 5 of the AN URSR (now ANU) history of Ukrainian art (1967, 1969–70).

**Tsymbal, Liudmyla** [Cymbal, Ljudmyla], b 12 October 1937 in Kharkiv. Physicist; AN URSR (now ANU) corresponding member since 1988. After graduating in 1958 from Kharkiv University, she joined the ANU Physical-Technical Institute in Kharkiv, where she has served as a division head since 1981. Her research is devoted to low-temperature physics of metals.

**Tsymbal, Tetiana** [Cymbal, Tetjana] (née Mykhailovska), b 20 March 1900 in Bratslav, Podilia gubernia. Civic activist; wife of V. *Tsymbal. After her studies at the Kiev Polytechnical Institute were interrupted by the First World War, she joined a partisan detachment led by I. Ukhov. She later fled to Rumania, where she taught for a brief period, and in 1923 she emigrated to Argentina. There she was involved in establishing Prosvita societies in Buenos Aires and its suburb of Berisso and was active in developing Ukrainian organizational life in Dock Sud and Valentin Alsina. After the Second World War she initiated a refugee aid committee in Argentina. In 1960 she moved to the United States, where she published two albums of her husband's works and wrote a book of recollections (1978).

Viktor Tsymbal and his *Ariel* in 1962

**Tsymbal, Viktor** [Cymbal], b 1 May 1902 in Stupychne, Zvenyhorodka county, Kiev gubernia, d 28 May 1968 in New York. Painter and graphic artist. A soldier of the UNR Army, he was interned by the Poles in 1920. Having escaped to Czechoslovakia in 1923, he studied in Prague at the Higher Art and Industrial School and the Ukrainian Studio of Plastic Arts. He designed many book covers and bookplates and illustrated children's books, primarily for the Svit Dytyny publishing house. In 1928 he emigrated to Argentina, where he designed neorealist commercial posters for Argentinian, American, and European companies and won six awards for his graphic work. Tsymbal was active in Ukrainian community organizations in Buenos Aires, designed Ukrainian-Argentinian periodicals and theatrical scenery, and painted icons for Ukrainian churches there. In 1960 he emigrated to the United States and worked as a commercial artist in Detroit (1961–6). Tsymbal also painted fantastical Patagonian landscapes and neosymbolist religious, historical, and mythical compositions, such as *People of the Stone Age, The Year 1933 (Famine), The Dnieper, 1941, The Creator, The Immaculate,* and *Ariel*. His mezzotint portraits of T. Shevchenko, V. Domanytsky, V. Lypynsky, T. Edison, A. Toscanini, D. Skoropadsky, B. Khmelnytsky, and I. Mazepa are noted for their detail and workmanship. His political caricatures appeared in Ukrainian émigré periodicals (eg, *Ukraïns'ka trybuna, Mitla*). Solo exhibitions of his works were held in Buenos Aires (1936, 1948, 1956, 1959), New York (1960, 1961), and Detroit (1961, 1963) and, posthumously, in Detroit, Philadelphia, and New York. An album of his graphic works and paintings (ed S. Hordynsky) was published

in New York in 1972, and an album of his caricatures (ed B. Pevny) in 1981.

S. Hordynsky

**Tsymbalist, Viktor** [Cymbalist], b 25 January 1930 in Chervone (now in Adrushivka raion, Zhytomyr oblast). Stage actor. He completed study at the Kiev Institute of Theater Arts (1952, class of H. Yura) and the Kiev Conservatory (1957, class of I. Patorzhynsky). In 1952 he joined the Kiev Ukrainian Drama Theater, where he has played both heroic and character roles, including Edmund in W. Shakespeare's *King Lear* (1959).

Bohdan Tsymbalisty          Yevhen Tsymbalisty

**Tsymbalisty, Bohdan** [Cymbalistyj], b 5 August 1919 in Bovshiv, Rohatyn county, Galicia, d 16 August 1991 in Port Jarvis, New York. Psychologist, community figure, and publicist; member of the American Psychological Association and the Ukrainian Academy of Arts and Sciences in the US. He studied at the universities of Lviv, Berlin, Göttingen (PH D, 1948), and Leuven. In 1951–9 he was an associate of the Centro de Estudios Orientales in Madrid (1951–9), editor of its journal *Oriente Europeo*, and director of the Ukrainian program on the Spanish national radio. In 1959 he emigrated to the United States. He was director of the psychology clinic at the New Jersey Training School for Boys. In 1978 he became chairman of the board of the Ukrainian Museum in New York. He published such essays as *Problema identychnosty* (The Problem of Identity, 1974), *Tavro bezderzhavnosty* (The Stigma of Statelessness, 1982), and *Growing Up in Two Cultures* (1987).

**Tsymbalisty, Yevhen** [Cymbalistyj, Jevhen], b 29 January 1909 in Bovshiv, Rohatyn county, Galicia, d 5 May 1967 in Munich. Conductor, composer, and teacher. He studied music at Lviv University and at the Szymanowski Conservatory in Lviv. In 1934 he moved to Berlin, where he continued his studies at the Hochschule für Musik. His works include the choral-orchestral *Suite of Traveling Songs, Suite of Love Songs,* and *Hunting Suite*; a cantata on the biblical text 'I Am the Beginning and the End'; and arrangements of Ukrainian and German folk songs for chorus.

**Tsymbalka kurhans.** Two burial mounds near Velyka Bilozerka, Kamianka-Dniprovska raion, Zaporizhia oblast. Both mounds were excavated in 1867–8 by I. Zabelin. The first kurhan (Velyka or Large Tsymbalka) contained a 4th-century-BC Scythian burial which included six horses (four with silver and two with gold trappings). Among the grave goods recovered were the remains of six horses (four with silver and two with gold accoutrements) and two gold forehead adornments, one with a figure of a dragonlike goddess and the other bearing the image of two gryphons. The second kurhan (Mala or Small Tsymbalka) contained a 9th-century-BC Bronze Age burial from which arrowheads, bronze fishing poles, and pottery were recovered.

*Tsymbaly*

***Tsymbaly*** (cimbalom or hammered dulcimer). A musical instrument whose strings are struck with two small padded sticks. It consists of a shallow rectangular or trapezoidal wooden sound box with 16–35 clusters of gut or wire strings stretched lengthwise across the deck. Its range is usually three octaves. Originating in Byzantium, it was brought to Europe by the Turks. During the 1600s the *tsymbaly* became widespread throughout Ukraine, supplanting even the *husli* (psaltery) in popularity. As an ensemble instrument it entered the tradition of *\*troisti muzyky*. Today it remains one of the basic instruments of all folk orchestras.

**Tsynkalovsky, Oleksander** [Cynkalovs'kyj] (Cynkałowski), b 9 January 1898 in Volodymyr-Volynskyi,

Oleksander Tsynkalovsky

Volhynia gubernia, d 19 April 1983 in Cracow. Archeologist. After teaching gymnasium in Volodymyr-Volynskyi (1919–25), he studied at Warsaw University and then worked for museums in Warsaw, Lviv, and Kremianets. Before the Second World War he undertook many fruitful archeological digs in Volhynia and Polisia and gathered information about their history and geography. In 1944 he returned to Warsaw to work in an archeological museum, and in 1952 he moved to Cracow as a research associate of the Polish Academy of Sciences Institute of Archeology. Although he could no longer continue his fieldwork in Volhynia and Polisia, he was able to publish *Materiały do pradziejów Wołynia i Polesia Wołyńskiego* (Materials Concerning the Prehistory of Volhynia and Volhynian Polisia, 2 vols, 1961, 1963) in Poland. His *Starovynni pam'iatky Volyni* (Ancient Monuments of Volhynia, 1975) and *Stara Volyn' i Volyns'ke Polissia* (Old Volhynia and Volhynian Polisia, 2 vols, 1984, 1986), an encyclopedic guide to the geography and history of the region, were published in Canada. He wrote many scholarly articles during his career and contributed regularly to Ukrainian periodicals in Poland, including *Nasha kul'tura, Ukraïns'kyi kalendar,* and *Tserkovnyi kalendar,* under the pseudonym O. Volynets.

**Tsypola, Gizelia** [Cypola, Giselja], b 27 September 1944 in Hat, Berehove raion, Transcarpathia oblast. Opera singer (lyric-dramatic soprano). A graduate of the Kharkiv Institute of Arts (1969), she is a soloist of the Kiev Theater of Opera and Ballet. Her operatic roles include Oksana in S. Hulak-Artemovsky's *Zaporozhian Cossack beyond the Danube,* Maryltsia in M. Lysenko's *Taras Bulba,* Ingigerda in H. Maiboroda's *Yaroslav the Wise,* Tatiana in P. Tchaikovsky's *Eugene Onegin,* Desdemona in G. Verdi's *Othello,* and the name-part in G. Puccini's *Madame Butterfly.* She also appears in concert. She performed in Canada in 1990.

**Tsys, Oleksander** [Cys'] (Tsyss; pseuds: Hurhurdiadko, (M.) Movchii, O. Ts ... batko), b and d ? Writer and cultural figure of the second half of the 19th century. The chief physician of the Odessa Military District and a member of the Old *\*Hromada of Kiev, he published poems in the Lviv newspapers *Meta* (1863), *Nyva* (1865), and *Pravda* (1867–8) and wrote the melodramas *Svatannia nevznachai* (A Sudden Betrothal, 1864) and *Iatrivka* (The Brother-in-law's Wife, 1864) and the drama *Hrikh zadlia lykha* (Sin out of Misfortune, 1865). He also organized and participated in theatrical performances (as a member of M. Kropyvnytsky's troupe) in Kiev and Poltava and wrote a dramatized history of Ukraine, *Starodavnia Ukraïna v dramatychnykh spravakh* (Old Ukraine in Dramatic Affairs, 1889).

**Tsys, Petro** [Cys'], b 1914 in Velyki Sorochyntsi, Myrhorod county, Poltava gubernia. Geographer. He graduated from Kharkiv University and then taught at higher educational institutions before becoming a professor at Lviv University in 1945. His major research interests include the geomorphology and physicogeographical regionalization of Ukraine.

**Tsyss, Hryhorii** [Cyss, Hryhorij], b 24 April 1869 in Poltava, d 1 January 1935 in Poltava. Painter. In 1900 he graduated from the St Petersburg Academy of Arts, where he studied under I. Repin. Eventually he returned to Poltava. He painted *The Sorochyntsi Tragedy* (1905) and many por-

Hryhorii Tsyss: *Portrait of a Woman* (oil, 1912)

traits. A catalog of his posthumous exhibition came out in 1956.

**Tsytsaliuk, Hryhorii** [Cycaljuk, Hryhorij], b 23 September 1929 in Podilske, Liatychiv county, Proskuriv okruha. Composer, conductor, and pedagogue. A graduate of the Lviv Conservatory (1953) in the composition class of S. Liudkevych, he has been a lecturer at the Kharkiv Institute of the Arts since 1962. His works include a symphony (1968), three symphonic poems (1956, 1963, 1974), incidental and chamber music, pieces for piano, choruses, art songs, and arrangements of Ukrainian folk songs.

**Tsytsurin, Fedir** [Cycurin], b 23 June 1814 in Biriuch, Voronezh gubernia, d 19 December 1895 in St Petersburg. Internal medicine specialist. A graduate of Kharkiv University (1835), he did his doctorate on typhoid fever at Dorpat University (1839–41) and worked in Germany, France, and England. He was the first professor of internal medicine at Kiev University (1844–57), where he founded the medical library and served as dean of the medical faculty (1847–50). He took part in the effort to control cholera in Kiev in 1847 and coauthored a report on it. From 1857 he was president of the Warsaw Medico-Surgical Academy, and from 1862, director of the medical department of the Ministry of War. Until his retirement he served as the tsar's personal physician (1865–80), and he was also physician to N. Gogol.

**Tuapse.** IX-20. A city (1990 pop 63,000) on the Black Sea and a raion center in Krasnodar krai, RF. It was founded in 1838 as the Russian military settlement of Veliaminovsk, was renamed in 1896, and became a city in 1916. Its development was influenced by the construction of a port and a railway station in Armavir. Tuapse is an industrial and health resort center. It has a natural-gas refinery, machine-building plants, ship repair docks, and a food industry. According to the census of 1926, Ukrainians represented 17 percent of the city's and 32.2 percent of the raion's population.

**Tuberculosis.** A highly variable infectious disease caused by several species of *Mycobacterium*, or the tubercle bacillus; in humans it is usually caused by the human (*M.* *tuberculosis*) and bovine (*M. bovis*) varieties of the bacillus. Tuberculosis is most prevalent and virulent where high population density, malnutrition, and poor hygiene exist side by side. Though it has steadily declined in the 20th century except during wars and other periods of catastrophe, tuberculosis is found worldwide, can be fatal, and has no safe or effective vaccine.

In Ukraine in the years just after the First World War, many dispensaries, sanatoriums, and sanitary stations were created to combat tuberculosis. The Scientific Research Institute of Tuberculosis and Thoracic Surgery was created in 1922 in Kharkiv (from 1982 the Kiev Scientific Research Institute of Tuberculosis, Pulmonology, and Thoracic Surgery). The Odessa Scientific Research Institute of Tuberculosis was founded in 1921. During and after the Second World War tuberculosis was again on a sharp increase. In the postwar years, with famine, inadequate housing, and rebuilding from the ruinous war, it was an ongoing cause of suffering and death well into the 1960s. The Lviv Scientific Research Institute of Tuberculosis was established in 1944; it includes an oblast-level dispensary. Specialized sanatoriums to treat tuberculosis in Ukraine exist on the Crimean coast and in Vorokhta and Yaremche, in the Carpathians.

Notwithstanding the continuing reduction in mortality from tuberculosis, the rate in the former USSR was 2 to 10 times higher than in other countries (combined rate of the United States, Japan, France, Germany, and Great Britain). In 1988, out of 42 (37.7 respiratory) cases first diagnosed per 100,000 population, the death rate was 7.6 (7 respiratory), or approx 20,000 of total deaths. In Azerbaidzhan, Ukraine, Turkmenia, and Kazakhstan the death rate exceeded the USSR level by 11–42 percent. At the beginning of 1990, curative institutions in the USSR had approx 603,000 patients on record as suffering from active tuberculosis. During 1981–8, however, the number of hospital beds for tuberculosis patients fell by 16 percent, and the number of medical specialists in the field decreased by 11 percent. In 1990 the supply of hospital beds in Ukraine, Estonia, Georgia, and Belarus was one-third lower than the norm, and antituberculosis dispensaries were poorly equipped, some with no fluorography or X-ray facilities.

BIBLIOGRAPHY
Fainshmidt, I.; Morozovskii, N. (eds). *Tuberkulez v gorode i na sele* (Kharkiv 1927)
Fainshmidt, I.; Morozovskii, N.; Ul'ianov, L. (eds). *Tuberkulez v gorode i na sele* (Kharkiv 1928)
Korchak-Chepurkivs'kyi, Iu. 'Iak vkorochuie zhyttia tuberkul'oza na Ukraïni,' *Profilaktychna medytsyna*, 1931, no. 5–6
Pilipchuk, N. *Tuberkulez* (Kiev 1977)
Iashchenko, B. *Aktual'nye voprosy tuberkuleza organov dykhaniia* (Kiev 1980)

P. Dzul

**Tuchapsky, Hryhorii** [Tučaps'kyj, Hryhorij], b 25 January 1877 in Krasnosilka, Chyhyryn county, Kiev gubernia, d 2 July 1956 in New York. Baritone singer and pedagogue. He studied at the Kiev Theological Seminary and the St Petersburg Conservatory (1900–3) and in Milan and Rome, and performed in operas in Moscow, St Petersburg, Kharkiv, Saratov, Baku, and Tbilisi. In 1918 he was a professor at the Lysenko Music and Drama Institute in Kiev, and in 1919 he became the singing instructor of the touring Ukrainian Republican Kapelle. From 1924 he lived in New York, where he trained many singers at his studio.

**Tuchapsky, Makarii** [Tučaps'kyj, Makarij], b ?, d 1549. Orthodox bishop. He served as administrator of Halych eparchy (1535–9) before being consecrated, in 1539, as bishop by Metropolitan Makarii II of Kiev, and thereby becoming the first bishop of the eparchy in 80 years. He was thrown into conflict with the Polish Catholic archbishop of Lviv, who had tried to install his own candidate in the position and exert control over the see. Tuchapsky called the Lviv sobor of 1539, which did much to improve affairs in the Lviv eparchy.

Pavlo Tuchapsky          Stepan Tudor

**Tuchapsky, Pavlo** [Tučaps'kyj], b 1869 in Besidka, Tarashcha county, Kiev gubernia, d 1922. Political leader. He studied at Galagan College and in higher institutions in Kiev. A supporter of M. *Drahomanov, he was one of the main founders of the Russian Social Democratic Workers' party and served as a delegate to its first congress in 1898, representing the Kiev Union of Struggle for the Liberation of the Working Class. In 1904 he was an activist and ideologue of the Ukrainian Social Democratic Association (*Spilka) and championed Ukrainian autonomy. In 1905 he edited the monthly *Pravda* in Lviv. In 1910 he quit the Bolsheviks and began working with Russian Mensheviks, which he continued to do during the struggle for Ukrainian independence (1917–20). In 1921–2 he was a librarian for the VUAN in Kiev. He wrote articles about Drahomanov in *Ukraïna* (1926, no. 2–3) and a brochure initially published in the journal *Narod* (under the pseudonym 'E.S.') on T. Shevchenko's ideals and Ukrainian reality. His memoirs were published by V. Dembo in 1923.

**Tuchkevych, Volodymyr** [Tučkevyč] (Tuchkevich, Vladimir), b 29 December 1904 in Ivanivtsi, Khotyn county, Bessarabia gubernia. Experimental physicist; full member of the USSR Academy of Sciences since 1970 and a member of its presidium since 1971. A graduate of Kiev University (1928), in 1931 he organized and then directed the All-Ukrainian Institute of Roentgenology in Kharkiv. While in Kharkiv, he also worked at the AN URSR (now ANU) Physical-Technical Institute with K. *Synelnykov and lectured at the Kharkiv Electrical Engineering Institute. In 1935 he joined the staff of the Leningrad Physical-Technical Institute, and in 1967 he became its director. Tuchkevych's major contributions are in the field of semiconductor devices, in particular semiconductor power rectifiers for long-distance direct-current power transmission.

Gen Myron Tarnavsky and other officers of the Ukrainian Galician Army in the Tuchola internment camp in 1920

**Tuchola.** A town (1989 pop 13,200) and county center in Bydgoszcz voivodeship, Poland. At the end of the First World War it was the site of a Polish internment camp, which held 700 officers and 500 soldiers of the Red Ukrainian Galician Army. The men had surrendered to the Poles in 1920 with the intention of helping them fight the Bolsheviks. Instead they were disarmed and imprisoned. In the summer of 1920 Gen M. Tarnavsky and other officers of the Ukrainian Galician Army were arrested in Lviv and brought to the camp. Some officers escaped to Germany, and the rest were released. In the winter of 1921 the camp was closed down.

**Tudor, Stepan** (real surname: Oleksiuk), b 25 August 1892 in Ponykva, Brody county, Galicia, d 22 June 1941 in Lviv. Writer. He graduated from Lviv University in 1926. He began publishing in 1925. He was persecuted by the Polish authorities for his communist agitation. He was one of the organizers of the union of Western Ukrainian revolutionary writers *Horno. In 1930 he began publishing and editing its organ, *Vikna*. A number of collections of his short stories have been published, including *Narodzhennia* (Birth, 1929), *Krok u Zhovten'* (The Step to October, 1953), and *Chervonyi usmikh* (The Red Smile, 1960). His published novels include *Mariia* (1930), *Moloshne bozhevillia* (The Insanity of Moloch, 1930), *Den' otsia Soiky* (Father Soika's Day, 1947), *Vybrane* (Selections, 1949), and *Tvory* (Works, vols 1–2, 1962). He was killed on the first day of the German-Soviet conflict, during an aerial bombardment of Lviv.

**Tuftina, Halyna,** b 14 October 1933 in Novosibirsk, RSFSR. Opera singer (mezzo-soprano). After graduating from the Leningrad Conservatory in 1960, she sang as a soloist with the Little Opera and Ballet Theater in Leningrad and, from 1961, with the Kiev Theater of Opera and Ballet. In 1981 she began to lecture at the Kiev Conservatory. Her main roles were Nastia in M. Lysenko's *Taras Bulba*, Solomiia in K. Dankevych's *Bohdan Khmelnytsky*, the Mother in H. Maiboroda's *Arsenal*, Liubasha in N. Rimsky-Korsakov's *Tsar's Bride*, Amneris in G. Verdi's *Aida*, and Carmen in G. Bizet's *Carmen*. She has also performed as a chamber singer.

**Tuhai-Bei** [Tuhaj-Bej], b and d ? 17th-century Tatar prince of Perekop. Under orders from the Crimean khan Islam-Girei III he brought 4,000 cavalry troops to the assistance of Hetman B. Khmelnytsky in 1648. His forces played a significant role in Cossack victories against the Poles during the battles of *Zhovti Vody and *Korsun.

Mykhailo Tuhan-Baranovsky    Metropolitan Yosyf Tukalsky-Neliubovych

**Tuhan-Baranovsky, Mykhailo** [Tuhan-Baranovs'kyj, Myxajlo], b 20 January 1865 in Solone, Kharkiv gubernia, d 21 January 1919 near Odessa. Economist, sociologist, and co-operation theoretician; full member of the Ukrainian Academy of Sciences. After graduating from Kharkiv University (1888) he received higher degrees from Moscow University (PH D, 1898) and lectured at St Petersburg University. In his first published article (1890) he presented a synthesis of the labor and the marginal-utility theories of value. His MA dissertation on industrial cycles in Britain (1894) proposed a disproportionality theory of business cycles and anticipated later discoveries of the multiplier effect. Although in the 1890s he was a proponent of legal Marxism, he rejected K. Marx's theories of the business cycle, the inevitable breakdown of capitalism, and class struggle. Under the influence of neo-Kantian ideas he turned his attention to co-operation as a vehicle of social justice and published a survey of the history of political economy (1901–2), a textbook of political economy (1907; Ukrainian translation 1919), a study of the theoretical foundations of Marxism (1905), a comparative study of contemporary socioeconomic ideals (1913), a theoretical analysis of the social foundations of co-operation (1916; abr Ukrainian version 1919), and an outline of the co-operative ideal (1918). His *Bumazhnye den'gi i metall* (Paper Money and Metal, 1917) demonstrated the limits of the quantity theory of money and anticipated J. Keynes's ideas on monetary policy. After returning to Ukraine in 1917, Tuhan-Baranovsky joined the Ukrainian Party of Socialists-Federalists and served as general secretary of finance in the UNR government (September–December 1917). He helped found the Ukrainian Society of Economists, the Ukrainian Academy of Sciences, and the Ukrainian State University in Kiev and served as chairman of the academy's socioeconomic department, dean of the university's faculty of law and social sciences, and editor of the journal *Ukraïns'ka kooperatsiia*. He died on his way to Paris, where he was to have represented the UNR at the peace conference. Published in English translation have

been his works *Modern Socialism in Its Historical Development* (1910, 1966) and *The Russian Factory in the 19th Century* (1970).

BIBLIOGRAPHY
Kondrat'ev, N. *Mikhail Ivanovich Tugan-Baranovskii* (Petrograd 1923)
Kowal, L. 'Economic Doctrines of M.I. Tugan-Baranovsky,' PH D diss, University of Illinois, 1965

L. Kowal

**Tukalsky-Neliubovych, Yosyf** [Tukal's'kyj-Neljubovyč, Josyf], b ? in the Pynske region, d 26 July 1675 in Chyhyryn. Orthodox metropolitan and political activist. He was archimandrite of the Holy Ghost Monastery in Vilnius in 1657–8, a candidate for the office of metropolitan of Kiev (1657), and a participant in the 1657 Cossack council in Pereiaslav that elected I. Vyhovsky as hetman. He was consecrated bishop of Orsha and Mstsislau (and Belarus), and in 1663 he was elected metropolitan of Kiev at a council of clergymen, nobles, and Cossacks in Korsun. The king of Poland, favoring another candidate (A. Vynnytsky), refused to confirm his election. In the resulting administrative division of the Ukrainian church province, Tukalsky presided over Right-Bank Ukraine, Belarus, and Lithuania but not over Galicia, Volhynia, and Podilia. Hetman P. Teteria and the Polish government conspired against him, and he was imprisoned in the Marienburg fortress (1664–6). Hetman P. *Doroshenko secured his release, whereupon he resumed his post as metropolitan and took up residence near the hetman in Chyhyryn. In 1668 the Patriarch of Constantinople confirmed his position as metropolitan and named him exarch. Tukalsky was a close adviser to Doroshenko; he counseled him to enter into an alliance with the Turks, and opposed alliances with Russia and Poland. In church affairs he rejected any rapprochement with the Moscow patriarchate and staunchly defended the independence of the Kiev metropoly. He was buried in the Mhar Transfiguration Monastery, and his valuable archive was transferred to the Kievan Cave Monastery. A selection of his epistles and correspondence was published in 1884 by Bishop F. Gumilevsky.

I. Korovytsky

*Tuk-tuk* (Knock-knock). A monthly illustrated magazine for preschool children, published in Kharkiv from November 1929 to September 1935 (a total of 83 issues) by the People's Commissariat of Education. From 1933 it was also an organ of the Communist Youth League of Ukraine. In 1935 it was merged with *Zhovtenia.

**Tulcea.** VIII-9. A city (1981 pop 70,000), district center, and fluvial port in northern *Dobrudja (Rumania), situated near the Danube Delta. An important fish-processing and shipbuilding center, it is situated at the heart of a settlement area that includes approx 26,000 Ukrainians in 20 surrounding villages, who constitute about 10 percent of the region's inhabitants. In 1950–60 there was a Ukrainian pedagogical school in Tulcea. It was converted into a Rumanian one.

**Tulchyn** [Tul'čyn]. V-9. A city (1989 pop 17,100) on the Silnytsia River and a raion center in Vinnytsia oblast. It was first mentioned in historical documents in 1607, as the

Tulchyn in the late 19th century

translations of 15 of T. Shevchenko's poems in the journal *Vestnik Evropy*. He also translated poems by Shevchenko that were forbidden by the tsarist censors; they appeared in I. Belousov's Russian edition of *Kobzar* (Moscow 1919).

Zinaida Tulub

**Tulub, Zinaida,** b 28 November 1890 in Kiev, d 26 September 1964 in Kiev. Writer. She graduated from the Higher Courses for Women in Kiev in 1913. She was first published in 1910 in Russian, and after the Revolution of 1917 she wrote in Ukrainian. In 1937 she was arrested and imprisoned in a labor camp in Kolyma, from which she was freed in 1947. She was allowed to return to Kiev from forced exile in Kazakhstan early in 1955. Tulub is the author of a large-scale historical novel set in 17th-century Ukraine during the time of Hetman P. Sahaidachny, *Liudolovy* (The People Hunters, 1934; repub 1937 and 1958), and of a novel based on the life of T. Shevchenko in exile, *V stepu bezkraïm za Uralom* (In the Boundless Steppe beyond the Urals, 1964), which was translated into English in *The Exile* (1988). She also wrote plays and film scenarios and translated foreign literature into Ukrainian.

**Tumansky** [Tumans'kyj]. A family line of officers and nobility, probably of Right-Bank origin. The first generations lived in Left-Bank Ukraine and were clergymen. Hryhorii Tumansky was an archpriest (1730–50) in Basan, Pereiaslav regiment. His sons studied at the Kiev Academy: Ivan went on to the St Petersburg Academic University; Vasyl (ca 1719–1809) was the last general chancellor of the Hetmanate (from 1762), a member of the Little Russian Collegium (from 1764), and vice-governor of Novhorod-Siverskyi vicegerency (1782–96); Osyp (1731–ca 1798) was a member of the General Court (1781–2) and head of the Novhorod-Siverskyi Chamber of Criminal Court (1783–95); and Ivan (b 1740, d after 1798) was senior secretary of the Senate in St Petersburg (until 1777), a member of the Little Russian Collegium (1777–82), and head of the Kiev Civil Court (1791–6), as well as a translator from German and French. The sons of Vasyl Tumansky, Mykhailo and Ivan, studied at Königsberg University; Mykhailo was a member of the Little Russian Collegium (1778–82), cataloged its archives, and collected Ukrainian historical material (particularly the works of S. Lukomsky). Osyp Tumansky's son was Fedir *Tumansky. In the 19th century the family also included the Russian poets Vasyl Tumansky (1800–1860) and Fedir Tumansky (1801–1853, who was also imperial consul general in Belgrade) and Oleksander Tumansky (1861–1920), a scholar

town of Nestervar. In 1648 it was liberated from Poland by M. Kryvonis and I. Hanzha, but in 1667 it was returned under the Treaty of Andrusovo. In 1672–99 Tulchyn was occupied by the Turks. A century later it rebelled against the Polish overlords. In 1787 the town was granted the rights of Magdeburg law. It was annexed by the Russian Empire in 1793 and became a county center of Bratslav vicegerency. By 1859 its population had reached 11,200, and by 1897, 23,300. At the beginning of the 20th century there were about 40 small enterprises in Tulchyn. Today it is an agricultural town with a mixed-feed factory, a cannery, a meat-packing plant, a footwear factory, and a furniture factory. Its chief architectural monuments are the remains of an 18th- to 19th-century palace, the Dormition Church and its bell tower (1789), an 18th-century Dominican monastery and church, and 18th- and 19th-century residential buildings.

**Tulip** (*Tulipa*; Ukrainian: *tiulpan* or *tulipan*). Perennial bulbous plants of the family Liliaceae, with a hollow, erect stem that ends in a single colorful flower. Tulips were first cultivated in Turkey in the 16th century. During the following century they were imported into Holland; today tulip species number over 140. In Ukraine they are grown to beautify cities, as spring flower beds and borders.

**Tulov, Mykhailo,** b 20 November 1814 in Hrodna, Belarus, d 11 May 1882 in Kiev. Pedagogue, linguist, and writer. After graduating from Kiev University (1839) he taught at the Nizhen Lyceum (1844–53), was the director of the Nemyriv Gymnasium, and served as deputy director of the Kiev school district. He was forced to resign the last position after he came out in opposition to the school reforms of D. Tolstoi. He helped organize the Sunday school movement and was an associate of *Osnova* (for which he wrote under the pseudonym Lineikin). His scholarly work dealt mainly with the Russian language, although he also examined Ukrainian ('Little Russian') orthography.

**Tulub, Pavlo,** b 24 February 1862, d 16 March 1923. Lawyer and writer; father of Z. *Tulub. The son of a member of the Cyril and Methodius Brotherhood, he worked as a lawyer in Kiev, Bratslav, and Tahanrih and wrote poetry in Russian. In the years 1904–8 he published Russian of the Orient, as well as a number of magnates and zemstvo activists in the Chernihiv and Poltava regions.

O. Ohloblyn

**Tumansky, Fedir** [Tumans'kyj], b 1757 in Hlukhiv, d December 1810 on the Rodionivka *khutir*, near Hlukhiv, Chernihiv gubernia. Historian, ethnographer, and community activist; corresponding member of the Russian Academy of Sciences from 1779. He studied at Königsberg University (1773–7) and was elected to the Royal Prussian Society. Upon returning to Ukraine he was made a fellow of the standard (1778–9). He organized a topographical study of the Hetmanate, drew up a wide-ranging plan for cultural and research work in Ukraine, and established standards for collecting historical, geographical, economic, ethnographic, anthropological, and environmental data. The data provided the basis for the topographic descriptions of Hetmanate territories published in the 1780s by D. Pashchenko, O. Shafonsky, P. Symonovsky, and others. Tumansky presented proposals in late 1779 and early 1780 for the establishment of an academic library in Hlukhiv and an academic society in Little Russia (as the genesis of a Ukrainian academy of sciences); only the former proposal was acted upon. He then decided to write a complete history of 'Little Russia,' for which he requested that the requisite archival materials be sent to him from St Petersburg, but the Russian academy quashed his project. After the liquidation of the Hetmanate he was a tsarist censor in Riga; thereafter he set up an active literary-publishing and research concern in St Petersburg. He published a 10-volume collection of various notes and monographs on Peter I; a number of periodicals, among them *Rossiiskii magazin* (1792–4), in which important Ukrainian historical material appeared, including the Hrabianka Chronicle (see H. *Hrabianka); and the monographs *Vypiska iz zapiski 1749 g.* (Extract from Notes on the Year 1749, 1792), *Manifest getmana Bogdana Khmel'nitskogo* (The Manifesto of Hetman B. Khmelnytsky, 1793), and *Letopisets Malyia Rossii ...* (Chronicler of Little Russia ..., 1793). His glossary appendix to the last work, titled 'Iziasnenie malorossiiskikh rechenii v predshedshikh listakh' (Explanations of Little Russian Expressions in the Preceding Pages), was one of the first Ukrainian historical dictionaries; it consisted of 333 words. In 1801 he retired and settled on his homestead near Hlukhiv, but he continued his literary and publicistic activity (eg, he wrote in defense of the aristocratic rights of the Ukrainian nobility).

A. Zhukovsky

**Tumbleweed** (Ukrainian: *perekotypole*). A steppe and desert herbaceous plant that breaks off at the base during the time of seed maturity and, blown about by the wind, scatters its seeds across large areas of open landmass. In Ukraine the following tumbleweeds can be found: Russian thistle (*Salsola kali*), *Ceratocarpus arenarius*, snakeroot (*Eryngium campestre*), and baby's breath (*Gypsophila paniculata*).

**Tuna, bluefin** (*Thunnus thynnus*; Ukrainian: *tunets zvychainyi* or *t. blakytnyi*). An oceanic fish of the family Scombridae, related to the mackerel. In Ukrainian waters bluefin tuna is found in the Black Sea and the Sea of Azov. Tuna is of great commercial value as food fish. Recent measurements of high mercury levels, however, have led to a decrease in the sales of tuna.

**TUP.** See Society of Ukrainian Progressives.

Metropolitan Dymytrii Tuptalo          Stepan Turchak

**Tuptalo, Dymytrii (Rostovsky)** (secular name: Danylo), b December 1651 in Makariv, Kiev region, d 8 November 1709 in Rostov, Russia. Saint, writer, theologian, and churchman. He studied at the Kievan Mohyla Academy in 1662–5 and entered St Cyril's Monastery in Kiev in 1668. In 1675 he was ordained a hieromonk by Archbishop L. Baranovych. During the next 30 years he was hegumen of several Ukrainian (Hustynia-Trinity, Trinity–St Elijah's, Yeletskyi Dormition, St Nicholas's in Baturyn, Novodvirske in Volhynia, Kievan Cave) and Belarusian (Vilnius and Slutsk) monasteries. In 1701 Tsar Peter I summoned him to Moscow, where he was consecrated metropolitan on 23 March 1701. He was assigned to the Tobolsk see but did not assume the post because of ill health. Instead, in 1702 he was sent to Rostov. Tuptalo was associated with a group of Ukrainian hierarchs in the Russian church, led by Metropolitan S. Yavorsky, who fought against the Old Believers and other sects that had left the church over reforms introduced under Tsar Aleksei. This group, however, did not accept the more radical changes favored by Peter, especially the subordination of the church to the state.

Tuptalo's first published work was *Runo oroshennoie* (The Bedewed Fleece, 1680; 7 edns by 1702), a collection of stories about miracles attributed to the icon of the Mother of God at the Chernihiv Trinity–St Elijah's Monastery. His most important work is his *menaion for daily reading, a major collection of the lives of saints. It was first published by the Kievan Cave Monastery in 1689–1705; at least 10 more editions followed in the 18th century. This collection is the best example of Ukrainian hagiography of the 17th and 18th centuries; it contains the lives of many early Ukrainian saints, based on various manuscripts and on adaptations from Greek and Latin sources. Tuptalo was a well-known orator, and a collection of his sermons (some of which criticized Peter's reforms), edited by A. Titov, appeared in 1909. He also wrote polemical attacks on the schism (*Rozysk o raskolnicheskoi brynskoi vere* [An Examination of the Schismatic Brynian Sect, 1709]), theological treatises (*Zertsalo pravoslavnogo ispovedaniia* [The Mirror of the Orthodox Faith, 1805]), and historical studies (*Letopis' izhe vo sviatykh ... ot nachala mirobytiia do Rozhdestva Khristova* [The Chronicle of Saints ... from the Beginning of Life on Earth to the Birth of Christ, 1784]). His literary works – including the spiritual dramas *Komediia na den' Rozhdestva Khristova* (A Comedy on the Day of Christ's Birth) and *Uspenie Bohorodytsi* (The Dormition of the Mother of God) – were baroque in style and influenced by Western writing. The language Tuptalo used in his theological works was Old Church Slavonic, but it contained many Ukrainianisms. His sermons and menaion, which were intended for a popular audience, were close to the vernacular; posthumous editions of the menaion, however, were Russified by order of the Holy Synod.

BIBLIOGRAPHY
Shliapkin, I. *Sv. Dmitrii Rostovskii i ego vremia (1651–1709)* (St Petersburg 1891)
Ilarion (Ohiienko, I.). *Sv. Dymytrii Tuptalo* (Winnipeg 1960)
A. Zhukovsky

**Tupyi.** [Tupyj]. V-4. A small mountain group in the Volcanic Ukrainian Carpathians between the Borzhava River in the northwest, the Tysa River in the south, and the Rika River and the Maramureş Lowland in the east. The tallest peak in the formation is Mount Tupyi (878 m).

**Tur, Nykyfor,** b ?, d 1599. Archimandrite of the Kievan Cave Monastery from 1593. In 1594 and 1595 he refused to submit to the authority of Metropolitan M. *Rahoza, basing his position on the monastery's right of stauropegion. At the church sobor in Berestia in 1596, he opposed the hierarchs who favored church union with Rome, and in October 1596 Rahoza and five bishops issued an anathema against him. Despite this pressure, which was encouraged by the Polish king, he kept the monastery Orthodox and even rejected a royal decree of November 1597 that handed the monastery over to Rahoza's jurisdiction. Tur also managed to safeguard the monastery's valuables. A monograph on Tur was written by M. Maksymovych in 1876.

**Tur Lake.** II-5. A low-lying lake in northwestern Volhynia oblast between the Buh River and the source of the Prypiat River. The lake is approx 13 sq km in area and has a prevailing depth of 2.6 m. It is linked to the Dnieper-Buh Canal system through the Tur and Orikhiv canals.

**Turau.** See Turiv.

**Turbai uprising.** A revolt in Turbai village, Myrhorod county, Katerynoslav vicegerency, in 1789–93, sparked by a dispute about Cossack status. Until 1727, when Hetman D. Apostol removed them from the register and listed them as his serfs, most of the town residents were Cossacks. After appealing to the colonel of Myrhorod, V. Kapnist, 76 of them were reregistered as Cossacks in 1738. In 1776 the Bazylevsky family purchased the town and raised demands on the serfs, who reacted by refusing corvée and petitioning the Russian Senate to restore their Cossack status. The Senate ruled in 1788 that the families of the 76 men who had been reregistered in 1738 possessed Cossack status. When the local authorities, prompted by the Bazylevsky family, delayed the implementation of the Senate decision, the people revolted. They stormed the manor, killed three members of the Bazylevsky family, took over Turbai and several adjacent villages, and elected their own local hetman, judge, and

secretary. Mindful of events in France, the authorities hesitated and attempted to negotiate a compromise. After long, futile talks they decided to make an example of the rebels and in 1793 moved in with a large force. The leaders of the uprising were sentenced to death (later commuted to life imprisonment in Siberia), secondary figures were subjected to public lashing, and the rest of the inhabitants (approx 2,300) were resettled in Kherson and Tavriia gubernias. The village was renamed and was known as Skorbne for almost two centuries. It is now in Hlobyne raion, Poltava oblast.

**Turbiv kaolin deposits.** Rich kaolin deposits located in Lypovets raion, Vinnytsia oblast. The estimated reserves of Turbiv's kaolin (1983) are 5,669,000 t. Seams of the substance 5–12 m in thickness (maximum, up to 22.8 m) are located 2.3–17.6 m underground. They were first mined in 1912. The kaolin from the region is used in the manufacture of rubber and leatherette.

**Turbot, Black Sea** (*Scophthalmus maeoticus* or *Rhombus maeoticus*; Ukrainian: *kalkan*). A broad-bodied, sedentary European flatfish of the family Scophthalmidae (or Bothidae), with both eyes on the left side of the head. In Ukraine it is found in the Black Sea and the Sea of Azov. It reaches a length of 1 m and a weight of 25 kg and is a valuable commercial fish.

**Turchak, Stepan** [Turčak], b 28 February 1938 in Matskovychi, Peremyshl county, Galicia, d 23 October 1988 in Kiev. Conductor. A graduate of the Lviv State Conservatory (1962) in the conducting class of M. Kolessa, he conducted the Lviv Theater of Opera and Ballet (1960–2), the Symphony Orchestra of the Ukrainian SSR (1963–7 and 1973–7), and the Kiev Theater of Opera and Ballet (from 1977). He also taught conducting at the Kiev State Conservatory (1966–74). As an orchestral and operatic conductor Turchak was a bold, searching, modern artist. His innovations were enthusiastically welcomed in Ukraine and during his tours of the USSR, Yugoslavia, Poland, Czechoslavakia, Hungary, Rumania, Germany, France, England, Spain, Italy, Japan, and elsewhere. His legacy includes definitive recordings of symphonic works by B. Liatoshynsky, V. Hubarenko, and H. Maiboroda.

**Turchaninov, Petro** [Turčaninov], b 1 December 1779 in Kiev, d 28 March 1856 in St Petersburg. Composer, conductor, and teacher. A student of G. Sarti and A. Vedel (1794–8), he became a priest in 1803 and after 1809 conducted the metropolitan's choir in St Petersburg. He subsequently taught singing at the imperial court kapelle (1827–41). As a composer of sacred choral music he followed the school of A. *Vedel. His harmonizations of melodies of Kievan, Bulgarian, and Greek monastic chants are characterized by simplicity, expressiveness, and masterly choral technique. His complete works were edited and published by A. Kastalsky (Moscow 1905–6) in five volumes. His autobiography, published in St Petersburg in 1863, is a valuable source on the life and music of his teacher Vedel.

**Turchenko, Yurii** [Turčenko, Jurij], b 7 November 1923 in Zhuky, Poltava okruha. Art historian and museologist; full member of the Shevchenko Scientific Society since 1982. A graduate of Kiev University (1950), he was a dep-

Yurii Turchenko        Osyp Turiansky

uty director (1950–2) responsible for scholarly work at the Kiev Museum of Ukrainian Art, a lecturer (1954–69) and professor (1969–74) in art history at Kiev University, scholarly secretary (1955–7) of the AN URSR (now ANU) Institute of Fine Arts, Folklore, and Ethnography and chairman (1960–74) of its Department of Art and Museology, editor in chief of the serial *Ukraïns'ke mystetstvoznavstvo* (1967–74), and chairman (1972–4) of the Republican Scientific Council on Problems of Museology and Museum Development. He received his doctorate in 1965. Turchenko has written many articles on Ukrainian art, museology, and art education and books on M. Murashko and his Kiev Drawing School (1956), Soviet Ukrainian graphic art (1957, with V. Kasiian), O. Slastion's portraits of Ukrainian kobzars (1961), Ukrainian pre-Soviet realist graphic art (1961, with V. Kasiian), and the Ukrainian print (1964). From 1961 he was a member of the editorial board of the ANU history of Ukrainian art (6 vols, 1966–70) and the editor in charge of its sixth volume (1968). In 1974 he accepted the position of chief of the UNESCO Museums Division in Paris. In 1977 he was appointed chief of the UNESCO Section for Research and Publications on Questions of Preserving the World Cultural Heritage. In December 1979 Turchenko and his wife defected and received asylum in France.

**Turchyniuk, Vasyl** [Turčynjuk, Vasyl'], b 1864 in Luh, Nadvirna county, Galicia, d 25 July 1939 in Luh. Wood carver and builder. He carved decorative and household articles and made wooden furniture with carved designs. His iconostases, bas-reliefs, wooden sculptures, and carvings decorated the wooden churches in Yablunytsia (1895–1904), Maidan (1932), Strymba (1930–2), Luh (1912–39), and Vorokhta (1936–8).

**Turchynovsky, Illia** [Turčynovs'kyj, Illja], b 30 July 1695 in Berezan, Pereiaslav regiment, d ? A traveling precentor. He studied at the Kievan Mohyla Academy. From 1710 he traveled in Ukraine and Belarus, where he worked variously as a teacher, precentor, secretary, singer, and church choir director. Toward the end of his life he became a priest. He wrote an autobiography, which is full of the details of everyday life of his time. It was printed in *Khrestomatiia davn'oï ukraïns'koï literatury* (Anthology of Old Ukrainian Literature, ed O. Biletsky, 1952).

**Turchynska, Ahata** [Turčyns'ka], b 11 February 1903 in Kulykiv, Zhovkva county, Galicia, d 22 August 1972 in Kiev. Poet and prose writer. She graduated from the Kiev Institute of People's Education in 1926 and belonged to the Zakhidnia Ukraina literary organization. Her collections of verse include *Izvory* (Brutes, 1929), *Urozhai* (The Harvest, 1939), *Pisnia pro druzhbu* (A Song about Friendship, 1946), *Dorohi zapovity* (Dear Testaments, 1958), and *Dumnyi potik* (The Pensive Stream, 1972). She is also the author of the short stories *Smok* (The Dragon, 1930) and *Buz'kove zillia* (The Stork's Magic Herbs, 1966), the novel *Druh mii Ashkhabad* (My Friend Ashkhabad, 1963), a libretto for H. Maiboroda's opera *Milana* (1957), and the dramatic poem *Zustrich z mavkoiu* (Meeting with a Forest Nymph, 1972).

**Turgenev, Ivan,** b 9 November 1818 in Orel, Russia, d 3 November 1883 in Bougival, France. Russian writer. He is the author of a number of novels that have become part of the Russian literary canon; all of them have been translated into Ukrainian. In the 1860s he became interested in Ukrainian literature and befriended T. Shevchenko (he wrote his memoirs of Shevchenko in 1876). He maintained a close friendship with M. *Vovchok and published Russian translations of her folktales (1859). Turgenev's works have been translated into Ukrainian by I. Franko, Lesia Ukrainka, M. Rylsky, and others. The many Ukrainian translations include *Poeziï v prozi* (Poetry in Prose, 1903), *Vybrani tvory* (Selected Works, 1937), *Opovidannia i povisti* (Stories and Novellas, 1949), *Dvorians'ke hnizdo* (A Nest of Gentlefolk, 1952), *Naperedodni* (On the Eve, 1954), and *Rudin* (1956).

**Turiansky, Osyp** [Turjans'kyj] (pseud: I. Dumka), b 22 February 1880 in Ohliadiv, Kaminka-Strumylova county, Galicia, d 28 March 1933 in Lviv. Writer and literary critic. While studying at Vienna University he published his first stories (novellas), in the 1908 almanac of the Sich student society. While working as a secondary-school teacher in Galicia he wrote an autobiographical antiwar novel, *Poza mezhamy boliu* (Beyond the Limits of Pain, 1921; English trans: *Lost Shadows*, New York 1935), the novelettes *Duma pralisu* (Duma of the Primeval Forest, 1922) and *Syn zemli* (Son of the Soil, 1933), the story collection *Borot'ba za velykist'* (The Struggle for Greatness, 1926), and the satirical comedy *Raby* (Slaves, 1927). In the late 1920s and early 1930s he contributed to the left-wing Lviv journal *Novi shliakhy*.

**Turiansky, Roman** [Turjans'kyj] (pseud of Roman Kuzma), b 25 May 1894 in Stryivka, Zbarazh county, Galicia, d 16 July 1940. Galician Communist leader and publicist. With O. Vasylkiv and R. Rozdolsky he founded the 'Drahomanovite' International Revolutionary Social Democratic Organization in Lviv (1915) and edited its publications. In 1919 he served as a physician in the Red Army and joined the CP(B)U. After the war he served as a Party official in Berdychiv okruha, chief of the Kiev gubernia branch of the Trade Union of Educational Workers, and a member of the Kiev Gubernia Trade Union Council and taught sociology and political economy. In 1924 he was elected to the CC of the *Communist Party of Western Ukraine (KPZU). He edited its organ *Nasha pravda* and served as a member of the KPZU Politburo responsible for

Roman Turiansky

Ivan Turianytsia

propaganda and the KPZU representative to the Polish section of the Comintern. He wrote most of the resolutions adopted at the 5th to 9th conferences, the Second Congress, and CC plenums of the KPZU. Together with the KPZU leaders K. Maksymovych and O. Vasylkiv he was expelled from the party in 1928 for supporting O. Shumsky's policies. In 1932 he was sent by the Comintern to work for the trade-union press in Moscow, and in 1933 he was arrested. His later fate is unknown; he probably died in a concentration camp or was executed.

**Turianytsia, Ivan** [Turjanycja], b 1901 in Mukachiv, d 27 March 1955 in Uzhhorod. Transcarpathian Communist figure. The Czechoslovak Communist party secretary in Mukachiv (1928–9) and Uzhhorod (1929–30), from 1930 he studied in the USSR, where he graduated from the Kharkiv Communist Institute of Journalism (1933). From 1934 to 1939 he was a trade-union activist in Transcarpathia. He fled to the USSR in 1939, and from 1941 to 1944 he was a Party official in the Third Czechoslovak Brigade. After returning to Transcarpathia he served as head of the *People's Council of Transcarpathian Ukraine and the Communist Party of Transcarpathian Ukraine (1944–6), the first CPU secretary and administration chief in Transcarpathia oblast (1946–8), and a member of the CC CPU and the Ukrainian Supreme Soviet Presidium (1947–55).

**Turiia River** [Turija or Tur'ja]. A right-bank tributary of the Prypiat River that flows for 184 km through Volhynia oblast and drains a basin area of 2,900 sq km. The river is 3–4 m wide in its upper reaches and 5–10 m wide along its lower course. It has a wide marshy valley and is a central feature in a regional drainage system. The river freezes over from December to late March. The town of Turiiske and the city of Kovel, which has a water reservoir, are situated on it.

**Turiiske** [Turijs'ke]. II-5. A town smt (1986 pop 5,500) on the Turiia River and a raion center in Volhynia oblast. It is first mentioned in the chronicles under the year 1097. From 1340 it belonged to Lithuania, and from 1569, to the Polish Commonwealth. It obtained the rights of *Magdeburg law in 1759. After the partition of Poland in 1795, Turiiske was annexed by Russia. In the interwar period it was occupied by Poland. After the Second World War it was incorporated into the Ukrainian SSR.

**Turiv** (Belarusian: Turau). I-8. A port on the right bank of the Prypiat River in eastern Polisia, now a town smt (1939 pop 5,500) in Zhytkavichy raion, Homel oblast, Belarus, on the Ukrainian ethnographic border. It was a medieval center in the territory of the Drehovichians, and is first mentioned in writing in the Primary Chronicle under the year 980. In the late 10th century it became the capital of *Turiv-Pynske principality and eparchy, and in the 12th century it was the residence of Bishop *Cyril of Turiv. In the late 13th and early 14th centuries Turiv belonged to the Grand Duchy of Lithuania. From the mid-15th to the mid-16th century it was ruled by the princes of Ostrih. It was attacked by the Crimean Tatars in 1502 and 1521. It was briefly a part of B. Khmelnytsky's Hetmanate in the 17th century. In 1793 it became part of Mozyr county, Minsk gubernia, in the Russian Empire. In 1918–20 it was part of the UNR, and in 1938 it was incorporated into the Belorussian SSR. Remains of its old fortifications are still standing.

**Turiv Gospel** (Turivske yevanheliie). An 11th-century Church Slavonic literary monument most likely transcribed in Ukraine. From the 16th century it belonged to the Transfiguration Church in Turiv. Fragments of the gospel (10 double pages) containing two charters (1508, 1513) granting land to local priests by Prince K. *Ostrozky, the owner of Turiv, are preserved at the library of the Lithuanian Academy of Sciences. The text and I. Sreznevsky's study of it were published in *Sbornik otdeleniia russkogo iazyka i slovesnosti Imperatorskoi akademii nauk* (vol 12, 1875).

**Turiv-Pynske principality.** An administrative territory of the 10th to 14th centuries in central Polisia. Its capital was *Turiv. The larger, northern part was settled by Drehovichians, and the smaller, southeastern part by Derevlianians. Its inhabitants, who lived by farming, hunting, fishing, and beekeeping, were protected from nomad attacks by thick forests and swamps. The land and water routes from Kiev to Poland and the land route from Kiev to Lithuania and the other Baltic countries contributed to the principality's economic and political importance. The oldest cities are mentioned in the medieval chronicles: Turiv (under the year 980), Pynske (1097), Berestia (1019), Chortoryisk (1110), Klechesk (Kletsk, 1128), Sluchesk (Slutsk, 1116), and Mozyr (1155). From the 9th century the territory was within Kiev's sphere of influence, and during the reign of Volodymyr the Great it became part of Kievan Rus'. The first ruler was Volodymyr's son, Sviatopolk I (988–1015). In the 11th century, because of its ties with the West, it was one of the more important principalities of Kievan Rus'. In 1052 Yaroslav the Wise installed his son Iziaslav there. Iziaslav was succeeded by his sons, Yaropolk (1078–86) and Sviatopolk II (1087–1113). Then the principality was ruled directly by the grand prince in Kiev until Yurii Yaroslavych, a descendant of Sviatopolk II Iziaslavych, wrested Turiv from Kiev's control (1157). In the second half of the 12th century, during Yurii's sons' reign, the principality declined and eventually was divided into appanages: Sviatopolk got Turiv, Ivan, Dubrovytsia, Yaropolk, Pynske, and others, Slutsk and Kletsk. In the second quarter of the 13th century those small principalities came under the influence of the Principality of Galicia-Volhynia, which was ruled by Danylo Romanovych. After the Mongol invasion of 1240 the area came under the control of the Golden Horde, and in the 14th century, under Lithuanian rule. In the mid-16th century the territory became part of the Polish Commonwealth.

BIBLIOGRAPHY
Dovnar-Zapol'skii, M. *Ocherk istorii Krivichskoi i Dregovichskoi zemel' do kontsa XII st.* (Kiev 1891)

M. Zhdan, A. Zhukovsky

**Turka.** IV-4. A town (1989 pop 7,800) on the Stryi River and a raion center in Lviv oblast. It was first mentioned in historical documents in 1431. It was granted the right of *Magdeburg law in 1730, while it was under Polish rule. In 1772 Turka was annexed by Austria, and after the First World War it was placed under Polish rule. Since 1944 it has been part of the Ukrainian SSR. Turka is an agricultural town with a light-fixtures factory, a gravel quarry, and a branch of the Boryslav Haberdashery Sewing Complex. It has three rare examples of Boiko wooden architecture: the Higher St Nicholas's Church (early 15th century), the Middle St Nicholas's Church (1739, by D. Prokopii), and the Dormition Church (1750). In the fall of 1744 the legendary outlaw O. *Dovbush staged an opryshok rebellion in the area.

Kost Turkalo                Lev Turkevych

**Turkalo, Kost,** b 20 August 1892 in Nemyryntsi, Proskuriv county, Podilia gubernia, d 17 October 1979 in New York. Chemical engineer and civic and political leader. A former member of the Central Rada, he became a research associate of the All-Ukrainian Academy of Sciences and editor of the technical department of the Institute of the Ukrainian Scientific Language (1922–9). In that capacity he prepared a number of technical dictionaries, the most notable (coauthored by V. Favorsky, 1928) dealing with agriculture. He was arrested repeatedly by the NKVD and was a defendant in the Stalinist show trial of the *Union for the Liberation of Ukraine (1930), at which he was sentenced to three years of imprisonment. He managed to flee from the USSR in 1943 and emigrated to the United States in 1949. In addition to articles on linguistic, political, and community issues he wrote two collections of autobiographical essays, *Tortury* (Tortures, 1963) and *Spohady* (Recollections, 1978).

**Turkestan** (also Turkistan). A historical and geographic territory in Central Asia, extending from Kazakhstan (in some calculations as far as Siberia) in the north to Iran and India on the south, and from the Caspian Sea in the west to China in the east. Inhabited predominantly by Turkic peoples, it increasingly fell under the domination of China and the Russian Empire in the 19th century. In 1865 its western reaches were given a Russian administrative apparatus and designated as Turkestan. By the end of the century Russia had fully subjugated the region, and the Chinese established the province of Sinkiang in 1884 in its eastern reaches. The initial Russian policy of agricultural colonization by Cossacks was later replaced by one of settlement by peasants, including Ukrainians, who were familiar with farming in steppe terrain. Turkestan did not manage to become independent after the revolution and civil war. It was gradually absorbed by the USSR in 1918–24, as the Turkestan Autonomous SSR, and was later divided into the Tadzhik, Turkmen, Uzbek, and Kirghiz Soviet republics. Northern Turkestan was joined to Kazakhstan. Together with other peoples under Soviet rule, Turkestanis participated in the *Promethean movement of the 1920s and 1930s. For information on Ukrainians in Turkestan, see *Kazakhstan, *Kirgizia, *Tadzhikistan, *Turkmenistan, and *Uzbekistan.

**Turkevych, Lev** [Turkevyč], b 4 May 1901 in Brody, Galicia, d 4 November 1961 in Toronto. Conductor, composer, teacher, and cellist. He graduated (1922) from the Szymanowski Conservatory in Lviv in the class of M. Soltys, and then studied composition in the class of J. Marks (1923–5) at Vienna Academy of Music and musicology at Vienna University. He conducted the Boian and Banduryst choruses in Lviv and, from 1927, conducted at opera theaters in Lviv, Warsaw, Poznań, and elsewhere. He was music director of the Lesia Ukrainka Drama Theater in Lviv (1939–41) and worked as both music director and conductor of the Lviv Opera Theater (1941–4). After emigrating to Germany he organized the male Vatra Chorus (1945), with which he successfully toured Switzerland, Germany, Austria, and North America (1946–51). From 1949 he lived in Canada, where he conducted the Chaika female chorus and the Prometheus male chorus (both in Toronto), as well as the Toronto Symphony Orchestra in a number of concerts. Turkevych's compositions include choral music, both secular and religious; new piano accompaniments to existing choral works; new orchestrations for stage works and for choral music; and independent symphonic music. A biography, by I. Bodrevych and L. Levytska, was published in Toronto in 1965.

**Turkevych-Lukiianovych, Stefaniia** [Turkevyč-Lukijanovyč, Stefanija], b 1908 in Lviv, d 8 April 1977 in Cambridge, England. Composer, pianist, and musicologist; sister of L. *Turkevych, wife of R. *Lisovsky, and mother of Z. *Lisovska. She studied at the Lysenko Higher Institute of Music, the University of Lviv, the University of Vienna, the Prague Conservatory, and the Ukrainian Free University in Prague (PH D in musicology, 1934). In 1935–9 she taught harmony and piano at the Lysenko Higher Institute of Music in Lviv, and in 1940–4 she was a lecturer at the Lviv Conservatory, an accompanist at the Lviv Opera, and a pianist for Lviv Radio. In 1945 she emigrated to England, where she spent most of her time composing. Her works include the opera-ballet *Mavka* (The Sylph), four symphonies, a liturgy, chamber music, pieces for piano, and art songs.

**Turkevych-Martynets, Iryna** [Turkevyč-Martynec'], b 1900 in Brody, Galicia, d 5 July 1983 in Winnipeg. Opera singer (lyric soprano); sister of L. Turkevych and wife of V. Martynets. She studied music at the Lysenko Higher Institute of Music and in Prague and Paris. In the Lviv Opera Theater she performed the name-parts in G. Bizet's *Carmen* and G. Puccini's *Tosca*. After emigrating to Canada in 1950, she was active in the Ukrainian Women's Organization and Ukrainian theater groups in Winnipeg, where she directed M. Arkas's *Kateryna* (1951) and the Ukrainian Children's Theater production of M. Lysenko's operetta *Billy Goat's Bluff*.

**Turkey.** A country in the Near East that occupies the peninsula of Asia Minor (97 percent of the country's territory) and a small corner of the Balkan Peninsula. It is bounded by the Black, Aegean, and Mediterranean seas, and shares boundaries with Georgia and Armenia (formerly with the USSR), Iran, Syria, Greece, and Bulgaria. It covers an area of 780,000 sq km and in 1990 had a population of 56.5 million. Turkey is Ukraine's neighbor to the south across the Black Sea. Until after the First World War it was identified with the Ottoman Empire, the multinational polity in which it played a dominant role. In some periods Turkey bordered directly on Ukraine or controlled sections of Ukrainian territory (particularly the southern steppe). Turkish vassal-states, such as the Crimean Khanate (see *Tatars), Moldavia, and Transylvania, were southern neighbors of Ukraine over the centuries. Turkey never controlled Ukrainian-inhabited territories for any extended period of time (with the exception of Bukovyna, which was part of the Ottoman-controlled *Moldavia principality in the 16th to 18th centuries).

Turkey played an important role in Ukrainian history. The rise of the *Cossacks was in part a reaction to Turkish expansion in Southern Ukraine beginning in the late 15th century. Once the Ukrainian Cossacks were established as a force in their own right, they occasionally sought to balance the power and territorial aspirations of Poland and Muscovy through alliances with Turkey. The (Islamic) Ottoman conquest of the Byzantine Empire was a critical factor in the development of Moscow's sense of mission as the Third Rome, the pre-eminent force of Orthdoxy that later was to subsume Ukraine. After the incorporation of Ukrainian lands into the Russian Empire the struggle against Turkey, now undertaken within an imperial context, became a popular cause among Ukrainians. In 1918 Turkey recognized the Ukrainian state as a signatory of the Treaty of Brest-Litovsk and established diplomatic relations with it. For several years after the inception of the Ukrainian SSR Turkey maintained separate economic and cultural relations with it.

**To the mid-17th century.** Over several centuries nomadic Turkic tribes worked their way westward from Outer Mongolia to Central Asia and beyond. Having adopted the Islamic faith, the Turks coalesced around the Seljuk dynasty and began to develop a territorial base in the Middle East. By the 12th century they had pushed forward in Byzantine-controlled Anatolia (present-day Turkey). The ruler of one of the numerous semi-independent principalities (emirates) within the Turkish realm, Osman (late 14th to early 15th century), began expanding his holdings and created the nucleus of what was to become a powerful empire (Osmanli to the Turks, Ottoman in the West). The Ottomans took over many former Byzantine lands, including Asia Minor and the southern Balkans, in the 14th and 15th centuries. They finally took Constantinople in 1453, renamed it Istanbul, and turned it into the capital of their empire. In the 16th century they seized Wallachia, Moldavia (including Bukovyna), Transcaucasia, and the countries of the Near East. From the 1470s on Turkey began to control the northern Black Sea coast. In 1475 it took the Genoese colonies in the Crimea (Teodosiia, Kaffa, Balaklava, Sudak, and Kerch). In 1478 the Crimean Khanate recognized the suzerainty of Turkey; that development allowed the Turks to establish military bases in Akkerman (1484), Kiliia (1484), Ochakiv (1480s), and Izmail (early 16th century) and control the Black Sea.

In the late 15th century the Crimean Tatars began a 200-year campaign of raids on Ukrainian territories, independently or jointly with the Turks, in pursuit of booty and slaves. The slaves were sold either in the large market of Kaffa or in Turkey, particularly *Istanbul. The Turks themselves first attacked Ukraine in 1498–9 (jointly with the Tatars) to punish King Jan Olbracht for interfering in Turko-Moldavian affairs. They plundered Podilia and Galicia and advanced as far as Peremyshl.

With the rise of the *Zaporozhian Sich in the middle of the 16th century the Cossacks mounted an organized resistance to the Turks and Tatars and staged retaliatory naval raids on Turko-Tatar centers in Southern Ukraine, such as Ochakiv (1589), Akkerman (1594, 1601), Kiliia (1602, 1606), Izmail (1609, 1621), and Kaffa (1616). In the 17th century the Cossacks began organizing large campaigns against Turkish cities. They captured Varna in 1604, Trabzon in 1614 and 1625, and Sinop in 1614 and even attacked Istanbul in 1615, in 1620, and three times in 1624.

The Cossacks could not stop Tatar and Turkish slave raids. The majority of the captives became forced laborers, galley slaves, or domestic workers. Young women and girls became concubines, and strapping boys were trained as *janissaries. A few Ukrainians attained success and prominence among their captors; for example, *Roksoliana became the principal wife of Sultan Süleyman I and a major power behind the throne. Notwithstanding such exceptions a harsh fate usually awaited Ukrainian captives, and the evils of Turkish enslavement was a major theme in the Ukrainian *dumas.

Until the mid-17th century the Ukrainians maintained a largely antagonistic relationship with Turkey. In spite of their geographic proximity the two did not engage directly in trade, and only minor cultural influences passed between them (most notably the *Turkisms that entered the Ukrainian language). The antagonism was made stronger when the Cossacks emerged as the self-styled defenders of Ukrainian Orthodoxy. Hetman P. *Sahaidachny considered combating the Muslim world to be the primary duty of Cossacks and attempted to organize an anti-Ottoman coalition. At the Battle of *Khotyn (1621), for example, a 40,000-strong Cossack force under the command of Sahaidachny was a decisive factor in the victory, which proved a major setback for the Ottoman Empire. Hetmans M. *Doroshenko (in 1625–8) and M. *Fedorovych (1630) continued the anti-Turkish policy and conducted further successful naval attacks.

**The Cossack state.** With the establishment of the Ukrainian Cossack state Ukraine's relations with Turkey took a dramatic turn: they were guided now by the interests of a nascent state and realpolitik rather than territorial defense, religious ideology, and adventurism.

The earliest approaches were made by B. Khmelnytsky in the wake of a tentative anti-Tatar agreement between Muscovy and the Polish Commonwealth arranged by A. Kysil in 1647. Seeking an ally against Poland, Khmelnytsky signed a treaty with the Crimea in late 1647 or early 1648 that enabled him to mount his large-scale offensives. A Ukrainian diplomatic mission headed by Col F. Dzhalalii (himself of Turkish origin) traveled to Istanbul in 1648 and concluded a treaty with the Ottomans that recognized Ukraine as a sovereign state and forbade the Crimean khan to plunder Ukrainian territory. Later the sultan signed a naval convention with the Zaporozhian army, which set out the terms of trade between Turkey and Ukraine. The Ukraino-Turkish alliance was sundered by Crimean opposition, notably that of Khan *Islam Girei III, whose demand that Tatars be given the exclusive right to 'oversee northern Ukrainian affairs' was accepted by Sultan Mehmed IV.

Direct negotiations with Turkey resumed only in 1650, when Turkey offered to make Ukraine its protectorate – a vassal-state similar to Moldavia or Wallachia. Despite opposition from the Ukrainian nobility (Kysil) and the clerical hierarchy (S. Kosiv) Khmelnytsky accepted Turkey's offer in 1651. The agreement was never fully implemented, however, and it proved generally unpopular. Moreover the Tatars proved to be unreliable allies, and Khmelnytsky found himself in increased political isolation as his plans for a Cossack-Moldavian alliance (even union) fell apart. Consequently, he reoriented himself and Ukraine to Muscovy with the Treaty of *Pereiaslav in 1654. Certain provisions of the treaty prohibited independent relations between Ukraine and Turkey, but those relations continued uninterrupted. A new Ukraino-Turkish agreement was signed the following year.

Relations and agreements with Turkey in the ensuing years followed a familiar pattern as a succession of hetmans looked to Turkey for assistance, particularly in times of need: I. Vyhovsky (1659), P. Teteria (1670), P. Doroshenko and Yu. Khmelnytsky (especially after the Treaty of Andrusovo in 1667), and I. Briukhovetsky (1668). Doroshenko's initiative had the greatest significance, when he established an alliance with Turkey (recognizing Ottoman suzerainty) and launched a joint military campaign with the Turks. The subsequent *Buchach Peace Treaty of 1672, concluded with Poland on 5 October, ceded Podilia to the Turks and Bratslav and southern Kiev voivodeships to the Cossacks under Turkish protectorship. Doroshenko's shaky hold on the territory ended with his resignation in 1676, at which time the Turks replaced him with Yu. *Khmelnytsky. Khmelnytsky's rule proved unsatisfactory to his Muslim overlords and they executed him in 1681 and replaced him by the Moldavian hospodar G. Duca. That year the Ottomans concluded the Treaty of Bakhchesarai with Muscovy, which recognized the basic delineation of Ukrainian territories and gave the Turks the Right-Bank possessions they had obtained in 1672. Those lands, now largely depopulated by the ongoing fighting

during the *Ruin, were taken back by Poland in 1699. The Ottomans did not commit major resources to that part of the empire, in the wake of their defeat in 1683 near Vienna (a battle in which an important role was played by the Ukrainian Yu. *Kulchytsky).

The tenures of I. Mazepa and P. Orlyk as hetmans saw the last independent diplomatic efforts dealing with the Ottoman Empire. In the initial phase of his hetmancy (pre–1700) Mazepa was outspoken in his anti-Turkish sentiment, and Ukraine participated in anti-Turkish campaigns. Mazepa personally commanded victorious military actions against Turkish fortifications on the lower Dnieper. After 1701 Mazepa sought a reconciliation with Turkey and assistance for his effort to break free of Moscow. His defeat at Poltava in 1709 ended those efforts. Mazepa and K. Hordiienko then sought asylum in the Ottoman realm. Orlyk led a joint military action with Ukrainian, Tatar, and Turkish forces in Right-Bank Ukraine against Russian forces in 1711. In 1712 he sought to revive a union with Turkey. Turkey recognized his title to Right-Bank Ukraine but did not offer him the support he needed to wrest the territories from Polish control. In 1722 Orlyk was interned at Salonika. He lived out his days (until 1742) in the Ottoman Porte, vainly expecting assistance for his designs on Ukraine. His gradual disillusionment became evident in the growing anti-Islamic sentiment evident in his writings.

**18th to 20th centuries.** Ukrainians took part in the various struggles related to the *Russo-Turkish wars, which in the 18th century (1735–9, 1768–74, and 1787–91) resulted in the expulsion of Ottoman forces from Southern Ukraine. In 1774 the triangle between the Dnieper and the Boh rivers was wrested from Turkish control, and the Crimean Khanate was made independent of Turkey (under the Peace Treaty of Küçük-Kaynarca). After the destruction of the Zaporozhian Sich in 1775, some Cossacks petitioned Turkey for refuge and were granted a settlement near the mouth of the Danube in northern Dobrudja. There they established the *Danubian Sich, which was active as an organized military unit until 1828. In 1783 Russia annexed the Crimean Khanate, and in 1791 (under the Treaty of Iaşi) it acquired the territory between the lower Boh and the Dniester rivers. That development effectively ended Turkey's presence on the northern Black Sea littoral. The Ottomans' last (albeit indirect) holding in Ukrainian territory, Bukovyna (under the vassal-state of Moldavia), was annexed by Austria in 1774 while Turkey was engaged in hostilities with the Russian Empire.

During the 19th century the Russo-Turkish wars continued, in 1806–12 (with the annexation of Bessarabia by the Russian Empire), in 1828–9, in 1853–6 (the Crimean War), and in 1877–8 (the Balkan campaign). Ukrainians sided almost universally against the Turks, particularly in the Balkan campaign. Even before the beginning of hostilities Ukrainian volunteers took part in the struggle of the South Slavs (Serbs and Bulgarians) against Turkish domination. Ukrainians gathered considerable financial support for that cause and organized a medical-relief effort in the region.

On the side of Turkey, however, Polish (or Polonized Ukrainian) émigrés, notably A. Czartoryski, led an anti-Russian movement in the mid-19th century that was partially sponsored by Turkey. M. *Czajkowski, a participant in the Polish Insurrection of 1830–1, emigrated to Istanbul in 1848, converted to Islam, and convinced the Porte to organize Cossack formations in the Turkish forces with Ukrainian volunteers from northern Dobrudja. Those units were active in the Crimean War and until 1861.

During the First World War Turkey fought on the side of the Central Powers against the Russian Empire. In November 1914 the Turkish interior minister met with a delegation from the Union for the Liberation of Ukraine (SVU) and promised support for the Ukrainian independence movement. M. Melenevsky headed an SVU mission in Istanbul, which published a pamphlet intended for Turkish servicemen (*Asker*), and *Ukrayna, Rusya, Türkiye, Magâlemer mecmu'asi* (1915), a handbook of general information.

In the spring of 1916 the Russian imperial army, which included Ukrainians, captured eastern Anatolia (centered on Trabzon), which it held until 1918. After the February Revolution of 1917 a Ukrainian Hromada was established in Trabzon, which published *Visti Ukraïns'koï hromady mista Trapezundu*, edited by H. Khymenko. In September 1917 the Central Rada appointed M. Svidersky as commissar of the Trabzon district. Entrusted with Ukrainizing local military units, he organized a military congress there in October 1917. In early 1918 the imperial army evacuated the city, and the Ukrainians returned to Ukraine.

A Turkish delegation that included the grand vizier and the minister of foreign affairs signed the Treaty of Brest-Litovsk on 9 February 1918, in which Turkey recognized the UNR as an independent and sovereign state. The treaty was ratified in Turkey on 22 August 1918, and Ukraine and Turkey set up diplomatic missions. The head of the Hetman government's mission in Istanbul was M. Sukovkin (1918), and of the UNR Directory, O. Lototsky (1919–20) and J. Tokarzewski-Karaszewicz (1920–1). Tokarzewski-Karaszewicz's aides included L. Kobyliansky and V. Mursky (who was later the UNR government-in-exile's envoy in Turkey until 1935). The Turkish envoy to the Hetman government in Kiev was A. Mukhtar Bey. Another handbook on Ukrainians, *Ukrayna ve Türkiye* (1919), was published in Istanbul. Mursky published his monograph *Ukrayna ve istiklâl müca hedeler* in 1930.

After the Ukrainian SSR was established in January 1922, a treaty was signed with Turkey concerning political, economic, and cultural relations as well as 'friendship and brotherhood.' Soviet Ukraine, however, never had a permanent diplomatic mission in Istanbul, and from 1923, relations were conducted only on an all-Union level. In 1926 the All-Ukrainian Learned Association of Oriental Studies maintained direct contact with Turkey and devoted considerable attention to its culture. In 1928–9 a delegation of Ukrainian scholars (O. Hladstern, O. Samoilovych, P. Tychyna, and V. Zummer) visited Turkey. In 1927–31 the association issued the journal *Skhidnii svit* (the last issue came out under the title *Chervonyi skhid*). After 1945 a Ukrainian Hromada was revived in Istanbul, headed by M. Zabillo. Diplomatic relations were once again established between Turkey and Ukraine after 1991.

Turkish-Ukrainian cultural relations were on the whole limited. There were some efforts on the part of Ukrainians to acquaint Turks with Ukrainian political and cultural concerns. Ukrainian writers translated or adapted Turkish folk or classical literature. Ukrainian publications on Turkish themes include studies by M. Drahomanov on Turkish anecdotes in the Ukrainian oral tradition and by

I. Franko on poems about the Russo-Turkish War of 1787–91; a grammar and basic language text by T. Hrunin (1930); A. Krymsky's translations of Turkish folk tales and songs (1890); Tychyna's translations of a variety of Turkish authors; and the anthology *Opovidannia turets'kykh pys'mennykiv* (Short Stories by Turkish Writers, 1955). There have been few Turkish translations of Ukrainian works. Some of T. Shevchenko's poems were translated by Krymsky and Nazim Hikmet, and translations of Tychyna's works appeared in the Turkish journal *Milliyet* in 1928. In the 1970s and 1980s several books of Turkish literature were translated into Ukrainian by H. Khalymonenko.

Until 1931 Krymsky headed the Turkological Commission of the All-Ukrainian Academy of Sciences, which published *Istoriia Turechchyny* (History of Turkey, 1924), *Tiurky, ïkh mova i literatura* (The Turks, Their Language and Literature, 1930), and other titles. Other Ukrainian scholars in the field at that time and since then include L. Bykovsky, V. Dubrovsky, O. Hanusets, Kh. Nadel, O. Pritsak, O. Samoilovych, Ye. Zavalynsky, L. Hajda, and V. Ostapchuk. The painter O. Hryshchenko worked in Turkey and published *Deux ans à Constantinople* (1930; Ukrainian trans 1961).

BIBLIOGRAPHY
Kostomarov, N. *Bogdan Khmel'nitskii, dannik Ottomanskoi Porty.* Vol 5 of his *Sobranie sochinenii* (St Petersburg 1905)
Zastyrets', I. 'Mazepyntsi v Turechchyni: Z paperiv Sadyk Pashi (Chaikovs'koho),' *Ukraïna,* no. 2 (1914)
Stübe, R. *Die Ukraine und ihre Beziehungen zum Osmanischen Reich* (Leipzig 1915)
Kryms'kyi, A. *Istoriia Turechchyny* (Kiev 1924)
Rypka, J. 'Aus der Korrespondenz der Hohen Pforte mit B. Chmelnicki,' *Z dějin Východni Europy a Slovanstva* (Prague 1928)
'Ukraïna ta Turechchyna,' *Skhidnii svit,* 1929, nos 7–8
Pritsak, O. 'Soiuz Khmel'nyts'koho z Turechchynoiu, 1648,' *ZNTSh,* 156 (1948)
– 'Das erste türkisch-ukrainische Bündnis (1648),' *Oriens,* 6, no. 2 (1953)
Apanovych, O. *Zaporozs'ka Sich u borot'bi proty turets'ko-tatars'koï ahresiï* (Kiev 1961)
Bartl, P. 'Der Kosakenstaat und das Osmanische Reich im 17 und in der ersten Hälfte des 18 Jahrhunderts,' *Südostforschungen,* no. 33 (1974)
Berindei, M. 'La Porte Ottomane face aux Cosaques Zaporogues 1600–1637,' *HUS,* 1, no. 3 (September 1977)

A. Zhukovsky

**Turkisms.** Loanwords from the Turkic languages became part of the Ukrainian vocabulary during the 10th to 18th centuries mostly as a result of the proximity of various Turkic peoples to Ukraine and their commercial, political, and cultural relations with it. Some Turkisms in the Ukrainian language were themselves originally loanwords from other languages (eg, *Iranianisms, *Hellenisms). A minority entered Ukrainian via the Polish, Russian, and other languages. The majority of Turkisms in the West Slavic languages entered them via the Ukrainian.

The earliest proto-Ukrainian–Turkic contacts took place in Common Slavic times. In the 6th century AD the Central Asian Turkic kaganate extended its influence to the Black and Azov seas. In the 7th and 8th centuries Turkic tribes that belonged to the Volga Bulgar and Khazar tribal unions penetrated into the Ukrainian steppe. It is possibly at that time that Turkisms such as *kahan* 'kagan, ruler', *bahatyr* 'hero', and *san* 'high rank' and the suffix *-čij* to form names of persons according to their occupation (eg, *k"nih"čij* 'scribe') originated. In the 9th century, Kievan Rus' had ongoing relations with the Turkic Khazar kaganate, whose influence extended to the Dnieper. In the 9th to 11th centuries, the nomadic Turkic Pechenegs, Torks, and Black Klobuk traversed the steppe from the Don to the Danube. In the 11th to 13th centuries they were succeeded by the Turkic Cumans. It was from those tribes (most certainly the Cumans) that the Turkisms found in the Rus' chronicles and the epic *Slovo o polku Ihorevi* (The Tale of Ihor's Campaign) were borrowed, including *bulat* and *xaraluh* (types of steel), *žemčuh* 'pearl', *kurhan* 'fortress, barrow', *šatro* 'tent', *japončycja* (later *opanča*) 'coat', *klobuk* (later *kovpak*) 'tall hat', *tovar* 'merchandise', *koščij* 'male captive', *čaha* 'female captive', *tlumač* 'interpreter', *lošad'* (later *loša*) 'horse', *borsuk* 'badger', *jaruha* 'large ravine', and *jevšan* 'wormwood'.

Many Turkisms date from the 13th- to 14th-century Mongol-Tatar invasion of Europe. They include *kozak* 'free person, Cossack', *vataha* 'band, herd', *saraj* 'palace (later barn)', *čardak* 'ship's bridge', *bazar* 'bazaar', *xarč* 'food', *bašlyk* 'hood', *kalyta* 'pouch, purse', *baryš* 'profit', *čaj* 'tea', *buhaj* 'bull', and *karyj* 'black, brown, dark'. The largest number of Turkisms were borrowed in the 15th to 18th centuries as a result of Turkish and Crimean Tatar relations with and influence in Ukraine. They include herding terms such as *čaban* 'shepherd', *otara* 'flock', *tabun* 'horse herd', *arkan* 'lasso', *torba* '(feed) bag, sack', *kaban* 'boar', *haida* (a herder's call), and the horse colors *bulanyj* 'light bay, fallow' and *čalyj* 'roan'; terms of the steppe environment and way of life, such as *bajrak* 'wooded valley', *komyš* 'bulrush', *lyman* 'estuary', *tuman* 'fog', *berkut* 'golden eagle', *sarana* 'locust', *harba* 'cart', and *kurin'* 'house' (later 'Cossack barrack' or 'detachment'); gardening terms such as *baštan* 'melon garden', *harbuz* 'gourd', *kavun* 'watermelon', and *tjutjun* 'tobacco'; Cossack military terms such as *kiš* 'encampment', *tabir* 'camp', *osavul* 'aide', *bunčuk* 'horse-tail standard', *čajka* 'boat', and *sa(ha)jdak* 'quiver'; clothing terms such as *haba* 'white cloth', *kuntuš* 'a kind of coat', *kaftan* 'caftan', *kobenjak* 'hooded coat', *šaravary* 'balloon pants', *štany* 'trousers', *očkur* 'rope belt', *sap'jan* 'morocco leather', *čoboty* 'boots', *postoly* 'bast shoes', *tas'ma* 'ribbon', and *serpanok* 'veil'; and commercial, manufacturing, and social terms such as *čumak* 'salt trader', *aršyn* 'arshin' (= 28 inches), *mohoryč* 'drinking to a bargain', *majdan* 'town or village square', *čavun* 'cast iron', *kazan* 'cauldron', *kylym* 'kilim', *tapčan* 'trestle-bed', *lokša* 'noodles', *kav'jar* 'caviar', *kava* 'coffee', *kobza* 'kobza' (lute), *ljul'ka* 'smoking pipe', *hajdamaka* 'brigand', *xarcyz* 'robber', *kančuk* 'whip', *kajdany* 'shackles', and *čuma* 'plague'. Many toponyms in the steppe regions of Ukraine are of Turkic origin, eg, Kremenchuk, Inhul, Izium, Kalmiius, Samara, and Saksahan.

BIBLIOGRAPHY

Miklosich, F. *Die türkischen Elemente in den Südost- und Osteuropäischen Sprachen (Griechisch, Albanisch, Rumunisch, Bulgarisch, Serbisch, Kleinrussisch, Grossrussisch, Polnisch)*, part 1 (Vienna 1884)

Makarushka, O. 'Slovar ukraïns'kykh vyraziv, pereiniatykh z mov turks'kykh: Prychynok do diial'nosty O. Ohonovs'koho,' *ZNTSh*, 5 (1895)

Kryms'kyi, A. *Tiurky, ïkh movy ta literatury* (Kiev 1930); repr in *A.Iu. Kryms'kyi: Tvory v p'iaty tomakh*, 4, *Skhodoznavstvo* (Kiev 1974)

Rohal', M. 'Tiurks'ki leksychni zapozychennia v ukraïns'kykh litopysakh XVII–pochatku XVIII st.,' in *Z istoriï ukraïns'koï ta inshykh slov'ians'kykh mov (Zbirnyk statei)* (Kiev 1965)

Baskakov, N. (ed). *Tiurkizmy v vostochnoslavianskikh iazykakh* (Moscow 1974)

Stryzhak, O. (ed). *Hidronimiia Ukraïny v ïï mizhmovnykh i mizhdialektnykh zv'iazkakh* (Kiev 1981)

V. Swoboda

**Turkmen.** An ethnic group whose religion is Sunni Muslim, and whose language belongs to the South Turkic or *Oghuz group. There are a total of 3.4 million Turkmen, of whom 2,729,000 live in the territories of the former USSR (1989 census), including 2,537,000 in Turkmenistan, 92,300 in Uzbekistan, 14,000 in Tadzhikistan, and 23,000 in Stavropol krai, Russia. Some also live in Iran (approx 350,000), Afghanistan (300,000), various Arab countries (150,000), and Turkey (80,000). *Turkmenistan was incorporated into the Russian Empire in the late 19th century.

Ukrainian-Turkmen relations have centered mainly on the translation of literary works. The works of T. Shevchenko, I. Franko, and contemporary Ukrainian writers have been translated into Turkmen, and Turkmen works by Maktumkuli, Kh. Ismailov, B. Soltanniazov, and R. Aliev have been translated into Ukrainian (by P. Tychyna, V. Sosiura, M. Rylsky, and others). In 1971 a Turkmen Literature Week was held in Ukraine, and in 1972 Ukrainian art and literature days were held in Turkmenistan. Among Ukrainian writers who have dealt with Turkmen subjects are M. Shumylo, A. Turchynska, L. Zabashta, D. Doroshko, and Ya. Shporta. The collection *Holosy Turkmeniï* (Voices of Turkmenistan) was published in 1978. In 1977 there were 37,000 Ukrainians living in the Turkmen SSR.

**Turkmenistan.** A republic (1989 pop 3,534,000) in the southwestern part of Soviet Central Asia (Turkestan), covering an area of 488,100 sq km. Its capital is Ashkhabad. The territory belonged to various states in the past: in the 16th and 17th centuries a part of it came under the Bukhara and Khiva khanates and another part under Persia; in the 1880s it was annexed by Russia; in 1917–21 its indigenous peoples resisted the Soviet invaders; in 1921 it became an oblast within the Turkestan ASSR; and in 1924 it was promoted to the status of a republic and became the Turkmen SSR. With the disintegration of the Soviet Union in 1991 Turkmenistan gained independence.

According to census figures, there were 6,780 Ukrainians in Turkmenistan in 1926, 21,000 (1.4 percent of the population) in 1959, 35,400 (1.6 percent) in 1970, and 37,000 in 1989. Its other inhabitants include (1979) 1,417,000 Turkmen, 313,000 Russians, 180,000 Uzbeks, 68,000 Kazakhs, and 36,000 Tatars. In 1970 most Ukrainians (29,500) lived in cities, 11,000 in Ashkhabad alone. Although 65 percent of the Ukrainians claimed Ukrainian as their mother tongue, only 8 percent were fluent in that language.

**Turko, Roman,** b 21 July 1906 in Starychi, Yavoriv county, Galicia, d 6 January 1984 in Toronto. Physician. A graduate of Lviv University (MD, 1934), he specialized in roentgenology at Cracow University (1938) and practiced medicine in Cherche, Yavoriv, and Stryi. In 1952 he emigrated to Canada, where he became head of the roentgenological department at Veterans' Hospital in Saint John, New Brunswick. In 1962 he founded the Montreal branch of the Ukrainian Medical Association of North America.

The Turkovychi icon of the Theotokos

Yevhen Turula

**Turkovychi** [Turkovyči]. III-4. A village in the Kholm region (now in Poland) and the site of a once-renowned monastery. According to legend, during the transfer of the famous icon of the Theotokos from Belz to Częstochowa (ca 1378) a similar icon appeared miraculously in the village. A monastery was built at the site. It was closed down in 1749, with only the small wooden church that housed the miraculous icon left. In 1901 an Orthodox nunnery with a teachers' seminary for girls and an orphanage was built there. It was closed by the Polish government in 1918: the church was leveled, and the other buildings were converted into a warehouse and a Roman Catholic church. In 1928 the Orthodox eparchy was permitted to build a wooden church in the partly intact cemetery. Until 1938, when the church was destroyed, it attracted large numbers of pilgrims from the Kholm and Volhynia regions.

**Turnip** (*Brassica rapa*; Ukrainian: *brukva, turneps, ripak*). A biennial plant, also called swede, of the family Cruciferae, related to *rape. It is grown in Ukraine for its fleshy edible root, principally to feed livestock. The early, round Volhynian variety is favored.

**Turovsky, Mykhailo** [Turovs'kyj, Myxajlo], b 8 May 1933 in Kiev. Graphic artist and painter of Jewish origin. He studied under O. Pashchenko at the Kiev State Art Institute (1954–60) and under M. Derehus at the USSR Academy of Arts (1965–7). In 1980 he emigrated to the United States. He has made several series of prints, including 'Pages of Struggle' (1960, lithographs) and 'Motherhood,' and illustrated over 200 books, including editions of V. Stefanyk's stories (1966), Lesia Ukrainka's *Lisova pisnia* (The Forest Song, 1967), and I. Franko's poetry (1969). He also painted a portrait of M. Hlushchenko. A catalog of an exhibition of his graphic works was published in Kiev in 1975. Since 1978 he has lived in the United States.

**Turtledove** (*Streptopelia*; Ukrainian: *horlytsia*). A reddish brown, migratory bird of the pigeon family Columbidae, up to 30 cm in body length, with a blue-gray head and a white-tipped tail. In Ukraine the only two species are the common turtledove (*S. turtur*) and a recent arrival, the collared turtledove (*S. decaocto*), which came from the west during the 1940s and settled as far east as Poltava, Kharkiv, and Kherson. Both are considered secondary game birds.

**Turula, Yevhen,** b 4 January 1882 in Berezhany, Galicia, d 3 December 1951 in Winnipeg. Greek Catholic priest, choir director, and composer. Educated at the theological seminary and the Conservatory of Music in Lviv, he was ordained in 1906. He worked as a religious instructor and army chaplain before emigrating to Winnipeg in 1923. There he conducted choirs for the Prosvita Society and the Ukrainian National Federation, staged operettas, operated a school of music, and composed original works for violin, piano, and chorus. He published numerous collections of music, which included carols, and dance, war, and historical songs.

**Turyn, Roman,** b 2 September 1900 in Sniatyn, Galicia, d 29 August 1979 in Lviv. Postimpressionist and realist painter. He studied at the Cracow Academy of Fine Arts (1921–5) and under W. Jarocki and Yu. Pankevych in Paris (1925–7). Having settled in Lviv, he painted landscapes, still lifes, and portraits, including ones of A. Drahomanova-Trush (1946), F. Kolessa (1947), V. Stefanyk (1948), and V. Shchurat (1950). Turyn discovered the Lemko primitive painter *Nykyfor and organized an exhibition of his works in Lviv. In 1933–5 he made the documentary film *Hutsul Fragments* and another about sports in Galicia.

**TUSM.** See Ukrainian Student Organization of Mikhnovsky.

**Tustan.** A Rus' fortress of the 9th to 13th century near Urych, Lviv oblast. Built on a rocky hill which rose sharply above the surrounding area, the fortress had a stone stronghold and wooden exterior walls up to 15 m high. The interior of the fortress had living quarters (with up to five levels in places) and a well and two cisterns to supply water. Documents of the 14th to 16th centuries note Tustan as an important regional center.

**Tustanovsky, Lavrentii.** See Zyzanii, Lavrentii.

**Tutkovsky, Mykola** [Tutkovs'kyj], b 17 February 1857 in Lypovets, Kiev gubernia, d 28 February 1931 in Kiev.

Mykola Tutkovsky

Composer, pianist, and pedagogue; brother of P. Tutkovsky. A graduate of the Russian Musical Society's school in Kiev (1880) and the St Petersburg Conservatory (1881), he studied piano with V. Pukhalsky and music theory with A. Kazbyriuk. In 1893 he opened his own music school in Kiev, where he worked until 1930. From 1920 he also taught at the Kiev Conservatory. His works include the opera *Buinyi viter* (The Wild Wind), symphonic and chamber music, pieces for piano, choruses, art songs, and arrangements of Ukrainian folk songs. He also wrote a textbook on harmony in 1905.

Pavlo Tutkovsky                Ivan Tverdokhlib

**Tutkovsky, Pavlo** [Tutkovs'kyj], b 1 March 1858 in Lypovets, Kiev gubernia, d 3 June 1930 in Kiev. Geologist; full member of the VUAN from 1919 and of the Academy of Sciences of the Belorussian SSR from 1928. After graduating from Kiev University in 1882, he taught secondary school and in 1914 was appointed a lecturer at Kiev University. He helped organize the All-Ukrainian Academy of Sciences and headed the physics-mathematics (1919–24) and geology departments.He was one of the founders of the academy's geological museum. He wrote numerous scientific works on mineralogy, petrography, geochemistry, paleontology, hydrogeology, geomorphology, and regional geology. He is the author of the eolian theory of loess formation and one of the founders of the micropaleontological method for studying sedimentary rocks. In 1895 he proposed a project for supplying Kiev with artesian water, which was later implemented. He wrote many textbooks of geology and geography and the first Ukrainian dictionary of geological terminology (1923).

**Tuwim, Julian,** b 13 September 1894 in Łódź, d 27 December 1953 in Zakopane, Poland. Polish poet, writer, book editor, and translator. During the Second World War he lived as an émigré in Brazil (1940–2) and New York City (1942–6). He translated into Polish the Rus' epic *Slovo o polku Ihorevi* (The Tale of Ihor's Campaign), poems by M. Rylsky and Ye. Malaniuk, and N. Gogol's *The Inspector General* (1929), and he adapted Gogol's *The Overcoat* for the Polish stage (1934). His poems have been translated into Ukrainian by K. Polishchuk, Rylsky, Yu. Shkrumeliak, V. Lesych, D. Pavlychko, M. Lukash, H. Kochur, Ye. Drobiazko, and L. Yatskevych. Yu. Bulakhovska's book about him was published in Kiev in 1960, and an edition of his selected poems in Ukrainian translation appeared there in 1963.

*Tvarynnytstvo Ukraïny* (Animal Husbandry of Ukraine). A monthly journal of scientific production, published since 1926 (except in 1941–4) by the Ministry of Agriculture of Ukraine, initially in Kharkiv and since 1935 in Kiev. In 1926 its title was *Ukraïnske skotovodstvo*; in 1931 it was changed to *Sotsialistychne tvarynnytsvo Ukraïny*, in 1934 to *Sotsialistychne tvarynnytstvo*, and in 1964 to the current one. (In 1933 one issue was published under the title *Kolhospna tvarynnyts'ka ferma*, and in 1941 six issues under the title *Naukovo-vyrobnychyi zhurnal*.) In 1950 the circulation was 13,900; it grew to 51,800 in 1970 and 68,000 in 1976. In 1980 the circulation dropped to 56,900, a reflection of the conscious effort on the part of the Soviet government to reduce the circulation of periodicals published in the Ukrainian language.

The journal reports on the newest developments in livestock breeding, the production of fodder, effectiveness of herd reconstitution, pedigree stock breeding, artificial insemination, improvements in productivity, and quality of work. Other topics dealt with include the technology and mechanization of production and issues of veterinary medicine.

**Tverdokhlib, Ivan** [Tverdoxlib], b 24 June 1899 in Dovzhyk, Kharkiv county, d 16 October 1986 in Odessa. Character and comic stage and film actor. His roles ranged from Voznyi in I. Kotliarevsky's *Natalka Poltavka* (Natalka from Poltava) to Falstaff in W. Shakespeare's *The Merry Wives of Windsor*. He played in the Kharkiv People's Theater (1923–4), the Shevchenko First Theater of the Ukrainian Socialist Republic (1925), the Kharkiv Children's Theater (1926–7), the Kharkiv Chervonozavodskyi Ukrainian Drama Theater (1927–9), and the Odessa Ukrainian Drama Theater (from 1929, with interruptions). He acted in the films *Perekop* (1930), *Koliïvshchyna* (1933), and *Dorohoiu tsinoiu* (At a High Price, 1957, based on M. Kotsiubynsky's story).

**Tverdokhlib, Mykola** [Tverdoxlib] (nom de guerre: Hrim), b 1911? in Petryliv, Tovmach county, Galicia, d 1951? in Stanyslaviv oblast. Senior UPA commander. A graduate of a Polish officer school, in early 1944 he became an instructor in the 'Oleni' officer school of the UPA-West. In the summer of 1945 he assumed command of the *Hoverlia (4th) Group of the UPA operating in the Fourth Military District (covering Stanyslaviv, Drohobych, and Chernivtsi oblasts). Some units of the group took part in two successful raids into Czechoslovakia (in September 1945 and April 1946) and one into Rumania (in June–July 1949). In 1948–9 Tverdokhlib commanded the last UPA units to be demobilized. In 1950 he was appointed chief of security for the Carpathian region, and a year later he was killed in battle by MVD troops.

**Tverdokhlib, Sydir** [Tverdoxlib], b 9 May 1886 in Berezhany, Galicia, d 16 October 1922 in Lviv. Writer and translator. After studying at Lviv and Vienna universities he worked as a gymnasium teacher in Lviv. There he belonged to the modernist group *Moloda Muza; his first poems and translations appeared in 1906 in its journal *S'vit*. A bilingual (Ukrainian-Polish) writer, Tverdokhlib published one small book of poetry, *V svichadi plesa* (In the Mirror of the River's Surface, 1908), and verse, novellas, and translations in both Ukrainian (*Nedilia, Iliustrovana Ukraïna, Dilo*) and Polish (*Krytyka, Przegląd Krajowy,*

Sydir Tverdokhlib

Pavlo Tychyna (portrait by
Mykhailo Zhuk, watercolor
and pencil, 1919)

*Widnokręgi*) periodicals. Tverdokhlib's translations introduced the Polish reading public to contemporary Ukrainian literature and were favorably received by critics.
Published separately were his Polish translations of three
books of M. *Yatskiv's novellas (1908, 1910, 1911), an anthology of modern Ukrainian poetry (1911; 2nd edn 1913),
and a book of T. Sevchenko's selected verse (1913). Tverdokhlib also translated Shevchenko's 'Haidamaky' into
German and J. Słowacki's poems into Ukrainian. From
1920 he and Yatskiv headed the small, unpopular Ukrainian Agrarian party, which co-operated with the Polish
occupational regime in Western Ukraine and published
the government-funded weekly *Ridnyi krai*. During the
Ukrainian general boycott of the 1922 elections to the Sejm
Tverdokhlib announced his candidacy and began campaigning. Consequently the underground Ukrainian Military Organization condemned him as a national traitor
and had him assassinated in Kaminka-Strumylova.

R. Senkus

**Tverdokhlibov, Oleksander** [Tverdoxlibov] (pseud:
Zemliak), b 1840, d 1918. Historian. He taught in Okhtyrka, Kharkiv gubernia, and contributed historical essays
and regional and ethnographic studies to the newspaper
*Iuzhnyi krai*, the journal *Kievskaia starina*, and the publications of the Kharkiv Gubernial Statistical Committee.

**Tverdovsky, Petro** [Tverdovs'kyj], b 1879 in the Poltava
region, d ? Political leader in the Far East. After graduating from cadet school in Irkutsk, he served in the Far East
as an officer in the Russian army. In 1917 he organized
Ukrainian military units in Manchuria and was elected
president of the Ukrainian Regional Council of Manchuria. In the spring of 1918 he was sent as the council's delegate to Kiev, where he was appointed as Ukraine's consul
in Harbin. The following year he was arrested by the
White forces in the Far East and tranferred to Omsk,
where he was released.

**Tvorydlo, Mykola,** b 4 April 1884 in Zashkiv, Lviv
county, Galicia, d ca 1952 in Lviv. Agronomist and co-operative leader. After completing his studies in Vienna
(1911) he undertook research in Germany and Switzerland. In 1912–19 he worked as an itinerant agricultural instructor for *Silskyi Hospodar, and in 1920 he became
director of an agricultural school in Mukachiv. He soon

returned to Galicia to become director of the head office of
the Silskyi Hospodar society in Lviv (1924–7), a member
of the board of directors of *Tsentrosoiuz in Lviv (1928–
39), and an active member of the Ukrainian National
Democratic Alliance (UNDO). In 1938 he was elected to the
Polish Senate as an UNDO representative, and during the
Second World War he was an agricultural specialist for
the Ukrainian Central Committee. He edited the monthly
*Hospodar* in Uzhhorod (1920) and wrote two handbooks
for farmers, *Shkidlyvi i korysni zviriata v hospodarstvi*
(Harmful and Useful Animals in Farming, 2 vols, 1923)
and *Praktychnyi hospodar* (The Practical Farmer, 1928). He
also wrote brochures and articles on economic questions.

**Twardowski, Samuel,** b ca 1595–1600 in Lutyn, near
Jarocin, or in the vicinity of Skrzypna and Twardów, near
Pleszew, Poland, d June 1661 in Zalesie Wielkie, Poland.
Polish baroque poet. From 1633 he lived at the court of the
magnate J. Wiśniowiecki. He wrote historical narrative
poems about K. Zbaraski's 1622–3 diplomatic mission to
the Ottoman Porte (1633), in which he took part, and
about the Polish 'civil war' with the Cossacks, Tatars,
Muscovites, Swedes, and Hungarians (4 pts, pub 1681).
They are of value to both literary scholars and historians.
The latter poem describes in detail the 1649 siege of
Zbarazh and the 1651 Battle of Berestechko during the
Cossack-Polish War. Part 1 of the poem was translated by
S. *Savytsky; S. *Velychko translated parts 2 and 3 and
used them as a source in his Cossack chronicle, as did H.
Hrabianka. An edition of Twardowski's collected works
was published in Wrocław in 1955.

**Tychyna, Pavlo** [Tyčyna], b 27 January 1891 in Pisky,
Kozelets county, Chernihiv gubernia, d 16 September
1967 in Kiev. Poet; recipient of the highest Soviet awards
and orders; member of the VUAN and AN URSR (now ANU)
from 1929; deputy of the Supreme Soviet of the Ukrainian
SSR from 1938 and its chairman in 1953–9; deputy of the
Supreme Soviet of the USSR from 1946; director of the ANU
Institute of Ukrainian Literature in 1936–9 and 1941–3;
and minister of education of the Ukrainian SSR in 1943–8.
He graduated from the Chernihiv Theological Seminary
in 1913. His first poems were in part influenced by O.
*Oles, M. *Vorony, and M. *Kotsiubynsky. His first extant
poem is dated 1906 ('Synie nebo zakrylosia' [The Blue Sky
Closed]), and the first one published ('Vy znaiete, iak lypa
shelestyt'?' [You Know How the Linden Rustles?]) appeared in *Literaturno-naukovyi vistnyk* in 1912. In 1913 Tychyna enrolled at the Kiev Commercial Institute, and
while a student, he worked on the editorial boards of the
newspapers *Rada* and *Svitlo*. Later he worked for the
Chernihiv zemstvo administration.

His first collection of poetry, *Soniashni kliarnety* (Sunny
Clarinets, 1918; repr 1990), is a programmatic work, in
which he created a uniquely Ukrainian form of *symbolism and established his own poetic style, known as *kliarnetyzm* (clarinetism). Finding himself in the center of the
turbulent events during Ukraine's struggle for independence, Tychyna was overcome by the elemental force of
Ukraine's rebirth and created an opus suffused with the
harmony of the universal rhythm of light.

During the early years of the Bolshevik occupation of
Ukraine, marked by terror, ruin, famine, and suppression
of the national uprising, Tychyna maintained his position
as an independent poet and quickly established himself as

the leading Ukrainian poet. His pre-eminence is evident in the collections *Zamist' sonetiv i oktav* (Instead of Sonnets and Octaves, 1920), *Pluh* (The Plow, 1920) and *V kosmichnomu orkestri* (In the Cosmic Orchestra, 1921), the poem 'Skovoroda' (the first part of which appeared in *Shliakhy mystetstva*, 1923, no. 5), and *Viter z Ukraïny* (The Wind from Ukraine, 1924), dedicated to M. *Khvylovy. In 1923 he moved to Kharkiv and joined the organization Hart and, in 1927, *Vaplite. His membership in the latter organization and his poem 'Chystyla maty kartopliu' (Mother Was Peeling Potatoes) provoked harsh official criticism, and he was accused of 'bourgeois nationalism.'

Soon after, Tychyna capitulated to the Soviet regime and began producing collections of poetry in the socialist-realist style sanctioned by the Party. They included *Chernihiv* (1931) and *Partiia vede* (The Party Leads, 1934). The latter collection has symbolized the submission of Ukrainian writers to Stalinism. The titles of his subsequent collections reflect the spirit of apologia for J. Stalin, including *Chuttia iedynoï rodyny* (Feelings of One Unified Family, 1938), for which he was awarded the Stalin Prize for literature in 1941, *Pisnia molodosti* (Song of Youth, 1938), and *Stal' i nizhnist'* (Steel and Tenderness, 1941). Abstract and expressionistic, his Stalinist poetry consists of kinetic iambs that push inexorably and bluntly forward, mimicking the Party line of the day.

The Second World War intensified those features of Tychyna's poetry, and gave rise to a patriotic combativeness, as manifested in *My idemo na bii* (We Are Going into Battle, 1941), *Peremahat' i zhyt'* (To Conquer and to Live, 1942), *Tebe my znyshchym – chort z toboiu* (We Will Destroy You – To Hell with You, 1942), and *Den' nastane* (The Day Will Come, 1943). The titles of Tychyna's many postwar collections suggest their content: *Zhyvy, zhyvy, krasuisia* (Live, Live, and Be Beautiful, 1949), *I rosty, i diiaty* (To Grow and to Act, 1949), *Mohutnist' nam dana* (Might Has Been Given Us, 1953), *Na Pereiaslavs'kii radi* (At the Pereiaslav Council, 1954), *My svidomist' liudstva* (We Are the Consciousness of Humanity, 1957), *Druzhboiu my zdruzheni* (By Friendship We Are Bound, 1958), *Do molodi mii chystyi holos* (My Clear Voice Speaks to Youth, 1959), *Bat'kivshchyni mohutnii* (To the Mighty Fatherland, 1960), *Zrostai, prechudovyi svite* (Grow, O Wonderful World, 1960), *Komunizmu dali vydni* (The Horizons of Communism Are in Sight, 1961), and *Topoli arfy hnut'* (Poplars Bend the Harps, 1963). He also wrote *Virshi* (Poems, 1968) and other collections.

Tychyna did not take part in the Ukrainian cultural revival of the late 1950s and early 1960s, and he even attacked the *shestydesiatnyky*. The poetry of the last decade before his death is full of glorification of the Party, of the new leader, N. Khrushchev, and of heroes of socialist labor, collective farms, and so on. During L. Brezhnev's repressive regime after Khrushchev's death Tychyna's creation sounded anachronistic and self-parodying. Occasionally, however, there were flashes of his former talent, as in the poem 'Pokhoron druha' (Funeral of a Friend, 1942) and some fragments in a collection published posthumously, *V sertsi moïm* (In My Heart, 1970), and particularly in the philosophical poem *Skovoroda*, which was never completed but was published posthumously, in 1971.

Tychyna's poetry before his capitulation to the regime represented a high point in Ukrainian verse of the 1920s. It is marked by a synthesis of 17th-century baroque and 20th-century symbolist styles. Some of the greatest advances in European poetry can be found in his 'clarinetism,' in its drawing upon the irrational elements of the Ukrainian folk lyric, its striving to be all-encompassing, its pervasive tragic sense of the eschatological, its play of antitheses and parabola, its asyndetonal structure of language, and other features.

BIBLIOGRAPHY
Nikovs'kyi, A. *Vita nova* (Kiev 1919)
Maifet, H. *Materiialy do kharakterystyky tvoriv Pavla Tychyny* (Kharkiv 1926)
Iurynets', V. *Pavlo Tychyna* (Kharkiv 1928)
Lavrinenko, Iu. *Tvorchist' Pavla Tychyny* (Kharkiv 1930)
Boiko, I. *Pavlo Tychyna: Bibliohrafichnyi pokazhchyk* (Kiev 1951)
Barka, V. *Khliborobs'kyi orfei, abo Kliarnetyzm* (New York 1961)
Novychenko, L. *Poeziia i revoliutsiia: Tvorchist' Pavla Tychyny v pershi pisliazhovtnevi roky*, rev edn (Kiev 1968)
– *Spivets' novoho svitu: Spohady pro Tychynu* (Kiev 1971)
Lavrinenko, Iu. *Na shliakhakh kliarnetyzmu* (New York 1977)
Halchenko, S. *Tekstolohiia poetychnykh tvoriv P.H. Tychyny* (Kiev 1989)
Tel'niuk, S. *Molodyi ia, molodyi: Poetychnyi svit Pavla Tychyny (1906–1925)* (Kiev 1990)

I. Koshelivets

**Tykhenko, Serhii** [Tyxenko, Serhij], b 6 June 1896 in Shemakha, Baku gubernia, Azerbaidzhan, d 19 October 1971 in Kiev. Jurist. A graduate of the law faculty of Petrograd University (1918), he worked at the Ukrainian Institute for the Study of Crime (1928–38) and then at the Kiev Scientific Research Institute of Forensic Experts (1935–41) and the Ukrainian Institute of Juridical Sciences (1938–41). After the Second World War he taught criminal law at Kiev University. As a member of the Supreme Court of the Ukrainian SSR (1947–52) he participated in drafting the 1960 Ukrainian criminal code. His publications deal with criminal law and criminology.

**Tykhomandrytsky, Matvii** [Tyxomandryc'kyj, Matvij], b 29 January 1844 in Kiev, d 1921. Mathematician. After completing his studies at St Petersburg University (1865) he taught there (1879–83), at Kharkiv University (1885–1904), and at Symferopil University. His contributions to mathematics are in higher algebra, elliptic functions, Abelian integrals, and the theory of probability. He wrote several textbooks on mathematical analysis and higher algebra.

**Tykhomel** [Tyxomel'] (aka Tykhoml or Tykhomlia). A fortified town built in the 10th century. It was an object of contention between the principalities of Halych and Volhynia. It was first mentioned in the chronicles under the year 1152. In 1199 it was annexed by the Principality of Galicia-Volhynia. After the Mongol invasion the town lost its importance, and in the 1340s it came under Lithuanian rule. The remains of the fortress in Bilohiria raion, Khmelnytskyi oblast, are believed to be Tykhomel's.

**Tykhonovych, Yosyp** [Tyxonovyč, Josyp], b ? in Kiev, d after 1855. Military physician. A graduate of Moscow University (1813), he worked in its medical faculty until 1828 (obtaining his doctorate of medicine in 1823), took part in the Russo-Turkish War (1828–9), practiced medicine in Kremenchuk and Lubni (1839–48), and was physician of the gubernial administration in Moscow (1848–55).

He wrote a two-volume work on health care for pregnant women and newborn infants (1825) and a description of surgical instruments (1838).

**Tykhorsky, Khoma** [Tyxors'kyj, Xoma], b 23 October 1733 in Domontiv, Pereiaslav regiment, d 14 February 1814 in St Petersburg. Physician; honorary member of the St Petersburg Academy of Sciences from 1798. After being educated at the Kievan Mohyla Academy (1750–6), the Medical School of the St Petersburg Admiralty Hospital (1756–9), and Leiden University (MD, 1765) he lectured on pharmacology in hospital schools in St Petersburg. He was senior physician at the St Petersburg Admiralty (1771–5) and Army (1776–1806) hospitals. He was a member of the Medical College (1779–99) and the medical council of the Moscow Police (1804–6). He translated a number of Medical Works into Russian and wrote a handbook on forensic medicine.

**Tykhorsky, Yepyfanii** [Tyxors'kyj, Jepyfanij], b ?, d 1731. Orthodox bishop. A former archimandrite of the Annunciation Monastery in Nizhen, he became the bishop of Belgorod in 1722. His tenure saw the extension of Ukrainian religious practices within the eparchy and the establishment of an eparchial seminary in 1722. The school was moved from Belgorod to Kharkiv in 1726 to become Kharkiv College.

**Tykhovsky, Pavlo** [Tyxovs'kyj], b 2 January 1867 in Pokaliv, Ovruch county, Volhynia gubernia, d 1938. Literary scholar and bibliographer. In the Soviet period he was an associate of the Kharkiv Institute of People's Education's department of literature. While researching the manuscripts of 19th-century Ukrainian writers, he discovered and published O. *Navrotsky's manuscripts. He also compiled a bibliography of Ukrainian translations of A. Mickiewicz's works (pub 1924) and contributed two articles to the Taras Shevchenko Scientific Research Institute's annuals, *Shevchenko* (1928, 1930). He fell silent during the Stalinist terror.

**Tykhovsky, Yuvenalii** [Tyxovs'kyj, Juvenalij], b 1882, d 1919. Teacher and literary critic. He contributed to *Volynskiia eparkhial'nyia vedomosti*. He published articles on *Slovo o polku Ihorevi* (The Tale of Ihor's Campaign), Ukrainian folk songs, the Kiev Chronicle, and the Pochaiv Monastery Press in *Kievskaia starina*, and an article on the Russian works of T. Shevchenko in *Ukraïns'ka khata*.

**Tykhy, Ivan** [Tyxyj], b 10 January 1927 in Savyntsi, Izium okruha, d 27 June 1982 in Kiev. Painter. In 1953 he graduated from the Kiev State Art Institute, where he studied under S. Hryhoriev and V. Kostetsky, and in 1964 he began teaching there. He painted landscapes and genre paintings, such as *The Happy Father* (1951), *Joining the Pioneers* (1953), *Motherhood* (1957), *Storks* (1960), *Native Land* (1963), *Eternal Fire* (1964–5), and *Greetings, Slavutych!* (1975).

**Tykhy, Naum** [Tyxyj] (pen name of Naum Shtilerman), b 28 May 1920 in Yemilchyne, Novohrad-Volynskyi county, Volhynia gubernia. Poet and writer of Jewish origin. Since 1947 he has published numerous poetry collections and the novels *V dorohu vykhod' na svitanni* (Set Out for the Road at Daybreak, 1959) and *Rakhunok za sontse* (A Bill for the Sun, 1979).

Oleksii Tykhy                          Ivan Tyktor

**Tykhy, Oleksii** [Tyxyj, Oleksij], b 27 January 1927 in Izhevka, Kostiantynivka raion, Donetske oblast, d 6 May 1984 in the Mordovian SSR. Dissident and political prisoner. A teacher in the Donbas, he was first arrested in February 1957, on a charge of 'Ukrainian nationalism,' and was sentenced in May to seven years in labor camps and five years' exile. After being released in 1964, he returned to the Donbas and worked there as a laborer. In November 1976 he became a founding member of the *Ukrainian Helsinki Group. He was arrested in February 1977, and sentenced in July to 10 years in a Mordovian camp and 5 years' exile. He did not survive his sentence. The transfer of his remains to Kiev and their interment at the Baikove cemetery in 1989 were accompanied by a massive procession. A collection of his dissident writings and of documents pertaining to his case was published in the United States in 1982.

**Tyktor, Ivan**, b 6 July 1896 in Krasne, Zolochiv county, Galicia, d 27 August 1982 in Ottawa. Publisher and community figure. In 1923 he founded in Lviv the *Ukrainska Presa publishing company, until 1939 the largest and most important and successful Ukrainian publishing house in Western Ukraine, which supplied the Ukrainian public with several nonpartisan periodicals and approx 400 books. During the Second World War he directed the trade department of the Ukrainske Vydavnytstvo publishing house and ran the religious publishing house Nove Zhyttia in Cracow (1939–41) and Lviv (1941) and the Volyn publishing house in Rivne (1941–3). As a postwar refugee in Austria, he headed the Ukrainian Students' Aid Commission there. In 1948 Tyktor emigrated to Canada and settled in Winnipeg, where he founded the Club of Friends of the Ukrainian Book, which revised and republished several of the most important books issued by Ukrainska Presa – including *Velyka istoriia Ukraïny* (The Great History of Ukraine, 1931, 1948), *Istoriia ukraïns'koho viis'ka* (The History of the Ukrainian Armed Forces, 1935, 1953), and *Istoriia ukraïns'koï kul'tury* (A History of Ukrainian Culture, 1937, 1964) – and approx 40 books of prose and poetry. A booklet about Tyktor and Ukrainska Presa by Ye. Yavorivsky was published in Winnipeg in 1953.

**Tylihul Estuary** [Tylihul's'kyj lyman]. VII–12. A saltwater lake at the mouth of the Tylihul River on the Black Sea coast along the border of Odessa and Mykolaiv oblasts. The estuary is 80 km long, generally about 3.5 km wide (as narrow as 0.2 km in places), and 3 m deep (up to 21 m maximum). Its area fluctuates between 150 and 170 sq km. It is fed by the Tylihul River and by seawater which seeps through the 4 km of sand deposits at its mouth. The estuary has a salinity of up to 13 per cent and contains a layer of black mire with medicinal qualities along its bottom. It is also fished.

**Tylihul River.** A river that flows for 173 km through Odessa oblast before emptying into the Tylihul Estuary on the Black Sea coast. It drains a basin area of 3,550 sq km. Quite narrow in its upper reaches, it is 10–20 m wide along its lower course and has a valley up to 3 km wide. It is fed mainly by meltwater and tends to dry up in sections during the summer. Two dams are situated on the river, which is also used for irrigation. The major centers along the Tylihul are Ananiv and Berezivka.

**Tylych Pass** [Tylyc'kyj pereval]. IV–2. A mountain pass situated in the western part of the Lemko region along the present-day Polish-Czechoslovakian border. The pass has an elevation of 683 m. It was part of a once-important travel route between Poland and Hungary that went through Bardejov.

**Tylyk, Volodymyr,** b 21 July 1938 in Dnipropetrovske. Composer and administrator. A graduate of the Kiev State Conservatory (1962) in the composition class of A. Shtoharenko, he has been music editor of the journal *Mystetstvo* (from 1967), a member of the editorial board of *Muzyka* (from 1969), and editor of the Muzychna Ukraina publishing house (1971–4). His compositions include an overture; suites for orchestra; piano, bandura, and soprano concertos; String Quartet (1967) and Trio (1976); Sonata (1965), *Watercolors* (1966), and *Preludes-Songs* (1969) for piano solo; and *Dances of Poltava* (1971) for folk instrument orchestra.

**Tymchenko, Marfa** [Tymčenko], b 55 March 1922 in Petrykivka, Novomoskovske county, Katerynoslav gubernia. Master of *Petrykivka painting; wife of I. *Skytsiuk. She studied at the Petrykivka School of Decorative Painting (1936–8) under T. Pata and at the Kiev School of Folk-Art Masters (1938–41) and worked at the Kiev Experimental Plant of Artistic Ceramics (1954–77), where she decorated clay, porcelain, and wooden tableware, vases, and other objects. She has also designed fabric, posters, books, and murals (eg, in the Kazka toy store in Kiev). She is best known for her paintings on paper and cardboard, such as *Blue Birds* (1966), *Bear Family* (1972–3), *Rain in Sedniv* (1975), *Strength and Tenderness* (1980), *Village under a Mountain, Bridge, Holosiieve Forest,* and *Flowering Birches.* An album of her works was published in 1974.

**Tymchenko, Yevhen** [Tymčenko, Jevhen], b 8 November 1866 in Poltava, d 22 May 1948 in Kiev. Linguist, translator and lexicographer; member of the Shevchenko Scientific Society and the Ukrainian Scientific Society in Kiev, and corresponding member of the USSR Academy of Sciences from 1929. While working in a lands office in

Marfa Tymchenko

Kiev (1891–2), the zemstvo administration in Chernihiv (1893–8), and the library of Kiev University (1898–1908), he belonged to the *Brotherhood of Taras and was active in the Kiev Prosvita society. After completing his studies at Kiev (1909–12) and St Petersburg (MA, 1914) universities, he taught at Warsaw University (1914–16) and Don University in Rostov-na-Donu (1916–18). In 1918 he was appointed a member of the Codification Commission under the UNR Ministry of Justice. While he was a professor of Ukrainian and linguistics at Kiev University (1918–20) and the Kiev Institute of People's Education (1920–32), he also headed the VUAN Permanent Commission for the Compilation of the Historical Dictionary of the Ukrainian Language. From 1932 he was persecuted by the Soviet regime, and in 1939 he was imprisoned. Exiled to Krasnoiarsk, Siberia, in 1941, he was released in 1944 and worked at the AN URSR (now ANU) Institute of Linguistics until his death.

Tymchenko's major works are a Russian-Ukrainian ('Little Russian') dictionary (2 vols, 1897, 1899); a scholarly Ukrainian grammar (1907, 1917, 1918) and a secondary-school grammar textbook (1918); a book-length program for the collection of Ukrainian dialectal particularities (with K. Mykhalchuk, 1910); a booklet of instructions on how to record Ukrainian dialectal materials (1925); a course book on the history of the Ukrainian language (1927; 2nd edn 1930); and monographs on the genitive case in the South Russian linguistic province (1913), and the Ukrainian locative (1924), nominative and dative (1925), vocative and instrumental (1926), and accusative (1928) cases. After 1932 only his article on a dialectal trait of the use of the morpheme *sja* (1948) was published. In his approach to modern literary Ukrainian, Tymchenko was the most typical representative of the archaizing ethnographic school, whose members propagated the notion of the independent development of Ukrainian on the basis of selectively chosen dialectal features. In studying the history of Ukrainian, he applied a neogrammarian approach. In an article on Slavic unity and the position of Ukrainian in the Slavic family (*Ukraïna*, 1924, no. 3) he came out against the hypothesis of a proto–East Slavic language.

From 1894 to 1898 Tymchenko worked on the preparation of a Ukrainian-Russian dictionary. Prepared in a Russian orthography, it was later converted to the Ukrainian orthography, augmented, and published by B. *Hrinchenko (4 vols, 1907–9). From 1901 Tymchenko collected materials for a historical dictionary of 14th- to 18th-century Ukrainian. Its prototype was to be published (but was not) as an appendix to Hrinchenko's. The first two fascicles of a vastly expanded version of the historical dictionary (*A–Zh*), prepared in collaboration with E. Voloshyna, K. Lazarevska, and H. Petrenko, were finally published in Kiev in 1930 and 1932 (repr, Munich 1985). The Stalinist suppression of Ukrainian culture permanently interrupted work on the dictionary, and a subsequent fascicle was destroyed at the imprimery. The dictionary's huge file (approx 313,000 cards) is preserved at the ANU Institute of Linguistics. Tymchenko translated into Ukrainian the Finnish national epic *Kalevala* (1901; rev edn 1928); parts of the Estonian epic *Kalevipoeg*; and stories by G. de Maupassant, M. Maeterlinck, and V. Hugo.

R. Senkus

**Tymchenko, Yosyp** [Tymčenko, Josyp], b 15 April or 26 November 1852 in Okip, Zolochiv county, Kharkiv gubernia, d 20 May 1924 in Odessa. Inventor and self-taught mechanical engineer. He studied in the machine shop of Kharkiv University, where he obtained some training in mechanics. In Odessa he worked in the factory of the Russian Society for Steamships and Trade and then established a physical-optical machine shop at the university (1880). Among his numerous inventions were a signaling device for railroads, an apparatus for the detection of defects in rails and cranes, and various meteorological instruments (new types of barograph, seismograph, etc). He built a working model of the first telephone switching station in the world. Tymchenko's most important invention was a 'stroboscope' (with the physicist N. Liubimov and the inventor M. Freidenberg). This device for projecting 'live pictures' was demonstrated in Odessa in November 1893 and at the Ninth All-Russian Congress of Naturalists and Physicians in Moscow in January 1894. Although it was critically acclaimed by the scientists, Tsar Nicholas II refused to sponsor it, and a similar device was patented by the Lumière brothers in France in 1895 and brought to Russia in 1896. Tymchenko's students later formed Kinap, the first movie company in the Soviet Union.

**Tymchuk, Roman** [Tymčuk], b 19 August 1909 in Volytsia, Galicia, d 21 January 1991 in Philadelphia. Stage actor and director. He acted in the Zahrava Theater (1931–2) and the Tobilevych Theater (1933–6), studied in the Ukrainian Drama School in Warsaw (1936–7), acted in Y. Stadnyk's troupe (1937–8), and directed in Ukrainian theaters in Stanyslaviv and Drohobych (1941–3). In 1947–50

he was a member of the Ensemble of Ukrainian Actors in Germany and the United States.

**Tymchuk, Viktor** [Tymčuk], b 10 October 1936 in Druzheliubivka, Kalynivka raion, Vinnytsia oblast. Writer. He has written the prose collections *Okraiets' syn'oho neba* (The Edge of the Blue Sky, 1965), *Den' bilykh kashtaniv* (Day of the White Chestnuts, 1973), *Ne huby peliustok, soniashnyku!* (Don't Lose Your Petals, Sunflower!, 1977), and *Uviidy v mii dim* (Come into My Home, 1979) and the mystery novel *Bez dozvolu na rozsliduvannia* (Without Permission to Investigate, 1982).

**Tymiak, Mariia** [Tym'jak, Marija], b 19 January 1889 in Kosiv, Galicia, d 1970 in Kosiv. Folk ceramist. She produced original earthenware, vases, and ram figurines decorated with geometric designs. Her works have been preserved in museums in Kiev and Lviv.

Ivan Tyminsky

**Tyminsky, Ivan** [Tymins'kyj], b 1852, d 1902. Bukovynian civic and political leader and government finance official. One of the region's leading populists, he helped to wrest control of the Ruska Besida (1884) and the Ruska Rada (1885) societies from the Russophiles. In 1884 he was one of the founders of the Ukrainian People's Home in Chernivtsi. He also helped to establish and edit the semimonthly *Bukovyna*, which in 1885 began publication in the vernacular. In 1890 he was elected to the Bukovynian Diet. His articles appeared in *Bukovyna* and *Dilo*.

**Tyminsky, Taras** [Tymins'kyj] (monastic name: Tyt), b 1858 in Piadykivtsi, Bukovyna, d 27 February 1927 in Roztoky, Bukovyna. Church and community activist; brother of I. *Tyminsky. He studied philosophy at Lviv University and theology at Chernihiv University, and served as a parish priest in Bukovyna. Before the First World War he was a leading member of several Ukrainian organizations. He defended the rights of Ukrainians in the metropoly and criticized attempts to Rumanianize the church, and contributed articles on church and community affairs to *Dilo*, *Bukovyna*, and the journal *Candela*. He also published a brochure criticizing the policies of the Rumanian metropolitan. In 1917–18 the Austrian authorities planned to divide the Bukovynian metropoly into separate Ukrainian and Rumanian eparchies. At this time Tyminsky was nominated to head the Ukrainian eparchy and made an archimandrite. With the establishment of Rumanian control over Bukovyna in late 1918, the plan was abandoned, and Tyminsky was removed from his posts. He then retired from public life.

**Tymkiv, Mykola,** b 26 February 1909 in Moskalivka, Kosiv county, Galicia, d 20 July 1985 in Kosiv. Master wood carver. He learned his craft from V. Devdiuk. He created wooden plates, caskets, writing instruments, album covers, and table lamps decorated with inlay or intarsia designs.

**Tymkovsky** [Tymkovs'kyj]. A family line of Cossack officers, established by Vasyl Tymchenko, a Cossack in Pereiaslav regiment (1740), and his grandson, Fedir Tymkovsky (1739–1790), a regimental osaul and postmaster of Pereiaslav regiment. Fedir's sons were cultural activists in Ukraine and Russia: the eldest was Illia *Tymkovsky, a scholar of classical literature; Roman Tymkovsky (1785–1820) was a philologist who taught at Moscow University, researched chronicles, and compiled and edited the notable *Letopis' Nestorova po drevneishomu spisku mnikha Lavrentiia* (The Chronicle of Nestor According to the Oldest Laurentian Manuscript, 1824); and Yegor Tymkovsky (4 May 1790–21 February 1875) was a sinologist and diplomat. Yegor's 1820–1 travelog (3 vols, 1824) was translated into French, German, and English (*Travels of the Russian Mission, through Mongolia to China, and Residence in Peking ... by E. Timkovskii*, 2 vols, 1827). His memoirs appeared in *Kievskaia starina* (1894). Their sister, Hlikeriia Tymkovska (1788–1829), was the mother of the historian Mykhailo *Maksymovych.

**Tymkovsky, Illia** [Tymkovs'kyj, Illja], b 26 July 1773 in Pereiaslav, d 27 February 1853 in Turanivka, Hlukhiv county, Chernihiv gubernia. Pedagogue and writer. After completing studies at the Kiev Academy (1789) and Moscow University (1797) he taught law in St Petersburg and worked for the Ministry of Justice, where he attempted the first codification of Russian law. He then moved to Kharkiv, where he was a supervisor of the regional school district (from 1803) and a professor of law, history, and literature (1805–11) at Kharkiv University. In 1825–38 he was director of the Novhorod-Siverskyi Gymnasium. Tymkovsky was an ardent promoter of education and played a vital role in the establishment of gymnasiums and regional schools in Kharkiv, Chernihiv, Katerynoslav, Voronezh, Novhorod-Siverskyi, and Odessa. He also assisted in the founding of Kharkiv University.

**Tymofieiev, Valentyn** [Tymofjejev], b 21 July 1927 in Odessa. Musicologist. He graduated from the Piano Department of the Odessa State Conservatory (1951) and completed postgraduate studies at the AN URSR (now ANU; 1961). He also taught at the Odessa State Conservatory (1951–8), worked as editor in chief of the Mystetstvo publishing house (1961–4), and served as editor in chief of the Music Repertoire–Editing Board of the Ministry of Culture of the Ukrainian SSR (1964–78); he has taught at the Kiev State Conservatory since 1978. His works include the monographs *Bela Rudenko* (1963, 1973) and *Ukrainskii sovetskii fortepiannyi kontsert* (The Ukrainian Soviet Piano Concerto, 1972), the brochure *Vokal'na muzyka* (1962), the libretto for the opera *Kinets' kazky* (The Tale's End, after Jack London; music by A. Krasotov, 1959), miscellaneous articles, and scripts for television.

**Tymofii, Petrovych** [Tymofij, Petrovyč], b and d ? Engraver. He created decorative wood engravings for the Kievan Cave Monastery Press's books on St John Chryso-

stom's discourses on 14 epistles of the apostles (1623) and his discourses on the Acts of the Apostles (1624).

**Tymokhin, Volodymyr** [Tymoxin], b 19 June 1929 in Dmytrivka, Zinovivske okruha (now Znamianka raion, Kirovohrad oblast). Opera singer (lyric-dramatic tenor). He studied at the Moscow and Leningrad conservatories (1951–5) and graduated from the Kiev Conservatory (1975). He was a soloist of the Leningrad Opera (1953–6) and the Kiev Theater of Opera and Ballet (1956–78). His operatic roles included Andrii in M. Lysenko's *Taras Bulba*, Lensky in P. Tchaikovsky's *Eugene Onegin*, and the name-part in R. Wagner's *Lohengrin*. In 1976 he began lecturing at the Kiev Conservatory. He has concertized abroad under the auspices of Ukrkontsert.

**Tymosh, Lidiia** [Tymoš, Lidija], b 12 December 1918 in Mykolaiv, Kherson gubernia. Stage actress. She completed study at the Odessa Theater Arts College (1941) and in 1945 joined the Kirovohrad Ukrainian Music and Drama Theater. She has played both heroic and character roles and was acclaimed for her performance in I. Franko's *Dlia domashn'oho vohnyshcha* (For the Home Hearth, 1976).

Yurii Tymoshchuk          Oleksander Tymoshenko

**Tymoshchuk, Yurii** [Tymoščuk, Jurij], b 23 April 1880 in Hrabiv, Rivne county, Volhynia gubernia, d ? Farmer and political activist. After completing study at a teachers' seminary in Rivne he worked as a rural teacher and served his term in the Russian army. From 1910 he worked in local agricultural institutions and co-operatives in Hrabiv. In 1912 he ran as a candidate for the Fourth State Duma. During the First World War he was assigned an office job in the Russian military. At the outset of the revolution he returned home and organized a military detachment, which was incorporated into the UNR Army. In 1922 he was elected to the Polish Sejm, where he sat on the Labor and Public Works Committee and then on the Communications Committee.

**Tymoshenko, Oleksander** [Tymošenko], b 1909 in Kiev, d 1973 in Washington, DC. Architect; son of Serhii *Tymoshenko. An interwar émigré, he studied at the Prague Polytechnic (1928–32) and worked as an architect in Rivne, Warsaw, and, during the Second World War, Berlin and Prague. A postwar refugee, in 1947 he emigrated to the United States, where he worked as an architect in New York City, California, and Washington. He designed a number of skyscrapers in New York and stations of the Washington subway. He was a founding member and president (1953–4) of the Ukrainian Engineers' Society of America and founded and headed its Washington chapter. He wrote articles on Ukrainian architecture and residential construction.

**Tymoshenko, Petro** [Tymošenko], b 20 June 1920 in Vilkhovets, Zvenyhorodka county, Kiev gubernia, d 29 April 1984 in Kiev. Linguist. After completing graduate studies in the Ukrainian language at Kiev University (1949) he taught Ukrainian linguistics there and received his candidate's degree in 1953. He wrote studies on subjects such as the history of the Ukrainian language and Ukrainian linguistics, and Ukrainian orthography, lexicology, phonetics, stylistics, dialectology, onomastics, and language teaching. He also compiled a methodological handbook for the study of the history of Ukrainian (1959) and an anthology of critical materials in the history of literary Ukrainian (2 vols, 1959, 1961).

**Tymoshenko, Semen** [Tymošenko], b 18 February 1895 in Furmanka, Odessa county, Kherson gubernia, d 31 March 1970 in Moscow. Marshal of the Soviet Union. In the interwar period he graduated from military academies and then commanded the Kharkiv (1937) and Kiev (1938) military districts. In September 1939 he was in charge of the army which occupied Western Ukraine. After being promoted to marshal of the Soviet Union (1940) he was commissar for the defense of the USSR (1940–1), deputy commissar of defense (1941), and commander of the western and southwestern fronts (1941–2). After the war he was in charge of several military districts until his retirement in 1960. In retirement he was chairman of the Soviet Committee of War Veterans and an inspector-general of the defense ministry.

Serhii Tymoshenko          Volodymyr Tymtsiurak

**Tymoshenko, Serhii** [Tymošenko, Serhij], b 4 February 1881 in Bazylivka, Borzna county, Chernihiv gubernia, d 6 July 1950 in Palo Alto, California. Architect and political leader; brother of V. and S. *Timoshenko. As a student at the Institute of Civil Engineering in St Petersburg he was active in the Ukrainian Student Hromada and the Northern Committee of the Revolutionary Ukrainian party. After completing his studies (1906) he worked as an architect and was noted for his Ukrainian styling. In Kovel he

built the Railway Ambulatory and the Pirogov Gymnasium, in Kiev, the Yurkevych and Lavrentiev residences, and in Kharkiv, the head office of the Northern Donets Railway Administration and the Popov and Boiko residences. He also drafted plans for three towns in Kharkiv gubernia. With the outbreak of the revolution in 1917 he became commissioner for Kharkiv gubernia and a member of the Central Rada. In 1919–20 he served as UNR minister of communications in I. Mazepa's, V. Prokopovych's, and A. Livytsky's cabinets and took part in the Second Winter Campaign. In 1921–4 he worked in Lviv, where he built churches in the suburbs and a Studite monastery in Zarvanytsia. Then (1924–9) he served as a professor of architecture at and rector of the *Ukrainian Husbandry Academy in Poděbrady and the Ukrainian Studio of Plastic Arts in Prague. In 1930 he was appointed chief architect of farm construction for Polish-ruled Volhynia. While working in Lutske he was active in the Volhynian Ukrainian Alliance, which he headed from 1935, in the Lutske Orthodox brotherhood, and in the Lesia Ukrainka Society. He was elected to the Polish Sejm in 1935 and to the Senate in 1938–9. From 1940 he lived in Lublin, and from 1944, in Germany. After emigrating to the United States in 1946, he resumed his architectural work and designed four Ukrainian churches in Canada and one in Argentina.

**Tymoshenko, Stepan.** See Timoshenko, Stephen.

**Tymoshenko, Volodymyr.** See Timoshenko, Vladimir.

**Tymoshenko-Polevska, Liudmyla.** See Polevska, Liudmyla.

**Tymtsiurak, Volodymyr** [Tymcjurak], b 18 May 1889 in Piilo, Kalush county, Galicia, d 11 November 1980 in Chicago. Lawyer and civic activist. After completing his law studies at Lviv University he served as captain in the Austrian army and then in the Ukrainian Galician Army. He headed the general department of the State Secretariat for Military Affairs of the Western Ukrainian National Republic, served as Ye. Petrushevych's adjutant, and belonged to the UNR military mission to Poland. After the First World War he was active in Ukrainian organizations in Stanyslaviv. In 1940–1 he represented the Ukrainian Central Committee in the Lublin district. After leaving Ukraine in 1945, he lived in Graz, Austria, and then emigrated to the United States in 1949.

**Typhus.** Epidemic typhus (Ukrainian: *vysypnyi tyf*) is an acute, human, fever-producing rickettsial disease transmitted by the body louse (*Pediculus humanus*). It is controlled by vaccination and delousing, but it still presents a potentially fatal threat to impoverished and destitute people in many parts of the world. The Ukrainian scientist Y. *Mochutkovsky studied epidemic typhus extensively and, in an 1876 experiment on himself, proved that its pathogen is found in the blood of the stricken. His contemporary G. *Minkh arrived at a similar conclusion. In Ukrainian the name *tyf* 'typhus' is also used for the endotoxic infections caused by salmonellae and spirochetes, including typhoid (*cherevnyi tyf*), paratyphoid (*paratyf*), and relapsing fever (*povorotnyi tyf*).

In the 19th century, the Napoleonic Wars, the Crimean campaign, and the Russo-Turkish wars, plus the years of famine throughout Europe, brought on virulent typhus epidemics in Ukraine. Particularly during the First World War and shortly thereafter Ukraine was devastated by epidemic typhus and typhoid and paratyphoid fever. It has been estimated that perhaps 25 million cases of epidemic typhus occurred in the Russian Empire during the war (11.3 per 10,000 in the army in 1914, and 22.3 in 1915). Because of evacuation from the western front the rate of infection was much higher in Ukraine (21.9 per 10,000 in 1917) than the average throughout the empire (8.3 in 1916). The generally ruinous conditions during the struggle for independence in 1919–20 sparked an increase of up to 340 per 10,000 infected by epidemic typhus in Ukraine (500 per 10,000 infected by all forms of typhus). In fact, the rates of infection were much higher than those released by the Soviet authorities. In the regions of Podilia and Right-Bank Ukraine under the jurisdiction of the Army of the UNR, one-half of the civilian population and up to 90 percent of the soldiers and officers of the Ukrainian Galician Army (of whom 25,000 died) were stricken with typhus. The disaster brought about a crisis in the Army of the UNR and the deterioration of the Ukrainian front.

With the stabilization of life the incidence of epidemic typhus declined, from 158.9 per 10,000 in 1921 to 1.5 in 1933, partly as a result of the work of sanitary-epidemiological stations (of which there were 40 in 1928). Some flare-ups occurred in the 1930s, particularly during the man-made famine of 1932–3, again during the German occupation of Ukraine, and right after the Second World War. Between the two world wars epidemic typhus was endemic in the villages of Western Ukraine, especially in the Hutsul region, which also had the highest mortality rate (26 percent of those diagnosed in 1933). In the postwar period sporadic cases of typhoid and paratyphoid occurred in the USSR (16,900 in 1980, 17,600 in 1985, and 11,500 in 1988), but wholesale morbidity was eradicated through drugs, lice control, and adequate sanitary conditions. Typhoid fever occurred 20 times more often in the USSR (3.2 cases per 100,000 pop in 1987) than in the United States (0.16 cases in 1984).

P. Dzul

**Typikon** (Ukrainian: *Typyk*). A book containing the rules to be observed for the Liturgy and Office of all feasts in the Eastern Christian church. In Ukraine the Studite *Typikon* (from the Byzantine monastery of St Theodore Studite) was used in monasteries from the time of *St Theodosius of the Caves (d 1074). In the 15th century it was replaced by the Jerusalem *Typikon* (from the St Sava Monastery near Jerusalem). A manuscript *Typikon* was also called *Ustav* (Rubric) or *Oko tserkovnoie* (The Eye of the Church). They were first printed as appendixes to liturgical books. The Ukrainian Catholic church adopted the *Typikon* published in part in 1766 by the Pochaiv Monastery Press and then in full as *Ustav tserkovnoho peniia* (Rubric of Church Singing) in 1780. Other editions published for the Ukrainian Catholic church included those prepared by Ya. Doskovsky in Peremyshl (1852; repr 1870, 1903) and O. Mykyta in Uzhhorod (1890, 1901). The best edition was the *Typik Tserkve Rus'ko-Katolicheskiia* (*Typikon* of the Ruthenian Catholic Church, 1899), by I. *Dolnytsky.

**Typographic Gospels** (*typohrafichni yevanheliia*). Two primary textual sources to the study of Old Ukrainian, once kept at the library of the Moscow Synodal Imprimery (*tipografiia*) and now preserved at the Tretiakov Gallery and the Central Archive of Ancient Documents in Moscow. They consist of a 12th-century manuscript (252 double pages) and a 13th-century manuscript (228 double pages), both of which were transcribed from the Bulgarian in Ukraine, most likely in Kiev. Fragments of their texts and a linguistic description were published by A. Sobolevsky (1884).

**Tyras** (aka Tira, Tiras). An ancient Greek city-state on the right bank of the Dniester Estuary at the site of present-day *Bilhorod-Dnistrovskyi. It was established in the 6th century BC by colonists from Miletus. By the 4th century BC it was a prosperous trading center, which even minted its own coinage. It was sacked in the mid-1st century BC by the Getae, but it revived. By the early 2nd century AD it was an important outpost on the frontier of the Roman Empire. In the late 3rd century it was destroyed by the Goths. The site was repopulated much later by the Tivertsians and Ulychians and named Bilhorod. Some preliminary archeological work was done at the site in 1927–32. Systematic excavations under the AN URSR (now ANU) Institute of Archeology commenced in 1945.

**Tyras River.** The ancient Greek name for the Dniester River. The city-state Tyras was built on the Dniester Estuary.

**Tyraspil** [Tyraspil'] (aka Tiraspol). VII-10. A city (1990 pop 184,000) and port on the Dniester River and a raion center in Moldova. It was founded in 1793 as a fortress on the site of the Moldavian settlement of Suklei. In 1806 it became a county center of Kherson gubernia. In 1924–40 it was part of the Moldavian ASSR (within the Ukrainian SSR), and from 1929, its capital. According to the census of 1926, Ukrainians represented 11.9 percent of the city's and 19.5 percent of the raion's population.

**Tyravska, Nataliia** [Tyravs'ka, Natalija], b 9 March 1924 in Kyvertsi, Lutske county, Volhynia gubernia. Choreographer. She was a soloist dancer with the Ukrainian Theater in Lutske (1941–4) and then a teacher-choreographer in Germany (1945–9). She emigrated to Sydney, Australia, in 1949 and established a Ukrainian dance group, which has won many awards over the years at international folk dancing competitions. She toured with the Veselka Ukrainian Dance Ensemble the United States and Canada (1986) and Ukraine (1990).

**Tys, Yurii** (pseud of Yurii Krokhmaliuk), b 27 October 1904 in Cracow. Writer, editor, and military historian. He graduated from the Vienna Technical Higher School (1928) and worked as an engineer in Galicia. During the Second World War he was a staff officer with the rank of major in the *Division Galizien. As a postwar refugee he was a cofounder of the Association of Ukrainian Scholars, Artists, and Litterateurs in Buenos Aires. After moving to Detroit he founded the Institute of Ukrainian Culture there, and he has been chief editor of the journal *Terem since 1962. A major émigré author of historical fiction, he wrote the novels *Pid L'vovom pluh vidpochyvav* (Near Lviv the Plow Rested, 1937), *Reid u nevidome: Dyvni pryhody znatnoho molodtsia pana Mykoly Predtvycha* (Raid into the

Yurii Tys

Unknown: The Strange Adventures of the Notable Young Noble Mykola Predtvych, 1955), *Zhyttia inshoï liudyny* (The Life of a Different Person, 1958), *Konotop* (1959), *Zvidun z Chyhyryna* (The Scout from Chyhyryn, 1961), *Na svitanku: Biohrafichna povist' z zhyttia Marka Vovchka* (At Daybreak: A Biographical Novelette from the Life of Marko Vovchok, 1961), and *K-7* (1964), and the story collections *Shliakhamy vikiv* (Along the Roads of Ages, 1951) and *Markiza* (The Marquise, 1954). He also wrote the reportage collection *Symfoniia zemli* (The Earth's Symphony, 1951), the Christmas mystery play *Ne plach, Rakhile* (Don't Cry, Rachel, 1952), the humorous autobiographical *Shchodennyk natsional'noho heroia Selepka Lavochky* (Diary of the National Hero Selepko Lavochka, 1954; 2nd edn 1982), and the monographs *Boï Khmel'nyts'koho* (Khmelnytsky's Battles, 1954), *La Batalla de Poltava* (1960), *Guerra y libertad: Historia de la Division 'Halychyna' (d.u.1) del Ejercito Nacional Ucranio (1943–1945)* (1961), and UPA *Warfare in Ukraine: Strategical, Tactical and Organizational Problems of Ukrainian Resistance in World War II* (1972). His belletristic, historical, and political writings have appeared in émigré periodicals such as *Vyzvol'nyi shliakh*, *Visti kombatanta*, and *Estafeta*.

R. Senkus

**Tysa Lowland** (Potyska nyzovyna). A major lowland in *Transcarpathia that borders the foothills of the Volcanic Ukrainian Carpathians. It is a continuation of the large Pannonian Lowland and covers a territory of almost 2,000 sq km (15 percent of the total area of Transcarpathia). Only the northern part of the lowland constitutes Ukrainian ethnic territory. The south is inhabited by Hungarians (with a few Ukrainian pockets); the west is located in Slovakia and is settled mostly by Slovaks (with an admixture of Ukrainians and Hungarians).

The Tysa Lowland is a monotonous flatland at an elevation of 100–130 m. It occupies a tectonic depression (Chop–Makaliv) overlaid with Neogene deposits and then tuff, clay, and sand. The Tysa River and its tributaries (the Borzhava, the Latorytsia, the Uzh, and the Liaborets) meander through the lowland, often changing their course and forming mud holes. The flat relief and the slow flow of the rivers, high groundwater level, and large spring runoffs (often with flooding) have caused the creation of wetlands, especially between Mukachiv and Berehove. They have (in part) been drained since the late 19th century. The lowland is dotted with some volcanic hills 200–360 m and even 560 m high.

The climate of the Tysa Lowland is warm and humid.

Annual temperatures average 8.5°C (in the north) to 10°C (in the south); they reach 20–21°C in July and drop to –3°C in January. The growing season (with temperatures over 5°C) is 230 to 240 days a year. Precipitation averages 600–700 mm a year, with 400 mm falling in the summer (peaking in June). The soil is of average fertility with high acidity. Commonly found are podzolized gleys and bog soils, with some better soils near the mountains. The flora is forest-steppe, with steppe admixtures, and includes oak forests dotted with meadows. Most of the forest has been cut back (only about 10 percent of the area remains forested), and over half the territory is under cultivation – primarily wheat, corn, and some industrial crops (notably sunflower and tobacco). Garden farming and grape growing are also practiced, and about one-quarter of the land is pasture or hayfields. Dairy farming is the most common form of animal husbandry. For the entire lowland population the density is about 100 persons/sq km. The largest settlements on the edge of the lowland include Uzhhorod, Mukachiv, and Vynohradiv. Within the lowland itself Berehove and Chop are the major centers.

V. Kubijovyč

The Tysa River

**Tysa River.** The largest left-bank tributary of the Danube River. It flows for 966 km through Ukraine (233 km) and Hungary and drains a basin area of 157,100 sq km (over 15,000 sq km of which is in Transcarpathia and 3,000 in the Prešov region). The Tysa is formed by the confluence of the Bila (White) Tysa and the Chorna (Black) Tysa, near Rakhiv. It has a typical mountain character in its upper reaches, with a drop of 4.5 m/km and a velocity of 3 m/sec. It widens out to 50–100 m, drops at 1.8 m/km, and moves at 2 m/sec or less as it flows through the Maramureş Basin. It then flows through the Ukrainian Volcanic Carpathians and eventually ends up in flatter terrain. The Tysa forms part of the border between Ukraine and both Rumania and Hungary. Rock salt, petroleum, and natural gas can be found in its basin.

**Tyshchenko, Anatolii** [Tyščenko, Anatolij], b 22 August 1943 in Tahanrih, Rostov oblast, RSFSR. Canoeing champion. He was the 1970 world champion in the men's kayak singles, the 1969 European champion in the 500-m singles and the 4 × 500-m singles relay, a silver and bronze medalist at numerous world and European championships, and a champion of Ukraine and the USSR many times.

**Tyshchenko, Mykola** [Tyščenko], b 16 January 1893 in Velbivka, Hadiache county, Poltava gubernia, d ? Historian and archivist. A graduate of Kiev University, in the 1920s he worked for the VUAN and the Central Archives in Kiev. He studied the mercantile history of 18th-century Ukraine, as well as archival history, and his scholarly works were published in the serials of the VUAN Historical-Geographical Commission and the Historical-Philological Section. After the Second World War he worked in Kamianets-Podilskyi. An article by him on 18th-century trade between Russia and Left-Bank Ukraine appeared in the journal *Ukraïns'kyi istorychnyi zhurnal* in 1963. Nothing further is known of him.

Yurii Tyshchenko          Mykhailo Tyshkevych

**Tyshchenko, Yurii** [Tyščenko, Jurij] (pseuds: Yu. Siry, Yu. Azovsky, Halaida, O. Kadylo, Yu. Soltychynsky), b 22 April 1880 near Berdianske, Tavriia gubernia, d 28 November 1953 in New York. Writer, journalist, publisher, and bookseller; full member of the Ukrainian Academy of Arts and Sciences in the US. Threatened with imprisonment for his involvement in the *Ukrainian Social Democratic Workers' party, he fled to Lviv in 1907. After returning illegally to Kiev under the assumed name P. Lavrov, he established the *Dzvin publishing house there in 1907 together with V. Vynnychenko and L. Yurkevych, ran the *Lan publishing house (1909–14), served as managing editor of *Selo (1909–11), and coedited Zasiv (1911–12) and *Literaturno-naukovyi vistnyk* (1911–14). He also opened bookstores in Kiev, Kharkiv, and Katerynoslav to sell publications of the Shevchenko Scientific Society, and contributed to periodicals such as *Ridnyi krai, Rada, Ukraïns'ka khata, Moloda Ukraïna, Dzvinok*, and *Dzvin*. In 1914, before the outbreak of the First World War, Tyshchenko visited the United States and worked as an editor for the Prosvita society in Jersey City. Following the February Revolution of 1917 he published educational materials and journals (eg, *Svitlo, Ukraïns'ka shkola*) in Kiev and edited *Vistnyk Heneral'noho Sekretariiatu Ukraïny* (1917–18), the official organ of the Ukrainian Central Rada government. In 1919 he

re-established Dzvin in Vienna and published numerous textbooks that were shipped to Ukraine and used in elementary schools until 1925, as well as a collection of his own novellas (1920). As a postwar refugee in Germany, he published a printing handbook (1948), wrote memoiristic articles, and headed the *Association of Ukrainian Writers for Young People (OPDL). He emigrated to the United States in 1950, and there he published more children's books and, together with A. Bilous, a 12-volume collection of works by Lesia Ukrainka; contributed to *Svoboda*; and again headed the OPDL.

**Tyshchynsky, Oleksander** [Tyščyns'kyj], b 17 July 1835 in Holubychi, Horodnia county, Chernihiv gubernia, d 9 February 1896 in Chernihiv. Civic and political activist and journalist. He was expelled from universities in Kharkiv, Kiev, and Dorpat in the latter 1850s for his political activities (as a member of the Kharkiv-Kiev Secret Society and coauthor of an 1860 Ukrainophile 'manifesto') and general insubordination. He was arrested in 1863 in conjunction with a Third Section investigation and imprisoned in the Peter and Paul Fortress. Subsequent ministerial orders gave him a bureaucratic position in Chernihiv under the watchful eye of the gubernial governor. There Tyshchynsky pressed hard for zemstvo reform. He put his ideas into practice as president of the Chernihiv county zemstvo for a nine-year period, until a conservative backlash forced him out of that post. He obtained a position as deputy director of the Chernihiv municipal bank, where he pursued a loans policy generally favorable to peasant needs. He was also active in numerous civic organizations and established a library and a bookstore in Chernihiv.

**Tyshevsky, Ivan** [Tyševs'kyj], b 1760 in Sachkovychi, Starodub regiment, d 19 August 1830 in Poltava. Physician. A graduate of Chernihiv College (1776–83) and the Medical School of the St Petersburg Army Hospital (1785), he served as the official doctor of Katerynoslav vicegerency (1792–4) and a county doctor in Poltava (from 1797), where he built and financed a hospital and pharmacy. From 1803 he was the obstetrician of the Poltava Gubernia Medical Board. He wrote on surgery and ergot poisoning.

**Tyshkevych, Mykhailo** [Tyškevyč, Myxajlo] (Tyszkiewicz, Michel), b 20 April 1857 in Andrushivka, Lypovets county, Kiev gubernia, d 3 August 1930 in Żydanowo, Poznań voivodeship, Poland. Count, diplomat, publicist, artist, and patron of Ukrainian culture. A descendant of a Polonized line of Lithuanian-Ukrainian nobility, he graduated from the St Petersburg Academy of Arts and studied abroad. After settling down on his estate in 1880, he devoted himself to the welfare of the peasants and became active in the Ukrainian populist movement. He established the Mykhailo Prize at the Prosvita society for the best historical novel or drama about Ukraine (1888), supported Ukrainian and Polish artists and writers, and donated 20,000 rubles to the Ukrainian Scientific Society in Kiev on the centennial of T. Shevchenko's birth (1914). He founded several societies, such as the Catholic Union, the Union of Nobles and Landowners (1906), and the Kiev Society of Peace Advocates (1907), to promote social and national progress. As a publicist he defended Ukrainian demands in Polish and Russian papers. In 1917 he was elected president of the Union of Ukrainian Catholics in Kiev. During the First World War he lived in Lausanne, where he actively supported the cause of Ukrainian independence by publishing articles in the Western press and corresponding with influential political figures of the Entente. He supported the weekly L'*Ukraine financially and helped establish the Ucraina information service. He was president of the Ukrainian-Lithuanian Society. In 1919 the UNR government appointed Tyshkevych chief of its diplomatic mission to the Vatican and then of the delegation to the Paris Peace Conference. From 1920 he lived on his son's estate near Poznań. He financed the publication of *Documents historiques sur l'Ukraine et ses relations avec la Pologne, la Russe et la Suède (1569–1764)* (1919) and wrote the brochure *L'Ukraine en face du Congrès* (1919). Excerpts from his memoirs appeared in *Literaturno-naukovyi vistnyk* in 1928 and 1929.

**Tyshynska, Evstakhiia** [Tyšyns'ka, Evstaxija], b 1872, d 1944. Galician civic leader. A teacher by vocation, she was a founder and the first president of the Buduchnist domestic servants' society in Lviv. She also headed the women's section of Catholic Action and developed a plan (ultimately unsuccessful) to restructure the Union of Ukrainian Women on a religious basis.

*Tysiacha*. In Kievan Rus' (9th–10th centuries) a *tysiacha* ('thousand') was a military unit, commanded by a trusted appointee of the prince called the *tysiatskyi*. Each large city with its adjoining territories constituted a *tysiacha*, subdivided into *sotni* ('hundreds'). Eventually the *tysiacha* became the largest administrative-military unit; it corresponded to a land or territory and was governed by a prince's appointee.

*Vasyl Tysiak*

**Tysiak, Vasyl** [Tysjak, Vasyl'], b 21 October 1900 in Veldizh, Dolyna county, Galicia, d 5 July 1967 in Toronto. Opera singer (lyric tenor). He studied singing in Warsaw (1927–9) and under E. Garbini in Milan (1930–2), and debuted with the Polish Opera in Lviv (1929). He was a soloist in the Warsaw Opera and the Lviv Opera Theater (1941–4). In 1944 he left Ukraine and concertized in France, Belgium, Spain, Algiers, and North America, and in 1950 settled in Canada. In concert he often performed songs of the Ukrainian Sich Riflemen.

*Tysiatskyi*. During the Princely era a higher territorial official and the prince's viceregent, authorized to rule during his absence. He was appointed by the prince from among his distinguished boyars. The *tysiatskyi* also headed the military levy called the *tysiacha* and executed general administrative and policing functions. In the Novgorod republic (11th–13th centuries) the *tysiatskyi* was an elected official, chosen from a council of boyars.

The Church of the Nativity of the Mother of God in Tysmenytsia (1736)

**Tysmenytsia** [Tysmenycja or Tys'menycja]. V-5. A town smt (1983 pop 8,500) on the Vorona River in Ivano-Frankivske raion, Ivano-Frankivske oblast. It was first mentioned in the Hypatian Chronicle under the year 1143. From the end of the 14th century the town was under Polish rule. It was an active trading and manufacturing center on a trade route from Lviv to Moldavia. In 1449 the town was granted the rights of *Magdeburg law. It was destroyed by the Turks and Tatars in 1515 and 1676. After the partition of Poland in 1772, it was annexed by Austria, and after 1919 it was under Polish rule. In 1939 it was incorporated into the Ukrainian SSR. Today its main industries are fur manufacturing and woodworking. Its chief architectural monument is a wooden church from the 18th century.

**Tysovsky, Oleksander** [Tysovs'kyj] (pseud: Drot), b 9 August 1886 in Bykiv, Sambir county, Galicia, d 29 March 1968 in Vienna. Educator and biologist; full member of the Shevchenko Scientific Society from 1927. A graduate of Lviv University, he taught natural science at the *Academic Gymnasium of Lviv (1911–39). Recognizing the shortcomings of the school system in building character, he adapted the scouting program to the needs of Ukrainian society and founded the first groups of the *Plast Ukrainian Youth Association (1911). After serving in the Austrian army during the First World War, he served as a

Oleksander Tysovsky          Serhii Tytarenko

professor of the *Lviv (Underground) Ukrainian University (1920–4), Lviv University (1939–41), and the Higher Agronomic Courses in Lviv (1941–3). As Plast developed into a national organization, he prepared its basic scouting handbook and presided over the Supreme Plast Council (1921–30). From 1944 he lived as an émigré in Vienna. In addition to scientific articles in botany and zoology (written in Ukrainian or German) his publications include *Plast* (1912), *Zhyttia v Plasti* (Life in Plast, 1921; 2nd rev edn 1961; 3rd edn 1969), and articles on education and upbringing.

**Tyssarovsky, Yeremiia** [Tyssarovs'kyj, Jeremija] (secular name: Yevstafii), b ?, d 1 March 1641 in Zolochiv, Galicia. Orthodox bishop. He succeeded H. Balaban as bishop of Lviv in 1607, at which time he promised the Polish king Sigismund III Vasa that he would join the Uniate church. After his consecration by Metropolitan Anastasii of Suceava, however, he remained Orthodox. In 1610–20 he was the only Orthodox bishop in the Polish-Lithuanian Commonwealth, and the patriarch of Constantinople appointed him his exarch. Tyssarovsky maintained good relations with the Lviv Dormition Brotherhood. In 1633, together with three other bishops, he consecrated P. *Mohyla bishop in Lviv.

**Tytarenko, Nadiia,** b 18 April 1903 in Makedony, near Potik, Kaniv county, Kiev gubernia, d 26 January 1976 in Kiev. Heroic stage actress. She began her career in Kyidramte (1920–1) and then acted in Berezil (1922–31), the Kharkiv Theater of the Revolution (1931–40), and the Kharkiv (1941–4) and Lviv (1944–52) Young Spectator's theaters.

**Tytarenko, Serhii,** b 1889 in Ichnia, Borzna county, Chernihiv gubernia, d ? in the United States. Journalist and publisher. In Kiev he was editorial secretary of the pedagogical journals *Svitlo* (1910–14) and *Vil'na ukraïns'ka shkola* (1917–19). In 1912 he cofounded the *Krynytsia publishing house, which he helped run until the First World War and after its revival in 1917–20. Under Soviet rule he directed the Kiev branch of the State Publishing House of Ukraine and the editorial staff of the *Knyhospilka publishing co-operative (1924–7) and was a member of the executive of Slovo publishers (1922–6). Tytarenko wrote several children's primers and readers. He was arrested in 1929 in connection with the Union for

the Liberation of Ukraine and exiled by administrative order to Voronezh for three years. There he translated works by N. Gogol and M. Kostomarov for the State Publishing Alliance of Ukraine, which were published under the pseudonym P. Vilkhovy. In 1943 he managed to return to Kiev. A postwar refugee in Germany, he emigrated to the United States.

Bohdan Tytla: *Early Spring* (watercolor)

**Tytla, Bohdan,** b 23 March 1928 in Pidhaitsi, Galicia. Painter and graphic artist; husband of H. Tytla. A postwar refugee, he has lived in the United States since 1950, and graduated from City University in New York (1957). He specializes in watercolor landscapes but also paints in oils and acrylics. He has designed book covers, including the collection *Pidhaiets'ka zemlia* (Pidhaitsi Land, 1980). Solo exhibitions of his work have been held in New York (1964, 1978), Washington (1973), Philadelphia (1974), Toronto (1979), and Ottawa (1982, 1984).

Halyna Tytla: icon of St Olha in the Ukrainian Catholic Church of the Immaculate Conception in Barnesboro

**Tytla, Halyna** (née Hrytsenko), b 28 November 1935 in Brno, Czechoslovakia. Graphic artist and iconographer; wife of B. Tytla. A postwar refugee, she has lived in the United States since 1949. She has worked as a book designer and has studied iconography under P. Kholodny, Jr. She painted the icons of SS Olha and Volodymyr in the Church of the Immaculate Conception in Barnesboro, Pennsylvania, the Good Friday holy shrouds in St Volodymyr's Church in Glen Spey and St Michael's Church in Yonkers, New York, and other icons. Solo exhibitions of her work have been held in Philadelphia (1976), Toronto (1979), and Ottawa (1982, 1984).

**Tytla, William** (Volodymyr), b 24 October 1904 in Yonkers, New York, d 30 December 1968 in East Lyme, Connecticut. Cartoonist. After graduating from the New York Evening School of Industrial Arts he studied sculpture in Paris. Upon returning to New York he worked as a draftsman for Paul Terry's Terrytoons and then for Walt Disney (1934–43). He was the animator of *Saludos Amigos* and *Victory through Air Power*; directing animator of *Snow White, Pinocchio,* and *Dumbo*; and animations supervisor of *Fantasia*. He created famous characters, such as the Seven Dwarfs, Stromboli, and Dumbo. He also did many shorts for Disney before moving to Famous Studios, Paramount, and Twentieth Century Fox, where he directed comedy series such as *Little Audrey, Little Lulu,* and *Popeye*. At the end of the 1950s he set up his own firm, Tytla Productions, and produced animated commercials.

**Tyvriv.** IV-9. A town smt (1986 pop 5,100) on the Boh River and a raion center in Vinnytsia oblast. It is first mentioned in historical documents in 1505, when it was under Lithuanian rule. In 1569 it was transferred to Poland. After the Cossack-Polish War it was restored to Poland by the Treaty of Andrusovo. A few years later Tyvriv was captured by the Turks (1672–99). During the 18th century its inhabitants rebelled against the Polish lords (1734, 1750). In 1793 the town was annexed by Russia and became a volost center in Vinnytsia county, Podilia gubernia. After the revolutionary period Tyvriv belonged to the Ukrainian SSR, except for a few years of Rumanian rule (1941–4). Today the town produces bricks, reinforced concrete, baked goods, and beer.

*Tyvun* (aka *tiun*). In Kievan Rus' a prince's servant, who on the ruler's instructions sometimes performed administrative and judicial duties. Some of the *tyvuny* were former slaves. The *tyvun* enjoyed certain privileges, and the penalty for killing a *tyvun* was a double *\*vyra*. Eventually boyar and episcopal households and monasteries had *tyvuny*. In the Grand Duchy of Lithuania the *tyvun* was a *volost* administrator and belonged to the nobility or the wealthy peasantry. In some localities he was an elected representative of a village *hromada*.

# U

**Ubid River** [Ubid']. A right-bank tributary of the Desna River that flows for 106 km through Chernihiv oblast and drains a basin area of 1,310 sq km. The river is 10–20 m wide and has a flat valley 2.5–3 km wide. It is used for water supply and serves as an outlet for a regional drainage system.

**Ubort River** [Ubort']. A right-bank tributary of the Prypiat River that flows for 292 km through Zhytomyr oblast and Homel oblast (Belarus) and drains a basin area of 5,820 sq km. The river is 10–20 m wide (up to 40 m in some places) and flows slowly. Its banks and the area surrounding them are quite marshy. The river is used for water supply and irrigation.

*Uchytel'* (Teacher). The first Ukrainian pedagogical journal in Transcarpathia, published weekly in Uzhhorod from April to December 1867 (a total of 26 issues). It published teaching materials and professional advice for teachers. *Uchytel'* was edited and published by A. *Ripai.

*Uchytel'* (Teacher). A newspaper published weekly in 1869–73 and then semimonthly in 1874 in Lviv (a total of 242 issues). Intended initially for teachers, it soon became a more general paper of pedagogy and enlightenment affiliated with the Russophile *Stauropegion Institute. It also published belles lettres and articles on cultural and economic affairs and the children's supplement *Lastivka*. The editor and publisher was M. Klemertovych. In 1880 publication of *Uchytel'* was renewed briefly.

*Uchytel'* (Teacher). A leading pedagogical journal published semimonthly and then monthly in Lviv in 1889–1914 by the Ruthenian Pedagogical Society (later *Ridna Shkola). It contained sample lessons and curricula for Ukrainian schools, articles on teaching methodology and the history of education, book reviews, and belles lettres. The journal did much to popularize pedagogical techniques developed in Western Europe and North America among Ukrainian teachers and educational theorists. It also devoted considerable attention to the development of education in Western and Russian-ruled Ukraine. In its last years it concentrated on primary education. *Uchytel'* was edited by I. Chapelsky, T. Hrushkevych (1890–2), V. Shukhevych (1893–1905), I. Kopach, V. Shchurat, O. Sushko, and I. Yushchyshyn (1911–14).

*Uchytel'* (Teacher). A monthly organ of the School Administration of Subcarpathian Ruthenia, published in 1920–36 in Uzhhorod. It was edited by I. Pankevych, S. Bochek, and Yu. Revai. It helped to instill Ukrainian consciousness among the population of Transcarpathia.

**Uchytelska Hromada society.** See Teachers' Hromada.

*Uchytel'* (first issue, 1889)

*Uchytel's'ke slovo* (Teacher's Word). A pedagogical journal published by the *Ukrainian Teachers' Mutual Aid Society in Lviv in 1912–39 (with some interruptions). The journal appeared semimonthly and then monthly and was edited by I. Kazanivsky, H. Koval, I. Lishchynsky, A. Zeleny, A. Dombrovsky, I. Yushchyshyn, and others. It also published the supplements *Metodyka i shkil'na praktyka* (1930–9) and *Shliakh vykhovannia i navchannia*. In 1930 *Uchytel's'ke slovo* appeared in a pressrun of 3,000 copies.

*Uchytel's'kyi holos* (Teacher's Voice). A monthly organ of the Teachers' Hromada of Subcarpathian Ruthenia, published in Uzhhorod and then in Mukachiv in 1930–8. It published articles on pedagogical and cultural affairs and was edited by O. Poliansky with the assistance of V. Svereniak, I. Vasko, and A. Shtefan.

*Ucrania Libre.* A Spanish-language quarterly and then semiannual journal, published by the Ukrainian Information and Publishing Institute in Buenos Aires from 1951 to 1960 (a total of 19 issues). Edited by Yu. *Tys, it contained articles on Ukrainian history, culture, religion, politics, and economics; on developments in Soviet Ukraine; and on Ukrainian life in Argentina. Many of the articles were translated from émigré periodicals published in North America and Western Europe.

**Udai River** [Udaj]. A right-bank tributary of the Sula River that flows for 327 km through Chernihiv and Poltava oblasts and drains a basin area of 7,030 sq km. The river is 5–10 m wide in its upper reaches and 20–40 m wide along its lower course. Wetlands are found in several sections of its basin. The river is used for industry, water supply, and fishing. The cities of Pryluka and Pyriatyn are situated along it.

**Udovenko, Levko,** b 19 August 1932 in Kiev. Film director. He completed study in the actor's (1954) and film director's (1959) faculties at the Kiev Institute of Theater Arts and became a director of popular-scientific films in the Kiev Artistic Film Studio (1959). Among them are *Nasha Ukraïna* (Our Ukraine, 1966), *Lesia Ukraïnka* (1968), and *Rushiï prohresu* (The Promoters of Progress, 1980).

Volodymyr Udovenko          Gen Mykola Udovychenko

**Udovenko, Volodymyr,** b 9 July 1881 in Kiev, d 8 December 1937. Medical scientist and political prisoner. In the 1920s he was a professor at the Kiev Medical and Art institutes and a member of the presidium of the VUAN medical section. He was arrested by the GPU on 22 November 1929 and sentenced to eight years' imprisonment at the 1930 show trial of members of the so-called *Union for the Liberation of Ukraine. Three days before his scheduled release he was sentenced to death by the NKVD and shot in a concentration camp in the Soviet Arctic.

**Udovychenko, Mykola** [Udovyčenko], b 17 May 1885, d 21 July 1937 in Homécourt, France. Military figure; brother of O. Udovychenko. An officer in the Russian army from 1905, during the First World War he commanded a battalion of the 129th Bessarabian Regiment in Kiev and then served on the southwestern front in the topography department of the General Staff. After the February Revolution he became the Ukrainian commissioner for review on the General Staff of the southwestern front of the Russian army and chief organizer of the UNR units there. He was a member of the Ukrainian General Military Committee. In January 1918 his detachment fought the Bolsheviks in Kiev. Thereafter he served as director of the personnel department in the Ministry of Military Affairs under the Central Rada, the Hetman government, and the UNR Directory. In 1920 he was interned with other UNR Army soldiers in a camp near Kalisz, Poland. In 1924 he emigrated to France.

**Udovychenko, Oleksander** [Udovyčenko], b 20 February 1887 in Kharkiv, d 21 April 1975 in Maintenon, near Paris. UNR Army field commander. After completing a course at the Nikolai Military Academy in St Petersburg, he held various staff positions in the Russian army. In 1917 he chaired the Ukrainian Council of the Third Caucasian Corps of the imperial army. In October he was called to Kiev to become S. Petliura's military adviser. In January–March 1918 he served as chief of staff in the *Haida-

Gen Oleksander Udovychenko

maka Battalion of Slobidska Ukraine and distinguished himself in fighting the Bolshevik insurrection in Kiev. He was assigned to the General Staff in April 1918 and soon promoted to colonel. After serving as general quartermaster of the southwestern front (November 1918–March 1919) he commanded the *Third Iron Rifle Division. Ill with typhus, Udovychenko was captured by A. Denikin's forces. He escaped in the spring of 1920 and once again took command of the reactivated Iron Division. From November 1920 he served as general inspector of Polish internment camps for UNR soldiers. After emigrating to France in 1924, he presided over its veteran Ukrainian Military Society (1927–75) and the European Federation of Ukrainian Veterans' Organizations (1953–75) and served as vice-president of the UNR government-in-exile and its defense minister (1954–61). He was promoted to major general by the government-in-exile. He wrote *Ukraïna u viini za derzavnist'* (Ukraine in the War for Statehood, 1954) and *Tretia zalizna dyviziia* (The Third Iron Division, 2 vols, 1971, 1982).

P. Sodol

**Udy River** (also Uda). A right-bank tributary of the Donets River that flows for 164 km through Belgorod oblast (RF) and Kharkiv oblast and drains a basin area of 3,893 sq km. Its source is in the Central Russian Upland, and it is fed by rain and meltwater. The river is used for irrigation and for water supply. The city of Kharkiv is situated at the point where the Lopan River empties into the Udy.

**UHA.** See Ukrainian Galician Army.

**Uhlytsky, Pavlo.** See Pecheniha-Uhlytsky, Pavlo.

**Uhlytsky, Teodosii** [Uhlyc'kyj, Teodosij], b in the 1630s in Ulaniv, Podilia, d 5 February 1696 in Chernihiv. Orthodox churchman and saint. He studied at the Kievan Mohyla Academy and then entered the Kievan Cave Monastery. After serving as a deacon at St Sophia Cathedral he resided at the monastery near Baturyn and then became hegumen of the Korsun St Onuphrius's (1662–4) and the Kiev Vydubychi (1664–88) monasteries. In 1688 he became archimandrite of the Yeletskyi Dormition Monastery in Chernihiv and assistant to Archbishop L. Baranovych. At the Chernihiv sobor of 1692 he was elected auxiliary bishop to Baranovych. He then traveled to Moscow to be consecrated by Patriarch Adrian. His consecration by Adrian helped to undermine the eparchy's relationship to the metropolitan of Kiev and increase the authority of the Moscow patriarch. Uhlytsky maintained good relations with Hetman I. Mazepa, however, who assisted in building new churches and monasteries. Uhlytsky also supported the *Chernihiv printing press. After his death his remains were associated with a number of miracles and healings, and he was canonized in 1896 (his feast day is 22 September [9 September OS]).

**Uhniv.** III-4. A town (1989 pop 1,400) on the Solokiia River in Sokal raion, Lviv oblast. It was first mentioned in historical documents in 1360. In 1528 it was granted the rights of *Magdeburg law. After the partition of Poland in 1772, it was annexed by Austria. In the interwar period it belonged to Poland. Today it is an agricultural town with a feed factory. A 17th-century Roman Catholic church, the Dormition Church, has been preserved there.

**Uhniv Brigade of the Ukrainian Galician Army** (Uhnivska [9] brygada UHA or Belzka [9] brygada UHA). Formed in April 1919 out of the Uhniv and Belz front units of the Northern Group, the brigade belonged to the First Corps of the UHA and was active in the Rava Ruska region. During the joint UHA and UNR Army offensive on Kiev in August 1919, the brigade fought at Zhmerynka, Kalynivka, and Berdychiv. Subsequently it fought against A. Denikin's army and was incorporated as an infantry regiment into the Second Brigade of the Red Ukrainian Galician Army. It ceased to exist following its surrender to the Polish army on 27 April 1920.

**Uholka Nature Reserve** (Uholskyi zapovidnyk). Established in 1964 by a decree of the Council of Ministers of the Ukrainian SSR to preserve the primeval beech forests of the Uholka Depression, the reserve covers 4,724 ha on the southern slope of Mount Menchul in the Polonynian Beskyd. In 1968 it became part of the *Carpathian Nature Reserve. Because of its unique plant species and disappearing English yew, the reserve has attracted much scientific attention.

Rev Mykola Uhorchak          Mykola Uhryn-Bezhrishny

**Uhorchak, Mykola** [Uhorčak] (pseuds: Mykola Pohidny, Mykola Skrypa Hedeon), b 22 December 1901 in Tysmenytsia, Tovmach county, Galicia, d 9 January 1982 in the United States. Catholic and Orthodox priest and children's writer. He studied at the Lviv (Underground)

Ukrainian University (1921–4) and the Greek Catholic Theological Seminary in Stanyslaviv (1924–8) and served as a Ukrainian Catholic priest and catechist in Kolomyia county from 1928. A postwar refugee, in 1948 he settled in the United States and converted to Ukrainian Orthodoxy. From 1931 he contributed over 60 stories, articles, and sermons to periodicals, such as *Pravda* (Lviv), *Promin'* (Winnipeg), *Tserkva i zhyttia* (Neu-Ulm and Chicago), *Veselka* (Jersey City), *Ukraïns'kyi holos* (Winnipeg), and *Ukraïns'ke pravoslavne slovo* (South Bound Brook). He published 10 books of children's stories, including *Pokotyhoroshok* (1946), *Het'mans'ka bulava* (The Hetman's Mace), *Sribna hryvna* (The Silver *Hryvnia*, 1951), and *Illia Muromets'* (1967), and a book of sermons (1959).

**Uhryn-Bezhrishny, Mykola** [Uhryn-Bezhrišnyj] (real name: Vengzhyn), b 18 December 1883 in Kupiatychi, Peremyshl county, Galicia, d 19 January 1960 in Neu-Ulm, Germany. Pedagogue, publicist, and journalist. In 1911, after studying at Lviv and Chernivtsi universities, he obtained a position at a gymnasium in Rohatyn. The experience he had gained in editing newspapers, such as *Bdzhola* (1908–9) and *Buduchnist'* (1909), and in writing prose and poetry afforded him the opportunity to work with the Ukrainian Sich Riflemen press corps and its publications. After returning to Rohatyn he resumed his teaching duties (until the 1940s), edited the local *Rohatynets'*, published *Narys istoriï Ukraïns'kykh sichovykh stril'tsiv* (An Outline History of the Ukrainian Sich Riflemen, 1923), and wrote plays, such as *Sofiia Halechko* (1924) and *Lytsari zaliznoï ostrohy* (Knights of the Iron Spur, 1938).

**Uhryn-Huzar, Kalyna** (Uhryn-Houzar, Kaléna), b 4 March 1939 in Paris. Translator and civic leader of Ukrainian origin. She was a founding member of the Organization of Ukrainian Youth in France (1956) and editor of *Bulletin franco-ukrainien* (1959–68) and *Echanges* (1971–81). She has translated many Ukrainian works into French, most notably M. Osadchy's *Cataracte* (1974), I. Dziuba's *Internationalisme ou russification?* (1980), and selections from O. Berdnyk entitled *La Confrérie étoilée* (1985). She is also the author of *La notion de 'Russie' dans la cartographie occidentale* (1975) and coauthored the monograph *Tarass Chevtchenko, sa vie et son oeuvre* (1964).

**UHVR.** See Ukrainian Supreme Liberation Council.

**Uiomov, Avenir** [Ujomov], b 4 April 1928 in Poreche, Ivanovo oblast, RSFSR. Philosopher. A graduate of Moscow University (1949), he completed postgraduate studies there under V. Asmus (1952) and taught philosophy at the Ivanovo Pedagogical Institute. Since 1964 he has chaired the philosophy department at Odessa University, and since 1973 he has headed the Department of Control Theory and Systems Analysis at the Odessa branch of the AN URSR (now ANU) Institute of Economics. The president of the Odessa branch of the Ukrainian Philosophical Society and one of the first Soviet advocates of *cybernetics as a distinct science, he has written over 300 works (10 of them monographs) on logic, the philosophy of science, cybernetics, and systems theory. His chief monographs are written in Russian and deal with logical errors (1958), things, properties, and relations (1963), the logical foundations of the modeling method (1971), logic and empirical knowledge (1972), and the systems approach and the general theory of systems (1978).

**Ukapisty.** See Ukrainian Communist party.

**Ukase.** In the Russian Empire the term was used for a wide variety of decrees, usually signed by the tsar or his plenipotentiaries. In the USSR the ukase was a decree passed by the Presidium of the Supreme Soviet of the USSR or of a Union republic. Two types of ukase were distinguished: (1) normative, that is, decrees that introduced legal norms, and (2) individual, that is, decrees that appointed people to government positions or bestowed awards and prizes. Normative ukases acquired the force of law after they were published and ratified by the appropriate supreme soviets. Individual ukases, however, did not have to be ratified by any soviet, and acquired the force of law during the period of time specified therein. The ukases of the Presidium of the Supreme Soviet of the USSR were automatically binding on all the republics. The ukases of the Ukrainian SSR were published in *Vidomosti Verkhovnoï Rady URSR*.

**Ukhiv, Ivan** [Uxiv], b 24 June 1897 in Bronnytsia, Mohyliv county, Podilia gubernia, d 24 February 1974 in the United States. Military officer and civic leader. During the First World War he advanced to the rank of staff captain in the Russian army. In 1917 he commanded a unit of Free Cossacks stationed in Mohyliv, and later he served under P. Shandruk in the UNR Army. He was wounded in combat at Vapniarka and was promoted to colonel. In 1923 he emigrated to Argentina. In Berisso he was a founder of Argentina's first Prosvita society (1923), and he helped organize an Orthodox parish in Buenos Aires.

**Ukhodnyky.** Persons of various classes – peasants, burghers, boyars, and even magnates – who traveled in the Ukrainian steppes in the 14th to 16th centuries in search of adventure and risk and to hunt, fish, and collect honey. The *ukhodnyky* ('frontiersmen') came from the steppe borderlands around Cherkasy, Kaniv, Kiev, and Bratslav in the spring, trekked to the southern reaches of the Dnieper River, and returned to their original settlements in the winter. Sometimes they paid tithes for their booty to local voivodes. Life in the steppes was dangerous, particularly because of the risk of clashes with the Tatars. The *ukhodnyky* joined to form bands of warriors (*vatahy*), which became highly organized and increasingly more powerful, to the point where they were able to wrest back the slaves and livestock taken by the Tatars. Over time they began to remain in the steppes, chiefly in the lower Dnieper regions, and were transformed into a distinct class of the Ukrainian population known as *kozaky* (see *Cossacks). Their life was described by A. Chaikovsky in *Na ukhodakh* (On the Frontier, 1921).

**Ukoopspilka** (full name: Ukrainska spilka spozhyvchykh tovarystv [Ukrainian Association of Consumer Societies]). The central co-ordinating body for Ukrainian consumer co-operatives, founded in June 1920. In 1971 it represented 25 oblast co-operative associations, 469 raion-level associations, over 3,300 local consumer societies, and almost 17 million shareholders. It organizes the distribution of manufactured goods through the local societies to consumers, primarily in the countryside, maintains village bakeries and other small food-processing facilities, and purchases agricultural products for sale in cities. In 1977 Ukoopspilka was responsible for 31 percent of all retail trade and 25 percent of all food sales in Ukraine. Until 1991 Ukoopspilka was under the authority of Tsentrosoiuz, the Central Union of Co-operative Societies in Moscow.

*Ukraïna* (Ukraine). A journal of Ukrainian studies, published in Kiev in 1907 (four issues). It was the continuation of *Kievskaia starina* and the first Ukrainian-language scholarly journal in Russian-ruled Ukraine. *Ukraïna* contained articles on history, literature, and culture, belles lettres, and surveys of Ukrainian literary and theatrical affairs and press. Among the contributors were I. Franko, I. Nechui-Levytsky, I. Steshenko, and V. Domanytsky. The editor and publisher was V. *Naumenko.

*Ukraïna* (Ukraine). A weekly newspaper published in Chernivtsi from April 1913 to early 1914. Edited by Z. Kuzelia, it supported S. Smal-Stotsky in his personal competition with M. Vasylko for the leadership of the Ukrainian movement in Bukovyna.

*Ukraïna* (Ukraine). An academic journal of Ukrainian studies that was published in Kiev from 1914 to 1930 (except in 1915–16 and 1919–23). The editor was M. *Hrushevsky. From 1914 *Ukraïna* was the official publication of the Ukrainian Scientific Society in Kiev, and from 1924 it was the official publication of the historical section of the VUAN. Altogether 43 issues were published (10 in 1914–18 and 33 in 1924–30). Until 1924 the journal was a quarterly publication, and after that it appeared bimonthly, with a pressrun of 1,700–3,000.

The journal's core section consisted of columns on history, archeology, economics, folklore, ethnography, language, literature, art, and regional studies of Ukraine. Hrushevsky was chief editor of that section and also wrote editorials on prominent cultural personalities and important events in the history of Ukraine. The journal also contained annotated primary sources and documents (memoirs, correspondence, previously unpublished literary works) concerning civic and cultural life in the 19th and early 20th centuries; documents pertaining to the history of Ukraine; criticism and bibliographies of important Ukrainian-studies publications, especially foreign-language publications in the field (Hrushevsky was editor of that section also); a chronicle of scholarly events; notices of the activities of the historical-philological division of the VUAN and its historical section; obituaries of persons in the field of Ukrainian studies; and, from 1927, a bibliographical overview (edited by Y. Hermaize).

Certain issues of *Ukraïna* were devoted to eminent cultural figures (T. Shevchenko, M. Kostomarov, P. Kulish, M. Maksymovych, I. Franko, O. Lazarevsky, M. Drahomanov, V. Antonovych, P. Tutkovsky), important events in the history of Ukraine (the Koliivshchyna rebellion, the Cyril and Methodius Brotherhood, the Revolution of 1905, the centenary of the Decembrist movement, the 10th anniversary of Ukraine's struggle for independence), and regional topics (Bukovyna, Galician–central Ukrainian relations, etc).

Hrushevsky edited *Ukraïnu* for 16 years (it was often referred to as Hrushevsky's *Ukraïna*). Among its writers and editors were M. Vasylenko, M. Vozniak, O. Hrushevsky, V. Doroshenko, I. Kamanin, O. Levytsky, K. Mykhalchuk (managing editor in 1914), M. Mochulsky, Ye. Onatsky, V. Peretts, and the non-Ukrainians G. Ilinsky, F. Korsh, and A. Shakhmatov. Among those who contributed to the journal from 1924 to 1930 were D. Bahalii, Vasylenko, Vozniak, Hermaize, O. Hrushevsky, H. Zhytetsky, S. Yefremov, A. Krymsky, P. Klepatsky, K. Koperzhynsky, I. Krypiakevych, P. Klymenko, M. Makarenko, V. Miiakovsky, Mochulsky, V. Novytsky, O. Novytsky, M. Petrovsky, Peretts, V. Romanovsky, O. Riabinin-Skliarevsky, F. Savchenko (who also served as editorial board secretary), O. Syniavsky, K. Studynsky, M. Tkachenko, P. Tutkovsky, S. Shamrai, S. Smal-Stotsky, V. Shcherbyna, V. Yurkevych, and B. Yakubsky.

*Ukraïna* was published under onerous censorship conditions, but it overcame the difficulties to present an objective picture of Ukraine's past. Along with *Kievskaia starina* and *Literaturno-naukovyi vistnyk*, *Ukraïna* was one of the most authoritative journals in the field of Ukrainian studies, and it has remained a good source for research, especially in the area of the national-cultural processes in the 19th and early 20th centuries. Toward the end of 1930 *Ukraïna* was forced to discontinue publication. The last issue (no. 44) was printed but not released. In its place the Party leadership of the VUAN began to issue a periodical titled *Ukraïna*, with the subheading *Zhurnal tsyklu nauk istorychnykh* (Journal of the Cycle of Historical Sciences). Edited by P. Shuran, that journal was of a totally different ideological nature. Its aim was to oppose national Ukrainian historiography, particularly the 'school of Hrushevsky.' In 1932 there were two issues of the new, replacement *Ukraïna* (no. 1–2 and no. 3); they contained essays sharply critical of M. Hrushevsky and Vasylenko (also essays by P. Kyianytsia and L. Okinshevych). Then the journal ceased publication.

BIBLIOGRAPHY
*Systematychnyi kataloh vydan' Vseukraïns'koï akademiï Nauk: 1918–1929, 1930* (Kiev 1930, 1931; repr, Chicago 1966)
Zhukovs'kyi, A. 'Mykhailo Hrushevs'kyi i zhurnal *Ukraïna*,' *UI*, no. 89–90 (1986)

A. Zhukovsky

***Ukraïna*** (Ukraine). A daily official bulletin of the UNR Army, published at its headquarters during 1919–20.

***Ukraïna*** (Ukraine). A popular illustrated magazine published in Kiev since May 1941, as a monthly to July 1955, then semimonthly, weekly from July 1963, semimonthly in 1991, monthly in 1992, and again weekly. During the Second World War it appeared in Moscow under the editorship of Yu. Smolych. It contains articles on culture, history, politics, economics, social issues, and sports, as well as art reproductions, prose, poetry, travelogues, translations, games, humor, and special features for children. Although many of the articles had propagandistic quality and stressed the achievements of Soviet culture, science, and scholarship, in the last years of Soviet rule the magazine began to examine objectively some of the negative aspects of Soviet life; it has published articles on the 'blank spots' in Ukrainian history and on cultural and historical figures repressed by or formerly out of favor with the regime, as well as literary works that were formerly banned

*Ukraïna*

or censored. In 1976 it was printed in a pressrun of 332,000; this figure had fallen to 230,000 by early 1980, 125,000 by 1988, and 116,000 by 1989. The current editor in chief is A. Mykhailenko.

***Ukraïna*** (Ukraine). An irregular journal of Ukrainian studies, published in Paris in 1949–53 (a total of 10 issues). It succeeded *Soborna Ukraïna*, four issues of which appeared in 1947. Edited by E. *Borschak and published with the financial support of Bishop I. Buchko, the journal devoted particular attention to historical topics, including the history of Ukrainian-French relations. It featured biographies of prominent Ukrainian political and cultural figures, materials on Hetman P. Orlyk, documents relating to Ukrainian history (particularly from French archives), bibliographies, book reviews, and memoirs by E. Batchinsky, B. Krupnytsky, D. Olianchyn, N. Polonska-Vasylenko, Yu. Tyshchenko, and others.

*Ukraïna i svit*

***Ukraïna i svit*** (Ukraine and the World). An irregular journal of cultural, literary, scholarly, and political affairs, published by I. Sapiha in Hannover, West Germany, in 1949–69 (a total of 28 issues). The journal devoted particular attention to Ukraine's cultural relationship with other nations. It published works on the archeology of the Black Sea region and on the history of Georgia, original literary contributions by contemporary émigré authors, and Ukrainian translations of European classics. V. Derzhavyn, I. Kostetsky, E. Kottmeier, M. Orest, and V. Barka were regular contributors.

**Ukraina Society** (aka Association for Cultural Relations with Ukrainians Abroad; Ukrainian: Tovarystvo Ukraina, or Tovarystvo kulturnykh zviazkiv z ukraintsiamy za kordonom). An organization formed in 1960 in Kiev out of the Ukrainian division of the USSR Return to the Homeland Committee. The Ukraina Society has institutional affiliates, such as artists' unions and business enterprises, as well as individual members, including prominent Ukrainian writers and artists. To strengthen cultural ties with Ukrainians abroad and to acquaint them with cultural developments in Ukraine the society organizes performances by Ukrainian ensembles from abroad in Ukraine and of Soviet Ukrainian groups abroad, hosts foreign students, and publishes two newspapers aimed at readers abroad, *News from Ukraine* and *Visti z Ukraïny*. Until Ukraine's independence the Ukraina Society was under the central, Moscow-based Rodina Association, which was responsible for furthering cultural ties with foreign compatriots of all of the peoples of the Soviet Union. Traditionally the Ukraina Society spread pro-Soviet propaganda and emphasized contacts with so-called progressive Ukrainian groups abroad. Under the influence of M. Gorbachev's reforms this emphasis was played down. The reforms also affected the society's publications, which have begun to cover a wider range of events both in Ukraine and in Ukrainian communities abroad. The presidents of the society have been L. Revutsky, Yu. Smolych, O. Pidsukha (from 1975), and V. Brovchenko (since 1979).

**Ukrainbank.** Ukrainian second-level credit co-operatives in interwar Galicia. Set up in county centers, they served as savings and loan associations for urban residents and community organizations and provided support for the Raiffeisen credit co-operatives in the countryside. The central co-ordinating body for these county credit associations was *Tsentrobank. By the end of the 1930s there were 115 Ukrainbank associations, in almost every major town in Galicia. Most of them were small; only 25 had an operating capital of 100,000 zlotys. In 1937 their total deposits came to just over 4.6 million zlotys. The typical loan was 300 to 500 zlotys. A major obstacle to their growth was their exclusion from Polish state banks' credit. Ukrainbank offices were closed down by the Soviet authorities in 1939. Seventy-one of them were reopened under the German occupation (1941–4).

**Ukrainbank** (full name: Ukrainskyi narodnyi kooperatyvnyi bank, or Ukrainian National Co-operative Bank). The central financial co-ordinating body for Ukrainian credit and agricultural co-operatives. It was founded in 1917 in Kiev with an initial capitalization of one million rubles. At the time its shares were valued at 250 rubles and were sold only to co-operatives. In July 1918 more shares were issued, to raise the capital fund to two million rubles. By the end of 1919 the capital reserve had reached 25 million rubles. The first director was F. Kryzhanivsky, and the first chairman of the board was Kh. Baranovsky. Ukrainbank was to regulate the finances for all Ukrainian co-operatives, attract capital for co-operatives from the money market and foreign sources, provide financing for manufacturing and marketing co-operatives, and arrange state loans for co-operatives. It had branches (16 in 1919) in most larger cities in Ukraine. In 1919 it had a total turnover of 286 million rubles. From its earnings it supported Ukrainian cultural and educational institutions, including Kiev University and the Ukrainfilm film studio.

The central building of Ukrainbank in Kharkiv

The Soviet authorities dissolved Ukrainbank in December 1920 and closed down all credit co-operatives during the period of War Communism. The bank was revived in 1922 but was placed under much stricter central control. By 1926 it had organized a system of 50 regional branches and affiliates, which served almost 5,800 credit co-operatives, and by 1929 it had reserves of over 130 million rubles. Its operations were restricted gradually until they consisted mostly of financing import and export trade. Ukrainbank was placed under the authority of the all-Union Commissariat of Finances and the central bank in Moscow, and in 1936 it was closed down.

**Ukraine** (Ukraina). The name of the territory settled by the Ukrainian nation. It originated from the Slavic word *ukraina* (from the Indo-European root *(s)krei-*, 'to separate' or 'cut'). In the literary and historical documents of the 12th to 15th centuries Ukraine meant borderland or bordering country as well as country (modern Ukrainian: *krai*). The Kiev Chronicle, recounting the death of Prince Volodymyr Hlibovych of Pereiaslav during his campaign against the Cumans in 1187, noted that 'for him Ukraine mourned greatly.' It also stated that Prince Rostyslav Berladnyk arrived in 'Galician Ukraine,' referring to the Dniester Lowland. The Galician-Volhynian Chronicle said that in 1213 Prince Danylo 'reunited Brest and Uhrovesk ... and all of Ukraine,' referring to the territory west of the Buh River (Kholm and Podlachia regions). It also contained the phrase 'in Ukraine' *na Vkrainie* (1280), *na Vkrainitsi* (1282). In all those examples Ukraine meant either borderland with respect to the center of the Kiev principality or the Principality of Galicia-Volhynia, or simply land or country.

Ukraine continued to mean 'land' well into the 15th and 16th centuries and even later. Documents referred to Podilian Ukraine, Bratslav Ukraine, and Kiev Ukraine. The records of the Polish Diet in 1585 referred to Podilia as Podilian Ukraina. With the rise of the Cossack Host in the 16th century, Ukraine came to mean the Cossack territory stretching along both sides of the Dnieper River and corresponding to Kiev voivodeship of the Polish Commonwealth. The term *Ukraina* was used in that sense in the writings of the Roman Catholic bishop of Kiev, J. Wereszczyński (end of the 16th century), the diaries of S. Bielski (1609) and S. Okolski (1638), and the letters of Hetman P. Sahaidachny and Bishop I. Kopynsky. In his letter to King Sigismund III Vasa (15 February 1622) Hetman Sahaidachny wrote of 'Ukraine, our rightful eternal homeland,' 'Ukrainian cities,' and 'Ukrainian people.' I. Kopynsky, in his letter to the patriarch of Moscow (4 December 1622), complained that 'all here, in Ukraine, in Kiev [voivodeship], are being hampered.' The concept of Ukraine was extended at that time beyond Kiev voivodeship to Left-Bank Ukraine, which was rapidly colonized by Ukrainians during the first half of the 17th century, and even to the territory of the Muscovite state (Slobidska Ukraine), which attracted Cossack settlers.

The name Ukraine acquired a specific political meaning as a result of Hetman B. Khmelnytsky's successful uprising and the rise of a Cossack state in central Ukraine. Although the official name of the new Hetman state of the 17th to 18th century was the Zaporozhian Host (in several variants), its territory was usually known in Ukrainian and Polish sources as Ukraine. The terms Ukraine, Ukrainian, and Ukrainian people were used more and more frequently in political and cultural contexts. They appear again and again in the proclamations and documents of Hetmans B. Khmelnytsky, I. Vyhovsky, P. Doroshenko, I. Samoilovych, I. Mazepa, and P. Orlyk. Doroshenko's staff secretary in a letter to the Zaporizhia (1671) wrote about 'the entire Ukraine,' 'our Ukrainian people,' and 'Ukrainian cities.' In a letter to V. Kochubei, L. Polubotok wrote (1685) of our 'fatherland Ukraine.' The anti-hetman P. Petryk declared that he concluded a treaty with the Crimean Khanate (1692) to 'free my dear homeland, Ukraine, from Muscovite rule.' In his proclamations and letters he used the phrase 'our Ukraine.' The name appears regularly in Orlyk's proclamations and letters. Both the Latin and the Ukrainian texts of the Constitution of Bendery (1710) use 'Ukraine,' 'into Ukraine,' and 'Kiev and other Ukrainian cities.' In a treaty with Crimea (1711) Orlyk styled himself 'duke of Ukraine' (*dux Ucrainae*). He and his fellow émigrés popularized the name Ukraine, which had been introduced by G. le Vasseur de *Beauplan in 1650 in Western Europe. In the 18th century the name appeared in various spellings on French, Italian, English, German, and other maps.

The partition of Ukraine between Muscovy and Poland in 1667 interrupted the evolution of the concept of Ukraine into an all-embracing national concept. To reflect the political division, adjectives such as 'this side' (*s'ohobichna*) and 'that side' (*tohobichna*) were introduced. Left-Bank Ukraine or the Hetmanate, a protectorate of Muscovy, was transformed in the 18th century into a province of the Russian Empire and became officially known in Russian as Malorossiia (Little Russia) and in Ukrainian as Malorosiis'ka Ukraïna. Ukraine began to be used as the name of a small geographic region. In the Samovydets Chronicle a locust infestation was reported to have occurred in 1690 'in Ukraine and near Starodub in Siveria.' In the second half of the 18th century, writers from Starodub used the name to refer to the central part of the Hetmanate, from Chernihiv and Nizhen to Pryluka, Lokhvytsia, and Hadiache.

Only in the 19th century, when the larger part of the Ukrainian territories was unified within the Russian Empire, did the name Ukraine begin to mean the Ukrainian national territory. T. *Shevchenko associated the name Ukraine with the Cossack past and the idea of national independence, the name Malorossiia with national humiliation and colonial status. From the beginning of the second half of the 19th century Ukraine began to be used by Ukrainians for the entire territory of the Ukrainian nation, and gradually it displaced all other names, particularly Malorosiia. After the declarations of autonomy (20 November 1917) and independence (22 January 1918) of the Ukrainian National Republic, the Ukrainian State (29 April 1918), and the Western Ukrainian National Republic (1 November 1918) and the unification of all Ukrainian lands in the new UNR (22 [but dated 25] January 1919), Ukraine became established as the official name of the state, and Ukrainian as the official name of its people. The official adoption of the name Carpatho-Ukraine (15 March 1939) put to rest any doubts as to the national identity of that part of the Ukrainian territory (see *Transcarpathia). Under the Soviet occupation Ukraine was named the Ukrainian Socialist Soviet Republic (6 January 1919) and then (31 January 1937) the Ukrainian Soviet Socialist Republic (USSR). In the declaration of independence of 24 August 1991 the new state adopted Ukraine as its official name.

BIBLIOGRAPHY
Dorošenko, D. 'Die Namen "Rus," "Russland," und "Ukraine" in ihrer historischen und gegenwärtigen Bedeutung,' *Abhandlungen des Ukrainischen Wissenschaftlichen Institutes*, vol 3 (Berlin 1931)
Shelukhyn, S. *Ukraïna – nazva nashoï zemli z naidavnishykh chasiv* (Prague 1936)
Sichyns'kyi, V. *Nazva Ukraïny: Terytoriia Ukraïny* (Prague 1944; 2nd edn, Augsburg 1948)
Andrusiak, M. *Nazva 'Ukraïna'* (Chicago 1951)
Rudnyćkyj. J. *The Term and Name 'Ukraine'* (Winnipeg 1951)
Simpson, G. *The Names 'Rus',' 'Russia,' 'Ukraine,' and Their Historical Background* (Winnipeg 1951)
Šerech, Yu. 'An Important Work in Ukrainian Onomastics,' *The Annals of the Ukrainian Academy of Arts and Sciences in the US*, vol 2, no. 4 (Winter 1952)

I. Stebelsky

**Ukraine.** An English-language illustrated magazine published quarterly from 1970 to 1980 and since then monthly in Kiev. Until 1989 it was a supplement to the magazine *Ukraïna*; since 1990 it has been published by the *Ukraina Society and the *Ukrainian Society for Friendship and Cultural Relations with Foreign Countries. *Ukraine* contains articles translated from *Ukraïna* as well as original pieces on political, historical, cultural, and social topics; art reproductions; and translations of Ukrainian literary works. Until recently it was a Soviet propaganda tool and was distributed widely, often free of charge, in the West and the Third World. It has persistently used an English transliteration based on the Russian spelling for Ukrainian names. The chief editors have been A. Bilenko, A. Mykhailenko, and V. Mokhurenko.

**L'Ukraine.** A monthly French-language journal published in Lausanne, Switzerland, from June 1915 to 1920. It informed the Western public about Ukrainian affairs and garnered support for the Ukrainian national movement and Ukrainian independence. *L'Ukraine* was edited by V. Stepankivsky with the assistance of M. Tyshkevych, who supported it financially.

*Die Ukraine*

**Ukraine, Die.** An organ of the *German-Ukrainian Society in Berlin, published in 1918–26 (a total of 40 issues). It contained articles on Ukrainian studies, the political situation in Soviet Ukraine, and German-Ukrainian relations. *Die Ukraine* was edited by A. Schmidt, and among its many German contributors were P. Rohrbach, E. Nolde, and B. Hann.

**Ukraine in Vergangenheit und Gegenwart.** A quarterly organ of the *German-Ukrainian Society, published in Munich in 1952–7 and 1962–8 (a total of 44 issues). Edited by H. Prokopchuk, the journal informed the West German public about Ukrainian politics, culture, scholarship, and émigré life; devoted considerable attention to German-Ukrainian relations; and contained a regular chronicle of Ukrainian affairs. It featured biographies of prominent Ukrainians and Germans, literary and art criticism (with many illustrations), and articles on the history of Ukraine.

**L'Ukraine libre.** A French-language monthly journal of politics and culture, published in Paris in 1954–5 by the Hromada Franco-Ukrainian publishing house. It was edited by I. Siletsky.

**Ukraine-Philatelisten Verband.** A society founded in 1920 by German philatelists in Berlin. Its original goal was the documentation of all the trident overprinted imperial Russian *postage stamps issued by a decree of the Ukrainian government of 20 August 1918. Many of its founding members had been in Ukraine at the time of Ukrainian independence and had brought such stamps with them upon returning to Germany. After 1934 the society also devoted itself to the promotion of Ukrainian philately and to the authentication of overprints and cancels. Under its longtime (35 years) head R. *Seichter, the society published the catalog *Sonder-Katalog Ukraine* and the philatelic journal *Der Ukraine-Philatelist*.

**Ukrainets** (The Ukrainian). A Russian and Ukrainian miscellany edited by M. *Maksymovych, two volumes of which appeared in Moscow in 1859 and 1864. The first volume contained an article on how to read Ukrainian and Maksymovych's Ukrainian translations of the Psalms and excerpts from *Slovo o polku Ihorevi* (The Tale of Ihor's Campaign), his recollections of the Poltava region, and his correspondence with M. Pogodin concerning B. Khmelnytsky. The second volume included Maksymovych's articles on the history of the Kiev region, Volhynia, and the Ostrozky family, an unsigned article on the Mezhyhiria Transfiguration Monastery, and several transcriptions of Ukrainian folk songs.

**Ukraïnets'** (The Ukrainian). A weekly newspaper for Ukrainian *Ostarbeiter in Germany, published in Berlin in 1942–5 by the *German Labor Front and edited by A. Lutsiv, B. Kravtsiv, O. Florynsky, and A. Drahan. A special page for women was edited by N. Snizhna in 1944–5.

*Ukraïnets' na Zelenomu Klyni*

**Ukraïnets' na Zelenomu Klyni** (The Ukrainian in the Far East). The first Ukrainian newspaper in the Far East, published weekly in Vladivostok from May 1917 to 1918 (?). It had a great impact on the development of Ukrainian political activity and national consciousness in the Far East. The publisher and editor was D. Borovyk. The paper published news and articles on political developments in the Far East, elsewhere in the former Russian Empire, and in Ukraine after the February Revolution of 1917. It printed the four universals of the Central Rada.

**Ukraïnets' u Frantsiï** (The Ukrainian in France). A nationalist newspaper published in Paris in 1945–9. Published by I. Popovych, it appeared monthly in 1945, semimonthly in 1946, and weekly from 1947 as the organ of the *Union of Ukrainian Workers in France. It was later called *Ukraïnets'*, and in 1949 it merged with the newspaper *Chas* to form *Ukraïnets'-Chas*.

**Ukraïnets' v Avstraliï** (The Ukrainian in Australia). A newspaper established in Melbourne in 1956 by K. Himmelreich and others. It was printed by B. Ihnativ, who later also became the newspaper's editor. Initially a four-page publication, it gradually expanded to six pages appearing fortnightly from October 1957. At the beginning of 1965 its format grew to eight pages. In addition to the news and views of the UNR government-in-exile, *Ukraïnets' v Avstraliï* covered Ukrainian religious and community life in Australia. Following years of financial difficulties and a transformation into a monthly magazine in the early 1980s, it ceased publication in January 1985.

**Ukraïnets'-Chas** (The Ukrainian-Time). A newspaper published in Paris from 1949 to 1960. It was created through the merger of *Ukraïnets'* (formerly *Ukraïnets' u*

*Frantsii*) in Paris with *Chas*, a newspaper published in Fürth, Bavaria. *Ukraïnets'-Chas* was edited by D. Shtykalo, D. Chaikovsky (1952–6), and B. Vitoshynsky (1956–60). It supported the OUN (Bandera faction).

**Ukrainian Academic Committee** (Ukrainskyi akademichnyi komitet, or UAK). An organization created in Prague in late 1924 on the initiative of O. *Shulhyn. Until June 1926 it was an autonomous body of the *Ukrainian Historical-Philological Society. Its purpose was to unite all Ukrainian scholars outside the USSR and to represent Ukrainian scholarship in the West. It was presided over by the rector of the *Ukrainian Free University of Prague. Its members were 17 Ukrainian émigré postsecondary institutions and learned societies in Czechoslovakia, the Shevchenko Scientific Society in Lviv, the Ukrainian scientific institutes in Warsaw and Berlin, and several individuals (I. Horbachevsky, O. Kolessa, O. Lototsky, M. Slavinsky, S. Smal-Stotsky, O. Shulhyn, A. Yakovliv). The UAK was recognized by the Commission for Intellectual Co-operation at the League of Nations in Geneva and was a member body of the league's International Institute of Intellectual Co-operation in Paris until the USSR joined the League of Nations in 1934. The UAK spoke out against the Polish pacification of Galicia (1930) and the Stalinist terror in Soviet Ukraine; participated in international congresses and conferences; organized two Ukrainian scholarly congresses (1926 and 1932) in Prague (over 130 émigré and Western Ukrainian scholars took part in the Second Congress); and published an informational bulletin in French edited by B. Martos (4 issues, 1929–31), as well as Ye. Chykalenko's memoirs of 1917 (1932), D. Doroshenko's book about Chykalenko (1934), and a detailed report of the Second Congress (1934). The committee arranged for the transfer of part of the archives of the Union for the Liberation of Ukraine to the Museum of Ukraine's Struggle for Independence in Prague, financially supported the Central Union of Ukrainian Students and several scholars, and created a commission to prepare an English-language encyclopedia of Ukraine. The UAK was forced to suspend its activity in 1940, during the German occupation of Prague.

**Ukrainian Academic Gymnasium.** See Academic Gymnasium of Lviv.

**Ukrainian Academic Hromada** (Ukrainska akademichna hromada v Chekhoslovachchyni). The oldest and largest Ukrainian students' organization operating in the interwar Czechoslovak Republic (CR). It was founded in November 1919 as the Ukrainian Academic Circle in Prague, and changed its name to the Ukrainian Academic Hromada in May 1920. Immediately after the First World War all Ukrainian students at Czechoslovakian and Ukrainian schools of higher education in the CR enrolled in the Hromada, with the result that in 1922 there were 1,258 members. By 1923, however, organizations based on regional affiliations, such as the Hromada of Students from Great Ukraine and the Union of Student-Emigrés from Northwestern Ukraine, or on political orientation had broken away and left it with only 321 members. Membership continued to decline steadily and in 1937 it could claim only 40 members. During the Second World War membership increased, and in 1943 there were 164 members. The Hromada had branches outside of Prague, in Josefov, Brno, Mělník, and Příbram. It had separate professional sections and cultural groups. By the late 1920s the Hromada had developed a nationalist orientation, the promoter of which was the *Group of Ukrainian Nationalist Youth. The Hromada formed the basis for the *Central Union of Ukrainian Students, all the presidents of which were members of the Hromada. In 1941 the Hromada was reorganized as a branch of the Nationalist Organization of Ukrainian Students in Germany, which lasted until the arrival of the Soviet army in 1945. The Hromada published the periodical *Ukraïns'kyi student* (1922–4) and the literary almanac *Sterni*. The leading activists in the Hromada were I. Kharak, M. Stakhiv, O. Boidunyk, R. Sushko, B. Oreletsky, O. Boikiv, M. Masiukevych, M. Mukhyn, O. Kandyba, M. Soroka, M. Ryndyk, M. Antonovych, and V. Kunda. Antonovych wrote a history of the Academic Hromada in 1941.

O. Skrypnyk

**Ukrainian Academic Press.** A division of Libraries Unlimited, an American publishing house in Littleton, Colorado, owned by B. *Wynar. Since 1972 the press has issued translations of Ukrainian works: V. Pidmohylny's *Little Touch of Drama* (1972), P. Kulish's *Black Council* (1973), *Modern Ukrainian Short Stories* (ed G.S.N. Luckyj, 1973), D. Čyževs'kyj's *History of Ukrainian Literature* (1975), Ye. Sverstiuk's *Clandestine Essays* (with the Harvard Ukrainian Research Institute, 1976), and M. Kotsiubynsky's *Shadows of Forgotten Ancestors* (1981). It has also published works in English, such as D.H. Struk's *Study of Vasyl' Stefanyk: The Pain at the Heart of Existence* (1973), the second edition of J. Armstrong's *Ukrainian Nationalism* (1980), and Wynar's *Ukraine: A Bibliographic Guide to English-Language Publications* (1990).

**Ukrainian Academic Society in Paris** (Ukrainske akademichne tovarystvo v Paryzhi). An organization founded in 1946 on the initiative of Ukrainian students in Paris. Originally a student aid society, it sponsored many public lectures, assemblies, and conferences on scholarly, cultural, and political topics, as well as concerts and commemorative and literary events, for Ukrainians living in and around Paris. The society was headed by Yu. *Rusov (1946), O. *Shulhyn (1946–60), O. *Kulchytsky (1960), and A. *Vyrsta (from 1960). A Literary and Artistic Club was part of the society from 1955; it was headed by M. Kalytovska (1956–66) and K. Mytrovych (from 1966). The society published an account of the first 12 years of its activity in 1958, and A. Zhukovsky wrote a history of the society in 1969.

**Ukrainian Academy of Agricultural Sciences** (Ukrainska akademiia silskohospodarskykh nauk, or UASHN). An institution of higher learning specializing in agriculture, established in Kiev in 1956. It was the third agricultural center of a national stature, succeeding the *Agricultural Scientific Committee of Ukraine (1918–28) and the *All-Ukrainian Academy of Agricultural Sciences (1926 to mid-1930s), neither of which was mentioned in Soviet sources. The UASHN directed and co-ordinated agricultural research in various teaching and research institutes and on experimental farms. It was divided into departments for crop growing, farm mechanization and electrification, animal husbandry, forestry, hydrotechnology and melioration, and economics and farm management. It oversaw 21 research institutes with their experimental farms and stations, 25 oblast research stations, and a central research library. It also included a teaching division that became the *Ukrainian Agricultural Academy. The staff of the UASHN consisted of 22 full members and 22 corresponding members. It published the bimonthly *Dopovidi UASHN* (from 1958) and the monthly *Visnyk sil's'kohospodars'koï nauky* (from 1957) and had its own publishing house. In 1962 the system of agricultural research was reorganized; research institutes in Ukraine were placed directly under the Ministry of Agriculture of the Ukrainian SSR, and the UASHN was dissolved.

**Ukrainian Academy of Arts.** See Ukrainian State Academy of Arts.

**Ukrainian Academy of Arts and Sciences.** The official English name of the Ukrainian Free Academy of Sciences (Ukrainska vilna akademiia nauk, or UVAN). UVAN is an academy of Ukrainian émigré scholars, founded in November 1945 in Augsburg, Germany. At its founding meeting UVAN was defined as the Ukrainian academy-in-exile, inheriting the traditions of VUAN, whose important work began in the 1920s and was quashed by the Stalinist terror (see *Academy of Sciences of the Ukrainian SSR [now the Academy of Sciences of Ukraine]). The first president of UVAN was the historian D. *Doroshenko. Initially it was made up of 17 professional groups, representing 150 scholars and scientists. It organized joint conferences and annual conferences in Shevchenko studies with the help of the Society of Friends of UVAN, directed by V. Mudry. The first UVAN publications were an informational bulletin (1946–7), a chronicle (1947–8), a book on Kiev's historical maps by P. Kurinny and O. Povstenko (1947), and a book on Hetman D. Apostol and his age by B. Krupnytsky (1948). In April 1948 the first 24 UVAN full members were elected at a conference in Regensburg.

After most postwar Ukrainian DPs and refugees emigrated from Germany to the New World in 1947–8, the UVAN center in Augsburg lost its importance. In 1949 the presidium was transferred to Winnipeg, where Doroshenko had settled, and named in English the Ukrainian Free Academy of Sciences in Canada. Doroshenko was succeeded as president by L. *Biletsky (1951–4), J. *Rudnyckyj (1954–74), A. *Baran (1974–7, 1980–3), J. *Rozumnyj (1977–80), and M. *Marunchak (since 1983). In the 1980s UVAN acquired its current English name. It was divided into social sciences, humanities, and mathematics and natural sciences sections and had its own library, archives, and Ukrainian War Museum (Gen M. Sadovsky's collection) in Winnipeg. It has published booklet series, such as Slavistica (begun in Augsburg, 87 issues, 1948–86), Onomastica (50 issues, 1951–76), Literatura (11 issues, 1949–70), Litopys (29 issues by 1983), and Ukraïnski vcheni (19 Issues, 1949–80), on Ukrainian scholars; Rudnyckyj and D. Sokulsky's annual bibliography *Ukrainica Canadiana* (1953–72); T. Shevchenko's *Kobzar* (4 vols, 1952–4), edited and annotated by Biletsky; Rudnyckyj's materials on Ukrainian-Canadian folklore and dialectology (9 fascicles, 1956–63) and *Etymological Dictionary of the Ukrainian Language* (2 vols in fascicles, 1962–75); Marunchak's *The Ukrainian Canadians: A History* (1970; rev edn 1982), studies on

The building of the Ukrainian Academy of Arts and Sciences in Manhattan

the history of Ukrainians in Canada (5 vols, 1964–80), book on Ukrainians in the USSR outside Ukraine (1974), and biographic dictionary of Ukrainian Canadians (1986); and several other publications and collections of articles. In 1989 UVAN in Canada had over 60 full members.

UVAN members who settled in the United States established their own organization (in English, the Ukrainian Academy of Arts and Sciences in the US) and foundation in New York City in 1950. UVAN groups were also organized in Detroit (1955), Denver (1955), Washington (1956), and Philadelphia (1970s). In 1961 UVAN purchased its own building in Manhattan. Its presidents have been M. *Vetukhiv (1950–9), G.Y. *Shevelov (1959–61, 1979–84), O. *Arkhimovych (1961–70), O. *Ohloblyn (1970–9), Ya. *Bilinsky (1984–90), and M. Boretsky (1990–2), and Marko *Antonovych (since 1993). The UVAN in the US has consisted of historical, ancient history, literary-philological, ethnographic, pedagogical, philosophical, bibliographic, economics-law, biological-medical, musicological, and physics-chemistry-mathematics-technology sections; a fine arts group; the Commission for the Preservation, Study, and Publication of the Heritage of V. Vynnychenko (chaired by H. Kostiuk); the Shevchenko Institute; and the Archeological-Anthropological Institute. In 1986 it had 64 full members (many of them professors at American universities), 80 corresponding members, and 23 scholarly associates. Its library (over 50,000 vols) and museum-archive (the most valuable archive outside Ukraine) have been directed by V. *Miiakovsky (who began them in Augsburg) and V. Omelchenko (since 1972).

The UVAN in the US has issued over 90 publications, including 16 volumes of its English-language *Annals (from 1951) and several other collections of articles; 10 issues of the annual *Shevchenko* (1952–64); O. Powstenkos's study *The Cathedral of St Sophia in Kiev* (1954); editions of V. Pidmohylny's *Misto* (The City, 1954) and M. Kulish's plays and letters (1955); Ye. Chykalenko's memoirs (1955); D. Chyzhevsky's history of Ukrainian literature (1956); editions of S. Petliura's articles and letters and documents pertaining to him (2 vols, 1956, 1979); Vynnychenko's previously unpublished works (1960, 1971–2, 1988) and diary (2 vols, 1980, 1983); editions of literary studies by M. Plevako (1961) and P. Fylypovych (1981); collections of Ukrainian folk melodies compiled by Z. Lysko (6 vols, 1964–71); books on the artists M. Radysh (1966), V. Tsymbal (1972), and P. Andrusiv (1980); I. Sonevytsky's book on A. Vedel and his musical legacy (1966); a collection of articles on the Silskyi Hospodar society (1970); O. Kosach-Kryvyniuk's chronology of the life and work of Lesia Ukrainka (1970); an edition of O. Koshyts's religious musical works (1970); V. Pavlovsky's book on V. Krychevsky (1974); S. Pohorily's book on Vynnychenko's unpublished novels (1981); and D. Doroshenko's book on Hetman P. Doroshenko (1985). The academy has also organized lectures, seminars, conferences, commemorative events, art exhibitions, concerts, recitals, and summer seminars (near Hunter, New York).

The few UVAN members who remained in Germany after 1948 were concentrated in Munich. They were led by P. *Kurinny until 1972, after which the European UVAN ceased activity. Yu. *Blokhyn has been the Munich representative of the UVAN in the United States since 1976.

BIBLIOGRAPHY
*Desiatylittia Ukraïns'koï vil'noï akademiï nauk u SShA, 1950–1960* (New York 1961)
*Iuvileine vydannia, prysviachene dvadtsiatylittiu diial'nosti UVAN, 1945–1965* (New York 1967)
*A Guide to the Archival and Manuscript Collection of the Ukrainian Academy of Arts and Sciences in the US, New York City: A Detailed Inventory*, comp Yu. Boshyk et al (Edmonton 1988)

**Ukrainian Academy of Sciences.** See Academy of Sciences of the Ukrainian SSR.

**Ukrainian Agrarian party** (Ukrainska khliborobska partiia, or UAP). A numerically small liberal-democratic party representing the national and class interests of the Ukrainian peasantry, founded in Polish-ruled Galicia in 1922. Its leading members were the writers M. *Yatskiv and S. *Tverdokhlib, Rev M. Ilkiv, and S. Danylovych, and its organs were *Ridnyi krai* (Lviv) and *Pravo narodu* (Kolomyia). Whereas all other Ukrainian parties and most Ukrainians in Galicia, regarding the Polish occupation of Galicia as illegal, boycotted the 1922 elections to the Polish Sejm, the UAP promoted co-operation with the Polish regime to bring about economic reconstruction and agrarian and political reforms, and, with government support, fielded candidates in the elections. While campaigning Tverdokhlib was assassinated by the underground Ukrainian Military Organization, but five UAP candidates (Rev Ilkiv, I. Dutchak, O. Zalutsky, I. Kravchyshyn, and S. Mel-

nyk) were elected to the Sejm, where they constituted the Ukrainian Agrarian Club. After the elections the party's support (primarily in Pokutia) rapidly declined. In mid-1924 the club in the Sejm split into anti- (Ilkiv, Dutchak) and pro-government (Zalutsky, Kravchyshyn, Melnyk) factions. The latter faction later left the club, and in 1926 Zalutsky and Kravchyshyn left the UAP and joined the Ukrainian People's Union (UPU), newly founded in Stanyslaviv by Danylovych. In the 1928 elections the UPU received a paltry 8,887 votes.

R. Senkus

The forestry building of the Ukrainian Agricultural Academy in Kiev

**Ukrainian Agricultural Academy** (Ukrainska silskohospodarska akademiia, or USHA). An institution of higher learning, formerly under the USSR Ministry of Agriculture. It was formed in Kiev in 1954 through the merger of the Kiev Agricultural Institute, which had been established in 1922 out of the agricultural department of the Kiev Polytechnical Institute (est 1898), and the Kiev Institute of Forest Management, which had been established in 1930 out of the forest engineering faculty (est 1923) of the Kiev Agricultural Institute. In 1957 the Kiev Veterinary Institute (est 1921) was brought under the USHA. The academy has 10 departments for agronomy, agricultural chemistry and soil science, plant protection, zoological engineering, veterinary medicine, the mechanization of agriculture, the automation of agriculture, the electrification of agriculture, forest management, and economics. It has a graduate school, three research stations (agronomy, animal husbandry, and forestry), a historical museum, and a botanical garden. Its library contains approx 900,000 volumes. The enrollment in 1986 was 14,000, half of whom were correspondence students, and the faculty members numbered close to 700. The USHA continues to publish the irregular collection *Naukovi pratsi*, inaugurated by the Kiev Agricultural Institute in 1940.

**Ukrainian Agricultural Bank** (Ukrainskyi silsko-hospodarskyi bank, or Ukrsilbank). A co-operative joint-stock bank established in Kharkiv in 1923 to provide financial assistance and credit for peasants and agricultural co-operatives. Its shareholders were the State Bank, the Ukrainian SSR people's commissariats of land affairs and finances, gubernia agricultural banks, the Central Agricultural Bank, and other institutions. In 1930 it was transformed into a branch of the All-Union Agricultural Co-operative Collective-Farm Bank, and in the succeeding year it was abolished.

**Ukrainian Alliance in Czechoslovakia** (Ukrainske obiednannia v Chekhoslovachchyni). A civic organization founded in 1928 in Prague by circles opposed to the Ukrainian Committee in Czechoslovakia. The alliance was dominated by UNR supporters, who worked closely with the *Museum of Ukraine's Struggle for Independence. It had branches in Poděbrady and Mělník. Its president until its dissolution in 1939 was A. Yakovliv.

*Ukrainian American, The.* A pro-Soviet monthly magazine founded in New York in 1965. In 1977 it merged with *Ukrains'ki visti*, and since then it has appeared as a monthly supplement to the paper. The editors have been E. Senuk and W. Kowalchuk.

**Ukrainian American Association of University Professors** (Ukrainska amerykanska asotsiiatsiia universytetskykh profesoriv). A professional association of Ukrainians teaching at American universities and colleges. Founded in 1961, it grew from 45 original members to 300 in 1980 and has been headed by M. Melnyk, M. Pap, P. Stercho, Ju. Fedynskyj, M. Stepanenko, I. Kamenetsky, and L. Wynar. In 1971 the association established a publication fund for its members and began publishing an irregular newsletter, *Profesors'ki visti*.

**Ukrainian American Bar Association** (Asotsiiatsiia ukrainsko-amerykanskykh advokativ). An organization of Ukrainian-American lawyers founded in September 1977. The organization has been involved in defending human-rights activists in Ukraine, opposing the denaturalization of wrongfully accused Ukrainians in the United States and the use of Soviet-supplied evidence in American courts, and lobbying the United States government to stop the transfer of estates to the USSR. The presidents of the organization have included V. Borowsky, M. Smorodsky, B. Porytko, and B. Shandor.

**Ukrainian American Coordinating Council** (Ukrainska amerykanska koordynatsiina rada, or UAKR). An umbrella organization of Ukrainian civic, cultural, and political associations in the United States, formed on 15 May 1983 by the Committee for Law and Order in the *Ukrainian Congress Committee of America (UKKA). The Committee for Law and Order was set up by the 27 organizations that walked out at the 13th Congress of Ukrainian Americans in Philadelphia (10–12 October 1980) in protest over what was regarded as an illegal seizure of power in the UKKA by the organizations of the *Ukrainian Liberation Front. When negotiations with the new executive of the UKKA to rectify the statutory and procedural violations perpetrated at the 13th Congress broke down, the Committee for Law and Order set up the UAKR to continue the tradition of the pre–13th Congress UKKA. This decision and the council's statute were approved by member organizations on 1 October 1983. UAKR was admitted to the World Congress of Free Ukrainians in November 1983. At the First Convention of the UAKR, held in Philadelphia on 1 October 1985, delegates of 49 national organizations and 22 branches elected a new executive with J. *Flis as president.

**Ukrainian American Veterans** (Ukrainsko-amerykanski veterany, or UAV). A national association of servicemen of Ukrainian descent who have served in the armed forces of the United States. It was founded at the First National Convention in Philadelphia in 1948 by several independent local organizations, the first of which was the Ukrainian American Veterans' League of Philadelphia (est in the 1920s by veterans of the Spanish-American War and the First World War). The UAV lobbies for veteran programs, preserves the memory of fallen soldiers, and co-operates with Ukrainian community organizations on cultural and educational projects. It is a member of the World Council of Ukrainian Combatant Organizations and until 1980 was a member of the Ukrainian Congress Committee of America. Today UAV represents 21 local posts in four states with almost 600 members. It published the monthly *Bugler* (est 1946) and has begun publishing the quarterly UAV *Tribune* (1989). Its presidents are elected at annual conventions and have included M. Chaika (1980–2), E. Zetick (1982–4), J. Brega (1984–6), A. Kobryn (1986–8), J. Fedoryczuk, and D. Bykovetz, Jr. The UAV National Ladies' Auxiliary was organized in 1974.

**Ukrainian American Youth for the Rebirth of Ukraine.** See Young Ukrainian Nationalists.

**Ukrainian Art Studio** (Ukrainska mystetska studiia). An art school established in Philadelphia in 1952. Its creation was initiated by V. *Galan, and for its first decade

A gathering of artists at the Ukrainian Art Studio in 1964. Sitting, from left: Sviatoslav Hordynsky, Oleksa Hryshchenko, Mrs Hryshchenko; standing: Petro Andrusiv, Stepan Rozhok, A. Kyryliuk, V. Doroshenko, R. Vasylyshyn-Harmash, Mykhailo Dmytrenko, Petro Mehyk, Petro Kapshuchenko

the studio was housed in the building of the United Ukrainian American Relief Committee. The studio's director until 1992 was P. *Mehyk. Its curriculum includes drawing, painting, printmaking, sculpture, modeling, ceramics, and art history. By 1980 it had 450 graduates, including the artists R. Luchakovska and S. Lada. Its faculty has included P. Andrusiv, A. Darahan, V. Doroshenko, P. Kapshuchenko, H. Luzhnytsky, M. Mukhyn, S. Rozhok, and V. Simiantsev. Exhibitions of works by over 75 artists and student shows have been held in the studio's building (bought in 1961). The school is supported by a group of patrons that has been headed by Rev Yu. Hirniak, B. Luchakovsky, I. Mazepa, and O. Zelinsky.

**Ukrainian Artistic Alliance** (Ukrainske mystetske obiednannia, or UMO). An organization of realist artists that was active in Kiev from 1929 to 1931. Its membership consisted of older artists who had left the *Association of Artists of Red Ukraine, such as F. Krychevsky, K. Trokhymenko, I. Izhakevych, M. Kozyk, F. Konovaliuk, V. Korovchynsky, H. Svitlytsky, O. Syrotenko, T. Tymoshchuk, I. Khvorostetsky, and I. Shulha. UMO promoted 'art among the masses.' This fact did not prevent its denunciation by Stalinist critics, who forced UMO to disband.

**Ukrainian Artists' Association in the USA** (Obiednannia mysttsiv ukraintsiv v Amerytsi, or OMUA). An organization of Ukrainian émigré artists, formed in New York in 1952 to promote Ukrainian art outside Ukraine. Its Philadelphia branch (est 1952) has overseen the *Ukrainian Art Studio and published the magazine *Notatky z mystetstva/Ukrainian Art Digest. Its New York branch (est 1954) has included the Society of Young Ukrainian Artists (est 1955) and a student section (est 1964). OMUA has organized annual group exhibitions, sometimes with the *Ukrainian Association of Creative Artists in Canada, and solo shows. It maintains a gallery on its premises in New York. In 1966 OMUA had 59 members. Its presidents have been S. Lytvynenko (1952–6 and 1963–4), S. Hordynsky (1956–63), P. Andrusiv (1964–5), L. Kuzma, and M. Chereshnovsky. Its secretaries have been R. Pachovsky (1953–65) and B. Vasylyshyn.

**Ukrainian Association of Artists** (Ukrainska spilka obrazotvorchykh mysttsiv, or USOM). An organization of Ukrainian émigré artists, established in Munich in January 1947. Most of the members were in *displaced persons' camps in Germany or Austria. They included P. Andrusiv, V. Balias, S. Burachok (vice-president), M. Butovych, V. Diadyniuk, J. Hnizdovsky, S. Hordynsky, M. Hotsii, M. Dmytrenko, I. Keivan, E. Kozak (president), H. Kruk, Yu. Kulchytsky, V. Lasovsky, O. Liaturynska, S. Lutsyk, S. Lytvynenko, H. Mazepa, P. Mehyk, M. (B.) Mukhyn, M. Novytska, A. Pavlos, L. Perfetsky, O. Povstenko, and V. Sichynsky. USOM had as its aim the preservation and cultivation of Ukrainian art forms banned under Soviet domination. It participated in the 1947 International Displaced Persons' Art Exhibition in Munich, for which it supplied 290 works by 48 artists; held several of its own exhibitions; and published the magazine Ukrains'ke mystetstvo (1947, 2 issues, ed Dmytrenko) and books on Ukrainian art and sculpture. USOM ceased functioning after most of its members emigrated to the New World, and it was officially dissolved in 1951.

**Ukrainian Association of Creative Artists in Canada** (Ukrainska spilka obrazotvorchykh mysttsiv v Kanadi, or USOM). An organization of Ukrainian émigré artists, established in 1955 out of the art section of the Ukrainian Literary and Artistic Club in Toronto. Branches were later founded in Montreal and Edmonton. The society has held art exhibitions, public lectures, and discussions on art. One of its founders, M. Dmytrenko, served as the first president. The other presidents have been B. Stebelsky, I. Keivan, and O. Telizhyn. In 1970 USOM had about 30 members, among them A. Kyryliuk, N. Mudryk-Mryts, D. Kravtsiv-Yemets, and M. Styranka. Most of the members lived in Toronto.

**Ukrainian Association of Disabled Veterans** (Ukrainska spilka voiennykh invalidiv). An organization of Ukrainian veterans founded in Kalisz, Poland, in 1920. It operated a home for disabled veterans and published the journal Ukraïns'kyi invalid. It had over 1,500 registered members and was active until 1939.

**Ukrainian Association of Marxist-Leninist Scientific Research Institutes.** See All-Ukrainian Association of Marxist-Leninist Scientific Research Institutes.

**Ukrainian Association of Victims of Russian Communist Terror** (Soiuz ukrainstsiv zhertv rosiiskoho komunistychnoho terroru, or SUZhERO). Initiated in 1950 in Toronto by S. *Pidhainy, its first head, the society consists of survivors of Soviet repression. It is dedicated to publicizing the misdeeds of the Soviet regime in Ukraine and has prepared The Black Deeds of the Kremlin: A White Book (2 vols, 1953) and other publications. The group has a democratic orientation and supports the UNR government-in-exile. At one time there were up to 15 branches in Canada.

**Ukrainian Autocephalous Orthodox church** (Ukrainska Avtokefalna Pravoslavna Tserkva, or UAOC). The national Ukrainian Orthodox church, independent (autocephalous) of all other church formations and with its own administrative structure and hierarchy.

The movement for an independent Ukrainian Orthodox church gained strength following the Revolution of 1917 and the rebirth of a Ukrainian state. The *All-Ukrainian Orthodox Church Council, with representatives of the clergy and laity from throughout Ukraine, began the process of Ukrainizing church life and establishing a permanent organizational structure for the Ukrainian church. The *autocephaly of the church was proclaimed at a May 1920 *sobor called by the All-Ukrainian Orthodox Church Council (a 1919 decree on church autocephaly by the Ukrainian National Republic had never been implemented owing to the upheavals of the Ukrainian-Soviet War). The church's leaders, however, could not find a bishop to assume spiritual leadership or consecrate a new hierarchy for the church. The difficulty was resolved only at the first All-Ukrainian Orthodox Church sobor in Kiev on 14–30 October 1921, when the delegates decided to revive an ancient Alexandrian rite, which did not require the participation of other bishops, to consecrate V. *Lypkivsky (as the church's first metropolitan) and N. *Sharaievsky. Soon after, these two bishops elevated several other bishops to the ranks of the new hierarchy.

Hierarchs of the Ukrainian Autocephalous Orthodox church in 1926

A period of rapid growth for the UAOC began. By early 1924 the church had approx 30 bishops, 1,500 priests and deacons, and 1,100 parishes. At its peak it had as many as 6 million followers in Ukraine. It also began to spread its influence to Ukrainian communities abroad; E. *Batchinsky was designated as its representative in Western Europe, and Bishop I. *Teodorovych was dispatched to minister to Ukrainians in North America. Administratively, it was divided into okruhas, each headed by a bishop and okruha sobor. The church was strongest in Podilia, Kiev, Uman, and Cherkasy okruhas and in the city of Kiev itself. In 1927–8 it published a monthly journal, *Tserkva i zhyttia.

The UAOC was closely allied with the Ukrainian national revival of the revolutionary period and the 1920s. It was primarily supported by the Ukrainian intelligentsia (and lower clergy) and envisioned playing a major role in raising the national consciousness of the masses. Politically it was committed to the social reforms of the UNR (V. *Chekhivsky, the most influential ideologue of the UAOC, had headed the Council of Ministers of the UNR). The theology and ecclesiology of the UAOC, as it evolved in the 1920s, was distinguished by several characteristics. One of the major tenets of the church was an insistence on the separation of church and state – largely a reaction to the state of affairs under tsarist rule, when the Orthodox church was essentially an arm of the state and a pillar of the autocratic system. Second, the leaders of the church were committed to the independence (autocephaly) of the UAOC; their argument was that the incorporation of the Ukrainian church into the Russian Orthodox church in the 17th century had been uncanonical. They called for jurisdictional independence from the Moscow patriarch and the creation of an independent hierarchy, equal to and recognized by the entire Orthodox community. A third feature of the new church was a commitment to conciliarism or *sobor rule. This concept stressed the complete democratization and decentralization of church life and the active participation of the laity in decision-making, with sobors, attended by elected delegates of lay and clergy, replacing bishops as the highest authority in the church. Another important feature of the UAOC was the Ukrainization of the church rite, including the use of the vernacular (in place of Church Slavonic) and the revitalization of Ukrainian liturgical and ecclesiastical traditions (see *Church rite). Finally, the ideology of the church stressed the Christianization of all aspects of life.

The canonical reforms adopted by the UAOC – the method used to consecrate its hierarchy, the introduction of an elected and married episcopate, the insistence on lay participation in church affairs, and so on – had tremendous ramifications for the church. These reforms, however, impeded relations with other Orthodox churches, even though the UAOC stressed its adherence to traditional Orthodoxy. The church was denounced as noncanonical by the Patriarchal Russian Orthodox church, and its leaders were ridiculed as *samosviaty* (self-consecrated). The Patriarchal church was especially concerned because the UAOC succeeded in acquiring many churches, including the St Sophia Cathedral in Kiev, and thereby posed a threat to its dominance.

From the outset the Soviet authorities sought to discredit all churches in Ukraine and limit their influence. The campaign against the UAOC involved exploiting internal divisions by supporting dissenting factions within the UAOC (eg, the Active Church of Christ) and favoring the more pro-Russian competing churches that emerged in the 1920s (eg, the *Living church, which initially sought to subsume the UAOC, and the *Sobor-Ruled Episcopal church). In 1926 a major GPU crackdown on the UAOC began, and V. Lypkivsky was arrested and placed under house arrest. At the Second All-Ukrainian Church Council he was replaced as metropolitan by M. *Boretsky. The repression was eased for a brief time but resumed in full force in 1929. The church was accused of collaborating with the *Union for the Liberation of Ukraine, and many of its leaders (including Chekhivsky) were arrested. At an extraordinary sobor held in January 1930 the UAOC formally abolished itself, although some 300 of its parishes reconstituted themselves as the Ukrainian Orthodox church under Metropolitan I. *Pavlovsky (this body was finally destroyed in 1936). The 1930s brought the physical liquidation of the entire hierarchy of the UAOC and many of its priests and faithful.

**The Second World War.** Although the UAOC was destroyed in Soviet Ukraine, Ukrainian Orthodoxy survived in those territories that came under Polish rule in the interwar period – Volhynia, Polisia, and the Kholm region. The *Polish Autocephalous Orthodox church, although not a specifically Ukrainian institution, permitted the use of the Ukrainian language and adherence to Ukrainian religious customs. One of its hierarchs, P. *Sikorsky, was of Ukrainian origin, and the metropolitan, D. *Valedinsky, supported the re-establishment of an independent Orthodox church in Soviet Ukraine. Following the German invasion of Ukraine in June 1941, efforts were immediately begun to revive the church there. Valedinsky assumed spiritual authority over the reborn UAOC, which was administered by Sikorsky (who was named metropolitan) and supported by Bishops I. *Ohiienko and P. Vydybida-Rudenko of the Orthodox church in Poland (within the Generalgouvernement). New hierarchs were consecrated in Kiev in February 1942 (N. Abramovych, who was designated head of the church in the Reichskommissariat Ukraine, and I. Huba) and in May 1942 (M. *Skrypnyk, M. Khoroshy, S. Haievsky, and H. Ohiichuk). The reborn UAOC, although disavowing the radical canonical reforms of its predecessor of the 1920s, made accommodations for surviving clergy of the church. It grew quickly and soon claimed some 500 parishes.

The UAOC faced competition from another church in Ukraine, the *Ukrainian Autonomous Orthodox church. Headed by Metropolitan O. *Hromadsky, this church rejected the UAOC of the 1920s as uncanonical and would not accept former clergy from that church unless they were re-ordained. The autonomous church also recognized the spiritual authority of the Moscow patriarch over Ukraine, but considered this authority suspended as long as the patriarch was under Soviet domination. In general this church appealed to the Russian and Russified population of Ukraine, while the UAOC was closely tied to the Ukrainian national movement. Although some attempts were made to unite the two jurisdictions in 1941–2, these ultimately failed.

**The diaspora.** With the Soviet reoccupation of all of Ukraine by mid-1944, almost all the bishops and many of the priests and faithful of the UAOC fled to the West, and all the remaining parishes were dissolved or forced to join the Russian Patriarchal church in Ukraine. The UAOC continued its activity among Ukrainian émigrés in Western Europe under the leadership of Sikorsky. By 1947 it numbered 71 parishes with 103 priests and 18 deacons. The *Theological Academy of the UAOC was established in Munich to train priests, and a theological institute was founded. The church split at the Ashchaffenburg Conference of August 1947, when a number of priests and faithful followed Archbishop H. Ohiichuk to form the *Ukrainian Autocephalous Orthodox Church (Conciliar). Followers of this church strictly adhered to the reforms of the UAOC of the 1920s, especially the principle of rule by the sobor, and rejected the authority of the Synod of Bishops of the UAOC, which had emerged as the church's highest authority.

The UAOC in Western Europe declined with the emigration of many Ukrainians to North America, where most Orthodox emigrants joined the existing *Ukrainian Orthodox Church of Canada or the *Ukrainian Orthodox Church in the USA (UOC-USA). New UAOC parishes, however, were established in Great Britain, Australia and New Zealand, and South America. Sikorsky, who died in 1953, was succeeded by N. Abramovych (1953–69) and then M. Skrypnyk, who is also metropolitan of the UOC-USA. Other hierarchs of the UAOC in the 1950s to 1980s included O. Ivaniuk (of Western Europe) S. *Haievsky, V. *Solovii, D. Burtan, I. Danyliuk (Australia and New Zealand), M. Solovii, O. Pylypenko (South America), and V. Didovych (Western Europe, Australia). In the late 1980s the UAOC had 30 parishes, 11 priests, and 8,000 faithful in Western Europe; 23 parishes, 8 priests, and 4,000 faithful in Great Britain; 15 parishes, 8 priests, and 4,200 faithful in Australia and New Zealand; and 22 parishes, 10 priests, and 30,000 faithful in South America and a hierarchy composed of Skrypnyk, Bishop A. *Dubliansky (of Western Europe), and Bishop P. Ishchuk (of South America). Church organs are *Ridna tserkva (Germany), *Vidomosti Heneral'noho tserkovnoho upravlinnia UAPTs u Velykii Brytanii (Great Britain), *Pratsia i zhyttia (Australia), and *Pravoslavne zhyttia (Belgium).

**Revival in Ukraine.** The political liberalization of the late 1980s permitted the rebirth of the UAOC in Ukraine. Beginning in 1987 with the parish of SS Peter and Paul in Lviv, a number of parishes and priests seceded from the official Russian Orthodox church (ROC) and re-established the UAOC. In October 1989 I. Bodnarchuk, a bishop of the ROC, announced his resignation from that church and agreed to head the UAOC. Subsequently, assisted by a retired bishop of the ROC, he consecrated several new bishops. Relations were established with the UAOC abroad, and Skrypnyk was elected Patriarch of Kiev and all Ukraine at the first sobor of the reborn UAOC, in June 1990 (he was installed the following November). By the end of 1990 the church hierarchy was composed of Patriarch Skrypnyk, Metropolitan Bodnarchuk of Lviv, and the bishops of Ternopil and Buchach, Ivano-Frankivske and Kolomyia, Bila Tserkva and Vyshhorod, Chernivtsi and Khotyn, Lutske and Volodymyr-Volynskyi, Uman, and Rivne and Ostrih. A seminary was established in Ivano-Frankivske in 1991, and several journals and other publications were initiated. That year the UAOC had 944 parishes in Ukraine.

BIBLIOGRAPHY

Heyer, F. *Die Orthodoxe Kirche in der Ukraine von 1917 bis 1945* (Köln–Braunsfeld 1953)

Yavdas, M. *Ukrainian Autocephalous Orthodox Church, 1921–1936* (Munich–Ingolstadt 1956)

Lypkivs'kyi, V. *Istoriia Ukraïns'koï Pravoslavnoï Tserkvy, rozdil 7: Vidrodzhennia Ukraïns'koï Tserkvy* (Winnipeg 1961)

Vlasovs'kyi, I. *Narys istoriï Ukraïns'koï Pravoslavnoï Tserkvy*, vol 4, pts 1–2 (South Bound Brook, NJ 1961, 1966)

Bociurkiw, B. 'The Ukrainian Autocephalous Orthodox Church, 1920–1930: A Case Study in Religious Modernization,' in *Religion and Modernization in the Soviet Union*, ed D. Dunn (Boulder, Colo 1977)

Armstrong, J. *Ukrainian Nationalism*, 2nd edn (Littleton, Colo 1980)

Zinkevych, O.; Voronyn, O. (eds). *Martyrolohiia ukraïns'kykh tserkov*, vol 1, *Ukraïns'ka Pravoslavna Tserkva* (Toronto–Baltimore 1987)

Burko, O. *Ukraïns'ka Avtokefal'na Pravoslavna Tserkva* (South Bound Brook, NJ 1988)

A. Zhukovsky

## Ukrainian Autocephalous Orthodox Church (Conciliar) (Ukrainska Avtokefalna Pravoslavna Tserkva – Sobornopravna, or UAOC[C]). A church formed in August 1947 in Aschaffenburg, Germany, following a split in the Ukrainian Autocephalous Orthodox church (UAOC). It rejected the authority of Metropolitan P. Sikorsky of the UAOC, who had disavowed many of the radical reforms adopted by the UAOC in the 1920s under Metropolitan V. Lypkivsky. Initially it submitted itself to the jurisdiction of Archbishop I. Teodorovych, but in October 1947 Archbishop H. *Ohiichuk became its ruling hierarch. It stressed its support for the reforms of the UAOC and especially the primacy of the church sobor or council as the highest authority in the church (over the episcopate). After the emigration of most of its supporters to the United States, Chicago became its center. In Great Britain six parishes, led by I. Hubarzhevsky and then Bishop I. Hrytsenko, also joined the UAOC(C), as did a few parishes in Australia (formerly led by Bishop D. Burtan) and South America. In the 1960s the church in the United States had 10 parishes served by 10 priests, and nearly 2,000 faithful. In 1973 it split into two factions, one under Ohiichuk and the other (the smaller) under Archbishop O. Pylypenko of Argentina and then Bishop P. Kolisnyk. The two factions reunited in 1983, and new bishops were ordained, but they subsequently split again. In 1989 the two factions of the UAOC(C) claimed 5 bishops, 15 parishes, 12 priests, 2 deacons, and a few thousand faithful. The official press organ of the majority faction of the church, *Pravoslavnyi ukraïnets'*, was published irregularly in Germany and then in Chicago and Detroit; the opposition faction, which was grouped around the Metropolitan Lypkivsky Ukrainian Orthodox Brotherhood, published the journal *Tserkva i zhyttia* (1957–77).

## Ukrainian Autocephalous Orthodox Church in Exile (Ukrainska Avtokefalna Pravoslavna Tserkva v Ekzyli). A church founded in New York in 1951 by Archbishop P. *Vydybida-Rudenko. It traced its roots to the Polish Au-

Participants in the 1976 sobor of the Ukrainian Autocephalous Orthodox Church (Conciliar) in Detroit. Sitting, in the center: Archbishop Oleksii Pylypenko and Bishop Petro Kolisnyk

tocephalous Orthodox church under Metropolitan D. Valedinsky. Vydybida-Rudenko questioned the canonicity of the Ukrainian Autocephalous Orthodox church and placed his church under the jurisdiction of the patriarch of Constantinople in 1954, thereby maintaining ties with the Standing Conference of Canonical Orthodox Bishops of America. The church based itself on the 1924 *Tomos* of the patriarch of Constantinople, which had granted autocephaly to the Orthodox church in Poland. In the 1960s it had 2 bishops (Vydybida-Rudenko and I. *Huba), 16 parishes, 25 priests, and close to 5,000 faithful, mainly postwar immigrants from Volhynia and central Ukraine. The church organ, *Zhyttia i tserkva* (1956–67), was edited by S. Kindzeriavy-Pastukhiv. After the deaths of Huba (1966) and Vydybida-Rudenko (1971), the church was administered by Kindzeriavy-Pastukhiv until 1980, when it ceased to exist and the majority of the clergy and faithful joined the Ukrainian Orthodox Church in the USA.

## Ukrainian Autonomists-Federalists' Association

(Spilka ukrainskykh avtonomistiv-federalistiv). An organization of liberal conservatives, with the largest proportion of professionals in its cadres of all the Ukrainian political parties. The association revived the program of the prewar *Ukrainian Democratic Radical party, which in 1908–17 had been a part of the Society of Ukrainian Progressives (TUP). At its congress on 7–8 April 1917 TUP transformed itself into the Ukrainian Autonomists-Federalists' Association, which took part in the early work of the Central Rada (April–June 1917) and later changed its name to the *Ukrainian Party of Socialists-Federalists. Among its leaders were S. Yefremov, A. Nikovsky, I. Shrah, O. Lototsky, and P. Stebnytsky.

## Ukrainian Autonomous Orthodox church

(Ukrainska Avtonomna Pravoslavna Tserkva). An Orthodox church jurisdiction that existed during the German occupation of Volhynia and eastern Ukraine in the Second World War. It was headed by Metropolitan and Exarch O. *Hromadsky, formerly a bishop of the Polish Autocephalous Orthodox church (PAOC). It was formed in August 1941 by a synod of bishops held at the Pochaiv Monastery. The church based itself on a 1918 statute of the Russian Orthodox church that had granted it some measure of autonomy. It accepted the canonical dependence of the Ukrainian church on the Moscow patriarchate, but considered this relationship suspended as long as the patriarch was subject to Soviet control. The Autonomous church attracted the conservative Orthodox faithful as well as the Russified segment of the population, especially the clergy. Its hierarchy (a total of 15 bishops) included bishops of the PAOC as well as several bishops consecrated by the Russian Orthodox church during the Soviet occupation of Western Ukraine (eg, P. Rudyk, archimandrite of the Pochaiv Monastery). Some monasteries of the Volhynia and the Dnieper regions also joined the Autonomous church, among them the Kievan Cave Monastery.

Throughout the war the Autonomous church competed with the *Ukrainian Autocephalous Orthodox church for predominance in Ukrainian Orthodox church life. The competition was encouraged by the German authorities, who generally favored the Autonomous church but feared the emergence of a united church. In October 1942 a joint conference of the two churches (attended by Metropolitan Hromadsky, Archbishop N. Abramovych, and Bishop M. Skrypnyk) was held at the Pochaiv Monastery. Steps were taken to unite the two jurisdictions. Union would have involved de facto recognition of the autocephaly of the Ukrainian Orthodox church and the calling of a joint synod of Ukrainian bishops. Most Autonomist bishops, however, as well as the German authorities, were hostile to the idea, and the plans were never realized. Hromadsky was unintentionally killed in an ambush of Ukrainian partisans in May 1943, and he was replaced by Archbishop Rudyk. Tensions continued between the churches until 1944, when the Soviet army retook Ukraine. Most of the Autonomous church bishops emigrated to the West and joined the Synodal Russian Orthodox Church in Exile. Those bishops and priests who remained in Ukraine joined the Russian Orthodox church under the Moscow patriarch.

A. Zhukovsky

**Ukrainian Auxiliary Police.** A security force established by the German occupational regime in the General-gouvernement. It was active from the end of 1939 (under the name Ukrainian Police) in areas with a predominantly Ukrainian population. The force was introduced into Galicia on 18 August 1941 (after the Generalgouvernement had expanded to incorporate Germany's new possessions) instead of a Ukrainian national militia. By the later phases of the war the Ukrainian Auxiliary Police numbered more than 5,000 men, including 120 officers. The intended number of 6,000 police for Galicia was never reached because of a dearth of volunteers.

The force functioned at a municipal level, and its jurisdiction was not limited to Ukrainians. Nevertheless it often found itself in conflict with other formations, such as the Bahnschutz or Werkschutz. Although it did not have a national command structure, the Ukrainian Auxiliary Police was ultimately responsible, as was the Polish militia, to the commandant of the German security police (Ordnungspolitzei, or ORPO) at the Generalgouvernement headquarters in Cracow. At a district level okruha and county (*povit*) commands were created for the auxiliary police, again responsible to regional ORPO centers. The force's highest-ranking officer was Maj V. Pitulei, the district commander of Lviv; his assistant was Capt L. Ohonovsky. In Lviv a special police academy headed by Capt I. Kozak trained recruits for the Ukrainian auxiliary force.

As representatives of the German occupational regime the Ukrainian Auxiliary Police were forced to participate in unpopular, repressive measures. Among the German authorities themselves, however, the police had low prestige. They were insufficiently armed, with one rifle for two policemen and 10 cartridges per rifle. The pay was also low for both officers and policemen, and protection for their families was virtually nonexistent.

L. Shankovsky

**Ukrainian Bandurist Chorus** (Ukrainska kapelia bandurystiv im. T. Shevchenka). The beginnings of this chorus lead back to the Banduryst Kapelle founded in 1923 in Poltava, which was succeeded in 1935 by the Ukrainian State Exemplary Banduryst Kapelle. In 1941 most of the ensemble members were incarcerated for several months by the German authorities. They were then

The Ukrainian Bandurist Chorus in 1955. Sitting, first and second from the right: Hryhorii Kytasty and Volodymyr Bozhyk

reorganized into the Shevchenko Ukrainian Banduryst Kapelle, and toured throughout Germany and the occupied eastern territories. After the Second World War the group remained in Germany, then emigrated en masse in 1949 to Detroit. There the group members generally took laboring jobs and continued their choral activities part-time. The ensemble subsequently has toured throughout the United States, Canada, Western Europe, and Australia to considerable acclaim. It has also trained or recruited new members to replace the original core group, and issued numerous LP records. In 1991 the ensemble toured Ukraine.

For several decades the most outstanding member of the ensemble was H. *Kytasty, who served as musical director, performing banduryst, and composer. The chorus has also been led by V. Bozhyk, H. Nazarenko, I. Zadorozhny, P. Potapenko, and V. Kolesnyk. The central place in the chorus's repertoire is held by Ukrainian folk songs, particularly historical songs as arranged by H. Khotkevych, K. Stetsenko, M. Leontovych, O. Koshyts, H. Kytasty, and others. (See *Bandurysts.)

BIBLIOGRAPHY
Samchuk, U. *Zhyvi struny* (Detroit 1976)
Wytwycky, W. *Ukrainian Bandurist Chorus* (Detroit 1976)
W. Wytwycky

**Ukrainian bilingual education** (*ukrainska dvomovna osvita*). A program in which Ukrainian is used along with English as a language of instruction in elementary and secondary schools. Bilingual schools exist in the three prairie provinces of Canada, Alberta, Manitoba, and Saskatchewan. Ukrainian bilingual education there has undergone two distinct stages of development.

From 1897 until the period of the First World War Ukrainians were able to take advantage of the educational concessions granted to French Catholics and other minorities in Manitoba to establish Ukrainian-English bilingual schools in rural bloc settlements in Manitoba. A severe shortage of English-speaking teachers (or their refusal to teach in the Ukrainian bloc settlements) and a concern with overcoming the reluctance of rural communities to provide schools initially made the bilingual-school option tolerable for the English-speaking majority. Ja. *Arsenych,

J. Baderski, and T. *Ferley were among those who played an active role in the development of Ukrainian bilingual education. As the proportion of immigrants in Manitoba grew, however, Canadian nativists became concerned with the threat to the Anglo-Canadian identity posed by the unassimilated immigrants. The pro-British fervor of the war years (1914–18) and the coincident increase in hostility toward foreigners aggravated the situation. On 8 March 1916 all Ukrainian bilingual schools in Manitoba were abolished. Before their dissolution there were 111 Ukrainian and Polish bilingual schools in Manitoba (lumped together in the 1915 report on their status), with 114 teachers and 6,513 pupils.

Inspired by the Manitoba model, Ukrainians in the provinces of Saskatchewan and Alberta also attempted to establish bilingual schools. In 1916 it was estimated that in 40 public schools in Saskatchewan, Ukrainian was used as the language of instruction. In 1919 the Saskatchewan government placed severe restrictions on French and banned the use of all languages other than English in schools for reasons similar to those of the Manitoba authorities.

In Alberta, bilingual schools did not formally exist, but Ukrainian was used in classrooms. The very limited supply of Ukrainian teachers, however, severely restricted the development of unofficial bilingual schools. In 1909–12 about a dozen Ukrainian teachers worked in Alberta under temporary teachers' permits and used both Ukrainian and English in instruction. The greatest setback to bilingual education in Alberta occurred in 1913, when the Department of Education canceled the permits of Ukrainian teachers trained in Saskatchewan and Manitoba. These teachers were accused of having raided schools in Alberta, of being poorly qualified, and of having been recruited by organizations promoting the use of Ukrainian in schools in Ukrainian bloc settlements. Department of Education pressure proved so effective in preventing the hiring of bilingual teachers that there was not even a need to repeal the regulations allowing Ukrainian instruction, as happened in Manitoba and Saskatchewan.

In all of the prairie provinces Ukrainian community pressure was unable to prevent the elimination of bilingual schools. Furthermore, in all three provinces the linguistic and cultural assimilation of immigrants became one of the main goals of the respective provincial systems of education.

The 1970s witnessed the rebirth of Ukrainian bilingual education in western Canada. Alberta took the lead in re-establishing Ukrainian-language instruction. Availing themselves of the legitimacy afforded to the linguistic and cultural aspirations of minorities by the Royal Commission on Bilingualism and Biculturalism, leading members of the Edmonton Ukrainian Professional and Businessmen's Club, including P. *Savaryn and M. *Lupul, lobbied successfully to have the Alberta School Act amended in 1971 to allow any language in addition to English to be used as a language of instruction. Saskatchewan (1974, 1978) and Manitoba (1979) introduced legislative changes modeled on Alberta's and permitted up to 50 percent of the school day to be devoted to instruction in languages other than English. The Ukrainian bilingual (or partial immersion) education program was established in Alberta in 1974 and in Saskatchewan and Manitoba in 1979. To facilitate Ukrainian bilingual education in all three provinces, a formal agreement, the Joint Ukrainian Bilingual Curriculum Project, was signed by education authorities in all three provinces in 1985 for the joint development and exchange of curriculum materials.

The objectives of contemporary Ukrainian bilingual education are, among others, to develop students' written and oral communication skills in Ukrainian and English, to familiarize them with Ukrainian culture in Canada, Ukraine, and other countries, and to give them an opportunity to learn French (Canada's second official language) as well as English. The programs attempt to develop positive attitudes toward learning other languages and understanding other cultures. The Ukrainian language itself is studied as a separate subject, Ukrainian language arts. In grades one through six, half of the day is devoted to instruction in Ukrainian. Social studies, art, music, physical education, health, and religion are taught in Ukrainian. Science, mathematics, and English language arts are taught in English. In grades 7 through 9 about 30 percent of instruction is in Ukrainian, and at the grades 10 to 12 level the instruction time in Ukrainian is reduced to about 18 percent. All teachers in the program are fully certified to teach in the public schools of their province. Currently, however, no formal program exists specifically for training Ukrainian bilingual teachers. The *Canadian Institute of Ukrainian Studies, University of Alberta, organizes summer courses on an occasional basis. Some teacher inservice and professional development is provided by local school boards and provincial departments of education.

The legislation governing bilingual programs in the three provinces is permissive. Local school boards may offer a program if there is sufficient parental interest, but they are not required to do so. Thus, the establishment and maintenance of programs depends on the organized support of parents. The Alberta Parents for Ukrainian Education (established in 1984) and the Manitoba Parents for Ukrainian Education (founded in 1980) are two umbrella organizations for parent groups in their respective provinces.

The lack of commercially available Ukrainian-language resources and textbooks in Canada and the ideological and pedagogical inappropriateness of resources from Ukraine, until recently, have necessitated Canadian production of textbooks. So far, the most ambitious projects have involved the Ukrainian community, the Alberta Department of Education, and the Ukrainian Language Education Centre at the Canadian Institute of Ukrainian Studies.

In 1989, 1,400 students were enrolled in Ukrainian bilingual, education programs in Alberta, 1,000 in Manitoba, and 160 in Saskatchewan. One of the main issues affecting the programs is the disproportionately low enrollment figures, given the demographic strength of Ukrainians in western Canada.

BIBLIOGRAPHY
Skwarok, J. *The Ukrainian Settlers in Canada and Their Schools* (Edmonton 1959)
Lupul, M. (ed). *Osvita: Ukrainian Bilingual Education* (Edmonton 1985)

J. Sokolowski

**Ukrainian Black Sea Institute** (Ukrainskyi chornomorskyi instytut). An émigré institution established on the initiative of Yu. *Lypa in Warsaw in 1940 to study and disseminate knowledge about the Black Sea and the Black Sea region. The institute was directed by I. *Shovheniv (1940–3) and I. Lypa (1943–4), and by M. Miller in Germany (1946–9). Its permanent secretary and chief organizer was L. Bykovsky. After 1945 the institute functioned (with interruptions) in the Hersfeld and Mainz-Kastel DP camps in Germany. It was renamed the Ukrainian Marine Institute in 1946, its secretariat moved to New York in 1948, and it was dissolved in 1949. The institute published a total of 11 volumes of its serial *Chornomors'kyi zbirnyk*, 27 offprint brochures, and 29 other publications (mostly brochures). Bykovsky's detailed article about the institute and its publications appeared in the Ukrainian Technical and Husbandry Institute's *Naukovi zapysky*, vol 22 (1970).

**Ukrainian Botanical Society** (Ukrainske botanichne tovarystvo). A scientific society, which formerly had been a branch of the All-Union Botanical Society of the USSR Academy of Sciences. It was organized originally in 1919 as a botanical subsection of the biology section of the Ukrainian Scientific Society and renamed in 1925. During the period 1921–9 the society published the botanical journal *Ukraïns'kyi botanichnyi zhurnal* (5 vols), and since 1959 it has published the annual *Shchorichnyk Ukraïns'koho botanichnoho tovarystva*. There are about 700 full and 300 corresponding members of the society.

**Ukrainian Branch of the Slovak Writers' Union** (Ukrainska filiia Spilky slovatskykh pysmennykiv). An organization founded in 1952. Its 30 to 40 members, most of whom live in the *Prešov region, produce 10 to 12 books per year. In 1969 some of them were expelled during the Czechoslovak regime's crackdown against the liberal supporters of the Prague Spring. The branch's official organ has been the bimonthly *Duklia. Periodically the union has awarded the Franko Prize for the best Ukrainian-language literary work to one of its members.

**Ukrainian Brazilian Central Representation** (Ukrainsko-brazyliiska tsentralna reprezentatsiia; Portuguese: Representaçao Central Ucraniano-Brasiliera). An umbrella organization for Brazilian Ukrainians established in 1985. The founding members of the group included the Union for Agricultural Education, Ukrainian-Brazilian Youth Association, Ukrainian-Brazilian Club, St John the Baptist Social Services Society, General Administration of the Ukrainian Autocephalous Orthodox church in Brazil, and 'Unification' (Sobornist) Society of Brazil. Except for the latter (centered in São Caetano do Sul–São Paulo), all the groups have their headquarters in Curitiba. The association's purpose is to represent the Ukrainian community before the government, institutions, and the general public; to provide advice and facilitate co-operation in the areas of cultural affairs and social services; and to defend the interests of the Ukrainian community by all legal means. The first president was A. Antoniuk; he was followed in 1989 by M. Czaikowski. Two organizations have subsequently joined the association, the Brazilian Center for Ukrainian Studies and the Society of Friends of Ukrainian Culture. Among the most impor- tant activities of the group has been the creation of the Ukrainian Brazilian Foundation (Fundaçao Ucraniano-Brasileira, known popularly in Ukrainian as the 'Dopomohova fundatsiia') to co-ordinate the social assistance rendered to Ukrainians in Brazil from other parts of the world. Its first president was H. Bezruchka. The Representation is a member of the World Congress of Free Ukrainians.

N. Kerechuk

***Ukrainian Bulletin, The.*** An English-language semimonthly newsletter published in New York from May 1948 to February 1970, when it merged with the \*Ukrainian Quarterly. The organ of the Pan-American Ukrainian Conference until September 1951 and then of the Ukrainian Congress Committee of America, it was edited by W. Dushnyck. The *Ukrainian Bulletin* reported mostly on political affairs concerning Ukrainians in the West and on political developments in the Ukrainian SSR. A total of 518 issues appeared.

**Ukrainian Bureau in London** (Ukrainske biuro v Londoni, aka Ukrainske presove biuro). An information office established and financed by Ya. \*Makohin to acquaint the British public with Ukrainian affairs. It operated in London under V. \*Kaye-Kysilewsky from 1931 to 1939. Its irregular *Bulletin* was mailed to 250 papers in Britain. As a result the number of articles on Ukrainian issues in the British press increased. (See \*Press and Information bureaus abroad.)

***Ukrainian Canadian, The.*** An English-language magazine published in Toronto by the \*Association of United Ukrainian Canadians semimonthly from September 1947 to 1969 and monthly until the end of 1991. It contains articles on Ukrainian culture, translations of Ukrainian literature, and reports on developments in the Ukrainian pro-Soviet community in Canada. While it devoted less attention to political affairs than most other Ukrainian pro-Soviet publications, it consistently supported the policies of the Communist Party of Canada, particularly concerning the peace movement. The editors of the *Ukrainian Canadian* included J. Weir, M. Sago, M. Skrypnyk, W. Szczesny, P. Prokop, and G. Moskal. In 1992 it was succeeded by the bilingual *Ukraïns'ko-kanads'kyi visnyk/Ukrainian Canadian Herald.*

**Ukrainian Canadian Archives and Museum of Alberta** (Ukrainsko-kanadskyi arkhiv-muzei Alberty, or UCAMA). The museum, located in Edmonton and based on the collections of S. and H. Yopyk, was founded on 31 October 1972 and officially opened on 17 October 1974. Its collection reflects the contribution of Ukrainian pioneers to the development of Canada and includes much material about Ukraine. The library contains more than 15,000 volumes and several archival collections, including those of M. \*Luchkovich. UCAMA also houses an extensive exhibit of photographs and documents of the Royal Canadian Legion, Norwood Branch 178 in Edmonton. UCAMA has held over 30 public exhibits including works by artists such as P. Shostak and J. Hnizdovsky. H. Yopyk was president of UCAMA until his retirement in 1988; he was followed by M. Kalinowsky (1988–90) and W. Chmiliar (1990–).

**Ukrainian Canadian Art Foundation** (Kanadsko-ukrainska mystetska fundatsiia, or KUMF). A nonprofit corporation established in 1975 in Toronto to promote Ukrainian art. Its founders, M. and Ya. Shafraniuk, donated their collection of Ukrainian art and a building to the foundation. The KUMF runs an art gallery. By 1989 it had

A display room in the gallery of the Ukrainian Canadian Art Foundation

hosted over 180 exhibitions there, including the 1982 Ukrainian Artists International Exhibit, to which 87 artists living in the West submitted their works. In recent years KUMF has sponsored exhibitions of works by artists living in Ukraine. It also organizes art lectures and literary readings and has published several art albums. Its permanent art collection includes over 200 paintings and sculptures, including works by M. Hlushchenko, J. Hnizdovsky, O. Hryshchenko, B. Kriukov, H. Kruk, M. Krychevsky, W. Kurelek, M. Levytsky, V. Makarenko, H. Mazepa, L. Molodozhanyn, V. Patyk, P. Shostak, A. Solohub, and V. Tsymbal.

**Ukrainian Canadian Citizens' League** (Ukrainsko-kanadiiskyi horozhanskyi komitet). A Ukrainian-Canadian organization founded in Winnipeg in December 1918 to assist the cause of Ukraine's independence by lobbying the Canadian government. It sent two delegates (I. Petrushevych and O. Megas) to the \*Paris Peace Conference. It also initiated the Ukrainian Red Cross Society. Because of religious differences a rival Catholic Ukrainian National Council was formed, but in 1920 the two briefly merged into the Ukrainian Central Committee to represent the community nationally.

**Ukrainian Canadian Committee.** See Ukrainian Canadian Congress.

**Ukrainian Canadian Congress** (Kongres ukraintsiv Kanady, or KUK). An umbrella organization of the Ukrainian community of Canada. It was formed as the Ukrainian Canadian Committee on 6–7 November 1940 in Winnipeg by a merging of two rival umbrella organizations established earlier that year – the Ukrainian Central Council of Canada and the Representative Committee of Ukrainian Canadians – that included the five major Ukrainian associations in Canada: the \*Ukrainian Catholic Brotherhood (BUK), the \*United Hetman Organization, the \*Ukrainian Self-Reliance League (SUS), the \*Ukrainian National Federation (UNO), and the \*Ukrainian Workers' League. As an ad hoc committee, KUK had the original purpose of uniting the Ukrainian community behind the Canadian war effort, and its establishment was fostered intensively by the Canadian government. The actual process of forming the group was aided in large measure by

The first KUK executive. First row, from left: S. Chwaliboga, Jaroslaw Arsenych, Rev Semen Sawchuk, Rev Vasyl Kushnir, Volodymyr Kossar, A. Malofie, Anthony Yaremovich; second row: Mykhailo Pohoretsky, Myroslaw Stechishin, Stepan Skobliak, Rev Stefan Semchuk, Taras Ferley, Paul Barycki, Andrii Zaharychuk; third row: I. Gulay, Vasyl Sarchuk, Boryslav Dyma, Evstakhii Vasylyshyn, Constantine Andrushyshen, T. Melnychuk

the intervention of T. *Philipps, a British specialist on Near Eastern and Eastern European affairs.

KUK was successful in getting young Ukrainians to enlist in the armed forces and in promoting the purchase of war bonds. After the war it continued its activities by responding to the plight of Ukrainian refugees in Western Europe. It set up the *Ukrainian Canadian Relief Fund and the Central Ukrainian Relief Bureau in London, thereby saving many refugees from forced repatriation to the Soviet Union, helping them materially, and resettling them in Canada. As the new immigrants set up their own organizations, KUK altered its constitution to admit them. By 1965 its membership increased to 30 organizations, although its structure and operations were effectively controlled by the so-called Big Six senior member groups – BUK, SUS, UNO, the *Ukrainian Canadian Veterans' Association, the *Canadian League for Ukraine's Liberation, and (later) the *Ukrainian Canadian Professional and Business Federation (UCPBF).

Prime Minister Louis St Laurent addressing the 4th KUK Congress (Winnipeg, July 1953)

KUK has promoted Ukrainian in public schools, universities, and in private schools run by Ukrainian organizations. Its recommendations on preserving the multicultural character of Canadian society helped shape government policy. In 1963 it set up the Ukrainian Canadian Foundation of Taras Shevchenko to support Ukrainian-Canadian cultural activities. It also played a major role in founding the *World Congress of Free Ukrainians in 1967.

Since its inception KUK has had a strongly anticommunist character and has steadfastly refused to co-operate with the pro-Soviet Association of United Ukrainian Canadians. During the 1970s KUK came under increasing criticism from its own member groups, particularly the Ukrainian Canadian Students' Union (SUSK) and the UCPBF, for its 'undemocratic' structure (manifested in the issue of veto power for each of the Big Six groups) and the actual ineffectiveness of its operations. Such concerns finally led to the establishment of KUK's *Ukrainian Community Development Committee (UCDC) in 1982 and the formation or revival of KUK provincial council structures in the four western provinces.

KUK has established its own Ukrainian Information Bureau in Ottawa (1987). It organized the celebrations of the millennium of Ukrainian Christianity (1988) and the centenary of Ukrainian settlement in Canada (1991–2). It has sponsored a Civil Liberties Commission (from 1985) whose first and paramount task was to respond to indiscriminate charges of war criminals among Ukrainian Canadians. KUK also undertook the issue of redress for the internment in Canada during the First World War of unnaturalized Ukrainian migrant laborers from Austrian-ruled Western Ukraine.

Today KUK has 30 member organizations and 35 local branches in six provinces. Work on the regional level is coordinated by five KUK provincial councils (British Columbia, Alberta, Saskatchewan, Manitoba, and Ontario). The head office in *Winnipeg is run by an executive director, a position filled by V. Kokhan (1948–66), S. Kalba (1966–81), A. Yaremovich (1981–5), Yu. Weretelnyk (1985–6), and W. Werbeniuk (1986–). The presidents of the UCC, elected at its congresses every three years, have been Rev V. *Kushnir (1940–53, 1958–71), A. Yaremovich (1953–6), Rev S. Sawchuk (1957), P. Kondra (1971–4), S. Radchuk (1974–80), J. Nowosad (1980–6), D. Tsipyvnyk (Cipywnyk) (1986–92), and O. Romaniw (1992– ). It adopted its present 'Congress' title in 1989.

BIBLIOGRAPHY
Zbirnyk materiialiv i dokumentiv u 25–littia diial'nosty KUK, 1930–1965 (Winnipeg 1965)
Kordan, B. 'Disunity and Duality: Ukrainian Canadians and the Second World War.' MA diss, Carleton University, 1981
Gerus, O. 'The Ukrainian Canadian Committee,' in A Heritage in Transition, ed M. Lupul (Toronto 1982)
Prymak, T. Maple Leaf and Trident: The Ukrainian Canadians during the Second World War (Toronto 1988)

O. Gerus

**Ukrainian Canadian Foundation of Taras Shevchenko** (Ukrainska Kanadska fundatsiia im. Tarasa Shevchenka). A Winnipeg-based nonprofit endowment fund incorporated in July 1963 by the Ukrainian Canadian Committee (now Congress) (KUK) to promote Ukrainian culture in Canada. Between 1964 and 1988 its capital assets reached 3,500,000 dollars and its grants exceeded 1,500,000 dollars in support of folk ensembles, institutes, museums, the Ukrainian press, language schools, research, and publications. Administered by a board of directors appointed by the KUK presidium, it has been headed by I. Hlynka (1964–83) and S. Radchuk (1983–).

**Ukrainian Canadian Professional and Business Federation** (Obiednannia ukrainskykh kanadskykh profesionalistiv i pidpryiemtsiv, or UCPBF). A national association of Ukrainian professional and business clubs in Canada. Founded by delegates from 12 clubs at the Ukrainian Canadian Congress in Winnipeg in October 1965, it was known originally as the Federation of Ukrainian Professional and Businessmen's Clubs of Canada. The federation represents the interests of the Ukrainian community in Canadian business and government circles and has played an influential role in Ukrainian-Canadian community affairs, particularly with the establishment of educational bodies, such as the Canadian Institute of Ukrainian Studies, the Canadian Foundation for Ukrainian Studies, and the Chair of Ukrainian Studies at the University of Toronto. Today it has about 20 member clubs in cities such as Toronto, Winnipeg, Ottawa, Regina, Saskatoon, Edmonton, Vancouver, Hamilton, and Calgary. It has published irregularly the magazines *Ukrainian Canadian Review* (since 1966) and *Panorama* (1972–8). At its biennial conventions the following have been elected president: V. Swystun (1965–6), S. Radchuk (1966–8), S. Frolick (1971–3), M. Lupul (1973–5), J. Karasevich (1975–7), G. Danyliw (1977–9), L. Decore (1979–81), J. Tutecky (1981–3), J. Slogan (1983–5), B. Shuliakevych (1985–7), P. Zakarow (1987–9), P. Ortynsky (1989–91), and E. Zalucky (1991–).

**Ukrainian Canadian Relief Fund** (Fond dopomohy ukraintsiv Kanady, or UCRF). An organization created in 1945 by the Ukrainian Canadian Servicemen's Association and the Ukrainian Canadian Committee (now Congress) to assist Ukrainian refugees in postwar Europe. Between 1945 and 1947 it gathered nearly 200,000 dollars. In Europe the UCRF was represented by a Relief Mission (B.G. *Panchuk, A. Crepleve, A. Yaremovich) which worked through the Canadian Red Cross and the International Relief Organization in the British zone of Germany to organize Ukrainian schools, resist forced repatriation, lobby for resettlement in Canada, and assist in family reunions. The Relief Fund was initially linked to the *Central Ukrainian Relief Bureau (CURB) but continued functioning after CURB was disbanded late in 1948. In 1962 the UCRF was reconstituted as *Ukrainian Canadian Social Services.

**Ukrainian Canadian Research and Documentation Centre** (Ukrainsko-kanadskyi doslidchyi i dokumentatsiinyi tsentr). A research center in Toronto that developed out of the Ukrainian Famine Research Committee (est 1982, renamed the Centre for Research on the Ukrainian Famine in 1986). It acquired its present name and an expanded mandate to examine Ukraine during the Second World War (together with other recent events in Ukrainian history) in 1988. The center collects official and personal documents, photographs, film footage, and newspaper articles; conducts audio and video oral history interviews; and organizes conferences and workshops relating to its areas of research. In 1984 it produced *Harvest of Despair*, an award-winning documentary about the man-made famine in Ukraine in 1932–3.

**Ukrainian Canadian Research Foundation.** A society founded in Toronto in 1957 to support the study of Ukrainians in Canada by assisting research and publication. The group's titles include *Early Ukrainian Settlements in Canada, 1895–1900* (1964) by V.J. Kaye; *A Ukrainian Canadian in Parliament* (1965), the autobiography of M. Luch-

kovich, edited by J.B. Gregorovich; *Persistence and Change* (1978), a sociological study of Ukrainian Canadians in Alberta by C.W. Hobart and W.E. Kalbach; *Dictionary of Ukrainian Canadian Biography: Pioneer Settlers of Manitoba, 1891–1900* (1975) by V.J. Kaye; and *Ukrainian Canadians in Canada's Wars* (1983) by V.J. Kaye. S. Pawluk was the foundation's first president.

Members of the Ukrainian Canadian Servicemen's Association in front of their building in London (November 1945)

**Ukrainian Canadian Servicemen's Association** (Soiuz ukrainskykh kanadskykh voiakiv, or UCSA). A service club established in 1943 in Manchester. Formed as a social group to provide a means for Ukrainian-Canadian service personnel overseas to gather with their kinsmen, the UCSA was underwritten by the Ukrainian Canadian Committee (now Congress). It established a Services Club in large rented premises in London, organized several major 'Get-Togethers' (initially in Britain and later on the Continent), published the UCSA *Newsletter*, and arranged the recruitment of Ukrainian chaplains for the Canadian troops. More significantly, UCSA members were among the first to become aware of the plight of Ukrainian *displaced persons in Europe during the war and played a leading role in efforts to prevent their forced repatriation to the Soviet Union by forming the *Central Ukrainian Relief Bureau as a parallel structure to their own for this purpose. The UCSA later laid the groundwork for the establishment of the Association of Ukrainians in Great Britain. The group disbanded shortly after the war and was succeeded in Canada by the Ukrainian Canadian Veterans' Association. Leading figures in the UCSA included B.G. *Panchuk, J. Yuzyk, and J. Swystun.

**Ukrainian Canadian Social Services** (Suspilna sluzhba ukraintsiv Kanady, or SSUK). A national welfare agency founded in 1962 to continue the charitable work of the *Ukrainian Canadian Relief Fund. Affiliated with the Ukrainian Canadian Congress, it works through its 12 local branches in the major Ukrainian communities in Canada, including Toronto, Winnipeg, Edmonton, Saskatoon, Montreal, and Vancouver. It has provided aid to needy Ukrainians (students, the elderly, and newcomers) in Canada as well as Ukraine, Poland, Argentina, Brazil, and Paraguay; to political prisoners in Soviet Ukraine; and to refugees from the Soviet bloc in Austria. The agency is a member of the World Council of Ukrainian Welfare and Social Services. Its head office was moved from Winnipeg to Toronto in 1972. The presidents of SSUK, elected at its triennial conventions, have been: R. Senchuk (1962–8), O. Zhuravsky (1968–71), S. Kharko (1971–4, 1983–9), Z. Duda (1974–80), I. Kushpeta (1980–3), and O. Danyliak (since 1989).

**Ukrainian Canadian Students' Union** (Soiuz ukrainskykh studentiv Kanady, or SUSK). A co-ordinating national organization of Canadian postsecondary students of Ukrainian descent. SUSK was founded at the first Congress of Ukrainian Canadian Students in Winnipeg (26–27 December 1953), under the auspices of the *Ukrainian Canadian Congress, of which it became a member organization. SUSK played an important role in the late 1960s and the 1970s in promoting multiculturalism and in defending political prisoners in Ukraine. In 1968 SUSK established a newspaper called *Student. In 1975–6 SUSK had member clubs at 18 Canadian universities, to which some 1,250 students belonged: in 1989 the organization had member clubs at 15 universities, involving almost 1,000 students.

**Ukrainian Canadian Veterans' Association** (Soiuz ukrainskykh kanadiiskykh veteraniv). A national association of Ukrainian veterans of the Canadian armed forces formed in Winnipeg in June 1945 to maintain the wartime camaraderie developed by members of the disbanded *Ukrainian Canadian Servicemen's Association. Prominent founders were B.G. *Panchuk, J. Yuzyk, J. Karasevich, and S. Kalin. The first organization in the postwar period to join the Ukrainian Canadian Committee (now Congress), the association opened its membership to Ukrainian veterans of other armies in 1965. It published a newsletter, *Opinion*, and became a member of the Royal Canadian Legion. Most of the group's functions are local in nature and are carried out by its branches.

**Ukrainian Catholic Brotherhood of Canada** (Bratstvo ukraintsiv katolykiv Kanady). A national lay organization for Ukrainian Catholics founded in 1932 in Saskatoon to strengthen the Ukrainian Catholic church in Canada. Guided for many years by Rev S. Samchuk, it published *Biuileten' Bratstva ukraïntsiv katolykiv Kanady* (1933–7) and *Buduchnist' natsiï* (1932–50) and sponsored the establishment of the Sheptytsky Institute in Saskatoon in 1935. One of the founding members of the *Ukrainian Canadian Committee (now Congress) in 1940, it had over 100 branches across Canada in 1982.

**Ukrainian Catholic church** (Ukrainska Katolytska Tserkva). The current name of the Ukrainian church that belongs to the group of Eastern or Byzantine rite churches that are in communion with the Roman Catholic church and recognize the spiritual and administrative authority of the pope. These Eastern churches are also called 'particular' (*pomisni*), because they are hierarchically, canonically, liturgically, and culturally autonomous, although they belong to the association of particular churches that forms the Universal Church. (For the history of Ukrainian Catholicism, see *Church, history of the Ukrainian.)

**Canonical aspects.** The name 'Ukrainian Catholic church' (UCC) has been used popularly and in official Vatican documents since the early 1960s to refer to all Ukrainian Catholics in the diaspora and the underground (until 1989) church in Ukraine. It replaced the term *'Greek

Ukrainian Catholic hierarchs at the Second Vatican Council. First row, from left: Bishop Nil Savaryn, Archbishop Ivan Buchko, Metropolitan Maksym Hermaniuk, Supreme Archbishop Yosyf Slipy, Metropolitan Ambrose Senyshyn, Archbishop Havryil Bukatko, Bishop Isidore Borecky; second row: Bishop Yosyp Martynets, Bishop Volodymyr Malanchuk, Bishop Avhustyn Horniak, Bishop Platon Kornyliak, Bishop Andrii Roboretsky, Bishop Joseph Schmondiuk, Bishop Ivan Prashko, Bishop Andrii Sapeliak, Bishop Yoakym Segedi

Catholic church,' which had been used since the 18th century, and the official term *Ecclesia Ruthena unita* used by the Vatican. UCC leaders favored the new term because it recognized the national character of the church; prevented the confusion that arose with such terms as 'Greek Catholic,' *Ruthenus*, or 'Ruthenian'; and implied the spiritual and administrative unity of Ukrainian emigrants with the church in Ukraine.

After the formal liquidation of *Halych metropoly at the *Lviv Sobor of 1946, those Ukrainian Catholic (then Greek Catholic) clergy and faithful who refused to convert to Russian Orthodoxy were severely persecuted, and most of the church's hierarchs died in concentration camps. In February 1963, however, Metropolitan Y. *Slipy was released from prison and permitted to emigrate. In October 1963, at the Second Vatican Council, he proposed the creation of a Kiev-Halych patriarchate for Ukrainian Catholics (see *Patriarch). The council did not resolve the matter, but in December 1963, as a result of the Decree on the Eastern Catholic Churches, the Vatican recognized the archbishop of Lviv as the major archbishop of the UCC. In 1975 Slipy began using the title 'Patriarch of Kiev and Halych and All Rus',' and many UCC bishops began to refer to him and his successor as 'patriarch'; this was done without the pope's consent, however, and the UCC has not been recognized as a patriarchal church by the Vatican. Nonetheless, Slipy secured official recognition of the *synodal structure of the UCC under the authority of the major archbishop, who has the right to convoke the synods of Ukrainian Catholic bishops and the Council of the UCC.

The UCC is formed by Halych metropoly (traditionally composed of *Lviv, *Stanyslaviv, and *Peremyshl [now primarily in Poland] eparchies) and all metropolies, eparchies, and exarchates in the diaspora (consisting mainly of Ukrainian immigrants from Galicia and their offspring) that participate in the synods of Ukrainian Catholic bishops.

Not all Ukrainian Catholics outside Ukraine belong directly to the UCC. Many Ukrainians in ethnically mixed borderlands west of Ukraine, for example, belong to Byzantine rite Catholic church eparchies not jurisdictionally

TABLE 1
The Ukrainian (Greek) Catholic church in Ukraine, ca 1944

|  | Bishops | Parishes | Churches | Priests | Seminaries | Faithful (in thousands) |
|---|---|---|---|---|---|---|
| *Halych metropoly* |  |  |  |  |  |  |
| Lviv eparchy | 4 | 1,267 | 1,308 | 1,061 | 2 | 1,300 |
| Peremyshl eparchy | 2 | 640 | 1,268 | 715 | 1 | 1,160 |
| Stanyslaviv eparchy | 2 | 455 | 886 | 531 | 1 | 1,000 |
| *Other* |  |  |  |  |  |  |
| Lemko apostolic administration | – | 129 | 198 | 135 | – | 128 |
| Mukachiv eparchy | 1 | 281 | 459 | 367 | 1 | 462 |
| Prešov eparchy | 1 | 150 | 298 | 247 | 1 | 321 |
| Volhynian visitature | 1 | 28 | – | 41 | – | 35 |
| Bukovyna-Maramureş vicarate | – | 35* | 40* | 35* | – | 55 |
| Total | 11 | 2,985 | 4,457 | 3,132 | 6 | 4,461 |

*Estimate

affiliated with the UCC. *Prešov eparchy in eastern Slovakia is one such eparchy. Forcibly converted to Orthodoxy in 1950, the eparchy was re-established as a Greek Catholic eparchy in 1968 for both Ukrainians and Slovaks. It has been subject to increasing Slovakization, and the Ukrainian hierarchs P. *Goidych and V. *Hopko, who were arrested when the eparchy was converted in 1950, were succeeded in 1968 by a Slovak. In Hungary, *Hajdúdorog eparchy and the exarchate of Miskolc include many Magyarized Transcarpathian Ukrainians. The *Lemko Apostolic Administration existed until most Ukrainians were deported from the Lemko region after the Second World War. In Rumania the Greek Catholic parishes in Bukovyna and the Maramureş region, which had been subordinated to Lviv archeparchy and then Stanyslaviv eparchy (from 1885) and consisted primarily of Ukrainians, were forcibly incorporated into the Rumanian Orthodox church on 1 December 1948. In the United States, Transcarpathian Ukrainian emigrants and their descendants belong primarily to *Pittsburgh metropoly, which is also a Byzantine rite province with four eparchies that do not fall under the UCC. Finally, in some countries with very small Ukrainian communities, individual Ukrainian Catholic parishes may exist, but they are under the jurisdiction of the local Roman Catholic hierarchy.

**In Ukraine.** Despite official persecution, the hierarchy, clergy, monastic orders, and theological seminaries of the UCC remained active in the underground after 1946; they conducted secret services, administered rites, and ordained priests and consecrated bishops. Many Ukrainian Catholic believers also attended Roman Catholic or Orthodox churches while retaining their traditional beliefs and convictions. It was only during the liberalization of the late 1980s that the UCC re-emerged in public. In October 1987 two bishops and several priests announced that they were coming out of the underground; they notified Pope John Paul II of their actions and asked for his protection. In 1989 six more people identified themselves as hierarchs of the UCC (from 1946 several other bishops had died in Ukraine without their identity being revealed; only Ya. Tymchuk [d 20 December 1988] was posthumously identified as a bishop). In a May 1989 open letter to President M. Gorbachev, leading members of the underground UCC (including Metropolitan V. Sterniuk, three bishops, and several priests) demanded that the church be legalized; that same month a major hunger strike was staged in Moscow to publicize these demands.

The movement for the legalization of the UCC quickly gained great momentum. Throughout western Ukraine, parishes, priests, and believers formally declared their allegiance to the church. Such actions were strongly supported by the Vatican and the UCC hierarchy outside Ukraine. In August 1989 the hierarchy in Ukraine met to re-establish the authorities of three individual eparchies. As of 1990 the hierarchy was headed by V. Sterniuk, ordinary of Lviv archeparchy (which includes that part of the former Peremyshl eparchy not in contemporary Poland) and acting metropolitan under the major archbishop (M. Liubachivsky). He was assisted by Bishops F. Kurchaba, M. Sapryha, and Yu. Voronovsky. The ordinary of Ivano-Frankivske (formerly Stanyslaviv) eparchy, Bishop S. Dmyterko, was assisted by Bishops P. Vasylyk (co-adjutor) and I. Bilyk, and the ordinary of Uzhhorod eparchy, Bishop I. Semedii, by Bishops Y. Holovach and I. Margitych. The last eparchy was newly created and based primarily on the former *Mukachiv eparchy, which had not been a part of Halych metropoly before its forcible conversion to Orthodoxy after the Second World War. In June 1990 the entire hierarchy met with Pope John Paul II in Rome.

Official permission to register UCC parishes was granted by the Council for Religious Affairs of the Ukrainian government in December 1989. By March 1992 more than 1,000 parishes in Lviv eparchy, 530 in Ivano-Frankivske eparchy, and 12 in Uzhhorod eparchy had declared themselves to be Ukrainian Catholic. The church included over 1,000 priests (including 350 former priests of the Russian Orthodox church), 700 nuns, and 400 seminarians. Official registration of the entire church as a legal entity, however, had still not been granted by the end of 1990. Moreover, several contentious questions were also unresolved, particularly the ownership and control of church properties. Neither this difficulty nor the unofficial measures used by the central government to hamper the church's growth have been able to stop the popular rebirth of the UCC. Many church publications and religious schools have been founded; several monasteries have been renewed under the UCC; and a variety of public demonstrations

Ukrainian Catholic hierarchs from Ukraine at the Vatican in June 1990. From left: Auxiliary Bishop Mykhailo Sapryha (Lviv), Auxiliary Bishop Ivan Margitych (Uzhhorod), Auxiliary Bishop Yuliian Voronovsky (Lviv), Auxiliary Bishop Pavlo Vasylyk (Ivano-Frankivske), Auxiliary Bishop Fylemon Kurchaba (Lviv), Cardinal Myroslav Liubachivsky (Rome), Pope John-Paul II, Auxiliary Bishop Yosyf Holovach (Uzhhorod), Metropolitan Volodymyr Sterniuk (Lviv), Bishop Ivan Semedii (Uzhhorod), Bishop Sofron Dmyterko (Ivano-Frankivske), Auxiliary Bishop Irynei Bilyk (Ivano-Frankivske)

have been held, including a large religious festival in September 1990 in Lviv. In the fall of 1990 the St George's Cathedral complex, the historic cathedral and residence of the metropolitan of Halych, was transferred back to the UCC from the Russian Orthodox church. Cardinal M. Liubachivsky moved from Rome to Lviv on 30 March 1991. A synod under his leadership took place on 16–31 May 1992 at St George's Cathedral in Lviv. The 28 bishops from Ukraine and the West who participated in the synod created new eparchies and metropolies and condemned the Lviv Sobor of 1946 as uncanonical.

**In Poland.** Following the Second World War, part of Peremyshl eparchy and the entire Lemko region were ceded to Poland. Most Ukrainians living in these regions were forcibly deported to the Ukrainian SSR or resettled in the western territories that Poland acquired from Germany. At the same time the Greek Catholic church was severely repressed. Bishop Y. Kotsylovsky of Peremyshl and his assistant, H. Lakota, were both deported to the USSR, where they subsequently died in prison, and most priests were deported or resettled along with their faithful. Liturgies in the Byzantine rite were forbidden, both by the authorities and by the Roman Catholic church; some Ukrainian priests conducted Latin liturgies as assistants to Polish clergymen.

From 1957 Ukrainian Catholic priests were again permitted to conduct Byzantine liturgies for Ukrainians in Poland. But they were allowed to establish only 'pastoral centers' attached to and dependent on local Roman Catholic churches and bishops, and not canonical parishes. By the end of 1977 there were 77 such centers, served by lay and Basilian priests. Also, from the 1950s the Sister Servants of Mary Immaculate, Sisters of Saint Joseph, and Basilian Sisters were re-established. In 1969 a Byzantine rite seminary was established at the Catholic University in Lublin. Graduates have been ordained by the Polish cardinal

S. Wyszyński and, since 1982, by Ukrainian hierarchs (including some from outside Poland, such as Archbishop M. Marusyn and Cardinal M. Liubachivsky). In general the Polish church has had a very ambivalent attitude toward Ukrainian Catholics; it has pressured them to adopt the Latin rite, disallowed them an independent hierarchy, and hindered their contacts with the UCC hierarchy in the West.

In 1949 Wyszyński was appointed by the Vatican as special delegate for Catholics of the Byzantine rite in Poland. He appointed V. Hrynyk, a former professor of the theological seminary in Peremyshl, as vicar-general for Ukrainian Catholics. In 1977 Hrynyk was succeeded by S. Dziubyna. In December 1981 Wyszyński's successor, Cardinal J. Glemp, appointed two vicars-general for Ukrainian Catholics: I. Martyniak was chosen to head the southern deaneries of Peremyshl and Wrocław, and Y. Romanyk was assigned to the Koszalin and Olsztyn deaneries in the north. Despite persecution by the government and the occasional prejudice of the Roman Catholic clergy, Ukrainian Catholics began to establish parishes, build chapels and churches, and renovate shrines that had been returned to them (especially in the Peremyshl and Lemko regions, to which many Ukrainians have returned in recent years). Finally, John Paul II consecrated I. Martyniak as the first Ukrainian Catholic bishop in Poland in September 1989, in the presence of Cardinals Glemp and Liubachivsky. At first Martyniak was an auxiliary bishop to the ordinary for Catholics of the Byzantine rite in Poland (Cardinal Glemp). In January 1991 he became bishop of the traditional Ukrainian Catholic see of Peremyshl. He has participated in the synods of the UCC since his consecration.

Estimates of the total number of Ukrainian Catholics in Poland range as high as 500,000, but since many identify themselves as Roman Catholics to avoid harassment, this number is uncertain. In 1987 there were 83 missions and pastoral centers served by 47 priests and 11 Basilian fathers. Their celebrations of the millennium of Christianity in Ukraine were very successful, and a large rally, attended by 70,000 Ukrainians from across Poland, was held in Częstochowa in September 1988. (See also *Poland.)

**In former Yugoslavia.** Ukrainian settlers from Transcarpathia and Galicia began arriving in Vojvodina and Croatia in the 18th century. The separate *Križevci eparchy was established for them in 1777. Today this eparchy includes all 50,000 Byzantine rite Catholics in former Yugoslavia, most of whom (35,000) are of Ukrainian descent. The bishop of the eparchy participates in synods of the UCC, and the eparchy's clergy is often trained in UCC seminaries and uses Ukrainian liturgical texts.

**In the United States.** The Ukrainian Catholic church in the United States was established after the arrival in 1884 of Rev I. Voliansky, who had been sent to minister to Ukrainian emigrants by Metropolitan S. Sembratovych of Lviv. The first bishop, S. *Ortynsky, arrived from Western Ukraine in 1907. He was under the authority of the Roman Catholic church until 1913, when a separate exarchate for all Greek Catholics in the United States was established. Soon after his death in 1916, the Vatican appointed two vicars-general for Byzantine rite Catholics, one for Galician Ukrainians (P. Poniatyshyn) based in Philadelphia, and one for Transcarpathian Ukrainians (H. Martiak) based in Pittsburgh; the latter eventually became Pittsburgh metropoly.

In 1924 the Holy See appointed K. *Bohachevsky exarch for the Galician Ukrainians, with his see in Philadelphia. In 1956 a second exarchate was established, in Stamford, Connecticut, to serve New York State and New England. In 1958 the church was reorganized as Philadelphia

TABLE 2
Status of the Ukrainian Catholic church outside Ukraine and the USSR, 1989

| Country/eparchy | Bishops | Parishes | Priests | Seminaries | Faithful (in thousands) |
|---|---|---|---|---|---|
| *Eastern Europe* | | | | | |
| Poland | 1 | 89 | 58 | 1 | 500[a] |
| Czechoslovakia (Prešov eparchy) | 2 | 200[a] | 232 | – | 286 |
| Yugoslavia (Križevci eparchy) | 3 | 54 | 46 | 1 | 49 |
| Total | 6 | 343 | 336 | 2 | 835 |
| | | | | | |
| *Western Europe* | | | | | |
| Great Britain | 1 | 27 | 15 | – | 25 |
| Germany | 1 | 19 | 28 | – | 29 |
| France, Benelux, Switzerland | 1 | 17 | 23 | – | 16 |
| Austria | – | 6 | 2 | – | 4 |
| Total | 3 | 69 | 68 | – | 74 |
| | | | | | |
| *United States* | | | | | |
| Philadelphia archeparchy | 2 | 80 | 82 | 1 | 78 |
| Stamford eparchy | 1 | 51 | 172 | 1 | 41 |
| Chicago eparchy | 1 | 32 | 46 | 1 | 17 |
| Parma eparchy | 1 | 35 | 39 | – | 12 |
| Total | 5 | 198 | 339 | 3 | 148 |
| | | | | | |
| *Canada* | | | | | |
| Winnipeg archeparchy | 1 | 133 | 53 | 1 | 55 |
| Edmonton eparchy | 1 | 94 | 41 | – | 41 |
| Saskatoon eparchy | 1 | 121 | 35 | – | 30 |
| Toronto eparchy | 1 | 86 | 99 | – | 80 |
| New Westminster eparchy | 1 | 19 | 19 | – | 20 |
| Total | 5 | 453 | 247 | 1 | 226 |
| | | | | | |
| *South America* | | | | | |
| Brazil (Curitiba eparchy) | 1 | 20 | 59 | – | 88 |
| Argentina (Buenos Aires eparchy) | 2 | 15 | 20 | – | 115 |
| Paraguay | – | 8 | 1 | – | 1[a] |
| Venezuela | – | 3 | 1 | – | 1[a] |
| Total | 3 | 46 | 81 | – | 205 |
| | | | | | |
| *Australia, New Zealand, Oceania* | | | | | |
| Melbourne eparchy | 1 | 15 | 14 | – | 30 |
| | | | | | |
| Grand Total | 23[b] | 1,124[c] | 1,085 | 6 | 1,518 |

[a]Estimate
[b]Includes Cardinal M. Liubachivsky and Archbishop M. Marusyn, secretary of the Holy Congregation of Eastern Churches; two bishops ordained by Cardinal Y. Slipy without the consent of the Vatican have not been included.
[c]Includes all missions

metropoly, and the exarchates were designated as eparchies (Philadelphia was raised to the status of archeparchy). Eparchies were established in 1961 in Chicago, to serve congregations in the western states, and in 1983 in Parma, Ohio, to serve parishes in the central and southern United States. In the mid-1970s there were approx 285,000 Ukrainian Catholics in the country. (See also *United States of America.)

**In Canada.** The first Ukrainian Catholic priests in Canada were N. Dmytriv, who arrived from the United States in 1897, and P. Tymkevych. The first bishop, N. *Budka, served in 1912–28; he was succeeded by V. Ladyka (1929–56). In 1943 the church was made an exarchate, and N. Savaryn was named as an assistant bishop to Ladyka. Two more exarchates were added, in 1948 and 1951. In 1956 the church was reorganized as Winnipeg metropoly under M. *Hermaniuk, with an archeparchy in Winnipeg and eparchies in Edmonton, Saskatoon, and Toronto; a fourth eparchy was established in New Westminster, British Columbia, in 1974. According to the 1981 Canadian census, there are 191,300 Ukrainian Catholics in Canada; a further 100,600 Ukrainians claimed Roman Catholicism as their religion. (See also *Canada.)

**In Brazil.** Although priests and monks accompanied the earliest Ukrainian immigrants to Brazil in the late 19th and early 20th centuries, it was not until 1952 that a separate apostolic exarchate was established for Byzantine rite faithful. The exarchate was initially headed by Archbishop J. Câmara, who appointed C. Preima as vicar for Ukrainians. In 1958 Y. *Martynets was appointed as the first bishop for Ukrainians, and in 1962 a separate Ukrainian exarchate was established, with its center in Curitiba. The exarchate was made an eparchy in 1971, and is now headed by Bishop Ye. *Kryvy. Although the Curitiba UCC eparchy is under the jurisdiction of the Curitiba Roman Catholic metropoly, its bishop participates in UCC synods. (See also *Brazil.)

**In Argentina.** Ukrainian Catholics in Argentina were served by Basilian priests from Brazil until 1909, when Ya. Karpiak arrived from Peremyshl. Soon afterward he was joined by I. Senyshyn and O. Ananevych from Stanyslaviv (Ivano-Frankivske) eparchy. In 1959 the Vatican designated the archbishop of Buenos Aires ordinary for all Byzantine rite Catholics in Argentina. He appointed Y. Halabarda to oversee Ukrainian congregations. The first Ukrainian bishop, A. *Sapeliak, was made apostolic visitator for Ukrainian Catholics in 1961. A separate Ukrainian exarchate was created in 1968 under Sapeliak, and in 1978 it was made an eparchy. There are approx 115,000 Ukrainian Catholics in the country. (See also *Argentina.)

**In Paraguay and Venezuela.** The small Ukrainian Catholic communities in these countries date only from the late 1940s and number only a few hundred faithful. Church services are generally conducted by visiting priests from other South American countries.

**In Australia and New Zealand.** When Ukrainian Catholics began to arrive in Australia in 1948, they were accompanied by several priests. The Vatican created an apostolic exarchate in 1958 encompassing all of Australia, New Zealand, and Oceania and appointed Bishop I. *Prashko as first exarch. In June 1982 the Vatican raised the exarchate to an eparchy. The eparchy serves approx 30,000 Ukrainians. (See also *Australia and *New Zealand.)

**In Germany.** In the interwar period the small Ukrainian community in Germany was initially served by a succession of priests assigned from Lviv eparchy. In 1927 Metropolitan A. Sheptytsky sent P. Verhun to Berlin as a permanent priest. During the Second World War, Ukrainian refugees and others arrived in large numbers in Germany. Because Verhun was unable to communicate regularly with Lviv, he turned to the Vatican, which named him apostolic visitator and administrator for Ukrainian Catholics in 1940. By the end of the war there were several hundred thousand Ukrainians, including many Catholics, throughout Western Europe, mainly in West Germany. In 1945 M. *Voiakovsky was appointed to assist Verhun, who was seized by the Soviets later that year and taken to Siberia. In 1946 the Vatican appointed Bishop I. *Buchko as apostolic visitator for Ukrainian Catholics in Western Europe, and Voiakovsky was made vicar-general for Germany. When Voiakovsky emigrated to the United States in 1949, he was succeeded by P. Holynsky in West Germany. In total, some 240 Ukrainian Catholic congregations, served by 300 émigré priests, were established in the displaced persons' camps. Voiakovsky established a theological seminary in Hirschberg, Bavaria, which was moved to Culemborg, Holland, in 1948. From 1948, however, church life declined as most DPs emigrated to North or South America. In 1959 Bishop P. *Kornyliak was appointed as exarch for Germany, with his see in Munich; in 1982 his responsibilities were extended to include Scandinavia. (See also *Germany.)

**In Great Britain.** The largest wave of Ukrainian immigrants in Britain arrived in 1947–50, among them many members and chaplains of the Division Galizien. Until 1956 they were under the jurisdiction of Bishop I. Buchko, who appointed V. Malanchuk (1949–50), O. Malynovsky (1950–7), and P. Maliuga (1957–62) vicars-general for Britain. The Roman Catholic bishop of Westminster, W. Godfrey, served as ordinary for Ukrainian Catholics from 1957. The first Ukrainian bishop, A. Horniak, served as an assistant to Godfrey (1961–3) and then as exarch. He was forced to resign in 1987 over controversies concerning the Ukrainian patriarchate, and the administration of the eparchy was given temporarily to the exarch of France and Benelux, Bishop M. Hrynchyshyn. In October 1989 Bishop M. Kuchmiak was installed as exarch. (See also *Great Britain.)

**In France, Benelux countries, and Switzerland.** Metropolitan A. Sheptytsky established the first Ukrainian Catholic mission in Paris in 1938, with J. Perridon as pastor. In 1946 Bishop I. Buchko, apostolic visitator for Ukrainian Catholics in Western Europe, made Perridon his vicar-general for France. In 1954 the archbishop of Paris was made ordinary for all Byzantine rite believers in France. A separate exarchate for Ukrainian Catholics in France, headed by Bishop V. *Malanchuk, was created in 1961. In 1982 he was succeeded by M. *Hrynchyshyn, and the exarchate was expanded to include the Benelux countries and Switzerland (from 1946 Ukrainian Catholics in these countries had been under the jurisdiction of Bishops I. Buchko and then M. Marusyn). (See also *France, *Belgium, and *Switzerland.)

**In Austria.** The first Greek Catholic church in Austria was *St Barbara's Church in Vienna, established in 1775; a parish has existed there since 1784. Many prominent church leaders and theologians have served there, including S. Lytvynovych, I. Olshavsky, Yu. Pelesh (bishop of Stanyslaviv and Peremyshl), and I. Snihursky. The parish has always been small; it has primarily served students and people working in the Austrian civil service. Many Ukrainian Catholic priests were trained at the Jesuit theological faculty in Innsbruck, and for a short time the *Barbareum seminary in Vienna trained priests. Immediately after the Second World War many parishes functioned in displaced persons' camps, but most Ukrainians soon emigrated to North America, and now the entire Ukrainian population of Austria is less than 5,000. In 1946 the Vatican designated the Roman Catholic archbishop of Vienna as ordinary for Byzantine rite Catholics; to this day there is no separate Ukrainian Catholic bishop resident in the country; M. Hornykevych serves as vicar general. (See also *Austria.)

**In Italy.** Rome emerged as a major center of the UCC after the Second World War and the suppression of the church in Western Ukraine. Archbishop I. Buchko resided there and served as the church's unofficial ambassador to the Vatican. Rome became the temporary residence of the archbishop of Lviv and metropolitan of Halych after Y. Slipy's release in 1963. A variety of educational institutions – St Josaphat's Pontifical College, a minor seminary, the Ukrainian Catholic University – as well as the secretariat of the synod of Ukrainian Catholic bishops, the headquarters of the Basilian and Studite monastic orders, and a number of other institutions are all located in Rome. (See also *Italy and the *Vatican.)

The accompanying tables provide data on the state of the UCC in 1944 and in 1989. All active and retired clergymen and members of the monastic orders are included under 'Priests,' and all churches and other pastoral centers are included under 'Parishes.' The tables are based on various *shematyzmy and church almanacs.

BIBLIOGRAPHY
Blažejovskyj, D. Byzantine Kyivan Rite Metropolitanates, Eparchies, and Exarchates: Nomenclature and Statistics (Rome 1980)
– Schematism of the Ukrainian Catholic Church: A Survey of the Church in Diaspora (Rome 1988)
– Ukrainian Catholic Clergy in Diaspora (1751–1988): Annotated List of Priests Who Served outside Ukraine (Rome 1988)
Bourdeaux, M. Gorbachev, Glasnost, and the Gospel (London 1991)
W. Lencyk, V. Markus

**Ukrainian Catholic Organization.** See Ukrainian Christian Organization.

**Ukrainian Catholic People's party** (Ukrainska katolytska narodnia partiia, or UKNP). A political party founded in Lviv in 1930 and known from 1932 as the Ukrainian People's Renewal (Ukrainska narodnia obnova). The UKNP promoted the principles of the Catholic church and opposed atheism and Freemasonry. To a large extent it superseded the Christian Social party. It demanded autonomy for the Ukrainian territories under Poland but remained loyal to the Polish state. The party operated under the care of Bishop H. *Khomyshyn and had more influence in his Stanyslaviv eparchy than in other regions of Galicia. From 1933 the president of UKNP was I. *Voliansky, who was also a deputy to the Polish Sejm. O. *Nazaruk was one of the party's leading members. Its organ was *Nova zoria. It usually succeeded in placing one of its members in the Sejm and the Senate, but it failed to attain much political power in interwar Galicia.

**Ukrainian Catholic Press Association** (Ukrainska katolytska asotsiiatsiia presy). An émigré organization founded in 1952. Centered in Philadelphia and since 1969 in Toronto, it has branches in Australia, Argentina, and Western Europe. The association has had close to 100 members and unites almost all Ukrainian Catholic publications; it is also a member of the International Catholic Press Union. The heads of the organization have included H. Luzhnytsky, L. Mydlovsky, Rev P. Khomyn, and V. Markus.

**Ukrainian Catholic Relief Committee** (Ukrainskyi katolytskyi dopomohovyi komitet, or UKDK). An agency set up by the Ukrainian Catholic hierarchy in Stamford, Connecticut, in 1946 to help and to resettle Ukrainian displaced persons and refugees in Western Europe. The committee was not an independent organization but a section of the National Catholic Welfare Council. With its founding the representatives of the Ukrainian Catholic church withdrew from the *United Ukrainian American Relief Committee. The UKDK was headed by Auxiliary Bishop A. Senyshyn and from 1961 by W. *Lencyk. Rev I. Stakh acted as its representative in Munich (1946–52). In the late 1940s and early 1950s it helped resettle about 40,000 refugees in the United States. Its activities ceased toward the end of the 1960s.

**Ukrainian Catholic Union** (Ukrainskyi katolytskyi soiuz, or UKS). A socioreligious organization founded in Lviv in 1931 through the initiative of Metropolitan A. *Sheptytsky. Its purpose was to ensure religion a proper role in public life and to promote the fully rounded social development of the Ukrainian people in a manner consistent with Christian principles. On political issues the UKS tacitly supported the Ukrainian National Democratic Alliance. It published the weekly *Meta, edited by V. Kuzmovych and M. Hnatyshak. The Meta publishing house, the journal Khrystos – nasha syla (edited by M. Hnatyshak), and the literary and public affairs monthly Dzvony (edited by P. Isaiv) co-operated with the union. The Polish authorities restricted its field of activity to Lviv archeparchy. By the end of 1935 the UKS had 416 organizational committees, 261 circles, and district councils in county centers. The first UKS president was V. *Detsykevych; he was followed in 1932 by Z. Lukavetsky. The Second World War put an end to the union's activity.

**Ukrainian Catholic University** (Ukrainskyi katolytskyi universytet im. sv. Klymentiia). An institution of

The building of the Ukrainian Catholic University

higher learning established in Rome on 25 November 1963 by Cardinal Y. *Slipy, who also served as its first rector. The university was built in 1965–6 on the grounds of the St Sophia Cathedral. At the time of its founding it had an academic staff of 24. At present the university serves as a seminary for candidates for the priesthood. It has a library, a museum, and a collection of paintings and icons, which are housed in the Church of the Zhyrovytsi Mother of God. Since 1970 the university has operated a summer school, and in 1981 a course for candidates for the diaconate was initiated. Branches of the university are located in Buenos Aires, Chicago, Washington, Philadelphia, Montreal, and London. The university has published 14 volumes of archival materials, 12 volumes of the collected works of Cardinal Y. Slipy, and other theological texts. It also publishes a periodical, *Blahovisnyk,* and a scholarly journal, *Dzvony.*

*Nasha doroha,* the journal of the Ukrainian Catholic Women's League of Canada

**Ukrainian Catholic Women's League of Canada** (Liga ukrainskykh katolytskykh zhinok Kanady). A religious and cultural organization formed in 1944 in Winnipeg from the women's sections of the *Ukrainian Catholic Brotherhood of Canada. The league undertakes cultural, educational, and charitable activities dedicated to strengthening the Ukrainian Catholic church in Canada. The league established eparchial museums in Edmonton, Saskatoon, and Toronto. In 1987 it had 152 parish branches with 6,200 members. Since 1970 it has published the quarterly magazine *Nasha doroha.* Its national presidents have been M. Dyma, K. Krouse, L. Wall, A. Pryma, S. Pototska, I. Pavlykovska, I. Malytska, V. Buchynska, M. Dolishna, A. Dudar, and Ya. Tatarniuk.

**Ukrainian Catholic Youth** (Ukrainske katolytske iunatstvo, or UCY). A Canadian organization for Ukrainian Catholic youth, founded in 1938 in Saskatoon. The group, guided in its formative years by Rev M. Horoshko, developed as an offshoot of the *Ukrainian Catholic Brotherhood to unite the various youth associations affiliated with church parishes. The UCY maintains a nonsecular profile and undertakes religious education as well as cultural activities. Each branch is organized around a church, with the parish priest as adviser.

**Ukrainian Catholic Youth League in America.** See League of Ukrainian Catholics.

Founding members of the Ukrainian caucus in the First Russian State Duma. Top row, from left: Mykola Onatsky, Vasyl Shemet, Pavlo Chyzhevsky; bottom row: Andrii Viazlov, Illia Shrah, Havrylo Zubchenko

**Ukrainian caucus in the Russian State Duma** (Ukrainskyi parliamentarnyi kliub; Ukrainska dumska/trudova hromada). The 497-member First Russian State Duma (1906) had 101 deputies from the nine Ukrainian gubernias, 63 of whom were nationally conscious Ukrainians. Most of the nationally conscious were peasants, and nearly half were members of the *Ukrainian Democratic Radical party (UDRP) or the liberal Russian *Constitutional Democratic party. To promote their goal of Ukrainian national-territorial autonomy and to represent more successfully Ukrainian national interests, 44 Ukrainian deputies from various parties constituted a caucus, the Ukrainian Parliamentary Club, chaired by I. Shrah. The caucus was assisted by an advisory committee of leading Ukrainian intellectuals in St Petersburg belonging to the *Society of Ukrainian Progressives; they established the caucus's organ, *Ukrainskii vestnik.* In the Second Duma (1907) the more radical 47-member caucus, the Ukrainian Duma Hromada, demanded democratic freedoms, autonomy for all the non-Russian peoples of the empire, the use of Ukrainian and other national languages in civic and government institutions, the reform of zemstvo and municipal governments, the distribution of all land to the peasants, an eight-hour workday, the abolition of capital punishment, and the introduction of Ukrainian-language elementary schools and teachers' colleges and of Ukrainian studies courses at Ukraine's secondary and post-secondary schools. The caucus was advised by P. Chyzhevsky, P. Stebnytsky, F. Vovk, and V. Domanytsky; Domanytsky edited the caucus's Ukrainian-language organ, *Ridna sprava – Dums'ki visti.* Duma members from the *Ukrainian Social Democratic Workers' party and

Founding members of the Ukrainian caucus in the Second Russian State Duma. Top row, from left: Yukhym Saiko, Vasyl Khvist, Nyfont Dovhopolov; bottom row: Mykola Rubis, Rev Antonii Hrynevych, Semen Nechytailo

*Spilka (14 members) did not join the UDRP-dominated caucus, which they labeled petit bourgeois. Because of the tsarist reaction and suppression of organized Ukrainian life, the 25 Ukrainian deputies (most of them right-wing 'Little Russians') in the conservative Third (1907–12) and Fourth (1912–17) Dumas did not form a caucus. Some, however, supported M. Onatsky's 1908 draft bill to introduce Ukrainian as the language of instruction in elementary schools, and protested against the banning of public commemorations of the centenary of T. Shevchenko's birth and the tsarist repressions in Galicia in 1914. (See *Duma, State.)

R. Senkus

**Ukrainian Center for Social Research** (Ukrainskyi sotsiolohichnyi instytut). An émigré institution founded in 1969. Initially an autonomous body within the Ukrainian Historical Association, it was incorporated in New York City in 1973. Works prepared by its members include R. Drazniowsky's physical map of Ukraine (1974); R. Tsybrivsky and I. Teslia's statistical study of Ukrainians in the United States and Canada identified in censuses (1975); a collection of articles on Ukrainians in American and Canadian society, edited by W. Isajiw (1976); a handbook on Ukrainian settlements outside Ukraine, edited by A. Milianych et al (1980); and *Ethnicity and National Identity: Demographic and Socioeconomic Characteristics of Persons with Ukrainian Mother Tongue in the United States*, edited by O. Wolowyna (1986). The center is preparing a new handbook on Ukrainian settlements. Its presidents have been Milianych and, since 1987, V. Bandera. Other members of the center include I. Huryn, M. Kots, A. Lencyk-Pavlichko, V. Nahirny, Yu. Pavlichko, and I. Zielyk.

**Ukrainian Central Civic Committee in France** (Ukrainskyi tsentralnyi hromadskyi komitet u Frantsii). An organization founded in Paris in 1948 for the co-ordination of Ukrainian community and cultural life and the representation of Ukrainians before the French government. Until 1985 it represented approx 20 organizations and institutions and was the only Ukrainian umbrella organization in the country. After 1985 the *Ukrainian Central Representation in France emerged as a parallel organization. The Civic Committee, now with 15 member organizations, belongs to the *World Congress of Free Ukrainians. The organization has been headed by S. Sozontiv (1948–70), O. Melnykovych (1970–9), Ya. Musianovych (1979–86), V. Malynovych (1986–9), and V. Mykhalchuk (since 1989). During the tenure of S. Sozontiv, the committee ensured that the French government officially recognized Ukrainians as one of the country's nationality groups.

**Ukrainian Central Committee** (Ukrainskyi tsentralnyi komitet, or UTsK). The only officially sanctioned Ukrainian political and community organization in the *Generalgouvernement (1939–45). Headed by V. *Kubijovyč, the UTsK oversaw virtually all secular Ukrainian activities following the closure of all other Ukrainian institutions in the Generalgouvernement. It also acted as a representative body that brought Ukrainian concerns to the attention of the German authorities. Its activities and structure were shaped by the occupation policies and the nature of the Nazi regime.

The building in Cracow where the Ukrainian Central Committee was housed

**History.** Shortly after the fall of Poland local Ukrainian committees sprang up in the Generalgouvernement to organize cultural-educational activities, manage economic affairs, and provide Ukrainians with representation before the German authorities. In November 1939 the idea of a central Ukrainian organization was put forward at a congress of local committee deputies in Cracow. R. Sushko, the chief OUN representative in the Generalgouvernement, set out the legal and organizational basis for such a central organization, and a conference in late November established the Ukrainian National Alliance (UNO) as the central body. Sushko nominated V. Kubijovyč to be its leader; the other members of the executive included O. Boidunyk, M. Khronoviat, I. Zilynsky, and Ya. Rak. The new organization was tolerated, but not officially recognized, by the German authorities.

Early in its existence the central organization developed a close working relationship with the *Ukrainske Vydavnytstvo (UV) publishing house, the only legally sanctioned Ukrainian press in the Generalgouvernement. It used the publisher to print Ukrainian textbooks, and the UV's *Krakivs'ki visti served as the unofficial organ of the UTsK.

The formal organizational structure of the UTsK began to take shape after a meeting of Ukrainian representatives in April 1940. The numerous local groups functioning under its umbrella were reconstituted as Ukrainian relief committees (Ukrainski dopomohovi komitety, or UDKs) in order to expedite official German recognition. The UTsK itself was formally constituted in June 1940 as the official umbrella body of the UDKs and as such received official sanction. It incorporated other Ukrainian organizations under its name in order to provide them with a measure of legal status. This arrangement later developed into a system of subsidiary *labor alliances that were linked to the various departments of the UTsK. It also established the *Ukrainian educational societies (Ukrainski osvitni tovarystva, or UOTs) as affiliated groups. They were granted official recognition in July 1940.

The UTsK executive was headed by Kubijovyč, with V. Hlibovytsky as deputy leader and executive officer. The UTsK departments and their heads consisted of the following: administration, O. Boidunyk, M. Tsenko (from 1941), and A. Figol (from 1943); finance, O. Zybenko, R. Mytsyk, and Omelian Tarnavsky (from 1942); social services, O. Malynovsky and Rev M. Sopuliak (from late 1941); culture, M. Duzhy and M. Kushnir; education, N. Hirniak, I. Teslia, and P. Isaiv; economic affairs, M. Khronoviat, A. Milianych, and O. Kotyk-Stepanovych; and youth, Ya. Rak, Yu. Tatomyr, S. Levytsky, and Z. Zeleny. The UTsK staff numbered 80 to 200 people in 1940–5. In the spring of 1941 it dealt with 26 UDKs, 33 rural-district delegations, and 100 local trustees. The UTsK also established a mission in Berlin (staffed initially by Figol and then by Kotyk-Stepanovych) in the spring of 1941. Offices were also opened in Vienna and, briefly, Bratislava in 1944 during the evacuation before oncoming Soviet troops.

The OUN maintained a close connection with the UTsK, a body in whose formation it had played a key role. Excluding Kubijovyč, many of the UTsK leaders and a significant number of its cultural and organizational cadres were OUN members. The UTsK maintained an ostensibly neutral position on the split within the OUN between the Bandera and Melnyk factions, although tacitly it supported the latter. With the outbreak of German-Soviet hostilities a large number of the OUN activists who had been working with the UTsK joined *OUN expeditionary groups. At the same time the UTsK declined to join the Ukrainian National Committee, established by the Bandera OUN faction in Cracow in late June 1941. It also refrained from involving itself in Galician affairs, although it did open the Work Bureau in Lviv (eventually with a branch in Rivne) to assist in the movement of refugees from the Generalgouvernement back to Galicia.

After the annexation of Galicia by the Generalgouvernement the UTsK did not agree with German demands that it expand its activities into Galicia, because of the political characteristics of that territory. In September 1941 the Germans established the *Ukrainian Regional Committee (UKK) to oversee the Distrikt Galizien, with statutes

The presidium of the Ukrainian Central Committee in 1943. Sitting, from left: Kost Pankivsky, Volodymyr Kubijovyč, Vasyl Hlibovytsky; standing: Zenon Zeleny, Rev Mykhailo Sopuliak, Petro Isaiv, Atanas Figol, Omelian Tarnavsky, Ya. Mazurak, Mykhailo Kushnir

similar to those of the UTsK. In its jurisdiction the Ukrainian okruha committees (UOKs) performed the same function as the UDKs. K. *Pankivsky was the head of the UKK.

In February 1942 the Germans dissolved the UKK and ordered the UTsK to expand its activities into Galicia. In March 1942 the Lviv executive branch of the UTsK began operations under K. Pankivsky, who then became the UTsK's deputy leader. The cultural and youth departments were transferred to Lviv. The UTsK's jurisdiction in Galicia was fairly narrow. Ukrainians assumed control over the lower administration, the commissioners of education, the lower courts, and the auxiliary police. That situation, however, did not prevent abuses by the German authorities, which the UTsK reported to Governor O. Wächter, Governor-General H. Frank, and the Gestapo chief in Berlin, H. Müller. Another aspect of German-Ukrainian co-operation was the creation, through the efforts of Wächter, of the *Division Galizien. The Military Board (the division's civilian advisory council) worked with the UTsK in this area.

The Germans agreed to limited Ukrainian involvement in the administration of Galicia, but both internal and external factors made Ukrainian participation difficult. In order to protect the civilian population the UTsK urged Ukrainians not to provoke the Germans and called for an end to revolutionary military resistance. At the request of the UTsK the Ukrainian Catholic hierarch (A. Sheptytsky) issued a proclamation to that effect.

The capture of eastern Galicia by Soviet armies in the spring of 1944 resulted in the partial evacuation of the UTsK and its workers to the western reaches of the Generalgouvernement; the central bureau continued to operate out of Cracow. A skeleton staff headed by Pankivsky continued to work in Lviv. The Soviet advance of the summer and fall into Galicia and the capture of Lviv resulted in further evacuations of people via Cracow to Germany. Temporary accommodations were found for nearly 10,000 people in Slovakia. In early 1945 there were 300,000 to 400,000 Ukrainians in Germany who required the legal and social services the UTsK could provide. Through an agreement with the Generalgouvernement administration a UTsK bureau headed by Pankivsky was opened in Lüben (now Lubin) in lower Silesia. The Cracow bureau was reduced, and the Berlin mission was expanded. The Vienna bureau was headed by Yu. Poliansky. The Ukrainske Vydavnytstvo and the editorial office of *Krakivs'ki visti* were also moved to Vienna.

To assist Ukrainian workers and refugees approx 20 local centers were set up by the UTsK in various German cities, and a conference of their directors was convened by the UTsK in Weimar in March 1945. When the *Ukrainian National Committee (UNK) was set up under the leadership of Gen P. *Shandruk, Kubijovyč, as the head of the UTsK, became its deputy leader, and the UTsK local centers became the primary network of the UNK. After the Allied occupation of Germany Kubijovyč dissolved the UTsK on 17 April 1945 in Aufkirchen (in southern Bavaria) and handed its assets over to V. Mudry's civic committee, which formed the basis for the *Central Representation of the Ukrainian Emigration in Germany.

**Activity.** From July 1940 until the outbreak of German-Soviet hostilities in June 1941 the UTsK leadership concerned itself mainly with reviving Ukrainian life in the territories that had been under Polish control. In virtually every village with a Ukrainian population, a Ukrainian school and a co-operative were established. A UOT (which functioned much as a Prosvita society) could be found in 80 percent of these villages, and approx 50 percent had youth groups and nursery schools. Much of this educational work was conducted by refugees from Galicia. In approx 70 percent of the villages a 'man of trust' could be found. The most active Ukrainian centers in the Generalgouvernement were Kholm, Jarosław, Peremyshl, Sianik, Krynytsia, and Cracow.

Social services were by far the most important UTsK function and consisted of public health care as well as assistance to children, the sick, invalids, students, and Ukrainian POWs. Dealing with these issues was made even more difficult by the constant interference of the German authorities.

Food supplies were distributed by the UDK-UOK network, which received additional rations for community kitchens, student residences, and rest homes for children and youths as well as for civil servants and teachers. In mountainous regions seasonal kitchens were set up to deal with food shortages in the spring. In late 1943 there were 1,366 Ukrainian kitchens, which fed nearly 100,000 people. The UTsK was particularly successful in providing aid to victims of a flood in the Subcarpathian region in 1941: in the spring of 1942 it saved approx 30,000 children from starvation by resettling them with peasant families in Galician Podilia and Pokutia.

The UTsK also cared for Ukrainian POWs captured during the German-Polish conflict. It arranged for the quick release of around 85,000 of them. Some returned to the Generalgouvernement; others remained as laborers in Germany. The fate of Ukrainians taken on the Soviet-German front was much worse. Only very few, mainly those from Galicia, were released. They were forced to return home by foot, and most of them were ill with typhus. The UTsK commissioner for POW affairs, R. Danylevych, toured virtually all the POW camps on Ukrainian territory, but he was powerless to stem the implicit German policy of exterminating Slavic POWs. The UTsK could do nothing for the staggering numbers of prisoners who died of disease, starvation, and exposure or were taken to labor camps in Germany.

The UTsK assisted in resettling approx 10,000 Ukrainians who took advantage of the Volksdeutsche provisions of the German-Soviet accord in camps (*Umsiedlungslager*) in Germany in 1939–40. The UTsK secured administrative positions for many people within the Generalgouvernement civil service or in other state institutions. Among them were a few Orthodox clergymen from Bukovyna, who assisted in the Ukrainization of the Orthodox church. The UTsK also managed to resettle nearly 600 families in the Kholm region after they had been evacuated to Germany. When the Germans set up artillery ranges in the Lviv region in 1943, they displaced several thousand of the local rural population. The UTsK, in concert with local UOKs, helped resettle those displaced people in other areas.

The UTsK helped Ukrainian laborers in Germany through Ukrainian organizations there. Its Berlin mission issued certificates of nationality to workers from the Generalgouvernement. The UTsK petitioned the German authorities concerning political prisoners, to whom it sent care packages. It also secured compensation for Ukrainian invalids of the German-Polish War and the war for Ukrainian independence in 1918–20.

The public health department of the UTsK was directed by V. Karkhut and later by R. Osinchuk. It worked with the Labor Alliance of the Medical-Sanitation Service to deploy medical personnel, establish medical clinics and disinfection centers, train auxiliary medical personnel, and open four rest resorts.

In education the UTsK was fairly limited because under Nazi rule all schools were state-run. The UTsK co-operated with the German authorities in forming new schools, finding teachers, and establishing curricula. The UTsK's education department organized training for those not qualified to teach in vocational schools and the retraining of teachers from gymnasiums. It also organized a preschool system and oversaw pupil residences (131 in 1943–4, which housed 7,000 pupils). Funds for these institutions were taken from the social services treasury. The department was aided by the Ukrainian Teachers' Labor Alliance.

The Ukrainian Students' Aid Commission (KODUS), funded by the social services treasury and private donations, was established in 1940. It issued 730 scholarships (valued at 1,350,000 zloty) in 1943, subsidized a student cafeteria in Lviv, and maintained an assistance fund for Ukrainian students. The *Labor Alliance of Ukrainian Students was the main Ukrainian student body in the Generalgouvernement.

The cultural department of the UTsK oversaw extramural education. In the fall of 1939 the Prosvita, Kachkovsky, and Ridna Khata (in Podlachia and the Kholm region) societies were revived throughout the Generalgouvernement. On 16–17 March 1940 the First Cultural-Educational Congress was held in Cracow. In July 1940 UOTs began to function largely independently of one another but were overseen by the UTsK cultural department and maintained a liaison with local UDKs. In March 1941 there were 808 UOTs with 46,000 members. The UTsK cultural department issued guidelines for the UOTs, prepared educational materials for them, published the monthly *Dosvitni vohni*, assisted in the assembling of libraries, and organized courses for UDK cultural officials.

After Germany took control of Galicia from the Soviet

Union all branches and reading rooms of the Prosvita society were reopened. The UTsK cultural department also oversaw the work of the Institute of Public Education (INO, headed by S. Volynets) and the Institute of Folk Art (INT, headed by S. Saprun). The INO aimed to train field workers and to provide them with instructional materials. The INT was divided into three virtually independent sections, music, theater, and folk arts. It oversaw 780 choirs and organized 10 conducting classes. It organized a festival of Ukrainian song in Lviv on 8 July 1943, in which over 1,200 singers participated. Art associations came under the umbrella of the Literary-Artistic Club. They included associations of painters, writers, journalists, musicians, actors, photographers, and scholars. A women's section, headed by M. Biliakova and M. Zaiachkivska, largely continued the work of the *Union of Ukrainian Women. On 2–3 March 1942 the first congress of deputies of the women's groups of the Generalgouvernement took place in Lviv. The women's organizations dealt mainly with social services.

The UTsK also tried to stimulate academic activity. There were some difficulties in this area. An Institute of Ukrainian Studies was planned to open in Cracow in 1941, but the plan was halted by the German-Soviet War. A Shevchenko Institute was to replace the banned Shevchenko Scientific Society, but it too was proscribed by Berlin. Nevertheless, the Labor Alliance of Academic Workers was established, the Ukrainske Vydavnytstvo publishing house remained active, and educational and vocational courses were taught. The UTsK also assisted Ukrainian academic institutions (such as the Ukrainian Free University) through the separate Academic Fund, headed by V. Simovych.

The youth department of the UTsK organized physical-education and sports clubs. Youth groups were divided according to age: 7 to 14, 14 to 18, and 18 to 24. In July 1941 the UOTs oversaw 52 school youth groups, 28 teen groups, 18 sports associations, and 46 fire brigades. The youth department organized camps, courses for cultural instructors, and jamborees (1,200 youths participated in one held in Kholm in 1941). Other youth organizations under the UTsK included the Ukrainian Youth Educational Societies (VSUM), which were similar to the scouting *Plast Ukrainian Youth Association. In 1944 they had over 2,500 members, in 60 groups. The youth department organized two Galician youth congresses in 1943 and set up a number of rest and instructional camps. Leading VSUM figures included R. Olesnytsky and K. Paliiv. When the German authorities established compulsory construction service (Baudienst), the UTsK secured the right to form a separate *Ukrainian Service to the Fatherland, headed by M. Rusnak.

The UTsK's economic activity was marginal owing to wartime conditions. During its existence, however, some co-operatives were reopened, and new ones were established. After considerable difficulties Ukrainian county associations and the so-called Society of Patrons of Ukrainian Co-operation, headed by Yu. Pavlykovsky, were set up. Co-operatives were kept under German control, however. The UTsK economic department called a congress of merchants and craftsmen and created the requisite labor alliances.

The UTsK was financed by a variety of means. The primary source was a budgetary allotment given by the Generalgouvernement, earmarked mainly for social services but also covering administrative costs. Significant contributions were also made through regular collections among Ukrainian citizens. Material assistance (food, clothing, medication) also arrived from the International Red Cross in Geneva, with which the UTsK was in constant contact. The deputy head of the financial department in Lviv was V. Pushkar.

The UTsK existed for over five years as the only Ukrainian social and community force during the Second World War that concerned itself with the vital interests of the Ukrainian people. For Ukrainians its activity was particularly significant in that it made possible the restoration of some national features to institutions that until then had been increasingly Polonized. These gains were made in spite of limitations imposed by the Nazi regime, such as the forbidding of all contact between the UTsK and Ukrainians in the Reichskommissariat Ukraine, Rumania, and other territories.

BIBLIOGRAPHY
Pan'kivs'kyi, K. Vid derzhavy do komitetu (lito 1941 r. u L'vovi) (Toronto 1957; 2nd edn 1970)
– Roky nimets'koï okupatsiï (New York–Toronto 1965; 2nd edn 1983)
Kubijovyč, V. Ukraïntsi v Heneral'nii hubernii, 1939–41: Istoriia Ukraïns'koho tsentral'noho komitetu (Chicago 1975)
                                                           V. Kubijovyč

**Ukrainian Central Committee in Poland** (Ukrainskyi tsentralnyi komitet u Polshchi, or UTsK). A central émigré organization, founded in Warsaw in 1921 and active until the fall of Poland in September 1939. The UTsK provided a community base in Poland for the Government-in-exile of the UNR, with which it co-operated closely. It conducted cultural and educational work and provided legal and other aid to its members. Most of the political and military leaders of the UNR who lived in Poland belonged to it. The Central Executive of the UTsK co-ordinated the work of 68 branches (1929), with a membership of approx 15,000, located in both central Poland and parts of Western Ukraine under Polish rule. In Kalisz the UTsK organized a rest station for 310 invalids and a Ukrainian gymnasium; in Peremyshl it founded the Petliura Student Residence for émigré children; in Warsaw it sponsored the Lysenko Ukrainian National Choir. The UTsK was headed throughout its existence by M. *Kovalsky. The executive members included V. Kushch, I. Zolotnytsky, M. Sadovsky, and V. Krasnopilsky. Policy was set by the UTsK Council, which was elected every three years at a congress of delegates of the Ukrainian political emigration in Poland. It included V. Andriievsky, M. Bezruchko, L. Chykalenko, Ye. Glovinsky, O. Halkyn, P. Kholodny, O. Kuzminsky, O. Lototsky, A. Lukashevych, Yu. Lypa, S. Pysmenny, M. Sereda, V. Sinkler, P. Shandruk, P. Shkurat, S. Shramchenko, R. Smal-Stotsky, V. Solsky, M. Tyshkevych, M. Yunakiv, O. Zahorodsky, and V. Zmiienko. The official organs of the UTsK in Poland were Visty (published 1923–8 in Warsaw), Shliakh nezalezhnosty (1929–31), and Za nezalezhnist' (1934–8). They were all edited by Shkurat.

The UTsK in Poland worked with other Ukrainian émigré organizations, in Czechoslovakia, Rumania, and France. Together they held congresses of the Ukrainian emigration (the first in 1929) and formed the *Supreme Emigration Council.

                                                           A. Zhukovsky

**Ukrainian Central Co-operative Committee** (Tsentralnyi ukrainskyi kooperatyvnyi komitet, or Kooptsentr, aka Central Ukrainian Co-operative Committee). The central organization of the *co-operative movement in Ukraine, established in Kiev as a temporary body in April 1917 and as a permanent body in September 1918. It represented the whole Ukrainian co-operative movement at home and abroad, defended the interests of co-operatives in government circles, trained co-operative workers, audited individual co-operatives, organized conferences and congresses, collected statistics on co-operatives, and developed and propagated the theory of co-operation. Its activities were organized into three sections, organizational-legal, economic-statistical, and cultural-educational. Membership was restricted to co-operative associations and unions. The board of directors was headed by M. *Tuhan-Baranovsky, assisted by K. Matsiievych; the executive was headed by B. Martos. By the end of 1918 Kooptsentr represented 45 credit, 110 consumer, 31 mixed, 4 agricultural, and 62 other co-operative unions. A year later there were almost 400 unions and 30,000 individual co-operatives in Ukraine. The committee published the journal *Ukraïns'ka kooperatsiia* and then, irregularly, a bulletin. In 1919 its courses were reorganized into the Tuhan-Baranovsky Co-operative Institute, the first school of its kind in the world. Kooptsentr was dissolved by the Soviet authorities in 1921.

**Ukrainian Central People's Council.** See Central Ruthenian People's Council.

**Ukrainian Central Rada.** See Central Rada.

**Ukrainian Central Relief Alliance in Austria** (Ukrainske tsentralne dopomohove obiednannia Avstrii, or UTsDOA; German: Ukrainische Zentralhilfsvereinigung in Österreich). A social-services organization founded in Innsbruck in February 1946 to care for and assist in the resettling of Ukrainian émigrés, DPs, and refugees, in co-operation with the United Ukrainian American Relief Committee, Caritas, the International Relief Organization, and other organizations. It also provided cultural-educational facilities and programs, established a network of schools (of all levels) and recreational camps, and tended Ukrainian burial sites. Later it co-ordinated the work of all Ukrainian organizations and institutions in Austria and represented the Ukrainian community before the Austrian government and other institutions. The UTsDOA membership consisted of nine provincial committees and a number of cultural and professional associations in Austria, and its activities were centered in Innsbruck, Salzburg, Linz, Graz, Villach, Klagenfurt, and (after its release from the Soviet zone in 1955) Vienna. The headquarters were moved to Salzburg in 1950, and to Vienna in 1965. In the 1940s the UTsDOA had approx 12,000 members and served over 30,000 Ukrainians. After the emigration of most Ukrainians from Austria by the early 1950s, the membership declined. In the early 1980s the membership stood at approx 800, and the alliance served nearly 5,000 Ukrainians. In the mid-1980s it began assisting a new wave of Ukrainian emigrants, particularly from Poland and also from the USSR and its satellites (Czechoslovakia, Yugoslavia, Rumania, Hungary, Bulgaria).

The UTsDOA has been headed successively by M. Rosliak, I. Kedryn, I. Tyktor, Ye. Glovinsky, M. Kurakh, V.

Bemko, D. Bobanych, M. Kovalevsky, I. Dashkovsky (1957–65), S. Naklovych (1965–71), and Yu. Kostiuk (1971–5). It has been headed by S. Naklovych since 1975.

BIBLIOGRAPHY
Maruniak, V. *Ukraïns'ka emigratsiia v Nimechchyni i Avstriï po druhii svitovii viini* (Munich 1985)

S. Naklovych

**Ukrainian Central Representation in Argentina** (Ukrainska tsentralna reprezentatsiia v Argentini; Spanish: Representación Central Ucraina en la República Argentina). An umbrella organization for Ukrainian associations in Argentina, established in 1947 in Buenos Aires. Inspired by the example of representative Ukrainian councils in Canada and the United States, the group managed to bring almost all the noncommunist Ukrainian-Argentinian societies into its ranks. Strong infighting, however, particularly between the Prosvita and Vidrodzhennia societies, was a major problem for the group and limited its effectiveness for many years. This tension subsided somewhat in the 1960s. The Representation is a member of the *World Congress of Free Ukrainians.

**Ukrainian Central Representation in France** (Ukrainske tsentralne predstavnytstvo u Frantsii). One of two émigré umbrella organizations in France, it was established in September 1985 as a breakaway body from the *Ukrainian Central Civic Committee in France. It represents seven organizations and institutions affiliated with or sympathetic to the *Ukrainian Liberation Front. It is headed by B. Kopchuk.

Members of the executive of the Ukrainian Christian Movement in 1963. From left: Volodymyr Kalvarovsky (secretary of the Supreme Council), Petro Zeleny (head in Belgium and 4th vice-president), Osyp Melnykovych (head in France and 2nd vice-president), Oleksander Kulchytsky (head of external relations), Volodymyr Yaniv (president), Hnat Martynets (head in Germany and 1st vice-president), Markiian Zaiats (secretary of the executive)

**Ukrainian Christian Movement** (Ukrainskyi khrystyianskyi rukh, or UKhR). A community and religious organization of Ukrainian Catholics in Western Europe, founded on the initiative of Archbishop I. *Buchko in 1955. V. Yaniv was appointed president, and M. Konovalets was made head of its council (later he was replaced by I. Holubovych). National chapters were established in Germany, France, England, and Belgium, headed by H.

Martynets, O. Melnykovych, R. Rudensky, and V. Popovych respectively. In seven other countries (four of which were outside Europe) trust groups were set up. As an organization with an ecumenical purpose, the UKhR invited Ukrainian Orthodox activists to participate.

The UKhR sought to expand lay participation in Ukrainian religious life. It organized pilgrimages to Rome and Lourdes for the millennium of Olha's baptism, the 15th anniversary of A. Sheptytsky's death, and other occasions. For the 10th anniversary of the Soviet arrest of the Ukrainian Catholic hierarchy and the 25th anniversary of the Soviet abolition of the Ukrainian Autocephalous Orthodox church, it compiled memorial booklets, which were distributed throughout the world. In 1962 the UKhR initiated a campaign for the release of Metropolitan Y. *Slipy. The UKhR participated officially in international Catholic organizations, particularly in World Congresses of the Lay Apostolate. It also organized study days in Rocca di Papa in Italy on the topic of Ukrainian laity in the life of the church. It supported a conference on religion in the life of the Ukrainian people, together with the Shevchenko Scientific Society (NTSh), the Ukrainian Free University (UVU), the Ukrainian Free Academy of Sciences (UVAN), and the Ukrainian Theological Scientific Society. The proceedings of both events were published. The UKhR also published *Informatyvnyi lystok zv'iazku*. Leading UKhR activists included D. Buchynsky, Ye. Glovinsky, V. Kachmar, O. Kulchytsky, I. Mirchuk, D. Pelensky, S. Shakh, and P. Zeleny. In the early 1970s UKhR activity dropped off, and its members joined the laymen's movement in support of a Ukrainian patriarchate.

V. Yaniv

## Ukrainian Christian Organization

(Ukrainska khrystyianska orhanizatsiia, or UKhO). A nonpolitical organization established in Lviv in 1925 for educating Ukrainian Catholics in a Catholic spirit and countering sectarian and communist influences. In 1930 it assumed the name Ukrainian Catholic Organization. It set up the newspaper *Nova zoria* (1926–38) and the Biblioteka UKhO publishing house. The organization remained loyal to the Polish state and favored a realistic policy aimed at winning autonomy for the Ukrainian territories under Poland. It opposed Ukrainian and Polish nationalism and criticized the Polish government for neglecting 'burning Ukrainian problems.' In the elections of 1928 it supported the Ukrainian National Democratic Alliance. The first president of UKhO was Rev T. *Halushchynsky, and its leading members included O. Nazaruk and S. Tomashivsky.

## Ukrainian Citizens' Committee

(Horozhanskyi komitet, or Ukrainskyi horozhanskyi komitet). A Ukrainian public body formed in Lviv in December 1918, after the evacuation of the Ukrainian government, for the purpose of representing the interests of the city's Ukrainian community before the Polish occupational authorities and providing relief to the victims of the military operations (particularly prisoners of war and political prisoners). The committee had several departments – charitable (Samaritan), legal aid, and clandestine operations for liaison with the Ukrainian army. The president of the committee was S. *Fedak, and its leading members were L. Hankevych, Rev L. Kunytsky, M. Panchyshyn, and O. Fedak-Sheparovych. Most of its membership consisted of women. The body was dissolved in September 1921.

The executive of the Ukrainian Civic Committee in Czechoslovakia. From left: Nykyfor Hryhoriiv, Mykyta Shapoval, Mykola Halahan

## Ukrainian Civic Committee in Czechoslovakia

(Ukrainskyi hromadskyi komitet v Chekhoslovachchyni, or UHK). An immigrant aid organization established in the summer of 1921 in Prague. The group was initiated by Mykyta *Shapoval, who used his connections with the Czechoslovak authorities to secure government funds for the committee's organizational and relief work. The committee had a medical and sanitary department under the leadership of S. Litov that ran a clinic and provided aid to invalids. It also initiated the establishment of the *Ukrainian Husbandry Academy in Poděbrady (1922) and the Ukrainian Higher Pedagogical Institute in Prague (1923). Initially the UHK represented all Ukrainians in Czechoslovakia, but eventually some émigré circles broke away from it because of ideological and political differences. In 1925 the Czechoslovak government withdrew its financial support, and the committee was replaced by several new organizations. The president of the UHK was M. Shapoval, and its most active members were N. Hryhoriiv and M. Halahan.

The logo of the Ukrainian Civic Publishing Fund (artist: Robert Lisovsky)

## Ukrainian Civic Publishing Fund

(Ukrainskyi hromadskyi vydavnychyi fond). A publishing house in Prague from 1923 to 1932. Initially part of the *Ukrainian Civic Committee in Czechoslovakia and then an independent institution, it was directed by a bureau headed by Ye. Vyrovy and consisting of Ye. Prykhodko, P. Bohatsky, H. Shcherbyna, and Mykyta Shapoval. It published approx

40 scholarly and popular-educational books on a variety of topics, including Ukrainian literary criticism (by L. Biletsky), Ukrainian ethnography and anthropology (F. Vovk), political economy (M. Tuhan-Baranovsky), Ukrainian theater and cultural history (D. Antonovych), philosophy (Ya. Yarema and D. Chyzhevsky), educational theory (S. Rusova), Ukrainian art (D. Antonovych, V. Sichynsky, and V. Shcherbakivsky), statistics (F. Shcherbyna), music (F. Yakymenko), and the pure and applied sciences (S. Ryndyk, F. Burian, A. Honcharenko, F. Yakymenko, M. Pavlichuk, M. Chaikovsky, M. Halahan, V. Harmashov, F. Frolov, R. Kakhnykevych, and L. Hrabyna). The fund also published a bulletin and editions of poetry by O. Oles, Yu. Darahan, and H. Chuprynka.

**Ukrainian Club** (Ukrainskyi klub). A literary and artistic society founded in Kiev in 1908 by various leading Ukrainian cultural figures, such as M. Starytsky, M. Sadovsky, O. Pchilka, O. Oles, and M. Lysenko. The club's literary-dramatic, musical, lecture, and library sections organized theatrical performances by Sadovsky's theater, literary-musical evenings which included artists from the Solovtsov theater and advanced students from Lysenko's music school, and public lectures by figures such as I. Franko, M. Kotsiubynsky, and Lesia Ukrainka. The tsarist authorities closed down the club in 1912. It was revived in 1913 as the Rodyna club, and it was disbanded again by the authorities at the outbreak of the First World War.

**Ukrainian Committee in Czechoslovakia** (Ukrainskyi komitet v Chekhoslovachchyni). A community organization established in Prague in 1926 after the dissolution of the *Ukrainian Civic Committee. Most members of the committee were Ukrainian émigré socialist revolutionaries, social democrats, radicals, or nonpartisan émigrés. The chairmen of its executive board were N. Hryhoriiv, M. Halahan, and S. Shelukhyn. The committee declined in the 1930s.

**Ukrainian Communist party** (Ukrainska komunistychna partiia, or Ukapisty). A Communist group of no more than 250 members who in 1920–4 supported Soviet rule but opposed Russian domination of Ukraine through the CP(B)U. Its most prominent leaders were Yu. *Mazurenko, Mykhailo Tkachenko, and A. *Richytsky.

In January 1919, at the Sixth Congress of the Ukrainian Social Democratic Workers' party, a group called the *nezalezhnyky* (see *Ukrainian Social Democratic Workers' Party [Independentists]) walked out and began to function as a separate party with its own press organ, *Chervonyi prapor*. It adopted an ideology of national communism, favoring a Soviet regime in Ukraine but rejecting both the UNR Directory and the CP(B)U. In June 1919 it formed a revolutionary committee under the protection of Otaman D. *Zeleny, who had revolted against the Bolshevik regime. In August the group split: its left faction joined the *Borotbists, and the majority co-operated in military matters with the Directory for a short period.

On 22–25 January 1920 the group held the founding convention of the Ukrainian Communist party in Kiev and appealed unsuccessfully to the Comintern for recognition as the legitimate representative of the Ukrainian proletariat. In the next few months it attracted Communists who opposed Russian domination. Yu. Lapchynsky joined the Ukapisty after his Federalist Opposition within the CP(B)U was defeated, and a number of former Borotbists went over to the Ukapisty when their group merged with the CP(B)U.

In 1919 V. *Vynnychenko organized an émigré branch of the Ukapisty in Vienna. In the summer of 1920 he visited Moscow and Kharkiv, ostensibly representing the Ukapisty, and was named Ukrainian Soviet deputy premier, but he soon realized that the Bolsheviks would not give him any real power. Vynnychenko left Ukraine and ended his association with the Ukapisty.

Thereafter the Ukapisty were tolerated as a legal but impotent opposition which objected to the economic exploitation of Soviet Ukraine by Russia. In 1921 Yu. Mazurenko and M. Yavorsky, both members of the party's Central Committee, left to join the CP(B)U. In 1923 a so-called Left Faction was formed with CP(B)U encouragement to subvert the Ukrainian Communist party from within, but it was expelled from the party. In August 1924 the Ukapisty again applied for admission to the Comintern, and the Left Faction was drawn into the discussions in order to discredit the Ukapisty. In December the Comintern Executive Committee ordered both the party and the faction to dissolve. They complied in January 1925. Their members were admitted into the CP(B)U, where they helped carry out the *Ukrainization policy. The leading Ukapisty members were appointed to high posts in Ukraine. Eventually most of them were charged with Ukrainian nationalism and executed by the NKVD.

BIBLIOGRAPHY
*Memorandum Ukraïns'koï komunistychnoï partiï Kongresovi III Komunistychnoho Internatsionalu* (Kiev 1920)
*Prohrama Ukraïns'koï komunistychnoï partiï* (Vienna–Kiev 1920)
Halahan, M. 'Likvidatsiia U.K.P.,' *Nova Ukraïna*, 1925, no. 1
*Kak i pochemu Ispolkom Kominterna raspustil UKP* (Kharkiv 1925)
Popov, M. *Narys istoriï Komunistychnoï partiï (bil'shovykiv) Ukraïny* (Kharkiv 1928)
*Dokumenty ukraïns'koho komunizmu* (New York 1962)
Mace, J. *Communism and the Dilemmas of National Liberation: National Communism in Soviet Ukraine, 1918–1933* (Cambridge, Mass 1983)
Maistrenko, I. *Istoriia moho pokolinnia* (Edmonton 1985)
J. Mace

**Ukrainian Communist Youth Association** (Ukrainska komunistychna yunatska spilka, or Ukrainska komunistychna robitnycha yunatska spilka). The youth organization allied with the *Ukrainian Communist party. It was founded in 1920 by some former members of the *Communist Youth Association and by the *Independent Social Democratic Youth Association. The new association was based in Kharkiv, and its leading members were Ya. Chmil and P. Syniavsky. The association competed with the Communist Youth League of Ukraine, which was allied with the CP(B)U for several years. In 1925 it was absorbed by the league.

**Ukrainian Community Aid in France** (Ukrainska hromadska opika u Frantsii). An organization founded in 1946 in Paris by former members of the Union of Ukrainian Emigré Organizations in France. It had 10 branches throughout the country. It was headed by S. *Sozontiv (1946–54) and S. Kachura (1954–68) and included Yu. Batsutsa and I. Kosenko among its active members. It ceased to exist in the late 1960s. The majority of its membership also belonged to the Society of Former Combatants of the Ukrainian Republican Democratic Army in France.

**Ukrainian Community Development Committee** (Ukrainskyi komitet suspilno-hromadskoho rozvoiu, or UCDC). A subcommittee of the National Executive of the Ukrainian Canadian Congress (UCC) established in May 1982. The group was established as a prairie-wide committee consisting of 15 members, five from each province, to provide the national UCC with concrete proposals for actions to meet the long-term needs of the Ukrainian community in Canada. In this regard it undertook a major survey of organized Ukrainian life in Alberta, Saskatchewan, and Manitoba and co-ordinated a series of 'needs-assessment' conferences in each of these provinces in 1984–5. The committee's findings were published as *Building the Future: Ukrainian Canadians in the Twenty-First Century* and submitted as a report to the UCC at its 1986 congress. By this time the UCDC had begun to function as a strategic development committee for the UCC provincial councils in Alberta and Saskatchewan and as the initiative group for the formation of UCC provincial councils in Manitoba and British Columbia. It has continued to serve in an advisory capacity to the national UCC. Chairpersons of the committee have included M. Lupul (1982–3), L. Melosky (1983–4), C. Devrome (1984–5), M. Spolsky (1985–6), T. Harras (1986–7), and R. Petryshyn (1987–8).

The seal of the Ukrainian Congress Committee of America

**Ukrainian Congress Committee of America** (Ukrainskyi kongresovyi komitet Ameryky, or UKKA). An umbrella organization of Ukrainian civic associations in the United States founded at the First Congress of Ukrainian Americans in Washington, DC, on 25 May 1940. Its chief promoters were four fraternal insurance associations: the *Ukrainian National Association (UNA), the Ukrainian Workingmen's Association (see *Ukrainian Fraternal Association [UFA]), the *Providence Association of Ukrainian Catholics in America, and the *Ukrainian National Aid Association. Besides them the committee represented, in 1980, about 70 political, social, scholarly, professional, economic, religious, women's, young people's, and veterans' organizations of a national status and 65 local branches. By 1990 membership had dropped to 42 organizations in 67 local branches as a result of a major rift and the establishment of the Ukrainian American Coordinating Council, a rival representative organization for Ukrainian Americans.

The governing bodies of the UKKA are the Congress of Ukrainians in the United States, held every four years (the 16th in 1992); the Presidium and Executive (30 members altogether); and the National Council (formerly the Political Council, the Audit Commission, and the Court), consisting of two representatives from each of the national organizations and one representative from each of the 12 largest local branches of the UKKA. The latter body was intended to serve as a kind of parliament between congresses, but it does not sit regularly and does not have the authority needed to fulfill this function. The presidents, elected at quadrennial congresses, have been M. Murashko (1940–4), S. Shumeyko (1944–9), L. *Dobriansky (1949–84), I. Bilynsky (1984–92), and A. Lozynsky. Executive directors have included Yu. Revai, V. Mudry, V. Bazarko, and Ya. Haivas. UKKA activists have included A. Batiuk, D. Halychyn, B. Hnatiuk, J. Lesawyer, O. Lototska, T. Mynyk, M. Piznak, I. Roberts, R. Smal-Stotsky, J. Flis, and S. Yarema.

The UKKA has consistently defended Ukraine's right to national independence and the interests of the Ukrainian people inside and outside Ukraine. As well, it has promoted recognition of the contribution of the Ukrainian community to American society. After the war the UKKA opposed the repatriation of Ukrainian displaced persons to the USSR and fought for their resettlement in the United States; it established the *United Ukrainian American Relief Committee for this purpose. It demanded that the United States establish diplomatic relations with Kiev and won the US president's annual proclamation of Captive Nations' Week. In the last three decades the UKKA has defended political dissidents and human rights activists in Ukraine. In 1944 the UKKA began to publish the *Ukrainian Quarterly* under the editorship of M. Chubaty and, later, W. *Dushnyck. It also issued the semimonthly *Ukrainian Bulletin* (1948–70) and numerous Ukrainian and English publications about Ukraine. A UKKA page has appeared occasionally in two Ukrainian-American dailies and two weeklies since 1975. An information bureau, directed by L. Dobriansky, was set up in Washington in 1977.

Much of the UKKA's energy is directed toward political goals and visible external events rather than internal community problems, such as generational changes, language retention and cultural awareness, and alienation among young people. It organized the celebration on a national scale of a number of important Ukrainian anniversaries: the centennial of T. Shevchenko's death (with the opening of his monument in Washington in 1964), the centennial of Ukrainian immigration to the United States (1976–7), and the millennium of Christianity in Ukraine (1988). It ensures that Ukrainian Independence Day is commemorated every 22 January by the US Congress, some state assemblies, and some municipal councils. The Educational Council, an autonomous body affiliated with the UKKA, which oversees Ukrainian Saturday schools (75 in 1970 and 40 in 1980), publishes textbooks (about 30 titles), approves school programs, and sponsors teacher training.

The UKKA supported efforts to organize and co-ordinate the activities of Ukrainian organizations abroad: it was one of the founders of the *Pan-American Ukrainian Conference and the *World Congress of Free Ukrainians. Maintaining a policy of consensus on political issues (up to 1980), it has tried to work with all noncommunist Ukrainian civic groupings. Occasional attempts by one group or another to seize control of the UKKA led to crises and factionalism. In 1966 an opposition group, the Committee for Community Unity, arose, and some of its members formed the Association of Ukrainians in America. Its conflict with the UKKA was finally settled, in 1978. A more serious crisis arose at the 13th Congress in 1980 in Philadelphia, when the organizations of the *Ukrainian Liberation Front and their allies stacked the gathering with their own candidates and used their majority to override the UKKA statute and procedures. Two fraternal associations (the UNA and UFA) and 25 national organizations walked out of the convention and formed the Committee for Law and Order in the UKKA, which, after more than two years of unsuccessful negotiation, gave birth to the *Ukrainian American Coordinating Council.

**Ukrainian Constituent Assembly.** See Constituent Assembly of Ukraine.

**Ukrainian Co-operative Council of Canada** (Ukrainska kooperatyvna rada Kanady). A national association of Ukrainian credit unions in Canada established in 1971. Its purpose is to co-ordinate the activities and plans of its members. In 1988 there were 28 member groups, with total assets of 564 million dollars. The council publishes a newsletter, *Koordynator*. Its presidents, elected at triennial conventions, have included V. Sytnyk (1971–88) and P. Mykuliak (1988–).

**Ukrainian Co-operative Insurance Union.** See Strakhsoiuz.

**Ukrainian Cossack Brotherhood.** See Ukrainian Free Cossacks.

Badges of the Ukrainian Council for Physical Culture (1–3) and member clubs

**Ukrainian Council for Physical Culture** (Rada fizychnoi kultury, or RFK). The central sports and physical-education organization for Ukrainian refugees in postwar Germany, founded in November 1945 in Munich-Karlsfeld. In 1946 the RFK represented 38 Ukrainian sports clubs in the DP camps of the American zone (2,873 members), 12 in the British zone (829 members), and 4 in the French zone. The various organized activities, such as soccer, track-and-field sports, swimming, volleyball, basketball, hockey, hiking, skiing, mountaineering, table tennis, boxing, weight lifting, swimming, and chess, came under eight departments. The RFK introduced a standard test for a physical fitness badge, which had been awarded to 1,003 individuals by the end of 1947; accredited 27 referees and judges; and organized an association and courses for them, as well as an instructors' school (in Mittenwald) and skiing, volleyball, and basketball training camps.

On the initiative of the RFK the International Committee of Political Refugees held a DP Olympiad in June–November 1948; Ukrainian athletes captured gold medals in soccer, men's volleyball, boxing, and the men's 4 × 100-m relay. The RFK also organized, as part of international refugee sports meets, games with German teams, and annual competitions among the various Ukrainian soccer, track-and-field, chess, and skiing clubs. After the mass emigration of refugees from Germany, the RFK wound down its activities in 1950. It was headed by A. Lukiianenko (1945–6), V. Blavatsky (1946–7), I. Krasnyk (1947–8), and S. Kikta (1948–50).

BIBLIOGRAPHY
*Al'manakh Rady fizychnoï kul'tury: Almanac of the Ukrainian Council for Physical Culture* (Munich 1951)

**Ukrainian Council of the National Economy** (Ukrainska rada narodnoho hospodarstva, or URNH). A central body for economic management and planning in Ukraine roughly analogous to the *Supreme Council of the National Economy, which was abolished in 1932. It was established in June 1960 to oversee the Ukrainian *regional economic councils, which were restored in May 1957 in the major economic reform initiated by N. Khrushchev. The URNH was responsible primarily for drafting and implementing yearly economic plans (long-term planning remained the prerogative of the *State Planning Committee of the USSR). Initially accountable only to the Council of Ministers of the Ukrainian SSR, in 1962 the URNH was subordinated also to the newly established USSR Council of the National Economy. The URNH was instrumental in decreasing the influence of central planners on the Ukrainian economy and in restoring some semblance of economic autonomy for the republic. Its first head was M. *Sobol. The council was dissolved in January 1966, following Khrushchev's fall from power.

**Ukrainian Council of Industrial Co-operation** (Ukrainska rada promyslovoi kooperatsii, or UKRPROMRADA). The central union of manufacturing co-operatives in Ukraine, established in 1932 with its head office in Kiev. It co-ordinated the activities of the oblast-level councils of manufacturing co-operatives. Unlike the various co-operative bodies of the 1920s, UKRPROMRADA was under stricter official control and served as an instrument of government and Party economic policy. By 1940, 26,700 enterprises were nominal members of the council. In 1960 UKRPROM-

RADA was dissolved, and its enterprises were transferred to various state farms and city soviets or to the ministries of Trade, Health Care, Transport, and Communal Housing.

The head office of the Ukrainian Credit Union in Toronto

The Ukrainian Crystalline Shield near Korostyshiv

**Ukrainian Credit Union** (Ukrainska kredytova spilka). The largest Ukrainian credit union in Canada, and the oldest in Toronto. It was established on 12 July 1944, as the Ukrainian (Toronto) Credit Union, with a membership of 42. By the end of the year it had 91 members and assets of 17,000 dollars. Its office was located on the premises of the Ukrainian National Federation and was open one evening per week. In 1949 a branch was set up in the west end of the city. The credit union grew rapidly in the 1950s. By 1969 it had 5,000 members and assets of 8 million dollars, and by 1991 it had over 14,000 members and assets of 168 million dollars. The union built its own office building in 1980 and by 1991 had two other branches in Toronto and one each in Mississauga, London, Oshawa, and Windsor. From its educational and cultural fund the union provides scholarships and sponsors summer camps, cultural events, and sports teams. Its presidents have been V. Sytnyk (1944–79) and M. Rebryk (1979–).

**Ukrainian Crystalline Shield** (aka the Ukrainian Massif or Azov-Podolian Shield). An uplifted block of outcropping crystalline rocks of the Precambrian age running through the central reaches of Ukraine mainly on the right bank of the Dnieper. It originally made up the southwestern portion of the Fennosarmatian paleocontinent and is now tilted toward the west. It extends in the form of a boomerang for some 1,000 km from the Horyn River in the northwest to the Azov Sea in the southeast and covers an area of about 200,000 sq km. Within the shield area the crystalline rocks outcrop in deeply incised river valleys (such as the Dnieper between Dnipropetrovske and Zaporizhia) in the form of picturesque cliffs and rapids. To the northwest the Ukrainian Crystalline Shield dips under the Hercynian structures of the Dnieper-Donets Trough (including the Donets Basin), without apparently being involved in their late Paleozoic structural deformation, and connects in the subsurface to the Voronezh Massif north of Vovcha and the iron-ore district of Belgorod. Elsewhere it dips under Alpine folded structures of late Mesozoic and early Cenozoic, in the Caucasus to the east, the Crimean Mountains to the south, and the Carpathian Mountains to the west.

The Ukrainian Crystalline Shield is made up of a folded basement broken up by deep meridional faults into a series of blocks: Volhynian-Podolian, Bila Tserkva–Odessa, Kirovohrad, and Dnieper-Azov. The shield is divided into an older Archean and a younger Proterozoic series of igneous and metamorphic rocks.

The Archean is represented predominantly by gneisses, granites, and green schists that are 3,500 to 1,900 million years old. A lower suite, the Dnieper series, 3,500 to 2,700 million years old, contains various gneisses and amphibolites and is intruded by pegmatites and aplites associated with migmatites. An upper suite, 2,700 to 1,900 million years old, consists of paragneisses, biotite, sillimanite and graphite schists, quartzites, marbles, and amphibolites intruded by monzonites, diorites, and either charnockitic or microcline-bearing granites. The degree of deformation increases to the southwest. Both the lithologic composition and the grade of metamorphism are distinctly different from rocks of the Lower Proterozoic and their precise subdivision is not generally accepted.

Wedged into the Archean and separated from it by angular unconformity are tight, long, narrow folds of Lower Proterozoic rocks (1,900–1,600 million years old) of a lower grade of metamorphism. Basal arkosic and conglomeratic sandstones are overlain first by phyllites and quartzose schists, then by talcose and actinolitic schists, and finally by ferruginous hornstones and jaspilites. The jaspilitic iron ores (banded iron formation) of the Kryvyi Rih series, composed of alternating laminae of chert and hematite, extend north to include the iron ores of Kremenchuk. Owing to intensive folding the ore-bearing sequence is never less than 50 m thick, and often exceeds 1,000 m.

The sequence is surrounded by Middle Proterozoic (1,600–1,300 million years ago) metamorphosed sediments and volcanics and is cut by postorogenic Rapakivi granites in plutons at Korosten, Korsun, and Novomyrhorod as well as an Azov complex of alkaline gabbros. They are covered by chloritic, carbonaceous, and quartz-mica schists with intercalations of dolomitic marble. The highest beds are quartzose schists.

The Upper Proterozoic (1,100–570 million years ago) is represented by the Ovruch series of quartzites, schists, and quartz porphyries as well as by muddy sandstones and volcanics. A sharp unconformity separates it from a thin covering of younger sedimentary rocks (Paleogene, Neogene, and Quaternary) that include the Dnieper Lignite Basin and the Nykopil manganese-ore deposit.

BIBLIOGRAPHY
Bezborod'ko, M. *Ukraïns'ka krystalichna smuha* (Kiev 1935)
Luchyts'kyi, V.; et al. *Ukraïns'kyi krystalichnyi masyv* (Kiev 1947)
*Platformennye struktury obramleniia Ukrainskogo shchita i ikh metallonosnost'* (Kiev 1972)

P. Sonnenfeld

The building and logo of the Ukrainian Cultural and Educational Centre

**Ukrainian Cultural and Educational Centre** (Oseredok ukrainskoi kultury i osvity, or Oseredok). Established in *Winnipeg in 1949 by the Ukrainian National Federation as a repository for Ukrainian historical and cultural artifacts, Oseredok consists of a museum, art gallery, 40,000-volume library, and archive containing important collections on wartime refugees, Ukrainian-Canadian organizations, and prominent individuals (Ye. Konovalets, O. Koshyts, I. Bobersky). The center also maintains an extension and educational program. It is governed by a board of directors and supported by a Canada-wide membership, its own foundation, and (since 1979) an operational grant from the province of Manitoba.

**Ukrainian Cultural Council** (Ukrainska kulturna rada, or UKR). A body set up in Vienna in 1915 to oversee cultural activity among Ukrainian émigrés. The president of the UKR was Yu. Romanchuk, but the actual director was O. *Kolessa. The council founded schools and reading

societies in several Ukrainian camps located in Austria (notably Gmünd and Wolfsberg) and sponsored education courses in Vienna. It ceased activity after the war.

**Ukrainian Cultural Festival in Czechoslovakia.** An annual three-day folk-art festival organized in late June by the *Cultural Association of Ukrainian Workers (KSUT; since 1990, the Union of Ruthenian Ukrainians) and other institutions and organizations in Slovakia. Known as the Festival of Song and Dance until 1977, it was held in 1955 in Medzilaborce and has been held since then in Svydnyk. The festival is usually attended by 20,000 to 40,000 people, who watch 40 to 60 independent folklore ensembles (1,500–2,500 performances). Besides the local Ukrainian ensembles and folklore groups an ensemble from each of the other nationalities in Czechoslovakia (Czech, Slovak, Hungarian, and Polish) and groups from neighboring countries (Poland, Hungary, and Ukraine) have participated in the festival. The *Duklia Ukrainian Folk Ensemble from Prešov appears every year, and the *Transcarpathian Folk Chorus from Uzhhorod is a frequent guest. The main festival is preceded by regional song and dance festivals in 12 localities inhabited by Ukrainians in the Prešov region.

In recent years the festival has consisted of eight distinct programs: choral ensembles, contemporary vocal and instrumental groups, children's collectives, folk groups, visiting ensembles, anniversary collectives, authentic folk art (in the setting of the Svydnyk Museum of Ukrainian Culture), and the final gala performances. Virtually all the programs are broadcast live or are recorded for radio, and an hour or two of the gala performance is televised.

Thematic exhibits at the Museum of Ukrainian Culture, talks with veterans of the struggle for national liberation, and a performance by the winner of the Dukhnovych Festival of Ukrainian Drama have been integral parts of the cultural festival.

M. Mushynka

**Ukrainian Cultural Heritage Village** (Selo spadshchyny ukrainskoi kultury). An open-air living history

Premier Peter Lougheed of Alberta unveiling the Ukrainian pioneer family monument (sculptor: Leonid Molodozhanyn) at the Ukrainian Cultural Heritage Village on 10 August 1980)

museum situated on 320 acres of land along the eastern boundary of Elk Island National Park approx 50 km east of Edmonton. The village was founded by the Ukrainian Cultural Heritage Society (est 1971) and in 1975 was purchased by the government of Alberta, which then developed it according to a master plan. The purpose of the village is to preserve and reconstruct pioneer farm and town buildings, collect artifacts and farm implements, and demonstrate practical skills and cultural traditions practiced by the pioneers. Administered by the Alberta Department of Culture and Multiculturalism, the museum conducts extensive research and uses dramatic presentations and skill demonstrations to convey to visitors the experience of Ukrainian pioneer life.

**Ukrainian Democratic Agrarian party** (Ukrainska demokratychno-khliborobska partiia, or UDAP). A conservative democratic nationalist party founded in Lubni, Poltava gubernia, in May 1917 as the Ukrainian Democratic party. Among the founding members were V. Andriievsky, M. Boiarsky, V. Chyhryn, L. Klymov, I. Korniienko, M. Makarenko, S. and V. Shemet, and V. Shkliar; M. Mikhnovsky, V. *Lypynsky, and D. Dontsov were prominent members. Its constituent congress in Lubni on 29 June 1917 was attended by 1,500 rich peasants and 20 landowning nobles. The UDAP adopted a program (written by Lypynsky) of Ukrainian national sovereignty and independence, the preservation of private property as the foundation of the national economy, the preservation of middle-sized landholdings, the resolution of the land question by a Ukrainian parliament on the basis of the mandatory state purchase of lands owned by the large landowners and the permanent leasing of parcels therefrom to the poor and landless peasantry, and an agrarian economy based on well-developed co-operatives. On 27 March 1918 a 200-man UDAP delegation lobbied the Central Rada and UNR Council of Ministers for the inclusion of UDAP members in the Rada, the repeal of the land-socialization law, and new elections to the Constituent Assembly of Ukraine. Because its demands were rejected, the UDAP welcomed Hetman P. Skoropadsky's coup d'état in April 1918. Later, however, it protested against the *Hetman government's reactionary and repressive policies and administrative abuses. At its second congress (Kiev, 26–28 October 1918) the UDAP was against Skoropadsky's declaration of federation with a non-Bolshevik Russia. It co-operated with, but did not officially vote in favor of joining, the anti-Hetman *Ukrainian National Union. In 1921 its émigré members (eg, S. Shemet, Lypynsky) helped to found the *Ukrainian Union of Agrarians-Statists.

R. Senkus

**Ukrainian Democratic Alliance** (Ukrainskyi demokratychnyi rukh). A political organization founded in New York in 1976 by the Ukrainian National Democratic Alliance, the Ukrainian Revolutionary Democratic party, and the Organization of Ukrainian Nationalists (Abroad). Its aims were to promote the development of the world Ukrainian community and to help the Ukrainian nation in its struggle for cultural and political rights. The alliance sought specifically to mobilize younger, highly educated Ukrainians of democratic persuasion who were not involved in established Ukrainian parties. Its first president was A. *Figol.

**Ukrainian Democratic party** (Ukrainska demokratychna partiia). A liberal democratic party that superseded the *General Ukrainian Non-Party Democratic Organization in 1904. Its members (V. Antonovych, V. Chekhivsky, O. Cherniakhivsky, Ye. Chykalenko, B. Hrinchenko, M. Komarov F. Matushevsky, M. Levytsky, V. Naumenko, T. Shteingel, I. Shrah, P. Stebnytsky, I. Steshenko, Ye. Tymchenko, S. Yefremov, and others) adopted a program calling for the overthrow of tsarist absolutism and its replacement by a constitutional democratic federation, Ukrainian autonomy, and the official use of Ukrainian in the schools, courts, public institutions, and government; a Ukrainian territorial diet would nationalize all land, transfer the ownership of industrial enterprises to the workers, and introduce an eight-hour workday, pensions for seniors and the handicapped, and a progressive tax system. Early in 1905 a left wing led by Hrinchenko left the party and founded the *Ukrainian Radical party. Both parties competed for support in the various local hromadas until they merged in December 1905 to form the *Ukrainian Democratic Radical party.

**Ukrainian Democratic Radical party** (Ukrainska demokratychno-radykalna partiia, or UDRP). A liberal nationalist party formed in Kiev in December 1905 out of the merger of the *Ukrainian Democratic and *Ukrainian Radical (URP) parties. It consisted primarily of members of the intelligentsia (eg, Ye. Chykalenko, P. Chyzhevsky, V. Domanytsky, B. Hrinchenko, M. Hrushevsky, M. Levytsky, F. Matushevsky, V. Shemet, I. Shrah, Ye. Tymchenko, A. Viazlov, F. Vovk, S. Yefremov) who were active in the Prosvita societies and the co-operative movement. The party adopted a revised version of the URP program, without the independence clause. Its organs were *Hromads'ka dumka*, *Rada*, and *Ridnyi krai*. Many members of the *Ukrainian caucus in the Russian State Duma (eg, three-quarters of the caucus in the Second Duma) belonged to the UDRP. In early 1908 the UDRP, many of whose members also belonged to the Russian *Constitutional Democratic party, fell apart, and most of its members joined the clandestine *Society of Ukrainian Progressives.

*Moloda Ukraïna*, the magazine of the Ukrainian Democratic Youth Association

**Ukrainian Democratic Youth Association** (Obiednannia demokratychnoi ukrainskoi molodi, or ODUM). A youth association in the United States and Canada established in 1950 in New York. The group was composed initially of the children of postwar refugees from Soviet Ukraine who were adherents of or sympathetic to the *Ukrainian Revolutionary Democratic party. It undertakes Ukrainian studies, sports, and performing-arts activities (it sponsors a number of dance, bandura, and music ensembles). With its centers of support in Ontario and the eastern United States, ODUM has a central committee and separate structures for each side of the border. It sponsors (since 1951) the monthly journal *Moloda Ukraïna* and has had pages in the Ukrainian-American newspapers *Ukraïns'ki visti* (Jersey City) and *Ukraïns'ke zhyttia* (Chicago). It also owns summer resorts in Acton, New Jersey, and London, Ontario, that are commonly used for summer camps and performing-arts workshops. ODUM has a total membership (1980) of approx 1,000. It published a commemorative almanac in 1965.

The Ukrainian Diocesan Museum of Stamford

**Ukrainian Diocesan Museum of Stamford** (Ukrainskyi muzei v Stemfordi). A museum in Stamford, Connecticut, established in 1935 by Bishop K. Bohachevsky. Since that time it has collected and preserved Ukrainian artworks, folk costumes, and handicrafts and has amassed a library with over 20,000 volumes, including rare books and incunabula. The Lemko Museum is also located there. The museum is housed in the residence of Bishop B. Losten. Since 1964 the director has been W. *Lencyk.

**Ukrainian Drama School** (Ukrainska dramatychna shkola). The first drama school in Ukraine, a department of the *Lysenko Higher Institute of Music in Lviv. Directed by M. *Vorony with the participation of O. *Zaharov, it offered a two-year program and was active in 1922–5.

**Ukrainian Economic Advisory Association.** See Ukrainian National Credit Union Association.

**Ukrainian Economic Bureau** (Ukrainske ekonomichne biuro, or UEB). A research office set up by eight Ukrainian economists in Warsaw in 1932 to publish an an-

nual Ukrainian statistical compendium. They also set up the Mediator legal and commercial consulting firm, which supported the UEB. It published four statistical collections in 1933–8 in printings of 2,000 to 3,000. In 1936 the Shevchenko Scientific Society consented to lend its name to the publication.

**Ukrainian Economic Council** (Ukrainska ekonomichna rada). An economic planning and administrative organ, under the Council of People's Commissars of the Ukrainian SSR. It was established in September 1923. Its primary task was to co-ordinate the economic plans of the various commissariats and prepare overall plans for the entire republic. The council was disbanded in 1936 and renewed briefly in 1940–1.

**Ukrainian Educational and Cultural Center** (Ukrainskyi osvitno-kulturnyi tsentr). A community center established in Philadelphia in 1980 for the promulgation of Ukrainian culture and heritage. Under the leadership of O. Chernyk, the center has become the focus of nearly all communal cultural, social, and educational life for the Ukrainians of Greater Philadelphia. Among the center's most valuable programs are the Ukrainian Heritage (Saturday) School, with over 350 children; an extensive library; and the Ukrainian Social Services, which helps senior citizens, needy families, and newly arrived immigrants. Nearly 50 organizations of different kinds are housed at the center. Some are branches of the Plast Ukrainian Youth Association, the Ukrainian Youth Association (SUM), the Ukrainian Women's League, the Ukrainian Engineers' Society, the Ukrainian Medical Association, and the Ukrainian Professional Society. B. Zakharchuk is the current director of the center.

**Ukrainian educational societies** (Ukrainski osvitni tovarystva, or UOTs). Local Ukrainian societies for popular education and cultural work that were active in the Generalgouvernement in 1940–4. They replaced the Prosvita, Ridna Khata, and Kachkovsky societies, which had been banned by the German authorities. The UOTs were independent organizations with no direct organizational connections to one another. Their work, however, was co-ordinated at a regional level by a district Ukrainian relief committee (UDK), which in turn reported to the cultural department of the *Ukrainian Central Committee (UTsK), which was based in Cracow. The UOTs provided the only legal means of carrying out broad-based educational and cultural work for the general Ukrainian population. Only a UOT, for example, could sponsor a women's or a youth group.

UOTs existed in virtually every locality of the Generalgouvernement which had Ukrainian inhabitants. By early 1943 there were 4,000 UOTs with a combined membership of 230,000. A third of them had their own buildings, and there were 2,200 libraries, holding over 360,000 volumes (the figure would have been higher if many books had not been destroyed in 1939–41 during the Soviet occupation). The UOTs had 1,770 drama groups (which gave approx 7,350 performances) and 870 choral groups in addition to women's groups and youth sections, kindergartens, and adult literacy courses. The heads of the UOTs were usually young local peasants. The UOTs received assistance from the cultural department of the UTsK, which prepared programs and materials for them and offered leadership training courses. The UDKs had permanent staffs who advised and helped co-ordinate the work of the UOTs. In many respects the UOTs resembled the prewar Prosvita societies.

After 1943 the activities of the UOTs declined as many of their leading figures were deported to Germany for forced labor or enlisted in the Division Galizien. With the second Soviet occupation of Galicia (and then Poland) in 1944, they ceased to exist.

V. Kubijovyč

**Ukrainian Emigrant Aid Society** (Tovarystvo opiky nad ukrainskymy emigrantamy). An organization founded in Lviv in 1925 to provide aid for and maintain contact with immigrants from central and eastern Ukraine. It published the magazine *Ukraïns'kyi emigrant* (from 1927). By the early 1930s the society had offices not only in Lviv but also in Ternopil, Sambir, and Stanyslaviv as well as a network of circles throughout Galicia. As the number of emigrants shrank in the 1930, the society's activity declined, and after the death of its only president, M. *Zaiachkivsky, in 1938, it was dissolved.

**Ukrainian Engineers' Society in Lviv.** See Ukrainian Technical Society.

**Ukrainian Engineers' Society of America** (Tovarystvo ukrainskykh inzheneriv Ameryky, or TUIA). A professional association of Ukrainian engineers, architects, and economists in the United States, established in 1948 to promote research and professional upgrading by means of scientific conferences, seminars, and publications. In 1990 the society had 30 branches, in the major cities of the United States. It is the largest of the constituent societies in the World Federation of Ukrainian Engineers' Societies (United States, Canada, Argentina, and Australia), which has over 1,500 members. With its head office in New York, the TUIA has standing committees on the technology and industry of Ukraine and on Ukrainian technical terminology. It has published the quarterly *Visti ukraïns'kykh inzheneriv* since 1950 and *Biuleten' TUIA* since the 1960s, as well as a number of separate publications, including a dictionary of selected terms and a history of the Ukrainian engineers' movement. Its presidents have been V. Bohachevsky, M. Lepkaliuk, P. Shokh, O. Tymoshenko, O. Balaban, R. Wolchuk, I. Zhukovsky, V. Ryzhevsky, R. Rohozha, R. Levytsky, M. Shul, E. Yarosh, P. Hrytsak, R. Halibei, V. Hnatkivsky, Ye. Ivashkiv, I. Mokrivsky, M. Boretsky, E. Zmyi, Yu. Bazylevsky, R. Havryliak (1989–91), and Yu. Honcharenko. With the *Society of Ukrainian Engineers and Associates in Canada, TUIA has organized international conferences of Ukrainian engineers. Particularly interested in automation and the use of Ukrainian in computer programming, TUIA sponsored a public conference on that theme in New York (1990) and initiated contacts and joint projects with the AN URSR (now ANU) Institute of Cybernetics and the Kiev Polytechnical Institute.

**Ukrainian Evangelical Alliance of North America** (Ukrainske yevanhelske obiednannia v Pivnichnii Amerytsi). A co-ordinating body of Ukrainian Presbyterian (Reformed) church congregations in North America. The group was formed in 1922 at an evangelical convention in Rochester, New York, in order to rejuvenate the flagging Evangelical movement, to combine forces in

The participants in the 1st convention of the Ukrainian Evangelical Alliance of North America (Rochester, 1922)

proselytizing efforts in North America, and to underline the Ukrainian character of the congregations represented so that they would not be lost in the milieu of the United church. It also resolved to undertake evangelical missionary work in Galicia, an action that imbued the new body with a stronger sense of purpose. The alliance's effort in establishing the *Ukrainian Evangelical Reformed church in Galicia, in fact, led to one of its greatest successes. It also arranged for the translation of the Bible into Ukrainian by I. Ohiienko (later Metropolitan Ilarion). The first leader of the alliance was V. Kuziv. Other notable figures in it were P. Krat, I. Kovalevych, V. Borovsky, V. Kupchynsky and V. Bahrii. Since 1961 the alliance has published the bimonthly *Ievanhel's'kyi ranok.*

**Ukrainian Evangelical Baptist Union of Canada** (Ukrainske yevanhelske baptystske obiednannia). A national religious organization established in 1959 in Winnipeg. Initiated and led (until 1972) by the pastor P. *Kindrat, the union brought together the Western and Eastern conferences of the Ukrainian Evangelical Baptist church. The union conducts radio programs, publishes *Khrystiians'kyi visnyk* in Winnipeg, and is closely associated with the Ukrainian Bible Institute in Argentina.

**Ukrainian Evangelical Church of the Augsburg Confession** (Ukrainska Yevanhelsko-Avgsburgska Tserkva). A Lutheran church active in Galicia during the interwar period. It was established in 1925 under the guardianship of the German Evangelical superintendent for Galicia, with its headquarters in Stanyslaviv (now Ivano-Frankivske). It made some inroads in the Ternopil region and Volhynia and had over 20 parishes, with nearly 5,000 faithful and 16 preachers, by the outbreak of the Second World War. The official organ of the church was the monthly *Stiah*, and its major figures included I. Shebets and T. Yarchuk (who later perished in a Soviet prison). It was disbanded by the Soviet authorities following the annexation of Western Ukraine.

**Ukrainian Evangelical Reformed church** (Ukrainska Yevanhelsko-Reformovana Tserkva). An Evangelical church active in Galicia during the interwar era. Formed in 1925 through the missionary efforts of the *Ukrainian Evangelical Alliance of North America, the church had its consistory in Kolomyia. In spite of efforts to attain organizational autonomy, it never attained official recognition by Polish authorities and was forced to remain affiliated first with the Ukrainian Evangelical Church of the Augsburg Confession and then with the Evangelical Reformed Church of Poland. By the outbreak of the Second World War the church consisted of 35 congregations, with 17

Leaders of the Ukrainian Evangelical Reformed church in Western Ukraine in 1922. First row, from left: Roman Didenko, Ivan Vynnychuk, Rev Mykola Zhurakovsky, Supt Stefan Skerski, Rev Lev Buchak, Rev Pavlo Krat, Roman Kvasniuk; back row: Rev Volodymyr Borovsky, Rev Petro Yaremko, Rev Teodosii Dovhaliuk

preachers and approx 5,000 adherents, and published the monthly *Vira i nauka*. Among its notable leaders were V. Kuziv, P. Krat, V. Fediv, and V. Borovsky. The church was liquidated by the Soviet authorities after the annexation of Western Ukraine. A number of its pastors were arrested and incarcerated; others fled to the West or joined the Russian Orthodox church.

**Ukrainian Federative Democratic party** (Ukrainska federatyvno-demokratychna partiia). A minor conservative party founded in December 1917 by former members of the Old *Hromada of Kiev, among them V. Naumenko, B. Kistiakovsky, I. Kviatkovsky, I. Luchytsky, and V. Ihnatovych. Their program for the transformation of the Russian Empire into a federation of autonomous lands and their passive opposition to Ukrainian independence won them little support, and the party had virtually no impact on revolutionary events in Ukraine.

The coat of arms of the Ukrainian Former Combatants in Great Britain

**Ukrainian Former Combatants in Great Britain** (Obiednannia buvshykh voiakiv ukraintsiv u Velykii Brytanii, or ObVU). An organization of veterans, mainly from the First Division of the *Ukrainian National Army, established in 1949 in London to perpetuate Ukrainian military traditions and soldierly brotherhood. It had a membership of 4,850 divided among 52 branches in 1952–

3, before many of its members departed for North America. Its structure stabilized in 1965–6, when there were 47 branches with 718 members. In 1989 there were still 47 branches (as well as an affiliate in Spain and six postings), albeit with a greatly reduced membership. In the 1950s the organization was strongly involved with sports; in the 1960s and 1970s it concentrated more on military studies.

From its beginnings ObVU devoted effort and resources to care for the chronically ill, the disabled, and war amputees. It also looked after military cemeteries in Austria and Italy. It has published 2 almanacs, 13 books, a number of anthologies, commemorative cards, brochures on history and military affairs, and V. Kubijovyč's *Etnichni hrupy Pivdennozakhidn'oï Ukraïny* (Ethnic Groups of Southwestern Ukraine, 1953). From 1955 to the early 1970s ObVU sponsored the military journal *Surmach*. In 1959 it assisted in establishing the Ukrainian Officers' Club and later the Ukrainian Former Combatants' Council. It also established Ukrainian branches of the British paramilitary Home Guard in Edinburgh, Bolton, and Manchester (1953–7). The association has been headed successively by M. Dliaboha, M. Bily-Karpynets, B. Mykytyn, and S. Fostun.

C. Zelenko

The seals of the Ukrainian Workingmen's and Ukrainian Fraternal associations

**Ukrainian Fraternal Association** (Ukrainskyi bratskyi soiuz, or UFA). A fraternal insurance association founded on 25 October 1910 in Scranton, Pennsylvania, as the Ruthenian National Association (Ruskyi narodnyi soiuz). Its founders (42 delegates from 34 branches) were former members of the Ruthenian National Association, which at its 11th Convention in Cleveland in 1910 had adopted the resolution to change its name to the Greek Catholic Ruthenian Association (Hreko-Katolytskyi ruskyi soiuz) and to limit membership to Catholics. This resolution was eventually overturned, but in the interim two organizations with the same (Ukrainian) name came into being. In 1918 the new association changed its name to the Ukrainian Workingmen's Association (Ukrainskyi robitnychyi soiuz), and in 1978 to the UFA.

The UFA has always been a democratic, nondenominational, all-Ukrainian organization, initially with an anticlerical and radical orientation based on the ideas of M. Drahomanov and I. Franko. Its leaders have been politically active in the larger Ukrainian community, and played a decisive role in combating communist influence among Ukrainians in both the United States and Canada. They organized the first all-Ukrainian congress in America (1915), supported the Federation of Ukrainians in the United States, provided the core of support for *Oborona

The main building of the UFA resort, Verkhovyna, in Glen Spey, New York

Ukrainy, and helped found the Ukrainian Congress Committee of America, the United Ukrainian American Relief Committee, and the World Congress of Free Ukrainians.

Besides meeting its basic duty of paying out insurance to families of deceased members and assisting disabled or unemployed members, the UFA (through its educational committee) has organized Ukrainian schools, orchestras, and drama groups at its branches and has financed publications, bookstores, and libraries. It published the newspapers *Shershen'* (1910) and *Narodna volia* (1911–) in Ukrainian, the English-language weekly *Ukrainian Life* (1941–3) and illustrated quarterly *Forum* (1967–), annual calendars or almanacs (1912–51), and popular books. Over the years it has disbursed over 300,000 dollars in scholarships. The head office and editor's office are housed in the association's own building in Scranton. In 1955 it purchased the Verkhovyna resort in Glen Spey, New York, where it conducts summer camps, cultural workshops, annual art festivals (since 1976), and sports competitions. In the interwar period the UFA offered financial aid to various institutions in Ukraine, including the All-Ukrainian Academy of Sciences in Kiev, the Ukrainian Workers' Home in Lviv, the Union of Ukrainian Progressive Youth, the Ridna Shkola society, and Prosvita reading halls.

From 1,800 members in 1910 the association grew to 6,800 in 1920, 15,800 in 1930, 19,100 in 1950, and 24,200 in 1960. In 1990 the group's membership stood at 22,000, and its assets came to approx 13 million dollars. Since 1932 it has recruited members in Canada.

The presidents of the UFA, elected at its quadrennial conventions, have been J. Ardan (1910–12), M. Semeniuk (1912–13), I. Artymovych (1913–16, 1922–5), O. Zaplatynsky (1916–19), Yu. Kraikivsky (1919–22, 1925–7), P. Duchak (1927–33, 1941–6), M. Sichynsky (1933–41), A. Batiuk (1946–73), and I. Oleksyn (1973–). Other important leaders of the association include M. Belia, O. Lenchytsky, S. Korpan, T. Mynyk, E. Popil, and R. Rychok.

BIBLIOGRAPHY
*Iuvileina knyha Ukraïns'koho robitnychoho soiuzu, 1910–1960* (Scranton 1960)

**Ukrainian Fraternal Society of Canada** (Ukrainske tovarystvo vzaiemnoi pomochi v Kanadi). A mutual benefit society founded by members of the Ukrainian National Home Association in Winnipeg in November 1921. In 1925 it obtained a Dominion charter and began to organize branches across Canada. Incorporation in 1943 has enabled it to offer a wide variety of life insurance plans. Among its leaders have been I. Trach, M. Stechishin, T. Dowhanyk, T.D. Ferley, J.H. Syrnick, and S. Radchuk. Intended initially to be a nonpartisan association, the society has maintained an informal affiliation with the Ukrainian Orthodox Church of Canada.

**Ukrainian Free Academy of Sciences.** See Ukrainian Academy of Arts and Sciences.

**Ukrainian Free Cossacks** (Ukrainske vilne kozatstvo, or UVK). An émigré military and educational society established in Munich in 1923 on the model of the Free Cossack units of Ukraine. The founder and first otaman of the UVK was I. *Poltavets-Ostrianytsia, who viewed the Cossacks as a paramilitary force. Branches of the organization were established in other European émigé centers. After 1946 the makeup of the group changed as new branches sprang up in the DP camps of Austria and Germany and then in Ukrainian communities overseas. Today the UVK has 39 branches (*kureni*) in eight countries (*palanky*). Since 1947 it has published the magazine *Ukraïns'ke kozatstvo*, which in 1968–80 appeared quarterly. It prints historical and literary materials about the Cossacks and their traditions. The society's other otamans have included I. Birchak-Voloshyn, Gen M. Omelianovych-Pavlenko, I. Voloshyn, P. Tereshchenko, I. Tsapko (1952–67), V. Diachenko, A. Kushchynsky, P. Korshun-Fedorenko, M. Kovalsky, and V. Riznyk.

**Ukrainian Free Society of America** (Ukrainska vilna hromada Ameryky, or UVHA). An ideological organization in the United States set up in 1949 by those members of the *Oborona Ukrainy society who rejected a pro-Soviet policy and remained committed to Ukraine's independence. In the 1950s some socialists among the new immigrants joined the society. The UVHA published the journal *Vil'na Ukraïna* (1954–70s) on an irregular basis, I. Makukh's valuable memoirs *Na narodnii sluzhbi* (In the People's Service, 1958), and the Politycho-naukova biblioteka (Political Science Library), a book series of over 30 works in 19 issues. In the 1970s the society dissipated. Its presidents included V. Dovhan, V. Lazechko, and I. Palyvoda. The group had close ideological ties with the Ukrainian Workers' League in Canada.

**Ukrainian Free University** (Ukrainskyi vilnyi universytet, or UVU). An institution devoted to the development of Ukrainian scholarship and postsecondary studies free of the political influences dominating Ukraine, inaugurated on 17 January 1921 in Vienna. It emerged through the initiative of the *Union of Ukrainian Journalists and Writers Abroad, the *Ukrainian Sociological Institute, and the Society of Friends of Education in Vienna and was to work parallel with the *Lviv (Underground) Ukrainian University. The initiative was supported by professors of former Austrian universities, who influenced its formation along traditional lines. O. *Kolessa was its first rector, and his traditionalism in education won out over the project of a people's university, put forward by M. Hrushevsky.

The faculty in the UVU's initial stages consisted of 12 professors and 3 lecturers. Initial enrollment was low (90 students) because the principal centers of Ukrainian emigration at the time were Prague and other Czechoslovak

Rectors of the Ukrainian Free University to 1986. Top row, from left: Oleksander Kolessa, Stanyslav Dnistriansky, Ivan Horbachevsky, Fedir Shcherbyna, Dmytro Antonovych, Andrii Yakovliv; middle row: Serhii Shelukhyn, Oleksander Mytsiuk, Ivan Borkovsky, Rev Avhustyn Voloshyn, Vadym Shcherbakivsky, Ivan Mirchuk; bottom row: Yurii Paneiko, Mykola Vasyliv, Oleksander Kulchytsky, Vasyl Oreletsky, Yurii Blokhyn, Volodymyr Yaniv

locales. The founders hoped to tap the potential in the Czechoslovak Republic for students and for financial support for the institution, which did not exist in Vienna. As a result of the efforts of V. *Starosolsky, the dean of the Faculty of Law, in conjunction with his association with J. *Nečas and the president of the Czechoslovak Republic and active supporter of Slavic studies T. *Masaryk, the UVU was relocated to Prague. Official negotiations of this transfer were carried out by Kolessa, S. *Dnistriansky, and the premier of the Czechoslovak Republic, J. Černý.

The Czechoslovak government guaranteed financial assistance (including scholarships for students) and the right to use the resources of Charles University. The UVU was also officially recognized by the Ministries of Foreign Affairs and Education (16 and 30 September 1921). Upon its transfer the university was limited to two faculties, philosophy and law. This structure has remained in place to this day.

In 1921–2 the faculty was expanded to include 16 professors, 4 docents, and 1 lecturer. By 1931 it had expanded to include 39 members. Enrollment had increased from the initial 702 to 874 by 1922–3, and many students studied at both the UVU and Charles University. As the first Ukrainian postsecondary institution in Prague, the UVU became the center of Ukrainian academic life in the Czechoslovak Republic, the point of departure for many postsecondary institutions, academic institutes, and scientific societies. Every rector of the UVU also served as head of the governing *Ukrainian Academic Committee. By the late 1920s the UVU's library had expanded to include 10,000 titles, and its press had issued 27 monographs. The latter included jubilee anthologies in honor of Masaryk and three collections of the faculty's works.

In the 1930s the institution underwent a crisis, because the Czechoslovak government's rapprochement with the Soviet Union and Poland resulted in limitations on the rights given to Ukrainian political émigrés. Saved from

dissolution through the efforts of its rector, I. *Horbachevsky, the UVU's financial resources forced it to cut back on publishing. Other difficulties arose because of a decline in enrollment, which fell to 61 in 1939. Some hope was rekindled when *Carpatho-Ukraine was granted autonomy in 1938.

After the partition of the Czechoslovak Republic the UVU was placed under the jurisdiction of the new, German rector of Charles University. Enrollment rose when students began arriving from the rest of the *Generalgouvernement (107 in 1940–1). As a result V. *Kubijovyč, head of the *Ukrainian Central Committee, secured monthly grants and financing for the institution's press. In the final stages of the UVU's stay in Prague, the faculty consisted of 20 professors, 10 docents, and 3 lecturers. In 1921–41, 37 doctorates in philosophy and 95 in law were conferred.

In the years 1921–45 the rectors were Kolessa (1921–2, 1925–8, 1935–7, 1943–4), Dnistriansky (1922–3), Horbachevsky (1923–4, 1931–5), F. *Shcherbyna (1924–5), D. *Antonovych (1928–30, 1937–8), A. *Yakovliv (1930–1, 1944–5), O. *Mytsiuk (1938–9, 1940–1), I. *Borkovsky (1939–40, 1941–3), and Rev A. *Voloshyn (1945). The institution's Prague period came to an end when the city was occupied by Soviet forces in May 1945. Yakovliv handed over the rectorship to Voloshyn (who believed in continuing activities in Czechoslovakia), and together with most of the faculty emigrated westward. Voloshyn's hopes proved illusory. He was arrested, and died in prison; the UVU was liquidated, and its assets plundered.

The building of the Ukrainian Free University in Munich

Through the initiative of V. *Shcherbakivsky and a group of scholars of the Ukrainian Scientific Institute in Berlin (including its director, I. *Mirchuk) the UVU was re-established in Munich in 1946. Its faculty was expanded to include émigré scholars from central and eastern Ukraine. In 1947 the faculty consisted of 44 professors, 16 lecturers, and 18 teaching assistants. The highest level of enrollment (493) was reached in 1947–8. The revival of the UVU was funded by donations from the Ukrainian Publishing House in Cracow and the Congregation of the Eastern Churches (gathered by Bishop I. *Buchko, who became the UVU's curator). Instruction continued in law and philosophy, as did publishing, which focused primarily on the printing of textbooks and original manuscripts (27 titles by 1950). In 1946–56, 206 doctorates and 103 masters degrees were conferred. On 16 September 1950 the Bavarian Ministry of Education and Religion officially recognized the UVU as a private university.

The monetary reforms in Germany, instituted in June 1948, complicated the financial status of displaced persons and prompted the emigration of professionals and students to North America. This course of events had a negative impact on the UVU, whose enrollment declined to 272 in 1949 and 137 in 1950. Classroom instruction was cut back sharply, and eliminated altogether in 1956. The UVU sought to compensate for this curtailment by establishing the Institute for Correspondence Education, establishing firmer ties with former faculty members in institutions in Canada, France, and the United States, and fortifying its publishing house. In 1957 it began publishing the journal *Zapysky Ukraïns'koho vil'noho universytetu*.

O. Kulchytsky of the UVU and others established the *Association for the Advancement of Ukrainian Studies in 1962, and the new association gave rise to greatly improved conditions for the institution. Yu. *Blokhyn (rector) was able to reintroduce classroom instruction in 1965, and V. *Yaniv (rector), to expand it further, to include summer and winter courses in general Ukrainian studies, pedagogy, basic linguistics, and Eastern European studies in English (in co-operation with Michigan State University). The faculty increased from 56 members in 1965 to 92 in 1990. Most members live outside of Munich but participate in summer instruction. In the years 1968–81, 1,585 students, from 17 countries, enrolled in UVU programs. The large increase in enrollment was made possible by the acquisition of a building for the university in 1974 with funds from a donation made by Cardinal Y. *Slipy, the expansion of a foundation in Canada and the United States, and contacts with non-Ukrainian scholars.

Between 1972 and 1989 the UVU organized 189 conferences, including a commemorative conference on H. Skovoroda held in co-operation with universities in Germany, France, and Austria. Contacts with Belarusian, Bulgarian, Czechoslovakian, Jewish, and Polish academics proved particularly important. The UVU also held numerous art exhibitions.

In all, the UVU has published 230 works since it established operations in Munich. In the years 1966–89 it conferred 116 doctoral and 44 masters degrees. In 1981 the Institute for the Study of Nationalities Problems was established, headed by Z. Sokoliuk.

Notable members of the UVU faculty have included the historians D. Doroshenko, B. Krupnytsky, O. Ohloblyn, N. Polonska-Vasylenko, and A. Zhukovsky; the geographers V. Kubijovyč and S. Rudnytsky; the philologists O. Horbach, O. Kolessa, J. Rudnyckyj, G. Shevelov, and S. Smal-Stotsky; the scholars in philosophy D. Chyzhevsky, O. Kulchytsky, I. Mirchuk, and V. Yaniv; the ethnographers Z. Kuzelia and V. Petrov; the art historians D. Antonovych and V. Zalozetsky-Sas; the church historians V. Bidnov, M. Chubaty, and O. Lototsky; the jurists S. Dnistriansky, O. Eikhelman, R. Lashchenko, L. Okinshevych, Ya. Padokh, V. Paneiko, V. Starosolsky, and A. Yakovliv; and the economists Ye. Glovinsky, O. Mytsiuk, and V. Timoshenko.

The rectors of the UVU since 1946 have been V. Shcherbakivsky (1946–7), I. Mirchuk (1947–8, 1950–5, 1956–61), Yu. *Paneiko (1948–50, 1961–2), M. *Vasyliv (1955–6), O. Kulchytsky (1963), V. *Oreletsky (1964, 1966–8), Yu. Blokhyn (1965–6), V. Yaniv (1968–86), T. *Ciuciura (1986–92), and P. Goy (since 1992).

BIBLIOGRAPHY
*Ukraïns'kyi vil'nyi universytet v Prazi v 1921–1931*, 2 vols (Prague 1931)
Narizhnyi, S. *Ukraïns'ka emigratsiia: Kul'turna pratsia ukraïns'koï emigratsiï mizh dvoma svitovymy viinamy* (Prague 1942)
'Z diial'nosty UVU za druhe desiatylittia isnuvannia (1931–1941),' *Naukovyi zbirnyk UVU v Prazi*, 3 (1942)
Mirchuk, I. 'Ukraïns'kyi vil'nyi universytet,' *Naukovyi zbirnyk UVU*, 5 (1948)
– *Ukraïns'kyi vil'nyi universytet: Korotkyi ohliad* (Munich 1958)
Holiat, R. 'Short History of the Ukrainian Free University,' *Papers of the Shevchenko Scientific Society*, no. 21 (New York 1964)
Janiw, W. *Ukrainische Freie Universität: Kurzgefasste, Geschichte, und dokumentarische Ergänzungen* (Munich 1976)
V. Yaniv

**Ukrainian Galician Army** (Ukrainska halytska armiia [UHA]). The regular army of the Western Ukrainian National Republic (ZUNR), known as the Galician Army (Halytska armiia). It was formed around a nucleus consisting of the Legion of Ukrainian Sich Riflemen and other Ukrainian detachments of the Austro-Hungarian army, which recognized the authority of the *Ukrainian National Rada and took part in the *November Uprising in Lviv in 1918.

The UHA was a well-organized and disciplined force. It was established as a regular army of the ZUNR by the law of 13 November 1918 on compulsory military service, which empowered the State Secretariat for Military Affairs (DSVS) to divide the country into military districts, to define an organizational structure for the army, and to call up Ukrainian males between the ages of 18 and 35 for military duty. Three military regions (Lviv, Ternopil, and Stanyslaviv) were introduced, each consisting of four districts (covering five to eight counties). The military commander of each district was responsible for recruitment, training, and combat readiness.

Until 9 June 1919 all military affairs of the ZUNR came under the jurisdiction of the DSVS, which was divided into a chancellery and 16 departments, and was headed initially by Col D. Vitovsky (to 13 February 1919) and then by Col V. Kurmanovych. With the installation of the Dictatorship of the Western Province of the Ukrainian National Republic, the functions of the DSVS were transferred partly to the Military Chancellery, directed by Lt Col K. Dolezhal, and partly to the Supreme Command of the Ukrainian Galician Army (NKHA).

The NKHA was set up in November 1918 in Lviv. Its chief, the UHA supreme commander, was appointed by the head of the Ukrainian National Rada and later by the dictator of the Western Province. All UHA units at the front came under its command; all other UHA units came under the district commands, and ultimately under the DSVS. When the DSVS was abolished, the NKHA assumed responsibility for supplies and training. The supreme commanders of the UHA were Col D. Vitovsky (29 October–5 November 1918), Col H. Kossak (to 9 November), Col H. Stefaniv (to 10 December), Brig Gen M. Omelianovych-Pavlenko (to 9 June 1919), Maj Gen O. Hrekov (to 5 July), Brig Gen M. Tarnavsky (to 7 November), and Brig Gen O. Mykytka (to 10 February 1920). The chiefs of the General Staff included Col M. Marynovych (to 5 November 1918), Maj S. Goruk (to 10 December), Col Ye. Myshkivsky (to 12 February 1919), Col V. Kurmanovych (to 7 June), Col A. Schamanek (to 7 November 1919, and 10 February–1 March 1920), and Gen G. Ziritz (to 10 February 1920).

The Supreme Command of the Ukrainian Galician Army (Khodoriv, 1919). Sitting, 5th through 7th from left, Gen Mykhailo Omelianovych-Pavlenko, Col Viktor Kurmanovych, Otaman Alfred Schamanek

The territory controlled by the UHA was divided into 13 military districts of four or five counties each: Berezhany, Chortkiv, Drohobych, Kolomyia, Lviv, Peremyshl, Rava Ruska, Sambir, Sokal, Stanyslaviv, Stryi, Ternopil, and Zolochiv. The commands of the districts, which grew out of military committees established in November 1918, were responsible for security and public order in the army's rear. They conducted drafts, trained draftees and organized them into infantry units, and protected government property.

The first regular UHA units were joined by worker and student detachments, which sprang up spontaneously to resist the Polish underground in Lviv and the Polish army invading Galicia. By December 1918 the Galician Army consisted of combat groups of different strength and profile – regular, semi-insurgent, and insurgent. The strongest were the Navariia, Stare Selo, and Skhid groups operating around Lviv. On the northern border of the ZUNR the Northern Group under Col O. Mykytenko was organized to repel the Polish offensive. The oblast command in Stryi, under Col H. Kossak, took charge of the groups that sprang up on the western front, including the Komancha, Liutkiv, Staryi Sambir, Hlyboka, Krukenychi, Rudky, South I, and South II groups. They did not form a continuous front and were rarely in contact with the NKHA or with each other. At the beginning of December 1918, when Gen M. Omelianovych-Pavlenko took command of the Galician Army, it numbered 30,000 officers and men, half of whom were combat-ready.

In December 1918 all field units were brought under the NKHA, and in January–February 1919 they were organized into three corps, each consisting of four brigades. A brigade generally had three to six infantry battalions (sometimes merged into two regiments), a cavalry company, a field artillery regiment with four to six batteries, a sapper company, and communications, auxiliary, and support groups. The First Corps, based in Kaminka-Strumylova and commanded by Col O. *Mykytka, consisted of the Sokal, Rava, Uhniv, and Yaniv brigades. The Second Corps, based in Bibrka and commanded by Col M. Tarnavsky, included the First Brigade of the Ukrainian Sich Riflemen and the Kolomyia, Third Berezhany, and Zolochiv brigades. The Third Corps, based in Stryi and commanded by Col H. Kossak and then Gen M. Gembachiv, encompassed the Lviv (initially named the Seventh Stryi Brigade), Sambir, Mountain, and Stryi (formed out of the Krukenychi and Hlyboka groups) brigades. The basic combat unit was the kurin (51 on the Polish front, 48 on the Soviet front), consisting of four companies (sotni), which were in turn divided into platoons (choty).

In June 1919 the UHA at its maximum strength numbered 70,000 to 75,000 men, including reserves. Its proportion of officers to men was very low, only 2.4 percent. To overcome the shortage of staff and higher officers, non-Ukrainian specialists of the Austrian-Hungarian army and officers of the UNR Army were recruited. To train young officers three infantry schools, an artillery, and a communications cadet school were set up in Galicia, and one infantry and artillery school in central Ukraine.

The bulk (67 percent) of the combat force was infantry. Each kurin had a machine gun company. About 10 percent of the soldiers belonged to artillery units, with 58 batteries on the Polish front and 47 on the Soviet front. The Galician Army also had two or three armored cars and two armored trains. Cavalry did not play an important role, because the DSVS preferred the tactics of positional warfare. On Gen O. Hrekov's recommendation a cavalry brigade and regiment were set up in June and July 1919 with a total of 1,340 sabers. The first air force unit was organized by Capt P. Franko in Krasne. With the help of former pilots of the Russian army, a flying regiment under Col B. Huber (later under Col D. Bulat Kanukov) was formed. Until April 1919 the UHA had an advantage in the air over the Polish forces, but it lost it as the Polish strength increased (150 Polish planes vs 40 Ukrainian). Four of the nine sapper companies were attached to the corps and five to the brigades. The companies were formed and trained by the reserve sapper kurin in Chortkiv, which was reorganized into a technical kurin under K. Kiziuk's command. Communications specialists were trained in Stanyslaviv. Each corps had two to five field hospitals and sanitary trains. Because of a severe shortage of medical personnel and supplies, medical care deteriorated quickly, and by the end of 1919 the army fell victim to typhus.

In the *Ukrainian-Polish War in Galicia (1918–19) the UHA scored some victories against the numerically stronger and better-equipped Polish forces. After the *Chortkiv offensive it retreated across the Zbruch River and joined up with the UNR Army to take part in the *Ukrainian-Soviet War. Reduced by typhus to a mere 5,000 combat-ready men, the UHA accepted absorption into the Red Army and became the *Red Ukrainian Galician Army. Having been thrown into battle against the Poles, its First Brigade was defeated and captured; its Second and Third brigades deserted the Red Army and allowed themselves to be disarmed by the Poles. By the end of April 1920 the UHA had ceased to exist.

BIBLIOGRAPHY

Sopotnicki, J. *Kampania polsko-ukraińska: Doświadczenia operacyjne i bojowe* (Lviv 1921)

Omelianovych-Pavlenko, M. *Ukraïns'ko-pol's'ka viina 1918–1919* (Prague 1929)

Shukhevych, S. *Spomyny z Ukraïns'koï halyts'koï armiï 1918–1920*, 5 vols (Lviv 1929)

Kuz'ma, O. *Lystopadovi dni 1918 roku* (Lviv 1931; 2nd edn, New York 1960)

Kutschabsky, W. *Die Westukraine im Kampfe mit Polen und dem Bolschewismus in den Jahren 1918–1923* (Berlin 1934)

Iaroslavyn, S. *Vyzvol'na borot'ba na zakhidn'o-ukraïns'kykh zemliakh u 1918–1923 rr.* (Philadelphia 1956)

Mykytiuk, D. (comp). *Ukraïns'ka halyts'ka armiia: Materiialy do istoriï*, 5 vols (Winnipeg 1958–76)

Hirniak, N. *Ostannii akt trahediï Ukraïns'koï halyts'koï armiï* (Perth Amboy, NJ 1960)

*Dennyk Nachal'noï komandy Ukraïns'koï halyts'koï armiï* (New York 1974)

Shankovs'kyi, L. *Ukraïns'ka halyts'ka armiia: Voienno-istorychna studiia* (Winnipeg 1974)

L. Shankovsky

## Ukrainian Geographical Society (Ukrainske heohrafichne tovarystvo).

An organization of professional and amateur scientists engaged in theoretical and applied research in geography. Its purpose is to co-ordinate geographical research and training, improve geographical education in high schools and postsecondary institutions, and popularize geographical knowledge. The society originated in 1947 as a branch of the Geographical Society of the USSR, which evolved from the Imperial Russian Geographical Society (est 1845). In 1958 it was reorganized into the Geographical Society of the Ukrainian SSR and placed under the jurisdiction of the Academy of Sciences in Kiev. In 1987 it had over 8,000 members grouped in 33 chapters throughout Ukraine. Its work was divided among 17 sections, specializing in such areas as physical geography, economic geography, cartography, paleo-

geography, geomorphology, meteorology and climatology, hydrology, medical geography, remote sensing, high-school geography, regional studies, tourism, and speleology. The society held scientific meetings and conferences, published collections of scientific papers, organized exhibitions of geographical publications and maps, and participated in organizing geographical contests for high-school students. In the absence of an institute of geography it played an important role in linking the many specialists in the field, but it did not participate as a separate entity in international geographical conferences or the congresses of the International Geographical Union. In 1990 the society asserted its independence from the all-Union geographical society and changed its name to the Ukrainian Geographical Society.

I. Stebelsky

## Ukrainian Geological Administration (Ukrainske heolohichne upravlinnia).

The chief government agency in charge of geological research and prospecting in Ukraine from 1918 to 1957. Its history goes back to the Ukrainian Geological Committee, which was formed in Kiev in 1918 on the initiative of V. *Luchytsky. The administration introduced a program of systematic geological surveying and mapping and published the first geological maps of Soviet Ukraine. Its prospecting work led to the development of many mineral deposits, such as coal, iron, titanium, nickel, and potassium salts. As part of the economic reforms of 1957 the Chief Administration for Geology and the Protection of Underground Resources was established under the Council of Ministers of the Ukrainian SSR, and the Ukrainian Geological Administration was reorganized into the Kiev Geological Administration, which was renamed the Kiev Geological Prospecting Trust in the subsequent year.

## Ukrainian Girls' Institute in Peremyshl (Ukrainskyi institut dlia divchat u Peremyshli).

A secondary school for young women, supported by private funds, in which education was provided in Ukrainian. It was opened in 1895; in 1903 the higher grades of the institute were transformed into a *lyceum, and in 1920 into a *gymnasium. The school, which boasted the first forced central air heating in Eastern Europe, a tennis court, a large library, and a massive three-story building that is still in use today, was the fruit of private initiative and fund-raising efforts. It was founded by Ukrainian parents and Ukrainian Catholic clergy who wanted to provide Ukrainian women with the opportunity to acquire a secondary education to prepare them for admission to university or teacher training institutes. The school accommodated about 200 boarders, and another 50 or so day students. It employed female and male faculty members and prided itself on progressive educational approaches, which included sports, foreign languages, and sciences. The school was closed down by Soviet authorities in 1939.

## Ukrainian Gold Cross (Ukrainskyi zolotyi khrest, or UZKh).

A humanitarian relief and educational organization of Ukrainian women in the United States. Founded in New York in 1931 as the women's auxiliary of the *Organization for the Rebirth of Ukraine (ODVU), it was renamed the Ukrainian Red Cross of the ODVU (1933) and incorporated in 1940 as the Ukrainian Gold Cross. In the interwar period UZKh provided help to Ukrainian war invalids and political prisoners in Polish-ruled Western Ukraine, and in 1938–9 sent supplies of food, clothing, and medicine to Carpatho-Ukraine. In 1940 it opened an office under O. Nyzhankivsky in Leysin, Switzerland, to help Ukrainian detainees in French and Swiss internment camps. After the war UZKh helped Ukrainians in DP camps and sponsored immigrants to the United States. In 1967 it set up a special Defense and Relief Committee to help Ukrainian political prisoners and their families in the USSR. The Ukrainian Gold Cross has also organized nurseries, summer camps for boys and girls, and exhibits of Ukrainian art and handicrafts. It grants scholarships to needy students in the United States and South America. It is a founding member of the United Ukrainian American Relief Committee, the World Federation of Ukrainian Women's Organizations, and the World Congress of Free Ukrainians. Besides publishing its own page in *Natsionalist* (1936), *Ukraïna*, and *Zhinochyi svit* and its own bulletin (1975–), it has published collections of O. Teliha's poetry (1977) and H. Cherin's humorous sketches (1974). The presidents of UZKh have been A. Hladun (1931–6, 1950–4), A. Sereda (1936–8), S. Halychyn (1938–40), M. Lechytska (1940–9), A. Levkut (1949–50), P. Riznyk (1954–8), M. *Kvitkovska (1958–82), and N. Ivaniv (since 1982–). A history of UZKh was published in 1981.

**Ukrainian Greek Orthodox Church of Canada.** See Ukrainian Orthodox Church of Canada.

**Ukrainian Gymnasium in Chernivtsi** (Ukrainska himnaziia v Chernivtsiakh). Founded in Chernivtsi in 1896 as the Ukrainian counterpart of the German-language gymnasium in the city, the institution provided Ukrainian-language instruction in all areas of study and had a predominantly Ukrainian staff. By 1913 it had 560 students and 34 teachers. After the Rumanian occupation of Bukovyna the gymnasium was Rumanianized. The name was changed in 1922 from the Ukrainian State Gymnasium to the Fourth Gymnasium, and in 1930 it became the Liceul Marele Voievod Mihai. In 1925–7 Rumanian became the language of instruction, and after 1927 even Ukrainian language courses were canceled. After the Soviet occupation of Bukovyna the gymnasium was turned into a *10-year school. Some of the notable figures who taught at the gymnasium were A. Artymovych, A. Klym, M. Korduba, V. Kmitsykevych, Yu. Kobyliansky, and M. Ravliuk.

**Ukrainian Gymnasium in Czechoslovakia** (Ukrainska himnaziia v Chekhoslovachchyni). Founded in Prague in 1925 on the initiative of the *Ukrainian Higher Pedagogical Institute. In 1926 it received official sanction as a realgymnasium, on the model of the Czech gymnasium system. In 1927 it was relocated to Řevnice, and in 1938 to Modřany, near Prague. In 1937–8 the gymnasium had 185 students and 33 faculty members. It had a dormitory which housed the majority of its students, who came mainly from Transcarpathia. It remained open until 1945. The directors were Ya. Yarema, A. Artymovych, I. Kobyzky, M. Khliur, H. Omelchenko (from 1936), and A. Shtefan (from 1940). A collection of articles (ed V. Maruniak) about the gymnasium was published in 1975.

**Ukrainian Helsinki Group** (aka Ukrainian Civic Group for Promoting the Implementation of the Helsinki

The 1928–9 report of the Ukrainian Gymnasium in Czechoslovakia

Accords; Ukrainian: Ukrainska helsinkska hrupa, or Ukrainska hromadska hrupa spryiannia vykonanniu Helsinkskykh uhod). A human rights committee founded on 9 November 1976 in Kiev by M. *Rudenko (head), O. *Berdnyk, P. *Grigorenko, I. *Kandyba, L. *Lukianenko, M. *Marynovych, M. *Matusevych, O. *Meshko, N. *Strokata, and O. *Tykhy. Its purpose was to monitor the implementation of the human rights provisions of the Helsinki Accords, signed in August 1975 by 33 European states, the United States, and Canada: freedom of conscience, the free flow of information, and freedom of travel. Although the USSR, not Ukraine, signed the accords, the provisions were binding on the Soviet authorities and could be used as a basis for demands for individual and national rights in Ukraine.

The group assumed three principal tasks: to monitor the implementation of the accords in Ukraine, to gather and disseminate information about their violation, and to secure an independent role for Ukraine in subsequent negotiations and in international affairs. In its memoranda and open letters to international agencies the group pointed out violations of human and national rights in Ukraine and showed how the people's aspirations for independence were being suppressed. It gave voice to the Ukrainian people's demands for political, cultural, and social freedom within the framework of the Soviet legal system.

In February 1977 the authorities began to arrest the group's members. Within two years all the founding members were tried and sentenced to imprisonment for 7 to 10 years and to exile. In defiance of the crackdown new members joined: V. Kalynychenko, Yu. Lytvyn, M. Melnyk, V. Ovsiienko, V. Striltsiv, P. and V. Sichko, and P. Vins. In 1979 V. Chornovil, O. Heiko-Matusevych, M. Horbal, Z. Krasivsky, Ya. Lesiv, V. Malynkovych, P. Rozumny, S. Shabatura, I. Sokulsky, V. Stus, and Y. Zisels became members. Early that year political prisoners in various labor camps declared their membership: S. Karavansky, O. Popovych, V. Romaniuk, B. Rebryk, I. Senyk, Yu. Shukhevych, and D. Shumuk. In 1983 the Estonian M. Niklius and the Lithuanian V. Petkus, both political prisoners, were accepted into the group. The new groups were punished promptly: in 1979–80 O. Berdnyk, V. Chornovil, O. Heiko-Matusevych, M. Horbal, V. Kalynychenko, Z. Krasivsky, Ya. Lesiv, Yu.

Lytvyn, V. Ovsiienko, P. Rozumny, P. and V. Sichko, and V. Stus were given sentences of 2 to 10 years' imprisonment, sometimes on trumped-up criminal, not political, charges. In 1978 the group's *Informatsiinyi biuleten'* began to appear. It was reprinted by the Smoloskyp publishing house in the United States in 1981, and the first two issues were translated into English.

By 1983 the group had 37 members, of whom 22 were in prison camps, 5 were in exile, 1 (M. Melnyk) had committed suicide, 3 had been released and were living in Ukraine, and 6 had emigrated to the West. Three members of the group subsequently died in concentration camps: O. Tykhy (1984), Yu. Lytvyn (1984), and V. Stus (1985).

In 1979 the Foreign Representation of the group was established in the United States under the leadership of P. Grigorenko (to 1987) and then M. Rudenko. N. *Svitlychna, who joined the group in the United States, edited *Visnyk represii na Ukraïni*. The Committee of Helsinki Guarantees for Ukraine, headed by A. Zvarun, was established in November 1976 in the United States. It staged a number of demonstrations at the Helsinki review conferences in Belgrade (1977), Madrid (1980), and Vienna (1986), demanding the inclusion of Ukraine in the Helsinki process and defending the imprisoned members of the Helsinki Group. The Helsinki Committee of the Ukrainian Congress Committee of America, the World Congress of Free Ukrainians, and Americans for Human Rights in Ukraine were particularly active in attracting international attention to the group.

In 1987–8, during the period of Perestroika and Glasnost, all imprisoned members of the group were released. Upon their return to Ukraine they revived the organization and elected a new leader, L. Lukianenko. They changed the group's name to the Ukrainian Helsinki Association (Ukrainska helsinska spilka) and they expanded it into a broad civic union. On 7 July 1988 they issued the Declaration of Principles of the new association and published its statutes. The goal of the association was to promote democratic reform in Ukraine and to achieve economic and political sovereignty for Ukraine.

In the succeeding year the association revised its program and activities. It became involved in the elections to the USSR Supreme Soviet and to the Ukrainian Supreme Soviet. It organized large demonstrations against repressive laws and measures and participated in organizing the *Popular Movement of Ukraine. Its branches in various parts of Ukraine established their own newspapers: *Holos vidrodzhennia* in Kiev, *Ekspres-khronika Ukraïns'koho visnyka*, *Informatsiinyi biuleten'*, and *L'vivs'ki novyny* in Lviv, *Informatsiinyi biuleten'* in Kharkiv, and *Vil'na dumka* in Volhynia. When the 1990 elections in Ukraine opened up new opportunities for political competition, the association was dissolved and replaced by the Ukrainian Republican party.

BIBLIOGRAPHY

Zinkevych, O. (ed). *Ukraïns'kyi pravozakhysnyi rukh: Dokumenty i materiialy kyïvs'koï Ukraïns'koï hromads'koï hrupy spryiannia vykonanniu hel'sinks'kykh uhod* (Baltimore–Toronto 1978)
Verba, L.; Yasen, B.; Zinkevych, O. (eds). *The Human Rights Movement in Ukraine: Documents of the Ukrainian Helsinki Group, 1978–1980* (Baltimore–Toronto 1980)
Zinkevych, O. (ed). *Ukraïns'ka hel'sinks'ka hrupa, 1978–1982: Dokumenty i materiialy* (Baltimore–Toronto 1983)

O. Zinkevych

**Ukrainian Hetman Organization of America.** See United Hetman Organization.

The seal of the Ukrainian Higher Pedagogical Institute

**Ukrainian Higher Pedagogical Institute** (Ukrainskyi vysokyi pedahohichnyi instytut im. M. Drahomanova). A pedagogical school in Prague, founded in 1923 by the Ukrainian Citizens' Committee. It received financial support from the Czechoslovak government and trained teachers for elementary and extramural education. In 1925 it increased the program of study from two to four years and in addition began training teachers for secondary schools. The institute had departments of literature-history, mathematics-sciences, and, from 1924, choral music. The faculty consisted of 78 members. Over the period of its existence the institute graduated 178 students, most of whom went on to teach in schools in Transcarpathia. In 1924 a gymnasium was attached, which in 1925 became the *Ukrainian Gymnasium in Czechoslovakia. The institute's publication activity consisted of 44 course outlines, 3 volumes of the journal *Pratsi* (1929–33) put out by its own publishing house, Siiach, and 11 other works published by the Ukrainian Publishing Fund in Prague. In 1933 the Czechoslovak government cut off funding, and the institute was forced to close. The rectors of the institute were L. *Biletsky, V. *Simovych, and V. *Harmashiv.

**Ukrainian Higher School of Economics** (Ukrainska ekonomichna vysoka shkola, or UEVS). An institute of higher education established in Munich in 1945 by Ukrainian displaced persons. Its mandate, from the American military authorities, was to prepare cadres for government, co-operative, and private-enterprise posts. The program at UEVS lasted for eight semesters and consisted of 58 subjects and three seminars. Subjects were divided into 10 departments: accounting, national and private husbandry, statistics, geographical economics, trade, public and private law, sociology, and co-operative theory. Among the professors at UEVS were M. Velychkivsky, I. Vytanovych, S. Drahomanov, I. Zamsha, B. *Martos, M. Stakhiv, and Yu. Studynsky. The rectors of UEVS were B. Martos (1945–9) and M. Kosenko (1950–1). The UEVS was liquidated in 1951 as a result of financial restraints and the emigration of both potential students and professors. In the six years that it operated it graduated some 280 students, among them one with a doctorate in economics.

**Ukrainian Historical Association** (Ukrainske istorychne tovarystvo, or UIT). A society of Ukrainian historians in North America and Europe founded in 1965 with an initial membership of 45. Since its inception it has published the quarterly *Ukraïns'kyi istoryk* and the book series Istorychni monohrafiï (Historical Monographs), Istorychni studiï (Historical Studies), Memuarystyka

(Memoirs), Ukraïns'ki vcheni (Ukrainian Scholars), Hrushevskiiana, and Ukraïns'ko-zhydivs'ki vzaiemyny (Ukrainian-Jewish Relations). By 1990 the association had published approx 70 Ukrainian and English titles. It is particularly interested in source material in Ukrainian history deposited in Western archives and libraries. The UIT is a member of the American Historical Association and a participant in various American and Canadian learned conferences. It collaborates with the Ukrainian Academy of Arts and Sciences in the US and the Shevchenko Scientific Society. The presidents of UIT have been O. Ohloblyn (1965–81) and L. *Wynar (1981–).

The seal of the Ukrainian Historical-Philological Society

**Ukrainian Historical-Philological Society** (Ukrainske istorychno-filolohichne tovarystvo). A Ukrainian learned society founded in Prague in 1923 and affiliated with the Ukrainian Free University. It held semimonthly sessions featuring scholarly lectures and published offset editions of its members' essays and five volumes of its proceedings (1926–44). Its members participated in European Slavic conferences. Most of its approx 50 members were specialists in Ukrainian history or philology and worked as scholars and teachers in Czechoslovakia. Its president was D. *Antonovych (1923–45), and its prominent members included O. Kolessa, V. Bidnov, and S. Narizhny. The society was disbanded when the Soviet army occupied Prague and was revived briefly in Munich in 1946 under the leadership of V. Shcherbakivsky.

**Ukrainian Hromada** (Ukrainska hromada). A civic and cultural association established in Berlin in 1919 by Ukrainian emigrants, many of whom were prisoners from the Russian Imperial Army, supporters of the *Union for the Liberation of Ukraine, or members of Ukrainian diplomatic missions. It was initially a nonparty organization but subsequently became associated with the hetmanite movement. It was active throughout the 1920s and into the early 1930s and had over 6,000 members. Its official organs were *Nove slovo* (1920) and *Ukraïns'ke slovo* (1921–3). Among its leaders were B. Lepky and Z. Kuzelia (1924–33). It was revived under the auspices of P. Skoropadsky, and was active in 1940–5 as one of two Ukrainian organizations permitted by the German authorities (along with the Ukrainian National Alliance). It was headed then by B. Homzyn, and its official organ was *Ukraïns'ka diisnist'*. It was dissolved when Germany was occupied in 1945 by the Allied forces.

**Ukrainian Hromada in Czechoslovakia** (Ukrainska hromada v Chekho-Slovachchyni). A cultural and educational organization of a nationalist profile established in 1927. Its membership was over 200 and consisted mostly

of veterans of the UNR Army and some Ukrainians from Transcarpathia. It had several branches and a head office in Prague. After the German occupation of Czechoslovakia in 1939, the Ukrainian Hromada merged with the Ukrainian National Alliance in Germany. The Hromada's president for the duration of its existence was M. Halahan.

**Ukrainian Hromada in France** (Ukrainska hromada u Frantsii). The first Ukrainian community-cultural organization to emerge in France after the First World War. It was established in 1924 in Paris, and its membership initially included émigrés of varying political and ideological leanings. Soon the Sovietophiles formed their own Union of Ukrainian Citizens in France (1925); the UNR supporters established the Union of Ukrainian Emigré Organizations in France (1926); and the nationalists founded the Ukrainian National Union in France (1932). Also known as the Shapoval Hromada, the UHF adhered to the political ideals of M. *Drahomanov and Mykyta *Shapoval. In the 1930s it had 22 branches, which sponsored reading rooms and Ukrainian language schools for children, with a membership of 600 to 1,200. The Hromada ceased its activities during the German occupation (1940–4) but revived after the war. It was headed successively by M. Kapustiansky (1924–9), Mykola Shapoval (1929–48), A. Shapoval (1948–53), I. Bodnar, and P. Turkevych. It published *Vistnyk ukraïns'koï hromady u Frantsiï* (1929–38, 68 issues), *Ukraïns'ka volia* (1938–9, 13 issues), and *Vistnyk* (1948, 3 issues). In 1976 the Hromada formally disbanded. That same year A. Zhukovsky wrote a brief history of the organization.

**Ukrainian Hromada in Paris.** See Circle of Ukrainians in Paris.

**Ukrainian Hromada in Venezuela** (Ukrainska hromada u Venesueli, or UHV; Spanish: Asociación de Ucranianos en Venezuela). A cultural organization founded in Caracas on 13 March 1949 as the central organization representing the whole Ukrainian community in Venezuela (at that time approx 3,400 individuals). It was based in Caracas and had branches in Valencia, Puerto Caballo, and Maracay. The Ukrainian Women's Alliance in Venezuela, the Ukrainian Reading Hall, the Society of Ukrainian Engineers, and the Plast Ukrainian Youth Association were affiliated with the Hromada. The society ran a kindergarten and a Saturday school; organized concerts, plays, and dances; and built its own hall, the Ukrainian People's Home. Its presidents have been I. Lazarenko, L. Stakhovsky, V. Koval, V. Vasiuk, R. Prypkhan, Yu. Hrytsyk, and I. Khomniak.

**Ukrainian Husbandry Academy** (Ukrainska hospodarska akademiia, or UHAK). A postsecondary school operating in Poděbrady, Czechoslovakia, from 1922 to 1935. It was founded by the *Ukrainian Civic Committee in Czechoslovakia, which was headed at the time by Mykyta Shapoval, and was financed by the Ministry of Foreign Affairs of the Czechoslovak Republic. The school's first constitution, which was approved by the Czechoslovak Ministry of Agriculture on 16 May 1922, defined an institution similar to Czechoslovak schools of higher learning. The UHAK consisted of three faculties subdivided into departments: (1) the faculty of agronomy and forestry, (2) the faculty of engineering, with departments of chemical-

The castle housing the Ukrainian Husbandry Academy

Members of the last senate of the Ukrainian Husbandry Academy (1934). From left: Isaak Mazepa, Volodymyr Cherediiv, Leonid Frolov, Borys Ivanytsky, Olgerd Bochkovsky, Vasyl Ivanys, Mykola Dobrylovsky, Leonid Hrabyna, Hryhorii Shyianiv

technology and hydrotechnology, and (3) the faculty of economics and co-operation, with departments of economics and statistics, and numerous co-operatives. Its supporting institutions included a library of 30,000 volumes, 33 special collections, 14 laboratories, several experimental farms, a tree farm, a meteorological station, and two training co-operatives. Most of these facilities were housed in the castle built by Jiři of Poděbrady (1420–71). The academy's three-year program led to an engineering degree and differed from the standard program in Czechoslovak schools only in offering courses in Ukrainian studies. In 1925 the program of study was extended to four years. The academy's program was overseen by the Ministry of Agriculture, its economic and administrative affairs by the Ministry of Foreign Affairs. The highest governing body of the UHAK was the Faculty Council and its presidium, consisting of the rector, prorector, and secretary of the council. The rectors were I. *Shovheniv (1922–5, 1926–7), B. *Ivanytsky (1925–6, 1928–35), and Serhii *Tymoshenko (1927–8).

In the first decade of its operation the school employed 118 teachers in total, 92 of whom were Ukrainians and 26 of whom were Czechs. At its peak (in 1928) the teaching staff numbered 96. Many of the faculty members were distinguished scientists, such as V. *Domanytsky and V. *Cherediiv (agronomists), B. Ivanytsky (forester), O. *Mytsiuk, V. *Sadovsky, and V. *Timoshenko (economists), S. *Borodaievsky and B. *Martos (co-operative organizers), F. *Shcherbyna (statistician), L. *Bych and O. *Eikhelman (jurists), O. *Bochkovsky (sociologist), and S. *Komaretsky (chemist).

The total enrollment over the years was 786, with a peak of 613 students in 1926–7. The student population was for the most part made up of Ukrainian émigrés. Most of the students were dependent on the government for financial assistance. A total of 559 students graduated with engineering degrees – 125 agronomists, 92 foresters, 58 chemical-technologists, 117 hydrotechnicians, and 167 economists. In the 1930s most of them worked in their professions in Western Ukraine.

The academy undertook a vigorous publishing program. It issued 698 scientific publications, including 229 books (of which many were the first technical higher education textbooks to appear in Ukrainian). The Terminological Commission worked to develop a consistent

Ukrainian technical terminology; in particular it published a German-Ukrainian forestry dictionary. Some 50 organizations, including 9 scientific and professional associations, sprang up at the academy.

In 1928, as financial support for the UHAK diminished, the Czechoslovak government ordered the academy not to admit any more new students and gradually to wind down its operation. In 1931 the Society of Friends of the Ukrainian Husbandry Academy (president, B. Matiushenko) was set up in Prague to save the academy. Enough funds could not be raised, and the academy closed in 1935. The society directed its efforts at the *Ukrainian Technical and Husbandry Institute, which had been established as a correspondence school at the academy in 1932.

BIBLIOGRAPHY
Narizhnyi, S. Ukraïns'ka emigratsiia (Prague 1942)
Ukraïns'ka hospdars'ka akademiia v Ch.S.R., 1922–1935 (New York 1959)

**Ukrainian Hygienic Society** (Ukrainske hihiienichne tovarystvo). An organization established in Lviv in 1929 to educate the community and improve the general level of hygiene. M. *Panchyshyn was the founding president and a patron of the society. With branches in most of the larger towns and circles in the smaller ones, the society organized popular lectures, exhibitions, first-aid courses, and courses for nurses and sanitary workers. It also published articles, leaflets, popular pamphlets, and the popular magazine Narodne zdorovlia (1937–9). To improve the general level of health it maintained clinics, tuberculosis dispensaries, a tuberculosis sanatorium in Hrebeniv, sports and eugenics consulting centers in Lviv, and vacation facilities for young people, including a climate station in Pidliute. Its activities came to an end with the Soviet occupation of Galicia in 1939.

**Ukrainian Independent Theater.** See Lviv Ukrainian Independent Theater.

**Ukrainian Information Agency (Ukrinform).** See Radio and Telegraph Agency of Ukraine.

**Ukrainian Institute for the Upgrading of Physicians** (Ukrainskyi instytut udoskonalennia likariv). A postgraduate medical education institution, until 1992 under the directorship of the Ministry of Health of the Ukrainian SSR. Established in 1923 in Kharkiv, it was reorganized in 1965 and subordinated to the All-Union Ministry of Health. The institute has faculties of internal medicine, surgery, pediatrics, and hygiene, 61 departments, and 2 laboratories, as well as a scientific society. In 1983, 500 physicians upgraded their qualifications there. Medical problems studied include arterial hypertension, arteriosclerosis, the diagnosis and treatment of malignant tumors, road accident traumas, and tissue degeneration. The institute has developed innovative procedures in the surgical treatment of spinal column disorders, the early diagnosis and treatment of tuberculosis in children and teenagers, and the treatment of wound infections, as well as improved noncorrosive materials for dentures and cryogenic treatment methods in stomatology. (See also *Kiev Institute for the Upgrading of Physicians.)

The Ukrainian Institute of America

**Ukrainian Institute of America** (Ukrainskyi instytut Ameryky). An educational and cultural foundation established in 1948 by W. *Dzus. Originally housed in the Parkwood Lakes estate at West Islip, Long Island, it was moved in 1955 to its present headquarters on 79th Street in Manhattan, a historical building owned previously by A. van Horne Stuyvesant. The institute collects and preserves works of Ukrainian artists, such as A. Archipenko, O. Hryshchenko, and H. Kruk; religious artifacts, such as icons and chasubles; patents of Ukrainian inventors; portraits of historical figures; and samples of folk art. Its library contains 22,000 volumes, and its Ukrainian Research and Documentation Center (est 1985) has an archival repository. The institute's cultural program includes concerts, lectures, art shows, and poetry readings. In the 1950s it granted prizes to artists and scholarships and loans to university students in addition to publishing a collection of M. Fomenko's songs titled *Ukrainian Youthful Melodies* (1957). In 1962 it had 26 individual and 17 association members. By 1988 it had 400 members. The presidents of the institute have included Dzus, T. Dzus (the founder's son), and W. Nazarewicz.

**Ukrainian Institute of Marxism-Leninism** (Ukrainskyi instytut marksyzmu-leninizmu, or UIML). A Party-sponsored educational and research institute in Kharkiv analogous to the Moscow-based Communist Academy. Its political patron was M. *Skrypnyk. The UIML arose out of the Ukrainian Institute of Marxism, which was established in November 1922 by a decision of the CP(B)U Organizational Bureau to train instructors in ideology for institutions of higher education. In 1924 its name was changed to the UIML. The institute was divided into three divisions – economics, history, and philosophy-sociology – each consisting of three departments. The economics department was headed by D. Naumov, the agrarian department by P. Liashchenko, and the co-operation and collectivization department by A. Lozovy. In the second division M. Yavorsky chaired the history of Ukraine department, H. Rokhkin the world history department, and S. Hopner the Party history department. The third division consisted of the philosophy department under S. Semkovsky, the sociology department under V. Yurynets, and the law department under Yu. Mazurenko. A special department on the nationality question was established in 1926 and headed by Skrypnyk. The institute's duties were expanded in 1925 to include not only the training of teaching cadres but also research.

The institute's prestige grew in the mid-1920s. Major Soviet political figures, such as N. Popov (1927–8), Skrypnyk (1928–30), and O. Shlikhter (1930–1), served as its directors. In 1923 its enrollment was 22. By 1931 it had 48 full members, 17 corresponding members, 29 research associates, and 165 graduate students. Beginning in 1927 the UIML published its own monthly, *Prapor marksyzmu-leninizmu*. From 1929 M. Yavorsky and V. Yurynets came under increasingly intemperate attack for Ukrainian nationalism, and the institute came to be portrayed as a hotbed of ideological heresy. Finally the CC CP(B)U ordered the UIML to be reorganized into a loose union of autonomous institutions called the *All-Ukrainian Association of Marxist-Leninist Scientific Research Institutes (VUAMLIN).

BIBLIOGRAPHY
Komarenko, N. *Ustanovy istorychnoï nauky v Ukraïns'kii RSR* (Kiev 1973)
Mace, J. *Communism and the Dilemmas of National Liberation: National Communism in Soviet Ukraine, 1918–1933* (Cambridge, Mass 1983)

J. Mace

**Ukrainian Institute of Modern Art** (UIMA; Ukrainskyi instytut modernoho mystetstva). A nonprofit, tax-exempt, cultural institution in Chicago, founded in 1971 to promote and collect contemporary Ukrainian art. Its creation was initiated by A. Khreptovsky (its principal benefactor) and the sculptors K. Milonadis and M. Urban. Since 1974 the UIMA president has been O. Koverko. Since 1978 the UIMA has been housed in a reconstructed building containing an exhibition gallery. An addition housing the UIMA permanent collection was opened in 1980, and two new galleries were added in 1991. The first and only UIMA curator (until 1982) was V. Kachurovsky. Since 1982 the art collection and art exhibitions (approx five a year) have been curated by a committee (K. Milonadis, A. Diachenko-Kochman, A. Koverko, I. Kuchma, and I. Kobyletsky). The UIMA has sponsored solo exhibitions of works by émigré, Ukrainian-American, and Ukrainian-Canadian art-

Part of the permanent collection of the Ukrainian Institute of Modern Art

ists, such as A. Archipenko (1971), H. Kruk (1972), Milonadis (1973), Urban (1974), A. Hunenko (1974, 1982), R. Kostyniuk (1974, 1988), P. Kolisnyk (1975, 1987), I. Dmytruk (1975), M. Andriienko-Nechytailo (1976), J. Hnizdovsky (1978, 1985), Koverko (1979), A. Olenska-Petryshyn (1980), J. Solovij (1980), W. Pura (1984), Diachenko-Kochman (1985), W. Kurelek (1987), and Kuchma (1989). The UIMA has also published exhibition catalogs and some monographs, presented concerts of contemporary music, and organized literary readings and art lectures.

**Ukrainian Institute of Sociology** (Ukrainskyi instytut hromadoznavstva). An émigré institution founded in November 1924 in Prague on the initiative of members of the Ukrainian Sociological Society (est October 1923 in Prague). The institute had 33 full members and 15 corresponding members. The director and leading figure was Mykyta *Shapoval; when he died in 1932, the institute virtually ceased to exist. The institute included in its program of research, lectures, and seminars all branches of the social sciences; maintained a library of 8,000 volumes (2,500 were from Shapoval's private collection); ran the Ukrainian National Museum and Archives in Prague (est 1923); and organized the Ukrainian Workers' University, a correspondence school with over 30 courses and some 300 students (primarily émigré workers and peasants). The journal *Nova Ukraïna* and the publishing house Vilna Spilka were associated with the institute. The institute published 46 studies and reports and the first Ukrainian sociological journal, *Suspil'stvo* (three issues, 1925–7), which contained contributions by Western Ukrainian sociologists.

**Ukrainian Institute of Water-Management Engineers** (Ukrainskyi instytut inzheneriv vodnoho hospodarstva). An institution of higher education under the jurisdiction of Ukraine's Ministry of Higher and Secondary Education. It was set up in Kiev in 1922 and was known until 1959 as the Kiev Tekhnikum of Engineering and Melioration. In 1959 it was moved to Rivne. It has 10 faculties and offers evening courses, correspondence courses, and a graduate program. Its library has 546,000 volumes (1983). In 1982–3 its enrollment was 9,300.

**Ukrainian Institution of Trust in the German Reich** (Ukrainska ustanova doviria v Nimetskomu Raikhu; German: Ukrainische Vertrauensstelle im Deutschen Reich). An agency established by the German government in 1938 to aid stateless Ukrainians in the Reich. With a head office in Berlin, it had branches in Vienna, Prague, and Łódź. The agency helped individuals, particularly migrant workers, to contact government institutions and obtain passports, visas, and temporary work permits and gave advice on various personal problems. Owing to its intervention almost 50,000 Ukrainian POWs were released. The agency also kept track of the activities of Ukrainian nationals. Similar agencies were established for other non-German groups, such as the Russians, Belarusians, and Caucasian peoples. The agency was headed by M. *Sushko until it was dissolved in April 1945.

**Ukrainian Insurgent Army** (Ukrainska povstanska armiia [UPA]). A Ukrainian military formation which fought from 1942 to 1949, mostly in Western Ukraine, against the German and Soviet occupational regimes. Its immediate purpose was to protect the Ukrainian population from German and Soviet repression and exploitation; its ultimate goal was an independent and unified Ukrainian state.

The first UPA units appeared in western Volhynia (now Volhynia and Rivne oblasts). They were organized independently by T. *Borovets (in spring 1942), the Bandera faction of the OUN (from October 1942), and the Melnyk faction of the OUN (in spring 1943). As resistance to the Germans intensified, the military forces of the Bandera faction grew rapidly and established their control over many districts of Volhynia. When talks on unification among the three groups failed, the most powerful group, the Bandera units, disarmed and absorbed the two other groups, in July and August 1943. K. *Savur, the leader of the OUN (Bandera faction) for northwestern Ukraine, became the commander in chief of the unified UPA.

German auxiliary police and guard units, composed not only of ethnic Ukrainians but also of other nationals who had served in the Red Army, defected to the UPA. The number of non-Ukrainian UPA soldiers grew rapidly, and peaked in the late fall of 1943. They were organized into separate national units, the largest of which were the Azerbaidzhani, Uzbek, Georgian, and Tatar. In the autumn of 1943 the UPA established a secret armistice with Hungarian units which guarded German communication lines in Volhynia. Recognizing the importance of national aspirations, the UPA organized on 21–22 November 1943 the Conference of the Oppressed Nations of Eastern Europe and Asia. It was attended by representatives of 13 nationalities, who resolved to support each other's liberation struggles.

Beginning in the summer of 1943, UPA units from the northwestern region conducted southward raids into Kamianets-Podilskyi and Vinnytsia oblasts to undermine German control of this territory and to build up local insurgency forces. By the late autumn a new military grouping was consolidated under the command of V. *Kuk, the OUN leader for central Ukraine.

In the first two years of the German occupation the OUN used Galicia as a training and supply area for the UPA. When a successful recruitment drive for the Division Galizien was launched, in May–June 1943, and a large detachment of Soviet partisans led by S. Kovpak made its way

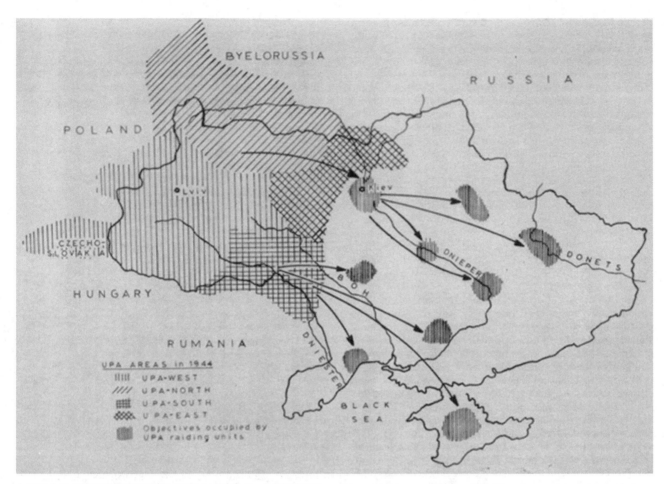

## AREAS WHERE THE UPA WAS ACTIVE
(reproduced from Yu. Tys-Krokhmaliuk, UPA *Warfare in Ukraine* [1972])

through Galicia into the Carpathian Mountains, in July 1943, the OUN decided to form military units in Galicia as well. Commanded by O. *Lutsky, these units were at first called the Ukrainian People's Self-Defense (UNS). As insurgent activity increased, the Germans placed Galicia under martial law, in October 1943. This only provoked stronger resistance.

A single command for all three regions of Ukraine, the Supreme Command of the UPA, was set up on or about 22 November 1943. The command consisted of the supreme commander and the Supreme Military Headquarters or General Staff, which was headed by the chief of staff (who was also the deputy commander) and was divided into six sections: operations, intelligence, logistics, personnel, training, and political education. Lt Col R. *Shukhevych was appointed commander in chief, and Maj D. Hrytsai became chief of staff. The original UPA in Volhynia was named officially the UPA-North, the insurgent units in central Ukraine became the UPA-South, and the UNS in Galicia was renamed the UPA-West. With Maj V. Sydor's appointment to commander of the new UPA-West in January 1944, the reorganization of the unified UPA was completed. Each of the three krais of the UPA was subdivided into military districts. At the beginning of 1944 there were at least 10 districts in total: 2 in the UPA-North, 6 in the UPA-West, and 2 in the UPA-South. In 1945 each district was subdivided

Members of the UPA Levy company

into tactical sectors. Every district and sector had its commander and headquarters analogous to the General Staff. This territorial organization of the UPA remained unchanged during the active combat period until 1949. To broaden the social and political base of the armed struggle for Ukraine's independence, the Supreme Command of the UPA took the initiative in setting up the *Ukrainian Supreme Liberation Council (est 15 July 1944), which served as a provisional government expressing the political will of the insurgency movement.

The basic combat unit during most of the UPA's history was a company of 120 to 180 men. The standard UPA company had three platoons each with three squads (10 to 12 men armed with a light machine gun, two or three automatic weapons, and seven or more rifles). In 1943–5 most companies were organized into kurins (two to four companies per kurin), and under special conditions two or more kurins were combined into a zahin. A kurin commander's staff included a political-education officer, an adjutant, a sergeant major, and sometimes a chaplain and a medical doctor. Regardless of size, all combat units within one military district formed a group (hrupa). The UPA did not receive aid from other countries; weapons, ammunition, medical supplies, and uniforms had to be seized from the enemy. Although it deployed some cavalry and artillery units during 1943–4, the UPA was basically an infantry force. According to some German intelligence reports in 1944, its strength was 200,000. According to a Soviet source (1988), in 1944–6 some 56,600 UPA soldiers were killed, 108,500 were captured, and 48,300 surrendered voluntarily. According to UPA historians in the West, at its peak in 1944 the army had at least 25,000 and at most 40,000 men.

The UPA made use of two rank systems, a functional one and a traditional formal one (see *Military ranks). The functional system was instituted because of an acute shortage of qualified and politically reliable officers during the early stages of organization. Those who demonstrated leadership ability were appointed to command positions regardless of formal rank or training. The most critical leadership shortages were found at the lower levels, ie, the platoon and squad. Almost every district organized its own NCO school, lasting four to six weeks, but the demand for qualified squad leaders could not be met. A severe shortage of medical officers was alleviated partly by enlisting Jewish doctors, who willingly joined the anti-Nazi resistance. The UPA also ran formal officer candidate schools, which produced approx 690 graduates. (For the UPA's award system see *Military decorations.)

Publishing was usually the responsibility of the political-education section. The UPA printed journals, such as Do zbroï (1943) and Povstanets' (1944–6); newspapers; military textbooks; pamphlets for youth; and leaflets. Some military districts and tactical sectors published their own irregular periodicals (eg, Shliakh peremohy, Chornyi lis, and Lisovyk). The best-known contributors to the UPA press were Ya. Busel, P. Poltava, O. Diakiv, and the artists N. Khasevych and M. Chereshnovsky.

During 1943 the UPA staged some successful ambushes and battles against the Germans, establishing its control of the countryside in Volhynia and leaving only the towns in German hands. At the same time it cleared some of the region of Soviet partisans and expanded its power southward and eastward. In 1944 it fought its largest engagements with German and Soviet forces. Retreating German units were frequently ambushed for their weapons and supplies. German attempts to secure areas of the Carpathian Mountains in the summer of 1944 led to several pitched battles with the UPA-West. But the main threat to the UPA was the Soviet NKVD combat troops that arrived in the rear of the advancing Red Army with the special task of re-establishing Soviet power. In the winter of 1944 and spring of 1945 numerous ambushes, skirmishes, and large-scale battles occurred between NKVD forces and the zahony of the UPA-North and UPA-South. In February Gen N. Vatutin, Soviet commander of the First Ukrainian

The first issue of the UPA organ Povstanets', containing the UPA soldier's oath

Front, was mortally wounded in an ambush. On 24 April 30,000 NKVD troops encircled and fought 5,000 soldiers of the UPA-South near Hurby. Modifying its tactics according to experience, the UPA gradually dispersed its larger units and operated mostly with companies which held specific territories and staged occasional propaganda raids into uncontrolled areas or neighboring countries. The first large-scale NKVD offensive against the UPA was conducted in the winter of 1944–5 in the Carpathian region. The UPA managed to preserve its control of the countryside and scored successful attacks against Soviet administrative centers and garrisons. With the ending of the war the returning Red Army divisions were turned against the UPA in the summer of 1945. The results were disappointing to the Soviet regime, but its offer of amnesty to soldiers surrendering by 20 July 1945 appeared more successful. Many men evading induction into the Red Army gave themselves up. The UPA used this opportunity to send home some discouraged or disabled soldiers. By 1949 there were at least four more amnesty calls.

The 'Great Blockade' in the Carpathians from January to April 1946 was the only successful Soviet offensive against the UPA. Special contingents of NKVD troops were stationed in all the towns and villages, and mobile combat units scoured the forests. Denied food and shelter, and forced to fight on the march at extremely low temperatures, the UPA experienced casualties of 40 percent. The Supreme Command decided to demobilize most combat units and ordered their surviving members to continue the struggle underground. The UPA command structure

A radio-communications station of the UPA-North

(krai, military district, and tactical-sector headquarters), however, continued to function.

The demobilization order did not apply to the forces of the Sixth Military District – the Sian Division of the UPA-West – which operated in Ukrainian ethnic territories that were annexed by Poland after 1944. The division defended the Ukrainian population from forced deportations to the USSR in 1945 and 1946. Having reached an understanding with the Polish Home Army, it conducted several joint operations against Polish security forces. On 28 March 1947 Gen K. Swierczewski, the deputy defense minister of Poland, was killed in an ambush by the Lemko Company under Lt S. Stebelsky ('Khrin'). In the spring and summer

Women soldiers of the UPA

of 1947 the Polish authorities staged Operation Wisła, in which the remaining Ukrainian population was deported by force to other parts of Poland. UPA battle losses went up sharply, and the surviving units were ordered either to cross into the USSR or to march across Czechoslovakia to West Germany. Remnants of Company 95, led by Lt M. Duda ('Hromenko'), reached West Germany on 11 September 1947.

Some UPA units continued to operate in 1948 and 1949 in the Carpathian Hoverlia Military District. They were usually composed of two platoons of two squads each, and had a total strength of 30 to 50 veteran noncommissioned officers. Except for two units, they were demobilized at the end of the summer of 1948. On 3 September 1949, R. Shukhevych ordered the command structure and the remaining combat units to be deactivated, and their members to be transferred to the underground network. After Shukhevych's death (5 March 1950) the underground continued the armed struggle under V. Kuk's ('Koval's') leadership until 1954.

BIBLIOGRAPHY
*Hrafika v bunkrakh UPA* (Philadelphia 1952)
Shankovs'kyi, L. 'Ukraïns'ka Povstancha Armiia,' in *Istoriia ukraïns'koho viiska* (Winnipeg 1953)
Tys-Krokhmaliuk, Yu. UPA *Warfare in Ukraine: Strategical, Tactical, and Organizational Problems of Ukrainian Resistance in World War II* (New York 1972)
Szczesniak, A.; Szota, W. *Droga do nikąd* (Warsaw 1973)
Shtendera, Ie.; Potichnyi, P. (eds). *Litopys UPA*, vols 1–18 (Toronto 1976–90)
Potichnyj, P.; Shtendera, Ye. (eds). *Political Thought of the Ukrainian Underground, 1943–1951* (Edmonton 1986)
Lebed', M. *Ukraïns'ka povstans'ka armiia* (1946; 2nd rev edn, np 1987)
Sodol, P. UPA: *They Fought Hitler and Stalin* (New York 1987)
P. Sodol

**Ukrainian Insurgent Army, Former Members of the** (Obiednannia kolyshnikh voiakiv UPA). A veterans' organization formed in Toronto in September 1966 out of a union of the Former Members of the UPA in the United States (est 1955 in New York) and the Former Members of the UPA in Canada (est 1951 in Toronto). Its purpose is to cultivate the military traditions of the UPA, to inform the West of Ukraine's struggle for independence, and to support the liberation struggle in Ukraine. The association (1981) has six branches in the United States and five branches in Canada. It has published several books about the UPA and military theory and a veterans' page in *Homin Ukraïny*, in addition to copublishing the magazine *Visti kombatanta* (1961–) and the documentary collection *Litopys UPA* (The UPA Chronicle, 1976–). Its presidents have included O. Gerega, M. Chuiko, P. Mykolenko, Ya. Strutynsky, M. Ripetsky (1983–6), M. Bokhno (1986–9), M. Kovalchyn (1986–9), and L. Futala (1989–92).

**Ukrainian Invalids' Aid Society** (Ukrainske tovarystvo dopomohy invalidam u Lvovi). An association set up in Lviv in 1922 to help invalid veterans of the Ukrainian Galician and the UNR armies. It assumed some of the tasks that until then had been performed by the social welfare section of the Ukrainian Citizens' Committee. In 1937 it had 2,016 registered clients, 434 of whom received regular monthly assistance. Others received less frequent aid. The society owned a large building in Lviv and ran a workshop employing invalids. For many years its president was I. Gyzha. The society was disbanded under Soviet rule.

**Ukrainian Journalists' Association Abroad** (Spilka ukrainskykh zhurnalistiv na chuzhyni). An organization of Ukrainian émigré journalists formed in June 1946 in Dillingen, Germany. Its original membership of about 100 declined gradually, to about 50 in 1954. Its presidents were S. Baran, M. Livytsky, M. Konovalets, D. Andriievsky, V. Stakhiv, Z. Pelensky, V. Shtelen, and M. Styranka. The association ceased its activities after 1986.

**Ukrainian Journalists' Association of America** (Spilka ukrainskykh zhurnalistiv Ameryky, or SUZhA). A professional organization founded in 1952 in New York to promote the interests of Ukrainian journalists. Consisting largely of émigré journalists, the association organized writing competitions, debates, and lectures and offered scholarships to students specializing in journalism. Together with a similar organization in Canada it formed (1966) the Federation of Ukrainian Journalists of the United States and Canada, which later founded the World Federation of Ukrainian Journalists. In 1967 the first federation began to publish a semiannual magazine, *Ukraïns'kyi zhurnalist*. The SUZhA has published a collection of materials on two of its conventions (1969) and Yu. Ternopilsky's *Ukraïns'ka presa z perspektyvy ïï 150-richchia* (The Ukrainian Press from the Perspective of Its 150th Anniversary, 1974). By 1976 it had 130 members. The association's presidents have included L. Myshuha (1952–8), R. Kupchynsky (1958–61), I. Kedryn (1964–7), M. Dolnytsky (1967–76), and O. Kuzmovych (1976–80). The organization has not met since 1980, when it failed to elect a new president, and has been in a process of decline.

Participants at the 2nd congress of the Ukrainian Journalists' associations of America and Canada (Toronto, 1966)

**Ukrainian Journalists' Association of Canada** (Spilka ukrainskykh zhurnalistiv Kanady, or SUZhK). A professional organization founded in Toronto in 1957 to promote the interests of Ukrainian journalists. In 1976 it had 90 members. To attract younger members it set up a youth section and provided scholarships to students of journalism. It has organized writing competitions, discussions, beauty pageants, and lectures. In 1966 it joined with its counterpart in the United States to form a federation, which published the semiannual *Ukraïns'kyi zhurnalist* (1967–76). The presidents of SUZhK have been V. Solo-

nynka, M. Sosnovsky, V. Levytsky-Sofroniv, O. Matla, N. Ripetsky, M. Lypovetsky, and V. Didiuk.

**Ukrainian Labor party** (Ukrainska trudova partiia, or UTP). A political party consisting largely of Ukrainian co-operators, established in Kiev on 18 October 1917. The UTP was ideologically similar to the Ukrainian Party of Socialist Revolutionaries. It was led by F. Kryzhanivsky, who was its representative to the Central Rada (where he was vice-president) and Little Rada, and later participated in the Ukrainian National Union. The UTP was a small and relatively insignificant party; it ceased to exist in 1918.

**Ukrainian Labor party** (Ukrainska trudova partiia, or UTP; also Labor Party, Ukrainian People's Labor party). Formerly the *National Democratic party, it was inaugurated as the UTP at a party congress on 28 March 1919 in Stanyslaviv. The UTP maintained its predecessor's basic profile and personnel. It was the strongest Galician party in the Ukrainian National Rada and the General Secretariat of the Western Ukrainian National Republic (ZUNR). Ye. Petrushevych and members of his government belonged to the UTP. Its publications included the dailies *Dilo*, *Ukraïns'ka dumka* (1920), and *Ukraïns'kyi vistnyk* (1921) as well as the weekly *Bat'kivshchyna*. The People's Committee of the UTP protested against the Treaty of Warsaw (1920) between the UNR government and Poland, which acknowledged Poland's claim to Galicia, as well as against the Peace Treaty of Riga (1921). The UTP protested Polish rule in Ukrainian lands on the ground that it was a foreign occupation, and recognized the ZUNR government-in-exile under Ye. Petrushevych. On 21 May 1923 the National Congress of the UTP protested against the 14 March ruling of the Conference of Ambassadors, which recognized Poland's control over Galicia. The reaction to that decision resulted in the UTP's split into three factions. The first, the so-called independent group (under Ye. Evyn, Rev O. Stefanovych, and others), rejected any attempt to harmonize Ukrainian-Polish relations and continued its support of Petrushevych. It published *Nash prapor*. The second, more influential group centered around the paper *Dilo* and stressed its independence from émigré government centers, particularly that of Petrushevych, who was moving politically to Sovietophilism. The third, nationalist faction, headed by S. Pidhirsky, D. Paliiv, and V. Kuzmovych, broke away altogether from the UTP and founded the Ukrainian Party of National Work. The split was not final. In 1924, talks took place between the groups regarding the consolidation of Ukrainian political forces, and the factions were reunited on 11 July 1925 as the *Ukrainian National Democratic Union.

V. Kubijovyč

**Ukrainian Labour-Farmer Temple Association** (Tovarystvo ukrainskyi robitnycho-farmerskyi dim, or ULF-TA). A nationwide Canadian pro-Communist organization active in the interwar era. Established in Winnipeg in March 1918 as the Ukrainian Labour Temple Association on the basis of a recently completed Ukrainian labor hall, the group built upon and expanded the network of organizations encompassed by the *Ukrainian Social Democratic Party of Canada. It obtained a Dominion charter in 1924, and in 1925 expanded its name to underline its desire to develop further in rural areas. Membership grew to

Delegates at the 5th convention of the Ukrainian Labour-Farmer Temple Association (Winnipeg, February 1924). Second row, 4th through 8th from left: Ivan Navizivsky, Danylo Lobai, Matthew Popovich, Myroslav Irchan, William Kolisnyk

2,650 in 88 branches in 1929 and to approx 10,000 in 201 branches (with 113 labor temples) in 1939. The association also developed women's and young people's sections; initiated and maintained a close affiliation with the *Workers' Benevolent Association and the Society for the Aid of the Liberation Movement in Western Ukraine; and operated an active publishing house, whose newspapers and journals included *Ukraïns'ki robitnychi visti, Robitnytsia, Svit molodi, and Farmers'ke zhyttia. The activities of ULFTA worked in tandem with an overriding political connection to the *Communist Party of Canada through the Communist-dominated ULFTA leadership. The group faced a major organizational crisis in 1935, when a group of ULFTA stalwarts led by D. *Lobai broke ranks over the issues of the ULFTA's bolshevization, the man-made famine in Ukraine, and the disappearance of two former ULFTA cultural activists, M. *Irchan and I. Sembai, during the Stalinist purges. Leading figures in the ULFTA included M. Popovich, M. Shatulsky, I. Navizivsky (J. Navis), and I. Boychuk (J. Boyd). The ULFTA was closed down under wartime regulations by Order in Council on 4 June 1940. It was succeeded in 1946 by the *Association of United Ukrainian Canadians.

BIBLIOGRAPHY
Al'manakh TURFDim, 1918–1929 (Winnipeg 1930)
Lobai, D. 'Komunistychnyi rukh sered ukraïntsiv Kanady,' in Propam'iatna knyha ukraïns'koho narodnoho domu v Vynypegu, ed D. Doroshenko (Winnipeg 1949)
Kravchuk, P. Na novii zemli (Toronto 1958)
Kolasky, J. Prophets and Proletarians: Documents on the Rise and Decline of Ukrainian Communism in Canada (Edmonton 1990)
J. Kolasky

**Ukrainian language.** See Language, Ukrainian.

**Ukrainian Language Association** (Tovarystvo plekannia ridnoi movy). An organization established in Winnipeg in 1964 to promote the proper use of Standard Ukrainian among Ukrainians in the West. The society's presidents have been C. Bida (1964–71), J. Rudnyckyj (1971–9, 1982–8), and O. Woycenko (1979–82). The society has had representatives in the United States (G.Y. Shevelov, P. Kovaliv), Australia (O. Pavlyshyn, P. Hrin, T. Babii), New Zealand (V. Krekhovets), Argentina (Ye. Onatsky, O. Bunii), Venezuela (V. Vasiuk, I. Polisky), and

Brazil (O. Borushenko, M. Kusa). Its official organ is the annual *Slovo na storozhi, edited by J. Rudnyckyj.

**Ukrainian Language Education Centre** (ULEC). A center established in Edmonton at the University of Alberta by the *Canadian Institute of Ukrainian Studies in June 1987. Endowed by the Ukrainian Professional and Business Club of Edmonton and the Government of Alberta, ULEC has dealt primarily with publishing a Ukrainian language series (Nova) for grades 1 to 12 in the Ukrainian-English bilingual education program. ULEC works in partnership with the Department of Education in Alberta, which sponsored the development of the series with some assistance from the province of Manitoba. ULEC also sponsors methodology workshops for teachers of the Ukrainian language. The center houses a library of print and audiovisual Ukrainian-language educational materials. ULEC also has a mandate to facilitate research in the area of bilingualism. The predecessor of the center was headed by O. Bilash, the originator of the Nova series. The coordinators of ULEC have been A. Biscoe (1987–9) and M. Petryshyn (1989–).

**Ukrainian Law Society** (Ukrainske pravnyche tovarystvo). An organization of Ukrainian lawyers, judges, and jurists founded in Kiev in May 1917. The president was V. Voitkevych-Pavlovych, and the vice-president was R. Lashchenko; other prominent members included H. Vovkushivsky, A. Viazlov, A. Yakovliv, M. Tkachenko, M. Korchynsky, and I. Shrah. The society was dissolved in 1920 after the Bolsheviks occupied Kiev. A branch of the organization existed in Poltava (1917–19).

**Ukrainian Law Society** (Ukrainske pravnyche tovarystvo). An organization of Ukrainian lawyers and jurists founded in 1922 in Prague to continue the work of the society with the same name that had existed in Kiev in 1917–20. It sponsored academic lectures and conferences and published R. Lashchenko's monograph on Lithuanian law and the text of Ruskaia Pravda. At its height in 1933, it had over 60 members, many of whom were teachers and professors of various Ukrainian higher schools in Czechoslovakia. It also included some corresponding members in Transcarpathia. The society's presidents were R. Lashchenko (1922–9), A. Yakovliv, K. Losky, and S. Dnistriansky. The society ceased functioning during the Nazi occupation.

**Ukrainian Lawyers' Association.** See Association of Ukrainian Lawyers.

**Ukrainian Learned Educational Society** (Ukrainske naukove osvitnie tovarystvo, or UNOT). An association in Belgium for promoting Ukrainian education and scholarship. It was founded in Brussels in 1947 as a section of the Ukrainian Relief Committee and in 1950 was reorganized into an independent organization. Its activities included the operation of Ukrainian Saturday schools and the publication of scholarly works in Ukrainian and French. Its presidents were Rev M. Hermaniuk, P. Zeleny, D. Andrievsky, I. Vytiaz, Rev B. Kurylas, and Rev I. Kit (1978–).

**Ukrainian Liberation Army** (Ukrainske vyzvolne viisko). The common name for various German auxiliary military units formed from among Ukrainian POWs interned by the Germans on the eastern front in 1941–3. The first units of this kind were created in the fall of 1941 by the Wehrmacht front commands and were used in the rear, in the Kharkiv region and the Donbas. They were usually organized as companies and were called Hilfswillige. A. Hitler ordered the Ukrainian units disbanded (but allowed units made up of Caucasian and Central Asian nationals). But as the Wehrmacht's manpower shortage became more acute, the army expanded its recruitment program, and by the end of 1942 it had about 300 so-called eastern battalions, 74 of which consisted mostly of Ukrainians. In 1944 there was an attempt to regroup these units into the Ukrainian Liberation Army, but they were never brought under a central command, and the name was used by the Wehrmacht largely for propaganda purposes. The total strength of all these units in 1945 was estimated at 75,000.

**Ukrainian Liberation Front** (Ukrainskyi vyzvolnyi front, or UVF). A coalition of community, youth, women's, and cultural organizations associated with the Bandera faction of the OUN. It incorporates approx 50 member groups in Great Britain (Association of Ukrainians in Great Britain and others), France (Union of Ukrainians in France), Belgium (Ukrainian Relief Committee), Germany (Ukrainian Youth Association [SUM]), Australia (League for the Liberation of Ukraine), Argentina (Prosvita society), Canada (Canadian League for Ukraine's Liberation), and the United States (Organization for the Defense of Four Freedoms for Ukraine), as well as representations in other countries. The combined membership of these groups is estimated at up to 30,000. They were formally organized as the World Ukrainian Liberation Front (SUVF) in 1973. A head office for the group was then established in Toronto. The SUVF has been headed by R. Malashchuk, B. Fedorak, and M. Andrukhiv. It is a member of the Anti-Bolshevik Bloc of Nations.

**Ukrainian Library Association of America** (Ukrainske bibliotechne tovarystvo Ameryky, or UBTA). An organization of Ukrainian-American professional librarians. Until 1974 it was called the Association of Ukrainian Librarians of America (TUBA). Its founding conference was held in Cleveland in 1961 on the initiative of B. Wynar, R. Kos, and O. Danko. The association's presidents were S. Volyniak (1961–3), R. Weres (1963–70), D. Shtohryn (1970–4), V. Luchkiv (1974–7), R. Drazniowsky (1977–9), and M. Kravchuk (from 1979). Its organs were the irregular *Biuleten' TUBA* (1962, 1965, 1969), an internal bulletin (from 1971), and the bibliographic quarterly *Ukraïns'ka knyha* (1971–82). In 1971 the association created the Ukrainian Bibliographical Reference Center (directed by Weres) at the Ukrainian National Museum in Chicago. It also co-sponsored the preparation of the biographical directory *Ukrainians in North America* (1975, ed by D. Shtohryn), and in 1974 it organized the First Congress of Ukrainian Librarians, Publishers, and Booksellers in the United States and Canada (held in Jersey City). Its approx 100 members – mostly in Metropolitan New York, but also in Urbana, Chicago, Bloomington, Philadelphia, Denver, and Washington – developed Ucrainica collections at many American university and reference libraries, cataloged Ukrainian-American community libraries, prepared bibliographies of Ukrainian publications as well as a catalog of Ucrainica in North American libraries and indexes of Ukrainian periodicals, and organized Ukrainian book exhibitions. The association has been inactive since the mid-1980s.

**Ukrainian Line.** A network of fortifications that was built at the behest of the Russian government to replace the Belgorod Line as the population of the Russian Empire expanded southward into Slobidska Ukraine. The Ukrainian Line was maintained from the 1730s to the 1760s as a defense against attacks by Crimean and Nogay Tatars. It extended for nearly 285 km from the Dnieper River along the Orel River and the tributary Berestova River, and further east along the Bereka River to its junction with the Donets River. Construction of the fortifications began in 1731, according to the design of General J.-B. von Weissbach, and proceeded intensively until 1733, but was not fully completed until well into the 1740s. Each year 20,000 Left-Bank Cossacks, 2,000 Cossacks from Slobidska Ukraine, and 10,000 common peasants worked on the building of the line. It consisted of 16 fortresses and 49 redoubts, connected by a large earthen rampart and deep ditches. Defensive forces included 20 regiments of land militia (14 cavalry and 6 infantry), totaling nearly 22,000 men, as well as 180 cannons and 30 mortars.

The construction, maintenance, and defense of the Ukrainian Line proved to be a heavy burden on the population of the Hetmanate and Slobidska Ukraine. Unfortunately the line was unable to defend Ukraine (particularly Slobidska Ukraine) from the incessant Tatar attacks, which frequently penetrated it. In the 1760s P. Rumiantsev set out to reorganize the system of defense, but by that time the Tatar threat had begun to subside.

The Ukrainian Line also had a policing function, in that it divided the Zaporizhia from the Hetmanate. It impeded the efforts of deserters to flee to the Zaporozhian Sich and the freedom of Cossacks in Slobidska and Left-Bank Ukraine to move from one place to another. The Ukrainian Line lost its strategic significance in the 1770s, when the border of the Russian Empire moved southward by 175–180 km, to where a new line, the *Dnieper Line, was built.

BIBLIOGRAPHY
Bahalii, D. *Zaselennia Pivdennoï Ukraïny (Zaporozhzhia i Novorosiis'koho kraiu) i pershi pochatky ïï kul'turnoho rozvytku* (Kharkiv 1920)
Polons'ka-Vasylenko, N. *The Settlement of the Southern Ukraine (1750–1775)*, vols 4–5 of AUA (1955)

A. Zhukovsky

**Ukrainian Medical Association of Czechoslovakia.** See Ukrainian Physicians' Association in Czechoslovakia.

**Ukrainian Medical Association of Lviv.** See Ukrainian Physicians' Society.

**Ukrainian Medical Association of North America** (Ukrainske likarske tovarystvo Pivnichnoi Ameryky, or UMANA). A professional and civic association of medical doctors and dentists. Founded as the Ukrainian Medical Association in New York in 1950, in 1953 it became the coordinating center for 17 branches in the United States and Canada, with a total membership of over 1,000. Since 1956

UMANA has sponsored annual or biennial scholarly conferences in major centers, such as Cleveland, Chicago, Toronto, Detroit, New York, Montreal, Philadelphia, Washington, DC, and Vienna, as well as in Australia and the Bahamas. The conferences are accredited by the American Medical Association. The UMANA quarterly journal *Likars'kyi visnyk* has been published since 1954. The association also published almanacs in 1958 (Chicago) and 1962 (Detroit) and *Materiialy do istoriï ukraïns'koï medytsyny* (Materials for the History of Ukrainian Medicine, 3 vols, 1975–90). In 1975 the headquarters was moved to Chicago. Since 1977 UMANA has collected a sizable medical library. Its archivist, P. Pundii, has re-edited old issues of medical publications and begun publishing an annual report of newly acquired materials. In 1991 M. Klodnytska-Protsyk was succeeded by A. Levytsky as president of UMANA. The executive board oversees a stipend fund, named after M. Panchyshyn, for deserving students.

## Ukrainian Medical Charitable Service (Ukrainska medychno-kharytatyvna sluzhba).

An organization for providing basic medical care and material aid to Ukrainian refugees in Germany. It was formed as the Sanitary Charitable Service (SKhS) in November 1945 out of former branches of the *Ukrainian Red Cross (closed down by the occupational authorities in Germany) and the Sanitary Charitable Service at the Apostolic Visitator's Office of the Greek Catholic Church for Germany. From 1945 the SKhS surreptitiously obtained supplies of food, medicine, and clothing from the Bavarian Red Cross, as well as donations from Ukrainian organizations in North America and from the Catholic church. To cover operating costs it collected membership fees from approx 14,000 members in 61 branches (1947) and organized charitable concerts. In 1948 (renamed the Ukr SKhS) it expanded its operations into the three western occupational zones of Germany and Austria. The SKhS had delegations and liaison officers in the United States, Canada, Australia, France, and Belgium. Medical care was dispensed through clinics in the DP camps; in 1946 there were 20 clinics, including 5 under the direct supervision of the SKhS, and after 1950 there was 1, in Munich. About 150 physicians worked in these clinics, and a number of nursing courses were conducted. The SKhS also had special departments for family search and reunion and aid for invalids, former soldiers of the Ukrainian Insurgent Army, and widows and orphans.

As more and more refugees were resettled, the SKhS curtailed some of its activities and redirected them to helping needy Ukrainians in Ukraine, Poland, Czechoslovakia, Yugoslavia, Rumania, and Argentina. In 1955 its name was changed from Ukrainian Sanitary Charitable Service to Ukrainian Medical Charitable Service. Presidents of the SKhS were B. Andriievsky (1945–51), I. Mirchuk (1951–5), H. Martynets (1955–68), and Ya. Kovalyk (from 1968); executive presidents were T. Vorobets (1945–8), Ya. Voievidka (1948–9), I. Mirchuk (1949–50), M. Khronoviat (1950–1), Ya. Hynylevych (1951–79), V. Mialkovsky, and V. Synyshyn (from 1979); from 1945 H. Komarynsky served as secretary. A separate organization called the Ukrainian Medical Charitable Alliance (Ukrainske medychno-kharytatyvne obiednannia) was founded at the first DP physicians' convention in Munich-Karlsfeld in May 1946, with Ya. *Voievidka elected president. Its 640 members were grouped into sections of physicians, dentists, pharmacists, and intermediary medical personnel. Two issues of its journal *Medychno-sanitarnyi visnyk* were published. At the second DP physicians' convention in Regensburg in December 1947, F. Bohatyrchuk succeeded Voievidka as president.

## Ukrainian Meteorological Service (Ukrainska meteorolohichna sluzhba, or Ukrmet).

A government agency established in Kiev in 1921 to monitor the weather and climate in Ukraine. It had sections for general meteorology, weather forecasting, and agricultural meteorology, and regional branches in Kiev (est 1912), Chernihiv (est 1922), Volhynia (est 1911), Podilia (est 1922), Poltava (est 1910), Kharkiv (est 1903), the Black Sea region (est 1912), Dnipropetrovske (est 1922), and Donetske (est 1923). In 1927 the Hydrometric Service of the Melioration and Water Management Department of the People's Commissariat of Agricultural Affairs, and the Boh and Dnieper hydrological research stations, were brought under Ukrmet, which was then reorganized into the Ukrainian Meteorological and Hydrological Service under the directorship of M. Sofoterov. Ukrmet published a bulletin and the popular magazine *Pohoda i zhyttia*.

## Ukrainian Military Club (Ukrainskyi viiskovyi kliub im. Hetmana Pavla Polubotka).

A military-political organization founded on 29 March 1917 at a conference of Ukrainian officers and soldiers of the Kiev Military District. Its chief founder was Lt M. *Mikhnovsky. The club organized Ukrainian volunteer regiments and military organizations. Thanks to its efforts, similar clubs sprang up on all the fronts, the *Khmelnytsky Regiment was formed in Kiev, and the First *All-Ukrainian Military Congress (18–21 May 1917) was held. Club members demanded a declaration of Ukraine's independence from the congress. The club's activities ceased in June 1917, when Mikhnovsky was transferred to the Rumanian front.

## Ukrainian Military Committee (Ukrainskyi viiskovyi komitet or Tsentralnyi viiskovyi komitet).

A clandestine organization of Ukrainian officers in the Austrian army formed in Lviv in September 1918. Working closely with the People's Committee of the National Democratic party, it made preparations to transfer power in Galicia to the Ukrainian people. In October 1918 representatives of the Legion of Ukrainian Sich Riflemen were added to the Military Committee, and Capt D. Vitovsky was elected chairman. On orders of the Ukrainian National Rada the committee carried out a coup d'état on the eve of the *November Uprising in Lviv and other cities. With the proclamation of the Western Ukrainian National Republic, the Military Committee was dissolved. Besides D. Vitovsky its more active members were P. Bubelia, T. Martynets, L. Ohonovsky, D. Paliiv, I.T. Rudnytsky, and V. Starosolsky.

## Ukrainian Military History Institute (Ukrainskyi voienno-istorychnyi instytut).

Founded in Toronto in 1952 as a continuation of the *Ukrainian Military History Society. It established a museum of the UNR Army and Navy and published two volumes of *Za derzhavnist'* (1964, 1966). It was headed by Gen M. Sadovsky until 1967 and then by Col M. Bytynsky. The institute was dissolved in 1969, and its museum was transferred to the Ukrainian Free Academy of Sciences, which reopened it in Winnipeg in 1981.

**Ukrainian Military History Society** (Ukrainske voienno-istorychne tovarystvo). A society of UNR Army veterans founded in Kalisz, Poland, in 1925. It published nine volumes of historical materials titled *Za derzhavnist'*. Its president was Gen M. Sadovsky. In 1939 the society was disbanded by the German authorities.

Participants at a conference of the command of the Ukrainian Military Organization in 1923. Sitting, from left: Volodymyr Bemko, Andrii Melnyk, Yevhen Konovalets, Volodymyr Tselevych, Yaroslav Selezinka, Yaroslav Indyshevsky; standing: Petro Bakovych, Yuliian Holovinsky, Ivan Reviuk, Pavlo Merkun

**Ukrainian Military Organization** (Ukrainska viiskova orhanizatsiia [UVO]). An underground revolutionary organization formed in 1920 to continue the armed struggle for an independent Ukrainian state. Its founders were former officers of the *Sich Riflemen and the *Ukrainian Galician Army, particularly its Rava Brigade. UVO members differed in political outlook but were bound by their participation in the 1917–20 wars for Ukrainian independence.

In September 1920 a provisional Supreme Collegium of the UVO, consisting of O. Navrotsky, M. Matchak, Ya. Chyzh, Yu. Poliansky, and V. Tselevych, was established in Lviv. On 20 July 1921 it was renamed the Supreme Command, and Ye. *Konovalets and Yu. Otmarshtain were appointed commander and chief of staff, respectively. Organizational, intelligence, operations, and propaganda-political departments were established. The main area of operations was Galicia, which was divided into 13 military districts and 58 counties, each with its own command.

The first phase of the UVO's history (1920–2) was devoted to organizing cadres, obtaining arms, and conducting terrorist operations. Its major actions included an unsuccessful attempt on J. *Piłsudski's life on 25 September 1921, a Galicia-wide arson campaign against Polish landlords and colonists in the autumn of 1922, and the assassination of S. *Tverdokhlib on 15 October 1922. The Polish government responded with a wave of arrests which shattered the UVO. Its leaders went underground, and some of them, including Konovalets, escaped abroad. At a conference near Danzig in early 1923, it was decided to move the Supreme Command to Berlin and to set up a home command in Lviv under A. *Melnyk. At the same time the UVO severed its ties with the Government-in-exile of the Western Ukrainian National Republic (ZUNR).

UVO operations in the Ukrainian SSR were planned by Otmarshtain and executed by Yu. *Tiutiunnyk. A number of officers, including I. Andrukh, M. Opoka, and V. Romanyk, were sent east to establish contact with insurgent forces. The prospects for UVO activity in Soviet Ukraine diminished as the partisan movement was brought under control, the NEP was introduced, and Ukrainization started. The UVO maintained several missions under different names outside Ukraine, including the Krai Command in Czechoslovakia, the External Delegation in Berlin, a group in Danzig, and the Ukrainian Circle of the Lithuanian-Ukrainian Society in Lithuania. Their tasks were to get official recognition for the UVO, cultivate contacts with government and other foreign circles, print UVO literature, purchase arms, and organize training for new cadres. UVO cells in North America organized larger civic institutions and provided financial support.

A prolonged power struggle within the UVO resulted in a serious setback for the organization. With the recognition of Poland's annexation of Galicia by the Conference of Ambassadors (15 March 1923), the ZUNR government, led by Ye. Petrushevych, lost its international status. To continue the struggle against Poland, President Petrushevych turned to the Soviet government, which made its aid conditional on his controlling the UVO and the removal of Konovalets from the leadership of the organization. After two years of internal fighting, Petrushevych's faction was forced out of the UVO. It formed a rival organization (14 May 1926), the Western Ukrainian National Revolutionary Organization, which published *Ukraïns'kyi revoliutsioner* in Berlin (1926–9). Lacking support in Ukraine, the organization eventually disintegrated.

As political conditions in Galicia changed, and open opposition to the regime through political parties and institutions became possible, many UVO veterans opted to work within legally recognized civic and political organizations. Weakened by arrests, internal dissension, and the loss of veteran cadres, the UVO limited its terrorist activities and emphasized intelligence gathering, political education, and training of new recruits. Training courses were conducted in the Carpathian Mountains, Czechoslovakia, Germany, and Danzig.

After an unsuccessful attempt on the life of the Polish president S. Wojciechowski on 5 September 1924, a small detachment known as the Flying Brigade was set up. For about two years it held up mail trucks and post offices to obtain sorely needed funds, and carried out other operations, such as the assassination of the Lviv school superintendent S. Sobiński on 19 October 1926. This activity gave the UVO notoriety and attracted young people into its ranks. Its contribution to mass political education was equally important. Its own magazine, *Surma*, published in Berlin (1927–8) and then in Kaunas, Lithuania (1928–34), had a run of 10,000. The organization also helped finance the publications *Literaturno-naukovyi vistnyk*, *Zahrava*, and *Novyi chas* and the *Chervona Kalyna publishing house. A special Political Collegium was set up in the Home Command of the UVO.

UVO activities were financed from a number of sources – eg, funds of former military units, donations from the UNR government-in-exile, donations from Ukrainians overseas, grants from Ukrainian financial institutions in Galicia, and expropriations. The UVO also received aid from foreign sources: Lithuanian government and military circles underwrote the publication and distribution of UVO publications, and German military circles financed training courses for its cadres.

After A. Melnyk, the home commanders of the UVO were Ya. Indyshevsky, Yu. Holovinsky, O. Senyk, R. Sushko, B. Hnatevych, and V. Horbovy.

Taking advantage of its prestige among young Ukrainian revolutionaries, the UVO played a key role in forging the *Organization of Ukrainian Nationalists (OUN) out of smaller nationalist youth groups. Konovalets, who assumed leadership in the OUN, regarded it at first as a political front for the UVO and as a pool for its cadres. The OUN, however, absorbed the UVO, appropriating its program and traditions. Without being dissolved formally, the UVO withered away in the early 1930s.

BIBLIOGRAPHY
Konovalets', Ie. *Prychynky do istoriï ukraïns'koï revoliutsiï* (Prague 1928)
Martynets', V. *Ukraïns'ke pidpillia: Vid UVO do OUN* (Winnipeg 1949)
Knysh, Z. (ed). *Sribna surma*, 2 vols (Toronto 1959, 1962)
Knysh, Z. *Vlasnym ruslom: UVO v 1922–1926 rr.* (Toronto 1966)
– *Dalekyi prytsil: UVO v 1927–1929 rr.* (Toronto 1967)
– *Na povni vitryla: UVO v 1924–1926 rr.* (Toronto 1970)
*Ievhen Konovalets' ta ioho doba* (Munich 1974)
Motyl, A. *The Turn to the Right: The Ideological Origins and Development of Ukrainian Nationalism, 1919–1929* (New York 1980)
Z. Knysh

**Ukrainian Mineralogical Society** (Ukrainske mineralohichne tovarystvo). A scientific association founded in 1970 in Kiev to co-ordinate research in the field, promote expeditions, and popularize results achieved in mineralogy. It was organized out of the Ukrainian Division of the All-Union Mineralogical Society (est 1954). One of the chief founders of the new society was Ye. *Lazarenko, who also served as its first president (1970–9). After him Yu. Melnyk was elected president. The society holds conferences, organizes lectures, and publishes scientific collections. In 1984 there were 18 branches, which represented 540 members altogether.

**Ukrainian Mohylo-Mazepian Academy of Sciences** (Ukrainska mohyliansko-mazepynska akademiia nauk, or UMMAN). A scholarly institution created in Warsaw in May 1938 by the Government-in-exile of the UNR. Its aim was to continue the work of the VUAN after it was shut down during the Stalinist terror, to revive its publications, and to inform the Western scholarly community about Ukraine and Ukrainian scholarship. UMMAN consisted of a Ukrainian studies division made up of 24 chairs and research groups. Its presidents were S. *Smal-Stotsky and I. Feshchenko-Chopivsky (from August 1938); the secretary was A. Yakovliv. UMMAN published three monographs before the 1939 German invasion of Poland forced it to suspend its activity. In the 1980s UMMAN renewed its activity in the diaspora, and J. Rudnyckyj was elected president. In 1992, with the revival of the Kievan Mohyla Academy in Kiev, UMMAN terminated its activites and encouraged its members to continue working with the renewed academy in Kiev.

**Ukrainian Museum** (Ukrainskyi muzei). A museum set up in New York in 1976 to house the folk-art and handicrafts collection of the *Ukrainian National Women's League of America. The core of the collection was acquired in 1933 from the Ukrainske Narodnie Mystetstvo co-operative in Lviv. It included weavings, embroidery pieces, folk dress, wood carvings, ceramics, metal artifacts, and Easter eggs. Besides that ethnographic collection the museum has built up collections of paintings and historical documents. It has presented special exhibitions of Ukrainian embroideries, folk ceramics, ceremonial *rushnyky*, and other folk art, exhibitions of individual painters, and thematic exhibitions of the lost architecture of Kiev, the Ukrainian emigration to America, and Ukrainian wooden churches. The museum has published catalogs and studies to accompany some of its exhibitions. Courses in traditional handicrafts are offered to the public from time to time. The museum has a membership of approx 1,500. Its most recent president has been T. Hewryk.

The Ukrainian Museum of Canada

**Ukrainian Museum of Canada** (Ukrainskyi muzei Kanady). Canada's first professional ethnic museum, founded in 1936 in Saskatoon by the *Ukrainian Women's Association of Canada (SUK) with branches in Vancouver, Edmonton, Winnipeg, and Toronto. The museum's main branch was housed at the *Mohyla Ukrainian Institute in Saskatoon for many years before acquiring its own building in 1980. It contains collections of Ukrainian embroidery, weaving, folk costumes, Easter eggs, domestic tools and farm implements, historical photographs and documents, and printed materials. Its gallery owns W. Kurelek's series of paintings of the Ukrainian pioneer woman. In addition to mounting touring exhibitions, the museum has offered courses in arts and crafts and published works such as *Ukrainian Embroidery: Designs and Stitches* (1957), *Pysanka: Icon of the Universe* (1977), and *Pobut: Folk Costume Patterns* (1986). A catalogue of its library and archival holdings was published in 1989 as *The Monograph Collection of the Ukrainian Museum of Canada*. Its directors have been L. Lazarovych (1973–80), M. Kishchuk (1981–4), A. Kachkowski (1984–9), and J. Zayachkowski (1989–91).

**Ukrainian Museum of the Liberation Struggle.** See Museum of Ukraine's Struggle for Independence.

**Ukrainian Museum-Archives** (Ukrainskyi muzei-arkhiv, or UMA). An archival repository and exhibiting museum in Cleveland. Originally established in 1952 by L.

*Bachynsky on the top floor of a community center as a repository for Plast memorabilia and other items of interest, the museum acquired a building of its own in 1977. It houses a library of over 14,100 separate volumes; 2,400 Ukrainian periodical titles from around the world; an archive; and fine art, stamp and coin, folk art, and Shevchenkiana collections. The UMA has published six volumes of *Bibliohrafichnyi pokazhchyk ukraïns'koï presy* (A Bibliographic Guide to the Ukrainian Press, 1966–78) and *Derzhavni hroshi Ukraïny* (Ukraine's State Currency, 1973); released the videotape *Muted Bells*, which deals with the suppression of the church in Western Ukraine; and held exhibits of paintings, folk art, and Shevchenkiana. Its presidents have been Bachynsky (1952–77), O. Fedynsky (1977–81), S. Kikta (1981–7), and A. Fedynsky (1987–).

**Ukrainian Music Institute of America** (Ukrainskyi muzychnyi instytut Ameryky, or UMIA). A Ukrainian music school established in New York in 1952, with branches subsequently located in Philadelphia, Washington, Baltimore, Cleveland, Detroit, Chicago, and other American cities. The UMIA was founded for the purpose of continuing and further developing the music program of the *Lysenko Higher Institute of Music. It offers a 10-year course of study with an introductory year for younger children, a 'concert performance' year for graduates, and (since 1972) a preschool music program. The UMIA also sponsors recitals of guest vocalists, thematic evenings, and concerts of Ukrainian music and is active in music publishing. The group's main organizer and first director (1952–9) was R. *Savytsky. Later directors include I. Sonevytsky (1959–61), Z. Lysko (1961–2), M. Bailova, T. Bohdanska, N. Kotovych, D. Karanovych, and K. Chichka-Andriienko (since 1981).

**Ukrainian Musicians' Alliance** (Obiednannia ukrainskykh muzyk, or OUM). An organization of Ukrainian professional musicians in Germany in 1946–50. With more than 60 members, the group was active in music education, musicological work, and musical performances for the community. Executive members of the alliance included Z. Lysko, W. Wytwycky, R. Savytsky, and A. Olkhovsky. The group disbanded after many of its key members emigrated to North America.

**Ukrainian Mutual Benefit Association of Saint Nicholas** (Bratstvo zapomohove sv. Mykolaia). The oldest Ukrainian mutual-aid society in Canada. It was founded by Rev T. Hura, V. Karpets, and N. Hladky at the Ukrainian Catholic St Nicholas Church in Winnipeg on 11 September 1905. At first there were 45 members. By 1931 it had 15 branches and 2,500 members, and by 1990 it had 24 branches and 1,200 members. Its assets total 3,588,000 dollars. Besides helping its members with funeral expenses and sickness benefits, the association supports Ukrainian cultural and educational institutions. The presidents of the association have been T. Hura, N. Kotliaryk, N. Hladky, I. Martsiniv, M. Havryliuk, S. Horbachevsky, Ya. Baryliuk, I. Zavidovsky, T. Stefanyk, I. Zarovsky (1923–38, 1940–60), T. Kozak, J. Nowosad (1960–70), J. Kozoriz (1970–83), and Bishop M. Daciuk (1983–).

**Ukrainian National Aid Association of America** (Ukrainska narodna pomich, or UNAAA). A fraternal-bene-

fit life-insurance society founded in 1914 and known until 1926 as the National Aid Association (Narodna pomich). Until the Second World War most of its members were Orthodox; in the postwar period it has been dominated by members of the Ukrainian Liberation Front. Since 1914 the UNAAA has published *Narodne slovo*, renamed *Ukraïns'ke narodne slovo* in 1959, as its official organ. The association also produces an annual almanac titled (since 1960) *Zolotyi homin* (The Golden Echo), as well as various books, plays, and songbooks. The association maintained contact with civic organizations in Western Ukraine and sent them financial aid. As a founding member of the Ukrainian Congress Committee of America and the *United Ukrainian American Relief Committee, it donated funds for the resettlement of Ukrainian displaced persons in the United States. In 1961 it expanded into Canada. In 1981 its head office was moved from Pittsburgh to Chicago. Today (1990) the UNAAA has 8,710 members in 161 branches. Its presidents have included D. Porada (1915–23), V. Sorochak (1923–34), M. Markiv (1934–42), V. Shabatura (1942–62), and V. Mazur (since 1966–90). In 1977 L. Poltava prepared *Istoriia Ukraïns'koï narodnoï pomochi v Amerytsi i Kanadi* (History of the Ukrainian National Aid Association in the United States and Canada).

**Ukrainian National Alliance** (Ukrainske natsionalne obiednannia, or UNO). An émigré organization centered in Berlin. Established in 1933, it was one of two Ukrainian community organizations tolerated by the Nazi regime (the other was the Ukrainian Hromada). It was active in central Germany and then expanded into Austria and the protectorates of Bohemia and Moravia in 1937–45. Its membership expanded markedly after it adopted a Ukrainian nationalist position in 1937. In spite of government restrictions, the UNO had 42,000 members in over 1,268 branches and lesser groups in 1942. Until 1937 it was headed by I. Koroliv and I. Drabaty, and in 1938–45 by T. Omelchenko. Members of the UNO executive included Yu. Artiushenko, M. Dorozhynsky, B. Kravtsiv, D. Kvitkovsky, V. Levytsky, V. Maruniak, M. Seleshko, P. Verzhbytsky, and V. Yaniv. The executive had active publicist departments in Berlin and ran a publishing house in Prague. The UNO's official press organ was the weekly *Ukraïns'kyi visnyk*. During the Second World War it also operated a Ukrainian Information Bureau out of Berlin, which informed Germans and other non-Ukrainians about Ukrainian affairs. Apart from its work in organizing lectures and classes, the UNO defended the interests of Ukrainian workers in Germany (forced and voluntary), assisted Ukrainian students, and gave aid to Ukrainian prisoners from Soviet and Polish units. During the course of the war the UNO published 13 educational brochures and 2 brochures on the rights and duties of Ukrainian workers. Lower-level UNO groups organized courses in Ukrainian studies, German language instruction, folk dancing, driving, and first aid; sponsored art workshops; and ran various libraries and reading rooms. In 1943–5 the Gestapo began persecuting its members. The UNO was finally forced to cease activities outright after the occupation of Berlin by Soviet forces in 1945.

A. Zhukovsky

**Ukrainian National Alliance** (Ukrainske natsionalne obiednannia, or UNO). A political organization of Transcarpathian Ukrainians, which replaced the Central Ruthenian People's Council in representing the interests of the region's Ukrainian inhabitants. It was founded in Khust on 18 January 1939, and its members were from all the Ukrainian parties and groups except the Communists. Its president was F. Revai (later Yu. Perevuznyk), and its general secretary was A. Voron. The UNO presented a single slate of 32 candidates in the elections to the Diet of Carpatho-Ukraine, all of whom were elected. Its daily organ was *Nova svoboda*. The UNO ceased its activities when Hungarian troops occupied Carpatho-Ukraine (March 1939).

## Ukrainian National Alliance in France (Ukrainska natsionalna yednist u Frantsii).

A civic and cultural organization founded in Paris in 1949 by supporters of the Organization of Ukrainian Nationalists (Melnyk faction) as the successor to the interwar *Ukrainian National Union in France. The alliance belongs to the world federation of Ideologically Allied Nationalist Organizations and works with the Ukrainian Central Civic Committee in France. The central executive in Paris co-ordinates the work of 12 branches (in the 1950s there were 22) in the major centers of Ukrainian settlement in France. It organizes annual courses in Ukrainian studies for young people (courses are also offered at the local level by the branches) and, together with the newspaper *Ukraïns'ke slovo*, publishes pamphlets and almanacs. The alliance also initiated the creation of the *Organization of Ukrainian Youth in France. Its presidents have been Ya. Musianovych (1949–61), V. Lazovinsky (1961–7), V. Malynovych (1968–70), L. Huzar (1970–1), Yu. Kovalenko (1972–6), V. Mykhalchuk (1976–8, 1984–6), A. Zhukovsky (1978–82), O. Korchak (1982–4), and V. Genyk (since 1986). V. Mulyk served as the alliance's longtime secretary.

## Ukrainian National Army (Ukrainska natsionalna armiia).

A military formation within the German armed forces at the end of the Second World War. On 12 March 1945 the Ukrainian National Committee, with the approval of the German government, announced the formation of the Ukrainian National Army (UNA), which was to group approx 220,000 Ukrainians serving in the German armed forces into one army. The committee hoped that after the defeat of the Germans the UNA would play an important role in establishing an independent Ukraine, an outcome made possible by postwar rivalry between the Western Allies and the Soviet Union. With the consent of the UNR government-in-exile, former UNR Army officers accepted key posts in the army, among them Gen P. Shandruk, as UNA commander, and Gen A. Valiisky, as chief of staff. The Division Galizien (approx 16,000 men) became the First Division of the UNA, and Col P. Diachenko's antitank brigade (approx 1,900 men) was to be the nucleus of the Second Division. Other units also volunteered to join the UNA, but military operations prevented their reassignment. By war's end the UNA headquarters still lacked operational control of the UNA units. The UNA surrendered to the British in Austria and was interned in *Rimini.

## Ukrainian National Association (Ukrainskyi narodnyi soiuz, or UNA).

The oldest and largest Ukrainian fraternal benefit association in North America, known until 1914 as the Ruthenian National Association (Ruskyi narodnyi soiuz). It was founded in Shamokin, Pennsylvania, on

The Ukrainian National Association building in Jersey City

22 February 1894 by several local brotherhoods, which had seceded from the Union of Greek Catholic Ruthenian Brotherhoods because of its conservative, pro-Hungarian and pro-Russian policies. The purpose of the UNA was to promote unity and education and to improve the material security of Ukrainian families in the United States through life and health insurance. The initiative for an organization of this type came from Rev H. *Hrushka and a group of Ukrainian Catholic clergy. Appeals first appeared in *Svoboda* (1893), which later became the paper of the UNA. The Brotherhood of SS Cyril and Methodius in Shamokin constituted the original nucleus of the association. It was joined by St Michael's Brotherhood (est 1885) in Shenandoah – the first Ukrainian organization in the United States – and by 11 other brotherhoods in the region. Later, brotherhoods in other states became branches of the association, and in 1906 its first Canadian branch was set up in Toronto. In 1990 there were 399 branches in North America.

Until 1910 the UNA was the only Ukrainian-American community fraternal association. That year an effort was made by Bishop S. *Ortynsky to give the association a confessional character. He spearheaded a resolution at the UNA's national convention to change its name to the Greek Catholic Ruthenian Association (Hreko-Katolytskyi ruskyi soiuz) and to limit its membership to Catholics. The legality of the resolution's adoption was successfully challenged by the UNA executive, and the group reverted to its former character. Before it had done so, however, a section of the UNA membership established a second fraternal association, the Ruthenian National Union (with the same Ukrainian title, Ruskyi narodnyi soiuz). It changed its name to the Ukrainian Workingmen's Association in 1918 and then to the *Ukrainian Fraternal Association in 1978. Ortynsky dropped his aspirations for control of the UNA and established a separate *Providence Association of Ukrainian Catholics in 1912. Another rival fraternal association was established in 1914 as the *Ukrainian National Aid Association of America.

Membership in the UNA has varied with the number of immigrants, the internal state of the Ukrainian community, and the insurance system. In 1894 the association had 439 members and assets of 220 dollars; in 1904 it had 9,000 members and assets of 46,000 dollars. Competition and changes in the fee schedule based on a theoretical mortality table adopted by the other fraternal associations led to a crisis in the UNA and a drop in membership in 1914–17 from 25,300 to 11,900. In the interwar period membership rose again: by 1946 UNA had 46,000 members and assets of 8.5 million dollars. With the influx of new immigrants after the war membership almost doubled: by 1971 it had reached over 88,000. In 1988 there were 74,000 members and total assets of approx 60 million dollars.

As a nonpartisan organization the UNA reflects the general sociopolitical opinion of the Ukrainian community: it stands for democracy, Ukrainian independence, and allegiance to the United States. It has initiated some of the main projects undertaken by the Ukrainian community. It played a leading role in founding Ukrainian umbrella organizations, such as the American Ruthenian National Council (1914), the Federation of Ukrainians in the United States (1915), the Ukrainian National Council (1916), the Ukrainian National Committee (1918), the United Ukrainian Organizations in America (1922), and the *Ukrainian Congress Committee of America (UKKA, 1940). It was instrumental in getting President W. Wilson to proclaim 21 April 1917 'Ukrainian Day' and permit a public collection in aid of the Ukrainian people. During the struggle for Ukraine's independence (1917–20) the UNA organized financial support for the Central Rada and the government of Western Ukraine, and in the interwar period it provided assistance for political and educational organizations in Polish-ruled Ukraine. After the Second World War it helped the United Ukrainian American Relief Committee (est 1944) resettle Ukrainian displaced persons in the United States. It supported the building of the T. Shevchenko monument in Washington, DC (1964), and the establishment of the Ukrainian studies program at Harvard University (1968–73). As the largest Ukrainian organization in the United States, the UNA played a leading role in the UKKA: its president traditionally held the post of executive vice-president and from 1976 shared it on a rotational basis with the presidents of the other three fraternal associations. When the social consensus that had held the UKKA together fell apart at the 13th Congress of Ukrainian Americans (1980), the UNA and many other organizations seceded from the UKKA and established the *Ukrainian American Coordinating Council (1983) as a new representative umbrella group.

The association's paper *Svoboda* played an important role in the development of the UNA and of the Ukrainian community as a whole. Some of its editors, such as Rev H. Hrushka, Rev N. Dmytriv, and L. *Myshuha, had a strong impact on the shaping of Ukrainian-American attitudes. In 1933 the UNA began to publish *The *Ukrainian Weekly*, and in 1954 the children's magazine *Veselka*. It has also published 80 almanacs (by 1990), over 20 English books about Ukraine, and the two-volume *Ukraine: A Concise Encyclopaedia* (1963, 1971). The UNA has also funded the publication of a multivolume index of selected articles from *Svoboda*. The index is being published by the Immigration History Research Center of the University of Minnesota.

Soiuzivka, the association's resort in Kerhonkson, New York, is used not only for sports and recreation but also for educational activities. The cultural commission of the UNA, set up in 1956, plans its cultural and educational program. Each year the association distributes scholarships to Ukrainian students: in 1992 it granted 229 scholarships worth 124,000 dollars.

Since the earliest days of the UNA, its head office has been located in Jersey City, New Jersey. The supreme ruling body of the association is its convention, which meets every four years (32 by 1990). It elects an executive committee, an auditing commission, and a board of directors to run the association. The presidents of the UNA have

been T. Talpash (1894–5), I. Glova (1895–8), Yu. Khyliak (1898–1900), Rev A. Bonchevsky (1900–2), Rev M. Stefanovych (1902–4), K. Kyrchiv (1904–8, 1917–20), D. Kapitula (1908–17), S. Yadlovsky (1920–5), T. Hrytsei (1925–9), M. Murashko (1929–49), D. *Halychyn (1950–61), J. *Lesawyer (1961–78), J. Flis (1978–90), and U. Diachuk (1990–; the first woman president). R. Slobodian served for over 50 years in various positions, including that of treasurer (1933–66).

BIBLIOGRAPHY
Myshuha, L. (ed). *Propam'iatna knyha vydana z nahody soroklitn'oho iuvileiu Ukraïns'koho narodnoho soiuzu* (Jersey City 1936)
Myshuha, L; Drahan, A. (eds). *Ukraïntsi u vil'nomu sviti: Iuvileina knyha Ukraïns'koho narodnoho soiuzu* (Jersey City 1954)

The delegation of the Ukrainian National Committee that went to Washington, DC, in 1919 to urge the US government to recognize the UNR. Rev Petro Poniatyshyn, the committee's president, is in the center.

**Ukrainian National Committee** (Ukrainskyi narodnyi komitet, or UNK). A political umbrella organization of Ukrainians in the United States in 1918–22 which rivaled the *Federation of Ukrainians in the United States. A coalition of church and community organizations that included the Ukrainian National Association, the UNK was headed by P. *Poniatyshyn (the administrator of the Greek Catholic church in the United States), with V. *Lototsky as its secretary. A 'people's congress' was held on 16–17 January 1919 to give the UNK a broader mandate. The UNK organized a wide range of activities in support of Ukrainian statehood, including publishing, fund-raising, lobbying the US government, and maintaining information bureaus in New York and Washington. The UNK was a member of the Eastern European Union (headed by T. Masaryk) and the League of Four Nations (Estonia, Latvia, Lithuania, and Ukraine). In 1919 the UNK sent its delegation (K. Bilyk and Congressman J.M. Hammill) to the Paris Peace Conference. The UNK was disbanded in 1922 in the interests of forming a larger organization, the *United Ukrainian Organizations in America.

**Ukrainian National Committee** (Ukrainskyi natsionalnyi komitet, or UNK). An administrative body formed in Cracow on the initiative of the Bandera faction of the OUN in an attempt to present a united Ukrainian national representation to the German occupying forces. A total of

113 people were individually selected from a range of political parties, community organizations, and economic firms for the association. As a nonpolitical institution the Ukrainian Central Committee decided not to join. At the inaugural meeting held on 22 June 1941 Gen V. Petrov was elected head of the committee in absentia, and V. *Horbovy was chosen to be acting leader until Petrov's acceptance. V. Andriievsky was second deputy leader. The committee's secretaries were S. Shukhevych and V. Mudry. The UNK sent a memorandum to A. Hitler in which it underscored the Ukrainian people's aspirations for independence and their readiness to fight against Moscow; at the same time it expressed the hope that Germany would respect the will of the Ukrainian people. It did not have a chance to develop any significant activity, because on 5 July the German security police arrested the nationalist organizers of the committee (M. Bohun, V. Horbovy, Ya. Rak, and V. Yaniv). Their action effectively abolished the group.

**Ukrainian National Committee** (Ukrainskyi natsionalnyi komitet, or UNK). A central political and civic body set up in Germany in October–November 1944 to defend Ukrainian interests before the German authorities. A change in German policy toward Eastern Europe and the release of Ukrainian political leaders, such as A. Melnyk and S. Bandera, from concentration camps paved the way for the founding of the committee. Besides the freed leaders, the committee's founders included A. Livytsky, president of the UNR government-in-exile, the Ukrainian Civic Committee (an organization of Ukrainians from central and eastern Ukraine), and the Ukrainian Central Committee. The founding of the Committee for the Liberation of the Peoples of Russia under Gen A. Vlasov, which claimed to represent all anti-bolshevik émigrés from the USSR, prompted Ukrainian leaders to set up their own organization. All Ukrainian political camps accepted Gen P. *Shandruk as president of the UNK, V. *Kubijovyč and O. Semenenko as vice-presidents, and P. Tereshchenko as secretary. At first the German authorities did not recognize the UNK and wanted it to be subordinate to A. Vlasov, but the Ukrainians refused to comply. Reichsminister A. Rosenberg officially recognized the UNK as the sole political representative only on 12 March 1945. In the name of the German government he also consented to having the UNK represent all the Ukrainian military formations in the German armed forces (the Ukrainian Liberation Army and the *Division Galizien). The presidium of the UNK issued a proclamation to the Ukrainian people and on 17 March 1945 appointed Gen P. Shandruk commander of the *Ukrainian National Army. On 25 April 1945, at the front, the Division Galizien took the oath of allegiance to the Ukrainian people and became the First Division of the Ukrainian National Army. Branches of the Ukrainian Central Committee functioned as local organizations of the UNK, and the daily *Ukraïns'kyi shliakh* (renamed from *Krakivs'ki visti*) in Vienna became its organ (five issues). The disintegration of Nazi Germany put an end to the committee's activities.

A. Zhukovsky

**Ukrainian National Council** (Ukrainska narodna rada). A representative committee formed early in 1919 in Winnipeg by Ukrainian Catholics who broke away from the *Ukrainian Canadian Citizens' League (UCCL). The council duplicated the efforts of the UCCL in fighting discrimination and promoting Ukrainian independence at the Paris Peace Conference. It collected funds for the Ukrainian Press Bureau in Paris and purchased supplies for Ukrainian prisoners of war in Italy. It also sought (unsuccessfully) to obtain government assistance to ship grain to Galicia. It was dissolved in the early 1920s.

**Ukrainian National Council** (Ukrainska natsionalna rada). A political and civil body established on 5 October 1941 in Kiev on the initiative of the OUN (Melnyk faction). Its presidium was headed by M. *Velychkivsky, and its secretaries were I. Dubyna and O. Boidunyk. At the end of 1941 the Reichskommissariat Ukraine banned the council, which thereupon functioned underground until 1943. On 29 April 1944 the council created the All-Ukrainian National Council (VUNR) in conjunction with the Ukrainian National Council in Lviv and representatives of the former Diet of Carpatho-Ukraine. Velychkivsky was elected president of the new council, and Metropolitan A. Sheptytsky and A. Shtefan were chosen vice-presidents. Efforts to create a common program for the VUNR and the Ukrainian Supreme Liberation Council in the fall of 1944 did not succeed. In 1946 the VUNR, whose members were now in the emigration, ceased to function.

Members of the Presidium and Executive Organ of the Ukrainian National Council in 1952. First row, from left: Gen Mykhailo Kapustiansky, Stepan Baran, Pres Andrii Livytsky, Ivan Bahriany, Mykhailo Khronoviat; second row: V. Hryhorenko, Spyrydon Dovhal, M. Khrobak, Yurii Blokhyn, Mykola Livytsky; third row: Mykhailo Voskobiinyk, Fedir Haienko, Oleksander Yurchenko, V. Dibert, Ivan Luchyshyn, Dmytro Andriievsky; fourth row: I. Inozharsky, Ya. Dziabenko, Col Mykola Stechyshyn, Yevhen Glovinsky, Col Mykola Shramenko

**Ukrainian National Council** (Ukrainska natsionalna rada). The parliamentary body of the *Government-in-exile of the UNR, established in 1947 as the result of a pact between émigré Ukrainian political parties. The aim of the council was to consolidate all independentist parties and organizations for the renewal of an independent Ukrainian state with a democratic order and to broaden the political base for the State Center of the Government-in-exile of the UNR. It established an executive organ functioning as a protoparliament or constituent assembly (that looked after the council's affairs between sittings) and a state auditing body and elected a president of the UNR-in-exile. The inaugural council had representatives from the OUN Melnyk faction, the OUN Bandera faction, the Ukrainian National State Union (UNDS), the Ukrainian National Democratic Alliance (UNDO), the Ukrainian Revolutionary Democratic party (URDP), the Ukrainian Revolutionary Democratic party (Socialist), the Ukrainian Party of Socialist Revolutionaries, the Ukrainian Socialist Radical party, and the Ukrainian Social Democratic Workers' party (USDRP).

After the second session of the council in 1950, the OUN Bandera faction left the parliament. At the fourth session in 1957, the Union of Lands of United Ukraine (the Peasant party) and the Union of Constructively Creative Forces of Ukraine joined the council. From October 1957 to 1961 the OUN Melnyk faction operated outside the council. In the meantime, there were schisms in the URDP and the UNDO. At the seventh session a breakaway URDP faction headed by M. Stepanenko and a UNDO faction headed by P. Kashynsky were officially recognized by the council. A range of amendments were brought into the council's statutes at its eighth session in 1979, one of which set the term of its sitting at five years (after the completion of the term, the parliament is dissolved by decree of the president, and the presidium and chairman hand over their positions), and another of which concerned the election of a president, vice-president, chairman, and presidium. In 1984–9 the council, after considerable effort, managed to consolidate and obtain the support of most of the émigré Ukrainian parties for the State Center of the UNR: the OUN Melnyk faction returned, as did the URDP led by M. Voskobiinyk, and the UNDO schism was resolved.

The council convened for 10 sessions: July 1948 in Augsburg, June 1949 in Leipheim, March 1954 in Munich, March 1957 in Munich, November 1961 in Munich, March 1967 in Munich, December 1972 in London, June 1979 in Munich, July 1984 in Toronto, and June 1989 in South Bound Brook, New Jersey. At the third session (1954) S. *Vytvytsky was elected to replace the recently deceased A. *Livytsky as president, and at the sixth session (1967) M. *Livytsky was elected president after Vytvytsky's death. After the death of M. Livytsky in December 1989, the vice-president, M. *Plaviuk, assumed the presidency. After the creation of the independent Ukrainian state in 1991, the council transferred its mandate to the Ukrainian government in 1992. The council's vice-presidents have included O. Udovychenko (1954–61), I. Bahriany (1961–3), M. Stepanenko (1967–84), Yu. Blokhyn (1984–8), J. Rudnyckyj (1988–9), and M. Plaviuk.

W. Zyla

**Ukrainian National Council in Lviv, 1941** (Ukrainska natsionalna rada, or UNC). A body formed in Lviv out of the Council of Seniors on 30 July 1941 to represent the interests of the Ukrainian population of Galicia, Volhynia, and the Kholm region before the German authorities. The Council of Seniors, convened on 6 July 1941 by the Bandera faction of the OUN, consisted of 16 members (30 by the end of July). The Melnyk faction did not participate in the UNC, although the council tried to embrace all political camps and professions. Its membership eventually rose to 45. The president of the council was K. *Levytsky; his deputies were Rev Yu. Dzerovych and L. Turchyn; the secretary was A. Bilenky (later H. Myketei). The other members included Archbishop Y. Slipy, Rev H. Kostelnyk, M.

Panchyshyn, V. Simovych, Yu. Pavlykovsky, A. Palii, M. Stefanivsky, M. Voloshyn, V. Zahaikevych, K. Pankivsky, B. Kozubsky, and S. Khrutsky, most of whom were members or supporters of the Ukrainian National Democratic Alliance. The patron and honorary president was Metropolitan A. Sheptytsky. The UNR recognized the OUN as the leading force in Ukrainian political life and supported the *Ukrainian State Administration, but it was critical of the strife between the two OUN factions. On 30 July the UNC protested to the German government the annexation of eastern Galicia by the Generalgouvernement. At the beginning of September it sent a memorandum to the governor general, H. Frank, defending the interests of Ukrainians in Galicia.

On 31 July the UNC set up a General Secretariat, headed by Pankivsky, to serve as its executive branch and to cultivate contacts with the German authorities. But after Levytsky's death (12 November) the German government made it increasingly difficult for the UNC to function. Finally, Sheptytsky's letter to H. Himmler (February 1942) protesting the genocide policy with respect to Jews provided the authorities with a pretext for banning the council (3 March). The job of maintaining contacts with the German government was assumed by the *Ukrainian Regional Committee.

**Ukrainian National Council in Petrograd** (Ukrainska natsionalna rada v Petrohradi). The council, established on 1 April 1917, consisted of Petrograd representatives of the Society of Ukrainian Progressives (TUP), Ukrainian Social Democrats, the Ukrainian Revolutionary Committee, Ukrainian factions of soviets of workers' and soldiers' deputies, Ukrainian students and workers, the Petrograd Hromada, and other groups. O. *Lototsky headed the executive committee. His deputy was M. *Korchynsky, and the secretary was P. *Stebnytsky (who was elected head in May). Other members of the executive were H. *Holoskevych, M. *Slavinsky, F. *Sliusarenko, and P. *Zaitsev. The council became formally associated with the Central Rada on 3 April. It also sent a delegation to the first head of the Provisional Government, G. Lvov, which submitted a memorandum concerning Ukrainian national rights and the Russian army's occupation of Galicia and Bukovyna. The council met with Metropolitan A. Sheptytsky (who had returned from exile) and acted as a liaison with the Provisional Government for the Central Rada. After the consolidation of the Central Rada's position in Kiev most members of the council left Petrograd, and the group's liaison functions diminished. After the Second Universal P. Stebnytsky, the Provisional Government's Ukrainian commissioner, assumed the council's liaison functions.

**Ukrainian National Credit Union Association** (Tsentralia ukrainskykh kooperatyv Ameryky, or TsUKA). A central organization of Ukrainian credit unions in the United States, founded in 1957 as the Ukrainian Economic Advisory Association (Tovarystvo ukrainskoi kooperatsii, or TUK) and renamed in 1974. Its purpose is to promote the development of Ukrainian credit unions and of the Ukrainian community as a whole. Its original members were seven credit unions in New York, Philadelphia, Baltimore, Chester, Jersey City, Detroit, and Chicago. In 1967 its head office was moved from New York to

Chicago. By 1970 TsUKA had 20 member unions with a membership of 24,000 and assets of 32 million dollars. By 1979 it had 35 member unions, and in 1988 it had 29 member unions with a membership of 57,000 and assets of 82 million dollars. Today it includes 32 separate financial insitutions with total assets approaching 300 million dollars. The association is a copublisher of the bimonthly magazine *Nash svit*. Since 1986 it has published an occasional page, 'Kooperatyvna trybuna,' in *Svoboda*. The presidents of TUK and TsUKA have included I. Sheparovych, O. Pleshkevych, and D. Hryhorchuk.

**Ukrainian National Defense** (Ukrainska natsionalna oborona, or UNO). A paramilitary organization established on the initiative of the OUN on 4 September 1938 in Uzhhorod, Transcarpathia. Its purpose was to prepare young men for service in a future Ukrainian army. It was headed first by V. Ivanovchyk, then by S. Rosokha. The first military unit of the UNO, a platoon, was commanded by M. Kolodzinsky. In November 1938 the UNO was transformed into the *Carpathian Sich.

**Ukrainian National Democratic Alliance** (Ukrainske natsionalno-demokratychne obiednannia, or UNDO). The main legal Galician Ukrainian political party of the interwar period. Established on 11 July 1925 by a merger of the *Ukrainian Labor Party, the *Ukrainian Party of National Work, and the Ukrainian deputies and senators from Volhynia, the Kholm region, and Podlachia, the party emerged as a broadly based centrist group and successor to the *National Democratic party. Its founding convention called for a struggle for the unification of Ukrainian lands into an independent state, demanded the right to self-determination for the Ukrainians in Poland, and rejected international decisions (from 1919 to 1923) concerning Galicia. It criticized the Soviet system but treated the Ukrainian SSR as 'a stage in the development of a single independent Ukrainian state.' It also supported the émigré representation headed by Ye. *Petrushevych.

The program prepared at the second UNDO convention on 19–20 November 1926 contained no positive statements about Soviet Ukraine and Petrushevych; instead it proclaimed the conviction that the best orientation for Ukrainians was a belief 'in their own strength.' The program defined the system of the future independent Ukrainian state as a parliamentary democracy and announced policies regarding a redistribution of land (without redemption) among Ukrainian peasants, the development of national industry, trade, and co-operatives, and the recognition of equal rights for all religions. At the same time it noted Christian morality as the spiritual foundation of the Ukrainian nation.

In the 1920s UNDO refused to recognize the legality of Poland's annexation of Ukrainian lands and opposed Polish settlement in the eastern regions of Western Ukraine, the school and language laws passed by the Sejm (July 1924), and the principles of the Polish land reform (July 1925).

The highest body of authority in UNDO was the People's Convention, held every two years, which elected a central (people's) committee whose work was directed by a presidium. The chairman of UNDO was D. *Levytsky (to 1935), the secretary was V. Tselevych, and some of the most important figures were V. Bachynsky, M. Halushchynsky, I.

Kedryn-Rudnytsky, K. Levytsky, O. Lutsky, V. *Mudry, S. Vytvytsky, and V. Zahaikevych. The official UNDO organ was *Svoboda*, although the party also received support from the papers *Dilo*, *Rada*, *Ukraïns'ke slovo*, and *Novyi chas*.

Legalism and organic work were key characteristics of UNDO's approach to politics. As a result it spread its influence over a broad spectrum of Ukrainian life in Galicia. It developed strong links with the majority of cultural-educational societies (*Prosvita, *Ridna Shkola), co-operative, credit, and economic institutions (the *Audit Union of Ukrainian Co-operatives, *Tsentrosoiuz, *Silskyi Hospodar), and even the sport association *Sokil. It was active mainly in Galicia but also had support in the towns of Volhynia.

UNDO considered itself to be the representative body of the entire Ukrainian community in interwar Poland, and did not co-operate with other Ukrainian parties (apart from early contacts with the leaders of the Ukrainian Military Organization). That self-perception, though somewhat inflated, was not entirely off base: UNDO enjoyed mass support and remained by far the strongest legal Ukrainian party. It also dominated the *Ukrainian Parliamentary Representation in the Sejm and Senate from 1928. In 1928 and 1930 UNDO took part in elections as a member of the Bloc of National Minorities.

Several splits occurred within UNDO before 1930. They established splinter groups but did not affect the main body of the party. In December 1926 a Polonophile group led by Bachynsky left the party; it was followed in April 1927 by supporters of an understanding with Soviet Ukraine, who founded the *Ukrainian Party of Labor.

In the summer of 1930, in connection with a campaign against the anti-Sanacja opposition and with the *Pacification, the Polish authorities took repressive steps against UNDO. In September a number of UNDO deputies were imprisoned in the Brest fortress, and in October a new wave of arrests (D. Levytsky, Mudry) took place. The government's hard new line and a perception that the tactics pursued up to that time had been futile prompted the leaders of UNDO to consider a compromise with the *Sanacja regime. Negotiations between the Ukrainian Parliamentary Representation and Non-Party Bloc for Co-operation with the Government (February 1931) were, however, unsuccessful.

The desire of the UNDO leadership to recognize the reality of the incorporation of Ukrainian lands by Poland without dismissing a pro-independence stance became a major item of party discussion in the first half of the 1930s. The representatives of one current of thought developed a minimal program of autonomy for Ukrainian lands. The chief opponents of a rapprochement left the party in July 1933 and founded the *Front of National Unity. Nevertheless the shift in UNDO policy continued, influenced now by dramatic new developments, such as the Polish-German agreement of January 1934, the denunciation by Poland of the Minorities Treaty in September 1934, and the repressions in Soviet Ukraine. It resulted finally in an agreement with the Polish government in the spring of 1935, the so-called *Normalization. The policy proved contentious among UNDO members and supporters. In October 1935 D. Levytsky and M. Rudnytska were expelled from the Central Committee, and Mudry became the new head of the party. The opponents of the tactics of the party gathered around the daily *Dilo*, and *Novyi chas* became the main periodical of UNDO.

Normalization proved to be an absolute debacle for UNDO, and by May 1938 its central committee had largely abandoned the policy. It once again demanded autonomy for Ukrainian lands. In December 1938 an understanding with D. Levytsky's group ended the split within the party.

In October 1938 UNDO welcomed the *Munich Agreement as a sign of the creation of new national states in Europe. But in the following months it became discouraged by the German policy with respect to Transcarpathia. On 24 August 1939, a day after the Molotov-Ribbentrop Pact was signed in Moscow, the UNDO Central Committee passed a resolution in which it proclaimed that despite unsolved political accounts with Poland, Ukrainians would defend the Polish state in case of war. After the takeover of Western Ukraine by the Soviet armies and the signing of the German-Soviet convention of 28 September 1939 UNDO was forced to cease all activity.

BIBLIOGRAPHY
Feliński, M. *Ukraińcy w Polsce Odrodzonej* (Warsaw 1931)
Holzer, J. *Mozaika polityczna Drugiej Rzeczypospolitej* (Warsaw 1974)
Kedryn, I. *Zhyttia-podiï-liudy: Spomyny i komentari* (New York 1976)

A. Chojnowski

**Ukrainian National Federation** (Ukrainske natsionalne obiednannia, or UNO). A national organization established in Edmonton in 1932 by members of the *Ukrainian War Veterans' Association of Canada who were seeking a means of expanding the base of support for the Ukrainian national cause in Europe. Major figures in the association during its early years included V. Kossar, A. Gregorovich, T. Pavlychenko, and M. Pohoretsky, the editor of its official newspaper, *Novyi shliakh*. Although it had greatest appeal for Ukrainians who had immigrated to Canada during the interwar period, UNO had some success in drawing the Canadian-born into its ranks. It grew throughout the 1930s and 1940s and eventually established 91 branches, with major bases of strength in Alberta, Saskatchewan, and Ontario. It also established the Ukrainian Women's Organization of Canada (OUK) and the Ukrainian National Youth Federation (MUNO) as auxiliary bodies. During the late 1930s UNO's connections with European-based Ukrainian groups (particularly the OUN) became an issue of concern to the Canadian authorities, although the group was never subjected to the damaging public scrutiny experienced by its US counterpart, the Organization for the Rebirth of Ukraine. In 1940 UNO became a founding member of the Ukrainian Canadian Committee (now Congress) (KUK). In the postwar period UNO aligned itself politically with the Melnyk faction of the OUN and took a significant portion of the new wave of Ukrainian immigrants into its ranks. UNO's cultural-educational program has included Ukrainian language schools, summer camps for youth, and dance groups and choirs, the best known being the Koshetz Choir in Winnipeg. It has also sponsored higher-education courses for its cultural activists and organized the *Ukrainian Cultural and Educational Centre (Oseredok) in Winnipeg in 1944. In 1980 the federation had 56 branches and about 6,200 members.

BIBLIOGRAPHY
Knysh, Z. (ed). *Na shliakhu do natsional'noï iednosty: Iuvileinyi zbirnyk UNO Kanady, 1932–1982*, 2 vols (Toronto 1982)

**Ukrainian National Front** (Ukrainskyi natsionalnyi front). A clandestine political organization founded in the mid-1960s in Ivano-Frankivske. In its journal, *Volia i bat'-kivshchyna* (15 issues, 1965–7), it propagated the idea of an independent, democratic Ukraine. Most of its members, including Z. Krasivsky, D. Kvetsko, M. Diak, H. Prokopovych, Ya. Lesiv, V. Kulynyn, M. Kachur, I. Hubka, and M. Melen, were arrested in 1966–7 and sentenced to long prison terms for 'anti-Soviet activity.'

Another organization with the same name and some 40 members was established in Ivano-Frankivske in the mid-1970s. Some of its members, including M. Krainyk and V. Zvarych, were arrested in 1979. I. Mandryka died in mysterious circumstances after his arrest. The group propagated the idea of Ukrainian independence in its journal, *Ukraïns'kyi visnyk*, and its almanac, *Prozrinnia*.

**Ukrainian National Museum** (Ukrainskyi natsionalnyi muzei-arkhiv). A Ukrainian museum and archive founded in Chicago in 1953. Its initial fund consisted of the private folk-art collection donated by O. and A. Kachan and the military artifacts and portraits donated by K. Lysiuk. M. *Simenovych-Simens provided the museum with a building. The museum consists of a folk-art section, a library of over 17,000 books, a military history collection, an archive of émigré materials, and a bibliographic and informational center. The presidents of the museum have been Yu. Kamenetsky (1953–62, one of its founders), Simenovych-Simens (1962–6), I. Mula, R. Weres, and E. Basiuk.

**Ukrainian National Museum.** See National Museum.

**Ukrainian National party** (Ukrainska natsionalna partiia, or UNP). The only legal Ukrainian political party in Rumania after the Ukrainian section of the Social Democratic Party of Bukovyna was disbanded. Continuing the traditions of the Ukrainian National Democratic party from the time of the Austro-Hungarian occupation of *Bukovyna, the UNP was centered in Chernivtsi, where it was active in 1928–38. It protested against the forced Rumanianization of the Ukrainian population, demanded that Ukrainian be taught in schools and used in churches, and promoted wide-ranging cultural and national development as well as agrarian reform. Its efforts to expand into Bessarabia and the Maramureş region were stymied by administrative edicts and by a lack of organization. The UNP drew on an electoral base of approx 32,000 voters, but because of Rumanian proscriptions it had to enter into coalitions with Rumanian parties (which it did with the national-peasant party, the liberal party, and the radical-agrarian party). It maintained good relations with parties that represented other minority groups in Rumania, including Jews, Germans, and Hungarians. UNP representatives, particularly its leader V. *Zalozetsky-Sas, participated in the Minorities Section of the League of Nations and spoke out about the oppression of Ukrainians under Rumanian, Polish, and Soviet rule. Yu. Serbyniuk was party secretary; other parliamentary representatives were V. Dutchak, D. Maier-Mykhalsky, and O. Shkraba. Other activists included T. Ivanytsky, L. Kohut, A.

Kyryliv, Yu. Lysan, I. Stryisky, M. Syvy, M. Vitan, R. Yasenytsky, and I. Zhukovsky. The UNP's official organ was the periodical *Rada*; periodicals affiliated with the party included *Ridnyi krai*, *Chas*, *Narod*, and *Narodnia syla*. The UNP was banned in 1938 along with all political parties in Rumania.

BIBLIOGRAPHY
Kvitkovs'kyi, D. 'Politychni partiï i rukhy,' in *Bukovyna, ïï mynule i suchasne*, ed D. Kvitkovs'kyi et al (Paris–Detroit–Philadelphia 1956)
Zhukovs'kyi, A. 'Rumuns'kyi period, 1918–40,' in ibid
A. Zhukovsky

**Ukrainian National Rada** (Ukrainska natsionalna Rada). A council formed in Lviv on 18 October 1918 to represent the Ukrainian ethnic territories within the Austro-Hungarian Empire in their quest for self-determination. Its membership included all Ukrainian deputies in both houses of the Austrian parliament and the diets of Galicia and Bukovyna, three representatives from each Ukrainian political party in the two crownlands, a group of nonpartisan specialists, and selected deputies from counties and towns. Several seats were reserved for representatives of national minorities, but they were never filled. The Rada's total membership was 150. On 9 November 1918 the Rada proclaimed the establishment of the *Western Ukrainian National Republic (ZUNR). With its legislative and review powers the Rada served as the parliament of ZUNR and the body to which the *State Secretariat (the latter's executive branch) was accountable. The plenum of the Rada elected an executive consisting of a president and nine members. It was responsible for key state functions, including installing the government, granting amnesties, appointing directors of higher state offices, and enacting legislation passed by the Rada. The post of president was filled first by K. Levytsky and then by Ye. Petrushevych. All constitutional powers were transferred to President Ye. Petrushevych as the 'dictator plenipotentiary' on 9 June 1919, when the government of the ZUNR was forced to quit the country and the *Ukrainian Galician Army retreated beyond the Zbruch River. Until the calling of the next plenum of the Ukrainian National Rada Petrushevych was invested with all military and civil executive powers (see *Dictatorship of the Western Province of the Ukrainian National Republic).

M. Dobriansky

**Ukrainian National Republic** (Ukrainska Narodnia Respublika, or UNR). The Ukrainian state, established at

Boundaries

| | |
|---|---|
| ·········· | Ukrainian ethnic territory |
| —·—·—·— | States (1. 7. 1914) |
| — — — — | Gubernia or province |
| — — — — | Ukrainian National Republic |
| ———————— | Autonomous Ukraine during the period of the Central Rada in 1917 |

Territories

| | |
|---|---|
| | Ukrainian National Republic in 1917–1920 |
| | Western National Republic |
| | Temporarily incorporated into the Ukrainian State in 1917–1919 |
| ⊙ | Center of gubernia or province |

The UNR diplomatic mission in Hungary in 1919–20. From left: Baron Mykola Vasylko, Otaman Symon Petliura, Gen Volodymyr Sikevych

Leading members of the Ukrainian National State Union with President Andrii Livytsky in 1946. Sitting, from left: Ivan Kabachkiv, Kost Pankivsky, Livytsky, Gen Mykhailo Omelianovych-Pavlenko; standing: Viktor Solovii, Gen Mykhailo Sadovsky, Mykhailo Vetukhiv, Col Mykola Stechyshyn

first on the territory of central Ukraine and then, as of 4 January 1919, also including the Western Ukrainian lands of the former Austro-Hungarian Empire. The UNR was first proclaimed in the Third *Universal of the Ukrainian *Central Rada on 20 November 1917. It was in federation with Russia until it declared complete independence in its Fourth Universal on 25 January 1918 (back-dated to 22 January). Under the Hetman government of P. *Skoropadsky the UNR was renamed the Ukrainian State (29 April to 14 December 1918). Under the *Directory the name UNR was restored. The UNR existed on Ukrainian territory until 1920, when the head of the Directory and the government of the UNR went into exile. The *Government-in-exile of the UNR was first in Poland and then, in 1939–40, in France. After the Second World War (1948) the *Ukrainian National Council was created as a preparatory parliament for the State Center of the Ukrainian National Republic, which continued the traditions of the national republican government of Ukraine until 1992.

**Ukrainian National Revolutionary party** (Ukrainska natsionalno-revoliutsiina partiia). A short-lived (July–August 1917) faction of the Ukrainian Party of Socialist Revolutionaries. Led by M. Liubynsky, it opposed the Central Rada's compliance with the 'Instruction' from the Provisional Government in Petrograd.

**Ukrainian National Society for Child and Adolescent Care** (Ukrainske kraiove tovarystvo okhorony ditei i opiky nad moloddiu, or UKTOD). A charitable organization founded in Lviv in 1917 through the efforts of V. *Detsykevych and Rev T. *Voinarovsky-Stolobut. Its chief patron and financial supporter was Metropolitan A. *Sheptytsky. The society had 31 branches throughout Galicia, which maintained 10 orphanages, 6 child shelters, 3 counseling centers for mothers, a publishing house in Lviv, and a children's library. The head office in Lviv operated another orphanage and an outpatient clinic; raised funds for summer camps, Plast Ukrainian Youth Association camps, and rest homes; managed organizational matters; and participated in international conferences. The first president of the UKTOD was M. *Karatnytsky. With the Soviet occupation of Ukraine in 1939, the society's activities ceased.

**Ukrainian National State Union** (Ukrainskyi natsionalno-derzhavnyi soiuz, or UNDS). An émigré political party established in 1946 in Neu-Ulm, Germany. It incorporated a number of groups, including interwar émigré activists; officials of the UNR government-in-exile; veterans of the Army of the UNR; post–Second World War émigrés from Soviet Ukraine (notably the so-called Kharkiv community, which included V. Dolenko and V. Dubrovsky); and political centrists from Western Ukraine (including M. Dobriansky, V. Kubijovyč, K. Pankivsky, and M. Shlemkevych), many of whom had been involved with the *Ukrainian Central Committee (UTsK). The party's official platform was written by M. Dobriansky. T. Olesiiuk was its first president, and V. Dolenko headed its executive council. The UNDS was a founding member of the Ukrainian National Council, and B. Ivanytsky, a UNDS activist, was elected as its chairman. At the second UNDS congress, in 1947, the structure of the party was changed, and a central committee headed by M. Oleksiiv was elected. In 1950 M. Livytsky was chosen as leader; he was succeeded by T. Leontii in 1967 and I. Samiilenko in 1982. Other active UNDS members included M. Omelianovych-Pavlenko, M. Sadovsky, A. Valiisky, O. Vyshnivsky, A. Yakovliv, and M. Yurchenko.

Several groups seceded from the UNDS coalition within a decade of its founding and established their own parties. In 1948 the Kharkiv representatives established the Union of Lands of United Ukraine (later known as the Peasant party). In 1950 K. Pankivsky, M. Shlemkevych, and M. Vetukhiv established the Union of Ukrainian National Democrats in the United States. A group of former UTsK adherents led by V. Kubijovyč also left the party. By 1956 only a core group of UNR supporters remained; T. Leontii, was the long-standing director of the UNR executive branch, and in 1965 the UNDS president, M. Livytsky, was elected as president of the UNR government-in-exile.

The official organ of the party, the monthly *Meta*, was published in Munich in 1952–82 (before being moved to Philadelphia) and served as the semiofficial voice of the UNR government-in-exile from the 1970s. In the 1950s the *Biuleten' UNDS* briefly appeared in the United States. The party also put out four issues of *Biblioteka ukraïns'koho derzhavnyka* (1946–9) and other publications.

A. Zhukovsky

**Ukrainian National Theater** (Ukrainskyi natsionalnyi teatr). A theater founded by the UNR government's Theatrical Committee in Kiev in April 1917, under the artistic directorship of I. Marianenko and with the executive members M. Hrushevska, M. Vorony, and O. Koshyts. The National Theater attempted to move away from the populist-ethnographical repertoire toward a more realistic and contemporary theater genre. Vorony directed its first productions – V. Vynnychenko's *Pryhvozhdzheni* (The Downtrodden) and S. Cherkasenko's *Khurtovyna* (The Snowstorm) – and H. Haievsky directed Vynnychenko's *Panna Mara* (Miss Mara), M. Starytsky's *Oborona Bushi* (The Defense of Busha), Molière's *Tartuffe*, and H. Sudermann's *Fires of St John*. Marianenko staged V. Samiilenko's *U Haikhan-Beia* (At Haikhan Bei's). Other directors included I. Zamychkovsky and M. Petliashenko. Economic and political difficulties led to the dissolution of the theater by the Hetman government in July 1918; its successors were the State Drama Theater and the People's Theater.

**Ukrainian National Theater.** See Prešov Ukrainian National Theater.

**Ukrainian National Union** (Ukrainskyi natsionalnyi soiuz, or UNS). An umbrella organization formed at the beginning of August 1918 as a successor to the Ukrainian National-State Union with the intention of establishing a democratic parliamentary system and consolidating Ukraine's independence. Its membership consisted of political parties, such as the Ukrainian Party of Socialists-Federalists, the Ukrainian Social Democratic Workers' party, the Ukrainian Party of Socialist Revolutionaries, and the Ukrainian Party of Socialists-Independentists, as well as civic and professional associations, such as the Peasant Association, the Teachers' Association, the Ukrainian Law Society, the Union of Railway Workers, the Postal-Telegraph Association, the Physicians' Association, the Prosvita society, and the All-Ukrainian Union of Zemstvos. It had branches in Odessa, Vinnytsia, Kremenchuk, Kamianets-Podilskyi, and Poltava. On 5 October 1918 a delegation of the UNS demanded of P. Skoropadsky that he reorganize his Hetman government and introduce Ukrainian ministers. The reformed government (from 24 October 1918) was headed by F. Lyzohub, and included several notable Ukrainian figures. Nevertheless it failed to win the confidence of the UNS. When the Hetman government proclaimed Ukraine's federation with Russia on 14 November 1918 and approved a cabinet of Russian monarchists headed by S. Gerbel, the UNS instigated an uprising against it, which was led by the UNR *Directory. The presidents of the UNS were A. Nikovsky (August to 18 September), V. Vynnychenko (18 September to 14 November), and Mykyta Shapoval (14 November 1918 to January 1919).

**Ukrainian National Union in France** (Ukrainskyi narodnyi soiuz u Frantsii, or UNSF). A nationalist community organization established in 1932 (with Paris as its center) as an umbrella group for local bodies, Prosvita societies, and clubs active among Ukrainians in France. It supported the idea of a unified Ukrainian state and was active in preserving national consciousness among Ukrainian émigré workers (particularly in preventing them

Members of the executive and audit commission of the Ukrainian National Union in France. Sitting, from left: ?, Ivan Stasiv, Gen Mykola Kapustiansky (president), Panas Zavorytsky, Oleksander Boikiv; standing: Khodan, ?, Kulchenko, Martyniuk, Pidkovych, Nedaikasha, Oleksander Kyselytsia

from becoming Polonized). It also strongly opposed the pro-UNR Union of Ukrainian Emigré Organizations, Mykola Shapoval's Ukrainian Hromada, and the Sovietophile Union of Ukrainian Citizens in France.

UNST began publishing the weekly *Ukraïns'ke slovo* in Paris in 1933 and supported the cultural and educational work of Paris's Ukrainian Students' Hromada in different parts of the country. It was formed initially by 13 groups; the number of its affiliates had risen to 50 by 1936 and to 87 by 1939 (with a total membership of 5,000). By that time it was the most influential Ukrainian émigré organization in Europe. The union was headed successively by Gen M. Kapustiansky (1932–8), P. Zavornytsky (1939–43), and O. Boikiv (after 1943). Active members included V. Fedoronchuk, L. Huzar, O. Kyselytsia, M. Nebeliuk, Z. Riznykiv, Yu. Soroko, I. Stasiv, T. Tsvikula, L. Verzhbitska, and P. Zakusylo. In early 1939 the UNSF waged a successful public campaign to encourage Ukrainians of Polish citizenship to join the French Foreign Legion rather than the Polish army – a considerable achievement in light of Poland's close ties with France. During the German occupation, UNSF activity dropped until the group was proscribed early in 1944. It revived after the war, but because of difficulties in registration the group soon dissolved. Its former members created the *Ukrainian National Alliance in France in 1949.

A. Zhukovsky

**Ukrainian National Women's League of America** (Soiuz ukrainok Ameryky, or SUA). A national organization formed in 1925 by the merger of five women's associations in and around New York. Its purpose is to promote Ukrainian national consciousness, organize educational programs, participate in the wider women's movement, and provide aid to Ukraine or Ukrainians in need. The league raised funds to help flood victims in the Carpathian region (1927), victims of the Polish Pacification (1930), war refugees in Germany and Austria (1946–8), widows with children resettled in the United States (1950), elderly women without families in Europe (1958), earthquake victims in Yugoslavia (1969), political prisoners and their families in the USSR, and needy families in Poland and Brazil. The SUA has supported Ukrainian schools in Austria and Germany (since 1954) and in Belgium

*Nashe zhyttia*, the magazine of the Ukrainian National Women's League of America

(since 1963) and has provided scholarships (141,000 dollars by 1986) to needy students in Europe and particularly in South America. Local branches run 26 nurseries in the United States. A collection of folk art purchased by the SUA in Galicia in 1932 became the core of its permanent exhibit at the Ukrainian Institute of America in 1967 and then of its Ukrainian Museum in New York (est 1976).

The league has published *Spirit of Flame* (1950), a collection of Lesia Ukrainka's poetry in translation; a second edition of the women's almanac *Pershyi vinok* (The First Garland, 1984); a collection of poetry by N. Livytska-Kholodna (1986); several albums of Ukrainian embroidery; and some cookbooks. It provides grants for scholarly research and prizes for scholarly books. In 1938 it began to publish a special page in *Ameryka*, and in 1944 the monthly *Nashe zhyttia*. The SUA was a founding member of the Ukrainian Congress Committee of America, the United Ukrainian American Relief Committee, and the World Federation of Ukrainian Women's Organizations. It is a member of the General Federation of Women's Clubs (since 1949) and the National Council of Women in the United States (since 1952). It has participated in various international women's conferences. Before the Second World War it maintained contacts with the Union of Ukrainian Women in Galica. Today the league has over 100 branches with a membership of approx 3,500. Its head office was moved to Philadelphia in 1943 and back to New York in 1975. The presidents of the SUA have been Yu. Shustakevych, Yu. Yarema (1925–31), O. *Lototska (1931–4, 1943–65), A. Kmets (1934–5, 1939–43), A. Wagner (1935–9), S. Pushkar (1965–71), L. Burachynska (1971–4), I. Rozhankovska (1974–87), and M. Savchak.

## Ukrainian National Youth Federation of Canada

(Molod ukrainskoho natsionalnoho obiednannia, or MUNO). The youth affiliate of the *Ukrainian National Federation, established in 1934 as Molodi ukrainski natsionalisty (Young Ukrainian Nationalists). During its earliest years MUNO was active in cultivating a nationalist consciousness among Ukrainian-Canadian youth, in attempting to counter the influence of the Ukrainian pro-communist left, and in providing youth with paramilitary training – most notably through the operation of a radio-telegraph school in Toronto (1935–9) and a flying school in Oshawa (1937–9). Led by the organizing efforts of president P. *Yuzyk (1936–7 and 1941–3), the group had established approx 50 branches throughout Canada by 1939. During the Second World War many of its rural branches

were dissolved, and MUNO's strength was thereafter concentrated in Ontario and the urban centers of western Canada. After the war MUNO was reconstituted with a strong cultural focus, largely through the efforts of M. Orychiwsky (national organizer, 1945–8, and president, 1956–9). It became particularly strong in the field of dance and spawned a number of (later independent) ensembles, including Cheremosh (Edmonton), Yevshan (Saskatoon), Rusalka (Winnipeg), and Kalyna (Toronto). It adopted its current Ukrainian name in 1963. The group published a separate page (with interruptions) in the newspaper *Novyi shliakh* in 1934–47. It then sponsored *Holos molodi* (1947–54) and *MUN Beams* (1955–66). Since 1977 it has published *New Perspectives* as a monthly supplement to *Novyi shliakh*.

## Ukrainian National-State Union

(Ukrainskyi natsionalno-derzhavnyi soiuz, or UNDS). A co-ordinating organization for Ukrainian parties of the center and right wing (Ukrainian Party of Socialists-Independentists, Ukrainian Party of Socialists-Federalists, Ukrainian Labor party, Ukrainian Democratic Agrarian party), as well as the Unified Council of Railways of Ukraine and the Postal-Telegraph Association. The UNDS was formed in Kiev in mid-May 1918 with the purpose of 'rescuing the threatened Ukrainian nationhood' from the encroachment of influential Russian monarchists in the Hetman government. In its manifesto of 24 May the UNDS expressed a vote of nonconfidence in the government of F. Lyzohub, protesting the anti-Ukrainian activities of some of its ministers and administration and demanding the Ukrainization of the government apparatus. The UNDS widened its scope at the end of July, when it included the left-wing formations of the Ukrainian Social Democratic Workers' party and the Ukrainian Party of Socialist Revolutionaries; subsequently it transformed itself into the *Ukrainian National Union.

## Ukrainian Native Faith church

(Ridna Ukrainska Natsionalna Vira or RUNVira). A Ukrainian religious body established in the West in 1964 by L. *Sylenko that combines Ukrainian pre-Christian beliefs with monotheism and nationalism. The teachings of RUNVira present the ancient Slavic god *Dazhboh generally as the 'consciousness of the world' and specifically as the Ukrainian

*Samobutnia Ukraïna*, an organ of the Ukrainian Native Faith church

conception of God (comparable to Brahma for a Hindu or Yahweh for a Jew). RUNVira adherents view the adoption of Christianity during Rus' times as an aberration from the 'native faith' of Ukrainians. RUNVira's sense of its 'native faith' as the natural religion of the Ukrainian people is reinforced by a strong affiliation with Ukrainian history and a marked disdain for all foreign invaders of Ukraine. This disposition is most evident in the major scriptural work of the group, *Maha vira* (The Great Faith), the magnum opus completed by Sylenko in 1979. In 1987 the church had 37 branches in the United States (where it has its major world center, in Spring Glen, New York), Canada, Great Britain, West Germany, Australia, and New Zealand. Since 1966 it has published a journal, *Samobutnia Ukraïna*.

**Ukrainian News.** See *Ukraïns'ki visti*.

**Ukrainian Onomastic Commission** (Ukrainska onomastychna komisiia). In 1960 the Commission on Toponymy and Onomastics was created within the AN URSR (now ANU) Social Sciences Section to organize and coordinate onomastic research, teaching, conferences, and publications in Ukraine. It was renamed in 1963. A member organization of the International Onomastic Committee, the commission has been headed by K. Tsiluiko (1960–81) and A. Nepokupny (since 1982). It has approx 30 members, who work at the ANU Institute of Linguistics. Its publications include 15 issues of *Povidomlennia* (1966–76); a prospectus for a hydronymic atlas of Ukraine (ed K. Tsiluiko, 1967); a dictionary of Ukraine's hydronyms (ed A. Nepokupny, O. Stryzhak, and K. Tsiluiko, 1979); and books on the hydronyms of the lower Dniester Basin (ed Yu. Karpenko, 1981), the interlingual and interdialectal aspects of Ukraine's hydronyms (ed O. Stryzhak, 1981), the hydronyms of western Podilia (L. Masenko, 1979), and Baltic–Northern Slavic linguistic ties (A. Nepokupny, 1976).

**Ukrainian Orthodox church** (Ukrainska Pravoslavna Tserkva). The general designation for a number of Orthodox churches that include Ukrainian believers, clergymen, and hierarchs. Although all of these churches have a common historical, liturgical, and theological tradition, and some are joined in a spiritual union, they are organized in separate jurisdictions. In addition to the church in Ukraine and the explicitly Ukrainian churches formed by Ukrainian emigrants in the West, some Ukrainians also belong to other Orthodox churches. (For the history of Ukrainian Orthodoxy, see *Church, History of the Ukrainian.)

The annexation of the Ukrainian church by the Russian Orthodox church under the patriarch of Moscow in the late 17th century was followed by the eradication of Ukrainian church autonomy and the increasing Russification of church life and practices. It was only after the fall of the tsarist regime in 1917 that the brief renaissance of Ukrainian statehood permitted the revival of an independent Ukrainian church. In January 1919 the government of the Ukrainian National Republic declared the *autocephaly of the Ukrainian church and its independence from the Moscow patriarch. Efforts to realize this independence in practice culminated in 1921 in the creation of the *Ukrainian Autocephalous Orthodox church (UAOC). This church, under the leadership of metropolitans V. Lypkivsky (1921–7) and M. Boretsky (1927–30), grew to encompass 30 bishops, 1,500 priests, and 1,100 parishes in 1924. But the radical reforms that the UAOC adopted (which stressed the participation of the laity in all aspects of church life), the untraditional rite of ordination that it used to consecrate its hierarchy, and especially its great popularity among the population and the threat it posed to the status of the Patriarchal Russian Orthodox church in Ukraine earned it the enmity of the conservative Russian hierarchy and some of the clergy, who denounced it as noncanonical, illegitimate, and a nationalist creation. The UAOC was also opposed by the Soviet regime, which in the 1920s tried unsuccessfully to undermine it by supporting the competing *Living church, the *Renovationist church, and the so-called Active Church of Christ. In the late 1920s the Soviet authorities decided to destroy all of these bodies, as well as the Patriarchal Russian church. The UAOC was decimated in the Stalinist terror, and all of its hierarchs and many of its priests were killed or died in concentration camps.

The partition of Ukrainian territories in the interwar period found many Ukrainian Orthodox believers living in the Polish state (in Volhynia, Polisia, and the Kholm region). There the *Polish Autocephalous Orthodox church, under Metropolitan D. *Valedinsky, was granted autocephaly by the patriarch of Constantinople in 1924. Despite strong Russifying and Polonizing pressures, many traditions of Ukrainian Orthodoxy survived, the Ukrainian language was introduced for services and church publications, and Ukrainian lay and church figures (eg, Bishop P. *Sikorsky) played a major role in the church.

In *Bukovyna the Orthodox church was initially established as a part of Halych metropoly. From the early 15th to the late 18th century a separate metropoly was centered in Suceava, then the capital of Moldavia. When all of Bukovyna came under Habsburg rule a separate eparchy, which became a metropoly in 1873, was established there. For most of its history this jurisdiction was dominated by Rumanians, but concessions were made to the large Ukrainian minority (in the interwar period there were 155 Ukrainian parishes and 135 priests in Bukovyna).

In the interwar period Orthodox churches were established by Ukrainian immigrants in North America. The *Ukrainian Orthodox Church of Canada (UOCC) was formed in 1918 (until 1990 known as the Ukrainian Greek Orthodox Church of Canada). It was under the spiritual authority of Metropolitan G. Shegedi of the Syrian Orthodox church in the United States until 1924, when Bishop I. *Teodorovych of the UAOC arrived in North America and assumed leadership of it and the *Ukrainian Orthodox Church in the USA (UOC-USA), which had been formed in 1920. Administratively these two churches remained totally independent, however, and the UOCC was actually run by the church's consistory in Winnipeg (Teodorovych had settled in Chicago and then Philadelphia). Both of these churches attracted many former Ukrainian Catholics, who opposed the Latinization of their church and rejected the authority of Roman Catholic hierarchs in North America. (For the same reasons, many immigrants from Transcarpathia established the American Carpatho-Russian Orthodox Greek Catholic church in 1936, but it does not consider itself a part of Ukrainian Orthodoxy.) The churches especially stressed their Ukrainian character (adopting the Ukrainian language for the liturgy) and conciliar organization. In 1928 many former Ukrainian Catholics in the United States established the *Ukrainian Orthodox Church of America. This group rejected the authority of Teodorovych and the canonical reforms of the UAOC, and placed itself under the jurisdiction of the patriarch of Constantinople. Many parishes left this church in the late 1940s and 1950s to join the UOC-USA. Now the church is administered as part of the Greek Orthodox exarchate of North and South America (it also maintains a few parishes in Canada).

Many Ukrainians in North America also joined other, non-Ukrainian, Orthodox jurisdictions. Before the First World War some 200,000 immigrants from Galicia and Transcarpathia in the United States joined the Russian Orthodox church that was under the patriarch of Moscow and was supported directly by the tsarist government. After the Russian Revolution of 1917 and the subjugation of the church to the Bolshevik regime, this church split. Most parishes were reconstituted in 1924 as the Russian Greek Catholic Orthodox church; it functioned, except for short interludes, as an independent church before being granted autocephaly in 1970 by the patriarch of Moscow and being renamed the Orthodox Church of America. Although many of this church's adherents are of Ukrainian origin, the church has little contact with the other Ukrainian churches, and a conscious attempt was made initially to Russify and recently to Americanize church practices and traditions. The other two jurisdictions to emerge from the pre–First World War Russian Orthodox church (the so-called Patriarchal church, which remained directly under the jurisdiction of the Moscow patriarch, and the Synodal church or Russian Orthodox Church outside Russia, which is under a synod of émigré bishops who do not recognize the patriarch) are much smaller. The Synodal church is predominantly Russian in constituency, though it has attracted some emigrants from eastern Ukraine. The Patriarchal jurisdiction in North America is predominantly composed of former Uniates from Western Ukraine (in the United States) or from Bukovyna (in Canada), but only in western Canada do its members retain links to the Ukrainian community.

During the Second World War the UAOC was revived in German-occupied territories under the spiritual authority of Metropolitan Valedinsky of the Polish Orthodox church and the leadership of P. Sikorsky. Several new bishops (including M. *Skrypnyk) were consecrated for the Reichskommissariat Ukraine (the former Soviet Ukrainian territories). At the same time, two Ukrainians, I. Ohiienko and P. Vydybida-Rudenko, were consecrated as bishops for the Orthodox Ukrainians in the Generalgouvernement. Sikorsky was named metropolitan of the UAOC, and attempts were made to absorb surviving clergy from the UAOC of the 1920s into the church, although its radical reforms were not affirmed. A competing body, the *Ukrainian Autonomous Orthodox church, was also organized in German-occupied Ukraine. This church, under Metropolitan O. Hromadsky, recognized the authority of the Moscow patriarch over the Ukrainian church, although it considered this authority suspended as long as the church remained under Soviet control, and was supported by the more conservative and Russified elements of the population. The German authorities encouraged

this division to prevent the emergence of a united church in opposition to their rule.

After Soviet rule was consolidated throughout Ukraine at the end of the Second World War, both the UAOC and the Autonomous church were destroyed, and most of the UAOC bishops and many priests fled to the West. The Ukrainian exarchate of the *Russian Orthodox church (ROC) remained as the only legal church entity in Ukraine, and it was closely controlled by the regime. At the *Lviv Sobor of 1946 the Ukrainian Greek Catholic church in Western Ukraine was forced to liquidate itself and join the ROC. The surviving hierarchy of the UAOC fled to Western Europe, where they re-established the church under Metropolitan Sikorsky. When they also did not affirm the most radical reforms of the UAOC of the 1920s, an opposition emerged, and in 1947 the *Ukrainian Autocephalous Orthodox Church (Conciliar) under the leadership of Bishop H. Ohiichuk split from the UAOC. Since then the UAOC (Conciliar) has also split and reunited itself several times. Another jurisdiction, the short-lived *Ukrainian Autocephalous Orthodox Church in Exile, was established under Bishop P. Vydybida-Rudenko in New York in 1951. Other bishops and priests of the UAOC also emigrated to North America, where they joined the UOCC or UOC-USA. In 1949 Archbishop Teodorovych underwent a reconsecration as part of an agreement to unite the Ukrainian Orthodox Church of America and the newly arrived followers of the UAOC with his church. Many parishes of the former and most of the clergy and believers of the latter took part in the unification, thereby creating the largest Ukrainian Orthodox jurisdiction in the United States, since 1970 headed by Metropolitan Skrypnyk.

Now, Skrypnyk is metropolitan of both the UOC-USA and the UAOC (which includes parishes in South America, Europe, and Australia), but the two bodies remain administratively independent. In 1960 the three largest jurisdictions – the UOCC, UOC-USA, and UAOC – at a joint sobor resolved that outside Ukraine there is a single Ukrainian Orthodox church, which is autocephalous and conciliar and consists of three independent metropolies that create a single spiritual whole. This sobor also took steps to standardize liturgical practices and the training of priests for the churches. The *Ukrainian Orthodox church in Australia, which dates only from the late 1940s, is split into two jurisdictions, one under the UAOC and the other under the Ukrainian Greek Orthodox Church in Canada.

After the Second World War the ROC, in addition to assuming total control over the church in Ukraine, extended its authority over the Orthodox church in Poland. Metropolitan Valedinsky was forced to resign his post and was replaced by a bishop from the ROC. At the same time the Moscow patriarch invalidated the 1924 *Tomos* of the patriarch of Constantinople granting autocephaly to the Polish church, and replaced it with its own grant of autocephaly. The Polish Autocephalous Orthodox church, however, remains a Russian-dominated institution with occasional Polonizing tendencies, despite the fact that the majority of its believers are Ukrainians or Belarusians, and in recent years it has begun to protest this situation. The small Orthodox church in Czechoslovakia has Ukrainian parishes in the Prešov region. The Rumanian Orthodox church, which has several parishes in the largely Ukrainian *Maramureş region and southern Bukovyna, is independent of Moscow. Since 1990 it has permitted an administration for Ukrainian believers. It also tolerates some practices of Ukrainian Orthodoxy and the limited use of the Ukrainian language in services, but has no Ukrainian hierarchs. In any case, none of the churches in the Ukrainian border states can be seen as national Ukrainian institutions.

The relative liberalization of the Gorbachev regime in the late 1980s permitted the rebirth of Ukrainian Orthodoxy in Ukraine. Several parishes and priests began to leave the official ROC and re-form themselves as a revived UAOC. In 1989 Bishop I. Bodnarchuk left the ROC to head a new UAOC hierarchy. The church sobor in June 1990 elected Metropolitan M. Skrypnyk as patriarch, and he was installed in October 1990. In response to these developments the ROC began granting its Ukrainian exarchate increased independence: it renamed it the Ukrainian Orthodox church and in October 1990 proclaimed that it was formally independent and administratively autonomous. The church was to be returned its right to choose its own metropolitan (although the candidate had to be approved by the patriarch of Moscow) and hierarchs; the head of the church, however, is the former exarch, Metropolitan F. *Denysenko. A struggle has developed between the two jurisdictions over parishes and other church property in Ukraine. In general the UAOC has greater support in western and central Ukraine, where it is supported as a national church; the other church enjoys its greatest support in the more Russified east and south.

A. Zhukovsky

## Ukrainian Orthodox church in Australia.

The first Orthodox parishes in Australia were founded in 1945 following the arrival of postwar immigrants from Soviet Ukraine and Bukovyna. These immigrants included several priests and Bishop S. Haievsky of the Ukrainian Autocephalous Orthodox church (UAOC). Other hierarchs in the 1950s to 1970s were Bishops I. Danyliuk, V. Solovii, and D. Burtan. The eparchy, with its see in Canberra, includes parishes in New Zealand. A split developed in the 1960s, and now there are two separate jurisdictions, the Ukrainian Autocephalous Orthodox church (which recognizes the authority of Metropolitan M. Skrypnyk) and the Ukrainian Orthodox church (which is affiliated with the Ukrainian Orthodox Church of Canada [UOCC] and recognizes that church's metropolitan as its spiritual head). From 1986 to 1990 Bishop V. Didovych headed the branch under the UAOC, which in 1989 had 9 priests, 10 parishes, and 2 small communities in New Zealand. The church's consistory has published the quarterly *Pratsia i zhyttia* since 1966. The branch under the UOCC has fewer parishes and no bishop of its own.

## Ukrainian Orthodox Church in the USA

(Ukrainska Pravoslavna Tserkva v SShA, or UOC-USA). The largest Ukrainian Orthodox church in the United States. It is in communion with the Ukrainian Orthodox Church of Canada and the *Ukrainian Autocephalous Orthodox church (UAOC) in Western Europe but is administered independently.

The first UOC-USA parishes were founded in 1919, mostly by former Ukrainian Catholics from Galicia or Orthodox from Transcarpathian Ukraine and Bukovyna. At that time several Catholic parishes founded as early as 1903 joined the new church. Influenced by the movement for an independent church in Ukraine, these parishes founded

The first synod (1924) of the Ukrainian Orthodox Church in the USA. Sitting in the center is Archbishop Ioan Teodorovych.

the independent UOC-USA at a national convention held in Newark in 1920. Its first administrator was Rev N. Kopachuk, an Orthodox priest from Bukovyna. This church organization proclaimed its unity with the UAOC in Ukraine. In 1924 Archbishop I. *Teodorovych was dispatched by the All-Ukrainian Orthodox Council in Kiev to serve as a hierarch for the new churches in the United States and Canada.

The UOC-USA grew quickly, and by 1932 it included 32 parishes and 25 priests. Some priests and faithful, however, questioned the canonicity of Teodorovych's episcopal ordination by the UAOC and formed the *Ukrainian Orthodox Church of America (UOCA) under the jurisdiction of the patriarch of Constantinople. In the late 1940s many parishes left the UOCA to join the UOC-USA, and attempts were made to unite the two jurisdictions. In 1949 Teodorovych even accepted a reconsecration to satisfy the demands of some elements of the UOCA, but the division remained. With the arrival of postwar immigrants the church grew, and many new parishes were founded. In 1950 a sobor in New York reorganized the church as a metropoly under Metropolitan Teodorovych, and in 1951 the see and the administrative offices were transferred to South Bound Brook, New Jersey, where a memorial church (St Andrew's), a museum, an archive and library, and a Ukrainian cemetery were all founded.

In the 1960s the UOC-USA had 93 parishes, 94 priests, and approx 100,000 faithful. Teodorovych was assisted by Archbishop M. *Skrypnyk, who became administrative head of the consistory. In 1967 three eparchies were established, in New York (Skrypnyk), Detroit (Archbishop V. Malets), and Chicago (Archbishop H. Shyprykevych). In 1975 St Sophia's Seminary was opened in the Ukrainian Orthodox center in South Bound Brook; it is affiliated with Rutgers University in New Brunswick. The church has published *Ukraïns'kyi pravoslavnyi kalendar* (1951–), *Ukraïns'ke pravoslavne slovo* (1951–), the English-language *Ukrainian Orthodox Word* (1967–), and *Dnipro* (1920–50). By 1990 the church had over 100 priests and parishes and over 100,000 adherents.

H. Myroniuk

**Ukrainian Orthodox Church of America** (Ukrainska Pravoslavna Tserkva v Amerytsi, or UOCA). A church founded in 1928 in Allentown, Pennsylvania, that is under the jurisdiction of the patriarch of Constantinople. Its predecessor was the American Greek Catholic church, founded in 1926 under the administration of Rev Y. Pelekhovych. The church attracted former Ukrainian Catholics who resented the Latinization of their church and the authority of Roman Catholic hierarchs in the United States (later it attracted some parishes in Canada formed by immigrants from Bukovyna). The church, priests, and faithful refused to join the *Ukrainian Orthodox Church in the USA because they questioned the canonicity of Archbishop I. Teodorovych's episcopal consecration. Rev Y. Zhuk (a Catholic priest from Galicia) was selected as the church's bishop in 1931 and consecrated in 1932 by the patriarch of Constantinople. He was succeeded by Bishop B. *Shpylka (consecrated in 1937), who later was named metropolitan. In the late 1940s some of the UOCA's parishes joined the church headed by Archbishop Teodorovych, and an attempt at uniting the churches was made in 1948, but Bishop Shpylka and some of the parishes refused to join the other group. In 1959 the UOCA had 37 parishes, 52 priests, and 40,000 faithful. Bishop A. *Kushchak headed the church from 1967 to 1986. In 1980 the church had 1 bishop and 26 parishes (including several organized in a Canadian administration). In 1983 it was elevated to the status of a metropoly. Since 1987 Bishop V. Maidansky has headed the church. The UOCA is administered as a part of the Greek Orthodox exarchate in the Americas. It publishes the quarterly newsletter *Ukrainian Orthodox Herald* (est 1928).

The consistory of the Ukrainian Orthodox Church of Canada in 1980. Sitting, from left: Rev Semen Sawchuk, Archbishop Mykola Debryn, Archbishop Borys Yakovkevych, Metropolitan Andrei Metiuk, Bishop Wasyl Fedak, Rev Hryhorii Udod

**Ukrainian Orthodox Church of Canada** (Ukrainska Pravoslavna Tserkva v Kanadi, or UOCC). The major Ukrainian Orthodox jurisdiction in Canada. The church was known as the Ukrainian Greek Orthodox Church of Canada until 1990, when the word 'Greek' was dropped from common use. (Officially, its charter was amended by Parliament only in 1991.) Until 1918 the spiritual needs of the Orthodox Ukrainians in Canada, mainly immigrants from Bukovyna, were met by the itinerant clergy of the Russian Orthodox mission in the United States, subsidized by the Russian government. Protestants also tried to penetrate the Ukrainian community in the guise of Orthodoxy through the *Independent Greek church, absorbed in 1912 by the Presbyterian church.

The formation in 1918 of a national Ukrainian Orthodox church resulted from a bitter conflict between Bishop N. Budka, head of the Ukrainian Catholic church in Canada, and a nationalistically minded segment of the Ukrainian intelligentsia associated with the *Mohyla Ukrainian Institute in Saskatoon and the weeklies *Ukraïns'kyi holos and *Kanadiis'kyi farmer. A range of controversial issues – the bishop's personality, parish property rights, a perceived Latinization of the Ukrainian Catholic church in Canada – led to a schism. In July 1918 a confidential conference of disenchanted lay Catholics from Manitoba, Saskatchewan, and Alberta created a Ukrainian Orthodox Brotherhood to organize the Ukrainian Greek Orthodox Church of Canada. The church placed itself under the temporary spiritual jurisdiction of Metropolitan G. Shegedi of the Syrian Orthodox church in the United States, who accepted the new church's administrative body, the elected consistory.

The new church was a distinct Canadian institution, unconnected with any Ukraine-based church. It accepted the traditional dogma and rites of Eastern Orthodoxy, including a married clergy. It also stressed that church property was to be owned by congregations (and not the bishop), and that the church was to be democratic and conciliar in organization. Theology classes were begun in Saskatoon in 1919, and the church's first three priests, S. *Sawchuk, P. Samets, and D. Stratychuk, were ordained by Shegedi in 1920. Large numbers of Ukrainians who had formerly belonged to the Russian Orthodox and Ukrainian Catholic churches joined the newly formed UOCC.

In 1924 Archbishop I. *Teodorovych of the *Ukrainian Autocephalous Orthodox church, formed in Kiev, became primate of the *Ukrainian Orthodox Church in the USA, and the church in Canada, with 14 priests, also accepted his primacy; the UOCC, however, insisted on retaining its administrative independence under Rev Sawchuk as church administrator and president of the consistory. The *Ukrainian Self-Reliance League, formed in 1927, became an effective lay arm for the UOCC and boosted its fortunes. By the end of 1928 the church had approx 64,000 followers, organized in 152 parishes served by 21 priests. It was strongest in Saskatchewan (81 parishes in 1940), Alberta (55 parishes), and Manitoba (53 parishes).

Serious internal conflict broke out in 1935–40 between the consistory and a group led by W. *Swystun and centered around the church's designated cathedral parish, St Mary the Protectress in Winnipeg. The group questioned Teodorovych's leadership and his desire for a closer relationship with other Orthodox churches, and the parish seceded. Despite its problems the church opened a theological school, *St Andrew's College, in 1946.

In 1947 Archbishop M. *Skrypnyk, newly arrived from Europe, succeeded Teodorovych, but policy differences with the consistory led to his resignation in 1950, and the church came under the temporary authority of Metropolitan P. Sikorsky of the *Ukrainian Autocephalous Orthodox church (UAOC) in Europe. In August 1951 Metropolitan I. *Ohiienko was elected primate, and Archbishop M. *Khoroshy became bishop of Toronto. At the same time the church was reorganized as a metropoly with three eparchies and two bishops; a self-contained and independent church able to perpetuate its own hierarchy was thereby created. By 1951 it had almost 300 congregations, 70 priests, and some 110,000 adherents. By 1963 the UOCC had four eparchies (Winnipeg, Toronto, Edmonton, and Saskatoon). Under Metropolitan Ohiienko

(1951–72) relations with the Ukrainian Catholic and Protestant churches improved. Ohiienko was succeeded by Khoroshy (1972–5), A. Metiuk (1975–85), and W. Fedak (1985–).

The quintennial councils or sobors represent the supreme decision-making body of the UOCC. Executive duties are shared between the council of bishops and the consistory, based in Winnipeg and composed of elected representatives of the laity and the clergy. The Ukrainian Self-Reliance League, with its component organizations, continues to play a leading role in church affairs at the local and national levels. In addition to St Andrew's College, the church is affiliated with three student residences: the Mohyla Ukrainian Institute in Saskatoon, St John's Institute in Edmonton, and St Vladimir Institute in Toronto. Its organ since 1924 has been *Visnyk*. Since 1978 several parishes of the Ukrainian Orthodox church of Australia have also been under the jurisdiction of the UOCC.

Data on membership are imprecise because many faithful have been classified as Greek Orthodox rather than Ukrainian. Historically, membership has been relatively stable, and has ranged between 20 and 25 percent of the total Ukrainian-Canadian population. In 1989 the church's estimated membership was 128,000, in 293 congregations with 99 clergy. Since 1960 the UOCC has been in spiritual union with the Ukrainian Orthodox Church in the USA and the UAOC, both of which are headed by Metropolitan Skrypnyk. In July 1990 the sobor of the UOCC ratified an agreement with the ecumenical patriarch of Constantinople that established a eucharistic union between the two churches. In 1990 the church had three bishops. (See also *Canada.)

BIBLIOGRAPHY
Trosky, O. *The Ukrainian Greek Orthodox Church in Canada* (Winnipeg 1968)
Yuzyk, P. *The Ukrainian Greek Orthodox Church of Canada, 1918–1951* (Ottawa 1982)
Mulyk-Lutsyk, Iu; Savchuk, S. *Istoriia Ukraïns'koï Hreko-Pravoslavnoï Tserkvy v Kanadi*, 3 vols (Winnipeg 1984–7)

O. Gerus

***Ukrainian Orthodox Herald/Ukraïns'kyi pravoslavnyi visnyk***. A bilingual English-Ukrainian illustrated quarterly organ of the Ukrainian Orthodox Church of America. Founded ca 1928, it appeared irregularly until 1967 as *Ukraïns'kyi visnyk*. It contains information about church affairs as well as articles on religious and cultural topics.

**Ukrainian Orthodox League of the USA** (Ukrainska pravoslavna liga ZSA, or UOL). An association of Ukrainian Orthodox laity founded in 1947 in New York for the purpose of propagating knowledge about Ukraine and its Orthodox church and involving young people in church activities. The league has organized annual summer camps, art and dance competitions, and basketball tournaments; published educational pamphlets on Ukrainian issues; granted scholarships to seminarians; and held annual conventions. In 1961 a junior division was formed. Today the senior division has 30 chapters, and the junior division has 20. Recent presidents of the UOL have included G. Woloschak and E. Skocypec.

**Ukrainian Orthodox (Synodal) church.** See Living church.

***Ukrainian Orthodox Word***. An English-language organ of the Ukrainian Orthodox Church in the USA, published quarterly in South Bound Brook, New Jersey, since 1967. It contains church news and articles on religion, history, and culture, many of which are translated from the church's Ukrainian-language publication, *Ukraïns'ke pravoslavne slovo*.

Members of the Ukrainian Parliamentary Representation and Ukrainian émigré leaders at a conference of the Interparliamentary Union held in Berlin in 1928. From left: Rep Antin Maksymovych, Zenon Kuzelia, Rep Dmytro Paliiv, Yevhen Konovalets, Rep Oleksander Vyslotsky, Rep Stepan Kuzyk, Dmytro Andriievsky, Rep Ivan Blazhkevych, Sen Ostap Lutsky, Rep Volodymyr Pellikh

**Ukrainian Parliamentary Representation** (Ukrainska parliamentarna reprezentatsiia). The Ukrainian caucus in the Polish Sejm and Senate in 1928–30. Similar in nature to the *Ukrainian caucus in the Russian State Duma, the representation was organized after the 1928 parliamentary elections. Its immediate precedent was the bloc of Ukrainian deputies from Volhynia and the Kholm region in the first Sejm (1922–7). In the campaign of 1928 the Ukrainian parties formed a coalition with the Belarusian and other minority groups to present a common slate of candidates. Ukrainians won 42 seats in the Sejm and 12 in the Senate. The majority of the Ukrainian deputies belonged to the representation, which was dominated by the Ukrainian National Democratic Alliance. It presented a common front on Ukrainian issues. After the 1930 election a joint Ukrainian representation did not take shape, because of Polish harassment and contention among Ukrainian parties.

**Ukrainian Party of Labor** (Ukrainska partiia pratsi, or UPP). A political party formed in Lviv on 7 May 1927 by the followers of Ye. Petrushevych as a breakaway group from the Ukrainian National Democratic Alliance (UNDO), largely in reaction to UNDO's growing anti-Soviet stance. The UPP remained to the left of the Galician political mainstream and was a strong opponent of the Polish state. The main item of its political platform was the unification of all ethnic Ukrainian lands into one independent country, although it relegated specific legal and state issues in that area to a secondary position. In its quest for a united Ukraine the party aligned itself to the national fortunes of the Ukrainian SSR, which it acknowledged as the core of the future state. Accordingly the UPP experienced a major crisis as a result of the arrest and subsequent show trial (March–April 1930) in Soviet Ukraine of 45 members of the so-called *Union for the Liberation of Ukraine. The party suffered a further setback with its poor success during the November 1930 elections to the Polish Sejm. It was dissolved almost immediately thereafter. The leaders of the UPP included V. Budzynovsky, M. Zakhidny, and M. Topolnytsky. It publications were the biweekly *Rada* and the weekly *Pratsia*.

**Ukrainian Party of National Work** (Ukrainska partia natsionalnoi roboty, or UPNR). A political party formed in Lviv on 24 April 1924 by a group of politicians originally affiliated with the *Ukrainian Labor party. They were joined by the editorial staff of the journal *Zahrava*, which was published by D. Dontsov. The executive committee consisted of O. Lutsky, D. Paliiv, S. Pidhirsky, K. Troian, and Yu. Sheparovych. Their political program maintained that the Ukrainian nation had been reduced by foreign elements controlling the cities into a dependent rural society. The party believed that effective counteraction could be developed only through a system of re-education of the younger generations, who would develop a sense of discipline and self-reliance. The group's rallying cry was 'Ukraine for the Ukrainians.' Its political platform also denounced unequivocally all doctrines of internationalism or cosmopolitanism. The party was never able to implement its ambitious goals, and was dissolved on 11 July 1925, when its members joined forces with the newly formed *Ukrainian National Democratic Alliance. Nonetheless the political program of the UPNR strongly influenced the shaping of the ideology of Ukrainian nationalism.

**Ukrainian Party of Socialist Revolutionaries** (Ukrainska partiia sotsiialistiv-revoliutsioneriv, or UPSR). A national-liberationist revolutionary socialist party that played an important role in Ukraine during the revolutionary period of 1917–20. Modeling themselves on the Russian Socialist Revolutionary party, small, clandestine cells of nationally conscious Ukrainian socialist revolutionaries were active in Symferopil and Odessa from 1905, in Kiev, Poltava, Chernihiv, Podilia, Kherson, and Tavriia gubernias from 1906, and in Kharkiv gubernia from 1907. In 1907 they held a conference and elected a Central Committee headed by Mykola *Zalizniak. In 1915 the Kiev group published five issues of *Borot'ba*, and in 1916 it issued a draft program. As a national party the UPSR held its founding congress in Kiev, on 17–18 April 1917. There it adopted resolutions calling for the national and territorial autonomy of Ukraine, convening of a Ukrainian constituent assembly, and socialization of all land; L. Bochkovsky, V. Ihnatiienko, P. Khrystiuk, Mykola Kovalevsky, K. Korzh, L. Kovaliv, I. Maievsky, O. Shleichenko, and V. Zalizniak were elected to the CC. At the second UPSR congress (28–31 July 1917) a radical socialist program was adopted, which provided for the transformation of the Russian Empire into a federation of national republics; I. Baziak, M. Chechel, D. Isaievych, I. Kovalenko, Kovalevsky (chairman), Korzh, S. Lymar, I. Lyzanivsky, H. Mykhailychenko, Yu. Okhrymovych, M. Panchenko, P. Plevako, A. Polonsky, M. Poloz, I. Puhach, P. Pylypchuk, M. Saltan, O. Sevriuk, Mykyta Shapoval, O. Shleichenko,

and M. Shrah were elected to the permanent CC. At the third congress (3–6 December 1917) the UPSR clarified its position on the need for social revolution in Ukraine and on government by democratic councils of the toiling masses.

In 1917–19 the UPSR was the leading spokesman of the Ukrainian peasantry. In its daily *Borot'ba*, its biweekly *Vil'na spilka*, and the co-operative daily *Narodnia volia* it promoted the slogan All Land to the Toilers without Redemption Payments and thus attracted mass support (by November 1917 it had nearly 75,000 members) and control of the influential Ukrainian *Peasant Association. It had the largest caucus in the Ukrainian *Central Rada; one of the vice-presidents, Shrah, was a member. In the *General Secretariat of the Central Rada the general chancellor Khrystiuk and the secretaries V. Holubovych, M. Savchenko-Bilsky, Kovalevsky, Shapoval, M. Stasiuk, O. Zhukovsky, and O. Zarudny were UPSR members; and the *Council of Ministers of the UNR formed after the declaration of Ukrainian independence in January 1918 included UPSR members, such as Holubovych (the prime minister), N. Hryhoriiv, Khrystiuk, Kovalevsky, M. Liubynsky, A. Nemolovsky, Shapoval, and Zhukovsky. Holubovych and Sevriuk headed the UNR delegation that signed the Peace Treaty of Brest-Litovsk, and Liubynsky and Poloz were members.

Under the right-wing 1918 Hetman government many UPSR leaders were arrested, and the party was forced to go underground. At its secret fourth congress near Kiev on 13–16 May 1918, ideological differences split the UPSR. The internationalist left wing (V. Blakytny [Ellansky], Kovaliv, P. Liubchenko, Yu. Mazurkevych, Mykhailychenko, Poloz, A. Prykhodko, O. Shumsky, A. Zalyvchy), which had repudiated the Central Rada and advocated co-operation with the Bolsheviks, gained control of the CC. A few weeks later the CC dissolved the UPSR and formed a new underground revolutionary organization that conducted political terror and organized a separate uprising against the government and the German occupation. The party's right wing (Chechel, Holubovych, Khrystiuk, D. Odryna, Saltan, Sevriuk, Shrah, A. Stepanenko, Zhukovsky) and center (Hryhoriiv, Lyzanivsky, Okhrymovych, Shapoval, O. Yanko) rebuilt the UPSR only after the left formed the separate pro-Bolshevik party of *Borotbists in March 1919. In the meantime the center played a key role in organizing the *Ukrainian National Union that co-ordinated the successful popular rebellion against the German-backed Hetman government, and after the UNR Directory took power in December 1918, a few of its members (O. Mytsiuk, S. Ostapenko, Shapoval, I. Shtefan) received portfolios in the renewed Council of Ministers of the UNR of December 1918 to February 1919. At the January 1919 legislative *Labor Congress UPSR delegates constituted the majority and pushed through resolutions on the socialization of land, the nationalization of the railways, sugar refineries, and industrial enterprises, and the transfer of power to collectives of representatives of the toiling masses. UPSR members did not take part in the pro-Entente Council of National Ministers in February to April 1919, and in protest against its policies the UPSR and other socialist parties formed in March the Committee for the Defense of the Republic. In the socialist Council of National Ministers headed by B. Martos (April to August 1919) and Isaak Mazepa (August 1919 to April 1920), however, UPSR members (T.

Cherkasky, Hryhoriiv, Kovalevsky, Lyzanivsky, Odryna, I. Palyvoda, L. Shramchenko) again held portfolios. Many members joined the ranks of the UNR Army and the *partisan movement that fought the Reds, Whites, and Allied expeditionary forces.

From late 1919 on, many UPSR leaders and a small number of members lived as émigrés in Polish-ruled Western Ukraine and in Central Europe, especially in Austria and Czechoslovakia. At the UPSR conference in Tarnów, Poland, a Foreign Committee led by Shapoval and consisting of Hryhoriiv, Mytsiuk, and H. Hrytsai was elected. The ideologues Shapoval and Hryhoriiv propagated the principle of the 'dictatorship of a democracy of toilers' in a sovereign pan-Ukrainian federal republic and elaborated a critique of the USSR as a state-capitalist, colonialist, totalitarian system. In Vienna M. Hrushevsky, Chechel, Shrah, Khrystiuk, and Isaievych founded the UPSR Foreign Delegation; its organ *Boritesia – poborete!* promoted the idea of transforming the UNR into a republic of workers' and peasants' councils and reaching an accord with Soviet Russia. From February to July 1920 it had a common 'soviet-revolutionary bloc' with V. Vynnychenko's Foreign Group of the *Ukrainian Communist party, with the aim of creating an independent Ukrainian soviet republic. The Foreign Delegation belonged to the Second International until January 1921, when it withdrew because the International did not support the principles of social revolution.

By January 1921 the émigré UPSR had split into mutually hostile factions: (1) the small Vienna-based Foreign Delegation, which supported recognition of Kh. Rakovsky's Soviet Ukrainian government; (2) Shapoval's anti-Soviet, revolutionary-socialist UPSR Foreign Committee (renamed the Foreign Organization in 1925) in Prague, which published the irregular organ *Vil'na spilka*, played a key role in the *Ukrainian Civic Committee and *Ukrainian Committee in Czechoslovakia, the *Ukrainian Institute of Sociology, and the monthly *Nova Ukraïna and strongly opposed the 'bourgeois' *Government-in-exile of the UNR; and (3) the right-wing UPSR Foreign Organizational Committee, headed by Kovalevsky and Mykola Zalizniak in Vienna, which had been purged from the UPSR in 1920 for supporting S. Petliura. In 1924 the members of the Foreign Delegation returned to Ukraine to help build a Ukrainian state; there, during the Stalinist terror, they were repressed. At the 1927 conference of the Foreign Organization a new provisional program by Shapoval was adopted. After Shapoval's death in 1932, the remaining factions reunited and established in Prague a common CC, which published the irregular *Trudova Ukraïna. Other leading members of the émigré UPSR were M. Balash, P. Bohatsky, S. Dovhal, Isaievych, K. Kobersky, L. Kobyliansky, M. Kosenko, V. Liakh, M. Mandryka, Palyvoda, S. Pilkevych, S. Ripetsky, M. Stakhiv, F. Sumnevych, B. Zalevsky, and A. Zhyvotko. The interwar *Ukrainian Radical party in Western Ukraine and the *Oborona Ukrainy organization in North America had close links with the émigré UPSR. After the Second World War the UPSR was reactivated in Western Europe under the leadership of Shapoval and Ya. Zozulia. In 1948 it joined the *Ukrainian National Council, and in 1950 it fused with other émigré parties to form the *Ukrainian Socialist party.

BIBLIOGRAPHY
Hrushevs'kyi, M. 'Ukraïns'ka partiia sotsiialistiv-revoliutsioneriv,' *Boritesia – poborete!*, 1 (1920)
Khrystiuk, P. *Zamitky i materiialy do istoriï ukraïns'koï revoliutsiï, 1917–1920 rr.* 3 vols (Vienna 1921; repr, New York 1969)
Shapoval, M. 'Narodnytstvo v ukraïns'komu vyzvol'nomu rusi,' *Vil'na spilka*, 3 (1927–9)
Zhyvotko, A. *50 rokiv: Do istoriï Ukraïns'koï partiï sotsiialistiv-revoliutsioneriv* (Prague 1936)
Majstrenko, I. *Borot'bism: A Chapter in the History of Ukrainian Communism* (New York 1954)
A. Zhukovsky

**Ukrainian Party of Socialist Revolutionary-Borotbists (Communists).** See Borotbists.

**Ukrainian Party of Socialists-Federalists** (Ukrainska partiia sotsiialistiv-federalistiv, or UPSF). A numerically small but influential liberal democratic party that superseded the *Society of Ukrainian Progressives (TUP) in April 1917. Until June 1917 it was called the Union of Ukrainian Autonomists-Federalists. The UPSF leader was S. *Yefremov. Its organ was the daily *Nova rada. Of all the Ukrainian political parties that arose after the February Revolution the UPSF had the largest number of experienced politicians and members of the elite intelligentsia, who had long been involved in national-cultural work. Its program was based on that of the *Ukrainian Democratic Radical party (1905–8), the predecessor of TUP.

In 1917–18 Yefremov was vice-president of the Ukrainian Central Rada, and he and other UPSF members, such as O. Shulhyn, P. Stebnytsky, O. Lototsky, and M. Tuhan-Baranovsky, held portfolios in its *General Secretariat; the latter two secretaries resigned after the proclamation of the Third *Universal in November 1917. In the 1918 *Council of National Ministers of the UNR portfolios were held by the UPSF members I. Feshchenko-Chopivsky, P. Kholodny, I. Kraskovsky, Lototsky, V. Prokopovych, S. Shelukhyn, and Shulhyn, and A. Yakovliv served as UNR emissary to Austria-Hungary. The UPSF boycotted the 1918 *Hetman government and took part in organizing the oppositional *Ukrainian National-State Union and *Ukrainian National Union. D. Doroshenko, however, resigned from the UPSF to become acting minister of foreign affairs, Shelukhyn chaired the government's peace delegation to Soviet Russia, Shulhyn served as ambassador to Bulgaria, and V. Leontovych, Lototsky, M. Slavinsky, Stebnytsky, and A. Viazlov participated in the government's Council of Ministers of October–November 1918. After the overthrow of the Hetman government in December, under the UNR Directory the UPSF members Feshchenko-Chopivsky, Kholodny, O. Korchak-Chepurkivsky, M. Korchynsky, D. Markovych, K. Matsiievych, and I. Ohiienko held portfolios in the revived UNR Council of National Ministers, until April 1919. Others served as UNR ambassadors to Greece (F. Matushevsky), Bulgaria (Shulhyn), Turkey (Lototsky), Czechoslovakia (Slavinsky), Rumania (Matsiievych), Sweden and Norway (K. Losky), and Holland and Belgium (Yakovliv), and as members of the UNR delegation at the Paris Peace Conference (Shulhyn, Shelukhyn, M. Kushnir).

Most UPSF members fled from the Bolshevik occupation of Ukraine in 1919–20. In Tarnów, Poland, Prokopovych became prime minister of the new UNR Council of National Ministers in May 1920, and Kholodny, Ohiienko, A. Nikovsky, and O. Salikovsky received portfolios. Feshchenko-Chopivsky headed the *Council of the Republic in 1921. In 1923 the émigré UPSF was renamed the Ukrainian Radical Democratic party (URDP). Lototsky was elected its leader. He and other members, such as P. Chyzhevsky, Matsiievych, Prokopovych, Shulhyn, Salikovsky, Slavinsky, and Yakovliv, played important roles in the *Government-in-exile of the UNR; Prokopovych served as prime minister (1926–39) and head of the UNR Directory (1939–40), and Lototsky was deputy prime minister. Other prominent UPSF/URDP members were V. Bidnov, Z. Mirna, I. Mirny, I. Shrah, and L. Starytska-Cherniakhivska. The URDP ceased functioning during the Second World War and was not revived.

A. Zhukovsky

### Ukrainian Party of Socialists-Independentists

(Ukrainska partiia sotsiialistiv-samostiinykiv, or UPSS). A numerically small nationalist party founded in Kiev on 30 December 1917 by members of the former *Ukrainian People's party and by UNR Army senior officers. In its weekly organ *Samostiinyk* (Kiev 1918) the UPSS demanded the immediate proclamation of Ukrainian independence. Although it advocated a social program based on the peasants' ownership of the land and the workers' ownership of industrial enterprises, it was in fact antisocialist and therefore opposed the General Secretariat of the Central Rada and criticized its land-socialization policies and its liberal position with respect to the ethnic minorities. It also opposed the succeeding 1918 Hetman government and took part in the creation of the *Ukrainian National-State Union and Ukrainian National Union. O. Andriievsky represented the UPSS in the UNR *Directory, and under its rule the UPSS members M. Bilynsky, M. Kryvetsky, I. Lypa, O. Osetsky, O. Shapoval, and D. Symoniv held portfolios in the UNR *Council of National Ministers until April 1919. Other prominent UPSS members were P. Bolbochan, I. Lutsenko, O. and P. Makarenko, and O. Stepanenko. Dissatisfied with the policies of the UNR government headed by B. Martos and supporting the idea of creating a military dictatorship to fight Soviet Russia, Andriievsky and the UPSS supported Otaman V. *Oskilko's failed coup in Rivne in April 1919. Thereafter the UPSS had negligible influence. Its émigré members joined a short-lived coalition of Ukrainian antisocialist opponents of S. Petliura in Vienna in 1921. In 1923 the émigré Ukrainian People's Party of Socialists-Independentists was founded by Oskilko in Polish-ruled Volhynia. In its government-funded organ, *Dzvin* (Rivne, 1923–8), it advocated co-operation with the Polish regime and therefore had little support. The party fell apart after Oskilko's death in 1926.

BIBLIOGRAPHY
Tymoshevs'kyi, V. *Istoriia ukraïns'koï vlady 1917–1919* (Vienna–Kiev 1920)
*Ukraïns'ka partiia samostiinykiv-sotsiialistiv* (Vienna 1920)

R. Senkus

### Ukrainian Patriarchal Society in the United States

(Ukrainske patriiarkhalne tovarystvo v Amerytsi, or UPT). An organization founded in 1965 to pursue the cause of establishing a Ukrainian Catholic patriarchate headed by Cardinal Y. Slipy. Until 1979 it was called the Society for the Promotion of the Patriarchal System in the Ukrainian Catholic Church. The UPT has organized petitions and demonstrations and copublished the monthly *Patriiarkhat* (until 1977 titled *Za patriiarkhat*) and other lit-

erature to promote the idea of self-government in the Ukrainian church. It has approx 30 branches and over 2,500 members. Its head office has moved from New York to Philadelphia to Detroit. The presidents of the UPT have included V. Kachmar, V. Shebunchak, V. Pasichniak, Z. Gil, M. Navrotsky, V. Lonchyna, O. Pryshliak, and R. Haida. Similar associations have arisen in Argentina, Australia, Canada, Germany, and France and are united with their American model group in the Ukrainian Patriarchal World Federation.

*Patriiarkhat*, the organ of the Ukrainian Patriarchal Society in the United States and the Ukrainian Patriarchal World Federation

### Ukrainian Patriarchal World Federation

(Ukrainske patriiarkhalne svitove obiednannia, or UPSO). An umbrella organization of Ukrainian patriarchal societies in the United States, Canada, Belgium, Germany, France, Britain, Australia, and Argentina as well as of some other Ukrainian Catholic organizations, such as Obnova and the Union of Brotherhoods and Sisterhoods in America. It was founded on 28–29 December 1974 in Washington, DC, to promote the introduction of the partiarchate system in the Ukrainian Catholic church. Besides organizing lay conferences, UPSO copublishes the monthly *Patriiarkhat* and publishes a book series, Biblioteka myrianyna (Laymen's Library). Its presidium has shifted between Europe and the United States.

### Ukrainian Peasants' and Workers' Party of Subcarpathian Ruthenia

(Ukrainska seliansko-robitnycha partiia Pidkarpatskoi Rusy). A short-lived nationalist party set up in Transcarpathia in 1936. It was headed by I. Nevytska, and its leading members included I. Hryts, M. Tulyk, and V. Kuzmyk. It published a semimonthly newspaper, *Narodnia syla* (1936–8), in Prešov. The party failed to attract support beyond student circles.

### Ukrainian Peasants' and Workers' Socialist Alliance. See Sel-Rob.

### Ukrainian Pedagogical Society. See Ridna Shkola society.

### Ukrainian Pedagogical Society in Prague

(Ukrainske pedahohichne tovarystvo v Prazi, or UTP). A society founded in 1930 by S. *Siropolko as a continuation of the Skovoroda Philosophical-Pedagogical Society, which had existed since 1925. It undertook practical measures to help teachers, most notably in attempting to secure for them teaching positions in Transcarpathia. One volume of *Pratsi UPT* (Works of the Ukrainian Pedagogical Society, 1932) appeared.

### Ukrainian People's Council of the Prešov Region

(Ukrainska narodna rada Priashivshchyny, or UNRP). A political and social body representing the indigenous Ukrainians of the Prešov region in eastern Slovakia. It was set up on 1 March 1945 in Prešov at a congress of delegates from Ukrainian villages and counties. Initially the UNRP favored the incorporation of the Ukrainian part of the Prešov region along with Transcarpathia in the Ukrainian SSR. Then it consented to remain within Czechoslovakia and assumed the task of defending the interests of the Ukrainian minority. The council did not succeed in winning de jure recognition as the political representative of a national group or cultural autonomy for the Ukrainian community. But it was recognized de facto as the voice for Ukrainians by the central government in Prague and the Slovak National Council, and appointed five deputies to the provisional assembly in Prague and the Slovak National Council in 1945–8. It published annual almanacs and the weekly *Priashevshchina* (1945–51), which contained Ukrainian- and Russian-language materials. Its work was conducted by the presidium and county committees. One of its jobs was to co-ordinate mass education in various villages. The first chairman of the UNRP was V. Karaman, and the general secretary was I. Rohal-Ilkiv. Its most active members were V. Kapishovsky, P. Babei, P. Zhydovsky, D. Roikovych, and S. Bunhanych. After the Communist coup in Czechoslovakia in 1948, the role of the council diminished, and it was forced to dissolve. It ceased all activities in 1951 and formally disbanded itself on 11 December 1952. In its place the *Cultural Association of Ukrainian Workers was set up.

### Ukrainian People's Democratic party

(Ukrainska narodno-demokratychna partiia, or UNDP). A political group established in 1942 among left-wing OUN members then fighting in Volhynia with T. Borovets's UPA. The UNDP was inspired by I. *Mitrynga, and the other leading members were V. Turchmanovych, V. Rybak, and B. Levytsky. The manifesto announcing its political program was critical of both the German occupation and the ideological foundations and political practices of the OUN. The new group failed to attract members and soon dissolved itself. After the war a number of its members in the West joined the left wing of the Ukrainian Revolutionary Democratic party (the *Vpered* group).

### Ukrainian People's Labor party. See Ukrainian Labor party.

### Ukrainian People's party

(Ukrainska narodna partiia, or UNP). A numerically small, clandestine organization of nationalistic intellectuals and students founded by M *Mikhnovsky in Kharkiv in 1902. Its members, among them Ye. Liubarsky-Pysmenny, O. Makarenko, S. and V. Shemet, and O. Stepanenko, rejected the socialist politics of the *Revolutionary Ukrainian party. A 1903 brochure containing the UNP 'ten commandments' deemed the Russians, Poles, Jews, Hungarians, and Rumanians enemies of the Ukrainian people for as long as they kept exploiting them; it advocated a 'Ukraine for the Ukrainians,' the expulsion of all foreigners, the creation of an independent, unitary, democratic, pan-Ukrainian republic, and the use of the Ukrainian language always and everywhere; and condemned marriage and fraternization with non-Ukrainians. Mikhnovsky's draft constitution for an independent Ukraine was published in 1905 in its Lviv organ, *Samostiina Ukraïna*. Because of its extremist views the UNP had negligible support. In 1906 an 'autonomist' faction left the 'independentist' UNP and formed the short-lived Ukrainian People's Democratic party. After Mikhnovsky left the UNP in 1907, it became inactive. In 1917, however, its former members established the *Ukrainian Party of Socialists-Independentists.

### Ukrainian People's Republic. See Ukrainian National Republic.

### Ukrainian People's Republican party

(Ukrainska narodno-respublikanska partiia, or UNRP). A political group founded in Ukraine toward the end of 1918. The UNRP followed a conservative line on agrarian and other matters, supported the Entente, and opposed socialism. Its leading members included Ye. Arkhypenko, P. Pylypchuk, and O. Kovalevsky. In April 1919 the UNRP played a key role in V. Oskilko's failed coup in Rivne.

### Ukrainian People's Revolutionary Army. See Polisian Sich.

### Ukrainian Philatelic and Numismatic Society

(UPNS). An international society devoted to the promotion of Ukrainian *philately and numismatics, founded in 1925 as the Society of Ukrainian Philatelists by I. Turyn in Vienna. The society published the Journal *Ukraïns'kyi filatelist* in 1925–39 before it was disbanded.

The society was renewed in the United States after the Second World War (in 1951), under its original name. E. Kotyk served as president and editor of its journal, *Filatelist*. The society prospered for a decade but started to fail financially during the 1960s. In 1971 the society was reorganized under a new president, G. Slusarczuk. The journal of the society again became *Ukrains'kyi filalelist*, and the society itself was renamed the Ukrainian Philatelic and Numismatic Society. A system of public auctions of philatelic materials, held under the supervision of V. Zabijaka, was instituted, and a biweekly newsletter, *Trident Visnyk*, was added to the society's publications. The society also holds UKRAINPEX as an annual exhibition and convention.

### Ukrainian Philatelic Society of Austria

(Ukrainske filatelistychne tovarystvo v Avstrii; German: Ukrainischer Briefmarkensammlerverein in Österreich, or UFTA). The organization, established in Vienna in 1967 by local Ukrainian philatelists, held its first philatelic exhibition that year and has continued to sponsor or to participate in philatelic exhibitions since then. Every UFTA exhibition has been commemorated by an official bilingual postal cancellation of the Austrian post office; there had been over 75 such cancellations by the end of 1988. The society also was responsible for the issue of two Austrian postal stamps (1979 and 1988) with Ukrainian icons. The society issues a journal and is active in the cultural life of Ukrainians in Austria. The group was first led by J. Kostiuk; other heads have included B. Jaminskyj and S. Marzinger-Romanyshyn.

**Ukrainian Philosophical Society** (Ukrainske filosofske tovarystvo). The organization of philosophers and teachers of philosophy in Ukraine, founded in June 1972. Based in Kiev, until late 1989 it was the Ukrainian Branch of the USSR Philosophical Society (est 1971), but it is now an independent organization. The society co-ordinates research, facilitates exchanges of ideas, fosters contacts with philosophers in other countries, and popularizes philosophical ideas. It is divided into thematic sections (dialectical materialism, historical materialism, scientific communism, the history of philosophy, logic, ethics, and esthetics) and, geographically, into locals (Kiev, Lviv, Kharkiv, Donetske, Zaporizhia, Mykolaiv, and Sevastopil). Membership, which is open to lecturers in philosophy and ideology at postsecondary institutions, numbers close to 3,000. Its executive is elected every five years. The presidents have been V. Shynkaruk (1972–86) and M. Popovych (since December 1986).

**Ukrainian Physicians' Association in Czechoslovakia** (Spilka ukrainskykh likariv u Chekhoslovachchyni). Founded in 1922 in Prague, the association aided émigré doctors in their professional endeavors. Its founder and first president was B. *Matiushenko (1922–35); he was followed by Yu. Dobrylovsky (1935–40) and M. Zavalniak. The association was disbanded in September 1940. Its membership was approx 120; in 1923–8 the members were allocated stipends by the Czechoslovakian government. Six issues of *Ukraïns'kyi medychnyi vistnyk* were published (1923–5), and in 1936 a Ukrainian-Latin medical dictionary appeared, compiled by M. Halych and edited by Yu. Matiushenko and V. *Nalyvaiko (re-edited in the United States by P. Dzul in 1969).

The association participated in medical conventions in Lviv and Prague, published scholarly articles in *Likars'kyi vistnyk* (Lviv), and edited the medical reference book 'Knyha zdorov'ia' (Book of Health), which went unpublished because of the Second World War. Members of the association participated in the founding and activities of the Ukrainian Scientific Society in Prague and played an active civic role in numerous Ukrainian organizations in Czechoslovakia (eg, in collecting funds for the construction of a Ukrainian hospital in Lviv). They took part in organizing conventions of the All-Slavic Medical League in Belgrade, Warsaw, and Prague. They were also active in non-Ukrainian organizations, in attending conventions, and in publishing in Czechoslovakian and German medical journals. In 1990 the association was revived (headed by Ya. Babiuk) as a member of the World Federation of Ukrainian Medical Associations.

P. Pundii

**Ukrainian Physicians' Society** (Ukrainske likarske tovarystvo, or ULT). A professional association of Ukrainian physicians in Western Ukraine, founded in October 1910 in Lviv by 63 members. Its aims were to promote the interests of Ukrainian physicians, raise their qualifications, and improve health care in Ukraine. Its precursor was the Medical Commission of the Shevchenko Scientific Society (est 1898). To raise the level of popular knowledge about sanitation and health the ULT published the monthly *Zdorovlie* (1912–24). With the Shevchenko Scientific Soci-

*Narodne zdorov'ia,* the paper of the recently revived Ukrainian Physicians' Society in Lviv

ety it published the scientific journal *Likars'kyi vistnyk* (1920–39). It was also instrumental in setting up the *Ukrainian Hygienic Society (1929) and worked closely with it. The membership of the ULT was 205 in 1925, and 289 in 1937 (268 in Galicia). The association held four scientific conferences (1927, 1931, 1933, and 1935). With the financial support of Metropolitan A. Sheptytsky it built the Ukrainian Hospital in Lviv (1935). The presidents of the ULT were Ye. *Ozarkevych, T. Burachynsky, and M. *Panchyshyn, and the membership included I. Horbachevsky, I. Kurivets, M. Muzyka, S. Parfanovych-Volchuk, and R. Osinchuk. The association was dissolved with the Soviet occupation of Galicia in 1939. It was revived in Lviv in April 1990; its new president is O. Kitsera.

**Ukrainian Planning Design-and-Technology Institute of Local Industry** (Ukrainskyi proektnyi konstruktorsko-tekhnolohichnyi instytut mistsevoi promyslovosti). A research institute under the jurisdiction of Ukraine's Ministry of Local Industry, established in Kiev in 1929 as a branch of the All-Union Scientific Research Institute of the Peat Industry. In 1933 it was reorganized into the Ukrainian Scientific Research Institute of Peat, and in 1978 it acquired its present name. The institute has 24 departments and laboratories, an experimental plant, and branches in Donetske and Dnipropetrovske. Its research is directed at the production of consumer and industrial goods made of metal, plastic, local raw materials, and industrial wastes; documentation for the manufacture of new products; and the technological improvement of local industry enterprises.

**Ukrainian Polytechnical Correspondence Institute** (Ukrainskyi zaochnyi politekhnichnyi instytut im. I. Sokolova). A higher educational institution established in Kharkiv in 1958, until 1992 under the Ministry of Higher and Secondary Special Education of the Ukrainian SSR. It has (1983) faculties for machine building, chemical technology, energy, electromechanics, and mechanical technology and four general technical faculties (in Kharkiv, Artemivske, Kostiantynivka, and Slovianske). It offers a graduate program. Enrollment in 1983 reached 13,000.

**Ukrainian Press** (Ukrainska drukarnia; French: Imprimerie ukrainienne; Russian: Ukrainskaia tipografiia). An imprimery in Geneva, founded in 1876 by M. *Drahomanov. From 1878 to 1918 its manager was A. *Lia-khotsky. Until approx 1890 it was called the Russian (Imprimerie russe), Rabotnik, Hromada, and Volnoe Slovo (La Parole libre) Press. Using funds provided by the *Hromada of Kiev, Drahomanov printed materials that were smuggled into Russian-ruled Ukraine after the Ems Ukase prohibited publishing in Ukrainian. In 1882 the Hromada withdrew its support, and left the press in difficult circumstances. Nonetheless, it continued operating. By the time Drahomanov moved to Sofia in 1889, it had printed his miscellany/journal *Hromada (1878–82) and nearly 70 books and brochures in Russian and Ukrainian, many of them by Drahomanov, but also by authors such as S. Podolynsky, T. Shevchenko, F. Volkhovsky, M. Pavlyk, and P. Myrny. Thereafter Liakhotsky printed other booklets by Drahomanov; editions of Shevchenko's banned poems (1890) and P. Kulish's duma collection (1893); and booklets, leaflets, and periodicals for various Russian and Ukrainian revolutionary groups, including Lesia Ukrainka and I. Steshenko's small Ukrainian Social Democracy group in Kiev and, during the First World War, the Union for the Liberation of Ukraine and L. Yurkevych (his paper *Borot'ba* [1916] and his brochure on the Russian Social Democrats and the national question [1917]). By the time the press ceased functioning in 1917, it had issued over 110 books and brochures. E. Batchinsky's detailed account of the press was published in *Naukovyi zbirnyk* II (1953) of the Ukrainian Academy of Arts and Sciences.

Easter at the Ukrainian Press Service in Berlin in 1934. Sitting, from left: Mykhailo Seleshko, Ivan Gabrusevych, Oleksander Vlasiv; standing: Yuliian Hoshovsky, Orest Semchyshyn, Mykola Mytliuk, Sydir Chuchman, Pavlo Turula, Orest Chemerynsky, Volodymyr Stakhiv

**Ukrainian Press Service** (Ukrainska presova sluzhba; German: Ukrainischer Pressedienst). An information bureau established in 1931 in Berlin by the OUN to inform the Western world, particularly the German government and public, about the Ukrainian question and the Ukrainian national movement. The director was R. *Jary. It published bulletins in Ukrainian (for the Western Ukrainian and émigré press) and German under the editorship of M. Seleshko (1931–4) and V. Stakhiv (1937–41). Editors at the service included A. Lutsiv, O. Chemerynsky, B. Kordiuk, and M. Prokop. The service maintained contacts with similar bureaus and offices maintained by the OUN in New York, Geneva, London, Paris, Rome, Prague, Madrid, Brussels, Vienna, and Kaunas (see *Press and information bureaus abroad). In 1938 it was renamed the Nationalist

Press Service, and after the outbreak of the Second World War it was moved to Rome, where it was directed by Ye. Onatsky until 1943.

**Ukrainian Printing Institute** (Ukrainskyi polihrafichnyi instytut im. I. Fedorova). The only postsecondary school in Ukraine for the training of skilled workers and managers in the publishing and printing industries. It was established in Kharkiv in 1930 out of faculties of the Kiev and Kharkiv art institutes. Since 1945 it has been located in Lviv, and until 1992 it was under the jurisdiction of the Ukrainian SSR Ministry of Higher and Secondary Special Education. The institute has a teaching staff of approx 250, in 5 faculties and 21 departments. Approx 4,000 students are enrolled in its three- and five-year programs each year. The institute also offers graduate and correspondence programs, upgrading courses, and, in Kiev, a six-year evening program. Over 13,000 specialists have graduated from the institute.

**Ukrainian Publishers Limited** (Ukrainska vydavnycha spilka, or UPL). The largest Ukrainian publishing house in Great Britain, founded in May 1949 by members of the émigré OUN (Bandera faction). In 1951 H. Markiv was elected chairman of its board of directors, and V. Oleskiv became UPL secretary. In 1951 UPL began publishing the monthly journal *Vyzvol'nyi shliakh. It has set and printed other periodicals, such as the weekly paper *Ukraïns'ka dumka, the quarterly journal *Ukrainian Review, the Catholic organ Nasha tserkva, the Orthodox organ Vidomosti UAPTs, the children's magazine Iuni druzi, the Ukrainian Youth Association's journal Avangard, and the Ukrainian Former Combatants' organ Surmach. UPL has also published dozens of books of political and belletristic writing by authors such as B. Antonenko-Davydovych, B. Bora, D. Dontsov, S. Karavansky, S. Mechnyk, P. Mirchuk, L. Orlyhora, V. Sichynsky, A. Svydnytsky, O. Voropai, and O. Zvychaina. Directors of UPL have included V. Yavorsky, R. Borkovsky, I. Ratushny, V. Vasylenko, and Ya. Deremenda.

**Ukrainian Publishing Institute** (Ukrainskyi vydavnychyi instytut). A publishing house of scholarly and popular-educational materials in Lviv from 1936 to the outbreak of the Second World War in 1939. Directed by M. Mykytchuk, V. Vytvytsky, and I. Fediv, it published V. Kubijovyč's atlas (1937) and geography (1938) of Ukraine and adjacent lands, a reference book for choir conductors, a collection of articles about Transcarpathia, and a series of educational titles.

***Ukrainian Quarterly, The.*** An English-language quarterly journal published since 1944 in New York by the Ukrainian Congress Committee of America (UCCA). It contains articles on Ukrainian history, culture, and political and economic developments and has been especially concerned with the national question in the USSR and with publicizing Ukrainian opposition to the Soviet regime, national-liberation struggles in Asia, and anticommunist movements throughout the world. After the Second World War the journal took up the cause of the *displaced persons and lobbied to have them admitted to the United States. Many prominent Ukrainian-American émigré and non-Ukrainian scholars have contributed to *The Ukrainian*

*The Ukrainian Quarterly*

*Quarterly*. Its chief editors have been N.(M.) Chubaty, W. Dushnyck (1957–84), and N. Bohatiuk (1985–). Others who have served on the editorial board include A. Drahan, M. Stakhiv, P. Stercho, R. Smal-Stotsky, S. Shumeyko, and Ye. Zyblikevych. Cumulative indexes to the journal for the years 1944–64 and 1965–70 have been published.

**Ukrainian Radical party** (Ukrainska radykalna partiia, or URP; originally the Ruthenian-Ukrainian Radical party, and from 1926 the Ukrainian Socialist Radical party, or USRP). A Western Ukrainian political party, formally established at a congress in Lviv on 4 October 1890. The URP could trace its descent from a movement of radical Galician young people influenced by M. *Drahomanov in the late 1870s. The founding members of the URP included V. *Budzynovsky, S. Danylovych, I. *Franko, Ye. *Levytsky, M. *Pavlyk, and K. *Trylovsky. Drahomanov considered the formation of a party premature but reconciled himself to the accomplished fact. He contributed regularly to the Radical press and helped to shape the party's ideology. His personal involvement was important in holding the young party together, and his death in 1895 accelerated a division into factions which culminated in party splits at the end of the 1890s.

The URP was the first modern Ukrainian political party with a defined program, a mass following, and a registered membership. The party program advocated socialism and a series of political reforms aimed at the extension of democracy and the improvement of the position of Ukrainians in Galicia. The URP called for the secularization of Ukrainian social and cultural life and opposed the influence of the Greek Catholic church and its clergy in national affairs. The party aimed its activities at peasants and, to a lesser extent, workers; it convened public assemblies (*vicha*) in small towns and villages, founded reading clubs (*chytalni*) and co-operatives, campaigned in elections, organized women's groups, and trained activists from among the peasantry. The Radicals were in opposition to the government as well as to the mainstream Ukrainian populists (*narodovtsi*); they were particularly successful in their opposition to the *New Era, the short-lived rapprochement between the populists and the Polish establishment in Galicia. In 1895 three Radical deputies were elected to the Galician Diet, and in 1897 two were elected to the all-Austrian parliament. At their 1895 congress in Lviv the Radicals passed a resolution in favor

of Ukrainian independence; the resolution was proposed by Yu. *Bachynsky, but the idea of independence had been championed in the party even earlier by Budzynovsky. At its 1897 congress the URP endorsed strikes for agricultural workers, and such strikes became an important feature of Galician life over the next decade. The Radicals also organized mass assemblies and demonstrations to demand universal suffrage.

From the mid-1890s there were three competing groups in the URP: the orthodox Radicals, who remained faithful to the ideas of Drahomanov; younger Radicals, who were influenced by Marxism and hoped that the URP would unite with Europe's social democratic parties in the Second International; and other Radicals who were becoming increasingly uncomfortable with the party's socialist program and more and more interested in purely national concerns. In 1899 the latter two groups left the URP. Yu. Bachynsky, M. Hankevych, S. Vityk, R. Yarosevych, and others founded the *Ukrainian Social Democratic party (USDP); Budzynovsky, Franko, Levytsky, V. Okhrymovych, T. Okunevsky, and others, together with the majority of the populists, founded the *National Democratic party (NDP). Thereafter the URP, which was now definitively a peasant party, was the second-largest Ukrainian political party in Galicia, after the NDP. In 1911 five Radicals were elected to the parliament in Vienna, and in 1913 six were elected to the Galician Diet. In the early 20th century, largely through the efforts of Trylovsky, the Radicals established the sporting society *Sich and, later (1913), the paramilitary Ukrainian Sich Riflemen.

With the proclamation of the *Western Ukrainian National Republic (ZUNR) the URP joined the *Ukrainian National Rada. The Radical L. Bachynsky was vice-president of the Rada, and the Radicals D. Vitovsky and I. Makukh served in the ZUNR's State Secretariat as military secretary and interior secretary respectively. After the collapse of the Ukrainian state the URP joined the *Interparty Council.

At its first congress after the war (1 April 1923) and at subsequent congresses the URP reworked its program. It defined itself as the party of the working masses of Ukraine; it aimed to implement a socialist program, including the socialization of the means of production, in an independent Ukrainian republic in which the working masses themselves would hold power. The URP distanced itself from the USDP, which in 1923 began to follow a pro-communist line. At its 1925 congress the URP passed a resolution against collaborating with Ukrainian 'bourgeois parties' and simultaneously condemned the colonialist policies of the Bolsheviks in Ukraine and endorsed the slogan All Land to the Peasants without Redemption. In 1926, after the Ukrainian Socialist Revolutionaries of Volhynia joined it, the party changed its name to the Ukrainian Socialist Radical party. In April 1931 the USRP joined the Second Socialist International. Together with other Ukrainian parties the URP boycotted the 1922 elections to the Polish Sejm. In 1928, 11 USRP candidates were elected to the Sejm, and 3 to the Senate. In the 1931 elections the USRP ran jointly with the *Ukrainian National Democratic Alliance and won one-fourth of the coalition's seats; the USRP's deputies formed separate clubs in the Sejm and Senate. The USRP boycotted subsequent elections because they regarded them as undemocratic. In 1934 the USRP had 20,000 members.

The leaders of the party were Franko, Pavlyk, M. Lahodynsky, L. Bachynsky, and Makukh. Other prominent Radical activists included I. Blazhkevych, K. Kobersky, D. Ladyka, V. Lysy, M. Matchak, O. Nazaruk (until 1922–3), O. Pavliv-Bilozersky, I. Popovych, M. Stakhiv, Trylovsky, and S. Zhuk. Some prominent writers were also associated with the URP: D. Lukiianovych, O. Makovei, L. Martovych, and V. Stefanyk.

The URP had its own youth and women's organizations, the *Union of Ukrainian Progressive Youth (Kameniari) and the *Union of Ukrainian Working Women (the Women's Hromada). The publishing house and people's university *Samoosvita (1930–9) was under the party's influence. The URP's official publishing house was Hromada (1922–39); its official organs included *Narod (1890–5) *Khliborob (1891–5), and *Hromads'kyi holos (1895–1939).

The USRP renewed its activities in the postwar emigration (1946) and took part in the formation of the Ukrainian National Council (1948). In 1950 the USRP joined with the USDP and other socialist parties to form the Ukrainian Socialist party. The radical leaders in the emigration included Lysy and Stakhiv.

BIBLIOGRAPHY
Badeni, J. *Radykali ruscy* (Cracow 1896)
Levyns'kyi, V. *Narys rozvytku ukraïns'koho robitnychoho rukhu v Halychyni* (Kiev 1914)
Vozniak, M. 'Ivan Franko v dobi radykalizmu,' *Ukraïna*, 1926, no. 6
Makukh, I. *Na narodnii sluzhbi* (Detroit 1958)
Himka, J.-P. *Socialism in Galicia: The Emergence of Polish Social Democracy and Ukrainian Radicalism (1860–1890)* (Cambridge, Mass 1983)

J.-P. Himka, I.L. Rudnytsky

**Ukrainian Radical party** (Ukrainska radykalna partiia, or URP). A numerically small, clandestine organization formed in Kiev in the spring of 1905 by a younger left-liberal group that had quit the *Ukrainian Democratic party (UDP). Most of its members were writers (eg, B. Hrinchenko, Modest Levytsky, F. Matushevsky, S. Yefremov). The URP concentrated on publishing antitsarist and socialist propaganda, and in 1905 it issued its platform and 15 other brochures by authors such as B. and M. Hrinchenko, Matushevsky, Yefremov, M. Drahomanov, A. Munko, and V. Durdukivsky, which were printed in Austrian-ruled Lviv and smuggled into Russian-ruled Ukraine. In its literature the URP advocated Ukrainian autonomy (and independence as a maximum goal), democratic rights, the abolition of private land ownership, the nationalization of industries, and the creation of industrial and agricultural co-operatives. Because it failed to recruit new members, the URP merged with the UDP in December 1905 to form the *Ukrainian Democratic Radical party.

**Ukrainian Red Cross** (Ukrainskyi chervonyi khrest). A voluntary nongovernmental organization for providing aid to victims of war or natural disasters and various medical services to the population. The Ukrainian Red Cross society was organized in April 1918 out of already-existing local branches of the Russian Red Cross society on Ukrainian territories. It was formed at the initiative of the All-Ukrainian Congress of Physicians in Kiev; its founders included Ye. Lukasevych and B. Matiushenko. The first president of the society was A. Viazlov; he was followed in 1919 by A. Nikovsky and in the 1920s by I. Kholodny.

The Ukrainian Red Cross established ties with the International Committee of the Red Cross in Geneva through its representative, E. Batchinsky, and sent missions to Germany (headed by I. Kholodny), Austria (A. Okopenko), Yugoslavia (D. Doroshenko), Poland (L. Starytska-Cherniakhivska and S. Rusova), and Italy. These missions obtained sorely needed medical supplies for the population in Ukraine and provided relief to Ukrainian internees in foreign countries. With the loss of Ukraine's independence the Ukrainian Red Cross continued to operate abroad but lost the right to belong to the International Red Cross. B. Matiushenko ran the foreign office of the Ukrainian Red Cross in Paris (1919–21). In 1931 the *Ukrainian Gold Cross was set up in the United States to furnish aid to Ukrainians, particularly political prisoners who were suffering under Polish or Soviet rule.

In 1941 another Ukrainian Red Cross organization was established, surreptitiously, in Lviv to provide relief and medical care to released Soviet political prisoners, prisoners of war, and displaced people. Its president was O. Kurchaba and then T. *Vorobets. Similar organizations, which co-operated with the office in Lviv, were formed later in Kiev (headed by F. Bohatyrchuk), Rivne (M. Kornyliv and Kh. Kononenko), and other cities. In 1942 the German authorities dissolved the Red Cross in Lviv, but its functions in the Generalgouvernement were assumed by the Department of Social Services of the Ukrainian Central Committee. An underground health service of the Ukrainian Insurgent Army, called the Ukrainian Red Cross, operated in 1943–9. It was headed for several years by K. *Zarytska.

In Germany and Austria several attempts were made to revive the Ukrainian Red Cross. A conference in Munich on 10 October 1945 elected the officers of a Red Cross organization (president, B. Andriievsky, and executive chairman, Vorobets), but under Soviet pressure the American occupational authorities prohibited the use of the name Red Cross (see *Ukrainian Medical Charitable Service).

Red Cross societies continued to operate in Soviet Ukraine as independent humanitarian organizations. Eventually they were brought under the People's Commissariat of Public Health and absorbed by the unitary Soviet Red Cross system. The Red Cross Society of the Ukrainian SSR had republican, oblast, and raion offices representing nearly 70,000 (1983) primary organizations with 24 million members. Like all so-called nongovernmental organizations in the USSR it was under the complete control of the state and the Party.

**Ukrainian regiments in 1812.** Temporary military formations raised in Ukraine during *Napoleon Bonaparte's Russian campaign. The governor-general of Left-Bank Ukraine, Prince Ya. Lobanov-Rostovsky, permitted a *levy en masse and the formation of regular Cossack regiments and promised to keep the Cossack units after the war as a permanent Cossack army. Influential Ukrainian leaders, such as D. Troshchynsky and V. Kapnist, persuaded the governor-general to give the regiments a Ukrainian character. The organizational scheme of the Cossack regiments was drafted by Senator M. Myklashevsky. In addition to Cossacks serfs volunteered for service to escape from their oppressive condition. Most of the regiments raised by the levy en masse came from the Poltava and Chernihiv regions. Cossack regiments, under the command of Count de Witte, also came from Kiev and Podilia gubernias. Among the organizers of the Cossack regiments in Poltava gubernia was I. *Kotliarevsky. The total number of troops, peasant and Cossack, was almost 75,000. They were supported (provided with horses, arms, uniforms, and supplies) mostly by the local population. The Russian command did not trust the Ukrainian regiments; hence, it did not use them at the front in Russia, but gave them an auxiliary role.

In 1813–15 some Cossack regiments took part in the war against Napoleon in central and western Europe and in the occupation of Paris. During that time they discovered Western ideas of individual liberty and human rights. After the war some of the regiments were converted into regular Russian units. The rest were demobilized, and returned to the peasant estate.

**Ukrainian Regional Committee** (Ukrainskyi kraiovyi komitet, or UKK). A body set up in Lviv in 1941 by the German authorities to represent the Ukrainian community, and the only legal Ukrainian civic institution in Galicia at the time. Its statute was similar to that of the *Ukrainian Central Committee (UTsK) in Cracow. The Germans approved the general secretary of the Ukrainian National Council, K. *Pankivsky, as chairman of the UKK. The vice-chairman and executive director was M. Dobriansky-Demkovych.

The departments of the UKK were organized in September–December 1941 and were headed by M. Rosliak and M. Tsenko (organizational), Yu. Savchak and V. Pushkar (financial), V. Lysy and M. Voloshyn (legal), Rev V. Lytsyniak and P. Sanotsky (social services), M. Bachynsky and then M. Mazuryk and P. Koniukh (economic), Z. Zeleny (educational), V. Zubrytsky (cultural), S. Levytsky (youth affairs), M. Biliak and M. Zaiachkivska (women's affairs), T. Vorobets and I. Cherkavsky (prisoners' aid), I. Tkach (labor), and D. Kvasnytsia (auditing). Ukrainian okruha committees (UOKs), which were comparable to the Ukrainian relief committees (UDKs) operating under the UTsK, were set up in the administrative areas introduced by the Germans, and trustees were installed in the villages.

The UKK assumed the tasks of furnishing relief to war victims, defending the Ukrainian population from arbitrary treatment by the occupational power, improving or at least tempering the difficult economic circumstances, widening the scope of its activities to support as many facets of national life as possible, and establishing as much influence as possible over government agencies which had an impact on the well-being of the population.

From the outset the UKK worked closely with the UTsK. Its activities ceased in March 1942, when the Generalgouvernement administration decreed that the UTsK in Cracow would assume its functions. The similarity of their structures facilitated the merging of the two bodies, and Pankivsky was subsequently made deputy head of the UTsK.

Besides its daily work in the fall of 1941 the UKK assisted in the return of Soviet officials to eastern Ukraine and in the release of Soviet POWs from Galicia; organized relief for inmates of POW camps; set up public, factory, and school cafeterias; and promoted the establishment of gymnasiums and professional schools.

M. Dobriansky

**Ukrainian Relief Committee in Belgium** (Ukrainskyi dopomohovyi komitet u Belhii). An organization founded in Brussels in 1945 to assist Ukrainian *displaced persons arriving in Belgium from Germany. From 1947 to 1949 the committee had 26 branches with approx 3,000 members; after large-scale emigration to North America, 10 branches with 380 members (1981) remained. The committee has published *Visti* (News) since 1945, initially as a semimonthly, later as a monthly, and since 1976 as a bimonthly. The presidents of the committee have been M. Hrab (1945–6), K. Mulkevych (1947), A. Kishka (1948), M. Dzoba (1949–51), V. Popovych (1952–86), and O. Koval (since 1986).

**Ukrainian Relief Committee in Rome** (Ukrainskyi dopomohovyi komitet u Rymi). A body formed by Bishop I. Buchko at the end of the Second World War (1945) to help Ukrainian refugees, POWs, and students in Italy. Headed by Bishop I. Buchko, it included Rev I. Prashko, Yu. Mylianyk, M. Vavryk, and P. Polishchuk (secretary). The Vatican provided funds for material aid in the form of clothes, food, and spending money. The committee helped the members of the *Division Galizien interned at Rimini by establishing contacts for them with the Vatican and with Italian and international circles, by providing postal services, and by supplying camp schools with textbooks and equipment. The committee ceased functioning in 1970. Thenceforth, the apostolic mission for Ukrainians in Western Europe, under Archbishop I. Buchko and Rev M. Marusyn (secretary), has fulfilled whatever charitable responsibilities have remained.

**Ukrainian Republican Council of Trade Unions** (Ukrainska respublikanska rada profesiinykh spilok, or URRPS). The central body co-ordinating and directing trade-union activities in Soviet Ukraine. Before the Second World War that function was fulfilled by the *All-Ukrainian Council of Trade Unions, which was dissolved in 1937 in an attempt to centralize all power in the All-Union Central Council of Trade Unions (VTsSPS) in Moscow. The first URRPS was elected in 1948 by a conference of Ukrainian trade unions in Kiev. The council was elected at trade-union congresses held every five years. Although formally it was an autonomous body, in fact it came under the VTsSPS and made few decisions itself. It was also closely tied to the Party, and helped implement Party economic and social policies. The presidents of the council were A. Kolybanov (1948–51), K. Moskalets (1951–60), M. Synytsia (1961–5), V. Klynenko (1966–71), V. Solohub (1971–90), and O. Kovalevsky.

**Ukrainian Republican Kapelle** (Ukrainska respublikanska kapelia). A state choir founded in Kiev in early 1919 by K. *Stetsenko and O. *Koshyts. The group had been commissioned by S. Petliura and charged with the task of propagating Ukrainian musical culture abroad. The kapelle, directed and conducted by O. Koshyts, consisted of 80 members in a mixed choir. In February 1919 it embarked on a major European concert tour through Czechoslovakia, Austria, Switzerland, France, Belgium, Holland, England, and Germany. When disbanded in Berlin in July 1920, its members formed three separate choirs. The core group, led by O. Koshyts, was reconstituted in Warsaw as the Ukrainian National Choir. Late in 1921 it

The Ukrainian Republican Kapelle in 1919. Sitting, 5th through 8th from left: Hryhorii Tuchapsky, Oleksander Koshyts, Platonida Shchurovska, Kyrylo Stetsenko

began a tour of Spain, France, Belgium, Germany, and the United States, where from October 1922 to March 1923 it performed in more than 100 concerts. A tour of Brazil, Argentina, Uruguay, and Cuba followed. In 1924 the Ukrainian National Choir disbanded, after having staged approx 900 concerts.

The kapelle and its successors had a significant impact in raising in the West an awareness of Ukrainian musical life. They also provided a training ground for many individuals who were later active in Ukrainian civic cultural societies. The most popular pieces in the repertoire of the kapelle were works by M. Leontovych (particularly 'Shchedryk,' later known as the 'Carol of the Bells'), M. Lysenko, K. Stetsenko, and O. Koshyts.

BIBLIOGRAPHY
Nejedlý, Z. *Ukrajinská republikanská kapela* (Prague 1921)
*Ukraïns'ka pisnia za kordonom* (Paris 1929)
Pelens'kyi, O. *Ukraïns'ka pisnia v sviti* (Lviv 1933)
Koshyts', O. *Z pisneiu cherez svit*, 3 parts (Winnipeg 1952, 1970, 1974)

W. Wytwycky

**Ukrainian Republican Regiment** (Pershyi ukrainskyi respublikanskyi polk). An infantry regiment organized in the fall of 1917 by Col P. Bolbochan. It consisted of volunteers from the Fifth Corps of the Russian army. In January 1918 it suffered heavy casualties defending Kiev from the invading Bolshevik army. Its surviving units re-formed as the Second Battalion of the Separate Zaporozhian Detachment and later expanded into the Second Infantry Regiment of the Zaporozhian Corps.

**Ukrainian research and documentation centers.** Centers established to collect historical materials of various forms, for the purpose of conducting directed research. A number of such centers have been founded in the West and financed by donations from the Ukrainian community. The *Lypynsky East European Research Institute was established in Philadelphia in 1963 to preserve the archives of V. Lypynsky and P. Skoropadsky and to publish materials from them. The Ukrainian Famine Re-

search Centre, founded in 1982 in Toronto to produce the documentary film *Harvest of Despair* in 1985, was reorganized in 1987 as the *Ukrainian Canadian Research and Documentation Centre. It is collecting materials on Ukrainian participation in the Second World War and on the effects of the war on Ukraine and its people and plans eventually to make a film on the subject. In 1987 the Ukrainian Research and Documentation Center was set up at the *Ukrainian Institute of America in New York to collect archives and documents on Ukrainians in the 20th century and, particularly, on the Soviet collectivization and 1932–3 man-made famine in Soviet Ukraine, the two world wars, the dissident movement, and diaspora institutions. The collection is to serve as the basis for research and documentary publications. Its director is T. Hunchak.

**Ukrainian Research and Information Institute** (Ukrainskyi publitsystychno-naukovyi instytut, or UPNI). An information organization founded in the United States on the initiative of M. *Shlemkevych in 1961 to inform the Ukrainian and the general public about current Ukrainian issues and to correct misinformation about Ukraine and Ukrainians. The first branch of the institute was formed in Chicago, where its head office, under T. Lapychak, was set up. Ten other branches were organized, in cities such as New York, Detroit, Newark, Trenton, and Winnipeg. It also had individual members in Europe and Australia. Its main publications were in English and included S. Goldelman's *Jewish National Autonomy in Ukraine, 1917–1920* (1968). It also published a series of brochures in Ukrainian and English. In 1976 the institute was dissolved.

**Ukrainian Research Station for Beekeeping** (Ukrainska doslidna stantsiia bdzhilnytstva). In 1920 the Kharkiv Oblast Beekeeping Research Station was organized and in 1924 it was relocated to the village of Artemivka, near Merefa, and renamed the Ukrainian Beekeeping Research Station, a research institution in the system of the Ukrainian SSR Ministry of Agriculture. In 1959 the station was transferred again, to the village of Cherniatyn, in Zhmerynka raion, Vinnytsia oblast. It consists of a biochemical laboratory and three research divisions – bee breeding and maintenance, procurement of food and pollination of agricultural plants, and research on bee diseases.

**Ukrainian Research Station for Floral and Ornamental Plants** (Ukrainska doslidna stantsiia kvitkovykh i dekoratyvnykh roslyn). A Kiev-based research institution, organized in 1946 on the basis of the former Kiev Floriculture Trust and placed under the jurisdiction of the Ukrainian Ministry of Public Economy. At present it has support bases in Odessa, Mykolaiv, Lviv, Kharkiv, Donetske, Dnipropetrovske, and Sevastopil. Its scientific program extends over the following areas: agricultural engineering and agricultural chemistry, selection and seed production, covered-ground floriculture, dendrology, plant protection, and the organization and construction of municipal and rural greenbelts. The station operates an ornamental plant nursery, an agricultural laboratory, a meteorological station, and a technical workshop.

**Ukrainian Research Station for Hop Growing** (Ukrainska doslidna stantsiia khmeliarstva). Organized in 1924 on the basis of the Experimental Hops Plantation of the Ukrainian SSR People's Commissariat of Agriculture, the station is now a research institution in the system of the Ukrainian Ministry of Agriculture, located in the village of Smykivka, Korostyshiv raion, Zhytomyr oblast. The station consists of three divisions (selection and seed production, agricultural engineering, and mechanization), four laboratories (plant physiology and agricultural chemistry, technology, entomology, and phytopathology), an economic and organizational group, a library, a museum, and a meteorological station. New, highly productive hops have been developed there, including Clone 18, Zhytomyr 5, and Zhytomyr 8. The research results are published in professional journals.

**Ukrainian Research Station for Orcharding.** See Mliiv Orcharding Research Station.

**Ukrainian Research Station for Silk Production** (Ukrainska doslidna stantsiia shovkivnytstva). A research facility under the Ministry of Agriculture of Ukraine, located in Merefa, Kharkiv oblast. It was established in 1933. The station has developed several new varieties of silkworms (Ukrainian 1, 9, and 107 and Kharkiv 3) and new techniques for producing natural silk for the *silk industry. It has departments of selection, agrotechnology, cultivation, diseases, economics, and mechanization, as well as chemical-technological and physiology laboratories.

**Ukrainian Research Station for Tobacco** (Ukrainska doslidna stantsiia po tiutiunu i makhortsi). Originally established in 1890 in Lokhvytsia (now in Poltava oblast), the institute was renamed in 1959 and moved to Pryluka (Chernihiv oblast). A component of the Ukrainian Ministry of Agriculture, it consists of a laboratory, a tobacco support base in Nova Ushytsia (Khmelnytskyi oblast), and departments of selection, agricultural engineering, and plant protection.

**Ukrainian Resource and Development Centre** (Ukrainskyi tsentr zasobiv i rozvytku, or URDC). Estab-

lished in 1987 at Grant MacEwan Community College in Edmonton, the URDC is the first Ukrainian center located in a Canadian community college. It deals with major provincial, national, and international projects in the fields of business, the arts, audiovisual communications, and community development. Members of its staff have been involved in projects with Ukrainian choirs and dance groups across Canada, with farmers in Ukraine, with an international network of Ukrainian businessmen, with the *Encyclopedia of Ukraine*, and with the Ukrainian Canadian Congress. It operates on funds derived from endowments established by the Ukrainian community and the governments of Canada and Alberta. R. Petryshyn has been the URDC's first director.

***Ukrainian Review, The.*** An English-language quarterly journal of politics, history, and culture, published since 1954 in London by the *Association of Ukrainians in Great Britain; since the mid-1960s the *Canadian League for Ukraine's Liberation and the *Organization for the Defense of Four Freedoms for Ukraine have been copublishers. The journal supports the OUN (Bandera faction) and the Anti-Bolshevik Bloc of Nations. It has covered political developments in the USSR, with particular focus on the national question and the plight of the non-Russian minorities; devoted considerable attention to the dissident and democratic movements in Ukraine; and published reviews of Soviet and non-Soviet books. The first editors were V. Derzhavyn and V. Oreletsky. Since 1965 S. Stetsko has served as chief editor and head of an editorial board that has had such members as V. Bohdaniuk, R. Yendyk, N. Chirovsky, L. Shankovsky, A. Bedrii, O. Romanyshyn, M. Savchuk, and M. Sosnovsky.

**Ukrainian Revolutionary Democratic party** (Ukrainska revoliutsiino-demokratychna partiia, or URDP). An émigré political party dedicated to the overthrow of the Soviet regime and the building of an independent and democratic Ukrainian state. It was founded officially in Regensburg, Germany, in August 1947 by émigrés from Soviet Ukraine who embraced the ideals of the Ukrainian national renaissance of the 1920s and by former members of the OUN who supported I. *Mitrynga. Charter members included I. Bahriany, H. Kostiuk, I. Maistrenko, B. Levytsky, S. Pidhainy, and R. Paladiichuk. Its first president was H. *Kostiuk, who in 1948 left the party with I. Maistrenko, B. Levytsky, R. Paladiichuk, and others to form the Left URDP. This faction published the monthly *Vpered* and, eventually, dissolved. I. *Bahriany was president for the longest term (1948–63); he was followed by F. Haienko (1963–7), M. Stepanenko (1967), V. Hrysko (1967–75), and M. Voskobiinyk (since 1975). Some of the leading members of the party were V. Bender, P. Volyniak, V. Holubnychy, Yu. Lavrinenko, I. Dubylko, O. Konoval, I. Korniichuk, A. Lysy, F. Pigido, and A. Riabyshenko. Stepanenko led a group that established a separate Right URDP in 1979. The URDP helped found the *Ukrainian National Council, in which it participated until 1968, and the *Ukrainian Democratic Alliance. Its members played key roles in the founding of the Ukrainian Association of Victims of Russian Communist Terror, the Symon Petliura Legion, and the Ukrainian Democratic Youth Association. Today the party has national offices in the United States, Canada, Britain, Belgium, Germany,

Australia, and Argentina, which sponsor or support a variety of publications. The official voice of the URDP is the irregular magazine *Nashi pozytsiï* (1948–). In 1990 the URDP changed its name to Ukrainian Democratic Republican party.

**Ukrainian Scholarly Association** (Ukrainska naukova asotsiiatsiia). A learned society founded in Prague in late 1932, at a time when the activity of Ukrainian émigré scholars and scholarly institutions in Bohemia was in a period of marked decline. Organized on the initiative of professors at the Ukrainian Husbandry Academy, the society aimed to unify all Ukrainian scholars in Bohemia. Its approx 50 members were headed by V. Ivanytsky and K. Matsiievych (from 1936). The association organized over 70 lectures in the years 1933–6.

**Ukrainian school in Polish literature.** The term was first used in 1837 by the Polish writer A. Tyszyński and came to be used widely to denote a group of Polish writers and poets of the Romantic era, who used Ukrainian historical subjects, Ukrainian folklore, customs, and landscapes in their work. The group included T. Padura, A. Malczewski, S. Goszczyński, J.B. Zaleski, J. Słowacki, W. Pol (geographic and ethnographic descriptions of the Ukrainian lands as a part of the Commonwealth in 'Pieśń o ziemi naszej' [Song about Our Land]), M. Czajkowski, M. Grabowski, and J. Korzeniowski. The traditions of the Ukrainian school have remained in the works of many Polish writers to this day, such as S. Vincenz, J. Jędrzejewicz, and J. Łobodowski.

**Ukrainian Scientific and Technical Society.** See Scientific-technical societies.

**Ukrainian Scientific Institute in Berlin** (Ukrainskyi naukovyi instytut u Berlini). An émigré institution established in Berlin in November 1926 on the initiative of Hetman P. Skoropadsky and with the support of Gen W. Groener. The institute's mandate was to represent Ukrainian scholarship, develop Ukrainian studies, disseminate information about Ukraine in Germany, study Ukraine's relations with Western countries (particularly Germany), and aid Ukrainian students and young scholars in Germany by granting scholarships and fellowships and running a student residence in Berlin. It also established a library, a Ukrainian-press archive, and an archive of foreign press clippings about Ukraine. Until 1931 the institute was funded by the Verein zur Förderung der ukrainischen Kultur und Wissenschaften. Its director was the historian D. Doroshenko. The chairman of its board of trustees was Groener, and the vice-chairman was O. Skoropys-Yoltukhovsky. Full members of the institute included Doroshenko, R. Dyminsky, B. Krupnytsky, Z. Kuzelia, V. Lypynsky, and I. Mirchuk. Other associates in Germany included M. Antonovych, O. Burghardt, E. Chykalenko-Keller, D. Chyzhevsky, V. Leontovych, and P. Verhun. In 1928 the institute took part in the International Press Exhibition in Köln and issued a catalog of Ucrainica in the German press and literature (compiled by M. Hnatyshak). By 1931 it had published three volumes of scholarly papers called *Abhandlungen* (1927, 1929, 1931) and two volumes of informational articles called *Mitteilungen* (1927–8).

From 1931, under the new director, Mirchuk, the insti-

tute was funded by the German Ministry of Education. In 1934 it received the status of a state institution affiliated with Berlin University. Groener was succeeded as chairman of the board of trustees by A. Palme (1934–9) and G. Gerullis (1939–45). In the 1930s the institute worked to bring the Ukrainian question to the fore of Central and Western European public attention. To this end it organized lectures (mostly at Berlin University) by Ukrainian and German scholars, offered German-language courses in Ukrainian studies (taught by Krupnytsky, Kuzelia, Leontovych, and Mirchuk), sent literature on Ukraine to German and foreign academic libraries, organized public exhibitions (eg, of Ukrainian graphic art [Berlin 1933] and of Ukrainian demographic, economic, and ethnographic maps [Berlin 1936]), and provided German institutions, publishers, and encyclopedias with information about Ukraine and Ukrainian issues. It expanded its library (est 1926) to nearly 35,000 volumes. After 1932 the institute issued informational and scholarly publications, including the brochure series Beiträge zur Ukrainekunde (mostly transcripts of the institute's lectures); exhibition catalogs; the bulletins *Visty Ukraïns'koho naukovoho instytutu u Berlini* (1933–8) and *Ukrainische Kulturberichte* (1933–40), edited by Kuzelia; an ethnographic map of Transcarpathia (1938); the encyclopedic *Handbuch der Ukraine* (1941), edited by Mirchuk; Krupnytsky's *Geschichte der Ukraine von den Anfängen bis zum Jahre 1920* (1939, 1943); J. Rudnyckyj's *Lehrbuch der ukrainischen Sprache* (1940, 1942, 1943); and several dictionaries, notably Kuzelia and Rudnyckyj's large *Ukrainisch-deutsches Wörterbuch* (1943).

After the Soviet occupation of Berlin in 1945, the institute was dissolved, and its library holdings perished.

V. Kubijovyč

**Ukrainian Scientific Institute in Warsaw** (Ukrainskyi naukovyi instytut u Varshavi). A research institution established in Warsaw in 1928 (formally in 1930) through the efforts of the Government-in-exile of the UNR. It was funded by the Polish Ministry of Religious Faiths and Education as an autonomous Ukrainian studies institute. The directors were O. Lototsky (until January 1939) and A. Yakovliv, the secretary-general was S. Smal-Stotsky, and the board of directors included B. Lepky, Ye. Glovinsky, and V. Sadovsky. The institute was divided into commissions and seminars, and most of its members were émigré or Galician scholars.

The institute supported research on topics in Ukrainian studies that it was not possible to pursue freely in Soviet Ukraine, and published more books (over 70 vols) than any other interwar émigré or Western Ukrainian scholarly publisher. In its series Pratsi Ukrainskoho naukovoho instytutu (55 vols) were D. Doroshenko's survey history of Ukraine (2 vols, 1932–3), Hetman P. Orlyk's diary (ed J. Tokarzewski-Karaszewicz, 1936), B. Krupnytsky's book on Orlyk (1938), the article and document collection *Mazepa* (2 vols, 1938), A. Yakovliv's book on 17th- and 18th-century Ukrainian-Russian treaties (1934), an annotated volume of M. Drahomanov's correspondence with the Old Hromada of Kiev (1938), O. Dotsenko's book on the 1920 Winter Campaign of the UNR Army (1932) and a collection of documents pertaining to the campaign (ed P. Shandruk, 1933), O. Lototsky's memoirs (3 vols, 1932–4) and books on the Ukrainian sources of canon law (1931) and on the principles and history of autocephaly (2 vols,

1935, 1938), a volume of memoirs by L. Wasilewski, M. Halyn, S. Stempowski, A. Topchibashi, and G. Tabouis (1932), K. Chekhovych's book on O. Potebnia (1931), I. Zilynsky's map of Ukrainian dialects with commentaries (1933), S. Smal-Stotsky's book of interpretations of T. Shevchenko (1935) and book on the Ukrainian language under Soviet rule (1936), a collection of memoirs and articles about the late 19th-century Ukrainian movement in the Russian empire (2 vols, 1939), collections of articles on Soviet Ukrainian demography (by T. Olesevych [Olesiiuk], O. Pytel, V. Sadovsky, and O. Chubenko, 1931) and economics (by Ye. Glovinsky, K. Matsiievych, and V. Sadovsky, 1931–6), a book of Soviet Ukrainian statistical tables (ed Olesevych, 1930), I. Ivasiuk's book on credit cooperatives in Ukraine (1933), V. Ivanys's two books on energy and industry in Ukraine and northern Caucasia (1933), I. Shovheniv's book on water management in the Dnieper Basin (1934), V. Sadovsky's book on agricultural labor in Soviet Ukraine (1935), S. Siropolko's book on public education in Soviet Ukraine (1934), L. Wasilewski's book in Polish on the Ukrainian question (1934), V. Sadovsky's book on Soviet nationality policy in Ukraine (1937), B. Ivanytsky's book on Ukraine's forests and forest economy (2 vols, 1936), D. Chyzhevsky's book on H. Skovoroda (1934), S. Kuczyński's book in Polish on the Chernihiv and Novhorod-Siverskyi lands under Lithuanian rule (1936), and T. Shevchenko's collected works with critical articles and notes (13 of 16 planned vols, ed P. Zaitsev, 1934–9), as well as Ukrainian translations of the Psalter (1936) and three liturgical books prepared by a commission headed by Metropolitan D. Valedinsky (1936–9). Other publications included a book of Shevchenko's poems in Polish translation (1936), two brochures on the institute's activities (in Ukrainian, Polish, and French, 1935, 1939) and two on the activities of its Economic Seminar (1935, 1936), and the *Bulletin de la commission pour l'étude des problèmes polono-ukrainiens* (5 issues, 1935–8). Approx 35 prepared volumes were never published. After the German occupation of Warsaw in 1939, the institute was closed down, and its valuable 10,000-volume library and archive holdings perished.

V. Kubijovyč

## Ukrainian Scientific Institute of Bibliology

(Ukrainskyi naukovo-doslidnyi instytut knyhoznavstva, or UNIK). A scholarly research institution established in Kiev in 1922 on the basis of the Supreme Book Chamber (est 1919). Under its director, Yu. *Mezhenko, UNIK undertook the study of general and Ukrainian bibliology and bibliography and the history of printing, developed library science methodology, offered courses in bibliography and library science, prepared various bibliographic guides to Soviet Ukrainian publications, and amassed a valuable catalog and library of Ukrainian publications. Its staff and research associates (approx 50 people) were divided into four sections: the history of the book (chaired by S. Maslov), the sociology of the book (D. Balyka), book art and technology (N. Makarenko), and bibliography (T. Aleksieiev and V. Shpilievych). UNIK published research in bibliography, library science, and the history of Ukrainian printing, the Ukrainian press, and Ukrainian book art in its serials *Bibliolohichni visti* (25 issues, 1923–30), *Trudy* (4 issues, 1926–30), and *Naukovi zapysky* (2 issues, 1933), and in over 60 books and brochures. Its activities declined with the onset of the Stalinist terror and the persecution

*Bibliolohichni visti*, the organ of the Ukrainian Scientific Institute of Bibliology

of its staff. Mezhenko was replaced as director by S. Yakubovsky in 1931, and UNIK was closed down in 1934.

## Ukrainian Scientific Research Institute of Agricultural Microbiology

(Ukrainskyi naukovo-doslidnyi instytut silskohospodarskoi mikrobiolohii). A research institute formed in Chernihiv in 1969 out of the Department of Agricultural Microbiology, Virology, and Immunology of the Ukrainian Scientific Research Institute of Land Cultivation and the Department of Agricultural Microbiology of the Chernihiv Oblast Agricultural Research Station. Until 1991 it was part of the Southern Branch of the All-Union Academy of Agricultural Sciences, and is now part of the new Ukrainian Academy of Agrarian Sciences. The institute has seven laboratories and a research farm. It researches problems of agricultural microbiology and virology and develops practical methods for increasing food production and improving the quality of agricultural produce. It also develops animal and plant antibiotics.

The Ukrainian Scientific Research Institute of Animal Husbandry of the Steppe Regions

## Ukrainian Scientific Research Institute of Animal Husbandry of the Steppe Regions

(Ukrainskyi naukovo-doslidnyi instytut tvarynnytstva stepovykh raioniv im. M. Ivanova). An agricultural institute located in the Askaniia-Nova Nature Reserve, in Kherson oblast. It was established in 1956 on the basis of the All-Union Scientific

Research Institute for the Hybridization and Adaptation of Animals. Studies are carried out on heredity patterns, livestock breeding, variability in traits, the care and feeding of sheep, and methods of the acclimatization, domestication, and hybridization of wild animals. Its scientific journal *Trudy* has been published since 1933. The institute also manages a zoo, a botanical garden, a technical information division, livestock breeding farms, and an experimental farm. Some of the achievements of the institute include improved Askaniia sheep, purebred multiparous Karakul sheep, a new breed of Red Steppe cattle, and new breeds of local swine. It has domesticated a number of wild animals and hundreds of plants. A graduate course is offered on a resident or correspondence basis.

**Ukrainian Scientific Research Institute of Coal Chemistry** (Ukrainskyi naukovo-doslidnyi vuhlekhimichnyi instytut). Until 1992 an institute of the USSR Ministry of Ferrous Metallurgy, founded in Kharkiv in 1930. From 1968 it played a key role in the Soviet coke-chemical industry. In 1984 it had 7 departments, 18 laboratories, an experimental factory, and a postgraduate studies program. Its main research areas are thermal coal conversion and the isolation and conversion of coking products. Since 1972 it has published collections of scientific articles.

**Ukrainian Scientific Research Institute of Experimental Veterinary Science** (Ukrainskyi naukovo-doslidnyi instytut eksperymentalnoi veterynarii). The main veterinary research center of the Ukrainian SSR and now Ukraine. Located in Kharkiv, it was formed in 1921 out of the bacteriological station (est 1889) of the Kharkiv Veterinary Institute. Until 1956 it was known as the State Institute of Scientific and Practical Veterinary Medicine. The institute consists of 18 departments and oversees four veterinary research stations, the Department of Noninfectious Farm-Animal Diseases in Kirovohrad, and the Leukemia Research Support Center in Luhanske. The purpose of the institute is to develop methods of preventing and treating diseases that afflict farm animals and bees. It has prepared a number of vaccines, serums, antigens, and other effective means of combating animal diseases. It also trains researchers and upgrades the qualifications of veterinary workers. It offers a graduate program. The institute publishes an interdepartmental collection of papers titled *Veterynariia* and has published a 20-volume collection of its scientific works.

**Ukrainian Scientific Research Institute of Forest Management and Agroforest Amelioration** (Ukrainskyi naukovo-doslidnyi instytut lisovoho hospodarstva ta agrolisomelioratsii im. H. Vysotskoho). An institute established in Kharkiv in 1929 under the Commissariat (now Ministry) of Forest Management of Ukraine. It was merged with the Ukrainian Institute of Forest Management in 1951 and with the Forestry Institute of the AN URSR (now ANU) in 1956. In 1980 the institute had 12 laboratories, 2 departments, and a Carpathian branch. It oversaw the work of four forestry stations, the Crimean Mountain Forestry Station, four agroforest amelioration stations, the Lower-Dnieper Sand Forestation and Viticulture Research Station, the Desna Soil Erosion Research Station, the Veseli Bokovenky Dendrological Selection Station, and the Danylivka Experimental Forest Farm. Its chief goals are to increase forest productivity and improve forest protection. The institute has a graduate program and publishes collections of scientific papers.

**Ukrainian Scientific Research Institute of Geography and Cartography** (Ukrainskyi naukovo-doslidnyi instytut heohrafii ta kartohrafii). A research institute under the People's Commissariat of Education of the Ukrainian SSR, founded in October 1927 in Kharkiv. Its director was S. *Rudnytsky, and its associates were geographers such as M. *Dmytriiev and K. Dubniak. Its objectives were to modernize fundamental research in geography, train professional geographers, develop geography curricula for secondary and higher schools, and prepare textbooks, maps, and atlases. It managed to publish two issues of *Zapysky* and a physiographic wall map of the Ukrainian SSR for schools before it was dissolved in 1934. Its director and some of its associates were charged with nationalism and repressed.

**Ukrainian Scientific Research Institute of Geological Prospecting** (Ukrainskyi naukovo-doslidnyi heolohorozviduvalnyi instytut). A research institute under the Ministry of Geology of Ukraine, dealing with oil and gas explorations in Ukraine. Established in Lviv in 1952, it was a branch of the All-Union Scientific Research Institute of Geological Prospecting for Petroleum until 1957. In 1978 the institute had 11 departments and branches in Kiev, Chernihiv, and Poltava. Its research deals mostly with the geology of petroleum and gas-bearing regions, prospecting methods, techniques and technologies for deep drilling, geophysical research methods, ways of estimating resources, and the economic analysis of geological prospecting. The institute participates in planning the development of the petroleum and gas industry in Ukraine and in international programs of petroleum and gas exploration. It publishes an annual collection of scientific papers.

**Ukrainian Scientific Research Institute of Irrigation Farming** (Ukrainskyi naukovo-doslidnyi instytut zroshuvanoho zemlerobstva). An institute established in Kherson in 1956 out of the Ukrainian Scientific Research Institute of Cotton Growing and until 1992 under the Southern Branch of the All-Union Academy of Agricultural Sciences. The earlier institute was formed in 1949 out of the Ukrainian Research Station of Cotton Growing, which grew out of the Kherson Research Station, which had been set up in 1910 on the basis of the experimental field of the Kherson Agricultural School (est 1889). The institute in 1979 had 19 departments, 2 research stations, 2 research farms, and 2 state farms. It researches the theoretical and practical aspects of irrigation farming and develops new techniques for effective irrigation. In 1972 a selection center for irrigated feed cultures was added to the institute. Since 1991 the institute has been part of the new Ukrainian Academy of Agrarian Sciences.

**Ukrainian Scientific Research Institute of Irrigation Orcharding** (Ukrainskyi naukovo-doslidnyi instytut zroshuvanoho sadivnytstva). A research institute of the Chief Administration of the Fruit-Preserving and Wine-Making Industry, established in 1972 in Melitopil, Zaporizhia oblast. It was formed out of the Melitopil Orcharding Research Station, which was based on a branch of the Mliiv Orcharding Research Station (1928–30). The institute in 1979 had 13 departments and specialized laboratories, a quarantine and introduction nursery, and 2 research farms. It studies the theoretical and practical aspects of irrigation orcharding and develops new farming techniques and new strains of fruit trees with higher yields.

**Ukrainian Scientific Research Institute of Land Cultivation** (Ukrainskyi naukovo-doslidnyi instytut zemlerobstva). An institution established in 1928 in the village of Chabany, Kiev oblast, on the basis of an agronomic laboratory. Until 1965 it was called the Ukrainian Scientific Research Institute of Socialist Land Cultivation, and until 1992 it was under the Southern Branch of the All-Union Academy of Agricultural Sciences. It is now part of the Ukrainian Academy of Agrarian Sciences. The institute has 22 departments and laboratories and a selection center of feed crops for Polisia and the forest-steppe region of Ukraine. It also maintains three research stations: for soil cultivation (in Drabiv, Cherkasy oblast), for meadowland management (in Kiev oblast), and for bog reclamation (in Panfyly, Kiev oblast); two research farms (in Kiev oblast); and several other research facilities. The main purpose of the institute is to develop the theoretical foundations and practical methods of land cultivation in the various agricultural regions of Ukraine. It also develops new plant strains and trains graduate students in agronomy. Research by its associates has been published in regular collections.

**Ukrainian Scientific Research Institute of Mechanized Wood Processing** (Ukrainskyi naukovo-doslidnyi instytut mekhanichnoi obrobky derevyny). A research institution, until 1992 under the Ministry of the Lumber and Woodworking Industry of the Ukrainian SSR. It was established in Kiev in 1930 as a branch of the Kharkiv Central Scientific Research Institute of Forest Management and the Lumber Industry and was given its present name in 1933. From 1975 it was the chief agency of the Ukrainian Scientific-Manufacturing Wood-Processing Consortium. Under the USSR Ministry of the Lumber and Woodworking Industry, it was the main agency for the standardization and metrology of sawdust materials, lumber, and wood products. The institute consists of 14 departments and a graduate school.

**Ukrainian Scientific Research Institute of Metals** (Ukrainskyi naukovo-doslidnyi instytut metaliv). A research institution established in Kharkiv in 1928 and until 1992 under the jurisdiction of the USSR Ministry of Ferrous Metallurgy. In 1980 it had 10 departments, 12 laboratories, an experimental plant, and a graduate program. Its research is devoted to increasing the range and quality of rolled steel, developing and applying the technology for manufacturing special steels and steel rollers, improving the technology for producing better-quality metals for railway use, implementing continuous steel pouring into the production process, and improving quality testing and control methods. The institute published three collections of scientific papers, in Russian: *Sortoprokatnoe proizvodstvo*, *Gnutye profili prokata*, and *Proizvodstvo zheleznodorozhnykh rel'sov i koles*.

**Ukrainian Scientific Research Institute of Orcharding** (Ukrainskyi naukovo-doslidnyi instytut sadivnytstva). A research institution established in 1930 in the village of Novosilky, Kiev oblast, known until 1954 as the All-Union Research Institute of Fruit and Vegetable Farming. Until 1992 it was under the USSR Ministry of the Food Industry. The institute has 11 departments, 9 laboratories, and 2 research farms. It studies new methods and techniques for orcharding and vegetable growing, and has developed 500 new strains of fruits and vegetables. It offers a graduate program and publishes collections of scientific papers.

**Ukrainian Scientific Research Institute of Plant Cultivation, Selection, and Genetics** (Ukrainskyi naukovo-doslidnyi instytut roslynnytstva, selektsii i henetyky im. V. Iurieva). A scientific-research institution in the system of the Ukrainian Ministry of Agriculture located in Kharkiv, established in 1956 by the union of the Kharkiv Selection Station (est 1909) and the AN URSR (now ANU) Institute of Selection and Genetics (est 1946). It consists of 5 departments, 12 laboratories, 3 seed farms, and a research farm and has a total area of some 30,000 ha. The divisions support the following programs: agriculture, agricultural ecology and plant resources, plant protection, seed production, and the economics of agriculture. The laboratories investigate the *selection of spiked-grain cultures, the selection of corn, grain, and cereal cultures, genetics, implantation and development, heterosis, physiology and biochemistry, agricultural chemistry, soil microbiology, and grain biochemistry.

**Ukrainian Scientific Research Institute of Refractory Materials** (Ukrainskyi naukovo-doslidnyi instytut vohnetryviv). A research institute established in Kharkiv in 1932 on the basis of the Scientific Research Institute of the Silicate Industry of the Ukrainian SSR. Until 1992 it was under the jurisdiction of the USSR Ministry of Ferrous Metallurgy. The institute consists of several departments, laboratories, an experimental plant, and a graduate school. It develops refractory materials for blast furnaces as well as auxiliary devices for coke, Martin, two-tank, and glass furnaces, such as air heaters and mixers, and studies the technology of refractory-materials production. The institute has published a collection of scientific papers since 1932.

**Ukrainian Scientific Research Institute of Scientific-Technical Information and Technical-Economic Research** (Ukrainskyi naukovo-doslidnyi instytut naukovo-tekhnichnoi informatsii i tekhniko-ekonomichnykh doslidzhen). An institution under the State Planning Committee of Ukraine, established in Kiev in 1966. It has 15 departments and controls 17 interbranch territorial centers for disseminating information and propaganda. It also maintains a library and offers courses on information processing and propaganda. The institute develops strategies and methods for informing the public and economic managers of the state's economic goals and plans and for encouraging the implementation of the plans.

**Ukrainian Scientific Research Institute of Soil Science and Agrochemistry** (Ukrainskyi naukovo-doslidnyi instytut hruntoznavstva i ahrokhimii im. O.N.

Sokolovskoho). An institute of the Southern Branch of the All-Union Academy of Agricultural Sciences (to 1992) and now the Ukrainian Academy of Agrarian Sciences, founded in Kharkiv in 1956 on the basis of the AN URSR (now ANU) Soil Science Laboratory. It consists of four departments (soil science, chemical soil melioration, antierosion melioration, and agrochemistry), each with its own laboratories. It houses Ukraine's soil science archives, and maintains an antierosion research station in Yasynuvata raion (Donetske oblast) and an experimental state farm in Korotych (Kharkiv oblast). The institute conducts large-scale studies of soil utilization by the collective and state farms, and provides them with soil analyses and recommendations for the prevention of soil erosion and the improvement of productivity. It offers postgraduate and correspondence programs, and has compiled and published soil charts of Ukraine and the serial collection *Ahrokhimiia i hruntoznavstvo*.

**Ukrainian Scientific Research Institute of the Economics and Organization of Agriculture** (Ukraïns'kyi naukovo-doslidnyi instytut ekonomiky i orhanizatsii silskoho hospodarstva im. O.H. Shlikhtera). A republican institute established in Kiev in 1956, which by 1963 had become the central institution for co-ordinated studies of agricultural problems in Ukraine. Until 1992 it was under the Southern Branch of the All-Union Academy of Agricultural Sciences, and is now part of the Ukrainian Academy of Agrarian Sciences. The institute studies theoretical and practical problems of agricultural economics and organization with the aim of increasing and accelerating agricultural production. It drafts proposals for rationalizing the labor process, establishing work norms and wages, and stimulating production. It also works out ways to improve farm management. In 1979 the institute had 10 departments, a computing center, and a graduate program. Its Department for the Organization of Agricultural Production is located in Kharkiv. It has three branches, in Tarashcha, Kiev oblast, Nykopil, Dnipropetrovske oblast, and Zhytomyr, and published the journal *Ekonomika i orhanizatsiia sil's'koho hospodarstva*.

**Ukrainian Scientific Research Institute of the Meat and Dairy Industry** (Ukrainskyi naukovo-doslidnyi instytut miasnoi i molochnoi promyslovosti). An institution established in Kiev in 1959. Until 1992 it was under the USSR Ministry of the Meat and Milk Industry. It had 7 departments, 17 laboratories, a construction office, experimental factories, and a graduate program for food workers. The institute was primarily concerned with improving meat- and milk-processing techniques in the USSR. It designed machinery and equipment used in the industry and new processing and packaging methods.

**Ukrainian Scientific Research Institute of the Printing Industry** (Ukrainskyi naukovo-doslidnyi instytut polihrafichnoi promyslovosti). A research institute of the Ukrainian State Committee on Publications, Printing, and the Book Trade. It was founded in Kharkiv in 1932 and was moved to Lviv in 1945. Since 1972 it has been the leading institute of the printing industry for problems of high-quality printing. The institute consists of nine departments, five laboratories, an experimental plant, a computing center, and a standardization group.

**Ukrainian Scientific Research Institute of the Spirits and Liqueur-Whiskey Industry** (Ukrainskyi naukovo-doslidnyi instytut spyrtovoi i likero-horilchanoi promyslovosti). A research institute formed in Kiev in 1958 out of the Kiev branch of the All-Union Scientific Research Institute of the Spirits Industry. Until 1992 it was under the jurisdiction of the USSR Ministry of the Food Industry. In 1982 the institute included 5 departments and 11 laboratories, a design and construction office, and 2 experimental distilleries, in Luzhany (Chernivtsi oblast) and Popivka (Sumy oblast). Its main areas of research are improved distilling technology; the complex processing of sugar-beet molasses into alcohol, baking and fodder yeasts, amino acids, and pharmaceuticals; improved industrial equipment; the automation of production; the mechanization of labor-intensive operations; and scientific work-planning and management. The institute also improves safety procedures and the control technology for chemical and microbiological processes. It studies more efficient ways to use raw materials and fuels.

**Ukrainian Scientific Research Institute of Viticulture and Winemaking** (Ukrainskyi naukovo-doslidnyi instytut vynohradarstva i vynorobstva im. V. Tairova). An institute established in 1931 on the basis of the Central Scientific Research Winemaking Station (est 1905). It is a component of the Ukrainian Ministry of Agriculture, located on the shores of the dry estuary southwest of Odessa. The institute consists of seven departments: agricultural engineering, wine production, *selection and studies of various grape varieties, plant protection, mechanization, economics and organization, and agricultural meteorology. In addition there are laboratories for plant physiology and biochemistry, agricultural chemistry, soil science and microbiology, and wine chemistry. It also manages the Donets Zonal Viticulture Research Station in Dokuchaievske and support bases in Kiev, Vinnytsia, and Bilhorod-Dnistrovskyi. The total area of the institute extends over 340 ha of grape fields, 100 ha of grafting vine nurseries, and 120 ha of orchards. New grape varieties developed by the institute include the Tairov, Sukholyman White, Early Odessa, and Ukrainian Beauty. Other innovations include the isolation of novel yeasts and improved wine storage technology.

**Ukrainian Scientific Society** (Ukrainske naukove tovarystvo, or UNT). The first Ukrainian-language and openly Ukrainophile learned society in Russian-ruled Ukraine. It was founded in Kiev on the initiative of V. *Naumenko in 1907, after tsarist restrictions on Ukrainian publishing were lifted. Its structure and activities were modeled on those of the *Shevchenko Scientific Society in Lviv, with which it maintained close ties. In 1912 the executive council members were M. Hrushevsky (president from 1908), O. Levytsky and I. Steshenko (vice-presidents), O. Cherniakhivsky (secretary), O. Shramchenko (treasurer), M. Biliashivsky, M. Lysenko, and I. Feshchenko-Chopivsky. The UNT was divided into historical, philological, natural sciences, and, later, technical, medical, archeological, pedagogical, and art sections and commissions on ethnography, linguistics, statistics-economy, and, from 1917, economic history, law, archeography, botany, and 11 other natural sciences. It maintained a library, an archeology and art museum, and the Museum of Ukrainian Personages in Kiev. The UNT held biweekly lecture meetings, organized scholarly conferences and public lectures, and published original research, surveys, reviews, and some primary-source materials in its serials *Zapysky Ukraïns'koho naukovoho tovarystva v Kyievi* (18 vols, 1908–14, 1917–18), *Ukraïna* (quarterly, 1914, 1917–18), and *Ukraïns'kyi naukovyi zhurnal* (2 vols, Moscow, 1915–16), a symposium dedicated to T. Shevchenko (1915), and several publications of the natural sciences, technical, and medical sections and the Ethnographic Commission. The UNT's activities were interrupted by the First World War and consequent tsarist restrictions, persecution, and censorship until 1917. After the 1917 Revolution the UNT was instrumental in the founding of the Ukrainian State University (see *Kiev University) and the UAN (see *Academy of Sciences of the Ukrainian SSR [now the Academy of Sciences of Ukraine]) in Kiev. It organized the first congress of Ukraine's natural scientists (1918), created the *Ukrainian Meteorological Service, and prepared many scientific terminological dictionaries.

The UNT grew from 54 members in 1908 to 98 members in 1912. In its first decade it elected 161 full members. Most of them lived in Kiev and elsewhere in Russian-ruled Ukraine, with only a few in Galicia. Among the members were K. and V. Antonovych, D. Bahalii, J. Baudouin de Courtenay, B. Bukreev, V. Danylevych, V. Domanytsky, V. Durdukivsky, I. Dzhydzhora, F. Ernst, I. Franko, D. Grave, M. Halyn (chairman of the medical section), B. Hrinchenko, O. Hrushevsky, I. Kamanin, P. Kholodny (chairman of the natural sciences and technical sections), B. Kistiakovsky, O. Kolessa, M. Komarov, O. Korchak-Chepurkivsky, F. Korsh, O. Kosach (Pchilka), V. Kostiv (Verkhovynets), P. Kozytsky, M. Kravchuk, A. Krymsky, K. Kvitka, O. Leontovych, A. Loboda, I. and V. Luchytsky, V. Modzalevsky, K. Mykhalchuk, V. Naumenko, I. Nechui-Levytsky, H. Pavlutsky, V. Peretts (chairman of the philological section), M. Petrov, M. Porsh, V. Riznychenko, O. Rusov (chairman of the Statistical-Economic Commission), D. Shcherbakivsky, V. Shcherbyna, A. Shakhmatov, M. Sharleman, Ya. Shulhyn, S. Smal-Stotsky, M. Stadnyk, L. Starytska-Cherniakhivska, M. Sumtsov, S. Tomashivsky, P. Tutkovsky, Ye. Tymchenko, M. Vasylenko (chairman of the historical section), V. Vernadsky, F. Vovk, M. Vozniak, A. Yakovliv, O. and N. Yanata, D. Yavornytsky, O. Yefymenko, D. and M. Zerov, and P. Zhytetsky. In 1918 the UNT had nearly 300 members. In 1921 the UNT sections, commissions, library, and museums were forcibly incorporated into the All-Ukrainian Academy of Sciences (VUAN). Its *Zapysky* and *Ukraïna* were revived in 1924 as the annual *Naukovyi zbirnyk* and quarterly/bimonthly *Ukraïna* (1924–30) of the VUAN historical section.

R. Senkus

**Ukrainian Self-Reliance League** (Soiuz ukraintsiv samostiinykiv, or SUS). An umbrella group of liberal nationalist Ukrainian-Canadian associations and institutions founded in 1927 at conventions in Edmonton and Saskatoon. The member groups of SUS include the Ukrainian Self-Reliance Association (Tovarystvo ukraintsiv samostiinykiv, or TUS); *Ukrainian Women's Association of Canada (SUK); *Canadian Ukrainian Youth Association (SUMK); *Union of Ukrainian Community Centres (SUND); Ukrainian student residences in Edmonton (*St John's In-

stitute), Saskatoon (*Mohyla Ukrainian Institute), and Toronto (*St Vladimir Institute); and *St Andrew's College in Winnipeg. The association grew out of an informal grouping of leading figures among the Ukrainian intelligentsia in Canada (including T. Ferley, J. Arsenych, W. *Swystun, P. Zvarych, and the three Stechishin brothers) which was centered around the newspaper *Ukrains'kyi holos* and which established the *Ukrainian Orthodox Church of Canada in 1918. Its ideology of self-reliance, articulated most clearly by Myroslaw *Stechishin and W. Swystun, has centered on the ideas of self-respect among individuals, organizations, and nations; self-sufficiency in politics, economics, and religion; and independence of thought and action. The application of these ideas has resulted in efforts to develop nonpartisan 'all-Ukrainian' community organizations among Ukrainians in Canada. SUS actively promoted strong civic involvement in Canada by its members. At the same time it wholeheartedly supported Ukrainian causes abroad, although it has consciously refrained from direct involvement with Old World political factions. The league was a founding member of the Ukrainian Canadian Committee (now Congress) in 1940.

**Ukrainian Service to the Fatherland** (Ukrainska sluzhba batkivshchyni; German: Ukrainischer Heimatsdienst). A German-run program established in late 1941 in the *Generalgouvernement to organize youths 19 and 20 years of age for work primarily in construction and road-building. In 1942 it was extended to include all males 18 to 60 years of age. From 1943 high-school students were required to do one year of service, and university students half a year. From the outset the *Ukrainian Central Committee attempted to modify the program. Initially Ukrainians were accepted as volunteer laborers rather than conscripts. They were organized into separate Ukrainian units and allotted time for physical exercise and relaxation. The committee's representative for the program was O. Rusnak. In 1943 leadership courses for Ukrainians were organized in Lviv. In total, over 10,000 Ukrainians served under the program. When the Soviet forces approached Galicia, the workers were assigned to the German army, to the Division Galizien, or to anti-aircraft units.

**Ukrainian Shield.** See Ukrainian Crystalline Shield.

**Ukrainian Sich Riflemen** (Ukrainski sichovi striltsi [USS], Legion USS). The only Ukrainian unit in the Austrian army. Organized in Galicia in August 1914 at the initiative of the Supreme Ukrainian Council, it was supervised by the Ukrainian Combat Board. The first volunteers were members of Ukrainian paramilitary organizations, such as Sich, Sokil, and Plast. In September 1914 only 2,500 of them were accepted into the army and sent to Transcarpathia for brief training. After two weeks, individual USS companies were moved to the Russian front in the Carpathian Mountains.

The USS was divided into ten companies, grouped initially into two and one-half battalions and then into three independent groups (commanded by Capt M. Voloshyn, Capt H. Kossak, and Maj S. Shukhevych). Placed under the operational control of the Austrian 55th Infantry Division, they were employed tactically as battalions or com-

The coat of arms of the Ukrainian Sich Riflemen

panies of the 129th and 130th Austrian brigades. The legion's commander was T. *Rozhankovsky, then M. *Halushchynsky. In March 1915 the post of legion commander was abolished, and the USS were divided into two independent battalions (commanded by H. Kossak and S. Goruk and, later, V. Didushok), a reserve company, and a training unit. The legion distinguished itself in battle at *Makivka (29 April–3 May 1915), Bolekhiv, Halych, Zavadiv, and Semykivtsi. Despite casualties, the force remained at eight infantry companies (in two battalions). In 1916 the battalions were merged into the First Regiment of the USS, under the command of Maj H. Kossak and then Lt Col A. Varyvoda. In August–September 1916 the regiment lost over 1,000 men at *Lysonia and was reduced to a battalion (commanded by Col F. Kikal). The USS suffered another severe loss at Koniukhy in July 1917. The survivors of the USS Hutsul Company and the USS Kish were reformed into a new battalion (commanded by D. Krenzhalovsky). In February 1918, under Maj M. Tarnavsky, it marched with the Austrian army to the Kherson region. In October it was transferred to Bukovyna. On 3 November, the USS arrived in Lviv, too late to hold the city against the Poles. By January 1919 the battalion was expanded into

The Combat Board of the Ukrainian Sich Riflemen. Sitting, from left: Volodymyr Starosolsky, Teofil Kormosh, Kyrylo Trylovsky, Stepan Tomashivsky, Dmytro Katamai; standing: Ivan Bobersky, Volodymyr Temnytsky, Lonhyn Tsehelsky

the First Brigade of the *Ukrainian Galician Army (UHA). Commanded by Maj S. Bukshovany, it consisted initially of one regiment. By June 1919 it had two infantry regiments, a cavalry troop, an artillery regiment, and other support units. When the UHA was reorganized into the *Red Ukrainian Galician Army, the USS became the First Infantry Regiment, under the command of Capt Z. Noskovsky and then M. Baran. In late April 1920 the regiment suffered heavy casualies in battle and was surrounded by the Polish army; on 2 May 1920 it was forced to capitulate.

The Legion USS was the first and most durable (5.5 years) Ukrainian military formation during and after the First World War. Its former officers became the organizers and leaders of the *Sich Riflemen in Kiev. Its officers also played an important role in the *November Uprising in Lviv. It had the best-trained troops of the UHA, and its officers were the army's top commanders.

BIBLIOGRAPHY
*Ukraïns'ki sichovi striltsi, 1914–1920* (Lviv 1935; 3rd edn, Montreal 1955)
Ripets'kyi, S. *Ukraïns'ke sichove striletstvo* (New York 1956)
                                                                P. Sodol

**Ukrainian Sich Riflemen, Brotherhood of** (Bratstvo ukrainskykh sichovykh striltsiv). A veterans' organization of former members of the Ukrainian Sich Riflemen (USS), founded at the first USS convention in Regensburg, Germany, in February 1948. Its original name, Union of Ukrainian Sich Riflemen, was changed at the next convention to the present one. Its eight local branches in Germany and Austria had a membership of over 200. As its members emigrated overseas, new branches were set up in the United States (5 in the 1950s), Canada (4), and Argentina (1). The brotherhood organized the Chervona Kalyna press (New York), which published the collection *Nash L'viv* (Our Lviv, 1953) and S. Ripetsky's *Ukraïns'ke sichove striletstvo* (The Ukrainian Sich Riflemen, 1956) and copublished the quarterly *Visti kombatanta*. Leading figures in the brotherhood included I. Porytko and N. Hirniak.

**Ukrainian Social and Cultural Society** (Ukrainske suspilno-kulturne tovarystvo, or USKT). Established in 1956, the USKT was the only community institution in postwar Poland allowed to engage in Ukrainian cultural and educational activities until the 1980s. In spite of its official sanction, the USKT functioned under surveillance by the Ministry of Internal Affairs.

In 1981 the USKT headquarters in Warsaw oversaw 170 groups with nearly 6,000 members, and in 1988, 180 groups with about 7,500 members, all of whom were spread throughout Poland. Of these, only 10 percent lived on traditional Ukrainian ethnographic territory. For a long time the USKT was barred from forming groups in the Kholm and Podlachia regions. The largest branches (1981 figures) were in Peremyshl (400 members), Gdańsk (250), Szczecin (250), Koszalin (200), Cracow, Katowice, Olsztyn, Słupsk, Warsaw, and Wrocław. The USKT was headed by S. Makukh, H. Boiarsky, M. Korolko, K. Lashchuk, Ye. Kokhan, and M. Verbovy. Despite the impediments created by the Polish authorities, it managed to organize 50 art collectives, establish the male choir Zhuravli in 1972, and stage Ukrainian song festivals every two years, as well as (since 1972) an annual festival of children's art collectives in Koszalin. Other aspects of the society's work include a wide-ranging program of lectures, dissemination of Ukrainian publications (in Olsztyn, Szczecin, and Warsaw), radio programs (in Koszalin, Olsztyn, Rzeszów, and Szczecin) in Polish about Ukrainian affairs, and work with Polish scholars in Ukrainian disciplines. It has published the weekly *Nashe slovo* (circulation, 10,000), with monthly supplements such as the scholarly-popular *Nasha kul'tura* and the children's *Svitanok*. It also publishes the weekly *Lemkivs'ka storinka* as well as the annual *Ukraïns'kyi kalendar*. Other publications include the literary anthology *Homin* (Echo, 1964); collections of poetry by Ya. Hudemchuk, Ye. Samokhvalenko, and I. Zlatokudra; and 19 school texts for Ukrainian language instruction in elementary schools.

Until 1989 a literary and artistic association with 40 members, including S. Demchuk (translator), P. Halytsky (prose writer), V. Hirny (prose writer), S. Kozak (literary scholar), O. Lapsky (poet), M. Lesiv (linguist), A. Mentukh (painter), H. Petsukh (sculptor), Ye. Samokhvalenko (poet), A. Serednytsky (literary scholar), T. Venhrynovych (painter), and S. Zabrovarny (historian), was affiliated with the executive. Other leading activists of the USKT have been R. Andrukhovych, O. Hnatiuk, S. Kontrolevych, M. Kovalsky, M. Kozak, P. Kreminsky, O. Laska, M. Serkiz, M. Syvitsky, and Ya. Zalitach. Its art collectives were headed by M. Duda, B. Fitsak, P. Lakhtiuk, E. Mohyla, Ya. Popovska, and O. Valkovska. Former activists now deceased include H. Dmytriieva, L. Gets, L. Hladylovych, A. Hoshovsky, Y. Kurochko, O. Kutynsky, K. Kuzyk, I. Markiv, and O. Vasylkiv.

In 1990 the USKT was reconstituted as the Alliance of Ukrainians in Poland (Obiednannia ukraintsiv v Polshchi).

M. Trukhan

**Ukrainian Social Democratic Association.** See Spilka.

**Ukrainian Social Democratic party** (Ukrainska sotsial-demokratychna partiia, or USDP). A socialist workers' party founded on 18 September 1899 by Ukrainian members of the Polish Social Democratic Party of Galicia and Silesia (PPSD) who had formed a Ukrainian social democratic organization in Lviv in 1897, and by a minority faction that split away from the *Ukrainian Radical party. The USDP was a national section of the federated Social Democratic Party of Austria. Its Austro-Marxist program advocated the equality and autonomy of all nations in the Austro-Hungarian and Russian empires and the creation of a pan-Ukrainian independent republic. The executive consisted of Yu. *Bachynsky, M. *Hankevych (the chairman), R. *Yarosevych (a member of the Austrian State Council), M. Novakivsky, and S. *Vityk. Hankevych and Vityk were the key leaders. Other prominent members were R. Dombchevsky, Ye. Kosevych, V. Levynsky, T. Melen, P. and S. Novakivsky, M. Ogrodnik, Ya. Ostapchuk, M. Sichynsky, I. Siiak, D. Starosolska, M. Vitoshynsky, and I. Vozniak. The USDP had ties with the Revolutionary Ukrainian party and Ukrainian Social Democratic Workers' party in Russian-ruled Ukraine. By concentrating on trade-union work among the Ukrainian rural proletariat and organizing strike committees during the 1902 *peas-

ant strikes in Galicia it fostered a national identity and class consciousness within the Ukrainian peasantry. The first USDP congress was held in Lviv in March 1903. A fraternal Ukrainian section of the Social Democratic Party of Bukovyna was founded in 1906 and was led by Y. Bezpalko.

Until 1907 the USDP was de facto a section within the PPSD. Its leaders Vityk and M. Hankevych were also members of that party (Hankevych headed the PPSD committee in Lviv). By mutual agreement the USDP did political work in the Galician Ukrainian villages, and the PPSD was active in urban centers. In 1906, however, Levynsky and other younger USDP members began demanding that the USDP do political work among the Ukrainian urban proletariat independently of the PPSD. Consequently, at the June 1907 USDP conference a new party statute was adopted, which made the USDP independent of the PPSD and instructed its members to begin organizing USDP committees, Volia workers' associations, and Ukrainian trade unions in urban centers; it also postulated the ethnic partitioning of Galicia. During the 1907 elections to the Austrian parliament the USDP received 8 percent of the Ukrainian vote and sent Ostapchuk and Vityk to the Chamber of Deputies. At the December 1911 USDP conference factional strife between the pro-PPSD leadership and the independentist 'young' faction (Bachynsky, P. Buniak, L. Hankevych, I. Kvasnytsia, Levynsky, V. Starosolsky, V. Temnytsky, Yarosevych) ended in the secession of the latter group. The USDP was not reunited until its fifth congress, in March 1914, which elected Temnytsky the new leader.

During the First World War USDP members were active in nation-building organizations such as the Supreme Ukrainian and General Ukrainian councils, the Combat Board of the Ukrainian Sich Riflemen, and the Union for the Liberation of Ukraine. In 1918 they took part in the first Ukrainian National Rada of the Western Ukrainian National Republic (ZUNR). Vityk was one of the Rada presidium's vice-presidents and a member of the executive; O. Ustyianovych was the presidium's deputy secretary; and V. Birchak, M. Boikovych, A. Chernetsky (also the first ZUNR state secretary of labor and social security), L. and M. Hankevych, I. Kalynovych, Y. Krupa, R. Kulytsky, I. Liskovatsky, H. Mariiash, and R. Skybinsky were Rada delegates. As early as December 1918, however, the USDP left the coalition government and joined the socialist opposition, the Peasants' and Workers' Union. The USDP supported the January 1919 unification of the ZUNR and UNR, however, and from April 1919 to May 1920 Y. Bezpalko, Temnytsky, and Vityk held portfolios in the UNR Council of National Ministers. Starosolsky served as a deputy minister.

In 1921, after the Soviet-Polish Peace Treaty of Riga partitioned Ukraine between the two powers and the UNR Army was routed in the Ukrainian-Soviet War, the USDP adopted a pro-Soviet Ukrainian-unification platform and remained openly hostile to both the Polish government and Ye. Petrushevych's Vienna-based ZUNR government-in-exile. In the early 1920s members of the Vasylkiv faction of the *Communist Party of Western Ukraine (KPZU) infiltrated the USDP upper echelons. Consequently, at its sixth congress, in Lviv in March 1923, the USDP adopted a Communist platform and removed M. and L. Hankevych, Skybinsky, Starosolsky, Buniak, and Kvasnytsia from the leadership. In 1922 the Volhynian USDP members A. Bratun, M. Chuchmai, S. Kozytsky, M. Lutskevych, V. Mokh-niuk, A. Pashchuk, Kh. Prystupa, Y. Skrypa, P. Vasyn-chuk, and Ya. Voitiuk were elected to the Polish Sejm. In November 1923 they met in Lutske with other representatives of Ukrainian socialist organizations and established a united front, which was named the USDP of Eastern Galicia, Volhynia, the Kholm Region, Polisia, and Podlachia in December.

On 30 January 1924 the Polish government proclaimed the USDP a threat to peace and order and outlawed it and its organs. Most USDP members then joined the underground KPZU. The Sejm members Mokhniuk, Pashchuk, Prystupa, Skrypa, and Voitiuk left the Ukrainian Parliamentary Representation, formed their own Ukrainian Social Democratic Club, and then in November joined the Communist caucus in the Sejm. The non-Communist USDP minority became involved in the Robitnycha Hromada cultural and educational society. L. Hankevych's *Vpered* group revived the USDP in 1928. Under his and, from 1933, Starosolsky's leadership the new USDP belonged to the Labour and Socialist International. In December 1934 it formed a Ukrainian Socialist Bloc with the Ukrainian National Democratic Alliance and the Ukrainian Socialist Radical party. By that time the USDP had few members and little political influence or support, and after the German invasion of Galicia in 1939, it became inactive. Postwar émigrés in Western Europe who had been USDP members helped to found the *Ukrainian Socialist party.

The USDP organs were *Volia* (1900–7), *Zemlia i volia* (1906–13, 1919–20, 1922–4), *Chervonyi prapor* (1906–7), *Nash holos* (1910–11), *Vpered* (1911–13, 1918–24), *Pratsia* (1914, 1918), and, in Bukovyna, *Borba* (1908–14, 1918), *Volia naroda* (1919–21), *Robitnyk* (1919–23), and *Borot'ba* (1925–8).

BIBLIOGRAPHY
Levyns'kyi, V. *Narys rozvytku ukraïns'koho robitnychoho rukhu v Halychyni* (Kiev 1914; rev edn, 1930)
– *Narys istoriï Ukraïns'koï sotsiial-demokratychnoï partiï* (Lviv 1921)
Papierzyńska-Turek, M. *Sprawa ukraińska w Drugiej Rzeczypospolitej 1922–1926* (Cracow 1979)
Petliura, S. 'Politychni ukraïns'ki partiï v Halychyni: 1. Ukraïns'ka partiia sotsiial-demokratychna,' in *Symon Petliura: Statti, lysty, dokumenty*, 2 (New York 1979)
Hornowa, E. 'Powstanie Ukraińskiej Partii Socjalno-Demokratycznej w Galicji Wschodniej,' *Zeszyty Naukowe Wyższej Szkoły Pedagogicznej im. Powstańcow Śląskich w Opolu: Historia*, 17 (1980)

R. Senkus

## Ukrainian Social Democratic Party of Canada

(Ukrainska sotsiial-demokratychna partiia v Kanadi, or USDPC). A socialist political organization established in 1914. Its organizational antecedents include the Taras Shevchenko Society, formed in Winnipeg in 1904; the Ukrainian branches of the Socialist Party of Canada, organized in Nanaimo, Portage la Prairie, and Winnipeg in 1907; and the Federation of Ukrainian Social Democrats, formed in 1909, whose biweekly newspaper, *Robochyi narod*, became the USDPC's official organ. The group's leaders included I. Navizivsky and M. Popovich. When banned in 1918 for antiwar agitation, the USDPC had about 1,500 members, mostly immigrant laborers in mining, lumbering, and construction. It was later reconstituted as the *Ukrainian Labour-Farmer Temple Association.

## Ukrainian Social Democratic Workers' party

(Ukrainska sotsiial-demokratychna robitnycha partiia, or USDRP). A clandestine party of the nationally conscious, revolutionary Marxist intelligentsia in Russian-ruled Ukraine that superseded the *Revolutionary Ukrainian party at the end of that party's third congress in December 1905. Prominent among the founding members were D. Antonovych, L. Bych, P. Diatliv, V. Doroshenko, D. Dontsov, M. Kovalsky, A. Livytsky, B. Martos, L. Matsiievych, Isaak Mazepa, P. Poniatenko, M. *Porsh (the first leader and ideologist), S. Petliura, V. Sadovsky, V. Stepankivsky, M. Tkachenko, M. Trotsky, S. Tymoshenko, V. Vynnychenko, L. Yurkevych, and A. Zhuk. The USDRP basically adopted the German Social Democratic Erfurt program. The approx 3,000 members of the USDRP did political work among the proletarianized peasantry of Chernihiv, Kharkiv, Kiev, Podilia, Poltava, and Volhynia gubernias and the Kuban. In 1906–7 the USDRP boycotted and condemned the 'bourgeois' *Ukrainian caucus in the Russian State Duma. From late 1906 on, the USDRP suffered mass arrests, repressions, and desertions, as well as internal conflicts. After its March 1907 congress the party was dormant, and its members co-operated with the Mensheviks and the Jewish Workers' Bund. Many leading members fled to Galicia and Central Europe, where they formally united with the *Spilka in late 1911. During the First World War several of them were active in the *Union for the Liberation of Ukraine. In the first decade of its existence the USDRP published the organs *Vil'na Ukraïna* (1906) and *Nasha Duma* (1907) in St Petersburg, *Borot'ba* (1906) and *Slovo* (1907–9) in Kiev, and *Sotsiial-demokrat* (1907) in Poltava. The USDRP Foreign Group, headed by Zhuk, published *Pratsia* (1909–10), *Robitnyk* (1910), and *Nash holos* (1910–11) in Austrian-ruled Lviv and *Borot'ba* (1915–16, ed Yurkevych) in Geneva.

The USDRP was reactivated as a public organization after the February Revolution. Until 1919 it published a daily paper, *Robitnycha hazeta*. At its conference in Kiev on 17–18 April 1917 it voted in favor of Ukrainian autonomy and federation with a democratic Russia. In July 1917 it dominated the First All-Ukrainian Workers' Congress. Although the USDRP had the most politically developed members (5,000 in October 1917) of all the Ukrainian left-wing parties, unlike the *Ukrainian Party of Socialist Revolutionaries it did not have mass support because of its cautious position on the socialization of land. It was on the executive level of the 1917–18 Central Rada and 1918–20 UNR coalition governments that the USDRP had the greatest influence. Vynnychenko was the Rada's vice-president and also headed the 1917 *General Secretariat of the Central Rada, and Petliura, Porsh, Sadovsky, and Tkachenko held portfolios in the latter body. In the first UNR *Council of National Ministers (CNM) Vynnychenko served as prime minister until 30 January 1918, and Antonovych, Porsh, Mazurenko, L. Mykhailiv, and Martos held portfolios. Under the right wing 1918 *Hetman government the USDRP suffered repression; Petliura, Vynnychenko, and other leaders were imprisoned. Forced to go underground, the party adopted a position in favor of Ukrainian independence and participated in the coalition *Ukrainian National Union that led the successful uprising against the Hetman government and the German army.

In the UNR *Directory that took power in December 1918, Vynnychenko was the head, and Petliura was commander in chief of the UNR Army. In the revived CNM V. Chekhivsky served as prime minister, and Antonovych, Martos, B. Matiushenko, V. Mazurenko, and Mykhailiv held portfolios until February 1919. At the fourth USDRP congress (10–12 January 1919) a split in the USDRP occurred. The left wing, which advocated rule by peasants' and workers' councils in an independent Ukrainian socialist republic and immediate peace with Soviet Russia, broke away and formed the separate *Ukrainian Social Democratic Workers' party (Independentists). The majority faction advocated a toilers' democracy, the gradual socialization of key economic sectors, and support for the Directory and the defense of the independent UNR against Soviet and Allied aggression. At the January 1919 *Labor Congress its delegates voted in favor of a democratic parliament, the implementation of major social reforms, the supreme authority of the Directory, and local rule by commissioners.

When the new prime minister, S. Ostapenko (not a USDRP member), began attempts at reaching an accord with the Entente Powers in February 1919, the USDRP instructed its members in the CNM to resign. Vynnychenko also resigned and emigrated with his followers. He was succeeded by Petliura, who resigned from the USDRP to become the new head of the Directory. A part of the USDRP remaining in Ukraine (including the Central Committee members A. Livytsky, I. Romanchenko, and M. Shadlun) continued supporting the Directory. In the CNM appointed in April 1919, Martos served as prime minister until August, and Livytsky (deputy prime minister), Mazepa, Shadlun, and H. Syrotenko held portfolios. Mazepa served as prime minister from August 1919 until May 1920. He added Tymoshenko to the CNM and appointed P. Fedenko a member of the Central Ukrainian Insurgent Committee. Livytsky signed the UNR-Polish Treaty of *Warsaw in April 1920, and from May 1920 only he, Mazepa, and Tymoshenko remained in the CNM.

The USDRP was banned in Soviet Ukraine. At the 9–13 September 1919 conference of USDRP émigrés in Vienna the Central Committee members P. Chykalenko, P. Didushok, Yu. Hasenko, I. Kalynovych, V. Levynsky, S. Mazurenko, H. Palamar, H. Piddubny, S. Vikul, and Vynnychenko demanded that the USDRP withdraw its support for Petliura's Directory and the CNM, and that its members resign from the CNM. After losing the vote on their motion they left the USDRP and constituted the so-called Foreign Group of the Ukrainian Communist party until 1921. The émigré majority formed the Prague-centered USDRP Foreign Group under the leadership of Mazepa. Y. Bezpalko, O. Bochkovsky, Fedenko, O. Kozlovsky, Matiushenko, and V. Starosolsky were prominent members. A member organization of the Labor and Socialist International, the group published the organs Vil'na Ukraïna (Lviv 1921), Sotsiialistychna dumka (Lviv and Prague 1921–3), and Sotsiial-Demokrat (Prague 1925–9; Poděbrady 1929–39?). Although it was not part of the UNR *government-in-exile, it remained loyal to it, and the former USDRP member Livytsky served as its prime minister until 1947. After the Second World War former USDRP members helped to found the émigré *Ukrainian National Council in 1947 and the *Ukrainian Socialist party in 1950.

BIBLIOGRAPHY
Stepaniuk, V.; Dovbyshchenko, Ia. Z istoriï ukraïns'koho sotsiial-demokratychnoho rukhu 1900–1918 rr. (Kharkiv 1918)
Khrystiuk, P. Zamitky i materiialy do istoriï ukraïns'koï revoliutsiï 1917–1920 rr., 4 vols (Vienna 1921–2; repr, New York 1969)
Hermaize, O. Narysy z istoriï revoliutsiinoho rukhu na Ukraïni, 1 (Kiev 1926)
Fedenko, P. Sotsiializm davnii i novochasnyi (London–Paris–Munich 1968)
Boshyk, G. 'The Rise of Ukrainian Political Parties in Russia, 1900–1907: With Special Reference to Social Democracy,' D Phil diss (Oxford University 1981)
Kuras, I. Povchal'nyi urok istoriï (Ideino-politychne bankrotstvo Ukraïns'koï sotsial-demokratychnoï robitnychoï partiï) (Kiev 1986)
R. Senkus, A. Zhukovsky

## Ukrainian Social Democratic Workers' party (Independentists)

(Ukrainska sotsiial-demokratychna robitnycha partiia-nezalezhnykh, or Nezalezhnyky). Originally a leftist faction within the *Ukrainian Social Democratic Workers' party (USDRP) and then a separate political party. In December 1918 the faction established its own Organizational Bureau in Kiev. It was opposed to both the Directory of the UNR and the CP(B)U and advocated an independent Soviet Ukrainian republic. It accused the CP(B)U of being an alien organization obsessed with violence, which substituted the dictatorship of the Party for the dictatorship of the proletariat and rejected the national rights of Ukrainians. The Independentists officially left the USDRP in January 1919, when the party's sixth congress rejected their motion to transform the UNR into a Soviet republic. As a party the Independentists patterned themselves on the Independent German Social Democratic party. Their leading ideologists were M. *Tkachenko and A. *Richytsky, and their official organ was Chervonyi prapor.

Initially the Independentists adopted a pro-Soviet program and welcomed the establishment of G. Piatakov's Bolshevik government in Ukraine. They tried to function as a legal opposition party but were soon disillusioned. Upon breaking with the Bolsheviks the Independentists set up the *All-Ukrainian Revolutionary Committee, which headed an anti-Bolshevik revolt from April to July 1919. The leading members of the committee (Yu. Mazurenko, A. Drahomyretsky, Richytsky, and M. Avdiienko), the Supreme Insurgent Council, and the General Insurgent Staff (Richytsky and Mazurenko) were prominent Independentists.

A tiny group within the party, the so-called Left-Independentist faction (Pankiv, Hurkovych, and Dihtiar), condemned the revolt, split off from the Independentists, and formed a separate party with the official organ Chervonyi stiah.

At the beginning of the revolt the Independentists opposed not only the Soviet Ukrainian and Russian governments but also the Directory of the UNR and co-operated with Otaman D. Zeleny's partisans. A short-lived modus vivendi with the UNR was reached in June 1919. In July the Independentists decided to call an end to their insurrection, which was making it easier for A. Denikin's forces to advance into Ukraine. The UNR government arrested some members of the General Insurgent Staff but soon released them. Mazurenko and Tkachenko fled to Moscow and tried to work with the Bolsheviks.

In August 1919 the Left-Independentists merged with the *Borotbists and formed the Ukrainian Communist party (of Borotbists); the Independentists became the Ukrainian Communist party, or Ukapisty, in January 1920. Both Communist parties criticized the CP(B)U and argued for an independent Soviet Ukraine with its own economic, political, and party centers. The Borotbists were dissolved in 1920, and the Ukapisty in 1924, and most of their members joined the CP(B)U. Many of the former Independentists, such as Richytsky, Yu. Lapchynsky, and B. Antonenko-Davydovych, became prominent Ukrainian cultural figures during Ukrainization and were later persecuted and even destroyed for their alleged nationalism.

BIBLIOGRAPHY
Maistrenko, I. *Istoriia Komunistychnoï partiï Ukraïny* (Munich 1979)
I. Myhul

**Ukrainian Socialist Alliance–Peasant Union.** See Sel-Soiuz.

**Ukrainian Socialist party** (Ukrainska sotsiialistychna partiia, or USP). A small revolutionary party founded in Kiev in 1900 by Polish students sympathetic to the Ukrainian cause and other Poles who considered themselves Ukrainian. The USP was led by B. *Yaroshevsky, and modeled its program on that of the Polish Socialist party. Its approx 15 active members propagated among the peasantry of Right-Bank Ukraine the overthrow of tsarist oppression and the creation of an independent, democratic socialist Ukraine. Its five pamphlets (including the first Ukrainian translation of K. Marx's *Communist Manifesto*), proclamations, and the organ *Dobra novyna* (1903, ed S. Vityk and M. Stanko) were published in Austrian-ruled Lviv with the help of the *Ukrainian Social Democratic party there. The USP merged with the *Revolutionary Ukrainian party (RUP) in the summer of 1903, but it seceded in December after the Lviv-based RUP Foreign Committee condemned its position on Ukrainian independence as chauvinist. The USP never officially disbanded, but by 1905 most of its members had joined other parties.

**Ukrainian Socialist party** (Ukrainska sotsiialistychna partiia). A union of émigré members of Ukrainian socialist parties from central (the Ukrainian Social Democratic Workers' party and the Ukrainian Party of Socialist Revolutionaries) and Western Ukraine (the Ukrainian Social Democratic party and the Ukrainian Radical party), formed in Augsburg, Germany, in 1950. The party supported the UNR government-in-exile and belonged to the *Ukrainian National Council. It represented Ukraine in international socialist party congresses in Europe. Its leaders included S. Dovhal, P. and B. Fedenko, I. Luchyshyn, V. Lysy, S. Ripetsky, and M. Stakhiv. With the death of most of its members, it ceased to be active. The party published several issues of an irregular organ, *Nashe slovo*, and several books by P. Fedenko.

**Ukrainian Socialist Radical party.** See Ukrainian Radical party.

**Ukrainian Society for Friendship and Cultural Relations with Foreign Countries** (Ukrainske tovarystvo druzhby ta kulturnoho zviazku z zarubizhnymy krainamy). An association for developing cultural contacts between Ukraine and other countries, with 12 oblast branches and nearly 2,000 affiliate members (local friendship societies and cultural organizations). First established in 1926 in Kharkiv as the Ukrainian Society for Cultural Relations with Foreign Countries, it assumed its present name in 1959. The society was a member of the Union of Soviet Societies for Friendship and Cultural Relations with Foreign Countries. In representing Soviet policy the Ukrainian Society served as a major source of propaganda. Its activities consisted of sponsoring foreign cultural and trade delegations; sending Ukrainian delegations abroad; organizing Ukrainian festivals, art and industrial exhibitions, lectures, film screenings, and theatrical events in other countries; sending books and periodicals about Ukraine abroad; and hosting similar events in Ukraine. The presidents of the Ukrainian Society have been K. Kolosov (1959–68), V. Dmytruk (1968–71), V. Shevchenko (1972–7), M. Orlyk (1977–8), and V. Osnach.

**Ukrainian Society for the Protection of Historical and Cultural Monuments** (Ukrainske tovarystvo okhorony pamiatok istorii ta kultury). A republican voluntary organization established in Kiev on 21 December 1966 with the purpose of involving the Soviet Ukrainian public in the finding and protection of monuments of history, archeology, architecture, art, literature, ethnography, and folk art. The society has been headed by K. Dubyna (1966–7) and P. Tronko (since 1968). It co-operated closely with the Communist Youth League, the Znannia Society, the Ministry of Culture, the Chief Archival Administration at the Ukrainian SSR Council of Ministers, and city planners. In 1986 it had nearly 18 million dues-paying individual members, in 75,293 workplaces and schools, who also donated over three million rubles to the society that year. The society's nearly 4,000 councils, research sections and commissions, and inspectorates function within the framework of state, oblast, raion, and city governments and employ more than 37,000 people, over 3,000 of them in administration. The society has devoted particular attention to protecting monuments of the Second World War. In 1981–5 it spent over 20 million rubles on the erection of new architectural monuments and the reconstruction and restoration of old ones. It organizes public events using the services of over 20,000 lecturers; operates some 700 'people's universities,' which educate new organizers, lecturers, guides, and inspectors; and publishes textbooks, guides, photo albums, methodological literature, and a quarterly magazine, *Pam'iatnyky Ukraïny* (est 1969), renamed *Pam'iatky Ukraïny* in 1988. It also convenes republican congresses (1966, 1971, 1976, 1981, 1986), has columns in more than 200 local newspapers and a regular radio broadcast, prepares television documentaries, and funds and runs the Museum of Folk Architecture and Folkways of Ukraine and a special restoration workshop.

**Ukrainian Society of Aid to Emigrants from Greater Ukraine** (Ukrainske tovarystvo dopomohy emigrantam z Velykoi Ukrainy). A relief and cultural organization established in Lviv in 1921, initially as a department of the *Ukrainian Citizens' Committee and then as an independent entity. It had active branches in Warsaw, Kalisz, and Częstochowa. The society provided a wide range of services to émigrés from Soviet Ukraine – financial support, legal aid, medical care, and cultural and educational development. It maintained a library, organized workshops and co-operatives, arranged concerts and lectures, and helped students to finish their education. Starting in 1922 it published the annual almanac *Dnipro*. The society's president was V. *Doroshenko, and its leading members were L. Biletsky, M. Dontsova, P. Kholodny, S. Fedak, and I. Kokorudz. After the Soviet occupation of Galicia in 1939 the society was dissolved.

**Ukrainian Society of Bibliophiles in Prague** (Ukrainske tovarystvo prykhylnykiv knyhy v Prazi). An association of bibliographers, librarians, publishers, and book lovers, founded in Prague in January 1927. It organized conferences and lectures on Ukrainian bibliography and publishing, book exhibits, and displays; compiled bibliographies of Ukrainian publications and Ucrainica; published the journal *Knyholiub* (1927–32); organized a large exhibition of Ukrainian book art in 1933; and, from 1934, sponsored annual awards for the five best-designed Ukrainian publications. The society maintained close contact with similar organizations in Czechoslovakia, Poland, Lviv, and (initially) Soviet Ukraine. In 1932 it had over 100 members. Its first head, S. *Siropolko, was succeeded in 1934 by V. *Sichynsky. The society ceased to exist in 1942.

**Ukrainian Sociological Institute** (Ukrainskyi sotsiolohichnyi instytut). An émigré institution founded in 1919 in Vienna by M. *Hrushevsky with the participation of other members of the *Ukrainian Party of Socialist Revolutionaries. In 1920–1 the institute organized public lectures on topics ranging from sociology to the history of the Ukrainian revolution and published 10 works, among them P. *Khrystiuk's classic collection of materials on the history of the 1917–20 Ukrainian revolution (4 vols, 1921–2), M. Lozynsky's book on Galicia in 1918–20 (1922), V. Starosolsky's *Teoriia natsii* (Theory of Nation, 1921), and a book on M. Drahomanov and the Geneva socialist circle (1922) edited by Hrushevsky. The institute ceased to exist when Hrushevsky and Khrystiuk returned to Ukraine in 1924.

**Ukrainian Soviet Socialist Republic** (Ukrainska Radianska Sotsialistychna Respublika, or URSR). A communist state proclaimed by the First All-Ukrainian Congress of Soviets in Kharkiv on 24–25 December 1917 and established through armed aggression against the UNR by Soviet Russia and local Bolshevik forces in 1917–20. At the end of 1922 it became one of the constituent republics of the USSR. Until 1937 it was called the Ukrainian Socialist Soviet Republic (Ukrainska Sotsiialistychna Radianska Respublika). The URSR ceased to exist on 24 August 1991, when its Supreme Soviet proclaimed the independent state of Ukraine.

The URSR bordered on the Black Sea and the Sea of Azov in the south, on Rumania, the Moldavian SSR (Moldova), and Hungary in the southwest, on Czechoslovakia and Poland in the west, on the Belorussian SSR (Belarus) in the north, and on the RSFSR (now Russian Federation) in the northeast and east. The total length of its borders was 6,466 km, of which 4,142 km were with other USSR republics, 1,271 km were with Eastern European countries, and the remaining 1,053 km were coast. Lying between 52°10′ and 40°23′ N latitude (893 km from north to south) and between 22°10′ and 40°15′ E longitude (1,316 km from west to east), the URSR had an area of 603,700 sq km. It was the third-largest USSR republic, after the RSFSR and the Kazakh SSR.

The population of the URSR, second only to that of the RSFSR, was 51.7 million according to the 1989 census; 34.6 million, or 67 percent of it, was urban. Less than three-quarters of the population was Ukrainian (72.7 percent), over one-fifth was Russian (22.1 percent), and other minorities accounted for the remaining 5.2 percent (including 0.95 percent Jewish, 0.86 percent Belarusian, 0.63 percent Moldavian, 0.45 percent Bulgarian, 0.43 percent Polish, 0.32 percent Hungarian, 0.26 percent Rumanian, 0.19 percent Greek, and 0.17 percent Tatar). For administrative purposes the URSR was divided into 25 oblasts, 479 raions, and 8,878 rural councils (*silrady*). Of its 434 cities 2 were subordinated directly to the republican government, 142 to the oblast governments, and 290 to the raion authorities. There were 927 urban-type settlements in 1989 (see the table). The borders of the URSR did not encompass the entire Ukrainian ethnic territory, which is one-quarter larger (750,200 sq km) than the national territory and contains 16 percent more people (60 million). The capital of the URSR was *Kharkiv, and from 1934, *Kiev.

The state emblem and red-and-blue flag of the Ukrainian SSR

**Political structure.** During the revolutionary period the Bolsheviks set up, on 25 December 1917, the Central Executive Committee of the Soviets of Ukraine as the government of Soviet Ukraine and formed, on 17 December, the People's Secretariat (headed by Ye. Medvediev and then M. Skrypnyk). The Bolsheviks had proclaimed Ukraine a republic of workers', soldiers', and peasants' soviets federated closely with Soviet Russia. Yet the URSR constitution of 10 March 1919 did not mention any federative links, and established a nominally independent state. In reality Moscow (the Party and government of Soviet Russia) controlled the URSR through the CP(B)U, which, except briefly, from its Tahanrih conference in April to its first congress in Moscow in July 1918, was a constituent part of the Russian Communist Party (Bolshevik).

The government institutions of the URSR were copies of the Russian institutions, and Ukrainian legislation merely echoed Russian laws. In fact, Russia's legislative acts were enforced automatically in Ukraine. The pretense of a separate Ukrainian state was maintained briefly to counteract the appeal of the UNR among the Ukrainian people. As soon as Soviet rule was established firmly in Ukraine, the URSR was turned into a constituent part of the federated state of the USSR.

In 1917–27 the highest governing body of Soviet Ukraine was the *All-Ukrainian Congress of Soviets. That body elected the *All-Ukrainian Central Executive Committee, which governed the country between sessions of the congress and appointed the *Council of People's Commissars as its executive organ. Similar bodies were established locally on the city, village, volost, county, and

Ukrainian SSR in 1920-1939

Incorporation of lands into the Ukr. SSR 1939

Northern Bukovyna, northern Bessarabia
and southern Bessarabia 1940

Transcarpatia 1945

Crimea 1954

0    100    200 km

Contemporary boundary
of Ukraine

International boundary

⊙    Administrative center

# UKRAINIAN SOVIET SOCIALIST REPUBLIC

gubernia level. Their members were selected through indirect elections, in which a worker's vote was worth more than a peasant's, and some citizens had no vote at all.

The URSR was absorbed into the RSFSR by the merging of their commissariats on the basis of so-called defensive or economic alliance treaties between two or more Soviet republics (1 June 1919 and 28 December 1920). The situation did not change when the URSR joined the USSR on 30 December 1922 as an equal partner of the RSFSR, the Belorussian SSR and the Transcaucasian SFSR. In the revised (May 1925) constitution of the URSR and its new version (1929) the governing bodies remained similar to the previous ones: the All-Ukrainian Congress of Soviets, the All-Ukrainian Central Executive Committee (headed by H. *Petrovsky), and the Council of People's Commissars (headed by V. *Chubar and later by P. *Liubchenko). The organs of the state administration, the people's commissariats, were of three types: (1) merged, which existed at the USSR level and had representatives in the republican governments; (2) joint, which existed in parallel at both the USSR and the republican levels; and (3) independent, which existed only at the republican level. In the Union agreement, five merged commissariats were created: foreign affairs, defense, foreign trade, transportation, and postal and tele-

graph service. Later, other commissariats were also merged. The new constitutions of the USSR (1936) and the URSR (1937) centralized the government system even further. A system of direct elections was introduced, and every citizen was given the vote. The Supreme Soviet, with its Presidium, became the highest governing body, and the Council of People's Commissars (from 1946, the Council of Ministers) became the highest executive organ. The people's commissariats were classified into (1) all-Union, (2) Union-republican, and (3) republican, and the number of all-Union and Union-republican commissariats was increased. The Constitution of 1 February 1944 gave the URSR new powers in foreign relations and defense by establishing Union-republican commissariats (later ministries) in those areas. The URSR did not establish its own embassies or armed forces, however. By the end of the 1940s Ukraine's Ministry of Defense had been abolished.

As the rights of the Union republics were expanded after J. Stalin's death, the URSR received in its revised constitution some new powers in administrative, judicial, and economic matters. In 1957, *regional economic councils were introduced in addition to the republican economic councils to strengthen republican autonomy. The URSR gained the right to pass its own laws in the field as long as

Administrative divisions and population of the Ukrainian ssr, January 1989

| Oblast | Raions | Rural soviets | Cities | Town smts | City raions | Population (1,000s) | (% urban) |
|---|---|---|---|---|---|---|---|
| Cherkasy | 20 | 489 | 16 | 16 | 2 | 1,532 | 53 |
| Chernihiv | 22 | 504 | 15 | 32 | 2 | 1,416 | 53 |
| Chernivtsi | 10 | 218 | 10 | 9 | 3 | 938 | 42 |
| Crimea | 15 | 243 | 16 | 56 | 17 | 2,456 | 70 |
| Dnipropetrovske | 20 | 260 | 19 | 54 | 18 | 3,883 | 83 |
| Donetske | 18 | 226 | 50 | 134 | 21 | 5,328 | 90 |
| Ivano-Frankivske | 14 | 383 | 14 | 25 | 0 | 1,424 | 42 |
| Kharkiv | 25 | 333 | 16 | 62 | 9 | 3,196 | 79 |
| Kherson | 18 | 249 | 9 | 30 | 3 | 1,240 | 61 |
| Khmelnytskyi | 20 | 485 | 13 | 24 | 0 | 1,527 | 47 |
| Kiev* | 25 | 574 | 25 | 32 | 14 | 4,542 | 80 |
| Kirovohrad | 21 | 346 | 12 | 26 | 2 | 1,240 | 60 |
| Luhanske | 18 | 189 | 37 | 109 | 4 | 2,864 | 86 |
| Lviv | 20 | 483 | 41 | 36 | 5 | 2,748 | 59 |
| Mykolaiv | 19 | 253 | 9 | 20 | 4 | 1,331 | 66 |
| Odessa | 26 | 393 | 17 | 33 | 8 | 2,642 | 66 |
| Poltava | 25 | 410 | 15 | 21 | 5 | 1,753 | 57 |
| Rivne | 15 | 319 | 10 | 17 | 0 | 1,170 | 45 |
| Sumy | 18 | 355 | 15 | 21 | 2 | 1,433 | 62 |
| Ternopil | 16 | 458 | 16 | 21 | 0 | 1,169 | 41 |
| Transcarpathia | 13 | 269 | 10 | 28 | 0 | 1,252 | 41 |
| Vinnytsia | 27 | 637 | 17 | 30 | 3 | 1,932 | 44 |
| Volhynia | 15 | 352 | 11 | 21 | 0 | 1,062 | 49 |
| Zaporizhia | 18 | 240 | 14 | 22 | 6 | 2,081 | 76 |
| Zhytomyr | 23 | 543 | 9 | 46 | 2 | 1,545 | 53 |
| Total | 481 | 9,211 | 436 | 925 | 120 | 51,704 | 67 |

*Includes city of Kiev

they were consistent with Union legislation and were called for by Union organs. On that basis a number of new URSR codes were worked out in the 1950s and 1960s. From the end of the 1960s the system of government was increasingly centralized: by 1978 there were 28 Union-republican ministries and 16 state committees, and only 6 republican ministries. As of June 1986 there were 23 Union-republican ministries and 14 state committees, and 6 republican ministries and 1 republican state committee. The last constitution of the URSR (1978), modeled on the USSR constitution (1977), reiterated the main articles of the latter and made only minor changes in the structure of government. Structural changes in the ministries could be made thenceforth by legislative enactment.

Both formally and actually the URSR was a unitary state without autonomous parts. Until 1940 it contained the Moldavian ASSR, which that year became a separate Union republic. In 1954 Crimea oblast was transferred from the RSFSR to the URSR. After a local referendum in January 1991, the Supreme Soviet of the URSR recognized the Crimea's autonomy. Until the end of 1991 the URSR was part of a broader federation of the USSR and its governing organs were subordinated to the governing organs of the USSR. Until 1990 the leading force in the political system in the URSR was the CPU, which was merely a branch of the CPSU.

**History.** (For the history of the URSR to the beginning of the 1980s see *History of Ukraine.) Under L. Brezhnev's aging successors Yu. Andropov (1982–4) and K. Chernenko (1984–5) it became increasingly clear that the repressive, corrupt regime established by Brezhnev was leading the USSR into bankruptcy. After assuming power in 1985,

M. Gorbachev tried to revive the stagnant economy by a program of restructuring (Perestroika) at home and a reduction of armaments and tensions abroad. But economic reforms threatened the existing power structure and could succeed only if extensive political reforms were introduced. Furthermore, the Chornobyl nuclear accident (26 April 1986) and its handling by the authorities undermined public confidence not only in Soviet technology but also in the Party, the central government in Moscow, and the old guard led by V. *Shcherbytsky in Kiev. The disaster convinced even many members of the privileged Soviet elite that the existing political system and its corrupt leadership endangered the very survival of the people.

Gorbachev's policy of Glasnost (openness) led to increasingly bolder criticism of the Party, the government, and Soviet society and demands for faster and more radical reform. Nonofficial and uncensored publications began to circulate widely, and unofficial organizations (see *Neformaly) sprang up to address cultural needs. National movements calling for greater local autonomy and less control from Moscow emerged in the Baltic and Caucasian republics and set an example for Ukraine. Recently released political prisoners reactivated the Ukrainian Helsinki Group at the end of 1987 and had reorganized it by mid-1988 into a broad political organization, the Ukrainian Helsinki Union, which spearheaded the national movement in Ukraine. The first unsanctioned public rallies were held in Kiev and Lviv in the summer of 1988.

Elections to the new USSR Congress of People's Deputies were held in March 1989. Although only a third of the deputies were elected by direct popular vote, some outspoken critics of the government won seats in the con-

A non-Party public rally in Lviv in July 1988

gress and turned it into a forum of debate over important issues. By September Shcherbytsky had retired as the first secretary of the CPU. The *Popular Movement of Ukraine was founded to unify the various streams of the national movement. In response to strong public protest the electoral law for the coming elections to the Supreme Soviet of the URSR in March 1990 was changed to make the election of all deputies subject to direct voting. Although the democratic movement lacked financial means and was poorly organized, it captured over a fifth of the seats in the Supreme Soviet and overwhelming majorities on the oblast and city councils in the three western oblasts of Ukraine (Lviv, Ternopil, and Ivano-Frankivske). Upon forming the National Council the 125 democratic deputies used the live radio and TV coverage of the parliamentary proceedings to raise the political consciousness of the Ukrainian people. A number of political parties appeared. On 16 July 1990 parliament passed the Declaration on Ukraine's State Sovereignty, which asserted the precedence of Ukrainian laws over Union laws and signaled Ukraine's intention to form its own army, create a banking system, and issue its own currency. A student hunger strike in October forced the resignation of Prime Minister V. Masol. In November the chairmen of the Ukrainian and Russian parliaments, L. Kravchuk and B. Yeltsin, signed a 10-year co-operation agreement between the two sovereign republics. To preserve the USSR, reactionary forces unleashed violence in the Baltic republics, which had declared their independence, and the Communist majority in the Ukrainian parliament passed undemocratic restrictions on political expression. In Ukraine there were protests in support of independent Lithuania and against Ukraine's signing of a new Union treaty. To build pressure for maintaining the Union, the central authorities held an all-Union referendum. In Ukraine 70 percent of the voters approved a new union of sovereign states, but at the same time 80 percent supported sovereignty as defined in the act of 16 July 1990. Negotiations between the central government and the sovereign republics continued until the attempted coup of 19–21 August in Moscow. On 24 August 1991 the Supreme Soviet of the URSR proclaimed Ukraine's independence, subject to a popular referendum to be held in December. Two days later the Supreme Soviet suspended the activities of the CPU, and shortly afterwards it banned the Communist party altogether. On 1 December 1991 over 90 percent of the voters

confirmed the declaration of independence and elected Kravchuk the first president of the new state, Ukraine. Ukraine was recognized immediately by Poland, Canada, Hungary, Russia, and the Baltic states. The referendum sealed the fate of the Soviet Union: without Ukraine a meaningful federation was not possible. On 8 December Ukraine, Belarus (formerly Belorussia), and Russia formed a Commonwealth of Independent States and declared the end of the USSR.

The state symbols of the URSR were a red and blue flag with a golden star, hammer and sickle on the red field, and an emblem with a golden hammer and sickle over a golden rising sun on a red shield surmounted by a red star and encircled in ears of wheat. Its anthem glorified the Soviet Union, V. Lenin's leadership, and the friendship of the Russian people.

(See also *International legal status of Ukraine.)

BIBLIOGRAPHY
Fedenko, P. *Ukraïna pislia smerty Stalina* (Munich 1956)
Zlenko, A. *Derzhavnyi ustrii Ukraïns'koï RSR* (Kiev 1959)
Sullivant, R. *Soviet Politics and the Ukraine, 1917–1957* (New York 1962)
Bilinsky, Y. *The Second Soviet Republic: The Ukraine after World War II* (New Brunswick, NJ 1964)
Lewytzkyj, B. *Die Sowjetukraine, 1944–1963* (Köln–Berlin 1964)
Potichnyj, P. (ed). *Ukraine in the Seventies* (Oakville, Ont 1975)
Krawchenko, B. (ed). *Ukraine after Shelest* (Edmonton 1983)
Lewytzkyj, B. *Politics and Society in Soviet Ukraine, 1953–1980* (Edmonton 1984)
*Istoriia gosudarstva i prava Ukrainskoi SSR*, 3 vols (Kiev 1987–)
Marples, D. *Ukraine under Perestroika* (Edmonton 1991)
Solchanyk, R. (ed). *Ukraine: From Chernobyl' to Sovereignty* (Edmonton 1992)

V. Markus, I. Stebelsky

**Ukrainian Sports Federation of the USA and Canada** (Ukrainska sportova tsentralia Ameryky i Kanady, or USTsAK). An umbrella organization of Ukrainian sports clubs and of teams sponsored by Plast and the Ukrainian Youth Association, founded in December 1955. It consists of three divisions: eastern United States (Newark, NJ, Philadelphia, New York City, Rochester, Yonkers), western United States (Chicago, Cleveland, Detroit), and Canada (Toronto, Montreal). USTsAK has run an annual summer sports school; trained referees and coaches; and organized annual soccer, skiing, volleyball, basketball, tennis, chess, swimming, and golf competitions, nearly 20 Ukrainian

Youth Sports Games, and Free Olympiads in Toronto (1980, 1984) and Philadelphia (1988), in which Ukrainians, Estonians, Latvians, Lithuanians, and Armenians living in North America competed. In 1981 it represented 20 clubs and sections and had a membership of 2,500. The first chairman of the board of directors was E. Zharsky. The presidents of the federation were I. Krasnyk, V. Levytsky, Ya. Khorostil, Y. Kosachevych, M. Snihurovych, W. Kizyma, R. Kucil, and M. Stebelsky.

**Ukrainian Sports Union** (Ukrainskyi sportovyi soiuz, or USS). An umbrella organization of Ukrainian sports clubs and sports sections of the Sokil and Luh societies in Galicia, founded in 1925. The USS oversaw sports and physical education programs in Galicia, organized annual competitions in various sports, introduced tests for a physical fitness badge (1934–9), organized medical care for athletes (with the co-operation of the Ukrainian Physicians' Society), and published sports magazines. In 1934 it represented 77 organizations with a combined membership of 2,053. Through its activities it contributed to the rise of national consciousness, and because of this it was abolished by the Polish authorities in 1937. The USS presidents were O. Navrotsky, Ye. Savchak, B. Hnatevych, S. Dmokhovsky, B. Makarushka, S. Shukhevych, and O. Radlovsky.

**Ukrainian State** (Ukrainska Derzhava). The official name of Ukraine under the *Hetman government of P. *Skoropadsky, formally announced on 29 April 1918 in the Manifesto to the Entire Ukrainian Nation and the Laws on the Provisional State System of Ukraine. The legal structure of the Ukrainian State was a distinctly Ukrainian variant of a constitutional monarchy, based on some aspects of the traditional Cossack Hetmanate of the 17th and 18th centuries. The name appeared on official seals and currency until the fall of the Hetman government on 14 December 1918.

**Ukrainian State Academy of Arts** (Ukrainska derzhavna akademiia mystetstv). The first Ukrainian postsecondary art school, established in Kiev by a commission created in August 1917 by I. *Steshenko, the Central Rada's general secretary of education, and headed by H. *Pavlutsky. The academy's statute was approved by the Central Rada on 18 November 1917. The academy was officially opened on 5 December 1917 in the Rada building (formerly the Pedagogical Museum). On 31 December the Rada adopted a law making the academy an autonomous state institution with an annual budget of 97,400 *karbovantsi* and the right to receive foreign books and artworks duty-free. In January 1918 the academy moved into the former Tereshchenko School. It was governed by a council, elected on 27 October 1917, that included D. Antonovych, P. Zaitsev, and D. Shcherbakivsky (learned secretary). The rectors were V. Krychevsky (1917–18), F. Krychevsky (1918 and 1920–2), H. Narbut (1919–20), and M. Boichuk (1920). Its original faculty consisted of Boichuk (fresco and mosaic), M. Burachek (landscape), V. Krychevsky (folk art, ornamentation, architecture, composition), F. Krychevsky (genre, portrait, and historical painting, sculpture), A. Manevich (landscape), O. Murashko (genre painting), M. Zhuk (portraiture), and Narbut (graphic art). Courses were also taught by F. Ernst, M. Makarenko, V. Modzalevsky, and Shcherbakivsky. In

Faculty members and important guests at the official opening of the Ukrainian State Academy of Arts in 1917. Sitting, from left: Abram Manevich, Oleksander Murashko, Fedir Krychevsky, President Mykhailo Hrushevsky, Secretary of Education Ivan Steshenko, Mykola Burachek; standing: Heorhii Narbut, Vasyl Krychevsky, Mykhailo Boichuk

April 1919 the academy's premises were closed down by the Bolshevik authorities. Courses were held in the professors' homes until October, when the academy moved into a building rented by the Dniprosoiuz co-operative union. In 1920 the sculptor B. Kratko replaced Manevich, and in 1921 L. Kramarenko (large-scale decorative painting), V. Meller (theatrical scenery), S. Nalepinska (xylography), Ye. Sahaidachny (sculpture), and A. Taran (mosaic) joined the faculty. The academy had 140 students in 1918–19, 253 in October 1919, and approx 400 in 1921–2. Among them were T. Boichuk, S. Kolos, O. Lozovsky, O. Pavlenko, I. Padalka, V. Sedliar, R. Lisovsky, O. Dovzhenko, V. Krychevsky, Jr, S. Pozharshy, M. Rokytsky, O. Saienko, M. Yunak, K. Antonovych, and O. Sakhnovska. In 1922–3 the Kiev Gubernial Department of Professional Education transformed the academy into the Kiev Institute of Plastic Arts, which in 1924 became the *Kiev State Art Institute. Its first rector was I. Vrona. The formerly independent Ukrainian Architectural Institute (est 1918) became a faculty of the new institute.

S. Bilokin

**Ukrainian State Administration** (Ukrainske derzhavne pravlinnia). A provisional regional administration set up by S. *Bandera in Lviv in 1941. At a public meeting of Lviv's Ukrainian residents at the Prosvita hall on 30 June 1941 (later referred to as the National Assembly), Ya. *Stetsko proclaimed Bandera's decree on the creation of the Ukrainian state in the western territories of Ukraine (see *Proclamation of Ukrainian statehood) and the creation of a regional administration headed by Stetsko. On 4 July the German police prohibited publication of the act. Nevertheless, people held spontaneous meetings in outlying areas, at which representatives of the OUN (Bandera faction) proclaimed the restoration of Ukrainian statehood. A few similar demonstrations also took place in Volhynia, which was cleared of Soviet troops. At the same time local administrations, which recognized the State Administration, sprang up in Galicia and were tolerated for a period by the German and Hungarian military authorities.

The composition of the government was set on 5 July: Stetsko, president; M. Panchyshyn, first vice-president and minister of health; L. Rebet, second vice-president; Gen V. Petriv, defense; V. Lysy, internal affairs; M. Lebed, state security; V. Stakhiv, foreign affairs; Yu. Fedusevych, justice; Ye. Khraplyvy, agriculture; I. Olkhovy, finance; A. Piasetsky, forestry; V. Radzykevych, education and religion; O. Hai-Holovko, information and propaganda; I. Klymiv-Legenda, political co-ordination; N. Moroz, post and telegraph; and M. Rosliak, state chancery. Deputy ministers and secretaries were appointed also. Some of those who had been appointed without consultation turned down their appointments. Metropolitan A. Sheptytsky agreed to become the honorary patron of the new body. The State Administration sat several times (although attendance was never full), published several declarations, and sent a memorandum to the German government. At its sitting of 11 July some members pressed the need to clarify the nature of the relationship between the German command and the administration. The matter was to be settled by a delegation made up of Stetsko, Rebet, Pankivsky, and Lysy.

On 12 July Stetsko and R. Ilnytsky were arrested in Lviv and Stakhiv in Berlin by the German political police. Thereupon the Ukrainian State Administration ceased to function. The Council of Seniors headed by K. Levytsky, which had been set up as a consultative body by the Bandera OUN at a public meeting on 6 July, assumed the role of a temporary Ukrainian representation. Eventually it was reorganized into the Ukrainian National Council in Lviv.

BIBLIOGRAPHY
Pan'kivs'kyi, K. *Vid derzhavy do komitetu (lito 1941 roku u L'vovi)* (New York–Toronto 1957)
Stets'ko, Ia. *30-oho chervnia 1941: Proholoshennia vidnovlennia derzhavnosty Ukraïny* (Toronto–New York–London 1967)

The Ukrainian State Museum of Ethnography and Crafts

**Ukrainian State Museum of Ethnography and Crafts** (Ukrainskyi derzhavnyi muzei etnohrafiï ta khudozhnoho promyslu). The principal museum of its kind in Western Ukraine. It was established in 1951 through the merger of the Museum of Handicrafts (est 1874) and the Ethnographic Museum of the Shevchenko Scientific Society (est 1895). The holdings of both museums suffered heavy losses during the two world wars. After the second war they were replenished with nationalized private and public collections. By 1974 the museum held almost 80,000 artifacts of material culture, which were divided into two collections, ethnographic and handicraft. The ethnographic collection encompasses articles from every region of Ukraine, but particularly Western Ukraine: farm implements, craft tools, weavings, folk costumes, embroidery, ceramics, wood-carvings, artistic metal products, toys, and Easter eggs. The handicraft collection includes articles not only from Ukraine but also from other territories, such as Russia, Central and Western Europe, and the Orient: porcelain, faience, fine furniture, belts, tapestries, and clocks. In 1967 a Department of Folk Architecture was set up. It oversaw the construction of the Lviv Museum of Folk Architecture and Folkways (opened in 1972). The Museum of Ethnography and Handicrafts supports a wide research and publishing program. It organizes expeditions, conferences, and seminars and provides methodological consultation for cultural institutions and manufacturing enterprises. It has published scholarly monographs, albums, and the collection *Materialy z etnohrafiï ta mystetstvoznavstva* (8 vols, 1954–63). In 1982 the museum became a subdivision of the AN URSR (now ANU) Institute of Fine Arts, Folklore, and Ethnography in Kiev. Its director since 1958 has been Yu. Hoshko.

**Ukrainian State Trio** (Ukrainske derzhavne trio). An instrumental group established in Kharkiv in 1926 and active until 1941. Its members were M. Polevsky (piano), L. Tymoshenko (cello), and O. Ilevych (violin). The trio performed classical chamber music and works of contemporary Ukrainian composers.

**Ukrainian State University of Kiev.** See Kiev University.

**Ukrainian Steppe Nature Reserve** (Ukrainskyi stepovyi zapovidnyk). A nature reserve established in 1961 as an amalgamation of three nature reserves, Khomutovskyi step (Khomutove Steppe), Kamiani Mohyly (Stone Graves), and Mykhailivska tsilyna (Mykhailivka Virgin Soil Preserve). The reserve is dedicated to preserving a portion of the original steppe environment. It has a total area of 1,634 ha. The largest (1,030 ha) of the components, Khomutivskyi step, is situated in Novoozivske raion, Donetske oblast, in the Black Sea Depression. It provides sanctuary for animals such as the European hare, the mole rat, the tiger weasel, the steppe viper, the black-headed bunting, the whip snake, marmots, and the like, some of which faced almost total extinction at the turn of the century. It also features approx 560 varieties of flora. The Kamiani Mohyly component of the reserve consists of two parallel granite ridges separated by a valley. With an area of 404 ha, it stretches across the border between Donetske and Zaporizhia oblasts in Volodarske and Kuibysheve raions. A variety of vegetation can be found in the reserve, including the European aspen, pears, hawthorns, spireas, the dog rose, and the blackberry cotoneaster. Several centaureas and yarrows unique to the region grow in the reserve. The Mykhailivska tsilyna component (202 ha) is situated farther to the north, in Lebedyn raion of Sumy oblast. Although in the forest-steppe zone, the Ukrainian Steppe Nature Reserve is primarily a steppe-type reserve. Among its 960 varieties of fauna are approx 40 rare plants, including several vetches, carnations, wedge larkspurs, and irises. The reserve also shelters 26 species of mammals, 115 of birds, and 10 of fish.

I. Masnyk

**Ukrainian Student Association in Germany** (Spilka studentiv-ukraintsiv u Nimechchyni). The first Ukrainian student organization in Germany. Founded in 1921 and based in Berlin, it had 11 branches with approximately 180 members in 1923. In the following decade approx 400 students were members of the association, of whom 140 completed their education. In the 1930s the association gradually dissolved.

**Ukrainian Student Hromada in Saint Petersburg** (Ukrainska studentska hromada v Peterburzi). An association of Ukrainian students attending the various institutions of higher learning in St Petersburg, founded in 1898. Its purpose was to raise the national consciousness of Ukrainian students. It had a student choir and maintained close ties with the Ukrainian community in St Petersburg. Its members were active in the *Revolutionary Ukrainian party and the *Society of Ukrainian Progressives. The membership in the Hromada grew steadily: in 1905 there were 60 members, in 1908, 100, and on the eve of the First World War, 300. The heads of the Hromada were S. Shemet, V. Mazurenko, D. Doroshenko, and Serhii Tymoshenko, among others. Active and noteworthy members were M. Maslov, D. Dontsov, Ye. Neronovych, M. Skrypnyk, B. Ivanytsky, and I. Kosenko. The Hromada published the magazine *Ukraïns'kyi student* (Ukrainian Student, 1913–14). In 1916 the Hromada ceased operations.

**Ukrainian Student Organization of Mikhnovsky** (Tovarystvo ukrainskoi studiiuiuchoi molodi im. M. Mikhnovskoho, known also as Ukrainian Students' Association of Mikhnovsky, or TUSM). A student organization with a nationalist ideological profile founded at a conference in Leipheim, Germany, in December 1949. Affiliated with the External Units (Bandera faction) of the *Organization of Ukrainian Nationalists, TUSM organizes ideological and political conferences. At its peak it had 300 to 350 members organized in several local branches (which in Canada and the United States come under national offices) and published the journal *Feniks. Its head office was in Munich until 1955, when it was moved to North America. In 1970 Senior TUSM, a support group consisting of former student members of TUSM, was organized; it was headed by M. Bohatiuk, K. Savchuk, and M. Sosnovsky. The national executives and the executive of Senior TUSM constitute the association's supreme executive. Its presidents have included H. Vaskovych, M. Kravchuk, V. Budziak, V. Kulchytsky, B. Futala, and A. Lozynsky.

**Ukrainian Students' Aid Commission** (Komisiia dopomohy ukrainskomu studentstvu, or KODUS). Founded in 1940 in Cracow by the Ukrainian Central Committee, it was transferred to Lviv in 1942. After 1945 it became an émigré group based successively in Fürth (Germany), Sarcelles (France, 1951–82), and Munich (since 1982). It has been headed consecutively by I. Hrynokh, Yu. Poliansky, Z. Kuzelia (1944–52), O. Kulchytsky (1952–80), I. Hrynokh (1982–9), and Z. Sokoliuk (from 1989). Its secretaries have been T. Voloshyn (1946–82), H. Komarynsky (1982–9), and V. Lenyk (from 1989). To date approx 2,600 students have received financial aid from the commission. These funds were drawn from community donations, the Ukrainian Central Committee (before 1945), the Ukrainian Catholic church (through the efforts of Archbishop I. Buchko), the United Ukrainian American Relief Committee, the Ukrainian Congress Committee of America, and the Ukrainian Canadian Relief Fund.

**Ukrainian Studies Centre** (Tsentr ukrainskykh studii). A scholarly institution established in March 1984 within the School of Modern Languages at Macquarie University in Sydney, Australia. In addition to a teaching program, the center undertakes research and publication in the areas of Ukrainian language, literature, history, political economy, and art. It is responsible for continuing education programs in Ukrainian studies and engages in community-related activities to attract support from outside the university. The center's operations are funded by the Ukrainian Studies Foundation (est 1974) in Australia. Its first director was I. Gordijew (1985–90).

**Ukrainian Studies Fund** (Fond katedry ukrainoznavstva, or FKU). A major funding body for Ukrainian studies in the United States. The fund was created in 1957 for the purpose of establishing and supporting Ukrainian scholarship at American universities. Headed by S. Khemych, the FKU has raised endowments for three chairs in Ukrainian studies at Harvard University, of history (1968), literature (1973), and linguistics (1973). The FKU has also endowed the *Harvard Ukrainian Research Institute at Harvard University. The endowments were the result of a community-wide effort during which 9,000 individuals and organizations donated over three million dollars.

Professors Robert Lisovsky, Ivan Kulets, and Kostiantyn Stakhovsky of the Ukrainian Studio of Plastic Arts

**Ukrainian Studio of Plastic Arts** (Ukrainska studiia plastychnoho mystetstva). A private postsecondary art school established in Prague in late 1923 by the émigré Ukrainian Society of Plastic Arts. D. *Antonovych, the society's president, was the studio's director. Graduates of its four-year program received the degree of master of arts. Enrollment reached its peak in 1925 (67 students). Until 1930 the studio received a small subsidy from the Czech government. From 1932 it was registered in the name of I. *Kulets. The faculty, who taught for free, consisted of I. Mirchuk (esthetics), S. Litov, and, from 1925, Yu. Rusov (anatomy), F. Sliusarenko (classical archeology), D. Antonovych (art history), Serhii Tymoshenko (architecture, to 1929), V. Sichynsky (perspective), K. Stakhovsky (sculpture), S. Mako, and, from 1924, I. Kulets (drawing, painting) and I. Mozalevsky and, from 1929, R. Lisovsky (graphic art). From 1925 the studio held annual exhibitions of its students' works (13 by 1939). It continued operating even under the German occupation. Its more noted graduates include K. Antonovych, Yu. Vovk, P. Hromnytsky, S. Zarytska, I. Ivanets, V. Kasiian, M. Krychevsky, O. Liaturynska, H. Mazepa, P. Omelchenko, I. Palyvoda, P. Kholodny, Jr, V. Khmeliuk, V. Tsymbal, and Ye. Biss. The studio was closed down by the communist regime in 1950.

**Ukrainian Supreme Emigration Council.** See Supreme Emigration Council.

**Ukrainian Supreme Liberation Council** (Ukrainska holovna vyzvolna rada, or UHVR). A body formed toward the end of the Second World War by members of the Ukrainian Insurgent Army (UPA) and the Organization of Ukrainian Nationalists (OUN) to provide political leadership for Ukrainian independentist forces. It proclaimed itself the 'supreme organ of the Ukrainian people in its war of revolutionary liberation.' The council's organizers hoped to establish a broader political and social base for armed resistance to both the German and the Bolshevik occupational forces and sought to attract support from outside the OUN, although the OUN would continue to serve as the UHVR's ideological and organizational foundation.

A bulletin of the Ukrainian Supreme Liberation Council

In January 1944 L. Shankovsky, as a leader of UPA forces, headed the initiating commission that established contacts with representatives of former Ukrainian political parties as well as nonpartisan activists. Representatives of the Melnyk faction of the OUN declined to participate in the undertaking. The founding meetings of the UHVR were held on 11–15 July 1944 near Nedilna, in the Sambir region, under the protection of UPA forces. There were 20 participants; another 5 people had agreed to accept mandates but were unable to attend. The majority at the founding meeting were not OUN members, and

10 of them were from the northwestern Ukrainian lands and central Ukraine. The proceedings, chaired by R. *Voloshyn, resulted in the election of a provisional executive (presidium), the formulation of a social and political platform, and the proclamation of a universal to the Ukrainian people. The UHVR resolved to adopt democratic principles of state and political life and outlined the social and economic policies it believed a future Ukrainian administration would institute. The presidium included the president, K. Osmak, of Kiev; the vice-president, V. *Mudry; the director of the general secretariat, R. *Shukhevych; I. *Hrynokh; and I. Vovchuk.

In Soviet-occupied Ukraine the UHVR co-ordinated armed resistance through the UPA and waged a political and propaganda campaign against the Soviet authorities through the OUN. It also aimed its propaganda at Red Army detachments in Western Ukraine. Its official publications were *Visnyk UHVR* (1944–5), *Biuro informatsiï UHVR* (9 issues, 1948–51), and *Samostiinist'* (1 issue, 1946). P. *Poltava headed the information bureau. In 1946 the UHVR organized a boycott of the Soviet-sponsored elections. It also opposed the forced liquidation of the Ukrainian Catholic church.

In October 1949 the UHVR, UPA, and OUN issued a joint communiqué, *Zvernennia voiuiuchoï Ukraïny do vsieï ukraïns'koï emigratsiï* (An Appeal of Fighting Ukraine to the Entire Ukrainian Emigration), as a call for people to mobilize around the independence issue beyond Ukraine's borders. After Shukhevych's death in 1950, V. *Kuk headed the general secretariat. According to Soviet sources, Kuk was captured in the mid-1950s. Likewise, most other members of the UHVR in Ukraine were either killed or arrested, and the organization was effectively eliminated there.

A number of UHVR members had left Ukraine in late 1944 and formed its External Representation (Zakordonne predstavnytstvo, or ZP UHVR), which was headed by Hrynokh. The general secretary was M. *Lebed, who served as the UHVR's external liaison officer and director of its information bureau. Lebed established contact with the Western Allied leadership in Italy in 1945. In the emigration the ZP UHVR issued a number of memorandums concerning the situation in Ukraine, including a submission (jointly with the UNR government-in-exile) to the peace conference in Paris. A Ukrainian press service was established, assistance was organized for UPA expeditionary forces that had worked their way to the West, and contacts were maintained (as far as possible) with the underground in Ukraine. A separate UPA mission was attached to the ZP UHVR.

The Bandera faction of the OUN supported the ZP UHVR until 1948. A number of tactical, ideological, and personal differences had emerged by 1954, and a splinter group of the Bandera OUN was formed, the OUN (Abroad); the new group became the main supporter of the ZP UHVR.

Attempts by the ZP UHVR to attract other organizations and parties to a popular front under its leadership were unsuccessful. After the establishment of the broadly based *Ukrainian National Council in 1947, the ZP UHVR formally renounced any intention of leading Ukrainian émigré political life; its focus was to serve as a representative of the revolutionary movement in Ukraine. The group co-opted a number of new members, formed a council, and established representative bodies in various countries.

From the mid-1960s the ZP UHVR held periodic conferences, at which new members were brought in and new executives were elected. In 1980 the group had over 20 members, of whom 10 were founding members. Original members of the UHVR who had died as émigrés included P. Chuiko, O. Malynovsky, Mudry, Z. *Pelensky, I. Simianchuk, Vovchuk, and Ye. *Vretsona.

The ZP UHVR began publishing the biweekly *Suchasna Ukraïna* and the monthly *Ukraïns'ka literaturna hazeta* in Munich in 1951. Those later provided the basis for the establishment of the journal *Suchasnist'*. In 1952, members of the ZP UHVR formed the research and publishing firm *Prolog, which issued the English-language journal *Prologue* (1957–61) and the monthly *Digest of the Soviet Ukrainian Press* (1957–77). The Suchasnist and Prolog publishing houses have issued more than 100 titles in history, political science, literature, and fine art. In the 1960s the ZP UHVR press bureau began publishing samvydav materials and popularizing the efforts of the Ukrainian dissident movement.

BIBLIOGRAPHY
*UHVR u svitli postanov Velykoho Zboru ta inshykh dokumentiv*
    (Munich 1956)
Prokop, M. 'Geneza, ustrii, i pliatforma UHVR,' *Suchasnist'*, 1978,
    no. 7–8
Rebet, D. 'Do pochatkiv UHVR (spohady, komentari, reflektsiï),'
    *Suchasnist'*, 1986, no. 7–8

V. Markus

**Ukrainian Teachers' Federation of Canada** (Obiednannia ukrainskykh pedahohiv Kanady). An association formed in Toronto in 1949 by post–Second World War immigrant teachers to develop a national curriculum for the Ukrainian Saturday school system in Canada. Headed for many years by Z. Zeleny, the association attempted to develop curriculum, texts, and teaching aids as well as a specific pedagogical philosophy. While not totally successful, the federation had some influence in Ontario through its journal *Ridna shkola* and its participation in the National Center of Ukrainian Educational Councils created by the Ukrainian Canadian Committee (now Congress).

**Ukrainian Teachers' Labor Alliance** (Ukrainske uchytelske obiednannia pratsi). An organization for Ukrainian teachers, founded in 1941 as one of the separate professional *labor alliances operating under the auspices of the *Ukrainian Central Committee. The Teachers' Labor Alliance was the largest of these unions. Its statutes were accepted by the *Generalgouvernement, with the alliance thereby receiving semiofficial status. It fulfilled the functions of the two prewar teachers' professional societies, the *Ukrainian Teachers' Mutual Aid Society and the *Teachers' Hromada. In addition to engaging in its own professional activities, the alliance co-operated with school authorities in creating curricula, collecting materials, overseeing teacher qualifications, organizing courses, and publishing the journal *Ukraïns'ka shkola*. It worked closely with the education section of the Ukrainian Central Committee. The headquarters was initially in Cracow, and from the autumn of 1941 the alliance also operated out of Lviv. It had over 8,000 members, and 80 percent of the Ukrainian teachers in the Generalgouvernement. The heads of the alliance were I. *Herasymovych, I. *Teslia, and S. *Levytsky.

**Ukrainian Teachers' Mutual Aid Society** (Vzaiemna pomich ukrainskoho vchytelstva, or VPUV). A professional organization of Ukrainian elementary-school teachers, founded in 1905. Initially it operated only in Galicia, but eventually it had four district branches in Bukovyna. Its membership in 1906 was 865 teachers out of a total possible membership of 4,000, and in 1914 some 710. In 1922 the society became a union of all the Ukrainian teachers in Polish-ruled Ukraine. In 1930 and after, because of the growth of the teachers' professional movement, the society expanded rapidly; that year it had 2,792 members out of a possible 3,500, and in 1938, 2,162 members, with 44 branches and 20 delegations. The headquarters was in Lviv. The society published the biweekly journal *Uchytel's'ke slovo, the pedagogical-methodological monthly, later a quarterly, *Shliakh vykhovannia i navchannia, and a series entitled Pedahohichna-metodychna biblioteka (A Pedagogical-Methodological Library). The society had a central pedagogical library, a research commission, a pedagogical consulting service, a credit union (Vzaiemna Pomich), relief funds for teachers, widows, and orphans, two buildings in Lviv, one building in Mushyna, and vacation resorts in Vorokhta and Cherche. Among the leading members of the organization were A. Alyskevych, I. Stronsky, M. Moroz, O. Vlasiichuk, I. Yushchyshyn, A. Zeleny, H. Koval, I. Lylyk, and D. Stelmakh. With the arrival of the Soviet army in 1939, the organization was disbanded. In 1941–4 the society operated as the *Ukrainian Teachers' Labor Alliance, a section of the Ukrainian Central Committee.

O. Skrypnyk

**Ukrainian Teachers' Publishing Company** (Vydavnycha spilka ukrainskoho vchytelstva). A publishing house in Kolomyia that existed from 1909 to 1928. It issued readers; popular books on Ukrainian history, culture, and ethnography; and a series of five books of selected works by Ukrainian writers. It also ran its own bookstore.

**Ukrainian Teachers' Union.** See Ukrainian Teachers' Labor Alliance.

**Ukrainian Technical and Husbandry Institute** (Ukrainskyi tekhnichno-hospodarskyi instytut, or UTHI; German: Ukrainisches Technisch-Wirtschaftliches Institut). A polytechnical institute established in November 1932 as a correspondence school of the *Ukrainian Husbandry Academy (UHA) in Poděbrady, Czechoslovakia. With the closing of the academy in 1935, the institute took over its scientific and educational functions. The UTHI was organized along the same lines as the UHA, with departments of agronomy and forestry, chemistry and technology, and economics and co-operatives. It also offered courses in practical fields, such as beekeeping, gardening, and soap making, a secondary-school program on the farming industry, and programs of Ukrainian studies, foreign languages, and journalism. The economics and co-operatives department attracted the most students; the other two departments were soon dissolved. To supply correspondence students with textbooks a publishing house was established. It published 77 textbooks, the journal *Zhurnal shkil'noho lystuvannia* (1932–3), and the bulletin *Visti UTHI*. In 1932–9 there were 87 faculty members, and 1,080 students (75 percent of them in Galicia) were registered at the institute. During the war (1940–5) enroll-

The first senate of the Ukrainian Technical and Husbandry Institute (1936). Top row, from left: Leonid Frolov, Borys Martos, Mykola Dobrylovsky; bottom row: Serhii Komaretsky, Volodymyr Cherediiv, Oleksii Kozlovsky

ment in the correspondence school increased to 7,000. The directors of UTHI were B. *Ivanytsky (1932–6), B. Martos (1936–7), L. Bych (1937–9), L. Frolov (1939–41), and S. Komaretsky (1941–5).

In April 1945 the institute's faculty fled from the advancing Soviet forces, leaving the library, press, and archive in Poděbrady. On 28 June 1945 the American authorities permitted the institute to resume its work in Regensburg, Bavaria. In addition to the three existing programs of study, courses were offered in veterinary science and medicine and pharmacology. The faculty and students were provided with food and lodgings by the United Nations Relief and Rehabilitation Administration, and then by the International Refugee Organization. In 1945–52, 1,290 students matriculated, 307 of them with diplomas: 91 agronomists, 34 foresters, 13 civil engineers, 32 veterinarians, 122 pharmacists, 6 chemists, and 9 economists. The faculty had 219 members: 62 full professors, 45 docents, 91 lecturers, and 29 assistants. Besides lectures the institute continued to offer correspondence courses, which had an enrollment of 1,500. It also organized vocational training in Ukrainian émigré centers in Germany and graduated over 2,300 skilled tradesmen. Forty-seven textbooks were published or reprinted, and the periodicals *Visti UTHI*, *Naukovi zapysky* (edited by R. Yendyk and then M. Korzhan), and *Naukovyi biuleten' UTHI* were issued. As Ukrainians emigrated from Germany UTHI was gradually transformed into a research institution. Its bimonthly *Biuleten'* (1980–5) was edited by I. Maistrenko, and its *Naukovo-tekhnichnyi visnyk* (1986) by M. Horbatsch. Since the war the rectors of the institute have been V. Domanytsky (1945–7), Ivanytsky (1947–52), P. Savytsky (1952–61), R. Yendyk (1961–74), M. Korzhan (1974–8), I. Kovalsky (acting rector 1978–9), Maistrenko (1979–84), and A. Figol (since 1985).

BIBLIOGRAPHY

*Ukraïns'kyi tekhnichno-hospodars'kyi instytut* (New York 1962)
*Ukraïns'ka hospodars'ka akademiia v Ch.S.R. i Ukraïns'kyi tekhnichno-hospodars'kyi instytut* (New York 1972)

**Ukrainian Technical Society** (Ukrainske tekhnichne tovarystvo, or UTT). A professional association of Ukrainian engineers, founded in Lviv in February 1909. The society's interests ranged from professional concerns to national issues. It participated in the development of Ukrainian industry and co-operatives, and the improvement of agriculture. To these ends the UTT organized conferences in Lviv in 1913 and in Stanyslaviv in 1919. After the First World War the UTT helped organize the Lviv (Underground) Ukrainian Higher Polytechnical School (1922–5), set up the Scientific Technical Commission of the Shevchenko Scientific Society (1929) and the Psychotechnical Commission (1930), and published the journal *Tekhnichni visty* (1925–39). Its membership grew from 65 (1913–23) to 366 (1930) and 532 (1935). During the Ukrainization drive in Soviet Ukraine, the UTT established contacts with professional societies such as the All-Ukrainian Association of Engineers in Kharkiv, the All-Ukrainian Intersectional Bureau of Engineers and Technicians, and the Scientific Technical Society of the VUAN. Some members of the UTT volunteered to work in Soviet Ukraine, and almost all of them perished there in the 1930s. In 1932 the UTT hosted the First Congress of Ukrainian Engineers in Lviv, which approved the charter of the Federation of Ukrainian Engineers' Organizations. The society's Commission for the Development of Ukrainian Industry (est 1932) promoted small businesses, worker training, and capital accumulation. The UTT was banned after the Soviet occupation of Western Ukraine. Many engineers fled from Galicia to the Generalgouvernement and established the Society of Ukrainian Engineers in Cracow (headed by Z. Kokhanovsky and R. Skochdopol). Under the German occupation of Galicia (1941–4) the Labor Alliance of Ukrainian Engineers (headed by P. Shokh and Ye. Perkhorovych) in Lviv co-operated with the Ukrainian Central Committee and promoted technical education. The presidents of the UTT were R. Zalozetsky-Sas (1909–19?), M. Gamota (1919–24), V. Manastyrsky (1925–6), P. Durbak (1926–7), A. Kornellia (1927–8), M. Pavlov (1928–30), V. Ryzhevsky (1930, 1935–8), Ye. Nahirny (1930), V. Levytsky (1930–2), O. Vasiuta (1932–5), and R. Vasylevych (1938–9). The society was reconstituted as the Ukrainian Engineers' Society in Lviv in 1990, under the directorship of V. Chaban; a similar society was founded in Kiev (1990), under the directorship of M. Zhurovsky.

Z. Kokhanovsky

**Ukrainian Technical Society of Canada.** See Society of Ukrainian Engineers and Associates in Canada.

**Ukrainian Technological Society.** A professional association set up in Pittsburgh in 1970 by M. Kotyk, P. Naber, M. Korchynsky, and M. Tymiak to help Ukrainian students attain higher education. It has organized concerts and other social events to raise funds for scholarships totalling more than 50,000 dollars over 20 years.

**Ukrainian Terminological Center of America** (Ukrainskyi terminolohichnyi tsentr Ameryky [UTTsA]). An institution established in New York City in 1965 under the aegis of the Shevchenko Scientific Society (NTSh) and the Ukrainian Academy of Arts and Sciences in the US to develop and popularize Ukrainian terminology. The initiator of the UTTsA was M. Pezhansky, and its first director was V. Davydenko (1965–78), who was followed by A. Wowk

(1978–92). The UTTsA bases its work on microfilms of almost all of the terminological dictionaries published in 1920–30 by the *Institute of the Ukrainian Scientific Language before its abolition by the Soviet authorities. The UTTsA assisted in preparing M. Danyliuk's *English-Ukrainian Dictionary of Medical Terms* (1970) and N. Chaplenko's terminological dictionary *Ukrainian Terms in Culinary Art and Nutrition* (1980). In 1982 the UTTsA published M. Pezhansky's *Materials for an Aeronautical Dictionary*. A. Wowk published the *English-Ukrainian Dictionary of Color Names and Color Science* in 1986. Also produced within the framework of the UTTsA was *A Selective English-Ukrainian Dictionary of Science, Technology, and Modern Living* by A. Wowk. The first volume (*A–M*) was published by the UTTsA in 1982, and the second volume was published in fascicles by the Ukrainian Engineers' Society of America in 1982–90.

**Ukrainian Theater Artists' Association** (Obiednannia mysttsiv ukrainskoi stseny, or OMUS). An actors' association organized in Augsburg, Germany, in 1946 under the chairmanship of V. *Blavatsky. OMUS members belonged to various theater troupes in the displaced persons camps of Germany and Austria and numbered 90 by 1948, the largest contingent coming from the Ukrainian Actors' Ensemble. OMUS published the magazine *Teatr*. With the postwar emigration of most members the association was inactive until 1971, when it was renewed with Yu. Kononiv as director. OMUS published the supplement *Holos aktora* in the newspapers *Ameryka* and *Svoboda*, organized theatrical festivals and conferences, and published a voluminous collection of historical essays and memoirs, *Nash teatr* (Our Theater, 1975), edited by H. Luzhnytsky.

**Ukrainian Theater in America** (Ukrainskyi teatr v Amerytsi). A theater founded in New York in 1954 from the main cast of the *Theater-Studio of Y. Hirniak and O. Dobrovolska. It was directed by V. Lysniak and L. Krushelnytska, and its repertoire included émigré Ukrainian plays – Dima's *Peresadzheni kvity* (Transplanted Flowers) and *Khmil'* (Hops) and I. Kernytsky's *Taina doktora Horoshka* (Dr Horoshko's Secret) – and Ukrainian and world classics with nontraditional staging – I. Karpenko-Kary's *Martyn Borulia*, Molière's *Tartuffe*, R. Burkner's *Kniazivna na horoshyni* (The Princess and the Pea), and the Dobrovolska productions *Moisei* (Moses, based on I. Franko's poem) and *Liudyna i heroi* (Man and Hero). The theater was active until 1964.

**Ukrainian Theater in Philadelphia** (Ukrainskyi teatr u Filiadelfii, formerly Ansambl ukrainskykh aktoriv). Formerly the Ensemble of Ukrainian Actors theater, created in 1945 in Germany from the former drama cast of the Lviv Opera House under the artistic direction of V. *Blavatsky. A touring theater based in Augsburg (until 1947) and Regensburg (until 1949), in its first two years it gave 309 performances in the DP camps, from its varied repertoire of 16 dramas, operettas, revues, and farces, including M. Kulish's *Narodnyi Malakhii* (The People's Malakhii), Yu. Kosach's *Voroh* (The Enemy) and *Order* (The Warrant), L. Kovalenko's *Domakha*, J. Anouilh's *Antigone*, and A. Obey's *Le viol de Lucrèce*. In 1949 the ensemble moved to the United States, where it continued performing with Y.

Shasharovsky as director (from 1953) as the Ukrainian Theater in Philadelphia until 1957 and as Teatr u Piatnytsiu (1963–74).

**Ukrainian Theater of the RSFSR.** See Moscow Ukrainian Theater of the RSFSR.

**Ukrainian Theatrical Society** (Ukrainske teatralne tovarystvo). A society subordinated to the Union of Theater Societies of the USSR and established under the auspices of the Ukrainian SSR Ministry of Culture in Kiev in 1944. It has branches in Kharkiv, Donetske, Lviv, Odessa, Dnipropetrovske, and Symferopil. By 1984 it had organized eight conferences to survey theatrical trends, discuss acceptable repertoire, and propagate K. Stanislavsky's acting method. It publishes *Ukraïns'kyi teatr* and *Teatral'no-kontsertnyi Kyïv* in Kiev and theatrical journals in Lviv, Odessa, and Kharkiv. Its directors have been I. Patorzhynsky (1948–54), N. Uzhvii (1954–73), and O. Kusenko (1973–87). In 1987 an extraordinary congress of the Ukrainian Theatrical Society was convened, which established the *Union of Theatrical Workers of Ukraine and elected its executive, headed by S. *Danchenko.

**Ukrainian Theological Academy.** See Theological Academy of the Ukrainian Autocephalous Orthodox church.

**Ukrainian Theological Scholarly Society** (Ukrainske bohoslovske naukove tovarystvo [UBNT]; Theologica Societas Scientifica Ucrainorum). An association for the advancement of Ukrainian Catholic theology, religious education, and scholarship. Until 1939 it was called the Theological Scholarly Society. It was founded in September 1922 in Lviv, and its statute was written by the society's key figure, Rev Y. *Slipy, and adopted in December 1923. The UBNT was housed at the Greek Catholic Theological Seminary in Lviv, and its presidents were the seminary's rectors, Rev T. Halushchynsky (1923–6) and Rev Slipy (1926–39). The general secretaries were Rev Y. Skruten (1923–5), Rev M. Galiant (1925–8), Rev P. Khomyn (1928–31), K. Chekhovych (1931–9), and Ya. Chuma (1939). The UBNT membership grew from 27 in 1923 to 236 in 1939; approx 80 percent were clerics. Its full members (17 in 1923, 52 in 1938) were grouped in four sections: biblical studies, philosophy and dogma, history and law, and practical (pastoral) theology. The UBNT published a theological quarterly, *Bohosloviia* (17 vols by 1939), edited by Slipy; the monograph series Pratsi Bohoslovs'koho naukovoho tovarystva (Works of the Theological Scholarly Society, 13 vols by 1939); the offprint and book series Vydannia bohoslovii (Publications of Theology, 29 issues by 1939); and the religious and community affairs monthly, *Nyva (1933–9). It also established a library and archive containing, by 1939, over 12,000 volumes; over 300 valuable manuscripts and old books; and icons, vestments, and other religious artifacts. From 1933 to 1938 the UBNT sponsored more than 120 public 'academic evenings for a Catholic world view' in Lviv and nine other Galician towns, and the scholarly 'Union Congress' in Lviv (December 1936). In September 1939 its library was destroyed by a German bomb, and the UBNT itself was abolished after the Soviet occupation of Galicia.

In October 1959 the Conference of Ukrainian Catholic

Bishops in Rome revived the UBNT. Since that time its presidents have been Rev A. Velyky (1960–4) and Rev I. Hrynokh and its general secretary, Rev I. Khoma. Major Archbishop Slipy became the society's patron in 1963. He housed it at the new Ukrainian Catholic University in Rome and revived the publication of *Bohosloviia*. Today the UBNT has over 140 members in the West and three sections: (1) biblical studies, theology, and philosophy (based in Canada), (2) law and pastoral theology (United States), and (3) history and Eastern Christian studies (Europe).

BIBLIOGRAPHY
Hlynka, L.; Chekhovych, K. *Bohoslovs'ke naukove tovarystvo u L'vovi v pershim desiatylittiu svoho isnuvannia (1923–1933)* (Lviv 1934)
Ianiv, V. 'Narys istoriï Ukraïns'koho bohoslovs'koho naukovoho tovarystva (z bibliohrafiieiu vydan') v 45-littia zasnuvannia,' in *Studiï ta materiialy do novishoï ukraïns'koï istoriï* (Munich 1970)
Senytsia, P. (ed). *Svityl'nyk istyny: Dzherela do istoriï Ukraïns'koï katolyts'koï bohoslovs'koï akademiï u L'vovi, 1928/29–1944*, vol 2 (Toronto–Chicago 1976)

W. Lencyk

## Ukrainian Theological Society. See Metropolitan Ilarion Theological Society.

## Ukrainian Touring Theater. See Stanyslaviv Ukrainian Touring Theater.

## Ukrainian Union. See Union for Agricultural Education.

## Ukrainian Union of Agrarians-Statists (Ukrainskyi soiuz khliborobiv derzhavnykiv, or USKhD).

An émigré monarchist organization founded in Vienna in February 1920 by V. *Lypynsky and S. *Shemet as the Union of Ukrainian Statehood (Soiuz ukrainskoi derzhavnosty). It was conceived as the body uniting all Ukrainian agrarians as a class in the pursuit of independent Ukrainian statehood, and in December 1920 it was renamed the USKhD and a statute and regulations were adopted. The USKhD consolidated the émigré members of the *Ukrainian Democratic Agrarian party and other supporters of Hetman P. *Skoropadsky. Lypynsky served as chairman of the Council of Jurors (Rada prysiazhnykh), the USKhD supreme council. A. Bilopolsky, D. Doroshenko, B. Homzyn, I. Mirchuk, N. Kochubei, V. Korostovets, S. Krylach (L. Sidletsky), V. Kuchabsky, O. Nazaruk, O. Shapoval, O. Skoropys-Yoltukhovsky, M. Tymofiiv, and V. Zalozetsky were other leading USKhD members. Lypynsky edited the USKhD organ, *Khliborobs'ka Ukraïna* (1920–5), and serialized therein his 'Lysty do brativ-khliborobiv' (Letters to [My] Brother Agrarians' (pub separately 1926), a 630-page discourse that served as the foundation of the USKhD ideology. It elaborated the idea of an independent, 'classocratic' (as opposed to democratic), pan-Ukrainian 'toilers' monarchy' without political parties, ruled by Skoropadsky (the embodiment of national unity) and his dynasty with the help of an agrarian aristocracy and the co-operation of the productive classes. Fraternal organizations of the USKhD were founded in Poland (the Union of Agrarians of Ukraine [est 1921], headed by M. Khanenko), Rumania (the Union of Ukrainian Agrarians in Bucharest [est 1921], headed by P. Novitsky), Germany, Czechoslo-

vakia, Bulgaria, Yugoslavia, Estonia (1921, headed by V. Pototsky), and North America (see *Sich society). At their joint June 1922 congress the Central Administration of United Ukrainian Agrarian Organizations, headed by S. Shemet, was appointed by Skoropadsky to assist him in Wannsee, near Berlin.

The USKhD prepared itself to take power in Ukraine after the collapse of Soviet rule, which it believed to be inevitable. It was hostile to the *Government-in-exile of the UNR and did not co-operate with that body's supporters. Because of political disagreements with Skoropadsky and his supporters in the Council of Jurors, in September 1930 Lypynsky announced the liquidation of the USKhD and founded in its place the short-lived Brotherhood of Ukrainian Classocrats-Monarchists Hetmanites (Bratstvo ukrainskykh kliasokrativ-monarkhistiv hetmantsiv). The majority of USKhD members disagreed with Lypynsky's actions, however, and after his death in 1931 the Council of Jurors revived the USKhD and elected Y. Melnyk the leader. Internal conflicts did not disappear, however, and the USKhD was formally dissolved without Skoropadsky's participation at a meeting of the Council of Jurors in Warsaw on 16 July 1937. It was replaced in September 1937 by the Union of Hetmanites-Statists. A fraternal North American organization by that name had been founded in 1934 and was called in English the *United Hetman Organization.

R. Senkus

## Ukrainian Veterinary Medical Association (Obiednannia ukrainskykh veterynarnykh likariv, or OUVL).

A professional organization established in Munich in 1946 with a membership of about 200. The first president was I. *Rozhin. In 1950 its head office was moved to Chicago. It has six branches in North America and individual members on other continents around the world. In 1967 its membership stood at 140. There is an active research group within the OUVL. The association published its journal *Informatyvnyi lystok OUVL* irregularly in Munich and then as a quarterly in Chicago (1950–63) and Saskatoon (1964–7). In 1981 it published an almanac, compiled by Ya. Geleta and edited by R. *Baranovsky.

## Ukrainian Veterinary Scientific Research Institute (Ukrainskyi veterynarnyi naukovo-doslidnyi instytut).

A research center under the Southern Branch of the All-Union Academy of Agricultural Sciences and, from 1991, the Ukrainian Academy of Agrarian Sciences. It was formed in Kiev in 1977 out of a branch of the *Ukrainian Scientific Research Institute of Experimental Veterinary Science. It has five departments with 20 laboratories, and three support centers. It also oversees the Poltava and Zhytomyr veterinary research stations and an experimental farm. Its purpose is to develop measures to prevent infectious diseases on industrial and specialized animal farms and to introduce sanitary inspection methods for farm products and quality-control methods for animal products. The institute developed ways to combat infectious hog diseases, a vaccine for hoof-and-mouth disease, and an improved diagnostic test for anthrax.

## Ukrainian Volcanic Carpathians. See Volcanic Ukrainian Carpathians.

Yevhen Konovalets with leading members of the Ukrainian War Veterans' Association of Canada in 1929. Sitting, from left: Pavlo Shtepa, Konovalets, Evstakhii Vasylyshyn; standing: Dmytro Gerych, Vasyl Topolnytsky, ?

## Ukrainian War Veterans' Association of Canada

(Ukrainska striletska hromada v Kanadi, or USH). A nationalist veterans' organization founded in 1928 in Winnipeg and incorporated in 1950 as an autonomous organization affiliated with the *Ukrainian National Federation (UNO). Its purpose was to cultivate Ukrainian military traditions and support the struggle for Ukrainian independence. From the beginning the USH maintained close contacts with the Ukrainian Military Organization (UVO), the Organization of Ukrainian Nationalists (OUN), and, after the war, the Melnyk faction of the OUN. In the 1930s it sent substantial sums to Western Ukraine to help war invalids and to defend political prisoners. It played a key role in the founding of the UNO. At first its membership (478 in 1928, 585 in 1931, and about 1,200 in 1939) consisted of former soldiers of the Army of the UNR and the Ukrainian Galician Army. There were 22 branches in the interwar period and 16 branches after the Second World War. After 1945 recent immigrants from Ukraine and veterans of the Canadian armed forces joined the USH. The head office was moved from Winnipeg to Saskatoon and, finally, to Toronto (1935). The presidents of the USH have included E. Vasylyshyn (1928–30, 1945–7, 1950–2), I. Guliai (1930–3, 1934–6, 1937–45), Yu. Diakunchak (1954–6, 1962–6), I. Nosyk (1956–62), and Yu. Temnyk (1966–71, 1972–5). To propagate its ideas the association published the monthly paper *Strilets'ki visti* (1930–1), a weekly page in *Novyi shliakh* (1932–9, 1949–50), and *Informator Holovnoï upravy USH* (1953–63).

BIBLIOGRAPHY
*Za chest', za slavu, za narod! Zbirnyk na zolotyi iuvilei Ukrïns'koï strilets'koï hromady v Kanadi, 1928–1978* (Toronto 1978)

## Ukrainian War Veterans' Association of the USA

(Ukrainska striletska hromada v ZDA). An organization of former soldiers of the Army of the UNR and the Ukrainian Galician Army founded in Philadelphia in 1925 for the purpose of cultivating Ukrainian military traditions, helping war invalids in Ukraine, and supporting the struggle for Ukrainian independence. The association collected

over 44,000 dollars in a decade and helped to finance the Ukrainian Invalids' Home in Lviv. Its first and longterm president was V. Galan. Upon organizing the United Ukrainian War Veterans in America in 1949, the association dissolved itself.

*Dorohovkaz*, the organ of the Ukrainian War Veteran's League of Canada, with a picture of the league's crest

## Ukrainian War Veterans' League of Canada

(Soiuz buvshykh ukrainskykh voiakiv). A veterans' organization founded in Montreal in 1936 to propagate Ukrainian national and military traditions. Composed primarily of former soldiers of the Army of the UNR, the group established six branches prior to the Second World War and several more after it. S. Waldstein served as the longtime head of the group during its early phase. In 1952 the organization's headquarters was moved to Toronto, where its leaders have included M. Sadovsky, I. Yanishevsky, I. Lypovetsky, and I. Roienko. The league published two quarterly journals, *Biuleten' Soiuzu buvshykh ukraïns'kykh voiakiv u Kanadi* (1959–64) and *Dorohovkaz: Orhan voiats'koï dumky i chynu* (1964–1970).

*The Ukrainian Weekly*

**Ukrainian Weekly, The.** An English-language weekly paper published in Jersey City, New Jersey, since October 1933. It succeeded the *Ukrainian Juvenile Magazine*, a quarterly supplement to the paper *Svoboda* that appeared from December 1927 to April 1931. The *Ukrainian Weekly* was also a supplement to *Svoboda* until the early 1970s. Since then it has been an independent paper published by the *Ukrainian National Association (UNA). Aimed at native Americans of Ukrainian descent, it has reported and commented on Ukrainian life in the United States and elsewhere and on developments in Ukraine, promoted Ukrainian culture and identity in the English-speaking world, and serialized English translations of Ukrainian prose. It has maintained high journalistic standards and has done much in recent years to increase its coverage of events and developments across North America through the use of local correspondents. The editors of the *Ukraini-*

*an Weekly* have been S. Shumeyko (1933–59), H. Perozak, W. Dushnyck, R. Chomiak, Z. Snylyk (1962–79), and R. Hadzewycz. The associate editors have included I. Dlaboha, G. Zarycky, I. Casanova, M. Kolomayets, and C. Lapychak. In 1986 the paper's circulation was 6,300.

**Ukrainian Women's Alliance in Belgium** (Obiednannia ukrainok Belhii, or OUB; Union des ukrainiennes en Belgique). A women's organization founded in 1948 as an autonomous section of the *Ukrainian Relief Committee in Belgium. It became an independent body in 1952. It was most active in 1948–52, with 15 branches and 500 members participating in the co-operative work of Belgian women's organizations, organizing exhibitions of Ukrainian folk art, and taking part in the congresses of the World Motherhood Movement. After the emigration of many of its members abroad, the OUB gradually restricted its activities largely to gatherings and commemorative events, day-care centers, social services, and the running of a radio program in the area of Hainaut and Centre. Today the OUB has five branches and fewer than 150 members. It has been headed by Z. Vytiaz and S. Sydor.

**Ukrainian Women's Alliance in Germany** (Obiednannia ukrainskykh zhinok u Nimechchyni, or OUZh; Ukrainische Frauenverband). An association formed in 1945 to serve the cultural, educational, and material needs of the Ukrainian *displaced persons in Germany. OUZh set up a network of nurseries and schools, trained nursery teachers, made contact with German and other émigré women's organizations, and published the monthly *Hromadianka* (1946–50) and quarterly *Zhinochyi informatsiinyi lystok* (1962–) as well as various brochures on Ukrainian women and folk art. In 1947 its membership peaked at 7,500 (72 branches); then it declined rapidly as many refugees emigrated overseas. In the 1960s OUZh had about 500 members organized in 16 branches, and in 1987 it had 186 members in 7 branches. Its head office is in Munich. It has financed two Ukrainian schools and three day-care centers; provided care for elderly members; sent parcels to political prisoners in the USSR and poor Ukrainian families in Poland, Brazil, and Yugoslavia; and given bursaries to Ukrainian student refugees from Poland and Ukraine. The presidents of the alliance have been I. Pavlykovska (1945–50), O. Pavlovska (1950–8), O. Sulyma-Boiko (1958–66), O. Yarymovych (1966–9), and O. Steiner (since 1969). A history of OUZh was published in Munich in 1980.

**Ukrainian Women's Alliance in Venezuela** (Obiednannia ukrainskykh zhinok Venesueli, or OUF). An autonomous women's section of the Ukrainian Hromada in Venezuela, founded in 1949 in Caracas. The alliance has organized national festivals, children's events, and recreational activities. It ran two kindergartens and a Saturday school and raised funds for building the Ukrainian People's Home. Its presidents have been H. Koval, E. Berezhna, E. Sliusar, O. Boshko, S. Prypkhan, L. Pochynok, and M. Mazniak.

**Ukrainian Women's Association in Australia** (Soiuz ukrainok Avstralii, or UWAA). Founded in 1949 by I. *Pelenska, the group held its first national conference in June 1951, with delegates from three states representing 400 members. In March 1989 the UWAA had 958 members in 19 branches. The UWAA promotes the cultural and educational development of women and the family as a whole, engages in social welfare work, and informs the general public about Ukraine. It maintains the Ukrainian Museum in Adelaide and is a member of the *World Federation of Ukrainian Women's Organizations and the National Council of Women of Australia. Its presidents have included I. Pelenska, S. Vavryk, L. Haievska-Denes, and (since 1983) O. Shevchyk. It has published the quarterly *Nashe slovo* since 1965. The first editor was L. Gordijew, who was followed by L. Haievska-Denes and in 1985 by S. Syvenka.

The central executive of the Ukrainian Women's Association of Canada in 1929. Sitting, from left: Savella Stechishin, Olena Kysilevska (guest from Ukraine), Anastasiia Ruryk; standing: Stefaniia Bubniuk, M. Hryniuk

**Ukrainian Women's Association of Canada** (Soiuz ukrainok Kanady, or UWAC). A national Ukrainian women's organization established in December 1926 in Saskatoon. Initiated by S. Stechishin, M. Madiuk, D. Yanda, and M. Hryniuk, the association organized Saturday and Sunday schools, sponsored concerts and lectures on topics of national concern and domestic matters, promoted the preservation of Ukrainian folk art traditions, and urged its members to become active in Ukrainian community affairs. It maintained ties with the Union of Ukrainian Women in Galicia, became a member of the National Council of Women (in Canada), and participated in national and international women's conferences. UWAC became part of the *Ukrainian Self-Reliance League in 1927. It has contributed a women's page to the newspaper *Ukraïns'kyi holos* since 1929 and began publishing its own monthly bilingual journal, * *Promin'*, in 1960. A history of the first 25 years of UWAC was published in 1952 under the editorship of N. Kohuska. The *Ukrainian Museum of Canada, begun by UWAC in 1936, is the group's most visible achievement. At present (1990) consisting of 160 branches, UWAC maintains a central office in its own building in Saskatoon. Its presidents have been S. Vasylyshyn, O. Woycenko, L. Ivasiuk, N. Kohuska, K. Miskiv, S. Paush, O. Svystun, S. Stechishin, M. Tkachuk, A. Tokaryk, L. Khorosh, D. Yanda, H. Romanchych, and A. Shemeliuk. UWAC is the only noncommunist Ukrainian women's organization in the West that does not belong to the *World Federation of Ukrainian Women's Organizations.

O. Woycenko

**Ukrainian Women's Association of France** (Soiuz ukrainok Frantsii; Association des femmes ukrainiennes). An organization established in Paris in 1945 with branches later in Lyon, Lille, and Metz. It has been active in educational and community work. It maintained contact with the World Movement of Mothers. Its membership has ranged from 50 to 100. It has been headed by H. Koval (1945–8), I. Knysh (1948–50), A. Saprun (1950–7), H. Pasternak (1957–74), M. Mytrovych (1974–89), and, since 1989, N. Tryndiak.

**Ukrainian Women's National Council.** See National Council of Ukrainian Women.

Some of the members of the first central executive of the Ukrainian Women's Organization of Canada

**Ukrainian Women's Organization of Canada** (Orhanizatsiia ukrainok Kanady im. Olhy Basarab, or OUK). A national organization established in 1934 in Saskatoon. It united the women's auxiliaries of the Ukrainian War Veterans' Association of Canada and became an affiliate of the *Ukrainian National Federation. OUK has focused largely on cultural and educational work, such as operating Saturday schools; organizing concerts, plays, and civic commemorations; and sponsoring lectures. Toward the end of the 1930s it also organized paramedical courses and formed locals of the Ukrainian Gold Cross.

OUK contributed to the Canadian war effort, and after the Second World War it was active in relief and resettlement work on behalf of Ukrainian displaced persons in Europe. The presidents of OUK have been A. Pavlychenko, M. Guliai, Ye. Sytnyk, A. Tarnovetska, O. Stebnytska, S. Savchuk, Ya. Zorych, L. Chaikovska, S. Protsiv, Y. Klymkiv, and M. Pidkovych. It has maintained approx 15 to 22 locals and contributed a women's page to the newspaper *Novyi shliakh* until 1950, when it began publishing the monthly *Zhinochyi svit*. The group published a 25th anniversary book in 1955, *Na sluzhbi ridnoho narodu* (In Service of Our People), under the editorship of I. Knysh.

The executive of the Ukrainian Women's Union in 1925. Sitting, from left: Mariia Levytska, Anna Zhuk, Mariia Krushelnytska, Olena Zalizniak; standing: Yaroslava Lahodynska, Olha Kossak, Mariia Plevako

**Ukrainian Women's Union** (Ukrainskyi zhinochyi soiuz, or UWU). A social-political, cultural-educational, and charitable organization. It was active in Vienna in 1920–38 and was renewed in 1957. A member group of the *National Council of Ukrainian Women, it participated in the congresses of the International League of Women for Peace and Freedom and of the International Council of Women. The UWU instituted literary and musical evenings and other such events, as well as courses in Ukrainian language, history, and art, and typing and stenography. Also active in the UWU was a section which assisted children and immigrants in Vienna (led by O. Halahan). The heads of UWU have included S. Maritchak, O. Zalizniak, A. Zhuk, and, from 1957, A. Saprun, D. Dzerovych, and S. Theil-Schwarz. Active members have included O. Basarab, M. Dontsova, M. Rudnytska, and M. Dnistrianska.

**Ukrainian Worker-Farmer Educational Society.** See Ukrainian Workers' League.

**Ukrainian Workers' and Peasants' Union** (Ukrainskyi robitnycho-selianskyi soiuz). A small clandestine group formed in Lviv in late 1959 to struggle by legal means for democracy and Ukraine's independence. It consisted of L. *Lukianenko, I. *Kandyba, S. Virun, O. Libovych, V. Lutskiv, Y. Borovnytsky, and I. Kipysh. Its draft program, prepared by L. Lukianenko, advocated Ukraine's secession from the USSR on the basis of a referendum. Before the draft could be revised and adopted, the group was betrayed by M. Vashchuk, and its members were arrested and charged with plotting the violent overthrow of the Soviet government. On 20 May 1961 L. Lukianenko was sentenced to death (later commuted to 15 years' imprisonment), I. Kandyba to 15 years', and the others to 10 years' imprisonment.

**Ukrainian Workers' League** (Ukrainska robitnycha orhanizatsiia, or URO). A socialist-oriented political and civic organization in Canada founded by defectors from the pro-communist *Ukrainian Labour-Farmer Temple Association (ULFTA). When the general convention of the ULFTA in 1935 refused to condemn the mass deportations, famine, and terror in Ukraine, five members of the executive (D. Lobai, T. Kobzei, T. Kulchytsky, S. Khvaliboga, and M. Smiiovsky) and their followers left the ULFTA. By January 1936 they had formed the Ukrainian Worker-Farmer Educational Society with branches in Winnipeg, Transcona, Portage la Prairie, Edmonton, and Calgary; the Ukrainian Educational Society in Montreal; and the Kameniari Society in Toronto. At the beginning of August 1936 these associations joined together to form the Federation of Ukrainian Worker-Farmer Organizations, which changed its name to the Alliance of Ukrainian Organizations (Soiuz ukrainskykh orhanizatsii) at its national convention in Toronto at the end of the year. In 1940 it adopted the name Ukrainian Workers' League. The leading members of the URO were D. Lobai (president, 1940–66), T. Kobzei, S. Khvaliboga, T. Kulchytsky, Yu. Elendiuk, T. Pylypas, and M. Kashchak. The league published the semimonthly *Pravda* (Winnipeg, 1936–8) and *Vpered* (Toronto, 1938–40), which were edited by D. Lobai. In 1940 the URO was one of the founders of the Ukrainian Canadian Committee (now Congress).

**Ukrainian Workingmen's Association.** See Ukrainian Fraternal Association.

**Ukrainian World Committee for Sport Affairs** (Ukrainskyi svitovyi komitet dlia sprav sportu). A body formed in 1956 in the United States under the name Ukrainian Olympic Committee in Exile and renamed shortly thereafter at the insistence of the International Olympic Committee (IOC). The committee arose after the suppression by Soviet authorities of a movement for separate Ukrainian representation at the *Olympic Games, which spread through Ukraine after the USSR first participated in the games in 1952. To publicize their demand in the West, the committee published the brochures *Ukraine and the XVI Olympic Games* (1956) and *Ukrainian Olympic Champions* (1968, 1972), a series of Ukrainian Olympic stamps, and the bulletin *Za uchast' Ukraïny v Olimpiis'kykh ihrakh* (For the Participation of Ukraine in Olympic Games). It sent numerous memoranda to the IOC and various national Olympic committees demanding Ukraine's separate and independent participation in the games. The press conferences organized by the committee (jointly with the Smoloskyp Organization for Defense of Human Rights in Ukraine) at the 1976 Summer Games in Montreal and the 1984 Summer Games in Los Angeles attracted international attention. At the latter conference, on the basis of documentation obtained from the USSR, the committee revealed that 59 Soviet Olympic athletes had died prematurely. These revelations prompted the Medical Commission of the IOC to investigate the illegal use of performance-enhancing drugs by Olympic athletes and to adopt strict

rules on the chemical testing of participants. In 1989 the movement for Ukraine's independent participation in the Olympics was revived in Ukraine, and this demand became part of the program of the *Popular Movement of Ukraine.

O. Zinkevych

**Ukrainian World Consolidation of Hutzuls [Hutsuls]** (Ukrainske svitove obiednannia hutsuliv, or USOH). An organization of Hutsuls founded in 1975 to maintain contacts among Hutsuls around the world and promote research on the culture and history of the Hutsul region. In 1985 the Conference of Hutsul Societies in the United States and Canada (est 1972), which was the successor of the Hutsul Council (1960s), joined the USOH. Today the association has six branches, five in North America and one in England. Since 1985 it has published the journal *Hutsul'shchyna*. Its presidents have been I. Havryliuk (1975–8), D. Tkachuk (1978–80), M. Belmega (1980–4), V. Borchuk (1984–7), V. Petryshyn (1987–9), and I. Andrusiak (1989).

**Ukrainian World Co-operative Council** (Ukrainska svitova kooperatyvna rada, or USKR). An umbrella organization of Ukrainian co-operatives set up on 31 October 1973 at the Second World Congress of Free Ukrainians in Toronto. It represented three national co-operative organizations – Council of Ukrainian Credit Unions in Canada, the Ukrainian National Credit Union Association of America, and the Council of Ukrainian Co-operative Societies of Australia – as well as other co-operatives; it has a combined membership of 120,000 and assets of 600 million dollars. Its presidents have been V. Sytnyk (1973–8) and O. Pleshkevych (since 1978).

*Ukrainian Youth.* An irregular organ of the Ukrainian Catholic Youth League in America. It was published from May 1934 to 1942 in Chicago, New York, and then Pittsburgh. The paper originally contained both Ukrainian-language (editor, B. Katamai) and English-language articles (editor, E. Piddubchyshyn), but later it appeared only in English.

**Ukrainian Youth Association** (Spilka ukrainskoi molodi, or SUM). An émigré youth organization established in Germany in 1946 by members of the Bandera faction of the OUN to attract those who did not already belong to other youth groups. Its initiators hoped to emulate the traditions of the Association of Ukrainian Youth in Ukraine, an organization allegedly active in Ukraine during the 1920s. In its statutes it sets itself forth as a patriotic organization whose slogan is God and Ukraine.

Initially SUM consisted of young men and women of 18 to 30 years of age. In 1948 groups of 12- to 18-year-olds were formed; they were followed by groups of 6- to 12-year-olds. In the 1950s members over 30 began to stay on, and the association came to consist of four age-groups: the junior youth (6–12), the senior youth (13–18), the *druzhynnyky*, or full members (19–35), and the senior members (over 35). It was soon organized along a three-level geographical scale, with local urban centers, national executives, and a central international executive that oversaw edification. In 1946–7 it was active mainly in Germany and Austria; it spread to Belgium in 1947, and then to Canada

The presidium at a national rally of SUM in Canada in the early 1950s. First row, from left: Yaroslav Stetsko, O. Kalynnyk, Rev Yaroslav Benesh, Slava Stetsko, Lev Husyn. The SUM emblem is in the background.

and Great Britain in 1948, the United States in 1949, and other countries (including Argentina, Australia, Brazil, France, and Paraguay) in subsequent years. In 1952 it was active in 14 countries and had a membership of more than 8,000. As a result of the gradual stabilization of émigré life in the West and extensive organizational efforts, SUM became the largest Ukrainian youth organization. In 1962 it had 10,500 members (of whom 3,200 were senior members and 7,300 were youth); in 1969, 13,700 members (with 4,500 and 9,200 respectively). Of the 1969 total, 1,800 senior members and 3,100 youths were active in the United States; 1,000 and 2,400 respectively in Great Britain; 750 and 2,500 in Canada; 430 and 570 in Australia; and 520 and 630 in other countries. By 1978 membership had declined to 11,780, and by 1987 to 7,290. The United States has consistently had the largest number of SUM members, followed by England, Canada, and Australia.

Every four years SUM sponsors world jamborees. These have taken place in Munich–Gomaringen–Rome (1972), Montreal (1976), Calgary (1980), Los Angeles (1984), and Rome (1988). Every summer the association runs summer camps in England, Belgium, France, the United States, Canada, Australia, and Argentina, using their own facilities.

The highest administrative body of the organization is the SUM Congress, elected by the Central Administration (before 1958, the Central Committee). Congresses were convened annually until 1949, after which they were held every three years. They are now held every five years. By October 1973, 10 congresses had been held. In 1946–9 the Central Committee was headed by M. Serdiuk; he was followed successively by S. Vozhakivsky, O. Kalynnyk, and M. Fil. The Central Administration of SUM has been headed by O. Koval (1958–78), Ye. Hanovsky (1978–88), and Y. Roshka (since 1988). In 1949 the Central Edifying Council (Vykhovna rada) was formed from the ranks of senior counselors and pedagogues to serve as an advisory body. It has been headed successively by P. Chuiko, M. Kushnir, D. Chaikovsky, Z. Sahan, B. Stebelsky, O. Koval (1978–88), and Ye. Hanovsky (1988–). In 1978 the headquarters of the Central Administration was moved from Brussels to New

Speakers at a SUM rally in the United States in the early 1950s

York. Other members of the central or national executives over the years included T. Buiniak (Canada), O. Chubaty (Australia), Ya. Deremenda (Great Britain), Ye. Hanovsky (United States), V. Kosyk (France), V. Lenyk (Germany), and H. Oshchypko (Belgium). Younger members who rose through the ranks of the organization and joined its executive at the 10th Congress included A. Bandera, M. Frankevych, R. Mirchuk, M. Pidhirna, R. Shuper, B. Yurkiv, and M. Yurkiv-Yavrotska. Many pedagogues and political activists also worked as counselors, editors of SUM publications, lecturers, and camp instructors, including P. Bashuk, M. Fostun, P. Kizko, V. Koval, I. Krushelnytsky, Y. Serbyn, P. Mirchuk, V. Mykula, L. Poltava, D. Shtohryn, S. Stetsko, H. Vashchenko, H. Vaskovych, and I. Vovchuk.

Publications of the SUM Central Comittee in 1947–52

The association's ideological and educational program combines Christianity and nationalism. Apart from helping its members develop religious and national consciousness, it encourages them to support Ukraine whether, as previously, in its liberation struggle or, as after 1991, in its drive for the democratization of the newly independent state. Attention is also paid to the teaching of Ukrainian history and culture. The organization's instructional methods are set out in various manuals, educational materials, and periodicals. Activities are conducted in groups of various sizes (junior youth are organized into *roï*, senior youth into *kureni*), as well as in the course of educational conferences, summer and winter camps, and sporting events.

SUM also provides the young with the opportunity to participate in choirs, dance and instrumental ensembles, theater groups, applied arts groups, and other cultural activities, as well as organizing sports competitions and clubs (soccer/football is particularly popular). Some SUM ensembles have gained wide popularity in the community and have traveled to émigré centers in various countries. These include the Prometei and Dibrova choirs, the Baturyn band (conducted by V. Kardash, M. Dlaboha, and O. Brezden), and the Verkhovyntsi dance ensemble (directed by Y. Klun) of Toronto; the banduryst kapelle of Detroit (V. Potapenko, conductor); the Krylati dance ensemble of Great Britain (O. Buriak, director); and the Krylati sports club of Chicago. SUM commonly takes part in national celebrations, anniversaries, and political demonstrations. Its members have also conducted mass actions in defense of Ukrainian political and religious prisoners.

SUM has acquired a number of facilities, such as meeting halls and summer camping grounds. The more notable include the resort in Ellenville, New York, the Veselka resort near Toronto, Verkhovyna near Montreal, Bilohorshcha near Sudbury, Tarasivka in Great Britain, Frankopole in Belgium, Tarasivka near Melbourne, Lemkivshchyna near Sydney, and Veselka near Buenos Aires. In some centers SUM has established and runs Ukrainian schools, of which there were nine in the United States in 1970.

SUM periodicals include *Avangard* (est 1947), the official organ of the Central Administration; *Na varti* (est 1949 in Canada); and *Krylati* (est 1963), a youth journal. In addition a number of émigré newspapers carry 'SUM pages,' including *Shliakh peremohy*, *Homin Ukraïny*, *Ukraïns'ka dumka*, *Svoboda*, *Ameryka*, *Vil'na dumka*, and *Ukraïns'ke slovo* (Argentina). Other materials are published by the Central Administration (such as *Biuleten' Tsentral'noï upravy SUM* and the irregular *Zapysky vykhovnyka*), national executives, and certain regional centers. The central SUM publishing house has published a number of works on edification of youth (particularly by H. Vashchenko), some fiction, and a series of youth-, children-, and family-oriented books.

Leading activists in SUM national centers through the 1980s have included A. Lozynsky, Ye. Kuzmovych, Ya. Petryk, Y. Roshka, and R. Zvarych (United States); Ye. Cholii, M. Figol, I. Mytsak, V. Okipniuk, and M. Shepetyk (Canada); M. Finiv, V. Karpynets, M. Matviivsky, and V. Shliakhetko (Great Britain); M. Duda, B. Kachmarsky, I. Khokholiak, Z. Koval, I. Levytsky, and P. Osmalsky (Belgium); A. and V. Haidamakha, S. Kostiuk, V. Panchuk, R. Shuper, and L. Vilych (Germany); I. Kopchuk, P. Naumiak, I. Pasternak, and L. Vitoshynska (France); I. Kohut, M. Moravsky, and S. Romaniv (Australia); and M. Rokush, R. Savchuk, and O. Stryga (Argentina).

BIBLIOGRAPHY
*SUM na chuzhyni: Zbirnyk-al'manakh* (London 1954)
*Pravyl'nyk iunatstva SUM* (Brussels 1961)
*Pravyl'nyk druzhyn SUM* (Brussels 1967)
*Materiialy 10-oho Kongresu SUM* (Brussels 1973)

H. Vaskovych

**Ukrainian Youth Educational Societies** (Vykhovni spilnoty ukrainskoi molodi, or VSUM). Youth organiza-

tions set up in the *Generalgouvernement between 1941 and 1944 at elementary and secondary schools. VSUM were modeled on the *Plast Ukrainian Youth Association, which was banned by the German occupational authorities. Among the chief organizers were K. *Paliiv, R. Olesnytsky, T. Samotulka, and I. Khoinatska-Chaikivska. The organ of VSUM was *Doroha*. In 1944 VSUM had a membership of over 2,500, organized in more than 60 cells.

**Ukrainian Youth for Christ** (Ukrainska Molod Khrystovi). A large festival for Ukrainian Catholic youths, held in Lviv in May 1933 on the occasion of the 1,900th anniversary of the death and resurrection of Christ. It was attended by over 100,000 people, including 50,000 youths. The festival was organized by I. Babii, V. Hlibovytsky, and R. Danylevych and held under the spiritual authority of Bishop I. Buchko and Metropolitan A. Sheptytsky. The program included a large public liturgy and procession through the streets of Lviv. To commemorate the 50th anniversary of the event, a festival for Ukrainian Catholic youths in the West was held in Stamford, Connecticut, in 1983, and subsequent gatherings were held in Stamford in 1985; in Parma, Ohio, in 1986; and in Philadelphia in 1987. Following the liberalization of the late 1980s another Ukrainian Youth for Christ festival was held in Lviv, in September 1990. It was attended by tens of thousands of participants from across western Ukraine, as well as several priests and lay persons from the West. The festival program included public liturgies, demonstrations, lectures, and other events.

**Ukrainian Youth League of North America** (Liga ukrainskoi molodi Pivnichnoi Ameryky). An umbrella organization of Ukrainian-American youth clubs founded in Chicago during the World's Fair, on 17 August 1933. Its purpose was to perpetuate Ukrainian traditions, disseminate knowledge about Ukraine among Americans, and promote the cause of Ukraine's independence. To this end it organized cultural activities, political rallies, sports competitions, and social events, including annual Ukrainian cultural courses at the Ukrainian National Association resort, Soiuzivka (1954–71); annual conventions; a Ukrainian-American Olympiad (1936); softball, basketball, and bowling tournaments (mainly in the 1950s); and sports rallies (1954–8). It published the quarterly magazine *Ukrainian Trend* (1937–1960s), the monthly newsletter *Trendette* (in the 1950s–1960s), and the book *Ukrainian Arts* (1951). In 1959 it made a color film for television, *With Faith, We Hope*, depicting Ukraine's struggle for independence. In the 1930s the league represented over 60 youth organizations. In time it added some Canadian member groups. Since 1971 the league has been inactive. A 1983 reunion of league members led to the creation of an offshoot organization, the Ukrainian Heritage Foundation, which has undertaken several video projects on cultural themes.

**Ukrainian-Polish War in Galicia, 1918–19.** The Ukrainian-Polish War broke out in late 1918 as a result of the Polish rejection of Ukrainian efforts to establish an independent state – the *Western Ukrainian National Republic [ZUNR] – in the wake of the dissolution of the Austro-Hungarian Empire. The major issue of dispute in the conflict was control over eastern *Galicia, a predominantly Ukrainian ethnic territory regarded by the Poles as an integral part of the historical Polish realm. As the boundaries of the new Polish state had not yet been established, and the ZUNR had not been granted international diplomatic recognition, the matter was ultimately reduced to a question of control by military force.

The outbreak of hostilites can be dated to 1 November, when Poles in Lviv organized resistance to Ukrainian efforts to take control of the city (see *November Uprising in Lviv). Similar resistance by Poles to the Ukrainian takeover followed in Drohobych, Sambir, Jarosław, and Peremyshl. The Ukrainian government, in response, established the *Ukrainian Galician Army (UHA) as its regular military force. Until the end of December the war remained a series of local skirmishes that developed into a standoff in which the Poles controlled Lviv and certain territories east of the city. The command of the UHA did not possess an overall operational plan, and the Poles simply tried to maintain their position. By January 1919 the front stretched from Balyhorod, in the Carpathian Mountains, along the Khyriv–Peremyshl railway line (with the Poles in possession of Peremyshl) to Lviv (in Polish hands) and then looped around in a clockwise direction to the Uhniv–Rava Ruska area, from which it went northward.

When the Polish government in Warsaw began to dispatch regular troops to eastern Galicia, the conflict assumed a new dimension. By January 1919, Polish numbers reached about 20,000 men. On 15 February the UHA (some 40,000 men) began a great offensive (the so-called Vovchukhy Operation) toward Lviv, the Peremyshl–Lviv railway line, Rava Ruska, and Belz. By the end of the month a short armistice was being enforced by the Entente (as a result of negotiations by the *Berthélemy Mission). On 2 March, however, the UHA renewed the attack and was able to encircle Lviv. On 19 March the Polish divisions broke through the Ukrainian lines in the region of Horodok and retook the Lviv–Peremyshl corridor.

On 2 April the Supreme Council of the Paris Peace Conference established a commission headed by Gen L. *Botha to arrange an armistice between Poland and Ukraine. The proposed demarcation line it suggested (Lviv to be on the Polish side, Drohobych and Boryslav, on the Ukrainian side) was accepted by the government of the ZUNR but rejected by the Polish government, which claimed the right to take over the whole of eastern Galicia.

By that time the Poles had acquired the means to enforce their will. On 17 March the Supreme Council in Paris had given permission for the army of Gen J. *Haller (six divisions, with about 68,000 men) to be transferred from France to Poland for the express purpose of securing a frontier against potential Bolshevik attack. It was moved in April. Although the Polish prime minister, I. Paderewski, had assured the council that the army would not be sent to eastern Galicia, the troops were nonetheless being deployed there by mid-May. On 14 May a Polish force of approx 50,000 men attacked from the regions of Peremyshl, Horodok, and Lviv; in six days it had occupied Turka, Drohobych, and Stryi in the south and Kaminka-Strumylova in the north (the Polish offensive also included Volhynia). By 27 May the Poles had taken Halych and Stanyslaviv and were making contact with the Rumanian troops which entered Pokutia. The protests of the Entente and the need to transfer the armed forces to the west (be-cause of fears of a German attack against Poland) stopped the Polish offensive on the Brody–Zolota Lypa River line.

On 7 June the reorganized UHA (with Gen O. *Hrekov as commander in chief from 9 June) embarked upon the *Chortkiv offensive, which in two weeks reached the Brody–Krasne–Peremyshliany–Hnyla Lypa River line. The UHA troops were now about 40 km from Lviv, but they began to run short of ammunition and provisions. At the same time the international situation of the ZUNR also changed for the worse: following the defeat of the UNR Army in Volhynia by the Red Army the Supreme Council empowered Poland (25 June) to take over the whole of eastern Galicia up to the Zbruch River in a move intended to block a potential Bolshevik onslaught to the west. The council, however, did not regard that resolution as a final decision on the political future of eastern Galicia.

After new Polish troops (under the command of J. *Piłsudski) were transferred to the east, they commenced a decisive offensive on 28 June. On 5 July the Poles reached the line of the Strypa River, and on 15 July they seized Ternopil and the area on both sides of the Seret River. Despite the defeat the UHA forces (about 80,000 men, including 36,000 in the first line of the front) retained their combat readiness and on 16–18 July crossed to the eastern side of the Zbruch, where the UNR Army was stationed. The government of the ZUNR also crossed the Zbruch to Kamianets-Podilskyi.

BIBLIOGRAPHY
Hupert, W. Zajęcie Małopolski Wschodniej i Wołynia w roku 1919 (Lviv 1929)
Omelianovych-Pavlenko, M. Ukraïns'ko-pol's'ka viina 1918–1919 (Prague 1929)
Krezub, A. [Dumin, O.] Narys istoriï ukraïns'ko-pol's'koï viiny 1918–1919 (Lviv 1933; repr, New York 1966)
Kutschabsky, W. Die Westukraine im Kampfe mit Polen und dem Bolschewismus in den Jahren 1918–1923 (Berlin 1934)
Iaroslavyn, S. Vyzvol'na borot'ba na zakhidno-ukraïns'kykh zemliakh u 1919–1923 rokakh (Philadelphia 1956)
Mykytiuk, D. (comp). Ukraïns'ka Halyts'ka Armiia: Materiialy do istoriï, 5 vols (Winnipeg 1958–76)
Hunczak, T. (ed). Ukraine and Poland in Documents, 1918–1922 (New York 1983)
Kozłowski, M. Między Sanem a Zbruczem: Walki o Lwów i Galicję Wschiodnią 1918–1919 (Cracow 1990)

A. Chojnowski

**Ukrainian-Polish War of 1648–57.** See Cossack-Polish War.

**Ukrainian-Ruthenian Publishing Company** (Ukrainsko-ruska vydavnycha spilka). A publishing venture established as a joint stock company in 1899 in Lviv. Initiated by M. *Hrushevsky, who also served as the first director, it published literary and scholarly works and literature in translation. The chief editors were I. Franko and V. Hnatiuk. In 1905 the company assumed responsibility for the publication of *Literaturno-naukovyi vistnyk from the Shevchenko Scientific Society. From 1907 to 1918 the company was based in Kiev. Renewed in 1922 in Lviv as the Ukrainian Publishing Company, it continued to function until 1932, but its output was minimal and of relatively little importance.

By 1917 the company had issued over 300 books in two major series. Its belletristic series included original and reprinted works by V. Vynnychenko, M. Kotsiubynsky, O.

Kobylianska, L. Martovych, V. Stefanyk, M. Cheremshyna, I. Franko, I. Nechui-Levytsky, M. Vovchok, and B. Lepky, and translations of W. Shakespeare, G. Byron, H. Heine, K. Hamsun, G. Hauptmann, E. Zola, G. de Maupassant, H. Pontoppidan, K. Gutzkow, L. Tolstoy, F. Dostoevsky, W. Orkan, V. Korolenko, and others. Its popular-scholarly series included primarily translations of historical, sociological, and philosophical works by authors such as J. Ingram, H. Taine, E. Kareev, A. Smith, F. Engels, and K. Kautsky.

**Ukrainians.** The East Slavic nation constituting the native population of Ukraine; the sixth-largest nation in Europe. According to the concept of nationality dominant in Eastern Europe the Ukrainians are people whose native language is Ukrainian (an objective criterion) whether or not they are nationally conscious, and all those who identify themselves as Ukrainian (a subjective criterion) whether or not they speak Ukrainian (see *Language, Ukrainian). Isolated attempts to introduce a territorial-political concept of Ukrainian nationality on the Western European model (eg, by V. Lypynsky) have been unsuccessful until the 1990s. Because territorial loyalty has also been manifested by the historical *national minorities living in Ukraine, the accepted view in Ukraine today is that all permanent inhabitants of Ukraine are its citizens (ie, Ukrainians) regardless of their ethnic origins or the language in which they communicate. The official declaration of Ukrainian sovereignty of 16 July 1990 stated that 'citizens of the Republic of all nationalities constitute the people (*narod*) of Ukraine.'

**The name.** The oldest recorded names used for the Ukrainians are *Rusyny*, *Rusychi*, and *Rusy* (from *Rus'), which were transcribed in Latin as *Russi*, *Rutheni*, and *Ruteni* (see *Ruthenians). In the 10th to 12th centuries those names applied only to the Slavic inhabitants of what is today the national and ethnic *territory of Ukraine. Later a similar designation was adopted by the proto-Russian Slavic inhabitants of the northeastern principalities of Kievan Rus' – *Russkie* (of Rus'), an adjectival form indicating that they were initially subjects of ('belonged to') Rus'. Beginning in the 16th century Muscovite documents referred to the Ukrainians as *Cherkasy, alluding perhaps to the fact that in and around the town of Cherkasy there were many Cossack settlements. In the 17th- and 18th-century Cossack Hetman state the terms *Malorosiiany* and *Malorosy*, from *Mala Rus'* (Rus' Minor, the name introduced by the patriarch of Constantinople in the 14th century to refer to the lands of Halych metropoly and reintroduced by Ukrainian clerics in the 17th century), became accepted by the inhabitants as their designation. Those terms were retained in a modified Russian form and used officially under tsarist rule and by foreigners until 1917 (see *Little Russia). By the 1860s, however, some opposition to the terms became evident in Russian-ruled Ukraine, on the ground that they were as pejorative as the term *khokhol.

The modern name *Ukraintsi* (Ukrainians) is derived from *Ukraina* (*Ukraine), a name first documented in the *Kiev Chronicle under the year 1187. The terms *Ukrainiany* (in the chronicle under the year 1268), *Ukrainnyky*, and even *narod ukrainskyi* (the Ukrainian people) were used sporadically before *Ukraintsi* attained currency under the influence of the writings of Ukrainian activists in Russian-ruled Ukraine in the 19th century. In late 18th- and early 19th-century tsarist nomenclature 'Ukrainians' was used only in reference to the inhabitants of Slobidska Ukraine. In 19th-century Polish usage the people so designated were the inhabitants of Kiev gubernia. Western Ukrainians under Austro-Hungarian rule used the term to refer to their ethnic counterparts under Russian rule but called themselves 'Ruthenians.' The appellation 'Ukrainian' did not take hold in Galicia and Bukovyna until the first quarter of the 20th century, in Transcarpathia until the 1930s, and in the Prešov region until the late 1940s. In the 20th century *Malorosiiany* or *Malorosy* has been a derogatory term used by Ukrainians to designate Ukrainians with little or no national consciousness.

**Population.** Until the final quarter of the 19th century the Ukrainians, with few exceptions, lived on their aboriginal lands, which now, basically, constitute Ukrainian ethnic territory. In the last few decades of the 19th century Ukrainians under Russian rule began a massive *emigration to the Asian regions of the empire, and their counterparts under Austro-Hungarian rule emigrated to the New World. The number of Ukrainians outside of their homeland had grown from 1 million in 1880 to over 14 million by 1989. Thus, approx one-quarter of all Ukrainians in the world today live outside of Ukraine. The greatest number live in Ukraine and elsewhere in Europe (44 million); they are followed in number by those in Asia (ie, within the former USSR, 5 million), North and South America (2.5 million), and Australia (35,000). (See table 1.) The constant pressure of Russification on Ukrainians in the USSR, especially those living outside Ukraine, who generally had an underdeveloped national consciousness, has resulted in a decline in the total number of Ukrainians and Ukrainians speaking Ukrainian (81.1 percent in 1989) on the territory of the former USSR, and a change in Ukraine's *national composition.

Table 2 illustrates the rather high natural population growth of Ukrainians (approx 18 to 20 per thousand per year) until 1914. Thereafter there have been exceptional decreases because of the First and Second *world wars, the Soviet famines of 1921–3, especially the Soviet man-made *famine of 1932–3, and the impact of *urbanization in the last 60 years. Since the Second World War the natural *population growth of Ukrainians has decreased, and since the mid-1980s it has been one of the lowest among the nations of Eastern Europe.

**Origins.** Archeological and linguistic evidence indicates that at the dawning of the Christian era the lands between the Oder or the Vistula and the middle Dnieper basins were inhabited by proto-Slavic tribes. The southern Ukrainian steppes were dominated by Iranian and then Turkic nomadic peoples, although some Slavic agrarian colonization occurred. From the 7th century AD on, proto-Ukrainian tribes are known to have inhabited Ukrainian territory: the *Volhynians, *Derevlianians, *Polianians, and *Siverianians and the less significant *Ulychians, *Tivertsians, and *White Croatians. The question of whether the Ukrainians of *Transcarpathia and the *Maramureș region were there before the Magyar expansion of the 9th and 10th centuries or arrived as colonists from Galicia or Podilia has not been settled. At any rate, they were already occupying those lands in the 13th century. The relatively late appearance of the *Lemkos has been attributed to a pastoral migration of the 13th to 15th cen-

TABLE 1
Ukrainians in the world in 1989

| | Soviet statistics | Encyclopedia of Ukraine |
|---|---|---|
| Ukrainian SSR | 37,500,000 | 37,400,000 |
| Russian SFSR | 4,400,000 | 8,000,000 |
| Belorussian SSR | 290,000 | 800,000 |
| Kazakh SSR | 900,000 | 900,000 |
| Moldavian SSR | 600,000 | 561,000 |
| Kirgiz SSR | 108,000 | 300,000 |
| Uzbek SSR | 154,000 | 154,000 |
| Latvian SSR | 92,000 | 92,000 |
| Georgian SSR | 52,000 | 52,000 |
| Estonian SSR | 48,000 | 48,000 |
| Lithuanian SSR | 45,000 | 45,000 |
| Tadzhik SSR | 41,000 | 36,000 |
| Turkmen SSR | 36,000 | 37,000 |
| Azerbaidzhan SSR | 32,000 | 26,000 |
| Armenian SSR | 8,000 | 9,000 |
| USSR total | 44,306,000 | 48,460,000 |
| Poland | 300,000 | 400,000 |
| Rumania | 55,000 | 160,000 |
| Czechoslovakia | 47,000 | 150,000 |
| Yugoslavia | 45,000 | 45,000 |
| Bulgaria | 2,000 | 2,000 |
| Hungary | 3,000 | 3,000 |
| Eastern Europe total | 452,000 | 760,000 |
| Germany | 20,000 | 20,000 |
| Great Britain | 30,000 | 30,000 |
| France | 30,000 | 30,000 |
| Austria | 5,000 | 5,000 |
| Belgium | 3,000 | 3,000 |
| Others | 5,000 | 5,000 |
| Western Europe total | 93,000 | 93,000 |
| United States | 500,000 | 1,350,000 |
| Canada | 530,000 | 750,000 |
| Brazil | 50,000 | 200,000 |
| Argentina | 100,000 | 200,000 |
| Paraguay | 10,000 | 8,000 |
| Uruguay | 8,000 | 6,000 |
| Venezuela | 2,000 | 2,000 |
| Americas total | 1,200,000 | 2,516,000 |
| Australia and elsewhere | 20,000 | 35,000 |
| Grand total | 46,071,000* | 51,864,000 |

*46,136,000, according to V. Naulko

TABLE 2
Ukrainians in the world in the 18th to 20th centuries (millions)

| Year | On ethnic Ukrainian territory | Outside Ukraine[e] | Total | Soviet sources[g] |
|---|---|---|---|---|
| 1719 | 4.91 | 0.83 | 5.74[a] | – |
| 1772–82 | 5.81 | – | 5.81[b] | – |
| 1795 | 8.70 | 1.74 | 10.44[a] | – |
| 1842 | 13.12 | – | 13.12[c] | – |
| 1858 | 12.78 | 3.24 | 16.02[a] | – |
| 1880 | 24.80 | 1.20 | 26.00[d] | – |
| 1897–1900 | 21.00 | 5.39 | 26.39[a] | – |
| 1914 | 35.90 | 4.30 | 40.20[d] | – |
| 1926–31 | 27.57 | 9.50 | 37.07[a] | – |
| 1933 | 38.20 | 6.30 | 44.50[d] | – |
| 1939 | 29.60 | 6.00 | 35.60[a] | – |
| 1959 | 32.16 | 11.00 | 43.16[e] | 38.30[a] |
| 1970 | 35.28 | 12.00 | 47.28[e] | 43.00[a] |
| 1979 | 36.49 | 13.00 | 49.49[e] | 44.08[a] |
| 1989 | 37.40 | 14.46 | 51.86[e] | 46.14[f] |

[a] S. Bruk and V. Kabuzan, 'Chislennost' i rasselenie ukrainskogo naseleniia v mire,' *Sovetskaia* etnografiia, 1981, no. 5; and V. Naulko, 'Etnichnyi sklad naselennia Ukraïny,' in *Radians'ka shkola*, 1990, no. 3
[b] J. Heym, *Versuch einer vollständigen geographisch-topographische Enzyklopädie des Russischen Reichs* (Göttingen 1796)
[c] P. Šafařík, *Slovenský národopis*, 4th edn (Prague 1955)
[d] *Ukraine: A Concise Encyclopaedia*, vol 1 (Toronto 1963)
[e] *Entsyklopediia ukraïnoznavstva*
[f] V. Naulko and N. Chorna, 'Dynamika chysel'nosti i rozmishchennia ukraïntsiv u sviti (XVIII–XX st.),' *NTE*, 1990, no. 5
[g] Using Soviet census statistics, which are based on respondents' self-definition

turies. Even more recent in origin is the population of *Southern and *Slobidska Ukraine, which arose out of ongoing colonization from the 16th to the 19th centuries.

That the Ukrainians share certain linguistic traits with the two other East Slavic nations, the Belarusians and Russians, has been interpreted variously. That the three nations shared a religion and a ruling dynasty in the time of Kievan Rus' has been used to hypothesize the existence of an 'ancient Rus'' nationality, that is, one proto-Rus' people, that disintegrated under the impact of Mongol, Lithuanian, and Polish domination during the 13th and 14th centuries. That originally Muscovite concept became dogma in the USSR and has often been repeated in the West; among Ukrainian scholars it was advocated by M. Korduba. A second theory states that a single, proto-Ukrainian people lived in the area from the Carpathian Mountains to the White Sea, and that the Russians and Belarusians later separated from it. That thesis has been supported by many Ukrainian scholars. A third hypothesis proposes that a complex interethnic process unifying as well as dividing the Ukrainians, Belarusians, and Russians occurred. The vast territory encompassed by the Kievan Rus' federation of principalities made the existence of a single people as well as political unity (with the exception of the reigns of Volodymyr the Great, Yaroslav the Wise, and Volodymyr Monomakh) virtually impossible, and from the very beginning there were territorially different cultural substrata: Iranian, Turkic, and perhaps even Thracian in Ukraine, Baltic in Belarus, and Finno-Ugric in Russia.

**Ethnocultural features.** The ethnocultural features of the Ukrainians are most evident when viewed historically and ethnographically by region. Yet there are features of folk culture and folkways common to all Ukrainians. Ukrainian *villages and *folk architecture were distinct from the Russian, as were certain implements (see *plow), various means of transportation (the chumak wagon, the Zaporozhian Cossack boat, Carpathian rafts), folk *dress and *folk musical instruments. With the advent of Christianity traditional and pagan practices were absorbed into the Christian calendar (see *Burial rites, *Christmas, *Demonology, *Easter, *Harvest rituals, *Kupalo festival, *New Year, *Spring rituals, and *Wedding); many are popular even today. The Ukrainians observed the spring ritual much more than did the other East Slavs. A unique feature of the Ukrainian folk tradition was the *kolodka, for which there is no analogous ritual among the other Slavs.

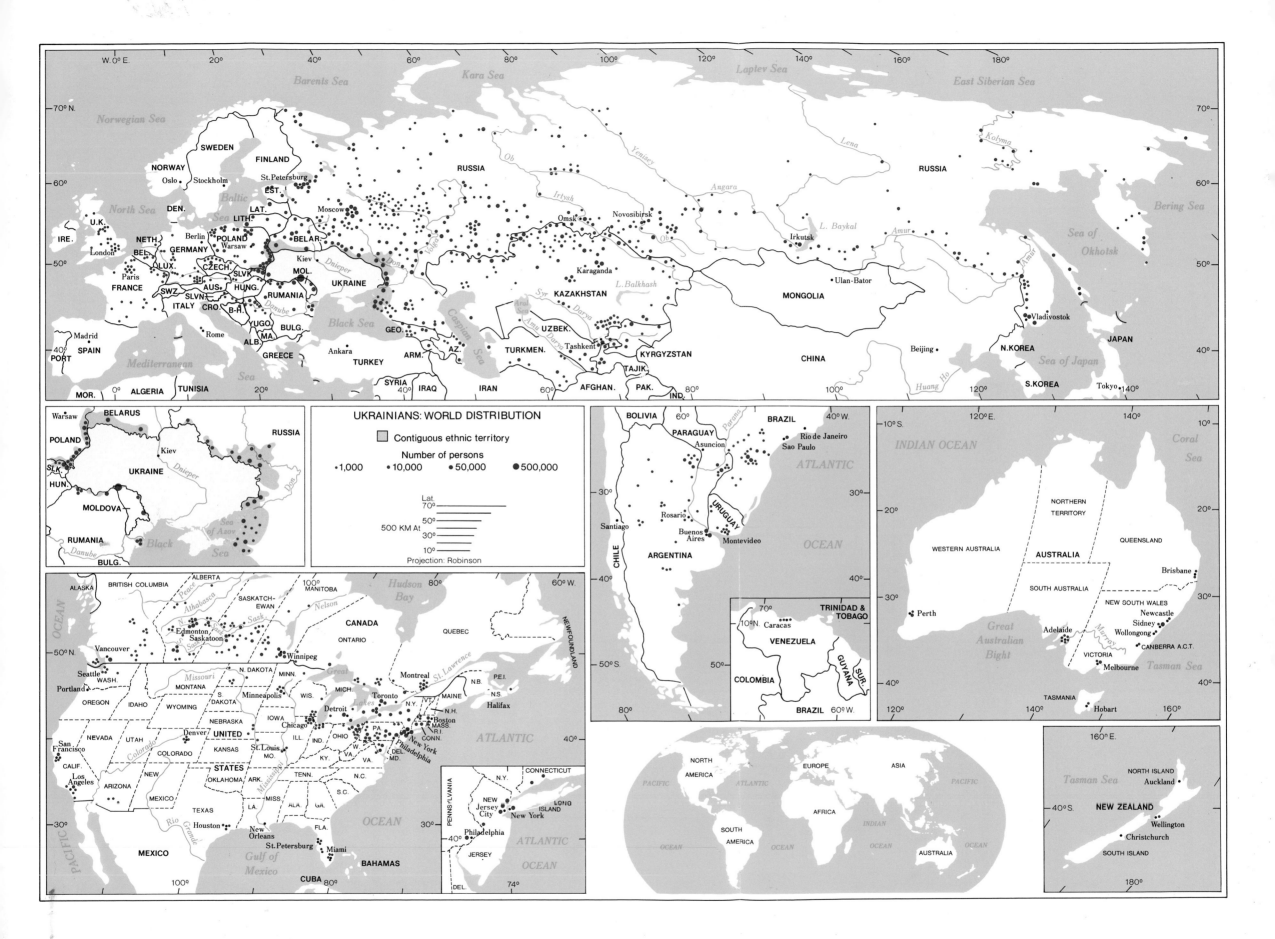

Ukrainian *folk oral literature and poetry (especially the *dumas), rich *embroidery, *ceramics, and other crafts and elaborate *folk dances are world-renowned.

The peasant commune, or *hromada, played a major role in Ukrainian life well into the 20th century. The large *clan, however, was abandoned by the Ukrainians sooner than by other Slavic nations. As early as the 18th century the small, two-generation family prevailed. Family customs and celebrations retained many unique features. Ukrainian *wedding traditions in particular had well-defined ceremonial stages (from betrothal to the post-wedding festivities) and involved ritual *foods (eg, the *korovai) and special musicians (*troisti muzyky) and songs. *Birth customs were more developed than among the Russians and Belarusians.

In the 20th century the Ukrainians have absorbed many features of modern European secular culture. Such modernization, coupled with rapid *urbanization, and the militant *atheism and *antireligious propaganda under Soviet rule, have resulted in the disappearance of many customs, widespread indifference to traditions, and spiritual impoverishment. In recent years, however, various attempts at reviving some of the lost customs have been made, particularly those connected with Christmas and Easter.

**National consciousness.** The people of Rus' did not have a common national consciousness, but they showed an allegiance to their rulers, their clans, their towns and regions, and later their church. They did know that they were different from their neighbors and their enemies, and they had a sense of loyalty and concern for the 'land of Rus',' judging by what was written in the extant literature and chronicles of the period. Some notion of a Rus' language also existed, as evidenced in Ilarion's Sermon on the Law and Grace, the Primary Chronicle, and the epic *Slovo o polku Ihorevi* (The Tale of Prince Ihor's Campaign). After the fall of the Principality of Galicia-Volhynia in the 14th century and its partition among Lithuania, Poland, Hungary, and Moldavia the Ukrainians began developing more than a territorial consciousness. Their awareness that they were a different people was reinforced by their distinct *church rite and use of the bookish *Slavonic-Ruthenian language. The common fate of the 'Ruthenian' Ukrainians and Belarusians in the Polish-Lithuanian Commonwealth resulted in the evolution of a cultural, religious, and partly national awareness that set them off from the neighboring 'Muscovites.' That Ruthenian identity became fragmented after the 1569 Union of Lublin. A rebirth of historical memory about Kievan Rus' occurred during the 'Orthodox Renaissance' of the late 16th and early 17th centuries, which revived the literary and architectural traditions of Kievan Rus'.

In the Cossack *Hetman state of 1648–1782 a 'Little Russian' or 'Cossack-Ruthenian' consciousness emerged. After the complete absorption of the Hetman state by the Russian Empire in the 1780s, the majority of the Left-Bank Cossack elite became loyal subjects of the empire. That did not exclude the nurturing of a local patriotism and culture (see, eg, I. *Kotliarevsky), but it resulted in the widespread growth of a *Little Russian mentality.

In Western Ukraine, after the partitions of Poland the indigenous elite (most of them clergy) rid themselves of Polish influence. They did not assume an Austrian identity, but they remained loyal subjects as long as the Austri-

ans kept the Poles in check. Unlike the 'Little Russian' elite, the *Old Ruthenians of Galicia and the assimilationist *Magyarones of Hungarian-ruled Transcarpathia did not participate in empire-building.

During the 19th century the former identification with the Ukrainian Cossack state was superseded by cultural *Ukrainophilism. The cultural rebirth that occurred was manifested primarily through the rise of a modern Ukrainian *literature. From the 1860s on, however, a *Russophile movement became prominent in Austrian-ruled Galicia, Bukovyna, and Transcarpathia. More an attempt at fending off Polish and Hungarian influences than a true acceptance of Russian hegemony, Russophile attitudes eventually gave way to populist and, later, nationalist ones.

The watershed in the development of modern Ukrainian national consciousness was the 1917–20 struggle for Ukraine's *independence. For the first time many Russified Ukrainians became aware they were not Russians, and the existence of a nation-state, albeit brief, consolidated Ukrainian national identity, and forced the Bolsheviks to create the Ukrainian SSR and even to accede to the policy of *Ukrainization in Soviet Ukrainian society through most of the 1920s.

A concerted effort to reverse the growth of Ukrainian national consciousness was begun by the Stalinist regime in the late 1920s, and continued with minor interruptions until the most recent times. The man-made *famine of 1932–3, the deportations of the so-called *kulaks, the physical annihilation of the nationally conscious intelligentsia, and *terror in general were used to destroy and subdue the Ukrainian nation. Even after J. Stalin's death the concept of a Russified though multiethnic *Soviet people was officially promoted, according to which the non-Russian nations were relegated to second-class status. The creation of a sovereign and independent Ukraine in 1991, however, pointed to the failure of the policy of the 'merging of nations' and to the enduring strength of the Ukrainian national consciousness.

National consciousness has not prevailed among all Ukrainian ethnographic groups. The inhabitants of the *Kuban, for example, have vacillated among three identities, Ukrainian, Russian (supported by the Soviet regime), and 'Cossack.' The linguistic and religious identities of some groups (eg, the *Latynnyky) have been in conflict. Not all so-called *Rusini* or *Rusnatsi* of Yugoslavia's *Bačka region consider their roots to be Ukrainian, nor do many immigrants from Transcarpathia and the Lemko and Prešov regions in the New World or, to a lesser extent, the inhabitants of those regions today. (See also *History of Ukraine, *Physical anthropology, and *Population of Ukraine.)

BIBLIOGRAPHY

Antonovych, V. 'Try natsional'ni typy narodni,' *Pravda*, 1888, no. 3

Hrushevs'kyi, M. 'Ukraintsy,' in *Formy natsional'nago dvizheniia v sovremennykh gosudarstvakh*, ed Kastelian (St Petersburg 1910; Ukrainian trans: 'Ukraïntsi,' in *Nauka i kul'tura: Ukraïna*, 24 [1990])

Rudnitsky [Rudnyts'kyi], S. *Ukraine, the Land and Its People: An Introduction to Its Geography* (New York 1918)

Rudnyts'kyi, S. *Osnovy zemleznannia Ukraïny*, 2, *Antropogeografiia Ukraïny* (Uzhhorod 1926)

Kostomarov, M. *Dvi rus'ki narodnosti* (Kolomyia nd [1927])

Smal'-Stots'kyi, S. *Rozvytok pohliadiv pro semiu slovians'kykh mov i ïkh vzaïmne sporidnennia*, 2nd rev edn (Prague 1927)

Fischer, A. *Rusini: Zarys etnografji Rusi* (Lviv, Warsaw, and Cracow 1928)

Vovk, Kh. *Studiï z ukraïns'koï etnohrafiï ta antropolohiï* (Prague 1928; New York 1976)

Iendyk, R. *Antropolohichni prykmety ukraïns'koho narodu* (Lviv 1934)

Shelukhyn, S. *Ukraïna* (Prague 1936–7)

Shcherbakivs'kyi, V. *Formatsiia ukraïns'koï natsiï: Narys praistoriï Ukraïny* (Prague 1941; New York 1958)

Petrov, V. *Pokhodzhennia ukraïns'koho narodu* (Regensburg 1947)

Rebet, L. *Formuvannia ukraïns'koï natsiï* (Munich 1951)

Diachenko, V. *Antropolohichnyi sklad ukraïns'koho narodu: Porivnial'ne doslidzhennia narodiv* URSR *i sumizhnykh terytorii* (Kiev 1963)

Chubatyi, M. *Kniazha Rus'-Ukraïna ta vynyknennia tr'okh skhid-n'oslov'ians'kykh natsii* (New York 1964)

Huslystyi, K. *Do pytannia pro utvorennia ukraïns'koï natsiï* (Kiev 1967)

Petrov, V. *Etnohenez slov'ian: Dzherela, etapy rozvytku i proble-matyka* (Kiev 1972)

Borysenko, V.; et al. *Ukraïns'ka narodnist': Narysy sotsial'no-ekonomichnoï i etno-politychnoï istoriï* (Kiev 1990)

Naulko, V.; et al. *Kul'tura i pobut naselennia Ukraïny* (Kiev 1991)

*Ukraïntsi: Skhidna diaspora (Atlas)* (Kiev 1992)

V. Kubijovyč, V. Naulko, B. Struminsky, A. Zhukovsky

**Ukrainian-Soviet War, 1917–21.** A military struggle for control of Ukraine waged intermittently in 1917–21 by Ukrainian independentist forces and pro-Bolshevik elements seeking to establish Soviet rule. The struggle began shortly after the *October Revolution of 1917. Notwithstanding the creation of the *Ukrainian National Republic (UNR) on 20 November 1917, the Bolsheviks planned to seize power in Ukraine with the aid of Russian or Russified urban elements, Russian garrisons, and army units stationed near the front. Their armed uprising in Kiev on 11 December 1917 was unsuccessful, however, and the Bolshevized army units were deported from Ukraine in stages. A pro-Bolshevik force under Ye. *Bosh moving in on Kiev was also disarmed by Ukrainian troops under P. Skoropadsky near Zhmerynka and then sent off to Russia.

**December 1917 to April 1918.** Hostilities broke out in Ukraine after a series of diplomatic maneuvers. On 17 December 1917 the Petrograd-based Soviet of People's Commissars issued an ultimatum demanding that Bolshevik troops be granted the legal right to be stationed on Ukrainian soil. The ultimatum was rejected by the UNR. The Bolsheviks countered by proclaiming their own Ukrainian government based in Kharkiv on 25 December, and then proceeded with a campaign to establish effective military control over Ukraine. The Ukrainian forces at that time consisted of a small volunteer detachment and several battalions of the *Free Cossacks. The pro-Soviet forces in Ukraine included Russian army regulars stationed at the front, a number of garrisoned units, and Red Guard detachments composed of laborers from Kharkiv gubernia and the Donbas. Their main strength, however, lay in a large force of Red Guards from Russia, which had been stationed along the Ukrainian border. On 25 December that 30,000-strong army, led by V. *Antonov-Ovsiienko, set off in four groups from Homel and Briansk toward Chernihiv–Bakhmach, Hlukhiv–Konotip, and Kharkiv–Poltava–Lozova.

The invasion by pro-Soviet forces was accompanied by uprisings initiated by local Bolshevik agitators in cities throughout Left-Bank Ukraine. The Bolshevik forces occupied Kharkiv (26 December), Lozova and Katerynoslav (now Dnipropetrovske, 9 January 1918), Oleksandrivske (now Zaporizhia, 15 January), and Poltava (20 January). The Briansk group captured Konotip (16 January) and Hlukhiv (19 January). On 27 January the Bolshevik army groups converged on Bakhmach and then set off under the command of M. *Muravev to take Kiev.

The Central Rada prepared for the defense of the capital by sending advance forces of volunteers to Poltava and Bakhmach. One of those, the Student Kurin, was annihilated by a vastly larger (4,000 troops) Bolshevik force at *Kruty, 130 km northeast of Kiev, on 29 January. As the Soviet advance continued, an attempt was made to take Kiev through an uprising organized by non-Ukrainian workers based at the *Arsenal plant. Fighting broke out on 29 January and continued until 4 February, when the revolt was put down by a newly formed contingent of the *Sich Riflemen and the Free Cossacks. Meanwhile the Bolshevik expeditionary force continued to move on the capital from Bakhmach and Lubni. On 8 February the Ukrainian government was forced to evacuate the city. Soviet troops under Muravev's command entered Kiev on 9 March and then carried out brutal reprisals against the Ukrainian civilian population.

After taking Kiev the Bolsheviks launched an offensive in Right-Bank Ukraine, where they were engaged in battle mainly with Free Cossack forces. They moved into Volhynia (led by the former Russian Seventh Army), where they took Proskuriv (now Khmelnytskyi), Zhmerynka, Koziatyn, Berdychiv, Rivne, and Shepetivka and forced the Ukrainians back to a Zhytomyr–Korosten–Sarny defensive line.

The tide changed following Ukraine's signature of the Peace Treaty of *Brest-Litovsk and the entry of German and Austrian troops into the conflict in late February as allies of the Central Rada. With a Ukrainian command of Gen K. Prisovsky and S. Petliura the combined force rolled the Bolshevik troops out of Right-Bank centers, such as Zhytomyr, Berdychiv, Koziatyn, and Bucha, before regaining Kiev on 1 March. Through March and April the German and Austrian armies took control of Left-Bank Ukraine, and the troops of P. *Bolbochan and V. *Sikevych took the Crimea and the Donets region. Alarmed by the changed military situation, V. Lenin ordered his representative in Ukraine, G. Ordzhonikidze, to Ukrainize (at least ostensibly) the predominantly Russian forces of Antonov-Ovsiienko and Muravev in a bid for more popular support. The maneuver proved unsuccessful. Continuing military setbacks gave Soviet Russia little choice but to comply with the articles of the Treaty of *Brest-Litovsk and to sign a preliminary peace with the Ukrainian government on 12 June 1918.

**December 1918 to December 1919.** The second phase of the Ukrainian-Soviet War began with the fall of the German-supported Hetman government to the forces of the UNR Directory. The Bolsheviks took advantage of the unsettled situation by forming a Provisional Workers' and Peasants' Government of Ukraine on 17 November 1918 and starting a military advance into Ukraine in December with an army led by Antonov-Ovsiienko, J. Stalin, and V. Zatonsky. The Directory protested the aggression, with diplomatic notes sent to the Soviet government on 31 December 1918 and on 3, 4, and 9 January 1919. Not having received a reply, the Directory was compelled to declare war against Russia on 16 January. The Ukrainian forces at that time consisted of two regular troop formations, the *Zaporozhian Corps and the Sich Riflemen, as well as partisan detachments led by otamans, such as N. *Makhno, N. *Hryhoriiv, and D. *Zeleny. The otamans, however, were politically unreliable and occasionally sided with the Bolsheviks.

In December 1918 and January 1919 the Bolshevik expeditionary force, aided by some of the otamans, captured Left-Bank Ukraine, and on 5 February it closed in on Kiev, where it forced the Ukrainian government once more to flee from the capital. The Soviet attack proceeded on several fronts. A northern group moved along a Mozyr–Korosten and Lunynets–Sarny–Rivne line in an attempt to cut off the UNR *Army from the *Ukrainian Galician Army (UHA) to the west. A southern group proceeded from the Kremenchuk-Katerynoslav region through Znamianka toward the Birzula–Koziatyn–Zhmerynka line in an effort to cut off the UNR troops from possible reinforcement by Entente forces. At a critical moment Otaman Hryhoriiv threw his support behind them. The third Bolshevik army group proceeded from Kiev to the Berdychiv–Koziatyn–Zhmerynka line in an effort to keep the northern and southern wings of the UNR Army divided.

The UNR Army launched a counteroffensive in March, in which it defeated the Soviet forces along the Berdychiv–Koziatyn line and advanced almost to Kiev, thereby effectively cutting off any possibility that the Soviets might march through Rumania to Hungary in order to aid the Béla Kun regime. The Bolshevik forces retaliated in April (after the withdrawal of Entente troops) by marching on Zhmerynka and dividing the UNR Army's southern flank from the force's main body. The southern group subsequently lost the support of Otaman O. Volokh and was forced to retreat into Rumania, where it was disarmed (eventually returning through Galicia to Volhynia). At the same time, the UNR Army was pushed back to a small parcel of territory approx 40–50 km wide in the Dubno-Brody region of southwestern Volhynia. Its position was weakened further with a coup attempt by one of its commanding officers, V. *Oskilko.

The UNR Army's fortunes improved as Ukrainian peasants, disgruntled by the Bolsheviks' anti-Ukrainian policy and high requisition quotas, started to replenish insurgent ranks. But before the army itself could regroup, it faced an assault by Polish forces in the Lutske region and advances from the Soviet troops in the north and southeast that took Rivne, Shepetivka, Proskuriv, and even Kamianets-Podilskyi. The UNR then reached a peace agreement with the Poles and reorganized its army into four groups – the Sich Riflemen and the Zaporozhian, Volhynian, and Southwestern corps – with a total of approx 15,000 soldiers. In early June the UNR forces launched an offensive which retook Podilia and Kamianets-Podilskyi. The Red Army retaliated at the end of the month with a campaign that regained Proskuriv (5 July) and approached Kamianets-Podilskyi, which had been made the UNR's provisional capital. The UNR was then strengthened by the arrival of Yu. *Tiutiunnyk with troops formerly under Hryhoriiv, who had worked his way through the Reds' southern flank. The UNR Army launched a campaign which pushed the Bolshevik forces back to the Horodok–Yarmolyntsi–Sharhorod–Dunaivtsi–Nova Ushytsia–Vapniarka line before being joined by UHA troops who had crossed the Zbruch River on 16–17 July; their arrival brought together a combined Ukrainian force of nearly 85,000 regulars and 15,000 partisans.

The subsequent campaign to take Kiev proceeded with victories in Vinnytsia (12 August), Khmilnyk, Yaniv, Kalynivka, and Starokostiantyniv (14 August), Berdychiv (19 August), and Zhytomyr (21 August). On 31 August the Ukrainian troops entered Kiev, only to discover that soldiers from A. *Denikin's Volunteer Army had arrived at the same time. Hostilities between the two forces were narrowly averted when the combined Ukrainian forces pulled out of the city. The Bolsheviks took advantage of the Ukrainians' standoff with Denikin's troops to move some of their forces from the Katerynoslav region to Zhytomyr. Meanwhile the leadership of the UNR and UHA split over how to deal with Denikin, a situation exacerbated by an outbreak of typhus among the troops. The UHA leadership finally made a separate peace with the Volunteer Army on 6 November. The military situation had worsened as Bolshevik forces, which had made substantial gains in Right-Bank areas formerly controlled by Denikin's troops, and the Poles moved into the western reaches of Ukraine. By the end of November the government and the UNR Army found themselves hemmed in by Soviet, Polish, and Volunteer Army troops. At a conference on 4 December the army decided to suspend regular military operations in favor of underground partisan warfare.

**December 1919 to November 1920.** The UNR Army under the command of M. *Omelianovych-Pavlenko carried out an underground operation known as the First *Winter Campaign in the Yelysavethrad (now Kirovohrad) region against the Soviet 14th Army from 6 December 1919 to 6 May 1920. In addition to that action the UNR government concluded the Treaty of *Warsaw on 22 April, and then launched a joint offensive with Polish troops against the Bolsheviks. By 7 May a Ukrainian division under the command of M. Bezruchko entered Kiev, but the success was short-lived. A Soviet counteroffensive led by S. Budenny pushed the combined forces back across the Zbruch and past Zamość toward Warsaw. After the decisive battle of 15 September the Polish-Ukrainian forces threw the Bolshevik contingent back as far as the Sharhorod–Bar–Lityn line in Podilia. The Poles concluded a separate peace with the Soviets on 18 October. The 23,000-strong UNR force continued fighting until 21 October, when its position became untenable. The UNR troops crossed the Zbruch into Polish-controlled Galicia, where they were disarmed and placed in *internment camps.

**November 1921.** The final military action of the UNR against the Soviets was a raid in November 1921 known as the Second Winter Campaign. The intent of the action was to provide a catalyst for the formation of partisan groups which would incite a general uprising against the Bolsheviks in Ukraine. The commander of the action was Tiutiunnyk. Two expeditionary forces were established, Podilia (400 men) and Volhynia (800 men). The Podilia group advanced as far as the village of Vakhnivka, in the Kiev region, before returning to Polish territory through Volhynia on 29 November. The Volhynia group took Korosten and advanced as far as the village of Leonivka in the Kiev region. On its return march it was intercepted by a Bolshevik cavalry force under the command of H. Kotovsky, however, and routed in battle near Mali Minky on

17 November. Of the 443 soldiers captured by the Soviets 359 were shot on 23 November near the town of Bazar, in the Zhytomyr region, and 84 were passed on to Soviet security forces.

The Second Winter Campaign brought the Ukrainian-Soviet War to a definite conclusion. The *partisan movement in Ukraine remained active until mid-1922, but conventional military action by regular troops had ceased.

BIBLIOGRAPHY
Kapustians'kyi, M. *Pokhid ukraïns'kykh armii na Kyïv-Odesu v 1919 r.: Korotkyi voienno-istorychnyi ohliad*, 3 pts (Lviv 1921–2; 2nd edn, Munich 1946)
Tiutiunnyk, Iu. *Zymovyi pokhid 1919–1922 rr.* (Kolomyia 1923)
Dotsenko, O. *Litopys ukraïns'koï revolitutsiï*, vol 2, bks 4–5 (Lviv 1923–4; repr, Philadelphia 1988)
Antonov-Ovseenko, V. *Zapiski o grazhdanskoi voine*, 4 vols (Moscow–Leningrad 1924–33)
Bezruchko, M. *Sichovi stril'tsi v borot'bi za derzhavnist'* (Kalisz 1932)
Shandruk, P. (ed). *Ukraïns'ko-moskovs'ka viina 1920 r. v dokumentakh* (Vienna 1933)
Stefaniv, Z. *Ukraïns'ki zbroini syly 1917–1921 rr.*, 3 vols (Kolomyia 1934–5)
Dotsenko, O. *Zymovyi pokhid Armiï* UNR (Vienna 1935)
Omelianovych-Pavlenko, M. *Zymovyi pokhid* (Prague 1940)
Udovychenko, O. *Ukraïna u viini za derzhavnist'* (Winnipeg 1954)
Mirchuk, P. *Ukraïns'ko-moskovs'ka viina 1917–1919* (Toronto 1957)
Shankovs'kyi, L. *Ukraïns'ka Armiia v borot'bi za derzhavnist', 1917–1920* (Munich 1958)
Skaba, A.; et al (eds). *Ukraïns'ka RSR v period hromadians'koï viiny 1917–1920 rr.*, 3 vols (Kiev, 1967–70)
Udovychenko, O. *Tretia zalizna diviziia*, 2 vols (New York 1971, 1982)
*La guerre polono-soviétique de 1919–1920* (Paris 1975)
A. Zhukovsky

***Ukrainische Blätter***. An irregular German-language periodical of the *Union for the Liberation of Ukraine, published by V. Kalynovych in Vienna in 1916–18 (a total of 42 issues). Edited by O. Hrytsai, it reported on Ukrainian political and cultural developments and the growth of the Ukrainian national movement.

***Ukrainische Korrespondenz***. A weekly informational organ of the *Supreme (later *General) Ukrainian Council, published in Vienna in 1914–18. Until 1916 it was called *Ukrainisches Korrespondenzblatt*. The publication informed the German and Austrian public and policymakers about Ukrainian affairs. It was specifically intended to garner support for the Ukrainian national movement and the cause of Ukrainian independence. The paper was published by K. Levytsky and edited by V. Paneiko, V. Singalevych, and V. Kushnir (1917–18).

***Ukrainische Kulturberichte***. An informational organ of the *Ukrainian Scientific Institute in Berlin. Published irregularly in 1933–40, it informed the German public about the work of the institute and other émigré scholars. It also devoted some attention to Soviet Ukrainian political, scholarly, and cultural affairs. The editors were Z. Kuzelia and M. Masiukevych.

***Ukrainische Nachrichten***. A German-language semimonthly and then weekly published by the *Union for the Liberation of Ukraine in Vienna from October 1914 to 1918 (a total of 100 issues). Originally a press bulletin, it later became a regular newspaper that provided German and Austrian newspapers, journalists, and political leaders with information on political developments in Ukraine and the growth of Ukrainian nationalism. *Ukrainische Nachrichten* was published by M. Trotsky and edited by O. Bachynsky and then an editorial board headed by V. Biberovych. The paper became popular; its circulation reached almost 4,000.

***Ukrainische Rundschau***. A German-language informational monthly published in Vienna in 1905–14. The continuation of *Ruthenische Revue*, it informed the Western public and policymakers about Ukrainian affairs in the Austro-Hungarian and Russian empires and was distributed free of charge to numerous newspapers, writers, and diplomats. Edited by V. *Kushnir, and in 1908–9 by O. *Turiansky, the publication was actively supported by members of the Ukrainian Parliamentary Representation in Vienna, particularly V. Yavorsky (the formal publisher), S. Dnistriansky, O. Kolessa, and Ye. Levytsky. Its other contributors included some of the most distinguished Ukrainian publicists and political figures of the time, such as Yu. Romanchuk, O. Turiansky, V. Shchurat, I. Krypiakevych, M. Korduba, B. Lepky, M. Lozynsky, I. Makukh, and V. Doroshenko, as well as many non-Ukrainians.

**Ukrainische Vertrauensstelle im Deutschen Reich.** See Ukrainian Institution of Trust in the German Reich.

**Ukrainischer Briefmarkensammlerverein in Österreich.** See Ukrainian Philatelic Society of Austria.

**Ukrainischer Pressedienst.** See Ukrainian Press Service.

**Ukrainization** (Ukrainizatsiia). A series of policies pursued by the CP(B)U in 1923–33 to enhance the national profile of state and Party institutions and thus legitimize Soviet rule in Ukrainian eyes. Ukrainization was the Ukrainian version of the all-Union policy of *indigenization.

Since Ukrainians were by far the largest non-Russian nation in the newly created USSR, indigenization went farther in Ukraine than in other national republics. It included the following measures: making Party and state cadres fluent in the Ukrainian language and familiar with Ukrainian history and culture; actively recruiting Ukrainians into the Party and state apparatuses; establishing separate Red Army units with Ukrainian as the language of command; financially supporting non-Communist cultural institutions, such as the All-Ukrainian Academy of Sciences; developing a Communist or pro-Communist Ukrainian intelligentsia to play, eventually, the leading role in the 'Ukrainian cultural process'; and vastly expanding education and publishing in Ukrainian to raise the social prestige of Ukrainian culture. Ukrainization evolved from an attempt to make the Soviet regime more palatable to the Ukrainian people into the larger project of de-Russifying the urban environment and establishing Ukrainian as the dominant language throughout society.

Ukrainization grew out of the weakness of early Soviet governments in Ukraine. As early as 1920 M. *Skrypnyk attributed this weakness to national hostility between the Ukrainian peasantry and the Russified workers, which was reflected in the Ukrainophobic policies of the Soviet authorities. The solution lay in the gradual de-Russification of the proletariat in Ukraine and its adoption of Ukrainian culture. The *Borotbists, led by O. *Shumsky, offered a similar analysis. Other Bolshevik leaders in Ukraine, such as Kh. *Rakovsky and D. Lebid, opposed any concessions to Ukrainian cultural aspirations.

In 1921 the 10th Congress of the Russian Communist Party (Bolshevik) (RKP[B]) proclaimed, along with the *New Economic Policy, the complete equality of national languages and cultures. The persistence of partisan activity in rural Ukraine, called 'kulak-banditry' in Soviet sources, and the Basmachi revolt in Central Asia forced the 12th Congress of the RKP(B) in 1923 to admit that its nationality policy was not working and to introduce the policy of indigenization, which was designed to give the Russian-imposed Soviet regimes in the non-Russian republics a veneer of national legitimacy. On 16 July 1923 Rakovsky was replaced as chairman of the Ukrainian Council of People's Commissars by V. *Chubar, a Ukrainian. On 27 July the council ordered the school system, except for schools serving national minorities, to be completely Ukrainized within the next two years. On 1 August the Ukrainian government decreed that all public officials master Ukrainian within two years, and that all official business be transacted in Ukrainian.

Despite widespread opposition to Ukrainization within the still largely Russian CP(B)U, ex-Borotbists, such as O. Shumsky, V. Blakytny, S. Pylypenko, and M. Semenko, were given considerable authority over Ukrainian cultural policy. Blakytny became editor of *Visti VUTsVK*, the organ of the government, and head of the mass literary organization *Hart. Pylypenko was editor of the newspaper *Selians'ka pravda* and head of the peasant literary organization *Pluh. Semenko founded Nova Generatsiia, an association of Ukrainian futurist writers. In 1923 Shumsky became editor of Soviet Ukraine's first and most prestigious 'thick journal,' *Chervonyi shliakh*, and in 1925, people's commissar of education responsible for the Ukrainization program and all cultural policy. Shumsky's appointment to this key post came shortly after the CP(B)U's Russophile leader, E. *Kviring, was replaced by L. *Kaganovich, who made it clear that no further foot-dragging on Ukrainization would be tolerated. Yet Shumsky called for Kaganovich's immediate replacement by an ethnic Ukrainian, V. Chubar, and an even faster pace of Ukrainization. In 1927 Shumsky was replaced by Skrypnyk, who had aligned himself against Shumsky with J. Stalin and Kaganovich, both of whom supported the policy but opposed any criticism of Russian interference. In 1927 S. *Kosior replaced Kaganovich as CP(B)U first secretary. Under Skrypnyk's supervision all postsecondary education was rapidly Ukrainized. He also oversaw Ukrainization in Ukrainian areas outside the Ukrainian SSR.

Ukrainization had a substantial impact on the national composition of Ukraine's cities, its proletariat, and the CP(B)U. The percentage of Ukrainian residency in Kharkiv grew from 38 in 1923 to 50 in 1933; in Kiev, from 27 to 42; in Dnipropetrovske, from 16 to 48; and in Odessa, from 7 to 17. The proportion of Ukrainians among Ukraine's 1.1 million workers grew from 55 percent in 1926 to 59 percent in 1931 and 60 percent in 1933. In 1922 CP(B)U membership was 23 percent Ukrainian and 54 percent Russian; in 1933 it was 60 percent Ukrainian and 23 percent Russian. But not all Ukrainians considered Ukrainian to be their native language or were literate in it. According to the 1926 census 45 percent of the population of the Ukrai-

nian SSR was literate (16 percent in the countryside and 50 percent in the cities). Of the 11.7 million literate inhabitants, 9.6 million were Ukrainians, of whom only 6.5 million were literate in Ukrainian. Slightly more of Ukraine's inhabitants were literate in Russian than in Ukrainian. The distinction between ethnicity and language literacy was particularly evident in the CP(B)U: in January 1927 Ukrainians accounted for 52 percent of the members and candidates, but only 31 percent gave Ukrainian as their native language. A mass literacy campaign, which was mostly Ukrainian, raised adult literacy in Ukraine to 74 percent in 1929. At the high point of Ukrainization, in the 1932–3 school year, 88 percent of all students were enrolled in Ukrainian-language schools. About 57 percent of trade-union members were Ukrainians in 1930, but only 44 percent claimed Ukrainian as their native language. In the crucial industrial sector the situation in 1929 was much worse: 48 percent of Ukraine's trade-union members in industry were Ukrainian by nationality, 32 percent spoke Ukrainian at home, 43 percent read Ukrainian, and 38 percent wrote Ukrainian. By 1933, 88 percent of all factory newspapers were published in Ukrainian, double the figure for 1928.

The policy of actively favoring Ukrainian over Russian led to resentment among some Russian-speakers. The view that Ukrainization violated the national rights of Ukraine's workers was articulated in 1925 by Yu. Larin. In 1927 G. *Zinovev, then in opposition to Stalin, denounced Ukrainization as a policy supporting S. Petliura's followers and encouraging Ukrainian chauvinism. Many Russian CP(B)U members felt excluded from the development of Ukrainian culture. Others, such as S. Dimanshtein, feared that the progress of Ukrainization would ultimately unleash centrifugal political forces. In the 1920s Stalin consistently supported Ukrainization and publicly denounced such views. But his attitude changed in the early 1930s.

The political justification for Ukrainization had been the need to placate the Ukrainian peasantry. The collectivization of agriculture, based on the massive application of force by central authorities against the peasants, eliminated any such need and bypassed the republic's leadership. When the Ukrainian elite, fostered by Ukrainization, attempted to defend the Ukrainian peasantry from the center's worst depredations, Stalin responded by eliminating the elite, its social base, and the Ukrainization policy which strengthened that social base. The state-ordered famine of 1932–3, P. *Postyshev's assignment to the position of second secretary of the CP(B)U, the 1933 purge of the CP(B)U, and the widespread repressions against Ukrainian cultural activists marked the end of Ukrainization. Rapid industrialization continued to draw Ukrainian peasants to the cities, mines, and factories, but means of preventing their denationalization were vastly diminished in Ukraine and completely eliminated in Ukrainian ethnic territories outside Ukraine.

BIBLIOGRAPHY

Dmytryshyn, B. *Moscow and the Ukraine, 1918–1953: A Study of Russian Bolshevik Nationality Policy* (New York 1956)
*Kul'turne budivnytsvo v Ukraïns'kii RSR: Vazhlyvishi rishennia Komunistychnoï partiï i Radians'koho uriadu, 1917–1959* (Kiev 1959)
Mace, J. *Communism and the Dilemmas of National Liberation: National Communism in Soviet Ukraine, 1918–1933* (Cambridge, Mass 1983)
Krawchenko, B. *Social Change and National Consciousness in Twentieth-Century Ukraine* (London 1985)

J. Mace

Lesia Ukrainka

**Ukrainka, Lesia** [Ukrajinka, Lesja] (pseud of Larysa Ko-sach-Kvitka), b 25 February 1871 in Zviahel (now Novo-hrad-Volynskyi), Volhynia gubernia, d 1 August 1913 in Surami, Georgia. Poet and playwright; daughter of O. Ko-sach-Drahomanova (O. *Pchilka). Lesia Ukrainka spent her childhood in Volhynia in the towns of Zviahel, Lutske, and Kolodiazhne and then moved to Kiev. Her views were particularly influenced by her mother's brother, M. *Drahomanov. Lesia Ukrainka achieved a broad educa-tion by self-tuition. She knew all of the major Western Eu-ropean languages as well as Greek and Latin and the Slavic languages (Russian, Polish, Bulgarian, and others). She was equally familiar with world history and at 19 wrote a textbook for her sisters, published in 1918 as *Starodavnia istoriia skhidnykh narodiv* (Ancient History of the Eastern Peoples). Lesia Ukrainka translated a great deal (eg, N. Gogol, A. Mickiewicz, H. Heine, V. Hugo, Homer). Suffering from tuberculosis, she traveled to Ger-many, Austria-Hungary, Italy, Egypt, and, several times, the Caucasus in search of a cure. Travel exposed her to new enriching experiences and broadened her horizons. Lesia Ukrainka began writing poetry at a very early age. At the age of nine she wrote the poem 'Nadiia' (Hope), and her first published poems, 'Konvaliia' (Lily of the Val-ley) and 'Safo' (Sappho), appeared in the Lviv journal *Zo-ria* in 1884. 1885 saw the appearance of her collection of translations of Gogol, which she prepared together with her brother, M. Kosach.

Lesia Ukrainka began to write more prolifically from the mid-1880s. In Kiev she joined the literary group *Pleiada and together with M. Slavinsky translated *Knyha pisen'* (Book of Songs, 1892) by H. Heine. Her first collec-tion of original poetry, *Na krylakh pisen'* (On Wings of Songs), appeared in Lviv (1893; 2nd edn, Kiev 1904). It was followed by the collections *Dumy i mrii* (Thoughts and Dreams, 1899) and *Vidhuky* (Echoes, 1902). Her early poems deal mainly with the beauty of nature, her love of her native land, personal experiences, the poet's vocation and the role of poetry, and social and community con-cerns. Epic features can be found in much of her lyric poetry, and reappear in her later ballads, legends, and the like – 'Samson,' 'Robert Brus, korol' shotlands'kyi' (Robert Bruce, King of Scotland), 'Vila-posestra' (Vila Sister), 'Odno slovo' (A Single Word).

Lesia Ukrainka reached her literary heights in her poetic dramas. Ukrainka's first drama was *Blakytna troianda* (The

Azure Rose, 1896), which describes the life of the Ukraini-an intelligentsia. In further dramatic works she developed a new genre, that of the 'dramatic poem.' The first such work was *Oderzhyma* (A Woman Possessed, 1901). Partic-ularly important among her works are the dramatic poems on the subject of prisoners in Babylon, which were meant to serve as symbols of the imprisonment of Ukrainians within the Russian Empire; among them are *Na ruïnakh* (Upon the Ruins, 1903), *Vavylons'kyi polon* (The Babylo-nian Captivity, 1903), and *V domu roboty – v kraïni nevoli* (In the House of Labor, In the Land of Slavery, 1906). In the dramatic poem *Kassandra* (1907) she portrayed the fate of Ukraine through the tragic history of long-lost Troy, and using Cassandra as her spokesperson, she challenged the Ukrainian people to shake off their apathy and inertia. In the dramatic poem *U katakombakh* (In the Catacombs, 1905) she also castigated the Ukrainian community for its com-promises and passivity. In the drama *Rufin i Pristsilla* (Rufinus and Priscilla, 1908) the shining image of the Christian woman is contrasted with the brutal strength of Imperial Rome. The dramatic poem *Boiarynia* (The Boyar Woman, 1910) illustrates most clearly Ukrainka's hostility to Russian imperialism; it maintains that only armed struggle can free the Ukrainian people from their Musco-vite prison. The theme of the poem *Orhiia* (The Orgy, 1912–13) concerns the poet's role in that ceaseless battle. In the dramatic poem *Kaminnyi hospodar* (The Stone Host, 1912) Lesia Ukrainka employs the Don Juan theme in an original presentation of the conflict between social conformity and personal freedom and responsibility. Her neoromantic work, the drama *Lisova pisnia* (The Forest Song, 1911), treats the conflict between lofty idealism and the prosaic details of everyday life. Lesia Ukrainka also wrote prose works. Her literary legacy is enormous, despite the fact that for most of her life she was ill and often was bedridden for months. The last few years of her life were spent con-valescing in Egypt and the Caucasus. The works of Lesia Ukrainka have been published many times. The most no-table editions, however, have been those of Knyhospilka (7 vols, 1923–5 and 12 vols, 1927–30), which include schol-arly introductions by M. Zerov, B. Yakubsky, M. Drai-Khmara, P. Rulin, Ye. Nenadkevych, O. Biletsky, and oth-ers. O. Kosach-Kryvyniuk's *Lesia Ukraïnka: Khronolohiia zhyttia i tvorchosty* (Lesia Ukrainka: A Chronology of Her Life and Works, New York 1970) is valuable for its bio-graphical and epistolary material.

BIBLIOGRAPHY
Muzychka, A. *Lesia Ukraïnka, ïï zhyttia, hromads'ka diial'nist' i poetychna tvorchist'* (Odessa 1925)
Drai-Khmara, M. *Lesia Ukraïnka: Zhyttia i tvorchist'* (Kiev 1926)
Odarchenko, P. *Lesia Ukraïnka i M.P. Drahomanov* (New York 1954)
Babyshkin, O.; Kurashova, V. *Lesia Ukraïnka: Zhyttia i tvorchist'* (Kiev 1955)
Babyshkin, O. *Dramaturhiia Lesi Ukraïnky* (Kiev 1963)
Avrakhov, H. *Khudozhnia maisternist' Lesi Ukraïnky* (Kiev 1964)
Kulins'ka, L. *Poetyka Lesi Ukraïnky* (Kiev 1967)
Bida, C. *Lesya Ukrainka: Life and Work*, with *Selected Works*, trans by V. Rich (Toronto 1968)
Kostenko, A. *Lesia Ukraïnka* (Kiev 1971)
Kulins'ka, L. *Proza Lesi Ukraïnky* (Kiev 1976)
Vyshnevs'ka, N. *Liryka Lesi Ukraïnky: Tekstolohichne doslidzhennia* (Kiev 1976)

P. Odarchenko

*Ukraïnka v sviti* (Ukrainian Woman in the World). An organ of the *World Federation of Ukrainian Women's Organizations, published in Philadelphia, then in Detroit, and since October 1963, in Toronto, three times a year at first and quarterly since 1965. Edited by a board headed by I. *Pelenska and, since 1982, by Ya. Zorych, it reports on the activities of the federation and its constituent organizations and on the women's movement in general. It also contains articles on issues of concern to women and on the status of women in Ukraine. An annual English-language issue, *Ukrainian Woman in the World*, has been published since 1973, edited by I. Pelenska, H. Mazurenko, and D. Rak.

**Ukrainophilism** (*ukrainofilstvo*). A cultural and political current sympathetic to Ukrainians. In its widest application the term can refer to any manifestation of sympathy for Ukrainians; it has been applied, for example, to 19th-century Polish and Russian writers who chose to work on Ukrainian themes. More narrowly, the word refers to the Ukrainian national movement in the Russian Empire from the 1860s to the 1880s, because Ukrainian activists in that period often referred to themselves and were referred to by others as Ukrainophiles (*ukrainofily* or *ukrainoliubtsi*). In the 1890s and 1900s the word acquired a negative connotation, when nationalist thinkers, such as B. *Hrinchenko and M. *Mikhnovsky, began to use the word Ukrainophiles to describe Ukrainians whose national consciousness had not developed beyond ethnographic appreciation. That refinement of the term, in part, reflected a generational difference between the revolutionary youth and their more moderate elders, the self-described Ukrainophiles. It also, however, reflected a more uncompromising national consciousness: the Ukrainophiles' critics presented themselves as consciously and exclusively Ukrainian and accused the Ukrainophiles of having a double national allegiance, Russian and Ukrainian; the very word Ukrainophile implied a sympathy with the Ukrainian nation perceived as other (ie, as not one's own). In English-language scholarly literature, and to some extent in Ukrainian political literature of the 1860s and 1870s, the term Ukrainophilism has also been used as a synonym for Western Ukrainian *populism (*narodovstvo*), to distinguish those who specifically allied themselves with the Ukrainian movement in the Russian Empire from the *Russophiles (and Rusynophiles) of Galicia, Transcarpathia, and Bukovyna.

J.-P. Himka

**Ukrainska Besida.** A Ukrainian cultural-educational club in Galicia in 1861–1939, known as Ruska Besida until the 1920s. The first Ukrainska Besida club was founded by Yu. *Lavrivsky in Lviv in 1861 and consisted of a group of local intelligentsia from the Moloda Rus' society. Ukrainska Besida provided a forum for social interaction and developed a program of literary and musical evenings, lectures, concerts, and commemorative observations. It also sponsored its own renowned theater group, *Ukrainska Besida Theater, and maintained a reading hall. In 1870–90 it provided a spiritual home for numerous Ukrainian student groups. As new organizations were established by the developing Ukrainian national movement in Galicia, Ukrainska Besida increasingly assumed a more social and recreational character. Ukrainska Besida clubs

were established in a number of Galician centers, including Peremyshl, Stanyslaviv, Ternopil, and Zhovkva. Notable leaders of the Ukrainian Besida in Lviv included Lavrivsky, V. Shukhevych (1895–1910), I. Kokorudz (1920–32), and I. Kopach.

**Ukrainska Besida Theater** (Teatr tovarystva Ruska Besida; also Ruskyi narodnyi teatr, Ukrainskyi liudovyi teatr). The first professional Ukrainian *touring theater, created in 1864 and subsidized by the Ruska Besida (see *Ukrainska Besida) Society in Lviv and occasionally supported by the Galician Diet. It served Galicia and Bukovyna, toured Poland and the Russian Empire, and was instrumental in the development of modern theater in all Ukraine. It performed mostly in the populist-realistic style and during its first years staged works from the Ukrainian classical repertoire (I. Kotliarevsky, H. Kvitka-Osnovianenko, T. Shevchenko, D. Dmytrenko, and O. Storozhenko) and the works of contemporary Galician dramatists (R. Mokh, I. Hushalevych, V. Kovalsky, and I. Naumovych). The director was O. Bachynsky; M. Verbytsky and I. Lavrivsky composed for the theater. After a hiatus (1867–9) the directors were A. Molentsky (1870–3), T. Romanovych (1874–80), M. Kropyvnytsky (1875), and I. Hrynevetsky (1878–89), jointly with I. Biberovych (1882–92).

During the 1870s and 1880s the theater introduced local historical dramas by O. Ohonovsky, K. Ustyianovych, and O. Barvinsky; populist-realistic comedies by H. Tsehlynsky; and plays by M. Kropyvnytsky, M. Starytsky, I. Karpenko-Kary, and P. Myrny. In the 1890s the theater staged I. Franko's realistic dramas, and after 1911, performances of V. Vynnychenko's psychological plays and V. Pachovsky's allegorical plays. While touring Ukraine it staged works by Western European playwrights – German (G. Lessing, A. Kotzebue, F. Schiller, F. Grillparzer, H. Kleist, K. Gutzkow, F. Hebbel, G. Hauptmann, and H. Sudermann), French (Molière, P. Beaumarchais, E. Scribe, G. Ohnet, and E. Rostand), Scandinavian (H. Ibsen and A. Strindberg), and Italian (C. Goldoni's comedies) – as well as Russian (N. Gogol, L. Tolstoi, A. Chekhov, M. Gorky) and Polish (A. Fredro, S. Przybyszewski) playwrights.

In addition to Ukrainian operas composed by S. Hulak-Artemovsky, M. Arkas, P. Bazhansky, D. Sichynsky, and Ya. Lopatynsky, the theater performed I. Vorobkevych's operettas and (in Ukrainian translation) C. Gounod's *Faust*, J. Offenbach's *Les Contes Hoffmann*, G. Bizet's *Carmen*, B. Smetana's *The Bartered Bride*, and S. Moniuszko's *Halka*. Many prominent actors appeared on its stage, among them T. Bachynska, M. Romanovych, I. and I. Biberovych, A. Osypovycheva, F. Lopatynska, S. Stadnyk, O. Pidvysotska, I. and K. Rubchak, S. Yanovych, V. Yurchak, A. Nyzhankivsky, V. Petrovych, M. Olshansky, and L. Kurbas, as well as visiting actors from Poland and Russian-ruled Ukraine.

In later years the directors of the Ruska Besida Theater were M. Hubchak (1901–4), M. Sadovsky (1905–6), Y. Stadnyk (1906–13), and R. Siretsky and S. Charnetsky (1913–14). The theater ceased activity with the start of the First World War. The members of its cast formed the nucleus of new theatrical collectives, including the *Theater of the Legion of Ukrainian Sich Riflemen (which used the name Ukrainska Besida Theater in 1916–18), Ternopilski Teatralni Vechory, the New Lviv Theater, and Y. *Stadnyk's touring theaters. In 1921–4 it existed as a resident theater in Lviv and then it was joined by the *Lviv Ukrainian Independent Theater.

BIBLIOGRAPHY
Charnets'kyi, S. *Narys istoriï ukraïns'koho teatru v Halychyni* (Lviv 1934)
Luzhnyts'kyi, H. 'Z istoriï ukraïns'koho teatru,' *Kyïv*, 2–4 (1953–4)

V. Revutsky

**Ukrainska biblioteka** (Ukrainian Library). A monthly book series issued by the *Ukrainska Presa publishing house in Lviv from 1933 to 1939. Eighty editions (a total of 230,000 copies by 1937) of literary works, including original works, reprints, and translations, appeared, under the editorship of M. Holubets. They were distributed free of charge to the subscribers of *Nash prapor*.

**Ukraïns'ka diisnist'** (Ukrainian Reality). An organ of the hetmanite *Ukrainska Hromada organization in Germany, published monthly and then semimonthly in Berlin in 1939–45. Until 1943 it included an economic supplement. The newspaper published reports on Ukrainian life in Germany, Czechoslovakia, and Austria and on developments in Soviet Ukraine. The editors were H. Derkach and M. Pasika, and I. Kalynovych was the publisher.

**Ukraïns'ka dumka** (Ukrainian Thought). A daily newspaper published in Lviv in October and November 1920 in place of the suppressed newspaper *Dilo*. It was edited by F. Fedortsiv.

**Ukraïns'ka dumka** (Ukrainian Thought). A weekly newspaper for Ukrainians in Great Britain, published in London since 1945. It has been the organ of the *Association of Ukrainians in Great Britain since 1947. The paper publishes news of the association and articles on Ukrainian political and community affairs in Great Britain and elsewhere; it supports the positions of the OUN (Bandera faction). It also devotes considerable attention to cultural issues and publishes literary works. At various times the paper has included pages devoted to the Ukrainian Youth Association, the Association of Ukrainian Women in Britain, and the Plast Ukrainian Youth Association. The paper has been edited by a board; since 1978 the board has been headed by S. Fostun. Circulation reached a high of over 4,000 in the late 1940s; since then it has dropped steadily.

**Ukraïns'ka hromada** (Ukrainian Community). A semimonthly organ of the *Oborona Ukrainy organization, published in New York in 1923–7 and in Detroit in 1930–1. The paper was edited by Ya. Chyzh and M. Tsehlynsky.

**Ukraïns'ka hromada** (Ukrainian Community). An illustrated weekly organ of the *Ukrainian National Democratic Alliance, published in Lutske from November 1926 to May 1929. Edited by M. Cherkavsky, S. Vyshnivsky, H. Hladky, and V. Ostrovsky, it published reports on political developments in Poland and abroad and was intended for the Ukrainian population of Volhynia. Like its forerunner *Hromada*, it was closed by the Polish authorities.

**Ukraïns'ka hromads'ka pora** (Ukrainian Community Time). A socialist weekly newspaper published in Detroit

from 1930 to 1952, initially as *Pora* (1930–6) and *Nova pora* (1937–40). Founded by T. Pochynok and edited by him and N. Hryhoriiv, it espoused the positions of the Ukrainian Party of Socialist Revolutionaries and the Ukrainian Socialist Radical party in Western Ukraine.

**Ukraïns'ka khata** (Ukrainian House [*UKh*]). A monthly journal of literature, criticism, and politics that appeared in Kiev from March 1909 to August 1914 (66 issues) under the editorship of P. *Bohatsky and Mykyta *Shapoval. A major forum of the younger democratic, nationally conscious Ukrainian intelligentsia after the Revolution of 1905, it published articles whose authors, particularly Shapoval (pseud: M. Sribliansky) and A. Tovkachevsky, formulated the foundations for a new Ukrainian national liberation ideology and national and social worldview. They promoted Nietzschean principles for the individual and the ideal of an independent, full-fledged Ukrainian culture free of external (ie, Russian and Polish) influences and inhumane materialism. They also attacked the moderate liberal Ukrainophile populists and their superficial ideas, political compromises, and slavish reliance on Russian 'higher culture' and social forces. In the esthetic realm they propagated the new trends of modernism and impressionism. The journal's literary critics, particularly Shapoval and M. *Yevshan, evaluated works on the basis of their esthetic value or their expression of the national ideal. A bitter rivalry and polemic arose between *UKh* and the more moderate paper *Rada*. S. Yefremov, for example, referred to the views expressed in *UKh* as those of refined, decadent burghers who had no principles.

*UKh* succeeded in attracting as contributors many prominent writers of the time. Translations of European contemporary works (by C. Baudelaire, K. Hamsun, P. Altenberg, J. Jakobsen, M. Maeterlinck, H. Mann, and others), notes on Ucrainica in the foreign press, and a literary chronicle were regular features. *UKh* was closed down by the tsarist authorities after Russia entered the First World War. A booklet of Bohatsky's and Shapoval's memoirs about *UKh* was edited by S. Zerkal and published in New York in 1955.

P. Bohatsky

**Ukraïns'ka knyha** (Ukrainian Book). A monthly journal of bibliography and bibliology published in Lviv in 1937–9 (21 issues) and in Cracow in 1943 (2 issues) by the Bibliographic Commission of the Shevchenko Scientific Society and the Ukrainian Society of Bibliophiles in Lviv. Edited by Ye. Pelensky, the journal contained articles on the history of Ukrainian books and libraries (by M. Andrusiak, V. Doroshenko, A. Gensorsky, M. Vozniak, I. Krypiakevych, P. Zlenko, T. Pachovsky, S. Siropolko, V. Sichynsky, A. Zhyvotko), on library science (L. Bykovsky), and on printing (V. Doroshenko and S. Yefremov). It also published lists of new Galician publications, and specialized military, literary, and regional studies bibliographies (P. Zlenko, B. Romanenchuk, M. Vozniak, and Ye. Pelensky). An entire issue was devoted to the history of Ukrainian publishing in Cracow.

**Ukraïns'ka knyha** (Ukrainian Book). A quarterly journal of bibliography and bibliology published in Philadelphia in 1971–82 by the Society of Ukrainian Bibliophiles, the Ukrainian Librarians' Association of America, and the

*Ukraïns'ka knyha*

Bibliographic Commission of the Shevchenko Scientific Society. Edited by B. Romanenchuk, V. Lev, and M. Kravchuk, it contained articles on the history of Ukrainian publishing, bibliographies, reviews of émigré and Soviet publications, biographies, and organizational news.

***Ukraïns'ka korespondentsiia*** (Ukrainian Correspondence). A newspaper published by H. Denysenko three times a week in Prague in 1930–1 to inform the Czech and Western European public about the brutal Polish *Pacification of Western Ukraine and suppression of Ukrainian activities there. It appeared in both Czech and Ukrainian. Although founded on the initiative of the Prague-based Ukrainian Party of Socialist Revolutionaries, it was an independent publication with a broad base of supporters. The editor was Ya. Zozulia.

***Ukraïns'ka lastivka*** (Ukrainian Swallow). An illustrated monthly children's magazine, published in Chernivtsi in 1933–9 by the Ridna Shkola society. It was edited by V. Yakubovych, O. Drachynsky, T. Bryndzan, M. Haras, and K. Horvatsky.

***Ukraïns'ka literatura.*** See *Vitchyzna*.

***Ukraïns'ka literaturna hazeta.*** A monthly paper of literature and art, which appeared from July 1955 until 1960 and was published by the Suchasna Ukraina publishing house in Munich. It was edited by I. *Koshelivets and Yu. *Lavrinenko. It was the unofficial organ of the *Slovo Association of Ukrainian Writers in Exile and aimed to reflect the literary and artistic processes in the emigration and in Soviet Ukraine. Since it was not a vehicle for any one ideology, it became a forum for the leading figures of the interwar (A. Zhuk, V. Doroshenko, Ye. Malaniuk, D. Chyzhevsky) and of the postwar emigration (Yu. Shevelov, V. Barka, H. Kostiuk, O. Izarsky, Y. Hirniak, and many others). The first works of writers of the younger generation, particularly of the *New York Group, also appeared in the journal. In 1961 the newspaper *Suchasna Ukraïna* and *Ukraïns'ka literaturna hazeta* merged to form the monthly *Suchasnist'*.

***Ukraïns'ka mala entsyklopediia.*** See Encyclopedias of Ukraine.

***Ukraïns'ka mova i literatura v shkoli*** (Ukrainian Language and Literature in Schools). A monthly pedagogical journal and organ of the Ministry of Education in Kiev. It was established in 1963 with the merger of two journals, *Ukraïnska mova v shkoli* (1951–62) and *Literatura v shkoli* (1951–62). The journal is aimed at secondary-school teachers of Ukrainian language and literature in *secondary general-education schools and *secondary special-education schools, and at lecturers in institutions of *higher education.

***Ukraïns'ka muzychna hazeta.*** See *Muzyka*.

***Ukraïns'ka muzyka.*** A monthly periodical published by the Union of Ukrainian Professional Musicians. It appeared from March 1937 in Stryi, and from March to June 1939 in Lviv. The editor in chief was Z. Lysko, and the members of the editorial board included V. Barvinsky, R. Savytsky, F. Steshko, and W. Wytwycky. Among the contributors were S. Liudkevych, A. Rudnytsky, M. Haivoronsky, and E. Tsehelsky. The periodical discussed music history, music criticism, the work of individual composers, and current musical affairs.

The logo of Ukrainska Nakladnia

**Ukrainska Nakladnia** (Ukrainian Publishing House). A publishing house owned by Ya. *Orenshtain. From 1903 to 1918 it operated in Kolomyia as Halytska Nakladnia (Galician Publishing House). From 1919 to 1932 it was located in Berlin. It issued hundreds of popular books: works on Ukrainian history and culture, illustrated editions of Ukrainian classics and contemporary Ukrainian literature, translations (eg, of Molière, R. Kipling, F. Nietzsche, A. France, L. Tolstoy), textbooks, atlases, musical scores, songbooks, and children's literature. Its Zahalna biblioteka (General Library) book series had 238 titles, of which 113 were published in Kolomyia and 125 in Berlin.

**Ukrainska Narodna Obnova.** See Ukrainian Catholic People's party.

***Ukraïns'ka nyva*** (Ukrainian Field). A newspaper published weekly and then semimonthly in Warsaw (1926–8) and semimonthly in Lutske (1929–36). Intended primarily for the Ukrainians of Volhynia and for émigrés from Soviet-occupied Ukraine, it promoted Polish-Ukrainian co-operation and supported the Government-in-exile of the UNR. The editors were P. Pevny, L. Musiievych, and V. Artsebka. In 1930 the paper had a pressrun of 2,000 copies.

It ceased publication in May 1936, but in June a weekly paper with the same name was established in Lutske. An organ of the *Volhynian Ukrainian Alliance, edited by A. Kokhanivsky, after 26 issues it was renamed *Volyns'ke slovo* (1937–9).

***Ukraïns'ka nyva*** (Ukrainian Field). An illustrated evangelical journal published quarterly (1947–58), monthly, and then annually (to 1966) in Saskatoon. It was the organ of the Ukrainian Missionary and Biblical Society in Canada and published articles on religious and theological topics. The editor was Ya. Homeniuk.

**Ukrainska politychna biblioteka** (Ukrainian Political Library). A series of political books and pamphlets edited by Mykola Zalizniak and printed between 1914 and 1917 in Vienna and Stockholm. Most were works by Ukrainian socialist writers, such as M. Drahomanov, S. Tomashivsky, and M. Lozynsky. They were distributed among Ukrainians in the Russian army interned in Austrian POW camps, and smuggled into Russian-ruled Ukraine.

***Ukraïns'ka pravoslavna nyva*** (Ukrainian Orthodox Field). The monthly organ of the General Church Administration of the Ukrainian Autocephalous Orthodox church in Brazil. Called *Lystok* in 1953–4 and then *Pravoslavna nyva* in 1954–5, it was published in Curitiba until 1974. The editors were Rev F. Kulchytsky (to 1963) and S. Plakhtyn.

The logo of Ukrainska Presa

**Ukrainska Presa** (Ukrainian Press). A major publishing house in interwar Lviv, owned and operated by I. *Tyktor from 1923 to the outbreak of the Second World War. It employed over 100 writers, editors, administrators, and printers, including some of the most prominent writers, journalists, and artists in Galicia. The press's publications did much to raise the educational level and national consciousness of Galicia's Ukrainian population. Foremost among them were the daily newspaper *Novyi chas*, the weekly *Narodnia sprava* for the rural population, the children's monthly *Dzvinochok*, the semimonthly *Nash prapor*, the satirical weekly *Komar*, and the semiweekly *Nash lemko*. Their combined pressrun was 92,600 in 1937 and 106,500 in 1938. Ukrainska Presa also published several annual almanacs, including *Zolotyi kolos* for the rural population from 1929 (approx 85,000 copies), *Kalendar dlia vsikh* from 1931 (renamed *Al'manakh Novoho chasu* in 1937), and the humorous *Komar* from 1935; and series of short books and pamphlets, which were sent free of charge to its

periodicals' regular subscribers: *Ukrainska biblioteka (Ukrainian Library), Novyi chas (New Times; 30 titles to 1933), Narodna sprava (National Cause; 18 titles to 1936), Ridne slovo (Native Word), Ranok (Morning), Amatorskyi teatr (Amateur Theater), Muzychna biblioteka (Musical Library), Biblioteka tserkovno-relihiinykh knyh (Library of Church and Religious Books), and Istorychna biblioteka (Historical Library), which included *Velyka istoriia Ukraïny* (The Great History of Ukraine), *Istoriia ukraïns'koï kul'tury* (The History of Ukrainian Culture), and *Istoriia ukraïns'koho viis'ka* (The History of the Ukrainian Army). Altogether, it published 400 titles.

The Ukrainska Radianska Entsyklopediia building

**Ukrainska Radianska Entsyklopediia** (Ukrainian Soviet Encyclopedia). An editing and publishing institution in Kiev established in 1957 by the AN URSR (now ANU) to prepare and publish general and specialized *encyclopedias and encyclopedic dictionaries in Ukrainian and Russian. It co-operated with other ANU bodies in the preparation of reference works, such as the multiauthor histories of Ukrainian art (6 vols, 1966–8), of Ukrainian cities and towns (26 vols, 1967–74), and of the AN URSR (2 vols, 1967). Its recent projects include the second edition of the Ukrainian Soviet encyclopedic dictionary (3 vols, 1986–7), a four-volume encyclopedia of Ukrainian literature (vol 1, 1988; vol 2, 1990), a three-volume geographic encyclopedia of Ukraine (vol 1, 1989; vol 2, 1990), and an as yet unpublished four-volume encyclopedia of Ukrainian art. In 1992 it was renamed Ukrainska Entsyklopediia (Ukrainian Encyclopedia).

***Ukraïns'ka reformatsiia*** (Ukrainian Reformation). An evangelical journal of religious and educational affairs published in Lviv in 1929–30 and Kolomyia in 1931. It began as a monthly and later appeared semimonthly. The journal worked to reconcile the two branches of the Evangelical movement in Western Ukraine, the *Ukrainian Evangelical Reformed church and the *Ukrainian Evangelical Church of the Augsburg Confession. *Ukraïns'ka reformatsiia* was edited by P. Yaremko, T. Yarchuk, Z.

Bychynsky, and V. Fediv; in 1930 it was published in a pressrun of 2,000 copies.

*Ukraïns'ka rodyna* (Ukrainian Family). A popular journal of literature and history, published monthly from October 1947 to August 1949 in Toronto (a total of 20 issues). It contained stories, fables, poems, biographies, and popular articles on Ukrainian history, primarily for children. The publisher and editor was O. Luhovy.

**Ukrainska Shkola.** A Ukrainian pedagogical association in Bukovyna, originally called Ruska Shkola (to 1910). Founded in 1887 as an offshoot of the *Ruska Besida society, the group developed as a regional counterpart to the Galician *Ridna Shkola society. It pursued the formation of state-supported Ukrainian schools, established private schools and courses, made efforts to upgrade the qualifications of Ukrainian teachers, and provided financial assistance for needy students. It sponsored a private teachers' seminary for girls in Chernivtsi, a (Realschule) gymnasium in Vashkivtsi, and a people's university in Chernivtsi. By 1914 it had 12 branches, with a total of 965 members. It published various journals (including *Nasha shkola* in conjunction with the Lviv-based Teachers' Hromada), school texts (30 titles by 1914), and two series of popular books for children, Kreitsarova biblioteka (The Kreutzer Library; 1902–8) and Dytiacha biblioteka (Children's Library; 1909–14). After the Rumanian occupation of Bukovyna, Ukrainska Shkola's undertakings suffered considerably as branches were closed down by the authorities, the central office was harassed, and Ukrainian schools were closed. After 1918 the group managed to print only three school texts. One successful aspect of its work was the summer courses in Ukrainian studies which it sponsored during the 1930s. Ukrainska Shkola was liquidated after the Soviet occupation of Bukovyna in 1940. The association's leaders included S. Smal-Stotsky (1887–91), O. Popovych (1891–1914), and A. Kyryliv (1919–40); among the prominent members were Ye. Pihuliak, I. Danylevych, I. Karbulytsky, I. Syniuk, M. Haras, and V. Yakubovych.

*Ukraïns'ka shkola* (Ukrainian School). A scholarly-pedagogical journal published with varying periodicity in Lviv in 1925–34 and 1938–9 by the *Teachers' Hromada. It contained professional news for Ukrainian teachers in Western Ukraine, book reviews, curricula, and articles on teaching methodology and the history of Ukrainian education. It was intended primarily for secondary-school teachers, and published a separate series of booklets and pamphlets. The editors of *Ukraïns'ka shkola* included H. Myketei, Yu. Rudnytsky, O. Makarushka, and Ya. Bilenky. In 1930 it appeared in a pressrun of 500 copies. During the Second World War the journal was briefly revived in Cracow (1942–3) under the editorship of I. Teslia and P. Isaiv.

*Ukraïns'ka stavka* (Ukrainian Card). A daily publication of the UNR Army Information Bureau during 1918–20. It was edited first by N. *Hryhoriiv, then by D. Budka.

*Ukraïns'ka trybuna* (Ukrainian Tribune). A newspaper published by Ye. Lukasevych six days a week in Warsaw from May 1921 to March 1922. It was edited by O. Salikovsky and supported the Government-in-exile of the UNR.

*Ukraïns'ka trybuna* (Ukrainian Tribune). One of the most widely read newspapers for Ukrainian displaced persons in postwar Germany. It was published in Munich, weekly in 1946–8 and then semiweekly to August 1949 (a total of 219 issues) by V. Pasichnyk under license from the US military authorities. *Ukraïns'ka trybuna* reported on developments in Soviet Ukraine, international politics, and Ukrainian émigré affairs and published a chronicle of life in the DP camps and documents from the nationalist resistance in Ukraine. At various times it included special sections devoted to literature and art, the émigré student movement, and the Ukrainian Youth Association. The first editors were Z. Tarnavsky and Z. Pelensky; they were assisted by M. Hlobenko, O. Lysiak, O. Pytliar, V. Stakhiv, D. Chaikovsky, B. Nyzhankivsky, and others. With time the paper came under the domination of the OUN (Bandera faction), and its quality declined as it became more partisan. In 1947–8 Ukrainska Trybuna publishers sublicensed the cultural magazine *Arka.

*Ukraïns'ka zahal'na entsyklopediia.* See Encyclopedias of Ukraine.

**Ukrainska Zakhoronka.** A society founded in 1901 in Lviv on the initiative of the *Club of Ruthenian Women, to hinder the trend of denationalization of Ukrainian children of preschool age in Polish-ruled Ukraine. In 1914 the society supported two nurseries operated according to Froebel techniques (see *Preschool education). By 1922 the society was responsible for 22 nurseries in Lviv and its surrounding area. The *Ridna Shkola society was responsible for the educational component of these nurseries. Leading members of the Ukrainska Zakhoronka included B. Kotsovska, S. Rakova, and M. Pasternak. In 1938–9 the society published the journal *Ukraïns'ke doshkillia*, devoted to preschool education. In 1939 the society was disbanded by the Soviet authorities, and the nurseries were incorporated into the Soviet preschool educational system.

*Ukraïns'ka zemlia.* See *Ukraïns'kyi selianyn*.

*Ukrainskaia literaturnaia letopis'* (Ukrainian Literary Chronicle). The first Ukrainian bibliological journal, published by O. *Lazarevsky in Chernihiv in 1856–8 (a total of five issues). It consisted of offprints from *Chernigovskie gubernskie vedomosti* of Lazarevsky's reviews of books and articles dealing with Ukrainian history, geography, ethnology, culture, language, literature, and religion.

*Ukrainskaia zhizn'* (Ukrainian Life). A Russian-language monthly journal published in Moscow in 1912–17 to inform the non-Ukrainian public in the Russian Empire about the Ukrainian question and the Ukrainian national movement, and to raise the level of Ukrainian national consciousness among Russified Ukrainians. It contained articles on the national question in Russia; chronicles of current events in Ukraine; reviews of articles in Russian, Polish, and other newspapers on Ukrainian topics; reports from Russian-ruled and Western Ukraine; polemics with the militant Russian nationalist and chauvinist press; critical articles on political, historical, cultural, and literary subjects; and book reviews. Although the formal editor and publisher was Ya. Sheremetsinsky, the real editors were S. Petliura and O. Salikovsky. Contributors included prominent Ukrainian and Russian figures.

**Ukrainske** [Ukrajins'ke]. V-18, DB III-2. A city (1989 pop 16,500) under the jurisdiction of the Selydove city council in Donetske oblast. It was founded as a mining town in 1952 and was first named Lisivka. In 1963 it was renamed and given city status. Ukrainske has two coal mines and a coal enrichment plant.

*Ukraïns'ke iunatstvo* (Ukrainian Youth). A Catholic monthly journal published by the *Orly Catholic Association of Ukrainian Youth in Lviv in 1933–9. It was edited by R. Danylevych and V. Hlibovytsky. A supplement, *Hotovs'*, published materials on work in the association's groups.

*Ukraïns'ke kozatstvo* (Ukrainian Cossackdom). An illustrated journal of the *Ukrainian Free Cossack, published irregularly (1964–70) and then quarterly (1971–80) in Chicago (a total of 63 issues). The chief editor was A. Kushchynsky. Seven more issues were published in Toronto in 1982–5 and edited by M. Huta. The journal contains articles and literary works on the history of the Zaporozhian Host, the Free Cossacks, and the UNR Army; a chronicle of the brotherhood and its branches; biographies; memoirs; military information; poetry; and song lyrics.

*Ukraïns'ke literaturoznavstvo* (Ukrainian Literary Scholarship, or UL). A scholarly serial published at Lviv University since 1966. It has been edited by a large board of literary scholars under the direction of F. Neboriachok (nos 1–17, 1966–72), I. Doroshenko (nos 18–48, 1972–87), and, since 1987, L. Mishchenko (nos 49–). Two issues have appeared annually except in 1967 (no issues), 1968 (three), 1969 (one), 1970 (five), 1971 (three), 1972 (three), and 1973 (three). UL is a major forum for scholars of Ukrainian literature. Theoretical and historical articles on prerevolutionary and Soviet Ukrainian writers and literary scholars (particular aspects of their lives and contributions in the context of Ukrainian and world literature, analyses of individual works) and on certain literary periodicals (eg, *S'vit, Narod*) and writers' groups (eg, Zakhidnia Ukraina), as well as bibliographies (eg, of M. Vozniak) and archival materials (writers' correspondence), have been published therein. Western Ukrainian literature, particularly I. *Franko, to whom every other issue has been devoted, has received the most attention.

*Ukraïns'ke muzykoznavstvo* (Ukrainian Musicology). An annual journal of the Academy of Sciences and the Ministry of Culture of Ukraine that has been published in Kiev since 1966. The journal, whose editorial board includes M. Hordiichuk, K. Maiburova, S. Pavlyshyn, M. Skoryk, and O. Shreier-Tkachenko, deals with the history and theory of music, music performance, folklore, esthetics, and music criticism. Some issues – most notably no. 6, which discusses Ukrainian musical culture in the 16th to 18th centuries – focus on a single theme.

*Ukraïns'ke mystetstvoznavstvo* (Ukrainian Art Studies). An annual publication of the AN URSR (now ANU) Institute of Fine Arts, Folklore, and Ethnography, published in Kiev in 1967–71 and 1974 (a total of six issues). It contained articles on the history of Ukrainian art, architecture, and folk art, and art criticism. It also published regular chronicles of art exhibitions and developments in the arts in Ukraine and comprehensive bibliographies in art studies. Among its contributors were some of the most distinguished art scholars in Ukraine, including H. Lohvyn, B. Butnyk-Siversky, V. Shcherbak, D. Stepovyk, and Yu. *Turchenko (editor in chief).

**Ukrainske Narodnie Mystetstvo** (Ukrainian Folk Art). A folk-art and handicrafts co-operative established in 1922 in Lviv. It operated workshops for Ukrainian handicrafts and organized courses to teach folk art. In 1936 its 13 workshops employed almost 500 workers. It also administered a system for the distribution and sale of folk art, especially embroidered and woolen goods and wood carvings. Ukrainske Narodne Mystetstvo worked with various local co-operatives in Lviv, Kosiv, Vilshany, and elsewhere and operated stores in Lviv and Warsaw. The co-operative also organized exhibitions of Ukrainian folk art in Stryi, Prague, and Chicago and sold goods at international trade shows. From 1925 it published the journal *Nova khata. Its board of directors was headed by S. Montsibovych and then I. Bonkovska. Its leading organizers included S. Pushkar, I. Pavlykovska, and S. Savytska. After the Soviet occupation of Galicia the co-operative and its workshops were transformed into artels.

*Ukraïns'ke narodne slovo* (Ukrainian National Word). A newspaper published by the *Ukrainian National Aid Association of America (UNAA). Founded in March 1914 as *Narodne slovo*, it was published weekly in McKees Rocks and, from 1921, Pittsburgh, Pennsylvania. It was renamed in 1959, and in 1969 it became a semimonthly (22–26 issues per year). Since 1981 it has been published in Chicago, where it now appears quarterly. In the interwar period the paper was closely aligned with the Ukrainian Orthodox church in the United States. It sought to raise the level of national consciousness of its readers and to instill the values of American patriotism. Since the 1950s it and the UNAA have been controlled by supporters of the OUN (Bandera faction). The chief editors have been H. Kysil (1914), Y. Kosovy (1914–17), D. Ivankiv (1917), M. Khavriuk (1917–20), M. Khandoha (1920–48), V. Kedrovsky (1948–50), R. Kryshtalsky (1950–2), M. Sydor-Chartoryisky (1952), P. Kravchuk (1952–9), V. Mazur (1959–61, 1963–5, 1974–), I. Vovchuk (1961–3), P. Marenets (1965–74), and L. Poltava. Recently the newspaper's circulation has been approx 5,000.

*Ukraïns'ke pravoslavne slovo* (Ukrainian Orthodox Word). A monthly organ of the Ukrainian Orthodox Church in the USA. It has been published since 1950, at first in New York and then, since 1951, in South Bound Brook, New Jersey. It succeeded *Dnipro as the official publication of the church. The editors of *Ukraïns'ke pravoslavne slovo* have included Yu. Bobrovsky, I. Hundiak, F. Istochyn, A. Kotovych, I. Kreta, H. Pavlovsky, Metropolitan M. *Skrypnyk, and P. Falko. *Ukraïns'ke pravoslavne slovo* had an English-language section from 1951; in 1967 it became a separate journal, *Ukrainian Orthodox Word. The journal includes pastoral letters; church news; and articles on religious, political, historical, and cultural topics. It is a valuable source of information on the history of the Ukrainian Orthodox church.

A Ukrainske Slovo publication (Viktor Andriievsky's memoirs)

The editorial board of *Ukraïns'ke slovo* in Berlin (1922). From left: Volodymyr Leontovych, Dmytro Doroshenko, O. Kryha, Ivan Herasymovych, Bohdan Lepky, Zenon Kuzelia, Stepan Tomashivsky

**Ukrainske Slovo** (Ukrainian Word). An émigré publishing house founded in Berlin in 1921. The director and chief editor was Z. Kuzelia. It published the weekly newspapers *Ukraïns'ke slovo* (1921–4) and *Litopys polityky pys'menstva i mystetstva* (1923–4) and over 70 books, including D. Doroshenko's book on the Slavic world in the past and present (3 vols); reprints of B. Hrinchenko's Ukrainian dictionary and M. Komarov's Russian-Ukrainian dictionary; an anthology of Ukrainian poetry edited by B. Lepky (2 vols); editions of works by P. Kulish, Ya. Shchoholiv, B. Lepky, V. Birchak, M. Kropyvnytsky, and H. Skovoroda; V. Yemets's book on the kobza and kobzars; S. Rudnytsky's monographs on Ukraine's national territory and the Ukrainian question from the perspective of political geography; V. Andriievsky's memoirs; books on the art of A. Archipenko and O. Novakivsky; M. Arkas's history of Ukraine; I. Herasymovych's *Hunger in der Ukraine*; a compendium on the Ukrainian Sich Riflemen; M. Drahomanov's selected works; O. Barvinsky's readers on world history and Ukrainian literature; a collection of M. Rudnytsky's literary essays; and M. Lozynsky's books on Polish and Russian revolutionary groups and Ukraine, M. Drahomanov, I. Franko, and M. Pavlyk. Ukrainske Slovo went bankrupt in 1926.

*Ukraïns'ke slovo* (Ukrainian Word). A daily newspaper published in Lviv from July 1915 to November 1918. Initially, under the editorship of F. Fedortsiv and S. Charnetsky, it supported the positions of the *General Ukrainian Council. I. Krypiakevych, M. Yatskiv, and H. Mykytei were regular contributors. In 1916 the newspaper's charter was acquired by Rev T. Voinarovsky-Stolobut, who had earlier published *Nove slovo*. Although Charnetsky continued to edit the paper, it changed its political orientation and began to support Ye. *Petrushevych in his opposition to the General Ukrainian Council. After Charnetsky S. Holubovych edited the paper. *Ukraïns'ke slovo* was closed down by the Polish authorities.

*Ukraïns'ke slovo* (Ukrainian Word). A hetmanite newspaper published in Berlin by the *Ukrainske Slovo publishing house. It appeared weekly in 1921–3 and six times a week in 1923–4 under the editorship of D. Doroshenko and Z. Kuzelia.

*Ukraïns'ke slovo* (Ukrainian Word). A weekly newspaper published in Lviv in 1922–5, in 1922–3 as *Slovo*. Edited by P. Seniuta and then I. Kuzmych, it was aimed at urban-

ized Ukrainians in Galicia, and supported Ye. Petrushevych's government-in-exile.

*Ukraïns'ke slovo* (Ukrainian Word). The first Ukrainian newspaper in Argentina, published in Buenos Aires since January 1928 weekly and now semimonthly. The organ of the Prosvita Ukrainian Cultural Association in Argentina, in the postwar period it has supported the émigré OUN (Bandera faction) and has included pages devoted to the Prosvita Women's Alliance, the Ukrainian Youth Association (SUM), the Ukrainian Student Organization of Mikhnovsky, and literature and art. The editors have been O. Vudkevych, S. Mandzii, M. Korytko, I. Kryvy, N. Blavatny, A. Bilopolsky, O. Shkeda, I. Mitrenga, I. Rybak, M. Kovalenko, N. Velychkovsky, O. Kuzmych, Yu. Serediak, I. Didenko, B. Vitoshynsky, I. Klymenko, H. Holiian, and M. Danylyshyn.

*Ukraïns'ke slovo* (Ukrainian Word). A newspaper published weekly in 1932–7 and semiweekly in 1938 in Uzhhorod. It supported the Ukrainian national revival in Transcarpathia and was one of the first papers there to appear from the outset in Standard Ukrainian. The newspaper was founded by Yu. Brashchaiko and edited by his brother, M. Brashchaiko. Frequent contributors included V. Grendzha-Donsky, V. Birchak, Rev K. Fedelesh, and I. Roman.

*Ukraïns'ke slovo* (*La Parole ukrainienne*, Ukrainian Word). A weekly newspaper published in Paris in 1933–40 and since 1948. It is closely allied with the OUN (Melnyk faction) and serves as an unofficial organ of the Leadership of Ukrainian Nationalists. The paper has been edited by O. Boikiv (1933–4), V. Martynets (1934–40), O. Shtul-Zhdanovych (1948–77), and M. Styranka (1977–92). Contributors have included some of the most prominent figures in the OUN, such as M. Stsiborsky, M. Kapustiansky, O. Olzhych, D. Andriievsky, Ye. Onatsky, and B. Kentrzhynsky. *Ukraïns'ke slovo* has been an excellent source of information on the Ukrainian nationalist movement before and after the Second World War. It has reported ex-

Kiev and Paris editions of *Ukraïns'ke slovo* in 1992

tensively on developments in the Ukrainian diaspora and in Ukraine. For some time the paper had special pages devoted to students, youth, military affairs, and culture. Until 1939 it was published by the *Ukrainian National Union in France. Since that time the publisher has been the First Ukrainian Press in France, which also issues the paper's annual almanacs and books. Since February 1992 the paper has had a Kiev edition.

***Ukraïns'ke slovo*** (Ukrainian Word). A daily newspaper published in Zhytomyr and then Kiev in September–December 1941 (a total of 100 issues). Edited by I. Rohach, P. Oliinyk, and O. Chemerynsky, all members of *OUN expeditionary groups (Melnyk faction), the newspaper advocated Ukrainian nationalism and independence and became one of the most influential and popular papers of its time; its pressrun was 20,000 to 50,000 copies. It also published a separate literary and artistic supplement. Because of the newspaper's outspoken views on Ukrainian independence, the German occupational authorities closed it down, arrested most of the editors, and executed them. In its place the pro-German *Nove ukraïns'ke slovo* was established.

***Ukraïns'ke slovo*** (Ukrainian Word). A weekly newspaper published in Stanyslaviv (now Ivano-Frankivske) in 1941–2. Edited by D. Gregolynsky, it was closed down by the German occupational authorities after 42 issues. It was succeeded in June 1942 by *Stanyslavivs'ke slovo* (1942–4), a newspaper published three times a week and edited by Gregolynsky and A. Kniazhynsky.

***Ukraïns'ke slovo*** (Ukrainian Word). A pro-Soviet weekly newspaper and the organ of the Association of United Ukrainian Canadians, published in Winnipeg from January 1943. Edited by M. Shatulsky and then M. Hrynchyshyn, the paper was intended mainly for Ukrainian farmers in western Canada, and published articles on the labor and farm movements, political and economic affairs, and cultural topics. It reached the height of its popularity during and after the Second World War, when it helped raise funds and supplies for the Soviet war and rebuilding efforts. At that time it had up to 15,000 subscribers. It constantly praised the Soviet Union and published regular attacks on Ukrainian 'bourgeois nationalists' in Canada. After the war it strongly criticized the Canadian government for allowing anti-Soviet Ukrainian displaced persons to immigrate to Canada. In 1965 the paper merged with *Ukraïns'ke zhyttia* to form *\*Zhyttia i slovo*.

**Ukrainske Vydavnytstvo** (Ukrainian Publishing House). A publishing house founded in March 1916 in Katerynoslav (now Dnipropetrovske). Directed by Ye. Vyrovy, by the end of 1916 it had published over a dozen children's and popular educational books. In 1919 it became a co-operative venture and printed its books in Kamianets-Podilskyi, Vienna, Leipzig, Berlin, and finally Prague. It was nationalized in 1921. By 1925 it had issued 68 titles with a combined pressrun of 591,200 copies. They included brief histories of Ukrainian culture (by I. Ohiienko) and literature (S. Yefremov), histories of Ukraine (D. Doroshenko) and ancient Rome and Greece (M. Kovalevsky), M. Levytsky's Ukrainian grammar, S. Ivanytsky and F. Shumliansky's Russian-Ukrainian dictionary, the *Iaryna* primer and reader by A. Voronets, pedagogical booklets and stories by S. Rusova, over 15 collections of children's stories and folktales, V. Simovych's edition of T. Shevchenko's *Kobzar*, and 10 stories and novelettes by A. Kashchenko.

Staff members of Ukrainske Vydavnytstvo. Sitting, from left: Lesia Khomiak, R. Hanas, R. Berezovsky, Lev Chubaty; standing: P. Dragan, Ivan K., V. Hryhorchak, Danylo Chaikovsky, Kateryna Huminilovych, V. Otchak, Mykola Denysiuk, V. Bilynsky

**Ukrainske Vydavnytstvo** (Ukrainian Publishing House [UV]). The only Ukrainian publishing house permitted by the German occupational authorities in the *Generalgouvernement of Poland during the Second World War, founded in Cracow in December 1939 as a limited company. V. *Kubijovyč was the major shareholder and chairman of the board of directors. UV had close ties with the *Ukrainian Central Committee (UCC), which Kubijovyč headed. The executive directors of UV were Ye. Pelensky (to May 1940), I. Kotsur (June 1940 to June 1941), I. Zilynsky (June 1941 to August 1944), and finally Omelian Tarnavsky. The assistant director was I. Fediv.

The first priority of UV was to supply books to the half-million Ukrainians of the Kholm, Podlachia, Lemko, and Sian regions, areas that had been denied Ukrainian-language publications by the Polish regime and in which the level of national consciousness was consequently low. UV concentrated on preparing and publishing textbooks and other educational materials for children and adolescents

(37 percent of its total output in 1940) and reading materials for peasants, which were distributed through the UCC-supervised *Ukrainian educational societies. It also published works by B. Lepky, V. Birchak, Lesia Ukrainka, B. Antonych, M. Cheremshyna, I. Vynnytska, R. Yendyk, and V. Karkhut, and issued 16 books about the aforementioned borderlands by M. Korduba, S. Liubarsky, V. Ostrovsky, V. Sichynsky, Yu. Tarnovych, and F. Kokovsky. Its largest editions were a history of Ukraine and T. Shevchenko's *Kobzar*. By mid-1941 UV had published 195 titles. It also printed the newspaper *Krakivs'ki visti* and the renewed children's monthly *Mali druzi* from January 1940, the literary-artistic monthly *Iliustrovani visti* from April 1940, and the renewed young people's monthly *Doroha* from October 1940.

After Lviv was taken by the Germans in July 1941, an independent UV publishing house was established there. By the end of 1941 it had published 37 books (textbooks, an orthographic dictionary, literary works, and books on historical and other topics) with a combined pressrun of over 857,000 copies. At the same time, however, the official German publishing house in the Generalgouvernement established a branch in Lviv and began publishing the daily *L'vivs'ki visti*. It tried, through official channels, to limit the distribution of the Cracow UV publications in Galicia and even have the house closed down. As a result of interventions by Ukrainian community leaders (K. Levytsky, K. Pankivsky, and Kubijovyč), however, the Cracow UV was permitted to sell and distribute in Galicia, to open a branch in Lviv with two printing shops, and to publish a literary-cultural monthly, *Nashi dni*. Thenceforth UV maintained its head office in Cracow (directed by I. Fediv), but the Lviv branch (directed by M. Matchak) printed most of the UV publications (except newspapers). Its publishing department was headed by M. Shlemkevych and included V. Simovych, Z. Khraplyvy, B. Hoshovsky, S. Hordynsky, Yu. Stefanyk, I. Krypiakevych, D. Shtykalo, and D. Kozii.

In 1942–3 UV issued 212 titles, 71 of them in Cracow and 141 in Lviv. A large part consisted of reprints of works by writers who had been repressed in Soviet Ukraine (eg, O. Vlyzko, B. Antonenko-Davydovych, O. Vyshnia, V. Pidmohylny, M. Kulish, M. Zerov, O. Slisarenko, I. Bahriany, T. Osmachka, V. Gzhytsky, V. Chaplenko, and M. Orest). It also published editions of the collected works of L. Martovych and V. Stefanyk, a few scholarly monographs by Ya. Pasternak and V. Kubijovyč, the mass-circulation monthly *Vechirnia hodyna*, and the Knyzhka dlia vsikh (A Book for Everybody) series (books devoted to Ukrainian history and Shevchenko studies). UV continued publishing *Krakivs'ki visti* and *Nashi dni* and introduced a weekly, *Kholms'ka zemlia* (1943–4), for the Ukrainians of the Kholm region. Its periodicals were distributed not only in Ukraine, but also among Ukrainians working in Germany and Czechoslovakia.

With the Red Army advance toward Lviv, the UV branch there was forced to curtail its activities, and finally cease publishing in April 1944. The Cracow head office continued functioning until August 1944, when it moved to Vienna and there published 26 more titles and, briefly, continued *Krakivs'ki visti*.

UV was undoubtedly the most prolific and important Ukrainian publisher of its time. Despite the financial and technical difficulties, strict German censorship, and paper shortages that plagued it throughout its existence, from 1940 to 1945 it published 544 titles (434 books) with a combined pressrun of nearly 5.8 million copies, and 1,839 issues of periodicals with a combined pressrun of 24.7 million copies.

BIBLIOGRAPHY
Pan'kivs'kyi, K. *Roky nimets'koï okupatsiï, 1941–1944* (New York 1965; 2nd edn, 1983)
Kubiiovych, V. *Ukraïntsi v Heneral'nii hubernii, 1939–1941: Istoriia Ukraïns'koho tsentral'noho komitetu* (Chicago 1975)

V. Kubijovyč

**Ukrainske Vydavnytstvo** (Ukrainian Publishing House). A publishing house established in Munich in 1954 by the OUN (Bandera faction). It has published its weekly organ *Shliakh peremohy*; Biblioteka ukrainskoho pidpilnyka (Library of the Ukrainian Underground Fighter), a series of documentary collections on the history of the OUN, the Ukrainian Insurgent Army, the Ukrainian Supreme Liberation Council, and the Anti-Bolshevik Bloc of Nations; books on political, historical, and ethnographic topics by authors such as N. Polonska-Vasylenko, O. Voropai, and P. Mirchuk; and literary works by O. Mak, V. Vovk, L. Khraplyva, P. Kizko, Yu. Tys, R. Yendyk, O. Berdnyk, and others.

*Ukraïns'ke zhyttia* (Ukrainian Life). A weekly newspaper published in Stanyslaviv in 1921 and 1922–3. Edited by I. Stavnychy, it focused on events in the Stanyslaviv region. The paper was twice banned by the Polish authorities.

*Ukraïns'ke zhyttia* (Ukrainian Life). A pro-Soviet newspaper published weekly from August 1941, then twice a week (1954–60), and then weekly again in Toronto. Sponsored initially by the Committee to Aid the Fatherland, the newspaper became the organ of the *Association of United Ukrainian Canadians. It published articles on economic and political topics, on the labor movement, and on culture. During the war it stressed the need to assist the Soviet war effort and helped to raise funds and supplies to be sent to the USSR. At that time it reached the height of its popularity, with between 12,000 and 15,000 subscribers. *Ukraïns'ke zhyttia* rarely strayed from the official Soviet line; it criticized Ukrainian 'bourgeois nationalists' and the acceptance of Ukrainian displaced persons into Canada after the war, and denied Russification and Soviet atrocities and terror at home. The paper was edited by S. Matsiievych, M. Hrynchyshyn, I. Stefanytsky, M. Korol, P. Krawchuk, and others. In 1965 the paper merged with *Ukraïns'ke slovo* to form *Zhyttia i slovo*.

*Ukraïns'ke zhyttia* (Ukrainian Life). A newspaper published weekly and then semimonthly and monthly in 1955–85 in Chicago. It was nonpartisan; it frequently criticized mainstream émigré organizations and promoted democratic ideals. It was generally less critical of Soviet Ukraine than other émigré papers and devoted considerable attention to cultural and political developments there. The paper was edited by a board headed for many years by T. Lapychak, who was also the main force behind the publication. Other editors and contributors included M. Semchyshyn, Yu. Stepovy, T. Kurpita, I. Yaremko, and A. Bilynsky, whose articles stressed the need for a rapprochement with Soviet Ukraine.

**Ukraïns'ki robitnychi visty** (Ukrainian Labor News). A pro-Communist newspaper published in Winnipeg; an organ of the *Ukrainian Labour-Farmer Temple Association. It appeared weekly from March 1919, twice a week from April 1920, and then three times a week from March 1924. In January 1935 it became the first and only Ukrainian-language daily newspaper in Canada. The paper published articles on political and economic topics and devoted considerable attention to the labor movement and trade unionism in Canada. It also published laudatory articles about developments in Soviet Ukraine and news of the international Communist movement, and made strident attacks on Ukrainian 'bourgeois nationalists.' The first editor was D. *Lobai, who was assisted by M. Shatulsky from 1920. In 1935 Lobai left the newspaper and split with the Communist movement over events in the Soviet Union. He was replaced by M. Popovich and, later, P. Krawchuk, A. Bilecki, and M. Hrynyshyn. In 1937 *Ukraïns'ki robitnychi visty* ceased publication and was succeeded by *Narodna hazeta. At the height of its popularity in 1929 the paper had a circulation of approx 10,000.

**Ukraïns'ki visti** (Ukrainian News). A pro-Soviet newspaper published weekly in New York and allied with the *League of American Ukrainians. In 1920 it succeeded *Robitnyk as the organ of the Ukrainian Federation of the Communist Party of America, and it appeared daily until 1956 as *Ukraïns'ki shchodenni visty*. It has reported on developments in the Soviet Union, the workers' movement in the United States and elsewhere, and cultural and community affairs. In the interwar period it devoted particular attention to events in Galicia. In the late 1920s the paper became Stalinist and criticized the more nationalistic elements in the Communist Party of Western Ukraine led by O. Vasylkiv. Since then it has rarely deviated from the official Soviet line, and has constantly praised the USSR and attacked Ukrainian 'bourgeois nationalists' in the West. It contains many reports of trips by Ukrainian Americans to Soviet Ukraine and literary contributions by Soviet Ukrainian writers. Editors and contributors have included M. Tkach, M. Andriichuk, M. Tarnovsky, M. Kniazevych, and D. Borysko. From 1956 until the mid-1980s the editor was L. Tolopko; he was succeeded by M. Hanusiak. Since 1977 *Ukraïns'ki visti* has published a monthly English-language edition, the *Ukrainian News*, which succeeded the *Ukrainian-American* (1965–77).

*Ukraïns'ki visti* (Neu-Ulm)

**Ukraïns'ki visti** (Ukrainian News). A newspaper published weekly (at times semimonthly) in Neu-Ulm, West Germany, from November 1945 to May 1978 and in Detroit since August 1978. It has been closely allied with the postwar émigré *Ukrainian Revolutionary Democratic party, and briefly published its ideological organ *Nashi pozytsiï*. The paper contains articles on politics, economics,

culture, and community affairs. It has devoted particular attention to developments in Soviet Ukraine. Until the 1960s it supported the Ukrainian National Council. In 1953 it published a semimonthly Russian-language supplement, *Osvobozhdenie*, edited by G. Aleksinsky. It has also published sections devoted to the Plast Ukrainian Youth Association, the Petliura Legion (veterans of the Army of the UNR), the Ukrainian Democratic Youth Association, and art and culture. In 1986 it had a circulation of approx 1,500. The initiator of the paper and a longtime chief editor (1946–7, 1954, 1957–62) was I. *Bahriany. Other chief editors have included P. Maliar (1945), Yu. Lavrinenko (1948), M. Voskobiinyk (1949), A. Romashko (1950–3), V. Bender (1955–6), V. Minialo, A. Hlynin (1963–74), F. Haienko (1975–8), and M. Smyk (since 1978).

*Ukraïns'ki visti/Ukrainian News* (Edmonton)

**Ukraïns'ki visti/Ukrainian News.** A newspaper published in Edmonton. It began to appear in 1928 as a weekly, under the name *Zakhidni visty*. Published by S. Fodchuk and then T. Tomashevsky, it was a general-interest paper concerned with economic and political affairs. Among its early editors and contributors were V. Kaye-Kysilewsky, M. Pohoretsky, and M. Koziak. In 1929 it was acquired by the Edmonton eparchy of the Ukrainian Catholic church, and in January 1932 it assumed its present name. The paper publishes articles on political, cultural, and historical topics; church news; and reports on current affairs, with a focus on developments in Alberta and western Canada. For many years after the Second World War the paper was edited by Rev M. Sopuliak. The newspaper's tone and appearance were modernized during the 1980s by its present editor (1991), M. Levytsky. It also adopted a bilingual English-Ukrainian format and became a monthly.

**Ukraïns'ki visti** (Ukrainian News). A semimonthly newspaper published in 1926–9 in Paris. The organ of the Sovietophile *Union of Ukrainian Citizens in France, it regularly criticized the Government-in-exile of the UNR, many leaders of which lived in Paris. The editor was E. Borschak.

**Ukraïns'ki visti** (Ukrainian News). An organ of the *Front of National Unity, published daily in 1935–9 in

Lviv. It was edited by I. Hladylovych with the assistance of D. Paliiv, M. Shlemkevych, S. Volynets, and V. Dzis. The newspaper reported extensively on political, economic, and Ukrainian community developments in Poland and abroad. From 1937 it published an illustrated weekly supplement and a page of news for workers. It did much to mobilize support for the national movement in Western Ukraine while criticizing both the pro-Polish policies of the Ukrainian National Democratic Alliance and the political terrorism of the OUN. Among its frequent contributors were Ya. Zaremba, O. Babii, M. Pasika, Z. Tarnavsky, O. Hubchak, and M. Levytsky.

*Ukrainskii al'manakh*

***Ukrainskii al'manakh*** (Ukrainian Almanac). The first Ukrainian literary miscellany, published in Kharkiv in 1831 by I. *Sreznevsky. It was edited by I. Roskovshenko, and contained poetry and prose in Ukrainian and Russian by writers of the *Kharkiv Romantic School, such as Roskovshenko, Sreznevsky, L. Borovykovsky, Ye. Hrebinka, O. Shpyhotsky, P. Morachevsky, and O. Afanasiev-Chuzhbynsky. It also published two dumas, nine folk songs, and translations of works by A. Pushkin and A. Mickiewicz. *Ukrainskii al'manakh* played an important role in the early development of Ukrainian literature and influenced many later writers. Although subsequent volumes were planned, a shortage of funds precluded their appearance.

***Ukrainskii biokhimicheskii zhurnal.*** See *Ukraïns'kyi biokhimichnyi zhurnal.*

***Ukrainskii domovod*** (Ukrainian Household Manager). A Russian-language journal, two issues of which appeared in Kharkiv in 1817 under the editorship of M.-H. Pilger. It provided practical advice on farming practices and especially veterinary medicine and the proper care of farm animals. The journal was closed down by the authorities for its criticism of official indifference to the plight of the peasantry.

***Ukrainskii fizicheskii zhurnal.*** See *Ukraïns'kyi fizychnyi zhurnal.*

***Ukrainskii khimicheskii zhurnal.*** See *Ukraïns'kyi khimichnyi zhurnal.*

***Ukrainskii matematicheskii zhurnal*** (Ukrainian Mathematical Journal, or *UMZh*). A scientific journal published by the Institute of Mathematics of the AN URSR (now ANU) on a quarterly basis in 1949–64 and a bimonthly basis until 1991. Initiated by A. Ishlinsky, its first editor, the journal was published in Russian until the 1970s, when it appeared briefly in both Ukrainian and Russian. In 1978 the Ukrainian edition was abolished. Since 1968 the journal has been translated into English in the United States. For many years it was edited by Yu. *Mytropolsky. The journal published primarily research papers in such fields as nonlinear mechanics and mathematical physics, theoretical physics, differential equations, algebra, geometry, topology, real and complex function theory, constructive function theory, functional analysis, and the theory of probability and mathematical statistics. Brief research notes and bibliographic information appeared also. The journal represented a good cross-section of mathematics in Ukraine. *UMZh* was the successor to *Zapysky Fizychno-matematychnoho viddilu* (1923–31), *Zhurnal matematychnoho tsyklu* (1931–4), *Zhurnal Instytutu matematyky* (1934–8), and *Zbirnyk prats' Instytutu matematyky* (1938–49).

***Ukrainskii narod v ego proshlom i nastoiashchem*** (The Ukrainian People in Its Past and Present). The first encyclopedic reference work on Ukraine. Initiated by O. Lototsky and M. Hrushevsky, it was originally conceived as an encyclopedic dictionary. A lack of contributors and other resources forced the editors to plan instead a four-volume reference work with long articles in Russian addressing the major areas of Ukrainian studies. The editorial board consisted of M. Hrushevsky, F. Vovk (Volkov), M. Kovalevsky, F. Korsh, A. Krymsky, M. Tuhan-Baranovsky, and A. Shakhmatov. The formal publisher was M. Slavinsky, and the managing editor was O. Lototsky. Contributors included leading Ukrainian scholars from Russian-ruled and Western Ukraine, and Russian academics. The first volume, published in Moscow in 1914, contained M. Hrushevsky's overview of the development of Ukrainian studies and his survey history of the Ukrainian people. The second volume, which appeared in 1916, contained articles by S. Rudnytsky (on Ukraine's geography), O. Rusov (on the demography of Russian-ruled Ukraine), V. Okhrymovych (on Galicia and Bukovyna), S. Tomashivsky (on Transcarpathia), P. Yefymenko (on Ukrainian customary law), F. Vovk (on Ukrainian anthropology and ethnography), and A. Shakhmatov (on the history of the Ukrainian language). Subsequent volumes, which never appeared because of the outbreak of the First World War and anti-Ukrainian tsarist policies, were to contain articles on Ukrainian culture, literature, architecture, art, music, economic history, religion, local government, political and national relations, and the social, political, and cultural life of Western Ukraine.

***Ukrainskii sbornik*** (Ukrainian Collection). The earliest Ukrainian literary periodical, published by I. *Sreznevsky. The first issue (1838, 88 pp) consisted of Sreznevsky's preface and postscript, I. *Kotliarevsky's drama *Natalka Poltavka* (Natalka from Poltava), and a short dictionary. The second (1841, 46 pp) consisted of Kotliarevsky's play *Moskal'-charivnyk* (The Soldier-Sorcerer).

*Ukrainskii vestnik*

**Ukrainskii vestnik** (Ukrainian Herald). One of the first journals in Ukraine, published in Kharkiv from 1816 to 1819 (a total of 16 large issues) under the editorship of H. Kvitka-Osnovianenko, R. Honorsky, and E. Filomafitsky. Although published primarily in Russian and initiated by I. *Sreznevsky, *Ukrainskii vestnik* was dedicated to publishing works on Ukrainian topics. It contained works on history, particularly the history of the Hetmanate and Slobidska Ukraine, by M. Markov, J. Vernet, M. Hrybovsky, and I. Kvitka; literary criticism by R. Honorsky and E. Filomafitsky; articles on Ukrainian ethnography by A. Levshin; commentaries by V. Karazyn, H. Kvitka-Osnovianenko, I. Voronov, and others; regular reports on cultural and intellectual life in Kharkiv; articles on prominent figures from Slobidska Ukraine, especially H. Skovoroda; original prose and poetry, in Ukrainian by P. Hulak-Artemovsky and H. Kvitka-Osnovianenko and in Russian by O. Somov; and translations of writings by Voltaire, J. Rousseau, and J. Milton. The tsarist Ministry of Education objected to the 'liberal' tendencies of the journal and eventually prevailed upon the local authorities to close it down.

**Ukrainskii vestnik** (Ukrainian Herald). A Russian-language weekly organ of the *Ukrainian caucus in the Russian State Duma, published in St Petersburg from June to September 1906 (a total of 14 issues). Published by N. Lototska and edited by M. Slavinsky, it contained articles on political, cultural, and economic affairs, and informed the public in the Russian Empire about the Ukrainian question and the autonomy movement. Regular contributors included Ukrainian figures such as M. Hrushevsky, D. Doroshenko (managing editor), O. Lototsky, M. Biliashivsky, B. Hrinchenko, S. Yefremov, L. Zhebunev, P. Zhytetsky, B. Kistiakovsky, M. Lozynsky, D. Markovych, I. Luchytsky, P. Stebnytsky, P. Chyzhevsky, V. Shemet, I. Shrah, F. Vovk, S. Rusova, M. Mohyliansky, D. Bahalii, M. Tuhan-Baranovsky, and O. Rusov. I. Franko and V. Hnatiuk contributed reports from Galicia, and the Russian writer D. Ovsianiko-Kulikovsky submitted an article on the psychology of national creativity. The paper stopped appearing after the First Duma was dissolved.

**Ukrainskii zhurnal** (Ukrainian Journal). A semimonthly Russian-language journal of literature, art, scholarship, and civic affairs, published by the Kharkiv University Press in 1824–5 (a total of 48 issues). It was edited by O.

Sklabovsky and appeared in a pressrun of 600 copies. From the end of 1824 important archival documents pertaining to the history of the Hetman state were published in a separate section called 'Little Russian Antiquities.' *Ukrainskii zhurnal* also contained ethnographic articles on Ukrainian towns and the Ukrainian language by J. Vernet and A. Levshin, and the first attempt at a synthetic assessment of Ukrainian poetry, by I. Kulzhynsky. The journal also reported extensively on educational, civic, and cultural affairs in Slobidska Ukraine.

**Ukraïns'kyi agronom** (Ukrainian Agronomist). A monthly organ of the agronomy section of the Ukrainian Bureau of the USSR Union of Agricultural and Forestry Workers. It appeared in Kharkiv in 1925–9 in place of *Zemel'nyk*, which had been published in 1924–5 before being split into *Ukraïns'kyi agronom*, *Ukraïns'kyi zemlevporiadnyk*, and *Ukraïns'kyi lisovod*. In 1930 the first two journals were succeeded by the semimonthly *Spetsialist sil's'koho hospodarstva Ukraïny*, which later became *Spetsialist sotsialistychnoho sil's'kohospodars'koho vyrobnytstva* (1931–2). *Ukraïns'kyi agronom* contained technical and scientific articles on agriculture and agronomy as well as articles on economic and political topics.

**Ukraïns'kyi agronomichnyi vistnyk** (Ukrainian Agricultural Herald). The only scholarly journal of agronomy published in Western Ukraine before the Second World War. It appeared quarterly in Lviv in 1934 and 1938 (a total of six issues). Its publisher and editor was Ye. *Khraplyvy.

**Ukraïns'kyi Beskyd** (Ukrainian Beskyd). A weekly Catholic, pro-hetmanite newspaper published by D. Gregolynsky in Peremyshl in 1933–9 as the continuation of *Beskyd*. It was edited by Yu. Kostiuk and appeared with the financial assistance of Bishop Y. Kotsylovsky of Peremyshl.

**Ukraïns'kyi biokhimichnyi zhurnal** (Ukrainian Biochemistry Journal). The oldest existing periodical devoted to biochemistry in the USSR, published bimonthly by the AN URSR (now ANU) Institute of Biochemistry. The continuation of *Naukovi zapysky Ukraïns'koho biokhemichnoho instytutu* (1926–34), it was originally called *Ukraïns'kyi biokhemichnyi zhurnal* (1934–7). Renamed *Biokhimichnyi zhurnal* (1938–41), it was revived under its current name in 1946. Since 1978 it has been published only in Russian, as *Ukrainskii biokhimicheskii zhurnal*.

**Ukraïns'kyi botanichnyi zhurnal** (Ukrainian Botanical Journal). A scientific quarterly published by the AN URSR (now ANU) Institute of Botany since 1940. It was founded in 1921 under the title *Zhurnal instytutu botaniky UAN*, and in the 1930s it was published as *Botanichnyi zhurnal AN URSR*.

**Ukraïns'kyi emigrant** (Ukrainian Emigrant). A monthly and then semimonthly and quarterly organ of the *Ukrainian Emigrant Aid Society, published in Lviv in 1927–39. Edited by V. Bachynsky, V. Konstantynovych, H. Rohozhynsky, and A. Hovynovych, it published reports on émigré life and developments in Western Ukraine. In 1930 it had a pressrun of 3,200 copies.

*Ukraïns'kyi filatelist* (Ukrainian Philatelist). A journal of the émigré Society of Ukrainian Philatelists, published in Vienna monthly from 1925 to 1930 and then bimonthly to 1939. Its first editor was I. Turyn. The journal sought to popularize Ukrainian affairs in philatelic circles, and published some articles in German.

*Ukraïns'kyi filatelist/Ukrainian Philatelist.* A journal of the *Ukrainian Philatelic and Numismatic Society, published annually and then semiannually since 1951 in the United States. Originally titled *Philatelist*, it was renamed the *Philatelic News/Filatelistychni visti* in 1962 and has appeared under its present name since 1963. The journal has published articles in both Ukrainian and English and has served as the main historical record of Ukrainian philately and numismatics in the world. The editors have been Ye. Kotyk (1951–61), I. Svit (1961–72), G. Slusarczuk (1972–5), S. Kikta (1975–6), J. Tkachuk (1976–85), and I. Kuzych (since 1985). By 1990, 58 issues had appeared.

*Ukraïns'kyi fizychnyi zhurnal* (Ukrainian Physics Journal). A scientific journal published by the AN URSR (now ANU) Physics and Astronomy Division, founded in 1956 at the initiative of V. *Lashkarev. A bimonthly until 1961, it has appeared monthly since 1962. From 1967 through 1977 the journal was published in parallel Ukrainian- and Russian-language editions. Since 1978 it has appeared only in Russian, as *Ukrainskii fizicheskii zhurnal*. It now publishes (since 1989) research papers in Russian, Ukrainian, and English, as submitted. The journal has published research papers in fields such as atomic and molecular physics, nuclear physics, field theory and elementary particles, elecromagnetic radiation and optics, plasma and gas dynamics, liquids and liquid crystals, solids, thermodynamics, statistical physics, quantum mechanics, and quantum optics; and brief research notes, letters, review articles, bibliographic information, and reviews. The chief editors have been V. Lashkarev, A. Simirnov, and O. Sytenko (since 1988).

*Ukraïns'kyi fol'klor* (Ukrainian Folklore). An illustrated popular scientific bimonthly periodical published in Kiev from 1937 to 1939 by the Institute of Ukrainian Folklore of the AN URSR (now ANU) and the Office for the Arts at the Council of People's Commissars of the Ukrainian SSR. It replaced *Etnohrafichnyi visnyk*, which had been discontinued in 1932. Ten issues appeared, containing articles mostly on 'Soviet folklore,' with examples of it and guidelines for creating it and recording it. The editor was A. Khvylia. In 1939 the periodical's name was changed to *Narodna tvorchist'*.

*Ukraïns'kyi holos* (Ukrainian Voice). A weekly newspaper published in *Winnipeg since March 1910; the oldest continuing Ukrainian newspaper in Canada. The paper was published by the Ukrainian Publishing Company (now *Trident Press), which was founded by a group of liberal-minded Ukrainians, many of them graduates of the *Ruthenian Training School. It was committed to the principles of popular enlightenment, education, economic self-reliance, Ukrainian nationalism (it was the first paper in Canada and one of the first in the world to call itself 'Ukrainian' instead of 'Ruthenian'), and loyalty to Canada. Initially it was supported by most liberal, na-

The first issue of *Ukraïns'kyi holos* (Winnipeg)

tionally conscious Ukrainians in Canada, by the emerging Prosvita movement and the various national homes and cultural societies across western Canada. The paper reported on Ukrainian-Canadian affairs and on developments in Western and Russian-ruled Ukraine. During the struggle for Ukraine's independence it supported the Central Rada and then the UNR. The paper also emerged as a major critic of the Ukrainian Catholic Church in Canada – engaging often in heated polemics on religious and church subjects – and (in the interwar era) of the Ukrainian Communist movement in Canada. Its first editor was V. *Kudryk (1910–21). Others involved in the early years of the paper included T. Ferley, W. Czumer, P. Woycenko, O. Zerebko, and J. Arsenych.

Early in its history, *Ukraïns'kyi holos* emerged as a major force behind the establishment of the *Ukrainian Orthodox Church of Canada, and it became the unofficial organ of the new church in 1918. Under its second editor, Myroslaw *Stechishin (1921–47), it worked to establish a new Orthodox lay organization, the *Ukrainian Self-Reliance League (SUS); it became that organization's organ in 1927. Since then it has reported extensively on the activities of SUS and its constituent organizations, the Canadian Ukrainian Youth Association, the Ukrainian Women's Association of Canada, the Union of Ukrainian Community Centres of Canada, and the four student residences affiliated with SUS. Until 1973 it included a monthly supplement devoted to literature, scholarship, and the arts. Since the Second World War the paper's editors have included I. Syrnyk, D. Lobai, S. Volynets, M. Hnativ, M. Hykavy, A. Kurdydyk, and P. Danyliuk.

In 1981 the newspaper *Kanadiis'kyi farmer* was merged with *Ukraïns'kyi holos*. Eight volumes of annals of Ukrainian life in Canada based on the contents of *Ukraïns'kyi holos* covering the period through the 1970s, prepared by O. Woycenko, appeared by 1992. The newspaper has published an annual almanac virtually from the time of its formation. The 1960 jubilee edition includes accounts of its history and development.

B. Balan

*Ukraïns'kyi holos* (Ukrainian Voice). A semiweekly organ of the Ukrainian Military Executive Council of the Northwestern Front, published from June to November 1917 (a total of 47 issues) in Riga, Valga, and Valmiera in Latvia, and in Pskov, Russia. It was edited by S. Pylypenko and K. Polishchuk.

***Ukraïns'kyi holos*** (Ukrainian Voice). An official daily newspaper of the *State Secretariat of the Western Ukrainian National Republic, published in November 1918 in Lviv and then, after the occupation of Lviv by Polish forces, to May 1919 in Ternopil. The editors were L. Tsehelsky (May 1918), P. Karmansky (November 1918 to February 1919), and M. Malytsky (February–May 1919). K. Hrynevych and S. Charnetsky were staff writers. The paper was succeeded by *Ukraïns'ki visty* (May–July 1919; 36 issues), edited by Malytsky, I. Halushchynsky, S. Sydorak, I. Brykovych, and F. Bulat.

*Ukraïns'kyi holos* (Peremyshl)

***Ukraïns'kyi holos*** (Ukrainian Voice). A weekly newspaper published in Peremyshl in 1919–32. Initially it backed the Ukrainian Labor party, but in 1920–9, under the editorship of D. Gregolynsky and then Ye. Zyblikevych, it supported the hetmanite movement. At this time it reached the height of its popularity and appeared in a pressrun of up to 17,000 copies. In 1929 it became the first legal, though unofficial, organ of the OUN; from then it was edited by Z. Pelensky (1929–30), Zyblikevych (1930–1), and V. Zubrytsky (1931–2). Issues of *Ukraïns'kyi holos* were frequently confiscated by the Polish authorities, particularly in 1920, when it appeared briefly under four different titles, and after 1929. The paper was finally closed down.

***Ukraïns'kyi holos*** (Ukrainian Voice). A newspaper published in Lutske during the German occupation. It appeared weekly from the fall of 1941 to October 1942 and then semiweekly to January 1944 (a total of 144 issues). The newspaper was edited by V. Postryhach and, from February 1942, by A. Dubliansky.

***Ukraïns'kyi holos na Dalekomu skhodi*** (Ukrainian Voice in the Far East). A newspaper published irregularly (usually three times a month) in Shanghai from November 1941 to July 1944. It reported on developments in Ukraine and the Far East, particularly on the Ukrainian nationalist movement and the struggle for Ukrainian independence. It carried on a lively polemic with anti- and pro-Soviet Russian émigré newspapers in China and criticized Nazi policies toward Ukraine. The newspaper was edited by M. Milko, O. Drobiazko, and I. Svit.

***Ukraïns'kyi invalid*** (Ukrainian Invalid). A biweekly and later irregular organ of the Ukrainian Association of Disabled Veterans, published in Kalisz, Poland, in 1923–31. It was intended for disabled veterans of the Army of the UNR living in Poland. The editors were V. Rohaza and M. Sadovsky. In 1937–9 a quarterly journal with the same title was published in Lviv by the Ukrainian Invalids' Aid Society.

*9'91*    *Ukraïns'kyi istorychnyi zhurnal*

***Ukraïns'kyi istorychnyi zhurnal*** (Ukrainian Historical Journal, or *UIZh*). An organ of the AN URSR (now ANU) Institute of History and of the Institute of Party History of the CC CPU (until 1991), published in Kiev bimonthly from 1957 and monthly since 1962. Its chief editors have been F. Shevchenko (1957–67, 1968–72), K. Dubyna (1967), P. Kalynychenko (1972–9), O. Kondufor (1979–88), and M. Koval (since 1988). During the Soviet period *UIZh* was the only historical journal in Ukraine, and it was in some ways the republican version of several Moscow-based historical journals, including *Voprosy istorii*, *Istoriia SSSR*, *Voprosy istorii KPSS*, and *Vestnik drevnei istorii*.

A great deal of space in *UIZh* was given to CP history, and comparatively little to the history of Ukraine. The journal mainly addressed the Soviet period and the socioeconomic history and workers' movement during the 19th and 20th centuries, and only marginally discussed the Cossack era and the history of Ukrainian culture. The Princely period was almost totally excluded from *UIZh*, and minimal attention was paid to world history. All the published material adhered ideologically and conceptually to Marxism-Leninism, and CP policies were strictly followed on national politics in Ukraine. During the 1960s there were attempts to broaden the scope of the journal and to rehabilitate the proscribed historical past, but those efforts were soon halted. Only a few prerevolutionary historians (O. Lazarevsky, D. Yavornytsky, A. Yefymenko, M. Drahomanov, and a few others) were partially accepted in the officially recognized historiography. In the mid-1970s *UIZh* came under severe CP restrictions, and a purge was carried out among the members of the editorial board and in the ANU Institute of History.

*UIZh* marked the great historical event of the millennium of Christianity in Ukraine with only one article, by M. Kotliar on the introduction of Christianity in Rus' (1988, no. 6). The reforms that began in 1985 had some slight effect on its orientation and contents (eg, the reprinting of M. Kostomarov's monograph 'Mazepa,' contradictory data on the 1932–3 man-made famine in Ukraine), but the journal continued to espouse, until the demise of the USSR, a conservative, dogmatic CP line and publish a minimal amount on the history of Ukraine. The standard sections of *UIZh* have included essays, announcements (including obituaries), history and source studies, notes, methodology and the methods of historical research ('to aid the lecturer on history'), documents, a historical calendar, relics of history and culture, reviews, annals, criticism and bibliography, and announcements of defenses of doctoral theses. Systematic guides to *UIZh* were published for the periods 1957–66 (1968), 1967–76 (1982), and 1977–86 (1987).

A. Zhukovsky

*Ukraïns'kyi istoryk*

**Ukraïns'kyi istoryk** (Ukrainian Historian, or *UI*). A quarterly journal on Ukrainian history published in one or two volumes per annum. The first three issues were published by Zarevo (1963–4), and the *Ukrainian Historical Association has published the journal since the fourth issue. The founder and chief editor of *UI* is L. *Wynar, who has been assisted by M. Antonovych. The journal was printed in the United States until 1964 and in Munich until 1986, and has again been printed in the United States since 1987. The language of the publication is primarily Ukrainian, although some papers are printed in the original English, German, or another language.

*UI* publishes research on the history of Ukraine and on related historical disciplines, as well as source materials, memoirs, epistolary documents, abstracts, reprints from other publications, reviews, annals, and so on. One of its major accomplishments has been its comprehensive illumination of the life and work of M. Hrushevsky (particularly by L. Wynar, who founded a section of *UI* dedicated to Hrushevsky studies). Separate volumes of the journal have focused on eminent Ukrainian historians (Hrushevsky, nos 9–10 and 81–4; O. Ohloblyn, nos 25–7; L. Wynar, nos 69–72; D. Doroshenko, V. Lypynsky, and M. Slabchenko, nos 75–7; and O. Kandyba, nos 85–8) and on historic jubilees and anniversaries (the centenary of the Shevchenko Scientific Society [NTSh], nos 37–8; the millennium of Christianity in Ukraine, nos 97–100). Some papers appearing in *UI* have been republished as monographs, including L. Wynar's essay on Hrushevsky and the NTSh in 1892–1930, Ya. Pasternak's historical, archeological, and linguistic study of early Slavs, and B. Wynar's examination of the development of economic thought in Kievan Rus'.

M. Antonovych

**Ukraïns'kyi khimichnyi zhurnal** (Ukrainian Chemistry Journal). A scientific journal published monthly in Kiev by the AN URSR (now ANU) Division of Chemistry and Chemical Technology. It succeeded *Ukraïns'kyi khemichnyi zhurnal*, a quarterly and then bimonthly published in 1925–6 and 1927–38 in Kharkiv. It was revived in Kiev in 1948 and has been published since then in Russian, as *Ukrainskii khimicheskii zhurnal*; since 1969 a Ukrainian edition has also been published. An English translation, ap-

pearing briefly in 1964 as *Ukrainian Journal of Chemistry*, has been marketed since 1966 by Allerton Press (New York) as *Soviet Progress in Chemistry*.

**Ukraïns'kyi khliborob.** See *Khliborob*.

**Ukraïns'kyi medychnyi vistnyk** (Ukrainian Medical Herald). An irregular medical journal published in Prague by the *Ukrainian Physicians' Association in Czechoslovakia in 1923–5 (six issues). During these years it was the only Ukrainian medical journal being published in the West, and its readership extended to Soviet Ukraine. Edited by B. *Matiushenko, the journal published articles on clinical and theoretical medicine, community hygiene, and eugenics. Besides scientific papers and professional news, it devoted much attention to the development of Ukrainian medical terminology. Its contributors included members of the association and doctors in Western and Soviet Ukraine.

**Ukraïns'kyi misionar** (Ukrainian Missionary; Portuguese: Missionário ucraino). A Ukrainian-Brazilian Catholic monthly, published in Prudentópolis by the Basilian order since 1911. Originally entitled *Misionar*, it was twice closed down by the Brazilian authorities (1918–34 and 1940–7) and replaced temporarily by the annual *Namirennia apostol'stva molytvy* under the editorship of Kh. Myskiv. It began appearing as *Ukraïns'kyi misionar* in 1935 and was later also called *Ukraïns'kyi misionar u Brazylii*. It contains a calendar of church events and dates, articles of general religious and national interest, and news from parishes from around the world. It has been edited by R. Krynytsky, I. Vihorynsky, and V. Zinko.

**Ukraïns'kyi myslyvets' i rybalka** (Ukrainian Hunter and Fisherman). A monthly organ of the All-Ukrainian Association of Hunters and Fishermen, published in Kharkiv in 1925–32 (a total of 98 issues). In 1925–6 it appeared in Russian as *Ukrainskii okhotnik i rybolov*. The journal was formed through the merger of two Russian-language journals founded in 1924, *Priroda i okhota na Ukraine* and *Ukrainskii okhotnichii vestnik*.

**Ukraïns'kyi pasichnyk** (Ukrainian Beekeeper). A monthly organ of the *Silskyi Hospodar society and *Rii beekeepers' co-operative society, published in Lviv in 1928–39 and 1942–4. It provided practical advice for beekeepers on producing and marketing honey. The editors were M. Borovsky (1928–38), Ye. Khraplyvy (1938–42), I. Drabaty, and S. Yatsura. The circulation in 1930 was 6,000.

**Ukraïns'kyi prapor** (Ukrainian Flag). An official organ of the *Dictatorship of the Western Province of the UNR, published in Vienna from August 1919 to October 1923. After the Dictatorship was dissolved, the paper moved to Berlin, where it continued to appear until 1932. In Berlin it attempted to influence Western European governments to support the cause of Ukrainian independence. *Ukraïns'kyi prapor* was published initially twice a week; then weekly from 1922, semimonthly from 1925, and monthly from 1929; and finally irregularly. Its editors included P. Lysiak, I. Nimchuk, and I. Prots (from 1923), and regular contributors included K. Levytsky, O. Nazaruk, and O. Hrytsai in Vienna and M. Lozynsky, R. Perfetsky, Yu. Bachynsky, and A. Zhuk in Berlin.

**Ukraïns'kyi pravoslavnyi visnyk.** See *Ukrainian Orthodox Herald*.

**Ukraïns'kyi Prometei** (Ukrainian Prometheus). A weekly newspaper published in Detroit in 1952–8, and then in New York in 1959–61 as *Prometei*. The unofficial organ of the *Ukrainian Revolutionary Democratic party, it was edited by P. Maliar, V. Hryshko, and M. Dziabenko.

*Ukraïns'kyi revoliutsioner*

**Ukraïns'kyi revoliutsioner** (Ukrainian Revolutionary). An organ of the clandestine émigré Western Ukrainian National Revolutionary Organization (ZUNRO) led by Ye. Petrushevych, the former president of the Western Ukrainian National Republic. The journal was printed in Berlin from July 1926 to August 1929 (a total of 24 issues) and smuggled into Polish-ruled Western Ukraine, where it was illegally disseminated. It advocated the revolutionary overthrow of Polish rule and the creation of a unitary pan-Ukrainian state. Because it and the ZUNRO were Sovietophile and condemned the legal Western Ukrainian parties and the much more influential Ukrainian Military Organization, they had little support in Western Ukraine, and disappeared.

**Ukrainskyi Robitnyk** (Ukrainian Worker). One of the four major publishing houses in Ukraine in the 1920s, founded in Kharkiv in July 1925 from the merger of the Ukrprofizdat publishing house of the All-Ukrainian Council of Trade Unions and the Rabochii Donbassa publishing house. Until October 1935 it published mass-distributed literature on industrial, technical, sociopolitical, and trade-union subjects, inexpensive series of prose and poetry (including Ukrainian literature in Russian translation), textbooks for vocational schools, and trade-union and cultural-educational journals, such as *Vestnik profdvizheniia Ukrainy* (1925–9), *Znanie* (1925–7), *Rabochii* (1925–6), *Rabochii klub* (1925–7), *Kul'trobitnyk* (1927–30), and *Kul'tfront* (1931–5). Major branch offices of the publishing house were located in Kiev, Odessa, Dnipropetrovske, and Kryvyi Rih. From late 1930 Ukrainskyi Robitnyk was part of the State Publishing Alliance of Ukraine.

**Ukraïns'kyi robitnyk** (Ukrainian Worker). A weekly organ of the *Sich society in Canada and then the *United Hetman Organization, published from January 1934 to August 1956 in Toronto. Splits in the hetmanite movement in the early 1950s led to several changes in the paper.

In July 1954 it was renamed *Ukraïns'kyi khrystyians'kyi robitnyk* to stress its anticommunist, Christian outlook, and in September of that year it became *Kanadiis'kyi horozhanyn*. The editors of *Ukraïns'kyi robitnyk* and its successors were I. Korchynsky, M. Hetman (1937–49; in 1952–5 he published a competing conservative newspaper, *Nasha derzhava*), Yu. Rusov, Yu. Tarnovych, V. Bosy, R. Domazar, and A. Kurdydyk.

*УКРАЇНСЬКИЙ САМОСТІЙНИК*
*UKRAINSKYJ SAMOSTIJNYK*
*Місячник політики, культури і суспільного життя*
*Monatsschrift für Politik, Kultur und Gesellschaftsleben, München 13, Heßstraße 50—52*

*Ukraïns'kyi samostiinyk*

**Ukraïns'kyi samostiinyk** (Ukrainian Independentist). The name of two related publications that appeared in Munich from 1950 to 1975. The first, a weekly newspaper of political news and commentary, was the semiofficial organ of the émigré OUN (Bandera faction) and was edited by K. Kononenko, S. Lenkavsky, D. Shtykalo, and Z. Pelensky. After the 1954 split in the faction, the paper became the organ of the newly formed OUN (Abroad) and was edited by Pelensky, L. Rebet, and B. Kordiuk. From September 1957 it appeared as a monthly journal of social and political thought. Edited by L. Rebet, V. Markus, B. Kordiuk, and A. Kaminsky, the journal espoused principles of democratic nationalism and provided a forum for more open discussion of political, social, cultural, and religious issues. It devoted particular attention to political developments in Soviet Ukraine, Ukrainian émigré politics, and the relationship between Ukraine and its neighbors. In 1975 it appeared quarterly. A total of 212 issues appeared before the journal merged with *Suchasnist'* in 1976.

**Ukraïns'kyi selianyn** (Ukrainian Peasant). A monthly organ of the *Union of Lands of United Ukraine. It succeeded the party's journal *Ukraïns'ka zemlia* (three issues in 1951–3) and was published in 1953 in New York and in 1954–62 in Munich. Edited by V. Dubrovsky (1954–5) and Yu. Semenko (1955–62), the paper was read primarily by émigrés from central and eastern Ukraine. Contributors included V. Dolenko, A. Vovk, Yu. Lavrinenko, T. Borovets, M. Kovalevsky, N. Pavlushkova, and V. Senyk. In the late 1970s the party revived *Ukraïns'ka zemlia* as an annual publication; no. 15 appeared in 1988.

**Ukraïns'kyi skytalets'** (Homeless Ukrainian). A newspaper published by émigré veterans of the Ukrainian Galician Army in the internment camps at Liberec (1920–2) and Josefov (1922) in Czechoslovakia, and then in Vienna. It appeared monthly and then semimonthly (with interruptions) from November 1920 to 1923 and was edited by P. Budz and I. Prots.

**Ukraïns'kyi teatr** (Ukrainian Theater). An illustrated bimonthly journal published under the auspices of the Ministry of Culture by the *Ukrainian Theatrical Society since 1970 in Kiev. It contains articles on the development of Soviet Ukrainian theater, the history of Ukrainian theater, the contemporary Soviet theatrical repertoire, public figures in the theater world, and the activities of 'progressive' foreign theaters. Its predecessor (1936–41) was *Teatr. In 1954–69 theatrical affairs were covered in the journal Mystetstvo.

**Ukraïns'kyi tyzhden'** (Ukrainian Week). A weekly newspaper published in Prague in 1933–8. Published and edited by P. Zlenko, it reported on Ukrainian life, particularly in Czechoslovakia and Prague.

**Ukraïns'kyi visnyk** (Ukrainian Herald). An organ of the *Ukrainian National Alliance in Germany, published in Berlin in 1936–45 irregularly, then monthly (from 1938), semimonthly, and three times a week, and finally weekly. A pro-OUN paper edited by T. Omelchenko, Yu. Artiushenko, V. Yaniv (1940), V. Panchenko-Yurevych, A. Bilynsky, and V. Maruniak (from 1941), and P. Bohatsky (1944), it contained articles on political and social issues and reports on Ukrainian émigré life in Germany and elsewhere and on the activities of the alliance. It also devoted considerable attention to developments in Ukraine. During the Second World War the paper had a pressrun of 15,000 copies; it was distributed throughout German-occupied Ukraine until distribution was forbidden by the Ostministerium.

A 1987 issue of the revived
Ukraïns'kyi visnyk

**Ukraïns'kyi visnyk** (Ukrainian Herald). An underground samvydav journal in Ukraine. The first eight issues (in six volumes) appeared in the early 1970s; all of them, except vol 5, were published in the West, and some were translated into English or French. The journal contained articles defending human rights in Ukraine and exposing *Russification and Russian chauvinism. The journal published much information on the illegal repressions against Ukrainian intellectuals, including reports on the closed trials and prison or camp conditions and the texts of defense speeches and protest letters. It presented the available evidence on the murder of A. Horska and the persecution of Ukrainian dissidents, such as V. Chornovil, M. Plakhtoniuk, S. Khmara, O. Shevchenko, V. Moroz, I. Svitlychny, Ye. Sverstiuk, S. Karavansky, and I. Sokulsky. Besides reports and materials on the human rights movement it published analytical articles on political questions and literary works by persecuted writers, such as V. Sy-

monenko, I. Kalynets, H. Chubai, and M. Kulchytsky. Issues 7–8, edited by the pseudonymous Maksym Sahaidak, differ from the previous issues in tone and in their more nationalistic positions. After a 13-year silence the journal was renewed, in 1987, with the appearance of issue 7 (the earlier issues 7–8 were not recognized by the journal's founders). A reflection of the more liberal atmosphere under M. Gorbachev, the editorial board was listed for the first time. It consisted of I. *Hel, V. *Barladianu, M. *Horyn, P. *Skochok, and V. *Chornovil (chief editor), all former political prisoners. For the most part issues published previously banned or censored literary works. Although the editors intended to publish monthly, no further issues have appeared. The journal was criticized severely in the Soviet press, and its editors were denounced as Ukrainian bourgeois nationalists and agents of Western imperialism.

B. Balan

**Ukraïns'kyi visnyk eksperymental'noï pedahohiky ta refleksolohiï** (Ukrainian Herald of Experimental Pedagogy and Reflexology). A scholary pedagogical journal published in Kharkiv from 1925 to 1930, until 1927 as Ukraïns'kyi visnyk refleksolohiï ta eksperymental'noï pedahohiky. It espoused modern Western methodologies in pedagogy and devoted much attention to psychology and behavioral science. The journal was closed down and replaced by the Stalinist *Za markso-lenins'ku pedahohiku.

**Ukraïns'kyi vistnyk** (Ukrainian Herald). A daily newspaper published in Lviv from January to September 1921 in place of *Dilo, which had been banned by the Polish authorities. It was edited by M. Strutynsky.

**Ukraïns'kyi zbirnyk.** See Institute for the Study of the USSR.

**Ukraïns'kyi zemlevporiadnyk** (Ukrainian Land Cultivator). A monthly organ of the land cultivation section of the Ukrainian Bureau of the USSR Union of Agricultural and Forestry Workers, published in Kharkiv in 1925–9. Until 1927 it appeared in Russian as Zemleustroitel' Ukrainy. It published scientific and technical articles about land melioration, irrigation, and drainage, and other aspects of land use. Ukraïns'kyi zemlevporiadnyk, *Ukraïns'kyi agronom, and the quarterly Ukraïns'kyi lisovod all succeeded Zemel'nyk (1924–5). In 1930 the first two journals were replaced by Spetsiialist sil's'koho hospodarstva Ukraïny, which later became Spetsiialist sotsialistychnoho sil's'kohospodars'koho vyrobnytstva (1931–2).

**Ukránia** (Ukraine). A popular monthly journal published in Hungarian in Budapest in 1916–17 (a total of 20 issues). Sponsored by the Hungarian government, it promoted the dismemberment of the Russian Empire by supporting the Ukrainian national movement there, and fostered Hungarian interest in the Ukrainian question by publishing articles on Ukrainian affairs and translations of Ukrainian literature. It did not, however, support the development of Ukrainian consciousness among Transcarpathia's Ukrainians. The editor was H. Strypsky.

**Ukrmet.** See Ukrainian Meteorological Service.

**Ulaszyn, Henryk,** b 19 January 1874 in Lykhachykha, Tarashcha county, Kiev gubernia, d 23 May 1956 in Łódź, Poland. Polish neogrammarian linguist and Slavist. He studied at Kiev (1895–7), Cracow (1897–1901), Vienna (1898–9), and Leipzig (1901–3; PH D, 1904) universities and then taught Polish at Kiev (1917–19), Lviv (1919–21), Poznań (1922–39, where he headed the Slavic Seminar and Slavic Society), and Łódź (1945–?) universities. He wrote over 1,000 works, including a textbook of Old Church Slavonic (1928); a historical study of Kievan contracts in 1798–1898 (1900); a study of the Polish criminal argot in Lviv (1902); a pamphlet on the origin of the ethnonym 'Ukrainian' (1947); and articles on the terms 'Ruthenian,' 'Little Russian,' and 'Ukrainian,' in *Dziennik Kijowski*. A bibliography of his works was published in *Rozprawy Komisji Językowej Łódzkiego Towarzystwa Naukowego* (2 [1955]).

**Ulianivka** [Uljanivka]. V-11. A city (1989 pop 11,000) on the Synytsia River and a raion center in Kirovohrad oblast. It was founded in the early 1880s and was first called Hrushky. It was renamed in 1924 and granted city status in 1974. Ulianivka is an agricultural center with a sugar refinery, juice factory, and dairy.

**Ulianov, Petr** [Uljanov], b 23 July 1899 in Patsyn, Smolensk gubernia, Russia, d 31 March 1964 in Kiev. Sculptor. After studying at the Kharkiv Art Institute (1919–27) and the Higher Art and Technology Institute in Leningrad (1927–31) he taught at the Kiev State Art Institute (1931–49) and Kiev Construction Institute (1936–64). His works include the monument to L. Hlibov in Chernihiv (1934), the bust *Red Army Soldier* (1934), and busts of Soviet political leaders, T. Shevchenko (1959), A. Mickiewicz, and M. Gorky.

**Ulizko, Yakiv** (Petrenko), b ?, d before 1686. Cossack officer. He was a military judge in I. Zolotarenko's army in Belarus (1654–5) and colonel of Korsun regiment (1660–4). With Yu. Khmelnytsky he switched his alliance to the Poles (1660) and was later captured by Muscovite forces (1665). In 1674 he was a general judge under P. Doroshenko, but then he threw his support behind I. Samoilovych and became judge of Starodub regiment (1676–8). Ulizko's descendants became members of the Chernihiv and Poltava nobility; his son, Tymish, was flag-bearer for Starodub regiment in 1686–7.

**Ulychians** (*ulychi, uhlychi, uluchi*). An East Slavic tribe that lived in the 6th to 9th centuries in the Dnieper River lowlands from the Ros River to the Black Sea, south of the Polianians. They were on friendly terms with the Tivertsians but warred with the Polianians and Kievan Rus'. In 885 Prince Oleh led a campaign against them. In the 10th century the Ulychians were pushed westward by the Pechenegs, and they settled in Bessarabia on the Boh and the Dniester rivers, where they extended as far as the Danube River and the Black Sea coast. Their capital was *Peresichen. In the mid-10th century, during the rule of Prince Ihor, the Ulychians were conquered by the voivode Svineld and absorbed by the Kievan Rus' state, along with the Tivertsians. With other *tribes they eventually became the original *Ukrainians. The Ulychians are not mentioned in chronicles after 940. Some scholars believe that, under Polovtsian pressure, they moved northward in the 12th century and settled near the Sluch and the upper Boh rivers (see *Bolokhovians).

**Ulynets, Oleksa** [Ulynec'], b 22 March 1903 in Tyshiv, Bereg county, Transcarpathia, d 25 November 1978 in Chynadiieve, Mukachiv raion, Transcarpathia oblast. Folk composer. While working as a laborer in various European countries in 1918–45 and, later, as a mechanic in Chynadiieve, he composed over 1,000 *kolomyika*-like songs. Many of them are addressed to his homeland, Ukraine.

The Uman Art Gallery

**Uman** [Uman'] (aka Human). V-11. A city (1990 pop 91,000) on the Umanka River and a raion center in Cherkasy oblast. It was first mentioned in historical documents in 1616, when it was under Polish rule. In 1648 it was liberated from the Poles by I. Hanzha, a colonel of B. Khmelnytsky, and became the administrative center of Uman regiment. After being returned to Poland in 1667, the town was abandoned by many residents, who moved to Left-Bank Ukraine. Under the ownership of the Potocki family of Polish magnates (1726–1832) the town grew in economic and cultural importance. A Basilian monastery and school were established. The Uman region was the site of the haidamaka rebellions in 1734, 1750, and 1768, when the town was captured by Maksym Zalizniak and I. Gonta. After the partition of Poland in 1793, Uman was annexed by Russia, and in 1797 it became a county center of Kiev gubernia. At the end of the 19th century Uman was linked by railway to Kiev and Odessa, and its manufacturing industries began to develop rapidly. Its population grew from 10,100 in 1860 to 29,900 in 1900 and over 50,000 in 1914. Today the city has optical and farm-machinery plants, a cannery, a brewery, a vitamin factory, a sewing factory, and a footwear factory. Its highest educational institutions are the Pedagogical and Agricultural institutes. The main architectural monuments are the catacombs of the old fortress, the city hall (1780–2), a Roman Catholic church in the classical style (1826), and 19th-century trading stalls. Uman has a rich regional museum and is the home of the famous *Sofiivka Park.

**Uman Agricultural Institute** (Umanskyi silskohospodarskyi instytut im. O. Horkoho). An institution of higher education, under the USSR Ministry of Agriculture until 1992. It is based on the Chief Orcharding School, the first

The Uman Agricultural Institute

school of its kind in the Russian Empire, established in Odessa in 1844 and transferred to the Sofiivka Park in Uman in 1859. The school was reorganized several times before acquiring its present name in 1929. The institute has faculties of agronomy, orcharding, economics, and the upgrading of agricultural specialists and managers. It also maintains an experimental farm. Its enrollment in 1986–7 was 3,475, including over 2,000 correspondence students. It publishes a bilingual, Ukrainian-Russian, collection of scientific papers.

**Uman Pedagogical Institute** (Umanskyi pedahohichnyi instytut im. P. Tychyny). An institution of higher learning, under the jurisdiction of the Ministry of Education. Founded in 1930 as one of the *institutes of social education with a three–year course of instruction, in 1933 it was reorganized as a pedagogical institute. In 1967 it was named after P. Tychyna. It has three faculties, natural sciences, elementary education, and technical education. The student enrollment in 1986–7 was 2,600. The library has a collection of 200,000 volumes.

**Uman regiment.** An administrative territory and military formation in Right-Bank Ukraine established in 1648 at the outbreak of the Cossack-Polish War. The regimental center, Uman, was well fortified and withstood a number of sieges by the Poles, including a major attack in 1653. The regiment was split during the 1670s as a result of factional fighting between its colonel, M. Khanenko, and Hetman P. Doroshenko and was disbanded in 1686. The regiment was revived under Hetman I. Mazepa in 1704 and dissolved in 1712.

**Uman Regional Studies Museum** (Umanskyi kraieznavchyi muzei). A museum founded in 1918 in Uman under the direction of P. Kurinny. Large archeological and ethnographic collections, a library, a collection of early books, and a picture gallery were created, including artworks and artifacts confiscated from local nobles. From 1922 to the mid-1930s the museum was called the Socio-Historical Museum of Uman Okruha. Its large collection of autographs was transferred to Kiev in the mid-1930s. In 1971 the museum had over 20,000 exhibit items, including objects of the prehistoric Trypilian, Bilohrudivka, and Cherniakhiv cultures and of the Scythians, a collection of 17th-century tiles, and materials pertaining to the Cossack Uman regiment. A guide to the museum was published in 1967.

**Umanets** [Umanec']. A Cossack *starshyna* family line from Right-Bank Ukraine that came into prominence during the B. Khmelnytsky period, when they moved to the Left Bank. Pylyp Umanets ('Pylypcha') was a captain in Hlukhiv company (1653–68) and the colonel of Nizhen regiment (1667 and 1669–74). The descendants of his only son, Demian Umanets, archpriest of Hlukhiv, were *town Cossacks and captains in Hlukhiv (1726–67) and Yampil (1772–81) companies. Some of them became regimental commanders; Vasyl Umanets was the flag-bearer of Nizhen regiment (1734 and 1736–8). That lineage also produced O. *Umanets, a physician and writer, and some important landowners in Chernihiv gubernia during the 19th century, especially the provincial activist F. *Umanets.

**Umanets, Fedir** [Umanec'], b 5 March 1841 in Yasnivka, Hlukhiv county, Chernihiv gubernia, d 1908. Liberal historian and civic figure. A law graduate of Moscow University, he served as a member of the agency for peasant affairs in Hlukhiv (1875–80) and the head of Hlukhiv county's zemstvo (1887–95) and Chernihiv gubernia's zemstvo administration (from 1896). He supported the Ukrainian national movement and secured zemstvo jobs for its members (B. Hrinchenko, M. Kotsiubynsky, M. Vorony, V. Samiilenko, and others). An active member of the Chernihiv Gubernia Scholarly Archival Commission, from the 1860s on he published historical and political articles on Ukrainian-Polish relations and other subjects in Russian journals, and books on public education in Russia (1871), the decline of Poland (1872), the colonization of unsettled lands in the Russian Empire (1884), and Hetman I. Mazepa (1897). Using archival and published sources, he was the first writer in Russian and Ukrainian historiography to evaluate positively Mazepa as a man and a statesman. He also wrote a study on Prince K. Ostrozky (*Russkii arkhiv*, 1904).

**Umanets, Oleksander** [Umanec'], b 23 October 1808 in Symferopil, Tavriia gubernia, d 26 December 1877 in St Petersburg. Epidemiologist with a specialization in quarantine. A graduate of Moscow University (1830), he was director of the Odessa Quarantine Office (1840–8). In 1842–3 he traveled to Egypt with a government commission to investigate heat disinfection of the clothes of plague victims. His report (1845) was translated into German and French. Later he published his memoirs of the trip to the Middle East (1850) and a survey history of the Black Sea coastal region (1887).

**Umanets, Vasyl** [Umanec', Vasyl'], b 2 May 1916 in Rubchenky, Skvyra county, Kiev gubernia. Composer, conductor, pedagogue, and musicologist. He graduated from (1945) and completed postgraduate work at (1948) the Kiev State Conservatory and taught (1944–56) in Kiev and Dnipropetrovske. Since 1956 he has taught singing at various schools in Kiev. His main works include the choral-symphonic suite *Na verkhovyni* (In the Highland, 1962); orchestral and chamber music; pieces for piano, violin, and bandura; solo songs to texts by T. Shevchenko, M. Rylsky, D. Pavlychko, R. Bratun, and others; children's songs; and folk song settings. He has also written musicological studies on the choral compositions of M. Lysenko, M. Leontovych, and others.

**Umansky, Morits** [Umans'kyj], b 8 March 1907 in Zhytomyr, d 19 December 1948 in Kiev. Theatrical and cinema designer. He was a student at the Kiev School of Industrial Art (1923–6) and completed his studies at the Kiev Art Institute (1926–30, pupil of V. Tatlin and K. Yeleva). He made designs for the Kiev Ukrainian and Russian drama theaters (1930–3) and then for the Kiev Artistic Film Studio (particularly for O. Dovzhenko's *Shchors*, 1935–7). A biography, by V. Nelli, was published in Kiev in 1967.

**Umansky, Oleksander** [Umans'kyj], b 2 February 1900 in Kiev, d 1973. Civil engineer. He studied at the Kiev Polytechnical Institute under Ye. *Paton, and in the period 1925–30 he designed a number of bridges in Ukraine. He was a professor at the Kiev Civil-Engineering Institute and the AN URSR (now ANU) Institute of Construction Mechanics and the Military Air Force Academy in Moscow (from 1935). He wrote numerous textbooks and monographs on floating bridges (1931, 1939), building mechanics (1934), the deformation of thin-walled aviation design parts (1939), the strength of materials (1952), and the engineering mechanics of airplanes (1957).

**Umantsev, Fedir** [Umancev], b 11 January 1914 in Udachne, Bakhmut county, Katerynoslav gubernia. Art scholar. He graduated from Kiev University in 1941. He wrote books on the Ukrainian painted portrait (1970, with M. Anikina) and the Trinity Church above the gate of the Kievan Cave Monastery (1970), introductions to and commentaries on several books, and chapters for a general history of art (1960), a history of Ukrainian art (1966), and the AN URSR (now ANU) history of Ukrainian art (vols 2–4, 1967–70).

**Unava River.** A right-bank tributary of the Irpin River that flows for 87 km through Zhytomyr and Kiev oblasts and drains a basin area of 680 sq km. The river is used for industry, water supply, irrigation, and fishing. Its channel has a general width of 2–10 m, and there are granite outcrops in its basin. The city of Fastiv is situated on it.

**Unbegaun, Boris,** b 23 August 1898 in Moscow, d 4 March 1973 in New York City. Russian émigré Slavist of German origin; full member of the Ukrainian Academy of Arts and Sciences in the US. He studied at the universities of Ljubljana and Paris (D LITT, 1935) and served as a professor at Brussels (1936–53), Strasbourg (1937–53), Oxford (1953–65), Columbia (1938–9, 1959–60, 1965–71), and New York (1965–73) universities. He wrote numerous works on Russian language and literature, Serbo-Croatian, and Slavic etymology and onomastics. His contributions to Ukrainian studies can be found in his *La Langue russe au XVIe siècle (1500–1550): La flexion des noms* (1935; repr 1978), and in his studies of the calque in the Slavic literary languages (1932); of the Church Slavonic and Hellenic names of towns founded in the 18th- and 19th-century Russian Empire, particularly in Ukraine (1936); of the origin of the name 'Ruthenians' (1949, 1950, 1953); of the Kaffa charters of 1502 (1950); of Ukrainian loanwords in 17th-century Russian (1960); and of Ukrainian surnames in the chapter 'Surnames of Ukrainian Origin' and elsewhere in his *Russian Surnames* (1972). His *Selected Papers on Russian and Slavonic Philology* appeared in 1969. In the journal *Revue des études slaves* he published annual surveys of publications in Ukrainian linguistics (1931–68).

**Underground economy.** Economic activity not sanctioned by the state and not subject to legislation and government control. Other terms used to describe the underground economy are the 'shadow' or 'alternative' economy and the 'black market.' The underground economy exists because of inadequacies in the official one, or because governments may define certain activities as illicit (eg, making, selling, and consuming *narcotics). The predominant role in modern economies has been played by the regular economy. Data for the early 1980s suggest that the underground economy generated the equivalent of 7.5 percent of the gross national product in Great Britain and of 10 percent of that in the United States. The size of the underground economy in the USSR and Ukraine has been difficult to establish because the underground economy has been so pervasive. In recent years, with increasing shortages, its size has grown. Rough estimates suggest that some 20 million people in the USSR were involved.

The means of production in the USSR were nationalized, and the state had a monopoly on most economic activity; much of the economic activity that was illegal would have been perfectly legal in a capitalist country. Unsanctioned economic activity, including production outside the state plan, was a punishable offense, and the death penalty was applied to major economic crimes.

The forms of exchange in the underground economy have been classified as gray, brown, and black markets. The gray market consists of money and barter transactions that are not officially recorded and are thus untaxed. They include renting apartments and houses, private tuition, and individual payment for services. The gray market is the most widespread. Sociological studies show that 83 percent of the Soviet population paid money for goods and services over and above the official state rate. In cities the gray market accounted for half of shoe repair, almost half of the repair of apartments, 40 percent of the repair of automobiles, a third of the repair of household appliances, and 40 percent of tailoring. The entire gray market of medical services was estimated as a 2.5- to 3-billion-ruble business. The USSR State Planning Committee estimated that the gray market turnover in the service sector was 14 to 16 billion rubles annually, or the equivalent of about 30 percent of the total value of paid services provided by the state.

The brown market is based on the unofficial redistribution of production. Because of chronic shortages in the USSR, demand has exceeded the supply of a commodity at its official price. Some commodities have vanished almost as soon as they came into the shops and have been sold illegally. The brown market has entailed the widespread corruption of employees in the distribution and retail sectors. In Ukraine in 1989–90, brown market prices for goods in short supply were 5 to 10 times higher than the official state price; in the early 1980s they were 1.5 to 2 times higher. The growth of the brown economy has resulted in a rapid increase in money supply, which in turn has fueled speculation.

The black market involves wide-scale speculation in illegally imported commodities, illegal goods (foreign currency, gold, and narcotics), prostitutes' services, privately distilled alcohol, goods stolen from state enterprises, and items produced from supplies pilfered from such enterprises.

Despite numerous state campaigns to stamp out the Soviet underground economy, it continued to flourish because of chronic shortages, and it has remained active since the collapse of Soviet rule. In recent years there have been many calls to legalize some of the activity that takes place in the underground economy. Privatization was suggested as a more rational solution to the economic problem but was resisted by the Soviet state, in part because it would entail higher prices, but also because state enterprises would then have to compete with private firms. The future of the underground economy in Ukraine and the other countries that made up the USSR will depend on the impact of the economic reforms introduced in 1992.

BIBLIOGRAPHY
Simis, K. USSR: Secrets of a Corrupt Society (London 1982)
Lane, D. Soviet Economy and Society (Oxford 1985)
Willis, D.K. Klass: How Russians Really Live (New York 1985)
Shmelev, N.; Popov, V. The Turning Point: Revitalizing the Soviet Economy (New York 1989)

B. Krawchenko

**Underground water.** Commonly known as groundwater, underground water is found in the soil pores and rock fissures beneath the land surface. It feeds wells and springs, maintains the dry-weather flow of streams, helps maintain the levels of lakes and ponds after overland runoff from rain or melting snow has ceased, and provides soil moisture during drought. Water from wells or springs is used for rural and urban domestic consumption, industrial processes, livestock watering, and crop irrigation. Groundwater is especially valued for its clarity, purity, cool temperature, and reliable, continuous supply, even in dry seasons and drought.

The presence, quantity, and quality of groundwater depend on a number of hydrogeological factors: climate (notably precipitation), morphology, and the nature of rocks and geologic structure. As those factors vary from place to place, they induce variations in hydrogeological conditions. In Ukraine the decline of precipitation and the rise in evaporation from the northwest to the southeast results in a corresponding decline in the quantity and quality of groundwater, especially in the strata nearest the surface. Despite the abundant precipitation in mountainous areas, steep slopes induce intensive runoff which hinders the formation of larger, water-bearing horizons called aquifers. In the steppe and forest-steppe, deep gullies and ravines tend to drain not only the surface but also groundwater, and thus lower the water table to far below the surface. Flat terrain and the shallow position of the impervious parent material are responsible for the poor drainage and marshy conditions of Polisia. Geological structure is responsible for the Dnieper-Donets, the Black Sea, and the Volhynian-Podilian artesian basins as well as for the poor supply of groundwater in the Donets Ridge and the Ukrainian Crystalline Shield.

In the Carpathian Mountains most of the precipitation runs off directly into the rivers, which are the main sources of water supply. Consequently there are few aquifers, or water-bearing strata. In Subcarpathia and in the Tysa Lowland fresh groundwater collects in the Quaternary alluvial deposits of the floodplains. Moreover, there are small artesian basins in the Tysa Lowland. Carbonated mineral waters come to the surface along the southwestern flank of the Carpathians (the Inner Carpathian Valley). Saline and alkaline mineral waters occur in the Tertiary deposits of the Subcarpathian Depression.

In the Crimean Mountains karst phenomena and underground drainage are common. Groundwater collects in several northward-sloping strata. Water is most abundant in the porous limestones and conglomerates that overlie impervious Tavriian shales. The lightly mineralized groundwater comes to the surface at the base of the mountains, where it feeds the streams and serves as a water supply.

The Black Sea Depression forms a large artesian basin. Since a large part of its surface is dissected by gullies and ravines, there are no continuous groundwater horizons near the surface. Instead there are artesian waters, found at considerable depths, with varying chemical characteristics. Mineralized waters prevail, with concentrations below 3 g/L on the border with the Ukrainian Crystalline Shield but increasing to above 5 g/L along the coasts of the Black Sea and the Sea of Azov. Fresh groundwater occurs in the western and eastern margins. Artesian waters (mostly brackish or salty) occur in over a dozen horizons at depths close to 300 m in the north and 100 m in the south. Fresh artesian water is obtained mostly from the Neogene deposits. In general that water supply is inadequate. Exceptional in this respect is the southern Kuban Lowland, which possesses Quaternary deposits rich in fresh artesian water.

Groundwaters of the Volhynian-Podilian artesian basin are generally fresh or lightly mineralized. In the severely dissected Podilian Upland the water table is found far below the surface. Artesian waters occur in deposits of Paleozoic, Mesozoic, and Cenozoic eras, but the highest-yielding strata are of the late Cretaceous period; they yield flows of up to 100 L/sec or more. The Tertiary period strata contain artesian waters with high concentrations of hydrogen sulfide.

The groundwater of the Ukrainian Crystalline Shield is variable. As a result of the intense development of gullies and ravines, the water table is usually found 20 m or more below the surface. In the interfluves the groundwater is usually saline. Potable water originates from sources along the sides of deep gullies and riverbanks and in wells on the bottom of ravines. In larger river valleys Quaternary alluvial deposits contain good drinking water. Limited quantities of groundwater occur in Paleogene deposits, in weathered deposits covering depressions in the Precambrian rock, and in fissures associated with tectonic dislocations or faults. Fissure waters, however, are usually highly mineralized.

In the Donets Basin groundwater is not abundant and is usually saline (with below 5 g/L of dissolved salts). The most accessible groundwater is obtainable from wells on the bottom of ravines or from sources along river valleys. Water under hydrostatic pressure may be found at greater depths, and the highest-yielding Cretaceous and Carboniferous deposits are located at considerable depths. The maximum yield of groundwater for those strata is estimated at 30–60 L/sec; the demand for industry, farming, and municipal uses is several times greater.

The Dnieper-Donets artesian basin occupies the Dnieper Lowland, the eastern margin of the Dnieper Upland, the Chernihiv section of Polisia, and a portion of Polisia northwest of Kiev. As a result of gullying on the higher elevations, the water table in those areas is found deep be-

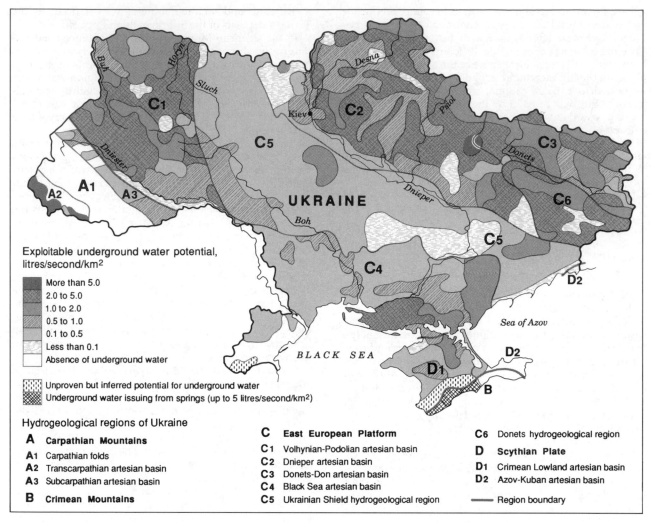

Exploitable underground water potential, litres/second/km²

- More than 5.0
- 2.0 to 5.0
- 1.0 to 2.0
- 0.5 to 1.0
- 0.1 to 0.5
- Less than 0.1
- Absence of underground water

Unproven but inferred potential for underground water
Underground water issuing from springs (up to 5 litres/second/km²)

**Hydrogeological regions of Ukraine**

**A  Carpathian Mountains**
A1  Carpathian folds
A2  Transcarpathian artesian basin
A3  Subcarpathian artesian basin

**B  Crimean Mountains**

**C  East European Platform**
C1  Volhynian-Podolian artesian basin
C2  Dnieper artesian basin
C3  Donets-Don artesian basin
C4  Black Sea artesian basin
C5  Ukrainian Shield hydrogeological region

**C6  Donets hydrogeological region**

**D  Scythian Plate**
D1  Crimean Lowland artesian basin
D2  Azov-Kuban artesian basin
—— Region boundary

# UNDERGROUND WATER

low the surface. Groundwaters are more commonly saline and are not abundant. The main sources of water supply for large cities, such as Kiev, Kharkiv, and, especially, Poltava, are the artesian waters obtainable from porous sandstones and marls of the Cretaceous, Jurassic, and Tertiary periods.

The southwestern perimeter of the Central Upland has a good supply of groundwater. Deep gullies and ravines, however, have reduced the water table to 25 or 30 m below the surface. Artesian water is available from several horizons in the Cretaceous, Carboniferous, and Devonian sedimentary rocks. More accessible groundwater is found in the Quaternary glacio-fluvial sands of larger river valleys.

As a result of poor drainage, groundwater in Polisia is closely related to surface water. Most of the water is mineralized with iron oxides or calcium oxides and, in peat bog areas, with hydrogen sulfide. In elevated areas good-quality water is obtainable from moraine sands. Artesian water is associated with Cretaceous and Jurassic deposits.

The increasing use of water by municipalities, industries, and agriculture has created a high demand for groundwater. In the mid-1980s, groundwater contributed

about 55 percent of the water consumed for various uses in the economy. About 80 percent of the water supply in the rural areas came from groundwater. Large-volume users, notably power generating stations and metallurgical plants, had to rely on surface water, for they could not obtain sufficient quantities of groundwater. Even very large cities had to develop systems of combined surface and groundwater sources. Groundwater supplies have been of good quality and adequate quantity only in the Dnieper Lowland, Polisia, and Western Ukraine. Elsewhere, notably in the Donets Basin and the Black Sea Lowland, the supplies were poor, and cities had to obtain additional surface water by means of long-distance transfers by canals and/or pipe. Meanwhile, groundwater supplies have shown signs of depletion where withdrawal rates have exceeded rates of recharge, even in areas with a good groundwater supply. Moreover, the top groundwater horizon has been subjected to pollution from fertilizers, herbicides and pesticides, chemical dumps, and, near Chornobyl, radionuclides. Consequently the wise management of groundwater has become complicated not only by the growing demand for water and the lack of correspondence between the location of good supplies and heavy demand, but also by the contamination of some of the groundwater supplies by human activities.

BIBLIOGRAPHY
*Pytannia vyvchennia pidzemnykh vod na Ukraïni: Zbirnyk* (Kiev 1959)
Babinets, A. *Podzemnye vody iugo-zapada Russkoi platformy* (Kiev 1961)
*Formuvannia resursiv pidzemnykh vod Ukraïny: Zbirnyk* (Kiev 1963)
Varava, K.; Vovk, I.; Nehoda, H. *Pidzemni vody chetvertynnykh vidkladiv platformennoï chastyny Ukraïny* (Kiev 1973)
Levkovskii, S. *Vodnye resursy Ukrainy* (Kiev 1979)
I. Stebelsky, I. Tesla

**UNDO.** See Ukrainian National Democratic Alliance.

**Unemployment.** A socioeconomic phenomenon wherein part of the population is not fully occupied in productive labor. The unemployed are those who want and are able to work but have lost their jobs and cannot find new ones. Unemployment was common in Ukraine before Soviet rule (it was common in Western Ukraine until 1939). Data on the total number of unemployed in this period are unavailable. Urban and especially rural unemployment and underemployment were mass phenomena. During the 1920s, under conditions of the *New Economic Policy, unemployment in Soviet Ukraine was significant, and labor exchanges and unemployment benefits were introduced by the state. According to the 1926 census 327,000 people were unemployed in Soviet Ukraine, and 475,000 others did not indicate an occupation. Official data did not register the large number of unemployed rural inhabitants because they indicated 'peasant' as their nominal occupation.

At the height of the First Five-Year Plan in late 1930, the Soviet regime announced that unemployment in the USSR had been eliminated. Labor exchanges were closed, assistance to the unemployed was abrogated, and everyone was obliged to work wherever he or she was assigned by the regime. From that time on, the Soviet regime continued maintaining that unemployment did not exist in the USSR and enacted laws punishing those who did not have work (eg, the law on 'parasitism'). In reality unemployment continued to be a problem, especially in the least industrialized regions of the USSR and Ukraine. A 1968 study of three towns in Rivne oblast, for example, found that 13 percent of the able-bodied population were unemployed. An analysis of the 1959 census showed that 21 million people were employed in Ukraine, whereas the average yearly number of blue-collar, white-collar, and agricultural workers was only 17 million. The difference of 4 million workers resulted primarily from underemployment, which affected 20 percent of all workers. It is true that a significant share of that number consisted of collective-farm workers, who had no retirement benefits and were forced to work to an advanced age. The 1979 census showed a similar discrepancy, of 1.5 million persons, or 6 percent. Just before the dissolution of the Union, the Soviet authorities admitted that the USSR had an unemployment problem. In 1990 it was revealed that some 2 million people were truly unemployed, and that another 8 to 10 million were underemployed.

Economic reforms designed to introduce market mechanisms have inevitably resulted in an increase in unemployment. The number of unemployed began to rise in 1989 with the introduction of self-financing enterprises and the cutback in the size of the white-collar force. According to specialists' estimates, market reforms will result in unemployment for 6 to 8 million people in what was until 1991 the USSR; some have given figures as high as 34 to 40 million. It has been estimated that 2 million people in Ukraine will be unemployed as a result of the closure of unprofitable plants. In 1990, draft legislation was prepared to establish labor exchanges and to provide unemployment benefits and job retraining. (See also *Work.)

A. Babyonyshev, B. Krawchenko

**União Agricola Instrutiva.** See Union for Agricultural Education.

**Uniates** (*uniiaty*). The popular term for Eastern Christians recognizing the authority of the papacy. In Ukraine and Belarus the term came into common use after the Church Union of *Berestia (1596), when some Orthodox Ukrainians and Belarusians united with Rome by accepting Catholic dogmas but retained their Byzantine rite and canonical peculiarities. In Catholic and Uniate writings those who rejected the Union were frequently called 'Disuniates.' The term 'Uniates' took on a negative coloration in Orthodox polemical literature, Ukrainian folk literature (dumas), and some modern Ukrainian writings (above all in the poems of T. Shevchenko). In modern times Ukrainian Catholics have objected to the term both for ecclesiological reasons and because of pejorative connotations it has taken on in writings of the Union's opponents.

**Unified Automated Gas Delivery System of the USSR** (Yedyna avtomatyzovana systema hazopostachannia USSR). A system integrating the facilities that produce, transport, and store gas with the automated systems which control those facilities. It covered the European part of the USSR, western Siberia, Central Asia, Kazakhstan, and Transcaucasia. It was established to ensure regular supplies of gas to consumers and industry. The first part of the system was completed in 1975. Ukraine's gas network is integrated with the system.

**Unified Electric Power System of the South** (Obiednana enerhetychna systema pivdnia). A power network consisting of power generating stations, including nuclear plants, and distribution lines in Ukraine and Moldavia. It was established in 1940. Its central control was in Kiev, and it was part of the *Unified Electric Power System of the USSR. The southern system is divided into nine regional electric power networks. One of them, the Lviv system, is integrated into the Mir international system serving Eastern Europe.

**Unified Electric Power System of the USSR** (Yedyna enerhetychna systema SRSR). A system integrating the regional electric power systems of the former USSR. It began to take shape in 1956, when the Unified Electric Power System of the European Part of the USSR was set up. Eventually the power networks of Kazakhstan and Siberia were connected with the latter. Some 1,000 power stations were part of the unified network, which generated and distributed almost 80 percent of the electricity produced in the USSR. The system was also connected to the former

COMECON countries through the Mir international electric power system. Its central control, known as the Central Distributing Administration, was in Moscow. The Unified Electric Power System of the Ukrainian SSR was integrated into the USSR network.

**Unified labor school** (*yedyna trudova shkola*). A system of public education established in the Ukrainian SSR in 1920. It existed as an independent system (with some changes) also known as the (H.) *Hrynko–(Y.) *Riappo system until 1932–3. The seven-year unified labor school was divided into two stages: grades one to four for children aged 8 to 12, also called elementary school; and grades five to seven for children aged 12 to 15, sometimes referred to as *incomplete secondary education. The system, developed by the Ukrainian Commissariat of Education, was at variance with the one in the RSFSR. The difference between the two systems was that the Ukrainian one stressed society's needs. The unified labor school tried to satisfy the specific demands of Ukraine, such as the dire shortage of skilled workers and specialists, and therefore introduced a polytechnical and vocational component at an early age. The emphasis on social education (understood as the active recruitment of children, the offer of protection to them in the school, and socialization was motivated by the fact that as a result of war, revolution, and famine, almost one million children had been left homeless or in single-parent families. In 1930 the Ukrainian SSR and the RSFSR commissars of education signed an agreement which paved the way for the creation of a single system of public education throughout the USSR; it was implemented in 1934. (See *Education.)

B. Krawchenko

**Unified military youth schools.** See Officer schools of the Army of the Ukrainian National Republic.

**Unified State Political Administration.** See GPU.

**Uniia** (Union; Hungarian: Unio). A publishing company in Transcarpathia, based in Uzhhorod, founded in 1902 in place of the *Society of St Basil the Great. Uniia was also active in cultural-educational activities. It published the periodicals *Nauka* (1897–1914, 1918–22), *Slovo Bozhe* (The Word of God), and the Hungarian-language *Görök-katholikus Szemle* as well as popular books. Uniia was active into the interwar period.

**Union, church.** See Berestia, Church Union of.

**Unión de Graduados Ucranios de la República Argentina.** See Society of Argentinian-Ukrainian Graduates.

**Union for Agricultural Education** (Khliborobsko-osvitnyi soiuz; Portuguese: União Agrícola Instrutiva). A community organization founded in 1922 as the Ukrainian Union at a congress of Ukrainians in Brazil in Dorizon. The group was organized by P. Karmansky as a central institution for cultural and educational activity among Brazil's Ukrainians. But the liberally minded union failed to attract the support of the Basilian clergy, who established a rival cultural-educational body, the Ukraina society, which gained the support of a majority of Brazil's Ukrai-

nians. Based initially in Porto União, Paraná, the union published *Ukraïns'kyi khliborob* *Khliborob from 1924, briefly operated a school (1925–9), and organized several cooperatives. It moved its headquarters to Curitiba in 1934 and changed its name to the present one in 1938 in an unsuccessful attempt to stave off its suppression (1940–7) during the Vargas regime's 'nationalization of culture' campaign. The group has been ideologically and politically identified with the Melnyk faction of the OUN since resuming its activities in 1947. The union's women's affiliate, the *Organization of Ukrainian Women in Brazil, maintains its own program and functions largely autonomously.

A youth section, Centro Lítero Esportivo Mocidade, was established in 1946. The renowned folk dance ensemble Barvinok was set up with union support in 1930. The union has maintained a students' residence in Curitiba and a press. Its branches are located throughout Paraná. It also has a twin organization, the Ukrainian-Brazilian Club (Clube Ucraíno-Brasileiro), which develops activities in tandem with the union. It has a library, a museum consisting largely of folk art, and a country resort in Curitiba. In 1985 it became a founding member of the *Ukrainian Brazilian Central Representation and offered its premises as a temporary headquarters.

N. Kerechuk

The presidium of the Union for the Liberation of Ukraine. From left: Andrii Zhuk, Volodymyr Doroshenko, Oleksander Skoropys-Yoltukhovsky, Mariian Melenevsky

**Union for the Liberation of Ukraine** (Soiuz vyzvolennia Ukraïny, or SVU). An organization of Ukrainian émigrés from the Russian Empire established in Austria-Hungary and Germany during the First World War as an organization representing Ukrainians under Russian domination. Its members were mostly socialists from central Ukraine who had either fled or been deported to Austrian territory. They sought to use the war, in which Austria-Hungary and Germany were pitted against the Russian Empire in the east, as a means of securing Ukrainian independence. Ultimately they hoped to establish a constitutional monarchy with a democratic structure and a unicameral legislature in Ukraine.

The SVU's presidium, initially headed by D. *Dontsov and Mykola *Zalizniak, consisted of V. *Doroshenko, M. *Melenevsky, O. *Skoropys-Yoltukhovsky, and A. *Zhuk. It was assisted by various Galician and Bukovynian activists, including I. Krypiakevych, B. Lepky, M. Lozynsky, S. Rudnytsky, V. Simovych, S. and R. Smal-Stotsky, and M.

Vozniak. The group was initially centered in Lviv, but moved to Vienna in August 1914. From its inception the SVU worked with the *Supreme Ukrainian Council (after May 1915, the *General Ukrainian Council) in Vienna, in which it was represented by Doroshenko, Skoropys-Yoltukhovsky, and Melenevsky.

Typesetters of the paper *Rozvaha* at the Union for the Liberation of Ukraine's press in the Freistadt POW camp. From left: Ovchynnyk, Dekhtiarenko, Kavun

The SVU undertook a wide-ranging campaign of distributing information and making representations to the Central Powers and neutral European nations. Its representatives were in Germany (Skoropys-Yoltukhovsky), Turkey (Melenevsky), Bulgaria and Rumania (L. Hankevych), Italy (O. Semeniv), Sweden and Norway (O. Nazaruk), and Switzerland (P. Chykalenko). It published the journal *Vistnyk Soiuza vyzvolennia Ukraïny* (edited by Doroshenko, Vozniak, and Zhuk) and the weekly *Ukrainische Nachrichten* in Vienna and *La Revue ukranienne* in Lausanne. It also issued about 50 books and 30 brochures about Ukraine in German, French, English, Italian, Turkish, Swedish, Rumanian, Croatian, Czech, and Bulgarian. Among the more important monographs it issued were Doroshenko's *Ukraïnstvo v Rosiï* (The Ukrainian Movement in Russia) and *Pivtorasta lit ukraïns'koï politychnoï dumky* (150 Years of Ukrainian Political Thought), V. Hnatiuk's *Natsional'ne vidrodzhennia avstro-uhors'kykh ukraïntsiv* (The National Revival of Austro-Hungarian Ukrainians), Krypiakevych's *Ukraïns'ke viis'ko* (The Ukrainian Military), Lozynsky's *Halychyna v zhytti Ukraïny* (Galicia in the Life of Ukraine), Rudnytsky's *Ukraina, Land und Volk*, M. Hrushevsky's *Geschichte der Ukraine*, and V. Temnytsky's *Ukraïns'ki sichovi stril'tsi* (The Ukrainian Sich Riflemen).

With the support of the Ukrainian community of Galicia and Bukovyna and the approval of the Austro-Hungarian and German military authorities the SVU provided medical, religious, and cultural services for Ukrainian prisoners of war of the Russian army held in camps in Austria (in Freistadt), Hungary (Duna-Serdagel), and Germany (Rastatt, Salzwedel, and Wetzlar). As a result of its efforts about 50,000 POWs in Germany and 30,000 in Austria were provided with hospitals, schools, libraries, reading rooms, choirs, orchestras, theaters, and courses in political economics, co-operative management, Ukrainian history and literature, and German language. Various newspapers were established, including *Rozsvit* (printed

in Rastatt), *Vil'ne slovo* (Salzwedel), *Hromads'ka dumka* (Wetzlar), *Rozvaha* (Freistadt), and *Nash holos* (Josefstadt). A number of educational brochures were also published.

In 1916 the SVU set up an office in Lviv, which established a private Ukrainian school system in those regions of Volhynia that had been occupied by Austria-Hungary. In the spring of 1917 the SVU organized a group of former Ukrainian POWs to set up about 100 schools (for about 5,500 pupils) and established the newspaper *Ridne slovo* (Biała Podlaska) in Podlachia, a region controlled by the German army at that time.

With the outbreak of the February Revolution in 1917, the SVU declared that its mandate extended beyond the supervision of POWs and the defense of Ukrainian territories under Austrian-Hungarian rule from Polish designs. As a result of SVU efforts two Ukrainian army divisions, the *Bluecoats (under the German army, commanded by V. Zelinsky) and the *Graycoats (under the Austro-Hungarians), were formed. They were later incorporated into the UNR Army.

The SVU was initially criticized by other central Ukrainians for its collaboration with the Central Powers, but its activities gradually earned acceptance, particularly as a result of its publishing. The supporters of the Entente and various Russian émigrés (including V. Lenin) were hostile to it. The Ukrainian Social Democratic journal *Borot'ba*, edited by L. *Yurkevych in Geneva, was also critical. The SVU was formally dissolved on 1 May 1918.

BIBLIOGRAPHY
*Pam'iatkova knyzhka SVU i kalendar na 1917* (Vienna 1917)
Terlets'kyi, O. *Istoriia ukraïns'koï hromady v Rashtati 1915–1918* (Leipzig 1919)
Skoropys-Ioltukhovs'kyi, O. 'Moï zlochyny,' *Khliborobs'ka Ukraïna*, nos 2–4 (Vienna 1920–1)
Bihl, W. *Österreich-Ungarn und der Bund zur Befreiung der Ukraina in Österreich und Europa* (1965)
Hornykiewicz, T. *Ereignisse in der Ukraine 1914–22*, vol 1 (Philadelphia 1966)
Rozdol's'kyi, R. 'Do istoriï SVU,' *Ukraïns'kyi samostiinyk*, 1969, nos 1–6
Fedyshyn, O. 'The Germans and the Union for the Liberation of the Ukraine, 1914–1917,' in *The Ukraine: A Study in Revolution*, ed T. Hunczak (Cambridge, Mass 1977)
*Soiuz vyzvolennia Ukrainy, 1914–1918, Viden'* (New York 1979)
A. Zhukovsky

**Union for the Liberation of Ukraine** (Spilka vyzvolennia Ukrainy, or SVU). A fictitious political organization invented by the GPU for the purpose of staging a show trial to intimidate the Ukrainian intelligentsia and put an end to Ukrainization. The trial of 45 non-Communist Ukrainian intellectuals was held in the Kharkiv Opera House from 9 March to 19 April 1930. Most of the defendants were associated with the VUAN: 2 of them (S. *Yefremov and M. *Slabchenko) were academicians, and 21 (Y. *Hermaize, O. *Cherniakhivsky, V. *Hantsov, H. *Ivanytsia, V. *Doha, K. *Shylo, H. *Holoskevych, H. *Kholodny, M. Kryvyniuk, V. *Strashkevych, V. *Sharko, V. *Durdukivsky, V. *Dubrovsky, K. *Turkalo, A. *Barbar, V. Udovenko, V. *Pidhaietsky, M. *Kudrytsky, V. *Otamanovsky, T. *Slabchenko, and A. *Nikovsky) were research associates. Many lectured at various institutes. The second-largest group consisted of educators of secondary and higher schools: Yu. Trezvynsky, O. *Hrebenetsky, N. Tokarevska, A. Zalesky, P. *Yefremov, L. Bidnova, V.

*Shchepotiev, M. Lahuta, Y. Karpovych, and K. Panchen-ko-Chalenko. Three defendants (M. *Pavlushkov, B. *Matushevsky, and M. Bily) were university students who were accused of organizing a youth branch of the SVU, the Association of Ukrainian Youth (SUM). Five were active in the co-operative movement: V. Sharko, A. *Bolozovych, M. Botvynovsky, P. *Blyzniuk, and Z. Morgulis. The brothers V. and M. *Chekhivsky were prominent leaders of the Ukrainian Autocephalous Orthodox church (UAOC). Two defendants were writers (L. *Starytska-Cherniakhivska and M. *Ivchenko), and one was a lawyer (V. Tovkach). Some of the accused had been active supporters of the UNR and had occupied high government posts in the revolutionary period. Besides the 45 accused who were put on trial, thousands of Ukrainians were arrested for 'belonging' to the SVU or SUM.

According to the prosecution the conspirators began to organize the SVU in 1926 on orders from the émigré L. *Chykalenko. Their purpose was to overthrow the Soviet regime and restore capitalism in Ukraine in 1930 or 1931 through an armed uprising of the kulaks and other capitalist elements. The rebellion was to be accompanied by an offensive by Poland and other capitalist powers. The SVU, it was alleged, had first hoped to restore the UNR and then opted for a fascist dictatorship headed by Yefremov. The police claimed to have uncovered 15 five-member cells in the VUAN, the UAOC hierarchy, the management of the rural co-operatives, and the school system, and among former 'bandits.' All the defendants were convicted, but they were given relatively lenient sentences ranging from 3 to 10 years' imprisonment. Ten were given conditional sentences and released, and seven were exiled from Ukraine for three years. In the next few years almost all of the defendants were rearrested, and perished in prison or a concentration camp.

Although the existence of the SVU and SUM as depicted at the trial has been unquestioned by Soviet historians and some opponents of the Soviet regime, most objective researchers of the period have recognized that the two organizations were contrived by the authorities for a political purpose. The SVU trial was one of the first show trials in the USSR to be aimed against the 'bourgeois nationalist intellectuals.' The specific targets of the SVU trial were the VUAN, the UAOC, and the Ukrainian co-operative movement – the three most important Ukrainian institutions that were beyond the Party's control. By linking concern for the Ukrainian language and culture with subversion, the trial established an association between national cultural assertion and treason, which would be used in the next decade to justify mass repressions against both non-Communist and Communist Ukrainian intellectuals.

On 11 August 1989 the Supreme Court of the Ukrainian SSR admitted that the charges against the 45 defendants at the SVU trial were groundless, and annulled their sentences.

BIBLIOGRAPHY
Kostiuk, H. *Stalinist Rule in the Ukraine: A Study in the Decade of Mass Terror (1929–1939)* (New York 1960)
Sniehir'ov, H. *Naboï dlia rozstrilu* (New York–Toronto 1980)
Mace, J. *Communism and the Dilemmas of National Liberation: National Communism in Soviet Ukraine, 1918–1933* (Cambridge, Mass 1983)

J. Mace

**Union Nationale Ukrainienne en France.** See Ukrainian National Alliance in France.

**Union of Agrarians-Statists.** See Ukrainian Union of Agrarians-Statists.

**Union of Architects of Ukraine** (Spilka arkhitektoriv Ukrainy, or SAU). A professional organization of architects, architectural conservators, and other specialists connected with architecture. It was created in 1933 by the Party in place of the Alliance of Contemporary Architects of Ukraine (OSAU), which had been founded in Kiev in 1928 and dissolved along with other Ukrainian organizations in April 1932. The union was a member of the Union of Architects of the USSR. Its highest governing body was the republican congress, held in 1937 and every five years after 1955. The congress elected the executive, and the executive selected the presidium. There were 28 oblast and city branches of the SAU. In 1983 their combined membership was over 2,600. The SAU has various sections, such as bridge construction, industrial architecture, architectural education, and theory. It has published the journals *Arkhitektura Radians'koï Ukraïny* (1938–41), *Arkhitektura i budivnytstvo* (1953–7), and, with the State Construction Committee, *Stroitel'stvo i arkhitektura* (est 1957). Its presidents have been H. Holovko (1937–75) and I. Sedak (elected in 1975). In the late 1980s the SAU freed itself of Party control. In 1992 it had 3,500 members, and its president was I. Shpara.

**Union of Artists of Ukraine** (Spilka khudozhnykiv Ukrainy). The only official organization of artists and art scholars in Soviet Ukraine since the Party banned all other artistic organizations in 1932 and set up an organizational committee. In 1938 the union was officially founded at its first congress. Subsequent congresses have been held every five or six years since 1956. The union has been divided into sections (painting, sculpture, poster design, graphic art, large-scale decorative art, applied art, artistic design, stage design) and commissions (art criticism and art scholarship). The Art Fund of the Ukrainian SSR has been administered by it. The union has been divided into 20 oblast organizations. In 1983 their combined membership was 2,200. The union's official organs have been *Maliarstvo i skul'ptura* and *Obrazotvorche mystetstvo*. Its presidents have been I. Boichenko (1938–41), O. Pashchenko (1941–4), V. Kasiian (1944–9), O. Shovkunenko (1949–51), M. Khmelko (1951–5), M. Derehus (1955–62), V. Borodai (1968–82), O. Skoblykov (1982–3), and O. Lopukhov (elected 1983). In the late 1980s the union freed itself of Party control, and it no longer propagates *socialist realism as the only artistic approach. Many of Ukraine's talented artists have never been members of the union. In 1992 the union had 3,600 members, and its president was V. Chepelyk.

**Union of Carpathian Youth** (Soiuz molodi Karpat). A youth organization founded in 1945 for Ukrainians of the Prešov region of Slovakia. In 1949 it had 20,000 enrolled members, with 225 branches. The leading members of the union were mainly Russophiles. The first head was I. Dzurenda; he was followed by A. Yedynak and A. Sushko. The union published the monthly *Kolokol'chik-dzvinochok* in Russian and Ukrainian and a supplement to the newspaper *Priashevshchina* called *Slovo molodezhy*. It ceased operations in 1950, and attempts to revive it in 1968 were unsuccessful.

**Union of Cinematographers of Ukraine** (Spilka kinematohrafistiv Ukrainy). An organization which unites film directors, screenwriters, film actors, cameramen, stage designers, sound producers, and technical staff, established in 1958 and subordinated until 1991 to the USSR Union of Cinematographers in Moscow. In 1988 it had over 7,000 members. It has commissions and sections of film dramaturgy, art cinematography, animation, documentary film, science film, theory and history of cinema, television, criticism, and actor training and publishes the journal *Novyny kinoekranu*. In 1992 the union had only 828 members, and its president was M. Bielikov.

**Union of Composers of Ukraine** (Spilka kompozytoriv Ukrainy). An administrative and policy-making body of composers and musicologists established in 1932 to replace Proletmuz and the All-Ukrainian Society of Revolutionary Musicians. The association, called the Union of Soviet Composers in 1932–57, sought to 'educate' its members politically and ideologically and to support them in their creative work. It has been headed by such musical luminaries as B. *Liatoshynsky (1939–41), L. *Revutsky (1944–8), H. *Verovka (1948–52), P. *Kozytsky (1952–6), K. *Dankevych (1956–67), H. *Maiboroda (1967–8), A. *Shtoharenko (1968–89), and Ye. *Stankovych (1989–91). The union administered the Ukrainian branch of the USSR Musical Foundation, publishes (since 1970) the journal *Muzyka*, and supported the work of the Music Society of the Ukrainian SSR. In 1992 it had 292 members, and its president was M. *Stepanenko.

**Union of Constructively Creative Forces of Ukraine** (Soiuz konstruktyvno-tvorchykh syl Ukrainy). An émigré Ukrainian organization established in Munich in 1948. Drawing upon Ukrainians who were not affiliated with any existing political party for its membership, the union sought to develop a high degree of economic independence for Ukrainian émigrés. Its president was T. Leontii, and its members included H. Prokopchuk, V. Horbachevsky, P. Kashynsky, and V. Odynsky. The union supported the Ukrainian National Council. It ceased to exist in the 1950s.

**Union of Contemporary Artists of Ukraine** (Obiednannia suchasnykh myttsiv Ukrainy, or OSMU). An association of Soviet Ukrainian artists, established in Kharkiv in 1927. Its members – L. Kramarenko, V. Palmov, A. Petrytsky, I. Pleshchynsky, Yu. Sadylenko, M. Sharonov, D. Shavykin, I. Shtilman, A. Taran, O. Zhdanko, and others – followed the newer schools of European modernist art, particularly those in France and the postfuturists. OSMU was disbanded in 1932 under pressure from the Stalinist regime.

**Union of Hetmanites-Statists.** See United Hetman Organization.

**Union of Industry, Trade, Finance, and Agriculture** (Soiuz promyshlennosti, torgovli, finansov i selskogo khoziaistva, or Protofis). An organization of Russian and Russified political activists in Ukraine, founded in the spring of 1918. The leaders of the organization included the banker and factory owner N. von Ditmar, the sugar-beet magnate A. Bobrinsky, and large landowners, such as A. Golitsyn and V. Kochubei. Protofis represented the conservative business elite of Ukraine and strongly supported the *Hetman government. Just prior to the German-sponsored coup d'état by Gen P. Skoropadsky it presented a series of demands to the Central Rada government, including closer economic ties between Russia and Ukraine, a greater say for representatives of industry and trade in government, and a reaffirmation of private ownership and an end to socialized industry and agriculture. Protofis also warned against the introduction of Ukrainian as the official language of the UNR; its claim was that such a measure would hurt economic growth and alienate the intellectuals. The organization held its first conference in Kiev on 15–18 May 1918. The conference attracted almost 1,000 delegates, including F. Lyzohub and S. Gutnik, both members of Skoropadsky's government. After the fall of the Hetman government the union suspended its activities, although it resumed them briefly during Gen A. Denikin's occupation of Kiev.

**Union of Journalists of the Ukrainian SSR** (Spilka zhurnalistiv URSR). The CPU-controlled organization of journalists, editors, and others working for newspapers, journals, publishing houses, news agencies, radio, and television in Ukraine, founded in 1959 as the Ukrainian branch of the USSR Union of Journalists. It is a voluntary organization; its goals were the improvement of journalism in Ukraine through the sponsorship of courses and conferences, the exchange of information among its members, and the fostering of relations with journalists in the rest of the USSR and the Soviet-bloc countries. Until recently an important agitation and propaganda tool of the Party, the union was organized into a republican administration, oblast sections, and over 540 primary organizations based at individual newspapers, journals, and television and radio stations. In 1987 it had over 11,200 members. Since 1964 it has awarded an annual prize for the best journalism, and since 1975 it has published a professional and methodological monthly journal, *Zhurnalist Ukrainy*. The presidents have been I. Syromolotny, I. Pedaniuk, Yu. Lazebnyk, Ya. Pashko, B. Sirobaba, and M. Shybyk. The union's seventh congress in October 1990 proclaimed the union's professional and creative independence, reconstituted it as a new organization free of Party and government control, and renamed it the Union of Journalists of Ukraine. I. Spodarenko was elected president.

**Union of Landowners.** See All-Ukrainian Union of Landowners.

**Union of Lands of United Ukraine** (Soiuz zemel sobornoi Ukrainy). A liberal émigré political party established in Aschaffenburg, Germany, in 1948. The group was renamed the Peasant party in 1950. V. *Dolenko was its main organizer and leader until his death in 1971. Then Yu. Semenko headed the group. Other figures associated with the party included V. Dubiv, V. Dubrovsky, and D. Melnyk. The party's head office was moved to New York; its journal, *Ukrains'kyi selianyn*, was published in Munich.

**Union of Peasant Associations** (Soiuz selianskykh spilok). An organization of Ukrainian peasants, established in Galicia in 1925. The Polish authorities suppressed its branches in Volhynia. The union's head office in Lviv co-ordinated the work of county and local associations. It organized life and livestock insurance, spearheaded strikes, and negotiated collective agreements for hired workers, especially for teamsters and lumbermen. The union co-operated with the Ukrainian Socialist Radical party and published a supplement, *Selians'ka spilka*, in the party's organ *Hromads'kyi holos*. The president of the union was M. Stakhiv, and the secretary was O. Pavliv-Bilozersky. The organization was dissolved in 1939, when Soviet troops occupied Western Ukraine.

**Union of Red Cross and Red Crescent Societies of the USSR** (Soiuz obshchestv Krasnogo kresta i Krasnogo polumesiatsa SSSR). An all-Union voluntary public organization, formed in 1923, that embraced the 11 republican Red Cross and 4 Red Crescent societies of the USSR. Its purpose was to co-ordinate their operations within and beyond the USSR, to address problems common to all the societies, and to defend the interests of the republican societies before the USSR government. The charter of the union was approved by the Council of People's Commissars on 1 September 1925. In 1934 the union was accepted into the League of Red Cross Societies. It published the journal *Sovetskii krasnyi krest* from 1951. Membership in the societies numbered several million volunteer nurses, health inspectors, and medical workers, who assisted government medical bodies to control infectious diseases, provide health care, improve working and living conditions, and furnish first aid in emergencies.

Members of the delegation of the Union of Ruthenians and Ukrainians of Croatia during their visit to the Presidium of the Supreme Soviet in Kiev in 1988. From left: the Presidium official Leonid Horovy, delegates Vasyl Sikorsky and Yuliiana Furmints, the Presidium secretary Mykola Khomenko, and the union's president Teodor Frytsky

**Union of Ruthenians and Ukrainians of Croatia** (Soiuz rusinokh i ukraintsokh Horvatskei, or Soiuz rusyniv i ukraintsiv Khorvatii). An umbrella organization representing four local cultural and educational societies in Croatia. It was established in 1968 in Vukovar, where it maintained its head office until Vukovar was destroyed by Serbian forces in 1992. Its purpose was to cultivate the Ukrainian language and Ukrainian folklore, arts, and historical research. It promoted theater and art groups, con-

certs, exhibits of folk costumes, and dance ensembles. The union published the journal *Nova dumka* (1971–91) and maintained a special library, an ethnographic collection, an artists' colony, a literary section, and a research commission on the history of Ruthenians and Ukrainians in Croatia. It published a number of books, including F. Labosh's *Istoriia rusinokh Bachkei, Srimu i Slavonii 1745–1918* (History of the Ruthenians of Bačka, Srem, and Slavonia, 1745–1918, 1979) and *Dumky z Dunaiu: Litopys Soiuzu rusyniv i ukraintsiv Khorvatii ta redaktsiï 'Novoï dumky'* (Thoughts from the Danube: A Chronicle of the Union of Ruthenians and Ukrainians of Croatia and the Editorial Office of *Nova dumka*, 1989).

**Union of Salvation** (Soiuz spaseniia). One of the first clandestine political organizations in the Russian Empire and a forerunner of the *Decembrist movement. It was founded in St Petersburg in February 1816 by a group of guard officers, including A. and N. Muravev, Prince S. Trubetskoi, and P. Pestel. Some of its 25 to 30 members were Ukrainian by descent or had close ties with Ukraine: M. and S. Muravev-Apostol, V. Volkhovsky, A. Poltoratsky, and M. Novikov. Its goal was to abolish serfdom and absolutism and to establish a constitutional monarchy. In the spring of 1817 the union was dissolved and replaced by the *Union of Welfare.

**Union of Song and Music Societies** (Soiuz spivatskykh i muzychnykh tovarystv). An organization for the promotion of music in Western Ukraine, founded in Lviv in 1903 by V. Shukhevych and A. *Vakhnianyn at the first convention of the Boian choruses. The union's main initiative was to open a school, which was reorganized into the Lysenko Higher Institute of Music (1912). In 1907 the association was renamed the *Lysenko Music Society.

**Union of Soviet Socialist Republics** (Soiuz Radianskykh Sotsialistychnykh Respublik, or USSR). A 20th-century federal state made up of 15 constituent socialist republics on the former territory of the Russian Empire. It was the largest state in the world, with a territory of 22,276,000 sq km (land area only), and spanned two continents, with 23 percent of its landmass in Europe and the remaining 77 percent in Asia. With a population exceeding 288 million (1 January 1990), it was, after China and India, the third most populous country in the world. During its existence from 1944 to 1991 the USSR incorporated 97 percent of the Ukrainian contiguous ethnographic territory and was the home of approx 93 percent of the Ukrainians in the world.

History. The assumption of power by Bolshevik forces in Russia in 1917 precipitated a civil war between Communist and anti-Communist forces (also known as the Whites), which lasted for three years, until the latter were defeated. At the same time the Bolsheviks waged war against non-Russian nations that had formed separate states after the collapse of the empire in 1917; one of the major conflicts was the *Ukrainian-Soviet War. By 1920 the Bolsheviks had assumed contol of virtually all the lands that formerly had constituted *Russia and the Russian Empire. The Baltic nations, Finland, and Poland were the only former imperial possessions to escape inclusion in the Soviet Union, and they emerged as independent states in their own right. Ukrainian and Belarusian lands were divided between Poland and the *RSFSR in 1921 by the Peace Treaty of *Riga, which concluded the Polish-Soviet War. After the Bolshevik victory the formerly independent national republics were converted into Soviet republics under the control of the RSFSR, and on 30 December 1922 they were formally linked together in a federative union, the USSR.

In their drive to power the Bolsheviks instituted a policy of *War Communism and practiced extensive terror (conducted by the secret police, the Cheka) to subdue the population. In order to consolidate its power and reconstruct the war-torn economy the Soviet government replaced those practices in 1921 with the concessions of the *New Economic Policy (NEP). Several years of relative peace followed, until the assumption of power by J. *Stalin, following the death of V. *Lenin in 1924, and his elimination of both the *Left and the *Right opposition (L. Trotsky, G. Zinovev, L. Kamenev, N. Bukharin, A. Rykov). In 1928-9 the NEP came to an end as the first *five-year plan was instituted in an effort to industrialize the Union and collectivize agriculture. The plan was accompanied in the late 1920s and especially in the mid-1930s by the growth of totalitarianism, the application of mass *terror by the secret police (the GPU, later the NKVD) against all groups of the population, the establishment of an enormous network of forced labor camps, the destruction of the peasantry as a class by means of forced collectivization and the liquidation of the so-called kulaks, and the destruction of non-Russian national intelligentsias. That first wave of Stalinist social policy, marked by collectivization, the enforcement of prohibitively high food procurements in the grain-producing regions, and open hostility toward the peasantry (particularly in Ukraine), culminated in the massive man-made *famine of 1932-3, which claimed millions of lives. At the same time the nominally federative nature of the Soviet Union was undermined, proponents of national communism arrested or eliminated, and an increasingly centralized state structure established. Stalinist repressions continued throughout the 1930s and resulted in the devastation of the national cultures of most non-Russian peoples in the USSR. Stalin also launched a wholesale attack on the Union's cultural, intellectual, military, and political elite that culminated in 1937-8 with the *Yezhov terror.

In the earliest years of its existence the USSR, as a state ostensibly based on the ideology of communism, was regarded as a pariah among world powers, and remained largely isolated. Nevertheless it maintained a loyal following among Communists and Communist sympathizers beyond its borders and played a dominant role in the affairs of the *Communist International (Comintern). In the 1930s the USSR began to seek rapprochement with Western democracies, particularly with the rise of anticommunist powers such as Nazi Germany, fascist Italy, and imperial Japan. It entered the League of Nations (1934), signed several nonaggression pacts (with Poland and France in 1932, Italy in 1934) and mutual assistance treaties (with France and Czechoslovakia in 1935), and pursued a policy of establishing united fronts. Unwilling to risk its own security, the USSR chose not to participate openly in the civil wars of China and Spain. It even came to terms with Nazi Germany by signing the *Molotov-Ribbentrop Pact in 1939, which established a nonaggres-

sion agreement between them and delineated their respective spheres of influence in Eastern Europe. The accord paved the way for the partitioning of Poland later that year. The USSR occupied the former western borderlands of the Russian Empire (Estonia, Latvia, Lithuania, a region of Finland, western Belarus, western Volhynia, western Polisia, and Bessarabia) and annexed Galicia and northern Bukovyna, lands that had never been part of the Russian Empire.

The German advance into Poland triggered the Second World War. On the eve of the conflict the USSR was militarily and politically weakened by the purges of 1937-8. Its loss of strength had already become apparent during a war with Finland, which country, despite territorial losses, had managed to defend its independence. During the first months of the German invasion the Wehrmacht defeated and captured a large portion of the Soviet army and advanced to the outskirts of Moscow and Leningrad. The German attack, launched on 22 June 1941, initiated a dogged war for the very existence of the USSR. Stalin and the Communist party of the USSR called it the Great Patriotic War and strove to harness Russian national sentiments (rather than a belief in communist ideals) to sustain their military efforts. Russian military tradition was rejuvenated, the Russian Orthodox church was used to promote patriotism, and the Comintern was abolished (1943). At the same time Soviet propaganda exploited the anti-German feelings of the non-Russian nations that were occupied and persecuted by the Nazis. Together with the Western Allies (the United States, Britain, France, and others) and with considerable material and technical assistance from the United States, the USSR came out of the war victorious. Its victory was also helped by the destructive and racist Nazi German policy toward Eastern Europeans, which gave rise to resistance on the part of both the non-Russian nations, particularly the Ukrainians (see *Organization of Ukrainian Nationalists, *Ukrainian Insurgent Army, and *Soviet partisans in Ukraine), and the Russians themselves, on the territory occupied by the Germans.

After the defeat of the Nazis the Soviets firmly re-established their authority in the parts of the USSR that had been overrun. The USSR increased its territory in Eastern Europe and the Far East through a series of agreements attained by means of a succession of tripartite meetings, notably the *Yalta Conference. Included in the gains were Western Ukrainian lands previously ruled by Poland, Czechoslovakia, and Rumania. A bloc of communist satellite countries was formed in Eastern and Central Europe, with which the USSR established treaties of friendship and mutual assistance (1948), economic integration (the Council for Mutual Economic Assistance, or Comecon, in 1949), and unified military command (the Warsaw Pact, 1955). Only Yugoslavia (1948) and Albania (1960) managed to slip out of Soviet control. There was considerable resistance to the extension of Soviet territory. The Ukrainians (in the western borderland regions) and the Balts continued guerrilla actions against the new regime until the mid-1950s. An anti-Soviet rebellion erupted in Hungary in 1956 and was suppressed by Soviet forces. Peaceful attempts to sever dependency in Poland (1956) and Czechoslovakia (1968) were also suppressed. The 'legitimacy' of Soviet interests in its Eastern European satellites was eventually provided by the so-called Brezhnev Doctrine, which provided an ideological justification for the 1968 invasion of Czechoslovakia.

As a result of its territorial expansion the Soviet Union emerged as a world superpower after the Second World War. Its cordial relations with its wartime allies, however, soured after a clerk in the Soviet embassy in Canada, I. *Gouzenko, after his defection in September 1945, revealed the extent and intentions of Soviet espionage in the West. The so-called Cold War between the USSR and the United States then erupted and was fought out for over four decades on political and propaganda fronts and occasionally in limited wars between their respective client states. The economic cost to the Soviet Union was enormous, as vast resources were allocated for military expenditures and economic and technical assistance for client states. The USSR managed to develop a formidible military and industrial capacity during that period, but it fell chronically short in providing its citizens with a high standard of housing, food stocks, medical service, and consumer goods.

Politically the USSR was totally dominated by Stalin and the Communist party in the immediate postwar period. Social control was maintained through an extensive internal security force (the *KGB), and large numbers of people were imprisoned for political reasons. Even laborers who had been forceably taken by the Germans and who after the war were subjected to *repatriation to the Soviet Union against their will were sent to labor camps, their 'crime' being the departure, no matter how forced, from the Soviet Union. The Party also sought to extend its tenets throughout society and launched a campaign spearheaded by A. Zhdanov against 'formalism, cosmopolitanism, and stooping to the decadent West.' Marked strongly by anti-Semitism and chauvinism, the policy provided a convenient means of expanding a policy of *Russification.

Stalin's death (1953) and a change of leadership (G. Malenkov, N. *Khrushchev) brought about a temporary détente or 'thaw' in Soviet life in 1956–9. Khrushchev's dramatic revelations about the extent of Stalin's crimes at the 20th Congress of the CPSU in 1956 provided a particularly important catalyst for the process. The successful removal of the 'anti-Party group' (Malenkov, V. Molotov, and L. Kaganovich) strengthened Khrushchev's position and allowed him to combine his function as first secretary of the CC of the CPSU with that of the premier or head of the government (in place of N. Bulganin, who had resigned). Setbacks in the economy (notably the costs of developing highly mechanized state farms and amenity-supplied agrocities, and the crop failures and dust storms in the virgin lands) and in foreign brinkmanship (the Cuban missile crisis, the border conflict with China), and, in particular, the strains on the Soviet bloc caused by liberalization in the USSR, prompted a reaction. In October 1964 Khrushchev was deposed and replaced by a 'collective leadership' headed by L. *Brezhnev. Like Khrushchev before him, Brezhnev gradually strengthened his position in party and government leadership. In 1973 and 1977 two Ukrainians were removed from the Politburo, P. *Shelest and M. *Pidhirny (Podgorny). Pidhirny lost his prestigious, albeit largely ceremonial, position as president of the Supreme Soviet to Brezhnev.

The Brezhnev leadership assumed a highly conservative course that in some respects returned to Stalin's methods (neo-Stalinism). The role of the KGB increased, and the military assumed an even greater influence on the armaments policy. The party apparatus and government bureaucracy grew in importance, and corruption, already well established in Soviet life, became rampant. The limited dynamism seen in cultural and intellectual life during the Khrushchev thaw was largely brought under control. The economy did not expand to any significant degree. Critics later characterized the Brezhnev regime as being afflicted with a particular malaise and referred to it as 'the period of stagnation.'

Political *dissidents in the Soviet Union were repressed during the Brezhnev era, as they had been under previous administrations. The methods of the state security organs, however, had become more refined, and the sort of mass terror experienced by Soviet society under Stalin was not repeated. Publications, however, that did not conform to official ideology were closed down, and their editors commonly jailed. Ukrainians and other non-Russian peoples in the USSR constituted a disproportionately high percentage of dissidents, for in addition to general political rights they were also often concerned about the national rights of their respective peoples. The issue became particularly acute in the 1970s, after Brezhnev's *nationality policy downplayed the existence of different peoples in the USSR and began to promote the concept of a *Soviet people. The regime also took a sharper course against religion. Under the combined pressure of internal protests and external diplomatic action, the emigration of Jews increased, and a number of dissidents, chiefly Russian, were exiled to the West.

While tightening up controls internally and maintaining a Cold War with China, the Soviet leadership began, in the early 1970s, a policy of détente with the West. Negotiations and agreements were concluded with the United States that limited nuclear armaments and broadened trade relations. The USSR obtained nearly 15 billion dollars' worth (1976) of credits from Western Europe, the United States, and Japan for the purchase of machinery and grain. Such help carried it through a series of poor harvests and aided its industries with modern Western technology. In 1976 the USSR signed the Helsinki Accord, which provided Western recognition of the post–Second World War boundaries in Eastern Europe. In return the Soviet Union and its satellite countries made certain human rights guarantees, agreed to broaden the access granted to Western media, and promised to allow greater emigration. The USSR did not abide by any of those commitments. Its failure to act was highlighted by dissident groups formed in 1976–7 in Moscow, Kiev, Vilnius, Tbilisi, and Yerevan to monitor the implementation of the Helsinki agreement. Three groups succeeded in gaining international publicity with their protests. In due course their leaders were arrested, and their activities repressed.

Brezhnev died in November 1982 and was succeeded, in rapid succession, by Yu. Andropov (who died in February 1984), K. Chernenko (who died in March 1985), and M. Gorbachev. Gorbachev initiated major disarmament measures that diffused Cold War tensions with the West. He also launched the policies of perestroika (Ukrainian: *perebudova*), or restructuring, in an effort to stimulate the Soviet economy, and of glasnost (Ukrainian: *hlasnist*), or openness, in order to allow for greater freedom of social and intellectual life in the Union. The Party was increasingly criticized in the media and challenged politically by a host of new parties and unsanctioned civic groups known (in Ukrainian) as *neformaly. National movements also threatened the power of the USSR. The competence of the Party and the Soviet system in general was particular-

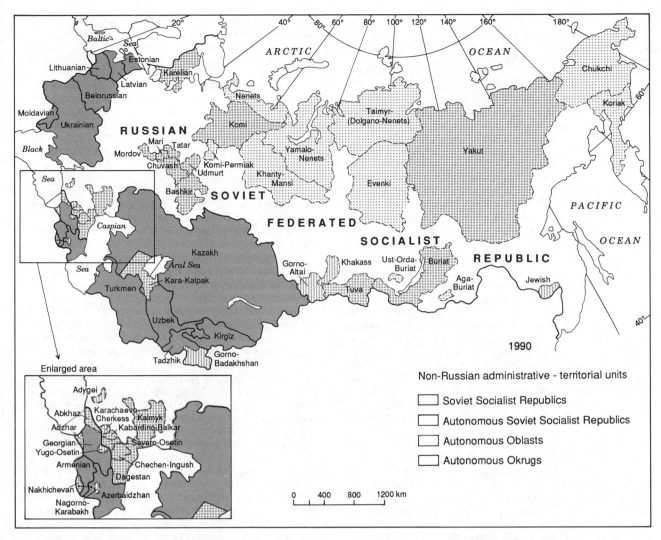

## UNION OF SOVIET SOCIALIST REPUBLICS, POLITICAL-ADMINISTRATIVE SUBDIVISION

ly brought into question as the cover-up of the Chornobyl nuclear disaster of 1986 came to light.

The visible collapse of the USSR began in 1989, when its satellite countries in Central and Eastern Europe (East Germany, Czechoslovakia, Hungary, Poland, and Rumania) swept out their Soviet-backed Communist governments in rapid succession. In 1990 the three Baltic states declared themselves independent of the Soviet Union, and the majority of republics made claims to sovereignty (by which their local laws took precedence over those of the USSR). The uncertainty of the political situation was accentuated by a growing economic crisis. Matters quickly came to a head after an abortive coup attempt led by G. Yanaev in August 1991. The Ukrainian SSR declared itself independent of the USSR (on 24 August); it was followed soon by most of the other Soviet republics. On 1 December 1991 Ukraine's declaration was confirmed by a decisive vote in a national referendum. It proved to be the deathblow to the Union. A week later, on 8 December 1991, L. Kravchuk (Ukraine), B. Yeltsin (Russia), and S. Sushkevich (Belorussia, now renamed Belarus) met in Minsk, ostensibly to discuss bilateral trading arrangements; they

emerged from the gathering with a blueprint for the establishment of a Commonwealth of Independent States (CIS) that would render the USSR obsolete. After a last-ditch effort to save the Union, Gorbachev accepted the CIS as a fait accompli and resigned from his position as president of the Soviet Union, on 25 December. The state was formally dissolved the following day (26 December 1991) during the final session of the Supreme Soviet. Subsequently the RSFSR (reconstituted as the Russian Federation) sought and obtained international recognition as the legal successor state to the USSR and assumed its seat at the United Nations; in addition it seized a large portion of the USSR's assets and appropriated numerous central institutions (bank, post office, and the like) directly into its own state structure.

**Administrative-political structure.** The existence of the RSFSR alongside a buffer of 'independent' Soviet republics tied to each other in a military, economic, and diplomatic union was considered by the Russian Communist party as a temporary phenomenon. It sought, in fact, to unite the Soviet republics tightly and to unify their internal and external policies under one monolithic leadership. The principle of unity was shared by many factions of the party, but there was no common concept as to how it should be achieved. The Russian centralists demanded the inclusion of the republics in the RSFSR as autonomous units (the so-called autonomy concept, represented principally by Stalin), whereas some national-Communists (such as M. *Skrypnyk, Kh. Rakovsky, P. Mdivani) desired a union of equal partners on the basis of confederation. An intermediate formula, that of a federative union, was supported by Lenin, and eventually won out. The founding act of the new state was the 'Declaration and Agreement Concerning the Establishment of the USSR,' approved at the First Congress of the Soviets of the USSR, 30 December 1922. The Second Congress, 31 January 1924, approved the 'Constitution of the USSR.' Despite the opposition of some non-Russian representatives, the constitution was formulated along the lines of a centralized federation.

The union and autonomous republics, autonomous oblasts, and autonomous okrugs were political-territorial units that formed the federative structure of the USSR. The krais (despite the presence of autonomous units within them) and the oblasts had only administrative-territorial significance. The chief criterion for the establishment and division of the political-territorial units was the presence of a particular nationality or people in a particular territory. The Soviet constitution provided the Union and autonomous republics with the characteristics of state structures, including their own constitutions. The Union republics thus had theoretical indicators of sovereignty. In that way the federal structure of the USSR was unique, and in many respects it evoked contradictory interpretations in constitutional law and political science (see *Federalism).

Initially the main Soviet principle of political order was considered to be the dictatorship of the proletariat, with the soviets (councils) as the organs of administration. Following the 22nd Congress of the CPSU the emphasis in guiding principles shifted to the 'general peoples' nature of the Soviet state and the strengthening of social democracy through the participation of social organizations and the masses in the administration.

The governing state organs of the USSR in 1923–36 were the Congress of Soviets of the USSR and the Central Executive Committee of the USSR. The executive and administrative power was wielded by the Soviet of People's Commissars (Sovnarkom), chaired first by Lenin and later by A. Rykov. Deputies to the All-Union Congress of the Soviets were selected by the republics by indirect vote, with one deputy per 25,000 electors in the cities and one per 100,000 in the rural areas.

The Central Executive Committee consisted of two chambers, the Soviet of the Union and the Soviet of the Nationalities. The Congress of the Soviets elected members to the Soviet of the Union in proportion to the population of each republic. The Soviet of the Nationalities consisted of delegates from the Union and autonomous republics (five from each), and the autonomous oblasts (one each). The Central Executive Committee met three times a year. Between sessions the Presidium performed legislative and control functions and could exercise the prerogative for negating the acts of the republican organs.

The Sovnarkom consisted of the all-Union people's commissars (External Affairs, Transport, Post and Telegraph, Army and Navy, and External Trade) and the uni-

fied or directive commissars (Supreme Council of the National Economy, Finance, Land Affairs, Labor, Worker-Peasant Control), who had counterparts in the Union republics. Matters of sociocultural or local significance were deferred to the republics to be managed by republican commissars along general guidelines established by the USSR government. The Supreme Court both served as the highest judicial body of the USSR and had some control functions over the republican courts. Legislation tended to be unified, but in many matters there were separate republican codes (civil and criminal codes and process, administrative law, and the like).

Some institutional changes were brought about by the new USSR Constitution of 5 December 1936. The functions of the All-Union Congress of the Soviets and the Central Executive Committee were taken over by the Supreme Soviet of the USSR, consisting of two chambers, the Soviet of the Union and the Soviet of the Nationalities. The Supreme Soviet convened two times a year for sessions, which were held either separately in each chamber or jointly in a plenary meeting. Between the sessions of the Supreme Soviet all the functions of the highest state organ were performed by the Presidium of the Supreme Soviet, with the president as its chairman. The highest executive-administrative organ of the government with broad managerial (in fact, legislative) functions became the Council of Ministers of the USSR (until 1946 the Council of People's Commissars), whose members were chosen by the Supreme Soviet or its Presidium. The individual ministries and bodies of state administration (committees, councils, administrations) were either all-Union, directly managing all matters throughout the USSR, or Union-republican, with respective organs at the republican level as well. The ministries encompassed almost all governmental, economic, cultural, and social matters and left the republics with jurisdiction over minor matters (usually of local significance). A movement to expand republican rights in the late 1950s and to decentralize the national economy through the establishment of regional economic councils (known as the Sovnarkhozy) was ended in the early 1960s.

The Supreme Court of the USSR was the highest court, and the USSR state public prosecutor and his prosecuting magistracy provided the central supervision of the execution of Soviet law. In October 1977 an extraordinary session of the Supreme Soviet of the USSR approved a new constitution for the USSR that broadened the prerogatives of the Union over the republics and strengthened the leading role of the Communist party in state affairs. Its provisions negated the previous constitutional right of Union republics to have their own national military units, although in practice the military forces of the USSR were strictly centralized and nationally mixed. It also repealed provisions that recognized most of the non-Russian languages as the official languages of their respective Union republics.

In accordance with the concept of democratic centralism, government administration in the USSR and the direction of its economy were highly centralized. The representative bodies of the government actually exercised nominal control; real power resided in smaller groups (such as the Presidium of the Council of Ministers) or individual administrators, who invariably were leading Party functionaries. Centralization among state political organs and administrative bodies was maintained through a tight chain of answerability.

The most characteristic trait of the Soviet political system was the leading role of the *Communist Party of the Soviet Union. Effectively it was a superior body that gave direction to and controlled the state from the outside. Its members held all the key positions at every level of government. The real and highest power in the USSR was concentrated in the Politburo and the Secretariat of the Central Committee of the CPSU. The secretariats of the CPSU and the CPU, and even those at the oblast and raion level of the party committees, had divisions structured parallel to the ministries and other government bodies. Those divisions carried out directives and maintained control functions over government establishments in addition to appointing people to leading posts or removing them from administrative responsibility.

The absolute political dominance of the Party (no other political organs or opposition was allowed), with its dogmatic ideology, control over economic resources, and monopoly over the means of communication, effectively rendered the Soviet Union a model totalitarian state. The CPSU was disbanded shortly after the abortive coup attempt of August 1991, and its assets were seized by republican governments.

**The Ukrainian diaspora in the USSR.** Although most Ukrainians lived within the limits of the Ukrainian SSR and in adjacent areas that constitute contiguous Ukrainian ethnographic territory, there were large numbers of Ukrainians who lived in other areas of the Soviet Union. The contiguous Ukrainian ethnic territory included (along with the Ukrainian SSR) the predominantly Ukrainian-settled territories in the bordering RSFSR, consisting of the southern parts of Belgorod, Kursk, and Voronezh oblasts (northern Slobidska Ukraine), part of Rostov oblast (the Donets-Don), and most of Krasnodar krai (the Kuban), as well as a southern wedge in the Belorussian SSR, incorporating most of Brest and the southwestern strip of Homel oblasts. Contiguous mixed Ukrainian-Russian territory (in which the Ukrainians constituted a minority) could be found in central and in a portion of eastern North Caucasia (the rest of Krasnodar krai and nearly all of Stavropol krai) as well as in the southern part of Briansk oblast north of Chernihiv. Because Soviet census figures after 1926 do not provide nationality and language characteristics of the population for units smaller than the oblast or krai, it is impossible to ascertain the status of the contiguous Ukrainian and mixed territories beyond the Ukrainian SSR in a definitive manner. The 1926 census itself also underestimates the number of USSR Ukrainians outside the Ukrainian SSR.

*To 1930.* The Ukrainian diaspora in the USSR was distributed in a geographical pattern established before the Revolution of 1917. The first Russian census in 1897 recorded that the Ukrainian diaspora numbered 1,560,000 in the Russian Empire, with 1,232,000 in the European part, 311,000 east of the Urals, and 17,000 south of the Caucasus. Between 1897 and 1914 a major shift occurred as Ukrainians emigrated in large numbers beyond the Urals (nearly 1.5 million, after taking returnees into account). By 1914 the number of Ukrainians in the Asian part of Russia had increased to approx 2 million. Meanwhile, in European Russia the assimilation of Ukrainians began to speed up, especially in those areas where they were not highly

concentrated, or were dispersed among the Russian population. During and immediately after the First World War Ukrainian emigration to the east was insignificant, and the geographical pattern of Ukrainian settlement there remained unchanged. Therefore, the 1914 situation was closely reflected in the 1926 census, even though it tended to understate the number of Ukrainians (for example, in the Central, or Industrial, region of Russia it identified only 41,300 Ukrainians, in spite of the fact that 121,000 persons indicated their place of birth as Ukraine). Nevertheless the 1926 census noted that 3,450,000 Ukrainians lived beyond contiguous Ukrainian ethnic territory, 1,310,000 in the European USSR and 2,140,000 in the Asian.

The distribution of the Ukrainian diaspora in the European USSR in 1926 was similar to what it had been in 1897. Nearly 340,000 Ukrainians lived in the RSFSR borderland regions, including 170,000 in Kursk gubernia, 69,000 in Voronezh gubernia, and 79,000 in the Donets subregion (later the western half of Rostov oblast). The largest number (771,000) lived along the Volga and in the foothills of the Southern Urals in large concentrations. Those concentrations included approx 440,000 in the Lower Volga region (15,000 in the Kalmyk Autonomous Oblast, 14,000 in Astrakhan gubernia, 141,000 in Stalingrad [later Volgograd] gubernia, 202,000 in Saratov gubernia, and 69,000 in the Volga German ASSR), 206,000 in the Middle Volga region (Samara and Orenburg gubernias), 77,000 in the Bashkir ASSR, and 48,000 in Ural oblast. Fully 92 percent of that Ukrainian diaspora was rural population.

Other large concentrations of Ukrainians were in North Caucasia, not far from the contiguous Ukrainian territory. The largest ones were at Rostov-na-Donu (59,200, but only 5,600 in 1897), Groznyi (8,800), Novocherkassk (7,500, with 2,600 in 1897), and Vladikavkaz (now Ordzhonikidze, 4,000).

In the rest of the European USSR there were almost 100,000 Ukrainians in the diaspora (nearly 10,000 in the Belorussian SSR and the rest in the RSFSR). They resided mostly in large cities and had come there as workers or employees. The largest concentration of Ukrainians was in Moscow (16,100 in 1926, 4,500 in 1897); it was followed by those in Leningrad (10,800 in 1926, 5,200 in 1897), Kaluga (7,000), Orenburg (3,500), Voronezh (3,400), and Kursk (2,400).

The Ukrainian diaspora in the Asian USSR was, by 1926, more numerous than that in the European. According to the 1926 census it had reached 2,160,000 (only 328,000 in 1897) and thus represented 62 percent of all the Ukrainian diaspora in the USSR (only 20 percent in 1897). In other words, the Ukrainian presence in Asia increased from 1.6 percent of all the Ukrainians in the Russian Empire in 1897 to 6.8 percent of all the Ukrainians in the USSR in 1926. Its share of all population in the Asian USSR also doubled, from 3.2 percent in 1897 to 6.4 percent in 1926. Within the borders of *Kazakhstan lived 861,000 Ukrainians, who constituted 13.2 percent of its population, within *Siberia there were 853,000 Ukrainians (9.5 percent of the Siberian population); in the Far Eastern krai there were 315,000 Ukrainians (16.8 percent of the Far Eastern population); in the Kirgiz SSR, 64,000 (6.5 percent); in the remaining Central Asian republics, 33,000 (0.5 percent); and south of the Caucasus, 35,000 (0.6 percent).

The Ukrainian population in Asia was not uniformly distributed. The Ukrainian peasants, who migrated beyond the Urals, searched for physical conditions comparable to those in Ukraine: they shunned arid deserts (in the south) and forests (in the north) and settled where possible in a forest-steppe or steppe zone. Consequently the Ukrainians were concentrated in two areas, the Far East and the Siberian-Kazakh steppe. The latter area, located in southwestern Siberia and northern Kazakhstan, is the eastern extremity of the broad zones of chernozem soils and the forest-steppe and steppe zones that extend all the way from Ukraine. In both the *Far East and the Siberian-Kazakh steppe the Ukrainians constituted a majority in some places. Ukrainians in the Asian USSR were almost exclusively rural (97 percent).

According to the 1926 census about one-quarter of the Ukrainian diaspora in the USSR claimed Russian as its native tongue. That indicator should be considered with caution, for linguistic Russification was impeded by the fact that 95 percent of the Ukrainians were rural and lived in large concentrations or villages with their own way of life, seldom intermarried with members of other nationalities, and were first- or sometimes second-generation immigrants from Ukraine.

As of 1 January 1933 the Ukrainian diaspora in the USSR was estimated at 4.5 million, or some 14 percent of all the Ukrainians in the USSR, with 3 million in Asia and 1.5 million in Europe. By comparison, at that time there were 1.2 million Ukrainians in North America and up to 0.6 million in Europe beyond the contiguous Ukrainian ethnic territories in Poland, Czechoslovakia, and Rumania.

*Changes after 1930.* Changes in the 1930s and later concerning the Ukrainian diaspora cannot be firmly documented because of scanty and less reliable subsequent census data (1959, 1970, 1979, and 1989). In the 1930s the Ukrainian diaspora in the European USSR suffered disruptions of the sort experienced by the Ukrainian population in its contiguous ethnic territory, though with proportionately smaller losses. Those disruptions included deaths resulting from repression, hunger, and deportations, escapes from repression to other parts of the USSR, and escapes, deportations, and deaths during the Second World War. Moreover, more individuals preferred not to identify themselves as Ukrainians, and succumbed to the increasing tempo of Russification. By contrast, the number of Ukrainians in the Asian USSR continued to grow as a result of new immigration from Ukraine. During the period of collectivization the immigrants were exiled peasants and those who saved themselves from hunger and repression by fleeing to industrial towns in Asia. Subsequent immigration included Second World War evacuees (only some of whom subsequently returned to Ukraine), exiles and prisoners of concentration camps (many of whom remained in Asia after their release), settlers recruited for the virgin lands program in the 1950s and for major construction and industrial projects, and those who migrated to the Asian USSR in search of higher income or better living conditions. Similar immigration processes (though much weaker) in the European part of the RSFSR involved the forced or voluntary migration of Ukrainians to the north or to industrial centers. The Soviet authorities also encouraged interrepublican transfers of population, with the migration of Ukrainians to other republics and a reciprocal movement of other populations to Ukraine.

The present state of the Ukrainian diaspora in the former USSR is the product of the aforementioned process-

es and of a constant and increasingly intense process of Russification. Beyond the borders of the Ukrainian SSR Ukrainians had no national rights, not even on the territory of the Kuban (part of the contiguous Ukrainian ethnic territory, where Ukrainians once constituted the majority of the population). There were no Ukrainian schools, societies, or organizations outside the Ukrainian SSR, and no newspapers or books published. The dissemination of printed matter in Ukrainian from the Ukrainian SSR as well as cultural contacts with the Ukrainian SSR was difficult. Such a state of affairs resulted in the linguistic and national Russification of the Ukrainian diaspora. The greatest losses within the Ukrainian diaspora (in census terms) occurred in the Ukrainian-Russian borderland, in those oblasts or krais which in whole or in part made up the contiguous Ukrainian ethnic territory beyond the Ukrainian SSR – Belgorod, Kursk, and Voronezh oblasts – and in Subcaucasia, which consisted of the Kuban, Stavropol, and, partly, Terek regions and is now encompassed by Krasnodar and Stavropol krais and Rostov oblast.

The Soviet census indicates a drop in the Ukrainian population in the Ukrainian northeastern borderlands by 1959 to 17 percent of the 1926 numbers, and a reduction in the use of Ukrainian as the mother tongue (among Ukrainians) from 84 to 8 percent. For the southeastern borderlands official Soviet figures indicate a Ukrainian population drop to 10.5 percent of 1926 numbers and a reduction in the use of Ukrainian as the mother tongue from 50 to 42 percent. The situation is comparable to that in the northern Chernihiv land, in the southern part of the present Briansk oblast, where the number of census Ukrainians declined from 128,000 in 1926 to 21,000 in 1970. A similar decline is indicated for that portion of Ukrainian Polisia that in 1939 was joined to the Belorussian SSR (nearly 600,000 Ukrainians): the proportion of Ukrainians there fell from 68.8 percent in 1931 (calculations by V. Kubijovyč) to 2.3 percent in 1959 (official Soviet figures).

The Ukrainians of the diaspora in the USSR living in the non-Russian republics tended to rely on the Russian language for communication with others rather than the language of the local national population. According to the 1979 census only 17 percent of the Ukrainians in the Belorussian SSR knew Belarusian, and 14 percent in the Moldavian SSR knew Moldavian. In the Baltic republics 17 percent in Lithuania knew Lithuanian, 7 percent in Latvia knew Latvian, and 6 percent in Estonia knew Estonian. In Central Asia the figure for those Ukrainians knowing the local language reached only 3 percent in the Uzbek SSR, 2 percent in the Kirgiz and Tadzhik SSRs, 1 percent in the Turkmen SSR, and scarcely 0.4 percent in the Kazakh SSR. Conversely, non-Russians settled in Ukraine commonly lacked a knowledge of the Ukrainian language and relied on Russian.

The Ukrainian diaspora in the USSR has changed dramatically, from being overwhelmingly rural (92 percent in 1926) to being predominantly urban (65 percent in 1970). Recently the level of urbanization of the Ukrainian diaspora exceeded the USSR average (56 percent in 1970) and especially that of the Ukrainians in the Ukrainian SSR (46 percent in 1970). The level of urbanization of the Ukrainian diaspora was not uniform: it was highest in the Baltic republics, the industrial regions of the RSFSR, and Transcaucasia, but it fell below the average in the Kirgiz SSR (51

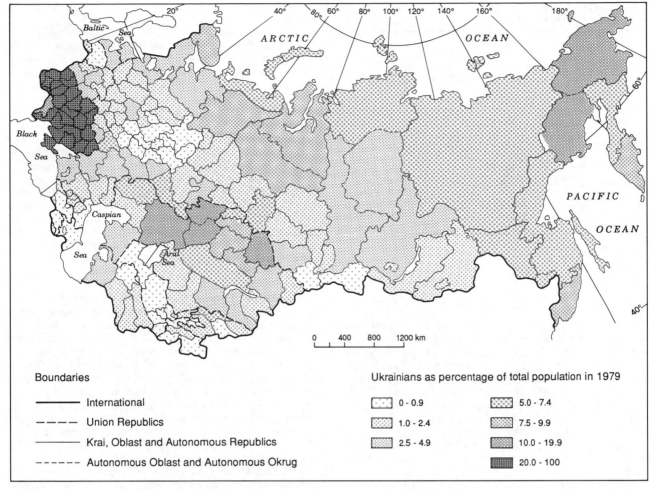

## UKRAINIANS IN THE USSR, 1979

**Boundaries**

—————— International

— — — — Union Republics

————— Krai, Oblast and Autonomous Republics

- - - - - Autonomous Oblast and Autonomous Okrug

**Ukrainians as percentage of total population in 1979**

| 0 - 0.9 | 5.0 - 7.4 |
| 1.0 - 2.4 | 7.5 - 9.9 |
| 2.5 - 4.9 | 10.0 - 19.9 |
| | 20.0 - 100 |

percent in 1970). It was particularly low in the Moldavian SSR (44 percent in 1970). The high levels of urbanization resulted in major changes in life-style, with an increased frequency of mixed marriages and accelerated Russification.

The largest Ukrainian concentration in the European USSR was found, as in 1926, in the Volga and Ural regions (771,000 in 1926, 779,000 in 1989). Ukrainian as the mother tongue was claimed by 41 percent of the people; an additional 12 percent claimed Ukrainian as their second language (1989). By 1970, 65 percent lived in cities, whereas in 1926 only 8 percent were urban. The distribution by oblast was also similar to that in 1926: the largest number (1989) lived in the oblasts of Cheliabinsk (110,000, or 3 percent of the population), Orenburg (102,000, or 5 percent), Saratov (102,000, or 4 percent), Sverdlovsk (82,000, or 1.8 percent), Kuibyshev (82,000 or 2.5 percent), Volgograd (79,000, or 3 percent), and in the Bashkir ASSR (75,000, or 2 percent).

A new concentration of the Ukrainian diaspora had emerged in the Central (Industrial) region of the RSFSR. In 1968–9 alone approx 96,500 persons migrated there from the Ukrainian SSR (in their place, the Central region provided 59,400 migrants to the Ukrainian SSR). The number of Ukrainians in the Central region had grown constantly, from approx 13,000 in 1897 to some 675,000 in 1989. The largest concentration of Ukrainians was in the city of *Moscow (253,000 in 1989). Of the Ukrainians living in the Central region, 86 percent (1970) were urban, with 44 percent declaring Ukrainian as their mother tongue, and another 22 percent declaring it as their second language (1989).

Similar conditions existed in the Western region. As in the Central region, the Ukrainian diaspora was more recent, having grown from 6,000 in 1897 to 293,000 in 1989, and was predominantly urban (88 percent in 1970). The main concentration of Ukrainians was in Leningrad (now St Petersburg; 151,000 in 1989, or 3 percent of the city's population, compared to approx 5,000 in 1897), although significant numbers were also found in Leningrad oblast (49,200, or 3 percent) and Kaliningrad oblast (formerly East Prussia, 62,800, or 7.2 percent). Some 42 percent (1989) indicated Ukrainian as their mother tongue, and another 22 percent declared it their second language.

Ukrainian settlement in the European north was also relatively recent. In 1926 approx 1,100 Ukrainians lived there, but by 1959 their number had grown to 194,000, and by 1970 to 230,200, mostly (78 percent) urban. Whereas the number of Ukrainians in the old-settled Vologda oblast was relatively small (13,000, or 1.4 percent of Vologda's population), the number increased to the north, in the

Union republics in the USSR: territory, total population, and
Ukrainian population, 1989

| Administrative unit | Territory in sq km | Total population in 1,000s | Ukrainians | |
|---|---|---|---|---|
| | | | 1,000s | % of total |
| USSR | 22,403,000 | 286,731 | 44,306 | 100.0 |
| Ukrainian SSR | 603,700 | 51,707 | 37,500 | 84.6 |
| RSFSR | 17,075,400 | 147,400 | 4,400 | 9.9 |
| Kazakh SSR | 2,717,300 | 16,536 | 900 | 2.0 |
| Moldavian SSR | 33,700 | 4,338 | 600 | 1.3 |
| Belorussian SSR | 207,600 | 10,200 | 290 | 0.6 |
| Uzbek SSR | 447,400 | 19,905 | 154 | 0.3 |
| Kirgiz SSR | 198,500 | 4,290 | 108 | 0.2 |
| Latvian SSR | 64,500 | 2,680 | 92 | 0.2 |
| Georgian SSR | 69,700 | 5,443 | 52 | 0.1 |
| Azerbaidzhan SSR | 86,600 | 7,038 | 32 | 0.07 |
| Estonian SSR | 45,100 | 1,573 | 48 | 0.1 |
| Turkmen SSR | 488,100 | 3,534 | 36 | 0.08 |
| Tadzhik SSR | 143,100 | 5,109 | 41 | 0.09 |
| Lithuanian SSR | 65,200 | 3,690 | 45 | 0.1 |
| Armenian SSR | 29,800 | 3,288 | 8 | 0.02 |

Karelian ASSR (27,400, or 3.8 percent), in Arkhangelsk oblast (51,200, or 3.7 percent), in Murmansk oblast (56,300, or 7 percent), and, especially, in the Komi ASSR (83,000, or 8.6 percent). Ukrainian males outnumbered females in the region two to one (1959), especially in older age cohorts; that fact indicated the substantial number of former prisoners of concentration camps (notably Vorkuta) and exiles. The number of Ukrainians continued to grow with immigration from the Ukrainian SSR. By 1989 there were 310,000 in the northern region (with increases to 104,200 in the Komi ASSR and 105,100 in the naval base of Murmansk).

Linguistically the Ukrainian diaspora in the European north was the least assimilated. In 1970 some 59 percent considered Ukrainian as their mother tongue, and 15 percent used Ukrainian as their second language; by 1989 the figures had declined to 47 and 17 percent respectively.

Among the other neighboring Union republics there was a very large Ukrainian presence in the Moldavian SSR (600,400 in 1989). In the Belorussian SSR the Ukrainians (according to the 1989 census) numbered 291,000 (2.9 percent of the republic's population), of whom 132,100 (45 percent) declared Ukrainian as their mother tongue. Most were urban residents, scattered through all the oblasts. Even in those regions that contained parts of the contiguous Ukrainian ethnic territory Ukrainians were identified by census figures as a tiny minority – in Brest oblast, 60,600 (4 percent) and in Homel oblast, 68,600 (4 percent).

Ukrainians came to live in the Baltic republics in substantial numbers only after the Second World War. Most (88 percent in 1970) have resided in cities, many as civil servants, notably the capital cities of Riga (43,600 in 1989, nearly half of the Ukrainians in Latvia and 4.8 percent of the city's population), Tallinn (24,200, or 50 percent of the Ukrainians of Estonia and 4.8 percent of the city's population), and Vilnius (13,300, or 30 percent of the Ukrainians in Lithuania and 2.3 percent of the city's population). A large proportion declared Ukrainian as their mother tongue (53 percent in 1970, 48 percent in 1979) or knew it

as their second language (15 percent in both 1970 and 1989).

Despite a large influx of Ukrainians into the Asian USSR census figures suggested only a slight absolute growth, from 2,160,000 in 1926 to 2,378,000 in 1959, and a declining share of the Ukrainian population, from 6.7 to 4.2 percent. Although increases in the numbers of Ukrainians in the Far East and especially in eastern Siberia were noted, the census suggested a decline in their number in western Siberia and the Kazakh SSR despite an influx of Ukrainian workers for the virgin lands program. By 1970, census figures indicated losses in the regions of western Siberia, eastern Siberia, and the Far East, thereby suggesting the continuing Russification of the second-generation Ukrainians. Meanwhile, the number of Ukrainians in the Asian north and northeast increased, from 4,000 in 1926 to 116,300 in 1970 and 252,100 in 1989. Many settled in the Yakut ASSR (in 1989, 77,100, or 7 percent of the ASSR's population), in Kamchatka oblast (43,000, or 9 percent), in Sakhalin oblast (46,200, or 6.5 percent), and, especially, in Magadan oblast (85,800, or 15.4 percent), with its infamous Kolyma. Magadan oblast represented the highest proportion of Ukrainian population in any oblast of the RSFSR. Clearly the Ukrainian element continued to play a prominent role among the exiles and workers of the north. Urbanization in Siberia and the Far East was above the USSR average, especially in the north, a trend that also pertained to Ukrainians (66 percent for all Siberia and the Far East in 1970). In all of Siberia and the Far East 44 percent of Ukrainians declared Ukrainian as their mother tongue, and 14 percent knew it as their second language, in 1989. The respective percentages for the three separate regions were 46.5 and 10.9 percent for western Siberia, 48.7 and 15.4 percent for eastern Siberia, and 37.4 and 16.7 percent for the Far East. (See also *Siberia and *Far East.)

In the Kazakh and Kirgiz republics the size of the Ukrainian diaspora (according to the official statistics) changed little over time: from 925,000 in 1926 to 1,007,300 in 1970 (largely in Kazakhstan, offset in part by a small decline in Kirgizia), followed by a decline, and then to 1,004,000 in 1989. The proportion of the Ukrainian population declined throughout the period, as both the Kazakh and Kirgiz populations experienced rapid growth. Urbanization among Ukrainians was not rapid, because many of the newcomers were settled on the virgin lands (54 percent in Kazakhstan and 51 percent in Kirgizia in 1970). Ukrainian as the mother tongue was claimed by 36.6 percent of the Ukrainians in Kazakhstan (1989); another 5.8 percent used Ukrainian as their second language; the respective indicators for Kirgizia were 34 and 6.0 percent. (See *Kazakhstan and *Kirgizia.)

Most Ukrainians in Central Asia (formerly Turkestan) settled there in the post–Second World War period. In 1926 the old settlers, mostly grain farmers in the border foothills or workers in the cities, numbered 33,000; by 1959 their number had grown to 136,000, by 1970 to 179,000, and by 1989 to 230,100, virtually all in the cities. The largest Ukrainian concentration in Central Asia is in the Uzbek SSR (153,200, or 0.8 percent of the republic's population in 1989). In 1970 approx 87 percent of the Ukrainians in the republic were urbanized. In the capital city of Tashkent lived 60,000 Ukrainians in 1989 (2.9 percent of the city's population), the largest known urban concentration of Ukrainians in the Asian USSR. In the Turkmen SSR there were 35,600 Ukrainians (1 percent of the republic's population) in 1989. Of those, 29,500 (82 percent) lived in cities, mainly (11,000) in the capital of Ashkhabad (where they constituted 4.3 percent of the city's population). In the Tadzhik SSR the 41,400 Ukrainians (0.8 percent) in 1989 indicated a rise from 31,700 (1.1 percent) in 1970, when 29,400 (92 percent) were urban, and 13,300 lived in the capital, Dushanbe (constituting 3.6 percent of the city's population). In sum, over one-third of all Ukrainians living in Central Asia resided in the capital cities of their respective republics. Since that diaspora was mostly recent, its language retention indicators were somewhat higher: 50.0 percent declared Ukrainian as their mother tongue, and 6.5 percent indicated Ukrainian as their second language.

In the Transcaucasian republics most Ukrainians lived in Georgia (52,400, or 1 percent of the population in 1989); it was followed by Azerbaidzhan (32,300, or 0.5 percent) and Armenia (8,300, or 0.3 percent). The largest urban concentration of Ukrainians in Transcaucasia was in Baku (14,400 in 1970); it was followed by Tbilisi (10,600) and Yerevan (2,600). Their linguistic retention was slightly better than that of their counterparts in Central Asia: in 1989 fully 59 percent declared Ukrainian as their mother tongue, and another 7.2 percent gave Ukrainian as their second language.

The census data provided only a sketchy indication of the status of the Ukrainian diaspora in the Asian USSR. The large migrations (until the 1960s) from Ukraine, along with a relatively high level of natural increase, presumably would have resulted in a population of Ukrainian origin in the Asian USSR of seven to eight million. As they stand, the official figures suggest that the majority of the migration had undergone extensive Russification.

BIBLIOGRAPHY
Shibaev, V. *Etnicheskii sostav naseleniia Evropeiskoi chasti Soiuza* SSR (Leningrad 1930)
Smal'-Stots'kyi, R. (ed). *Ukraïns'ka liudnist' v SSSR* (Warsaw 1931)
Pipes, R. *The Formation of the Soviet Union: Communism and Nationalism, 1917–1923* (Cambridge, Mass 1954)
*Itogi Vsesoiuznoi perepisi naseleniia 1959 g.* (Moscow 1962–3)
Strong, J. (ed). *The Soviet Union under Brezhnev and Kosygin* (New York 1971)
*Itogi Vsesoiuznoi perepisi naseleniia 1970 goda*, vol 4, *Natsional'nyi sostav naseleniia SSSR* (Moscow 1973)
Marunchak, M. *Ukraïntsi v SSSR poza kordonamy URSR* (Winnipeg 1974)
Lewis, R.; Rowland, R.; Clem, R. *Nationality and Population Change in Russia and the USSR: An Evaluation of Census Data, 1897–1970* (New York 1976)
Carrère d'Encausse, H. *L'Empire éclaté: La révolte des nations en URSS* (Paris 1978)
*Chislennost' i sostav naseleniia SSSR: Po dannym Vsesoiuznoi perepisi naseleniia 1979 goda* (Moscow 1984)
Kort, M. *The Soviet Colossus: A History of the USSR*, 2nd edn (Boston 1987)
Westwood, J. *Endurance and Endeavour: Russian History, 1812–1986*, 3rd edn (London–New York 1987)
Treadgold, D. *Twentieth Century Russia*, 7th edn (Boulder, Colo 1990)
*Natsional'nyi sostav naseleniia SSSR po dannym vsesoiuznoi perepisi naseleniia 1989 g.* (Moscow 1991)
V. Kubijovyč, V. Markus, I. Stebelsky

**Union of Struggle for the Liberation of the Working Class** (Russian: Soiuz borby za osvobozhdenie rabo-chego klassa). An underground organization in Kiev, founded in March 1897 by Russian and Polish social democrats. Initially the union had 30 members. Among the most active were P. Belousov, B. Eidelman, and P. Tuchapsky. The union issued revolutionary leaflets, brochures, and a newspaper, maintained a library, and had contacts with other Marxist groups in the Russian Empire. The First Congress of the *Russian Social Democratic Workers' party in March 1898 in Minsk was called at the union's insistence. Shortly after the congress 142 of the union's members were arrested by the tsarist police and banished to Siberia, whereupon the union ceased to exist.

**Union of Subcarpathian Ukrainian Students** (Soiuz pidkarpatskykh ukrainskykh [ruskykh] studentiv). A Ukrainophile student organization that existed in Czechoslovakia in the interwar period from 1920. It organized cultural-educational activities (such as a traveling theater) in Prague and Subcarpathia, belonged to the *Central Union of Ukrainian Students, and from 1933 published the journal *Proboiem*.

**Union of the Archangel Michael** (Russian: Soiuz Mikhaila Arkhangela; aka the Russian People's Union of the Archangel Michael). A reactionary, anti-Semitic, Russian chauvinist organization founded in March 1908 by a group that broke away from the *Union of the Russian People. It was led by a Bessarabian landowner, V. Purishkevich, and received financial support from official tsarist circles. Like the Union of the Russian People, the union defended tsarist autocracy, Orthodoxy, Russification, and a centralized Russian Empire. It terrorized and assassinated liberals, revolutionaries, Jews, Ukrainians, Poles, and other non-Russians considered enemies of the regime. It did not, however, boycott the Third Russian State Duma (although it demanded nonsuffrage for Jews and limits on the number of non-Russian representatives), and it supported the Stolypin agrarian reforms. In Ukraine the union had particularly strong branches in Odessa and Kiev. It was banned soon after the February Revolution of 1917. (See also *Black Hundreds.)

**Union of the Free Press** (German: Verband der Freien Presse; Ukrainian: Soiuz vilnoi presy). An organization of Eastern European and Soviet émigré publishers and journalists in postwar Germany. It was established on the initiative of Ukrainian journalists in Augsburg in 1947 to provide the Western world with objective information about and analyses of events in Soviet-occupied Europe and the USSR. Initially it had members from 6 nations; the 6 had grown to 23 by the 1960s. The union published the monthly *Freie Presse-Korrespondenz* from 1952 (with interruptions) and informational brochures, and in 1962 it initiated the creation of the Bonn-based Federation of Exiled Journalists in Europe. It became inactive in the 1970s. Ukrainians who served as its presidents were R. Ilnytsky (the first president) and V. Lenyk (1962–74).

**Union of the Russian People** (Russian: Soiuz russkago naroda). The largest and most extremist of the Russian *Black Hundreds organizations, founded in St Petersburg in October 1905. It was led by A. Dubrovin and, from 1910, N. Markov. It fanatically defended tsarist autocracy, an indivisible Russian Empire, and Orthodoxy, and its members terrorized and murdered 'traitors' and enemies: Jews, liberals, socialists, revolutionaries, and participants in the non-Russian national movements. Enjoying the moral and financial support of Tsar Nicholas II, the government, the police, and even Russian Orthodox bishops and members of the Holy Synod, the union founded 900 branches throughout the Russian Empire and published a daily, *Russkoe znamia*, and other reactionary propaganda. In Ukraine, where it was particularly strong in the cities of Odessa, Kiev, and Chernihiv and at the Pochaiv Monastery in Volhynia gubernia, it disseminated militantly anti-Semitic and anti-Ukrainian views through periodicals such as its own *Pochaevskii listok* and the right-wing Kiev daily, *Kievlianin*. During the Revolution of 1905–6 the union's 'combat bands,' consisting mostly of lumpen and criminal elements, instigated many vicious anti-Semitic *pogroms, particularly in Odessa, Yalta, and Chernihiv gubernia. In the 1907–12 Third Russian State Duma at least 32 deputies were union members. From 1908 on the union increasingly lost popular support, and several factions (eg, the *Union of the Archangel Michael) broke away from it. In 1913 the union inspired the infamous anti-Semitic *Beilis affair in Kiev. It was banned after the February Revolution of 1917.

R. Senkus

### Union of Theatrical Workers of Ukraine (Spilka teatralnykh diiachiv Ukrainy, or STD).

An organization established at an extraordinary congress of the *Ukrainian Theatrical Society (UTT) in Kiev in 1987. A 95-member executive was elected, headed by S. *Danchenko (artistic director of the Kiev Ukrainian Drama Theater). The resolutions of the UTT congress defined the main objectives of the STD: to carry out Party policy in this branch of the arts (an objective abandoned in 1991), to promote high idealism and esthetic quality in theater, to support the search for new masters of the stage, and to take responsibility for all theater issues in Ukraine. In 1992 the STD had 6,000 members, and its president was L. *Taniuk.

### Union of Ukrainian Autonomists-Federalists.
See Ukrainian Party of Socialists-Federalists.

### Union of Ukrainian Citizens in France (Soiuz ukrainskykh hromadian u Frantsii, or SUHUF).
A Sovietophile organization founded in 1925 in Paris. It opposed other Ukrainian émigré groups, particularly UNR government-in-exile circles, and the state of Poland (for which it gained favor among some expatriate Galicians). Some members traveled to Soviet Ukraine and became disillusioned; others continued returning there even after 1945. Leading activists included E. *Borschak, A. Halip, M. Norych-Dzikovsky, N. Okhrym, O. Savchyn, O. Sevriuk, and I. Zhahaidak. Its official organs were *Ukraïns'ki visty* (1926–9, edited by E. Borschak) and *Vistnyk SUHUF* (1929–30). It became particularly popular during the period of Ukrainization in the Ukrainian SSR. In 1927 it included 16 branches with approx 800 members, but its membership declined after the onset of the Stalinist terror in Ukraine. In 1929 the organization experienced a split during which leading figures, such as Borschak and Sevriuk, left, and in 1932 it ceased its activity.

### Union of Ukrainian Community Centres of Canada (Soiuz ukrainskykh narodnykh domiv, or SUND).
A national association of Ukrainian community centers (*narodni domy*) under the umbrella of the *Ukrainian Self-Reliance League (SUS). Established in 1927 as an integral part of the SUS organizational structure, the union was formally incorporated in 1928. T. *Ferley was the first official president of the national association, which provided support for the member groups of SUS and sponsored Ukrainian Saturday schools. The extensive depopulation of rural areas inhabited by Ukrainians that accompanied urbanization in the 1950s caused its decline.

### Union of Ukrainian Emigrant Engineers and Technicians in Poland (Spilka inzheneriv i tekhnikiv ukraintsiv-emigrantiv u Polshchi).
A professional organization founded in Warsaw in 1927. Its membership rose from an initial 17 to 174 in 1930. The union had four branches and a head office in Warsaw. Until 1939 it promoted scientific work, supported students by means of scholarships, and published its own bulletin, *Visty* (1928–9). The leading members of the union were I. Shovheniv, A. Lukashevych, Ye. Glovinsky, M. Shtanko, L. Panasenko, V. Shevchenko, and M. Teliha. It ceased its activity after the Nazi invasion of Poland.

The executive of the Union of Ukrainian Emigrant Women in Poland in 1932–3. Sitting, from left: O. Sadovska, V. Zavadska, M. Livytska, N. Salikovska; standing: K. Chaikivska, O. Lukasevych, E. Kmet, M. Shevchenko

### Union of Ukrainian Emigrant Women in Poland (Soiuz ukrainok emigrantok u Polshchi, or SUEP).
The organization originated in 1921 as a women's section of the *Ukrainian Central Committee in Poland. Headed by O. Lukasevych, it was reorganized in 1924 as the Women's Hromada under the presidency of N. Salikovska, and in 1927 as the SUEP under the leadership of M. Livytska. The union had a branch in Lviv. At first the union was involved mostly in charity work, but later it also organized literary readings, choirs, theatrical performances, and embroidery. It was disbanded in 1939.

### Union of Ukrainian Emigré Organizations in France (Soiuz ukrainskykh emigrantskykh orhanizatsii u Frantsii).
An organization founded on 3–4 January 1925 in Paris. It consisted of groups that supported the UNR government-in-exile, mainly political emigrants from central Ukraine. Notwithstanding its posture as an umbrella group for Ukrainians in France, the union maintained an intense rivalry with the Sovietophile *Union of Ukrainian Citizens in France, the *Ukrainian Hromada in France,

and the *Ukrainian National Union. In the 1930s the union co-ordinated the work of 56 community associations and seven Plast scouting groups. Fifteen of its affiliates offered Ukrainian language instruction for youth. It held 16 general assemblies and published the *Biuleten'* (later it provided columns in the weekly *Tryzub*). Throughout its existence the union was headed by M. *Shumytsky; other activists included Yu. Batsura, M. Kovalsky, I. Kosenko, B. Lototsky, M. Shulhyn, and P. Verzhbytsky. It belonged to the *Supreme Emigration Council. The union ceased activities in 1940. In 1946 many of its former members established the *Ukrainian Community Aid Society in France.

**Union of Ukrainian Engineers' Organizations Abroad** (Soiuz orhanizatsii inzheneriv ukraintsiv na emigratsii, or SOIU). An umbrella organization of Ukrainian engineering associations outside Ukraine. It was founded on 15–17 November 1930 in Poděbrady by delegates of 10 engineering and technical societies in Poland, Czechoslovakia, and France. Later, societies in Argentina and Belgium became members. By 1931 the union represented 556 individual members. It established contacts with other Ukrainian scientific societies and non-Ukrainian professional associations. In 1931–4 it published four issues of *Ukraïns'kyi inzhener*. The head office was in Poděbrady, and the president was V. *Ivanys. When the Czechoslovak government withdrew its support of Ukrainian scientific and educational institutions, many engineers were forced to leave the country, and in 1937 the union ceased its activities.

**Union of Ukrainian Evangelical-Baptist Churches in Australia.** A federation of four churches (Sydney, Melbourne, Brisbane, Perth). Ukrainian Evangelical-Baptist church services were first celebrated in Sydney in 1959. Pastor M. Yatsyshyn replaced Pastor L. Semenets as chief pastor in 1985 in the Sydney Ukrainian Evangelical community. Pastor I. Podolak conducts services in Melbourne, which formed a religious community in 1960. Church services were first celebrated in Brisbane and in Perth in 1955. The Evangelical-Baptist communities in both of the last-named cities have their own prayer halls. W. Tereshchuk is pastor in Brisbane; F. Baranenko performs pastoral duties in Perth. The union has published the quarterly magazine *Dobra novyna* since 1960.

**Union of Ukrainian Foresters and Woodsmen in the USA** (Obiednannia ukrainskykh lisnykiv i derevnykiv, or OBULID). A professional organization of Ukrainian émigré foresters, originally founded in 1946 in Germany. The group sponsored technical courses in forestry, sought accreditation from Western technical institutes for studies completed in Ukraine, and pursued various possibilities for finding jobs or professional contacts for émigré Ukrainian foresters. It ceased operations in Germany in 1948 and was reconstituted in the United States in 1949. The group's official organ was *Visnyk OBULID* (edited by Ya. Zubal), which was published irregularly. It also sponsored a Ukrainian forestry almanac (1958) to commemorate the group's 10th anniversary. By this time, however, the union was moribund. Its presidents included B. Luchakovsky (1946–8), I. Vintoniak (1949–52), and P. Piasetsky (1954–6).

**Union of Ukrainian Journalists and Writers Abroad** (Soiuz ukrainskykh zhurnalistiv i pysmennykiv na chuzhyni). A professional association founded in Vienna on 12 September 1919 to inform the Western press and public about developments in Ukraine, to defend the professional interests of its members, and to give financial help to needy writers. In 1920 the union set up a lecture program, which in the following year was reorganized as a series of university courses under the name of the *Ukrainian Free University. In 1925 its head office was moved to Prague. In the 1930s it had 50 to 70 members and was active in disseminating information about Polish and Soviet repressions in Ukraine. Its presidents included V. Kushnir, O. Oles, and S. Siropolko. The group was disbanded in 1940.

**Union of Ukrainian Lawyers** (Soiuz ukrainskykh advokativ, or SUA). A professional organization of Ukrainian lawyers in interwar Poland. Established in 1923, it had its headquarters in Lviv and local branches in most towns with a district court. The union succeeded the Collegium of Advocates (1919–21), which was the legal section of the Ukrainian Citizens' Committee. The SUA defended the professional interests of Ukrainian lawyers in Poland and the use of the Ukrainian language in courts and official institutions, and organized the defense of Ukrainians involved in political trials. Together with the Society of Ukrainian Lawyers, it published the legal quarterly *Zhyttia i pravo* (1928–39). The SUA published an almanac commemorating its 10th anniversary (1934), and R. Dombchevsky's *Za prava ukraïns'koï movy* (For the Rights of the Ukrainian Language, 1936). By 1939 it had a membership of almost 400 lawyers and 300 articling students, almost three-quarters of all the Ukrainian lawyers in Poland. The presidents of SUA were L. Hankevych and K. Levytsky (1924–39). The society was dissolved in 1939, when the Soviets occupied Western Ukraine.

The first council of the Union of Ukrainian Merchants and Entrepreneurs in Lviv (1928)

**Union of Ukrainian Merchants and Entrepreneurs** (Soiuz ukrainskykh kuptsiv i promyslovtsiv, or SUKP). An organization of Ukrainian businessmen in Western Ukraine, established in 1923 with headquarters in Lviv. Until 1933 it was called the Union of Ukrainian Merchants. SUKP represented businessmen and entrepreneurs, encouraged the development of the private sector in the Ukrainian economy, organized exhibitions of goods manufactured by Ukrainians, defended the interests of the Ukrainian business community before the Polish government, helped organize *Prombank, published the semimonthly *Torhovlia i promysl and an almanac, and assisted the Ukrainian cooperative movement. The Polish government permitted it to operate only in Galicia, but the union accepted members from Volhynia and even from abroad. In 1937 it had 29 branches and 3,137 members (in 1934 the respective figures were 10 and 521). Separate sections were established in the organization for manufacturers, retailers, young businessmen, restaurateurs, and so on. SUKP was headed by Ye. Martynets, R. Zubyk, H. Hanuliak (1928–34), and Ya. Skopliak; other leading figures in the organization included Ye. Hovykovych, V. Ryzhevsky, S. Herasymovych, Ye. Dumyn, M. Zaiachkivsky, D. Koniukh, Yu. Tys, and V. Lazorko. After the Soviet occupation of Western Ukraine in 1939, SUKP suspended its activities. The Labor Alliance of Merchants and Entrepreneurs under the Ukrainian Central Committee continued the work of the SUKP in the German-run Generalgouvernement.

BIBLIOGRAPHY
Nestorovych, V. Ukraïns'ki kuptsi i promyslovtsi v Zakhidnii Ukraïni, 1920–1945 (Toronto–Chicago 1977)

**Union of Ukrainian National Democrats** (Soiuz ukrainskykh natsionalnykh demokrativ, or SUND). A political organization founded in New York in 1950. The group was established by post–Second World War émigrés who hoped to develop a nonpartisan center-left coalition to support the cause of Ukrainian independence and to counterbalance the perceived extremism of the existing nationalist and socialist Ukrainian-American organizations. The initiators of and main figures in the group were K. *Pankivsky and M. *Shlemkevych. The union published its own Biuleten' and then Informatsiinyi lystok, although its members also used the journal *Lysty do pryiateliv as a forum for expressing their views. The SUND was centered in and around New York City and initially generated some interest in establishing branches in other locations. These hopes were never realized, and the group dissolved itself in 1966.

**Union of Ukrainian Nationalist Youth** (Soiuz ukrainskoi natsionalistychnoi molodi, or SUNM). A coordinating body for Ukrainian nationalist youth groups in Galicia, formed in 1926 out of the *Group of Ukrainian National Youth. SUNM sought to activate Ukrainians (particularly youths) in the nationalist cause. The union had its greatest strength in Lviv (with headquarters in the *Academic Gymnasium), although its members frequently toured villages with plays, public lectures, concerts, and the like. The union quickly assumed a leading role in the Ukrainian nationalist movement and became one of the founding members of the *Organization of Ukrainian Nationalists, after the establishment of which, in 1929, SUNM disbanded. The union published the newspaper *Smoloskypy in 1927–8. Leading SUNM figures included O. Bodnarovych, I. Habrusevych, B. Kravtsiv, S. Lenkavsky, S. Okhrymovych, and M. Dobriansky-Demkovych.

**Union of Ukrainian Private Office Employees** (Soiuz ukrainskykh pryvatnykh uriadovtsiv, or SUPRUHA). A professional organization of Ukrainian office workers in Galicia, founded in 1914 in Lviv. By 1939 it had 13 branches and over 1,100 members. It also owned a bank, called SUPRUHA, which financed the union's Suspilnyi Promysl co-operative (est 1932). The latter ran a factory that produced a coffee substitute. The union published a monthly, *Sluzhbovyk. SUPRUHA was dissolved by the authorities following the Soviet occupation of Western Ukraine in 1939. Its last president was L. *Yasinchuk.

**Union of Ukrainian Professional Musicians** (Siouz ukrainskykh profesiinykh muzyk, or SUPROM). A music society active in Lviv in 1934–9. The union was active in the fields of composition, musicology, and musical performance. It sponsored the periodical Ukraïns'ka muzyka, selected the items to be included in the collection Velykyi spivannyk Chervonoï kalyny (The Great Songbook of Chervona Kalyna), published Dyrygents'kyi poradnyk (The Conductor's Adviser), and organized a competition for young performers. Among the leading figures in the union were N. *Nyzhankivsky, V. *Barvinsky, Z. *Lysko, R. *Savytsky, and W. *Wytwycky.

**Union of Ukrainian Progressive Youth** (Soiuz ukrainskoi postupovoi molodi im. M. Drahomanova 'Kameniari'). A Galician youth organization founded in 1929 and popularly known as the Kameniari (Stonecutters) after the poem by I. *Franko. The organization had a radical-democratic and ethical-socialist ideology and was under the influence of the *Ukrainian Radical party. Its headquarters was in Lviv. In 1930 the union had 48 branches throughout Galicia, in 1933, 108 branches, and in 1936, 291 branches, with over 15,000 members. Local branches organized study circles, sports activities, theatrical groups, and choirs. Annual district sports meets were organized at the district level. The union had two journals, *Kameniari and Molodi kameniari, and published several organizational handbooks. The union belonged to the International Workers Sports Union (headquarters in Brussels) and participated in two of its olympiads. The head of the union was A. *Hryvnak, and the secretary-general was P. Kostiuk. The organization ceased to exist with the Soviet occupation of Galicia in 1939.

**Union of Ukrainian Student Organizations in Germany and Danzig** (Soiuz ukrainskykh studentskykh orhanizatsii u Nimechchyni ta v misti Dantsigu, or SUSOND). A student umbrella organization founded in Berlin in August 1924. It united six student organizations in Berlin, Danzig, and Königsberg, of which the largest was the *Osnova Union of Ukrainian Students in Danzig. In its cultural activities SUSOND collaborated with similar German, Lithuanian, Bulgarian, Turkish, and Estonian student organizations. In the 1930s its membership decreased. In 1938 it accepted student associations in Austria (the Sich student societies in Vienna and Graz), and in 1939 the Ukrainian Academic Hromada in Prague. In 1941 the union was reconstituted as the *Nationalist Organization of Ukrainian Students in Germany. Presidents of SUSOND included M. Milko, M. Kachmar, and A. Kishka.

**Union of Ukrainian Student Organizations in Rumania** (Soiuz ukrainskykh studentskykh orhanizatsii u Rumunii, or SUSOR). A student umbrella organization established in 1929 to represent various Ukrainian student societies in Rumania. It co-ordinated the work of the Zaporozhe, Chornomore, and Zalizniak student fraternities in Chernivtsi; the Bukovyna society in Bucharest; and the Hromada in Iași. It organized Ukrainian national celebrations and demonstrations, such as the protest in 1933 against the man-made Soviet famine, and published a supplement, *Students'ki visty* (Student News, 1935–7), in the papers *Chas* and *Samostiinist'*. It raised funds to provide health care for Ukrainian students. The union represented about 160 students. From 1929 it was a member of the Central Union of Ukrainian Students. Although the Rumanian authorities banned SUSOR activities in 1937, it continued its formal existence until 1940. Its presidents were L. Romanovsky, V. Yakubovych, O. Popovych, M. Ivanovych, and Ya. Baver.

Members of the executive of the Union of Ukrainian Student Organizations under Poland in 1931–2. Sitting, from left: Bohdan Zanko, Mykola Duzhy, Anna Chemerynska, Volodymyr Yaniv, Olha Prystai, Yaroslav Hladky, Yaroslav Rak; standing: Bohdan Dorotsky, Andrii Marchenko, Ivan Maliutsa, Bohdan Romanenchuk, Vasyl Miliianchuk

**Union of Ukrainian Student Organizations under Poland** (Soiuz ukrainskykh studentskykh orhanizatsii pid Polshcheiu, or SUSOP). A semilegal union of Ukrainian student groups in Poland. Active in 1931–9, SUSOP united Ukrainian students from 5 university cities and 65 district sections; the total membership was nearly 2,500, approx 83 percent of the Ukrainians in postsecondary schools in Poland. SUSOP was formed at a meeting of the Central Student Committee in Lviv in 1931, where it established its plans to undertake cultural-educational work as a means of strengthening the national consciousness of the Ukrainian masses. In 1933 SUSOP assumed a portion of the mandate of the *Central Union of Ukrainian Students, and its journal, *Students'kyi shliakh*, became the official voice of both co-ordinating bodies. Strongly influenced by the temper of the times, SUSOP sought to instill a nationalist spirit in its members. The Polish government retaliated in 1934 with repressive measures: the organization's first three presidents were arrested, and publication of the SUSOP journal was prohibited (it resumed publication under a new name only in 1938). In 1939 all the delegates to the organization's Seventh Congress were arrested. Notable members of SUSOP included V. Yaniv, D. Shtykalo, R. Voloshyn, and V. Rudko.

**Union of Ukrainian Student Societies in Europe** (Soiuz ukrainskykh studentskykh tovarystv v Evropi, or

SUSTE). A Ukrainian student umbrella organization established in 1963 in Paris. It had over 250 members grouped in Ukrainian student clubs in Britain, France, Germany, Belgium, Austria, and Italy. SUSTE organized conferences and student meets. In 1975 it began to publish *Informatyvnyi lystok* irregularly. Its presidents have included F. Tatarchuk, I. Hirna, A. Rebet, B. Drozdovsky, and T. Lonchyna.

**Union of Ukrainian Veterans** (Soiuz ukrainskykh veteraniv, or SUV). An émigré association of former Ukrainian soldiers in various armies. It was founded in Neu-Ulm, Germany, in 1945 to cultivate Ukrainian military traditions and provide aid to needy members. In 1948 it had over 2,000 members in more than 50 branches. As Ukrainians emigrated from Germany, branches of the SUV sprang up in Austria, Britain, Belgium, Holland, Argentina, and Australia. The head office is in Munich. Ten issues of the union's magazine, *Ukraïns'kyi kombatant*, were published. The presidents of SUV have included Gen M. Omelianovych-Pavlenko, Col V. Tatarsky, Col M. Stechyshyn, and R. Debrytsky.

**Union of Ukrainian War Invalids** (Soiuz ukrainskykh voiennykh invalidiv). A charitable organization founded in 1947 in Augsburg to aid Ukrainian invalids in Germany and Austria. Its list of dependents has gradually diminished from over 500 in 1952 to 280 in 1958 and 80 in 1983. Funds are donated by Ukrainian veterans' organizations and Ukrainian welfare services in Canada, the United States, and Australia. The union's head office is in Munich. Its presidents have been I. Marchuk, I. Nebola, M. Stechyshyn (1955–71), and R. Debrytsky (since 1971).

The presidium of the Union of Ukrainian Women in 1937. Sitting, from left: Olena Fedak-Sheparovych, Iryna Prisnevska, Natalia Livytska-Kholodna, Zinaida Mirna, Sofiia Rusova, Milena Rudnytska, Konstantyna Malytska, Olena Shtohryn, Olha Tsipanovska; standing: Antonina Horokhovych, Myroslava Mryts

**Union of Ukrainian Women** (Soiuz ukrainok, or SU). The largest Ukrainian women's organization in Western Ukraine during the interwar period. A successor to the *Women's Hromada in Lviv, the group was established in December 1921 at a women's conference in Lviv. It sought to improve the educational and economic status of Ukrainian women, and to involve them in civic affairs. It undertook activities related to community sanitation, social welfare, the co-operative movement, and the research and development of Ukrainian folk arts.

The SU had a three-tiered structure, with a central executive in Lviv, branch organizations in larger cities and towns (67 in 1936), and village circles (1,101 in 1936). The Polish authorities deliberately limited the scope of its activities to Galicia. The SU branches represented approx 30 percent of all Ukrainian settlements there, and its membership of 45,000 constituted about 5 percent of the female Ukrainian population. The SU was particularly successful in extending its influence into the countryside by dealing with issues of concern to rural women and by using its branches as regional organizational and programming centers for the village circles. The constitution of the SU was ratified in 1917 (wartime circumstances delayed its formal implementation until 1921) and amended in 1933.

The work of the SU proceeded in several directions and at several levels. One of the earliest concerns was the adaptation of Ukrainian folk arts to urban uses; it was followed by the improvement of life among rural women as well as an involvement in the international women's movement. The organization's work in the early 1920s focused largely on postwar reconstruction and the establishment of branches. In 1922 the *Ukrainske Narodnie Mystetstvo co-operative was founded under the auspices of the SU as a means of popularizing and marketing Ukrainian folk-art items. To develop cadres to work in the field, training courses were organized in 1927, 1929, 1932, and 1937. Besides explaining the aims and methods of the SU the specialists lectured on topics such as the operating of co-operatives and nursery schools, housekeeping and garden tending, and the basics of hygiene. Course attendees (approx 200 graduates) were mainly young women who had completed secondary school and were looking for employment. The most capable of these were posted in SU branches; others organized courses in the villages. In 1937 alone the SU sponsored 177 courses in various Galician villages, 81 on cooking, 13 on housekeeping, 52 on knitting and crocheting, 21 on pattern-making and sewing, and 7 on embroidery. The SU also added the organization of summer preschool programs for children and the establishment of youth affiliates around village circles to its activities.

The work of the central organization was divided into sections. The organizational section was headed by O. *Kysilevska, who contributed the SU circulars to the popular weekly *Zhinocha dolia. The co-operative section was headed by I. Blazhkevych and, later, I. Hladka; it was responsible for disseminating information about co-operatives and keeping a close liaison with county unions of co-operatives. The health section was headed by S. Parfanovych and, later, S. Korenets; it worked in co-operation with the Ukrainian Hygienic Society. The folk-art section was headed by I. Hurhula, and its activities were linked with those of the Ukrainske Narodnie Mystetstvo co-operative. The recruiting section was headed by O. Tsipanovska, who was also responsible for Ukrainian studies, Ukrainian embroidery, and housekeeping programs. In the mid-1930s there were 142 girls' groups organized around the village circles.

The growth of the SU was stimulated by the Ukrainian Women's Congress, which it sponsored in June 1934 in Stanyslaviv, on the occasion of the 50th anniversary of the founding of the first Ukrainian women's association. The gathering attracted not only a large portion of the SU membership but also representatives of many other women's groups. The agenda of the congress included presentations on all areas of SU activity. During the congress the idea of a World Union of Ukrainian Women, which would unite all such women's organizations under one superstructure, was discussed. Although set in motion later, in 1937, the proposition was not realized because of the disbanding of the SU by the Polish authorities and the outbreak of the war.

The SU published the biweekly *Zhinka (edited by M. *Rudnytska from 1935) and the monthly Ukraïnka (1938–9, ed M. Strutynska), which was particularly popular among village women. SU members were also avid readers of other women's periodicals, including the monthly Nova khata and the weekly Zhinocha dolia.

Relations between the SU and other Ukrainian organizations were generally good through the 1920s, and the involvement of women in Ukrainian civic life was viewed as desirable. The union maintained a high degree of internal cohesion by concentrating on specific programs and immediate concrete issues and maintaining a moderate political stance, which effectively put theoretical questions of ideology in a secondary position. In the 1930s the situation changed dramatically. The Union of Working Women was formed in 1931 (initially as the Women's Hromada) under the auspices of the Ukrainian Socialist Radical party as a breakaway group of political radicals from the SU. The Ukrainian Catholic church defended the traditional role of women and linked the sort of female consciousness demonstrated by the SU with socialism and atheism as well as with the destruction of the family and the moral fiber of society. In the 1930s an increasing number of Catholic lay bodies were formed, and competed for the loyalties of Ukrainian women. The OUN, also a proponent of a conservative role for women in society, likewise engaged large numbers of potential SU recruits (particularly among the young). Finally, in the mid-1930s a drive by the co-operative society *Silskyi Hospodar to increase its female membership throughout the countryside was launched before discussions regarding SU co-operation had been completed. Relations between the two groups soured as a result.

The SU executive maintained ties with international women's organizations. In 1923 the SU became a member of the International Women's Union and participated in its congresses in Rome (1923), Paris (1926), Berlin (1929), and Marseille (1933). The SU had a section in the International Women's League of Peace and Freedom (WLPF) headed by B. Baran. An official WLPF representative, M. Sheepshanks, attended the 1934 Stanyslaviv congress. The co-operative section of the SU was also a member of the Women's Co-operative Guild and participated in its congresses in Vienna (1931), London (1933), and Paris (1937).

In 1938 the Polish authorities disbanded the SU. The SU executive then founded *Druzhyna Kniahyni Olhy to maintain some organizational continuity until it was possible to operate legally again. The new organization had a predominantly political profile and appealed mainly to the SU leadership and intelligentsia. Rank-and-file members usually joined local community associations (particularly Silskyi Hospodar and Prosvita) until the SU was again allowed to function. The SU was disbanded following the Soviet occupation of Galicia in 1939.

The presidents of the SU were Ye. Makarushka (1917–22), K. Hrynevycheva (1923–4), M. Biletska (1924–5), O. Fedak-Sheparovych (1925–6), M. Dontsova (1926–7), I. Vitkovytska (1927–8), and M. Rudnytska (1928–39). Also prominent in the association were M. Biliak, K. Malytska, Ya. Ostrovska, I. Pavlykovska, M. Bilozor, O. Dzhydzhora-Dzoba, A. Horokhovych, Hurhula, and N. Selezinka.

Among the notable branch heads were S. Olesnytska and A. Rubleva (Stanyslaviv), M. Vesolovska (Stryi), S. Chorpita (Kalush), M. Martynyk (Staryi Sambir), O. Malko (Velyki Mosty), S. Hryniv (Buchach), and M. Khoptiak (Rohatyn).

The SU was revived on 21 February 1990 at a conference in Lviv. At the constituent congress held in Kiev in December 1991, A. Pashko was elected president of the SU.

BIBLIOGRAPHY
Bohachevsky-Chomiak, M. *Feminists Despite Themselves: Women in Ukrainian Community Life, 1884–1939* (Edmonton 1988)
L. Burachynska

**Union of Ukrainian Women of Volhynia** (Soiuz ukrainok Volyni). Established in 1921 and disbanded by the Polish government on 3 June 1938, this organization of women considered itself part of the *Union of Ukrainian Women in Galicia, although a formal merger of the two organizations was prohibited by the Polish government. The union, which in the early 1920s showed signs of becoming a mass organization, had been reduced to 500 members by 1936. It promoted modernization in the villages through a network of village circles, established day-care centers and summer camps, organized trade courses, and promoted a program that enabled Volhynian girls to study in Ukrainian schools in Galicia. Among the most active women in the union were P. Bahrynivska, O. Pidhirska, M. Volosevych, I. Prisnevska, and O. Levchanivska.

**Union of Ukrainian Workers in France** (Obiednannia ukrainskykh robitnykiv u Frantsii, or OURF). A community, cultural, and professional organization established in 1945. Over 6,000 Ukrainians have belonged to the union. It was most active in 1950–1, when it had 63 branches, 3,617 members who belonged to various trade unions, and 402 free members. Its official press organ in 1945–60 was the weekly *Ukraïnets' u Frantsiï (later Ukraïnets')*. Working in co-operation with French Christian trade-union organizations, the OURF initiated the Ukrainian émigré trade-union movement. In 1949 it established the Confederation of Ukrainian Free Professional Organizations (KUVPO), which joined the International Confederation of Christian Trade Unions in 1951. Leading members of OURF included O. Forsyk, V. Nesterchuk, P. Polishchuk, I. Popovych, and Yu. Zablotsky. Because of large-scale emigration to North America in the 1950s, OURF membership declined. After the French Christian Trade Union (CFTC) split up in 1964, the union declined until it ceased activities in 1971.

**Union of Ukrainian Working Women** (Soiuz ukrainskykh pratsiuiuchykh zhinok). A central women's organization which was active in Galicia in 1931–9 and was linked ideologically and organizationally with the Ukrainian Socialist Radical party (see *Ukrainian Radical party). Established initially as the Women's Hromada, it had county branches and local women's hromadas numbering 148 in 1939. The Polish authorities banned the organization from Volhynia and restricted it to Galicia. Its membership reached 7,800, of which almost 95 percent were peasant or working-class women. The hromadas organized cultural events and circles of the Samoosvita popular university. The union published the semimonthly

*Zhinochyi holos*. Its leadership consisted of I. Blazhkevych (president), N. Mykytchuk and L. Muryn (vice-presidents), and F. Stakhiv (secretary).

**Union of Ukrainians in Poland** (Obiednannia ukraintsiv v Polshchi). See Ukrainian Social and Cultural Society.

**Union of Ukrainians of France** (Obiednannia ukraintsiv u Frantsii, or OUF). A cultural and social organization established in 1948. Until 1965 it co-operated closely with the *Union of Ukrainian Workers in France (OURF) by concentrating on social development while the latter developed trade-union programs. In 1965 the OUF had about 300 members and 250 supporters; branches in Sochaux, Thionville, Rombas, Mulhouse, Metz, Le Cateau, Denain, Lyon, and Vésines-Chalette; and affiliates in Sarrebourg and Villetupt. In 1989 it had about 200 members and 200 supporters. It owns a building in Sochaux and in December 1978 bought a vacation resort named Verkhovyna in Rosey, near Vesoul. In 1986 the French Ministry of Youth and Sports officially recognized the OUF as a popular educational association. In 1953–67 the union ran a publishing operation, which was taken over by L'Est Européen publishers in 1967. The presidents of the OUF have been V. Nesterchuk (1949–54), O. Melnykovych (1955–60), and V. Kosyk (1961–).

**Union of Welfare** (Russian: Soiuz blagodenstviia). A clandestine political organization which arose out of the *Union of Salvation at the beginning of 1818 in St Petersburg. Its goal was to abolish serfdom and absolutism and to transform the Russian Empire into a constitutional monarchy or (from 1820) a centralized republic. The union was headed by a central executive to which local executives were subordinate. In Ukraine there was a local branch in Tulchyn, and branches were to be set up in Poltava and Odessa. The union had about 2,000 members. Among its Russian members were M. Orlov, N. Turgenev, P. Pestel, N. and A. Muravev, Prince S. Trubetskoi, Prince S. Volkonsky, and M. Lunin. Some members were Ukrainians by descent or were closely linked with Ukraine, among them S. and M. Muravev-Apostol, S. Krasnokutsky, V. Lukashevych, O. Yakubovych, O. Myklashevsky, S. and O. Kapnist, P. Horlenko, A. Rodzianko, L. and V. Perovsky, N. Fylypovych, V. Davydov, and M. Novikov. After January 1821 the union was replaced by the two main Decembrist organizations, the *Southern and the Northern societies.

**Union of Writers of Ukraine.** See Writers' Union of Ukraine.

**Union of Young Artists of Ukraine** (Obiednannia molodykh mysttsiv Ukrainy, or OMMU). An artists' organization established in 1929 by graduates of the Kiev State Art Institute who rejected the tenets of the Association of Artists of Red Ukraine and the *Association of Revolutionary Art of Ukraine and promoted, instead, 'utilitarian revolutionary art.' As a group OMMU first appeared before the public at the Second All-Ukrainian Art Exhibition held in several cities in 1929. Among its members were S. Raievsky, O. Pashchenko, S. Hryhoriev, and H. Pyvovarov. OMMU was dissolved by the Party in 1932.

**Unions of zemstvos and cities.** Organizations in the Russian Empire set up after the outbreak of the First World War for the purpose of assisting the Russian army with supplies and road-building in the war zone and aiding wounded soldiers and (beginning in 1915) war refugees. Until July 1915 the All-Russian Zemstvo Union (Vserossiiskii zemskii soiuz) and the All-Russian Union of Cities (Vserossiiskii soiuz gorodov) acted independently of each other. Then their work was co-ordinated by the United Committee of Unions. Each union had its head office in Moscow, which represented a network of county, gubernia, and war-front committees. In Ukraine the Union of Cities of the Southwestern Front was headed by T. Shteingel, and numbered among its employees M. Biliashevsky, A. Viazlov, D. Doroshenko, I. Kraskovsky, V. Leontovych, F. Matushevsky, A. Nikovsky, and V. Ulianytsky. The Zemstvo Union of the Southwestern Front was headed by S. Shlykevych. From 1916 S. Petliura was plenipotentiary of the unions of zemstvos and cities at the western front. Subsidized by the government, the unions helped the population of Galicia and Bukovyna during the Russian occupation as well as refugees from Galicia. Ukrainian women organized a number of hospitals (even in Petrograd) for Ukrainian soldiers. Hundreds of Ukrainians worked in the unions and acquired managerial and administrative skills, which later proved useful in the setting up of a Ukrainian state. The zemstvo and city unions in Ukraine continued their work in a modified form under the Central Rada and Hetman regimes. Until June 1915 their main offices were in Lviv and then Kiev.

**Uniontown.** A city (1988 pop ca 35,000) in southwestern Pennsylvania, with approx 1,500 residents of Transcarpathian origin. The first Ruthenian church, St John the Baptist, was established in 1921. A convent of the Sisters of St Basil the Great was built on Mount St Macrina in 1934, and eventually it became the motherhouse of the order's Ruthenian province. A senior citizens' home (1947), a nursing home (1970), and a novitiate were added to the convent, which today houses about 50 nuns. The bilingual (Ruthenian-English) monthly *Voice from Mount St Macrina* (1948–70) was published there. Mount St Macrina is a site of annual pilgrimages.

**Unitarians.** See Socinians.

**United Hetman Organization** (Soiuz hetmantsiv derzhavnykiv, or SHD). A Ukrainian monarchist organization dedicated to the restoration of a Ukrainian hetman state under P. *Skoropadsky, which developed independently in Canada and the United States during the interwar era. The organization grew out of *Sich sporting societies that had been formed in North America in the early part of the century. The impetus for their transformation came from the influence of O. *Nazaruk, a leading conservative Ukrainian ideologue, who came to North America in the early 1920s. Both in Canada and the United States the hetman movement had the implicit support of the Ukrainian Catholic church.

In Canada the SHD was preceded by the *Canadian Sitch organization. Proclaiming a clearly monarchist ideology, the group published *Probii*, *Kanadiis'ka Sich*, and (from 1934) *Ukraïns'kyi robitnyk*. It acquired real estate holdings and spread to western Canada after V. Bosy obtained a

The central executive of the United Hetman Organization of America and Canada in 1937–8. Sitting, from left: Stefan Muryn, Anna Matychak, Bohdan Pelekhovych, Supreme Otaman Mykola Hul, Col Oleksander Shapoval, Ivan Duzhansky, Hryhorii Matviiv; standing: Mykhailo Soltys, Mykhailo Baran, Mykola Kulak, Mykola Moranets, Petro Luchkiv, Tymko Kryvoviaz, Vasyl Sydoruk

teaching position in Yorkton, Saskatchewan. Its members devoted much energy to military training and even acquired several aircraft. In 1934 the group formally reconstituted itself as the SHD. It reached the height of its development around the time of the visit of D. *Skoropadsky, the hetman's son and successor, to North America in 1937–8. In 1940 it became one of the founders of the Ukrainian Canadian Congress, but then declined during the war. A split in the group in 1952 further weakened it, and *Ukraïns'kyi robitnyk* ceased publication in 1958. The SHD subsequently published *Nasha derzhava* and *Bat'kivshchyna*.

In the United States the Sich societies began a process of centralization and militarization that culminated in the election of S. *Hrynevetsky as supreme otaman (head) at the 1922 convention, where resolutions were passed mandating the transformation of each branch into a *sotnia* (company) and each branch head into a *sotnyk* (captain or company commander). Hrynevetsky subsequently expanded the association's paramilitary trappings and developed its monarchist ideological character (the group was now called Hetman Sich). In 1924 Hrynevetsky received his *bulava* of office and pledged fidelity to Hetman P. Skoropadsky. With tacit support from the Ukrainian Catholic church, the Hetman Sich established a Ukrainian 'liberation army.' In 1930 hundreds of Sich members joined the American militia (now the National Guard). Permitted to form their own separate companies, they believed their American-trained force would someday become part of a Ukrainian liberation army. The final step in the development of a Ukrainian fighting force was the creation of a Ukrainian 'air corps.' During the 1930s the Hetman Sich obtained three airplanes – two biplanes and a four-passenger monoplane – named *Ukraina*, *Lviv*, and *Kiev*. In spite of substantial opposition and defections (with many previous supporters becoming adherents of the Organization for the Rebirth of Ukraine), the group continued its activities, and its members increasingly began to seek military training within the US National Guard or with their own resources. In 1930 the Sich organization was formally reconstituted as the SHD. In 1938 the SHD was investigated by the (congressional) Dies Committee, and in 1940 by the FBI, for possible subversive activities. Although no direct charges were ever laid, the probes undercut member support drastically and resulted in the group's dissolution in 1942. A successor body of sorts (the Ukrainian Hetman Organization of America) was established in 1943 by figures such as O. Bilovus, M. Simenovych-Simens, and P. Zaporozhets, but failed to generate mass support.

**United Nations** (Obiednani natsii). An international organization set up by charter on 24 October 1945 for the purpose of preserving peace and security through co-operation among nations and international justice based on the principles of equal rights and the self-determination of nations. The United Nations (UN) is the successor of the *League of Nations. The Ukrainian SSR was one of its 51 founding members.

The Ukrainian delegation was one of three Soviet delegations to the founding conference in San Francisco. Its head, D. *Manuilsky, chaired the commission writing the preamble and the first section of the UN Charter. The Ukrainian SSR took part in many UN conferences, such as the 1949 Geneva conference on war victims, the 1954 Hague conference on protecting cultural property during armed conflict, the 1958 and 1960 conferences on maritime law, and the 1961 conference on diplomatic relations. It served twice as a nonpermanent member on the Security Council (1947–9, 1985–7) and once on the Economic and Social Council (1946). It was a coauthor and cosponsor of many resolutions during the first decade of the UN. The Ukrainian SSR was a member of nine UN agencies: the International Atomic Energy Agency, International Labour Organization (ILO), International Telecommunication Union, United Nations Educational, Scientific and Cultural Organization (UNESCO), UN Industrial Development Organization, Universal Postal Union, World Health Organization, World Organization for the Protection of Intellectual Property, and World Meteorological Organization. Its most active role was in UNESCO. Ukraine was conspicuously absent from the major international bodies, however. In 1945 the Ukrainian SSR and the USSR jointly ratified the statute of the International Court of Justice but refused to submit to the court's compulsory jurisdiction. Similarly, Ukraine accepted ILO labor conventions, but Soviet trade unions refused to apply them. Finally, the Ukrainian SSR was represented on some committees and commissions established by UN agencies or intergovernmental organizations outside the UN system.

The Ukrainian SSR signed some 120 treaties, agreements, conventions, declarations, and acts. The most important among them, besides the UN charter itself, are the *Paris Peace Treaties of 1947, the Universal Declaration of Human Rights (1948), and the Moscow Treaty limiting the testing of nuclear weapons (1963). (See also *Treaties.)

Despite the aforementioned activities, until Ukraine's declaration of independence in August 1991 its role in the UN amounted to little more than one of assisting Soviet diplomacy. L. Kravchuk's appearance at the UN in October 1991 signaled the future independent status of Ukraine among the nations of the world. The first independently appointed Ukrainian representative to the UN was V. Batiuk (1992–).

T. Kis

**United Nations Educational, Scientific, and Cultural Organization** (UNESCO). A United Nations agency established on 4 November 1946 to facilitate international co-operation in nonpolitical endeavors. It had 158 member countries and approx 250 nongovernmental organizations with consultant status by 1987. UNESCO's main offices, located in Paris, include a publishing house (Office des Presses de l'Unesco), which produces 26 periodicals in various languages. The Ukrainian SSR, as a full member of the *United Nations (UN), joined UNESCO on 12 May 1954. It was represented by Yu. Kochubei (later deputy minister for external affairs of the Ukrainian SSR and deputy director general of UNESCO), M. Reshetniak, A. Zlenko, V. Skofenko, and O. Slipchenko. In 1980–5 the representative of the Ukrainian SSR, H. Tsvetkov, was a member of the Executive Board. In 1974–9 the UNESCO museum division was headed by Yu. Turchenko. In 1956 the Council of Ministers of the Ukrainian SSR created the UNESCO Commission of the Ukrainian SSR, which includes over 50 representatives of state educational and civic institutions. The commission drafted plans for UNESCO work and co-ordinated the work of UNESCO committees on scientific programs (geological co-operation, hydrological program, the oceanographic commission, the study of Slavic cultures, and so forth) in the Ukrainian SSR.

An international UNESCO conference of Slavists (with approx 200 participants) took place in Kiev in 1979. The *Biuleten' Komisiï URSR u spravakh IuNESKO* was published in many foreign languages from 1970. As well, the pamphlet *Ukraïna – chlen IuNESKO* (Ukraine: A Member of UNESCO, 1966), by M. Petrachkov and T. Kovalenko-Kosaryk, and A. Zlenko's UNESCO *and Problems of the Present* (1984) have appeared in print. As part of its work, UNESCO has produced the following: G. Chevchuk, *La politique culturelle dans la République socialiste soviétique d'Ukraine* (1981; also in English), the album *Sculpture et architecture de bois* (1981), L. Novychenko's *Taras Chevtchenko* (1982), and *Antolohiia ukraïns'koï radians'koï poeziï* (Poetry of Soviet Ukraine's New World: An Anthology, 1986). UNESCO has celebrated the 150th and 175th anniversaries of the birth of T. Shevchenko, the 250th anniversary of the birth of H. Skovoroda, and the centenary of the birth of Lesia Ukrainka, I. Franko, and Ye. Paton, and has staged a festival of films by O. Dovzhenko (1984). In 1983 UNESCO took part in the celebration of the 1,500th anniversary of the founding of Kiev, and in 1988 the commemoration of the millennium of Christianity in Ukraine.

Before Ukraine declared its independence the UNESCO representatives of the Ukrainian SSR, like those in other international organizations, followed closely a common Soviet policy.

A. Zhukovsky

**United Nations Relief and Rehabilitation Administration** (UNRRA). An international organization created by the Allied and associated powers to plan, co-ordinate, and administer relief (food, fuel, clothing, shelter, medical, and other essential services) for victims of war in areas controlled by the Allied powers. Its objectives also included assistance in returning prisoners and exiles to their homes and help in the re-establishment of agricultural and industrial production. These goals were broadly outlined in the General Agreement signed on 9 November 1943 by 44 governments. The UNRRA was governed by a council, a central committee (initially consisting of representatives from China, the USSR, the United Kingdom, and the United States), a committee on supplies, regional and other special committees, and a director general with the authority to carry out relief operations. Because of special circumstances the Ukrainian and the Belorussian SSR were admitted to the council on 13 August 1945.

Ukrainian children in the Munich-Freimann DP camp

The UNRRA conducted operations only in the occupation zones of the Western powers, since Soviet authorities did not invite the agency into their occupation zones in Germany and Austria. In providing assistance UNRRA officials worked closely with many voluntary relief agencies, which were granted a special status. Neither the *United Ukrainian American Relief Committee nor the *Ukrainian Canadian Relief Fund was approved by the UNRRA, because a number of its members, including the governments of Canada and the United States, found their anticommunist political activities to be unacceptable. At the peak of its operation, in August 1946, the UNRRA employed a staff of 24,976 and operated 29 servicing or supply offices and 16 missions in receiving countries. Its total resources, based on contributions and receipts, were almost four billion US dollars. It took two years to dismantle the UNRRA and to transfer its functions to new international agencies, such as the World Health Organization (WHO), Food and Agriculture Organization (FAO), International Children's Emergency Fund (UNICEF), and *International Refugee Organization (IRO). The UNRRA was closed formally in September 1948.

**The Ukrainian SSR.** Prior to the Third Council Session (August 1945) the Soviet Union applied to the UNRRA for 700 million dollars' worth of relief and rehabilitation supplies. After surveying conditions in the USSR, American, British, Canadian, and Soviet representatives agreed on a substitute program for Ukraine and Belorussia worth 250 million dollars: 189 million dollars for Ukraine and the rest for Belorussia. The allocations were free, because neither republic had any foreign reserves. The formal agreement between Ukraine and the UNRRA was signed on 18 December 1945 by Director General H. Lehman and A. Baranovsky, a member of the UNRRA Council for the Ukrainian SSR; the target date for the completion of the aid program was 1 July 1946. The UNRRA mission did not arrive in Kiev until 20 March 1946. It was headed by M. MacDuffie (to June 1946) and then by P. White (August 1946 to August 1947) and consisted most of the time of seven members, including a supply officer and a medical officer. The UNRRA mission at Kiev was slotted for a staff

of 15, but a full complement was never realized; at its peak, personnel at the Ukraine mission numbered 10. UNRRA agricultural and industrial rehabilitation specialists were turned down, supposedly because Soviet experts were better acquainted with Soviet practices and needs.

The mission's chief task was to monitor the distribution of UNRRA supplies. Distribution decisions were worked out not by the mission, but by the host government Supplies Administration and the individual ministries. Approximately 55 percent of all UNRRA goods were allocated for sale, and the remaining 45 percent were distributed free in the most devastated areas. Since most rural districts were considered self-sufficient, the food was directed mainly to urban areas. The food that was sold was offered at fixed prices to ration-card holders. Both prices and rations were determined by USSR authorities. Ration scales were in place throughout 1946 and most of 1947. Information on food rationing was never released to the UNRRA mission because it was considered strategic data. According to UNRRA estimates approx 10 percent of the food imported was distributed to welfare institutions, particularly to children's homes.

Food imports comprised slightly more than 50 percent of the total dollar value of relief and rehabilitation provided for Ukraine (see table 1). Since Ukraine was considered self-sufficient in grain production, wheat or wheat flour was not included in the program, despite the bad harvest of 1946–7. Next in dollar value came industrial rehabilitation goods, notably 'protocol goods,' such as power stations, that had been ordered from Britain in 1942, as well as items such as locomotives, trucks, bulldozers, cranes, integrated plants, and raw metals for repairing telecommunications and electrical systems. Agricultural rehabilitation included 18,240 gross long tons of seeds (vegetable, grass, and clover) and 1,500 tractors. Medical supplies constituted the smallest share of the commodities, and all of them were delivered by March 1947: drugs, chemicals, field-hospital equipment, X-ray and dental equipment, and major components for a penicillin plant.

TABLE 1
UNRRA supply deliveries to Ukraine

| Category | US dollar equivalent | Gross long tons |
|---|---|---|
| Food | 99,437,700 | 315,748 |
| Clothing, textiles, and footwear | 17,207,700 | 16,225 |
| Medical and sanitation | 2,445,500 | 1,037 |
| Agricultural rehabilitation | 16,988,900 | 38,069 |
| Industrial rehabilitation | 52,119,500 | 95,970 |
| Total | 188,199,300 | 467,049 |

The UNRRA wanted public recognition of its contribution to Ukraine's rehabilitation. Since no provision for acknowledgment was made in the agreement except for a clause concerning UNRRA labels on goods, little press was given to the UNRRA relief effort in Ukraine.

**Displaced persons**. In 1946, after the initial stage of repatriation, an estimated 1.2 million *displaced persons remained in Europe. Nearly 200,000 of them were Ukrainians. Thanks to resettlement, by 1947 the number had been reduced to approx 125,000. As a rule they lived in displaced persons' camps in the Western occupation

TABLE 2
Displaced persons under UNRRA care or supervision

|  | December 1945 | September 1946 | June 1947 |
|---|---|---|---|
| **In Germany:** |  |  |  |
| Ukrainians* | – | – | 99,078 |
| Poles | 427,407 | 302,725 | 136,180 |
| Balts | 132,098 | 176,362 | 148,776 |
| Yugoslavs | 18,029 | 14,439 | 9,324 |
| Jews | 14,000 | 120,849 | 134,864 |
| Others | 85,874 | 81,255 | 30,629 |
| **In Austria:** |  |  |  |
| Ukrainians† | 9,190 | – | 7,471 |
| Poles | 11,236 | 9,239 | 2,899 |
| Balts | 1,594 | 2,270 | 1,841 |
| Yugoslavs | 14,877 | 8,479 | 6,959 |
| Jews | 4,361 | 10,400 | 5,723 |
| Others | 8,524 | 9,808 | 3,166 |

* Included under Poles and/or others in December 1945 and September 1946

† Reported mainly under Poles and partly under Yugoslavs and others in September 1946

zones of Germany and Austria. In June 1947 about 106,500 Ukrainians were under the care or supervision of the UNRRA (see table 2).

*Repatriation became a most difficult issue for the UNRRA. The USSR authorities, in keeping with the council's resolutions, demanded that assistance be withheld from displaced persons who refused to be repatriated. Under the expanded legal definition of Soviet national, which embraced Ukrainian inhabitants of prewar Poland, most Ukrainian displaced persons were subject to repatriation. The Ukrainians, Balts, and so-called *Volksdeutsche* who refused to be repatriated found some support among council members. After long debate UNRRA assistance was extended to this category of refugees. Bowing to Soviet pressure, the UNRRA, however, promoted repatriation by removing practical obstacles, providing personal information to governments of origin, removing UNRRA personnel who opposed repatriation, and expelling from its camps activists resisting repatriation.

Since supplies were controlled by the military, the primary function of the UNRRA was to distribute the goods. The military was also responsible for health care. Supervision of the medical and sanitation program was assumed at the end of 1945 by the UNRRA. The agency developed a comprehensive vocational training program which equipped several thousand Ukrainians with the skills necessary to emigrate overseas as contract laborers. Since American authorities were opposed to using UNRRA funds for academic or religious instruction, academic education was organized by self-governing bodies set up within the various DP camps. Over a hundred Ukrainian elementary schools and some 35 Ukrainian gymnasiums were opened. The daily regimen of camp life was administered by self-governing bodies which technically were subordinate to the UNRRA. An international university, UNRRA University, was organized in Munich, and many Ukrainians taught or studied there. In this context social, cultural, religious, and political life among the Ukrainian refugees flourished. Recreational associations and theatrical groups proliferated, churches sprang up, and a publishing

center prospered in Neu-Ulm. When the UNRRA was dissolved, its functions were assumed by the IRO.

B. Kordan

**United Societies of Greek Catholic Religion in the USA** (Sobraniie greko-kafolicheskikh tserkovnykh bratstv). A fraternal organization founded in 1903 as a breakaway group from the *Greek Catholic Union of the USA (GCU). It was established by Transcarpathian Ukrainian immigrants who were opposed to the GCU's openly antagonistic stance toward the Greek Catholic church leadership in the United States. Based in the Pittsburgh suburb of McKeesport, it has published the newspaper *Rusin* (1910–16) and its successor *Prosvita* (from 1917). In 1982 the group had 3,900 members in 58 lodges.

**United States of America.** A federal republic on the North American continent with an area of 5,797,472 sq km. In 1990 the official US population was 248,709,873. The 740,803 Americans of Ukrainian origin (0.30 percent of the total) form the 26st-largest American ethnic group.

**Immigration.** Isolated individuals from what is today Ukraine began arriving with the first white settlers in the New World. Ukrainian-sounding names appear in references to and in the records of the Jamestown colony in Virginia and of New Amsterdam (now New York), in the rolls of the American revolutionary army, and in the US census of 1790.

Rev Ahapii Honcharenko and visitors on his homestead in Hayward, California, in the late 1880s

The first documented Ukrainian on American soil was Rev A. *Honcharenko, an Orthodox priest. After arriving in 1865 and settling eventually in San Francisco, he began publishing the *Alaska Herald*, a bilingual (Russian-English) newspaper aimed at the Slavic inhabitants of America's newly acquired territory. The first issue of his publication contained a short article about Taras Shevchenko and his ideals as well as a Russian-language translation of the United States Constitution.

The first wave of mass Ukrainian immigration to the United States began in the late 1870s and ended in 1914. The majority of the approx 250,000 immigrants who arrived during this period were single young men. Most of the earliest arrivals came from the Ukrainian borderland region of Transcarpathia, then under Hungarian rule. They possessed little awareness of a Ukrainian national identity and generally regarded themselves, in a regional sense, as 'Rusyns' (*Ruthenians) or 'Uhro-Rusyns' (Hungarian-Ruthenians). After 1900 a greater number of immigrants began to arrive from the more nationally conscious region of Galicia. The primary goal of both types of Ukrainian immigrants was economic improvement in the face of land shortages and a chronically depressed agrarian economy.

A second wave of mass Ukrainian immigration began in 1920 and ended in 1939. Immigration restrictions imposed by the US Congress in 1921 and 1924 limited the number of Ukrainians immigrating to the United States during this period to approx 20,000. Although most of the new arrivals came to improve their economic situation, some were political refugees fleeing persecution by the Soviet, Polish, Rumanian, or Czechoslovakian authorities. The second wave differed from the first in that it included people who had participated in Ukraine's struggle for national independence, were keenly aware of their Ukrainian heritage, and, generally, were literate.

The third wave of Ukrainian immigrants to the United States arrived between 1947 and 1955. Almost all were *displaced persons from the refugee camps of Austria and Germany. The *United Ukrainian American Relief Committee, a charitable organization founded in 1944, had sponsored some 33,000 incoming Ukrainians by 1952. Relaxed immigration restrictions provided by the Displaced Persons Act of 1948 permitted a total of approx 85,000 new Ukrainian immigrants to enter the United States. The majority were from Western Ukraine, most were literate, and a relatively high percentage (compared to the previous immigrations) had had some higher education.

No more than 7,000 Ukrainians have immigrated to the United States since 1955. With the exception of Ukrainian Jews and a few human-rights dissidents, who arrived from Soviet Ukraine, most recent Ukrainian immigrants have resettled from other countries, primarily Argentina, Brazil, Chile, Paraguay, Australia, and Venezuela.

**Population.** Because the earliest Ukrainian immigrants had little sense of their national identity, and the concept of Ukrainians as a distinct people was largely unknown in the United States prior to 1917, Ukrainians were often labeled by immigration officials as Austrians, Hungarians, Poles, or Ruthenians. Furthermore, US census statistics have been suspect until recent times, when mother-tongue and ethnic ancestry questions have been added to census forms. As a result, tallying the number of Ukrainians in the country has been problematic. The 1930 census, for example, listed 68,500 Ukrainians at a time when Ukrainian scholars, such as Y. Chyz and W. Halich, were estimating the total Ukrainian population as between 650,000 and 900,000. The 1950 census listed 79,800 Ukrainians, half of them American-born. The 1960 census recorded 107,000 persons who listed Ukrainian as their mother tongue, and in 1970 the number jumped to 249,351. The 1980 census, which included an ethnic ancestry question, counted 730,056 Ukrainians. Only 52 percent (381,054), however, claimed single Ukrainian ancestry. V. Kubijovyč estimated that there were up to 1.5 million Ukrainians in the United States.

**Settlement and distribution.** Most Ukrainians who immigrated to the United States prior to the First World War settled in Pennsylvania and, in smaller numbers, in New York, New Jersey, Michigan, Ohio, Illinois, Connecticut, Massachusetts, and Rhode Island, where they usually worked in factories. With the exception of the growing Ukrainian population in the warmer states of Florida

TABLE 1
Percentage of Ukrainians in the United States by state, selected years, 1930–90

| State | 1930 | 1940 | 1970 | 1980 | 1990 |
|---|---|---|---|---|---|
| Pennsylvania | 22.4 | 32.0 | 19.8 | 19.7 | 17.5 |
| New York | 28.4 | 23.3 | 20.9 | 17.5 | 16.4 |
| New Jersey | 10.1 | 9.4 | 13.3 | 11.1 | 10.0 |
| Michigan | 6.7 | 8.9 | 7.3 | 6.5 | 5.9 |
| Ohio | 6.3 | 8.3 | 7.5 | 6.3 | 5.9 |
| Illinois | 5.9 | 4.1 | 7.9 | 5.6 | 5.2 |
| Connecticut | 3.5 | 2.9 | 3.9 | 3.5 | 3.2 |
| Massachusetts | 3.2 | 2.9 | 1.7 | 2.3 | 2.4 |
| Minnesota | 1.2 | 1.2 | – | 1.3 | 1.4 |
| Rhode Island | 1.0 | 1.3 | – | 0.5 | 0.5 |
| Missouri | – | 0.6 | – | 0.6 | 0.6 |
| California | – | – | 4.4 | 6.8 | 7.6 |
| Florida | – | – | 1.3 | 3.5 | 4.6 |
| North Dakota | – | 1.4 | – | 0.4 | 0.5 |
| Maryland | 0.6 | – | – | 1.9 | 2.1 |

(where some Ukrainians have established retirement communities) and California (where employment rates are usually high), this pattern of settlement has remained relatively stable (see table 1). Only a small number of Ukrainians have followed agricultural pursuits. Prior to the First World War Ukrainian farm communities were established in North Dakota, Wisconsin, Michigan, Virginia, Maryland, Connecticut, Georgia, and Texas. Ukrainians also lived in Hawaii as contract workers, often under abominable conditions.

Some of the first Stundists who emigrated from Russian-ruled Ukraine in North Dakota in the late 1890s. From left: Ivan Sypchenko, Havrylo Kuzenny, Ivan Yukhymiv, Yukhym Sych

During the First World War many Ukrainian workers were attracted to the cities by war industries; Ukrainian communities in Allentown-Bethlehem (Pennsylvania), Baltimore, Boston, Buffalo, Chicago, Cleveland, Detroit, Minneapolis, Newark (New Jersey), New Haven (Connecticut), Rochester (New York), Youngstown (Ohio), and Wilmington (Delaware) consequently developed or expanded. Most of these centers continued to grow during and after the Second World War as a result of both the

TABLE 2
Estimated number of Ukrainians in the most populous
US metropolitan areas, 1980

| | | |
|---|---|---|
| 1. | New York | 56,340 |
| 2. | Philadelphia | 52,740 |
| 3. | Chicago | 37,420 |
| 4. | Detroit | 34,640 |
| 5. | Pittsburgh | 34,200 |
| 6. | Newark | 23,920 |
| 7. | Cleveland | 20,220 |
| 8. | Los Angeles | 19,660 |
| 9. | Nassau-Suffolk, NY | 18,440 |
| 10. | NE Pennsylvania | 14,420 |
| 11. | Allentown-Bethlehem | 11,440 |
| 12. | New Brunswick (PA)–Sayreville (NY) | 11,200 |
| 13. | Washington, DC | 10,180 |
| 14. | Buffalo, NY | 10,020 |
| 15. | Youngstown-Warren, OH | 9,460 |
| 16. | Rochester, NY | 8,860 |
| 17. | Minneapolis–St Paul, MN | 7,720 |
| 18. | Syracuse, NY | 7,420 |
| 19. | Boston, MA | 7,060 |
| 20. | Baltimore, MD | 7,020 |
| 21. | Albany–Schenectady–Troy, NY | 6,840 |
| 22. | San Francisco–Oakland | 6,700 |
| 23. | Fort Lauderdale–Hollywood, FL | 6,180 |
| 24. | Patterson–Clifton–Passaic, NJ | 5,820 |
| 25. | Anaheim–Santa Ana–Garden Grove, CA | 5,720 |
| 26. | Tampa–St Petersburg, FL | 5,180 |
| 27 | Jersey City, NJ | 5,120 |
| 28. | Long Branch–Asbury Pk, NJ | 4,480 |
| 29. | San Diego, CA | 4,440 |

burgeoning war economy and the influx of new immigrants. Visible Ukrainian communities also emerged in San Francisco, San Diego, Los Angeles, Phoenix, Denver, Tampa–St Petersburg, Miami, Fort Lauderdale, Houston, and Washington (DC).

In 1980 the largest concentrations of Ukrainians were found in the metropolitan areas of New York City, Philadelphia, Chicago, Detroit, Pittsburgh, Cleveland, and Newark (see table 2). Distinct Ukrainian neighborhoods were fading, however. In New York (between East 2nd and East 14th Streets in Lower Manhattan) and Chicago (between Rockwell, Damen, Superior, and Division) one can still find local churches, stores, youth and community centers, banks and credit unions. In Detroit and Cleveland, however, the center of Ukrainian life has shifted to the suburban towns of Warren and Parma respectively.

**Socioeconomic development.** According to US immigration records, 97.2 percent of the 174,375 'Ruthenians' who arrived in the United States between 1899 and 1910 had been peasant farmers, unskilled laborers, or servants. A mere 0.06 percent (109 persons) claimed to be professionals or business people. Not surprisingly, fewer than 1 percent went into business, usually a grocery store, butcher shop, or tavern.

After the First World War the number of Ukrainians who went into business increased. Grocery stores predominated (some 2,000 in 250 communities were recorded in 1934), but bakeries, restaurants, pharmacies, hardware stores, funeral homes, service stations, barber and beauty salons, laundries, and window-cleaning establishments were also owned and managed by Ukrainians. According to a survey conducted by W. Halich, there were some 1,207 professionals in the United States in 1937. Of this

number, 625 were clergymen, 262 teachers, 68 attorneys, 66 nurses, 61 physicians, and 34 engineers.

The socioeconomic profile of the third immigration revealed a greater number of professionals and persons with skills. Among the Ukrainians living in Germany's displaced persons camps in 1948 (many destined to move on to the United States), 12.3 percent were professionals, business people, or administrators; 26.6 percent skilled laborers; and 61 percent unskilled or farm workers. By 1965 there were 1,200 Ukrainian physicians in the United States, 700 engineers, 150 lawyers, almost 2,000 school teachers, 250 college and university professors, nearly 200 librarians, and over 100 veterinarians. According to the 1970 census 22.4 percent of Ukrainian-American males were either professionals or administrators, 23.7 percent craftsmen, 20.4 percent skilled laborers, 22.5 percent unskilled laborers, and 11 percent service or farm workers. The annual median income for Ukrainian-American males, however, was only 6,200 dollars, 500 dollars less than the US average. For Ukrainian-American females, in contrast, the annual median income was 3,000 dollars, 900 dollars more than the US average. In terms of education, 9.1 percent of Ukrainian-American males and 2.5 percent of Ukrainian-American females had completed 17 or more years of schooling.

The 1980 census identified groups according to ancestry, and so gave a more complete and accurate socioeconomic profile of Ukrainians. In 1980, 10.2 percent of Ukrainian-American males held managerial positions; 8.5 percent were professionals; 5.3 percent were in education at all levels; 5.9 percent were artists, athletes, or technicians; 27.7 percent were in direct sales or sales-related fields; 12.3 percent were in the service industry; 1.3 percent were employed in agriculture and mining; 24.3 percent were skilled laborers; 4.2 percent were unskilled laborers; and 0.4 percent were unemployed. The 1980 educational picture showed that 11.1 percent of Ukrainian males and 5.6 percent of Ukrainian females had completed 17 or more years of schooling; this figure was above the US national average of 10.2 and 5.3 percent respectively. Individual income for males was 13,150 dollars (958 dollars above the US average) and 6,123 dollars for females (861 dollars above the US average).

The first Ukrainian business ventures were grocery stores established in Shenandoah, Pennsylvania, in 1887. The stores were later combined to form the so-called Co-operative General Store, which had expanded to five neighboring cities by 1889. The co-op movement began to decline after 1910 and by 1936 Ukrainian co-ops existed in only four American centers. Ukrainians, however, excelled as private entrepreneurs. From an early date Ukrainians owned boardinghouses, saloons, grocery stores, bakeries, and steamship agencies. By 1936 there were 2,723 Ukrainian-owned enterprises, including 847 grocery stores, 487 restaurants, 307 hotels, 46 window-cleaning establishments, and 11 financial establishments. Consumer co-operative stores were opened in Chicago and Philadelphia after the Second World War, but the co-operative movement became static as Ukrainians continued to concentrate on the professions and small business. A few Ukrainians succeeded in establishing or owning their own corporations. Before the Second World War, Dr S. Sochotzky established the Zellotone Chemical Company in New York City; P. Yarosh owned a canning factory near

Orange, Connecticut; and W. Dzus founded a company in West Islip, New York, to produce the industrial fastener he invented. Since the war Ukrainians have established successful engineering firms, tool companies, printing shops, and construction firms.

Ukrainian banking began after 1919 with the establishment of building and loan associations. Usually associated with neighborhood churches, some were able to survive the Great Depression and to re-establish themselves later in new, modern facilities as savings and loan associations. Among those that thrived during the 1950s were Parma Savings and Loan in Cleveland (founded in 1915), Ukrainian Savings and Loan in Philadelphia (1918), Trident Savings and Loan in Newark, New Jersey (1924), and Trident Savings and Loan in Chicago (1935). In 1964 Security Savings and Loan was established in Chicago; the name was changed to First Security Savings Bank in 1984, and by the end of 1988 the institution had assets of 136 million dollars. During the 1950s a number of Ukrainian federal credit unions were opened in major cities throughout the United States. In 1989 the *Ukrainian National Credit Union Association included 32 separate financial institutions, with total assets approaching 300 million dollars.

The first organization of Ukrainian businessmen was established in New York City in 1890. By 1942 it had over 100 members and was called the Association of Ukrainian Businessmen. A Ukrainian Graduates' Club (open to all college graduates) was founded in Detroit in 1939. The Ukrainian Professional Association was established in 1933. Called the Ukrainian Professional Society of North America after the Second World War, the organization faded out of existence in the early 1970s after various professional groups created separate organizations. The Ukrainian Engineers' Society of America and the *Ukrainian Veterinary Medical Association were both founded in 1948. Ukrainian professional groups formed later included the *Association of Ukrainian Lawyers, founded in 1949 and reorganized as the *Ukrainian American Bar Association in 1977; the *Ukrainian Medical Association of North America (1950); the *Ukrainian Journalists' Association of America (1952); the *Ukrainian Catholic Press Association (1952); the *Ukrainian Library Association of America (1961); the *Ukrainian American Association of University Professors (1961); and the Ukrainian Teachers' Association of the USA (1966). Among the most active of all professional groups are the medical doctors, lawyers, and university professors. During the 1980s local professional and business clubs were created in New York, New Jersey, and Washington, DC.

**Participation in American political life.** Ukrainians were not active in American political life until recently, largely because they lacked the numerical and financial strength to launch successful campaigns for the US House or Senate. Of the 435 congressional districts, Ukrainians are statistically referenced in only 44: 16 in Pennsylvania, 12 in New York, 9 in New Jersey, 3 in Ohio, and 2 each in Illinois and Michigan. Of these 44 districts, Ukrainians account for 1 percent or more of the total population in only 8 (see table 3). Despite the odds, Ukrainians have run for congressional seats in Pennsylvania, Ohio, Illinois, Michigan, and Florida.

A number of Ukrainians have been appointed to significant posts in the federal government. Of these, Dr G. *Kistiakowsky served as a special adviser to President D.

TABLE 3
Congressional districts in which Ukrainians account for 1 percent or more of the population, 1980

| State | District no. | Area | Percent Ukrainian |
|---|---|---|---|
| Pennsylvania | 3 | Northeast Philadelphia | 1.3 |
| Pennsylvania | 6 | Reading | 1.1 |
| Pennsylvania | 10 | Scranton | 1.0 |
| Pennsylvania | 11 | Wilkes-Barre | 1.3 |
| Pennsylvania | 15 | Allentown-Bethlehem | 1.2 |
| New Jersey | 6 | New Brunswick–Perth Amboy | 1.2 |
| Ohio | 20 | Cleveland (central and west) suburbs | 1.1 |
| Illinois | 8 | Chicago (north and northwest) | 1.2 |

Eisenhower for science and technology (1959–61), J. Charyk was an air force undersecretary (1960–3) during the J. Kennedy administration, Dr M. *Yarymovych was deputy director of the Energy Research Development Agency (1975–77), and Dr M. *Kuropas served in the White House under President G. Ford as special assistant to the president for ethnic affairs (1975–6). C. *Warvariv was agency director of UNESCO Affairs in the Department of State (1978–9) during the J. Carter years. Dr L. *Dobriansky was appointed US ambassador to the Bahamas in 1982–6 by President R. Reagan. B. Futey was appointed a federal judge in the US Foreign Claims Court by President Reagan in 1987. D. Bonior (Democrat, Michigan) was elected House majority whip in July 1991.

Ukrainian-American leaders have encouraged involvement in local American politics since the early 1900s. *Svoboda*, the oldest Ukrainian newspaper in North America, urged the creation of local political clubs in every Ukrainian community followed by the establishment of a national political federation. The idea was never realized, and the few chapters that were organized accomplished little. An exception was the Ukrainian American Citizens' Club of Philadelphia, organized in 1909 with the help of Bishop S. *Ortynsky. The First World War and the hope of Ukrainian independence mobilized the Ukrainian community to organize a national political lobby. A 'Ukrainian Day' was proclaimed by President W. Wilson for 21 April 1917, largely as a result of Ukrainian efforts. Ukrainian Americans have lobbied in Washington, DC, ever since then. In 1959 the Ukrainian Congress Committee of America (UKKA) was instrumental in having the US Congress pass Public Law 86–90, which mandated the annual observance of Captive Nations Week during the third week of July. The Ukrainian National Association (UNA) and the UKKA combined forces to press for a statue of Taras Shevchenko on public land in Washington, DC. The statue was unveiled in 1964 during a ceremony which included participation by former President Eisenhower and approx 100,000 Ukrainian Americans. The most successful recent lobbying effort was conducted by Americans for Human Rights in Ukraine on behalf of a US commission to study the 1932–3 famine in Ukraine. The commission was established in 1984, monies were authorized in 1985, and a staff headed by Dr J. Mace was hired in 1986. In 1988 the commission presented a 524-page report to Congress documenting the nature of the famine.

A rally of some 18,000 Ukrainian Americans commemorating the 1932–3 man-made famine in Soviet Ukraine at the Washington Monument on 2 October 1983

Republicans and Democrats have had Ukrainian affiliates since the 1920s, but their effectiveness within both the party and the community has been minimal. Ukrainian Republicans created the Ukrainian Republican Federation in 1969, with 20 state organizations from New York to California. But with the advent of television advertising during national campaigns, the need for special-interest political affiliates has waned. This change in approach has not diminished Ukrainian lobbying activities in the capital, however. The UKKA opened a Washington office in 1977, and the UNA opened its office in Washington in 1988.

**Religion.** The early immigrants from Western Ukraine were predominantly Greek Catholic (now 'Ukrainian Catholic') in religion. Because early immigrants had no churches of their own, they initially attended the Roman Catholic churches of Poles and Slovaks. They petitioned Metropolitan S. Sembratovych of Lviv for priests from Galicia or Carpatho-Ukraine to serve them, and in 1884 Rev I. Voliansky arrived in Shenandoah, to organize America's first Ukrainian community. Because he was a married priest, Archbishop P. Ryan of Philadelphia petitioned Rome to recall him, thereby opening a struggle between American Roman and Greek Catholics over celibacy that has lasted to the present day. During Voliansky's five years in the United States, he established parishes in five Pennsylvania towns (Kingston, Freeland, Olyphant, Shamokin, and Wilkes-Barre) as well as in Jersey City, New Jersey, and Minneapolis, Minnesota. In 1890 the Roman Curia approved a prohibition against married Ukrainian priests' holding parishes in North America. As a result many priests and parishioners joined the Russian Orthodox church, following the lead of Rev A. Toth, the first cleric to convert. Centered in Minneapolis, the new Russian Orthodox Greek Catholic church had converted over 7,000 Ruthenians to Russian Orthodoxy by 1900.

Despite the substantial loss of clergy and parishioners, the Ukrainian (Greek) Catholic church survived. By 1894 there were 30 Greek Catholic priests in the United States, 26 from the eparchies of Mukachiv and Prešov in Carpatho-Ukraine and 4 from the eparchy of Lviv in Galicia. The most consciously Ukrainian of them was the small contingent from Galicia, which was later to play a critical role in the development of a Ukrainian community in America. Other priests arrived with different loyalties. After 1892, pro-Magyar Greek Catholic priests from the Carpatho-Ukrainian eparchies were instructed by the Hungarian government to remain 'faithful Magyars' in America and to remember their Hungarian homeland. Because of their numbers, the Hungarian-Ruthenian clergy dominated the Ruthenian-American community, at least initially. Like their Russian counterparts, they opposed the Ukrainian national revival.

In the 1890s eight ethnonationally conscious priests from Galicia arrived in the United States: Revs I. Konstankevych, N. Dmytriv, M. Stefanovych, I. Ardan, A. Bonchevsky, S. Makar, M. Pidhoretsky, and P. Tymkevych. Called the *'American Circle' by their supporters, they stemmed the Russian and Hungarian-Ruthenian tides and helped to establish a distinctly Ukrainian Catholic community in the United States, primarily by taking control of *Svoboda* and the Ukrainian National Association from the Russophiles and expanding reading rooms, Ukrainian schools, publications, and choirs. The American Circle introduced the term 'Ukrainian' into Ruthenian social consciousness by publishing the poems of T. Shevchenko and I. Franko, by explaining political developments in Galicia in the pages of *Svoboda*, and by elaborating on the idea of a united and free Ukraine. In 1901 the circle established the *Association of Ruthenian Church Communities in the United States and Canada. Renamed the Ruthenian Church in America in 1902, this society organized a convention in Harrisburg, Pennsylvania, which called for the appointment of a Greek Catholic bishop for Ruthenians in the United States.

A struggle between the American Circle and the Hungarian-Ruthenian clergy for control of the Ruthenian Catholic church ensued for the next five years. In 1907 the Holy See appointed S. Ortynsky, a Basilian monk from Galicia, the first Greek Catholic bishop in America. The Ruthenian-American community, while highly supportive of Ortynsky's appointment, did not like *Ea Semper*, the papal bull, that defined the bishop's prerogatives. Ortynsky had to obtain permission from local Latin rite bishops before visiting Ruthenian parishes in their dioceses; he had to file a full report with the Latin bishop after each visit; and he could not allow his Ruthenian priests to administer confirmation. In mixed Catholic marriages the primacy of the Latin rite was maintained. In 1913 the situation was rectified, when Rome granted Ortynsky 'full and ordinary jurisdiction over all Greek Catholics coming from Galicia and Podcarpathia [Subcarpathia].' A year later the Holy See issued *Cum Episcopo Graeco*, another papal bull, which removed the more offensive canons of *Ea Semper*.

After Ortynsky's death in 1916, the Holy See created two Greek Catholic jurisdictions in the United States, one for the Ukrainians and another for the Ruthenians (Carpatho-Rusyns). Rev P. Poniatyshyn was appointed administrator of the Ukrainian parishes. The division was reconfirmed in 1924, when two exarchates were established along the same administrative lines. Bishop K. *Bohachevsky was appointed bishop of an exarchate that included 144 parishes, 102 priests, and 237,445 faithful. V. *Takach, the Ruthenian exarch, received 155 parishes, 129 priests, and 288,390 faithful. The division between the two ethnically identical groups has remained to the present.

The Ukrainian Orthodox movement in America began in Chicago in 1915, when a group of disgruntled parishioners left St Nicholas's Ukrainian Catholic church to form the Independent People's Church. They were soon joined by other disaffected Catholics and former Ukrainian adherents of Russian Orthodoxy, and in 1919 established the *Ukrainian Orthodox Church in the USA, which was affiliated with the recently established Ukrainian Autocephalous Orthodox Church in Ukraine. In 1924 the All-Ukrainian Orthodox Church Council in Kiev appointed Archbishop I. *Teodorovych the first hierarch of America's newly created Ukrainian Orthodox community. In the late 1920s more Catholics joined the diocese, which by 1939 consisted of 24 parishes, 22 priests, and 19,000 faithful. Concerned by doubts of the canonicity of Teodorovych's consecration in Kiev, another group of ex-Catholic priests and laity met in Allentown, Pennsylvania, in 1929 and founded a second Orthodox diocese, the Ukrainian Orthodox Church of America, which was headed for a time by Y. Zhuk and later by B. *Shpylka. The second diocese included 43 parishes and 36 priests by 1939.

Ukrainian Protestantism in the United States began in the 1890s, when a group of Baptists (*Stundists) from villages in the Kiev region settled first in Virginia and later in North Dakota. Converted from Orthodoxy by German colonists in Ukraine, they had fled religious persecution by the tsar. The spread of Protestantism in Ukrainian-American urban centers benefited from the religious conflicts among Ruthenian Catholics, Ukrainian Catholics, and Russian Orthodox, and before the First World War Baptist groups emerged in Illinois and Pennsylvania, and a Presbyterian congregation was established in Newark, New Jersey (1909). In addition Bloomfield College (New Jersey) and the University of Dubuque (Iowa), two institutions which prepared Presbyterian ministers, offered Ukrainian language, history, and literature courses. In 1922 the Ukrainian Evangelical Alliance of North America was formed, and a group of Presbyterian parishes established the Ukrainian Evangelical Reformed church.

All Ukrainian religious denominations benefited from the influx of new immigrants after the Second World War. The third immigration followed the pattern of church membership established earlier. Ukrainians from Galicia generally joined Catholic parishes; Ukrainians from Bukovyna, Volhynia, and eastern Ukraine usually joined the Orthodox. In 1954 the Vatican elevated Bohachevsky to the rank of archbishop and the exarchate to the status of an eparchy. Two years later a second Ukrainian Catholic eparchy was created. Headed by Bishop A. *Senyshyn, whose seat was in Stamford, Connecticut, the new jurisdiction comprised all the New England states and the state of New York, with 53 parishes, 101 priests, and 86,324 faithful. The Philadelphia eparchy was headed by an auxiliary bishop (J. *Schmondiuk became the first American-born Ukrainian Catholic bishop on 8 November 1956) and included 122 parishes, 93 priests, and 219,720 faithful. In 1958, when Bohachevsky was elevated to the rank of metropolitan, the Ukrainian Catholic Church in America had 300 priests, 2 bishops, 223 churches or chapels, 2 orphanages, 3 homes for the aged, 2 colleges, 4 high schools, and 32 parochial day schools. Bohachevsky died in 1961 and was succeeded by Senyshyn. In the same year Schmondiuk moved to Stamford, and a third eparchy was established to include Ukrainian Catholics in Michigan and all states west of the western boundaries of Ohio, Kentucky, Tennessee, and Mississippi. J. *Gabro, with his episcopal seat in his native Chicago, was consecrated in 1961 to oversee 31 parishes and 20,439 faithful.

During the 1960s the Ukrainian Catholic church in the United States suffered a serious rift. In Chicago, Bishop Gabro changed the religious calendar from Julian to Gregorian, thereby creating a split among the parishioners of St Nicholas's Cathedral, with the result that half of the congregation built a new church, SS Volodymyr and Olha.

Metropolitan Senyshyn died in 1976 and was succeeded by Schmondiuk. When Schmondiuk died unexpectedly in 1979, he was succeeded by M. *Liubachivsky. When the pope convened a synod of Ukrainian bishops in 1980, Liubachivsky was selected coadjutor to the aging Cardinal Y. *Slipy. He was replaced in Philadelphia by Rev S. *Sulyk, who was consecrated on 31 March 1981. Two days later he participated in the consecration of Rev I. *Lotocky as successor in Chicago to Gabro, who had died the previous year. In 1983 a fourth Ukrainian eparchy, headed by Bishop R. *Moskal, was created for the 60,000 Ukrainian Catholics living in western Pennsylvania, Ohio, West Virginia, Kentucky, Tennessee, Georgia, and Florida. Although the Ukrainian Catholic church maintains the heritage of the Greek Catholic (Uniate) church in Ukraine, Old Church Slavonic, which until the 1960s was used exclusively as the liturgical language, was to a great extent replaced by the vernacular in 1965.

The Ukrainian Orthodox Church in America also experienced a period of expansion immediately after the Second World War. In 1947 a synod of Ukrainian Orthodox bishops was convened in Germany under the leadership of Metropolitan P. Sikorsky. Hoping to unite the Ukrainian Orthodox in North America, the synod delegated Archbishop M. *Skrypnyk to approach Metropolitan Teodorovych to effect his reconsecration. The two newly constituted Orthodox groups attempted to unite at a 1948 conference in Allentown, Pennsylvania, with Archbishop Skrypnyk as the head of a Ukrainian Orthodox church. Bishop Shpylka's refusal to join prompted some of his parishes to place themselves under Skrypnyk's jurisdiction, thereby creating a third Orthodox diocese. On 27 August 1949 Teodorovych was reconsecrated by a Syrian exarch, and in 1950 Skrypnyk's parishes came under Teodorovych's jurisdiction. A 1950 synod in New York City constituted the hierarchy of the newly unified Ukrainian Orthodox church, with Teodorovych as its head and Skrypnyk head of the consistory. Also included in the hierarchy were Archbishops V. *Malets and H. Shyprykevych. By 1964 the Ukrainian Orthodox Church in the USA consisted of 104 churches, 127 clergy, and 87,200 faithful. Metropolitan Teodorovych died in 1971 and was succeeded by Skrypnyk, who headed an archdiocese centered in South Bound Brook, New Jersey, with two dioceses (one in Chicago headed by Archbishop C. *Buggan, the other in New York headed by Bishop A. Scherba) consisting of 90 parishes with 80,000 faithful. The administrative offices, along with a museum, publishing house, memorial church, and central cemetery, are located in South Bound Brook. Ukrainian is used predominantly in the Divine Liturgy, although English services and sermons are occasionally given in some parishes to accommodate the younger generation. In 1990 Metropolitan Skrypnyk became the patriarch of the Ukrainian Autocephalous Orthodox church and was succeeded as American metropolitan by Archbishop Buggan in 1992.

Bishop B. Shpylka, head of the Ukrainian Orthodox Church of America, died in 1965 and was succeeded by

Archbishop P. Vydybida-Rudenko and, in 1967, by Bishop A. *Kushchak. Consecrated a metropolitan in 1983, Kushchak died in 1986 and was succeeded by Bishop V. Maidansky, whose diocese remains under the canonical jurisdiction of the patriarch of Constantinople. The church includes 22 parishes and 22 priests. Old Church Slavonic is used in the Divine Liturgy exclusively.

The influx of new immigrants from Ukraine also helped strengthen the Ukrainian Protestant churches in the United States. After 1950, new Baptist congregations were established in Hartford, Cleveland, Philadelphia, Minneapolis, Milwaukee, Pittsburgh, Seattle, and the California cities of Los Angeles, Santa Barbara, and Hemet. Today there are 30,000 Ukrainian Protestants in the United States, most of whom belong to congregations organized into two national federations. The largest is the Ukrainian Evangelical Baptist Convention, headed by Rev O. Harbuziuk, with 24 churches and some 10,000 faithful. Baptist leaders are visible in mainstream Ukrainian-American life as well as in Ukraine itself. A daily radio broadcast, the 'Ukrainian Voice of the Gospel,' was initiated in 1952. In addition the Baptist Convention has delivered some 250,000 Ukrainian-language religious books to Ukraine in recent years, including 10,000 copies of the New Testament in 1988. The other Protestant group, the *Ukrainian Evangelical Alliance of North America, once included some 12 Presbyterian parishes (Reformed confession). Since the death of its head, Rev. V. *Borovsky, in 1987, however, most of the parishes have ceased to exist. Ukrainians in the United States are also Pentecostals (many of whom are recent émigrés), Methodists, Lutherans, and Seventh Day Adventists.

All three of the major Ukrainian religions in the United States are losing members because of intermarriage, changing values, and migration among the younger generation (see table 4).

**Civic and political organizations.** The oldest and most significant civic organizations in the Ukrainian-American community are the fraternal insurance associations established prior to the First World War, whose major purpose was to provide low-cost insurance to Ukrainian immigrants, most of whom had limited savings and little income. They continue to provide insurance plus a variety of benefits to their members and to the Ukrainian community to the present day.

TABLE 4
Ukrainian-American church membership, 1967 and 1988

| Church | Diocesan/ eparchial seat | Membership 1967 | 1988 |
|---|---|---|---|
| Ukrainian Catholic church | Philadelphia, Stamford, Chicago, Parma | 281,253 | 147,533 |
| Ukrainian Orthodox Church of the USA | South Bound Brook, NJ | 87,000 | 45,000* |
| Ukrainian Orthodox American-Ecumenical patriarchate | New York | 30,000 | 5,310 |
| Protestant denominations | | 50,000* | 30,000* |

*Estimates; no reliable statistics are available.

The first fraternal insurance association, the Brotherhood of St Nicholas, was established by Rev Voliansky in 1885, but dissolved soon after he returned to Ukraine. The first permanent fraternal society was the *Greek Catholic Union of the USA (GCU), which was founded in 1892. Although membership was open to all Ruthenians, disputes over finances and national orientation resulted in an exodus of the Galician leadership and the establishment in 1894 of the Ruthenian National Association (renamed the *Ukrainian National Association [UNA] in 1914). From its inception the UNA represented a Ukrainian perspective, while the GCU initially supported the Hungarian-Ruthenian point of view. Both fraternal societies aided their respective churches – the formation of a local UNA branch was often a prelude to the establishment of a local parish – and developed various educational means to promote their ethnic identity. The fraternal newspapers were the most influential in developing popular public opinion. The GCU published *Amerikanskii russkii viestnik*; the UNA was responsible for *Svoboda*. Today the GCU does not have an active ethnocultural orientation, but focuses its resources on spiritual and social programs.

In 1908 the UNA convention proclaimed Bishop Ortynsky as 'patron' of the organization. In his capacity as chairman of the bylaws committee at the 1910 convention, Ortynsky, despite strong lay opposition, pushed through resolutions which changed the name of the organization to the Greek Catholic Ruthenian Association, subordinated the renamed fraternal society to the bishop's office, restricted the election of future convention delegates to Catholics exclusively, and obligated all members to attend confession at least once a year, during Easter. The bishop's action, subsequently approved by the majority, led to the first serious split in the Ukrainian/Ruthenian camp. Delegates from 14 branches walked out and, with other newly established local brotherhoods, called a convention which in 1911 gave birth to the Ukrainian Workingmen's Association (today the *Ukrainian Fraternal Association [UFA]). In 1912 an all-Catholic fraternal organization, the *Providence Association of Ukrainian Catholics in America, appeared. A fourth fraternal society, the *Ukrainian National Aid Association (UNAA), was established two years later. Each fraternal society supported Ukraine's struggle for freedom during the First World War by organizing political action committees and raising thousands of dollars in support of this cause. Ideological differences during the interwar period put a temporary end to such co-operation. In 1940, however, the four organizations set aside their political differences to form the *Ukrainian Congress Committee of America (UKKA), an all-Ukrainian coalition to lobby on behalf of Ukrainian interests in Europe. The four fraternal societies helped establish the *United Ukrainian American Relief Committee (1944) and fully supported its later efforts to resettle Ukrainian refugees at the end of the Second World War. The united fraternal front collapsed in 1980, when the UNA and the UFA withdrew from the UKKA in response to attempts by the militant nationalist wing of the community to extend its control over the body. In 1983 the two fraternals were instrumental in establishing the *Ukrainian American Coordinating Council (UACC), a parallel umbrella organization.

The UNA, with headquarters in Jersey City, New Jersey, has approx 60,000 members and remains the largest and most influential Ukrainian fraternal benefit society in

America. The UFA, with headquarters in Scranton, Pennsylvania, has some 18,000 members. The Providence Association of Ukrainian Catholics has 17,000 members and headquarters in Philadelphia. With a national membership of 8,000, the Ukrainian National Aid Association, centered in Chicago, is the smallest of the 4 Ukrainian fraternal organizations. A major concern of fraternal executives is declining membership. Although assets and insurance in force have increased, membership, usually measured in terms of certificates in force, dwindled by an average of 1 percent per year in 1977–87 (see table 5).

The first political ideology to influence the thinking of American Ruthenian-Ukrainians was socialism. Under the leadership of the American Circle, the political posture of the community essentially reflected the ideology of the Ruthenian-Ukrainian Radical party in Galicia. After the Radicals split into Social Democrats and National Democrats in 1899, the UNA leadership leaned toward the more moderate National Democrats. The first socialist organization to appear in the Ukrainian-American community was *Haidamaky, in 1907. An even more radical group, the Ukrainian Workers' party, formed in 1909, was dissolved a short time later. With Ukrainian socialist organizations multiplying, a convention in 1915 established the Ukrainian Federation of Socialist Parties of America (UFSPA).

The first Ruthenian-Ukrainian national congress was held in Jersey City on 1 January 1900, with subsequent congresses in 1903, 1904, and 1905. At the last congress the organization was renamed the Society of Ruthenian Patriots. Disagreements between social and national democrats within the society continued to escalate, however, and the fledgling organization soon ceased to exist.

The First World War and the Ukrainian liberation struggle galvanized the Ukrainian-American community and strengthened its sense of ethnonational identity. Following a meeting of fraternal society leaders after the onset of hostilities, an all-Ukrainian national organization was created on behalf of Ukrainians in the United States and Europe. In late October 1915 a convention in Philadelphia established a new, national umbrella organization, the *Federation of Ukrainians in the United States, with Dr V. Simenovych as president. Almost from its inception internal strife between those who supported social reform in Ukraine and those whose first priority was national independence made the federation ineffective. In 1916 the UNA withdrew from the federation and joined forces with the Providence Association to create a second all-Ukrainian umbrella organization, the Ukrainian Alliance of America, which was headed by Rev P. *Poniatyshyn. The feder-

Members of the Ukrainian-American Citizens' Association in Philadelphia in 1916

ation's main base was thus reduced to Haidamaky, the UFA, and socialists.

Both the federation and the alliance competed for the loyalty of the community, now fully conscious of its Ukrainian identity. Representatives of both organizations urged the White House and Congress to assist a war-torn Ukraine. In response to a congressional resolution, President Wilson issued a proclamation on 2 March 1917 which designated 21 April 1917 as 'Ruthenian (Ukrainian) Day' in the United States. The alliance also succeeded in creating a Washington office in the Capitol building suite of Congressman J.A. Hammil (Democrat, New Jersey), one of the most articulate allies the Ukrainian-American community has ever had in Washington. On 18 November 1918 the alliance changed its name to the Ukrainian National Committee, realigned its executive to include disenchanted former federation members, and embarked on a new phase of international lobbying, still under the leadership of Poniatyshyn.

At the second convention of the UFSPA, held in 1917, participants were split between the 'internationalists,' who believed the first priority for Ukraine should be economic reform, and the Social Patriots, who were more nationalistic in their orientation. With the internationalists in the majority, resolutions were passed calling for the destruction of capitalism. In August 1919 an official delegation of UFSPA officers attended the first convention of the Communist Party of America, and a month later the UFSPA was renamed the Ukrainian Federation of the Communist Party of America. This development forced the Social Patriots to form a new socialist organization, *Oborona Ukrainy.

Ukrainian Communist activity in the United States

TABLE 5
Statistics of Ukrainian fraternal benefit societies in the United States, 1977 and 1987

| Name | Insurance in force (in dollars) | | Certificates in force | | Lodges | |
|---|---|---|---|---|---|---|
| | 1977 | 1987 | 1977 | 1987 | 1977 | 1987 |
| Ukrainian National Assn | 92,399,396 | 100,266,521 | 81,076 | 67,644 | 459 | 415 |
| Ukrainian Fraternal Assn | 22,108,312 | 27,716,406 | 22,546 | 18,434 | 261 | 215 |
| Providence Assn | 14,950,219 | 17,390,302 | 18,694 | 17,179 | 210 | 213 |
| Ukrainian Natl Aid Assn | 9,721,822 | 19,098,913 | 8,802 | 7,942 | 171 | 159 |
| Greek Catholic Union | 93,557,407 | 129,035,779 | 48,385 | 43,256 | 421 | 213 |

flourished following the creation of the United Ukrainian Toilers Organization (SURO) in 1924. Its growth was dramatic. By the fifth SURO convention in 1932, its network included 2,750 members in 112 branches, 3,400 members in affiliated front organizations, 12 Young Pioneer branches (with some 300 children), 36 Ukrainian schools, 64 reading rooms, 35 drama groups, 17 choirs, 12 mandolin orchestras, and 23 owned or rented 'labor temples.' The Communists expanded their activities during the 1930s, especially after the United States extended diplomatic recognition to the Soviet Union. In 1932, Ukrainian Communists established their own fraternal insurance society by creating separate Ukrainian branches of the International Workers' Order. By 1938 there were some 15,000 Ukrainian members of the order, including 3,000 children. During the late 1930s and all through the early 1940s America's Ukrainian Communists were engaged in a vicious and continuous polemics with most other Ukrainian associations in the country. Ukrainian Communist influence in the United States all but disappeared with the end of the Second World War (see *League of American Ukrainians).

Members of the Sich society in New York in 1917

The first political organization to counter the Communists was the Hetman Sich, which consisted of individuals loyal to Hetman P. *Skoropadsky. The *Sich society movement began in the United States in 1902, when Rev M. Strutynsky established the first Sich Athletic Society in Olyphant, Pennsylvania. By 1918 there were 14 Sich branches on the eastern seaboard, all dedicated primarily to bodybuilding. During the First World War some Sich members attempted to organize a Ukrainian military legion to fight for Ukrainian independence. The project failed, but the idea lived on. Militarization began with the introduction of uniforms and the election of S. Hrynyvetsky as supreme otaman at the 1922 convention. Sich began to change ideologically soon after O. Nazaruk, a leading monarchist theorist, convinced Hrynyvetsky that monarchism was the only viable ideological alternative to the increasingly popular Bolsheviks. The Sich came under attack during the 1930s when Ukrainian-American Communists and others alleged that it was a Nazi underground organization serving Germany. Even though the FBI could substantiate none of the charges, the cloud of accusation caused a serious setback for the group. When the Second World War began, the Communist network in the United States accused Sich (renamed the *United Hetman Organization, or UHO) of conducting espionage to sabotage the American war effort. Although another FBI investigation, which continued until 1943, completely exonerated the UHO, the barrage of negative commentaries heard on radio and published in American books, newspapers, and magazines made UHO members fearful

that their activity might someday lead to deportation to the USSR, and caused them to leave the organization in droves. The UHO Supreme Executive voted for dissolution on 7 March 1942.

The second anticommunist political organization to emerge in the United States between the two world wars was the *Organization for the Rebirth of Ukraine (ODVU). Founded in 1930 with moral assistance from the Organization of Ukrainian Nationalists (OUN), ODVU was by 1939 the single most powerful anticommunist political organization in the Ukrainian-American community. Two other affiliated organizations came into being during the early 1930s, the *Ukrainian Gold Cross (a women's society) and the *Young Ukrainian Nationalists (MUN). The first All-American Congress of Ukrainian Nationalists took place in 1935, with 223 delegates representing ODVU, the Gold Cross, MUN, the Black Sea Sich, and the Ukrainian War Veterans' Association of the USA in attendance. By 1938 the combined ODVU network – some 70 ODVU branches, 70

A mass demonstration of Ukrainian Americans in Philadelphia protesting the Polish Pacification of Western Ukraine in December 1930

Gold Cross branches, and 41 MUN branches – had a total American membership estimated to be over 10,000.

Meanwhile, the dissolution of the Federation of Ukrainians in 1919, coupled with the subsequent decline of the *Ukrainian National Committee in 1922, prompted another attempt to form a truly representative umbrella political organization for all Ukrainians. On 26–27 October 1922, 130 delegates representing 176 Ukrainian organizations established the *United Ukrainian Organizations in America (UUOA), which survived for 18 years. The UUOA was soon under attack by the Communists, and the executive was forced to reconstitute the organization under a new name.

Ukrainian Americans in the US Armed Forces taking part in a flag-blessing ceremony at St George's Ukrainian Catholic Church in Manhattan in 1943

In May 1940, 805 delegates from 168 different communities met in Washington, DC, and formed the *Ukrainian Congress Committee of America (UKKA). Included were practically all the organizations that had once belonged to the UUOA. In 1944 the UKKA established the United Ukrainian American Relief Committee (ZUADK) to aid Ukrainian displaced persons. Between 1947 and 1957 the ZUADK helped resettle approx 60,000 Ukrainian refugees in the United States. With the exception of the Communists, all segments of Ukrainian-American society – religious, political, cultural, and social – belonged to the UKKA. In 1967 it helped to organize the first *World Congress of Free Ukrainians (SKVU), in New York City. During the 1970s the UKKA increasingly fell under the direction of the *Ukrainian Liberation Front, a post–Second World War coalition of OUN (Bandera faction) organizations which included the *Organization for the Defense of Four Freedoms for Ukraine (OOChSU), the OOChSU Women's Society, the *Ukrainian Youth Association (SUM), and the *Ukrainian Student Organization of Mikhnovsky (TUSM). The Liberation Front arrived at the 1980 UKKA convention with a majority of delegates and took total control of the organization. As a result, delegates from 27 national organizations walked out of the conclave. Led by the UNA, the dissidents included the UFA, the Ukrainian National Women's League of America (SUA), the Ukrainian American Veterans, ODVU, the Gold Cross, MUN, the Plast Ukrainian scouting organization, the Organization of Democratic Ukrainian Youth (ODUM), most professional

and scholarly societies, and a number of smaller organizations. Remaining within the UKKA were the Providence Association, the UNAA, OOChSU, TUSM, SUM, OOChSU Women's Society, and the Association for the Liberation of Ukraine. Subsequent compromise talks failed, and on 1 October 1983 approx 100 delegates from the UNA, UFA, ODVU, and many (but not all) other dissenting societies came together in Washington, DC, to form the UACC.

The first Ukrainian women's organization in the United States was the Sisterhood of St Olha, a fraternal insurance society established in 1897 in Jersey City, New Jersey. The second national women's organization was the Ukrainian Women's Alliance of America, established in Chicago as a fraternal benefit society in 1917. Both organizations dissolved within a few years. The Ukrainian Women's Society of New York, established in 1921, lasted longer. In 1925 the society founded the first Ukrainian women's confederation, changed its name to the *Ukrainian National Women's League of America (SUA), and began establishing branches on the east coast. A national congress of Ukrainian women was held in New York City in 1932, with 68 delegates in attendance. By 1940 the SUA had 61 branches throughout the United States, organized into three regional councils. With the arrival of the third immigration, the SUA enjoyed unprecedented growth, and by 1984 there were 120 branches from New York to California. Other national Ukrainian women's organizations in the United States include the Ukrainian Gold Cross (est 1931), the *United Ukrainian Orthodox Sisterhoods (est 1961), and the OOChSU Women's Society (est 1967).

The first Ukrainian youth organization in the United States was Sokil, a gymnastic society. Patterned after its European counterpart, the first branch was organized by Rev P. Tymkevych in Yonkers in 1902. That same year Rev M. Strutynsky established the first Sich branch in Olyphant. Sokil eventually faded, and Sich became associated with the political agenda of Hetman Skoropadsky and eventually evolved into an adult-dominated political organization.

The lack of viable youth organizations was not perceived as a problem by community leaders until the 1930s, when the generation born during and after the First World War was in its early teens. Hoping to activate the younger generation, many organizations began forming youth affiliates. The first to develop youth cadres was the Ukrainian Orthodox community. In 1932 the League of Ukrainian Clubs (LUK) was created. Three years later there were some 20 LUK clubs throughout the United States. The LUK eventually disappeared; it was replaced in 1941 by the Organization of Ukrainian Orthodox Youth (renamed the *Ukrainian Orthodox League of the USA [UPL] in 1947).

The most successful early coalition of secular, nonpartisan youth groups was the *Ukrainian Youth League of North America (UYLNA), which emerged in 1933. At a constitutional convention during Ukrainian Week at the Chicago World's Fair, delegates established a North American organization that sought to hold annual youth conventions, sponsor annual sports rallies, publish a cultural monthly in the English language (*Trend*), and form local clubs. By 1939, 69 American and Canadian youth organizations were affiliated with the UYLNA. Except for the war years, the UYLNA held annual conventions until the 1970s, when it ceased to exist.

In 1933 the Ukrainian Catholic church established the Ukrainian Catholic Youth League, renamed the Ukrainian

Catholic Youth League of North America (UCYLNA) in 1938, when the Ukrainian Catholic Brotherhood of Canada joined its ranks. In 1939 it consisted of 60 clubs. With support from the Providence Association and the church, the UCYLNA held annual conventions and sponsored track and field events. In 1962 the name was changed to the *League of Ukrainian Catholics of America (LUC), a reflection of its aging membership. Conventions are still held annually.

Ukrainian political organizations also created youth affiliates. The UHO established 'Junior Siege' (ie, Junior Sich) branches, whose activities included flying lessons, horseback riding, track and field events, and baseball. The Junior Siege disappeared when the UHO was dissolved. The first nationalist youth organization was MUN, founded in New York City in 1933. Activities included military drill, drama, basketball, baseball, writing articles for the *Trident*, and glider and airplane flying. With support from ODVU (which became associated with the OUN [Melnyk faction] after the war), MUN survived as a national organization until the early 1960s. Communist youth affiliates, the Young Pioneers, were prevalent before the war, but all but disappeared completely during the Cold War era of the 1950s. With many Ukrainian young people serving in the armed forces during the Second World War, all Ukrainian youth organizations suffered major drops in membership.

While prewar Ukrainian youth organizations struggled to survive in the postwar era, three new youth organizations founded by the third immigration flourished. SUM, established in 1949, claimed 4,100 members in 34 local branches and 5 summer camps in 1984. Today it is the largest and most affluent Ukrainian youth organization in America. Part of the Liberation Front network, SUM is a member of the UKKA. ODUM was created in 1950. It claimed 450 members in 1984, with local branches in the larger cities and a summer camp in New York State. A member of the UACC, ODUM is associated with the 'democratic' political network composed mostly of the Second World War immigrants from eastern Ukraine. A virtual transplant of the Ukrainian scouting organization founded in Western Ukraine in 1912, the *Plast Ukrainian Youth Association was established in the United States in 1951. In 1984 it claimed some 4,000 members, 27 local chapters, and 5 summer camps. Politically, Plast is nonaligned.

Although several Ukrainian student clubs existed prior to 1940, it was only after the arrival of the third immigration that a national effort was made to organize Ukrainian college students. The *Federation of Ukrainian Student Organizations of America (SUSTA) was founded in 1953 and by 1971 had approx 30 university campus branches. The most successful endeavor initiated by SUSTA was the creation of the *Ukrainian Studies Fund in 1957. Other student organizations established after the war include TUSM, associated with the OUN (Bandera faction); the *Zarevo Ukrainian Student Association, associated with the OUN (Melnyk faction); and the *Obnova Society of Ukrainian Catholic Students.

**Education.** The first Ukrainian heritage school was established in Shenandoah, in 1888 by Rev I. Voliansky, and a second was begun in Shamokin, Pennsylvania, in 1893 by Rev I. Konstankevych. Within a year similar part-time heritage classes existed in Mt Carmel, Wilkes-Barre, and Olyphant in Pennsylvania, and in Minneapolis. By 1913 most large Ukrainian-American communities had such schools, thanks largely to the efforts of priests who viewed the expansion of Ukrainian education among youth as part of their ministry. During the early days of the movement, texts were substandard, there was no co-ordinated curriculum, and the facilities were poor, with many classes held in damp church basements. Reform measures began in 1913, soon after the Ruthenian Greek Catholic Teachers' Association was created, and in 1918 proficiency exams for teachers were introduced. A new teachers' organization, *Ridna Shkola, was established in 1927. By 1939 there were 86 Ukrainian heritage schools in the United States, with 56 taught by the precentors, 18 by Basilian sisters, and 12 by the Sisters of the Immaculate Conception. The third immigration increased school enrollments and improved curriculum co-ordination under the auspices of the UKKA Educational Council (established in 1953), which also provided school accreditation. By 1971 there were some 150 Ukrainian heritage schools. Approximately half were under the jurisdiction of the Educational Council; the others were administered by Catholic and Orthodox parishes.

The first Ukrainian college, Ruska Kolegiia, was opened in Shamokin in 1905. Organized on the European gymnasium model, it accepted all students who had the equivalent of an American high-school education. The school folded after a year, but college-level courses were later established at Bloomfield College in Bloomfield, New Jersey, and at the University of Dubuque, in Iowa, two institutions that had once trained Presbyterian missionaries for work among Ukrainian immigrants. Bloomfield offered courses in Ukrainian language, history, and literature from 1910 to 1920, and Dubuque offered them from 1912 to 1935. During the 1970s approx 20 American universities and colleges were offering courses in the Ukrainian language. Today the Ukrainian Catholic church operates Manor Junior College for Girls in Jenkintown, Pennsylvania, and St Basil's Ukrainian Catholic Seminary for Boys in Stamford. Both offer courses in Ukrainian language and culture. The most comprehensive program of Ukrainian studies can be found at Harvard University.

The first boarding school (for boys) was established in Yonkers, New York, by Rev P. Tymkevych in 1904. Opened as a high school, it lasted less than two years. The first permanent boarding school was an orphanage opened by Bishop Ortynsky in 1912 in Philadelphia. In 1931 the first accredited Ukrainian high school, St Basil's Academy for Girls, was dedicated by Bishop Bohachevsky in Fox Chase, Pennsylvania. A Catholic preparatory school for boys opened in Stamford in 1933. A third high school for boys and girls was established in 1951 in Hamtramck, Michigan.

Bishop Bohachevsky opened the first permanent Ukrainian parochial day school in 1925. Six years later he initiated a national campaign to build schools which resulted in full-time elementary classes in Pittsburgh (1933), New Kensington, Pennsylvania (1936), Chicago (1936), Hamtramck (1936), Newark (1939), and Watervliet, New York (1940). The influx of immigrant children in the postwar era resulted in the opening of more schools. By 1967 there were 33 elementary schools, 3 high schools, and 2 college-level institutions. Twenty years later the elementary-school population had dropped by more than 50 percent (see table 6).

**Press.** Ukrainian press history in the United States began in 1868, when Rev A. Honcharenko brought out the

TABLE 6
Ukrainian Catholic elementary and secondary schools and enrollments, 1967 and 1987

| Eparchy | No. of elementary schools | | Elementary school population | | No. of secondary schools | | Secondary school population | |
|---|---|---|---|---|---|---|---|---|
| | 1967 | 1987 | 1967 | 1987 | 1967 | 1987 | 1967 | 1987 |
| Philadelphia | 19 | 12 | 4,119 | 1,489 | 1 | 1 | 285 | 360 |
| Stamford | 10 | 6 | 2,406 | 594 | 1 | 1 | 74 | 95 |
| Chicago | 4 | 2 | 1,702 | 480 | 1 | 0 | 207 | 0 |
| Parma | – | 2 | – | 446 | – | 0 | – | – |
| Total | 33 | 22 | 8,227 | 3,009 | 3 | 2 | 566 | 455 |

*Alaska Herald*. In the same year he added *Svoboda* (Liberty), a supplement that included articles about Ukraine written in Russian. The first Ukrainian-language newspaper in America was *Ameryka*, first published by Rev I. Voliansky in Shenandoah, on 15 August 1886. It lasted until 1890. Two other early Ukrainian publications were *Ruske slovo* and *Novyi svit*, both of which came into existence in 1891 and folded the same year.

The first permanent Ukrainian newspaper in the United States was *\*Svoboda*, today the world's oldest continuously published Ukrainian-language daily newspaper. First published by Rev H. *\*Hrushka on 15 September 1893, *Svoboda* became the official press organ of the Ukrainian National Association in 1894. Between 1886 and 1934, 79 different Ukrainian periodicals were established in the United States, most of them short-lived. Those that survived were usually backed by fraternal or religious organizations.

*Shershen'*, a twice-monthly literary journal which first appeared as a satirical periodical in 1908, became the official organ of the Ukrainian Workingmen's Association (UWA) in 1910. It was replaced in 1911 by a new UWA publication, *Narodna volia*, which today is published weekly in Ukrainian and English. The Providence Association began to publish the newspaper *Ameryka* (not to be confused with Voliansky's) in 1912. *Narodne slovo* (*Ukraïns'ke narodne slovo* from 1959) made its appearance in 1914 as the organ of the Ukrainian National Aid Association.

In 1908–21 a group of Ukrainian Presbyterians brought out *Soiuz*. *Pislanets' pravdy*, a Baptist periodical first published in Ukraine in 1927, was revived as a US publication in 1947. The Ukrainian Evangelical Alliance of North America began publishing *Ievanhel's'kyi ranok* in 1961.

In 1909 Rev P. Poniatyshyn started *Dushpastyr*, a Catholic monthly which soon became the official organ of Bishop Ortynsky. The Ukrainian Catholic exarchate began publishing *Shliakh* in 1940. The Ukrainian Catholic eparchy of Chicago has published the bilingual weekly *Nova zoria* since 1965. In 1967 the *\*Ukrainian Patriarchal Society in the United States began publishing *\*Patriarkhat*, a quarterly magazine.

Two widely read Ukrainian Orthodox periodicals, *Dnipro* (1920–50) and the *Ukrainian Orthodox Herald* (from 1935), were published prior to the Second World War. The Ukrainian Orthodox Church in the USA began publishing *Ukraïns'ke pravoslavne slovo* in 1950 and its English edition in 1967. Another periodical, *Pravoslavnyi ukraïnets'*, was published by the Ukrainian Autocephalous Church (Conciliar) from 1952.

Ukrainian socialists began publishing *Khlops'kyi para-*

*graf* and *Haidamaky* in 1909. The latter periodical survived until 1916. Another early socialist weekly was *Robitnyk*, founded in 1914. It was replaced by *Ukraïns'ki shchodenni visty* in 1920, soon after the formation of the Ukrainian Federation of the Communist Party of America. It is still published in New York City as *Ukraïns'ki visti*.

The Sich organization began publishing *Sichovi visty* in 1918, renamed *Sich* in 1924 after the monarchists took over. As the official organ of the UHO, during the 1930s it was renamed *Nash stiah*.

The ODVU began publishing *Vistnyk ODVU* in 1932, and in 1935 created *Natsionalist*, a bilingual paper (Ukrainian-English) whose name was later changed to *Ukraïna*. In 1939 the ODVU took over publication of the *Trident*, an English-language monthly periodical initiated by MUN in 1936. After the Second World War the ODVU began publishing *Samostiina Ukraïna*, initially as a monthly and then as a quarterly. It now appears irregularly as a journal of political opinion. MUN resurrected the *Trident* as a quarterly in 1960, but publication was discontinued in 1962.

The Liberation Front has published *Visnyk OOChSU* since 1947. UKKA has published the *Ukrainian Quarterly* since 1944. The latter also sponsored the *Ukrainian Bulletin* between 1948 and 1970.

The Ukrainian Women's Alliance of America published

Some of the Ukrainian-American newspapers published in the 1930s

Some of the Ukrainian-American journals and magazines published in the postwar period

*Rannia zoria* between 1918 and 1920. The oldest women's journal in the United States, *Zhinochyi svit*, was first published in 1933 by the Ukrainian National Women's League of America (SUA). SUA began publication of *Nashe zhyttia/Our Life* in 1944.

Periodicals exclusively for Ukrainian youth began appearing in the 1930s. Among them were *Junior Siege*, published by the UHO; the *Trident* (1936–41), initially published by MUN; the *Ukrainian Trend* (1937–69), the official organ of the UYLNA; and *Ukrainian Youth* (1934–42), a periodical of the UCYLNA. Postwar youth publications include *Krylati* (1951–), published by SUM; *Hotuis'* (1953–), published by Plast; and *Veselka* (1954–), a children's magazine published by the UNA.

The most successful English-language periodicals are the UNA-sponsored *Ukrainian Weekly*, which first appeared in 1933 as a youth-oriented newspaper, and *Forum*, published by the UFA.

One of the most popular periodicals was *Lys Mykyta* (a regular publication from 1951 until 1990), a satirical journal edited by E. Kozak.

Today the Ukrainian press in the United States includes some 53 Ukrainian-language periodicals, 23 bilingual publications, and 15 English-language publications. These include 1 daily publication, 10 weekly, and 20 monthly; the remainder appear less frequently. The estimated readership for all Ukrainian periodicals is 208,000.

Particularly popular among Ukrainian Americans are the *calendars or almanacs published annually by the three major Ukrainian churches, the four fraternal societies, and other organizations. In addition to such periodicals, books, pamphlets, and other literature are produced regularly by publishing houses and cultural and scholarly institutions. These include the four fraternal societies, the three major churches, the Shevchenko Scientific Society, the Ukrainian Academy of Arts and Sciences, Prolog Research Corporation, the Ukrainian Academic Press, Smoloskyp publishers, Bulava, and Chervona Kalyna.

**Literature.** Ukrainian-American literature began with the development of the Ukrainian press in the 1890s. Many editors and contributors to *Svoboda* wrote dramas, short stories, essays, and poetry, as well as journalistic articles. Among the pioneers in this field were Rev H. Hrushka, who wrote poetry and short stories; Rev S. Makar, who was renowned for his short stories about the perils of assimilation and the demoralizing aspects of American life (his 'American Boy' is an early classic); Rev N. Dmytriv, who provided factual and fictional accounts

of immigrant life; and S. Chernetsky, a poet and satirist. Most early immigrant literature focused on the hardships of life in the United States and on a romanticized version of life in the old country.

During and immediately after the First World War Ukrainian immigrant literature was devoted to patriotic themes reflecting Ukraine's struggle for independence. Poets who emerged during this period included S. Musiichuk, D. Zakharchuk, and M. Kostyshyn. A central literary figure was A. *Granovsky, a professor of entomology at the University of Minnesota. Granovsky published three separate collections of lyric poetry between 1910 and 1914 while still in Ukraine. In the United States his poetry became more patriotic, in keeping with his work as an American activist in Ukraine's liberation struggle. Some writers who tried their hand at prose during this period were M. Biela, Zh. Bachynsky, M. Strutynsky, and Yu. Chupka. All wrote on social themes centered around immigrant life.

In contrast the literary works of American-Ukrainian writers (approx 150 in number) after the Second World War tended by and large to ignore immigrant life and to focus on more universal themes. Among the most noteworthy are the poets Ye. Malaniuk, T. Osmachka, V. Barka, O. Tarnavsky, B. Boychuk, B. Rubchak, and G. Tarnawsky; the humorists M. Ponedilok and I. Kernytsky; the novelists Yu. Kosach and D. Humenna; the dramatist L. Poltava; and the literary critics Yu. Sherekh (Shevelov), Yu. Lavrinenko, and H. Kostiuk. The writers organized themselves into literary societies, the most notable being the *Slovo Association of Ukrainian Writers in Exile. Founded in 1954, it publishes *Slovo*, a periodical devoted to new literary works and criticism, and sponsors literary evenings and conferences. Another postwar group, the *Association of Ukrainian Writers for Young People, was transplanted from Germany during the 1950s and has edited the Ukrainian children's magazine *Veselka*. A circle of younger writers constituting the so-called *New York Group introduced modernist trends into the Ukrainian literary process. It published *Novi poeziï* on an annual basis in 1959–79.

The Shevchenko Scientific Society, the Ukrainian Academy of Arts and Sciences in the US, and the Ukrainian studies program at Harvard University provide studies on literary topics, usually in the form of conference proceedings. Also enhancing Ukrainian literary life in America are such small literary groups as Svitannia and Volosozhar, and literary discussion clubs in New York, Philadelphia, Chicago, Detroit, Minneapolis, and Los Angeles. Two Ukrainian writers who have succeeded in the American literary market are M. Bloch and Ya. Surmach-Mills, both of whom write children's stories.

**Scholarship.** Among Ukrainians who excelled in the American academic world prior to the Second World War were G. Kistiakowsky, a chemist and researcher in atomic energy at Harvard University; S. Timoshenko, a pioneering scientist in strength of materials at the University of Michigan and Stanford University; the historian G. Vernadsky, at Yale; the entomologist A. Granovsky, at the University of Minnesota; and the geneticist T. Dobzhansky of Columbia University. Among the Ukrainians who gained national and international renown as scholars after the Second World War were the Byzantologist I. Ševčenko and the Turkologist O. Pritsak of Harvard; the political scientists and historians J. Reshetar of the University of Washington in Seattle and A. Motyl at Columbia University; the linguist and Slavist G.Y. Shevelov of Columbia University; the political scientist Ya. Bilinsky of the University of Delaware; the historians R. Szporluk of the University of Michigan and Harvard University and J. Pelenski of the University of Iowa; the archeologist and art historian R. Holod of the University of Pennsylvania; the scientists O. Smakula, R. Jackiw, and D. Sadoway of the Massachusetts Institute of Technology, L. Romankiv of the IBM T.J. Watson Research Center, O. Bilaniuk of Swarthmore College, N. Holoniak of the University of Illinois, L. Dmochowski of Baylor University, S. Trofimenko of Du Pont Experimental Station, and M. Kasha of Florida State University; and the literary scholars B. Rubchak at the University of Illinois and G. Grabowicz at Harvard.

Oleh Bilorus (left), Ukraine's first ambassador to the United States, his wife, and Viktor Batiuk, Ukraine's first ambassador to the United Nations, at Kennedy International Airport on 28 April 1992

A valuable contribution of the third immigration has been the formation of research institutions. These include organizations with European antecedents, such as the Shevchenko Scientific Society, which publishes its *Proceedings* in English and *Zapysky* in Ukrainian, and the Ukrainian Academy of Arts and Sciences, which publishes its *Annals* in English. Societies founded in the United States include the Lypynsky East European Research Institute (Philadelphia), the Ukrainian Historical Association (Kent, Ohio), the Ukrainian Center for Social Research (New York), and the Ukrainian Research and Documentation Center (New York).

**Music.** The first Ukrainian choir in America was established in Shenandoah, by V. Simenovych in 1887. Choral ensembles were later organized in Shamokin, Olyphant, and Mayfield. Even though they were enthusiastically supported by the local community, most early choral ensembles were mediocre. Choral performances improved dramatically after 1900 when a number of fully qualified cantors came to the United States and took up residence in parishes that could afford their services. By the beginning of the First World War good choirs existed in Chicago, Pittsburgh, Philadelphia, Newark, New Haven, New York City, and Perth Amboy, New Jersey.

The arrival of the Ukrainian National Chorus under O. Koshyts (formerly the *Ukrainian Republican Kapelle) was a milestone in Ukrainian-American musical history. In 1922 and 1923 the chorus toured North America and set a new standard for Ukrainian choral performance. By 1936 former chorus members were directing outstanding choral ensembles in Newark, Cleveland, and Chicago. Ukrainian music was also being recorded during this period by such American companies as Columbia and RCA Victor. Between 1923 and 1952 Columbia released 430 separate Ukrainian recordings, and Victor produced over 100. Two of the most popular Ukrainian recording artists of the time were the fiddler P. Humeniuk, whose *Ukraïns'ke vesil'ia* (Ukrainian Wedding) became a classic, and W. Gula and his Trembita Orchestra, who recorded for Columbia.

The highly professional character of Ukrainian choral music was maintained after the Second World War by choruses in New York City (Dumka), Philadelphia (Prometheus and Kobzar), Detroit (Trembita), Cleveland (Dnipro), and Chicago (Surma). Today the best-known Ukrainian choral ensemble in the United States is the Ukrainian Bandurist Chorus in Detroit.

Ukrainian vocal performers who have excelled in the American music world in recent years include the Metropolitan Opera star P. Plishka, who has starred in over 40 roles, and A. Dobriansky, who has sung with the Met since the 1969–70 season.

Ukrainian instrumental music also dates back to the days of the early immigrants. The first Ukrainian band was organized in Shamokin in 1891, and within a few years marching bands, often with elaborate uniforms, existed in Olyphant, Mayfield, Shenandoah, Braddock, Pittsburgh, and Cleveland. As interest in marching bands waned after the First World War, the popularity of mandolin orchestras increased. A Ukrainian Conservatory of Music existed in New York City during the 1920s. The Association of Friends of Ukrainian Music was established in New York in 1934 and contributed greatly to the growing popularity of Ukrainian instrumental music. String orchestras were established in New York (under the direction of the composer M. Haivoronsky) and in Chicago during the 1950s. The *Ukrainian Music Institute of America was created in 1952 and soon had 16 branches throughout the country. In recent years bandura ensembles have become a popular form of instrumental expression, especially among the young. Ukrainian Americans who have enjoyed the most success in American music circles include M. Malko, who was director of the Chicago Symphony Orchestra from 1945 to 1957; V. Baley, conductor of the Las Vegas Symphony; and the concert pianist L. Artymiw.

**Theater, film, and dance.** The first drama troupes were established in Shamokin and Olyphant in 1880 and were soon followed by ensembles in other Ukrainian communities of eastern Pennsylvania. The first performance of the popular Ukrainian opera *Zaporozhets za Dunaiem* (Zaporozhian Cossack beyond the Danube) was staged in New York City in 1910. By 1940 such classic Ukrainian operas as *Natalka Poltavka*, *Kateryna*, and *Taras Bulba* were seen regularly on Ukrainian-American stages. Most dramatic productions, however, dealt with local themes, such as those by Rev S. Makar, who wrote *Amerykans'kyi shliakhtych* (American Noble) and *Skupar* (Miser). Both were pop-

President Leonid Kravchuk of Ukraine (left) meeting with President George Bush, Secretary of State James Baker, and National Security Adviser Brent Scowcroft at the White House on 6 May 1992

ular productions prior to the First World War. Efforts to establish permanent drama societies in major Ukrainian cities persisted through the 1920s and 1930s. Most troupes, however, were short-lived. Ukrainian theater in the United States greatly improved following the arrival in the 1950s of the Ensemble of Ukrainian Actors, under the direction of V. Blavatsky, in Philadelphia and the *Theater Studio of Y. Hirniak and O. Dobrovolska. Both companies staged a series of popularly acclaimed productions during the 1950s and 1960s. Since 1965 their theatrical tradition has been continued by the drama school of L. *Krushelnytska in New York City.

During the 1930s Ukrainian amateur film studios under the direction of V. *Avramenko produced films such as *Natalka Poltavka, Marusia,* and *Zaporozhets za Dunaiem.* Ukrainian filmmaking has recently improved, with the emergence of S. Nowytski of Minneapolis, who has produced such prizewinning films as *Pysanka, Harvest of Despair* (a documentary about the man-made famine in Ukraine), and *Helm of Destiny* (the story of America's Ukrainians). Ukrainian Americans who have pursued successful film careers in Hollywood include A. Sten, N. Adams, J. Hodiak, M. Mazurki, J. Palance, and the director E. Dmytryk.

Like the early choirs, Ukrainian dance ensembles prior to the First World War were supported by a handful of enthusiastic supporters. This changed soon after the arrival in 1928 of V. Avramenko, a dance master from Ukraine. After settling in New York City, Avramenko began his American dance career by advertising dance lessons in *Svoboda.* Supported almost entirely by contributions from the community, Avramenko began visiting Ukrainian communities and by 1936 had organized over 50 dance troupes throughout the country. A high point in his career came on 25 April 1931, when approx 500 of his dancers performed at the Metropolitan Opera House.

Ukrainian dance troupes proliferated in the United States after the Second World War; some may have been given new impetus by the tour of P. Virsky's *State Dance Ensemble of Ukraine in 1966. Today outstanding dance groups perform in Miami, Chicago, Milwaukee, New York, Detroit, and Cleveland. As in the past, Ukrainian dance remains the single most effective vehicle for retaining the interest of young people in Ukrainian culture.

**Fine arts, architecture, and folk art.** Early Ukrainian artists in the United States were icon painters, such as Rev H. Verkhovsky, who painted the sanctuary of St Nicholas's Cathedral in Chicago, and E. Vasylenko. American-born painters who emerged between the two world wars, such as M. Myrosh and I. Kuchmak, devoted much of their time to creative painting. Others became involved with film illustration (A. Palyvoda), graphic arts (N. Bervinchak), and commercial illustration (J. Rosol). The most celebrated Ukrainian artist in the United States was the European-born A. Archipenko, internationally acclaimed as one of the great innovators of modern sculpture. During his American period he produced over 750 pieces, many of which can be found in major museums throughout the world.

Roman Popadiuk being sworn in at the White House on 27 May 1992 as the first American ambassador to Ukraine

Some 100 Ukrainian painters and sculptors immigrated to the United States after the Second World War. In 1952 they founded the *Ukrainian Artists' Association in the USA. Centered in New York City, the association sponsors art exhibits and individual showings. Similar local art groups exist in Chicago (home of the *Ukrainian Institute of Modern Art), Minneapolis, and Detroit. Among the individual Ukrainian artists who have exhibited in many American cities in the postwar period, the most consistently popular have been M. Moroz, L. Hutsaliuk, M. Butovych, E. Kozak, and J. Solovij. The best-known Ukrainian artist in recent years has been the late J. Hnizdovsky, whose unique graphic art is part of many museum and private collections. Ukrainian religious art has been preserved by such artists as S. Hordynsky, M. Dmytrenko, and P. Kholodny. Other Ukrainian artists work as illustrators (Ya. Surmach-Mills) or art instructors (N. Brytsky, J. Gaboda, and A. Olenska-Petryshyn). Perhaps the most commercially successful artist was cinematographer W. Tytla, who spent many years working for Walt Disney Studios in Hollywood. Ukrainian sculptors who have gained renown in America include S. Lytvynenko, M. Mukhyn, K. Milonadis, M. Chereshnovsky, and A. Darahan.

Another aspect of the Ukrainian artistic experience in the United States is Ukrainian church architecture. Noteworthy examples of traditional styles include Chicago's St

Nicholas's (Catholic) Cathedral, modeled after the St Sophia Cathedral in Kiev; the neo-Byzantine St Andrew's (Orthodox) Church in Bloomingdale, Illinois; the Cossack-baroque St Andrew's (Orthodox) Memorial Church in South Bound Brook; and Sacred Heart (Catholic) Church in Johnson City, New York. Churches built in a more modern style include St Joseph's (Catholic) Church in Chicago; Holy Trinity (Catholic) Church in Kerhonkson, New York; and St Josaphat's (Catholic) Church in Rochester, New York. A unique blend of traditional and innovative architectural styles can be found in the Ukrainian Catholic Church Shrine in Washington, DC, and in the Holy Ascension Ukrainian Orthodox Church in Clifton, New Jersey.

Ukrainian folk art – *pysanky*, wood carvings, ceramics, embroidery, kilims – is much in demand in cities with large Ukrainian populations. Most of these cities have retail stores which market such products. The recent availability of Easter egg–making kits has meant that this ancient folk art can be passed on more easily from one generation to another.

The most significant cultural achievement of the Ukrainian community prior to the Second World War was the 1933 erection of a Ukrainian pavilion at the Chicago World's Fair. The displays featured folk and modern Ukrainian art from Europe and the United States, highlighted by the works of the sculptor A. Archipenko. Another major cultural accomplishment was the Ukrainian Cultural Gardens in Cleveland. Dedicated on 2 June 1940, the gardens eventually were the site of statues of Volodymyr the Great, T. Shevchenko, I. Franko (all sculpted by A. Archipenko), and Lesia Ukrainka (rendered by M. Chereshnovsky). After some of the art was stolen or destroyed by vandals during the 1970s, the remaining statues were removed. Since the Second World War, memorial statues to T. Shevchenko have been erected in Washington, DC (1964), and Elmira Heights, New York (1981).

**Archives, museums, libraries.** Prior to the Second World War most Ukrainian archival materials were found in the private collections of older immigrants who appreciated the significance of historical documentation. Unfortunately many archives were either lost or destroyed after the collectors died. Only more recently large depositories have been established at the Ukrainian Academy of Arts and Sciences in the US; at the Ukrainian museums-archives in Cleveland, South Bound Brook, and Detroit; at the Ukrainian National Museum in Chicago; at the *Ukrainian Diocesan Museum of Stamford; and at the Ukrainian Cultural Institute at Dickinson State College, Dickinson, North Dakota. The most extensive collection of archival materials for all periods can be found at the Immigration History Research Center at the University of Minnesota.

The creation of museums was pursued particularly strongly by the third immigration. Ukrainian museums now exist in New York, Chicago, Philadelphia, Cleveland, Detroit, South Bound Brook, and Stamford. Of special significance is the Ukrainian Institute of America, founded by the millionaire W. Dzus and housed in a New York City landmark mansion. The institute features a permanent collection of paintings and occasional exhibits of Ukrainian fine and folk art.

Extensive Ukrainian book collections can be found at the Library of Congress in Washington, DC, the New York Public Library, and the libraries of Columbia University, Harvard University, the University of Illinois in Champaign–Urbana, the University of Chicago, and the Hoover Institution at Stanford University.

**Sport.** In the interwar period Sich societies established their own track and field, swimming, volleyball, soccer, softball, basketball, bowling, and tennis clubs and competitions. Ukrainian youth athletic competitions were held in Philadelphia in 1935 and 1936. Young athletes from the United States and Canada competed in the first Ukrainian-American Olympiad, held in Philadelphia in 1936. In 1938 the Ukrainian National Association founded a baseball league; by 1940 it had 28 teams.

After the mass emigration of refugees to the New World in the late 1940s, new Ukrainian sports clubs were founded. Soccer, tennis, volleyball, and swimming have been particularly popular. The *Ukrainian Sports Federation of the USA and Canada was founded in 1953–4. In 1980 it organized, with other émigré communities of the captive nations of the USSR, the Free Olympiad in Toronto. The Ukrainian delegation won 11 gold, 8 silver, and 7 bronze medals and took second place overall.

**Assimilation.** Statistics showing lower church and organizational membership and decreased language retention suggest that Ukrainians are assimilating rapidly into mainstream American society. Tables 4 and 5 examine church and fraternal-benefit society membership; the 1980 US census revealed that Ukrainian language use among Ukrainian Americans in the country stood at only 17 percent. Among certain professional groups the percentage is even lower (see table 7). No solution to the steady decline in language use has been found, nor does there appear to be any antidote for assimilation. Recent events in Ukraine, however, and the intensification of contacts with the mother country may slow down this process.

TABLE 7
Language retention among Ukrainian-American professionals, 1980

| Profession | Total number | Number speaking Ukrainian | % |
|---|---|---|---|
| Manager/administrator | 32,980 | 3,720 | 11 |
| Engineer | 10,820 | 1,060 | 9 |
| Sales representative | 8,040 | 980 | 12 |
| College teacher | 4,380 | 580 | 13 |
| Physician | 3,560 | 640 | 17 |
| Lawyer/judge | 3,160 | 260 | 8 |
| Natural scientist | 2,260 | 400 | 17 |
| Editor/reporter | 1,520 | 280 | 18 |
| Librarian | 1,320 | 420 | 31 |
| Dentist | 1,160 | 120 | 10 |

BIBLIOGRAPHY
Bachyns'kyi, Iu. *Ukraïns'ka imigratsiia v Z'iedynenykh derzhavakh Ameryky* (Lviv 1914)
Halich, W. 'Economic Aspects of Ukrainian Activity in the United States,' PH D diss, State University of Iowa, 1934
– *Ukrainians in the United States* (Chicago 1937)
Chyz, Ya. *The Ukrainian Immigrants in the United States* (Scranton 1939)
Mamchur, S.W. 'Nationalism, Religion, and the Problem of As-

similation among Ukrainians in the United States,' PH D diss,
Yale University, 1942

Czuba, N.A. *History of the Ukrainian Catholic Parochial Schools in
the United States* (Chicago 1956)

Dragan, A. *Ukrainian National Association: Its Past and Present,
1894–1964* (Jersey City 1965)

Procko, B. 'Pennsylvania: Focal Point of Ukrainian Immigration,'
in *The Ethnic Experience in Pennsylvania*, ed by J.J. Bodnar
(Lewisburg, Pa 1973)

*Proceedings of the Conference on Carpatho-Ruthenian Immigration, 8
June 1974*, ed by R. Renoff (Cambridge, Mass 1975)

Dyrud, K.P. 'The Rusin Question in Eastern Europe and in America, 1890–World War I,' PH D diss, University of Minnesota,
1976

Shtohryn, D. 'Ukrainian Literature in the United States: Trends,
Influences, Achievements,' in *Ethnic Literatures since 1776: The
Many Voices of America*, ed W.T. Zyla and W.M. Aycock (Lub-
bock 1978)

Magocsi, P.R. (ed). *The Ukrainian Experience in the United States: A
Symposium* (Cambridge, Mass 1979)

Gronow, P. 'Ethnic Recordings: An Introduction,' in *Ethnic Recordings in America: A Neglected Heritage*, ed A. Jabbour (Washington 1982)

Procko, B. *Ukrainian Catholics in America: A History* (Washington
1982)

Kuropas, M.B. 'Ukrainian Chicago: The Making of a Nationality
Group in America,' in *Ethnic Chicago*, ed P. d'A. Jones and M.
Holli (Chicago 1984)

Wynar, L. 'American Slavic and East European Press: A Brief
Survey Report,' *Ethnic Forum* 4, nos 1–2 (Spring 1984)

Procko, B. 'The Ukrainian Press,' in *The Ethnic Press in the United
States*, ed S.M. Miller (New York 1987)

Wolowyna, O. (ed). *Ethnicity and National Identity: Demographic
and Socioeconomic Characteristics of Persons with Ukrainian
Mother Tongue in the United States* (Cambridge, Mass 1986)

Kuropas, M.B. *The Ukrainian Americans: Roots and Aspirations,
1884–1954* (Toronto 1991)

M. Kuropas

## United Ukrainian American Relief Committee

(Zluchenyi ukrainskyi amerykanskyi dopomohovyi komitet, or ZUADK). A Ukrainian charitable organization established on 20 June 1944 under the name Ukrainian
Relief Committee by a commission set up at the Second
Congress of the Ukrainian Congress Committee of America in January 1944. On 9 November 1944 it merged with
Ukrainian War Relief, a committee in Detroit headed by J.
*Panchuk, and adopted its current name. The purpose of
the committee was to help Ukrainians in the homeland
and displaced Ukrainians outside Ukraine, particularly
with respect to resettlement.

Because the Soviet authorities would not permit direct
contact with institutions and individuals in Ukraine,
ZUADK concentrated its efforts on helping Ukrainian political refugees and *displaced persons in Western Europe.
In 1945 it was recognized as a relief organization by the US
government, and joined the American Council of Voluntary Agencies for Foreign Service and the Cooperative
for American Remittance to Europe. It collaborated with
international relief organizations, such as the *United
Nations Relief and Rehabilitation Administration, the *International Refugee Organization, and, later, the Intergovernmental Committee for European Migration and the UN
High Commission for Refugees. The ZUADK raised funds
through membership fees from various Ukrainian organizations, local fund-raising committees, and appeals to the
public. To channel its aid to Ukrainian refugees and displaced persons in Europe, ZUADK (in co-operation with the

Volunteers preparing clothing parcels for Ukrainian refugees in
Europe at the New York warehouse of the United Ukrainian
American Relief Committee after the Second World War. Among
them is the committee's executive director, Volodymyr Galan

Ukrainian Canadian Relief Fund) helped to set up the
*Central Ukrainian Relief Bureau in London (1945) and
then its own European Representation (1947) in Munich,
with branches in Salzburg, Paris, Brussels, Trieste, and
Berlin, as well as local offices in German towns with sizable Ukrainian communities.

The committee's efforts in 1947–57 were concentrated
on resettling Ukrainian refugees and displaced persons
overseas: it helped almost 60,000 of them to emigrate to
the United States. To achieve this end ZUADK fought to put
an end to the forced repatriation of Soviet citizens, to win
recognition of the national status of Ukrainian refugees,
and to gain immigration rights to the United States for
veterans of the Division Galizien and the Ukrainian Insurgent Army. After the period of immigration the committee continued to support Ukrainian organizations, arts
ensembles, nurseries, and schools in Europe. In the late
1960s ZUADK sent food, clothes, and medical supplies to
Ukrainian earthquake victims in Yugoslavia. Since then it
has helped Ukrainian political prisoners and their families
in the USSR. In the 1980s the committee helped resettle political refugees from Poland and set up (1985) and funded
a land-purchasing program for needy peasant families in
Brazil. It has published its own *Visti* ZUADK. Its head office
has been in Philadelphia. The presidents of the committee
have been V. Galan (1944–7, 1955–78), J. Panchuk (1947–
53), L. Myshuha (1953–5), M. Stakhiv (1955), and O. Bilyk
(1978–). The executive directors have been V. Galan, V.
Mudry, O. Tarnavsky, and I. Skalchuk.

BIBLIOGRAPHY
Tarnavs'kyi, O. *Brat–bratovi: Knyha pro* ZUADK (Philadelphia 1971)
M. Kuropas

## United Ukrainian Organizations in America

(Obiednannia ukrainskykh orhanizatsii v Amerytsi, or
OUO). A Ukrainian-American umbrella organization, set
up by the Ukrainian National Congress, which convened
in Philadelphia on 26–27 October 1922 for the purpose of
promoting Ukrainian education in the United States, helping Ukrainian institutions in the homeland, and publiciz-

ing Ukraine's right to independence. Its seven charter members included the Ukrainian National Association, the Providence Association of Ukrainian Catholics, and the Ukrainian National Aid Association. The OUO raised about 250,000 dollars to help Ukrainian organizations in Western Europe and in Western Ukraine and organized protest campaigns against the Polish *Pacification in Galicia and the 1933 man-made famine in Soviet Ukraine. It published several books on Ukraine for the American reader, including *Polish Atrocities in Ukraine* (1931), a book on the famine, and *Spirit of Ukraine: Ukrainian Contribution to the World Culture* (1935) by D. Snovyd (Dontsov). Its presidents were Rev L. Levytsky (1923–4), Rev V. Spolitakevych (1924–6), O. Reviuk (1927–39), and M. Murashko (1939–40). From 1924 its secretary was L. Myshuha. With the establishment of the *Ukrainian Congress Committee of America in 1940 as the main Ukrainian representative body in the United States, the OUO was dissolved.

**United Ukrainian Orthodox Sisterhoods** (Obiednannia ukrainskykh pravoslavnykh sestrytstv, or OUPS). A national women's organization established in 1961 to represent and co-ordinate the work of Ukrainian Orthodox parish sisterhoods in the United States. The OUPS provides scholarships, social services to senior citizens, and financial aid to needy Ukrainians in Europe and South America. It has also participated in campaigns for human rights and the defence of Ukrainian political prisoners in the USSR. It has organized cultural events, such as concerts of church music and literary evenings. Its organizational news and views were first published in a page devoted to women's issues in *Ukraïns'ke pravoslavne slovo* and then in the quarterly *Vira*, edited by H. Petrenko (1975–). Its major contribution to Ukrainian education has been the publication of a junior encyclopedia titled *Ukraïna* (1971), which was translated into English as *Ukraine: A Concise Encyclopaedia* (1988). As a member of the World Federation of Ukrainian Women's Organizations and the World Congress of Free Ukrainians it participates in the projects of the world bodies. The first president of OUPS was L. Ivchenko ([L. *Kovalenko] 1961–9); she was followed by O. Selepyna (1969–74 and 1977–8), H. Petrenko (1974–7), and V. Kuzmych (1978–present). Today (1989) the association represents 48 parish sisterhoods.

**United Ukrainian Toilers Organization.** See League of American Ukrainians.

**United Ukrainian War Veterans in America** (Obiednannia buvshykh voiakiv ukraintsiv v Amerytsi, or OBVUA). The largest Ukrainian veterans' association in the United States, formed in New York on 9 October 1949 out of the Ukrainian War Veterans' Association of the USA (est 1924) and Ukrainian veterans who had recently arrived in the United States. Its head office is in Philadelphia. In 1964 it had 17 branches with a membership of 850, consisting of former soldiers of the *Army of the UNR, the *Ukrainian Galician Army, and of foreign armies, and of members of the autonomous Brotherhood of *Ukrainian Sich Riflemen. By 1990 there were 6 branches remaining, with approx 200 members. The OBVUA has set up the Combatants' Welfare Service (1953) to help needy Ukrainian veterans and is a copublisher, with the Brotherhood of Former Sol-

diers of the First Ukrainian Division of the Ukrainian National Army, of the quarterly *Visti kombatanta*. Other veterans' organizations, such as the Former Members of the Ukrainian Insurgent Army, Brody-Lev, the Ukrainian War Veterans' Association of Canada, and the Ukrainian American Veterans, maintain friendly relations with the OBVUA. The presidents of the association have been D. Halychyn (1949–53), V. Galan (1953–80), Y. Vyshnevetsky (1980–6), and O. Trush (1986–).

The Univ Dormition Monastery

**Univ.** Formerly an important Galician monastic center (pop 1,300) with a thriving publishing industry. After the Second World War it was renamed Mizhhiria; it is now a village in Peremyshliany raion, Lviv oblast.

In the 14th century the Orthodox church founded the Univ Dormition Monastery, and it was built with fortified walls. In 1618 the hegumen K. *Stavrovetsky-Tranquillon began issuing the expository *Zertsalo bohosloviia* (Mirror of Theology) on the monastery's mobile printing press. The monastery's permanent press was brought from Lviv by Bishop A. *Zhelyborsky. The leading printer A. *Skulsky worked there from 1646, and a psalter and acathistus were published in 1660. In 1670–1710 the monastery's overseer was the archimandrite V. Sheptytsky, under whom S. and V. *Stavnytsky printed *Vyklad o tserkvi sviatoi* (An Essay on the Holy Church, 1670) and D. Kulchytsky printed a psalter (1678). Also at the Univ Monastery Press, the Moldavian metropolitan D. Barila published the important versified psalter *Psaltirea pre versuri tocmită* (1673, modeled on J. Kochanowski), an acathistus (1673), and a liturgicon (1679), all in Cyrillic Rumanian, translated from Ukrainian texts.

The Univ Dormition Monastery came under the jurisdiction of the Basilian monastic order in 1700–90. During the tenure of Bishop A. Sheptytsky (1722–46) the chronicle *Sobranie prypadkov* (Collection of Events, 1732) was published, as were liturgicons in 1733, 1740, and 1747.

In all, about 60 books were published by the Univ Monastery Press, and the printing remains an example of typographic excellence. In 1770 the press went into decline because of a clash with the Lviv Dormition (Stauropegion) Brotherhood. In 1919 Metropolitan A. Sheptytsky transferred the Studite Fathers' hegumenate to Univ. They founded a painting school and a bookbindery, and published the monthly *Prominchyk sontsia liubovy* (1935–9). When Soviet forces occupied Galicia in 1939, the Univ

Dormition Monastery's cells were turned into prison cells, and the rest of the buildings were converted into an asylum for the aged.

BIBLIOGRAPHY
Petrushevich, A. 'Istoricheskiia izvestiia o drevnei Arkhimandrii chinu sv. Vasyliia Velykogo v sele Uneve, okruga Zolochevskogo,' *Pchola*, 1849
Butsmaniuk, I. *Univ i ioho monastyri* (Zhovkva 1904)
Ohiienko, I. 'Univs'ka drukarnia,' in *Istoriia ukraïns'koho drukarstva* (Lviv 1925)

B. Kazymyra

**Universal** (from the Latin *litterae universales*). An act issued by a government as a proclamation of a certain position, as a political resolution, or for the conferral of privileges. In 17th- and 18th-century Ukraine, various hetmans, members of the General Officer Staff, and colonels followed the example of Polish kings and the Sejm in issuing universals, which dealt with military affairs (eg, the beginning of a campaign, a duty roster), land affairs (eg, the recognition of land claims, distribution of holdings, setting of boundaries, enserfment of peasants), appointments to government positions, the levying of taxes, and declarations of foreign policy (eg, the appointment of envoys, signing of treaties). Some universals served as certificates of personal protection.

Universals were written largely in the hetman's or a colonel's chancellery. The preamble contained the names of the issuing party and the addressee, and the end section included the place and date of issue and a signature. Most universals were disseminated through local administrative offices (one per company), and some were read in public squares or in churches.

One of the first hetmans to issue a universal directly to the Ukrainian population was P. Pavliuk in 1637. Thereafter virtually every hetman, including K. Rozumovsky, issued universals (see *Hetman manifestos). Also notable was the universal issued on 22 July 1655 by A. Zolotarenko, the wife of B. Khmelnytsky, in defense of the estate of the Hustynia Trinity Monastery.

Later, political documents and addresses to the population by leaders of revolutionary movements also came to be called universals. The leaders of the Koliivshchyna rebellion, for example, issued a universal in 1768, calling the peasantry to revolt against the Polish nobility. In 1917–18 the Ukrainian struggle for *independence culminated in the proclamation of the four *universals of the Central Rada.

A. Zhukovsky

**Universal'nyi zhurnal** (Universal Journal, or *UZh*). An illustrated journal for the general educated reader. It was edited by a board consisting of O. Vyshnia, M. Bazhan, M. Yohansen, Yu. Smolych, and O. Slisarenko, and it appeared monthly in Kharkiv from November 1928 to August 1929. *UZh* published works by the aforementioned writers and by M. Kulish, O. Dosvitnii, V. Gzhytsky, M. Semenko, V. Vrazhlyvy, O. Vlyzko, L. Chernov, N. Zabila, L. Pervomaisky, K. Kotko, Yu. Gedz, S. Chmelov, Yu. Shovkoplias, and M. Skazbush. It included literary translations; articles on civic matters, politics, international affairs, literature, art, film, science, and technology; humorous and travel sketches; and a chronicle of cultural events. It was illustrated by V. Krychevsky, I. Padalka, A.

Petrytsky, L. Kaplan, O. Dovhal, B. Fridkin, and other artists; it also published photographs.

Mykhailo Hrushevky's booklet on the Ukrainian Central Rada and its first two universals (1917)

**Universals of the Central Rada.** In 1917–18 the Ukrainian *Central Rada (CR) adopted and promulgated four edicts possessing the significance of fundamental laws and reflecting the evolution of the Ukrainian state, from autonomy within Russia to independence. Like the edicts of the 17th- and 18th-century Hetman state, they were called *universals. The universals were published in the official CR organ, *Visty z Ukraïns'koï Tsentral'noï Rady*, and most newspapers, broadcast by radio, and posted throughout Ukraine on placards printed in Ukrainian, Russian, Polish, and Yiddish. The author of the First Universal was V. *Vynnychenko; he also coedited the Second and Third universals. The Fourth Universal was cowritten by M. *Hrushevsky, Mykyta *Shapoval, and Vynnychenko. The First Universal was proclaimed at the Second All-Ukrainian Military Congress; the Second, at a CR session. The Third and Fourth universals were voted on as bills and passed at sessions of the Little Rada.

In the First Universal (23 June 1917) the CR proclaimed Ukraine's autonomy ('from this day on we alone will create our life'). Referring to the hostility of the Russian *Provisional Government's (RPG) rejection of the demands put to it by the CR delegation in Petrograd, it stated, 'without seceding from all of Russia ... let the Ukrainian people have the right to manage its own life on its own soil,' and called for the creation of a democratically elected all-Ukrainian people's assembly, which would have the sole right to draft laws that would be confirmed later by the *All-Russian Constituent Assembly. It appealed to the national minorities for support and co-operation and introduced a special public tax as the basis of the CR treasury. Five days later the first government of autonomous Ukraine, the *General Secretariat (GS) of the Central Rada, was appointed.

The Second Universal (16 July 1917) reflected the results of the 12–13 July negotiations between the GS and RPG representatives in Kiev. Addressed to the 'citizens of the Ukrainian land' instead of, as in the First Universal, 'the Ukrainian people,' it proclaimed that the CR would be expanded to include representatives from the national minorities, and would thereby become 'the single supreme body of revolutionary democracy in Ukraine.' A new GS would be appointed and would be 'subject to confirmation by the RPG as the repository of the highest regional authority of the RPG in Ukraine.' The CR would 'prepare drafts of legislation for Ukraine's autonomous structure,' would submit them for confirmation to the All-Russian Constituent Assembly, and would not take any steps to establish Ukrainian autonomy until the assembly was convoked. The formation of separate Ukrainian military units would be subject to the approval of the Russian minister of war.

The Third Universal (20 November 1917) was issued after the Bolshevik coup in Petrograd. Addressed to 'the Ukrainian people and all the peoples of Ukraine,' it proclaimed the creation of the *Ukrainian National Republic within a federated Russia of equal and free peoples. The UNR would be governed by the CR and GS until the convocation of the Constituent Assembly of Ukraine. The universal abolished capital punishment and the ownership of land by nontoilers; declared all land the property of the working people without compensation to its former owners; introduced an eight-hour workday and state control over all production; stated that the CR would 'use resolute means to force ... both allies and enemies to begin peace negotiations at once'; granted full amnesty to all political prisoners and *national-personal autonomy to Ukraine's national minorities; directed the GS to strengthen and broaden the local self-government rights; affirmed the freedom of speech, the press, religion, assembly, and association, the right to strike, and the inviolability of the person and the home; called upon all citizens to 'struggle decisively against all anarchy and destruction' (ie, the Bolsheviks); and set 9 January 1918 as the date for election of the *Constituent Assembly of Ukraine and 22 January as the day of its convocation.

The Fourth Universal (22 January 1918) was issued after the *Ukrainian-Soviet War began. Denouncing the Bolshevik aggression and expressing the desire for peace, it proclaimed the UNR an 'independent, subject to no one, free, sovereign state of the Ukrainian people.' The universal renamed the GS the *Council of National Ministers (CNM) of the UNR, directed it to negotiate an independent peace treaty with the Central Powers and to 'struggle firmly against all counterrevolutionary forces,' and called on all citizens to defend their welfare and liberty and to drive out the Bolsheviks. It announced an immediate end to the war and promised that the army would be replaced by a people's militia after the ratification of the peace treaty; prescribed new elections to rural-district, county, and urban popular councils; affirmed that a land law would soon be ratified and that all land would be transferred from the land committees to the people before spring tilling; nationalized all natural resources and the most important branches of commerce; directed the CNM immediately to change over industry to peacetime production, to increase the industry of the state, to solve unemployment, and to ensure the welfare of the handicapped; introduced state supervision of imports, exports, and monopolies to prevent speculation and excessive profits by the bourgeoisie; imposed state control over banks so that loans could thenceforth 'primarily ... support the working population and the economic development of the UNR'; and reaffirmed all democratic freedoms and national-personal autonomy. Although the universal was antedated to the day the Constituent Assembly of Ukraine was to convene but could not, it was in fact passed by the Little Rada on 25 January 1918.

BIBLIOGRAPHY

Hrushevs'kyi, M. Ukraïns'ka Tsentral'na Rada i ïï universaly pershyi i druhyi, 3 edns (Kiev 1917)
– Na porozi novoï Ukraïny: Hadky i mriï (Kiev 1918)
Khrystiuk, P. Zamitky i materiialy do istoriï ukraïns'koï revoliutsiï 1917–1920 rr., vols 1–2 (Vienna 1921; repr, New York 1969)
Doroshenko, D. Istoriia Ukraïny 1917–1923 rr., vol 1, Doba Tsentral'noï Rady (Uzhhorod 1930; repr, New York 1954)
Kostiv, K. Konstytutsiini akty vidnovlenoï ukraïns'koï derzhavy 1917–1919 rokiv i ïkhnia politychno-derzhavna iakist' (Toronto 1964)
Hunczak, T. (ed). The Ukraine, 1917–1921: A Study in Revolution (Cambridge, Mass 1977)

A. Zhukovsky

**Universita Cattolica Ucraina.** See Ukrainian Catholic University.

**Universities of Marxism-Leninism** (*universytety marksyzmu-leninizmu*). Communist educational institutions, established in the USSR in 1938. These universities were organized by city Party committees at larger enterprises. Their purpose was to train propagandists for the system of political education. Courses were scheduled in the evening or offered by correspondence so that students could continue their education 'without withdrawing from the production process.' In 1981–2 there were 26 such universities in Ukraine, with 62,400 students, of whom 44,700 were Party members.

**University.** An institution of higher learning offering programs of study in all of the major academic disciplines. In Ukraine there are 10 universities to date (1991), with a total enrollment of 110,000. They are the *Chernivtsi, *Dnipropetrovske, *Donetske, *Kharkiv, *Kiev, *Lviv, *Odessa, *Symferopil, *Uzhhorod, and *Zaporizhia universities. The normal program of study lasts five to five and a half years. Until 1992 universities were under the jurisdiction of the USSR Ministry of Higher and Specialized Secondary Education, and the *Supreme Attestation Commission in Moscow was the body which conferred all university degrees and academic appointments in Ukraine, and which designated fields in which each institution could conduct degree training. In recent years university students and staff have challenged the absence of university autonomy. (See *Higher education.)

**Unkovsky, Grigorii** [Unkovskij, Grigorij], b and d ? A 17th-century Muscovite diplomat. He was sent by the tsar to Ukraine in 1649 to negotiate with Hetman B. Khmelnytsky. His message was that Moscow could not render military assistance to Ukraine in securing its northwestern frontier, as that would contravene its peace treaty with Poland. Moscow's offer of economic aid and trade concessions provoked the Poles into attacking Ukraine. Soviet scholars have interpreted Unkovsky's mission as a success by regarding the discussions as an important step in the process of the 'reunification' of Ukraine with Russia.

**UNO.** See Ukrainian National Federation.

**UNR Army.** See Army of the Ukrainian National Republic.

**UPA.** See Ukrainian Insurgent Army.

**Upenyk, Mykola,** b 14 June 1914 in Platove-Ivanivka, Tahanrih circle, Don Cossack province. Socialist-realist poet. A former editor of *Pravda Ukrainy*, deputy chief editor of *Radians'ke mystetstvo* and *Vsesvit*, and managing editor of *Kul'tura i zhyttia* (1960–2), since 1935 he has published numerous poetry collections, a collection of song lyrics, children's books, and a book of articles.

**Uplands** (*vysochyny*). Parts of the earth's surface that rise above surrounding plains. Uplands on dry land usually rise 200–600 m above sea level. They are areas subjected to intensive erosive forces, which commonly carry materials from them (mostly by flowing water) onto adjacent lowlands. Uplands may be characterized morphologically as hilly, rolling, flat, or incised, according to the forces sculpting the surface.

The formation of uplands on the territory of Ukraine is associated with geological structure and tectonic movements of the earth's crust. The southern spurs of the Central Upland mark the upwarp of the Voronezh Massif. The Donets Ridge corresponds to a remnant of the main Donets Basin anticline. Neotectonic uplift (300–350 m) of portions of the southwestern slope of the East European Platform resulted in the formation of the inverted morphostructures of the Volhynia-Kholm Upland and the Podolian Upland. Neotectonic uplift (200–300 m) of individual blocks of the Ukrainian Crystalline Shield gave rise to the Dnieper Upland and the Azov Upland.

The uplands of Ukraine form two distinct belts. In the northeast is the Central Upland, the southern spurs of which (rising to 200 m above sea level or more) enter the territory of Ukraine. Its extension to the southeast forms the Don Ridge. Through the middle extends a belt of uplands, tapering off to the east. In its western reaches are the Volhynia-Kholm Upland (200–300 m above sea level); the Podolian Upland (200–400 m, reaching 471 m at Mt Kamula) with its western extensions, the Opilia Upland (250–400 m) and the Roztochia (300–390 m); and, south of the Dniester River, the Pokutian-Bessarabian Upland (200–400 m, reaching 516 m at Mt Berda). In the center of Ukraine are the Dnieper Upland (180–320 m) and the Zaporozhian Ridge (150–200 m), which straddles the Dnieper River at the rapids. The Azov Upland (200–250 m, reaching 327 m at Mt Mohyla-Belmak) is found in the southeast, and the Donets Ridge (150–300 m, reaching 367 m at Mt Mohyla-Mechetna) in the east.

Among the uplands of Ukraine the gently rolling Volhynia-Kholm Upland and especially the plateaulike Podolian Upland are severely eroded. The depths of the incised valleys and ravines range from 50 to 100 m, and along the Dniester River the valleys form gorges 150–200 m deep. Along the Dnieper River the rolling Dnieper Upland is incised with ravines and tributary valleys 100–150 m deep, and the hilly Azov Upland is carved up with ravines and valleys 150–200 m deep. In the northeast the southern spurs of the rolling Central Upland have a dense network of ravines and gullies, joining river valleys 200–250 m below the general level of the upland.

I. Stebelsky

**Upper elementary school** (*vyshcha pochatkova shkola*; Russian: *vysshee nachalnoe uchilishche*). Four-year schools established in 1912 in the Russian Empire to replace *city schools. They were created in order to facilitate admission to secondary schools for the less-privileged social groups. The program of upper elementary schools resembled that of the four lower classes of secondary schools, except for the fact that foreign languages were not part of the curriculum. Upon graduation from upper elementary schools students could enter the fifth grade of the secondary-school system upon successful completion of foreign-language entry examinations. Tuition fees were charged, and all instruction was in Russian. In some schools supplementary one- or two-year vocational courses were organized. In 1917 there were 312 upper elementary schools in Ukraine, and in 1920, 1,210. The schools were abolished with the Soviet Ukrainian education reform of 1920.

**Urals.** The popular name for the Ural Mountains as well as for the geographic and economic territory that makes up the southern reaches of the range and the foothills (mostly rolling plains) to the east, west, and south. Ukrainians live in the southern section of the Urals (an area of 355,500 sq km), in Cheliabinsk and Orenburg oblasts and the Baskhir AR. In 1980 the population of the area was 9.5 million, of whom 64 percent lived in cities. The southeastern section of the Urals (Ural oblast) lies in Kazakhstan. The regions in which Ukrainians reside are in the steppe and forest-steppe zones and have chernozem soils. The climate is continental, with mean January temperatures of –14 to –18° C, July temperatures of 17 to 21° C, and an annual precipitation of 300–700 mm.

Ukrainians began settling in the Urals in the 18th century, at around the same time as they were moving into the Volga regions. Virtually the entire immigrant population worked in agriculture. Census figures show that by 1897 there were 49,000 Ukrainians in the region. Immigration to the Urals subsequently increased, and the number of Ukrainians had reached 236,000 by 1926. They settled mostly in the southeastern section of what is now Cheliabinsk oblast. They formed a majority in many settlements; their presence is reflected in place-names such as Poltava, Dvorianske, and Kharkivskyi Khutir.

The condition of the Ukrainians in the Urals changed considerably in the 1930s and more so after the Second World War. Cut off from further sources of immigration and deprived of any national rights, local Ukrainians became denationalized. Loss of linguistic fluency was a particular problem. In addition many moved to the cities, and large urban concentrations of Ukrainians emerged in Cheliabinsk, Magnitogorsk, Orenburg, and other locales. By 1970, 51 percent of the Ukrainians in the region lived in cities.

According to the 1970 census there were 76,000 Ukrainians in the Bashkir ASSR, 113,000 in Orenburg oblast, and 115,000 in Cheliabinsk oblast (a total of 304,000). The largest ethnic group in the Ural region was Russian (42.6 percent of the population). Other groups included the Bashkir, Mordovian, and Belarusian people. The impact of denationalization on local Ukrainians was marked. In 1970, 64.2 percent of Ukrainians gave Ukrainian as their mother tongue. Of the rest, only 18.7 percent were also fluent in Ukrainian. Certainly elements of folklore (songs in particular) and dress seemed to persist longer than sentiments of nationality or facility with language.

V. Kubijovyč

**Urazovsky, Serhii** [Urazovs'kyj, Serhij], b 8 October 1903 in Rivenky, Tahanrih district, Don Cossack province (now Luhanske oblast), d 13 January 1961 in Kharkiv. Physical chemist; AN URSR (now ANU) corresponding member from 1943. A graduate of Kharkiv University (1927), he taught at the Kharkiv Chemical Technology Institute (1930–50) and chaired departments at the ANU Institute of Physical Chemistry (1941–2), the Kharkiv Chemical Technology Institute (1942–50), the Kharkiv Polytechnic Institute (from 1950), and Kharkiv University. Specializing in the physical chemistry of surface phenomena, Urazovsky originated the theory of molecular polymorphism and wrote a monograph about it (1956).

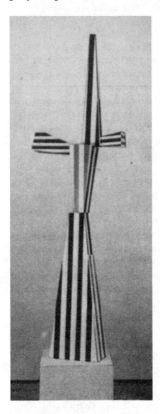

Mykhailo Urban: *Playful Forms* (painted plywood, 1976)

**Urban, Mykhailo,** b 27 September 1928 in Luka, Galicia. Sculptor and painter. A resident of the United States since 1950, he studied at the School of the Art Institute of Chicago, the University of Chicago (BFA, 1959) and the University of Notre Dame (MFA, 1972). He has been active in the Ukrainian Institute of Modern Art in Chicago. Most of Urban's work has been nonrepresentational. The arrangement of his spatial plywood sculptures results in a constructionist unity of forms and colored surfaces (eg, *Pulsating Form*, 1969). His tubular steel sculptures, such as *Parallel Counterpoint* (1971) and *Mahamudra* (1981), reveal the artist's planar concerns. Urban's paintings (mostly acrylic) are hard-edged, abstract compositions with flat areas of clearly defined and undifferentiated hues (eg, the series 'Exploration I, II, and III,' 1972). Solo exhibitions of his works have been held in Chicago (1965, 1973), Urbana, Illinois (1970), and elsewhere, and he has taken part in many group exhibitions.

**Urban economy.** See Municipal services.

**Urban planning.** The design and construction of cities and other urban settlements. The spontaneous growth of the earliest cities was restricted mostly by defensive needs. In Europe deliberate attempts to lay out streets and public buildings date back to the medieval period.

Urban planning in Ukraine can be traced to the second half of the 16th century. (For the earlier history of urban settlements see *Cities and towns.) Many cities founded or rebuilt at that time by the Polish magnates of Right-Bank Ukraine, including Zamość (1580), Sharhorod (1585), Brody (1586), and Zhovkva (1597), bore features of the Italian Renaissance. Zamość was designed by B. Morano of Padua, who lived in the city from 1579 to 1600, and its construction took 50 years. The old town has survived almost intact and is one of the finest examples of Renaissance urban planning. Brody was planned as a rectangular city with a standard grid of streets and two markets. The castle of its owner, S. Koniecpolski, was situated at the hub of the city's fortifications. Some of the cities resembled fortresses. Stanyslaviv (now Ivano-Frankivske), founded in 1662 by A. Potocki, consisted of a few blocks of houses, a marketplace, a castle, and a church, all surrounded by defensive walls. Continual warfare hampered the growth of cities in Ukraine.

In Left-Bank Ukraine the character of urban design was influenced by the cultural and spiritual role of the settlements. Many cities were dominated by large monasteries and were important religious and educational centers. Generally trade and manufacturing were poorly developed. The cities of the Hetman state remained quite small, usually having under 10,000 inhabitants. Their main architectural style was the Cossack baroque.

The towns of Slobidska Ukraine were designed primarily as armed outposts. They were built at strategic sites, usually in unsettled territory on routes used by the invading Nogay and Crimean Tatars. Sumy (est 1650s), for example, was built on a spit and surrounded by three rivers, a palisade, and earthen walls. Its gridiron of streets and squares permitted a high population density within the fortified center and gave the settlement a city appearance. In one of the corners of the city stood the citadel, the city's main stronghold. The irregular streets in the suburbs outside the city walls sprang up spontaneously, without formal planning.

Beginning in the mid-17th century the tsarist government attempted to regulate urban planning throughout the empire but had limited success. The first truly planned city in the empire was St Petersburg, built in the first decades of the 18th century. City planning became a regular feature in the development of the new territories annexed by Russia. In Southern Ukraine, which had been inhabited by nomadic Tatars and was captured by the Russian Empire in the second half of the 18th century, there were no urban centers. Unrestrained by established norms or traditions, the state could create cities according to its own designs. City planning was strongly supported by Peter I and especially Catherine II. In 1762 a special commission was set up by the central government to draw up plans for over 400 cities throughout the empire. Most of the plans were prepared by foreign-born architects and engineers. Generally the cities were laid out in a geometric pattern. Their gridiron of streets was usually rectangular and occasionally radial. In some cases plans were imposed on a previously settled territory without consideration for local traditions or geographic conditions. Often only a plan's central core, dealing with government and public buildings, was implemented. A certain code of esthetics played a major role in city design: broad avenues with grand views lined with uniform buildings were officially prescribed. Generous provisions were made for parks and greenery. A special district was set aside for industry, and residential areas were segregated by class. Ukrainian cities that were planned and built in the late 18th and early 19th centuries include Katerynoslav (by I. Starov and V. Geste), Mykolaiv (by I. Kniazev), Kherson, and Odessa (by F. de Voland and J. de Ribas). Odessa was noted for its European appearance.

The government continued to regulate urban planning throughout the 19th century. The pace of urbanization, however, especially in the developing mining and manufacturing areas of the Donets Basin, often precluded the possibility of conscious planning and design of cities. Little thought was given to public utilities or the rational use of space in the developing industrial cities, and in the suburban districts of established cities.

In the Soviet period urban planning developed rapidly throughout the USSR. According to Marxist ideology social and economic planning are feasible and desirable, a doctrine that has important implications for city planning. Ambitious renewal projects for many old cities were drafted, and new model centers of industry and culture were designed.

The best example of the new approach to urban planning in Soviet Ukraine was Kharkiv, the country's first capital. Under I. Voitkevych's direction an ambitious plan was drawn up: a new city center with a square of over 11 ha and a variety of official buildings, mostly in the constructivist style, were to be built. Although P. Aloshyn's innovative design for a new residential district was neglected, much work was completed before the capital was transferred to Kiev in 1934.

In June 1933 the Soviet government issued a decree on the design and reconstruction of cities, and in July 1935 it adopted a general plan for the reconstruction of Moscow. Similar plans were to be drawn up for all the cities of the USSR. At that time the Ukrainian Institute of City Planning in Kiev played an important role in the development of urban planning. From 1930 to 1934 it prepared plans for the reconstruction of 38 cities, including 27 Ukrainian ones. Uncontrolled population growth in the cities and a failure to appreciate the role of automotive transport caused many problems. Many roads in the old city were transformed into monumental boulevards or squares which hampered effective movement. Not enough new housing was constructed, but many pompous office buildings were erected in the official socialist-realist style. The reconstruction of the cities led to the demolition of many historical and architectural monuments. Many old cities, such as Kiev and Poltava, began to lose their distinctive character.

Although it has long been widely recognized that urban planning and construction require a comprehensive approach, city planning in Ukraine was often fragmentary and incomplete. Many cities have no general development plan, or have an outdated plan; of the 331 cities in Ukraine, including Kiev and Odessa, in 1960, for example, 187 did not have a general plan. City planning was complicated by the fact that local planning had to be compatible with the all-Union economic plan. Furthermore, city administrations were often influenced by interests that conflicted with the interests of the industrial enterprises on their territory. Professional city planners were often unqualified, and qualified ones were in short supply. The methodology of city planning was undeveloped. The problem of rapid urban growth was tackled by the introduction of urban microregions and satellite settlements. Satellite cities were laid out 10–20 km from the main cities, beyond the greenbelts that ring the metropolitan centers. Most new Ukrainian cities are in the Donets Basin: 18 new cities were registered there in 1959–70. The location of the new cities indicates that the chief factor in siting was accessibility to sources of raw materials.

In general recent city planning in Ukraine has been fairly well developed compared with Western practices. The lack of financial resources and poor quality control, however, have been much graver problems in Ukraine. Official buildings and hotels in the city centers, and sporting facilities, have been built with greater care than most buildings. The over-centralized nature of city planning has resulted in monotonous buildings and city layouts, particularly in new districts. Another distinctive feature of Soviet planning was high population density. New cities and new housing districts of old cities are compact and easily accessible to pedestrians and public transport. In planning new housing districts, some provision was made for private housing, but not for sewers and water supply for the private housing. For economic and ideological reasons most new housing was concentrated in microregions, which hold 5,000 to 10,000 inhabitants and cover an area of 30–50 ha. Communal housing is still claimed to be the optimal form of living. The architectural style of new Ukrainian cities is contemporary modernism. Buildings are up to 24 stories high.

BIBLIOGRAPHY
Parkins, M. *City Planning in Soviet Russia, with an Interpretative Bibliography* (Chicago 1953)
Orekhov, V.; et al. *Opyt proektirovaniia gorodov Ukrainy i Moldavii* (Kiev 1965)
Zabolotnyi, H.; et al. *Misto krokuie v maibutnie* (Kiev 1967)
Pitiurenko, Iu. *Rozvytok mist i mis'ke rozselenniia v Ukraïns'kii RSR* (Kiev 1972)
Bater, J. *The Soviet City: Ideal and Reality* (London 1980)
Morton, H.; Stuart, R. (eds). *The Contemporary Soviet City* (Armonk, NY 1984)
T. Hewryk

**Urban transit.** The transportation of passengers within a given city or town or between a city and its suburbs. The most common modes of transport used for this purpose are buses, trolleybuses, tramways (horse, steam, or electric – also called streetcars or trolley cars), subways (metros), and suburban railways.

The first modern urban transport system in Ukraine was established in Odessa in 1880, where a 8.5 km steam tramway line was built between Kulykove Pole and the Great Fountain. Then the first horse-drawn tramway was introduced, in Lviv in 1886. Kiev was the first city in Ukraine to introduce electric tramways (1892), petrol-rail buses (1912), trolleybuses (1936), a subway (1960), a monorail (1971), and light-rail transit (1982). Kharkiv was the first to establish a regular suburban railway network, in 1975. Its example was followed quickly by Kiev and Kryvyi Rih.

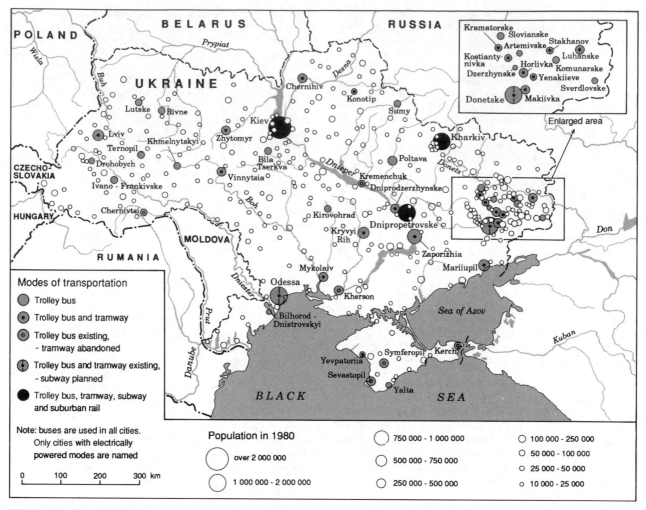

Modes of transportation

- Trolley bus
- Trolley bus and tramway
- Trolley bus existing, - tramway abandoned
- Trolley bus and tramway existing, - subway planned
- Trolley bus, tramway, subway and suburban rail

Note: buses are used in all cities. Only cities with electrically powered modes are named

0   100   200   300 km

Population in 1980

over 2 000 000

1 000 000 - 2 000 000

750 000 - 1 000 000

500 000 - 750 000

250 000 - 500 000

100 000 - 250 000

50 000 - 100 000

25 000 - 50 000

10 000 - 25 000

## URBAN TRANSIT

The scale of urban transit in Ukraine is enormous. Over two-thirds of the republic's 50 million people live in urban areas. A very large urban cluster has emerged in the Donbas region around Donetske (Makiivka, Yenakiieve, Horlivka, Komunarske, Lysychanske, Sverdlovske, Luhanske, Stakhanov, Dzerzhynske, Artemivske, Kostiantynivka, Kramatorske, Krasnyi Luch, and Slovianske). Slightly smaller conurbations have developed around Kiev, Kharkiv, and Dnipropetrovske. Since there are relatively few private automobiles, most people have to commute by public transit. The number of daily passenger trips in Ukraine increased sixfold between 1950 and 1980, and the trend is still growing. The number of transit systems has also increased (see table 1).

Meanwhile the growth of traffic and changes in transport modes have produced some unintended consequences. Bus services have grown at a rate exceeding the officially approved level. Traffic congestion and pollution, associated particularly with buses, are considered sufficiently serious to require a complete overhaul of transport policy. Transport authorities are planning to increase and extend urban electric transport and cut back on bus traffic. Since subways and suburban railways are expensive and take a long time to build, the preferred solution is to revi-

TABLE 1
Growth of transit systems by transport mode in Ukraine, 1914–88

| Mode | 1914 | 1940 | 1963 | 1970 | 1984 | 1988 |
|---|---|---|---|---|---|---|
| Suburban railways | – | – | – | – | 2 | 3 |
| Subways | – | – | 1 | 1 | 2 | 3 |
| Tramways | 14 | 26 | 26 | 25 | 24 | 23 |
| Trolleybuses | – | 4 | 20 | 30 | 39 | 41 |
| Buses | – | 63 | 264 | 320 | 436 | 460 |

talize the tramway in the form of a light-rail system (basically a rapid tramway with its own right-of-way). Kiev was the first city to build a light-rail line, in 1982. Despite government commitment to the policy the share of urban traffic carried by electric transport has not changed significantly. Not only are buses cheaper and simpler to operate, but their cost has risen less rapidly than that of other modes. In the past 25 years tramways have been replaced by buses in Chernivtsi, Kerch, Kherson, Kremenchuk, Sevastopil, and Symferopil (see table 2). Still, completely new tramway systems have been built in Stakhanov and Yenakiieve. Light-rail systems have been introduced in

TABLE 2
Cities of Ukraine with electric transit systems in 1988

| City | Trolley-buses | Tram-ways | Sub-ways | Suburban railways |
|---|---|---|---|---|
| Artemivske | C | | | |
| Bila Tserkva | C | | | |
| Bilhorod-Dnistrovskyi | C | | | |
| Chernihiv | C | C | | |
| Chernivtsi | C | A | | |
| Dniprodzerzhynske | | C | | |
| Dnipropetrovske | C | C | C | C |
| Donetske | C | C | P | |
| Drohobych | C | | | |
| Dzerzhynske | C | | | |
| Horlivka | C | C | | |
| Ivano-Frankivske | C | | | |
| Kerch | C | A | | |
| Kharkiv | C | C | C | C |
| Kherson | C | A | | |
| Khmelnytskyi | C | | | |
| Kiev | C | C | C | C |
| Kirovohrad | C | | | |
| Komunarske | C | | | |
| Konotop | | C | | |
| Kostiantynivka | | C | | |
| Kramatorske | C | C | | |
| Kremenchuk | C | A | | |
| Kryvyi Rih | C | C | | |
| Luhanske | C | C | | |
| Lutske | C | | | |
| Lviv | C | C | | |
| Makiivka | C | C | | |
| Mariiupil | C | C | | |
| Mykolaiv | C | C | | |
| Odessa | C | C | P | |
| Poltava | C | | | |
| Rivne | C | | | |
| Sevastopil | C | A | | |
| Symferopil | C | A | | |
| Slovianske | C | | | |
| Stakhanov | C | C | | |
| Sumy | C | | | |
| Sverdlovske | C | | | |
| Ternopil | C | | | |
| Vinnytsia | C | C | | |
| Yalta | C | | | |
| Yenakiieve | | C | | |
| Yevpatoriia | | C | | |
| Zaporizhia | C | C | | |
| Zhytomyr | | C | | |

C = currently operating; A = abandoned; P = planned.

Kiev, Kryvyi Rih, Lviv, and Mariiupil. The subways in Kiev and Kharkiv are being extended gradually, and a new system opened recently in Dnipropetrovske. Subways for Donetske and Odessa are in the planning stage.

BIBLIOGRAPHY
Lehnhart, H.; Jeanmaire, C. Strassenbahn-Betriebe in Osteuropa, vol 2 (Villingen 1977)
Kuhlman, B. Stadt-Schnellbahnen der Sowjetunion (Vienna 1981)
Saitta, J. Traction Yearbooks (Merrick 1981–5)
Baddeley, G. The Continental Steam Tram (London 1982)
Taplin, M.; et al. Light Rail Transit Today (London 1982)
Vlassov, V. 'Light Rail in the USSR,' Modern Tramway, December 1985
Jane's Urban Transport Systems (London 1987)

B. Myndiuk

**Urbanization.** A process of population concentration whereby the ratio of urban dwellers in the total population of a country increases. The growth of *cities and towns is closely linked to economic development and social modernization. The fact that until the early 1960s the majority of Ukraine's population lived in rural areas is indicative of the country's economic underdevelopment. Urbanization has loomed large as a problem in Ukraine's national development because until the 1930s the majority of urban residents were non-Ukrainian.

A striking characteristic of urbanization in Ukraine was that there was less of it at the beginning of the 19th century than in the second half of the 17th century. It has been estimated that in the mid-17th century Ukraine had 1.2 million urban residents, which figure represented 10 percent of the total population. By the beginning of the 19th century Ukraine's cities and towns had only 375,000 inhabitants, or 5 percent of the total population. The deurbanization of Ukraine that occurred in the second half of the 17th and in the 18th centuries was a consequence of the socioeconomic policies of the Russian and Polish rulers, such as the enserfment of the peasants, which restricted their ability to migrate to urban centers, the ruin of Ukraine's trade and industry by Russian mercantilist policies, and discriminatory measures applied against Ukrainian urban dwellers by the Polish authorities. Only after the abolition of serfdom and the development of trade and industry in the 1870s and 1880s, spurred by foreign investment, did the urban population begin to grow again. By 1897 Ukraine had 3 million urban inhabitants, representing 13.2 percent of the total population.

The urbanization of Ukraine that occurred in the 19th century proceeded largely without the participation of Ukrainians. As a consequence, with little more than 5 percent of their numbers living in towns in 1897, they were the least urbanized national group in their native land. By contrast, 38 percent of Russians and 45 percent of Jews living in Ukraine in 1897 were urban dwellers. In 1897, Ukrainians formed 30 percent of the urban population of Russian-ruled Ukraine. The weak Ukrainian presence in towns, combined with discriminatory tsarist policies aimed at stultifying the Ukrainian language and culture, meant that the cities provided a milieu for the *Russification of the relatively few Ukrainians living there. As a result, in the course of the 1917–21 struggle for independence the Ukrainian national movement was weakest in the urban centers. That weakness made an important contribution to its defeat. Symptomatic of the problems the movement faced was the fact that in 1917 only 16 percent of Kiev's population was Ukrainian.

The collapse of Ukraine's economy and industry during the revolutionary period of 1917–21 resulted in a decline in the urban population. By 1920, the cities and towns in what was to become Soviet Ukraine counted 4.1 million inhabitants, 1.5 million fewer than the 1914 figure of 5.6 million. During the 1920s, urban centers began recouping their population losses. In 1926, 18.5 percent of Ukraine's population lived in urban centers, and Ukrainians accounted for 47 percent of the urban population. During the second half of the 1920s the Ukrainian presence in the urban centers was strengthened. The growth was brought about by the sizable in-migration of Ukrainian peasants; by *Ukrainization policies, which halted the Russification process in urban centers and created employment opportunities for Ukrainian-speakers; by the spread of literacy in rural areas; and by the rise in the expectations of village youths, who had been most affected by the mobilization of 1917–21. A 1927 study of migration into the cities of Odessa, Kiev, and Dnipropetrovske found that three out of four residents were from Ukraine and that 77 percent of those were from the countryside.

The industrialization of the 1930s resulted in rapid urban growth: Ukraine's urban population increased from 5.4 million in 1926 to 11.2 million in 1939, and the proportion of urban residents increased from 18.5 to 32.6 percent of the total population in the same period. Because Ukraine's industrialization was centered on the development of mining and heavy industry, the Donbas and Dnieper Industrial Region accounted for three-quarters of the increase. Industrialization thus created serious regional imbalances in Ukraine's urban network. The urban population of Right-Bank Ukraine stagnated during the 1930s.

The devastation of the countryside during *collectivization accelerated the migration of peasants to the city and changed the national composition of Ukraine's urban population. The number of Ukrainians in the towns increased from 2.5 to 6.8 million between 1926 and 1939, and the rate of urbanization among Ukrainians had risen to 29 percent by 1939, almost triple the 1926 figure. By 1939, Ukrainians had emerged as a majority of the urban population, 58.1 percent. The increase in the Ukrainian urban population would have been much higher had it not been for the 1932–3 man-made *famine. To combat the spontaneous process of immigration, a series of laws regulating migration were passed in 1931 and 1932, and on 27 December 1932 the internal passport was introduced. By making peasants apply for passports in their villages and report their destinations, the authorities artificially controlled the migration to towns.

There was little industrial development in Western Ukraine until the period after the Second World War, and Ukraine's western oblasts remained predominantly rural until the 1980s. In 1931 only 18.5 percent of the 9.1 million inhabitants of the Ukrainian lands under Polish rule (Galicia, Volhynia, Polisia) lived in towns and cities, and only 28 percent of the urban population was Ukrainian. In 1930, only 17.5 percent of the 1.2 million inhabitants of Rumanian-ruled Bukovyna were urban dwellers, and Ukrainians there represented 31 percent of the urban population. In 1930, 18 percent of the inhabitants of Transcarpathia under Czechoslovak rule lived in urban centers, and Ukrainians represented 38 percent of the urban population. After the Second World War Ukrainians increased their share of the urban population of those regions in the wake of the departure of the members of the former ruling nations. By 1959 the overwhelming majority of urban residents of the western oblasts were Ukrainians.

During the Second World War Ukraine's cities bore the brunt of military confrontations. Ukraine's urban centers accounted for 40 percent of the population of the USSR left homeless by the war. Between 1946 and 1951, however, Ukraine received only 15 percent of Soviet construction funds to rebuild its cities. The central government's neglect of investment in Ukrainian urban construction meant that as late as 1950 Ukraine's towns had 12.8 million people, well below the 1940 total of 13.8 million, and two-thirds of the republic's population lived in the countryside, just as in 1940.

Real urban growth did not begin until the 1960s: the number of urban residents grew from 19 million in 1959 to 26 million in 1970. Ukraine had an urban population exceeding half of the total population by 1966 (but the number of Ukrainians in the urban population was not proportionately equivalent). That Ukraine reached the benchmark a full decade behind the RSFSR pointed to major problems in the republic's urbanization. The gap in the rate of urbanization between Ukraine and Russia developed under Soviet rule; Ukraine had been more highly urbanized than Russia at the beginning of the 20th century. The gap reflected the unequal industrial investment policies of the central government in Moscow. Because major industrial investment decisions were the monopoly of the all-Union government in Moscow, Ukraine suffered from discriminatory practices in the location of new plants and factories. The republic's economic development was also affected by the substantial drain of capital. It has been calculated that Ukraine lost 34 percent of the total receipts of its budgetary system between 1959 and 1970. The net capital outflow represented 20 percent of Ukraine's reported national income.

The Ukrainians' rate of urbanization increased from 37 to 46 percent between 1959 and 1970. In 1959, Ukrainians accounted for 62 percent of the republic's urban population. Because during the 1960s there was a large-scale in-migration of Russians into Ukraine (approx 750,000 Russians settled in its cities), the Ukrainians' share of the urban population remained largely stagnant between 1959 and 1970. In 1970, Ukrainians still accounted for only 63 percent of the urban population. The Russification of Ukrainians in the urban centers, especially in eastern Ukraine, reduced the size of the Ukrainian urban population. Russian in-migration also stymied Ukrainian urbanization because it forced Ukrainians to compete with Russians for jobs and housing.

Between 1970 and 1989 Ukraine's urban population grew from 25.7 to 34.5 million, or from 55 to 67 percent. The level of urbanization in Russia (74 percent in 1989) was much higher than in Ukraine. Ukraine's western oblasts remain characterized by a relatively low level of urban development; in 1989 only Lviv oblast had more than 50 percent of its inhabitants living in urban areas.

In 1979, 53 percent of Ukrainians lived in urban areas, and Ukrainians represented 63 percent of the urban total, a figure unchanged from 1970. The linguistic and cultural Russification of many Ukrainians and large-scale Russian in-migration into Ukraine's cities accounted for the failure of Ukrainians to improve their share of the republic's urban population. In 1989, Ukrainians represented 65 percent of the republic's urban population.

BIBLIOGRAPHY

Vologodtser, I. Osobennosti razvitiia gorodov Ukrainy (Kharkiv 1930)

Dotsenko, A. 'Heohrafichni osoblyvosti protsesiv urbanizatsiï na Ukraïni (XIX–XX st.),' Ukraïns'kyi istoryko-heohrafichnyi zbirnyk, 2 (Kiev 1972)

Lewis, R.; Rowland, R. Population Redistribution in the USSR: It's [sic] Impact on Society, 1897–1977 (New York 1979)

Krawchenko, B. Social Change and National Consciousness in Twentieth-Century Ukraine (London 1985; Edmonton 1987)

Zastavnyi, F. (ed). Rasselenie: Voprosy teorii i razvitiia (na primere Ukrainskoi SSR) (Kiev 1985)

Kovtun, V.; Stepanenko, A. *Goroda Ukrainy (ekonomiko-geograficheskii spravochnik)* (Kiev 1990)
Balan, B. 'Urbanization and the Ukrainian Economy in the Mid-Nineteenth Century,' in *Ukrainian Economic History: Interpretive Essays*, ed I.S. Koropeckyj (Cambridge, Mass 1991)
For additional bibliography, see *Cities and towns.)

B. Krawchenko

**Urban-type settlement** (*selyshche miskoho typu*, or smt). A special type of town introduced into the administrative-territorial system of the USSR in 1925. According to a decree of the Presidium of the Supreme Soviet of the Ukrainian SSR on the administrative-territorial structure of the republic (28 June 1965), an smt is a populated area around an industrial plant, construction site, railway junction, educational institution, research station, sanatorium, or other stationary medical or convalescent establishment that has state housing and over 2,000 residents, 60 percent of whom are wage or salaried workers or members of their families. In an exceptional case an smt may have fewer than 2,000 residents, if it is likely to develop soon into a full-fledged smt. Urban-type settlements are classified into three types: worker smt (no fewer than 3,000 residents), resort smt (no fewer than 2,000), and cottage smt (no more than 25 percent of the adults occupied in agriculture). The number of smts in Ukraine has increased steadily: there were 459 in 1940, 478 in 1950, 823 in 1960, 861 in 1970, 901 in 1980, and 927 in 1990.

*Urbarium.* A contract form for landowners and peasants in Hungary printed in the 1770s as a result of Maria Theresa's reforms. It outlined the obligations and rights of the peasants and was to be supplemented locally with precise details concerning each village. Printed in the different languages used in Hungary, it was, according to A. Petrov, who discovered and studied it from the historical and linguistic perspectives, the first printed document in the Ukrainian vernacular of Transcarpathia. It was reprinted in 1908 in *Sbornik Otdeleniia russkogo iazyka i slovesnosti Imperatorskoi akademii nauk*, no. 84. The replies of peasants to questions in the *Urbarium* were written down word for word in the Cyrillic or Latin alphabet. The notes from 212 villages have been preserved and are valuable dialectological materials, containing many geographical and personal names. They have been investigated and published in part by L. Dezső in *Studia Slavica Hungarica*, vols 3, 11; *Die Welt der Slaven*, vol 10; and *Slavica* (Debrecen), vol 10; and by I. Cherednychenko in *Naukovi zapysky Chernivets'koho universytetu*, no. 31.

*Uriadovyi vistnyk Pravytel'stva Karpats'koï Ukraïny* (Administrative Herald of the Government of Carpatho-Ukraine). An official organ of the government of *Carpatho-Ukraine, five issues of which appeared from 20 October 1938 to March 1939. Initially it was published in Ukrainian and Russian and titled *Uriadovyi vestnik Pravitel'stva Pidkarpats'koï Rusi*. From the third issue it appeared only in Ukrainian, and it was renamed with the fourth issue (21 January 1939). The first issue appeared in Uzhhorod under the editorship of F. Skral. From the second issue (15 November) it was published in Khust and edited by V. Grendzha-Donsky.

**Uruguay.** A country in northern South America (1989 pop 3,017,000), with an area of 176,215 sq km (1989). Montevideo is its capital.

It is possible that a New Israel Orthodox sect from the Kuban region, which fled religious persecution at home and founded the colony of San Javier in the province (department) of Rio Negro in 1913, included many ethnic Ukrainians. Mass Ukrainian immigration did not commence until 1924–31, however, when several thousand, almost exclusively from the Western Ukrainian regions of Volhynia, Polisia, Galicia, Transcarpathia, and Bukovyna, arrived. In addition a small number (approx 50) of immigrants came from displaced persons' camps after the Second World War. From the 1950s to the 1970s the community experienced considerable out-migration to Argentina, North America, Australia, and even Ukraine in response to recurring economic crises. Conservative contemporary estimates of the size of the community have generally agreed on 8,000, which figure makes Ukrainians the largest single Slavic group in Uruguay.

Approximately half the country's Ukrainians live in Montevideo, and most of the others in cities such as Salto, Florida, and Paysandu. Few Ukrainians were able to establish themselves on the land owing to difficulties in gaining access to vacant tracts. Nevertheless, one group of approx 500 persons from Volhynia was able to found a colony in the department of Salto. Otherwise, those Ukrainians who elicited a livelihood from agriculture usually did so by becoming tenant farmers on the estates of wealthy landowners. The majority of the Ukrainian immigrants were employed as laborers in the frozen meat industry or in construction. Those who became farmers brought a new dimension to Uruguayan agriculture by introducing sunflowers and new varieties of wheat to the country. An insignificant number of Ukrainians started their own businesses, and a small percentage are now engaged in the liberal arts professions. Nearly all Ukrainians are home owners.

The first known Ukrainian organization was the Taras Shevchenko Workers' Society, which was founded in 1928. It assumed a pro-communist posture and gradually evolved into the Ukrainian-Belarusian Citizens' Cultural and Educational Organization. In 1934 the Prosvita society was founded, and functioned as a branch of the Prosvita society of Buenos Aires. It acquired its own premises in 1946 and maintained a part-time school. Among its achievements is the naming of one of the capital city's streets 'Ukrania.' Shortly after its founding, a split in the ranks of the Prosvita society resulted in the formation of a short-lived rival nationalist group, Vidrodzhennia, which modeled itself after the organization of the same name in Buenos Aires.

For a long time Ukrainians in Uruguay were without religious institutions of their own. In 1948 the Prosvita society contacted the Basilian Fathers in Argentina, and the result was the establishment of a Ukrainian Catholic parish in 1952. The parish ceased to exist in 1967, when its priest, Rev I. Maika, died. The Ukrainian Orthodox community was organized around a brotherhood in Montevideo, but was unable to sustain a parish for an extended period of time owing to the acute shortage of Orthodox priests in South America.

Among other Ukrainian organizations which were briefly active in Uruguay were the Committee to Assist the Ukrainian National Rada and the Committee for the Struggle against Communism.

In mid-1942 the All-Slavic Committee (ASC) was created in Moscow, and published a periodical (in Russian) called *Slaviane*, which was disseminated throughout the Americas. The ASC established its co-ordinating committee in Montevideo and in 1943 founded the Unión Eslava. The Soviet consul in Montevideo, V. Riabov, played a crucial role in its formation. In the 1940s the Unión Eslava consisted of approx 40 Slavic associations, mainly in Argentina and Uruguay, many of them Ukrainian. This pan-Slavic movement affected a considerable segment of the Ukrainian immigration in Uruguay, and those Ukrainian organizations that supported it soon lost their strictly Ukrainian character. During the 1940s the pro-communist Ukrainian organizations merged with like-minded Belarusian and Russian groups to found the Maxim Gorky Society (Centro Cultural Maxim Gorki), which maintained direct links with the USSR and had branches outside Montevideo. Since the 1960s, however, both this organization and Prosvita have had to contend, unsuccessfully, with the rapid assimilation, indifference, or disappearance of their constituencies. Neither group is very active today.

BIBLIOGRAPHY
Strelko, A. *Slavianskoe naselenie v stranakh Latinskoi Ameriki* (Kiev 1980)
Vasylyk, M. 'Ukraintsi v Urugvaiu,' in *Ukraïns'ki poselennia*, ed A. Milanych et al (New York 1980)

S. Cipko

**Uruski, Bill** [Urus'kyj, Vasyl'], b 27 July 1942 in Poplarfield, Manitoba. Canadian politician of Ukrainian descent. Uruski served as a Royal Canadian Mounted Police constable (1962–7) before his election to the Manitoba legislature in 1969 as the New Democratic party member for Interlake constituency. He was re-elected in 1973, 1977, 1981, 1986, and 1988. He was minister responsible for the Manitoba Public Insurance Corporation (1973–6, 1987–8), minister responsible for the Motor Vehicle Branch (1973–5), minister of municipal affairs and minister responsible for the Civil Service Act (1976–7), and minister of agriculture (1981–7).

**Usatove culture**. A Neolithic culture of the late 3rd millennium BC that existed in southwestern Ukraine along the lower Dniester River and the area near the Dniester Estuary. It takes its name from a site excavated by M. *Boltenko in Odessa oblast in 1921. Although classified as a late Trypilian culture, the Usatove culture had developed enough distinctive cultural traits through contact with steppe tribes, northern Caucasia, and the Mediterranean world to be considered a separate archeological entity. Its people engaged in animal husbandry and fishing and (to a lesser degree) agriculture. Excavations at sites revealed surface dwellings with stone walls, pottery with corded and painted ornamentation, earthenware figurines of women, and copper weapons and adornments. Eighteen Usatove kurhans, surrounded by cromlechs, have been unearthed. The deceased were buried in a flexed position on their sides; tribal leaders were in the central chambers of the structures. Common grave goods included weapons and adornments.

**Usenko, Ivan,** b 27 March 1906 in Keleberda, Zolotonosha county, Poltava gubernia. Geologist; corresponding member of the ANU (formerly AN URSR) since 1967. He graduated from the Kiev Institute of Mining and Geology (1932) and worked for the ANU Institute of Geological Sciences. In 1969 he became section head at the ANU Institute of Geochemistry and the Physics of Minerals. Usenko's research was in the areas of the petrography and mineralogy of various rock formations in the Ukrainian Shield, and also in the stratigraphy of Precambrian deposits in Ukraine. He developed criteria useful in exploration for nickel-ore deposits and also introduced a classification for the geological formations of the shield.

Pavlo Usenko

**Usenko, Pavlo,** b 23 January 1902 in Zaochipske, now in Tsarychanka raion, Dnipropetrovske oblast, d 4 August 1975 in Kiev. Poet and Komsomol activist. He was one of the founders of the organization *Molodniak and was editor of its official organ, *Molodniak*. His first published work appeared in 1922. His collections of poetry include KSM (Communist Youth League, 1925), *Poeziï* (Poems, 1932), *Lavy idut' Ka-eS-eM-ovi* (The KSM Ranks March On, 1934), and others dedicated to the Komsomol. During the Second World War he published a number of collections of war poetry, including *Za Ukraïnu* (For Ukraine, 1941), *Klianys'* (Swear!, 1942), *Vesna* (Spring, 1943), and *Z vohnyshch borot'by* (From the Fires of Battle, 1943). His later collections were typically socialist-realist, such as *I s'ohodni vesna, iak uchora* (And Today It Is Spring, Just like Yesterday, 1957) and *Vesen nezviianyi tsvit* (The Unblown Bloom of Springs, 1960). Editions of his works appeared in 1966 (2 vols) and 1982 (4 vols). Usenko also published collections of essays, including *Polustanok* (Whistle-stop, 1929) and *Liudy Bilomorbudu* (The People of the White Sea–Baltic Canal Construction, 1934) and wartime notes and poetry for children, *Dva svity* (Two Worlds, 1933) and *Sanochky skrypuny* (The Creaking Sleigh, 1941).

**Usha River.** See Uzh River.

**Ushakevych, Vasyl** [Ušakevyč, Vasyl'], b and d ? Wood engraver. He prepared illustrations for liturgical books which were printed at various times by the Lviv Dormition Brotherhood Press: Pentekostarions (1663, 1667, 1688), Triodions (1664, 1699, 1717, 1753), an *Apostol* (1666, 1772), and Sacramentarions (1668, 1682, 1717, 1719, 1761).

**Ushakov, Nikolai** [Ušakov, Nikolaj], b 6 June 1899 in Rostov, Russia, d 17 November 1973 in Kiev. Russian writer and translator. He graduated from the Kiev Institute of the National Economy (1924) and spent most of his life in Kiev. The first of his numerous collections appeared in 1927. He wrote many poems on Ukrainian subjects and a book of sketches about Kiev (1960). He was a coeditor of Russian editions of T. Shevchenko's *Kobzar* (1939), Shevchenko's collected works (5 vols, 1948–9), and M. Kotsiubynsky's works (3 vols, 1951–2). He wrote theoretical articles about translating Shevchenko and translated into Russian some 40 of his poems. He also translated into Russian I. Franko's Boryslav stories, Kotsiubynsky's *Fata Morgana* and *Tini zabutykh predkiv* (Shadows of Forgotten Ancestors), prose by Yu. Yanovsky and A. Holovko, and poems by Franko, Lesia Ukrainka, M. Rylsky, P. Tychyna, V. Sosiura, M. Bazhan, L. Pervomaisky, A. Malyshko, and other Ukrainian poets. He was awarded the Shevchenko Prize in 1973.

**Ushinsky, Konstantin** [Ušyns'kyj], b 2 March 1824 in Tula, Russia, d 3 January 1871 in Odessa. Educator and pedagogue; one of the founders of pedagogy as an independent discipline in the Russian Empire. Ushinsky regarded upbringing as a social phenomenon determined by history, and undertook a broad examination of humanity in light of the information provided by all human sciences, thereby laying the foundations of pedagogical anthropology. He developed an integrated system of didactics that presented principles for selecting the content of education and adapting it to the needs of children to help organize their cognitive activity. He emphasized the importance of knowledge of the natural sciences and opposed focusing on the classics in the teaching of the humanities. He was an ardent advocate of the use of the native language in schools and opposed tsarist prohibitions on the use of Ukrainian in the education system. He argued for the integration of national traditions into the school system and demanded universal compulsory education for children of both sexes. Ushinsky wrote the primer *Rodnoe slovo* ([Our] Native Language, 1864), which was used in schools in Russian-ruled Ukraine.

**Ushytsia River** [Ušycja]. A left-bank tributary of the Dniester River that flows for 122 km through Khmelnytskyi oblast and drains a basin area of 1,420 sq km. Fed by rain and meltwater and characterized by a narrow, ravinelike valley (0.3–1.3 km), the river is 10–15 m wide. It is used for irrigation and fishing.

**Uskiw, Samuel** (Jus'kiv, Semen), b 18 October 1933 in East Selkirk, Manitoba. Canadian politician of Ukrainian descent. Uskiw was elected to the Manitoba legislature in 1966 as the New Democratic party member for the Lac du Bonnet constituency and was re-elected in 1969, 1973, 1977, and 1981. He served as minister of agriculture (1969), minister of co-operative development (1971–5), minister of highways and transportation (1981–3), minister of business development and tourism and minister responsible for the Manitoba Telephone Act (1983–5), and minister of natural resources (1985). He did not stand for re-election in the 1986 general election.

*Uspenskii sbornik* (The Dormition Collection). A 304-folio manuscript collection of the late 12th and early 13th centuries, containing primarily lives of saints from the May cycle and sermons, especially of St John Chrysostom. Most of the texts were translated from Byzantine originals in Bulgaria; some, including the oldest extant Life of St Methodius, may have been done in Moravia. The collection also contains many of the earliest original Kievan Rus' texts, among them *Skazaniie i strast' i pokhvala sviatuiu muchenyku Borysa i Hliba*, the Tale of the Miracles of Princes Roman and Davyd, and Life of St Theodosius of the Caves. The manuscript was found by O. Bodiansky in 1855 in the Dormition Cathedral in Moscow (hence its name) and is now preserved at the Central Historical Museum in Moscow. A facsimile edition was published in Moscow in 1971. V. Jagić, A. Sobolevsky, A. Shakhmatov, and other scholars believe the manuscript was compiled in Ukraine, most likely in Kiev. Its language has been studied by A. Popov, Shakhmatov, Sobolevsky, A. Lukianenko, I. Popova, R. Aitzetmüller, and others.

**Ussuriisk.** A city (1983 pop 152,000) and raion center of Primorskii krai in Russia's Far East. It was founded in 1866 and was known as Nikolsk-Ussuriisk until 1935. Then it was renamed Voroshilov. Its current name was adopted in 1957. It has a large food-processing and machine-building industry. In 1926 there were about 3,600 Ukrainians (10 percent of the population) living there. On 11 June 1917 the First Far Eastern Ukrainian Congress was held there. A local and regional Ukrainian council was formed, and Prosvita societies were organized in the villages around Ussuriisk. The Haidamaka co-operative, the Siaivo publishing house, and the head office of the Far Eastern Artistic Union operated in the city during the revolutionary period.

*Ustav.* A law or collection of laws that regulated a specific area of legal relations; or an important legislative act which constituted a source of law in Kievan Rus'. The most famous *ustavy* of the Princely era were *Volodymyr Monomakh's Statute and statutes of Volodymyr the Great and Yaroslav the Wise. In the Grand Duchy of Lithuania, some legislative acts, such as *land charters, were also called *ustavy*. In Poland the *voloka* land reform was based on an *ustav* issued in 1557 by King Sigismund II Augustus. In the Russian Empire, the new relations between the landowners and the peasants after emancipation in 1861 were regulated by *statutory deeds. Today the term is sometimes used to refer to a statute or constitution of an institution.

*Ustav* script. The earliest Cyrillic script. It was created in Bulgaria in the early 10th century on the basis of the Greek majuscular uncial script, which had been used in Greek church books and transcriptions of the New Testament since the 4th century.

The oldest dated manuscript written in the *ustav* in Ukraine is the *Ostromir Gospel (1056–7). It contains typical characteristics: the letters are drawn precisely between two lines, beyond which only the descenders of the letters *d, z, r, u, x, c,* and *šč* extend; the letters are vertical and have angular lines and curves; their average width approximately equals their height, giving them a square appearance; the distances between letters are generous;

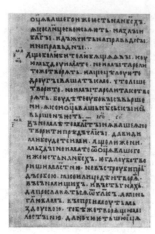

The *ustav* script of the 1144 Halych Gospel

there are no word breaks; except in a few titles, there are almost no diacritics; and the letters are 6–7 mm in height. The *\*Izbornik* of Sviatoslav of 1073 is written in a smaller *ustav* with smaller spaces between letters and some right-slanted letters and accents. Other extant manuscripts written in the *ustav* include the \*Halych Gospel (1144) and the \*Pandects of Antiochus (11th–12th centuries).

The change from parchment to paper, the increased demand for books, and the requirements of chancery writing forced changes in the *ustav* beginning in the 13th century. Texts had to be written more quickly, and haste led to a decline in the precise geometric written forms of the letters, to their simplification, reduction in size, and slanting. The script evolved through an intermediary stage, large *pivustav* (semi-uncial) (eg, the \*Krekhiv *Apostol* [1563–72]), into the \*pivustav script of the late 15th and 16th centuries. Nonetheless, a modified *ustav* script (containing *pivustav* elements) was still used in some liturgical books, eg, the \*Peresopnytsia Gospel (1556–61).

V. Swoboda

**Ustava na voloky.** See *Voloka* land reform.

**Ustavni hramoty.** See Statutory deeds.

**Ust-Kamianka kurhans.** Bronze Age and 1st- to 2nd-century Sarmatian burial mounds near Ust-Kamianka, Apostolove raion, Dnipropetrovske oblast. Twenty Sarmatian kurhans at this site were excavated in 1951, revealing 31 burials. Most of the deceased were buried with their heads facing south. Common grave goods included animal bones, pottery, knives, daggers, and bronze mirrors. Traces of a Bronze Age and an early Scythian settlement were found adjacent to the burial mounds.

**Ustryky Dolishni** [Ustryky Dolišni] (Polish: Ustrzyki Dolne). IV-3. A town (1967 pop 3,700) in Krosno voivodeship, Poland. It was first mentioned in historical documents in 1727. Until 1939 it was known for its cattle markets. In 1945–51 Ustryky Dolishni was included in the territory of the Ukrainian SSR.

**Ustyianovych, Kornylo** [Ustyjanovyč], b 1839 in Vovkiv, Lviv district, Galicia, d 22 July 1903 in Dovhe, Stryi county, Galicia. Painter, writer, and journalist; son of M. \*Ustyianovych; founding member of the Shevchenko Society (1873). After studying at the Vienna Academy of

Kornylo Ustyianovych: *Hutsul Woman* (oil, 1891)

Fine Arts (1858–63) he worked in Vienna and throughout Galicia and Bukovyna, where he painted icons for over 50 churches, 15 iconostases, 11 church murals, and 7 religious canvases, including *Christ before Pilate* (1880), in Vienna; *Moses* (1887), in the Transfiguration Church in Lviv; and *Baptism of Rus'*, *Christ in the Desert*, *Volodymyr the Great*, and *St Olha*, in the Vistova village church, near Kalush. Among his 40 portraits are ones of M. Ustyianovych, S. Kachala (1871), P. Bazhansky, Yu. Lavrivsky (1887), and A. Vakhnianyn (1895). He also did paintings on historical themes, such as *Prince Vasylko of Terebovlia* (1866), *Shevchenko in Exile* (1880), *Nestor the Chronicler* (1901), *Yaroslavna's Lament*, and *Cossack Battle* (1890); ethnographic paintings, such as *Boiko Couple* and *Hutsul;* and a few landscapes, such as *The Black Sea*, *Sunset*, and *Morning*. His portrait drawings of Galician princes were printed in the journal *Pryiatel' ditei* (1881–3). Ustyianovych's works conform to the principles of \*academism but reveal a romantic bent.

Ustyianovych's first poems were written in \**yazychiie* and published in 1861. During his studies in Vienna he evolved from a Pan-Slavist into a Ukrainian populist. From 1872 he contributed articles, humorous feuilletons, accounts of his travels, and several stories in the Ukrainian vernacular to Galician periodicals, such as *Halychanyn*, *Slovo*, *Zoria*, *Pravda*, *Dilo*, *Ruslan*, and *Osnova*. In the 1870s he published his historical poems 'Iskorosten',' 'Vadym,' and 'Sviatoslav Khorobryi' (Sviatoslav the Brave). He worked as a scenery designer for the Ruska Besida Theater in Lviv, and his tragedies *Iaropolk I Sviatoslavych* (1877) and *Oleh Sviatoslavych* (1876) were performed there (1878, 1883). In 1882–3 he edited and illustrated the satirical magazines *Zerkalo* and *Nove zerkalo*. Three volumes of his writings were published in 1875–7, and his memoirs about M. Raevsky and Russian Pan-Slavism appeared in 1884. A book about Ustyianovych by Ya. Nanovsky was published in Kiev in 1963.

Rev Mykola Ustyianovych    Mykola Ustymovych, the first head of the Hetman government

**Ustyianovych, Mykola** [Ustyjanovyč] (pseuds: Drotar, Yor, Naum, Nykola(i) (i)z Nykolaieva, N.U.), b 7 December 1811 in Mykolaiv, Stryi circle, Galicia, d 3 November 1885 in Suceava, Bukovyna. Writer, priest, and civic figure; father of K. *Ustyianovych. A graduate of the Greek Catholic Theological Seminary in Lviv (1835–8), he served as a pastor in Slavsko, Stryi circle (1841–9, 1850–70), and Suceava (1870–85). In 1848 he was one of the initiators and organizers of the *Congress of Ruthenian Scholars, as a member of which he championed the use of the vernacular in literature. In 1849–50 he edited the paper *Halychoruskii vistnyk* in Lviv and adapted J. Korzeniowski's *Karpaccy górale* (The Carpathian Highlanders) for the Galician stage under the title 'Verkhovyntsi Beskydiv' (Highlanders of the Beskyds). From 1861 to 1866 he was a member of the first Galician Diet.

Ustyianovych wrote his first Ukrainian poem in 1836 under the influence of his friend M. Shashkevych and joined the *Ruthenian Triad circle. Because of sanctions against those writing in the vernacular, his next three poems appeared only in 1847, in the almanac *Vinok rusynam na obzhynky*. During the Revolution of 1848–9 he began publishing Romantic poetry on patriotic, social, lyrical, historical, and folkloric (Boiko) subjects, prose based on Galician ethnography and history, and articles on political and cultural issues in *Zoria halytska* and *Halycho-ruskii vistnyk* in Lviv and *Vistnyk* and *Otechestvennyi sbornik* in Vienna. His poems 'Verkhovyno, svitku ty nash' (O Highland, Our Little World) and 'Hei, brattia opryshky' (Hey, Fellow Opryshoks) became popular songs. From 1861 on, having become a Russophile, he wrote poems, stories, and articles in the artificial *yazychiie and in Russian (in

Suceava). Published separately were a volume of his poems (1860), his story *Staryi Iefrem* (Old Yefrem, 1874), and a book (1879) consisting of 'Mest' verkhovyntsia' (The Highlander's Revenge) and 'Strastnyi chetver' (Passion Thursday), two of the best Galician novelettes until the 1860s. The fullest edition of his poems (together with A. Mohylnytsky's) appeared in Lviv in 1913.

R. Senkus

**Ustyluh.** III-5. A city (1989 pop 2,600) on the Buh River at the mouth of the Luha River in Volodymyr-Volynskyi raion, Volhynia oblast. From the 9th century a fortified settlement stood at the site. It belonged to Kievan Rus' (10th–11th centuries), Volodymyr-Volynskyi principality (12th century), and the Principality of Galicia-Volhynia (13th century). In 1240 it was razed by the Mongols. In the medieval period Ustyluh was a prosperous river port and trade center that exported foodstuffs to the Baltic towns. From the mid-14th century the town belonged to the Grand Duchy of Lithuania, and from 1569, to the Polish Commonwealth. A Capuchin monastery was built there at the beginning of the 18th century, and a Roman Catholic church in 1747. The town was annexed by Russia in 1795, and became a tariff collection post. In 1875 M. Biliashivsky excavated some of the kurhans in its vicinity. In the interwar period the town was under Polish rule. It was occupied by the Soviet army in 1939 and granted city status in 1940. Today it is an agricultural center with a workshop of the Volodymyr-Volynskyi Sewing Factory and some rest homes in the vicinity.

**Ustymovych** [Ustymovyč] (Sakhno-Ustymovych). A Cossack *starshyna* family line from Khorol, in the Poltava region. They were descended from the *town Cossack captain Sofon (Sakhno) Ustymovych, who was killed near Chyhyryn in 1678, and his son, Ustym (Sokhnovych, Sokhnenko) Ustymovych (d 1727), who was a captain in Vlasiv (1704–5) before becoming a monk (Ilarion) and serving as the superior of the Motronynskyi Trinity Monastery. His descendant, Prokip Ustymovych (b ca 1756, d ca 1814), was a regimental secretary and a member of a historical committee on the Hetmanate (1780) and later a department director in the imperial Naval Ministry in St Petersburg. Prokip's son, Adriian Ustymovych (b ca 1797, d 1851), was an aide-de-camp to the Little Russian military governor, Prince N. Repnin, took part in the formation of Cossack regiments in 1831–2, and later served as civil governor of Kursk gubernia. His marriage with the daughter of H. Myloradovych linked him with the Polubotok and Apostol lines. Adriian's son, Mykola (b 1832, d 1891), was an active participant in the peasant reforms of 1861 in the Poltava region; he was also the grandfather (through his daughter) of O. Shulhyn. Other members of the Ustymovych family were Petro (b ca 1786, d after 1865), who was a Decembrist from 1821, and Mykola (b 1863, d 1918), who was an engineer and the first head (otaman) of the Council of Ministers of Ukraine's Hetman government (1918).

A. Zhukovsky

**Ustymovych, Mykola** [Ustymovyč] (Sakhno-Ustymovych), 1863–1918. Ukrainian government figure. An engineer and landowner in the Poltava region, on 29 April 1918 he became the first head (otaman) of the Council of Ministers of the *Hetman government. Little known among Ukrainian circles, he failed in his primary task of attracting moderate Socialists-Federalists into the new government. He was forced to resign on 30 April 1918. His successor, M. Vasylenko, was no more effective in bringing representatives of the major Ukrainian political parties into the cabinet. Ustymovych was killed during the uprising that brought the Directory of the UNR into power.

**Ustynivka.** VI-13. A town smt (1986 pop 3,800) on the Berezivka River and a raion center in Kirovohrad oblast. It was founded in the 1740s by settlers from Poltava gubernia. Today it is an agricultural town with a cheese factory and a poultry incubation station.

**Usyk, Yakiv,** b 9 February 1872 in Marianske, Myrhorod county, Poltava gubernia, d 6 February 1961 in Myrhorod, Poltava oblast. Wood carver. In the 1920s he was a member of the Association of Artists of Red Ukraine. His works include portraits of Ukrainian, Georgian, and Russian writers, such as T. Shevchenko (1943), M. Gorky (1946), I. Kotliarevsky (1947), D. Guramishvili (1949), A. Pushkin (1953), and I. Franko (1955), and thematic compositions, such as *The Pereiaslav Council* (1953) and *B. Khmelnytsky Meeting Russian Envoys* (1954).

Oleksandr Usykov

**Usykov, Oleksandr** (Usikov, Aleksandr), b 11 January 1904 in Yankivka, Bohodukhiv county, Kharkiv gubernia. Radio physicist; AN URSR (now ANU) full member since 1964. A graduate of the Kharkiv Institute of People's Education (1929), he worked in Kharkiv at the ANU Physical-Technical Institute (1936–55) and as director (1955–73) and a department head at the ANU Institute of Radio Physics and Electronics. In 1966–78 he was a member of the ANU presidium. Usykov made an important contribution to the invention of the impulse magnetron generator of decimeter and millimeter radio waves and to their application in radiolocation. He studied the absorption and diffusion of radio waves and new methods of radio communication. In 1944 he developed a radiolocation method of uncovering damage in power lines, and in 1960 he proposed a way of using the lens effect of the earth's ionosphere in refractor radio telescopes.

**Utevsky, Aron** [Utevs'kyj], b 20 June 1904 in Konotip, Chernihiv gubernia. Biochemist; AN URSR (now ANU) corresponding member since 1939. A graduate of the Kharkiv Institute of People's Education (1924), he continued his studies at the Kharkiv Biochemical Institute (1925–8) and

taught there and at the Kharkiv Medical Institute, where he chaired the biochemistry department from 1932. A professor since 1932 (doctorate, 1935), he became head of the neurohumoral systems department at the ANU Institute for Problems of Cryobiology and Cryomedicine in Kharkiv. Utevsky's research has dealt with problems of intracellular carbohydrate exchange; metabolic processes in the endocrine glands; the biochemistry of enzymes and hormones (especially catecholamines), where he introduced methods to study their metabolic intermediates; and the biochemistry of vitamin deficiency. In addition to over 140 scientific papers, he has published articles on the history and philosophy of science, short stories, and a play in Russian.

**UTHI.** See Ukrainian Technical and Husbandry Institute.

**Utilities, public.** See Municipal services.

**Utliuk Estuary** [Utljuc'kyj lyman]. VII-16. A bay situated at the northwestern corner of the Sea of Azov off the coast of Zaporizhia and Kherson oblasts. Separated from the Sea of Azov by Fedotova Spit and Byriuchyi Island, the estuary is 45 km long, 2–20 km wide, and up to 3.5 m deep. The Velykyi Utliuk and the Malyi Utliuk rivers empty into it. A section of the estuary is within the Azov-Syvash Game Preserve.

*Utrenniaia zvezda*

**Utrenniaia zvezda** (The Morning Star). A literary miscellany published by I. Petrov and I. Sreznevsky in two volumes in Kharkiv in 1833–4. The miscellany was initiated by H. *Kvitka-Osnovianenko, and the first volume, published in Russian, contained Russian folk songs, Sreznevsky's notes on H. Skovoroda, a translation of a folktale by O. Somov, and poems by Petrov and P. Inozemtsev. The second volume contained Kvitka-Osnovianenko's first Ukrainian-language tale, 'Saldats'kyi patret' (The Soldier's Portrait), his 'supplication' to the publisher in which he justified the right of the Ukrainian people to have a national literature, an excerpt from I. Kotliarevsky's *Eneïda* (Aeneid), poetry by Ye. Hrebinka, Sreznevsky, and P. Hulak-Artemovsky, historical folk songs, music to poems by Kotliarevsky, and drawings of Skovoroda and views of Kharkiv.

Myron Utrysko

**Utrysko, Myron,** b 30 August 1908 in Lviv, d 14 October 1988 in Edmonton. Civic leader and journalist. In 1934 he completed law studies in Lviv. After emigrating in 1952 to the United States he founded and directed a Ukrainian radio program in Philadelphia. In 1977 he began to edit the journal of regional studies *Litopys Boikivshchyny,* and in 1980 he edited and published *Monohrafiia Boikivshchyny* (Monograph of the Boiko Region). In addition to other regional, memorial, and commemorative articles he wrote *Viden' 1683 – Kozaky i Kul'chyts'kyi* (Vienna 1683 – The Cossacks and Kulchytsky, 1983).

**Uvarov, Aleksei,** b 12 March 1825, d 10 January 1885. The son of a Russian minister of education and grandson of K. *Rozumovsky, he graduated from St Petersburg University (1845) and then worked in the Russian diplomatic corps while continuing his studies in Berlin and Heidelberg. He undertook archeological research first in Southern Ukraine, where he conducted studies at Olbia, Chersonesus, and Neapolis, and then in Vladimir and Moscow gubernias. He published *Issledovaniia o drevnostiakh Iuzhnoi Rossii i beregov Chérnogo moria* (Studies of the Antiquities of Southern Russia and the Black Sea Coast) in two volumes (1851, 1856). Uvarov was instrumental in organizing many archeological conferences, forming archeological societies in Moscow and St Petersburg, and establishing the Moscow Historical Museum.

**Uvarov, Mykola,** b 1861 in Bohodukhiv, Kharkiv gubernia, d 1942. Painter and graphic artist. He studied at the Kharkiv Painting School and St Petersburg Academy of Arts (1882–90). He took part in painting the murals inside the Poltava Zemstvo Building (1903–8) by collaborating with S. Vasylkivsky on *The Election of Col Pushkar.* He also painted portraits of T. Shevchenko, I. Franko, M. Lysenko, D. Bahalii, and S. Vasylkivsky and made prints, particularly satirical prints on biblical themes. Later he worked as a restorer in a Kharkiv museum.

**UVO.** See Ukrainian Military Organization.

*Uvyvanets.* A folk dance performed by many pairs. It has a quick 2/4 beat and demands great dexterity, as the pairs of lovers wind (*uvyvaiutsia*) themselves around each other. The dance is mostly comical in effect but has some lyrical moments. It has been popular in Western Ukraine.

**Uzbekistan.** A republic (1989 pop 19,905,000) in Central Asia formerly the Uzbek SSR. It borders on Kazakhstan in the north, Turkmenistan in the southwest, and Kirgizia in the east and has an area of 447,400 sq km. The capital is Tashkent. The area was absorbed by the Russian Empire in the 1860s and 1870s and reconstituted as a Soviet republic in 1924. Native Turkic-speaking Uzbeks account for about two-thirds of the population. There are 153,000 Ukrainians in Uzbekistan (1989), most of whom live in the cities, including 60,000 in Tashkent. There are approx 20,000 Uzbeks in Ukraine.

*UZh.* See *Universal'nyi zhurnal.*

**Uzh River** [Už]. A left-bank tributary of the Laborets River that flows for 133 km along the Tysa Lowland in Transcarpathia oblast and western Czechoslovakia and drains a basin area of 2,750 sq km. It has a valley 2–3 km wide. It is used for industry, water supply, and irrigation. A hydroelectric station is situated on it. Sources of mineral water are found in the river's basin. The city of Uzhhorod is located in its middle reaches.

**Uzh River** [Už]. A right-bank tributary of the Prypiat River that flows for 256 km through Zhytomyr and Kiev oblasts and drains a basin area of 8,080 sq km. It is 5–40 m wide and has a valley width of 1–7 km. The river is used for industry, water supply, irrigation, and log rafting. It freezes over from December to late March. Granite outcrops can be found in its basin. The city of Korosten is situated near its upper reaches.

**Uzhevych, Ivan** [Uževyč] (Ioann), b and d ? The 17th-century author of the Latin 'Hrammatyka slovenskaia/Grammatica sclavonica,' the first grammar of the Ruthenian bookish (non–Church Slavonic) language used by both Ukrainians and Belarusians. He studied at Cracow University (1637–ca 1641) and at the Sorbonne (1643–5). There are only two manuscripts of his grammar, one (1643) at the National Library in Paris and the other (1645) at the Municipal Library in Arras in northern France. A photoreproduction of the two manuscripts, together with a Ukrainian translation of the Paris manuscript, notes, index, and bibliography by I. Bilodid and Ye. Kudrytsky, was published in Kiev in 1970. The grammar has been studied by A. Sobolevsky, V. Jagić, E. Borschak, and M. Zhovtobriukh.

**Uzhhorod** [Užhorod] (Hungarian: Ungvár; Czech: Užhorod). A city (1989 pop 117,000) on the Uzh River and the capital of Transcarpathia oblast. It is a major economic and cultural center of the Carpathian region. Its name means 'city (*horod*) on the Uzh.'

According to the archeological evidence the site was inhabited as early as the Stone Age. A Slavic tribe founded a fortified settlement there in the 8th or 9th century. Early in the 10th century it was controlled by the Hungarians and then by Kievan Rus'. Hungary regained control of the town in the 11th century and remained the dominant influence there until the 20th century. Uzhhorod was sacked by the Tatars in 1242, and its fortress was destroyed. Its economy was initially based on wine-making, agriculture, and animal husbandry. Trade and manufacturing, stimulated by the town's military and administrative needs, developed through the 15th to 18th centuries. The religious struggle of the 17th century culminated in the *Uzhhorod Union of 1646. In the late 1770s Bishop A. Bachynsky

Uzhhorod and the Uzh River

transferred the seat of Mukachiv eparchy to Uzhhorod. By the end of the century a theological seminary and teachers' college had been established there.

The Austrian Habsburgs won control of Uzhhorod in 1691, and the city became involved in Hungarian attempts to throw off Austrian rule – in the Rákóczi uprising of 1703–11 and the Revolution of 1848–9. With the defeat of the revolution the Ukrainian cultural movement in Uzhhorod gained strength for a time. The *Society of St Basil the Great, the *Uniia publishing society, and Ukrainian schools were established. Most of the movement's leaders worked in Uzhhorod, although they found little support there, for the city was inhabited mostly by Hungarians, Jews, and Slovaks.

In 1848 the city was granted self-government, and began the process of modernization. A sewage system was built in 1855, and a rail link with Chop was established in 1872. A new gymnasium was erected in 1894. The wine-making industry was expanded, and new manufacturing industries (furniture-making, woodworking, brick-making) were introduced. Trade and commerce increased. The population grew from 3,000 in 1800 to 9,750 in 1860 and 14,700 in 1900.

With Transcarpathia's incorporation into Czechoslovakia after the First World War, Uzhhorod became the capital of Subcarpathian Ruthenia, the seat of the governor and the administration, and a center of Ukrainian life. Ukrainian cultural organizations, such as the Prosvita society, the Russophile Dukhnovych Society, and the Ruthenian People's Theater, and economic institutions, such as the Subcarpathian Bank and the Co-operative Union, set up their regional centers in Uzhhorod. In the 1930s a new administrative district was developed on the right bank of the Uzh. There was a Ukrainian gymnasium in the city.

When Uzhhorod was transferred to Hungary in accordance with the Vienna award of 2 November 1938, the government of autonomous Carpatho-Ukraine moved to Khust. In 1939–44 the city continued to be a center of Ukrainian cultural and civic life.

Uzhhorod was occupied by Soviet forces in November 1944 and became the seat of the People's Council of Transcarpathian Ukraine, which called for the territory's unification with the Ukrainian SSR. In January 1946 it became the capital of Transcarpathia oblast. New cultural institutions, many of them regional in scope, were established in the city, including a philharmonic orchestra, a folk-song and -dance ensemble, a theater company, a regional studies museum, a picture gallery, Uzhhorod University, and a publishing house (later renamed Karpaty). Later a museum of folk architecture and folkways was set up.

Today the city is an industrial and communications center. It has strong machine-building (Uzhhorodprylad), woodworking (plywood and furniture manufacturing complex), light (footwear and clothing), food (winery, cannery, meat packers, distillery), and building-materials (reinforced concrete, brick, tiles) industries. A hydroelectric power station provides energy to run the industries. Tourism plays an important role in the local economy.

In addition to the university there are five vocational and five specialized secondary schools in the city. A number of research institutions, such as branches of the Institute of Nuclear Research and the Institute of Social and Economic Problems of Foreign Countries, are located in

Uzhhorod, with the Cathedral of the Elevation of the Cross (1644) in the background

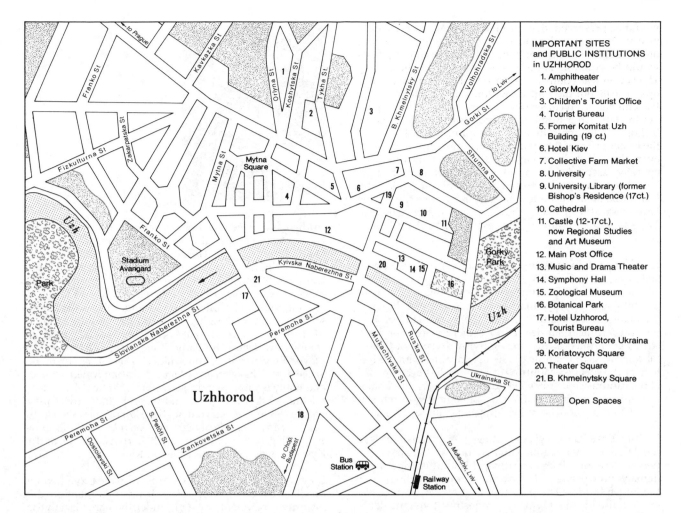

IMPORTANT SITES
and PUBLIC INSTITUTIONS
in UZHHOROD

1. Amphitheater
2. Glory Mound
3. Children's Tourist Office
4. Tourist Bureau
5. Former Komitat Uzh
   Building (19 ct.)
6. Hotel Kiev
7. Collective Farm Market
8. University
9. University Library (former
   Bishop's Residence (17ct.)
10. Cathedral
11. Castle (12-17ct.),
    now Regional Studies
    and Art Museum
12. Main Post Office
13. Music and Drama Theater
14. Symphony Hall
15. Zoological Museum
16. Botanical Park
17. Hotel Uzhhorod,
    Tourist Bureau
18. Department Store Ukraina
19. Koriatovych Square
20. Theater Square
21. B. Khmelnytsky Square

Open Spaces

Uzhhorod. The main architectural monuments are the fortress (built in 1598 and reconstructed in the 17th century), the episcopal palace (1646, now the university library), the cathedral (17th century), the Roman Catholic Cathedral of the Elevation of the Cross (1644), the gymnasium (1784), the town hall (1810), and the former synagogue (1904, now the philharmonic hall).

BIBLIOGRAPHY
Hranchak, I.; Pol'ok, V. *Misto nad Uzhem* (Uzhhorod 1973)
Kushnir, B.; Uhliai, A. *Uzhhorod: Narys-putivnyk* (Uzhhorod 1990)

**Uzhhorod gymnasium** (Uzhhorodska himnaziia). One of the oldest secondary schools in Ukraine, established in 1649 on the basis of an earlier Jesuit college. Until 1778 Jesuits continued to teach in the gymnasium, using Latin as the language of instruction (except for religion classes, which were taught in the Ukrainian redaction of Church Slavonic). In the 18th century approx 150–200 students attended the school. In 1778 it was given the status of an Austrian royal gymnasium; the primary language of instruction was (until 1790) German, then Latin again (until 1796), and finally Hungarian. Two extra grades of philosophy were added to the course of study in 1856, the number thereby being raised to eight. In the 1880s strong pressures were exerted to make the gymnasium a totally Hungarian institution despite the fact that most of the staff and students were Ukrainian. During the interwar period the gymnasium was first Ukrainized and later Russified, according to the desires of the directors and regional education supervisors (who were alternately Ukrainophile or Russophile in orientation). Approx 800 students attended the school at that time. In 1945, after the Soviet occupation of Transcarpathia, the gymnasium was turned into a *ten-year school. One of the school's most notable directors was A. Alyskevych.

**Uzhhorod *polustav*** (Uzhhorod Semi-Uncial). A 209-folio Church Slavonic manuscript of the late 14th to early 15th centuries containing one of the oldest extant East Slavic books of monastic rule. According to O. Kolessa it was first composed in Kiev and then copied in eastern Transcarpathia, possibly at the Hrusheve Monastery. For many years the manuscript was stored in the library of the Prosvita society in Uzhhorod. Now it is preserved at the Transcarpathian Regional Studies Museum in Uzhhorod.

**Uzhhorod Union of 1646.** An act under which 63 Transcarpathian Orthodox priests joined the Catholic church on the model of the Church Union of *Berestia. It was signed in Uzhhorod by the Roman Catholic bishop of Eger, and was initiated on the Ukrainian side by the Basilian order under the leadership of P. Partenii. Its main provisions were that the Eastern or Byzantine church rite would be preserved; that the eparchy of Mukachiv would reserve the right to choose bishops, and Rome would have only the right of confirmation; and that the Uniate priests would be equal in status to the Roman Catholic priests. The Union was confirmed by a synod of Hungarian bishops in 1648, but the Vatican withheld ratification because Partenii had been consecrated by an Orthodox metropolitan in 1651. After Rome finally confirmed Partenii as the bishop of Mukachiv in 1655, the union was extended to the eastern part of the eparchy; it was not until 1721, however, that all Transcarpathian Ukrainians in Mukachiv eparchy accepted it. In 1949 the Soviet authorities had the Union revoked, and created the Orthodox Mukachiv-Uzhhorod eparchy, under the patriarch of Moscow. In the late 1980s the Uniate church was re-established in Transcarpathia, following the easing of Soviet religious persecution.

**Uzhhorod University** (Uzhhorodskyi universytet). A state university established in 1945. In 1982–3 the university had 11 faculties: history, philology, Romano-Germanic philology, physics, mathematics, chemistry, biology, medicine, evening studies, correspondence studies, and general technical studies. In 1988 there were over 7,800 students enrolled at the university. A division of the AN URSR (now ANU) Institute of History (dealing with the history of the socialist countries of Europe) has been housed at the campus since 1969. The university operates a botanical garden and a mountainside biological research station. Its library collection has approx 1 million volumes.

**Uzhok Pass** [Užoc'kyj pereval]. V–3. A mountain pass in the High Beskyd region situated on the boundary between Lviv and Transcarpathia oblasts (historically the demarcation between Galicia and Transcarpathia) near the Polish border. The pass stands at an elevation of 889 m. A railroad and highway connecting Lviv and Uzhhorod go through it.

**Uzhvii, Nataliia** [Užvij, Natalija], b 8 September 1898 in Liuboml, Volodymyr-Volynskyi county, Volhynia gubernia, d 29 July 1986 in Kiev. Stage and screen actress. She

Nataliia Uzhvii

studied and acted in the Shevchenko First Theater of the Ukrainian Soviet Republic (1922–5) and then acted in the Odessa State Drama Theater (1925–6), Berezil (1926–34; later the Kharkiv Ukrainian Drama Theater), and the Kiev Ukrainian Drama Theater (from 1936). In Berezil she played a wide range of roles (from heroic to character), including Sadie in J. Colton and C. Randolph's *Sadie Thompson* (based on S. Maugham's *Rain*, 1926), Auntie Motia in M. Kulish's *Myna Mazailo* (1929), and Larysa in M. Irchan's *Pliatsdarm* (The Battle Zone, 1932). Elsewhere she played Elizabeth in F. von Schiller's *Don Carlos* (1936), Beatrice in W. Shakespeare's *Much Ado about Nothing* (1940), and many leading female characters in dramas by O. Korniichuk, O. Levada, M. Zarudny, and other Soviet playwrights. She also starred in the films *Taras Shevchenko* (1926), *Taras Triasylo* (1927), and *Raiduha* (The Rainbow, 1943). Biographies of Uzhvii, by R. Bernatska (1958) and Y. Kyselov (1978), were published in Kiev.

**Uzyn.** IV-11. A city (1989 pop 11,800) on the Uzyn River in Bila Tserkva raion, Kiev oblast. It was first mentioned in historical documents in 1651, under the name Uzenytsia. From 1773 it was called Tembershchyna, and since the end of the 18th century, by its current name. After the partition of Poland in 1793, the village was annexed by the Russian Empire. In 1971 it was granted city status. Today it has a large sugar refinery, a canning factory, and a brick plant.

# V

**Vacation.** A period of exemption from work granted to an employee for rest or relaxation. Mandatory vacations regulated by law have become common in developed countries only in the 20th century. In the Russian Empire before 1917, senior government officials received two-month vacations once every two years.

Vacations in Soviet Ukraine were regulated by various acts and statutes governing labor relations. From 1968 the minimum vacation throughout the USSR was 15 working days annually. It was granted after at least 11 months of uninterrupted service at the same place of employment. Employees were guaranteed their jobs when they returned from vacation and could not be fired during that time. Vacation time could not be replaced by extra pay. Workers employed under special conditions received extra vacation time; academics and teachers, for example, were entitled to 24 to 48 working days of vacation, and lumbermen to 24 days. Workers in difficult jobs, such as mining, qualified for an extra 6 to 36 working days in addition to the normal 15 days of vacation. People who worked with handicapped children got premiums of 12 working days, and workers in the metallurgical industry got 3 to 9 days extra. Vacation time increased with seniority, and workers under the age of 18 also were given extra time off.

**Vacation Resort Society** (Tovarystvo vakatsiinykh osel). A charitable society in Lviv, active in 1905–39 under the patronage of Metropolitan A. *Sheptytsky, which sponsored country vacations for children aged 7 to 14. The society organized summer expeditions for over 200 children to resorts in Myluvannia, Tovmach county, and Korshiv, Kolomyia county. Major figures in the group included O. Bachynska and Y. Pankivska.

**Vagner, Ivan** (Wagner, Johann), b 7 November 1833 in Riga, d 1892. Anatomist. A graduate of Dorpat (Tartu) University (1857), he taught there and at Kharkiv University (from 1861, as professor from 1871) and conducted research on cattle vaccination in Kharkiv. His publications include monographs on anatomy written in German and a translation of J. Henle's book on human anatomy into Russian (1881).

**Vahylevych, Ivan** [Vahylevyč] (pseuds: Dalibor, Volk Zaklyka), b 2 September 1811 in Yasen, Stanyslaviv circle, Galicia, d 10 May 1866 in Lviv. Romantic poet, philologist, and ethnographer of the Galician revival. In the years 1829–39, while studying at Lviv University and at the Greek Catholic Theological Seminary in Lviv, he associated with M. Shashkevych and Ya. Holovatsky, and the three of them formed the *Ruthenian Triad. During that time he repeatedly interrupted his studies to conduct archeological and ethnographic fieldwork in Western Ukrainian villages. Because of his populist activities, cul-

Ivan Vahylevych

tural nationalist views, and correspondence with scholars in the Russian Empire, such as M. Pogodin, I. Sreznevsky, and the Ukrainians M. Maksymovych and O. Bodiansky, he suffered harassment by the church and Austrian civil authorities. He was ordained in 1846, and served as pastor in Nestanychi, Zolochiv circle. During the Revolution of 1848–9, as a supporter of a democratic Polish-Ukrainian political federation, he accepted the *Ruthenian Congress's invitation to edit its weekly, *Dnewnyk Ruskij, in Lviv. Later that year he left the Uniate church in protest against the hierarchy's sanctions against him and converted to Lutheranism. Ostracized by most Ukrainians and by the church because of his 'pro-Polish' politics and his conversion, he was unable to find steady work until 1862, when he was appointed city archivist in Lviv.

Vahylevych wrote poetry in Polish in the years 1829–41. In 1836 he wrote a Ukrainian vernacular prose rendition of the Rus' epic Slovo o polku Ihorevi (The Tale of Ihor's Campaign, pub 1884). He coedited the first Galician Ukrainian almanac, *Rusalka Dnistrovaia (1836). He contributed pioneering articles on the Hutsuls (1838–9), vampires and witches (1840), and the Boikos (1841) to the annual, Časopis, of Prague's Czech Museum, and other ethnographic articles to Polish periodicals (Przegląd Naukowy, Biblioteka Warszawska, Biblioteka Ossolińskich). In 1840, with A. Bielowski, he translated into Polish and annotated the Rus' Primary Chronicle (pub 1864). In an unpublished treatise (1841–9) on the Ukrainian ('Southern Rus'') language, he was one of the first to treat that language as distinct from Russian and Polish; he divided it into Galician and Kievan dialectal groups. Those views were also expressed in his published Polish grammar of the 'Little Ruthenian' language in Galicia (1845) and 'Little Ruthenian' grammar for elementary schools (1846), which were modeled on the grammar of the Russian N. Grech. In them he employed a 16th- and 17th-century orthography rather than one based on the vernacular, because he believed it to be 'pure Ruthenian.' In 1848 in Dnewnyk Ruskij, Vahylevych published political articles on Ukraine as a separate cultural entity, on the need for education in the vernacular, and on the need for Ukrainian-Polish co-operation on the basis of democracy, autonomy, and equality, and he provided one of the earliest surveys of Ukrainian literature. He also wrote a pioneering booklet on the *Maniava Hermitage (1848). Among his unpublished works are a dictionary with over 10,000 Ukrainian words (1834–44), materials for a Ukrainian-German-Latin dictionary and for books on Carpathian ethnography and Lviv's historical monuments, studies of Slavic demonology, symbolism, and wedding and birth rituals, collections of songs about the opryshoks, and a collection of Ukrainian Christmas carols (of which he had gathered 280). Although he wrote mostly in Polish, he remained true to his Ukrainophile and democratic principles to the end of his life.

The fullest editions of Vahylevych's works were published together with Shashkevych's and Holovatsky's in Lviv in 1913 and in Kiev in 1982. O. Dzoban's guide to Vahylevych's unpublished manuscripts and biographical materials appeared in Lviv in 1986.

BIBLIOGRAPHY
Brock, P. 'Ivan Vahylevych (1811–1866) and the Ukrainian National Identity,' in *Nationbuilding and the Politics of Nationalism: Essays on Austrian Galicia*, ed A. Markovits and F. Sysyn (Cambridge, Mass 1982)
Shalata, M. (ed). *Narodni pisni v zapysakh Ivana Vahylevycha* (Kiev 1983)

R. Senkus

**Vainshtein, Moisei** [Vajnštejn, Mojsej], b 20 February 1940 in Druzhkivka, Donetske oblast, d 26 May 1981 in Kiev. Painter and sculptor of Jewish origin. A graduate of the Kiev State Art Institute (1965), throughout his brief life he alternated between painting pictures demanded by socialist realism, such as *Liknep* (1967) and *First Day: Lenin at the 2nd Congress of Soviets* (1980), and works inspired by his quest to express himself, such as the heavily textured *Mountain Ash* (1966) and *The Sun Has Set* (1976). In most of his landscapes the oil pigments are applied with relish and with great sensitivity to hues. Although most of his work was figurative, some of his paintings, such as *Spring* (1968), are reminiscent of abstract expressionism in their gestural application of paint. In some of his final works, such as *Evening, Lviv Square*, and *Kiev* (1979), representation once more yields to a vibrating surface of colors. His first solo exhibition was held posthumously in Kiev in 1987.

**Vaišvilkas** (Ukrainian: Voishelk Mindovhovych), b ?, d 1268. Grand duke of Lithuania; son of *Mindaugas. Having converted to Orthodoxy, he gave up his holdings in Chorna Rus' to *Roman, the son of Danylo Romanovych of Galicia (thus cementing a peace treaty between the two powers, 1255), and became a monk. He was brought into power after his father and two brothers were assassinated in 1263 by rebel Lithuanian princes. In 1267 he abdicated in favor of his brother-in-law, *Shvarno Danylovych, and returned to the monastery. He was killed by Shvarno's older brother, Lev Danylovych, who resented not being chosen to reign over Lithuania.

**Vakhnianyn, Anatol** [Vaxnjanyn, Anatol'] (also Natal), b 19 September 1841 in Siniava, Peremyshl circle, Galicia, d 8 March 1908 in Lviv. Composer, conductor, writer, and

Anatol Vakhnianyn

civic figure. He studied at the Lviv Theological Seminary, graduated from the University of Vienna (1868), and then taught (from 1870) at the Academic Gymnasium in Lviv. His civic and cultural activity was extensive and included the founding or cofounding of the Sich student society of Vienna (1867), the musical associations *Torban (Lviv, 1869) and *Boian (Lviv, 1891), and the *Lysenko Higher Institute of Music (1903 in its nascent form), which he directed in 1903–6. He also served as the first head of the *Prosvita Society in Galicia (1868–70). He was elected to the Galician Diet and the Austrian parliament (1894–1900). His musical works include *Kupalo*, the first opera in Western Ukraine (to his own libretto, 1870–92); music to plays by T. Shevchenko, F. Zarevych, O. Ohonovsky, and K. Ustyianovych; original choral scores to texts by Yu. Fedkovych, I. Hushalevych, O. Levytsky, and others; and choral arrangements of Ukrainian folk songs. He wrote four novels, and tales, poems, and articles, in addition to translating works by N. Gogol and I. Turgenev. His memoirs were published in Lviv in 1908, and a biography, by I. Hrynevetsky, appeared in Kiev in 1961.

**Vakhnianyn, Ostap** [Vaxnjanyn], b 1890 in Lviv, d 31 August 1924 in Uzhhorod, Transcarpathia. Educator and cultural activist; son of A. *Vakhnianyn. After graduating from Lviv University he taught briefly at a Lviv gymnasium and then joined the Ukrainian Sich Riflemen. In Uzhhorod he was one of the founders of the Prosvita Society Theater in 1921. He also founded a branch of the *Plast Ukrainian Youth Association in Uzhhorod, published its paper *Plastun*, and wrote two handbooks, *Plast* and *Plastovyi pidruchnyk* (Plast Handbook).

**Vakhrusheve** [Vaxruševe]. V-19, DB III-5. A city (1989 pop 19,600) on the Khrustalna and the Miiusyk rivers in Luhanske oblast, under the jurisdiction of the Krasnyi Luch city council. It was founded in 1954 and granted city status in 1963. The city's chief enterprises are three coal mines and a coal enrichment plant, a machine repair plant, and a workshop of the Luhanske Sewing Consortium.

**Vaks, Borys,** b 25 May 1912 in Zhytomyr, Volhynia gubernia. Painter. In 1948 he graduated from the Kharkiv Art Institute, where he had studied with S. Prokhorov, O. Kokel, and M. Derehus. He painted genre paintings, such as *On the Virgin Land* (1961), the triptych *Bread* (1967), and

*Miners Resting* (1976), and collaborated on monumental paintings such as the frieze *Coal Donbas* in the Horlivka Palace of Culture (1960) and the panel *Builders* in the Krasnodon Building of Culture (1966). He also collaborated on a lithograph series of prints devoted to T. Shevchenko (1964).

**Vakulenchuk, Hryhorii** [Vakulenčuk, Hryhorij], b 1877 in Velyki Korovyntsi, Zhytomyr county, Volhynia gubernia, d 27 June 1905. Seaman and revolutionary. Upon finishing military training in 1900, he was assigned as a gunner on the battleship *Potemkin*. He headed a cell of the Russian Social Democratic Workers' party on the ship and became an organizer of the Sevastopil Seamen's Central, which was preparing a general uprising of the Black Sea Fleet. A mutiny broke out on the *\*Potemkin* sooner than anticipated, and Vakulenchuk was killed at the beginning of the uprising. His funeral in Odessa on 29 June 1905 turned into a political demonstration.

Metropolitan Dionisii          Gen Arkadii Valiisky
Valedinsky

**Valedinsky, Dionisii** [Valedinskij, Dionisij] (secular name: Konstantin), b 16 May 1876 in Murom, Russia, d 15 March 1960 in Warsaw. Russian Orthodox hierarch. After graduating from the Kazan Theological Academy he spent most of his early career in Ukraine, where he served as a rector of the Kholm Theological Seminary (1903–11) and then as bishop of Kremianets (from 1913). In 1918 he supported the creation of an independent Ukrainian church and participated in the All-Ukrainian Church Sobor in Kiev. In 1919 he became acting bishop of Polish-occupied Volhynia, and in 1923, metropolitan of the Orthodox church in Poland, with his see in Warsaw. In this capacity he encouraged the revival of Ukrainian church traditions and approved the translation of liturgical texts into contemporary Ukrainian and their use in services. Under his leadership the *\*Polish Autocephalous Orthodox church was formally granted autocephaly by the patriarch of Constantinople in 1924. During the Second World War Valedinsky gave his blessing to the revival of the *\*Ukrainian Autocephalous Orthodox church and designated P. *\*Sikorsky as administrator of the church. After the war he was interned by the Polish communist government, which stripped him of the title of metropolitan in 1945. He was also excommunicated by the Russian Orthodox church. After several years under house arrest (at Sosnowic) he was allowed to return to Warsaw, where he died in poverty.

**Valerian** (*Valeriana*; Ukrainian: *valeriana*). A perennial grassy herb of the teasel family Valerianaceae. Of its 200 species worldwide there are 13 known in Ukraine; the most widely distributed in the wild is the medicinal or common valerian (*V. officinalis*), also known as the garden heliotrope. Its roots and rhizomes contain volatile oils, acids, alkaloids, tannic substances, and sugar. Extracts of valerian are used as tranquilizing agents to control excitement, insomnia, neuroses of the cardiovascular system, spasms, and so on. A relaxant tea is brewed from its roots. Cultivated species in Ukraine include *V. nitida*, *V. rossica*, and *V. stoionifera*.

**Valiashko, Mykola** [Valjashko], b 1 April 1871 in Kupianka, Kharkiv gubernia, d 25 January 1955 in Kharkiv. Organic chemist. A professor at Kharkiv University from 1909 and the Kharkiv Polytechnical Institute from 1919, he researched the chemistry of pharmaceutical materials and the ultraviolet spectroscopy of aromatic and heterocyclic compounds, including the effect of solvents on their spectra. In 1910 he established the first spectroscopic laboratory in the Russian Empire.

**Valiisky, Arkadii** [Valijs'kyj, Arkadij], b 8 February 1894 in Chernihiv gubernia, d 16 September 1976 in New York. Military officer. In 1918–19 he served in Zhytomyr as a company commander and then as an instructor in the UNR Army officer school. In 1920 he was a company commander at the unified military youth school in Kamianets-Podilskyi and then an instructor in the Kalisz internment camp. In 1924 he became chief of the Operations Section at the UNR Ministry of Military Affairs, and in 1927 he was contracted by the Polish army. In 1936–9 he was chief of staff in the UNR Ministry of Military Affairs in Warsaw. At the outbreak of the Second World War he was interned by the Germans. In the spring of 1945 he served, at the rank of colonel, as chief of staff of the Ukrainian National Army. After the war, he emigrated to the United States (1951), where he was active in veterans' organizations and the defense department of the UNR government-in-exile, which promoted him to brigadier general.

**Valky.** IV-16. A city (1989 pop 10,300) on the Mozh River and a raion center in Kharkiv oblast. It was founded in 1646 as a fort to defend Muscovy's southern border against Crimean and Nogay Tatars. A settlement sprang up around the fort, and in 1740 it was granted town status. It served as a company center in Kharkiv regiment and then as a county center in Kharkiv vicegerency (1780–96) and Kharkiv gubernia (1802–1923). By the end of the 19th century its population had reached 7,900. It was granted city status in 1938. Today Valky is an agricultural town with a building-materials plant, a sewing factory, and a branch of the Mechyk Furniture Factory.

**Valleys** (*dolyny*). Linear-shaped areas of lower elevation on the surface of the earth commonly formed by the erosive action of flowing water. All valleys consist of slopes (along the sides) and a bottom. In Ukraine valley slopes typically are asymmetrical, often with a high right bank and a low left bank. The asymmetry can be attributed to the endogenic processes and the lithology of parent material, while the manner of the erosion and aggradation of the country's rivers have resulted from fluctuations in the level of the Black Sea and changes in climate.

River valleys in Ukraine are usually classified into three types, lowland (which constitute an overwhelming majority), mountain, and submontane (as in the Dniester Basin). The number of their terraces varies not only from one river valley to another but also within the same river valley. Lowland river valleys predominantly contain aggradational type terraces consisting of fine particles (usually sand). Such terraces are also found in the submontane valleys, together with erosive-aggradational types made up of water-sorted gravels. The erosive terraces (including boulder pavements and rock sculpting) prevail in the mountain valleys.

The river valleys of Ukraine evolved in several geomorphological stages. Broad river valleys with large floodplains were formed at the end of the Pliocene epoch, when the Black Sea stood approx 50 m above its present level. Their remnants may still be seen in the form of broad terraces along the left bank of the Dnieper as well as in the Donets, the Dniester, and the Prut river valleys.

Intensified or rejuvenated river erosion in the early Pleistocene epoch, caused by a drop in the landlocked sea (80–100 m below the present level) resulting from neotectonic uplift, deepened valleys and sculpted landforms. The submarine valleys of the old Dnieper, Dniester, and Danube rivers were created in consequence. The valleys may still be detected on the shelf bottom of the Black Sea, but their surfaces have been modified by subsequent marine deposits. Climatic cooling in the Dnieper age of the Pleistocene brought on the maximum extent of continental glaciation, in which the ice cap depressed the landmass and caused the Black Sea to rise 20 m above its present level. Its rising provided conditions for the formation of liman valleys along the coast. As well, meltwaters from the ice cap produced ponding, with excess water that either spilled over the low points of divides or flowed along the ice margin into valleys that channeled it toward the Black Sea. Glacial spillways were thereby created, some of which still serve as parts of existing river valleys, and others of which have become dry. Examples include the spillways between the Styr and the Slovechna rivers (over 400 km) and between the Sian and the Dniester, and the shorter but more numerous spillways that cross the Dnieper Upland from north to south or connect the left-bank tributaries of the Dnieper. The subsequent isostatic recovery of the landmass and the adjustment of the Black Sea to the present level rejuvenated erosive forces. River channels cut deeper valleys and left remnants of the Pleistocene alluvial deposits visible as terraces. Former river channels of the Pleistocene Dnieper delta dried up to form some of the depressions known as *pody*.

BIBLIOGRAPHY
Gerenchuk, K. *Tektonicheskie zakonomernosti v orografii i rechnoi seti Russkoi ravniny* (Lviv 1960)
Tsys', P. *Heomorfolohiia URSR* (Lviv 1962)
Sokolovs'kyi, I. *Zakonomirnosti rozvytku rel'iefu Ukraïny* (Kiev 1973)

I. Stebelsky

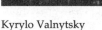
Kyrylo Valnytsky        Rev Maurice Van de Maele

**Valnytsky, Kyrylo** [Val'nyc'kyj], b 1889, d ? Galician Russophile and socialist leader. He founded (ca 1908) and then headed the *People's Will party in Lviv. He edited (1921–8) the Lviv Russophile newspaper *Volia naroda* and its Sovietophile Ukrainian-language successor, *Volia narodu*. Valnytsky and his group supported the Galician Ukrainian boycott of the 1922 Sejm elections and established a chair of Russian culture and language at the Lviv (Underground) Ukrainian University. By 1924 their views had changed from Russophile to Ukrainophile, pro-Soviet Marxist. In 1925 and early 1926 Valnytsky debated the Ukrainian question with R. *Turiansky in *Volia narodu*. When the People's Will party merged with the Sel-Soiuz to form the *Sel-Rob party, Valnytsky was elected to its Central Committee. As a leader of the pro-Comintern, anti-Vasylkiv faction he played a key role in the Sel-Rob split, and in 1928 he became the head of the 'reunited' Sel-Rob–Yednist federation, editor of its organ *Sel'-Rob*, and a member of the Communist Party of Western Ukraine. Until 1930, when he fled to the USSR, he represented Lviv voivodeship at the Sejm. He perished in a Soviet concentration camp.

**Valuev, Petr** [Valujev], b 22 September 1815 in Tsaritsyno, near Moscow, d 27 January 1890 in St Petersburg. Russian statesman and writer. As tsarist minister of internal affairs (1861–8; also responsible for press censorship from 1862) he implemented the legislation that emancipated the peasantry, introduced the zemstvo government reform, and expanded the powers of the bureaucracy and police. Having been alarmed by the spread of peasant dissatisfaction, student unrest, and Polish separatist, *khlopoman, and other populist and revolutionary activity, in 1862 he closed down all *Sunday schools on the ground that they were seditious, and had several hromada leaders (eg, O. Konysky, P. Chubynsky, S. Nis, P. Yefymenko) arrested as subversives and exiled to Siberia. In the wake of the *Polish Insurrection of 1863–4 in Right-Bank Ukraine and in response to official fear of 'separatist' *Ukrainophiles, he reacted to the application to print P. *Morachevsky's Ukrainian translation of the New Testament by banning it and all other publications in Ukrainian except belles lettres. In his 30 July 1863 secret instruction informing the minister of education of the ban, he gave the mo-tive for his decision: 'No separate Little Russian language has [ever] existed, does exist [now], and can [ever] exist, and the dialect used by the common folk is the very same Russian language, only adulterated by the influence on it of the Polish language ... The all-Russian language is just as understandable for Little Russians as it is for Great Russians, and even more understandable than the so-called Ukrainian language, presently fabricated for them by certain Little Russians, and in particular the Poles.' Valuev's instruction was echoed by that of the Holy Synod to its censors and was followed by a vicious campaign in the Russian press (including *Vestnik Iugo-zapadnoi Rossii, Kievlianin,* and *Trudy Kievskoi dukhovnoi akademii*) against the Ukrainophile movement as a Polish intrigue.

Valuev later served as a member of the State Council (from 1868) and on D. Tolstoi's commission for gymnasium reform, and as minister of state domains (1872–9). He also headed a commission on the 'peasant question' (from 1872) and was chairman of the Committee of Ministers (1877–81). He chaired several bodies concerned with suppressing the revolutionary movement, created governors-general with extraordinary powers, and published a government-funded counterrevolutionary weekly, *Otgoloski* (1879–81). His diaries of the years 1847–60 (in *Russkaia starina,* 1891, nos 5–11), 1861–76 (2 vols, Moscow 1961), and 1877–84 (Petrograd 1919) were published.

R. Senkus

**Vampire** (*upyr, opyr, opyrytsia*). A dead person believed to rise from the grave at night and to suck the blood of sleeping people, particularly children. According to Ukrainian folk belief vampires can also be living people, and they can cause droughts and epidemics. They are distinguished by their red faces and a tiny tail. Vampires are former criminals, suicides, victims of a spell, or improperly buried people. They can be destroyed by being exhumed and having a stake driven through their bodies. Living vampires must be pierced by a stake or buried. References to vampires occur in Ukrainian literature of the 13th to 17th centuries and in the works of Romantic writers.

**Van de Maele, Maurice,** b 5 April 1892 in Alveringem, Belgium, d 19 May 1970 in Belgium. Belgian Redemptorist. In 1917 he was ordained, and in 1922 he adopted the Byzantine Ukrainian rite and became a missionary in Western Ukraine. Until the Second World War he served as a priest and hegumen of several Redemptorist monasteries in Galicia and Volhynia; later he was dean of Ukrainian parishes in the Rzeszów region (1944–6). In 1946 he returned to Belgium. Until December 1952 he ministered to Ukrainian Catholics in Belgium, Holland, and Scandinavia, and from 1953 to 1961 he served as vicar-general for Ukrainian Catholics in France.

**Vanchenko, Kostiantyn** [Vančenko] (pseud: Pysanetsky), b 1863 in Zhytomyr, d 18 July 1928 in Tashkent. Actor, singer (baritone), director, and playwright. He worked in M. Starytsky's (1883–90) and H. Derkach's (1898–1900) troupes and later led his own. He is the author of many plays, including *Muzhychka* (The Peasant Girl, 1893), *Nedoliudky* (The Brutes, 1906), and the adaptations of N. Gogol, *Taras Bul'ba pid Dubnom* (Taras Bulba at Dubno, 1891) and *Zaporoz'kyi klad* (The Zaporozhian Treasure, 1898).

**Vanchenko, Petro** [Vančenko], b 1898 in Zhuky, Poltava gubernia, d 1937? Writer and satirist. A member of the writers' group Hart in the 1920s, from 1924 on he published stories (many of them satirical) in journals such as *Literatura, nauka, mystetstvo, Zoria, Vsesvit, Hart,* and *Chervonyi shliakh* (*ChSh*). Published separately were his prose collections *Zhyva rekliama* (The Live Advertisement, 1928), *Muzhnist'* (Manhood, 1928), *Obov'iazok* (Duty, 1929), *Try pal'tsi* (Three Fingers, 1929), and *Klopit tsyrul'nyka Emilia Termana* (Barber Emil Terman's Trouble, 1930) and the novelettes *Povist' bez nazvy* (A Tale without a Name, 1930) and *Onoprii Kud'* (1933). His 'Opovidannia pro hnidu kobylu' (Story of a Bay Mare, *ChSh*, 1929, no. 3) was condemned by Party critics. Vanchenko was arrested in 1934 and sentenced to 10 years of imprisonment. His further fate is unknown; he most likely perished in the Stalinist terror. He was rehabilitated posthumously. Posthumous editions of his works, also called *Onoprii Kud'*, appeared in Ukrainian in 1968 and in Russian in 1971.

Vancouver's Ukrainian Canadians taking part in the 1936 Pacific Exhibition parade

**Vancouver.** The third largest city (1981 metropolitan pop 1,250,000) in Canada, situated in the southwest corner of British Columbia. Vancouver's natural harbour has made it a major port and railway terminal. Its chief industries are transportation and trade. Although Ukrainians started coming to the area around the turn of the century, their numbers remained small until after the Second World War (1,800 in 1941, 7,200 in 1951). Its first Catholic parish, the parish of the Holy Eucharist, was established in the suburban city of New Westminster in 1952 and became the see of a new Ukrainian Catholic eparchy in 1975. Since then three new Catholic churches (St Mary's, Holy Cross, and Assumption) and one Ukrainian Orthodox church (SS Peter and Paul) have been built. A branch of the Ukrainian National Federation was organized in 1937 and became the center of cultural (choir, drama club) and educational (elementary school, lectures) activities. In 1970 it absorbed the New Westminster branch (est 1951). The local Ukrainian Canadian Professional and Business Club (est 1960) has helped to establish Ukrainian language courses at the University of British Columbia. A provincial council of the Ukrainian Canadian Congress was created in Vancouver in 1990. The area's Ukrainian population stood at 47,620 in 1981, a figure that included many former Alberta and Saskatchewan Ukrainians. In 1991, 6,745 of them claimed Ukrainian as their sole mother tongue.

**Vano, Teodor** [Van'o], b 1880 in Buzk, Kaminka-Strumylova county, Galicia, d ca 1958–9 in Nesterov (Zhovkva), Lviv oblast. Lawyer and civic and political leader. In 1910, after obtaining a law degree at Lviv University and a doctorate at Vienna University, he opened a law office in Zolochiv. He organized Prosvita reading rooms, Silskyi Hospodar circles, and credit unions in the county. A candidate of the National Democratic party, he was elected to the Galician Diet in 1913, and during the First World War he served as a captain in the Austrian army. A member of the Ukrainian National Rada, he was placed in charge of food procurements in 1919 by the State Secretariat of the Western Ukrainian National Republic. Having been deported by the Poles, he returned to Zolochiv in 1921 and there resumed his law practice and played a leading role in most of the county's organizations. In 1944 he was imprisoned in Siberian labor camps by the Soviets. He returned to Ukraine in the 1950s.

**Vanotti, Jacob-Ludwig,** b 1773 in Freiburg im Breisgau, d 14 February 1819 in Kharkiv. Physician. A graduate of Freiburg University (MD, 1798), he practiced medicine in Lviv and worked at Kharkiv University (from 1805), where he set up an anatomy theater and cabinet and taught pharmacology and the history of medicine (from 1810, as professor from 1812). He wrote on smallpox vaccination and field medicine.

**Vanzetti, Tito,** b 29 November 1809 in Venice, d 7 June 1888 in Padua. Surgeon. He graduated from Padua University (1832) and came to Odessa in 1834. In 1837 he received a doctoral degree from Kharkiv University and was appointed to the chair of eye surgery. In 1848 he performed the first ovariotomy operation in the Russian Empire and published *Annales scholaeclinicae chirurgicae cesareae universitatis Charcoviensis*. He returned to Padua in 1853.

**Vaplite** (full name: Vilna akademiia proletarskoi literatury [Free Academy of Proletarian Literature]). A writers' organization which existed in Kharkiv from 1925 to 1928. While accepting the official requirements of the Communist party, Vaplite adopted an independent position on questions of literary policy and supported M. *Khvylovy in the *Literary Discussion of 1925–8. Vaplite proposed to create a new Ukrainian literature based on the writers in its ranks who strived to perfect their work by assimilating the finest masterpieces of Western European culture. J. Stalin interpreted that goal as a betrayal of the aims of the Party and accused Khvylovy and Vaplite of working under the slogan Away from Moscow. The association rejected decisively the policy of mass participation (*masovism*) in proletarian writers' organizations, which were supported by the Communist party. Khvylovy was the actual leader of Vaplite; its official president was first M. Yalovy (Yu. Shpol) and then M. Kulish, and its secretary was A. Liubchenko. Its members were M. Bazhan, V. Vrazhlyvy, I. Dniprovsky, O. Dosvitnii, H. Epik, P. Ivanov, M. Yohansen, O. Kopylenko, H. Kotsiuba, M. Maisky, P. Panch, I. Senchenko, O. Slisarenko, Yu.

Members of Vaplite in 1926. Sitting, from left: Pavlo Tychyna, Mykola Khvylovy, Mykola Kulish, Oleksa Slisarenko, Maik Yohansen, Hordii Kotsiuba, Petro Panch, Arkadii Liubchenko; standing: Mykhailo Maisky, Hryhorii Epik, Oleksander Kopylenko, Ivan Senchenko, Pavlo Ivanov, Yurii Smolych, Oles Dosvitnii, Ivan Dniprovsky

Smolych, P. Tychyna, and Yu. Yanovsky. The association published the almanac *Vaplite* (1926), devoted mostly to literary problems, and five issues of the journal *Vaplite* (1927). Vaplite's position on literary issues was supported by the *Neoclassicists (M. Zerov in particular) and by other Ukrainian writers.

The ideas of Khvylovy and Vaplite came under vehement criticism not only from their literary rivals and key Soviet leaders of Ukraine (eg, V. Chubar, V. Zatonsky, M. Skrypnyk, T. Taran, and A. Khvylia) but also from the Communist Party of Ukraine. Neither the admission of political 'errors' by Khvylovy and others in December 1926 nor the expulsion of Khvylovy, Yalovy, and Dosvitnii from Vaplite in January 1927 could save the organization. Khvylovy's novel *Val'dshnepy* (The Woodcocks, first part pub in *Vaplite*, no. 5, 1927) came under particularly severe criticism. The sixth and last issue of *Vaplite*, containing the continuation of the novel, was confiscated at the printing office and Vaplite was forced to dissolve. Members of the association continued their literary work in association with the journal *Literaturnyi iarmarok and in the organization *Prolitfront.

BIBLIOGRAPHY
Leites, A.; Iashek, M. (eds). *Desiat' rokiv ukraïns'koï literatury (1917–1927)*, vol 2 (Kharkiv 1928)
Hordyns'kyi, Ia. *Literaturna krytyka pidsoviets'koï Ukraïny* (Lviv 1939)
Luckyj, G.S.N. *Literary Politics in the Soviet Ukraine, 1917–1934* (New York 1956)
Luts'kyi, Iu. (ed). *Vaplitians'kyi zbirnyk* (Oakville, Ont 1977)
                                                    M. Hlobenko

**Vaplite.** The official organ of *Vaplite. Its editorial board consisted of M. *Kulish, I. *Senchenko, O. *Slisarenko, P. *Tychyna, and M. *Yohansen. Only an almanac and five issues of a journal appeared. The almanac (1926) consisted of articles on cultural politics and literary topics submitted by five members of Vaplite and the Comintern figure V. Serge (Kibalchich), Vaplite's statute, and a literary chronicle. The journal issues (1927) contained poems and prose by Vaplite members and other writers (eg, N. Surovtsova, V. Stefanyk, N. Shcherbyna, K. Hordiienko,

The cover of the first Vaplite almanac and the Vaplite logo

D. Falkivsky, H. Koliada); polemical and theoretical articles and literary criticism (including articles by nonmembers, such as Y. Aizenshtok, Ye. Kruk, R. Yakobson, A. Pavliuk, L. Kurbas, I. Vrona, H. Maifet, and V. Derzhavyn); an article on literary Paris by the Russian writer A. Gatov; literary translations by A. Liubchenko, P. Tychyna, V. Pidmohylny, and A. Pavliuk; a literary chronicle (probably by A. Leites); book reviews; and Vaplite's resolutions (1927, no. 2). The journal and its contributors were constantly attacked by Party critics belonging to the *All-Ukrainian Association of Proletarian Writers and *Molodniak, particularly by V. Koriak. The Party forced *Vaplite* to cease publication after it printed former Vaplite member M. *Khvylovy's novel 'Val'dshnepy' (Woodcocks, pt 1) and a literary article by the nonmember P. *Khrystiuk. The sixth issue of *Vaplite*, containing the continuation of Khvylovy's novel, was confiscated by the authorities at the printing office.

R. Senkus

**Vapniarka** [Vapnjarka]. v-9. A town smt (1988 pop 9,200) in Tomashpil raion, Vinnytsia oblast. It emerged in the 1870s as a railway settlement. As a railway junction, in 1919 it was contested by the UNR Army, the Ukrainian Galician Army, the Red Army, and A. Denikin's forces. Today its main enterprises belong to the railway industry, but it also has a large baking complex and a lime factory.

**Vapniarka Hill** [Vapnjarka]. IV–6. One of the tallest elevations (460 m) of the Voroniaky section of the Podolian Upland, situated on the watershed between the Styr and the Seret rivers. With distinctive formations cut into its sandy limestone faces, the hill is a local attraction.

**Varangian route.** A medieval trade route extending from Scandinavia through Kievan Rus' to the Byzantine Empire, mentioned in chronicles as the route 'from the Varangians to the Greeks.' The trade route consisted of a series of waterways and portages covering nearly 3,000 km from the Baltic ('Varangian') to the Black seas. It began near present-day Stockholm and crossed the Baltic Sea and the Gulf of Finland, followed the Neva River, Lake Ladoga, the Volkhov River, Lake Ilmen, and the Lovat River, and connected with the *Dnieper River by way of the Western Dvina River. The route continued all the way along the Dnieper directly to the Black Sea and then followed its western coast to Constantinople.

The Varangian route was first used in the 9th century. It played a major role not only in the development of trade in the Kievan Rus' territories but also in the cultural and political transformation of East Slavic tribes into the Rus' state with its center in Kiev. Among the cities founded

VARANGIAN ROUTE

along the Varangian route were Ladoga, Novgorod, Smolensk, Liubech, Vyshhorod, Kiev, and Kaniv. Voyaging in the southern Ukrainian portion of the route was difficult owing to raids by nomadic tribes in the region, and by the early 12th century an alternate trade route into western Europe was being used that followed the Prypiat, the Buh, and the Vistula rivers. The Varangian route is described in the Primary Chronicle and is mentioned by Constantine VII Porphyrogenitus in his *De administrando imperio* (948–52).

A. Zhukovsky

**Varangians** (from Norse *waering* 'one who has taken an oath of allegiance' or *war* 'oath, sworn fidelity'; Ukrainian: *variahy*). Nordic warrior-traders who established themselves in Rus' after first appearing there in the early 9th century. Known as Normans or Vikings in other parts of Europe, those adventurers were called Varangians in Eastern Europe and Byzantium. In the 9th to 11th centuries Varangians served as key mercenary troops for Rus' princes (eg, Ihor, Volodymyr the Great) and also hired themselves out to Byzantine emperors (eg, Basil II). They occupied key administrative positions in Kievan Rus' and engaged in trade in the towns. The Varangians are associated particularly with the use of the *Varangian route, which provided an eastern access for traders from Scandinavia through Kievan Rus' to the Byzantine Empire.

The extent of Varangian influence in Rus' has been debated for several centuries in connection with the controversial *Normanist theory. The kernel of the debate is accounts of contemporary chroniclers that credit the Varangians with establishing a state structure in ancient Rus'. Certainly the Varangians assumed a leading role in the running of the Rus' state; the *Riurykide dynasty, in fact, is descended from a Varangian. But the extent of their influence beyond that is difficult to ascertain, notably because the Varangians assimilated rapidly with the local population; their influence in Rus' was particularly evident in military organization and in personal names. In Novgorod they built a church which is mentioned in chronicles as the Varangian Church. Later archeological expeditions unearthed large Varangian grave sites in the Kiev and Chernihiv (Shestovytsia) regions containing well-preserved caches of grave goods and weapons.

BIBLIOGRAPHY
Bjorner, E. *Schediasma historico geographicum de varegis, heroibus scandianis, et primis Russiae dynastis* (Stockholm 1743)
Gedeonov, S. *Variagi i Rus'*, 2 vols (St Petersburg 1876)
Thomsen, V. *The Relations between Ancient Russia and Scandinavia and the Origin of the Russian State* (1877; repr, New York nd)
Stender-Petersen, A. *Varangica* (Aarhus 1953)
Łowmiański, H. *Zagadnienie roli Normanów w genezie państw słowiańskich* (Warsaw 1957)
Pound, D. *Varangian Political Influences on Kievan Rus'* (College Park, Md 1970)
Rydzevskaia, E. *Drevnaia Rus' i Skandinaviia v IX–XIV vv: Materialy i issledovaniia* (Moscow 1978)

A. Zhukovsky

**Varavva, Oleksii.** See Kobets, Oleksii.

**Varchenko, Vasyl** [Varčenko, Vasyl'], b ?, d 1770. Banduryst. He took part in the Koliivshchyna rebellion in 1768. He joined Rémeza's detachment and with his songs encouraged the haidmakas to battle. He was executed by the Poles in Kodnia.

The 27-ft-high, 12-ft-wide, 3-t fiberglass 'perogy' erected in Glendon, Alberta, in 1991

**Varenyky.** Boiled dumplings consisting of a dough shell filled with meat, mashed potato, cheese, fruit, or other filling. They are a popular Ukrainian dish. Traditionally they were eaten as a festive dish at weddings or on holidays. In Galicia *varenyky* were indispensable parts of the Christmas Eve and Epiphany meals, and in many regions of Ukraine they played a symbolic role in the wedding ritual. They have been popular among Ukrainian immigrants in North America. Since the 1960s they have become popular even among non-Ukrainians in Canada and the United States, where they are usually known as 'perogies' (*pyrohy*), and are manufactured as a commercial product.

**Varenytsia Uprising.** A peasant and Cossack revolt in Right-Bank Ukraine in 1664–5. The uprising took place several years after the Right Bank had been returned to the Polish overlords under the Treaty of Slobodyshche. It was preceded by a revolt in Pavoloch regiment led by I. Popovych in 1663. The 1664–5 uprising broke out in the Dnieper region and quickly spread throughout the Right Bank. Its leaders were V. Varenytsia, the colonel of Kalnyk regiment, and a Cossack named Sulymka. The rebels were soon joined by Zaporozhian forces under I. Sirko. After the Poles crushed the rebellion they meted out harsh punishments to its perpetrators and supporters. Sulymka was executed; Varenytsia died in battle near Kalnyk in 1665.

**Varetska, Valentyna** [Varec'ka] (née Sofiienko), b 17 December 1900 in Ivano-Kepyne near Snihurivka, Kherson county, d 3 January 1981 in Kharkiv. Stage and film actress. She began her theatrical career in the Kherson Theater (1919) and then was a leading actress in the Kiev Ukrainian Drama Theater (1922–31) and the Kharkiv Theater of the Revolution (1931–5) and in Ukrainian troupes in Poltava, Ternopil, Kharkiv, and Drohobych (until 1950). Her noted roles included Donna Anna in Lesia Ukrainka's *Kaminnyi hospodar* (The Stone Host) and the title role in V. Vynnychenko's *Nad* (Nad[ia]). She acted in the film *Order na aresht* (The Warrant for Arrest, 1927).

**Variah** (Varangian). A publishing house in Warsaw, established in 1933 by émigré writers grouped around the journal *My*. It published *My* and books by S. Hordynsky, N. Livytska-Kholodna, B. Olkhivsky, A. Kryzhanivsky, and Ya. Dryhynych. The publishing house closed down in late 1939.

**Varlaam,** b ? in Kiev, d 19 November 1065 in Volodymyr-Volynskyi. Churchman and saint. The son of the boyar Ivan Vyshatych, he was tonsured in 1056, and lived with St Anthony of the Caves and became the first hegumen of the *Kievan Cave Monastery. During his tenure the wooden Dormition Church was built, in 1058. In 1062 Prince Iziaslav Yaroslavych established a church and monastery that later became known as *St Michael's Golden-Domed Monastery, and invited Varlaam to become its hegumen. Varlaam twice went on pilgrimages to Jerusalem and other places in the Holy Land. On his way back to Kiev he fell ill, and died in the Zymne Monastery near Volodymyr-Volynskyi. He was buried in the Kievan Cave Monastery. He was canonized in the 11th century; his feast day is 2 December (19 November OS).

**Varlaam i Ioasaf** (Barlaam and Joasaph). A medieval philosophical narrative about the conversion to Christianity of the Indian prince Joasaph (or Josaphat) under the influence of the hermit Barlaam, who told him many parables. Modeled on Indian tales about Buddha, it was written in Greek by a monk called John at the St Sava Monastery near Jerusalem ca 630 AD and translated, with various revisions and additions, into Persian, Arabic, Hebrew, Ethiopian, Armenian, and Georgian in the 1st millennium AD. A new Greek version was adapted from the Georgian text at Mt Athos at the beginning of the 11th century. Latin translations (1220–33) of the Greek became popular throughout Western Europe and were translated, in turn, into German, French, Italian, and other languages. A Church Slavonic translation from Greek was made in Kiev no later than the 12th century. Thereafter the tale was widely read in Ukraine. It was transcribed over 1,000 times, in many variants; themes from it were depicted in icons, murals, and miniatures; and parables from it were included in numerous religious didactic collections (eg, the *Menaion and *Prolog). *Cyril of Turiv used it as a source for one of his tales. The first printed Ruthenian translation, made by Y. Polovko using J. Billio's Latin version, appeared in 1637 at the Kutein Epiphany Monastery near Orsha, in Belarus; its text is notable for its incorporation of details of 16th- and 17th-century Ukrainian folkways. The tale left a distinct mark in 17th- and 18th-century Ukrainian literature (eg, in the works of S. Kosiv and L. Baranovych, the *Bohohlasnyk*) and folklore. Verses from it were sung by lirnyks. In the 19th century I. Franko rendered its parables into poetry and, in 1897, published a monograph about it (his PH D diss, reprinted in Franko's collected works, vol 30 [Kiev 1981]). The full Old Slavonic text with I. Lebedeva's long scholarly introduction and annotations appeared in Moscow in 1985.

R. Senkus

**Varnak, Okhrim.** See Vasylenko, Onoprii.

**Vartovy, P.** See Hrinchenko, Borys.

**Varva.** III-13. A town smt (1988 pop 9,100) on the Udai River and a raion center in Chernihiv oblast. In 1079 Volodymyr Monomakh defeated the Cumans at Varyn fortress, which stood near the site of the present town. Varva was destroyed by the Mongols in 1239 and by the Tatars in 1482. From 1569 the territory around Varva belonged to the Polish Commonwealth. Under the Hetman state Varva was a company center of Pryluka regiment (1649–1781). In 1658 Hetman I. Vyhovsky defeated the Russian army commanded by Prince G. Romodanovsky at Varva. In the 19th century the town belonged to Lokhvytsia county in Poltava gubernia. In 1960 it was granted smt status. Today it is an agricultural town with a dairy, a building enterprise, and a machine repair shop.

**Varvariv, Victoria** [Varvariv, Viktorija], b 21 June 1954 in New York. Painter; daughter of C. *Warvariv. She studied drawing, sculpture, and mosaics at l'Ecole nationale supérieur des beaux arts and art history at the American College in Paris and the Sorbonne (PH D, 1984). She also paints on silk and glass. She has had over 20 solo exhibitions (eg, in Paris, Geneva, New York, Washington, San Francisco, and Toronto).

**Varvarivka settlement.** A settlement of the 4th to 3rd century BC near Varvarivka, near Mykolaiv, Mykolaiv oblast, on the Boh River. Excavations in 1938–9 uncovered stone surface dwellings and over 70 pits. Most of the pits

were used for storing grain, although eight functioned as dwellings (some even being linked by underground walkways). Pottery, millstones, and the bones of a variety of domestic animals were also unearthed. A Scythian burial site was located adjacent to the settlement.

Otaman Antin Varyvoda          Hryhorii Vashchenko

**Varyvoda, Antin,** b 10 January 1869 in Seret, Bukovyna, d 12 March 1936 in Vienna. Senior army officer. During the First World War he was a regular officer in the Austrian army and commanded the Legion of Ukrainian Sich Riflemen (14 January 1915 to 30 November 1916). During 1918–19, at the rank of colonel, he was a member of the Western Ukrainian National Republic mission in Vienna. Later he served briefly as a senior officer of the Ukrainian Galician Army at the internment camp in Josefov, Czechoslovakia.

**Varzar, Vasilii,** b 16 December 1851 in Lublin, now in Poland, d 28 September 1940 in Leningrad. Russian economist and one of the first industrial statisticians in the Russian Empire. After graduating from the St Petersburg Polytechnical Institute in 1874, he worked with P. Chervinsky and O. Rusov in the statistical bureau of the Chernihiv zemstvo. After 1890 he worked as an economist in the Ministries of Finance and Trade and Industry in Moscow. After the Revolution of 1917 he served as a statistics professor at Moscow University. He wrote some important statistical studies of the cottage industry in Chernihiv gubernia (1880) and of the economies of Novozybkov and Oster counties (1881), of the factory industries of the Russian Empire (1912), and of factory strikes in Russia in 1895–1904 (1905). He also prepared a textbook on industrial statistics in two volumes (1925, 1927).

**Vashchenko, Hryhorii** [Vaščenko, Hryhorij], b 5 May 1878 in Bohdanivka, Pryluka county, Poltava gubernia, d 4 May 1967 in Munich. Pedagogue. A graduate of the Moscow Theological Academy (1903), he taught at various schools in Ukraine and Russia until 1918, when he started lecturing at the teachers' institute in Poltava. He was purged from the Poltava Institute of People's Education in 1933, and he obtained a post at the Stalingrad Pedagogical Institute in 1936. After the war he settled in Munich, where he lectured (from 1945) at the *Ukrainian Free University and the *Theological Academy of the Ukrainian Autocephalous Orthodox Church. In 1950 he became the rector of the latter institution. Vashchenko wrote several short stories and a novel, *Do gruntu* (To the Foundation, 1912), as well as pedagogical works, including *Zahal'ni metody navchannia* (General Methods of Teaching, 2 vols, 1949).

**Vashchenko, Oleksander** [Vaščenko], b 1909 in Poltava gubernia, d 21 June 1974 in Curitiba, Brazil. Journalist. After emigrating to Brazil in 1948, he was editor of the weekly *Khliborob*, published by the Union for Agricultural Education, from 1953 to the end of his life. He also contributed reports and articles to *Svoboda* under the pen name Mykhailo Kylymny.

**Vashchenko, Vasyl** [Vaščenko, Vasyl'], b 1850, d 1918. Beekeeper. He set up and directed a beekeeping school in Boiarka, Kiev gubernia. He invented an improved beehive and proposed a number of effective methods of beekeeping.

**Vashchenko, Vasyl** [Vaščenko, Vasyl'], b 11 March 1905 in Nizhen, Chernihiv gubernia. Linguist. A graduate of the Dnipropetrovske Institute of People's Education (1930), from 1933 he lectured at Dnipropetrovske University, eventually chairing the department of Ukrainian language. He has written numerous works, including a Ukrainian grammar (1938); textbooks on Ukrainian stylistics (1958), the Ukrainian language (1959, 1961), and Ukrainian stylistic morphology (1970); monographs on the Poltava dialects (doctoral diss, 1957), the dialectal lexicon of the middle and lower Dnieper region (1962), T. Shevchenko's language (1963), the linguistic geography of the Dnieper region (1968), and the stylistics of the Ukrainian sentence (1968); and a dictionary of the Poltava dialects (1960); and has prepared a scheme for a dictionary of Ukrainian synonyms (1969). He also edited the AN URSR (now ANU) dictionary of Shevchenko's language (2 vols, 1964) and books on the folk and contemporary dialects of the Dnieper region (1969).

Mykhailo Vashchenko-Zakharchenko

Viacheslav Vaskivsky (self-portrait, wood engraving)

**Vashchenko-Zakharchenko, Mykhailo** [Vaščenko-Zaxarčenko, Myxajlo], b 12 November 1825 in Maliivka, Zolotonosha county, Poltava gubernia, d 27 August 1912 in Kiev. Mathematician. After studying at Kiev University, the Sorbonne, and the Collège de France (1847–8) he graduated from Kazan University in 1854 and taught at

the Kiev Cadet School (1855–62) and Kiev University (1863–1902). Vashchenko-Zakharchenko made significant contributions to the theory of linear differential equations, operational calculus, theory of probability, and the history of mathematics. His master's dissertation was the first treatise in Russian on the operational method and its application to the solution of linear differential equations (1862). He wrote a monograph on the history of mathematics to the 15th century (1883) and a historical survey of the development of analytic geometry. He was the author of 12 textbooks in various fields of mathematics. As one of the first proponents of non-Euclidean geometry in the Russian Empire, he exerted considerable influence on the development of mathematics in Ukraine and Russia.

**Vashetko, Mykola** [Vašetko], b 18 February 1880 in Mykolaivka, Borzna county, Chernihiv gubernia, d 6 September 1960 in Kiev. Pathophysiologist. A graduate of Kiev University (1908), he chaired departments at Kiev University (1918–21) and the Kiev and Donetske (1931–6) medical institutes, the Kiev Veterinary Institute (from 1936), and the Ukrainian Agricultural Academy (from 1957). His publications dealt with toxicoses, urologic pathology, and the role of the nervous system in regulating metabolism.

**Vashkivtsi** [Vaškivci]. V-6. A city (1989 pop 6,300) on the Cheremosh River in Vyzhnytsia raion, Chernivtsi oblast. It was first mentioned in historical documents in 1431, when the village belonged to the Principality of Moldavia. In 1774 it was annexed by Austria. In 1903 it was promoted to the status of a county administrative center. In the interwar period Vashkivtsi was occupied by Rumania. After the war it became part of the Ukrainian SSR. It was granted city status in 1940. Today it is an industrial and agricultural town with a distillery, a canning factory, and a branch of the Chernivtsi Handicrafts Factory.

**Vasilev, Leonid** [Vasil'ev], b 1880, d 1920. Russian linguist. He studied under A. Sobolevsky at St Petersburg University and taught there until approx 1913. He was an expert on the manuscripts of Kievan Rus'; his careful analysis of them shed new light on Old Ukrainian phonetics (the softness or hardness of consonants before *e* and nasal *e*, the new *jat'*, the softening of *n*) and changes in Slavic stress. A bibliography of his works was published in *Slavia* (1926, no. 4).

**Vaskivsky, Viacheslav** [Vas'kivs'kyj, Vjačeslav], b 15 February 1904 in Rivne, Volhynia, d ? Artist and educator. In the late 1920s he studied art at the Warsaw Academy of Fine Arts and belonged to the Spokii art group. In 1937 he began teaching at the academy. Besides drawing, painting, and using traditional graphic techniques, he experimented widely with xylotype, colored aquatype, deep linocut, and engraving in various plastic media. His works, many of which deal with Ukrainian subjects (landscapes and portraits), are found in museums in Warsaw, Cracow, New York, Chicago, Moscow, Leningrad, and Kaniv.

**Vasko, Havrylo** [Vas'ko], b 1820 in Korop, Krolevets county, Chernihiv gubernia, d after 1878. Painter. He learned to paint by copying works by the masters. He

Portrait of a girl by Havrylo Vasko (oil, 1840s)

Yuliian Vassyian

taught drawing at Kiev University and headed its painting art museum (1847–63). He specialized in painting portraits; among his works are ones of B. and V. Tomara (1847) and Tsar Nicholas I and a series (now lost) of Cossack hetmans for V. Tarnovsky's museum in Chernihiv.

**Vasmer, Max,** b 28 February 1886 in St Petersburg, d 30 November 1962 in Berlin. German Slavist; member of several German academies of science, the Shevchenko Scientific Society, and the USSR Academy of Sciences. A graduate of St Petersburg University (PH D, 1915), he lectured in Slavic philology at Saratov (1915–17), Dorpat (1918–21), Leipzig (1921–5), and Berlin (1925–56) universities. He was a founder and editor of *Zeitschrift für slavische Philologie*. His main interests were Slavic etymology and ethnogenesis. His *Russisches etymologisches Wörterbuch* (1950–8) contains much material on Ukrainian etymology, although the material is not always complete and verified. He tried to locate the original homeland of the Slavs (1923, 1926) on the basis of Slavic hydronyms and other historical data, and compiled *Wörterbuch der russischen Gewässernamen* (1960–73) and *Russisches geographisches Namenbuch* (1962–81), which fully cover Ukrainian geographical names (except for Transcarpathia). He devoted separate articles to Ukrainian subjects, such as the names of the Sea of Azov (1930), the Desna River (1930), and the Psol River (1932); Queen Anna Yaroslavna's signature (1927, 1931); and other subjects. At his request V. *Hantsov wrote a fundamental survey of Ukrainian dialectology.

**Vassyian, Yuliian** [Vassyjan, Julijan], b 12 January 1894 in Kolodentse, Zhovkva county, Galicia, d 3 October 1953

in Chicago. Nationalist ideologue and philosopher. His studies at Lviv University were interrupted by the First World War and Ukrainian-Polish War in Galicia, during which he was an officer in the Ukrainian Sich Riflemen and Ukrainian Galician Army. After his release from a Polish POW camp, he studied at the Lviv (Underground) Ukrainian University (1922–4), Prague University (PH D, 1929), and the Ukrainian Higher Pedagogical Institute in Prague, and was active in nationalist student groups. As chairman of the Ideological Commission, he was elected to the OUN Leadership at its founding congress in 1929. After returning to Galicia in 1930, he worked as an editor of the weekly *Ukraïns'kyi holos* in Peremyshl and was imprisoned by the Poles for his political activities (1931–5, 1939). In 1944 he was imprisoned by the Gestapo. A postwar refugee in Germany, he emigrated to the United States in 1950. Vassyian contributed articles defining nationalist ideology to *Natsional'na dumka, Rozbudova natsiï*, and *Samostiina Ukraïna*. Some of his philosophical essays, dealing with Ukrainian history, the Ukrainian national character, and the role of the individual, were published posthumously in the collections *Odynytsia i suspil'nist'* (The Individual and Society, 1957), *Suspil'no-filosofichni narysy* (Socio-Philosophical Essays, 1958), and *Tvory* (Works, 1972). Many of his manuscripts remain unpublished.

T. Zakydalsky

**Vasyl** [Vasyl']. The 13th archimandrite of the Kievan Cave Monastery (1182–97), and before that a priest at the church on Shchekavytsia Hill in Kiev. During his tenure the monastery was greatly expanded, and several new churches were established, including St Basil's in Kiev (1184) and the Church of the Holy Apostles in Bilhorod, near Kiev (1197).

**Vasyl of Lviv** [Vasyl'], b and d ? Painter at the court of King Jan III Sobieski in Zhovkva. Between 1659 and 1687 he painted a portrait of Jan III (now in the Uffizi Gallery in Florence), murals depicting the Polish-Turkish War (in the Roman Catholic church in Zhovkva), and icons for the Krekhiv Monastery.

**Vasylashchuk, Hanna** [Vasylaščuk], b 2 November 1924 in Sheshory, Kosiv county, Galicia. Weaver. She has woven decorative *rushnyky*, curtains, furniture, covers, skirts, and pillowcases. Her colors and designs are characteristic of Hutsul folk weavings. An album of her work was published in Kiev in 1985.

Stepan Vasylchenko

Mykola Vasylenko

**Vasylchenko, Stepan** [Vasyl'čenko] (pseud of Stepan Panasenko), b 8 January 1879 in Ichnia, Borzna county, Chernihiv gubernia, d 11 August 1932 in Kiev. Writer, teacher, and journalist. He became well known for his short stories, which were published in the collections *Eskizy* (Sketches, 1911) and *Opovidannia* (Short Stories, 1915). Vasylchenko's short stories are filled with humanism and a gentle sense of humor. They are marked by a combination of realism and fantasy (eg, 'V tiniakh lypnevoï nochi' [In the Shadows of the July Night], 'Kriz' drimoty' [Through Slumber], 'Solov'ï' [Nightingales]) and by the richness of a language gleaned from folk poetry. Vasylchenko was also the author of numerous plays, which were published in the collection *Dramatychni tvory* (Dramatical Works, 1917). He could not countenance Soviet rule and consequently turned to writing stories for children. Vasylchenko's works have been republished a number of times; the most complete editions are *Povna zbirka tvoriv* (Complete Collection of Works, vols 1–4, 1928–30) and *Tvory* (Works, vols 1–4, 1960).

**Vasylchykov, Dmytro** [Vasyl'čykov], b 7 November 1884 in Rostov, Don Cossack region, d 20 February 1960 in Kharkiv. Actor. From 1906 he worked in various Ukrainian touring troupes. In 1929 he was one of the founders of the Kharkiv Theater of Musical Comedy, where he worked until 1940 (in 1945–7 as administrative director).

**Vasylenko, Andrii,** b 4 November 1891 in Bilenke, Oleksandrivske county, Katerynoslav gubernia, d 5 July 1963 in Kiev. Mechanical and agricultural engineer, specialist in agricultural machinery; full member of the AN URSR (now ANU) from 1948. He studied at the Kiev Polytechnical Institute and worked at agricultural institutes in Kiev, Kharkiv, Moscow, and other cities. He contributed significantly to the development of new agricultural machinery, particularly sugar-beet planters (1930), harvesters (1933 and 1935), and loaders and special types of mechanized plows.

**Vasylenko, Mykola,** b 14 February 1866 in Esman, Hlukhiv county, Chernihiv gubernia, d 3 October 1935, probably in Kiev. Historian, legal scholar, and community and political leader; husband of N. *Polonska-Vasylenko. He studied medicine and then history and philology at Dorpat (now Tartu) University in 1885–90. He taught in gymnasiums in Kiev (1892–1902), served in the Russian Ministry of Internal Affairs (1902–5), worked as a journalist and editor of *Kievskie otkliki* (1905–6), and coedited *Kievskaia starina*. He was imprisoned for his editorship of the *Kievskie otkliki*, and while incarcerated, took to studying law. In 1907 he graduated with a law degree from Odessa University, and he practiced law until 1917. He was elected to the Ukrainian Scientific Society in Kiev (UNTK) in 1908, headed its historical section, and edited its *Zapysky*. He was also made a lecturer at Kiev University but was barred from teaching by the government. He became a full member of the Shevchenko Scientific Society (NTSh) in 1911. He was a member of the Old Hromada of Kiev, joined the Society of Ukrainian Progressives (TUP), and in 1910 became active in the Russian Constitutional Democratic party (Kadets).

In April 1917 Vasylenko was appointed curator of the Kiev school district (which included Kiev, Volhynia, Podilia, Chernihiv, and Poltava gubernias) by the Provisional Government, and that year he became an associate minister of national education in Petrograd. In January 1918 he became a member of the collegium of the Ukrainian General Court. In the Hetman government he was head of the Council of Ministers and then minister of education (until 18 October), and in August 1918 he was also made president of the State Senate. As minister of education he encouraged the formation of the Ukrainian state universities in Kiev and Kamianets-Podilskyi and the establishment of the UAN (November 1918) and the National Library.

In 1920 he became a full member of the VUAN, and in 1921 he was made its head, although the appointment was not confirmed by the Soviet authorities. In 1922–9 he was head of the socioeconomic division of the VUAN, as well as head of the Commission for the Study of the History of Western-Ruthenian and Ukrainian Law and a member of the Archeographic Commission and the Ukrainian Historiographic Commission. In 1924 he was sentenced at a show trial to 10 years' imprisonment but was granted amnesty. In 1929 he was barred from holding directorial positions within the VUAN.

Vasylenko's scholarly work continued the work of O. Lazarevsky in the field of general Ukrainian history and Ukrainian legal history; he undertook studies of Left-Bank Ukraine and published a host of primary documents. By the time of the Revolution of 1917 Vasylenko had already contributed significantly to the literature of his field, with numerous articles in *Kievskaia starina* and *Ukrainskaia zhizn'*, and in the Russian encyclopedia published by Brockhaus and Efron and *Ocherki po istorii Zapadnoi Rusi i Ukrainy* (Studies in the History of Western Rus' and Ukraine, 1916). Vasylenko published *Materialy dlia istorii ekonomicheskogo, iuridicheskogo i obshchestvennogo byta staroi Malorossii* (Materials for the Economic, Juridical, and Political Life of Old Little Russia, 3 vols, 1901–8) as well as studies on the holdings of Hadiache and Kiev regiments. His essays on such Ukrainian historians and scholars as O. Bodiansky, O. Levytsky, I. Kamanin, B. Kistiakovsky, I. Balinsky, and M. Semevsky (the editor of *Kievskaia starina*) are valuable historiographical sources.

In the 1920s Vasylenko headed the group of scholars who formed the VUAN Commission for the Study of the History of Western-Ruthenian and Ukrainian Law, and was editor of seven volumes of its *Pratsi* (1925–30) and of six volumes of *Zapysky Sotsiial'no-ekonomichnoho viddilu*

VUAN (1923–7). The VUAN also published a number of his monographs, including *Pavlo Polubotok* (1925), *Iak skasovano Lytovs'koho statuta* (How the Lithuanian Statute Was Abolished, 1926), *O.M. Lazarevs'kyi* (1927), and *Terytoriia Ukraïny 17-oho viku* (The Territory of Ukraine in the 17th Century, 1927); 'Zbirka materiialiv do istoriï Livoberezhnoï Ukraïny ta ukraïns'koho prava XVII–XVIII vv.' (A Collection of Materials for the History of Left-Bank Ukraine and Ukrainian Law in the 17th and 18th Centuries), in *Ukraïns'kyi arkheohrafichnyi zbirnyk*, vol 1, 1926, and as a separate publication; 'Pravne polozhennia Chernihivshchyny za pol's'koï doby, 1618–1648' (The Legal Status of the Chernihiv Region in the Polish Era, 1618–48), in *Chernihiv i pivnichne Livoberezhzhia* (1928); and *Materiialy do istoriï ukraïns'koho prava* (Materials in the History of Ukrainian Law, vol 1, 1929).

His scholarly works were harshly criticized by the Soviet historian S. Ivanytsky-Vasylenko in 1932, and Vasylenko was subsequently forbidden to publish his works.

L. Okinshevych, A. Zhukovsky

Onoprii Vasylenko

**Vasylenko, Onoprii** (pseuds: Okhrim Varnak, Onysko Vasiuta), b 15 June 1861 in Kovrai, Zolotonosha county, Poltava gubernia, d 20 December 1921 in Zolotonosha. Writer and community figure. A career officer-bureaucrat in the tsarist engineering corps, he was posted in Sevastopil (1890–4), Symferopil (1894–1900), Warsaw (1900–2), Brest-Litovsk (1902–14), and Babruisk (1914–17). He began publishing poems, stories, and correspondence in *Zoria* and other Lviv periodicals in 1890. He dedicated a few poems to T. Shevchenko and wrote articles about him. In 1892 his accounts of his trip from Sevastopil to Zolotonosha appeared in the Chernivtsi paper *Bukovyna*. In 1893 he published *Musii Krynytsia*, a story about Kovrai peasants struggling to open a school. His story about the oppression of military service, 'Z pryntsypa' (Out of Principle, *Literaturno-naukovyi vistnyk*, 1901), was well received by critics. During the Revolution of 1905 he disseminated antitsarist literature among the troops in Brest-Litovsk. There in 1907–8 he directed a soldiers' choir and actors' troupe, which staged Ukrainian plays. From 1904 to 1914 he played a key role in finding and restoring O. \*Storozhenko's grave. He organized illegal commemorations of T. Shevchenko's centenary in Brest-Litovsk in 1914. In 1918 he returned home, and in 1920–1 he edited the Zolotonosha newspaper.

**Vasylenko, Petro,** b 17 October 1900 in Myhiia, Yelysavethrad county, Kherson gubernia. Mechanical engineer, specialist in agricultural machinery; corresponding member of the ANU (formerly AN URSR) since 1939. He studied at agricultural institutes in Luhanske and Kiev and from 1937 was a professor at the Kiev Agricultural Institute. He contributed to the theoretical and mathematical modeling of various agricultural machines and developed the equations for calculating the dynamics of such machinery.

**Vasylenko, Petro** (noms de guerre: Volosh, Poltavets, Hetmanets), b 1921 in Viitovtsi, Poltava gubernia, d 21 May 1946 in the Liubachiv region. UPA officer. After joining the UPA in 1944, he served initially as a political instructor and later as an OUN propaganda officer. He edited the periodical *Lisovyk* and wrote a collection of poetry, *Moï povstans'ki marshi* (My Insurgent Marches, 1946) and a collection of combat reports titled *U borot'bi za voliu pid boiovymy praporamy UPA* (In the Struggle for Freedom under the Combat Flags of the UPA). He was killed in battle with the Polish army.

**Vasylenko, Rostyslav,** b 27 June 1920 in Kiev. Stage actor and director, reciter, and pedagogue. He completed study in the drama studio at the Kiev Ukrainian Drama Theater (1941) and then worked in the Poltava and Mykolaiv Ukrainian drama theaters (until 1944) and in the Ensemble of Ukrainian Actors in Germany (1946–9). He emigrated to Australia and became artistic director of the Ukrainian Theater of Small Forms in Adelaide (1949–50). In 1957 he moved to Canada.

**Vasylenko, Viktor,** b 12 February 1839 in Poltava gubernia, d ? Economist and ethnographer. He worked as a statistician in the Poltava zemstvo and the Poltava peasant land bank and collected statistical and ethnographic materials on Poltava gubernia. His articles on topics such as brotherhoods and guilds, folk meteorology, student residences, peasant markets, land leasing, games of peasant children, farming associations, and the 1785 register of Hadiache Regiment appeared in *Kievskaia starina* and other journals and papers.

**Vasylevska, Liudmyla.** See Dniprova Chaika.

**Vasylevska, Vanda.** See Wasilewska, Wanda.

**Vasylevsky, Radomyr** [Vasylevs'kyj], b 27 September 1930 in Cheliabinsk, RSFSR. Cameraman and film director. He completed study at the State Institute of Cinema Arts in Moscow (1954) and has worked in the Kishinev Artistic Film Studio and, since 1955, the Odessa Artistic Film Studio. He has filmed or directed about 20 films. His children's film *Kvity dlia Oli* (Flowers for Olia) received a prize at the Republican Cinema Festival in Kiev (1976).

**Vasylevsky, Serhii** [Vasylevs'kyj, Serhij], b 21 March 1917 in Khotin, Sumy county, Kharkiv gubernia. Architect. After graduating from the Kharkiv Civil-Engineering Institute (1947) he worked in Zaporizhia and eventually became the city's chief architect. He designed the metallurgical tekhnikum in Zaporizhia (1954) and planned the reconstruction of the city center (1960). He also designed a residential complex and park (1952) in Osypenko and a block of three-story residential buildings in Tokmak (1955).

**Vasylevsky, Teofan** [Vasylevs'kyj] (pseud: Sofron Krut), b ?, d 13 April 1915. Populist activist and publicist; husband of *Dniprova Chaika. As a student at Odessa University he belonged to the Odessa Hromada. Later he studied at Prague University but interrupted his studies to fight as a volunteer in the Hercegovinian uprising against Turkey in 1876 and to help M. Drahomanov publish *Hromada* in Geneva in 1877. He published several articles about the Balkan situation in Galician periodicals, such as *Molot, Pravda,* and *S'vit* (1878–81). In 1879 he returned to Ukraine and worked as a village scribe. From the 1880s on he was a zemstvo statistician in Kherson. A book about his experiences in the Balkans was published in Lviv in 1905 with a preface written by I. Franko. Vasylevsky committed suicide.

**Vasyliev, Vasyl** [Vasyl'jev, Vasyl'], b 20 March 1890 in Yelysavethrad, Kherson gubernia, d 14 August 1956 in Kiev. Metallurgist; corresponding member of the AN URSR (now ANU) from 1939. He studied at the Kiev Polytechnical Institute and taught there from 1918. He worked at the All-Union Institute of Ferrous Metallurgy (1939–49) and the ANU Institute for Problems of Casting (from 1950). He was instrumental in the introduction of new chemically stable alloys and magnesium steels.

**Vasyliev, Vsevolod** [Vasyl'jev], b 28 February 1935 in Voronezh, RSFSR. Scientist in the field of electronics and modeling; corresponding member of the ANU (formerly AN URSR) since 1981. He studied in Tahanrih and since 1981 has worked at the ANU Institute for Problems of Modeling in Energetics. He has made significant contributions in the field of modeling energy control systems, constructions, and so forth.

**Vasylieva, Antonina** [Vasyl'jeva], b 27 December 1910 in St Petersburg. Ballerina and pedagogue. In 1930 she completed study at the Leningrad Choreography School (pupil of A. Vaganova). She was a soloist in the Kirov Ballet (1930–5), the Odessa Theater of Opera and Ballet (1935–7), and the Kiev Theater of Opera and Ballet (1937–56), and then worked as a teacher (1956–62) and as artistic director (1963–72) of the Kiev Choreography School.

**Vasyliev-Sviatoshenko, Matvii** [Vasyl'jev-Svjatošenko, Matvij], b 30 August 1863 in Smolensk, Russia, d 14 February 1961 in Chernihiv. Conductor and composer. From 1882 he worked as conductor with the M. Kropyvnytsky, M. Sadovsky, and L. Sabinin theater troupes. With some interruptions he served in 1935–48 as music director of the Chernihiv Ukrainian Music and Drama Theater. His major works consist of music to classical Ukrainian plays, such as I. Kotliarevsky's *Natalka Poltavka* (Natalka from Poltava, 1882), H. Kvitka-Osnovianenko's *Shel'menko-denshchyk* (Shelmenko the Orderly, 1882), P. Myrny's *Lymerivna* (The Saddler's Daughter, 1884), I. Karpenko-Kary's *Beztalanna* (The Fortuneless Maiden, 1887), and M. Starytsky's *Tsyhanka Aza* (The Gypsy Aza, 1892). In the Soviet period he wrote music for some contemporary plays, including O. Korniichuk's *Pravda* (Truth, 1939) and *V stepakh Ukraïny* (On the Steppes of Ukraine, 1943).

Matvii Vasyliev-    Osyp Vasylkiv
Sviatoshenko

**Vasyliv, Mykhailo** [Vasyljiv, Myxajlo], b 1863 in Lebedyn, Kharkiv gubernia, d 10 May 1912. Ethnographer and engineer; member of the Ukrainian Scientific Society from 1909. A graduate of the St Petersburg Institute of Technology, he specialized in sugar refining and wrote over 50 works in the field. He also collected folklore and ethnographic materials. In the 1880s and 1890s he contributed articles on folk songs, folk theater, funeral rites, and folk beliefs to *Kievskaia starina* and *Etnograficheskoe obozrenie*.

**Vasyliv, Mykola** [Vasyl'jiv], b 22 June 1901 in Kiev, d 19 March 1961 in Oberammergau, Germany. Economist and pedagogue; full member of the Shevchenko Scientific Society from 1947; son of Mykhailo *Vasyliv. After graduating from the Kiev Institute of the National Economy (1922) and Kiev University (1924) he studied under K. Vobly at the VUAN. In 1930–41 he was an associate and academic secretary of the Kiev Scientific Research Institute of the Food Industry. A postwar émigré, he was a professor (from 1946) and rector of the *Ukrainian Free University in Munich. He wrote studies of the food industry in Ukraine, of the theory of value, and of the history of cooperatives in France.

**Vasyliv.** A village (1969 pop 1,300) on the right bank of the Dniester River in Zastavna raion, Chernivtsi oblast. One of the oldest settlements in Bukovyna, it is mentioned in the Hypatian Chronicle under the year 1230. In medieval times it was a trading center on the route from Halych principality to the Black Sea. It declined after the Mongol invasion of 1240. In 1958–9 and 1967 archeologists uncovered the remains of a 12th- to 13th-century wooden church, a pagan temple, 12 stone sarcophagi, and many imported artifacts.

**Vasyliv.** See Vasylkiv.

**Vasylivka.** VI-16. A city (1989 pop 17,200) on the Kakhivka Reservoir and a raion center in Zaporizhia oblast. It was founded by Cossacks and runaway serfs at the end of the 18th century. In 1957 it was granted city status. Today it has a shoe factory, an automotive repair plant, a metal-products factory, and a brick factory.

**Vasylivka burial sites.** Burial ground near Vasylivka, Synelnykove raion, Dnipropetrovske oblast, in use during the Mesolithic and Neolithic periods. Excavations in 1950 uncovered numerous Mesolithic burials covered in red ocher. Among the skeletal remains uncovered, arrowheads or spear tips were frequently encountered embedded in the bones. The most common grave goods recovered were pendants with deer or fish teeth and bone bracelets with geometric ornamentation.

**Vasylkiv, Osyp** [Vasyl'kiv] (pseud of Osyp Krilyk), b 22 July 1898 in Krakovets, Yavoriv county, Galicia, d ? Western Ukrainian Communist leader. As a law student at Lviv University he, together with R. Rozdolsky and R. Turiansky, was one of the founders and leaders of the 'Drahomanovite' International Revolutionary Social Democracy. In 1920 he and Rozdolsky organized communist circles among their fellow internees of the Ukrainian Galician Army in Czechoslovakia and established a Committee to Aid the Revolutionary Movement in Eastern Galicia in Prague and the Foreign Committee of the Communist Party of Eastern Galicia (KPSH) in Vienna. After returning to Lviv in late 1920, he became a KPSH CC secretary and a leader of its partisan movement opposed to the Polish occupation of Galicia. From 1921 he was a prominent 'secessionist' who advocated a KPSH independent of the Communist Workers' Party of Poland (KPRP). He was a principal defendant in the *Saint George Trial of 39 Communists in Lviv. From 1923 he was a CC secretary of the *Communist Party of Western Ukraine (KPZU) and a member of the CC KPRP. In 1927 he became a KPRP Politburo member and the KPZU representative to the Polish section of the Comintern. Vasylkiv headed the national-communist majority faction in the KPZU (popularly known as the Vasylkivtsi) that supported the policies and views of O. *Shumsky. Consequently he was expelled from the Stalinist-dominated Comintern in 1928. In 1932, after emerging from a Polish prison (arrested in 1929), he emigrated with his family to Soviet Ukraine and worked for the Chief Administration of Literary Affairs and Publishing in Kharkiv. In May 1933 he was arrested. He was last seen in 1938, in a concentration camp in Karelia.

R. Senkus

**Vasylkiv** [Vasyl'kiv]. III-11. A city (1989 pop 35,700) on the Stuhna River and a raion center in Kiev oblast. According to the chronicles it was founded in 988 by Volodymyr the Great – who, it is believed, was christened there – and was named Vasyliv after his new Christian name. In the 11th century a fort was built there, and the town became an important defense and trade center. In 1240 it was destroyed by the Mongols, and declined to village size. In 1648 Vasylkiv became a company center of Kiev regiment. In 1796 it was promoted to city status and made a county center of Kiev gubernia. In 1825 the local units of the Cherkasy regiment took part in the Decembrist revolt. By the mid-19th century the town was an active manufacturing and trading center with a population of 11,000. Today it is an industrial city with a refrigerator plant, an electric-appliance factory, and a leather factory. Its architectural monuments include the baroque SS Anthony and Theodosius Church and bell tower (1756–9) and St Nicholas's Church (1792).

**Vasylkiv Board.** See Southern Society.

St Nicholas's Church (1792) in Vasylkiv

**Vasylkivka** [Vasyl'kivka]. V-17. A town smt (1988 pop 12,500) on the Vovcha River and a raion center in Dnipropetrovske oblast. It was founded in the 18th century as a winter settlement of the Zaporozhian Cossacks. In the 19th century it was a farming village in Pavlohrad county, Katerynoslav gubernia. Today the town is an agricultural center with a cheese and a canning factory.

**Vasylkivsky, Serhii** [Vasyl'kivs'kyj, Serhij], b 19 October 1854 in Izium, Kharkiv gubernia, d 7 October 1917 in Kharkiv. Painter and art scholar. He studied at the St Petersburg Academy of Arts (1876–85) and in France (1886–8). He also painted in Italy, Spain, northern Africa, and Britain. After settling in Kharkiv in 1888, he was active in Ukrainian artistic circles and headed the architectural and art society there. He produced over 3,000 realist and impressionist works. They include a few portraits; historical paintings, such as *Zaporozhian Skirmish with Tatars* (1892), *Cossacks in the Steppe* (1915), and *Cossack Campaign* (1917); genre paintings, such as *Cossack and Girl* (1894) and *Market in Poltava* (1902); and many landscapes, such as *Cossack Meadow* (1893), *Dnieper Floodplains* (1896), and *Along the Donets* (1901). In 1901–8 Vasylkivsky painted murals and ornamental wall panels for the Poltava Zemstvo Building, which perished in the Second World War; they included *The Chumak Romodan Route*, *The Cossack Holota*, and *The Election of Colonel Martyn Pushkar*. He copublished, with M. *Samokysh, an album of Ukrainian folk ornamental motifs (1912), for which he painted over 100 designs, and

Serhii Vasylkivsky: *Rendezvous* (oil, 1894)

an album on Ukrainian antiquity (1900, text by D. Yavornytsky), for which he did 27 historical portraits. Albums of Vasylkivsky's works were published in 1970 and 1987, and books about him have been written by O. Nikolaiev (1927), K. Slipko-Moskaltsiv (1930), M. Bezkhutry (1954, 1967), and I. Ohiievska (1980).

Mykola Vasylko                Vasyl Vasylko

**Vasylko, Mykola** [Vasyl'ko], b 21 March 1868 in Chernivtsi, Bukovyna, d 2 August 1924 in Bad Reichenhall, Germany. Diplomat, parliamentarian, and Bukovynian civic figure. He belonged to the Vasylko family line of nobility in Bukovyna. He studied at the Theresianum in Vienna. He was chosen mayor of Lukavets, in Vyzhnytsia county, Bukovyna, and then elected to the Bukovynian diet and the Austrian parliament (1898–1918). Together with Rumanian (A. Onciul), Jewish (B. Straucher), and Armenian (S. Stefanowicz) politicians he formed the Freethinking Union, which assisted Ukrainians in making gains in the administrative, cultural, and church realms. Some of those included the recalling of the unpopular president of Bukovyna, F. Bourgignon (1903), the founding of a Ukrainian gymnasium in Vyzhnytsia (1908), and the division of the Bukovynian metropoly into Ukrainian and Rumanian parts (1916). He organized a Hutsul-Bukovynian Kurin (1915–16) as an Austrian volunteer unit, founded and served as deputy leader of the General Ukrainian Council in Vienna (1915), and served in the Ukrainian National Rada in Lviv (1918). In the Austrian parliament he was deputy leader of the Ukrainian Club and a noted defender of Ukrainian rights. He addressed issues such as changes in voter registration (1901), the opening of a Ukrainian university in Lviv (1901), and the peasant strikes of 1902. He was an active foe of Russophilism and of the Rumanianization of Bukovyna. He was a proponent of the so-called Austro-Ukrainian scheme, which provided for (in the event of a victory by the Central Powers in the First World War) the addition of Volhynia and Podilia to Galicia and Bukovyna to form a revived Galician-Volhynian state as an autonomous territory within Austria-Hungary. During the First World War Vasylko assisted refugees from Bukovyna and Galicia who were interned in Austria and rescued many Ukrainians from the *Thalerhof camp. Through diplomatic efforts and by direct participation he contributed to the signing of the Treaty of *Brest-Litovsk (9 February 1918) between Ukraine and the Central Powers. He was diplomatic representative of the ZUNR government in Austria (1918–19) and ambassador of the UNR in Switzerland and Germany (1919–24). A collection of his speeches titled *Posol's'ka diial'nist' v Derzhavnii Radi i v Kraievim Soimi v rokakh 1901–3* (Deputy Activity in the State Council and the Provincial Diet in 1901–3) came out in 1904.

A. Zhukovsky

**Vasylko, Vasyl** [Vasyl'ko, Vasyl'] (real name: Miliaiev), b 7 April 1893 in Burty, Cherkasy county, Kiev gubernia, d 18 March 1972 in Odessa. Theatrical director and actor. He began his stage career in Sadovsky's Theater (1912) and then performed in Molodyi Teatr (1916–19), Kyidramte (1920–1), and *Berezil (1922–6). In 1929–32 he lectured at the Kharkiv Music and Drama Institute. He was artistic director of the Odessa Ukrainian Music and Drama Theater (1926–8, 1938–41, and 1948–56), the Kharkiv Chervonozavodskyi Ukrainian Drama Theater (1928–33), and theaters in Donetske (1933–8) and Chernivtsi (1944–8). Vasylko debuted as a director in Berezil in 1925, with *Za dvoma zaitsiamy* (After Two Hares, based on M. Starytsky). He also staged I. Kocherha's *Marko v pekli* (Marko in Hell, 1928), W. Shakespeare's *Macbeth* (1938), and his own adaptations of O. Kobylianska's *Zemlia* (The Land, 1947) and *U nediliu rano zillia kopala* (On Sunday Morn She Gathered Herbs, 1955). As a character actor he appeared in varied roles, from H. Kvitka-Osnovianenko's Shelmenko to Shakespeare's Banquo. Vasylko helped initiate the Kiev Museum of Theater Arts. A biography, by P. Kravchuk, was published in Kiev in 1980, and his memoirs were published in 1984.

**Vasylko Romanovych** [Vasyl'ko Romanovyč], b 1199, d 1271. Rus' prince; son of Roman Mstyslavych. After the death of his father (1205) he and his mother and brother, Danylo, were exiled to Poland. Taking advantage of the power struggles involving Galician boyars, Hungarians, and Poles, the brothers undertook the process of reclaiming the Principality of Galicia-Volhynia. In 1227 Vasylko was granted rule over Lutske, Peresopnytsia, and Brest by Danylo, and in 1238 he received western Volhynia as his realm, including the capital, Volodymyr. He was forced to acknowledge Tatar suzerainty after the Tatars' invasion of Rus', although he continued to rule largely unimpeded. In

1259 he was ordered to burn all his fortifications except Kholm. After Danylo's death in 1264 Vasylko became the eldest representative of the Romanovych dynasty and the de facto ruler of all Galicia-Volhynia.

**Vasylko Rostyslavych** [Vasyl'ko Rostyslavyč], b ?, d 28 February 1124. Rus' prince; son of Rostyslav Volodymyrovych. He and his brothers, Volodar and Riuryk, are regarded as the cofounders of Halych principality. They formed a loose alliance with Byzantium and the Cumans in order to maintain their independence from the grand prince of Kiev to the east and from Hungary and Poland to the west. Vasylko became the prince of Terebovlia in 1092. He was blinded by *Davyd Ihorevych in Zvenyhorod (other sources say in Bilhorod) in 1097 after the Liubech congress of princes. The instigator of the assault, the Kievan prince *Sviatopolk II Iziaslavych, then invaded Volhynia (1100) but was unable to seize power in the Rostyslavych realm. Vasylko was defended by Volodymyr Monomakh and Davyd and Oleh Sviatoslavych, and ruled Terebovlia until he died. He probably founded the town of Vasyliv at the confluence of the Seret and the Dniester rivers.

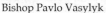
Bishop Pavlo Vasylyk          Evstakhii Vasylyshyn

**Vasylyk, Pavlo,** b 8 August 1926 in Boryslavka, Peremyshl county, Galicia. Ukrainian Catholic bishop. He was tutored in theology by V. Pynyla and I. Hotra. After being arrested in 1947, he was held in a number of concentration camps in Central Asia. He was ordained a deacon in 1950 in Kazakhstan. Upon his release in 1956 he settled in Buchach, Ternopil oblast, where he was ordained a priest of the underground Ukrainian Catholic church by Bishop M. Charnetsky. He was rearrested in January 1959 and imprisoned in Mordovia until 1964. In 1974 he was consecrated assistant bishop of Ivano-Frankivske eparchy by Bishop Y. Fedoryk. Following the policies of perestroika and new religious tolerance, he was the first Ukrainian Catholic bishop openly to proclaim his status; he emerged from the underground in August 1987.

*Vasylykha.* A folk dance for girls performed in a circle with one or two people in the middle. The *vasylykha* is a slow dance which begins in 3/4 time and increases in tempo to 2/4 time. It originated in the Kiev region.

**Vasylyshyn, Evstakhii** [Vasylyšyn, Evstaxij], b 24 December 1897 in Ternopil, Galicia, d 29 June 1974 in Winnipeg. Community leader in Canada. He joined the Ukrainian Sich Riflemen in 1918 and was wounded in the battle for Lviv. After the war he was a member of the Ukrainian Military Organization. Having emigrated to Canada in 1924, he became a founder and president (1928–30, 1945–7, 1950–2) of the *Ukrainian War Veterans' Association of Canada. He was also a founder of the Ukrainian Canadian Committee (now Congress) and the Ukrainian Cultural and Educational Centre in Winnipeg. As director (1949–50) of the European office of the Ukrainian Canadian Relief Fund, he helped to resettle many Ukrainian war refugees in Canada.

Antin Vasynchuk          Pavlo Vasynchuk

**Vasynchuk, Antin** [Vasyn'čuk] (Vasylchuk), b 1885 in Kholm, d 13 May 1935 in Kholm. Agronomist and civic and political leader; brother of P. *Vasynchuk. In the revolutionary period he was a member of the Central Rada and the UNR government's director of repatriation for the displaced inhabitants of the Kholm and Podlachia regions. He was a founder and president of the Ridna Khata society (1920) and copublisher of the weekly *Nashe zhyttia* (1921–8) in Kholm. He also set up Ukrainian co-operatives. In 1922 he was elected to the Polish Sejm, where he presided over the Ukrainian caucus (1922–4).

**Vasynchuk, Pavlo** [Vasyn'čuk] (Vasylchuk), b 2 August 1893 in Kholm, d 1944 in Kholm. Lawyer, economist, and civic and political leader; brother of A. *Vasynchuk. A graduate of the Kiev Commercial School and the law faculty of Kiev University, he participated in the revolutionary events in Kiev in 1917 and worked as director of the press office of the UNR Ministry of Food Supplies. At the beginning of 1918 he represented the UNR government on the international repatriation commission in Kovel. After returning to Kholm he copublished *Nashe zhyttia* with his brother and in 1920 was arrested with him for bringing out its eighth issue. In 1922 and 1928 he was elected to the Polish Sejm. He was a founder and the first president of the *Sel-Soiuz party (1924). A convinced socialist who opposed communism, he did not support Sel-Souiz's merger into *Sel-Rob. Breaking ranks with the latter group in December 1926, he reconstituted Sel-Soiuz and established *Selians'kyi shliakh as its organ. In 1944 he acted as a representative of the UNR government-in-exile and as the Ukrainian liaison of the clandestine Polish home government. He was murdered by the Polish underground.

**Vatchenko, Oleksii** [Vatčenko, Oleksij], b 25 February 1914 in Yelyzaveto-Kamianka, Katerynoslav gubernia, d 22 November 1984 in Kiev. Stalinist CPU and government leader. A graduate of Dnipropetrovske University (1938), he worked as a teacher and then an education official in Dnipropetrovske. In the 1950s he rose through the Party hierarchy to the positions of first secretary of Khmelnytskyi (1959–63), rural Dnipropetrovske (1963–4), Cherkasy (1964–5), and Dnipropetrovske (1965–7) oblast Party committees; member of the CC CPU (1960–84) and its Politburo (1966–84); and CC CPSU candidate (1961–6) and member (1966–84). He served as president of the Ukrainian and a vice-president of the USSR supreme soviets (1976–84). A protégé of L. Brezhnev and a close associate of V. Shcherbytsky, in 1968 he initiated the Party campaign to ban O. Honchar's novel *Sobor* (The Cathedral), and in 1971–2 he helped engineer the downfall of CPU first secretary P. Shelest, whose policies he opposed.

Pope John Paul II and Cardinal Myroslav Liubachivsky paying their respects to the late Cardinal Yosyf Slipy

**Vatican.** A city-state in Rome and the center of the Catholic church. It was recognized as an independent state under the terms of the Lateran Treaty of 1929 between the Italian government and the Holy See. It covers a territory of approx 0.4 sq km and includes St Peter's Basilica, the papal palaces, the Vatican Library, Vatican Radio, a number of other buildings, and properties outside the city (eg, Castel Gandolfo, the pope's summer residence).

According to tradition, ties between the papacy and Ukrainian territory date from the 1st century, when the Roman emperor Trajan exiled *St Clement I to Crimea. Clement died a martyr in Chersonese Taurica, and some of his relics were reputedly taken to Kiev and deposited in the Church of the Tithes. After the adoption of Christianity in Kievan Rus', Popes John XV (988 and 991) and Sylvester II (1000) sent emissaries to Kiev, and Prince Volodymyr the Great sent representatives to Rome (991 and 1001). Bruno von Querfurt, while traveling on a mission to the Pechenegs ca 1006, visited Volodymyr in Kiev. Prince Iziaslav Yaroslavych sent his son Yaropolk to Rome in 1075 to enlist the help of Pope Gregory VII in his fight for control of Kiev. G. da Pian del Carpini headed a mission

from Pope Innocent IV to the Mongols in 1245–7 and began negotiations with Princes Danylo and Vasylko Romanovych that led to the 1253 coronation of Danylo by an apostolic delegate. In the 15th century the Kievan metropolitan *Isidore lived in Rome, and Yu. *Drohobych published *Judicium prenosticon Magistri Georgii Drogobicz de Russia*, the first book written by a Ukrainian, there in 1483. It contained a dedication to Pope Sixtus IV.

A new era in Ukrainian relations with the Vatican began in 1595, when several Ukrainian and Belarusian bishops wrote to the Holy See to initiate the Church Union of *Berestia. Since then there has been close contact between the Ruthenian or Ukrainian Catholic church and the Vatican. Many bishops and metropolitans (eg, Y. Rutsky, R. Korsak, M. Terletsky, Ya. Susha) traveled regularly to Rome, which served as the legal center of the Halych metropoly following the destruction of the Catholic church in Ukraine in 1946. The Ukrainian Catholic church has been formally represented at the Vatican since 1626 by a procurator of the Kievan metropolitan and Basilian order, who was based at the Church of SS Sergius and Bacchus from 1639 to 1880. Beginning with I. Morokhovsky (1596) and Y. Rutsky (1599), many Ukrainians attended St Athanasius Greek College, founded in the mid-16th century to train Eastern rite theologians. Over 50 Ukrainian Basilian theologians were educated in the international college of the Congregation for the Propagation of the Faith, which was responsible for the affairs of the Uniate church from 1622 until the creation of the *Congregation for Eastern Churches in 1917. From 1845 Ukrainian Catholic priests were trained at the Greek College, which was called the Greek-Ruthenian College until 1897, when Pope Leo XIII sanctioned the establishment of *St Josaphat's Ukrainian Pontifical College. The college was based near the Church of SS Sergius and Bacchus until 1932, when Pope Pius XI had a new building constructed outside the Vatican, and the original premises became a study center for the Basilian order. In the 1960s the building came to house the parish offices and a museum of Ukrainian art.

In addition to these older bodies, several other institutions of the Ukrainian Catholic church were moved to the Vatican after the liquidation of the church in Ukraine, or established there or near there since then. These include the headquarters of the Sisters Servants of Mary Immaculate and of the Basilian order of nuns, the Ukrainian Minor Pontifical Seminary, the Studite Monastery in Castel Gandolfo, the *Ukrainian Catholic University, and St Sophia's Church. Important Ukrainian church figures (or their relics) are buried at the Vatican, including St Yosafat Kuntsevych (in St Peter's Basilica), R. Korsak (in SS Sergius and Bacchus Church), and Y. Sembratovych (in the crypt of St Sophia's Church).

The Vatican library and archives contain many documents and monuments relating to Ukraine. These include papal correspondence concerning Ukrainian affairs, beginning with letters from Pope Gregory VII to Prince Iziaslav Yaroslavych from 1075. There are also many reports and documents from papal nuncios in Poland and elsewhere who were charged with gathering information for the Vatican. The archives of the congregations for the Propagation of the Faith and the Eastern Churches are especially rich in these materials, as are the holdings of the Greek College and the various monastic orders or congregations. Many of the first works dealing with Ukrainian church history to be published abroad (eg, biographies of Y. Kuntsevych [1643] and Ya. Susha [1665] and I. Kulchytsky's outline history of the Ukrainian Catholic church [1733–4]) were published at the Vatican, and major series of Vatican documents pertaining to Ukraine were initiated in the 19th century and especially in the interwar period. These resources and the other notable structures at the Vatican have attracted Ukrainian scholars and artists, and other Ukainians, since the 18th century.

The Vatican has been the site of several conclaves of Ukrainian bishops (held in 1929, 1932, 1955, and regularly since the late 1960s), and since 1946 the apostolic visitator for Ukrainians in Western Europe has been based there.

**Vatican-Ukrainian diplomatic relations**. The Vatican maintains diplomatic relations with various states (currently 132). In November 1918, after the dissolution of the Austro-Hungarian Empire, Pope Benedict XV issued a directive calling for the establishment of friendly relations with all the nations of the empire (including Ukraine) that had formed independent states. Prior to that, in April 1918, he had sent A. Ratti as an apostolic visitator to Poland and Lithuania to study Ukrainian affairs. Relations were maintained through the apostolic delegates in Constantinople, Washington, and Rome before M. Tyshkevych arrived in February 1919 and was formally accredited as a consul to the Holy See from Ukraine (he had been sent by the Directory government). He was succeeded by Rev F. Bonne; P. Karmansky represented the Western Ukrainian National Republic. In 1920 Ratti was succeeded by G. Genocchi as apostolic visitator to Ukraine. He was never permitted to visit Soviet Ukraine, and carried out his duties from Poland. After the consolidation of Soviet power in eastern Ukraine and the conclusion of the 1925 concordat with Poland, which implicitly recognized Polish control over Western Ukrainian territories, the Vatican cut off formal diplomatic relations with Ukraine until Ukraine's renewed independence in 1991. Archbishop A. Franco became the first papal nuncio to Ukraine in 1992. (See also *Italy, *Ukrainian Catholic church, and *Church, history of the Ukrainian.)

BIBLIOGRAPHY
Stehle, H. *Eastern Politics of the Vatican, 1917–1979*, trans S. Smith (Athens, Ohio 1981)
Moroziuk, R. *Politics of a Church Union* (Chicago 1983)
Khoma, I. *Apostol's'kyi Prestil i Ukraïna, 1919–1922* (Rome 1987)
Dunn, D. 'The Vatican, the Kremlin and the Ukrainian Catholic Church,' in *The Ukrainian Religious Experience: Tradition and the Canadian Cultural Context*, ed D. Goa (Edmonton 1989)

**Vatra**. The name of several Ukrainian student organizations. The most renowned Vatra student society was formed in Lviv in 1892. It merged with the socialist *Academic Brotherhood in 1896 and formed the *Academic Hromada. A group of Ukrainian students studying mining engineering in Příbram (Czechoslovakia) named themselves the Vatra society in 1898–1914, as did a group of students of veterinary medicine in Lviv in 1926–39.

**Vatra** (Bonfire). A publishing house of the Plast scouting organization in Transcarpathia, founded in Uzhhorod by L. Bachynsky. In the years 1924–9 it issued 25 booklets, with a combined pressrun of 38,000 copies. Among them were several plays by S. Cherkasenko, Plast handbooks by Bachynsky, and translations of stories by E.T. Seton and S.

Lagerlöf. Vatra closed down after Bachynsky was expelled from Czechoslovakia.

*Vatra* (1887)

**Vatra** (Bonfire). A literary miscellany published in Stryi in 1887 and edited by V. Lukych to commemorate the 25th anniversary of T. Shevchenko's death and 25 years of Yu. Fedkovych's literary career. Published therein were original contributions and some reprints: stories by D. Mordovets, P. Myrny, I. Franko and V. Luchakovsky; poems by O. Psol, O. Konysky, S. Rudansky, V. Samiilenko, P. Kulish, M. Starytsky, V. Kotsovsky, U. Kravchenko, S. Vorobkevych, and Fedkovych; biographical sketches of Konysky by V. Hrechulevych, P. Ohiievsky-Okhotsky, O. Shyshatsky-Illich, P. Morachevsky, P. Kuzmenko, and A. Svydnytsky; Mordovets's autobiography; articles by M. Drahomanov (on an old verse about the destruction of Hell by Christ), O. Barvinsky (on the lives and works of Shevchenko and Fedkovych), M. Kostomarov (on the destruction of Baturyn), D. Lepky (on folk beliefs about domestic animals), Konysky (on archives in Ukraine), M. Sumtsov (on Ukrainian surnames), and V. Lukych (on Hungarian-ruled Ruthenia); book reviews (O. Ohonovsky on a novel by Konysky; Franko on Mordovets's writings); and several pages of literary and historical notes by V. Lukych.

**Vatulia, Oleksii** [Vatulja, Oleksij], b 14 August 1891 in Trubaitsi, near Khorol, Poltava gubernia, d 20 May 1955 in Kiev. Stage and film actor. He completed study at the Ly-

Oleksii Vatulia

senko Music and Drama School in Kiev (1916) and then played in Molodyi Teatr (1917–19) and was one of the founders and a leading actor of the Kiev Ukrainian Drama Theater (1920–55, except 1927–8, when he worked in the Kharkiv Chervonozavodskyi Ukrainian Drama Theater). His repertoire ranged from roles in ethnographic plays to the title roles in Sophocles' *Oedipus Rex* and E. Toller's *Hinkemann*. He acted in the films *Kira Kiralina* (1928) and *Neskoreni* (The Undefeated, 1945) and was well known as a reciter, particularly of T. Shevchenko's poetry.

**Vatutine** or **Vatutyne**. IV-12. A city (1989 pop 20,700) on the Shpolka River in Zvenyhorodka raion, Cherkasy oblast. It was founded in 1946 as the workers' settlement Shakhtynske, was renamed in 1949, and was granted city status in 1952. It is an industrial center with lignite, granite, and kaolin mines, a briquette factory, and a refractory-materials plant.

Nikolai Vavilov            Rev Mykhailo Vavryk

**Vavilov, Nikolai,** b 25 November 1887 in Moscow, d 26 January 1943 in Saratov, Russia. Russian geneticist; full member of the AN URSR (now ANU), the USSR Academy of Sciences, and the All-Union Academy of Agricultural Sciences (VASKhNIL) from 1929. He is considered to be the Soviet Union's most prominent plant breeder and is referred to as the 'Mendeleev of biology.' A graduate of the Moscow Agricultural Institute (1911), he taught at Saratov University (1917–21) and directed the All-Union Institute of Plant Cultivation (1924–40). He rose to prominence during the period of collectivization and was the founder and first director of VASKhNIL. In 1935 T. *Lysenko's attack on genetics as a bourgeois, capitalist, and idealist science useless to agriculture led to Vavilov's demotion to vice-president of VASKhNIL. Vavilov was harassed, and openly broke with Lysenko in 1939. He was arrested in August 1940 while on a collecting expedition in Western Ukraine and was found guilty of espionage and sabotaging Soviet agriculture. His death sentence was commuted, but he died of malnutrition in a Saratov prison. In 1955 he was posthumously rehabilitated, and in recent years he was portrayed as a hero in Soviet publications.

**Vavryk, Mykhailo** (Wawryk), b 16 December 1908 in Laskivtsi, Terebovlia county, Galicia, d 1 March 1984 in Hawthorne, New York. Basilian priest and scholar; full

member of the Shevchenko Scientific Society from 1961. He completed his term in the novitiate at the Krekhiv Monastery and studied at the Pontifical Oriental Institute (1934–7) and the Pontifical Institute of Christian Archaeology (1937–9) in Rome. He served as vice-rector of *St Josaphat's Ukrainian Pontifical College (1938–48), director of the Ukrainian program on Vatican Radio (1939–42), and a chaplain for the interned members of the Division Galizien after the war. In 1948–60 he taught theology and did missionary work in North America. He then returned to Rome to become chaplain of St Josaphat's College and then general consultor of the Basilian order (1963–76). Vavryk was a specialist on the history of the Ukrainian church and of the Basilian order. His publications include *Po vasyliians'kykh monastyriakh* (At Basilian Monasteries, 1958); *Narys rozvytku i stanu vasyliians'koho chynu XVII–XX st.* (A Survey of the Development and Status of the Basilian Order of the 17th–20th Centuries, 1979); and articles in *Analecta Ordinis S. Basilii Magni / Zapysky ChSVV* (which he also helped edit), the *Encylopedia of Ukraine*, and elsewhere.

**Vazhynsky, Porfyrii** [Važyns'kyj, Porfyrij] (Skarbek-Vazhynsky), b 5 August 1732 in Ashmiany, near Vilnius, d 9 March 1804 in Kholm. Uniate bishop. He studied in Rome before becoming a professor of philosophy in Polatsk and then rector of Basilian schools in Buchach and Volodymyr-Volynskyi. He was protoarchimandrite of the order in 1772–80 and 1788–89, and was consecrated bishop of Kholm in 1789. As bishop he was active in the efforts to revive Halych metropoly.

**VChK.** See Cheka.

**Vdovychenko, Maksym** [Vdovyčenko] (pseud of Maksym Havryliuk), b 4 May 1876 in Zozivka, Lypovets county, Kiev gubernia, d 2 January 1928 in Aubun-la-Tiche, France. Poet and translator. He contributed to *Literaturno-naukovyi vistnyk* (1900–10), *Maiak* (1913), and *Rada* (1913, under the pseud Syvy). His collection *Na khvyliakh smutku* (On the Waves of Sorrow) was published in Kiev in 1911.

*Vecherniaia Odessa* (Evening Odessa). A Russian-language organ of the Odessa City Council and, until 1992, the city Party committee, published six days a week since July 1973. In 1980 the newspaper appeared in a pressrun of 123,000.

*Vechernii Donetsk* (Evening Donetske). A Russian-language organ of the Donetske City Council and, until 1992, the city Party committee, published six days a week since July 1973. In 1980 the newspaper appeared in a pressrun of 230,000.

*Vechernytsi* (aka *vechornytsi, dosvitky, priadky, popriakhy, odenky*). Evening or night gatherings of young men and women, usually at the home of a childless widow, an *otamansha*, who was responsible for keeping moral standards and order on such occasions. The girls paid her for use of the house's fuel and food and sometimes for her labor. The *vechernytsi* season lasted from the end of the fieldwork in the fall until Lent. There were two types of gatherings: working *vechernytsi*, at which the young women

*Vechernytsi* (oil, 1881) by Ilia Repin

spun or embroidered, and recreational *vechernytsi*, with music and dancing. The latter gatherings usually took place just before or during a holiday. *Vechernytsi* often began with work and ended with eating, games, singing, and dancing. In some localities the young men and women stayed all night, sleeping in pairs on the straw-covered floor. The chief purpose of the *vechernytsi* was to enable the participants to work in a group and to enable young people who lived in remote parts of the village or on distant farmsteads to become acquainted with each other. During the work the participants told stories and anecdotes, shared the latest news, sang songs, and told fortunes. Most courtships, leading eventually to marriage, began at such gatherings. For this reason the community tolerated a certain amount of sexual freedom at *vechernytsi*. The church, however, regarded them as sinful and opposed them. When factory products made home production, particularly spinning, obsolete, the *vechernytsi* lost their work-related function and became simply recreational. During the Soviet period they virtually disappeared and were replaced by dances in the village clubs or buildings of culture. The *vechernytsi* are frequently described in Ukrainian literature and staged in theater.

M. Mushynka

**Vechernytsi** (Evening Get-togethers). A Ukrainophile literary weekly 'for amusement and learning.' It was edited and published in the vernacular by F. *Zarevych in Lviv from 1 February 1862 to 2 May 1863 (59 eight-page issues). With the 35th issue V. *Shashkevych became the main collaborator, and he edited the last nine issues. Published therein were poems, stories, literary and publicistic articles, historical articles, editorials, notes, and correspondence, and dictionary materials by V. Shashkevych, I. Verkhratsky, and others. Works by writers from Russian-ruled Ukraine were taken (and translated, if necessary) from *Osnova* (St Petersburg) and other sources. The magazine had 600 subscribers.

**Vechirnia hodyna** (Evening Hour). A monthly popular literary magazine published in Cracow from November 1942 to 1944 by the Ukrainske Vydavnytstvo publishing house in a pressrun of up to 15,000 copies. The editors were S. Hordynsky and V. Chaplenko.

**Vechirnii Kharkiv** (Evening Kharkiv). An organ of the Kharkiv City Council and, until 1992, the city Party com-

mittee, published six days a week since 1969. Its pressrun increased from 100,000 in 1970 to 158,000 in 1979. In 1980, however, probably as a result of official restrictions imposed on the growth of the Ukrainian-language press, its run was reduced to 84,000.

*Vechirnii Kyïv*

**Vechirnii Kyïv** (Evening Kiev). A former organ of the Kiev City Council and the city Party committee, published six days a week since 1951. It succeeded the Russian-language *Vechernii Kiev* (1927–30) and the Ukrainian-language *Bil'shovyk* (1932–9). *Vechirnii Kyïv* has been one of the most widely read newspapers in Ukraine. Its pressrun increased from 100,000 in 1960 to 367,000 in 1975. In the late 1970s, however, as a result of the official imposition of restrictions on the growth of the Ukrainian-language press and policy of Russification, its pressrun was reduced, to 200,000 by 1980. In 1983 a parallel Russian-language edition was established with an initial pressrun of 47,000, and the pressrun of the Ukrainian edition was reduced to 188,500. By 1989, only 130,000 copies of the Ukrainian edition were being printed, while the pressrun of the Russian edition was 330,000. Since 1990 it has been an independent commercial paper edited by V. Karpenko, a member of the Ukrainian Supreme Council. In 1991 the pressrun was 500,000, and subscriptions to the Ukrainian edition increased to 300,000.

**Vedel, Artem** [Vedel'] (born Vedelsky), b 13 April 1767 in Kiev, d 26 July 1808 in Kiev. Composer, conductor, singer (tenor), and teacher. After studying at the Kievan Academy he went to Moscow in 1787 to conduct the choir of Governor-General P. Yeropkin. In 1792 he returned to Kiev to conduct General A. Levanidov's private choir and in 1796 accompanied Levanidov to Kharkiv to conduct the collegium choir there. This period (1792–8) saw the height of Vedel's musical creativity. In 1798 Levanidov was removed from his post by Paul I, leaving Vedel without a benefactor. He returned to Kiev in search of a choir posting and even contemplated joining a monastery to achieve this end. Instead he was banished to a mental asylum in 1799 after church authorities attributed to him some irreverent marginal notes scribbled in a religious book. The incarceration ended Vedel's creative work and led to his premature death.

Vedel, whose musical legacy consists entirely of church

music for choir a cappella, is considered the chief representative of the Cossack baroque style in Ukrainian music. More than 80 of his compositions have been identified, including sacred concertos, one liturgy, one all-night vigil, works in honor of the Virgin Mary and the Nativity, and paschal hours. Vedel's most popular works are his concerto *On the Rivers of Babylon* and his trio *Open the Gates of Repentance*. A selection of his compositions is included in I. Sonevytsky's anthology, *Sacred Choral Music a Cappella of A. Vedel* (New York 1990).

BIBLIOGRAPHY
Sonevyts'kyi, I. *Artem Vedel' i ioho muzychna spadshchyna* (New York 1966)
Kozyts'kyi, P. *Spiv i muzyka v Kyïvs'kii akademiï za 300 rokiv ïï isnuvannia* (Kiev 1971)

I. Sonevytsky

**Vedmitsky, Oleksander** [Vedmic'kyj] (pseuds: Meteorny, Ol. Meteor, O. Sashko), b 22 December 1894 in Pryluka, Poltava gubernia, d 18 October 1963 in Orsk, Siberia. Writer. A teacher from 1913, he graduated from the Poltava Teachers' Institute in 1918. In 1924 he took up journalism and joined the peasant writers' group Pluh. Later he was an associate of the Taras Shevchenko Scientific Research Institute (Kharkiv), where he completed his graduate studies in 1932. He began publishing in a Pryluka newspaper in 1917. His poems, humorous sketches, stories, literary criticism, and scholarly articles appeared in Soviet Ukrainian periodicals from 1924 to 1933. Published separately were his poetry collections *Pid zahravoiu povstan'* (Under Red Skies of Insurrections, 1923), *V oreoli: Ahitkartyny* (In the Halo: Agitpictures, 1924), *Shumyt' topolia* (The Poplar Rustles, 1927), *Pokosy* (Hay Gatherings, 1929), and *Vuhil'* (Coal, 1931); the feuilleton collection *Z lykhtarem po selakh* (Around Villages with a Lantern, 1925); the humor book *Ahitatory* (Agitators, 1927); the story collection *Khalabuda i strybunets'* (The Hut and the Jumper, 1930); and studies of the Literary Discussion of 1925–8 (1932) and Soviet literature in the period of socialist reconstruction (1932). He became a literature docent in 1934, headed the department of literature at the Orsk Pedagogical Institute in the 1950s, and published a Russian book on T. Shevchenko's exile in Orenburg (Orenburg 1960).

**Vegetable farming** (*horodnytstvo*). A branch of agriculture involved in the growing of vegetables. It is labor-intensive and consequently employs many field-workers. It forms a basis for the development of the vegetable-processing industry (canning and freezing).

The vegetables grown in Ukraine belong to various botanical families domesticated in different parts of the world and brought to Ukraine by many routes. The most widespread in Ukraine (1981) are tomato (24.4 percent), cabbage (19.2 percent), cucumber (17 percent), red beet and carrot (11.9 percent), and onion, all of which together occupy over 80 percent of the area sown to all vegetables (491,000 ha). Potatoes, which form a separate category not included among vegetables in agricultural statistics, occupy a considerably larger area (1,653,000 ha in 1981). Less widespread vegetables in Ukraine are radishes, turnips, swedes, celery, pepper, garlic, horseradish, brussels sprouts, kohlrabi, eggplant, asparagus, and squash. Garden herbs, seeds, and spices are considered a category of vegetables. The more common ones in Ukraine are poppy, dill, caraway, origanum, anise, and fennel. Garden-grown legumes (pulses, lentils, beans, and green peas), sweet corn, and gourds (melons, watermelons, and pumpkins) are generally included, but field-grown legumes, gourds, and corn (generally used for feed) are considered separate categories. (In 1981, field-grown legumes occupied 1,415,000 ha, field-grown roots and gourds for feed, 726,000 ha, corn for grain, 1,866,000 ha, and corn for silage and green fodder, 3,396,000 ha.) In 1988, vegetables occupied 498,000 ha, or 1.5 percent of the total sown area of Ukraine. Their concentration was more pronounced on irrigated land in the southern steppe, where they occupied 179,000 ha, or 7.7 percent of the sown area.

Among the vegetables grown in the Princely era were pulses, peas, lentils, onion, garlic, celery, carrots, and cabbage. In general, however, vegetable farming was poorly developed. The first improved vegetable gardens were cultivated by monasteries, such as the Kievan Cave Monastery. New families of vegetables, including cucumbers, muskmelons, and watermelons, began to spread in the 15th century. By the 16th century parsley, parsnips, kohlrabi, and lettuce had arrived, mostly from Italy. In the 17th century cauliflower, radishes, spinach, and beans were added; in the 18th century potatoes were introduced; and in the 19th century eggplant, peppers, and tomatoes began to be grown in Ukraine.

Before the First World War and until collectivization vegetable farming was largely a peasant enterprise with little, if any, commercial significance. Commercial vegetable farming arose mainly around large cities (Kiev, Kharkiv, Odessa, Mykolaiv, Kryvyi Rih, Kherson, Dnipropetrovske, and in the Donbas), resorts, and hospitals and sanatoriums. A few small rural areas also developed a specialty in vegetable farming. Commercial vegetable farming was usually conducted by Germans, Russian Old Believers, and Bulgarians. After collectivization a number of state farms were set up to replace the private entrepreneurs in commercial vegetable farming, but the overwhelming bulk of the vegetables continued to be produced on the subsidiary gardens of the collective farmers and state-farm workers and the private plots of other individuals. Only after the Second World War was a concerted effort made to produce more vegetables on specialized state farms. The proportion of the private plots in the sown area of vegetables then fell from 56 percent in 1940 to 45 percent in 1955, 36 percent in 1960, and 27 percent in 1987.

The total area sown to vegetables has grown over time. From 196,000 ha in 1913 (within Ukraine's 1938 borders), it grew to 402,000 ha in 1928, declined during collectivization, and then expanded again to 488,000 ha in 1940. In addition about 70,000 ha were acquired with the annexation of Western Ukraine. The Second World War brought another reduction; the area had failed to recover its former size by 1950 and was still marginally short in 1960 and 1970; it surpassed the 1940 level only in 1973. Yields, like the sown area, have increased over time, though they were also reduced by calamities such as collectivization and the Second World War. The harvests followed a similar pattern. In the postwar period the harvest per person (a measure of the physical availability of vegetables for the population) has indicated an overall improvement. Only 1940 was an anomalously abundant year, when the private farms of Western Ukraine were incorporated into the republic's total output.

Vegetable production: sown areas, yield, harvest, 1913–87

|  | 1913 | 1940 | 1950 | 1960 | 1970 | 1980 | 1987 |
|---|---|---|---|---|---|---|---|
| **Sown areas (1,000 ha)** | | | | | | | |
| Ukraine | 267 | 486 | 374 | 474 | 466 | 498 | 513 |
| USSR | 648 | 1,507 | 1,303 | 1,476 | 1,499 | 1,715 | 1,713 |
| **Yield (centners/ha)** | | | | | | | |
| Ukraine | na | 113 | 62 | 103 | 120 | 138 | 157 |
| USSR | 84 | 91 | 72 | 111 | 138 | 150 | 159 |
| **Harvest (million t)** | | | | | | | |
| Ukraine | na | 5.5 | 2.3 | 4.9 | 5.8 | 7.2 | 8.1 |
| USSR | 5.5 | 13.7 | 9.3 | 16.6 | 21.2 | 27.3 | 29.2 |

The Ukrainian SSR accounted for about 30 percent of the USSR area sown to vegetables. The Ukrainian SSR produced considerably more vegetables per person than did the USSR (see the table). The per capita consumption in the Ukrainian SSR was also higher, but not to the same degree. The difference indicates that about one-fifth of the harvested vegetables were shipped out of Ukraine to other republics, chiefly the RSFSR. The shipment of vegetables to Russia (notably to Moscow and St Petersburg) was common even before the revolution, especially in the spring and early summer (vegetables can be harvested in Ukraine one to two months earlier than in Russia).

The comparative climatic advantage as well as the presence of local urban markets stimulated vegetable farming in specific regions of Ukraine. The heat-loving melons, for example, are grown predominantly in the steppe, the Left-Bank forest-steppe, and, beyond the borders of Ukraine, in the Kuban region. State farms whose specialties include the production of field tomatoes are also located mostly in the steppe. The highest share of sown area devoted to vegetables is found in raions adjacent to large cities, in the cities of the Donbas, and around food-processing centers in cities such as Cherkasy, Kherson, Dzhankoi, Symferopil, and Izmail. Some areas developed a specialty in a particular vegetable, such as the Nizhen region in cucumbers and onions, the Oleksandriia region in watermelons and muskmelons, the Stryi region in cabbage, the Zalishchyky region in early tomatoes, and the Kuty area (south of Kolomyia) in onions.

In addition to field cropping there was considerable development of early vegetable production in greenhouses or under cold frames, especially near Kiev and Kharkiv and in the Donbas. More recently the production has been expanded with the use of long, semicylindrical structures under polyethylene cover (a technique less expensive than greenhouses) and of individual plant or row coverings in the fields (a technique requiring less work and capital expenditure than with cold frame coverings).

The production of selected seeds for vegetable farming in Ukraine before the First World War was inadequately developed. Seed supply had to be supplemented with imports from abroad, notably from Germany. In Ukraine under Russian rule, agricultural extension service was provided by the zemstvos through their instructors, courses, and schools in Uman, Kiev, and Poltava. In Western Ukraine under Austria-Hungary, the *Silskyi Hospodar agricultural society in Lviv supported vegetable growers through its gardening-orcharding section and sponsored vegetable gardening and orcharding courses, exhibitions, and contests for young people. After the Revolution of 1917 agricultural experimental research in Ukraine was reorganized, and the production of selected seeds was improved to the extent that Ukraine was able to satisfy its own needs and even provide seed material for the Russian SFSR. The main scientific research center for the development of regionalized varieties of vegetable and melon seeds is the Ukrainian Scientific Research Institute of Vegetable and Melon Growing in Merefa. It co-ordinates the efforts of scientists involved in selecting and testing seeds at a network of research stations, in Kiev, Odessa, Voznesenske, Kherson, Symferopil, Melitopil, Dnipropetrovske, Donetske, Luhanske, Poltava, Sumy, Nizhen, Chernihiv, Mliiv (west of Cherkasy), and other locations.

BIBLIOGRAPHY
*Ovochivnytstvo zakrytoho i vidkrytoho hruntu* (Kiev 1965)
*Ekonomika kolhospnoho ovochivnytstva* (Uzhhorod 1969)
Bilets'kyi, P. *Ovochivnytstvo* (Kiev 1970)

I. Stebelsky

**Vegetable-oil industry.** A branch of the *food industry that processes *oil plants (primarily sunflowers) to make vegetable oil, margarine, mayonnaise, glycerol, soap, fat concentrates, and other products. The production of oil from plants has a long history in Ukraine, but until the 20th century it was a poorly developed industry. As late as 1913 there were only five factories employing over 50 workers in the industry in Ukraine; they produced only 6.3 percent of the vegetable oil in the Russian Empire. Since the 1920s the industry has grown substantially. The output of vegetable oil increased from 158,700 t in 1940 to 449,200 t in 1960 and 1,071,300 t in 1970. Then it declined to 941,300 t in 1980 and 846,300 t in 1985, but it increased again, to 1,057,600 t in 1990. In the mid-1960s Ukraine accounted for over one-third of the vegetable-oil production in the USSR. The output of margarine products increased steadily, from 15,200 t in 1940 to 82,200 t in 1960, 151,400 t in 1970, 263,900 t in 1980, and 288,500 t in 1990. The output of soap (with a minimum content of 40 percent vegetable oil) also increased, from 99,200 t in 1940 to 226,400 t in 1970 and 278,200 t in 1982. The vegetable-oil industry in Ukraine is most developed in the south and east. Major factories and manufacturing complexes are located in Donetske, Odessa, Kharkiv, Poltava, Dnipropetrovske, Zaporizhia, Vinnytsia, and Chernivtsi oblasts. The industry is also well developed in the Kuban.

**Vegetation regions.** Geographical areas characterized by distinct assemblages of plant communities. Ukraine is divided into four broad vegetation zones: (1) the European broad-leaved forest region, (2) the European-Siberian

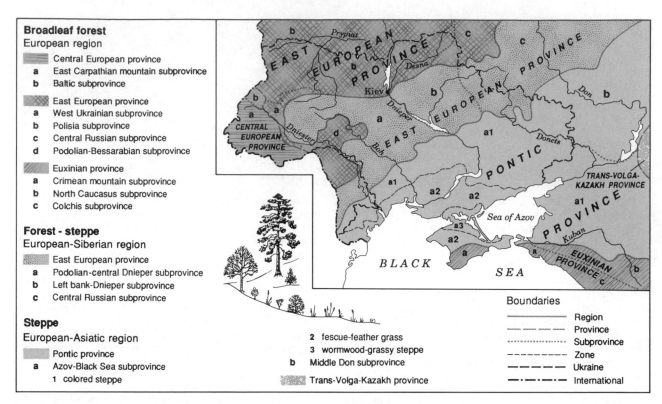

**Broadleaf forest**
European region

| | Central European province |
| --- | --- |
| a | East Carpathian mountain subprovince |
| b | Baltic subprovince |

| | East European province |
| --- | --- |
| a | West Ukrainian subprovince |
| b | Polisia subprovince |
| c | Central Russian subprovince |
| d | Podolian-Bessarabian subprovince |

| | Euxinian province |
| --- | --- |
| a | Crimean mountain subprovince |
| b | North Caucasus subprovince |
| c | Colchis subprovince |

**Forest - steppe**
European-Siberian region

| | East European province |
| --- | --- |
| a | Podolian-central Dnieper subprovince |
| b | Left bank-Dnieper subprovince |
| c | Central Russian subprovince |

**Steppe**
European-Asiatic region

| | Pontic province |
| --- | --- |
| a | Azov-Black Sea subprovince |
| 1 | colored steppe |
| 2 | fescue-feather grass |
| 3 | wormwood-grassy steppe |
| b | Middle Don subprovince |
| | Trans-Volga-Kazakh province |

Boundaries

| | |
| --- | --- |
| ———————— | Region |
| — — — — | Province |
| ·················· | Subprovince |
| – – – – – | Zone |
| — — — — | Ukraine |
| –·–·–·– | International |

# VEGETATION REGIONS

forest-steppe region, (3) the Eurasian steppe region, and (4) the Euxinian province of the European broad-leaved forest region. Within those zones anomalies exist that are governed by other factors, such as soils and elevation. Thus, in northern and northwestern Ukraine (Polisia), where sandy soils prevail, the broad-leaved forest zone contains pine and oak-pine forests. The mountains are characterized by altitudinal zonation of vegetation, in response to increasingly colder and wetter conditions with higher elevations. Thus, the broad-leaved forests of lower elevations merge, at higher elevations, into coniferous forests and then, at the highest elevations of the Carpathians and the Caucasus Mountains, give way to alpine meadows.

Plant communities in Ukraine have evolved and changed over time. In the Eocene period the territory of what is now Ukraine consisted of shallow seas and low islands covered by subtropical vegetation (palms, laurels, myrtles, eucalypti, sequoias, and cypress). Increasing continentality following the rise of the Carpathian Mountains and the disappearance of the Paratethys Sea during the Pliocene brought about a change in vegetation: representatives of the subtropics were gradually displaced by deciduous broad-leaved species (beech, oak, chestnut, walnut, and tulip tree). In the south, drier conditions gave rise to the prevalence of grassland.

During the Pleistocene epoch of the Quaternary period a significant cooling (the Dnieper glaciation) caused the impoverishment of forests and a reduction of their area. In northern Ukraine the pine-birch forests prevailed. Broad-leaved species survived in refuge areas (the Carpathian foothills, the Volhynia-Podilia and the Dnieper uplands, the Donets Ridge, the Crimean Mountains, and the Cauca-

sus). The forest-steppe (with the presence of pine, larch, and birch) survived near the ice front; to the south of it the steppe vegetation was even less significantly affected by glaciation.

In the postglacial (Holocene) period the climatic warming gradually restored most broad-leaved trees and grasses of the steppe from their areas of refuge to areas that almost corresponded to their previous extent. In the mid-Holocene mixed needle-leaved and broad-leaved forests were common, with pine, oak, linden, willow, elm, hazel, and (in swampy areas) alder. In the Carpathian Mountains the pine was replaced by the spruce. By the late Holocene the forest communities were enriched by moisture-loving species such as the beech, fir, and spruce. In Western Ukraine hornbeam gained significant distribution. In Subcarpathia and in the Carpathian Mountains beech and coniferous forests with spruce and fir became established. A more humid climate during the late Holocene was conducive to considerable expansion of peat bogs in the northern and northwestern part of Ukraine. The steppe attained its northern limits during the middle Holocene period.

With the agricultural colonization of the steppes from the 10th century, field crops replaced much of the grasslands and non-native plants were introduced into the region. Today most of the land area of Ukraine is covered by vegetation planted or sown by people. In 1981, of the total land area of Ukraine (60.4 million ha), 70.5 percent (42.5 million ha) was agricultural lands, either cropped or used for hay and pasture (see *Land use). The nonagricultural lands, some 24.8 percent of the total land area, may be considered as still supporting natural vegetation. Such remnant areas of natural vegetation, although modified by centuries of human activity, provide some clues as to what the plant communities must have been like on most of the remaining land areas. Of particular importance in this respect are the forests, which constitute a significant share of the land area in Polisia (26 percent), the Carpathians (39 percent), and the Crimean Mountains (36 percent).

The first attempts to regionalize the vegetation of Ukraine were made by O. Fomin (1925) and Ye. Lavrenko (1927). They were soon followed by schemes for the regionalization of the forests (P. Pohrebniak, 1928), steppes (Yu. Kleopov and Lavrenko, 1933) and wetlands (V. Matiushenko, 1925; D. Zerov, 1938) of Ukraine. Further work on the regionalization of vegetation was conducted after the Second World War by Lavrenko (1947), Zerov (1949), M. Popov (1949), V. Povarnitsyn (1957), H. Bilyk and Ye. Bradis (1962). The most recent geobotanical regionalization of Ukraine (accomplished within the broader framework of the European part of the USSR) was worked out by Lavrenko and T. Isachenko (1977) and then modified by Yu. Sheliah-Sosonko and T. Andriienko (1985).

BIBLIOGRAPHY
Ianata, O. (ed). *Heobotanichna raionizatsiia Ukraïny z mapoiu* (Kharkiv 1927)
Zerov, D.; et al. *Flora URSR*, 12 vols (Kiev 1936–65)
*Heobotanichne raionuvannia Ukraïns'koi RSR* (Kiev 1977)
Sheliag-Sosonko, Iu.; Osychniuk, V.; Andrienko, T. *Geografiia rastitel'nogo pokrova Ukrainy* (Kiev 1982)

I. Stebelsky

**Velehrad congresses.** International gatherings held in 1907, 1909, 1911, 1924, 1927, 1932, and 1936 in Velehrad, Moravia, the missionary center of SS Cyril and Methodius and the burial place of St Methodius. The congresses, which were attended by Catholic and Orthodox theologians, church historians, bishops, and other church figures from the various Slavic nations, were devoted to the study and advancement of the idea of church unification. The first three congresses were initiated and chaired by Metropolitan A. *Sheptytsky. Other prominent Ukrainian Catholic participants were Bishops Y. Kotsylovsky, M. Charnetsky, P. Goidych, D. Niaradi, and Y. Stoika and Revs Y. Slipy, P. Verhun, and A. Khira (there was no formal participation by Ukrainian Orthodox leaders). Materials from the congresses were published mostly in Latin (the official language of the congresses) in *Acta Conventus Velehradensis*, *Acta Academiae Velehradensis*, and *Opera Academiae Velehradensis* (publications of the Velehrad Academy, an institution founded at the 1911 congress), and the journal *Slavorum litterae theologicae*.

**Veles** (aka Volos). The old Slavic god of cattle, wealth, and trade. He was one of the chief deities in the pantheon of pagan Rus'. In concluding treaties with the Byzantines the Kievan princes swore an oath to Perun and Veles. With the adoption of Christianity St Vlas (Vlasii) replaced Veles as the protector of livestock.

**Veliaminov, Stepan** [Vel'iaminov], b and d ? 18th-century Russian general; head of the first *Little Russian Collegium. He was sent by Peter I to Ukraine in 1722, ostensibly to direct the collegium, and also to usurp the authority of the hetman and the Cossack *starshyna*. He was recalled to St Petersburg in 1727, when the collegium was abolished.

**Vellansky, Danylo** [Vellans'kyj] (real name: Kavunnyk), b 11 December 1774 in Borzna, Nizhen regiment, d 15 March 1847 in St Petersburg. Physician and philosopher. He studied at the Kievan Mohyla Academy (1789), at the St Petersburg Medico-Surgical Academy (1796–1802), and abroad in Jena and Würzburg, where he attended lectures by F. *Schelling and L. Oken. After returning to St Petersburg in 1805, he served as a lecturer and eventually professor (1814–37) at the Medico-Surgical Academy. He wrote, in Russian, over 20 works on medicine, physics, and philosophy, including books on medicine as a fundamental science (1805), physiology (1812), Oken's system (1815), and experimental, observational, and speculative physics (1831). Vellansky accepted Schelling's *Naturphilosophie* uncritically and applied his chief ideas (ie, the unity and evolution of nature, the struggle of opposites, and the three-stage dialectic) to systematize the empirical materials in medicine, physiology, and physics. In epistemology he admitted the need for experience but stressed the contribution of reason. His writings influenced the Russian thinkers M. Pavlov and V. Odoevsky, as well as M. Maksymovych and some Ukrainian Romantics. Vellansky and his contributions are discussed in Z. Kamensky's book on Russian philosophy and Schelling (Moscow 1980).

Mykola Velychkivsky

**Velychkivsky, Mykola** [Velyčkivs'kyj], b 1 February 1882 in Zhytomyr, Kiev gubernia, d 17 July 1976 in Irvington, New Jersey. Economist and community leader; member of the Shevchenko Scientific Society from 1963 and of the Ukrainian Academy of Arts and Sciences in the US. A graduate of the Kiev Commercial Institute (1914), in the 1920s he held the chair of agricultural sciences at the Kamianets-Podilskyi Agricultural Institute, the chair of statistics at the Luhanske Co-operative Institute, and then the chair of agricultural sciences at the Zhytomyr Institute of Technical Cultures. In the 1930s he occupied similar positions in Voronezh, Novocherkassy, and Rostov-na-Donu. He returned to Ukraine during the Second World War, becoming a professor at Kiev University and rector of the Kiev Polytechnic Institute. In 1941 he was elected president of the Ukrainian National Council in German-occupied Ukraine. A postwar refugee in Germany, he taught at the Ukrainian Higher School of Economics in Munich before emigrating to the United States. Velychkivsky authored many works on Soviet agricultural policy and Ukraine's economy, including *Sil's'ke hospodarstvo Ukraïny i koloniial'na polityka Rosiï* (The Agriculture of

Ukraine and the Colonial Policy of Russia, 1959) and *Nashi vtraty v lisyvnytstvi* (Our Losses in the Forest Industry, 1959).

**Velychko, Hryhorii** [Velyčko, Hryhorij], b 1863 in Mykolaiv, Stryi circle, Galicia, d 1932 in Kharkiv. Economist and historian; member of the Shevchenko Scientific Society from 1899. He taught in Galician gymnasiums and published many popular works and articles on Ukrainian geography and economics, including an article on the political and trade relations between Rus' and Byzantium in the 10th and 11th centuries (*ZNTSh*, vol 6, 1891), a demographic map of the Ukrainian-Ruthenian people (1896), and an entry on Galicia in the Russian-language encyclopedia published by Brockhaus and Efron (vol 14, 1892).

The title page of Samiilo Velychko's chronicle (1720)

**Velychko, Samiilo** [Velyčko, Samijlo], b 1670 in the Poltava region, d after 1728 in Zhuky, Poltava region. Cossack chronicler and political activist. He studied at the Kiev Mohyla Academy and mastered the Latin, German, and Polish languages. He served as general secretary to V. Kochubei in Dykanka, and in 1705 he transferred to the General Military Chancellery. He was relieved of his post after the execution of Kochubei in 1708; thereafter he lived in Zhuky, where he devoted himself to writing and teaching. He translated into Ukrainian the German anthology *Cosmography*, which he published with an introduction in 1728. Velychko's principal work was a chronicle (4 vols, 1720) describing the events of 1620–1700; it has not been preserved in full.

The first volume examines the events of 1648–59; the second volume, those of 1660–86; and the third, of 1687–1700. The fourth volume, the largest (2,041 pages), contains various documents from the 17th century. This first systematic history of the Cossack state refers to contemporary sources, Ukrainian (S. Zorka's *Diiariiush*, I. Gizel's *Sinopsis*, the works of I. Galiatovsky), Polish (S. Okolski, S. Twardowski), and German (S. Puffendorf), and quotes from many documents. The first volume contains a number of distortions as well as plagiarisms from other histories. The second and third volumes are based on Velychko's personal observations and partly on documents of the General Military Chancellery.

Velychko's chronicle was written in the Ukrainian bookish language of the 18th century, with clearly dis-

cernible elements of dialect. Stylistically it is highly rhetorical and patriotic. In one place the author describes himself as 'a true son and servant of Little Russia.' Velychko paints a moving picture of the era of the *Ruin, and he portrays the Cossacks as righteous defenders of Ukraine and B. Khmelnytsky as a second Moses. The chronicle contains many anecdotes and stories that enhance its literary value. The manuscript was illustrated by 10 portraits of hetmans, from B. Khmelnytsky to I. Mazepa. Some historians, such as M. Kostomarov, S. Solovev, M. Maksymovych, V. Antonovych, O. Levytsky, D. Bahalii, and P. Klepatsky, have considered Velychko's chronicle a reliable historiographical source; others, including G. Karpov, V. Ikonnikov, M. Petrovsky, I. Krypiakevych, and O. Ohloblyn, have viewed with skepticism its stated sources, particularly the accounts of S. Zorka.

The chronicle was published by the Kiev Archeographic Commission as *Letopis' sobytii v Iugo-Zapadnoi Rossii v XVII v.* (Chronicle of Events in Southwestern Russia in the 17th Century, 4 vols, 1848–64). The first volume was reprinted by the Archeographic Commission of the VUAN as *Skazanie o voine kozatskoi s poliakami* (Account of the Cossack War with the Poles, 1926). It was translated into contemporary Ukrainian by Valerii Shevchuk and published in the journal *Kyïv* (1986, nos 10–11 and 1987, nos 1–5, 7, 10, 12; with an introduction by V. Krokoten) and separately (vol 1, 1991).

BIBLIOGRAPHY
Ikonnikov, V. *Opyt russkoi istoriografii*, vol 2 (Kiev 1908)
Doroshenko, D. *Ohliad ukraïns'koï istoriohrafiï* (Prague 1923)
Petrovs'kyi, M. 'Psevdo-diiariiush Samiila Zorky,' *ZIFV*, 17 (1928)
Marchenko, M. *Ukraïns'ka istoriohrafiia: Z davnikh chasiv do seredyny XIX st.* (Kiev 1959)
Dzyra, Ia. 'Tvorchist' Shevchenka i litopys Velychka,' *Vitchyzna*, 1962, no. 5
– 'Samiilo Velychko ta ioho litopys,' in *Istoriohrafichni doslidzhennia v Ukraïns'kii RSR*, 4 (Kiev 1971)

A. Zhukovsky

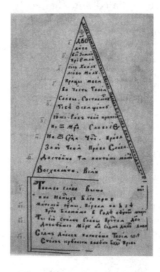

A figural poem from Ivan Velychkovsky's 'Mleko'

**Velychkovsky, Ivan** [Velyčkovs'kyj], b ?, d 1726. Poet and archpriest of Poltava. He wrote *Virshi het'manovi Samoilovychevi* (Poems for Hetman Samoilovych) and two manuscript collections of Ukrainian poetry, 'Zegar ...' (Clock ..., 1690) and 'Mleko ...' (Milk ..., 1691). His works ably capture the stylistic qualities of the baroque era. He also wrote panegyrics in Polish and Latin, some on the subject of L. Baranovych (published in Chernihiv ca 1680–3). His works were erroneously attributed (by M. Petrov) to his brother Lavrentii, but subsequent scholars (V. Peretts, D. Chyzhevsky) rectified the mistake. A full collection of his unpublished poetry was published in 1972.

Archimandrite Paisii          Bishop Vasyl Velychkovsky
Velychkovsky

**Velychkovsky, Paisii** [Velyčkovs'kyj, Pajisij] (secular name: Petro), b 21 December 1722 in Poltava, d 15 November 1794 in Neamţ Monastery, Rumania. Orthodox monk, ascetic, and writer; son of I. *Velychkovsky. He studied at the Kievan Mohyla Academy (1735–9) but withdrew in order to devote himself completely to monastic life. He visited a number of monasteries in the Kiev and Chernihiv regions and became a novice at the St Anthony of the Caves Monastery in Liubech before being tonsured at the St Nicholas Monastery near Medvedivka (1741). After brief stays at the Kievan Cave Monastery and the Motronynskyi Trinity Monastery, he moved to Wallachia, where he stayed at monasteries in Trăisteni (near Focşani), Cîrnul, and Poiana Mărului. In 1746 he traveled through Constantinople to Mt Athos, where he was accepted into the Monastery of Christ Pantocrator. In 1750 he was raised to the second degree of monasticism and took the name Paisii, and in 1758 he was ordained a priest (hieromonk). At Mt Athos Velychkovsky began attracting a number of Slavic and Wallachian monks, and together they founded the St Elijah's Hermitage in 1757 under the Christ Pantocrator Monastery.

While on Athos, he studied the works of the church fathers and translated several from Greek into Ukrainian and Rumanian. Although most of these works remained in manuscript, some were published in the 19th century, including his translation of the ascetic work *Dobrotoliubie* (The Love of Goodness, 1793); prologues, translations, and comments on various lives of saints; and his autobiography (English trans, by J. Featherstone, *The Life of Paisij Velyčkovs'kyi*, 1989).

In 1763 the Moldavian hospodar invited Velychkovsky to reform monastic life in Moldavia. Together with 64 other monks, he left Athos and settled in the monastery in Dragomirna (in Bukovyna). From there he and 350 monks moved to the Secul Monastery in 1775. Finally, in 1779, Velychkovsky moved to the most important Moldavian monastery, in Neamţ, where he was made archimandrite in 1790. He reorganized Moldavian monastic life, stress-ing asceticism, poverty, communal living, and intellectual work. His translation into Slavonic of the *Philocalia* revived the Hesychast tradition throughout Moldavia, Ukraine, and Russia, and under his leadership the Neamţ Monastery emerged as an important center for Slavonic theology and philosophy.

Velychkovsky stands as one of the major figures of Orthodox spirituality in the 18th century, and he is considered to be the father of the Orthodox monastic revival. His labors and example influenced generations of clergy, both monastic and secular, as well as laity, throughout the 19th and 20th centuries. He was canonized by the Russian Orthodox church in June 1988 on the occasion of the millennium of the Baptism of Rus'.

BIBLIOGRAPHY
*Zhitie i pisaniia moldavskogo startsa Paiisiia Velichkovskogo* (Moscow 1892)
Ilarion (Ohiienko, I.). *Starets' Païsii Velychkovs'kyi* (Winnipeg 1975)
Metrophanes. *Blessed Paisius Velichkovsky* (Platina, Calif 1976)
Chetverikov, S. *Starets Paisii Velichkovskii: His Life, Teachings, and Influence on Orthodox Monasticism* (Belmont, Mass 1980)
Tachios, A.E. *The Revival of Byzantine Mysticism among Slavs and Romanians in the XVIIIth Century: Texts Relating to the Life and Activity of Paisy Velichkovsky (1722–1794)* (Thessalonica 1986)
A. Zhukovsky

**Velychkovsky, Vasyl** [Velyčkovs'kyj, Vasyl'], b 1 June 1903 in Stanyslaviv (now Ivano-Frankivske), d 30 June 1973 in Winnipeg. Redemptorist priest and bishop of the underground Ukrainian Catholic church. He took monastic vows, was ordained (1925), and served as a missionary priest in Volhynia (1925–35) before being named hegumen in Stanyslaviv. When the Soviet authorities liquidated the Ukrainian Catholic church after the war, he was arrested for refusing to convert to Russian Orthodoxy and sentenced to 10 years' hard labor in the gulag. After he was released in 1955, he lived under KGB surveillance. In 1959 he was secretly consecrated bishop of Lutske by Y. Slipy in Moscow. In 1968 he was again arrested and sentenced to three years of strict-regime imprisonment in the Donetske region. Upon his release in 1972, he was permitted to emigrate to his family in Yugoslavia. From there he moved to Rome and then Canada. Velychkovsky is the subject of a biography by S. Bakhtalovsky (1975).

**Velyhorsky, Ivan** [Velyhors'kyj], b 9 June 1889 in Serafyntsi, Horodenka county, Galicia, d 21 July 1955 in Toronto. Linguist and pedagogue; member of the Shevchenko Scientific Society (NTSh). He studied at Vienna University (1910–14; PH D, 1923) and from 1921 taught in gymnasiums in Chortkiv, Stanyslaviv, and Yavoriv. In the 1930s he published articles on Serafyntsi's Pokutian dialect and family names, V. Stefanyk's and M. Cheremshyna's use of the Pokutian dialect, children's vocabulary, and diminutive and augmentative words in *Ridna mova* (Warsaw). In 1949 he emigrated to Canada from Germany. He was secretary of the NTSh in Canada, contributed articles on the etymology of first names to *Ukraïns'kyi robitnyk* (1951), and wrote the brochure *The Term and Name 'Canada'* (1955).

**Velyka Bahachka** [Velyka Bahačka]. IV-14. A town smt (1988 pop 5,700) on the Psol River and a raion center in Poltava oblast. It arose at the beginning of the 17th century and was called Bahachka until 1925. In 1649 it became a company center of Myrhorod regiment. In the 19th century it was a village in Myrhorod county, Poltava gubernia. In 1925 the town was made a raion center. Today it is an agricultural town with a mixed-feed factory and a flour mill.

**Velyka Blyznytsia.** A Scythian burial ground of the late 4th to early 3rd century BC located on the Taman Peninsula. It was excavated in 1863–6 and 1883–5. The site appears to have been the burial plot of a wealthy family that adhered to the cult of Demeter.

**Velyka Homilsha fortified settlement.** A Scythian fortress settlement of the 5th to 3rd century BC near Velyka Homilsha, Hotvald raion, Kharkiv oblast. Excavated in 1949 by S. *Semenov-Zuser and in 1967–8 by B. *Shramko, the settlement covers an area of 7 ha and was surrounded by a thick wall and trenches. Remains of handmade pottery, milling devices, bronze arrowheads, and Greek amphoras were found at the site. A burial ground, where researchers excavated 10 Scythian kurhans, was located near the settlement.

**Velyka Kamianka River** [Velyka Kam'janka]. A right-bank tributary of the Donets River. It is 100 km long and drains a basin area of 1,810 sq km. The river is situated in southern Luhanske oblast and a short stretch of Rostov (RF) oblast and is used for water supply. It passes through the city of Krasnodon.

**Velyka Lepetykha** [Velyka Lepetyxa]. VI-14. A town smt (1988 pop 10,800) on the Kakhivka Reservoir and a raion center in Kherson oblast. It was founded by a French landowner in 1792, and developed into a farming and trading center. In the 19th century it belonged to Mariiupil county, Tavriia gubernia. Today it is a river port with a grain elevator and a creamery.

**Velyka Mykhailivka** [Velyka Myxajlivka]. VI-10. A town smt (1988 pop 6,000) on the Kuchurhan River and a raion center in Odessa oblast. It was founded at the end of the 18th century and was called Hrosulove (Grosulove) until 1945. Today it is an agricultural town with a number of food-processing enterprises.

**Velyka Novosilka.** VI-17. A town smt (1988 pop 7,800) on the Mokri Yaly River and a raion center in Donetske oblast. It was founded in 1779 and was called Velykyi Yanysol until 1946. In 1965 it was granted smt status. It is a farming town with a dairy, a bakery, and a canning factory.

**Velyka Oleksandrivka.** VI-14. A town smt (1988 pop 7,800) on the Inhulets River and a raion center in Kherson oblast. It was founded in 1784 and was called Novooleksandrivka for a few decades. In the 19th century it was part of Kherson county, Kherson gubernia. Today it has a canning factory, winery, and vegetable-oil factory.

**Velyka Pysarivka.** III-16. A town smt (1988 pop 5,900) on the Vorskla River and a raion center in Sumy oblast. The village of Pysarivka arose in 1709 and is first mentioned in a historical document of 1732 as Velyka Pysarivka. In the second half of the 18th century the village

provided care for blind bandura players. In the 19th century it belonged to Bohodukhiv county, Kharkiv gubernia. Because of poor soil many inhabitants engaged in the trades. In 1959 the village was given smt status. It is an agricultural town with a starch and a mixed-feed factory and a branch of the Okhtyrka creamery.

**Velyka Rika River.** See Rika River.

**Velyka Vys River** [Velyka Vys']. A river that flows for 166 km through Kirovohrad oblast and along the border of Cherkasy oblast before converging with the Hnylyi Tikych to form the Syniukha River. It drains a basin area of 2,860 sq km. The city of Novomyrhorod is situated on it.

Dmytro Velykanovych

**Velykanovych, Dmytro** [Velykanovyč], b 1886, d ? Educator and civic and political leader in Galicia. A gymnasium teacher, he organized Ukrainian teachers' associations and was active in the Ukrainian Teachers' Mutual Aid Society. In the 1930s he was a member of the Central Committee of the Ukrainian National Democratic Alliance (UNDO). From 1928 to 1939 he served as an UNDO deputy to the Polish Sejm and secretary of the Ukrainian Parliamentary Representation. In 1940 he was arrested and deported by the Soviets. He died in a prison camp.

***Velyke zertsalo*** (The Great Mirror). The title of a manuscript collection of 273 tales, apocrypha, legends, religious and historical teachings, anecdotes, and other texts that circulated among preachers (eg, I. Galiatovsky, A. Radyvylovsky) in Ukraine in the mid-17th century. It was a translation of selections from the Polish *Wielkie żwierciadło przykładów* (Cracow 1621 and 1633), which itself was a translation of the Latin *Speculum exemplorum*, published in the Netherlands in 1481 and revised by J. Meyer as *Speculum Magnum exemplorum* (1605). The tales were used to reinforce the church's teachings and morality, and several became part of Ukrainian oral literature.

**Velyki Mosty.** III-5. A city (1989 pop 6,500) on the Rata River in Sokal raion, Lviv oblast. It was first mentioned, as Mosty or Mostky, in historical documents in 1472. In 1559 it was granted the rights of *Magdeburg law and was renamed. After the partition of Poland in 1772, it was transferred to Austria. It was restored to Poland only in the interwar period. In 1939 it was incorporated into the Ukrainian SSR and in 1940 it was granted city status. Today it has a haberdashery factory and a brick plant.

The iconostatis inside the Church of the Transfiguration in Velyki Sorochyntsi

**Velyki Sorochyntsi** [Velyki Soročynci]. III-14. A village (1967 pop 5,300) on the Psol River in Myrhorod raion, Poltava oblast. It was first mentioned in historical documents in the 1720s. The village boasts the baroque Church of the Transfiguration (built in 1732), with a wooden iconostasis, and a literary museum dedicated to N. Gogol, who was born in Velyki Sorochyntsi.

**Velykoanadol Forest Project** (Velykoanadol'skyi lisovyi masyv). A man-made forest complex situated approx 50 km from Donetske. The project was started in 1843 by V. Graff, a recent graduate of the St Petersburg Forestry Institute, as a research center dealing with steppe afforestation. Graff worked there until 1866 before moving to teach elsewhere. The project was established as a scientific research center in 1893 in conjunction with V. Dokuchaev's research into drought prevention. Its organizer and first director was Yu. Vysotsky. The center's purpose was to create and study a variety of forests in a steppe environment. Research has continued at the site to the present day. The site now has a total area of 2,920 ha, of which 2,200 ha are forested.

**Velykodolynske** [Velykodolyns'ke]. VII-11. A town smt (1988 pop 8,700) in Ovidiopil raion, Odessa oblast. It was founded in 1803 and was known as Velyka Akarzha until 1944. Its factories make reinforced-concrete products and structures and ceramic products.

**Velykodolynske archeological site.** An upper Paleolithic camping ground near Velykodolynske, Ovidiopil raion, Odessa oblast. Excavations in 1959 and 1961 by P. Boryskovsky recovered nearly 19,000 flint pieces and the bones of wild animals which served to provide a valuable body of data concerning the prehistory of this region.

Protoarchimandrite Atanasii Velyky

**Velyky, Atanasii** [Velykyj, Atanasij] (Welykyj, Athanasius G.), b 5 November 1911 in Turynka, Zhovkva county, Galicia, d 24 December 1982 in Rome. Churchman and historian; member of the Shevchenko Scientific Society from 1953. He studied philosophy and theology in Krystynopil (1938–40) and at the Ukrainian Free University in Prague (PH D, 1944) and the Gregorian University in Rome (TH D, 1948). He also studied the history of the Eastern church at the Pontifical Oriental Institute (1946–8) and paleology at the Vatican. He joined the Basilian monastic order in 1933, and was ordained in 1946. He was vice-rector (1948–53 and 1955–60) and prorector (1961–3) of St Josaphat's Ukrainian Pontifical College in Rome. From 1960 to 1965 Velyky served as president of the Ukrainian Theological Scholarly Society and secretary of the Vatican's Preconciliar and Conciliar Commission on the Eastern Churches. Thanks to his efforts the commission adopted a resolution on the need for establishing a Kievan patriarchate. He was superior general (1963–76) and then consultant general of the Basilian order. He was also a consultant to the Congregation for Eastern Churches and the Commission for the Revision of the Canon Law of the Roman and Eastern Churches. He headed the Bible commission of the Basilian order that prepared the first Ukrainian translation of the Bible from the original languages.

In 1949 Velyky revived and expanded *Analecta Ordinis S. Basilii Magni*. He published a number of important documentary collections: *Actae S. Congregationis de Propaganda Fide, 1622–1862* (5 vols, 1953–5), *Documenta Pontificum Romanorum Historiam Ucrainae Illustrantia, 1075–1953* (2 vols, 1953–4), *Litterae S. Congregationis de Propaganda Fide, 1622–1862* (7 vols, 1954–7), *Epistolae Metropolitarum Kioviensium Catholicorum, 1613–1839* (9 vols, 1956–80), *Litterae Nuntiorum Apostolicorum, 1550–1900* (14 vols, 1959–77), *Documenta Unionis Berestensis eiusque Auctorum, 1590–1600* (1970), *Litterae Episcoporum, 1600–1900* (5 vols, 1972–81), and *Litterae Basilianorum, 1601–1760* (2 vols, 1979). He established the series Ukrainska dukhovna biblioteka (The Ukrainian Spiritual Library), which published over 70 titles, 17 of which he wrote. His book on religious persecution in Ukraine, *Bila knyha* (The White Book, 1952), was translated into German, English, and Spanish. He also wrote a history of the Sisters Servants of Mary Immaculate (1968), *Svitla i tini* (Lights and Shadows, 1969), *Ukraïns'ke khrystyianstvo* (Ukrainian Christianity, 1969), and *Z litopysu khrystyians'koï Ukraïny* (From the Chronicle of Christian Ukraine, 9 vols, 1968–77). He contributed many entries to *Entsyklopediia ukraïnoznavstva* and *Encyclopedia of Ukraine* and drafted the missive from the Ukrainian Catholic hierarchy on the anniversary of St Olha and the official statement issued by the Ukrainian bishops regarding the release from Siberia of Metropolitan Y. Slipy.

I. Patrylo

**Velykyi Bereznyi** [Velykyj Bereznyj]. V-3. A town smt (1988 pop 6,600) on the Uzh River and a raion center in Transcarpathia oblast. It was first mentioned in historical documents in 1427, when it was under Hungarian rule. At the end of the 17th century the village was annexed by Austria, and in the interwar period it belonged to Czechoslovakia. In 1945 it was transferred from Hungary to the Ukrainian SSR. The town manufactures kitchen furniture and canned foods and bottles mineral water. It has a fine park, planted in the 19th century.

**Velykyi Burluk** [Velykyj Burluk]. III-18. A town smt (1988 pop 4,600) on the Velykyi Burluk River and a raion center in Kharkiv oblast. It was mentioned in historical documents in the 1670s. Today it is an agricultural town with a cheese factory and bakery. The village church built in the 1830s has been preserved.

**Velykyi Burluk River** [Velykyj Burluk]. A left-bank tributary of the Donets River that flows for 93 km through Kharkiv oblast and drains a basin area of 1,130 sq km. The river has its source along the southern slopes of the Central Upland. Parts of it are used for water supply.

**Velykyi Bychkiv** [Velykyj Byčkiv]. VI-5. A town smt (1988 pop 9,200) on the Tysa River in Rakhiv raion, Transcarpathia oblast. It was mentioned in historical documents at the end of the 14th century. In the interwar period it was an active center of the Ukrainian nationalist movement in Transcarpathia. Under Soviet rule it was promoted to smt status (1947). Today it is an industrial town with a wood-chemicals manufacturing complex (est 1868), forest-products manufacturing complex, canning factory, and handicrafts factory.

**Velykyi Dil** [Velykyj Dil]. V–4. A Volcanic Carpathian mountain group located between the Liatorytsia and the Borzhava rivers in Transcarpathia oblast. The highest peak in the group is Mt Buzhora (1,085 m). The slopes of the mountains in the group are covered with beech forests and are sparsely populated. In contrast, the lowland area surrounding the group is heavily populated and is an active center of viticulture.

**Velykyi Kuialnyk River** [Velykyj Kujal'nyk]. A river that flows for 150 km through Odessa oblast before emptying into the Kuialnyk Estuary on the Black Sea coast. It drains a basin area of 1,860 sq km. Sections of the river commonly dry out during summers of low precipitation and leave behind a series of individual ponds.

**Velykyi Luh.** The floodplains of the Dnieper River south of Khortytsia Island. They were covered with forests, meadows, and marshes and were used by the Zaporozhian Cossacks in the 16th to 18th centuries as a refuge and hunting ground. In folk songs the region was called *batko* (father), and symbolized security and freedom.

**Velykyi Utliuk River** [Velykyj Utljuk]. A river that flows for 83 km through southwestern Zaporizhia oblast before emptying into the Utliuk Estuary along the Sea of Azov coast. It drains a basin area of 810 sq km. The river is used in part for industry. Sections of it tend to dry out seasonally.

**Velykyi Yanysol.** See Velyka Novosilka.

**Vendzylovych, Myron** [Vendzylovyč], b 26 August 1919 in Solynka, Lisko county, Galicia. Architect. A graduate of the Lviv Polytechnical Institute (1949), he has designed many buildings in Lviv, including the physics complex at Lviv University (1967), the computing center (1968), the Dynamo sports complex (1970), and the Institute of Applied and Decorative Arts (1972).

**Venedi.** Numerous tribes that occupied the territory between the Oder and the Vistula rivers in the first centuries AD and then moved along the Buh and the Sian rivers into the Dniester River region. The Venedi are mentioned by the ancient historians Pliny the Elder, Tacitus, Ptolemy, and Jordanus. Copying German archeologists, some historians in the past incorrectly called them Vandals. Most Slavic archeologists, including the Ukrainians Ya. Pasternak and M. Smishko, considered the Venedi to be ancestors of the West Slavs and identified them with members of the Przeworsk culture. Other scholars (including Soviet ones) took 'Venedi' to be the primordial name of the Slavs who inhabited the forest-steppe belt and Polisia between the Dnieper River and the Carpathian Mountains, as well as the southern part of Poland to the Oder River, at the beginning of the millennium.

**Venedyktov, Lev,** b 6 October 1924 in Tambov, Russia. Choir conductor. In 1949 he graduated from the Kiev Conservatory and after a decade joined its faculty. From 1941 he worked as a conductor with army ensembles at the front and the Red Flag Song and Dance Ensemble of the Kiev Military District, and in 1953–86 as chief choirmaster of the Kiev Theater of Opera and Ballet. In 1986–91 he was the theater's director. He took part in such operas as H. Maiboroda's *Yaroslav the Wise*, D. Shostakovich's *Katerina Izmailova*, P. Tchaikovsky's *Queen of Spades* and *Eugene Onegin*, and M. Mussorgsky's *Boris Godunov*.

**Venelin, Yurii** (nom de plume of Heorhii Hutsa), b 3 April 1802 in Velyka Tybava, Transcarpathia, d 7 April 1839 in Moscow. Slavist; member of Moscow University's Society of Russian History and Antiquities from 1833. An early Transcarpathian *Russophile, he studied at the Uzhhorod gymnasium and theological seminary and at Lviv University (1822–3). After emigrating illegally to Russian-ruled Bessarabia in 1823, he worked there as a teacher at the Kishinev seminary until 1825 and researched the folkways of the Bulgarian colonists. Having found a patron in I. *Orlai, he studied medicine at Moscow University (1825–9). One of the 'spiritual fathers' of the Russian

Yurii Venelin

*Slavophiles, he also collected Ukrainian folk songs and corresponded with the Ukrainian scholars M. Maksymovych and I. Sreznevsky. Six of his articles were published in I. Svientsitsky's 1906 book of materials on the history of the Transcarpathian Ruthenian revival. T. Baitsura's Ukrainian-language monograph about Venelin was published in Bratislava in 1968.

**Venereal diseases.** The name given to a group of contagious diseases spread through sexual intercourse, including *syphilis, gonorrhea, lymphogranuloma venereum, chankroid, and AIDS (Ukrainian: SNID – *syndrom nabutoho imunodefitsytu*). The stigma and shame associated with sexually transmitted diseases makes them hard to acknowledge, treat, or eradicate. As with most infectious diseases, they are most virulent in times of physical and economic hardship. In Ukraine wars, mobilization of armies, and population migration (eg, the industrialization of the Donbas) have all served to increase the incidence of venereal diseases.

In Western Ukraine under Austro-Hungarian rule, medical dispensaries were organized to deal with venereal diseases. At the end of the 19th century 2 percent of the Hutsul region population was registered as infected with syphilis. In Russian-ruled Ukraine there were no specific medical institutions to deal with the overall question of venereal diseases before 1917, and aid was given on a small scale in general medical institutions. The first *polyclinic specifically for the treatment of venereal and dermatological diseases was founded in Odessa in 1917. Also at that time medical institutes, societies, scientific research centers, medical dispensaries, and venereological stations were established in Kharkiv, Kiev, and smaller towns and villages throughout the country, particularly in the Donbas. By 1927 there were 80 venereological dispensaries for the urban and 125 for the rural population. Research is still conducted at the Kharkiv *Scientific Research Institute of Dermatology and Venereology (est 1924 on the basis of an existing polyclinic), which publishes the collection *Dermatologiia i venerologiia*.

The Ministry of Health in the Ukrainian SSR had the legal right to force those infected with venereal diseases into treatment and hospitalization, to register all cases of venereal disease, to follow up with inquiries into the family life of the infected, and to bring to justice those who knowingly spread venereal diseases (up to five years' detention, one year's hard labor, or a strict fine). A sharp increase in reported cases (a fraction of the estimated total), mainly among teenagers, young adults, and homosexuals, has

been noted in recent years. The cases of acute and chronic gonorrhea in the Ukrainian SSR per 100,000 population numbered 99.5 (148 in the USSR) in 1980, 82.7 (113) in 1985, and 73.5 (86.3) in 1987.

The Soviet Union was slow to acknowledge the presence of AIDS victims within its borders. The USSR Ministry of Health in early 1990 admitted that 28 patients had contracted AIDS, and that 19 of them had died. The number of HIV carriers was recorded at 457, of whom more than 200 were children. It was estimated that by 1992 the number of HIV carriers would be 24,000. The Soviet Union imposed mandatory testing for the AIDS virus on African (sometimes all) foreign students and all visitors staying longer than three months, and reserved the right to demand that they leave the country. The puritanical stance of the USSR and the state of its *public health system made it difficult to educate the public at large, particularly teenagers, about the dangers of AIDS. In Odessa a Prophylactic Center against AIDS was opened in October 1991.

P. Dzul

Ukrainian-Venezuelan members of the Plast and SUM Ukrainian youth associations at a public meeting to commemorate Gen Roman Shukhevych

**Venezuela.** A country in South America (1990 pop 19,405,429), with an area of 912,050 sq km. Caracas is the capital. There were few Ukrainians in Venezuela prior to the Second World War. Between 1947 and 1950 approx 3,400 Ukrainians arrived from displaced persons' camps in Europe; they were joined by a small number of Ukrainians from Czechoslovakia, Yugoslavia, France, and Colombia. Many of the displaced persons quickly departed to North America and left the number of Ukrainians in Venezuela (including the native-born) at an estimated 1,500 in 1968. Of this number, 800 resided in Caracas, and a total of approx 350 in the cities of Valencia, Puerto Caballo, and Maracay. The remainder are dispersed elsewhere. Still further departures had reduced the community in the whole of Venezuela to approx 800 by 1987. No municipalities bear Ukrainian names, although there are two streets in the Alta Vista and Los Magallanes districts of Caracas which (from 1950) bear the name 'Ucrania.' All Ukrainians in Venezuela are naturalized citizens.

Ukrainians in Venezuela are predominantly urbanized (90 per cent). Many had tried settling on the land, but unaccustomed to farming in tropical conditions, most of them soon moved to the cities. In the late 1960s about 40

Ukrainian-Venezuelan 'Cossacks' during carnival festivities in Caracas

percent of the Ukrainians were unskilled and semiskilled laborers; another 35 percent were engaged as merchants, artisans, and entrepreneurs; 15 percent were in the liberal arts professions; and 10 percent were farmers and rural laborers. The majority were home owners.

The *Ukrainian Hromada (Spanish: Asociación de Ucranianos en Venezuela) was established in 1948 and obtained state approval as a nonpolitical organization and as the legal representative body for Ukrainians in Venezuela. The hromada maintained branches outside Caracas in Valencia, Maracay, and Barquisimeto. Its headquarters are situated in the organization's own Ukrainian People's Home in Caracas. The following groups have also been active in Venezuela: the Federation of Ukrainian Women, the Society of Ukrainian Youth, the Plast Ukrainian Youth Association, the Ukrainian Youth Association (SUM), the Society of Ukrainian Engineers, the Association of Ukrainian Veterans, the Chornomortsi Sports Society, the Committee for the Liberation of Ukraine, and the Prosvita reading club. Ukrainian-language programs have been broadcast in Caracas.

Ukrainian Catholics constitute (1980) approx 58 percent of the Ukrainian community in Venezuela. The remainder are Orthodox (approx 38 percent) and Protestant. Both the Catholics and the Orthodox founded their parishes in 1948. The Ukrainian Autocephalous Orthodox church has two churches, one in Caracas and one in Valencia.

The Ukrainian community in Venezuela, particularly in Caracas and Valencia, has a fairly high level of identity retention, although the number of Ukrainians not fluent in the Ukrainian language is considerable. Some of the more noted Ukrainians who lived in Venezuela were P. Horsky, O. Halchenko, V. Krychevsky, H. Mazepa, K. Belsky, V. Yemets, L. Martyniuk, and K. Koliankivska.

BIBLIOGRAPHY
Panchyshyn, O. *Ukraïntsi u Venesueli* (Chicago–Caracas 1988)
S. Cipko

**Venglovsky, Ivan** [Vengl'ovs'kyj], b 1884, d ? Lawyer and civic and educational activist in Bibrka county, Galicia. He was a member of the Central Committee of the Ukrainian National Democratic Alliance. In 1939 he was deported by the Soviets. He disappeared in the labor camps.

**Venhlovsky, Yurii** [Venhlovs'kyj, Jurij] (Wenhlowsky, Yuriy), b 4 December 1921 in Berteshiv, Bibrka county, Galicia. After emigrating to Australia in 1949, he became a church and OUN activist. He was the founder of the Prosvita firm in Melbourne as well as manager, writer, and editor of the weekly *Tserkva i zhyttia*.

**Venhlovsky, Yurii, Jr** [Venhlovs'kyj, Jurij] (Wenhlowsky, Juri), b 1945 in Ulm, Germany. Diplomat; son of Yu. *Venhlovsky. He moved to Australia in 1949 and became an officer (lt-col) in the Australian army after graduating from cadet school. He saw service in Vietnam (1968–70) and was awarded the Military Cross. He later graduated from the military academy and rose to the rank of adjutant general at army headquarters. In 1987 he was appointed defense attaché to Korea and Australia, UN national senior adviser, and Commonwealth Alliance officer.

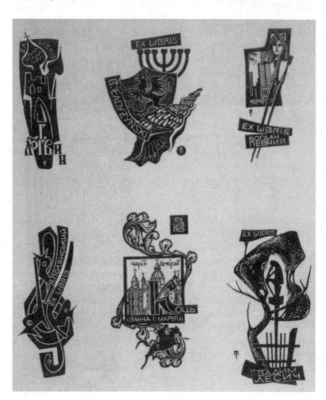

Bookplate designs by Tyrs Venhrynovych

**Venhrynovych, Tyrs** [Venhrynovyč] (Wenhrynowycz), b 21 September 1924 in Drohobych, Galicia. Graphic artist and painter of Ukrainian origin in postwar Poland. Since graduating from the Cracow Academy of Fine Arts (1952) he has directed the drawing department of the Institute of the History of Material Culture of the Polish Academy of Sciences in Cracow and devoted his free time to art. As a member of the Union of Polish Artists he has had over 50 solo exhibitions in Poland and has also exhibited in Edmonton, New York City (1986), Brockport, New York (1987), and Lviv (1989). A master of line, wood, metal, and plaster engraving, he has illustrated books and created many prints and over 500 bookplates. A series of 120 prints depicts Lemko and Boiko churches. As a painter he has done mostly landscapes, particularly of the Lemko region and Cracow, but also genre paintings and icons.

**Vepr River** (Polish: Wieprz). A right-bank tributary of the Vistula River. It is 234 km long and drains a basin area of 10,422 sq km. The upper reaches of the river flow through the southern part of the Kholm region.

**Verba, Antin.** See Serednytsky, Antin.

**Verba, Prokip,** b 7 July 1919 in Tokarivka, Kharkiv county, Kharkiv gubernia, d 20 July 1988 in Kharkiv. Economist; corresponding member of the AN URSR (now ANU) from 1972. A graduate of the Kharkiv Financial-Economic Institute (1941) and the Leningrad Financial Academy (1952), he worked in the Kharkiv branch of the State Bank (1945–50), the Kharkiv oblast Higher Party School, the Kharkiv branch of the Odessa Credit-Economic Institute, and finally, Kharkiv University, where he held the chair of finance and credit (1966–88). He wrote or coauthored monographs and many articles on finance, economic management, and administration, including *Rentabel'nost' promyshlennogo predpriiatiia i puti ee povysheniia* (The Profitability of the Industrial Enterprise and Ways to Increase It, 1967) and *Effektivnost' i kachestvo* (Efficiency and Quality, 1977).

**Verbytsky, Andrii** [Verbyc'kyj, Andrij], b 1788, d 27 April 1859. Scholar and litterateur. A professor at Kharkiv University (1816–39), from 1811 to 1829 he published, in Russian, the first almanacs in Ukraine, a handbook subtitled 'Ukrainian Notes' (1821), and the daily newspaper *Khar'kovskie izvestiia* (1817–18). He wrote textbooks on Russian literature and grammar and Latin versification.

Mykhailo Verbytsky

**Verbytsky, Mykhailo** [Verbyc'kyj, Myxajlo], b 1815 in Uliuch, Sianik circle, Galicia, d 7 December 1870 in Mlyny, Yavoriv county, Galicia. Composer, conductor, and Catholic priest. Typical of the semiprofessional composers in 19th-century Galicia, he studied in the Peremyshl Cathedral Music School with A. Nanke and later took private lessons with F. Lorenz. He is best known for composing the Ukrainian national anthem *Shche ne vmerla Ukraïna* (Ukraine Has Not Yet Perished, to a text by P. Chubynsky). His other significant contributions consist of church music for mixed and male choir; music for 18 plays, operettas, and vaudevilles; a number of overtures and polonaises for orchestra; and choral music to texts by T. Shevchenko, I. Hushalevych, Yu. Fedkovych, and M. Shashkevych.

**Verbytsky, Mykola** [Verbyc'kyj] (pseuds: Mykolaichyk Bilokopyty, M. Antiokhov, Chernihovets Ya., Tsybulka), b 13 February 1843 in Chernihiv, d 10 December 1909 in Chernihiv. Writer, publicist, and teacher. He studied at the universities of Kiev (1859–60, 1861–4) and St Petersburg (1860–1). In 1863 he took part in an underground satirical journal, *Pomyinytsia*. He then taught in gymnasiums in Poltava (1864–5) and Chernihiv (1865–74). While in Chernihiv he was active in the Hromada of Kiev, edited the Chernihiv zemstvo miscellany, was a town councillor, and published feuilletons in *Kievskii telegraf*, *Nedelia*, and the local press. His first few Ukrainian poems, written in the style of T. Shevchenko, and a story appeared in 1862 in *Osnova* and *Chernigovskii listok*. From 1904 he published a few poems in *Literaturno-naukovyi vistnyk* and Ukrainian literary almanacs and miscellanies.

**Verbytsky, Oleksander** [Verbyc'kyj], b 27 September 1875 in Sevastopil, Crimea, d 9 November 1958 in Kiev. Architect; full member of the USSR Academy of Architecture. A graduate of the St Petersburg Institute of Civil Engineers (1898), he moved to Kiev, where he worked as an architect for the Southwestern Railway (1901–33). He designed railway stations, depots, warehouses, hospitals, many country villas, and some apartment buildings in Kiev in the Moderne style. He helped set up the Kiev Architectural Institute in 1918 and taught there (1918–24) and at the Kiev State Art Institute (1924–30, 1937–53) and Kiev Civil-Engineering Institute (1930–7). He also designed the large hotel in what is now Khmelnytsky Square in Kiev, a bridge across the Volga in Gorkii (with Ye. Paton), the Kiev Railway Station (built in 1927–33), a grain elevator in Odessa, a sugar refinery in Verkhniachka, and a paper factory in Malyna. He enjoyed painting and produced many oils and watercolors. A book about Verbytsky by S. Kokhan and S. Kilesso was published in Kiev in 1966.

**Verbytsky, Tymofii** [Verbyc'kyj, Tymofij], b ?, d ca 1642. Early printer. He probably worked at K. Stavrovetsky's itinerant press in Pochaiv and Rokhmaniv in Volhynia (1618–19) before joining the Kievan Cave Monastery Press (1621–4). In 1624 he established his own press in Kiev with the assistance of Metropolitan Y. Boretsky and printed a Horologion (1625, 1626) and a Psalter (1628), and the first primer printed in Kiev. From ca 1635 he ran the press in Câmpulung, which had been given to the Wallachian hospodar M. Basarab by Metropolitan P. Mohyla, and printed a Sacramentarion there.

**Verekundova, Nataliia,** b 13 May 1908 in Pavlovskoe, Voronezh gubernia, Russia, d 10 February 1987 in Kiev. Ballerina. She completed study at the Leningrad Choreography School (1926) and then was the leading soloist in the Kiev Theater of Opera and Ballet and, from 1949, its ballet master. From 1946 she taught in the Kiev Choreography School.

**Veres, Roman.** See Weres, Roman.

**Veresaev, Vikentii** [Veresajev, Vikentij] (pen name of Smidovich, Vikentii), b 16 January 1867 in Tula, Russia, d 3 June 1945 in Moscow. Russian writer. In the years 1890–2 he worked as a physician in Yuzivka (now Donetske) and wrote a book of sketches about the miners there

(1892). Later he edited the Russian edition of *Pesni Tarasa Shevchenka* (The Songs of Taras Shevchenko, 1911) and the important collection *Gogol' v zhizni* ([N.] Gogol in [His] Life, 1933). His autobiographical *Zapiski vracha* (A Doctor's Notes, 1901) appeared in a Ukrainian translation in Lviv in 1903 and in Kharkiv in 1929. A Ukrainian edition of his selected works (2 vols) was published in Kiev in 1956.

Ostap Veresai

**Veresai, Ostap** [Veresaj], b 1803 in Kaliuzhyntsi, Pryluka county, Poltava gubernia, d April 1890 in Sokyryntsi, Pryluka county, Poltava gubernia. Kobza player and singer (tenor). A peasant who became blind in his early youth, he studied from 1818 with S. Koshovy and other kobzars. By the 1860s he was the most renowned performer of Ukrainian epic and historic songs. In 1873 he appeared in recital for the Southwestern Branch of the Imperial Russian Geographic Society and in 1875 concertized in St Petersburg. His repertoire included the dumas *Kinless Fedir, Three Brothers from Azov,* and *Oleksii Popovych.* Veresai's artistry was studied by ethnographers such as O. Rusov and P. Chubynsky, as well as by M. Lysenko, who wrote a monograph on the works in Veresai's repertoire (1873, 1978).

**Vereshchagin, Leonid** [Vereščagin], b 29 April 1909 in Kherson, d 20 February 1977 in Moscow. Physicist; full member of the USSR Academy of Sciences from 1966. A graduate of the Odessa Institute of People's Education (1928), he worked at the Ukrainian Physical-Technical Institute in Kharkiv (1934–9) and the Institute of Organic Chemistry of the USSR Academy of Sciences in Moscow (1939–54), and directed the academy's High Pressures Laboratory (from 1954) and its Institute of High-Pressure Physics (from 1958). His chief publications deal with the physics of superhigh pressures and the methods of measuring physical properties under high pressures. Under his supervision the first synthetic diamonds in the USSR were produced in 1960. An edition of his selected works was published in Moscow in 1982.

**Vereshchahin, Fedir** [Vereščahin], b 30 May 1910 in Mykolaiv, Kherson gubernia. Stage director. He completed study at the Kiev Institute of Theater Arts (1941) and during the war worked in the theater of the 21st Red Army at the front. Then he worked in the Kirovohrad Ukrainian Music and Drama Theater (1944–5), in the Izmail Ukrainian Music and Drama Theater (1945–8), and, as artistic and administrative director, in the Vinnytsia Ukrainian Music and Drama Theater (1948–86).

**Vereshchak, Vadym** [Vereščak], b 6 May 1914 in Pryluka, Poltava gubernia. Film and television cameraman. He completed study at the State Institute of Cinema Arts in Moscow (1947) and worked in the Riga Artistic Film Studio (1947–53, pupil of E. Tisse) and then in the Kiev Artistic Film Studio, notably on the film production of O. Korniichuk's *Zahybel' eskadry* (The Destruction of the Squadron, 1966).

**Vereshchynsky, Yosyf** [Vereščyns'kyj, Josef] (Wereszczyński, Józef), b 1530? in Zbarazh, d 1 February 1599. Roman Catholic bishop of Kiev. An aide to the Orthodox bishop of Kholm, he converted to Roman Catholicism and became (1581) abbot of a Benedictine monastery in Poland and later (1589) the Catholic bishop of Kiev. The author of theological and satirical works, he was particularly renowned for tracts urging war against the Turks and Tatars and supporting Polish colonization of the steppe.

**Vereshchytsia River** [Vereščycia]. A left-bank tributary of the Dniester River that flows southward for 91 km through Lviv oblast and drains a basin area of 955 sq km. The river has small weirs constructed at intervals for almost its entire length. The town of Horodok is situated along it.

**Veretenchenko, Oleksa** [Veretenčenko], b 25 October 1918 in Bilyi Kolodiaz, Vovchanske county, Kharkiv gubernia, d 15 March 1993 in Detroit. Poet. From 1925 he lived in Kharkiv, where he studied at the Kharkiv Pedagogical Institute. A postwar refugee, since 1949 he has lived in Detroit. He began publishing in 1935 and is the author of the poetry collections *Pershyi hrim* (First Thunder, 1941), *Dym vichnosty* (The Smoke of Eternity, 1951), and *Zamors'ki vyna* (Overseas Wines, 1974) and the historical narrative poem *Chorna dolyna* (The Black Valley, 1953). He also translated G. Byron's *Mazeppa* into Ukrainian (1959) and edited the first posthumous edition of V. Svidzinsky's poetry (1975).

**Vergennes, Charles de,** b 28 December 1717 in Dijon, France, d 13 February 1787 in Versailles. French diplomat. He financially sponsored the émigré supporters of Hetman I. Mazepa. His friend H. Orlyk recommended him for the position of French ambassador to Constantinople (1754–68). There de Vergennes played a role in Turkey's protest against the formation of New Serbia in Ukraine (1753) and its declaration of war on Russia (1768).

**Verhanovsky, Volodymyr** [Verhanovs'kyj], b 7 March 1876 in Lukavytsia Vyzhnia, Stryi county, Galicia, d 26 November 1946 in Pramer, Austria. Jurist and law scholar; from 1914 full member of the Shevchenko Scientific Society. After graduating in law from Lviv University (LLD, 1900) he conducted research in Berlin and Vienna and in

1908 began lecturing on Austrian civil law at Lviv University. In the interwar period he was a professor and dean of the law faculty at the Lviv (Underground) Ukrainian University (1921–3) and, from 1929, a member of the highest court of appeal in Galicia. He taught law at Lviv University (1939–41). His publications include *Pro pobichnu interventsiiu* (On Lateral Intervention, 1903) and *Zmina pozovu* (Altering the Summons, 1912).

Rev Petro Verhun while in Soviet exile

**Verhun, Petro,** b 18 November 1890 in Horodok, Galicia, d 7 February 1957 in Angar, Krasnoiarsk krai, RSFSR. Ukrainian Catholic priest. He studied theology in Prague and completed a D TH at the Ukrainian Free University (1926) before being ordained in 1927 in Lviv. That year he moved to Berlin to serve as pastor for Ukrainian Catholics throughout Germany, and in 1940 he became apostolic visitator there. For many years the only Ukrainian Catholic priest in Germany, he was an active preacher, published religious pamphlets, and issued a newsletter. Verhun was arrested by the Soviets in June 1945 and exiled to Siberia, where he was imprisoned until 1955. A biography, by P. Romanyshyn, was published in 1988.

**Verkhatsky, Mykhailo** [Verxac'kyj, Myxajlo], b 17 May 1904 in Lokhvytsia, Poltava gubernia, d 16 February 1973 in Kiev. Stage director, pedagogue, and theatrical historian. He completed study at the Kharkiv Music and Drama Institute (1930, pupil of L. Kurbas) and then worked in Berezil (1926–33, from 1929 as assistant director), Veselyi Proletar, and the Kharkiv Young Spectator's Theater (1934–41) and taught in the Kharkiv (1930–3), Tashkent (1945–52), and Kiev (1952–72) institutes of Theater Arts.

**Verkhivsky, Oleksander** [Verxivs'kyj], b 1827 in the Chernihiv region, d 1882. Church historian and biblical scholar. He served as a regimental physician and devoted his spare time to historical and biblical studies. He compiled (but did not complete) a dictionary of biblical history (5 vols, 1871–6) and a dictionary of church history (1881–). He knew 12 ancient and modern languages.

**Verkhivtseve** [Verxivceve]. V-15. A city (1989 pop 11,700) in Verkhnodniprovske raion, Dnipropetrovske oblast. It was founded in 1884 as a railway station on the Donbas–Kryvyi Rih and the Katerynoslav–Dolynska lines. Until 1904 the settlement was called Liubomyrivka. In 1956 its was granted city status. Most of its enterprises belong to the railway industry, and many of its residents work in Dniprodzerzhynske.

**Verkhnia Lypytsia settlement.** A settlement of the 1st to 2nd century near Verkhnia Lypytsia, Rohatyn raion, Ivano-Frankivske oblast. Excavations in 1960–4 uncovered the remains of eight pit and semi-pit dwellings with hearths and storage pits. Other artifacts found included pottery, tableware, iron knives, and Roman coins.

**Verkhnia Tersa River** [Verxnja Tersa]. A left-bank tributary of the Vovcha River that flows for 107 km through Zaporizhia and Dnipropetrovske oblasts and drains a basin area of 1,680 sq km. The river is 15–20 km wide and has a valley 1.5–2.5 km wide. It is used for water supply and irrigation (although it becomes very shallow in the summer).

**Verkhnii Rohachyk** [Verxnij Rohačyk]. VI-15. A town smt (1988 pop 7,300) and a raion center in Kherson oblast. It was founded in 1786 and granted smt status in 1967. It is an agricultural town with a mixed-feed factory and a creamery.

**Verkhnii Saltiv.** A village in Vovchanske raion, Kharkiv oblast, where Alan catacomb tombs of the 6th to 9th century were discovered. They were excavated in 1904–20 and in 1946. Virtually every tomb had three or four people buried in it with a variety of grave goods, including pottery vessels, iron swords, battle axes, knives, and jewelry.

**Verkhnodniprovske** [Verxn'odniprovs'ke]. V-15. A city (1989 pop 23,900) on the Dniprodzerzhynske Reservoir and a raion center in Dnipropetrovske oblast. It was established by the Zaporozhian Cossacks in the 17th century as a winter settlement. By 1780 it had developed into the village of Hryhorivka, which in 1785 was renamed Novohryhorivka, and in 1806, Verkhnodniprovske. In 1956 it was granted city status. Today the city is an industrial center with a cast-iron foundry, automobile repair plant, paper factory, and dairy.

**Verkhnodniprovske Mining and Metallurgical Complex** (Verkhnodniprovskyi hirnycho-metalurhiinyi kombinat). An enterprise of the metallurgical industry, located in Vilnohirske, Dnipropetrovske oblast. Construction of the first upgrading plant began in 1956 and was completed in 1961. A second plant was opened in 1968. The complex processes zirconium, rutile, and ilmenite concentrates, zirconium dioxide, and other metals and alloys. The primary source of raw materials is a local deposit of titanic sand.

**Verkhovyna** [Verxovyna]. A common designation for the highland region of the Middle-Carpathian Depression in the upper reaches of the Stryi, the Opir, the Liatorytsia, and the Velyka Rika river basins. The Verkhovyna area is inhabited by the Boikos, although local people also refer to themselves as *verkhovyntsi*, or Highlanders. A number of popular Ukrainian folk songs praise the Verkhovyna region and its natural beauty.

**Verkhovyna** [Verxovyna]. V-5. A town smt (1988 pop 5,800) on the Chornyi Cheremosh River and a raion center in Ivano-Frankivske oblast. Known as Zhabie until 1962, it was first mentioned in historical documents in 1424. Until 1772 it was under Polish rule, and subsequently under

A view of Verkhovyna

Austrian and Polish (1919–39) rule. After the Second World War it became part of the Ukrainian SSR. In 1962 the village was granted smt status. It has a forest-products manufacturing complex and a mineral-water bottling plant.

**Verkhovyna Regional Studies Museum.** See Stryi Regional Studies Museum.

**Verkhovyna Subcarpathian Song and Dance Ensemble** (Prykarpatskyi ansambl pisni i tantsiu Verkhovyna). A professional performing collective founded in Drohobych in 1946. The ensemble consists of a chorus, dance troupe, and folk orchestra. It collects and performs folk music of the Subcarpathian region as well as contemporary works of Soviet Ukrainian composers. Its artistic directors have been O. Korchynsky (1946–70), O. Volynets (1970–81), and M. Duda (since 1983).

Vasyl Verkhovynets          Ivan Verkhratsky

**Verkhovynets, Vasyl** [Verxovynec', Vasyl'] (pseud of Vasyl Kostiv), b 5 January 1880 in Staryi Mizun, Dolyna county, Galicia, d 11 April 1938 in Kiev. Composer, ethnographer, conductor, folklorist, and teacher. He taught singing at the Poltava Pedagogical Institute and the Lysenko Music and Drama Institute in Kiev and chaired the Department of Fine Art at the Poltava Institute of People's Education (1919–32). Verkhovynets is the author of the first Ukrainian ethnochoreographic textbooks, *Ukraïns'ki narodni tantsi* (Ukrainian Folk Dances, 1913) and *Teoriia*

*ukraïns'koho narodnoho tanka* (Theory of the Ukrainian Folk Dance, 1919; four later edns). His collection *Vesnianochka* (Spring Song, 1925) includes descriptions of 210 children's games with 226 songs and melodies. He wrote numerous popular songs and choral works based on Lesia Ukrainka's, I. Franko's, M. Rylsky's, and his own poems. He also arranged many folk songs, dance tunes, and theater pieces. In 1912 he wrote a detailed account of a traditional wedding in Shpychyntsi village, Skvyra county, Kiev gubernia, which included 140 wedding songs and 70 melodies. The wedding was staged that year in the Sadovsky Theater, and an account was published with historical notes in 1914.

**Verkhovynka, Lesia** [Verxovynka, Lesja] (pseud of Yaroslava Kuchkovska, née Lahodynska), b 3 March 1903 in Diliatyn, Nadvirna county, Galicia, d 21 February 1936 in Diliatyn. Writer. Her poems and stories appeared in *Moloda Ukraïna*, *Novi shliakhy*, *Nova khata*, *Svit dytyny*, and other Galician periodicals. She also wrote a cycle of stories about Hutsul life, among them *Stare lykho* (Old Evil, 1923) and *Nevistka* (Daughter-in-law, 1929); plays for children, such as 'Imenyny Vlodka' (Vlodko's Name Day); and a number of autobiographical stories, such as 'Kazka mynulykh lit' (A Story of Bygone Years, 1923) and 'Probudzhennia' (Awakening, 1930).

**Verkhovynsky, Andrii.** See Voloshyn, Avhustyn.

**Verkhrata** [Verxrata]. A village on the Rata River in the Roztochia Upland, now in Lublin voivodeship, Poland. It was the site of a Basilian monastery (1678–1806), which was known for its miracle-working icon of the Holy Theotokos. With the closing of the monastery, the icon was transferred in 1810 to Krekhiv.

**Verkhratsky, Ivan** [Verxrats'kyj] (pseuds: Ivan Chaika, Liubart Horovsky, Losun, Petro Pravdoliub, Liubart Spivomyr, Ivan Shchypavka), b 26 April 1846 in Bilche Zolote, Borshchiv county, Galicia, d 29 November 1919 in Lviv. Natural scientist and philologist; full (and later honorary) member of the Shevchenko Scientific Society (NTSh) from 1899 and the first chairman of its Mathematical–Natural Science–Medical Section. He studied at Lviv University (1865–8) and in Cracow (1874), worked as a Realschule and gymnasium teacher in Drohobych (1868–71), Lviv (1871–9, 1891–1908), and Stanyslaviv (1879–90), and founded the natural science cabinet at the Academic Gymnasium in Lviv and the NTSh Ethnographic Museum. He specialized in the flora and fauna, especially insects, of Galicia. He wrote numerous works, including the first Ukrainian high-school textbooks in zoology (1895, 1906) and botany (1905); the first Latin-German-Ukrainian dictionary of natural science nomenclature and terms (7 fascicles, 1864–1908); materials for a Ukrainian dictionary (1877); a register of vernacular botanical terms and nomenclature (1892); materials on mineralogical terminology (*Zbirnyk Matematychno-pryrodnycho-likars'koï sektsiï NTSh*, vol 13 [1909]); pioneering studies of the Maramureş (1883), Sian (1894, 1900), Transcarpathian (1901), Lemko (1902), Bukovynian (1908), and Dniester (1912) dialects; and liberal-populist polemical articles criticizing the Galician Russophiles and their use of the *yazychiie. His attempts at classifying and determining the etymologies of the dialects were dilettantish, but his descriptions of them and data about their lexicon remain an important empirical source. In the 1870s Verkhratsky also wrote poetry and translated Polish verse into Ukrainian, and in 1880 he published the Stanyslaviv literary-scholarly newspaper *Dennytsia*, in which he included his own poems, stories, and articles under various cryptonyms.

R. Senkus

Boris Verkin     Ivan Vernadsky

**Verkin, Boris,** b 8 August 1919 in Kharkiv, d 12 June 1990 in Kharkiv. Low-temperature physicist; AN URSR (now ANU) full member from 1972. A graduate of Kharkiv University (1940), he joined the ANU Physical-Technical Institute in Kharkiv and served as its director in 1960–88. There in 1949 he discovered, with B. *Lazarev, quantum oscillations of magnetic susceptibility. He initiated the establishment of the ANU Physical-Technical Institute of Low Temperatures in Kharkiv in 1960 and was its director until 1988. Cryogenic instrumentation and superconducting magnets, in the development of which Verkin actively participated, have played an important role in low-temperature materials science and in cryomedicine.

**Verlan,** b and d ? 18th-century haidamaka leader. A captain of manorial Cossacks in the service of Prince Lubomirski in the Sharhorod district, he emerged as a leading figure in the uprising which engulfed most of Podilia early in 1734. By the summer the rebel forces, organized in a regiment, had taken Brody, Zhvanets, and Kremianets and were advancing on Kamianets-Podilskyi and Lviv. A large Polish force then quelled the rebellion. Verlan and a number of his supporters fled to Moldavia; his subsequent fate is unknown.

**Vermenych, Andrii** [Vermenyč, Andrij], b 4 July 1897 in Hradyzke, Kremenchuk county, Poltava gubernia, d 20 September 1979 in Dnipropetrovske. Stage actor and singer (baritone). He began his career in D. Haidamaka's troupe (1916) and worked in various Ukrainian touring troupes until 1930. Then he was an actor in the Donbas Theater of Musical Comedy. In 1934 he completed study at the Moscow Theater Institute (by correspondence) and joined the Dnipropetrovske Ukrainian Music and Drama Theater.

**Vermenych, Volodymyr** [Vermenyč], b 3 August 1925 in Borysy, Kremenchuk okruha, d 11 December 1986 in

Kiev. Composer, conductor, and teacher. A graduate of the conducting (1954) and composition (1970) faculties at the Kiev State Conservatory in the class of M. Dremliuha, he taught singing and led school choruses in Kiev (1952–60) and lectured at the Kiev Pedagogical Institute (1963–5) before devoting himself exclusively to composing. His works include the cantata for chorus and orchestra *Song about the Stormy Petrel* (1970); choruses to texts by I. Nekhoda, L. Tatarenko, and A. Kaspruk; and solo songs to texts by M. Synhaivsky, V. Korotych, and others.

**Verna, Petro,** b 5 January 1877 in Hora, Pereiaslav county, Poltava gubernia, d 3 April 1966 in Hora. Wood carver. He carved portraits of T. Shevchenko (1912) and I. Kotliarevsky (1950) and compositions inspired by the works of N. Gogol (*Taras Bulba with Sons* [1913]), Shevchenko (*Perebendia* [1947], *My 13th Year Was Coming to an End* [1947]), and Kotliarevsky (*The Aeneid* [1948]). K. Promenetsky's book about him was published in 1958.

**Vernadsky, George** [Vernads'kyj, Jurij], b 20 August 1897 in St Petersburg, d 12 June 1972 in New Haven, Connecticut. Historian; son of V. *Vernadsky. He studied in Moscow and St Petersburg. Having emigrated to the United States via Prague (1926–7), he joined the history department at Yale University and was a full professor there in 1946–56. He was instrumental in developing the university's Slavic holdings and gained renown as one of the foremost English-language Russian historians. His major achievement was the five-volume *History of Russia*, which included *Ancient Russia* (1943), *Kievan Russia* (1948), *The Mongols and Russia* (1953), *Russia at the Dawn of the Modern Age* (1959), and *The Tsardom of Moscow* (1967). Although of Ukrainian descent and well versed in Ukrainian history, he integrated the history of the Ukrainians into his general scheme of Russian history. His most Ukrainophile work was a biography of Hetman B. Khmelnytsky, *Bohdan, Hetman of Ukraine* (1941). A festschrift in his honor was published in 1964.

**Vernadsky, Ivan** [Vernads'kyj], 24 May 1821 in Kiev, d 27 March 1884 in St Petersburg. Economist; father of V. *Vernadsky. He studied philosophy and Slavic philology at Kiev University and political economy at St Petersburg University. He taught at Kiev University and completed his PH D dissertation on the Italian school of political economy at Moscow University (1849). He taught political economy at Moscow University (1851–6), served as an adviser to the Ministry of Internal Affairs in St Petersburg (1857–67), and was director of the Kharkiv branch of the State Bank (1868–76). He published and edited the weekly paper *Ekonomicheskii ukazatel'* (later *Ukazatel' politiko-ekonomicheskii: Statisticheskii i promyshlennyi zhurnal*, 1857–61) and a supplement (1859–61) devoted specifically to economic topics, which became a separate, but irregularly published, journal titled *Ekonomist* (1861–5).

As an economist Vernadsky was interested in a variety of problems, including the history of economic thought, methodology, theoretical and practical statistics, international trade, and agriculture. His many publications include *Ocherk teorii potrebnostei* (An Outline of the Theory of Needs, 1857), *Istoricheskii ocherk prakticheskoi statistiki* (A Historical Survey of Practical Statistics, nd), *Politicheskoe ravnovesie v Anglii* (Political Balance in England, 1855), *Ocherk istorii politicheskoi ekonomii* (An Outline of the History of Political Economy, 1858), and *O mene i torgovle* (On Barter and Trade, 1865). Vernadsky also wrote many publicistic articles on economic, social, and political topics. He argued for the complete emancipation of the peasants and the introduction of individual, capitalist farming and advocated a laissez-faire approach to all economic issues.

Volodymyr Vernadsky

**Vernadsky, Volodymyr** (Vladimir) [Vernads'kyj], b 12 March 1863 in St Petersburg, d 6 January 1945 in Moscow. Pioneering geochemist, mineralogist, and crystallographer, philosopher of science, political activist, and politician; full member of the Russian (later USSR) Academy of Sciences from 1912, the VUAN from 1918, and the Czechoslovak and Yugoslav academies of sciences from 1926, corresponding member of the French Academy of Sciences from 1928, and member of the Ukrainian Scientific Society in Kiev, the Poltava Prosvita society, the Shevchenko Scientific Society, and the Volhynian Scientific Society; son of I. *Vernadsky and father of G. *Vernadsky. After graduating from St Petersburg University (1885) he did graduate work there and in Munich and Paris (1888–9) and was elected president (1886) of the United Council of Regional Student Organizations in the Russian Empire. He taught at Moscow University (1891–1911; professor from 1898) and was a member of the Russian State Council (1906–11). Vernadsky had close genealogical, personal, and intellectual links to Ukraine. From 1889 to 1918 he spent part of nearly every summer in Poltava gubernia. In 1890 he researched the soils of Kremenchuk county as a member of V. *Dokuchaev's soil-science expedition.

After the February Revolution of 1917 Vernadsky chaired the Agricultural Scholarly Committee of the Russian Ministry of Agriculture, returned to Moscow University as chairman of its department of mineralogy and geology, and was appointed (in August) the Russian deputy minister of education in charge of all universities and scientific institutions. After the Bolshevik coup he fled to Ukraine. In 1918, at the behest of M. Vasylenko and the Hetman government, he headed the group of Ukrainian scholars that drafted the detailed project for founding the UAN. In 1918–19 he served as the first UAN president, organized the UAN chemical laboratory and Commission for the Study of Ukraine's Natural Productive Forces, was active in the geological and agricultural scholarly committees of Ukraine, and lectured at Kiev University. Although he was a liberal supporter of the idea of 'Russian' unity

and a vocal opponent of the Bolsheviks, Whites, and the UNR Directory, he resigned from the Russian Constitutional Democratic party because of the Russian chauvinism of its Ukrainian wing. In 1919, while visiting Rostov, he was unable to return to Ukraine and ended up in the White-controlled Crimea, where he was a professor and rector of Tavriia University in Symferopil in 1920.

In 1921 Vernadsky returned to Petrograd and organized the Radium Institute there. In 1922 he went to Paris to work with M. Curie and lecture at the Sorbonne. In 1926 he returned to Russia, and from 1928 until his death he directed the USSR academy's Radium Institute and Laboratory for Geochemical Problems, the precursor of the Institute of Geochemistry and Analytical Chemistry (est 1947), in Leningrad. Under Soviet rule Vernadsky was a spokesman for preserving the academy's autonomy and for freedom of thought and travel. In the 1930s he headed the academy's new commissions on the Permafrost and Heavy Water, began the building of the first Soviet cyclotron, and oversaw the development of Soviet radiogeology and biochemistry. In 1940 he cofounded the academy's Uranium Commission and was elected its vice-chairman.

Vernadsky's ideas became the core of new directions in geology, mineralogy, and hydrogeology, and he is regarded as the founder of Soviet geochemistry and biogeochemistry. He wrote extensively about philosophical issues in science, popularized the concepts of the biosphere and noosphere, and developed radiogeological and radiochemical concepts. Vernadsky's scholarly works include books of lectures on crystallography (1894) and mineralogy (1908), a classic study on the fundamentals of crystallography (1904), an unfinished descriptive mineralogy of the Russian Empire (vol 1, pts 2 [1909], 4–5 [1912, 1914], vol 2, pt 1 (1918]), two volumes of studies and speeches (1922), a history of the minerals of the earth's core (4 vols, 1923, 1927, 1933–4), the pioneering *La Géochemie* (1924) and *La Biosphère* (1929), and a book of biochemical studies conducted in 1922–32 (1940). The summation of his life's work, a monograph on the chemical structure of the earth's biosphere and its surroundings, was published in censored form in 1965, 20 years after his death. Also censored were his 'thoughts of a naturalist' on space and time in nature and on scientific thought (2 vols, 1975).

Vernadsky has been a very popular figure in Russia and Ukraine, particularly since the 1960s. Many books and articles about him have appeared, as have posthumous Russian editions of his collected works (5 vols, 1954–5, 1959–60), selected works (1959), collected works on biogeochemistry (1967), the history of science (1981), and crystallography (1988), and writings on the history of science in Russia (1988). A Ukrainian edition of his selected works was published in Kiev in 1969.

BIBLIOGRAPHY
Balandin, R. *Vladimir Vernadsky* (Moscow 1982) [in English]
Shcherbak, N. *Vladimir Ivanovich Vernadskii*, 2nd rev edn (Kiev 1988)
Sytnik, K.; Apanovich, E.; Stoiko, S. *V.I. Vernadskii: Zhizn' i deiatel'nost' na Ukraine*, 2nd rev edn (Kiev 1988)
Bailes, K.E. *Science and Russian Culture in an Age of Revolutions: V.I. Vernadsky and His Scientific School, 1863–1945* (Bloomington and Indianapolis 1990)

S. Trofimenko

**Vernydub.** A mythical character in Ukrainian folktales. Vernydub (literally, 'oak uprooter') is a giant who can uproot mighty oaks and use them as weapons or roadblocks. He often appears with other heroic figures, such as Vernyhora ('Mountain Mover'), Lomykhashcha ('Bush Thrasher'), Misyzalizo ('Iron Kneader'), Tovchykamin ('Stone Crusher'), and Valybuk ('Beech Breaker').

**Vernyhora.** A mythical figure in Ukrainian folktales. Vernyhora is a giant who can level mountains with a push of his shoulder. He usually appears in the role of the protagonist's ally and helps him to free his fiancée or to defeat a dragon or a witch. Vernyhora is also the name of a legendary figure in the historical novels of Polish writers of the Ukrainian school (M. Czajkowski, J. Słowacki, S. Wyspiański, and others), in which he is depicted as a peasant seer of the 18th century who foresaw the future of Poland and Ukraine.

**Vernyhora.** A publishing house founded by P. *Kashynsky in 1916 in Kiev. By the end of 1917 it had issued some 30 publications: popular books and pamphlets on Ukrainian history and culture, a school grammar, fables, poetry, stories, political pamphlets, a map of Ukraine, placards, and translations of D. Defoe's *Robinson Crusoe*, Molière's *Tartuffe*, and F. Nietzsche's *Thus Spoke Zarathustra*. It continued operating in Kiev until 1921. A branch of Vernyhora functioned in Vienna from 1918 to 1923. Kashynsky renewed the press in Munich in 1946 and published a few more works there until 1948 (eg, M. Dolnytsky's geography of Ukraine, I. Krypiakevych's history of Ukraine, and M. Terletsky's histories of the Middle Ages and the modern world).

**Vernyvolia.** See Konysky, Oleksander and Simovych, Vasyl.

**Veronica.** See Speedwell.

Hryhorii Verovka

**Verovka, Hryhorii** [Ver'ovka, Hryhorij], b 25 December 1895 in Berezna, Chernihiv county, Chernihiv gubernia, d 21 October 1964 in Kiev. Composer, conductor, and pedagogue. He began his musical studies at the Chernihiv seminary, learned composition theory from B. Yavorsky (1918–21), and graduated from the Kiev Conservatory (1933). He taught at the Lysenko Music and Drama Institute (1923–7) and the Kiev Conservatory (1931–64). Verovka achieved his renown as artistic director and principal conductor of the Ukrainian (later *Verovka) State Chorus, from 1943 until his death. In 1948–52 he also headed the

*Union of Composers of Ukraine. His works include the cantatas *Tam na hori za Dniprom* (There, on the Hill beyond the Dnieper, 1924), *To ne viter* (It Is Not the Wind, 1941), and *Ne spochyvaite* (Do Not Rest, 1956); chamber music; pieces for folk orchestra; choruses; songs; and arrangements of Ukrainian folk songs.

The Verovka State Chorus

**Verovka State Chorus** (Derzhavnyi akademichnyi ukrainskyi narodnyi khor im. H. Verovky). A professional performing collective founded as the Ukrainian State Choir in Kharkiv in 1943 and based in Kiev since 1944. The ensemble consists of a mixed chorus, dance troupe, and folk orchestra. Its repertoire includes traditional and recent Ukrainian folk songs, works of contemporary Ukrainian composers, and classical music, and its style is based on a refined form of traditional Ukrainian folk harmonizations. The ensemble is the largest collective of its kind in Ukraine and the most influential in artistic terms. Notwithstanding a routine amount of propaganda in its performances, during the Soviet period the ensemble fostered traditional forms of music-making and supported Ukrainian folk artists, such as N. *Matviienko, V. Martynenko, I. Melnychenko, P. Pavliuchenko, N. Tsiupa, and V. Boiko. The chorus has made numerous recordings on the Melodiya label and has concertized throughout the former USSR and abroad. Its artistic directors have been H. *Verovka (1943–64), E. *Skrypchynska (1964–6), and A. *Avdiievsky (since 1966). The group was named after Verovka in 1964.

**Versailles, Treaty of.** The treaty negotiated at the 1919 *Paris Peace Conference between the victorious Allied and Associated Powers and the new Polish and Czecho-Slovak republics on the one hand, and Germany on the other. It was signed at Versailles on 28 June 1919 and was in many respects identical to the Treaty of *Saint-Germain with Austria. The Treaty of Versailles went into effect on 10 January 1920. The Allied Powers reiterated their recognition of Poland's sovereignty and independence, its membership in the League of Nations, and its incorporation of portions of the former German Empire defined in the treaty with Germany. Persons habitually resident in Polish-occupied territories were recognized as Polish nationals, but they could abandon Polish nationality within two years after the coming into force of the treaty. Poland agreed to articles guaranteeing all of its citizens basic human, civil, and political rights and freedoms and providing its minorities (Germans, Ukrainians, Jews, Belarusians) with adequate facilities for the use of their language before the courts; with the right to use their own language and to exercise their religion in their own charitable, religious, and social institutions, schools, and other educational establishments; with public education facilities adequate for ensuring that in the primary schools instruction would be given to their children in their own language; and, in towns and districts where there was a considerable proportion of such minorities, with an equitable share of public funds for educational, religious, or charitable purposes. A separate article stated that the aforementioned stipulations constituted obligations of international concern and should be placed under the guarantee of the League of Nations, and that any dispute arising therefrom would be referred to the Permanent Court of International Justice. Chapter 2 of the treaty defined Poland's diplomatic and commercial relations with the Allied and Associated states and its adherence to existing telegraphic and radio-telegraphic, railway, sanitary, and other conventions.

R. Senkus

**Vershigora, Petr** [Veršigora, Pjotr], b 16 May 1905 in Severynivka, near Rybnytsia, Bessarabia, d 27 March 1963 in Moscow. Soviet Russian actor, military figure, and writer. He graduated from the Odessa Conservatory (1930) and worked as an actor. He became a director at the Kiev Artistic Film Studio in 1939. During the Second World War he was a Soviet partisan commander with the rank of major-general. He wrote three books of reminiscences about S. Kovpak's partisan forces in Western Ukraine.

**Versification.** Excluding folk poetry and recently discovered examples dating back to Kievan Rus', the first documentary evidence of versification in Ukraine dates from the late 16th century. It includes the poems in the Ostrih Bible (1581) and A. Rymsha's *Khronolohiia* (Chronology). In the early 17th century, verse began to develop rapidly. Initially, Ukrainian poetry consisted of syllabic verse, usually with 11, 12, or 13 syllables, with a caesura after the 6th or 7th. The rhyme scheme was predominantly contiguous and based on verbal endings. That pattern persisted until the late 18th century.

In the late 18th century (I. Kotliarevsky's period), syllabo-tonic verse appeared; it has been the dominant form in Ukrainian poetry since then. Iambic dimeter and tetrameter are the most common forms (Kotliarevsky wrote in the latter measure, as did T. Shevchenko in some works). Iambic unrhymed pentameter was also used (in Lesia Ukrainka's dramatic poems). The *Neoclassicist group of poets used Alexandrine iambic hexameter. Although less common, trisyllabic meter (dactyls, amphibrachs, anapests) is also used in Ukrainian poetry – dactylic hexameter with trochees, for example. M. Zerov used the last-named form, as well as combinations of pentameter and hexameter.

Polymetric forms with no set number of syllables in feet, or feet per line, have come to dominate modern poetry; they are known as *vers libre* or free verse. Such forms combine feet of varying lengths and often border on rhythmic prose (the early works of P. Tychyna provide an example). *Dolnyk*s (fixed stress lines – usually three) are also used. The stress remains constant per line of verse by singling out individual words regardless of the number of their constituent syllables (eg, in O. Vlyzko's works).

The use of strophes in Ukrainian poetry is rich and varied, although odd-numbered strophes are avoided because they are asymmetrical. Two-line strophes are very rare in modern poetry, as are three-line strophes, which are more often used in chain rhymes (*aba*, *bcb*, etc) and in

tercets of iambic pentameter (I. Franko, Yu. Klen, M. Orest). The most widely used strophe is the quatrain, which is the dominant form in folk songs. The most common rhyme schemes are the *abab* or *abcb* patterns (the latter is typical of folk songs and of some of Shevchenko's poetry). The five-line strophe occurs rarely but is used by Franko, Lesia Ukrainka, and most often, Tychyna. More common is the iambic pentameter or hexameter six-line strophe. Seven-line strophes are also rare but occur in Lesia Ukrainka's poetry. The eight-line strophe, or octave, occurs widely; in its canonic form it bears an *abababcc* rhyme scheme. That pattern appears in the work of P. Kulish, V. Samiilenko, Franko, the Neoclassicists, T. Osmachka, and others. Nine-line and 10-line strophes occur rarely, although Kotliarevsky's *Eneïda* (Aeneid) is written in a 10-line form (*ababccdeed*). The 20th century has seen the appearance of heterometric strophes, such as those in Tychyna's works. More infrequent are complex strophic (logaoedic) forms derived from ancient classical poetry, such as Alcaic, Asclepiadean, and Sapphic, which appear in the work of Zerov and Orest.

Poetic forms that appeared in medieval Romance poetry, such as the sonnet, triolet, rondelle, rondo, and sestina, were not represented in Ukrainian verse until much later. The first sonnets in Ukrainian poetry were written in the mid-19th century, and the form was subsequently developed by Franko, M. Cherniavsky, and succeeding generations of writers. In the 20th century the sonnet became common and was brought to a high level of sophistication by Zerov and M. Rylsky. Sonnetoids (sonnets with departures from the standard metrical arrangement and rhyme scheme) have also been written in Ukrainian (most recently by E. Andiievska). Sonnet cycles have been written by M. Zhuk, V. Bobynsky, O. Tarnavsky, and I. Kalynets. Triolets have been written by M. Drai-Khmara, Tychyna, M. Vorony, and D. Zahul; sestinas, by M. Zhuk and L. Mosendz.

In the early 1930s, versification went into decline as a result of pressures exerted on Ukrainian literature and culture in general. The efflorescence of poetic devices during the 1920s was denounced as a feature of formalism and suppressed in favor of the primitivistic mimicry of folk poetry as practiced by a younger generation of writers.

BIBLIOGRAPHY
Iakubs'kyi, B. *Nauka ukraïns'koho virshuvannia* (Kiev 1922)
Zahul, D. *Poetyka* (Kiev 1923)
Chaplia, V. *Sonet v ukraïns'kii poeziï* (Kharkiv 1930)
Hordyns'kyi, S. *Ukraïns'kyi virsh* (Munich 1947)
Koshelivets', I. *Narysy z teoriï literatury* (Munich 1954)
Kachurovs'kyi, I. *Strofika* (Munich 1967)
– *Narys komparatyvnoï metryky* (Munich 1985)
I. Koshelivets, D.H. Struk

**Versta.** See Weights and measures.

**Vertebny, Vadym** [Vertebnyj], b 11 September 1930 in Kiev. Nuclear physicist. A graduate of Kiev University (1952), in 1970 he joined the AN URSR (now ANU) Institute for Nuclear Research, where he has worked on cross sections of neutron-induced reactions and nuclear-reactor design and development. Since 1976 he has also been a professor at Kiev University.

A *vertep*

**Vertep.** A venerable form of Ukrainian *puppet theater, regarded as distinct from the Polish *szopka*, the Belarusian *betleika*, and the Russian *petrushka*. The origins of the name *vertep* may be related to the verb *vertitysia* 'to whirl,' as do rays about a star. The *vertep* performance is a standardized enactment of the Nativity with merry interludes depicting secular life, in the style of an *intermede. There are 10 to 40 *vertep* characters, typically among them a sacristan, angels, shepherds, Herod, three kings, Satan, Death, Russian soldiers, gypsies, a Pole, a Jew, a peasant couple, and various animals. All the hand puppets are usually operated by one person, the *vertepnyk*. The *vertep* is also the two-level stage in the form of a building in which the performance takes place, the religious part on the upper level and the secular part on the lower.

*Vertep* performances date back to the late 16th century. They reached their height in popularity in the second half of the 18th century. Many students from the Kievan Mohyla Academy contributed to the development of *vertep* puppet theater; its two-part performance was in part a reflection of the academy's style of theatrical productions. Itinerant precentors were also responsible for popularizing *vertepy*. In time the specifications as to *vertep* stage architecture; the number, character, and construction of the puppets; and costumes, music, and scripts became well defined. The foremost village *vertepy* were in Sokyryntsi, Baturyn, and Mezhyhiria. The secular part in *vertep* performances often contained references to contemporaneous events; a Zaporozhian Cossack puppet, for example, appeared during the reign of Catherine II.

*Vertep* theater declined in the mid-19th century. It has retained a symbolic significance, as in the miniature Nativity scene displayed in Ukrainian homes during the Christmas season and in the Christmas carolers dressed up as *vertep* characters. In the 20th century *vertep* theater

has been revived as a *zhyvyi* 'live' *vertep*, with live actors faithfully re-creating the traditional village *vertepy*, by, for example, L. Kurbas's Molodyi Teatr, the Lviv Ukrainian Drama (Zankovetska) Theater, the Avant-Garde Ukrainian Theater in Toronto, and the New Generation Theater in Cleveland.

BIBLIOGRAPHY
Markovs'kyi, Ie. *Ukraïns'kyi vertep: Rozvidky i teksty* (Kiev 1929)
Fedas, I. *Ukraïns'kyi narodnyi vertep* (Kiev 1987)

V. Revutsky

Dziga Vertov

Yevhen Vertyporokh

**Vertov, Dziga** (real name: Kaufman Denys), b 2 January 1896 in Białystok, Poland, d 12 February 1954 in Moscow. Film director and cinema theoretician. From 1926 he worked in the All-Ukrainian Photo-Cinema Administration, where he produced the films *Odynadtsiatyi* (The Eleventh, 1928) and *Liudyna z kinoaparatom* (Man with a Movie Camera, 1929) and his first sound movie, *Symfoniia Donbasu* (Symphony of the Donbas, 1930). He used split screens, multiple superimpositions, and variable speeds in an attempt to support his theoretical claim concerning the power of the camera eye – techniques which influenced international filmmakers. Accused of formalism in 1937, he subsequently worked mainly on Soviet documentaries and newsreels.

**Vertyporokh, Yevhen** [Vertyporox, Jevhen], b 17 April 1898 in Liashky Korolivski, Peremyshliany county, Galicia, d 12 January 1973 in Toronto. Organic chemist and community leader; full member of the Shevchenko Scientific Society (NTSh) from 1934. A graduate of the Danzig Polytechnic (1926; doctorate, 1929), he worked there in the department of organic chemistry and technology (1926–34), headed the Ukrainian Hromada in Danzig (1932–4), and was a department head in the largest Polish pharmaceutical company in Warsaw (1935–41). He chaired the general chemistry department of the Lviv Medical Institute and was dean of the Lviv Pharmaceutical Institute (1942–4). A postwar refugee, he was a professor of chemistry at the UNRRA University in Munich (1946–7) and dean of the pharmaceutical faculty at the Ukrainian Technical and Husbandry Institute there (1947–8). In 1948 he settled in Toronto, where he founded and was the long-term president of the NTSh in Canada (1949–73). In 1966 he was elected a fellow of the Chemical Institute of Canada.

**Verv.** A clan-territorial rural unit in ancient Ukraine, consisting of one or more villages and peasant homesteads. Smaller than a volost, the *verv* corresponded to the Polish *opole*, the Serbian *okolyna*, and the Novgorod-Muscovite *pogost*. Originally the *verv* might have been a clan unit, which developed on a territorial basis after the dissolution of the clan system and the advancement of civic relations over kinship relations. The *verv* also encompassed newcomers, foreigners, and tradesmen who lived on its territory. All its members were called *liudiie*.

The *verv* was governed by the *kopa* or *\*viche*. It was also an administrative entity and had a \*community court, whose members were bound by collective responsibility (see \*Hromada). If a crime was committed, the *verv* was responsible for conducting the investigation (*honyty slid*), and if it failed to find the culprit, the community assumed responsibility for the crime committed on its territory. The *verv* performed the duties of a tax collector for the prince and constituted a military defense unit. In the Christian period the *verv* became an administrative unit with its own church.

The main source of information about the *verv* is *Ruska-ia Pravda*, which includes 15 articles on the subject. Another source is the Polatsk Statute (15th–17th centuries). Among scholars K. Bestuzhev-Riumin and A. Yefymenko emphasize the clan character of the *verv*, and M. Vladimir-sky-Budanov, V. Sergeevich, and R. Lashchenko argue for its territorial-civic character.

V. Markus

**Vervain** (*Verbena*; Ukrainian: *verbena, telezniak*). Annual and perennial grasses and small shrubs with showy, phloxlike flowers in various shades of blue, purple, yellow, and white. Large-flowered plants are usually called verbenas. Medicinal or European vervain (*V. officinalis*) grows in Ukraine as a weed. It was used in folk medicine to treat a number of ailments, including kidney stones. Another native species is *V. supina*. *V. hybrida* is cultivated for decoration in parks and gardens.

Hryhorii Verves              Mykhailo Verykivsky

**Verves, Hryhorii,** b 15 April 1920 in Petrove, Oleksandriia county, Kherson gubernia. Slavist; AN URSR (now ANU) corresponding member since 1978. In 1942 he graduated from the Unified Ukrainian University in Kzyl Orda, Kazakhstan (see \*Kiev University), and in 1945 he began postgraduate studies at the Institute of Literature of the ANU. Subsequently he became a scholarly secretary, senior associate, and department head at the institute. He is a specialist on Ukraine's literary relations with the rest of the Slavic world, particularly with Poland, and has written many articles and books, on topics such as A. Mickiewicz in Ukrainian literature (1955), I. Franko and the question of Ukrainian-Polish literary and civic relations from the 1870s to 1890s (1957), the main problems in 19th-century Ukrainian-Polish literary relations (1958), J. Słowacki and Ukraine (1959), W. Orkan and Ukrainian literature (1962), T. Shevchenko and Poland (1964), the traditional and the innovative in 20th-century Slavic poetry (1968), M. Rylsky in the circle of Slavic poets (1972), Ukrainian literature in a general Slavic context (1978), J. Iwaszkiewicz (1978), Mickiewicz (1979), and Polish literature and Ukraine (1985). Editions of his literary essays have been published in Polish (1972) and Ukrainian (1976, 1983). Verves edited a book of essays on literary relations among the socialist countries (1980) and was chief editor of the Institute of Literature's edition of articles on Ukrainian literature in a general Slavic and world literary context (5 vols, 1987–).

R. Senkus

**Veryha, Vasyl,** b 3 January 1922 in Kolodribka, Zalishchyky county, Galicia. Librarian, community activist, and journalist; member of the Shevchenko Scientific Society. A veteran of the Division Galizien, he emigrated to Canada in 1951, where he worked as a librarian at the University of Toronto (1961–87). He has played an active role in Ukrainian community affairs, particularly in Ukrainian veterans' associations (co-editor of *Visti kombatanta* in 1965–74), and contributed to the Ukrainian press. He published an English-language booklet on the status of national languages in Soviet television broadcasts (1972), a monograph on the Galician Socialist Soviet Republic of 1920 (1986), and several books dealing with the history of the Division Galizien, including *Dorohamy druhoï svitovoï viiny* (Along the Roads of the Second World War, 1981) and *Pid sontsem Italiï* (Under the Sun of Italy, 1984). In 1988 he was elected secretary general of the World Congress of Free Ukrainians.

**Verykivsky, Mykhailo** [Verykivs'kyj, Myxajlo], b 20 November 1896 in Kremianets, Volhynia gubernia, d 14 June 1962 in Kiev. Composer, conductor, and teacher. He graduated from the Kiev Conservatory (1923) in the composition class of B. Yavorsky and then conducted the Kiev Opera (1926–8), the Kharkiv Opera (1928–35), and symphony orchestras in Kiev, Kharkiv, Moscow, and Ufa. He also taught at the Lysenko Music and Drama Institute and the Kiev Conservatory. His works include the ballet *Pan Kanovsky* (1930, 2nd edn 1953); the Shevchenko-based operas *The Captain* (1938) and *The Servant Girl* (1940; premiered 1943); operas to texts by L. Hlibov, M. Kotsiubynsky, and O. Vyshnia; an oratorio on Marusia Bohuslavka; five cantatas; a concerto for piano and orchestra (1950); a number of orchestral works; a large body of piano music; chamber and church music; original choral works and arrangements of Ukrainian folk songs for chorus; about 70 original solo songs and settings of Ukrainian folk songs for voice and piano; children's songs; and music for radio and films. N. Zhurova published a monograph about Verykivsky in 1972.

**Verzylov, Arkadii,** b 22 December 1867 in Kovchyn, Chernihiv county, Chernihiv gubernia, d ? Historian. A pupil of V. Antonovych, in the 1920s he taught at an agricultural tekhnikum in Chernihiv and did research at the historical-philological division of the VUAN. His scholarly publications include a study of trade in Ukraine in 1480–1569 (in *Zemskii sbornik Chernigovskoi gubernii*, 1898, nos. 1–4, and separately, 1899), a description of daily life in the medieval period in the Chernihiv region, and an account of the Chernihiv Hromada (both in *Chernihiv i pivnichne Livoberezhzhia*, 1928). His recollections about M. Kostomarov and V. Antonovych appeared in *Ukraïna* (1928, no. 6).

*Vesela bryhada* (Happy Brigade). A children's magazine published by the Communist Youth League of Ukraine and the People's Commissariat of Education, semimonthly in 1931–3 and then monthly to 1937 in Kharkiv. It contained materials on extracurricular activities and education. In August 1937 it was merged with *Pioneriia*.

**Vesele.** VI-15. A town smt (1988 pop 11,900) and raion center in Zaporizhia oblast. It sprang up in 1812 as a village of runaway serfs and army recruits. In 1957 it was granted smt status. The town has a powdered-milk factory, a grain elevator, a canning factory, and an asphalt plant.

**Veseli Bokovenky** [Veseli Bokoven'ky]. A dendrological park situated along the Bokovenka River valley in Dolynska raion, Kirovohrad oblast. Established in 1893 according to a design by the fresco painter I. *Padalka, the park initially consisted of 109 ha of landscaped area. In 1924 it was nationalized, and in 1962 a selection station for the Ukrainian Scientific Research Institute of Forest Management and Agroforest Amelioration was added to it and the park area thereby increased to 543 ha. Veseli Bokovenky contains over 960 species and varieties of local and imported trees and bushes, including rare specimens of mountain oak, yellow cypress, and yellow poplar.

**Veselka** (Rainbow). A publishing house of children's literature in Kiev. It was founded in 1934 as Dytvydav. It ceased functioning after the German invasion of 1941, renewed operations in 1956, and was renamed in 1964. Veselka has published books of prose, poetry, folktales, proverbs, science fiction, popular-educational literature, songs, and games for children and teenagers. These include anthologies and single-author editions of works by Soviet Ukrainian and Russian writers, reprints of Ukrainian and Russian classics, and anthologies and single-author editions translated from the literatures of the USSR (especially Russian) and other countries. Since 1976 Veselka has published an annual collection of articles about Ukrainian children's literature and writers, *Literatura, dity, chas* (Literature, Children, Time). In 1981–5 Veselka issued 1,230 titles with a combined pressrun of 206 million copies. A 631-page bibliography of the books it and Dytvydav published in the years 1934–84 appeared in Kiev in 1985.

*Veselka* (Rainbow). A literary monthly published in 1922–3 in the internment camp for veterans of the Army of the UNR in Kalisz, Poland. It contained literary contributions and articles on culture and the arts, primarily by internees in the camp. The journal was edited by a board

that included Ye. Malaniuk, M. Selehii, I. Zubenko, A. Korshnivsky, F. Krushynsky, and A. Padolyst. Writers associated with the journal also organized literary evenings, acting courses, and other events.

*Veselka* (Rainbow). A semimonthly for Ukrainian children in the Prešov region of Slovakia, published by the Czechoslovak Youth League. It first appeared in Russian in September 1951 as *Pionerskaia gazeta*. From 1953 it was published in Ukrainian as *Pioners'ka hazeta*, and since 1968 it has been called *Veselka*. Initially the magazine was published in Bratislava, but since 1965 it has appeared in Košice. Among its editors have been A. Konchok, Z. Hanudel, L. Starunska, V. Bodnar, and M. Bobak.

Various covers of *Veselka*

*Veselka* (Rainbow). A monthly children's magazine published in Jersey City, New Jersey, since September 1954 by the Ukrainian National Association. Edited by V. Barahura, B. Hoshovsky, R. Zavadovych, and other members of the Association of Ukrainian Writers for Young People, it contains fairy tales, stories, poems, games, puzzles, and songs. The magazine's subscriptions dropped from a high of approx 6,000 in 1954 to approx 1,000 in 1984.

**Veselovska, Zinaida** [Veselovs'ka, Zinajida], b 4 July 1900 in Kharkiv, d ? Linguist. After completing her graduate studies at the Kharkiv Institute of People's Education (1920s) she taught at Kharkiv University. She wrote articles on the language of H. Kvitka-Osnovianenko (1927), the language and stress in P. Berynda's lexicon (1927, 1929), Ukrainian and Russian vernacular terms used in hemp and flax cultivation (1929), and the grammar of workers' speech (1934) and was a coauthor of an advanced course book on the Ukrainian language edited by L. Bulakhovsky (1929). Her research in the 1950s and 1960s culminated in a monograph on stress in East Slavic languages from the late 16th to the early 18th century.

**Veselovsky, Aleksandr** [Veselovskij], b 16 February 1838 in Moscow, d 23 October 1906 in St Petersburg. Russian literary scholar and ethnographer; corresponding member from 1876 and full member from 1881 of the Russian Academy of Sciences. He graduated from Moscow University in 1859. He worked in Spain and studied in Berlin, Prague, and Italy before becoming a professor at St Petersburg University in 1872. In his writings on Slavic and world literature he combined the historical-cultural and comparative approaches. He analyzed many Rus' legends, literary monuments, and apocrypha in a European context and described the literary influence of the Byzantine Empire on medieval Europe as an intermediary between the West and the East. Using parallels in Slavic, Byzantine, and Western European sources, he produced a comparative structural analysis of the *bylyny* (Rus' epics) against the background of Ukrainian folklore and constructed a genre of 'Kievan *bylyny*' that had once existed in southern Rus'. Among his many works are books on Slavic tales about Solomon and Kitovras and the Western legends of Morolf and Merlin (1872, his PH D diss) and on the southern Rus' *bylyny* (1885), a series of investigations of Rus' spiritual poems, and reviews of ethnographic studies by V. Antonovych, M. Drahomanov, and P. Chubynsky. An edition of his collected works (vols 1–6, 8, 16, 1908–38), a book of his selected articles (1939), and his book on historical poetics (1940) were published posthumously. A bibliography of his works is found in a collection of articles published in his memory in Prague in 1921. Books about him have been written by B. Engelgardt (Petrograd 1924) and I. Gorsky (Moscow 1975).

R. Senkus

**Veselovsky, Nikolai** [Veselovskij, Nikolaj], b November 1848 in Moscow, d 12 April 1918 in St Petersburg. Russian archeologist. He graduated from St Petersburg University (1873) and taught there from 1890. Although a specialist in Oriental studies, he made some valuable archeological finds in Southern Ukraine, particularly the *Solokha kurhan and *Kamiana Mohyla. He posited that the numerous *stone *baby* in the region were Turkic in origin.

**Veselovsky, Roman** [Veselovs'kyj], b 1 February 1937 in Tashkent, Uzbekistan. Chemist. A graduate of the Kazan Chemical Technology Institute (1959), since 1959 he has worked at the AN URSR (now ANU) Institute of the Chemistry of Large-Molecule Bonds. In 1978 he became a department head. A specialist in adhesion phenomena in polymer systems, he developed the theory for new biodestructive polymers and created the technology to produce and apply them in medicine.

**Veselovsky, Serhii** [Veselovs'kyj, Serhij], b ca 1878 in Podilia, d ? Economist and politician. Before the Revolution of 1917 he graduated from the Kiev Polytechnical Institute. A member of the Revolutionary Ukrainian party and then the Ukrainian Social Democratic Workers' party, in 1917 he sat on both the Central and the Little Rada. In 1918 he was appointed consul in Petrograd by the Hetman government and then a professor of statistics at the new Ukrainian State University of Kiev. In the 1920s he headed the Agricultural Scientific Committee of Ukraine, taught at the Kiev Agricultural Institute (formerly a department of the Polytechnical Institute), and chaired the Department of Agricultural Economics. He was repressed during the Stalinist terror of the 1930s and fled to the West during the Second World War.

**Veselyi Lviv.** A theater of small forms, established in Lviv in 1942 under the artistic direction of playwright Z. *Tarnavsky. Its predecessors were the theaters Tsvirkun (1930–1) and Bohema (1933–4). Veselyi Lviv performed humorous and satirical sketches, monologues, songs, and dances with its own dance group, female quartet, and orchestra. It was active until 1944; its scope and style were revived by O. *Lysiak in the United States (1958–70).

**Veselynove.** VI-12. A town smt (1988 pop 7,400) on the Chychykliia River and a raion center in Mykolaiv oblast. It was founded at the end of the 18th century and named after its owners, the Veselynov family. In the 19th century the village belonged to Ananiv county, Kherson gubernia. In the second half of the century it was called Oleksandrivka. The town was granted smt status in 1960. Today it has a powdered-milk factory, a mixed-feed factory, and a hemp-processing mill.

**Veshniak, Fedir** [Vešnjak], b ?, d 1650. Cossack officer. A registered Cossack, he became colonel of Chyhyryn regiment at the beginning of the Cossack-Polish War in 1648. He was a trusted adviser to Hetman B. Khmelnytsky and wielded great influence in the military and organizational affairs of the Hetmanate. He carried out diplomatic missions for Khmelnytsky, including discussions in Warsaw in 1648 and Moscow in 1649, and was acting hetman on several occasions.

A painting depicting *vesnianky-hahilky* by Ivan Trush (oil, 1905)

**Vesnianky-hahilky** (also known in Galicia as *haïvky, iahilky, hahulky, halahilky, iaholoiky, maivky,* and *rohulky*). Ritual folk songs sung by girls in conjunction with ritual dances and games from early spring until the Feast of the Holy Trinity, particularly at Easter. In some regions they were sung only at Easter. They were performed in the village street, churchyard, cemetery, or pasture. Originally their purpose was to persuade the mysterious forces of nature to provide the people with a bountiful harvest and a happy life. The magical function of the songs was eventually forgotten, and they became entertainment.

The *vesnianky* season opened as a rule with a farewell to winter, which took place on Candlemas, the day marking the meeting of winter and summer and their strength, or at the first sighting of migratory birds. A straw or wooden image of winter called *Smert* (Death), *Mara* (Specter), or *Kostrub* (Slob) was burned or drowned to the singing of *vesnianky*, and then spring, sometimes personified by a girl in a flower and herb wreath, was welcomed with ritual dances, such as *Mosty* 'Bridges' and *Vorotar* 'Gatekeeper'. The dialogue, 'O beautiful spring, what have you brought us?' – 'I have brought you summer, a pink flower, winter wheat, and all sorts of fragrant things,' was sung. In some localities bird-shaped bread was baked and tossed by children into the air to represent birds in flight. Many *vesnianky* were addressed to birds, groves and woods, and trees and flowers, asking them to assist the coming of spring.

The oldest *vesnianky* are those associated with ritual portrayal of plant growth and farm work (*Mak* 'Poppy', *Proso* 'Millet', *Ohirochky* 'Cucumbers', *Khmil'* 'Hops', *Khrin* 'Horseradish', *Hrushka* 'Pear', *L'on* 'Flax') and the behavior of birds (*Horobchyk* 'Sparrow', *Soloveiko* 'Nightingale', *Husky* 'Geese', *Kachky* 'Ducks', *Kachuryk* 'Drake'), animals (*Vovk* 'Wolf', *Lysytsia* 'Fox', *Zaichyk* 'Bunny'), domestic animals (*Baran* 'Ram', *Kozel* 'Goat'), and insects (*Zhuk* 'Beetle'). Most of the *vesnianky* that have survived include motifs of courtship, the invitation to dance, female charms, true love, and the marriage proposal, but they also include mockery and satiric couplets about young men and women. These songs are of more recent origin. Sometimes they are accompanied a dance or game. Their purpose is to attract young suitors. These *vesnianky* are closely related to *wedding songs and *lyrical songs; they are a kind of prologue to forthcoming weddings. Many of them contain echoes of ancient family and social practices, such as the abduction and ransoming of girls, and the decisive role of the girl's mother in the setting up of the marriage. Some *vesnianky* contain references to the Princely era, mention of Dazhboh, images of Prince Roman, talk of tribute in honey, and battle accounts. The Cossack era is depicted in many songs about the wanderings of the peasant Cossacks, the campaigns, the Cossack's separation from his beloved, and various Cossack exploits. The genre reflects many historical periods and often deforms the concrete details. Some *vesnianky*, such as *Dunai, Vorotar*, and *Mosty*, originated in Western Europe and were brought to Ukraine. The songs are rich in imagery, associations, antitheses, similes, and especially psychological parallelism. The simple but moving melodies have a deep rhythmic structure punctuated with frequent exclamations. *Ryndzivky*, a form of *vesnianky*, were sung at Easter by young men in the Yavoriv area in Galicia.

In Soviet Ukraine the *vesnianky* began to disappear after the revolution and were completely gone by the end of the famine of 1933. Today they are sung only by professional and amateur ensembles. In the Ukrainian communities of Western Europe and North and South America they remain a part of the Easter celebrations. They continue to be performed by young people in the churchyard after the blessing of the Easter bread.

The *vesnianky* began to be recorded systematically only in the mid 19th century. They can be found in almost every song collection: there are 91 in Ya. Holovatsky's *Narodnye pesni z Galitskoi i Ugorskoi Rusi* (Folk Songs of Galician and Hungarian Ruthenia, 1878) and 184 (and 108 melodies) in V. Hnatiuk's *Haïvky* (1909). To date the fullest collection is O. Dei's *Ihry ta pisni* (Games and Songs, 1963), which contains 368 texts and 129 melodies. The *vesnianky* had an important influence on the development of lyric poetry in Ukrainian classical literature (H. Skovoroda, M. Shashkevych, T. Shevchenko, I. Franko, Lesia Ukrainka).

In music they were exploited by P. Nishchynsky, M. Lysenko, M. Leontovych, S. Liudkevych, and others. They were presented on stage in the ethnographic-realist plays of M. Starytsky, I. Karpenko-Kary, and I. Tobilevych and were depicted on canvas by I. Trush, O. Kulchytska, Ya. Surmach, and others. In recent times they have made their way onto film and television. In 1988 Czechoslovak television filmed *Lety mii vinochku* (Fly, My Wreath), with screenplay by M. Mushynka, based on the Ukrainian *vesnianky* of the Prešov region.

BIBLIOGRAPHY
Potebnia, A. *Obiasnenie malorusskikh i srodnykh narodnykh pesen*, 2 vols (Warsaw 1883, 1887)
Anichkov, E. *Vesennyia obriadovyia pesni na zapade i u slavian*, 2 vols (St Petersburg 1903, 1905)
Voropai, O. *Zvychaï nashoho narodu*, vol 1 (Munich 1958)
Kylymnyk, S. *Ukraïns'kyi rik u narodnikh zvychaiakh v istorychnomu osvitlenni*, vol 2 (Winnipeg 1959)
Sokolova, V. *Vesenne-letnyie kalendarnye obriady russkikh, ukraintsev i belorusov XIX–nachalo XX v.* (Moscow 1979)

M. Mushynka

The Vesnivka choir

**Vesnivka** (Spring Song). A female choir of about 60 singers in Toronto. Founded in 1964 as a church choir for the St Nicholas Ukrainian Catholic parish, the group has staged concerts in Toronto, Rome, Chicago, Montreal, and New York. It has toured Canada (1976); Britain (1980); Germany, Austria, and France (1983); Brazil (1986); and Ukraine (1991). Its repertoire includes Ukrainian and French-Canadian folk songs, classical music by composers such as W. Mozart, F. Schubert, and J. Brahms, and modern music. A. Hnatyshyn wrote a Liturgy for the choir in 1968. The choir performed M. Lysenko's operetta *Koza Dereza* (Billy Goat's Bluff) in 1973 and 1979. The ensemble took first place in the CBC Radio choir competitions in 1984 and 1986. Since the beginning the choir's founder, K. *Zorych-Kondracki, has served as its conductor and musical director.

**Vesolovsky, Bohdan** [Vesolovs'kyj], b 30 May 1915 in Vienna, d 17 December 1971 in Montreal. Composer of light music. He studied music at the Lysenko Higher Institute of Music. Displaced by the Second World War, he emigrated to Canada in 1949. He became famous because of the many highly popular dance tunes (tangos and slow waltzes) he composed, such as 'Pryide shche chas' (The Time Will Come), 'Namaliui meni nich' (Paint Me a Night), and 'Lety tuzhlyva pisne' (Fly Sorrowful Song). His dance tunes were performed best by the baritone A. Derbish.

**Vesolovsky, Yaroslav** [Vesolovs'kyj, Jaroslav], b 1881, d 21 June 1917 in Vienna. Journalist and political leader. He edited *Postup (1903–5) in Kolomyia and then *Bukovyna (1904–6) in Chernivtsi. From 1907 he worked in Lviv, where he contributed to and then edited *Dilo and *Pys'mo z Prosvity (1907–8). During the First World War he was an official of the Ministry of Foreign Affairs in Vienna in charge of the Ukrainian and Russian press, as well as a member of the Presidium of the General Ukrainian Council.

**Vestments** (*ryzy*). Garments worn by clergymen or their assistants while conducting church services. In the Ukrainian church they are modeled on vestments used in the Byzantine church. They are most commonly made of gold or silver brocade, although the Ukrainian church occasionally uses vestments made out of linen decorated with embroidery. The style of vestments worn corresponds with the rank of the clergyman, more elaborate vestments and a greater number of them being worn by the higher clergy. A deacon's vestments consist of a deacon's sticharion, a sacklike tunic with brocaded sleeves; an orarion, a long cincture which is passed under the right arm and over the left shoulder; and maniples, or brocaded cuffs. A priest's vestments consist of a priest's sticharion, a long shirtlike tunic; an epitrachelion, a silk stole representing the priest's authority which is worn around the neck and then along the front of the sticharion; a cincture (or zone), a belt made of the same material as the stole and used to secure it; maniples; and a chasuble, or phelonion, a large capelike outer garment, usually with extensive and rich brocade work. A bishop's vestments include a priest's sticharion, stole, cincture, and maniples together with a *nabedrenyk*, a diamond-shaped piece of stiff brocade attached to the cincture on the right side, symbolizing the word of God or, more concretely, a 'spiritual sword'; a saccos, a sacklike chasuble which resembles the outer garments worn by Byzantine emperors; an omophorion, or bishop's orarion, a wide band of brocade which is wrapped about the shoulders and hangs both in front and in back; and a mantle which is used for processions.

The color of vestments used during a church service varies according to the observance. White or gold is worn on Sundays, feast days, and holy days; red is worn for a funeral or the feast day of a martyr; purple is worn during Lent; green is worn on Pentecost and on all days of the week following it; and blue is worn on Marian feast days. The vestments are put on by a priest one at a time, to the accompaniment of prayers noting their symbolism. The vestments worn by the Ukrainian Catholic and Ukrainian Orthodox clergy are similar in form, particularly the deacon's sticharion, the chasuble, and the omophorion.

BIBLIOGRAPHY
Bulgakov, S. Nastol'naia kniga dla sviashchenno-tserkovno-sluzhitelei (Kharkiv 1900)
Trenkle, E. Liturgische Geräte und Gewänder der Ostkirche (Munich 1962)
Walter, C. Art and Ritual of the Byzantine Church (London 1982)

**Vetch** (*Vicia*; Ukrainian: *vyka*). A grassy plant of the pea family Fabaceae (Leguminosae), also known as tare. In Ukraine the cultivated annual species are the most important – the spring or common vetch (*V. sativa*) and the winter or hairy vetch (*V. villosa*). They are planted mixed with oats or barley to yield highly nutritional green fodder, silage, and hay. Early feed is obtained by mixing vetch with winter wheat and rye. Like other legumes vetch adds nitrogen to the soil. All vetch species are valuable nectar bearers.

**Veterinary Code of the Ukrainian SSR** (Veterynarnyi kodeks URSR). A code of laws on the state veterinary service adopted by the All-Ukrainian Central Executive Committee on 13 March 1925. It consisted of 112 articles grouped into four sections: (1) the organization and tasks of the veterinary service, (2) methods of dealing with epidemic and infectious animal diseases, (3) veterinary-sanitary care, and (4) government agencies and the rights and duties of veterinary officials. As Soviet administrative law became centralized, the code was repealed by the Central Executive Committee, on 20 January 1937, and replaced by the Veterinary Statute of the USSR, passed on 27 October 1936. A new Union statute of nine sections and 62 articles was adopted on 22 December 1967. The first three sections deal with the organization and duties of veterinary workers, sections four and five with quarantine, sections six and seven with veterinary inspection of transported and slaughtered livestock, section eight with the use of chemical substances in veterinary practice, and section nine with sanctions for violating the law.

**Veterinary medicine.** A discipline which deals with the diagnosis, treatment, and prevention of animal diseases as well as the study of their continuous relationship to human beings. In Ukraine, from the prehistoric period up to the beginning of the 19th century, veterinary science as a branch of *folk medicine was practiced by soothsayers, local healers, shepherds, furriers, blacksmiths, and barbers. Veterinary medicine as a profession emerged in Rus' in the 10th to 13th centuries, and some laws were passed to combat epizootics in the 16th and 17th centuries.

Veterinary hospitals appeared in the first half of the 19th century as parts of military bases and commands. In Ukraine under Russian rule, veterinary dispensaries or hospitals in urban or rural areas were controlled by gubernial veterinary inspectors of the Veterinary Administration of the Ministry of the Interior or, in the case of the military, by the Military Veterinary Department of the Military Medicine Command. A similar system of inspectors existed in Western Ukraine under Austro-Hungarian rule. In the late 1880s, veterinary medicine was still in a relatively primitive state, although it had been taught as a subject at Kharkiv University as early as 1805. In 1835 a veterinary technical school was established in conjunction with Kharkiv University, in 1852 the Veterinary School of Higher Learning was founded, and in 1871 the Kharkiv Institute of Veterinary Science was created. Veterinary institutes were founded in Lviv (1880) and Kiev (1920).

Despite some progress in the academic branch, there was no organized network for the sanitary inspection of meat, and only after 1879 was a concerted attempt made to control epizootic disease by transferring the administration of meat inspection to the zemstvos. In the system of *zemstvo medicine a network of veterinary stations was created, and many veterinary schools and laboratories were founded, of which the biggest were located in Kherson and Katerynoslav. By the beginning of the 1890s the cattle plague had been almost eliminated, but debilitating diseases of domestic animals, such as tuberculosis, leptospirosis, brucellosis, salmonellosis, and hoof-and-mouth disease, were still widespread. The years of the revolution saw the return of the epizootic diseases, including the cattle plague.

From the 1920s, veterinary medicine was administered by the veterinary department of the Commissariat of Agriculture of the Ukrainian SSR. It consisted of numerous veterinary departments, scientific and educational institutions, and production entities for drugs and instruments. Regional veterinary departments were made up of a network of dispensaries, veterinary-bacteriological laboratories, high schools and seminars, senior personnel of veterinary doctors and inspectors in cities, veterinary stations, and hospitals. The growth and development of the veterinary network in 1923–8 was abruptly halted by forced collectivization and the liquidation of private farms. In 1934, measures were again taken to re-establish the veterinary network. In 1937 the government in Moscow centralized all Soviet administrative law by abolishing the Veterinary Code of the Ukrainian SSR and substituting for it the Veterinary Code of the USSR. The decree of the Council of Ministers of the USSR and the CC of the CP in 1953 to transfer the zootechnical and veterinary personnel from their regional administrations to the machine and tractor sections brought about a crisis in agriculture in the Ukrainian SSR.

In Western Ukraine under Polish rule (1920s to 1930s), veterinary medicine was the responsibility of the veterinary department of the Ministry of Agriculture. That ministry controlled the voivodeship inspectors and the regional veterinary doctors, as well as an independent group of veterinary doctors who belonged to self-governing organizations. These institutions admitted very few Ukrainians. At the initiative of the *Silskyi Hospodar society a network of Ukrainian veterinary doctors was formed in 1933 in conjunction with the dairies of the *Maslosoiuz. After the Second World War the Soviet Union annexed Western Ukraine and abolished all existing organizations.

Today veterinary research is conducted at the *Ukrainian Scientific Research Institute of Experimental Veterinary Science, at the *Ukrainian Veterinary Scientific Research Institute, at the Ukrainian Agricultural Academy, at the Kharkiv and Lviv Zootechnical-veterinary institutes, and in departments of veterinary science at Odessa University and the Bila Tserkva Agricultural Institute. The journals *Visnyk silʹskohospodarsʹkoï nauky* and *Tvarynnytstvo Ukraïny* and the collection *Veterynariia* publish research and works pertaining to veterinary science in Ukraine.

BIBLIOGRAPHY
Petrenko, B. *Dosiahnennia radiansʹkoï veterynariï* (Kiev 1958)
Bondarenko, H.; Didovetsʹ, S. *Orhanizatsiia veterynarnoï spravy* (Kiev 1972)

P. Dzul

**Vetlyna.** See Borduliak, Tymotei.

**Vetukhiv, Mykhailo** [Vetuxiv, Myxajlo], b 25 July 1902 in Kharkiv, d 11 June 1959 in New York. Biologist, geneticist, and civic figure; member of the Shevchenko Scientific

Mykhailo Vetukhiv          Oleksa Vetukhiv

Society from 1947; son of O. *Vetukhiv. After graduating from the Kharkiv Agricultural Institute (1923), he taught (1926–34) at the Poltava Agricultural Institute, the Kharkiv Veterinary Institute, and Kharkiv University. In 1934 he was forced to move to Moscow, where he taught at the Moscow Veterinary-Zootechnical Institute and headed the genetics section of the All-Union Institute of Experimental Veterinary Medicine. After returning to Kharkiv in 1941, he was rector of the university there (1942–3). In 1944 he emigrated to Germany and cofounded the Ukrainian Free Academy of Sciences (UVAN). He served in Germany as a minister for the UNR government-in-exile (1945). Later, in the United States, he was executive vice-president of the Ukrainian Congress Committee of America (1949–55) and head of UVAN in the United States (from 1950). He prepared analyses of Soviet scientific research for the Institute for the Study of the USSR. His postulate, known as Vetukhiv's breakdown, notes the substantial loss of breeding potential among second-generation hybrid plants.

**Vetukhiv, Oleksa** [Vetuxiv], b 27 March 1869 in Ternova, Vovchanske county, Kharkiv gubernia, d 1941. Ethnographer and linguist. A student of O. *Potebnia, in the 1920s he was a professor at the Kharkiv Institute of People's Education and director of the ethnography and regional studies section of the Department of the History of Ukrainian Culture. He belonged to the Kharkiv Historical-Philological Society and the Potebnia Committee. His special interests were the dialects of Slobidska Ukraine and methodology. His chief work was *Zagovory, zaklinaniia, oberegi i drugie vidy narodnogo vrachevaniia, osnovannye na vere v silu slova* (Charms, Incantations, Precautions, and Other Forms of Folk Healing Based on Faith in the Power of the Word, 2 vols, 1902, 1907). He also wrote many articles and several textbooks in linguistics, in which he propagated Potebnia's ideas.

**Vexillology.** The study of the history, symbolism, use, design, manufacture, and other aspects of *flags. Vexillology is a relatively new science and is closely related to *heraldry. Ukrainian flags were first mentioned in a 14th-century Spanish book. A great deal of valuable information about them is found in Polish works, particularly J. Długosz's *Insignia seu clenodia incliti Regni Poloniae* (15th century) and K. Niesiecki's *Korona Polska ...* (The Polish Kingdom ..., 4 vols, 1728–43), and in old Ukrainian and

Cossack chronicles. Vexillology in Ukraine was begun at the start of the 20th century by the historians D. Yavornytsky and I. Krypiakevych. The independent Ukrainian governments of 1917–21 sparked an interest in such studies, but contributions were mostly of a popular nature. Several scholarly studies, particularly of Cossack flags, were published in Soviet Ukraine. In the 1930s S. Shramchenko published studies on Ukrainian naval flags of 1917–20 in Galician periodicals. Postwar émigré scholarship was initiated by M. Bytynsky and continued by R. Klymkevych, V. Trembitsky, and others.

**Viacheslav Volodymyrovych** [Vjačeslav Volodymyrovyč], b 1083, d 1155. Kievan Rus' prince; son of Volodymyr Monomakh, brother of Yaropolk and Hlib Volodymyrovych and Yurii Dolgorukii. He ruled in Smolensk (from 1107), Turiv (1125–32, 1134–46), and Pereiaslav (1132–4, 1142). He was briefly in Kiev (18 February to 5 March 1139) after Yaropolk died, but was ousted by Vsevolod Olhovych. In 1142 he reclaimed Pereiaslav and turned over its rule to his cousin, Iziaslav Mstyslavych, who later ousted him from Turiv. Viacheslav is mentioned in chronicles as the ruler of Peresopnytsia in 1149. Yurii granted him the rule of Vyshhorod ca 1150. That year also Viacheslav became a coruler of Kiev with Iziaslav, and after Iziaslav's death in 1154, Viacheslav coruled with Rostyslav Mstyslavych.

**Vialov, Oleh** [Vjalov], b 23 January 1904 in Tashkent, Turkestan general gubernia, d 1 June 1988 in Kiev. Geologist; member of the AN URSR (now ANU) from 1948, and president of the Ukrainian Paleontological Society from 1977. After graduating from Leningrad University in 1928, he worked in the city at the Geological Committee, the All-Union Scientific Research Institute of Geological Prospecting for Petroleum, the Leningrad Mining Institute, and Leningrad University. After the war he chaired the paleontology department at Lviv University (1945–59) and headed the tectonics department of the ANU Institute of the Geology and Geochemistry of Fossil Fuels (1949–87). He took part in geological expeditions in the Carpathian Mountains, the Crimean peninsula, and the Antarctic. Vialov published numerous papers in regional geology, tectonics, stratigraphy, paleontology, and hydrogeology.

**Viatichians** (*viatychi*). A Slavic tribe that lived in the basin created by the upper and middle sections of the Oka River and the upper Don River. According to the Primary Chronicle they were descendants of the *Liakhs. In the 9th and 10th centuries the Viatichians paid tribute to the Khazars, and in the 10th and 11th centuries they were a part of Kievan Rus'. The cities of Moscow, Koltesk, Didoslav, and Nerinsk were established in the territories inhabited by the Viatichians in the 11th and 12th centuries. In the mid-12th century their lands were divided between Suzdal and Chernihiv principalities. After the 14th century the Viatichians were no longer mentioned in chronicles because they mixed with Finnish tribes and became the Russian people.

**Viazlov, Andrii** [Vjazlov, Andrij], b 1862 in Volhynia, d 16 October 1919 in Kamianets-Podilskyi, Podilia gubernia. Lawyer and civic activist. A civil judge and a member of the circuit court, he was a deputy to the First Russian State

Andrii Viazlov

Duma in 1906 and a member of the Ukrainian caucus there and the Autonomists' Union. During the First World War he served on the *Committee for the Relief of the Population of Southern Russia Suffering from Military Actions and played an important role in determining its plan of action. He was a member of the Society of Ukrainian Progressives and from 1917 sat on its council. Later he joined the Ukrainian Party of Socialists-Federalists. During the rule of the Central Rada he was the gubernial commissioner for Volhynia (1917) and then a general judge (1918). Under the Hetman government he was appointed senator and, in October 1918, minister of justice in F. Lyzohub's cabinet. With the hetman's downfall he left politics and assumed the presidency of the Ukrainian Red Cross. While retreating with the UNR Army he died of typhus.

A metal badge of the Sich Riflemen corps incorporating a cluster of viburnum berries (1919)

**Viburnum** (*Viburnum*; Ukrainian: *kalyna*). A deciduous shrub and small tree of the honeysuckle family Caprifoliaceae, with ornamental leaves and white or pink flowers. Of the approx 200 species of viburnum 2 are native to Ukraine. The most abundant is the common *viburnum* (*V. opulus*), also known as the European cranberry, highbush cranberry, or water elder, a small tree reaching 4–5 m in height. It has maplelike leaves that turn red in autumn and clusters of shiny, bright, translucent red, edible berries. A widely cultivated sterile variety (*V. opulus* var. *roseum*) is known as snowball or guelder rose. The wood of viburnum is used in the manufacturing of small articles. The sap extracted from the bark in early spring is used as a hemostatic. Fresh berries, which contain vitamin C, are used as a cold remedy. The European wayfaring tree (*V. lantana*; Ukrainian: *hordovyna*) grows west of the Dnieper River. In Ukrainian folklore the viburnum is a popular subject of many songs, and it is also used as a national symbol, especially in the folksong 'Hei u luzi chervona kalyna pokhylylasia' ('O, in the Meadow the Red Viburnum has Bowed Low'), where *kalyna* symbolizes Ukraine.

**Vicegerency** (Ukrainian: *namisnytsvo*; Russian: *namestnichestvo*). A territorial-administrative unit introduced in the Russian Empire in the late 18th century by Catherine II. In Ukraine the following vicegerencies were set up: Kharkiv in 1780, Kiev, Novhorod-Siverskyi, and Chernihiv in 1781, Katerynoslav in 1783, Voznesenske in 1795, and Iziaslav (renamed Volhynia in 1795), Bratslav, and Podilia in 1793. The districts were administered by vicegerents, who had the powers of a governor-general. In 1797 the vicegerencies were abolished and replaced by gubernias. The term was also used to note the office of the Galician vicegerent.

**Vicegerent** (*namisnyk*). A high administrative official who governs a country or a province as the sovereign's direct deputy. In Kievan Rus' vicegerents governed the regions outside cities and towns. In the Grand Duchy of Lithuania they initially had broad powers, but by the 15th century they were merely managers of the royal estates. In the Russian Empire vicegerents were the tsar's deputies in cities and counties. When Catherine II reformed the territorial system in 1775, vicegerents became equal to governors or governors-general. In the Austrian Empire the vicegerent was the highest royal administrator of a crownland (called *gubernator* before 1848). In 1866–1914 all the vicegerents of Galicia were appointed from the Polish nobility. During the war the position was filled by Austrian generals.

*Viche* (Russian: *veche*). A general meeting of the citizens of a Kievan Rus' town or city that was called to discuss important matters facing the community. The origins of the *viche* were in a tribal *court system, which was a characteristic governing entity for all East Slavic peoples. In terms of its legal authority the *viche* was a manifestation of popular rule, analogous to the popular meetings held in the cities of ancient Greece and in Western European cities during the Middle Ages. In the larger ('senior') *cities and towns of the various principalities, the *viche* evolved into a high-level body that competed in jurisdiction with the offices of the prince and of the *Boyar Council. It also gained importance after the waning of the princes' authority in the late 11th century and later, as the role of the general citizenry in the political life of the principalities increased in importance.

The first *viche* to be chronicled was held in Bilhorod in 997; it was followed by others in Novgorod the Great (1016), Kiev (1068), Volodymyr-Volynskyi (1097), Zvenyhorod (1147), Rostov (1157), Pereiaslav (1175), and Smolensk (1185). Others were held in smaller cities (*pryhorody*), where they were largely limited to municipal administrative matters. Members of a *pryhorod* had the right to take part in the *viche* of their senior city; eventually they came to be represented by a *tysiatskyi (deputy of 1,000 citizens).

The *viche* was called irregularly, as required, by the prince or one of the boyars or at the initiative of a group of citizens. It was usually attended by the prince, boyars, the bishop, and members of the clergy. It was held on the grounds of the prince's estate or in the church square or market square; in Kiev it was held in the court of the St Sophia Cathedral. The order of business was conducted by the prince or the bishop (in Kiev by the metropolitan), or occasionally by a *tysiatskyi*; there were no standard rules for debate, however, or for the adoption of resolutions. In principle resolutions were adopted unanimously, but actually they were decided by a democratic majority of those in attendance.

The jurisdiction of the *viche* was also not rigidly defined, though certain matters were undoubtedly within its prerogative. They included matters of war and peace (particularly a levy en masse), some matters of foreign policy, the *election of a prince to the throne (if he was not an heir apparent or a conqueror) or his expulsion therefrom, the drawing up of agreements (*riady*) with the prince, and the ratification of laws (see *Legislation). Occasionally the *viche* would demand the removal of certain officials of the prince's government or become a court in the event of abuses of political power. The decisions of the *viche* in senior cities were binding on the whole principality.

As an organ of state power the *viche* was not as influential in Ukrainian principalities as it was in Novgorod, Polatsk, or Pskov. In contrast to those northern principalities, however, where the prince usurped all power for himself, the *viche* in Ukraine remained equal in power to other governing bodies. Only in Halych principality was it subject to the higher authority of the Boyar Council. The *viche* declined after the absorption of Ukraine by the Grand Duchy of Lithuania and by Poland, where it was replaced by *dietines of the nobility. In the 16th to 18th centuries the *viche* functioned as a *community court and served as a model for the proceedings of the *General Military Council of the Hetmanate. In the late 19th century the term *viche* was revived in Galicia as the name for large public assemblies called to discuss Ukrainian politics.

BIBLIOGRAPHY
Sergeevich, V. *Veche i kniaz'* (Moscow 1867)
Linnichenko, I. *Veche v Kievskoi oblasti* (Kiev 1881)
Lashchenko, R. *Lektsiï po istoriï ukraïns'koho prava* (Prague 1923)
L. Okinshevych

*Vidhuky*

*Vidhuky* (Echoes). A student journal published in Lviv in 1913 (a total of four issues). Edited by I. Chmola, it criticized the ideological tone and socialist views of *Zhytie*, the major Ukrainian student organ of the time, and advocated a program of physical fitness and military training for students, in preparation for a possible war that would decide the fate of Ukrainian independence.

**Vidomosti Heneral'noho tserkovnoho upravlinnia UAPTs u Velykii Britaniï** (News of the General Church Administration of the Ukrainian Autocephalous Orthodox Church [UAOC] in Great Britain). An official quarterly publication of the UAOC in Britain, published in London since 1950.

**Vidomosti Verkhovnoï Rady Ukraïns'koï Radians'koï Sotsialystychnoï Respubliky** (News of the Supreme Soviet of the Ukrainian Soviet Socialist Republic). An official organ of the Supreme Soviet of the Ukrainian SSR, published in Kiev from 1941. Interrupted by the war, its publication was resumed in 1944, first monthly and then weekly. Published in parallel Ukrainian and Russian editions, it contains new laws and resolutions passed by Ukraine's Supreme Soviet, and decrees and proclamations of the Presidium of the Supreme Soviet. It also published the texts of international treaties and agreements ratified by the presidium, information about the work of the permanent committees of the Supreme Soviet, and details about changes in the administrative-territorial division of the Ukrainian SSR. It is now called *Vidomosti Verkhovnoï Rady Ukraïny.*

**Vidriz.** See Weights and measures.

**Vidro.** See Weights and measures.

**Vidrodzhennia** (Rebirth). A democratic, nonpartisan daily newspaper published in Kiev in 1918. The editor was P. Pevny.

**Vidrodzhennia** (Rebirth). A temperance journal published monthly in 1928–39. In 1928–9 it was called *My molodi*, and appeared in Rohatyn under the editorship of M. Chaikovsky and Yu. Kamenetsky. In 1930 it became the organ of the *Vidrodzhennia society and was renamed. Thenceforth it was published in Lviv and edited by Kamenetsky and then S. Parfanovych-Volchuk. The journal condemned smoking as well as drinking and advocated a healthy lifestyle. In 1930 it appeared in a press-run of 4,000 copies.

**Vidrodzhennia society** (Rebirth). A Ukrainian temperance society founded in 1909 in Lviv in response to a resolution of the First Educational-Economic Congress. Its purpose was to discourage the Ukrainian population from consuming alcohol and smoking. Since alcohol and tobacco were state monopolies, its temperance message coincided with the struggle of the Ukrainians against the Polish occupation of Galicia, and in the 1930s its activities expanded considerably. The society's head office was in Lviv. By 1937 it had a membership of 6,400, organized in 18 branches and 122 circles in the towns and villages of Galicia. In addition to conducting anti-alcohol courses, lectures, public meetings, and anti-alcohol plebiscites, it published the monthly *Vidrodzhennia* (1928–39), the youth supplement *My molodi*, and a series of popular brochures. Its chief activists were I. Rakovsky, S. Parfanovych, Yu. Kamenetsky, P. Vovchuk, I. Kostiuk, I. Herasymovych, and M. Tsenko.

**Vidrodzhennia society** (Spanish: Renacimiento). A Ukrainian-Argentinian educational society established in Buenos Aires in 1939. The group had its genesis in a number of Sokil sports associations and Riflemen hromadas (modeled on the Ukrainian War Veterans' Association of Canada) that were established from the early 1930s. In 1938 these groups organized an Argentinian wing of the *Organization for the Rebirth of Ukraine (ODVU). In order to deflect the possibility of suppression, the overtly political ODVU was dissolved in 1939 and reconstituted as Vidrodzhennia. After the Second World War Vidrodzhennia and the Prosvita society in Argentina established a relief committee to help displaced persons resettle in Argentina. The Vidrodzhennia society is affiliated with the Melnyk faction of the OUN. In 1952 it founded the first Ukrainian credit union in the country, which later set up two additional branches. The association has published *Nash klych since its inception, and it established a women's section in 1974. In the 1980s the society maintained a central office with four branches. It has also sponsored choirs, drama groups, dance troupes, and Saturday schools.

**Vidrodzhennia Ukraïny** (Rebirth of Ukraine). A Ukrainian-language organ of the press bureau of the Austrian Ministry of War, published in Vienna in 1918. Initially it was called *Vidrodzhennia*. The editor was I. Nimchuk.

**Vidumershchyna.** In Kievan Rus', the land or other property left by a deceased *smerd without a male heir. This property was transferred to the prince, and if the smerd had any daughters, they received some compensation from him. From the 14th century the prince did not take *vidumershchyna* if the smerd's daughter married someone capable of military service. *Vidumershchyna* also applied to some extent to deceased boyars' estates. In the Cossack period the state took the estate only if the deceased had no relatives, or if he died intestate. In medieval times under Polish rule, livestock was transferred to a noble instead of *vidumershchyna* when a peasant died.

Pupils and teachers of the Ukrainian school in Vienna in 1957. Sitting, from left: A. Hnatyshyn, M. Dzerovych, Yu. Kostiuk, Rev M. Hornykevych, Rev V. Gavlich, Mrs Gross, Mr Kolotylo, Mr Tarko

**Vienna.** The capital of Austria (1988 pop 1,482,825), situated on the Danube River. It is a national and international political center with a vibrant cultural history.

Before 1772 Ukrainian contact with the city was sporadic. Trade relations with Ukraine had existed since the

Princely era. Ukrainians (notably the Transcarpathian polemicist M. Andrella) had studied at the University of Vienna since the 16th century. In 1683 Yu. *Kulchytsky was instrumental in lifting the Turkish siege of the city, while Hetman S. Kunytsky led a Cossack force into battle against the Turks on its outskirts. Kulchytsky later founded Vienna's first coffeehouse, had a street named after him, and had a monument erected in his honor in 1885.

With the Austrian annexation of Galicia (1772) and Bukovyna (1774) Ukrainian ties with the city increased substantially. Vienna served as a training ground for Ukrainian parliamentarians and civil servants as well as for the Ukrainian Greek Catholic clergy. In 1774 Empress Maria Theresa and Emperor Joseph II established an 'Oriental Academy' that was to serve as a school for Eastern rite clergymen. This was the first *Barbareum. It had trained many theological and lay scholars by the time it was supplanted by the Greek Catholic Theological Seminary in Lviv in 1784. That same year St Barbara's Church was organized as a Ukrainian Catholic parish; it soon became a center of Ukrainian community life in Vienna. A crown boarding school where lay students of various nationalities and Ukrainian candidates for the clergy stayed and studied together was established in the city in 1804. When it was closed in 1847, 30 Ukrainians were living there. The facilities subsequently housed the Central Theological Greek Catholic Seminary (the so-called Second Barbareum), which was attended by an average of 50 students annually until its liquidation in 1892.

The Ukrainian community in Vienna consisted of government officials, among them figures such as A. Dolnytsky, O. Haninchak, M. Harasymovych, I. Kopystiansky, O. and Ye. Lopushansky, T. Luchakivsky, V. Mykhalsky, Yu. Romanchuk, I. Savytsky, A. and I. Vitoshynsky, Yu. Vyslobotsky, and R. Zalozetsky; general laborers who were permanent residents; students and military personnel who were temporarily in the city; various politicians (including members of the Austrian parliament) and journalists; and those who came to local sanatoriums. There were also some emigrants (such as A. Rozumovsky) from Russian-ruled Ukraine. At the outbreak of the First World War there were 3,000 Ukrainians living in Vienna. Before 1914 Vienna University (particularly the Slavists F. Miklosich and V. Jagić) trained a number of Ukrainian scholars, including I. Franko, O. Ohonovsky, M. Osadtsa, and S. Smal-Stotsky. Other notable graduates were the optometrist M. Borysykevych, the urologist T. Hrynchak, the chemist I. Horbachevsky, and the physicist I. Puliui.

The number of Ukrainian students in the city increased consistently over the years. In 1868 they established Sich, the oldest Ukrainian students' society. R. Sembratovych established the monthly *X-Strahlen* in 1900 and then joined with V. Yavorsky to edit *Ruthenische Revue* (1903–5), which was later renamed *Ukrainische Rundschau* (1906–14). Ya. Vesolovsky, a former editor of *Dilo*, worked as the Ukrainian and Russian press commissioner for the Austrian Ministry of Foreign Affairs. Community organizations included the student Sich, the workers' society Rodyna, the St Barbara's Brotherhood, the Zemliaky society, and the Ukrainska Besida society.

After the outbreak of the First World War the number of Ukrainians in Vienna increased to 15,000 because of the Russian occupation of Galicia and Bukovyna. The city briefly served at this time as a virtual capital of Ukrainian political and cultural life. The Supreme Ukrainian Council (established in 1914, renamed the General Ukrainian Council on 5 May 1915), the *Union for the Liberation of Ukraine, the Military Executive of the Ukrainian Sich Riflemen, the Ukrainian Parliamentary Representation, and the editorial offices of countless transplanted Ukrainian newspapers from Galicia and Bukovyna were all active in the city. New periodicals were established (published in Ukrainian and German), including *Vistnyk Soiuza vyzvolennia Ukraïny*, *Ukrainische Nachrichten* (1914–16), and *Ukrainische Korrespondenz*. New organizations included the Ukrainian Cultural Council, the Ukrainian Relief Committee, and the Ukrainian Women's Union.

After the signing of the Treaty of Brest-Litovsk the UNR government maintained an embassy in Vienna (staffed by H. *Sydorenko and A. *Yakovliv), as did the Hetman government (V. *Lypynsky was ambassador) and the Western Ukrainian National republic (ZUNR; represented by V. *Singalevych and M. *Vasylko). H. Besidovsky and Yu. *Kotsiubynsky served as consular officials for the Soviet Ukrainian republic in Vienna.

After the dissolution of the Austro-Hungarian Empire the Ukrainian population in Vienna dropped briefly, but it rebounded after the arrival of the ZUNR government under Ye. *Petrushevych in late 1919. In 1920–3 Vienna vied with Prague in importance as a Ukrainian émigré center. New organizations emerged, including Yednist, Postup, the Ukrainian Club, and the Union of Ukrainian Journalists and Writers. The Ukrainian Free University and the Ukrainian Sociological Institute were established initially in Vienna, in 1920–1 (both later moved to Prague). About 400 students attended various Viennese institutions of higher education in this period. The headquarters of many political parties also moved to Vienna and published various periodicals, including *Ukraïns'kyi prapor* (the organ of ZUNR), *Boritesia – poborete!* (the organ of M. Hrushevsky's Socialist Revolutionaries), S. Vityk's Sovietophile *Nova hromada*, V. Vynnychenko's *Nova doba*, V. Vyshyvany's *Soborna Ukraïna*, *Na perelomi* (edited by O. Oles), and the nonpartisan *Volia* (published by V. Pisniachevsky). V. Lypynsky published his series Khliborobs'ka Ukraïna (Agricultural Ukraine) in Vienna, and T. Savula opened his bookstore in the city. The Dzvin, Vernyhora, Dniprosoiuz, Zemlia, Chaika, and other publishing houses issued numerous titles, ranging from textbooks to fiction. Most of these were banned from distribution in Ukraine.

After the Polish annexation of Galicia in 1923, much of the Western Ukrainian emigration moved back to Galicia. The result was the closure of many Ukrainian presses and publishing houses and most community organizations in Vienna. The number of Ukrainians in the city declined to 3,000 or 4,000, mainly workers, pensioners, and lesser civil servants, and some professionals. Ukrainian community life continued in the form of various jubilees, civic meetings, and demonstrations. The last included assemblies and actions against the *Pacification in 1930, against religious persecution in the USSR, and against the man-made famine in Ukraine in 1933 (Cardinal T. Innitzer, the archbishop of Vienna, led a multidenominational and international committee formed to provide relief for its victims). In 1929 the Congress of Ukrainian Nationalists was held in Vienna, at which the *Organization of Ukrainian Nationalists (OUN) was formed. The writer O. *Hrytsai worked in Vienna in 1914–45.

After the annexation of Austria by Germany in 1938, the Nazi authorities abolished the 15 existing Ukrainian organizations and societies. In their place branches of the *Ukrainian National Alliance and the *Ukrainian Institution of Trust in the German Reich were formed.

During the Second World War the number of Ukrainians in the city increased again, particularly after 1944, when a wave of refugees arrived and increasing numbers were conscripted for forced labor. In 1944 and early 1945 representatives of the Cracow-based Ukrainian Central Committee and the Ukrainske Vydavnytstvo publishing house published *Krakivs'ki visti* in Vienna. Soviet forces captured the city on 15 April 1945 and immediately began repatriating those citizens who had not managed to flee to the West. Among those deported were V. Kurmanovych, S. Naklovych, T. Voloshyn, W. Habsburg-Lothringen (V. Vyshyvany), and Mykola Zalizniak. After the signing of a peace treaty between Austria and the USSR on 15 May 1955, some former residents returned to Vienna following a 10-year period of incarceration.

After 1955 Vienna once again became an émigré center and the headquarters of the Coordinating Council of Ukrainian Organizations of Austria and the Ukrainian Central Relief Alliance in Austria. Other active community organizations included the Ukrainian Women's Union in Austria, the Union of Ukrainian Philatelists, and the Bukovyna society. Individuals active in the immediate postwar period have included S. Bush, M. Ivanovych, Yu. Kostiuk, S. Naklovych, D. Rakhlitsky, V. Zalozetzky-Sas, B. Yaminsky, and I. and O. Zhupnyk. St Barbara's Church has a renowned choir conducted by A. Hnatyshyn and a church brotherhood led by I. Zhupnyk. According to the parish records of 1989, there are 1,400 Ukrainians living in Vienna. Many of them, particularly the young, have been entirely assimilated. Ukrainian Catholics in the city are served by Rev O. Dzerovych, and the Orthodox by Rev P. Dubytsky.

Many libraries, archives, and museums in Vienna have valuable holdings of materials on Ukraine and Ukrainians, particularly the National Library, which preserves Ukrainian publications of Bukovyna and Galicia from 1772–1918 as well as a large collection of maps.

M. Hornykevych, A. Zhukovsky

**Vienna, Congress of.** A conference of representatives of the major powers involved in the Napoleonic Wars, which met in Vienna from September 1814 to June 1815 to settle the boundaries of the European states after Napoleon's defeat. The congress decided to turn the *Congress Kingdom of Poland, including the Kholm and Podlachia regions, over to the Russian Empire. The Ternopil region, which in the Treaty of Schönbrunn (1809) had been transferred to Russia, was returned to Austria. A key figure in the Russian imperial delegation to the congress was A. *Rozumovsky.

**Vienna Arbitration.** The name given to two agreements signed in Vienna by Germany and Italy in 1938 and 1940 repealing the Treaty of *Trianon and ceding considerable territory from Czechoslovakia and Rumania to Hungary. The first of the agreements (2 November 1938) compelled Czechoslovakia to surrender to Hungary the southern areas of Slovakia and parts of Ukrainian Transcarpathia. The latter area constituted 1,545 sq km of territory, with a population of 182,000 (of whom 30,000 were Ukrainians), and included the region's capital, Uzhhorod, as well as the cities of Mukachiv and Berehove. The second arbitration (30 August 1940) saw northern Transylvania ceded by Rumania to Hungary and did not affect Ukrainians specifically. The Vienna arbitrations were annulled in the Paris peace treaties of 1947.

**Vigenère, Blaise de,** b 1533, d 1596. French diplomat and historian; secretary to the duke of Nivernais and inventor of a cryptographic substitution system. He wrote *La description du royaume de Pologne et pays adjacents ...* (1573), in which he recorded accurate descriptions of Galicia, Volhynia, and Podilia. K. Antonovych, the wife of V. Antonovych, translated Vigenère's work into Russian and published it in Kiev as 'Opisanie pol'skogo korolevstva i porubezhnykh s nim stran' in *Memuary otnosiashchiesia k istorii Iuzhnoi Rusi* (Memoirs Dealing with the History of Southern Rus', ed V. Antonovych, 1890).

**Vihorlat Mountains** [Vyhorlat] (aka Vihorlat-Huta). An effusive mountain belt situated in eastern Slovakia between the valleys of the Laborets and the Uzh rivers. Reaching elevations of over 1,000 m, the group is deeply dissected by valleys. Its main peaks are Vihorlat (1,074 m) and Snynskyi Kamin (1,007 m), both extinct volcanoes with remains of craters and lakes. The mountains are covered with beech forests. The area is sparsely populated except for the Uzh Valley and a small belt of viticulturists along the mountain approaches. The Vihorlats are situated in Ukrainian ethnic territory.

**Vii** [Vij]. A figure from Ukrainian demonology. As described in N. Gogol's short story, he was covered with earth and had an iron face and long eyelids drooping to the ground. He could see things invisible to ordinary humans.

***Viis'ko Ukraïny*** (Ukraine's Army). A journal of military science and military history published in Kiev since 1992. It was established by the Chief Administration of the Ukrainian National Guard and the Association of Officers of Ukraine and is supported financially by the 'For Ukraine's Democratization' fund and the Society of Veterans of the Ukrainian Insurgent Army in the United States. Its first editors in chief are V. Korkodym and V. Labunsky.

***Viis'kovo-naukovyi vistnyk heneral'noho shtabu*** (Military-Scientific Herald of the General Staff). A monthly organ of the General Staff of the Ukrainian army, published in Kiev in 1918 under the *Hetman government.

***Viit*** (Polish *wójt*, from Old German *Voit*, from Latin [ad]-*vocatus*). The head of a town self-governed by *Magdeburg law in 14th- to 18th-century Ukraine. The position was initially a hereditary one. The *viit* was responsible to the town's owner (usually the monarch or a magnate) and was appointed by him, usually from among the rich burghers. He presided over the town's administration, treasury, lands, properties, police, and *lava* court, and shared his powers with the town council (see *Magistrat*), whose members were elected by agreement of the *viit* with the burghers. For his services he received part of the town's taxes and court payments. The *viit* could pass on or sell his position to someone else. If the town purchased it, the *viit* was thenceforth elected by the burghers. In the 17th- and 18th-century Hetman state the *viit* was elected, but the election was subject to ratification by the hetman or his representative. Under tsarist rule the position was abolished together with Magdeburg law in 1831. In Western Ukraine, under Austrian rule the *viit* was the head of a village *\*hromada*, and under interwar Polish rule he was the chief administrator of a *\*gmina*. A study of Kiev's *viity* is found in V. Shcherbyna's collection on Kiev's history (1926).

**Viitovych, Petro** [Vijtovyč], b 1862 in Peremyshl, Galicia, d 1936 in Lviv. Sculptor. After graduating from the Vienna Academy of Arts (1890) he settled in Lviv, where he produced many decorative sculptures for building façades and interiors. His early works include *Persius, Slave, Spear Thrower, Kidnapping of a Sabine Woman* (1888), and *After Bathing* (1888). He sculpted the façade and the allegorical figures *Trade* and *Labor* at the Main Railway Station in Lviv (1900–4), sculptures on the façade of and inside the Lviv Opera (eg, *Glory*), the crucifixion scene and figures inside St Elizabeth's Church in Lviv, and reliefs inside the Dominican church in Lviv.

Staff members of the Vik publishing house in 1903. Sitting, from left: Oleksander Lototsky, Vasyl Domanytsky, Serhii Yefremov; standing: Fedir Matushevsky, Volodymyr Durdukivsky

**Vik** (Era). A publishing house established in Kiev in 1895 by several students (future political and cultural leaders V. Domanytsky, O. Lototsky, F. Matushevsky, V. Durdukivsky, S. Yefremov, V. Prokopovych, and others) under the influence of O. Konysky. In 1896–7 it issued only five short stories and tales in pamphlet form, most of which were reprinted from the journal *Osnova* (1861–2) and earlier periodicals. Over time it published a series of 23 books of poetry and prose by Konysky, T. Shevchenko, A. Krymsky, I. Franko, I. Nechui-Levytsky, L. Hlibov, S. Rudansky, M. Vovchok, M. Kotsiubynsky, V. Stefanyk, and others with a combined pressrun of 73,000 copies; 70 books and brochures aimed at enlightening the peasantry (375,000 copies); 21 books and pamphlets on political topics (25,000 copies); 10 editions of the selected works of Nechui-Levytsky, Franko, P. Myrny, B. Hrinchenko, I. Karpenko-Kary, and other writers (30,000 copies); and 16 books (50,000 copies) not part of any series, including the massive literary anthology *Vik* (3 vols, 1900, 1902), compilations of some of the best and most important literary works of the 19th century, and an anthology commemorating I. Kotliarevsky, *\*Na vichnu pam'iat' Kotliarevs'komu* (In Eternal Memory of Kotliarevsky, 1904). Despite the strict tsarist censorship of Ukrainian-language works and the official persecution of the Ukrainian cultural movement, Vik managed to publish 91 books by 1905 (when the Ems Ukase was rescinded) and 140 by 1918, with a combined pressrun of approx 560,000 copies. Its books contributed to the growth of national consciousness among many Ukrainians under tsarist rule.

*Vikna*

**Vikna** (Windows). A Sovietophile literary, art, and political monthly published in Lviv from November 1927 to September 1932. In 1929 it became the organ of the writers' group *\*Horno. Among the contributors were its editors, V. *\*Bobynsky and S. Tudor, and other Western Ukrainian left-wing writers, such as Ya. Halan, O. Havryliuk, A. Ivanchuk, P. Kozlaniuk, Ya. Kondra, S. Masliak, A. Mykhailiuk, V. Myzynets, D. Osichny, M. Sopilka, and K. Tkach. The journal also printed works and reviews by Soviet Ukrainian writers and critics. *Vikna* included translations of Soviet Russian and Belarusian literature by Bobynsky, Halan, Kozlaniuk, and M. Yohansen; book reviews; a theater supplement; articles criticizing D. Dontsov, the *Vistnyk* group, and the Polish regime; a literary and art chronicle; and news of cultural and political developments in Soviet Ukraine. *Vikna* was subject to censorship and confiscation and was finally closed down by the Polish authorities. O. Kizlyk's systematic index of its contents (Lviv 1966) and Y. Tsokh's bibliography of Western Ukrainian belletristic works in it (Kiev 1981) have been published.

**Vikonska, Dariia** [Vikons'ka, Darija] (pseud of Ivanna-Karolina Malytska, née Fedorovych), b 1892 in Vienna, d 23 October 1945 in Vienna. Writer; daughter of V. *Fedorovych and wife of M. *Malytsky. She was educated in England, and traveled widely in Western Europe. Her sketches and articles on art appeared in *Literaturno-naukovyi vistnyk* from 1922 on. She also used the pseudonym I. Fedorenko. In the 1930s she contributed to *Dazhboh* and *Zhinocha dolia*. She wrote a collection of poetic dialogues about art and love, *Rais'ka iablinka* (The Crab Apple Tree, 1931), a book about J. Joyce (1934), and the book *Za sylu i peremohu* (For Power and Victory, 1938).

**Viktiuk, Yurii** [Viktjuk, Jurij], b 28 August 1944 in Lviv. Graphic artist. Since graduating from the Lviv Institute of Applied and Decorative Arts (1974) he has concentrated on Ukrainian ethnographic themes and experimented with folk-art motifs and their adaptations. Line is the dominant element in most of his works, such as the 1970 linoprint series 'Folk Talents,' his illustrations to Ukrainian folk songs (1983), and the 'Seven Strings' series of illustrations to the poetry of Lesia Ukrainka (1986).

Iryna Vilde                    Oleksander Vilinsky

**Vilde, Iryna** [Vil'de] (pseud of Daryna Polotniuk), b 5 May 1907 in Chernivtsi, d 30 October 1982 in Lviv. Writer. She graduated from Lviv University in 1933 and then worked as a teacher and contributed to the journal *Zhinocha dolia* in Kolomyia (1933–9). Under Soviet rule she wrote for *Pravda Ukraïny* as a special correspondent and headed the Lviv branch of the Writers' Union of Ukraine. Her work was first published in 1930. Some of her works from the prewar period are *Povist' zhyttia* (The Novelette of Life, 1930), the anthology of short stories *Khymerne sertse* (The Whimsical Heart, 1936), the novelettes *Metelyky na shpyl'kakh* (Pinned Butterflies, 1936) and *B'ie vos'ma* (The Clock Strikes Eight, 1936), and novelettes based on the life of the intelligentsia and students, such as *Povnolitni dity* (Grown-up Children, 1939). Her postwar works include *Istoriia odnoho zhyttia* (The History of One Life, 1946), *Nashi bat'ky roziishlysia* (Our Parents Have Separated, 1946), *Stezhynamy zhyttia* (Along the Paths of Life, 1949), *Iabluni zatsvily vdruhe* (The Apple Trees Have Blossomed Again, 1949), *Kury* (Chickens, 1953), *Nova Lukavytsia* (1953), *Zhyttia til'ky pochynaiet'sia* (Life Is Just Beginning, 1961), and *Troiandy i ternia* (Roses and Thorns, 1961). In all of those works Vilde showed herself a master at describing the life of Galicians from a variety of social classes. The work

most highly rated by literary critics is the novel *Sestry Richynski* (The Richynsky Sisters, 2 vols, 1958, 1964), in which she portrays the intelligentsia and townspeople from a wide range of social backgrounds. A collected edition of Vilde's works, *Tvory* (Works, 4 vols, 1967–8), has been published, as well as a Russian translation in five volumes (1958).

BIBLIOGRAPHY
Val'o, M. *Iryna Vil'de* (Kiev 1962)
Val'o, M.; Lazeba, E. *Iryna Vil'de: Biohrafichnyi pokazhchyk* (Lviv 1972)

I. Koshelivets

**Vilensky, Dmytro** [Vilens'kyj], b 18 June 1892 in Shepetivka, Iziaslav county, Volhynia gubernia, d ? Soil scientist and geobotanist. In the late 1920s and the 1930s he chaired the melioration subdepartment at the Ukrainian Institute of Applied Botany and the geobotanical section of the chair of soil studies at the Kharkiv Agricultural Institute. Then he moved to Kiev and Moscow to work in research institutions. His scholarly publications included a botany textbook (1928) for use in agricultural institutes and articles on soil salinity.

**Vilensky, Illia** [Vilens'kyj, Illja], b 14 March 1896 in Kremenchuk, Poltava gubernia, d 28 February 1973 in Kiev. Composer. He studied composition with V. Kalafati at the St Petersburg Conservatory (1914–18) and later was affiliated with the Kiev Young Spectator's Theater. His works include the operas *Horbokonyk* (The Hunchbacked Horse, 1936) and *Ivasyk Telesyk* (1949, 2nd edn 1971), the musical comedies *Sorochyntsi Fair* (1935) and *Shelmenko the Orderly* (1962), orchestral suites, incidental and chamber music, film scores, choruses, art songs, and arrangements of Ukrainian folk songs.

**Vilinska-O'Connor, Valeriia.** See O'Connor-Vilinska, Valeriia.

**Vilinsky, Mykola** [Vilins'kyj], b 14 May 1888 in Holta (now part of Pervomaiske), Ananiv county, Kherson gubernia, d 9 September 1956 in Kiev. Composer and pedagogue. He graduated from (1919) and then worked at (1920–41) the Odessa Conservatory. He later taught in Tashkent (1941–4) and Kiev (1944–56) and headed the Faculty of Composition at the Kiev Conservatory from 1948. His works include the cantata *Moldavia* (1939), three symphonic suites (1932, 1933, and 1944), chamber music, pieces for piano, and songs. He also edited the piano works of M. Lysenko for publication in the 1950s.

**Vilinsky, Oleksander** [Vilins'kyj], b 1872, d 1928 in Poděbrady, Czechoslovakia. Mechanical engineer and civic leader. He lectured (from 1908) at the Kiev Polytechnical Institute and other schools. He was a member of the Society of Ukrainian Progressives and the Ukrainian Scientific Society in Kiev. In 1917 he became a member of the Central Rada and was appointed director of the Department of Vocational Education at the UNR General Secretariat of Public Education. In 1918 he was appointed consul general for Ukraine in Geneva. From 1923 he taught at the Ukrainian Husbandry Academy in Poděbrady, from 1925 as a professor of mechanical engineering. His publications include technical papers in Ukrainian, German, and Russian and the textbook *Narysna heometriia* (Projective Geometry, 1923).

**Vilkhivsky, B.** See Hrinchenko, Borys.

**Vilkhovy, Petro** [Vil'xovyj], b 25 September 1900 in Viazivok, Pavlohrad county, Katerynoslav gubernia, d 14 October 1975. Writer. After completing journalism courses sponsored by the CP(B)U Central Executive Committee in 1925, he worked as an editor of the newspaper *Kolhospne selo*. From 1935 to 1940 he was an editor at the Derzhlitvydav publishing house. From 1945 to 1959 he was a plenipotentiary with the Council for Religious Cults of the Ukrainian SSR Council of Ministers. He began publishing prose in 1921, and in the 1920s he belonged to the writers' group Pluh. Among his works are the prose collections *Zubata baba* (The Toothy Granny, 1927), *Tryfonove ozero* (Tryfon's Lake, 1962), *Sertsem do sertsia* (Heart to Heart, 1965), and *U Topolynomu* (In Topolyne, 1966) and the novels *Neboiany* (1928), *Zelena fabryka* (The Green Factory, 2 vols, 1930, 1934), and *Na berehakh dvokh rik* (On the Banks of Two Rivers, 1956).

**Village** (*selo*). A rural settlement, the inhabitants of which are occupied primarily in agriculture. The legal definition of village and the classification criteria for settlements in Ukraine have changed considerably over time. Hence, it is difficult to compare the number or distribution of villages in different historical periods. Since 1965 the legal definition of village has been based on Ukraine's Code on the Method for Transforming, Evaluating, Naming, and Registering Certain Settlements, which essentially treats villages as settlements that are neither *cities nor *urban-type settlements. It was Soviet policy for 70 years to obliterate the difference between rural and urban life. Yet there are still significant differences between villages and cities in Ukraine.

The village Snizhkiv in Valky raion, Kharkiv oblast

In medieval times most rural inhabitants in Ukraine lived on individual or family homesteads ranging from a *dym to a *dvoryshche*, which consisted of 40 to 50 members of an extended family. In the 16th century, villages – that is, larger and more complex settlements of unrelated individuals – began to emerge. The process was promoted by the spread of the seigneurial economy, the intensification of *serfdom, population growth, and the need for protection against Tatar raids. Formerly separate homesteads

and other small settlements merged into villages to form unified economic and social entities. The pace of the process was rapid in Galicia and Right-Bank Ukraine, where the population density was relatively high, and serfdom was most intensive, and slower in Left-Bank Ukraine, which was colonized in the late 16th and the 17th centuries by runaway peasants from the Right Bank. The threat of Tatar raids in Left-Bank and Southern Ukraine was the strongest impetus to compact settlement. Yet the colonists often set up family homesteads in the sparsely settled territory. Even in the late 18th century it was not uncommon for several conjugal families to live together in a single economic unit. When the Tatar threat was removed toward the end of the 18th century, the steppes were settled in a planned manner by large landholders who brought in whole peasant colonies. Thus villages became common in steppe Ukraine. After the emancipation of the serfs in 1861, many peasants in the region left the villages to settle on individual farmsteads (see *khutir).

A street in an old village in Left-Bank Ukraine

Villages in Ukraine are laid out in a number of patterns depending largely on the terrain and natural environment: linear, chain, complex linear, irregular, radial, and regular. In the linear or 'ribbon' layout the cottages are evenly spaced on one or both sides of the road, and the gardens stretch at right angles from the road. The form is common in Belarus, Russia, and western Polisia in Ukraine. The chain village is similar to the linear one: the houses, less regularly spaced, are strung along a road that is usually winding and long. Chain settlements are characteristic of the Carpathian Mountains and foothills, except for the Hutsul region. There are several variants of the complex linear layout. The multistreet variant consists of two or more parallel streets with houses situated on one or both sides. Horseshoe-shaped villages sprang up along river bends or on small lakes. Fork- or star-shaped settlements developed at road or river junctions. The most common village form in Ukraine is the irregular one, particularly the cluster (*hurtove*) variant. It is characterized by crooked streets running in an irregular pattern and eventually leading to an open yard. Usually the shape of the village is roughly circular or elliptical. The radial village is built around an open core, usually a common square or plaza. The regular village has a grid layout and is square or rectangular in shape. Such settlements devel-

oped mostly in the 19th century in the open steppes of southern Ukraine.

Four distinctive settlement zones can be distinguished in Ukraine: the northwest (particularly Polisia), the Carpathian, the forest-steppe, and the southern steppe. In each zone the location and layout of the villages are different. In the northwest, villages are set far away from bodies of water because of poor drainage and swampy conditions. Because of the scarcity of arable land, the settlements are small and spaced far apart. The linear village is the most common type in the region. The mountainous terrain of the Carpathians ruled out large farm settlements. Villages are mostly located in the valleys and are usually built in chain formation. Some nucleated settlements can be found on terraces along the southern slopes of mountains or hills. The forest-steppe zone was settled before the development of guidelines or regulations; its favorite form is the irregular cluster village. Radial settlements are also common in the region, because the central square often functioned as a defense zone from the raiding Tatars. Southern Ukraine, which was colonized only after the 18th century, is marked by planned regular villages.

The collectivization of agriculture in Ukraine under the Soviet regime resulted in some significant changes in village life and layout. The *machine tractor stations (MTS) quickly appropriated certain political and administrative functions and thus undermined the traditional government of the village. Without radically altering the physical appearance of the village the change to collectivized farming brought in its wake new facilities and buildings at the outskirts of existing villages. New construction practices gave rise to a preference for the grid pattern.

The village has long been an important symbol in Ukrainian literature and culture. Glorification of rural life and the extensive use of themes and images from Ukrainian folklore were characteristic of Romantic and realist writers and artists (eg, T. Shevchenko, P. Kulish, I. Nechui-Levytsky), most of whom were of rural origin, from the early 19th century on. Since the cities and much of the elite of Ukraine were either Russified or Polonized, the village and the peasantry came to represent the Ukrainian nation. The village was portrayed as the cradle of the Ukrainian national renaissance, an idealization that remained a facet of Ukrainian life well into the 20th century. In early Ukrainian political thought the village was idealized by M. Kostomarov, especially in his 'Dve russkie narodnosti' (Two Rus' Peoples), which stressed the uniqueness of the Ukrainian village vis-à-vis the Russian village.

(For the structure and government of the village community see *Hromada.)

BIBLIOGRAPHY

Huslystyi, K. (ed). Ukraïntsi (Kiev 1959)
Blum, J. Lord and Peasant in Russia from the Ninth to the Nineteenth Century (Princeton 1961)
Stel'makh, H. Istorychnyi rozvytok sil's'kykh poselen' na Ukraïni (Kiev 1964)
Cybriwsky, R. 'The Pre-Soviet Village in Ukraine,' Yearbook of the Association of Pacific Coast Geographers, 34 (1972)
Kononenko, P. Selo v ukraïns'kii literaturi: Literaturno-krytychnyi narys (Kiev 1984)
                                                B. Balan, A. Makuch

**Village assembly** (silskyi skhod). In Russian-ruled Ukraine a general meeting of the household heads that was the chief governing body of the village *hromada. From 1797 it was restricted to appanage and state peasants. In 1861 the newly emancipated serfs were allowed to participate. The assembly had limited powers: it divided land under its jurisdiction among its members, distributed the tax burden, and elected village officials, such as the starosta and *sotskyi*.

In the Soviet period the village assembly was a general meeting of the residents of a rural district governed by a rural council.

**Village center** (*selianskyi budynok* or *selbud* 'peasants' building'). A rural cultural and extramural educational institution established in Soviet Ukraine by the regime in the 1920s to compete with the local *Prosvita society branch. In 1921 there were 4,007 Prosvita branches and 116 village centers. After the liquidation of the Prosvita society by the Bolsheviks in 1922, the communist-dominated village centers expanded rapidly, to 4,550 by 1929. Usually each center maintained a library, and the larger ones had auditoriums for theatrical performances and facilities for various artistic, educational, and sports activities. During collectivization the village centers were replaced by collective-farm clubs and by rural 'palaces of culture' run by the Ministry of Culture. (See also *Reading house.)

*Vil'na dumka* (Free Thought). The first Ukrainian-language newspaper in Australia. It was founded by V. Shumsky, O. Pytliar, B. Podolianko, and O. Siversky, and has been published in Sydney since July 1949, biweekly to October 1950 and then weekly. Since the early 1950s Shumsky has been the chief editor and the publisher. From April 1956 to January 1957 the paper was called *Vil'na dumka – Ukraïns'kyi shliakh*.

*Vil'na spilka* (Free Association). A semimonthly organ of the *Ukrainian Party of Socialists-Federalists, published in Kiev in 1917.

*Vil'na Ukraïna* (Free Ukraine). A monthly journal of literature, politics, and scholarship, published by A. Shablenko in St Petersburg in 1906 as an organ of the *Ukrainian Social Democratic Workers' party. It was edited by I. Lychko (nos 1–2) and then by S. Petliura, M. Porsh, and P. Poniatenko. The journal was closed down by the tsarist authorities after they confiscated issue no. 5–6. At the same time, Shablenko was sentenced to a year in prison for his revolutionary activities.

*Vil'na Ukraïna* (Free Ukraine). An organ of the Union of Ukrainian Autonomists-Federalists (later the *Ukrainian Party of Socialists-Federalists), published in Uman in 1917 under the editorship of A. Kaminsky.

*Vil'na Ukraïna* (Free Ukraine). The official newspaper of the Lviv city and oblast Party committees and soviets, published five days a week in Lviv from November 1939 to June 1941 and from 1944 to 1991. The newspaper's pressrun was increased from 88,000 in 1960 to 230,000 in 1980, but by 1990 it had been reduced to 192,000. By contrast, the pressrun of the Russian-language newspaper of the Lviv oblast Party Committee and Soviet, *L'vovskaia pravda* (est 1946), was increased from 38,000 in 1960 to 111,250 in 1980.

*Vil'na Ukraïna* (Free Ukraine). A journal published by the *Ukrainian Free Society of America in Detroit and, from 1961, New York City. Edited by a board headed for

*Vil'na Ukraïna* (Detroit)

many years by V. Lysy, it appeared quarterly from 1954 to 1967 and then once or twice a year to 1972 (a total of 67 issues). The journal contained valuable articles and memoirs pertaining to the history of Ukrainian socialism, the revolutionary period of 1917–20, the OUN, and the Ukrainian Insurgent Army; analyses of Soviet Ukrainian politics, economics, education, and demographic changes; and critiques of Ukrainian émigré politics, particularly of the OUN (Bandera faction), the Ukrainian Congress Committee of America, and the Ukrainian National Council.

*Vil'na ukraïns'ka shkola* (Free Ukrainian School). An organ of the *All-Ukrainian Teachers' Association, published in Kiev in 1917–19. It published articles on pedagogy and teaching methodology and devoted particular attention to the development of a modern Ukrainian education system. The editors were S. *Cherkasenko and then O. *Doroshkevych, and prominent contributors included V. Durdukivsky, O. Muzychenko, S. Rusova, S. Siropolko, P. Kholodny, Ya. Chepiha-Zelenkevych, and I. Yushchyshyn.

*Vil'ne slovo* (Free Word). A newspaper published by the *Union for the Liberation of Ukraine for Ukrainians serving in the Russian army interned in the POW camp in Salzwedel, Germany, in 1916–18. It appeared semimonthly, weekly, and then semiweekly under the editorship of P. Karmansky and, in 1918, Z. Kuzelia. It was succeeded by *Shliakh*, the organ of the Ukrainian government's commission for the repatriation of prisoners.

*Vil'ne zhyttia* (Free Life). A daily newspaper published by the Prosvita society in Odessa in 1918. It was edited by V. Chekhivsky and V. Ponomarenko.

*Vil'ne zhyttia* (Free Life). A newspaper of the Ternopil oblast and city councils and, until 1991, Party committees, published five days a week in Ternopil from October 1939 to June 1941 and since 1944. Its pressrun was increased from 45,000 in 1960 to 99,000 in 1970, 128,000 in 1980, and 131,000 in 1988.

**Vilner, Volodymyr** [Vil'ner], b 21 March 1885 in Hrodna, Belarus, d 9 August 1952 in Kiev. Stage director of Lithuanian origin. He completed drama courses at St Petersburg University (1912) and acted in the St Petersburg Novyi Teatr (from 1911). Then he worked as a director in

Kharkiv (1918–20) and as principal stage director in the Kiev Ukrainian Drama Theater (1938–41) and the Kiev Theater of Musical Comedy (1947–50).

**Vilnianske** [Vil'nians'ke]. VI-16. A city (1988 pop 17,800) on the Vilnianka River and a raion center in Zaporizhia oblast. It was founded in 1840 and named Sofiivka. In 1935–66 it was called Chervonoarmiiske. It was given city status and renamed Vilnianske in 1966. Its factories manufacture tableware, instruments, and plastics.

**Vilnius** (Ukrainian: Vilna; Polish: Wilno). The capital (1989 pop 582,000) of *Lithuania, situated at the confluence of the Vilnia and the Neris rivers. Vilnius was founded in the 13th century and became the capital of the Grand Duchy of Lithuania in 1323. From 1795 to 1915 it was a gubernial center in the Russian Empire. From 1920 to 1939 it was occupied by Poland, and from 1940 to 1991 it was the capital of the Lithuanian SSR. In 1991 Vilnius became the capital of independent Lithuania.

In the 16th and early 17th centuries Vilnius was a major center of Ruthenian (Ukrainian and Belarusian) and Polish cultural and religious life. It was the cradle of Ruthenian printing: F. *Skoryna established a press there ca 1520. P. Mstsislavets produced an edition of the four Gospels (1575) and a psalter (1576) there. His press was later taken over by the *Mamonich brothers. The works of the Orthodox polemicist S. *Zyzanii, L. *Zyzanii's Slavonic grammar (1596), and M. *Smotrytsky's *Threnos* (1610) were also published there.

In the late 16th century there were 14 Catholic and 9 Orthodox churches and monasteries in Vilnius. The most famous was the Holy Spirit Monastery (est 1584, founded by the Vilnius Brotherhood), which received the right of stauropegion in 1588 from Patriarch Jeremiah. S. *Kosiv, K. *Stavrovetsky-Tranquillon, and I. *Kozlovsky-Trofymovych studied at the Vilnius Brotherhood School attached to the monastery, and M. Smotrytsky taught there. Y. *Kuntsevych was a monk and archimandrite at the Basilian monastery in Vilnius. The Jesuit college in Vilnius also attracted many Ukrainians. P. *Skarga was its rector in 1574–9 and became the rector of its successor, the Vilnius Academy.

In 1829–30 T. *Shevchenko lived in Vilnius. In 1986 a statue of him was erected on the campus of Vilnius University. In the 1920s, under Polish rule, over 200 Western Ukrainians studied at Vilnius University and were active in a Ukrainian student hromada there, which frequently collaborated with Belarusian students in Vilnius. Until 1939 Vilnius was a major Eastern European studies center. The collections of documents published by the Vilnius Archeographic Commission (39 vols, 1865–1915) are a valuable source for the study of Ukrainian history, as are materials preserved in Vilnius's museums, libraries, and archives (particularly of the monasteries).

In 1989 some 13,000 Ukrainians lived in Vilnius. There they founded the main branch of the Hromada of Ukrainians of Lithuania in December 1988. The Vilnius branch runs an amateur choir and a Sunday school (est 1989) that provides lessons in Ukrainian and Lithuanian history and in the Ukrainian language. It also publishes the Hromada bulletin *Prolisok*, which contains articles on Ukrainian history, culture, and literature and on current events. The branch organizes lectures by speakers and performances by actors and singers from Ukraine. A Ukrainian program is broadcast monthly by Lithuanian state radio in Vilnius.

BIBLIOGRAPHY
Kraszewski, J. *Wilno od początków jego do roku 1750*, vol 4 (Vilnius 1842)
Milovidov, A. *Opisanie staropechatnykh knig Vilenskoi publichnoi biblioteki* (Vilnius 1908)
Hrushevs'kyi, M. *Kul'turno-natsional'nyi rukh na Ukraïni v XVI–XVII vitsi* (Lviv and Kiev 1912, 1919)
Šapoka, A. *Vilnius in the Life of Lithuania* (Toronto 1962)
Jurginis, J.; Merkys, V.; Tautavičius, A. *Vilniaus miesto istorija* (Vilnius 1968)

A. Zhukovsky

**Vilnohirske** [Vil'nohirs'ke]. V-15. A city (1989 pop 24,000) in Verkhnodniprovske raion, Dnipropetrovske oblast. It was founded in 1956 as a workers' settlement and was granted city status in 1964. It is an industrial city that manufactures electrovacuum glass, reinforced-concrete products, silicate brick, and canned foodstuffs. It is the home of the *Verkhnodniprovske Mining and Metallurgical Complex.

**Vilny, Volodymyr** [Vil'nyj], b 13 February 1921 in Velykomykhailivka, now in Pokrovske raion, Dnipropetrovske oblast, d 2 October 1981 in Kiev. Writer. He graduated from the Kiev Pedagogical Institute in 1946. His poetry was first published in 1938. The poetry collections *Liubliu zhyttia* (I Love Life, 1949), *Dai ruku, tovarysh* (Give Me Your Hand, Comrade, 1957), and others appeared thereafter. In later years Vilny wrote mainly prose: the novelettes *Zdrastuite, mamo!* (Greetings, Mother, 1964), *Tak pochynalos' kokhannia* (Thus Love Began, 1969), and *Den' neskinchenyi* (The Unfinished Day, 1974); the novels *Ty na sviti odna* (You Are the Only One in the World, 1963), *Zhytni hory* (Mountains of Rye, 1972), *Vohnenni troiandy* (Fiery Roses, 1976), *Komu spivaiut' zhaivoronky* (For Whom the Larks Sing, 1976); and other works. Vilny also wrote publicistic prose.

*Vil'nyi holos* (Free Voice). A daily newspaper published in Poltava in 1918.

*Vil'nyi kozak* (Free Cossack). An organ of the Central Council of the *Free Cossacks, published in 1917–18 in Uman and Bila Tserkva. The editors were M. Levytsky and S. Kinash.

**Vilshanka** [Vil'šanka]. V-11. A town smt (1988 pop 5,600) on the Syniukha River and a raion center in Kirovohrad oblast. It was founded at the end of the 17th century by Cossacks and runaway serfs and was called Maslove. In the 1740s it was renamed Vilshanka and made part of Myrhorod regiment. A large Bulgarian colony was settled there in 1774. In 1967 the village was granted smt status and made a raion center. It is an agricultural town with a mixed-feed factory.

**Vilshanka, Treaty of.** An agreement between the Cossacks and Poles reached in October 1617 at Sukha Vilshanka (near Tarashcha), in the Kiev region. The Cossack *starshyna*, headed by Hetman P. *Sahaidachny, and the commissioners of Crown Hetman S. Żółkiewski ended their negotiations with two separate declarations, in which there were some discrepancies. The number of registered Cossacks was to be determined by the Polish Sejm; the decision was made, however, to exclude townsmen (tradesmen, merchants, tavern keepers, reeves, and burgomasters) who had joined the Cossack Host within the previous two to three years. The registered Cossacks were allowed to elect their hetman, and their choice was to be confirmed by the Polish king. The Cossacks were to stay in their usual localities without migrating into the free lands, and they were to desist from attacking the Crimea and Turkey.

**Vilshanka River** [Vil'šanka] (aka Vilshana). A right-bank tributary of the Dnieper River that flows for 100 km through Cherkasy oblast before emptying into the Kremenchuk Reservoir. It drains a basin area of 1,260 sq km. Sections of the river are used for water supply and irrigation. The city of Horodyshche is situated on its middle course.

**Vilshany** [Vil'šany]. III-16. A town smt (1988 pop 9,100) on the Losyk River in Derhachi raion, Kharkiv oblast. It was founded in the 1650s by refugees from the Kiev region led by Capt S. Kovalevsky. The town received smt status in 1938. It has a furniture, a sewing, and a brick factory.

**Vilshenko, Yaroslav.** See Lototsky, Antin.

**Vilshyna, Ostap** [Vil'šyna] (pseud of Yurii Panteleichuk), b 14 March 1899 in Rohizna (now part of Chernivtsi), d 15 May 1924 in Lenkivtsi (now part of Chernivtsi), Bukovyna. Poet. During and after the First World War he studied at the Chernivtsi Teachers' Seminary. There he organized a secret Ukrainian literary circle in 1919. To avoid Rumanian military service he fled to Uzhhorod, in Transcarpathia, in 1921, where he worked for the Committee of Ukrainian Refugees. When he returned to Bukovyna in 1922, he was imprisoned for two months and then forced to do military service in Bessarabia. He deserted and died soon thereafter of an illness. As a poet he was influenced by Yu. Fedkovych, T. Shevchenko, and I. Franko. His patriotic and lyrical poems appeared from 1921 in periodicals published in Chernivtsi (eg, *Kameniari, Promin'*), Lviv (*Svit dytyny*), and Uzhhorod. He also wrote poetry for children.

**Vilshytsky, Fedir.** See Potushniak, Fedir.

**Vimina, Alberto** (Bellunese or da Ceneda; assumed names of Michele Bianchi), b 1 March 1603 in Belluno, Republic of Venice, d 1667 in Italy. Italian adventurer, diplomat, and travel writer. In 1650 he was engaged by the Venetian consul to Vienna and the papal nuncio to approach Hetman B. Khmelnytsky in Chyhyryn about forming an anti-Ottoman coalition. In 1656, after returning to Lviv, Vimina prepared several accounts of his journey (one of which was published in 1890 as *Relazione dell' origine e dei costumi dei Cosacchi* and reprinted in Russian translation in *Kievskaia starina*, 1899) and wrote a broader survey of the Cossack-Polish War titled *Historia della guerre civili di Polonia*, which was published posthumously in Venice in 1671 (repr, Milan 1861).

**Vinaikin, Vasyl** [Vinajkin, Vasyl'], b 9 January 1924 in Shamkino, Chuvash Autonomous oblast, RSFSR. Sculptor. In 1953 he graduated from the Kiev State Art Institute, where he studied under M. Lysenko. He sculpted a statue of B. Khmelnytsky (1954) and *Youth* (1957) and collaborated on the monument commemorating the 'reunification' of Ukraine and Russia in Pereiaslav-Khmelnytskyi (1961) and the monument to Soviet victims of the Nazis erected in Kiev's Darnytsia raion (1970).

**Vincenz, Stanisław,** b 30 November 1888 in Sloboda Rungurska, Kolomyia county, Galicia, d 28 January 1971 in Lausanne, Switzerland. Polish writer and essayist. He spent his childhood and youth in the Hutsul Region. He studied at Vienna University and worked for a few years as a journal editor in Warsaw. Later he lived in Hungary (1940–6) and Germany (1946–7), near Grenoble, France (1947–64), and in Lausanne. From 1947 he contributed to the Polish journal *Kultura (Paris). Fluent in the Hutsul dialect and well versed in Hutsul folkways and lore, he wrote an epical tetralogy about the Hutsul region's past and present, *Na wysokiej połoninie: Obrazy, dumy i gawędy z Wierchowiny Huculskiej* (In the High Mountain Pasture: Pictures, Elegies, and Tales from the Hutsul Highland, 1936 [rev edn 1956], 1970, 1974, 1979; repr 1983). An abridged English translation of the first volume, *On the High Uplands*, was published in New York in 1955, and Ukrainian translations of it were serialized in the Lviv journal *Zhovten'* (1969–71). Several editions of Vincenz's philosophical, cultural, and political essays and reminiscences were published in the West and in Poland between 1965 and 1983; they include *Wspomnienia o Lwowie* (Reminiscences of Lviv, 1967) and *Dialogi Lwowskie* (Lviv Dialogues, 1968).

Mykola Vinhranovsky

**Vinhranovsky, Mykola** [Vinhranovs'kyj], b 7 November 1936 in Pervomaiske, Mykolaiv oblast. Writer, actor, film director, and translator. He graduated from the All-Union Institute of Cinematography (1960) in Moscow and has worked at the Kiev Artistic Film Studio, where he played the lead role in Yu. Solntseva's film *Povist' polumianykh lit* (The Tale of Flaming Years, 1961). He has written film scripts and directed the feature films *Eskadra povertaie na zakhid* (The Squadron Turns Westward, 1967), *Bereh nadiï* (The Shore of Hope, 1967), *Duma pro Brytanku* (Duma about Brytanka, 1969), and *Klymko* (1984) and several documentaries. Vinhranovsky gained prominence in the early 1960s as a leading poet of the *shestydesiatnyky*. He has published the poetry collections *Atomni preliudy* (Atomic Preludes, 1962), *Sto poezii* (A Hundred Poems, 1967), *Poezii* (Poems, 1971), *Na sribnim berezi* (On the Silver Shore, 1978), *Kyïv* (Kiev, 1982), *Hubamy teplymy i okom zolotym* (With Warm Lips and a Golden Heart, 1984), and *Kin' na vechirnii zori* (The Horse on the Evening Star, 1987); over 20 stories, including *V hlybyni doshchiv* (In the Depth of the Rains, 1980; about the making of a film); and, since 1970, several poetry books for children, for which he was awarded the Shevchenko Prize in 1984. Editions of his selected prose (1985; 1987 in Russian translation) and poetry (1986) have been published.

**Vinkivtsi** [Vin'kivci]. IV-8. A town smt (1988 pop 6,500) on the Kalius River and a raion center in Khmelnytskyi oblast. It was first mentioned in historical documents in 1493, when wat was under Polish rule. In 1672–99 it was occupied by Turkey. After the partition of Poland in 1793, it was annexed by Russia. The village was granted smt status in 1957. It has a canning, a cheese, a mixed-feed, and a brick factory.

The Jesuit college (1617) in Vinnytsia

**Vinnytsia** [Vinnyc'ja]. IV-9. A city (1990 pop 379,000) on the Boh River and an oblast and raion center since 1932. It was first mentioned in historical documents in 1363, as a Lithuanian fortress. The settlement gradually developed from a farming village into a manufacturing and trade center. By the 16th century it held regular fairs, had several guilds, and traded with cities on the Black Sea coast. As a frontier town Vinnytsia was exposed to Tatar attack: between 1400 and 1569 it was raided 30 times. In 1558 a new fortress was built on a river island, and then a new town sprang up on the right bank. From 1569 Vinnytsia was under Polish rule. In 1598 it was made the administrative center of Bratslav voivodeship, and in 1640 it was granted the rights of *Magdeburg law. An Orthodox brotherhood was set up by the burghers in the 1570s. It sponsored a school, which operated for almost two centuries. In 1632 a college was set up at the brotherhood Monastery of the El-

A bridge in Vinnytsia

evation of the Cross. At the same time the Poles established two monasteries and a Jesuit college (1642). After being liberated from the Poles by M. Kryvonis in 1648, Vinnytsia became a regimental center (1653–67). Under I. Bohun's command it withstood a major Polish siege in 1651. After being reoccupied by Poland in 1667, it was captured by the Turks, and entered a period of economic decline (1672–99) until it once more came under Polish control. In the 18th century its inhabitants revolted repeatedly against their Polish overlords and with the help of the haidamakas seized the town in 1702–4, 1734, 1750, and 1764. In 1793 Vinnytsia was annexed by the Russian Empire and became the administrative center of Bratslav vicegerency and a county center in Podilia gubernia (1797–1925). It developed rapidly in the second half of the 19th century. The Kiev–Balta railway line (1871) linked the town with Kiev, Odessa, St Petersburg, and Moscow. Vinnytsia became the gubernia's leading exporter of foodstuffs and trading center. The population grew from 10,000 in 1860 to 30,000 in 1897. About 35 percent of the population was Jewish in 1897 (45 percent in 1910).

During the revolutionary period the city changed hands several times. In 1919 it was the seat of the Supreme Command of the Ukrainian Galician Army. At the beginning of 1920 the Revolutionary Committee of the Red Ukrainian Galician Army was stationed there. Then the

The Mykhailo Kotsiubynsky Literary Memorial Museum in Vinnytsia

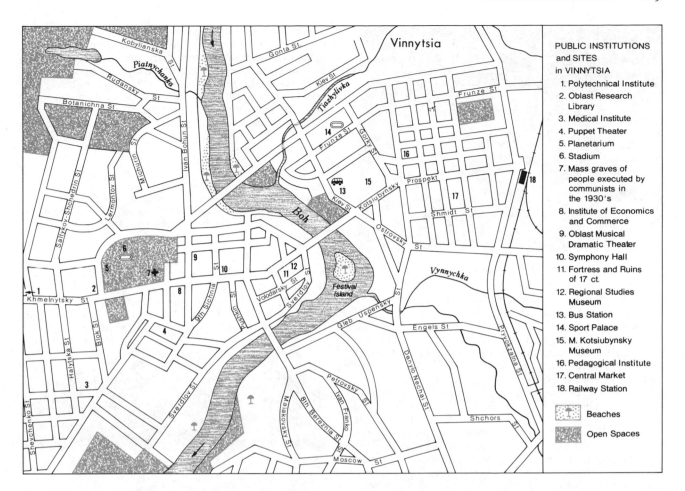

PUBLIC INSTITUTIONS and SITES in VINNYTSIA

1. Polytechnical Institute
2. Oblast Research Library
3. Medical Institute
4. Puppet Theater
5. Planetarium
6. Stadium
7. Mass graves of people executed by communists in the 1930's
8. Institute of Economics and Commerce
9. Oblast Musical Dramatic Theater
10. Symphony Hall
11. Fortress and Ruins of 17 ct.
12. Regional Studies Museum
13. Bus Station
14. Sport Palace
15. M. Kotsiubynsky Museum
16. Pedagogical Institute
17. Central Market
18. Railway Station

Beaches

Open Spaces

government of the UNR stayed there for a brief period. Under the Soviet regime Vinnytsia became an important cultural center. It was the home of the Cabinet for the Study of Podilia (est 1924), which was tied to the VUAN, and the Vinnytsia Branch of the National Library of Ukraine. Under the German occupation (1941–4) the atrocities committed by Soviet security forces were exposed (see *Vinnytsia massacre), but new crimes were committed by the Nazi forces, particularly against the Jewish population.

After the Second World War the city developed into a large industrial and communications center. Its population rose from 93,000 in 1939 to 211,400 in 1970 and 314,000 in 1979. Vinnytsia accounts for nearly 50 percent of the oblast's industrial output. Its machine-building and metalworking enterprises produce instruments, radio devices, ball bearings, and tractor assemblies. The main chemical plants produce superphosphate fertilizer and paint. The large food industry consists of meat packing, oil and fat processing, canning, confectionery manufacture, distilling, and brewing. The largest enterprises of the light industry are the clothing and footwear consortia. The building-materials industry produces reinforced concrete and bricks. Woodworking and furniture manufacturing make a sizable contribution to the economy.

The city's educational facilities include 9 secondary special schools and 12 vocational schools, 3 institutes (pedagogical, polytechnical, and medical), and branches of the Ukrainian Agricultural Academy (est 1982) and the Kiev Trade and Economics Institute (est 1969). Its chief cultural institutions are the Ukrainian Music and Drama Theater, a puppet theater, a philharmonic society, a literary museum dedicated to M. *Kotsiubynsky, who was born in Vinnytsia, and a regional studies museum. The N. Pirogov Museum (est 1947) is just outside the city. The main architectural monuments are the Dominican (est 1624), Jesuit (1610–17), and Capuchin (1760) monasteries and the wooden churches of St George (1726) and St Nicholas (1746).

**Vinnytsia Chemical Plant** (Vinnytskyi khimichnyi zavod). A chemical industry plant located in Vinnytsia. Built in 1912 to produce superphosphates (10,000 t in 1914), the plant was expanded after the Revolution of 1917 and especially after the Second World War. It is an important producer of mineral fertilizers (817,000 t in 1977) and detergents.

**Vinnytsia Instrument Plant** (Vinnytskyi instrumentalnyi zavod). A machine and instrument factory founded in Vinnytsia in 1946. The plant was totally rebuilt and modernized in 1958–67. It produces mainly metal-cutting machines, including reamers, mills, countersinks, and over 1,500 other specialized and standard products.

**Vinnytsia massacre.** A series of executions of thousands of citizens of the city of Vinnytsia and its surrounding area, perpetrated in 1937–8 by the NKVD during the

A mass grave of victims of the Vinnytsia Massacre

*Yezhov terror. The massacre was not the only action of its kind; many were carried out by the Soviet state security in prisons throughout the Ukrainian SSR. But the Vinnytsia massacre gained particular notoriety because of the extent to which it was made public. In an attempt to discredit the previous Soviet regime by highlighting the atrocities it had perpetrated, the German occupational forces, following the lead of various witnesses, exhumed the bodies of the massacre's victims between May and July 1943. To supplement the examinations made by German and Ukrainian doctors, the German authorities invited an international commission of medical experts to investigate the corpses found in 66 mass graves in the Vinnytsia area. Forensic scientists from Belgium, Bulgaria, Croatia, Finland, France, Hungary, Italy, Holland, Rumania, Sweden, and Slovakia participated in July 1943. It was reported that a total of 9,439 bodies (including 169 women) were recovered. Most of the victims had been shot in the back of the head; some had been buried alive. Only 10 percent of them were identified, largely on the strength of documents found on their persons, items of clothing, body markings, or other documents interred by the NKVD at another site. Among those identified were persons whose

Foreign physicians performing an autopsy of the remains of a victim of the Vinnytsia Massacre

families had been told they had been sent to prison camps without right of correspondence. According to the testimony of Vinnytsia's citizens there were other graves, but the Germans were unable to investigate because they were eventually forced to retreat. The fact that the German Gestapo itself used the NKVD prisons and installations for mass murder prevented a comprehensive investigation of the NKVD's actions in other cities, towns, and villages, both in the 1937–8 period and during the Soviet retreat of 1941.

BIBLIOGRAPHY
*Massenmord von Winniza* (Berlin 1944)
*Le crime de Moscou à Vinnytzia* (Paris 1953)
Kamenetsky, I. (ed). *The Tragedy of Vinnytsia: Materials on Stalin's Policy of Extermination in Ukraine (1936–1938)* (Toronto–New York 1989)

M. Stakhiv

**Vinnytsia oblast.** An administrative territory in central Ukraine, formed on 27 February 1932. It has an area of 26,500 sq km and a population (1990) of 1,925,600. The oblast is divided into 26 raions, 17 cities, 29 towns (smt), and 615 rural councils. The capital is *Vinnytsia.

The Rosava Valley in Vinnytsia oblast

**Physical geography.** The oblast consists largely of a rolling plain which slopes down toward the south and southeast. The southwestern part consists of the Podolian Upland, and the northeastern part, of the Dnieper Upland. The climate is temperate continental: the average January temperature is −5°C, and the average July temperature is 19.6°C. The annual precipitation ranges from 480 to 590 mm. The Boh River, the tributaries of which include the Zhar, the Riv, the Selnytsia, the Dokhna, the Sob, the Snyvoda, and the Udych, runs through the oblast in a southeasterly direction. The Dniester, the tributaries of which include the Murafa, the Liadova, the Nemiia, the Rusava, and the Markivka, flows along the oblast's southern border. Chernozems are the main soil type in the northeastern part of the oblast; gray, heavy gray, and light gray soils predominate in the central part; and deep chernozems and podzolized chernozems are common in the southeast and the Dniester region. Part of the forest-steppe belt, the oblast has maintained some forests of oak, hornbeam, maple, ash, and linden.

**History.** The territory was inhabited as early as the Paleolithic period. From the 10th to 12th centuries it was part of Kievan Rus', and in the 13th century, part of the Principality of Galicia-Volhynia. In the 13th century it came under the Golden Horde. The Grand Duchy of Lithuania gained control of the region in the 14th and 15th centuries and in 1569 transferred the territory to the Polish Commonwealth, where it formed part of Bratslav voivodeship. Vinnytsia regiment (1648–67) was part of the Hetman state, before it was recaptured by Poland and then conquered by Turkey (1672–99). In 1793, after almost another century of Polish rule, the territory was annexed by the Russian Empire in 1793 and absorbed into Podilia gubernia (1797–1925). Under the Soviet regime Vinnytsia okruha was set up in 1925, dissolved into raions in 1930, and reconstituted as an oblast in 1932.

**Population.** The majority of the oblast's population in 1989 was Ukrainian (91.5 percent). The largest minority was Russian (5.9 percent). The most densely populated parts are around Vinnytsia and along the Dniester River. About 45 percent of the population is urban. The major city is Vinnytsia, and *Zhmerynka, *Mohyliv-Podilskyi, *Koziatyn, *Haisyn, *Khmilyk, *Tulchyn, and *Ladyzhyn represent significant secondary centers.

**Industry.** The main industries in the oblast are food processing (41.8 percent of the industrial output in 1983), machine building and metalworking (22.6 percent), light industry (11.6 percent), and electric power (5.7 percent). The food industry consists mostly of sugar refining: there are 39 refineries in the oblast, the largest ones being in Haisyn, Kyrnasivka, Bershad, and Pohrebyshche. The by-products are used by distilleries in such centers as Bar, Kalynivka, and Trostianets. The largest meat packers are in Vinnytsia, Trostianets, Haisyn, Bar, Koziatyn, and Tulchyn. Dairy products, fruit canning, flour milling, and brewing are also important branches of the food industry. Machine-building plants manufacture tractor parts in Vinnytsia, sugar refining machinery in Kalynivka, instruments in Vinnytsia, and other kinds of machinery in Bar, Mohyliv-Podilskyi, and Turbiv. The main branch of light industry is clothes manufacturing; there are 39 sewing factories, of which the largest are in Vinnytsia, Mohyliv-Podilskyi, Bar, Haisyn, Khmilnyk, and Koziatyn. The other important branches are footwear, fur, and knitwear manufacturing and handicrafts. The electric energy to run industry is supplied by the Dniester Hydroelectric Complex near Mohyliv-Podilskyi, the thermoelectric plant in Ladyzhyn, and the thermoelectric substation in Vinnytsia. Other significant industries in the oblast are the chemical industry (fertilizers, consumer products, cleaning substances), furniture-making, and the building-materials industry.

**Agriculture.** About 62 percent of the oblast's gross output consists of agricultural production. In 1986 there were 577 collective and 101 state farms in the oblast. The total area devoted to agriculture was 2,044,000 ha, of which 89.8 percent was cultivated, and the rest was hayfield and pasture. Drained land amounted to 36,900 ha, and irrigated land, 32,000 ha. Of the cultivated land 50.6 percent was devoted to grain crops, mostly winter wheat and barley, but also legumes, corn, oats, and buckwheat; 14.2 percent to industrial crops (sugar beets, sunflowers, and tobacco); 27.9 percent to feed crops; and 7.3 percent to vegetables, melons, and potatoes. The Dniester region is known for its orchards (apples, pears, apricots, and cherries). Animal husbandry consists of beef- and dairy-cattle farming, hog raising, and sheep and goat farming. Poultry farming, beekeeping, and fish farming are supplementary branches.

**Transportation.** In 1989 there were 1,262 km of rail track, 163 km of which were electrified, in the oblast. The main lines running through the oblast are Kiev–Odessa, Kiev–Lviv, Vapniarka–Znamianka, Vapniarka–Yampil, Koziatyn–Berdychiv–Kalynkovychi, Koziatyn–Pohrebyshche–Uman, and Vinnytsia–Haivoron. The main junctions are Vinnytsia, Zhmerynka, and Vapniarka. The highway network consisted of 9,500 km of road, 8,200 km of which were paved. The major highways in the oblast are Kiev–Zhytomyr–Vinnytsia–Khmelnytskyi, Vinnytsia–Nemyriv–Mohyliv-Podilskyi, Nemyriv–Yampil, and Nemyriv–Uman. Both the Boh and the Dniester rivers are navigable. Vinnytsia and Mohyliv-Podilskyi serve as river ports. An airport is situated in Vinnytsia. The Urengoi–Uzhhorod gas pipeline passes through the oblast.

BIBLIOGRAPHY
*Istoriia mist i sil URSR: Vinnyts'ka oblast* (Kiev 1972)

**Vinnytsia Pedagogical Institute** (Vinnytskyi pedahohichnyi instytut). An institute of higher learning for training teachers under the jurisdiction of the Ministry of Education of Ukraine. Established in 1938 as the Vinnytsia Pedagogical Institute, the school had earlier been a *teachers' institute (1912–20 and 1934–8), a *pedagogical tekhnikum (1921–30), and one of the *institutes for social education (1930–4). It has seven faculties: history, philology, physics-mathematics, English language, natural science–geography, music education, and physical education. A total of 4,260 students attended classes in 1976–7, 2,660 as day students. The library has nearly 500,000 volumes. In 1937 the institute was named after N. Ostrovsky.

**Vinnytsia Polytechnical Institute** (Vinnytskyi politekhnichnyi instytut). An institute of higher learning under the jurisdiction of the Ministry of Higher and Secondary Special Education of Ukraine. It was established in 1974 on the basis of a branch of the Kiev Polytechnical Institute. The institute has six faculties: energetics, machine construction, computing technology, radio technology, civil engineering, and general technology. It offers evening and correspondence courses as well as a graduate program. In 1977–8 a total of 6,594 students were registered in courses.

**Vinnytsia regiment.** An administrative territory and military formation set up in 1649 in Right-Bank Ukraine. Its first center was Kalnyk; hence, it was known initially as Kalnyk regiment. The regiment was divided into 19 companies, which numbered 2,000 registered Cossacks. In 1653 the regimental center was transferred to Vinnytsia. The regiment was devastated in the 1670s by factional fighting among Right-Bank Cossacks. In 1678 it was incorporated into Bratslav regiment. I. Mazepa and I. Skoropadsky made unsuccessful attempts to revive the regiment. Its most famous colonels were I. Bohun (1651–8) and I. Sirko (1658–60).

**Vinnytsia Regional Studies Museum** (Vinnytskyi kraieznavchyi muzei). A museum founded in 1919 as the Vinnytsia Historical and Folkways Museum. In 1978 it had 50,000 items, including valuable archeological, numismatic, and ethnographic collections and artworks, exhibited in natural science, pre-Soviet history, Soviet society, and fine art sections. Museums dedicated to the history of the Decembrist movement (in Tulchyn) and the Soviet-French partisan V. Poryk (in Poryk, Khmilnyk raion) are also sections of the museum, and the Mohyliv-Podilskyi Regional Studies Museum is a branch. Guides to the museum were published in 1972 and 1984.

**Vinnytsia Ukrainian Music and Drama Theater**
(Vinnytskyi ukrainskyi muzychno-dramatychnyi teatr im. M. Sadovskoho). A theater established in 1940. It has staged classical Ukrainian and Russian and Soviet plays, G. Lessing's *Emilia Galotti*, an adaptation of V. Hugo's novel *Notre-Dame de Paris*, B. Brecht's *Der kaukasische Kreidekreis*, and M. Arkas's *Kateryna*. Among its members have been F. Vereshchahin, A. Ovcharenko, M. Pedoshenko, I. Sadovsky, and I. Sikalo.

*Vinnyts'ka pravda* (Vinnytsia Truth). A newspaper of the Vinnytsia oblast and city Party committees and councils, published six days a week from 1944 to 1991. The Podilia Gubernia Party Committee began publishing a paper in Russian in 1917. It changed names several times before switching to Ukrainian as *Chervonyi krai* (1924–31) – under which name it was published three and, from 1926, two times a week as the paper of the Vinnytsia and Tulcha okruha Party committees – and then as *Bil'shovyts'ka pravda* (1932–41), the paper of the Vinnytsia Oblast Party Committee. The paper's pressrun increased from 35,000 in 1950 to 135,000 in 1970 and 213,000 in 1980.

*Vino.* In medieval Rus', a payment from a bridegroom to the parents or relatives of the bride. It is mentioned in *Povist' vremennykh lit* and other early sources. Initially, this was a significant sum, but with time it was reduced to a symbolic value. In *Kormchaia kniga* and according to Lithuanian-Ruthenian law until the 16th century, *vino* is the dowry the bride brings into the marriage. The dowry usually consisted of both money and goods, such as livestock and clothing. In *Ruskaia Pravda* and the Lithuanian Statute, the term is used to identify the property given by the bridegroom to his bride in compensation for her dowry. The property was used jointly during the marriage, but in the event of the husband's death it remained with the widow.

*Vinochok dlia podkarpats'kykh ditochok* (Garland for Subcarpathian Children). A children's magazine published semimonthly in 1920 and monthly in 1921–3 in Uzhhorod by the Subcarpathian Ruthenian school board. In 1924 it appeared as a supplement to *Nash ridnyi krai* in Tiachiv. The editors were I. Pankevych, Ya. Rozvoda, and A. Markush.

*Vinok rusynam na obzhynky*
(pt 1)

*Vinok rusynam na obzhynky* (A Garland for Ruthenians during the Harvest). The title of two miscellanies published in Vienna in 1846 and 1847 by I. Holovatsky. They were among the first Ukrainian-language literary publications and played an important role in the early development of Ukrainian literature. The first contained A. Dobriansky's article on the Christianization of Rus', Ya. Holovatsky's articles on M. Shashkevych and Serbian folk songs and his translations of over 20 songs, I. Danylovych's article on Lithuanian-Ruthenian law, and over 25 poems and poetic translations by Shashkevych. The second volume included A. Mohylnytsky's article on the duties of Austrian subjects; stories and poems by I. Vahylevych, M. Ustyianovych, I. Holovatsky, Mohylnytsky, and L. Dankevych; and poems, articles on ethnographic and historical subjects, translations, and transcriptions of folktales by Holovatsky.

Pastor Georgii Vins     Aleksandr Vinter

**Vins, Georgii,** b 4 August 1928. Prisoner of conscience. The secretary of the Council of Churches of Evangelical Christians and Baptists and a Baptist pastor in Kiev, he was imprisoned in labor camps in 1966–9 for his religious activities. He was rearrested in March 1974, and sentenced in 1975 to five years in camps in the Yakut ASSR and five years' exile. He was released in April 1979 as a result of an agreement between the US and USSR governments, and given asylum in the United States. There he founded and heads the International Evangelical Christian Baptist Representation and published the *Prisoners' Bulletin: Voice of the Persecuted Church in the Soviet Union.*

**Vinter, Aleksandr,** b 10 October 1878 in Staroseltsi (now Stara Wieś), Siedlce gubernia (now in Poland), d 9 March 1958 in Moscow. Specialist in energetics; full member of the USSR Academy of Sciences from 1932. He studied at the Kiev Polytechnical Institute and in St Petersburg. He designed and built the first peat-burning electric generating station in the Russian Empire. After the First World War he directed the construction of many major electric power stations in the USSR (including the Dnieper Hydroelectric Station, the largest power station in Europe at the time), the Dnieper Industrial Complex, and the Dniprobud trust. After 1944 he held important positions in the energy hierarchy of the USSR and contributed significantly to its energy planning, including the planning of the energy complexes of central Ukraine.

**Vintskovsky, Dmytro** [Vinckovs'kyj] (pseuds: D[imitrii] or D[mytro] iz O[stry], D[mytro] iz nad D[nestra]), b 15 November 1846 in Ostra, Bukovyna, d 25 October 1917 in Kiev. Writer. He published his first story in *Nedilia* in 1865 while still a student at the Drohobych gymnasium. He worked as a teacher in Suceava (1973–4), Chernivtsi (1875–7), and Lviv (1877–83) and from 1884 as a bank clerk in Lviv. His popular articles and pedestrian poems and stories appeared in various Russophile periodicals, including those of the Kachkovsky Society and the Stauropegion Institute. The Kachkovsky Institute published his educational brochures for the peasantry in the 1880s.

**Vintskovsky, Yaroslav.** See Yaroslavenko, Yaroslav.

**Violet** (Ukrainian: *fiialka*). The common name for annual and perennial plants of the family Violaceae, representing over 500 species of herbs and low shrubs worldwide. Over 30 species grow in Ukraine in forests, meadows, and marshes, with multicolored, violet, yellow, or white flowers. The sweet violet (*Viola odorata*) and the weedy *V. tricolor* grow wild and are also cultivated as ornamentals. The European tricolor violet and the Asiatic *V. altaica* served as parent species of the most popular garden violet, the pansy (Ukrainian: *bratky, bratchyky*), a hybrid developed centuries ago.

**Violin** (*skrypka*). A bowed string instrument. Older types of this instrument existed in Ukraine as early as the 9th century. The *hudok* (medieval fiddle) is depicted on an 11th-century fresco in Kiev's St Sophia Cathedral. In the territories of Western Ukraine a three-stringed fiddle (*skrypytsia*) was known from the 14th century. The modern violin, developed in Italy, was introduced into Ukraine at the beginning of the 17th century and became extremely popular as a folk instrument in ensembles of *troisti muzyky*. Vibrato, a modern violin technique, originated in Western Ukraine and Poland and was first described by M. Praetorius in *Syntagma musicum* (1618). During the 17th and 18th centuries interest in the violin led to the growth of Western-style orchestras in Ukraine. In the early 19th century H. *Rachynsky became Ukraine's first touring concert violinist, and in the 20th century O. *Krysa and S. *Staryk have emerged as outstanding Ukrainian violinists. Well-known contemporary Ukrainian violin makers include T. Pidhorny and V. Mochalov.

**Viper.** See Snake.

**Viper's bugloss** (*Echium*; Ukrainian: *syniak*). A coarse, bristly Old World weed or shrub of the family Boraginaceae, a valuable nectariferous plant and a source of beebread. All parts of this plant are poisonous, including the showy, blue, tubular flowers. In Ukraine the bugloss, or blueweed (*E. vulgare*), grows everywhere. Its seeds contain nearly 30 percent oil, used in the manufacturing of paints. The red tower-of-jewels (*E. roseum*, formerly *E. rubrum*) grows on the steppes, in pine forests, and in forest clearings; the bark of its roots was used to obtain a carmine red textile dye.

**Vira** (Faith). A co-operative savings and loan association established in Peremyshl in 1894 by T. Kormosh. It became a model for several other co-operatives established in Galicia, especially the Provincial Credit Union (later Tsentrobank). Vira was dissolved by the Soviet authorities in 1939.

*Vira i kul'tura* (Faith and Culture). A journal of religious thought published in 1953–67 in Winnipeg by the Ukrainian Theological Society. The publication was the successor to *Nasha kul'tura* (1947–51) and *Slovo istyny* (1951–3). Edited by Metropolitan Ilarion (I. *Ohiienko), it dealt with theological, religious, and historical topics related to the Ukrainian Orthodox church. It also contained chronicles of religious life in Ukraine and the West; book reviews; and essays on literature, philosophy, art and architecture, and ethnography. After Ilarion's death in 1972 the theological society was revived and renamed in his honor (see *Metropolitan Ilarion Theological Society). It has published a number of *Vira i kul'tura* annuals which deal with many of the same topics as its namesake.

*Vira i nauka* (Faith and Science). An organ of the Ukrainian Evangelical Reformed church, published in Stanyslaviv (now Ivano-Frankivske) in 1925 and Kolomyia in 1926–39. It appeared monthly and, for a short time, semimonthly. The journal published articles on religious topics and on the Evangelical movement in Western Ukraine, North America, and elsewhere. Its editors were P. Krat, V. Fediv, L. Buchak, V. Mykytchuk, and M. Kostiv. In 1930 it appeared in a pressrun of 2,000 copies.

*Vira ta derzhava* (Faith and the State). An official biweekly publication of the Hetman government's Ministry of Religious Denominations. Edited by V. Rybynsky, the publication appeared briefly in Kiev in 1918, in a bilingual Ukrainian-Russian format.

**Virah, Yulii,** b 13 September 1880 in Khust, Transcarpathia, d 22 March 1949 in Mukachiv, Transcarpathia oblast. Painter. He studied at the Munich Academy of Arts (1898–1903) and in Budapest and Paris. He painted the murals inside the church of the Chernecha Hora monastery, near Mukachiv (1906–13), and portraits and genre paintings, such as *I Will Not Be a Monk* (1911), *Portrait of Mother* (1929), *Old Man with a Hat* (1932), and *From the Market* (1937). A catalog of his memorial exhibition was published in 1950.

**Virgin lands** (*tsilynni zemli*). Uncultivated land suitable for agriculture. Except for official preserves and sanctuaries there are no virgin lands in Ukraine today. Until the second half of the 18th century virtually all of Southern Ukraine and the Kuban was virgin land. At the end of the 18th century 90 percent of the land in those regions was still untilled; by mid-19th-century, 50 percent; and by the beginning of the 20th century, 20 percent. Much of the virgin land was used for sheep and cattle grazing. By the 1940s the last tracts of virgin land in Ukraine and the Kuban had been brought under cultivation.

In the late 19th century Ukrainian peasants from Russian-ruled Ukraine settled and brought under cultivation virgin lands in Central Asia and the *Far East. Peasants from Western Ukraine brought much of the prairie land of western Canada under the plow.

In 1953 N. Khrushchev initiated a major virgin lands campaign to increase agricultural production in the USSR. By 1964 almost 42 million ha had been brought under cultivation in Central Asia, the Volga and Ural regions, western Siberia, and the Far East. The campaign involved a massive propaganda effort and an unprecedented mobilization of labor and technical resources throughout the USSR. By 1956 some 80,000 young Ukrainians had 'volunteered' to work in Kazakhstan and Siberia. In addition two-thirds of all graduates of Ukrainian agricultural institutes were sent to work in the east, and tens of thousands of students worked there during summer vacations. The whole campaign was only a partial success: much of the land was of marginal quality, the climate was not always suited to agriculture, and some of the topsoil was blown away. The failure of the campaign was one of the pretexts for ousting Khrushchev from power in 1964, and the entire policy was abandoned soon afterward.

**Virnyk, Davyd,** b 22 July 1898 in Uiaryntsi, Vinnytsia county, Podilia gubernia. Economic historian. After graduating from the Kiev Co-operative Institute in 1926, he taught at various institutes of higher education in Kiev and directed a department of the AN URSR Institute of Economics (1936–68). From 1966 he held the chair of political economy at the Ukrainian Agricultural Academy. Virnyk is known for his works in the history of Ukrainian economic thought, which follow the Party line and stress Soviet economic achievements, Russian-Ukrainian brotherhood, and Ukrainian indebtedness to Russian scholarship. He coauthored or coedited several works, including the two-volume *Rozvytok narodnoho hospodarstva Ukraïns'koï RSR* (The Development of the National Economy of the Ukrainian SSR, 1967) and *Narysy z istoriï ekonomichnoï dumky na Ukraïni* (Essays in the History of Economic Thought in Ukraine, 1956).

**Virology** (*virusolohiia*). The branch of microbiology that studies viruses. The bacteriologist D. Ivanovsky observed that the agent that caused the tobacco mosaic disease could pass through the finest filter whereas bacteria could not; he wrote his doctoral thesis on the experiment at Kiev University in 1903. Modern virology began when W. Twort in 1915 and F. d'Hérelle in 1917 independently discovered viruses that infect bacteria. In the 1930s V. Ryzhkov and other scientists at Kharkiv University again studied the tobacco mosaic disease. In 1934, 40 types of bacteriophages were described and studied at the AN URSR (now ANU) Institute of Microbiology and Epidemiology (est 1928), renamed the ANU Institute of Microbiology and Virology in 1963, when a department of virology was created there. Entomopathogenic viruses have been studied at the ANU Institute of Zoology since 1953. Studies in medical virology have been carried out at the Kharkiv Scientific Research Institute of Microbiology, Vaccines, and Serums (est 1908), the Odessa Scientific Research Institute of Virology and Epidemiology (est 1920), and the Kiev Scientific Research Institute of Infectious Diseases (est 1949).

Scientists working with viruses have included H. Ruchko, F. Serhiienko, H. Frenkel, and S. *Moskovets. The study of viral diseases of farm animals resumed after the Second World War in Kharkiv at the Institute of Zoology under S. *Hershenzon and continued at the *Kharkiv Zootechnical-Veterinary Institute under M. Revo, the *Ukrainian Scientific Research Institute of Experimental Veterinary Science under I. Kulesko, and the Ukrainian Agricultural Academy under V. *Nikolsky. Questions of virology are dealt with in the journal *Microbiologicheskii zhurnal*, published in Russian by the ANU.

BIBLIOGRAPHY
Diachenko, S. 'K istorii mikrobiologii na Ukraine,' in *Ocherki istorii meditsinskoi nauki i zdravookhraneniia na Ukraine* (Kiev 1954)
Kvasnykov, Ie. 'Mikrobiolohiia,' in *Istoriia Akademiï nauk Ukraïns'koï RSR* (Kiev 1982)

P. Dzul

Pavlo Virsky

**Virsky, Pavlo** [Virs'kyj], b 25 February 1905 in Odessa, d 5 July 1975 in Kiev. Ballet dancer, ballet master, and choreographer. He completed study at the Odessa Music and Drama School (1927) and studied in the Moscow Theater Tekhnikum (1927–8). He was a soloist and ballet master in the Odessa Theater of Opera and Ballet (1923–31); ballet master in the Kharkiv, Odessa, Dnipropetrovske, and Kiev theaters of opera and ballet (1931–7) and the Ensemble of Song and Dance of the Kiev Military District (1939–42); and artistic director of the ballet group of the Red Army Ensemble (1942–55). He organized the *State Dance Ensemble of Ukraine in 1937 and was its ballet master and artistic director from 1955. In 1962 his ensemble toured the United States and Canada. In 1977 the ensemble was named after him. Virsky's biography, by Yu. Stanishevsky, was published in Kiev in 1962.

**Virzhykovsky, Roman** [Viržykovs'kyj], b 28 July 1891 in Poti, Georgia, d 5 October 1938. Geologist. He graduated from Kiev University in 1916. In 1928 he was appointed a professor at the Kiev Hydromelioration Institute and head of the Ukrainian Scientific Research Institute of Hydraulics and Melioration. After moving to Kharkiv in 1935, he served as a government consultant on hydrogeological research. He was the author of a Ukrainian textbook in hydrogeology (1932) and of several geological maps of Podilia and Moldavia. He was arrested during the Stalinist terror in 1938, and died in prison.

*Visnyk* (Herald). A Ukrainian Orthodox newspaper published in Winnipeg since April 1924. Until 1928 it appeared monthly and was called *Pravoslavnyi vistnyk*. Since then it has appeared semimonthly, from 1954 as the official organ of the Ukrainian Orthodox Church of Canada. The editors have included Revs S. Savchuk, V. Kudryk, Ye. Hrytsyna, and S. Yarmus.

*Visnyk* (Herald). A monthly (in 1951–2 quarterly) organ of the Organization for the Defense of Four Freedoms for Ukraine published in New York since 1947. It contains nationalistic articles on political, cultural, and historical topics and reports on the activities of the organization. The journal has a circulation of approx 2,000.

***Visnyk Akademiï budivnytstva i arkhitektury
URSR*** (Herald of the Academy of Construction and Architecture of the Ukrainian SSR). A quarterly published in
Kiev from 1958 to 1964 by the Academy of Construction
and Architecture. The journal's predecessors were *Visnyk
Akademiï arkhitektury* URSR (1946–52) and *Arkhitektura i
budivnytstvo* (1953–7). *Visnyk* contained scholarly articles
on construction and architecture and surveys of developments in those fields in Ukraine and abroad. Its editor was
I. Litvinov.

***Visnyk Akademiï nauk Ukraïns'koï RSR*** (Herald of
the Academy of Sciences of the Ukrainian SSR). A monthly
journal of the AN URSR (now ANU), published in Kiev under
that title from 1947 until 1991, when it became the *Visnyk
Akademiï nauk Ukraïny*. The journal began to appear irregularly (from 1 to 12 times a year) in Kiev in 1928 as *Visti
Vseukraïns'koï akademiï nauk*. In was titled *Visti Ukraïns'koï
akademiï nauk* in 1935 and *Visti Akademiï nauk* URSR in 1936–
46, and for some time was incorporated into *Dopovidi AN
URSR*. The journal documents the organization of scholarship in Ukraine in articles on the planning and co-ordination of research and the training of academics, devotes
considerable attention to the practical application of scholarship in the economy and the development of technology
and industry, and reports on scientific discoveries and
achievements, scholarly bodies, and scholarly conferences
and symposia. In 1990 its editor in chief was I. Lukinov.

***Visnyk radians'koï iustytsiï*** (Herald of Soviet Justice).
An organ of the People's Commissariat of Justice of the
Ukrainian SSR and the Society of Ukrainian Jurists, published in Kharkiv (a total of 185 issues) from 1922 to 1930.
It appeared in Russian as *Vestnik sovetskoi iustitsii na
Ukraine* (1922–8) and then in Ukrainian (1929–30), first
monthly (1922–3), then semimonthly. It published theoretical articles on Soviet law, official pronouncements and
documents of Soviet legal bodies, and articles on the administration of justice in Ukraine. In 1931 it was merged
with *Chervone pravo* to form \**Revoliutsiine pravo*.

***Visnyk sil's'kohospodars'koï nauky*** (Herald of Agricultural Science). A monthly agricultural journal published by the Ministry of Agriculture of Ukraine in Kiev
since 1957. It has popularized developments in agricultural sciences and assisted in improving farming practices in
Ukraine. The journal saw a steady decrease in its pressrun, from 5,400 in 1960 to 2,900 in 1980. Ca 1991–2 it was
renamed *Visnyk ahrarnoï nauky*.

***Visnyk Ukraïns'koï Hreko-Katolyts'koï Tserkvy v
Zakhidnii Evropi*** (Herald of the Ukrainian Greek Catholic Church in Western Europe). A monthly religious journal published in Paris in 1940 and 1945–52, originally as
*Visnyk Ukraïns'koï Hreko-Katolyts'koï Tserkvy u Frantsiï*. Edited by Rev I. Yatskiv, it contained church news and articles on religious and other topics.

***Visti*** (News). A weekly political newspaper published in
Lviv in 1933–4 and edited by R. Kulchytsky and B. Kravtsiv. Because it was pro-OUN, issues were frequently confiscated by the Polish authorities, and the paper was
eventually suppressed. It was succeeded in July 1936 by
\**Holos natsiï*.

*Visti* (1933–4)

***Visti*** (News). A weekly newspaper for Galician Ukrainians forced to work in Germany, published in Berlin in
1942–5 by B. Kravtsiv. The chief editor was H. Stetsiuk.

***Visti*** (News). A newspaper published since 1945 in Brussels by the Ukrainian Relief Committee in Belgium, semimonthly and then monthly to 1973, twice in 1974, and
bimonthly since 1976. The editors have included K.
Mulkevych, M. Dzoba, Ya. Pryshliak, and V. Popovych.

***Visti***. See *Muzychni visti*.

***Visti Bratstva kolyshnikh voiakiv I Ukraïns'koï
dyviziï UNA.*** (Herald of the Brotherhood of Former Soldiers of the First Ukrainian Division of the Ukrainian National Army). A press organ of the veterans of the Division
Galizien, established in October 1950 in Munich. Initially
it was a monthly journal of 4 to 12 pages; in December
1951 it became a bimonthly of 24 to 40 pages. Its editors
were O. Lesniak, O. Horbach, and L. Ortynsky (from
1952). It was succeeded by *Visti kombatanta*.

*Visti kombatanta*

***Visti kombatanta*** (Veterans' News). A journal published since 1961 by the United Ukrainian War Veterans in
America and the Brotherhood of Former Soldiers of the
First Ukrainian Division of the Ukrainian National Army
in association with the Brotherhood of Ukrainian Sich Riflemen, Former Members of the Ukrainian Insurgent
Army, and the Ukrainian War Veterans' Association of
Canada. It appeared quarterly in New York City until
1964; since 1965 it has been published bimonthly in Toronto. The editors have been I. Kedryn-Rudnytsky (since
1961), Yu. Tys-Krokhmaliuk (1961–4), V. Veryha (1965–
74), and M. Maletsky (since 1974). The journal contains articles and memoirs pertaining to Ukrainian military formations in the years 1917–21 and 1939–50, and articles on
military strategy, the Western and Soviet armed forces, in-

ternational and Soviet politics, and contemporary Ukrainian affairs. Its more than 325 contributors include V. Fedorovych, O. Horodysky, R. Kolisnyk, A. Komarnytsky, F. Korduba, R. Krokhmaliuk, Ya. Kurdydyk, B. Pidhainy, V. Simiantsiv, P. Samutyn, M. Sulyma, and V. Trembitsky. An author and subject index to the journal for the years 1961–85 was published in 1987.

***Visti Tsentral'noho komitetu Komunistychnoï partiï (bil'shovykiv) Ukraïny*** (News of the Central Committee of the Communist Party [Bolshevik] of Ukraine). A CP(B)U information bulletin founded in Kharkiv in April 1921. Until March 1928 it came out in Russian, and then in Ukrainian. The magazine published the decisions, directives, instructions, and reports of the CC as well as articles on Party work. In March 1930 it was reorganized and renamed *Partaktyvist*, then *Partrobitnyk Ukraïny* (Kharkiv–Kiev, 1933–41, 1945–6), and finally *Partiine zhyttia* (Kiev, 1946–9).

***Visti ukraïns'kykh inzheneriv*** (Ukrainian Engineers' News). A quarterly (initially monthly, then bimonthly) journal published in New York since 1950 by the Ukrainian Engineers' Society of America and the Ukrainian Technical Society of Canada (from 1956). It is the official organ of the World Federation of Ukrainian Engineers' Societies. It contains articles on various aspects of science and technology, especially developments in these fields in Soviet Ukraine. The editors have been R. Wolchuk, Z. Turkalo, S. *Protsiuk, S. Genyk-Berezovsky, Ya. Verhanovsky, O. Moroz, and Yu. Honcharenko.

***Visti Vseukraïns'koï akademiï nauk.*** See *Visnyk Akademiï nauk Ukraïns'koï RSR.*

The *Visti VUTsVK* supplements *Literatura, nauka, mystetstvo* and *Kul'tura i pobut*

***Visti VUTsVK*** (VUTsVK News). The major newspaper of the Soviet Ukrainian government, published daily in May–September 1919 in Kiev, from May 1920 to November 1934 in Kharkiv, and then again in Kiev to May 1941. Called *Visty VUTsVK* until 1929, it was the organ of the *All-Ukrainian Central Executive Committee (VUTsVK) and, from 1937, the *Supreme Soviet of the Ukrainian SSR.

It contained republican, all-Union, and world news, official Party government pronouncements, and political analyses and commentaries. Under its first editors, V. *Blakytny and Ye. Kasianenko, it also devoted considerable attention to cultural issues and emerged as one of the most influential organs supporting the *Ukrainization policy of the 1920s. At that time, contributors included prominent writers and political figures, many of whom were former *Borotbists or former members of other Ukrainian parties. The weekly cultural and literary supplements *Literatura, nauka, mystetstvo* (1923–4) and *Kul'tura i pobut* (1924–8) published some of M. Khvylovy's most important contributions to the *Literary Discussion of 1925–8, and writings by other members and supporters of the writers' group Vaplite. *Visti VUTsVK* also published contributions to the forthcoming official conference on Ukrainian orthography held in Kharkiv in 1927, and a supplement on co-operative affairs (1927–8). In the late 1920s it was one of the most influential and popular papers in Ukraine; it reached a daily circulation of 74,000 in 1929, at a time when only 48,000 copies of the official *Pravda*, the central Party organ in Moscow, were sold in the Ukrainian SSR.

Under Stalinist rule the quality of the paper rapidly declined, and severe restrictions on its freedom of expression reduced it to a tool of the totalitarian state. By 1938 almost all of its former editors and contributors had fallen victim to the terror. That year the paper was renamed *Visti Rad trudiashchykh URSR*, and in 1941 it was amalgamated with *Komunist* (renamed *Radians'ka Ukraïna*).

***Visti z Ukraïny.*** See *News from Ukraine.*

*Vistnyk* (Vienna)

***Vistnyk*** (Herald). An official government newspaper for Ukrainians in the Austrian Empire, published in Vienna from February 1850 to 1866 as the continuation of *Halycho-ruskii vistnyk*. Frequent subtitle changes included *Povremenne pis'mo ... rusynov austriiskoi derzhavy* (1850–1), *Dlia rusynov austriiskoi derzhavy* (1852), *Chasopys' politicheskaia dlia rusynov austriiskoi derzhavy* (1857), and *Chasopys' uriadova ... dlia rusynov austriiskoi derzhavy* (1865). It contained decrees and laws passed by parliament and articles on political, religious, and educational issues. The paper appeared three times a week (1850–1, 1861–2), semiweekly (1852–60, 1863–5), and weekly (1866). It was edited by I. Holovatsky (1850–2) and, later, by Yu. Vyslobotsky.

***Vistnyk*** (Herald). A monthly journal of politics, literature, culture, scholarship, and community affairs published in Lviv in 1933–9 as the continuation of *Literaturno-naukovyi vistnyk*. Under D. *Dontsov, its publisher and chief editor, *Vistnyk* became one of the most influential journals in Western Ukraine, especially among students and young adults. It propagated a militant nationalist ide-

Vistnyk (Lviv)

ology, advocating the 'national-political slogans of the new Europe and the psychological rebirth of the nation,' and strongly condemned Marxism, communism, the Soviet Union, freemasonry, Russophiles, and even Ukrainian liberal-democrats and socialists. Articles, prose, and poetry were contributed by many prominent Western Ukrainian and émigré writers and publicists. *Vistnyk* attracted 1,500 subscribers. From 1934 it published a separate quarterly book series, with pressruns of up to 5,000 copies, featuring works by Dontsov and biographies of European nationalist and fascist leaders. The journal ceased publication in September 1939 with Dontsov's arrest by the Polish authorities.

***Vistnyk Derzhavnoho sekretariiatu osvity i viroispovidannia*** (Herald of the State Secretariat of Education and Religion). An irregular organ of the State Secretariat of Education and Religion of the Western Ukrainian National Republic, published in Stanyslaviv in 1919. It contained official decrees and communiqués of the secretariat.

***Vistnyk Derzhavnoho sekretariiatu viis'kovykh sprav*** (Herald of the State Secretariat of Military Affairs). An official organ of the Ministry of Military Affairs of the Western Ukrainian National Republic, published from December 1918 to the end of May 1919. From July 1919 to the end of 1919 it was published as *Vistnyk ukraïns'koho viis'ka*. Its editor was Lt I. Bobersky.

Vistnyk derzhavnykh zakoniv i rozporiadkiv Zakhidnoï Oblasty Ukraïns'koï Narodnoï Respublyky

***Vistnyk derzhavnykh zakoniv i rozporiadkiv Zakhidnoï Oblasty Ukraïns'koï Narodnoï Respublyky*** (Herald of State Laws and Regulations of the Western Province of the Ukrainian National Republic). The official gazette of the National Rada and State Secretariat of the Western Province of the UNR, published in Stanyslaviv in 1919 (a total of 11 issues). It succeeded *Zbirnyk zakoniv, rozporiadkiv, ta obizhnykiv proholoshenykh Derzhavnym Sekre-*

tariiatom Zakhidnoï Oblasty Ukraïns'koï Narodnoï Respublyky, one issue of which appeared in December 1918.

***Vistnyk Heneral'noho Sekretariiatu Ukraïny*** (Herald of the General Secretariat of Ukraine). The official gazette of the General Secretariat of the Central Rada, published in Kiev from fall 1917 to early 1918 as the successor to *Visty z Ukraïns'koï Tsentral'noï Rady*. It contained official proclamations of the government and articles on political and economic affairs. Its editor was Yu. Tyshchenko. In early 1918 it was succeeded by *Vistnyk Rady Narodnikh Ministriv Ukraïns'koï Narodn'oï Respubliky*.

***Vistnyk Holovnoho Komisariiatu Uriadu Ukraïns'koï Narod'noï Respubliky*** (Herald of the Chief Commissariat of the Government of the UNR). The official gazette of the UNR government, published in Zhytomyr in 1920 during the joint Polish-Ukrainian offensive against the Bolsheviks.

***Vistnyk Kholms'koho huberniial'noho starostva*** (Herald of the Kholm Gubernial Starostvo). A newspaper published in Brest, Belarus, by the Kholm gubernial starosta of the Hetman government in 1918. It published news and articles about developments in the Kholm region and Podlachia. The editor was I. Bazylevych.

***Vistnyk Narodnoho doma*** (Herald of the People's Home). A Russophile organ of the *People's Home in Lviv published monthly in 1882–1914 and then irregularly in 1921 and 1924. The journal began to appear after Russophiles had gained control of the People's Home and appeared initially in *yazychiie before switching to literary Russian. It contained reports on the home's activities, literary works (primarily by Russian authors), and articles on scholarly and cultural topics. Many of the most prominent Russophiles of the time edited the journal and contributed articles to it.

***Vistnyk Odesy*** (Odessa Herald). A daily newspaper published in Odessa in 1918.

***Vistnyk ODVU*** (ODVU Herald). An organ of the *Organization for the Rebirth of Ukraine (ODVU), published monthly in New York in 1932–4 and then semimonthly in Philadelphia to June 1935. Edited by Ye. Skotsko, it contained news of the organization and articles on political affairs written mainly from an OUN perspective. It was succeeded by *Natsionalist and Ukraïna.

***Vistnyk Rady Narodnikh Ministriv Ukraïns'koï Narodn'oï Respubliky*** (Herald of the Council of National Ministers of the UNR). The official gazette of the UNR cabinet, published in early 1918 in Kiev. It contained official proclamations and articles on political and economic topics. When the Hetman government was established in April 1918, it was replaced by *Derzhavnyi vistnyk*.

***Vistnyk Soiuza vyzvolennia Ukraïny*** (Herald of the Union for the Liberation of Ukraine). An organ of the *Union for the Liberation of Ukraine, published in Vienna semimonthly and then weekly from October 1914 to November 1918 (a total of 226 issues); in 1918 it was titled *Vistnyk polityky, literatury i zhyttia*. The paper propagated

Vistnyk Soiuza vyzvolennia
Ukraïny

Ukrainian independence, the interests of which, it argued, would be served by the defeat of the Russian Empire by the Central Powers. It remains an excellent source of information about political developments in Western and Russian-ruled Ukraine during the First World War and after the February Revolution of 1917. *Vistnyk* reported extensively on Ukrainian life in German and Austrian POW camps and in Central Europe, and on foreign attitudes toward the Ukrainian question. It also published prose, poetry, and literary and art criticism. The editors were V. Doroshenko, M. Vozniak, and A. Zhuk.

**Vistnyk Ukraïns'koho viddilu Narodn'oho komisariiatu u spravakh natsional'nykh** (Herald of the Ukrainian Section of the People's Commissariat for Nationality Affairs). The official gazette of the RSFSR People's Commissariat for Nationality Affairs, published in Ukrainian from 23 July 1918 to 18 February 1919 in Moscow (10 issues). It contained official resolutions, decrees, and appeals of the commissariat and of the newly formed Soviet Ukrainian government, and articles on political and current affairs.

**Vistnyk Ukraïns'koho viis'kovoho heneral'noho komitetu** (Herald of the Ukrainian Military General Committee). A periodical of the Ukrainian Military General Committee under the Central Rada, published from May to November 1917.

**Vistnyk Ukraïns'koï Narodn'oï Respubliky** (Herald of the Ukrainian National Republic). An official organ of the UNR government, published in Kiev, Vinnytsia, and Kamianets-Podilskyi in 1918–19. It contained official orders, decrees, and texts of all UNR laws. In 1919 it was called *Vistnyk derzhavnykh zakoniv*. The publication also appeared in 1920 in Tarnów, Poland, after the evacuation of the UNR government from Ukraine.

**Vistula River** (Ukrainian: Vysla; Polish: Wisła). The largest river in Poland, which flows for 1,068 km and empties into the Baltic Sea. The river drains a basin area of 194,300 sq km, nearly 35,000 sq km of which are in Ukrainian ethnic territory (approx 15,000 sq km of that area are in Ukraine). A number of its major tributaries, including the Sian and the Buh, originate in Ukraine or near its border. The Vistula is connected with Ukraine's inland water system through the Dnieper-Buh Canal.

**Visty z Luhu** (News from Luh). A monthly organ of the *Luh sports society, published in Lviv in 1926–39. It was

edited by R. Dashkevych, F. Fedorchak, and A. Kurdydyk. In 1930 it appeared in a pressrun of 1,000 copies.

Visty z Ukraïns'koï Tsentral'noï Rady

**Visty z Ukraïns'koï Tsentral'noï Rady** (News from the Ukrainian Central Rada). An irregular organ of the *Central Rada, published in Kiev from April to the autumn of 1917. It contained the Rada's proclamations, government news, and reports on political developments throughout Ukraine and the Russian Empire. It is an excellent source of information on the early struggle for Ukrainian independence. The paper was edited by several Rada functionaries, including M. Yeremiiv, I. Steshenko, O. Vus, and V. Skrypnyk. *Visty* was succeeded by *Vistnyk Heneral'noho Sekretariiatu Ukraïny*. The first nine issues of *Visty* were reprinted in the émigré journal *Ukraïns'kyi istoryk* (1978–9, 1981, 1984, 1986).

**Visty z Zaporozha** (News from the Zaporizhia). A monthly journal published and edited in Lviv in 1910–14 by S. Demydchuk and then I. Bobersky. It contained articles on sports, hiking, physical fitness, and hunting aimed at members of the *Sich and *Sokil societies.

**Vitalii** [Vitalij], b ?, d ca 1640. Writer and translator. A hieromonk at the Dubno Monastery, he died there as its hegumen. He was the author of *Dioptra ...* (Dioptry ..., 1612), a collection of his bookish religious, philosophical, and didactic poems and elegies and translations of moral rules from Greek and Latin. The collection was popular in the 17th century and was reprinted several times elsewhere.

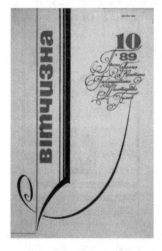

Vitchyzna

**Vitchyzna.** A literary, art, and political monthly publication of the Writers' Union of Ukraine. It was founded in response to the resolution of the CC of the All-Union Communist Party (Bolshevik) of 23 April 1932 regarding the dissolution of literary organizations. Under the title *Radians'ka literatura* it was published in Kharkiv in 1933 and in Kiev from 1934 until the outbreak of the Second World War. In 1941 its office was evacuated to Ufa, where the journal was published as *Ukraïns'ka literatura*. From November 1943 it was published in Moscow, and in March 1944 it was once again published in Kiev under the editorship of Yu. *Yanovsky. During that second Kiev period the content of the journal benefited from the temporarily liberal censorship brought about by wartime conditions. Since January 1946 the journal has been published as *Vitchyzna*. In a resolution of 4 January 1946 the CC of the CP(B)U harshly criticized the publication for its nationalist tendencies of the previous period and changed the members of the editorial board. Following Yanovsky, the editors of *Vitchyzna* were O. Honchar, L. Novychenko, V. Kozachenko, O. Poltoratsky, D. Kopytsia, who was fired in 1962 for lack of 'political attentiveness,' and his replacement, L. Dmyterko. After Dmyterko's death in 1985, O. Hlushko became editor of *Vitchyzna*. During the 1930s many of those who wrote for *Vitchyzna* were killed in the Stalinist terror (among others, the editor–in–chief, I. Kulyk, and the members of the editorial board M. Khvylovy [who committed suicide] and I. Mykytenko). Until the mid-1980s the journal adhered to the official Party line and had little popularity – a circulation of barely 20,000. Only in 1985, when the movement for the rebirth of the Ukrainian language and Ukrainian culture gained momentum, did *Vitchyzna* begin to print previously banned writers. By 1989 its circulation had grown to 40,000.

I. Koshelivets

**Viticulture.** A branch of agriculture dealing with the cultivation of grapes. Grape-growing in Ukraine dates back at least 2,500 years. Until the end of the 15th century, when it was conquered by the Turks and Tatars, the Black Sea coast was known for its viticulture and wine making. The Moslem religion of the newcomers banned both industries. They were restored in Southern Ukraine in the 18th century, when Russia won control of the Black Sea coast. Catherine II encouraged not only Ukrainians and Russians but also Germans and Austrians to settle the region. Colonists experienced in viticulture were in particular demand.

Grape harvest time at the Koktebel state farm in the Crimea

The distribution of viticulture in Ukraine is determined largely by temperature. In most regions the soil and precipitation are suitable for viticulture, but the ripening period for grapes limits commercial viticulture largely to the area south of the 48th parallel. Except for Transcarpathia and the *Crimean southern shore, which are protected by high mountains from the cold northern winds, all vineyards in Ukraine have to be covered with earth to prevent freezing during the winter.

The phylloxera, which devastated vinifera grapes throughout the world, arrived in Ukraine toward the end of the 19th century and by 1914 had infested all southwestern Ukraine. To overcome the problem peasants and small landowners planted resistant vines, such as American varieties and French-American hybrids. Quality and productivity were not high. In spite of repeated efforts to eradicate American and hybrid varieties, they are still an important part of Ukrainian vineyards. The costlier method, of grafting vinifera vines onto phylloxera-resistant American rootstocks, guaranteed consistent production of high-quality grapes but was affordable only by the larger landowners.

Until 1980 Ukraine had the largest area of vineyards in the Soviet Union. From 1986 it was in third place, after Azerbaidzhan and Moldavia. The reduction in vineyard area resulted largely from the discontinuation of low-quality and unproductive vineyards devoted mostly to American and hybrid varieties. In 1990 there were 176,000 ha of vineyards in Ukraine, 143,000 of which were productive. The gross harvests of grapes in the last 50 years are given in the table.

Grape harvests in Ukraine, 1940–90

|  | 1940 | 1960 | 1970 | 1980 | 1985 | 1990 |
|---|---|---|---|---|---|---|
| Gross output (in 1,000 t) | 161 | 423 | 904 | 886 | 430 | 836 |
| Yield (in centners per ha) | 21.8 | 34.3 | 37.6 | 49.3 | 30.9 | 57.4 |

There are three major viticultural regions in Ukraine, each with its microregions: the steppe, the Transcarpathian, and the Crimean region. The first is divided into many subregions. The Odessa subregion, with 78,000 ha of vineyards, 4,000 of which are irrigated, consists of two zones, the viticultural area of Odessa oblast east of the Dniester River, and the area between the Dniester and Danube rivers. The 12 state farms in the first zone produce varieties such as Hybrids, Rkatsiteli, Aligote, Johannisberg Riesling, Cabernet Sauvignon, Leanka, Pinot, and Italian Riesling. The 13 state farms in the second zone produce Hybrids, Rkatsiteli, Aligote, Cabernet Sauvignon, Johannisberg Riesling, Leanka, and Sereksiia grapes. The Mykolaiv-Kherson subregion covers Mykolaiv oblast and the Right-Bank portion of Kherson oblast. It has 17,000 ha of vineyards, belonging to 16 state farms and producing grapes such as Aligote, Rkatsiteli, Johannisberg Riesling, Cabernet Sauvignon, and Hybrids. The Left-Bank Kherson subregion covers the Left-Bank portion of Kherson oblast. Largely phylloxera-free, its 26,000 ha of vineyards occupy the sandy soil of the Lower Dnieper River. The region produces varieties such as Kabassia, Johannisberg Riesling, Plavai, and Cabernet Sauvignon. The Zaporizhia subregion includes two viticultural areas in Zaporizhia oblast, located on the left bank of the Dnieper River and on the Azov Sea coast. It has 4,000 ha of vineyards.

The Transcarpathian region is a relatively narrow belt at an altitude of 200–250 m, running southeast from Uzhhorod to Vynohradove and on to the Tysa River. Its 11,000 ha of vineyards are divided among 11 state farms. The

VITICULTURAL REGIONS in UKRAINE

‒‒‒‒‒ Boundary of the region

● Oblast center

━━━ Boundary of Ukraine

Research: Robert W. Hutton

0    100    200 km

grapes cultivated there include Leanka, Italian Riesling, Rose Traminer, Muller Thurgau, Furmint, Harslevelu, and Isabella. The Crimean region includes 85,000 ha of vineyards, 11,000 of which are irrigated. It is divided into two subregions by the Yaila Mountains and into 24 microregions. The three major viticultural enterprises in the region are the Masandra Wine-Making Complex, based in Yalta and covering the southern shore, the Zolota Balka Wine-Making Complex, based at Sevastopil and covering the southwestern part of the Crimea, and the Crimean Wine Trust, which includes viticultural areas in the steppe region of the Crimea. The grapes grown in the Crimea include Aligote, Cabernet Sauvignon, Merlot, Saperavi, Rkatsiteli, Johannisberg Riesling, White Muscat, Rose Muscat, Sercial, Verdelho, and Feteasca. The other viticultural areas of Ukraine account for only 1 percent of the commercial grape output.

The main viticultural research institutions in the Steppe region are the *Ukrainian Scientific Research Institute of Viticulture and Wine Making in Odessa, the Zaporizhia Oblast Agricultural Experimental Station in Zaporizhia, the Lower Dnieper Scientific Research Station for Sands Afforestation and Viticulture in Tsiurupynske, Kherson oblast, the *Odessa Agricultural Institute, the Kherson Agricultural Institute, the (formerly All-Union) Antiphylloxera Scientific Research Station of the (formerly) All-

Union Research Institute of Plant Protection in Odessa, and the Dniester Experimental Station of Horticulture and Viticulture in Chernivtsi. In the Crimea the main research institutions are the (formerly All-Union) Scientific Research Institute of Viticulture and Wine Making in Yalta and the Crimean Agricultural Institute in Symferopil. In Transcarpathia the oblast agricultural experimental station in Berehove does research on grape growing. (See also *Grapes and *Wine-making industry.)

BIBLIOGRAPHY
Okhremenko, N. *Vinodelie i vina Ukrainy* (Moscow 1966)
*Entsiklopediia vinogradarstva*, 3 vols (Kishinev 1986–7)
R. Hutton

**Vitkovsky, Ivan** [Vitkovs'kyj], b 1777, d ca 1844 in Kharkiv. Composer, violinist, conductor, and educator. He studied with J. Haydn in Vienna and then taught music at Kharkiv University and the institute for daughters of the nobility (1805–15, 1821–30). He organized the first public concerts and set up the first music store (1812) and the first piano factory (1813) in Kharkiv. His compositions include an oratorio (1805) and six fantasies for violin and piano (1807).

**Vitkovsky, Oleksander** [Vitkovs'kyj], b 1888 in eastern Podilia, d 1945 in Harbin, Manchuria. Ukrainian community leader in Manchuria. He emigrated to Manchuria in 1932 and became the last president of the Ukrainian National Colony, an umbrella organization founded in 1935 in Harbin. He was arrested and executed by Soviet troops who occupied Manchuria in 1945.

**Vitoshynsky, Aital** [Vitošyns'kyj, Ajtal'], b 1875 in Galicia, d 1937. Lawyer. He was a member of the Supreme Court in Vienna until 1918 and then presided over the Military Codification Commission of the UNR in Kiev. In 1919 he was appointed legal adviser to the Ukrainian diplomatic mission in Prague, and in 1923, counsel to the Government-in-exile of the Western Ukrainian National Republic in Vienna.

**Vitoshynsky-Dobrovolia, Yosyp-Mykhailo** [Vitošyns'kyj-Dobrovolja, Josyp-Myxajlo], b 1857, d 1931. General of the Austrian army. A brigadier general, he was one of the four Ukrainians to hold general officer rank in the Austrian army. During the First World War he commanded the 130th Brigade on the eastern front. His brigade was part of the corps that included the Legion of Sich Riflemen. He was with the Ukrainian Galician Army in central Ukraine during 1919–20, but did not occupy any official position.

Otaman Dmytro Vitovsky    Semen Vityk

**Vitovsky, Dmytro** [Vitovs'kyj], b 8 November 1887 in Medukha, Stanyslaviv county, Galicia, d 8 July 1919 near Ratibor, Silesia, Germany. Military officer. A student activist at Lviv University, he later organized educational and paramilitary organizations in Stanyslaviv. During the First World War he served in the Legion of Ukrainian Sich Riflemen as a company commander and carried out special assignments. He was chairman of the *Ukrainian Military Committee, which staged the *November Uprising in Lviv. He was briefly (1–5 November 1918) the first commander of the Ukrainian Galician Army and then minister of defense of the Western Ukrainian National Republic (until 13 February 1919). On 1 January 1919 he was promoted from major to colonel. After serving on the Ukrainian National Rada (February–April 1919) he attended the Paris Peace Conference as a member of the Western Ukrainian delegation. On the return flight his plane crashed, and he was killed.

**Vityk, Semen,** b 1876 in Drohobych county, Galicia, d 1937. Galician trade union organizer and political leader. He was a founding member of the Ukrainian Social Democratic party and the leader of the wing that collaborated with the Polish Socialist party. In 1907 and 1911 he was elected to the Austrian parliament, where he began increasingly to stress Ukrainian national rather than class interests. In 1918–19 he became a member and vice-president of the Ukrainian National Rada and of the presidium of the Labor Congress in Kiev. After emigrating to Vienna in 1919, Vityk developed pronounced Sovietophile sympathies and opposed both Ukrainian governments-in-exile. He published the monthly *Nova hromada* (1923–5). He emigrated to Soviet Ukraine in the late 1920s and was given a number of important journalistic posts in Kharkiv. In March 1933 he was arrested, and he disappeared in prison.

**VKP(B).** See Communist Party of the Soviet Union.

**Vlachs** or **Wallachians** (*volokhy*). An eastern Romance people, the ancestors of the *Rumanians, who lived in the territories of what is now *Rumania and south of the Danube River from ca 500 AD. The earliest mention of the Vlachs is in the Primary Chronicle under the year 898. Because of invasions by the Tatars the Vlachs continued to move from beyond the Carpathian Mountains to the territory between the Carpathians and the Dniester River, the Prešov region, and *Moldavia, and thus displaced the Slavic population. The independent Vlachian principalities of Wallachia (Muntenia) and Moldavia arose in the 14th century. Although the Ukrainian term Voloshchyna (Wallachia) designates the entire ancient territory of Rumania, in Ukrainian historiography it often refers specifically to Moldavia.

**Vladimir.** See Volodymyr the Great.

Mikhail Vladimirsky-Budanov

**Vladimirsky-Budanov, Mikhail** [Vladimirskij-Budanov], b 1838 in Borozdino, Tula gubernia, d 7 April 1916 in Kiev. Russian historian. He studied at Kiev University (1868) and was a professor of the history of Russian law there from 1875. He was also editor in chief for the Kiev Archeographic Commission (from 1882) and head of the Historical Society of Nestor the Chronicler (from 1887). Among his important works are *Nemetskoe pravo v Litve i Pol'she* (German Law in Lithuania and Poland, 1868; repr in Ukrainian translation in the series Ruska istorychna biblioteka [Ruthenian Historical Library], vols 23–4), *Ocherki iz istorii litovsko-russkogo prava* (Essays in the History of Lithuanian-Ruthenian Law, 1882), *Istoriia universiteta sv. Vladimira* (A History of St Vladimir [Kiev] University, 1884), and the major study *Obzor istorii russkogo prava* (A Survey of the History of Russian Law, 1886; 6th rev edn 1909). He also compiled an anthology in the history of Russian law (3 vols, 1872–5), which served as the basic source book in its field until the 1950s.

Leaders of the Ukrainian community in Vladivostok in 1920. Sitting, from left: Vasyl Shkalych, Kutenko, Yurii Hlushko-Mova, Col Fedir Steshko, Ivan Tadzaman, Oleksii Makarenko, Mykola Kobliansky; standing: Orlyk, Hnat Kyselytsia, Vitalii Zhuk, Kost Strelbytsky, Teodosii Kovtun, Mykola Novytsky, Shkliarenko, Lemishko, Hryhorii Kucherenko

**Vladivostok.** A city (1989 pop 648,000) on the Pacific coast, and the administrative center of Primorskii krai in Russia. It is the eastern terminal of the Trans-Siberian Railway and an important commercial and naval port on Zolotoi Rog Bay. Its growth was spurred by the building of the railway: its population rose from 66,000 in 1914 to 108,000 in 1926 and 206,000 in 1939. A Ukrainian colony existed in Vladivostok from its very beginning (1860) and by 1914 exceeded 2,000. In 1907–8 a Ukrainian student hromada was organized at the Oriental Institute. There was also a clandestine Ukrainian political circle in the city. With the outbreak of the revolution Vladivostok became a center of the Ukrainian movement in the Far East. At the beginning of 1917 a local hromada, with over 1,500 members, sprang up. In the next three years a Prosvita society, the Ukrainska Khata club, the Ukrainian Colony, and the Union of Oil and Telegraph Workers were founded. The Far Eastern Territorial Council established its secretariat in Vladivostok and held its third session there in November 1920. The city was the seat of the Vladivostok Okrug Council. The weekly \**Ukraïnets' na Zelenomu klyni* and the daily *Shchyre slovo* came out in the city. When the Soviets occupied Vladivostok in 1922, Ukrainian political organizations were suppressed. According to the 1926 census there were 6,000 Ukrainians in the city.

**Vladko, Volodymyr,** b 8 January 1901 in St Petersburg, d 21 April 1974 in Kiev. Writer. In the 1920s he studied at the Voronezh Institute of People's Education. After the Second World War he headed the Main Repertoire Committee of the Ukrainian SSR (1947–51) and was chief editor of *Radians'ke mystetstvo* (1947–8) and director of the Ukrainian department of *Literaturnaia gazeta* (Moscow, 1951–6).

Volodymyr Vladko

He began publishing sketches, feuilletons, and theater reviews in 1922. Between 1930 and 1932 he published several popular booklets about Ukraine's industries, the collection of travel stories *Troie za odnym marshrutom* (Three on One Itinerary, 1931), and the science-fiction novel *Idut' robotari* (The Robots Are Coming, 1931). He is known as the Ukrainian Jules Verne for his widely read science-fiction novels *Arhonavty Vsesvitu* (Argonauts of the Universe, 1935; rev edn 1956), *Chudesnyi henerator* (The Miraculous Generator, 1934), *Syvyi kapitan* (The Gray Captain, 1959), *Pozychenyi chas* (Borrowed Time, 1962), *Fioletova zahybel'* (Violet Annihilation, 1965), and *Zaliznyi bunt* (Iron Rebellion, 1967). He also wrote the best-selling historical fantasy novel *Nashchadky skifiv* (Descendants of the Scythians, 1939; rev edn 1958; English trans 1986) and the story collections *Dvanadsiat' opovidan'* (Twelve Stories, 1936) and *Charivni opovidannia* (Spellbinding Stories, 1962) and translated English and Russian literature into Ukrainian. An edition of his works in five volumes appeared in 1970–1.

**Vladych, Leonid** [Vladyč] (né Ioann Roizenberg), b 17 November 1913 in Zhytomyr, d 5 June 1984 in Kiev. Art historian and critic. A graduate of the Leningrad Institute of Painting, Sculpture, and Architecture (1958), he taught at the Kiev State Art Institute from 1960 and received his candidate's degree in 1964. He wrote many articles and introductions to exhibition catalogs and compiled many art albums. He wrote books about the artists O. Pashchenko (1947, 1957), I. Izhakevych (1955), T. Yablonska (1958), O. Shovkunenko (1960, 1983), L. Pozen (1961), and V. Kasiian (1978) and about T. Shevchenko's album *Zhivopisnaia Ukraina* (Picturesque Ukraine, 1963) and self-portraits (1973), and books of essays about Soviet Ukrainian graphic book art (1967) and Soviet Ukrainian poster artists (1989).

**Vlasenko, Nataliia,** b 3 January 1929 in Kharkiv. Experimental solid-state physicist. A graduate of Kharkiv University (1952), in 1966 she joined the AN URSR (now ANU) Institute of Semiconductors in Kiev as head of the department conducting research in photo- and electroluminescence. Vlasenko has designed a number of novel solid-state light sources and devices, including an electroluminescent solid-state laser.

**Vlasenko, Paraska,** b 10 November 1900 in Skoptsi (now Veselynivka), Pereiaslav county, Poltava gubernia, d 6 October 1960 in Kiev. Master of decorative folk painting. She designed kilims and embroidery patterns, paint-

Paraska Vlasenko in front of    Petro Vlasiuk
one of her wall paintings

ed decorative panels, tiles, and vases, and took part in decorating the walls of the Ukrainian pavilion at the All-Union Agricultural Exhibition in Moscow (1938–40), the Palace of Culture in Nova Kakhivka, and other buildings. In 1937 she won a silver medal at an international exhibition in Paris. She taught (1939–49) at what is now the Kiev School of Applied Art and worked as a designer at the Institute of Monumental Art of the Academy of Architecture of the Ukrainian SSR (1949–57).

**Vlasenko, Vasyl,** b 16 September 1921 in Yablunka, Kiev county. Chemist; AN URSR (now ANU) corresponding member since 1976. A graduate of the Kiev Polytechnical Institute (1948), he has worked since 1958 at the ANU Institute of Physical Chemistry. His research involves process technology as applied to industrial catalysis, with emphasis on the fundamental problems of the selection and preparation of heterogeneous catalysts. He has made significant contributions to the elucidation of mechanisms in important industrial catalytic processes.

**Vlasenko-Bojcun, Anna,** b 15 February 1917 in Ponykovytsia, Brody county, Galicia. Philologist, journalist, and community figure. She studied at Lviv (M PHIL, 1942), Syracuse (1964), and the Ukrainian Free (PH D, 1965) universities. Since emigrating to the United States in 1949 she has taught at Mary College (Bismarck, ND, 1966–70) and the Ukrainian Catholic University (since 1972). She has published collections of onomastic and literary studies (1977), essays and reviews (1983), travel accounts (1984), and *Onomastic Works* (1984, with a bibliography of her works).

**Vlasiuk, Dmytro** [Vlasjuk], b 25 July 1902 in Odessa. Scenery designer. He studied at the Kiev State Art Institute (1921–7, class of V. Meller) and worked in Berezil and then as a designer in the Kharkiv, Kiev, and Odessa Ukrainian drama theaters. He also taught at the Kharkiv Theater School (from 1931) and the Kharkiv Theater Institute

**Vlasiuk, Petro** [Vlasjuk], b 16 February 1905 in Chemeryske, Zvenyhorodka county, Kiev gubernia, d 20 March 1980 in Kiev. Agrochemist, plant physiologist, and soil scientist; full member of the AN URSR (now ANU) and the All-Union Academy of Agricultural Sciences from 1948. He graduated from the Uman (1926) and Leningrad (1930) agricultural institutes and then taught at the former institute (1931–47) and at Kiev University (1947–56). He

went on to serve as director of the ANU Institute of Plant Physiology and Agrochemistry and was president of the Ukrainian Academy of Agricultural Sciences (1956–62). Vlasiuk published numerous scientific and popular articles dealing with agrochemistry, plant physiology, and soil science. He showed that manganese acts as a strong oxidizing agent during ammonia feeding of plants but as a strong reducing agent during nitrate nourishment, and that manganese increases the efficiency of carbon dioxide transformation during photosynthesis. He introduced the use of industrial wastes as a source of microelements in fertilizers and contributed to the applications of radioactive labeling in plant research and the use of radiation methods for inducing plant mutation.

**Vlasov, Aleksandr,** b 1 November 1900 in Kosha, Tver gubernia, Russia, d 25 September 1962 in Moscow. Russian architect; president of the USSR Academy of Architecture (1955–6) and vice-president of the Academy of Construction and Architecture of the Ukrainian SSR (1956–62). After graduating from the Moscow Higher Technical School (1928) he worked as an architect, taught at the Moscow Architectural Institute (from 1931), and studied at the upgrading faculty of the USSR Academy of Architecture (to 1936). After the Second World War he served as chief architect of Kiev (1944–50) and Moscow (1950–5). He supervised the reconstruction of the Khreshchatyk in Kiev and the general plan for the rebuilding of Kiev (1945–7).

**Vlasov, Andrei,** b 1 September 1900 in Lomakino, Nizhnii Novgorod gubernia, Russia, d 2 August 1946 in Moscow. Soviet Russian military commander; the highest-ranking Soviet collaborator with the Germans during the Second World War. In January 1942 he was promoted to lieutenant general, and in March he took command of the Second Shock Army, which had been encircled during its advance toward Leningrad. Despite the army's starvation and imminent annihilation, J. Stalin refused to allow it to retreat. It was finally routed in June 1942, and Vlasov was taken prisoner on 11 July and sent to a POW camp near Vinnytsia.

Incensed by Stalin's disastrous military direction and already aggrieved by the Stalinist collectivization, terror, and military purges of the 1930s, Vlasov turned against Stalin and co-operated with the Wehrmacht and A. Rosenberg's Ostministerium as a propagandist. Consequently nearly 1 million Russian, Ukrainian, and other Soviet soldiers in German POW camps enlisted to fight in Wehrmacht units (Osttruppen) on the eastern front, and thousands of others deserted from the Red Army to do so. A. Hitler, pathologically mistrustful of the *Untermenschen* and Vlasov's intentions, suspended Vlasov's propaganda in June 1943, and in September he had all Osttruppen transferred to the western front.

The impending defeat of Germany again altered the Nazi leaders' attitude. In September 1944 H. Himmler promised Vlasov Waffen SS support to create, train, and command a genuine liberation army from among the Soviet citizens in the Wehrmacht and over 3 million prisoners of war and *Ostarbeiter*. Vlasov formed and chaired the independent Committee for the Liberation of the Peoples of Russia (KONR) in Prague in November 1944 with the aim of uniting all anti-Bolshevik forces of Soviet citizens in the German-occupied territories. The *Ukrainian National Committee and other non-Russian organizations, however, refused to join the KONR; they rejected its Russian imperialist, nationalist ideology and Vlasov's claim to speak on behalf of the non-Russians, and disbelieved its promise that the non-Russians would have national self-determination after the destruction of Bolshevism (in response to which mistrust the KONR established its own eight-member Ukrainian Committee, chaired by F. Bohatyrchuk). Approx 300,000 men, 30–40 percent of them ethnic Ukrainians, were transferred to the Armed Forces of the KONR, more popularly known as the *Russian Liberation Army (ROA). Only one 20,000-man division, commanded by Col S. Buniachenko, became fully operational; it fought briefly along the Oder River in mid-April 1945. Vlasov and the division then headed west to avoid the advancing Red Army and surrendered with other ROA units to American forces on 11 May. The next day the Soviet authorities stopped an American convoy and removed Vlasov from it without opposition. He, Buniachenko, and 10 other members of his staff were hanged after over 14 months of imprisonment and a three-day closed trial for treason, espionage, and terrorism by the Military Collegium of the Soviet Supreme Court. Hundreds of thousands of surrendered ROA personnel were forcibly repatriated to the USSR, with American and British military collusion, and deported to Soviet concentration camps. (See also *Repatriation.)

BIBLIOGRAPHY
Steenberg, S. Vlasov (New York 1970)
Strik-Strikfeldt, W. Against Stalin and Hitler: Memoir of the Russian Liberation Movement, 1941–1945 (London 1970)
Thorwald, J. The Illusion: Soviet Soldiers in Hitler's Armies (New York 1975)
Andreyev, C. Vlasov and the Russian Liberation Movement: Soviet Reality and Emigré Theories (Cambridge 1987)

R. Senkus

Ivan Vlasovsky　　　　　Orest Vlokh

**Vlasovsky, Ivan** [Vlasovs'kyj] (Wlasowsky), b 15 August 1883 in Vilshany, Kharkiv county, Kharkiv gubernia, d 10 October 1969 in Toronto. Orthodox church historian and theologian, and civic leader. A graduate of the Kiev Theological Academy (1908), he taught (1908–18) in various gymnasiums in the Poltava region (Lokhvytsia, Zolotonosha, Konotop) before becoming principal of a gymnasium in Lutske (1918–26). In the interwar period he worked on the Ukrainization of the Orthodox church in Volhynia. With A. Richynsky he organized the Ukrainian church council in Lutske in 1927. He was a member of the commission for the translation of liturgical texts into Ukrainian (1932–9), general secretary of the Mohyla Society in Lutske and editor of its organ Za sobornist', a member of the Metropolitan's Council of the Polish Autocephalous Orthodox church and editor of the journal *Tserkva i narid (1935–8), and secretary of the Volhynia Theological Consistory in Kremenets (1934–9). He was one of the founders of the Prosvita society in Lutske and a deputy to the Polish Sejm (1928–30) from the Ukrainian Socialist Radical party. For his political activities he was imprisoned by the Polish authorities several times.

During the Second World War, Vlasovsky assisted in the rebirth of the *Ukrainian Autocephalous Orthodox church (UAOC) in Ukraine, and served as adviser to Metropolitan P. Sikorsky and secretary of the administration of the UAOC in Lutske (1942–3). He fled from the advancing Soviet army to Prague and then Munich in 1945, where he was director of the chancellery of the UAOC Synod and of the Theological Academy of the UAOC. In 1948 he emigrated to Canada. In Winnipeg he was a professor of St Andrew's College (1949–50) and edited the renewed journal Tserkva i narid (1949–51) before moving to Toronto. Vlasovsky authored numerous works on church history and other subjects, including Kanonichni i istorychni pidstavy dlia avtokefalii Ukraïns'koï Pravoslavnoï Tserkvy (The Canonical and Historical Bases for the Autocephaly of the Ukrainian Orthodox Church, 1948), Korotka istoriia Pravoslavnoï Tserkvy (A Brief History of the Orthodox Church, 1948), Narys istorii Ukraïns'koï Pravoslavnoï Tserkvy (An Outline of the History of the Ukrainian Orthodox Church, 4 vols in 5 books, 1955–66; the first 2 vols in English as Outline History of the Ukrainian Orthodox Church, 1956, 1979), and Kyievo-Pechers'ka Lavra ta iï istorychne znachennia (The Kievan Cave Monastery and Its Historical Significance, 1966). A memorial book in his honor, containing a bibliography of his works, was published in Toronto in 1974.

A. Zhukovsky

**VLKSM.** See Communist Youth League of Ukraine.

**Vlokh, Orest** [Vlox], b 2 July 1934 in Lviv. Solid-state physicist and civic activist. A graduate of Lviv University (1957), he has worked as a researcher and now is a professor of physics and the holder of the chair of nonlinear optics there. In his research on nonlinear optical effects in crystals, Vlokh has obtained significant results on the role of spatial dispersion in electromagneto- and piezo-optical effects. He has done pioneering work on electrogyration, a nonlinear parametric effect in dielectrics, and has written a monograph on the effects of spatial dispersion in parametric crystal optics (1984). In 1989 he became head of the Popular Movement of Ukraine in Lviv oblast, and in 1990 he was elected deputy to the Supreme Council of the Ukrainian SSR.

**Vlyzko, Oleksa** [Vlyz'ko], b 17 February 1908 in Korosten, Novgorod gubernia, Russia, d 14 December 1934 in Kiev. Poet. He studied at the philological faculty of the Kiev Institute of People's Education. He belonged to the literary organizations Molodniak and the All-Ukrainian Association of Proletarian Writers and later worked on the futurist journal Nova generatsiia. His first published poem was 'Sertse na nord' (Heart to the North) in the journal Hlobus (1925.) Although Vlyzko paid the obligatory tribute to the Soviet way of life, his poetry was character-

Oleksa Vlyzko                    Kostiantyn Vobly

ized by a search for new socialist forms of artistic expression, a cheerful romanticism, a love of the sea as a primal element, and interest in the adventures and passions of people of strong character. Vlyzko's poetry appeared in such collections as *Za vsikh skazhu* (I'll Speak on Everyone's Behalf, 1927), *Poeziï* (Poems, 1927), *Zhyvu, pratsiuiu* (I Live and I Work, 1930), *Knyha baliad* (The Book of Ballads, 1930), and *P'iatyi korabel'* (Fifth Ship, 1933). In December 1934 he was arrested, accused of counterrevolutionary diversionary activities, and shot along with 28 other writers and cultural activists. During the Khrushchev 'thaw' he was rehabilitated. A posthumous collection was published in 1963, *Vybrani poeziï* (Selected Poems).

**VOAPP.** See All-Union Alliance of Associations of Proletarian Writers.

**Vobly, Kostiantyn** [Voblyj, Kostjantyn], b 27 May 1876 in Tsarychanka, Kobeliaky county, Poltava gubernia, d 12 September 1947 in Kiev. Economist, statistician, and geographer; full member of the VUAN and AN URSR (now ANU) from 1921. After completing study at the Kiev Theological Academy (1900) he graduated from Warsaw University and worked with the Warsaw statistical committee. From 1906 he lectured at Kiev University, where he wrote his MA thesis, *Ocherki po istorii pol'skoi fabrichnoi promyshlennosti* (Outlines of the History of Polish Factory Industry, 1909). His research in Berlin, Vienna, and Paris culminated in a PH D dissertation on the third professional-industrial census in Germany at Kiev University (1911). Before the Soviet period he lectured at Kiev University and the Kiev Co-operative Institute (director in 1917–19). From its inception Vobly was involved with the VUAN: he was head of its social-economic division from 1925, president of its Society of Economists, vice-president of the academy (1928–30), chairman of the Commission for the Study of the Economy of Ukraine (1927–30), chairman of the chair of commercial trade and industrial economics, chairman of the Department of Economic Geography (1939–42) at the Institute of Economics, and the institute's director (1942–7).

Vobly was a prolific writer who published numerous separate works on political economy, economic geography, economic theory, the agrarian question, industry, trade, and finance. His monographs include *Statistika* (Statistics, 1908; 6 edns), *Osnovy ekonomii strakhovaniia* (The Foundations of Insurance Economics, 1915; 2 edns), *Nachal'nyi kurs politicheskoi ekonomii* (A Beginning Course

in Political Economy, 1918; 2 edns), *Ekonomicheskaia geografiia Ukrainy* (The Economic Geography of Ukraine, 1919; 5 edns), *Narysy z istoriï rosiis'ko-ukraïns'koï tsukrovo-buriakovoï promyslovosty* (Essays in the History of the Russian-Ukrainian Sugar-Beet Industry, 3 vols, 1928–31; 2 more volumes remain unpublished), and *Organizatsiia truda nauchnogo rabotnika* (The Organization of the Work of the Scientific Worker, 1943).

BIBLIOGRAPHY
Virnyk, D.; Kuhukalo, I. *Kostiantyn Hryhorovych Voblyi* (Kiev 1968)
Koropets'kyi, I. 'Ekonomichni pohliady Kostiantyna Vobloho pered 1917 rokom,' *JUS*, 12, no. 2 (Winter 1987)

**Vocational-technical education** (*profesiino-tekhnichna osvita*). An educational network of programs for the training of the work force and for the upgrading of its skills, established during the Soviet period. Vocational-technical education is provided in *vocational-technical schools, *tekhnikums, *technical schools, and institutions offering *secondary special education. There are also numerous schools and courses organized at the enterprise level which provide on-the-job training. Instruction at the individual brigade level is also widely practiced. Some 8.6 million workers and white-collar staff have received training at the enterprise or collective farm to upgrade their qualifications. (See also *Professional and vocational education.)

**Vocational-technical schools** (*profesiino-tekhnichni uchylyshcha*, or PTU). Educational institutions established in 1958 under the jurisdiction of the Chief Administration for Professional and Technical Education of the Council of Ministers of Ukraine. They offer vocational education for young people joining the labor force after completing eight years of general education. The schools, which have day and evening programs, tend to recruit young people with low academic achievement levels. PTU specialize according to branches of production. There are urban and rural vocational-technical schools affiliated with various enterprises to provide practical experience. There is a unified curriculum established for each individual occupation. Vocational training forms 60–70 percent of the curriculum, the remaining time being spent on general education subjects. Urban PTU have one- to three-year programs of study; rural PTU have one- to two-year programs. In 1965 there were 754 PTU in Ukraine with an enrollment of 284,000. Between 1959 and 1964 a network of *technical schools was established. The PTU provide practical training and the final two years of compulsory general education for students with an incomplete secondary education (see *Eight-year school). After three years of study and practical work students who pass their final examinations are awarded both a general education certificate and a vocational diploma. The PTU network has grown rapidly in recent years. In 1986 there were 1,100 such schools, with 742,000 students. PTU still exist to provide pupils with basic work training without the general education component. The majority of PTU courses are evening and shift courses that allow workers to study at times compatible with their work shifts.

B. Krawchenko

**Vodiany, Mykhailo** [Vodjanyj, Myxajlo] (Vodianoi), b 23 December 1924 in Kharkiv, d 13 September 1987 in

Odessa. Stage actor and comedian. In 1939–41 he studied in the Leningrad Theatrical Institute, and in 1943–5 he worked in the Piatigorsk Operetta Theater. In 1945–6 he performed in the Lviv Philharmonic and in 1947–53, in the Lviv Theater of Musical Comedy. From 1954 he worked in the Odessa Theater of Musical Comedy.

*Vodianyk.* See Demonology in Ukraine.

**Vodianytsky, Volodymyr** [Vodjanyc'kyj], b 6 January 1894 in Konstiantynohrad (now Krasnohrad), Poltava gubernia, d 30 November 1971 in Sevastopil, Crimea. Zoologist and hydrobiologist; corresponding member of the AN URSR (now ANU) from 1957. A graduate of Kharkiv University (1916), he founded the Novorossiisk Biological Station (1921), taught at Rostov-na-Donu University (1939–42, 1944–5), and directed the ANU Sevastopil Biological Station (1945–62) and the ANU Institute of the Biology of Southern Seas (1963–8). He researched the acclimatization of invertebrates in Ukrainian reservoirs and the productivity of the Black Sea.

**Vodolazhchenko, Olha** [Vodolažčenko, Ol'ha], 1888–? Historian. A scholarly associate of the Kharkiv Scientific Research Chair of the History of Ukrainian Culture during the 1920s, she wrote on the history of Ukraine and the history of education in Slobidska Ukraine. She was arrested and deported to Siberia ca 1937–8.

**Vohni** (Fires). A publishing co-operative established in Lviv in 1929 to publish works and manuals by writers belonging to the Plast scouting association (eg, B. Kravtsiv, A. Richynsky, Ye. Pelensky, I. Manastyrsky). After Plast was banned by the Polish authorities in 1930, Vohni continued to propagate the organization's ideology through the journal *Vohni* (1931–9), edited by Pelensky, J. Rudnyckyj, V. Karkhut, and Ya. Hladky. Vohni also published the monthly magazine *\*Na slidi*.

**Voiakovsky, Mykola** [Vojakovs'kyj], b 12 June 1899 in Bohdanivka, Skalat county, Galicia, d 12 May 1972 in Brooklyn, New York. Ukrainian Catholic priest and community activist. A graduate of the Lviv Theological Seminary, he was ordained in 1925 and then served as a parish priest in Galicia. At the outset of the Second World War he fled to Vienna and then went to serve Ukrainian workers in the Sudetenland. In 1945–8 he served as acting apostolic visitator and administrator of Ukrainian Catholics in Germany. He organized religious life for Ukrainian refugees in the displaced persons' camps in Germany; organized the theological seminary in Hirschberg; and published the church organ, liturgical books, and a *shematyzm* of the church in Germany (1947). In 1949 he moved to the United States. Voiakovsky was a prolific writer who frequently contributed articles to religious periodicals in Ukraine and the United States. He also published three volumes of his collected sermons (1949, 1954, 1969), several short monographs on religious topics, and a collection of his writings and memoirs (1971).

**Voice of America** (VOA). A US government agency that broadcasts news and entertainment worldwide. Administered by the US Information Agency and closely tied to the State Department, VOA emerged at the end of the Second

World War from several offices and departments that had been established to broadcast American war propaganda and news to Nazi-occupied Europe. After the war VOA began devoting most of its efforts to countering communist influence around the world (especially in the Third World and Soviet-occupied Eastern Europe). VOA has provided an American perspective on international affairs, served as an alternative source of news about international and internal developments in other countries, and informed foreigners about life in the United States in English (some programs are read in a special simplified English) and dozens of other languages. With the intensification of the Cold War, VOA began beaming signals directly to the USSR from transmitters in the United States, Western Europe, and Asia. Russian-language broadcasts were begun in February 1947. Much of the programming commented on Soviet affairs and exposed the totalitarian nature of the Soviet system. In response, the Soviet authorities began electronically jamming VOA signals in February 1948. In November 1949 daily half-hour Ukrainian programs were begun; they were followed in the next few years by broadcasts in the Baltic languages, Armenian, Georgian, Tatar, Azeri, and Turkic. By December 1954 the Ukrainian program was one hour daily, and the broadcasts were specially beamed to Ukrainians in Soviet Central Asia as well as in Ukraine. There have been several directors of the Ukrainian section of Voice of America, including N. Hryhoriiv, V. Kedrovsky, Ye. Zelevska, M. Terpak, O. Drahan, M. Frantsuzhenko, and V. Biliaiv.

**Voice of Canada.** See Radio Canada International.

**Voievidka, Yaroslav** [Vojevidka, Jaroslav], b 5 March 1882 in Petranka, Kalush county, Galicia, d 30 March 1920 in Pishchanka, Balta county, Podilia gubernia. Army officer. After serving in the Austrian army during the First World War, he joined the Ukrainian Galician Army in December 1918 and organized the First Artillery Regiment of the First Brigade of the Ukrainian Sich Riflemen. As commander of the regiment he was promoted on 22 June 1919 to major. He was killed by the Bolsheviks.

Yaroslav Voievidka

**Voievidka, Yaroslav** [Vojevidka, Jaroslav], b 26 October 1909 in Chernivtsi, Bukovyna, d 25 January 1981 in Reno, Nevada. Obstetrician and gynecologist. A graduate of Cracow University (1934), he served as a specialist in its hospital clinic. He was deputy director from 1941 and director from 1943 of the gynecological and obstetrical clinic of the Lviv Medical Institute. A postwar refugee in Germany from 1945, he was president of the *Ukrainian Medical Charitable Service (1948–9), president of the Ukrainian Physicians' Association in Germany, and director of the Ukrainian polyclinic in Munich. In 1950 he emigrated to the United States, where he ran his own clinic in New York, helped found the Ukrainian Medical Association of North America, and was its president (1955–7) and editor of its journal (1956–7). His publications dealt with hysterectomy and the history of Ukrainian medical organizations.

**Voin** [Vojin']. A fortress town in Kievan Rus', located in Pereiaslav principality, on the right bank of the Sula River approx 1.5 km from its junction with the Dnieper River (near present-day Voinska Hreblia, Hlobyne raion, Poltava oblast). Voin had a strategic importance in the system of fortified towns which was built by Vsevolod Yaroslavych in the 980s along the Sula River as a line of defense against marauding nomadic tribes to the south. Voin was first mentioned in a chronicle under the year 1055 as the site of a victory by the prince of Pereiaslav, Vsevolod Yaroslavych, over the Torks. It was again mentioned under the year 1079 in conjunction with the internecine warfare among Rus' princes, in which the Cumans also took part; under the year 1110, when Rus' forces met the Cumans outside its walls; and under the year 1147, when Voin was the site of a peace treaty between the Kievan prince Iziaslav Mstyslavych and the Cumans.

The Voin fortress and harbor (diorama by O. Kazansky)

The exact location of Voin was discovered in 1897 by V. *Liaskoronsky, and the site was excavated in 1956–9 under the direction of the AN URSR (now ANU) Institute of Archeology. It was situated on a terrace, well protected by waterways, and consisted of a fortress surrounded by a moat and double-constructed walls of wood and earth. Together with the open-air trade and crafts district beyond its walls, the site covered 27.6 ha. The inside of the fortress was a protected area in which the traders kept their stores. It also housed a garrison of soldiers. To the west of the settlement was a burial ground. Excavations at the site unearthed armor and weapons (swords, spears, battle-axes), personal items (knives, scissors, keys, bone combs, clasps, bracelets, rings, crosses, bronze Byzantine coins), tableware (jars, amphorae, iron pots, glass dishes), and work articles (hammers, nails, blacksmiths' tongs, wire, carpenters' axes, a loom).

Voin existed as an important economic and military center in Rus' for nearly three centuries. It was sacked in 1186 during a major offensive by the Cumans on military installations along the Sula River. Subsequently Voin was partially rebuilt, only to be razed in 1240 by the Tatars. Today its ruins are submerged beneath the waters of the Kakhivka Reservoir.

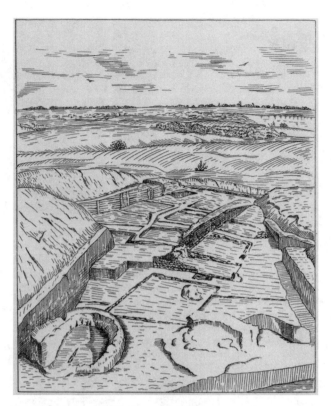

A reconstruction of Voin's western *ditynets

BIBLIOGRAPHY
Makarenko, N. *Gorodishcha i kurgany Poltavskoi gubernii* (Poltava 1917)
Dovzhenok, V.; Honcharov, V.; Yura, R. *Drevn'orus'ke misto Voïn'* (Kiev 1966)

A. Zhukovsky

**Voinar, Meletii.** See Wojnar, Meletius.

**Voinarovsky, Andrii** [Vojnarovs'kyj, Andrij], b ca 1689, d ca 1740 in Yakutsk, Siberia. Hetman state political and military figure. He was the son of a highly placed Volhynian aristocrat and O. Mazepa, the sister of Hetman I. Mazepa. He completed his studies at the Kievan Mohyla Academy. He was considered to be one of Mazepa's most trusted aides and his confidant. The hetman sent him on various special missions, including an attempt to allay Russian suspicions in October 1708 by visiting A. Menshikov's headquarters in the Siversk region and explaining the gradual approach of Mazepa's army. When Mazepa made his break with Muscovy, Voinarovsky became the primary liaison officer between the Ukrainian and the Swedish armies. After the defeat at Poltava he conveyed Charles XII to Turkey. After Mazepa's death he inherited the hetman's estate. This precipitated a break with other *starshyna* and P. Orlyk. In 1711–12 he lived in Istanbul as the special envoy of Charles XII. He remained in Turkish-controlled territories until 1715, with sojourns in Wrocław and Vienna. On 12 October 1716, en route to Sweden, he was seized by agents of Peter I and handed over by the Hamburg Senate to the Russian authorities. He was taken to St Petersburg and imprisoned in the Peter and Paul Fortress. In 1723 he was exiled to Yakutsk, where

Andrii Voinarovsky

Rev Tyt Voinarovsky-Stolobut

Petro Voinovsky

Yakiv Voitiuk

he lived in penury for 16 years. He was last heard from in 1737. The Decembrist K. Ryleev wrote a poem about him, which was translated into German by S. Chamisso and into Ukrainian by S. Hordynsky.

BIBLIOGRAPHY
Borshchak, I. *Voinarovs'kyi – sestrinok het'mana Ivana Mazepy, druh Avrory Kenigsmark i sybirs'kyi v'iazen'* (Lviv 1939)
Vynar, L. *Andrii Voinarovs'kyi: Istorychnyi narys* (Munich–Cleveland 1962)

A. Zhukovsky

**Voinarovsky-Stolobut, Tyt** [Vojnarovs'kyj-Stolobut], b 16 February 1856 in Liatske Shliakhetske, Tovmach county, Galicia, d 21 February 1938 in Lviv. Greek Catholic priest, economist, and civic leader. After graduating in theology from Lviv University (1878) he was ordained, and served as parish priest in various villages in Kolomyia county. In 1907 he was elected as a candidate of the National Democratic party to the Austrian parliament. To promote land distribution he inspired the founding of the Zemlia society in 1908 and the Land Mortgage Bank in 1909. Having been appointed canon of the metropolitan chapter and general administrator of the metropolitan's estates he moved in 1910 to Lviv, where he persuaded Metropolitan A. Sheptytsky to donate estates in Korshiv and Myluvannia to farming schools. He was also active in the *Silskyi Hospodar society as its vice-president (1918–21) and president (1929–36) and was vice-president of the Lviv Agricultural Chamber (1934–6). He devoted much of his time to economics and (usually under the pseudonym Danylo Zhuravel or T. von Slepowron) wrote articles and books on economic questions. For these and other works he was awarded an honorary doctorate by the Ukrainian Husbandry Academy. His memoirs were published in *Istorychni postati Halychyny XIX–XX st.* (Historical Figures of Galicia in the 19th and 20th Centuries, 1961).

**Voinovsky, Petro** [Vojnovs'kyj], b 8 September 1913 in Stanivtsi Dolishni, Bukovyna. OUN leader and military officer. He joined the OUN in 1933 and rose to deputy (1940) and then chief of the OUN in Bukovyna. In 1941 he prepared an anti-Soviet revolt and organized the *Bukovynian Battalion, which marched to Kiev. The leadership of the OUN (Melnyk faction) appointed Voinovsky chief military co-ordinator for central Ukraine and military representative on the Ukrainian National Council in Kiev (1941–2). During 1943 he served at the OUN military headquarters in Lviv. After being arrested by the Gestapo in January 1944, he spent over eight months in the Bratz concentration camp. In 1949 he emigrated to the United States, where he was active in the Ukrainian community, especially in veterans' organizations. In 1973 the UNR government-in-exile promoted him to colonel.

**Voishelk Mindovhovych.** See Vaišvilkas.

**Voitenko, Vasyl** [Vojtenko, Vasyl'], b 13 January 1881 in Volokytyne, Putyvl county, Kursk gubernia, d 16 June 1951 in Kharkiv. Opera singer (dramatic tenor). From 1912 he appeared on the stages of St Petersburg, Baku, Kharkiv, and Kiev. He was a founder and soloist of the Dnipropetrovske Opera and Ballet Theater (1930–41), and taught at the Kharkiv Conservatory (1944–51). His main roles were Andrii in M. Lysenko's *Taras Bulba*, Grigorii in I. Dzerzhinsky's *Tikhii Don* (The Quiet Don), and Hermann in P. Tchaikovsky's *Queen of Spades*.

**Voitiuk, Yakiv** [Vojtjuk, Jakiv], b 1894 in Siltse, Kholm county, d 1937 on Solovets Islands. Civic and political leader. He studied in the historical-philological faculty of Moscow University for two years and belonged to a socialist student circle. During the First World War he served in the Russian army in the Ternopil region, and in 1919 he organized the Polisia Sich in Kobryn to fight the Poles. In 1922 he was elected to the Polish Sejm, where he was secretary of the Ukrainian Parliamentary Representation and then founder and chairman of the Ukrainian Social Democratic caucus (1924) and chairman of the Communist parliamentary faction. In 1928 he emigrated to Soviet Ukraine. He was arrested in 1933 and sentenced to 10 years but then executed in 1937 for 'belonging to a counterrevolutionary organization.'

**Voitkevych-Pavlovych, Vasyl** [Vojtkevyč-Pavlovyč, Vasyl'], b ?, d 1920? Lawyer and legal scholar. He helped found the Ukrainian Law Society in Kiev (1917–20) and later served as its president. He lectured at the Ukrainian State University of Kiev (1918–19). In 1920 he served as legal adviser to the VUAN and as member of its Commission on Legal Terminology.

**Voitkovsky, Vasilii** [Vojtkovskij, Vasilij], b ?, d 1904. Russian church figure and publicist. From 1850 to 1869 he served as pastor of the Russian Orthodox church in Üröm, near Budapest. During that time he was a member of M. *Raevsky's coterie and was instrumental in the spread of Russophile tendencies among Transcarpathia's Ruthenians. He had a great influence on Rev I. *Rakovsky, a leader of the Transcarpathian revival, and became his main adviser. Under Voitkovych's de facto editorship Rakovsky published the papers *Zemskii pravitel'stvennyi vestnik dlia Korolevstva Ugorskago* (1850–9) and *Tserkovnaia gazeta* (1856–8). Rakovsky and Voitkovych reworked the manuscript of O. Dukhnovych's grammar of the Transcarpathian dialect and published it as a grammar of literary Russian. As a professor of church history and theology at New Russia (Odessa) University from 1869, Voitkovych maintained contacts with Transcarpathian scholars and teachers, particularly those who had emigrated to the Russian Empire. He wrote in Russian about the Uniate church under Austria, the religious movement in Galicia, and the church-rite issue in Galicia, and translated into Russian Dukhnovych's history of Prešov eparchy (1877).

**Voitsekhivka burial site.** A Copper and Bronze Age burial ground near Voitsekhivka (now Kolosivka), Polonne raion; Khmelnytskyi oblast. Excavations in 1924 and 1949 revealed a burial site of an entire family of the *Globular Amphora culture – one man, two women, six children, and a slave. Individual, pair, and group burials from the *Komariv culture were uncovered in the sites dating from the Bronze Age. Grave goods included pottery and bronze and stone items.

**Voitsekhivsky, Osyp** [Vojcexivs'kyj], b 1793 in Ivanivka, Uman county, Kiev vicegerency, d 17 November 1850 in Kazan, Russia. Physician and sinologist. A graduate of the Kievan Mohyla Academy and the St Petersburg Medico-Surgical Academy (1819), he worked in China as a physician (1819–32). In 1829 a monument was erected to Voitsekhivsky in Peking for his dedicated fight against cholera and other epidemics. He served at Kazan University as the first professor of Chinese and Manchurian literature in Russia. He translated a number of works by Chinese thinkers into Russian and compiled a Chinese-Manchurian-Russian dictionary.

**Voivode** (Ukrainian: *voievoda*; Polish: *wojewoda*; Russian: *voevoda*). An ancient Slavic term for the leader of *voï* ('warriors'). He was elected by the tribal assembly in times of war. In Kievan Rus' the term referred initially to the commander of a prince's Varangian guard and then to the commander of his army in times of war or to his vicegerent and garrison commander in a particular town. In the 13th- and 14th-century Western Ukrainian principalities it occasionally designated the joint administrator and military commander of a certain territory.

In the Grand Duchy of Lithuania and the Lithuanian-Ruthenian state a voivode was a noble appointed for life by the grand duke to be the governor and military commander of a province, called a *zemlia* ('land') or, beginning in 1413, a *voivodeship (palatinate), in accordance with the Polish model; he was simultaneously a member of the *Council of Lords. Towns self-governed by *Magdeburg law were exempt from his powers. In the 14th- to 16th-

century Polish Kingdom and, after the 1569 Union of Lublin, the Polish-Lithuanian-Ruthenian Commonwealth, a voivode was a lord appointed for life by the king to govern a voivodeship; he was simultaneously a member of the Royal Council and its successor, the Senate. His authority was weakened after the creation of starostas and noble dietines. The starosta assumed the role of commander of the royal army and chief justice in the voivodeship, and the voivode was responsible for leading the levy en masse among the nobility, trying Jews, regulating commercial prices, and controlling weights and measures there. The position was abolished after the partition of Poland in 1772.

In Muscovy a voivode was a regimental commander and, from the early 17th century, the tsar's chief administrator and military commander in a province or county and its capital, usually for a term of one to three years. After the Treaty of Pereiaslav in 1654, the term was applied to the commanders of the fortresses and Russian garrisons of Kiev, Pereiaslav, Chernihiv, Uman, Nizhen, and, during the hetmancy of I. Briukhovetsky, Hadiache, Poltava, Myrhorod, Lubni, Hlukhiv, and other towns in Ukraine. The voivodes were subordinated to the *Little Russian Office and to the tsar himself. The military rank of voivode was abolished in 1708, during the reign of Peter I, but the term was retained as a designation of government rank. From 1718–20 on a voivode was the administrator, chief of police, and chief justice (from 1722) in a gubernial subunit, the *provintsiia*. From 1730 he was appointed for two years, and from 1760, for five years. The position was abolished in most of Russian-ruled Ukraine in 1775 and in Slobidska Ukraine in 1780–2.

In interwar Poland, which occupied most of Western Ukraine, a voivode was the state-appointed governor of a province called a voivodeship. The position was abolished in the Polish People's Republic in 1950.

R. Senkus

**Voivodeship** (*voievodstvo*; Polish: *województwo*). An administrative-territorial unit equivalent to a palatinate in the 13th- to 16th-century Kingdom of Poland and the 16th- to 18th-century Polish-Lithuanian Commonwealth. It was governed by a *voivode with the help of several castellans and other officials. After the introduction of *dietines each voivodeship was an autonomous unit and a separate electoral region with its own noble assembly, court, administration, army, and taxes. After the Union of Lublin Ukrainian ethnic territory was divided among Belz, *Bratslav, *Kiev, *Podlachia, *Podilia, *Rus', and *Volhynia voivodeships under Polish rule, and Berestia voivodeship under Lithuanian rule. *Chernihiv voivodeship was added in 1635. From 1815 to 1837 the Congress Kingdom of Poland was divided into eight commission-governed voivodeships; Lublin and Podlachia voivodeships included Ukrainian ethnic territories. The interwar Polish Republic was divided into provinces called voivodeships. Western Ukrainian ethnic territories were located in Lviv, Stanyslaviv, Ternopil, Volhynia, and Polisia voivodeships and parts of Cracow, Lublin, and Białystok voivodeships. (See also *Administrative territorial division.)

**Vojvodina.** See Bačka and Serbia.

**Volcanic Ukrainian Carpathians.** The southwestern-most belt of the *Carpathian Mountains, located between the Tysa Lowland and the Polonynian Beskyd and Inner Carpathian Valley. The mountains rise steeply for 600–900 m above the Tysa Lowland to an elevation of 900–1,100 m. They consist mostly of effusion centers joined by lava streams that were created during the sinking of the Inner Carpathians through volcanic eruptions during the Miocene epoch. The volcanic deposits include trachytes, andesites, rhyolites, and tuffs.

The Volcanic Carpathians stretch from the Laborets River in the northwest to the northern Rumanian border (south of the Maramureş Basin) in the southeast. Transverse valleys of the Tysa River and its tributaries divide the mountains into the following groups: the Vyhorlat (1,074 m), Makovytsia (978 m), Syniak (1,014 m), Velykyi Dil (1,086 m), Tupyi (878 m), and Hutyn (1,093 m) mountains. The massive and broad ranges are dotted with picturesque volcanic rings (the remains of craters) and cones. The mountains are almost unsettled and are covered with oak and beech forests.

The foothills of the Volcanic Carpathians form a narrow band to the west. They are formed of tuffs and andesites. The land is highly productive – corn, wheat, and grapes are all grown there – and densely populated. The most important cities of Transcarpathia (Mukachiv, Vynohradiv, Uzhhorod) are found in the passes formed by rivers through the foothills. A few isolated volcanic regions are found in the vicinity of Berehove, in the Tysa Lowland.

V. Kubijovyč

**Volchuk, Roman.** See Wolchuk, Roman.

**Vole** (Ukrainian: *polivka, norytsia*). Any of the numerous rodents of the family Cricetidae, most particularly of the genus *Microtus*; also known as the meadow vole, field vole, or meadow mouse. Because it feeds on various plants and often damages crops and trees, the vole is one of the worst agricultural pests in Ukraine. Species include the common grey vole (*M. arralis*), the social vole (*M. socialis*), the steppe vole (*Lagurus lagurus*), the underground vole (*M. subterraneus*) in Western Ukraine, the snow vole (*M. nivalis*) in Caucasia, and the water vole or water rat (*Arvicola terrestris*; Ukrainian: *ondatra*), which lives a semi-aquatic life and is hunted for its fur. Some voles are carriers of disease organisms.

**Volga Bulgars.** Turkic-speaking nomads from Asia who appeared with the Huns in the Black Sea steppes in the 5th century AD and set up a confederation in the middle Volga and Kama region in the 10th century. After migrating into the region between the Sea of Azov and the northern Caspian they were attacked by the Avars in 558 and then subjugated by the Turkic Kaganate. Under the leadership of Kubrat the Bulgar tribes formed a union and established a state in the 630s with Phanagoria as capital. After Kubrat's death (ca 650) the tribes divided into two rival hordes. Weakened by internal fighting, the Bulgars were displaced by the Khazars: some of them fled to the Danube region and occupied the eastern Balkans, others moved east to the Volga-Kama region, and the third and smallest group, known as the Black or Inner Bulgars, stayed in the Azov steppe.

At first the Volga Bulgars were subject to the Khazar Kaganate. In 922 Khan Almas, the ruler of Bulgar city, began uniting the Bulgar tribes against the Khazars. After Prince Sviatoslav Ihorevych conquered the Khazars (965) the Bulgar confederation flourished as a major trading power. The Bulgars conducted a considerable amount of trade with Kievan Rus'. The princes of Rus' conducted several campaigns (in 977, 985, 994, and 997) against the Volga Bulgars and concluded a treaty in 1006 that gave Rus' merchants access to Bulgar markets. In the 12th century Bulgar trade was redirected northward toward Vladimir-Suzdal. The Bulgars were subdued by the Tatars in 1236–41, and continued their commercial activities under the Golden Horde. In the 1390s they were weakened by Tamerlane's invasion, and in the 1430s they succumbed to attacks from Muscovy.

**Volga German ASSR.** An autonomous Soviet republic formed in 1924 out of the Volga German Autonomous Oblast (est 1918). The region, covering 28,200 sq km along the Volga River, was colonized by *Germans beginning in the 1770s. Its capital was Pokrovsk (renamed Engels in 1931). According to the Soviet census of 1926 most of the republic's population (66.4 percent) was German (379,600); after the Russian minority (20.4 percent), the second-largest minority was Ukrainian (12 percent, or 68,600 people). The Ukrainian population lived in compact islands and constituted the largest ethnic group in Pokrovsk (51.3 percent) and Staraia Poltavka (44.8 percent) raions. In September 1941 the German population was deported to the east, and in 1945 the republic was abolished.

**Volhynia** (Ukrainian: *Volyn*). A historical region of northwestern Ukraine, located north of Podilia, south of Polisia, east of the Buh River, and west of the upper parts of the Teteriv and the Uzh rivers. Its area is approx 70,000 sq km, and its population exceeds 4 million. Volhynia's borders have changed considerably over the centuries, shifting consistently from west to east. In the 12th century the principality of Volhynia was larger than the present region. It extended to the Wieprz River in the west and to the Narev and the Yaselda rivers in the northwest and thus encompassed the present *Kholm region and *Podlachia. Until 1170 it also encompassed the *Belz land in the south. Under Poland the smaller *Volhynia voivodeship (1569–1793) did not reach west beyond the Buh River, but included new territory to the east and southeast. Within the Russian Empire *Volhynia gubernia consisted approx of the same territory, except for the Zbarazh region, but expanded east to the upper Teteriv and the Uzh rivers. Even its capital, Zhytomyr, belonged once to Kiev, not Volhynia principality. After the 1921 partition of Volhynia between Poland and the Ukrainian SSR the western part became Volhynia voivodeship. Today Volhynia encompasses most of Volhynia, Rivne, and Zhytomyr oblasts, and parts of the former Volhynia gubernia belong to other oblasts – the Kremianets region, to Ternopil oblast, and the Zaslav (now Iziaslav) and the Starokostiantyniv regions, to Khmelnytskyi oblast. Berdychiv and Radomyshl counties of the former Kiev gubernia now belong to Zhytomyr oblast. Volhynia is usually associated with the territory of the former Volhynia gubernia, which covered 71,700 sq km and in 1914 had a population of 4,190,000. The present Volhynia, Rivne, and Zhytomyr oblasts cover

70,200 sq km and have a total population of 3,777,000 (1989 census).

**Physical geography.** Volhynia is the meeting ground of two distinct landscapes: the glacial, characteristic of *Polisia, and the plateau, characteristic of *Podilia. From south to north the following landscape zones appear: (1) the *Podolian Upland, (2) *Little Polisia, (3) the *Volhynia-Kholm Upland, and (4) Volhynian Polisia. East of Slavuta the zone of depressions that forms Little Polisia disappears, leaving only two zones. The northward-flowing Ikva and Horyn rivers have cut deeply into the Podolian plateau and turned it into an eroded upland with mesas and pinnacles. The *Kremianets Mountains, rising to 407 m above sea level, are the most picturesque part of Volhynia. The Podolian Upland is separated from the Volhynia-Kholm Upland by a zone of depressions. The upper *Buh Depression and the depressions of the Styr, the Ikva, and the Horyn rivers, all ranging in elevation from 200 to 220 m, are separated by low divides. Although they are of tectonic origin dating back to the Paleozoic era, their present appearance is attributed to the Pleistocene period, when meltwaters, blocked by the continental glacier, ponded in the upper Buh Depression and spilled eastward, leaving behind fluvioglacial deposits. As a result depressions are outwash plains, particularly in Little Polisia, east of the Ikva River at the foot of the Kremianets Mountains, where the depression changes to a broad valley. The Volhynia-Kholm Upland rises some 40–80 m above the depressions. The undulating plain has an elevation of 240–300 m. It is built of chalk in the west and granite in the east and is overlain with a thick layer of loess. In the north it descends abruptly to Volhynian Polisia.

**Prehistory.** The earliest settlements in Volhynia date back to the Lower Paleolithic period. Flint tools of the Acheulean culture have been uncovered in the Kremianets region. There are more finds from the Upper Paleolithic (around Kremianets, Dubno, Rivne) and even more from the Mesolithic period (tools of the Swiderian and its successor, the Campignian, cultures). During the Neolithic (5000–2500 BC) and the Eneolithic (2500–1800 BC) periods Volhynia was relatively densely peopled by an agricultural tribe that developed flint tools and linear-band pottery (the Buh culture). Then the first immigrants from the south (the Trypilian culture), from Silesia (the Volute Pottery culture), and from the northwest (the Stone-Cist Grave culture) appeared. In the Bronze Age (1800–800 BC), the population of Volhynia quickly assimilated immigrants from Silesia (Lausitz culture), and adopted from them the cremation of the dead. It established trade with Transcarpathia, where it acquired bronze weaponry. Toward the end of the Bronze Age the culture evolved into the Vysotske culture. Its carriers, according to Herodotus, were the Nevrians. In the Sarmatian-Roman period (50 BC to 200 AD) Volhynia's contacts with the Dniester and Dnieper regions and the Roman trading stations on the Black Sea increased.

**History.** The first historical name of the people of Volhynia was *Dulibians. In the 10th century that name was replaced by *Buzhanians (found also in Western sources) and *Volhynians.

The name Volhynia (*Volyn*) probably comes from a fortified town from before the 10th century, located at the confluence of the Buh and the Huchva rivers. Archeologists have discovered many artifacts from the 6th to 9th

Western Volhynia

centuries, including Roman and Arab coins, at the site. The Arab geographer Mas'ūdī (10th century) called Volhynia Valinana, its inhabitants, the Dulaba, and their king, Vand Slava.

In the 9th century Volhynia came under the sway of the Great Moravian state. By the beginning of the 10th century the Dulibians were subject to Kiev. In 981 and 993 Prince Volodymyr the Great secured the lands along the Sian River and beyond the Buh River and built Volodymyr-Volynskyi (988), which he gave to his son, Vsevolod. In the 990s a Volhynian eparchy was established. From 1015 to 1030 Volhynia was the battleground of Polish-Rus' wars. After the death of Yaroslav the Wise Volhynia was inherited by Ihor Yaroslavych and then by Iziaslav Yaroslavych, his son Yaropolk (d 1087), and his grandson, Yaroslav Sviatopolkovych (d 1123). During that period Volhynia acquired political individuality. In the 1120s it passed into the hands of the Monomakh dynasty, and in 1154, to the Iziaslav dynasty (Mstyslav and Yaroslav).

Having subordinated the Galician boyars and beaten foreign invaders Roman Mstyslavych established a large state encompassing Volhynia, Galicia, and Kiev and known as the Principality of Galicia-Volhynia. After protracted wars with Hungary and Poland his son Danylo reclaimed all of Volhynia (1227) and Galicia (1230s) and granted western Volhynia to his brother, Vasylko. Galicia-Volhynia survived the Mongol invasion (1240–1). After Danylo's death (1264) eastern Volhynia was ruled by his son, Mstyslav, and after Vasylko's death western Volhynia was inherited by his son, Volodymyr (d 1288). After Volodymyr's death Mstyslav Danylovych briefly brought most of Volhynia under his rule. In the second half of the 13th century Mazovia principality became subject to Volhynia.

At the beginning of the 14th century Volhynia and Galicia were reunited under Yurii Lvovych and maintained under the rule of his grandson, Yurii. In 1349, however, the state was partitioned, and Volhynia fell under the control of *Liubartas. By the beginning of the 15th century Volhynia was a distinct principality within the Grand Duchy of Lithuania. Its local princes supported Švitrigaila in his bid to gain the Lithuanian throne. From 1452 to 1569 Volhynia was a province of the Grand Duchy of Lithuania consisting of Volodymyr, Lutske, and Kremianets starostvos. It came under increasing Polish administrative and economic influence, but maintained the church traditions, customs, and way of life of the Princely era. In the 15th

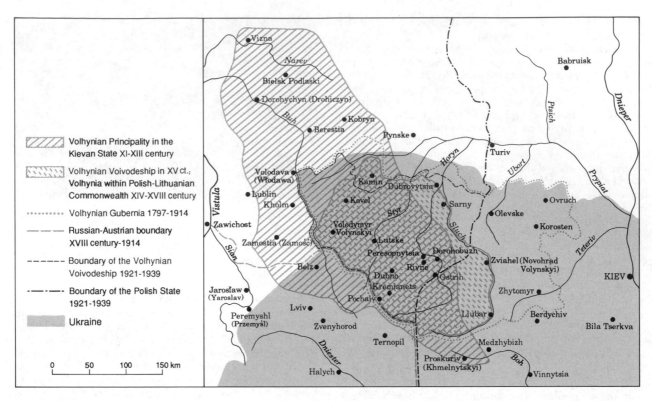

Volhynian Principality in the Kievan State XI-XIII century

Volhynian Voivodeship in XV ct.; Volhynia within Polish-Lithuanian Commonwealth XIV-XVIII century

Volhynian Gubernia 1797-1914

Russian-Austrian boundary XVIII century-1914

Boundary of the Volhynian Voivodeship 1921-1939

Boundary of the Polish State 1921-1939

Ukraine

0    50    100    150 km

# VOLHYNIA

and 16th centuries the princely and noble families, who led a continuing struggle against the Tatars, consolidated their privileged positions in society. As the Turks and Tatars blocked access to the Mediterranean markets, Volhynia strengthened its trade with the Baltic ports. In the 16th century the flow of Polish nobles and tradesmen into Volhynia, which was one of the most densely populated Ukrainian regions, increased. As Polish influence grew, the condition of the Volhynian peasantry became more difficult.

After the Union of *Lublin (1569) Volhynia became a Polish crown voivodeship without losing its internal autonomy and Ukrainian character. The union, however, accelerated the Polonization of the administration and the upper estates of Volhynia. The struggle against Roman Catholicism and the Ukrainian national-cultural movement at the beginning of the 17th century was expressed in the writings of the opponents and the supporters of the Church Union of *Berestia (1596), the Orthodox opposition to the Reformation in Hoshcha, Lutske, and elsewhere, the activities of the Orthodox brotherhoods in Ostrih, Volodymyr, and Lutske, and the founding of the *Ostrih Academy, schools in Volodymyr-Volynskyi, Lutske, Dubno, and elsewhere, and printing presses in Ostrih, Pochaiv, Derman, Kremianets, Kostiantyniv, and Chetvertnia.

The insurrections of K. Kosynsky (1591–3) and S. Nalyvaiko (1595) received wide support in Volhynia. During B. Khmelnytsky's uprising rebel groups led by M. Kryvonis, I. Donets, and M. Tyt were active there. Some of the battles of the *Cossack-Polish War of 1648–57 took place in Volhynia (Zbarazh, Vyshnevets, Brody, and Berestechko). Nevertheless Volhynia never became part of the Hetman state but remained a province of Poland. After B. Khmel-

nytsky's death heavy Polish oppression and Tatar raids forced much of the Ukrainian population to emigrate to Left-Bank Ukraine. The Ukrainian nobility in Volhynia lost its political significance. As the Uniate church spread, the Polish authorities granted the Uniate Lutske eparchy jurisdiction over the remaining Orthodox clergy. In the 18th century the *haidamaka uprisings (1734, 1768) received popular support in Volhynia.

After the partitions of Poland (1772, 1793, and 1795) Volhynia, with the exception of the southern part of Kremianets county, which was taken by Austria in 1772, became part of the Russian Empire. At the beginning of the 19th century Volhynia gubernia, with Zhytomyr as its capital, was set up. But the region continued to be dominated by the Polish nobility, and the position of the Ukrainian peasantry remained unchanged. The Polish language prevailed. The school superintendent, T. Czacki, opened many Polish schools, and the Kremianets Lyceum (1819–31) served as a Polish educational center.

The Polish Insurrection of 1830–1 provoked the Russian government to introduce an anti-Polish Russification policy, particularly in Volhynia, which was part of Kiev general gubernia. The Kremianets Lyceum, Polish schools, and many Roman Catholic and Uniate monasteries were closed down. In 1838 the Uniate Church in Volhynia was abolished. The Lithuanian Statute was replaced by Russian law, and Russian became the language of the courts and government. The emancipation of the serfs (1861) and another Polish uprising (1863) weakened the Polish nobility. In the 1860s a program of rapid and comprehensive Russification was launched. Russian official circles set up a center for Black Hundreds propaganda at the Pochaiv Monastery. Volhynia was cut off from the Ukrainian national revival of the late 19th and early 20th centuries. Until 1911 it did not even have zemstvos, which in other gubernias provided a measure of self-government and within permitted limits supported Ukrainian cultural expression.

The process of national rebirth began in Volhynia only with the Revolution of 1917. A. Viazlov, a native of Volhynia, was appointed gubernia commissioner by the Central Rada. Networks of Ukrainian schools, Prosvita reading rooms, and co-operatives were organized. With the Bolshevik advance against Ukraine, in February 1918 Volhynia became the battleground of UNR forces and the Seventh Russian Army. Zhytomyr served as a temporary seat of the Central Rada. In the spring of 1919 Rivne became a temporary capital of the UNR, whose army fought the Bolsheviks in eastern Volhynia, then the Poles in western Volhynia, and again the Bolsheviks in 1920. In November 1921 the Volhynian military group under Gen Yu. Tiutiunnyk staged a raid which inspired many popular revolts against the Bolsheviks (see *Winter campaigns).

In 1921 Volhynia was partitioned according to the Peace Treaty of Riga: the eastern part was annexed by the Ukrainian SSR, the western part by Poland. Eastern Volhynia experienced the same changes as the rest of Soviet Ukraine. In the early 1920s much of the evacuated population returned to Volhynia. The Volhynian intelligentsia was active in the Ukrainization movement of the 1920s, but became a victim of Stalinist terror in the 1930s. Collectivization and industrialization changed the economic and social profile of Volhynia.

The position of western Volhynia was unique. In the 1920s the national rebirth was promoted by a sizable group of Ukrainian intelligentsia, who had close contact with activists in the Kholm region, Podlachia, and Galicia. There was a united and fairly strong Ukrainian representation from Volhynia in the Polish Sejm and Senate. Volhynian and Galician political groups worked closely together. Ukrainian co-operatives in the two voivodeships were linked organizationally, and their Prosvita societies co-operated with one another in spite of official prohibition and the establishment of the Sokal border. Nevertheless the authorities managed to fragment and then influence the Ukrainian political movement in Volhynia. The *Volhynian Ukrainian Alliance advocated loyalty and collaborated with the Polish regime. The Polish government's *Pacification and policy of terror in the 1930 elections weakened the Ukrainian parties. The governor of Volhynia, H. Józewski, tried to isolate Volhynia from Galicia. The authorities took strong measures to suppress Ukrainian national and cultural activity: in 1928–32 they closed down the Prosvita societies in Kremianets, Ostrih, Dubno, Rivne, Kovel, Volodymyr, and Lutske (along with 134 branches). On the eve of the Second World War there were only 8 Ukrainian elementary schools in Volhynia, compared to 443 in 1922–3, 1,459 Polish schools, and 520 bilingual schools, where most subjects were taught in Polish. There were three Ukrainian private secondary schools, but not one state school. Printed matter from Galicia was not allowed into Volhynia. In 1934, Volhynian co-operatives were subordinated to Polish co-operatives. In the border zone, which covered about one-third of Volhynia, the terror against Ukrainians was intensified: political activists were imprisoned, and people were forcibly converted to Roman Catholicism or to the Uniate church. The OUN reacted to the repressions by stepping up its activities, and Ukrainian deputies from Volhynia,

such as Mstyslav *Skrypnyk, protested strenuously in the Sejm.

In 1939 western Volhynia was occupied by the Soviet armed forces and annexed by the Ukrainian SSR. Two oblasts, Volhynia and Rivne, were formed out of it, and the Kremianets region was attached to Ternopil oblast. In 1941, as Soviet forces retreated, they committed mass murders in the prisons of Lutske, Dubno, and other cities. Initially the German occupational authorities that replaced them tolerated the revival of Ukrainian civic and religious life. But as soon as the Reichskommissariat Ukraine had been set up, in the fall of 1941, the German terror intensified. The Ukrainians of Volhynia responded with armed resistance. The Germans secured the cities and railway lines, but not the countryside. They staged punitive raids on the villages, which they burned and killed their defenseless inhabitants. In the spring of 1944 the resistance was redirected against the Soviet occupational forces.

Volhynia played an important role in the recent history of the Ukrainian Orthodox church. In the early 1920s a group of Ukrainian Orthodox priests and laity in Volhynia began to Ukrainianize the Orthodox eparchy that had been Russified until 1917. The Mohyla Society in Lutske and a number of church brotherhoods were active in the work. The Kremianets Seminary and the Orthodox faculty at the University of Warsaw trained Ukrainian Orthodox priests. When the Bolsheviks dissolved the Ukrainian Autocephalous Orthodox church (UAOC) in 1930, Polish-ruled western Volhynia became its chief stronghold. After the German occupation of that part of Volhynia Bishop P. *Sikorsky of Lutske became metropolitan (1942) and revitalized the UAOC. In 1943 the hierarchy of the UAOC fled to the West. Under Soviet rule the Orthodox parishes of Volhynia were forced to submit to the patriarch of Moscow.

**Population.** The average population density of Volhynia is 54 persons per sq km (1989 figures). The highest densities occur in the southern (80 persons/sq km) and central (65 persons/sq km) parts of Volhynia, average densities in the zone of depressions (55 persons/sq km), and the lowest densities in Polisia (40 persons/sq km). Because of lagging industrialization the proportion of the population that is urban is one of the lowest in Ukraine. In western Volhynia it was 12.1 percent in 1931 and 46.6 percent in 1987; in eastern Volhynia it was 20.5 percent in 1939 and 51.2 percent in 1987. In all of Volhynia it was only 8 percent in 1897, 17 percent in 1939, and 48 percent in 1987. The largest cities in Volhynia are (1989 figures) Zhytomyr (292,000), Rivne (228,000), Lutske (198,000), Berdychiv (92,000), Korosten (72,000), Kovel (69,000), Novovolynske (53,500), and Novohrad-Volynskyi (55,000).

Until the mid-19th century non-Ukrainians accounted for nearly 20 percent of the population. Among them were Jews, Poles, Ukrainian-speaking Roman Catholics, and a few Russians. After the abolition of serfdom the landlords sold some of their estates and deforested lands to colonists. Some 20,000 Czechs settled in Volhynia (mostly in Dubno, Zdolbuniv, and Rivne counties), nearly 100,000 Germans (usually on newly cleared land) in Volodymyr-Volynskyi, Lutske, Zhytomyr, and Zviahel counties, and Poles mostly in Volodymyr-Volynskyi, Kostopil, and Zviahel counties. The proportion of the Ukrainians in the population declined to 70 and even 65 percent. During the First World War the Russian government deported some

Traditional Volhynian dress

TABLE 1
Ethnic composition of Volhynia, 1897–1931 (percentages)

| | Western Volhynia 1931 | Eastern Volhynia 1926 | All Volhynia 1897 | All Volhynia 1931 |
|---|---|---|---|---|
| Ukrainians | 70.4 | 68.6 | 70.1 | 69.9 |
| Jews | 9.8 | 9.0 | 12.2 | 9.5 |
| Poles and Ukrainian-speaking Roman Catholics | 15.2 | 11.7 | 6.2 | 13.9 |
| Russians | 1.1 | 2.5 | 3.7 | 1.5 |
| Germans | 2.2 | 7.3 | 5.7 | 3.9 |
| Czechs | 1.1 | 0.4 | 0.9 | 1.0 |
| Others | 0.2 | 0.5 | 1.2 | 0.3 |

of the German colonists. After 1920 the number of Poles in western Volhynia increased (see table 1).

The Second World War changed the national composition of Volhynia (see table 2). Most Jews not evacuated by the Soviets were killed by the Germans. At the end of the war almost all the Germans and Czechs left, and many Poles, particularly from western Volhynia, changed places with Ukrainians living in Poland. An increasing influx of Russians and Belarusians strengthened the influence of the Russian language in the region.

**Economy.** Volhynia is an agrarian land with low industrial development, especially in the western part. At the beginning of the 1930s some 78 percent of the population was employed in agriculture, and only 8 percent in industry. In 1987, 52 percent of the population was rural, and most of it based its livelihood on agriculture.

Most of the sown area in 1940 was devoted to grain (73 percent), including rye (29 percent), oats (15 percent),

wheat (14 percent), and barley (9 percent). Feed crops occupied 11 percent, potatoes, 9 percent, and industrial crops (sugar beets, flax, hemp, hops, and tobacco), 7 percent of the cultivated land. By the 1970s grain accounted for only about 44 percent of the sown area and feed crops had increased to 32 percent, potatoes and vegetables, to 14 percent, and industrial crops, to 10 percent. Grain yields rose from about 12 centners per ha in 1940 to over 20 centners per ha in the 1970s. Southern Volhynia produced a grain and hop surplus. In northern Volhynia forestry and animal husbandry (dairying and hog farming) prevailed.

Industrial development in Volhynia has been hampered by lack of energy resources, by competition from the more developed central regions of the Russian Empire, the USSR, and Poland, and by the region's exposed position between two unfriendly powers. After the Second World War the political and economic conditions for industrialization along the western Soviet frontier improved. The development of the *Lviv-Volhynia Coal Basin has strengthened the local base for power generation. The Rivne and Khmelnytskyi nuclear power stations have made Volhynia a power exporter. Pipelines feed the major cities of Volhynia with natural gas for industrial as well as domestic use. The oil pipeline crossing Volhynia transported only Soviet crude oil to the West and contributed nothing to Volhynia's economy.

The most important industry in Volhynia is the food industry. Based on local raw materials, it accounts for over one-third of the value of industrial goods. Its major branches are grist milling, sugar refining, liquor distilling, brewing, fruit and vegetable canning, meat packing, milk processing, and butter making. Sugar refining has expanded to western Volhynia. Berdychiv has the only malt kiln in Ukraine. Other food-processing operations are more or

TABLE 2
Ethnic composition of Volhynia after the Second World War (percentages)

| | Western Volhynia[1] 1959 | 1970 | 1979 | Eastern Volhynia[2] 1959 | 1970 | 1979 | All Volhynia 1959 | 1970 | 1979 |
|---|---|---|---|---|---|---|---|---|---|
| Ukrainians | 93.9 | 94.1 | 93.9 | 84.5 | 85.1 | 84.9 | 89.5 | 90.1 | 90.0 |
| Russians | 4.2 | 4.2 | 4.5 | 5.4 | 6.2 | 7.0 | 4.8 | 5.1 | 5.6 |
| Belarusians | 0.8 | 0.9 | 1.0 | 0.4 | 0.4 | 0.5 | 0.6 | 0.7 | 0.8 |
| Poles | 0.6 | 0.4 | 0.3 | 6.4 | 5.6 | 5.2 | 3.3 | 2.7 | 2.4 |
| Jews | 0.3 | 0.2 | 0.1 | 2.6 | 2.2 | 1.8 | 1.4 | 1.1 | 0.9 |
| Others | 0.2 | 0.2 | 0.2 | 0.7 | 0.5 | 0.6 | 0.4 | 0.3 | 0.3 |

[1]Rivne and Volhynia oblasts
[2]Zhytomyr oblast

less ubiquitous. Second in importance are the lumber, woodworking, furniture, wood-chemical, and pulp and paper industries. The large woodworking plants and furniture factories in Kovel, Lutske, Rivne, Sarny, Zhytomyr, Korosten, and Malyn are based on the forest resources of Volhynian Polisia. The Kostopil prefabricated-house-building plant is the largest of its kind in Ukraine. Paper mills at Korostyshiv, Malyn, Myropil, and Chyzhivka account for 20 percent of the forest-based industrial output of the region. Third in importance, light industry accounts for less than one-quarter of the region's industrial output. The machine-building and metalworking industries have developed only in the last three decades. They produce equipment for the chemical and food-processing industries (Berdychiv, Korosten), metal-cutting machines (Zhytomyr, Berdychiv), road-building (Korosten) and farm machinery (Novohrad-Volynskyi, Kovel, Rivne), tools (Zhytomyr, Lutske, Rivne), automobiles (Lutske), and railway equipment (Kovel). Volhynia's chemical industry produces fertilizers (Rivne), synthetic fibers (Zhytomyr), pharmaceuticals (Zhytomyr) and plastics (Lutske). The building-materials industry is well developed and supplies other regions. Crushed stone and asbestos-cement (Zdolbuniv) are used for prefabricated cement products. Granite, labradorite, basalt, and other rock quarrying provides fine building stone. Local kaolin clays and sand are used for manufacturing pottery, china, and glass, particularly in a cluster of small towns between Zhytomyr and Rivne. The mining of bog iron ores is obsolete, but the discovery and development of ilmenites has given rise to nonferrous metallurgy at Irshanske, which produces titanium dioxide and phosphate fertilizers. The most important industrial centers in Volhynia are *Zhytomyr, *Rivne, *Lutske, *Novohrad-Volynskyi, *Kovel, and *Zdolbuniv.

BIBLIOGRAPHY
Antonovich, V. 'Arkheologicheskaia karta Volynskoi gubernii,' *Trudy 11 arkheologicheskogo s"ezda* (Moscow 1901)
*Trudy Obshchestva issledovatelei Volyni*, 1–13 (Zhytomyr 1902–15)
*Rocznik Wołyński*, 1–8 (Rivne 1930–9)
Richyns'kyi, A. *Staryi horod Volyn'* (1938)
Levkovych, I. *Narys istorii Volyns'koi zemli* (Winnipeg 1953)
*Litopys Volyni*, 1–15 (New York–Winnipeg 1953–88)
Baranovich, A. *Magnatskoe khoziaistvo na iuge Volyni v XVIII v.* (Moscow 1955)
*Starodavnie naselennia Prykarpattia i Volyni: Doba pervisnoobshchynnoho ladu* (Kiev 1974)
Tsynkalovs'kyi, O. *Stara Volyn' i Volyns'ke Polissia*, 2 vols (Winnipeg 1984, 1986)
P. Hrytsak, V. Kubijovyč, Ya. Pasternak, I. Stebelsky

**Volhynia eparchy.** An Orthodox eparchy with its see in Zhytomyr. It was created at the turn of the 19th century, after the Russian Empire acquired Volhynia in the partitions of Poland. It comprised the territory of Volhynia gubernia and included most of the former eparchies of *Volodymyr-Volynskyi and *Lutske. In the 19th century it was one of the largest and wealthiest eparchies of the Russian Orthodox church, with over 1,800 parishes (1907) and 4 women's and 10 men's monasteries, including the *Pochaiv Monastery. In 1917, in addition to the titular bishop, the eparchy had three vicar bishops (in Volodymyr-Volynskyi, Kremianets, and Ostrih). In the early 20th century, under Bishop A. *Khrapovitsky, the eparchy became a major center of Russian ultranationalism, and many clergymen and monks there supported the Black

Hundreds movement. The *Volynskie eparkhial'nye vedomosti*, the official eparchial organ published from 1861 to 1917, contains much information about the eparchy and its history (including the history of Volodymyr-Volynskyi and Lutske eparchies), and M. Teodorovych published a five-volume history and description of the eparchy in 1888–1903.

In the interwar period most of the territory of Volhynia eparchy was in Poland. In the 1930s the bishop of Volhynia, O. Hromadsky, had his see in Kremianets and vicars in Lutske (P. Sikorsky) and Ostrih (S. Ivanovsky). Many Ukrainian church organizations were active in the eparchy, including the *Mohyla Society, and several publications appeared there.

During the Second World War the *Ukrainian Autocephalous Orthodox church (UAOC) established the eparchy of Lutske and Kovel (under Sikorsky), with vicars in Rivne (Bishop P. Artemiuk) and Dubno (Bishop V. Lisytsky). With the rebirth of the UAOC in the early 1990s, two eparchies (Rivne-Zhytomyr and Lutske) have been re-established.

**Volhynia gubernia.** An administrative-territorial unit in Russian-ruled Right-Bank Ukraine that replaced *Volhynia vicegerency in 1797. The gubernial capital was Novohrad-Volynskyi and, from 1804, *Zhytomyr. From 1799 the gubernia's territory (71,737 sq km) was divided among 12 counties: Dubno, Kovel, Kremianets, Lutske, Novohrad-Volynskyi, Ostrih, Ovruch, Rivne, Starokostiantyniv, Volodymyr-Volynskyi, Zaslav, and Zhytomyr. The gubernia's population grew from 1,212,800 in 1811 to 1,314,100 in 1838, 1,469,400 in 1851, 1,602,700 in 1863, 2,196,000 in 1885, 2,989,500 in 1897, and 4,189,000 in 1914. In 1897 the population was 70.1 percent Ukrainian, 13.2 percent Jewish, 6.2 percent Polish, 5.7 percent German, 3.5 percent Russian, 0.9 percent Czech, and 0.1 percent Belarusian. Only 7.8 percent of the population was urban, of which nearly 51 percent was Jewish and 7.6 percent Polish. In 1914 the gubernia had the lowest percentage (8.4 percent) of urban dwellers among the nine Ukrainian gubernias.

In 1905 almost half of the gubernia's land was still owned by the gentry, of which 69 percent was Polish in 1885. Land hunger and poverty forced many peasants to resettle in Siberia or to emigrate to North America. Industry – consisting primarily of sugar-beet refining, distilling, weaving, flour milling, and tanning – occupied only 7.4 percent of the population and was generally poorly developed, although the gubernia was the primary producer of woolen cloth in Ukraine. Under Soviet rule the gubernia's western counties were ceded to Poland in the 1921 Peace Treaty of Riga. In 1925 the gubernia was abolished, and the territory of the remaining counties (31,860 sq km) was distributed among Korosten, Shepetivka, and Zhytomyr (later Novohrad-Volynskyi) okruhas.

R. Senkus

**Volhynia oblast.** An administrative territory (1989 pop 1,062,000) in northwestern Ukraine, formed on 4 December 1939. It has an area of 20,100 sq km and is divided into 15 raions, 11 cities, 21 towns (smt), and 352 rural councils. The capital is *Lutske.

**Physical geography.** The territory of the oblast consists largely of a flat plain which slopes down from 190–200 m in the south to 140–150 m in the north. The central and northern parts are covered by the Polisian Lowland and are marked by extensive floodplains, rivers and lakes, forests, and swamps. The terrain is flat, with some gentle rolling and moraine hills. The southern part of the oblast lies in the Volhynia-Kholm Upland and is dissected by ravines and valleys. The oblast has a moderate continental climate: the average January temperature is –4.5°C, and the average July temperature is 19°C. The annual precipitation is 550–660 mm. Much of the oblast's territory (32.4 percent) is forested. The more common trees are spruce, pine, oak, linden, and hornbeam. There are 224 lakes, covering an area of 14,429 ha. The oblast lies along the watershed between the Baltic and Black Sea basins, but most of its rivers belong to the latter. The major rivers are the Buh, the Prypiat, the Turiia, the Stokhid, and the Styr. Podzolized dark gray soils and chernozems are prevalent in the southern part of the oblast, and soddy podzolic, soddy, and meadow soils are common in the central and northern regions. Extensive coal deposits are found in the Lviv-Volhynia Coal Basin.

**Population.** The majority of the oblast's population is Ukrainian (94.6 percent in 1989), and the main minority is Russian (4.4 percent). The southern part of the oblast is settled more densely than the northern part. Urban dwellers account for 51.9 percent of the population. The major cities are Lutske, *Kovel, *Volodymyr-Volynskyi, and *Novovolynske.

**Industry.** The main industries are food processing (29.4 percent of the industrial output in 1983), light industry (25.7 percent), machine building and metalworking (21.7), forestry and woodworking (7.1) and building-materials manufacturing (5.4 percent). The major branches of the food industry are sugar refining (Volodymyr-Volynskyi, Lutske, Ivanychi), meat packing (Lutske, Novovolynske, Kovel), canning (Lutske, Volodymyr-Volynskyi, Ivanychi), and dairy goods. The light industry consists of footwear, linen (Kovel, Manevychi, Stara Vyzhivka), textile (Lutske, Novovolynske, Kovel), and artificial leather (Lutske, Novovolynske, Kovel, Volodymyr-Volynskyi) plants. Instruments, electrical equipment, agricultural machinery, automobiles, and ball bearings are the major products of the machine-building industry, which is concentrated in Lutske, Kovel, Novovolynske, and Rozhyshche. Furniture-making is the main branch of the woodworking industry; its main centers are Kyvertsi, Tsuman, Kovel, Lutske, Volodymyr-Volynskyi, and Manevychi. The oblast also has a large coal industry and a building-materials industry which produces bricks, reinforced concrete, and sheet roofing.

**Agriculture.** In 1986 farming accounted for 60 percent of the oblast's output. There were 341 collective and 46 state farms and 2 poultry factories. About 1,073,000 ha of land were devoted to agriculture, of which 62.4 percent was cultivated, and 37 percent was hayfield and pasture. Of the agricultural land 343,000 ha were drained, and 2,600 ha were irrigated. The major drainage projects are on the Tsyr, the Melnytsia, and the Turiia rivers. The cultivated land was devoted mostly (41.7 percent) to grain crops (rye, wheat, barley, buckwheat), followed by fodder crops (36.1 percent), industrial crops (sugar beets and flax, 9.3 percent), and potatoes and vegetables (12.9). Animal husbandry produced 49.8 percent of the farm output. It is concentrated on beef- and dairy-cattle raising and hog farming. Sheep and poultry are raised also.

**Transportation.** In 1986 there were 621 km of rail track in the oblast. The main lines running through the oblast are Kiev–Kovel–Brest, Kovel–Lutske–Lviv, Kiev–Zdolbuniv–Lutske, and Kovel–Lublin. The largest junction is Kovel. The highway network consists of 5,800 km of road, of which 4,600 km are paved. The major highways are Kiev–Rivne–Lutske–Kovel–Brest, Kiev–Korosten–Kovel–Kholm, Kovel–Novovolynske–Lviv, and Lutske–Lviv. The Styr River is navigable and feeds into the Dnieper-Buh Canal system. Lutske serves as a river port. It also has an airport.

(For the history of the oblast see *Volhynia.)

BIBLIOGRAPHY
*Istoriia mist i sil* URSR: *Volyns'ka oblast'* (Kiev 1970)
*Pryroda Volyns'koï oblasti* (Lviv 1975)

**Volhynia Research Society** (Russian: Obshchestvo issledovatelei Volyni). A regional studies society in Zhytomyr from 1900 to 1917. Its chairman was the governor of Volhynia gubernia, M. Melnikov. The vice-chairman was P. *Tutkovsky. Members of the society's council were O. *Fotynsky, V. *Kravchenko, V. Dvernytsky, Yu. Shulikov, A. Księżopolski, N. Bellonin, R. Renning, and T. Zakusylo. The treasurer was A. Brzozowska. The society published the serial *Trudy* (13 vols, 1902–15), containing studies of Volhynia's geography, geology (mainly by Tutkovsky), natural environment, ethnography, and history. In 1902 it established what is now the *Zhytomyr Regional Studies Museum. Part of the society's library is preserved at the ANU Central Scientific Library in Kiev.

**Volhynia vicegerency.** An administrative unit established in 1793 after Russia's annexation of Volhynia from Poland. The vicegerency consisted of the entire Volhynia voivodeship and the southern portion of Kiev voivodeship. Until 1795 its capital was Iziaslav; hence, it was known as Iziaslav vicegerency. Then the capital was moved to Novohrad-Volynskyi, and the vicegerency was renamed. When the vicegerencies were replaced by gubernias in 1797, the largest part of the territory was included in Volhynia gubernia. Only Radomyshl county was transferred to Kiev gubernia.

**Volhynia voivodeship.** An administrative territory of the Polish Commonwealth in the 16th to 18th centuries. The voivodeship was formed after the Union of Lublin (1569) and divided into Lutske, Volodymyr, and Kremianets counties. Its capital was Lutske. Most of the land in the province was owned by either Polish or Polonized Ukrainian magnates, such as the Ostrozky, Wiśniowiecki, Zasławski, Lubomirski, and Sanguszko families. The peasants and townsfolk took part in B. Khmelnytsky's uprising in 1648 and the haidamaka rebellions of the 18th century. After the partition of Poland in 1793, the territory was annexed by Russia. In the interwar period (1919–39) the territory was again under Polish control and was called a voivodeship. When Western Ukraine was annexed by the USSR in 1939, the voivodeship was divided into Volhynia and Rivne oblasts.

**Volhynia-Kholm Upland.** The most northwesterly section of the Volhynian Upland region. With a length of approx 200 km and a width of 80 km, the formation has an average elevation of 220–250 m and rises to 342 m at its highest point. It slopes downward from its southern to its northern reaches. The upland contains a number of plateaus, which are dissected by the Buh, the Styr, and the Horyn rivers as well as their tributaries and lie on top of Cretaceous deposits. In its western reaches the deposits sit on top of the carboniferous Lviv-Volhynia Coal Basin. Karst landscape formations are found in the region; the natural vegetation is generally of a broadleaf forest variety.

**Volhynian Chronicle.** See Galician-Volhynian Chronicle.

**Volhynian dialects.** See South Volhynian dialects.

**Volhynian Regional Studies Museum** (Volynskyi kraieznavchyi muzei). A museum founded in Lutske in 1929 on the basis of local archeological and ethnographic collections. During the Second World War its entire holdings were either plundered or destroyed. After the war the museum was rebuilt. In the mid-1970s over 47,000 exhibit items were held in its natural science, pre-Soviet history, Soviet history, atheism, and art sections. The Partisan Glory Memorial Complex in Lobna (Liubeshiv raion), the Partisan Glory Museum in Kivertsi raion, and the Volodymyr-Volynskyi Historical Museum are also sections of the museum, and the Lesia Ukrainka Literary Memorial Museum in Kolodiazhne (Kovel raion, est 1949) is a branch. A guide to the museum was published in 1967, and guides to the Lesia Ukrainka museum appeared in 1969, 1971, 1976, and 1984.

**Volhynian Ukrainian Alliance** (Volynske ukrainske obiednannia). A pro-government political party in Polish-ruled western Volhynia in the 1930s. It was set up by Ukrainian émigrés from central and eastern Ukraine with the help of the Polish voivode H. Józewski. Its candidates, who ran on the list of the Polish Nonparty Bloc of Co-operation with the Government, won some seats in the Polish Sejm and Senate, where they formed a faction separate from the Ukrainian Parliamentary Representation. For its loyalty to Poland the alliance looked to gain some concessions from the government, particularly in church and cultural affairs, but it had little success. The alliance had little influence among the local Ukrainian population. The presidents of the party were P. Pevny and (from 1935) S. Tymoshenko. The chief activists included M. Bury, M. Volkov, O. Kovalevsky, and S.(M.) Skrypnyk. The party published *Ukraïns'ka nyva* and (from 1936) *Volyns'ke slovo*.

**Volhynian Ukrainian Music and Drama Theater** (Volynskyi ukrainskyi muzychno-dramatychnyi teatr im. T. Shevchenka). A theater established in 1940 in Lutske. Its repertoire has consisted mostly of Ukrainian and Russian classical and Soviet plays. Since 1978 its artistic director has been Ye. Olshevsky.

**Volhynians** (*volyniany*). An East Slavic tribe that inhabited Volhynia, northeastern Galicia, and the Buh River basin from the prehistoric period. According to some scholars, the tribe was known at one time as the *Dulibians. In the 9th and 10th centuries the Volhynians came under Kievan Rus', and thereafter they were gradually integrated into the Ukrainian nation.

**Volhynia-Podilia Plate** (also 'Platform'). A Precambrian geological formation underlying the Volhynia-Kholm and Podilian uplands. With a crystalline foundation of up to almost 200 m in its western reaches, the plate has several layers of subsequent sedimentary deposits and contains coal and basalt.

The Volhynia-Podilia Upland

**Volhynia-Podilia Upland.** A name used to designate a series of uplands in the Dnieper's right-bank region. They include the Podolian and Volhynia-Kholm uplands, the Roztochia, and the Pokutian-Bessarabian and Dnieper uplands.

**Volia**. A cultural-educational society sponsored by the Ukrainian Social Democratic party (USDP) of Galicia in 1903–24. Volia was formed in an attempt by the USDP to counter the Polonization of Ukrainian workers. The first (and central) branch was established in Lviv, and by 1909 there were branches in eight other Galician and Bukovynian centers. Early in 1924 the Polish government outlawed the group. The longtime leader of Volia was P. *Buniak.

**Volia** (Freedom). A voluntary organization in Lviv of Ukrainian domestic and security workers for the defense of their professional interests. It was active from 1932 to 1944, with a brief interruption during the first Soviet occupation of Galicia in 1939–41. In 1939 it had 1,500 members. The president of Volia was I. Zhminkovsky.

*Volia* (Freedom). A semimonthly organ of the *Ukrainian Social Democratic party, published in Lviv in 1900–4 and 1905–7 by M. Hankevych. Edited by Hankevych (to 1905), V. Levynsky (to 1906), A. Zelib (1903), and S. Vityk (1906–7), the paper advocated co-operation between Ukrainian and Polish socialists. *Volia* was succeeded by *Zemlia i volia.

*Volia* (Freedom). A political weekly published in Vienna from June 1919 to November 1921; the last three issues appeared as *Volia Ukraïny*. Edited by V. Mursky, Z. Adelsberger, L. Shopak, and V. Pisniachevsky (pseud: A. Horlenko), *Volia* reported extensively on political developments in Ukraine and is a good source of information on the last years of the struggle for Ukrainian independence. It also covered Ukrainian émigré affairs and Western policies toward Ukraine, and published excerpts from

German, French, and British papers; reviews; and a chronology of events.

*Volia naroda* (Will of the People). A weekly newspaper published by Galician Russophile socialists in Lviv in 1921–8. It succeeded the newspaper *\*Prikarpatskaia Rus'* and initially used a Russified etymological orthography. After the final defeat of the Whites, *Volia naroda* supported Soviet rule in Ukraine. Gradually, probably on orders from the Comintern, the newspaper was Ukrainized in an attempt to appeal to Ukrainian socialists in Galicia. In 1923 it appeared twice a week in Russian and once in Ukrainian, and from 1924 it appeared only in Ukrainian. From 1926 it was the organ of \*Sel-Rob. It criticized both Ukrainian nationalists and Russophile conservatives who opposed the USSR, but it did not support the Soviet Ukrainization policy. The editors were K. Pelekhaty and K. Valnytsky.

**Volian, Vasyl** [Voljan, Vasyl'], b 1832 in Nynovychi, Sokal county, Galicia, d October 1899 in Vienna. Physician and Bukovynian civic leader. A resident of Chernivtsi from 1866, he was a populist who eventually joined the Russophile camp. In 1890 he was elected to both the Bukovynian Diet and the Austrian parliament. His support of the Rumanian faction in the diet from 1898 turned the Ukrainian public against him. In his will he left his fortune to the Ukrainian tradesmen of Chernivtsi.

**Volianske Lake** [Voljans'ke ozero]. II–5. A lake situated in the northern part of Volhynia oblast near the Belarusian border. The lake, 4–6 m deep, is 2.5 km long and an average of 1.6 km wide, with an area of 4.05 sq km. It is connected by canals with both the Prypiat River and the Dnieper-Buh Canal.

Rev Ivan Voliansky

**Voliansky, Ivan** [Voljans'kyj] (Wolansky), b 1857 in Yabloniv, Husiatyn county, Galicia, d 1926 in Dychkiv, Ternopil county. The first Ukrainian Greek Catholic priest in the United States. He was sent to the United States in 1884 by Metropolitan S. Sembratovych at the request of the Ukrainian community in Shenandoah, Pennsylvania. There he established the first Ukrainian Greek Catholic parish and built a church. He also organized a branch of the Brotherhood of St Michael; a church choir; a reading room; a school; and a printing house, where he began publishing the newspaper *\*Ameryka* in August 1886. In 1889 he returned to Galicia, and in 1896–8 he did mission-ary work among Ukrainians in Brazil. In 1917–20 he was a missionary in the Kholm region. Although he had intended to return to the United States after the war, doing so did not prove feasible, and he remained as the pastor of Dychkiv.

**Voliansky, Ivan** [Voljans'kyj], b 1887, d 1950s in Argentina. Lawyer and political leader in Galicia. A lawyer in Stanyslaviv, he was active in the Ukrainian community. For many years he served as president of the county branch of the Ridna Shkola society and director of a branch of the Land Mortgage Bank. From 1933 he headed the Ukrainian Catholic People's party, and in 1935–9 he was its representative in the Polish Sejm.

**Voliansky, Oleh** [Voljans'kyj] (Wolansky), b 15 April 1914 in Kolomyia, Galicia. Psychiatrist. A graduate of Poznań University (MD, 1939), he emigrated to the United States in 1950. He worked as a psychiatrist in state hospitals and schools in New York, was an active member of the Ukrainian Medical Association of North America (president in 1971–2), and contributed regularly to *Likars'kyi visnyk* and *Svoboda*.

**Voliansky, Pavlo** [Volians'kyj], b 27 January 1888 in Otynia, Tovmach county, Galicia, d 30 June 1944 in Poznań. Pedagogue and community activist. He graduated from Chernivtsi University in 1913, having specialized in the Ukrainian and German languages. From 1916 he taught at the \*Peremyshl State Gymnasium and played an active role in local Ukrainian musical and theatrical circles. He was forced into retirement in 1937 by the Polish authorities, ostensibly for medical reasons. In 1939 he moved to Poznań to work in the university library. During the war he sheltered and assisted numerous Western Ukrainian intellectuals who had fled the Soviet occupation of their homeland.

**Volk, Ihor,** b 12 April 1937 in Zmiiv, Kharkiv oblast. Pilot and cosmonaut. He studied in Kirovohrad, Moscow, and Ordzhonikidze. He was a member of the Soviet cosmonaut group from 1978, and was on the flight of the Soiuz T-12 spacecraft (17–29 July 1984) which successfully docked with Saliut-7 and Soiuz T-11.

**Volkhovsky, Feliks** [Volxovs'kyj], b 15 March 1846 in Poltava, Poltava gubernia, d 3 August 1914 in London. Revolutionary populist and writer. After graduating from the Richelieu Lyceum in Odessa (1863) he audited law courses at Moscow University and joined the Ukrainian Student Hromada in Moscow. In 1867, after the hromada had been investigated and banned by the authorities, he founded the Ruble Society. The society was to hire itinerant teachers to spread literacy in rural areas and collect ethnographic, historical, and economic data. In 1875 Volkhovsky wrote in Ukrainian a populist propagandist brochure for the peasantry printed by O. Terletsky in Vienna. Volkhovsky was often detained for investigation (1866, 1868, 1869–71, and 1874–8) and was finally exiled to Siberia. He escaped in 1889 and made his way to London, where he wrote revolutionary pamphlets and edited the monthly *Free Russia*. He corresponded with M. Drahomanov, M. Pavlyk, I. Franko, M. Vovchok, Lesia Ukrainka, who translated one of his pamphlets into Ukrainian, and M. Kotsiubynsky, whose *Tini zabutykh predkiv* (Shadows of Forgotten Ancestors) Volkhovsky translated into Russian (1912).

**Volkhv.** A pagan priest in pre-Christian Rus'. *Volkhvy* were believed to possess mystical powers, particularly the ability to predict the future. The first literary reference to a *volkhv* occurs in the Primary Chronicle under the year 912; there, the priest-soothsayer predicts Prince Oleh's death. With the adoption of Christianity the pagan priests came under persecution and sometimes tried to channel social discontent against the church.

Dmytro Volkov

Mykola Volkovych

**Volkov, Dmytro** (Dmitrii), b 3 July 1925 in Leningrad. Theoretical physicist; AN URSR (now ANU) corresponding member since 1976 and full member since 1988. A graduate of Kharkiv University (1952), in 1956 he joined the ANU Physical-Technical Institute in Kharkiv, where he is now head of the theoretical physics department. Most of Volkov's research deals with the quantum electrodynamical basis for the phenomenology of fundamental particles and their interactions. He has done pioneering work in the new fields of supersymmetry and superspace, and has contributed significantly toward a unified theory of fundamental interactions.

**Volkov, Fedir.** See Vovk, Fedir.

**Volkov, Sergei,** b 16 November 1935 in Moscow. Chemist; AN URSR (now ANU) corresponding member since 1978. After graduating from the Moscow Chemical-Technological Institute in 1959 he joined the ANU Institute of General and Inorganic Chemistry. His research has dealt with high-temperature inorganic chemistry, especially with inorganic and co-ordination compounds in ionic or molecular melts and in the gas phase; gas transport reactions involving co-ordination compounds; and the quantum chemistry of inorganic compounds. He has contributed to the furthering of chemical processes by means of laser beams.

**Volkovych, Ioanykii** [Volkovyč, Joanykij]. Seventeenth-century Lviv priest and lecturer at the Lviv Dormition Brotherhood School. He was the author of a passion play titled *Rozmyshlian'ie o mutsie Khrysta Spasytelia nasheho* (Reflections on the Sufferings of Christ Our Saviour,

1631). Written in verse as a dialogue, it is one of the earliest examples of dramatic literature in the Ukrainian language.

**Volkovych, Mykola** [Volkovyč], b 8 December 1858 in Horodnia, Chernihiv gubernia, d 11 July 1928 in Kiev. Surgeon; full member of the VUAN in 1928. A graduate of Kiev University (1882), he was a professor there (1903–22) and head of the medical research department of the Kiev division of the Chief Science Administration of the People's Commissariat of Education (1922–8). A pioneer of modern surgery in Ukraine, he founded the Kiev Surgical Society (1908), established a school of surgeons, invented special instruments for treating fractures, introduced an osteoplastic operation for tibiofibular joint tuberculosis and plastic closure of a vesicovaginal fistula, performed a laminectomy (1894) and intracapsular resection of a knee joint (1896), and designed an incision for appendectomy (1898) and the tyre for shoulder joint immobilization (Volkovych tyre, 1908). He wrote numerous works on the surgical treatment of rhinoscleroma, gallstones, appendicitis, bone and joint injuries, and throat cancer.

**Volksdeutsche.** In Nazi terminology Germans who resided outside German territory. Under the provisions of the Nazi-Soviet pacts of 18 September 1939 and 5 September 1940 Germany was granted the right of repatriation of Germans who lived in the Western Ukrainian territories that had been incorporated into the Ukrainian SSR. Over 250,000 of them moved. A number of Ukrainians (about 10,000) who were able to convince the resettling committees of their mixed parentage, or who presented some other claim, left with the Volksdeutsche. Once in Germany the Ukrainians were housed in temporary camps. Some of them took German citizenship, but most remained active in Ukrainian circles in the Generalgouvernement. Some Poles who resettled as Volksdeutsche worked in the German administration in Ukrainian territory, where they displayed anti-Ukrainian attitudes. In time the administrative positions of the German occupation were handed over to actual Volksdeutsche.

**Volleyball** (*vidbyvanka, sitkivka, voleibol*). In the 1920s volleyball quickly became one of the most popular sports in Ukraine. In 1927, 64 teams competed for the championship of the Ukrainian SSR. A year later the Ukrainian team captured first place at the first All-Union Spartakiad. In 1948 the USSR Volleyball Federation (est 1932) joined the International Volleyball Federation. Today over 1 million people in Ukraine play volleyball. The European Cup-Winners' Cup was captured by the Odessa women's team Burevisnyk in 1961, the Luhanske men's team Zirka in 1973, and the Luhanske women's team Iskra in 1976. Ukrainian volleyball teams took first place at the Spartakiads of the Peoples of the USSR in 1956, 1967, and 1975. Ukrainian players were also part of the men's volleyball teams that won Olympic gold medals in 1964, 1968, and 1980.

In interwar Galicia the Ukrainian Sports Union conducted national volleyball competitions every year. Abroad, the *Ukrainian Sports Federation of the USA and Canada has staged annual competitions since 1957. In 1975 the Ukraina (Toronto) men's volleyball team won the Canadian national championship.

**Volnenko, Anatolii,** b 21 November 1902 in Kharkiv, d 21 August 1965 in Kiev. Scenery designer. He studied at the Kharkiv Art Institute (1921–9, pupil of S. Prokhorov and O. Khvostenko-Khvostov) and then worked in the Kharkiv Theater of Opera and Ballet (1925–35), in theaters in Russia (1936–50), and in the Kiev Theater of Opera and Ballet (from 1951). He also illustrated the journal *Chervonyi perets'*.

*Vol'noe slovo* (Free Word). A political newspaper published by Russian democratic émigrés in Geneva from August 1881 to April 1883. It advocated political freedom and constitutionalism in the Russian Empire. Because it also denounced radical socialism and the terrorism practiced by Russian revolutionary groups, some historians believe that it was actually supported by the Russian government or individuals close to it. *Vol'noe slovo* was initially edited by A. Malshinsky. He was closely assisted by M. *Drahomanov, who submitted articles on the Ukrainian question and other topics, and became the editor in 1883. Under Drahomanov's editorship *Vol'noe slovo* stressed federalist and socialist ideals. The paper ceased publication because of a lack of funds.

**Volnovakha** [Volnovaxa]. VI-18, DB IV-2. A city (1989 pop 25,300) and a raion center in Donetske oblast. It originated in 1881 as a railroad settlement during the construction of the Olenivka–Mariiupil branch line and developed into a major railway junction. In 1938 it was granted city status. Its main industry is railway transportation, which its metalworking and building-materials industries serve.

**Volobuiev, Mykhailo** [Volobujev, Myxajlo], b 24 January 1900 in Mykolaiv, Kherson gubernia, d 1932. Economist of Russian origin. A lecturer at the Kharkiv Tekhnikum of the National Economy, he published a major article, 'Do problemy ukraïns'koï ekonomiky' (On the Problem of the Ukrainian Economy), in *Bil'shovyk Ukraïny* (1928, nos 1–2), the main theoretical journal of the CC CP(B)U. Rejecting the view that the Russian Empire was a unified economic system, he argued that Ukraine should be studied as a separate national-economic entity with its own path of de-velopment, and that its separateness should be respected under the Soviet regime. He defended Ukraine's right to control its economic development and its national budget. Volobuiev showed how central control of the economy combined with Russian chauvinism resulted in exploitation of Ukraine. His arguments gained wide support in Ukraine but were attacked vehemently by Party authorities as 'bourgeois nationalist' and anti-Soviet. He was forced to recant his ideas in a letter to *Komunist* (1928) and in a two-part article in *Bil'shovyk Ukraïny* (1930) titled 'Proty ekonomichnoï pliatformy natsionalizmu (Do krytyky volobuïvshchyny)' (Against the Economic Platform of Nationalism [Toward a Criticism of Volobuievism]). He was arrested eventually and perished in the Soviet terror of the 1930s.

**Volobuiev, Yevhen** [Volobujev, Jevhen], b 30 July 1912 in Varvarivka, Vovchanske county, Kharkiv gubernia. Painter. In 1940 he graduated from the Kiev State Art Institute, where he studied under F. Krychevsky. He painted landscapes and genre paintings, such as *At Noon* (1947), *Springtime* (1949), *Morning* (1954), *On an Animal Farm* (1957), *On the Dnieper* (1960), and *First Greenery* (1975).

*Volochinnia.* A ceremonial visit on Easter Monday paid to relatives, friends, priests, midwives, and other community figures by young people. The visitors brought greetings and presents of small Easter breads (*kolachi*) and Easter eggs and sang ritual carol-like songs known as *ryndzivky*. This originally pagan custom was opposed by the church and was gradually eliminated. Some remnants of it survived in Yavoriv county in Galicia until the end of the 19th century.

**Volochyske** or **Volochyska** [Voločys'ke or Voločys'ka]. IV-7. A city (1989 pop 23,600) on the Zbruch River and a raion center in Khmelnytskyi oblast. It was first mentioned in historical documents in 1463, as the settlement of Volochyshche. The current name goes back to 1545. From 1569 to 1793 it was under Polish rule, and then, under Russian rule. A border town, it was a crossing point between the Russian and Austrian empires and, in the interwar period, between the USSR and Poland. In November 1920 it was a battleground between UNR and Bolshevik forces. In 1970 it was granted city status. Today the city has a metalworks, canning factories, and a sugar refinery.

**Volodar Rostyslavych** [Rostyslavyč], b ?, d 19 March 1124. Rus' prince; son of Rostyslav Volodymyrovych. Volodar and Davyd Ihorevych of Volhynia invaded Tmutorokan on 18 May 1081 and ruled there until they were ousted by Oleh Sviatoslavych in 1083. Volodar and his brothers, Vasylko and Riuryk, ruled Halych principality from ca 1084. He was granted the rule of Peremyshl by Vsevolod Yaroslavych after Riuryk died (1092). He and Vasylko defeated the Kievan prince, *Sviatopolk II Iziaslavych, in 1097 and the Hungarians in 1099 in a critical battle near Peremyshl. They formed an alliance with Byzantium and the Cumans, which was cemented in 1104 by the marriage of Volodar's daughter, Iryna, to the son of the Byzantine emperor Alexis Comnenus.

**Volodarka.** IV-10. A town smt (1988 pop 7,300) on the Ros River and a raion center in Kiev oblast. It was first mentioned in historical documents, as Volodarev, in 1150. There are several kurhans from the Kievan Rus' era in the vicinity. It has a cheese and a brick factory.

**Volodarske** [Volodars'ke]. VI-18. A town smt (1988 pop 9,600) on the Kalets River and a raion center in Donetske oblast. It originated in the early 19th century as the *khutir* of Y. *Hladky, named after the otaman of the Azov Cossacks. In 1855 the name was changed to Nikolske, and in 1924, to Volodarske. The village was granted smt status in 1965. It has several food-processing enterprises and a regional museum.

**Volodarske-Volynske** [Volodars'ke-Volyns'ke]. III-9. A town smt (1988 pop 8,200) on the Irsha River and a raion center in Zhytomyr oblast. It was first mentioned in historical documents in 1545, as Oleksandropil. Later it was called Horoshky (1607–1912), Kutuzove (1912–21), and Volodarske (1921–7). For two centuries (1569–1793) it was under Polish rule. In 1683–99 the village was visited by S. Palii's and Z. Iskra's Cossack detachments, who stirred up resistance to the Polish landowners. In 1793 Horoshky was annexed by the Russian Empire and granted to M. Kutuzov. In 1924 the village was given smt status. Until the 1930s there were many German colonies in its vicinity. Today it is a mining center for granite, quartz, labradorite, and topaz. The town has a mineralogical museum.

**Volodava** (Polish: Włodawa). II-4. A town (1989 pop 15,000) on the Buh River and a county center in Chełm voivodeship, Poland. It has a 17th-century castle which belonged to the Potii family. On the eve of the Second World War approx 27 percent of the county's population was Ukrainian, 30 percent *kalakut*, 33 percent Polish, and 10 percent Jewish. After the war all the Ukrainians were forcibly resettled.

**Volodkovych, Fylyp** [Volodkovyč], b 6 June 1697 in Navasëlki, near Vilnius, d 2 February 1778 in Uman. Uniate bishop. He joined the Basilian order and studied theology at the papal seminary in Braunsberg. He was superior of the monastery and school in Volodymyr-Volynskyi and then hegumen of a monastery in Lublin. In 1730 he became archimandrite of the Dubno and Derman monasteries, and in 1731 he was consecrated bishop of Kholm and Belz. In 1755 he was appointed coadjutor to Metropolitan F. Hrebnytsky despite opposition from the Polish nobility. He became bishop of Volodymyr-Volynskyi the next year, and in 1762 he succeeded Hrebnytsky as metropolitan of Kiev and titular archimandrite of the Kievan Cave Monastery, although he remained in Volodymyr-Volynskyi. During his tenure as metropolitan, Catherine II of Russia actively sought to destroy the Uniate church throughout Right-Bank Ukraine. Volodkovych also faced opposition from the haidamakas and went into hiding during the Koliivshchyna revolt.

**Volodymyr, son of Algirdas** (Volodymyr Olhierdovych), b ?, d 1394. Prince of the Gediminas dynasty. He ruled from 1362 as the first Lithuanian prince of Kiev. During his reign he was compelled to recognize the suzerainty of the Tatar khan, and his coins bore a Tatar seal. When Kiev was taken by Vytautas, Volodymyr was replaced by Skirgaila, and fled to Moscow. He returned to Lithuania ca 1398, went into Vytautas's service, and was granted a small holding in Belarus.

**Volodymyr Andriiovych** [Andrijovyč], b ?, d 28 January 1170. Rus' prince; son of Andrii Volodymyrovych the Good. In 1146 he received towns in the Volodymyr principality from his uncle, Viacheslav Volodymyrovych, but he was ousted by Iziaslav Mstyslavych shortly thereafter. In the subsequent struggles for Kiev with Yurii Dolgorukii of Suzdal, Volodymyr shifted loyalties and was granted Dorohobuzh, Peresopnytsia, and lands up to the Horyn River by Yurii (1157). In 1159 he supported Rostyslav Mstyslavych's bid to rule Kiev. In 1169 (after Rostyslav's death) he intended to take the Kievan throne, and he blocked Mstyslav Iziaslavych by joining Andrei Bogoliubskii's coalition, which plundered Kiev in 1169. In retaliation Mstyslav waged a campaign through Volodymyr's territories and elevated his son, Volodymyr (Mstyslavych), to rule after Volodymyr died.

**Volodymyr Davydovych** [Davydovyč], b ?, d 12 May 1151. Rus' prince; elder son of Davyd Sviatoslavych. He received lands in the Siversk principality from his cousin, Vsevolod Olhovych, in 1127. After helping Vsevolod take the Kievan throne in 1139, he was granted the Chernihiv principality, which he ruled until his death. In 1142 Vsevolod also gave Volodymyr and his brother, Iziaslav, several towns, including Dorohychyn. When Iziaslav Mstyslavych became grand prince of Kiev in 1146, tensions between the Olhovych and Monomakh princely families continued to rise. In 1148 Iziaslav surrounded Chernihiv and ravaged a large part of the principality. Volodymyr then joined Yurii Dolgorukii of Suzdal in his fight against Iziaslav. Volodymyr was killed in battle near the Ruta River.

**Volodymyr Ihorevych** [Ihorevyč], b 8 October 1171, d 1212. Rus' prince; son of Ihor Sviatoslavych. The Hypatian Chronicle mentions him as ruler of Putyvel in 1185. He was taken prisoner during his father's campaign against the Cumans, and escaped to Siversk after two years of captivity. After the death of Roman Mstyslavych in 1205, Volodymyr was chosen by Galician boyars to rule the Principality of Galicia, to which he lay claim through his mother, Yevfrosyniia, the sister of the last Rostyslavych ruler in Galicia, Volodymyr Yaroslavych. Galician boyars and his brother, Roman of Zvenyhorod, organized a Hungarian-backed revolt against Volodymyr in 1207 (or 1209), and he escaped to Putyvel. An attempt to retake Galicia resulted in his being ousted by Danylo Romanovych (1211).

A *hryvnia* minted during the reign of Voldymyr Monomakh

**Volodymyr Monomakh** [Monomax] (Volodymyr I Vsevolodovych), b 1053, d 19 May 1125 in Kiev. Grand prince of Kiev (1113–25); son of *Vsevolod Yaroslavych. He was named Monomakh after his mother, who was the daughter of the Byzantine emperor Constantine Monomachos (some 20th-century historians dispute the relation, alleging that Soviet scholars invented it for their own purposes). While his father was alive, Volodymyr ruled the Smolensk (from 1067) and Chernihiv (1078–94) principalities, led 13 successful military campaigns in his father's name, and participated in diplomatic missions. He became prince of Pereiaslav in 1094. After the death of Sviatopolk II Iziaslavych and the Kiev Uprising of 1113, he ascended to the Kievan throne.

Volodymyr was one of the outstanding statesmen of the medieval period in Ukraine. He sought to strengthen the unity of Rus' and the central authority of the Kievan prince. He struggled against the deterioration of dynastic solidarity in Kiev and attempted to unite the princes against the Polovtsian (Cuman) threat. He initiated the *Liubech congress of princes (1097), at which the order of succession (*rota* system) was radically reformed, and he organized the congresses of princes in Vytychiv (1100) and Dolobske (1103), at which joint campaigns against the Polovtsians were agreed upon.

During his tenure in Kiev, Volodymyr introduced a number of legal and economic reforms. He called a meeting to address the social problems which had caused the Kiev uprising of 1113, and issued *Volodymyr Monomakh's Statute (which was added to *Ruskaia Pravda*). The reforms, including the limitation of interest on loans and the abolition of servitude as a method of debt payment, brought about radical improvements to terms of credit in Rus'. Volodymyr was also the author of *Poucheniie ditiam* (Instruction to [My] Children, ca 1117), which was entered into the Laurentian Chronicle along with a letter he wrote to Oleh Sviatoslavych, the prince of Chernihiv. His *Poucheniie* was a didactic and autobiographical work of high literary quality, in which he condemned the internecine struggles of princes and promoted the idea of a unified state. The narrative voice of the testament is that of a courageous warrior and a wise and judicious ruler.

Volodymyr married *Gytha, the daughter of the English king Harold II, and founded the Kievan, Smolensk, and Suzdal lines of the *Riurykide dynasty. In 1966 *Debrett's Peerage, Baronage, Knightage, and Companionage* published the statement that Queen Elizabeth II was descended from Volodymyr Monomakh. He was the last prince of Rus' to preside over a unified state. He is buried in the St Sophia Cathedral in Kiev.

BIBLIOGRAPHY
Shliakov, N. *O Pouchenii Vladimira Monomakha* (St Petersburg 1900)
Ivakin, I. *Kniaz' Vladimir Monomakh i ego Pouchenie*, part 1 (Moscow 1901)
Orlov, A. *Vladimir Monomakh* (Moscow–Leningrad 1946; repr, The Hague–Paris 1969)
Sakharov, A. 'Vladimir Monomakh,' in *Polkovodtsy Drevnei Rusi* (Moscow 1985)

A. Zhukovsky

**Volodymyr Monomakh's Statute** (Ustav Volodymyra Monomakha). A legal code drafted by Prince Volodymyr Monomakh, representatives of the boyars, and several officials during the *Kiev Uprising of 1113. It contained several concessions to the burghers and lower estates of the city, made to appease the rebellious commoners. It regulated and improved the status of the *zakupy, thereby restricting the power of the boyars. It banned usury (limiting interest rates to 25 percent per annum) and prohibited the enslavement of an indebted merchant whose indebtedness was accidental. It also defined the status of *kholopy. The text of the statute, composed of 69 articles, is contained in the expanded version of *Ruskaia Pravda*. It was an important source for criminal, civil, and procedural law in Kievan Rus'.

**Volodymyr Mstyslavych** [Mstyslavyč], b 1132, d 30 May 1171 in Kiev. Rus' prince; son of Mstyslav I Volodymyrovych. He supported his brother Iziaslav Mstyslavych as prince of Kiev in 1146–54, and was granted in return the Osterskyi Horodets (now Oster) lands in 1147 and Dorohobuzh in 1153. After his brother Sviatopolk died in 1154, Volodymyr ruled in Volodymyr-Volynskyi,

but he was chased out by his nephew, Mstyslav Iziaslavych. He ruled in Slutske, Riazan, and, again, Dorohobuzh before being proposed by Rostyslavych dynasty members as grand prince of Kiev in 1171. He held that position for only four months before his death.

**Volodymyr Riurykovych** [Rjurykovyč], b 1187, d ca 1239. Rus' prince; son of Riuryk Rostyslavych. He ruled in Pereiaslav (1206) and Smolensk (1215), and he became grand prince of Kiev in 1223. His reign was threatened in 1235 by the invasion of Mykhail Vsevolodovych of Chernihiv and Iziaslav Volodymyrovych, which he repelled with the aid of Danylo Romanovych of Galicia. He was captured by the Cumans in 1235 as the struggle for Kiev continued, and in 1236, after his freedom was purchased, he deposed Yaroslav Vsevolodovych and returned to the Kievan throne.

A silver coin minted during the reign of Volodymyr the Great

**Volodymyr the Great** (Valdamar, Volodimer, Vladimir), b ca 956, d 15 July 1015 in Vyshhorod, near Kiev. Grand prince of Kiev from 980; son of *Sviatoslav I Ihorevych and *Malusha; half-brother of *Yaropolk I Sviatoslavych and *Oleh Sviatoslavych; and father of 11 princes by five wives, including *Sviatopolk I, *Yaroslav the Wise, *Mstyslav Volodymyrovych, and *Saints Borys and *Hlib Volodymyrovych. In 969 Grand Prince Sviatoslav I named his son Volodymyr the prince of Novgorod, where the latter ruled under the guidance of his uncle, *Dobrynia. In 977 a struggle for power broke out among Sviatoslav's sons. Yaropolk I, who was then the grand prince of Kiev, seized the Derevlianian land and Novgorod, thereby forcing Volodymyr to flee to Scandinavia. In 980 Volodymyr returned to Rus' with a Varangian force, expelled Yaropolk's governors from Novgorod, and took Polatsk after a battle in which Prince Rogvolod of Polatsk was slain. Volodymyr took Rogvolod's daughter, *Rohnida, as his wife. Later that year he captured Kiev and had Yaropolk murdered, thereby becoming the grand prince, and married Yaropolk's Greek widow.

Over the next 35 years Volodymyr expanded the borders of *Kievan Rus' and turned it into one of the most powerful states in Eastern Europe. After taking the *Cherven towns and Peremyshl from Poland (981) and waging successful wars against the *Viatichians (981–2) and *Radimichians (984) he united the remaining East Slavic tribes, divided his realm into lands, and installed his sons or viceroys to govern them, dispense princely justice, and collect tribute. In 983 Volodymyr waged war against the *Yatvingians and thereby gained access to the Baltic Sea. In 985 he defeated the *Khazars and *Volga Bulgars and secured his state's eastern frontier. Volodymyr devoted considerable attention to defending his southern borders against the nomadic *Pechenegs and *Chorni Klobuky. He had lines of fortifications built along the Irpin, the Stuhna, the Trubizh, and the Sula rivers and founded fortified towns (eg, Vasyliv, Voin, and Bilhorod) that were joined by earthen ramparts.

Volodymyr attributed his victory over Yaropolk to the support he received from pagan forces, and had idols of the deities Perun, Khors, Dazhboh, Stryboh, Simarhl, and Mokosh erected on a hill overlooking his palace in Kiev. Later he became convinced that a monotheistic religion would consolidate his power, as Christianity and Islam had done for neighboring rulers. His choice was determined after the Byzantine emperor Basil II turned to him for help in defeating his rival, Bardas Phocas. Volodymyr offered military aid only if he was allowed to marry Basil's sister, Anna, and Basil agreed to the marriage only after Volodymyr promised to convert himself and his subjects to Christianity. Volodymyr, his family, and his closest associates were baptized in December 987, when he took the Christian name Vasylii (Basil). Soon afterward he ordered the destruction of all pagan idols. The mass baptism of the citizens of Kiev took place on 1 August 988 (see *Christianization of Ukraine), and the remaining population of Rus' was slowly converted, sometimes by force. In 988 Volodymyr sent several thousand warriors to help Basil regain power and married Anna, and in 989 he besieged Chersonese Taurica, took it from Bardas Phocas, and returned it to Basil.

The Christianization of Rus' was essentially engineered by Byzantium. Byzantium supplied the first hierarchs and other missionary clergy in Rus' and introduced Byzantine art, education, and literature there. During Volodymyr's reign the first schools and churches were built, notably the Church of the *Tithes in Kiev. The adoption of Christianity as the official religion facilitated the unification of the Rus' tribes and the establishment of foreign dynastic, political, cultural, religious, and commercial relations, particularly with the *Byzantine Empire, *Bulgaria, and *Germany. Relations with Poland improved after Volodymyr's son Sviatopolk I married the daughter of Prince Bolesław I the Brave in 992. Volodymyr received papal emissaries in 986, 988, 991, 992, and 1000 and sent his own envoys to Rome in 993 and 1001.

After Anna's death in 1011, Volodymyr married the daughter of Count Kuno von Enningen. Toward the end of his life his sons Sviatopolk of Turiv and Yaroslav of Novgorod challenged his rule. Having defeated Sviatopolk, Volodymyr died while preparing a campaign against Yaroslav and was buried in the Church of the Tithes. He was succeeded briefly by Sviatopolk.

The Rus' clergy venerated Volodymyr because of his support of the church, but he was canonized only after 1240. Thereafter he was referred to as 'the holy, equal to the Apostles, grand prince of Kiev.' The oldest extant mention of him as St Volodymyr is found in the Hypatian Chronicle under the year 1254, and his feast day, 28 July (15 July OS), was first celebrated in 1263.

BIBLIOGRAPHY
Zavitnevich, V. *Vladimir Sviatoi kak politicheskii deiatel'* (Kiev 1888)
Nazarko, I. *Sviatyi Volodymyr Velykyi, volodar i khrystytel' Rusy-Ukraïny (960–1015)* (Rome 1954)
Poppe, A. 'The Political Background to the Baptism of Rus': Byzantine-Russian Relations between 986 and 989,' *Dumbarton Oaks Papers*, no. 30 (1976); repr in his *Rise of Christian Russia* (London 1982)
Volkoff, V. *Vladimir the Russian Viking* ([London] 1984)
A. Zhukovsky

**Volodymyr Vasylkovych** [Vasyl'kovyč], b ?, d 10 October 1289 in Luboml. Rus' prince; son of Vasylko Romanovych. He was prince of Volhynia from 1270 or 1272, described in the Galician-Volhynian Chronicle as a 'great bibliophile and philosopher' who built towns, castles, and churches, promoted ecclesiastical art and literature, and compiled a large library. During his rule Volhynia enjoyed a period of prosperity and expansion into Belarusian territories, as well as the acquisition of Mazovia. Volodymyr refrained from the political intrigues undertaken by his cousin, the Galician prince Lev Danylovych, although he was forced to repulse several incursions by Lithuanian princes in the 1270s and to provide auxiliary support for Tatar incursions into Poland in 1280, 1283, and 1287. In 1288 he turned over his authority to his cousin, Mstyslav Danylovych. The Galician-Volhynian Chronicle ends with Volodymyr's death.

**Volodymyr Yaroslavych** [Jaroslavyč], b 1151, d ca 1199. Rus' prince; son of Yaroslav Osmomysl of Halych and Olga, the daughter of Yurii Dolgorukii. After Yaroslav's death in 1187, Volodymyr received the Peremyshl land. He forced his stepbrother, Oleh, out of Halych and claimed the Galician throne in 1188. He was ousted by the boyars, who wished to invite Roman Mstyslavych of Volhynia to rule, and sought refuge in Hungary. The Hungarian king Béla III imprisoned Volodymyr and sent his own son, Andrew, to govern Galicia. Volodymyr escaped in 1189 and returned to Galicia with the assistance of King Frederick Barbarossa. The boyars and the local population welcomed his return and incited a popular revolt. Volodymyr regained his authority and ruled as the last of the Rostyslavych dynasty in the Principality of Galicia-Volhynia. He maintained friendly relations with Riuryk Rostyslavych of Kiev and Vsevolod Sviatoslavych of Suzdal.

**Volodymyrets** [Volodymyrec']. II-7. A town smt (1988 pop 8,000) and raion center in Rivne oblast. It was first mentioned in historical documents in 1570, when it belonged to the Czartoryski family of Polish magnates. After the partition of Poland in 1793, it was annexed by Russia and assigned to Lutske county in Volhynia gubernia. In the interwar period Volodymyrets was occupied by Poland. In 1943 a company of the Ukrainian Insurgent Army under Lt I. Perehiiniak operated in the vicinity and fought the Germans. Today the town has a starch and syrup factory, a flax-processing plant, and a dairy. There is a historical museum and a park dating back to 1827.

**Volodymyrivka.** A multi-occupational site along the tributary of the Boh near Volodymyrivka, Novoarkhanhelske raion, Kirovohrad oblast. Excavated in the 1930s and

1940s by S. Magura, T. Passek, among others, the site yielded eight Paleolithic occupations and a large Trypilian settlement. The artifacts uncovered included many fine pottery pieces, earthenware figures of women, models of homes, bones of wild and domestic animals, and various flint, horn, and bone items. The excavation of the entire Trypilian settlement, the only Trypilian site to be totally excavated, uncovered the remains of some 200 structures arranged into five concentric circles. The immense size of the site, in which all structures appear to have been used contemporaneously, suggests that the larger Trypilian sites may have served as proto-urban centers.

**Volodymyrko** (Volodymyr Volodarovych), b 1104, d February 1153. Rus' prince; son of Volodar Rostyslavych and father of Yaroslav Osmomysl. He became prince of Zvenyhorod and Belz in 1124 and then began a campaign to bring all the lands in Galicia under his control. He attempted to wrest Peremyshl from his brother, Rostyslav, in 1125–6 but did not succeed. In 1141, after his cousin, Ihor (Ivan) Vasylkovych, died, Volodymyrko established Halych as the capital of his principality, but he faced incursions by Poles (1142) and Bulgars (1144) as well as an uprising of his subjects (1144). He captured Pryluk in 1146 and successfully defended it and Zvenyhorod against Vsevolod Olhovych. Looking to expand his holdings further, in 1149 he sided with Yurii Dolgorukii of Suzdal against Iziaslav Mstyslavych of Kiev. The alliance resulted in attacks on Galicia by Iziaslav's ally, King Géza of Hungary, which lasted until 1152, when Volodymyr managed to establish peace with the king through diplomacy and bribes.

**Volodymyrsky, Adriian** [Volodymyrs'kyj, Adrijan], b 16 April 1875 in Lypovets, Kiev gubernia, d 18 January 1936 in Rostov-na-Donu, RSFSR. Specialist in congenital diseases. A graduate of Kiev University (1900), he conducted research on the development and education of children with physical and psychological handicaps. In 1917 he lectured at the Pedagogical Academy in Kiev, and in the 1920s he served as a professor at the Kiev Medical Institute and the Kiev Institute of People's Education. His publications dealt with reflexology and educational hygiene.

**Volodymyr-Volynskyi** [Volodymyr-Volyns'kyj]. III-5. A city (1989 pop 40,900) on the Luha River and a raion center in Volhynia oblast. One of Ukraine's oldest cities, it is first mentioned in the chronicles under the year 988, as the fortified trading town of Volodymyr and the seat of an eparchy. In the 12th century it was the center of a principality, and in 1199 it became part of the Principality of Galicia-Volhynia. Frequent Tatar attacks (1240, 1260, 1491, and 1500) brought about its decline. In the late 14th century it came under Lithuanian rule, and in 1431 it obtained the rights of *Magdeburg law. From 1569 the town belonged to the Polish Commonwealth. Prince K. Ostrozky set up a school there in 1577, and a Basilian college operated there in the 18th century. In 1795 the town was annexed by the Russian Empire. It was renamed Volodymyr-Volynskyi, and served as a county center in Volhynia gubernia. During the First World War the Ukrainian Sich Riflemen opened the first Ukrainian school there, in 1916, and the Graycoats division was stationed there, in 1918. In the spring of 1919 the town was captured by the Polish army. In the interwar period Volodymyr-Volynskyi was a

Volodymyr-Volynskyi, with the Dormition Cathedral (1160) and its campanile (1494) in the foreground

county center under Polish rule. In 1943–6, units of the Ukrainian Insurgent Army operated in the surrounding forests. Today the city is an industrial and communications center. It has a sugar refinery, canning plant, winery, dairy-products plant, sewing factory, flax-processing plant, and furniture factory. Its chief architectural monuments are the remains of the 12th- to 13th-century fortifications, the foundations of 10th- to 14th-century residential buildings, the Dormition Cathedral (1160, restored at the end of the 19th century), St Basil's Church (13th–14th century), and the Renaissance bishops' palaces (16th century). Hermit cells and an old monastery complex have been preserved in nearby *Zymne.

**Volodymyr-Volynskyi eparchy.** One of the oldest eparchies of the Ukrainian church and by tradition second in importance only to the eparchy of Kiev. The first mention of an eparchy with its see in Volodymyr-Volynskyi and comprising much of the territory of the principality of Volodymyr-Volynskyi dates from 992. The first known bishop was Stefan. At various times the eparchy included much of the territory of Right-Bank Ukraine and Belarus. In 1596 the bishop of Volodymyr-Volynskyi, I. *Potii, joined the Uniate church. Although Orthodox forces continued to struggle for control of the eparchy and even had Y. Kurtsevych consecrated as Orthodox bishop of Volodymyr in 1620, the eparchy remained Uniate until the end of the 18th century. Prominent Uniate bishops in that period included L. Zalensky (1679–1708), L. Kishka (1711–28), and P. Volodkovych (1758–78). With the partitions of Poland the territory of the eparchy came under Russian rule. The Uniate church was soon destroyed there, and the new Orthodox eparchy of Volhynia, comprising the territory of Volhynia gubernia, was established, with its see in Zhytomyr.

**Volodymyr-Volynskyi principality.** A principality of medieval Rus', covering the upper and middle reaches of the Buh River and the tributaries of the Prypiat. It was formed in the 10th century out of territories inhabited by the Volhynians. Vsevolod, the son of Volodymyr Sviatoslavych, was its first ruler. The Liubech congress of princes in 1097 awarded the principality to Davyd Ihore-vych, and the Vytychiv congress of princes in 1100 over-turned that decision in favor of Sviatopolk II Iziaslavych. Volodymyr Monomakh seized the territory and placed it under his son, Andrii (1118–34). Then it was ruled by Iziaslav Mstyslavych for two decades (1134–54). After his death the principality was divided among his sons, and became independent of Kiev. Volodymyr-Volynskyi principality reached its apex under Roman Mstyslavych (1170–1205), who strengthened the power of the prince over the boyars and merged the principality with Halych principality in 1199, thereby creating the Principality of *Galicia-Volhynia.

**Volodyslav Kormylchych** [Kormyl'čyč], b and d ? 12th- to 13th-century Galician boyar. He opposed the establishment of a central leadership in Galicia. Roman Mstyslavych banished him from Galicia, but when he died in 1205 Volodyslav returned and began inciting the boyars to strengthen their hold on power. Roman's sons were forced to flee to Hungary, and the sons of Ihor Sviatoslavych were invited to rule as nominal figure-heads. After they were ousted in 1211, Volodyslav himself made an attempt to take over (1213), but the Hungarian king Andrew invaded Galicia and placed his own son, Kálmán, on the throne. Volodyslav was taken to Hungary (1214), where he died.

*Voloka.* See Weights and measures.

*Voloka* **land reform.** A *land reform introduced in 1557 in Ukrainian and Belarusian territories, during the rule of the Polish king Sigismund II Augustus, through laws known as *ustavy na voloky*. It had been initiated by Sigismund I in the early 16th century, and continued into the early 17th century. It consisted of a redistribution, consolidation, and revaluation of state-owned, communal, and individual peasant lands and resulted in increased income for the state treasury. The reform established the first official land registry in the Polish-Lithuanian Commonwealth and aimed to standardize peasant landholdings and obligations. Free peasants received one *voloka* (33 *morgy*, or approx 20 ha) and bonded peasants (*otchychi*) received one-third of a *voloka*. *Putni* and *pantsyrni* boyars and starostas received two *voloky*. Noblemen were entitled to compensation (*odminy*) for reallocated land, but peasants were not. In addition parcels of approx 20 *voloky* were set aside for export grain production. Initally the *voloka* land reform was implemented on state-owned lands; then it was carried out on aristocratic holdings. Peasants who participated in the new *land tenure system were subjected to new duties. It was opposed by them because it disrupted old forms of ownership and agricultural practice, and because it did away with communal land use (as in the *dvoryshche*) and their freedom of movement.

BIBLIOGRAPHY
Picheta, V. *Agrarnaia reforma Sigizmunda-Avgusta v Litovsko-Russkom gosudarstve* (Moscow 1958)

A. Zhukovsky

**Volokh, Omelian** [Volox, Omeljan], b 1886 in Kalnybolotska *stanytsia*, Kuban, d November 1937 in Solovets Islands. Revolutionary military figure. He was an otaman commanding the Second Ukrainian Regiment (1917), the Haidamaka Regiment (1918), and the Zaporozhian Corps and Haidamaka Brigade (1919). On 1 December 1919 he attempted an uprising against the Directory. Although it was unsuccessful, he made away with the treasury and went over to the Bolshevik side.

**Volokh, Petro** [Volox], b 1699 in Wallachia, d May 1768 in Kiev. Jeweler. He worked at the Kievan Cave Monastery. His most important work is the Royal Gate for the iconostasis of Kiev's St Sophia Cathedral, designed by S. Taranovsky and made by Volokh and I. Zavadovsky in 1747. The now nonexistent silver gate was carved with plant ornamentation and bas-reliefs of the Annunciation, Christ's Presentation at the Temple, the Evangelists, King David, and other biblical figures.

**Volokh, S.** See Prokopovych, Viacheslav.

Pavel Volokidin (self-portrait, oil, 1921)

**Volokidin, Pavel,** b 22 December 1877 in Arkharovo, Orel gubernia, Russia, d 16 March 1936 in Kiev. Painter. He studied at the Odessa Art School (1898–1905) under K. Kostandi and G. Ladyzhensky and at the St Petersburg Academy of Arts (1905–6). A member of the *Society of South Russian Artists in Odessa from 1910, he taught at the Odessa Art Institute (1918–34) and at the Kiev State Art Institute (1934–6). Volokidin painted expressive portraits and colorful landscapes and still lifes, including *Woman in a Black Dress* (1908–11), *Reflection in the Water* (1915), *Still Life with a Red Tray* (1927), *Peonies* (1928), portraits of I. Severyn (1919), Z. Haidai (1935), and O. Syrotenko (1935), several portraits of his wife, and *Woman in a Shawl* (1935). An album of his works was published in Moscow in 1981.

**Volosenko, Pavlo,** b 1876 in Tysmenytsia, Tovmach county, Galicia, d 27 April 1958 in Flushing, New York. Engineer and civic activist; corresponding member of the Shevchenko Scientific Society. As a student of mechanical engineering at the Lviv Polytechnic he was active in student organizations and took part in the student *secession of 1901. After completing his studies in Vienna, Zurich, and Lviv he worked on the staff of *Hromads'kyi holos*, the organ of the Ukrainian Radical party. In 1909 he moved to Kharkiv, where he set up his own office of sanitation technology. He joined the Osnova and Prosvita societies and was active in Ukrainian community life. During the First World War he was deported by the Russian authorities to Kazan. In 1918 he held an important post in the UNR Ministry of Highways. In 1922 he was elected president of the Society of Ukrainian Engineers in Lviv, and from 1926 he managed his own sanitation and construction firm in that city. After emigrating to the United States following the Second World War, he wrote a number of memoirs.

**Voloshchak, Andrii** [Vološčak, Andrij] (pseuds: Vasyl Boiko, Ivan Kos), b 31 August 1890 in Mshanets, Turka county, Galicia, d 6 August 1973 in Lviv. Poet. He studied at the Peremyshl gymnasium (1904–12) and at Lviv (1912–14, 1918–19) and Prague (1916–18) universities. He was blinded while in the Austrian army in 1914. His first poem appeared in *Dobra novyna* (Lviv) in 1909. In the interwar years he lived in Drohobych, Peremyshl, Staryi Sambir, and, from 1933, Lviv. In the 1930s he belonged to the writers' group Horno and contributed to *Vikna* and *Znannia*. His first collection, *U t'mi horiu* (In the Darkness I Burn), was published in 1934. Under Soviet rule (in 1941 and from 1946 on) he published over 10 poetry collections. Editions of his selected poems appeared in 1961, 1971, and 1974.

**Voloshchak, Ostap** (Evstakhii) [Vološčak], b 1 October 1835 in Yavoriv, Galicia, d 10 July 1918 in Vienna. Botanist; member of the Shevchenko Scientific Society from 1914 and of the Vienna and Cracow academies of science. A graduate in law and biology of Vienna University, he was a founding member of the *Sich student society of Vienna in 1868. From 1884 he was a professor of zoology and botany at the Lviv Polytechnical Institute. He researched the flora of the Carpathian Mountains, particularly the Eastern Carpathians and Pokutia.

**Voloshenko, Inokentii** [Vološenko, Inokentij] (pseuds: Petro Vovk, Pavlov, Vishniakov), b 1848, d 1908 in Poltava. Revolutionary populist. He studied at Odessa University. In 1876 he spread revolutionary literature among the Kuban Cossacks. In 1879, as a member of V. *Osinsky's terrorist group in Kiev, he was arrested and sentenced to 10 years of hard labor in Siberia. He escaped in transit in 1880, was captured one month later, and had 11 years added to his sentence. After being transferred to the Peter and Paul Fortress in St Petersburg in 1882, he was returned to Siberia in 1884. From 1890 he lived in exile in Transbaikal oblast, and in 1906 he returned to Ukraine.

**Voloshkevych, Heorhii** [Vološkevyč, Heorhij], b 1 August 1911 in Zhytomyr, Volhynia gubernia. Metallurgist and specialist in welding technology. He studied in Kiev and since 1941 has worked at the Institute of Electric Welding of the AN URSR (now ANU). He has developed a number of new electric welding processes, including an electro-flux method of welding, and an extensive theoretical basis for studying such processes.

**Voloshko, Yevhen** [Vološko, Jevhen], b 16 March 1927 in Luhanske. Literary scholar and critic. A graduate of the Voroshylovhrad Pedagogical Institute (1951), he has been a candidate of sciences since 1968. He taught for 10 years in secondary schools in the Donbas and was a lecturer in Ukrainian literature at the Co-operative Institute and Higher Military-Political School in Donetske. Since 1980 he has chaired the department of Ukrainian literature at Donetske University. He has written, in Russian, four books on the literature and writers of the Donbas (1961, 1968, 1975, 1980), including Greek and Jewish writers and Ukrainian-Russian literary relations, and one book on the

birth and development of proletarian poetry in Ukraine (1966). He has also edited a collection of Ukrainian writings about the Russian writer M. Sholokhov (1985). In recent years he has studied the life and works of B. Lepky.

Rev Avhustyn Voloshyn

**Voloshyn, Avhustyn** [Vološyn], b 17 March 1874 in Kelechyn, Transcarpathia, d 1946 in a Soviet prison. Greek Catholic priest and leading cultural and political figure in Transcarpathia. A graduate of the Uzhhorod Theological Seminary and the Higher Pedagogical School in Budapest, he served as a professor (1900–17) at and director (1917–38) of the Uzhhorod Teachers' Seminary. He edited and published *Nauka (1903–14), the only Ukrainian newspaper in Ukrainian lands under Hungarian rule, *Svoboda* (1922–38), and the annual *Misiatsoslov* (1901–21). In 1922 he helped found *Blahovistnyk. His Hungarian-language practical grammar of the Little Russian (Ruthenian) Language (1907; repr 1920), which was awarded a prize by the Academy of Sciences in Budapest, defended the vernacular and the view that it was part of the Ukrainian language.

As a founding member of the Ruthenian People's Council in Uzhhorod and then president of the *Central Ruthenian People's Council Voloshyn played an important role in Transcarpathia's process of national self-determination in 1918–20. In 1919–20 he sat on the provisional autonomous executive of Subcarpathian Ruthenia. He was one of the founders and the president (1923–39) of the *Christian People's party. In 1925 he was elected as its candidate to the Czechoslovak parliament. At the same time he was a leading member of various cultural and economic institutions: president of the Pedagogical Society of Subcarpathian Ruthenia, an organizer of the Teachers' Hromada of Subcarpathian Ruthenia, honorary president of the Uzhhorod Prosvita society, and a founder of the Subcarpathian Bank and the Co-operative Union. His role in the building of the Carpatho-Ukrainian state was critical. On 26 October 1938 he was appointed premier of an autonomous government by the president of Czechoslovakia, and on 15 March 1939 the Diet of *Carpatho-Ukraine elected him president of an independent state. After the Hungarian invasion Voloshyn emigrated to Prague and devoted himself to research and teaching at the Ukrainian Free University. On 21 May 1945 he was arrested by the Soviet secret police and deported to the USSR, where he soon died in prison.

Voloshyn wrote a number of elementary- and secondary-school textbooks in grammar, physics, and chemistry (coauthor, M. Velyhorsky), readers, and pedagogical textbooks for teachers. Later, in Prague, he wrote a general survey of pedagogy in several volumes. He was the author of other books, such as *O pys'mennom iazytsi podkarpatskykh rusynov* (On the Literary Language of Subcarpathian Ruthenians, 1921), *Spomyny* (Recollections, 1923, 1959), and *Dvi politychni rozmovy* (Two Political Conversations, 1923). His contributions to belles lettres were signed with the pseudonym A. Verkhovynsky and include two populist plays, *Marusia Verkhovynka* (Marusia from the Highlands, 1931) and *Bez Boha ni do poroha* (Not Even a Start without God, 1935).

V. Markus

**Voloshyn, Ivan** [Vološyn], b 10 October 1905 in Kiev, d 15 August 1973 in Kiev. Writer. He began publishing in 1925 in Kiev periodicals. From 1928 on he wrote sketches for newspapers and worked as a graphic artist. He was also a researcher at the AN URSR (now ANU) Institute of Ukrainian Folklore (1938–42, 1945–51). Among his works are the prose collections *Sady tsvitut'* (The Orchards Are Blooming, 1950), *Samotsvity* (Gems, 1952), *Naddniprians'ki vysoty* (The Dnieper Heights, 1953), *Z moria narodnoho* (From the People's Sea, 1955), *Dni khudozhnyka* (Days of the Artist, 1958), *Ozero sered dibrovy* (The Lake amid the Grove, 1959), *Misiachne sriblo* (Lunar Silver, 1961), and *Sontse u rosi* (The Sun in Dew, 1964); and the novels *Khudozhnyky* (Artists, 1963) and *Sashko Roden'* (1966).

Mykhailo Voloshyn          Rostyslav Voloshyn

**Voloshyn, Mykhailo** [Vološyn, Myxajlo], b 1878, d 29 July 1943 in Lviv. Lawyer. In the 1930s he was a member of the Lviv Chamber of Advocates, and he acted for the defense in many political trials. He served on the Central Committee of the Ukrainian National Democratic Alliance (1925–39) and on the boards of several Ukrainian cooperatives. For many years he conducted the *Boian chorus in Lviv. During the German occupation he presided over the Lviv Chamber of Advocates.

**Voloshyn, Rostyslav** [Vološyn] (pseuds: A.S. Borysenko, Pavlenko), b 1911 in Volhynia gubernia, d 22 August 1944 in Drohobych oblast. Revolutionary and political leader. He was a founding member of the OUN and its organizer in Volhynia, and for his political activities he was imprisoned by the Polish authorities. During the German occupation he was one of the principal organizers of the UPA (1942–3) and a member of the OUN (Bandera faction)

Leadership (1943–4). In August 1943 he chaired the Third OUN Congress, in November 1943 the First Conference of the Captive Nations of Eastern Europe and Asia, and in July 1944 the First Congress of the *Ukrainian Supreme Liberation Council (UHVR). He was elected general secretary of internal affairs in the UHVR. He was killed in combat with NKVD troops.

**Volosiansky, Ivan** [Volosjans'kyj], b 1861 in Staryi Sambir, Sambir county, Galicia, d 19 April 1930 in Sokal, Galicia. Greek Catholic priest, cultural figure, and ethnographer. After graduating from the Greek Catholic Theological Seminary in Lviv, he was ordained in 1885 and served as pastor in various villages of Sambir county. He organized reading rooms, temperance societies, and rural schools. In politics he supported the populists and was a member of the National Democratic party. His main ethnographic interest was the life of tradesmen and guilds, and his studies appeared in *Zoria* from 1886. After being assigned to Krakovets parish in Yavoriv county in 1898, he organized and headed the local branch of the Prosvita society, helped to establish a Ukrainian gymnasium in Yavoriv, and campaigned for electoral reform in 1905–7.

*Volost* (Russian: *vlast*). In Old Ukrainian the term meant 'power' or 'government.' During the Princely era it was also used, like the earlier term *zemlia*, to refer to the princely state, especially in relation to the appanage principalities, and sometimes to its population. In the 11th to 13th centuries a *volost* was an administrative-territorial division consisting of several *hromady*, headed by a *volostel* or starosta. The *volost* center was usually called a *pryhorod*, headed by a *horodnychyi*.

As the medieval Ukrainian states disintegrated, the term fell out of use. In 1861 the *volost* (or *gmina*) was introduced by Alexander II in the Russian Empire as an administrative unit of rural self-government; it was composed of several village *hromady* and had limited administrative and judicial powers. The *volost* was governed by a board which included the *volost starshyna*, village starostas, tax collectors, and a scribe. The *volost* assembly, which included those officials plus deputies of the rural population (1 per 10 farmsteads), oversaw the elections of local officials, candidates to county zemstvo assemblies, and members of the *volost* court, which settled minor disputes. Under the Ukrainian national government in 1917–20, the *volost* was implemented as a secondary self-governing entity, between the *zemlia* and the *hromada*. *Volosti* continued to function under the Soviet regime until the administrative reform of 12 April 1923, when they were replaced by raions. The 1,989 *volosti* of the Ukrainian SSR were then reorganized into 706 raions.

A. Zhukovsky

*Volost* **court.** A rural court for peasants in the Russian Empire. *Volost* courts were established in 1861 with the emancipation of the serfs. Until then, justice was administered by the landowners. *Volost* courts were composed of a president and from 3 to 11 judges, all of whom were elected by *volost* assemblies for a one-year term. They handled disputes and litigations between peasants involving sums of less than 100 rubles, and punished minor offenders. They also had the authority to mete out corporal punishment. The *volost* courts were abolished in 1918.

**Volove.** See Mizhhiria.

Carpathian highlands in Volovets raion

**Volovets** [Volovec']. V-4. A town smt (1988 pop 6,200) on the Vicha River and a raion center in Transcarpathia oblast. It was first mentioned in historical documents in the 15th century, when it was under Hungarian rule. From the end of the 17th century the village belonged to Austria, and in the interwar period, to Czechoslovakia. In 1957 it was granted smt status. The town has a mineral-water bottling factory, a lumber mill, and a compression station on the Urengoi–Uzhhorod gas pipeline. The folk-art gallery and Plai tourist base attract visitors from outside the region to the town.

**Volovyk, Hryhorii,** b 29 May 1902 in Konotip, Chernihiv gubernia, d 7 July 1967 in Lviv. Stage director. He completed study at the Lysenko Music and Drama Institute (1923) and then worked as artistic director of the Chernihiv Ukrainian Music and Drama Theater (1926–41, with interruptions) and the Transcarpathian Ukrainian Music and Drama Theater in Uzhhorod (1948–53). He also staged plays in Kirovohrad, Vinnytsia, and other cities.

**Volska, Frantsishka** [Vol's'ka, Franciška] (née Lekhno-Vasiutynska), b 1863, d 1930. Community activist in Kiev. During the First World War she organized relief for Galician prisoners in Russian-ruled Ukraine, and in 1917 she founded the Hromada of Ukrainian Catholics. She published Ukrainian-language children's literature and edited the magazine *Voloshky* (1917).

**Volsky, Serafym** [Vol's'kyj], b 13 January 1911 in Svirneve, Balta county, Podilia gubernia. Historian. He graduated from Odessa University (1940), worked as a CP functionary (1940–53), and headed the Department of

CPSU History at the Odessa Institute of Naval Engineers (from 1953). He was an author in the collective work *Ukraïns'ka RSR u Velykii vitchyznianii viini Radians'koho Soiuzu 1941–1945 rr.* (The Ukrainian SSR in the Great Patriotic War of the Soviet Union of 1941–5, 1967).

**Voluntary Society for Assistance to the Army, Air Force, and Navy** (Dobrovilne tovarystvo spryiannia armii, aviatsii i flotu; Russian: Dobrovolnoe obshchestvo sodeistviia armii, aviatsii i flotu, or DOSAAF). A mass organization in the USSR that promoted military knowledge and training among civilians, especially young people, under the guidance of the CPSU and Komsomol. Established in 1927 as the Society for the Promotion of Defense and Aviation and Chemical Construction, it was split in 1948 into three societies paralleling the three main branches of the armed forces, which were merged as the DOSAAF in 1951. The DOSAAF provided, through local clubs, paramilitary and civil-defense instruction, disseminated patriotic propaganda, and promoted military sports, such as flying, helicoptering, gliding, parachuting, driving, motorcycling, cross-country skiing, shooting, and the martial arts. In Ukraine the DOSAAF was headed by a CC usually chaired by a general. It published the weekly *Patriot Bat'kivshchyny*.

**Volunteer Army.** See Denikin, Anton.

**Volunteer regiments** (*okhotnytski polky*). Military units in Left-Bank Ukraine from the 1670s to 1770s, formed of volunteers who were paid, armed, and provisioned by the Hetmanate government. They were divided into infantry (see *Serdiuk regiments) and cavalry (see *Mercenary regiments). The volunteer regiments were not named after their territory, as the town regiments were, but after their commanders, as in Novytsky's, Maksymiv's, Yavorsky's, and Kozhukhovsky's regiments. They were not attached to a particular territory, and frequently changed the location of their headquarters. In general the number of Cossacks in volunteer regiments was lower than in town regiments. At the beginning of the 18th century the Hetmanate had seven volunteer regiments.

**Volykivska, Iryna** [Volykivs'ka] (real surname: Pidopryhora), b 5 May 1902 in Zasullia, Romen county, Poltava gubernia, d 29 January 1979 in Odessa. Opera singer (dramatic soprano). She studied acting under P. Saksahansky and graduated from the Lysenko Music and Drama Institute (1928). She sang with opera companies in Kiev, Kharkiv, Tbilisi, Moscow, Alma-Ata, and Odessa (1929–30, 1936–41, 1944–57). Her repertoire included Natalka in M. Lysenko's *Natalka from Poltava*, Odarka in S. Hulak-Artemovsky's *Zaporozhian Cossack beyond the Danube*, Myroslava in B. Liatoshynsky's *Zolotyi obruch* (The Golden Ring), Tatiana in P. Tchaikovsky's *Eugene Onegin*, Yaroslavna in A. Borodin's *Prince Igor*, and Aida in G. Verdi's *Aida*.

**Volyn** (Volhynia). A publishing house founded in August 1941 in German-occupied Rivne by a former member of the Polish Sejm, S. Skrypnyk (now Patriarch Mstyslav). It was managed by O. Petliura and, from November 1941, the prominent publisher in interwar Lviv, I. Tyktor. Volyn published the nationalist weekly and then semiweekly

*Volyn'*

newspaper *Volyn'* (1941–4, 233 issues), edited by U. Samchuk and then Ye. Mysechko and P. Zinchenko, with the assistance of Ye. Lazor, R. Bzhesky, and V. Shtul; the monthly children's magazine *Orlenia* (1941–3), edited by P. Zinchenko; the farming journal *Ukraïns'kyi khliborob* (1942–3, 10 issues), edited by P. Kolisnyk; books that had been banned under Soviet rule; and anticommunist brochures. *Volyn'* was widely read in Volhynia, and its press-run grew from 20,000 in 1941 to 102,000 in 1942. Tyktor and many of Volyn's staff were imprisoned by the Gestapo in 1942–3; six of them (including Kolisnyk) were executed.

**Volyn.** See Volhynia.

Ananii Volynets          Stepan Volynets

**Volynets, Ananii** [Volynec', Ananij], 1894–1939. Ukrainian partisan activist. An agronomist by profession, during the revolutionary period in Ukraine he commanded troops in Haisyn county, Podilia gubernia, and was an organizer of the Free Cossacks. He published the newspaper *Povstanets'* and participated in the 1919 uprising which overthrew the Hetman government and in the anti-Bolshevik *partisan movement in Ukraine until the end of 1920. Then he lived in western Volhynia. He was executed by the Soviet occupation forces.

**Volynets, Ivan** [Volynec'], b 1896 in Peremyshl, Galicia, d 22 February 1956 in São Caetano do Sul, Brazil. Wrestler. In interwar Galicia he was a popular wrestler; he worked in the Lviv and Peremyshl regions as a coach for the Ukrainian Sports Union and organizer for the Luh society. A postwar refugee, he emigrated to Brazil, where he served as president of the Sobornist society in São Paulo, for which he acquired the first People's Home there.

**Volynets, Stepan** [Volynec'], b 22 January 1895 in Lviv, d 10 April 1969 in Winnipeg. Journalist and civic and political leader. During the revolutionary period he fought in the ranks of the Ukrainian Sich Riflemen and in the UNR Army. In the 1920s he completed his education at the Lviv (Underground) Ukrainian University and Vienna University. He held high posts in the Communist Party of Western Ukraine. In 1928–30 he was a deputy to the Polish Sejm and secretary of its Sel-Rob caucus. His political sympathies later shifted, and from 1933 he was active in the Front of National Unity and its publications *Bat'kivshchyna*, *Ukraïns'ki visty*, and *Peremoha*. During the Second World War he directed the Institute of Public Education under the Ukrainian Central Committee and sat on the Military Board of the Division Galizien. After leaving Ukraine in 1944, he edited the paper *Ukraïns'ke slovo* in Blomberg, Germany. In 1949 he settled in Canada, and in 1957 he was appointed editor of *\*Ukraïns'kyi holos*. He wrote *Peredvisnyky i tvortsi lystopadovoho zryvu* (The Precursors and Creators of the November Uprising, 1965).

Petro Volyniak

**Volyniak, Petro** [Volynjak] (pseud: Chechet), b 29 September 1907 in Korets, Novohrad-Volynskyi county, Volhynia gubernia, d 29 December 1969 in Toronto. Journalist, writer, and political figure. He made his debut as a writer in the early 1930s with stories in the Kiev journals *Zhyttia i revoliutsiia* and *Molodyi bil'shovyk*. He was arrested in the mid-1930s and sentenced to forced labor on the White Sea–Baltic Waterway. After his release in 1941, he returned to Ukraine. A postwar refugee, he founded the Novi Dni publishing house in Salzburg, Austria, which issued the daily *Ostanni novyny*, the weekly *Novi dni*, the literary monthly *Litavry*, and other periodicals and books, and wrote the story collections *Zemlia klyche* (The Land Beckons, 1947) and *Pid Kyzhurtom* (Beneath Kyzhurt, 1947), children's books and readers, and *Kuban': Zemlia ukraïns'ka, kozacha* (Kuban: A Ukrainian, Cossack Land, 1948). In 1949 he emigrated to Canada. In Toronto he published and edited the monthly magazine *\*Novi dni* from 1950, was the deputy leader of the émigré *\*Ukrainian Revolutionary Democratic party, and published Ukrainian schoolbooks and belletristic works. A posthumous collection of his articles and stories appeared in 1975.

***Volyns'ka nedilia.*** See *Nedilia*.

**Volynsky, Petro** [Volyns'kyj], b 13 February 1893 in Olyka, Lutske county, Volhynia gubernia, d 12 April 1982 in Kiev. Literary scholar and teacher. He graduated from the Nizhen Historical Philological Institute (1916) and worked as a teacher. In the 1920s he lectured in Ukrainian literature at the Nizhen Institute of People's Education, and from 1929, at the Kiev Institute of People's Education and the Kiev Pedagogical Institute. He was made a professor in 1954, and headed the department of Ukrainian literature at the Kiev Pedagogical Institute (1947–76). He published studies of the history of Ukrainian literature of the 19th and early 20th centuries (especially the works of I. Kotliarevskyi, T. Shevchenko, I. Franko, and Lesia Ukrainka). The following monographs have appeared: *Ivan Kotliarevskyi: Zhyttia i tvorchist'* (Ivan Kotliarevsky: Life and Works, 1951), *Teoretychna borot'ba v ukraïns'kii literaturi: Persha polovyna XIX st.* (The Theoretical Struggle in Ukrainian Literature: The First Half of the 19th Century, 1959), and *Ukraïns'kyi romantyzm u zv'iazku z rozvytkom romantyzmu v slov'ians'kykh literaturakh* (Ukrainian Romanticism in Relation to the Development of Romanticism in Slavic Literatures, 1963). He also published the textbooks *Istoriia ukraïns'koï literatury* (The History of Ukrainian Literature, 3 vols, 1964–9) and *Osnovy teoriï literatury* (The Fundamentals of the Theory of Literature, 1962), among others.

**Volyntseve.** A Slavic settlement of the 7th to 8th century near Volyntseve, Putyvl raion, Sumy oblast. Excavations in 1948, 1953, and 1965–6 uncovered the remains of 35 pit dwellings with hearths, three workshops, and three ritualistic burials of adolescents in grain storage pits at the settlement site. Excavations of the burial site revealed 19 earthenware cremation urns buried in plots without kurhans. Pottery fragments, knives, sickles, arrowheads, bronze and silver adornments, and items of daily use were also found.

**Volyntsivske Reservoir** [Volyncivs'ke vodosxovyšče]. A water reservoir on the Bulavynka River in Donetske oblast. The reservoir has a surface area of 320 ha, a volume of 13.6 million cu m, and a usable volume (in dry years) of 8 million cu m. It was constructed in 1936 to regulate water supply for the city of Yenakiieve. It was rebuilt in 1946 after the Second World War and then used for reserve water supply and irrigation after Yenakiieve started obtaining its water through the Donets-Donbas Canal system. The banks of the reservoir have been seeded with trees to provide a shelterbelt.

**Vonatovych, Varlaam** [Vonatovyč] (Vanatovych, secular name: Vasyl), b ca 1675 in Jarosław, Galicia, d 17 January 1751 in the Tikhvin Monastery, near Novgorod, Russia. Orthodox church leader. After completing his theology training in Moscow he entered the service of the Russian Orthodox church and became archimandrite of the Tikhvin Monastery in 1719. Along with several other Ukrainian churchmen he participated in drawing up the reforms of the Russian church that culminated in the adoption of the *Dukhovnyi reglament* and the creation of the Holy Synod. In 1722 Vonatovych was named archbishop of Kiev and Halych. This appointment was a great blow to the Ukrainian church because it meant that the eparch of Kiev no longer had the dignity of metropolitan, and that his jurisdiction was limited to Right-Bank Ukraine and did not include the Ukrainian eparchies in the Hetmanate. Vonatovych continued to press for the re-

turn of the metropolitan's title and authority over the rest of the Ukrainian church province. He also attempted to maintain control over the Kievan Mohyla Academy and to prevent the secularization of Ukrainian monasteries. In 1730 he was arrested on trumped-up charges of treason by local Kievan authorities supported by T. *Prokopovych, and was defrocked and imprisoned in St Cyril's Monastery in Belozersk. After he was pardoned and released in 1740, he retired to the Tikhvin Monastery. A comprehensive biography of Vonatovych was published by A. Rybolovsky in *TKDA* (1908, nos 2–3).

**Voritskyi Pass** [Voric'kyj pereval] (aka Veretskyi or Tukholskyi pereval). V–4. A pass (elevation 841 m) in the High Beskyds situated on the watershed between the Stryi and the Liatorytsia rivers along the border between Lviv and Transcarpathia oblasts. An important historical road linking Mukachiv and Stryi runs through the pass.

**Vorkuta.** A city (1989 pop 116,000) situated north of the Arctic Circle on the Vorkuta River in the Komi AR, in northern Russia. It was founded in 1931 as a center of the Pechora Coal Basin and was granted city status in 1943. The region was developed mostly by penal labor from the nearby concentration camps filled with political prisoners and common criminals. Almost half the inmates were Ukrainians. After the Second World War many of the prisoners were Soviet soldiers who had been German POWs and nationalist resistance fighters from Western Ukraine. The prison population at this time was estimated at approx 90,000 (compared with 30,000 inhabitants of the city). At the end of the 1940s two clandestine organizations were formed in the camps, the Ukrainian Liberation Organization and the Ukrainian Cossack Front. When the release of political prisoners and improvements in camp regime introduced in 1954 were rescinded, the prisoners staged an uprising (1955). An account of life in the Vorkuta camps is provided in H. Kostiuk's memoirs *Okaianni roky* (The Accursed Years, 1978).

**Vorobets, Toma** [Vorobec'] (Thomas Worobec), b 1 July 1899 in Peremyshliany, Galicia, d 16 February 1986 in Chicago. As a volunteer to the Ukrainian Sich Riflemen he fought in defense of the Lviv citadel. After completing his medical studies at the Lviv (Underground) Ukrainian University and Prague University (MD, 1928) he practiced medicine in Terebovlia and founded the Ukrainian Hygienic Society there. He was director of the tuberculosis dispensary and the Ukrainian Red Cross in Lviv (1940–1), and a lecturer at the Lviv Medical Institute and director of its tuberculosis clinic (1941–4). He was president of the Ukrainian Medical Charitable Service in Germany (1945–8) and then emigrated to the United States, where he became head of the Department of Pulmonary Diseases at Veterans' Hospital in Downey, Illinois (1954). He wrote in English and Ukrainian on tuberculosis chemotherapy.

**Vorobiov, Anatolii** [Vorobjov, Anatolij], b 30 November 1900 in Mytrofanivka, near Salhyr, Perekop county, Tavriia gubernia, d 26 October 1955 in Kiev. Physiologist; corresponding member of the AN URSR (now ANU) from 1951. A graduate of the Kharkiv Medical Institute (1926), he taught at the Kharkiv Stomatology Institute (from 1936) and the Lviv Medical Institute (from 1945) and then became director of the ANU Institute of Physiology (1952). His research mainly concerned the physiology of digestion and nerve function.

**Vorobiov, Mykola** [Vorobjov], b 12 October 1941 in Melnykivka, Smila raion, Cherkasy oblast. Poet of the *shestydesiatnyky* generation. He began publishing in Soviet periodicals in 1962. In 1970 the publication of his first collection was canceled by Soviet censors for political reasons, and he was blacklisted until 1984, when some of his poems appeared in *Ukraïna*. A selection of his poems appeared in the émigré journals *Suchasnist'* (1971) and *Vyzvolnyi shliakh* (1972). He has published several collections of lyric poetry: *Pryhadai na dorohu meni* (Remind Me for the Road, 1985) and *Misiats' shypshyny* (Moon of the Wild Rose, 1986), *Obrii ozhyny* (The Horizon of a Blackberry, 1987), *Prohulianka odyntsem* (A Walk Alone, 1990), and a volume of selected poems, *Verkhovnyi holos* (The Supreme Voice, 1991). He has also published verses for children, *Luhova krynychka* (A Meadow Well, 1987) and *Zeleni traviani zaichyky* (Green Grass Bunnies, 1991). A selection of his poetry appeared in Toronto in 1992 in a bilingual Ukrainian-English edition, *Misiats' shypshyny/Wild Dog Rose Moon*.

Volodymyr Vorobiov     Hryhorii Vorobkevych

**Vorobiov, Volodymyr** [Vorobjov] (Vorobev, Vladimir), b 27 July 1876 in Odessa, d 31 October 1937 in Kharkiv. Anatomist; full member of the AN URSR (now ANU) from 1934. A graduate of Kharkiv University (1903), he served as a department chairman at the Kharkiv Women's Medical Institute (1910–17), Sofia University (1919–21), and the Kharkiv Medical Institute (1921–37) and as scientific director of the Ukrainian Institute of Experimental Medicine (1927–37). One of the pioneers of the functional approach to anatomy, he founded a large school of Soviet anatomists, investigated the innervation of organs, developed the macro-microscopic method of determining the anatomic structure of an organ, and embalmed V. Lenin. He wrote *Anatomiia liudyny* (Human Anatomy, vol 1, 1934) in Ukrainian and compiled the first Soviet *Atlas anatomii cheloveka* (Atlas of Human Anatomy, 5 vols, 1946–8). In 1936 his work was attacked by the Party, but later the USSR Academy of Medical Sciences created an anatomy award in his name. Monographs about him to mark the centenary of his birth appeared in 1976, by K.

Kulchytsky et al (in Ukrainian) and A. Novominsky (in Russian).

**Vorobkevych, Hryhorii** [Vorobkevyč, Hryhorij] (pseud: Naum Shram), b 10 January 1838 in Chernivtsi, d 24 November 1884 in Chernivtsi. Poet, priest, and community leader; brother of S. *Vorobkevych. He graduated from the Chernivtsi Orthodox Theological Seminary in 1860. He was ordained, and served as a pastor in Horoshivtsi (to 1867), Lviv (1867–70), and Toporivtsi (1881–4) and was also a spiritual adviser at the Chernivtsi seminary (from 1870), a catechist and teacher at the Chernivtsi Orthodox Realschule (from 1872), and an active member of the Ruska Besida and Ruska Rada societies in Chernivtsi. From 1868 on he published poems in Galician and Bukovynian periodicals (eg, *Pravda, Rodimyi listok*). He wrote narrative poems about the B. Khmelnytsky era, such as 'Bohun,' 'Bohdan pido L'vovom' (Bohdan [Khmelnytsky] at the Gates of Lviv), and 'Berestechko,' and patriotic and lyrical verse. He also translated from Russian into Ukrainian M. Kostomarov's study of B. Khmelnytsky. An edition of his poetry appeared in Chernivtsi in 1904.

Sydir Vorobkevych

**Vorobkevych, Sydir** [Vorobkevyč] (Isydor; pseuds: Danylo Mlaka, Demko, Demko Makoviichuk, Morozenko, Isydor V., S. Volokh, Semen Khrin), b 17 May 1836 in Chernivtsi, d 19 September 1903 in Chernivtsi. Writer, composer, and community figure in Bukovyna; honorary member of the Shevchenko Scientific Society. He was ordained after completing his studies at the Chernivtsi Orthodox Theological Seminary in 1861, and then served as a parish priest in Davydeny and Ruska Moldavytsia. He completed studies at the Vienna Conservatory in 1868 and returned to Chernivtsi to teach music and singing in the seminary. In 1875 he became a professor of theology at Chernivtsi University. From 1878 to 1884 he was president of the Ruska Besida society in Chernivtsi. Vorobkevych played an important role in the Ukrainian national revival in Bukovyna in the late 19th century through his literary and musical activity.

As a composer Vorobkevych was best known for his popular works, such as the operettas *Kaspar Rumpel'maier* (1874), *Zolotyi mops* (The Golden Pug, 1879), and *Pani moloda z Bosnii* (The Bride from Bosnia, 1880). He also composed liturgical songs, music for psalms, choral pieces to words by T. Shevchenko, and original songs for solo voice. His writings on musical topics included a cycle of sketches of Ukrainian composers and textbooks on music theory and harmony.

Vorobkevych's literary work was published first in 1863, in B. Didytsky's *Halychanyn*, and later in *Pravda*, *Zoria*, *Bukovyna*, and numerous other periodicals. His sojourn in Kiev in 1874 greatly influenced his literary development. As a writer Vorobkevych was noted for his lyric poetry (over 1,000 works); poems in German; historical poems, such as 'Kyfor i Hanusia' (1868), 'Nechai' (1877), and 'Tymosh Khmel'nyts'kyi' (1885); and short stories and historical dramas, such as *Vasyl'ko Rostyslavych* (1882), *Petro Sahaidachnyi* (1884), and *Kochubei i Mazepa* (1891). He also wrote two volumes of sermons, *Nauka dlia naroda* (Teachings for the People) and *Nadhrobni propovidi* (Grave-side Sermons), and edited the Ukrainian section in the church periodical *Candela* in Chernivtsi. Collections of his works include *Tvory* (Works, 3 vols, 1909–21), *Tvory* (Works, 1986), and *Vybrani tvory* (Selected Works, 1987).

A. Zhukovsky

Vorokhta in 1920

**Vorokhta** [Voroxta]. V-5. A town smt (1988 pop 4,900) on the Prut River in Yaremche raion, Ivano-Frankivske oblast. It was founded in the 17th century and was granted smt status in 1960. Surrounded by coniferous and beech forests, the town is a popular tourist resort. It has sanatoriums for tuberculosis patients, a sports base, and a wooden church from the 18th century.

**Vorona, Oleksander,** b 25 May 1925 in Skadovske, Tavriia gubernia. Graphic artist and mural artist. He studied under O. Shatkivsky, V. Manastyrsky, and R. Selsky at the Lviv Institute of Applied and Decorative Arts (1948–51) and under V. Myronenko at the Kharkiv Art Institute (1951–4). He has designed political posters; stained-glass windows, such as *Native Land*, in the Building of Culture in Verhuny, Cherkasy raion (1970, codesigner); large murals, such as *Revolution*, *Science*, *Victory*, and *Labor*, at Kiev University (1967, with A. Bazylevych and Yu. Ilchenko); and mosaics, such as *Science*, on the façade of the Zhytomyr Polytechnical Institute (1976).

**Voronets, Petro** [Voronec'], b 8 July 1871, d 27 October 1923. Mathematician and mechanician. After completing his studies at Kiev University in 1896, he taught there (professor from 1908). Voronets made contributions to differential equations, vector analysis, dynamics, analytic mechanics, and, in particular, nonholonomic mechanics. In 1909 he derived the equation of motion of nonholonomic systems in a form which included functions depending

Petro Voronets

only on time, generalized co-ordinates, and certain linear functions of generalized velocity. He obtained his famous equation through the generalization of the Hamilton-Ostrohradsky principle for nonholonomic systems and used it to solve a number of problems in mechanics and other fields.

**Voronezh Massif.** A tectonic formation in Voronezh and Kursk oblasts consisting of Precambrian crystalline rock that surfaces near the Don River between Pavlovske and Bohuchar. It includes Devonian, Jurassic, Cretaceous, and Paleogene formations. The massif was separated from the Ukrainian Crystalline Shield in the Upper Devonian period by the appearance of the Dnieper-Donets Trough. It forms part of the Central Upland and is rich in iron-ore deposits.

**Voronezh region.** The northeastern region of *Slobidska Ukraine, which in the 19th and early 20th centuries constituted Voronezh gubernia and in 1934 was reorganized into Voronezh oblast of the Russian SFSR (68,400 sq km; 1939 pop 3,550,000). The southern part of the oblast, including the cities of Valuiky, Ostrohozke, Rozsosh, and Bohuchar, was in Ukrainian ethnographic territory (31,300 sq km). In 1926, 1,009,000 of the 1,450,000 inhabitants of that territory (69.6 percent) were Ukrainians. In 1954 the southwestern part of Voronezh oblast was transferred to the newly created Belgorod oblast; Voronezh oblast was left with 52,400 sq km (1985 pop 2,460,000), of which the Ukrainian ethnographic territory covered 16,000 sq km (1979 pop 135,200 Ukrainians).

**Voroniaky** [Voronjaky]. A section of the Holohory-Kremianets Ridge in the Podolian Upland that runs from east to west for approx 70 km from upper Zolochivka to the Ikva River in Lviv and Ternopil oblasts. With a prevailing elevation of 350–400 m, the formation drops off sharply in the northwest when it reaches Little Polisia. Its highest point is Vapniarka Hill (467 m). It is dissected by tributaries of the Buh, the Styr, and the Ikva rivers. Its plateaus are generally arable, and oak and beech forests are found along its ridges and ravines. Meadows and marshes are located along the banks of the rivers that run through the formation.

**Voronin, Prokhor,** b 3 July 1885 in Tsvizhyn, Vinnytsia county, Podilia gubernia, d 24 April 1940, Kiev. Writer. He was expelled from the Kamianets-Podilskyi Teachers' Seminary in 1904 for his involvement in a Ukrainian revolutionary circle. From 1906 on he published stories under various pseudonyms in *Hromads'ka dumka*, *Rada* (1907–13), *Ukraïns'ka khata* (1909–14), *Moloda Ukraïna* (1911), and *Dzvinok* (1912–13). The collections *Iak ia vyhrav u tovarysha vchytelia samovara* (How I Won from My Friend the Teacher's Samovar, 1909) and *Shchaslyvyi den' Flora* (Flor's Lucky Day, 1910) appeared separately. In the 1920s he lived in Kharkiv, belonged to the writers' group *Pluh, and contributed to periodicals for the peasantry. A large collection of his stories, *Na zazhynkakh* (At the Harvest), was published in 1927. He disappeared during the Stalinist terror.

St Michael's Church (1776) in Voronizh

**Voronizh** [Voroniž]. II-14. A town smt (1988 pop 9,700) on the Osota River in Shostka raion, Sumy oblast. The town mentioned in the chronicles under the year 1177 was destroyed. At the beginning of the 17th century a *khutir* arose on its site. It grew quickly; by 1654 it was a company town of Nizhen regiment. With the abolition of the Hetman state Voronizh became part of Hlukhiv county in Novhorod-Siverskyi vicegerency, then Little Russia gubernia (1796–1802), and then Chernihiv gubernia. Two sugar refineries were built in the 19th century. Today it produces sugar and mixed feed. Its 18th-century St Michael's Church is a tourist attraction.

**Voronko, Platon** [Voron'ko], b 1 December 1913 in Chornechchyna, Okhtyrka county, Kharkiv gubernia, d 10 August 1988 in Kiev. Poet and children's writer. A former Soviet partisan commander, after the Second World War he was an editor of *Dnipro*, the vice-chairman of the Writers' Union of Ukraine and vice-chairman of its Kiev branch, and a deputy to the Ukrainian Supreme Soviet (from 1980). From 1944 on he published over 30 collections of civic and lyric poetry and over 30 books of poems, tales, and plays for children. Much of his writing reflects

his love for and knowledge of Ukrainian folklore and folk songs. He was awarded the Stalin Prize in 1951, the Shevchenko Prize in 1972, and the Lesia Ukrainka Prize in 1976. Many articles and three books, by P. Serdiuk (1963), S. Rusakiiev (1973), and L. Horlach (1973), have been written about him. An edition of his works in four volumes appeared in 1982–3.

**Voronovych, Mykhailo** [Voronovyč, Myxajlo], b ?, d 1918. State figure. A large landowner and former governor of Bessarabia, he was one of the key participants in the coup which put P. Skoropadsky in power on 29 April 1918, and president of the congress of the All-Ukrainian Union of Landowners at which the Hetman government was proclaimed. He served as an associate to the minister of internal affairs in F. Lyzohub's cabinet and as minister of information in the S. Gerbel government. He was killed in late 1918 during the uprising which toppled the Hetman government.

**Voronovytsia** [Voronovycja]. IV-9. A town smt (1988 pop 6,900) in Vinnytsia raion, Vinnytsia oblast. It was first mentioned in a historical document in 1545. In 1956 it was granted smt status. The town has a canning plant, a sugar refinery, and brick, asphalt, and sewing factories. Its 18th-century palace and aviation and astronautics museum are tourist attractions.

**Voronovytsia archeological sites.** A group of Paleolithic sites along the Dniester River near Voronovytsia, Kelmentsi raion, Chernivtsi oblast. Excavations in 1951–3 revealed hearths, many flint pieces, and the bones of wild animals. The sites are best known for the discovery of the first Paleolithic dwellings in Ukraine.

**Vorontsov, Danylo** [Voroncov], b 23 December 1886 in Propoisk, Mahiliou gubernia, Belarus, d 12 July 1965 in Kiev. Physiologist; member of the AN URSR (now ANU) from 1957. After graduating from St Petersburg University (1912) he worked at the Moscow laboratories of M. Vvedensky (1912–16) and at Odessa University (1916–22). He taught at Smolensk University (1922–30), the Kazan (1930–5) and Kiev medical institutes (1935–41), and Kiev University (from 1944). He established and directed the electrophysiology laboratory at the ANU Institute of Physiology (1956). He wrote *Obshchaia elektrofiziologiia* (General Electrophysiology, 1961) and cowrote *Fizicheskii elektroton nervov i myshts* (Physical Electrotonus of Nerves and Muscles, 1966).

**Vorontsov, Mikhail** [Voroncov, Mixail], b 30 May 1782 in St Petersburg, d 18 November 1856 in Odessa, Kherson gubernia. Russian statesman and military figure. He was raised in England (educated at Cambridge University) and possessed huge tracts of land in Cherkasy county and the Crimea. He attained the rank of major general in 1812 and commanded the Russian troops occupying France in 1815–18. He was governor-general of New Russia oblast (from 1823) and Bessarabia oblast (from 1828) until 1844. Although he opposed the revolutionary movement, he maintained an effective liberal bureaucratic structure. During his tenure the population of Odessa nearly doubled, agricultural development in Southern Ukraine increased dramatically, and a host of public institutions and civic societies were established in the region. In 1844–54

Prince Mikhail Vorontsov

Heorhii Vorony

Marko Vorony

Mykola Vorony (portrait by
Mykhailo Zhuk, watercolor
and pencil, 1917)

Vorontsov was vicegerent of Caucasia. His grandiose palace at Alupka, in the Crimea, was turned into a museum. A. Rhinelander published a full account of his life and career in *Prince Michael Vorontsov: Viceroy to the Tsar* (1990).

**Vorony, Heorhii** [Voronyj, Heorhij] (also Yurii), b 28 April 1868 in Zhuravka, Pyriatyn county, Poltava gubernia, d 20 November 1908 in Warsaw. Mathematician; corresponding member of the St Petersburg Academy of Sciences from 1907. A graduate of St Petersburg University, he taught at the University of Warsaw from 1894. His fundamental works are devoted to the theory of numbers. His first major results were obtained in the theory of algebraic numbers, particularly in the theory of irrationalities of the third degree, where he made an exhaustive analysis of the problem concerning the basis of a cubic field and developed the necessary computational methods for determining the decomposition of various classes of real numbers. He also developed algorithms which provide a generalization of continuous fractions. In 1894–1908 he made significant contributions to the arithmetic theory of quadratic forms and the analytic theory of numbers. Together with H. Minkowski, Vorony is regarded as the founder of the geometric theory of numbers. Many of Vorony's ideas and his work were developed further by some members of D. Grave's Kiev school of algebra, such as B. Delone. Most of Vorony's work was not published during his lifetime and appeared only in 1952–3 in the three-volume complete collection of his writings. It is only recently that he has received the recognition he deserves.

W. Petryshyn

**Vorony, Marko** [Voronyj], b 5 March 1904 in Chernihiv, d 3 November 1937 in the Solovets Islands. Poet; son of M. *Vorony. In the mid-1920s he published his poems in *Literaturno-naukovyi vistnyk* in Lviv, under the pseudonym Marko Antiokh. Under the same name he later published verse in *Chervonyi shliakh*, *Zhyttia i revoliutsiia*, *Hlobus*, and other journals. Collections of his poetry include *Chervoni kravatky* (Red Ties, 1930) and *Forvard: Chotyry zoshyty virshiv* (Forward: Four Notebooks of Poetry, 1932). He was arrested in March 1935 and was sentenced to eight years' imprisonment in the Solovets Islands. On 9 October 1937 he was resentenced by an NKVD tribunal to death by firing squad.

**Vorony, Mykola** [Voronyj] (pseuds: Arlekin, Vishchy Oleh, Homo, Siriuk, Kondratovych, and others), b 7 December 1871 in Rostov-na-Donu, Don Cossack province, d 7 June 1938 in Odessa. Poet, journalist, and theater director. He studied at the Kharkiv and Rostov pedagogical institutes, but his studies were interrupted by his arrest for political activity. He remained under tsarist police surveillance for three years and then emigrated to study at Vienna and Lviv universities. He became director of the Ukrainian theater in Ternopil. In 1897 he returned to Russian-ruled Ukraine, acted in the troupes of M. Kropyvnytsky and P. Saksahansky, and joined the Revolutionary Ukrainian party. In 1901 he worked in the Chernihiv zemstvo administration and wrote drama criticism. After the February Revolution Vorony directed the National Theater in Kiev. In 1920–1 he was a senior attaché with the UNR government-in-exile in Warsaw, and then moved to Lviv, where he taught at the Lysenko Higher Institute of Music and its drama school. He emigrated to Soviet Ukraine in 1926, taught at the Kharkiv Music and Drama Institute, and worked as a screenwriter, critic, and translator in Kiev.

Vorony began writing poetry while he was still a student. He was one of the first Ukrainian modernists; his modernist manifesto of 1901 provoked a lively discussion. One of his most prominent opponents was S. Yefremov. Vorony consciously opposed the realist and folkloric poetry; he introduced the motifs of the city and a subjective mood and worked with a variety of strophes and meters. He was criticized, however, for his superficial 'cult of beauty' and for a paucity of themes and images. Collections of his verse include *Lirychni poeziï* (Lyrical Poems, 1911), *V siaivi mrii* (In the Aura of Dreams, 1913), *Za Ukraïnu* (For Ukraine, 1921), and *Poeziï* (Poems, 1929). His works on theater include *Teatr i drama* (Theater and Drama, 1913, 1989 and *Dramatychna prima donna* (A Dramatic Prima Donna [a study of L. Linytska], 1924).

In 1934 Vorony was arrested by the NKVD and exiled for three years to Voronezh. From 1937 he lived in Hlyniane, now in Dobrovelychkivka raion, Kirovohrad oblast. He was rearrested there, and on 29 April 1938 he was sentenced to death by firing squad. After J. Stalin's death he was rehabilitated, and in 1959 a collection of his poetry, *Vybrani poeziï* (Selected Poems), was published.

I. Koshelivets

**Vorony, Yurii** [Voronyj, Jurij], b 1895 in Poltava gubernia, d ? Surgeon; son of the mathematician H. *Vorony. In the 1920s he lectured at the Kharkiv Medical Institute and was a member of the editorial board of *Ukraïns'kyi medychnyi arkhiv*. Then he became a professor at the Kiev Medical Institute. His publications dealt with the influence of the nervous system on the development of tumors.

**Voropai, Oleksa** [Voropaj], b 9 November 1913 in Odessa, d 20 July 1989 in Leeds, England. Ethnographer and writer; member of the Ukrainian Academy of Arts and Sciences. A graduate in agronomy (1940), he emigrated to England after the Second World War and obtained doctoral degrees in Slavic ethnology (1957) and biology (1961) at the University of London. He published collections of Ukrainian folk songs (1952), Ukrainian folk riddles (1955), and calendric rituals – *Zvychaï nashoho narodu* (The Customs of Our People, 2 vols, 1958, 1966). He wrote four books of recollections, beginning with *V dev'iatim kruzi* (1953; trans: *The Ninth Circle*, 1954), which deals with the famine of 1933.

**Voroshilov, Kliment** [Vorošilov], b 4 February 1881 in Verkhnie (now a part of Lysychanske), near Luhanske, Slovianoserbske county, Katerynoslav gubernia, d 2 December 1969 in Moscow. Soviet Russian political and military leader. In 1918 he commanded detachments of Red Army partisans recruited from miners of the Donets Basin. In November 1918 he was appointed people's commissar of internal affairs of the Ukrainian SSR and commander of the Kharkiv Military District. In May 1919 he suppressed N. Hryhoriiv's anti-Bolshevik uprising. After the imposition of Soviet rule he was the USSR people's commissar of military and naval affairs (from 1925) and of defense (from 1934), as well as marshal of the Soviet Union (from 1935). In 1942–3 he co-ordinated Soviet partisan activity on German-occupied territories in Ukraine and Belarus. He was a steadfast supporter of J. Stalin, a member of the Politburo of the CC CPSU (1926–60), vice-chairman of the Council of Ministers of the USSR (1946–53), and chairman of the Presidium of the Supreme Soviet of the USSR (1953–60). For his opposition to N. Khrushchev's policies he was removed from his post in 1960, along with other leading Stalinists. He was rehabilitated under L. Brezhnev, and the city of Luhanske, which had been called Voroshylovhrad in 1935–58, was again renamed Voroshylovhrad in 1970 (reinstated as Luhanske in 1990).

BIBLIOGRAPHY
Kardashev, V. *Voroshilov* (Moscow 1976)
Kalintsev, Iu.; Kryzhanivs'kyi, V. 'Diial'nist' K.Ie. Voroshylova na Ukraïni,' *UIZh*, 1981, no. 1

A. Zhukovsky

**Voroshylovhrad.** See Luhanske.

**Voroshylovhrad Agricultural Institute.** See Luhanske Agricultural Institute.

**Voroshylovhrad Machine-Building Institute.** See Luhanske Machine-Building Institute.

**Voroshylovhrad Pedagogical Institute.** See Luhanske Pedagogical Institute.

**Voroshylovske.** See Komunarske.

**Vorozhba** [Vorožba]. II-15. A city (1989 pop 8,900) on the Vyr River in Bilopillia raion, Sumy oblast. It was settled by peasants from Right-Bank Ukraine. It was first mentioned in a historical document in 1653. At the end of 1917 it was the staging point for the Bolshevik army that invaded Ukraine. It obtained city status in 1959. The city is a railway junction. Most of its inhabitants work in transportation. Its metalworking plants serve the needs of the railway industry.

The Vorskla River

**Vorskla River** (also Vorsklo). A left-bank tributary of the Dnieper River that flows for 452 km through Belgorod (RF), Sumy, and Poltava oblasts and drains a basin area of 14,700 sq km. The river valley in Ukraine ranges from 10 to 12 km in width. The right bank of the river is quite high and is marked by numerous gullies; the left bank is low-lying. The floodplain is covered with meadows, deciduous forest, and some marshland. The river itself contains numerous shoals and sandbars. The average discharge near its mouth is 36 cu m/sec. The Vorskla freezes over from early December to March and is used for water supply and irrigation. The major centers along the river include Poltava and Kobeliaky. The main tributaries are the Vorsklytsia and the Boromlia on the right and the Merlo, the Kolomak, and the Tahamlyk on the left.

**Vorzel** [Vorzel']. III-11. A town smt (1988 pop 9,100) under the jurisdiction of the Irpin municipal council in Kiev oblast. It was founded in 1900 and granted smt status in 1938. Surrounded by forests, Vorzel is a resort town. It has 7 sanatoriums, 4 of them for children, 5 rest homes, and 15 campsites.

**Voskobiinyk, Mykhailo** [Voskobijnyk, Myxajlo] (Voskobiynyk, Michael), b 21 November 1918 in Myrhorod, Poltava gubernia. Historian, journalist, and po-

Mykhailo Voskobiinyk          Marko Vovchok (portrait by
                              Mykhailo Zhuk, lithograph,
                              1925)

litical activist; full member of the Shevchenko Scientific Society. A graduate of Kharkiv University (1941), he fled to Germany during the Second World War and then emigrated to the United States and completed his studies at Syracuse University (1964) and the University of Pennsylvania (PH D, 1972). He edited *Ukraïns'ki visti* (1945–53) in Neu-Ulm. He taught history at Syracuse University (1958–64) and Central Connecticut State University (1966–87). He also served as president of the *Ukrainian Revolutionary Democratic party (1975–) and chairman of the council of the Ukrainian Democratic Alliance. In 1989 he became head of the *Ukrainian National Council.

**Voskoboinykov, Mykhailo** [Voskobojnykov, Myxajlo], b 28 April 1873 in Pavlovsk, Voronezh gubernia, Russia, d 1942. Zoologist. A graduate of Moscow University (1896), he worked with O. Severtsov at Tartu (1899–1903) and Kiev universities, where he specialized in the comparative anatomy of vertebrates and functional evolutionary morphology. He headed Kiev University's vertebrate zoology section (1917–42) and was founding director of the morphology section of the VUAN and AN URSR (now ANU) Institute of Zoology (1927–42).

**Voskrekasenko, Serhii,** b 19 October 1906 in Lazirtsi, Kaniv county, Kiev gubernia, d 16 May 1979 in Kiev. Poet and journalist. He began publishing in the Komsomol press in 1928. In the years 1931–76 he published 30 collections of poetry, much of it humorous and satirical. He also translated Soviet Russian and Belarusian poetry into Ukrainian. Posthumous editions of his works appeared in 1980 and 1984.

**Votchal, Yevhen** [Votčal, Jevhen], b 26 October 1864 in Borzna, Chernihiv gubernia, d 1 April 1937 in Kiev. Plant physiologist; full member of the VUAN and AN URSR (now ANU) from 1921. A graduate of Kazan University (1889), he was a professor at the Kiev Polytechnical Institute (1898–1932) and one of the organizers of the Scientific Institute of Selection (1922, later the All-Union Scientific Research Institute of Sugar Beets). Votchal studied transpiration in agricultural plants and the physiological principles underlying selection, and contributed to the development of the Soviet turpentine industry. He established the Ukrainian school of *plant physiology.

**Vovcha River** [Vovča]. A left-bank tributary of the Samara River that flows for 323 km through Donetske and Dnipropetrovske oblasts and drains a basin area of 13,300 sq km. It has 19 tributaries that are over 10 km in length, most of which dry up in the summer months. The river is used for industry and irrigation. The city of Pavlohrad is situated on it.

**Vovchak, Nestor** [Vovčak] (Volchak), b 1903 in Ustie Ruske, Gorlice county, Galicia, d 11 June 1958 in Toronto. Lemko activist. After emigrating to Canada (1924) he became active in communist organizations and helped organize the first branch of the Lemko Association in Winnipeg (1929). Later, after moving to Toronto, he organized new branches of the association and supported the purchase of the Carpathian People's Home. He served as general secretary of the Carpatho-Ruthenian Society.

**Vovchanske** [Vovčans'ke]. III-17. A city (1989 pop 24,100) on the Vovcha River and a raion center in Kharkiv oblast. It was founded in 1674 as the Cossack *sloboda* of Vovchi Vody. In the 18th century its military significance declined, and it became a county administrative center. In 1780 it was granted city status, and in 1776 its name was changed from Vovcha to Vovchanske. In the middle of the 19th century the town had eight or nine fairs a year. The main commodities were cattle and sheep. In the second half of the century it developed as an industrial center. Today the city's factories produce building materials, asphalt, vegetable oil, cotton thread, and furniture.

**Vovchok, Marko** [Vovčok] (pseud of Mariia Vilinska), b 22 December 1834 in Ekaterininskoe, Orel gubernia, Russia, d 10 August 1907 in Nalchik, in Caucasia. Writer. In 1851 she married Opanas *Markovych, who had been a member of the Cyril and Methodius Brotherhood, and moved from Orel to Ukraine. From 1851 to 1858 she lived in Chernihiv, Kiev, and Nemyriv and studied the Ukrainian language and Ukrainian traditions and folklore and wrote *Narodni opovidannia* (Folk Stories), which was published in 1857. It met with immediate acclaim in Ukrainian literary circles, particularly from T. Shevchenko and P. Kulish, and in Russia (it was translated into Russian and edited by I. *Turgenev as *Ukrainskie narodnye rasskazy* [Ukrainian Folk Tales, 1859]). In 1859, after a short stay in St Petersburg, Vovchok moved to Germany. She spent some time in Switzerland, England, and Italy but stayed the longest in Paris. In 1862 a two-volume edition of *Narodni opovidannia* was published, and individual works were published in the journals *Osnova, Meta,* and *Vechernytsi.* From 1867 to 1878 Vovchok lived in St Petersburg, where owing to the prohibition against the Ukrainian language she wrote and translated for Russian journals. She wrote in Russian *Zhivaia dusha* (The Living Soul, 1868), *Zapiski prichetnika* (The Notes of a Participant, 1870), *V glushi* (In the Backwoods, 1875), and several other novels. From 1878 Vovchok lived in northern Caucasia, and in 1885–93 in Kiev gubernia, where she continued her work on Ukrainian folklore and a dictionary. At the beginning of the 1900s she renewed her contact with Ukrainian publishers.

Elements of realism appear mainly in her short stories about Ukrainian peasants living under serfdom and about the difficult plight of women. Other works continue the tradition of ethnographic romanticism and are typified by strong characters and willful heroes. Also in that tradition are the children's stories 'Dev'iat' brativ i desiata sestrytsia Halia' (Nine Brothers and the Tenth Sister Halia, 1863), 'Karmeliuk' (1865), and 'Marusia' (1871), the last-named of which was popular for some time in France in the translation of P.J. *Stahl (*Maroussia, d'apres la légende de Marko Wovzog*, 1878). Vovchok's prose markedly influenced the development of the Ukrainian short story in the second half of the 19th century. Editions of Vovchok's works have been published in Ukrainian in Kiev in 7 vols (1964–7) and 3 vols (1975). Several books about Vovchok have been written by her grandson, B. Lobach-Zhukenko, and an edition of her *Ukrainian Folk Stories* (trans N. Pedan-Popil) was published in Saskatoon in 1983.

M. Hlobenko

Ivan Vovchuk                     Gen Andrii Vovk

**Vovchuk, Ivan** [Vovčuk] (Wowchuk), b 12 September 1902 in Kharkiv, d 14 May 1979 in Pittsburgh. Journalist and political activist. After graduating in agronomy from Kharkiv University (1926) he worked as a research associate of the Kharkiv Plant Breeding Institute. In 1944 he was elected vice-president of the Ukrainian Supreme Liberation Council. As an émigré he was active in the Bandera faction of the Organization of Ukrainian Nationalists and served as president of the *Central Representation of the Ukrainian Emigration in Germany (1949–50) and editor of the paper *Natsional'na trybuna* (1950–2). In 1953 he emigrated to the United States, where he became a leading figure in the *Organization for the Defense of Four Freedoms for Ukraine and edited its *Visnyk*. His articles on political issues appeared in various nationalist newspapers and journals.

**Vovchyi Grot.** A middle Paleolithic (Mousterian culture) cave shelter near Nova Mazanka, Symferopil raion, Crimea. Discovered in 1880 and excavated in 1936–7 by O. Bader, the site yielded the remains of hearths, flint tools (mainly for scraping and cutting), and the bones of mammoths, cave bears, and other wild animals.

**Vovk, Andrii,** b 15 October 1882 in Delky, Poltava gubernia, d 11 February 1969 in Neu-Ulm, West Germany. Senior army officer. A regular officer in the Russian army during the First World War, in 1917 he Ukrainianized

Russian army units on the Rumanian front and then joined the UNR Army. He was commander of the Fifth Infantry Rural Division (1918) and the Fourth Rifle Division (1919), and deputy commander of the Kiev Division during the First Winter Campaign. In the summer of 1920 he briefly commanded the Kiev Division. He was one of the founders of the Society of Former Soldiers of the UNR Army (1924) and first president of the *Ukrainian Military History Society (1925). In 1940–2 he was president of the Ukrainian Hromada in Germany, and after the war he remained in West Germany. He was promoted to brigadier general by the UNR government-in-exile, and headed its military department (1957–61).

Fedir (Khvedir) Vovk

**Vovk, Fedir (Khvedir)** (Volkov), b 17 March 1847 in Kriachkivtsi, Pyriatyn county, Poltava gubernia, d 30 June 1918 in Zhlobin, near Homel, Belarus. Ethnographer, anthropologist, and archeologist; member of the Shevchenko Scientific Society (NTSh) from 1899. A graduate of the Nizhen gymnasium and Odessa and Kiev universities (1871), he was active in the Kiev Hromada and a founder of the Southwestern Branch of the Imperial Russian Geographic Society (1873). After spending two years abroad he did archeological research in Kiev gubernia and Volhynia (1878–9) and then fled abroad again because of tsarist persecution. From 1887 he studied anthropology, comparative ethnography, and archeology in Paris. In 1905 he was permitted to return to Russia to become custodian of the Aleksander III Ethnographic Museum and lecturer in anthropology at St Petersburg University. He established a Ukrainian section at the museum and was active in the Imperial Russian Geographic Society, particularly in preparing an ethnographic, anthropological, and archeological map of Russia. His doctoral dissertation, *Variations squelettiques du pied chez les primates et chez les races humaines* (Paris 1900), was awarded the Godard Prize. In 1904–6 he participated, along with I. Franko, I. Rakovsky, Z. Kuzelia, and L. Hankevych, in several anthropological and ethnographic expeditions in Galicia, Bukovyna, and Transcarpathia. Assisted by his students, he amassed vast collections of ethnographic materials and anthropological measurements from various regions of Ukraine, on which he built the geography and anthropology cabinet at St Petersburg University. He was a member of the Ukrainian Scientific Society in Kiev (from 1907) and of many European learned societies. He was appointed a professor at Kiev University in 1917 but died on his way to Ukraine.

Vovk's main contributions to anthropology were 'Ukraintsy v antropologicheskom otnoshenii' (Ukrainians with Respect to Their Anthropology, *Ukrainskii vestnik*, 1906; German trans in *Ukrainische Rundschau*, 1908), 'Antropometrychni doslidy ukraïns'koho naselennia Halychyny, Bukovyny, i Uhorshchyny: Hutsuly' (Anthropometric Research on the Ukrainian Population of Galicia, Bukovyna, and Hungary: The Hutsuls, 1908), and 'Antropologicheskie osobennosti ukrainskogo naroda' (Anthropological Peculiarities of the Ukrainian People, in *\*Ukrainskii narod v ego proshlom i nastoiashchem*, 2 [1916], and *Materiialy do ukraïns'koï etnologiï*, 10 [1908]). In these works he argued that Ukrainians are a separate group of Slavs, related to the Southern Slavs (Dinaric type). His chief ethnographic works were 'Etnograficheskie osobennosti ukrainskogo naroda' (Ethnographic Peculiarities of the Ukrainian People, in *Ukrainskii narod v ego proshlom i nastoiashchem*, 2 [1916]), 'Rites et usages nuptiaux en Ukraine' (*L'Anthropologie*, 2–3 [1891–2]), 'Le traineau dans les rites funéraires de l'Ukraine' (*Revue de traditions populaires*, 9 [1895]), 'Zadunaiskaia Sech po mestnym vospominaniiam i razskazam' (The Danubian Sich in Local Recollections and Stories, *Kievskaia starina*, 1883, nos 1, 2, 4), and 'Russkie kolonii v Dobrudzhe' (Russian Colonies in Dobrudja, *Kievskaia starina*, 1889, nos 1–3). He contributed also to the study of archeology, botany, geography, and literary scholarship. He was a founder of the Ethnographic Commission of the NTSh, its chairman for several years, and editor of its *Materiialy do ukraïns'koï etnolohiï*. His students included some well-known scholars such as I. Rakovsky, L. Chykalenko, A. Nosiv, and P. Yefymenko. A selection of his work was published in Ukrainian in Prague, as *Materiialy do ukraïns'koï etnohrafiï ta antropolohiï* (Materials in Ukrainian Ethnography and Anthropology, 1928). A bibliography of his works was published in Kiev in 1929.

M. Mushynka

Ivan Vovk                Vira Vovk

**Vovk, Ivan** (professional name: S. Jascove), b 25 September 1921 in Kryvchunka, Tarashcha county, Kiev gubernia. Composer and pianist. He studied at the Odessa Conservatory (1935–9). Having emigrated in 1945, he graduated (1954) from the César Franck music school in Paris and then worked as a piano teacher in San Francisco (1955–77) and Curitiba, Brazil. His works include the opera *Zakhar Berkut*, a concerto for violin and orchestra, and a score of a liturgy for mixed choir, as well as music to V. Sosiura's poem 'Liubit' Ukraïnu' (Love Ukraine).

**Vovk, Nataliia,** b 13 October 1896 in Skoptsi (now Veselynivka), Pereiaslav county, Poltava gubernia, d 16 October 1970 in Kiev. Master kilim weaver. She wove ornamental kilims, using traditonal motifs, and thematic kilims designed by professional artists, such as *K. Voroshilov and S. Budenny Reviewing a Parade of Red Cossacks* (1936), *T. Shevchenko* (1938), and *Unification of the Ukrainian People* (1954).

**Vovk, Vira** (pseud of Vira Selianska), b 2 January 1926 in Boryslav, Drohobych county, Galicia. Writer, literary scholar, and translator. Having been forced to emigrate by the Second World War, Vovk studied German language and literature in Germany, at Tübingen and Munich universities (1945–9), and completed her studies with a doctorate in 1950 at the Catholic University of Rio de Janeiro, where she remained as a lecturer and, in 1968–80, professor of comparative literature. Since 1980 she has taught at the Federal University in Rio. Vovk writes in three genres: poetry, prose, and drama. By far the most voluminous is her poetic output. Eight collections have appeared so far: *Iunist'* (Youth, 1954), *Zoria providna* (The Leading Star, 1955), *Elehiï* (Elegies, 1956), *Chorni akatsiï* (Black Acacias, 1961), *Liubovni lysty kniazhny Veroniky do kardynala Dzhovannibattisty* (Love Letters of Princess Veronika to Cardinal Giovannibattista, 1967), *Kappa Khresta* (Kappa of the Cross, 1969), *Meandry* (Meanders, 1979), and *Mandalia* (Mandala, 1980). The poetry, which began as often derivative, formally unsophisticated lyricism, developed in her later collections into the highly complex and rhythmical free verse of her 'elegies' and the intricate multirhythms of her 'ballads,' in which she mixes dialogue with narration and bilingual texts. Two major motifs flow through her poetry, exotic geography (the result of displacement) and religious mysticism. The interest in mysticism and myth carries over into her less-voluminous prose, which consists of the collections *Legendy* (Legends, 1954), *Kazky* (Fairy Tales, 1956), *Dukhy i dervishi* (Spirits and Dervishes, 1956), and the novel *Vitrazhi* (Stained-Glass Windows, 1961). Of special interest are her bilingual prose works, such as *Sviatyi hai* (The Holy Grove, 1983) and *Karnaval* (Carnival, 1986). In the realm of poetic drama Vovk has written *Smishnyi sviatyi* (The Funny Saint, 1968), *Tryptykh* (Triptych, 1982), and *Ikonostas Ukraïny* (Iconostasis of Ukraine, 1988). Most of her publications, from the 1970s on, are exquisite esthetic productions with hand-inserted illustrations by Ukrainian artists (Z. Lisovska, M. Dzyndra, J. Solovij, and others) or Vovk's own paper cutouts.

Vovk has devoted a great deal of time to translation into Ukrainian and into Portuguese and German. An annotated anthology of modern Portuguese and Brazilian poetry, *Zelene vyno* (Green Wine), appeared in 1964. She also collaborated in an anthology of Quebec poetry (1972) and in translations of F.G. Lorca with W. Burghardt, H. Kochur, and others. In addition to many of her own poems, she has rendered into Portuguese *Antologia da Literatura Ucraina* (1959), several anthologies of Ukrainian stories and folktales (*Lendas Ucranianas* [1959], *A Canoa no mar* [1972], *Galos bordados* [1972], *Contos populares ucranianos* [1983]), and a series of translations of some individual Ukrainian works by H. Skovoroda (1978), T. Shevchenko (1980), I. Franko (1981), V. Stefanyk (1982), and Lesia Ukrainka (1983). Her scholarly writing is mostly in Portuguese and German.

D.H. Struk

**Vovk, Yurii,** b 21 March 1899 in Kiev, d 14 November 1961 in Prague. Graphic artist and painter. He studied at the Ukrainian State Academy of Arts in Kiev (1918–20) and in Rome (1920–2). In 1922 he settled in Prague, where he graduated from the Ukrainian Studio of Plastic Arts. He served on the executive of the Scythians, an international artists' association, and exhibited his works at its show in Prague (1931). Vovk worked as a book illustrator for publishing houses in Prague. He illustrated novels by I. Franko, A. Kashchenko, and B. Lepky, published in Czech translation; story collections by Yu. Borolych (1953, 1956, 1960) and F. Ivanchov (1954, 1957); a collection of V. Zozuliak's plays (1955); and a novel by M. Shmaida (1957). He did many portraits in pencil and charcoal, including ones of A. Procházka (1953), K. Stakhovsky (1954), and inhabitants of the Prešov region.

**Vovk-Karachevsky, Vasyl** [Vovk-Karačevs'kyj, Vasyl'], b 8 May 1834 in Brytany (now Duboluhivka), Nizhen county, Chernihiv gubernia, d 8 March 1893 in Kiev. Civic figure, writer, and physician. He graduated from the medical faculty of Kiev University (1856) and then worked as a justice of the peace and judge. He was involved with the Old Hromada of Kiev, which often met at his home, and contributed to journals, such as *Osnova* and *Pravda*. His major writings consisted of translations for several volumes of O. Barvinsky's series, Rus'ka istorychna biblioteka (The Ruthenian Historical Library). He also published original historical essays and publicistic works. His reminiscences appeared in *Kievskaia starina* in 1901.

**Vovkushivsky, Hryhorii** [Vovkušivs'kyj, Hryhorij], b 1866, d ? Lawyer. He was secretary of the Commission on Legal Terminology of the Social-Economic Division of the VUAN, and served on the editorial board of *Rosiis'ko-ukraïns'kyi slovnyk pravnychoï movy* (The Russian-Ukrainian Dictionary of Legal Language, 1926).

**Vovky** (Wolves). An UPA battalion in the Hrubeshiv-Kholm region. In the spring of 1944 a company was originally formed to defend the Ukrainian population against the Polish Home Army, Soviet partisans, and Nazi police. In 1945 the unit grew into a battalion, and by 1946 it consisted of three combat companies. Its chief mission became to defend the population against the Polish regime and Soviet border troops. The Vovky Battalion operated in the 28th Tactical Sector of the Sixth Military District of the UPA-West. It became known for its frequent raids, a rocket attack on a Polish police garrison, and a joint operation with the underground Polish Home Army against Soviet and Polish government forces in Hrubeshiv in May 1946. Its commanders were Maj A. Sydoruk (nom de guerre: Yahoda, 1944–5), Capt Ye. Shtendera (Prirva, 1945–6), and Capt V. Sorochak (Berkut, 1946–7). The unit suffered heavy casualties during *Operation Wisła and was demobilized in September 1947. A chronicle of its operations, titled *Vovky*, was published in 1948.

**Vovnyhy burial sites and settlement.** Two Upper Paleolithic burial grounds of the late 4th to early 3rd millennium BC near Vovnyhy, Solone raion, Dnipropetrovske oblast. Excavations in 1949 and 1952 revealed the remains of 161 individuals, all of whom were covered with a thick layer of red ocher. Grave goods recovered included pottery sherds, flint fragments, and pendants with deer teeth.

**Voynich, Ethel Lillian** (née Bull), b 11 May 1864 in Cork, Ireland, d 28 July 1960 in New York. English writer, and author of articles on Eastern Slavic folklore and Slavic music. She corresponded with M. Pavlyk. Her first published writings were translations from Russian writers. She then learned Ukrainian and began translating Ukrainian folk songs ('Oi hore tii chaitsi' [O Woe to the Seagull] and others). In 1911 she published a collection of translations (of six poems) of T. Shevchenko and his biography, *Six Lyrics from the Ruthenian of T. Shevchenko*. Her novel *The Gadfly* was published twice in Ukrainian translation (*Ovid*, 1929 and 1985), and a translation of her novel *Jack Raymond* was published in 1930.

**Vozhakivsky, Symon** [Vožakivs'kyj], b 1911, d 6 June 1984 in Irvington, New Jersey. Nationalist revolutionary and community figure. In 1941 he established contact with an OUN expeditionary force in the Kirovohrad region and helped to organize an OUN underground network and the nucleus of what became the UPA-South. As a postwar refugee in Germany, he was one of the founders of the *Ukrainian Youth Association (SUM) and its president in 1949. After emigrating to the United States he headed SUM (1952–3) and was active in other Ukrainian-American organizations of the Banderite faction. He also chaired the Commission on Culture and Science of the Ukrainian Congress Committee of America.

**Voznesenka hoard.** A cache of approx 1,400 silver and gold items found near Voznesenka (now part of Zaporizhia). Found in 1930 in a 7th- to 8th-century Slavic military fortress during the building of the Dnieper Hydroelectric Station, the hoard included such items as numerous weapons (swords, arrowtips, knives), horse trappings, and valuable adornments, including a silver eagle and lion from the tops of standards. The total weight of the hoard's gold items is 1.246 kg; its silver items weigh 1.782 kg.

**Voznesenske** [Voznesens'ke]. VI-12. A city (1989 pop 44,500) on the Boh River and a raion center in Mykolaiv oblast. The city was founded by a decree of Catherine II in 1795 at the site of a Cossack winter settlement called Sokoly. During the 19th century Voznesenske developed into an important manufacturing and trading center of New Russia gubernia. It held three fairs a year and traded in lumber and salt. It was granted city status in 1938. Today it is an industrial center and railway junction. It is the home of a leather-manufacturing consortium, a conveyor-belt plant, a winery, and sewing, musical-instruments, canning, cheese, and meat-processing factories.

**Voznesenske vicegerency.** An administrative territory set up in 1795 out of a part of Katerynoslav vicegerency and lands recently acquired from Poland and Turkey. The capital was at first Novomyrhorod and then Voznesenske. In 1797 the vicegerency was abolished, and its territory was distributed among New Russia, Kiev, and Podilia gubernias.

**Vozniak, Ivan** [Voznjak], b 1865, d 1914. Civic activist. He was director of the Shevchenko Scientific Society printing press in Lviv. A founder of the *Ukrainian Social Democratic party, he served as chairman of its executive council and president of the Volia workers' society.

Mykhailo Vozniak

**Vozniak, Mykhailo** [Voznjak, Myxajlo], b 3 October 1881 in Vilky-Mazovetski (now Volytsia), Rava Ruska county, Galicia, d 20 November 1954 in Lviv. Literary scholar. He graduated from Lviv University in 1908, was a professor there from 1939, and was director of the department of Ukrainian literature at that university from 1944. He was a full member of the VUAN from 1929 (which later became the AN URSR and is now the ANU), was barred from membership during the 1930s, and was reinstated as a full member in 1939. He began to publish his work in 1902, and for many years he worked on Shevchenko Scientific Society publications and commissions. He is the author of many studies on the history of Ukrainian literature (he adhered to the historical-cultural approach), in particular on the Galician rebirth during the 19th century, including *Pysannia Markiiana Shashkevycha* (The Writings of Markiian Shashkevych, 1911) and *Prosvitni zmahannia halyts'kykh ukraïntsiv 19 v.* (The Enlightenment Efforts of Galician Ukrainians in the 19th Century, 1912), and on Ya. Holovatsky, I. Vahylevych, and M. Ustyianovych. His works include *Rizdviani i velykodni virshi – Oratsiï zi zbirnyka kintsia XVII–pochatku XVIII v.* (Christmas and Easter Poems: Orations from a Collection of the Late 17th and Early 18th Centuries, 1910), *Materiialy do istoriï ukraïns'koï pisni i virshi* (Materials for the History of the Ukrainian Song and Verse, 3 vols, 1913–25), and *Pochatky ukraïns'koï komediï (1619–1819)* (The Beginnings of Ukrainian Comedy [1619–1819], 1919). Vozniak's most notable work is *Istoriia ukraïns'koï literatury* (The History of Ukrainian Literature, 3 vols, 1920–4) from its beginnings to the 18th century. Vozniak published the anthology *Stare ukraïns'ke pys'menstvo* (Old Ukrainian Literature, 1929) and many popular publications, notable among which are *Kyrylo-metodiïvs'ke bratstvo* (The Cyril and Methodius Brotherhood, 1921) and *Iak probudylosia ukraïns'ke narodne zhyttia v Halychyni za Avstriï* (How Ukrainian National Life Awakened in Galicia under Austrian Rule, 1924). He also published a great number of works on folklore and on old and modern literature. A posthumous collection of Vozniak's articles about the literary work of I. Franko, *Z zhyttia i tvorchosty I. Franka* (From the Life and Works of I. Franko), was published in 1955.

I. Koshelivets

**Voznyi.** See *Ditskyi.*

**Voznytsky, Borys** [Voznyc'kyj], b 16 April 1926 in Ulbarove (now Nahirne), Dubno county, Volhynia. Art gallery director. Since graduating from the Leningrad Institute of Painting, Sculpture, and Architecture (1962) he has directed the *Lviv Art Gallery. A member of the International Council of Museums (ICOM) and vice-president of its Soviet section, he is a dedicated collector of the art treasures of Galicia and Volhynia, and has built a fine collection of contemporary Lviv painting at the gallery and directed the restoration of the Olesko Castle as a branch of the gallery. As an art historian he specializes in 17th- and 18th-century Western Ukrainian art, particularly the work of Y. Kondzelevych, and in 18th-century sculpture, with a concentration on J. Pinzel. For his contributions he was awarded the 1990 Shevchenko State Prize.

**Vpered** (Forward). A weekly organ of the 'independent' faction of the *Ukrainian Social Democratic party (USDP) in Galicia, published by P. Buniak in Lviv from December 1911 to March 1913. Its primary aim was to build support for the trade union movement among Ukrainian workers. *Vpered* was edited by V. Levynsky, Yu. Bachynsky, and A. Chernetsky. The paper was renewed in late 1918 and appeared daily and then semimonthly to 1924. Until 1923 it provided general coverage of political and economic developments. In this period its editors included L. Hankevych, Buniak, Chernetsky, I. Ivashko, I. Kvasnytsia, S. Pashkevych, and A. Holovka. In 1923–4 *Vpered* again served as a pro-Soviet USDP organ, under the editorship of M. Parfanovych, S. Volynets, and S. Rudyk.

**Vpered** (Forward). A weekly (at times semiweekly) organ of the Social Democratic party of Subcarpathian Ruthenia, published in Uzhhorod in 1922–38 as the successor to *Narod.* Until 1926 it appeared in the Transcarpathian dialect, and from then in literary Ukrainian. *Vpered* was edited by Ye. Puza, S. Klochurak, D. Nimchuk, and S. Dovhal.

**Vpered** (Forward). A monthly paper for Ukrainian workers, published by the left Vpered faction of the *Ukrainian Revolutionary Democratic party in Munich from April 1949 to December 1959. It contained articles on developments in Soviet Ukraine, international politics, and Ukrainian émigré life written from a democratic socialist perspective. The editors were I. Maistrenko, V. Holubnychy, B. Levytsky, E. Bobykevych, and V. Ryvak. H. Kostiuk and V. Sabal (pseud: V. Chorny) were regular contributors.

**Vpered.** See *Pravda.*

**Vrabel, Mykhailo** [Vrabel', Myxajlo] (Vrábely, Mihály) (pseuds: Ivan Hazda, Vorobei), b 1866 in Vyrava, Zemplén komitat, Transcarpathia, d 4 January 1923 in Budapest. Transcarpathian folklorist, teacher, and journalist. After graduating from the Uzhhorod Teachers' Seminary he taught in the Prešov region and in Ruski Krstur, in the Bačka region. He collected Transcarpathian folklore and published a collection of folk verses, *Russkii solovei* (The Ruthenian Nightingale, 1890), and one of the Maramureş region's songs and *kolomyiky, Uhroruski narodni spivanki* (Hungarian-Ruthenian Folk Songs, 1901). He was editor of the weekly *Nedilia* (1899–1918) for Transcarpathia's Ruthenians. In 1898 he published a primer which was used in Ruthenian schools in the Bačka region and Transcarpathia and was reprinted several times.

**Vrabel, Oleksander** [Vrabel'], b 26 February 1931 in Ivanivtsi, Transcarpathia. Opera singer (baritone). He graduated from the Lviv Conservatory (1960). In 1957 he joined the Lviv Theater of Opera and Ballet, where he has been appearing in the lead roles in P. Tchaikovsky's *Eugene Onegin*, W. Mozart's *Don Giovanni*, and G. Verdi's *Rigoletto*, and as Hnat in K. Dankevych's *Nazar Stodolia* and Hurman in Yu. Meitus's *Stolen Happiness*.

Vasyl Vrazhlyvy          Ivan Vrona

**Vrazhlyvy, Vasyl** [Vražlyvyj, Vasyl'] (pseud of Vasyl Shtanko), b 1903 in Opishnia, Zinkiv county, Poltava gubernia, d 8 December 1937 in the Solovets Islands. Writer. He was a member of the literary organizations Vaplite and Prolitfront. His first collection of short stories was *V iaru* (In the Ravine, 1924). Subsequently he published *Zemlia* (Earth, 1925), *Zhyttia biloho budynku* (The Life of a White Building, 1927), *Vovchi bairaky* (The Wolf Thickets, 1927), *Molodist'* (Youth, 1927), *Shist' opovidan'* (Six Stories, 1930), *Hlyboki rozvidky* (Deep Inquiries, 1932), *Peremoha* (Victory, 1932), a long novelette, *Bat'ko* (Father, 1929), and a novel, *Sprava sertsia* (A Matter of the Heart, 1933). In December 1934 he was arrested, and in 1935 he was sentenced to 10 years' imprisonment in a concentration camp. He was subsequently resentenced, to death by firing squad.

*Vremennik Stavropigiiskogo instituta s mesiatsoslovom* (Periodical of the Stauropegion Institute with a Menology). A serial of the *Stauropegion Institute in Lviv that appeared annually in 1864–1915 and 1923–39. It contained valuable articles on history and culture by A. Petrushevych, Ya. Holovatsky, P. Svystun, and other leading Russophiles in Galicia.

**Vretsona, Hryhorii** [Vrec'ona, Hryhorij], b 8 October 1839 in Vynnyky, Lviv county, Galicia, d 2 November 1901 in Lviv. Pedagogue and education activist. He taught in Galician village schools (1862–77) until moving to Lviv, where he was a teacher from 1877. He was active in Ukrainian community affairs in Lviv and was a member of many organizations, including Prosvita, Narodna Torhovlia, and the Shevchenko Scientific Society. He wrote extensively for Galician newspapers and journals, and edited and published *Shkol'na chasopys'* in 1880–9.

**Vretsona, Yevhen** [Vrec'ona, Jevhen], b 1 October 1905 in Vynnyky, Lviv county, Galicia, d 4 February 1975 in Basel. Political leader of the OUN and the Ukrainian Supreme Liberation Council (UHVR). After graduating in chemistry from the Higher Technical School in Prague (1933) he edited the sports weekly *Hotovi* in Lviv and contributed to *Tekhnichni visti*. As an OUN member he participated in organizing the Carpathian Sich (1938–9). After the Second World War he was active in the External Representation of the UHVR and contributed to *Suchasna Ukraïna* and *Suchasnist'*.

**Vrona, Ivan**, b 29 September 1887 in Otroch, Kholm county, Lublin gubernia, d 5 January 1970 in Kiev. Art scholar and critic, and political figure. After serving two years of exile in Siberia for revolutionary activities he studied law at Moscow University (1910–14) and art at K. Yuon's studio in Moscow (1912–14) and in schools in Kiev (1918–19). In 1918 he joined the *Borotbists, and in 1920 the CP(B)U. In 1921 he was elected to the All-Ukrainian Central Executive Committee. In the 1920s Vrona helped organize the *Kiev State Art Institute and served as its first rector; he taught there later (1930–3, 1945–8). He was also a founder and leader of the *Association of Revolutionary Art of Ukraine (ARMU), whose program he defined in his *Mystetstvo revoliutsiï i ARMU* (The Art of the Revolution and ARMU, 1926), and served as director of the Kiev Museum of Western and Eastern Art and chief inspector of art education of the People's Commissariat of Education. His art criticism was published in *Zhyttia i revolutsiia* and *Krytyka*. In 1933 Vrona was arrested and sent to a western Siberian labor camp. He was released in 1936 and rehabilitated in 1943. After being allowed to return to Ukraine in 1944, he became a research associate of the AN URSR (now ANU) Institute of Fine Arts, Folklore, and Ethnography and wrote monographs on the artists Karpo Trokhymenko (1957), M. Derehus (1958), and A. Petrytsky (1968) and two chapters for vol 5 of the ANU history of Ukrainian art (1967).

**Vronchenko, Mykhailo** [Vrončenko, Myxajlo], b 1801 in Kopys, Mahiliou gubernia, Belarus, d 26 October 1855 in Kharkiv. Geodesist and army general. He enlisted in the Russian army before completing his studies at Moscow University. His main achievements were a topographic survey of Moldavia, Wallachia, and Rumania (1828–33), a two-volume geographic survey of Asia Minor (1838–40), and a major survey of Southern Ukraine in 1848–54. He also translated some of W. Shakespeare's tragedies and G. Byron's poems.

**Vronsky, Makar** [Vrons'kyj], b 14 April 1910 in Barysau, Minsk gubernia, Belarus. Sculptor. He studied under M. Helman and M. Lysenko at the Kiev State Art Institute until 1945 and taught there from 1949. His sculptures include compositions, such as *Lesia Ukraïnka* (1947) and *Ustym Karmaliuk* (1948); portraits of I. Kavaleridze (1957) and M. Amosov (1961); the monuments to T. Shevchenko in Palermo, Ontario (1950, with O. Oliinyk), and Shevchenko, Kazakhstan (1982); and the Eternal Glory monument in Lutske (1977).

**Vronsky, Vakhtanh** [Vrons'kyj, Vaxtanh] (real surname: Nadiradze), b 28 August 1905 in Tbilisi, d 27 February 1988 in Kiev. Ballet dancer, ballet master, and choreographer. In 1923 he completed study at the Tbilisi Ballet School. Until 1940 he worked outside Ukraine. In 1940–54 he was the principal ballet master in the Odessa and in 1954–73 in the Kiev theater of opera and ballet. In 1961–73 he worked simultaneously as principal ballet master and artistic director of the Kiev Ballet on Ice, and in 1977–80, the Moscow Ballet on Ice. Since 1981 he has been the artistic director of the Kiev Theater of Classical Ballet. In 1959 he made (with V. Lapoknysh) a film of K. Dankevych's ballet *The Lily*.

Mikhail Vrubel: the *Theotokos* in the iconostasis of St Cyril's Church in Kiev

**Vrubel, Mikhail** [Vrubel', Mixail], b 17 March 1856 in Omsk, Russia, d 14 April 1910 in St Petersburg. Russian painter and designer; member of the St Petersburg Academy of Arts from 1905. After graduating from the St Petersburg Academy of Arts in 1884, he lived in Kiev. There he supervised the restoration of the frescoes in St Cyril's Church by the students of the Kiev Drawing School and restored several sections himself. He painted the church's

icons and frescoes *Theotokos and Child*, *Descent of the Holy Ghost*, *St Cyril*, *St Athanasius*, and *Mourning at the Sepulcher*; the ornamental designs in the side naves of St Volodymyr's Cathedral (his mural sketches were turned down); and oils and watercolors, such as *Girl against the Background of a Persian Carpet* (1886), *Oriental Fairy Tale* (1886), and *Hamlet and Ophelia* (1888). From 1889 he lived in Moscow. He was obsessed with the Demon figure as a symbol of individual pride and rebellion and painted several versions of it. Many of his secular works are fine examples of Russian symbolism.

**Vruchyi.** See Ovruch.

**Vsekhsviatsky, Sergei** [Vsexsvjatskij, Sergej], b 20 June 1905 in Moscow. Astrophysicist. A graduate of Moscow University (1925), he taught in institutes in Moscow and Kalinin. In 1939 he joined the faculty of Kiev University. He has written over 270 works on the physics of comets and solar activity, including the monograph *Physical Characteristics of Comets* (1958; English trans 1964), shorter books on that subject (1974, 1979), and a monograph on the nature and origin of comets (1967).

*Vsesvit*

**Vsesvit.** A political, community, literary, and art illustrated journal published in Kharkiv in 1925–34, at times as a weekly, at others as a biweekly. One of its founders was V. *Blakytny; the editor–in–chief was Ye. Kasianenko, and the managing editor was O. Kopylenko. The staff of illustrators included O. Dovzhenko, A. Petrytsky, and V. Kasiian. The journal was revived in July 1958 under the editorship of O. Poltoratsky. Subsequent editors have been D. *Pavlychko, V. *Korotych, and O. *Mykytenko. It was the only publication in Soviet Ukraine devoted to foreign literature, and it featured, until recently, primarily translations of Communist and 'progressive' authors in the West and of writers in other socialist countries and the Third World. Since for a long time it was the only source of contact with Western literature, it has been widely popular. It has been published with the co-operation of the *Ukraina Society for Friendship and Cultural Relations with Foreign Countries and the Writers' Union of Ukraine.

**Vsesvitnia Biblioteka** (Universal Library). A publishing house in Zolochiv, Galicia, founded and operated by

I. Kalynovych. In 1913–14 and 1918–26 it published popular educational pamphlets and booklets and translations of literary classics, including an edition of A. Pushkin's plays (1914) and the *Song of Roland* (1918).

**Vseukrainskyi strakhovyi soiuz.** See Strakhsoiuz.

**Vsevolod Olhovych** [Ol'hovyč], b ?, d 1 August 1146 in Vyshhorod, north of Kiev. Rus' prince; son of Oleh Sviatoslavych. He succeeded his father in Novhorod-Siverskyi in 1115 and successfully forced his uncle, Yaroslav Sviatoslavych, out of Chernihiv in 1127. With the support of the Cumans he displaced the ineffectual Viacheslav Volodymyrovych from the Kievan throne in 1139, after the death of Yaropolk II Volodymyrovych, and turned over Chernihiv to his cousin, Volodymyr Davydovych. Vsevolod was the first of the Sviatoslavych dynasty to rule in Kiev, and he maintained his grip on power by manipulating rival princely factions. Dissatisfaction arose among his subjects because of his exploitive rule, and his main administrative officials in Kiev, Ratsha and Tudor, were accused of ruining the city. Vsevolod also clashed with the Kievan metropolitan, Mykhail, over the question of appointing bishops. In 1145 Vsevolod appointed his brother, Ihor, as his successor, hoping thereby to establish a family claim to the principality. When he died the following year, a popular revolt broke out in Kiev against the Olhovych family and their officials, and the throne was claimed by the Monomakh descendant, Iziaslav Mstyslavych.

**Vsevolod Sviatoslavych** [Svjatoslavyč] (Bui-Tur), b ?, d 17 May 1196. Rus' prince; grandson of Oleh Sviatoslavych. He took part in numerous battles against the Cumans, including the campaigns led by his brother, Ihor, in 1185 and 1191. His gallantry was celebrated in *Slovo o polku Ihorevi* (The Tale of Ihor's Campaign), which mentions that he was the prince of Kursk; the Hypatian Chronicle describes him as the ruler of Trubchevsk (or Trubetsk, on the Desna River).

**Vsevolod Sviatoslavych Chermny** [Svjatoslavyč Čermnyj], b ?, d 1212 or September 1215. Rus' prince; son of Sviatoslav III Vsevolodovych and father of Mykhail Vsevolodovych. He took part in campaigns against the Cumans in 1183 and 1191. He became prince of Chernihiv ca 1204, probably after the death of his brother, Oleh. In 1206–10 he unsuccessfully fought Riuryk Rostyslavych and Mstyslav Romanovych for the Kievan throne.

**Vsevolod Yaroslavych** [Jaroslavyč], b 1030, d 13 April 1093. Rus' prince; fifth (and favorite) son of Yaroslav the Wise and father of Volodymyr Monomakh. He received lands in the Pereiaslav, Upper Volga, Rostov-Suzdal, and Belozersk regions after his father's death in 1054 and for nearly two decades maintained the peace of the realm through close co-operation with his elder brothers, Iziaslav and Sviatoslav II Yaroslavych. One of the crowning achievements of that period was the confirmation in 1072 of the so-called *Pravda Iaroslavychiv* (see *Ruskaia Pravda*), an extensive revision of their father's law codes. Fighting between the princes started in 1073, when Vsevolod rose up against Iziaslav at Sviatoslav's bidding. Iziaslav then fled abroad, Sviatoslav emerged as the grand prince of Kiev, and Vsevolod took the throne of Cherni-

hiv. Upon Sviatoslav's death in 1077, Iziaslav returned to Kiev, but he died the following year while helping Vsevolod to defend Chernihiv from their nephew, Oleh Sviatoslavych. Vsevolod then ascended the Kievan throne (1078) and placed his own son, Volodymyr Monomakh, in Chernihiv. The remainder of Vsevolod's reign saw continued fighting among the Rus' princes, although without serious challenges to Vsevolod's own position. It also witnessed considerable artistic and cultural development, including the building of the *Vydubychi Monastery near Kiev.

**VUAMLIN.** See All-Ukrainian Association of Marxist-Leninist Scientific Research Institutes.

**VUAN.** See Academy of Sciences of the Ukrainian SSR.

**VUFKU.** See All-Ukrainian Photo-Cinema Administration.

**Vuhlehirske** [Vuhlehirs'ke]. V-19, DB III-4. A city (1989 pop 12,800) under the jurisdiction of the Yenakiieve city council in Donetske oblast. It originated in 1879 as the railway settlement of Khatsapetivka. It was renamed in 1957 and promoted to city status the following year. It has a coal mine and a coal enrichment plant.

**Vuiakhevych-Vysochynsky, Mykhailo** [Vujaxevyč-Vysočyns'kyj, Myxajlo] (religious name: Meletii), b ca 1625, d 1697. Cossack officer and church figure, descended from Ukrainian Galician nobility. He was a scribe at the Kievan Cave Monastery (1654) and then served as general chancellor under hetmans Ya. Somko (1661–2) and P. Doroshenko (1669–76), general judge under I. Samoilovych and I. Mazepa (1683–91), and acting hetman in the field (1689). From 1691 he was archimandrite of the Kievan Cave Monastery.

*Vuiko*

**Vuiko** (Uncle). A humoristic magazine published semimonthly in Winnipeg from May 1924 to mid-1925 by Ya. *Maidanyk. It chronicled the humorous misadventures of Vuiko Shtif Tabachniuk (Uncle Steve Tabachniuk), an ignorant and boorish Ukrainian-immigrant comic-strip character Maidanyk had introduced to the Ukrainian-Canadian press. It satirized the low level of culture among Ukrainian pioneers as well as the pretensions of Anglo-Canadian society. The journal was especially noted for its illustrations (by Maidanyk himself) and for its humorous language, a rich mixture of Ukrainian, English, and other languages filled with slang, Galicianisms, and jargon. One issue of the *Vuiko kalendar* also appeared. After the demise of the magazine, a 'Vuiko Shtif' comic strip appeared as a supplement to *Kanadiis'kyi ukraïnets'* (1927–9).

Yurii Vukhnal

**Vukhnal, Yurii** [Vuxnal', Jurij] (pseud of Ivan Kovtun), b 5 October 1906 in Chornobaivka, Izium county, Kharkiv gubernia, d 15 July 1937. Writer and humorist; member of the writers' groups Pluh, Molodniak, Prolitfront, and the All-Ukrainian Association of Proletarian Writers. He lived in Kharkiv from 1923, and from that time he began to publish his humorous stories in the newspapers *Sil's'ko-hospodars'kyi proletar* and *Komsomolets' Ukraïny* and in periodicals such as *Chervonyi perets'* and *Molodniak*. Among his works published separately were the collections of humorous stories *Chervoni parostky* (Red Shoots, 1925), *Tovarysh i tovaryshok* (The Comrade and the Little Comrade, 1926), and *Zhyttia i diial'nist' Fed'ka Husky* (The Life and Deeds of Fedko Huska, 1929) and the novels *Iastruby* (Hawks, 1929), *Aziiats'kyi aerolit* (The Asiatic Aerolite, 1931), and *Iunbund* (Youth League, 1932). In 1936 Vukhnal was arrested, and he was shot in a prison. In the 1950s he was rehabilitated, and editions of his selected works, *Zhyttia i diial'nist' Fed'ka Husky* (1960) and *Tovarysh i tovaryshok* (1963), were published.

**Vukoopspilka.** See All-Ukrainian Association of Consumer Co-operative Organizations.

**VUTsVK.** See All-Ukrainian Central Executive Committee.

**VUZ.** See Higher educational institution.

**Vydubychi Monastery** (Vydubetskyi or Vydubytskyi manastyr). An architectural monument of the 11th to 18th century in Kiev. The monastery known as Vydubychi was founded ca 1070 by Grand Prince Vsevolod Yaroslavych on the southern edge of Kiev by the Dnieper River. Vsevolod and his descendants (eg, Grand Prince Volodymyr Monomakh) were the monastery's principal patrons. In 1088 the stone St Michael's Cathedral was completed at the monastery. The monastery was damaged by the Cumans in 1096. A century later P. Mylonih built a support wall under the monastery's slope to prevent landslides. In the early 17th century (until 1637) the monastery belonged

The Vydubychi Monastery, with St George's Cathedral in the center

to the Uniate church; then it reverted to the Orthodox church. The eastern part of St Michael's Cathedral collapsed after the Dnieper flooded it in the 1580s, and was rebuilt with the financial support of Metropolitan P. Mohyla as a two-story wooden structure. It was rebuilt again in its present form in 1766–9 by M. Yurasov. The present monastery complex dates back to the late 17th and early 18th century, when the baroque St George's Cathedral (containing a magnificent iconostasis with five rows of icons) and a refectory building (containing the Trinity Church), financed by Col M. Myklashevsky (1696–1701), and a campanile, financed by Hetman D. Apostol (1727–33), were built. In the 19th century the monastery ran a hospital for clerics, a school, an orphanage, and a home for retired priests. Many luminaries were buried in its cemetery. In the 1920s the monastery was abolished, and its buildings and churches were used by workers' clubs and, later, converted into military warehouses by the Soviet authorities. The monastery's iconostases and cemetery were destroyed. Today the ANU Institute of Archeology has use of the buildings, all of which were restored in 1967–82. In 1968–9 the restricted archive kept in St George's Cathedral, which contained over 500,000 books, incunabula, prerevolutionary periodicals, and UNR and ANU documents, was destroyed by four mysterious fires that ravaged the building.

**Vydybida-Rudenko, Palladii** (secular name: Petro), b 29 June 1891 in Strilchyntsi, Bratslav county, Podilia gubernia, d 1 September 1971 in Sea View, Staten Island, New York. Orthodox church and community leader. He graduated from the Kamianets-Podilskyi Theological Seminary and the mathematics faculty of Kiev University (1916) and then worked in the co-operative movement in Vinnytsia. An active member of the Society of Ukrainian Progressives and a delegate to the Central Rada, he was made director of the finance department of the UNR government in November 1918 and deputy finance minister in 1919. After moving to Polish-occupied Volhynia, he was ordained in 1921 and served as a parish priest and member of the church consistory. In 1934 he moved to Warsaw and became secretary of the metropolitan's office and administrator of the Polish Autocephalous Orthodox church's pension fund. In 1935 Vydybida-Rudenko took monastic vows and was named an archimandrite soon after. In February 1941 he was ordained in Warsaw as archbishop of Cracow and the Lemko region. He was subsequently also named bishop of Lviv, and was elected chancellor of the Autocephalous Orthodox church in the Generalgouvernement. A postwar refugee, he lived in Germany from 1944 (in Passau, Munich, and Regensburg), before settling in the United States in 1950. From 1951 to his death he headed the *Ukrainian Autocephalous Orthodox Church in Exile.

**Vyhonivske Lake** [Vyhonivs'ke ozero]. I–6. A lake situated in northwestern Polisia in southern Belarus near the Ukrainian border. The lake has a surface area of 26.5 sq km and a depth of 2.7 m.

**Vyhovsky** [Vyhovs'kyj]. Descendants of a boyar family line from Ovruch county. Ostap Vyhovsky (d 1663) was vicegerent of the Kiev fortress under the voivode A. Kysil and a member of the Kiev Epiphany Brotherhood. His sons were Hetman Ivan *Vyhovsky, Danylo *Vyhovsky, and Kostiantyn Vyhovsky, a colonel of Turiv-Pynske regiment and general quartermaster (from 1658). Vasyl Vyhovsky (a colonel) and his relatives were also members of the line. Illia and Yurii Vyhovsky were exiled to Siberia in 1659. Some members of the family were hierarchs of the Catholic church, among them Oleksander Vyhovsky (b 1649, d 1714) and Yosyf *Vyhovsky. In the early 20th century descendants of the Vyhovsky line lived in Volhynia, Podilia, and Kiev gubernias.

**Vyhovsky, Danylo** [Vyhovs'kyj], b ?, d 1659. Cossack officer. The son-in-law of B. Khmelnytsky, he occasionally undertook some diplomatic missions for the hetman. In 1655 he laid siege to Lublin, and in 1659 he expelled a Muscovite force from Kiev. He was captured by the Muscovites and tortured to death in Kaluga.

Hetman Ivan Vyhovsky

**Vyhovsky, Ivan** [Vyhovs'kyj], b ?, d 19 March 1664 in Olkhivka, near Korsun. Hetman of Ukraine in 1657–9 and close confederate of B. Khmelnytsky. He studied at the Kievan Mohyla Academy, worked in the Kiev civic court, and joined the Lutske Brotherhood. Before the Khmelnytsky uprising he was secretary to a Polish starosta in Lutske, and in 1648 served in a crown force under the command of S. Potocki. He was captured by the Tatars at the Battle of Zhovti Vody. His release was arranged by Khmelnytsky, who admired his learning and experience. Vyhovsky then joined forces with the hetman, together with his brothers, Danylo and Kostiantyn (colonel of Pynske-Turiv Regiment). He became the military chancellor and then general chancellor; he participated in diplomatic negotiations and drafted some of the more im-portant treaties of the time. After Khmelnytsky's death he became the guardian of and second-in-command to Yu. Khmelnytsky. He was chosen hetman at the Korsun Council in 1657, and immediately entered into an agreement with Charles X Gustav of Sweden in the hope of establishing an independent Ukraine that would extend as far as the Vistula River. He was assisted in those negotiations by Yu. *Nemyrych. At the same time Vyhovsky understood the relative weakness of the fledgling Ukrainian state and was willing to consider a rapprochement with the Polish Commonwealth.

Vyhovsky ran into problems when internal opposition to his command began to grow. A revolt, led by the Zaporozhian otaman Ya. *Barabash and the colonel of Poltava regiment, M. *Pushkar, culminated in a bloody confrontation near Poltava in June 1658. Vyhovsky, who emerged victorious but weakened, decided to sever his ties with Muscovy and concluded the Treaty of *Hadiache with Poland on 16 September 1658. The agreement proposed to bring Ukraine back into the Commonwealth as the autonomous Grand Duchy of Rus'. In response to the signing of the treaty Muscovy sent a large force under Prince A. Trubetskoi to stop the hetman. Vyhovsky annihilated the Muscovite troops on 8 July 1659 near Konotip, with Polish and Tatar aid. The victory was short-lived. Widespread dissatisfaction with the Hadiache agreement and the possibility of renewed Polish influence in Ukraine gave rise to a revolt headed by T. Tsiutsiura, V. Zolotarenko, and others, who were supported by the Zaporozhian leader, I. Sirko. Vyhovsky was forced to flee to Hermanivka, in the Kiev region, in September 1659, and his title of hetman was officially revoked at a council in Bila Tserkva. He was later made voivode of Kiev and starosta of Bar by the Polish king. He joined the Lviv Dormition Brotherhood in 1662 and actively defended the interests of the Ukrainian Orthodox citizenry. He was later denounced by P. Teteria as a leader of a Cossack insurrection, and was shot by the Poles near Korsun.

Vyhovsky has been considered in Ukrainian historiography a leading statesman who strove for the freedom and independence of Ukraine. Soviet historians, however, have portrayed him as a traitor of his people.

BIBLIOGRAPHY
Herasymchuk, V. 'Vyhovs'kyi i Iurii Khmel'nyts'kyi: Istorychna studiia,' ZNTSh, 59–60 (1904)
Budzynovs'kyi, V. Hadiats'ki postuliaty i Het'man Vyhovs'kyi (Lviv 1907)
Herasymchuk, V. 'Vyhovshchyna i Hadiats'kyi traktat,' ZNTSh, 87–9 (1909)
Lypyns'kyi, V. Ukraïna na perelomi (Vienna 1920)
Seniutovych-Berezhnyi, V. 'Rid i rodyna Vyhovs'kykh,' UI, nos 25–7 (1970)

B. Krupnytsky, A. Zhukovsky

**Vyhovsky, Yosyf** [Vyhovs'kyj, Josyf], b 1657 in Zamość, d 17 January 1730 in Rozhyshche, Volhynia. Uniate bishop; nephew of Hetman I. Vyhovsky. He joined the

Uniate church and entered the Basilian monastery in Suprasl. In June 1710 King Augustus II nominated him as bishop of Lutske and Ostrih to succeed Bishop D. Zhabokrytsky, who had been exiled to the Solovets Islands by Peter I of Russia. He was ordained bishop of Mstsislau in 1713 and became bishop of Lutske and Ostrih after Zhabokrytsky's death in 1715. In Lutske he convinced the Brotherhood of the Elevation of the Cross to accept church union. He rebuilt the cathedral in Lutske and introduced strict discipline among the clergy. He participated in the Zamostia Synod of 1720. In 1727 he introduced mandatory celibacy for the clergy of his eparchy, although he agreed to ordain married candidates for the priesthood if they divorced their wives.

One of Vylkove's canals

**Vylkove.** VIII-10. A city (1989 pop 11,500) in the Danube River delta in Kiliia raion, Odessa oblast. Because of its numerous streams and canals it is known as the 'Ukrainian Venice' or 'Venice on the Danube.' It was founded in 1746 as the settlement of Lypovanske in territory that was under Turkish rule, and in 1762 was granted city status. In 1812 it was awarded to the Russian Empire and was renamed. In the interwar period (1918–40) it was occupied by Rumania. The city's main industry is fishing. It has a branch of the Antarktyka fishing consortium, a boat repair yard, and a research base of the ANU Institute of Hydrobiology. Nearby is a state preserve called Dunaiski Plavni.

**Vynnychenko, Volodymyr** [Vynnyčenko], b 27 July 1880 in the village Velykyi Kut, Yelysavethrad county, Kherson gubernia, d 6 March 1951 in Mougins, France.

Volodymyr Vynnychenko        Volodymyr Vynnychenko
                             (self-portrait)

Writer, statesman, and politician. Vynnychenko began to study law at Kiev University in 1901 but, owing to his expulsion in 1902 for 'revolutionary' activities, he never completed his studies. He was a member of the *Revolutionary Ukrainian party (RUP) and, later, the executive committee of the *Ukrainian Social Democratic Workers' party (USDRP) and editor of its journal *Borot'ba*. To avoid arrest for his political activities Vynnychenko fled abroad many times between 1903 and 1917 and returned clandestinely to Ukraine or Russia. An unsuccessful clandestine return earned him a year in prison (1903–4). During the First World War Vynnychenko lived in Moscow illegally, and in 1917 he returned to Ukraine to take part in the struggle for Ukraine's independence. As leader of the USDRP he was chosen one of two vice-presidents of the Central Rada and then the first president of the *General Secretariat, the autonomous government of Ukraine. During the Hetman government he headed the oppositional *Ukrainian National Union, and then, from its creation in 1918 until February 1919, the *Directory of the Ukrainian National Republic. Upon disagreeing with the rightist and pro-Entente politics of the Directory Vynnychenko left for Vienna, where he tried to mobilize Ukrainian socialists abroad and to negotiate with V. Lenin an independent socialist Ukrainian state. His attempts in 1920 to reach a similar end while in Ukraine also proved unsuccessful, and Vynnychenko emigrated and finally settled in France. Though he maintained contact with some Soviet Ukrainian leaders he never returned to Ukraine. He devoted himself almost exclusively to his literary career.

Vynnychenko began writing while he was a student, during which time he produced stories depicting the working-class milieu, which he knew best. His first story, 'Krasa i syla' (Beauty and Strength, 1902), created a sensation and brought him almost immediate recognition. In both his heroes (the working classes, the déclassé, petty criminals, and, finally, revolutionaries) and his themes he abandoned the former populist didactic piety for the more risqué contemporary revolutionary life, which is often tinged with explicit sexual tensions and wry humor, and is presented in a dynamic, impressionistic narrative style and a language bold enough to use the most current patois (*surzhyk*). His short stories were extremely popular as a result. More a poser of problems than a stylist, Vynnychenko did not polish his work; often it seems hurried and even tendentious. The desire to postulate solutions to various social and moral problems led Vynnychenko to drama, where he could more readily examine, as if in a moral laboratory, the consistency of human behavior with the accepted morality, especially the morality of the 'new revolutionary man.' In the 20 plays he wrote (many of them translated and staged in various theaters of Europe) Vynnychenko examined closely the frequent disparity between deed and 'noble word,' aim and moral code. The proclaimed equality of the sexes is debunked in *Bazar* (Bazaar, 1910), the notion of spiritual love, in *Dysharmoniia* (Disharmony, 1906), the acceptability of 'surrogate motherhood,' in *Zakon* (The Law, 1923), and the belief that 'a noble end justifies the means,' in *Hrikh* (The Sin, 1920). Other no less interesting plays are *Velykyi Molokh* (The Grand Moloch, 1907), *Brekhnia* (The Lie, 1910), and *Chorna pantera i bilyi vedmid'* (The Black Panther and the White Bear, 1911). Having found that moral codes were often set to protect the interests of a dominant group, Vynnychenko sought to find a way in which humans could live a truly moral life, and came to the notion 'To thine own self be true' as the only viable moral law. Promulgated best in his novel *Chesnist' z soboiu* (Honesty with Oneself, 1906), the notion provoked misunderstanding and criticism. Vynnychenko was accused of strict individualism and total amorality.

In all, 11 novels appeared during Vynnychenko's lifetime, of which *Zapysky kyrpatoho Mefistofelia* (Notes of Pug-nosed Mephistopheles, 1917) and *Soniashna mashyna* (The Sun Machine, 1928; the first Utopian novel in Ukrainian literature) stand out. Of the three novels which appeared posthumously, *Slovo za Toboiu, Staline* (It's Your Word Now, Stalin, 1971) is interesting as an example of Vynnychenko's political thinking after he developed his own moral world order, which he called 'concordism.' He propagated that concept in the novel *Nova zapovid'* (The New Commandment, 1949). Throughout his life Vynnychenko kept a detailed diary, of which two volumes have been published (*Shchodennyk* [Diary, vol 1, 1980; vol 2, 1983]). They provide some insight into his artistic, personal, and political life. Of historical interest is Vynnychenko's three-volume memoir of the struggle for Ukraine's independence, *Vidrodzhennia natsii* (Rebirth of a Nation, 1920).

Until recently Vynnychenko was proscribed in Ukraine, and his works have not been republished since the 24-volume edition of 1926–30. In the West interest in him was maintained primarily as a result of the efforts of H. *Kostiuk, under whose guidance the standing Commission for the Study and Publication of the Heritage of Volodymyr Vynnychenko was established at the Ukrainian Academy of Arts and Sciences in the US. The commission is the custodian of the Vynnychenko archives, housed at Columbia University in New York.

BIBLIOGRAPHY
Kostiuk, H. *Volodymyr Vynnychenko ta ioho doba* (New York 1980)
Articles in Part III of *Studies in Ukrainian Literature*, ed B. Rubchak.
  Vol 16 of *AUA* (1984–5)
Stel'mashenko, V. (comp). *Volodymyr Vynnychenko: Anotovana bibliohrafiia* (Edmonton 1989)

D.H. Struk

Ivanna Vynnykiv: *Flowers* (oil)

**Vynnykiv, Ivanna** (née Nyzhnyk), b 7 August 1912 in Lviv, d 10 January 1993 in Mougins, France. Painter and ceramist. She studied at the Novakivsky Art School in Lviv. In the 1930s she was a member of *RUB and the *Association of Independent Ukrainian Artists and took part in their exhibitions. Her portraits, landscapes, and still lifes combined an impressionist use of color with an expressionist brush stroke. A postwar refugee, Vynnykiv came to Paris to study art in 1948. She exhibited at the Salon d'Automne and Salon des Artists Indépendants. From 1958 she lived in Mougins, near Cannes, in V. Vynnychenko's former home. There she founded a ceramics atelier with Yu. *Kulchytsky in 1960. More recently Vynnykiv created impressive, colorful wall hangings, using various fabrics. Some (eg, *Yaroslavna*) have a Ukrainian theme; others (eg, *Wedding Party* and *Three Riders*, in the Mougins town hall) treat more universal subjects.

**Vynnykiv, Nataliia,** b 1920, d 1942. Nationalist figure. In 1941 she was one of 59 OUN members arrested by the Soviet police and sentenced at a show trial in Lviv. Her death sentence was commuted to life imprisonment. After the German invasion of Ukraine she was released, but later she was executed by the Gestapo in Kiev.

**Vynnyky.** IV-5. A city (1989 pop 12,100) on the Marunka River just outside Lviv in Lviv oblast. It originated in the second half of the 13th century and attained city status in the late 19th century. Vynnyky is an industrial center with a tobacco factory, a branch of the Yunist Textile and Haberdashery Consortium, and a workshop of the Kharchoprodukt canning factory. It was one of the first places in Galicia to erect a statue of T. Shevchenko. A Roman Catholic church in the baroque style (1737) has been preserved there.

**Vynnytska, Iryna.** See Pelenska, Iryna.

**Vynnytsky, Antin** [Vynnyc'kyj], b?, d 1679. Orthodox bishop. In 1650 he was consecrated bishop of Peremyshl, and in 1663 he was elected metropolitan of Kiev and exarch of the patriarch of Constantinople in Ukraine by the pro-Polish supporters of Hetman P. Teteria, who sought to block the candidacy of Y. *Neliubovych-Tukalsky, a supporter of P. Doroshenko. The latter candidate was also elected metropolitan (he served in 1663–75), however, and the two hierarchs divided the metropoly, with Vynnytsky gaining jurisdiction over the western Ukrainian eparchies (Galicia, Podilia, Volhynia) and Neliubovych-Tukalsky administering Right-Bank Ukraine, Belarus, and Lithuania. Vynnytsky remained in Galicia throughout his term. In 1667–8 he also served as administrator of Lviv eparchy. After the death of Neliubovych-Tukalsky he tried to assume control over the entire metropoly but was opposed by Moscow.

**Vynnytsky, Inokentii** [Vynnyc'kyj, Innokentij], b ?, d 1700. Bishop of Peremyshl. He was ordained by Y. Shumliansky as the Orthodox bishop of Peremyshl in 1680, and he secretly joined the Uniate church in 1681. The public declaration of his action and the open conversion of his eparchy were delayed, however, because of Vynnytsky's desire to be the sole Uniate bishop there. The 1691 transfer of the sitting Uniate bishop of Peremyshl, I. Malakhovsky, resolved the issue, and the whole eparchy formally joined the union in 1692. A biography of Vynnytsky by B. Balyk appeared in *AOBM* (1978).

Sydir Vynnytsky

Metropolitan Yurii Vynnytsky

**Vynnytsky, Sydir** [Vynnyc'kyj], b 1839, d 1922. Civic and political leader in Bukovyna. An active participant in the populist movement, he helped the populists gain control of the Ruska Rada society in 1885 and served as president of the People's Home in Chernivtsi (1887–98). In 1897–1901 he was a deputy to the Austrian parliament.

**Vynnytsky, Yurii** [Vynnyc'kyj, Jurij] (secular name: Havryil), b ?, d 22 November 1713. Uniate metropolitan. He studied at the Jesuit college in Peremyshl before entering the monastery in Lavriv in 1700. Later that year he was

consecrated bishop of Peremyshl. Vynnytsky reformed his eparchy, which had joined the Uniate church in 1692. He was administrator of Mukachiv eparchy from 1707 and of Lviv eparchy from 1708. In 1708 he was nominated as metropolitan of Kiev, but his installation was delayed until 1710 because his candidacy was opposed by the pope.

An 18th-century Catholic monastery in Vynohradiv

**Vynohradiv.** V-4. A city (1989 pop 25,200) on the Tysa River and a raion center in Transcarpathia oblast. Until 1946 it was known as Sevliush or Sevlus. The settlement originated in the 9th century around the Slavic fortress of Kanko. At the end of the 11th century it came under Hungarian rule and was renamed Sevliush. At the end of the 17th century it was annexed by Austria, and in 1919 it was awarded to Czechoslovakia. Officially part of Ukraine since 1945, it was granted city status in 1946. Today the city is an industrial and communications center. It is the home of the Elektron Manufacturing Consortium, a plastic sanitary-products plant, and sewing, footwear, canning, and cheese factories. Its architectural monuments include the remains of the medieval castle, the Perényi palace (15th century), a Franciscan church (14th–15th century), and a 16th-century church.

**Vynohradov, Andrii,** b 14 October 1875 in Suzdal, Vladimir gubernia, Russia, d 2 November 1933 in Donetske. Metallurgist. He studied in Katerynoslav (now Dnipropetrovske) and taught at the Dnipropetrovske (1908–31) and Donetske (from 1931) mining institutes. He made important discoveries and inventions in the field of the granular structures of steel. In particular he obtained a fundamental physical and structural understanding of the grain structure of high-strength Damascus-type steels. He also developed a basic theoretical concept of the effect of the laminar structure in steel on its wear resistance, and the effect of rolling on the laminar structure. A biography of Vynohradov, by E. Shevchenko, was published in Kiev in 1951.

**Vynohradsky, Serhii** [Vynohrads'kyj, Serhij] (Winogradsky, Sergei), b 13 September 1856 in Kiev, d 31 August 1946 in Brie-Comte-Robert, near Paris. Microbiologist; corresponding member of the Russian Academy of Sciences from 1894, honorary member of the USSR Academy of Sciences from 1923, and member of the French Academy of Sciences (Institut de France), the Royal Society of London, and scientific societies in Germany, Sweden, Italy, Czechoslovakia, Holland, India, and the United States. After graduating from the natural sciences faculty of St Petersburg University (1881, PH D 1884) he did research on the physiology of sulfur bacteria at Strasbourg University (1885–8) and discovered the phenomenon of autotrophism (1887). At Zürich University (1888–91) he studied microbial agents in oxidization and nitrification and isolated two new genera (*Nitrosomonas* and *Nitrosococcus* or *Nitrobacter*) in the latter process. Vynohradsky was head of the microbiology division at the Institute of Experimental Medicine in St Petersburg (1891–1905, director from 1902), where he discovered that certain anaerobic organisms use atmospheric nitrogen in metabolic processes. With V. Omeliansky and D. Zabolotny he analyzed the hydrolysis of cellulose. From 1922 he led the agricultural microbiology laboratory of the Pasteur Institute in Paris. His discoveries concerning the physiology of nitrification and nitrogen fixation by soil bacteria helped to establish bacteriology as a major biological science.

Ye. Roslytsky

**Vynohradsky, Vitalii** [Vynohrads'kyj, Vitalij], b 24 October 1925 in Lebedyn, now in Sumy oblast. Writer. A former editor of the papers *Prykarpats'ka pravda* (Ivano-Frankivske) and *Literaturna Ukraïna* (1975–80), he is the author of the prose collections *Hlybynni shliakhy* (Interior Roads, 1966), *Katrusyna dolia* (Katrusia's Fate, 1967), *Chekai mene na svitanku* (Await Me at Dawn, 1973), and *I nastav svitanok* (And Dawn Arrived, 1979, 1986).

**Vynokurov, Serhii,** b 4 May 1899 in Odessa, d 1955. Physician and biochemist. In the 1920s he conducted research in the department of pathophysiology at Odessa University and in the Ukrainian Biochemical Institute in Kharkiv. He was the founder and director of the Kharkiv Institute of Nutrition. He was a professor at medical institutes in Kharkiv (1932–8) and Kiev (1938–55) and headed the vitamin laboratory of the AN URSR (now ANU). He wrote numerous scientific works, including textbooks on the physiology of digestion.

**Vynsky, Hryhorii** [Vynskyj, Hryhorij], b 1752 in Pochep, Starodub regiment, d after 1818. Writer. A Ukrainian petty noble, he studied at the Kievan Mohyla Academy. Vynsky served in the Russian army in St Petersburg (1770–5) and lived there until 1779, when he was imprisoned for his freethinking (he translated and disseminated

works of the French Enlighteners) and was forced to live in exile in Orenburg gubernia. He stayed there after being amnestied in 1805. Late in his life he wrote his memoirs, *Moë vremia* (My Time, pub 1914); they are a valuable source for the study of Ukrainian society in the late 18th century.

*Vyra.* The highest monetary penalty imposed for the killing of a free man in Kievan Rus'. It was paid to the prince by the transgressor who had escaped blood vengeance. With the abolition of vengeance, it became the only penalty for killing, and was imposed by the ruler on the murderer, or on the community if the offender was unidentified (it was then called a *verv*). The rate was 40 *hryvni* for killing a free man; 80 *hryvni*, an official of the prince; and 20 *hryvni*, an unfaithful wife or a handicapped individual. There was no *vyra* for a slave, only compensation for loss of property. *Ruskaia Pravda* mentions a *vyra* for libel. The *vyra* was collected by a special official known as a *vyrnyk*.

**Vyrhan, Ivan** (pseud of Verhun), b 1 June 1908 in Matviivka (now Klishchyntsi), Zolotonosha county, Poltava gubernia, d 12 January 1975 in Kharkiv. Poet and prose writer. He was a member of the literary organization *Pluh and began to publish his work in 1927. He was arrested in 1940, and from 1941 to 1944 he was imprisoned in labor camps in the Soviet Arctic. He published the collections of verse *Ozbroiena liryka* (Armed Lyricism, 1934), *Sad druzhby* (The Garden of Friendship, 1935), and *Shchastia-dolia* (Fortune-Fate, 1938). His collections of verse from the postwar period include *Povorot sontsia na lito* (The Return of the Sun to Summer, 1947), *Kvituchi berehy* (The Blossoming Banks, 1950), *V rozpovni lita* (In the Fullness of Summer, 1959), *Nad Suloiu shumliat' iavory* (The Maples are Rustling on the Banks of the Sula, 1960), and *Sertse* (Heart, 1969). He also published the collections of short stories *Vasylyna* (1960), *Darynka z bratykom* (Darynka and Her Brother, 1961), and *Krasa* (Beauty, 1966). He compiled a Ukrainian-Russian phraseological dictionary together with his wife, M. Pylynska, which was published in the journal *Prapor*.

Yevhen Vyrovy (portrait by Kateryna Antonovych)

**Vyrovy, Yevhen** [Vyrovyj, Jevhen], b 26 February 1889 in Smila, Cherkasy county, Kiev gubernia, d 17 May 1945 in Prague. Educator and civic activist. After graduating from a teachers' institute in Hlukhiv he taught in a commercial school in Katerynoslav (1910–19). He presided over the local Prosvita society, belonged to the Society of Ukrainian Progressives, and contributed to the paper *Dniprova khvylia*. In 1919 he chaired the cultural-educational commission of the Labor Congress in Kiev. He was the founder and director of *Ukrainske Vydavnytstvo in Katerynoslav, and he continued to publish books even after he had left for Kamianets-Podilskyi and emigrated to Berlin and then Prague. He also directed the *Ukrainian Civic Publishing Fund in Prague. He contributed articles to *Knyholiub* and edited several stamp albums. His collection of Ukrainian stamps was displayed at international exhibitions and became widely known. As NKVD agents arrived at his apartment to arrest him, Vyrovy committed suicide.

Arystyd Vyrsta

**Vyrsta, Arystyd** (Wirsta, Aristide), b 22 March 1922 in Barbivtsi, Bukovyna. Musicologist, teacher, and violinist; member of the Shevchenko Scientific Society (since 1977). He received his PH D degree in musicology from the Sorbonne (1974). In 1950 he was engaged as concertmaster by the Belo Horizonte Symphony Orchestra in Brazil. He was subsequently soloist of chamber orchestras in Vienna, Rome, and Paris. He was on the music faculty of the Sorbonne (1975–87), where he lectured on musicology. Since 1976 he has been a professor at the Ukrainian Free University (Munich). Vyrsta has contributed articles on Ukrainian music and musicians to French, German, and English music encyclopedias.

**Vyrsta, Temistokl** (Wirsta, Themistocle), b 15 October 1923 in Ispas, Bukovyna. Painter; brother of A. Vyrsta. He studied architecture at the Royal Academy in Bucharest and art at the Academy of Fine Arts in Paris. A postwar refugee, since 1950 he has lived in Paris, where he worked as an architect until the late 1950s. His early paintings were figurative. Later he became a lyrical expressionist, stressing color rather than form or composition, and ultimately he evolved into an abstractionist. Some of his works depict imaginary landscapes and flowers and employ various light effects. Solo exhibitions of his works have been held in Paris (1959), Bern (1964), Ancona, Italy (1967), Montreal (1970), Detroit (1970), New York (1982), and Toronto (1982). An album of his works was published in Paris in 1975.

**Vyshcha Shkola** (Higher School). A state publishing conglomerate founded in 1973, consisting of the Vyshcha

An acrylic painting by Temistokl Vyrsta

Shkola publishing house (est 1968) in Kiev, which maintains editorial offices at Donetske and Odessa universities; the university publishing houses of Kiev (est 1949), Kharkiv (est 1949), and Lviv (est 1946); and the Chief Editorial Office of the Ukrainska Entsyklopediia. The conglomerate prints and publishes educational and research materials, textbooks, scholarly monographs, and serials (eg, *Ukraïns'ke movoznavstvo, Ukraïns'ke literaturoznavstvo, Inozemna filolohiia, Problemy slov'ianoznavstva, Zhurnalistyka, Bibliotekoznavstvo i bibliohrafiia,* and *Polihrafiia i vydavnycha sprava*) produced by faculty members of, and used at, Ukraine's postsecondary, technical, and specialized secondary schools, as well as reprints of classic and representative works of Ukrainian, Russian, and foreign literature. In 1979 the Vyshcha Shkola publishing house issued 650 books and brochures with a combined pressrun of 5.3 million copies.

**Vyshensky, Ivan** [Vyšens'kyj] (pseud: Feodul), b ca 1550 in Sudova Vyshnia, Galicia, d after 1620 in Mt Athos, Greece. Orthodox monk and polemicist. Biographical information on him is sparse. He passed some of his youth in Lutske and was connected with the *Ostrih Academy scholars (eg, H. Smotrytsky). Ca 1576–80 he entered a monastery at Mt Athos. There are 15 known works by Vyshensky: seven epistles, six treatises, a dialogue, and a story. His most important works were directed against the Church Union of *Berestia and were written in the late 1590s. In 1600–1 he prepared a collection of the 10 works he had written by then and sent it to the Lviv Dormition Brotherhood, probably in the hope of having it printed. Titled 'Knyzhka' (Book), it did not appear in print at that time, but its transcriptions circulated widely in Ukraine. In 1604–6 he visited Ukraine and quarreled with the leaders of the Lviv Brotherhood.

Vyshensky's writings stand out among Ukrainian polemical works of the 16th and 17th centuries by virtue of both their literary merit and their ideological content. He did not simply reject the Uniate church and Catholicism.

Grounded in Byzantine asceticism, he sharply criticized temporal life and the entire church and secular hierarchy and urged a return to the simplicity of old Christian brotherhood in order to bring about God's Kingdom on earth. He rejected as pagan both secular education and learning on the one hand and old, pre-Christian folk traditions on the other. Stylistically, Vyshensky drew upon the traditional forms of the epistle dialogue and polemical treatise and often mixed these genres. In strong, colorful language he depicted the moral decadence of the upper classes, particularly of the clergy, and contrasted them with poor peasants and simple monks. Exalted feelings alternate with harsh satire and sarcasm. An abundance of epithets and similes, the dramatic use of rhetorical questions and exhortations, ironic portrayals of everyday detail, a rich vocabulary, and the use of the vernacular make his writings lively and persuasive. His style owes much to Byzantine sermons and is closely related to the polemical writings of his Ukrainian (M. Smotrytsky) and Polish (P. Skarga, M. Rej) contemporaries. It is one of the finest examples of the baroque style. Published first in *Arkhiv Iugo-Zapadnoi Rossii* (1887), his works were studied by I. Franko, A. Krymsky, I. Zhytetsky, M. Sumtsov, M. Hrushevsky, M. Vozniak, D. Chyzhevsky, V. Peretts, O. Biletsky, L. Makhnovets, A. Pashuk, S. Pinchuk, P. Yaremenko, and Valerii Shevchuk, among others. I. Eremin prepared two editions of Vyshensky's works (1955, 1959), and Shevchuk has translated them into contemporary Ukrainian (1986).

BIBLIOGRAPHY
Franko, I. *Ivan Vyshens'kyi i ioho tvory* (Lviv 1895)
Pinchuk, S. *Ivan Vyshens'kyi: Zhyttia i tvorchist'* (Kiev 1968)
Gröschel, B. *Die Sprache Ivan Vyšenskyjs* (Vienna 1973)
Iaremenko, P. *Ivan Vyshens'kyi* (Kiev 1982)
M. Hlobenko, A. Zhukovsky

**Vyshhorod** [Vyšhorod]. III-11. A city (1989 pop 18,700) on the Dnieper River and a raion center in Kiev oblast. It is first mentioned in the chronicles under the year 946, as the residence of Princess *Olha. Vyshhorod was a strategic fortress that defended the northern approach to Kiev. It repelled Cuman attacks in 1093, 1136, and 1146. In 1240 it was destroyed by the Mongols. In the 15th and 16th centuries Vyshhorod was merely a village owned by the Mezhhiria Transfiguration Monastery. In 1934–37 and 1947 archeologists uncovered the remains of houses and smithing, bronzing, and pottery implements. In 1968 Vyshhorod was promoted to city status. It is the site of the Kiev Hydroelectric Station and of the first accumulation power station built in the USSR..

**Vyshkivskyi Pass** [Vyškivs'kyj pereval] (aka Torunskyi pereval). V–4. A Carpathian mountain pass (elevation 988 m) between the Rika and the Mizunka rivers along the border between Ivano-Frankivske and Transcarpathia oblasts. A highway connecting Dolyna and Khust passes through it.

**Vyshkove** [Vyškove]. A town smt (1988 pop 8,300) on the Tysa River in Khust raion, Transcarpathia oblast. It was first mentioned in historical documents in 1271. In 1976 the village was given smt status. Surrounded by oak and beech forests, it is the home of the Transcarpathian Mercury Research and Application Complex and quarries

of building stone. Archeologists have discovered the remains of a Ukrainian settlement from the 13th and 14th centuries in the town.

**Vyshnevetska, Raina** [Vyšnevec'ka, Rajina] (née Mohylianska), b 1589, d 1619. Distinguished Ukrainian benefactor in the 17th century; daughter of the Moldavian hospodar J. Movilă; first cousin of the Kiev metropolitan P. Mohyla. She married Prince *Michał Korybut Wiśniowiecki, the palatine of Kiev; J. *Wiśniowiecki was their son. Vyshnevetska opposed the Polish persecution of the Ukrainian Orthodox church and supported the Orthodox clergy, especially I. Kopynsky. She was a patron of monasteries in Pryluka, Hustynia, Ladan, and Lubni.

**Vyshnevetsky.** See Wiśniowiecki.

Prince Dmytro Vyshnevetsky

**Vyshnevetsky, Dmytro** [Vyšnevec'kyj] (Wiśniowiecki), b ?, d 29 October 1563 in Istanbul. The first Cossack otaman in the history of Ukraine, a founding member of the Cossack nobility, and a landowner in southern Volhynia; nephew of K. Ostrozky. In the 1550s he was starosta of Cherkasy and Kaniv. He built a fort (ca 1552) on the island of Mala *Khortytsia, in the Dnieper River. He recruited Cossacks for war against the Tatars, which he waged with the help of Lithuania and Muscovy, and he traveled to Turkey to enlist the aid of the Ottoman Empire in 1553. In 1557–61 he served the Muscovite government and then again organized wars against the Tatars, but his attempts to form an alliance to do battle in the Crimea failed in 1561. In 1563, during a military campaign in Moldavia, he was defeated, taken prisoner by the Turks, and executed. Vyshnevetsky is the hero of the folk song about Baida. Soviet historians disputed the fact that he founded the *Zaporozhian Sich and that he is the folk hero Baida.

BIBLIOGRAPHY
Storozhenko, A. 'Kniaz' Dmitrii Ivanovich Vishnevetskii po narodnomu Baida,' *KS*, 1894
Hrushevs'kyi, M. 'Baida-Vyshnevets'kyi v poezii i istorii,' *ZNTK*, 3 (1909)
Lutsiv, V. 'Kniaz' Dmytro Vyshnevets'kyi-Baida,' *Vyzvol'nyi shliakh*, 1958, no. 3
Vynar, L. *Kniaz' Dmytro Vyshnevets'kyi* (Munich 1964)
A. Zhukovsky

**Vyshnevetsky, Mykhailo.** See Michał Korybut Wiśniowiecki.

**Vyshnevsky, Ahapyt** [Vyšnevs'kyj] (Antonii), b 16 July 1867 in Volhynia, d 1926? Ukrainian bishop of the Russian Orthodox church. A graduate of the Kiev Theological Academy (1896), he served as bishop of Uman (from 1902), Chyhyryn (from 1908), and Katerynoslav (from 1911). After 1917 he supported the movement for the autocephaly of the Ukrainian church and the Ukrainization of his eparchy. He also took part in meetings with the government of the Ukrainian National Republic and S. Petliura, which participation led a Russian ecclesiastical court to relieve him of his duties and force his retirement. He was arrested by the Soviet authorities in 1922 and died in incarceration.

**Vyshnevsky, Dmytro** [Vyšnevs'kyj], b 1871, d ? Historian; specialist in the history of education in Ukraine. He wrote *Kievskaia akademiia v pervoi polovine 18 st.* (The Kiev Academy in the First Half of the 18th Century, 1903) and a series of articles in *Kievskaia starina* on the life of the students of the Kievan Mohyla Academy (1896, nos 1–3), the wages of the professors (1896, no. 6), and the general educational policy of the academy (1904, no.2).

**Vyshnevsky, Karl** [Vyšnevs'kyj], b 11 October 1805, d 3 April 1863 in Verbka, Liatychiv county, Podilia gubernia. Veterinarian. A graduate of Vilnius University (1830), he was a professor at Kharkiv University (from 1837) and founder of its practical veterinary school (1839). He was the first in the Russian Empire to raise the issue of insuring livestock. His publications in Russian, Polish, and Latin dealt with cattle plague, glanders, and influenza.

**Vyshnevsky, Volodymyr** [Vyšnevs'kyj], b 20 July 1897 in Tesluhiv, Dubno county, Volhynia gubernia, d 5 July 1961 in Paris. Orthodox church leader. A graduate of the Orthodox theological faculty of Warsaw University (1928), in 1928–39 he served as a priest in Podlachia and carried out missionary work in 50 parishes in the region. During the Second World War (1941–3) he administered 84 parishes of the *Ukrainian Autocephalous Orthodox church (UAOC) in the Kovel region and then became secretary to Archbishop N. Abramovych (1944). From 1948 he was a parish priest in Paris; later he was administrator of the UAOC in France (from 1950) and in Switzerland, Italy, and Spain (from 1953). Vyshnevsky was also secretary of the Synod of the UAOC (from 1952) and a member of the Higher Council (1956).

**Vyshnia, Ostap** [Vyšnja] (pseud of Pavlo Hubenko), b 11 November 1889 in Chechva (now Hrun), Zinkiv county, Poltava gubernia, d 28 September 1956 in Kiev. Writer, humorist, and satirist. He participated in the struggle for Ukrainian independence in 1917–20 and moved to Kamianets-Podilskyi with the UNR government in 1919, where he began publishing a column in Ukrainian newspapers. He was imprisoned by the Soviets in 1920 and released in 1921 as a result of the intervention of V. *Blakytny. He continued publishing his feuilletons, in the newspapers *Visti, Selians'ka pravda*, and *Radians'ke selo* and in the journal *Chervonyi perets'*. From 1920 to the early 1930s Vyshnia published a number of collections of his writings, including *Dila nebesni* (Heavenly Doings, 1923), *Komu vesele, a komu sumne* (For Some It's Funny, For Some It's Sad, 1924), *Rep'iashky* (Little Burrs, 1924), *Lytsem do sela* (Facing the Village, 1926), and *Ukraïnizuiemos'* (We Are

Ostap Vyshnia

Becoming Ukrainized, 1926). There was also a series of thematic collections, including *Vyshnevi usmishky sil's'ki* (Vyshnia's Rural Merriment, 1923), *Vyshnevi usmishky kryms'ki* (Vyshnia's Crimean Merriment, 1925), *Vyshnevi usmishky literaturni* (Vyshnia's Literary Merriment, 1927), *Vyshnevi usmishky teatral'ni* (Vyshnia's Theatrical Merriment, 1927), and *Vyshnevi usmishky zakordonni* (Vyshnia's Merriment from Abroad, 1930). Owing to his popularity among the peasantry, Vyshnia's works had one of the largest pressruns among Ukrainian writers in the 1920s.

In 1933 Vyshnia was charged with nationalism and plotting terrorist actions against the Party leadership. He was arrested and imprisoned in various northern concentration camps, whence he was released in 1943. His collection of war writings, *Zenitka* (The Anti-Aircraft Gun, 1944), those directed against Ukrainian nationalists, *Samostiina dirka* (The Independent Little Hole, 1945), and his later works, including *Vesna – krasna* (Spring Is Beautiful, 1949), *Mudrist' kolhospna* (Collective-Farm Wisdom, 1952), *A narod viiny ne khoche* (But the People Don't Want a War, 1953), and *Velyki rostit'* (May You Prosper, 1955), were written in the spirit of the official Party line and were not as well received as those of the 1920s. Several editions of Vyshnia's complete works have been published, including *Usmishky* (Merriment, 4 vols, 1928), and *Tvory* (Works, 2 vols, 1956; 7 vols, 1963–5; and 5 vols, 1974–5). A small selection of his stories appeared in English translation as *Hard Times* (1981).

I. Koshelivets

**Vyshnivets** or **Vyshnevets** [Vyšnivec' or Vyšnevec']. IV-6. A town smt (1988 pop 4,100) on the Horyn River in Zbarazh raion, Ternopil oblast. It was first mentioned in historical documents in 1395. For about two centuries (mid-16th to 1744) it was the residence of the *Wiśniowiecki family, who built a castle (1640), a Carmelite monastery (17th century), and a palace (1720) there. It was captured by B. Khmelnytsky's Cossacks in 1648 and destroyed by the Tatars in 1653, 1666, and 1672. At the partition of Poland in 1793, the village became part of Kremianets county in Volhynia gubernia. In 1846 it was visited by T. Shevchenko, and in 1848, by H. de Balzac. It became a town smt in 1960. Today its old park, palace, and 17th-century castle ruins are tourist attractions.

**Vyshnivsky, Oleksander** [Vyšnivs'kyj], b 12 August 1890 in Zalyvna, Oleksandrivske county, Katerynoslav gubernia, d 12 October 1975 in Detroit. Senior army officer. A regular officer in the Russian army during the First World War, he joined the UNR Army in 1917. In the

Col Oleksander Vyshnivsky      Dmytro Vyslotsky

following three years he commanded, at the rank of colonel, the First Regiment of the Bluecoats, the Seventh Regiment of the Third Iron Rifle Division, and the Third Separate Cavalry Regiment. He distinguished himself and was seriously wounded in action near Vapniarka in July 1919. In the interwar period he lived in Poland, and after the Second World War he emigrated to the United States. He was promoted to major general by the UNR government-in-exile. He wrote *Povstans'kyi rukh i otamaniia* (The Partisan Movement and Warlordism, 1973) and *Trahediia 3-oï dyviziï Armiï UNR* (The Tragedy of the Third Division of the UNR Army, 1963).

**Vyshyvany, Vasyl.** See Habsburg-Lothringen, Wilhelm.

**Vyslotsky, Dmytro** [Vysloc'kyj] (pseud: Vano Hunianka), b 4 November 1888 in Labova, Nowy Sącz county, Galicia, d 27 December 1968 in Lviv. Lemko community leader, journalist, and writer. As a law student at Lviv University he edited the socialist paper *Lemko* (1912), in which he printed his own verses, stories, and articles. During the war he was imprisoned in the *Thalerhof concentration camp and sentenced to death. Saved by a general amnesty, he emigrated to Canada (1922) and then to the United States (1927), where he set up the semimonthly *Lemko*. He was one of the founders of the first branch of Lemko-Soiuz in Winnipeg. At the first national convention of Lemko-Soiuz in 1931 he was elected secretary and editor of its weekly paper *Lemko*. Besides editing *Lemko* and its successor, *Karpats'ka Rus'* (1939–45), he wrote plays, short stories, songs, and political pamphlets in the Lemko dialect. In 1946 he returned to Ukraine and settled in Uzhhorod, where he continued to write articles and literary pieces for the communist press in the United States.

**Vyslotsky, Oleksander** [Vysloc'kyj], b 1897 in Hai Starobridski, Brody county, Galicia, d ? Civic and political activist. During the First World War he served in the Ukrainian Sich Riflemen and then headed the Brody county branch of the Ukrainian National Democratic party. In 1928 he was elected to the Polish Sejm. In 1940 he was arrested by the Soviet secret police and disappeared in prison.

**Vysochan, Hnat** [Vysočan], b and d ? A 17th-century Galician peasant leader. Born in Vyktoriv village near Halych, he founded the villages of Sloboda Vysochanska and Bodnariv, and he is mentioned in municipal documents of Halych (1609). In the early 1620s he organized a peasant detachment, which attacked Tatar raiding parties on their way to the Crimea and freed their captives. The force also staged rebel actions against local feudal lords. It was active for over 20 years and grew to approx 15,000 in number. With the outbreak of the Cossack-Polish War in 1648, Vysochan sided with B. Khmelnytsky against the Poles and led an uprising in the Pokutia region, during which he was seriously wounded. His son, Semen, then took over the detachment.

**Vysochan, Semen** [Vysočan], b ? in Vyktoriv near Halych, Galicia, d 1666. Cossack officer; son of H. Vysochan. A graduate of the Lviv Dormition Brotherhood school, he succeeded his father as leader of a guerrilla regiment consisting of approx 15,000 peasants, which operated in Pokutia in 1648 and was headquartered in Otynia (Hutsul region). Despite some initial successes the uprising in Galicia was quelled by Polish forces, and Vysochan and a number of his followers were forced to retreat to Bratslav. He later distinguished himself at the siege of Vinnytsia in 1651, and in 1661 he became colonel of Lysianka regiment. He was arrested by I. Briukhovetsky in 1666 and exiled to Siberia. Vysochan's exploits provided the basis for T. Mykytyn's historical novel *Polkovnyk Semen Vysochan* (Colonel Semen Vysochan, 1968).

**Vysochansky, Pavlo** [Vysočans'kyj], b June 1892 in Viknyne, Zvenyhorodka county, Kiev gubernia, d ? Organizer and historian of the co-operative movement. From 1915 he organized Ukrainian co-operatives in the Poltava region. Then he served on the executives of the Dniprosoiuz co-operative (1919–21), the All-Ukrainian Association of Consumer Co-operative Organizations (1922–3), and the Ukrainbank. From 1927 he directed the Kiev Co-operative Institute. He wrote several works on the Ukrainian co-operative movement, including *Nacherk rozvytku ukraïns'koï spozhyvchoï kooperatsiï* (An Outline of the Development of Ukrainian Consumer Co-operatives, 2 vols, 1925), *Korotka istoriia kooperatyvnoho rukhu na Ukraïni* (A Short History of the Co-operative Movement in Ukraine, 1925), *Kooperatyvnyi prodazh* (Co-operative Selling, 1928), and *Kooperatyvnyi kredyt* (Co-operative Credit, 1929). He was arrested in 1930 and exiled to Saratov. After serving his term he directed the financial department of a mining concern in Karaganda. He was last heard from in 1941.

**Vysokopillia** [Vysokopillja]. VI-14. A town smt (1988 pop 5,000) and raion center in Kherson oblast. It was founded in 1869 by German colonists from Tavriia gubernia and was called Kronau until 1915. Today it is an agricultural town with several food-processing enterprises.

**Vysokovych, Volodymyr** [Vysokovyč], b 28 January 1854 in Haisyn, Podilia gubernia, d 26 May 1912 in Kiev. Anatomical pathologist, bacteriologist, and epidemiologist. A graduate of Kharkiv University (1876), from 1895 he was a professor at Kiev University. He helped organize and taught at the Women's Medical Courses in Kiev and directed efforts to control the plague and cholera in

Kharkiv (1892), Bombay (1896), Odessa (1902, 1910), and Kiev (1906). His chief achievement was the discovery of the reticuloendothelial system, and he wrote *O kholere* (On Cholera, 1907) and *Patologicheskaia anatomiia* (Pathological Anatomy, 2 vols, 1911, 1913).

**Vysokyi** [Vysokyj]. A town smt (1988 pop 14,100) in Kharkiv raion, Kharkiv oblast. It was founded in 1903. Most of the residents work in Kharkiv. The town has two children's sanatoriums, a rest home, and several camping grounds.

**Vysotske culture**. A late Bronze to early Iron Age culture of the 10th to 6th centuries BC that existed in the area of Lviv and Ternopil oblasts. It was named in the 1930s after a site excavated near Brody. The people of this settlement lived in unfortified settlements located along rivers in semi-pit dwellings. Major economic activities included agriculture, animal husbandry, and metalworking. Full body burial with the deceased placed in a supine position was the culture's norm, although cremation was also common. Artifacts unearthed at excavations included tulip-shaped and biconical pottery, earthenware sculptures decorated with bird images, stone and metal implements and weapons, and bronze adornments.

**Vysotsky, Serhii** [Vysoc'kyj, Serhij], b 15 July 1923 in Poltava. Historian and archeologist. After graduating from Kiev University (1956) he worked at the St Sophia Museum and the AN URSR (now ANU) Institute of Archeology (from 1967; as a section head from 1981). He has specialized in the history and culture of Kievan Rus', particularly graffiti and frescoes, and he was one of the managers of the restoration of Kiev's *Golden Gate. His works include *Zolotye vorota v Kieve* (The Golden Gates in Kiev, 1982) and *Kievskie graffiti XI–XVII vv.* (Kievan Graffiti of the 11th–17th Centuries, 1985).

Yurii (Heorhii) Vysotsky     Illia Vytanovych

**Vysotsky, Yurii** [Vysoc'kyj, Jurij] (Heorhii), b 19 February 1865 in Mykytivka, Hlukhiv county, Chernihiv gubernia, d 6 April 1940 in Kharkiv. Forester and soil scientist; full member of the All-Union Academy of Agricultural Sciences from 1934 and of the AN URSR (now ANU) from 1939. He graduated from the Petrovskoe Agricultural Academy near Moscow in 1890. He joined V. Dokuchaev's expedition to study the causes of drought in Southern Ukraine and oversaw the forestation works at the *Ve-

lykoanadol Forest Project in the Mariiupil region (1892–1904). He taught at Kiev University (1917–19) and was appointed a professor at Tavriia University, the Crimean Agricultural Institute, and the Belarusian Agricultural Institute in Minsk (1923–6). He served as a department head at the Kharkiv Institute of Agriculture (1926–30) and as consultant at the All-Union Scientific Research Institute of Forest Management and Agroforest Amelioration in Kharkiv (1930–40). He was a leading authority on steppe soils and a founder of soil hydrology in arid regions. Vysotsky introduced the oroclimatic classification table for soils, first calculated the forest and field moisture balance, and developed the theory of the transgressive role of forests. His numerous scientific works include *Pokrovovedenie* (Topsoil Science, 1925) and *Materialy po izucheniiu vodookhrannoi i vodoreguliruiushchei roli lesov i bolot* (Materials for the Study of the Water-Conserving and Water-Regulating Role of Forests and Marshes, 1937). Collections of his selected works were published in 1960 and 1962.

**Vysova** (Polish: Wysowa). IV-2. A Lemko village on the Ropa River, now in Gorlice county, Nowy Sącz voivodeship, Poland. Because of its mineral springs it developed into a health resort in the 19th century. In the 1930s an average of 700 patients a year visited Vysova. A Lemko wooden church from the early 19th century has been preserved there. In 1939, 890 of Vysova's 1,020 inhabitants were Ukrainian.

**Vysun River** [Vysun']. A right-bank tributary of the Inhulets River that flows for 196 km through Mykolaiv oblast and drains a basin area of 2,670 sq km. The river is up to 20 m wide and 0.8 to 1.5 m deep, with a valley (in its lower reaches) up to 3 km wide. It is used for water supply and irrigation, although sections of it dry up routinely in the summer months.

**Vytanovych, Illia** [Vytanovyč, Illja], b 9 August 1899 in Burshtyn, Rohatyn county, Galicia, d 30 December 1973 in New York. Historian, pedagogue, and co-operative activist; member of the Shevchenko Scientific Society from 1933. He served in the ranks of the Ukrainian Sich Riflemen, the Ukrainian Galician Army, and the Army of the UNR. He studied at Lviv (Underground) Ukrainian University and Lviv University (1923–7), taught at the economic school of the Ridna Shkola society (1927–37), and directed the Co-operative Lyceum in Lviv (1937–40). A postwar refugee, he was a professor at the Ukrainian Technical and Husbandry Institute and the Ukrainian Free University in Munich from 1946 and then emigrated to the United States in 1949. He was a longtime associate of *Entsyklopediia ukraïnoznavstva* (Encyclopedia of Ukraine) and a founding member of the Ukrainian Historical Association. He wrote on economic history, in which field is his major work, *Istoriia ukraïns'koho kooperatyvnoho rukhu* (History of the Ukrainian Co-operative Movement, 1964). He also wrote studies of the Cossack army under Hetman P. Sahaidachny and of the methodology and historiography of M. Hrushevsky.

**Vytautas the Great** (Polish: Witold; Ukrainian: Vytovt), b 1350 in Lithuania, d 27 October 1430 in Trakai fortress, on an island in Lake Galvė, Lithuania. Grand duke of Lithuania from 1392; grandson of Gediminas and brother of *Žygimantas. Vytautas stood for Lithuanian independence and allied with the *Teutonic Knights to oppose the union with Poland that was advocated by his cousin, King Jagiełło (Jogaila). In 1384, fearing the growing power of the order, he was reconciled with Jagiełło, who granted him the rule of Hrodna, Brest-Litovsk, and Podlachia. After the death of Liubartas (1385) he annexed Volhynia, including Lutske and Volodymyr. When Jagiełło chose *Skirgaila to rule Lithuania (1387), however, Vytautas again enlisted the support of the Teutonic Knights, as well as Muscovy. He besieged and devastated Vilnius, and in 1392 he was again reconciled with Jagiełło, whereupon he was granted the rule of the whole Grand Duchy of Lithuania.

In order to strengthen his position Vytautas began taking over the lands of Ukrainian and Belarusian appanage princes, and in 1396 he deposed Jagiełło's brother, the Kievan prince Volodymyr (son of Algirdas). He also defeated the princes of Podilia, Volhynia, and Chernihiv and became resolutely anti-Muscovite in his policies. He signed treaties with the Russian princes of Tver, Riazan, and Pronsk, who were against Moscow's centralist policy, and in 1395 he took over Smolensk, an important strategic and commercial center. Vytautas built fortifications in the south and expanded the borders of the *Lithuanian-Ruthenian state, particularly to the south and east, where they reached the Black Sea between the lower Dnieper and the Dniester rivers. He was defeated in 1399, however, at the Vorskla River in a joint Ukrainian-Belarusian-Lithuanian campaign against the Tatars, and the defeat forced him into another alliance with Poland. It took Vytautas nearly 10 years to regain control of the eastern lands. He recaptured Smolensk in 1404, and in 1410 he and Jagiełło crushed the Teutonic Knights at Tannenberg and halted their eastward advance. The joint victory strengthened the Polish-Lithuanian union, and the formal Union of *Horodlo was signed in 1413. During the remainder of his rule Vytautas contributed to the expansion of trade and artisanship in Lithuanian-ruled territory, and he introduced *Magdeburg law in many of its cities. But the limitation of the political rights of Orthodox citizens aroused considerable hostility against Vytautas among Ukrainian and Belarusian noblemen, who turned to *Švitrigaila for support.

A. Zhukovsky

**Vytvytsky, Ivan** [Vytvyc'kyj], b 1901 in Vytvytsia, Dolyna county, Galicia, d late August 1939. Journalist. A veteran of the Ukrainian Galician Army, after the First World War he studied law at Lviv University and became a member of the Ukrainian Military Organization. While working as an editor for the newspaper *Novyi chas* in Lviv, he received a scholarship from I. Tyktor to study journalism in Berlin. After returning to Lviv in 1934, he wrote on international politics for *Novyi chas*. In his articles and public talks he especially criticized Hitler's *Mein Kampf*. In the general panic that preceded the Nazi invasion of Poland he was arrested by the Polish police and shot.

**Vytvytsky, Stepan** [Vytvyc'kyj], b 13 March 1884 in Uhornyky, Tovmach county, Galicia, d 19 October 1965 in New York. State figure and political activist. While studying law at the universities of Lviv and Vienna he headed the Academic Hromada in Lviv and the Sich society in Vi-

Stepan Vytvytsky

enna. He was a cultural and civic activist in Drohobych county. In 1915–18 he was a member of the editorial board of the newspaper *Dilo*, editor of the weekly *Svoboda* in Lviv, a member of the Ukrainian *National Democratic party and of the political committee which prepared the declaration of 1 November 1918 by the *Ukrainian National Rada, and secretary of the Rada. As a member of the delegation from the Western Ukrainian National Republic (ZUNR) to the Labor Congress in Kiev he participated in the ratification of the union of the UNR and ZUNR on 22 January 1919. He became state secretary of external affairs, and he represented the Western Province of the UNR in negotiations with the Entente for a truce with Poland. In November 1919 he was deputy to the head of the UNR Directory's mission in Warsaw, a position from which he resigned in protest against the Treaty of Warsaw (1920). Vytvytsky directed the Department of External Affairs of the ZUNR government-in-exile in Vienna, and in 1921–3 he headed the ZUNR missions in Paris and London. In 1924–39, after returning to Galicia, he worked as a lawyer and was active in the leadership of the *Ukrainian National Democratic Alliance (UNDO) in Drohobych. He was an UNDO representative to the Polish Sejm (1935–9) as well as deputy head of UNDO and of the *Ukrainian Parliamentary Representation (from 1938). As a postwar refugee Vytvytsky was vice-president of the *Central Representation of the Ukrainian Emigration in Germany (1945) and participated in establishing the *Ukrainian National Council; he became vice-president of its executive organ and director of its office of external affairs in 1949. In 1951 he emigrated to the United States, and he represented the executive organ there. He was elected president of the *Government-in-exile of the UNR in 1954 and re-elected at its fifth session in 1961.

A. Zhukovsky

**Vytvytsky, Vasyl.** See Wytwycky, Wasyl.

**Vytvytsky, Yosyp Dominik** [Vytvyc'kyj, Josyp], b 1813 in Volhynia gubernia, d 20 February 1866 in Kiev. Composer, pianist, and pedagogue. He studied music with his father, an organist in Berdychiv, and then worked as a music teacher in Podilia and Volhynia gubernias. In 1840–65 he taught piano at the finishing institute for the daughters of the nobility in Kiev. His works consist largely of piano pieces based on Ukrainian, Polish, and Russian folk themes, such as *The Ukrainian Girl*, *Chumak*, and *The Neighbor's House Is White*.

**Vytychiv congress of princes.** A conference of Kievan Rus' princes that took place on 10 August 1100 in Vytychiv, 40 km south of Kiev on the right bank of the Dnieper River. It was called by *Volodymyr Monomakh to settle differences among the princes and unite them in battle against the Cumans. The Primary Chronicle states that among the assembled were Sviatopolk II Iziaslavych of Kiev, Volodymyr Monomakh, Oleh Sviatoslavych of Chernihiv, and Davyd Ihorevych of Volhynia (who blinded Vasylko Rostyslavych of Terebovlia). For his violation of a treaty signed at the Liubech congress (1097), which had caused much internal strife, Davyd was forced to give up Volodymyr-Volynskyi. The chronicle describes Volodymyr's call for unity and Davyd's antagonism. A number of successful campaigns against the Cumans, fought by a united force, followed the Vytychiv congress.

**Vyzhnytsia** [Vyžnycja]. V-6. A city (1989 pop 5,500) on the Cheremosh River and raion center in Chernivtsi oblast. It was first mentioned in historical documents at the end of the 15th century, when it was part of the Moldavian principality. In 1774 it was annexed by Austria. An opryshok band was active in the area in 1817–30. In 1867 Vyzhnytsia obtained the rights of a trading town. During the interwar period the town was occupied by Rumania. It was granted city status in 1940. Today it is a resort center and is known for its handicrafts (kilim weaving, embroidery, wood carving, and metalworking). It has a historical and a decorative art museum.

*Vyzvol'na polityka* (Liberation Politics). A journal of the émigré OUN (Bandera faction). Approx 20 issues were published in 1946–9 in Germany. It was edited by I. Vovchuk and M. Myronenko.

*Vyzvol'nyi shliakh* (Liberation Path). A monthly serial of the émigré OUN (Bandera faction) in Great Britain, founded in January 1948. Except for the first few issues, it has been published in London. Until 1950 it was available only to the faction's members. Since April 1951 it has been

*Vyzvol'nyi shliakh*

published by Ukrainian Publishers Ltd, and since 1954 it has appeared in a journal format. It contains the faction's programmatic documents and ideological articles; journalistic and scholarly articles on Soviet Ukrainian politics and economics, international politics, and the history of the OUN and Ukrainian Insurgent Army; articles on Ukrainian history, archeology, society, literature, music, and art; prose and poetry by émigré writers and members of the OUN underground; literary translations; historical and political memoirs; reprints of works by Soviet Ukrainian writers of the 1920s and the *shestydesiatnyky*; samvydav literature and political documents; book reviews; news and analyses of the Ukrainian national opposition in Ukraine; and a chronicle of life in Ukraine and the émigré community. The journal was edited initially by a board consisting of P. Oliinychenko, R. Borkovsky, I. Ratushny, and V. Vasylenko. H. Drabat was managing editor from 1948 and chief editor from 1955 to 1977. He was succeeded by S. Halamai and, in 1979, by an editorial board headed by I. Dmytriv. In the 1950s and 1960s L. Poltava and V. Derzhavyn served as literary editors. Among the contributors have been many publicists, writers, and scholars, most of them affiliated with the Bandera faction.

# W

**Wächter, Otto von,** b 8 July 1901 in Vienna, d 1949 in Rome. A Nazi functionary. A baron and a lawyer by profession, in 1934 he was the political leader of the failed Austrian SS putsch in Vienna. During the Second World War Wächter served as an SS Brigadeführer and (from April 1944) Gruppenführer. As governor of Cracow (from 1939) and the Distrikt Galizien (from November 1941) in the German-occupied *Generalgouvernement of Poland Wächter was more sympathetic to the *Ukrainian Central Committee and the Galician Ukrainians' national aspirations than were other Nazi administrators, and he removed many aggressively anti-Ukrainian bureaucrats under his command. In 1943 he conceived the idea of creating the Waffen SS *Division Galizien and convinced the SS Reichsführer, H. Himmler, to agree to it; he failed, however, to convince Himmler that it should be called the Division Ukraine. Wächter appointed the members of the *Military Board of the Division Galizien and generally had good relations with them. In 1945 he was the commander in chief of all Waffen SS divisions made up of non-Germans. After Germany's capitulation he received asylum at the Maria dell'Anima Monastery in Rome.

**Wadowice.** A town (1983 pop 14,600) and county center in Bielsko-Biała voivodeship, Poland. In 1919–20 it was the site of a concentration camp in which the Polish regime kept Ukrainians from Galicia. Almost 1,500 of the 15,000 prisoners died of typhus. Then the camp held interned soldiers of the UNR Army. As in other internment camps, the Ukrainian internees organized a cultural and educational program that included literacy and Ukrainian studies courses, choirs, a theater, a library, and a credit union.

**Wages.** A payment on a regular basis for labor or services according to a contract. In the USSR wages were regulated by the state. The USSR Council of Ministers established a general wage fund with separate pools and rates for every republic, ministry, economic branch, and individual job category. The trade unions were only consulted as to the setting of the rates. At the local level the enterprise administration classified workers by category and established the specific rates. Workers dissatisfied with their classification could appeal to a wage-rate commission at the enterprise but did not have the practical right to strike. By establishing the general wage fund for the entire USSR and the individual republics, the central government regulated the basic wages of the entire work force and the proportion of wages to the GNP. It also allowed the government to use wage rates to influence other economic policies.

Immediately following the Revolution of 1917, during the period of War Communism, wages were often paid in goods and services rather than money, owing to the debasement of Soviet currency and the influence of radical economic ideas that rejected money as an exchange medium. Under the New Economic Policy monetary wages were reintroduced. They remained low because services such as lunch and housing continued to be subsidized by the employer or state. Wages in the co-operative or private sectors were generally higher.

With the introduction of rapid industrialization in the late 1920s, wages rose quickly. At the same time the gap between wages paid to unskilled workers and skilled workers, technicians, managers, and Party and government officials widened, especially after J. Stalin's criticism of egalitarianism in 1931. Wage differentials, it was believed, would increase productivity and worker discipline. The other important features of Stalinist wage policy were the conversion to piecework, which became widespread after 1934, and the use of bonuses to reward workers. By the 1950s over 70 percent of all industrial workers in Ukraine were paid on a piecework basis; at the same time, some 35 percent of all wages were paid as bonuses for overtime work or for overfulfilling quotas in either quantity or quality of production. In general, workers in heavy industry received higher wages than workers in light industry, trade, and services. The most disadvantaged sector was agriculture, where wages were calculated on the basis of the *workday.

In absolute terms wages rose steadily from the 1930s to the mid-1950s. Average monthly wages for all industrial workers and managers (before taxes and social security deductions) increased from 52 rubles in 1925 to 115 in 1932, 237 in 1937, 319 in 1940, and 643 in 1953. Their real value, however, probably decreased, because the ruble's buying power was reduced by price inflation and the shortage of consumer goods (see *Standard of living). At the same time wage differentials continued to increase. In 1955, for example, whereas workers with average qualifications at medium-sized factories in Ukraine earned about 800 rubles a month, chambermaids received 450, secretaries 780, teachers 1,300, doctors 1,400, accountants 1,650, engineers 1,780, army generals 3,850, university professors 5,000, academicians 6,800, directors of medium-sized factories 7,400, and ministers 10,500 rubles. The differentials were intended to secure the support of privileged segments of the population and to encourage development in certain sectors of the economy.

In 1955–64, after N. Khrushchev's consolidation of power, a major reform of the wage system was undertaken. Rates were standardized to remove wage discrepancies between workers in similar jobs, differentials were reduced somewhat, a higher minimum wage was introduced (300 rubles a month in urban and 270 rubles in rural areas), some extremely high wage rates were reduced, and piecework and bonuses were partially eliminated or reduced. For the next two decades the wage system changed little, although some Soviet economists urged greater differentials.

Average monthly wage (in rubles) of blue- and white-collar workers in Ukraine, 1960–90

| Sector | 1960 | 1970 | 1980 | 1990 |
|---|---|---|---|---|
| Industry | 93.2 | 130.1 | 176.9 | 277.5 |
| Agriculture | 53.7 | 96.0 | 136.3 | 260.3 |
| Transportation | 78.3 | 120.9 | 168.2 | 257.0 |
| Communications | 59.7 | 92.3 | 134.8 | 217.8 |
| Construction | 85.6 | 135.0 | 175.7 | 308.7 |
| Trade | 54.1 | 88.0 | 125.4 | 213.4 |
| Information computing | – | 87.7 | 119.6 | 222.5 |
| Consumer services | 52.5 | 87.5 | 123.3 | 185.7 |
| Health care | 55.6 | 85.0 | 115.3 | 162.7 |
| Education | 71.9 | 105.0 | 130.2 | 176.1 |
| Culture | 44.9 | 77.1 | 102.7 | 143.2 |
| Art | 56.6 | 86.8 | 129.1 | 176.6 |
| Scholarship | 90.0 | 126.4 | 164.0 | 312.8 |
| Credit and insurance | 66.6 | 103.7 | 147.8 | 366.2 |
| State administration | 78.8 | 114.1 | 144.4 | 304.9 |
| All workers in Ukraine | 78.3 | 115.2 | 155.1 | 247.3 |
| All workers in USSR | 80.6 | 122.0 | 168.9 | – |

The table above shows the average pretax wage by branch of the economy in Ukraine since 1960 (the currency reform in 1961 exchanged 10 old for 1 new ruble; the figures for 1960 have been converted into new rubles). Overall, average wages in the state sector in Ukraine were lower than for the entire USSR: the ratio between average annual wages in Ukraine and in the USSR as a whole was 0.97 to 1 in 1960 and 0.92 to 1 in 1980. The difference is partly attributable to the preponderance of lower-paying jobs in the Ukrainian economy, especially in the agricultural, service, and light-industrial sectors. Ukrainian wages, however, were considerably lower than those in the Russian SFSR: the ratio between wages in Russia and in the USSR as a whole was 1.03 to 1 in 1960 and 1.07 to 1 in 1987. Throughout the USSR wages for women were lower than for men, because the economic sectors employing mostly women offered the lowest wages.

BIBLIOGRAPHY

Tsentral'ne statystychne upravlinnia USRR. *Dyferentsiiatsiia zarobitnoï platy v promyslovosti Ukraïny v 1928–1929 rr.* (Kharkiv 1930)

Bukhanevich, B.; Sonin, M. 'O mezhraionnom regulirovanii zarabotnoi platy v SSSR,' *Voprosy ekonomiki*, 1957, no. 1

Matthews, M. *Class and Society in Soviet Russia* (London 1972)

Schroeder, G. 'Consumption and Personal Incomes,' in *The Ukraine within the USSR: An Economic Balance Sheet*, ed I. Koropeckyj (New York 1977)

Manykina, I.; et al (eds). *Trud v SSSR: Statisticheskii sbornik* (Moscow 1988)

B. Balan, V. Holubnychy

**Wagner, Marcel** (né Shevchynsky), b 2 June 1904 in Dorohiv, Stanyslaviv county, Galicia, d 24 November 1973 in Hillside, New Jersey. Lawyer; first American state legislator of Ukrainian origin. He emigrated to the United States with his family in 1905, graduated from Fordham University (1926), and then practiced law in Jersey City. In the 1940s he served four terms in the New Jersey state assembly; later he held various state appointments, one as a compensation judge (1962–73). His community involvements included acting as legal counsel to the Ukrainian Congress Committee of America during its formative years and to the Ukrainian American Relief Committee.

**Wagtail** (*Motacilla*; Ukrainian: *plyska*). A slender songbird of the family Motacillidae that constantly pumps its long tail up and down. Its body length is 18–20 cm, and its weight 16–25 g. Four species are known in Ukraine: the white (*M. alba*) and yellow (*M. flava*) wagtails nest all over Ukraine, the gray wagtail (*M. cinerea*) favors the Crimean and Carpathian mountains, and the yellow-headed wagtail (*M. citreola*) is a migrant bird that visits Ukraine in summer. Wagtails nest on the ground but roost in trees. They feed on insects, spiders, and butterflies and so are considered to be valuable birds.

**Walawa** (Ukrainian: Valiava). A village in the Peremyshl area (now in Poland), near which a small Rus' fortified settlement and burial site were found. The site was excavated in 1939 by Ya. Pasternak. Earlier (1926) a unique find had been made in the region when a Paleolithic skull was washed up by the Sian River. In 1939, 740 of Walawa's 760 inhabitants were Ukrainian.

William Wall                    Alexander Walter

**Wall, William** [Voloxatjuk, Vasyl'], b 11 July 1911 in Ethelbert, Manitoba, d 7 July 1962 in Winnipeg. Canadian senator of Ukrainian origin. Wall was educated at the University of Manitoba (M ED, 1939) and served as a school principal and administrator for the Winnipeg school board. He was the first Ukrainian to be appointed to the Canadian Senate, in 1955 as a Liberal from Manitoba. He was also president of the Ukrainian Catholic Council of Canada (1946–53).

**Wallachia** or **Walachia**. See Rumania.

**Wallachian Church.** See Dormition Church in Lviv.

**Wallachian law** (*voloske pravo*). Customary law that in the 14th and 15th centuries governed settlements in Wallachia and spread to pastoral communities in Galicia and Transcarpathia. The name is associated with the migration of Wallachian shepherds through the Carpathian Mountains as far west as Moravia. Wallachian law does not have any determinate national traits, and little is known about the nationality of its original carriers. Because of the small number of ethnic Wallachians in the area, it is reasonable to assume that, long ago, Ukrainian communities were also founded on Wallachian law. The law arose out of a pastoral way of life. The village community was headed by a hereditary *kniez* (literally, 'prince'), who convened the *viche* (assembly) to decide communal issues. Several villages governed by the law formed a *kraina*, a judicial-administrative district headed by a *krainyk*. The *krainyk* presided over semiannual judicial assemblies. The community was collectively responsible for the wrongdoings of its members and for various levies. Taxes and other fees were usually paid in kind, in livestock, cheese, or wool; a third went to the *kniez*, and the rest to the village's owner. The inhabitants of many villages under Wallachian law were required to do military service. Eventually, many became serfs of the gentry.

**Wall-materials industry.** A branch of the construction-materials industry that produces materials for making interior and exterior walls. Wall materials are produced by the *brick, *building-ceramics, *asbestos-cement, and *reinforced-concrete industries.

**Walnut** (*Juglans regia*; Ukrainian: *horikh voloskyi* or *horikh hretskyi*). A deciduous tree of the family Juglandaceae, 20–30 m tall, and with a thick, rounded crown, large aromatic leaves, and edible fruit (nut). In Ukraine walnuts grow from northern Polisia south to the shores of the Black Sea. They grow well in moist, sunny places and can withstand temperatures of −35°C. One tree yields 65–100 kg of edible nuts rich in oil (up to 77 percent), which is used in the production of high-quality printing inks and varnishes. Walnut wood is used in the manufacture of furniture and in the production of dyes and india ink. Walnut leaves and husks yield some medicinal preparations and tannin. The ripe walnut kernels are consumed whole and in baked goods.

**Walter, Alexander,** b 9 January 1818 in Revel, Estonia, d 1889. German anatomist and physiologist. A graduate of Tartu University (1841), he lectured on physiological anatomy at Kiev University (1843, as professor from 1847). In 1874 he was appointed medical inspector of civilian hospitals in Warsaw. In his numerous publications he dealt with the physiological effects of heat and cold in organisms, the production of heat in animals, and the sympathetic nervous system. His *Kurs anatomii chelovecheskogo tela* (A Course in the Anatomy of the Human Body, 1852) went through several editions, and he was the founder and editor of the paper *Sovremennaia meditsina* (1860–81).

**Walter, Anton,** b 24 December 1905 in St Petersburg, d 13 July 1965 in Kharkiv. Experimental physicist; AN URSR (now ANU) full member from 1951. A graduate of the Leningrad Polytechnical Institute (1926), in 1930 he joined the Ukrainian Physical-Technical Institute (renamed the ANU Physical-Technical Institute) in Kharkiv, where he became centrally involved in the development and construction of nuclear-particle accelerators. In 1932 Walter was a member of the research group (with G. *Latyshev, A. *Leipunsky, and K. *Synelnykov) that accomplished for the first time in the USSR the transmutation of one stable nucleus (lithium) into another (helium). Walter became a leading specialist in accelerator design and in associated vacuum and high-voltage technology. In 1937, together with K. Synelnykov, he built a 2.5-MeV electrostatic particle accelerator, which at the time was the most powerful in Europe. After the Second World War, Walter contributed significantly to the design of the Kharkiv 2-GeV linear

Anton Walter

electron accelerator. From 1937 he was a professor at Kharkiv University.

**War Communism.** A term used to describe the Soviet economic policy from June 1918 to March 1921. The policy was designed to abet the Bolshevik war effort by means of state control over all sectors of the economy and forced *agricultural procurement. In Ukraine the system came into operation between 1919 and 1921. Factories, enterprises, trade, and transport were nationalized, and all market and labor relations were regulated by the state. Able citizens between the ages of 16 and 50 were eligible for compulsory labor conscription. Trade unions were stripped of their independence in April 1919, when the Bolsheviks convoked the First All-Ukrainian Trade Union congress to subordinate them to the state; that was followed by their absorption into all-Russian bodies. Such measures, coupled with the disorders caused by the Ukrainian-Soviet War and the Allied blockade, resulted in general economic chaos. Real wages fell, an extensive black market emerged, and inflation soared; the situation was particularly exacerbated when the Commissariat of Supplies began to dispense food free of charge, from December 1920. Such conditions encouraged a flight of workers from Ukrainian cities; thus, by 1921 there were only 260,000 factory workers left in Ukraine (half the pre-revolution figure).

War Communism also provoked chaos in the countryside. *Committees of Poor Peasants (*komnezamy*) were set up and charged with the forced collection of foodstuffs for the state. Members of those *komnezamy* were allowed to retain for themselves up to 25 percent of what was collected. Subsequently squads were sent across the countryside to fulfill grain deliveries. The requisitions were met with fierce resistance by the peasantry. During the course of 1920 about 1,000 food requisitioners were killed by peasants in Ukraine. The policy was largely unsuccessful: of the 2,624,000 t of grain demanded from Ukrainian sources in 1920, only 159,000 t were extracted. It has been argued that the requisition measures were a factor contributing to the famine of 1921. The discontent and disorder that War Communism bred impelled the Bolsheviks to abandon the policy in favor of the *New Economic Policy.

S. Cipko

**Warbler.** A small (to 25 cm), insectivorous, migratory songbird of the family Sylviidae, consisting of several genera. Its drab plumage is brownish with a lighter underside; males and females look alike. Warblers build their nests in shrubs, reeds, and bushes, and on the ground. In Ukraine they live in Polisia, in Carpathian forests, in the forest-steppe zone, and in the Crimea. Eleven species of reed, bush, tree, and grasshopper warblers (Ukrainian: *ocheretianka*) are represented by the genera *Acrocephalus*, *Locustella*, *Phragmaticola*, *Cettia*, and *Horeites*; five species of leaf or willow warblers (Ukrainian: *vivcharyk*) by the genus *Phylloscopus*; and five species of tree and scrub warblers (Ukrainian: *slavka*) by the genus *Sylvia*.

Patricia Warren

**Warren, Patricia** (pseud: Patricia Kilina [Patrycija Kylyna]), b 21 June 1936 in Helena, Montana. Poet, translator, and writer. Warren studied English literature and worked as an editor for *Reader's Digest* (1959–80). After marrying G. *Tarnawsky she learned Ukrainian and began to appear in print under her Ukrainian pseudonym. She is the author of three collections of Ukrainian poetry, *Trahediia dzhmeliv* (Tragedy of Bees, 1960), *Legendy i sny* (Legends and Dreams, 1964), and *Rozhevi mista* (Roseate Cities, 1969). Her poetry is characterized by striking imagery and a certain estrangement evolving from a non-native approach to the Ukrainian language. Warren also wrote in English the novel *The Last Centennial* (1972) and, together with Tarnawsky, translated *Ukrainian Dumy* (1979).

The Ukrainian Chamber Choir of Warsaw (director: Yaroslav Poliansky)

**Warsaw** (Polish: Warszawa). The capital and largest city (1988 pop 1,651,200) of Poland, located in the center of the country on the Vistula River. As the capital of the Polish-Lithuanian Commonwealth Warsaw long attracted Ukrainian nobles (the Sviatopolk-Chetvertynsky, Ostrozky, Urusky, and other families had palaces there until 1944),

Cossacks, and merchants (who had warehouses on the Vistula). The members of those strata were particularly numerous in Warsaw, but clergymen and burghers (representatives of the *brotherhoods) were also present in the city during sessions of the Diet. Since 1721 there has been a Basilian monastery in Warsaw; it once owned the Łazienki park.

After Warsaw became part of the Russian Empire in the early 19th century, many Ukrainian activists spent time there. At the beginning of the 20th century, when Ukrainian cultural and political life was undergoing intense development, links with Ukraine became stronger. In that period many Ukrainians studied at Warsaw University, because of government restrictions on enrollment in institutions of higher education in Ukraine. A Ukrainian student hromada was formed, with 120 to 150 members. In 1910 Ukrainian students formed an illegal revolutionary organization, the Union of Ukrainian Youth of Poland. The increasing activization of the Ukrainian movement contributed to the awakening of national consciousness among the numerous imperial civil servants of Ukrainian origin, both in Warsaw and in other Polish cities. In Warsaw there was also a fairly large colony of Ukrainians from the nearby Kholm region and Podlachia.

In the 1920s and 1930s Warsaw became one of the centers of the Ukrainian political emigration, particularly for émigrés associated with the UNR. In the fall of 1919 a UNR diplomatic mission was in Warsaw, where it signed in the name of the Directory the Treaty of *Warsaw with Poland. The former president of the UNR, M. Hrushevsky, stayed in Warsaw briefly (fall 1919), and the UNR's supreme otaman, S. Petliura, lived there from 1920 to 1923. Petliura's deputy A. Livytsky settled permanently in Warsaw, as did some other members of the UNR's government-in-exile and UNR civilian and military activists. After the conclusion of the Peace Treaty of Riga a diplomatic mission from the Ukrainian SSR, headed by O. Shumsky, was also in Warsaw. Warsaw was the center of the *Ukrainian Central Committee in Poland, which was a vital organization for Ukrainian emigrants. Other groups active in Warsaw included the Ukrainian Military History Society, the Union of Ukrainian Emigrant Women in Poland, the Union of Ukrainian Engineers and Technicians in Emigration, the Ukrainian Juridical Society, the Society of Ukrainian Veterans, the Society of Friends of the League of Nations, the Society to Aid Students of Higher School, and the Women's Hromada (est 1924). In time the Ukrainian colony in Warsaw grew to 2,000 or 3,000 owing largely to the arrival of workers and students from Galicia and the so-called northwestern lands. Warsaw was the temporary home of Ukrainian Sejm deputies and senators as well as Ukrainian journalists. The Ukrainian Student Hromada was revived, and the fraternity Zaporizhia was established; a social center, the Ukrainian Club, came into existence in 1928. The Promethean League of Nations Enslaved by Moscow (see *Promethean movement) was centered in Warsaw and had a Ukrainian section. Church life centered around the Orthodox cathedral in the Praga section of Warsaw and around the Greek Catholic church and Basilian monastery on Miodowa Street. From 1929 scholarly life centered around the *Ukrainian Scientific Institute in Warsaw, with its valuable library and publications. Warsaw University had a department of Orthodox theology and chairs of Ukrainian language and history. Also important for Ukrainian studies were the Polish Oriental Institute and the *Institute for Nationalities Research. In 1932 the Ukrainian Economic Bureau was established, which published statistical yearbooks. Valuable archival and museum materials for Ukrainian studies were preserved in the Orthodox Metropolitan Archive-Museum, in the Zamoyski and Krasiński libraries, and in the Archiwum Akt Dawnych; many Ukrainian-related archival materials perished, however, in 1944. The Ukrainian scholars who lived in Warsaw included P. Andriievsky, S. Balei, V. Bidnov, L. Chykalenko, D. Doroshenko, M. Korduba, O. Lototsky, I. Ohiienko, I. Shovheniv, R. Smal-Stotsky, and P. Zaitsev; the writers included N. Livytska-Kholodna, Yu. Lypa, Ye. Malaniuk, and O. Teliha; and the painters, P. Andrusiv, N. Khasevych, P. Kholodny (the younger), P. Mehyk, graduates of and lecturers at the Academy of Arts, and members of the artists' group *Spokii. Between 1918 and 1939 over 40 Ukrainian periodicals appeared in Warsaw. In 1921–2 Warsaw had a daily Ukrainian newspaper, *Ukraïns'ka trybuna, edited by O. Salikovsky; and in 1926–7 it had the newspaper *Ukraïns'ka nyva. Prior to 1939 Ukrainian journals published in Warsaw included *Za nezalezhnist', *Za derzhavnist', the monthlies *Nasha kul'tura and *Ridna mova, the literary-artistic bimonthly *My, and *Biuletyń Polsko-Ukraiński. V. Ostrovsky's publishing firm and the publishing houses Variah and Nasha Kultura were located there. In Warsaw appeared Studiï do ukraïns'koï hramatyky i filolohiï (edited by Smal-Stotsky and later also Ohiienko), the publications of the Ukrainian Scientific Institute, numerous Orthodox publications (from the metropolitan printing press), the series Biblioteka ukraïns'koho derzhavnyka (The Library of the Ukrainian State-Builder), and the publications of Spokii.

During the Second World War the Ukrainian Relief Committee, a branch of the *Ukrainian Central Committee in Cracow, was active in Warsaw, with numerous sections and organizations. The Ukrainian colony in Warsaw grew rapidly when Ukrainians fled there to escape communist rule.

After the war and the establishment of a communist government in Poland Ukrainian activity in Warsaw declined notably, both because of the numerical decrease of Warsaw's Ukrainian population and because of the restrictions put on associations and the press, especially Ukrainian ones, by the communist regime. The situation of Ukrainians was particularly bleak in the first decade after the war, when Poland was combating the *Ukrainian Insurgent Army on its territory and Stalin was still alive. In 1956 Ukrainians in Poland were allowed to have an organization, albeit under the control of the Ministry of Internal Affairs – the *Ukrainian Social and Cultural Society (as of 1990 the Alliance of Ukrainians in Poland [OUP]), with headquarters in Warsaw. Warsaw also revived as a center of publishing for Ukrainians in Poland. The weekly newspaper *Nashe slovo began to appear in 1956, as did its supplements, the cultural review Nasha kul'tura (since 1958) and the children's periodical Svitanok. The OUP calendar as well as the Orthodox church calendar (in the Ukrainian language until 1977, since then multilingual) has been published in Warsaw; since 1988 a Ukrainian Catholic church calendar has also appeared. Since 1953 there has been a department of Ukrainian philology at Warsaw University. Warsaw has developed as a center of Ukrainian studies. Scholars, mainly Polish, who have

been active in the field since the Second World War include the historians A. Chojnowski, Ye. Misylo (a Ukrainian), M. Papierzyńska-Turek, A. Poppe, J. Radziejowski, R. Torzecki, and Ż. Wójcik; the literary historians M. Jakóbiec, S. Kozak (a Ukrainian), A. Serednytsky (a Ukrainian), E. Wiśniewska, V. Nazaruk (a Ukrainian), T. Holynska (a Ukrainian), and F. Nieuważny; and the linguists P. Zwoliński and Z. Stieber. As in the interwar period the Orthodox cathedral remained a center of Ukrainian religious life. In spite of intense persecution in the late 1940s, Ukrainian Catholicism in Warsaw survived into the postwar period; both a Ukrainian Catholic community and the Basilian monastery continued to exist, although the monastery converted to the Latin rite in order to do so.

With the end of communist rule in Poland in 1989, Ukrainians in Warsaw undertook new initiatives. In 1989 the Basilian fathers published the first issue of a scholarly journal devoted to Ukrainian studies, Varshavs'ki ukraïnoznavchi zapysky.

M. Kovalevsky, J.-P. Himka, A. Zięba

**Warsaw, Grand Duchy of.** An administrative territory in Poland set up by Napoleon in 1807. It was formed out of the Polish regions of the Kingdom of Prussia, to which were added in 1809 the regions acquired by Austria under the Second Partition of Poland, including Zamość and Cracow. After Napoleon's defeat the Congress of Vienna divided the grand duchy. A small portion (Poznań) was awarded to Prussia, Cracow and its environs were set up as a free state (under an allied protectorate), and most of the territory was reconstituted as the *Congress Kingdom of Poland under the indirect jurisdiction of the Russian Empire.

**Warsaw, Treaty of.** An agreement between the Polish government and the government of the Ukrainian National Republic (UNR), signed in Warsaw on 21 April 1920. The pact centered on the promise of Polish military assistance to the UNR in exchange for a recognition of Poland's claims to the western Ukrainian lands. It was signed under desperate circumstances by the Directory of the UNR, and caused a major falling out between Galician Ukrainians and the UNR.

Despite a formal merger of the UNR and the Western Ukrainian People's Republic (ZUNR) in January 1919, the two republics held differing opinions regarding Poland. For the leaders of the ZUNR Poland remained the foremost enemy; the leaders of the UNR perceived their main threat to be Russia. In January 1919 the first mission of the UNR (V. Prokopovych) arrived in Warsaw to test the possibility of an anti-Bolshevik agreement. The issue became particularly pertinent after the Red Army seized Kiev on 5 February 1919; UNR troops were driven back to Volhynia and Podilia, and the *Ukrainian-Soviet War increased in intensity.

On 25 May B. Kurdynovsky, a representative of the Directory, and Prime Minister I. Paderewski signed an agreement which foresaw the recognition by Poland of an independent Ukraine; military assistance was promised by Poland in exchange for a renunciation by the UNR of all claims to eastern Galicia and a portion of Volhynia west of the Styr River. As a result of the intensification of combat in eastern Galicia in conjunction with the *Ukrainian-Polish War the convention was never realized.

Subsequent negotiations with Poland were tempered by the UNR's changing military fortunes and its relations with the ZUNR and the Ukrainian Galician Army (UHA). On 7 June 1919 a delegation of the Polish Supreme Command and a military delegation of the UNR commenced negotiations in Lviv concerning an armistice. The command of the UHA did not feel obliged to observe those negotiations, and at the same time it launched a counterattack on the Galician front (the *Chortkiv offensive). The campaign faltered, however, and by July the Poles had forced the UHA and the ZUNR out of Galicia. The UHA forces then joined the UNR Army in a successful campaign that had taken Kiev by the end of August. The UNR's military fortunes then declined drastically. On 1 September an armistice was signed between the Polish command and that of the UNR. On 21 October the UNR concluded a secret agreement with the Poles which made it possible for its troops to cross into the territory occupied by Polish divisions in order to regroup and receive additional arms. By late 1919 the Ukrainian forces were no longer capable of continuing the war. On 5 December Petliura left for Warsaw, where he hoped to obtain support for a renewed campaign from Poland and possibly, through Poland, the Entente powers. He met in the Polish capital with a UNR diplomatic mission led by the UNR's deputy prime minister, A. Livytsky, which had arrived earlier in October.

The Livytsky mission had already issued a declaration, on 2 December, regarding the principles of a political and military convention with Poland, which noted, among other items, the willingness of the UNR to renounce its claims to the territories west of the Zbruch River. The declaration, which foreshadowed the agreement of 21 April 1920, met with sharp protests from the Galician members of the mission. It was also criticized harshly by a gathering of Galician Ukrainian politicians in Vienna on 9 December 1919.

The next stage of the Polish-Ukrainian talks began in January 1920. The Poles exerted great pressure on the Ukrainian delegation and played on the military and political weakness of the UNR government. They also made it difficult for the ministers of the UNR government to maintain contacts with members of the Directory who were in Poland. On 22 January Petliura and Livytsky presented J. Piłsudski with a list of complaints concerning the conduct of the Polish authorities.

The final edition of the text of the treaty was drafted in April. The main points of the agreement, signed by Livytsky and J. Dąbski, resolved that (1) Poland would recognize the independence of Ukraine and the Directory of the UNR under Petliura's leadership as its legitimate government; (2) the Polish-Ukrainian frontier would run along the Zbruch River, following the former Austrian-Russian frontier, across the Kremianets Mountains, along the eastern boundary of Rivne county, and then along the Prypiat River; (3) both governments would not enter into any conventions with third parties contrary to the treaty; (4) the Polish and Ukrainian minorities in both countries would be granted reciprocal national and cultural rights; and (5) the land question in Ukraine would be resolved by a constituent assembly, and in the interim the interests of Polish landowners in Ukraine would be dealt with through separate accords. The treaty also noted that a military convention was to follow, and that it was to be regarded as an integral part of the agreement. On 24 April a

military convention concluded that the Ukrainian and Polish armies would act as allies, but under Polish command; the Ukrainian side would organize its own administration in the liberated territories; Poland would equip three Ukrainian divisions, for which it would later be reimbursed; Ukraine would supply food for the armies operating in Ukraine; and Polish evacuation from Ukraine would begin at the request of one of the sides of the treaty.

The Treaty of Warsaw brought protests from the Galician leaders as well as from leading Ukrainian political authorities (M. Hrushevsky, V. Vynnychenko). The UNR government of I. Mazepa resigned in protest, and was replaced by the cabinet of V. Prokopovych in May 1920. Four days after the signing of the Treaty of Warsaw (25 April 1920) Polish and Ukrainian troops (two divisions) began marching on Kiev.

BIBLIOGRAPHY

Shelukhyn, S. *Varshavs'kyi dohovir mizh poliakamy i S. Petliuroiu 21 kvitnia 1920 roku* (Prague 1926; repr, London 1966)

Knysh, Z. *Varshavs'kyi dohovir v svitli natsionalistychnoï krytyky* (Winnipeg 1950)

Hunczak, T. *Ukraine and Poland in Documents, 1918–1922*, 2 vols (New York 1983)

A. Chojnowski

Constantine Warvariv at the 17th session of the UNESCO General Assembly

**Warvariv, Constantine** [Varvariv, Konstantyn], b 4 November 1924 in Povorske, Kovel county, Volhynia gubernia, d 6 April 1982 in Washington, DC. American diplomat. A postwar refugee, after graduating in international law from Heidelberg University (1949) he emigrated to the United States and continued his studies in public law at Columbia University (MA, 1952). He joined the State Department in 1961 and was promoted to the offices of deputy director for UNESCO affairs (1971), deputy representative to UNESCO (1974), and director of transportation and communication at the State Department's Bureau of International Organizations. In 1977 a KGB attempt to blackmail him into working for Soviet intelligence was unsuccessful and provoked official American protest. Warvariv pursued an interest in the diplomatic history of Ukrainian-American relations and wrote a number of articles in this field.

**Washington, DC.** The capital (1990 pop 606,900; 1980 metropolitan pop 3,060,000) of the United States. In 1988

The unveiling of the Taras Shevchenko monument in Washington by President Dwight Eisenhower in June 1964

there were approx 4,900 Ukrainians living in the area. The Ukrainian community in Washington dates from the late 1930s, when federal jobs began to attract Ukrainians from other states. By 1940 there were over 30 families in the district, and the American-Ukrainian Society was formed. In 1949 the Alliance of Ukrainians in Washington assumed leadership in local Ukrainian cultural and social life. The community grew rapidly through the 1950s and 1960s as new immigrants and American-born Ukrainians assumed professional positions at the Ukrainian section of the Voice of America, the Library of Congress, and various federal agencies. A monument to T. Shevchenko was unveiled in 1964. The Ukrainian Catholic parish of the Holy Family and the Ukrainian Orthodox Church of St Andrew were organized, and St Josaphat's Ukrainian Catholic Seminary was transferred to Washington from Philadelphia. In the 1970s a branch of the Ukrainian Catholic University was founded, and in the 1980s the Ukrainian National Shrine of the Holy Family was built. The \*Washington Group, a local association of Ukrainian-American professional and business people, was inaugurated in 1984. As the capital of the country, Washington has been the scene of Ukrainian-American lobbying efforts since the formation of the first representative Ukrainian associations in 1915 and 1916. In 1977 these efforts were supplemented by the establishment of an information bureau in the capital by the Ukrainian Congress Committee of America.

**Washington Group, The** (TWG). The group, established as the Association of Ukrainian-American Professionals in 1984 in Washington, DC, provides a forum for activities that preserve and promote Ukrainian heritage. With its headquarters in the capital of the United States, TWG focuses much of its activity on informing the public and the government about issues of concern to Ukrainian Americans. It publishes a monthly newsletter, submits letters and articles to the media, sponsors the Distinguished Speaker Series, and holds annual leadership conferences. The membership of TWG grew from 54 in 1984 to nearly 400 in 1991. Its president is Lydia Chopivsky-Benson.

**Wasik, Walter** [Vasik], b 1 May 1930 in Sambir, Galicia. Photographer and film producer. After emigrating to

Canada in 1948, Wasik studied at the Brooks Institute of Photography in California (1955–6) and at the Institute of Photography in New York (1961–3). He organized the Ukrainian Film Club of Oshawa, Ontario, and the Canukr film production company. He made several short documentary films and produced three full-length feature films, *Zhorstoki svitanky* (Cruel Dawns, 1965), *Nikoly ne zabudu* (I Shall Never Forget, 1969), and *Marichka* (1974).

**Wasilewska, Wanda** [Vasylevs'ka, Vanda], b 21 January 1905 in Cracow, d 29 July 1964 in Kiev. Polish communist writer; daughter of L. Wasilewski and wife of O. \*Korniichuk. She moved to Kiev from Lviv in 1939. In 1944 she was deputy leader of the Committee for the National Liberation of Poland, and later she was a deputy to the Supreme Soviet of the USSR. Her first published work appeared in 1921. Together with Korniichuk she wrote the libretto to K. Dankevych's opera *Bohdan Khmelnytskyi*. She received the Stalin Prize in 1943. Most of her novels and stories have been translated into Ukrainian, and an edition in eight volumes was published in 1966–8.

Leon Wasilewski

**Wasilewski, Leon,** b 24 August 1870 in St Petersburg, d 10 December 1936 in Warsaw. Polish political activist and journalist. A prominent figure in the Polish Socialist party and editor of its official organ *Przedświt*, he studied, among other places, at the University of Lviv. There he developed a firsthand understanding of Ukrainian concerns. He published articles on Ukrainian issues in the Polish, Russian, and Ukrainian press. He advocated the idea that co-operation was necessary among the peoples oppressed by the tsarist regime. After the establishment of a Polish state Wasilewski was called upon on numerous occasions to deal with Ukrainian and Soviet issues. In 1919 he led negotiations with V. \*Prokopovych in Warsaw and H. Sydorenko in Paris. He participated in the preparation of the Peace Treaty of Riga (1921). During the years 1921–3 he was leader of the Polish delegation to settle Polish-Soviet and Polish-Rumanian border disputes. In 1926 he headed a government committee on the eastern provinces and national minorities, which argued against the policy of national assimilation. Wasilewski even proposed to divide eastern Galicia into Polish and Ukrainian regions. He maintained connections with Ukrainians through the \*Promethean movement (as a member of the Promethean Club in Warsaw), the Polish-Ukrainian Society, and the *Biuletyn Polsko-Ukraiński*. His writings include several works on nationality issues in Eastern Europe, particularly Ukrainian affairs, among them *Sovremennaia Galitsiia* (Contemporary Galicia, 1898), *Ukraina i sprawa ukraińska* (Ukraine and the Ukrainian Question, 1919), *Ukraińska sprawa narodowa w jej rozwoju historycznym* (The Ukrainian National Question in Its Historical Development, 1925), and *Sprawa ukraińska jako zagadnienie międzynarodowe* (The Ukrainian Question as an International Issue, 1934).

A. Zięba

**Wasteland.** See Land use.

**Water management.** An important branch of the national economy, concerned with the rational use of *water resources and the prevention of damage caused by water. Water management developed in Ukraine only in the 20th century, although some branches of it can be dated back to earlier times. Hydraulic structures were built in the ancient cities of the Black Sea coast and later in Kiev and other cities of Kievan Rus'. Water power began to be used in flour mills and sawmills in the 13th century. In the 15th century, ponds were dug and rivers dammed to provide more waterpower. In the late 18th century a number of canals were constructed to connect the Dnieper River with the rivers of the Baltic Basin. The first hydroelectric power station, the Tyvriv Station, was built in 1912 on the Boh River.

In the forest and forest-steppe belts subterranean waters were the main source of supply. In the south, rivers also served that purpose, and water was stored in artificial ponds and dams before the streams ran dry. Wells and water-carriers were used to supply water. Modern pumping stations began to be built only in the 1870s, in Kiev, Lviv, Odessa, Kharkiv, and Chernihiv. By 1915 only 33 cities in Russian-ruled Ukraine had such stations. Sewerage and water purification were limited. In that respect Galicia was ahead of all other regions. *Irrigation was not widely used, except in some areas near southern Ukraine's larger cities. Drainage of land began in the 19th century.

Land development and deforestation disrupted the country's water system in the 19th century. The need for water management became apparent. Erosion spread and flooding became common as rivers became shallower and the water flow irregular. In the south the land area requiring irrigation grew larger and larger. At the end of the 19th century, research in water management and systematic irrigation and drainage work were started in Ukraine. Major contributions in the field were made by V. Dokuchaev, Yu. Vysotsky, P. Kostyshev, B. Williams, and M. Maksymovych. Little hydrotechnical work was accomplished before 1914, however. Plans to flood the Dnieper Rapids, build hydroelectric stations, and construct navigable canals to connect the Dnieper and Desna rivers, the Donets River, and the Donets Basin were interrupted by the First World War. By 1917 only 17,400 ha in Ukraine had been irrigated, and only 454,000 ha had been drained.

In 1918–19, during the period of Ukrainian independence, water-management plans were drafted. A department of water management was established in the Ministry of Transport and was headed by I. Shovheniv. The Hydrology Commission of the Ukrainian Academy of Sciences did research that was relevant to water management.

An ambitious project for using the water resources of the Dnieper Basin for transportation, irrigation, and power generation was worked out in the 1920s. Called the Great Dnieper Project (see *Dnieper River), it was connected with a large-scale electrification plan prepared by *GOELRO. Its first stage was completed with the construction of the *Dnieper Hydroelectric Station (1927–32) and involved the flooding of the Dnieper Rapids. The plans for *land melioration were not implemented, and the excessive deforestation and destruction of small ponds resulted in water shortages.

During the Second World War water installations were almost totally destroyed. In the 1950s work on the Great Dnieper Project was resumed. Hydroelectric power stations were built at Kakhivka (1950–6), Kremenchuk (1954–60), Dniprodzerzhynske (1956–64), Kiev (1960–8), and Kaniv (1963–75), and the *Dnieper Cascade of Hydroelectric Stations was thereby completed. The six reservoirs thus created hold 43.8 billion cu m of water. At the same time a number of irrigation canals were built in southern Ukraine. By 1965, 540,000 ha had been irrigated. With further intensive development, by 1985 the republic had 2.4 million ha under irrigation. Considerable work was also done on the reclamation of marshes and swampland, and by 1985, 2.9 million ha had been reclaimed (see *Drainage of land). Flood-control projects, especially in the mountainous areas of western Ukraine, were co-ordinated with power generation, water-supply, and land reclamation projects. Ukraine has 871 reservoirs, holding 51.7 billion cu m of water, and over 24,000 ponds.

Water shortage is a serious problem in Ukraine. In the past Soviet authorities regarded environmental protection as an unnecessary burden on the economy. Until the last two decades Soviet water management was based on the assumption that some natural resources were virtually inexhaustible. The planners of vast hydroelectric energy programs gave little consideration to unavoidable water loss. It was only in the 1970s that alarm about limited water resources was raised. Water management in Ukraine is complicated by the number of poorly co-ordinated agencies in the field and the lack of suitable legislation. In the debate on water management the powerful agricultural and industrial ministries, which are the main water users, have generally rejected the calls for conservation and pollution control.

BIBLIOGRAPHY
Tolmazin, D. *Degradation of Ukrainian Water Resources* (Edmonton, forthcoming)

B. Krawchenko

**Water pollution.** See Pollution.

**Water polo** (*vodnyi miach, vodne polo*). In Ukraine, water polo became popular in the early 1920s, in the southern cities of Odessa and Mykolaiv and in the Crimea. In the 1930s it spread to Kiev, Kharkiv, and Dnipropetrovske, and intercity competitions were held. In 1948 the USSR Water Polo Federation was founded and joined the International Federation of Amateur Swimming. Several Ukrainians, such as O. Zakharov and V. Rozhkov, played on the USSR teams that captured the gold medal at the 1972 and 1980 Olympics, the world championship in 1975, and the European championship in 1966 and 1970.

**Water reservoir** (*vodoskhovyshche, vodoimyshche*). Artificial water reservoirs are created to control flooding, to regulate water flow for hydroelectric generation and other uses, to store drinking water, and for *irrigation. In Ukraine the largest reservoirs, created during the construction of the *Dnieper Cascade of Hydroelectric Stations, are found along the Dnieper River. The Dnieper Reservoir (Dniprovske vodoskhovyshche), created in 1932 during the construction of the *Dnieper Hydroelectric Station, covers an area of 410 sq km. The other reservoirs on the river are the *Kaniv, *Kakhivka, *Kiev, *Kremenchuk, and *Dniprodzerzhynske reservoirs. Smaller reservoirs along the Donets and the Dniester rivers mostly store drinking water. In recent years some small reservoirs have been created for fish farming. In 1988 there were 1,057 reservoirs in Ukraine containing an estimated 55 billion cu m of water.

**Water resources.** The combined amount of surface water (in seas, *rivers, *lakes, *water reservoirs, and canals) and groundwater (see *Underground water). Whereas surface water is renewed rapidly through hydrologic cycling, groundwater is renewed slowly, the rate depending on hydrological conditions. The main source for both is precipitation, of which most evaporates or infiltrates the ground, leaving in Ukraine about 16 percent as runoff.

Major water reservoirs in Ukraine

| Name of reservoir | River | Surface area (sq km) | Capacity (cu km) in use | full |
|---|---|---|---|---|
| Kiev | Dnieper | 922 | 1.17 | 3.78 |
| Kaniv | Dnieper | 582 | 0.28 | 2.48 |
| Kremenchuk | Dnieper | 2,252 | 9.10 | 13.50 |
| Dniprodzerzhynske | Dnieper | 567 | 0.27 | 2.45 |
| Dniprovske | Dnieper | 410 | 0.84 | 3.30 |
| Kakhivka | Dnieper | 2,155 | 6.80 | 18.20 |
| Dniester | Dniester | 142 | 2.00 | 3.00 |
| Pechenihy | Donets | 86.2 | 0.34 | 0.38 |
| Chervonyi Oskil | Oskil | 122.6 | 0.44 | 0.47 |
| Ladyzhyn | Boh | 20.8 | 0.13 | 0.15 |
| Starobesheve | Kalmius | 9 | 0.03 | 0.04 |
| Karachunivske | Inhulets | 44.8 | 0.29 | 0.31 |
| Symferopil | Salhyr | 3.23 | 0.03 | 0.04 |

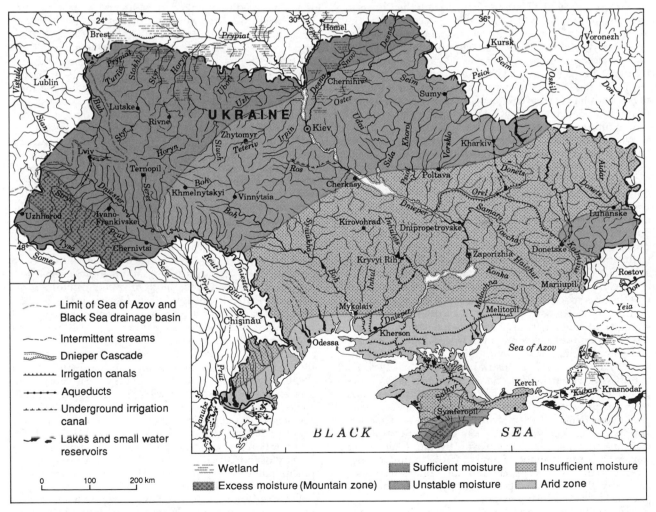

WATER RESOURCES

The water resources of Ukraine are scanty. On a per capita basis in Ukraine surface runoff constitutes only 1,000 cu m/person/year, one of the lowest rates among the republics of the former USSR. That meager water supply supports 51.7 million people (1989 census).

Historically, territorial patterns of industrial and agricultural demand in Ukraine were never in close accord with the geographical distribution of surface water (see the map). The notable exceptions are in the mountainous areas, where precipitation exceeds evaporation by two to three times, and also in Subcarpathia, western Podilia, Volhynia, and Polisia, where precipitation generally exceeds evaporation. Many industrialized areas, such as the Donbas and the metropolitan areas of Kharkiv and Kryvyi Rih, have notoriously low water availability. The major agricultural areas located in the Black Sea Lowland and the Crimean Lowland are characterized by a semiarid climate with very low moisture supply during the vegetative period.

There are only three major rivers in Ukraine suitable for multipurpose river basin development: the Dnieper, with an average flow of 40–42 cu km/yr; the Dniester (only its upper and middle courses, as well as a small delta, for the rest of the river passes through the Moldova), discharging 7–8 cu km/yr into the Dniester Estuary; and the Donets (a tributary of the Don River), releasing 4–5 cu km/yr. The Boh River (approx 2–3 cu km/yr) has an intermittent flow and is used solely for local water supply. Only the Dniester, in its upper and middle courses, has a well-developed tributary drainage system. With the exception of the Inhulets River, the Dnieper (downstream of Kiev) and the Donets do not have stable tributary influx. Those rivers flow through semiarid lands, with a few small tributaries providing only meager seasonal inflow.

Water quantity and quality in the drainage system of Ukraine are experiencing increasing degradation. The degradation is only marginally related to the disparity in location between the availability of river water and the demand for it. The ongoing depletion and worsening water quality in the Ukrainian watercourses has been closely related to the political system instituted by the Soviet regime. The roots of present-day water resources mismanagement may be found in the accelerated industrialization and all-out collectivization policies that began at the end of the 1920s. The sweeping program for hydroelectric dam construction and river navigation initiated at that time had poor, if any, scientific and technical justification, and served mostly propaganda purposes. Numerous storage reservoirs with large evaporation surfaces (6 large reservoirs on the Dnieper, 1 on the Don, 1 on the Kuban, and 3 smaller ones on the Dniester), as well as flow diversions to the Donbas for industrial and municipal uses and to the Crimea for irrigation and water supply, severely depleted water reserves, and pollution sharply worsened their quality. Average water withdrawals from the Dnieper have reached 31–32 cu km/yr, and from the Dniester, approx 4–5 cu km/yr. The Donets has been completely used up, and its flow is controlled by interbasin water transfer from the Dnieper. Some of the withdrawn water returns to the rivers via point and nonpoint sources, carrying deadly contaminants, such as cyanides, ammonia, phenols, PCBs, and heavy metals.

Irreversible losses and the pollution of fresh water have become even more dramatic as a result of Soviet agricultural policies. Following collectivization and the manmade *famine (which resulted in the loss of 6 to 9 million lives), the most experienced farmers, who over the centuries had developed highly productive dry farming practices, disappeared. Facing an imminent crisis in farm production, the postwar leaders expanded irrigation agriculture to the point where it became (by 1975) the prime water user. A huge network of highly inefficient irrigation systems (160,000 km of unlined canals) was built in southern Ukraine. Now, more efficient closed conduits (41,000 km) are also in place. Although agricultural output was raised at the cost of high capitalization and water demand, the food supply could not satisfy the growing population because of mismanagement and alarming losses. Still, the environmental impact from large-scale irrigation has been disastrous. Rivers and aquifers have become polluted by fertilizers and organic wastes. Eutrophication, oxygen depletion, and mass fish kills have occurred nearly every summer. More energy and machinery are necessary for water purification if the resources are to be made suitable for drinking and irrigation.

At the same time decreased river flows have reduced the energy output from hydroelectric plants, and shoreline erosion has increased the siltation of the reservoirs, thereby impeding navigation. More and more water has to be withdrawn for purposes of washing out the salts brought to the soil surface by saline seeps from irrigation and for ameliorating deep salty aquifers. Some small rivers (the Kalmiius, the Inhulets, the Samara, the Oskil, and the Donets) have been turned into industrial sewers devoid of life. Many others have become silted up, and their watercourses have disappeared.

The estuaries have been most severely affected. The reduction or elimination of the annual spring floods, the intrusion of salt water from the sea, and pollution have had deleterious effects on the reproduction of anadromous and semianadromous fish. Practically no commercial fishery now exists in the Dnieper and the Dniester estuaries.

Since 1973 the formerly healthy coastal waters of the northwestern Black Sea have been affected by near-bottom hypoxia (or even anoxia), which has turned richly populated bottom areas into fetid deserts each summer. Since 1987 the famous Odessa beaches have been closed to all recreational activities except sailing. In 1980, fish losses were estimated at approx 46 to 51 million rubles a year. The only relatively healthy habitat remains in the Danube Delta. The effects of river basin development have spread far into the Black Sea and have impeded fish migration from the Mediterranean.

Past and present freshwater management practices have affected huge areas and have caused disruptions in potable water supply, acute and chronic toxic contamination, and even outbreaks of epidemics (notably cholera in 1970–1). Some regions, such as the Donbas and the Kherson Steppe, have been brought to the brink of water shortages that prevent the normal functioning of society. Even severe rationing of water cannot ensure the uninterrupted activity of industries and municipalities. Above-average precipitation in the years 1986–8 brought only temporary relief from water shortages.

Ukraine is now recognized as an area with a water resources crisis. It suffers from a legacy of indiscriminate exploitation, driven by ambitious plans to increase output by transforming the environment. In recent years water deficiency in Ukraine has been meliorated by an above-average atmospheric moisture supply, but dry years are bound to bring about serious hardships. The demand for water is continuing to rise, pollution from point and non-point sources is increasing, treatment facilities are scarce and outdated, effective environmental legislation and regulatory agencies are lacking, and prices that would reflect the scarcity of resources have not yet been introduced. Unless water resource management is improved quickly, Ukraine's water resource situation will likely worsen. (See also *Rivers, *Underground water, and *Wetlands.)

BIBLIOGRAPHY
*Kompleksne vykorystannia vodnykh resursiv Ukraïny* (Kiev 1959)
*Ispol'zovanie i okhrana vodnykh resursov* (Kiev 1979)
Levkovskii, S. *Vodnye resursy Ukrainy* (Kiev 1979)
Tolmazin, D. 'Rozbazariuvannia ta vysnazhennia vodnoho bahatstva Ukraïny,' *Suchasnist'*, 1986, no. 2
*Priroda Ukrainskoi SSR: Moria i vnutrennye vody* (Kiev 1987)
D. Tolmazin

**Water spangle** (*Salvinia*; Ukrainian: *salviniia*). Tiny aquatic ferns in the family Salviniaceae, also known as gloating moss. They have a whorl of three leaves, two of them round and emergent and the third submerged and finely divided, functioning as a root. There are 10 species of *Salvinia* worldwide; only *S. natans* (Ukrainian: *salviniia plavaiucha*) is found in Ukraine, where it grows in slowly moving rivers and lakes. It is a rare plant, listed as an endangered species in Ukraine.

**Water sports.** See Rowing and canoeing, Swimming, Water polo, and Yachting.

**Water transportation.** See River transportation and Sea transportation.

**Watermelon** (*Citrullus*; Ukrainian: *kavun*). A sweet fruit of the gourd family Cucurbitaceae. The plant's vines grow along the ground, with branched tendrils, deeply cut leaves, and yellow flowers. The sweet, juicy flesh of the fruit may be white, reddish, or yellow. Watermelons range in weight from 1 or 2 kg to 20 kg or more. The fruit consists of up to 88 percent water and is thirst-quenching; it also contains much sugar (from 5 to 13 percent) and some vitamin A and C. Of the three known species, table watermelon (*C. vulgaris* or *C. lanatus*) and *C. colocynthoides* (used for feed) grow in Ukraine, primarily in Zaporizhia, Kherson, Dnipropetrovske, and Odessa oblasts.

Several Ukrainian varieties have been developed. They are very popular among Ukrainians and are eaten fresh as a dessert or even as a main course, pickled, candied, or boiled to make juice. (See also *Melon.)

**Wawrykow, Mary** [Vavrykiv] (née Zakus), b 1912 in Wakaw, Saskatchewan, d 15 April 1977 in Winnipeg. Ukrainian-Canadian community leader and judge. Wawrykow completed her education at the University of Manitoba (L LB, 1934) and worked as a lawyer until her appointment as a family court judge in Winnipeg in 1968. She was prominent in Ukrainian Catholic activities and in the women's sections of the Ukrainian Canadian Committee (now Congress). She was appointed Queen's Counsel in 1965.

**Waxwing** (*Bombycilla*; Ukrainian: *omeliukh, svyrystel*). An elegant-looking, crested songbird of the family Bombycillidae, 20 cm long. The Bohemian waxwing (*B. garrulus*), which winters in Ukrainian territory, is gray-brown with yellow, red, and white markings.

**Weatherfish** (*Misgurnus fossilis*; Ukrainian: *viun*). An elongated, scaly, whiskered Old World fish of the carp family Cobitidae, found in almost all Ukrainian fresh waters, especially in small stationary reservoirs. Also known as loach, weatherfish are not numerous and hence are of little commercial value, but they are widely used in laboratories for gonadotropic research.

**Weaving** (*tkatstvo*). Weaving has been practiced in Ukraine for many centuries. Using flax, hemp, or woolen thread, weavers have produced various articles of folk *dress, towels, *kilims, blankets, tablecloths, sheets, and covers. The colors, ornamentation, and even the techniques of weaving varied from region to region. By the 14th century weaving had developed into a cottage industry. Weavers' guilds modeled on Western European examples were founded in Sambir (1376), Lviv, and elsewhere in Galicia. They tried to improve weaving techniques and the quality of the products. Later, artistic textiles and kilims were manufactured by small enterprises established by magnates in Brody (1641), Lviv, Nemyriv, Zalishchyky, Korsun, Korets, Kiev, and Horokhiv. In 17th-century Left-Bank Ukraine the Cossack *starshyna* established similar enterprises to make decorative furnishings on order for the nobility and churches, using imported silk and gold thread. Eventually such thread was manufactured in Ukraine. Weaving manufactories flourished from the mid-17th to the mid-19th century. Their owners sometimes imported weavers from Turkey, Armenia, and Persia. Thus Oriental designs became popular in Ukraine. In the 17th century Emmanuel of Corfu (Korfynsky) established a factory for luxurious silk and gilded textiles in Lviv. Many weavers were trained there, and they disseminated their craft throughout Ukraine. In the 18th century large decorative weaving factories sprang up in Kholm, Buchach, Brody, Sokal, Medzhybizh, and Stanyslaviv. From the 1650s on the development of weaving as a cottage *textile industry intensified in Ukraine. The town of *Krolevets became one of the largest centers of artistic folk weaving. Ukrainian textiles were popular abroad, where they were called 'Ruthenian textiles' by foreign merchants. Hetman K. Rozumovsky's factory in Baturyn manufactured a wide assortment of artistic textiles, including tapestries with floral designs for his palaces in Baturyn, Hlukhiv, and Kozelets and colorful wool cloth for the uniforms of his Cossack guard units. In the mid-19th century commercial weaving began declining. To reverse the trend and to improve the technology and the artistic level of weaving, various zemstvos created weaving schools (eg, in Dihtiari and Shylovychi, in Chernihiv gubernia) and weaving departments in technical-industrial schools. In late-19th-century Austrian-ruled Galicia, renewed interest in folk-weaving techniques and designs prompted the opening of weaving schools and kilim-weaving shops in villages such as Vikno, Kosiv, and Hlyniany. To promote the merits of Galician folk weaving, exhibits of their wares were included in industrial and agricultural expositions. There they won awards and attained a reputation as far abroad as North America.

In early Soviet Ukraine efforts were made to revive handicraft and commercial artistic weaving. The School of Ukrainian Folk Masters was set up in Kiev in 1920 and then reorganized into the Kiev State School of Applied Art. It gathered together many noted folk artisans, who passed on their skills and knowledge to their students. Since the 1930s the main centers of artistic weaving in Soviet Ukraine have been *Bohuslav and Pereiaslav-Khmelnytskyi in Kiev oblast, Krolevets in Sumy oblast, *Dihtiari in Chernihiv oblast, and Reshetylivka and Velyki Sorochyntsi in Poltava oblast. After the Second World War weaving artels were organized in those centers and in Galicia (particularly Lviv, Kosiv, and Yavoriv), Bukovyna, and Transcarpathia, where artistic commercial and domestic weaving has continued developing. Weavers are trained at tekhnikums of folk handicrafts; designers are educated at schools of applied art in Lviv, Vyzhnytsia, and Krolevets or at departments of artistic textiles at institutes of decorative and applied art in Kiev, Kharkiv, and Lviv. Mass-produced woven ornamental articles are made at the Kherson, Donetske, and Ternopil cotton-manufacturing complexes, the Kiev, Darnytsia, and Lutske silk-manufacturing complexes, and the Kyianka Kerchief Factory in Kiev. (See also *Kilim weaving and *Textile industry.)

BIBLIOGRAPHY
Sichyns'kyi, V. *Narysy istoriï ukraïns'koï promyslovosty* (Lviv 1937)
Kolos, S.; Khurhin, M. *Dekoratyvni tkanyny* (Kiev 1949)
Manucharova, N. (ed). *Ukraïns'ke narodne mystetstvo*, vol 1, *Tkanyny ta vyshyvky* (Kiev 1960)
Zhohol', L. *Tkanyny v inter'ieri* (Kiev 1968)
Zapasko, Ia. (ed). *Narysy z istoriï ukraïns'koho dekoratyvnoho prykladnoho mystetstva* (Lviv 1969)
Sydorovych, S. *Khudozhnia tkanyna zakhidnykh oblastei URSR* (Kiev 1979)
Zhuk, A. *Suchasni ukraïns'ki khudozhni tkanyny* (Kiev 1985)
Bushyna, T. *Dekoratyvno-prykladne mystetstvo Radians'koï Bukovyny: Naukovo-populiarnyi narys* (Kiev 1986)
Bilash, R.; Wilberg, B. (eds). *Tkanyna: An Exhibit of Ukrainian Weaving* (Edmonton 1988)
Nykorak, O. *Suchasni khudozhni tkanyny Ukraïns'kykh Karpat* (Kiev 1988)

V. Hodys

**Weber, Friedrich Christian,** b and d ? Envoy from Brunswick-Hannover to the Russian Empire in 1714–20. His reminiscences, which provide a valuable source of information about Ukraine in the period shortly after Hetman I. Mazepa, were published in French (*Memoirs*, 1720) and German (*Das veränderte Russland*, 1721).

**Wedding.** The marriage ceremony with its accompanying festivities. In Ukraine the traditional wedding was a well-planned ritual drama, in which the leading roles were played by the bride and bridegroom, called princess and prince, and the other clearly defined roles (matchmaker, groomsman, bridesmaids) by the couple's parents, relatives, and friends. The wedding combined the basic forms of folk art – the spoken word, song, dance, music, and visual art – into a harmonious whole. It was reminiscent of an ancient theatrical drama with chorus, whose spectators were also actors. The rituals date back to pre-Christian times (traces of *matriarchy, the abduction of

the bride) and were influenced extensively by medieval practices (ransoming the bride, simulating a military campaign, the fighting between two camps, addressing the guests as princes and boyars, and the church ceremony). The ceremony included traces of ancient customs, which had lost their original, mainly magical, significance and had become mere play. Gradually the church ceremony assumed the central role in the wedding.

Amvrosii Zhdakha: *Ukrainian Wedding: Greeting of the Bride* (watercolor, 1890s)

The traditional Ukrainian wedding usually took place in the early spring or the autumn and lasted several days. It was divided into many acts or episodes: (1) the matchmaking (*svatannia*) – discussions about the marriage between the bridegroom's representatives (*starosty* or *svaty*) and the bride's parents or relatives; (2) the inspection (*ohliadyny, obzoryny, rozhliadyny*) – a visit by the bride's relatives to the bridegrooms's house for the purpose of assessing his wealth; (3) the betrothal (*zaruchyny, rukovyny, khustky*) – the marriage agreement between the young couple, symbolized by the joining of hands; (4) the branch (*hiltse viltse*) – a ceremonious dressing of a green tree with flowers, ribbons, and ears of wheat; (5) the wreaths (*vinky*) – a ritual making of wreaths using periwinkle, the symbol of virginity; (6) the invitation (*zaproshuvannia*) of guests to the wedding; (7) the seating (*posad*) of the betrothed couple in the place of honor at the table; (8) the unbraiding (*rozpleteny*) – the ritual combing of the bride; (9) the wedding bread (*korovai*) – the baking and decorating of the ritual bread from flour donated by all the wedding participants; (10) the blessing (*blahoslovlennia*) of the couple by the bride's parents before the couple's departure for church; (11) the marriage ceremony (*vinchannia*) in church, usually on a Sunday; (12) the return (*povernennia*) to the bride's house; (13) the fetching (*poïzd*) – the arrival of the bridegroom's relatives at the bride's house to claim her, and their cold reception; (14) the introduction (*predstavliuvannia*) – an attempt by the bride's relatives to substitute other girls for the bride; (15) the reconciliation (*pomyrennia*) – the presentation of gifts to the bride's parents and the establishment of peace between the two families; (16) the division (*rozpodil*) – the cutting and distributing of the wedding bread among the wedding guests; (17) the departure (*vid'ïzd*) of the bride with her belongings to her husband's house; (18) the interception

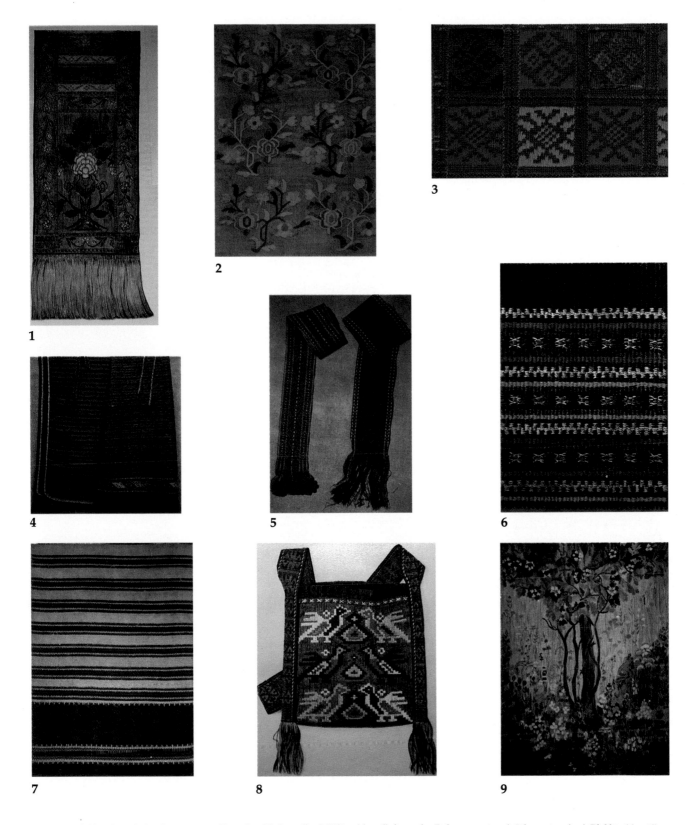

WEAVING  1) Slutsk sash (18th century, silk and gold thread). 2) Kilim (detail) from the Poltava region (18th century). 3) *Plakhta* (detail) from the Sumy region (19th century). 4) *Zapasky* from Sheshory (Hutsul region, 1920s). 5) Hand-woven men's wool sashes (early 20th century) from Krasnostavtsi (Hutsul region) and Ispas (Bukovyna). 6) *Rushnyk* from eastern Podilia (early 20th century). 7) *Pavolochka* (detail) from Kopachyntsi (Hutsul region, early 20th century, linen and wool). 8) *Taistra* (Chernivtsi region, 20th century). 9) L. Zhohol: *There Will Be Life* (wool hand weaving, 1987).

(*pereima*) – the capture of the bride by a group of young people, and her ransoming; (19) the reception (*zustrich*) – the welcoming of the bride in her new home by her mother-in-law; (20) the chamber (*komora*) – the defloration of the bride in the bridal chamber; (21) the invitation (*perezva*) – the public announcement of the bride's virginity and invitation of her parents to the bridegroom's house; (22) the supplements (*prydatky*) – a visit of the bride's relatives to the bridegroom's house, marking the climax of the wedding; (23) the toasting (*perepii*) – the postwedding feast at the house of the bride's parents; and (24) the gypsying (*tsyhanshchyna*) – the collecting of means for further merrymaking by the wedding guests throughout the village. This wedding 'scenario' became well established in the 16th to 19th centuries and had many regional variations. Each act in the drama involved magic ceremonies, wedding songs, and rituals.

A wedding in Mykolaiv oblast in 1986

After the revolution the Soviet regime treated the traditional wedding, with its church ceremony, as a bourgeois vestige and launched a campaign against it. The concept of 'free love,' which was widely promoted in its place, proved to contribute to the dissolution of family life; hence, in the early 1920s marriage registration was made compulsory, and to give the event some solemnity, people were urged to combine the registration with a 'red wedding.' This ceremony, it was hoped, would supplant the traditional wedding. In essence the 'red wedding' was another public meeting, featuring a presidium, speeches, and a march with red banners and slogans. The ceremony did not catch on and by the late 1920s had been forgotten. In the countryside young people continued to hold the traditional wedding, and members of the intelligentsia and most urban residents simply registered marriages without any ceremony.

Forced collectivization, man-made famine, and terror, followed by the Second World War, led to the disappearance of the traditional wedding in Soviet Ukraine. It was revived after the war and provoked a reaction from the regime. The authorities encouraged 'red weddings,' 'Komsomol weddings,' 'collective-farm weddings,' and other forms of wedding, incorporating in them certain old traditions that appeared 'progressive.' But these new weddings failed to catch on. To divert young people from church marriages, the Communist party and the government decided to build 'marriage palaces,' later renamed

'happiness palaces.' The first marriage palace was opened in Kiev in July 1960, and by 1963 there were a hundred of them in Ukraine. Five thousand clubs and palaces of culture, also, were adapted for marriage registration ceremonies. Folklore specialists at the Academy of Sciences, the universities, and other institutions were instructed to design a 'contemporary Soviet wedding,' composers, to write new wedding songs, and poets, to write special wedding verses.

On 15 July 1972 the Presidium of the Supreme Soviet of the Ukrainian SSR adopted a law on the official marriage ritual: the marriage registration ceremony would be conducted by the 'ritual matchmaker' – a member of the Soviet of Workers' Deputies – assisted by the staff of the civil registry office. The law specified how the officials were to be dressed, how the hall was to be decorated, and what the speeches were to contain. Couples who agreed to a Komsomol wedding were rewarded handsomely: often the entire cost of the wedding was covered by the couple's collective farm, plant, or institution, and the couple was given access to a special store stocked with generally unavailable goods. Despite these incentives the imposed wedding ceremony was not accepted widely in Ukraine. The 1986–8 campaign for an 'alcohol-free wedding' was also a failure. Most young people, especially in the villages, continue to prefer the traditional wedding with a church ceremony. A good number of those who went through a Komsomol wedding also married secretly in a church. Many of the traditional wedding rituals are no longer practiced, and those that have been preserved (the blessing, the wedding bread) are considerably simplified.

In Ukrainian communities abroad the traditional wedding has retained some archaic elements; in the 1950s, for example, Ukrainians in Rumania still practiced the ritual of abduction of the future bride. Guests at a Ruthenian wedding in Yugoslavia, where weddings of 500 guests are not uncommon, are still decorated with *rushnyky* (see *Rushnyk*). Ukrainians in Canada and the United States hold on to some elements of the traditional wedding as an expression of national identity.

The earliest references to Ukrainian folk weddings can be found in medieval chronicles, church sermons, and religious works of the 11th to 15th centuries. There are descriptions of weddings from the 16th to 18th centuries, written mostly by foreign visitors to Ukraine (J. Lasitzki, G. de Beauplan, G. Kalinovsky). In the 19th and early 20th century, detailed descriptions of weddings in various regions of Ukraine were published. F. Vovk's historical study of the Ukrainian wedding, however, remains unsurpassed. Among recent books published in Ukraine on the traditional and contemporary wedding M. Shubravska's work is noteworthy. The traditional wedding is described frequently in Ukrainian literature – in H. Kvitka-Osnovianenko's *Marusia* and *Svatannia na Honcharivtsi* (Matchmaking at Honcharivka), for example; T. Shevchenko's *Nazar Stodolia* and *Naimychka* (The Hired Girl); Yu. Fedkovych's *Liuba-zhuba* (Love Is Fatal), *Sertse ne povchyty* (You Can't Teach the Heart), and *Beztalanne zakokhannia* (Hapless Love); I. Franko's *Velykyi shum* (The Great Noise) and *Ukradene shchastia* (Stolen Happiness); M. Kotsiubynsky's *Tini zabutykh predkiv* (Shadows of Forgotten Ancestors); and in the works of Ukrainian Soviet writers, such as M. Stelmakh, L. Kostenko, and I. Chendei. It has been depicted since the 18th century by Ukrainian painters, such as K. Trutovsky, M. Pymonenko, I. Izha-kevych, A. Zhdakha, A. Bazylevych, V. Zadorozhny, T. Yablonska, H. Yakutovych, F. Humeniuk, and I. Marchuk, and by non-Ukrainian painters, such as M. Shibanov, V. Tropinin, I. Sokolov, and J. Brandt.

BIBLIOGRAPHY
Kalinovskii, G. *Opisanie svadebnykh ukrainskikh prostonarodnykh obriadov v Maloi Rossii i Slobodskoi ukrainskoi gubernii* (St Petersburg 1776)
Volkov, T. [Vovk, F.]. 'Rites et usages nuptiaux en Ukraine,' *L'Anthropologie*, 2–3 (1891, 1892); Ukrainian trans: 'Shliubnyi rytual ta obriady na Ukraïni,' in his *Studiï z ukraïns'koï etnohrafiï ta antropolohiï* (Prague 1928; repr, New York 1976)
Chubinskii, P. *Trudy Etnografichesko-statisticheskoi ekspeditsii v Zapadno-russkii krai*, vol 4 (St Petersburg 1877)
Grinchenko, B. *Etnograficheskie materialy, sobrannye v Chernigovskoi i sosednikh s nei guberniiakh*, 3 vols (Chernihiv 1895–9)
Iashchurzhinskii, Kh. 'Svad'ba malorusskaia, kak religiozno-bytovaia drama,' *KS*, 1896, no. 11
Hnatiuk, V. 'Ukraïns'ki vesil'ni obriady i zvychaï,' *Materiialy do ukraïns'koï etnolohiï*, 19–20 (Lviv 1919)
Bielichko, Iu.; V'iunyk, A. *Ukraïns'ke narodne vesillia v tvorakh ukraïns'koho, rosiis'koho ta pol's'koho obrazotvorchoho mystetstva XVIII–XX stolit'* (Kiev 1970)
Shubravs'ka, M. *Vesillia*, 2 vols (Kiev 1970)
Zdoroveha, N. *Narysy narodnoï vesil'noï obriadovosti na Ukraïni* (Kiev 1974)
Borysenko, V. *Nova vesil'na obriadovist' v suchasnomu seli* (Kiev 1979)
– *Vesil'ni zvychaï ta obriady na Ukraïni (Istoryko-etnohrafichne doslidzhennia)* (Kiev 1988)
                                                            M. Mushynka

**Wedding songs.** Ritual songs that accompany the different stages of a traditional *wedding. They form the largest subgroup of lyrical folk songs on family life. The earliest reference to wedding songs in the written sources dates back to 1096, and the first published samples of wedding songs appeared in 1820. Since then they have been included in virtually every anthology of Ukrainian folk songs. The AN URSR (now ANU) collection *Vesil'ni pisni* (Wedding Songs, 1982) contains 2,256 songs, 1,662 of them with the melody. No Slavic nation has a larger repertoire of wedding songs. Although all ritual songs have gradually lost their magical meaning, wedding songs retained such a meaning longer than other songs. They can be divided into four groups according to their role in the wedding: songs that are closely tied to only one event in the wedding, for example, the wedding bread, branch, or wreath rituals; songs that accompany several stages of the wedding; songs that may be sung during various parts of the wedding; and songs whose relation to the wedding has been forgotten. Songs of the first group are the oldest. Wedding songs can also be divided according to the various stages of the wedding. M. Shubravska divided them into 45 groups and some subgroups. In fact there is no wedding ritual without an accompanying song. The majority of wedding songs deal with family life, and many of them contain traces of the primeval matriarchal order. But there are also reminders of later epochs. The basic themes are the hardships awaiting the young couple, particularly the bride in her new home with the groom's parents; separation from one's beloved; the forced marriage to a repugnant man; the understanding mother; the cruel mother-in-law; and the tender feelings of the young cou-

ple. Many of the songs have melancholy melodies similar to those of carols and laments. Today wedding songs have disappeared almost completely from the wedding ceremonies. They are performed only on stage in a stylized and dramatized form by folk ensembles. Attempts to replace the traditional songs with 'contemporary' ones have been unsuccessful.

BIBLIOGRAPHY
Shubravs'ka, M.; Ivanyts'kyi, A. (comps). *Vesil'ni pisni u dvokh knyhakh* (Kiev 1982)
                                                            M. Mushynka

**Weevils.** See Seed beetles.

**Węgliński, Lew,** b and d ? Polish poet in 19th-century Galicia. In 1858 he published in the Latin alphabet a three-volume collection of poems written in Ukrainian, *Nowyi poezyi małoruskii* (New Little Russian Poems). In 1885 he published two poetry books in Cracow titled *Zvuky od nashykh sel i nyv* (Sounds from Our Villages and Fields) under the pseudonym Lirnyk Naddnistrianskyi and a collection of satirical stories, *Hirkyi smikh* (Bitter Laughter), under the pseudonym Kost Pravdoliubets.

Olympic champion Ihor Rybak

**Weight lifting** (*vazhka atletyka*). The first weight-lifting circle in Ukraine was founded in Kiev in 1895 by Ye. Harnych-Harnytsky. At the turn of the century the Kievan physicians V. Kramarenko and A. Anokhin did much to promote the sport in Russian-ruled Ukraine. The first competition in the Southwestern krai of the Russian Empire was held in 1908, and many Ukrainian athletes took part in the All-Russian Olympiads in Kiev (1913) and Riga (1914). World records in the snatch, clean and jerk, and press in various weight categories were set by the Ukrainians K. Pavlenko (1914), M. Urytsky (1914), F. Hrynenko (1914), and S. Tonkopei (1917).

In the early years of Soviet rule, weight lifting became a popular sport. At the first All-Ukrainian Olympiad in 1922, the champions in three weight categories were Krylov, Lukashevych, and Bohdanov. The 1924 USSR weight-lifting championships were held in Kiev, and Kiev athletes placed second overall. In the 1930s the Ukrainian G. Popov established many world, USSR, and Ukrainian records, and from 1935 Ukrainian athletes were part of USSR teams sent to international weight-lifting competitions. In 1937 the Ukrainian team took first place overall at a USSR championship for the first time, and in 1938 Ya.

Kutsenko became the first Ukrainian athlete to lift a combined total of over 400 kg in the snatch, clean and jerk, and press. At the 1938 USSR championships Ukrainians set five of eight possible all-Union records, and on the eve of the Second World War, H. Novak became one of the leading weight lifters in the world. By 1939, out of 35 Soviet records (27 of them higher than world records), 17 had been set by Ukrainian athletes.

Since 1952, Ukrainians have taken part in the *Olympic Games as part of the USSR team. In 1956 I. Rybak from Kharkiv became the first Ukrainian to win an Olympic gold medal in weight lifting (lightweight). Ukrainians who have become world champions in various weight categories are L. Zhabotynsky (four times), P. Korol (three times), Yu. Zaitsev (twice), S. Rakhmanov (twice), V. Kryshchyshyn, H. Ivanenko, V. Ustiushyn, S. Poltoratsky, A. Pysarenko, V. Beliaev, and H. Novak. Eighty-six USSR records have been set by H. Novak, 58 by Ya. Kutsenko, 24 by M. Kasianyk, 23 by V. Kryshchyshyn, and 20 by L. Zhabotynsky. In the postwar period new world records in various weight categories have been set by Ya. Kutsenko (1946), I. Maltsev (1948), O. Donskoi (1949), V. Piven (1949), P. Kirshon (1954), F. Osypa (1955), P. Matiukha (1957), V. Tymoshenko (1958), A. Zhytetsky (1958), V. Beliaev (1962), L. Zhabotynsky (1963), V. Berlizov (1963), H. Troitsky (1964), V. Andreev (1965), V. Shishov (1967), O. Kidiaev (1968), V. Kryshchyshyn (1969), B. Pavlov (1969), S. Batishchev (1970), and Yu. Yablonovsky (1970).

BIBLIOGRAPHY
Draha, V.; Kotko, D. Bohatyri Ukraïny (Kiev 1972)
Nartovskii, B. Tiazheloatlety Ukrainy (Kiev 1979)

O. Zinkevych

**Weights and measures.** As agriculture, manufacturing, and commerce evolved in Ukraine from medieval times, so did various means of measuring their output and value. Weights and measures were not standardized, however; they were approximate, and varied spatially and temporally until the rise of modern centralized states. In medieval Ukraine, as elsewhere, a popular metrology was well developed. Units of linear measurement were originally named after parts of the human body and their dynamics: palets ('finger' [digit]); likot ('elbow' [cubit]); stopa ('foot'); krok ('step'); mala piad ('small palm' [the span of the extended thumb and forefinger]); velyka piad ('large palm' [the span of the extended thumb and little finger]); and sazhen or siazhen (from the verb siahaty ['to reach']), measured variously as the breadth of the horizontally extended arms (makhovyi sazhen), two large steps, or the distance between the toes of the left foot and the fingertips of the vertically raised right arm (kosovyi or kosyi sazhen). Large distances were measured in units called verstva or versta (a 'small' verstva equaling 500 sazhni and a 'large' verstva equaling 1,000 sazhni), popryshche (ie, 1,000 steps), perestril (ie, the distance an arrow shot from a bow could travel, roughly 60–70 m), and hin (originally the length of a plowed field), which came to equal 60 sazhni (a 'small' hin), 80 sazhni (a 'middle' hin), and 240 large steps or 185 m (a 'large' or 'good' hin, corresponding to the Roman stadium).

Area was measured in units of desiatyna ('tenth' or 'tithe' of a sq verstva), vyt (6–8 desiatyny), and sokha ('plow', ie, 400–600 desiatyny). Mass was measured in units of zolotnyk (named after a gold coin equaling the weight of a 10th- to 11th-century Byzantine solidus, or 4.3 g), pochka (ie, 1/20 zolotnyk), hryvnia (literally 'fur collar' [cf German Griff], ie, 96 zolotnyky or 1 Byzantine litra, which was then also used in Ukraine), ansyr (ie, 128 zolotnyky [approx 546 g], cf German Ganzer), pud (ie, 40 hryvni or 1 Hellenic gold talent), kentar or kontar (ie, 3 pudy), and berkovets (ie, 10 pudy, named after the Viking trade center of Birka, in Sweden), and kap (4 pudy of silver). Various Byzantine weights, such as the didrachm (approx 2 zolotnyky), were also used in the 11th and 12th centuries.

Volume, particularly of grain, was measured out in units of horst ('handful') and in various wooden domestic receptacles: oslynka, lukno (possibly equaling the later harnets), vidro ('pail'), chetveryk (corresponding to a Roman quadrant), korets (cf Greek choros, later also a unit of mass [approx 50 kg under Polish rule and 6 pudy, ie, approx 100 kg, under Russian rule], mishok ('sack'), and mirka ('measure', approx 6 pudy and later approx 12.5 kg under Polish rule). Salt was measured out in receptacles called holovazhnia and puz, and honey and mead were measured out in large receptacles called koloda ('log', ie, 10–12 vidra) and provara. Liquids were measured out in receptacles called kobel (cf German Kübel), skord, vidro (approx 12 L), bochka ('barrel'), and kad (or okova, an iron-banded barrel weighing 12–14 pudy). Grain sheaves, fruits, vegetables, eggs, coins, and other items were measured out in quantities of kopa (ie, 60 pieces) and polukopa (polukipok for sheaves, ie, 30 pieces).

Under Lithuanian and Polish rule German commercial units of measurement were widely used in Ukraine in addition to customary units. The tsal (Polish: cal, from German Zoll), equaling the width of the thumb (later 24.8 mm), became the basic linear measurement; 12 tsali equaled a stopa, and 24, a likot (Polish: łokieć). Distances were measured in miles of various lengths: 7,422 m (the German Meile), 9,278 m (the Ukrainian mylia), and 5,566 m (the Polish mila). Land area was measured in units of morg (Polish: mórg, from German Morgen); originally designating the size of a field that could be plowed using a pair of oxen in a morning, a 'royal' morg equaled 0.5985 ha, and a 'Lithuanian' morg, 0.7123 ha; they were divided into 300 pruty ('rods', Polish: pręty). Land was also measured in units of lan (Polish: łan, German: Lehen, from Latin laneus); a small ('Flemish' or 'Chełmno') lan was 30 morgy (approx 16.8 ha), and a large ('Franconian') lan was 43.5 morgy (approx 25 ha). With the introduction of the *voloka land reform, from 1557 on land was measured in units of voloka (Polish: wołoka), that is, the amount of land a peasant could harrow in a day (30 [later 33] morgy). Mass was measured in units of funt ('pound', German: Pfund); weighing from 398 g (the 'Cracow' funt) to 405.5 g (the 'Szczecin' funt), the funt was divided into 2 hryvni (Polish: grzywna), or 32 luty (Polish: łut), or 8,400 asy. Thirty-two funty made up a 'Warsaw' kamin ('stone', Polish: kamień), and 26, a 'Cracow' kamin; 5 kamini made up a tsentnar (German: Centner, Polish: centnar). The basic unit of volume was the harnets (Polish: garniec, approx 3 L), which was divided into 4 kvarty ('quarts') or 16 kvatyrky. Seventy-two harntsi made up a bochka ('barrel'). Quantities were measured out in dozens (tuzin, from French douzaine).

In the Ukrainian lands that came under Russian rule a standardized Russian metrology, developed in the early part of the 18th century, was introduced and retained, with some minor changes, until 1927. A verstu (1,066.8 m) had 500 sazhni; 1 sazhen (2.133 m) had 3 arshyny; and 1 ar-

*shyn* (originally a Turkic measure, Russian: *arshin*, 71.1 cm) had 16 *vershky* (1 vershok equaled 4.44 cm). Alternately, 1 *sazhen* had 7 *futy*; 1 *fut* ('foot', 30.48 cm) had 12 *diuimy*; 1 *diuim* ('inch', cf Dutch *duim*, 2.54 cm) had 10 *linii*; and 1 *liniia* ('line', 2.54 mm) had 10 *tochky* ('points'). Land area was measured in *desiatyny*: from 1753, 1 *desiatyna* was 2,400 sq *sazhni* (1.09 ha), and 1 sq *sazhen* (4.55 sq m) was 9 sq *arshyny* or 49 sq *futy*. The basic unit of dry volume was the *chetvert* (209.9 L), which had 2 *miry*, or 8 *chetvertyky*, or 64 *harntsi*. Liquids were measured in units of *bochka* (491.96 L), which had 40 *vidra*; 1 *vidro* (12.3 L) had 10 *kukhli* ('ladles') or 20 *pliashky* ('bottles'); 1 *pliashka* (0.61 L) had 5 *charky* ('cups') or 10 *shkalyky* ('half-cups'). Mass was measured in units of *berkovets* (163.8 kg), which had 10 *pudy*; 1 *pud* had 40 *funty*; 1 *funt* (409.5 g) had 32 *loty*; 1 *lot* (12.8 g) had 3 *zolotnyky*; and 1 *zolotnyk* (4.27 g) had 96 *doly* (1 equaled 44.4 mg).

In the Western Ukrainian lands that fell under Austrian imperial rule, Lower Austrian metrology was introduced and became the only legal system in 1855. Lengths were measured in units of *sazhen* (1.9 m) and *likot* (77.8 cm); 1 *sazhen* had 6 *stopy* (1 equaled 31.6 cm). Distances were measured in 7.58-km postal miles. Agricultural land was measured in 0.575-ha units of *morg* (German: *Joch*).

Many other measurements were also used in 19th- and 20th-century Ukraine. Lengths, particularly of cloth, were measured in units of *mira* (76 cm), which had 30 *tsali*; of *stina* or *stinka* (approx 7 m); and of *postav* (approx 28 m). Several other land measurements were widespread: *chvertka* (8–10 *desiatyny*), *zahin* (5–6 *desiatyny*), *vidriz* (3 *desiatyny*), *riza* (2 *desiatyny*), *polurizka* (0.25 *zahin* or 1.50 *desiatyny*), *pishak* (11 *morgy*), *klitka* (12 *morgy*), *den* ('day'), that is, the amount of land that could be plowed in a day (approx 0.75 *desiatyna*), and *upruh*, that is, the amount of land that could be plowed using a pair of oxen in a third of a day. Large volumes, particularly of lumber, were measured in cu *sazhni*. In Southern and Western Ukraine the *oko* (originally a Turkic unit, 1,248–1,283 g or 1–1.5 L) was used and, for weighing wax, lead, sugar, and tobacco, the *kamin* (24, 30, 32, or 36 *funty*).

Most of the old units of measurement gradually fell into disuse after the official adoption of the metric system in the Austro-Hungarian Empire in 1875, partially in the Russian Empire in 1899, and in the USSR in 1925.

BIBLIOGRAPHY

Kaufman, I. *Russkii ves, ego razvitie i proiskhozhdenie*, 2nd edn (St Petersburg 1911)

Beliaev, N. 'O drevnikh i nyneshnikh russkikh merakh protiazheniia i vesa,' *Seminarium Kondakovianum*, 1 (Prague 1927)

Ierofeïv, I. 'Do pytannia pro stari ukraïns'ki miry, vahu ta hroshovyi oblik,' *Roboty z metrolohiï*, no. 2 (Kharkiv 1927)

Stamm, E. *Miary długości w dawnej Polsce* (Warsaw 1938)

Rybakov, V. 'Russkie sistemy mer dliny XI–XV vv.,' *Sovetskaia etnografiia*, 1949, no. 1

Ianin, V. *Denezhno-vesovye sistemy russkogo srednevekov'ia: Domongol'skii period* (Moscow 1956)

*Spravochnik mer* (Moscow 1960)

Hratsians'ka, L. 'Narodna lichba ta miry na Ukraïni,' in *Z istoriï vitchyznianoho pryrodoznavstva* (Kiev 1964)

Kamentseva, E.; Ustiugov, N. *Russkaia metrologiia* (Moscow 1965)

Sydorenko, O. *Istorychna metrolohiia Livoberezhnoï Ukraïny XVIII st.* (Kiev 1975)

Himka, J.-P. *Galicia and Bukovina: A Resource Handbook about Western Ukraine, Late 19th–20th Centuries*. Alberta Historic Sites Service Occasional Paper, no. 20 (Edmonton 1990)

                                        B. Kravtsiv, R. Senkus

**Weir, John** [Vyvjurs'kyj, Ivan], b 23 October 1906 in Broad Valley, Manitoba, d 23 November 1983 in Toronto. Journalist, publicist, and community leader. Weir was a member of the Communist Party of Canada from 1927 and sat on its central committee after 1934. He edited the Party's newspapers *Worker* (1935–6), *Daily Clarion* (1936–9), and *Canadian Tribune* (1943–6, 1970–3) as well as the procommunist *Svit molodi* (1927–9) and *Ukrainian Canadian* (1947–54). He was on the executive of the *Association of United Ukrainian Canadians and national secretary of the Canadian Slav Committee (1958–61). In 1940–2 he was interned by the Canadian government. Weir translated works by T. Shevchenko, I. Franko, and Lesia Ukrainka into English.

**Welding** (*zvariuvannia*). Research on electric welding in Ukraine was begun early in the 20th century by specialists such as M. *Benardos, M. Slavianov, and D. Dulchevsky. By the end of the 1920s V. Nikitin in Dnipropetrovske, R. Lashkevych in Kharkiv, and V. Nauman in Mariiupil had organized welding into a systematic science. In 1929, on Ye. *Paton's proposal, the department of engineering structures was set up in the VUAN (now ANU) in Kiev. In 1934 the department was reorganized into the *Institute of Electric Welding, which in the 1950s became the chief center of welding research in the USSR; the laboratories of the leading plants in Ukraine came under its supervision. Welding research is also carried out at the *Institutes of Electrodynamics of the ANU, the institutes of ferrous metallurgy in Dnipropetrovske (est 1953) and Donetske (est 1960), and the *Ukrainian Scientific Research Institute of Metals. In 1939–40 Ukrainian scientists invented a method of constructing all-welded bridges. In 1953 the largest such bridge in the world was built over the Dnieper River in Kiev.

Welding and related research has been done in Ukraine by Paton and V. Shevernytsky (the strength of welded structures), K. *Khrenov, N. Kytsiak, and M. Matiiko (underwater welding and cutting of metals), H. *Voloshkevych (welding metal in the vertical position), Paton and Voloshkevych (electro-slag welding, which can join metals of any thickness), D. *Dudko (welding in carbon dioxide settings), V. *Lebedev, S. *Kuchuk-Yatsenko, I. Chernenko, and V. Cherednychok (continuous flash welding for joining rails and serial production), A. Asnis, B. Kasatkin, and M. Hapchenko (the vibrational immunity of welded joints and structures), Khrenov, V. Moravsky, and S. Svechnikov (electric condensation welding of small-gauge metals), and H. Raievsky and O. Rozenberg (the assembly of petroleum tanks from sheet metal).

Ukrainian scientists, such as S. Hurevych, O. *Romaniv, and V. Volkov, were the first to introduce in industry the welding of titanium and its melt under flux. D. Rabkin developed the mechanized welding of aluminum and its melt under flux, and B. *Medovar the mechanized welding of rust-resistant and thermal steels, and copper. B. Lebedev and V. Sosnovsky mechanized welding tasks in the construction of smelting furnaces and applied complex mechanization in the construction of the largest blast furnace in the world (No. 9 of the Kryvyi Rih Metallurgical Plant). Plasma-arc and electronic-radiation recasting were tested in ferrous and nonferrous metallurgy by B. *Movchan. Articles on welding technology have appeared in the specialized journal *Avtogennyi rabotnik* (1932–9) and the monthly *Avtomaticheskaia svarka* (1948–), published in Kiev by the Institute of Electric Welding and translated into English in Cambridge, UK.

**Welling, Gottard,** 1624–59. Swedish diplomat. He was sent to Ukraine in 1657 for discussions with Hetman B. Khmelnytsky. His personal account of the mission confirms that Khmelnytsky set his policies and conducted his affairs independently of Muscovy. A full account of the proceedings was provided by a second Swedish legate, J. Hildebrandt (published as *Dreyfache Koenigl. Schwed. Legations-Reiss-Beschreibung in Siebenbuergen, die Ukrain ... den Legaten An 1656 et 1657*, 1937).

**Welykyj, Athanasius.** See Velyky, Atanasii

**Wenhlowsky, Juri.** See Venhlovsky, Yurii, Jr.

**Weres, Roman** [Veres], b 27 November 1907 in Paryshchi, Nadvirna county, Galicia, d 11 January 1980 in Chicago. Librarian; member of the Shevchenko Scientific Society. He was educated at Lviv (1930) and the Ukrainian Free (1947) universities. He emigrated to the United States in 1955 and obtained an MLS from Western Michigan University (1958). He worked in libraries in Adrian and Chicago, Michigan, and became president of the Ukrainian National Museum in Chicago and the Ukrainian Library Association of America. He compiled *Ukraine: Selected References in the English Language* (2nd edn, 1974) and *Index of Ukrainian Essays in Collections Published outside the Iron Curtain* (9 vols, 1967–75).

**Werewolf** (*vovkulaka*). A mythological creature who changes from a man into a wolf at night to eat animals, humans, or corpses and returns to human form at sunrise. According to folk beliefs, some persons, whose mothers had unexpectedly seen a wolf, had eaten meat from an animal killed by a wolf, or had been impregnated during a religious ban on sexual activity, were born werewolves. Others were changed into werewolves by a witch's or sorcerer's spells. Ukrainian beliefs about werewolves were similar to those of other European peoples.

**Werkschutz.** A paramilitary formation organized by the German authorities in occupied territories during the Second World War for guarding industrial sites, particularly plants involved in war production. The *Werkschutz* units had a military structure and were commanded by locally recruited officers who were subordinate to German commanders or administrative bodies. The first Ukrainian units arose in 1940 in the Generalgouvernement to guard the steel mills in Stalowa Wola and Starachowice. They were formed mostly of officers and soldiers of the former Legion of Ukrainian Nationalists. Later, similar units were organized in other towns of the Generalgouvernement and, from 1941, in the Galicia district and Reichskommissariat Ukraine.

**Westerfeldt, Abraham van** (Westervelt), b ?, d between 24 and 30 April 1692 in Rotterdam. Dutch artist. While in the service of the Lithuanian hetman J. Radziwiłł (1649–53), he witnessed the Cossack-Polish War and depicted it in his paintings. Eighteenth-century copies of some of these works have been preserved. They include *Cossack Envoys*, *Audience with Radziwiłł*, *General View of Kiev from the Dnieper*, and *Defeat of the Lithuanian Flotilla by the Cossacks on the Dnieper*. He also sketched lanscapes in Kiev, including views of the Golden Gate, the St Sophia Cathedral, and the Kievan Cave Monastery. It has been conjectured that W. Hondius's engraving of B. Khmelnytsky was copied from a portrait by Westerfeldt.

**Western Beskyd.** The part of the Carpathian *Beskyds lying between the Biała and Topla river valleys in the west, the Slanské Mountains to the south, and the Low Beskyds in the east. Only the eastern reaches of the Western Beskyds lie in ethnic Ukrainian territory, in a region in southern Poland and northeastern Czechoslovakia. Within that area a number of notable mountain and mountain groups are located, including the Yavoryna group (1,116 m) and the Cherhiv Mountains (with Mt Menchil at 1,157 m) and the *Spišská Magura (1,158 m) and the Levoča Mountains (up to 1,300 m). Those two main areas are separated by a rocky plain. The ridges of the formation generally are broad and smooth, sparsely populated, and covered with woods and meadows. Most of the area's population can be found in its lower-lying reaches. The Ukrainian inhabitants of the Western Beskyd, generally *Lemkos, were forcibly resettled after the Second World War and can be found today only in the Prešov region of Slovakia.

**Western Buh River** (Zakhidnyi Buh). The official Soviet name of the *Buh River, used to differentiate it from the Southern Buh (*Boh) River.

**Western Caucasia** (Zakhidnii Kavkaz). The western section of the Great Caucasus Range. It runs for approx 500 km from the Kerch Strait in the northwest to the source of the Kuban River in the southeast. The Black Sea area of Western Caucasia (in the RF) has extensive Ukrainian settlement (see *Kuban) whereas only the northwestern corner of the Abkhaz AR (also included in this geographic zone) has any significant Ukrainian population. (See also *Caucasia.)

**Western Province of the Ukrainian National Republic** (Zakhidnia oblast Ukrainskoi Narodnoi Respubliky, or ZOUNR). The name assumed by the Western Ukrainian National Republic after the proclamation of union with the UNR. According to the resolution of the Ukrainian National Rada, passed in Stanyslaviv on 3 January 1919, and the proclamation of the Directory of the UNR, issued on 22 January 1919, the two states merged into one, with ZOUNR preserving its territorial autonomy. The final union of the two states was to be settled by the Constituent Assembly of Ukraine. Until then the Ukrainian National Rada and the State Secretariat were invested with civil and military power on the territory of the ZOUNR. Only the commands of the armed forces at the front were merged, a joint delegation was sent to the Paris Peace Conference (1919–20), and a common currency was introduced. For a brief while Ye. *Petrushevych, the president of the Ukrainian National Rada, was a member of the Directory. The Directory set up a special ministry for the ZOUNR, which was later abolished. When the UNR mission to Warsaw declared on 2 December 1919 that the government of the UNR had no interest in the territory of Western Ukraine, the government of the ZOUNR (see *Dictatorship of the Western Province of the UNR), including its delegation in Paris, rejected the joint institutions with the Directory and began to conduct its own, independent policy. At the beginning of 1920 the ZOUNR government-in-exile and its delegation in Paris returned to the former name of the state, the Western Ukrainian National Republic, and began to call its territory Eastern Galicia, because that name had been used in mid-1919 in the documents of the Paris Peace Conference.

M. Stakhiv

**Western Ukraine** (Zakhidnia Ukraina). The designated name of the territories of the renewed Ukrainian state created in what had been part of the Austro-Hungarian Empire, defined by the Ukrainian National Rada (UNRada) in a resolution of 19 October 1918 in Lviv. Western Ukraine encompassed 'Eastern Galicia bordered by the Sian River, but including the Lemko region; northern Bukovyna, including the towns of Chernivtsi, Storozhynets, and Seret; and the Ukrainian region of northeastern Hungary' (Article 1, Resolutions of the UNRada). That entity became the *Western Ukrainian National Republic (ZUNR) by the constitution of 13 November 1918.

The term 'Western Ukraine' was also used popularly to designate the ZUNR or to describe all the Ukrainian territories occupied by Poland, Czechoslovakia, and Rumania in the interwar period. After 1939 'Western Ukraine' referred to the Ukrainian territories which in that year became part of the Ukrainian SSR, as distinct from central and eastern Ukraine, which were a part of the Ukrainian SSR in 1920–39. In Soviet terminology 'Western Ukraine' designated the historical or geographic territories that became the Lviv, Ivano-Frankivske, Ternopil, Volhynia, and Rivne oblasts.

The Government-in-exile of the Western Ukrainian National Republic in Vienna in 1920. Sitting, from left: Lev Petrushevych, Lev Syroichkovsky, Kost Levytsky, Pres Yevhen Petrushevych, Volodymyr Singalevych, Roman Perfetsky, Yaroslav Selezinka, Myron Havrysevych; standing behind Perfetsky is Olha Basarab.

**Western Ukrainian National Republic** (Zakhidno-Ukrainska Narodnia Respublika, or ZUNR). A nation-state established on the Ukrainian ethnic territory of former Austria-Hungary on 19 October 1918 by the Ukrainian National Rada in Lviv. The Constitution of 13 November 1918 determined its name and defined the territory of the ZUNR as that which encompassed the Ukrainian regions of the Austrian crownlands of Galicia and Bukovyna and the Transcarpathian komitats of Szepes, Sáros, Zemplén, Ung, Bereg, Ugocsa, and Máramoros. A Ukrainian government took power on 1 November 1918 in Galicia, on 6 November in Bukovyna, and on 19 November in Transcarpathia. The governments in the last two territories were short-lived. In spite of the Ukrainian-Polish War

(November 1918 to July 1919) the government of the ZUNR held out longest in eastern Galicia.

The *Ukrainian National Rada, a legislative council, was the state's ruling body before the calling of the Constituent Assembly of the ZUNR. The *State Secretariat was its executive branch. Its power was eventually transferred to the *Dictatorship of the Western Province of the Ukrainian National Republic.

On 1 December 1918 the State Secretariat of the ZUNR concluded a preliminary agreement with the Directory of the UNR on the union of the two Ukrainian states. The agreement was approved by the Ukrainian National Rada on 3 January 1919 and by the Directory on 22 January. The union was proclaimed in a special proclamation of 22 January. Thenceforth the ZUNR assumed the name *Western Province of the Ukrainian National Republic. But the union was not fully implemented: the government bodies of the ZUNR continued to operate separately (see *Dictatorship of the Western Province of the UNR). When the UNR government recognized Polish rule in Ukrainian territory west of the Zbruch River, the ZUNR government rejected its policies completely.

In July 1919 Poland occupied most of the territory of the ZUNR and tried to get Entente recognition for its rule in Galicia. Although the Supreme Council of the Peace Conference representing the Entente instructed Poland on 25 June to occupy Ukrainian Galicia temporarily, it recognized Galicia's special status. On 20 November it drafted a treaty with Poland on the autonomy of eastern Galicia under the higher administration of Poland for 25 years, but the Poles rejected that treaty. The *Conference of Ambassadors of the great powers of the Entente finally recognized (12 March 1923) the Polish occupation, albeit with the provision that eastern Galicia was to remain autonomous.

BIBLIOGRAPHY
Lozyns'kyi, M. *Halychyna na myrovii konferentsiï v Paryzhi* (Kamianets 1919)
– *Halychyna v rr. 1918–1920* (Vienna 1922; repr, New York 1970)
Levyts'kyi, K. *Velykyi zryv* (Lviv 1931)

V. Markus, M. Stakhiv

**Wetlands** (*bolota*). Land areas with excessive moisture that provide a habitat for moisture-loving plants, the remains of which often accumulate to form peat. Wetlands may form along watercourses with impeded drainage, in and around shallow bodies of water with low shorelines, and in areas of humid climate (even away from bodies of water) where the soil is inadequately aerated, and decaying processes are impeded. Wetlands may be classified into three types according to the supply of water-borne minerals, the type of peat cover, and the nature of the vegetation: lowland (eutrophic), upland (oligotrophic), and transitional (mesotrophic).

Wetlands in Ukraine belong principally to the lowland and the transitional types. Upland wetlands make up no more than 10 percent of its wetlands by area alone. Ukrainian wetlands may also be subdivided according to vegetation into three types, sphagnum, grassy, and wooded. Sphagnum wetlands (which correspond to the upland wetlands) are found mostly in western Polisia and the Carpathian Mountains. Among the grassy wetlands the most widespread are sedge wetlands; they are followed closely by high grass wetlands consisting of reeds, cattails, and rushes. High grass wetlands are widespread in the floodplains of the forest-steppe and steppe zones. Wooded wetlands, including the alder, birch, and willow-pine subtypes, are found mainly in Polisia.

Wetlands occupy about 1 million ha, or 1.7 percent of the land surface of Ukraine. They claim the most significant share of the territory in the forest belt (5–30 percent of a given raion), much less in the Left-Bank forest-steppe (2–5 percent), even less in the Right-Bank forest-steppe (up to 2 percent), and the least in the steppe (up to 1 percent). The most extensive wetlands are found in Polisia, along both sides of the Prypiat River, especially in its western reaches (Volhynia and Rivne oblasts), where they occupy large expanses and extend along river valleys. Grassy wetlands known as *hala* occupy up to 90 percent of the wetlands in that region. Central Polisia has fewer wetlands, particularly along the Dnieper River. More wetlands are found in the Chernihiv Polisia, notably on the Dnieper-Desna Divide (the Zamhlai Marsh) and on the floodplains of little rivers. In Western Ukraine pockets of wetlands occur along rivers such as the Buh, the Styr, the Dniester (the Sambir Marsh), and the Tysa (the Chorne Boloto or Black Marsh). The Left-Bank forest-steppe has wetlands mostly in the floodplains of rivers such as the Sula, the Udai, and the Khorol. In the Right-Bank forest-steppe isolated wetlands are encountered in only a few river valleys. In the steppe zone the typical wetlands are found in floodplains known as *plavni*. Those reach their largest expanses in the mouths of major rivers, notably the Danube, the Dnieper, and the Kuban.

The economic exploitation of wetlands in their natural state for agriculture or forestry has offered limited returns. Hay harvested from grassy wetlands has generally been coarser than that from meadows, and wooded wetlands have yielded relatively low value in small trees. The harvesting of reeds, cattails, and berries has provided only marginal income to those engaged in handicrafts or food processing. Only the extraction of peat for fuel has provided a major industrial benefit. Furthermore, wetlands hindered transport and were conducive to the breeding of locusts and mosquitoes. Accordingly, the drainage of wetlands in Ukraine was considered to be a wise economic policy (see *Drainage of land).

The amount of drained agricultural land in Ukraine surpassed three million hectares in 1987. Some of the drained areas have been retained as hayfields; others have been plowed for the growing of crops, such as oats, buckwheat, cabbage, potatoes, and clover. As a consequence of the drainage the area of wetlands declined to approx one million hectares in the 1980s.

The combined effect of drainage and the reduction in area of the wetlands has increased spring flooding and reduced the summer flow of the Prypiat and other rivers that were formerly flanked by wetlands. Wetlands not only act like a sponge, regulating the water flow of rivers, but also serve as a buffer against shoreline and riverbank erosion. Furthermore, wetland vegetation (notably reeds and cattails) has a high capacity to act as a pollution filter (an important consideration when surface water is to be used for drinking). Finally, wetlands serve as refuges for wildlife, which is becoming impoverished as a result of the extinction of species. Because of their valuable ecological functions, wetlands are now being viewed as natural ecosystems that should be subject to conservation.

BIBLIOGRAPHY
Zerov, D. *Bolota* URSR: *Roslynnist' i stratyhrafiia* (Kiev 1938)
Bradis, Ie.; Bachuryna, H. *Bolota* URSR (Kiev 1969)
*Torfovo-bolotnyi fond* URSR, *ioho raionuvannia ta vykorystannia* (Kiev 1973)
*Tipy bolot* SSSR *i printsipy ikh klassifikatsii* (Leningrad 1974)

I. Stebelsky

Part of the monument to Ukrainian soldiers who died in the Wetzlar POW camp (sculptor: Mykhailo Parashchuk, limestone and sandstone, 1918)

**Wetzlar.** A town (1990 pop 51,400) on the Lahn River in Hessen, Germany. During the First World War a POW camp for soldiers of the Russian army was established there. There were over 10,000 Ukrainians among its inmates. Supported by the *Union for the Liberation of Ukraine, the camp's educational department set up an elementary school, an amateur theater, a library, and a press (*Prosvitnii lystok* and then *Hromads'ka dumka*) for the Ukrainians. A Sich society and Orthodox and Methodist congregations were also active there.

**Wheat** (*Triticum*; Ukrainian: *pshenytsia*). A cereal grass of the Gramineae (Poaceae) family, one of the oldest and most important cereal in *crop cultivation, particularly in Europe and North America. Of the thousands of known species of wheat by far the most common is bread wheat (*T. vulgare* or *aestivum*; Ukrainian: *pshenytsia miaka*); it produces a soft grain that is used for making bread flour. Durum, or macaroni, wheat (*T. durum*; Ukrainian: *pshenytsia tverda, boroshno*) yields a hard grain used in making pastas; club wheat (*T. compactum*) is used to make flour for cakes, crackers, and pastries.

Most wheat is grown for human food. Some 10 percent is retained annually for seed, and small quantities are used in making starch, paste, malt, dextrose, gluten, alcohol (see *Liquor and spirits distilling), and other products. The former USSR was the world's largest single producer of wheat, with Ukraine accounting for the major share. Ukraine is popularly known as 'the breadbasket of Europe.'

Wheat has been known in Ukraine since the Neolithic period (5th to 4th millennium BC), when it was grown along the Buh and Dniester rivers. By the 6th century BC it was an important export from southern Ukraine to Greece and Rome. In the early Princely era it was partially displaced in importance by *barley and *rye. Conditions were favorable in the steppe and eastern Ukraine for large-scale commercial farming of wheat. The steppe proved to be well suited to growing superior winter wheats (spring wheat had predominated in western and central Ukraine).

Wheat production (see *Grain production) has generally expanded during the 20th century – except following the forced *collectivization of agriculture in the late 1920s and early 1930s and the subsequent man-made *famine in Soviet Ukraine – although the total area sown with wheat has declined from 8,858,000 ha in 1913 to 7,568,000 ha in 1990. The decline has been accomplished primarily through a significant increase in average yields: in 1913 grain yield in centners per hectare was 11.8 for winter wheat and 7.5 for spring wheat, and by 1986–90 the respective figures were 36.4 and 27.3. New varieties of wheat and more effective farming techniques (see *Agriculture) in the south, relying on extensive *irrigation, have been developed. Some 7,970,000 t of wheat was harvested in 1913; in 1986–90 average annual harvests equaled 23,510,000 t. In Soviet Ukraine wheat production was concentrated on large state farms in Odessa, Mykolaiv, Kherson, Kirovohrad, and Crimea oblasts. Production of spring wheat was negligible; it had been displaced by hardier winter wheat strains.

An important scientific research establishment is the *Myronivka Institute of Wheat Selection and Seed Cultivation. There were 11 varieties of spring and 34 varieties of winter wheat in Ukraine in 1983. The most common varieties of winter wheat grown in Ukraine are Bezostaia 1 and Myronivka 808. Other popular soft winter wheat varieties are Myronivka Jubilee, Odessa Jubilee 16 and 55, and Illich. The *selection and development of new wheat strains has a long history in Ukraine; many Ukrainian varieties are also grown in other countries. The famous Red Fife wheat, which emerged as the most important wheat in Canada in the mid to late 19th century and has set world standards for hard winter wheat, was based on a wheat that was developed in Galicia.

BIBLIOGRAPHY
Ozyma pshenytsia na Ukraïni (Kiev 1965)
Pshenytsi Ukraïns'koï RSR ta ïkh iakosti (Kiev 1965)
Pshenitsa (Kiev 1977)

V. Kubijovyč

**Wheel- and wagon-making.** Wheeled vehicles and sleds have been built in Ukraine since ancient times. In the 19th century wheelwrights were found in virtually every village, although many practiced their craft seasonally. In some parts of the country the craft was especially well developed: in Zinkiv, Lubni, and Hadiache counties of Poltava gubernia; in Starobilske, Okhtyrka, and Bohodukhiv counties of Kharkiv gubernia; and, to a lesser degree, in Radomyshl, Chyhyryn, and Tarashcha counties of Kiev gubernia. Wheels and wagons from those areas were sold in Southern Ukraine and other regions where local craftsmen could not meet the demand. With the modernization of transport in the 20th century, wheel- and wagon-making declined in importance.

**White Croatians** (bili khorvaty). A proto-Slavic tribe that was part of an alliance of *tribes in Subcarpathia. They migrated westward and to the Balkan Peninsula in the 7th century. They are believed to be the ancestors of certain *Ukrainians, specifically the *Hutsuls. In the Primary Chronicle they are mentioned twice in an undated tribal survey and also, later, as Oleh's allies in his Byzantine campaign (907) and as the target of a campaign by Volodymyr the Great (993). There has been much controversy about the origin and migrations of the White Croatians. Among Ukrainian historians Ya. Holovatsky, O. Partytsky, M. Hrushevsky, Ya. Pasternak, and M. Smishko have written about the tribe.

**White Sea Canal.** A slave-labor project. A massive subarctic construction project, it was one of the most ambitious showpieces of the First Soviet Five-year Plan. It also marked the first use of forced labor in the Soviet Union for a large-scale economic undertaking. In just 20 months, from September 1931 to April 1933, prisoners using primitive technology excavated over 2.5 billion cu m of rock in a stretch of approx 227 km to connect Lake Onega with the White Sea. There are no accurate figures on how many people perished; the literature speaks of over 100,000 or even a quarter of a million deaths. Among the victims were numerous Ukrainians, such as activists arrested in connection with the show trial of the *Union for the Liberation of Ukraine and, especially, deported *kulaks.

**Whitefish** (Coregonus; Ukrainian: syh, riapushka, peliad). A valuable silvery food fish of the family Salmonidae, generally found in cold northern lakes, often in deep water. Whitefish (C. peled) was introduced in Ukraine in 1929; it acclimatized well in local ponds, where it matures earlier than in lakes. Commercial whitefish breeding was established in *Pushcha-Vodytsia.

**Wiart, Adrian Carton de,** b 5 May 1880 in Brussels, d 5 June 1963 in Cork county, Ireland. British military and diplomatic figure. In 1918 he was appointed second-in-command of the British military mission in Poland, and in 1919–24 he led the mission. In January 1919 he mediated negotiations between the Poles and the Western Ukrainian National Republic, in which S. Petliura also participated. His experiences in Poland and Ukraine are noted in his autobiography, Happy Odyssey (1950).

**Wild horse** (Equus coballus; Ukrainian: tarpan). An extinct predecessor of the domestic horse, measuring 107–136 cm at the shoulders. It was gray with a black mane, a black tail, and a black stripe down its back. Once wild horses were commonly found in the steppes and forest-steppes of Ukraine, but because of land cultivation and natural displacement they disappeared completely. The last specimen was caught in 1886 near the village of Novovorontsovka, Kherson gubernia. Some experts claim that tarpan and the Przewalski horse are of the same species. Tarpan horses were rederived in the 1930s by selection of primitive horses and are preserved in the *Bilovezha Forest.

**Wildlife protection and management.** See Environmental protection, Nature preserves, and Wildlife refuge.

**Wildlife refuge** (zakaznyk). An area of land or a body of water designated for the purpose of protecting some specific plants or animal species. Such areas do not constitute fully rounded natural complexes, as in nature preserves (zapovidnyk). The most common wildlife refuges were established to protect valuable wild animals and birds by means of the prohibition of hunting on their territory for

10 years or more. Fishing refuges protect spawning grounds or young fish. A landscape refuge may protect a picturesque river valley or lake so that its esthetic qualities will be maintained for the benefit of outdoor recreation and tourism. Small plots of forest, steppe, or wetlands may be designated as plant refuges for the purpose of protecting their unique flora. Geological features such as caves or sites rich in fossils may also be protected. Even a site of historical significance may be designated as a *zakaznyk*.

Wildlife refuges were established on the basis of decisions made by the Council of Ministers of Ukraine or by local (oblast or even raion) councils. Activities on their sites were regulated by the republican government, the organs responsible for the protection of nature, and the executive committees of local councils. Legislation concerning the refuges was adopted by all USSR republics. Hunting, fishing, logging, grazing, hay cutting, and mining were usually prohibited on the refugees. In 1986 the Ukrainian SSR had 1,490 *zakaznyky* of various kinds, occupying a total area of 597,600 ha. (See also *Nature preserves.)

I. Stebelsky

**Willow** (*Salix*; Ukrainian: *verba*). A shrub or tree of the family Salicaceae, valued for ornamentation, shade, timber, and erosion control. Pussy willow, the male form of several shrubby species, has woolly catkins that harbinger the coming of spring. In Ukraine pussy willow branches are used on Palm Sunday instead of palm fronds. At least 30 species of willow are found in Ukraine, where they grow along riverbanks and canal banks, road ditches, and dam slopes. Willow wood is light and soft; it rots easily. It is used for making hand-carved articles, cores for veneers, furniture, barrels, boxes, crates, and some musical instruments, including the *bandura. Twigs of the common or silky osier (*S. viminalis*) are used for basket weaving and fence construction. In unforested areas willow is used as a construction material. Goats and sheep feed on the leafy branches of young willows. The bark is used in tanning leather. The hybrids with droopy branches are called weeping willows (*S. babylonica*). Certain willows are the source of salicylic acid, used in the manufacture of pain relievers.

**Wilson, Thomas Woodrow,** b 28 December 1856 in Staunton, Virginia, d 3 February 1924 in Washington, DC. Democratic president of the United States (1913–21). Rev P. *Poniatyshyn's efforts resulted in Wilson's signing on 2 March 1917 a public law resolution to designate a day on which funds could be raised in the United States for the relief of the Ukrainians, 'especially ... in war-stricken Galicia, Bukovina, and other Provinces of Austria.' Wilson proclaimed 21 April 1917 as Ukrainian Day in the United States. On 22 March 1917 his government was the first to recognize formally the Russian Provisional Government, and later it advanced it nearly 188 million dollars. It persistently refused, however, to do or say anything that would recognize Ukrainian national aspirations.

In his famous Fourteen Points Address to Congress on 8 January 1918, Wilson offered peace between the United States and the Central Powers based on the 'evacuation of all Russian territory' by the forces of the Central Powers and the preservation of the territorial integrity of the Russian Empire (point 6), on the 'freest opportunity of autonomous development' for 'the peoples of Austria-

Hungary' (point 10), and on the establishment of an independent Polish state on territories 'inhabited by indisputably Polish populations' (point 13).

From December 1918 to June 1919 Wilson headed the American delegation at the *Paris Peace Conference. There he labored to convince Britain and France to accept his Fourteen Points; succeeded in incorporating in the Treaty of Versailles a provision for the creation of the *League of Nations; drew up the 'Prinkipo proposal' for an immediate end to the Russian Civil War and the convocation of a peace conference (accepted only by the Bolsheviks); vehemently objected to the enlargement or prolongation of Allied military intervention in 'Russia'; and advocated a plebiscite in eastern Galicia to resolve the Ukrainian-Polish War. Wilson betrayed his imperative principle of national self-determination, however, by his stubborn commitment to the preservation of 'Russia's' territorial integrity (without, however, recognizing the Soviet government). He did not recognize the January 1918 UNR declaration of independence, and agreed to recognize Poland's annexation of eastern Galicia in 1919 on the condition that Ukrainians there would have autonomy.

R. Senkus

**Wind energy.** The harnessing of wind power by means of windmills has been practiced in Europe since the 11th century. Windmills were also known in Ukraine, especially in the forest and forest-steppe regions. They were used to power grain mills and sometimes to pump water. The first windmills appeared in Ukraine in the late 16th century. Some windmills are still used today. The first modern electicity generator using wind power in Ukraine was built in the 1930s near Sevastopil under the direction of Yu. *Kondratiuk; it had a capacity of 100 kW. In the late 1980s there were approx 9,000 wind generators in the former USSR (some 600,000 in the world in 1967). They serve mostly very small localities with no other sources of electricity and account for an insignificant share of Ukraine's total power output.

**Windsor.** A city (1981 pop 192,000; metropolitan pop 246,000) on the Detroit River in southwestern Ontario. Ukrainian workers were attracted to Windsor in the 1920s by the automobile industry. In 1925 the Ukrainian Catholic parish of SS Volodymyr and Olha was organized, and in 1939 it completed its church. The Orthodox community set up a parish in 1927 and built St Volodymyr's Church in 1937. The Ukrainian People's Home (est 1926) and the Prosvita society (est 1932) organized plays, concerts, and Ukrainian schools. Politically active émigrés from Galicia set up a branch of the Ukrainian National Federation and its affiliate veterans' and women's associations in the mid-1930s. Postwar émigrés established a branch of the Canadian League for Ukraine's Liberation (1953). The Ukrainian Credit Union in Windsor has grown steadily since 1946. Ukrainian businessmen and professionals organized their own association in 1952. In 1981 the city's Ukrainian population stood at 8,100. But only 1,430 inhabitants claimed Ukrainian as their sole mother tongue in 1991.

**Wine-making industry.** Modern wine making in Ukraine began at the end of the 18th century, shortly after the Black Sea region was annexed by Catherine II. After 1860 the imperial household department purchased land

A reserve of 1905 Tokay wine
at the Masandra winery

on the south shore of the Crimea that was suited for viticulture. The Livadiia estate near Yalta soon became the
leading wine-making center in Ukraine. The department's
estates became the nucleus of the *Masandra Wine-
Making Complex, which dominated the Crimean southern shore after the 1917 Revolution. Wine making in the
steppe region was undertaken primarily by large landowners or German colonists, who were selected partly for
their wine-making ability. Wine making in the Transcarpathian region developed as part of the larger Hungarian
wine-making industry.

Today there are 123 primary wineries in the three wine
regions of Ukraine. Most of them belong to state farms
that process their own grapes and those from neighboring
collective farms. There are several secondary wineries,
where wine from the primary wineries is further processed and bottled. The most important are located in
Kiev, Dnipropetrovske, Symferopil, Odessa, Kherson,
Lviv, Donetske, Makiivka, and Yalta. The champagne industry, which has plants in Kiev, Kharkiv, Odessa,
Artemivske, Sevastopil, and Novyi Svit, is a separate industry.

In 1985 over 488 million L of more than 208 different
named wines were produced in Ukraine, in addition to
492 million L of several varieties of champagne. By 1990
the quantity had dropped to 267 million L of wine and 488
million L of champagne. Some 77 of them were branded
wines – high-quality wines, which are aged under special
conditions. The rest were ordinary wines, which normally
are bottled and sold within a year after harvesting. White
wines outnumber red wines, because in most regions it is
difficult to grow red grapes with sufficient color for a
proper red wine. Unlike wines from Right-Bank Ukraine,
wines made in Left-Bank Ukraine, including the Crimea,
do not have a stable acid level and require the addition of
citric acid for proper taste.

The steppe region produces 11 branded wines. The

WINERIES in UKRAINE

●   Important primary wineries

◉   Secondary wineries

Y   Champagne plants

──   Boundary of Ukraine

Research: Robert W. Hutton

0     100     200 km

Odessa region produces three white wines, Leanka Ukrainska, Perlyna Stepu, and Sylvaner Dnistrovskyi, and one red, Oksamyt Ukrainy. The Kherson region produces two whites, Naddniprianske and Rkatsiteli Beryslav; a white dessert wine, Beryslav Dessert; and a rosé dessert wine, Lydia Kakhovska. The Izmail region has a red table wine, Shabo, and a rosé dessert wine, Starokozache, and the Zaporizhia region has a white dessert wine, Berdianske.

Transcarpathia produces nine branded wines. The Berehove microregion makes two white table wines, Berehovske and Transcarpathian Riesling, and the Vynohradiv microregion produces the whites Kvity Polonyny, Promenyste, and Zakarpatske. The Serednie microregion has a white, Serednianske. Perlyna Karpat is made throughout Transcarpathia. The Mukachiv microregion makes a rosé, Rozheve stolove, and a white, Troianda Zakarpattia.

The Crimea produces 54 branded wines. The white table wines are Feteasca Krymska, Kokur Nizhnohorskyi, Kuldzhinskyi, and Sylvaner Feodosiiskyi. The white fortified wines are Madeira Al'Minska and Sherry Krymskyi. The Zolota Balka Wine-Making Complex produces five branded wines: the white table wines Aligote Zolota Balka, Riesling Al'Kadar, and Rkatseteli Inkerman, the red table wine Cabernet Kachynske, and the red dessert wine Al'Minsk. On the south shore 43 branded wines are produced, 29 by the Masandra Wine-Making Complex, and 14 by the Maharach Experimental Station. Masandra produces the red table wine Alushta; the white dessert wines Kokur Dessert Surozh, Muscat Koktebel, Muscat White Dessert, Muscat White Pivdennoberezhnyi, Muscat White Chervonyi Kamin, Muscat White Livadiia, Pinot Gris Ai-Danil, Soniashna Dolyna, and Tokai Pivdennoberezhnyi; the rosé dessert wines Muscat Rosé Dessert, Muscat Rosé, and Pivdennoberezhnyi; the white fortified wines Madeira Krymska, Madeira Masandra, Port White Pivdennoberezhnyi, Port White Krymskyi, Port White Surozh, and Sherry Masandra; and the red fortified wines Port Red Pivdennoberezhnyi, Port Red Krymskyi, Port Red Livadiia, and Port Red Masandra. Maharach produces experimental quantities of the red table wine Rubinovyi Maharach; the white dessert wines Maharach no. 25, Muscat White Maharach, Pinot Gris Maharach, and Serdolik Tavridy; the red dessert wine Bastardo Maharachskyi; the rosé dessert wine Muscat Rosé Maharach; the white fortified wines Maharach no. 23, Maharach no. 24, Port White Maharach, and Sertsial; and the red fortified wines Maharach no. 22 and Port Red Maharach. (For bibliography see *Viticulture.)

R. Hutton

**Winnipeg.** The capital of and the largest city (1989 pop 564,474) in *Manitoba, situated at the confluence of the Red and Assiniboine rivers. After the Canadian Pacific Railway reached it in 1885, it became the central railway and immigration dispersal point through which European immigrants passed en route to settling in western Canada.

Winnipeg was the main center of Ukrainian life in Canada before the Second World War. It had the first newspapers: the Liberal *Kanadiis'kyi farmer* (est 1903), the Protestant *Ranok* (1905), the socialist *Robochyi narod* (1909), the communist *Ukraïns'ki robitnychi visty* (1919), the Orthodox *Ukraïns'kyi holos* (1910), and the Catholic *Kanadiis'kyi rusyn* (1911). The first Ukrainian urban cultur-

Prime Minister John Diefenbaker at the unveiling of the Taras Shevchenko monument outside the Manitoba Legislative Building in Winnipeg in July 1961; at the far left is Sen Paul Yuzyk.

al society in Canada, the Shevchenko Reading Association, was formed in Winnipeg in 1899. Equally important were several community organizations which developed varying degrees of national status: the Ukrainian National Home, Ukrainian Canadian Citizens' Committee, Ukrainian National Committee, Ukrainian Central Committee, and Ukrainian Labour Temple. The co-ordinating body of the majority of organized Ukrainians, the *Ukrainian Canadian Committee (now Congress), was formed in 1940, in the city its headquarters since then. Winnipeg's pre-eminent position during this period reflected the fact that its Ukrainian community was up to five times larger than that in any other Canadian city. This situation changed considerably after the Second World War, and by 1971 both Edmonton and Toronto had Ukrainian populations roughly equal in number and influence to Winnipeg's.

The Ukrainian presence in Winnipeg was initially concentrated almost exclusively in the city's multiethnic and working-class districts: the North End, Point Douglas, and Brooklands. Although largely unskilled and frequently discriminated against, the city's Ukrainians had made respectable advances by 1939 in the retail trade, the service industry, manufacturing, transportation, and the professions, especially education and law. In 1943 the Ukrainian Professional and Businessmen's Club was organized. The city's Ukrainian population grew (according to census figures) from 3,600 (1911) to 7,000 (1921), 21,459 (1931), 28,162 (1941), 41,997 (1951), 53,918 (1961), and 64,305 (1971). The 1981 figures show a total of 79,350 Ukrainians in Winnipeg. In 1991, 18,590 of the inhabitants claimed Ukrainian as their sole mother tongue. Since the 1940s Ukrainians have constituted 10 percent or more of the city's total population.

The first Ukrainian alderman (T. Stefanyk) was elected in 1911, and the first city-based Ukrainian members of the provincial legislature (W. Kardash and S. Krawchyk) in 1941. Among the city politicians of Ukrainian ancestry, the best known was undoubtedly Mayor S. *Juba (1956–77), who in 1973 twinned Winnipeg with the city of Lviv.

Winnipeg regularly hosts triennial conventions of the Ukrainian Canadian Congress (KUK) and is the headquarters of the Ukrainian Catholic and Orthodox churches of

St Nicholas's Ukrainian Catholic Church in Winnipeg

Canada as well as of KUK. It is also the home of the *Ukrainian Cultural and Educational Centre (Oseredok), *St Andrew's College, the *Ukrainian Academy of Arts and Sciences in Canada, the O. Koshets Choir, the Rusalka dance ensemble, and the Osvita Foundation. It boasts a monument to Taras Shevchenko on the grounds of the Manitoba legislature, a monument to community victims of the 1932–3 Soviet Ukrainian man-made famine on the grounds of city hall, and 15 Ukrainian Catholic and 4 Ukrainian Orthodox churches. Since 1979 a Ukrainian-English bilingual program has been offered in a number of Winnipeg schools. Ukrainian language and literature are taught at the University of Manitoba.

O. Gerus

**Winter, Eduard,** b 16 September 1896 in Grottau (now Hrádek), Bohemia, d 3 March 1982 in East Berlin. German historian; full member of the East German Academy of Sciences (EGAS) from 1948. A graduate of Innsbruck University and the German-language Ferdinand University in Prague, he was a professor at Ferdinand University (1922–45), Martin Luther University in Halle (1946–51; rector, 1948–51), and Humboldt University in East Berlin (from 1950). At the EGAS he headed the Institute of USSR History, the history department of the Institute of Slavistics, and the Working Group for the History of the Slavic Peoples. He wrote many works on East European cultural and religious history, among them *Byzanz und Rom im Kampf um die Ukraine, 955–1939* (1942; Ukrainian trans 1944), as well as a monograph on the papacy and tsarism and Vatican policy vis-à-vis the USSR (1961; Russian trans 1964, 1977). He also edited *Die Deutschen in der Slowakei und in Karpathorussland* (1926), coedited an edition of I. Franko's selected German writings on Ukrainian history and culture (1963), and contributed to an East German collection of essays on T. Shevchenko (1976). Festschrifts in his honor were published in 1956 and 1966.

**Winter campaigns.** Offensives of the Army of the Ukrainian National Republic behind the lines of the Volunteer (White) and Bolshevik armies in 1919–20 and 1921.

The First Winter Campaign lasted from 6 December 1919 to 6 May 1920. As conventional military action in the

*Ukrainian-Soviet War became impossible, the UNR government decided to demobilize those units unfit for battle and to send its battle-ready troops behind enemy lines to conduct partisan warfare until it could set up a regular front. The participating UNR troops were commanded by Gen M. *Omelianovych-Pavlenko. His assistant was Gen Yu. *Tiutiunnyk, and his chief of staff was Col A. Dolud. Permanent political officers were assigned to the army to maintain liaison among the government, the troops, and the civilian population. Prime Minister Isaak Mazepa kept in touch with the army and even accompanied it for a while. The combat troops consisted of the following groups (renamed divisions in February 1920): Zaporizhia (commanded by Gen A. Huly-Hulenko), formed from the remnants of the Zaporozhian Corps; Kiev (commanded by Gen Tiutiunnyk), formed from the remaining troops of the Sich Riflemen; and Volhynia (commanded by Gen O. Zahrodsky). At first the units operated in the Yelysavethrad region between the Red Army and A. Denikin's forces. When the Bolshevik-Denikin front moved southward, the Ukrainian units penetrated east behind the Bolshevik lines, and in February 1920 they crossed the Dnieper River into the Zolotonosha region. In April the raiding army fought its way back to the Ukrainian forces on the Polish-Bolshevik front, which it reached finally on 6 May in the vicinity of Yampil.

The participants in the First Winter Campaign marched almost 2,500 km and fought for the following locations: Lypovets, Zhashkiv, Uman, Kaniv, Cherkasy, Smila, Zolotonosha, Olviopil, Holovanivske, Haisyn, Voznesenske (capturing major items from the 14th Soviet Army), Ananiv, and Balta. Estimates of the number of officers and men who took part in the campaign range from 3,000 to 6,000.

The Second Winter Campaign (also known as the Ice Campaign or the November Raid) took place in November 1921, while the UNR government and its disarmed army were in Poland, and the partisan movement was still active in Ukraine. The goal of the raid behind the Bolshevik lines was quite bold: to unify the partisan operations and to sweep the Soviet regime from Ukraine. Detachments of volunteers from the interned soldiers of the UNR in Poland formed what was called the Ukrainian Insurgent Army. It was commanded by Gen Tiutiunnyk, and its chief of staff was Col Yu. Otmarshtain.

The main Volhynia group (800 men) was commanded by Tiutiunnyk, and the Podilia group (400 men), by Lt Col M. Palii and, later, Col S. Chorny. Gen Huly-Hulenko's Bessarabia group did not undertake any serious operations and after a few days returned from Ukraine to Rumanian territory. The men in all the groups were poorly armed and clothed. The Podilia group set out on 25 October and fought its way through Podilia, where it crushed a Soviet cavalry regiment and transformed itself into a cavalry group. It reached the village of Vakhnivka, 60 km north of Kiev, and then returned through Volhynia to cross the Polish border on 29 November. The Volhynia group set out on 4 November and captured Korosten on 7 November but was unable to defend it. The group then moved as far east as the village of Leontivka. Having lost any hope of meeting with the Polisia group and replenishing supplies, it turned west. During the return march it was encircled by H. Kotovsky's cavalry near the town of Bazar, in the Zhytomyr region. Many of its men were killed in battle at Mali Mynky on 17 November, but the majority (443) were captured: 359 of them were executed at Bazar on 23 November, and the rest (84) were handed over to Bolshevik police. Only 120 men and the staff broke out of the encirclement, and they had fought their way to the Polish border by 20 November. The Second Campaign was the last operation of the UNR Army against the Bolshevik forces occupying Ukraine.

BIBLIOGRAPHY
Tiutiunnyk, Iu. *Zymovyi pokhid 1919–1920 rr.* (Kolomyia 1923)
*Bazar: Zbirnyk Instytutu Voienno-istorychnoho tovarystva* (Kalisz 1932)
Omelianovych-Pavlenko, M. *Zymovyi pokhid* (Kalisz 1932)
Dotsenko, O. *Zymovyi pokhid* (Warsaw 1935)
Mazepa, I. *Ukraïna v vohni i buri revoliutsiï 1917–1919*, vol 2 (Munich 1951)

**Wirsta.** See Vyrsta.

**Wisła.** A Polish scientific journal of ethnography and folklore, published in Warsaw in 1887–1905 and 1916–17. It printed studies in ethnology, comparative folklore, and the relation of folklore to literature and folklore materials of various genres. Many Ukrainian scholars, including I. Franko, M. Storozhenko, M. Sumtsov, and M. Yanchuk, contributed articles and materials to the journal. It published samples of Ukrainian folklore – legends, sayings, dumas, songs, tales, and magic spells – as well as notices and reviews of books on Ukrainian ethnography and folklore.

**Wisła River.** See Vistula River.

**Wisłok River** (Ukrainian: Vyslok or Vyslik). A left-bank tributary of the Sian River that flows for 228 km through Slovakia and Poland and drains a basin area of 3,540 sq km. In Rus' times most of the river and its basin area formed part of the Kievan or Galician-Volhynian realm. Ukrainians inhabited the upper part of the river (in addition to forming a few pockets of Ukrainian settlement between the Wisłok and the Sian) until the late 1940s, when they were forcibly resettled during *Operation Wisła.

**Wisłoka River** (Ukrainian: Vysloka). A right-bank tributary of the Vistula River that flows for 163 km through Poland. The upper reaches of the river are situated in the Lemko region.

**Wiśniewska, Elżbieta,** b 18 January 1931 in Radziwiłłów Mazowiecki, Poland. Slavist. She received her M PHIL in Ukrainian literature from Warsaw University (1955) and has worked as an assistant at the Polish-Soviet Institute in Warsaw (1955–7) and as a scholarly associate of the Institute of Slavic Studies of the Polish Academy of Sciences (since 1958). Since 1957 she has contributed articles on I. Franko, M. Kotsiubynsky, V. Stefanyk, Lesia Ukrainka, and other Ukrainian writers to *Slavia Orientalis, Vsesvit, Radians'ke literaturoznavstvo*, and the Ukrainian Warsaw paper *Nashe slovo*. She is the author of Polish monographs on Kotsiubynsky (1973; her 1970 doctoral diss) and on Stefanyk and his relations with Polish modernists (1986).

**Wiśniowiecki (Vyshnevetsky)** [Vyšnevec'kyj]. A branch of the Nesvitsky Ukrainian princely family from Volhynia, that is, the Turiv-Pynske *Riurykide dynasty. Prince Fedir Nesvizky is considered the progenitor and ancestor of four princely families: Vyshnevetsky (Wiśniowiecki), *Zbaraski, Porytsky, and Voronetsky. The surname Vyshnevetsky derives from *Vyshnivets in Volhynia. Among the members of the Vyshnevetsky family were Ivan Vyshnevetsky, the starosta of Propoisk and Chechersk (1536–43); Andrii Vyshnevetsky, the castellan of Volhynia (1569) and voivode of Bratslav; Prince Dmytro *Vyshnevetsky (Baida), who founded the Zaporozhian Sich; Kostiantyn Vyshnevetsky, the starosta of Zhytomyr (1583); and Kateryna Vyshnevetska, who married the grand hetman of Lithuania, Hryhorii Khodkevych.

Between the late 16th and the early 17th centuries the Vyshnevetsky family converted to Catholicism and became Polonized. In the 17th century its members held key posts in the Polish government, notably Jeremi *Wiśniowiecki and his son, *Michał Korybut Wiśniowiecki. The Vyshnevetsky (Wiśniowiecki) family line ended in 1744 with the death of the Lithuanian grand hetman, Michał Serwacy Wiśniowiecki (1680–1744). Polish chroniclers (M. Stryjkowski and B. Paprocki) incorrectly linked the family of Prince Fedir Nesvizky with the family of Fedir Korybutovych. That error resulted in the legend of the Lithuanian-Ruthenian origins of the Vyshnevetsky family from the descendants of Gediminas. It was later corrected by historians such as W. Semkowicz and V. Seniutovych-Berezhny.

BIBLIOGRAPHY
Dlugopol'skii, A. 'Vishnevets i ego kniaz'ia,' *Vestnik Zapadnoi Rossii*, 1868, nos 6–8

L. Wynar

Jeremi Wiśniowiecki

**Wiśniowiecki, Jeremi,** b 1612, d 20 August 1651 near Pavoloch. Polish magnate, starosta of Ovruch, and voivode of Rus' voivodeship (from 1646); father of *Michał Korybut Wiśniowiecki. He studied in Rome, Padua, Bologna, and the Netherlands. He colonized large estates in the Lubni region and neighboring territories in Left-Bank Ukraine. The region, including 50 cities, towns, and villages, became known as Vyshnevechchyna. In 1640 it had 7,630 homesteads; by 1645 it had a population of 230,000 and 38,000 parcels of land and supported a garrison of 12,000 soldiers. In the 1630s Wiśniowiecki gained notoriety for persecuting the Ukrainian Orthodox population, and in 1637 he suppressed a Cossack rebellion. In 1648, in the early stages of the *Cossack-Polish War, he was expelled from Vyshnevechchyna. In the course of the war against B. Khmelnytsky he fled with his forces from Pyliavtsi and was assigned to defend Lviv. He fled again to Zamostia in 1648 and was one of the commanders of the defense of Zbarazh in 1649. He opposed the chancellor J. Ossoliński and attempted to impede the signing of the Treaty of *Zboriv. He distinguished himself in the Battle of Berestechko (1651). He opposed any negotiations with the Cossacks and supported harsh reprisals against insurrectionists. His unprecedented cruelty was particularly felt in Volhynia. In general, Polish histories have portrayed Wiśniowiecki as a hero, and he was depicted as such by H. Sienkiewicz in the novel *Ogniem i mieczem* (With Fire and Sword, 1884). But 20th-century historiographers have taken a more critical view of him.

BIBLIOGRAPHY
Tomkiewicz, W. *Jeremi Wiśniowiecki, 1612–1651* (Warsaw 1933)
Widacki, J. *Kniaź Jarema*, 2nd edn (Katowice 1988)

A. Zhukovsky

**Wiśniowiecki, Michał.** See Michał Korybut Wiśniowiecki.

**Witch** (*vidma*). According to folk beliefs a woman with magical powers to harm people and animals. Ukrainians attributed various evils to witches – hailstorms, droughts, lack of milk in cows, diseases, and crop failure. Witches were portrayed as beautiful young women or ugly old hags. Some were born witches; others acquired the art from other witches or devils. Flying on brooms, witches gathered after major Christian feasts on Lysa Hora (Bald Mountain) near Kiev. Although witches were widely feared, there was no systematic or large-scale persecution of them in Ukraine. Unlike the Catholic church authorities in medieval Europe, the church authorities in Ukraine never showed any interest in such actions. Private actions against witches usually led to lenient verdicts. The peasants used various spells and rituals to safeguard themselves and their livestock from witches.

**Witer, Andrew** [Viter, Andrij], b 23 February 1946 in Leonberg, Germany. Canadian management consultant and politician. A graduate in economics of Sir Wilfrid Laurier University, he served as MP from the Progressive Conservative party in Toronto's High Park constituency in 1984–8. During his term of office he was instrumental in representing to the federal government Ukrainian-Canadian concerns over unsubstantiated allegations stemming from the creation of the Deschênes Commission of Inquiry on War Criminals. Witer has been active in the World Congress of Free Ukrainians.

**Witkowski, Wiesław,** b 7 January 1927 in Warsaw. Polish Slavist. After graduating from Cracow University (1952) he lectured in its department of Russian philology (full professor in 1978). His works include monographs on the phonetics of P. Berynda's 1627 Slavonic-Ruthenian lexicon (doctoral diss, 1964) and the language of I. Galiatovsky's works against the background of 17th-century Ukrainian literature (habilitation diss, 1969), an anthology of Rus' and Russian historical-linguistic texts (with T. Lehr-Spławiński, 1965), a booklet on the Ukrainian language (1968), a survey article on the Ukrainian language in a Polish handbook on Ukraine (ed M. Karaś and A. Podraza, 1970), and a survey of Polish studies of Ukrainian linguistics in *Studia z filologii rosyjskiej i słowiańskiej* (14 [1987]).

**Witos, Wincenty,** b 1 January 1874 in Wierzchosławice (near Tarnów), Poland, d 3 October 1945 in Cracow. Polish political figure. A self-educated peasant, Witos was a member of the Galician provincial diet (1908–14) and the Austrian parliament (1911–18). He was a cofounder and leader of the Piast Polish Peasant party in Galicia, and he emerged as an important political figure in the interwar Polish state, in which he served as longtime member of the Sejm (1919–33) and as prime minister three times (1920–1, 1923, 1926). He maintained a strongly anti-Ukrainian position throughout his political career. He supported the colonization and Polonization of eastern Galicia and Volhynia. In 1923 he introduced provisional courts in Volhynia and proscribed the use of the word 'Ukrainian' in all official terminology. He was an opponent of the federalist concepts of J. Piłsudski and a supporter of the restriction of the electoral and educational rights of the Ukrainian minority in Poland. From 1933 to 1939 he was an émigré in Czechoslovakia, from which he issued statements in opposition to the so-called *Normalization policy. His views on Ukrainians are expressed in (among other works) his autobiography, *Moje Wspomnienia* (My Memoirs, 3 vols, 1964–5).

**Witte, Jan de,** b ca 1716, d 22 December 1785 in Kamianets-Podilskyi. Flemish engineer and architect. As a military engineer in the Polish army, he designed the Dominican Church in Lviv (1749), the barracks and command headquarters in Kamianets, and the fortifications and church of the Carmelite monastery in Berdychiv (1754). From 1768 he commanded the Kamianets-Podilskyi fortress.

**Władysław II Jagiełło.** See Jagiełło.

**Władysław III Warneńczyk,** b 31 October 1424 in Cracow, d 10 November 1444 near Varna, Bulgaria. King of Poland and Hungary; son of Władysław II Jagiełło. He ascended to the throne in 1434 while still a minor, and gained the Hungarian crown in 1440, largely owing to the efforts of his manipulative adviser, Z. Oleśnicki, the bishop of Cracow. Władysław led a major campaign against the Turks in the Balkans in 1443, which ended in a rout at the Battle of Varna, in which he died fighting.

**Władysław IV Vasa,** b 19 April 1595 in Łobzów, near Cracow, d 20 May 1648 in Merecz, Lithuania. Polish king (1632–48); son of Sigismund III Vasa. In need of assistance in his wars against Muscovy (1612 and 1617–18) and the Ottoman Empire (1621), he ignored the Polish Senate's opposition and forged an alliance with the Ukrainian Cossacks, in which he arranged to satisfy their religious demands. At the elected Sejm of 1632 he headed the commission which drafted the 'Measures for the Appeasement of the Ruthenian People of the Greek Faith that Live in the Kingdom of Poland and the Grand Duchy of Lithuania,' by which Ukrainian Uniate and Orthodox metropolies were both granted legal jurisdiction (the latter had been outlawed by the Polish authorities in 1596). After the cessation of hostilities with Muscovy, however, Władysław did not honor those measures. Cossack armies commanded by I. Sulyma destroyed Kodak in 1635; the P. Pavliuk rebellion erupted in 1637; and D. Hunia and Ya. Ostrianyn led an insurrection in 1638. All those were brutally suppressed, and through the 'ordination' of 1638 the

Cossacks were put under the command of Polish officers. In 1646 Władysław initiated secret talks with Cossack leaders (especially B. Khmelnytsky), in preparation for an anti-Turkish war. He again promised to renew the Cossacks' privileges, but neither the plans for war nor the promises were realized.

BIBLIOGRAPHY
Śliwiński, A. *Król Władysław IV* (Warsaw 1925)
Czapliński, W. *Na dworze Władysława IV* (Warsaw 1959)
A. Zhukovsky

**Władysław Łokietek,** b ca 1260–1, d 2 March 1333 in Cracow. King of Poland from 1320. He actively engaged in external politicking and had several clashes with the Teutonic Knights. He brought a number of regions in Great and Little Poland, Pomerania, and Danzig under his control. The Galician prince Lev Danylovych provided him with military support during his campaign to seat himself in Cracow. The alliance between the two leaders was further strengthened through a dynastic marriage between Władysław's sister, Eufemia, and Lev's son, Yurii Lvovych.

**Władysław Opolczyk,** b ?, d 8 May 1401. Galician ruler of Silesian Piast origin. In 1372–8 he governed as prince of Galicia (Halych-Ruthenia) by the authority of the Hungarian king Louis I.

**Włodawa.** See Volodava.

**Wójcicki, Kazimierz-Władysław,** b 3 March 1807 in Warsaw, d 2 August 1879 in Warsaw. Polish writer, publisher, archeologist, and ethnographer. After taking part in the 1830 Polish uprising he moved to the Pokutia region, where he studied the customs and lore of the local people, developed connections with Polish Ukrainophiles in Lviv, and followed the growth of the Ukrainian national movement. He published the materials he had collected in *Pieśni ludu Biało-Chrobatów, Mazurów i Rusi znad Bugu* (Songs of the White Croatian, Mazovian, and Ruthenian People from along the River Buh, 1836) and *Klechdy starożytne, podania i powieści ludu polskiego i Rusi* (Old Folk Legends, Stories, and Tales of the Polish People and Ruthenia, 1837) and wrote an essay on the historical and agricultural proverbs of the people of Poland and Ruthenia (1840). After returning to Warsaw in 1843, he worked as an archivist, a newspaper editor, and a publisher.

**Wójcik, Zbigniew,** b 29 October 1922 in Warsaw. Polish historian. A graduate of Warsaw University (PH D, 1947), he served in Warsaw on the chief directorate of the state archives (1950–9), directed the Office of Scientific Works (1953–9), and taught at the Institute of History of the Polish Academy of Sciences (from 1959, as professor from 1971) and became chairman of its Scholarly Council (1981). He has written books in Polish on the 1667 Treaty of Andrusovo and its origin (1959), the Cossacks in the Polish Commonwealth (1960; 3rd edn 1968), the 16th- to 18th-century Polish diplomatic service (1966), Polish-Russian relations in 1667–72 (1968), the history of Russia from 1533 to 1801 (1971), 16th- to 17th-century world history (1973), Polish foreign policy vis-à-vis Turkey and Russia in 1674–9 (1976), and King Jan III Sobieski (1983). He also edited, with an introduction, a Polish edition of E. Lassota

von Steblau and G. Le Vasseur de Beauplan's descriptions of Ukraine (1972).

Rev Meletius Wojnar                Col Arnold Wolf

**Wojnar, Meletius** [Vojnar, Meletij], b 15 October 1911 in Bosko (Besko), Sianik county, Galicia, d 22 July 1988 in Glen Cove, New York. Basilian scholar; member of the Shevchenko Scientific Society from 1966. He studied at the Basilian Fathers' seminary and college and the Gregorian University in Rome (JCD, 1949). He was ordained in 1938, and became rector of St Josaphat's Ukrainian Pontifical College (1953–4) in Rome and a professor of Oriental canon law at the Catholic University of America (1954–74). He wrote several authoritative studies of the Basilian order in Ukraine, including *De Regimine Basilianorum Ruthenorum a metr. J. V. Rutskyj restauratorum* (1949), *De Capitulis Basilianorum* (1954), *Vasyliiany v ukraïns'kim narodi* (The Basilians within the Ukrainian Nation, 1955), and *De Protoarchimandrita Basilianorum (1617–1804)* (1958), and articles on Eastern canon law in *Analecta Ordinis S. Basilii Magni/Zapysky ChSVV* and elsewhere.

**Wolchuk, Roman** [Volčuk], b 22 February 1922 in Łańcut, Poland. Ukrainian civil and structural engineer. He studied in Lviv, Vienna, and Graz and emigrated to the United States in 1949. From 1959 he worked as a consultant in New York, where he established his own company, Wolchuk and Mayrbaurl (1963–82). Among his important projects were the design of the KCS railroad bridge over the Arkansas River in Oklahoma, the rebuilding of the Benjamin Franklin suspension bridge in Philadelphia and the Triboro Bridge in New York, and the first orthotropic steel plate redecking of the Champlain Bridge in Montreal and other major steel bridges in America. He prepared the AISC *Design Manual for Orthotropic Steel Plate Deck Bridges* and wrote other manuals and numerous technical papers. He was president of the Ukrainian Engineers' Society of America and editor of *Visti ukraïns'kykh inzheneriv* (1950–60).

**Wolf, Arnold,** b 1877 in Prostějov, Moravia, d 24 November 1924 in Prostějov, Czechoslovakia. Senior commander of the Ukrainian Galician Army (UHA), of German origin. While on duty in the Austrian army in the Sian region, he came in contact with Ukrainians and developed a sympathy for their aspirations. In November 1918 he traveled to Western Ukraine and volunteered for service in the UHA. Assigned as commander of the Berezhany (3rd) Brigade, in July 1919 he took command of the Second Galician Corps and in August he led the Northern Army Group during the offensive on Kiev. For his bravery and command performance Wolf was promoted to the rank of colonel and, later, brigadier general. In 1920, together with A. Kravs, he led the remainder of his troops into Czechoslovakia, where they were interned for several years; he was the senior commander of UHA veterans in Czechoslovakia until 1923.

**Wolf** (*Canis lupus*; Ukrainian: *vovk*). The largest of the wild members of the dog family Canidae. A powerful and intelligent social animal, the wolf inhabits both open and timbered areas throughout Ukraine (except the Crimea). Wolves are common in the forests of north Polisia, in steppe gullies, and in the Carpathian Mountains; they hunt in pairs or packs, mostly at night. As carnivores wolves perform the important natural function of controlling the population of herbivores, but they also kill domesticated animals; for that reason wolf hunting is permitted year round.

**Woloshyn, George** [Vološyn, Jurij], b 15 October 1943 in Kupnovychi, Rudky county, Galicia. Lawyer and administrator. After serving in the US army (1969–71) he completed his professional studies at the City University of New York (MBA, 1972) and Fordham Law School (1974). He was active in Ukrainian-American student life and the *Organization for the Defense of Four Freedoms for Ukraine. He worked as finance manager for the New York Transit Authority and associate director for the US Office of Personnel Management, and headed the National Preparedness Directorate, which is responsible for industrial mobilization, telecommunications, and warning in major emergencies. In 1988 he was received into the Sovereign Military Order of the Temple of Jerusalem in recognition of his contribution to NATO and free-world security.

**Wołoszynowski, Joachim,** b 1870 in the Podilia region, d ? Co-operative organizer, of Polish descent. He was director of the Hurt co-operative union in the Lutske region, which included local Ukrainian co-operative ventures that had separated from their central body in Lviv. He also organized a number of small village co-ops throughout the district and published the regional co-op journal *Svitova zirnytsia* in 1906–13. With the beginning of the revolution Wołoszynowski developed an ever-increasing Polonophile perspective that estranged him from the *Ukrainian co-operative movement.

**Women.** In Russian-ruled Ukraine in 1897, for every 1,000 men there were 1,008 women. That near balance was broken by the loss of many male lives during the First World War and ensuing Ukrainian-Soviet and Ukrainian-Polish wars. Consequently, for every 1,000 men over 20 years old in Soviet Ukraine in 1926, there were 1,090 women. A still greater imbalance developed as a result of Soviet repression and the Second World War, the primary victims of which were men. In the early 1990s in Ukraine, women constituted the majority (54 percent) of Ukraine's population. In Ukrainian immigrant communities in the West, however, they constituted a minority.

The social role and position of women vary greatly, according to the level of cultural development of a particular society. In 20th-century Ukraine women's rights and obligations have been, de jure if not de facto, nearly equal to men's, with the exception of certain religious functions. Women have been exempt from military service, and only in times of war have they been recruited to fulfill certain duties. The laws of most European and other Western countries recognize a range of privileges for women (special working conditions, maternity leave, and protection of the mother, etc), but a significant number of women have been and remain economically dependent on men, and in places their dependence has been reinforced by legislation.

**From ancient times to the 20th century.** In primitive societies the position of women was equal and at times even superior to that of men (see *Matriarchy). The prehistoric cultures of Ukraine were matriarchal, as is confirmed by archeological findings and ethnographic research. After patriarchy took hold, women were forced into a subordinate position and were even treated as men's property. During the transition from a tribal society to rule by a Christian princely state in medieval Kievan Rus', the primitive view of women as property disappeared. Various sources attest to the consolidation and regulation of monogamous bonds between men and women. In the family the role of the mother in raising and educating children became equal to that of the father.

The *Ruskaia Pravda* reflected the legal norms and societal view of women's status, marriage, and family in Rus'. According to that document the murderer of a woman was judged and punished in the same manner as the murderer of a man. In contrast to Roman and Germanic law, Rus' law did not delimit women's status and privileges. A widow was not assigned a legal guardian, as in other medieval states, but acted in place of her deceased husband. A guardian was assigned only to her children, and only if she remarried. As long as a widowed woman was the head of the family, she retained all rights, including the right to decide (if it was not stated in the father's will) when to grant sons their independence and patrimony. Once the family property was divided, the mother kept and governed her share; she could not, however, give it to someone outside the family. Daughters fared worse: they were excluded from inheritance and were entitled only to an allowance. If a woman slave bore her owner's child, she and the offspring were granted their freedom but were not eligible to inherit from the owner's estate. The liberal treatment of women in *Ruskaia Pravda* stemmed from East Slavic customary law.

Women's legal status in Rus' was linked to their socioeconomic status. Working alongside her peasant, merchant, or noble husband, a woman had the knowledge and experience to be capable of managing all their property after the husband's death. Noble women wielded influence in state affairs, and some became regents – Princess *Olha in Kiev, Anna (the widow of Prince Roman Mstyslavych) in Halych, and Yanka (the daughter of Prince Vsevolod Yaroslavych, hegumen of St Andrew's Monastery in Kiev), who traveled to Constantinople to invite a metropolitan to Kiev. Many European princesses were wed to Kievan grand princes (eg, a Byzantine princess, Anna, married Volodymyr the Great; Ingigerth, the daughter of Olof Skötkonung of Sweden, married Yaroslav the Wise; and Gytha, the daughter of Harold II of

England, married Volodymyr Monomakh), and Rus' princesses married foreign monarchs (eg, *Yelysaveta Yaroslavna married Harald III of Norway, *Anna Yaroslavna married Henry I of France, Anastasia Yaroslavna married Andrew I of Hungary, *Yevpraksiia Vsevolodivna married Henry IV of Germany, and *Yevfrosyniia Mstyslavna married Géza II of Hungary).

During the period of the Lithuanian-Ruthenian state women's legal status was defined by the *Lithuanian Statute, which incorporated the principle of gender equality into its criminal and civil articles. Like men, women were the subject of specific laws and regulations, and they were granted legal rights without any basic restrictions. Criminal norms guaranteed the complete protection of women and in particular cases specified special protection (eg, during pregnancy). To protect her dowry a husband gave his wife a writ guaranteeing her ownership of one-third of his immovable property and thus securing her financial independence. Daughters were not eligible to inherit immovable property, however, because land ownership derived from military service.

The Cossack period, with its constant wars and uprisings, like the earlier period of the Mongol-Tatar invasion, gave rise to a new type of woman, who ran the domestic economy and defended her home and family with arms while her husband was away at war (eg, O. *Zavisna). Women also fought in insurgent units during the Cossack-Polish War. Many women were captured by the Tatars and sold as slaves for Turkish harems. In Turkish captivity some used their talents to exercise considerable influence over their husbands (eg, *Roksoliana, the wife of Sultan Süleyman I Canuni).

The socioeconomic status of most women was shaped by the increasing enserfment of the lower classes. The absence of men as a result of frequent wars made women more responsible than men for supporting a family. They also carried more of the burden of corvée. Of Ukrainian noblewomen, many became Polonized. Others, however, actively supported the Ukrainian church and their own culture. Eminent examples were A. Olshanska, who funded the translation of the Peresopnytsia Gospel; Ye. *Hulevychivna, who donated her property to the Kiev Epiphany Brotherhood Monastery; and R. Vyshnevetska, O. and S. Chartoryska, and A. Hoiska, who were benefactors of various monasteries.

In the Cossack Hetman state women's legal status was still defined by the Lithuanian Statute and by certain local customary norms, until the adoption of the *Code of Laws of 1743. The code specified harsher penalties for killing or insulting a woman than a man, holding that a woman was physically less able to defend herself. The murderer of an unmarried woman, however, as of a slave, serf, or prisoner of war, was subject only to a monetary fine, or *holovshchyna*.

Women's economic standing was determined by their social estate. Wives of free peasants toiled together with their husbands and were basically their social equals. Women serfs, however, were the principal victims of exploitation and had no legal protection. Male serfs could often flee to the free lands of the Zaporozhian Cossacks, but female serfs were forced to remain behind and fulfill onerous corvée and eke out a living to support their families. The lives of peasants improved during and after the Cossack-Polish War of 1648–57, when latifundia were abolished in Left-Bank and, for a while, Right-Bank Ukraine. At that time the development of artisanship and manufacturing intensified, and as a result numerous female peasants and burghers were employed in weaving, pottery, and kilim enterprises. An important role in the growth of artistic crafts was played by nuns, who developed the production of vestments and other items for religious use.

In the Hetman state many women of Cossack *starshyna* families played important roles in social and political life. Hanna, the wife of Hetman B. Khmelnytsky, for example, was influential in the final years of his rule and even issued *universals. Hetman I. Mazepa often turned to his mother, Maryna, for counsel, and the wife of S. Palii effectively commanded the Bila Tserkva regiment during her husband's absence. In the 17th and 18th centuries many such women were persecuted and punished by the Russian state. P. Myloradovych, the widow of a Pereiaslav colonel and mother of émigré Mazepists, for example, spent several decades in Siberian exile.

The dissolution of Cossack society under Russian rule led to a decline in the leadership role of women. After the loss of a native elite, and with Russification (or Polonization, in the cities of Western Ukraine), national consciousness was most preserved among the peasantry. The primary conduits of that consciousness were women, who through their story-telling and singing imparted knowledge of Ukrainian history and culture to their children.

From the end of the 18th century, when Ukraine was partitioned between the Russian and Austro-Hungarian empires, women's status was determined by the Russian law code, which was based on the Napoleonic Code, and the Austrian civil code, which was based on Roman law. The lot of noblewomen improved because they were allowed to inherit land and estates. Middle-class women were generally dependent on their fathers, brothers, and husbands and did not earn incomes outside the home. The worst oppression remained the fate of serf women. They had no legal protections and were oppressed by their husbands as well as their owners, and bore the brunt of exploitative corvée, domestic chores, and work in the cottage industry.

During the Ukrainian social and cultural revival of the 19th century many middle-class women gained prominence as writers, actors, and cultural activists. Many more were teachers and contributed to the growth of literacy and elementary education. Before the First World War women did not have suffrage or many of the other fundamental rights, such as the right to higher education, the freedom to enter and work in the professions, and political equality. Those became the main goals of the *women's movement, which emerged in the late 19th century. Women were granted suffrage only in 1914 in Austrian-ruled Galicia and Bukovyna and only after the February Revolution in Russian-ruled Ukraine. The UNR Constitution of April 1918 proclaimed complete gender equality and rejected any differences in rights or obligations between men and women.

**Soviet Ukraine**. All Soviet constitutions and laws have proclaimed and defined equality between men and women. For example, Article 33 of the 1978 Constitution of the Ukrainian SSR stated that women are guaranteed equal access to higher education and professional training and equality in work, wages, advancement opportunity, and civic and cultural activity. Special provisions addressed the protection of women's health and work and ensured conditions whereby women could combine work with maternity, through moral and material support, such as paid maternity leaves and other perquisites for pregnant women and mothers, and a shorter workday for mothers of infants.

After the October Revolution the Soviet state announced that women's emancipation was one of its most important goals. Hidden behind the declaration was the practical consideration that women would play an important role in the work force because of the shortage of men brought about by the human losses of the First World War and revolutionary upheavals of 1917–21. The need for a female work force became particularly pronounced following the adoption of rapid industrialization policies in 1928, and the Stalinist state began promoting the cult of the large family and motherhood by initiating a system of prizes and awards for women producing many children ('mother-heroines'). The campaign was at odds with the earlier Soviet legalization of *abortion in 1920 and the ideas and practice of sexual liberation that gained currency in the 1920s. Eventually Stalinist conservatism and the unrestricted expansion of labor resources triumphed, and abortion was made illegal in 1936; it was not legalized again until 1955.

Women suffered the same mass-scale repressions as men during the collectivization of agriculture and the man-made famine and Stalinist terror of the 1930s. Many peasant women actively opposed the regime and led uprisings against the local authorities (the so-called *babski bunty*), especially after many of the men had been deported or killed. In the postwar period a significant number of women were active in the *dissident movement, which began in the 1960s, and were unjustly persecuted, incarcerated, and abused.

The Soviet state consistently denied women access to political and economic leadership positions. In 1990, for example, women constituted only 28.5 percent of CPU members, and at the final (28th) CPU congress, only 7 percent of delegates. In 1990 as well, women accounted for only 5.3 percent of Ukraine's industrial senior management. The participation of women in various Soviet elected Party and state organs never exceeded 30 percent. In 1988, women accounted for only 26.5 percent of all full and candidate members of the CPU CC and CPU oblast committees and 30.4 percent of all full and candidate members of CPU raion and city committees. As a rule, in the Party apparatus women were usually involved in ideological work, which was considered secondary to work in industry or agriculture. With the decline of communist power and the rise of alternative political forces after 1985, women failed to compete successfully with men, and their share in elected organs even declined.

Under Soviet rule no women served as government ministers or senior diplomats in Ukraine. Women rarely occupied senior positions in scholarship, despite the fact that in 1987, for example, the 81,582 women employed in science and scholarship constituted 38 percent of the work force in that sector. In education and medicine, sectors in which women have dominated and account for almost 80 percent of the work force, only some 20 percent were in leadership positions. Women were almost completely absent from leadership positions in cultural and art institutions and professional organizations, and from chief editor positions of newspapers and journals, despite the fact that many women made important contributions to literature, art, culture, and science.

Throughout the Soviet period the economic and political equality of men and women remained an ideological myth. Statistics show that women belonged to the exploited stratum of Soviet Ukrainian society. In present-day Ukraine the role of women has not changed. They constitute 52 percent of Ukraine's entire work force, which is higher than the highest percentage among all developed countries, that of the United States (45 percent). Women account for 80 percent of Ukraine's workers performing heavy physical labor. Because such labor requires minimal qualifications and is the lowest paid, women's wages are on average 25–30 percent lower than men's. Over 25 percent of the female work force is employed in the construction industry, and millions of women work on night shifts and in conditions formally banned by labor legislation.

Soviet women were officially organized in the Committee of Soviet Women, which had branches in all Soviet republics, including Ukraine. Special journals devoted to women's issues (see *Women's press) were published in the interwar period. From 1946 *Radians'ka zhinka* appeared monthly; in the late 1980s it became possible for that journal to begin devoting serious attention to the social, economic, domestic, and sexual exploitation of women in Soviet society. Issues of concern in Western feminism and radicalism and the struggle for true political equality, however, have never really been raised, let alone discussed, in Ukraine. Feminist organizations do not exist, feminist theory is not part of political science and sociology, and there have been no serious studies on the economic, political, social, and cultural dimensions of the women's question. Women did, however, become increasingly involved in the restructuring democratization processes of the late 1980s and early 1990s and joined the new political parties, social organizations, and ecology movement. Their activization and election to political leadership positions has been slow, however. Of the 1,109 delegates at the constituent congress of the *Popular Movement of Ukraine (Rukh) in September 1989, only 89 (8 percent) were women.

Only three women were elected to the Rukh executive. At the 1990 Rukh congress only 10.24 percent of the 2,020 delegates were women, and only 2 of 45 executive positions were filled by women. Women constituted only 16.3 percent of the deputies from Ukraine elected to the USSR Congress of People's Deputies in 1989 and only 13 (2.9 percent) of the 450 deputies elected to the Ukrainian Supreme Soviet in 1990. Patriarchal, sexist, and even misogynist attitudes and hostility to the ideas of feminism and women's emancipation are widespread in Ukrainian society, even among supposedly enlightened strata, including various leaders of Rukh and the many new political parties.

(See also *Education of women, *Marriage, *Prostitution, *Sexual life, and *Women's movement.)

BIBLIOGRAPHY
Luhovyi, O. *Vyznachne zhinotstvo Ukraïny: Istorychni zhyttiepysy v chotyr'okh chastynakh* (Toronto 1942)
Chyz, M. *Woman and Child in the Modern System of Slavery – USSR*

(Toronto and New York 1962); French translation as *Savez-vous, a l'Ouest?* (Montreal 1965)

Polons'ka-Vasylenko, N. *Vydatni zhinky Ukraïny* (Winnipeg and Munich 1969)

Atkinson, D.; Dallin, A.; Warshofsky Lapidus, G. (eds). *Women in Russia* (Stanford 1977)

Warshofsky Lapidus, G. *Women in Soviet Society: Equality, Development, and Social Change* (Berkeley 1978)

Blekher, F. *The Soviet Woman in the Family and in Society (A Sociological Study)* (Jerusalem 1979)

Warshofsky Lapidus, G. (ed). *Women, Work, and Family in the Soviet Union* (Armonk, NY 1982)

Steshenko, V. (ed). *Trudovaia aktivnost' zhenshchin* (Kiev 1984)

Koval's'ka, N.; Oleksandrova, T. *Zhinky Radians'koï Ukraïny* (Kiev 1990)

M. Kobrynska, S. Pavlychko, N. Polonska-Vasylenko, O. Trofymovska

**Women's Association of the Canadian League for Ukraine's Liberation** (Obiednannia zhinok Ligy vyzvolennia Ukrainy). An organization formed in 1952 out of the Women's Section (est 1949) of the *Canadian League for Ukraine's Liberation. It has carried out various cultural and educational work and contributed a page to the Toronto weekly *Homin Ukraïny*. In 1988 the association had 21 branches (14 in Ontario) and some 1,000 members. Its presidents have been M. *Solonynka (1952–75), O. Zaverukha (1975–81), M. Shkambara (1981–7), and L. Shust (1987–).

**Women's education.** See Education of women.

**Women's Hromada in Bukovyna** (Zhinocha hromada na Bukovyni). A cultural and charitable organization of Ukrainian women active in Bukovyna in 1906–40. By 1918 it had 14 branches and approx 600 members throughout the region. The society organized nurseries, an orphanage, a tailor's workshop and sewing school, a girls' residence, and folk-art workshops in Chernivtsi. It also published Hutsul and Podilian embroidery designs; participated in arts and crafts exhibitions in Chernivtsi (1912), Vienna (1912), The Hague, and Kiev (1913); and organized exhibitions of Hutsul handicrafts (1927) and Bukovynian folk costumes (1935) in Chernivtsi. The leading members of the Women's Hromada were E. Kumanovska, K. *Malytska, E. Smal-Stotska, K. Kostetska, Z. Hrushkevych, Ye. Halip, Ye. Korduba, E. Sterniuk, M. Levytska, V. Lukashevych, O. *Huzar, A. Fedorovych, and I. Hordiichuk.

**Women's Hromada in Kiev** (Zhinocha hromada). A clandestine women's group founded in the autumn of 1901 by prominent members of Kiev's nationally conscious Ukrainian intelligentsia: M. Chykalenko (Ye. Chykalenko's wife), L. Drahomanova (M. Drahomanov's wife), M. *Hrinchenko, O. *Romanova, L. Shulhyn (Ya. Shulhyn's wife), L. *Starytska-Cherniakhivska, M. Stepanenko (Ivan Steshenko's sister), M. Tymchenko (Ye. Tymchenko's wife), and V. Zhytetska. Younger women, such as H. *Chykalenko-Keller and V. Chykalenko (M. Chykalenko's daughters), M. Hozhenko (later B. Matiushenko's wife), N. Hrinchenko (B. and M. Hrinchenko's daughter), I. Kosach (Lesia Ukrainka's sister), M. and Ye. Livytska (A. Livytsky's wife and sister), K., H., and Mariana *Lysenko (Mykola Lysenko's daughters), Ye. Shcherbakivska (D. and V. Shcherbakivsky's sister and later M. Pavlovsky's and V. Krychevsky's wife), N. Shulhyn (L.

and Ya. Shulhyn's daughter), O. *Steshenko, and K. Yarmut (later Ye. Holitsynsky's wife) also joined the Hromada. The members secretly collected dues, distributed Ukrainian educational pamphlets and books in the Ukrainian countryside, and materially supported and helped several talented young peasant women while they trained in Kiev to become village teachers. The Hromada ceased functioning during the Revolution of 1905, which made its conspiratorial activities redundant.

**Women's Hromada in Lviv** (Zhinocha hromada). A women's organization that arose out of the merger of the *Club of Ruthenian Women and the *Circle of Ukrainian Women in 1909. In Lviv the Hromada organized public lectures, founded a girls' dormitory, ran subsidized cafeterias and emergency kitchens, expanded the activity and branches of the Trud women's co-operative, and popularized the Domestic Servants' Aid Society and the Ukrainska Zakhoronka nursery school society. It and its branches in 14 Galician counties and smaller village groups conducted cultural, educational, and charity work among Galicia's Ukrainian women and waged a campaign for women's suffrage. The Hromada's first head was M. Biletska. Prominent members were K. *Malytska, O. Luchakovska, O. Budzynovska, O. Zalizniak, O. Krushelnytska-Okhrymovych, E. Verhanovska, M. Mudrak, and M. Izhytska. On Malytska's initiative, in 1912 the Hromada proposed the creation of the For Ukraine's Needs fund, which gave considerable support to the Ukrainian Sich Riflemen. In 1917 the Hromada was transformed into the *Union of Ukrainian Women.

**Women's movement.** In Ukraine the development of organized groups of women sharing common goals and common interests was hampered by the nonexistence of a Ukrainian state and the severe limitations placed upon Ukrainian community organizations by various foreign authorities. Nevertheless, from the 1880s on, Ukrainian women managed to create effective organizations under all the states that occupied Ukraine – the Russian and Austro-Hungarian empires and interwar Poland, Rumania, Czechoslovakia, Hungary, and even the USSR. Women's organizations were also established by immigrant women in Europe and the New World. Ukrainian women's organizations were primarily self-help and community-oriented in nature. The members were not initially interested in feminism, women's liberation, or traditional women's causes such as the struggle against prostitution and the promotion of philanthropy, education, and suffrage. Instead the thrust of the women's movement in Ukraine was similar to that under all colonial regimes: it addressed the needs of the entire community, and not only of women. Organized Ukrainian women sought to expand the role of women in existing institutions and the national-liberation struggle and to ameliorate poverty, disease, and illiteracy. They adapted to existing institutions and mores and, instead of challenging society, highlighted the importance of the family and of the economic and socializing role of the mother. They also, however, maintained their political independence and did not become adjuncts of male-dominated political parties. As the women's organizations grew, opposition forced women to articulate a feminist agenda. Interest in feminism among those women developed as a result of their activism.

The beginnings of the Ukrainian women's movement date from the tsarist suspension of university courses for women in Kiev in 1883. The ban led to the creation of the first independent women's study circle, on the initiative of O. Dobrohaieva. The society was informal because all organizations had to be sanctioned by the police. Attempts by Kievan women to gain permission for the creation of a ladies' club from the 1880s on succeeded only after the Revolution of 1905. Women in Kiev and Kharkiv established branches of imperial women's organizations, such as the Society of Mutual Aid for Working Women and the Society for the Protection of Women. The Ukrainian branches developed distinctive forms of activity. In Kharkiv women founded schools under the aegis of the *Kharkiv Literacy Society. There Khrystyna *Alchevska became the major spokesperson for adult education and ran the oldest and largest adult literacy school in Ukraine. In the 1870s, women in Kiev organized the Hospice for Children of the Working Class; it functioned until 1917.

The women's movement in Kiev was characterized by close co-operation between Ukrainian, Jewish, and Russian women. There in 1901 an exclusively Ukrainian women's organization, the *Women's Hromada in Kiev, was founded. Because specifically Ukrainian organizations were banned by the tsarist regime, the hromada, and other such groups that sprang up in the major cities of Russian-ruled Ukraine and in St Petersburg (where there was a large Ukrainian community), functioned clandestinely and met under the guise of ladies' teas. After the Revolution of 1905, when public organizations were legalized, the hromada's members functioned openly; they successfully lobbied the Union of Equality for Women for recognition of the rights of non-Russian women and for a federal structure in the imperial organization. Women joined *Prosvita societies and the *co-operative movement that sprang up following the revolution and frequently established women's sections in local Prosvita and co-operative branches.

In Austrian-ruled Galicia community organizations were able to develop legally. Institutes for widows and orphans, founded under Austrian pressure by Ukrainian Catholic clergy in the early 1800s, sought to alleviate the position of women in priests' families. The institutes accustomed women to take interest in public and economic concerns. In some Galician towns, such as Peremyshl, the institute and the women connected with it were instrumental in establishing schools for girls. In 1868, when the first *Prosvita society was created in Galicia, women created an unofficial auxiliary force to it. The first woman formally inducted into the Prosvita society was I. Sembratovych-Osterman, in 1871. The first separate women's organization with a formal statute and structure was the *Society of Ruthenian Ladies, founded on 14 December 1878 in Lviv. The society remained technically in existence until 1939, but in the early 1880s it came under the domination of a conservative faction who sought to circumscribe the role and activities of women.

On 8 December 1884 N. *Kobrynska, under the influence of moderate socialism and J.S. Mill's *On the Subjection of Women*, organized the first public meeting of Galician women in Stanyslaviv (now Ivano-Frankivske). About 100 women from various Galician towns and villages attended the meeting and officially established the short-lived Society of Ruthenian Women. In 1887 Kobrynska

and O. Kosach, who wrote under the pen name of O. *Pchilka, published, with the help of I. Franko, the first literary miscellany by Ukrainian women living under both Austrian and Russian rule, *Pershyi vinok* (First Wreath). Kobrynska's feminist socialism was not popular, however, and her subsequent publishing and organizational ventures had little support. But the Society of Ruthenian Women, with its program of the enlightenment of women, the creation of community day-care centers, and publishing for women, caught the imagination of Western Ukrainians. Branches of the society were formed, and other women's organizations with similar programs later emerged in several Galician towns. The most influential were the *Club of Ruthenian Women, founded in Lviv in 1893 and modeled on British ladies' clubs, and the Circle of Ukrainian Girls, founded in Lviv in 1901 and renamed in October 1905 the *Circle of Ukrainian Women. Affiliates of both organizations were established in the towns and villages of Galicia, and the two organizations fused in 1909 into the *Women's Hromada in Lviv. The *Women's Hromada in Bukovyna was created in 1906 in Chernivtsi.

Women were also the prime, although not the sole, force behind the formation of the Ukrainska Zakhoronka society for day-care centers in 1901 and the Domestic Servants' Aid Society in 1903. Ukrainian women were among the first in the Austrian Empire to draft petitions for the right of women to attend state gymnasiums and universities and to organize prosuffrage rallies (some of them jointly with Polish and Jewish women). Between March and December 1908 they published the socialist women's journal *Meta* (revived in 1919–20 as *Nasha meta*). They also edited a supplement to the most influential Galician Ukrainian newspaper, *Dilo*, under the title *Zhinoche dilo*.

The women set up day-care centers, sewing and other trade courses, and co-operatives; experimented with cooking, gardening, and poultry-raising courses in the villages; ran subsidized cafeterias and emergency kitchens; and founded dormitories for girls. Societies for domestics were established in the towns to help peasant girls adjust to urban life. Sometimes Greek Catholic parish priests initiated the creation of women's social clubs in an attempt to offset Polonization. The first *Marian society was founded in Lviv in 1904, and spread to other cities; its members engaged in Christian philanthropy and self-betterment.

Organized women repeatedly discussed the need for unity, and a number of conferences were held in attempts to initiate it. The women also expected to be included in the leadership of the Ukrainian movement in Galicia. After Ukrainian community leaders refused to have women's organizations represented at a major gathering, representatives of leading women's organizations, reinforced by Ukrainian women university students, held a clandestine meeting of their own on 14 December 1912, at which they expressed the need for organized armed struggle for Ukraine's independence in case of war and set up a national emergency fund and first-aid and military training for women.

During the First World War Western Ukrainian women served as nurses in the Austrian army and fought in the ranks of the *Ukrainian Sich Riflemen. During the First World War under Russian rule, Ukrainian women ran hospitals under the auspices of the Tatiana Society and the Society to Aid Victims of War in Southern Russia. They also helped the many Western Ukrainians who were forcibly evacuated east during the Russian occupation of Galicia.

After the February Revolution of 1917, women on the territory of the UNR organized the All-Ukrainian Women's Hromada, whose members were active in community and relief work, education, public health, and care of orphans. That organization affiliated itself with the International Council of Women and sought outside medical aid for the epidemic-ravaged country. In the Western Ukrainian National Republic a similar organization of women arose, and the two attempted to work together. Ukrainian independence did not last long enough for the organization to develop fully. During the Ukrainian-Soviet War many women were engaged in combat and military reconnaissance activity; some even headed their own units and became legendary figures.

Ukrainian delegates at the 1921 congress of the International Women's League for Peace and Freedom held in Vienna. First row, from left: Kharytia Kononenko, Nadiia Surovtsova, Valeriia O'Connor-Vilinska, Oksana Khrapko-Drahomanova, Milena Rudnytska; second row: N. Tabakar, Olha Halahan, Olena Zalizniak, Ivha Loska, Oksana Lototska-Tokarzewski, N. Kovaliv; third row: Olena Sichynska-Levytska, N. Daskaliuk, N. Udovychenko, Blianka Baranova (Bachynska)

Under Bolshevik rule all independent women's organizations were disbanded and banned, and women who had been in their forefront (eg, O. Pchilka) were excluded from public life. The only sanctioned organizations were those that were affiliated with the CP(B)U and had as their goal the mobilization of support for the Party. Russian and Jewish Bolshevik women, who were not, by and large, sympathetic to Ukrainian autonomy and culture, were brought into the countryside to work with the peasants. They experienced serious opposition, especially from peasant women who did not understand Russian. Only in 1924, when M. Levkovych became head of the Women's Section (Zhinviddil) of the CP(B)U, did those organizations make headway in the villages. They sought to politicize women through mass rallies, introduced literacy programs, initiated two women's journals, *Selianka Ukraïny* (1924–31) and the Russian-language *Rabotnitsa*, and provided programs of health care and hygiene and information on the new law codes legalizing gender equality. The Zhinviddil also used women to glean information on anti-

Soviet conspiratorial activities and to find out which peasants hid food and harbored priests. In 1926 Levkovych was replaced by the Russian O. Pilatskaia so that any collusion between Ukraine's increasingly vocal and popular National Communists and women would be prevented. In 1930 the Zhinviddil and its locals were disbanded, and the women's question was proclaimed solved in the Soviet Union.

Ukrainian peasant women were in the forefront of spontaneous resistance to forced *collectivization and grain-requisitioning campaigns. Millions died in the manmade *famine of 1932–3 or were sent during the terror of the 1930s to concentration camps, where they perished.

Under Soviet rule women gained formal equality, but not real autonomy or full human rights. In 1945 the All-Union Soviet Women's Society was established, mainly to participate for propaganda purposes in international gatherings of women. Women in Soviet society, while legally equal, in effect bore the double burden of the need to work outside the home and at the same time to care for the family and the home in conditions of extreme want, with shortages of basic necessities and food. Many of the laws benefiting women were abolished in the 1930s, and thereafter the traditional role of the woman as mother was bolstered by a series of incentives and distinctions awarded to women who bore six or more children ('mother-heroines').

In the late 1980s, women became actively involved in Ukrainian political life. In early 1990 new women's organizations were founded: the Union of Ukrainian Women, which focuses on national rather than women's concerns and promotes traditional Ukrainian family values; the Women's Hromada of the Popular Movement of Ukraine, which focuses on ecological issues and issues of political independence; and the Organization of Soldiers' Mothers of Ukraine, which has publicly protested against violations of human rights in the armed forces and the sending of Ukrainian soldiers to serve outside Ukraine. The first non-communist women's newspaper in Soviet Ukraine, *Halychanka,* began publication in Lviv in October 1990 with a circulation of 10,000 copies. In 1993 the All-Ukrainian Women's Hromada was founded; M. Drach is the president, and L. Skoryk is the honorary president.

In Polish-, Czechoslovak-, and Rumanian-ruled Western Ukraine and in countries where Ukrainian emigrants settled in the interwar period, Ukrainian women established politically autonomous organizations. The Lviv-based *Union of Ukrainian Women (UUW, 1921–39) was the largest per capita women's organization in Europe. Founded through the fusion of a number of existing women's organizations, it and related organizations outside Galicia developed an effective system of self-help and modernization programs in towns and villages. Under the dynamic leadership of M. *Rudnytska the UUW spread to encompass over 100,000 members in Galicia. It organized day care, trade courses, agricultural programs, dormitories, and fresh air funds and instituted *women's press publications. Through involvement in the union, women became accustomed to political work. In 1928 Rudnytska was elected to the Polish Sejm, where she was a spokesperson for the Ukrainian cause and was particularly effective in the Educational Commission. Two women, O. *Levchanivska and O. *Kysilevska, were elected to the Polish Senate. The *Union of Ukrainian Women of Volhynia (1921–38) and similar organizations in Bukovyna and Transcarpathia co-operated closely with the Union of Ukrainian Women.

The cover of the official publication of the First Ukrainian Women's Congress (Stanyslaviv, 1934)

The presidium of the First World Congress of Ukrainian Women (Philadelphia, 1948)

The work of the UUW was so effective that other politically diverse women's organizations emerged. All of them, including the *Union of Ukrainian Working Women (1931–9), the Nasha Khata co-operative, and the Marian societies, co-operated with the UUW. Most rallied to its defense when it was attacked in the mid-1930s by the Western Ukrainian political right. The *Union of Ukrainian Emigrant Women in Poland (1921–39) and in Rumania (1923–40) and the *Ukrainian Women's Union in Austria (1920–38) and Czechoslovakia (1923–?) had close relations with the UUW. Women's clubs in Canada and the United States fused to create the Ukrainian National Women's League of America (UNWLA, est 1925) and the *Ukrainian Women's Association of Canada (UWAC, est 1926), which worked closely with the UUW, patterned their community organizations and self-help programs closely upon those of UUW, and materially aided the European groups. In 1937 the *World Union of Ukrainian Women was formally inaugurated to co-ordinate the work of all women's organizations outside the USSR.

During the Second World War all independent women's organizations were dissolved. Under German rule Ukrainian women managed to create in Lviv the *Women's Service to Ukraine, which provided the little help it could to children, women, and forced laborers sent to Germany, until it was disbanded by the German occupational authorities.

After the war Rudnytska sought to resurrect the Union of Ukrainian Women in the *displaced persons' camps in Germany and Austria. She was edged out, however, and a new organization, the *Ukrainian Women's Alliance in Germany, was established in 1945 through the efforts of I. *Pavlykovska, who objected to Rudnytska's refusal to have women support the émigré political parties. Fraternal organizations were soon created in the refugees' new host countries: the *Ukrainian Women's Association in France, the *Ukrainian Women's Alliance in Belgium, the *Association of Ukrainian Women in Great Britain, the *Ukrainian Women's Association of Argentina, the *Ukrainian Women's Association in Australia, and the *Ukrainian Women's Alliance in Venezuela. The UNWLA and the new émigré organizations joined together to create the *World Federation of Ukrainian Women's Organizations (SFUZhO) in 1948. That body has since then united all Ukrainian women's organizations in the West, except the UWAC and the women's section of the pro-communist *Association of United Ukrainian Canadians.

Other SFUZhO members are the *Ukrainian Women's Organization of Canada (est 1934), the *Ukrainian Catholic Women's League of Canada (est 1944), and the *Women's Association of the Canadian League for Ukraine's Liberation (est 1952); in the United States, the *United Ukrainian Orthodox Sisterhoods (est 1961) and the Women's Association of the *Organization for the Defense of Four Freedoms for Ukraine (est 1967); the Society of Ukrainian Women (est 1951) of the *Federation of Ukrainians in Great Britain; the *Organization of Ukrainian Women in Brazil (est 1952); and in Argentina, the women's sections (est ca 1939) of the Prosvita and *Vidrodzhennia societies.

Halychanka, the organ of the recently revived Union of Ukrainian Women

BIBLIOGRAPHY
Iuvileina knyha Soiuzu ukraïnok Ameryky, 1925–1940 (New York 1941)
Kohus'ka, N. Chvert' stolittia na hromads'kii nyvi, 1926–1951: Istoriia Soiuzu ukraïnok Kanady (Winnipeg 1952)
Knysh, I. (ed). Na sluzhbi ridnoho narodu: Iuvileinyi zbirnyk Orhanizatsiï ukraïnok Kanady im. Ol'hy Basarab u 25-richchia vid zasnuvannia (1930–1955) (Winnipeg nd)

Pavlykovs'ka, I. *Na hromads'kyi shliakh: Z nahody 70-littia ukrain-s'koho zhinochoho rukhu* (Philadelphia 1956)

Sez', H.; Marchenko, N. (eds). *Vidrodzhennia na chuzhyni: 15-littia diial'nosty OUZh u Velykii Brytanii, 1948–1963* (London 1967)

Stites, R. *The Women's Liberation Movement in Russia: Feminism, Nihilism, and Bolshevism, 1860–1930* (Princeton 1978)

Rebet, D.; et al (eds). *35 rokiv Ob'iednannia ukrains'kykh zhinok u Nimechchyni, 1945–1980* (Munich 1980)

Zorych, Ia.; Knysh, I.; Mazurenko, H. (eds). *Na sluzhbi ridnoho narodu: Iuvileinyi zbirnyk Orhanizatsii ukrainok Kanady im. Ol'hy Basarab u 50-richchia vid zasnuvannia (1956–1980)* (Toronto 1984)

Zorych, Ia. (ed). *P'iatyi kongres Svitovoi federatsii ukrains'kykh zhinochykh orhanizatsii, 26–29 lystopada 1987, Toronto, Ontario, Kanada* (Toronto nd)

Bohachevsky-Chomiak, M. *Feminists despite Themselves: Women in Ukrainian Community Life, 1884–1939* (Edmonton 1988)

M. Bohachevsky-Chomiak

**Women's press.** In Ukraine, as in other countries, the *women's movement found it necessary to establish its own press organs, in which it could discuss issues of interest to women and encourage women to take part in the national liberation movement and be active in community affairs.

The literary miscellanies *Pershyi vinok (The First Wreath, 1887) and *Nasha dolia (Our Fate, 3 vols, 1893, 1895–6) were the precursors of women's periodicals. Published by the pioneering Western Ukrainian feminist N. Kobrynska, they elucidated the theoretical foundations of feminism, the social and political status of women, and their most immediate tasks. The first feminist journal, *Meta, was published by the Circle of Ukrainian Women, in Lviv in 1908. It was followed by *Zhinoche dilo*, a supplement to the Lviv daily *Dilo* in 1912, edited by O. Kysilevska; *Zhinochyi vistnyk*, a semimonthly published by the Ukrainian Women's Union in Kiev in 1917; *Nasha meta, a journal published by the Ukrainian Social Democratic party in Lviv in 1919–20; and *Zhinochyi vistnyk*, a weekly supplement to *Dilo* in 1921, edited by M. Rudnytska.

As women's organizations in Western Ukraine expanded in the 1920s, the demand for women's periodicals increased. In 1925, O. Kysilevska and the Kolomyia branch of the Union of Ukrainian Women (SU) began publishing the monthly (later biweekly) *Zhinocha dolia, and the Ukrainske Narodne Mystetstvo co-operative association began publishing the magazine *Nova khata in Lviv. Both periodicals continued to appear until the outbreak of the Second World War. In the 1930s openly partisan journals were established. The Union of Ukrainian Working Women affiliated with the Ukrainian Socialist Radical party issued *Zhinochyi holos (1931–9), and the SU published an official semimonthly, *Zhinka (1935–8), which supported the Ukrainian National Democratic Alliance; *Ukrainka (1938–9), a popular magazine for peasant women, edited by M. Strutynska; and *Hromadianka (1938–9).

Until 1990 the few women's periodicals in Soviet Ukraine served as communist propaganda tools. They include the magazines for peasant women *Komunarka (1920–34), *Selianka Ukrainy (1924–31), and *Kolhospnytsia Ukrainy (1932–41) in Kharkiv; *Rabotnitsa i domashniaia khoziaika (1926–7, 7 issues), a supplement to *Shkval*, the Russian-language journal published in Odessa; and the republican monthly *Radians'ka zhinka (now *Zhinka*), published in Kiev since 1946. The first independent women's periodical was *Halychanka* (est October 1990), the biweek-ly paper of the revived Union of Ukrainian Women in Lviv.

In Canada the first Ukrainian separate women's periodicals were the communist *Holos robitnytsi* (1923–4) and *Robitnytsia* (1924–37) in Winnipeg. From 1934 to 1949 the Ukrainian Women's Organization of Canada published a regular section in the pro-OUN weekly *Novyi shliakh* in Winnipeg, and since 1950 it has issued its own monthly magazine, *Zhinochyi svit. From 1929 to 1959 the Ukrainian Orthodox church–affiliated Ukrainian Women's Association of Canada published a special page in another Winnipeg weekly, *Ukrains'kyi holos*; since then it has issued its own monthly magazine, *Promin'. In 1970 the Ukrainian Catholic Women's League of Canada began publishing its quarterly magazine, *Nasha doroha*, in Winnipeg, edited by A. Baran and V. Buchynska.

In the United States the first Ukrainian periodicals for women were *Rannia zoria* (1919–20) in Chicago, edited by V. Simenovych; the Ukrainian National Women's League of America's (UNWLA) monthly magazine *Zhinochyi svit* (1933-4) in Pittsburgh; and *Zhinka* (1939–40) in Detroit, edited by M. Beck. In 1938 the UNWLA began publishing a page of news in the Philadelphia paper *Ameryka*; since 1944 it has published its own monthly magazine, *Nashe zhyttia, in Philadelphia and, since 1975, New York. From 1949 the World Federation of Ukrainian Women's Organizations published a page in *Nashe zhyttia. In 1963 it established its own quarterly, *Ukrainka v sviti, and since 1973 it has published an English-language annual issue, *Ukrainian Woman in the World. In 1975 the United Ukrainian Orthodox Sisterhoods began publishing a quarterly magazine, *Vira*, in South Bound Brook, New Jersey, edited by H. Petrenko. Since late 1975 the *Ukrainian Gold Cross has issued an irregular bulletin in Rochester, New York, edited by M. Povkh.

Elsewhere in the Western world, Ukrainian women published eight issues of the journal *Ukrainka* (1945–6) in Hannover, Germany. The Ukrainian Women's Alliance in Germany published the monthly *Hromadianka* (1946–50) in Augsburg, edited by L. Kovalenko and M. Dontsov, and an irregular informational leaflet. In England the O. Teliha Ukrainian Women's Association has published an irregular magazine, *Lastivka*, edited by V. Smereka, and a page in the bulletin of the Federation of Ukrainians in Great Britain. The Ukrainian Women's Association in Australia published a quarterly magazine, *Nashe slovo*, in Sunshine, Victoria, in 1966–77. Women's pages are also published in weeklies such as *Ukrains'ka dumka* in London (by the Association of Ukrainian Women in Great Britain), *Nash klych* in Buenos Aires (by the Vidrodzhennia Organization of Ukrainian Women), *Ukrains'ke slovo* in Buenos Aires (by the Prosvita Alliance of Ukrainian Women), *Homin Ukrainy* in Toronto (by the Women's Association of the Canadian League for Ukraine's Liberation), and *Nashe slovo* in Warsaw.

O. Zalizniak

**Women's Service to Ukraine** (Zhinocha sluzhba Ukraini). A women's association established in Lviv just after the Soviet retreat from Galicia in June 1941. Its purpose was to render social assistance to the needy, particularly to political prisoners, prisoners of war, and starving children. The organization was inspired by K. Malytska and was headed by M. Biliak. Following directives from the German authorities the association was absorbed by the *Ukrainian Central Committee, and ceased to operate as an independent body.

**Wood carving** (*rizblennia khudozhne*). One of the chief branches of the decorative and applied arts in Ukraine. For many centuries the common people carved wooden plates, spoons, bowls, canes, furniture, cards, sleds, gates, beams, and gables and decorated them with designs organically linked with the practical function of those objects. Richly carved crosses and three-armed candlesticks played an important role in family and religious rituals. The carving of iconostases and church objects, which flourished particularly in the 16th and 17th centuries, was distinct from the popular form of the art. It was mostly thematic and large-scale, and its ornamentation, unlike folk ornamentation, was mostly floral and done in relief. Very few examples of pre-19th-century carving have survived. In the 19th century the influence of larger market forces was profound: carvers began producing purely decorative objects, and middlemen, who organized the distribution of such objects, began demanding new and alien designs. Under Soviet rule wood carving had been a highly organized handicraft industry, supported and exploited commercially by the state.

A carved wooden cross (1872) from the village of Stari Kuty (now in Kosiv raion, Ivano-Frankivske oblast)

Because of its remoteness, its forest resources, and the artistic talent of its inhabitants the *Hutsul region has been by far the leading center of wood carving in Ukraine. The distinctive, traditional Hutsul style was developed further in the 19th and 20th centuries by master carvers, such as the *Shkribliak family, M. *Mehedyniuk, and V. *Devdiuk. The ornamentation of Hutsul wood carving is flat-carved and geometric. It is enriched with inlays of colored wood, bone, metal wire, mother-of-pearl, and beads. The works of contemporary Hutsul masters, such as the *Korpaniuk family, I. *Balahurak, M. *Tymkiv, and the *Toniuk family, have been sold throughout the world.

In central and eastern Ukraine, folk designs are flat-carved with mostly geometric (rosettes, zigzags, and semicircles) and occasional floral motifs. The incisions are

deeper, and the relief is higher. The folk tradition of the Poltava region was popularized in the 19th century by the *Yukhymenko family. In the 20th century a number of folk masters turned to thematic carving. P. *Verna, for example, carved portraits of literary characters.

A carved wooden cheese box with brass inlay and embossing (1971) by Volodymyr Guz of Kosiv

In Transcarpathia V. *Svyda has developed a distinct style based on the local tradition of wood carving. He has also inspired and trained a younger generation in this art. The Lemko tradition of wood carving is known for its animal figures and floral ornamentation. Many families (eg, the *Odrekhivskys, Sukhorskys, and Orysyks) have won recognition for their artistic work.

BIBLIOGRAPHY
Lapa, V. *Poltavs'ki riz'biari* (Kiev 1937)
Pan'kiv, V. *Lemkivs'ki maistry riz'by po derevu* (Kiev 1953)
Budzan, A. *Riz'ba po derevu v zakhidnykh oblastiakh Ukraïny* (XIX–XX st.) (Kiev 1960)
Iurchenko, P.; Budzan, A.; Zholtovs'kyi, P. (eds). *Ukraïns'ke narodne mystetstvo: Riz'blennia ta khudozhnii metal* (Kiev 1962)
Zapasko, Ia. (ed). *Narysy z istoriï ukraïns'koho dekoratyvno-prykladnoho mystetstva* (Kiev 1969)
Drahan, M. *Ukraïns'ka dekoratyvna riz'ba* XVI–XVIII st. (Kiev 1970)
Mozdyr, M. *Ukraïns'ka narodna derev'iana skul'ptura* (Kiev 1980)
Bushyna, T. *Dekoratyvno-prykladne mystetstvo Radians'koï Bukovyny: Naukovo-populiarnyi narys* (Kiev 1986)
Zakharchuk-Chuhai, R. (ed). *Narodni khudozhni promysly* URSR: *Dovidnyk* (Kiev 1986)

**Woodcock, Eurasian** (*Scolopax rusticola*; Ukrainian: *slukva, valdshnep, valiushen*). A long-billed, squat game bird related to the snipe, in the family Scolopacidae, with mottled brown plumage well suited to camouflage among dead leaves. In Ukraine the Eurasian woodcock is found in damp mixed and deciduous forests of the Polisia region, in the Carpathian Mountains, in the Crimea, and occasionally in the forest-steppe. A favorite of hunters, it averages 34–38 cm in length and weighs 200–460 g. Eurasian woodcocks feed mainly on earthworms and thus must migrate south with the onset of frost.

**Woodcut** (*derevoriz*). A pictorial design from a block of wood incised with the grain. With the introduction of the printing press woodcuts were used widely for book *illustration. In the late 18th and early 19th century, wood engraving, in which the design is incised in the end grain, became the chief method of illustration, but soon it was displaced by other techniques. From then the woodcut was used mostly in *printmaking. Today it is one of the main forms of *graphic art.

**Woodpecker** (Ukrainian: *diatel*). A tree-dwelling, insectivorous bird of the family Picidae, including the genera *Dendrocopus* (*Dryobates*) and *Picus*, with a straight and powerful bill and an extensible barbed tongue. Approximately 10 species can be found in the forests of Ukraine, among them the great spotted woodpecker (*D. major*), green woodpecker (*P. viridis*), gray woodpecker (*P. canus*), northern three-toed woodpecker (*P. tridactylus*), Syrian woodpecker (*D. syriacus*), white-back woodpecker (*D. leucotos*), and medium and small woodpeckers (*D. medius* and *minor*). Woodpeckers are beneficial to the forest industry.

**Woodwaxen** (*Genista*; Ukrainian: *drik*). A small, yellow-flowered shrub of the family Leguminosae. In Ukraine the dyer's greenweed (*G. tinctoria*) is widespread; it grows in rocky soil in the steppe and forest-steppe zones. A yellow dye for textiles can be obtained from its leaves, stems, and flowers. The smaller thorny woodwaxen (*G. germanica*) is rarer. A tea made of woodwaxen has been used in folk medicine as a purgative and diuretic.

**Woodworking industry.** A branch of industry that processes wood for use in the *furniture, *construction, and other industries. Rough-cut wood supplied by the *lumber industry is processed to make finished and semifinished wood products, including veneers. Woodworking emerged as a modern industry only in the late 19th century. The first factories of the industry made furniture, matchsticks, and cabinets. In Russian-ruled Ukraine there were approximately 274 woodworking plants in 1913. They were mostly small enterprises concentrated near Kiev and Sumy.

The industry grew and modernized in the 20th century. Its relative weight in the economy is small, in that it accounts for only a small proportion of the GNP. Its modest size is due primarily to the scarcity of wood resources in Ukraine. Moreover, what lumber is harvested is often transported to mills and factories in Russia for processing. The annexation of Western Ukraine during the Second World War added some forested regions to Ukraine's resources, particularly in Ivano-Frankivske, Lviv, Transcarpathia, and Chernivtsi oblasts. The addition gave rise to a dramatic increase in the output of wood products. Today most of the industry's approx 5,000 factories are organized into manufacturing complexes or consortia that make a wide assortment of wood products. Factories in the southwestern economic region accounted (in 1968) for over half of the industry's output. Ukraine's share in the former USSR output remained low, less than 10 percent of most wood products.

**Wool industry.** A branch of light industry that processes wool for use in the textile industry. *Sheep farming in Ukraine dates back to the Neolithic period. Mostly coarse-haired sheep were raised to provide individual peasant households with raw wool. Processing was done at home,

usually as a handicraft. Only in the 19th century, when large numbers of sheep were raised in the newly acquired steppe region, was large-scale wool processing begun. During that period the industry was primitive, and its washing and spinning factories were small. Much wool was exported from Ukraine to Western Europe or to Russia in a semiprocessed state. Before the First World War the wool industry was concentrated in eastern Podilia; the Chernihiv region, especially in the vicinity of Klintsy (now in the RFR), where there were seven large textile factories; Kharkiv; and Kherson gubernia. In Russian-ruled Ukraine there were, altogether, 3 wool-washing and almost 40 small wool-processing factories, employing some 5,800 workers; that figure does not include the many peasant artisans and craftsmen who processed wool locally. Ukraine's share in the empire's wool output in 1913 was tiny, only 3.4 percent.

The wool industry was partially reorganized in Soviet Ukraine in the 1930s. Raw wool ceased to be imported, and since then only domestically produced wool has been processed. At the same time some synthetic wool factories were built. In 1940 the total wool output was 13,500 t. It increased, to 27,600 in 1960. Since then wool production has stagnated: it fell to 24,800 t in 1970 and then rose to 27,200 t in 1980 and 29,000 t in 1987. In 1987 most of the wool was produced on collective (19,300 t) or state (6,800 t) farms; only 2,700 t was produced by private producers. The wool industry in Ukraine now processes mostly fine wool from Merino and other fine-wooled sheep. (See also *Light industry and *Textile industry.)

B. Balan, B. Wynar

**Woolly rhinoceros** (*Coelodonta antiquitatis*; Ukrainian: *volokhatyi nosorih*). An extinct Pleistocene rhinoceros. It was a massive animal (over 2 m high at the shoulders) covered in thick, dark brown, woolly hair, with two horns on the anterior skull (the front one up to 1 m long). It fed on grasses, pine needles, and the saplings of young trees. Two carcasses were discovered in Western Ukraine, well preserved in ozocerite, near Starunia, Bohorodchany raion, Ivano-Frankivske oblast. Individual bones have been excavated in many parts of Ukraine. Cave rock paintings and sculptures of the animals have been preserved in several areas.

**Work.** The history of work in Ukraine has still not been adequately studied. Under Soviet rule all men aged 16 to 59 and women aged 16 to 54 were officially considered employable (see *Labor resources). People formally considered employed were those who earned incomes outside their homes and family *private plots, including underaged and officially retired people working full-time. Formally unemployed people included those between jobs, the ill, the handicapped, military conscripts, students, housewives, and women tending private plots. Growth in the work force has been due largely to the ever-increasing involvement of women therein, from 21 percent of all nonagricultural employees in 1921 to 37 percent in 1940, 50 percent in 1970, and 52 percent in 1987. (In 1987, women constituted 45 percent of Ukraine's collective-farm workers.) The share of women has increased because of high male mortality in the Second World War, male *migration to other Soviet republics, and the inadequacy of a single income for maintaining an entire family.

In 1969, occupations with the highest percentages of women involved were health services (84 percent), banking (76 percent), trade and food services (75 percent), education (71 percent), communications (66 percent), the civil service (58 percent), and public housing services (50 percent). Young people who do not pursue postsecondary studies have constituted another important labor source, particularly since the early 1950s. In 1969, for example, only 20.9 percent of the 371,400 students who completed grade 10 went on to postsecondary institutions.

Under Soviet rule allocation of workers was controlled centrally in Moscow and Kiev. From 1931 annual economic plans projected the number of workers needed by every enterprise and every profession. Vocational and professional schools trained graduates to fulfill these plans, and the USSR and Ukrainian ministries placed graduates in positions they were obliged to occupy for at least three to four years. All-Union ministries often assigned graduates of schools they ran to positions outside Ukraine. Another form of labor allocation was the *organized recruitment of workers system under which local soviets and their employment commissions found work for youths. In the Ukrainian SSR the system was co-ordinated by the Republican Commission for Youth Job placement. At the all-Union level the State Committee for Labor Affairs and Wages of the USSR Council of Ministers and state committees for exploiting the labor resources of individual republics oversaw most matters relating to work.

Officially *unemployment did not exist from 1930 until the late 1980s in the USSR. Consequently, public unemployment records were not available, and *social security was not available to the unemployed. Under Stalinism employees who came to work late or were absent were liable to imprisonment. The communist state exercised absolute control over the population through repression and the internal passport system. *Forced labor was widespread. Between 1940 and 1956, workers could change jobs only with the permission of the management. From 1956, people could change without permission with two weeks' (later a month's) notice, but lost seniority, on which the amount of the retirement *pension they received was based. Dismissal by the management of an enterprise was legally allowed only if the position was eliminated or if there was a general reduction in staff, and only with the approval of the enterprise's trade-union committee. If dismissal occurred for economic reasons (eg, automation), the management was required to find the employee another position with equal pay. As a result many enterprises were saddled with superfluous employees, and the introduction of new technologies was retarded. Employees, however, enjoyed considerable job security, which was considered one of the greatest achievements of communism.

Between 1969 and 1985 the percentage of employees involved in mechanized labor and mechanical repair increased from 42 to 65 percent of Ukraine's nonagricultural work force. The percentage of agricultural workers using or repairing machines and mechanical devices remained low (eg, only 28 percent of all state farmers and 32 percent of collective farmers in 1985). Productivity was very low. In 1969, for example, for every single unit of production four to five times as many workers were required in Ukraine as in the United States and three times as many as in Western Europe. The productivity of skilled industrial workers in Ukraine was 65 percent of that in the United States in 1970, and the corresponding figure for auxiliary workers was only 15–20 percent. According to official statistics labor productivity in Ukraine was 25 percent lower than in the RSFSR.

According to Soviet economic doctrine, labor productivity should have increased more rapidly than wages. In practice it did not always do so, however, and the methods used to calculate labor productivity were proved faulty. In 1933 the USSR government issued decrees on wages and production norms for the Donbas mines that initiated the centralized regulation of wages. To that date, wages had been arrived at through collective agreements. In 1934 the Soviet Ukrainian government decreed that when employees failed to meet their set production norms, their wages would be determined according to the quantity and quality of production achieved and without a guaranteed minimum wage. Thereafter a minimum wage was not set until 1957 (30 rubles per month, which was gradually increased). In 1971, 40 percent of Ukrainian workers still earned minimum wages.

In 1934 a wage system based on piecework and bonuses was introduced. In 1969 still only 43.8 percent of Ukraine's industrial workers received hourly wages, despite the fact that both K. Marx and V. Lenin had stated that piecework was exploitative and should not exist under socialism. To raise production norms and to force workers to work more intensively J. Stalin introduced '*socialist competition,' 'Stakhanovism,' and 'shock work,' and under N. Krushchev 'communist labor brigades' were created.

In 1922 an hourly wage tariff with 17 levels was introduced for blue- and white-collar workers, with a ratio of highest to lowest pay of eight to one. Later the ratio widened because the wages of state and Party bureaucrats grew much faster than those of the rest of the population. Industrial workers, in fact, saw their pay ranges shrink from a ratio between the highest and lowest pay of 3.6 to 1 in 1931, to 3 to 1 in 1951, and 2 to 1 in 1963. Wage reforms in 1962 introduced a six-level tariff for industrial workers. Under Khrushchev the wages of senior bureaucrats were reduced, but after his ouster they were raised again. In 1970 the basic monthly wage for blue- and white-collar workers was 60 and 450 rubles respectively, not including bonuses. Not only did the upper echelon of the *nomenklatura receive substantial premiums ('blue packets'), they could also buy goods in special 'closed' stores that stocked items that were generally unavailable and were, in addition, untaxed. The difference in wages among the Soviet republics and various occupations was arbitrarily set by the USSR State Committee for Labor and Wages. The most highly paid were miners, fishermen, steelworkers, scientific workers, artists, clock workers, and construction workers. Among the lowest paid were postal workers, telephone operators, doctors and other hospital personnel, state farmers, librarians, teachers, and workers in the sugar and light industries.

In 1741 the workday of industrial workers in Ukraine was 14 to 15 hours six days a week; in 1841, 12 hours; and in 1881, 12 or more hours, usually including overtime (see *Factory legislation). An 1897 tsarist decree limited the workday to 11.5 hours, but that law was widely ignored. During the Revolution of 1905–6, strikes brought about a reduction of the workday to 10.9 and even 8 hours, but by 1908 the 11.5-hour workday had been restored. In 1917 the

Third Universal of the Central Rada declared an eight-hour workday. In 1919 the People's Commissariat of Labor also declared an eight-hour workday and a six-hour workday for 14- to 16-year-olds. In 1929–33 the workday in Soviet industry was reduced to seven hours, and the workweek to five days (four days of work and a day off), because of the massive influx of the peasant labor force into the cities and for antireligious purposes, to force people to work on Sundays. In the 1930s the six-day week was reintroduced, and the eight-hour workday was restored in 1940. During the war years of 1943–5 the workday was extended to 11 hours, and vacations were suspended until 1947. In 1960 the workday for blue- and white-collar workers was shortened to seven hours (Saturdays, to six hours), and in 1967 the five-day workweek with Saturdays and Sundays off was introduced. In the 1970s and 1980s the average workweek in Ukraine was 39.2 hours (except for collective farmers) and 40.5 hours for industrial workers. Although overtime had been banned in 1921 as exploitative, it continued to be practiced because employees wanted to earn more, and management had to fulfill and even overfulfill their quotas. In 1930, blue- and white-collar workers received 12 days of annual paid *vacation; in 1958, 18 days; and in 1960, 20 days. In the late 1980s all employees received a minimum of 15 days of vacation and an average of 22 days.

*Overtime work and vacations were set according to a scale agreed upon by the enterprise's management and trade-union committee. *Trade unions had an important say in collective agreements and the distribution of work-related leaves, housing, and goods and services. Conflicts between management and workers were resolved by special commissions and people's courts. *Strikes were banned under Soviet rule until 1990, except during the brief interval of the *New Economic Policy (NEP) in the 1920s. The rationalization was that workers could not strike against a 'workers' state.' Various strikes occurred nevertheless and were until recently violently suppressed. In 1990 some 130,000 workers struck against about 260 enterprises.

Work safety in Ukraine was poor and ignored completely in many cases (notably the 1986 Chornobyl nuclear accident), despite comprehensive *labor laws. Inspection of factories was created in 1882, but inspectors were and continued to be few and for the most part corrupt. During the NEP, statistics were published on the incidence of work-related accidents, but thereafter, until 1986, the information was a state secret. It was known, however, that the highest number of accidents occurred in mining, construction, and agriculture. Occupational diseases were widespread, particularly in the chemical industry and in mercury, uranium, coal, and iron mines. Average annual absenteeism in Ukraine's industry in 1960–9 was 15 workdays.

In 1987 Ukraine had a work force of 20.7 million people, 14.43 million of them blue-collar workers. Of the total, 7.53 million worked in industry; over 5 million, in agriculture (3.78 million on collective farms); and 1.25 million, in construction. Ethnic Ukrainians constituted 70 percent of the total work force. In industry they made up 68 percent; in agriculture (excluding collective farms), 79 percent; in transportation and communications, 71 percent; in construction, 69 percent; in trade and food services, 73 percent; in public housing management and the nonmanu-

facturing service sector, 68 percent; in public health, fitness, and social security, 68 percent; in education, 74 percent; in culture and art, 70 percent; in science, scholarship, and their services, 59 percent; and in the government apparat, 73 percent. Of the total ethnic Ukrainian work force, 37 percent worked in industry and 2–9 percent worked in each of the remaining sectors (excluding collective farms).

BIBLIOGRAPHY
Sadovs'kyi, V. *Pratsia v USSR* (Warsaw 1932)
Schwarz, S. *Labor in the Soviet Union* (New York 1951)
Kahan, A.; Ruble, B. (eds). *Industrial Labor in the U.S.S.R.* (New York 1979)
Sacks, M. *Work and Equality in Soviet Society: The Division of Labor by Age, Gender, and Nationality* (New York 1982)
Yanowitch, M. *Work in the Soviet Union: Attitudes and Issues* (Armonk, NY and London 1985)
Lane, D. (ed). *Labour and Employment in the USSR* (Brighton, Sussex 1986)
Vitruk, L. *Uluchshenie sotsial'no-bytovykh uslovii zhizni trudiashchikhsia USSR (60–80-e gg.)* (Kiev 1986)
Manykina, I.; et al (eds). *Trud v SSSR: Statisticheskii sbornik* (Moscow 1988)
Porket, J. *Work, Employment, and Unemployment in the Soviet Union* (Houndsmills and London 1989)
                                                    V. Holubnychy

**Work people** (*robitni liudy*; Russian: *rabochie liudi*). A term first applied in the early 18th century to state peasants and *posad people mobilized by the tsarist state to construct canals and wharves. Later, until the mid-19th century, it denoted *possessional peasants and, particularly from the 1760s on, freely hired factory and water-transportation workers. The 'work people' were mercilessly exploited and abused as a labor force in areas where there were few serfs, particularly in the state-owned salt factories of Tor (Slovianske) and Bakhmut (Artemivske) in the Donbas.

**Workday** (*trudoden'*). A device outside the regular wage system for determining compensation to collective-farm workers for their labor. It was introduced in the USSR in 1930–1 during the forced collectivization of agriculture. Farm jobs were divided into seven to nine categories, based on difficulty or importance. An average job was worth one workday, a job of the first category as little as half a workday, and a job of the ninth category (the operation of heavy machinery) as much as four and a half workdays. In addition workers were rewarded with extra workdays for especially good work or penalized with workday deductions for poor performance. At the end of each year the collective-farm administration divided the farm's profits (in kind and cash) among its members according to the number of workdays accumulated by each worker. Because the farm's income depended largely on the state-set quota of produce that it had to sell the state at artificially low prices, the farm workers were exploited severely in the drive to finance rapid industrialization. In 1932 the average workday for the USSR was worth only 0.42 rubles, in 1937, 0.85 rubles, and in 1952, 1.4 rubles. Farm profits and the value of a workday for each farm were unpredictable from year to year; hence, there was little incentive to work.

In the second half of the 1950s monetary payments replaced payments in kind in the agricultural system, a change that brought about a rising demand for consumer goods among farm workers. In 1986 the CC CPSU and the USSR Council of Ministers finally decided to abolish the workday and to introduce a guaranteed wage for collective-farm workers.

**Workers' and collective-farm theaters** (*robitnychokolhospni teatry*). *Touring theaters, usually organized by state political education administrations, and known as workers' and peasants' theaters until the 1930s. The first such theater in Ukraine was the Franko First Ukrainian Workers' and Peasants' Theater in Odessa (est 1924 by L. Predslavych). It was followed by the Zatyrkevych-Karpynska Touring Workers' and Peasants' Theater in Romen (est 1925) and the Tobilevych Workers' and Peasants' Theater in Lokhvytsia (est 1925). Workers' and peasants' theaters were organized in Zinovivske in 1926 and in Kiev, Kharkiv (Veselyi Proletar), and Zaporizhia in 1927. The Kiev Theater of the Oblast Council of Trade Unions performed in the Donbas from 1929, and the *Lviv Workers' Theater was active in Galicia. Their repertoire consisted mostly of Ukrainian populist-ethnographic classics, with some world classics and contemporary Soviet dramas. From 1929 Soviet dramaturgy became dominant in the repertoire of workers' and collective-farm theaters and consisted mostly of plays published in the magazines *Sil'-s'kyi teatr* and *Masovyi teatr*. In 1930 workers' and collective-farm theaters were created in Okhtyrka and Artemivske, and in 1932 in Nizhen (*see Nizhen Ukrainian Drama Theater). Their number had reached 22 by 1933, and in 1937–9 there were 29 Ukrainian, 4 Russian, and 1 each of Moldavian, Bulgarian, German, Greek, Jewish, and Polish such theaters. After the Second World War there were only 17 in all, ethnic-minority workers' and collective-farm theaters were eliminated, and the number of Russian theaters increased. In 1961 workers' and collective-farm theaters became oblast theaters.

V. Revutsky

**Workers' and Peasants' Alliance Treaty between the RSFSR and the Ukrainian SSR.** A state treaty signed by the representatives of the RSFSR and the Ukrainian SSR on 28 December 1920 dealing with common defense and economic development. It recognized 'the independence and sovereignty of each of the parties to the treaty.' The following people's commissariats were to be shared: military and naval affairs, economic affairs, financial affairs, roads, post and telegraph, and labor. These commissariats came under the RSFSR Council of People's Commissariats and had representatives on the Ukrainian Council of People's Commissars. Other commissariats were to be the exclusive responsibilities of the respective republics. In practice the joint commissariats ignored the central organs of the Ukrainian SSR and dealt directly with local authorities. The treaty was an important step toward the creation of the USSR in 1923.

**Workers' and Peasants' Government of Ukraine.**
See Provisional Workers' and Peasants' Government of Ukraine.

**Workers' Benevolent Association** (Robitnyche zapomohove tovarystvo, or WBA). A pro-communist fraternal association established in Winnipeg in 1922. Closely allied with the *Ukrainian Labour-Farmer Temple Association, the association provided sick and death benefits to its members and operated a retirement home and orphanage in Parkdale, Manitoba, in 1930–8. Its membership grew from 700 in 20 branches in 1924 to approx 7,000 in 114 branches in 1930 before dropping, as a result of the Depression, to 3,500 in 76 branches and picking up in 1937. After the Second World War the WBA continued to expand its operations, and by 1954 it had 12,478 members, a level it maintained for just over a decade. As the WBA's Ukrainian membership started to decline during the 1950s, it increasingly recruited Russians, Ruthenian immigrants from Transcarpathia, and Poles into its ranks. In 1963 it absorbed the Independent Mutual Benefit Federation, with its Hungarian, Slovak, and Czech members. These practices failed to stem a steady decline in membership that began in the 1970s.

**Workers' control.** The power of workers to manage the factories or plants in which they work. This power has been sought by socialist and even trade-union movements and has been achieved to some degree in certain countries. A workers' control movement developed in Russia and in Ukraine between 1917 and 1920. Immediately after the fall of the tsarist regime, in March and April 1917, factory committees and other workers' organizations were established in most of the large enterprises in Ukraine. Their purpose was to negotiate with the managers and owners and to dissuade them from acting against the workers. In a number of cities local and regional factory committees as well as workers' soviets were established. In the summer of 1917 trade unions were organized in various branches of industry, and factory committees were turned into trade-union locals at the factory level. When in the course of negotiations managers and enterprise owners refused to make concessions to workers' demands, the factory committees began to take control over the administration, financial records, and order fulfillment. Eventually they began to participate directly in the management of the enterprises. By the spring of 1918 workers' control had been introduced in most of the large enterprises in Ukraine. In its Third and Fourth universals the Central Rada supported the trade unions and proposed to set up organs of state and popular control over the economy in order to deal with the collapse of the economy. This proposal, however, was never realized. Because of the revolutionary turmoil and war many factory owners closed their enterprises and fled the country. Such enterprises were taken over by workers, declared to be under workers' control, and nationalized. In their declarations the Bolsheviks supported workers' control but considered it as only a stage on the route to state ownership and control. The Bolsheviks argued that the rapidly deteriorating economic situation made it necessary to centralize economic power in the hands of the state. In Ukraine workers resisted centralization and tried to retain control of the enterprises. It was this conflict that gave rise to the Workers' Opposition in 1919. After the opposition was defeated and the trade unions were purged, workers' control was abolished. By 1921 all key sectors of the economy were under the control of the state.

In recent years the question of workers' control has reemerged. Mistrust of the bureaucratic apparatus's management of the economy and of individual enterprises has spurred the demand for it. In 1990, during the October strikes in support of Ukraine's independence, the Kiev Strike Committee and other committees demanded workers' control over factories. Some workers' groups have argued that workers' control can be realized by the sale of factories to the employees.

BIBLIOGRAPHY
*Robitnychyi kontrol' i natsionalizatsiia promyslovosti na Ukraïni* (Kiev 1957)

V. Holubnychy, B. Krawchenko

**Workers' faculties** (*robitnychi fakultety* or *robitfaky*). General education schools for adults in the USSR that were designed to prepare students for institutions of *higher education and at the same time train politically dependable cadres. Both daytime (three–year) and evening (four–year) programs were available. Established in Moscow in 1919 and in the Ukrainian SSR in 1921, the faculties were jointly operated by higher educational institutions and the government commissariats in charge of different sectors of the economy. The faculties were limited to workers and peasants nominated by Party, Komsomol, and trade-union organizations. Admission requirements were minimal: the ability to read and write, the ability to perform the first four arithmetical operations, and a basic understanding of political developments. Although the academic background of students in these faculties was poor, almost all graduates of the program could transfer (without entrance examinations) into regular programs in institutions of higher learning. In 1929 workers' faculties in Ukraine had 14,553 students, of whom 51.8 percent were Ukrainians and 24.1 percent were Russians. Members and candidate members of the Communist party represented 35.8 percent of the total enrollment, Komsomol members, 38.6 percent, and students not belonging to the Party, 25.6 percent. Ukrainian was the language of instruction in 62 percent of the workers' faculties. The faculties were closed in 1940.

In 1969 workers' faculties were reopened at institutions of higher education to educate working-class and peasant youths who had completed secondary-school education, and demobilized army personnel.

I. Bakalo, B. Krawchenko

**Workers' universities** (*robitnychi universytety*). Institutions offering a general continuing education that existed in the USSR and in the Ukrainian SSR from 1925 to 1931. In Ukraine the institutions were under the jurisdiction of the Main Political-Educational Committee of the People's Commissariat of Education of the Ukrainian SSR, which was charged with the development of adult education. The universities offered an evening program designed to upgrade workers' political awareness, educational level, and job-related skills. They also prepared working-class cadres for managerial positions in the economy, trade unions, and political institutions. Established in large industrial enterprises and drawing on the staff of institutions of higher learning, these universities had two departments, socioeconomic and technical, with a two- and three- year program of study respectively. Classes were held four times a week in four-hour sessions. Workers' universities were closed in 1931 with the development of new adult education programs. (See also *People's universities.)

**Working Alliance of Progressive Students** (Dilove obiednannia postupovoho studenstva, or DOPS). A semilegal Sovietophile union of Western Ukrainian students which existed in 1924–8. The alliance was formed in 1924 when five delegates walked out of a conference of the *Central Union of Ukrainian Students (being held in Poděbrady, Czechoslovakia) because of political disagreements and formed their own students' union. DOPS had branches in Berlin, Vienna, Cracow, and Prague. It was based initially in Prague and later in Lviv. The group maintained a strong pro-Soviet stance and was linked with the Communist Party of Western Ukraine. Among active members of the alliance were B. Dudykevych and S. Oleksiuk.

**Working class.** Traditionally the working class has been defined as a social *class made up of wage laborers (and their dependents) engaged in material production in *industry or *agriculture who do not own the means of production they use in their labor. The working class thus differs from artisans (see *Crafts), *peasants, and the *intelligentsia. Soviet statistics agencies defined the working class as an aggregate of persons involved in predominantly physical labor in the nationalized sector of the economy. According to that criterion junior service personnel and guards were included in the working class, as were state farmers. Collective farmers were not, because they formally owned the means of production, except the land.

There has been much debate on how to define the working class. Many sociologists in Ukraine and the USSR have argued that collective farmers should be included in definitions of the working class because the division between collective and state farmers is artificial; that is, the ownership of the means of production on a *collective farm is fictitious, and the work performed by collective and state farmers is similar. Moreover, sociologists have argued that the traditional boundaries between white-collar and blue-collar workers must be re-examined in view of recent changes in the economy and because the intellectualization of physical labor (eg, an increase in the number of skilled workers in automated plants) and the proletarianization of intellectual labor (eg, the existence of a large number of low-grade engineers with only specialized secondary educations) have undermined the usefulness of the key criterion used in defining the working class in the USSR, namely, 'predominantly physical labor.' Some sociologists have called for more all-inclusive definitions of the working class that emphasize control over the labor process. According to such definitions all wage laborers excluded from control over the labor process would be considered part of the working class.

**Russian-ruled Ukraine to 1917.** Because of the late development of capitalism in Ukraine, a modern working class was formed there only in the mid-19th century. Of course, there existed a work force in industry earlier. In the 16th century some free labor (drawn from among peasants, artisans, and Cossacks) was already employed in premanufacturing and manufacturing enterprises (paper, potash and saltpeter works, foundries, and mines). At that time wide use was made of bonded and, later, serf labor in enterprises belonging to *landowners and monasteries. The reintroduction of *serfdom in Ukraine in the late 17th century by Polish and Russian rulers blocked the development of free labor, which is a precondition for the rise of a working class as a separate social group. In the 18th and the first half of the 19th centuries, most factories in Ukraine utilized bonded or serf labor and were manorial enterprises owned by nobles. State enterprises that used some free labor were rare, and there were relatively few enterprises owned by merchants or foreign colonists that also used free labor. As a result most of the labor force in Ukraine was closely tied to agriculture.

In the mid-19th century, in connection with the expansion of industry and the increase in its mechanization, wage labor became more widespread on manorial enterprises. Besides using the labor of serfs under the corvée system of feudal obligations, landowners began offering wages to some of the serfs. The development of the sugar industry and the appearance of large mechanized sugar refineries created new demands for additional labor, which the landowners filled by renting serfs from neighboring estates or by hiring free labor. The growth of industry and the increasing unprofitability of serf labor vis-à-vis free labor undermined the institution of serfdom and hastened the rise of capitalist relations in industry and agriculture and the formation of a working class.

Tsarist government statistics show that in 1825 there were some 15,000 workers in industry in Russian-ruled Ukraine. (The data are incomplete because they do not include workers in distilleries and mines or the work force of Tavriia guberniia.) Almost 60 percent of those workers were concentrated in Kiev, Poltava, Kharkiv, and Chernihiv gubernias. Free wage laborers formed only 25 percent of workers in industry in 1828. Sixty-one percent of the working class in that period worked in fulling mills and the textile industry; 10 percent, in metallurgy and metalworking; 9 percent, in saltpeter works; 5 percent, in paper works; and 15 percent, in other sectors. By 1860 the working class in industry (as defined above) had grown to 85,000 because of the expansion of the labor-intensive sugar industry; 77 percent was concentrated in the aforementioned guberniias. In 1861, free workers constituted 75 percent of all workers.

The figures just given underestimate the real size of Russian-ruled Ukraine's working class. In the mid-19th century the gathering of labor statistics was in its infancy in Europe in general and in the Russian Empire in particular. Moreover, it was difficult to establish the size of the working class because many workers retained their ties to the village economy. O. Hurzhii estimates the size of the working class in 1861 as approx 200,000: 45,000 in the sugar industry, 25,000 in distilleries, 10,000 in the textile industry, 70,000 in water transportation, and 5,000 in mining, to name some of the major sectors. Not included in the figure were hundreds of thousands of agricultural *migrant workers, many of whom traveled long distances to work in Southern Ukraine.

The early working class, especially serf laborers, worked under appalling conditions. The entrepreneurial landowners had the right to punish their serfs, and beatings were common, despite the efforts of some government officials to limit abuses. The average working day was 12 to 15 hours, and payment, especially for serf labor, was minimal. The highest-paid workers were locksmiths and blacksmiths. Labor conditions were best in the newly established machine-building plants and engineering works.

Before 1861 the vast majority of workers in Russian-

ruled Ukraine were Ukrainian. The skilled sectors of that early working class were formed out of urban and rural artisans, many of whom were of Cossack origin, whereas the mass of unskilled workers were from the peasantry. In that period Russians did not predominate in the working class, although many Russians worked in Ukraine, especially as itinerant craftsmen. In 1845 in Kiev gubernia, for example, Russians made up one-third of the 6,000 craftsmen.

The national composition of Ukraine's working class altered dramatically in the second half of the 19th century, because in the postemancipation period (from 1861) industrial capitalism developed much faster in Ukraine than in Russia. The growth was spurred by large-scale foreign investment in Ukrainian industry, particularly in mining and metallurgy. With rapid industrial development a distinct social group of nonagricultural wage laborers came into being. Technicians and engineers arrived from Europe, and the bulk of the labor force, especially in key industrial sectors, was recruited from Russia because suitable labor was in short supply in Ukraine.

Between 1861 and 1870 the average annual number of workers in the nine gubernias of Russian-ruled Ukraine was 142,600. Only 13 percent were located in the steppe gubernias of *Southern Ukraine and the *Donets Basin. By 1900 the working class had grown to 327,400, 46 percent of it in the steppe gubernias. (The figures include only workers in industrial enterprises with motor power with at least 16 workers, or those without motor power with at least 30 workers.) In 1897 there were 425,000 industrial workers in Russian-ruled Ukraine, almost half of them in the steppe gubernias. Over 65,000 workers were employed in mining and metallurgy. The industrial working class made up 7 percent of the employed population. By 1913 a further concentration of workers in mining and metallurgy had taken place. That year the working class numbered 642,308; 45 percent worked in mining and metallurgy.

Census data give some idea of how much of industry's labor needs were met by Russian labor. According to M. Porsh's analysis of the data, 42 percent of the 425,000 industrial workers in Russian-ruled Ukraine were born beyond its borders. Two-thirds of those migrants settled in the industrial south and gravitated toward the large enterprises. In 1892, for example, 80 percent of the labor force in the mines and factories of Yuzivka (now Donetske) had come from the Moscow area. In 1897 Ukrainians formed 32 percent of the industrial working class, and a quarter worked in the mines, and a third, in metallurgy. Data suggest that the rate of the Ukrainians' industrial *migration tended to increase as the economy grew, and as mechanized agriculture made them increasingly superfluous as an agricultural labor force. In 1871, for example, only 14 percent of Donbas miners originated from the Ukrainian gubernias. By 1914 almost half the new recruits in the mines were Ukrainian. Such changes, however, did not occur on a large enough scale to alter the national composition of the working class before the Revolution of 1917.

The total number of workers in Russian-ruled Ukraine in 1897 (including all nonindustrial sectors except agriculture) is estimated at 1.5 million, of whom 44 percent were Ukrainians. (Seasonal agricultural workers in that period numbered approximately 2 million.) Ukrainians tended to predominate in the most unskilled sectors; over half of the day laborers were Ukrainian. The vast majority of Ukrainian workers were located in the Right-Bank and Left-Bank gubernias rather than the steppe gubernias. Only a small proportion of Ukrainian workers worked in towns; most labored in enterprises located in rural areas. Russian-ruled Ukraine was characterized by an unusually high proportion of temporary workers in its factory proletariat. Studies of the Donbas reveal that almost all temporary workers there were Ukrainian. Women represented 9.3 percent of industrial workers in 1897; the vast majority worked in the clothing industry, where they accounted for one-third of the total number of workers (including nonindustrial ones).

The working class in the steppe gubernias reflects the uneven industrial development of Ukraine. Enterprises in Katerynoslav gubernia (including the Donbas) were relatively modern, utilized much greater horsepower per worker than industries in Russia proper, and employed very large work forces. In 1902, for example, 69 percent of all industrial workers in Russian-ruled Ukraine laboring in factories with over 1,000 employees were in that gubernia. As early as 1894, two-thirds of all enterprises in the gubernia employed not fewer than 500 workers, and the highest-paid workers in the Russian Empire (excluding Finland) worked in the gubernia. Wages in Right-Bank and Left-Bank Ukraine (except in the city of Kharkiv), however, were among the lowest in the empire, and compared to that in Western Europe, the standard of living of workers in Ukraine was very low. In 1910 the average wage of industrial workers in Russian-ruled Ukraine was less than one-quarter that of their Western European counterparts. Housing and working conditions, especially in the mining areas, were among the worst in Europe. In 1897, 52 percent of Ukraine's industrial working class were illiterate (among metallurgists, 33 percent).

The expansion of the Russian defense industry during the First World War resulted in the growth of Ukraine's industrial working class from 631,000 in 1914 to 812,500 in 1916. Using contemporary Soviet definitions, M. Rubach calculated that in 1917 the working class in Ukraine numbered 3.6 million, of whom 893,000 were industrial workers, 121,000 were railway workers, 230,000 were employed in urban artisan production, 300,000 worked in construction, 444,000 labored in village artisan enterprises, 365,000 were servants, 59,000 were employed in trade and urban transportation, and 1.2 million were agricultural laborers. With their dependents the working class thus broadly defined numbered 6.5 million people, or 20.8 percent of the total population of Ukraine in 1917.

**Interwar Soviet Ukraine.** During the Ukrainian-Soviet War of 1917–21 much of Ukraine's industry was destroyed, and economic chaos resulted in massive deproletarianization of the population. Soviet compulsory mobilizations of workers and the general militarization of labor did not stop the flight from factories. In 1921 Soviet Ukraine had only 260,000 factory workers, who constituted little more than 1 percent of the total population. During the period of the *New Economic Policy (NEP) economic recovery began, and the working class began to reconstitute itself. The number of factory workers had increased to 360,000 by 1924 and 675,000 by 1927. The total work force (industry, transportation, and communication) more than doubled between 1924 and 1927, from 1.2 to 2.7 million. In 1927, women made up 14 percent of all workers. What was significant about the new working class was that for the first time in the history of the country the majority of new recruits were Ukrainian.

Trade-union membership data show that the number of Ukrainians had increased from 41 percent of the total membership in 1923 to 57 percent by the autumn of 1929. The most complete record of the working class is provided by the 1926 general population census. It reveals that 55 percent of Soviet Ukraine's 1.1 million workers were Ukrainians, 29 percent were Russians, and 9 percent were Jews. Ukrainians formed 43 percent of the 509,000 workers in industry and manufacturing, 66 percent of the 143,000 workers in transportation, and 81 percent of the 160,000 agricultural workers. During the upsurge in the economy in the second half of the 1920s, the weight of Ukrainians in the working class increased. According to a trade-union census, between the winter of 1926 and the autumn of 1929 the number of Ukrainians in industry increased from 41 to 48 percent; among miners, an occupation Ukrainians traditionally eschewed, it increased from 36 to 40 percent. In the younger age-groups Ukrainians predominated, and they constituted 62 percent of all industrial trainees.

In the tsarist era most workers never attended a Ukrainian-language school or read a Ukrainian-language newspaper or book, and acquired their literacy and elementary exposure to culture in the Russian language. As a result the working class was by and large Russified. During the 1920s, however, as a result of the policy of *Ukrainization, the use of Ukrainian and the popularity of Ukrainian culture increased substantially within the working class. Between 1926 and 1929 the proportion of workers in industry who read Ukrainian publications increased from 22 to 43 percent. By the autumn of 1929 half of the industrial trade unions were conducting their business in Ukrainian.

The new agrarian conditions under the NEP forced many peasants to seek nonagricultural employment to supplement their meager incomes. Between 1926 and 1929, for example, 23 percent of workers in metallurgy still owned land. Because wages in industry were much higher than agrarian incomes, however, and industrial workers had the added advantage of social security and a shorter workday, nonagricultural employment became the chief source of livelihood.

During the First *Five-Year Plan (1928–33) the working class in Ukraine expanded rapidly. Escaping *collectivization and attracted by the higher standard of living and the opportunities for social mobility offered by industrial employment, hundreds of thousands of peasants moved en masse into urban centers and filled the labor needs of rapidly growing industry. By 1930, for example, almost 80 percent of the new recruits in the Donbas mines were Ukrainian peasants. The workers entering industry were also very young. By 1933, 40 percent of Soviet Ukraine's working class were less than 23 years old.

The number of workers in *heavy industry had expanded from 607,000 in 1929 to 1.1 million by 1933 and 1.4 million by 1939. In 1940 the number of workers in Ukraine in all sectors was 4.6 million. Between 1926 and 1939 the social weight of the working class increased in Soviet Ukrainian society from 6.2 percent of the economically active population to 37 percent. By 1939, 29 percent of ethnic Ukrainians were part of the working class and constituted 66 percent of all workers.

The working class that came into existence during the early years of industrialization was formed when Ukrainization was still in force. At that time the influx of ethnic Ukrainian workers gave fresh impetus to the Ukrainization of the *trade unions. By 1932, for example, 56 percent of trade unionists in the Donbas were Ukrainian. By 1933, 88 percent of all factory newspapers, double the figure for 1928, were being published in Ukrainian. In 1933, however, Ukrainization policies implemented within the working class were attacked as counterrevolutionary. The end of Ukrainization coincided with the introduction of a totalitarian factory regime. The working class, like other social classes, became highly atomized and ceased to exist as an interest group.

**Western Ukraine to 1939.** Under Austro-Hungarian rule Western Ukraine remained economically underdeveloped, even in comparison with Russian-ruled Ukraine. Only at the beginning of the 20th century did some industrial development occur, primarily in Galicia through foreign investment in the petroleum industry. In ethnic Ukrainian eastern Galicia the working class in industry, construction, transportation, and trade numbered 66,100 in 1869 and 75,000 in 1902, not including day laborers and agricultural workers. In 1902 the working class numbered 7,000 in Transcarpathia and 6,000 in Bukovyna.

There were many seasonal migrant workers and day laborers in Western Ukraine. At the beginning of the 20th century, for instance, there were only 4,000 full-time workers in the petroleum industry, but 10,000 seasonal workers. The landless and land-poor peasantry also formed a large corps of agricultural day laborers and seasonal workers. In addition, some 75,000 Ukrainians left Galicia each year between 1907 and 1912 to work on a seasonal basis in Germany (primarily Prussia), Czechoslovakia, Denmark, and Rumania. Some 700,000 to 800,000 emigrated to the United States, Canada, and Brazil.

Ukrainians were poorly represented among full-time workers. In Galicia in 1900, they formed only 15–18 percent of the 20,000 full-time workers, whereas Poles made up 56 percent, and Jews, 25 percent. Women in Galicia in 1900 formed only 9 percent of workers. In Transcarpathia Ukrainians accounted for 20 percent of the permanent labor force.

The standard of living of workers in Western Ukraine was very low. They received subsistence wages and lived in primitive housing. In Lviv in 1910, for example, 48 percent of workers lived in rooms without beds. Seasonal workers, the overwhelming majority of whom were Ukrainians, lived in even worse material conditions.

In the interwar period, conditions in Galicia and Volhynia deteriorated under Polish rule. Emigration abroad was reduced, and there was little industrial development to absorb the surplus rural population. Mass unemployment ensued, especially during the Great Depression. Between 1929 and 1933 the real *wages of workers declined by 45 percent. In 1931 there were 393,700 workers in industry, of whom 34 percent were Ukrainians. Ukrainians accounted for 62 percent of all 341,400 agricultural workers.

**Ukraine since 1940.** In 1940 there were 4.6 million workers on the territory of present-day Ukraine. During the Second World War some one million were drafted into the Red Army, and many others were evacuated by the Soviets to the east. More than two million people were taken by the Nazis to work in Germany (see *Ostarbeiter).

During the war Ukraine's economy was devastated, and by 1944 there were only 615,000 workers in Ukraine. Because millions of men died in the war, there was an acute shortage of able-bodied male workers. Thus, in the postwar reconstruction period *women became a major source of industrial labor. By 1950, 38 percent of Ukraine's industrial workers were women. The authorities made access to higher education more difficult in order to stream young people into the working class (see *Social mobility). Through the *organized recruitment of workers over two million workers were placed in jobs between 1946 and 1962, and 812,000 were sent to work outside Ukraine elsewhere in the USSR.

Ukraine's working class numbered 7.9 million by 1960 and 11.6 million by 1970. The number of workers in agriculture (state and collective farmers) declined, however, from 8.7 million in 1959 to 5.8 million in 1970. In 1970 the largest nonagricultural sector of the working class was in trade and the services industry (3.0 million), followed by machine building and the metalworking industry (2.8 million), transportation and communications (2.2 million), construction (1 million), and light industry (960,000). Ukraine's working class was highly concentrated, with two-thirds employed in factories containing over 1,000 workers. Indicative of larger economic problems was the fact that the rapid growth of Ukraine's working class was brought about to a significant degree by a level of productivity much below the USSR norm. What that fact pointed to was inadequate industrial investment and poor mechanization, which in turn produced a conflicting factory regime. In the Donbas, for example, because new investment in mining was meager, workers' safety was allowed to deteriorate, and major unrest occurred as a result. Such inadequacies existed because between 1959 and 1970 half the total capital formed in Ukraine was reinvested in the USSR outside the republic. Consequently the earned income of workers in Ukraine slipped from sixth place among 15 Soviet republics in 1960 to ninth place in 1970.

In the post-Stalin period many of the Draconian labor laws introduced in the 1930s were abolished, and their abolition paved the way for greater labor turnover and mobility – a principal mechanism for expressing workers' dissatisfaction with their pay and working conditions. In 1970, for example, almost 30 percent of workers changed jobs. Moreover, because of the influx of young educated workers into the labor force, the working class as a whole had higher expectations. In 1970, one-third of all workers in Ukraine, and 46 percent of machine-building and metal workers, were under the age of 29. Ukraine's working class was among the best educated in the USSR. In 1979, for example, 28.8 percent of all workers in Russia had secondary educations, and 8.5 percent had either incomplete higher or specialized secondary educations. In Ukraine the corresponding figures were 40 and 9.8 percent, and 63 percent of young people entering the blue-collar work force for the first time had secondary educations.

Women formed 48 percent of Ukraine's working class in 1970. One-third of all workers in Ukraine that year were located in the western or central-western oblasts of the republic. In 1959, 70 percent of the working class was Ukrainian. By 1970 their share had increased to 74 percent. By the mid-1960s, 70 percent of all industrial workers in the republic, 78 percent of railway workers, 72 percent of workers in the chemical industry, and 70 percent of machine-building and metal workers were ethnic Ukrainians.

In 1980 there were 14.1 million workers in Ukraine, and in 1988, 14.3 million. In 1979, 55 percent of Ukraine's population was classified as belonging to the working class, and 56 percent of ethnic Ukrainians in the republic belonged to that category. In 1987 there were 6.2 million industrial workers in the republic. The average monthly wage for both white- and blue-collar workers in Ukraine in 1987 was 185 rubles. That was below the USSR monthly wage of 202.9 rubles and the RSFSR wage of 216.1 rubles. The per capita family income of Ukraine's industrial workers was 163 rubles in 1988. The largest expense for a working-class family has been food. In 1988 over 35 percent of family income was spent on food.

In recent years, especially since the late 1980s, Ukraine has seen the rise of a working-class movement independent of official trade unions. *Strikes have become a common form of protest against difficult living conditions and shortages of all kinds. Workers challenged the monopoly of power that the Communist party enjoyed until September 1991 and have called for *workers' control, protested the privileges of the elite, supported demands for social and political reform, and, especially in western Ukraine, played an important role in the national movement. Today the working class faces uncertainty with the transition from a command to a market economy. Among the most worrisome consequences of present economic reform is the threat of large-scale *unemployment.

(See also *Labor law, *Labor productivity, *Labor resources, *Overtime work, *Socialist competition, and *Work.)

BIBLIOGRAPHY
Porsh, M. 'Robitnytstvo Ukraïny: Narys po statystytsi pratsi,' ZNTK, 10–12 (1913)
– Ukraïna i Rosiia na robitnychomu rynku (Kiev 1918)
Sadovs'kyi, V. Pratsia v USSR (Warsaw 1932)
Hurzhii, I. Zarodzhennia robitnychoho klasu Ukraïny (kinets' XVIII–persha polovyna XIX st.) (Kiev 1958)
Iatskevych, Ie. Stanovyshche robitnychoho klasu Halychyny v period kapitalizmu (1848–1900) (Kiev 1958)
Nesterenko, O. Rozvytok promyslovosti na Ukraïni, 2 vols (Kiev 1958, 1962)
Koshik, A. Rabochee dvizhenie na Ukraine v gody pervoi mirovoi voiny i Fevral'skoi revoliutsii (Kiev 1965)
Skliarenko, Ie. Robitnychyi klas Ukraïny v roky hromadians'koï viiny (1918–1920 rr.): Narysy (Kiev 1966)
Los', F.; Hurzhii, I.; et al (eds). Istoriia robitnychoho klasu Ukraïns'koï RSR, 2 vols (Kiev 1967)
Kizchenko, V. Kul'turno-osvitnii riven' robitnychoho klasu Ukraïny naperedodni revoliutsii 1905–1907 rr. (Kiev 1972)
Romantsov, V. Robitnychyi klas Ukraïns'koï RSR (1946–1970 rr.) (Kiev 1972)
Reznitskaia, M. Rabochii klas v period sotsialisticheskoi rekonstruktsii narodnogo khoziaistva (1926–1937): Ocherk istoriografii problemy (Kiev 1977)
Kul'chitskii, S.; Likholat, A.; et al (eds). Istoriia rabochikh Donbassa, 2 vols (Kiev 1981)
Bojcun, J.M. 'The Working Class and the National Question in Ukraine, 1880–1920,' PH D diss, York University, 1985
Klopov, E. Rabochii klas SSSR (tendentsiia razvitiia v 60–70-e gody) (Moscow 1985)
Krawchenko, B. Social Change and National Consciousness in Twentieth-Century Ukraine (London 1985; Edmonton 1987)
Danilenko, V. Rabochii klas i kul'turnaia revoliutsiia na Ukraine (Kiev 1986)
Friedgut, T.H. Iuzovka and Revolution, vol 1, Life and Work in Russia's Donbass, 1869–1924 (Princeton 1989)

B. Krawchenko

**World Anti-Communist League** (WACL). An alliance of anticommunist organizations based in over 60 countries, founded in 1967 in Taipei, Taiwan. One of its founding members is the *Ukrainian Liberation Front; the Ukrainian Youth Association (SUM) has been a member since 1968. The other members include the *Anti-Bolshevik Bloc of Nations (ABN), the Asian Pacific Anti-Communist League, the European Freedom Council, and the American Council for World Freedoms. S. *Stetsko has been a permanent delegate of the ABN to WACL. The league holds annual conferences. Its purpose has been to remind the democratic countries of the threat of communism and to struggle for the liberation of nations living under communist subjugation. Reports on the WACL are published in *ABN Correspondence*.

A mass rally at Toronto's Maple Leaf Gardens sponsored by the World Congress of Free Ukrainians during its second convention (November 1973)

**World Congress of Free Ukrainians** (Svitovyi kongres vilnykh ukraintsiv, or SKVU). An umbrella organization of Ukrainian organizations and institutions in the West, founded on 16–19 November 1967 in New York. Its purpose is to co-ordinate the activities of its member organizations and to support the striving of the Ukrainian people for national independence. Its members include national umbrella organizations, such as the *Ukrainian Congress Committee of America and the *Ukrainian American Coordinating Council (both in the United States), the *Ukrainian Canadian Congress, the Co-ordinating Center of Ukrainian Community, Central, and National Instituns in Europe, the *Federation of Ukrainian Organizations in Australia, the *Ukrainian Central Representation in Argentina, the *Ukrainian Brazilian Central Representation, and the *Ukrainian Hromada in Venezuela; Ukrainian world organizations, such as the *World Federation of Ukrainian Women's Organizations and the *Central Union of Ukrainian Students; various national Ukrainian associations; and the Ukrainian Catholic, Orthodox, and Protestant churches. The presidium of the SKVU has set up special committees to co-ordinate activities in certain fields: the World Council of Ukrainian Social Services to help Ukrainian refugees and needy

Ukrainian communities around the world, the Human Rights Commission to defend political prisoners in the USSR, the World Ukrainian Coordinating Educational Council to set program guidelines and prepare textbooks for Ukrainian schools, the World Council on Scholarship to stimulate and plan research, the World Council for Cultural Affairs to register and encourage development in the arts, the Co-ordination of Ukrainian Youth Organizations to organize youth conferences, the Council of Ukrainian Veterans' Organizations to follow the activities of veterans' associations, and the Ukrainian World Co-operative Council to monitor the development of Ukrainian credit unions in various countries. The Information Service of the SKVU has published a quarterly, *Visnyk SKVU* (since 1974), and a bimonthly *Newsletter* (since 1980). The presidents of the World Congress have been Rev V. Kushnir (1967–77), M. Plaviuk (1978–81), V. Bazarko (1981–3), P. Savaryn (1983–8), and Yu. Shymko (1988–).

**World Federation of Ukrainian Medical Associations.** See Medical scientific societies.

**World Federation of Ukrainian Women's Organizations** (Svitova federatsiia ukrainskykh zhinochykh orhanizatsii, or SFUZhO). A women's umbrella organization in the West, founded on 13 November 1948 by the First World Congress of Ukrainian Women in Philadelphia for the purpose of representing Ukrainian women in the Ukrainian community and in international organizations and for promoting the cause of Ukrainian independence. The ten founding members were the *Ukrainian National Women's League of America, the *Ukrainian Women's Organization of Canada, the *Ukrainian Women's Association in France, the *Association of Ukrainian Women in Great Britain, the *Ukrainian Women's Alliance in Germany, the *Ukrainian Women's Alliance in Belgium, the *Ukrainian Catholic Women's League of Canada, the *Ukrainian Gold Cross, the Ukrainian Women's Association of Argentina, and the *Organization of Ukrainian Women in Brazil. In 1959 four more organizations joined the federation: the *Women's Association of the Canadian League for Ukraine's Liberation, the *Ukrainian Women's Union in Austria, the *Ukrainian Women's Alliance in Venezuela, and the *Ukrainian Women's Association in Australia. Today the federation embraces 22 organizations, with a total membership of about 25,000. It conducts a wide-ranging program through different committees: the Educational Committee has designed programs for parents' seminars, lectures, kindergartens, and children's libraries; the Cultural Committee has encouraged the organization of choirs, book clubs, festivals, and exhibits and created a special Mary *Beck literary award; the Welfare Committee ensures support from national welfare programs or directly from the federation; and the Press and Publishing Committee has published a regular page in the monthly *Nashe zhyttia* (since 1949) and *Zhinochyi svit* (since 1975) and its own bulletin, *Zhinka v sviti* (since 1963). In 1956 it published a short history of the Ukrainian women's movement, I. Pavlykovska's *Na hromads'kyi shliakh* (On the Community Way).

The SFUZhO has been active on the international stage: it is an associate member of the General Federation of Women's Clubs in the United States and an affiliate of the Mouvement Mondial des Mères, the International Women's Alliance, and the World Council of Women and par-

ticipates regularly in international conferences. It has sent petitions and appeals to various international organizations in defense of politically persecuted Ukrainian women, the families of political prisoners, women's rights, and the suppressed Ukrainian churches. The SFUZhO was a founding member of the World Congress of Free Ukrainians and has a representative on its executive. Its head office is in Philadelphia. The federation's presidents have been O. *Kysilevska (1948–56), O. *Zalizniak (1956–69), O. *Lototska (1969–71), S. Savchuk (1971–7), L. *Burachynska (1977–82), M. *Kvitkovska (1982–92), and O. Bryzhun-Sokolyk.

BIBLIOGRAPHY
*P'iatyi kongres Svitovoï federatsiï ukraïns'kykh zhinochykh orhanizatsii* (Toronto 1988)

**World Union of Ukrainian Women** (Svitovyi soiuz ukrainok; also known as Vseukrainskyi zhinochyi soiuz). An international representative body of Ukrainian women's organizations, established in Lviv in October 1937. Early in its existence the *National Council of Ukrainian Women (NRUZh) had hoped to assume a central co-ordinating role, but the unwillingness of the *Union of Ukrainian Women (SU) to affiliate itself with an émigré association made this arrangement impossible. The idea received fresh impetus in 1934 at the Ukrainian Women's Congress in Stanyslaviv. Women's groups in Galicia (the SU), Europe (the NRUZh), Volhynia, Transcarpathia, Rumania, Poland, Canada, and the United States were brought together as founding members. M. *Rudnytska was elected president, Z. Mirna, secretary, and S. *Rusova, honorary president. The closing down of the SU (the union's strongest and most important member) by the Polish authorities in 1938 and the outbreak of the Second World War in 1939 rendered the union stillborn.

**World wars.** Two major international conflicts which punctuated 20th-century history and entailed unprecedented destruction and sociopolitical upheaval. Dozens of countries participated in each of the world wars, but the principal belligerents were as follows: in the First World War (1914–18), the Entente (Great Britain, France, Russian Empire), which was joined by the United States in 1917, and the Central Powers (Germany, Austria-Hungary, Turkey, Bulgaria); in the Second World War (1939–45), the Allies (England, France; joined by the USSR and the United States in 1941) and the Axis (Germany, Italy, Japan). Both wars profoundly affected Ukraine.

**First World War.** Among the primary causes of the First World War was the rivalry between the Habsburg monarchy and the Russian Empire, which between them ruled all Ukrainian lands. Although the main source of Austro-Russian rivalry was a conflict of interests in the Balkans, there was also tension over the Ukrainian question. Russian adherents of *Pan-Slavism had long anticipated the 'reunification' of Habsburg-controlled Galicia and Transcarpathia with Russia, and the imperial authorities had subsidized the activities of *Russophiles there for many years. In the decade preceding the outbreak of war the Russian government spent large sums of money on pro-Russian propaganda in Galicia, Bukovyna, Transcarpathia, and among Ukrainian emigrants in North America.

In December 1912, by which time the outbreak of a European war seemed to be only a matter of time, representatives of the three major Ukrainian political parties in Galicia, *National Democratic, *Ukrainian Radical, and *Ukrainian Social Democratic, met in Lviv and unanimously agreed that in the event of war the Ukrainian people would support Austria against Ukraine's greatest enemy, the Russian Empire. The same sentiments were expressed by an emigrant from Russian-ruled Ukraine, D. *Dontsov, at a student congress in Lviv in 1913. When war finally broke out in the east in August 1914, the three representative Galician parties formed the *Supreme Ukrainian Council, which pledged its loyalty to the Central Powers and expressed the hope that all of Ukraine would be delivered from Russian rule in the course of the war. Within weeks the council established the *Ukrainian Sich Riflemen, a volunteer unit in the Austro-Hungarian army. Political émigrés from central Ukraine formed the pro-Austrian *Union for the Liberation of Ukraine in Lviv in August.

Ukrainian activists in the Russian Empire feared that the outbreak of war would provide the tsarist authorities with a pretext for the complete suppression of the Ukrainian movement. They therefore hastened to present themselves as loyal to the empire and its war effort. S. *Petliura wrote a declaration of loyalty, which was published in the journal Ukrainskaia zhizn'. Another prominent Ukrainian periodical, the Kiev daily *Rada, also published a declaration of loyalty. The pre-eminent spokesman of the Ukrainian movement in the Russian Empire, the historian M. *Hrushevsky, was in Lviv (in the Habsburg monarchy) when war erupted; he left for Kiev and there distanced himself publicly from the anti-Russian activities of the Union for the Liberation of Ukraine. In spite of those protestations of loyalty a wave of repression engulfed the Ukrainian movement. The authorities closed down most Ukrainian periodicals, including Rada, arrested Hrushevsky, and deported him to the interior of Russia.

In August and September 1914 a Russian offensive resulted in the occupation of much of Galicia, including its capital, Lviv, as well as all of Bukovyna. Many prominent Ukrainians fled to Vienna, and the Supreme Ukrainian Council (expanded in May 1915 and renamed the *General Ukrainian Council) and other Ukrainian organizations and periodicals transferred their activities to the Austrian capital as well. Retreating before the rapid and powerful Russian advance, the Austro-Hungarian military authorities proceeded to blame their defeat on the alleged treason of the Ukrainian population, which purportedly sympathized with the Russians. Tens of thousands of Ukrainians, only a minority of whom were actually Russophiles, were brutally repressed; many were shunted off to concentration camps in Austria, including the notorious *Thalerhof, and many others were summarily executed. (A few thousand Ukrainians in Canada were also placed in *internment camps, but because of purported sympathies with the Austrians.)

The Russian occupation of Galicia and Bukovyna was characterized by a pogrom against the Ukrainian movement, complete with mass arrests and deportations, the closing down of newspapers, and the burning of Ukrainian books; among those arrested was the Greek Catholic metropolitan A. *Sheptytsky, who spent most of the rest of the war in a monastery prison in Russia. The Russian occupation authorities, particularly Bishop E. *Georgievsky, persecuted the Greek Catholic church and attempted to convert Galician Ukrainians to Russian Orthodoxy. The Russian administration was aided in all its anti-Ukrainian efforts by the Carpatho-Russian Liberation Committee, a group of Galician Russophiles based in Kiev which returned to Lviv with the conquering Russian army. In large measure the harshness of the occupational regime had its roots in ideology: the Russians regarded Galicia not as a foreign territory but as a natural part of their realm (denied to them for centuries because of Polish influence). Furthermore, in Austrian-ruled Galicia and Bukovyna the Ukrainian movement had developed relatively freely, and exerted considerable influence on Russian-ruled Ukraine, where the members of the Ukrainian movement were persecuted. The imperial authorities wished to stifle the Ukrainian movement there in order to destroy the source of what they considered pernicious 'Mazepist' thinking.

The Russians were driven from Galicia and Bukovyna in the first half of 1915, but returned a year later. The second Russian occupation was somewhat milder, but its essential anti-Ukrainian character remained unaltered until the overthrow of tsarism in March 1917. Shortly thereafter the Russian *Provisional Government appointed the Ukrainian historian and activist D. *Doroshenko as its commissioner for Galicia and Bukovyna. An Austrian administration returned to the region in the summer of 1917.

The interior of the Peremyshl fortress after the German occupation during the First World War

The Central Powers maintained a more positive relationship with the Ukrainian movement after 1914, although they were far from willing to satisfy Ukrainian aspirations. At first Vienna and then Berlin financed the Union for the Liberation of Ukraine, which published many informative brochures on the Ukrainian question and also conducted educational work among Ukrainians from the Russian Empire held in Austrian and German *prisoner of war camps, in an effort to develop their national consciousness. To increase support for the war effort the Austrian central government held out the prospect of concessions to all of Austria's nationalities. It proved impossible, however, to reconcile conflicting national claims, notably those of the Ukrainians and Poles. In late 1915 and early 1916 Prime Minister K. von Stürgkh of Austria promised the General Ukrainian Council that Ukrainian-inhabited eastern Galicia would become a separate province from Polish western Galicia; that territorial division had been a demand of the Galician Ukrainian movement since 1848. The promise was superseded, however, in November 1916, when Emperor Franz Joseph promised the Poles that the unity of the province would be preserved, and that it would in fact be granted greater autonomy from Vienna – a long-standing political goal of the Polish national movement. In protest the General Ukrainian Council dissolved itself. In its place appeared the Ukrainian Parliamentary Representation, which initially adopted a cooler attitude to Austria than its predecessor had had.

The war had a corrosive effect on the stability of almost all the belligerent states, but it caused the greatest disintegration in the Russian Empire. Largely owing to revolutionary unrest generated by the war, Tsar Nicholas II abdicated in March 1917. In the wake of this democratic revolution the *Central Rada emerged in Kiev as the focus of Ukrainian political activity. The Central Rada took steps to create Ukrainian armed forces, including the *Khmelnytsky Regiment, which fought on the world-war front in the fall of 1917. Beginning in May 1917 the Rada also convened a series of *all-Ukrainian military congresses, which passed resolutions essentially supporting the Provisional Government's continuation of the war against the Central Powers. Only small groups on the extreme left of Ukrainian political life (L. *Yurkevych in exile in Switzerland and the International Revolutionary Social Democratic Youth in Galicia) held a position of principled opposition to what they considered an imperialist war.

Continuing the war proved to be a grave error on the part of the Russian Provisional Government; just as the war had contributed to the collapse of tsarism, so too it was a major factor in the victory of the *October Revolution, which swept the Russian Provisional Government from power and brought the Bolsheviks to the helm of the Russian state. As a result of the revolution hostilities were halted on the Russian and Ukrainian fronts. Also as a result the Central Rada called into being the *Ukrainian National Republic in November 1917. In December the UNR found itself at war with Soviet Russia (see *Ukrainian-Soviet War). In January 1918 it declared its full independence from Russia, and in February it concluded separately the Peace Treaty of *Brest-Litovsk with the Central Powers. By that agreement the UNR officially withdrew from the First World War.

In the wake of the treaty the German army helped the UNR forces to reconquer Ukraine. Germany hoped to pressure Soviet Russia to make peace so that it could concentrate its forces on the western front; more important, Germany wanted large quantities of food from Ukraine in order to maintain its increasingly restive population for the duration of the war. To facilitate the extraction of foodstuffs, the Germans deposed the Rada in April 1918 and replaced it with the authoritarian regime of Hetman P. *Skoropadsky. German backing kept Skoropadsky in power, but his position was seriously undermined by the defeat of Germany on the western front in November 1918. Almost immediately the *Directory of the UNR launched an uprising against the hetman, and in December he was deposed.

The defeat of the Central Powers also resulted in the collapse of the Habsburg monarchy and the establishment of the *Western Ukrainian National Republic in November 1918.

Soldiers of the Russian army fraternizing with captured soldiers of the Austrian army near Lviv during the First World War

Because the front moved back and forth across Ukrainian territory, the war brought much physical destruction to Ukraine and crippled its economy for years to come. Much of the damage occurred in Galicia and Bukovyna, which constituted the southern reaches of the Austro-Hungarian eastern front for a long period of time. The political upheaval initiated by the war and the diffusion of weapons as a result of the disintegration of the armies unleashed chaos and civil war.

The peace that followed the First World War was precarious, and undermining it was dissatisfaction with the peace settlement on the part of a number of the nationalities of East Central Europe. Among them were the Ukrainians, who now found themselves divided among the Ukrainian SSR, Poland, Rumania, and Czechoslovakia. The incorporation of Ukrainian territories that had formerly been under Austria-Hungary into the latter three countries was sanctioned by the *Paris Peace Conference and the *Conference of Ambassadors.

**Second World War.** The prelude to the outbreak of the Second World War was A. Hitler's dismemberment of Czechoslovakia, initiated by the *Munich Agreement of September 1938. The Ukrainian-inhabited province of Czechoslovakia, Subcarpathian Ruthenia (known also as *Carpatho-Ukraine), became autonomous in October 1938. In November large parts of Carpatho-Ukraine were ceded to Hungary on the basis of the *Vienna Arbitration. Though truncated, Carpatho-Ukraine was still regarded by Ukrainians in Poland as a potential Piedmont, the nucleus of a future Ukrainian state. J. Stalin assessed the situation in the same way and let it be known that his attitude to Hitler's Germany would depend in part on the evolution of events in Carpatho-Ukraine. In March 1939, when Hitler did away completely with the Czechoslovak state, he awarded Carpatho-Ukraine to Hungary, which occupied the area and repressed its Ukrainian movement. Thereafter, representatives of Stalin and Hitler began exploratory talks that culminated in the *Molotov-Ribbentrop Pact of 1939.

A secret codicil of the pact provided for the division of Eastern Europe between Germany and the Soviet Union. The first step in the division, and also the start of the Second World War, was the German invasion of Poland on 1 September 1939, following which Britain and France declared war on Germany. Soon thereafter, on 17 September, the Soviet Union occupied Galicia, western Volhynia, and Polisia, areas that had been under Polish rule since the end of the First World War. In November those territories were incorporated into the Ukrainian SSR. Many Ukrainian political activists fled Soviet rule, and Cracow, in the German sector of former Poland, became an important center of Ukrainian émigré life. There the *Ukrainian Central Committee was formally established in the spring of 1940. In June 1940 the Soviets incorporated northern Bukovyna and northern and southern Bessarabia, formerly held by Rumania, into the Ukrainian SSR.

Ukrainians being evacuated to the Soviet interior in 1941

Nazi-Soviet collaboration ended with the German invasion of the Soviet Union on 22 June 1941. The Germans took Lviv in June, Kiev in September, and Kharkiv in October. Ukrainian Galicia was incorporated as a separate administrative district into the *Generalgouvernement (the name which the Germans gave to the bulk of the territory of the former Polish state). Northern Bukovyna and Bessarabia were reincorporated by Germany's ally Rumania. Rumania also occupied Transnistria, the territory between the Dniester and the Boh rivers, including the port of Odessa. Most of the rest of Ukraine became the *Reichskommissariat Ukraine, except for the easternmost parts of Ukraine, which were under direct military occupation, and the Crimea, which was under a separate jurisdiction.

The Second World War in general was characterized by unheard-of violence outside the fields of battle. The violence was particularly brutal in Ukraine. When the Soviets withdrew from Western Ukrainian territory in June 1941, they shot, murdered, or burned to death nearly 20,000 inmates of NKVD prisons. *Nazi war crimes in Ukraine were on a yet greater scale. The Germans killed hundreds of thousands of Ukrainian POWs by starvation, gassing, and other methods. Millions of civilians were also murdered. The Nazis systematically executed members of the former Communist apparatus of Ukraine and randomly killed many other Ukrainians. The Reichskommissar of Ukraine, E. *Koch, for instance, authorized the mass murder of Ukrainians living in an area he wished to make into a hunting preserve. Over two million Ukrainians were also deported to Germany to work as forced laborers, the so-called *Ostarbeiter. Forced labor also existed in Ukrainian territory. The Germans' refusal to permit the dismantling

of collective farms and their massive food requisitions also contributed to the misery of Ukraine's population.

The Nazis singled out the Jews for extermination. Within the first weeks of their invasion of Ukraine the Germans orchestrated a series of pogroms against the Jews in which tens of thousands perished; the Nazis recruited elements of the local population to conduct these first actions against the Jews. Thereafter, the destruction of the Jews became more systematic and was carried out primarily by the Germans themselves. In the Reichskommissariat Ukraine mobile killing units (Einsatzgruppen) went from locality to locality and shot the Jewish population. One of the most notorious of their killing grounds was situated at *Babyn Yar in Kiev. In the district of Galicia the Jews were, in the main, transported to killing centers, such as Auschwitz (*Oświęcim concentration camp). The Ukrainian Catholic metropolitan A. Sheptytsky condemned the genocide and registered his protest with Himmler. After the war Nazi leaders were prosecuted at the *Nuremberg trials for their war crimes and crimes against humanity, including those perpetrated in Ukraine.

In spite of the great brutality of the Nazi occupation there was a degree of ambivalence toward it on the part of some sectors of Ukrainian society. The murderous nature of the Nazi regime did not become patently evident until after the attack on the Soviet Union in the summer of 1941. Until that time the majority of Ukrainian nationalists felt that Germany could be an important ally against what seemed the greater evil – the lawless terror of the Soviet Union. That belief was encouraged by the fact that the Soviet regime had clearly revealed its attitude toward Ukrainians, whereas the Germans were still (at least in Ukraine) an unknown quantity. Illusions about the Nazis continued to be fostered by the German minister for the occupied eastern territories, A. *Rosenberg, who held out the prospect of an end to the brutalities as well as the establishment of a Ukrainian state under German protection. There were also certain areas of policy in which the Germans were more tolerant than the Soviets had been. Many churches were reopened during the occupation, and it was possible under the Germans to investigate and publicize some Stalinist crimes (as in the exhumation of the mass graves that bore witness to the *Vinnytsia massacre, and the publication of memoirs concerning the repression of the Ukrainian intelligentsia).

Ukrainians fought on both sides in the Second World War. By far the majority of the Ukrainians, about 4.5 million, fought in the Red Army against the Germans. Others joined the Communist partisans, who included the prominent commander S. *Kovpak. There were also Ukrainian volunteer units in the German army, however, specifically the *Legion of Ukrainian Nationalists (the Nachtigall and Roland units, which marched into Lviv in June 1941 together with the Germans) and the Waffen SS *Division Galizien (est April 1943). By the time the latter unit was formed Ukrainians had no illusions about the nature of the Nazi regime; it seemed likely, however, that Germany was going to lose the war, and Ukrainian nationalists wanted to have trained troops and weapons ready for an eventual confrontation with the Soviets. There were also Ukrainians who fought against both Nazis and Soviets during the war, the members of the *Ukrainian Insurgent Army (UPA). Originally founded by T. *Borovets in 1941, the UPA grew rapidly in the spring of 1943, by which time

## THE SECOND WORLD WAR IN UKRAINE

it had come under the political control of the Bandera faction of the Organization of Ukrainian Nationalists (OUN). The UPA continued guerrilla warfare against the Soviet authorities into the mid-1950s. A significant number of Ukrainians, many of them former POWs, ended up in A. Vlasov's *Russian Liberation Army or in the auxiliary units that constituted the *Ukrainian Liberation Army. Ukrainians also served in various Allied formations. Many Galician Ukrainians could be found in the *Polish Second Corps, and a large number of Ukrainian Americans and Ukrainian Canadians served in the wartime armies of their respective countries. The latter group formed the London-based *Ukrainian Canadian Service-

men's Association, which was to play a critical role with respect to displaced Ukrainians at the end of the war.

Ukrainian political and cultural aspirations were frustrated by the Nazi administration. On 30 June 1941 the Bandera faction of the OUN proclaimed an independent Ukrainian state (see *Proclamation of Ukrainian statehood), hoping thereby to place before the Germans a fait accompli. In July, however, the Germans responded by arresting S. *Bandera, Ya. *Stetsko, and many other prominent nationalists of the Bandera faction; others went underground. Both the Bandera and the Melnyk factions of the OUN organized clandestine *OUN expeditionary groups to travel into Eastern Ukraine and agitate among the population. Most of the Ukrainian organizations that sprang up spontaneously in the wake of the Soviet withdrawal were closed down by the Germans. The legal centers on which Ukrainian cultural and political life focused were the Ukrainian Central Committee in Cracow and the *Ukrainian Regional Committee in Lviv. The primary aim of those committees was to intervene with the German authorities to preserve Ukrainian culture and to mitigate the sufferings of the Ukrainian population. The Germans also maintained a tight control over Ukrainian life outside Eastern Europe, by allowing only selected organizations to continue their activities (eg, the Ukrainian Hromada and *Ukrainian National Alliance) and establishing the *Ukrainian Institution of Trust in the German Reich as a liaison body.

Ukrainian *Ostarbeiter* being herded onto a Germany-bound train in Kiev in 1941

The Germans began to lose the war after the Battle of Stalingrad in the fall and winter of 1942–3. By August 1943 the Soviets had recaptured Kharkiv, and by November they had taken Kiev. In the summer of 1944 the Soviets reached Galicia. A decisive battle for the fate of Galicia was fought at *Brody in July; the German forces, and with them the Division Galizien, were routed. By the fall virtually all of Ukraine was under Soviet control. Germany capitulated on 8 May 1945, but the war against Japan continued until September.

Before the end of the war the territory of the Ukrainian ssr was expanded. The Ukrainian territories that had been taken from Polish and Rumanian rule in 1939–40 were reincorporated as they were reconquered; in addition, Czechoslovakia ceded Transcarpathia to the Ukrainian ssr in June 1945.

The destruction and dislocation in Ukraine caused by the Second World War surpassed even that of the First World War. An estimated 6.8 million Ukrainians were killed, and direct material damage came to 285 billion rubles (1941 prices). About 200,000 Ukrainian *displaced persons ended up in the emigration in the West; the vast majority were returned to Soviet rule through forced *repatriation. The extermination of much of the Jewish population during the war and a series of wartime and postwar population transfers and deportations introduced changes in the national demography of Ukraine. After the expulsion and emigration of most Poles the cities

An example of Nazi scorched-earth tactics in Ukraine (1943)

of Western Ukraine became Ukrainianized and for the first time developed a Russian minority. The once substantial German settlements in Ukraine, particularly in the south, as well as those of the Tatars in the Crimea, disappeared; Ukrainians in the Lemko region were deported from their ancestral territories into the new lands that Poland acquired from Germany (see *Operation Wisła).

A machine-gun nest of the Division Galizien during the Battle of Brody (July 1944)

The victory against the Nazis in 1941–5 became an important source of legitimation for the Soviet regime and figured prominently in its propaganda at home and abroad. The Soviets referred to the war as the Great Patriotic War (Velyka Vitchyzniana viina) and made its commemoration ubiquitous: statues, monuments, and military hardware (tanks, airplanes) could be found in public places throughout the USSR (even in villages); Soviet literature and film produced a torrent of factual and fictional works about the war; veterans were granted a prominent place in public celebrations; Stalin was elevated to the stature of a military genius, and his successors (N. Khrushchev and L. Brezhnev) were also given inflated reputations for the roles they had played in the war effort; and 9 May (Victory Day) was declared an all-Union holiday commemorating the German surrender (the calendar date a day later than in Western Europe because of a time

A technician attaching a bomb with the inscription For Ukraine to a Soviet bomber (1944)

difference between Berlin and Moscow). An enormous monument and museum commemorating the Second World War were erected in 1982 near the Kievan Cave Monastery.

In the Ukrainian SSR the 'official' memory of the war was accompanied by an ongoing smear campaign against nationalist opponents of the Soviet regime that sought to portray the nationalists as Nazi collaborators and war criminals. The purpose of the campaign was not to provide a factual account of deeds that had been done during the war years, but to besmirch Ukrainian patriotism of any sort as bourgeois nationalism (and to underscore its incompatibility with Soviet *nationality policy). Consistent targets of official criticism included the Division Galizien, Metropolitan A. Sheptytsky, and the OUN. The UPA could not be dealt with in such a simplistic manner and became conspicuously absent from Soviet Ukrainian publicism and historiography. The UPA was vilified, however, in Polish postwar historiography.

(See also *History of Ukraine.)

BIBLIOGRAPHY

Levyts'kyi, K. Istoriia vyzvol'nykh zmahan' halyts'kykh ukraïntsiv z chasu svitovoï viiny 1914–1918, 3 pts (Lviv 1928–30)

Kamenetsky, I. Hitler's Occupation of Ukraine (1941–1944): A Study of Totalitarian Imperialism (Milwaukee 1956)

Ilnytzkyj, R. Deutschland und die Ukraine 1934–1945: Tatsachen europäischer Ostpolitik, 2 vols (Munich 1958)

Rudnyts'ka, M. (ed). Zakhidnia Ukraïna pid bol'shevykamy, IX. 1939–VI. 1941 (New York 1958)

Hornykiewicz, T. (ed). Ereignisse in der Ukraine 1914–1922: Deren Bedeutung und historische Hintergründe, 4 vols (Philadelphia 1966–9)

Ukraïns'ka RSR u Velykii Vitchyznianii viini Radians'koho Soiuzu 1941–1945 rr., 3 vols (Kiev 1967–9)

Borowsky, P. Deutsche Ukrainepolitik 1918 unter besonderer Berücksichtigung der Wirtschaftsfragen (Lübeck and Hamburg 1970)

Fedyshyn, O.S. Germany's Drive to the East and the Ukrainian Revolution, 1917–1918 (New Brunswick, NJ 1971)

Torzecki, R. Kwestia ukraińska w polityce III Rzeszy (1933–1941) (Warsaw 1972)

Boshyk, Y. (ed). Ukraine during World War II: History and Its Aftermath: A Symposium (Edmonton 1986)

Gross, J.T. Revolution from Abroad: The Soviet Conquest of Poland's Western Ukraine and Western Belorussia (Princeton 1988)

Horak, S.M. The First Treaty of World War I: Ukraine's Treaty with the Central Powers of February 9, 1918 (New York 1988)

Sword, K. (ed). The Soviet Takeover of the Polish Eastern Provinces, 1939–41 (London 1991)

J.-P. Himka

**Wormwood** (*Artemisia*; Ukrainian: *polyn*). Perennial or annual plants of the Compositae family, also known as absinthe. In Ukraine there are 23 species, some cultivated for medicinal purposes, some used decoratively, and some growing as weeds. Mountain wormwood (*A. absinthium*) grows wild and is used to improve appetite and stimulate the digestive system. Crimean wormwood (*A. taurica*; Ukrainian: *polynok, yevshan*) is found along the Crimean coast. Also found in Ukraine are *A. pseudofragrans, A. boschniakiana*, and tarragon (*A. dracunculus*), which in its cultivated form contains essential oil, and the leaves and stems of which are used for pickling. Annual wormwood (*A. annua*) grows wild and is cultivated for its fragrance. In Ukrainian folk tradition the fragrance of the wormwood (*yevshan-zillia*) produces nostalgia for the native land.

Lieut-Gov Stephen Worobetz      Anatole Wowk

**Worobetz, Stephen** [Vorobec, Stefan], b 26 December 1914 in Krydor, Saskatchewan. Surgeon of Ukrainian descent. Educated at the universities of Saskatchewan (1935) and Manitoba (MD, 1940), during the Second World War he was awarded the Military Cross for heroism. Worobetz served as lieutenant governor of Saskatchewan in 1970–6, making him the first Ukrainian Canadian appointed to a viceregal position. In 1984 he was awarded an honorary LLD degree from the University of Saskatchewan.

**Wowk, Anatole** [Vovk, Anatol'], b 11 March 1921 in Ukraine, d 9 November 1992 in Edison, New Jersey. Chemist and lexicographer; member of the Shevchenko Scientific Society. A graduate of the Lviv Polytechnical Institute (1944), he emigrated to the United States in 1948, where he worked as a research chemist. Besides contributing research articles to *Analytical Chemistry*, he compiled *A Selective English-Ukrainian Dictionary of Science, Technology, and Modern Living* (2 vols, 1982, 1990) and *English-Ukrainian Dictionary of Color Names and Color Science* (1986). He was one of the cofounders (1965) of the *Ukrainian Terminological Center of America and was its president from 1978.

**Wowk, Wira.** See Vovk, Vira.

Ol'ha Woycenko

**Woycenko, Ol'ha** [Vojcenko], b 25 July 1909 in Winnipeg. Editor and researcher. A longtime associate of *Ukraïns'kyi holos* (Winnipeg) and the Trident Press (1927–72), Woycenko was national president of the *Ukrainian Women's Association of Canada (1948–54) and of the women's section of the Ukrainian Canadian Committee (now Congress) (1959–62). The compiler of the monumental *Litopys ukraïns'koho zhyttia v Kanadi* (Annals of Ukrainian Life in Canada, 8 vols, 1961–92), based on information gleaned from the newspaper *Ukraïns'kyi holos*, she also wrote *The Ukrainians in Canada* (1967) and *Slovians'ka literatura v Kanadi* (Slavic Literature in Canada, 1969).

**Wrangel, Petr,** b 27 August 1878 in Mukuliai, Kaunas gubernia (Lithuania), d 25 April 1928 in Brussels. Russian military and political figure. Following a distinguished career in the Russian imperial army, Wrangel moved to the Crimea when the monarchy was overthrown, in 1917. During the German occupation of Ukraine in 1918, he was invited by Hetman P. Skoropadsky to become his chief of staff, but refused. Instead he became one of the organizers of the loyalist 'White' Volunteer Army headed by A. *Denikin. As a lieutenant general he earned himself an unsavory reputation for his ruthlessness. Wrangel succeeded Denikin as head of the White forces in April 1920. With the Bolsheviks busy fighting an invading Polish army, Wrangel decided to launch an offensive into Ukraine from the Crimea in the summer of 1920. The offensive advanced northward toward the Donbas and Katerynoslav, but peace in the war with Poland in September freed the bulk of Bolshevik troops to meet it. Wrangel's army, harassed also by the forces of N. Makhno's partisans, was pushed back to the Crimea by November 1920. That month he ordered a mass evacuation of his army and sympathizers. In exile he continued his anti-Bolshevik political activities.

**Wrestling** (*borotba*). In turn-of-the-century Ukraine several prominent Ukrainian wrestlers became internationally known: I. *Piddubny, who scored 11 victories at a tournament in Paris in 1903 and remained an international champion until the 1920s; O. Harkavenko, who competed in Europe and the United States; D. Posunko, whom the Polish world champion, S. Cyganiewicz, was unable to

Viktoriia Kobzarenko (right), winner of the women's 72-kg-weight category at the European Sambo Federation championships held in Kiev in 1992

defeat during a three-hour match in Poltava in 1915; the world champion Z. Yalov; and I. Kalashnykov.

The modern international styles of wrestling – Greco-Roman, freestyle, judo, and sambo – all have had practioners in Soviet Ukraine. Soviet wrestlers have belonged to the International Amateur Wrestling Federation (IAWF) since 1947. Ukrainian Greco-Roman wrestlers who have won Olympic gold medals are Ya. Punkin (1952, featherweight); I. Bohdan (1960, heavyweight), also the 1958 and 1961 world champion; and O. Kolchynsky (1976 and 1980, super-heavyweight), also the 1978 world champion. V. Trostiansky won an Olympic silver medal (1964, featherweight). Ukrainians who have become Greco-Roman world champions are S. Rybalko (1962 and 1965), O. Kucherenko (1988, light flyweight), and A. Ihnatenko (1988, flyweight).

Ukrainian freestyle wrestlers who have won Olympic gold medals are O. Ivanytsky (1964, heavyweight); O. Medvid (1964, light heavyweight; 1968, heavyweight; 1972, super-heavyweight); B. Hurevych (1968, middleweight), also the 1967 and 1969 world champion; P. Pinigin (1976, lightweight), also the 1975 and 1977–8 world champion; A. Beloglazov (1980, flyweight); I. Mate (1980, heavyweight); and S. Beloglazov (1980 and 1988, bantamweight), also the world champion in 1982 (featherweight) and in 1983 and 1985–8 (bantamweight). V. Syniavsky won a silver medal (1960, lightweight).

Soviet athletes have belonged to the International Judo Federation since 1962. Olympic medals in judo have been won by A. Novikov (1972 bronze, light middlweight); S. Novikov (1976 gold, heavyweight), also the 1973–4 and 1976 European champion; V. Dvoinikov (1976 silver, middleweight); and O. Yatskevych (1980 bronze, middleweight). A. Bondarenko, S. Melnychenko, and V. Saunin have been Soviet and/or European judo champions.

Sambo (an acronym for the Russian *samozashchita bez oruzhiia* 'self-defense without weapons') is a distinctive form of Soviet self-defense wrestling based on over 20 different styles of wrestling native to the USSR. It was created by A. Kharlampiev in the 1930s and was officially adopted in 1938 when the USSR Sambo Federation was founded. Sambo wrestlers wear special costumes and compete on a round carpet 6–9 m in diameter. A round lasts 4–6 minutes. There are 10 classes by weight (48 kg to over 100 kg). From 1955 the sport was part of the Ready for Labor and Defense of the USSR mass fitness program, and since 1966 it has been recognized by the IAWF). In 1971 sambo was included in the Spartakiad of the Peoples of the USSR. At the fifth Spartakiad the Ukrainian team won first prize. European sambo championships were introduced in 1972, and world competitions in 1973. The Ukrainians V. Saunin (1974), M. Yunak (1973), and M. Levytsky (1980) have been world champions, S. Novikov was a 1973 European champion, and V. Kobzarenko was a 1992 European champion.

R. Senkus

**Writers' Union of Ukraine** (Spilka pysmennykiv Ukrainy, or SPU). An organization of poets, prose writers, dramatists, and translators. From 1932 until 1991 it was the only litterateurs' organization legally permitted in Soviet Ukraine. It was founded on 23 April 1932 following a resolution of the CC of the All-Union Communist Party (Bolshevik), 'On the Reconstruction of Literary and Artistic Organizations.' In accordance with the resolution all previously existing literary organizations were dissolved (in Ukraine, the All-Ukrainian Assocation of Proletarian Writers, Pluh, Molodniak, Zakhidnia Ukraina), and a preparatory founding committee was formed to create the single Writers' Union (SP) of the USSR and its republican branches. In the new organizational structure the writers' unions of the republics were subordinated to the SP of the USSR and, thus, dependent on Moscow. Consequently the literatures of the nations of the USSR began to lose their previous national independence. The SP USSR and the SPU were formally established in 1934 at the first All-Union and the first Ukrainian congresses of Soviet writers, respectively. The statute of the SP of the USSR accepted at that meeting bound Soviet writers to active participation in building socialism and loyalty to Soviet state and Party policies. The statute specified that the only method in Soviet literature permitted was that of *socialist realism.

The highest body of the SPU has been the Republic Conference. Beginning with the fifth conference (1966), it has been called every five years. At those conferences the executive administration of the SPU is elected. Members nominate from among themselves a presidium and secretariat, chaired by the first secretary, to deal with current business. The SPU has been headed by I. Kulyk (1934), I. Mykytenko (1934–8), O. Korniichuk (1938–41, 1946–53), M. Rylsky (1943–6), M. Bazhan (1953–9), O. Honchar (1959–71), Yu. Smolych (1971–3), V. Kozachenko (1973–8), P. Zahrebelny (1978–86), and Yu. Mushketyk (since 1986).

In 1934, as a result of the terror of the early 1930s, the membership of the SPU numbered only 206 writers. In 1945 there were 250, in 1958, 500, and during the seventh conference (1976), 922. Its members have been writers who live in the territory of the Ukrainian SSR (now Ukraine), regardless of nationality. The members include a small number of Jews, Belarusians, and Moldavians, and a rather large number of Russians: by 1991 they constituted approximately 20 percent of the total membership. The SPU has had its own publications: *Literaturna Ukraïna*, *Vitchyzna*, *Kyïv*, *Zhovten'* (now *Dzvin*), and *Prapor* (*Berezil* since 1991). Together with the Ukrainian Society for Friendship and Cultural Relations with Foreign Countries, it publishes *Vsesvit*, and with the Institute of Literature of the AN URSR (now ANU), it publishes *Slovo i chas* (*Radians'ke literaturoznavstvo* until 1991) and the Russian-language *Raduga*. Among the assets of the SPU were the publishing house Radianskyi Pysmennyk and the *Literary Fund. Until 1991 the CPU directed the SPU through the Communist faction in the SPU, and the KGB played a more direct role in controlling the SPU. From 1971 the members of the SPU at the writers' conferences were forced to elect KGB officers to so-called secretarial positions in the SPU for 'organizational matters' and thereby give the KGB control over the activities of the SPU and its affiliates. In 1971 Col I. Soldatenko was elected to a secretarial post; he was succeeded by P. Shabatyn in 1976.

The SPU was an organization with privileges based on *nomenklatura* and was directed by the Party. Until the late 1980s it adhered to official Party policy. With its help the post-Stalinist literary revival was quashed, particularly the *shestydesiatnyky, and the policy of Russification was implemented in the Ukrainian SSR. The SPU did not defend the activists of the opposition movement, and it banned from membership those writers (eg, M. Lukash, O. Berdnyk, H. Kochur, and others) who opposed Russification and defended freedom of speech, Ukrainian language rights, and so forth.

Membership in the SPU continues to increase. At the 1986 conference there were close to 1,100 members. During that conference the policy of the Executive of the SPU changed radically owing to the newly proclaimed policies of Perestroika and Glasnost. Since then, among official organizations, the SPU has led the movement for the rebirth of Ukrainian culture and language, has initiated the foundation of native-language societies, and has actively worked to fill in the so-called blank spots in history and literature (the rehabilitation of B. Hrinchenko, M. Hrushevsky, V. Vynnychenko, M. Khvylovy, H. Mykhailychenko, and many others, and the partial reprinting of their works). In the process those writers previously denied membership in or excluded from the SPU have been granted memberships, and émigré writers have been inducted as members. Among the writers and literary scholars involved in that work have been O. Honchar, D. Pavlychko, I. Drach, Mushketyk, Yu. Shcherbak, S. Plachynda, M. Zhulynsky, and V. Drozd. The 10th conference, in 1991, re-elected Mushketyk as head and declared the Writer's Union separate and independent of the Writer's Union of the USSR. In 1992 the SPU had 1,243 members.

BIBLIOGRAPHY
Garrard, J.; Garrard, C. *Inside the Soviet Writers' Union* (London 1991)

I. Koshelivets

**Wyczółkowski, Leon,** b 11 April 1852 in Huta Miastkowska, Poland, d 27 December 1936 in Warsaw. Polish painter and graphic artist. He studied art in Warsaw, Munich, and Cracow. From 1879 to 1893 he lived mostly in Ukraine. He painted many landscapes, genre scenes, and portraits of peasants in Ukraine, such as *Fishermen* (1891), *Tilling in Ukraine* (1892), and *Sower* (1896). Among his many series of lithographs are the 'Hutsul Portfolio' (1910) and 'Ukrainian Portfolio' (1910) of landscapes, portraits, buildings, and still lifes.

Bohdan Wynar

Lubomyr Wynar

**Wynar, Bohdan** [Vynar], b 7 September 1926 in Lviv. Economist, bibliographer, and publisher; full member of the Ukrainian Academy of Arts and Sciences in the US and the Shevchenko Scientific Society; brother of L. Wymar. A postwar refugee, he graduated from the University of Munich (PH D, 1950) and the University of Denver (1958). He taught library science before becoming director of library education (1966–7) and dean of library science (1967–9) at the State University of New York College at Geneseo. Since 1969 he has been president of Libraries Unlimited, a major publisher of library reference materials and bibliographies, and of the *Ukrainian Academic Press. Wynar wrote several monographs in Ukrainian economic history, including *Ekonomichnyi koloniializm v Ukraïni* (Economic Colonialism in Ukraine, 1958), *Ukraïns'ka promyslovist': Studiia soviets'koho koloniializmu* (Ukrainian Industry: A Case Study in Soviet Colonialism, 1964), *Materiialy do istoriï ekonomichnykh doslidiv na emigratsiï, 1919–1964* (Materials in the History of Economic Studies in the Emigration, 1919–64, 1965), and *Rozvytok ekonomichnoï dumky u Kyïvs'kii Rusi* (The Development of Economic Thought in Kievan Rus', 1974), and articles on economics and other subjects for various journals and for the *Entsyklopediia ukraïnoznavstva* and the *Encyclopedia of Ukraine*. He has also written, edited, and compiled numerous works in library science and bibliographies.

**Wynar, Lubomyr** [Vynar, Ljubomyr], b 2 January 1932 in Lviv. Historian and bibliographer; member of the Shevchenko Scientific Society and the Ukrainian Academy of Sciences in the United States; brother of B. Wynar. He earned degrees in Munich at the Ukrainian Free University (PH D, 1957) and in Cleveland (bibliographic studies) and then taught at the Case Institute of Technology (1959–62), the University of Colorado (1962–5), and Bowling Green State University (1965–9) in Ohio before becoming a professor of ethnic studies and library science at Kent State University since 1969 in Ohio. He was a co-founder of the *Ukrainian Historical Association (1965), which he served as academic secretary and has headed since 1981. He has also been the founder and director of the Bibliographical Research Center at Bowling Green State University (1965–9) and the Center for the Study of Ethnic Publications at Kent State University (since 1971). He headed the scholarly council of the World Congress of Free Ukrainians in 1984–8.

Wynar has been the editor of *Ukraïns'kyi istoryk* since

1963. He established 'Ethnic Forum' (now an independent journal) in the *Journal of Ethnic Studies* and has edited it since 1970, and is the editor of the Ukrainian-Jewish Studies Series (since 1984), *Hrushevs'kiana* (since 1980), and *Social Sciences Reference Guide* (since 1986). He has written extensively on a variety of Ukrainian historical and bibliographic topics. Among his more important works are *Ostap Hrytsai* (1960), *Andrii Voinarovs'kyi: Istorychna studiia* (Andrii Voinarovsky: A Historical Study, 1962), *History of Early Ukrainian Printing, 1491–1600* (1962), *Kniaz' Dmytro Vyshnevets'kyi* (Prince Dmytro Vyshnevetsky, 1964), *Istorychnyi atlas Ukraïny* (A Historical Atlas of Ukraine, 1980), *Mykhailo Hrushevs'kyi, 1866–1934: Bibliographical Sources* (1985), *Naivydatnishyi istoryk Ukraïny, Mykhailo Hrushevs'kyi (1866–34)* (The Most Eminent Historian of Ukraine, Mykhailo Hrushevsky [1866–1934], 1986), and *Ukrainian Scholarship in Exile: The DP Period, 1945–52* (1989). He has also prepared a variety of guidebooks to and compilations of source materials on ethnic groups in the United States and contributed to the *Encyclopedia of Ukraine*.

M. Antonovych

**Wyspiański, Stanisław,** b 15 January 1869 in Cracow, d 28 November 1907 in Cracow. Polish modernist poet, dramatist, painter, and designer. From 1902 he taught at the Cracow Academy of Fine Arts. A friend of the Ukrainian writers V. Stefanyk and B. Lepky, he introduced Ukrainian themes in his plays *Legion* (Legion, 1900) and *Bolesław Śmiały* (Bolesław the Bold, 1903) and set his play *Sędziówie* (The Judges, 1907) in the Hutsul region. In 1887 he traveled in Galicia and sketched its architectural monuments and landscapes. He knew the collection of Ukrainian art at the Cracow National Museum well. His play *Wesele* (Wedding) influenced V. Pachovsky to write *Son ukraïns'koï nochi* (The Dream of a Ukrainian Night), and his paintings influenced the Ukrainian artists O. Novakivsky, M. Holubets, I. Severyn, and M. Zhuk.

BIBLIOGRAPHY
Hordyns'kyi, Ia. 'Stanyslav Vyspians'kyi i Ukraïna,' *ZNTSh*, 155 (1937)

Wasyl Wytwycky

**Wytwycky, Wasyl** [Vytvyc'kyj, Vasyl'], b 16 October 1905 in Kolomyia, Galicia. Musicologist, composer, and teacher; full member of the Shevchenko Scientific Society since 1960. He studied musicology at Cracow University (graduating in 1932) and theory at the Cracow Conservatory before becoming a teacher and director of the Peremyshl branch of the Lysenko Higher Institute of Music. He was also active in the *Union of Ukrainian Professional Musicians and its publication *Ukraïns'ka muzyka* as well as editor of *Dyrygents'kyi poradnyk* (The Conductor's Handbook) in Lviv. Following the Soviet occupation of Galicia he taught in Lviv, worked in the music section of Lviv Radio, and briefly (1939–41) held a position with the AN URSR (now ANU) Institute of Ukrainian Folklore. Emigrating at the end of the war, he lived in Germany, where he headed the Ukrainian Musicians' Alliance, and from 1949 in Detroit. Wytwycky has written extensively on various aspects of Ukrainian music for the periodical press in Ukraine, Germany, the United States, and Canada and has served as subject editor of music for *Entsyklopediia ukraïnoznavstva* and the *Encyclopedia of Ukraine*. His published works include monographs on M. Berezovsky (1974) and M. Haivoronsky (1954), as well as his own memoirs, *Muzychnymy shliakhamy* (Along Musical Paths, 1989). His compositions include *Diptych* for string orchestra; two string quartets; a piano trio; *Suite for Youth* for violin, cello, and piano; the piano *Sonatina* for four hands; music to the children's plays of N. Zabila and N. Buryk; marches to the words of H. Chuprynka, I. Bahriany, and others; and arrangements of Ukrainian folk songs for choir.

R. Savytsky

# Y

**Yablochyn Saint Onuphrius's Monastery** (Yablochynskyi manastyr sv. Onufriia). An Orthodox men's monastery located near Bielsk Podlaski (Bilske), in Podlachia (now in Białystok voivodeship, Poland). It was founded in the late 15th century. In the 17th century a larger church, a bell tower, and monks' cells were constructed, and in 1838–40 the complex was surrounded by a stone wall. Until 1914 courses for precentors and catechism teachers were held there, as well as a three-year agriculture program. The monastery was partly destroyed during the First World War, and in the interwar period the Polish government confiscated the school buildings and most of the monastery's land. More damage occurred during the Second World War. Today it is the only functioning Orthodox monastery in Poland. Its library houses a collection of old icons (including one of St Onuphrius from the 15th century) and manuscripts, and since 1974 senior students of the Warsaw Orthodox Theological Seminary have completed their education there. It also holds precentors' courses, and retired priests often live on the premises. In *Pravoslavna tverdynia Pidliashshia* (The Orthodox Citadel of Podlachia, 1984) M. Syvitsky gives the history of the monastery.

Sofiia Yablonska

**Yablonska, Sofiia** [Jablons'ka, Sofija] (Jablonska-Oudin, Sophie), b 15 May 1907 in Hermaniv, Lviv county, Galicia, d 4 February 1971 on Île de Noirmoutier, France. Writer and architect. From 1915 to 1921 she lived with her Russophile parents in Russia. In 1927 she left Galicia for Paris. There, under the influence of her friend S. *Levynsky, she decided to travel. Accounts of her exotic travels were published in the Galician women's periodicals *Zhinocha dolia* and *Nova khata* and as the well-received books *Char Marokka* (The Charm of Morocco, 1932), *Z kraïny ryzhu ta opiiu* (From the Land of Rice and Opium, 1936), and *Daleki obriï* (Distant Horizons, 2 vols, 1939). In 1950 Yablonska returned with her French husband and three sons to France and lived in Paris and on Île de Noirmoutier, where she designed and supervised the construction of villas. Published posthumously were her prose collection *Dvi vahy – dvi miry* (Two Weights, Two Measures, 1972) and autobiographical novel *Knyha pro bat'ka: Z moho dytynstva* (Book about [My] Father: From My Childhood, 1977), and M. *Kalytovska's French translations of her works, *L'année ensorcelée: Nouvelles* (1972), *Le charme du Maroc* (1973), *Les horizons lointains* (1977), *Mon enfance en Ukraine: Souvenirs sur mon père* (1981), and *Au pays du riz et de l'opium* (1986).

Tetiana Yablonska: *Betrothed* (1966)

**Yablonska, Tetiana** [Jablons'ka, Tetjana], b 24 February 1917 in Smolensk, Russia. Ukrainian painter and teacher, of Belarusian descent; full member of the USSR (now Russian) Academy of Arts since 1975. She studied at the Kiev State Art Institute (1935–41) under F. Krychevsky and later taught there (1944–52, 1966–73). Her canvases, most of which are painted in the realist tradition, are often bathed in light and show a highly developed sense of color. They have more in common with impressionism than with socialist realism, even though some have depicted happy collective-farm workers (eg, her famous *Bread*, 1949) and workers (eg, *Evening on the Dnieper*, 1946). In the 1960s, as a result of her interest in Ukrainian folk art and ethnography, her paintings became more decorative, with simplified forms and flattened space (eg, *Young Mother*, 1964; *Summer*, 1967). Ukrainian elements appeared in works such as *Betrothed* (1966) and *Swans* (1966). By 1969 Yablonska was creating canvases that synthesized her two previous styles, a synthesis that culminated in the powerful, symbolic *Youth* (1969) and *Silence* (1975). In the last decade she has created portraits and numerous landscapes, including *Winter in Old Kiev* (1975) and *Old Apple Tree* (1986), peaceful compositions painted in a subdued, pearly gray palette. A monograph about her by E. Korotkevich was published in Moscow in 1980, and a large retrospective of her paintings was held at the Kiev Museum of Ukrainian Art in 1987.

D. Zelska-Darewych

**Yablonsky, Anatol** [Jablons'kyj, Anatol'], b 3 July 1912 in Kiev, d 11 July 1954 in Paris. Painter. An interwar émigré, he studied art in Lviv and, with the financial support of Metropolitan A. Sheptytsky, Paris. He was a member of the Association of Independent Ukrainian Artists in the 1930s and the Labor Association of Ukrainian Pictorial Artists in 1941–4. A specialist in church fresco and icon painting in the Byzantine style, he painted frescoes in the churches of the Studite monasteries in Lviv, Lavriv, and Uhniv, the Studite nunnery in Sukhovolia, and the Basilian nunnery in Lviv, and 18 iconostases for churches and chapels in Galicia and outside Ukraine. Yablonsky often collaborated with P. Kovzhun and M. Osinchuk. A postwar refugee in Germany, in 1950 he settled in Paris. There he illustrated editions of *Slovo o polku Ihorevi* (The Tale of Ihor's Campaign) and I. Franko's *Lys Mykyta* (The Fox Mykyta), prepared albums of drawings of Ukrainian princes and hetmans and of Ukrainian folk costumes, painted icons for Paris's St Volodymyr's Church, and did portraits and landscapes on commission.

**Yablonsky, Martyn** [Jablons'kyj], b 1801 in Hlohiv in the Lviv region, d after 1875 in Lviv. Painter. He studied art in Lviv, Warsaw, Cracow, and Vienna. He settled in Lviv, where he painted mostly portraits, including ones of his father and son, *Girl with Breakfast on a Tray*, and *Woman's Portrait*. He also painted the iconostasis for the Dormition Church in Lviv and some religious compositions, and restored paintings. He set up a printing shop in Lviv in 1850 and there made lithographs.

**Yabluniv kurhans.** A group of kurhans of the 1st millennium BC to the 5th century BC near Yabluniv, Kaniv raion, Cherkasy oblast. Excavations in 1876 revealed that all eight kurhans, most of which were Scythian in origin, had been looted long ago, but remains of a funeral feast, local and Greek pottery, and gold, silver, and bronze adornments were recovered.

**Yablunivka** [Jablunivka]. A village (1972 pop 1,100) in Buchach raion, Ternopil oblast. It was known as Yazlovets until 1947 and was once an important trading town on the Lviv–Moldavia route. The earliest references to it appear in documents in the first half of the 14th century. A prosperous Armenian colony was established in the town. Its magnate owners built a castle there. In the 16th and early 17th centuries they added a Roman Catholic church and a Dominican monastery. After being occupied by the Turks (1672–83), the town never recovered its commercial importance. The 17th-century Armenian cathedral, which was converted into St Michael's Church, was destroyed during the Second World War, but the ruins of the castle (from 1646) and St Anne's Roman Catholic Church have been preserved.

**Yachting** (*vitrylnyi sport*). The first yacht club in Ukraine was founded in Odessa in 1875. Since then, yacht clubs have been founded in Mykolaiv, Sevastopil, Kherson, Kiev, Dnipropetrovske, and Zaporizhia. In 1913 the first all-Russian yachting competitions were held in Kiev.

Yacht racing was a part of the USSR Spartakiad Games since 1928. The All-Union Sailing Section was set up in 1936 and was renamed the Soviet Federation of Yacht Racing in 1959. It competed in the Olympic Games from 1952 and was a member of the International Yacht Racing Union from 1956. Ukrainian Olympic gold medalists include V. Mankin in the Finn (1968), Tempest (1972), and Star class (1980) and V. Dyrdyra in the Tempest class (1972).

Semen Yadlovsky        Pavlo Yakhno

**Yadlovsky, Semen** [Jadlovs'kyj], b 1879 in the Lemko region, d late August 1929 in Mukachiv, Transcarpathia. Civic leader. After emigrating to the United States in 1890, he became active in the *Ukrainian National Association (UNA) and served as secretary (1904–21), president (1920–5), and administrator of *Svoboda*. In 1915–20 he was involved at the executive level with the UNA-backed Ukrainian-American co-ordinating committees. He died during a visit to Transcarpathia.

**Yahn, Aleksandr** [Jahn], b 11 March 1848 in Penza, Russia, d 10 February 1922 in Veisbakhivka (now Bilorichytsia), Pryluka county, Poltava gubernia. Architect and ceramist. After graduating from the Moscow School of Painting, Sculpture, and Architecture (1863) he studied at the Rome Academy of Arts. From 1876 he lived in Ukraine. He applied the Moderne style in his designs of M. Kochubei's residence in Voronky, Chernihiv gubernia, the Kapnist family's buildings in Velyka Obukhivka, Poltava gubernia, A. Gorchakov's buildings in Tashan, Poltava gubernia, the burial chapel of the Kochubei family in Yaroslavets, Chernihiv gubernia, and A. Rakhmanova's pavilion (1878) and palace (1886) in Veisbakhivka. He organized folk-handicrafts workshops in Voronky, where he revived the making of pottery with Ukrainian folk ornamentation.

**Yahniatyn settlement.** A *Cherniakhiv culture settlement of the 2nd to 6th century near Yahniatyn, Ruzhyn raion, Zhytomyr oblast. Discovered in 1927 and excavated in 1946–7, the site produced evidence of 10 surface dwellings with wood frames and clay walls along with the remains of 2 two-room pottery workshops (one of which contained traces of a single-layered kiln). Artifacts uncovered at the site include local pottery, imported 4th- to 5th-century amphoras, knives, swords, clasps, and 2nd-century Roman coins.

**Yahorlyk Bay** [Jahorlyc'ka zatoka]. VII–12. A Black Sea bay situated along the west coast of Kherson oblast. Located between the Kinburn Spit and the Yahorlyk Kut Peninsula, it is 15 km wide at its entrance, 26 km long, and up to 5 m deep. It has a salinity of 14–15 per cent and freezes up only in unusually harsh winters. A number of islands are situated in the bay, with Dovhyi Island in the middle of its entrance. A section of the bay (including a stretch of shoreline) is within the *Black Sea Nature Reserve.

**Yahotyn** [Jahotyn]. III-12. A city (1989 pop 23,300) on the Supii River and a raion center in Kiev oblast. It was founded in 1552 by Cossacks and peasants fleeing Polish oppression. At the beginning of the 17th century it came under Polish rule and became part of Pereiaslav county in Kiev voivodeship. In 1648 the town became a company center in Pereiaslav regiment. A century later Empress Elizabeth granted the town to Hetman K. Rozumovsky. In 1820 it passed through marriage to Prince N. *Repnin, whom T. Shevchenko visited there several times in the 1840s. In the 19th century the town belonged to Pyriatyn county in Poltava gubernia. Today the city is an agricultural center with several food-processing enterprises, including the Tsukor Research and Refining Consortium, and a building-materials industry. It has a historical museum and an art gallery.

**Yahupolsky, Lev** [Jahupol's'kyj], b 6 February 1922 in Uman, Kiev gubernia. Organic and fluorine chemist. A graduate of Kiev University (1947), since 1951 he has worked at the AN URSR (now ANU) Institute of Organic Chemistry, where he became a department head in 1965 and a professor in 1967. He has made significant contributions to fluorine chemistry, mainly the study of fluorocyanines and aromatic compounds with diverse fluorinated substituents.

**Yaila** [Jajla]. The main range of the Crimean Mountains. Its name is sometimes applied to the mountains as a whole. (See *Crimean Mountains.)

**Yakemchuk, Roman** [Jakemčuk] (aka Yakemtchouk, Romain), b 23 September 1925 in Lviv. Legal scholar; member of the Royal Academy of Sciences Overseas. After emigrating from Ukraine during the war, he completed his studies in Belgium and lectured in political science and international law at the Catholic University in Leuven. A noted specialist in African political and economic development, he has written several monographs on Africa and has been a visiting professor at the University of Zaïre. His works on Ukrainian topics include *L'Ukraine en droit international* (1954), *The Foreign Policy of Soviet Russia* (1956), *L'Ukraine sur le plan diplomatique* (1957), *La ligne Curzon et la IIe Guerre Mondiale* (1957), and *Ukraïna iak pidmet mizhnarodnoho prava* (Ukraine as the Subject of International Law, 1962)

**Yakhnenko** [Jaxnenko]. A family of wealthy industrialists and sugar refiners descended from well-to-do serfs of Count Samoilov in Smila, in the Cherkasy region. Having purchased their own freedom, they gained a fortune through the wholesale trading of industrial products, livestock, and grain. In the 1820s and 1830s, two Yakhnenko brothers (one of them Kindrat Yakhnenko [b 1790, d 1868]) leased mills in Smila and Uman together with F.

*Symyrenko. In the early 1840s they founded the company Braty Yakhnenky i Symyrenko, and in 1843 they built the first steam-powered sugar refinery plant in Ukraine, in Tashlyk. The company expanded its operations to include heavy-machinery production and contributed to the increase in shipping on the Dnieper River. In 1861 the company's assets stood at 4 million rubles. It owned a refining plant (in Horodyshche, Kiev gubernia), sugar refineries (in Ruska Poliana and Tashlyk), ships, mills, and major buildings (in Kiev, Kharkiv, Odessa, and Rostov). As a result of a crisis in the *sugar industry and the lack of credit common in the postreformation period, the company became moribund in the mid-1860s.

**Yakhno, Bohdan** [Jaxno], b 1899 in Galicia, d 21 September 1984 in Buenos Aires. Co-operative leader and civic activist. During the First World War he fought in the ranks of the Ukrainian Sich Riflemen. After the war he organized consumer co-operatives in Zalishchyky county and worked at the Pokutia Credit Union in Kolomyia. After emigrating to Argentina following the Second World War, he helped organize the Vidrodzhennia Ukrainian Co-operative there and served as its director for many years. He was a member of the OUN Leadership (Melnyk faction), the governing bodies of the *Vidrodzhennia society, and Ukrainian veterans' organizations.

**Yakhno, Pavlo** [Jaxno], b 1895, d ? Civic leader in the Far East. In 1918, after participating in the revolutionary events in Ukraine, he went to the *Far East and became an official of the Far Eastern Ukrainian Secretariat in *Vladivostok (1918–21). He was tried and imprisoned by the Soviets in Chita (1923–4), and then settled in Manchuria. He was director of the Ukrainian People's Home in *Harbin, manager of *Man'dzhurs'kyi vistnyk* (1932–7), and a leading member of the Ukrainian National Colony.

**Yakhymovych, Fedir** (Teodor) [Jaxymovyč], b 11 March 1800 in Belzets, near Zolochiv, Galicia, d 14 April 1889 in Vienna. Scenery designer and painter. A graduate of the Vienna Academy of Arts (1827), he worked in Vienna's theaters and as chief designer at the Royal Vienna Opera (1851–71). He painted portraits, landscapes, religious, historical, and genre paintings, miniatures on ivory, and icons for iconostases in the Greek Catholic churches in Vienna and Cracow and in a Greek monastery in Lebanon. In the last years of his life he worked as an artist at the Royal Gallery in Vienna and painted the interior of the university church (eg, the painting *Banishment from Eden*). His best-known canvases are *The Heroism of David* (1841), *Mary Magdalene* (1842), *Interior of the Piarist Church in Vienna*, *The Baptism of Christ* (1849, until 1944 in the Greek Catholic Episcopal Residence in Peremyshl), and *Interior of St Stephen's Church in Vienna* (1860).

**Yakhymovych, Hryhorii** [Jaxymovyč, Hryhorij], b 16 February 1792 in Pidbirtsi, Lviv circle, Galicia, d 17 April 1863. Ukrainian Catholic metropolitan, professor, and civic activist. After completing a doctorate of divinity in Vienna (1818) he taught religion and pedagogy at Lviv University and was rector of the Greek Catholic Theological Seminary and a canon of the metropolitan chapter. In 1841 he was consecrated bishop of Lviv and suffragan to Metropolitan M. Levytsky. In 1849–59 Yakhymovych was the bishop of Peremyshl, and in 1860–3 metropolitan of

Metropolitan Hryhorii
Yakhymovych

Dmytro Yakimishchak

Halych. In 1848–51 Yakhymovych assumed the leadership of the *Supreme Ruthenian Council and became the main spokesperson for Ukrainian interests in Galicia during the crisis period of the 1848 revolutions. He was loyal to the Habsburg monarchy and concerned about the social position of the Ukrainian Catholic clergy. Yakhymovych won some short-lived concessions from the monarchy, but failed to realize a major Ukrainian goal – the partition of Galicia and the creation of a separate Ukrainian crownland. At the same time he was instrumental in keeping revolutionary fervor from spreading into eastern Galicia, and thus helped Ukrainians gain a loyalist reputation within the empire as the 'Tyroleans of the East.'

**Yakimishchak, Dmytro** [Jakymiščak] (Yakimischak), b 7 October 1888 in Zarichia, Nadvirna county, Galicia, d 18 July 1958 in Winnipeg. Lawyer and political and civic activist. He emigrated to Canada with his parents in 1898, became one of the first Canadian public school teachers of Ukrainian origin, and took part in the first Ukrainian-Canadian teachers' convention (1907). He graduated in law from the University of Manitoba and was one of the few Ukrainians with a law practice at the time. A member of the Ukrainian Canadian Citizens' League and a founder of the Ukrainian economic association Lantsiuh, he was elected in 1920 and 1922 to the Manitoba legislative assembly as an independent farmer candidate from Emerson district.

**Yakir, Yona** [Jakir, Jona], b 15 August 1896 in Kishinev, Bessarabia, d 11 June 1937 in Leningrad. Soviet military and political figure. He commanded Red Guard units in Moldavia and southern Ukraine and then led several Red Army units against the Whites and the Army of the UNR. During the Ukrainian-Soviet War of 1920 he served on the southwestern front, and from December 1920 he commanded the 14th Army. After the war he commanded several military districts, including the Kiev Military District (from 1935). He was elected to the CC CP(B)U several times and became a candidate (1927) and full member (1930) of its Politburo. In 1937, after being appointed commander of the Leningrad Military District, he was arrested in the purge of the Red Army and executed.

**Yakovchenko, Mykola** [Jakovčenko], b 3 May 1900 in Pryluka, Poltava gubernia, d 11 September 1974 in Kiev. Stage and film actor. He began his career in an amateur circle in Pryluka (1918) and in various Ukrainian touring troupes (1920–7) and then joined the Kiev Ukrainian Drama Theater. He acted in the films *Ukradene shchastia* (Stolen Happiness, 1952), *Martyn Borulia* (1953), and *Zakhar Berkut* (1972).

Hryhorii Yakovenko

Archbishop Borys Yakovkevych

**Yakovenko, Hryhorii** [Jakovenko, Hryhorij], b 2 December 1895 in Katerynivka, Katerynoslav gubernia, d 27 April 1940 in Donetske. Writer. He was a member of the literary organization *Pluh. He is the author of the novels *Praporshchyk Holobuzenko* (Warrant Officer Holobuzenko, 1925), *Verbivchany* (1928), *Try elementy* (Three Elements, 1930), and *Borot'ba tryvaie* (The Struggle Continues, 1931). Yakovenko made his mark in literary history with an article attacking M. Khvylovy, which began the *Literary Discussion of 1925–8.

**Yakovenko, Valentyn** [Jakovenko], b 11 November 1859 in Poltava gubernia, d 20 March 1915. Journalist and publisher, and popularizer of T. Shevchenko's works. While working as a statistician in Russia in the 1880s, he contributed articles on economic and social problems to progressive Russian journals. He wrote a popular biography of Shevchenko (1894) and published in 1910 the third edition of *Kobzar, edited by V. Domanytsky, and in 1911 the most complete edition (2 vols) of Shevchenko's works to that date.

**Yakovenko, Volodymyr** [Jakovenko], b 1857, d 1923. Psychiatrist. He worked in zemstvo hospitals in Ukraine and Russia and directed the psychiatric hospital he built in Meshcherske, Podilia gubernia (1894–1907). He was dismissed from that position for political reasons. He wrote works on psychiatry and psychiatric care and initiated the first survey of the mentally ill in the Russian Empire.

**Yakovkevych, Borys** [Jakovkevyč], b 8 December 1901 in Mala Klitynka, Starokostiantyniv county, Volhynia gubernia, d 24 March 1984 in Edmonton. Ukrainian Orthodox hierarch. A graduate of the Kremianets Theological Seminary (1923), he served in the Polish army (1924–5), was ordained (1930), completed a master's degree in theology in Warsaw (1934), and then undertook pastoral work in the Kholm region and Volhynia. During the Second World War he was active in the Ukrainian Social Welfare Committee and helped to save several hundred soldiers imprisoned by the Germans in Volodymyr-Volynskyi. This work, as well as his ties with the Ukrainian Insurgent Army, sent Yakovkevych and his father to a Gestapo prison, from which they managed to escape during the confusion of the German retreat. Yakovkevych settled in Canada in 1948. He was consecrated as bishop of Saskatoon eparchy in 1963 and as archbishop of Edmonton and Western Canada in 1975.

**Yakovkin, Avenir** [Jakovkin], b 21 May 1887 in Blagoveshchenskii zavod (now Blagoveshchensk), Ufa gubernia, Russia, d 18 November 1974 in Kiev. Astronomer; AN URSR (now ANU) corresponding member from 1951. A graduate of Kazan University (1910), he worked at the Kazan Astronomical Observatory (1910–37) and was a professor at Sverdlovsk (1937–45) and Kiev (1945–51) universities. From 1951 to 1967 he worked at the ANU Main Astronomical Observatory near Kiev, which he served as director in 1952–9. His main contributions were in the study of the motions of celestial bodies, particularly the moon. He discovered the asymmetry of the lunar disc, developed novel methods of measuring the moon's libration, worked out mathematical models of perturbations in the moon's motions, and designed special apparatus for the study of the moon.

Andrii Yakovliv          Feliks Yakubovsky

**Yakovliv, Andrii** [Jakovliv, Andrij], b 11 December 1872 in Chyhyryn, Kiev gubernia, d 14 May 1955 in New York. Legal scholar and civic and political leader; full member of the Ukrainian Scientific Society in Kiev and the Shevchenko Scientific Society (NTSh, from 1926) and director of the law section of the Ukrainian Academy of Arts and Sciences in the US. After graduating from the law faculties of Yurev (1903) and Kiev (1904) universities, he worked in Kiev as a civil servant and in the treasury department. From 1908 he maintained a legal practice and conducted research in the Kiev archives. During the Ukrainian struggle for independence he was a member of the Central Rada (1917–18, delegate of the cultural organization of Kiev) and the Little Rada (director of its bureau)

and consul extraordinary to Austria-Hungary (1918); under the Hetman government he was director of international relations in the external affairs ministry; and under the Directory he was head of the extraordinary diplomatic mission of the UNR in Holland and Belgium (January 1919).

Yakovliv lived as an émigré in Prague from 1923. He served as a professor at the Ukrainian Free University (rector in 1930–1 and 1944–5), a professor of law at the Ukrainian Husbandry Academy in Poděbrady, head of the society of the Museum of Ukraine's Struggle for Independence, and head of the Ukrainian Academic Committee in Prague. In 1939 he became director of the Ukrainian Scientific Institute in Warsaw. After the Second World War he lived in Belgium, and in 1952 he moved to the United States.

Yakovliv ranks as one of the leading researchers in the field of the history of Ukrainian law. Among his works (written in Ukrainian, Russian, French, German, and English) are *Dohovir het'mana B. Khmel'nyts'koho z Moskvoiu r. 1654* (Hetman B. Khmelnytsky's 1654 Treaty with Moscow, 1927), *Pro kopni sudy na Ukraïni* (About Community Courts in Ukraine, 1931), *Ukraïns'ko-moskovs'ki dohovory 17–18 vv.* (Ukrainian-Muscovite Treaties of the 17th–18th Centuries, 1934), *Osnovy Konstytutsiï UNR* (The Foundations of the UNR Constitution, 1935), *Das deutsche Recht in der Ukraine* (1942), and *Dohovir Het'mana B. Khmel'nyts'koho z moskovs'kym tsarem Oleksiiem Mykhailovychem 1654: Istorychno-pravnycha studiia* (The 1654 Treaty of Hetman B. Khmelnytsky with the Muscovite Tsar Aleksei Mikhailovich: A Historical-Juridical Study, 1954), as well as articles in *Zapysky* NTSh on Muscovite treaties with Hetman I. Vyhovsky (1933), on the authorship of the historical-political tract *Istoriia Rusov* (1937), and on the history of the Ukrainian Code of Laws of 1743 (1949). In his series of studies on 17th-century Ukrainian-Muscovite relations, Yakovliv defended the theory that the Pereiaslav Treaty of 1654 created the conditions for a vassalage relationship akin to that of a protectorate between Ukraine and Russia. Yakovliv was also a philatelist; under the pseudonym Andrii Chyhyrynets he published *Poshtovi marky Ukraïny 1918–1943* (Postage Stamps of Ukraine in 1918–43, 1948).

A. Zhukovsky

**Yakubovsky, Feliks** [Jakubovs'kyj], b 25 September 1902 in Kiev, d 25 September 1937. Literary scholar and critic. He graduated from the Kiev Institute of People's Education (1926) and worked at the Kiev branch of the Taras Shevchenko Scientific Research Institute. He was a member of the literary organization Zhovten and, later, of the All-Ukrainian Association of Proletarian Writers. He wrote many articles and introductory essays to literary publications. He published the monographs *Syliuety suchasnykh ukraïns'kykh pys'mennykiv* (Silhouettes of Contemporary Ukrainian Writers, 1928), *Vid noveli do romanu* (From Short Story to the Novel, 1929), *Stepan Vasyl'chenko* (1930), and *Za spravzhni oblychchia* (For Real Faces, 1931). He was arrested by the NKVD in 1937 and shot.

**Yakubovsky, Volodymyr** [Jakubovs'kyj] (nom de guerre: Bondarenko), b 1915 in Zaliztsi, Zboriv county, Galicia, d 17 June 1947 in Kozova raion, Ternopil oblast. Senior UPA commander. In 1942–3 he organized military training for OUN members, and in December 1943 he be-

Maj Volodymyr Yakubovsky

came chief of staff of the Third Military District (Ternopil oblast) of the UPA-West. In 1944 he also directed a non-commissioned officer school in his district and led a UPA battalion on a combat raid. Then he commanded the Lysonia Group in the Third Military District (1945–7) and was promoted to major. He was killed in combat with MVD troops.

**Yakubsky, Borys** [Jakubs'kyj], b 27 September 1889 in Illintsi, Lypovets county, Kiev gubernia, d ? Literary scholar and critic. He joined the Bolshevik party in 1905 but left it in 1919. A graduate of Kiev University (1908–14), he was a full member of the VUAN Historical and Literary Society (from 1918), the Ukrainian Scientific Society in Kiev (from 1919), and the scientific research chairs of linguistics, art studies, and Marxism-Leninism in Kiev, and an associate of the VUAN Commission for the Publication of Monuments of Modern Ukrainian Literature and of the Kiev branch of the Taras Shevchenko Scientific Research Institute. Yakubsky was one of the first scholars to apply the sociological method in studying Ukrainian literature. An associate of the *Neoclassicists, he published books on the science of versification (1922), the sociological method in literature (1923), and S. Vasylchenko (1928). His articles on the form of T. Shevchenko's poems (1921), Shevchenko's style (1924) and rhythm (1926), and the sociology of Shevchenko's epithets (1928) appeared in Shevchenko studies compendiums. Yakubsky also published articles in literary theory, on D. Zahul (1928), M. Vorony (1928), Lesia Ukrainka (1928), and Soviet Ukrainian literature, in periodicals such as *Hlobus*, *Literaturna hazeta*, *Zhyttia i revoliutsiia*, *Chervonyi shliakh*, and *Krytyka*. He also edited, with introductions, the collected works of Lesia Ukrainka (7 vols, 1923–5), an anthology of 20th-century Galician and Bukovynian poetry (1930), a subsequently banned AN URSR (now ANU) edition of Shevchenko's complete works (2 vols, 1939), and other works. Though reviled as a formalist, Yakubsky survived the Stalinist terror of the 1930s and was still alive in Kiev in 1943. His subsequent fate is unknown. Despite his contributions he has barely been mentioned in Soviet publications since the 1930s.

R. Senkus

**Yakutiia.** An autonomous republic in northeastern Siberia and the largest member of the Russian Federation. Until 1991 it was known as the Yakut ASSR (est 1922). Its territory covers 3,103,200 sq km, and its population in 1989 was 1,081,000. The capital is Yakutsk.

In 1989 Ukrainians accounted for 7 percent of Yakutiia's population. They are predominantly highly skilled specialists who work there on a temporary basis. There are also exiles or descendants of exiles deported there by the Soviet or the tsarist regime as far back as the 17th century (see *Siberia). In 1990 the Ukrainian community in Yakutiia set up the Shevchenko Social and Cultural Association in Yakutsk. Its president is V. Taniuk, Yakutiia's deputy minister of culture.

Heorhii Yakutovych: *The Arkan* (linocut, 1960)

**Yakutovych, Heorhii** (Yurii) [Jakutovyč, Heorhij], b 14 February 1930 in Kiev. Graphic artist; corresponding member of the USSR (now Russian) Academy of Arts since 1983. He studied at the Kiev State Art Institute (1948–54) under V. Kasiian and I. Pleshchynsky and taught there in 1954–7 and 1961–2. A master of different graphic techniques from woodcut to metal engraving, he blends realism with formal experimentation to create a thoroughly modernist impression. The influence of Hutsul folk art is evident in his use of geometric forms. Yakutovych has illustrated editions of M. Kotsiubynsky's novels *Fata morgana* (1957) and *Tini zabutykh predkiv* (Shadows of Forgotten Ancestors, 1966), I. Kocherha's plays *Iaroslav Mudryi* (Yaroslav the Wise) and *Svichchyne vesillia* (Svichka's Wedding, 1962), I. Franko's novel *Zakhar Berkut* (1972), the epic *Povist' pro Ihoriv pokhid* (The Tale of Ihor's Campaign, 1977), V. Stefanyk's story collection *Klenovi lystky* (The Maple Leaves, 1978), the epic *Slovo mynulykh lit* (The Tale of Bygone Years, 1981), and N. Gogol's *Vii* (1985). Many of his prints have been widely reproduced. They include the series 'Ancient Ukrainian Music' (1957), 'Ivan Vyshensky' (1959), 'Oleh Horyslavych' (1959), and 'Arkan' (1960) and two series of postcards on folk-song themes (1960, 1963). Yakutovych served as artistic consultant for the films *Tini zabutykh predkiv* (Shadows of Forgotten Ancestors, 1965; director, S. Paradzhanov) and *Zakhar Berkut* (1971). Books about Yakutovych have been written by Yu. Belichko (1968) in Ukrainian and I. Verba (1970) and L. Popova (1988) in Russian.

W. Wytwycky

**Yakutovych, Serhii** [Jakutovyč, Serhij], b 21 November 1952 in Kiev. Graphic artist; son of H. Yakutovych. He studied at the Moscow Printing Institute (1973–7) and graduated from the Kiev State Art Institute (1980). Although he works in a figurative manner, there are elements of surrealism in his etchings and lithographs (eg, *Time,* 1979). The series 'Chords of War' (1980) and 'Foreboding' (1982) reveal his concern with moral issues and judgments and make a statement against the horrors of war and the destruction of humankind.

Fedir Yakymenko          Mykhailo Yalovy

**Yakymenko, Fedir** [Jakymenko] (also Akymenko), b 20 September 1876 in Pisky, outside Kharkiv, d 8 January 1945 in Paris. Composer, pianist, and teacher; brother of Ya. *Stepovy. At 10 years of age he was sent to St Petersburg, where he sang in the court kapelle; he studied piano with M. Balakirev (1886–95) and graduated (1900) from the St Petersburg Conservatory in the composition class of N. Rimsky-Korsakov and A. Liadov. He then worked as a music teacher in Tbilisi (1901–3), Paris (1903–6), and Kharkiv before returning to St Petersburg to lecture (1914–23) at the conservatory. He emigrated to Prague in 1923 and headed the music section of the Ukrainian Higher Pedagogical Institute. Z. Lysko and M. Kolessa were among his students. He performed as a concert pianist, conducted choirs in tours through Western Europe, and prepared *Praktychnyi kurs harmonii* (A Practical Course in Harmony, 1926). From 1928 he lived in France (Nice, Paris). As a composer Yakymenko belonged to a 20th-century neoromantic school which was influenced by impressionist techniques. His major compositions were instrumental; they include two symphonies, symphonic poems, an orchestral suite, an overture, a trio for strings, a sonata for cello, sonatas for violin, and numerous works for piano (sonatas, sonatas-fantasias, *Ukrainian Suite,* preludes, and études). He also composed works for solo voice (notably to the words of O. Oles), church music, and choir arrangements of Ukrainian folk songs. Many of Yakymenko's works have appeared in German, French, Russian, and Ukrainian publications. His biography, by P. Matsenko, appeared in Winnipeg in 1954.

**Yakymenko, Yakiv.** See Stepovy, Yakiv.

**Yakymivka** [Jakymivka]. VII-16. A town smt (1986 pop 12,800) on the Malyi Utliuk River and a raion center in Zaporizhia oblast. In 1833 a colony of state peasants from Tambov and Kursk gubernias was settled there. In the

1870s the town was linked by rail to the ports of the Black Sea, and began to export grain. Today it is the administrative center of an agricultural region with several food-processing plants and a cast-iron foundry.

**Yakymovych, Bohdan** [Jakymovyč], b 29 January 1952 in Serafyntsi, Horodenka raion, Ivano-Frankivske oblast. Historian and civic figure. A graduate of the Kiev Polytechnical Institute (1974), he has been a scholarly associate of the AN URSR (now ANU) Institute of Social Sciences in Lviv since 1986. He has compiled books on I. Franko in postcards (1987) and the paintings of I. Marchuk (1990), edited and annotated an uncensored edition of I. Krypiakevych's history of Ukraine (1990), edited the UNESCO collection of materials on Franko and world culture (3 vols, 1990), and written articles on Ukrainian history and culture (eg, Ukraine's national symbols, the Ukrainian Sich Riflemen, the Cossacks and their role, the preservation of cultural monuments). Since 1992 he has been head of the Lviv branch of the *Ukraina Society.

**Yakymovych, Tetiana** [Jakymovyč, Tetjana], b 20 September 1905 in Kiev. Literary scholar. She graduated from the Kiev Institute of People's Education (1926) and worked at the Kiev Pedagogical Institute. In 1931 she began teaching at Kiev University, and from 1949 to 1976 she headed the department of foreign literature there. A former member of the editorial board of *Vsesvit,* she has written books on the French satirical press in the years 1830–5 (1961), the French realist sketch in the years 1830–48 (1963), contemporary French dramaturgy and theater (1968, 1973); the young E. Zola (1971); a book of essays about 19th- and 20th-century French writers (1981); and numerous articles.

**Yalovy, Mykhailo** [Jalovyj, Myxajlo] (pseud: Yuliian Shpol), b 5 June 1895 in Dar-Nadezhda, Kostiantynohrad county, Poltava gubernia, d 9 October 1937 in Lodeinoe Pole, northern Russia. Poet, prose writer, and dramatist. He began to publish his work in 1920 in the journals *Shliakhy mystetstva, Chervonyi shliakh,* and *Vsesvit.* Yalovy was one of the founders and the first president of *Vaplite. He wrote the poetry collection *Verkhy* (The Peaks, 1923), the comedy *Katyna liubov, abo Budivel'na propahanda* (Katia's Love, or Building Propaganda, 1929), and the novel *Zoloti lyseniata* (Golden Fox Cubs, 1928). In May 1933 Yalovy was arrested, sentenced to 10 years of imprisonment, and dispatched to the labor camps of Siberia. He was resentenced by a special tribunal in 1937 and shot. The arrest of Yalovy marked the beginning of the P. Postyshev pogrom against the Ukrainian intelligentsia.

**Yalpukh Lake** [Jalpux] (also Yalpuh). VIII-9. A lake in Odessa oblast situated along the Danube River Delta. The lake is 39 km long and up to 5 km wide, with a prevailing depth of 2 m and a surface area of 149 sq km. Its steep eastern and western sides are dissected by gullies, and the southern end facing the Danube is sandy and low-lying. The lake is fed directly by the Yalpukh River and indirectly (through seepage) by the Danube. Over 40 types of fish and several varieties of waterfowl can be found there. Yalpukh Lake is used for water supply and irrigation. The town of Bolhrad is situated at its northern end.

**Yalta** [Jalta]. IX–15. A city (1989 pop 89,000) on the southern shore of the Crimean Peninsula. The earliest recorded

Yalta

reference to settlement on the site is a reference to a Greek colony named Yalita (Halita) in the 1st century BC. Control of the area later passed to Byzantium. By the 12th century Yalta (called Dzhalita) had become an established port and fishing village. Genoese traders had control of the town (known as Etalita) in the 13th to 15th centuries, until they were succeeded by the Turks in 1475. Yalta fell under Russian control in 1783 with the annexation of the Crimea. At that time the region around it began to be colonized by estate owners. In 1823 the governor-general of the region, Prince M. Vorontsov, decided to cultivate Yalta as the major settlement on the Crimean south shore. It was not until 1838, however, that it was established officially as a town. Yalta began to expand considerably in the later 19th century because of its growing popularity as a resort and sanatorium center. By 1885 its population was approx 5,000, and by 1895, nearly 10,000. The city came under Soviet control in 1920 and was the site of the *Yalta Conference in 1945.

Yalta is nestled in a scenic location between the Black Sea and the Crimean Mountains. It is particularly noted for its Mediterranean climate, and the city and its surrounding environs have (1975) 65 sanatoriums, 18 health resorts, and 8 boarding hotels with a summer capacity of approx 39,000 beds. Yalta is also a wine-making center; other major economic activities include fish and food processing, tobacco fermentation, and the production of beer and nonalcoholic beverages. A number of notable architectural monuments are situated in and around the city, including the Tavrida Hotel, the Vorontsov Palace, and the ruins of the medieval Isar fortifications and a Byzantine cave church. Also located in the city are a statue of Lesia Ukrainka and the grave of S. Rudansky.

**Yalta Conference.** The conference of the 'Big Three' Allied leaders held in Yalta, in the Crimea, on 4–11 February 1945. There F.D. Roosevelt, W. Churchill, J. Stalin, and their foreign ministers, military chiefs of staff, and other advisers planned the final defeat of Nazi Germany and determined the political order of postwar Europe. Among the most important decisions reached were those concerning the dismemberment of Germany and Austria into military-occupation zones of the United States, Great Britain, France, and the USSR; the reparations to be imposed on Germany; the prosecution of Nazi war criminals; the *repatriation of American prisoners of war and displaced Soviet citizens (*Ostarbeiter*, prisoners of war, and collaborators with the Germans); Soviet entry into the war against Japan within three months after Germany's defeat

(a top secret protocol); the redrawing of Poland's borders (ie, Poland's withdrawal east of the *Curzon Line, with digressions in some areas of 5–8 km in Poland's favor, in exchange for the incorporation of Germany's eastern borderlands within Poland); the establishment of the Moscow-sponsored Polish Provisional Government of National Unity; the convocation of the *United Nations Conference on International Organization in San Francisco on 25 April 1945; the admission of Soviet Ukraine and Belarus in addition to the USSR as members of the proposed UN General Assembly; and the principle of unanimity and veto in the UN Security Council.

The conference's 'Declaration on Liberated Europe' allowed the USSR to interpret broadly its 'aid' to the countries it 'liberated'; the result was the Sovietization of Eastern Europe and the Cold War. Stalin and his advisers maximally exploited the Soviet military victories against Germany, the Soviet military occupation of most of Eastern Europe, and the need for Soviet participation in the war against Japan to gain an upper hand in the conference's decisions. Roosevelt yielded to most of the Soviet demands. Soviet historians have viewed the conference as the greatest success of Soviet foreign policy. It formally recognized the Soviet annexation of eastern Galicia and Volhynia and western Belarus (ie, half of prewar Poland's territory), sealed Eastern Europe's fate within the Soviet sphere of influence, and strengthened the position of the USSR in world politics.

BIBLIOGRAPHY
Stettinius, E.R. *Roosevelt and the Russians: The Yalta Conference* (New York 1949)
McNeill, W.H. *America, Britain, and Russia: Their Co-operation and Conflict, 1941–1946* (Oxford 1953; repr, New York 1970)
Clemens, D.S. *Yalta* (New York 1970)
Iakovlev, A. (ed). *Ialtinskaia konferentsiia 1945: Uroki istorii* (Moscow 1985)

V. Markus

**Yalta Mountain and Forest Nature Reserve** (Yaltynskyi hirsko-lisovyi zapovidnyk). Established in 1973 to preserve the forests of the main range of the *Crimean Mountains, the reserve extends for 40 km along the southern shore of the Crimea from Aiu-Dag to Cape Foros and covers an area of 14,600 ha on the mountains' southern slopes. It encompasses some unique landforms: gentle, clay-schist slopes alternate with steep cliffs and exposed magmatic layers. Its rich flora (1,360 species) consists mostly of oak, pine, and beech forests (11,000 ha) and includes some rare plants, such as the English yew and the wild pistachio. Approx 115 plant species are endemic. The most common animals are the red deer, roebuck, boar, badger, and marten. The most scenic sites in the reserve are the Uchansu and Yauzlar waterfalls and the Tarak-Tash and Stavri-Kaia cliffs.

**Yalynsky, Semen** [Jalyns'kyj], b ?, d after 1695. Printer and engraver. He served as Archbishop L. Baranovsky's secretary and became technical director of the Novhorod-Siverskyi Press (1674–9) and Chernihiv Press (1679 to ca 1684). Besides liturgical books, polemical literature, and moralistic works by L. Baranovych and other writers, he printed school grammars and primers. He signed his illustrations, headpieces, and tailpieces with the initials 'SM.' His *Punkty* (Agreement) with his employer, L. Baranovych, is an important document for the history of printing in Ukraine.

**Yama.** See Siverske.

**Yamnychenko, Ivan** [Jamnyčenko], b 31 August 1909 in Reshetylivka, Poltava county, Poltava gubernia. Geologist. After graduating from the Kiev Institute of Mining Geology (1935) he worked at the AN URSR (now ANU) Institute of Geological Sciences. His works deal with the stratigraphy and fauna of Mesozoic strata in Ukraine. They include *Struktura i sutnist' biostratyhrafichnoho metodu* (The Structure and Essence of the Biostratigraphic Method, 1976).

**Yampil** [Jampil']. V-9. A town smt (1986 pop 11,400) at the junction of the Rusava and the Dniester rivers and a raion center in Vinnytsia oblast. It was first mentioned in historical documents in the 16th century, as a trading center of Bratslav voivodeship. At the beginning of the 17th century it was acquired by J. *Zamoyski, who built a castle there. During B. Khmelnytsky's rule it became a company town of Mohyliv and then Bratslav regiment. After being destroyed by S. Lanckoroński's troops in 1651, the town declined to a village. During the 18th century it belonged to the Potocki family. It was annexed by Russia in 1793, and became a county town in Podilia gubernia. Today it is an agricultural center of which the main industry is food processing.

**Yampil.** [Jampil']. II-14. A town smt (1986 pop 5,700) on the Ivotka River and a raion center in Sumy oblast. It originated at the beginning of the 17th century and was called Klyn until 1674. From the mid-1680s to 1709 and from 1722 to 1781 it was a company town of Nizhen regiment. An agricultural center, it has a dairy and a flax-processing factory.

Stefan Yampolsky

Oleksander Yanata

**Yampolsky, Stefan** [Jampol's'kyj], b 21 December 1906 in Izium, Kharkiv gubernia. Economist; full member of the AN URSR (now ANU) since 1967. After graduating from the Kharkiv Industrial-Engineering Institute (1932) he worked at several large enterprises and served as rector of the institute (1938–41). After the war he was rector of the Lviv Polytechnical Institute (1944–53) and Odessa Polytechnical Institute (1957–65) and director of the ANU Insti-

tute of Economics (1965–70). He chaired the ANU Council for the Study of the Productive Resources of Ukraine (1970–2) and then the Department of Machine-Building of the Institute of Economics. He was chief editor of the journal *Ekonomika Radians'koï Ukraïny* (1965–74) and of *Entsyklopediia narodnoho hospodarstva Ukraïns'koï RSR* (Encyclopedia of the National Economy of the Ukrainian SSR, 4 vols, 1969–72). Yampolsky is the author of numerous scholarly works, including *Voprosy skorostnogo proektirovaniia i osvoeniia novykh konstruktsii v mashinostroenii* (Questions of Rapid Designing and the Assimilation of New Constructions in Machine Building, 1944), *Skorostnoe osvoenie novykh proizvodstv* (The Rapid Assimilation of New Manufactures, 1949), *Ekonomika osvoeniia novykh konstruktsii mashin* (The Economics of the Assimilation of New Machine Constructions, 1964), *Ekonomicheskie problemy upravleniia nauchno-tekhnicheskim progressom,* (Economic Problems of Managing Scientific and Technological Progress, 1976), and *Ekonomicheskoe upravlenie sozdaniem sistem mashin* (Economic Management through the Creation of Machine Systems, 1981).

B. Wynar

**Yanata, Oleksander** [Janata], b 9 June 1888 in Mykolaiv, d 1938 in the Kolyma region. Botanist and agronomist of Czech origin; full member of the Shevchenko Scientific Society from 1923 and corresponding member of the VUAN. A graduate of the Kiev Polytechnical Institute, he taught at Kiev University (from 1928) and was secretary of the Ukrainian Scientific Society and a cofounder of *Ukraïns'kyi botanichnyi zhurnal*. Before its liquidation in 1928 he was scientific secretary of the Agricultural Scientific Committee of Ukraine, chairman of its botany section, and editor of *Visnyk sil's'ko-hospodars'koï nauky.* In Kharkiv he organized and directed departments of Applied Botany and Plant Cultivation at the Kharkiv Agricultural Institute. He was arrested in 1933, and died in a labor camp. Yanata's scholarly work dealt with the botany of southern Ukraine and the Crimea, botanical regionalization, and Ukrainian botanical terminology. Much of it has remained unpublished, and his authorship of the first volume of *Flora URSR* (published after his arrest) was uncredited.

**Yanchevsky, Mykola** [Jančevs'kyj], b 1888, d ? Army officer. During the First World War he served in the Russian army, and in 1917 he helped Ukrainianize units of the 12th Cavalry Division, which joined the Odessa Haidamaka Battalion organized by I. *Lutsenko in late 1917. In 1918–19 he served in other UNR Army units. He was promoted to brigadier general in 1920 and worked in the UNR defense ministry. After emerging from the internment camp in Kalisz, Poland, he was active in the Orthodox church brotherhood and edited the journal *Tabor* in Warsaw.

**Yanchuk, Mykola** [Jančuk], b 29 November 1859 in Kornytsia, in the Podlachia region of Lublin gubernia, Congress Kingdom of Poland, d 6 December 1921 in Moscow. Folklorist, ethnographer, and playwright. After graduating from Moscow University (1885) he served as editor of *Etnograficheskoe obozrenie* (1889–1916) and custodian of the ethnographic departments at the Dashkov and Rumiantsev museums. In 1921 he became a professor of Belarusian literature and ethnography at Minsk University. He wrote in Russian, Belarusian, and Ukrainian. He is the author of *Malorusskaia svad'ba v Kornytskom prikhode, Konstantinovskogo uezda Sedletskoi gubernii* (The Little Russian Wedding in Kornytsia Parish, Kostiantyniv County, Siedlce Gubernia, 1886). In 1901 he set up the Musical Ethnography Commission at the ethnographic section of the Society of Lovers of Natural Science, Anthropology, and Ethnography, which popularized Ukrainian musical folklore. The members of its expedition to Poltava gubernia recorded, in May 1912, over 300 Ukrainian songs. Yanchuk wrote some plays in Ukrainian, such as 'Pylyp muzyka' (Pylyp the Musician, 1887), 'Vykhovanets'' (The Pupil, 1899), and 'Ne pomozhut' i chary' (Even Charms Will Not Help, 1891).

M. Mushynka

**Yanchukov, Oleksander** [Jančukov], b 28 December 1910 in Kharkiv, d 18 June 1982 in Lviv. Stage actor. He began his career in the Kharkiv Young Spectator's Theater (1934) and then joined the Lviv Young Spectator's Theater (1944). He played the title role in Yu. Kostiuk's drama *Taras Shevchenko*.

Mykhailo Yanhel

Volodymyr Yaniv

**Yanhel, Mykhailo** [Janhel', Myxajlo] (Yangel, Mikhail), b 7 November 1911 in Zirianova, near Irkutsk, Siberia, d 25 October 1971 in Moscow. Mechanical engineer, specialist in spacecraft design; full member of the AN URSR (now ANU) from 1961 and of the USSR Academy of Sciences from 1966. He studied in Moscow and worked in various aviation plants, construction offices, and rocket institutes. Most of his later work, particularly in the Soviet space program, remains secret. He is reported to have headed the Soviet space effort, including all the manned and unmanned spaceflights and the spacecraft design bureau, after the death of S. *Korolov. He was prominent in the political elite of the Soviet technical establishment. His main published technical contributions were in the area of applied mechanics and rocket technology.

**Yanishevsky, Vasyl** [Janiševs'kyj, Vasyl'] (Janischewskyj, Wasyl), b 21 January 1925 in Prague. Engineer and Plast activist; member of the Shevchenko Scientific Society and the Ukrainian Academy of Arts and Sciences. He graduated from the University of Toronto (1954) and taught electrical engineering there, as full professor since 1970. His publications deal with high-voltage transmis-

sion, radio interference by high-voltage corona, fault behavior of complex electric power systems, methods of testing underground cables, lightning studies, microgap discharges, and TV interference. He has been president of the *Plast Ukrainian Youth Association in Canada (1968–71) and head of its world executive as well as president of the *Ukrainian Canadian Research and Documentation Centre in Toronto.

**Yaniv, Sofiia** [Janiv, Sofija] (née Moiseiovych), b 14 November 1908 in Lviv. Civic activist; wife of V. *Yaniv; corresponding member of the Shevchenko Scientific Society (NTSh). As a member of the OUN and its Home Executive she was imprisoned three times by the Polish authorities. Since 1947 she has worked with the NTSh as the secretary of the editorial board of *Entsyklopediia ukraïnoznavstva* (Encyclopedia of Ukraine, 1949 and 1955–90) and as a subject editor for the *Encyclopedia of Ukraine* (vols 1–2, 1984, 1988). She served as the first director of the museum of the Ukrainian Catholic University in Rome (1963–72).

**Yaniv, Volodymyr** [Janiv] (Janiw, Wolodymyr), b 21 November 1908 in Lviv, d 19 November 1991 in Munich (buried in Sarcelles, near Paris). Political, community, and scholarly figure; full member of the Shevchenko Scientific Society (NTSh, from 1950; honorary member from 1987), the Ukrainian Theological Scholarly Society (UBNT, from 1960), the Ukrainian Academy of Arts and Sciences (UVAN in the US, from 1977; and honorary member of the Canadian UVAN from 1988). He studied history and psychology at Lviv University (1927–34), joined the underground Ukrainian Military Organization (in 1927) and OUN (in 1929), and was active in the Plast scouting organization and the Union of Ukrainian Nationalist Youth. In Lviv he headed the branch of the *Mohyla Scholarly Lectures Society (1930–2); was the first president of the *Union of Ukrainian Student Organizations under Poland (1931–2); edited *Students'kyi shliakh* (1932–4), *Nash klych* (1933), and other nationalist and student periodicals; and was a member of the OUN Home Executive in charge of political affairs (1932–4). For his OUN involvement he was imprisoned by the Polish authorities five times in 1928–33, and from June 1934 to August 1937 he was incarcerated in the Bereza Kartuzka concentration camp and the Lviv Brygidky prison. After the 1939 Soviet occupation of Galicia he moved to Berlin, where he resumed his studies and edited *Ukraïns'kyi visnyk* (1940). In June 1941 he became a member of the *Ukrainian National Committee in Cracow, for which act he was imprisoned by the Gestapo. He was released in September 1942 through the efforts of the Ukrainian Central Committee in Cracow and thereupon banished from German-occupied Galicia. He returned to Berlin, where he wrote his PH D dissertation (1944) on the psychological effects of imprisonment.

Yaniv was a prominent figure in the postwar Ukrainian émigré community in Western Europe. He played a key role in the political unification of the *Central Union of Ukrainian Students in 1947 and in the organization of the 1948 ideological congress of émigré Ukrainian student organizations. His primary involvement was with the Ukrainian Free University (UVU) in Munich, where he taught psychology and sociology from 1946 (as a professor from 1955) and was rector from 1968 to 1986, and the

NTSh, in which he served as Philosophical-Pedagogical Commission secretary (1947–50). He was an executive board member (1949–55) and the scholarly secretary of the European NTSh center in Sarcelles (1952–68), and the Historical-Philosophical Section secretary (1955–73), vice-president (1968–85, from 1987), and president (1985–7) of the European NTSh. Yaniv edited *Visti NTSh, Khronika NTSh,* and *Zapysky NTSh* (vols 169, 181, 186) and organized NTSh and UVU scholarly conferences and sessions and a scholarly congress on the millennium of the Christianization of Rus'. He was also president of the *Ukrainian Christian Movement (from 1955) and a professor (from 1963) and dean of the philosophy faculty (1963–72) at the Ukrainian Catholic University in Rome, and the Ukrainian representative in international Catholic organizations.

Yaniv began publishing poetry in Galician periodicals in 1926. His political and prison experiences are reflected in his collection *Sontse i graty* (Sun and [Prison] Bars, 1941) and the autobiographical sketches *Lystopadovi fragmenty* (November Fragments, 1941). His religious and introspective lyrical poems and epic ballads appeared separately in the émigré collections *Shliakhy* (Roads, 1951) and *Zhyttia* (Life, 1975). Yaniv also wrote articles on socio- and ethnopsychology. He wrote a booklet (1948) and articles on Nazi concentration camps and their psychological consequences, a habilitation dissertation on Ukraine's psychological Westernness (1949), an UVU mimeographed textbook on sociology (1949), the booklet *The Battle of Kruty* (1958), surveys of Ukrainian culture (1953, 1961), articles on Soviet society, on the Ukrainian student and scouting movements, and on Ukrainian nationalist leaders, scholars, and religious figures, and a history of the UBNT (1970). His selected studies and materials on modern Ukrainian history were published by the UVU in two volumes (1970, 1983). Several articles about him and a bibliography of his works were published in the festschrift *Symbolae in honorem Volodymyri Janiw* (1983).

O. Horbach

**Yaniv Brigade of the Ukrainian Galician Army** (Yanivska [10] brygada UHA, aka Yavoriv Brigade). A unit of the First Corps of the UHA, formed in January 1919 from contingents that belonged to the Northern Group commanded by Maj A. Dolud. The brigade consisted of four infantry battalions, a machine-gun company, and a technical company. It fought against Polish forces at Briukhovychi, Kulykiv, and Belz, and then at Terebovlia and Ternopil during the Chortkiv offensive. During the Kiev offensive in August 1919 it captured Vinnytsia and Kalynivka from the Bolsheviks, and later it engaged A. Denikin's Volunteer Army in a number of battles in the Haisyn region. In 1920 the brigade was integrated into the Red Ukrainian Galician Army as the Fifth Infantry Regiment, and after revolting against the Bolsheviks it surrendered to the Poles in late April 1920.

**Yaniv Cemetery** (Yanivskyi tsyntar). A major cemetery in Lviv established in 1883. During the First World War the northern part of the cemetery was reserved for interned soldiers who had died of epidemic diseases. Almost 1,000 soldiers of the Ukrainian Galician Army, who died in the Ukrainian-Polish War of 1918–9, are buried there. A special square was set aside for 648 graves of members of the *Ukrainian Sich Riflemen, each marked

A vandalized grave of a soldier of the Ukrainian Galician Army at the Yaniv Cemetery

with a concrete military cross designed by P. Kholodny, Jr, and L. Lepky. Some prominent Ukrainian figures, such as M. Sosenko, Gen O. Tarnavsky, and O. Basarab, were buried at the cemetery. In the interwar period the Ukrainians of Lviv held annual memorial services there for those who had died fighting for Ukraine's independence. In 1971 the Lviv Oblast Executive Committee ordered the graves of the Ukrainian Sich Riflemen to be bulldozed, and the crosses destroyed. Only the graves of O. Tarnavsky and K. Levytsky were left untouched, but even they had their crosses removed. In the late 1980s the national revival in Lviv began with the restoration of some of the graves and commemorative ceremonies at Yaniv Cemetery.

**Yanivsky, Bohdan** [Janivs'kyj], b 4 July 1941 in Lviv. Composer and pianist. He graduated from the piano faculty (1967) and the composition faculty (1978) of the Lviv Conservatory. Since 1967 he has served as musical director of the Lviv Young Spectator's Theater. His compositions include more than 100 scores for plays, cartoons, and television films, as well as scores for symphonies, instrumental chamber music, and popular songs.

**Yanko, Dmytro** [Janko], b 19 October 1930 in Zachepylivka, Novi Sanzhary raion, Poltava oblast. Art scholar. In 1959 he graduated from Kiev University. He has written books about the sculptors O. Kovalov (1977) and O. Skoblykov (1979) and about the memorials and monuments of Kiev (1974) and Ukraine (1982).

**Yanko, Oleksander** [Janko], b 1882 in Novi Sanzhary, Kobeliaky county, Poltava gubernia, d ? Revolutionary leader. After the February Revolution he returned from political exile in Siberia and was elected to the CC of the *Ukrainian Party of Socialist Revolutionaries (UPSR) and as a representative from Poltava gubernia to the Ukrainian Central Rada (at the All-Ukrainian Peasants' Congress in June 1917) and the Russian Constituent Assembly (in November 1917). He headed the UPSR caucus in the Little Rada. He was one of the leaders of the centrist faction at the Fourth UPSR Congress in May 1918, and he played an important role in the November 1918 uprising against the Hetman government as a member of the *Ukrainian National Union and head of the *Peasant Association and

UPSR Organizational Committee. From January 1919 he supported the position of government by workers' and peasants' councils based on the UPSR concept of the 'toiling masses.'

**Yankovsky, Marko** [Jankovs'kij], b 17 October 1915 in Astrakhan, Russia, d 27 April 1980 in Symferopil, Crimea. Stage designer. A graduate of the Astrakhan Art School (1938) and Kharkiv Art Institute (1941), where he studied under O. Khvostenko-Khvostov, in 1945–52 he worked at theaters in Nalchik, in Subcaucasia, and Tomsk, in Siberia. From 1953 to 1980 he was principal stage designer at the Crimean Russian Drama Theater in Symferopil.

Liubov Yanovska          Feofil Yanovsky

**Yanovska, Liubov** [Janovs'ka, Ljubov], b 30 July 1861 in Mykolaivka, Borzna county, Chernihiv gubernia, d 1933 in Kiev. Writer and community activist. She worked as a teacher in Lubni county, Poltava gubernia, and founded Sunday schools. From 1905 she lived in Kiev. She initially wrote in Russian and then changed to Ukrainian. Her first short story in Ukrainian was 'Zlodiika Oksana' (Oksana the Thief, 1897). Yanovska wrote over 100 short stories, novelettes, and novels, most of which were not published during her lifetime, and some of which were never finished. Her works deal with the life of the peasants and the intelligentsia, are written in a realist style, and reflect a populist philosophy. The publication of her first short story was followed by the drama *Povernuvsia z Sybiru* (He Returned from Siberia, 1897), the novelette *Horodianka* (The Townswoman, 1900), and the comedy *Na zelenyi klyn* (To the Far East, 1900). Many of her works were reprinted or first published during the period of Ukrainian statehood in 1918 and in the early years of the Soviet regime, in particular the plays *Lisova kvitka* (Forest Flower, 1918), *Zhertvy* (Sacrifices, 1918), *Liuds'ke shchastia* (Human Happiness, 1918), *Na sinozhati* (At the Haying Meadow, 1918), and *Dzvin, shcho do tserkvy sklykaie, ta sam u nii nikoly ne buvaie* (The Bell That Calls People to Church but Never Goes There Itself, 1918). Yanovska ceased writing after 1916, but her works, greatly influenced by I. Nechui-Levytsky, P. Myrny, and to a lesser degree, M. Kotsiubynsky, remained popular for many years. The collected works of Yanovska were published in 1930, 1959, 1991.

I. Koshelivets

**Yanovsky, Amvrosii** [Janovs'kyj, Amvrosij], b 1810, d 1884. Galician educator and political leader. He served as director of the *Academic Gymnasium of Lviv and gymnasium inspector in Galicia. For many years he sat in the Galician Diet (1861–83) and the Austrian parliament. He chaired the textbook commission for Ukrainian gymnasiums (from 1862) and was the first president of the Ruthenian Pedagogical Society (later *Ridna Shkola).

**Yanovsky, Borys** [Janovs'kyj], b 31 December 1875 in Moscow, d 19 January 1933 in Kharkiv. Composer, conductor, and music critic. A graduate of Kiev University (1903), he studied music privately with E. Ryb and was a conductor and music critic in Kiev until 1910. He then (1910–18) worked as a conductor and critic in St Petersburg and Moscow. In 1918 he settled in Kharkiv, where he taught at the music tekhnikum and the music and drama institute. His compositions include 10 operas, notably *Sorochyntsi Fair* (1899) and *Black Sea Duma* or *Samiilo Kishka* (1927); two ballets; orchestral pieces; chamber works; violin and piano music; works for chorus; art songs; and settings of Ukrainian folk songs.

**Yanovsky, Feofil** (Teofil) [Janovs'kyj], b 24 June 1860 in Mynkivtsi, Nova Ushytsia county, Podilia gubernia, d 8 July 1928 in Kiev. Internal medicine specialist; full member of the VUAN from 1927. After graduating from Kiev University (1884) he worked in its medical faculty and then served as a professor at the internal medicine clinic of Odessa (1904–5) and Kiev (1905–19) universities. He was director of the internal medicine clinic of Crimea University (1919–21) and headed the internal medicine department at the Kiev Medical Institute (from 1921). His publications dealt with the clinical treatment of tuberculosis and diseases of the lungs, kidneys, gastrointestinal tract, and circulatory system. He established a school of internal medicine specialists and was a longtime president of the All-Ukrainian Congress of Therapeutists. He initiated the establishment of many tuberculosis sanatoriums in Ukraine, and the Kiev Tuberculosis Institute was named in his honor (1928).

**Yanovsky, Oleksii** [Janovs'kyj, Oleksij], b 1739, d ? Architect. After graduating from the St Petersburg Academy of Arts (1764) he worked as a builder for Hetman K. Rozumovsky. In 1765–71 he built a palace and church designed by J.-B.-M. Vallin-Delamothe in Pochep. Governor-General P. Rumiantsev invited him, in 1778, to design the Trinity Church, the residence of the governor-general, and the court buildings in Hlukhiv.

**Yanovsky, Volodymyr** [Janovs'kyj], b 15 April 1876 in Ortalan, Symferopil county, Tavriia gubernia, d 14 November 1966 in Bakhchysarai, Crimea oblast. Painter. After graduating from the St Petersburg Art School of the Society for the Promotion of the Arts in 1899, he returned to Crimea and settled in Yalta. He painted landscapes and genre paintings, using mostly watercolors. They include *Ochakiv in Flames* (1905), *View of Bakhchysarai* (1948), and *Flowering Orchards* (1957).

**Yanovsky, Yurii** [Janovs'kyj, Jurij], b 27 August 1902 on Maierove *khutir* (now Nechaivka), Yelysavethrad county, Kherson gubernia, d 25 February 1954 in Kiev. Writer.

Yurii Yanovsky          Stepan Yanovych

From 1927 Yanovsky lived in Kharkiv, and from 1939, in Kiev. He began publishing poems in Ukrainian in 1924, and in 1927 the poetry collection *Prekrasna Ut* (The Beautiful Ut) appeared, after which he began writing prose. The neoromantic short stories from Yanovsky's early period have been published as *Mamutovi byvni* (The Mammoth's Tusks, 1925) and *Krov zemli* (The Blood of the Earth, 1927). Yanovsky is considered, with M. Khvylovy, one of the best neoromantic writers in Ukrainian literature in the first half of the 20th century. The sea, which he portrayed romantically, was his favorite subject, as is most clearly seen in his first novel, *Maister korablia* (The Shipbuilder, 1928). He subsequently published *Chotyry shabli* (Four Sabers, 1931), which was harshly criticized and was banned for a long time. In that novel he described in a Romantic manner the spontaneous popular movement in reborn Ukraine during the period of the struggle for independence. Yanovsky returned to the same subject in *Vershnyky* (1935; English trans: *The Horsemen*, 1989), although there, owing to the pressure of Stalinist censorship, he applied the official interpretation. The work is a finely wrought novel composed of short stories. One of the short stories, 'Podviine kolo' (Double Circle), deals with the tragedy of fratricidal conflict during the time of the Revolution.

In the period prior to the Second World War Yanovsky wrote several film scenarios (eg, *Hamburg*, *Fata morgana*, and *Sertsia dvokh* [The Hearts of Two]), the plays *Zavoiovnyky* (The Conquerors, 1931) and *Potomky* (The Descendants, 1940), among others, and *Korotki istorii* (Brief Histories, 1940), a collection of witty short stories. During the war Yanovsky was an army war correspondent and an editor of the journal *Ukraïns'ka literatura*. In 1945 he covered the Nuremberg Trials. Yanovsky's best work from the postwar period is *Zhyva voda* (Live Water, 1947), in which the image of the undying nation, reborn after the catastrophe of war, appears. The work was harshly criticized as 'nationalist,' and Yanovsky was forced to rewrite it in accordance with the principles of *socialist realism and to republish it in a weaker version under a different title, *Myr* (Peace, 1956). Yanovsky capitulated as an artist only toward the end of his life, when he produced *Kyïvs'ki opovidannia* (Kiev Stories, 1948), a collection of mediocre quality. Yanovsky's early works are classics of the Ukrainian literary rebirth of the first half of the 20th century. His writings have been published individually and in several editions of collected works: (4 vols, 1931–2; 2 vols, 1954; 5 vols, 1958–9, 1982–3).

BIBLIOGRAPHY
Babyshkin, O. *Iurii Ianovs'kyi* (Kiev 1957)
Trostianets'kyi, A. *Kryla romantyky* (Kiev 1962)
Plachynda, S. *Maisternist' Iuriia Ianovs'koho* (Kiev 1969)
*Lyst u vichnist': Spohady pro Iuriia Ianovs'koho* (Kiev 1980)
I. Koshelivets

**Yanovych, Stepan** [Janovyč] (real surname: Kurbas), b 28 October 1862 in Kuropatnyky, Berezhany county, Galicia, d 10 September 1908 in Staryi Skalat, Skalat county, Galicia. Actor, singer (tenor), and stage director; father of L. *Kurbas. In 1884–98 and 1900 he worked as an actor in the Ruska Besida Theater (from 1891 also as director), and in 1898–9 he led his own troupe (with K. Pidvysotsky) in Kamianets-Podilskyi. As an actor he played a range of roles, from those in Ukrainian populist plays to those in classical operettas. As a director he staged I. Franko's *Uchytel'* (The Teacher) and F. von Schiller's *Die Räuber* (where he played the role of Karl Moor). He retired in 1902 as a result of illness.

**Yanovych, Volodymyr** [Janovyč], b 1869 in Solotvyna, Nadvirna county, Galicia, d 22 December 1931 in Stanyslaviv, Galicia. Physician and civic and political leader. After completing his studies at Vienna University he practiced medicine in Vienna and, from 1902, in Stanyslaviv. For 30 years he played a leading role in most of the local Ukrainian organizations and institutions: he served as president of the Stanyslaviv branch of the *Prosvita society (1904–30) and founded the local branch of Sokil (1902), the Ukrainska Khata society, the Ukrainska Mishchanska Kasa co-operative, the Narodnyi Dim Credit Association, and the Zoria trades society. He supported many of these organizations financially and donated buildings to house their offices, schools, and residences. During the First World War he was deported by the Russians, but he returned in 1918. In the 1920s he was a leading member of the Ukrainian National Democratic Alliance. For his contribution to Ukrainian society he was elected an honorary member of the Prosvita society in 1929.

**Yanovycheva, Vanda** [Janovyčeva] b 11 November 1867 in Chernivtsi, d 24 August 1950 in Kharkiv. Stage actress; wife of S. *Yanovych and mother of L. *Kurbas. She worked in the Ruska Besida Theater (1885–98), in S. Yanovych's theater (1898–9), and in Kyidramte (1920–1).

**Yanushevych, Hanna** [Januševyč], b 27 December 1907 in Haivoron, Haisyn county, Podilia gubernia, d 25 December 1983 in Chernivtsi. Stage and film actress. She completed study at the Lysenko Music and Drama Institute in Kiev (1928) and then acted in the Kiev Ukrainian Drama Theater (1927–31), the Kharkiv Theater of the Revolution (1931–8), and the Chernivtsi Oblast Ukrainian Music and Drama Theater. She appeared in the film *Zemlia* (The Land, adaptation of O. Kobylianska's novel, 1954).

**Yanzhul, Ivan** [Janžul'], b 14 June 1845 in Vasylkiv county, Kiev gubernia, d 1914. Economist; full member of the Russian Imperial Academy of Sciences from 1893. After completing his master's dissertation on English indirect taxation (1874) he was appointed a lecturer in financial law at Moscow University. Two years later he wrote a doctoral dissertation on English free trade (pub, 2 vols, 1882). Besides teaching he served as factory inspector of the Moscow district (1882–7) and sat on commissions preparing factory legislation. A prolific writer, he published many articles in the Russian press about economic developments and thinking in Britain and the United States, a collection of essays on economic policy and legislation (2 vols, 1884), a history of factory industry in Poland (1887), and a textbook of financial law. He advocated government intervention in the economy.

**Yarema, Mariia** [Jarema, Marija] (Jarema, Maria), b 24 November 1908 in Staryi Sambir, Galicia, d 1 November 1958 in Cracow. Sculptor and painter. After studying at the Cracow Academy of Arts under X. Dunikowski (1929–35) she lived in Paris and Vienna. She belonged to the Cracow Group of artists (1933–9) and evolved as a sculptor from expressionism to abstractionism (eg, *Nude* [1938] and *Dance* [1955]). After the Second World War she was one of the leading members of Poland's Group of Modern Plastic Artists. She also used watercolors and tempera, and in the course of her experimentation with monotype and mixed media (monotype and tempera) she created surreal (eg, *Horses, Dancers, Knights*) and abstract works. In her monotypes she explored motion through overlapping surfaces (eg, *Filters, Rhythms* [1956], *Penetrations*, and *Spins*). From 1935 she worked as a scenery designer and actor with the Cracow experimental Cricot theater.

**Yarema, Oleksa** [Jarema], b 1855, d 1930. Educator and civic activist in Galicia. He taught classical languages at the Academic Gymnasium of Lviv (1885–91) and the Peremyshl State Gymnasium (1892–1909) and then served as principal of the Ukrainian Girls' Institute in Peremyshl (1910–21). He was also president of a number of Ukrainian organizations, including the Peremyshl branch of Prosvita. He was a deputy of the Ukrainian National Rada of the Western Ukrainian National Republic.

Yakym Yarema

**Yarema, Yakym** [Jarema, Jakym], b 23 March 1884 in Arlamivska Volia, Mostyska county, Galicia, d 15 December 1964 in Lviv. Psychologist, philosopher, literary scholar, and educator. A graduate of Graz University (1908), he was a professor at the Ukrainian Higher Pedagogical Institute in Prague (1923–30) and director of the Ukrainian Gymnasium in Czechoslovakia (1925–7). After returning to Galicia he taught at the Ridna Shkola gymnasium in

Ternopil. After the Second World War he headed the Department of Foreign Languages at the Lviv Veterinary Institute. He wrote an introductory philosophy textbook (1924), a psychology textbook (1925), a book on educational psychology (1926), studies of T. Shevchenko, I. Franko, M. Shashkevych and T. Masaryk, and *Ukrains'ka dukhovist' v ïï kul'turno-istorychnykh vyiavakh* (Ukrainian Spirituality in Its Cultural-Historical Manifestations, 1937).

The Hutsulshchyna tourist lodge in Yaremche

**Yaremche** or **Yaremcha** [Jaremče or Jaremča]. V-5. A city (1989 pop 9,400) in the Prut River Valley in Ivano-Frankivske oblast. It was founded in 1895, and incorporated the villages of Yamna and Dora, which date back to the end of the 16th century. In 1738–45 O. *Dovbush and his opryshok band were active in the vicinity. In 1963 Yaremche was granted city status. Situated 665 m above sea level and surrounded by mountain peaks, the town is famous for its health and recreational resorts. A third of its inhabitants are employed in the tourist industry. There are 2 tourist bases, a youth camp, 6 rest homes, and 2 sanatoriums specializing in the treatment of tuberculosis, rheumatism, and nervous disorders.

**Yaremenko, Hnat** [Jaremenko], b 9 February 1874 in Bakhmach, Konotip county, Chernihiv gubernia, d 8 August 1915 in Bakhmach. Painter and graphic artist. He graduated from the Kiev Drawing School (1897) and the St Petersburg Academy of Arts (1904), where he studied under V. Makovsky. He painted portraits of family members and O. Lazarevsky (1900), self-portraits, still lifes, such as *Still Life with a Melon*, and landscapes, such as *Volodymyr's Hill in Kiev*. He produced a series of satirical paintings and caricatures during the Revolution of 1905.

**Yaremenko, Vasyl** [Jaremenko, Vasyl'], b 1 November 1895 in Rohyntsi, Romen county, Poltava gubernia, d 6 March 1976 in Lviv. Stage and film actor. He played in a semiprofessional troupe in Romen under I. Kavaleridze (1918–21) and then became one of the founders of the Zankovetska Theater in Kiev (since 1944 the Lviv Ukrainian Drama Theater) and worked in it until his death. His large repertoire (over 150 roles) included Iago in W. Shakespeare's *Othello* and Taras Shevchenko in V. Malakov and D. Shaknevsky's *Peterburz'ki nochi* (Petersburg Nights). He also acted in K. Hubenko and V. Kharchenko's literary-musical composition *Ukraïna v borot'bi* (Ukraine in Struggle, 1944) and in the film *Nazar Stodolia* (1954).

**Yaremenko, Vasyl** [Jaremenko, Vasyl'], b 12 February 1932 in Sianno, Vitsebsk oblast, Belarus. Literary scholar. He received a candidate's degree from the Kiev Pedagog-

Vasyl Yaremenko (1895–1976)    John Yaremko

Archbishop Oleksander
Yareshchenko

Rev Stepan Yarmus

ical Institute in 1964. Since 1973 he has been a docent of Ukrainian literature at Kiev University. In 1989 he was elected vice-president of the newly created Ukrainian Language Society and a member of the Kiev Regional Co-ordinating Council of the Popular Movement of Ukraine. He has written nearly 200 scholarly articles and a history of Ukrainian journalism (1983), and he has edited, in most cases with introductions and notes, the works of B. Hrinchenko (2 vols, 1963), M. Kulish (1968), P. Kulish (1970), O. Oles (1971), M. Pavlyk (1985), and V. Svidzinsky (1986), and anthologies of folk dumas, songs, and ballads (1970), 17th- and 18th-century Kievan poets (1982), and Ukrainian poetry of the 16th (1987) and 17th (1988) centuries.

**Yaremko, John** [Jaremko], b 10 August 1916 in Welland, Ontario. Lawyer and politician of Ukrainian descent. He graduated from Osgoode Hall Law School in Toronto and was called to the Ontario bar in 1944. He was the first Ukrainian Canadian elected to the Ontario legislature, as the Progressive Conservative member for Bellwoods in 1951. Re-elected in 1955, 1959, 1963, and 1971, Yaremko held numerous cabinet posts, including minister of transportation (1958–60), provincial secretary and minister of citizenship (1960–6), minister of public welfare (1966–7), minister of family and social services (1967–71), provincial secretary (1971–2), and solicitor general (1972–6). He was appointed Queen's Counsel in 1953.

**Yaremych, Stepan** [Jaremyč], b 3 August 1869 in Halaiky, Tarashcha county, Kiev gubernia, d 14 October 1939 in Leningrad. Art scholar and artist. He graduated from the Kievan Cave Monastery Icon Painting Studio (1887) and the Kiev Drawing School (1894) and studied under N. Ge. In 1900 he moved to St Petersburg, where from 1918 he worked as a curator and restorer at the Hermitage. Under M. Vrubel's supervision he painted murals in St Volodymyr's Cathedral in Kiev. His landscapes include *Kniazha Hora, near Kaniv, View of the Dnieper,* and *Field.* He wrote the first book about M. *Vrubel (1911) and articles on 16th- and 17th-century art at the Kievan Cave Monastery (1900) and St Andrew's Church in Kiev (1903).

**Yareshchenko, Oleksander** [Jareščenko], b 12 September 1890 in the Poltava region, d ca 1938. Archbishop of the *Ukrainian Autocephalous Orthodox church (UAOC). He graduated from the Moscow Theological Academy

and the Institute of Road Engineering in St Petersburg and then became head of the Poltava railway (1920–1). At the UAOC sobor of 1921 Yareshchenko was consecrated bishop of Poltava. He worked in Lubni (1921–3), where he organized 50 Ukrainian parishes and the okruha council of the UAOC for the district. Then he became archbishop of Kharkiv (1923–6) and organized the UAOC in Slobidska Ukraine. Yareshchenko was vice-chairman of the All-Ukrainian Orthodox Church Council and a member of the Ideological Commission of the UAOC (1924–6). An accomplished preacher who strongly opposed communism, in 1926 he was one of the first UAOC hierarchs to be arrested and imprisoned (in Moscow, then sent to Tashkent). He was released briefly in 1934, and lived in Kursk. He was then exiled to Siberia, where he died.

**Yarkovsky, Pavlo** [Jarkovs'kyj], b 1781, d 24 May 1845 in Kiev. Librarian and bibliographer. He is considered to be the first Ukrainian library scientist. He headed the libraries of the Volhynia Gymnasium (Kremianets Lyceum) and Kiev University and taught the first courses in library science. His bibliography course was described by R. Rozet in *Sovetskaia bibliografiia* (no. 42 [1956]).

**Yarmachenko, Mykola** [Jarmačenko], b 6 September 1928 in Cheremoshna, now in Poliske raion, Kiev oblast. Pedagogue. He graduated from the Kiev Pedagogical Institute (1951). He taught there until 1973 and served as prorector (from 1968). A specialist on education for the deaf, in 1973 he became director of the Scientific Research Institute of Pedagogy of Ukraine.

**Yarmolyntsi** [Jarmolynci]. IV-7. A town smt (1986 pop 8,500) near the Ushytsia River and a raion center in Khmelnytskyi oblast. It was first mentioned in a historical document in 1400, when it was under Polish rule. In 1445 a castle was built there, and in 1455 the town was granted the rights of *Magdeburg law. After the partition of Poland in 1793, it was annexed by Russia and became part of Proskuriv county in Podilia gubernia. In July 1919 Yarmolyntsi was the site of battles between the UNR and Bolshevik armies. Today the town has several food-processing plants and two brick factories.

**Yarmus, Stepan** [Jarmus'] (Jarmus), b 25 May 1925 in Lidykhiv, Kremenets county, Volhynia gubernia. Orthodox church leader. He emigrated from Ukraine in 1944 and settled in England in 1947. There he studied pastoral theology and was ordained in 1956. He continued his study of theology at St Andrew's College, the University of Winnipeg, and the San Francisco Theological Seminary (PH D, 1981). He served as a parish priest in Saskatchewan before becoming a lecturer (1969) and then a professor (1977) at St Andrew's College, and editor of *Visnyk*, the official church bulletin (1969–75), and *Vira i kul'tura* (from 1981). From 1983 to 1990 he served as head of the presidium of the Ukrainian Orthodox Church of Canada consistory. Yarmus has written several works on the history of Ukrainian philosophy, including a study of the 19th-century philosopher P. Yurkevych (1979) and a monograph on the spirituality of the Ukrainian nation (1983). He has also published collections of Yurkevych's writings, textbooks on homiletics and general theology, and works on church history.

**Yaropolk Iziaslavych** [Jaropolk Iziaslavyč], b ?, d 22 November 1086. Prince of Volhynia and Turiv; son of the Kievan prince *Iziaslav Yaroslavych. He married Iryna (Kunigunde), the daughter of Count Otto of Orlamünde-Reichlingen. In 1073 he and his father and brother, Sviatopolk, were expelled from Kievan Rus'; they traveled to Poland and then to Germany. In 1075 Yaropolk petitioned Pope Gregory VII for support and was officially recognized as the 'King of Rus'.' The petition was recorded, along with miniatures of Yaropolk and his wife, in the *Trier Psalter.

In 1077 Yaropolk returned to Kiev with his father and was granted the rule of Vyshhorod volost. In 1078 he mounted a campaign against Oleh Sviatoslavych of Chernihiv, in which his father was killed. That event marked the separation of Volhynia (with Volodymyr-Volynskyi and Turiv-Pynske) from Kiev principality. Yaropolk ruled Volhynia with the agreement of the Kievan prince Vsevolod Yaroslavych, but he faced constant conflicts with the Rostyslavych dynasty. In 1084 his rule in Volhynia was overthrown by them and Davyd Ihorevych. In 1085 he petitioned Vsevolod to grant him Dorohobuzh and was refused; he took up the sword against Vsevolod but was forced to retreat from Volodymyr-Volynskyi and Lutske into Poland. He was killed by the assassin Neradets (who was probably a secret agent of Riuryk Rostyslavych) and buried in the Church of St Peter in Kiev.

A. Zhukovsky

**Yaropolk I Sviatoslavych** [Jaropolk Svjatoslavyč], b ca 958–60, d 980 (possibly 11 June). Grand prince of *Kievan Rus'; eldest son of Sviatoslav I Ihorevych. He ruled the Kiev principality from 970, and when his father died in 972 he became ruler of all Rus'. He maintained ties with Western Europe and with Emperor Otto I the Great. In 973 his emissaries participated in the parliament in Quedlinburg, and in 979 he received a papal delegation in Kiev. He took a Greek wife and had good relations with Byzantium. Yaropolk's wish to unite all of Rus' under his rule gave rise to conflicts with his brothers, *Oleh Sviatoslavych and *Volodymyr the Great. In 977, when Oleh murdered the son of Yaropolk's voivode Svineld, Yaropolk killed Oleh in a battle near Ovruch, and thus gained control of the *Derevlianian territories. He captured Novgorod in 980 and drove out Volodymyr, who

enlisted the aid of the *Varangians, regained Novgorod in the same year, and took over Kiev soon thereafter. Yaropolk fled to Roden, where he was murdered at Volodymyr's behest. In 1044 Yaroslav the Wise transferred Yaropolk's remains (and those of Oleh), having baptized them, to the Church of the Tithes in Kiev.

**Yaropolk II Volodymyrovych,** b 1082, d 18 February 1139 in Kiev. Prince of Pereiaslav (1113–32) and grand prince of Kiev (1132–9); son of Volodymyr Monomakh. He participated in his father's campaigns against the Polovtsians (Cumans) in 1103, 1109, 1111, and 1113 and defeated them roundly in 1116 and 1120. Yaropolk lived in harmony with his father and his older brother, Mstyslav I Volodymyrovych the Great. As grand prince Yaropolk minded the unity of the Kievan state and battled with the Olhovych family of Chernihiv princes (particularly Vsevolod II Olhovych), who desired to capture the Kiev throne and enlisted the aid of the Polovtsians in their attempt to do so. As mentioned in the chronicles, Yaropolk distinguished himself by his courage and won great fame for his successful campaigns against the Polovtsians. He married Olena, the daughter of an Ossetian prince, whom he had taken prisoner during one of the campaigns against the Polovtsians. Yaropolk was buried in the Yanchyn Monastery in Kiev.

Roman Yarosevych

**Yarosevych, Roman** [Jarosevyč], b 1861 in Bedrykivtsi, Zalishchyky county, Galicia, d 28 May 1934 in Stanyslaviv, Galicia. Physician and political activist. After graduating in philology from Lviv University he taught at a gymnasium in Kolomyia. He then studied medicine in Cracow and, finally, opened an office in Borshchiv. A member of the Ukrainian Radical party and then the Ukrainian Social Democratic party, he was elected in 1897 to the Austrian parliament. In 1908 he chaired the clandestine committee which organized M. *Sichynsky's escape from prison. In the 1920s he was elected president of the Alliance of Railway Physicians of the Stanyslaviv Directorate of Polish State Railways.

**Yaroshchuk, Vadym** [Jaroščuk], b 2 April 1966 in Kryvyi Rih. Swimmer. A member of the USSR swimming team since 1984, he set USSR records in the 400-m individual medley (IM) in 1985 and 1987, the 200-m IM in 1986 and 1987, and the 200-m butterfly in 1987; was the 1986 and 1987 USSR champion in the 200- and 400-m IM; and won silver and bronze medals at the 1986 world swimming championships and at the 1987 European championships, two gold medals at the 1987 ESSO International Swim Meet in Toronto, and two 1988 Olympic bronze medals (the 200-m IM and the 4 × 100-m medley relay).

Mykola Yaroshenko

Volodymyr Yaroshenko (1898–1937)

**Yaroshenko, Mykola** (Nikolai) [Jarošenko], b 13 December 1846 in Poltava, d 7 July 1898 in Kislovodsk, Stavropol krai. Painter. He audited courses at the St Petersburg Academy of Arts (1867–74) and became a leading member of the *Peredvizhniki society (from 1876). His genre paintings, such as *Stoker* (1878), *Prisoner* (1878), *Student* (1881), *Life Is Everywhere* (1888), and *Peasant Girl* (1891), depict social problems. He produced genre paintings, portraits of famous Russians, and many Caucasian landscapes. While staying in Poltava in 1865 and 1876 and Kiev in 1874, 1876, and 1878–9, he painted genre scenes, such as *Blind Cripples near Kiev* (1879) and *Beggars at the Kievan Cave Monastery* (1879–80). His *Village Choir* (1894) is also a Ukrainian genre scene, and his *Student* (1881) depicts a Ukrainian, P. Chyrko. Many of his works were bequeathed to the Poltava Art Museum. Books about Yaroshenko have been written, in Russian, by V. Prytkov (1960), V. Porudominsky (1979), and I. Polenova (1983).

**Yaroshenko, Mytrofan** [Jarošenko], b 1858 in Vradiivka, Ananiv county, Kherson gubernia, d 18 September 1926 in Chernihiv. Actor and theater director. He worked in the troupes of M. Kropyvnytsky (1883–4), M. Starytsky (1885–94), and O. Sukhodolsky (1894–8) and led his own troupe (1899–1915), which toured (besides Ukraine) Moldavia, the Kuban, and Crimea.

**Yaroshenko, Semen** [Jarošenko], b 1846 in Kherson, d 1917. Mathematician. After graduating from Odessa University (PH D, 1871), he worked there as a professor (from 1871) and rector (1881–90). He wrote many articles on differential equations, especially on solving equations of the first order, and prepared the first Russian-language monograph on descriptive geometry (1880).

**Yaroshenko, Volodymyr** [Jarošenko], b 4 July 1888 in Myrhorod, Poltava gubernia, d 2 July 1957 in Kiev. Linguist. A graduate of St Petersburg University (1912), from 1926 to 1934 he was a VUAN research associate and compiled dictionaries. He wrote the first detailed study of the Ukrainian language in 14th- and 15th-century Moldavian charters (1909; pub 1931) and articles on the phonetic transcription of Ukrainian (1919) and Ukrainian medical terminology (with I. Kyrychenko, 1934), and he coedited the VUAN Russian-Ukrainian dictionary (vol 2, fasc 2–3, 1932–3).

**Yaroshenko, Volodymyr** [Jarošenko], b 1898 in Yakhnyky, Lokhvytsia county, Poltava gubernia, d 13 July 1937 in Kiev. Poet, prose writer, and playwright. He began to write in Russian, and his poetry was first published in 1915. His first collection of poetry, *Stikhi* (Verses), was published in 1917. After the revolution he wrote in Ukrainian and belonged to the literary organizations *MARS and Pluh. His poetry was published in the collections *Luny* (Echoes, 1919), *Shcho do choho* (What Belongs Where, 1924), *Cherez resheto* (Through the Sieve, 1924), *Bozha kooperatsiia* (God's Co-operation, 1925), *Dobre roby – dobre i bude* (Work Well – Things Will Be Fine, 1925), and *Baiky* (Tales, 1926). He also published a collection of short stories, *Kryminal'na khronika* (A Criminal Chronicle, 1927), the novel *Hrobovyshche* (The Cemetery, 1928), film scenarios, and translations from Russian. In the early 1920s Yaroshenko's drama *Shpana* (Riff-Raff) achieved popularity; it was staged in 1922–3 in the Berezil theater. Yaroshenko was arrested on 26 February 1933 and accused of membership in a nonexistent nationalist organization, but he was released owing to lack of evidence. He was rearrested on 3 November 1936, interrogated, accused of counterrevolution, and shot.

**Yaroshevsky, Bohdan** [Jaroševs'kyj] (pseud: Stepan Zahorodny), 1869–1914. Ukrainian political activist and writer. Descended from Polonized Ukrainian nobility, he joined the Ukrainian national movement but maintained close ties with Polish socialist circles. He was the leader of the *Ukrainian Socialist party, which attracted Ukrainianized Poles, and editor of its periodical *Dobra novyna*. His political articles appeared in *Przegląd krajowy*, *Przedświt*, *Naprzód*, and *Krytyka*, and his poems and short stories, in *Rada*, *Hromads'ka dumka*, and *Literaturno-naukovyi vistnyk*.

**Yaroshevsky, Oleksander** [Jaroševs'kyj], b 25 August 1887 in Pryluka, Poltava gubernia, d 11 November 1977 in Prague. Construction engineer. After completing his studies at the Ukrainian Husbandry Academy in Poděbrady (1931), he worked on many road, bridge, and water-diversion projects in Czechoslovakia. In 1939 he patented an accumulative central heating radiator. He was also a strong supporter of the Ukrainian branch of the Slovak Pedagogical Society in Bratislava and translated a number of Slovak-language textbooks into Ukrainian.

**Yaroshevsky, Yurii** [Jaroševs'kyj, Jurij] (secular name: Hryhorii), b 18 November 1872 in the Podilia region, d 8 February 1923 in Warsaw. Orthodox hierarch and pedagogue. A graduate of the Kiev Theological Academy (1896), he contributed to *ZNTSh* in Lviv. He was tonsured in 1898 and became rector of the Tula Theological Semi-

Metropolitan Yurii Yaroshevsky

Yevheniia Yaroshynska

nary. After being consecrated as a bishop in 1906, he served as vicar of Tula and Poltava eparchies, rector of the St Petersburg Theological Seminary (1910), bishop of Kaluga and then Minsk (1913), and archbishop of Kharkiv (1919). He emigrated to Italy by way of Serbia in 1920, and moved to Poland in 1921 to administer a portion of Minsk eparchy that had come under Polish control. He was elevated to the office of metropolitan of Warsaw by Patriarch Tikhon in 1922. As metropolitan he sanctioned the publication of *Pravoslavna Volyn'* as a Ukrainian-language church organ, allowed the introduction of vernacular Ukrainian into liturgical services, and initiated translations into Ukrainian of church texts. He also supported the granting of autocephaly to the Orthodox church in Ukraine, although he questioned the canonicity of the Ukrainian Autocephalous Orthodox church. He was murdered at his residence in Warsaw by the fanatic Russian monk Smaragd, a former rector of the Kholm Theological Seminary who opposed Yaroshevsky's efforts to break ties with the Moscow patriarchate.

**Yaroshevych, Andrii** [Jaroševyč, Andrij], b 1875, d ? Economic geographer and historian, and statistician. In the 1920s he was a professor at the Kiev Institute of the National Economy. He wrote on the economic history of Ukraine and on the history of the *khutir* in the Kiev region; his history of the potash industry in Ukraine remained unpublished. He was fired from his job in the early 1930s, and disappeared during the Stalinist terror.

**Yaroshevych, Hryhorii** [Jaroševyč, Hryhorij] (real surname: Manko), b 30 November 1885 in Pidlypne, Konotip county, Chernihiv gubernia, d 1974 in Toronto. Singer (baritone) and actor. He began his theatrical career in M. Kropyvnytsky's troupe (1905) and worked in O. Suslov's and other troupes and then was a soloist at the Kharkiv Theater of Opera and Ballet (1925–7), the Kharkiv Chervonozavodskyi Ukrainian Drama Theater (1928–33), and the Kiev Theater of Opera and Ballet (1934–41). He also acted in the film *Natalka Poltavka* (Natalka from Poltava, 1936). After the Second World War he emigrated to Canada.

**Yaroshynska, Yevheniia** [Jarošyns'ka, Jevheniia], b 18 October 1868 in Chunkiv, Bukovyna, d 21 October 1904 in Chernivtsi. The first Ukrainian woman writer and folklor-

ist in Bukovyna. In 1882 she began writing stories in German, two of which she published in a Viennese periodical (1886–7). From 1886 on she published, in Ukrainian, stories about the peasantry and intelligentsia, feminist and populist articles, and literary translations in Chernivtsi and Lviv periodicals (*Biblioteka dlia molodizhi, Bukovyna, Bat'kivshchyna, Narod, Zoria, Dzvinok, Literaturno-naukovyi vistnyk, Promin'*) and in the annual *Bukovyns'kyi kalendar*. A self-educated person, she worked as a teacher in Bridok (1893–5) and Raranchi (now Ridkivtsi, 1896–9) and was active in the Ruska Shkola society. Published separately were three booklets of her children's stories (1901–2) and a novel about the corrupt, Rumanianized Orthodox clergy, *Perekynchyky* (Turncoats, 1903). She also collected embroidery and Easter egg designs, which she published in German and Czech periodicals, and wrote an article about Bukovynian wedding rituals. For her collection of 450 Bukovynian folk songs (pub finally in 1972) she received a silver medal and a monetary award from the Russian Geographic Society in 1888. Editions of her works were published in Kiev in 1958 and 1968. V. Holubets's bibliography of works by and about her appeared in Lviv in 1969.

**Yaroslav.** See Jarosław.

**Yaroslav, Battle of.** A clash between the army of the Galician-Volhynian prince, *Danylo Romanovych, and Hungarian-Polish forces near Yaroslav (now *Jarosław), Galicia, on 17 August 1245. Hungary and Poland took advantage of the weakened condition of the Principality of *Galicia-Volhynia after the Tatar invasion of 1241 to seize Ukrainian territories. They exploited the hostility of Galician boyars toward Prince Danylo and invaded Galicia, led by the expelled prince of Chernihiv, Rostyslav Mykhailovych (son-in-law of the Hungarian king, Béla IV). In the summer of 1245 Béla joined with Polish forces and Galician boyars under Rostyslav's command and besieged Yaroslav. Danylo's army, along with a detachment of Polovtsians (Cumans), set out from Kholm to defend Yaroslav, and proved victorious in a battle on the Sian River. The Hungarian voivode Fila was slain, and the boyar leader Volodyslav was taken prisoner and later executed. Danylo's definitive victory quelled Polish and Hungarian aggression and boyar rebellions. It also enabled Danylo to strengthen his authority and to raise the principality's prestige.

**Yaroslav Iziaslavych** [Jaroslav Izjaslavyč], b ?, d ca 1180. Prince of Turiv, Novgorod, Volodymyr-Volynskyi, and Lutske; son of the Kievan prince Iziaslav Mstyslavych and brother of Mstyslav Iziaslavych. In 1173–4, aided by the Rostyslavych family, he controlled the Kievan throne and extracted heavy tributes from the population, including the clergy, monasteries, and resident foreign merchants. The burden he imposed aroused considerable hostility, and Yaroslav was deposed. In Lutske he contributed to the establishment of a local bishopric. He married the daughter of the Czech king Vladislav II.

**Yaroslav Osmomysl** [Jaroslav], b ?, d 1 October 1187 in Halych. Galician prince; son of *Volodymyrko. He is first mentioned in the chronicles under the year 1150, when he married Olga, the daughter of *Yurii Dolgorukii. In *Slovo*

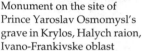

Monument on the site of
Prince Yaroslav Osmomysl's
grave in Krylos, Halych raion,
Ivano-Frankivske oblast

The marble sarcophagus of
Grand Prince Yaroslav the
Wise inside Kiev's St Sophia
Cathedral

o polku Ihorevi (The Tale of Ihor's Campaign) Yaroslav is given the appellation Osmomysl (possessed of eight senses, ie, wise and perceptive). Upon his assumption of the throne in 1153, Halych principality was in conflict with Kiev principality and a number of Volhynian cities. Yaroslav was ready to accept the primacy of *Iziaslav Mstyslavych of Kiev, but the Galician boyars were opposed. Iziaslav launched a campaign against the Galicians and defeated them at Terebovlia, on the Seret River.

Iziaslav's death in 1154 ushered in a period of peace between Kiev and Galicia, apart from the tenure of Iziaslav III Davydovych (1158–61), whom Yaroslav defeated with the assistance of Mstyslav Iziaslavych in 1159. That year Yaroslav also fought against his cousin, Ivan Rostyslavych *Berladnyk, who made an unsuccessful attempt from the Danube lowlands to conquer Galicia. Yaroslav maintained good relations with Yurii Dolgorukii and participated in campaigns against the Polovtsians (about which an account is given in Slovo o polku Ihorevi). He also lived in relative harmony with his neighbors in Poland and Hungary, the Byzantine emperor, and Frederick I Barbarossa. Yaroslav did not interfere in the conflict between Byzantium and Hungary, but after he harbored his relative, Andronicus I Comnenus (cousin of the Byzantine emperor, Manuel I), in 1164, his relations with Constantinople soured. In 1174 he supported Yaroslav Iziaslavych's ascent to the Kievan throne.

Yaroslav expanded his principality by annexing the territories between the Dniester River and the Carpathian Mountains and the Danube lowlands. His large standing army made him one of the mightiest princes of Rus'. Many Galician cities were built up and fortified during his reign. In 1153–7 the Dormition Cathedral was built in princely *Halych.

The Galician boyars initially aided Yaroslav, particularly in his war with Iziaslav, but as they grew richer through trade, they transformed themselves into a hereditary aristocracy and began interfering in Yaroslav's state and personal affairs. In 1172 he left his wife, Olha, and took a boyar's daughter, Nastasiia, as his mistress. The boyars rebelled and forced him to reinstate Olha, and had Nastasiia

burned as a witch. Olha withdrew to a convent in Suzdal and died in 1182. Yaroslav's last wishes were to grant *Oleh Yaroslavych (Nastasiia's son) the rule of Halych, and Peremyshl to Volodymyr, Olha's son, but the boyars expelled Oleh after Yaroslav died.

BIBLIOGRAPHY
Pasternak, Ia. 'Sarkofah Iaroslava Osmomysla,' in Staryi Halych (Cracow–Lviv 1944)
Hrytsak, P. Halyts'ko-Volyns'ka derzhava (New York 1958)
A. Zhukovsky

**Yaroslav Sviatopolkovych** [Jaroslav Svjatopolkovyč] (Yaroslavets Sviatopolchych), b ?, d 15 August 1123. Rus' prince; son of Sviatopolk II Iziaslavych and son-in-law of Mstyslav I Volodymyrovych. In 1100 (or 1097) he was placed in Volodymyr-Volynskyi by his father, who wished to replace the insubordinate Davyd Ihorevych; Sviatopolk's decision was ratified at the *Vytychiv congress of princes. In 1117 Yaroslav refused to recognize the suzerainty of the Kievan prince Volodymyr Monomakh and was forced to flee to Poland and then Hungary. He reestablished himself in Volodymyr-Volynskyi in 1118 with the aid of Hungarian troops, but was again challenged following a revolt by his boyars, who supported Volodymyr. In 1123 Yaroslav, with the help of Hungarian and Polish forces, laid siege to Volodymyr-Volynskyi, where he was killed in battle.

**Yaroslav the Wise** [Jaroslav Volodymyrovyč 'Mudryj'], b 978, d 20 February 1054 in Kiev. Grand prince of Kiev from 1019; son of Grand Prince *Volodymyr the Great and Princess *Rohnida of Polatsk; half-brother of *Sviatopolk I, *Mstyslav Volodymyrovych, and *Saints Borys and *Hlib Volodymyrovych; father of seven princes, including *Iziaslav, *Sviatoslav II, and *Vsevolod Yaroslavych. During his father's reign Yaroslav governed the lands of Rostov (from ca 988) and Novgorod (from 1010). While ruling Novgorod, which became his main power base, he rebelled against his father by refusing to pay the yearly tribute of 2,000 silver hryvni to Kiev. His father died in 1015 while preparing an expedition to subdue Novgorod, and after his death Yaroslav waged war against his brother Sviatopolk I for the Kievan throne. He defeated Sviatopolk and his Pecheneg allies at Liubech in 1015 and assumed the title of grand prince. In 1018, however, Sviatopolk and his father-in-law, Bolesław I of Poland, defeated Yaroslav's army at the Buh River and drove Yaroslav from Kiev. In 1019 Yaroslav and his Novgorodian army routed Sviatopolk at the Alta River and regained the Kievan throne.

To retain his authority in northern Rus', in 1021 Yaroslav fought and defeated his cousin Briachyslav Iziaslavych of Polatsk, thereby gaining his loyalty. Yaroslav's half-brother Mstyslav Volodymyrovych of Tmutorokan and Chernihiv, who was vying for control of southern Rus', proved to be a more stubborn opponent. After being defeated by him at Lystven, near Chernihiv, in 1024, Yaroslav was forced to cede to Mstyslav all of Left-Bank Ukraine except Pereiaslav principality. An accord between them was reached in Horodok in 1026, and Yaroslav assisted Mstyslav in his 1029 campaigns against the *Yasians and Kasogians, thereby extending his realm to the Caucasus. Mstyslav in turn helped Yaroslav consolidate his power west of the Dnieper. In 1030 Yaroslav conquered lands between Lake Peipus and the Baltic Sea and founded there the city of Yurev (named after Yaroslav's Christian name, Yurii-Georgii), now Tartu in Estonia. In 1030–1, with Mstyslav's help, he regained the *Cherven towns from Bolesław I and annexed the Polish-ruled lands between the Sian and the Buh rivers, where he founded Yaroslav (now *Jarosław).

After Mstyslav's death in 1036, Yaroslav annexed his lands and became the unchallenged ruler of Kievan Rus' except the Polatsk land, which remained under Briachislav. In 1038–42 he waged successful campaigns against the Lithuanian *Yatvingians, Mazovia (as the ally of his brother-in-law, Casimir I of Poland), and the Baltic Yamians and Chudians. In 1043, however, his military expedition against Constantinople, led by his son Volodymyr of Novgorod and the chiliarch Vyshata, ended in disastrous defeat.

To defend his state from the attacks of nomadic tribes, Yaroslav fortified the southern frontier by building along the Ros, the Trubizh, and the Sula the towns of Korsun, Kaniv, Pereiaslav, Lubni, and Lukoml and lines of ramparts, castles, and outposts. In 1037 he routed an army of *Pechenegs that had attacked Kiev, and initiated construction of the St Sophia Cathedral to commemorate his victory. During Yaroslav's reign the cities of *Kiev, Novgorod, Chernihiv, Pereiaslav, Volodymyr-Volynskyi, and Turiv were considerably transformed. Over 400 churches were built in Kiev alone, which was turned thereby into an architectural rival of Constantinople. Yaroslav's walled inner city in Kiev covered an area of nearly 60 ha. It was entered through the *Golden, Polish, and Jewish Gates, and the St Sophia Cathedral stood in the center, encircled by large palaces.

To strengthen his power and provide order in social and legal relations in his realm, Yaroslav arranged for the compilation of a book of laws called 'Pravda Iaroslava' (Yaroslav's Justice), the oldest part of the *Ruskaia Pravda. During his rule Christianity spread and grew stronger in Rus' (he actively suppressed paganism), and the organizational and hierarchical structure of the Rus' church was established. In 1039 the existence of the *Kiev metropoly was confirmed in writing as being under the jurisdiction of the Patriarch of Constantinople. Yaroslav issued a statute defining the rights of the church and clergy. Apart from Constantinople's right to confirm the appointment of the metropolitan, the Rus' church was autonomous, and in 1051 Yaroslav initiated the sobor of bishops that chose *Ilarion as metropolitan of Kiev. The first *monasteries in Rus' were formally established during Yaroslav's reign. He founded a primary school and library at the St Sophia Cathedral and sponsored the translation of Greek and other texts into Church Slavonic, the copying of many books, and the compilation of a chronicle (1037–9).

Yaroslav strengthened the international role of Kievan Rus' through dynastic unions. He married Ingigerd, the daughter of King Olaf Skötkonung of Sweden, and arranged marriages for his daughters *Yelysaveta, *Anna, and Anastasiia with Kings Harald III of Norway, Henry I of France, and Andrew I of Hungary respectively. His son Iziaslav married Gertrude, the daughter of Mieszko II of Poland; Vsevolod, the Byzantine princess Maria, of the Monomachus line; Sviatoslav, the granddaughter of Emperor Henry II; and Volodymyr, Oda, the daughter of Count Leopold von Stade. The monarchs Olaf II Haralds-

son and Harald III of Norway and Edmund II Ironsides of England sought asylum at Yaroslav's court, and he concluded alliances with Emperors Henry II, Conrad II, and Henry III.

During Yaroslav's reign the influence of the *Varangians was limited exclusively to the military; administrative and governing functions were assumed largely by indigenous viceroys (eg, Vyshata, I.Tvorymyrych, Dobrynia's son Kosniatin [Kostiantyn]). As a European power Kievan Rus' reached its zenith under his rule. To ensure the unity of his state, Yaroslav introduced primogeniture, according to which his eldest living son, Iziaslav of Turiv, was to succeed him as grand prince and ruler of the Kiev and Novgorod lands; Sviatoslav would rule the Chernihiv land to Murom, and Tmutorokan; Vsevolod, the Pereiaslav and Rostov lands; Ihor, the Volodymyr-Volynskyi land; and Viacheslav, the Smolensk land. As a result Kievan Rus' would never again be united.

Yaroslav was buried in the St Sophia Cathedral, where his marble sarcophagus has been preserved.

BIBLIOGRAPHY
Polons'ka-Vasylenko, N. *Kyïv chasiv Volodymyra ta Iaroslava* (Prague 1944)

A. Zhukovsky

**Yaroslav Vsevolodovych** [Jaroslav Vsevolodovyč], b 1139, d 1198. Rus' prince; son of Vsevolod Olhovych. He ruled in Starodub after the death of his father. He is mentioned in the Hypatian Chronicle under the year 1159 as the ruler of Ropesk, which was in the Snov River basin in Chernihiv lands. He was granted the rule of Chernihiv principality ca 1177–9 by his brother, Sviatoslav Vsevolodovych. Yaroslav threatened the unity of Rus' by refusing to participate in joint campaigns against the Polovtsians in 1184 and 1185, and he even caused one to be scuttled in 1187. After the death of Sviatoslav Yaroslav supported Riuryk Rostyslavych in his campaign to take the Kievan throne.

**Yaroslavenko, Yaroslav** [Jaroslavenko, Jaroslav] (actual surname: Vintskovsky), b 30 March 1880 in Jarosław, Galicia, d 26 June 1958 in Lviv. Composer, music publisher, and conductor. He studied music at the Lviv Conservatory (1898–1900) and then completed a degree (1904) in engineering (his subsequent profession) at the polytechnical institute. Yaroslavenko conducted two choruses in Lviv, Sokil and Zoria, and helped organize (1906) the music publishing house *Torban, which he directed for more than three decades. His compositions include the opera *The Witch* and three operettas; pieces for piano, including songs of the Sich Riflemen; choral works to texts by T. Shevchenko, I. Franko, U. Kravchenko, and others; solo songs to texts by T. Shevchenko, I. Franko, and others; and church music. He is best remembered in Western Ukraine for his patriotic 'Sokil March' and the Ukrainian Plast (scout) anthems 'Flower of Ukraine' and 'Hey, Plastuny.'

**Yaroslavska, Dariia** [Jaroslavs'ka, Darija] (pseud of Dariia Stoliarchuk; née Borodaikevych), b 25 April 1905 in Stanyslaviv (now Ivano-Frankivske). Writer. Her first novel, *Polyn pid nohamy* (Wormwood Underfoot), appeared in Lviv in 1938. As a postwar émigré in the United States she has contributed to Ukrainian periodicals there and written six novels about the experiences of displaced

Dariia Yaroslavska

Sylvester Yarychevsky

persons: *Pomizh berehamy* (Between Shores, 1953), *V obii-makh Mel'pomeny* (In Melpomene's Embrace, 1954), *Ïi N'iu-Iork* (Her New York, 1959), *Povin'* (The Flood, 1964), *Ostriv Di-Pi* (DP Island, 1969), and *Pid chuzhi zori* (Toward Foreign Stars, 1971). A collection of her short prose, *Prapor* (The Banner), appeared in 1981.

**Yaroslavsky, Petro** [Jaroslavs'kyj], b 1750 in Okhtyrka, Slobidska Ukraine, d after 1810. Architect. He studied art at Kharkiv College and architecture under V. Bazhenov in Moscow (1773–5). From 1781 he was assistant architect of Kharkiv vicegerency (later gubernia). He prepared the city plans for Kharkiv and other towns of the vicegerency, and he designed the vicegerent's hall (1782–5), the food warehouse (1785–7), the post office (1804), and residential buildings in Kharkiv. Among his important works are the churches in Babai (1782), Okhtyrka (1783), Sumy (1790), Kostiantynivka (1797), and Parkhomivka (1808). He also designed government buildings in Kursk and in Cherni-hiv and Novhorod-Siverskyi. His buildings show the in-fluence of the Ukrainian baroque and classical traditions.

**Yarovy, Mykhailo** [Jarovyj, Myxajlo], b 12 February 1864 in Moshny, Cherkasy county, Kiev gubernia, d 18 February 1940 in Kiev. Painter and graphic artist. A graduate of the Moscow School of Painting, Sculpture, and Architecture (1888), he painted portraits and genre paintings, such as *In-spection at the Betrothed's*, *Meeting of Cyclists*, *Lirnyk*, and *Two Generations* (1894). His works were displayed at exhi-bitions of the Moscow Society of Friends of the Arts and the Society of Kiev Artists (1891–1916). He was one of the first illustrators of A. Chekhov's stories (1903–9).

**Yarovynsky, Borys** [Jarovyns'kyj], b 11 March 1922 in Poltava. Composer and conductor. A graduate of the Mos-cow (1942) and Kharkiv conservatories (1949), he has served as a conductor and music consultant for a variety of music and drama groups in Kharkiv. His main compo-sitions include the opera *Lieutenant Schmidt* (1970), the bal-lets *The Seasons* (1959) and *Maryna* (1967), the musical comedy *The Magic Ray* (1976), symphonies (1948, 1960, 1964, and 1980), oratorios, cantatas, concertos, film scores, art songs, and arrangements of Ukrainian folk songs. In 1979 he edited and reorchestrated the national anthem of the Ukrainian SSR and orchestrated K. Dankevych's opera *Bohdan Khmelnytsky*.

**Yarrow** (*Achillea*; Ukrainian: *derevii, kryvavnyk*). A peren-nial medicinal herb of the family Asteraceae, with clusters of small white or pink flowers and aromatic fernlike leaves. Of the 23 species in Ukraine the common yarrow or milfoil (*A. millefolium*) grows as a weed. Liquid extract of its leaves and inflorescence has anti-inflammatory and hemostatic properties; it was used in folk medicine to stimulate the appetite. Endemic to Ukraine is the yellow-flowered 'naked' yarrow (*A. glaberrima*), which grows only on the granite rocks in the Kamiani Mohyly Nature Reserve in Donetske oblast.

**Yarychevsky, Sylvester** [Jaryčevs'kyj, Syl'vester] (pseuds: Landsman, Leonyd, Shalvyr), b 14 January 1871 in Rohatyn, Galicia, d 30 March 1918 in Seret, Bukovyna. Writer. He studied at Lviv (1891–4) and Vienna (1896–1901) universities. In 1891 he joined the Ruthenian Radical party. In 1909 he moved to Seret to teach and to run a residence for Ukrainian students. During the First World War he was Seret's burgomaster. From 1891 on he published stories (in-cluding some of the first Western Ukrainian stories dealing with urban themes and Vienna), poems, articles, and feuil-letons in many Western Ukrainian periodicals, mostly in *Bukovyna*. In 1906 he contributed translations of contem-porary German poetry to *S'vit*. Published separately were his dramatic allegory *Nebesni spivtsi* (Heavenly Bards, 1902), his prose-poem collection *Sertse movchyt'* (The Heart Stays Silent, 1903), his novella collections *Na fyliakh zhyttia* (On Life's Waves, 1903) and *Mizh terniam i tsvitom* (Between Thorns and the Bloom, 1905), his poetry collection *Pestri zvuky* (Varied Sounds, 1904), his fairy tale in verse *Horemyr* (1906), and his five-act play *Pochatok kintsia* (Beginning of the End, 1913). A two-volume edition of most of his extant poetry, prose, and dramas (some previously unpublished), edited with an introduction by M. Laslo-Kutsiuk, was pub-lished in Bucharest (1977, 1978).

**Yaryhina, Antonina** [Jaryhina], b 8 March 1908 in Kiev. Ballerina and pedagogue. She completed study at the Kiev (1924) and Leningrad (1929) choreography schools, and then danced in the opera and ballet theaters in Kiev (1924–32 and 1936–41), Odessa (1932–5), and Lviv (1944–6). She taught at the Odessa (1932–5) and Kiev (1946–51) choreog-raphy schools and at the Kiev Institute of Theater Arts (1951–72).

**Yarylo** [Jarylo]. The Rus' god of the spring sun, who awakens summer, love, and passion. Although extant ac-counts from Rus' times provide little information about Yarylo, they underline the fact that he was regarded as a major deity and a symbol of spring and rebirth. Many of his magical functions were transferred to *St George fol-lowing the Christianization of Ukraine. Traces of the cult of Yarylo could be found in parts of Ukraine (particularly Podilia) until the early 20th century, most notably his rit-ual burial in the spring. Nevertheless, these were quite weak in Ukraine and actually better preserved in eastern and central Russia and parts of Belarus. Linguists have noted that the *yar* stem of Yarylo's name is used widely in the Ukrainian language, for a variety of words invoking light, warmth, or strength.

**Yarymovych, Michael** [Jarymovyč, Myxajlo], b 13 Oc-tober 1933 in Białystok, Poland. Ukrainian-American

Michael Yarymovych     Vasyl Yashchun

aeronautical engineer; fellow of the American Institute for Aeronautics and Astronautics and member of the American Astronautical Society, the French Academy of Air and Space, the NASA Advisory Council, the Shevchenko Scientific Society, and the Ukrainian Academy of Arts and Sciences. After studying at New York University and Columbia University (DE, 1959) he worked in private industry and for the US federal government. He was director of the NATO Advisory Group for Aerospace Research and Development, chief scientist of the US Air Force, deputy for requirements for research and development of the air force, technical director of the Manned Orbiting Laboratory Program, chief of systems engineering in NASA's Apollo Applications Program, and assistant director for flight systems in NASA's Office of Manned Spaceflight. In 1977 he joined Rockwell International Corporation and managed research and engineering programs involving the Space Shuttle, rocket propulsion, satellites, high-energy lasers, and military and executive aircraft. From 1981 he was in charge of advanced systems development for the corporation, and since 1986 he has been associate director of its Strategic Defense Center.

**Yaryn, Viacheslav** [Jaryn, V'jačeslav], b 3 October 1883 in St Petersburg, d 30 March 1968 in Kiev. Civil engineer and specialist in reinforced concrete; member of the Ukrainian SSR Academy of Construction and Architecture from 1954. He studied in St Petersburg and worked at railroad offices in Galicia and Kiev (1915–19). He taught at the Kiev Polytechnical Institute (1921–30) and the Kiev Civil-Engineering Institute (from 1930). He directed the construction of a bridge over the Dnieper River (1928–9).

*Yaryzhka* **alphabet.** The derogatory name for the Russian alphabet in which, according to the Ems Ukase (1876), all Ukrainian-language publications in the Russian Empire had to appear. This regulation remained in effect until 1905. The *yaryzhka* is named after *yery*, the name of the Russian letter ы. Its orthography was phonetic, with the exception of the etymological *jer (ъ) at the end of words after a consonant.

**Yasenytsky, Volodymyr** [Jasenyc'kyj], b 1844 in Sambir, Galicia, d 31 August 1934 in Chernivtsi. Judge and civic leader. In 1868 he was one of the founders of the

Prosvita society in Lviv. From 1873 he worked in Chernivtsi as an assistant judge and played an important role in developing Ukrainian institutions, such as Ruska Besida, the People's Home, and the Fedkovych Bursa. As a member of the municipal council (1890–1918) he defended the interests of the Ukrainian community. In 1915 he was elected to the General Ukrainian Council in Vienna.

**Yashchun, Vasyl** [Jaščun, Vasyl'] (Jaszczun, Wasyl), b 24 January 1915 in Shnyriv, Brody county, Galicia. Philologist, pedagogue, and poet; full member of the Shevchenko Scientific Society. In 1949, after studing Slavic philology at Karl Franz University in Graz (PH D, 1948), he emigrated to the United States, where he served as a professor of Slavic languages and literatures at Pittsburgh University (1965–81) and was a member of its senate. His scholarly works deal mainly with linguistics and include *A Dictionary of Russian Idioms and Colloquialisms* (1967) and *Hovir Bridshchyny* (The Dialect of Brody County, 1972). His published collections of verse include *Diisne i mriine* (The Real and the Dreamed, 1981), *Z nyv i dorih zhyttia* (From the Fields and Roads of Life, 1986), and *Do svitla* (To the Light, 1988). The 216th vol of *ZNTSh* (1991) contains the selected papers of Yashchun in Slavic studies.

**Yashchurzhynsky, Khryzant** [Jaščuržyns'kyj, Xryzant], b 1852, d ? Archeologist and ethnographer. He studied at Kiev and Warsaw universities and then taught Russian in Odessa's secondary schools. He was a member of the Odessa Hromada. He published a study of J. Hus's teachings and a comparative study of Ukrainian and Russian folk songs (1880); articles on Ukrainian folk songs, tales, and rituals in *Kievskaia starina* (1888–98) and *Iuzhnyi sbornik* (Southern Anthology, 1892); and archeological notes in *Izvestiia Tavricheskoi uchenoi arkhivnoi komissii* and *Iz mira iskusstva i nauki* (From the World of Art and Science, 1887).

**Yashek, Mykola** [Jašek], b 23 November 1883 in Paniutyne, Pavlohrad county, Katerynoslav gubernia, d 17 August 1966 in Kharkiv. Bibliographer and literary critic. A graduate of Kharkiv University (1909), he worked as a librarian and bibliographer in various academic institutions in Kharkiv. In the 1920s he published a bibliography of materials in the years 1903–21 (1921) and over 10 articles in Shevchenko studies in *Znannia, Chervonyi shliakh,* and other journals. Together with A. *Leites he compiled *Desiat' rokiv ukraïns'koï literatury (1917–1927)* (Ten Years of Ukrainian Literature [1917–27], 2 vols, 1928), an important biobibliographic and documentary source and his most important contribution to Ukrainian bibliography. In 1929, with Yu. *Mezhenko, he copublished a bibliography of translated literature. His last major work was a bibliography of V. Lenin's writings on culture and literature (1933). During the Stalinist repressions Yashek stopped publishing; he was rehabilitated in 1963, and published an article on Shevchenko in 1964.

**Yasians** (*yasy*). Old Rus' name for the *Alans, ancestors of the Ossetes, a Sarmatian people who spoke a northern Iranian language. In the 1st centuries BC and AD they settled the expanses of Eastern European steppe lands between the Dnieper River and Subcaucasia. They established their own distinct culture, of which traces remain in burial mounds and catacombs of the 2nd to 4th centuries. Initially the Yasians were nomadic shepherds and gatherers, but later they settled and established a reputation for artisanship in ceramics, jewelry, and metalworking. In the 4th century they were ruled by the Huns, and some Yasians moved westward with the Vandals (as far as Spain and northern Africa); others moved to the Caucasian interior. The territories of the remaining Yasians were occupied by Avars in the 6th century and by Khazars in the 7th to 10th centuries. In the 9th and 10th centuries Christianity spread among the Yasians from Byzantium and Georgia. They recognized the suzerainty of Sviatoslav I Ihorevych in 963. In 1024 they fought alongside Mstyslav I Volodymyrovych against Yaroslav the Wise, only to be conquered by Mstyslav in 1029. In the 13th century a new wave of Yasians appeared in the Black Sea coastal steppes and established settlements in the Crimea and Moldavia (the city of Iaşi was probably named after them). Their state and culture were annihilated by the Mongols. Archeological research confirms that they maintained wideranging international relations with their neighbors, including Kievan Rus'.

BIBLIOGRAPHY
Miller, V. *Osetinskie etiudy*, no. 3 (Moscow 1887)
Kulakovskii, Iu. *Alany po svedeniiu klassicheskikh i vizantiiskikh pisatelei* (Kiev 1889)
Beninger, E. *Der westgotisch-alanische Zug nach Mitteleuropa* (Leipzig 1935)
Abaev, V. *Osetinskii iazyk i fol'klor* (Moscow–Leningrad 1949)
Paloczi-Horvath, A. *Pechenegs, Cumans, Iasians: Steppe Peoples in Medieval Hungary* (Budapest 1989)

A. Zhukovsky

Lev Yasinchuk

**Yasinchuk, Lev** [Jasinčuk], b 30 July 1882 in Bilobozhnytsia, Chortkiv county, Galicia, d 12 October 1963 in Brooklyn, New York. Pedagogue and community activist. He taught in a succession of village schools in Galicia and Bukovyna in 1905–14, having been dismissed several times for his community work. In 1923, after serving in the Ukrainian Galician Army and then being arrested twice in Bukovyna under the Rumanian regime, he moved to Galicia. There he served as administrative director of *Ridna Shkola in 1923–39 and played an important role in its organizational expansion. He also served as the last head of the Union of Ukrainian Private Office Employees and traveled twice to Canada and the United States as a representative of Ridna Shkola. He was inspector of Polish schools in Lviv (1939–40) and then of elementary schools

in Galicia (1941–4). He emigrated to Austria in 1945 and to the United States in 1949. His writings include the memoirs of his travels abroad, *Za okeanom* (Across the Ocean, 1930); *50 lit Ridnoï shkoly, 1881–1931* (50 Years of Ridna Shkola, 1881–1931, 1931); *Ridna shkola v ideï i zhytti* (Ridna Shkola in Concept and in Reality, 1934); *Ukraïns'ke doshkillia* (Ukrainian Preschool, 1936); and submissions about education in Bukovyna and Lviv to regional and municipal histories. He also wrote numerous articles for professional journals in Galicia and Bukovyna and for newspapers in Kiev (*Rada*), the United States (*Svoboda*), Canada, and Argentina.

**Yasinia** [Jasinja]. V-5. A town smt (1986 pop 7,900) on the Chorna Tysa River in Rakhiv raion, Transcarpathia oblast. It was first mentioned in a historical document in 1583. On 9 November 1918 the Hutsul Republic, which was part of the Western Ukrainian National Republic, was declared in Yasinia. Today the town is a manufacturing center for forest products and a tourist center with three tourist bases. It has a wooden church built in 1824.

**Yasnikov, Aleksandr** [Jasnikov], b 25 July 1923 in Milovskoe, Vladimir gubernia, Russia. Chemist; AN URSR (now ANU) corresponding member since 1969. A graduate of the Ivanovo Chemistry and Technology Institute (1947), he joined the ANU Institute of Organic Chemistry in 1950. His research has dealt with the mechanism of chemical and biochemical reactions and the synthesis of organic analogs mimicking the activity of enzymes in photosynthesis processes. He established the mechanism of photophosphorylation in plant chloroplasts.

**Yasnopolsky, Leonid** [Jasnopol's'kyj], b 1 February 1873 in Kiev, d 23 May 1957 in Moscow. Economist; full member of the VUAN and AN URSR (now ANU) from 1925; son of M. *Yasnopolsky. A graduate of St Petersburg University (1895), he taught economics there (1895–1902). After the Revolution of 1917 he worked for the government of the UNR and served as its economic consultant in negotiations with the Bolsheviks. He also taught at Kiev University and the Kiev Institute of the National Economy. In 1926–30 he headed the VUAN Commission for the Study of the Productive Resources of Ukraine and edited many of its publications. After the destruction of the VUAN he moved to Moscow. He returned to Kiev only after the war, to work at the ANU Institute of Economics. Yasnopolsky was a prolific writer. His more important works are *Ocherki russkogo biudzhetnogo prava* (Essays on Russian Budgetary Law, 1912), *Vosstanovitel'nyi protsess v nashem denezhnom obrashchenii i zadachi valiutnoi politiki* (The Reconstruction Process in Our Monetary Circulation and the Tasks of Monetary Policy, 1927), and studies of the mineral resources and economic development of the Donets and Dnieper basins.

**Yasnopolsky, Mykola** [Jasnopol's'kyj], b 1846 in Kiev, d 1920? Economist and statistician. After graduating from the law faculty of Kiev University he taught political economy at the Novo-Aleksandriia Agricultural and Forestry Institute, the Nizhen Lyceum, and the Kiev Higher Courses for Women. Then he served as a professor of commercial law at Kiev University (1889–1914). His major work was the two-volume *O geograficheskom raspredelenii gosu-*

*darstvennykh dokhodov i raskhodov Rossii* (On the Geographic Distribution of State Income and Expenditures in Russia, 1891–7), which showed how the peripheral territories were exploited by the tsarist capitals. He also wrote a number of important articles on the economic backwardness and future of Ukraine (1871), the railway lines from Ukraine to the Baltic (1868), and Ukraine's trade with Poland and the Baltic countries (1873).

**Yasny, Oles.** See Savytsky, Oleksii.

**Yastreb, Liudmyla** [Jastreb, Ljudmyla], b 10 April 1945 in Krasnikovka, Saratov oblast, Russia, d 8 August 1980 in Odessa. Painter. She graduated from the Odessa Art School (1964) and worked for the Art Fund. She took part in some of the exhibitions held in private apartments in Odessa in the 1970s and in the 1975 and 1976 exhibitions of Ukrainian nonconformist artists held in a private apartment in Moscow. Yastreb organized a solo exhibition of 100 of her paintings in her own studio in 1976. Women, her favorite subject, dominated her work. Her early paintings, such as *Women in Red, Blue, and Yellow* (1975), tended to be figurative but were not realistic. Later her work became more and more abstract, as in *Large Bathers* (1979). Some of her best canvases were painted near the end of her brief life. They were large overall compositions, full of light and painted with spontaneous, energetic brush strokes in the manner of American abstract expressionism (eg, *Bright Composition*, 1978). A posthumous exhibition of her works was organized in 1983. The studio of Yastreb and her husband, V. *Maryniuk, was a gathering place for Ukrainian artists in Odessa.

**Yastrebov, Fedir** [Jastrebov], b 28 November 1903 in Sudogda, Vladimir gubernia, d 30 June 1973 in Kiev. Historian. He graduated from Kiev University (1926) and then worked at the All-Ukrainian Association of Marxist-Leninist Scientific Research Institutes, the VUAN (in the Department of Marxism-Leninism), and the AN URSR (now ANU) Institute of History (1936–63). He researched the sociopolitical history of Ukraine in the 19th century, especially Ukrainian revolutionary movements. He also coauthored general surveys of Ukrainian history, including *Kyïvs'ka Rus' i feodal'ni kniazivstva XII–XIII st.* (Kievan Rus' and the Feudal Principalities of the 12th–13th Centuries, 1939; with K. Huslysty), *Narys istoriï Ukraïny* (Outline of the History of Ukraine, 1942; with L. Slavin and K. Huslysty), and *Istoriia Ukraïny: Korotkyi kurs* (History of Ukraine: A Brief Course, 1941; with S. Belousov, K. Huslysty, O. Ohloblyn, M. Petrovsky, and M. Suprunenko), in which he wrote the chapters on Ukraine in the early 19th century and on the development of capitalism in Ukraine. In 1947 he was criticized by the CC CP(B)U for 'examining the history of the Ukrainian people independently from the history of other peoples of the Soviet Union.' After the Second World War Yastrebov contributed chapters on 18th- and 19th-century Ukraine to two editions of *Istoriia Ukraïns'koï RSR* (The History of the Ukrainian SSR, vol 1, 1953; 2nd edn 1967) and chapters on the sociopolitical movements in 19th-century Kiev to *Istoriia Kyieva* (History of Kiev, vol 1, 1960).

A. Zhukovsky

**Yastrebov, Vladimir** [Jastrebov], b 18 July 1855 in Krivaia Luka, Samara gubernia, Russia, d 2 January 1899

in Kherson. Ethnographer and archeologist. After graduating from the University of Odessa (1876) he taught history in Yelysavethrad, conducted archeological research in Kherson gubernia, and collected ethnographic material. He published articles on the archeological treasures of Kherson gubernia (1893), Chersonese Taurica (1883), and the kurhans in Smila, and two collections – *Malorusskiia prozvishcha Khersonskoi gubernii* (Little Russian Surnames of Kherson Gubernia, 1893) and *Materialy po etnografii Novorossiiskago kraia* (Materials in the Ethnography of New Russia Krai, 1894).

Yuliian Yastremsky

**Yastremsky, Yuliian** [Jastrems'kyj, Julijan] (Jastremsky, Julian), b 1910 in Winnipeg. Architect; full member of the Shevchenko Scientific Society. After graduating from the University of Manitoba (1932) and Columbia University (1942) he worked as an architect at the National Housing Agency and the Bethlehem Steel Co in New York. He set up his own firm in New York in 1947 and went on to erect buildings such as the Cathedral of the Immaculate Conception and Christ the King Church in Philadelphia, St John the Baptist Church in Newark, New Jersey, a traditional Ukrainian wooden church in Barnesboro, Pennsylvania, the Holy Trinity Church in Westfield, New Jersey, St Mary's Church in Vancouver, British Columbia, St John the Baptist Cathedral in Ottawa, Ontario, the building of the Ukrainian National Association in Jersey City, New Jersey, St Josephat's Seminary in Washington, DC, and St Basil's Seminary in Stamford, Connecticut. A number of his articles on Ukrainian church architecture were published in *Arka* (1947–8).

**Yastrub.** See Karpenko, Dmytro.

**Yasynovsky, Mykhailo** [Jasynovs'kyj, Myxajlo], b 13 May 1899 in Odessa, d 29 August 1972 in Odessa. Internal medicine specialist; full member of the USSR Academy of Medical Sciences from 1963. After graduating from the Odessa Medical Institute in 1922, he taught there (as professor from 1934). He was chief physician of internal medicine of the Black Sea Fleet (1943–5). From 1959 he chaired a department of the Ukrainian Scientific Research Institute of Health Resort Science in Odessa. His publications dealt with viral hepatitis, rheumatism, and disorders of the blood-forming organs. A biography of him was published in Kiev in 1977.

**Yasynsky, Mykhailo** [Jasyns'kyj, Myxajlo] (Michail Jasinskij), b 11 October 1862 in Mezhyrich, Kaniv county,

Kiev gubernia, d 25 September 1935 in Nis, Yugoslavia. Jurist and legal historian. He graduated from Kiev University and became a docent there and then a professor in 1901. He was a member of the *Kiev Archeographic Commission and edited two collections of documents on 16th-to 18th-century courts for its *Arkhiv Iugo-Zapadnoi Rossii* (Archives of Southwestern Russia). He also served as secretary of the Historical Society of Nestor the Chronicler. By 1917 he had published several works on *Lithuanian-Ruthenian law, including studies of local statutes of the Lithuanian-Ruthenian state (1897), the court system (1901), and the Lutske Tribunal (1900), and works on the peasant movement in Russia (1890) and the *zakupy (1904). After the Revolution of 1917 Yasynsky emigrated to Yugoslavia, where he became a professor at Ljubljana University and wrote on Serbian and Slovenian legal history. Yasynsky's archives are preserved at the Central Scientific Library of the ANU and in Prague. Bibliographies of his works were published in St Petersburg in 1904 and Belgrade in 1931.

**Yasynsky, Mykhailo** [Jasyns'kyj, Myxajlo], b 21 November 1889 in Kiev, d 12 May 1967 in Kiev. Bibliographer and historian. He graduated from Kiev University (1914), and after the Revolution of 1917 he directed the Ucrainica division of the National Library of Ukraine (now the *Central Scientific Library of the ANU). He published articles on bibliographic methodology and Ukrainian bibliography in *Bibliotechnyi zbirnyk* (1927–8), *Metodolohichnyi zbirnyk* (1927), and elsewhere. He was arrested during the Stalinist terror in 1936 but was eventually released and rehabilitated. In 1965 he published a biography of the ethnographer M. Komarov.

Metropolitan Varlaam
Yasynsky

**Yasynsky, Varlaam** [Jasyns'kyj], b ca 1627 in Right-Bank Ukraine, d 22 August 1707. Orthodox churchman and Kievan metropolitan. He was rector of the Kievan Mohyla College (1665–73) and hegumen of the Kiev Epiphany Brotherhood (1665–73), St Michael's Golden-Domed (1673–7), and St Nicholas's (1680–4) monasteries. As hegumen of the Kievan Cave Monastery (1684–90) he defended the independence of the monastery from the Kievan metropolitan and accepted stauropegion from the Moscow patriarch. During his tenure as Kievan metropolitan (1690–1707) he did much to raise the level of education among the clergy in his see. With the support of Hetman I. Mazepa he also was able to defend many rights and privileges for the Kiev metropoly vis-à-vis Moscow, and to improve the teaching and the level of students at the Kievan Mohyla College, which was given the status of an academy in 1694. But he was not able to prevent the spread of the Church Union of Berestia to the remaining three Orthodox eparchies in Right-Bank Ukraine, or to stem the influence of the Moscow patriarchate in Chernihiv eparchy.

**Yasynuvata** [Jasynuvata]. V-18, DB III-3. A city (1989 pop 39,300) on the Kryvyi Torets River and a raion center in Donetske oblast. It was founded as a railway station in 1872 and was given city status in 1938. Today the city is an important railway junction. Its machine-building and metalworking plants serve the railway industry. It also manufactures reinforced-concrete products.

**Yatran River** [Jatran']. A right-bank tributary of the Syniukha River that flows for 104 km through Cherkasy and Kirovohrad oblasts and drains a basin area of 2,170 sq km. Two water reservoirs and a hydroelectric station are located on the river, which is also used for industry, water supply, irrigation, and fishing.

**Yatsenko, Oleksander** [Jacenko], b 19 January 1898 in Hovtva, Kobeliaky county, Poltava gubernia, d 31 January 1978 in Kharkiv. Biologist. A graduate of the Kharkiv Agricultural Institute (1928), he worked at the Scientific Research Institute of Animal Husbandry of the Forest-Steppe and Polisia of the Ukrainian SSR (1931–78). He codeveloped the Lebedyn breed of *great horned cattle.

**Yatsenko, Oleksander** [Jacenko], b 11 October 1929 in Snizhne, Donets okruha, d 6 January 1985 in Kiev. Philosopher. A graduate of Kiev University (1954), he taught at the Zhytomyr Agricultural Institute (1959–66) and Kiev University (1966–9) and was a senior associate at the AN URSR (now ANU) Institute of Philosophy (1969–80). From 1980 he headed the philosophy department of the Institute for the Upgrading of Social Science Lecturers at Kiev University. A specialist in Marxism-Leninism as a worldview, he wrote, in Russian, on goal positing and values (1977), on the worldview content of the categories and laws of the materialist dialectic (1981, coauthor), and on the humanism of the dialectico-materialist worldview (1984, coauthor).

**Yatsenko, Volodymyr** [Jacenko], b 21 April 1915 in Savkivka, Zolotonosha county, Poltava gubernia. Painter and art scholar. A graduate of the Kharkiv Art Tekhnikum

Volodymyr Yatsenko: *Wind* (1969)

(1937), he completed his studies at the Kharkiv Art Institute while it was based in Samarkand (1942). He has served as director of the Kharkiv Art Museum (1944–52) and the Kiev Museum of Ukrainian Art (1970–88). He has painted landscapes and historical canvases, such as *T. Shevchenko among Peasants* (1940), *Ustym Karmaliuk* (1947), *On the Dnieper* (1957), *On Chernecha Hora* (1960), *New Buildings in Kiev* (1965), *Dnieper Banks* (1967), *Beginning of March* (1979), and *Native Fields* (1984). He wrote a book about M. Samokysh (1945) and edited an album of his works (1979).

Rev Ivan Yatsentii                    Mykhailo Yatskiv

**Yatsentii, Ivan** [Jacentij], b 7 March 1896 in Cherniv, Rohatyn county, Galicia, d 9 December 1970 in Oshawa, Ontario. Evangelical pastor and community leader. After emigrating to the United States he studied theology at the Bloomfield Seminary in New Jersey. He served as a pastor in Passaic, New Jersey, and, from 1939, in Oshawa. Yatsentii was first elected vice-president of the *Ukrainian Evangelical Alliance of North America in 1926. He served for many years on the executive in a variety of positions, including that of president (from 1964). He was also a longtime member of the presidia of the Ukrainian Canadian Committee and the World Congress of Free Ukrainians.

**Yatskiv, Mykhailo** [Jackiv, Myxajlo] b 5 October 1873 in Lesivka, Stanyslaviv county, Galicia, d 9 December 1961 in Lviv. Writer; member of the modernist group *Moloda Muza. Yatskiv began his literary career in 1900 with a collection of prose miniatures, *V tsarstvi satany: Ironichno-sentymental'ni kartyny* (In the Kingdom of Satan: Ironic-Sentimental Scenes), which was influenced by Western modernists, and in particular C. Baudelaire and E.A. Poe and their predilection for the 'darker' elements in life. Yatskiv transformed these motifs into naturalistic sketches of the brutality of life. Besides other collections of miniatures and short stories (*Kazka pro persten'* [Tale of a Ring, 1907], *Chorni kryla* [Black Wings, 1909], *Adagio Consolante* [1912]) Yatskiv wrote the novelette *Ohni horiat'* (Fires Are Burning, 1902), the social study *Blyskavytsi* (Lightning Rods, 1913), and the novel *Tanets' tinei* (Dance of Shadows, 1916–7; repub as *V labetakh* [In the Clutches, 1956]). His longer works are on the whole weaker than his miniatures, especially the pretentious *Blyskavytsi* and the rather publicistic *Tanets' tinei*, where there is more disenchantment with the bureaucratic milieu of the Dnister Insur-

ance Society, where Yatskiv worked, than artistic creativity. In 1921 Yatskiv edited the newspaper *Ridnyi krai*, and after the Soviet takeover of Western Ukraine he worked in the Lviv Library of the AN URSR (now ANU). A volume of his collected works, *Muza na chornomu koni* (Muse on a Black Horse), appeared in 1989.

D.H. Struk

Yaroslav Yatskiv                    Petro Yatsyk (Jacyk)

**Yatskiv, Yaroslav** [Jackiv, Jaroslav], b 25 October 1940 in Danylche (now part of Kalynivka), Rohatyn raion, Stanislaviv oblast. Astronomer; AN URSR (now ANU) corresponding member since 1979 and full member since 1985. A graduate of the Lviv Polytechnical Institute (1960) and Moscow University, he worked at the Poltava Gravimetric Observatory (1960–2). He has been at the ANU Main *Astronomical Observatory near Kiev since 1962, and became its director in 1975. A specialist in astrometry, geodynamics, and earth rotation, he has developed novel methods of measuring earth rotation using laser beams from artificial satellites; has made very accurate measurements of the earth's poles; has compiled a catalog of 'inherently weak' stars; and was the first scientist to analyze completely the free nutation of the earth. He headed the Soviet program for tracking the comet Galileo during its recent flyby. Yatskiv has been vice-president of the International Astronomy Union (1982–9), head of the ANU Commission for Space Research, head of the Science and Culture Committee for Relations with Ukrainians Abroad, and chief editor of the journal *Kinematika i fizika nebesnykh tel*.

**Yatsko** [Jac'ko], b and d ? Icon painter in Vyshnia, Galicia, in the middle of the 17th century. He worked in the Boiko region. He painted the iconostasis of the church in Dnistryk, near Staryi Sambir (1653), and the icons *The Last Judgment* (1656) and *Crucifixion* (1656) in the church in Domashyn, Transcarpathia.

**Yatsyk, Petro** [Jacyk] (Jacyk, Peter), b 7 July 1921 in Synevidsko Vyzhnie, Stryi county, Galicia. Businessman, civic activist, and patron of Ukrainian learning. After emigrating to Canada in 1949, he established a successful building and land development firm. He was a founding member of the Patronat NTSh and a supporter of the *Entsyklopediia ukraïnoznavstva* project in Sarcelles. From the 1960s he assisted the Harvard Ukrainian Research Institute by donating money, raising funds, and serving on the institute's visiting committee. He financed the Peter

Jacyk Collection of Ukrainian Serials at the University of Toronto Library. In 1989 the Peter Jacyk Centre for Ukrainian Historical Research was established at the University of Alberta with a one-million-dollar donation from Yatsyk and a double matching grant from the province of Alberta. Through the Peter Jacyk Education Foundation he has supported other initiatives in Ukrainian scholarship and education, including the endowment of the Peter Jacyk Lectureship in Ukrainian Studies at the University of London (1991).

Kostiantyn Yatsymyrsky     Yakiv Yatsynevych

**Yatsymyrsky, Kostiantyn** [Jacymyrs'kyj, Kostjantyn] (Yatsimirsky, Konstantin), b 4 April 1916 in Polohy, Haisyn county, Podilia gubernia. Analytical, inorganic, and physical chemist; AN URSR (now ANU) corresponding member since 1961 and full member since 1964. A graduate of Tashkent University (1941), he taught at the Ivanovo Chemistry and Technology Institute (1946–62), directed a laboratory at the ANU Institute of General and Inorganic Chemistry (1962–9), became a professor at Kiev University in 1962, directed the ANU Institute of Physical Chemistry (1969–82), and headed a department there from 1983. From 1963 he was a member of the ANU presidium and an academic secretary, and from 1965 he was editor in chief of the journal *Teoreticheskaia i eksperimental'naia khimia.* Yatsymyrsky's research has dealt primarily with the coordination chemistry of metal complexes, especially thermochemistry, and the use of spectroscopic and radiospectroscopic methods of determining their structure and bonding parameters. He studied the structure and properties of lanthanide complexes in aqueous and nonaqueous media, invented an original method for determining stability constants, and devised original catalytic methods for the determination of trace quantities of various elements. His most recent work was in bioinorganic chemistry. He has published over 280 papers and 5 books, among them *Kinetic Methods of Analysis* (English trans 1966) and *Instability Constants of Complex Compounds* (coauthor; English trans 1960).

S. Trofimenko

**Yatsynevych, Yakiv** [Jacynevyč, Jakiv], b 27 October 1869 in Bila Tserkva, Kiev gubernia, d 25 April 1945 in Kropotkin, Stavropil krai. Conductor, composer, and teacher. A student at the Kiev Theological Seminary, he took private music lessons with M. Lysenko. He served as accompanist and assistant conductor of Lysenko's chorus in Kiev (1891–1904), conductor of the Kiev University Chorus (1899–1912), musical director of several Ukrainian theaters (1906–17), conductor of the Odessa Choral Association (1924–30), music teacher in Zaporizhia (1930–40), and folk ensemble director in Maikop (1940–5). His works include the symphony *The Year 1905*, the oratorio *Pièta* (text by P. Tychyna), instrumental music for violin and piano, choral songs (to texts by B. Hrinchenko, O. Oles, Lesia Ukrainka, and others), solo songs (to texts by Lesia Ukrainka and others), and church music.

**Yatvingians** (*yatvingy, yatviahy*; Polish: *Jaćwingowie*). One of four Lettish tribes that lived on the frontiers of Kievan Rus', northwest of the Ukrainian tribes. Ethnically similar to the Lithuanians, the Yatvingians settled mainly between the middle Neman and the upper Narva rivers, in a territory known as Sudovia. They are first mentioned in a treaty between Rus' and Byzantium dated 944. The Yatvingians were warlike and frequently engaged the armies of Kievan princes. The Kievan campaigns against them included those of Volodymyr the Great (983), Yaroslav the Wise (1038, 1040, 1044), and Volodymyr Monomakh (1112–13). The Galician-Volhynian princes Roman and Danylo, allied with the princes of Mazovia, finally subdued them. From 1283 most of the Yatvingian territory was occupied by the *Teutonic Knights. The rest became part of the Grand Duchy of Lithuania, and its inhabitants were assimilated into the Lithuanian people; others had been Polonized (in Mazovia) by the 15th century.

Rev Mytrofan Yavdas

**Yavdas, Mytrofan** [Javdas'], b 17 June 1903 in Yakymove, Myrhorod county, Poltava gubernia, d 29 December 1966 in Waterbury, Connecticut. Orthodox priest and church leader. He studied at the Poltava Institute of People's Education before being ordained a priest in the Ukrainian Autocephalous Orthodox Church (UAOC) in 1925. In 1929 he was arrested by the GPU and sentenced to seven years in a hard labor camp. He returned to Ukraine in 1937. During the wartime German occupation of Ukraine he assisted in the rebirth of the UAOC in the Dnipropetrovske region before fleeing to the West. As a postwar refugee in Germany he joined the UAOC (Conciliar) in 1947, served as administrator of the church in Western Europe from 1950, organized pastoral courses, and published the church's bulletin. Yavdas moved to the United States in 1957. There he served as pastor in Waterbury, helped organize the Metropolitan Vasyl Lypkivsky Orthodox Brotherhood, and edited its organ *Tserkva i zhyttia*. In 1956 he published *Ukraïns'ka Avtokefal'na Pravoslavna Tserkva/The Ukrainian Autocephalous Orthodox Church, 1921–36*.

The former town hall (now a secondary school) in Yavoriv

**Yavoriv** [Javoriv]. IV-4. A town (1989 pop 14,200) on the Shklo River and a raion center in Lviv oblast. It was first mentioned in a historical document in 1408, when it was under Polish rule. The town developed into a prosperous manufacturing and trading center on the Lviv–Jarosław trade route, and in 1569 it was granted the rights of *Magdeburg law. After being captured by anti-Polish rebels in 1648, the town was retaken and fortified by its Polish owner. With the partition of Poland in 1772, it was annexed by Austria. Many German colonists settled there. In the 19th century Yavoriv became a county center. The development of the railways ushered in its economic decline. The town maintained its reputation for fine handicrafts, however. In the interwar period it was under Polish rule. Today the town is an industrial center with a plastics and a canning factory. It has a historical and an ethnographic museum and two wooden churches, the Dormition Church (17th century) and the Church of the Nativity of Christ, with a bell tower (1760).

**Yavorivsky, Volodymyr** [Javorivs'kyj], b 11 October 1942 in Teklivka, Kryzhopil raion, Vinnytsia oblast. Writer and political figure. He graduated from Odessa University (1963) and has worked as a newspaper editor, television scenarist, and, most recently, deputy chief editor of the Kiev journal *Vitchyzna*. As a writer he gained prominence in the late 1970s. He is the author of the prose collections *A iabluka padaiut'* (Meanwhile Apples Fall, 1968), *Hrono styhloho vynohradu* (A Cluster of Ripe Grapes, 1971), *Kryla, vyhostreni nebom* (Wings Sharpened by the Sky, 1975), *Tut, na zemli* (Here, on Earth, 1976), and *Z vysoty veresnia* (From the Height of September, 1984); the publicism collections *I v mori pam'iataty dzherelo* (Even in the Sea to Remember the Source, 1980) and *Pravo vlasnoho imeni* (The Right of One's Own Name, 1985); and the novels *Lantsiuhova reaktsiia* (Chain Reaction, 1978), *Ohlian'sia z oseni* (Look Back from Autumn, 1979), *Avtoportret z uiavy* (Self-Portrait from Imagination, 1981), *A teper – idy* (And Now, Go, 1983), and *Vichni Kortelisy* (Eternal Kortelisy,

Volodymyr Yavorivsky          Dmytro Yavornytsky

1988). His recent work about the Chornobyl nuclear disaster appeared in English translation under the title 'Maria and Wormwood at the End of the Century' in *Soviet Literature* (1988, no. 2). In the late 1980s he was active in the Ukrainian national revival and was elected as a deputy to the Ukrainian parliament, where he has belonged to the opposition group Narodna Rada and chaired the commission on the consequences of the Chornobyl disaster.

**Yavorivsky, Yevhen** [Javorivs'kyj, Jevhen], b 19 September 1893 in Kolomyia, Galicia, d 11 November 1954 in Detroit. Journalist and civic activist. He completed philological studies at Vienna University in 1914. After the First World War he taught secondary school in Chortkiv and Yavoriv (1922–30). After being dismissed from his teaching position for political reasons he worked in Lviv for the newspaper *Novyi chas* and for Samoosvita publishers. He was a member of the chief executive of the Ukrainian Socialist Radical party and was active in its youth organization, Kameniari. After emigrating to the United States in 1950, he joined the editorial board of *Vil'na Ukraïna* and a number of Ukrainian civic and cultural organizations. In addition to journalistic articles he wrote a book on Greek mythology, the collection of short stories *Sered kul' i granat* (Amid Bullets and Grenades, 1922), the tragedy *Zradnyk* (Traitor, 1923), and the novel *Zaky more perelechu* (By the Time I Fly across the Sea, 1938).

**Yavornytsky, Dmytro** [Javornyc'kyj] (Evarnitsky), b 7 November 1855 in Sontsivka (now Borysivka), Kharkiv county, d 5 August 1940 in Dnipropetrovske. Historian, ethnographer, and lexicographer; full member of the Shevchenko Scientific Society from 1914 and of the VUAN from 1929. He studied at Kharkiv University (1877–86) and taught Russian history in gymnasiums in Kharkiv (1881–6) until he fell out of favor with the local authorities because of his 'separatist' (pro-Ukrainian) tendencies. He then taught in St Petersburg (1896) and Moscow (as a lecturer on the history and archeology of the Ukrainian Cossacks at Moscow University from 1897) and became director of the Museum of Antiquities of Katerynoslav Gubernia (later the *Dnipropetrovske Historical Museum) in 1902, a position he held for the rest of his life. He also worked at the Dnipropetrovske Institute of People's Education (1920–33, as head of its Chair of Ukrainian

Studies in 1925–9) and co-ordinated archeological and documentational work undertaken in the areas to be flooded by the building of the Dnieper Hydroelectric Station (1927–32).

Yavornytsky's scholarly interest, the history of the Zaporozhian Cossacks, earned him the nickname 'Father of the Zaporozhians.' During the 1880s he wrote many articles for *Kievskaia starina* and the preface for the 1885 edition of T. Shevchenko's *Haidamaky*. He published several major works about the Cossacks, including *Ivan Dmitriievich Sirko* (1894) and *Istoriia zaporozhskikh kozakov* (History of the Zaporozhian Cossacks, 3 vols, 1892–7; 2nd trans edn: *Istoriia zaporiz'kykh kozakiv*, 1990–1). His *Iz ukrainskoi stariny* (From the Ukrainian Past, 1900; 2nd trans edn: *Z ukraïns'koï starovyny*, 1991) was illustrated by S. Vasylkivsky and M. Samokysh. He used both primary and archival sources in his research and published a selection of them as *Istochniki dlia istorii zaporozhskikh kozakov* (Sources for the History of the Zaporozhian Cossacks, 2 vols, 1903). As director of the Katerynoslav museum he undertook numerous field expeditions and archeological digs, by means of which he increased the museum holdings from 5,000 to 80,000 items; after his death the museum was named in his honor. He also wrote several regional studies, including *Zaporozh'e v ostatkakh stariny i predaniiakh naroda* (The Zaporizhia in Relics of the Past and Legends of the People, 1888; illus by I. Repin) and *Do istoriï stepovoï Ukraïny* (Toward the History of Steppe Ukraine, 1929).

Yavornytsky also had a strong interest in ethnography, folklore, and lexicography. He published the valuable collection *Malorossiiskie narodnye pesni, sobrannye v 1878–1905 gg.* (Little Russian [Ukrainian] Folk Songs, Collected in 1878–1905, 1906; repub: *Ukraïns'ki narodni pisni, naspivani D. Iavornyts'kym: Pisni ta dumy z arkhivu vchenoho* [Ukrainian Folk Songs, Collected by D. Yavornytsky: Songs and Dumas from the Archives of a Scholar, 1990]). He contributed to B. Hrinchenko's Ukrainian dictionary and published *Slovnyk ukraïns'koï movy* (Dictionary of the Ukrainian Language) as an addendum to it in 1920.

Yavornytsky was a friend of I. Repin, who painted his portrait as the scribe in his monumental *Zaporozhian Cossacks Write a Letter to the Turkish Sultan* (1886). Although his scholarly works were often criticized as romantic and unsystematic, his promotion of the Zaporozhian past influenced the development of national consciousness in Ukraine in his day. In the late 1980s and early 1990s there was a great upsurge of interest in Yavornytsky and his works in Ukraine.

BIBLIOGRAPHY
Doroshenko, D. 'Dmytro Ivanovych Iavornyts'kyi,' *LNV*, 1913, no. 12
Shapoval, I. *V poshukakh skarbiv* (Kiev 1965)
Hapusenko, I. *Dmytro Ivanovych Iavornyts'kyi* (Kiev 1969) [with bibliography]
Shubravs'ka, M. *D.I. Iavornyts'kyi* (Kiev 1972) [with bibliography]
    A. Makuch

**Yavorsky, Boleslav** [Javors'kyj], b 22 June 1877 in Kharkiv, d 26 November 1942 in Saratov, RSFSR. Musicologist, pianist, and educator. He graduated from the Kiev Music School (1898) and the Moscow Conservatory (1903), and served as professor of the Kiev Conservatory (1916–21) and the Lysenko Music and Drama Institute (1918–21) and director of the People's Conservatory in Kiev (1917–21). He was appointed professor at the Moscow Conservatory (1938–42). His students included M. Leontovych, H. Verovka, M. Verykivsky, P. Kozytsky, V. Verkhovynets, and E. Skrypchynska. His musical theories are promulgated in *Stroenie muzykal'noi rechi* (The Structure of Musical Speech, 3 vols, 1908) and *Struktura melodii* (The Structure of Melody, 1929) and analyzed in G. McQuere's *Russian Theoretical Thought in Music* (1983). He also composed an opera, *The Tower of October* (1930), and some piano and vocal music.

**Yavorsky, Fedir** [Javors'kyj], b 1780 in Kiev, d 21 April 1828 in St Petersburg. Physician. After being educated at the Kievan Mohyla Academy and the St Petersburg Medico-Surgical Academy (1802–7), he worked as P. *Zahorsky's assistant (1807–10) and became chief surgeon of the St Petersburg Admiralty Hospital (1813–21), chief physician of the Caucasian health resort (1821–4), and municipal physician of St Petersburg (1827–8). He performed the first successful ligation of the popliteal artery in the Russian Empire.

**Yavorsky, Ivan** [Javors'kyj], b 1856, d 23 April 1930 in Strilbychi, Sambir county, Galicia. Greek Catholic priest active in Galician civic and political life. A leading member of the National Democratic party, he served as a deputy to the Galician Diet and fought for the improvement of Ukrainian schools and the founding of a Ukrainian gymnasium in Stanyslaviv. He was an organizer of the agrarian strike in 1902 and of the mass campaign for a universal, secret, and direct vote to the Austrian parliament (1905–6). He founded many Prosvita reading rooms in Sambir county. In 1918–19 he was a member of the Ukrainian National Rada.

Matvii Yavorsky

**Yavorsky, Matvii** [Javors'kyj, Matvij], b 27 November 1885 in Korchmyn, Rava Ruska county, Galicia, d 3 November 1937. Historian; full member of the VUAN and the Belarusian Academy of Sciences from 1929. Yavorsky graduated in law from Lviv University (1910). A former officer of the Ukrainian Galician army, he joined the CP(B)U in 1920. Although originally trained in law, he became a Marxist historian, much influenced by the Russian historian M. Pokrovsky. He headed the historical section of the *Ukrainian Institute of Marxism-Leninism (UIML) and, from 1926, Ukrholovnauka, a body that supervised all scholarly work in Soviet Ukraine. He was also a member of the VUAN Presidium and the secretary of its Historical-Philological Divison. Among his major works are *Narys istoriï Ukraïny* (Outline History of Ukraine, 2 vols, 1923–4; repr, Adelaide, Australia 1986), *Narysy z istoriï revoliutsiinoï borot'by na Ukraïni* (Sketches of the History of the Revolutionary Struggle in Ukraine, vol 1, 1927; vol 2, pt 1, 1928), *Ukraïna v epokhu kapitalizmu* (Ukraine in the Epoch of Capitalism, 3 vols, 1924–5), and *Istoriia Ukraïny v styslomu narysi* (History of Ukraine in a Concise Outline, 1928). Veteran Ukrainian historians, such as D. Bahalii, considered his work too dogmatic and marred by the subordination of facts to theoretical constructs. Stalinist Party leaders and historians, however, began to criticize his work at the end of 1928, by charging that he gave primacy to national concerns over class, and that he viewed Ukrainian history as a process distinct from Russian history. His theory of the origins of Ukrainian communism was criticized with particular severity. The 11th Congress of the CP(B)U, held in June 1930, condemned the 'anti-Marxist theory of Yavorsky' and equated it with the national deviations of O. Shumsky, M. Khvylovy, and M. Volobuiev. Yavorsky was purged from the CP(B)U in 1930 and arrested in March 1931 and charged with membership in a fictitious underground military organization. He was exiled to a labor camp on the Solovets Islands, where he was executed by the NKVD in 1937. He was rehabilitated in 1989.

J.-P. Himka

Oleksa Yavorsky                Metropolitan Stefan Yavorsky

**Yavorsky, Oleksa** [Javors'kyj], b 25 March 1896 in Kotuziv, Pidhaitsi county, Galicia, d 11 April 1987 in Toronto. Lawyer and political and civic activist. A veteran of the Austrian army and the Ukrainian Galician Army in 1919, he worked as a notary upon his return to civilian life in 1920. At the same time he studied law at the Lviv (Underground) Ukrainian University and then at Cracow University (1925–9) and was active in various local organizations in Pidhaitsi. He belonged to the Ukrainian Military Organization and served as chairman of the county committee and as member of the Central Committee of the *Ukrainian National Democratic Alliance (UNDO). In 1928 and 1930 he was elected as a candidate of UNDO to the Polish Sejm. After opening his own law office in Pidhaitsi in 1935, he defended Ukrainian political activists in the courts. In 1944 he was entrusted with the welfare of the families of Division Galizien soldiers. In 1948 he emigrated to Canada, where he was active in émigré political organizations.

**Yavorsky, Stefan** [Javors'kyj] (secular name: Semen), b 1658 in Yavoriv, Galicia, d 27 November 1722 in Moscow. Orthodox hierarch, theologian, poet, and philosopher. A graduate of the Kievan Mohyla College (ca 1684), he completed his education in Polish Jesuit colleges: he studied philosophy in Lviv and Lublin and theology in Poznań and Vilnius. After returning to Kiev in 1687, he renounced Catholicism, became an Orthodox monk (1689), and taught rhetoric (1690), philosophy (1691–3), and theology (1693–8) at the Mohyla College. He was hegumen of St Nicholas's Monastery in Kiev from 1697; in 1700 he was appointed metropolitan of Riazan and Murom in Russia, and on 1 December 1701, exarch in Moscow of the Russian Orthodox church, by Emperor Peter I. Yavorsky helped Peter to reform the church and education. Eventually his defense of church autonomy, criticism of Peter, opposition to T. *Prokopovych, and intolerance of Protestantism cost him the tsar's favor. In 1712 he was forbidden to preach, and in 1718 he was forced to live in St Petersburg and subjected to constant harassment and political inquiry. In 1721 Peter appointed him president of the *Holy Synod, an institution Yavorsky abhorred. Yavorsky wrote religious verses and panegyrics (eg, to Hetman I. Mazepa and Peter I), polemical treatises, and baroque sermons. His major work is the anti-Protestant dogmatic treatise *Kamen' very* ... (The Faith's Rock ..., written 1718, published 1728, and reprinted 1729, 1730, 1749, and 1841–2). In his philosophical lectures in Kiev he presented the scholastic systems of logic, physics, and metaphysics; he often sided with J. Duns Scotus and William of Ockham against the Thomists.

BIBLIOGRAPHY
Ternovskii, F. 'Mitropolit Stefan Iavorskii (Kratkii biograficheskii ocherk),' TKDA, 1864, nos 1, 3, 6
Iavorskii, S. *Ritoricheskaia ruka*, trans from Latin by F. Polikarpov (St Petersburg 1878)
Samarin, Iu. *Sochineniia*, vol 5, *Stefan Iavorskii i Feofan Prokopovich* (Moscow 1880)
Zakhara, I. *Bor'ba idei v filosofskoi mysli na Ukraine na rubezhe XVII–XVIII vv. (Stefan Iavorskii)* (Kiev 1982)
Iavors'kyi, S. *Filosofs'ki tvory*, 3 vols, ed I. Zakhara (Kiev 1992–3)
T. Zakydalsky

Vasyl Yavorsky

**Yavorsky, Vasyl** [Javors'kyj, Vasyl'], b 1854 in Yavora, Turka county, Galicia, d 22 May 1926 in Nowy Sącz, Galicia. Lawyer and political and civic leader in Galicia. He collaborated with A. Chaikovsky in organizing the Ukrainian community of Berezhany and represented the town in the Austrian parliament (1900–7). As parliamentary deputy he exposed the tax machinations of Polish magnates in Galicia and defended the Sich societies from Gov A. Potocki's persecution. With R. Sembratovych and A. Kos he founded the journals *Ruthenische Revue (1903–5) and *Ukrainische Rundschau 1905–15) to inform the general public about Ukrainian issues. After retiring from politics he settled in Nowy Sącz, where he founded the Lemko Bank, a student residence, and a branch of the Prosvita society. At his initiative a Greek Catholic church was also built there. He made generous donations to Ukrainian organizations.

Volodymyr Yavorsky    Mykola Yefremov

**Yavorsky, Volodymyr** [Javors'kyj], b 27 July 1876 in Ropcha, Chernihiv gubernia, d 24 September 1942 in Ufa, Bashkiria. Organic chemist; AN URSR (now ANU) full member from 1934. A graduate of Kiev University (1901), he worked and taught there (1901–21, 1935–9) and at the Kiev Polytechnical Institute (1921–35), where he chaired the department of organic chemistry. He directed the Sector of Organic Chemistry at the ANU Institute of Chemistry and the ANU institutes of Organic Chemistry and Technology (1939–41) and Inorganic and Organic Chemistry (1941–2). Yavorsky researched mainly the synthesis of unsaturated alcohols and alkenes using Grignard reagents, and also organic azides and their transformations into triazoles, tetrazoles, and triazenes.

**Yazlovets.** See Yablunivka.

**Yazlovsky, Borys** [Jazlovs'kyj], b 1 September 1894 in Kiev, d ? Legal historian. In the early 1920s he taught law at the Kiev Institute of the National Economy. He also served as secretary of the Society of Ukrainian Jurists and as a member of the VUAN Commission for the Study of Ukraine's Customary Law. Two of his articles were published in the commission's *Pratsi* (1925, 1928). He was arrested in 1929 and again in 1937; his subsequent fate is unknown.

*Yazychiie.* The derogatory name for the bookish language in which the Galician, Bukovynian, and Transcarpathian *Russophiles wrote in the 19th and early 20th centuries. Based on the earlier bookish *Slavonic-Ruthenian language, the *yazychiie* was a combination of Church Slavonic and Russian that included Western Ukrainian vernacular elements and Polonisms and had a Ukrainian

pronunciation. It was used in Lviv periodicals, such as *Slovo* (1861–87), *Naukovyi* (later *Literaturnyi*) *sbornik''* (1865–73, 1885–90, 1896–7), *Vremennik'' Stavropigiiskogo instituta* (1864–1915), and *Věstnik'' Narodnoho doma* (1882–1914), as well as in two Bukovyna periodicals: *Pravoslavnaia Bukovina* (1893–1904) and *Bukovinski vědomosti* (1895–1909). The Galician Populists and Radicals (eg, I. Franko) condemned its use.

**Ych Oba.** See Trybratni Mohyly.

**Yedynets, Yosyp** [Jedynec', Josyp], b and d ? Lviv builder in the first half of the 18th century. He built Lviv's St George's Monastery (1732–8) and took part in preparing the foundations of St George's Cathedral in 1744.

**Yefimov, Viktor** [Jefimov], b 5 March 1921 in Nykopil, Katerynoslav county, Katerynoslav gubernia. Metallurgist specializing in metal casting; full member of the ANU (formerly AN URSR) since 1973. He studied in Dnipropetrovske and has worked at the ANU Institute for Problems of Casting since 1964, as director since 1966. He has contributed to research on physicochemical, hydrodynamic, and thermodynamic aspects of casting and crystallization processes in castings.

**Yefrem** [Jefrem]. Church hierarch of the late 11th century. A monk from the Kievan Cave Monastery, he traveled to Constantinople, where he acquired a copy of the Studite monastic rules that were adopted at the Kievan Cave Monastery. He later became bishop of Pereiaslav. According to some sources, he subsequently became the second locally born metropolitan of Kiev, ca 1089–97.

**Yefremov, Ernest** [Jefremov], b 14 November 1934 in Staline (now Donetske). Mining engineer; corresponding member of the ANU (formerly AN URSR) since 1985. He graduated from the Dnipropetrovske Mining Institute (1957) and has worked at the ANU Institute of Geotechnical Mechanics since 1962. His main research interests are the mechanics of blasting and new technologies for mineral extraction.

**Yefremov, Fedir** [Jefremov], b 1874, d 1947 in Odessa. Forester and land meliorator. He worked at the Ukrainian Scientific Research Institute of Forest Management and Agroforest Amelioration in Kharkiv (1931–6) and lectured at the Odessa Agricultural Institute (1937–47). His research dealt with shelter belts and the stabilization of shifting sands and slopes. He wrote numerous works, mostly in Ukrainian.

**Yefremov, Mykola** [Jefremov] (Efremov, Nicholas), b 7 May 1904 in Myshkovske, d 13 September 1962 in New York. Geologist and mineralogist; full member of the Ukrainian Academy of Arts and Sciences in the US and the Shevchenko Scientific Society from 1949. After graduating from the Don Polytechnic Institute in Novocherkassk in 1929, he completed graduate studies at the Leningrad Mining Institute in 1938. During his exile in Siberia he worked as a geologist-prospector (1930–3). Then he taught at Rostov University (1935–8, 1941–3) and the Institute of Geology in Moscow (1938–9) and worked as a mineralogist at the Lviv Museum of Natural History (1943–5). He emigrated from Ukraine after the Second World War and taught at the UNRRA University in Munich (1945–8) and the Ukrainian Technical and Husbandry Institute (1945–51). He was a senior fellow in various research programs on the USSR in the United States and in 1958 he joined the faculty of the Middlebury College Institute of Soviet Studies.

Yefremov researched various aspects of geology in Northern Caucasia and the Mariiupil region and studied the iron-ore deposits of the Taman and Kerch peninsulas. He discovered 12 new minerals, one of which, yefremovite, was named after him. He wrote numerous works on economic geology, geochemistry, crystallochemistry, mineralogy, the processing technology of mineral raw materials, and agrochemistry.

Petro Yefremov                     Serhii Yefremov

**Yefremov, Petro** [Jefremov], b 24 December 1883 in Palchyk, Zvenyhorodka county, Kiev gubernia, d ? Literary scholar; brother of S. *Yefremov. In the 1920s he was a professor of Ukrainian literature at the Dnipropetrovske Institute of People's Education, a member of the Dnipropetrovske Scientific Society of the VUAN, and the first editor of the Dnipropetrovske journal *Zoria. From 1905 he contributed to the journals *Kievskaia starina, Literaturno-naukovyi vistnyk, Svitlo, Knyhar,* and *Zoria*; the almanacs *Rada, Nova rada,* and *Sich*; and the literary and artistic collection *Vyr revoliutsiï* (The Vortex of Revolution, 1921). He explored the problems of naturalism and studied the development of the historical novel in Ukrainian literature. He wrote articles about the works of T. Shevchenko, P. Kulish, M. Drahomanov, I. Karpenko-Kary, D. Markovych, L. Yanovska, B. Lepky, P. Karmansky, A. Krymsky, and many others. He was arrested in 1929 and sentenced at the 1930 show trial of the *Union for the Liberation of Ukraine. His further fate is unknown. He was rehabilitated in 1989.

**Yefremov, Serhii** [Jefremov, Serhij] (Iefremov), b 18 October 1876 in Palchyk, Zvenyhorodka county, Kiev gubernia, d 10 March 1939 in Vladimir prison, Russia. Literary journalist, historian, critic, and political activist; member of the Shevchenko Scientific Society from 1923 and the VUAN from 1919. He studied law at Kiev University before devoting himself to literary scholarship. He was a leading member of the *Ukrainian Democratic Radical party and its successor, the *Society of Ukrainian Progressives (TUP),

which he transformed into the *Ukrainian Party of Socialists-Federalists (and then headed). His contributions on political and literary topics to publications such as *Zoria, Pravda, Zapysky NTSh, Literaturno-naukovyi vistnyk, Kievskaia starina, Nova hromada, Hromads'ka dumka, Rada, Nova rada, Ukraïna, Zapysky Istorychno-filolohichnoho viddilu VUAN,* and *Literatura* were highly regarded. Yefremov served as vice-president of the VUAN governing council, secretary of its historical-philological division, and member of many of its commissions (notably the commission for publishing the classics of modern Ukrainian literature). He was also one of the directors of the Vik publishing house (1895–1918). He suffered several arrests under the tsarist regime for his writings and political activity.

In 1917 Yefremov became a member of the *Central Rada and its deputy head, a member of the Little Rada, general secretary of international affairs in the General Secretariat, and a member of the Ukrainian delegation that negotiated with the Provisional Government. Yefremov was the chief defendant in the 1929 show trial of the so-called *Union for the Liberation of Ukraine, which he was accused of heading. The death sentence he received in 1930 was later commuted to 10 years' imprisonment. He served the first seven of those in the Yaroslavl political prison and the remainder in the Vladimir prison. He died several months before the end of his sentence.

As a literary critic Yefremov was the most prominent representative of the late populist or neopopulist current, which, despite fierce criticism from those who stressed the primacy of sociological or esthetic criteria, enjoyed widespread support during the revolutionary years and still exerts an influence today. Claiming that the esthetic principle was completely inappropriate for a history of Ukrainian literature, he outlined three governing ideas in the development of that literature: (1) 'the element of personal freedom, a continuous emancipatory current'; (2) 'the idea of national liberation'; and (3) 'the progressive populist current in content and form.' Using service to the nation and norms of the literary language as criteria upon which to judge literature, Yefremov placed little value on the writing of the 17th and 18th centuries, which he considered artificial, scholastic, and divorced from 'real life.' He concentrated his attention on the history of modern literature, in which field he published a series of important monographs, chiefly on writers of the 19th century: *Marko Vovchok* (1907), *Shevchenko* (1914), *Spivets' borot'by i kontrastiv* (Singer of Struggle and Contrasts 1913; *Ivan Franko* in the 1926 edition), *Mykhailo Kotsiubyns'kyi* (1922), *Karpenko-Karyi* (1924), *Ivan Nechui-Levyts'kyi* (1925), and *Panas Myrnyi* (1928). He is responsible for editing many classics of Ukrainian literature (again primarily of the 19th century), for which he provided introductions, and notes: by L. Hlibov, Y. Hrebinka, T. Shevchenko, O. Konysky, I. Kotliarevsky, M. Kotsiubynsky, B. Hrinchenko, and others. One of his most important publications is the academic edition of Shevchenko's *Diary* and *Letters* (1927–8), which contain Yefremov's articles and commentary.

In an article that appeared in *Kievskaia starina* in 1902, Yefremov voiced his hostility toward the modernists. Using the works of H. Khotkevych, O. Kobylianska, N. Kobrynska, K. Hrynevycheva, and others as examples, Yefremov condemned what he regarded as 'modish currents,' 'caricaturish form,' enthusiasm for symbolism and decadence, and, above all, a failure to delve deeply into life in order to 'expose social sores' and heal them. In the 1924 edition of his *Istoriia ukraïn'skoho pys'menstva* (History of Ukrainian Writing) Yefremov devoted a new chapter to the 'revolutionary' literature of 1919–24 in which he modified his populist methodology by accepting the importance of formal considerations, and made insightful comments on Soviet writers. From the 1930s Soviet literary criticism never acknowledged Yefremov's contributions to literature and wrote practically nothing about him. Yefremov's views on literature are most fully expressed in his *Istoriia ukraïns'koho pys'menstva* (1911), the third edition (1917) of which became the most widely read literary-scholarly work of the revolutionary years.

BIBLIOGRAPHY
Kryms'kyi, A. 'Zhyttiepys i literaturna diial'nist' S.O. Iefremova,' *ZIFV*, 2–3 (1920–3)
– 'Spys prats' Iefremova,' ibid
Ovcharenko, M. 'Serhii Iefremov iak literaturoznavets',' *ZNTSh*, 173 (1962)
'Do stolittia narodzhennia Serhiia Iefremova,' *Suchasnist'*, 1976, no. 10 (three articles by P. Odarchenko, Iu. Boiko, and H. Hrabovych)

I. Koshelivets, M. Shkandrij

Col Serhii Yefremov          Aleksandra Yefymenko

**Yefremov, Serhii** [Jefremov, Serhij], b 1893, d 18 December 1966 in Astoria, New York. Senior army officer. Serving as an officer in the Russian army, in 1917 he Ukrainianized Russian army units in the Katerynoslav region and was sent as a delegate to the First and Second All-Ukrainian military congresses. In 1918 he commanded a regiment, which fought the Red Army around Katerynoslav. Then he served, at the rank of lieutenant colonel, as a special staff officer at the UNR Army headquarters. In the interwar period he lived in Transcarpathia, and in March 1939 he served, at the rank of colonel, as commander of the Carpathian Sich. After the Second World War he emigrated to the United States, where he was a founding member of the United Ukrainian War Veterans in America.

**Yefym** [Jefym], b and d ? Wood engraver at the Kievan Cave Monastery Press in the second half of the 18th century. He illustrated and decorated books, such as *Akafisty i kanony* (Akathists and Canons, 1783 and 1786) and *Sluzhby prepodobnym otsem pecherskim* (Services by the Venerable Father of the Caves, 1785), and made prints on religious themes, such as *The Great Martyr Barbara* (1781) and *Dormition* (1785).

**Yefymenko, Aleksandra** [Jefymenko] (Russian: Efimenko; née Stavrovskaia), b 30 May 1848 in Varzuga, Kola county, Arkhangelsk gubernia, Russia, d 18 December 1918 on Lubochka *khutir*, near Pysarivka, Vovchanske county, Kharkiv gubernia. Russian historian and ethnographer; full member of the Imperial Russian Geographic, Moscow Psychological, Kharkiv Historical-Philological, and Kiev Juridical societies and honorary member of the Poltava Learned Archival Commission. She worked as a teacher in Kholmogory. There she married the exiled P. *Yefymenko in 1870 and was consequently forbidden to teach. Instead she researched and published studies on the dialect, socioeconomic history, and folkways of Arkhangelsk gubernia and on Russian customary law. In the 1880s and 1890s Yefymenko was an active member of the Kharkiv Historical-Philological Society. She published book-length articles on the history of Ukrainian-Polish conflicts, the history of Right-Bank Ukraine, and Ukrainian church brotherhoods and guilds, and shorter ones in defense of the Ukrainophiles and on customary law (including the role of women in peasant families), community courts, and peasant relations in Ukraine, the haidamakas, the Little Russian Collegium, the Turbai uprising, the nobility in the Hetman state, dress and household items in Slobidska Ukraine, the Ukrainian language in elementary schools, and Ukrainian writers, such as H. Skovoroda, I. Kotliarevsky, N. Gogol, T. Shevchenko, and V. Antonovych. Twenty-four of her articles were reprinted as the collection *Iuzhnaia Rus'* (Southern Rus', 2 vols, 1905) by the St Petersburg Shevchenko Society. Her monographs in Russian on the history of the Ukrainian people (2 pts, 1906; 2nd edn 1990; Ukrainian trans 1922, ed D. Bahalii) and the history of Ukraine and its people (1907) were widely read. In 1903 she delivered the first speech at the unveiling of Kotliarevsky's monument in Poltava. From 1907 to 1917 she taught Russian and Ukrainian history at the Bestuzhev Higher Courses for Women in St Petersburg. She was the first woman in the Russian Empire to be awarded an honorary PH D (in Russian history, by Kharkiv University, 1910). Yefymenko was murdered by bandits, together with her daughter, Tatiana, at their homestead. In 1919 Bahalii's annotated bibliography of her works was published by the UAN in the *Zapysky* of its historical-philological section, and her elementary-school textbook on Ukrainian and Russian history was published in Russian and Ukrainian in Kharkiv. P. Markov's book about her appeared in Kiev in 1966.

R. Senkus

**Yefymenko, Heorhii** [Jefymenko, Heorhij], b 30 January 1917 in Katerynoslav (now Dnipropetrovske). Metallurgist; corresponding member of the ANU (formerly AN URSR) since 1973. He studied and taught at the Dnipropetrovske Metallurgical Institute, where he also served as rector. From 1951 he was a functionary in the CC of the CPU. He was assistant to the minister (1955–9) and then minister (1973–84) of higher and specialized secondary education for the Ukrainian SSR. He contributed some technical work in the field of iron smelting and other areas of ferrous metallurgy.

**Yefymenko, Petro** [Jefymenko], b 1835 in Velykyi Tokmak, Berdianske county, Tavriia gubernia, d 20 May 1908 in St Petersburg. Historian and ethnographer; husband of

Petro Yefymenko, Sr      Petro Yefymenko, Jr

A. *Yefymenko and father of P. *Yefymenko. He studied at Kharkiv and Moscow universities (1855–7) and belonged to clandestine student circles. He wandered through Ukraine gathering historical and ethnographic materials. In 1859 he was arrested and exiled for 10 years to Perm and then Arkhangelsk. Upon returning to Ukraine in 1876, he settled in Kharkiv and devoted himself to historical and ethnographic research. In 1884–8 he was editor of *Khar'kovskii kalendar*, in which he opened a special bibliographic section and published a list of P. Chubynsky's works. He contributed articles to *Osnova*, *Chernigovskii listok*, and *Kievskaia starina* on folk spells (1874), the cottage industry of the Sumy region, and folkways in the 17th and 18th centuries and compiled a bibliography of Ukrainian literature. Under the pseudonym P. Odinets he wrote a booklet on Ukrainian populism (1906).

**Yefymenko, Petro** [Jefymenko], b 21 November 1884 in Kharkiv, d 18 April 1969 in Leningrad. Archeologist; full member of the AN URSR (now ANU) from 1945; son of A. and P. *Yefymenko. After graduating from St Petersburg University (1912), he travelled through Europe, Africa, and the Orient, and then (1917–19) worked at museums in Moscow and Leningrad. While a research associate with the Leningrad Institute of the History of Material Culture (1919–46), he also served as a lecturer (1924–39) and then professor (1939–46) at Leningrad University. A specialist in the Paleolithic, he led archeological expeditions in east central Ukraine and the Don region. He became director of the ANU Institute of Archeology in 1945. During his tenure (to 1955) the institute launched new periodicals and published the first general survey of Ukrainian archeology, *Narysy starodavn'oï istoriï Ukraïns'koï RSR* (Essays on the Ancient History of the Ukrainian SSR, 1959).

**Yehorov, Yevhen** [Jehorov, Jevhen], b 17 May 1917 in Lyman (now Krasnyi Lyman), Izium county, Kharkiv gubernia. Painter and graphic artist. After graduating from the Kharkiv Art Institute (1949) he taught at the Kharkiv Industrial Design Institute and in 1972 became its rector. His prints include lithograph portraits of V. Myronenko (1954), I. Franko and M. Cheremshyna (1956), and T. Shevchenko (1961). He has painted series, such as 'Through France' (1961–2), 'Party Veterans' (1967), and 'My Comrades in Arms' (1975–80), and murals, in the Horlivka Palace of Culture.

**Yeia River** [Jeja]. A river in northern Kuban that flows for 311 km through Krasnodar krai before emptying into the Yeiske Estuary along the coast of the Sea of Azov. It drains a basin area of 8,650 sq km. It is well stocked with fish. Sections of the river usually dry up during the summer, although its lower reaches are quite marshy.

**Yeiske** [Jejs'ke] (Russian: Eisk). VII-19. A city (1990 pop 79,000) on the Sea of Azov and a raion center in Krasnodar krai, RF. It has a port, which exports grain and fish, a large machine-building and metalworking industry, and a popular health resort. According to the 1926 census, Ukrainians represented 42 percent of the city's population and 74 percent of the raion's population.

**Yeiske Estuary** [Jejs'kyi lyman]. VII-19. An estuary situated at the mouth of the Yeia River along Tahanrih Bay in the Sea of Azov. The estuary is nearly 20 km long and 12 km wide and is sheltered from the sea in part by the Yeiske Spit. The city of Yeiske is situated on its west side.

**Yelanets** [Jelanec']. VI-12. A town smt (1985 pop 4,900) on the Hnylyi Yelanets River and a raion center in Mykolaiv oblast. It was founded at the beginning of the 19th century as a peasant colony and called Hnylyi Yelanets. In 1810–58 it was known as Novomoskovske, and until 1925 it was part of Yelysavethrad county in Kherson gubernia. Today it is a farming center with several food-processing enterprises.

**Yelchenko, Yurii** [Jel'čenko, Jurij], b 23 July 1929 in Kaharlyk, Kiev okruha. CPU and government leader. After graduating from the Kiev Polytechnical Institute (1952) he rose in the Komsomol to the positions of secretary (1958–9), second secretary (1959–60), and first secretary (1960–8) of the Ukrainian organization. As a CC CPU member since 1961, he has served the Party as head of its Department of Agitation and Propaganda (1973–80), first secretary of the Kiev Party Committee (from 1980), secretary for ideology (1988–9), and chairman of the new CC CPU Commission for Internationality Affairs (from 1989). He was a member of the CPU Politburo from 1981 and of the CC CPSU from 1981. He served one term as Ukraine's minister of culture (1971–3).

**Yeletskyi Dormition Monastery** (Yeletskyi Uspenskyi manastyr). One of the oldest monasteries in Ukraine, situated in Chernihiv; founded in 1069 by Sviatoslav II Yaroslavych on the site of an apparition of an icon of Mary in a fir tree (the name of the monastery derives from the Old Church Slavonic *yel'* 'fir'). The monastery was sacked in 1239 during the Tatar invasion, and not restored until 1445–99. It was damaged again in the early 17th century when the Poles occupied Chernihiv. At that time it was also put under Uniate control. After the Khmelnytsky uprising the monastery returned to Orthodoxy and underwent a revival under Archimandrite L. Baranovych (1657–69) and Archimandrite I. *Galiatovsky (1669–88). The complex was restored, and a bell tower, refectory, and other buildings were added. In the late 18th century the monastery's properties were nationalized by the Russian state, and the monastery was granted first-class status. It was closed under Soviet rule and severely damaged during the Second World War. Restored in the early 1950s, it is now a museum preserve.

The cathedral of the Yeletskyi Dormition Monastery

The central feature of the monastery is the Cathedral of the Dormition, which was built in the late 11th century. It is a three-nave structure typical of the Chernihiv architectural style of that time. The original single cupola was complemented in the 17th century by three smaller cupolas. At the same time, a baroque façade and a side altar (where the monastery's patron, Ya. *Lyzohub, was buried) were added to the structure. The bell tower is hexagonal in shape, built in three layers with a single dome on top. Other surviving structures include three buildings containing the monks' cells.

BIBLIOGRAPHY
Dobrovol'skii, P. *Chernigovskii Ieletskii Uspenskii pervoklassnyi monastyr': Istoricheskoe opisanie* (Chernihiv 1900)

**Yeleva, Kostiantyn** [Jeleva, Kostjantyn], b 17 May 1897 in Kiev, d 19 November 1950 in Kiev. Graphic artist and theatrical scenery designer. After graduating from the Kiev State Art Institute (1922) he taught there. He was a member of the *Association of Revolutionary Art of Ukraine (1925–32) and contributed articles on art to *Hart*. He designed the scenery for L. Kurbas's staging of *Haidamaky* (1920) and propaganda posters; created several colored-pencil print series, such as 'Samarkand' (1941–3), 'Zagorsk' (1944), and 'Kiev – Kaniv' (1945–50); and did paintings, such as *The Strike Is Broken*, *Portrait of a Typist* (1927), *Portrait of M. Helman* (1943), and landscapes. A catalog of an exhibition of his paintings came out in 1955.

**Yelizarov, Viktor** [Jelizarov] (Elizarov), b 7 August 1911 in Pashkovo, Tula gubernia, Russia. Architect; full member of the Academy of Building and Architecture of Ukraine since 1958. In 1937 he graduated from the Moscow Architecture Institute. After the war he collaborated with a team of architects in planning and developing the Khreshchatyk (1949–57) and designing the communications center (1952), the Exhibition of Economic Achievements of the Ukrainian SSR (1951–8), the Khreshchatyk metro station (1960), and the Dnipro Hotel (1964), all in Kiev.

**Yelovych-Malinsky, Ostafii** [Jelovyč-Malins'kyj, Ostafij], b and d ? Greek Catholic bishop of Lutske in 1607–21. He was a Volhynian nobleman and a supporter of unification. His tenure as bishop was marked by stormy relations between Orthodox and Catholic supporters in the region, which ultimately rendered his position untenable.

**Yelyniak, Vasyl.** See Eleniak, Wasyl.

**Yelysaveta Yaroslavna** [Jelysaveta Jaroslavna], b ?, d 1076. Rus' princess; elder daughter of Yaroslav the Wise. In 1044 she married the renowned Norse warrior-prince (and king of Norway from 1047) *Harald III Hardraade, who had been a member of Yaroslav's retinue in the early 1030s. She retained her name and her faith while in Scandinavia and reportedly had two daughters (Ingrid and Maria) with Harald. After his death in 1066, she married Harald's Danish rival, Sweyn II.

**Yelysavethrad.** See Kirovohrad.

**Yemchenko, Andrii** [Jemčenko, Andrij], b 28 October 1893 in Mykhailivka, near Kamianka, Chyhyryn county, Kiev gubernia, d 18 February 1964 in Kiev. Physiologist; corresponding member of the AN URSR (now ANU) from 1957. A graduate of the Kiev Medical Institute (1925), he was head of the human and animal physiology department at Kiev University (1933–64). A specialist in the physiology of heart and higher nervous activity and digestion, he wrote the handbook *Fiziolohiia tvaryn i liudyny* (The Physiology of Animals and Man, 1952) with D. Vorontsov.

**Yemelianenko, Pavlo** [Jemeljanenko], b 5 July 1905 in Bobrykova-Petrivska stanytsia, Tahanrih county, Don Cossack province, d 13 November 1947 in Moscow. Specialist in the production processes of pipes; corresponding member of the AN URSR (now ANU) from 1939. He studied and taught at the Dnipropetrovske Metallurgical Institute. From 1941 he headed various all-Union pipe production facilities and contributed significantly to pipe manufacturing research, particularly in the development of seamless pipes, pipe welding, and numerical methods of the optimization of pipe dimensions.

**Yemelianov, Oleksandr** [Jemel'janov], b 30 October 1932 in Kharkiv. Economist; corresponding member of the AN URSR (now ANU) since 1979. Since graduating from the Kharkiv Industrial-Engineering Institute in 1955, he has worked at the All-Union Institute of the Coal Industry (1956–8), the Kharkiv Industrial-Engineering Institute (1958–62), and the Scientific Research Institute of Economics of the State Planning Committee of Ukraine (1965–), where he was appointed director in 1971. His scholarly works deal with economic planning and the improvement of economic performance. They include the monographs *Obshchestvennoe proizvodstvo: Dinamika, tendentsii, modeli* (Social Production: Dynamics, Tendencies, Models, 1980) and *Ekonometriia i prognozirovanie* (Econometrics and Prognostication, 1985).

Fedir Yemets (right) and his students in his studio in Salzburg (1947)

**Yemets, Fedir** [Jemec'], b 1894 in Sharivka, Bohodukhiv county, Kharkiv gubernia, d ? Sculptor; brother of V. *Yemets. An interwar émigré, he graduated from the Berlin Academy of Arts in 1929 and served as an assistant and then a professor there. A postwar refugee in Austria, in 1949 he emigrated to Venezuela. He worked in various media, particularly bronze. He created busts (eg, of H. Skovoroda) and large sculptures, such as *Dying Otaman, Dance, Bath, Sleeping Lion*, and *Mother*, in a classical-realist style.

Vasyl Yemets                    Rostyslav Yendyk

**Yemets, Vasyl** [Jemec', Vasyl'] (Yemetz, Wassyl), b 2 August 1890 in Sharivka, Bohodukhiv county, Kharkiv gubernia, d 6 January 1982 in Los Angeles. Bandura player; singer and teacher. He learned how to play the bandura from blind kobzars living near his family's holdings and started to perform when he entered university in Kharkiv (and later Moscow) in 1911–12. He organized and

directed the first banduryst chorus in Ukraine in Kiev in 1918 and (after emigrating in 1920) an ensemble in Prague. He taught students in Poděbrady. He toured extensively throughout Western Europe, the United States, and Canada, finally residing in Hollywood from 1937. He authored the book *Kobza i kobzari* (The Kobza and Kobza Players, 1923) and wrote articles on the bandura and bandurysts in Ukrainian, Czech, and French. A collection of memoirs, photographs, press clippings, and articles about or in praise of him was published in 1961 as *Vasyl' Iemets': U zolote 50-richchia na sluzhbi Ukraïni* (Vasyl Yemets: On His Golden 50th Anniversary of Serving Ukraine).

**Yemilchyne** [Jemil'čyne]. III-8. A town smt (1985 pop 7,200) on the Ubort River and a raion center in Zhytomyr oblast. It was first mentioned in 1585, as the village of Mezhyrichka, owned by Prince K. *Ostrozky. Until 1793 it was under Polish rule. It was annexed by Russia, and became part of Novohrad-Volynskyi county in Volhynia gubernia. Its current name has been in use since the end of the 19th century. Yemilchyne has a flax-processing factory and some food-processing enterprises.

**Yenakiieve** [Jenakijeve]. V-19, DB III-4. A city (1990 pop 120,000) on the Bulavyn River in Donetske oblast. It was founded in 1883 as a coal-mining town. In 1925 it was granted city status. Today it is one of the largest industrial centers in the Donbas. Besides 10 coal mines it has a large metallurgical plant, a coke-chemicals plant, a cement factory, a pipe plant, light industry, and some food-processing enterprises.

**Yenakiieve Metallurgical Plant** (Yenakiivskyi metalurhiinyi zavod). A large metallurgical plant located in Yenakiieve, in the Donets Basin. It was established by a Russian-Belgian company in 1895 and went into production in 1897. It produced steel, cast iron, and rolled metal and by 1913 was one of the largest metallurgical plants in the Russian Empire. Until 1921 it was called the Petrovskii Plant. It was destroyed during the Second World War and then rebuilt. It continues to produce steel, cast iron, and rolled metal. In the 1970s the plant employed almost 1,700 workers.

**Yendyk, Rostyslav** [Jendyk], b 28 April 1906 in Zaluche, Kolomyia county, Galicia, d 16 February 1974 in Munich. Anthropologist, belletrist, and publicist; full member of the Shevchenko Scientific Society from 1933. He received a PH D in anthropology from Lviv University. As a postwar émigré he was a professor at and rector (1961–74) of the Ukrainian Technical and Husbandry Institute in Munich and a member of the Ukrainian National Council. He wrote books on the anthropological traits of the Ukrainian people (1934) and the racial structure of Ukraine (1949) and numerous other studies in anthropology and demography; a novella about O. Dovbush, *Proklin krovy* (The Curse of Blood, 1934); books about A. Hitler (1934) and D. Dontsov (1955); the poetry collections *Bili nochi* (White Nights, 1936), *Tytan* (Titan, 1948 [long poems]), and *Triolety* (Triolets, 1953); the prose collections *Rehit Aridnyka* (The Devil's Laughter, 1937), *V kaidanakh rasy* (Fettered by Race), *Zov zemli* (Call of the Earth, 1940), and *Zhaha* (Desire, 1957); and a book of nationalist essays, *Slovo do brativ* (A Word to [My] Brothers, 1955).

**Yenina, Vira** [Jenina], b 2 May 1906 in Novotroitske, Berdianske county, Tavriia gubernia, d 26 November 1977 in Kiev. Writer. She graduated from the Kiev Art Institute (1929) and worked for publishing houses in Kharkiv and Kiev. She wrote the novels *Holubyi potik* (The Azure Stream, 1948), *Rozstupylysia hory* (The Mountains Parted, 1951), *Nahoroda* (The Award, 1955), *Nova trembita* (The New *Trembita*, 1955), *Ukraïns'ka kvitka* (A Ukrainian Flower, 1959), *Vyrok vvazhaty umovnym* (Consider the Sentence Conditional, 1962), *Mynule ne mynaie* (The Past Does Not Pass, 1965), and *Istyny rozkryvaiut'sia povoli* (Truths Reveal Themselves Slowly, 1971); three story collections (1958, 1967, 1970); and a book of memoirs about the Second World War (1974).

**Yenkovsky, Avgustyn** [Jenkovs'kyj], b 18 October 1833 in Sachuriv, Transcarpathia, d 1923 in Steblivka, Transcarpathia. Inventor; member of the French Academy of Sciences from 1893. A priest by training, he completed theological studies in Uzhhorod and served as a priest in Mukachiv eparchy. In the 1860s he invented a machine for reaping and binding sheaves. He took it to Kostroma in 1873 for manufacturing, but the factory could not fulfill his technical requirements. Yenkovsky had insufficient funds to patent his device; a nearly identical reaping machine was produced soon afterward by the McCormick Company in the United States. The prototype of Yenkovsky's steamship, submitted for patenting in Berlin in 1896, is in the Berlin Patent Museum. He also invented a regulated weaving loom.

**Yeremenko, Terentii** [Jeremenko, Terentij], b 21 April 1902 in Novovelychkivska stanytsia, near Katerynodar, Kuban oblast. Specialist in petroleum and natural gas and doctor of technology. He studied at the Don Polytechnical Institute. He taught at the Lviv Polytechnical Institute (1945–63) and worked at the Ukrainian Scientific Research and Planning Institute of the Petroleum Industry in Kiev. His main contributions are in the area of pipelines for petroleum and natural gas drilling and exploration.

**Yeremenko, Valentyn** [Jeremenko], b 12 August 1911 in Kreminna, Kupianka county, Kharkiv gubernia, d 31 October 1992. Physical chemist and material scientist; AN URSR (now ANU) full member since 1969. A graduate of Kharkiv University (1936), he taught there (1939–41) and at Kiev University (from 1944) and worked at the ANU institutes of Ferrous Metallurgy (1940–53), Metalloceramics and Special Alloys (1953–60), and Problems of Material Science (1960–5). He developed theories on the wetting of solids (metals, alloys, oxides, carbides, borides) by molten metals, studied the surface properties of pure metals and binary alloys (including titanium) at various temperatures, constructed phase diagrams of binary and ternary metallic systems, and made contributions to chemical thermodynamics and heterogeneous equilibria.

**Yeremenko, Vasyl** [Jeremenko, Vasyl'], b 16 December 1919 in Dmytrivka, Oleksandriia county, Kherson gubernia. Scenery designer. In 1944 he joined the Kirovohrad Ukrainian Music and Drama Theater, and in 1966 he became its principal designer, noted for his brightly colored scenery.

**Yeremenko, Viktor** [Jeremenko] (Eremenko), b 26 July 1932 in Kharkiv. Experimental solid-state physicist; AN URSR (now ANU) full member since 1978. After graduating from Kharkiv University (1955) he worked at the ANU Institute of Physics in Kiev. In 1961 he returned to Kharkiv to head the magneto-optical research department at the ANU Physical-Technical Institute of Low Temperatures. Yeremenko discovered and investigated exciton and exciton-magnon processes in antiferromagnetic crystals, light dispersion on parametric spin waves in nonlinear antiferromagnetic resonance, and the linear dependence on the magnetic-field strength of the double diffraction of light (a codiscovery). He is a leading authority on the interaction of electromagnetic waves with magneto-ordered crystals.

**Yeremiichuk-Yeremiiv, Denys** [Jeremijčuk-Jeremijiv], b 27 January 1866 in Novi Mamaivtsi (now Novosilka), Bukovyna, d ? Church activist and professor of theology. He graduated in theology from Chernivtsi University in 1890 and was ordained a priest the same year. He taught theology at a gymnasium in Chernivtsi before becoming a professor of pastoral theology at Chernivtsi University (1899–1936); there he taught his subject in Ukrainian until the 1920s and in Rumanian thereafter. He headed the Association of Ukrainian Orthodox Priests in Bukovyna and, with Ye. Vorobkevych, wrote a number of religious textbooks for primary schools.

Mykhailo Yeremiiv

**Yeremiiv, Mykhailo** [Jeremijiv, Myxajlo], b 7 February 1889 in Novoselytsia, Zhytomyr county, Volhynia gubernia, d 16 September 1975 in Geneva. Journalist and civic leader. As a student at the Kiev Polytechnic Institute he was twice arrested for his Ukrainian activities. In April 1917 he became a student representative to the Central Rada and then a member of its executive committee (representing the Ukrainian Social Democratic Workers' party [USDRP]) and secretary to the Central Rada (1917–18). He was editor in chief of \**Visty z Ukraïns'koï Tsentral'noï Rady* (1917–18) in Kiev and a board member of the USDRP's daily newspaper *Robitnycha hazeta* (1917–19). An opponent of the Hetman government in 1918, he was assigned in 1919 by the UNR Directory as secretary of the UNR mission in Rome, where he edited *La Voce del Ucraïna* (1919–20).

From 1920 Yeremiiv lived abroad: in Vienna, where he wrote for the journal *Volia*; in Prague; in Poděbrady, where he lectured at the Ukrainian Husbandry Academy (1924–6); and, from 1926, in Paris, where he was a professional journalist and worked with the \*Promethean movement. In 1928 he founded the \*Ofinor press agency, of which he was director and editor in chief (1928–44). Because of Soviet diplomatic pressure he was forced to leave France in 1936. He emigrated to Geneva, where the head office of Ofinor was relocated. During the Second World War he founded a Ukrainian refugee aid committee, which was subsequently named Comité Suisse d'Aide aux Réfugiés Ukrainiens. Even in his later years Yeremiiv continued to work with Ukrainian and non-Ukrainian newspapers and published many informational pamphlets on nationalities issues in the USSR, the 1917 Revolution, and Bolshevism.

A. Zhukovsky

Vasyl Yermakov

Vasyl Yeroshenko

**Yermakov, Vasyl** [Jermakov, Vasyl'] (Ermakov, Vasilii), b 11 March 1845 in Tserukha, Mahiliou gubernia, Belarus, d 16 March 1922 in Kiev. Ukrainian mathematician; corresponding member of the St Petersburg Academy of Science from 1884. He graduated from Kiev University in 1868 and taught there and at the Kiev Polytechnical Institute (from 1899). His contributions are in the fields of analysis, differential equations, mechanics, and the theory of functions.

**Yermilov, Vasyl** [Jermilov, Vasyl'] (Ermilov, Vasilii), b 22 March 1894 in Kharkiv, d 4 December 1967 in Kharkiv. Painter and graphic designer. He studied at the Art Trade School Workshop of Decorative Painting in Kharkiv (1905–9), the Kharkiv Art School (1910–11), and the Moscow School of Painting, Sculpture, and Architecture (1912–13). In 1918 he joined the avant-garde Union of Seven group in Kharkiv and designed the script for its album *Sem' plius tri* (Seven Plus Three, 1918). Under Soviet rule Yermilov designed posters, 'agit-trains,' street decorations, billboards, the interiors of public buildings (eg, the murals in the foyer of the Kharkiv Circus and the Red Army Club in Kharkiv), theatrical sets, displays, packaging, and journal and book covers; he also directed the art department of the All-Ukrainian Bureau of the Russian Telegraph Agency (1920–1) and taught at the Kharkiv Art Tekhnikum (1921–2) and Kharkiv Art Institute (1922–35). He received several international prizes for his graphic designs, including a gold medal at the 1922 Leipzig International Graphics Exhibition and an award at the 1928 Köln International Press Exhibition. While a member of the *Avanhard group (1926–9) he was graphic designer of its newspaper *Doba konstruktsiï*, its journal *Mystets'ki materiialy Avanhardu*, and, with V. *Polishchuk, the three issues of *Biuleten' Avanhardu*. From 1927 he was also a

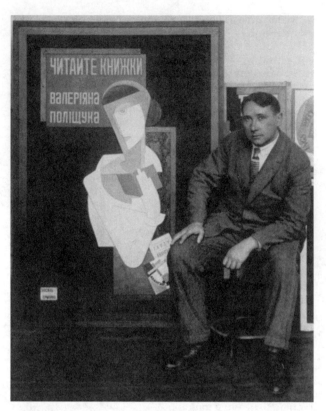

Vasyl Yermilov and one of his designs

member of the *Association of Revolutionary Art of Ukraine. Yermilov's synthesis of formalist esthetics, folk designs, and traditional painting methods (including egg tempera) was an important contribution to the development of Ukrainian design of the 1920s. His distinctive style of constructivist collage and typographic design, called constructive-dynamism or spiralism, developed distinctly and in parallel with Russian constructivism. Because of his formalist interests Yermilov was forced out of the Soviet art arena in the late 1930s. In the last years of his life he again taught at the Kharkiv Art Institute (1963–7). A book about him by Z. Fogel was published in Moscow in 1975.

N. Mykytyn

**Yermoliev, Yurii** [Jermol'jev, Jurij] (Ermolev), b 3 February 1936 in Karachev, Briansk oblast, Russia. Mathematician and cyberneticist; corresponding member of the AN URSR (now ANU) since 1976. Since completing his studies at Kiev University in 1959, he has worked at the Computing Center and the Institute of Cybernetics of the ANU in Kiev. He has contributed to the theory of graphs, optimal control of deterministic and stochastic systems, and stochastic programming.

**Yerofeiv, Ivan** [Jerofejiv], b 8 October 1882 in Andrushivka, Berdychiv county, Kiev gubernia, d 27 November 1953 in Vorzel, near Irpin, Kiev oblast. Writer, literary scholar, historian, and ethnographer. A graduate of Kiev University (1907), he lectured at higher educational institutions in Kiev and Kharkiv and worked in the 1920s as a research associate of the Department of the History of Ukrainian Culture at the All-Ukrainian Academy of Sciences. He was repressed in the 1930s, and resumed his scholarly activities in the 1940s. He wrote a book on the dumas (1910), articles on N. Gogol, H. Skovoroda, and T. Shevchenko, and the novel *Oleksa Dovbush* (1945); and compiled, with Ye. Cherkaska, a collection of documents on U. Karmaliuk.

**Yeroshenko, Vasyl** [Jerošenko, Vasyl'], b 13 January 1890 in Obukhivka, Belgorod county, Kursk gubernia, d 23 December 1952 in Obukhivka. Writer, poet, and pedagogue, whose works were written in Japanese and Esperanto. He was blinded at the age of four. He completed studies at a Moscow school for the blind (1908) and later studied at the Royal College for the Blind in Norwood, England. Through his studies Yeroshenko mastered English, Esperanto, French, German, Russian, and Swedish. In 1914 he was sent to Japan by the Russian Esperanto Society to teach Esperanto at Tokyo University. There he mastered Japanese and began to publish his verses, stories, and plays in the Japanese press. He traveled extensively in the Far East and taught Esperanto in Shanghai (1921) and Beijing (1922), and from 1923 he taught Japanese and other Oriental languages at the Communist University of the Workers of the East in Moscow. During the Stalinist terror he was arrested in 1929; he was imprisoned for 5 years in the Chukhotka labor camp and for another 11 years in Turkmenistan, and was released in 1945. He was reimprisoned for his refusal to work as a translator for the NKVD and was not released until 1951. He died soon afterward of cancer. Three collections of his works were published in Japan in the 1920s, and a three-volume collection was published there in 1959 (repr 1961). A volume of his works in Ukrainian translation was published under the title *Kvitka spravedlyvosti* (Flower of Justice, 1969). Biographical novels about Yeroshenko have been written by I. Takasugi in Japanese (1982) and by A. Kharkovsky in Russian (1978).

**Yeroshevych, Petro** [Jeroševyč], b 1870, d 1945. Senior army officer. A regular officer in the Russian army, by 1917 he commanded, at the rank of major general, the Ninth Russian Army Corps on the Russian southwestern front. He completely Ukrainianized his corps, but the Central Rada government ordered it demobilized. In August 1919 in the Kiev offensive, he commanded a two-division group. He was deputy defense minister in the UNR government and inspector-general of the UNR Army. From 1921 he lived in Poland, until he was arrested by the NKVD in 1945. His recollections of the wars for Ukrainian independence were published in *Za derzhavnist'*, vols 8 and 9 (1938, 1939).

**Yershov, Anatolii** [Jeršov, Anatolij], b 10 January 1899 in Tolkachevka, Lgov county, Kursk gubernia, Russia, d ? Historian and numismatist. In the 1920s he taught at the Nizhen Institute of People's Education and was an associate of the Kharkiv Institute of the History of Ukrainian Culture. His articles on guilds and currency in 17th- and 18th-century Left-Bank Ukraine and on the historiography of several Cossack chronicles appeared in the *Zapysky* collections of the Nizhen institute, the Shevchenko Scientific Society, and the Historical-Philological Division of the VUAN. He disappeared during the Stalinist terror of the 1930s.

**Yershova, Yevheniia** [Jeršova, Jevhenija], b 25 December 1925 in Smila (now in Cherkasy oblast). Ballerina. She studied at the Kiev Choreography School. In 1944–65 she was a soloist in the Kiev Theater of Opera and Ballet, where she danced leading roles in H. Zhukovsky's *Rostyslava*, K. Dankevych's *The Lily*, and M. Skorulsky's *The Forest Song*.

**Yerzhykovsky, Serhii** [Jeržykovs'kyj, Serhij], b 23 March 1895 in Vilnius, d 15 December 1989 in Kiev. Painter. He graduated from the Kiev State Art Institute (1928), where he studied under F. Krychevsky, and taught there for many years (1935–69). His works include *Love* (1934), *Artillerymen at Stalingrad* (1945), the portraits *Tetianka* (1965) and *O. Shovkunenko* (1970), wartime caricatures and drawings (1941–4), and landscapes (eg, *Morning on the Dnieper*, 1957). An album of his works came out in 1977.

**Yeselson, Boris** [Jesel'son], b 8 May 1917 in Mariiupil. Experimental low-temperature physicist. A graduate of Kharkiv University (1939), from 1938 he worked at the AN URSR (now ANU) Physical-Technical Institute in Kharkiv. In 1963 he became a department head at the ANU Physical-Technical Institute of Low Temperatures in Kharkiv. Yeselson has investigated the temperature dependence of quantum fluids and quantum crystals, and codiscovered quantum diffusion in solid helium. He has also contributed to the improvement of cryotechnology.

**Yeshchenko, Vadym** [Ješčenko], 1878–? Engineer. A member of the Ukrainian Party of Socialists-Independentists, he was head of railway transportation in eastern Ukraine, general secretary of roads in the General Secretariat of the Central Rada (1917–18), deputy minister of roads under the Hetman government, and director of the UNR Ministry of Roads (1918).

**Yevdokymov, Mykola** [Jevdokymov] (Evdokimov, Nikolai), b 7 April 1868 in Kharkiv, d 5 April 1940 in Kharkiv. Astronomer. A graduate of Kharkiv University (1890), he worked at the Kharkiv Astronomical Observatory from 1893 and was its director from 1917 to 1930. From 1914 he was also a professor at Kharkiv University. His main contributions were in measuring parallaxes of celestial objects and in developing instrumentation for such measurements. In 1935 he headed the effort in Kharkiv to establish a Unified Time Service. Yevdokymov wrote a practical astronomy handbook and a series of popular-science books.

**Yevfrosyniia Mstyslavna** [Jevfrosynija], b and d ? Rus' princess; granddaughter of Volodymyr Monomakh. She married King Géza II of Hungary ca 1145, thereby cementing an alliance that provided Hungarian support for her brother, Iziaslav Mstyslavych, in his campaign against Volodymyrko of Galicia.

**Yevmynka settlement.** A Trypilian settlement of the mid-3rd millennium BC near Yevmynka, Kozelets raion, Chernihiv oblast. Excavations in 1925–6 and 1965 uncovered a pit dwelling with a hearth in a corner, flint, stone, and bone tools, and fragments of ornamented pottery painted black and red.

The entrance to an arcade complex built in Yevpatoriia in the 19th century

**Yevpatoriia** [Jevpatorija]. VIII-14. A city (1990 pop 109,000) and port on the coast of the Black Sea in the Crimea. In the 6th and 5th centuries BC the Greek colony of *Kerkinitidis stood at the site. In the 2nd century BC it was captured by the Scythians. At the end of the 15th century the Turks built a fortified town there. Called Hezlev (Kozlov in Russian), it developed into a trading center and became the target of Zaporozhian raids (1588, 1675). After Russia's annexation of the Crimea the town was renamed Yevpatoriia, and a port was constructed. In the 19th century the town exported grain and farm products and manufactured salt. It has been an important resort, transportation, and manufacturing center. Almost 60 percent of its residents are employed in over 100 sanatoriums, rest homes, and recreational resorts in the vicinity. Sunbathing, mud baths (Mainak Lake), and hot saltwater baths are used to treat bone tuberculosis, rheumatism, respiratory ailments, and skin diseases. There are metalworking, food-processing, textile, and furniture plants in the city. A mosque built in 1552 has been preserved.

**Yevpraksiia Mstyslavna** [Jevpraksija], 1108–72. Rus' princess; granddaughter of Volodymyr Monomakh. She was renowned for her study of medicine, which she undertook from an early age. For applying her knowledge of anatomy, hygiene, diagnosis, and therapy among the nobility as well as the peasantry, she was given the appellation 'Dobrodiia' (Benevolent). She prepared the first medical text written in Rus', titled *Mazi* (Ointments), on the basis of information compiled from many sources. The work was all the more notable because it avoided ritualistic medical practices and superstitions that were common at that time, and instead relied on techniques of folk medicine and early principles of pharmacology. In 1122 Yevpraksiia married the Byzantine prince Alexius, son of John II Comnenus.

**Yevpraksiia Vsevolodivna** [Jevpraksija] (Prakseda, also Adelheid or Adelaïde), b 1071 in Kiev, d 9 June 1109 in Kiev. Daughter of the Kievan prince Vsevolod Yaroslavych; sister of Volodymyr Monomakh. She was the wife of Henry the Tall of Northern Saxony, and after he died she married the German emperor Henry IV in Köln in 1089. He treated Yevpraksiia with extreme brutality. In 1090, during a campaign in Italy, he had her imprisoned in Verona. In 1093 she escaped to Canossa (northern Italy),

to her husband's foes, Conrad and Mathilde of Tuscany. Through their intercession, she obtained the protection of Pope Urban II. In 1095 she publicly denounced Henry at the councils of Constanza and Piacenza for his immorality and depravity; he was anathematized and eventually forced to abdicate. Yevpraksiia returned through Hungary to Ukraine (1096) and entered a convent in Kiev (1106). She was buried in the Kievan Cave Monastery. Her biography inspired a wealth of literature, including P. Zahrebelny's novel *Ievpraksiia* (1975), which appeared in French translation as *Eupraxie: Princesse kiévienne* (1984). Most German historians condemn her conduct because it was exploited by Henry's enemies.

BIBLIOGRAPHY
Richter, G. *Annalen der deutschen Geschichte*, vol 2 (Halle 1898)
Ediger, T. *Russlands älteste Beziehungen zu Deutschland, Frankreich und der römischen Kurie* (Halle 1911)
Joukovsky, A. *La Rus' kiévienne et l'Occident aux X-ème–début XIII-ème siècles* (Paris 1983)

A. Zhukovsky

Mykola Yevshan

**Yevshan, Mykola** [Jevšan] (né Fediushka; other pseuds: Lebedyk, Yavir), b 19 May 1890 in Voinyliv, Kalush county, Galicia, d 23 November 1919 in Vinnytsia. Literary critic. Yevshan studied German and Ukrainian at Lviv University and supported his studies by employment in the Shevchenko Scientific Society's [NTSh] library, as the society's secretary and as personal secretary of M. *Hrushevsky. After being expelled from Lviv University for political reasons he continued his studies at the University of Vienna. His scholarly career was interrupted by the First World War. He served in the Ukrainian Galician Army and died from typhus during the Ukrainian-Polish War.

Yevshan began his critical writings very early and soon was a regular contributor to *Ukraïns'ka khata* and to *Literaturno-naukovyi vistnyk*, of which he became a coeditor. His critique of I. Franko in *Bdzhola* (1908) brought him notoriety, but it was his insistence on the esthetic values of literature that made him appear on the side of the nascent 'modernist' tendencies and in opposition to the populism of the established literary masters. Although accused of propagating 'art for art's sake,' Yevshan was a follower of the esthetic philosophy of J.-M. Guyau as espoused in Guyau's *Les problèmes de l'esthétique contemporaine* (1884, translated into Ukrainian in 1913). In his major critical work, *Pid praporom mystetstva* (Under the Flag of Art, 1910), Yevshan follows Guyau in stressing that humans possess a creative altruistic life force, and that to create the beautiful and the ennobling is their need and imperative. Yevshan thus denigrates literary writing without esthetic values to the level of publicistic pamphlets and praises authors, such as V. Stefanyk, in whose writings he sees the true merging of social purpose and esthetic form. Yevshan's other critical writings were few; they consisted of various articles in journals as well as the more substantive pamphlet *Kudy my pryishly* (To Where We Have Come, 1912) and a monograph on T. Shevchenko (1911).

D.H. Struk

**Yevsuh River** [Jevsuh] (also Yevsiuh). A left-bank tributary of the Donets River that flows southward for 82 km from a source in the Central Upland through Luhanske oblast and drains a basin area of 1,190 sq km. It has a water reservoir and is used for irrigation.

**Yevtymii** [Jevtymij]. Bishop of Chernihiv in the 15th century. As the only Ukrainian bishop not to recognize the authority as metropolitan of Kiev of Hryhorii II Bolharyn, who had been nominated by Pope Callistus III and confirmed by the pro-Union patriarch of Constantinople Gregory Mammas, he was forced to flee from his eparchy to Muscovy in order to escape persecution.

**Yevtymiia Volodymyrivna** [Jevtymija] (Yevfymiia), b ?, d 4 April 1139. Rus' princess; daughter of Volodymyr Monomakh. She was married to the Hungarian king Kálmán in 1112 in a bid to strengthen Rus'-Hungarian diplomatic relations, but was sent back to Kiev in 1113. Their son, Borys, was not recognized by Kálmán as an heir to the Hungarian throne. Nevertheless Borys pursued the title over a long period of time after he came of age.

**Yevtymovych, Varfolomii** [Jevtymovyč, Varfolomij], b 28 August 1888 in Perehonivka, Vasylkiv county, Kiev gubernia, d 8 February 1950 in Mittenwald, Germany. Military figure. A lieutenant colonel in the UNR Army, in early 1918 he commanded a company of Free Cossacks in the defense of Kiev. Later he served as a staff officer in the Zaporozhian Corps of the UNR Army. As an interwar émigré he was active in the hetmanite movement, and he published a book of recollections (1937) and articles about the 1917–20 revolutionary period in Galician and émigré periodicals. During the Second World War he was in charge of the *Military Board of the Division Galizien.

**Yew, English** (*Taxus baccata*; Ukrainian: *tys yahidnyi, nehnii-derevo*). An ornamental evergreen, a shrub or tree of the family Taxaceae. The yew is a slow-growing tree that is long-lived, tall (reaching heights of 20–30 m), and rot resistant. The foliage and seeds contain a toxic alkaloid that can harm some animals, especially horses. In Ukraine the English yew grows in the Carpathian and Crimean mountains. One of the oldest representatives of Ukrainian flora, it is slowly disappearing and is at present under state protection. Its hard, fine-grained, lustrous, reddish wood is valued in cabinetmaking and underwater construction.

**Yezhov terror** (*yezhovshchyna*). The mass repressions in the Soviet Union in 1937–8 conducted by N. Yezhov (b 1895, d 1939?) as commissar of internal affairs (head of the NKVD). The reasons for the mass terror have never been fully explained. It began with a resolution of the CC of the All-Russian Communist Party (Bolshevik) in March 1937 calling for wider repressions. According to N. Khrushchev, in the course of 1937 the number of arrests increased tenfold compared to 1936. Testimony and evidence about the subversive activities of the detainees and the existence of various underground and intelligence organizations were fabricated by the secret police. Bolshevik leaders, such as G. Piatakov, K. Radek, N. Bukharin, and A. Rykov, were tried and executed. A group of military officers, including Marshal M. Tukhachevsky, were shot. Throughout the USSR about 300,000 people were executed, and 3,500,000 deported to concentration camps.

In Ukraine 162,000 members of the CP(B)U, representing 35 percent of its total, disappeared during the Yezhov terror. About 98 percent of the Party's Central Committee and Ukraine's government and 80 percent of the oblast committees of the party and the oblast executive committees of the oblast soviets were arrested. The ranks of lecturers in higher educational institutions, teachers, physicians, agronomists, engineers, and technicians were decimated. Prominent Party and government officials in Ukraine, such as P. Postyshev, S. Kosior, V. Zatonsky, M. Popov, O. Shlikhter, A. Khvylia, and V. Balitsky, vanished. H. Hrynko, I. Dubovy, and Y. Yakir were executed. P. Liubchenko, the prime minister of Ukraine, committed suicide. The academicians M. Kravchuk and Ye. Oppokiv were sent to labor camps. Writers such as I. Mykytenko, I. Kulyk, B. Kovalenko, I. Kyrylenko, and M. Filiansky disappeared without a trace.

**Yezupil.** See Zhovten.

**Yiddish.** A language based primarily on several Middle High German dialects with significant influences from Hebrew, Aramaic, and Romance and Slavic languages. It is written using a slightly modified Hebrew alphabet. The Yiddish spoken by Jews living in Ukrainian ethnolinguistic territory is clearly distinguished from the northeastern dialect (characteristic of Belarus, Lithuania, and Latvia) and the central dialect (characteristic of Poland and west Galicia).

Often referred to as the southeast dialect, Ukrainian Yiddish is profoundly marked by the influence of the Ukrainian language. In terms of grammar, for example, Yiddish shows evidence of a form of the Ukrainian aspect, which is absent from Middle High German (*ikh hob geshribn* 'I have written' versus *ikh hob ongeshribn* 'I have completed writing'). Yiddish also has absorbed a multitude of Ukrainian conjunctions, prepositions, and adverbs, such as *i ... i, take, nu* 'both ... and, indeed, well'. The rich variety of Ukrainian diminutives was adapted to Jewish names (eg, *Moyshenyu, Khayimke,* diminutive of *Moyshe* and *Khayim*), and Ukrainian names were sometimes given to Jewish children, particularly girls (eg, *Badane,* from *Bohdana*). The Yiddish vocabulary has also been enriched by countless Ukrainian words, such as *khrayn* (from *xrin,* 'horseradish'), *zayde* (from *did,* 'grandfather'), and *nudnik* (from *nudnyj,* 'boring'). Although several attempts have been made to classify the areas of human activity in which Ukrainian words penetrated Yiddish, the influence extended perhaps too widely to allow such classification, from the profane (*paskudne,* from *paskudnyj* 'loathsome') to the sacred (*praven,* from *pravyty* 'to perform [a religious ceremony]').

The flowering of Yiddish literature in Ukraine is exemplified by one of the greatest writers in this language, *Sholom Aleichem (1859–1916). He legitimized the Ukrainian dialect by writing almost exclusively in that medium. The years he spent in the townlet of Voronkiv have been immortalized in his characters of the fictional Kasrilevke in *Fiddler on the Roof*.

With the establishment of Soviet Ukraine, Yiddish was made the official language of the Jewish proletariat to the exclusion of the classical Jewish language, Hebrew. A Yiddish press and theater briefly flourished in the 1920s, but the alphabet was 'modernized' by the removal of terminal forms of five letters, and great effort was expended to remove all Hebrew and Aramaic 'bourgeois' influences from Yiddish. Beginning in the 1930s, Yiddish was increasingly proscribed by Soviet authorities. With the loss of hundreds of thousands of Ukrainian Jews in the Holocaust, and the postwar harassment of Yiddish writers, Ukrainian Jewry turned increasingly to Ukrainian and Russian as vernacular languages. As a direct result of the most recent changes, a handbook of Yiddish (including rudiments of morphology, an anthology of literary work, short biographies of famous authors, and a brief history of Jews in Ukraine) was published in Kiev in 1991.

BIBLIOGRAPHY
Swoboda, V. 'Ukrainian in the Slavic Element of Yiddish Vocabulary,' *HUS*, 3–4 (1979–80)
Weinreich, M. *History of the Yiddish Language*, trans S. Noble (Chicago 1980)
Liptzin, S. *A History of Yiddish Literature* (New York 1985)
H. Abramson

**Yoffe, Abram** [Joffe], b 29 October 1880 in Romen, Poltava gubernia, d 14 October 1960 in Leningrad. Physicist; full member of the USSR Academy of Sciences from 1929 and the Shevchenko Scientific Society from 1929. A graduate of the St Petersburg Technological Institute (1902) and Munich University (doctorate, 1905), he was a physics professor at the St Petersburg (later Leningrad) Polytechnical Institute (1913–48) and the Crimean University in Symferopil (1918–25). He was also director of the Physical-Technical Institute (1944–51) and Institute of Semiconductors (1955–60) of the USSR Academy of Sciences. As early as 1931 he recognized the role of electrons in semiconductors and laid the foundation for the technology of thermoelectric cooling devices and thermoelectric generators. It was on Yoffe's initiative and with his direct involvement that physical-technical institutes were established in Kharkiv (1928) and Dnipropetrovske (1933). Yoffe's monographs published in English translation include *The Physics of Crystals* (1955–60), *Semiconductor Thermoelements and Thermoelectric Cooling* (1957), and *Physics of Semiconductors* (1960).

**Yohansen, Maik** [Johansen, Majk] (Mykhailo) (pseuds: V. Vetselius, M. Kramar), b 5 November 1895 in Kharkiv, d 27 October 1937 in Kiev. Poet, prose writer, screenwriter, translator, literary theorist, and linguist. He wrote in Russian until 1917, and wrote only in Ukrainian after 1919. He belonged to the writers' organizations Hart and *Vaplite. His collections of poetry include *D'hori* (To the Pinnacle, 1921), *Revoliutsiia* (The Revolution, 1923), *Proloh do komuny* (Prologue to the Commune, 1924), *Krokoveie kolo* (The Dancing Circle, 1923), *Dorobok* (The Gain, 1924), *Iasen* (The Ash, 1930), and *Poezii* (Poems, 1933). He wrote

Maik Yohansen

interesting experimental prose, using the technique of *uchudnennia*, that is, of making the ordinary appear strange or miraculous, and rendering his subject with a humorous edge. His collections of stories include *17 khvylyn* (Seventeen Minutes, 1925), *Podorozh doktora Leonardo po Slobozhans'kii Shvaitsarii* (Doctor Leonardo's Travels through the Switzerland of Slobidska Ukraine, 1928), and *Podorozh liudyny pid kepom* (The Journey of a Man under a Cap, 1932). His works in literary theory include *Elementarni zakony versyfikatsii* (Elementary Rules of Versification, 1922) and *Iak buduvaty opovidannia* (How to Construct a Story, 1926).

Yohansen studied linguistics under L. Bulakhovsky and A. Syniavsky and wrote studies on phonetics (descriptions of literary and dialectal Ukrainian pronunciation, particularly of the Shyshaky and Myrhorod regions) and on the compilation of dictionaries. He compiled a Russian-Ukrainian dictionary with M. Nakonechny, K. Nimchynov, and B. Tkachenko (1926) and a Russian-Ukrainian dictionary of folk sayings with Mlodzinsky. He participated in the creation of a standard *orthography in 1928 and worked on a project for the Latinization of Ukrainian script. He was arrested during the Yezhov terror and was sentenced to death by firing squad. He was posthumously rehabilitated.

I. Koshelivets

**Yonker, Anna** [Jonker] (née Huminilovych), b 25 December 1888 in Kalush, Galicia, d 6 May 1936 in Winnipeg. Community figure and patron of Ukrainian organizations. After emigrating to Canada early in the century, she lived in Winnipeg. There she organized relief for war victims in Galicia as a member of the Central Committee of the Ukrainian Red Cross Society of Canada. She also made generous donations to the Mohyla Ukrainian Institute, the Ukrainian Red Cross, and various cultural groups in Winnipeg and was the leading figure in an independent women's hromada in Winnipeg.

**Yorkton.** A city (1981 pop 15,000) in southeastern Saskatchewan, founded in 1882. The first Ukrainian colony of 51 families was established in the area in 1897. As the heavy influx of immigrants continued, Ukrainians began to constitute a majority of the local population. In 1904 a group of Belgian *Redemptorist Fathers led by Rev A. Delaere came to serve the Ukrainian community in Yorkton. They built a monastery (1913) and St Mary's Church

The Ukrainian Catholic Church of Our Lady of Perpetual Help (1914; enlarged 1954–5) in Yorkton

(1914) and set up a minor and major seminary and a printing press at the monastery. Besides books the Redemptorists published a monthly magazine, *Holos spasytelia*, and a theological quarterly, *Lohos*. Until 1957 Yorkton was the provincial house of the Ukrainian Redemptorist order. The Ukrainian Orthodox parish of the Holy Transfiguration (est 1920) hosted, in 1924, the Fourth Sobor of the Ukrainian Greek Orthodox Church of Canada. Two Catholic boarding schools (eventually high schools) were founded by Bishop N. Budka, the Sacred Heart Institute (est 1916, renamed Academy in 1945) for girls, run by the *Sisters Servants of Mary Immaculate, and St Joseph's College (1920–72) for boys. In the 1980s a Ukrainian cultural center was built by the Catholic community.

**Yorysh, Volodymyr** [Joryš], b 25 November 1899 in Katerynoslav, d 21 June 1945 in Kiev. Composer and conductor. He was educated in Katerynoslav, where he graduated in piano (1917) from the music school and in conducting and composition (1917–24) from the music tekhnikum. In 1928–34 he conducted opera theaters in the city and from 1934 the Kiev Theater of Opera and Ballet. Among his works are four operas, including *Karmeliuk* (1930) and *Poem about Steel* (1932); the ballet *The Devil's Night* (1943); *Ukrainian Bazaar* for symphony orchestra; and a string quartet. He was also the author of unsuccessful and unstylish remakes of M. Lysenko's *Natalka from Poltava* and S. Hulak-Artemovsky's *Zaporozhian Cossack beyond the Danube*.

**Yosyfovych, Dmytro** [Josyfovyč] (pseuds: O[rest] D[ubensky], Or. D-b, Vasyl R[ilenko]), b 6 November 1867 in Novi Skomorokhy, Rohatyn county, d 28 November 1939 in Khitar, Stryi county, Galicia. Writer. From 1888 on he contributed poems and stories to Western Ukrainian periodicals, such as *Zoria*, *Dilo*, *Dzvinok*, *Bukovyna*, *Literaturno-naukovyi vistnyk*, and *Nedilia*. He translated into Ukrainian J.W. von Goethe's *Iphigenie auf Tauris* (1895), ballads by F. von Schiller, and stories by V. Korolenko and G. Danilevsky.

**Young naturalists** (*iuni naturalisty* or *iunaty*). Young students, 10 to 15 years of age, who participated in an organized extramural program that deepened their knowl-

edge of the life sciences and developed their farming skills. The movement dates back to 1918, when the first groups of Nature's Friends arose. Members were organized into groups, societies, or clubs linked with schools, Pioneer palaces, or agricultural teaching institutions. *Stations of young naturalists played an important role in the movement. The activities of the groups consisted of experiments and practical projects conducted in laboratories, or on experimental plots or farms under the supervision of biology teachers, scientists, and agricultural specialists. Exceptional young naturalists took part in agricultural exhibitions, and the Exhibition of Economic Achievements of the USSR in Moscow maintained a permanent young naturalist pavilion. In the early 1960s the Union-wide movement had a membership of about two million students, organized in close to 60,000 groups. In Ukraine there were about 600,000 members, in 25,000 groups. The magazine *Iunyi naturalist* was published in Russian for members of the movement.

**Young spectator's theater** (*teatr yunoho hliadacha*). The official Soviet designation for a professional drama theater that performed for children and youth.

In Ukraine at the end of the 19th century, amateur and professional theaters staged productions for children, among them M. Lysenko's children's operas *Koza dereza* (Billy Goat's Bluff, 1888), *Pan Kots'kyi* (Sir Catsky, 1891), and *Zyma i vesna* (Winter and Spring, 1892) and M. Kropyvnytsky and K. Stetsenko's rhymed folktale plays *Lysychka, kotyk, i pivnyk* (The Vixen, Cat, and Rooster), *Po shchuchomu velinniu* (At the Pike's Behest), and *Ivasyk Telesyk* (all in 1906–7). The UNR government created a Commission for the Organization of Children's Theaters. The first Ukrainian professional children's theater existed in Kiev in 1918–19, but its activities were limited.

After the establishment of Soviet rule the first children's theaters in the USSR were in Petrograd, Saratov, Katerynodar, and Kiev. Children's theaters in Ukraine were founded in Kharkiv (1920, since 1945 the *Lviv Young Spectator's Theater), Kiev (1924, today the *Kiev Young Spectator's Theater), Dnipropetrovske (the Pioneer Pedagogical Children's Theater, 1927–39), Mykolaiv (1927, today the *Mykolaiv Ukrainian Theater of Drama and Musical Comedy), Odessa (1931, today the *Odessa Young Spectator's Theater), and Luhanske (the Donets Young Spectator's Theater, 1931–9; since 1945 the Kirovohrad Russian Drama Theater). Their repertoire consisted largely of dramatizations of stories and folktales. The first Soviet plays for children appeared in the late 1920s, written by authors such as O. Biletsky, I. Kocherha, S. Vasylchenko, O. Kopylenko, A. Shyian, and P. Voronka.

The programming of young spectator's theaters was controlled by the Moscow Central Children's Theater and integrated with the Soviet educational system and the Komsomol. Productions are geared to the age-group of the audience: preschool children attend dramatizations of children's stories and fairy tales, such as C. Perrault's *Puss 'n Boots* and *Little Red Riding Hood*, H.C. Andersen's *The Nightingale*, A. Biletsky's *Khubeana*, and D. Shkliar's *Bula i Yula*; primary schoolchildren attend adventure, historical, and biographical plays, such as V. Sukhodolsky's *Taras's Youth*, E. Shvarts's *The Dragon*, A. Yakovlev's *Pioneer Pavlik Morozov*, and A. Shyian's *Flying Ship*; and secondary-school students attend plays from the Soviet repertoire and world and Ukrainian classics, including O. Kobylianska's *Zemlia* (The Land), I. Kocherha's *The Black Waltz*, F. Schiller's *Wilhelm Tell*, and H.B. Stowe's *Uncle Tom's Cabin*. After the Second World War an emphasis was placed on 'ideological' plays about heroic fighting, the friendship of nations, or young people working in commerce and scholarship.

Additional young spectator's theaters appeared in Ukraine – the *Kharkiv Young Spectator's Theater (est 1960), the Dnipropetrovske Young Spectator's Theater (est 1963), the Donetske Oblast Russian Young Spectator's Theater (est 1971 in Makiivka), the *Zaporizhia Young Spectator's Theater (est 1979), and the Sumy Theater for Children and Youth (est 1981). In 1987 there were nine young spectator's theaters in Ukraine (13 in 1964). As theatrical entertainment for children, they have been less popular than *puppet theaters.

V. Revutsky

**Young Ukrainian Nationalists** (Molodi ukrainski natsionalisty, or MUN; also known as Molod ODVU, or Ukrainian American Youth for the Rebirth of Ukraine). A national youth association in the United States affiliated with the *Organization for the Rebirth for Ukraine (ODVU) and embracing the ideology of the OUN. It was founded in 1933 as a means of involving American-born youth in Ukrainian activities. Its aims were to aid the liberation struggle in Ukraine and to inform the American public about Ukraine's fight for independence. Branches of MUN were set up in 10 US cities during the 1930s. Typical local activities included sports and paramilitary drills as well as the staging of plays. The association published the quarterly *Trident* and, in the 1960s, the internal newsletter *MUN Beams*.

Holy Trinity Ukrainian Catholic Church in Youngstown

**Youngstown.** A city (1980 pop 115,000) in Pennsylvania at the heart of a steel-manufacturing region, with a Ukrainian population of approx 9,500. Immigrants from the Lemko region and Transcarpathia began to settle in the city during the 1880s, their influx peaking in the early 1900s. The first Greek Catholic parish was established by immigrants from Transcarpathia at the beginning of the century, and the second by immigrants from Galicia in 1909. The first Ukrainian Orthodox parish arose in 1922. By the end of the 1930s the city had approx 6,000 to 7,000 Ukrainians. This figure doubled after the Second World War. In the interwar period a Ukrainian National Day and a Ruthenian Day were held annually. At the end of the 1940s a local branch of the Ukrainian Congress Committee of America, the Plast Ukrainian Youth Organization, the Ukrainian Youth Association, and the Ukrainian Catholic Youth League in America were set up. Today there are 12 branches of Ukrainian fraternal associations as well as several church choirs and Ukrainian schools active in the city.

**Yovenko, Svitlana** [Jovenko], b 20 September 1945 in Kiev. Lyric poet, literary critic, and translator. She graduated from Kiev University (1968) and worked as an editor for the Dnipro publishing house (1968–77). Since 1977 she has been poetry editor of the journal *Vitchyzna*. She is the author of the poetry collections *Holube polum'ia* (Azure Flames, 1969), *Oblychchia vitru* (Face of the Wind, 1975), *Buzok u sichni* (Lilac in January, 1977), *Dialoh* (Dialogue, 1978), *Oblychchia spravzhnia myt'* (A Face's True Moment, 1979), *Mist cherez osin'* (Bridge across Autumn, 1981), *Ty – khto poruch* (You, Who Are Close By, 1983), *Chas liubovi* (Time of Love, 1984), *Nerozkrytyi konvert* (Unopened Envelope, 1987), and *Vich-na-vich* (Eye to Eye, 1989).

Valentyna Yudina

**Yudina, Valentyna** [Judina], b 7 May 1904 in Kiev, d 14 February 1984 in Kiev. Musicologist. After graduating from the Lysenko Music and Drama Institute (1930) she continued her studies there and at the Kharkiv Music and Drama Institute until 1934. She worked as a music editor in radio broadcasting and in theaters. The collected works of M. Lysenko (20 vols, 1950–9), K. Stetsenko (5 vols, 1963–6), Ya. Stepovy (3 vols, 1964–6), and V. Kosenko (1966–8) were prepared for publication by her. She prepared the piano scores of S. Hulak-Artemovsky's *Zaporozhian Cossack beyond the Danube*, M. Lysenko's *Natalka from Poltava*, and K. Stetsenko's *Matchmaking at Honcharivka*, in addition to publishing articles and reviews.

**Yugoslavia.** A country in southeastern Europe (1989 pop 23,710,000), with an area of 255,800 sq km. Established in 1911, from 1945 to 1992 Yugoslavia was a federation of six socialist republics: *Bosnia and Hercegovina (capital, Sarajevo), Macedonia (Skopje), Slovenia (Lubljana), *Croatia (Zagreb), Montenegro (Titograd), and *Serbia (Belgrade), which includes the autonomous territories of Vojvodina (capital, Novi Sad) and Kosovo (Priština). Its population is multinational and incorporates the major southern Slavic peoples. In 1981 it was home to 8.2 million Serbs, 4.5 million Croats, 2.0 million Bosnian Muslims, 1.8 million Slovenians, 1.8 million Albanians, 1.4 million Macedonians, 600,000 Montenegrins, and smaller minorities of Hungarians, Gypsies, Turks, Slovaks, Bulgars, Rumanians, and others. There are about 50,000 Ukrainians living in Yugoslavia, most of them in the *Bačka region of Serbia, the eastern reaches of Croatia, and northern Bosnia. Their (noncontiguous) settlements lie along an axis running roughly from Banja Luka to Novi Sad.

St Nicholas's Church in Ruski Krstur

**Yugoslavian-Ukrainian relations.** Relations between Southern Slavs (particularly Serbs, Croats, and Slovenes) and Ukrainians have existed since the days of Kievan Rus' and the first southern Slavic states. Contacts were maintained through the activities of such figures as Andrii of Sianik, D. Kantakuzin, S. Nemanjić, V. Nykolsky of Transcarpathia, P. Serb Logotet, I. Serbyn, L. Serbyn, and Yelysei of Kamianets-Podilskyi. Many Southern Slavs were later found in the ranks of the Ukrainian Cossacks, and in the late 18th century a substantial colony of Serbs settled in Southern Ukraine (see *New Serbia). The national revival of the Southern Slavic peoples in the 17th to 19th centuries was greatly influenced by the Kievan Cave

Monastery (and its publishing house) and the Kievan Mohyla Academy. Among the influential activists of the academy were L. Baranovych (bishop of Chernihiv) and his Serbian translator, G.S. Venclović. Serbian graduates of the academy included Metropolitan V. Jovanović, Bishop S. Končarević, D. Novaković, J. Rajić, A. Stojkov Tarbuk, and G. Zelić. In the 19th century the works of V.S. Karadžić and T. Shevchenko proved influential in the relations between Ukrainians and Serbs. Ukrainian activists, including V. Antonovych, M. Drahomanov, Yu. Fedkovych, I. Franko, V. Hnatiuk, F. Kolessa, Lesia Ukrainka, M. Lysenko, M. Maksymovych, O. Navrotsky, M. Starytsky, and the *Ruthenian Triad, also contributed to such relations through their written works or activities. Those who have either translated Ukrainian works or examined them in scholarly treatments include D. Ilić, S. Novaković, and S. Rašković (Serbians); V. Jagić, A. Harambašić, and A. Šenoa (Croatians); and J. Abram (a Slovene).

Serbian-Ukrainian relations increased during and immediately after the First World War. In August 1916 two Serbian volunteer divisions were formed in Odessa from groups of prisoners of war. After seeing action in Dobrudja, they were transferred to Salonika and became part of the Serbian army. From June 1917 to March 1918, the Yugoslavian Revolutionary Union was active in Ukraine among the approx 20,000 POWs from Yugoslavia interned

The Ukrainian Catholic church in Lipovljani

by the Russians. Headed by M. Čanak, most of the union's members sided with the Bolsheviks after the October Revolution, and many of them joined the Red Guards and fought against the Central Rada. In June–July 1919 a Yugoslavian Soviet of Workers' and Soldiers' Deputies was based in Kiev.

As the Soviet state emerged surrounded by a *cordon sanitaire* of countries hostile to it, enmity between Eastern and Southern Slavs grew significantly. The foreign and domestic policies of the Southern Slavic kingdoms were anti-Soviet and anticommunist, and Yugoslavia became a haven for émigrés from the former Russian Empire. Many of these émigrés were Ukrainians who had been military and civilian supporters of the White Russian forces, although some had been activists of the UNR and Western Ukrainian National Republic (ZUNR) governments, or hetmanites. Because of the greater influence exercised by the émigré Russian nationals on the Yugoslavian government and the king, most Ukrainians quickly moved on to Western Europe and the Americas. Those who remained usually assimilated with the Russian émigré community or were dispersed among the Ukrainian settlements in Vojvodina, Bosnia, and Croatia.

Some efforts at establishing government contacts between Ukraine and Yugoslavia were made in 1919. The ZUNR government had a mission in Belgrade that actively worked for the normalization of relations, but it had no success in gaining diplomatic recognition.

A Ukrainian military-medical mission established in Belgrade in the spring of 1919 (headed by a Dr Verbenets, assisted by P. Franko and V. Hankivsky) likewise was not officially recognized, although its activities were tolerated. The mission was eventually turned over to D. Doroshenko and renamed the Ukrainian Red Cross in the Balkans. Its most important undertaking was arranging for the transport of Ukrainian prisoners and providing assistance to refugees. It remained active until October 1919, when it was moved to Bucharest.

The blessing of Easter food baskets in Devjatina (1969)

In the interwar era the Serbian Orthodox church oversaw the Ukrainian Orthodox congregations in Transcarpathia (to 1945) and established the Orthodox Mukachiv-Prešov diocese. Yugoslavian cultural and academic circles maintained relations with their Ukrainian counterparts, particularly the Shevchenko Scientific Society (NTSh) in Lviv. Serbs who were accepted as full members of the NTSh included A. Belić, S. Bošković, J. Erdeljanović, J. Cvijić, D. Goranović-Kramberger, F. Ilešič, T. Maretić, S. Novaković, M. Petrović, B. Popović, and Ð. Šurmin. After the crisis over Carpatho-Ukraine in 1938–9 many refugees from Carpatho-Ukraine went (via Rumania) to Yugoslavia, where they received assistance and shelter from the local government and Ukrainian community.

Postwar ties between Yugoslavia and Ukraine depended on relations with the USSR as a whole. The first treaty of friendship, mutual assistance, and postwar co-operation between the two states was signed on 11 April 1945. Until the break between the Soviet Union and Yugoslavia in 1948, relations were lively but were conducted mainly through the central governments. This pattern was resumed after a normalization of relations that resulted from a declaration signed on 2 April 1955.

There were general cultural and economic relations between the Ukrainian SSR and the constituent Yugoslavian republics, particularly Croatia. Delegations from the Ukrainian SSR represented the Soviet Union at international trade fairs in Zagreb in 1961, 1974, and 1980. A treaty on economic, academic, and cultural co-operation was signed by Croatia and Ukraine. In 1979, days of Ukrainian culture were held in Croatia, and in the following year Croatian culture was celebrated in Ukraine.

Since 1945 the works of I. Franko, O. Honchar, L. Kostenko, M. Kotsiubynsky, Lesia Ukrainka, D. Pavlychko, T. Shevchenko, V. Stefanyk, M. Stelmakh, M. Vovchok, and Yu. Yanovsky have been translated into the various languages of Yugoslavia; the works of Serbian (I. Andrić, B. Ćiplić, R. Domanović, D. Maksimović, P. Nehoš, B. Nušić, and S. Sremac), Croatian (M. Krleža, V. Novak, A. Šenoa), Slovene (I. Cankar, F. Prešeren, O. Župančić), and Macedonian (S. Janevski and others) writers have been translated into Ukrainian.

A. Menac (of Zagreb) and A. Koval (of Kiev) jointly published the *Ukraïns'ko-khorvats'kyi abo serbs'kyi slovnyk* (Ukrainian-Croatian or Serbian Dictionary, 1979). A seven-volume history of world literature published in Zagreb (1977) contains a comprehensive survey of Ukrainian literature from its origins to the present day, written by S. Subotin.

P. Mitropan, a Yugoslavian literary scholar of Ukrainian origin, produced editions of T. Shevchenko's *Kobzar* (1969, 1980). A collection of works by Lesia Ukrainka, *Lomykamen* (Stone Breaker, 1971), was published in Požarevac. In 1980 the Institute of Literature and Art in Belgrade, the Serbian Matica association, and the Serbian People's Theater in Novi Sad jointly published V. Erčić's monograph *Manuil (Mihail) Kozačinskij i njegova tragedokomedija* (Mykhail Kozachynsky and His Tragicomedy, 1980). A selection of poetry by V. Holoborodko, translated by S. Rašković, was included in the two-volume anthology of contemporary world poetry published in Belgrade in 1983.

Leading contributors to the popularizing of Ukrainian literature in Yugoslavia have been J. Badalić, R. Bordon, D. Davidov, F. Dobrovoljc, A. Flaker, S. Hasparević, D. Grujić, J. Hrvaćanin, B. Kreft, D. Maksimović (recipient of the I. Franko Prize of the Ukrainian SSR in 1982), D. Medaković, A. Menac, M. Mitropan, J. Moder, V. Nedić, M. Nikolić, R. Pajković, M. Pavić, S. Rašković, S. Subotin, and F. Vurnik.

Those who have popularized Yugoslavian literature in Ukraine include I. Aizenshtok, O. Biletsky, I. Bilodid, Y. Chykyrysov, M. Drai-Khmara, Z. Honcharuk, A. Horetsky, V. Hrymych, M. Huts, A. Lirnychenko, R. Lubkivsky, M. Lukash, A. Lysenko, A. Malyshko, N. Neporozhnia, D. Palamarchuk, S. Panko, Ye. Pashchenko, D. Pavlychko, L. Pervomaisky, V. Polishchuk, M. Rylsky, S. Sakydon, F. Shevchenko, M. Yohansen, I. Yushchuk, and O. Zholdak.

Yugoslavia and Ukraine have also established exchanges of performing groups as well as of individual artists. The Slovene National Opera Theater of Lubljana, the Chamber Ensemble, the Kolo dance ensemble, and M. Cangalović, O. Marković, M. Radev, and others have performed in concert tours in Ukraine. The actors of the Kiev State Opera and Ballet Theater, as well as various choirs and dance groups, have staged productions in Yugoslavia. The Yugoslavian Dramatic Theater of Belgrade (1956, 1965), the Serbian National Theater of Novi Sad (1966), the Atelier 212 Experimental Theater of Belgrade (1968), and the Montenegrin National Theater of Titograd (1973) have all staged productions in Ukraine. The Kiev Ukrainian Drama Theater company took part in an international theater festival held in Belgrade in 1982, where it put on I. Franko's *Ukradene shchastia* (Stolen Happiness) as translated by S. *Rašković. In 1980, an exhibition of Croatian sculpture was held in Kiev.

**Ukrainians in Yugoslavia.** About 40,000 Ukrainians settled in Yugoslavia, after arriving as groups of farmers, in the Bačka region (Ruski Krstur, 1746; Koćura, 1765; Novi Sad, 1780; Stari Vrbas, 1848; Đurđevo, 1870; Gospođinci, 1870; Orahovo, Kula, Novi Vrbas, Bođani, after 1945) and the Srem region (Šid, 1800; Petrovce, 1836; Bačinci, 1850; Mikluševci, 1858; Berkasovo, 1880; Sremska Mitrovica, 1886; Rajevo Selo, 1889; Piškorevci, 1900; Andrijaševci, 1900; Inđija, 1946). Other settlements were established in Slavonia (Magič-Mala and Sibinj, 1900; Lipovljani and Kaniža, after 1900) and southwestern Bosnia (Kozarac near Prijedor, 1890; Devetina, 1898; Prnjavor, Derventa, Kamenica, Lipnica, Hrvaćani, Stara Dubrava, Lišnja, Cerovljani near Bosanska Gradiška, Banja Luka, 1910).

All of these settlements were Greek Catholic, but they differed in ethnic background and dialect and consisted of two main groups. Some are the Bačka-Srem Rusyns (Ruthenians; around 30,000) who settled in the Bačka region from 1745, upon arriving from the Zemplén, Borsod, Abaúj-Torna and Sáros komitats. In the early 20th century they elevated their transitional mixed Ukrainian-Slovak dialect to the status of a literary language, which is now used in schools, the press, radio programs, church services, and sermons. The others are Bosnian-Slavonian and Bačka Ukrainians (about 15,000) who arrived from 1898 to the 1900s from eastern Galicia and the Lemko region. Most of them speak Ukrainian. The political and economic conditions of the Second World War caused many of the latter group to migrate to Slavonia (Vukovar, Mikluševci, and Petrovci), Srem (Sremska Mitrovica), and Bačka (Bođani, Kula, Novi Vrbas, Savino Selo, and Zmajevo).

The first settlers of the Bačka region in the 18th century were free peasants who settled on state-owned land, paid tithes, and performed corvée labor. Their numbers were increased by new immigrants who arrived after the abolition of serfdom in the Austrian Empire in 1848 and helped to create new settlements in the Bačka and Srem regions. The original Bačka settlers were sheltered from Hungarianization or Serbianization through a government-supported network of church parishes and schools, and maintained enough dynamism to assimilate the later arrivals as far as language is concerned.

Until the First World War Ukrainian community life was centered around the church. Priests and, later, teachers were the only members of the intelligentsia. Initially the Bačka parishes were under the authority of the Hungarian Roman Catholic diocese of Kalocsa, but in 1778 they were joined to the newly established Croatian Uniate eparchy of Križevci (which already ran a theological seminary in Zagreb). Its bishops included Transcarpathian (H. Palkovych and Y. Drohobetsky) and Bačka (H. Bukatko, Y. Herbut, A. Horniak-Kukhar, S. Miklovsh, and D. Niaradi) Ukrainians, who looked after the development of Ukrainian cultural life as well as the conduct of religious services. In 1919 the Ruthenian Popular Enlightenment Society was established (under the auspices of the clergy) in Novi Sad and headed by Rev M. Mudry. It sponsored theatrical and choral groups, reading rooms, and educa-

tion courses and grew to include branches in numerous villages. The founder of its printing press in Ruski Krstur was Bishop D. Nariadi. In 1921–41 Rev Y. Bindas edited the annual *Ruski kalendar*. Other publications included the weekly *Ruski novini* (1921–41), the children's monthly *Nasha zahradka* (1937–41), almanacs, individual literary works, textbooks for primary school, and religious publications. All such activity was proscribed by the occupying Hungarian authorities in 1941–44, and existing publications were destroyed. A group of the secular intelligentsia, supported by Transcarpathian and Serbian Russophiles, established the Cultural-National Alliance of Ruthenians (Rusyns) in Yugoslavia in 1933 in Vrbas. In 1934–41 they published their weekly, *Russkaia zaria*, edited by Y. Kočiš, and in 1935–40 an annual, *Russki narodni kalendar Zaria*, edited by N. Olear. These were printed in the local Bačka dialect and in Russian. In 1945 members of this group worked to remove the Ukrainophile clerical intelligentsia.

Ukrainian settlers in northern Bosnia came mostly from Galicia (and, infrequently, from Transcarpathia) in the late 19th or early 20th century and set up on poor land that often had to be cleared of forests. Thus, it was not until the 1930s that their work resulted in any significant economic improvement. Community activities centered on the establishing of churches, reading rooms, credit unions, and co-operatives. Courses in Ukrainian were also taught, initially by the clergy but later also by Ukrainian students returning from Zagreb. The first Ukrainian clergyman to serve among the people in this region was A. Segedi (1897–1909). Metropolitan A. Sheptytsky came to the area in 1902 and 1913. In 1907 Y. Zhuk was made vicar general for the Ukrainian settlements under the auspices of the Roman Catholic archdiocese of Sarajevo. In 1910 a Studite monastery was established in Kamenica, to which many priests from Galicia came, but it was closed down in 1922. Kamenica was also the site of the apostolic administrative offices (headed by Rev O. Baziuk, 1914–24), a state of affairs which set the stage for the joining of these parishes with *Križevci eparchy.

The Ukrainian community in urban centers, such as *Zagreb, Sarajevo, and *Banja Luka, consisted largely of former officials of the Austrian administration and, later, of Ukrainian government officials, in exile or as diplomatic representatives. The ZUNR government had a mission in Zagreb in 1919 headed by D. Lukiianovych. In 1922 the *Prosvita society established headquarters in Zagreb (headed successively by A. Kravets and V. Voitanivsky), with branches in Ukrainian settlements in Bosnia, Slavonia, and Srem and also in Belgrade. The community in Zagreb was involved mainly with establishing relations with Croats and disseminating political and cultural information about Ukrainians. This included *Spomenitsa* (Memorial Book, 1922), a commemorative volume published on the 60th anniversary of Shevchenko's death, and articles in the Croatian press (*Hrvatska smotra*, *Hrvatska straža*, *Hrvatska revija*, *Hrvatski dnevnik*, *Hrvatski narod*, *Novi vijek*, and *Obzor*). In 1932 a group of students from Prague established a students' hromada affiliated with the Prosvita in Zagreb. Proboiem, a student nationalist organization founded in 1937, assembled a choir conducted by M. Vintoniv. It embarked on a tour of many Ukrainian settlements and did much to raise local Ukrainian national consciousness.

New Ukrainian publications began appearing in Yugoslavia from the 1930s. *Ridne slovo* was published in 1933–41 under the editorship of M. Firak, and in 1937–41 O. Biliak edited a Ukrainian almanac. *Dumka* (est 1936), the official organ of the local Ukrainian nationalist movement, was initially a bimonthly and then a biweekly in 1942–4. It appeared in Zagreb and Ruski Krstur in standard Ukrainian and in the Bačka dialect; the editors were S. Salamon and M. Buchko. From 1941 it served also as the official organ of the Ukrainian Representation in Croatia, headed by V. Voitanivsky, and was associated with the Melnyk faction of the OUN. During the Second World War a Ukrainian Legion (with approx 1,500 men) was organized by the Ukrainian Representation to fight on the Eastern front under the Croatian Home Army. The Germans, however, decided to use it for action in Croatia. The legion was partially wiped out in the process, and then fell apart. Its soldiers and their families were later subject to reprisals. After the war the Tito administration and Soviet security forces used the legion as a pretext to attack the Ukrainian intelligentsia and clergy; as a result Ukrainian community groups in Zagreb and Belgrade were disbanded. As well, a large number of Ukrainians migrated within Yugoslavia from Bosnia to the Srem or Bačka regions or emigrated to Poland or (illegally) to Australia and South America. In the 1950s, Ukrainian cultural and educational institutions in Bosnia began to revive under the auspices of official Ukrainian educational councils in Prnjavor and Banja Luka. In 1966 they managed to establish a Ukrainian radio program in Banja Luka and initiated Ukrainian language courses in schools in Prnjavor and Lišna. All the same, the center of Ukrainian cultural life had shifted markedly to the Bačka region.

About 1,500 Bačka-Srem Ukrainians had taken part in the Titoist resistance. In the postwar period, therefore, the Yugoslavian authorities supported the Bačkans' cultural activities within certain limits. The Bačka dialect was introduced in nine elementary schools, at the gymnasium in Ruski Krstur, and in local churches. In 1949 a radio station in Novi Sad began broadcasting a program in the Bačka dialect, and since then Bačka television programming has been introduced. A lectureship in the Bačka-Rusyn (Ruthenian) language was established at the university in Novi Sad. The church, however, faced strong repression, and clergymen were removed from their traditional position as community leaders. Anti-Ukrainophile sentiments were expressed openly (albeit only occasionally) in official reports or the press.

New publications, such as the weekly *Ruske slovo* (since 1945), the children's monthly *Pionerska zahradka*, the literary quarterly *Shvetlosts*, and *Nova dumka*, were established to continue the activities of earlier newspapers or journals (albeit in a manner that followed a new official line).

H. *Kostelnyk initiated Bačka literature with his poem-idyll *Z moioho valala* (From My Village, 1904) and his subsequent emotional and philosophical verse. He also wrote works on religion and ethnography, in addition to publishing (with D. Bindas) a collection of Bačka folk songs (1927). Other Bačka works published in the interwar years include Ya. Feisa's collection of poetry, *Pupche* (The Bud, 1929), and *Rus'ko-ukraïns'kyi al'manakh* (Ruthenian-Ukrainian Almanac, 1936), an anthology of prose. A number of Ukrainian and Russian plays were also translated into the dialect. P. Riznych (also a translator) and Ye. Sherehii staged many such productions in 1939–41, as well as many of their own plays (mostly melodramas). After 1945 literature and the-

ater became dominated by the motifs of socialist realism and memoirs of the war. Typical works were *Orache* (The Tillers, 1954) and *Na shvytaniu* (At Dawn, 1952) by M. *Kovach, *Vona n'evynovata* (She Is Not to Blame, 1954) by E. Kočiš, and *Ohen' v notsy* (Fire in the Night) by J. Sabadoš. A number of collections of poetry have been published, including *Antologyia poezyï bachvansko-srymskykh ruskykh pysatel'okh* (Anthology of Poetry of Bačka-Srem Rusyn/Ruthenian Writers, 1963) and *Antologyia dzetsyn'skei poezyï* (Anthology of Children's Poetry, 1964). *Odhuk z rovnïny, zbornik prypovedkokh, 1941–61* (A Call from Level Ground: A Collection of Proverbs, 1941–61, 1961) is an anthology of prose works.

The linguistic norms of Bačka Ukrainians are set out in *Hramatyka bachvansko-ruskei besedy* (Grammar of the Bačka Ruthenian Language, 1923) by H. Kostelnyk and in *Gramatyka* (Grammar, 1965) by M. Kočiš.

The leading compiler of Bačka Ukrainian folklore was V. Hnatiuk, who published a study of Ruthenian settlements in the Bačka region in the *Zapysky* (1898) of the Shevchenko Scientific Society and an ethnographic study of Hungarian Ruthenia in *Etnohrafichnyi zbirnyk* (vol 9, 1900; vol 25, 1909; vol 30, 1911). O. Tymko published a collection of folk songs with transcriptions of melodies, *Nasha pisnia* (Our Song, 3 vols, 1953–4), and an anthology of children's songs, *Maly solovei* (The Little Nightingale, 1953). V. Gzhanets published a collection of choral arrangements, *Pysnï iugoslavianskykh rusynokh* (Songs of Yugoslavian Rusyns [Ruthenians], 1946).

BIBLIOGRAPHY
Hrods'kyi, I. *Polozhennia rusyniv v Bosniï* (Lviv 1910)
Huts', M. *Serbo-khorvats'ka narodna pisnia na Ukraïni* (Kiev 1966)
Marunchak, M. *Ukraïntsi v Rumuniï, Chekho-Slovachchyni, Pol'shchi, Iugoslaviï* (Winnipeg 1969)
Flaker, A. *Ukrajinska literatura u Hrvatskoj* (Zagreb 1970)
Ramach, L. *Rusyny-ukraïntsi v Iugoslaviï* (Winnipeg 1971)
Pashchenko, E.; Rashkovich, S. [Rašković]. *Ukrajinci i srpska narodna pesma* (Belgrade 1978)
Rashkovich, S. [Rašković]. *Putevy y raskrshcha nashe ukrajinistike i prevodne knizhevnosti sa ukrajinskoh jezyka. Zbornyk radova ...* (Tetovo 1978)
Labosh, F. *Ystoryia rusynokh Bachkei, Srymu y Slavonyï 1745–1918* (Vukovar 1979)
Biljnja, V. *Rusini u Vojvodini: Prilog izučavanju istorije rusina Vojvodine (1918–1945)* (Novi Sad 1987)
Rudiakov, P. *Ukraïns'ko-khorvats'ki literaturni vzaiemyny v XIX–XX st.* (Kiev 1987)

O. Horbach, S. Rašković

**Yuhasevych-Skliarsky, Ivan** [Juhasevyč-Skljars'kyj], b 1741 in Príkra, Prešov region, Slovakia, d 15 December 1814 in Nevytske, Transcarpathia. Folklorist. He studied in Lviv and from 1775 taught church music and served as a church administrator and village elder in Nevytske, near Uzhhorod. The three collections of music compiled by him included secular songs and 30 *hirmoi* and were richly illustrated with his own drawings. The last collection, compiled in 1811, contained 224 folk songs, including many humorous and satirical songs. He also prepared several handwritten calendars. The one for 1809 contained 370 folk sayings and was the first collection of Ukrainian proverbs. It was edited by I. Pankevych and published in a collection of the Slavic Institute in Prague (1946) and then as part of Ye. Nedzelsky's *Z ust narodu* (From the People's Mouth, 1955).

**Yukhnove culture**. An archeological culture of the 6th to 2nd century BC which existed along the upper reaches of the Desna and Seim rivers. It was identified by M. Voevodsky in the 1940s and named after a site excavated in the Novhorod-Siverskyi region by D. Samokvasov in the 1870s. The people of this culture engaged mainly in agriculture, animal husbandry, hunting, fishing, and bronze and iron metal-working. Their southern settlements also traded with northern Black Sea centers and had contacts with the tribes of the forest-steppe region of Left-Bank Ukraine. Excavations at culture sites revealed the remains of wooden fortifications, bone, iron, and bronze implements and weapons, and pottery.

Ihor Yukhnovsky          Mariia Yunak

**Yukhnovsky, Ihor** [Juxnovs'kyj], b 1 September 1925 in Kniahynyne, Dubno county, Volhynia. Theoretical physicist; AN URSR (now ANU) full member since 1982. Since graduating from Lviv University (1951) he has taught there and, from 1959, directed the department of theoretical physics. Since 1969 he has headed the Lviv branch of the ANU Institute of Theoretical Physics, which in 1991 became a separate ANU institute. As a result of his research, a school of statistical condensed-matter physics arose in Lviv. Under his guidance and with his full participation, in research using the collective-variables method, the first microscopic treatment of electrolytic solutions including all interparticle forces was carried out, and resulted in a comprehensive theory of electrolytes. He achieved breakthroughs in the elaboration of a microscopic theory of phase transitions. Yukhnovsky worked out a quantum-statistical method of collective variables and formulated a quantitative theory of helium IV. Significant results have also been obtained by Yukhnovsky and his school in the theory of metals and in crystal optics. His monograph *Phase Transitions of the Second Order: Collective Variables Method* (1987) has been published in English. Since 1990 Yukhnovsky has been a member of the Ukrainian Supreme Council, where he has headed the People's Council opposition. He has played a key role in the revival of the Shevchenko Scientific Society, has directed the Lviv-based Western Scientific Center of the ANU, and has been a member of the ANU presidium. In October 1992 he was appointed first deputy prime minister of the Ukrainian government. In March 1993 he resigned from this position.

O. Bilaniuk

**Yukhymenko** [Juxymenko]. A family of master wood carvers. Fedot (b 2nd half of the 19th century in Velyki Budyshcha, Zinkiv county, Poltava gubernia, d early 20th century in Budyshche) sculpted figures in the round, large wooden statues for the Kochubei palace in St Petersburg, iconostases, furniture, and household articles. At his workshop he trained carvers, such as V. Harbuz, P. Krempokha, and V. Reva. His son, Prokip (b 20 July 1870 in Budyshche, d January 1931 in Poltava), specialized in bas-reliefs (eg, *Cossack, Banduryst*, 1902), sculptures in the round, furniture, and album covers. He carved the choir balustrades and columns for the Poltava Zemstvo Building (now the Poltava Regional Studies Museum) and the decorative cartouches on the exterior of the Museum of the History of the Battle of Poltava (1908–9). He also taught at the Poltava Tekhnikum of Industrial Co-operation (1928–31).

**Yukhymenko, Ivan** [Juxymenko], b 14 October 1892 in Kharkiv, d 6 February 1943 in Kazan, RSFSR. Stage director and pedagogue. He began his career in Russian troupes in Ukraine (1915) and then played in Molodyi Teatr in Kiev (1917–18) and in the State Drama Theater (1918–19). In 1920 he moved to Kharkiv and founded a theater-studio with Ya. Mamontov, and from 1925 he taught in the Kharkiv Music and Drama Institute and directed in the Kharkiv Workers' and Peasants' Theater. He directed in the Leningrad Zhovten Theater (1928) and was artistic director of the Dnipropetrovske (1929–32) and Odessa (1933–7) Ukrainian drama theaters. He was accused of nationalism and was arrested, and probably died in prison.

**Yunak, Mariia** [Junak, Marija], b 15 February 1902 in Kiev, d 1 August 1977 in Kiev. Painter and muralist. She studied at the Ukrainian State Academy of Arts, Kiev Institute of Plastic Arts, and Kiev State Art Institute under M. *Boichuk (1920–7). She was an instructor at Boichuk's studio in Kiev and was part of the groups he led that painted the frescoes in the Peasant Sanatorium in Odessa (1928) and the Kharkiv Chervonozavodskyi Ukrainian Drama Theater (1934). From the early 1930s Yunak worked as a graphic artist and designed posters, books, and textiles, and also as a film animator, muralist, and magazine illustrator. From 1947 she worked at the Institute of Monumental Art and Sculpture of the Academy of Architecture of the Ukrainian SSR. Her early works show the influence of the Byzantine icon and Ukrainian folk art. They include *Fairy Tale* (1921), *Girl in a Kerchief* (1921), and *Ukrainian Women* (1921).

**Yunakiv, Mykola** [Junakiv], b 6 December 1871 in Chuhuiv, Kharkiv gubernia, d 1 August 1931 in Tarnów, Poland. Military leader. He studied at the Nikolai Academy of the General Staff in St Petersburg (1894–7), defended his dissertation on the Swedish campaign in Ukraine in 1708–9 (1910), and became a professor of military history (1911), which post he was forced to resign in 1914 for attempting to implement teaching reforms at the academy. During the First World War he was chief of staff of the Russian Fourth Army and commander of the Eighth Army on the Rumanian front. In December 1917 Yunakiv joined the Ukrainian army and headed the main educational administration of the defense ministry. In August 1919 he was appointed chief of the joint staff of the UNR Army and the Ukrainian Galician Army, and co-ordinated

Gen Mykola Yunakiv          Hnat Yura

the advances on Kiev and Odessa. On 10 October 1919 he was promoted to the rank of major general, the highest in the UNR Army. During 1920 Yunakiv briefly headed the defense ministry and the Supreme Military Council of the UNR under S. Petliura. He emigrated to Poland, where he contributed to the Ukrainian Military History Society, worked as a member of the editorial collective of *Za derzhavnist'*, and published 'Materiialy dlia moho zhyttie-pysu' (Materials for My Autobiography, in *Tryzub*, no. 289/290 [1931]).

A. Zhukovsky

**Yunge, Ekaterina** [Junge], b 5 December 1843 in St Petersburg, d 1 February 1913. Russian painter. The daughter of Count F. *Tolstoi, she met T. Shevchenko at her father's home in St Petersburg and received art lessons from him. From 1882 to 1887 she taught art in Kiev. Her reminiscences about Shevchenko and M. Kostomarov were published in a volume of her memoirs of the years 1843–60 (1913).

**Yunokomunarivske** [Junokomunarivs'ke]. V-19, DB III-4. A city (1989 pop 25,100) on the Bulavynka River in Donetske oblast, under the jurisdiction of the Yenakiieve municipal council. It was founded in 1908 as a mining settlement called Buhne. In 1924 it was renamed Yunkom, and in 1965 it was granted city status and given its current name. The city is an industrial center with three coal mines.

**Yunytsky, Anatolii** [Junyc'kyj, Anatolij], b 31 March 1912 in Nizhen, Chernihiv gubernia, d 12 May 1976 in Lutske, Volhynia oblast. Stage actor. He began his career in the amateur theater Chervonyi Zhovten (1932) and in various workers' and collective-farm theaters. From 1945 he acted in the Volhynian Ukrainian Music and Drama Theater.

**Yupko, Lev** [Jupko], b 29 October 1911 in Kramatorske, Izium county, Kharkiv gubernia. Metallurgical engineer. He studied in Moscow, the Donbas, and Zaporizhia. From 1956 he served as director of the giant metallurgical concern Zaporizhstal, where he introduced many innovative modern processes in iron smelting and steel production, particularly the use of natural gas in the manufacturing of iron.

**Yura, Hnat,** b 8 January 1888 in Fedvar (now Pidlisne), Oleksandriia county, Kherson gubernia, d 18 January 1966

in Kiev. Theatrical director and actor. He began his professional career in S. Maksymovych's troupe in 1907 and then worked in the Ruska Besida Theater (1913–14) and in Molodyi Teatr (1917–19), in which he led the traditional (non-experimental) faction. He helped found the touring Franko New Drama Theater in Vinnytsia in 1920 and was its artistic director until 1961 (see *Kiev Ukrainian Drama Theater). Yura often staged productions from the repertoire of Molodyi Teatr, and he also staged numerous plays from the contemporary European repertoire. As an actor he was best known in the role of simpletons, including Tereshko and Kramariuk in I. Karpenko-Kary's *Suieta* (Vanity) and *Zhyteis'ke more* (The Sea of Life), Kopystka in M. Kulish's *97*, Luka in M. Gorky's *Na dni* (The Lower Depths), and Schweik in *Pryhody bravoho soldata Shveika* (The Adventures of the Brave Soldier Schweik, based on J. Hašek). He also acted in the films *Prometheus* (1936), *Zaporozhian Cossack beyond the Danube* (1937), *Karmeliuk* (1938), and *Taras Shevchenko* (1950). In 1945–61 Yura taught a t the Kiev Theater Institute. His autobiography is titled *Zhyttia i stsena* (Life and the Stage, 1965); a biography, by Yu. Boboshko, was published in Kiev in 1980.

V. Revutsky

**Yura, Terentii** [Jura, Terentij], b 22 April 1884 in Fedvar (now Pidlisne), Oleksandriia county, Kherson gubernia, d 9 May 1973 in Kiev. Actor; brother of H. Yura and O. Yura-Yursky. He played in the Ukrainian touring troupes of S. Maksymovych, O. Sukhodolsky, T. Kolesnychenko, and others in 1907–17 and then led his own troupe, Surma, in Oleksandriia (1917–20) and was a leading actor in the Kiev Ukrainian Drama Theater (1921–57). He played various roles, from the Zaporozhian Cossack Tur in O. Korniichuk's *Bohdan Khmel'nyts'kyi* to Moliere's Tartuffe. He also acted in O. Dovzhenko's film *Ivan* (1932).

**Yurasov, Mikhail** [Jurasov, Myxajlo], b and d ? Architect. He built a number of 18th-century buildings in Kiev. These fine examples of the baroque style include the student residence at the St Sophia Monastery (1763–7), the altar chamber of St Michael's Cathedral at the Vydubychi Monastery (1770–5), and the hegumen's residence at that monastery (1770–5).

**Yura-Yursky, Oleksander** [Jura-Jurs'kyi], b 23 June 1895 in Fedvar (now Pidlisne), Oleksandriia county, Kherson gubernia, d 30 December 1968 in Kiev. Actor, stage director, and reciter. He acted in Molodyi Teatr (1917–19) and then with his brother, H. *Yura, founded the Franko New Drama Theater in Vinnytsia (1920; later the Kiev Ukrainian Drama Theater), where he was a leading actor until 1948 (except in 1925–7, when he worked as stage director in the Donetske Theater). His large repertoire extended from the role of Makar in I. Karpenko-Kary's *Suieta* (Vanity) to the title role in W. Hasenclever's *Ein besserer Herr*. From 1948 he worked in the Kiev State Philharmonic Society as a reciter.

**Yurchak, Vasyl** [Jurčak, Vasyl'], b 26 August 1876 in Skala-Podilska, Borshchiv county, Galicia, d 28 September 1914 in Terebovlia, Galicia. Actor and singer (tenor). He began his career in the choir of the Ruska Besida Theater (1896), soon made his stage debut as Andrii in S. Hulak-

Vasyl Yurchak

Oleksander Yurchenko

Artemovsky's *Zaporozhets' za Dunaiem* (Zaporozhian Cossack beyond the Danube), and stayed with that theater until his death. In his acting he combined profound lyricism with utmost simplicity and was a master of complete transformation in character and comic roles. Among them were Kuksa in M. Kropyvnytsky's *Poshylys' v durni* (They Made Fools of Themselves), Zahonystyi and Mykola in I. Franko's *Uchytel'* (The Teacher) and *Ukradene shchastia* (Stolen Happiness; for this role he was highly praised by the author), and Sirko in V. Pachovsky's *Sontse ruiny* (Sun of the Ruin). A biography, by S. Charnetsky, was published in Lviv (1916).

**Yurchakova, Hanna** [Jurčakova], b 22 December 1879 in Terebovlia, Galicia, d 6 July 1965 in Lviv. Stage actress; wife of V. Yurchak. She worked in the Ruska Besida Theater (1899–1914), Ternopilski Teatralni Vechory (1915–17), K. Rubchak's troupe (1918–20), and the New Lviv Theater. In 1922–35 she led amateur groups in Ternopil and Lviv.

**Yurchenko, Liudmyla** [Jurčenko, Ljudmyla], b 14 March 1943 in Kharkiv. Opera singer (mezzo-soprano). After graduating from the Kiev Conservatory (1969) she joined the Kiev Theater of Opera and Ballet as a soloist. She has appeared in roles such as Aksinia in I. Dzerzhinsky's *Tikhii Don* (Quiet Don), Liubasha in N. Rimsky-Korsakov's *The Tsar's Bride*, Carmen in G. Bizet's *Carmen*, and Orpheus in C. Gluck's *Orpheus and Eurydice*.

**Yurchenko, Oleksander** [Jurčenko], b 18 November 1904 in Kiev, d 26 June 1962 in Munich. Historian of law, Sovietologist, and civic figure; member of the Shevchenko Scientific Society from 1958. A graduate in law from the Kiev Institute of the National Economy (1926) and the Kiev Institute of Trade and Distribution (1933), he worked as a researcher for the VUAN Commission for the Study of the History of Western-Ruthenian and Ukrainian Law (1926–1) and taught in secondary schools and institutes of higher education (1926–41). A postwar refugee in Germany, he became a professor of Soviet law at the Ukrainian Free University in Munich as well as an associate of the Institute for the Study of the USSR (from 1954), an activist in the Ukrainian National State Union party, and an executive member of the Ukrainian National Council (1952–4 and 1957–62). He wrote a number of studies about the le-

gal status of the Ukrainian SSR and the nature of Soviet federalism, including a posthumously published monograph entitled *Ukraïns'ko-rosiis'ki stosunky pislia 1917 r. v pravnomu aspekti* (Ukrainian-Russian Relations after 1917 from a Legal Aspect, 1971).

**Yurchenko, Petro** [Jurčenko], b 22 August 1900 in Medvyn, Radomysh county, Kiev gubernia, d 23 June 1972 in Kiev. Architect and art scholar. He graduated from the Kiev State Art Institute in 1928, and until 1941 he taught there and at the Kiev Civil-Engineering Institute (1928–41). He codesigned the Ukrainian Government Building (1927) and Promin apartment subdivision (1929) in Kharkiv and the Kursk Railway Station in Moscow (1932). In Kiev he designed the second story of the Askoldova Mohyla rotunda (1935) and the amphitheater near it (1936–7). He studied Ukraine's architectural monuments together with H. Lohvyn and Yu. Nelhorovsky and reconstructed many of them (eg, A. Kysil's palace, the Kiev city hall, and the campanile of St Michael's Golden-Domed Monastery). He wrote articles and books on the folk dwellings of Ukraine (1941) and the wooden architecture of Ukraine (1949, 1970) and contributed chapters to books on the history of architecture in Ukraine (vol 1, 1957), the history of Ukrainian art (vols 3 and 5, 1968, 1967), and Ukrainian folk art (vol 3, 1962).

**Yurchenko, Vasyl** [Jurčenko, Vasyl'], b 26 May 1950 in Dnipropetrovske. Canoeing champion. He won world championships in the 10,000-m Canadian singles in 1973, the 1,000-m singles in 1974, the 1,000-m and 10,000-m singles in 1975, and the 1,000-m pairs in 1977; the 1976 Olympic silver medal in the 1,000-m singles; and many Ukrainian and USSR championships.

**Yurchuk, Vasyl** [Jurčuk, Vasyl'], b 19 August 1921 in Brodetske, Berdychiv county, Kiev gubernia. Soviet historian and CP activist. A graduate of Kiev University (1942), he taught the history of the CPSU there (1949–52, 1954–5) and at Ulan Bator University (1952–4) and then headed the department of CPSU history at the Ukrainian Agricultural Academy (1955–74) and directed the CC CPU Institute of Party History (1974–89). He wrote 'Borot'ba KP Ukraïny za vidbudovu i rozvytok narodn'oho hospodarstva, 1945–1952' (The Struggle of the CPU for the Rebuilding and Development of the National Economy in 1945–52, 1965 [PH D diss]), *Diial'nist' M.V. Frunze na Ukraïni* (The Activities of M. Frunze in Ukraine, 1952), and *Dvadtsiatyi z'ïzd KP Ukraïny* (The 20th Congress of the CPU, 1961); contributed to collective works on the history of the CPU (1971, 1977), the history of the Kiev oblast CP organization (1967), and the history of the Komsomol in Ukraine (1971); and served on the editorial board of the journal *Komunist Ukraïny*.

**Yurchuk, Vira** [Jurčuk], b 6 May 1941 in Lublin, Poland. Painter. A postwar refugee, she has lived in Canada since 1949. She graduated from the Ontario College of Art (1963). Most of her better-known works, such as *Inheritors of the Earth* (1982) and *Angel over Toronto* (1983), are acrylics on canvas, but she has also done mixed-media works, such as *Growing* (1980) and *Autumn Landscape* (1980), holographs, such as *Profiles* (1981) and *Window* (1981), and several murals, including *Ukrainians in Canada*, at the St Demetrius Residence in Toronto (1982). In the 1960s she did illustrations for the Plast children's magazine *Hotuis'*. Thematically her work has evolved from abstract landscapes and still lifes to symbolic compositions on womanhood and her Ukrainian heritage. Solo exhibitions of her works have been held in Toronto (1967, 1980) and Ottawa (1977), and she has participated in many group shows.

**Yurchyshyn, Volodymyr** [Jurčyšyn], b 9 March 1925 in Zaiachivka (now part of Klekotyna, in Sharhorod raion, Vinnytsia oblast). Economist and agronomist; corresponding member of the All-Union Academy of Agricultural Sciences since 1975. After graduating from the Uman Agricultural Institute (1953) he worked at the Ukrainian Academy of Agricultural Sciences, where he served as rector in 1968–76. Since then he has chaired a department at the Ukrainian Scientific Research Institute of the Economics and Organization of Agriculture. Yurchyshyn's works deal with the economy and organization of fruit farming and the management of agricultural production complexes.

**Yurev.** See Tartu.

**Yurevych, Mykhailo** [Jurevyč, Myxajlo], b 1707, d ? Kievan jeweler. His works include the silver Royal Gates (1748) and altar decorations (1751) in the Dormition Cathedral of the Kievan Cave Monastery.

Vasyl Yuriev             Lev Yurkevych

**Yuriev, Vasyl** [Jur'jev, Vasyl'], b 20 February 1879 in Ivanovska Virga, Penza gubernia, Russia, d 8 February 1962 in Kharkiv. Selection and plant cultivation scientist; full member of the AN URSR (now ANU) from 1945. A graduate of the Kharkiv Agricultural Institute (1905), he worked at the Kharkiv Selection Station (1909–56, from 1944 as director), taught at the Kharkiv Agricultural Institute (from 1937), and headed the ANU Institute of Genetics and Selection (1946–56) and the Ukrainian Scientific Research Institute of Plant Cultivation, Selection, and Genetics (from 1956). He was one of the founders of the Soviet selection and seed cultivation industry and the creator of many productive varieties of winter and spring wheat.

**Yurii Dolgorukii** [Jurij Dolgorukij] (Yurii I Volodymyrovych), b ca 1090, d 15 May 1157 in Kiev. Rus' prince; sixth son of *Volodymyr Monomakh and *Gytha. His appellation, 'the Long-handed,' was assigned posthumously by chroniclers who deplored his interventions in the affairs of Kiev principality. While his father was alive, Yurii brought the Rostov-Suzdal territories in the north firmly under his control. In 1125, upon the death of his father, Yurii transferred his capital to Suzdal and became the sovereign ruler of Rostov-Suzdal principality. After the death of his elder brother, Mstyslav I Volodymyrovych (1132), Yurii seized Pereiaslav by force; after eight days he was ousted by his brother Yaropolk II Volodymyrovych (then the prince of Kiev). The takeover of Pereiaslav resulted in a conflict between Yurii and his brothers which ended in his defeat in 1135. He was compelled to relinquish all of his southern land claims and return to Suzdal.

During Yurii's reign the economic and political might of the northern principalities grew. The cities of Pereiaslavl-Zaleskii, Yurev (now Tartu), and (allegedly) Kostroma were built by him. Yurii is considered to be the founder of Moscow, which is first mentioned in 1147 and which he fortified in 1156. He formed appanage principalities in northeastern Rus', which he divided among his sons, and he established the Moscow branch of the *Riurykide dynasty. The Rostov-Suzdal principality ruled by Yurii later became the nucleus of *Russia.

In 1149, taking advantage of the internecine strife in Kievan Rus' to the south, Yurii allied himself with the Polovtsians (Cumans) and set out on a campaign against *Iziaslav Mstyslavych. He defeated Iziaslav and took over Kiev, but in 1150 he had to relinquish the city. He returned to Kiev, but Iziaslav II defeated him decisively in 1151 at the Ruta River and sent him back to Suzdal. Yurii captured Kiev a third time in 1155 and remained there. In order to strengthen his position in the south he granted his sons appanages in those territories. He was not liked by the Kievan citizens; he was poisoned at a banquet hosted by the Kievan boyar Petrylo. He was buried in the Transfiguration Church in Berestove. After his death the local population rose in rebellion against the remnants of his rule. The north-south hostilities intensified under the rule of Yurii's son, *Andrei Bogoliubskii.

BIBLIOGRAPHY
Ianovskii, A. *Iurii Dolgorukov* (Moscow 1955)

A. Zhukovsky

**Yurii II Boleslav** [Jurij] (Troidenovych), b ca 1306, d 7 April 1340 in Volodymyr-Volynskyi. Last ruler of the Principality of Galicia-Volhynia (1323–40); son of Trojden II of Mazovia and grandson of Yurii Lvovych. He was initially known as Bolesław and raised as a Catholic, but he converted to Orthodoxy, and he ascended to the throne of Volodymyr-Volynskyi principality. He maintained relations with Lithuania (he married Yevfymiia-Ofka, daughter of the grand duke of Lithuania, Gediminas) and the Teutonic Knights, with whom he signed treaties in 1325, 1327, 1334, 1335, and 1337. He was met with hostility by Poland and Hungary, however. Yurii sought to strengthen his rule by supporting towns and burghers, protecting German colonists, and encouraging the influx of foreigners. Under his rule Sianik was granted rights under *Magdeburg law. The boyars rebelled against him, and he was poisoned in suspicious circumstances. His death marked the end of the Romanovych dynasty of Galician-Volhynian princes as well as the end of the *Princely era of Ukraine.

**Yurii Lvovych** [Jurij L'vovyč], b ca 1252–7 (or 1262), d 23 April 1308 (or 1315). Ruler of the Principality of Galicia-Volhynia; son of *Lev Danylovych. He ruled in Kholm and Podlachia, and after his father's death he united all the lands of Galicia-Volhynia into a principality, with its capital in Volodymyr-Volynskyi. During his tenure Poland regained the Lublin region (1302), and Hungary seized a part of Transcarpathia, but his reign was largely peaceful, and his principality flourished economically. His title was 'King of Rus', Prince of Lodomeria.' Yurii enjoyed favorable foreign relations; he maintained a particularly close alliance with the princes of Kujavia, in Poland, and married Eufemia (Yevtymiia), the sister of Władysław Łokietek. When the Kievan metropolitan moved his see north to Vladimir, Yurii obtained the assent of Constantinople to establish *Halych metropoly (1303), in which the eparchies of Halych, Volodymyr-Volynskyi, Peremyshl, Lutske, Kholm, and Turiv were included. Yurii was succeeded by his sons, Andrii and Lev Yuriiovych.

Yurii's Temple

**Yurii's Temple** (Yuriieva bozhnytsia). A medieval architectural monument in Oster, Chernihiv oblast. Named in honor of Prince *Yurii Dolgorukii, it is the only remnant of St Michael's Church, which was built ca 1098, during the reign of Prince Volodymyr Monomakh. The original church was destroyed during the Mongol invasion in 1240. It was rebuilt, but it was closed after being hit by lightning in 1753 and was later dismantled. The temple consists of a single rectangular room with a large semicircular apse containing two high, arched windows. There are two large pillars on the west wall, and a system of arched vaults is attached to the walls. The structure is capped by a vaulted wooden roof. The only surviving example of the medieval Pereiaslav style of church architecture, the temple was restored in 1907, 1924, and 1950. Its most significant feature is its three frescoes, which were painted between 1098 and 1125 in the Kievan style. The one placed highest portrays the Orante with two archangels garbed in ornamental gowns with pearls. Under it is a scene of the Eucharist with two figures of Christ, and under that is a depiction of the apostles. The frescoes were restored in 1977–80 by V. Babiuk.

**Yurk, Yurii** [Jurk, Jurij], b 5 May 1905 in Mykolaivka, Katerynoslav county, Katerynoslav gubernia, d 16 January 1976 in Symferopil. Geologist and mineralogist. After graduating from the Kharkiv Institute of Vocational Education in 1932, he was a research associate of the AN URSR (now ANU) Institute of Geological Sciences. He became the director (1956–73) and then a department head (1973–6) of the Institute of Mineral Resources. Most of his research was devoted to the geology and mineralogy of the Ukrainian Crystalline Shield and to the genesis and commercial potential of various minerals.

**Yurkevych, Lev** [Jurkevyč] (pseuds: L. Rybalka, E. Nicolet), b 1884 in Kryve, Skvyra county, Kiev gubernia, d late 1917 or early 1918 in Moscow. Ukrainian Marxist; son of O. *Yurkevych. He joined the clandestine *Revolutionary Ukrainian party in 1904 and was a founding member of the *Ukrainian Social Democratic Workers' party (USDRP) in 1905. Later he was elected a USDRP CC candidate member. He went abroad in 1907 to complete his university studies, which he had begun at Kiev University in 1903. After his father's death in 1911, he lived in France, Lviv, and Switzerland (from 1914). Using his sizable inheritance, he funded and edited the Lviv USDRP monthly *Nash holos (1910–11) and subsidized the Kiev journal *Dzvin (1913–14). Under the pseudonym L. Rybalka he wrote and published brochures in Kiev on the national question and the working class (1913) and classes and society (1913). In Dzvin, his brochures, and Borot'ba (7 issues, 1915–16), the Geneva-based organ he funded and edited under the pseudonym E. Nicolet, Yurkevych polemicized against D. Dontsov's 'bourgeois nationalist' proposal that Ukraine separate from Russia and federate with Austria, and condemned the Ukrainian bourgeoisie in the Russian Empire (as servile supporters of tsarism) and the émigré *Union for the Liberation of Ukraine (as agents of Austrian and German imperialism). His open letter to the Second International Socialist Conference in Kienthal in 1916 was published in Lausanne as the brochure L'Ukraine et la guerre.

Yurkevych also criticized the chauvinist, centralist thinking of the Russian Bolsheviks and advocated the need for Ukrainian autonomy and a separate Ukrainian proletarian revolution and Ukrainian social democratic workers' party. V. Lenin denounced his views and in 1914 conspired to undermine his influence. In 1917 in Geneva, Yurkevych published a brochure in Russian on the Russian Social Democrats and the national question that was one of the earliest critiques of Lenin's positions on democratic centralism and the national question (English trans in Journal of Ukrainian Studies, Spring 1982). Yurkevych died after the February Revolution before being able to return to Ukraine. A biography of him, by V. Levynsky, was published in Lviv in 1927.

M. Yurkevich

**Yurkevych, Osyp** [Jurkevyč], b 12 February 1855 in Kryve, Skvyra county, Kiev gubernia, d 24 November 1910 in Kiev. Community leader and co-operative organizer. After graduating in medicine from Kiev University (1881) he practiced in Kharkiv, in the Chernihiv region, and in Kornyn, Kiev gubernia. He was a member of the Old Hromada of Kiev. Beginning in 1901 he organized consumer co-operatives in Kornyn, Kryve, and other towns. With the appearance of a Ukrainian press after the

1905 Revolution, he contributed articles on co-operatives and rural life to various journals and papers. Some of them came out in the collection *Suchasni sil's'ki maliunky: Pershyi rik spivrobitnytstva u vil'nii presi* (Contemporary Village Paintings: The First Year of Contributions to the Free Press, 1907). He served on the board of directors of the Kiev Credit Union and on the auditing commission of the Kiev Consumers' Union.

Pamfil Yurkevych　　　　　Anatol Yuryniak

**Yurkevych, Pamfil** [Jurkevyč], b 28 February 1826 in Lipliave, Zolotonosha county, Poltava gubernia, d 16 October 1874 in Moscow. Philosopher and educator. After graduating from the Kiev Theological Academy (1851) he was appointed supervisor of the philosophy class, assistant inspector (1854–6), lecturer in philosophy and German (1857), and associate professor of philosophy (1858) there. From 1861 he served as professor of philosophy at Moscow University and taught pedagogy at a teachers' seminary.

Although Yurkevych wrote little in philosophy (only 6 articles and 1 review out of a total of 7 articles, 3 reviews, and 2 books), his writings are noted for their originality, critical insight, and lucid style. His purpose was to reconcile and unify into one worldview faith and knowledge, metaphysics and science, and rationalism and empiricism. To this end he subjected the dominant movements in modern philosophy to a profound and severe critique in which he pointed out the strengths and weaknesses of the idealist tradition (1859) and exposed the failings of materialism as metaphysics (1860). He rejected the rationalist tendency to reduce all mental life to thought and argued for the diversity and depth of the human spirit. In his most interesting and sophisticated work, on reason according to Plato's teaching and experience according to I. Kant's teaching (1865–6), he pinpointed the source of Kant's errors and showed the necessity of reinstating Platonism (or rather his version of Platonism) as the foundation of knowledge. Although Yurkevych did not work out a philosophical system that would satisfy his philosophical demands, he indicated how and where adequate solutions must be sought. His philosophical program and many of his ideas were adopted by his student, V. Solovev, who constructed the most comprehensive and systematic philosophical theory in the history of Russian thought. Yurkevych also published a book of lectures on education (1865) and the best textbook on pedagogy (1869) in the Russian Empire at the time.

BIBLIOGRAPHY
Solov'ev, V. 'O filosofskikh trudakh P.D. Iurkevicha,' *Zhurnal Ministerstva narodnago prosveshcheniia*, no. 178 (1874)
Shpet, G. 'Filosofskoe nasledstvo P.D. Iurkevicha,' *Voprosy filosofii i psikhologii*, no. 125 (1914)
Iurkevych, P. *Tvory*, ed with an intro by S. Jarmus (Winnipeg 1979)
Pietsch, R. *Beiträge zur Entwicklung der Philosophie bei den Ostslawen in 19. Jahrhundret – Pamifil D. Jurkevyč (1826–1874)* (Ulm 1992)

T. Zakydalsky

**Yurkevych, Viktor** [Jurkevyč], b 7 January 1899 in Aleksandropol (now Leninakan), Armenia, d ? Historian. In the 1920s he studied under M. Hrushevsky at the Kiev Scientific Research Chair of the History of Ukraine, and from 1927 he worked for the VUAN Commission for the Study of Modern Ukrainian History. He was a specialist in 16th- and 17th-century Ukrainian social history. He contributed articles to VUAN serials and wrote a monograph about the eastward migration of Ukrainians and the colonization of Slobidska Ukraine in the time of Hetman B. Khmelnytsky (1932). He was arrested during the Yezhov terror of 1937 and sent to a concentration camp, where he perished.

**Yurko, William** [Jurko, Vasyl'], b 11 February 1926 in Hairy Hill, Alberta. Politician and nuclear engineer of Ukrainian-Rumanian origin. Yurko was educated at the universities of Alberta and Michigan. He was elected in 1969 to the legislature of Alberta as the Progressive Conservative member for Strathcona East, and re-elected in 1971 and 1975. While serving as minister of the environment (1971–5) and minister of housing and public works (1975–8) he played a large role in the establishment of the *Ukrainian Cultural Heritage Village as a provincial historic site. He was elected to the federal House of Commons in 1979 as member for Edmonton East and was re-elected in 1980. Yurko is the author of *Parliament and Patriation: The Triumph of Unilateralism* (1984).

**Yurynets, Volodymyr** [Jurynec'], b 1891 in Olesko, Zolochiv county, Galicia, d 1937. Philosopher and literary critic; VUAN full member from 1929. He studied mathematics and philosophy at Lviv, Berlin, Paris, and Vienna (PH D) universities. After graduating from the Institute of Red Professors in Moscow (1924) he lectured at the Communist University of the Eastern Peoples and Moscow University. In 1925 he moved to Kharkiv, where he taught dialectical materialism and chaired the sociology department at the Ukrainian Institute of Marxism-Leninism. From 1931 he chaired the philosophy department at the All-Ukrainian Association of Marxist-Leninist Scientific Research Institutes (VUAMLIN). Yurynets knew 10 languages and was familiar with the history of and current developments in Western thought. His articles in *Pod znamenem marksizma* on E. Husserl's phenomenology (1922, nos 11–12) and S. Freud's methodology (1924, nos 8–9) attracted wide attention. He expounded K. Marx's and F. Engels's doctrines of dialectical and historical materialism and defended them from 'bourgeois nationalist' criticisms (*Prapor marksyzmu*, 1927, no. 1; 1929, no. 6), and coauthored a textbook on dialectical materialism (1932). His chief ambition, however, was to develop a Marxist esthetics, and to this end he explored critically G. Lessing's esthetic theory (*Krytyka*, 1929, no. 3), I. Kant's theory of judgment (*Hart*, 1927, nos 2–3), and G. Plekhanov's contribution to the sociology of art (*Molodniak*, 1927, no. 5). He argued that universal esthetic criteria were possible only in a classless society. Yurynets also took a keen interest in Ukrainian literature: he participated in the *Literary Discussion of the 1920s, in which he criticized M. Khvylovy and the Vaplite writers' group, and wrote a book on P. Tychyna's poetry (1928). In 1933 Yurynets was branded as a 'bourgeois idealist,' expelled from the Party, and removed from his academic posts. About a year later he was denounced by the Party as an enemy of the state and was arrested. He perished in a Soviet prison or labor camp. Although he was posthumously rehabilitated in the 1960s, he has hardly been discussed, and his works have not been republished.

BIBLIOGRAPHY
Ivan'o, I. 'Volodymyr Iurynets' – doslidnyk mystetstva,' *Filosofs'ka dumka*, 1970, no. 5

T. Zakydalsky

**Yuryniak, Anatol** [Jurynjak, Anatol'] (pseud: B. Syvenko), b 8 December 1902 near Proskuriv (now Khmelnytskyi), Podilia gubernia. Pedagogue and writer. As a postwar refugee he worked as an editor of *Ukraïns'ki visti* in Neu-Ulm. A resident of the United States (Detroit, Chicago, and Los Angeles) since 1949, he has contributed to Ukrainian periodicals there and has been active in the Ukrainian Democratic Youth Association, the Ukrainian Orthodox church, and the Ukrainian Cultural Center in Los Angeles. Published separately have been his plays *Na dalekykh shliakhakh* (On Distant Roads, 1955) and *Spravzhnia narechena* (A Real Fiancée, 1967); the collections of literary criticism and publicism *Literaturnyi tvir i ioho avtor* (The Literary Work and Its Author, 1955) and *Krytychnym perom* (With a Critical Pen, 2 vols, 1974, 1987); the textbooks *Tvorchi komponenty literaturnoho tvoru* (Creative Components of a Literary Work, 1964), *Zasoby i sposoby poetychnoho vyslovu* (Devices and Means of Poetic Expression, 1966), *Literaturni zhanry* (Literary Genres, 1979), and *Literaturni zhanry maloï formy* (Small-Form Literary Genres, 1981); the poetry collection *Liudiam i sobi* (For People and Myself, 1964); and the prose collection *Kamikadze padaie sam* (Kamikadze Falls Alone, 1973).

R. Senkus

**Yurzhenko, Oleksandr** [Jurženko], b 29 August 1910 in Barativka, Kherson county. Physical chemist. A graduate of the Vologda Technological Institute (1932), he taught at postsecondary schools from 1935 (from 1949 as a professor) and was a prorector at Lviv University (1957–60) and rector of Odessa University (1960–70). From 1971 he taught in Kiev. His research dealt with the mechanism and kinetics of olefin polymerization processes in emulsions, and with hydrocarbon oxidations.

**Yushanly River** [Jušanly]. A left-bank tributary of the Molochna River that flows westward for 94 km in southern Zaporizhia oblast and drains a basin area of 700 sq km. Its water level drops considerably during the summer, and some sections of the river routinely dry out.

**Yushchenko, Kateryna** [Juščenko], b 8 December 1919 in Chyhyryn, Kiev gubernia. Mathematician and cyberneticist; corresponding member of the AN URSR (now ANU) since 1976. After graduating from the University of Central Asia in 1942, she worked at the ANU Institute of Mathematics (1946–57) and then at the Institute of Cybernetics and Kiev University. Yushchenko has made significant contributions to the theory of probability and obtained important results in the area of local limit theorems for multidimensional distributions as well as the development of algorithms connected with language programming.

**Yushchenko, Oleksa** [Juščenko], b 2 August 1917 in Khoruzhivka, Sumy county, Kharkiv gubernia. Writer. From 1945 to 1987 he published poetry collections, books of poetry for children, a book about the Soviet Ukrainian song (1964), a collection of songs (1967), a book of humor and satire (1973), and books of sketches, essays, and memoirs titled *Bezsmertnyky* (The Immortal, 3 vols, 1974, 1978, 1982) and *V pam'iati moïi* (In My Memory, 1986). He has written the lyrics to many Soviet Ukrainian songs. In 1983 he was awarded the Tychyna Prize.

**Yushchenko, Oleksander** [Juščenko], b 3 December 1869 in Vodotecha *khutir*, near Hlukhiv, Chernihiv gubernia, d 13 June 1936 in Kharkiv. Psychiatrist; full member of the AN URSR (now ANU) from 1934. A graduate of Kharkiv University (1893), he worked in Kharkiv, Warsaw, and St Petersburg (to 1897), was a professor at Tartu, Voronezh, and Northern Caucasia universities (1916–30), and worked at the Kharkiv Institute for the Upgrading of Physicians and the Ukrainian Institute of Clinical and Social Psychohygiene (from 1930) and at the Ukrainian Psychoneurological Academy (from 1932). One of the founders of the biochemical approach in psychiatry, he studied reflexes of the sympathetic nervous system in animals and humans, the relation of nutrition and blood chemistry to childhood paralysis, various nervous and mental diseases, and the delineation of various psychic types.

**Yushchyshyn, Ivan** [Juščyšyn], b 1883, d ? Educator. While working as an elementary-school teacher in the villages of Zbarazh county, Galicia, he served as secretary of the Ukrainian Teachers' Mutual Aid Society in Lviv and chairman of its Pedagogical Research Commission as well as editor of the journal *Uchytel'* (1911–14). During the First World War he was deported to Irkutsk by Russian authorities. In 1918 he directed the Department of Public Education in the Ministry of Education in Kiev and edited *Derzhavnyi vistnyk* there. After the war he continued to teach in Zbarazh county, edited *Uchytel's'ke slovo* for many years, and wrote articles on educational theory and methodology. His fate after 1939 is unknown.

**Yushkov, Serafim** [Juškov], b 4 May 1888 in Trofimovshchina, Penza gubernia, Russia, d 18 August 1952 in Moscow. Russian historian; corresponding member of the AN URSR (now ANU) from 1939. He taught at the universities of Moscow and Leningrad and worked at the ANU Institute of History. He specialized in medieval states and law and published a number of works on the Princely era of Ukraine, including ones on the statute of Grand Prince Volodymyr the Great (1925), the *Ruskaia Pravda* (1935, 1950), and the history of feudalism in Kievan Rus' (1939).

**Yushkov, Stanislav** [Juškov], b 21 March 1950 in Kasli, Cheliabinsk oblast, RSFSR. Painter. Since 1953 he has lived in Ukraine. A graduate of the Kharkiv Industrial Design Institute (1972), he has worked as a stained-glass artist. Yushkov paints mainly in watercolors, because he likes to work

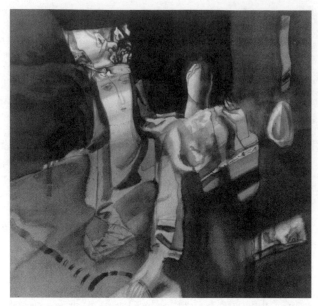

Stanislav Yushkov: *Understanding Each Other* (watercolor, 1986)

quickly to capture his prevailing mood. Such compositions as *Broken Line* (1985) and *Dialogue with Time* (1988) are indicative of the symbolic themes and language of his work.

**Yuskiv, Teodor** [Jus'kiv] (pseud: Teren), b 1911 in Potochyshche, Horodenka county, Galicia. Opera singer (baritone). He studied voice with A. Didur in Lviv and made his debut with the Lviv Opera in G. Donizetti's *La Favorita* in 1937. He performed in such operas as G. Verdi's *La Traviata* and *Rigoletto*, G. Rossini's *The Barber of Seville*, W. Mozart's *The Marriage of Figaro*, and G. Bizet's *Carmen*, in Poland, Germany, Norway, and France. After the war he gave concerts in Germany, and in 1949 he emigrated to the United States. He wrote *Natsional'no-derzhavna motyvatsiia tvorchosty S. Liudkevycha* (The National-Statist Motivation of the Work of S. Liudkevych, 1984) and contributed music reviews to the Ukrainian press.

**Yuz Oba.** A group of hills south of Kerch in which a number of 4th-century BC kurhans were found. Excavations of the kurhans in 1858–60 and in the 1880s revealed that they housed the remains of nobles from *Panticapaeum, the capital of the Bosporan Kingdom. Most of the kurhans were 8.5–12 m tall and 160–200 m wide and were stone vaulted. In one of the kurhans the remains of a priestess of the cult of Demeter were recovered. Among the grave goods found were carved wooden sarcophaguses (some inlaid with amber), gold crowns, jewelry, mirrors, and high-quality vases.

**Yuzefovich, Mikhail** [Juzefovič, Mixail], b 29 June 1802, d 2 June 1889. Russian administrator and cultural ac-

tivist in Kiev. He was a trustee of the Kiev school district (1842–58) and head of the Kiev Archeographic Commission (1857–89). As one of the founders of the *Southwestern Branch of the Imperial Russian Geographic Society he presided over the commission in charge of building the monument to B. Khmelnytsky in Kiev. He was fiercely opposed to the Ukrainophilism of many of the branch's members, and in May 1875 he submitted a memorandum to the tsarist authorities in St Petersburg denouncing the group and its work as subversive. His action resulted in the establishment of an imperial commission (of which he was a key member), whose recommendations lay the groundwork for the repressive *Ems Ukase of 1876, also commonly known as Yuzefovich's Law.

**Yuzivka.** See Donetske.

Sen Paul Yuzyk

**Yuzyk, Paul** [Juzyk, Pavlo], b 24 June 1913 in Pinto, Saskatchewan, d 9 July 1986 in Ottawa. Scholar and Canadian senator. The son of a Ukrainian immigrant coal miner, Yuzyk was educated at the University of Saskatchewan and the University of Minnesota (PH D, 1958). He taught Slavic studies and history at the University of Manitoba (1951–63) and Soviet and Eastern European studies at the University of Ottawa (1963–78). Appointed to the Canadian Senate in 1963 as a Progressive Conservative for Manitoba, Yuzyk was a major advocate of multiculturalism and a key figure in its establishment as a state policy in Canada. He was active in international parliamentary organizations and often represented Canada abroad. He was president of the *Ukrainian National Youth Federation (MUNO, 1934–6) and of the *Ukrainian Cultural and Educational Center (Oseredok) in Winnipeg (1955–71). His historical writings, notably *The Ukrainians in Manitoba: A Social History* (1953, 1977), were among the earliest efforts to present the viewpoint of Ukrainians on their history in Canada. His other works include *Ukrainian Canadians: Their Place and Role in Canadian Life* (1967), *A Statistical Compendium on the Ukrainians in Canada, 1891–1976* (1980, with W. Darcovich), and *The Ukrainian Greek Orthodox Church of Canada, 1918–1951* (1981).

# Z

**Z nevoli** (From Captivity). A literary miscellany published in 1908 in St Petersburg. It contained poetry and prose by O. Kovalenko, M. Cherniavsky, K. Maksymenko, P. Kapelhorodsky, Yu. Budiak, Kh. Alchevska, Lesia Ukrainka, A. Krymsky, P. Tenianko, A. Kashchenko, M. Kotsiubynsky, S. Cherkasenko, B. Hrinchenko, I. Lypa, O. Lutsky, N. Onatsky, and others. The collection was interpreted as antitsarist and was banned by the authorities; most of the copies were confiscated and destroyed.

**Z potoku zhyttia** (From the Stream of Life). A literary miscellany published in Kherson in 1905. Edited by M. Kotsiubynsky and M. Cherniavsky, it contained original poetry and prose by Kotsiubynsky, Cherniavsky, L. Yanovska, I. Franko, P. Myrny, A. Chaikovsky, A. Krymsky, N. Kybalchych-Kozlovska, O. Kobylianska, I. Nechui-Levytsky, M. Vorony, O. Lutsky, B. Hrinchenko, H. Hryhorenko, L. Starytska-Cherniakhivska, M. Verbytsky, and M. Starytsky. The contributions were written in response to Kotsiubynsky and Cherniavsky's appeals to Ukrainian writers to transcend peasant themes.

**Za derzhavnist'** (For Statehood). A serial published by the Ukrainian Military History Society in Kalisz and Warsaw (9 vols, 1925–39) and later by the Ukrainian Military History Institute in Toronto (2 vols, 1964, 1966). The editor of the entire collection was Gen M. *Sadovsky. It is an important source for the history of the struggle for Ukraine's independence. It consists of recollections, eyewitness accounts, materials on the different units of the UNR Army, and photographs.

**Za markso-lenins'ku pedahohiku** (For a Marxist-Leninist Pedagogy). A pedagogical journal and the organ of the *Scientific Research Institute of Pedagogy of the Ukrainian SSR, published in Kharkiv in 1931–2. It replaced *Ukraïns'kyi visnyk eksperymental'noï pedahohiky ta refleksolohiï and followed the Stalinist line in education. It favored the Russification of the Ukrainian school system and stressed Communist ideology and practice in education.

**Za nezalezhnist'** (For Independence). A bulletin of the *Ukrainian Central Committee in Poland, published monthly in Warsaw in 1934–6 and then every two months to 1939. Edited by P. Shkurat, it primarily reported on the activities of the committee.

**Za Radians'ku Ukraïnu!** (For Soviet Ukraine!). An organ of the CC CP(B)U and Supreme Soviet of the Ukrainian SSR, published three times a week in 1941–3 in various places, during the German occupation of Ukraine. One to two million copies were dropped from airplanes behind the German lines each month. The chief editor was the poet M. Bazhan; he was assisted by prominent writers and cultural figures, such as W. Wasilewska and O. Korniichuk.

**Za sobornist'** (For Unity). An irregular journal of the Mohyla Society in Lutske, nine issues of which appeared in 1932–5, under the editorship of I. *Vlasovsky. The journal supported the establishment of an autocephalous Ukrainian Orthodox church under the aegis of the patriarchate of Constantinople, and close ties to other Orthodox churches. It published some articles in Belarusian and Russian.

**Za sto lit: Materialy z hromads'koho i literaturnoho zhyttia Ukraïny XIX i pochatku XX stolittia** (In One Hundred Years: Materials from the Community and Literary Life of Ukraine in the 19th and Early 20th Centuries). A serial published in Kiev by the Commission for the Study of Modern Ukrainian History (est 1926) of the historical section of the VUAN. Six volumes of Za sto lit were issued from 1927 to 1930. They were edited by M. *Hrushevsky, and their authors included H. Zhytetsky, M. Vozniak, V. Miiakovsky, S. Shamrai, Y. Hermaize, F. Savchenko, B. Sheveliv, S. Rusova, T. Slabchenko, S. Kozub, Yu. Tsyhanenko, O. Riabinin-Skliarevsky, and Ya. Aizenshtok. They are valuable sources for Ukrainian historiography.

Liubov Zabashta

**Zabashta, Liubov** [Zabašta, Ljubov], b 3 February 1918 in Pryluka, Poltava gubernia. Writer. She graduated from the Odessa Water Institute (1941) and has worked as an engineer. She began publishing in 1935. Since 1950 she has published over 15 poetry collections, the narrative poem *Oleksa Borkaniuk* (1954), a collection of plays and dramatic poems (1963), two books of poetry for children, and the novels *Kryla Arsena Dorosha* (The Wings of Arsen Dorosh, 1968), *Tam, za rikoiu – molodist'* (There, across the River, Is

Youth, 1970), *Budynok moho dytynstva* (The Building of My Childhood, 1983), and *Krylati moï korabli* (My Winged Ships, 1983). Three of her more recent dramatic poems are about T. Shevchenko, Lesia Ukrainka, and the legendary Marusia Churai. Editions of her selected works appeared in 1958, 1968, 1977, 1982, and 1987.

**Zabashta, Vasyl** [Zabašta, Vasyl'], b 11 June 1918 in Babenkove, Izium county, Kharkiv gubernia. Painter. A graduate of the Kiev State Art Institute (1951), he joined its faculty in 1955. He has painted portraits and genre paintings in the socialist realist manner, such as *P. Tchaikovsky at the Home of M. Lysenko* (1954), *In the Years of the Underground* (1955), *Recollections of Ukraine* (1964), *Kulak Vengeance* (1971), *Victory Salute* (1975), and *The Banduryst H. Tkachenko* (1978).

**Zabashtansky, Volodymyr** [Zabaštans'kyj], b 5 October 1940 in Brailiv, Zhmerynka raion, Vinnytsia oblast. Poet of the *\*shestydesiatnyky* generation. At the age of 18 he lost his sight and both arms in an industrial accident. He is the author of the collections *Nakaz kameniariv* (The Order of the Quarriers, 1967), *Vira v liudynu* (Faith in Man, 1971), *Moia vuz'kokoliika* (My Narrow-Gauge Railroad, 1973), *Hranitni krapli* (Granite Droplets, 1975), *Syni skeli* (Blue Cliffs, 1978), *Krytseiu riadka* (With the Steel of a Line, 1977), *Vaha slova* (The Weight of the Word, 1980), and *Treba stoiaty* (One Must Stand, 1986). In 1986 he was awarded the Shevchenko Prize. An edition of his selected works appeared in 1988.

**Zabelin, Ivan,** b 29 September 1820 in Tver (now Kalinin), d 13 January 1909 in Moscow. Russian historian and archeologist; honorary member of the Russian Academy of Sciences from 1907. He worked in the Kremlin armory (1837–59), served on the Imperial Archeological Commission (1859–76), and taught Russian history and antiquity at Moscow University (1879–88). Among his works on the history of material culture is *Istoriia russkoi zhizni s drevneishikh vremen* (History of Russian Life from the Earliest Times, 1876–9; 2nd edn 1908–12). During expeditions to Ukrainian territories he studied several sites of note, including the Tsymbalka kurhans, Chortomlyk (1862–3), and Velyka Blyznytsia (1864). Zabelin was one of the driving forces behind the establishment of the Moscow Historical Museum, of which he was the de facto director in 1883–4.

**Zabila.** A family line of nobility and Cossack officers from the Chernihiv region. It was established by Petro \*Zabila, who was a general quartermaster in the Hetmanate. His descendants were notable political and cultural activists of the 17th to 19th centuries. Petro's sons were Stepan \*Zabila, Vasyl Zabila, who was a general flag-bearer in 1690, and Taras Zabila, whose son, Mykhailo, was a general judge in 1728–40. The poet Viktor \*Zabila and the wood-carver Parmen \*Zabila also belonged to the line.

**Zabila, Natalia,** b 5 March 1903 in St Petersburg, d 6 February 1985 in Kiev. Poet, prose writer, and playwright. She studied at the Kharkiv Institute of People's Education and worked first as a teacher and then in the editorial office of various journals; for some time she was editor of the periodical *Barvinok*. She began to publish her own

Natalia Zabila

work in 1924. Zabila wrote her first poetry in a modernistic style, which she was forced to abandon in response to Soviet political pressure. Her poetry appeared under the following titles: *Dalekii kraï* (Distant Lands, 1927), *Soniashni reli* (Sunny Lyres, 1928), and *Budivnyche* (Constructional, 1930). From the 1930s on she wrote mainly for children: *Iasochchyna ialynka* (Weasel's Christmas Tree, 1934), *Veseli maliuky* (Happy Youngsters, 1951), *Opovidannia, kazky, povisti* (Stories, Tales, and Novels, 1962), *Dyvovyzhni pryhody khlopchyka Iurchyka ta ioho dida* (The Strange Adventures of Little Boy George and His Grandfather, 1964), *Pro babyni kazky* (About Grandmother's Tales, 1978), *Try chverti viku* (Three-Quarters of an Age, 1978), and many others. Zabila also retold in verse *Slovo o polku Ihorevi* (The Tale of Ihor's Campaign, 1940) and translated A. Pushkin, M. Lermontov, and N. Nekrasov from Russian. The most complete edition of her collected works is *Tvory v chotyr'okh tomakh* (Works in Four Volumes, 1971–3).

**Zabila, Parmen** (Zabello), b 9 August 1830 in Monastyryshche, Nizhen county, Chernihiv gubernia, d 25 February 1917 in Lausanne. Sculptor. A graduate of the St Petersburg Academy of Arts (1857) and a member of the academy from 1869, he sculpted bas-relief portraits of the Kochubei family, busts of T. Shevchenko (1869, 1872), portraits of M. Saltykov-Shchedrin (1879), V. Makovsky (1894), and V. Borovykovsky, the statue of A. Herzen at his grave in Nice (1872), and a bust for the monument to N. Gogol in Nizhen (1881).

**Zabila, Petro,** b 1580 in Borzna, Chernihiv region, d 1689. Cossack leader. An administrator of Polish crownlands, he switched loyalties in 1648 and joined B. Khmelnytsky's forces. He was made colonel of Borzna regiment (1649, 1654–5) and captain of Borzna company (1652–61), which position his descendants inherited and held until the abolition of the Hetmanate. In 1654 and 1655 he traveled to Moscow as the emissary of I. Zolotarenko, the acting hetman of Ukrainian Cossacks in Belarus. He supported I. Vyhovsky and served as general judge (1663–9) under I. Briukhovetsky, whom he represented in Moscow (1665). Under D. Mnohohrishny he was general quartermaster (1669–87) and also served as Mnohohrishny's representative in Moscow. In 1672 Zabila participated in a plot against Mnohohrishny, aiming to seize power himself. His plan failed, and I. Samoilovych became hetman.

**Zabila, Stepan,** b and d ? 17th-century Cossack officer; son of Petro Zabila. A veteran of the Chyhyryn and Crimean campaigns as well as an envoy to Moscow for I. Samoilovych in 1672, he was a captain in Borzna company (1674–7) and then general flag-bearer (1678–83) and colonel of Nizhen regiment (1687–94).

**Zabila, Viktor,** b 1808 on the Kukurivshchyna estate (now Zabilivshchyna), Borzna county, Chernihiv gubernia, d 1869 in Borzna. Romantic poet. From the early 1830s he lived on his father's estates, where he was visited by T. Shevchenko, V. Shternberg, and M. Glinka. He began to publish his work in the 1830s, in *Lastôvka* (1841). In 1906 I. Franko published Zabila's collection *Pisni kriz' sl'ozy* (Songs through Tears). Zabila's poetry, with its motifs of sorrow and sadness, was neither highly original nor of great significance, but his songs 'Hude viter vel'my v poli' (The Wind Is Blowing Much in the Field) and 'Ne shchebechy soloveiku' (Don't Sing, Nightingale), set to music by Glinka, achieved great popularity. Zabila also wrote music to some of his own works and performed them with bandura accompaniment. Glinka and Shevchenko wrote about him in their memoirs.

Lidiia Zabiliasta                    Danylo Zabolotny

**Zabiliasta, Lidiia** [Zabiljasta, Lidija], b 8 September 1953 in Oleno-Kosohorivka, Kirovohrad raion. Opera and concert singer (soprano). In 1979 she graduated from the Kiev State Conservatory in the vocal class of Z. Khrystych and began singing with the Kiev Theater of Opera and Ballet. She has won numerous music competitions, including a first prize and gold medal at the 1982 Tchaikovsky International Competition in Moscow, and has toured France, Finland, Canada, and the United States. Among her major roles are Marguerite in C. Gounod's *Faust*, Mimi and Chio-Chio-San in G. Puccini's *La Bohème* and *Madame Butterfly*, Tatiana in P. Tchaikovsky's *Eugene Onegin*, Natalka and Maryltsia in M. Lysenko's *Natalka from Poltava* and *Taras Bulba*, and Oksana in S. Hulak-Artemovsky's *Zaporozhian Cossack beyond the Danube*.

**Zablonsky, Kostiantyn** [Zablons'kyj, Kostjantyn], b 18 June 1915 in Khrystynivka, Cherkasy county, Kiev gubernia. Mechanical engineer and specialist in the design and theory of machines. He studied and worked at the Odessa Polytechnical Institute, as rector from 1969. He developed a mathematical theory that allows exact calculations for mechanical transmission systems.

**Zablotsky-Desiatovsky, Pavlo** [Zabloc'kyj-Desjatovs'kyj], b 15 July 1814 in Chernihiv gubernia, d 14 July 1882 in Krymky, Zvenyhorodka county, Kiev gubernia. Physician; full member of the Russian Imperial Academy of Sciences. A graduate of Moscow University (1835), he was an adjunct professor of surgery (1842–6) and a professor of forensic medicine (1846–69) at the St Petersburg Medico-Surgical Academy and served as court physician (1843–9). In 1847 he was the first to use chloroform as an anesthetic in the Russian Empire. The founding president of the Russian Surgeons' Society (1882), he wrote scientific works on surgery and venereology, including *Rukovodstvo k izucheniiu i lecheniiu sifiliticheskikh boleznei* (A Guide to the Study and Treatment of Syphilitic Diseases, 1857).

**Zabłudów** (Ukrainian: Zabludiv). A town (1983 pop 1,800) in northern Podlachia in Białystok voivodeship, Poland. During 1567–8 a printing press was founded there and was run by I. *Fedorovych and P. Mstsislavets. The first printed works to come out were the *Zabłudów Gospel (1568–9) and a psalter with breviary (1570).

**Zabłudów Gospel.** The first published Church Slavonic didactic gospel. It was printed in 1568–9 by I. *Fedorovych and P. Mstsislavets at the press of the Lithuanian grand hetman H. Khodkevich in Zabłudów (Ukrainian: Zabludiv) in northern Podlachia. Khodkevych wanted the gospel to be published in the vernacular so that it would be comprehensible to the common people, but Fedorovych and Mstsislavets printed it in Church Slavonic.

**Zaboi.** A literary organization of the Donbas region, founded in 1925. It initially consisted of Russian writers and was led by the critic O. Selivanovsky. When Ukrainization was at its peak, it began attracting Ukrainian writers. Its membership included I. Le, H. Bahliuk, V. Haivoronsky, K. Herasymenko, B. Pavlivsky, V. Ivanov-Kramatorsky, M. Rud, A. Trylisky, M. Sobolenko, B. Semenov, P. Chebalin, and D. Tkach. During the attacks on Ukrainian culture in the 1930s, most of its members were shot or arrested and exiled. Its official organ was a journal of the same name. When the Writers' Union of Ukraine was formed in 1932, Zaboi ceased to exist.

*Zaboi.* A literary journal (141 issues) of Donetske writers, established in 1923 by the Artemivske newspaper *Kocheharka*. It was initially published in Russian, and then Ukrainized in the mid-1920s. In 1924 it was made the official organ of the organization of the same name and was edited by H. Bahliuk. In 1932 the journal was renamed *Literaturnyi Donbas.*

**Zabolotny, Danylo** [Zabolotnyj], b 28 December 1866 in Chobotarka (now Zabolotne), Olhopil county, Podilia gubernia, d 15 December 1929 in Kiev. Microbiologist and epidemiologist; full member of the VUAN from 1922 and its president in 1928–9; full member of the USSR Academy of Sciences from 1929. A graduate in physics and mathematics of Odessa University (1891) and in medicine of Kiev University (1894), he was the founding director of the first bacteriology department in the Russian Empire, at the St

Petersburg Women's Medical Institute (1898–1928), and of the first epidemiology department in the world, at Odessa University (1920). He was rector of the Odessa Medical Institute (1921–4), taught at the Leningrad Military Medical Academy (1924–8), and founded and directed the VUAN Institute of Microbiology and Virology (1928). Zabolotny achieved important results in his research on plague, cholera, syphilis, gangrene, diphtheria, typhus, and dysentery; he conducted expeditions to India, Mongolia, and China to study the plague. He discovered (with I. *Savchenko) bacilli-carrying and vibrio cholera (1893), and proved (1911) that the bacteria causing plague are transmitted to humans by wild rodents. A cofounder of the International Society of Microbiologists, Zabolotny wrote *Osnovy epidemiologii* (Fundamentals of Epidemiology, vol 1, 1927). Compilations of his studies were published as *Izbrannye trudy* (Collected Works, 2 vols, 1956–7) and *Vybrani pratsi* (Selected Works, 1969). Biographies of him have been written by H. Golubev (1962), V. Bilai (1966), and Ye. Kryzhanivsky (1971), and there is a museum in his honor in Zabolotne, where he is buried.

Volodymyr Zabolotny

Metropolitan Rafail Zaborovsky

**Zabolotny, Volodymyr** [Zabolotnyj], b 13 August 1898 in Karen, Pereiaslav county, Poltava gubernia, d 3 August 1962 in Kiev. Architect; president of the Academy of Architecture of the Ukrainian SSR (1945–56) and full member of the USSR Academy of Construction and Architecture from 1950. After graduating from the Kiev State Art Institute in 1927, he joined its faculty and in 1940 became a professor. He supervised the design and construction of over 70 blocks in interwar Kiev and many urban housing developments and workers' settlements in the Donbas and Kryvyi Rih region (1929–33), and designed the Palace of Culture at the Dzerzhinsky Metallurgical Plant in Dniprodzerzhynske (1932) and the Building of the Supreme Soviet in Kiev (1936–9). He wrote studies on Ukrainian architecture, including a book on the first 30 years of Soviet architecture in Ukraine (1948). A booklet about him by L. Hrachova was published in Kiev in 1967.

**Zaborovsky, Rafail** [Zaborovs'kyj, Rafajil] (secular name: Mykhailo), b 1677 in Galicia, d 22 October 1747 in Kiev. Orthodox bishop. He studied at the Kievan Mohyla Academy and the Moscow Theological Academy, where

he later taught rhetoric (1718). After serving as a chaplain in the Russian navy he became archimandrite of the Tver Monastery and a member of the Holy Synod in 1723. In 1725 he was consecrated bishop of Pskov. He was elevated to the office of archbishop of Kiev by the tsar in 1731, and he later convinced the church authorities to restore Kiev eparchy as a metropoly, whereupon he took the title 'Metropolitan of Kiev, Halych, and Little Russia' in 1743. A supporter of Archbishop T. *Prokopovych, Zaborovsky carried out the Russian government's policy of destroying the autonomy of the Ukrainian church by instituting the *Dukhovnyi reglament* of 1721 and other synodal ukases. He did, however, raise the academic standards and improve the economic standing of the *Kievan Mohyla Academy. He published a new statute for the academy, reformed the curriculum (adding new courses in more modern disciplines), and provided much money for the expansion of the academy's buildings and for scholarships for poor students. The academy even briefly became known as the Mohyla-Zaborovsky Academy. The bell tower of the Kievan Cave Monastery (1736–45), the bell tower of the St Sophia Cathedral, the baroque *Zaborovsky Gate, and a number of other buildings were constructed during his tenure as metropolitan. A biography of him by P. Orlovsky appeared in *TKDA* (1908).

A. Zhukovsky

The Zaborovsky Gate

**Zaborovsky Gate** (Zaborovskoho brama). The main entrance to the grounds of the former residence of the metropolitan of Kiev. It was built in 1746–8 in the baroque style by J. Schädel in the wall encircling the St Sophia Cathedral and was financed by Metropolitan R. Zaborovsky. The gate had columns with Corinthian capitals, volutes, mascarons, and acanthus leaves. In the 1920s its opening was walled up, and its façade was reconstructed by V. Krychevsky. It was restored again in 1946–8.

**Zaborowski, Tymon,** b 18 April 1799 in Lychkivtsi near Husiatyn, Galicia, d 20 or 28 March 1828 in Lychkivtsi. Polish pseudoclassical and Romantic poet in Galicia; a representative of the *Ukrainian school in Polish literature. He studied at the Kremianets Lyceum (1810–17), where he belonged to the so-called Writers' Club along with J. Korzeniowski. Many of his works are on Ukrainian themes and Ukrainian-Polish relations. They include the narrative poems 'Bolesław Chrobry, czyli zdobycie Kijowa' (Bolesław the Brave, or the Conquest of Kiev) and 'Bojan,' the patriotic collection 'Dumy podolskie za czasów panowania tureckiego w tej ziemi' (Podilian Dumas from the Time of Turkish Rule in That Land, pub in *Haliczanin*, vol 2, 1830), and the dramatic poems 'Bohdan Chmielnicki' (Bohdan Khmelnytsky) and 'Tajemnica, czyli Borys i Milwiana' (The Secret, or Borys and Milwiana), about the era of Yaroslav the Wise. An edition of his collected writings was published in Warsaw in 1936.

**Zabuzky, Semen** [Zabuz'skyj] (also Zabusky), b and d ? 17th-century Cossack officer. Prior to the Battle of Pyliavtsi in 1648, he defected from B. Khmelnytsky's Cossack army to the Poles. In the summer of 1649 he was designated hetman of Ukraine by Jan II Casimir Vasa, who hoped to replace Khmelnytsky with a loyal leader. Toward the end of 1650 he was instructed to amass a mercenary army to take into Ukraine, but the campaign did not materialize. Historical sources provide no information about Zabuzky's subsequent fate.

**Zachariasiewicz, Jan,** b 1 September 1825 in Radymno, Peremyshl circle, d 7 May 1906 in Kryvcha, Peremyshl county, Galicia. Polish Galician writer and radical democrat. In the years 1844–9 and 1851–65 he worked as a journalist and newpaper editor in Lviv. He wrote many publicistic novels about Galician society. They include 'Uczony' (The Scholar, 1855), based loosely on the life of I. Vahylevych, *Święty Jur* (St George's Cathedral, 3 vols, 1862), in which he criticized the Uniate clergy, and *Jarema* (Yarema, 1863), about conflicts between the Polish gentry and the Ukrainian peasantry. He was a popular writer in his time. An 11-volume edition of his collected works was published in 1886–8.

**Zacharjewicz, Juljan,** b 17 July 1837 in Lviv, d 27 December 1898. Polish architect. He was educated in Lviv and Vienna, and served as a railway engineer in Austria and Galicia (1858–71) before becoming a professor of the Lviv Polytechnic. In Lviv he designed the buildings of the Polytechnic (1872–7), the Industrial Museum (1874), the Savings Bank (1888–91), the Franciscan Church, and buildings in the Kostolivka district. He also restored a Roman Catholic church in Stryi and the castle in Husiatyn.

**Zachepylivka** [Začepylivka]. IV-16. A town smt (1990 pop 5,100) on the Berestova River and a raion center in Kharkiv oblast. It was founded in the first half of the 17th century by the Cossacks. From 1802 it was a *volost* center in Kostiantynohrad county, Poltava gubernia. The town was raised to smt status in 1968. It has a food industry and an embroidery workshop of the Kharkiv Handicrafts Consortium.

**Zadeka, Martyn.** See Hak, Anatol.

**Zaderej, Andrew** [Zaderej, Andrij], b 1921 in Yampil, Podilia gubernia. Engineer and inventor; member of the New York Academy of Sciences since 1980. He studied at the Kiev Polytechnical Institute but was displaced by the Second World War, and emigrated to the United States in 1949. He founded the Monitron and Unitron electronics companies in Indiana. Zaderej works in the fields of electronic and computer technology, bioelectronics, and medical electronics. He invented the first three-dimensional vector electrocardioscope and an electrogenic seed-treat-

ing machine, which is in worldwide use. His numerous electronic devices and systems also include an all-electric automobile, high-efficiency electric lamps, a sound-recorder, single-phase inductors, a solid state ignition, and thermally activated switches.

**Zadniprovsky, Mykhailo** [Zadniprovs'kyj, Myxajlo], b 9 January 1924 in Kamianka (now in Cherkasy oblast), d 9 June 1980 in Kiev. Stage and film actor. He completed study at the Kiev Institute of Theater Arts (1950) and then worked in the Kiev Ukrainian Drama Theater, where he played the title roles in T. Shevchenko's *Nazar Stodolia* and A. D'Ennery and F. Dumanoir's *Don Cezar de Bazan*. He also acted in the film *Dolia Maryny* (Maryna's Fate, 1953).

**Zadontsev, Anton** [Zadoncev], b 16 August 1908 in Stavydla, Oleksandrivske county, Katerynoslav gubernia, d 5 December 1971 in Dnipropetrovske. Biologist; corresponding member of the AN URSR (now ANU) from 1951 and full member of the All-Union Academy of Agricultural Sciences from 1960. A graduate of the Bila Tserkva Agricultural Institute (1929), he worked at the All-Union Scientific Research Institute of Corn (1932–71, from 1941 as director). His research mainly concerned the agrophysiological aspects of the hardiness and productivity of winter wheat.

Dezyderii Zador

**Zador, Dezyderii** [Dezyderij], b 20 October 1912 in Uzhhorod, d 16 September 1985 in Lviv. Composer, pianist, pedagogue, and conductor. A graduate of the Prague Conservatory (1934), he studied composition with V. Novak and piano with V. Kurz and then concertized in Czechoslovakia, Hungary, and Rumania. From 1945 he was a key figure in organizing musical life in Transcarpathia, as director of the Uzhhorod Music School and artistic director of the Transcarpathian Philharmonic Orchestra. In 1963 he moved, to teach at the Lviv Conservatory. His works include the cantata *The Carpathians* (1959), the symphonic poem *Verkhovyna* (1971), concertos for piano (1965) and for dulcimer (1982), incidental and chamber music, pieces for piano, choruses, art songs, and arrangements of folk songs.

**Zadoretsky, Petro** [Zadorec'kyj], b ? in Strilychi, Bibrka county, Galicia, d 9 May 1967 in New York. *Sich organizer and community activist. As a young man he set up a Sich society in his village, and after emigrating to the

United States in 1896 he organized and led a Sokil society (renamed Sich in 1914) in New York. He subsequently was active in establishing a network of Sich societies and served as supreme otaman in 1918–19. During the interwar period he was a strong supporter of the Organization for the Rebirth of Ukraine.

Ivan Zadorozhny                    Bishop Maksym Zadvirniak

**Zadorozhny, Ivan** [Zadorožnyj], b 10 March 1916 in Horodenka, Galicia, d 11 February 1972 in Stamford, Connecticut. Conductor and singer (baritone). He studied at the Greek Catholic Theological Academy in Lviv and the Lysenko Higher Institute of Music before emigrating to Germany (1944) and then to the United States (1949). There he appeared in opera productions and conducted church choirs and choruses such as Dumka (New York) and Prometheus (Philadelphia). He achieved his greatest renown as conductor of the Ukrainian Bandurist Chorus (Detroit).

Valentyn Zadorozhny: *Mother* (1969)

**Zadorozhny, Valentyn** [Zadorožnyj], b 7 August 1921 in Kiev, d 21 October 1988 in Kiev. Painter. In 1951 he graduated from the Kiev State Art Institute, where he studied under K. Yeleva, A. Petrytsky, and O. Shovkunenko. He has painted stylistically original historical and genre canvases, such as *Bohdan Khmelnytsky Leaving His Son Tymish as Hostage with the Crimean Khan* (1954), *Kobzar's Song* (1962–4), *At the Site of Past Battles: My Countrymen* (1964–5), the triptych *Mother* (1969), *My Village and I* (1975–7), *Marusia Churai* (1972–8), and *Soldiers' Mothers* (1985–6). He has also designed posters and the stained-glass triptych *T. Shevchenko and the People*, at Kiev University (1967), the mosaic panel *My Fatherland*, at the Dormash Plant's Palace of Culture in Kremenchuk (1969), and the stained-glass window *Cosmos* (1974) and mural *Birth of Technical Thought* (1975), in the Pavlohrad Palace of Culture.

**Zadunaiska Sich.** See Danubian Sich.

**Zadvirniak, Maksym** [Zadvirnjak], b 1882 in Podilia gubernia, d ? Bishop of the Ukrainian Autocephalous Orthodox church. He was ordained in 1915 and became bishop of Proskuriv in 1923. He was arrested in 1930 and sent to the Solovets Islands, where he died.

**Zafiiovska, Liubov** [Zafijovs'ka, Ljubov] (Safiowska, Lubow), b 25 June 1901 in Kielce, Poland, d 20 April 1969 in New York. Ukrainian botanist and cytologist; member of the Shevchenko Scientific Society from 1950. A graduate of Kiev University (1930, 1937), she worked at the VUAN Institute of Botany (1930–3) and taught at Kiev University (1933–42) and Poznań University (1942–5). After emigrating to the United States in 1951, she did research on embryology and the cell physiology of plants at Chicago (1958–9) and Fordham (from 1961) universities.

**Zagórski, Tadeusz,** b 1866, d 1934. Polish activist in Western Ukraine. A lawyer by profession, he was head of the Polish People's Committee in Ruthenia and J. Piłsudski's representative to the General Staff of the UNR Army (1919–20). He later lived in Volhynia, where he edited the newspaper *Przegląd Wołyński.*

**Zagreb.** The capital (1990 pop 649,586) of Croatia and its chief cultural and educational center. It is also a religious and educational center of *Križevci eparchy, which has jurisdiction over Greek Catholic Ukrainians in the Bačka region and Slovenia. SS Cyril and Methodius's Church and Greek Catholic Seminary, with a secondary school, are located in Zagreb. In 1981 there were 381 Ukrainians in the city (120 of whom were listed as Ruthenians).

In 1919 a mission of the Western Ukrainian National Republic, headed by D. *Lukiianovych, was stationed in Zagreb. After the First World War a small community of Ukrainian émigrés formed there, and the university attracted some young people from Galicia. In the interwar period a Prosvita Society (est 1922), the Union of Ukrainian Students (1927), and the Dnipro student society were active there. The student community helped publish the bimonthly *Dumka*. In 1941–4 a quasiconsular representation headed by V. Voitanivsky was maintained in Zagreb by the OUN (Melnyk faction). Today a Ukrainian cultural-educational association is active in the city. Since 1966 guest

ss Cyril and Methodius Church and Seminary in Zagreb

lecturers from Ukraine have taught Ukrainian language and literature at the department of Russian philology of Zagreb University. As well, an exchange program exists between Kiev and Zagreb universities, and occasional cultural exchanges take place between the two cities.

**Zahaikevych, Bohdan** [Zahajkevyč], b 5 February 1887 in Ternopil, Galicia, d 20 August 1967 in Irvington, New

Bohdan Zahaikevych        Volodymyr Zahaikevych

Jersey. Educator, collector, and civic activist; brother of V. *Zahaikevych; member of the Shevchenko Scientific Society and the Ukrainian Academy of Arts and Sciences in the US. After graduating from Lviv University he taught secondary school in Peremyshl. During the First World War he served in the Ukrainian Galician Army. In 1922 he returned as a teacher to Peremyshl, where he also became director of the Stryvihor Museum and president of the Boian society. After emigrating to the United States in 1950, he devoted his time to the Shevchenko Scientific Society's regional studies series of regional collections and was editor of the Peremyshl volume.

**Zahaikevych, Volodymyr** [Zahajkevyč], b October 1876 in Ternopil, Galicia, d 7 June 1949 in Mittenwald, Bavaria, West Germany. Lawyer and political leader; brother of B. *Zahaikevych. A graduate of Lviv University, he opened a law office in Peremyshl in 1909 and played a leading role in the economic and political life of the region. A member of the National Democratic party, he became a deputy to the Austrian parliament in 1912. With the disintegration of the Austrian Empire he was elected to the Ukrainian National Rada and a month later was imprisoned in a Polish concentration camp for a year. In the interwar period he acted as defense counsel in many political trials and was elected as a candidate of the Ukrainian National Democratic Alliance to the Polish Sejm in 1928 and 1930. He was deputy speaker of the Sejm (1928–30). During the Second World War he served on the court of appeal in Cracow. In 1944 he left Ukraine for Vienna and then Bavaria.

**Zahalna Knyhozbirnia** (General Library). A publishing house owned and operated in Kolomyia, Galicia, by D. Nykolyshyn from 1914 to 1935. It published 36 books of literature, primarily by Nykolyshyn and U. Kravchenko; reprints of T. Shevchenko's works; and translations of classical literature (eg, by Plato, Ovid, Cicero, and Demosthenes) by Nykolyshyn.

Oleksander Zaharov

**Zaharov, Oleksander** (real surname: Fessing), b 17 January 1877 in Yelysavethrad, Kherson gubernia, d 12 November 1941 in Saratov, Russia. Theatrical director and actor. After graduating form the Moscow Philharmonic School he began his career in various Russian theaters in Moscow and St Petersburg. He moved to Kiev and became artistic director of the *State Drama Theater (1918–

19) and the Shevchenko First Theater of the Ukrainian Soviet Republic (1919–21). Subsequently he became artistic director of the Ukrainska Besida Theater (1921–3) in Lviv and the Ruthenian Theater of the Prosvita Society (1923–5) in Uzhhorod. After returning from Prague (where he had worked with M. *Sadovsky) to Ukraine in 1926, Zaharov worked in the Zankovetska Theater (until 1927) and directed the Kharkiv Chervonozavodskyi Ukrainian Drama Theater (until 1928). A director of the realistic-psychological school, in Ukrainian theaters he successfully staged plays by V. Vynnychenko, Lesia Ukrainka, Ya. Mamontov, H. Ibsen, G. Hauptmann, and W. Shakespeare. He was severely criticized for his productions of L. Starytska-Cherniakhivska's *Rozbiinyk Karmeliuk* (The Robber Karmeliuk) and Vynnychenko's *Hrikh* (Sin), and left Kharkiv to work in Russian provincial theaters. Zaharov lectured at the Kiev Music and Drama Institute and the Ukrainian Drama School in Lviv. A biography by N. Nikeiev was published in Kiev in 1969.

V. Revutsky

**Zahirnia, Mariia.** See Hrinchenko, Mariia.

**Zahirny, Nykolai.** See Kachala, Stepan.

**Zahorianska, Kateryna** [Zahorjans'ka, Kateryna], b 8 September 1898 in Odessa, d 2 April 1985 in Kiev. Stage actress. She completed study at the Lysenko Music and Drama Institute (1920) and acted in the Shevchenko First Theater of the Ukrainian Soviet Republic (1919–25) and in the Odessa Ukrainian Music and Drama Theater (1925–60, with interruptions).

**Zahorodia** [Zahoroddja]. The higher (elevations up to 180 m) and dryer section of Polisia, situated between the Pyna and the Yaselda rivers in southern Brest oblast, Belarus. The region consists of a slightly rolling plain. Its soils (clays, moraines, and sands), generally better than those in the rest of Polisia, allow for extensive agricultural development and a greater population density. The inhabitants of the region are predominantly Ukrainian. Its main center is Pynske.

**Zahorovsky** [Zahorovs'kyj]. A Ukrainian noble family from Volhynia. The family was founded by Petro (d 1546), a mayor of Lutske and the father of V. *Zahorovsky. O. Fotynsky wrote *Iz semeinoi khroniki dvorian Zagorovskikh vo vtoroi polovine XVI v.* (From the Family Chronicle of the Nobles Zahorovsky in the Second Half of the 16th Century, 1900).

**Zahorovsky, Mykola** [Zahorovs'kyj], b 16 July 1893 in Odessa, d 1934. Hydrobiologist. A professor at the Odessa Institute of People's Education and the Institute of the National Economy in the 1930s, he was a pioneer in the study of the biocenosis of the Black Sea.

**Zahorovsky, Oleksander** [Zahorovs'kyj], b 1850 in the Kiev region, d 1919 in Odessa. Law historian. A graduate of Kiev University (1871), he served as a professor at Kharkiv (1880–92) and Odessa (1892–1919) universities. The most important of his works are *Istoricheskii ocherk zaima po russkomu pravu do kontsa 13 st.* (Historical Survey of Credit According to Russian Law to the End of the 13th Century, 1875), *O razvode po russkomu pravu* (On Divorce According to Russian Law, 1884), and *Kurs semeinogo prava* (A Course in Family Law, 1902; 2nd edn 1909).

**Zahorovsky, Vasyl** [Zahorovs'kyj, Vasyl'], b ?, d 1577 or 1580 in the Crimea. Volhynian nobleman; son of P. Zahorovsky. He worked in Volhynia as a tax official for the Polish kingdom and as vicegerent of Bratslav, in Podilia. During the Crimean Tatars' invasion of Volhynia (1576) he was taken captive. In confinement he recorded his testament (1577), in which he paid particular attention to the upbringing of his children. That cultural-historical document was published in *Arkhiv Iugo-Zapadnoi Rossii* (1859). Zahorovsky died in captivity.

**Zahorska, Melaniia** [Zahors'ka, Melanija] (née Khodot), b 1837 in Pokoshychi, Krolovets county, Chernihiv gubernia, d 1892 in Pokoshychi. Popular singer (soprano). Lacking formal training, she frequently performed in the Chernihiv amateur theater (directed by O. Markovych) and at folk song concerts. Much of her Ukrainian folk song repertoire was written down by M. Lysenko, and part was published in his *Zbirnyk ukraïns'kykh narodnykh pisen'* (A Collection of Ukrainian Folk Songs, vol 3, 1876).

**Zahorsky, Ivan** [Zahors'kyj], b 26 November 1858 in Bobrynets, Kherson gubernia, d 24 August 1904 in Katerynoslav (now Dnipropetrovsk). Comic actor. He began his career in Russian provincial touring troupes and then worked in M. Kropyvnytsky's (1889–1900) and P. Saksahansky's troupes (1900–3).

**Zahorsky, Ivan** [Zahors'kyj] (real surname: Podzikunov), b 1861 in Kharkiv, d 20 April 1908 in Odessa. Comic actor. He began his career in the Savin Russian Theater in Kharkiv (1879) and then worked in M. Kropyvnytsky's (1880–8) and M. Sadovsky's (1888–1900) troupes, on the Russian stage (1900–6), in O. Suslov's troupe (1907), and in Sadovsky's Theater (1907–8).

**Zahorsky, Petro** [Zahors'kyj], b 20 August 1764 in Ponornytsia, Novhorod-Siverskyi county, Chernihiv gubernia, d 1 April 1846 in St Petersburg. Anatomist and physiologist; full member of the Russian Imperial Academy of Sciences. Educated at Chernihiv College (1776–82) and the St Petersburg Army Hospital Medical School (1784–5), in 1797 he was appointed an adjunct professor (from 1880 professor) of the St Petersburg Medico-Surgical Academy. He discovered the nuclei of the abducent, accessory, and hypoglossal cranial nerves. He established the first school of anatomists in the Russian Empire and wrote the first anatomy textbook, *Sokrashchennaia anatomiia, ili rukovodstvo k poznaniiu stroeniia chelovecheskogo tela* (An Abridged Anatomy, or Guide to the Study of the Structure of the Human Body, 1801).

*Zahrava* (Crimson Sky). A semimonthly political journal published in Lviv by D. *Dontsov from April 1923 to mid-1924. Initially it was financially supported by the Ukrainian Military Organization (UVO), and its regular contributors were UVO members (eg, D. Paliiv, V. Kuchabsky, M. Matchak, and V. Kuzmovych). Aimed at a peasant readership, the journal propagated an uncompromising form of integral nationalism. In 1924 Dontsov and *Zahrava*'s supporters organized a distinct political party, the *Ukrainian Party of National Work. The journal served as its organ.

*Zahrava* (1923–4)                    Pavlo Zahrebelny (1924–)

**Zahrava** (Crimson Sky). A literary and artistic monthly published by the DP Association of Ukrainian Writers and Journalists in Augsburg, Germany, in 1946. Four issues appeared.

**Zahrava Theater.** The foremost theater in Western Ukraine during the interwar period, organized by V. *Blavatsky in Peremyshl in 1933 from the cast of an extant Zahrava theater (est 1931 by O. Stepovy) and from part of the cast of the *Tobilevych Theater. Zahrava continued the innovative experimentation of *Berezil: it introduced the chorus in its adaptations of V. Stefanyk's *Zemlia* (The Earth) and plastic-mass scenes in B. Lepky's *Baturyn*; modernized the text of M. Starytsky's *Oi, ne khody, Hrytsiu ...* (Don't Go to the Party, Hryts ...); performed new Ukrainian dramas of national-political, historical, and religious significance, such as O. Oles's *Obitovana zemlia* (The Promised Land), Z. Tarnavsky's *Taras Shevchenko*, and H. Luzhnytsky's *Duma pro Nechaia* (Duma about Nechai) and *Holhota* (Golgotha); and staged modern European plays, including M. Pagnol and P. Nivoix's *Les Marchands de gloire* and S. Maugham's *The Sacred Flame*. In 1938 Zahrava united with the Tobilevych Theater to form the Kotliarevsky Theater (later the *Lesia Ukrainka Theater).

**Zahrava Theater.** See Toronto Zahrava Theater.

**Zahrebelny, Oleksander** [Zahrebel'nyj], b 24 February 1937 in Dnipropetrovske. Opera singer (bass). After graduating from the Kiev Conservatory (1968) he joined the Kiev Theater of Opera and Ballet as a soloist. His repertoire includes the name-parts in M. Glinka's *Ruslan and Liudmila*, M. Mussorgsky's *Boris Godunov*, and H. Maiboroda's *Yaroslav the Wise*, as well as Mephistopheles in C. Gounod's *Faust* and Boris Timofeevich in D. Shostakovich's *Katerina Izmailova*. Zahrebelny also performs as a chamber singer.

**Zahrebelny, Pavlo** [Zahrebel'nyj], b 25 August 1924 in Soloshyne, now in Kobeliaky raion, Poltava oblast. Writer and community and political activist. His first published work appeared in 1949, and his first collection of stories was *Kakhovs'ki opovidannia* (Kakhivka Stories, written with Yu. Ponomarenko, 1953). In addition to other collections of stories he began writing novels, which were set during the Second World War and were mostly propa-

gandistic. They included *Evropa-45* (Europe-45, 1959; English trans 1977), *Evropa: Zakhid* (Europe: The West, 1961), and *Shepit* (The Whisper, 1966). Also propagandistic are his novels with contemporary settings, which are uneven and filled with seemingly irrelevant information: *Den' dlia pryideshn'oho* (A Day for the Future, 1964), *Z pohliadu vichnosti* (From the Point of View of Eternity, 1970; English trans 1978), *Perekhodymo do liubovi* (We Turn to Love, 1971), *Rozhin* (The Acceleration, 1976), *Levyne sertse* (Lionheart, 1978), and others. Zahrebelny also wrote a number of historical novels in which history is rather freely interpreted, including *Dyvo* (The Apparition, 1968), *Smert' v Kyievi* (Death in Kiev, 1973), *Ievpraksiia* (1975), and *Roksolana* (1979). His best work is a historical novel in the form of a monologue, *Ia, Bohdan* (I, Bohdan, 1983), about Hetman B. Khmelnytsky. In it he employs a rich lexicon and shows a mastery of style. Because it was a novel written under pressure of the official Soviet theme of the 'unification of peoples,' however, it suffers from historical falsification. Zahrebelny has also written essays, plays, and screenplays. He has been active in the administration of the Writers' Union of Ukraine, in which he served as first secretary (1979–86).

BIBLIOGRAPHY
Shakhovs'kyi, S. *Romany Pavla Zahrebel'noho* (Kiev 1974)
Fashchenko, V. *Pavlo Zahrebel'nyi: Narys tvorchosti* (Kiev 1984)
I. Koshelivets

**Zahrebelny, Pavlo** [Zahrebel'nyj], b 22 June 1934 in Rozhdestvenske, now in Drabiv raion, Cherkasy oblast. Stage actor and director. He completed study at the Kiev Institute of Theater Arts (1960) and then worked as an actor in the Ternopil Music and Drama Theater and, since 1974, as its principal stage director. He played the title role in M. Rylsky and B. Tiahno's *Taras Bulba*.

**Zahretsky, Dmytro** [Zahrec'kyj], b 8 September 1924 in Odessa, d 5 March 1980 in Odessa. Choir conductor. Upon graduating from the Odessa Conservatory in 1949, he joined its faculty and became artistic director and chief conductor of the choir kapelle of the Odessa Philharmonia (1949–55). Then he served as chief choirmaster of the Odessa Opera and Ballet Theater, at which he helped stage more than 50 operas. He was a coauthor of *Khorove aranzhuvannia* (Choir Arranging, 1977).

**Zahrodsky, Andrii** [Zahrods'kyj, Andrij], b 2 December 1886 in Zelenkiv, Uman county, Kiev gubernia, d 30 November 1948 in Kiev. Philologist. After graduating from Warsaw University (1912) he taught Russian and Ukrainian in Kiev. He was a docent at Kiev University (1938–41, 1944–8) and worked at the Institute of Pedagogy in Kiev (1943–8). He wrote a Ukrainian grammar for use in high schools (1938), which was reprinted annually until 1959, and articles on Ukrainian orthography and the methodology of teaching Ukrainian.

**Zahrodsky, Oleksander** [Zahrods'kyj], b 10 April 1889 in Zelenkiv, Uman county, Kiev gubernia, d 4 August 1968 in New York. Senior military officer. After joining the UNR Army in 1918, he commanded a battalion, a regiment, and a division of the *Zaporozhian Corps and served as a deputy corps commander (1919). In the First Winter Campaign (1919–20) he was in charge of the Second Volhynian

Gen Oleksander Zahrodsky

Dmytro Zahul (portrait by
Mykhailo Zhuk, crayon, 1919)

Division, and on his return he served as deputy commander of the UNR Army. He attained the rank of brigadier general. During his service he participated in about 100 battles and was wounded five times. In the Polish internment camp at Kalisz he was active in the educational and cultural program for Ukrainian soldiers. After the Second World War he emigrated to the United States, where he continued to be active in the Ukrainian community, veterans' organizations, and the military staff of the UNR government-in-exile, which promoted him to major general and lieutenant general.

**ZAHS** (Zapys aktiv hromadianskoho stanu; Russian: Zapis aktov grazhdanskogo sostoianiia, or ZAGS). The office of the Registry of Documents of Civil Status in the USSR, run by the MVD and oblast, raion, city, and rural soviets. ZAHS offices registered all births, deaths, marriages, divorces, adoptions, and name changes. They were created in Soviet Russia in 1918 and in Ukraine in 1919 as a replacement for *church registers. All ZAHS offices were under the jurisdiction of the *NKVD until 1931, when the central office in Soviet Ukraine came under the jurisdiction of the Presidium of the Central Executive Committee of the Ukrainian SSR, and other offices were placed under the executive committees of oblast, raion, city, and rural soviets. In 1941 all ZAHS offices were again placed under the jurisdiction of the NKVD, and for the first time a central USSR office was created at NKVD headquarters in Moscow. In 1946 the MVD replaced the NKVD. From 1958 the Ministry of Justice of the Ukrainian SSR was responsible for training ZAHS staff in procedures. Civil registration in the USSR did not escape political interference. During the 1932–3 man-made famine in Ukraine, for example, ZAHS offices falsified death certificates to hide the real scope of the catastrophe.

**Zahul, Dmytro** (pseuds: I. Maidan, B. Tyverets), b 28 August 1890 in Miliieve, Bukovyna, d 1944 in Kolyma. Writer. He belonged to the *Muzahet group of symbolist poets. He later joined the *Zakhidnia Ukraina group. His first published works appeared in the newspaper *Bukovyna* in 1907. Later he published in *Hart*, *Hlobus*, *Zhyttia i revoliutsiia*, *Chervonyi shliakh*, and other journals and almanacs. Collections of his poetry include *Z zelenykh hir* (From the Green Mountains, 1918), *Na hrani* (On the Edge, 1919),

*Nash den'* (Our Day, 1923), *Motyvy* (Motifs, 1927), and the posthumous *Vybrane* (Selections, 1961). He also wrote a textbook, *Poetyka* (Poetics, 1923), a collection of essays in literary criticism, *Literaturna chy literaturshchyna?* (Literature or Literary Hackwork?, 1926), and a collection of translations, *Vybir nimets'kykh baliad* (A Selection of German Ballads, 1928). He was arrested on 26 February 1933 and sentenced to 10 years' imprisonment in concentration camps. An edition of his poems was published in Kiev in 1990.

Mykola Zaiachkivsky

**Zaiachkivsky, Mykola** [Zajačkivs'kyj], b 21 November 1870 in Tyshkivtsi, Horodenka county, Galicia, d 11 February 1938 in Lviv. Civic and business organizer. A graduate in theology and law of Lviv University, he was director of the Ukrainska Besida Theater (1900) and inspector and then director of Narodna Torhovlia in Lviv. During the First World War he was deported to Siberia by the Russian authorities (1914–17). With the outbreak of the revolution he worked in the co-operative movement in Kiev (1917–18). After the war he served as president of a number of organizations, such as the Burgher Brotherhood, the Ukrainian Emigrant Aid Society (1925–38), Sokil (1922–33), and the Ridna Shkola society (1936–8). He was a member of the Trade and Industry Chamber in Lviv and an honorary member of the Union of Ukrainian Merchants and Entrepreneurs.

**Zaiachkivsky, Myron** [Zajačkivs'kyj] (pseud: Kosar), b 18 November 1897 in Kolomyia, Galicia, d 1937. Communist organizer. During the First World War he was captured and interned in a Russian POW camp. In 1920 he fought in the Red Army and joined the CP(B)U. After the war he worked as a lecturer and edited a Party newspaper in Berdychiv and then headed the Department of Agitation and Propaganda of the Uman Okruha Party Committee (1924–6) and the CC CP(B)U Department of Agitation in Kharkiv (1926–8). Upon returning to Galicia for underground work he was elected to the CC of the Communist Party of Western Ukraine, and directed its operations from the Party center in Berlin. After the purge of the Vasylkiv faction from the Party he was promoted to its Politburo. In 1933 he was called to Moscow. He was arrested in 1934 and sent to a concentration camp, where he was executed by the NKVD.

**Zaiachkivsky, Tyt** [Zajačkivs'kyj], b 1846 in Lopianka, Stryi circle, Galicia, d 25 March 1926 in Dora, Nadvirna county, Galicia. Judge and civic figure; son of Rev Y. *Zaiachkivsky. He studied law at Lviv University and then worked in several smaller centers before returning to Lviv, where he eventually became a judge. Continually active in local Ukrainian civic life, he served as a deputy to the Galician Diet in 1895–1901.

Rev Yosyp Zaiachkivsky (1810–94)

Mykola Zaitsev

**Zaiachkivsky, Yosyp** [Zajačkivs'kyj, Josyp], b 1810, d 1894. Greek Catholic priest and civic activist in Galicia. In 1848 he was a member of the Ruthenian Council in Stryi. During the 1860s he (together with S. Kachala) was a leading figure in the nascent Ukrainian national movement in Galicia and one of the founders of the *Prosvita society. He was elected honorary member of Prosvita.

**Zaiachkivsky, Yosyp** [Zajačkivs'kyj, Josyp], b 14 June 1889 in Bilobozhnytsia, Chortkiv county, Galicia, d 20 March 1952 in Merano, Italy. Basilian priest. He was hegumen of the Basilian monasteries in Dobromyl (1920–7) and Drohobych (1927–30) and then secretary (1930–49) and general consultator (1949–52) of the Basilian order in Rome. He also served as rector of *St Josaphat's Ukrainian Pontifical College (1948–52) and as a member of the commission responsible for codifying Eastern rite canon law.

**Zaiats, Mykhailo** [Zajac', Myxajlo], b 18 December 1899 in Horozhanka Mala, Rudky county, Galicia, d 1941. Lawyer and political activist. While working as a lawyer in Lviv he belonged to a Russophile Marxist group associated with the paper *Volia naroda*. He served on the secretariat of the People's Will party (PNV) from April 1926 and on the Central Committee of Sel-Rob, which originated from PNV's merger with Sel Soiuz, from October 1926. Eventually he became a member of the Communist Party of Western Ukraine, and he was arrested by the Polish authorities several times in the 1930s. After the occupation of Galicia by Soviet forces in 1939, Zaiats was an editor of *Vil'na Ukraïna* until June 1941, when he was arrested by the Soviet secret police. He died in a labor camp.

**Zaiats, Yuliian** [Zajac', Julijan], b 30 May 1880, d 2 September 1971 in Lviv. Legal adviser to the Greek Catholic metropolitan consistory in Lviv. He was a member of the Supreme Administrative Tribunal in Warsaw and president of the Court of Appeal in Lviv (1941–4).

**Zaifert, Ihor** [Zajfert], b 7 December 1909 in Ukraine, d 3 October 1972 in Detroit. Opera and concert singer (tenor). He graduated from the Kharkiv Conservatory and then performed in the Kharkiv (1942–3) and Poltava opera theaters and the Ukrainian Opera Ensemble in Germany (1946–8). He made recordings of arias from G. Verdi's *Rigoletto* and R. Leoncavallo's *I Pagliacci*, as well as of art songs by M. Lysenko and D. Sichynsky. Zaifert was a leading soloist in the Ukrainian Bandurist Chorus.

**Zaika, Viktor** [Zajika], b 2 May 1936 in Ulan-Ude, Buryat ASSR. Hydrobiologist; corresponding member of the AN URSR (now ANU) since 1978. A graduate of Leningrad University (1958), he worked at the ANU *Institute of the Biology of Southern Seas (1962–82, from 1977 as director). His major research interests include marine parasitology (particularly with respect to fish), the theory of animal growth, biological productivity, and biocenology. Zaika wrote *Chornoe more* (The Black Sea, 1983) and *Scientific Production of Aquatic Anvertebrates* (English trans, 1973).

**Zaikevych, Anastasii** [Zajkevyč, Anastasij], b 1842 in Lubni, Poltava gubernia, d 1931? in Lubni. Agronomist and plant physiologist. A graduate of Odessa University (1870), he taught at Kharkiv University (1877–1919). He was a key figure in the development of scientific agricultural research in the territories of the Russian Empire. He founded the Poltava and Solonytsia experimental farms, the Kharkiv Selection Station, and the Lubni Research Station of Medicinal Plants.

**Zaikin, Viacheslav** [Zajikin, Vjačeslav], b 1896, d ? Legal and church historian. His works on the Ukrainian church and church law include a series of articles on Christianity in Kievan Rus' (1926–30) and the monographs *Uchastie svetskogo elementa v tserkovnom upravlenii, vybornoe nachalo i 'sobornost' v Kievskoi mitropolii v XVI i XVII vekakh* (The Participation of the Secular Element in Church Administration, The Electoral Principle, and 'Conciliarity' in Kiev Metropoly of the 16th and 17th Centuries, 1930), *K voprosu o polozhenii pravoslavnoi tserkvi v pol'skom gosudarstve v XIV–XVII vekakh* (On the Question of the Status of the Orthodox Church in the Polish State in the 14th–17th Centuries, 1935), and *Zarys dziejów ustroju Kościoła wschodniosłowiańskiego* (An Outline of the History of the Structure of the Eastern Slavic Church, 1939).

**Zaitsev, Mykola** [Zajcev], b 5 November 1894 in Pisky, Kharkiv gubernia, d 30 May 1978 in New Jersey. Chemical engineer; full member of the Shevchenko Scientific Society from 1947. A graduate of the Prague Polytechnic, he taught at the Ukrainian Technical and Husbandry Institute (UTHI) in Poděbrady, Czechoslovakia (1924–35) and was the chief chemist at the Kosmos-Werke chemical concern in Czechoslovakia (1937–45). A postwar refugee, he was a professor and prorector at the UTHI in Regensburg, West Germany (1945–57), and then emigrated to the United States, where he worked as a research chemist. He contributed to various areas of organic chemistry, particularly the chemistry of fats.

Pavlo Zaitsev

Vasyl Zakharchenko

**Zaitsev, Pavlo** [Zajcev], b 23 September 1886 in Sumy county, Kharkiv gubernia, d 2 September 1965 in Munich. Literary scholar and political figure; member of the Shevchenko Scientific Society from 1938. After completing his studies in law (1908) and Slavic philology (1913) at St Petersburg University he worked as a gymnasium teacher in Petrograd, researched the life of T. *Shevchenko, and belonged to the Society of Ukrainian Progressives. In 1917 he moved to Kiev and became a member of the Central Rada. He was head of the chancery of the General Secretariat of Education in 1917, director of the general department in the Hetman government's Ministry of Education and Art in 1918, and head of the cultural-educational department of the UNR Army in 1920. He was also a lecturer at the Ukrainian Scientific Pedagogical Academy (1917), a member of the Council of the Ukrainian Scientific Society in Kiev (1918–20), and editor of the quarterly *Nashe mynule (1918–19), other publications of the Drukar publishing house (as chief editor), and vol 1 of the VUAN Zapysky Istorychno-filolohichnoho viddilu (1918).

From 1913 on Zaitsev was a recognized authority in the field of Shevchenko studies. He found many of Shevchenko's unpublished writings and drawings and wrote numerous textual and biographical studies, a book on Shevchenko and the Poles (1934), and an important biography of Shevchenko (1955; abridged English trans 1988). He also edited the 1914 Petrograd edition of Shevchenko's *Kobzar. From 1921 to 1941 he lived in Warsaw, where he was a regular contributor to Ukraïns'ka trybuna under the pseudonym L(uka) Hrabuzdov(ych), an associate of the Ukrainian Scientific Institute, and chief editor of its canonical edition of T. Shevchenko's works (13 vols, 1934–8). From 1941 on he lived in Germany. In 1948 he became director of the Shevchenko Studies Institute at the Ukrainian Free Academy of Sciences and a professor at the Ukrainian Free University in Munich.

R. Senkus

**Zaitsev, Yuvenalii** [Zajcev, Juvenalij], b 18 April 1924 in Mykolaivka-Novorosiiska, now in Sarata raion, Odessa oblast. Hydrobiologist; corresponding member of the AN URSR (now ANU) since 1969. A graduate of Odessa University (1949), he was director of its hydrobiology station (1949–56) and worked at the Odessa branch of the ANU Institute of the Biology of Southern Seas (1958, from 1972 as

director). His research interests include hydrobiology, ichthyology, and the conservation of organic marine resources. He discovered neuston complexes of organisms.

**Zaitseva, Tetiana** [Zajceva, Tetjana], b 31 December 1898 in Velykomykhailivka, Oleksandrivske county, Katerynoslav gubernia, d 24 March 1964 in Kiev. Linguist and lexicographer; wife of the historian I. *Boiko. After graduating from the Kharkiv Institute of People's Education (1927) she continued her graduate studies at the Kharkiv branch of the VUAN Institute of Linguistics. She wrote her candidate's dissertation on the syntax of T. Shevchenko's Kobzar (1943) and after the war worked as a senior associate at the Institute of Linguistics in Kiev. Her articles deal with Ukrainian stylistics, T. Shevchenko's language, and the history of Ukrainian lexicography. She was a coeditor of the AN URSR (now ANU) Ukrainian-Russian dictionary (6 vols, 1953–63).

**Zaitsiv, Dmytro** [Zajciv], b 1897, d ? Zoologist and entomologist; full member of the Shevchenko Scientific Society from 1943. A lecturer at the Kharkiv Agricultural Institute during the 1930s, he studied beetles in various regions of the USSR as well as in the Lemko region and identified a large number of species in Ukraine. After the Second World War he was a displaced person in Germany and then emigrated to Brazil.

*Zakarpats'ka pravda* (Transcarpathian Truth). An organ of Transcarpathia oblast Party committee and soviet, published six days a week in Uzhhorod from November 1944 to 1991. It succeeded *Karpats'ka pravda. Since 1946 and 1960 respectively, Hungarian- and Russian-language editions of the newspaper were also published. In 1980 the pressruns of the three editions were as follows: 158,000 Ukrainian, 158,000 Russian (up from 55,000 in 1976), and 38,000 Hungarian.

**Zakerzonnia.** The popular name used for the territories west of the *Curzon Line that were inhabited by Ukrainians. Zakerzonnia included the *Lemko and *Sian regions, parts of Liubachiv, Rava Ruska, and Sokal counties, the *Kholm region, and *Podlachia. During the Second World War the OUN and UPA military units in Zakerzonnia were commanded by Ya. Starukh (code name: Stiah). After the Second World War those lands (approx 19,000 sq km) were transferred to Poland, according to the Soviet-Polish agreement of 16 August 1945. Virtually all the Ukrainians in Zakerzonnia (approx 1,500,000) were then forcibly resettled to other regions of Poland, during *Operation Wisła.

**Zakhara, Ihor** [Zaxara], b 27 December 1943 in Lviv. Philosopher. After graduating from Lviv University he taught there. He now works at the ANU Institute of Social Sciences in Lviv. A specialist in the history of 16th- to 18th-century Ukrainian philosophy, he has contributed many articles to journals and collections, written a monograph on S. *Yavorsky and his philosophy (1982), and prepared and annotated a collection of Yavorsky's philosophical works in Ukrainian translation (3 vols, 1992–3).

**Zakharchenko, Vasyl** [Zaxarčenko, Vasyl'], b 13 January 1936 in Hutyrivka, Poltava raion. Writer, journalist, and political prisoner. He wrote the prose collections Spi-

*vuchyi korin'* (The Singing Root, 1964), *Tramvai o shostii vechora* (The Tram at Six in the Evening, 1966), *Stezhka* (The Path, 1968), *Dzvinok na svitanni* (The Bell at Dawn, 1981), *U p'iatnytsiu pislia obidu* (Friday after Lunch, 1982), and *Lozovi koshyky* (Willow Baskets, 1986). In 1972 he was expelled from the Writers' Union of Ukraine for participating in the Ukrainian national movement. Later that year he was arrested and sentenced to five years in labor camps in Perm oblast. There he participated in various prisoners' protests. In July 1977 he issued a public recantation and was released and 'rehabilitated.'

**Zakharchuk, Yevhen** [Zaxarčuk, Jevhen], b 1 June 1886 in Romanove Selo, Zbarazh county, Galicia, d 15 July 1936 in Kiev. Actor and singer (baritone). He began his theatrical career in the Ruska Besida Theater (1901–6) and then worked in Sadovsky's Theater (1906–18), the State People's Theater in Kiev (1918–19), the Kharkiv Ukrainian People's Theater (1924–8), and the Kharkiv Chervonozavodskyi Ukrainian Drama Theater. He was arrested in 1933, and died in a Soviet prison.

**Zakharenko, Ivan** [Zaxarenko], b 1839, d 1908. Theater director and playwright. He managed an amateur theater in Osnova, near Kharkiv (1899), and later led his own troupe. He wrote the dramas *Chervoni cherevychky* (The Red Shoes, based on an N. Gogol story), *Kliate sertse* (The Cursed Heart), and *Zakliuvana holubka* (The Pecked Dove).

**Zakhariiasevych, Teodor** [Zaxarijasevyč], b 1759, d 1808. Ukrainian Catholic priest and professor. A vice-rector of the Greek Catholic Theological Seminary in Lviv, he taught church history at the Studium Ruthenum and translated into Ukrainian the standard church history text then used in the Austrian empire, M. Dannenmayer's *Institutiones historiae ecclesiasticae Novi Testamenti*. His translation was published in Lviv in 1790.

Halyna Zakhariiasevych-Lypa: *Crowd* (watercolor, 1959)

**Zakhariiasevych-Lypa, Halyna** [Zaxarijasevyč-Lypa], b 28 April 1910 in Rakhynia, Dolyna county, Galicia, d 10 June 1968 in Lviv. Graphic artist, wife of Yu. *Lypa. A graduate of the Vienna School of Applied Arts (1938), after the Second World War she studied music and singing at the Lviv Conservatory (1945–8). In 1951 she found work as a textile designer. Her drawings, watercolors, and batiks are often based on Ukrainian folklore and are lyrical in mood. She did a postcard series and a series of illustrations to I. Franko's poem 'Kameniari' (The Stonecutters).

**Zakharivka.** See Frunzivka.

**Zakharko, Ivan** [Zaxarko], b 1851 in Lviv, d 25 September 1919 in Chernivtsi. Actor, theater director, and publisher. He worked as an actor in O. Bachynsky's troupe (until 1893) and in the Polish Theater in Cracow (1893–1900) and led the Bukovynian People's Theater (1900–10). In Chernivtsi he kept a printing shop, where he published Ukrainian literature.

**Zakharov, Fedor** [Zaxarov], b 25 September 1919 in Aleksandrovskoe, Smolensk gubernia, Russia. Painter. A graduate of the Moscow Art Institute (1950), he has lived in Yalta and painted colorful landscapes, such as *Alushta* (1953), *Before the Storm* (1954), *Evening in Sudak* (1957), *Blooming Almond* (1961), *Sedniv Vistas* (1964), *Early Spring* (1968), *Autumn Snow* (1970), *Autumn Evening* (1977), and *Stormy Sea* (1984).

*Zakhidni visty.* See *Ukraïns'ki visti.*

**Zakhidnia Ukraina.** An organization of revolutionary writers. It was established in Kiev in 1925, as a division of the organization *Pluh, and existed as an independent entity from 1926. It consisted largely of writers originally from Western Ukraine, among them V. Atamaniuk, D. Bedzyk, V. Bobynsky, M. Hasko, D. Zahul, P. Hirniak, V. Gadzinsky, V. Gzhytsky, L. Dmyterko, Y. Zazuliak, M. Irchan, M. Kachaniuk, M. Kichura, M. Kozoris, M. Marfiievych, H. Piddubny, D. Rudyk, I. Tkachuk, A. Turchynska, A. Shmyhelsky, M. Sopilka, and Rostyslav Zaklynsky. Upon the formation of the Writers' Union of Ukraine (1932–4), it was liquidated, and most of its members were either repressed or shot.

The organization controlled a publishing house and issued a publication of the same name, in which the works of its members were published. From 1930 to 1933 a number of Soviet publicist and fictional works were published in the Masova biblioteka (Mass Library) book series.

*Zakhidnia Ukraïna*

*Zakhidnia Ukraïna* (Western Ukraine). A magazine dealing with art, literature, politics, and community news in Kharkiv. It was published irregularly in 1927 and monthly from 1930 to 1933. It was the official organ of the literary organization of the same name and was edited by V. Atamaniuk, who was followed by M. Irchan, I. Tkachuk, V. Gzhytsky, Y. Zazuliak, and D. Zahul. The contributors, primarily members of the organization, wanted 'to emphasize the proletarian class direction and to relay the class struggle of workers in Western Ukraine in their works.' The magazine's illustrators were V. Kasiian, B. Kriukov, and Ya. Strukhmanchuk.

Mykhailo Zakhidny        Bohdan Zaklynsky

Kornylo Zaklynsky          Kornylo Zaklynsky
(1857–84)                       (1889–1966)

**Zakhidny, Mykhailo** [Zaxidnyj, Myxajlo], b 9 June 1885, d 17 October 1937 in Berezhany, Galicia. Lawyer and political leader. While practicing law in Berezhany he was president of the local branch of the Prosvita society. In 1927 he assumed leadership of the *Ukrainian Party of Labor, a Sovietophile organization, and in the following year he was elected as its candidate to the Polish Sejm. Eventually he dropped his pro-Soviet sympathies.

**Zaklynsky, Bohdan** [Zaklyns'kyj], b 9 August 1886 in Stanyslaviv (now Ivano-Frankivske), d 12 April 1946 in Lviv. Teacher and ethnographer; son of Roman Zaklynsky. A teacher (from 1910) in Ukrainian schools in Galicia and Transcarpathia, he prepared textbooks (including primers) and methodological works concerning styles of writing for children. While teaching in various villages, he conducted ethnographic field research, much of which remains in manuscript form in the libraries of the AN URSR (now ANU). He also gathered items for the ethnographic museum of the Shevchenko Scientific Society in Lviv. In 1917 he wrote a popular study of Ukrainian folk dwellings, *Zhytie ukraïns'koho naroda* (The Life of the Ukrainian People), which was published in Vienna. From 1944 Zaklynsky worked in the Lviv branch of the Institute of Fine Arts, Folklore, and Ethnography of the ANU.

**Zaklynsky, Kornylo** [Zaklyns'kyj], b 1857 in Mariiampil, Stanyslaviv circle, Galicia, d 13 February 1884 in Lviv, Galicia. Historian; brother of Roman Zaklynsky. He attended the gymnasium in Stanyslaviv (1869–77) and cofounded a branch of the Prosvita society there. In 1877 he moved to Lviv to further his studies in history, with a specialization in Cossack history. He founded a literary-historical circle and became a member of Ruska Besida and the Academic Brotherhood. He contributed articles on Cossack history, particularly the foreign relations of the Cossacks, and reworkings of historical articles by V. Antonovych and M. Kostomarov to *Zoria, Dilo, Vesna,* and other Galician periodicals. Zaklynsky died of tuberculosis; much of his research and literary work remains unpublished.

**Zaklynsky, Kornylo** [Zaklyns'kyj], b 1 August 1889 in Lviv, d 1 April 1966 in Prague. Pedagogue and literary critic; son of Roman Zaklynsky. In the early 1920s, after studying at Vienna and Lviv universities, Zaklynsky was forced to move to Transcarpathia because of political circumstances. There he became a teacher at the Berehove gymnasium (1920–38) and an active promoter of the *Plast Ukrainian Youth Association and the *Prosvita society. In 1939 he was arrested and imprisoned briefly by the Hungarians, and then moved to Prague. There he taught at the Ukrainian gymnasium and was the director of a Ukrainian museum. He wrote scholarly articles (particularly in Czech journals) about Ukrainian literary figures from Transcarpathia and the Prešov region as well as several school texts. Zaklynsky was a strong supporter of the *Museum of Ukrainian Culture in Svydnyk, to which he donated his personal library.

**Zaklynsky, Oleksii** [Zaklyns'kyj, Oleksij], b 27 March 1819 in Ozeriany, Stanyslaviv circle, Galicia, d ca 1894 in Bohorodchany Stari, Stanyslaviv county, Galicia. Greek Catholic priest and civic and political activist. He was a member of the Supreme Ruthenian Council and its delegate to the Slavic Congress in Prague (1848). In 1873–9 he was a deputy to the Austrian parliament. His memoirs were published in 1890 as *Zapiski Alekseia Zaklinskogo prikhodnika Starykh Bogorodchan* (Notes of Oleksii Zaklynsky, Pastor of Stari Bohorodchany).

**Zaklynsky, Roman** [Zaklyns'kyj], b 1852, d 1931. Western Ukrainian pedagogue and education activist. Zaklynsky was a founding member of the *Ridna Shkola society and a coeditor of the society's educational publication series, Biblioteka dlia ditei (Library for Children). He wrote many books for popular consumption, including *Heohrafiia Rusy* (The Geography of Rus', 1887).

**Zaklynsky, Rostyslav** [Zaklyns'kyj] (pseud: Viun), b 20 October 1887 in Stanyslaviv (now Ivano-Frankivske), Galicia, d 18 September 1974 in Lviv. Literary scholar and publicist; son of Roman *Zaklynsky and brother of Kornylo and Bohdan. He was active in the Ukrainian Radical party. From 1910 he contributed to Lviv periodicals, such as *Hromads'kyi holos, Shliakhy,* and *Iliustrovana Ukraïna,* and he was an editor of the dailies *Nove zhyttia* (1918–19)

Rostyslav Zaklynsky

and *Narod* (1919) in Stanyslaviv. From 1920 on he lived in Soviet Ukraine. He taught in postsecondary schools in Kamianets-Podilskyi and Kiev and belonged to the writers' group *Zakhidnia Ukraina. He contributed articles about Galician writers and book reviews to journals such as *Zhyttia i revoliutsiia* and *Zakhidnia Ukraïna*. In 1933 he was arrested and sent to a labor camp in the Soviet Arctic. He was released in 1946, and returned to Lviv. He continued to teach in Ivano-Frankivske oblast (from 1948 to 1956) and in Lviv (from 1957).

*Zakon i pravo* (Law and Jurisprudence). (Law and Jurisprudence). Monthly legal journal published in Kiev by the Chas publishing house and edited by M. Kushnir. Only a few issues appeared, starting in November 1918. They contained articles on Ukrainian legal history and legal theory, bibliographies, professional news, and statutes passed by the UNR government.

*Zakon sudnyi liudem* (The Law for Judging People). A 9th-century compilation of laws based on the Byzantine legal manual *Ecloga* and adapted for use by the Southern Slavs. It was commonly referred to in Rus' as 'Constantine's missal' (*Sluzhebnyk Konstantyna*) and was accepted as an unofficial source of Byzantine law. The code had an influence on the development of Rus' law.

**Zakovorot, Petro,** b 1871 in Kupievakha-Huty, Bohodukhiv county, Kharkiv gubernia, d 5 March 1951. One of the founders of the Soviet school of fencing. In 1899 and 1900 he won the world fencing championship. After the 1917 Revolution he taught fencing and trained many famous fencers and coaches. In 1935 he won the Ukrainian fencing championship.

**Zakrevsky** [Zakrevs'kyj]. A family line of Cossack officers that originated with Yosyp Zakrevsky, a general standard-bearer (1762) and general quartermaster (he was married to the sister of K. Rozumovsky). Yosyp's son, Andrii Zakrevsky (b 1742, d 1804), was director of the Academy of Art (1783) and head of the Medical Collegium (1789) in St Petersburg. Yosyp's great-grandsons were Viktor (b 1807, d 1858), Mykhailo (nd), and Platon (b 1801, d 1882) Zakrevsky; they were estate owners in Pyriatyn county (Poltava gubernia), members of the *Mochemordy Society, friends of Ya. de Balmain, and noteworthy progressives. They were also friends of T. Shevchenko, who painted a renowned portrait of Platon's wife, Hanna

Zakrevska, in 1843. The jurist Hnat Zakrevsky and the historian-ethnographer Mykola *Zakrevsky were also part of the family line.

**Zakrevsky, Mykola** [Zakrevs'kyj] (pseud: N. Shaginian), b 21 June 1805 in Kiev, d 10 August 1871 in Moscow. Historian, ethnographer, and writer. A graduate of Kharkiv University, he continued his studies at Dorpat University, worked as a teacher in Revel (now Tallinn), and lived in Moscow from 1859. He wrote *Ocherk istorii g. Kieva* (An Outline of the History of the City of Kiev, 1836), *Letopis' i opisanie g. Kieva* (A Chronicle and Description of the City of Kiev, 1858), and *Opisanie Kieva* (A Description of Kiev, 2 vols, 1868). He also researched Ukrainian folklore and published a collection of dumas, songs, proverbs, and riddles in *Starosvetskii bandurista* (Old World Banduryst, 3 vols, 1860–1), the third volume of which contained a dictionary of Little Russian idioms (over 11,000 words). Part of his collected data, including materials for two dictionaries, remained in manuscript form in Katerynoslav (Dnipropetrovske). Zakrevsky was an ardent defender of the right of Ukrainians to literature in their native language.

**Zakrzhevsky, Yuliian** [Zakrževs'kyj, Julijan] (Zakrevsky), b 29 September 1852 in Kosiv, Galicia, d 8 May 1915 in Kazan, Russia. Opera singer (tenor). He studied music in Lviv and Italy. He sang as a soloist with the Italian Opera in Kiev (1878–82) and with the Bolshoi Theater in Moscow (1882–4). He also sang in Prague, Vienna, Cracow, Kazan, Kharkiv (1893–5), and Perm. His repertoire included Hermann in P. Tchaikovsky's *The Queen of Spades*, Jontek in S. Moniuszko's *Halka*, and Rademes in G. Verdi's *Aida*. In his concerts he popularized Ukrainian songs.

**Zakup.** A semifree bondsman in Kievan Rus' (11th–12th centuries) and later in the Grand Duchy of Lithuania (14th–16th centuries). Legally the *zakupy* were free people, but in actual fact they were equal in status to slaves as a result of their voluntarily assumed dependence on their landlord or a particular institution. People became *zakupy* by agreeing to a loan (*kupa*), with their personal bondage as a guarantee. *Ruskaia Pravda* defined the relationship of the *zakup* with the landlord and categorized the *zakupy* into those who worked in the households (*dvirni*) and those who worked in the fields (*roleini*). The landlord had the right to mete out corporal punishment, but he could not kill or sell a *zakup*. The *zakup* had the right to bring charges against the landlord before the prince's court, to own property, to enter into agreements, and to appear in court as a witness. The repayment of the debt made the *zakup* a free man, but an attempt to escape before repayment could reduce him to a slave (*kholop*).

Under Lithuanian rule in Ukraine the *zakupy* were debtors, known as *zakupni* (equivalent to the *dvirni*) or as *liudy v peniazikh* (equivalent to the *roleini*). Relations between the landlord and the *zakup* were based on a bilateral private legal agreement, and the Lithuanian Statute only stated the amount which the *zakup* was obliged to repay annually. The *zakupni* would repay their debt by labor, whereas the *liudy v peniazikh* would repay an equivalent value from the yearly harvest. *Zakupy* who did not manage to repay their debt would become serfs (*nepokhozhi seliany*). (See also *Feudalism and *Land tenure system.)

V. Markus

**Zalensky, Lev** [Zalens'kyj], b 1648 in Liubechi, near Lutske, Volhynia, d 1708 in Volodymyr-Volynskyi, Volhynia. Uniate metropolitan of Kiev. A nobleman, he joined the Basilian order as a novice in the Byten Monastery. He then studied in Olmouc, in Moravia, in Vilnius, and at the Gregorian University in Rome (1673–6). In 1678 he became bishop of Volodymyr after the death of his uncle, V. Korchak-Hlynsky. In 1694 he succeeded K. Zhokhovsky as metropolitan of Kiev while retaining his position as bishop of Volodymyr. During his tenure the bishops of Lviv (Y. Shumliansky) and Lutske (D. Zhabokrytsky) joined the Uniate church. Zalensky fled to Saxony during the Russian-Swedish War, when Muscovite armies occupied Volhynia.

**Zalensky, Volodymyr** [Zalens'kyj], b 7 February 1847 in Shakhvorostivka, near Myrhorod, Poltava gubernia, d 21 October 1918 in Sevastopil. Zoologist and embryologist; member of the St Petersburg Academy of Sciences from 1897. A graduate of Kharkiv University (1867), he was a professor at Kazan (from 1871) and Odessa (from 1882) universities and director of the Zoological Museum in St Petersburg (from 1897). He specialized in the comparative embryological development of invertebrates and chordates.

Irena Zaleska          Osyp Zalesky

**Zaleska, Irena** [Zales'ka] (née Kobziar), b 1918 in Lviv, d January 1988 in Australia. Actress. Together with her husband, S. *Zalesky, she studied drama with Y. Hirniak and O. Dobrovolska and performed at the Lviv Opera theater in the 1940s. They continued their acting careers in Germany after the Second World War. In Australia they cofounded the Les Kurbas Theater in Melbourne in 1950 and toured the country with their productions. They appeared in several Ukrainian-Australian TV specials, and they presented the first Ukrainian-language radio program in Melbourne in 1966. Noted for her poetic recitals, Zaleska toured the United States and Canada in 1973 with great success. She taught Ukrainian dancing in her Rhythmo Plastic Dance Studio in Melbourne for 25 years.

**Zaleski, Józef Bohdan,** b 14 February 1802 in Bahatyrka, Tarashcha county, Kiev gubernia, d 31 March 1886 in Villepreux near Paris. Polish Romantic poet; an early, major representative of the *Ukrainian school in Polish literature. From 1812 he studied at the Basilian school in Uman. There he befriended S. Goszczyński and M.

Grabowski and formed with them the group Za-Go-Gra. In 1820 he moved to Warsaw. After participating in the Polish Insurrection of 1830–1 he fled to France. Most of Zaleski's Byronic lyrics, historical elegies (eg, about K. Kosynsky, I. Mazepa, and the Battle of Khotyn), and narrative poems and ballads (eg, 'Rusałki' [The Water Nymphs], 'Duch od stepu' [Spirit from the Steppe]) reflect his idealized love and longing for an idyllic Ukrainian land. Many of his poems are stylized imitations or reworkings of Ukrainian folk songs. In 1866 he published a poem dedicated to the recently deceased T. Shevchenko. He also wrote some poems in Ukrainian; they were first published in the 1890 Cracow edition of his works. The fullest editions of his works (4 vols, 1877) and correspondence (5 vols, 1900–4) were published in Lviv. J. *Tretiak wrote a major critical biography of him (3 vols, 1911, 1913, 1914).

**Zaleski, Wacław,** b 18 September 1799 in Olesko, Galicia, d 24 February 1849 in Vienna. Polish folklorist and writer. A graduate of Lviv University, he served in the civil service, taught mathematics, wrote verses and plays, and collected folklore. His *Pieśni polskie i ruskie ludu galicyjskiego* (Polish and Ruthenian Songs of the Galician People, 1833), published under the pseudonym Wacław z Oleska, was one of the first collections of Ukrainian folk songs. It contains an instrumental score by K. Lipiński. The work was regarded highly, and it encouraged the development of Ukrainian ethnography. Later it was criticized for its use of Latin script for Ukrainian transcription. Zaleski also translated Ukrainian folk poetry into German (1861).

**Zalesky, Mykola** [Zales'kyj], b 1835, d ? Pharmacologist. After graduating from Kharkiv University in 1860, he worked in its therapy and obstetrics clinic. For several years he specialized in medical chemistry abroad. In 1868 he was appointed a docent of toxicology and forensic medicine, and in 1885, a professor of pharmacology, at Kharkiv University. His publications dealt with the composition of human and animal bones and the role of the kidneys in producing urea.

**Zalesky, Osyp** [Zales'kyj], b 16 April 1892 in Trostianets Malyi, Zolochiv county, Galicia, d 13 March 1984 in Buffalo. Musicologist, educator, conductor, and composer. He completed studies in musicology with A. Chybinsky at the Lviv Conservatory (1911–14) and then worked as a gymnasium teacher. He founded, directed, and taught at the Stanyslaviv branch of the Lysenko Higher Institute of Music; conducted choruses in Lviv, Stanyslaviv, Yaroslav, and Vienna; and owned (1913–30) the musical publishing house Lira. From 1955 he taught music theory at the Buffalo branch of the Ukrainian Music Institute of America. Zalesky's writings include the pioneering *Pohliad na istoriiu ukraïns'koï muzyky* (A Look at the History of Ukrainian Music, 1916), *Muzychnyi slovnyk* (A Music Dictionary, 1925), *Korotkyi narys istoriï ukraïns'koï muzyky* (A Concise Sketch of the History of Ukrainian Music, 1951), *Zahal'ni osnovy muzychnoho znannia* (General Principles of Musical Knowledge, 1958), and *Mala ukraïns'ka muzychna entsyklopediia* (A Small Ukrainian Music Encyclopedia, 1971). He also composed choral works, solo songs, and piano miniatures.

**Zalesky, Petro** [Zales'kyj] (also Zalisky), b 1867 in Slobidska Ukraine, d 1929 in Yugoslavia. Ukrainian civic and political figure. The Hetman government appointed him as starosta of Kharkiv gubernia in 1918, but later removed him for his reluctance to implement the use of Ukrainian in his administration. During the 1920s he wrote several works regarding military tactics (particularly cavalry), as well as an essay on governing in Ukraine for *Khliborobs'ka Ukraïna* (1925).

**Zalesky, Stepan** [Zales'kyj], b 16 December 1915 in Lviv, d 31 October 1970 in Melbourne. Stage actor. He worked in the Lviv Opera Theater and studied in the Lviv Theatrical Studio (1942–4) and then was a leading actor in the Theater-Studio of Y. Hirniak and O. Dobrovolska in West Germany (1945–9). He moved to Australia in 1950, where he acted in the Les Kurbas Theater and, from 1958, taught in his own Theater Studio.

**Zalesky, Viacheslav** [Zales'kyj, V'jačeslav], b 3 September 1871 in Kharkiv, d 10 November 1936 in Kharkiv. Physiologist and plant biochemist; corresponding member of the VUAN from 1925. He graduated from Kharkiv University in 1893 and was a professor there from 1903 until his death. He researched the manner of and conditions for protein synthesis in plants, phosphorus metabolism, and the role of iron. He proved that plants can synthesize proteins from nitrate and carbohydrates in the absence of light, and was the first to isolate the enzyme carboxylase in plants.

Zalishchyky

**Zalishchyky** [Zališčyky]. V-6. A town (1989 pop 13,200) on the Dniester River and a raion center in Ternopil oblast. It was first mentioned in a historical document in 1340. From the 15th century the town was under Polish rule. In 1766 it was granted the rights of "Magdeburg law. After the partition of Poland in 1772, it was annexed by Austria, and in 1868 it became a county center of Galicia. In the interwar period (1919–39) it was again occupied by Poland. Today it is a river port and a climatological resort area that attracts 10,000 visitors a year. Zalishchyky has three resorts, a children's tuberculosis sanatorium, and a tourist base. Grapes, peaches, morels, and tobacco are grown in its vicinity. The chief architectural monuments are a 17th-century Roman Catholic church and an 18th-century city

hall, palace, and park. In 1927 a large settlement of the Trypilian culture was discovered there.

Maksym Zalizniak (portrait from the Motronynskyi Trinity Monastery)

Mykola Zalizniak

**Zalizniak, Maksym** [Zaliznjak], b ca 1740 in Medvedivka, Chyhyryn region, d ? Haidamaka leader of the *Koliivshchyna rebellion. In response to the Confederation of *Bar and the Polish vendetta against the Ukrainian peasantry, he organized a rebel group of Zaporozhian Cossacks in *Kholodnyi Yar. By late May 1768 they controlled Medvedivka, Zhabotyn, Smila, Cherkasy, Korsun, Kaniv, Bohuslav, Moshny, Fastiv, Kamianyi Brid, Lysianka, and Zvenyhorodka. Together with I. *Gonta's forces they captured Uman (the trading center of Right-Bank Ukraine) on 20–21 June 1768. Zalizniak was proclaimed hetman and began governing the territories according to the Cossack order. On 8 July 1768 he and virtually all of his leading *starshyna* were arrested by Gen M. Krechetnikov, who was commissioned by Empress Catherine II. Zalizniak was given a life sentence of hard labor in the ore mines of Nerchinsk, where he probably died. He became the subject of Ukrainian historical songs and epic literary works, including T. Shevchenko's 'Haidamaky,' 'Kholodnyi iar,' and 'Nevol'nyk' (The Captive) and Yu. Mushketyk's novel *Haidamaky* (1957).

BIBLIOGRAPHY
Antonovych, V. 'Neskol'ko dannykh o sud'be Zhelezniaka posle aresta v Umani,' *KS*, 1882, no. 2
Markovych, O. 'Do biografiï haidamakiv Zelïzniaka i Chorniaia,' *ZNTSh*, 45 (1902)
Golobutskii, V. *Maksim Zhelezniak* (Moscow 1960)

B. Krupnytsky

**Zalizniak, Mykola** [Zaliznjak], b 1888 in Melitopil, Tavriia gubernia, d 1950. Civic and political activist; husband of O. *Zalizniak. During the First World War he worked in Vienna as a journalist and publisher and was active in the *Union for the Liberation of Ukraine. He headed the UNR mission in Finland in 1919–20 and then returned to Vienna. In 1945 he was arrested by the Soviet secret police and sentenced to 15 years in prison, where he perished. He translated popular scientific works and wrote articles and numerous pamphlets about Ukraine and contributed to a collection of memoirs about the Peace Treaty of Brest-Litovsk (1928).

Olena Zalizniak                    Saint Yov Zalizo

**Zalizniak, Olena** [Zaliznjak] (née Okhrymovych), b
1886 in Senechiv, Dolyna county, Galicia, d 12 June 1969
in Montreal. Educator and civic leader; sister of Yu.
*Okhrymovych and wife of M. *Zalizniak. While studying
at Lviv University she was active in student organizations
and the Circle of Ukrainian Women. Upon graduating in
1913, she taught at the girls' gymnasium of the Basilian
Sisters and the teachers' seminary of the Ukrainian Pedagogical Society. During the First World War she made her
way to Vienna, where she was active in the Society for
Aiding Wounded and Imprisoned Soldiers and then
served as president of the Ukrainian Women's Union
(1920–2). After returning to Lviv in 1926, she was appointed director of the trade school at the Trud women's co-operative. At the beginning of the Second World War she
fled to Vienna, and in 1950 she emigrated to Canada,
where she was active in the Ukrainian Women's Organization of Canada. In 1956–69 she served as president of
the *World Federation of Ukrainian Women's Organizations. Her articles appeared in women's magazines, such
as *Nova khata*, *Zhinka*, *Zhinochyi svit*, and *Nashe zhyttia*.

**Zalizniak.** A student society active in Chernivtsi in the
mid-1930s. Established in July 1934 by a breakaway faction of the *Chornomore student society, the group espoused a militant nationalist orientation. Its members
were involved in legal and clandestine publishing and
were supporters of the newspaper *Samostiinist'* in Chernivtsi. It was closed by the Rumanian authorities in March
1937 following a demonstration at an anniversary commemoration of T. Shevchenko, and its leaders (including
D. Kvitkovsky, V. Todoriuk, and M. Nadasiuk) were tried
and sentenced to prison terms.

*Zaliznyi strilets'* (Iron Rifleman). A newspaper pub-
lished three times a week in 1920–2 by the soldiers of the
Third Iron Rifle Division in the Polish internment camp in
Kalisz. Its editor was Capt I. Zubenko.

**Zalizo, Yov** (Zhelizo; secular name: Ivan), b 1551 in the
Kolomyia region, d 28 October 1651 in Pochaiv. Monk and
saint of the Ukrainian Orthodox church. He was tonsured
at the Transfiguration Monastery in Uhornyky when he
was 12 years old, and made a hieromonk in 1581. In 1584
Prince K. Ostrozky invited him to become hegumen of the

Dubno Monastery. There he founded a brotherhood
whose members transcribed church books. Ca 1597 he left
for the *Pochaiv Monastery, where he served as hegumen
for the next 50 years. He introduced a strict *Studite monastic order at the monastery and continued administrative and educational activities. Under his leadership the
monastery was expanded, and gained fame throughout
Ukraine. He persuaded the Orthodox magnates F. and Ye.
Domashovsky to fund the building in 1649 of the Church
of the Holy Trinity, in which a miracle-working icon of the
Mother of God was placed. Zalizo actively defended the
Orthodox church, and in 1628 he participated in the Kiev
synod that condemned M. Smotrytsky's attempts to extend the church union. He translated much patristic literature and composed sermons. A selection of these works
was published in *Kievskaia starina* in 1885; the originals
were taken from the monastery in 1932 to Warsaw, where
they subsequently perished.

Zalizo was greatly revered during his life, and many
miracles were associated with him. His relics were discovered in 1659 by Metropolitan D. Balaban, who had him
canonized. He was known popularly as the Venerable
Yov; his feast is celebrated several times during the year.
His life, by the monk Dosyfei, was published in Pochaiv in
1791.

A. Zhukovsky

**Zalozetsky, Mykola** [Zalozec'kyj], b 21 October 1895 in
Nyrkiv, Zalishchyky county, Galicia, d 13 January 1993 in
Winnipeg. Pharmacist, community leader, and journalist.
He emigrated in 1906 with his parents to Canada, where
he graduated from the University of Manitoba (1925) and
was active in the Ukrainian community in Winnipeg. He
served as president of St Andrew's College (1946–70), the
Winnipeg branch of the Mohyla Society, the Ukrainian
National Home (1967–9), and the Friends of the Ukrainian
National Council (1976–7). He was a founder of the Order
of St Andrew. His articles and verses appeared under various pseudonyms in the Ukrainian press, including
*Ukraïns'kyi holos*, *Novyi shliakh*, and *Promin'*.

Roman Zalozetsky-Sas

**Zalozetsky-Sas, Roman** [Zalozec'kyj-Sas], 1861–1918.
Engineer and civic leader; full member of the Shevchenko
Scientific Society, son of V. *Zalozetsky-Sas. He completed his university studies in Lviv, Vienna, and Zurich and
served as a professor at the Lviv Polytechnical Institute.

He was president of the *Silskyi Hospodar society, a founder and director of the Prosvita society's Commercial School in Lviv (1911–15), and a member of the Galician Diet (1913–15). In 1915 he was appointed councillor at the Ministry of Public Works in Vienna. He served as an agent of French and British oil companies and was granted the honorary title of British consul for Lviv in 1904. His publications dealt with technological questions, particularly of the petroleum industry, and economic problems.

**Zalozetsky-Sas, Vasyl** [Zalozec'kyj-Sas, Vasyl'] (pseud: Panko iz Halychanova), b 7 February 1833 in Pohorilivka, Bukovyna, d 2 February 1915 in Hirne, Stryi county, Galicia. Greek Catholic priest and writer in Galicia. He contributed poems and historical stories to Russophile periodicals, such as *Slovo, Halychanyn, Halytskaia Rus', Rodimyi listok,* and *Prolom.* An edition of his complete works (3 vols, 1907–9) was published in Lviv.

Volodymyr Zalozetsky-Sas (1884–1965)    Volodymyr Zalozetsky-Sas (1896–1959)

**Zalozetsky-Sas, Volodymyr** [Zalozec'kyj], b 28 July 1884 in Chernivtsi, d 13 July 1965 in Ysper, Niederösterreich, Austria. Bukovynian political, cultural, and civic leader, diplomat, and art scholar. He studied at the universities of Chernivtsi, Vienna, Munich, and Florence and obtained doctorates in law as well as archeology and art history. From 1910 he served as a member of the Austrian central committee for the preservation of art and historical monuments in Vienna and as chief conservator of historical relics and art in the non-Germanic provinces of the monarchy. Having been mobilized to serve in the Austrian army in 1914, he was captured by Russian forces. In the fall of 1918 he returned to Bukovyna, where he became a member of the Ukrainian Regional Committee and of the Bukovynian delegation to the Ukrainian National Rada of the Western Ukrainian National Republic (ZUNR). On 10 November 1918 he became head of the Ukrainian government in Bukovyna, and in 1919 the ZUNR government appointed him to take part in the talks with the so-called Little Mission of the Entente powers. This appointment led to his position as councillor and chargé d'affaires of the Extraordinary Diplomatic Mission of the ZUNR in Bern.

In 1920 Zalozetsky-Sas returned to Bukovyna. He became involved in political work and was cofounder and head of the *Ukrainian National party (UNP) in Bukovyna

(1927–38) as well as official Ukrainian representative to the Rumanian government. He was elected a senator (1928–32 and 1934–8) and member of parliament (1932–4). A champion of the political, cultural, and religious rights of the Ukrainians under Rumanian rule, he served as a delegate to the national minorities section of the League of Nations in Geneva in 1928–38. In 1940 Zalozetsky-Sas headed the Ukrainian National Hromada in Rumania, and in 1944 he moved to Vienna, where he remained active in community and cultural affairs.

Zalozetsky-Sas was honorary president of many Bukovynian cultural and civic organizations as well as founder and head of the Ukrainian Museum of Ethnology in Chernivtsi (1927–40). He researched the art and ethnography of Bukovyna and wrote *Künstler oder Kunsthistoriker* (1924), *Die Ostereier der ukrainischen Huzulen* (1942), and *Ein Huzulenteller* (1944) as well as the play *Henii narodu* (The People's Genius, 1932).

A. Zhukovsky

**Zalozetsky-Sas, Volodymyr** [Zalozec'kyj-Sas] (Zaloziecky, Wladimir), b 10 July 1896 in Lviv, d 12 October 1959 in Graz, Austria. Art historian; son of R. *Zalozetsky-Sas; member of the Shevchenko Scientific Society from 1932. After graduating from Vienna University (PH D, 1918) he taught there and worked for the UNR diplomatic mission in Vienna. He served on a Czechoslovak government board for the preservation of cultural monuments in Uzhhorod (1922–4), lectured at the Ukrainian Free University in Prague (1924–6), and held the chair of art history at the Ukrainian Scientific Institute in Berlin (1926–39) and Greek Catholic Theological Academy in Lviv (1930–9). From 1939 he lectured at Vienna University, and from 1947 he was a professor at Graz University. He was a founder of the Österreichisch-Byzantinische Gesellschaft in Vienna (1945). He wrote many articles and books, among them *Gotische und barocke Holzkirchen in den Karpathenländern* (1926), *Oleksa Novakivs'kyi* (1934), *Die Sophienkirche in Konstantinopel und ihre Stellung in der Geschichte der abendländischen Architektur* (1936), *Geschichte der altchristlichen Kunst* (1936), *Byzanz und Abendland im Spiegel ihrer Kunsterscheinungen* (1936), *Geschichte der altchristlichen Kunst* (1936), and *Die byzantinische Baukunst in den Balkanländern und ihre Differenzierung unter abendländischen und islamischen Einwirkungen* (1955).

**Zalozny, Petro** [Zaloznyj], b 1 January 1866 in Rashivka, Hadiache county, Poltava gubernia, d 8 April 1921 in Rashivka. Pedagogue and linguist. A graduate of Kiev University (1889), he worked as a teacher in his home village. He wrote *Korotka hramatyka ukraïns'koï movy* (A Short Grammar of the Ukrainian Language, 2 vols, 1906, 1913), a work which assisted considerably in standardizing Ukrainian grammatical terminology, and contributed poetry to Ukrainian almanacs and periodicals.

**Zaloznyi route.** A surface trade route from Kiev to the Middle East. There are two major theories as to the origin of the name: from *za lozy* (beyond the willows), and from *zavoloznyi* (trans-Volga). The route is mentioned in historical sources of the 11th and 12th centuries, and according to archeological evidence it was already in existence in the 8th century. Known also as the Kiev–Azov route, it ran from Kiev along the left bank of the Dnieper River through Pereiaslav, Lukoml, and Ltava (Hovtva) to the upper Mozh River (a right tributary of the Donets River) and then to the upper Samara River and along the upper Kalmiius River to the mouth of the Don River and along the Azov Sea to Tmutorokan. From there it continued on to Asia Minor and the Middle East. The Zaloznyi route is mentioned in the Primary Chronicle under the years 1168, 1170, and 1185. It was not a safe route; frequently cut off by steppe hordes, it required fortified defenses in order to be maintained by the Rus' rulers.

**Zalukva.** A village, now in Halych raion, in Ivano-Frankivske oblast, near which a Rus' settlement site was excavated in 1883 by I. Sharanevych and Rev L. Lavretsky. The stone foundation of an ancient church (Holy Redeemer), a stone sarcophagus, bronze pendant crosses, and the lead seal of Bishop Kosma of Halych (1160s) were found at the site.

**Zalutsky, Vasyl** [Zaluc'kyj, Vasyl'] (real name: Orobets), b 30 January 1895 in Zaluche, Sniatyn county, Galicia, d 15 July 1973 in Edmonton. Painter and graphic artist. During the First World War he served in the Ukrainian Sich Riflemen, and in 1918 he fought with them in central Ukraine, where he stayed. After graduating from the Kiev Printing Institute he worked as a book illustrator in Kiev, Kharkiv, and Moscow. A postwar refugee in Germany, at the Augsburg DP camp he illustrated *Syn Ukraïny* (Son of Ukraine), U. Samchuk's *Iunist' Vasylia Sheremety* (Youth of Vasyl Sheremeta), and *Tysiacha i odna nich* (A Thousand and One Nights), designed theatrical scenery, and began painting oils. In 1949 he emigrated to Canada. In Edmonton he designed scenery, painted icons for St George's Church, and created greeting cards depicting Ukrainian folk customs.

Opanas Zalyvakha: *Self-Portrait*

**Zalyvakha, Opanas** [Zalyvaxa], b 26 November 1925 in Husynka, now in Kupianka raion, Kharkiv oblast. Nonconformist artist. Zalyvakha grew up in the Far East, where his parents resettled in 1933. He was expelled from the Leningrad Art Institute in 1947 for not conforming to socialist realism but was readmitted after J. Stalin's death, and graduated in 1960. He then headed the art council in Tiumen, Russia, where his first solo exhibition was held, in 1961. In December 1961 he moved to Ivano-Frankivske.

There his second solo exhibition (April 1962) was closed down by the Party authorities for 'decadent tendencies.' In 1964 Zalyvakha, A. *Horska, and L. *Semykina were commissioned to create a stained-glass panel for the vestibule of Kiev University's main building. Depicting T. Shevchenko embracing a woman, it was destroyed on orders of Kiev's Party secretary, V. Boichenko. Zalyvakha was arrested in August 1965 and sentenced at a closed trial in March 1966 to five years in a hard-labor camp in Mordovia for disseminating samvydav literature. After his release in 1970, he was forced to work as a laborer in Ivano-Frankivske, but continued painting. The first solo exhibition of his paintings, sculptures, and ceramics in 26 years was held in Lviv in December 1988 at the Ukrainian State Museum of Ethnography and Crafts. A second was held in Ivano-Frankivske in May 1989. Throughout the years Zalyvakha has experimented. Despite stylistic variation, from the figurative (*Woman from the Poltava Region*, 1965) to the abstract (*Primeval-Mother*, 1975) and the stylized (*Skovoroda*, 1977), his subject matter has remained deeply rooted in his Ukrainian heritage and in Ukrainian history, as is evident in works such as *Chumak Supper* (1970) and *Berestechko* (1980s). Zalyvakha has painted numerous icons of the Mother of God, including *Carpathian Mother of God* (1960s), *Cossack Madonna* (1970s), and *The Protectress* (1988). He has used the three-faced compositions of 18th-century icons of the Trinity to create contemporary secular icons, such as *Crying Ox* (1975), in which two human faces are intertwined with that of a beast of burden. He has painted many portraits of T. Shevchenko, of friends, and of family. Concerns about his fate and his nation's fate have resulted in works such as *Lira Player, 1933* (1973) and *Fate* (1982).

D. Zelska-Darewych

**Zalyvchy, Andrii** [Zalyvčyj, Andrij], b 26 October 1892 in Mlyny, Hadiache county, Poltava gubernia, d 13 December 1918 in Chernihiv. Political activist. For his membership in the Kharkiv cell of the Socialist Revolutionary party he was arrested in 1915 and exiled to Turgansk, Siberia. In early 1917 he returned to Ukraine, where he served as a member of the Central Rada, representing the *Ukrainian Party of Socialist Revolutionaries (UPSR). He was one of the founders of the left faction of the UPSR, which later founded the *Borotbist party. His collection of autobiographical stories, *Z lit dytynstva* (From Childhood Years, 1919), was published posthumously.

**Zamishantsi.** The Lemko name for the inhabitants of 10 Ukrainian villages (1939 pop 7,300) between Rzeszów and Krosno, about 30 km away from Ukrainian ethnic territory. Their dialect is close to the eastern Lemko dialect, except that it has some Boiko elements and a heavily Polonized lexicon. It was studied by I. Verkhratsky and I. Zilynsky.

**Zamorii, Petro** [Zamorij], b 25 June 1906 in Vysunske, Kherson county, Kherson gubernia, d 26 March 1975 in Kiev. Geologist and geomorphologist. He graduated from the Kherson Agricultural Institute in 1926. He became section head at the AN URSR (now ANU) Institute of Geological Sciences in 1941, a professor at Kiev University in 1950, and served as president of the Ukrainian Geographical Society (1956–64). He primarily studied Quaternary deposits and the geomorphology of Ukraine and the Urals and explained the effect of neotectonics on the relief of Quaternary deposits. He established the basic genetic types of scattered mineral deposits. He edited the periodical *Fizychna heohrafiia ta heomorfolohiia* (1973–5) and wrote numerous books on Quaternary deposits in Ukraine (1961).

The main square and town hall of Zamość

**Zamość** (Ukrainian: Zamostia). III-4. A city (1989 pop 60,700) in the southwestern Kholm region, at present the administrative center of Zamość voivodeship in Poland. Zamość was founded in 1580 by the Polish chancellor J. Zamoyski, and quickly became an important economic, military, and cultural center (particularly with the establishment of the *Zamostia Academy in 1594). The town was besieged by B. Khmelnytsky in 1648 and taken by I. Mazepa in 1705. It was incorporated into the Russian Empire as part of Kholm gubernia. The 1918 Peace Treaty of Brest-Litovsk was to have made Zamość part of Ukraine, but subsequent events established it as part of Poland. In 1920 Zamość was the site of a battle between the Sixth Division of the Sich Riflemen under M. Bezruchko and the Bolshevik cavalry army under S. Budenny. A small number of Ukrainians lived in Zamość until 1944; in 1945 there were approx 8,000 Ukrainians and over 10,000 Polonized Ukrainians living in the surrounding county.

Zamość was an important religious center in Ukrainian history. In 1589 Zamoyski allowed the Orthodox residents of the town to build the Church of St Nicholas, which became renowned for its iconostasis painted by masters from Constantinople. A brotherhood established by the church was sanctioned by the patriarch Theophanes. The brotherhood sponsored a school. In 1699 the brotherhood adopted the Catholic faith, and the church was given to the Basilian monastic order, which ran a monastery there in 1706–1864. The Synod of *Zamostia took place in 1720. A second Ukrainian church, the Church of the Dormition, was built in Zamość in 1592 and was taken over by the Basilians in 1758.

A. Zhukovsky

**Zamostia, Synod of.** A church synod held in August–September 1720 in Zamość (Zamostia), during the tenure of Metropolitan L. Kyshka. It was a provincial synod of the Kiev Uniate metropoly, the goal of which was to review church life and the liturgical customs of the Ukrainian and Belarusian Catholic church. Preparations for it began in 1715; it was initially to have been held in Lviv but

was moved because of an epidemic. The synod was approved by the pope and presided over by his nuncio, Grimaldi. It was attended by the metropolitan, 7 bishops, and 129 priests and monks, and the Lviv Stauropegion Institute sent 2 lay representatives. Metropolitan Kyshka and Bishop A. Sheptytsky were particularly influential participants in the deliberations. The synod condemned the Russian Filipian heresy, widespread in Ukraine and Belarusia at the time. It also ratified several important changes concerning *church rite and discipline, including the addition to the *Creed of the *filioque* clause used in the Roman Catholic church, and commemoration of the pope. The synodal decrees upheld the strong Latinization trend in the church, and were approved by the Holy See in 1724. The synod regulated church administration, made efforts to improve the education of priests, and ordered all Uniate monasteries in the province to join the Basilian order. Most of the resolutions were reconfirmed by the *Lviv Synod of 1891.

The Synod of Zamostia resolutions entered the canon of basic church law. The act and resolutions were published as *Synodus Provincialis Ruthenorum habita in civitate Zamosciae anno 1720* (1724 and several subsequent edns).

BIBLIOGRAPHY
Khrustsevich, G. *Istoriia Zamoiskago sobora (1720)* (Vilnius 1880)
Bilanych, I. *Synodus Zamostiana a. 1720* (Rome 1960)

I. Patrylo

The mace of the Zamostia Academy

**Zamostia Academy** (Zamostska or Zamoiska akademiia). An institution of higher education founded in 1595 by J. Zamoyski, chancellor of the Kingdom of Poland; located in Zamostia (Zamość), a city in the Kholm region. The academy was operated by Jesuits, but initially it had a secular program of studies. Talented scholars were recruited to the school, and for many years it was the best educational institution of its kind in the Polish Commonwealth. Seven chairs of study were established there: civil law, Polish law, moral philosophy, physics and medicine, logic and metaphysics, mathematics, and rhetoric. Additional courses included readings from the authors of antiquity, beginner's rhetoric, syntax, grammar, and orthography. The study of Latin, Greek, and Polish was compulsory. In addition to Poles, Lithuanians, Prussians, Livonians, and other foreigners, many Ukrainians (both Catholic and Orthodox) studied at the academy and later became prominent church or cultural leaders (figures of note include S. Kosiv, I. Kozlovsky-Trofymovych, and K. Sakovych). After the death of its founder and benefactor in 1605, the academy lost its initial dynamism and became increasingly clerical in its orientation. In 1784 the Austrian government closed the academy and replaced it with a secondary school.

**Zamoyski.** A family line of Polish magnates, originating with Tomasz Łaziński, who purchased a large estate in the Stara Zamość region (hence the Zamoyski name) in the early 15th century. Members of the family occupied important state positions in the Polish kingdom and played a significant role in Ukrainian affairs. The most notable family figure was Jan Zamoyski (1542–1605), the Polish chancellor and royal grand hetman. He was a close political adviser to Stephen Báthory and later a supporter of Sigismund III Vasa (although he eventually came into conflict with him). He also founded the Zamostia Academy in 1595.

**Zamoyski, Jan,** b 19 March 1542, d 3 June 1605 in Zamość, Poland. Polish magnate and statesman; father of T. Zamoyski. He was a major force in Polish politics, a close adviser to King Sigismund II Augustus and Stephen Báthory, and, later, a strong opponent of Sigismund III Vasa. He was named crown chancellor in 1578 and head of the army in 1581. He established an academy in Zamość in 1595.

**Zamoyski, Tomasz,** b 1591, d 1638. Polish nobleman; son of J. Zamoyski. A graduate of the Zamostia Academy, he was a voivode of Podilia (1618) and Kiev (1618–29), crown vice-chancellor (1629–35), and crown chancellor (from 1635). In his official capacities he concluded a treaty with the Cossacks in 1619 and conducted negotiations with them in 1625. He supported the promotion of the Ukrainian statesman A. *Kysil.

Ivan Zamsha               Ivan Zamychkovsky

**Zamsha, Ivan** [Zamša], b 8 October 1895 in Rozkishna, Tarashcha county, Kiev gubernia, d 15 November 1978 in New York. Economist and co-operative organizer. From 1918 he was active in the co-operative movement in Kiev. In 1922 he was appointed assistant head and then head of the financial department of the All-Ukrainian Association of Consumer Co-operative Organizations (Vukoop-

spilka). After graduating from the Kiev Co-operative Institute in 1923, he taught there and at other institutions. He was arrested in 1930 and 1931 but subsequently released, and he continued to teach in Kiev. During the war he headed the financial department of the Vukoopspilka in Kiev. A postwar émigré in Germany, he oversaw the financial department of the Central Ukrainian Relief Committee and helped found the Ukrainian Higher School of Economics in Munich, at which he served as a professor and chairman of the economic planning department. In 1952 he emigrated to the United States, where he managed the finances of the Ukrainian Academy of Arts and Sciences and continued his research. He published some articles on the history of the Ukrainian co-operative movement, the Vukoopspilka, M. Tuhan-Baranovsky, and economics in the USSR.

**Zamychkovsky, Ivan,** b 8 January 1869 in Kiev, d 15 July 1931 in Kiev. Stage and film actor. He began his career in the Kiev Russian Operetta Theater under I. Setov (1887). In 1896 he led an amateur theatrical group in Kiev. He was an actor in the Ukrainian National Theater (1917–18), the State Drama Theater (1918–19), the Shevchenko First Theater of the Ukrainian Soviet Republic (1919–25), and the Odessa Ukrainian Drama Theater (1925–31). He also acted in the films *Taras Shevchenko* (1926), *Taras Triasylo* (1927), and *Dva dni* (Two Days, 1927). A biography, by I. Duz, was published in Kiev (1962).

**Zamyrailo, Viktor** [Zamyrajlo], b 23 November 1868 in Cherkasy, d 2 September 1939 in Petrodvorets, Leningrad oblast, Russia. Graphic artist and theatrical scenery designer. He studied at the Kiev Drawing School (1881–4) and under M. Vrubel in Kiev. He took part in painting the murals in St Volodymyr's Cathedral in Kiev (1885–90). In 1897 he began designing Russian posters and books, including editions of N. Gogol's works (1913), J. Swift's *Gulliver's Travels* in Russian (1918), and A. Blok's *Dvenadtsat* (Twelve, 1924). Later he turned to designing scenery. In the Soviet period he served as a professor at the Higher State Artistic and Technical Institute in Leningrad (1925–9).

**Zander.** See Pike perch.

Mariia Zankovetska

**Zankovetska, Mariia** [Zan'kovec'ka, Marija] (neé Adasovska; married name: Khlystova), b 4 August 1854 in Zanky, now in Nizhen raion, Chernihiv oblast, d 4 October 1934 in Kiev. Actress, singer, and theater activist.

Zankovetska was educated in a Chernihiv private school and at the Helsinki Conservatory. She debuted in 1882 in I. Kotliarevsky's *Natalka from Poltava* as a member of M. Kropyvnytsky's troupe, which production heralded the rebirth of Ukrainian professional theater, heavily repressed since the Ems Ukase of 1876. Zankovetska performed as leading actress in the troupes of Kropyvnytsky (1882–3, 1885–8, 1899–1900), M. Starytsky (1883–5), and M. Sadovsky (1888–98), in Saksahansky's Troupe (1900–3), in O. Suslov's troupe (1903–4), in the Society of Ukrainian Actors (1915–17), and in the State People's Theater (1918–22). She appeared at the All-Russian Congress of Stage Workers in 1897, where she demanded the termination of censorship in Ukrainian theater. In 1909–15 she directed amateur groups in Nizhen and Krolevets. Her last performance on stage was in Kiev in 1922, and that same year a theater in her name was founded. Zankovetska's stage career spanned over 30 dramatic-heroic roles from the populist-ethnographical repertoire, which she played with innate subtlety and intelligence. Among them were Olena in M. Kropyvnytsky's *Hlytai, abo zh pavuk* (The Profiteer, or the Spider), Katria and Aza in M. Starytsky's *Ne sudylos'* (Not Destined) and *Tsyhanka Aza* (The Gypsy Aza), Sofiia and Kharytyna in I. Karpenko-Kary's *Bezta-lanna* (The Hapless Maiden) and *Naimychka* (The Hired Girl), Natalia in P. Myrny's *Lymerivna* (The Saddler's Daughter), and Zinka in L. Yanovska's *Lisova kvitka* (The Forest Flower). Her best performances were opposite M. Tobilevych (Sadovsky), and her talent was praised by K. Stanislavsky. She was less successful in comic roles and in the non-Ukrainian repertoire. She starred in the films *Natalka from Poltava* (1910) and *Ostap Bandura* (1923). She was the author of a book of memoirs, and biographies of her have been published in Kiev (1950, 1953, 1982). In 1964 a museum in her honor was established in Zanky.

V. Revutsky

**Zankovetska Theater.** See Lviv Ukrainian Drama Theater.

**Zaozirny, John** [Zaozirnyj], b 26 June 1947 in Calgary. Lawyer and politician of Ukrainian descent. He was educated at the University of Calgary, University of British Columbia (LLB, 1972), and London School of Economics (LLM, 1973). In 1979 he was elected to the legislature of Alberta as Progressive Conservative member for Calgary Forest Lawn. He was re-elected in 1982, at which time he was appointed minister of energy.

**Zap, Karel Vladislav,** b 8 January 1812 in Prague, d 1 January 1871 in Benešov, Bohemia. Czech writer, historian, and geographer. In the years 1836–44 he worked as a civil servant in Lviv. There he studied Ukrainian history, ethnography, and literature and had ties with leaders of the Galician revival (eg, M. Shashkevych, I. Vahylevych, Ya. Holovatsky, D. Zubrytsky). He published articles about Galician affairs and ethnography in Czech periodicals and wrote books on life in Eastern Europe (1843) and his travels in Galicia (1844); the travel book is a valuable ethnographic source. He was critical of the Polish landowners' oppression of the Ukrainian peasantry and considered the Ukrainians a distinct nation. He also translated N. Gogol's *Taras Bul'ba* and articles by Holovatsky, Vahylevych, and P. Kulish into Czech.

**Zapałowicz, Hugo,** b 15 November 1852 in Lublin, d 20 September 1917. Polish botanist. He studied the phytogeography of the flora of the Beskyds and the Pokutia and Maramureş regions of the Carpathian Mountains and wrote *Krytyczny przegląd roślinności Galicji* (A Critical Survey of the Vegetation of Galicia, 3 vols, 1906–11).

**Zapasko, Yakym,** b 28 August 1923 in Rozsishky, Uman county, Kiev gubernia. Art historian. He graduated from the Ukrainian Printing Institute in Lviv in 1950 and received his candidate's degree in 1958. Zapasko has taught at the Lviv Institute of Applied and Decorative Arts since 1959 and now heads its Department of Art History. He has written monographs on the ornamentation of Ukrainian manuscript books (1960), the first Ukrainian printer, I. Fedorov (1964), book art in 16th- to 18th-century Ukraine (1971), the Ukrainian folk kilim (1973), I. Fedorov's artistic heritage (1974), and old printed books published in Lviv (1983, with O. Matsiuk), and many articles on the history of Ukrainian book art and Ukrainian decorative and applied arts. Zapasko and Ya. Isaievych compiled a valuable catalog of old printed books published in Ukraine in 1574–1800 (3 vols, 1981, 1984).

*Zapiski Imperatorskogo Khar'kovskogo universiteta* (Annals of the Imperial Kharkiv University). A scholarly journal published quarterly by Kharkiv University from 1874 to 1917, with an interruption from 1884 to 1893. It contained much information about *Slobidska Ukraine and the Kharkiv region. Among its editors was D. *Ovsianiko-Kulikovsky (1894–1904).

*Zapiski Imperatorskogo Novorossiiskogo universiteta* (Annals of the Imperial New Russia University). A scholarly journal published by the Richelieu Lyceum and then Odessa (New Russia) University from 1853. Initially the journal published articles from all disciplines, especially historical linguistics and literature. After 113 volumes had appeared, the journal was divided into separate series: history-philology (14 vols of which appeared in 1909–18), physics-mathematics (12 vols in 1910–19), law (14 vols in 1909–17), and medicine (9 vols in 1909–19). Among its editors in the 19th century were A. Pavlov, S. Yaroshenko, and A. Kochubinsky.

*Zapiski Imperatorskogo Odesskogo obshchestva istorii i drevnostei* (Notes of the Imperial Odessa Society of History and Antiquities). A publication of the Odessa Society of History and Antiquities, which appeared irregularly in 1844–1919, altogether in 33 volumes. It contained articles on archeology, epigraphy, numismatics, history, ethnography, geography, and the economy of Southern Ukraine, as well as reports of the activities of the society. Also published was M. Popruzhenko's index to vols 1–30 (1914).

*Zapiski o Iuzhnoi Rusi* (Notes on Southern Russia). A two-volume collection of materials concerning the Cossack period, published by P. *Kulish in 1856–7 with the financial assistance of two magnates of the Chernihiv region, H. Galagan and V. Tarnovsky. The first volume consists of dumas, songs collected by Kulish, and legends about B. Khmelnytsky, S. Palii, leading Zaporozhians, Cossack battles against the Tatars, and struggles of the

Cossacks against the Church Union of Berestia. The second volume contains folktales recorded by L. Zhemchuzhnikov, an account of a meeting with the kobzar O. Veresai, accounts of haidamaka campaigns (the manuscript of S. Zakrevsky), a number of articles on history, ethnography, and linguistics, and a series of documents on the history of the Hetmanate in the 18th century. Because of censorship T. Shevchenko's poem 'Naimychka' (The Hired Girl) was first published in the collection, as a work of an unknown author. M. Kostomarov and Shevchenko greeted the collection with enthusiasm; M. Maksymovych met it with guarded criticism.

Florian Zapletal

Frederick Zaplitny

**Zapletal, Florian,** b 10 June 1884 in Bochoř, Moravia, d 16 October 1969 in Prague. Czech scholar and journalist. He studied at Prague, Vienna, Moscow, and Petrograd universities. In 1919–21 he served as chief of the press service in Transcarpathia and collected historical and ethnographical materials there. He wrote over 160 articles on the history, culture, architecture, and politics of Transcarpathia and the books *Rusini a naši buditelé* (Ruthenians and Our Awakeners, 1921), *Horjanská rotunda* (The Horiany Rotunda, 1923), and *A.I. Dobrjanskij a naši rusini r. 1849–51* (A.I. Dobriansky and Our Ruthenians in 1849–51, 1929). In 1967 he turned over part of his valuable archive and library to the Svydnyk Museum of Ukrainian Culture, and in 1973 his widow entrusted over 500 of his photographic glass plates from the 1920s to M. Mushynka in Prešov. An album based on these plates, *Wooden Churches in the Carpathians*, was published in 1982 with the help of P. Magocsi.

**Zaplitny, Antin** [Zaplitnyj], b 14 June 1890 in Hlibiv, Skalat county, Galicia, d 1 July 1968 in Detroit. Lawyer and civic leader; member of the Shevchenko Scientific Society from 1963. A graduate of Vienna University, he served as Terebovlia county commissioner for the Western Ukrainian National Republic (1919). He opened a law office in Terebovlia in 1926 and presided over the local branches of the Prosvita society, the Ridna Shkola society, and the Ukrainian National Democratic Alliance. In 1944 he fled to Germany, and in 1950 he emigrated to the United States, where he continued to be active in the Ukrainian community.

**Zaplitny, Frederick** [Zaplitnyj, Fedir], b 9 June 1913 in Oak Brae, Manitoba, d 19 March 1964 in Dauphin, Manitoba. Canadian politician of Ukrainian descent. After graduating from the teachers' college in Dauphin, he became active in the Co-operative Commonwealth Federation (CCF). In 1945 and 1953 he was elected an MP for the Dauphin riding, and in 1950–2 served as a councillor in Dauphin. In Ottawa he took an active interest in Ukrainian affairs.

**Zaporizhia** [Zaporižžja]. The name of the military and political organization of the Ukrainian *Cossacks and of their autonomous territory (approx 80,000 sq km) in *Southern Ukraine from the mid-16th century to 1775. The name was derived from the territory's location 'beyond the [Dnieper] Rapids' (*za porohamy*). Its center was the *Zaporozhian Sich. The Zaporizhia's territory – the 'Liberties of the [Cossack] Host beyond the [Dnieper] Rapids' – was situated to the south and east of Polish-ruled *Right-Bank Ukraine, from which it was separated by the Boh River, its tributaries the Syniukha and the Velykyi Vys, and the Tiasmyn River, a tributary of the Dnieper. To the northeast it bordered on the Left-Bank *Hetman state along the Dnieper River and its tributary, the Orel. To the east it was separated from Russian-ruled *Slobidska Ukraine by the Donets River. To the southeast it bordered on the lands of the Don Cossacks along the Kalmiius River. The Zaporizhia extended southward deep into the steppe, where it bordered on the *Crimean Khanate and reached, between the Berda and the Kalmiius rivers, the Sea of Azov.

The Cossacks gained renown in the late 15th century as defenders of the Lithuanian-Ruthenian state against the Crimean Tatars, while serving the Cherkasy and Kaniv starostas and living as free brigands in the uncolonized steppe frontier of the Polish state. The rise of the Zaporizhia resulted from the increasing colonization of that frontier by Ukrainians fleeing serfdom and other Polish-Lithuanian oppression. There they established homesteads and, to defend themselves from Tatar raids, built fortified camps (*sichi*), which were later united to create a central fortress, the Zaporozhian Sich, under the leadership of D. *Vyshnevetsky on the island of Mala Khortytsia (ca 1552). The anti-Polish Cossack rebellions of the 1590s, 1620s, and 1630s originated in the Zaporizhia and resulted in the growth of the military and political strength of the *Zaporozhian Host.

The Zaporizhia played a key role in the early period of the *Cossack-Polish War of 1648–57. During the following period, of the so-called *Ruin, it influenced the course of events, if at times only negatively, particularly during the hetmancy of I. Briukhovetsky and when I. *Sirko was the Zaporozhian otaman (1660–80). The politically unsophisticated Zaporozhian leaders were often exploited by Muscovy and Ottoman Turkey and the Crimean Khanate, which succeeded in pitting the Zaporizhia against the Hetman state. With the *Eternal Peace of 1686 the Zaporizhia became a Muscovite protectorate; it retained its autonomy while recognizing the authority of the hetman. Soon Russian armed forces appeared in the Zaporizhia, and with time they established their own forts to control the Cossacks, notably a fort 2 km from the *New Sich (1735).

Under Otaman K. *Hordiienko the Zaporizhia became an ally of Hetman I. *Mazepa and Charles XII in 1709. In retaliation Russian forces destroyed the *Chortomlyk Sich and, after their victory at the Battle of Poltava, mercilessly persecuted the Zaporozhians, thereby forcing them to flee to Crimean Tatar territory, where the Zaporozhians founded the new *Oleshky Sich. After Hordiienko's death in 1734, the Zaporozhians, having fared badly under the Tatars and not having their ranks replenished with new refugees from Ukraine, once again accepted Russian suzerainty and returned to their former lands. Thenceforth the Zaporizhia and the *New Sich were directly under the control of the Russian governor-general of Kiev. In 1752 the Russian government designated areas of Serbian colonization on Zaporozhian territory – *New Serbia in the northwest and *Sloviano-Serbia in the northeast – and used the colonists to subdue the Cossacks.

By the late 17th century a unique sociopolitical order had evolved in the Zaporizhia; with certain changes, it existed until the end of the 18th century. The order was based on the political equality of all Zaporozhian Cossacks regardless of their social origins. The principle of general elections was applied to all representative bodies, including the supreme *Sich Council, the central administrative body, known as the Kish of the Zaporozhian Sich, the *Kish otaman and his *starshyna* (the Kish judge, chancellor, osaul, and quartermaster), and the otamans of the Zaporozhian *kurins. Those elected figures constituted the Council of Officers, a collegial administrative body. Outside the Sich appointed colonels commanded districts called *palankas (eight in the 18th century).

At the Sich the Zaporozhian Host (army) was traditionally divided into 38 kurins (the number of kurins was actually higher, because several existed outside the Sich), each with several hundred Cossacks. Numerous homesteads (see *Zymivnyk) on the territory of each palanka were inhabited by married Cossacks (since only unmar-

ried Cossacks could dwell at the Sich) and peasants, who engaged in individual farming. Collective farming was undertaken by each kurin. Fishing, hunting, and cattle raising were the chief occupations in the Zaporizhia. Agriculture became particularly developed under its last otaman, P. *Kalnyshevsky (1765–75), when peasants were readily welcomed as free settlers. The Zaporizhia also played an important commercial role because of its location on the trade route from the Crimea to Poland, the Hetman state, and Russia.

Although Zaporozhian society was originally egalitarian, by the mid-18th century a higher stratum of *znatni* or *starshi tovaryshi* ('notable' or 'senior fellows') had come into being. Most Cossack officers were elected from among them. The 'fellows' accumulated wealth on their *zymivnyky* and were able to hire both free peasants and *Cossack helpers to work for them. The Cossacks and peasants did not constitute closed estates. Movement from one to the other was possible and was regulated by the Kish according to its military and war needs. In 1762 nearly 33,700 Cossacks and over 150,000 peasants lived on Zaporozhian territory. By the time it was abolished, over 200,000 peasants lived there. As a result of the stratification that occurred in the 18th century, there was frequent popular unrest among the commoners and even several uprisings (the largest in 1768). The Zaporizhia supported the *haidamaka uprisings and the *Koliivshchyna rebellion in Polish-ruled Ukraine; the rebellion was led by a Zaporozhian Cossack, M. Zalizniak.

In the second half of the 18th century the Zaporozhian Cossacks were forced to struggle constantly against the encroachments of the mainly Serbian and Rumanian colonists sponsored by the Russian government. The tsarist state increasingly limited the Zaporozhians' rights, freedoms, and self-government, particularly after the aboli-

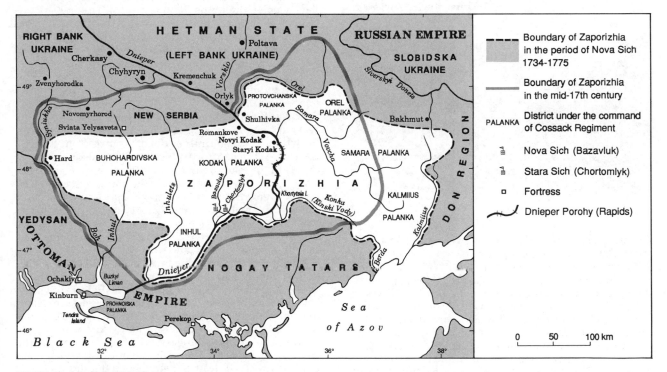

THE ZAPORIZHIA

tion of the Hetman state in 1764. On 15–16 June 1775, on orders from Catherine II, the Russian army under Gen P. Tekeli razed the New Sich. In her manifesto of 14 August 1775 Catherine officially abolished the Zaporozhian Host, calling it a 'political monstrosity.' Many of the Zaporozhians were forced into *military settlements, and later became *state peasants. Some 10,000 fled to Ottoman territory and founded the *Danubian Sich there. From among those who remained under Russian rule the *Boh Cossack Army and, later, the *Black Sea Cossacks were formed. The lands of the Zaporizhia were incorporated into *New Russia and *Azov gubernias and distributed among the Russian and Ukrainian landowners.

(See also *History of Ukraine, *Poland, *Russia, and *Turkey.)

BIBLIOGRAPHY
Maksimovich, M. 'Istoricheskiia pis'ma o kozakakh pridneprovskikh,' in his Sobranie sochinenii, vol 1 (Kiev 1876)
Skal'kovskii, A. Istoriia Novoi Sechi ili posledniago kosha zaporozhskago, 3 vols, 3rd edn (Odessa 1885–6)
Evarnitskii [Iavornyts'kyi], D. Vol'nosti zaporozhskikh kozakov (Moscow 1890)
– Istoriia zaporozhskikh kozakov, 3 vols (St Petersburg 1892, 1895, 1897; Kiev 1990–1; Ukrainian trans, Lviv 1990–1)
– Istochniki dlia istorii zaporozhskikh kozakov, 2 vols (Vladimir 1903)
Slabchenko, M. 'Sotsiial'no-pravova orhanizatsiia Sichy Zaporoz'koï,' Pratsi Komisiï dlia vyuchuvannia istoriï zakhidn'o-rus'koho ta ukraïns'koho prava, 3 (Kiev 1927)
Stöckl, G. Die Entstehung des Kosakentums (Munich 1953)
Golobutskii, V. Zaporozhskoe kazachestvo (Kiev 1957)
Holobuts'kyi, V. Zaporiz'ka Sich v ostanni chasy svoho isnuvannia: 1734–1775 (Kiev 1961)
Polons'ka-Vasylenko, N. Zaporizhzhia XVII stolittia ta ioho spadshchyna, vol 1 (Munich 1965)
Apanovych, O. 'Peredumovy ta naslidky likvidatsiï Zaporiz'koï Sichi,' UIZh, 1970, no. 9

B. Krupnytsky, A. Zhukovsky

Downtown Zaporizhia

**Zaporizhia** [Zaporižžja]. VI-16. A city (1990 pop 891,000) on the Dnieper River and the administrative center of an oblast and raion. It is a river port, a railway junction, and the second-largest industrial city in the *Dnieper Industrial Region. Until 1921 the city was called Oleksandrivske.

The city grew up around Oleksandrivske fortress, which was built in 1770, and which formed a link in the defensive front (the Dnieper Line) against the Tatars. The vicinity, situated at the southern end of the Dnieper Rapids, had long been a stopping point for travelers and traders on the Dnieper route. The Cossack stronghold of

*Khortytsia had been located on the island opposite the new settlement. After Russia's annexation of the Crimea in 1783, the fortress lost its military importance. Many of its demobilized soldiers settled in or around Oleksandrivske, which became a small administrative-commercial town. From 1806 it was a county center in Katerynoslav gubernia. Its agriculture-based economy grew slowly: the town's population increased from 1,700 in 1824 to only 3,700 in 1861. Oleksandrivske's rapid growth did not begin until the 1870s. After being linked by rail to Moscow in 1873 and Sevastopil in 1875, the town became a major transfer point, at which commodities (notably grain) were transferred from rail to river barges for shipment downriver to the seaports. At the same time its own industry, particularly farm-machine building, developed. By 1910 there were three large machine-building plants in Oleksandrivske. The completion of a railway line from the Donbas to Kryvyi Rih in 1902 stimulated the growth of metallurgy. The city's population grew from approx 7,000 in 1885 to 19,000 in 1897 and 38,000 in 1910. The city in 1897 was 43 percent Ukrainian, 28 percent Jewish, and 25 percent Russian.

During the revolutionary period the city was heavily damaged before Soviet rule was entrenched in 1920. It was rapidly rebuilt, and expanded northward and to the western bank of the Dnieper. The construction of the Dnieper Hydroelectric Station nearby provided the energy for the extensive growth of the metallurgical industry in the 1930s. Using iron ore from Kryvyi Rih, manganese ore from Nykopil, and coal from the Donbas, Zaporizhia soon became the second-largest (after Dnipropetrovske) metallurgical center in the Dnieper region. Some of its major enterprises were expanded or founded during the interwar period, including the Komunar machine (now automobile) plant, the Zaporizhstal metallurgical plant, the Instrumental Steels Plant (later Dniprospetsstal), and the Dnieper Aluminum Plant (est 1930). The city's population rose abruptly, from 56,000 in 1926 to 290,000 in 1939. During the Second World War much of the city, including the hydroelectric station, was destroyed. It was occupied by the Germans in October 1941 and recaptured by the Soviet army in October 1943. Its industry and power station were rebuilt and expanded during postwar reconstruction.

Today Zaporizhia is the sixth-largest city in Ukraine. The old town is spread out along a low-lying terrace on the left bank of the Dnieper directly across from Khortytsia Island. The new town is situated several kilometers to the north. Its main street runs south for more than 10 km from the hydroelectric dam to the railway station. The area between the old and new towns has slowly been built up with residential districts. The city encompasses Khortytsia Island and the right bank. There are rest homes and sanatoriums on Khortytsia Island. Public transport consists of streetcars, buses, and trolleybuses.

Metallurgy and machine building are the main industries of Zaporizhia. They include some giant plants, such as the Zaporizhstal and Dniprospetsstal steel mills, the Dnieper Aluminum Plant, the titanium-magnesium plant, the Zaporizhia Transformer Plant, the Komunar Automobile Plant, an engine plant, and an electric instruments factory. The chemical industry, which sprang up after the last war, includes the Kremniipolimer plant, which manufactures synthetic leather, petroleum refineries, and anti-

The Dnieper Hydroelectric Station dam in Zaporizhia

biotic and yeast factories. The building-materials industry produces reinforced-concrete structures, bricks, and prefabricated wall sections. The food industry includes confectionery factories, two breweries, and meatpacking plants. The light industry produces mainly clothing and footwear.

The city is an educational and research center. It has a university and 3 institutes (the Machine-Building, the Medical, and the Industrial), 14 secondary special schools, and 25 vocational schools. There are many research institutes specializing in areas such as transformer design, titanium, special alloys, and ferrous metals. The city's cultural facilities include a regional studies museum, an art museum, a philharmonic society, and three theaters (Ukrainian music and drama, puppet, and young spectator's). The chief architectural monuments are the remains of the Sich fortifications (1735–9) on Khortytsia Island, the zemstvo building (1912), and the Dnieper Hydroelectric Station dam.

**Zaporizhia Art Museum** (Zaporizkyi khudozhnii muzei). A museum established in 1971 in Zaporizhia. It is divided into two departments, fine art and decorative and applied art. In its collection are works by painters, such as M. Pymonenko, S. Svitoslavsky, A. Petrytsky, O. Shovkunenko, M. Hlushchenko, and T. Yablonska, and decorative artists, such as D. Holovko, T. Pata, and Yu. Korpaniuk.

**Zaporizhia Dniprospetsstal Electrometallurgical Plant** (Zaporizkyi elektrometalurhiinyi zavod Dniprospetsstal im. A.M. Kuzmina). An enterprise of the ferrous metallurgical industry, built in Zaporizhia in 1929–32. Until 1939 it was part of the Dnieper Industrial Complex; then it became a separate enterprise. It was evacuated during the war, and resumed production only in 1948. Equipped with the latest technology, it produces various steel alloys, high-grade rolled steel, and forged steel.

**Zaporizhia Iron-ore Complex** (Zaporizkyi zalizorudnyi kombinat). An iron-ore-mining and -processing complex located near Dniprorudne, Zaporizhia oblast. Construction of the plant began in 1960, and it opened in

1969. It processes iron ore from the Bilozerka Iron-ore Basin. The ore is found at a depth of 243–280 m and has an iron content of 46–69 percent. The complex has a processing capacity of 7 million t of ore annually.

Zaporozhets cars at the Zaporizhia Komunar Automobile Plant

**Zaporizhia Komunar Automobile Plant** (Zaporizkyi avtomobilnyi zavod Komunar). An automobile plant established in Zaporizhia in 1958 on the basis of an agricultural-machinery enterprise that had been created in 1923 by the merging of four older factories. In 1930 it was the first factory in the USSR to build combines. After the Second World War the plant produced combines, seeders, reapers, and other agricultural machines. In 1958 it was converted to produce four-passenger subcompact cars. Since 1963 it has built the popular Zaporozhets, the Tavriia, and four car models for the handicapped. Its output increased rapidly from 40,600 cars in 1965 to 150,000 cars in 1978. In 1977 the plant was joined with automobile plants in Lutske, Melitopil, and Dnipropetrovske to form the AvtoZAZ Automobile Manufacturing Consortium.

**Zaporizhia oblast.** An administrative territory (1989 pop 2,081,000) in southern Ukraine, formed on 10 January 1939. It has an area of 27,200 sq km and is divided into 18 raions, 14 cities, 22 towns (smt), and 240 rural councils. The capital is *Zaporizhia.

**Physical geography.** Most of the oblast lies within the Ukrainian Crystalline Shield. Its northeastern part lies in the Dnieper Lowland, its southern part, in the Black Sea Depression, and its southeastern part, in the Azov Upland. Its surface is lightly dissected and slopes gently from the northwest to the southeast. The Azov coastline is marked by a number of spits. The oblast is rich in mineral resources: coal, iron and manganese ore, natural gas, and building materials (granite, limestone, clay). The soils are mostly (75 percent) chernozems, common chernozems in the north and saline chernozems in the south. The oblast has a moderate continental climate with cold, dry winters and hot, dry summers. The average January temperature is –4°C in the south and –5°C in the north, and the average July temperature is 24°C and 23°C respectively. The annual precipitation is 400–500 mm in the north and 300–350 mm in the south. Some of the smaller rivers dry up during the summer. The main rivers are the Dnieper, the Molochna, the Obytochna, the Berda, and the Utliuk. The oblast lies in the European forest-steppe geobotanical province. Most of its arable land is cultivated; only 3–4 percent of the surface, mostly ravines and swampy bays on the coast, is covered with natural steppe vegetation. Forests (mainly white acacia, maple, oak, ash, and elm) cover 3.4 percent of the oblast's area and are located largely in the eastern part.

**History.** The territory of the oblast was inhabited as early as the Paleolithic period. From the 7th century BC it was controlled by the Scythians. They were forced by the Sarmatians to retreat southward in the 3rd and 2nd centuries BC. After the Sarmatians the Huns, Avars, and Khazars dominated the steppes. Kievan Rus' was unable to establish effective control of the region after it vanquished the Khazars in 965. Control fell to the Pechenegs and Cumans and then the Tatars and the Crimean Khanate. In the 16th century the Zaporozhian Cossacks established themselves in the region along the Dnieper Rapids and for centuries resisted Turkish and Polish attacks. By the end of the 18th century Russia, with the help of the Cossacks, defeated the Turks and Tatars and promptly crushed the Zaporozhian Sich. It annexed the territory and assigned it to New Russia gubernia (1797–1802) and then divided it between Katerynoslav gubernia and Tavriia gubernia. In the revolutionary period the territory was divided among many local otamans, including the most prominent of them, N. *Makhno, and witnessed much violence.

**Population.** According to the 1989 census, Ukrainians accounted for 63.1 percent of the oblast's population, Russians for 32 percent, Bulgarians for 1.7 percent, and Jews for 0.7 percent. The population density was 76.5 people per sq km. The highest density is in the industrialized northwestern part. About 76 percent of the population is urban. The largest cities are Zaporizhia, *Melitopil, and *Berdianske.

**Industry.** Almost 82 percent of the oblast's total output is produced by its industries. The major industries are machine building and metalworking (42.1 percent of the industrial output), ferrous and nonferrous metallurgy, food processing, and light industry. The largest machine-building and metalworking plants are Zaporizhia's transformer, automobile, and grinding-tools plants and Berdianske's road-building machine and cable plants. Zaporizhia is the chief center for metallurgy. The chemical and petrochemical industry, which is concentrated in Zaporizhia and Berdianske, produces polymers, petroleum grease, varnishes, and enamels. The main branches of light industry are sewing (Melitopil and Zaporizhia), footwear manufacturing (Zaporizhia, Berdianske, Vasylivka), and knitwear (Melitopil and Berdianske). The food industry processes oils and fats, flour, meat, fruit, and fish. Its main centers are Zaporizhia, Melitopil, Berdianske, Vasylivka, Tokmak, and Huliai Pole. The building-materials industry is concentrated in Zaporizhia, Polohy, Melitopil, Dniprorudne, Berdianske, and Tokmak.

**Agriculture.** In 1989 there were 276 collective farms and 109 state farms in the oblast. The total area of farmland was 2,243,000 ha, of which 86.7 percent was cultivated, 9 percent was pasture, and 2.2 percent was hayfield. A total of 273,000 ha were irrigated, mainly by the Kakhivka Reservoir. Over half of the sown area (51.8 percent) was devoted to grain crops (winter wheat, spring barley, and corn). The other main crops were industrial (11.6 percent), mostly sunflowers, fodder (32 percent), and melons, veg-

etables, and potatoes (4.6 percent). There are some large vineyards in the south. Truck farming is well developed in suburban regions. Animal husbandry accounts for 59.6 percent of the agricultural output. Its main branch is beef- and dairy-cattle farming. Overfishing and pollution have put an end to fishing in the Sea of Azov.

**Transportation.** In 1989 there were 993 km of railroad track in the oblast, of which 287 km were electrified. The main railway junctions are Zaporizhia, Polohy, Melitopil, and Tokmak. The trunk lines that cross the oblast are Moscow–Symferopil, Volnovakha–Zaporizhia–Nykopil, and Zaporizhia–Berdianske. The highway network consisted of 6,700 km of road, of which 6,400 km were paved. The main highways are Moscow–Symferopil, Zaporizhia–Mariiupil, and Zaporizhia–Berdianske. Zaporizhia is the main river port, and Berdianske the main sea port, of the oblast. Both cities have an airport.

BIBLIOGRAPHY
*Istoriia mist i sil URSR: Zaporiz'ka oblast'* (Kiev 1970)

**Zaporizhia Regional Studies Museum** (Zaporizkyi kraieznavchyi muzei). A museum founded in Zaporizhia in 1920 as a historical museum, under the direction of Ya. Novytsky. From 1927 to 1929 it was called the Museum of the Revolution. The museum was devastated during the Second World War, but it was subsequently rebuilt, and opened as a regional studies museum in 1948. In 1979 it had nearly 70,000 exhibit items in its four divisions – natural sciences, archeology, prerevolutionary history, and Soviet history – including valuable objects from the Cossack period and materials pertaining to the construction of the Dnieper Dam. The museum oversees smaller museums in Husarka (Kuibyshev raion) and Polohy, and the state historical preserve on Khortytsia Island is a branch. A guidebook to the museum was published in 1972.

**Zaporizhia Transformer Plant** (Zaporizkyi transformatornyi zavod). A plant of the power industry, built in Zaporizhia in 1947–9. It produces over 600 products, particularly high-power transformers with a capacity of 100 kW to 1 million kW, transformer parts, and other machinery used to transmit electricity for domestic and industrial use.

**Zaporizhia Ukrainian Drama Theater.** See Lviv Ukrainian Drama Theater.

**Zaporizhia Ukrainian Music and Drama Theater** (Zaporizkyi ukrainskyi muzychno-dramatychnyi teatr). A theater established in 1929 as the Kiev Theater of Small Forms. In 1930 it was reorganized into the second Kiev Oblast Touring Theater. In 1932–41 it was in Zhytomyr, and since 1944 it has been in Zaporizhia. Its repertoire has consisted mostly of Soviet and world classics. Among its leading members have been V. Mahar, S. Smiian, M. Ravytsky, M. Hrynko, Yu. Lishansky, A. Morozova, K. Parakoniev, A. Troshchanovsky, and Ye. Khutorna.

**Zaporizhia University** (Zaporizkyi universytet). The university was established in Zaporizhia in 1984 on the basis of the Zaporizhia Pedagogical Institute (founded in 1930). In 1985–6 it had five faculties and 3,249 students, and in 1988 it had 4,510 students.

**Zaporizhia Young Spectator's Theater** (Zaporizkyi teatr yunoho hliadacha). A theater established in 1979 as an oblast touring theater. It has staged Ya. Stelmakh's *Pryvit, synychko* (Welcome, Titmouse) and K. Chukovsky's *Mukha-tsokotukha* (The Chatterbox Fly).

Molten pig iron being poured into an oven at the Zaporizhstal mill

**Zaporizhstal** (from *zaporizhska stal* 'Zaporizhia steel'). One of the largest steel plants in Ukraine. It was built in Zaporizhia in 1930–3. By the Second World War the plant had 4 blast and 10 Martin furnaces in operation. The machinery was evacuated at the outset of the war, and the plant was rebuilt in 1944–7. Since then it has been considerably expanded and modernized. The factory produces cold and hot rolled and sheet steel, iron slabbing and castings, and various specialized metal products. It was the first plant in the USSR to practice continuous steel-pouring. In the 1970s the plant employed over 7,000 workers. It is the source of much air pollution.

**Zaporizka Sich.** A military unit of the Army of the UNR organized in November 1918 in Katerynoslav. Its initial cadres came from the Railway Guard Corps. In April 1919 it was reorganized into the Second Sich Division. It was commanded by Otaman Yu. Bozhko. Its top combat strength was 1,200 soldiers. The division suffered heavy losses during 1919. Some of the survivors took part in the First Winter Campaign (1919–20) in the ranks of the Volhynian Division.

**Zaporozhchenko, Ivan** [Zaporožčenko], b 24 February 1872 in Artiukhivka, Romen county, Poltava gubernia, d 11 March 1932 in Olava, Romen raion, now in Sumy oblast. Kobzar. After being blinded at the age of six, he learned to play the bandura and then wandered through Ukraine, the Crimea, and the Kuban. He supported the revolutionary movement in the early 1900s and disseminated revolutionary literature. He composed approx 60 songs about the 1905 Revolution, the First World War, and the 1917 Revolution.

Participants in the celebration of Zaporozhe's centenary in Vienna in 1961

**Zaporozhe.** The oldest Ukrainian student fraternity, active in Chernivtsi in 1906–40. The group was founded by Ukrainian students who were active in non-Ukrainian (German, Rumanian) fraternities but desired one of their own. Fencing was initially the focal point, but over the years Zaporozhe sponsored an active cultural and social program that included a choir, a traveling drama ensemble, dance classes and social evenings, and community activity (particularly in organizing co-operatives, reading societies, and *Sich societies in villages in Bukovyna). The group also provided the impetus for the formation of a popular local Ukrainian sports club, *Dovbush. Zaporozhe fraternities were also formed in Lviv, Warsaw, Danzig (now Gdańsk), Prague, and Vienna. In 1931 they all met in Stanyslaviv (Ivano-Frankivske) for a conference that established a co-ordinating body for the fraternities. The group was banned in 1925 after an incident with a Rumanian school inspector at a Ukrainian concert, but it was reconstituted in 1928 after a nominal name change from academic society (*tovarystvo*) to Cossack fellows (*kozatstvo*). In 1937, activities sponsored by Zaporozhe were prohibited after another incident involving fraternity members and the Rumanian authorities. Zaporozhe was liquidated after the Soviet occupation of Bukovyna in 1940 but was re-established by former members in the West after the war.

**Zaporozhets, Oleksander** [Zaporožec'], b 12 November 1905 in Kiev, d 1981 in Moscow. Psychologist; full member of the USSR Academy of Pedagogical Sciences (APN) from 1968. In 1922–3 he studied acting in Kiev and appeared in four Berezil productions. He graduated from Moscow University (1930), worked at the Ukrainian Psychoneurological Institute in Kharkiv, and held the chair of psychology at the Kharkiv Pedagogical Institute (1933–41). After the Second World War he directed the laboratory of preschool-child psychology at the APN Institute of Psychology in Moscow, and in 1960 he became director of the APN Institute of Preschool Education in Moscow. His doctoral dissertation (1958) on the development of voluntary movements was published in 1960. He wrote many pioneering works on child psychology (on the development of perception, reasoning, and the psyche and on the

Oleksander Zaporozhets

origin and nature of emotions), motor functions, and preschool education, including a psychology textbook for preschool teachers (1953, 1955, 1961, 1965) that was translated from Russian into Ukrainian (1961), Czech (1954), Bulgarian (1954), Polish (1954), Latvian (1955), Slovak (1958), and Lithuanian (1969). Some of his studies appeared in English. A two-volume posthumous edition of his works was published in Moscow in 1986; it includes a bibliography of his works and his reminiscences about L. Kurbas.

The right and left sides of the flag of the 2nd Infantry Regiment of the Zaporozhian Corps

**Zaporozhian Corps.** One of the regular formations of the *Army of the Ukrainian National Republic in 1918–20. It varied in strength, from 3,000 to 15,000, and structure, from a detachment to a brigade, division, corps, and group.

At first the unit was known as the Separate Zaporozhian Detachment, which was formed on 9 February 1918 out of several small military entities. It consisted of two infantry and one cavalry battalion, an artillery company, and support units and was commanded by Brig Gen K. Prisovsky. The detachment took part in the first phase of the Ukrainian-Soviet War.

In March–April 1918 it was expanded into a brigade and a separate division, both under Brig Gen O. Natiiv. The division consisted of four infantry regiments (under Cols O. Zahrodsky, P. Bolbochan, O. Shapoval, V. Sikevych) as well as cavalry (Col V. Petriv), engineering (Col O. Kozma), artillery (Col O. Parfeniv), mobile artillery (Col O. Almazov), armored-car (Capt O. Boldyriv), and aviation (Col M. Baraniv) regiments. With the support of German troops it cleared Left-Bank Ukraine, the Donets region, and the Crimea of Bolshevik forces, and then in June–November 1919 guarded the Ukrainian-Russian border. In the anti-Hetman revolt the division threw its support behind the UNR Directory.

In November–December 1918 the division was reorga-

nized into a two-division corps under the command of P. *Bolbochan, who was also the commander of the anti-Bolshevik front in Left-Bank Ukraine. The division commanders were O. Zahrodsky and V. Osmolovsky. After intense fighting against Soviet forces the corps was cut off from the UNR Army in April 1919 and had to cross Rumanian territory to reach Galicia and Volhynia. En route all its supplies were confiscated by the Rumanians. After O. Volokh's brief command, Col I. Dubovy conducted the retreat through Rumania. In May 1919 the corps was restructured into the Zaporozhian Group, under Capt V. Salsky's, then Gen M. Omelianovych-Pavlenko's, command. It consisted of the Sixth Division (under O. Zahrodsky), the Seventh Division (V. Osmolovsky), and the Eighth Division (Col H. Bazylevsky).

Modified for partisan warfare, the group took part in the First Winter Campaign (1919–20). After the campaign it was redesignated the First Zaporozhian Rifle Division and placed under the command of Brig Gen A. Huly-Hulenko (replaced later by Brig Gen H. Bazylevsky). The chief of staff was Col M. Stefaniv. Its subordinate units included three infantry brigades (commanded by I. Dubovy, I. Lytvynenko, and I. Trotsky), an artillery brigade (Col S. Loshchenko), the Black Zaporozhian cavalry regiment (Col P. Diachenko), a technical batallion (Col M. Herasymiv), an officer school (Col Rymarenko-Lymarenko), and a reserve brigade (Col V. Osmolovsky). The division took part in all the battles of the UNR Army before it crossed the Zbruch River into Western Ukraine under Polish rule on 21 November 1920.

BIBLIOGRAPHY
Petriv, V. *Spomyny z chasiv ukraïns'koï revoliutsiï (1917–1921)* (Lviv 1927–31)
Monkevych, B. *Spomyny z 1918 r.* (Lviv 1928)
Stefaniv, Z. *Ukraïns'ki zbroini syly 1917–1921*, 2 vols (Kolomyia 1934–5)

Z. Stefaniv

**Zaporozhian Cossacks.** See Cossacks, Zaporizhia, and Zaporozhian Sich.

**Zaporozhian Host** (Viisko Zaporizke). The name of the armed forces of the *Zaporizhia in the 16th to 18th centuries and the official name used by the Cossacks for the *Hetman state. B. Khmelnytsky's title of 'hetman of the Zaporozhian Host' signified that he was the head of state.

**Zaporozhian Lowland.** See Black Sea Lowland.

**Zaporozhian Ridge** (Zaporizka hriada). A narrow belt of crystalline rocks in the Dnieper channel that connects the Dnieper Upland with the Azov Upland.

**Zaporozhian Sich** (Zaporizka Sich). The name of several Cossack keeps on the Dnieper River that were the centers of the *Zaporizhia. The first Sich was established ca 1552 by Prince D. *Vyshnevetsky on Mala Khortytsia Island in the Dnieper River, near present-day Zaporizhia. It was besieged and destroyed by Crimean Tatars in 1558. The new *Tomakivka Sich was built 60 km to the south on a now-inundated island near present-day Marhanets. It was also razed by Tatars, in 1593, and a new Sich was built on Bazavluk Island, now also inundated, farther south near the mouths of the Chortomlyk and the Pidpilna

A Zaporozhian Cossack (19th-century lithograph)

The naval flag of the Zaporozhian Host (18th century)

The Zaporozhian Sich (drawing by an unknown artist)

rivers. A fourth Sich was built at nearby Mykytyn Rih, the site of present-day Nykopil; it is first mentioned in 1628 and was captured by Hetman B. Khmelnytsky in 1648. The *Chortomlyk Sich was also built nearby, at the mouth of the Chortomlyk, in 1652. It was destroyed by a Russian force on 25 May 1709, after Otaman K. Hordiienko and his Zaporozhian Host allied with Hetman I. Mazepa and Charles XII of Sweden against Peter I. The Zaporozhians then built a Sich at the mouth of the Kamianets River, but it was destroyed in 1711. Zaporozhian Cossacks who escaped from Russian persecution to lands controlled by the Crimean Khanate built the *Oleshky Sich on the lower Dnieper in 1711. In 1734 they returned to Russian-controlled Ukraine and built the *New Sich on the Pid-pilna River. That last Sich was destroyed by a Russian army on 15–16 June 1775.

Five of the eight Siches, including the most historically important ones, were located on or near floodplains of the Dnieper. All of them were protected by ramparts topped by a palisade with towers and openings for cannons. In-side was a square bounded by the barracklike Cossacks' quarters (see *Kurin). A church, a school, officers' resi-dences, and other administrative and military buildings stood in the middle of the square. The church and its clergy were under the authority of the archimandrite of Kiev's Mezhyhiria Transfiguration Monastery. The area in front of the church was the center of social and political life and the place where the Sich councils were held. A bazaar situated outside the ramparts attracted Zaporo-zhian traders and merchants from other parts of Ukraine, Poland, and Russia. The *kish*, or garrison, at the Sich num-bered in the thousands, at times even tens of thousands.

Coat of arms of the Zaporo-zhian Host (wood engraving from a 1622 edition of Kasiian Sakovych's poems)

BIBLIOGRAPHY

Evarnitskii, D. 'Zhizn' zaporozh'skikh kozakov po razskazu sovremennika ochevidtsa,' *KS*, 1883, no. 11
– 'Chislo i poriadok zaporozhskikh Sechei,' *KS*, 1884, no. 4
Holobuts'kyi, V. 'Vynyknennia Zaporiz'koï Sichi,' *Knyha dlia chytannia z istoriï URSR*, 1 (Kiev 1960)
Kytsenko, M. 'Pro mistse i rol' Khortytsi v istoriï zaporiz'koho kozatstva,' *UIZh*, 1968, no. 8
Pukha, I. 'Pro shkoly v Zaporiz'kii Sichi,' *UIZh*, 1969, no. 3

March, G.P. *Cossacks of the Brotherhood: The Zaporog Kosh of the Dniepr River* (New York 1990)

A. Zhukovsky

*Zaporozhskaia starina*

**Zaporozhskaia starina** (Zaporozhian Antiquity). A folkloric journal published in Kharkiv from 1833 to 1838 (six issues altogether). Edited by I. *Sreznevsky, it contained historical songs, stories, dumas, and other materials on the history of the Cossacks. Although much of the material was apocryphal and several of the dumas forged, the journal stimulated interest in Ukrainian history and the Cossacks. According to its editor *Zaporozhskaia starina* was intended to demonstrate the importance of Ukrainian folk literature and its relationship to historical chronicles and legends. The journal was closely associated with the *Kharkiv Romantic School.

**Zaporoz'ka dumka** (Zaporozhian Thought). A semi-weekly paper published in 1921–3 by UNR Army soldiers held in the Polish internment camp at Wadowice.

**Zapysky Chyna sv. Vasyliia Velykoho.** See *Analecta Ordinis S. Basilii Magni/Zapysky ChSVV.*

**Zapysky Fizychno-matematychnoho viddilu VUAN** (Annals of the VUAN Physical-Mathematical Division). A scholarly serial (16 issues) published in Kiev in 1923–31. Edited by M. Krylov, P. Tutkovsky, O. Fomin, I. Shmalhauzen, and M. Kholodny, it contained articles on mathematics, physics, chemistry, and biology in Ukrainian, German, and French, and reported on international developments in these fields and on the work of the various VUAN institutes and commissions involved in theoretical and applied science.

**Zapysky Istorychno-filolohichnoho viddilu VUAN** (Annals of the Historical-Philological Division of the VUAN). A serial published irregularly in Kiev in 1919–31 (27 volumes in all) by the VUAN. The editors in chief were A. Krymsky and M. Hrushevsky. It contained articles and materials on the history of Ukraine up to 1917 and the history of Ukrainian culture, folklore, and ethnography, as well as on art, linguistics, literary scholarship, and Slavic

studies. It also contained official notices and minutes of the meetings of the historical-philological division, reports on the work of the historical section, bibliographic surveys, and book reviews. Separate volumes were devoted to the literary or scholarly contributions of T. Shevchenko, V. Antonovych, M. Sumtsov, M. Biliashivsky, D. Bahalii, and A. Krymsky. Volumes 6, 11, 17, 20, and 24 were published as *Pratsi Istorychnoï sektsiï VUAN*. With the purge of the academy in 1931, the *Zapysky* were discontinued.

**Zapysky Naukovoho tovarystva im. Shevchenka** (Annals of the Shevchenko Scientific Society [NTSh]). A scholarly journal of the NTSh, published from 1892 until the Second World War in Lviv. The first four issues, under the de facto editorship of O. Konysky, appeared irregularly until 1894. Under the editorship of M. *Hrushevsky (1895–1913; also one of the most prolific contributors), *Zapysky NTSh* became a prominent quarterly, then bimonthly, publication, dealing with all areas of Ukrainian studies and publishing some works in other disciplines. Most of its articles dealt with history, philology, and ethnography, and its notable sections were the bibliographies, book reviews, and chronicles of scholarly affairs. A catalog of its first 20 volumes was published in Lviv in 1898. An index to the volumes (1892–1982) was prepared by M. Boiko in 1984.

Contributors to the *Zapysky* included the Western Ukrainian scholars and publicists B. Barvinsky, M. Vozniak, V. Herasymchuk, V. Hnatiuk, I. Dzhydzhora, M. Zubrytsky, O. and F. Kolessa, O. Konysky, M. Korduba, I. Krevetsky, I. Krypiakevych, Z. Kuzelia, S. Rudnytsky, I. Svientsitsky, I. Sozansky, K. Studynsky, S. Tomashivsky, I. Franko, and V. Shchurat, and the central Ukrainian scholars V. Peretts, O. Hrushevsky, V. Modzalevsky, O. Lototsky, S. Maslov, and V. Lypynsky.

After the First World War the publication was transformed into an irregular series of scholarly collections and monographs. In 1924 *Zapysky NTSh* was split into two separate subseries: works of the historical-philosophical section (ed I. Krypiakevych) and works of the philological section (ed K. Studynsky, Ya. Hordynsky, and V. Simovych). In the interwar period, in addition to the older scholars who began publishing works before the war, contributors included M. Andrusiak, A. Androkhovych, E. Borschak, I. Bryk, Ya. Hordynsky, I. Zilynsky, I. Ohiienko, Ya. Pasternak, M. Tershakovych, and M. Chubaty. Until the onset of Stalinism a few Soviet Ukrainian scholars were also permitted to publish their works (eg, K. Hrushevska and F. Savchenko).

In total 155 volumes of the *Zapysky* appeared in Lviv before 1939. After the Second World War the publication was renewed at first in Germany and then in other countries where the NTSh was established (the United States, Canada, Australia). Over 60 volumes have appeared, covering a wide range of topics. The renewed NTSh in Lviv (see *Shevchenko Scientific Society) took over the publication of *Zapysky NTSh* (from vol 221, ed O. Kupchynsky and M. Ilnytsky).

**Zapysky Nizhens'koho instytutu narodnoï osvity** (Annals of the Nizhen Institute of People's Education). A scholarly journal, 12 issues of which appeared in 1925–33. It contained articles on Ukrainian and world history, literature, and ethnography, written by V. *Riezanov, M.

Petrovsky, K. Shtepa, A. Yershov, and others. Some historical documents also appeared in the journal, as well as articles on scientific topics and pedagogy. Riezanov and Petrovsky were its editors. The journal was renamed *Zapysky Nizhens'koho instytutu sotsiial'noho vykhovannia* in 1932 and *Zbirnyk Nizhens'koho instytutu sotsiial'noho vykhovannia* in 1933.

***Zapysky Sotsiial'no-ekonomichnoho viddilu VUAN*** (Annals of the Social-Economic Division of the VUAN). A scholarly serial published in Kiev in 1923–7 (altogether, six volumes in four books). It contained articles on Ukrainian economic history, on economic, legal, and social theory, and on contemporary economic developments. It also published biographies and obituaries of prominent Ukrainian economists (eg, M. Tuhan-Baranovsky, B. Kistiakovsky, V. Hordon, and I. Kamanin) and reviews of Western and Soviet works on economics, law, and sociology. Contributors included academics such as M. Vasylenko, M. Ptukha, Ye. Slutsky, B. Landau, F. Taranovsky, and A. Kryster. The editor was M. Vasylenko.

***Zapysky Ukraïns'koho naukovoho tovarystva v Kyievi*** (Annals of the Ukrainian Scientific Society in Kiev, or ZNTK). An irregular publication of the *Ukrainian Scientific Society in Kiev, 18 volumes of which appeared between 1908 and 1918, most of them edited by M. *Hrushevsky. The journal contained articles in almost all areas of Ukrainian studies, especially history, literature, and linguistics. Among its many prominent contributors were V. Peretts, O. Levytsky, I. Kamanin, M. Vasylenko, M. Biliashivsky, M. Petrov, B. Buchynsky, M. and O. Hrushevsky, B. Hrinchenko, V. Modzalevsky, V. Dobrovolsky, V. Shcherbyna, and the Russians A. Shakhmatov and G. Ilinsky. In 1924 ZNTK was renewed as a subseries of *Zbirnyk Istorychno-filolohichnoho viddilu VUAN*, under the editorship of M. Hrushevsky and with the numeration continued. The collections *Za sto lit* also appeared as part of the series.

**Zaremba, Volodyslav** (Zaręba, Władisław), b 27 June 1833 in Dunaivtsi, Ushytsia county, Podilia gubernia, d 24 October 1902 in Kiev. Composer, pianist, and pedagogue of Polish descent. He studied music with A. Kocipiński in Kamianets-Podilskyi and from 1862 taught piano and choral singing in girls' schools in Kiev. His works include *Muzyka do* Kobzaria (Music to the *Kobzar*), a collection of 30 songs to words by T. Shevchenko, and piano pieces based on Ukrainian folk songs.

**Zaretsky, Viktor** [Zarec'kyj], b 8 February 1925 in Bilopillia, Sumy okruha, d 23 August 1990 in Kiev. Painter. A graduate of the Kiev State Art Institute (1953), he taught there and worked as a graphic artist. He painted realistic genre canvases in the Donbas and in Chornobyl raion, such as *Flax Gathering* (1960) and *Girls* (1962). He collaborated with his late wife, A. *Horska, and other artists in creating large mosaics and mixed-media murals, such as *Prometheus*, *Earth*, and *Fire*, in Secondary School No. 47 in Donetske, *The Tree of Life* and *Dream-Bird*, in the Ukraina restaurant in Mariiupil, and *The Flag of Victory*, in the Young Guard Museum in Krasnodon. For signing a public letter protesting against the political trials of Ukrainian artists and intellectuals in 1965–6 he was reprimanded by the Party and ostracized by the Union of Artists. In the

Viktor Zaretsky: *Green (The Future)* (oil, 1987–8)

1970s he abandoned socialist realism in favour of an art nouveau style. His favorite themes became women and nature. The threat of ecological disaster is expressed sharply in his paintings *Beauty Abandons the Earth, Sign of Calamity, Ozone Hole,* and *Atomic Winter.* His recent works include Klimtesque paintings, such as *Angels* (1988) and *Portrait of Liudmyla Kozachenko* (1987). A catalog of his works was published in 1991.

**Zarevo** (The Glow). An artists' group formed by graduates of the Cracow Academy of Fine Arts. It was active from 1933 to 1936 and organized annual exhibitions. The president was D. Ivantsev, and the members included Ye. Bozhyk, O. Vynnytsky, O. Kasarab, Yu. Kulchytsky, N. Kysilevsky, A. Nakonechny, and V. Prodan.

**Zarevo Ukrainian Student Association.** A Ukrainian student organization formed in 1949. Ideologically aligned with the OUN (Melnyk faction), this nationalist group promoted the concept of 'national solidarism' and published the newspaper *Rozbudova derzhavy*. An offshoot of its activity in the United States was *Smoloskyp, an activist group formed to address the human rights issue in Ukraine. The more prominent members of Zarevo have been M. Antonovych, P. Stercho, M. Plaviuk, A. Zhukovsky, B. Wynar, and P. Dorozhynsky.

**Zarevych, Fedir** [Zarevyč] (pseuds: Yurko Vorona, Fedko Klepailo, F.Z., V., V.Yu., Yu.V.), b 30 September 1835 in Slavske, Stryi circle, d 12 January 1879 in Skole, Stryi county, Galicia. Writer and journalist. He began publishing in 1860 and edited the first Galician Ukrainian journal, *Vechernytsi (1862–3), and the anti-Russophile newspaper *Rus' (1867). He contributed political articles and nearly 20 stories (eg, 'Khlops'ka dytyna' [The Peasant Child]) and novellas (eg, 'Syn opryshka' [The Opryshok's Son], 'Zahubydush' [The Cutthroat]) on social themes to those periodicals and to *Meta, Nyva, Osnova, Pravda,* and *Rusalka.* He also wrote a drama, 'Bondarivna' (The Cooper's Daughter, 1872). As a publicist he championed the Ukrainian peasantry and criticized the Poles, the Russophiles, and Austrian policies. In 1872 he became a member of the executive board of the Prosvita society, and he served for a year as director of the Ruska Besida Theater. As a cultural and political figure he followed in the footsteps of the Ruthenian Triad and was a precursor of I. Franko. An edition of his works was published in Lviv in 1901.

**Zarichia** [Zariččja]. The southwestern area of Polisia, situated within the triangle formed by Kovel, Brest, and Pynske. The region consists of treeless marshland (42 per cent), wetland forest (20 per cent), dry forest (24 per cent), and a small portion of dry arable land (14 per cent). Its marshy regions are located near the Prypiat, the forests in its western reaches, and its arable areas to the south. A number of smaller centers are found there (Ratne, Kamin-Koshyrskyi, Liubeshiv); no major cities are situated in the region.

**Zarichne** [Zarične]. II-7. A town smt (1990 pop 6,600) on the Styr River and a raion center in Rivne oblast. It is first mentioned in a historical document in 1480, as Pohost or Pohost Zarichnyi. In 1569 it was transferred from Lithuanian to Polish rule. After the partition of Poland in 1795, it was annexed by Russia and belonged to Pynske county in Minsk gubernia. In the interwar period Zarichne was occupied by Poland. In 1946 it was renamed Zarichne, and in 1959 it was granted smt status. Besides a small food industry it has a flax-processing plant and a lumber mill.

Yefrosyniia Zarnytska

**Zarnytska, Yefrosyniia** (Zinaida) [Zarnyc'ka, Jefrosynija Zinajida] (real surname: Azhuridi), b 16 February 1867 in Odessa, d 30 June 1936 in Pervomaiske, Mykolaiv oblast. Stage actress and singer (soprano). She completed musical school in Odessa (1886) and then acted in the troupes of M. Kropyvnytsky (1888–93), O. Suslov and O. Sukhodolsky (1894–8), Suslov again (1898–1909), and B. Orshanov (1909–14) and in the Petrograd Ukrainian Drama Theater (1919–24) and the Kharkiv Chervonozavodskyi Ukrainian Drama Theater (1927–30). As a singer she performed in ethnographical plays as well as in classical operettas.

**Zarub.** A fortified city of Kievan Rus' (11th–13th centuries) located near the present village of Zarubyntsi,

Pereiaslav-Khmelnytskyi raion, Kiev oblast. Built on the right bank of the Dnieper River opposite the mouth of the Trubizh River, it probably served as an important river crossing. It is mentioned in the chronicles under the years 1096, 1146, 1151, 1156, and 1223 in connection with campaigns against the Cumans. The site was excavated first in 1899 by V. Khvoika, who unearthed a burial site that gave its name to the *Zarubyntsi culture. Later excavations in 1948 undertaken by the AN URSR (now ANU) Institute of Archeology discovered the remains of two stone churches decorated with frescoes, mosaics, and tiles that belonged to the local monastery (11th–12th centuries).

**Zarubin, Aleksandr,** b ca 1881, d January 1920 in Rostov. Russian political figure. He was a leading member of the Russian Party of Socialist Revolutionaries in Ukraine, which he represented in the Central Rada in 1917. He was appointed minister of postal and telegraph services in the UNR by the Little Rada, and resigned in January 1918 following the declaration of independence of the UNR.

**Zarubyn, Ivan,** b 1835, d 1904. Surgeon. A graduate of Kharkiv University (1856), he completed his doctoral thesis (1861) and specialized abroad. He was a professor (from 1865) of theoretical surgery at Kharkiv University and organized a hospital clinic at the university, therapy and surgery clinics at the Alexandrian Hospital, and a hospital for the poor.

**Zarubyntsi culture.** An archeological culture of the mid-3rd century BC to early 2nd century AD which existed along the middle reaches of the Dnieper River and in areas along the Boh, Seim, and Tiasmyn rivers. It was named after a site excavated by V. *Khvoika in 1899. The people of this culture lived in (usually) fortified settlements in surface and semi-pit dwellings with hearths. They engaged in agriculture, animal husbandry, hunting, fishing, and craft production and traded with Black Sea centers. Cremation was the usual form of burial, with remains placed in urns and buried in shallow graves along with bronze adornments, glass jewelry, pottery, implements, and weapons. The culture maintained a patriarchal social order. Scholars regard these people as proto-Slavs. Major sites of the culture found in Ukraine include the Korchuvate burial site, Pylypenko's Hill, and the Sakhnivka settlements.

**Zarudny** [Zarudnyj]. A family line descending from Cossack *starshyna* holding posts in Myrhorod and Izium regiments. It was established in the mid-17th century by Fedir Zarudny. His son, Hryhorii Zarudny, was an osaul (1688–90) and judge (1690–1708) in Myrhorod regiment. Hryhorii's son, Ivan Zarudny (d 1748), was a captain of Izium regiment; his descendants were estate owners in Poltava and Kharkiv gubernias. The brother of Serhii *Zarudny, Mytrofan (b 1834, d 1883), was a lawyer who worked for the imperial Senate, the Ministry of Justice, and the Odessa court in the 1860s and wrote the legal guidebook *Zakon i zhizn'* (The Law and Life).

**Zarudny, Ivan** [Zarudnyj], b ?, d 1727 in St Petersburg. Architect and wood sculptor. He studied at the Kievan Mohyla College and worked as an architect for Hetman I. Mazepa in Baturyn. In 1690 Mazepa sent him to Moscow.

The Campanile Church of the Archangel Gabriel in Moscow designed by Ivan Zarudny

There Zarudny built Mazepa's home and the arch of triumph (1696) commemorating the Russian victory at Azov. He then studied abroad, and in 1701 he returned to Moscow, where he became the chief architect. He introduced various Ukrainian architectural forms and methods in Russian architecture. In Moscow he designed and supervised the building of the famous Campanile Church of the Archangel Gabriel (1704–7) commissioned by Count A. Menshikov, the Trinity Cathedral at the Zaikonospasskii Monastery, the Church of St John the Warrior, several other arches of triumph, a hospital (1706), and the building of the Holy Synod (1723). In 1707 the Holy Synod appointed Zarudny director of icon and all other painting in the Russian Empire. Zarudny himself designed several iconostases, including ones in the Transfiguration Cathedral in Tallinn (1719) and in the cathedral at the Peter and Paul Fortress in St Petersburg (1722–7).

**Zarudny, Mykola** [Zarudnyj], b 25 September 1859 in Hriakove, near Chutove, Poltava county, d 19 March 1919 in Tashkent. Zoologist and ornithologist. He undertook 17 research expeditions (from 1879) through Central Asia and Persia, and from 1906 he worked in Tashkent. He published numerous works in ornithology and some works in geography. His biography was written by N. Bobrynsky (1940).

**Zarudny, Mykola** [Zarudnyj], b 20 August 1921 in Orikhovets, Skvyra county, Kiev gubernia, d 25 August 1991 in Kiev. Socialist-realist novelist and popular dramatist. He is the author of the novels *Moï zemliaky* (My Countrymen, 1950), *Na bilomu sviti* (In the Wide World, 1967), *Uran* (Uranium, 1970), and *Hileia* (1973) and of over 20 plays, notably *Veselka* (The Rainbow, 1958), *Mertvyi boh* (The Dead God, 1960), *Dorohy, iaki my vybyraiemo* (Roads We Choose, 1971), *Pora zhovtoho lystia* (The Time of Yellow Leaves, 1972), *Pid vysokymy zoriamy* (Under the High Stars, 1976), *Tyl* (The Rear, 1977), *Rehion* (The Region, 1981), *Bronzova vaza* (The Bronze Vase, 1985) and *Porom* (The Ferry, 1987). He was awarded the Shevchenko State Prize in 1978 for *Tyl*. A four-volume edition of his works (1981–2) and D. Shlapak's book about his dramaturgy (1981) were published in Kiev.

**Zarudny, Oleksander** [Zarudnyj], b 1891, d February 1918 in Kiev. Political and state figure. A leading member in the left wing of the Ukrainian Party of Socialist Revolutionaries, he was a representative to the Central Rada and a minister of land affairs in the UNR. He was shot by Bolsheviks engaged in reprisals after M. Muravev seized Kiev.

**Zarudny, Serhii** [Zarudnyj, Serhij], b 29 March 1821 in Kharkiv gubernia, d 30 December 1887 near Nice, France. Legal scholar of Ukrainian descent, senator, and prominent jurist. After graduating in mathematics from Kharkiv University (1842) he took a position in the justice ministry in Moscow and, in 1849, became its chief consultant. He played a key role in the judicial reform of 1864, which liberalized the Russian legal system. He wrote a number of studies, including *Sudebnye ustavy s rassuzhdeniiami, na koikh oni osnovany* (Court Statutes with the Reasoning on Which They Are Based, 1866) and *Grazhdanskoe ulozhenie italianskogo korolevstva i russkie grazhdanskie zakony* (The Civil Code of the Italian Kingdom and Russian Civil Laws, 1870), and translated Beccaria and Dante.

**Zarulsky, Stanislav** [Zarul's'kyj], b and d ? Historian of Polish origin. He was a captain in the Russian army in the later 18th century. His *Opisanie o Maloi Rossii i Ukraine* (A Description of Little Russia and Ukraine), based largely on Polish and Russian sources, provided a short survey of Ukrainian history from antiquity until 1775, from a markedly conservative, pro-Russian, and monarchist point of view. It was published as part of the *Chteniia* of the Moscow University Historical Society (1848, no. 8).

**Zarvanytsia** [Zarvanycja]. IV-6. A village (1973 pop 650) on the Strypa River in Terebovlia raion, Ternopil oblast. It was first mentioned in a historical document in 1458. Its 13th-century icon of the Theotokos attracted many pilgrims. A Trypilian culture settlement of the 3rd millennium and two Scythian burials of the 7th and 6th centuries BC have been discovered in its vicinity.

**Zarytska, Kateryna** [Zaryc'ka], b 5 November 1914 in Kolomyia, Galicia, d 29 August 1986 in Lviv. Civic and nationalist leader; daughter of M. Zarytsky. She became a member of the OUN underground in 1930. In 1934, while a student of mathematics at the Lviv Polytechnical Institute, she was arrested by the Polish authorities for her involvement in the assassination of B. *Pieracki and sentenced at the Warsaw Trial to a four-year prison term. Shortly after

Kateryna Zarytska          Yevheniia Zarytska

her release in 1939, she married M. *Soroka. In 1940 she was again arrested, that time by the Soviet authorities, and imprisoned for her membership in the OUN. Having been released after the German occupation of Western Ukraine, she became the regional co-ordinator of the OUN women's section and head of the *Ukrainian Red Cross. She was arrested by the MGB in 1947 and sentenced to a 25-year term, which she served in Russian prisons (to 1968) in Verkhnouralsk and Vladimir and in a concentration camp in Mordovia. After her release in 1972 she lived in Ternopil oblast.

Sofiia Zarytska: *Loneliness* (oil, 1952)

**Zarytska, Sofiia** [Zaryc'ka, Sofija], b 21 August 1903 in Peremyshl, Galicia, d 17 April 1972 in Chennevières, France. Painter and graphic artist; cousin of Ye. *Zarytska. She studied art under O. Novakivsky in Lviv (1920–3) and at the Prague Academy of Arts (1924–8). After moving with her husband, P. *Omelchenko, to Paris she joined the Salon des Artists Indépendants and displayed her works at its annual exhibitions and at exhibitions of the Salon d'Automne in Paris and the Association of Independent Ukrainian Artists in Lviv. After the Second World War her work was shown at group exhibitions almost annually in Paris and the United States. Emphasizing line rather than color, she expressed herself in oil, tempera, and monotype. The main themes of her work were motherhood, childhood, and female friendship. Representative of her work are paintings such as *Woman and Girls* (1950) and monotypes such as *Girl's Head* (1950) and *Two Girls* (1954). Zarytska, together with many of her and Omelchenko's works, perished in a house fire.

**Zarytska, Yevheniia** [Zaryc'ka, Jevhenija] (Zareska, Eugenia), b 9 November 1910 in Rava Ruska, Galicia, d 5 October 1979 in Malmaison, near Paris. Opera and concert singer (mezzo-soprano). She studied under A. Didur at the Lviv Conservatory and made her debut at the Lviv Opera (1937) as Leonora in G. Donizetti's *La Favorita*. She also studied in Vienna, where she won first prize in the International Festival of Song (1938), and from 1939 she lived in Italy, where she performed at La Scala as Dorabella in W. Mozart's *Cosi fan tutte* and appeared in Italian feature films. She sang throughout Europe and North America, under the conductors P. Hindemith, I. Stravinsky, W. Furtwängler, E. Ormandy, and C. Guilini. Her operatic repertoire consisted of over 30 roles, including the Countess in Tchaikovsky's *The Queen of Spades*, the name-part in G. Bizet's *Carmen*, Margaret in A. Berg's *Wozzeck*, and Martha in M. Mussorgsky's *Khovantchina*.

Zarytska recorded for many international labels. She sang the role of Marina in the award-winning HMV recording of M. Mussorgsky's *Boris Godunov*. Her album of Ukrainian songs, titled *Chants d'Ukraine* (issued in 1956 by Paris Columbia), includes works by M. Lysenko, K. Stetsenko, M. Verykivsky, L. Revutsky, B. Kudryk, V. Barvinsky, N. Nyzhankivsky, V. Baltarovych, and M. Kolessa.

**Zarytsky, Ivan** [Zaryc'kyj], b 24 January 1929 in Hlobyne, Kremenchuk okruha. Glass artist. After graduating from the Kiev School of Applied Art (1948) and the Lviv Institute of Applied and Decorative Arts (1954) he worked at the Kiev Artistic Glass Plant. His works include plates, vases, table sets (*Wedding Set* [1975] and *Spring Set* [1977]) and glass sculptures, such as *Odarka and Karas* (1965).

**Zarytsky, Myron** [Zaryc'kyj], b 23 May 1889 in Mohylnytsia, Terebovlia county, Galicia, d 19 August 1961 in Lviv. Mathematician. After completing his studies at Vienna (1907) and Lviv (1912) universities, he worked as a gymnasium teacher in Galicia and then lectured at Lviv (1939–50) and Uzhhorod (1950–5) universities. He made contributions to set theory, mathematical logic, the theory of probability, and function theory.

**Zasenko, Oleksii**, b 4 October 1907 in Liubartsi, Pereiaslav county, Poltava gubernia. Literary scholar. He graduated from Kiev University in 1934. After the Second World War he was director and chief editor of the Radianskyi Pysmennyk publishing house and a department head at the Derzhlitvydav publishing house. The deputy director of the AN URSR (now ANU) Institute of Literature from 1950 to 1973, he also taught at the Kiev Pedagogical Institute. In 1963 he became a doctor of philological sciences. Among his works are a book of critical essays (1962) and monographs on M. Vovchok and foreign literature (1958), Vovchok's life and works (1964), O. Makovei (1968), and M. Cheremshyna (1974). In 1983 he published a book of memoirs about his contemporaries.

**Zasiadko, Oleksander** [Zasjadko], b 1779 in Lutenka, near Hadiach, in the Poltava region, d 8 June 1837 in Kharkiv. Inventor and innovator, rocketry expert, military engineer and major-general. He studied at a military academy and served as an artillery officer in the Russian army. Zasiadko was one of the first persons in Europe to see the value of rockets in combat. In 1815, on his own initiative, he started to experiment with gunpowder-propelled rockets and developed many types of combat and signaling rockets and mobile rocket launchers, including the first multiple-rocket launcher. His rockets were used successfully in 1825 in the Caucasus; after they were accepted for use by the Russian army, they were mass-produced in St Petersburg. Zasiadko was appointed director of an artillery school and a rocketry factory and received other important positions. In 1827 he was put in command of the artillery forces of the Russian army. During the Russo-Turkish War of 1828–9 his rockets were used to break the sieges of Varna and other Turkish cities. Zasiadko's inventions had a profound influence on the further development of military rocketry. A crater on the back side of the Moon is named after him.

L. Onyshkevych

*Zasiv* (Sowing Time). A weekly newspaper published in Kiev in 1911–12 (a total of 65 issues). It was the continuation of *Selo* and had the same basic orientation and major contributors. A popular publication intended for peasants and workers, it reported primarily on developments in the Ukrainian countryside and on the growth of the Ukrainian national movement. *Zasiv* was initiated and edited in 1911 by M. Hrushevsky; in 1912 the paper was published by O. Stepanenko and edited by him, O. Oles, and Yu. Tyshchenko (Siry). The tsarist authorities confiscated issues and frequently imposed fines, and thereby forced the paper to go bankrupt.

**Zaskalna archeological site.** A multi-occupational Paleolithic site near Bilohirske, Crimea. Excavations in 1969–78 produced numerous flint tools and weapons and wild animal bones. The site is best known for the discovery of a Neanderthal burial and the recovery of fragments of a Neanderthal skull.

**Zaslav.** See Iziaslav.

**Zaslavsky, David** [Zaslavskij], b 13 January 1880 in Kiev, d 28 March 1965 in Moscow. Journalist of Jewish origin. A graduate of Kiev University (1908), he contributed feuilletons and articles to Russian and Yiddish periodicals from 1904. In 1903 he joined the Jewish Workers' Bund

and became involved in Jewish socialist politics in Kiev. Zaslavsky published one of the first Soviet biographies of M. Drahomanov (1924). His second book on Drahomanov (1934) was Stalinist in approach; it viciously maligned him and the entire Ukrainian national movement, including the national Communists. A third book on Drahomanov (1964), cowritten in Ukrainian with I. Romanchenko, was more liberal in tone and interpretation. From 1926 Zaslavsky was a staff writer for *Izvestiia* and *Pravda* and lived in Moscow. His memoirs and several collections of his Stalinist, anti-Zionist, and anti-Israel writings were published posthumously in Moscow.

**Zaslavsky, Evgenii** [Zaslavskij], b 1 January 1845 in Voronezh, d 25 June 1878 in St Petersburg. Russian revolutionary. He was a student activist in Moscow and St Petersburg, and in the early 1870s he worked in Poltava gubernia, where he spread revolutionary propaganda among the peasants. In 1872 he moved to Odessa, where he founded a workers' library and a printery (1874), spread revolutionary propaganda, and did clandestine educational work among the workers. In May 1875 he founded and led the anarcho-socialist *South Russian Union of Workers. In May 1877, after being arrested in December 1875, he was sentenced to 10 years of hard labor. He died of tuberculosis in a prison hospital. Yu. Bocharov's book about him was published in Moscow in 1926.

**Zaslavsky, Mykhailo** [Zaslavs'kyj, Myxajlo], b 25 January 1925 in Zvenyhorodka now in Cherkasy oblast, d 24 July 1976 in Lviv. Ballet master. He completed study in the ballet studio of the Moscow State Theater Institute (1955) and then worked as principal ballet master in the Ulan-Ude Musical Theater Mongolia and the Lviv Theater of Opera and Ballet (1962–76).

**Zasławski.** A family line of Ukrainian nobles that had a common origin with the *Ostrozky family in the person of Vasyl Fedorovych (d 1461). His older son, Yurii (Heorhii), inherited the town of Zaslav (also Iziaslav), in Volhynia, and adopted the name Zasławski; his younger son, Ivan, inherited the town of Ostrih. The Zasławski family owned large tracts of land in Volhynia, Podilia, and Bratslav. Other notable family figures included Janusz Zasławski, the voivode of Podlachia (1591) and Volhynia (1604, 1620), his son Oleksander (d 1629), who was a Volhynian palatine (1605) and a voivode of Bratslav (from 1615) and Kiev (from 1628); and Oleksander's son, Władysław-Dominik *Zasławski. The family line died out with Władysław-Dominik's son, Oleksander, in 1673, and its fortunes went to the Lubomirski family.

**Zasławski, Władysław-Dominik,** b ca 1617–18, d 5 April 1656 in Stare Selo near Lviv. Polish magnate. A major landowner in Volhynia, he occupied army positions from 1636 and was voivode of Sandomierz (from 1645) and Cracow (from 1649). He was one of three commanders designated to lead Polish forces against B. Khmelnytsky's Cossack forces in 1648. His ineptitude and indolence (Khmelnytsky referred to him derisively as *peryna*, or the 'feather-bed') helped bring about the Polish army's crushing defeat at Pyliavtsi in 1648.

**Zastavna.** V-6. A city (1989 pop 8,300) and raion center in Chernivtsi oblast. It was first mentioned in a historical document in 1583. Until 1774 it was part of the Moldavian principality, and later, of the Austrian Empire and Rumania (1918–40). Under the Soviet regime it was granted city status (1940). Its main industries are food processing and communications. Three 12th- to 13th-century Rus' settlements have been uncovered in the town.

**Zastyrets, Yosyp** [Zastyrec', Josyp], b 15 August 1873 in Koniushkiv, Brody county, Galicia, d 15 January 1943 in Lviv. Greek Catholic priest, educator, and writer. After graduating from Lviv University (1899) he taught at gymnasiums in Berezhany, Lviv, Buchach, and Ternopil. During the First World War he completed a doctoral thesis on the Crimean War at Vienna University and conducted teachers' courses for Galician and Bukovynian students in Vienna. In 1917 he returned to Lviv, where he taught at the Ukrainian Academic Gymnasium (until 1933) and edited the daily *Nova rada* (1919–20). He wrote short stories, humorous sketches, and articles on historical, educational, and theological issues.

**Zatenatsky, Yakiv** [Zatenac'kyj, Jakiv], b 6 November 1902 in Velyka Kokhnivka (now part of Kremenchuk), Poltava gubernia, d 27 May 1976 in Kiev. Art historian. In 1931 he graduated from the Artem Communist University in Kharkiv. He wrote books on the artists M. Pymonenko (1955) and T. Shevchenko (1961) and on Shevchenko and Russian art (1964), Soviet Ukrainian painting (1961), and Ukrainian art in the first half of the 19th century (1965). He also contributed to the fullest edition of Shevchenko's artistic legacy (4 vols, 1961–4) and was a member of the editorial board of the AN URSR (now ANU) history of Ukrainian art (6 vols, 1966–70).

**Zatkovich, Gregory Ignatius.** See Zhatkovych, Hryhorii.

**Zatonsky, Dmytro** [Zatons'kyj], b 2 July 1922 in Odessa. Literary scholar; corresponding member from 1969 and full member since 1990 of the AN URSR (now ANU); the son of V. *Zatonsky. He graduated from Kiev University (1950), and taught there from 1956 to 1961. He has worked at the Department of the Literature of Western Europe and America of the Institute of Literature of the ANU (1961–74, director since 1986) and was an associate of the Institute of World Literature in Moscow (1974–5). A leading Soviet specialist on 20th-century Western (especially German) literature, he has written many articles; Russian monographs on F. Kafka and the problems of modernism (1965), the art of the novel and the 20th century (1973), and 19th-century European (French) realism (1984); four collections of theoretical essays in Russian; and four collections in Ukrainian, *U poshukakh sensu buttia* (In Search of the Meaning of Existence, 1967), *Pro modernizm i modernistiv* (On Modernism and Modernists, 1972), *Shliakh cherez XX stolittia* (The Path through the 20th Century, 1978), and *Mynule, suchasne, maibutnie* (The Past, Present, and Future, 1982). Some of his works were translated into German and published in East Germany.

**Zatonsky, Volodymyr** [Zatons'kyj], b 8 August 1888 in Lysets, Nova Ushytsia county, Podilia gubernia, d 29 July

Volodymyr Zatonsky                Hanna Zatyrkevych-
                                  Karpynska

1938. Ukrainian Bolshevik leader; VUAN and AN URSR (now ANU) full member from 1929. A graduate of Kiev University (1912), he taught physics at the Kiev Polytechnical Institute. He joined the Bolsheviks in early 1917 and by May was a Presidium member of the Kiev Party Committee and a deputy to the Kiev Council of Workers' Deputies. After the Bolshevik coup in Petrograd he headed the Bolshevik committee and organized an uprising in Kiev. He was secretary of education in the first Bolshevik government in Ukraine (December 1917 to April 1918), and in January 1918 he was appointed its plenipotentiary in Moscow. From late March to mid-April 1918 he also headed the Bolshevik Central Executive Committee in Ukraine. He played a key role in the creation of the CP(B)U at the *Tahanrih Bolshevik Conference and was elected to the CP(B)U Organizational Bureau. From November 1918 he was a member of the *Provisional Workers' and Peasants' Government of Ukraine (in which he supported the Russian-Ukrainian federalist position), and from December 1920, people's commissar of education. From July to September 1920 he also headed the *Galician Revolutionary Committee in Ternopil.

After the consolidation of Soviet rule Zatonsky was a CC CP(B)U member (1918–27, 1934–7) and a candidate (1923–4) and member (1924–37) of its Politburo. He headed the *All-Ukrainian Association of Consumer Co-operative Organizations (1921–2), the People's Commissariat of Education (1922–3), and the political administration of the Ukrainian Military District (1924–5). He replaced O. *Shumsky as editor of *Chervonyi shliakh* (1926–30) and served as deputy chairman of the Council of People's Commissars and director of the government's Institute of Soviet Construction (1927–33), and chairman of the government's Chemical Engineering Committee (1928–34). In 1933 he replaced M. *Skrypnyk as the people's commissar of education, and in 1934 he became a candidate to the CC of the All-Union Communist Party (Bolshevik). Although Zatonsky did not belong to any national 'deviation' in the CP(B)U and toed the Party line, he gave qualified support to Ukrainization. He wrote a book on the national problem in Ukraine (1926; 2nd edn 1927) and valuable memoirs about the revolutionary period (1929). A collection of his speeches on education was published in 1935. He was arrested by the NKVD together with his wife in November 1937 and later executed.

V. Holubnychy

**Zatula, Dmytro,** b 11 February 1923 in Baba *khutir*, near Bulatselivka (now Shevchenkove), Zmiiv county, Kharkiv gubernia, d 10 June 1987. Microbiologist; corresponding member of the AN URSR (now ANU) from 1973. A graduate of Kharkiv University (1952), he worked at the Kiev Institute of Epidemiology, Microbiology, and Parasitology (1953–62), the ANU Institute of Microbiology and Virology (1970–7, from 1972 as director), and the ANU Institute for Problems of Oncology. Zatula mainly researched microbiological aspects of malignant tumors.

**Zatulyviter, Volodymyr,** b 1 March 1944 in Yabluchne, Velyka Pysarivka raion, Sumy oblast. Poet and translator. He graduated from the Sumy Pedagogical Institute (1966) and has worked as a German teacher and journalist. Since 1986 he has been an editor for the Dnipro publishing house. He is the author of the poetry collections *Teoriia kryla* (Theory of the Wing, 1973), *Teperishnii chas* (Present Time, 1977), which won an award, *Tektonichna zona* (Tectonic Zone, 1982), *Pam'iat hlyny* (Memory of Clay, 1984), *Zoriana rechovyna* (Stellar Matter, 1985), *Polotno* (Cloth, 1986), which also won an award, *Chuttia iedynoï rodyny* (Feeling of a Single Family, 1987), and *Pochatkova shkola* (Primary School, 1988).

**Zatyrkevych, Mykhailo** [Zatyrkevyč, Myxajlo], b 1831 in the Chernihiv region, d 1893. Historian and lawyer. He was a professor at the Nizhen Lyceum (1859–75), where he wrote *O vliianii bor'by mezhdu narodami i sosloviiami na obrazovanie stroia russkogo gosudarstva v domongol'skii period* (The Influence of the Struggle between Peoples and Estates on the Formation of the Russian State System in the Pre-Mongol Period, 1874).

**Zatyrkevych-Karpynska, Hanna** [Zatyrkevyč-Karpyns'ka] (née Kovtunenko), b 20 February 1855 in Sribne, Pryluka county, Poltava gubernia, d 12 September 1921 in Romen, Sumy county, Kharkiv gubernia. Theater actress. She made her professional debut in M. Kropyvnytsky's troupe in 1883. She worked in M. Starytsky's (1883–5), Kropyvnytsky's (1885–92 and 1896–8), and M. Sadovsky's (1892–6) troupes, as well as in (from 1904) those of D. Haidamaka, O. Suslov, and O. Sukhodolsky; then in Sadovsky's Theater (1917–18) and the State People's Theater (1918–19); and, during her last year, in O. Korolchuk's troupes. An actress of great insight and simplicity, she performed in over 100 roles, the best of which were from the populist-ethnographic repertoire. Among them were Ahrafena in H. Kvitka-Osnovianenko's *Shel'menko-denshchyk* (Shelmenko the Orderly), Stekha in T. Shevchenko's *Nazar Stodolia*, and Hapka and Ryndychka in M. Kropyvnytsky's *Zaidyholova* (The Dreamer) and *Po revizii* (After the Inspection). In the non-Ukrainian repertoire she successfully played the character roles of Poshlepkina in N. Gogol's *Revizor* (The Inspector General) and Dulska in G. Zapolska's *Moralność pani Dulskiej* (Madame Dulska's Moral Code). Biographies of Zatyrkevych-Karpynska were published in Kiev in 1956 and 1966.

V. Revutsky

**Zauze, Volodymyr** (Vladimir), b 18 May 1859 in St Petersburg, d 26 June 1939 in Odessa. Painter and graphic artist. A graduate of the Stroganov School in Moscow (1879), he worked for a while in Dubno and Mykolaiv. In

Volodymyr Zauze: *In the Village* (1916)

1885 he settled in Odessa, where he joined the *Society of South Russian Artists in 1893 and cofounded the *Kostandi Society of Artists in 1922. From 1920 he taught at the Odessa Art Institute. At the beginning of his career he painted mostly watercolor landscapes, such as *First Snow* (1851), *Birch Forest* (1897), and *Autumn* (1897). In the early 20th century he began creating etchings and aquatints depicting landscapes, still lifes, and genre scenes, such as *Noon: Falling Shadows* (1904), *In the Village* (1916), *Woman Feeding Chickens* (1918), *Woods: Tree above a River* (1923), *Chumaks* (1929), *Geese* (1931), *Winter in Ukraine* (1935), and *River* (1936), and line engravings and monotypes, such as *Guarding Soviet Borders* (1931) and *Barricades: 1905* (1925). Ye. Davydova's book about Zauze was published in Kiev in 1966.

**Zavadovsky** [Zavadovs'kyj]. A family line of Ukrainian nobility and Cossack officers from the Chernihiv region. Yakiv Zavadovsky was a member of I. Samoilovych's court and a judge (1703–5) and acting colonel (1693, 1703–4) in Starodub regiment. His son, Vasyl, and his grandson, Vasyl, took part in the Polish and Turkish campaigns of the 1730s and were fellows of the standard; the latter Vasyl's sons became counts. One of them, Petro *Zavadovsky, was a noted imperial Russian government official; another, Yakiv Zavadovsky, was the last colonel of Starodub regiment (1778–82) and governor of Novhorod-Siverskyi (1794).

**Zavadovsky, Ivan** [Zavadovs'kyj], b and d ? Kievan goldsmith. In 1747 he and P. *Volokh carved the silver Royal Gates for the iconostasis of the St Sophia Cathedral from a copper model by S. Taranovsky.

**Zavadovsky, Ivan** [Zavadovs'kyj], b 16 January 1887 in Galicia, d 21 April 1932 in Dnipropetrovske. Linguist and pedagogue. A graduate of Vienna University (1915), he taught Greek and Latin in gymnasiums in Yavoriv and Lviv in Galicia and Tarashcha in Kiev gubernia (1918–23). From 1923 he taught Ukrainian at the Dnipropetrovske Institute of People's Education, where from 1928 he was a professor, dean of the language and literature faculty, and chairman of the Department of Ukrainian Linguistics. He wrote textbooks on the Ukrainian language (1927) and on the foundations of linguistics for students (1928) and teachers (1930; 2nd edn 1931, with L. Bulakhovsky).

Ivan Zavadovsky: *Pines* (tempera, 1974)

**Zavadovsky, Ivan** [Zavadovs'kyj], b 1937, d 1983 in Lviv. Painter. He graduated from the Lviv Institute of Applied and Decorative Arts in 1964. In the 1960s he experimented with surrealism (eg, *Composition with Donkey's Head*, 1966) and abstraction (*Laughter*, 1967). His later portraits, figural compositions, and landscapes were painted in an expressionistic manner (*Portrait of the Artist*, 1983).

**Zavadovsky, Petro** [Zavadovs'kyj], b 1739 in the Chernihiv region, d 22 January 1812 in St Petersburg. Ukrainian official in the imperial government, who descended from a Cossack *starshyna* family in the Starodub region. A graduate of the Kievan Mohyla Academy (1760), he was secretary of the Little Russian Collegium (1767) and later worked for the governor-general of Little Russia, P. Rumiantsev. In 1768–74 he was director of the secret chancellery and (according to one biographer) editor of the Treaty of *Küçük Kaynarca (1774). From 1774 he was secretary to and a favorite of Catherine II. He was given large estates in Ukraine and Belarus (his favorite being Lialychi, near the original family estate), and served as a senator, minister of education (1802–10), and honorary head of the State Council's Department of Laws (1810). He introduced a number of reforms, including the granting of autonomy to universities, and was instrumental in establishing Kharkiv University (1805) and a number of other educational institutions in Ukraine.

**Zavadovsky, Yevstakhii** [Zavadovs'kyj, Jevstaxij] (Zavadov), b and d ? Wood engraver of the second half of the 17th and the beginning of the 18th century. He worked in Kiev and Lviv, where he decorated and illustrated Psalters, 1677, 1697, 1703, 1708), Liturgicons (1681), an Octoechos (1686), a Gospel (1690), an Anthologion (1694), an *Apostol* (1696), and a daily prayer book (1701). His works include engravings of the evangelists Matthew (1681),

John (1683), and Luke (1744), the Crucifixion (1691), God on His Throne (1697), and Christ (1712). He signed his works with the initials EZ.

Roman Zavadovych          Ivan Zavalykut

**Zavadovych, Roman** [Zavadovyč] (pseuds: Roman zi Slavnoi, Fortissimo, R. Rolianyk, M. Mamorsky), b 18 December 1903 in Slavna, Zboriv county, Galicia, d 31 May 1985 in Chicago. Writer. He graduated from Lviv University (M PHIL, 1938). From 1920 on he contributed poems, stories, fairy tales, and plays for children to periodicals such as *Svit dytyny* and *Moloda Ukraïna* in Lviv, *Mali druzi* in Lviv, Cracow, and Augsburg, *Sonechko* in Ellwangen, *Mii pryiatel'* in Winnipeg, and *Veselka* in Jersey City. He also contributed lyric poetry for adults to *Literaturno-naukovyi vistnyk*, *Dzvony*, and *Dazhboh* and articles to *Zyz* (1929–32). After being displaced by the Second World War he emigrated from a DP camp in Germany to the United States in 1949. He was active in the Ukrainian community in Chicago and regularly contributed articles on educational and cultural topics to the daily *Svoboda*. In 1953 he became the honorary president of the *Association of Ukrainian Writers for Young People, which he cofounded in 1947. In 1954 he became a coeditor of the children's magazine *Veselka*. Published separately were 33 of his children's books, among them *Pryhody Gnomyka Romtomtomyka* (Adventures of the Little Gnome Romtomtomyk, 1940,1964), *Zymovi tsarivny* (Winter Princesses, 1942, 1956), *Charodiini muzyky* (Magic Musicians, 1942,1970), *Khloptsi z zelenoho boru* (Boys from the Green Wood, 1948, 1973), *Perepolokh* (Fright, 1951), *Soika-shtukarka i inshi opovidannia* (The Trickster Jay and Other Stories, 1953), *Marushka-Chepurushka i Les' Pobihdes' ta inshi veseli opovidannia* (Marushka-Chepurushka and Les Pobihdes and Other Merry Stories, 1969), and *Karpats'kyi charivnyk* (The Carpathian Sorcerer, 1981). He also wrote a collection of religious poems, *Z budniv u sviato* (From Workdays into a Holy Day, 1978).

R. Senkus

**Zavadsky, Edvald** [Zavads'kyj, Edval'd], b 2 June 1927 in Millerovo, Rostov oblast. Solid-state physicist; AN URSR (now ANU) corresponding member since 1978. A graduate of the Orsk Pedagogical Institute (1955), since 1966 he has worked at the ANU Physical-Technical Institute in Donetske. There he has researched the effects of intense magnetic fields on phase transitions in magnetic materials.

Together with O. Halkin, Zavadsky showed that magnetic phase transitions are affected by pressure. He discovered the possibility of inducing new stable phases not attainable under normal conditions.

**Zavadsky, Mykhailo** [Zavads'kyj, Myxajlo] (Zawadzki, Michał), b 7 August 1828 in Mykhalkivtsi, Liatychiv county, Podilia gubernia, d 19 March 1887 in Mykhalkivtsi. Composer, pianist, and pedagogue of Polish descent. In 1862–3 he studied at Kiev University, and then he taught music in Kiev and Kamianets-Podilskyi. He wrote more than 500 pieces for piano, all of them based on Ukrainian folk themes. These included dumas, shumkas, Cossack marches, rhapsodies, and songs such as 'The Zaporozhian.' He also left an unfinished opera, *Maria*.

**Zavadsky, Viktor** [Zavads'kyj], b 23 October 1886 in the Poltava region, d 8 May 1973 in Toronto. Jurist. After graduating in law from Kiev University (1909) he worked as a judge in Omsk and then Kiev. During the revolutionary period he was a member of the Central Committee of the Ukrainian Party of Socialists-Federalists. Under the UNR Directory he headed the law department of the Ministry of Justice. He went into exile with the UNR government and in 1929 settled in Warsaw, where he received a judicial appointment. In 1944 he fled to Germany, and eventually he emigrated to Canada. In Ukraine and later in Canada he contributed articles to the Ukrainian press.

**Zavaliv.** A village (1973 pop 1,300) on the Zolota Lypa River in Berezhany raion, Ternopil oblast. It was first mentioned in historical records in the second half of the 15th century. The remains of a Basilian monastery and a fortress from the 16th century are found there. In August 1915 an Austrian division and the Ukrainian Sich Riflemen broke through the Russian front at Zavaliv.

**Zavallia Graphite Complex** (Zavallivskyi hrafitovyi kombinat). A graphite-processing complex built in 1931 in Zavallia, Kirovohrad oblast. Its first enrichment plant opened in 1934. The plant was rebuilt and expanded after the Second World War. Since 1958 the graphite ore has been mined in open pits. In 1977, 961,000 t of ore was processed, to produce 58,000 t of graphite.

**Zavallia graphite deposit** (Zavallivske rodovyshche hrafitu). The largest graphite deposit in Ukraine, located in the western part of Kirovohrad oblast. It was discovered in 1931 and has been mined since 1934. The graphite is found in crystalline veins up to 80 m wide in Precambrian gneisses. The deposit has reserves of approx 25 million t of graphite. The ore is processed at the Zavallia Graphite Complex.

**Zavalykut, Ivan,** b 1884 in Husiatyn county, Galicia, d 21 March 1975 in Syracuse, New York. Lawyer and civic and political leader. Upon graduating from Lviv University (1911) he practiced law in Husiatyn and then fought in the ranks of the Ukrainian Galician Army. He practiced law in Kopychyntsi, Kolomyia, and Stanyslaviv and played a leading role in local civic life. A candidate of the *Ukrainian National Democratic Alliance, he was elected to the Polish Sejm in 1928 and 1935. After emigrating to the United States in 1950, he was an active organizer for the Ukrainian Congress Committee of America.

**Zavarov, Aleksei,** b 17 March 1917 in Kolomenskoe, Moscow gubernia. Architect. A graduate of the Kiev State Art Institute (1948), he has worked for various architectural institutions in Kiev. He collaborated on the design and construction of Khreshchatyk Blvd (1949–50), the Green Theater, overlooking the Dnieper (1950), the building of the City Council (1953–6), the October Palace of Culture (1956), the pedestrian bridge over the Dnieper (1957), the Sports Palace (1960), and several residential subdivisions (1957–70).

Anna Zavarykhin

**Zavarykhin, Anna** [Zavaryxin] (née Indzhilova), b 23 January 1889 in Kishinev, d 11 July 1972 in Toronto. Ballerina. She completed choreography school in Petrograd (1916). In 1922–39 she performed as soloist in Constantinople, Bucharest, France, London (Covent Garden), the Far East, and Latin America. She was a founder of and teacher at the ballet studio Apollon in Toronto (1953–69).

**Zavhorodnii, Anatolii** [Zavhorodnij, Anatolij], b 28 December 1929 in Znamenka, Altai krai. Artist. He has painted oils, such as *Before the Hunt* (1961), and gouaches, such as the series 'Mykolaiv, Land of Ships' (1966–70), and designed the Victory Park monument in Mykolaiv (1965) and the stained-glass windows of the Palace of Happiness and department store in Mykolaiv (1965–6).

**Zavisna, Olena** (Zavysna, Mariana), b ?, d November 1654 in Busha, Podilia. During the siege of the fortified town of Busha by a large Polish expeditionary force she took over the command of the garrison after her husband, Mykhailo, was killed. When it was no longer possible to hold out, she set fire to the munitions stockpile and razed much of the town, thereby annihilating the last of the defenders and a large number of the enemy. She was later celebrated in works of historical fiction, notably in a novella and a play by M. Starytsky.

**Zavitnevych, Vasyl** [Zavitnevyč, Vasyl'], b 24 April 1899 in Zamistia, Pryluka county, Poltava gubernia, d 25 March 1983 in New York City. Educator, lawyer, and musicologist. He worked as a teacher in Kiev from 1924 and studied law at the Kiev Institute of the National Economy (1924–5). He graduated from the Kiev Institute of People's Education (1929), worked as a legal consultant to the VUAN, and joined the VUAN Commission for the Study of

Vasyl Zavitnevych

Ukraine's Customary Law. In the 1930s he taught Ukrainian language and literature at postsecondary institutes in Kiev. He emigrated to the United States in 1948, where he served as president of the Scholarly Theological Institute (est 1952) of the Ukrainian Orthodox Church in the USA. He published two studies of Ukrainian customary law (1928), compiled nine volumes of Ukrainian liturgical choral music, and contributed articles to émigré periodicals, such as *Ukraïns'ke pravoslavne slovo* and *Novi dni*. His archives are preserved at the Ukrainian Orthodox Museum in South Bound Brook, New Jersey.

**Zavitnevych, Volodymyr** [Zavitnevyč], b 14 April 1853 in Litsviany, Minsk gubernia, Belarus, d February 1927. Historian and archeologist of Belarusian descent. He graduated from the St Petersburg Theological Academy (1879) and studied at the Warsaw Theological School (until 1883). He was a professor of Russian history at the Kiev Theological Academy (1884–1911), a member of the Historical Society of Nestor the Chronicler, and a contributor to *Trudy Kievskoi dukhovnoi akademii* (*TKDA*). In 1918 he sat on the Scientific Committee of the Ministry of Religions of the Ukrainian State. Zavitnevych conducted archeological excavations in Belarus and Polisia near the Prypiat River, as well as in the Kiev, Kharkiv, and Poltava regions. He wrote studies of the Princely era on the basis of his explorations, such as 'Vladimir Sviatoi kak politicheskii deiatel'' (St Volodymyr as a Political Figure, *TKDA*, 1880; pub separately in 1890) and 'Proiskhozhdenie i pervonachal'-naia istoriia imeni Rus'' (The Origin and Primordial History of the Name Rus', *TKDA*, 1892). Among his other works are *Palinodiia Zakharii Kopystenskogo i ee mesto v istorii zapadno-russkoi polemiki XVI i XVII vv.* (Z. Kopystensky's *\*Palinodiia* and Its Place in the History of Southern Russian [Ukrainian] Polemics in the 16th and 17th Centuries, 1883), *Religiozno-nravstvennoe sostoianie N.V. Gogolia v poslednie gody ego zhizni* (The Religious and Moral State of N. Gogol in the Last Years of His Life, 1902), and *Aleksei Stepanovich Khomiakov* (2 vols, 1902–3).

A. Zhukovsky

**Zbanatsky, Yurii** [Zbanac'kyj, Jurij], b 1 January 1914 in Borsukiv, now in Kozelets raion, Chernihiv oblast. Writer. During the Second World War he served as a partisan

commander and was decorated as a Hero of the Soviet Union. His first published work appeared in 1944. His novels, short stories, and documentary essays devoted to the war include *Taiemnytsia Sokolynoho boru* (The Secret of Sokolyne Forest, 1949), *Lisova krasunia* (The Forest Beauty, 1955), *Iedyna* (The Only One, 1959), and *My – ne z legendy* (We Are Not from a Legend, 1972). His novels *Malynovyi dzvin* (The Crimson Bell, 1958), *Kuiut' zozuli* (The Cuckoos Are Calling, 1975), *Lito v Sokolynomu* (A Summer in Sokolyne, 1953), *Pryvitaite mene druzi* (Greet Me, My Friends, 1956), *Kuriachyi boh* (The Chicken God, 1966), and others are written for young readers. His contemporary, mostly rural-set novels include *Peredzhnyv'ia* (Before the Harvest, 1955) and *Khvyli* (The Waves, 1967).

**Zbaraski.** A family of Ukrainian nobles in Volhynia that took their name from the town of Zbarazh. According to Polish heraldists the family was descended from Korybut, son of Algirdas, and had a common origin with the Nesvitsky family. Notable family members included Andrii Zbaraski, the founder of the line; his son, Stefan Zbaraski (d 1586), a voivode of Trakai; Andrii's grandson, Janusz *\*Zbaraski; and Janusz's son, Jerzy (Yurii) *\*Zbaraski. The Zbaraski line ended in 1631, and its assets were taken over by the Wiśniowiecki family.

**Zbaraski, Janusz,** b ?, d 1608. Polish military figure. He was voivode of Bratslav and a participant in numerous military campaigns, including a 1575 expedition which defeated a large Tatar force near Zbarazh, the siege of Pskov (1581), the suppression of the revolt led by S. Nalyvaiko (1594–6), and joint Polish-Swedish interventions against Muscovy in the early 17th century. In 1577 Zbaraski sent I. *\*Pidkova to his death at the hands of Stephen Báthory.

**Zbaraski, Jerzy,** b 1580, d 1631. Polish civic and military figure. He was castellan of Cracow and an authority on the Cossacks. His extensive correspondence, compiled by A. Sokolowski and published as *Listy ks. Jerzego Zbaraskiego, kasztelana krakowskiego z lat 1621–31* (1878), is a valuable source of information about the Cossacks.

**Zbarazh** [Zbaraž]. IV-6. A city (1989 pop 15,000) on the Hnizna River and a raion center in Ternopil oblast. It is first mentioned in the chronicles under the year 1211 as

An 18th-century church housing the Zbarazh Regional Studies Museum

the center of an appanage principality in the Principality of Galicia-Volhynia. From the 14th century it was under Polish rule. The fortress and town were destroyed by the Tatars in 1474 and 1598. Owned by J. Wiśniowiecki, the castle was captured by B. Khmelnytsky's forces in 1648 and besieged unsuccessfully in 1649. After the partition of Poland in 1772, Zbarazh was annexed by Austria, and served as a county center (1867–1918). In the interwar period it was under Polish rule. It was occupied by Soviet troops in 1939, and granted city status. Today it an agricultural center with a sugar refinery, winery, brick factory, foundry, and brewery. Its architectural monuments, including a fortress built by V. Scamozzi (1626–31), the Bernardine monastery (1627–30), and two 18th-century churches, are tourist attractions. The remains of a 15th-century fortress and the Transfiguration Church (1600) are found 3 km south of Zbarazh, in Staryi Zbarazh.

**Zbihlei, Yosyf** [Zbihlej, Josyf] (pseud: Yosyf Dubrova), b 13 March 1938 in Stebník (Stebnyk), Bardejov circle, Slovakia. Poet. He completed medical studies at the Prešov campus of Košice University (1962) and is a practicing physician. A leading 'modern' poet of the Prešov region, he has published poetry since 1955; he has written the collections *Zeleni neony* (Green Neons, 1964), *Vikna bez nizhnosti* (Windows without Tenderness, 1969), *Kosmichni vidlunnia* (Cosmic Echoes, 1980), *Zakruty* (Bends, 1983), *Tak, nespokii* (Yes, Disquietude, 1986), and *Oberezhno – sny!* (Careful, Dreams!, 1987).

**Zbirnyk Filolohichnoï sektsiï NTSh** (Collection of the Philological Section of the Shevchenko Scientific Society). An irregular scholarly series, 23 volumes of which appeared in Lviv in 1899–1937. Since the Second World War another 11 volumes (as of 1984) have appeared in the West. The series consists of monographs and collections of articles on Ukrainian linguistics and the history of Ukrainian literature.

*Zbirnyk Istorychno-filolohichnoho viddilu VUAN* (Collection of the Historical-Philological Division of the VUAN). An irregular serial of research and documents from various fields of Ukrainian studies. In 1921–31 104 issues and 115 volumes were published, including research in the following areas: the history and historiography of Ukraine (D. Bahalii, M. Hrushevsky, T. Sushytsky, V. Shcherbyna, V. Danylevych, V. Kordt, V. Modzalevsky, P. Klymenko), literature (V. Naumenko, V. Riezanov, M. Markovsky, S. Yefremov, V. Peretts, Hrushevsky, V. Sypovsky, P. Lavrov, V. Petrov), languages (O. Kurylo, Ye. Tymchenko, V. Hantsov, P. Buzuk, V. Rozov), folklore and ethnography (K. Hrushevska, E. Kagarov, K. Kvitka, M. Levchenko), education (F. Titov, O. Savych), art (H. Pavlutsky), and Oriental studies (A. Krymsky). Anniversary collections were dedicated to Bahalii, Hrushevsky, and Mykola Lysenko. The *Zbirnyk* ceased publication when the historical-philological division of the VUAN was abolished in 1931.

**Zbirnyk Istorychno-filosofichnoï sektsiï NTSh** (Collection of the Historical-Philosophical Section of the NTSh). A series published irregularly by the Shevchenko Scientific Society (NTSh) in Lviv. It began to appear in 1898 at the initiative of M. *Hrushevsky. Altogether 16

volumes came out, 14 of them edited by Hrushevsky. Seven volumes and the first part of the eighth volume of Hrushevsky's *Istoriia Ukraïny-Rusy* (History of Ukraine-Rus') appeared in the series. The 5th volume of the series contained materials from the history of religious life in Galicia in the 18th and 19th centuries; the 15th volume contained B. Barvinsky's biography of Yu. Tselevych, the first head of the NTSh; and the 16th volume contained O. Novytsky's study of T. Shevchenko as a painter.

**Zbirnyk Matematychno-pryrodopysno-likars'koï sektsiï NTSh** (Collection of the Mathematical–Natural Sciences–Medical Section of the Shevchenko Scientific Society). An irregular scholarly series, 32 volumes of which appeared in Lviv in 1897–1938. The series included monographs and collections of articles on scientific topics by a wide variety of scholars. Most of the volumes were edited by I. Verkhratsky, V. Levytsky, and Ye. Ozarkevych.

**Zbirnyk Sotsiial'no-ekonomichnoho viddilu VUAN** (Collection of the Social-Economic Division of the VUAN). A scholarly series, 37 volumes of which were published in Kiev in 1925–31. The series included several monographs, among them books by Y. Malynovsky (on the history of state institutions among the Slavs), M. Tuhan-Baranovsky (on political economy, esthetics, and philosophy), O. Baranovych (on the settlement of Volhynia in the 17th century), V. Rieznikov (a bibliography of works on Ukrainian demography), K. Vobly (a two-volume history of the sugar-beet industry in Ukraine), and L. Okinshevych (on the institutions of the Hetman state). Several commissions of the academy published collected works and monographs in the series, including the Commission for the Study of the History of Western-Ruthenian and Ukrainian Law (7 vols, edited by M. Vasylenko), the Commission for the Study of Ukraine's Customary Law (3 vols, edited by A. Kryster and then Y. Malynovsky), the Commission for the Study of Financial Issues (5 vols, edited by L. Yasnopolsky), the Commission for the Study of the Economy of Ukraine (7 vols, edited by Vobly), and the Demographic Institute (1 vol, edited by M. Ptukha).

**Zbiruisky, Dionysii** [Zbirujs'kyj, Dionisij] (secular name: Dmytro Hrytskovych), b ?, d 18 November 1603. Bishop of Kholm in 1585–1603. He supported church union with Rome and participated in the 1596 sobor that culminated in the Church Union of *Berestia.

**Zboriv.** IV-6. A town (1989 pop 6,200) on the Strypa River and a raion center in Ternopil oblast. It was first mentioned in historical documents in the 15th century. In the 16th century it was owned by the Zborowski family of Polish magnates, and from 1624, by J. Sobieski. In 1648 its inhabitants revolted against the Poles, and in 1649 B. Khmelnytsky's Cossacks encircled the Polish army in Zboriv. The town was granted the rights of *Magdeburg law in 1689. At the partition of Poland in 1772, the town was annexed by Austria, and eventually it became a county center (1904). In the interwar period it was under Poland. Today it is an agricultural center with a fruit-processing plant and a brick factory. Its baroque church was built in the late 18th century.

Zboriv

The last page of the Zboriv Cossack Register

**Zboriv, Battle of.** A victory scored by the armies of B. Khmelnytsky over Polish forces led by Jan II Casimir Vasa, near Zboriv, on the Strypa River, on 15–17 August 1649. After the invasion of Ukrainian territory by a Polish army in the spring of 1649, Khmelnytsky mobilized nearly 360,000 Cossacks. .After Khmelnytsky's forces laid siege to Zbarazh, battle lines between Cossack and Polish troops were drawn near Zboriv. The Polish army escaped complete destruction because of the treachery of the Crimean Tatar khan, Islam-Girei III, who feared the rise of Cossack might and forced Khmelnytsky to halt military actions and sign the Treaty of *Zboriv.

**Zboriv, Treaty of.** A pact between B. Khmelnytsky and Poland, signed on 18 August 1649 near Zboriv. Besides Khmelnytsky, the Ukrainian side was represented by I. Vyhovsky, and the Polish side was represented by A. Kysil, J. Ossoliński, J. Radziwiłł, and W.-D. Zasławski. The central provisions of the pact were the Polish king's affirmation of all Cossack rights and freedoms; the increase of the Cossack register to 40,000, with the provision that peasants who participated in the war but were not accepted into the register were to return to the estates of their landlords (that provision engendered considerable disappointment and the flight of many peasants to Slobidska Ukraine); the transfer of Bratslav, Chernihiv, and Kiev voivodeships to the Cossack administration headed by Khmelnytsky; denial of access to those territories for Polish armies; and the filling of all official positions by Ukrainian Orthodox noblemen, who were elevated to equal status with Catholics. The question of the abolition of the church union, as well as the question of the return of all rights and assets of the Orthodox church, was to be submitted to the Polish Diet for debate. The Orthodox metropolitan of Kiev was to be granted a seat in the Polish Senate. In accordance with an agreement in the treaty the register of the entire Zaporozhian army was accepted by Jan II Casimir Vasa and written down on 16 October 1649. (The register was published in 1874 by O. Bodiansky in *Chteniia v Imperatorskom obshchestve istorii i drevnostei rossiiskikh*.) Although the Zboriv Treaty was ratified by the Diet in January 1650, Poland never complied with it.

A. Zhukovsky

**Zborowski, Samuel,** b ?, d 26 May 1584. Polish magnate. In 1582 he was sent by the king of Poland, Stephen Báthory, to the Zaporozhian Sich in order to seek Cossack aid for Polish forces fighting in the Livonian wars. The mission failed, and Zborowski fled the Sich in fear of his life.

**Zbruch idol** (Zbrutskyi idol). A stone statue of an ancient Slavic god (commonly believed to be Sviatovyt, the god of war) discovered in 1848 in the Zbruch River near Horodnytsia, Husiatyn raion, Ternopil oblast. Erected in the 9th or early 10th century, this statue was probably thrown into the river after the Christianization of Rus'. It is basically a tall square pillar standing on a small base (with a total height of approx 2.7 m). At the top of the structure are four facial images set in each cardinal direction and wearing a single noble-style Rus' hat. On the sides are three layers of images that illustrate mythological beliefs of the time: the heavens with the (Slavic) gods living in them; the Earth inhabited by people; and an underworld dominated by evil forces. Since 1851 the idol has been in the Cracow Archeological Museum. Full-size replicas of it can be seen in the Kiev and Moscow historical museums.

**Zbruch River** [Zbruč]. A left-bank tributary of the Dniester River that flows southward for 244 km along the border between Khmelnytskyi and Ternopil oblasts and drains a basin area of 3,395 sq km. The river is 5–10 m wide in its upper region and 15–20 m (with a 50-m maximum width) in its lower part and has an average depth of

The Zbruch River in Ternopil oblast

1.5–2 m. The river is notable for its meandering course. A water reservoir and small hydroelectric station are situated on it. The Zbruch formed part of the border between the Russian Empire and Galicia (then in the Austrian Empire) in 1772–1917 and then between the Ukrainian SSR and Poland in 1921–39.

**Zbura, Ivan,** b 1859 in Zvyniach, Chortkiv circle, Galicia, d 28 October 1940 in Edmonton. Pioneer. After emigrating to Canada in 1898, Zbura settled near Star, Alberta. In February 1899 his poem 'Kanadiis'ki emigranty' (Canadian Emigrants), commonly regarded as the first piece of Ukrainian verse written in Canada, was published in *Svoboda* (Jersey City).

**Zderkovsky, Myroslav** [Zderkovs'kyj], b 1865 in Beneva, Pidhaitsi county, Galicia, d 30 January 1929 in Peremyshliany, Galicia. Lawyer and civic activist. After serving as a judge for many years, he resigned and opened a law of-

The Zbruch idol

fice in Mostyska. Now free to pursue political interests, he was active in the National Democratic party. In 1918–19 he was a member of the Ukrainian National Rada, and subsequently he went into exile with the government of the Western Ukrainian National Republic. After returning to Galicia in 1921, he practiced law in Mostyska and then Peremyshliany and was active in the Ukrainian National Democratic Alliance and civic organizations.

**Zdolbuniv.** III-7. A city (1989 pop 28,000) on the Ustia River and a raion center in Rivne oblast. It was first mentioned in a historical document in 1497. From 1569 it belonged to the Polish Commonwealth, and from 1793, to the Russian Empire. In the 19th century it was part of Rivne county in Volhynia gubernia. In the interwar period it was occupied by Poland. It was taken by Soviet troops in 1939 and granted city status. Today it is a railway junction with coach and locomotive repair shops, a plastics plant, and a cement factory.

*Zdorovlie* (Health). A monthly journal of the *Ukrainian Physicians' Society in Lviv, devoted to problems of sanitation and hygiene, published in 1912–14. Its editor was Ye. *Ozarkevych, and its contributors included I. *Horbachevsky.

**Zdvyzh River** [Zdvyž]. A right-bank tributary of the Teteriv River that flows for 145 km through Zhytomyr and Kiev oblasts and drains a basin area of 1,770 sq km. The river reaches a width of 20 m with a valley of 4 km. It is used for industry, water supply, and irrigation, and a water reservoir is situated on it.

**Zdykhovsky, Oleksander** [Zdyxovs'kyj], b 12 September 1907 in Muravev-Amursk, Far East, Russia. Opera director. A graduate of the Vinnytsia Music Tekhnikum (1929), he worked as a soloist and stage director at the Second Traveling Opera of Right-Bank Ukraine and the Luhanske Opera and Ballet Theater (1932–41). He was chief stage director of the Donetske Opera and Ballet Theater (1948–68) and artistic director of the Donetske Oblast Building of Cultural Workers. He staged operas such as M. Lysenko's *Taras Bulba*, S. Hulak-Artemovsky's *Zaporozhian Cossack beyond the Danube*, Yu. Meitus's *The Young Guard*, P. Tchaikovsky's *Mazeppa* and *Little Shoes*, M. Mussorgsky's *Boris Godunov*, G. Bizet's *Carmen*, and C. Gounod's *Faust*.

**Zdziarski, Stanisław,** b 17 November 1878 in Ternopil, Galicia, d 2 December 1928 in Warsaw. Polish ethnographer and literary scholar. After completing his studies in Lviv, he collected ethnographic materials in Pokutia and published a collection of Pokutian folktales. His major work, *Pierwiastek ludowy w poesji polskiej XIX wieku* (The Folk Element in Polish Literature of the 19th Century, 1901), contains numerous references to Ukrainian folklore.

**Zelenak, Edward,** b 9 November 1940 in St Thomas, Ontario. Sculptor of Ukrainian origin. He studied at the Meinszinger School of Art in Detroit, the Fort Worth Art Center, and the Ontario College of Art. Toward the end of the 1960s he began making large-scale compositions built of fiberglass modules in the form of cylinders, spheres, and elbows (*Stoattalos, Traffic* [1968], *Slingshot* [1969], and

Edward Zelenak with tubular fiberglass works in progress

*Untitled #2* [1972]). Since 1961 he has participated in over 30 group exhibitions in Canada, the United States, Paris, Lausanne, and Bologna. Solo exhibitions of his works have been held in Ottawa (1969, 1972), Toronto (1969, 1970), and Washington, DC (1971). In 1972 he was one of five Ukrainian-Canadian artists to exhibit his work at the Ukrainian Institute of Modern Art in Chicago. He teaches art at the University of Western Ontario.

**Zelenchuk rivers** [Zelenčuk]. Left-bank tributaries of the Kuban River that flow through the Karachai-Cherkess Autonomous Oblast and Stavropol krai. The rivers, the Zelenchuk Velykyi and the Zelenchuk Malyi, are 180 and 140 km long respectively. Their sources are in the Caucasus Mountains.

**Zeleni sviata.** See Rosalia.

**Zelenin, Dmitrii,** b 2 November 1878 in Liuk, Riazan gubernia, d 31 August 1954 in Leningrad. Russian ethnographer and dialectologist; corresponding member of the USSR Academy of Sciences from 1925. A graduate of Yurev (now Tartu) University (1904), he taught at the universities in Kharkiv (1916–25) and Leningrad. His chief works, *Bibliograficheskii ukazatel' russkoi etnograficheskoi literatury o vneshnem byte narodov Rossii, 1700–1910* (A Bibliographic Guide to Russian Ethnographic Literature on the External Life of the Peoples of Russia, 1700–1910, 1913) and *Russische (Ostslavische) Volkskunde* (1927), contain much information about Ukrainian ethnography. He also wrote several articles on the historical relations between the Ukrainian and Russian cultures.

**Zeleniv, Ivan,** b 1861, d 1918. Venereologist. He served as a professor at Kharkiv (1897–1910) and Moscow universities and as editor of the first venereological journal in the Russian Empire, *Russkii zhurnal kozhnykh i venericheskikh boleznei* (1901–17). He was a founder of the Dermatological Society in Kharkiv (1900) and the All-Russian League for Venereological Diseases (1914). Zeleniv established a school of dermatologists and venereologists in Ukraine.

**Zelenodolske** [Zelenodol's'ke]. VI-14. A town smt (1990 pop 15,700) in Apostolove raion, Dnipropetrovske oblast. It was founded in 1961 in conjunction with the build-

ing of the Kryvyi Rih Power Station. The town is on the Dnieper–Kryvyi Rih Canal.

**Zelenohorsky, Fedir** [Zelenohors'kyj], b 1839, d 1909. Philosopher. In 1868 he graduated from Kazan University, where he had studied under M. Troitsky and inherited from him a deep respect for British empiricism. After obtaining a PH D in 1878, he was appointed professor of philosophy at Kharkiv University. He wrote a master's thesis on Aristotle's doctrine of the soul in comparison with the doctrines of Socrates and Plato (1871). In his major work, on the mathematical, metaphysical, inductive, and critical methods of research and proof (1877), he admitted the importance of the inductive method and adopted many empiricist doctrines, such as D. Hume's doctrine of causality, but argued against Troitsky that the other three methods have a legitimate place in philosophy and science. In the 1890s he turned his attention to the history of philosophy in Ukraine and published articles on the influence of H. Skovoroda, J. Schad, and F. Schelling at Kharkiv University.

**Zelensky** [Zelens'kyj]. A family line of Cossack *starshyna* from Right-Bank that resettled in Left-Bank Ukraine. The notable family members included the brothers Mykhailo and Andrii Zelensky. Mykhailo was colonel of Bratslav and Dniester regiments under B. Khmelnytsky. Andrii was colonel of Podilia regiment and a supporter of I. Vyhovsky and Yu. Khmelnytsky; he eventually became a staunch P. Doroshenko loyalist and an envoy to the Crimea. Dmytro *Zelensky also came from the line.

**Zelensky, Dmytro** [Zelens'kyj], b and d ? Cossack officer, descended from Right-Bank nobility. A military fellow (1689) and colonel of Lubni regiment (ca 1700–9), he was a relative and trusted adviser of Hetman I. Mazepa. At the Battle of Poltava (1709) he surrendered to the Russians, who imprisoned him and then in 1711 sent him to Siberia, where he died.

**Zelensky, Viktor** [Zelenskij], b 18 February 1929 in Surochi (now Tabunovka), Balashov raion, Saratov oblast, RSFSR. Materials scientist and solid-state physicist; AN URSR (now ANU) corresponding member since 1978 and full member since 1988. Since graduating from Kharkiv University (1952), he has worked at the ANU Physical-Technical Institute in Kharkiv, where he was appointed an assistant director in 1974 and director in 1988. His main contributions have been in the area of radiation damage to materials, particularly to semiconductors.

**Zeleny, Andrii** [Zelenyj, Andrij], b 1882 in Kamianka Voloska, Rava Ruska county, Galicia, d 28 August 1937 in Lviv. Pedagogue and education activist. Upon graduation from teachers' college in Lviv, he taught in a number of village schools, where he actively promoted organizations such as the *Prosvita society and *Silskyi Hospodar. During the First World War he worked as a mobilization commissioner, and during the postwar struggle for independence he was a school inspector for the Lviv school district. In 1921 he became director of the *Ukrainian Teachers' Mutual Aid Society. He was also active in the *Ridna Shkola society as an associate editor of the publications *Uchytel'*, *Uchytel's'ke slovo*, and *Shliakh navchannia i vykhovannia*. He was a leading member of the *Ukrainian National Democratic Alliance.

**Zeleny, Danylo** [Zelenyj] (pseud of Danylo Terpylo), b 1883 in Trypilia, Kiev county, Kiev gubernia, d November 1919. One of the best-known otamans (warlords) during the Revolution of 1917–21. Zeleny was associated with the left-wing of the *Ukrainian Social Democratic Workers' party (USDRP) (Independents). When that faction broke with the UNR Directory in January 1919, Zeleny led a revolt against the Directory in the vicinity of Obukhiv. The rebellion soon spread from Kiev gubernia to the neighboring Poltava and Chernihiv gubernias. At the peak of his movement Zeleny is said to have commanded over 30,000 troops. In addition to the Directory his troops fought the Bolsheviks and Whites (the Volunteer Army) in 1919. The movement issued several manifestos which reflected the influence of the ideology of the USDRP. Zeleny fell in battle against White forces.

**Zeleny, Pavlo** [Zelenyj], b 1839, d 1912. Writer and civic activist. He published the paper *Odesskii vestnik* (1877–87) and served as mayor of Odessa (1878). He was a strong supporter of public education and initiated the building of a public library.

**Zeleny, Petro** [Zelenyj], b 13 October 1908 in Vysloboky, Lviv county, Galicia, d 4 June 1991 in Antwerp, Belgium. Agronomist; full member of the Shevchenko Scientific Society from 1953. He completed his studies at the Lviv Polytechnical Institute (1932) and worked for Silskyi Hospodar (1933–9) as a district agronomist and publications editor. In 1940 he became a research associate at the department of animal physiology at Berlin University, and in 1946 a lecturer at the Ukrainian Technical and Husbandry Institute in Regensburg and Munich. From 1948 he directed a dairy research station in Belgium. Zeleny wrote numerous scholarly articles, in Ukrainian, Polish, German, and Flemish.

Zenon Zeleny

**Zeleny, Zenon** [Zelenyj], b 2 September 1901 in Dobriany, Lviv county, Galicia, d 2 February 1973 in Toronto. Pedagogue. A graduate of Lviv University (1930), he taught in secondary schools and gymnasiums in Lviv until the Second World War. In 1941–3 he headed the educational committee of the *Ukrainian Central Committee (UTsK), and from 1943, its youth welfare division. In 1948

he emigrated to Canada, where he taught physics and mathematics in secondary schools in Toronto and the surrounding area. He also headed the Association of Ukrainian Pedagogues in Canada and was an active member of the educational council of the *World Congress of Free Ukrainians. In 1965 he published *Ukraïns'ke iunatstvo v vyri druhoï svitovoï viiny* (Ukrainian Youth in the Whirlwind of the Second World War), which details his UTsK work among Ukrainian young people.

**Zelenyi Klyn.** See Far East.

*Zelenyi svit*, the newspaper of the Zelenyi Svit association

**Zelenyi Svit** (Green World, or ZS). An ecological association initiated by the writer Yu. *Shcherbak and established in December 1987 under the aegis of the Ukrainian Committee in Defense of Peace. Shcherbak was elected the first chairman, and D. *Hrodzinsky, V. Sakhaev, and Yu. Tkachenko were elected his deputies. In its first year ZS operated as one of the *neformaly that drew public attention to Ukraine's ecological plight. In November 1988 it was one of the initiators of the first major ecological demonstration in Kiev, which led to new investigations of the Chornobyl nuclear accident. From the outset ZS supported Ukrainian control over energy issues and chemical plants in Ukraine. It sought to educate the public about alleged violations of ecological laws by Moscow-based USSR ministries and advocated a nuclear-free Ukraine and the total shutdown of the Chornobyl and the nearly completed Chyhyryn and Crimean nuclear power stations.

The founding congress of ZS took place in Kiev on 28–29 October 1989. The statute it adopted noted that ZS was a voluntary association of ecological cells and collective members headed by its Green Council and its Control and Inspection Committee. The executive body was declared to be the ZS congress, which was to meet every two years or more frequently if convoked by one-third of the cells.

Initially ZS stated that it would remain apolitical. In practice, however, it soon acquired a political dimension because its activity interfered directly with CPSU, CPU, and USSR government control of Ukraine's economic life. In the spring of 1989 the ZS leader, Shcherbak, was elected a deputy of the USSR Congress of People's Deputies, despite an intensive Party campaign directed against him.

Although ZS has taken an interest in many areas – such as the alopecia outbreak among children in Chernivtsi oblast, the construction of the Danube-Dnieper and other canals, the location of a radar station in Transcarpathia, the relatively short life span of Ukraine's citizens, the depletion of agricultural land through industrial expansion, and water and air pollution – the Chornobyl issue has remained predominant, and it acted as a catalyst in the formation of the *Popular Movement of Ukraine (Rukh), in which ZS has played a part. ZS has organized two major international 'Eurochornobyl' conferences on the effects of Chornobyl (1989, 1991). The politicization of the issue resulted in the division of ZS on 26 April 1990 and the creation of the Green Party of Ukraine, which was modeled to some extent on the German Green party. Shcherbak resigned as chairman of ZS to head the Green party. In 1991 he was also appointed Ukraine's minister of the environment.

D. Marples

**Żeligowski, Edward Witold** (pseud: Antoni Sowa), b 20 July 1816 in Mariampol (now Kapsukas), Lithuania, d 28 December 1864 in Geneva. Polish poet. He was exiled for his Polish revolutionary involvement to Petrozavodsk, Orenburg, and Ufa (1851–7). While in exile he developed an epistolary friendship with T. Shevchenko, a fellow exile, and wrote a poem dedicated to him. After his release, until 1860 he lived in St Petersburg, where he copublished the political paper *Słowo* (1859–60) and met Shevchenko. Shevchenko dedicated his poem 'Posadzhu kolo khatyny' (I'll Plant by the Cottage) to Żeligowski and translated several of his poems.

Gen Viktor Zelinsky         Daria Zelska-Darewych

**Zelinsky, Viktor** [Zelins'kyj], b 1867 in Katerynoslav gubernia, d 14 December 1940 in Sopot, Poland. UNR Army general. In 1918 he was an organizer and commander of the First Division of the *Bluecoats. During 1919–20 he served as chief of the UNR military mission in Poland. After the Ukrainian-Soviet War he was promoted to lieutenant general by the UNR government-in-exile. His memoirs are titled *Syn'ozhupannyky* (Bluecoats, 1938).

*Zeliznychnyk* (Railwayman). A Ukrainian-language monthly organ of the organization of railway workers, published briefly in Chernivtsi (1910) and then in Lviv (1910–18). Edited by O. Bezpalko, V. Levynsky, T. Melen, and A. Chernetsky, the paper contained articles on political and labor topics.

**Zelska-Darewych, Daria** [Zel's'ka-Darevyč, Darija], b 12 February 1939 in Włocławek, Poland. Ukrainian-Cana-

dian art historian and critic. A graduate of the University of London (PH D, 1990) and a specialist in contemporary Soviet Ukrainian painting, since 1982 she has curated over 16 exhibitions of Ukrainian artists, including the traveling Contemporary Artists from Ukraine exhibition (1982–4) and the M. *Levytsky retrospective in Toronto and Winnipeg, and has written articles about Ukrainian artists in Ukraine, France, Germany, and Canada, a monograph about M. Levytsky (1985), and many entries for the *Encyclopedia of Ukraine*, for which she was the art subject editor (vols 3–5).

**Zemanchyk, Ivan** [Zemančyk] (Zemansky, Semantiuk), b ?, d 1822. Naturalist and pedagogue. He was raised in Transcarpathia. He became a professor (1787–1804) at Lviv University, where he taught mathematics and physics in Ukrainian at the *Studium Ruthenum. In 1793 he was dean of the Faculty of Philosophy, and in 1803–4 rector of the university. He later became a professor at Cracow University.

**Zembnytsky, Yakym** [Zembnyc'kyj, Jakym], b 1784 in the Chernihiv region, d 18 November 1851 in St Petersburg. Geologist and educator; full member of the Russian Academy of Sciences. After graduating from the Chernihiv Theological Seminary and the Main Pedagogical Institute in St Petersburg (1807) he taught in several schools in St Petersburg and then obtained a position at St Petersburg University (1819). Under his presidency (1827–42) the Imperial Mineralogy Society expanded its activities and publishing program. He wrote many articles on mineralogy and paleobotany, including an introductory survey of the fossil plants known in his day (1832).

**Zemhano, Ihor** (real surname: Yutsevych), b 1904 in Kharkiv. Stage and film director. After a brief stay in Berezil, he was a director in the Kharkiv Chervonozavodskyi Ukrainian Drama Theater (1928, 1931), the Kharkiv Theater of the Revolution (1931–7), and the Odessa State Jewish Theater (1938–41). After 1944 he worked in film and television. His film *Ukraïns'ki melodiï* (Ukrainian Melodies, 1945) was criticized for 'nationalism.'

**Zemka, Tarasii**, b ?, d 13 September 1632 in Kiev. Churchman, poet, and printer. He became preacher at the Kievan Cave Monastery in 1625, and hegumen of the Kiev Epiphany Brotherhood Monastery, a teacher at the brotherhood school, and director of the Kievan Cave Monastery Press in 1627. An erudite scholar who knew Greek, Latin, Church Slavonic, and Ukrainian, he edited or translated several Greek theological texts and liturgical books into Ukrainian, including a *Triodion* (1627), *Nomacanon* (1629), and *Liturgicon* (1629). A number of these works included his prefaces or commentary and several of his poems.

*Zemlia* (Land). A weekly newspaper for Galician Ukrainians forced to work as agricultural laborers in Germany. It was published in 1942–5 by a German farmers' organization in Plauen. The editor was S. Nykorovych.

**Zemlia i Volia** (Land and Freedom, or ZiV). The name of two Russian revolutionary organizations. The first was founded in St Petersburg in late 1861. It loosely united several conspiratorial groups of the socialist, democratic, and liberal intelligentsia in various cities of the Russian Empire. In Ukraine ZiV had several small groups, notably in Poltava. The clandestine Warsaw-based Committee of Russian Officers in Poland, headed by the Ukrainian A. *Potebnia, joined ZiV in 1862. ZiV propagated the overthrow of tsarism by a peasant revolution, the abolition of redemption payments, military conscription, and government bureaucracy, and the introduction of peasant, county, and gubernial self-rule and government by a democratically elected, federal popular assembly. It issued several proclamations and two leaflets before it fell apart in the spring of 1864, after most of its members were arrested in the wake of the suppression of the Polish Insurrection of 1863–4.

The second ZiV was formed in 1876 by Russian *populists in St Petersburg. Called originally the Northern Revolutionary Populist Group, the conspiratorial party became known as ZiV after its organ *Zemlia i volia* (1878–9). The goals of the *Southern Rebels group (1875–7) in Ukraine, led by Ya. Stefanovych and V. Debohorii-Mokriievych, were similar to those of the ZiV, and after the group's suppression several of its members (eg, Stefanovych, L. Deich, M. Frolenko, V. Zasulich) joined ZiV. Tsarist repression and arrests defeated the ZiV strategy of agitation and settlement in the villages, and in late 1877 those of its members who were still at large in Kiev, Kharkiv, Mykolaiv, and Odessa began using terrorism as a political weapon against tsarist officials. In August 1879 ZiV split into the terrorist *Narodnaia Volia, headed by A. Zheliabov, and the less violent Chernyi Peredel (Black Repartition) group, headed by G. Plekhanov, which lasted until the mid-1880s.

BIBLIOGRAPHY
Popov, M. *Zemlevol'tsi na Ukraïni* (Kharkiv 1930)
Zhuchenko, V. *Sotsial'no-ekonomichna prohrama revoliutsiinoho narodnytstva na Ukraïni* (Kiev 1969)
Rud'ko, M. *Revoliutsiini narodnyky na Ukraïni (70-ti roky XIX st.)* (Kiev 1973)

R. Senkus

*Zemlia i volia* (Chernivtsi)

***Zemlia i volia*** (Land and Freedom). A weekly (later semimonthly and then irregular) organ of the *Ukrainian Social Democratic party, published in Chernivtsi in 1906 and in Lviv in 1907–13, 1919–20, and 1922–4. It was edited in 1906 by M. Ogrodnik; in 1907–13 by M. Hankevych, V. Levynsky, S. Vityk, V. Starosolsky, Yu. Bachynsky, and P. Buniak; and in 1919–22 by M. Filts, P. Buniak, I. Kvasny-

tsia, and A. Chernetsky. From the fall of 1923 it was controlled by a group of supporters of O. Shumsky, a prominent leader of the CP(B)U, and edited by S. Volynets. The paper was closed down by the Polish authorities in January 1924, after it openly voiced support for the platform of the Comintern.

***Zemlia i volia*** (Land and Freedom). An underground organ of the *Communist Party of Western Ukraine (KPZU), published irregularly in 1925–9. Issues were printed mostly in Germany, but also by an illegal KPZU press near Warsaw, and smuggled into Western Ukraine. For a short time in 1929 both major factions of the KPZU published a journal with the same name.

***Zemlia i volia*** (Land and Freedom). An organ of the Ukrainian section of the Czechoslovak Agrarian party in Transcarpathia, published in Mukachiv semimonthly in 1934–6 and then weekly to 1938. It was edited by S. Klochurak and Yu. Latsanych. In 1935 it published *Molodyi pluhar* as a biweekly supplement for youths.

**Zemliak, Vasyl** [Zemljak, Vasyl'] (pseud of Vasyl Vatsyk), b 23 April 1923 in Koniushivka, now in Lypovets raion, Vinnytsia oblast, d 17 March 1977 in Kiev. Writer. He graduated from the Zhytomyr Agricultural Institute (1953) and from 1958 worked in publishing. From 1963 to 1966 he was editor in chief at the Kiev Artistic Film Studio. He first published his writings in 1945. Subsequently he became popular as a result of his works on modern village life, such as the novelettes *Ridna storona* (Native Lands, 1956), *Kam'ianyi Brid* (1957), and *Hnivnyi Stration* (The Angry Stration, 1960). He went on to publish the novelette *Pidpolkovnyk Shymans'kyi* (Lieutenant Colonel Shymansky, 1966), the novels *Lebedyna zhraia* (The Swan Flock, 1971; English trans 1982) and *Zeleni Mlyny* (1976), and the play *Prezydent* (The President, 1975), about S. Allende. Several films based on Zemliak's work have been made.

**Zemplén komitat** (Ukrainian: Zemplyn). Until 1918 an administrative territory in northern Hungary, with Sátoralja-Ujhely (Nové Mesto) its center. The northern part of the komitat was populated mainly by Ukrainians, and the southern part by Slovaks and Hungarians. In 1910 the region settled by Ukrainians (1,650 sq km) had a population of 48,000, 77 percent of whom were Ukrainian. Since 1919 the Ukrainian and Slovak regions have been part of Slovakia (see *Prešov region).

**Zemstvo.** A gubernia and county institution for municipal self-government that existed in most European gubernias of the Russian Empire from 1865 until the Bolshevik Revolution. Under pressure from liberal nobles and the intelligentsia, Tsar Alexander II confirmed the Zemstvo Statute on 1 January 1864. Electoral institutions, specifically gubernia and county zemstvo assemblies (decision-making bodies) and zemstvo boards (executive bodies), were introduced in 1865. The jurisdiction of the zemstvos included municipal, economic, social, and educational affairs. They were to manage property, build and maintain roads, undertake measures for the improvement of agriculture, trade, and industry, and oversee medical services, sanitation, public education, veterinary services, insurance, fire prevention, and other activities. The work was financed by special taxes on agricultural land, commercial and industrial properties, and business and guild licenses, as well as direct government subsidies (the latter initially constituted only a small portion of revenues, but increased substantially after 1905). Provincial zemstvo organizations were established in 1865 in Chernihiv, Kharkiv, Kherson, and Poltava gubernias and in 1866 in Katerynoslav and Tavriia gubernia. They were not introduced in Right-Bank Ukraine (Kiev, Volhynia, and Podilia gubernias) until 1911 because of official concerns about extending local institutions of self-government into areas where a large portion of the nobility was Polish (particularly after the Polish Insurrection of 1863–4).

The zemstvo consisted of a mix of appointed and elected delegates. Separate electoral bodies existed for three classes of delegates, landowners, merchants and industrialists, and peasants. Those provisions were modified in 1890 in a revised Zemstvo Statute, which limited landowner representation to the nobility and turned over the selection of peasant representatives to the provincial governor. Orthodox clergymen and Jews were also forbidden to hold zemstvo offices at that time. All zemstvo positions had a three-year term, and the zemstvo assemblies usually sat once a year. In spite of provisions for representation from various estates, the zemstvo structure was dominated by the gentry both in absolute numbers and in leadership positions. As a rule the delegates from the nobility had more than half the votes in county zemstvo assemblies. They tended to have an even greater representation on the county executive boards and in the gubernia zemstvo organizations. In 1903 the county zemstvo councils in Ukrainian gubernias consisted of 83 percent nobility, 9.3 percent peasantry, and 7.7 percent others. In Kherson gubernia the county councils consisted entirely of nobility. After 1890 the appointed heads of zemstvo administrations were ratified by the governor (for county administrations) and by the minister of the interior (for gubernia administrations). The various zemstvo institutions were placed under the control and supervision of the state administration: all decisions of the zemstvo had to be ratified by the governor or the minister of the interior, who also had the power to nullify them; and elected zemstvo clerks were included in the general state administrative system.

Notwithstanding those limitations the zemstvos carried out a great deal of work in numerous areas of municipal management. They contributed significantly to the development of agriculture in Ukraine by creating a network of county and gubernia agronomists, introducing much-needed agricultural innovations (notably in machinery and equipment, seed, and fertilizer), launching a popular-education movement among the rural population (exhibitions, courses, lessons, popular brochures), establishing a series of agricultural schools, initiating agronomic projects (research stations, soil research, and the like), setting up insurance schemes, organizing a veterinary service, promoting the development of livestock breeding, supporting the co-operative movement, and assisting in the establishment of co-operative credit institutions serving the needs of the peasantry, village tradesmen, and others (see *Agriculture, *Agronomy, and *Agronomy, state and social). Zemstvo institutions built roads and organized the so-called zemstvo post (in areas

not reached by state postal service). Their work in public education was widespread; it started with the establishment of a network of primary schools, which was followed later by secondary and vocational schools (see *Zemstvo schools). Zemstvos commonly supported popular education (Sunday schools, rural and village libraries, vocational courses, public lectures, and the like). They are credited with the introduction of public health programs (see *Zemstvo medicine) in the countryside.

The work of the zemstvos in gathering statistical data and economic information about various regions of Ukraine resulted in the preparation of over 100 studies. In their day those had practical applications and, in some cases, political implications. Today they constitute a valuable source of historical information (see *Statistics).

In spite of their political domination by the nobility and attempts by the state to confine or control their activities, zemstvos developed into a liberal institution. They often attracted liberal nobles and the intelligentsia into their structure. They employed a large number of professional people (frequently referred to as 'the third element') and represented the most viable source of employment for educated persons outside official state service in the bureaucracy or military. Because they were mandated to provide services at a local, county, or gubernia level, the zemstvos commonly developed a greater loyalty to their region and its inhabitants than to the imperial bureaucracy, which functioned as the arm of a highly centralized government. The zemstvos' implicit political potential was already becoming obvious in the 1870s, when they frequently petitioned the tsar to establish a constitution for the empire. In the period of reaction following the assassination of Alexander II in 1881, the functions of local institutions, including the zemstvo, were reviewed. The review ultimately gave birth to the revised Zemstvo Statute of 1890, which increased state control over zemstvo activities. The zemstvo, nevertheless, maintained its liberal character and continued to engage or employ people regarded as politically suspect. The implicit political functions of the zemstvos were assumed by the political parties that emerged in the Russian Empire after the Revolution of 1905.

As an institution of local self-government the zemstvo often reflected the characteristics of its own region. In that respect the zemstvos of Ukraine could claim certain distinctive features, and some (notably those in Chernihiv and Poltava) could be called Ukrainophile in their orientation. The Poltava zemstvo initiated the building of a monument to I. Kotliarevsky in Poltava in 1903. The Poltava Zemstvo building (1905) was deliberately designed in a Ukrainian style by B. Krychevsky. Among the zemstvo employees in Ukraine were Ukrainian intellectuals, many of whom were ill disposed to the tsarist regime. For a good number of them the zemstvo institution served as a school for future involvement in the 1917–20 Ukrainian state. Among the eminent Ukrainian zemstvo activists in the Poltava region were P. Chyzhevsky, F. Lyzohub, B. Martos, O. Obolonsky, I. Prysetsky, and V. Shemet. Notables in the Chernihiv region included P. Doroshenko, I. Petrunkevych, O. Rusov, M. Savytsky, I. Shrah, O. Tyshchynsky, and F. Umanets.

The zemstvos functioned largely independently of one another. The Zemstvo Alliance was formed by zemstvo employees after a congress in Moscow in 1879, but the zemstvo institutions were not united until 1914. Even then the All-Russian Union of Zemstvos was created to co-ordinate medical aid for the empire's war effort rather than to expedite common zemstvo policy.

After the outbreak of the Revolution of 1917 the zemstvos became full-fledged institutions of municipal self-government. According to resolutions passed by the Provisional Government (21 May and 9 June 1917), district zemstvo institutions were established, and any citizen could be elected to them. Zemstvo institutions also gained the right to pass binding legislation, and the supervision of the state administration was limited to a review of the legality of their activities. Public safety (the militia) came under their jurisdiction. In Ukraine the zemstvos started a process of Ukrainianization and filled their ranks with Ukrainian political activists. The Kiev newspaper *Zems'ka hazeta* began to publish in Ukrainian.

The All-Ukrainian Union of Zemstvos, founded in April 1918, linked gubernia zemstvo administrations under S. Petliura. The zemstvo institutions later were opposed to the Hetman government, which had begun to assert greater administrative control over them. On 5 September 1918 the Zemstvo Statute was altered, and a curial system of elections was reintroduced. The electoral reform was only partly implemented before the Ukrainian-Soviet War caused the zemstvos to curtail their activities. The UNR government then dissolved the zemstvo assemblies until their re-election and transferred their competency to the appropriate state administrations. The legislation was stillborn, however, as Bolshevik troops established effective control over Ukraine shortly thereafter. The zemstvos were then dissolved, and their functions were assumed by local Soviet councils (soviets).

BIBLIOGRAPHY
Dragomanov, M. *Liberalizm i zemstvo v Rossii* (Geneva 1889)
Veselovskii, B. *Istoriia zemstva za 40 let*, 4 vols (St Petersburg 1909–11; repr, Cambridge 1973)
Doroshenko, V. *Z istoriï zemstva na Ukraïni* (Lviv 1910)
Shcherbina, F. *Istoriia poltavskogo zemstva* (Poltava 1915)
V. Markus

**Zemstvo agronomy.** See Agronomy, state and social.

**Zemstvo head** (Russian: *zemskoi nachalnik*). A judicial and administrative position established in the Russian Empire in 1889. The zemstvo head performed some of the functions of a justice of the peace (particularly in regard to criminal cases) and tried civil cases involving sums up to 3,000 rubles. He also had the authority to impose direct fines and to arrest people. He oversaw the administration of villages and *volosti*. Candidates for the post were chosen from among the local landowners by the governor and were appointed by the minister of the interior.

**Zemstvo medicine.** A system of medical and sanitary services in Ukraine under Russian rule, implemented as part of the *land reforms in 1865, except in the gubernias of Kiev, Volhynia, and Podilia, where it was implemented in 1911.

Zemstvo physicians gradually established a network of stationary dispensaries, medical clinics, and hospitals, mostly for the peasant population. They were financed by the collection of taxes from the whole population. Medical services were free, with some exceptions where small fees were charged. Zemstvo physicians also took over the care

and treatment of the mentally ill. They were responsible for the control of epidemics of cholera, diphtheria, and syphilis. Smallpox vaccination was also under their jurisdiction. Since they were also responsible for the training of medical personnel, mainly medics and doctors' assistants, zemstvo physicians founded schools for medics, including institutes of bacteriology in Odessa, Katerynoslav, and Chernihiv. Despite the shortcomings of the system and the relatively small number of medical institutions, which could not possibly serve the large population and such a large area, zemstvo medicine played an important part in the growth of medical science and health care in Ukraine. It established and developed, as far as was possible, the stationary medical care unit for the local population, introduced the prophylactic approach to health care, and initiated the recording of sanitation statistics.

BIBLIOGRAPHY
*Trudy XI-go gubernskago s''ezda zemskikh vrachei i predstavitelei zemskikh uchrezhdenii Ekaterinoslavskoi gubernii 20–29 marta 1914 goda*, vol 1 (Katerynoslav 1914)
Bortkevich', Ia. *Zemskaia meditsina v Verkhnedneprovskom uezde za 1913 god* (Verkhnodniprovske 1915)
*Zemsko-meditsinskii otchet Volynskoi gubernii za 1915 god* (Zhytomyr 1917)
Igumnov, S. *Ocherki razvitiia zemskoi meditsiny v guberniakh, voshedshikh v sostav USSR, v Bessarabii i v Krymu* (Kiev 1940)
P. Dzul

**Zemstvo schools** (*zemski shkoly*). Elementary and, later, secondary and vocational schools in the Russian Empire, established and financed by *zemstvo authorities. Zemstvo schools were established in 1864 in the wake of the agrarian reform and existed until 1917. They played a significant role in democratizing and improving the quality of public education, particularly in the villages. In general, reactionary forces in the tsarist government and the Holy Synod disapproved of the work done by zemstvos in the sphere of public education. Zemstvo schools compared favorably both with schools run by the Ministry of Education and with *parochial schools. The literacy rate was 19.9 percent in 1897 in zemstvo gubernias, and 16.9 percent in non-zemstvo gubernias. Though the zemstvo authorities had the sole responsibility for the organizing and funding of zemstvo schools, the administration of the schools was entirely in the hands of the central government. The zemstvos had no direct jurisdiction over curriculum, teaching methods, or hiring practices. Zemstvo representatives were outnumbered on the district and gubernia school councils created by the state to supervise the zemstvo schools. In 1874 the zemstvos were granted the right to nominate candidates for teaching positions in zemstvo schools. District zemstvos were responsible for the founding of elementary zemstvo schools, and gubernia zemstvos did the organized training courses for teachers, founded museums, libraries, and bookstores to serve zemstvo teachers, and established professional zemstvo schools. In 1898 there were 3,117 zemstvo schools in Ukraine. The figure increased in the period 1900–10 to 4,700 schools, with 460,000 pupils and 8,458 teachers. In 1914, in Tavriia gubernia there were 827 zemstvo schools, in Kherson gubernia, 1,087, in Kharkiv gubernia, 1,248, and in Katerynoslav gubernia, 945. In Right-Bank Ukraine, where the zemstvo structure was not introduced until 1911, the numbers were much lower. By 1912, in

Kiev gubernia there were 149 zemstvo schools, and in Podilia and Volhynia gubernias, only a few isolated schools. Because their formation depended on local initiative, zemstvo schools were often unevenly distributed.

Initially zemstvo schools had a three-year program. In the 1890s a fourth year was added, and by the time zemstvo schools were abolished in 1917, some seven-year schools had been established. The curriculum consisted of religion, reading, writing, arithmetic, and sometimes singing. Texts used at the zemstvo schools were superior to those used at their Ministry of Education and parochial school counterparts and included the primer *Rodnoe slovo* (Native Word) by K. *Ushinsky, the primer *Azbuka* (Alphabet) and simple readers by L. Tolstoy, and *Nash drug* (Our Friend) by N. Korf. Both Ushinsky, a well-known teacher, and Korf, a landowner in Oleksandriia county, Katerynoslav gubernia, were instrumental in the establishment of zemstvo schools. Korf pioneered the economical one-room school system in which a single teacher taught pupils of all ages in a single classroom. Between 1867 and 1872 Korf founded 80 new zemstvo schools in his gubernia.

Although most zemstvo schools were elementary schools, zemstvos at the gubernia level also founded some professional schools. Among them were the Industrial Arts and Ceramics School in Myrhorod and vocational schools in Novomoskovske and Poltava. In the 1870s a zemstvo seminary to train teachers was founded in Chernihiv, but it was closed in 1878 at the insistence of the Ministry of Education. Some zemstvos also established gymnasiums. The first was the Hlukhiv county zemstvo progymnasium, founded in the 1860s, which became a gymnasium in 1876.

County and gubernia zemstvos often came into conflict with the government over the use of Ukrainian in zemstvo schools. In 1870 zemstvo activist M. Konstantynovych raised the language issue at a meeting of the Chernihiv district zemstvo. It was broached again in 1881, at a session of the Chernihiv gubernia zemstvo, by N. Korf. In 1895 the Yelysavethrad zemstvo discussed the use of Ukrainian. In 1904–5, zemstvos passed resolutions concerning the Ukrainian language, but these were rejected by the government. Teachers who used Ukrainian as a teaching aid in zemstvo schools were dismissed.

C. Freeland, S. Siropolko

**Zemstvo statistics.** See Statistics.

**Zenkovsky, Vasilii** [Zen'kovskij, Vasilij], b 1881 in Podilia gubernia, d 5 August 1962 in Paris. Russian philosopher and theologian of Ukrainian descent. After graduating from Kiev University (MA, 1912) he taught philosophy there (1912–19) and directed the Institute for Preschool Education. In the 1918 Hetman government he served as minister of religious affairs in F. Lyzohub's cabinet. A White émigré from 1920, he lived in Belgrade (to 1923); in Prague, where he founded the Russian Pedagogical Institute; and in Paris, where he served as a professor and dean at the Russian Theological Institute. Suspected of pro-German sympathies, in 1939–40 he was imprisoned in a French concentration camp. In 1942 he was ordained an Orthodox priest. Early in his career he wrote on the mind-body problem and defended the theory of interactionism. In the interwar period he contributed to the Russian émigré press and published several monographs in

educational psychology. His chief contribution lies in his studies in the history of Russian philosophy, which encompassed many Ukrainian thinkers: *Istoriia russkoi filosofii* (A History of Russian Philosophy, 2 vols, 1948, 1950; English trans 1953), *Russkie mysliteli i Evropa* (Russian Thinkers and Europe, 1926; 2nd edn 1955; English trans 1953), and *Aus der Geschichte der ästhetischen Ideen in Russland im 19. und 20. Jahrhundert* (1958). He also wrote a book on N. Gogol (1961).

**Zerkal, Sava** [Zerkal'], b 18 April 1896 in Khmeliv, Romen county, Poltava gubernia, d ? Educator and agronomist. During the First World War he served in the UNR Army. After emigrating to Czechoslovakia, he graduated from the Ukrainian Husbandry Academy in Poděbrady (1928) and worked as an agronomist in Bratislava (1928–45). He founded the *Society of Ukrainian Engineers in Prague (1929). After the Second World War he lectured at the Ukrainian Technical and Husbandry Institute in Munich. In 1949 he emigrated to the United States, where he lectured at the Ukrainian Technological Institute in New York and published the magazine *Ukraïns'ke hromads'ke slovo* (1953–8). He wrote many journalistic articles, a few booklets on Transcarpathia, and *Ruïna kozats'ko-selians'koï Ukraïny* (The Destruction of Cossack-Peasant Ukraine, 1968).

**Zerkalo** (Mirror). A semimonthly illustrated humor magazine published in Lviv in 1882–6 (in 1883–5 as *Nove zerkalo*). Editors and regular contributors to both magazines included K. Ustyianovych (who also illustrated the journal), V. Nahirny, K. Levytsky, Ye. Olesnytsky, I. Hrabovych, V. Kotsovsky, V. Liskovatsky, V. Masliak, and I. Franko. *Zerkalo* directed most of its satire against the Russophile movement in Western Ukraine.

**Zerkalo** (Mirror). A semimonthly political humor magazine published in Lviv in 1889–93. It was edited by V. Levytsky and then I. Krylovsky.

**Zerkalo** (Mirror). A semimonthly humor magazine published in Lviv in 1906–10. It claimed to be the continuation of the magazine with the same title published to 1893, and retained the same numbering system. The editor was O. Dembitsky. In 1910 it appeared as *Nove zerkalo*.

Dmytro Zerov                    Mykola Zerov

**Zerov, Dmytro,** b 20 September 1895 in Zinkiv, Poltava gubernia, d 20 December 1971 in Kiev. Botanist, brother of M. *Zerov; full member of the AN URSR (now ANU) from 1948. A graduate of Kiev University (1922), he taught there (1920–57) and worked for the VUAN and ANU (from 1921), as director of the Institute of Botany in 1946–63. He wrote *Torfovi mokhy Ukraïny* (Peat Mosses of Ukraine, 1928) and *Bolota URSR* (Wetlands of the Ukrainian SSR, 1938) and edited the journal *Ukraïns'kyi botanichnyi zhurnal*, the multivolume *Flora URSR, Vyznachnyk roslyn Ukraïny* (Field Guide to Plants of Ukraine, 1965), and *Vyznachnyk hrybiv Ukraïny* (Field Guide to Fungi of Ukraine, 1967).

**Zerov, Mykola,** b 26 April 1890 in Zinkiv, Poltava gubernia, d 3 November 1937 in the Solovets Islands. Poet, translator, and literary historian. He studied philology at Kiev University. From 1917 to 1920 he edited the bibliographical journal *Knyhar*. He was a professor of Ukrainian literature at the Kiev Architectural Institute (1918–20), the Kiev Co-operative Tekhnikum (1935–5), and the Kiev Institute of People's Education (1923–35). He also taught the theory of translation at the Ukrainian Institute of Linguistic Education (1930–3). He was arrested by the NKVD in April 1935 and sentenced to 10 years' imprisonment in the Solovets Islands. On 9 October 1937 he was resentenced, to death by firing squad.

Zerov's literary activity, both as a poet and as a translator, was in complete harmony with his ideals and theoretical postulates. An avowed classicist and Parnassian, he became the leader of the *Neoclassicists. He concentrated on the sonnet and Alexandrine verse and produced excellent examples of both forms. He translated numerous works of Latin poetry. He also devoted attention to sonnets in other literatures and translated the works of J.-M. Hérédia, P. de Ronsard, J. Du Bellay, A. Mickiewicz, I. Bunin, and others. He wrote criticism on contemporary Soviet Ukrainian literary works, articles on literary translation, and introductions to editions of Ukrainian classics; edited anthologies; and took part in the *Literary Discussion. His published translations include *Antolohiia rym-s'koï poeziï* (An Anthology of Roman Poetry, 1920), *Kamena* (1924; 2nd edn 1943), and J. Słowacki's *Mazepa* (1925). Among his poetic works published posthumously and abroad are *Sonnetarium* (1948), *Catalepton* (1952), and *Corollarium* (1958). His literary histories include *Nove ukraïns'ke pys'menstvo* (New Ukrainian Writings, vol 1, 1924), *Do dzherel* (To the Sources, 1926; 2nd edn 1943), *Vid Kulisha do Vynnychenka* (From Kulish to Vynnychenko, 1928), and *Lektsiï z istoriï ukraïns'koï literatury* (Lessons on the History of Ukrainian Literature, 1977). In 1958 Zerov was formally rehabilitated, and *Vybrane* (Selections) of his poetry was published in 1966, but a full rehabilitation was blocked by hostility from official critics, such as L. Novychenko and M. Shamota. In the late 1980s, on the initiative of H. Kochur, Zerov's works began to be collected seriously for publication. The fullest edition of his works was published in 1990 in two volumes.

V. Derzhavyn, I. Koshelivets

**Zhabche** [Žabče]. A village in Lutske county, Volhynia, which became notorious for Polish persecution of Orthodox believers. In the winter of 1929 the parish priest, V. Sahaidakivsky, and 152 parishioners locked themselves in the church for 10 days. The Polish militia broke into the church, arrested them, and delivered them to the prison in Lutske. The incident aroused protests from Ukrainian delegates in the Sejm representing the Ukrainian National Democratic Alliance (S. Biliak, O. Vyslotsky, I. Zavalykut). Zhabche came to symbolize the struggle of Ukrainians in Volhynia against Polonization.

**Zhabie.** See Verkhovyna.

**Zhabie-Selietyn Depression.** A section of the Middle-Carpathian Depression centered in the area between the Cheremosh and the Suceava rivers. The formation is 10–12 km wide and sits at an elevation of 600–1,000 m. The area is relatively flat and has a high population density. Most of the inhabitants in the region are Hutsuls. Its major centers include Verkhovyna (formerly Zhabie), Selietyn, Storozhynets, and Putyliv.

Rev Lev Zhabko-Potapovych    Vladimir Zhabotinsky

**Zhabko-Potapovych, Lev** [Žabko-Potapovyč, Lev], b 1890, d 8 November 1975 in Crum Lynne, Pennsylvania. Ukrainian Baptist leader and civic activist. The head of the Ukrainian Baptist Missionary Society and the pastor of a church in Lviv during the interwar era, he sought to infuse the Baptist movement there with a strong sense of Ukrainian national identity. He later served as a pastor in Chester, Pennsylvania; edited the newspaper *Pislanets' pravdy*; and wrote *Khrystove svitlo v Ukraïni* (Christ's Light in Ukraine, 1952), a history of the Ukrainian Baptist movement.

**Zhabokrytsky, Denys Dionysii** [Žabokryc'kyj], b 1652, d 1715 in Moscow. Uniate bishop. He was nominated as Orthodox bishop of Lutske by King Jan III Sobieski in 1695 and consecrated by the bishop of Maramureş, Y. Stoika, in 1696. In 1702 he joined the Uniate church and was reconsecrated by Metropolitan L. Zalensky. Tsar Peter I had him arrested and exiled in 1709, first to Kiev and then to Moscow, where he died in prison. S. Kurganovich published a study of him in Kiev in 1914.

**Zhabotinsky, Vladimir** [Žabotinskij] (Jabotinsky, Ze'ev), b 18 October 1880 in Odessa, d 4 August 1940 near Hunter, New York. Writer, journalist, and Zionist activist. He worked in Bern and Rome as a foreign correspondent for the newspapers *Odesskii listok* and *Odesskie novosti* and then continued his journalistic activity in Odessa, where he became an active Zionist. From 1903 he lived in St Petersburg, where he espoused a strong Zionist viewpoint in the journals *Evreiskaia zhizn'* and *Razsvet* and undertook extensive organizational work among Jewish journalists and politicians. With the outbreak of the First World War Zhabotinsky approached Britain with a proposal for the creation of a Jewish Legion, in the belief that such an organization would assist in the eventual creation of a Jewish homeland in Palestine. His idea was accepted, although it did not have the impact he had anticipated. After the war Zhabotinsky continued to write and promote the idea of massive Jewish emigration to Palestine.

Zhabotinsky's writings were largely devoted to the national question. He was favorably disposed to Ukrainian national concerns, which he saw as compatible with Jewish ones, and he developed links with Ukrainian activists. Those links caused a falling out with Zionist leaders in 1921, after he had negotiated an arrangement with his friend M. Slavinsky (a representative of the UNR government-in-exile) to have a Jewish gendarmery follow an anticipated invasion force (led by S. Petliura) into Ukraine in order to protect the Jewish population from possible pogroms. Ultimately the controversy prompted Zhabotinsky to resign from the executive of the World Zionist Organization. A collection of his works was published in Ukrainian translation as *Vybrani statti z natsional'noho pytannia* (Selected Articles on the National Question, 1983).

BIBLIOGRAPHY
Brenner, L. *The Iron Wall: Zionist Revisionism from Jabotinsky to Shamir* (London 1984)
Schechtman, J. *The Vladimir Jabotinsky Story*, 2 vols (1956, 1961); repub as *The Life and Times of Vladimir Jabotinsky*, 2 vols (Silver Spring, Md 1986)

A. Makuch

**Zhabotyn kurhans and settlement.** Early Scythian kurhans and a settlement of the 7th to 6th century BC near Zhabotyn, Kamianka raion, Cherkasy oblast. The kurhans were excavated in the late 19th to early 20th century, and the settlement, in 1951–8. The kurhans contained the burials of military and clan nobility in a variety of wooden crypts. Common grave goods included weapons and armor, horse trappings, pottery, and adornments with zoomorphic designs. Excavations of the settlement revealed surface and pit dwellings, religious structures with the remains of sacrificial altars, pottery, and a variety of adornments that testify to local trade ties with the northern Black Sea and Caucasus regions.

Leonid Zhabotynsky

Edvard Zharsky

**Zhabotynsky, Leonid** [Žabotyns'kyj], b 28 January 1938 in Krasnopillia, Sumy oblast. Heavyweight weightlifting champion. He was the 1964 and 1968 Olympic gold medalist, the 1965 and 1966 world champion, and the 1966 and 1968 European champion. He won many Ukrainian and USSR championships and set 17 world records in 1963–70 and 1973.

**Zhabyntsi.** A multi-occupational archeological site located near Zhabyntsi, now in Husiatyn raion, Ternopil oblast. Excavations in the late 19th century by A. *Kirkor and G. *Ossowski uncovered the remains of settlements from Trypilian to Rus' times.

*Zhalo* (Sting). A semimonthly humor and satire magazine. It appeared under the editorship of S. Terletsky, P. Buniak, O. Liubomir, and M. Holubets in Lviv weekly in 1913 and semimonthly in 1914. In 1923 the magazine was briefly renewed by Buniak.

**Zhar River** [Zhar]. A right-bank tributary of the Boh River that flows eastward for 95 km through Khmelnytskyi and Vinnytsia oblasts and drains a basin area of 1,170 sq km. The river is 5–10 m in width (maximum 40 m) and 0.5–1.5 m in depth, with a valley up to 4 km wide. It is used for water supply, pisciculture, and irrigation.

**Zharko, Fedir** [Žarko], b 17 June 1914 in Mykhailivka, Cherkasy county, Kiev gubernia, d 17 July 1986 in Kiev. Banduryst. He graduated from the Cherkasy Pedagogical Institute in 1936 and sang as a soloist with the State Banduryst Kapelle of the Ukrainian SSR (1946–74). His repertoire included folk songs, dumas, and songs by Soviet composers. He compiled two collections of songs, which he arranged for voice with bandura accompaniment under the title *Ukraïns'ki narodni pisni* (Ukrainian Folk Songs, 1967 and 1969).

**Zharsky, Edvard** [Žars'kyj], b 1906. Zoologist, ichthyologist, and pedagogue; full member of the Shevchenko Scientific Society from 1960. A director of research fisheries in Galicia, he wrote *Zoloto z hlyny* (Gold from Clay, 1937), *Ryby richok Ukraïny* (Fish of Ukraine's Rivers, 1947), and *Atlas ryb* (Atlas of Fish, 1948). After emigrating to New York in 1949, he taught at the Ukrainian Technological Institute in New York and contributed to *Entsyklopedia ukraïnoznavstva* (1955–84), *Ukraine: A Concise Encyclopaedia* (1963, 1971), and *Encyclopedia of Ukraine* (vols 1–2, 1984, 1988).

**Zharsky, Yevhen** [Žars'kyi, Jevhen], b 1834 in Chertizh, now in Zhydachiv raion, Lviv oblast, d 1892 in Lviv. Pedagogue and writer. A teacher of Ukrainian language and literature in Ternopil (from approx 1865), he wrote two epic poems (*Sviatyi vechir* [Christmas Eve] and *Marusia Bohuslavka* [1862]), literary critiques, and numerous articles published in Ukrainian newspapers and journals in Galicia, including *Zoria halytska*, *Vechernytsi*, and *Meta*. He also translated works by J.W. von Goethe and H. Heine into Ukrainian, and in 1877 he published the collection *Poeziï* (Poems). In the 1880s he moved to Lviv, where he joined the *Russophiles.

**Zhashkiv** [Žaškiv]. IV-11. A city (1989 pop 16,900) on the Torch River and a raion center in Cherkasy oblast. It was first mentioned in historical documents at the beginning of the 17th century, when it belonged to the Ostrozky family. In 1648 it threw off Polish rule and became part of Uman regiment. Zhashkiv was returned to Poland in 1667 and captured by the haidamakas in 1738. After the partition of Poland in 1793, it was annexed by Russia, and in 1840 it became a volost center in Tarashcha county, Kiev gubernia. In the second half of the 19th century the town had a sugar refinery, brewery, and winery. The construction of a rail link with Pohrebyshche in 1927 encouraged further industrial development. It was granted city status in 1956. Today the city's factories produce sugar, powdered milk, bricks, clothing, and bread.

Hryhorii Zhatkovych

**Zhatkovych, Hryhorii** [Žatkovyč, Hryhorij] (also Zsatkovich, Gregory Žatkovich), b 1886 in Holubyne, Bereg county, Transcarpathia, d 26 March 1967 in Pittsburgh. Lawyer and political leader. He emigrated in 1891 with his parents to the United States, where he completed law studies and worked for General Motors. Although Zhatkovych himself was not actively involved in community affairs, he had some profile among the immigrant population through the activities of his father, an editor of *Amerikanskii russkii viestnik*. Consequently, in 1918 he was asked by the American Council of Uhro-Rusins to serve as spokesman of its delegation to the Mid-European Democratic Union in Philadelphia. He later went to Uzhhorod to follow through on the results of the plebiscite held by the *American National Council of Uhro-Rusins in 1918, which called for an autonomous Transcarpathia federated with Czechoslovakia. In the summer of 1919 he negotiated the terms of federation in Prague and Paris and on 12 August 1919 became president of the Directorate of Subcarpathian Ruthenia. He was appointed the first governor of Transcarpathia in April 1920, but he resigned a year later over the central government's refusal to grant full autonomy to the region. He returned to the United States, where he wrote several books critical of Czechoslovak policy. During the Second World War he changed his mind and again supported the aim of Transcarpathia's incorporation within Czechoslovakia.

**Zhatkovych, Yurii** [Žatkovyč, Jurij] (Zsátkovics, Kálmán], b 14 October 1855 in Dravtsi, near Uzhhorod, d 25 September 1920 in Stroine, Berehove county, Transcarpathia. Ukrainian historian, writer, and translator; member of the Shevchenko Scientific Society. Most of his scholarly articles deal with the history of Transcarpathia,

particularly its church figures, eparchy, and monasteries. He was elected to the Hungarian Historical Society for his lengthy study of the struggle between the Eger and Mukachiv dioceses (1884). Under V. *Hnatiuk's influence he became interested in Transcarpathian ethnography and published some articles on the subject in Ukrainian periodicals. He wrote short stories about the life of the common people and translated some works by Marko Vovchok, I. Franko, O. Makovei, O. Storozhenko, and M. Kotsiubynsky into Hungarian. He translated E. Egán's brochure on the economic situation of the Ruthenian peasants in Hungary (1901) into Ukrainian. On the language issue he took a conservative position, although he used a variant of *yazychiie that was close to the popular vernacular. His textbooks for Transcarpathian Ukrainian schools were banned, but three of them (in geography, history, and social studies) were reprinted 14 times in Slovak. Many of his works remain unpublished.

M. Mushynka

Amvrosii Zhdakha: a postcard drawing illustrating a Ukrainian folk song

**Zhdakha, Amvrosii** [Ždaxa, Amvrosij] (pseud of Smahlii, Amvrosii), b 18 December 1855 in Izmail, Bessarabia gubernia, d 8 September 1927 in Odessa. Graphic artist. His formal art education was limited to a brief period at the Odessa Drawing School in 1881. He taught at the Volhynian Eparchial School for Women in Kremianets (1908–10), the Odessa Trade and Industry School (1921–4), and the Odessa Art Institute (1924–7). While working as a bank clerk he was active in the Odessa Hromada and devoted his spare time to painting and to collecting Cossack weapons and folk art. From 1893 to 1914 he painted several series of watercolor illustrations to Ukrainian folk songs. Two of these series (20 pictures) were reproduced in Kiev in 1911–12 as postcards, together with words and scores. Zhdakha also designed book covers and illustrated editions of P. Kulish's *Chorna rada* (Black Council, 1901), M. Komarov's *Opovidannia pro Antona Holovatoho* (Stories about Antin Holovaty, 1901), Ye. Hrebinka's *Chaikovs'kyi*, and T. Shevchenko's *Kobzar* (30 unpublished illustrations).

**Zhdanov, Andrei** [Ždanov, Andrej], b 26 February 1896 in Mariiupil, Katerynoslav gubernia, d 31 August 1948 in Moscow. Russian Bolshevik and Party functionary. He was J. Stalin's close confidant. After the Second World War he was placed in charge of Soviet cultural policy. His 1946 attacks on the literary journals *Zvezda* and *Leningrad* opened a campaign to rid Soviet culture of 'servility before the West' and 'cosmopolitanism.' In the 'Zhdanovshchina' period, Russian culture was promoted and 'Zionism' and 'bourgeois nationalism' were singled out for repression. In Ukraine such works as M. Petrovsky's *Istoriia Ukraïny* (History of Ukraine, 1943) and S. Maslov and Ye. Kyryliuk's *Narys istoriï ukraïnskoï literatury* (Outline of the History of Ukrainian Literature, 1945) were criticized for nationalism. Ukrainian writers were roundly criticized: A. Malyshko, Yu. Yanovsky, O. Kundzich, S. Oliinyk, T. Masenko, L. Smiliansky, O. Dovzhenko, M. Rylsky, V. Sosiura, and O. Vyshnia suffered repression. The editorial staffs of the Ukrainian journals *Vitchyzna* and *Dnipro* were replaced. Similar actions were taken in other spheres of Ukrainian culture. The main effect of this campaign was to push Ukrainian culture closer to Russian. In June 1990 the CC CPU admitted that the Party's cultural policy in the late 1940s and early 1950s had been 'politically incorrect,' and rehabilitated many of the Ukrainian writers who had been prosecuted.

**Zhdanov.** See Mariiupil.

**Zhdanov Azovstal Metallurgical Plant.** See Mariiupil Azovstal Metallurgical Plant.

**Zhdanovych, Antin** [Ždanovyč], b in the early 17th century, d after 1657. Cossack officer and diplomat. He was a captain of the registered Cossacks in Chyhyryn regiment (to 1648) and then served under B. Khmelnytsky as colonel of Kiev regiment (1649–53 and 1656–7), Cossack envoy to Turkey (1650 and 1651), Poland (1653), and Muscovy (1654), and general judge (1656). During a critical phase of the Cossack-Polish War in 1651 (the Battle of Bertestechko) Zhdanovych was put in charge of defending Kiev from the advancing Lithuanian army of J. Radziwiłł. He gave up the city without a fight after consulting with Metropolitan S. Kosiv about how best to minimize destruction. In 1657 he was appointed acting hetman over an expeditionary force of 20,000 Cossacks sent by Khmelnytsky to support his allies Charles X Gustav of Sweden and György I Rákóczi of Transylvania. The combined army occupied Łańcut, Cracow, Brest, and Warsaw. By the summer of that year the situation had changed, and a

mutiny fomented by Muscovite informers erupted among the Cossacks and brought about the voluntary return of many of them to Ukraine. Zhdanovych also switched his loyalties to I. Vyhovsky and Yu. Khmelnytsky until 1659, when Russian pressure on the Cossack leadership forced his abdication.

**Zhdanovych, Oleh.** See Shtul, Oleh.

**Zhebelev, Sergei** [Žebelev, Sergej], b 22 September 1867 in St Petersburg, d 28 December 1941 in Leningrad. Soviet Russian historian and archeologist; member of the USSR Academy of Sciences (AN SSSR) from 1927. He graduated from St Petersburg University (1890) and taught there (1899–1927, as professor from 1904) and worked at the AN SSSR Institute of the History of Material Culture (from 1927) as director of research on antiquities of the northern Black Sea coast. A collection of his essays was published posthumously as *Severnoe Prichernomor'e* (The Northern Black Sea Coast, 1953), and a festschrift in his honor was published in 1968.

Leonid Zhebunev

**Zhebunev, Leonid** [Žebunev], b 1851 in Oleksandrivske county, Katerynoslav gubernia, d 1919 near Katerynoslav. Revolutionary and civic figure. For his populist involvement he was imprisoned in Katerynoslav (August 1874 to January 1875) and Odessa (December 1881 to April 1883) and then banished to eastern Siberia for five years. After returning to Ukraine he was involved briefly in the Kharkiv Literacy Committee. Around 1900 he became a radical Ukrainophile in Kharkiv (influenced by P. Yefymenko). From 1903 he was active in the Hromada organizations and the Ukrainian Democratic and Democratic Radical parties in Poltava, and Kiev. He became a member of the Society of Ukrainian Progressives in 1908 and contributed to *Literaturno-naukovyi vistnyk*, *Ukrainska-ia zhizn'*, and *Rada*.

*Zhelekhivka.* A revised version of the phonetic *\*kulishivka* orthography, introduced by Ye. *Zhelekhivsky in his Ukrainian-German dictionary (2 vols, 1885–6; repr 1982). Its 34-letter alphabet officially replaced *etymological spelling in Galician and Bukovynian schools in November 1892, and its orthographic and lexical norms (many of them based on the *southwestern dialects) were laid out in S. Smal-Stotsky and F. Gartner's 1893 Ruthenian school grammar. The *zhelekhivka* was retained in Galicia until the early 1920s. In Russian-ruled Ukraine it was used after 1905 mainly by M. *Hrushevsky in editing *Literaturno-naukovyi vistnyk* and in his own works. It did not become widely accepted there, however, because of the impact of the orthography propagated by B. *Hrinchenko in his seminal Ukrainian-Russian dictionary (4 vols, 1907–9).

The *zhelekhivka*'s main phonetic and morphological traits were (1) *je* and *ji* (*i*) after dentals (eg, *njis* 'he carried' [but *nis* 'nose'], *ljektsija* 'lesson') to indicate soft pronunciation; (2) the soft sign within the consonant clusters *sv, cv, zv* before *ja* and *i* to indicate soft pronunciation (eg, *s'viatyj, c'vit, z'vir* 'holy, bloom, animal'); (3) '*o* and, elsewhere, *ë* after dentals and instead of *jo* to indicate soft pronunciation (eg, *l'on, sëmu* 'flax, this (dative)'; (4) an apostrophe after the prefixes *z-/s-* before vowels (eg, *z'java, z'oraty* 'apparition, to plow'); (5) separation of the reflexive particle *sja* from the verb; (6) *g* and *l'* in Greek, Latin, and German loanwords (eg, *fil'ol'ogija* 'philology'); (7) *v* instead of postvocalic *l*, corresponding to the dialectal pronunciation of *l* as *ŭ* (eg, *horivka* 'whiskey'); (8) hardened (dialectal) suffixes *-skyj, -zkyj, -ckyj, -sko*, and a softened *n'* before them (eg, *ruskyj, don'skyj* 'Ruthenian, Don'); (9) *y-* instead of *i-* in the initially stressed position (eg, *ýnčyj* 'different'); (10) neuter noun endings *-nje, -tje* instead of *-nnja, -ttja* (eg, *pysanje, žytje* 'writing, life'); (11) the endings *-nyje, -anyje* in Church Slavonicisms (eg, *voznesenyje* 'ascension'); (12) *-yja* instead of *-ija* in loanwords (eg, *stacyja, sesyja* 'station, session'); (13) *-y* instead of *-i* in all singular nouns in the locative case and in feminine nouns in the dative case (eg, *na kony, na zemly, na poly* 'on the horse, on the land, on the field)'; (14) the endings *-y, -yj, -em, -ex* in feminine plural nouns of the third declension and in a separate group of plural nouns (eg, *visty, vistyj, liudem, v očex* 'news (nom), news (gen), people (dat), in the eyes (loc)'); (15) hard endings in third-person verb forms (eg, *xodyt, xodjat* 'he walks, they walk'); (16) *-a-* instead of *-o-* in the roots of imperfective verbs (eg, *zarabljaty* 'to earn'); (17) the archaic infinitive ending *-čy* in verbs with the laryngeal *-h-*, and the velar *-k-* (eg, *sterečy, pečy* 'to guard, to bake') and archaic retention of *-h-, -k-* in the first person singular (eg, *mohu, peku* 'I can, I bake'); and (18) in past-tense verbs (and in the present tense of *buty* 'to be'), the first- and second-person singular and plural endings *-jem, -jes', -s'mo, -s'te* (eg, *buvjem, buvjes', bulys'mo, bulys'te* 'I was, you [sing] were, we were, you [pl] were'). (See also *Orthography.)

O. Horbach

**Zhelekhivsky, Andrii** [Želexivs'kyj, Andrij], b 11 December 1892 in Kiev gubernia, d 1943. Physicist. A longtime head of the physics department at Kharkiv University and the All-Ukrainian Association of Physicists (est 1926), he wrote several monographs and a university-level physics textbook. In 1943 he was executed by Soviet authorities.

**Zhelekhivsky, Yevhen** [Želexivs'kyj, Jevhen] (Zhelekhovsky), b 24 December 1844 in Khyshevychi, Lviv circle, Galicia, d 2 March 1885 in Stanyslaviv, Galicia. Lexicographer, folklorist, and community figure. After graduating from Lviv University (1869) he taught languages at Ukrainian gymnasiums in Peremyshl (1870–2) and Stanyslaviv (1872–85). He was a founding member of the Prosvita so-

Yevhen Zhelekhivsky

cieties in Lviv and Stanyslaviv. Zhelekhivsky is renowned for his *Ukrainisch-Deutsches Wörterbuch*, one of the most important Ukrainian lexicographical works of the 19th century. Letters *A–O* were published in fascicles from 1882 on and in one volume in Lviv in 1884. Letters *P–Ja* were edited and supplemented by S. *Nedilsky and published posthumously as a second volume in 1886. The dictionary, which he began to compile in 1869, has approx 65,000 words and is based on the earlier Ukrainian dictionaries of M. Zakrevsky, M. Levchenko, F. Piskunov, and K. Sheikovsky; on published ethnographic collections; on contemporary literary and scholarly works and grammars; and on vernacular lexical data recorded by 92 correspondents, mostly from the *southwestern dialects. It also includes puristic terminological neologisms, many of them nonproductive. With its phonetic orthography it played a key role in forcing out the etymological orthography and *yazychiie* in Galicia and Bukovyna (see *Zhelekhivka). The dictionary was reprinted in Munich in 1982.

R. Senkus

**Zhelekhovsky, Yustyn** [Želexovs'kyj, Justyn], b 1821, d 1910. Greek Catholic priest and educator. He taught at a gymnasium in Peremyshl and contributed to Russophile periodicals in Galicia. He wrote a biography of Bishop I. Snihursky (1894) and articles in church history. His memoirs were published in *Vistnyk Narodnoho doma* in 1909–10.

**Zheliabov, Andrei** [Željabov, Andrej], b 17 August 1851 in Mykolaivka, Teodosiia county, Tavriia gubernia, d 15 April 1881 in St Petersburg. Russian revolutionary populist of Ukrainian and Russian background. A graduate in law (1871) of Odessa University, Zheliabov is best known as a leading member of the populist terrorist organization *Narodnaia Volia and as one of the driving forces behind the assassination of Tsar Alexander II in 1881. He coauthored some of the group's programmatic proclamations, organized student, worker, and military circles of Narodnaia Volia, and edited its newspaper, *Rabochaia gazeta*. He maintained contacts with the Ukrainian Hromadas in Odessa and Kiev and with M. Drahomanov. Zheliabov was arrested in February 1881, shortly before the assassination of the tsar; he was later tried and executed for his participation in the plot.

**Zheliabuzhsky, Ivan** [Željabužskij], b 1638, d after 1709. Russian diplomat and statesman. In 1667 he participated in the conclusion of the Treaty of Andrusovo. In 1684 he was sent by Tsar Peter I to obtain an oath of allegiance from Hetman I. Samoilovych, and later that year he was appointed voivode of Chernihiv. His *Zapiski* (Notes, 1840) provide a reliable record of the workings of the Russian state in the late 17th century, particularly in the years 1694–1700.

**Zheliezniak, Omelian** [Željeznjak, Omeljan], b 21 August 1909 in Hrybova Rudnia, Horodnia county, Chernihiv gubernia, d 21 June 1963 in Kiev. Master of ceramic sculpture. He created ceramic toys; animal figurines; genre and historical compositions, such as *Gonta and His Sons* (1956), *Farewell to a Cossack*, and *Kozak-Mamai* (1962); and compositions inspired by the works of T. Shevchenko and N. Gogol, such as *I Was Nearly Fourteen* (1949) and *The Smith Vakula Riding on the Devil* (1954). P. Musiienko and N. Fedorovna's monograph about him was published in Kiev in 1970.

**Zheliezniak, Yakiv** [Željeznjak, Jakiv], b 10 April 1941 in Odessa. Marksman. He won the 1972 Olympic gold medal in the running-boar event; was a member of the USSR team that won world championships in 1962, 1966, and 1973–5; and was a European champion in 1965 and 1972–3 and a USSR champion in 1965–7 and 1971–6.

**Zheltvai, Viktor** [Željtvaj], b 1890 in Krachunovo, Transcarpathia, d 1974 in Uzhhorod, Transcarpathia oblast. Greek Catholic priest, educator, and civic activist. A graduate of the Uzhhorod Theological Seminary and the Budapest Pedagogical Academy, he served as director of the Uzhhorod Teachers' Seminary for Women (until 1934). He was a member of the Christian People's party and helped edit its newspapers *Nauka* (1919–22) and *Svoboda* (1922–38). A member of the Ruthenian Club (1919) and the Uzhhorod Prosvita society, he was closely associated with A. Voloshyn and other Transcarpathian Ukrainophiles. He wrote articles and popular brochures, such as *Rozdumai to dobre!* (Think It through Well!, 1921).

**Zhelyborsky, Arsenii** [Želybors'kyj, Arsenij] (secular name: Andrii), b 1618, d 1663. Orthodox bishop of Lviv (1641–63). He established a printing press at the St George's Cathedral in 1645, oversaw the publication of many church books there, and wrote *Pouchenie novosviashchennomu iereevi* (Instructions to a Newly Consecrated Hierarch, 1642). He also provided the first printing press for the Univ Monastery Press. In 1648 he was rumored to have sent material support to the B. Khmelnytsky forces, but during Khmelnytsky's siege of Lviv in 1648, he and his brother, Adam, served as Polish royal emissaries to the Cossacks. In 1658 he assisted Hetman I. *Vyhovsky in writing the Treaty of Hadiache.

**Zhemchuzhnikov, Lev** [Žemčužnikov], b 14 November 1828 in Pavlovka, Orel gubernia, Russia, d 6 August 1912 in Tsarskoe Selo, Russia. Russian painter and graphic artist; grandson of Count A. Rozumovsky. A graduate of the St Petersburg Academy of Arts (1852), he lived in Chernihiv and Poltava gubernias in 1852–6 and collected folklore there. He corresponded with and helped the exiled T. Shevchenko. Some of Zhemchuzhnikov's best works are devoted to Ukraine and are influenced by Shevchenko's poetry and art. They include the paintings *Kobzar by the Road* (1854), *Lirnyk Indoors* (1857), and *Cossack*

Lev Zhemchuzhnikov: *Kobzar by the Road* (watercolor, 1854)

*Riding to the Sich* (1887); the ink drawing *Woman Reaper* (1851); the watercolor portrait *Khymka Zabyiachykha* (1853); the sepia *Cossack in the Steppe* (1853); and the etchings *Ukrainian Girl* (1860), *Ukrainian Man* (1862), and *Abandoned Girl* (1869). Zhemchuzhnikov contributed to *Osnova* (1861–2) and put together an album of his own and other artists' etchings, as a supplement to *Osnova*; it was called *Zhivopisnaia Ukraina* (Picturesque Ukraine) in homage to Shevchenko's album of the same title. From 1875 to 1892 Zhemchuzhnikov was secretary of the Moscow Art Society. A book about him by L. Popova was published in Kiev in 1961, and his memoirs were published in Leningrad in 1971.

**Zhenetsky, Stepan** [Ženec'kyj], b 28 December 1913 in Mosty Velyki, Zhovkva county, Galicia. Journalist and writer. In the 1930s he contributed to Lviv papers, such as *Narodnia sprava* and *Novyi chas*, and was an assistant editor of *Nove selo*. As a postwar émigré he has been a leading member of the Organization for the Defense of Lemkivshchyna, has edited its organ *Holos Lemkivshchyny* (1958–64) in Yonkers, New York, and has contributed hundreds of articles, humorous stories, and reviews to various Ukrainian-American periodicals. Published separately were his humor and satire collection *Natsiia v pokhodi* (Nation on the Offensive, 1958) and the story collection *Hory mstiat'sia* (The Mountains Take Revenge, 1961).

**Zherebko, Orest** [Žerebko] (Zerebko), b 15 September 1887 in Horodenka, Galicia, d 23 February 1943 in Blaine Lake, Saskatchewan. Community leader. Zherebko arrived in Canada in 1900 and received a BA from Manitoba College in 1913, the first degree awarded to a Ukrainian in Canada. He continued his studies in Vienna (1913–16). Stranded by the First World War, he worked for the Vienna-based Union for the Liberation of Ukraine (SVU) and was reputed to have written the brochure *Ukraïntsi v Amerytsi* (Ukrainians in America) under the name O. Kyrylenko. He returned to Canada in 1917, and in 1938 was elected Liberal member of the Saskatchewan legislature for the Redberry constituency. An adherent of the hetmanite philosophy of V. *Lypynsky, he supported the Khliborobska Ukraina publishing house in Vienna and

Orest Zherebko

Archbishop Yurii
Zhevchenko

helped finance the publication of Lypynsky's *Lysty do brativ khliborobiv* (Letters to Brother Agrarians, 1926).

*Zherela do istoriï Ukraïny-Rusy* (Sources on the History of Ukraine-Rus'). An 11-volume series published by the Archeographic Commission of the Shevchenko Scientific Society in Lviv from 1895 to 1924. The chief editor was M. Hrushevsky. Four volumes contain *lustrations*, detailed 16th- and 17th-century surveys of properties and economic and social conditions in Polish-ruled Western Ukrainian territories. Three contain documents pertaining to Galicia during the 1648–57 Cossack-Polish War. Three others contain documents on the history of the Cossacks to 1632, including reports from papal nuncios in Ukraine at the time. The final volume contains part of Ya. Markovych's diary from 1735 to 1740. Each of the volumes also contains a scholarly introduction and analyses by the volume editors, Hrushevsky, M. Korduba, S. Tomashivsky, and I. Krypiakevych.

**Zheriv River** [Žeriv] (also Zherev). A left-bank tributary of the Uzh River that flows eastward for 96 km in Zhytomyr oblast and drains a basin area of 1,470 sq km. The river, up to 5 m wide, has a meandering course. It is used for water supply and irrigation.

**Zhevaho, Mykola** [Ževaho], b 1907 in Kharkiv gubernia, d 1947 in Germany. Painter. He graduated in 1932 from the Kharkiv Art Institute, where he studied under M. Burachek, and he taught there in 1939–41. He painted landscapes, genre and historical paintings, and portraits, illustrated an edition of T. Shevchenko's 'Haidamaky,' and painted frescoes.

**Zhevchenko, Yurii** [Ževčenko, Jurij], b 17 February 1885 in the Yelysavethrad (now Kirovohrad) region, d ca 1938. Archbishop of the Ukrainian *Autocephalous Orthodox church (UAOC). A graduate of the Yelysavethrad Theological Seminary and Odessa University, he was ordained in 1911 and served as a chaplain in the Russian army (1914–17). During the period of Ukrainian statehood he organized church life in Kiev and was a member of the SS Cyril and Methodius Brotherhood. In 1919 he was chaplain at the Engineering Officer School in Kamianets-Podilskyi. In 1920 he was one of the organizers of the All-

Ukrainian Orthodox Church Council. He was consecrated in 1922 and served as a bishop of the UAOC in Svyra (to 1924), Poltava (1924–7), and Odessa (1928–9). In 1929 he was arrested and sentenced to eight years' hard labor in Karaganda. His sentence was extended in 1937.

**Zhezhava.** A multi-occupational archeological site near Zhezhava (now Zelenyi Hai, Zalishchyky raion, Ternopil oblast). It was excavated in 1877 and 1882 by A. Kirkor and others and in 1931 by T. *Sulimirski. Remains of a Trypilian culture settlement, early and late Bronze Age burials, a 9th- to 7th-century BC settlement, an early Slavic settlement of the 6th to 7th century, and three Rus' burial grounds were unearthed at this site.

**Zhezherin, Borys** [Žežerin], b 27 July 1912 in Kiev. Architect. A graduate of the Kiev Civil-Engineering Institute (1937), he helped plan the reconstruction and expansion of Zhytomyr (1946) and Korosten (1948). He designed the sanatorium complex in Koncha-Zaspa (1949–50) and the Central Pavilion of the Construction Industry at the Republican Exhibition of Economic Achievements in Kiev (1956–7), and codesigned the Zhytomyr Ukrainian Music and Drama Theater (1966) and the Dnipropetrovske Opera and Ballet Theater (1974).

*Zhinka* (Woman). A monthly and then semimonthly newspaper of the *Union of Ukrainian Women, published in Lviv from January 1935 to May 1938. It contained articles on politics, culture, feminism, education, health, hygiene, home economics, fashion, and child rearing; prose; poetry; and reports on the activities of the union and the women's movement in Western Ukraine and elsewhere. *Zhinka* was edited by O. Fedak-Sheparovych and M. Rudnytska. Regular contributors included S. Rusova, Z. Mirna, K. Hrynevycheva, S. Parfanovych, I. Gurgula, M. Strutynska, and I. Nevytska. *Zhinka* was subject to Polish censorship, and in 1938 it and the union were suppressed by the Polish authorities. In its place *Hromadianka* was published in 1938–9.

*Zhinocha dolia* (Woman's Fate). A monthly (1925–6) and semimonthly women's magazine published and edited by O. Kysilevska in Kolomyia in 1925–39. It contained articles on the women's movement in Western Ukraine and elsewhere, feminism, health and hygiene, farming, home economics, child rearing, cultural and political issues, and the women's question in Soviet Ukraine. It also published a separate section about Ukrainian women in North America; the biweekly supplement *Zhinocha volia* (1932–9) for peasant women, edited by M. Stavnycha; the monthly *Svit molodi* (1934–9) for young people, edited by I. Vilde; and four annual almanacs (1927–30). Contributors included U. Kravchenko, S. Rusova, S. Parfanovych, N. Koroleva, M. Duchyminska, M. Omelchenko, D. Vikonska, and S. Yablonska. In 1930 the magazine had a circulation of 2,500.

*Zhinochyi holos* (Woman's Voice). A women's journal published monthly in Lviv in 1931–5 as a supplement to *Hromads'kyi holos*, and then monthly (to 1937) and semimonthly to 1939 as the organ of the Union of Ukrainian Working Women, an organization affiliated with the Ukrainian Socialist Radical party. Edited by F. Stakhova with the assistance of I. Blazhkevych, N. Mykytchuk, and I. Muryn, it was concerned primarily with organizing working women in Western Ukraine and published articles on political affairs, child rearing, health, and hygiene, as well as literary works.

Various covers of *Zhinochyi svit*

***Zhinochyi svit*** (Woman's World). A monthly organ of the Ukrainian Women's Organization of Canada, published in Winnipeg from January 1950 to 1973 and in Toronto since then. Before 1950 it appeared as a regular section in the newspaper *Novyi shliakh*. It contains reports on the organization's activities; articles on culture, history, and the women's movement; and a separate page devoted to children. The first editors included K. Kandyba-Lazor, N. Syniavska, and S. Bubniuk. The journal is now edited by a board.

***Zhinochyi vistnyk.*** See Women's press.

***Zhivaia mysl'*** (Living Thought). A Russophile monthly journal published from September 1902 to October 1905 in Lviv (a total of 25 issues). It argued that Ukrainians were part of the Russian nation, and it appeared in literary Russian, unlike many other Galician Russophile publications, which were printed in the artificial Ukrainian-Russian *yazychiie*. The editor was I. Svientsitsky, and the publisher was I. Savchak.

***Zhivopisnaia Ukraina*** (Picturesque Ukraine). A series of etchings by T. *Shevchenko depicting Ukrainian landscapes, significantevents in Ukrainian Cossack history,

The title page of *Zhivopisnaia Ukraina* (etching by Lev Zhemchuzhnikov, 1861)

and scenes from peasant life. Only one album, of six etchings with commentary by Shevchenko, was published, in St Petersburg in 1844. Shevchenko planned to publish more albums but was unable to do so. In 1861–2 L. Zhemchuzhnikov published, under the same title, an album of 49 etchings by Russian and Ukrainian artists, such as I. Sokolov, K. Trutovsky, A. Beideman, and V. Vereshchagin, as a supplement to the St Petersburg journal *Osnova.

**Zhluktenko, Yurii** [Žluktenko, Jurij], b 31 August 1915 in Oleksandrivka, Novomoskovske county, Katerynoslav

The cover of Yurii Zhluktenko's book on the Ukrainian language in Canada (1990)

gubernia, d 4 February 1990 in Kiev. Linguist and translator. After graduating from Kiev University (1946) he completed his graduate studies at the Moscow Pedagogical Institute of Foreign Languages (1954) and lectured at the Kiev Polytechnical Institute and the Kiev Institute of the National Economy, and served as dean of the Faculty of Romance-Germanic Philology (1968–75) and chairman of the English philology department, which he developed, at Kiev University. In 1975–80 he chaired the Romance-Germanic linguistic section he had helped found at the AN URSR (now ANU) Institute of Linguistics. He was one of the founders of comparative and social linguistics in Ukraine. Specializing in English-Ukrainian linguistic relations, he wrote books on the comparative grammar of English and Ukrainian (1960), Ukrainian contacts with English in the United States and Canada (1964), and the Ukrainian language in Canada (1990), and cowrote a book on the comparative grammar of English, Ukrainian, and Russian (1981) and on English neologisms (1983). Many of his articles deal with the syntactic and lexical influence of English on the mother tongue of Ukrainian immigrants in North America. As an educator he coauthored a textbook on Ukrainian for foreign students (1973, 1978) and edited a collection of articles on foreign-language teaching methods (1979). He was a founder (1979) of the translation periodical *Teoriia i praktyka perekladu* and translated Frisian prose and poetry into Ukrainian (*Vsesvit*, 1983, 1984).

T. Zakydalsky

**Zhmailo, Marko** [Žmajlo], b and d ? Cossack leader. On 5 November 1625 he headed a rebel army against Polish troops under the command of S. Koniecpolski which had been sent to enforce Polish authority in Ukraine. The insurgent group was composed largely of non-registered Zaporozhian Cossacks who were veterans of the Khotyn campaign of 1621. Although the uprising failed to destroy the Polish force, it resulted in the adoption of the Treaty of Kurukove as a compromise with the Cossack *starshyna*. Zhmailo's subsequent fate is unknown.

**Zhmerynka** [Žmerynka]. IV-9. A city (1989 pop 43,100) and raion center in Vinnytsia oblast. It originated as a railway settlement during the construction of the Kiev–Balta railway line (1865). It was granted city status in 1903. During the revolutionary period Zhmerynka was a staging point of the Bolshevik forces advancing on Kiev (1917) and the site of Ukrainian-Bolshevik battles (1919). Today the city is an important railway junction, of several trunk lines. Besides various yards and plants servicing the railway, the city has a winery, a dairy, and a tobacco factory.

**Zhohol, Liudmyla** [Žohol', Ljudmyla], b 23 May 1930 in Kiev. Textile artist and art scholar. She studied at the Kiev State Art Institute (1948–50), graduated from the Lviv Institute of Applied and Decorative Arts (1954), and received her candidate's degree in 1965. She has designed decorative drapery and cover fabrics and created tapestries, such as *Sun* (1970), *Peacocks* (1970), *Ukrainian Autumn* (1975), *Beloved City* (1976), and *Native Spaces* (1982); batik panels, such as *Oranta* (1969), *Flowers* (1970), and *Birds* (1970); and the kilim *Wedding Wreath* (1971). She has written articles on decorative and applied art and books on textiles in interior design (1968) and decorative art in the contemporary interior (1986).

Archbishop Kypriian Zhokhovsky (engraving by Oleksander Tarasevych)

**Zhokhovsky, Kypriian** [Žoxovs'kyj, Kyprijan], b 1635 near Polatsk, Belarus, d 1693. Uniate metropolitan. He joined the Basilian order as a novice in Byten. From 1658 he studied in Rome, where he earned a doctorate in philosophy and theology and was ordained in 1663. He was in Ukraine from 1665, where he was archimandrite in Derman and then Dubno. In 1671 he was consecrated titular bishop of Vitsebsk; archbishop of Polatsk; and coadjutor to the Kievan metropolitan H. Kolienda (despite opposition from other bishops), whom he succeeded in 1674. As metropolitan he received confirmation for all the rights and privileges of the Uniate church from King Jan III Sobieski and oversaw the conversion of Lutske, Peremyshl, and Lviv eparchies to Catholicism. He was committed to improving the education of priests; renewing the seminary in Minsk; and founding a printing press in Vilnius, where liturgical and theological books and sermons would be printed. He also encouraged the cult of Y. *Kuntsevych. In 1680 he helped organize the Colloquium Lublinense, a conference of Uniate and Orthodox representatives called by King Jan III Sobieski to attempt to resolve the religious divisions in Ukraine.

Pavlo Zholtovsky (portrait by M. Shymchuk, tempera 1984)

**Zholtovsky, Pavlo** [Žoltovs'kyj], b 8 December 1904 in Mysliatyn, Iziaslav county, Volhynia gubernia, d 30 August 1986 in Moscow. Art scholar. He graduated from the Kiev State Art Institute in 1932 and received his candidate's degree in 1955. An associate of the Lviv branch of the AN URSR (now ANU) Institute of Fine Arts, Folklore, and Ethnography, he wrote many articles on Ukrainian art and books on the artistic monuments of the liberation struggle of the Ukrainian people in 16th- to 18th-century Ukraine (1958), artistic metalwork (1972), artistic metal casting in 14th- to 18th-century Ukraine (1973), 17th- and 18th-century Ukrainian painting (1978), the arts in the 16th to 18th centuries (1983), the paintings of the Kievan Cave Icon Painting Studio (1982), and mural painting in 16th- to 18th-century Ukraine (1988). He registered, measured, and photographed hundreds of architectural monuments and acquired many artistic monuments for Ukraine's museums.

Oleksander Zholud: *Self-Portrait* (oil, 1989)

**Zholud, Oleksander** [Zholud'], b 1951 in Murom, Russia. Painter. He has lived in Ukraine since 1968 and graduated from the Kharkiv Industrial Design Institute in 1973. In the 1980s he began experimenting with intense colors and an expressionist brush stroke. His style has been influenced by the paintings of P. Picasso, M. Chagall, H. Matisse, F. Léger, and Ukrainian, Mexican, Indonesian, and African folk art. His recent works include *Faith, Hope,*

*Love* (1988), *Atelier* (1988), *Three Models* (1988), *Beauty Contest in a Provincial Town* (1989), and *Emancipation* (1989).

**Zhorna** (Millstones). A satirical magazine published semimonthly in Lviv in 1933–4. It was edited by R. Pashkivsky and illustrated by R. Chornii and L. Senyshyn.

**Zhovkva.** See Nesterov.

The Zhovkva Monastery

**Zhovkva Monastery** (Zhovkivskyi manastyr). A Basilian monastery and religious publishing center in Zhovkva (now Nesterov), Galicia. It was founded in 1682 on the initiative of the bishop of Lviv, Y. Shumliansky, and suffered a major fire in 1690. Rebuilt with the support of the Polish king Jan III Sobieski, it slowly gained stature through the 18th century. The monastery's most important period, however, was in 1895–1946, when it was the site of the Basilians' publishing activity (among the works published was the popular monthly journal *Misionar and the scholarly *Analecta Ordinis S. Basilii Magni*). In 1939 approx 35 monks ran the monastery's press. The success of its publishing ventures allowed the monastery to undertake extensive renovations from 1907 and to engage Yu. Butsmaniuk during the 1930s to paint the church interior. After the Soviet occupation of Galicia, the monastery and press were closed down, and the monks living there were arrested. A catalog of the Monastery press's publications was published in *Analecta Ordinis S. Basilii Magni* (vol 5, 1967).

**Zhovkva School of Artists.** In the 17th and 18th centuries Zhovkva (now Nesterov) was one of the main art centers in Western Ukraine. Icon painters, such as D. Roievych, I. Rutkovych, T. Styslovych, V. and K. Petranovych, V. Biliansky, I. Starzhevsky, I. Poliakhovych, M. Krosovsky, and Mykolai, and wood sculptors, such as S. Piatynsky, S. Putiatytsky, Yu. Mykhailovych, and I. Stobensky, worked there. A biographical dictionary of Zhovkva masters was compiled by V. Svientsitska and published in *Ukraïns'ke mystetstvoznavstvo* (1967, no. 1).

**Zhovnir, Ivan** [Žovnir], 1855–1928. Civic and political figure. An early supporter of the Ukrainian socialist movement among workers in Galicia, he was a member of the CC of the Ukrainian Social Democratic party (1918–19) and a leading exponent of its independentist faction (the Vpered group). He was also a representative in the Ukrainian National Rada of the Western Ukrainian National

Republic and an organizer of the Sich Riflemen in the Peremyshl region.

**Zhovten** [Žovten']. IV-5. A town smt (1988 pop 3,600) on the Bystrytsia River in Tysmenytsia raion, Ivano-Frankivske oblast. It was first mentioned in a historical document in 1435. Until it was burned down by the Turks in 1594, it was called Cheshybisy. A new village, Yezupil, was built at the site. In 1939 it was renamed Zhovten and promoted to smt status. The town is a railway junction. Neolithic and Trypilian culture settlements and the remains of a medieval rotunda have been uncovered nearby.

**Zhovten** (October). A small organization of 'workers of proletarian culture,' founded in Kiev in 1924 by former members of the *Association of Panfuturists. Its declaration, signed by V. Desniak, V. Deviatnin, N. Denysenko, Ye. Kaplia-Yavorsky, Khrystyn, I. Le, S. Novin, T. Sliusarenko, Ya. Savchenko, V. Shum (Usenko), M. Tereshchenko, F. Yakubovsky, Yu. Yanovsky, and V. Yaroshenko, stated that the members could not support the writers' groups Pluh and Hart, because neither had a clearly defined program and therefore could not guarantee the full development of a proletarian culture in Ukraine. Zhovten failed to develop a group profile and disintegrated in 1926. Most of its members joined the *All-Ukrainian Association of Proletarian Writers.

*Zhovten'* (right) and *Dzvin*

**Zhovten'** (October). The monthly journal of the Writers' Union of Ukraine in Lviv. It was first published, from September 1940 to June 1941, under the name *Literatura i mystetstvo*. It was revived in July 1945 as *Radians'kyi L'viv*, and it was renamed *Zhovten'* with the February 1951 issue. The chief editors have been O. Desniak (1940–1), M. Bazhan (1945–51), Yu. Melnychuk (1951–63), R. Bratun (1963–6), M. Romanchenko (1966–8), and R. Fedoriv (since 1968); R. Lubkivsky (1966–80) and M. Ilnytsky (since 1980) have served as deputy chief editors. *Zhovten'* has published prose, poetry, humor, satire, literary translations (eg, of S. Lem, P. Verlaine, T.S. Eliot, B. Brecht, R.M. Rilke, G. Lessing, W. Faulkner, Michelangelo, Petrarch, C.-P. Baudelaire, R. Frost, J.W. von Goethe), articles on Western

Ukrainian literary and cultural figures, reminiscences, archival materials by and on deceased writers, literary criticism, book reviews, articles on Ukrainian ethnography, art, and theater, commentaries on social issues, news of cultural events and developments, and critiques and exposés of 'Ukrainian bourgeois nationalism.' Among its contributors have been many prominent Soviet Ukrainian writers born or living in the western Ukrainian oblasts. P. Kozlaniuk, P. Panch, M. Stelmakh, H. Tiutiunnyk, I. Vilde, V. Gzhytsky, P. Zahrebelny, R. Ivanychuk, Fedoriv, Valerii Shevchuk, V. Yavorivsky, S. Pushyk, and N. Bichuia originally published one or more of their major novels in *Zhovten'*. Since the mid-1980s the journal has played an important role in filling in the 'blank spots' in Western Ukrainian literature and history. It was renamed *Dzvin* in 1990.

R. Senkus

**Zhovten Theater in Petrograd-Leningrad.** A theater established as the Petrograd Ukrainian Drama Theater in November 1917 on the initiative of the local Ukrainian Hromada. In 1919–24 the theater had the name Shevchenko Ukrainian Communist Theater. In 1924 it joined with the Petrograd Ukrainian Drama Theater (est 1923) to form the Unified Ukrainian Theater, and staged classical and contemporary Ukrainian dramas. In 1929 it ceased its activities, but later that year it was reconstituted as the Leningrad Zhovten Theater, under the auspices of the RSFSR People's Commissariat of Education. Its repertoire consisted mostly of contemporary Ukrainian plays, as well as L. Kurbas's adaptation of T. Shevchenko's poem *Haidamaky* and O. Vyshnia's adaptation of S. Hulak-Artemovsky's opera *Zaporozhian Cossack beyond the Danube*. Leading members were D. Rovynsky, Ye. Kokhanenko, F. Levytsky, Ye. Sydorenko, D. Shostakivsky, and the musicians Yu. Meitus and P. Kozytsky. The Zhovten Theater was active until 1932.

*Zhovtenia* (Child of [the] October [Revolution]). A monthly magazine for young children, published in Kharkiv (1928–9) and Kiev (1929–41) by the Central Bureau of the Communist Children's Movement, the Communist Youth League of Ukraine, and the People's Commissariat of Education. In 1935 the magazine *Tuktuk* was merged with it.

**Zhovti Vody** [Žovti Vody]. V-14. A city (1989 pop 62,400) on the Zhovta River in Dnipropetrovske oblast. It originated as a mining town at the end of the 19th century and was first called Zhovta Voda. In 1957 the town was given city status and was renamed. Its main industry is iron-ore mining. It also manufactures radios and synthetic furs.

**Zhovti Vody, Battle of.** A battle between B. Khmelnytsky's forces and the Polish army, on 16 May 1648, in the swampy upper reaches of the Zhovta River (an eastern tributary of the Inhulets River), near what is now Oleksandriia. Khmelnytsky commanded 8,000 Zaporozhian Cossacks, 4,000 to 5,000 registered Cossacks (who joined him after his first victories over the Poles), and approx 4,000 Crimean Tatars led by Tuhai-Bei. The Polish army, commanded by S. Potocki and J. Szembek, was surrounded and defeated; approx 3,000 Poles were taken prisoner, along with two commanding officers. The victory heralded Cossack successes in the *Cossack-Polish War.

Mykhailo Zhovtobriukh        Andrii Zhuk

**Zhovtobriukh, Mykhailo** [Žovtobrjux, Myxajlo], b 17 November 1905 in Ruchky, Hadiache county, Poltava gubernia. Linguist. A graduate of the Dnipropetrovske Institute of People's Education (1929), he worked at the AN URSR (now ANU) Institute of Linguistics from 1959 to 1988 and served as head of its Department of Ukrainian Language Theory and Structural-Mathematical Linguistics. He has written over 300 works, including textbooks on modern Ukrainian (1949, 1961), a history of Ukrainian phonetics (1956), and books on the language of the Ukrainian press to the mid-1890s (doctoral diss, 1963) and in the late 19th and early 20th centuries (1970) and on literary Ukrainian (1984). He is the coauthor of textbooks on the Ukrainian language (1st edn 1959) and Ukrainian historical grammar (1957, 1962) and of books on Ukrainian and Russian comparative grammar (1957, 1962, 1978), modern Ukrainian phonetics (1969) and vocabulary and phraseology (1973), modern Ukrainian morphology (1975), the syntax of the word group and the simple sentence (1975), the history of Ukrainian phonetics (1979), word formation in modern Ukrainian (1979), and the East Slavic languages (1987). He also edited a dictionary of H. Kvitka-Osnovianenko's language (1978) and coedited a collection of 18th-century Ukrainian private letters (1987).

**Zhuchenko, Fedir** [Žučenko], b ? in Poltava, d 1709 in Paris. Political activist. He is mentioned in the 'Register of the Entire Zaporozhian Army' as a Cossack who participated in the B. Khmelnytsky uprisings. In 1659 he spoke out against I. Vyhovsky, and in 1659–91 he intermittently held the post of colonel of Poltava regiment. He supported Yu. Khmelnytsky and I. Samoilovych and participated in the 1678 Chyhyryn campaign and the 1687 and 1689 Crimean campaigns. He opposed I. Mazepa and supported V. Kochubei and I. Iskra. For his support of P. Petryk he was removed from his post, but he remained a 'notable and recognized military fellow.'

**Zhuchenko, Mykhailo** [Žučenko, Myxajlo], b 1840, d 1880. Lawyer and civil activist. As a law student at Kharkiv University he was active in the Ukrainophile movement and organized Sunday schools. After becoming a lawyer he often defended populists against political charges. He was one of the founders and chief financial supporters of the *Shevchenko Scientific Society in Lviv.

**Zhuk, Andrii** [Žuk, Andrij] (pseuds: A. Andriienko, A. Ilchenko, A. Khrushch, A. Vovchansky), b 14 July 1880 in Vovchyk, Lubni county, Poltava gubernia, d 3 September 1968 in Vienna. Political and co-operative activist and journalist. He was active in the *Revolutionary Ukrainian party (1901–5) and a key organizer of the Union of Ukrainian Railwaymen in Kharkiv. For his involvement he was imprisoned from December 1903 to July 1904. He was elected secretary-general of the *Ukrainian Social Democratic Workers' party (USDRP) at its founding congress in December 1905, and he contributed to the party's organs *Sotsiial-demokrat*, *Vil'na Ukraïna*, *Borot'ba*, and *Slovo*. After being imprisoned again, from August 1906 to January 1907, he was released on bail, and he evaded his trial by escaping in October 1907 to Austrian-ruled Galicia.

While living in Lviv Zhuk headed the USDRP Foreign Group until 1911 and edited the co-operative journal *Ekonomist* (1909–14) and its monthly supplement *Samopomich*. He was active in the Prosvita and Silskyi Hospodar societies and contributed to social democratic organs, such as *Zemlia i volia* and *Pratsia*, and to the Ukrainian dailies *Dilo* in Lviv and *Rada* in Kiev. In 1912 he initiated the creation of the Ukrainian Information Committee, dedicated to popularizing the Ukrainian cause in Europe, and was elected its secretary. That year he was expelled from the USDRP.

From 1914 Zhuk lived in Vienna, where he cofounded the *Union for the Liberation of Ukraine, directed its Central Bureau, and managed its publications and contacts with Galicia's Ukrainians. He also served as a member of the *Supreme Ukrainian Council (1914–15), the *General Ukrainian Council (1915–16), and the Central Administration of the Ukrainian Sich Riflemen (1917–22), and as a special commissioner of the Hetman government (1918) and director of the Vienna office of the UNR Ministry of Foreign Affairs (1918–20). Zhuk was also a member of the executive of the *Union of Ukrainian Journalists and Writers Abroad and vice-president of the Committee for the Defense of Western Ukrainian Lands (est 1922). From 1930, in Lviv, he was director of the Bureau of Co-operative Statistics of the *Audit Union of Ukrainian Co-operatives, a member of the executive and the editor of the *Khortytsia co-operative publishing house, secretary of the *Society of Ukrainian Co-operative Leaders (1936–9), and editor of *Kredytova kooperatsiia* (1938–9), the organ of Tsentrobank in Galicia. After fleeing the Soviet occupation of Galicia in 1939, from 1940 he again lived in Vienna. Zhuk wrote many articles on ideological, political, economic, and co-operative topics, as well as firsthand accounts of the Ukrainian national movement before 1920. He also wrote brochures on Ukrainian co-operatives in Galicia (1913), the Ukrainian economic and co-operative press (1931), and Ukrainian co-operatives in Poland (1934) and edited a collection of reminiscences about S. Petliura in his youth (1936). The Andrii Zhuk Collection of books and invaluable documents and archival materials amassed by him is preserved at the Public Archives of Canada.

R. Senkus

**Zhuk, Anna** [Žuk] (née Nedilko), b 1882 in Vytivka, Poltava county, d 17 January 1976 in Vienna. Political and community figure. While working as a teacher in Kharkiv gubernia in the 1900s, she was a member of the clandestine Revolutionary Ukrainian party and the Ukrainian

Social Democratic Workers' party. For her involvement she spent over a year in a tsarist prison around 1907–8. An émigré from 1909, she married A. *Zhuk and lived in Lviv and Vienna. In Vienna she cofounded the *Ukrainian Women's Union, which she headed in 1922–7 and again in 1963–4.

**Zhuk, Irenei.** See Zuk, Ireneus.

**Zhuk, Liuba.** See Zuk, Luba.

Mykhailo Zhuk          Semen Zhuk

**Zhuk, Mykhailo** [Žuk, Myxajlo], b 2 October 1883 in Kakhivka, Tavriia gubernia, d 7 June 1964 in Odessa. Painter, graphic artist, and writer. He studied at the Kiev Art School (1896–9), the Moscow School of Painting, Sculpture, and Architecture (1899–1900), and the Cracow Academy of Fine Arts (1900–4). From 1905 he taught art in Chernihiv. Zhuk produced many portraits, some of which incorporated cubo-futurist faceting of surfaces (eg, his 1919 portraits of P. Tychyna and L. Kurbas). While teaching at the Odessa Art School (1925–53) he produced a series of 20 lithographic portraits of Ukrainian writers (1925–6), including H. Skovoroda, T. Shevchenko, P. Kulish, I. Franko, M. Kotsiubynsky, and M. Zerov, using formalistic simplification of volumes; created a portrait etching series of Ukrainian artists (1932), including V. Borovykovsky, O. Novakivsky, F. and V. Krychevsky, H. Narbut, and M. Boichuk; and designed posters, bookplates, and book covers, and ceramic designs inspired by folk art.

Zhuk also wrote the poetry collection *Spivy zemlï* (Singings of the Earth, 1912) and contributed poems, stories, fairy tales, plays, and criticism to Ukrainian journals. An album of his works, edited by I. Kozyrod and S. Shevelov, was published in Kiev in 1987.

**Zhuk, Radoslav.** See Zuk, Radoslav.

**Zhuk, Roman** [Žuk], b 1955 in Kolomyia, Ivano-Frankivske oblast. Postmodernist painter. He graduated from the Lviv Institute of Applied and Decorative Arts (1978) and taught there in 1978–82. Influenced by both Renaissance and postmodern art, he has created oil paintings in which the symbolism is multifaceted. They include *Chickens* (1972), *She Who Sleeps* (1982), *My Parents* (1987), *Chameleons* (1987), *Cats* (1988), *Nude Woman* (1988), and *Amazon* (1988). He had a solo exhibition in Lviv in 1989.

Roman Zhuk: *Cats* (oil, 1988)

**Zhuk, Semen** [Žuk], b 16 May 1893 in Kremianets county, Volhynia gubernia, d 26 June 1941 in Sambir, Galicia. Civic and political leader, journalist, and co-operative organizer. A former member of the Ukrainian Party of Socialist Revolutionaries, he was vice-president of the Ukrainian Socialist Radical party and its deputy to the Polish Sejm (1928–30). After serving a prison term for his political activities (1931–3), he was director of the Ukrainian Co-operative Bank in Pochaiv. At the beginning of the German invasion of Soviet Ukraine he was shot by the retreating Soviet secret police.

**Zhuk, Serhii** [Žuk, Serhij], b 19 October 1885 in Shvaikyna Balka, near Poltava, d in the 1950s in Germany. Sculptor and writer. He became interested in painting and sculpting as a student at St Petersburg University and produced his first sculptures in 1907. In 1916 he founded the Ukrainian Literary and Artistic Society in St Petersburg. After returning to Kiev in 1918, he taught art there and helped set up the Ukrainian State Academy of Arts. In the interwar period he produced many monuments and wrote poetry, stories, and reviews. In 1943 he moved to Lviv. He was a postwar refugee in Vienna and Augsburg. Among his works are busts of Christ, M. Kropyvnytsky, and M. Zankovetska.

**Zhuk, Serhii** [Žuk, Serhij], b 4 April 1892 in Kiev, d 1 March 1957 in Moscow. Specialist in hydrology and hydro-technology; full member of the USSR Academy of Sciences from 1953. He studied in St Petersburg and was a major general of engineering units in the Red Army. Zhuk headed numerous major hydro-engineering projects, including the Moscow Canal, the Volga-Don Complex, the Volga-Baltic Waterway, and the Lenin Hydroelectric Station on the Volga, as well as the Uglich, the Rybinsk, and other hydroelectric stations. In 1942 he became director of the All-Union Hydroelectric Project Surveying and Scientific Research Institute, which in 1957 was named after him.

**Zhuk, Yosyf** [Žuk, Josyf], b 1872 in Galicia, d 23 February 1934 in St Petersburg, Florida. Orthodox bishop. He completed a D TH and was ordained a Greek Catholic priest in 1899. He served as prefect (from 1902) and then rector (1907–8) of the Greek Catholic Theological Seminary in Lviv before becoming Greek Catholic vicar-general in Bosnia (1908–14) and then pastor of St Barbara's Church in Vienna (1914–20). He emigrated to North America, where he served as a priest in Toronto (1921–2), Montreal, and Philadelphia (1923–4). A popular priest with a large following, he rejected the Latinizing policies of Bishop K. Bohachevsky and in 1927 led a group of 26 priests in demanding Bohachevsky's removal. He subsequently concentrated on organizing the new Ukrainian Orthodox Church of America, which recognized the authority of the patriarch of Constantinople. In 1932 he was consecrated as the first bishop of the jurisdiction by two Syrian bishops.

**Zhukov, Georgii** [Žukov, Georgij], b 1 December 1896 in Strelkovka, Kaluga gubernia, d 18 June 1974 in Moscow. Marshal of the Soviet Union. He commanded the Soviet troops fighting the Japanese in Mongolia in 1939 and then was in charge of the Kiev Military District. In 1941 J. Stalin selected him to be chief of general staff and deputy defense minister. When Gen N. Vatutin was mortally wounded by a UPA unit, Zhukov was given command of the First Ukrainian Front (March–May 1944). He formally accepted Germany's surrender and became the supreme Soviet commander in Germany. In 1946 he was commander of Soviet land forces and deputy defense minister. Having played an important role in the power struggle after Stalin's death, he was forced into retirement in 1957.

**Zhukov, Konstantin** [Žukov], b 1873, d 7 March 1940. Russian architect. In 1887 he graduated from the Moscow School of Painting, Sculpture, and Architecture. In the early 1900s he designed several buildings in Crimea. He also designed the building of the Kharkiv Art School (1913), which has characteristic features of the Ukrainian Moderne, and residential buildings in Vovchanske and Kharkiv.

**Zhukovich, Platon** [Žukovyč], b 26 September 1857 in Pruzhany, Hrodna gubernia, Belarus, d 13 December 1919 in Petrograd. Belarusian church historian; full member of the Shevchenko Scientific Society from 1910 and of the St Petersburg Academy of Sciences from 1918. He graduated from the St Petersburg Theological Academy in 1881 and taught at seminaries in Polatsk (1881–3) and Vilnius (1883–91) before becoming a lecturer (1891–4) and then professor (1894–1918) at the St Petersburg Theological Academy. His major work was *Seimovaia bor'ba zapadno-russkogo dvorianstva s tserkovnoi uniei* (The Parliamentary Struggle of the Western-Ruthenian Nobility against the Church Union, 6 parts, 1901–12). He also wrote articles on the Church Union of Berestia and on Y. Kuntsevych, K. Ostrozky, and Y. Rutsky, and published an important collection of materials on the Lviv and Kiev church sobors of 1629 (*Zapiski Akademii nauk po Istoricheskofilologicheskom otdelenii*, vol 7, no. 15). A bibliographical article on Zhukovych by K. Kharlampovych appeared in ZIFV, vol 6 (1925).

**Zhukovsky, Antin** [Žukovs'kyj] (Anthony Zukowsky), b 27 September 1904 in Pomoriany, Zboriv county, Galicia, d 8 January 1984 in Warren, Michigan. Physician and civic leader. A graduate of Cracow University (1936), he practiced medicine in Zolochiv, Brody, and Radekhiv counties. Because of his political and civic work he was ar-

Antin Zhukovsky          Arkadii Zhukovsky

rested twice by the Polish authorities and imprisoned in Bereza Kartuzka. Having been conscripted by the Germans, he served as a regimental doctor in the Division Galizien. A postwar refugee in Germany, he organized the *Ukrainian Medical Charitable Service and directed a DP hospital in Dillingen. In 1949 he emigrated to the United States and settled in Steele, North Dakota, where he was president of the local branch of the Ukrainian Congress Committee of America.

**Zhukovsky, Arkadii** [Žukovs'kyj, Arkadij] (Joukovsky), b 12 January 1922 in Chernivtsi, Bukovyna. Historian; member of the Shevchenko Scientific Society (NTSh) since 1972, and foreign member of the Ukrainian Academy of Sciences since 1991. A postwar émigré, he was active in Ukrainian student organizations, particularly as head of the Union of Ukrainian Student Societies in Austria (1947–9) and member of the executive of the Central Union of Ukrainian Students (from 1948), and completed his studies in Graz (1949). He was head of Zarevo (1955–8) and general secretary of the Ukrainian Academic Society in Paris (from 1959). He continued his studies at the Ukrainian Free University (PH D, 1969) and the Sorbonne (PH D, 1976). In 1960 he began teaching at the Institut national des langues et civilisations orientales in Paris, and in 1969, at the Ukrainian Free University in Munich, where he later became prodean of the Faculty of Philosophy. From 1968 he was scientific secretary of NTSh in Europe, and in 1987 he became its head. In 1983 he became president of the *Petliura Ukrainian Library in Paris.

Zhukovsky is renowned as a historian of Bukovyna and of the Ukrainian Autocephalous Orthodox church, which appointed him as a member of its Metropolitan's Council. His publications in those areas include the sections on Bukovynian history in *Bukovyna: Ï mynule i suchasne* (Bukovyna: Its Past and Present, 1956); a report on the state of religion in the Ukrainian SSR (*ZNTSh*, vol 181 [1966]); and the introduction to *Martyrolohiia ukraïns'kykh tserkov* (Martyrology of the Ukrainian Churches, vol 1 of the encyclopedic *Ukraïns'ka Pravoslavna Tserkva* [The Ukrainian Orthodox Church], 1987). He also wrote the monograph *Petro Mohyla i pytannia iednosty Tserkov* (P. Mohyla and the Question of Union of the Churches, 1969) and a critical analysis of Mohyla's *trebnyk* in the republished *Trebnyk Petra Mohyly* (1988). Other works by Zhukovsky in the field of history include 'Contributions à l'histoire de l'Académie de Kiev (1615–1817), centre culturel et d'enseignement en Europe Orientale' (PH D diss, 1976) and 'L'Ukraine dans les années 1917–1933: Aspect historique' in *Actes du colloque La Renaissance nationale et culturelle en Ukraine de 1917 aux années 1930* (1986, which he also co-edited), as well as articles on the Ukrainization policy, the 1932–3 man-made famine in Ukraine, M. Hrushevsky and the journal *Ukraïna*, and the nationalist polemics of M. Drahomanov and B. Hrinchenko.

A longtime associate of *Entsyklopediia ukraïnoznavstva* (or *EU*, Encyclopedia of Ukraine, 10 vols, 1955–84), Zhukovsky became a member of its editorial board in 1971 and its editor in chief after the death of V. Kubijovyč in 1985. As member of the *Encyclopedia of Ukraine* (or *AEU*, 5 vols, 1984–93) editorial board from 1976 and subject editor for religion and history, he contributed a multitude of entries to that work. Zhukovsky and O. Subtelny's article on the *history of Ukraine in *AEU* (vol 2, 1988) was translated, updated, and published in Lviv as *Narys istoriï Ukraïny* (1991).

D.H. Struk

Herman Zhukovsky          Col Oleksander Zhukovsky

**Zhukovsky, Herman** [Žukovs'kyj], b 13 November 1913 in Radzyviliv (now Chervonoarmiiske), Dubno county, Volhynia oblast, d 15 March 1976 in Kiev. Composer and pedagogue. He graduated from the Kiev Conservatory (1941) in the composition class of L. Revutsky and later (1951–8) taught music theory at the same institution. His works include the operas *Maryna* (1939), *From a Sincere Heart* (1951), and *First Spring* (1959); the ballets *Rostyslava* (1955), *The Forest Song* (1961), and *The Maiden and Death* (1971); and symphonic suites, cantatas, chamber music, choruses, art songs, arrangements of Ukrainian folk songs, and film scores.

**Zhukovsky, Ivan** [Žukovs'kyj], b 1810, d 1884 in Pidbereztsi, Lviv county, Galicia. Ukrainian Catholic priest and pedagogue. A graduate of Lviv (1830) and Vienna (1834) universities, he was a priest in Lviv and a teacher at the Academic Gymnasium of Lviv (1848–52). At the *Congress of Ruthenian Scholars in 1848, he presented a project for a Ukrainian orthography based on a phonetic system of transcription. This project was rejected, and the congress instead advocated the adoption of the *Maksymovychivka* etymological orthography. Zhukovsky later served as canon of the metropolitans' consistory and then as a parish priest in Pidbereztsi.

**Zhukovsky, Ivan** [Žukovs'kyj], b 4 March 1901 in Kitsman, Bukovyna, d 4 December 1980 in New York. Architect and civil engineer. He studied in Prague (1926) and had his own architectural office in Chernivtsi (1930–41), where he reconstructed the theater of the People's Home. He emigrated to Germany and then to the United States (1950), where he was active in Ukrainian community life. He served as president of the Ukrainian Engineers' Society of America (1958–9) and taught at the Ukrainian Technical Institute in New York. He designed the St John the Baptist Ukrainian Catholic Church in Hunter, New York, and the SS Peter and Paul Ukrainian Orthodox Church in Glen Spey, New York. He published a number of books, including Ukrainian-German dictionaries.

**Zhukovsky, Oleksander** [Žukovs'kyj] (Zhukivsky), b 1884, d 1925. Colonel of the Army of the UNR and political activist. He was a 'centrist' member of the Ukrainian Party of Socialist Revolutionaries (UPSR) and a member of the Central Rada and the General Military Committee in 1917. He became an adjutant to the UNR minister of defense and the minister of labor in January 1918, and in February he himself became minister of defense. In early 1919 he commanded an independent border corps and led the Kamianets-Podilskyi garrison. He emigrated in 1919 to Prague and then to Vienna, where he became secretary of the Foreign Delegation of the UPSR and worked closely with M. Hrushevsky.

**Zhukovsky, Vasilii** [Žukovs'kyj, Vasilij], b 9 February 1783 in Mishenskoe, Tula gubernia, Russia, d 24 April 1852 in Baden-Baden. Russian Romantic poet and translator. As a tutor at the tsar's court from 1815 to 1839, he used his influence to help buy T. Shevchenko's freedom from serfdom. In fact, it was a portrait of Zhukovsky, painted by K. Briullov, which was raffled to collect the necessary funds. Shevchenko dedicated the poem 'Kateryna' to him. Zhukovsky's works have been translated into Ukrainian by P. Hrabovsky and M. Rylsky.

**Zhukovsky, Yevhen** [Žukovs'kyj, Jevhen], b 1868 in Kitsman, Bukovyna, d 7 April 1944 in Chernivtsi. Agronomist, teacher, and community activist. A graduate of the Higher School of Agriculture in Vienna, he served as director of the agricultural school in Kitsman, the only secondary school of agronomy in Galicia and Bukovyna, in 1896–1918. He then held a post in the Ukrainian Bukovynian government. After being released from his post by the Rumanian authorities he continued to be active in various community and cultural organizations. He published *Uchebnyk ril'nytstva* (Textbook of Agriculture, 1903), which provides a valuable compendium of Ukrainian terminology. He also published numerous articles on agriculture in Ukrainian and German.

**Zhuky** [Žuky]. A village 10 km north of Poltava. In 1658 Hetman I. Vyhovsky's forces crushed those of Col M. Pushkar, a supporter of Muscovy, at Zhuky. From April to July 1709 the Swedish king Charles XII made his headquarters there. S. Velychko lived in Zhuky in 1708–28 and wrote some of his chronicle in the village.

**Zhuliany** [Žuljany]. III-11. The southwestern district of Kiev. The settlement Zhelannia was situated there during the period of Kievan Rus'. During the 17th and 18th centuries the land there was owned by the Kievan St Sophia Monastery. In the fall of 1918 the Sich Riflemen fought the troops of the Hetman government on the site. On 29 August 1919 the united forces of the UNR Army and the Ukrainian Galician Army routed the Bolsheviks at Zhuliany before taking Kiev. During the Soviet period the airport at Zhuliany (est 1924) serviced only internal flights connecting Kiev with the oblast centers of Ukraine.

**Zhulkevsky, Ivan** [Žulkevs'kyj], b 17 August 1919 in Proskuriv (now Khmelnytskyi), Podilia gubernia. Actor. He has worked in the Khmelnytskyi Ukrainian Music and Drama Theater (1947–52, and since 1963), the Stryi Ukrainian Music and Drama Theater (1952–9), and the Lviv Philharmonic (1959–63).

Mykola Zhulynsky              Col Dmytro Zhupinas

**Zhulynsky, Mykola** [Žulyns'kyj], b 25 August 1940 in Novosilky, Mlyniv raion, Rivne oblast. Literary scholar and critic; full member of the ANU since 1992. He graduated from Kiev University in 1968 and completed postgraduate studies at the Institute of Literature of the AN URSR (now ANU). In 1991 he was appointed director of the Institute of Literature, and in 1992 he was appointed state adviser to Ukraine on policies pertaining to the humanities and then a deputy prime minister. He is the author of a number of critical essays in Russian and Ukrainian, published in the collection *Nablyzhennia* (The Approach, 1986), and from the mid-1980s he was one of the leading scholars who demanded that works excised from the Ukrainian canon under L. Brezhnev and J. Stalin be once again brought into prominence. His numerous articles on V. Vynnychenko, M. Khvylovy, M. Ivchenko, and others have been published mainly in *Literaturna Ukraïna*, and he has delivered papers at plenums of the Ukrainian Writers' Union. In 1992 he was awarded the Shevchenko State Prize for his latest book of literary history, *Iz zabuttia v bezsmertia* (From Oblivion to Immortality, 1990).

**Zhupa.** The Slavic word for the territorial-administrative districts in Hungary and Czechoslovakia known as *komitats.

**Zhupa** (Polish: *żupa*). The name given to the larger salt mines and salt-processing facilities in medieval Poland. They were owned by the crown and administered by appointed officials called *zhupnyky* or leased out to church-

men or other notables. Brine from underground pools was evaporated in large cauldrons, and the remaining salt was shaped in conical forms. On Ukrainian territories there were *zhupy* in Sambir, Peremyshl, and Sianik.

**Zhupinas, Dmytro** [Župinas], b 1892, d ? Military commander. A lieutenant colonel in the UNR Army, he commanded the 1st Odessa and the 24th Sahaidachny Zaporozhian infantry regiments and the Combined Zaporozhian Cavalry Regiment in the First Winter Campaign, as well as the 2nd regiment of the Separate Cavalry Division. He emigrated to the United States in 1952.

**Zhurakhovych, Semen** [Žuraxovyč], b 6 November 1907 in Sokilka, Kobeliaky county, Poltava gubernia. Writer. Since 1948 he has published many books of stories and novelettes, the most recent being in 1987, and the novel *Kyïvs'ki nochi* (Kievan Nights, 1964). He was awarded the Yanovsky Prize in 1985, and a two-volume edition of his selected works appeared in 1987.

**Zhurakovsky** [Žurakovs'kyj]. A family line of noblemen and Cossack *starshyna* in Left-Bank Ukraine. Mykhailo Zhurakovsky was a captain of Sosnytsia regiment (1649). His son, Yakiv Zhurakovsky (d 1704), was a captain of Hlukhiv company and then colonel of Nizhen regiment (1678–85); he fought in the *Chyhyryn campaigns of 1677–8. Yakiv's sons were Lukiian (colonel of Nizhen regiment in 1701–18) and Vasyl *Zhurakovsky. Lukiian's grandson was Andrii Zhurakovsky, the last colonel of Nizhen regiment (1774–82). Also a member of the line was Irodion Zhurakovsky (d 1736), the bishop of Chernihiv in 1722–33.

**Zhurakovsky, Vasyl** [Žurakovs'kyj, Vasyl'], b ?, d 1730. Cossack leader. He was general osaul (1710–24) under Hetman I. Skoropadsky and a close associate of P. Polubotok. After Polubotok's departure for St Petersburg in 1723, Zhurakovsky and the general standard-bearer Ya. Lyzohub governed the Hetmanate. He relayed the *Kolomak Petitions to Polubotok in St Petersburg, with the consequence that Polubotok was taken into custody in 1723. The Rusian investigator A. Rumiantsev charged Zhurakovsky with conspiracy to promote the autonomy of Ukraine, and Zhurakovsky was imprisoned in St Petersburg (1724–5), after which period he lived in exile in Moscow. Through the intercession of D. Apostol he was allowed to return to Ukraine in 1728.

**Zhuravel, Andrii** [Žuravel', Andrij], b 1892, d after 1938. Physician. In 1918 he was a member of the Central Rada and of the Ukrainian Sanitation Commission in Berlin. In the 1930s he was a docent at the Ukrainian Tuberculosis Institute in Kharkiv. He was arrested in 1938, and his further fate is unknown.

**Zhuravli** (The Cranes). A male chorus, founded 1972 in Warsaw by Ya. *Poliansky, the ensemble's first artistic director and conductor. Since 1983 the chorus has been conducted by R. Revakovych. The chorus is affiliated with the Ukrainian Social and Cultural Society in Poland. It has appeared in Warsaw and other Polish cities and has toured Czechoslovakia, the United States, Canada, and Ukraine. Its repertoire incorporates a variety of eras and genres, including folk and historic songs, church music, classical and romantic pieces, and contemporary works. The group performs compositions by D. Bortniansky, A. Vedel, M. Lysenko, M. Leontovych, K. Stetsenko, I. Vorobkevych, P. Nishchynsky, and P. Maiboroda and arrangements of Ukrainian folk songs by O. Koshyts, A. Avdiievsky, and Ya. Poliansky. It has released several recordings.

**Zhuravlivka, Battle of.** A military engagement on 26 December 1919 at Zhuravlivka village, Bratslav county, Podilia gubernia, in which the Third Iron Division of the UNR Army defeated the 45th Division of the Red Army and forced it to retreat toward Tulchyn.

**Zhuravno, Treaty of.** A peace agreement between Poland and Turkey signed on 27 October 1676 at the town of Zhuravno (now in Zhydachiv raion, Lviv oblast). It canceled the annual tribute that had been imposed on Poland by the Buchach Peace Treaty of 1672. By the new agreement Poland recognized the Turkish annexation of Podilia and Hetman P. Doroshenko's right to most of Right-Bank Ukraine, except for the territory of the former Bila Tserkva and Pavoloch regiments. The Polish Sejm refused to ratify the treaty, however, and hostilities between Poland and Turkey continued until 1699.

**Zhuravsky, Dmytro** [Žuravs'kyj], b 1810 in Mahiliou gubernia, Belarus, d 23 November 1856 in Kiev. Statistician and economist. A graduate of the St Petersburg Cadet school (1829), he worked as a civil servant in Kamianets-Podilskyi and Kiev. In 1851 he was appointed to the position of academic secretary of the Commission for Describing Gubernias of the Kiev District at Kiev University. He edited the commission's works, including the three-volume *Statisticheskoe opisanie Kievskoi gubernii* (A Statistical Description of Kiev Gubernia, 1852), and wrote *O kreditnykh sdelkakh v Kievskoi gubernii* (On Credit Agreements in Kiev Gubernia, 1856), *Ob istochnikakh i upotreblenii statisticheskikh svedenii* (On the Sources and Use of Statistical Information, 1846), and *Statisticheskoe obozrenie raskhodov na voennyia potrebnosti v 1711–1825 g.* (A Statistical Survey of Expenditures on Military Needs in 1711–1825, 1859). Zhuravsky's theoretical and empirical works had an important impact on the development of the fields of statistics and economics in the Russian Empire. M. Ptukha wrote a biography of Zhuravsky in 1951.

**Zhurba, Andrii** [Žurba, Andrij], b ?, d July 1768 in Bloshchyntsi near Bila Tserkva. Cossack rebel leader. He led a detachment of 300 haidamakas during the Koliivshchyna rebellion of 1768. Aided by forces under M. Shvachka, they took the fortified town of Fastiv and raided the estates of Right-Bank landowners. Zhurba was killed in battle with Russian troops dispatched by Catherine II to suppress the uprising. He was celebrated in folk dumas as a counselor to M. Zalizniak.

**Zhurba, Halyna** [Žurba] (pseud of Halina Dombrowska), b 29 December 1888 in Teplyk, Haisyn county, Podilia gubernia, d 9 April 1979 in Philadelphia. Writer. The daughter of a Polish noble and a Polonized mother, she was Ukrainianized by the rural environment of her childhood. In 1909 her first, critically acclaimed story collection, *Z zhyttia* (From Life), was published in Odessa. She contributed several stories to the journal *Ukraïns'ka khata*; a

Halyna Zhurba

1912 issue of the journal was confiscated by the tsarist censors because of her story 'Koniaka' (The Horse). From 1912 she lived in Kiev and was part of the *Ukraïns'ka khata* circle. From 1917 to 1919 she was an editor of the daily *Nova rada*. In 1919 she belonged to the writers' group Muzahet and published her second story collection, *Pokhid zhyttia* (The March of Life). Having fled from Soviet rule in 1920 to the Polish internment camp in Tarnów, in the interwar years she lived with her husband, A. *Nyvynsky, in Zdolbuniv, Volhynia, in Lviv, and in Warsaw. She published the plays *Malanka* (1921) in Tarnów and *Metelytsia* (The Blizzard) and *V pereleti vikiv* (As Years Fly By) in Prague, in M. Shapoval's journal *Nova Ukraïna*. She also published a story in the Soviet journal *Vsesvit* (1925, no. 20). Her major works, two award-winning novels about the Revolution of 1917 in Volhynia, *Zori svit zapovidaiut'* (Stars Forecast the World, 1933) and *Revoliutsiia ide* (The Revolution Is Coming, 2 vols, 1937–8), were published in Lviv. In 1943 her 'sensational' novel *Doktor Kachioni* (Doctor Caccioni) was published in Cracow. As a postwar émigrée Zhurba lived in Germany. After emigrating to the United States in 1950, she published an autobiographical account of her childhood, *Dalekyi svit* (A Distant World, 1955), the first volume of a planned semi-autobiographical trilogy, *Todir Sokir* (1967), and essays, stories, and temperamental articles in émigré periodicals. She insisted on using an idiosyncratic phonetic orthography and many little-known, archaic words in her later works.

R. Senkus

**Zhurba, Vasyl** [Žurba, Vasyl'], b and d ? Rebel leader. A native of Ukraine who had settled in the Volga region, he was colonel of a rebel detachment in the uprising led by the Don Cossack E. Pugachev (1773–4). He fled to Ukraine to avoid capture by tsarist troops, and he organized and led rebel groups in Left-Bank and Slobidska Ukraine and the Voronezh and Rostov-na-Donu regions which were active for over a year.

**Zhurlyva, Olena** [Žurlyva] (pseud of Olena Kotova), b 24 June 1898 in Smila, Kiev gubernia, d 10 June 1971 in Kirovohrad. Poet and pedagogue. She graduated from the Kiev Institute of People's Education in 1922 and taught in secondary schools in Kiev, Kharkiv, Dnipropetrovske, Moscow, and Kirovohrad. Before the revolution she published her work in *Literaturno-naukovyi vistnyk* and *Ukraïns'ka khata*, and after, in *Chervonyi shliakh*, *Hlobus*, and other periodicals. She was arrested in 1938 by the NKVD and imprisoned from 1939 to 1944 in labor camps in the Altai region. Collections of her poetry include *Bahrianyi svit* (The Crimson World, 1930), *Virshi* (Poems, 1958), *Zemlia v tsvitu* (The Earth in Bloom, 1964), and *Chervone lystia* (Red Leaves, 1964). She also wrote children's verse and translated Lesia Ukrainka and V. Stefanyk into Russian.

**Zhurman, Illia** [Žurman, Illja], b ?, d 1783. Cossack officer and state figure in the Russian Empire. He was a leading civil administrator in Ukraine (1769–74), K. Rozumovsky's deputy to St Petersburg (1750, 1751), and a general judge in the Hetmanate (1756–82). In 1782–3 he was the first governor of Novhorod-Siverskyi vicegerency.

*Zhurnal bibliotekoznavstva ta bibliohrafiï*

***Zhurnal bibliotekoznavstva ta bibliohrafiï*** (Journal of Library Science and Bibliography). An annual publication of the National Library of Ukraine in Kiev (now the Central Scientific Library of the Academy of Sciences of Ukraine) in 1927–30. It contained articles on theoretical and practical issues in library science and management. It was edited by S. Posternak, M. Saharda, and V. Kozlovsky.

**Zhvanchyk River** [Žvančyk]. A left-bank tributary of the Dniester River that flows southward for 107 km in Khmelnytskyi oblast and drains a basin area of 769 sq km. The river is 3–5 m wide in its upper course and eventually widens to 10–35 m. It has a drop of 1.9 m/km, with several areas of rapids and waterfalls. Its waters are harnessed for electricity and used for pisciculture.

**Zhvanets** [Žvanec']. V-7. A village (1972 pop 1,500) near the junction of the Zhvanchyk and the Dniester rivers in Kamianets-Podilskyi raion, Khmelnytskyi oblast. It was first mentioned in a historical document in 1431. At the end of the 16th century the Poles built a castle there, which was destroyed by the Turks in 1620. It was rebuilt, and by 1646 the town had obtained the rights of *Magdeburg law. In 1653 B. Khmelnytsky laid siege to Jan II Casimir Vasa in the castle and was betrayed by his Tatar ally. In 1672–99 the town was occupied by the Turks, and subsequently it declined to a village. In 1793 it was annexed by Russia. Today the ruins of the 16th-century fortress and a 17th-century Roman Catholic church testify to Zhvanets's historical importance.

**Zhvanets fortified settlement.** A fortified Trypilian culture settlement of the early 3rd millennium BC located near Zhvanets, Kamianets-Podilskyi raion, Khmelnytskyi oblast. Excavations in the 1960s revealed that the massive earthen defensive walls were built over a stone base. Located outside the defensive perimeter was a pottery-making complex with seven double-ledged kilns. The pottery fragments found in this area were often decorated with images of humans, animals, birds, and hunting scenes.

**Zhydachiv** [Žydačiv]. IV-5. A town (1989 pop 11,200) on the Stryi River and a raion center in Lviv oblast. One of the oldest towns in Ukraine, it is first mentioned in the chronicles under the year 1164, as Udech. At different times it has also been known as Sudachiv, Zidachiv, and Zudechiv. The town was an important trading center on the routes between the Principality of Galicia-Volhynia, Kievan Rus', Western Europe, and the Black Sea. In 1241 it was sacked by the Tatars, and 10 years later it was recaptured by Danylo Romanovych. From the mid-14th century it was under Polish rule, and in 1393 it was granted the rights of *Magdeburg law. The townsmen rebelled against the Polish overlords in 1648 but were soon subjugated. An Orthodox brotherhood arose to resist union with the Roman Catholic church. A cholera epidemic in 1676 reduced the population by half. By the end of the century the town had declined to a village. After the partition of Poland in 1772 Zhydachiv was annexed by Austria, and in 1867 it became a county center in Galicia. In the interwar period Zhydachiv was under Polish rule. Today it is a transportation and industrial center. It has a cellulose and carton, a brick, and a cheese factory.

**Zhydiata, Luka** [Žydjata], b ?, d 15 October 1060 in Novgorod. The first locally born bishop of Novgorod (1036–55 and 1058–60). He was nominated as bishop by Prince Yaroslav the Wise. After the death of Yaroslav, Zhydiata was called to Kiev by Metropolitan Yefremii and imprisoned for three years. When the accusations against him proved to be false, he was freed, and returned to his cathedral. During his tenure the stone St Sophia Cathedral was constructed (1051), the Novgorod Chronicles were compiled, and the Ostromir Gospel was copied. Two of his sermons have survived, and were published in the 19th century.

**Zhydove** [Žydove]. A district in the northwestern part of medieval Kiev, settled by Jews. It was entered through the Jewish Gate (1037) in the walled city of Yaroslav the Wise (see the map of *Kiev in the 10th–12th centuries).

**Zhydychyn St Nicholas's Monastery** (Zhydychynskyi manastyr sv. Mykolaia). A monastery located near Lutske, Volhynia. Records of it date from as early as the 13th century. After the Church Union of Berestia it joined the Uniate church, and in 1608–1826 it was the residence of the Uniate bishop of Lutske-Ostrih, who also served as its archimandrite. The main church and bishop's residence were built in 1723. The monastery was closed in 1839 by Nicholas I.

**Zhyhadlo, Ivan** [Žyhadlo], b 1876, d? Jurist, teacher, and court official in Poltava gubernia. He was one of the founders of the Ukrainian Law Society in Poltava (1918).

Tried in 1930 for belonging to the *Union for the Liberation of Ukraine, he was exiled to Kazakhstan. In 1943 he emigrated, and in 1958 he settled in the United States. He compiled a Russian-Ukrainian legal dictionary (3 edns, 1918–19) and wrote articles on education and popular scientific topics, and recollections.

**Zhyla, Volodymyr.** See Zyla, Wolodymyr.

**Zhylenko, Iryna** [Žylenko], b 28 April 1941 in Kiev. Poet. She graduated from Kiev University (1964), and has worked as a newspaper and journal editor in Kiev. She began publishing in 1962. Among her works are the sketch collection *Bukovyns'ki balady* (Bukovynian Ballads, 1964) and the poetry collections *Solo na sol'fi* (A Solo in Sol-fa, 1965), *Avtoportret u chervonomu* (Self-Portrait in Red, 1971), *Vikno u sad* (Window onto the Orchard, 1978), *Kontsert dlia skrypky, doshchu i tsvirkuna* (Concert for Violin, Rain, and a Cricket, 1979), *Dim pid kashtanom* (The House under the Chestnut, 1981), *Iarmarok chudes* (The Market of Wonders, 1982), and *Ostannii vulychnyi sharmanshchyk* (The Last Street Barrel Organist, 1985). She has also written children's poetry books, such as *Dostyhaiut' kolosochky* (The Little Grain Ears Are Ripening, 1964) and *Vulychka moho dytynstva* (The Little Street of My Childhood, 1979).

**Zhylko, Fedot** [Žylko], b 14 March 1908 in Solovtsovtsy, Penza gubernia, Russia. Ukrainian dialectologist. A graduate of the Kiev Institute of Professional Education (1932), he taught Ukrainian language and dialectology in Kiev's postsecondary schools (1938–51). He has headed the AN URSR (now ANU) Institute of Linguistics Dialectology Division since 1950. The coauthor of programs for collecting dialectal data (1939, 1948), he has written a textbook on Ukrainian dialectology (1951), a prospectus for a Ukrainian dialectological atlas (1952), monographs on Ukrainian dialectology (doctoral diss, 1955; rev edn 1966) and the Ukrainian dialects (1958), and many dialectological articles. He edited the periodicals *Ukraïns'ka mova v shkoli* (1951–60) and *Dialektolohichnyi biuleten'* (nos 6–9, 1956–62), collections of the proceedings of the 10th, 11th, 12th, and 13th republican dialectological conferences (1961, 1965, 1971, 1970), and collections of articles on the Middle Dnieper dialects (1960), Ukrainian linguistic geography (1966), and Ukrainian dialectal morphology (1969). In his dissertation he posited the existence of three original Ukrainian dialectal groups: northern, southwestern, and southeastern.

**Zhylko, Yurii** [Žylko, Jurij] (pseuds: Istyk, Izhak, Ostiuk Navisny, Yurii Pluzhanyn, Selianyn Yurchyk), b 28 February 1898 in Pidluzhne, Rivne county, Volhynia gubernia, d May 1938 in Poltava. Writer. In 1923 he graduated from the Poltava Institute of People's Education, worked as a teacher, and belonged to the peasant writers' organization Pluh. From 1922 on his poems and stories appeared in periodicals, such as *Pluh*, *Pluzhanyn*, *Hlobus*, *Molodyi bil'shovyk*, and *Zoria*. His poetry collection *Polustanok* (The Whistle-stop) appeared in 1930. He died during the Stalinist terror of the 1930s.

**Zhylytsky, Petro** [Žylyc'kyj], b 9 June 1920 in Kiev, d 30 April 1970 in Kiev. Architect. He graduated from the Kiev Civil-Engineering Institute (1950) and worked in Kiev. He

helped design and build the administration building in Donetske (1954–5), the residential building for Kryvorizhstal in Kryvyi Rih (1956), the Palace of Culture in Novoekonomichne (1956–7), and the building of the State Construction Committee (1965) and Ukraina Palace of Culture in Kiev (1970).

Hnat Zhytetsky

**Zhytetsky, Hnat** [Žytec'kyj] (Ihnatii), b 15 February 1866 in Kamianets-Podilskyi, d 8 April 1929 in Kiev. Historian, literary critic, and librarian; son of P. *Zhytetsky. A graduate of Kiev University (1890), he taught in Petrograd until 1918. After returning to Kiev he worked in the National Library of Ukraine from 1921 as its senior librarian and from 1922 as director of its manuscript division. He contributed to the journal *Kievskaia starina* (KS), served as its editorial secretary in 1888, edited its Ukrainian-Russian history section in 1893–1903, and wrote many articles for the Prosveshcheniie edition of the *Bol'shaia entsiklopediia* (The Great Encyclopedia). In 1919 Zhytetsky established a VUAN journal of the National Library of Ukraine and edited two volumes of the collection *Knyzhnyi vistnyk*. He contributed to M. Hrushevsky's journal *Ukraïna* when it was revived, and served on the historical commission of the VUAN. His works on the social and cultural history of 19th-century Ukraine include *Literaturnaia deiatel'nost' Ioanna Vyshenskogo* (The Literary Activity of Ivan Vyshensky, KS, no. 6, 1890), *Order Rumiantseva 1737 roku i reskrypt imp. Pavla 1800 roku* (Rumiantsev's Order of 1737 and the Rescript of Emperor Paul of 1800, KS, no. 11, 1886). In *Ukraïna* he published articles on KS in 1883–7, while it was under the editorship of F. Lebedyntsev (1925), on the Southwestern Branch of the Imperial Russian Geographical Society in Kiev (1927), on the Hromada of Kiev in the 1860s (1928), and on efforts to organize a historical society in Kiev (1929). He also wrote essays on M. Maksymovych, M. Kostomarov, T. Shevchenko, P. Kulish, A. Svydnytsky, F. Vovk, and P. Lukashevych.

BIBLIOGRAPHY
Karachkivs'kyi, M. 'Soroklitnii iuvilei I.P. Zhytets'koho v Istorychnii sektsiï VUAN,' *Ukraïna* 1928, no. 4
A. Zhukovsky

**Zhytetsky, Irodion** [Žytec'kyj], b 20 April 1851 in Zaliniine, Kostiantynohrad county, Poltava gubernia, d 1913. Ethnographer and civic activist. After graduating from Kiev University (1875) he lectured at the Hlukhiv Teachers' Institute and was active in the Old Hromada of

Kiev. In 1878 he was expelled from the university for his involvement in student protests, which he described in his *Martovskoe dvizhenie studentov Kievskogo universiteta 1878 g.* (The March Movement of Kiev University Students in 1878, 1878), written under the pseudonym M. Tkachenko. Having been exiled to Viatka (1879–82) and then Astrakhan (1882–5) gubernias, he studied the local people and wrote two books on the Kalmyks of Astrakhan (1892, 1893). He contributed a study of nationalities in Ukraine to *Kievskaia starina* (1883, nos 5–6, 8–9, 11).

Pavlo Zhytetsky                   *Zhytie i slovo*

**Zhytetsky, Pavlo** [Žytec'kyj], b 4 January 1837 in Kremenchuk, Poltava gubernia, d 18 March 1911 in Kiev. Philologist and ethnographer; member of the Imperial Russian Geographic Society from 1873, the Historical Society of Nestor the Chronicler from 1879, the Shevchenko Scientific Society from 1903, the Ukrainian Scientific Society in Kiev from 1907 (first honorary member from 1908), and corresponding member of the Russian Academy of Sciences from 1898; husband of V. Zhytetska and father of H. *Zhytetsky. He studied at the theological seminary in Pereiaslav (1851–7), the Kiev Theological Academy (1857–60), and Kiev University (1860–4; M PHIL, 1878) and taught Russian language and literature in gymnasiums in Kamianets-Podilskyi (1865–8) and Kiev (1868–80), at Galagan College (1874–80, 1882–93), in military schools, at St Petersburg University (1880–2), and at the St Vladimir Cadet School in Kiev (1882–93). As a Ukrainophile and a leading member of the Old *Hromada of Kiev from the 1860s and a founding member of the *Southwestern Branch of the Imperial Russian Geographic Society (1873–6), he was kept under constant police surveillance and denied a university career. He was in charge of the Hromada's Ukrainian dictionary project, and from 1902 he was a consultant to B. *Hrinchenko on the preparation of the Ukrainian-Russian dictionary. In 1908 he received an honorary doctorate from Kiev University.

Zhytetsky's first work, an article entitled 'Russian patriotism' (*Osnova*, 1862, no. 3), argued for the viability of an independent Ukrainian literature and culture. The first historian of literary Ukrainian, he wrote (in Russian) the first complete and systematic (but soon obsolete) history of Ukrainian sounds (1876) and a pioneering survey of 17th- and 18th-century literary Ukrainian with an appendix consisting of *Synonima slavenorosskaia* (1889; Ukraini-

an trans 1941). For these books he was awarded the Uvarov Prize (1877, 1890). He also wrote a book of studies of Ukrainian folk dumas (1893; Ukrainian trans 1919); textbooks on the theory of creativity (8 edns, 1895–1911), the theory of poetry (8 edns, 1898–1913), and the history of poetry (6 edns, 1898–1913); a book on I. Kotliarevsky's *Eneïda* (Aeneid) and 18th-century Ukrainian literature (1900; Ukrainian trans 1919); and studies of the Peresopnytsia Gospel (1876), W. Humboldt (1900), O. Storozhenko's stories (1903), and Ukrainian translations of the Gospels (1905). In 1883 Zhytetsky rejected M. Pogodin's and A. Sobolevsky's hypothesis that medieval Kiev was ethnically Russian, and argued that Kievan Rus' was the cradle of the Ukrainian nation, and that Ukrainian linguistic traits were already present in 12th-century literary monuments. Zhytetsky's letters were published in a 1937 Warsaw edition of the Old Hromada's correspondence with M. Drahomanov. V. Plachynda's biography of Zhytetsky and an edition of his selected works (ed L. Masenko) were published in Kiev in 1987. The valuable archive of his papers is preserved at the ANU Central Scientific Library.

R. Senkus

**Zhytie** (Life). An irregular socialist youth journal published in Lviv in 1912–14. It was edited by S. Danylovych. Among its contributors were O. Bordun, R. Zaklynsky, I. Franko, O. Bezpalko, and M. Pavlyk.

**Zhytie i slovo** (Life and Word). A bimonthly journal published in Lviv from February 1894 to June 1897. It was edited by I. Franko and published by his wife, O. Franko. *Zhytie i slovo* contained belles lettres, literary criticism, and book reviews; articles on history, politics, and culture; and materials on ethnography and folklore. It also contained translations of Western European and Russian literature and regular reports on political and intellectual developments in Russian-ruled Ukraine. After a six-month interruption, from July 1896 it emphasized political and economic issues and published commentaries and analyses from a decidedly socialist, anti-imperialist perspective. Although the journal never attracted more than 400 to 500 subscribers, the high quality of its contents made it one of the more influential Ukrainian journals of the time. An index to *Zhytie i slovo* compiled by P. Babiak and edited by M. Humeniuk was published in Lviv in 1968.

**Zhytomyr** [Žytomyr]. III-9. A city (1990 pop 296,000) on the Teteriv River and an oblast and raion center. It was founded, according to local legend, by a favorite of Askold and Dyr, Zhytomyr, in 884. It is first mentioned in the chronicles under the year 1240, when the town was destroyed by the Mongols. In 1320 Gediminas annexed it to the Grand Duchy of Lithuania and fortified it against the Tatars, who besieged it in 1399, 1469, 1482, and 1606. In 1444 Zhytomyr was granted the rights of *Magdeburg law, and in 1471 it became a county center of Kiev province. In 1569 it became part of the Polish Commonwealth. Its inhabitants revolted against their Polish overlords in 1594–6, 1618, and 1648. Under B. Khmelnytsky's rule the town served briefly as a company center of Kiev regiment. In 1667 it was restored to Poland by the Treaty of Andrusovo, and in the following century it developed into an important Polish cultural center. It was the seat of a Ro-

Zhytomyr's Victory Square

man Catholic diocese and the home of a Jesuit college (1720) and monastery (1724), a Bernardine monastery (1761), and a convent of the Sisters of St Vincent (1766). Its inhabitants joined the haidamaka rebellions in 1750 and 1768. After the partition of Poland in 1793, the town was annexed by Russia, and in 1804 it was made into the administrative center of *Volhynia gubernia. In the 19th century Zhytomyr developed into a regional manufacturing and trading center. Its main industries were candle and soap making, distilling, brewing, brick-making, milling, and tanning. Toward the end of the century farm-machine building, metalworking, and tobacco manufacturing were added. The number of enterprises rose steadily, from 14 in 1834 to 33 in 1861, 46 in 1898, and 63 in 1914. A railway link to Berdychiv was completed in 1896 and to Korosten during the First World War. By 1900 the town had a boys' and a girls' gymnasium, a free public library (1896), a theological seminary, a city theater, a museum (1900), and a municipal hospital. Its population grew steadily, from 5,400 in 1798 to 16,700 in 1840, 38,400 in 1863, and 65,400 in 1897. The ethnic composition of the town at the end of the 19th century was: Jews, 36.7 percent, Ukrainians and Russians, 35.9 percent, and Poles, 13.4 percent.

At the beginning of 1918 Zhytomyr served briefly as the seat of the UNR government. In August 1919 the Second Corps of the Ukrainian Galician Army fought the Red Army in the vicinity. During the Second World War the city was occupied by the Germans, and suffered considerable damage. It was reconstructed in the postwar period. By 1971 its population had grown to 167,000 and by 1979, to 244,000.

Today Zhytomyr is a major industrial and transportation center. Its chief industries are machine building and metalworking; they include the Elektovymiriuvach instrument manufacturing consortium, the Avtozapchastyna automobile-parts plant, and the automatic machine-tool plant. The largest enterprises of light industry are the Linen Manufacturing Complex and clothing, footwear, and hosiery factories. The food industry consists of large meat-packing, confectionery, flour-milling, baking, distilling, and brewing enterprises. There are several building-materials manufacturers, a synthetic-fabrics plant, and a paper factory. The woodworking industry manufactures furniture, musical instruments, toys, and souvenirs. The city's educational facilities include a pedagogical and an agricultural institute, a branch of the Kiev Polytechnical Institute, 10 specialized secondary schools, and 15 vocational schools. There are several research institutes, such as the Institute of Hop Growing. Besides a regional studies museum there are literary memorial museums dedicated to M. Kotsiubynsky and V. Korolenko and a memorial museum devoted to S. Korolov. The cultural facilities include a picture gallery, a puppet theater, the Ukrainian Music and Drama Theater, and a philharmonic society. The chief architectural monuments are the Jesuit monastery, a Roman Catholic church (1744), the Assumption Church (1752), the Transfiguration Cathedral (1866–74), the city hall (1789), and the circuit court (1898, now the Agricultural Institute).

**Zhytomyr Agricultural Institute** (Zhytomyrskyi silskohospodarskyi instytut). A higher educational institution, until 1991 under the jurisdiction of the USSR Ministry of Agriculture. It was formed in 1935 out of the Zhytomyr Agricultural Institute of Industrial Crops, which had developed out of the Volhynia Agricultural Tekhnikum (est 1920). The institute has three faculties – agronomy, zoological engineering, and economics – as well as a correspondence school. The regular program requires four years and the correspondence program 5 years. About half the enrolment (2,700 in 1979) consists of correspondence students. Some research is done at the institute's experimental farm and laboratory, particularly on farming techniques suitable for Polisia. The institute publishes research studies.

**Zhytomyr Furniture Manufacturing Complex** (Zhytomyrskyi meblevyi kombinat). An enterprise of the woodworking industry, established in 1933. It produces wooden chairs, tables, and beds, as well as some wooden souvenirs. In 1974 it joined the Zhytomyrderev woodworking consortium, which consists of five furniture factories and a lumber mill.

**Zhytomyr kurhans.** Rus' burial mounds of the 11th to 12th century located outside Zhytomyr. Excavations in 1886–7 uncovered a total of 77 small (up to 2 m) kurhans. They contained single burials housed in wooden coffins with grave goods such as tableware, iron and bronze tools, and glass, silver, and carnelian jewelry.

**Zhytomyr Linen Manufacturing Complex** (Zhytomyrskyi lonokombinat). A textile factory built in Zhytomyr in 1958–61. It produces linen tablecloths, napkins, bed sheets, tent cloth, and fabrics for special uniforms. In 1977 it produced over 39 million sq m of fabric.

**Zhytomyr oblast.** An administrative territory (1989 pop 1,545,000) formed on 22 September 1937. It has an area of 29,900 sq km and is divided into 23 raions, 9 cities, 46 towns (smt), and 543 rural councils. Its capital is *Zhytomyr.

**Physical geography.** The oblast is divided between the Dnieper Upland (elevations up to 300 m) in the southwest and the Polisian marshes in the north. The northwestern part is marked by the Ovruch Ridge (elevation up to 300 m). The surface slopes down toward the north and northeast. Podzolized chernozems and gray forest soils are common in the southern part of the oblast; soddy, peat, clayey, and sandy soils are found in the north. The climate is moderate continental, with mild winters and wet summers. The average January temperature is –5.7°C, and the average July temperature is 18.9°C. The annual precipitation ranges from 600 mm in the north to 570 mm in the south. Approx 28 percent of the surface is covered with forest. In the marshy north the forests consist mostly of pine, oak, and birch. In the south oak and hornbeam prevail. The oblast is rich in mineral resources, such as coal, peat, granite, quartz, titanium, iron, and lead. The main rivers are the Teteriv, the Sluch, and the Uzh.

**History.** The territory was inhabited as early as the Paleolithic period. Toward the end of the 1st century AD it was occupied by the Derevlianians. In the 10th to 12th centuries it was part of Kievan Rus' and then of Volodymyr-Volynskyi and Galicia-Volhynia principalities. In 1362 the Grand Duchy of Lithuania took control of the territory. After the Union of Lublin it belonged to the Polish Commonwealth. With the partition of Poland in 1793, it was annexed by the Russian Empire, and became part of Volhynia and Kiev gubernias. Soviet control was established in 1919–20.

**Population.** According to the 1989 census 84.9 percent of the oblast's population was Ukrainian, 7.9 percent, Russian, 4.5 percent, Polish, and 1.4 percent, Jewish. The population density was 52.1 persons per sq km; the highest density was in the southwest, and the lowest in the northwest. Slightly over half of the population (53 percent) was urban. The largest cities are Zhytomyr, *Berdychiv, *Korosten, and *Novohrad-Volynskyi.

**Industry.** Over 70 percent of the oblast's production is industrial. The main industries are machine building and metalworking, which have expanded rapidly in the last 30 years. Their largest plants build equipment for the chemical industry (Berdychiv, Korosten), machine tools (Zhytomyr, Berdychiv), road-building machines (Korosten), farm machinery (Novohrad-Volynskyi), tractor parts (Olevske, Malyn), and power tools and equipment (Zhytomyr, Korosten). Sugar refining is the most important branch of the food industry. Its largest refineries are in Berdychiv, Andrushivka, Chervone, and Ivanopil. Other branches, such as distilling, brewing, meat packing, dairy products, and canning, are widely distributed. Ukraine's only malt factory is located in Berdychiv. The oblasts's light industry is known for its linen manufacturing. Footwear and leather (Berdychiv, Zhytomyr), musical instruments (Zhytomyr), and clothing (Zhytomyr, Korosten, Novohrad-Volynskyi, Malyn) are manufactured in the oblast. The local forests serve as a base for the paper (Zhytomyr, Malyn, Korostyshiv) and furniture industries. Building materials, such as reinforced-concrete products, brick, asphalt, and lime, are produced in Berdychiv, Malyn, Chudniv, and Cherniakhiv, and various stones are quarried in Korostyshiv, Malyn, Korosten, and Cherniakhiv raions. Glass factories are located in Romanivka and Zhytomyr.

**Agriculture.** In 1989 there were 419 collective farms, 87 state farms, and 3 poultry factories in the oblast. Approx 73 percent of the oblast's area was farmland. Of the farmland 78.4 percent was cultivated, 10.9 percent was hayfield, and 9.6 percent was pasture. A total of 380,100 ha of land were drained; the largest systems are located in the west and northwest. The sown area amounted to 1,312,000 ha. Much of it (40.9 percent) was devoted to grain crops, such as winter wheat, winter rye, legumes, barley, buck-

wheat, and millet. Feed crops occupied another 41.3 percent of the sown land. The rest was planted with industrial crops (8.5 percent), mostly sugar beets and flax, and potatoes and vegetables. Animal husbandry accounted for 45 percent of the agricultural output. It consists mostly of beef- and dairy-cattle raising and some hog and poultry farming.

**Transportation.** In 1989 the railway network consisted of 1,125 km of track. The trunk lines running through the oblast are Kiev–Lviv, Kiev–Brest, and Odessa–St Petersburg. The main junctions are Zhytomyr, Korosten, Berdychiv, Novohrad-Volynskyi, and Ovruch. The highway network had 8,100 km of road, 7,300 of which were paved. The major highways crossing the oblast are Kiev–Zhytomyr–Lviv, Kiev–Korosten–Kovel, and St Petersburg–Izmail. There is an airport in Zhytomyr.

BIBLIOGRAPHY
*Istoriia mist i sil URSR: Zhytomyrs'ka oblast'* (Kiev 1973)

**Zhytomyr Pedagogical Institute** (Zhytomyrskyi pedahohichnyi instytut im. I. Franka). A higher educational institute, under the jurisdiction of the Ministry of Education of Ukraine. Founded in 1919, the institute was named after I. Franko in 1926. It has four faculties: philology, foreign languages, physics-mathematics, and natural sciences. The institute specializes in preparing teachers for elementary education. In 1978–9 approx 3,180 students took classes there (2,215 of them full time), and the library contained nearly 300,000 titles.

**Zhytomyr Regional Studies Museum** (Zhytomyrskyi kraieznavchyi muzei). A museum founded in Zhytomyr in 1900 by the *Volhynia Research Society on the basis of an earlier museum created in 1865. Ecclesiastical and historical divisions with valuable artifacts, documents, and manuscripts were created there. In 1911 it was renamed the Central Volhynian Museum. Under interwar Soviet rule, as the Volhynian State Museum, it contained over 180,000 exhibit items and over 1,000 paintings (including those of the former museum [est 1893] of the Church Archeology Society of Volhynia Eparchy and others confiscated from local nobles), a botanical garden, an orangery, a laboratory, and a library with over 100,000 books (including the expropriated holdings of the Volhynia Theological Seminary Library). The museum was devastated during the Second World War and later rebuilt, and in 1979 it had nearly 60,000 exhibit items in its three divisions (natural sciences, history, and art). Memorial museums dedicated to Vladimir Korolenko (est 1973) and Serhii Korolov (est 1970) in Zhytomyr and to Lesia Ukrainka (est 1963) in Novohrad-Volynskyi are its branches. Guidebooks to the museum were published in 1972 and 1975.

**Zhytomyr Ukrainian Music and Drama Theater** (Zhytomyrskyi ukrainskyi muzychno-dramatychnyi teatr im. I. Kocherhy). A theater established in 1944. Its repertoire consists of world classics – including W. Shakespeare's *The Merry Wives of Windsor* and H. de Balzac's *La Marâtre* – and Ukrainian, Russian, Belarusian, and Latvian plays.

***Zhyttia*** (Life). An irregular socialist student journal published in Prague in 1924–5. Among its editors and contributors were K. and O. Kobersky, M. Kurakh, S. Ripetsky, and M. Stakhiv.

**Zhyttia** (Life). A monthly organ of the Basilian monastic order in Argentina published from 1948 to 1979. It first appeared in Buenos Aires, and then moved to Apóstoles in 1950. The journal contained church news and articles on religious and other topics. The editors included Revs O. Dub, I. Patrylo, V. Zinko, and V. Kovalyk.

**Zhyttia i mystetstvo** (Life and Art). A monthly journal of literature, culture, and the arts, published in Lviv in 1920. It was edited by F. Fedortsiv and M. Strutynsky.

**Zhyttia i pravo** (Life and Law). A quarterly journal of the Society of Ukrainian Lawyers and the Union of Ukrainian Lawyers, published in Lviv in 1928–39. Edited by K. Levytsky, it published articles on Ukrainian legal history and legal theory. Its regular contributors included Yu. Zaiats, L. Hankevych, Ya. Levytsky, M. Voloshyn, A. Paventsky, M. Hlushkevych, and O. Nadraga. In 1930 its circulation was 1,000.

Zhyttia i revoliutsiia

Zhyttia i znannia

**Zhyttia i revoliutsiia** (Life and Revolution, or *ZhR*). A monthly journal of politics, culture, scholarship, and civic affairs for the educated reader, published in Kiev from January 1925 to 1933. It was edited by writers such as M. Bazhan, O. Doroshkevych, I. Lakyza, I. Le, Yu. Savchenko, M. Tereshchenko, and others. With its sixth issue it began publishing belles lettres, literary criticism, poetry translations, and reviews. Like its Kharkiv counterpart *Chervonyi shliakh*, *ZhR* was a national forum for various writers, including those already established before the Soviet period (eg, M. Vorony, S. Vasylchenko) and the new postrevolutionary writers belonging to writers' groups such as *MARS, the *Neoclassicists, and the overtly communist *Zakhidnia Ukraina and *All-Ukrainian Association of Proletarian Writers. *ZhR* devoted much attention to the history of Ukrainian literature, art, theater, and music and to language and literary theory and debates. It published contributions by scholars and critics such as P. Balytsky (bibliology), Doroshkevych, M. Drai-Khmara, P. Fylypovych, M. Hladky (literary language), Ye. Kyryliuk, Lakyza, A. Leites, H. Maifet, Yu. Mezhenko (bibliography), M. Mohyliansky, Yu. Mykhailiv (art), A. Muzychka, B. Navrotsky, L. Pidhainy, V. Pidmohylny, V. Pokalchuk, D. Rudyk, P. Rulin (theater), S. Rodzevych (surveys of European literature and its translation into Ukrainian), S. Savchenko (foreign literature), Ya. Savchenko, S. Shchu-

pak, Ye. Shabliovsky, Yu. Smolych (theater), I. Vrona (art), F. Yakubovsky, B. Yakubsky, T. Yakymovych (foreign literature), Ya. Yurmas (music), D. Zahul, and M. Zerov.

*ZhR* played a prominent role in promoting the development of new Ukrainian literature in the 1920s. Because the editors pursued a course that often diverged from the interests of the Bolshevik party, during the Stalinist campaign against Ukrainian culture that began in the late 1920s, they were increasingly forced to admit their 'errors' and to renounce their ways. Party control over the journal grew; it became the organ of the Federation of Soviet Writers of Ukraine in 1932 and the Organizing Committee of the All-Ukrainian Union of Soviet Writers in 1933. With the full-fledged onslaught of the terror in Ukraine, the journal was shut down, and most of its contributors were repressed. N. Reva's systematic (but censored) index to its contents was published in Lviv in 1970.

I. Koshelivets

**Zhyttia i slovo** (Life and Word). A monthly and then bimonthly socialist newspaper, published in Drohobych in 1937–8 by I. Yurkiv and edited by R. Rozdolsky.

**Zhyttia i slovo** (Life and Word). A quarterly Catholic journal published in Innsbruck, Austria, in 1948–9 (four issues). It contained poetry, prose, articles on theological and cultural issues and the history of the Ukrainian Catholic church, and book reviews. The editor was O. Mokh.

**Zhyttia i slovo** (Life and Word). A pro-Soviet newspaper published weekly in Toronto from November 1965 to December 1991 in place of *Ukraïns'ke zhyttia and *Ukraïns'ke slovo. The organ of the *Association of United Ukrainian Canadians (AUUC), it contained political and economic news; reports on the Communist and labor movement in Canada; laudatory articles about developments in Soviet Ukraine, particularly in the field of culture; and reports on the activities of the AUUC and the related Workers' Benevolent Association. Although the paper published articles, especially in the 1960s, criticizing Russification in Ukraine, until recently it rarely strayed from the official Soviet line on other issues and ignored topics such as the dissident movement, the famine of 1932–3, and the crimes of Stalinism. The paper was edited by a board headed by M. Hrynchyshyn; the managing editor was P. Krawchuk. In 1992 *Zhyttia i slovo* and the AUUC monthly magazine the *Ukrainian Canadian* were replaced by a biweekly, bilingual tabloid, *Ukrainian Canadian Herald*.

**Zhyttia i znannia** (Life and Knowledge). A monthly self-educational magazine published by the Prosvita society in Lviv from October 1927 to August 1939 (a total of 143 issues). It contained popular articles in the fields of medicine and hygiene, the natural and technical sciences, farming, geography (descriptions of foreign countries), and Ukrainian history, literature, language, theater, music, and civic life; biographies and obituaries of prominent Ukrainians; some prose and poetry; occasional travel accounts; information about Prosvita and other community institutions; and book notes. *Zhyttia i znannia* was edited by M. Halushchynsky (1927–31), I. Bryk (1931–3), and V. Simovych (1933–9). In 1930 it had a pressrun of 2,500 copies.

*Zhyttia Podillia* (Life of Podilia). A daily newspaper published in Kamianets-Podilskyi from December 1918 to the end of April 1919. It was initiated by the Podilia gubernia executive and local Prosvita society; its first editors were L. Biletsky and V. Sichynsky. It was soon taken over by local members of the Ukrainian Socialist Revolutionary party and was edited by M. Hrushevsky and A. Zhyvotko.

*Zhyttia Pokuttia* (Life of Pokutia). A newspaper published weekly and then semimonthly in Kolomyia in 1931–4. The editors were Z. Stefaniv and D. Korbutiak.

*Zhyttie i znannie* (Life and Knowledge). A journal of health, hygiene, medicine, and popular science, published by a local society of feldshers and midwives from June 1913 to mid-1914 in Poltava (a total of 14 issues). The editor was H. Kovalenko.

Arkadii Zhyvotko

Mykola Ziber

**Zhyvotko, Arkadii** [Žyvotko, Arkadij] (pseuds: A. Pukhovsky, A. Pukhalsky), b 3 March 1890 in Pukhove, Voronezh gubernia, d 12 June 1948 in Aschaffenburg, Germany. Historian of the Ukrainian press, educator, journalist, and civic activist; full member of the Ukrainian Academy of Arts and Sciences. He graduated in 1917 from the Psychoneurological Institute in St Petersburg, where as a student he had been active in the Ukrainian Party of Socialist Revolutionaries. In 1917–18 he represented the Voronezh region on the Central Rada. When the Bolsheviks occupied Ukraine, he fled to Kremianets, where he worked as a teacher and was active in the local Prosvita. After emigrating to Czechoslovakia in 1923, he lectured at the Ukrainian Higher Pedagogical Institute in Prague and directed the archives of the Ukrainian Civic Committee in Czechoslovakia (which became the Ukrainian Historical Cabinet). After the war he was director of the Aschaffenburg branch of the Museum-Archive of the Ukrainian Academy of Arts and Sciences. In addition to poems and articles on public issues, literature, and education he wrote studies of the history of the Ukrainian press, most notably *Istoriia ukraïns'koï presy* (The History of the Ukrainian Press, 1946; repr 1990).

**Zhyvotovsky, Pavlo** [Žyvotovs'kyj], b ?, d 1699. Cossack officer. He was colonel of Myrhorod regiment and supported the election of Ya. Somko as hetman at the Nizhen Council of 1661. Later he was I. Hetman Briukhovetsky's general judge (1664–9). He also distin-guished himself in the defense of Hlukhiv from the Poles in 1664 and of Chyhyryn from the Turks in 1678.

**Ziber, Mykola**, b 10 March 1844 in Sudak, the Crimea, d 28 April 1888 in Yalta. Prominent Marxist economist. After graduating in law from Kiev University (1866) he continued his studies in Western Europe (1871–3). On his return to Ukraine he lectured on political economy at Kiev University, collaborated with the *Southwestern Branch of the Imperial Russian Geographic Society (for which he prepared a program for collecting statistical data), and contributed to *Kievskii telegraf*. In 1875, after the dismissal of his friend M. Drahomanov from Kiev University, Ziber resigned and emigrated to Switzerland. From there he contributed articles to Russian (eg, *Znanie, Slovo, Otechestvennyia zapiski, Vestnik Evropy, Russkaia mysl'*), French, and Swiss journals and to Drahomanov's *Hromada*, and developed close ties with younger Ukrainian intellectual and student circles in Lviv and Vienna. In 1884 he returned to the Crimea, where he died, probably of advanced syphilis of the central nervous system.

Ziber was the first popularizer of K. Marx's ideas in Ukraine and the Russian Empire. Although he agreed with Marx's theory of value and critique of capitalism, in his own works, such as his books on D. Ricardo's theory of value and capital (MA diss, 1871), primitive economic culture (1883), and the socioeconomic studies of Ricardo and Marx (1885), he stressed the evolutionary social development conditioned by changes in the relations of production. His writings exerted a great influence on Russian economic theorists well into the early 20th century. A champion of the idea of economic co-operation, in 1869 he was elected chairman of the board of the first consumer co-operative in Kiev and wrote a pamphlet on consumer societies. Two-volume editions of his works were published in Moscow in 1900–1 and 1959.

BIBLIOGRAPHY
Kleinbort, L. *Nikolai Ivanovich Ziber* (Petrograd 1923)
Koropeckyj, I. 'Academic Economics in the Nineteenth-Century Ukraine,' in *Selected Contributions of Ukrainian Scholars to Economics*, ed I. Koropeckyj (Cambridge, Mass 1984)
Scazzieri, R. 'Ziber on Ricardo,' *Contributions to Political Economy*, 6 (March 1987)

I. Vytanovych

**Zilberfarb, Moishe** (Silberfarb, Moses), b 1876 in Rivne, d 1934 in Warsaw. Jewish political activist in Ukraine. A leader of the United Jewish Socialist Workers' party, Zilberfarb became the Jewish deputy of the *Central Rada's general secretary for nationality affairs on 27 July 1917, a member of the *Committee for the Defense of the Revolution on 7 November, general secretary for Jewish affairs on 22 November, and, finally, minister for Jewish affairs on 22 January 1918; he resigned from the government as of 29 January 1918. Zilberfarb had been a long-standing proponent of Jewish autonomism before the revolution and therefore welcomed the Rada's and UNR's policies of national-personal autonomy for minorities in Ukraine; he drafted legislation regarding Jewish autonomy in Ukraine. In 1918–20 Zilberfarb headed the Jewish People's University and Cultural League in Kiev. In 1921 he left Ukraine for Warsaw. Zilberfarb published, in Yiddish, an account of the Jewish ministry and Jewish national autonomy in Ukraine (1919). His collected works were published in 2 vols (1935, 1937).

**Zilbershtein, Andrii** [Zil'berštejn, Andrij], b 1897, d ? Pedagogue. In the early 1930s he taught at the Kharkiv Institute of People's Education and worked as an associate of the Scientific Research Institute of Pedagogy of the Ukrainian SSR. He wrote *Systema narodnoï osvity* (The System of People's Education, 1929).

Ivan Zilynsky

**Zilynsky, Ivan** [Zilyns'kyj] (pseud: Ivan Korostensky), b 22 May 1879 in Krasna (Korostenka), Krosno county, Galicia, d 23 April 1952 in Prague. Phonetician and dialectologist; member of the Shevchenko Scientific Society (NTSh) from 1917, the VUAN Dialectological Commission from 1927, and the Language Commission of the Polish Academy of Arts and Sciences from 1927; father of O. *Zilynsky. Born Ivan Kobasa, he began using his mother's family name as a student at Lviv (1900–2) and Vienna (1903–7) universities. After receiving a PH D in 1907, he taught at gymnasiums in Berezhany, Stanyslaviv, and Lviv (1913–14, 1921–6) and lectured at the Lviv (Underground) Ukrainian University (1921–5) and Cracow University (1926–39), where he became a professor of East Slavic and Ukrainian linguistics in 1931. He was a member of the Commission for Research on Ukrainian-Polish Relations of the Ukrainian Scientific Institute in Warsaw and contributed to the Polish linguistic atlas of Subcarpathia (1934). During the Second World War he was in charge of cultural and educational affairs at the *Ukrainian Central Committee (1939–40) and chief editor (1940–1) and director (1941–4) of the *Ukrainske Vydavnytstvo publishing house in Cracow. From 1944 he served as a professor of Slavic philology at Prague University. Zilynsky contributed valuable studies on the Lemko, Boiko, and Sian dialects and on Ukrainian phonetics and linguistics to Western Ukrainian, Polish, and émigré Ukrainian periodicals. He devoted his energy to gathering materials for a linguistic atlas of Galicia. These materials were later edited by Y. Dzendzelivsky and M. Karas and published as *Studia nad dialektologią ukraińską i polską* (Studies in Ukrainian and Polish Dialectology, 1975). Zilynsky was also the author of booklets on the classification of Ukrainian dialects (1914, 1926) and the orthography adopted by the NTSh (1922); a map of the Ukrainian dialects (1933); and a book of Ukrainian orthography (4 edns, 1941–3), which was used by Ukrainian schools and publishers in German-occupied Galicia. His most important work, first published in Polish in 1932, was revised and translated as *A Phonetic Description of the Ukrainian Language* in 1979. K. Kysilevsky wrote a booklet about him and his work in 1962.

R. Senkus

**Zilynsky, Orest** [Zilyns'kyj], b 12 April 1923 in Krasna (Korostenka), Krosno county, Galicia, d ca 17 July 1976 near Vinné (Vynne), Michalovce county, Slovakia. Slavist; member of the International Commission for the Study of the Folk Culture of the Carpathians and Balkans; the son of I. *Zilynsky and husband of Ye. *Biss. From 1941 he studied Slavic philology at the Ukrainian Free University in Prague. After the Second World War he studied at Prague University under O. Kolessa and I. Pankevych (1945–9; PH D, 1949) and then taught Polish, medieval Rus' literature and folklore, and Soviet literature at Olomouc University, helped prepare teaching programs and textbooks for Ukrainian schools in the Prešov region in the early 1950s, and compiled two pioneering school anthologies of Ukrainian literature (1952).

Zilynsky was a central figure in Ukrainian literature and folklore studies in postwar Czechoslovakia. He published numerous articles (on 19th-century Ukrainian writers [especially T. Shevchenko and I. Franko], O. Oles, B.I. Antonych, Soviet Ukrainian writers of the 1920s and 1960s, Czech-Ukrainian literary relations, Ukrainian and West Slavic folk songs and games, folklore and folklorists, and Ukrainian dumas and folk ballads) in Czech, Soviet Ukrainian and Russian, and Polish scholarly serials and in Ukrainian periodicals published in Prešov and Warsaw. The foremost popularizer of Ukrainian literature in Czechoslovakia, he helped translate and wrote postscripts to Czech editions of works by M. Rylsky (1947), Yu. Yanovsky (1949, 1960, 1966), I. Kotliarevsky (1955), I. Nechui-Levytsky (1960), M. Bazhan (1963), I. Drach (1964), M. Kotsiubynsky (1964), and Ye. Hutsalo (1965); and he compiled and edited Czech anthologies of Ukrainian folk poetry (1950), Ukrainian poetry (1951), and poetry by new Soviet Ukrainian writers of the 1960s (1965), and an invaluable bibliographic compendium on 150 years of Czech-Ukrainian literary ties (1968). He also edited and published together N. *Koroleva's novels *Son tini* (Dream of the Shadow) and *1313* (1966). In addition to writing insightful articles on Ukrainian literature and writers in postwar Czechoslovakia, he edited the first synthetic compendium on that subject (1968).

Despite his contributions Zilynsky did not escape political persecution, particularly before 1954 and after the suppression of the Prague Spring in 1968. From 1969 his literary criticism was not published in Prešov's Ukrainian periodicals, and the publication of his massive annotated collection of Transcarpathian folk ballads was halted by the censors in Prešov in 1971. The circumstances of Zilynsky's death remain unclear. He was found dead in the Vihorlat Mountains of Slovakia on 17 July 1976 and was buried in Svydnyk. His valuable archive of folkloric materials is preserved at the Museum of Ukrainian Culture there. The first volume of his anthology of Ukrainian lyric poetry (to 1919) was published in Toronto in 1978. Many of his other manuscripts, including two monographs he prepared on West and East Slavic ritual games (his revised 1966 candidate's diss) and Ukrainian dumas for the Harvard Ukrainian Research Institute, have not been published. M. Mushynka's biography and bibliography of Zilynsky was published in South Bound Brook, New Jersey, in 1983.

R. Senkus

Col Petro Zilynsky-Sodol     Osyp Zinkevych

**Zilynsky-Sodol, Petro** [Zilyns'kyj-Sodol'], b 14 July 1893 in Vyrva, Radomyshl county, Kiev gubernia, d 18 May 1987 in Albany, New York. Army officer and community leader. An officer of the Russian army, he received four awards for bravery during the First World War and in October 1917 joined the UNR Army. He was a company commander in the Zaporozhian Corps, commander of the 41st Infantry Regiment, a battalion commander in the Sich Riflemen Corps, garrison commander in Yampil, and a participant in the First Winter Campaign (1919–20). After escaping from Polish internment in 1921, he lived in Galicia. During the Second World War he was an instructor in the OUN officer school in Lviv (July–August 1941). He emigrated to the United States in 1949, where he was active in the hetmanite movement and founded and headed the Bolbochan Society of Zaporozhians. He was promoted to colonel by the UNR government-in-exile.

**Zimorowicz, Józef Bartołomiej** (pseud of Józef Ozimek), b 20 August 1597 in Lviv, d 14 October 1677 in Lviv. Polish poet and historian of Armenian origin; brother of S. Zimorowicz. From 1620 he held several positions in Lviv's municipal government, and from 1648 he served as burgomaster a number of times. In 1672 he organized Lviv's defense during the Turkish siege. He is the author of the satirical narrative poem *Żywot Kozaków Lisowskich* (The Life of the Lisovsky Cossacks, 1620), the poetry collection *Sielanki nowe ruskie* (New Ruthenian Idylls, 1663), in which he depicted Hetman B. Khmelnytsky's siege of Lviv, and several Latin works on the history of Lviv, including *Leopolis triplex* (Polish trans 1835). He introduced the haidamaka theme into Polish poetry.

**Zimorowicz, Szymon** (pseud of Szymon Ozimek), b 1608 or 1609 in Lviv, d 21 June 1629 in Cracow. Polish poet of Armenian origin; brother of J. Zimorowicz. In 1629 he wrote a famous cycle of 69 baroque love poems celebrating his brother's marriage, *Roxolanki, to jest ruskie panny* (Roxolankas, That Is, Ruthenian Maidens, pub 1654). In their form and structure they indicate the strong influence of the Ukrainian folk song.

**Zinchenko, Petro** [Zinčenko], b 14 July 1903 in Nikolaevskaia Sloboda, Astrakhan gubernia (now Nikolaevsk, Volgograd oblast, Russia), d 17 February 1969 in Kharkiv. Psychologist. He graduated from the Kharkiv Institute of People's Education (1930), taught in postsecondary schools, and worked at research institutions in Kharkiv and Kiev, including the Scientific Research Institute of Psychology in Kiev. From 1960 he headed the department of psychology at Kharkiv University. A leading authority on the psychology of memory, he wrote *Neproizvol'noe zapominanie* (Involuntary Memorization, 1961, based on his 1958 doctoral dissertation at Moscow University) and co-authored a book on memory development (1965).

**Zinchyshyn, Vasyl** [Zinčyšyn, Vasyl'] (Zinchesin, William), b 11 January 1919 in Sheho, Saskatchewan, d 21 March 1966 in Toronto. Community leader. Zinchyshyn graduated with a medical degree from the University of Toronto in 1945. Active in Ukrainian Orthodox community life, he was a driving force behind the construction of the St Volodymyr Cathedral in Toronto and the initiator of the purchase of the Kiev community property in Oakville. In 1954 Zinchyshyn founded the So-Use Credit Union in Toronto; he guided its successful development during his eight years as president.

**Zinina, Olena** (née Maksymovych), b 11 February 1867 in Lubni, Poltava gubernia, d 24 October 1943 in Kiev. Stage actress. She began her career in M. Starytsky's troupe (1887) and then worked in Saksahansky's troupe (1893–5), M. Yaroshenko's troupe (1896–1914, with interruptions), and the Zankovetska Theater in Dnipropetrovske and Zaporizhia (1925–35).

**Zinkevych, Osyp** [Zinkevyč] (Zinkewych), b 4 January 1925 in Mykulyntsi, Sniatyn county, Galicia. Chemist, editor, and publisher. Having been active in the OUN underground during the war, he emigrated to the United States after the war and completed his education at the Ecole supérieure de chimie (BS, 1956) in Paris. He became a prominent figure in émigré Ukrainian student life (vice-president and general secretary of the Central Union of Ukrainian Students in 1950–6 and an executive member of the *Zarevo Ukrainian Student Organization in 1954–64). In 1957 he settled in the United States. In 1968 he set up the *Smoloskyp publishing house and the Smoloskyp Ukrainian Information Service, which he has served as president and chief editor. In addition to compiling and editing many important collections of materials on the Ukrainian human rights movement, the Ukrainian Catholic and Orthodox churches, and the student movement, he has written a book about the critics I. Dziuba and I. Svitlychny, *Z generatsiï novatoriv* (From the Generation of Innovators, 1967), and *Ukrainian Olympic Champions* (1968; 3rd edn 1984).

**Zinkiv** [Zin'kiv]. III-15. A town (1989 pop 12,100) on the Tashan River and a raion center in Poltava oblast. It was first mentioned in a historical document in 1604. After B. Khmelnytsky's uprising it was fortified, and became a company center in Poltava and then Hadiache regiment. For a while it was a regiment center (1660–71) before returning to the status of a company town of Poltava regiment (1671–1764). In the mid-18th century Elizabeth I granted the town to Hetman K. Rozumovsky. M. Zalizniak's haidamakas were active in the area in 1768. In the 19th century Zinkiv was a county center in Poltava gubernia and a flourishing manufacturing and trading town. Today the town has a food industry, a brick factory, and a workshop of the Poltavchanka handicrafts consortium.

St Michael's Church (1769) in Zinkiv (Khmelnytskyi oblast)

**Zinkiv** [Zin'kiv]. IV-8. A village (1972 pop 3,600) on the Ushytsia River in Vinkivtsi raion, Khmelnytskyi oblast. It was first mentioned in a document in 1404. A fortress was built there, and in 1458 the town was granted the rights of *Magdeburg law. Its inhabitants joined B. Khmelnytsky's uprising in 1648 and rebelled against the Polish overlords in 1702 and 1734. In the 18th century Zinkiv was one of the larger and more prosperous towns of Podilia. It was known for its pottery and handicrafts. At the partition of Poland in 1793 it was annexed by Russia, and in the 19th century it was part of Letychiv county in Podilia gubernia. Today it is an agricultural settlement with a brewery and a machinery repair shop. Remnants of the old triangular fortress as well as the oldest three-nave stone church in Ukraine (1521), a Roman Catholic church (1450), and a synagogue in the Renaissance style have been preserved.

**Zinkiv regiment.** An administrative territory and military formation in Left-Bank Ukraine. In 1648 Zinkiv became a company center in Hadiache regiment, and in 1649, in Poltava regiment. From 1662 to 1672 it was the center of a regiment consisting of 12 companies. Then Zinkiv returned to being a company center in Poltava regiment.

**Zinkivsky, Trokhym** [Zin'kivs'kyj, Troxym] (pseuds: Horlytsia, T. Zvizdochot, T. Povny, P Z , T Z., M. Tsupky), b 4 August 1861 in Berdianske, Tavriia gubernia, d 21 June 1891 in Berdianske. Populist writer. He graduated from the higher military law academy in St Petersburg and was active in the St Petersburg Ukrainian Hromada. While working for the Kiev Military District court he published poems, fables, stories, literary criticism, publicistic articles about the necessity for Ukrainian autonomy, and the play 'Sumlinnia' (Conscience) in the Lviv periodicals *Zoria* and *Pravda*. Published separately were his story collections

Trokhym Zinkivsky

*Maliunky spravzhn'oho zhyttia* (Pictures of Real Life, 1889), *Baiky M. Tsupkoho* (M. Tsupky's Fables, 1889), and *Verba i zirka* (The Willow and the Star, 1890). A posthumous edition of his works (2 vols, 1893, 1896) edited by B. Hrinchenko appeared in Lviv; it includes a major study of the Stundists in Ukraine.

**Zinovev, Grigorii** [Zinovjev, Grigorij] (pseud of Ovsel Radomyslsky), b 23 September 1883 in Yelysavethrad, Kherson gubernia, d 25 August 1936 in Moscow. Revolutionary and Soviet government official. A follower of V. Lenin from 1903, he was a member of the first Politburo. As general secretary of the Communist International (1919–26) he opposed giving the *Borotbists and the Ukrainian Communist party the status of separate members and succeeded in forcing them to join the CP(B)U. In 1923, when Lenin became incapacitated by a stroke, Zinovev, J. Stalin, and L. Kamenev formed a triumvirate that ruled the Party and state until 1926. The United Opposition of Zinovev and L. Trotsky against Stalin was defeated quickly, and the two leaders had been expelled from the Party by the end of 1927. Zinovev recanted and was readmitted to the Party, only to be expelled again in 1932. After S. Kirov's murder in December 1934, Zinovev was imprisoned on charges of complicity. In 1936 he was tried for treason, condemned, and executed.

**Zinovivske.** See Kirovohrad.

**Zionist movement.** A Jewish political movement formed in the last quarter of the 19th century for the purpose of bringing Jews back to Zion (ie, Jerusalem, the land of Israel). Zionism was born in Ukraine and flourished there despite Soviet persecution.

The first Jewish organization intent on systematic settlement of Palestine, then part of the Ottoman Empire, was established in Kharkiv in the wake of the pogroms that followed the assassination of Alexander II. A group of students created BILU (the Hebrew acronym of Isaiah 2:5, 'House of Jacob, Let us Go') and in the summer of 1882 sent a band of settlers to Palestine, where the newcomers founded Rishon L'Tzion and G'dera. Another movement, known as Hibbat Zion (Love of Zion), also became popular in Ukraine. Odessa was a center of Zionist activity. Important early Zionists in Ukraine include L. Pinsker, an Odessa physician who wrote the classic *Autoemancipation*, and Ahad Ha'am (Hebrew for 'One of the People,' pseud of A. Ginsberg), the founder of Cultural Zionism. Ukrainian Zionists played a decisive role in defeating the so-called Uganda scheme, a plan to settle East Africa instead of Palestine. M. Ussishkin organized a conference in Kharkiv in 1903 to protest the Uganda plan.

Under T. Herzl's leadership Zionism soon became popular in Western Europe. A wide range of Zionist ideologies were represented in Ukraine. After the fall of the tsar several world Zionist parties flourished in Ukraine, and Zionism was the most popular ideology of the politically conscious elements of Ukrainian Jewry. Besides the so-called General Zionists, Ukrainian Jews supported Mizrachi ('East,' a religious Zionist party), Zeire Zion ('Young Zion,' a socialist-oriented Zionist party), and *Poale Zion ('Workers of Zion'). During the revolutionary period the Zionists participated in the Central Rada, yet their bitter conflict with Jewish socialist parties precluded their involvement in higher levels of government. The left-leaning Poale Zion co-operated with the Jewish socialists, however, and several Jews from that party (S. Goldelman, A. Revusky) were influential in the Ukrainian National Republic.

Under the Soviets Zionism was mercilessly attacked as a 'tool of British imperialism' and decried as Jewish bourgeois nationalism. According to Soviet nationality policy Soviet Jews were not part of world Jewry and could have no desire to emigrate to a non-Soviet Jewish land. Futhermore, their immigration represented a security risk for the Soviet Union. To divert the Zionist aspirations of Ukrainian Jewry a Jewish autonomous region (Birobidzhan) was carved out of the RSFSR in the Far East, and Soviet Jews were encouraged to settle there. In the terror of 1937–8 Zionists and reputed Zionists were increasingly isolated and persecuted.

Except for a brief respite in 1948–9, when the Soviet Union officially supported the establishment of the state of Israel, Zionism continued to be suppressed. Jews who expressed Zionist sympathies were discriminated against, particularly the so-called Refuseniks (Jews who had been refused exit visas to emigrate to Israel). In 1982 there were an estimated 2,574 Refuseniks in Ukraine.

During the 1980s Ukrainian Jews continued to press for permission to emigrate to Israel and other countries and achieved increasing success. In late 1989 and early 1990 relaxed emigration laws allowed an unprecedented number of Jews to leave Ukraine for Israel.

H. Abramson

**Ziritz, Gustav,** b 15 February 1872 in Szatmár, Hungary (now Satu Mare, Rumania), d August 1920 in Moscow. Ukrainian military officer of Hungarian origin. During the First World War he served as chief of staff of the 43rd and 29th infantry divisions and the Second Corps of the Austrian army. In February 1919 he became, at the rank of colonel, the deputy state secretary for military affairs of the Western Oblast of the UNR in Stanyslaviv, and in November, at the rank of brigadier-general, chief of the General Staff of the Ukrainian Galician Army. In February 1920 the Supreme Revolutionary Committee of the Red Ukrainian Galician Army handed him over to the Bolsheviks. He refused to serve in the Red Army and was executed, along with Gen O. Mykytka, by the Cheka.

*Zirka* (The Star). A weekly republican newspaper published from 1925 to 1991 by the CC of the Communist

Youth League and the Republican Council of the Pioneer Organization in Kharkiv (to 1934) and Kiev. Until 1941 it was called *Na zminu*. Russian-language equivalents of the paper have been published under the titles *Iunyi spartak* (1922–4), *Iunyi leninets* (1924–8 and since 1944), and *Iunyi pioner* (1938–41). In 1960 *Zirka* had a pressrun of 1,000,000, and *Iunyi leninets*, one of 500,000; in 1980 the respective pressruns were 1,454,000 and 1,456,000.

Yosyf Zisels

**Zisels, Yosyf,** b 2 December 1946 in Tashkent. Jewish dissident and political prisoner. A graduate of Chernivtsi University (1969) and an employee of Chernivtsi television, he was expelled from the Komsomol for his human rights activities in 1972. He joined the *Ukrainian Helsinki Group in October 1978, was arrested in December, and was sentenced for 'anti-Soviet agitation and propaganda' in April 1979 to three years in a labor camp in Chernivtsi oblast. After being released in December 1981, he was re-arrested in Chernivtsi in October 1984, and sentenced in April 1985 to three more years in a camp. He was amnestied in 1987, and since that time he has been active in the Ukrainian Helsinki Union and has promoted Ukrainian-Jewish co-operation.

**Zisman, Marko,** b 19 March 1909 in Odessa, d 12 January 1985 in Kiev. Poet and translator. He graduated from the Ukrainian Institute of Linguistic Education (1933) and worked as a journal and newspaper editor in Kiev and Lviv. He wrote three poetry collections in the 1930s and *Riznolittia* (Various Ages, 1973) and *Riast* (Corydalis, 1979). From 1934 on he translated into Ukrainian Russian, Belarusian, Polish, Bulgarian, German, and Yiddish literary works, among them works of M. Lermontov, A. Tolstoi, Ya. Kupala, J. Słowacki, I. Vazov, J.W. von Goethe, H. Heine, F. von Schiller, and B. Brecht.

*Zlataia tsip* (Golden Chain). A collection of original and translated sermons popular in medieval Ukraine. Several different editions of the manuscript have survived. Topics covered in the sermons include faith, love, fasting, and refraining from usury. *Zlataia tsip* had an important impact on the development of Ukrainian *homiletics.

*Zlatnyk.* The first gold coin minted in Kievan Rus'. It was in circulation in the late 10th and early 11th centuries.

**Zlatopil.** See Novomyrhorod.

*Zlatostrui* (Golden Stream). A collection of sermons attributed to *St John Chrysostom. It is believed to have been translated into Old Church Slavonic under Tsar Simeon of Bulgaria in the 10th century. The oldest manuscripts copied in Ukraine, dating from the 12th century, suggest that the language and content of the sermons had been considerably revised. Their poetic qualities made the sermons popular in Ukraine, and they had an important influence on early Ukrainian literature. Two editions of the *Zlatostrui* are known, a full edition with 138 sermons and an abridged version with 67 sermons.

*Zlatoust* (Chrysostom). A compilation of popular sermons attributed to St John Chrysostom, which had been circulated widely in Ukraine by the 16th century. The standard compendium consisted of Old Church Slavonic translations of 112 sermons. Other editions included an abridged version for Lent; a 'Pentecost' edition, which was a slightly expanded version of the Lenten *Zlatoust*; and a 'study' version of the standard compendium, which provided expositions to the sermons. Some versions of the *Zlatoust* included sermons by local preachers, notably Cyril of Turiv.

**Zlenko, Petro,** b 1891, d ? Emigré bibliographer in interwar Bohemia. He worked as a librarian at the Slavonic Library in Prague and edited the Prague weekly *Ukraïns'kyi tyzhden'*. He contributed to the bibliological journals *Knyholiub* (*KL*, Prague) and *Ukraïns'ka knyha* (*UK*, Lviv). He was secretary of the Library-Bibliographic Commission of the Ukrainian Society of Bibliophiles in Prague, and he compiled valuable bibliographies of Revolutionary Ukrainian party publications (*KL*, 1930, no. 1), scholarly works by Ukrainian émigrés published in 1920–31 (1932; repub by the Canadian Institute of Ukrainian Studies [Research Report No. 39]), materials on the Ukrainian Sich Riflemen (*Za derzhavnist'*, vols 5–7 [1935]), and periodicals published in central Ukraine in 1918 (*UK*, 1938, nos 6–7). He wrote surveys of Ukrainian publications in Bohemia (*KL*, 1930, no. 4) and 11th- to 18th-century Ukrainian private libraries (*UK*, 1937, nos 1–10), and articles in Ukrainian encyclopedias published in Lviv (1939) and Munich (1949).

**Zlobyn, Mykola,** b 1874, d 1933. State and military figure. He held a number of posts in the government of the UNR, particularly the Ministry of Marine Affairs, and served as head of the Military Naval Board.

**Zlochevsky, Petro** [Zločevs'kyj], b 25 May 1907 in Kiev, d January 1988. Scenery designer. He studied with F. Krychevsky, K. Yeleva, and V. Tatlin at the Kiev State Art Institute (1927–31) and worked at the Voroshylovhrad Music and Drama Theater (1931–41). From 1944 he worked at the Odessa Opera and Ballet Theater, where he designed sets for S. Hulak-Artemovsky's *Zaporozhian Cossack beyond the Danube* (1945), K. Dankevych's *Bohdan Khmelnytsky* (1954) and *Nazar Stodolia* (1960), A. Borodin's *Prince Igor* (1967), and M. Lysenko's *Taras Bulba* (1971).

**Zlotsky, Teodosii** [Zloc'kyj, Teodosij], b 11 October 1846 in Osii, Bereg komitat, Transcarpathia, d 1926 in Drahove, Transcarpathia. Ukrainian writer, folklorist, and ethnographer. After completing his theological studies he served as a village priest and contributed articles on popular superstitions, rites, customs, legends, folk games,

songs, tales, charms, and proverbs to journals such as *Svit*, *Novyi svit*, *Kelet*, and *Etnographia*. For his work he was elected to the Hungarian Ethnographic Society. He founded a Ruthenian branch of the society in Uzhhorod. A book of selected verses by Zlotsky appeared in 1923. Most of his work remains unpublished, including a historical grammar of the Carpatho-Ruthenian language (written in 1883). His collection of proverbs was published in 1955.

**Zloty** (Polish: *złoty* 'golden'). A Polish monetary unit, the name of which is derived from the calque for various gold ducats, florins, and guldens that circulated in the 14th- and 15th-century Polish Commonwealth, including Ukraine. From 1493 it was worth 30 silver groszy (cf German *groschen*) and had a weight value of 30 g. From 1661, zlotys were minted on a large scale in Lviv, Cracow, and Bydgoszcz as silver coins equaling one-third of a *taler. In the 18th century 1 pre-Partition zloty (*złotówka*) was worth 30 copper groszy or 4 silver groszy. From 1786, zlotys (worth 15 Austrian kreuzers) did not circulate in Austrian-ruled Galicia. In the Congress Kingdom of Poland they were worth one-sixth of a taler. In Russian-ruled Poland 1 zloty was worth 15 kopecks from 1832. Since 1924, 1 zloty has equaled 100 groszy. The zloty was reintroduced in 1924 as the chief monetary unit of Poland. In the interwar years approx 5 zloty equaled 1 US dollar.

**Zlupko, Stepan,** b 16 July 1931 in Dorozhiv, Sambir county, Galicia. Economic historian; full member of the Shevchenko Scientific Society since 1990. A graduate of Lviv University (candidate's degree, 1960), he has worked at the Lviv branch of the AN URSR (now ANU) Institute of Economics as a specialist in Western Ukrainian economic history and thinkers. He has written books on the ideological struggle over the agrarian question in late 19th- and early 20th-century Galicia (1960), the history of economic thought in 19th-century Western Ukraine (1969), S. Podolynsky (1990), and I. Franko (1992). In recent years he has been active in the Lviv branches of the Ukrainian Language Society and the Popular Movement of Ukraine (Rukh).

*Zmah* (The Competition). A weekly sports paper published in Peremyshl (February–April 1937) and then Lviv (to November 1938). The chief editor was Ye. Zyblikevych.

**Zmiienko, Vsevolod** [Zmijenko], b 29 November 1884 in Odessa, d 30 October 1938 in Warsaw. Senior UNR Army officer. He served as chief of staff of various divisions in

Gen Vsevolod Zmiienko

the UNR Army: the Odessa Haidamaka Division (1917), the Third Kherson Corps (1918), the First Division of Sich Riflemen (1919), and the Sixth Sich Rifle Division (1920). He was promoted to brigadier general in the UNR Army. During the interwar period he was a founder and active member of the *Ukrainian Military History Society.

**Zmiievyky.** Amulets made of gold, silver, or bronze and worn in Kievan Rus' as charms against evil. Round or oval in shape, they had a sacred image (a saint, the Theotokos, etc) on one side and a dragon (*zmii*, hence the name *zmiievyk*) or medusa on the other. Such medallions were discovered in archeological digs in Chernihiv and Bilhorodka near Kiev.

**Zmii-Myklushyk, Yosyf** [Zmij-Myklušyk, Josyf] (Miklovshii), b 20 March 1792 in Slovinky, Slovakia, d 1 December 1841. Painter. He studied at the Vienna Academy of Arts (1814–22). He painted commissioned portraits and genre scenes and attracted attention with his portrait of Francis Joseph I (1835). In 1830 he was appointed official icon painter of Prešov eparchy and began painting iconostases and murals in village churches in the Prešov region. He painted murals in the side chapels of the Prešov Cathedral in 1835.

**Zmiinyi Island** [Zmijnyj ostriv] (also Zmiievyi and Fidonisi). An island within Odessa oblast situated in the northwestern part of the Black Sea, 37 km from the mouth of the Danube River. The island is 1.5 sq km in area and has a steep shoreline. It was known in Greek times as Levkoi and was the site of a temple to Achilles. A major naval battle during the Russo-Turkish wars took place near the island in 1788.

**Zmiiovi Valy.** A series of earthen wall fortifications whose furthest western reaches are located along a Zhytomyr–Cherkasy axis and whose eastern reaches run along the left bank of the Dnieper River south of Kiev. The walls are 8–22 m in width and approx 9 m high, with a cumulative length of at least 950 km (some estimates run as high as 2,000 km); a moat was dug out along the exterior (usually southerly-oriented) elevation. Notwithstanding their impressive size and extent, little is definitively known about these fortifications. Archeological evidence indicates that they are older than the *Trajan's Wall built further southwest in Ukraine, while historical documents indicate that Prince Volodymyr the Great (ruled 980–1015) built walls in at least the Pereiaslav-Khmelnytskyi area. It seems most likely that they were built over the course of the 2nd–12th centuries and at the time of their widest development served as frontier fortifications of the Kievan Rus' state against the incursions of steppe nomads. The walls took their name (literally meaning 'serpentine') from a folk legend that depicted them as being furrows made by a dragon that had been conquered by a Rus' warrior-hero and harnessed to a plow.

**Zmiiv.** See Hotvald.

**Znachko-Yavorsky, Melkhysedek** [Značko-Javors'kyj, Melxysedek] (secular name: Matvii), b ca 1716 in Lubni, Chernihiv region, d 14 June 1809 in Hlukhiv, Chernihiv regiment. Orthodox churchman. He studied at the Kievan Mohyla Academy before being tonsured in 1738 at the *Motronynskyi Trinity Monastery, where he served as hegumen in 1753–68. From 1761 he also served as administrator of the Orthodox churches and monasteries in Polish-ruled Right-Bank Ukraine, which belonged to Pereiaslav eparchy. In this capacity he fought against exploitation by the Polish gentry and against attempts to introduce the Uniate church throughout the area. He also supported the haidamaka uprisings. In 1768 he was accused of aiding M. *Zalizniak and of stirring up the peasantry against the Poles; he was arrested, but was released on the intervention of Bishop Hervasii of Pereiaslav. Under pressure from the Polish gentry, however, the Russian government removed him from his position at the Motronynskyi Monastery in 1768 and assigned him to Left-Bank Ukraine. Znachko-Yavorsky then served as hegumen at the Pereiaslav (1769–71), Vydubychi (1771–81), Mhar Transfiguration (1781–6), and Hlukhiv (1786–1809) monasteries. In 1771–83 he was also vicar of the St Sophia Cathedral in Kiev. A biography of Znachko-Yavorsky by T. Lebedyntsev and documents relating to his life appeared in *Arkhiv Iugo-Zapadnoi Rossii* (1864).

**Z-nad khmar i z dolyn** (From above the Clouds and from the Valleys). One of the first anthologies of Ukrainian modernist poetry and prose, published in Odessa in 1903. It was compiled and edited by M. *Vorony, and contained works by him, I. Franko, Lesia Ukrainka, B. Hrinchenko, H. Khotkevych, P. Hrabovsky, O. Kobylianska, N. Kybalchych-Kozlovska, M. Kotsiubynsky, N. Kobrynska, P. Karmansky, M. Starytsky, M. Cherniavsky, V. Shchurat, A. Krymsky, V. Samiilenko, A. Krushelnytsky, O. Romanova, and others. It influenced the subsequent development of modernist literature in Ukraine.

**Znamia kommunizma** (The Banner of Communism). A Russian-language organ of the Odessa oblast and city Party Committees and Soviets, published six days a week from April 1944 to 1991. In 1960 it had a pressrun of 52,000 while its Ukrainian-language equivalent, *Chornomors'ka komuna*, had 42,000; in 1980 their pressruns were 236,000 and 80,000 respectively.

**Znamianka** [Znamjanka]. V-13. A city (1989 pop 28,100) and raion center in Kirovohrad oblast. It was founded in 1869 as a railway settlement on the Kharkiv–Odessa line, and got its name from the nearby village of Znamianka. The Znamianka–Mykolaiv line and the Znamianka–Fastiv line were opened in 1873 and 1876 respectively, and the town developed into an important junction. In 1938 it was granted city status. The city is a railway center with repair yards and metalworking factories. It also has a food industry.

**Znannia** (Knowledge). A popular magazine published by the People's Commissariat of Education in Kharkiv (1923–34) and Kiev (from 1934–5). It appeared weekly in 1923–5 and then semimonthly. Until May 1924 it was called *Znattia*, and until 1927 it appeared in both Russian and Ukrainian. Its editors included A. Prykhodko and I. Nemolovsky.

**Znannia** (Knowledge). A pro-Soviet weekly newspaper published In Buenos Aires from late 1949 to March 1961. It succeeded the paper *Svitlo, which was banned by the Argentinian government. The paper popularized Soviet achievements in politics and culture and supported Soviet actions in foreign and domestic politics. Many articles were reprinted from Soviet Ukrainian journals. *Znannia* was succeeded by *Ridnyi krai*.

**Znannia Society.** A civic education and enlightenment organization based in Kiev. It was founded in 1947 as the Society for the Dissemination of Political and Scientific Knowledge, a 'voluntary' organization for the dissemination of communist and *antireligious propaganda under the guise of 'scientific knowledge' (*znannia*). A constituent member of the USSR Znanie Society, it was renamed the Znannia Society of the Ukrainian SSR in 1963. In 1979 it had 684,700 members, in 28,336 primary organizations. The society runs 24 stationary lecture halls, 10 planetariums, the Republican Building of Economic and Scientific-Technical Propaganda in Kiev, and a branch of the building in Sevastopil. It organized millions of public lectures and events throughout Ukraine, offered courses at over 7,500 *people's universities, conducted nature schools, and published the popular-educational and propaganda monthlies *Nauka i suspil'stvo* (since 1951), *Liudyna i svit* (since 1960), and *Trybuna lektora* (since 1965), the annual compendium *Nauka i kul'tura* (since 1966), and 12 brochure series. Reflecting the democratization of the late 1980s, the society reconstituted itself in November 1990 as the Znannia Society of Ukraine and adopted a new statute.

*Znannia ta pratsia* (Knowledge and Work). A popular science magazine for children published by the CC of the Communist Youth League of Ukraine. It appeared monthly (1929–30, 1936–41) and semimonthly (1931–5) in Kharkiv from 1929 to mid-1941, and was renewed as a monthly in Kiev from 1957 to 1991. The magazine contains articles and literary works, especially science fiction. Its pressrun was reduced from 50,000 in 1975 to 30,000 in 1984.

**Znoba, Ivan,** b 25 November 1903 in Novomykolaivka, Katerynoslav county, d 10 September 1990 in Kiev. Sculptor; father of V. *Znoba. In 1941 he graduated from the Kiev State Art Institute. He has done portraits of heroes of labor and created the T. Shevchenko monument in Dnipropetrovske and, with V. Znoba, *T. Shevchenko in Exile* (1958) and the liberation monument at the Slovak-Ukrainian border (1970) near Uzhhorod. An album of his works was published in 1970.

Valentyn Znoba at work on a portrait of Mykhailo Yanhel

**Znoba, Valentyn,** b 10 January 1929 in Sofiivka, Katerynoslav okruha. Sculptor. He learned to sculpt from his father, I. *Znoba, and I. Severa and studied at the Kiev State Art Institute (1947–53) under M. Lysenko. He has sculpted portraits, including ones of O. Veresai (1954) and H. Skovoroda (1960); monuments to the Soviet hero V. Poryk, in France (1967, with H. Kalchenko), to U. Karmaliuk, in Letychiv, to those who died in the Nazi concentration camps, in Darnytsia (1968), and to I. Mechnikov, at the Pasteur Institute in Paris; the liberation monument at the Ukrainian-Slovak border near Uzhhorod (1970, with I. Znoba); the Battle for the Dnieper monument in Bukryn; and the Eternal Glory monuments in Khmelnytskyi and Kherson.

Oleksander Znosko-Borovsky

**Znosko-Borovsky, Oleksander** [Znosko-Borovs'kyj], b 27 February 1908 in Kiev, d 8 March 1983 in Kiev. Composer and violinist. He graduated (1932) from the Lysenko Music and Drama Institute in the composition class of L. Revutsky, served as music consultant for feature films at the Ukrainfilm studio in Kiev (1931–41), and then (1945–63) worked as music editor for the Mystetstvo publishing house. His compositions include the cantata *Our Victory* (1946) for chorus and orchestra; three symphonies (1958, 1960, and 1967) and other works for orchestra; concertos for violin (1951), cello (1968), French horn (1976), and trombone (1975); works for chamber ensemble, chorus, piano, violin, and trombone; pieces for band; art songs and folk song settings; and music for radio and films. His musicological works include brochures on A. Shtoharenko (1946), M. Mussorgsky (1949), and A. Borodin (1959), as well as articles in journals.

**Zobkiv, Mykhailo,** b 1864 in Galicia, d 7 December 1928 in Mostar, Yugoslavia. Jurist; full member of the Shevchenko Scientific Society from 1899. A graduate of Lviv University, he submitted his doctoral dissertation at Zagreb University (1894) and taught civil law there. He became president of the Supreme Court of Bosnia and Hercegovina in Sarajevo. His publications include *Die Teilpacht nach dem römischen und österreichischen Recht* (1894) and articles on legal issues in *Chasopys' pravnycha* and Austrian legal journals.

**Zograf, Aleksandr,** b 10 March 1889 in Moscow, d 17 January 1942 in Leningrad. Russian archeologist and numismatist. Upon graduating from Moscow University (1912), he worked in the Moscow Museum of Fine Arts and then (from 1922) in the numismatics division of the Hermitage in Leningrad (from 1935 as its head). Taking part in archeological excavations in Olbia and Kerch, he studied coins excavated in the Black Sea region and developed a thorough classification scheme for them. His major work on this topic is *Antichnye monety* (Ancient Coins, 1951).

**Żółkiewski.** A Polish magnate family, some of whose members played an important role in Ukrainian history. Mikołaj (end of the 15th century) was voivode of Belz. His son, Stanisław (d 1588), converted from the Orthodox to the Roman Catholic faith and became voivode of Belz in 1582 and voivode of Rus' in 1586. Stanisław's son, S. *Żółkiewski, was a Polish grand hetman and chancellor. His nephew, Łukasz (b 1594, d 1636), served as voivode of Bratslav in 1636 and then as starosta of Pereiaslav. He financed a Jesuit church and college in Pereiaslav.

**Żółkiewski, Stanisław,** b 1547 in Turynka (near Lviv), d 7 October 1620 near Cecora, Moldavia. Polish state and military figure. His crown positions included field hetman (from 1588), grand hetman (from 1613), castellan of Lviv (from 1590), and chancellor (from 1618). He led the Polish expeditionary force that brutally suppressed the uprisings led by S. Nalyvaiko, H. Loboda, and others at the Battle of *Solonytsia in 1596. He was killed fighting the Turks at the Battle of Cecora.

**Zolne burial site.** The grave of an 8th- to 7th-century BC warrior located near Zolne, Symferopil raion, Crimea; excavated in 1959. The deceased had been buried in an earlier-constructed Pit-Grave culture kurhan. Items found in his grave included an iron sword, a whetstone, bronze, iron, and bone arrowheads, pottery fragments, and elegant horse trappings made of bronze and bone.

**Zolochiv** [Zoločiv]. IV-5. A city (1989 pop 21,300) on the Zolochivka River and a raion center in Lviv oblast. It was first mentioned in a document in 1442. By the end of the 15th century it was an important trade center in western Podilia, and in 1523 it obtained the rights of *Magdeburg law. The town was protected with a castle and walls. In 1672 it was captured by the Turks and burned to the ground. After the partition of Poland in 1772, it was annexed by Austria, and served as a county center in Galicia. In the interwar period (1919–39) it was occupied by Poland. Today it is an industrial center with a branch of the Maiak Sewing Consortium, a carton and furniture factory, a radio factory, and a sugar refinery. Its chief architectural monuments are the 16th-century castle (rebuilt in 1634–6), the Church of the Resurrection (1604), St Nicholas's Church (end of the 16th century, reconstructed in 1767), and a Roman Catholic church (1726–33).

**Zolochiv** [Zoločiv]. III-16. A town smt (1990 pop 12,900) on the Udy River and a raion center in Kharkiv oblast. It was founded in 1677 by Cossacks from Right-Bank Ukraine, and became a company center in Kharkiv regiment in 1685. In 1780 it became a county center in Kharkiv vicegerency. Today the town is an agricultural center with a railway station, a grain elevator, and several food-processing enterprises.

The castle in Zolochiv (Lviv oblast) and its plan

**Zolochiv Brigade of the Ukrainian Galician Army** (Zolochivska [4] brygada UHA). A unit of the Second Corps of the UHA, formed out of the Eastern Group in January 1919. It consisted of four infantry battalions, a cavalry machine-gun company, and two artillery regiments. In June the brigade scored victories against the Poles at Chortkiv, Terebovlia, Berezhany, and Pomoriany, and in August it marched with the UNR Army to Kiev, defeating the Bolsheviks at Proskuriv, Starokostiantyniv, Shepetivka, Zhytomyr, and Korosten. In the fall of 1919 it was deployed against A. Denikin's army, and in the spring of 1920 it fought on the Polish front. The brigade commanders were Col Didiukiv, Maj S. Shukhevych (February–May 1919), Col S. Chmelyk (May–July 1919), Maj Liaskovsky, and Maj B. Shashkevych.

**Zolota Balka settlement.** A large Scythian-Sarmatian trade and craft center of the 2nd century BC to 2nd century AD on the Dnieper River near Zolota Balka, Novovorontsovka raion, Kherson oblast. Excavations in 1951–63 revealed the remains of stone wall fortifications, dwellings with stone and clay outbuildings, grain storage pits, ironworks, and a pottery workshop. The settlement's inhabitants engaged in agriculture and various crafts and traded with northern Black Sea coast centers, particularly Olbia. A burial site with 86 individual and group graves without kurhans was discovered near the settlement.

**Zolota Lypa River.** A left-bank tributary of the Dniester River that flows southward for 126 km through Lviv, Ternopil, and Ivano-Frankivske oblasts and drains a basin area of 1,440 sq km. The river is 5–15 m in width (maximum 50 m) and 0.5–2 m in depth. It is used for water supply and irrigation and has a water reservoir. The town of Berezhany is situated on it.

**Zolota Mohyla.** A Scythian kurhan of the 5th century BC located near Symferopil, Crimea; also known as Zolotyi Kurhan. The kurhan was built over a Bronze Age burial site that contained corpses in a flexed position with red ocher sprinkled over them. It housed a Scythian warrior in iron armor decorated in bronze, silver, and gold, as well as an iron sword, a leather scabbard, and a quiver with 180 arrows.

**Zolota Mohyla.** A burial mound of a 4th-century BC Bosporan Kingdom nobleman located near Kerch, Crimea. It was excavated in 1832. The kurhan was approx 21 m high and 240 m long with stone blocks placed around its base. A long, narrow corridor led to three stone burial vaults which had been robbed prior to excavation. The largest of the burial vaults had stone block walls that gradually closed in overhead to form a high (approx 9 m) dome.

**Zolotarenko.** A family line of Cossacks from Korsun that later resettled in Nizhen, in Left-Bank Ukraine. Its notable members included the brothers Vasyl *Zolotarenko, Ivan *Zolotarenko, and Tymish Zolotarenko, all of whom served as colonels of Nizhen regiment; their sister, Hanna Nykyforivna, the third wife of B. Khmelnytsky (married in 1651), who entered a nunnery after his death; Vasyl's son, Ostap (Evstafii) Zolotarenko (Vasiutenko), who was the Kish otaman of the Zaporozhian Sich (1667) and colonel of Nizhen regiment (1669–70); and Yakiv Zolotarenko (d 1721), a captain of Pryluka regiment (1690–1709), who was exiled to Moscow in 1717 for supporting I. Mazepa. Yakiv left some of his estate to the Hustynia Trinity Monastery.

**Zolotarenko, Ivan,** b ?, d 15 November 1655 in Staryi Bykhau, Belarus. Cossack leader. He served as colonel of Nizhen regiment (1652–5), and in 1654 he led an army of 20,000 Cossacks to Smolensk to join with a Muscovite army led by Tsar Aleksei Mikhailovich in a campaign to wrest Belarus from Polish control. Most of Lithuania fell to the Muscovites, and Zolotarenko occupied southern Belarus (1654–5), where he established a Cossack administration. His doing so put him in direct conflict with Moscow, which had designs on the territory, and he was killed during a siege of Staryi Bykhau.

**Zolotarenko, Vasyl,** b ?, d 28 September 1663 in Borzna, Chernihiv region. Colonel of Nizhen regiment (1655–6, 1659–63). He was a leader of the mutiny that deposed Hetman I. Vyhovsky in 1659. He secured Left-Bank Ukraine with Ya. *Somko and handed it over to Prince A. Trubetskoi upon his arrival in Nizhen. Zolotarenko's ambition for the hetmancy made him envious of Somko, on whom he informed to the Russian tsar. At the *Chorna rada in 1663, the newly elected hetman I. Briukhovetsky ordered the execution of both Somko and Zolotarenko.

**Zolotarev, Aleksandr,** b 1880, d ? A leader of the Jewish Social Democratic *Bund in Ukraine. After the February Revolution of 1917 he was elected a Bund representative to the Central Rada. In July 1917 he was appointed a member of its Little Rada. In January 1918 he replaced M. Rafes as the Bund representative in the UNR General Secretariat, in which he spoke out against a separate UNR peace treaty with the Central Powers. After the proclamation of Ukraine's independence he was appointed UNR state comptroller but was ordered to resign by the Bund, which opposed Ukrainian independence. Later he joined the Bolshevik party. He was arrested during the Stalinist terror of the 1930s and probably executed.

**Zolotarev, Vasilii,** b 7 March 1872 in Tahanrih, d 25 May 1964 in Moscow. Russian and Ukrainian composer and educator. A graduate of the St Petersburg Conservatory (1900) in the composition class of N. Rimsky-Korsakov, he was professor at the conservatory in Odessa (1924–6) and the Lysenko Music and Drama Institute in Kiev (1926–31). He also taught at the Minsk Conservatory (1933–41). His works include the opera *Khvesko Andyber* (on Ukrainian themes, with a libretto by M. Rylsky, 1928); the *Shevchenko Suite* for chorus and orchestra (1909); art songs to texts by I. Franko, O. Oles, and others; and *30 Little Pieces*, a cycle of Ukrainian songs for piano four hands. Among his students were K. Dankevych, V. Femelidi, and K. Dominchen.

**Zolotcha.** A locality on the left bank of the Dnieper River opposite Kiev, where the princes of Kievan Rus' met in conference in 1101. The purpose of the conference was to work out a plan for a common campaign against the Cumans.

**Zolote.** V-19, DB II-5. A city (1989 pop 23,600) on the Komyshuvakha River in Luhanske oblast. It was founded in 1878 as a mining settlement. In 1938 it was granted city status. Today Zolote has five coal mines and an enrichment factory.

*Zolotnyk.* See Weights and measures.

**Zolotnytsky, Illia** [Zolotnyc'kyj, Illja], b 22 July 1870 in Poltava gubernia, d 5 November 1930 in Warsaw. Judge and state figure. In 1918–20 he filled a number of legal positions, including head of the Supreme Military Tribunal (at the rank of colonel), head of the General Administration of Prisons, and associate of the Ministry of Justice. He later emigrated to Warsaw, where he was active in Ukrainian community affairs.

**Zolotnytsky, Volodymyr** [Zolotnyc'kyj] (also Vasyl), b 1741, d ? Military figure, writer, and philosopher. A graduate of the Kievan Mohyla Academy and Moscow University, he worked as a cadet school teacher and translator. He returned to army service in 1771 as colonel of the Dnieper Engineering Regiment. His works include translations of Seneca and philosophical studies about ethics, the immortality of the soul, and natural law.

**Zolotonosha** [Zolotonoša]. IV-13. A city (1989 pop 30,900) on the Zolotonoshka River and a raion center in Cherkasy oblast. It was first mentioned in a document in

1576, as a fortified town. In 1640 it was acquired by J. Wiśniowiecki. After throwing off Polish rule in 1648, Zolotonosha became a company center in Cherkasy and, in the 1660s, in Pereiaslav regiment. In 1781 it was given city status and made a county center of Kiev vicegerency. In the 19th century it was part of Poltava gubernia. By 1885 there were 30 manufacturing enterprises in the city. The Bakhmach–Krasne railway (1897) ran through Zolotonosha and gave it access to agricultural markets. Today its main industry is food processing. It also has a large building-materials factory, a perfume factory, and a sewing plant. Its chief architectural monument is the Church of the Transfiguration (1760–7), built by I. Hryhorovych-Barsky.

**Zolotonoshka River** [Zolotonoška] (also Zolotonosha). A left-bank tributary of the Dnieper River that flows southward for 88 km in Cherkasy oblast before emptying into the Kremenchuk Reservoir. It drains a basin area of 847 sq km. The river, approx 5 m in width, has a valley which is marshy in places. It is used for water supply, irrigation, and pisciculture. The city of Zolotonosha is situated on it.

**Zolotov, Grigorii**, b 24 January 1882 in Pervoe Plesno, Voronezh gubernia, Russia, d 15 April 1960 in Pavlohrad, Dnipropetrovske oblast. Painter and graphic artist. He studied under M. Pymonenko and I. Seleznov at the Kiev Drawing School (1913–16) and at H. Narbut's studio in Kiev (1919). Besides portraits and historical and genre paintings, such as *Peter I Making a Print* (1912), *Triumph of Victory* (1945), and *Harvest Festival* (1945), he did murals in the church in Bilousivka, Podilia gubernia (1914), in workers' clubs in Pavlohrad (1920–3), and in the Pioneer Palace in Dnipropetrovske (1934). He did illustrations to T. Shevchenko's poem 'Kateryna' and P. Tychyna's poem 'Na maidani' (In the Square, 1934) and designed the magazines *Iskusstvo i pechatnoe delo* (1909), *Iskusstvo. Zhivopis'. Grafika. Khudozhestvennaia pechat'* (1911), and *Iskusstvo v Iuzhnoi Rossii* (1913).

**Zolotova, Yevheniia,** b 12 December 1928 in Synelnykove (now in Dnipropetrovske oblast). Stage director. Since completing study at the Kiev Institute of Theater Arts (1950) she has worked in the Chernivtsi Oblast Ukrainian Music and Drama Theater. Among her notable productions was B. Brecht's *Mutter Courage und ihre Kinder* (1965).

**Zolotyi Potik** [Zolotyj Potik]. V-6. A town smt (1990 pop 2,500) in Buchach raion, Ternopil oblast. It was founded at the end of the 14th century. Called Zahaipole at first, it was renamed in 1570. Today it has a branch of the Ternopil Cotton-Spinning Complex and a branch of the Monastyryska Sewing Consortium. The remains of a 17th-century fortress and a Roman Catholic church are tourist attractions.

**Zolozova, Tetiana** (née Andrushchak), b 1 December 1941 in Kiev. Musicologist. She studied violin at the Kiev Conservatory (1960–5) and then musicology (1965–70). Since 1969 she has taught at the Kiev Conservatory (professor from 1991). Her numerous works, mostly articles, are in the area of music history and theory; they include a monograph on the instrumental music of postwar France.

**Zoogeography.** See Zoology.

**Zoological gardens and parks.** Cultural and educational establishments in which wild and sometimes domesticated animals are kept for display, scientific research, and reproduction. The only difference between gardens and parks is in their size and the extent of their collections. In recent times zoological gardens have become responsible for the preservation and even breeding of rare or endangered species of animals; others have undertaken the task of acclimatizating animals to new geographic environments, research on various diseases and their prevention, and so on. In Ukraine the first zoological park was organized in 1875 in what is now the *Askaniia-Nova Nature Reserve. Others followed in Kharkiv (1896), Mykolaiv (1901), Kiev (1908), Odessa (1936), the city of Mena in Chernihiv oblast (1977), and Cherkasy (1979). The largest of these is the zoological park in Kiev, covering an area of 40 ha, where over 1,600 animals representing more than 240 species are kept. In Kharkiv 300 elephants were bred in captivity, and in Mykolaiv 300 lions are regularly bred. (See also *Nature preserves.)

**Zoological museums.** Institutions in which animal collections are assembled for scientific, educational, and cultural purposes, for exhibition and research. The oldest Ukrainian zoological museum (est 1919) is in Kiev, under the auspices of the AN URSR (now ANU) *Institute of Zoology. Other museums have been established at the universities in Lviv, Odessa, Kharkiv, Dnipropetrovske, and Chernivtsi. Zoological museums carry out extensive research on topics such as taxonomic descriptions of *fauna, zoogeography, the history of the animal world, and comparative anatomy. Expeditions are organized to enrich current knowledge of zoology. The staff is often involved in consultations on medical, agricultural, forestry, or hunting problems concerning various specimens of the local fauna.

**Zoology.** A complex biological science that studies the diversity of animals, their relationship to the environment, their activities, their evolutionary development, and their interaction with the human species.

There are three identifiable periods in the development of zoology in Ukrainian history: (1) the period of isolated early works, (2) the period of systematic studies of Ukrainian fauna, and (3) the modern period, which reflects the political upheavals of the 20th century.

Early treatises on Ukrainian *fauna by local writers and foreign travelers, supplemented by ancient chronicles of the Kievan Rus' period, provide a wealth of information about Ukrainian animals – wild bull, bison, elk, stag, chamois, wild boar, bear, lynx, fox, beaver, ermine, otter, swan, crane, black grouse, hazel grouse, wild horse, and others, some of them now extinct species. Some animals were drawn on pottery or on building walls. There is little material from the period between the end of the Halych principality and the 18th century except for the memoirs and diaries of Western European travelers. During that time yearly Turkish and Tatar raids on Eastern Europe had a detrimental effect on any scholarly ventures.

Toward the end of the 18th century the first systematic studies of Ukrainian natural sciences began to appear, spearheaded by graduates of the Kievan Mohyla Academy – A. *Prokopovych-Antonsky, P. *Prokopovych, and

M. Terekhovsky – as well as by G. Zhonchynsky, H. Yunker, F. Herman, B. *Hacquet, and others. The tsarist government began to support expeditions to catalog the fauna of its empire, including Ukrainian territory. The treatises of S. Gmelin, J. *Güldenstädt, and P. *Pallas provided valuable data on the animals of the steppe zone, the Crimea, and Caucasia. The fauna of Western Ukraine was studied by the faculty at the Kremianets Lyceum, A. *Andrzejowski, W. *Besser, F. Bauer, K. Eichwald, A. Behr, A. Demidov, J. Blazius, and G. Belke.

The establishment of Ukrainian universities gave fresh stimulus to Western methods of investigating various zoological problems in Ukraine. Numerous scholars did research: at Kiev University, K. Kessler (birds, reptiles, amphibians, and fish of the Kiev region), O. Kovalevsky (embryology and physiology; in 1871 he established the first marine hydrobiological station, in Sevastopil), K. Rumshevych (the embryology of the development of the eye), M. *Bobretsky (the embryology of invertebrates), V. *Bets (anatomy), L. Artemovsky (the histology of bone marrow), A. *Walter (the nerves regulating circulation of blood), A. Korotniv (lower marine animals), and S. Kushakevych (the simplest animals); at Kharkiv University, I. *Krynytsky (spiders and birds of Ukraine), A. *Chernai (fauna of the Kharkiv region and southeastern Ukraine), whose students included O. *Maslovsky (histology and embryology), V. Yaroshevsky (dipterology), V. Reinhardt (histology), P. Stepaniv (parasitology), and I. *Mechnikov, and the physiologists V. *Danylevsky, M. Biletsky, I. Kalynychenko, O. Nykolsky, P. Sushkin, N. Somov, and T. Tymofiiv; at Odessa University, where research centered on Black Sea fauna along with that of the Crimea and the nearby steppes, O. Nordman, V. Shmankevych, V. Zalensky, O. *Brauner, and the ornithologists B. Walch, I. Podushkin, and H. Borovikov.

A special role in the development of zoology in Ukraine was played by research associations organized in the 1870s – the *Kiev Society of Naturalists (which established the Dnieper River Biological Station in 1909), the *Kharkiv Society of Naturalists, and the Odessa Society of Naturalists, which studied the fauna of the Black Sea and its estuaries.

In Western Ukraine the development of zoology was centered at Lviv University and, to some extent, at the Dzieduszycki Museum and the Copernicus Society of Naturalists in Lviv. At a later stage the mathematical–natural sciences–medical section of the Shevchenko Scientific Society in Lviv took over the leadership in those efforts. Individual scientists active during the period were A. Zavadsky (vertebrates of Galicia and Bukovyna), R. Kner (local fish life), Z. Syrsky (the reproductive organs of eels), B. Dybovsky (morphology and anatomy), J. Nusbaum-Hiliarovych (animal histology), the cytologists and embryologists Ya. Hirshler, K. Sembrat, Ya. Poliushynsky, and M. Monne, and the entomologists M. Novytsky, M. Lomnytsky, H. Kinel, R. Kuntse, and Ya. Noskevych. Significant contributions to Ukrainian terminology were made by I. *Verkhratsky.

After the First World War the Ukrainian Academy of Sciences (UAN) gave a significant impetus to the development of modern zoology in Ukraine, especially with its *zoological museum (est 1919). A number of zoological organizations, museums, and institutions were established. Several journals were published by the UAN – *Zoolohichnyi zhurnal Ukraïny* (1921–3), *Zbirnyk prats' Biolohichnoho instytutu* (1926–32), *Zbirnyk prats' Zoolohichnoho muzeiu* (1926–63), and *Zbirnyk prats' Dniprovs'koï biolohichnoï stantsiï* (1926–31), renamed *Trudy hidrobiolohichnoï stantsiï* (1934–40), and *Trudy Instytutu hidrobiolohiï/Trudy Instituta gidrobiolohiï* (1947–61).

During the 1920s and 1930s the number of Ukrainian zoologists increased greatly in the Ukrainian SSR. The following is a partial list of investigators who were active: in the field of physiology, N. Bordzylovska, M. Zelynska, K. Kzhyshkovsky, V. *Radzymovska, V. *Pravdych-Nemynsky, and O. *Skovoroda-Zachyniaiev; in cytology, B. Aleksenko, M. *Bilousiv, S. Velish, and S. Shakhiv; in genetics, T. Dobzhansky, M. *Vetukhiv, and H. Karpechenko; in pathophysiology, O. *Bohomolets; in comparative anatomy, I. *Shmalhauzen, D. *Tretiakov, V. Balynsky, and M. *Voskoboinykov; in the simplest animals, S. Kushakevych and S. *Krasheninnikov; in zooplankton, H. Vereshchagin, Yu. Markovsky, V. *Roll, and H. *Melnykov; in sponges, M. Hrymailivska; in insects, S. Paramoniv, I. Bilanovsky, V. Gross-Haim, F. *Kyrychenko, V. Sovynsky, Yu. *Kleopov, V. Khranevych, L. *Sheliuzhko, H. Artobolevsky, S. Medvediev, V. *Karavaiv, and O. Makariv; in beetles, D. *Zaitsiv, M. Taran, H. Petrushevsky, and Ye. Savchenko; in mollusks, S. Panochini and V. Lindholm; in ichthyology, D. Beling, M. *Ovchynnyk, Ye. *Slastenenko, F. Velykokhatko, P. Balabai, F. Ovsiannykov, K. Tatarko, O. Isachenko, and I. Syrovatsky; in amphibians and reptiles, F. Sukhov and B. Voliansky; in birds, M. *Sharleman, O. Kistiakivsky, V. Herchner, M. Burchak-Abramovych, L. Portenko, M. Shcherbyna, M. Havrylenko, and V. *Artobolevsky; and in mammals, V. Khranevych, I. Tarnani, V. *Averin, O. *Myhulin, I. Barabash-Nikiforov, Ya. Zubko, B. Bilsky, and I. *Pidoplichko.

The terror of the 1930s and ensuing Second World War arrested the further development of Ukrainian science in general, including zoology. The autonomous Ukrainian scientific organizations were subordinated to the USSR All-Union Academy of Sciences in Moscow; publication of most of the professional journals was terminated. Many leading scientists were committed to hard-labor camps or executed.

In Western Ukraine entrance to Lviv University was closed for Ukrainians by the Polish government. Active scientific programs were initiated only after 1945, when Western Ukrainian territories were incorporated into the Ukrainian SSR.

The postwar period witnessed a switch to practical applied zoology, with a concentration on agricultural problems, *veterinary science, and evolutionary issues. Scientists worked in the following fields: leguminous plant pests, O. Petrukha; sugar beet pests, M. Ulashkevych, O. Zhytkevych, B. Bilsky, and Ye. Zvirozomb-Zubovsky; parasitology, O. Stankov, N. Shchupak, M. Pyvynsky, O. Prendel, R. Reinhard, and O. *Markevych; comparative anatomy and morphology, V. *Kasianenko, D. Dombrovsky, K. Tatarko, and P. Balabai; histology, O. *Leontovych, D. Tretiakov, Ye. Malovichko, and V. *Rubashkin; regeneration, E. Umansky, M. *Savchuk, H. Mashtaler, and N. Shevchenko; and zoogeography, M. Sharleman, O. Myhulin, V. Zhadin, and O. Kistiakivsky.

The principal centers of zoological studies are the ANU (formerly AN URSR) *Institute of Zoology, *Institute of Hydrobiology, and Institute of Ecology, the Kharkiv University Institute of Biology, the Ukrainian Scientific Research Institute of Fish Farming in Kiev (est 1930), the Azov–

Black Sea Scientific Research Institute of Fish Farming and Oceanography in Kerch, and the Odessa and Sevastopil biological stations.

In Western Ukraine zoological work is carried out at Chernivtsi, Uzhhorod, and Lviv universities, and the zoological departments of some pedagogical institutes and scientific research institutions, where there is concentration on specific local fauna. Principal investigators in this group include O. Markevych, I. Andreiev, O. Kistiakivsky, M. Kucherenko, F. Strautman, V. Abelentsev, I. Sokur, and K. Tatarynov.

A number of noted zoologists emigrated from Ukraine, beginning in the 1920s and continuing after the Second World War, including T. Dobzhansky, M. Vetukhiv, F. Velykokhatko, E. *Zharsky, Yu. *Rusov, Ye. Slastenenko, A. *Granovsky, S. Paramonov, D. Zaitsiv, V. Lazorko, and S. Krasheninnikov. Many of them continued their work at the *Ukrainian Technical and Husbandry Institute.

BIBLIOGRAPHY
Zbirnyk prats' Zoolohichnoho muzeiu AN URSR, 32 vols (Kiev 1926–63)
Sharleman', M. Zooheohrafiia URSR (Kiev 1937)
Fauna Ukraïny (Kiev 1956–)
Markevych, O. Zoolohichni doslidzhennia na Ukraïni za roky radians'koï vlady (Kiev 1957)
Zoologi Sovetskogo Soiuza: Spravochnik (Moscow–Leningrad 1961)
Kornieiev, O. Vyznachnyk zviriv URSR (Kiev 1965)
Biologi: Biograficheskii spravochnik (Kiev 1984)
Topachevs'kyi, V. (ed.) Zhivotnyi mir (Kiev 1985)

I. Masnyk

**Zootechny.** The technology of *animal husbandry, which incorporates *selection, breeding, *genetics, *nutrition, and housing. Zootechny has existed in various forms since the advent of animal domestication, although it has been developed extensively as a scientific undertaking only in modern times. In Ukraine zootechny was practiced in the Kievan Rus' era, when the breeding of horses (commonly used for military purposes) was well developed. During the Cossack era the stables of the Kochubei family were renowned. The early 18th century witnessed considerable developments in *sheep farming in Ukraine, when experienced breeders were brought in from other countries and certain industry norms and practices were implemented.

The origins of contemporary Ukrainian zootechny can be traced to the 1860s and 1870s, when two lines of thought regarding the best method of animal breeding were proposed: the first, to mix local breeds with known Western European ones; the second, to concentrate on the maintenance, improvement, and exploitation of local breeds. Most of the research in the field was undertaken by private scholars working in institutions, such as the Kharkiv Veterinary Institute, the Kiev Polytechnical Institute, and the Askaniia-Nova Nature Reserve. (See also *Cattle raising and *Goat farming.) No single authoritative body existed to administer the zootechny practices, and local efforts on the zemstvo level were attempted. In Western Ukraine some work was done by individual scholars at the Lviv Polytechnical Institute and by the agricultural society *Silskyi Hospodar, but there was no systematic institutional support in Galicia.

With the establishment of a Ukrainian state in 1917–18 an animal husbandry division was formed within the *Agricultural Scientific Committee of Ukraine. It co-ordinated theoretical and practical zootechnical research in Ukraine until the scientific committee was abolished in 1928. Animal husbandry virtually disappeared during the collectivization campaign and the man-made famine in Ukraine. It fully re-established itself only after the Second World War, under the auspices of the Animal Husbandry Board of the Ukrainian Ministry of Agriculture. Its major concerns include breed development, the exhibition of animals, and the maintenance of accurate pedigree records. In addition a variety of Ukrainian scientific research institutes deal with regional aspects of animal husbandry in the forest-steppe and Polisia, Western Ukraine, and the steppe regions. The major forum in Ukraine for zootechny has been the monthly journal *Tvarynnytsvo Ukraïny.

**Zoreslav.** See Sabol, Sevastiian-Stepan.

**Zoria.** An association of Ukrainian tradesmen, manufacturers, and merchants, founded in Lviv in 1884. Continuing the traditions of the old Ukrainian brotherhoods, the association promoted vocational education and technical training. It set up a special section for young tradesmen and a residence for apprentices and vocational students (1896). The organization expanded to the larger towns in Galicia: by 1932 it had 12 branches and over 10,000 members. The founder and longtime president of Zoria was V. *Nahirny. He was succeeded by Yu. Sydorak, the director of the Dilo printing press. Zoria was dissolved in 1939, when Soviet forces occupied Galicia. It was revived briefly under the German occupation (1941–4), when it was known as the Labor Alliance of Ukrainian Tradesmen (Obiednannia pratsi ukrainskykh remisnykiv) and operated under the umbrella of the Ukrainian Central Committee.

Zoria (Lviv)

**Zoria** (Star). A semimonthly literary and scholarly journal published in Lviv in 1880–5 by O. Partytsky and in 1885–97 by the Shevchenko Scientific Society. One of the most important journals of its time, it was devoted to pan-Ukrainian issues and topics, and united writers and subscribers from both Austrian- and Russian-ruled Ukraine. In 1891 it switched from using etymological spelling to a phonetic orthography. Zoria contained literary studies by I. Franko, M. Hrushevsky, V. Kotsovsky, A. Krymsky, O. Ohonovsky, K. Studynsky, and V. Shchurat, and articles on historical, ethnographic, and economic topics by K. Zaklynsky, O. Levytsky, O. Kalytovsky, I. Sharanevych, Franko, D. Lepky, S. Zhuk, and B. Poznansky. Several biographies and memoirs, as well as the correspondence of prominent individuals, also appeared in the journal. *Zoria* was edited by O. Partytsky (to 1885), O. Kalytovsky, O. Borkovsky (1886, 1888–9, 1897), H. Tsehlynsky (1887–8), P. Skobelsky (1889–90), V. Tysovsky (1890–1), and V. Lukych (1890–7). From 1885 Franko was managing editor. *Zoria* was succeeded by *Literaturno-naukovyi vistnyk*. A systematic index to it was published in Lviv in 1988.

*Zoria* (Star). A popular monthly magazine published in Kolomyia in 1902–3. It was edited by K. Trylovsky and P. Olearchuk. Each issue contained a relatively long literary work by writers such as Yu. Fedkovych, T. Yanytsky, B. Lepky, and K. Ustyianovych; articles on political issues and Ukrainian history and culture; and reports on the Sich and Sokil societies and the temperance movement in Western Ukraine.

*Zoria* (Star). A Ukrainian-language literary journal published in March–April 1906 in Moscow (a total of eight issues). It contained works by I. Franko, O. Kovalenko, B. Hrinchenko, M. Starytsky, B. Hrinchenko, Kh. Alchevska, and I. Nechui-Levytsky; art reproductions; articles on Ukrainian history and culture; and the text of the first part of a practical course on the Ukrainian language by A. Krymsky. The editor was I. Oppokov.

*Zoria* (Star). The first Ukrainian newspaper in Brazil. It was published semimonthly by the Prosvita society in Curitiba in 1907–9 and irregularly in 1910. The editor was S. Petrytsky.

*Zoria* (Star). A semimonthly Russophile newspaper published in 1920–31 in Uzhhorod by the Subcarpathian Popular Enlightenment Union. It appeared in the Transcarpathian dialect and was edited by K. Kokhanny-Goralchuk and then P. Fedor.

*Zoria* (Star). A weekly newspaper published in Chernivtsi in 1923–5. Edited by V. Rusnak, it managed to attract only 250 subscribers.

*Zoria* (Star). An illustrated monthly journal of literature, culture, and politics, published in Dnipropetrovske from January 1925 to October 1934. From 1927 it was the organ

*Zoria* (Dnipropetrovske)       *Zoria halytska*

of the Dnipropetrovske branch of the *All-Ukrainian Association of Proletarian Writers, and in 1925–9 it was edited by P. Yefremov and I. Tkachuk. *Zoria* published works by local writers, members of the *Zakhidnia Ukraina writers' group (eg, Tkachuk, M. Irchan, and V. Bobynsky), and pro-communist Ukrainian immigrants (eg, M. Tarnovsky in the United States and A. Pavliuk in Czechoslovakia). The monthly *Shturm* appeared in place of *Zoria* from January 1935 to April 1937.

*Zoria halytska* (Galician Star). The first Ukrainian-language newspaper, published in Lviv weekly from May 1848, semiweekly in 1849–52, and then weekly again to 1857 (a total of 717 issues). As the organ of the *Supreme Ruthenian Council until 1850, the paper stressed the separateness of the Ukrainian nation and the ethnic unity of Ukrainians in the Austro-Hungarian and Russian empires. In 1850–4 *Zoria halytska* was funded by the *Stauropegion Institute and controlled by *Russophiles. Throughout most of this period it was called *Zoria halytskaia* and was published in the artificial Ukrainian-Russian *yazychiie*. It was a journal from 1853. In late 1854 it was taken over by Ukrainophiles, but financial difficulties forced it to fold. *Zoria halytska* published news and articles on political, economic, religious, and community affairs. From 1850 it devoted much attention to literature. It was actively supported by the Greek Catholic clergy, and in 1853–4 it published a religious supplement, *Poucheniia tserkovnyia*. The paper was edited by A. Paventsky (1848–50), M. Kosak (1850), I. Hushalevych (1850–3), B. Didytsky (1853–4), S. Shekhovych (1854), P. Kostetsky (1855–6), and M. Savchynsky (1857).

*Zoria/Hajnal* (Star). A scholarly journal of the *Subcarpathian Scientific Society, published in Uzhhorod in 1941–3, during the Hungarian occupation of Transcarpathia, in the local Transcarpathian dialect and in Hungarian. Edited by I. Haraida, it advocated the existence of a separate 'Rusyn' (Ruthenian) nation and culture with close ties to Hungary.

**Zorka, Samiilo**, b and d ? According to S. Velychko he was a Cossack chronicler and a scribe at the Zaporozhian Sich, and later he became senior secretary to Hetman B. Khmelnytsky. He reportedly wrote a *Diiariiush* (Chronicle-Diary) of the events of 1648–57 in Ukraine, which has not been preserved, but which Velychko claims to quote in his own work. Velychko's chronicle also contains Zorka's eulogy delivered at Khmelnytsky's funeral. Certain scholars (I. Franko, V. Ikonnikov, I. Krypiakevych, M. Marchenko, and M. Petrovsky) claim that Zorka was a fictional personality, and therefore that his chronicle never existed, but others (V. Antonovych, O. Levytsky, M. Maksymovych, and K. Zaklynsky) maintain that he was a real person.

**Zörnikau, Adam** (Zernikav), b 1652 in Königsberg, Germany, d 1691 in Baturyn, Left-Bank Ukraine. Orthodox monk and theologian. A wandering German intellectual who had lived and studied throughout Western Europe, he became convinced that he would find spiritual truth in Orthodoxy and set off for Moscow in 1679. En route he stopped in Chernihiv, where Bishop L. Baranovych baptized him into the Orthodox faith and placed him as an army engineer for Hetman I. Samoilovych. A trip to Moscow in 1683 disillusioned Zörnikau completely and persuaded him to remain in Ukraine. After the fall of Samoilovych in 1687, he took monastic vows and settled in Baturyn. Zörnikau is renowned for a series of tracts written in Latin in 1682 under the title *De processione Spiritus Sancti*, which argue that the Holy Spirit descended from God the Father. The work was published in 1774 in Königsberg, translated into Ukrainian in the mid-18th century by monks at the Kievan Cave Monastery, and published in Russian translation in two volumes in 1902 (Pochaiv) and 1906 (Zhytomyr).

**Zorych-Kondracki, Kvitka** [Zoryč-Kondrac'ka], b 9 March 1944 in Lviv. Conductor and music teacher. She emigrated to Canada with her parents in 1948. She graduated from the Faculty of Music of the University of Toronto (BM, 1968) and then taught music in secondary schools. In 1965 she founded the *Vesnivka Choir, which she has since served as conductor and musical director. She is also a founding member of the Ukrainian Canadian Choral Society.

**Zorynske** [Zoryns'ke]. V-19, DB III-5. A city (1989 pop 9,600) in Perevalske raion, Luhanske oblast. It originated in the 1930s with the merging of the railway settlement of Manuilivka (est 1878) and the Nykanor mining settlement and was called Olenivka. In 1963 the town was renamed and raised to city status. Zorynske is an industrial center with two coal mines.

**Zoshchenko, Mikhail** [Zoščenko, Mixail], b 10 August 1895 in Poltava, d 22 July 1958 in Leningrad. Russian writer-humorist of Ukrainian origin. He belonged to the literary association Serapion Brothers. He published a number of collections of satirical stories and novels, including the biographical novel *Taras Shevchenko* (1939). In 1946 he was criticized for political deviation and was expelled from the Soviet Writers' Union. He was rehabilitated after J. Stalin's death.

**Zosymovych, Volodymyr** [Zosymovyč], b 30 October 1899 in Shapovalivka, Borzna county, Chernihiv gubernia, d 18 January 1981 in Kiev. Biologist; corresponding member of the AN URSR (now ANU) from 1961. A graduate of the Kiev Agricultural School (1926), he worked at the All-Union Scientific Research Institute of the Sugar Industry (1930–60), the Central Republican Botanical Garden of the ANU (1960–3), the ANU Institute of Botany (1963–7), and the ANU Institute of Molecular Biology and Genetics (from 1967). His research centered on the cytogenetics and polyploidy of sugar beets.

**ZOUNR.** See Western Province of the Ukrainian National Republic.

**Zozulia, Yakiv** [Zozulja, Jakiv], b 31 March 1893 in Lebedyn, Kharkiv gubernia, d 6 February 1984 in New York. Jurist, publicist, and political activist; member of the Ukrainian Academy of Arts and Sciences. He began to take an active part in Ukrainian political and cultural life in 1910 and joined the Ukrainian Party of Socialist Revolutionaries. He was a member of the Central Rada (1917–18) and a departmental director in the UNR Ministry of Economic Affairs. He emigrated to Czechoslovakia and graduated in law from Charles University in Prague (1928). In

Yakiv Zozulia

1938–9 he worked on the legal commission of the government of Carpatho-Ukraine, and in 1943 he became a professor of law at the Ukrainian Technical and Husbandry Institute; he published a guidebook to the institute's regulations and curriculum in 1947. He emigrated to the United States thereafter and taught at the Ukrainian Technological Institute in New York from 1954. He served as vice-president of the Association of Ukrainian Lawyers in New York (1955–62). He compiled a chronology of events during the struggle for Ukrainian independence (February 1917 to March 1918) and published popular articles on Ukrainian émigré schools (1958) and Ukrainian statehood (1967), as well as the monograph *Hroshi ukraïns'koï derzhavy* (Currency of the Ukrainian State, 1972; with B. Martos).

**Zozuliak, Vasyl** [Zozuljak, Vasyl'], b 19 September 1909 in Chertizhne, Zemplén county, Transcarpathia. Writer. He graduated from the Mukachiv Teachers' Seminary (1937) and worked as a teacher. He became the cultural-educational secretary of the Ukrainian People's Council of the Prešov Region (1947–9) and the Association of Czechoslovak-Soviet Friendship (1949–52) and then served, until his retirement, as director of the publishing house of the Cultural Association of Ukrainian Workers and of the Ukrainian department of the Slovak Publishing House of Artistic Literature. He first wrote in Russian, in which language he published two books of plays (1953) and a novel (1956). From the mid-1950s he wrote, in Ukrainian, many didactic plays, collected in the book *Za chyste nebo* (For a Clear Sky, 1983); the satire, humor, and play collection *Buvaie i tak* (It Also Happens Thus, 1957); the epic novel *Neskoreni* (The Undaunted, 3 vols, 1962, 1966, 1974); the novelette collections *Na krutykh povorotakh* (On Sharp Turnarounds, 1975) and *Nezlamni kryla* (Unbreakable Wings, 1977); the story collections *Svitlo i tini* (Light and Shadows, 1971) and *Khmary i zori nad Beskydom* (Clouds and Stars over the Beskyd, 1986); and the novel *Metamorfozy* (Metamorphoses, 1979). His plays have been staged by the Prešov Ukrainian National Theater.

**Zozulyntsi settlement.** A multi-occupational site near Zozulyntsi, Zalishchyky raion, Ternopil oblast. Studies revealed the remains of a Paleolithic camping ground, a Trypilian culture settlement (in which zoomorphic earthenware figurines were found), an early Slavic grave site, and a Rus' settlement.

*Źródła dziejowe* (Historical Sources). A collection of historical materials (22 volumes in all) published by the Polish historians A. Jabłonowski and A. Pawiński in 1876–99. Several volumes, subtitled *Ziemie ruskie* (Rus' Lands), were devoted to Right-Bank Ukraine, and contained valuable materials on the settlement, administrative system, and economic life of the region under Polish rule.

**Zsatkovich, Gregory.** See Zhatkovych, Hryhorii.

**ZUADK.** See United Ukrainian American Relief Committee.

Marco Zubar: *Portrait of Maria Lalevich* (oil and tempera, 1963)

**Zubar, Marco,** b 31 March 1925 in Dnipropetrovske, d 28 November 1990 in Philadelphia. Sculptor and painter. A postwar refugee, he graduated from the Düsseldorf Academy of Fine Arts (1951) and then emigrated to the United States. He studied architecture at Princeton University and worked for a firm in Philadelphia as a designer of church interiors. He designed stained-glass windows at the Randolph Macon Women's College in Lynchburg, Virginia, at St Josaphat's Ukrainian Catholic Church in Rochester, New York, and at the Boys Town Chapel in Boys Town, Nebraska. He built monumental metal sculptures, such as the bronze Eternal Flame, added to the Tomb of the Revolutionary Soldier in Washington Square; a light-sculpture for the Beth Zion–Beth Israel Temple, and a steel sculpture in Philadelphia at the Awbury Recreation Center. He also created original ceramic icons, using a technique of his own invention, and painted modernist portraits and compositions, such as *Madam M*, *God the Son, Prophet, Girl's Dance,* and *First Flower.*

Halyna Zubchenko: *Legend about Loyalty* (tempera, watercolor, gouache, 1978)

**Zubchenko, Halyna** [Zubčenko], b 19 July 1929 in Kiev. Mosaicist, muralist, stained-glass artist, and painter. A graduate of the Kiev State Art Institute (1959), she has created many large-scale decorations, including the mosaic wall in the Café Lybid in Kiev (1963), the folksy ceramic-bowl wall in the restaurant of the Hotel Dnipro in Kiev (1964), the murals for School No. 47 in Donetske (1965–6, with H. Synytsia, A. Horska, V. Zaretsky, and H. Marchenko), and several mosaic walls with her husband, H. *Pryshedko. The figures in her compositions tend to be heroic and idealized, in keeping with *socialist realism. Zubchenko has, however, made continuing use of Ukrainian folk-art motifs and mythology and has adapted them effectively to large architectural surfaces. The palette of her easel temperas is as radiant and intense as that of her wall decorations. She has painted a series of sensitive and ethnographically interesting portraits of Hutsuls in their native dress (eg, *Hanusia*, 1962; *Malva of the Carpathians*, 1965) and brooding landscapes of the Carpathian Mountains (eg, *Chornohora: Spring*, 1964).

**Zubenko, Artem,** b 2 November 1890 in Mali Budyshcha, Hadiache county, Poltava gubernia, d 26 August 1963 in New York. Engineer and community figure. After serving in the Russian army he joined the *Zaporozhian Corps and eventually was interned in Wadowice, Poland. He subsequently obtained an engineering degree in Prague (1928) and worked in Czechoslovakia (until 1945) He arrived in the United States in 1945, where he edited the bulletin of the *Ukrainian National State Union in 1952–60 and its organ *Tryzub* in 1960–3.

**Zubenko, Ivan,** b 1889 in Kherson gubernia, d 1940. Writer and journalist. The editor of the UNR Army paper *Zaliznyi strilets'* (1920–2) in Kalisz, Poland, from 1926 he lived in Kolomyia and coedited the women's journal *Zhinocha dolia*. His plays *Divcha z leliieiu* (Girl with a Lily) and

*Orlenia* (The Baby Eagle) were staged in Galicia. He wrote the novelettes *Fatum* (Fate, 1934), *Halyna* (1934), and *Kvitka na bahni* (A Flower on the Marsh, 1937) and the novella collection *Za kulisamy zhyttia* (Behind the Stage of Life, 1937).

**Zuber, Rudolf,** b 18 September 1858 in Orlat, Rumania, d 7 May 1920 in Lviv. Geologist. In 1896 he was appointed a professor at Lviv University. He specialized in petroleum exploration and the geology of the Carpathian Mountains. Volumes 2 and 17 of the multivolume *Atlas geologiczny Galicji* (The Geological Atlas of Galicia, 1888, 1905) were prepared by him. He was the author of *Geologia pokładów naftowych Karpat galicyjskich* (The Geology of the Petroleum Strata of the Galician Carpathians, 1899).

**Zubkov, Serhii,** b 25 September 1919 in Orchykova Cherneshchyna, Kostiantynohrad county, Poltava gubernia. Literary scholar. A graduate of the Kiev Pedagogical Institute (1951), he specialized in prerevolutionary Ukrainian literature and has written monographs on Ye. Hrebinka (1962), H. Kvitka-Osnovianenko (1978), and the Russian prose of Kvitka-Osnovianenko and Hrebinka in the context of Russian-Ukrainian literary relations (1979). He served as head of the manuscript and textology department of the AN URSR (now ANU) Institute of Literature (1951–74), director of the ANU Institute of Fine Arts, Folklore, and Ethnography (1974–87), and editor of *Narodna tvorchist' ta etnohrafiia* (1974–88).

**Zubkovsky, Heorhii** [Zubkovs'kyj, Heorhij], b 15 August 1921 in Bekhtery, Oleshky county, Tavriia gubernia. Graphic artist. In 1951 he graduated from the Kiev State Art Institute, where he studied under I. Pleshchynsky, A. Sereda, and V. Kasiian. He has created the oil series 'Donbas, Shaft 17–17 bis' (1951), the lithograph series 'Soviet Boryslav' (1957), and the linocut series 'On Guard for Peace' (1965) and has designed and illustrated editions of Yu. Zbanatsky's *Peredzhnyv'ia* (Preharvest Time, 1968), O. Makovei's *Iaroshenko* (1967), and a collection of Cossack songs (1969).

**Zubkovsky, Panas** [Zubkovs'kyj], b 1855 in Myrhorod, Poltava gubernia, d 22 December 1921 (or spring 1924) in Tomsk, Siberia. Populist revolutionary. He studied at the Poltava Theological Seminary and Kiev University and was involved in revolutionary circles close to *Zemlia i Volia and V. *Osinsky's group. He was one of the organizers of the assassination of Gov D. Kropotkin in Kharkiv in February 1879. After being arrested in Zasullia, Romen county (May 1879), he was sentenced by a military court in St Petersburg (November 1880) to 15 years of hard labor in eastern Siberia. In 1886 his sentence was commuted to permanent exile. In the 1890s he worked for the paper *Pribaltiiskii listok* in Riga, Latvia, and edited the paper *Sibirskii listok* in Tobolsk, Siberia. Under Soviet rule he worked in financial institutions in Omsk and Tomsk.

**Zubrytsky, Denys** [Zubryc'kyj] (Zubrzycki, Dyonizy; pseud: Denis Veniava iz Zubritsy), b 1777 in Batiatychi, Zhovkva circle, Galicia, d 16 January 1862 in Lviv. The first professional Ukrainian historian and archivist in Galicia; corresponding member of the St Petersburg Archeographic Commission from 1842 and the Russian

Denys Zubrytsky

Academy of Sciences from 1855, and honorary member of the Kiev Archeographic Commission from 1844 and the Moscow Society of Russian History and Antiquities from 1846. He graduated from a Lviv gymnasium (1795) and worked as a civil servant in Brzezowa (Sianik circle) and elsewhere in Galicia. From 1829 to 1847 he held various elected offices at the *Stauropegion Institute in Lviv, including vice-chairman and director of its press, archive, and library. In 1843–4 he was commissioned to put the Lviv municipal archive in order and to write a description of it.

Zubrytsky was greatly influenced by the Russian historian M. *Pogodin's theory of one Russian-Ukrainian nation. He in turn influenced the views of the Galician Russophile scholars. An opponent of the Polish nobility and of Polish domination in Galicia, Zubrytsky idealized the tsarist autocracy while remaining loyal to the Austrian crown. During the Revolution of 1848 he supported the Supreme Ruthenian Council but opposed the abolition of serfdom.

Zubrytsky did substantial archival research and in 1823 published a pioneering article on Galician folk songs in *Der Pilger von Lemberg*. He wrote a Polish book of historical studies on Ruthenian-Slavonic printeries in Galicia (1836), a survey history of the Ruthenian people and the church hierarchy in Galicia from 988 to 1340 (1837), a chronicle of the city of Lviv (1844), a pamphlet on the Ruthenian-Polish ethnic border in Galicia (1849; German trans 1849), and historical articles, published mostly in the Lviv journal *Rozmaitości*. Zubrytsky's Russian-language magnum opus on the history of the Principality of Galicia-Volhynia (3 vols, 1852, 1855) had a great impact on his Galician contemporaries. Instead of a fourth volume he published a book of excerpts from the medieval chronicles of Janko of Czarnków and J. Długosz with his Russian translations and critical commentaries and notes (1855).

Zubrytsky's letters appeared in editions of the correspondence of Pogodin (1880), V. Hanka (1905), and Ya. Holovatsky (2 vols, 1905, 1909). A selection of his correspondence in 1840–53 was published by K. Studynsky in *Zapysky NTSh* (vol 43 [1901]), and his correspondence with J. Kopitar was published by F. Svystun in *Vestnik 'Narodnago doma'* (vol 24 [1906]).

R. Senkus

**Zubrytsky, Dionisii** [Zubryc'kyj, Dionisij] (pseud: Torysyn), b 20 June 1895 in Dachiv, Prešov region, d 15 April 1949 in Prešov. Writer, artist, and publicist. He worked as a teacher and later became director of the Prešov Ruthenian Municipal School. In his time he was one of the few writers in the Prešov region who wrote in Ukrainian in addition to the *\*yazychiie*. In the 1920s and 1930s his prose, poems, and publicistic and literary articles were published in Transcarpathian and Prešov periodicals, such as *Nash ridnyi krai, Vinochok dlia podkarpats'kykh ditochok, Pchilka, Russkaia molodezh, Pidkarpats'ka Rus', Slovo naroda,* and *Russkoe slovo* (of which he was an editor) and in the almanacs of the Prešov Prosvita society, in which he was active in the 1930s. He promoted the literary use of the vernacular and a Ukrainian identity in the Prešov region.

**Zubrytsky, Mykhailo** [Zubryc'kyj, Myxajlo], b 22 October 1856 in Kindrativ, Turka county, Galicia, d 8 April 1919 in Berehy Dolishni, Lisko county, Galicia. Historian, ethnographer, and Greek Catholic priest (from 1883); member of the Shevchenko Scientific Society from 1904. He attended the gymnasium in Drohobych with I. Franko and later studied at the Lviv and Peremyshl theological academies. He researched the history of Galicia in the 19th century and published a wealth of materials on the history of the Galician village (*ZNTSh*, vols 70–9 [1906–7]), the years 1846–61 in Galicia (*ZNTSh*, vol 26 [1898]), recruitment in Galicia from the end of the 18th century to the middle of the 19th century (*ZNTSh*, vol 42 [1901]), the Ruthenian clergy in Galicia in 1820–53 (*ZNTSh*, vol 88 [1909]), the village clergy in Galicia in the 17th and 18th centuries (*ZNTSh*, vol 51 [1903]), and parish libraries of the Peremyshl eparchy (*ZNTSh*, vol 90 [1909]). He also researched the ethnology of the Boiko region and contributed articles to the journals *Zhytie i slovo* and *Dilo*.

**Zubrytsky, Nykodym** [Zubryc'kyj], b 1688, d 1724. Engraver. He worked for the presses in Krekhiv, Lviv (1691–1702), Pochaiv (1704), Kiev (1705), and Chernihiv (1709–24). Almost 400 of his engravings have been preserved, including 67 illustrations and ornaments etched in copper for *\*Ifika iieropolitika* (1712), some illustrations and ornaments for an edition of the New Testament (1717), and the print *Turkish Siege of Pochaiv* (1704). The themes of his genre prints were often taken from folk stories and legends.

Volodymyr Zubrytsky

**Zubrytsky, Volodymyr** [Zubryc'kyj], b 1888, d ? Pedagogue. A teacher in the Peremyshl State Gymnasium, he was an active promoter of education in the Sian region. In 1928–30 he was elected to the Polish Sejm. In 1944 he was sent to a Soviet labor camp, where he disappeared.

Nykodym Zubrytsky: engraved title page of a didactic gospel printed in Univ (1696)

**Zubyk, Roman,** b 1902, d 1940? Economic historian; member of the Shevchenko Scientific Society. He worked in Lviv and researched the history of prices from the 15th to 17th centuries. He was arrested in 1940, and perished at the hands of the NKVD.

**Zuev, Vasilii,** b 12 January 1754 in St Petersburg, d 18 January 1794. Russian natural scientist and traveler; member of the Russian Academy of Sciences from 1779. In 1768–74 he took part in research expeditions into the Urals and Siberia sponsored by the academy, and in 1781–2 he undertook a trip of his own through Ukraine. He noted his observations in the book *Puteshestvennye zapiski ot Sankt-Peterburgu do Khersona v 1781 i 1782 gg* (Travel Notes from St Petersburg to Kherson in 1781 and 1782, 1787). Zuev provided the first descriptions of the iron-ore deposits in the Saksahan River valley in the Kryvyi Rih region and the saltwater lakes between Poltava and Kremenchuk. He also prepared a map of the Dnieper Estuary.

**Zuhres.** V-19, DB III-4. A city (1989 pop 23,800) on the Krynka River in Donetske oblast, under the jurisdiction of the

Khartsyzke city council. It was founded as a workers' settlement in 1929–32 during the construction of the Zuivka Thermoelectric Station. Today its residents work at the thermoelectric station (DRES no. 2) and its experimental center and in the city's machine-building and brick factories.

Oleh Zuievsky

Luba Zuk

**Zuievsky, Oleh** [Zujevs'kyj] (Zujewskyj), b 16 February 1920 in Khomutets, Myrhorod county, Poltava gubernia. Scholar and poet. Zuievsky was educated at the Kharkiv Institute of Journalism. After being displaced by the Second World War he emigrated to the United States in 1950. He completed his studies at the University of Pennsylvania (PH D, 1962) and taught Russian language and literature at Fordham University in New York (1960–3) and Rutgers University in New Jersey (1963–6) and at the University of Alberta (1966–90). Two collections of his poems were published, *Zoloti vorota* (The Golden Gates, 1947) and *Pid znakom feniksa* (Under the Sign of the Phoenix, 1958). He has translated from French, English, and German poetry into Ukrainian and has published (with I. Kostetsky) *Vybranyi Stefan George po ukraïnskomu ta inshymy, peredusim slovians'kymy movamy* (Selected Stefan George [translated] into Ukrainian and Other, Especially Slavic, Languages, 2 vols, 1968, 1971). His translation of S. Mallarmé's *Poésies*, with an introduction and notes, was published in 1990.

**Zuikha, Yavdokha** [Zujixa, Javdoxa] (pseud of Syvak, Yavdokha), b 1 March 1855 in Kushchyntsi, Haisyn county, Podilia gubernia, d 19 January 1935 in Ziatkivtsi, Haisyn raion, Vinnytsia oblast. Folk singer. Over a period of 12 years H. *Tantsiura wrote down her repertoire of 1,008 folk songs with melodies, 400 proverbs and sayings, 156 tales, many riddles, and other ethnographic materials. His notations have been preserved in the manuscript collection of the AN URSR (now ANU) Institute of Fine Arts, Folklore, and Ethnography. The nonreligious songs (925 in all) were published in the collection *Pisni Iavdokhy Zuïkhy* (The Songs of Yavdokha Zuikha, 1965), and some of the remaining material appeared in the series Ukraïns'ka narodna tvorchist (Ukrainian Folk Art).

**Zuivka** [Zujivka]. V-19, DB III-4. A town smt (1985 pop 5,400) on the Krynka River in Donetske oblast, under the

jurisdiction of the Khartsyzke city council. It was founded in 1775. It is the site of the Vilkhivka Reservoir.

**Zuk, Ireneus** [Žuk, Irenej], b 5 August 1943 in Liubachiv, Galicia. Concert pianist and educator; brother of L. and R. Zuk. A graduate of the Peabody Conservatory in Baltimore (PH D, class of L. Fleischer, 1985), he has served on the faculties of McGill and Queen's universities in Canada. He has performed in recitals, often with his sister L. *Zuk, and as a soloist with the Montreal Symphony Orchestra, Radio-Canada CBC Orchestra, and other ensembles. His Ukrainian repertoire includes works by M. Lysenko, V. Kosenko, L. Revutsky, and A. Kos-Anatolsky.

**Zuk, Luba** [Žuk, Ljuba], b 5 April 1930 in Liubachiv, Galicia. Concert pianist and educator. She studied at the Graz Conservatory and in Montreal at McGill University before graduating from the Conservatory of Quebec. Since the 1950s she has taught at McGill University, and since 1965 at the Ukrainian Free University as a visiting lecturer. A popularizer of Ukrainian piano music in the West, she regularly interprets works by M. Lysenko, V. Barvinsky, F. Yakymenko, M. Verykivsky, M. Fomenko, V. Hrudyn, N. Nyzhankivsky, and I. Sonevytsky. She has appeared in piano duo recitals with her brother I. *Zuk premiering works by G. Fiala, M. Kouzan, I. Bilohrud, F. Yakymenko, and others.

Radoslav Zuk, architect: St Michael and the Angels Ukrainian Catholic Church in Tyndall, Manitoba

**Zuk, Radoslav** [Žuk], b 13 September 1931 in Liubachiv, Galicia. Architect and educator; brother of I. and L. Zuk. A graduate of McGill University (B ARCH, 1956) and the Massachusetts Institute of Technology (M ARCH, 1960), he has been a professor of architecture at the University of Manitoba (1960–6) and McGill (since 1976) and a designer with the Montreal firm of Gorman, Mixon, and Blood. A fellow of the Royal Architecture Institute of Canada since 1987, he has designed seven Ukrainian churches in Canada (St Michael's [1963] in Tyndall, Manitoba, Holy Family [1963] and St Joseph's [1964] in Winnipeg, St Michael's [1966] in Transcona, Manitoba, Holy Eucharist [1967] in Toronto, Holy Cross [1968] in Thunder Bay, and St Stephen's [1982] in Calgary) and two in the United States (Holy Trinity [1976] in Kerhonkson, New York, and St Josaphat's [1979] in Rochester). All of Zuk's designs have an impressive silhouette and evoke the traditional wooden architecture of Western Ukraine but remain contemporary and responsive to their surroundings. He received the Governor-General's Medal for Architecture for St Stephen's Church in Calgary, in which his intention was to capture the unique cultural character of the various historical periods of Ukrainian architecture mainly through volumetric articulation.

**ZUNR.** See Western Ukrainian National Republic.

**Zvarych, Andrii** [Zvaryč, Andrij] (Svarich, Andrew), b 1 October 1886 in Tulova, Sniatyn county, Galicia, d 23 May 1977 in Vegreville, Alberta. Community activist. An immigrant to Canada with his parents in 1900, he served as director of the National Co-operative Company (Ruska Narodna Torhovlia, 1910–23) and was the first Ukrainian to serve on the municipal council (1914). Active in the Ukrainian community, he was a founding member of the Ukrainian Orthodox church of Canada, the Hrushevsky Institute in Edmonton, and the Ukrainian People's Home in Vegreville.

Petro Zvarych

**Zvarych, Petro** [Zvaryč] (Svarich, Peter), b 24 March 1877 in Tulova, Sniatyn county, Galicia, d 30 June 1966 in Vegreville, Alberta. Community leader. He completed study at a gymnasium, emigrated to Canada in 1900, and settled in the Vegreville area after working at a variety of odd jobs for several years. In 1909 he was one of the founders of the National Co-operative Company (Ruska Narodna Torhovlia), which developed into a chain in the Ukrainian districts of east central Alberta. Zvarych became a leading figure in the Ukrainian Orthodox Church of Canada and the Ukrainian Self-Reliance League. As well, he was a strong supporter of the Mohyla Ukrainian Institute and a frequent contributor to *Ukraïns'kyi holos*. The first part of his memoirs was published in 1976 as *Spomyny, 1877–1904* (Reminiscences, 1877–1904).

**Zveno** (Link). A journal of literature, art, and criticism, published by the Central Union of Ukrainian Students and, later, the MUR association in Innsbruck. Seven issues appeared in 1946–7 under the editorship of V. Krymsky, the later ones with the assistance of Yu. Dyvnych (Lavrinenko) and Yu. Klen. Among the contributors were prominent postwar émigré writers.

**Zvenyhorod.** IV-5. A village in Pustomyty raion, Lviv oblast, approx 20 km southeast of Lviv. It is also called

Zvenyhorod Halytskyi, to distinguish it from Zvenyhorod Kyivskyi, which was a town south or southwest of Kiev during the era of Kievan Rus' (probably destroyed by Tatars in 1240). The Galician village site has been settled continuously since the Paleolithic period and is one of the oldest such sites in Galicia. Zvenyhorod is first mentioned in ancient chronicles under the year 1087, when it was the seat of Prince Volodar Rostyslavych. In 1124–41 his son, Volodymyrko, governed there, and after he moved to Halych, Ivan Rostyslavych (1144) and Roman Ihorevych (1206–12) ruled there. The town derived its importance from its position at the intersection of east–west and north–south trade routes. The fortress, built on a low hill surrounded by the marshes of the Bilka River, was virtually inaccessible. After it was burned down by the Tatars in 1240, Zvenyhorod declined to an ordinary village, and its leading role passed to Lviv. Excavations were conducted at Zvenyhorod by I. Sharanevych (1885), M. Hrushevsky (1899), N. Mykyta (1907), I. Bilynkevych (1920s), L. Chachkovsky (1932), Ya. Pasternak (1937), and I. Sveshnikov (1970–81). Among the retrieved artifacts the most historically valuable are samples of Roman provincial ceramics imported from Gaul and the lead seals of Metropolitan Constantine and Prince Vasylko of Terebovlia. Some traces of a court church built of white stone have been found.

BIBLIOGRAPHY
Sharanevich, I. *Raskopki v drevnem Zvenigorode* (Lviv 1885)
Hrushevs'kyi, M. *Zvenyhorod halyts'kyi* (Lviv 1899)
Pasternak, Ia. *Terra sigilliata iz Zvenyhorodu* (Lviv 1931)
Vlokh, M. *Vynnyky, Zvenyhorod, Uhniv ta dovkil'ni sela* (Chicago 1970)

A. Zhukovsky

**Zvenyhorod.** A fortress somewhere to the south or southeast of Kiev that protected the capital of Rus' from nomadic hordes. To distinguish it from other medieval towns of the same name, it is usually called Zvenyhorod Kyivskyi. Its exact location has not been determined. The fortress is mentioned in the Hypatian Chronicle as the site of *Vasylko Rostyslavych's blinding in 1097, as an object of contention between Yurii Dolgorukii and Iziaslav Mstyslavych in 1150–1, and as the site of a battle with the Cumans in 1234. The fortress was probably destroyed by the Mongols in 1240.

**Zvenyhorod principality.** An appanage principality of Kievan Rus' that emerged toward the end of the 11th century. Its capital was Zvenyhorod, near Lviv. It was ruled by Volodar Rostyslavych and then by his son, Volodymyrko, who by 1144 had formed a unified Halych principality out of the appanage principalities of Zvenyhorod, Halych, Peremyshl, and Terebovlia. After his death (1152) Zvenhorod principality was annexed by Terebovlia principality. In 1206 it was restored as a separate principality. During the reign of Danylo Romanovych Zvenyhorod principality became part of the Principality of Galicia-Volhynia.

**Zvenyhorodka.** IV-11. A city (1989 pop 22,400) on the Hnylyi Tikych River and a raion center in Cherkasy oblast. It dates back to the time of Kievan Rus'. It was destroyed by the Mongols in 1240 and, subsequently fortified, suffered from Tatar attacks in the 15th and 16th centuries. In 1648 it threw off Polish rule, but it was restored to Poland under the Treaty of Andrusovo. Haidamakas captured it in 1737, 1743, and 1768. Zvenyhorod was annexed by Russia in 1793, and it obtained the rights of *Magdeburg law (1795) and became a county center of Kiev gubernia. During the revolutionary period the Zaporizhian Mazepa Regiment scored a victory over the Bolshevik forces there on 1 February 1918. Today the city has a well-developed food industry, a sanatorium, a regional studies museum, and three historical parks.

**Zviahel.** See Novohrad-Volynskyi.

**Zviahel regiment.** An administrative territory and military formation of the Hetman state in Volhynia. It was formed in 1648 out of peasants and townsmen who joined the Cossack uprising. Under Col M. Tysha its troops captured the Ostrih fortress from the Poles. The regiment was abolished in 1649 and revived for a brief period in 1657–8. It was commanded by I. Tarnavsky and had eight companies.

**Zvirozomb-Zubovsky, Yevhen** [Zvirozomb-Zubovs'kyj, Jevhen], b 3 March 1890 in Kiev, d 21 April 1967 in Kiev. Entomologist; corresponding member of the AN URSR (now ANU) from 1939. A graduate of Kiev University (1916), he conducted research in Kiev, Voronezh, Rostovna-Donu, and Moscow and was associate director of the ANU Institute of Zoology and associate director (1946–8), director (1949–50), and laboratory director (1950–6) of the ANU Institute of Entomology and Phytopathology. He also taught at Kiev University (1946–8) and was founding president of the Ukrainian Entomological Society (1946–56). His major published work was *Vrediteli sakharnoi svekly* (Sugar Beet Pests, 1928; 2nd edn 1956).

Karlo Zvirynsky: *Interior* (1960)

**Zvirynsky, Karlo** [Zviryns'kyj], b 14 August 1923 in Lavriv, Turka county, Galicia. Painter and educator. He studied at the short-lived Lviv Academy of Art in 1943 under V. Krychevsky, graduated in 1953 from the Lviv Institute of Applied and Decorative Arts, where he studied under R. *Selsky, and taught at the institute (1958–79). Zvirynsky has experimented with the formal aspects of composition, form, line, texture, and color. Some of his works of the 1960s parallel the formal achievements of Western abstractionists. Zvirynsky has also painted semiabstract landscapes (eg, *Forest Motif*, 1966) and complex still lifes, in which an assortment of objects fill the canvas (eg, *Small Objects*, 1982). His numerous collages and relief constructions on panels explore the formal relationships of form and color.

**Zvychaina, Olena** [Zvyčajna], b ?, d 8 January 1985 on Staten Island, New York. Writer. She wrote the novelettes *Zolotyi potichok z holodnoho Kharkova* (A Golden Stream from Hungry Kharkiv, 1947) and *Myrhorods'kyi iarmarok* (Myrhorod Fair, 1953), the story collection *Ohlianuvshys' nazad* (Looking Back, 1954), and the novels *Selians'ka sanatoriia* (The Peasant Sanatorium, 1952), *Strakh* (Fear, 2 vols, 1957, 1958), *Voroh narodu* (Enemy of the People, 2 vols, 1966, cowritten with her husband O. Mlakovy), and *Ty* (You, 1982). All of her works are set in interwar and wartime Soviet Ukraine.

**Zwoliński, Przemysław,** b 26 September 1914 in Opava, Czechoslovakia, d 4 November 1981 in Warsaw. Polish Slavist. A graduate of Lviv University (MA, 1937), he worked there as an assistant (1939–41). After the war he lectured at Wrocław (1945–6), Cracow (1947–52), and Warsaw universities. In 1953 he set up the Ukrainian philology department at Warsaw University, which he chaired until 1970. He wrote articles on the development of Ukrainian from the 14th to the 18th century (1956), I. Franko as a linguist (1956), T. Shevchenko's language (1964), P. Hulak-Artemovsky's imitation of J. Kochanowski's psalms (1965), and I. Kotliarevsky's work (1970–1) and coedited a Ukrainian-Polish dictionary (1957).

Orest Zybachynsky          Yevhen Zyblikevych

**Zybachynsky, Orest** [Zybačyns'kyj] (pseud: Orlan), b 15 May 1912 in Chernivtsi, Bukovyna. Political activist and publicist. He studied law at Chernivtsi University. In 1934–40 he oversaw all OUN activity in Bukovyna, Bessarabia, and the Maramureş region in Rumania. He participated in OUN expeditionary groups (Melnyk faction) and co-organized the Bukovynian detachment that was active in Southern Ukraine, OUN forces in the Donbas region (1941–2) and in Volhynia and Polisia (1942–3), and the military wing of the Oborona Ukrainy organization (1943). He emigrated to Munich in 1945, where he founded the political organization *Freedom International and acted as its general secretary in 1946–9. In 1949 he moved to Sydney, Australia. He published collections of political essays, including *Svobodarnist'* ([combination of *svoboda* and *solidarnist*] Freedom and Solidarity, 1955), *Integral'na revoliutsiia* (The Integral Revolution, 1960), *Renesans – Reformatsiia – Revoliutsiia* (Renaissance, Reformation, Revolution, 1968), *Svobodarnyi manifest* (Manifesto of Freedom and Solidarity, 1978), *Mech dukha* (Sword of the Spirit, 1980), *Misteriia svobody* (The Mystery of Freedom, 1985), and *Volia do svobody* (The Will to Freedom, 1988).

**Zybenko, Oleksander,** b 12 November 1893 in Maiorske, Mariiupil county, Katerynoslav gubernia, d 7 June 1960 in Australia. Agronomist and co-operative organizer. After studying at the Kiev Polytechnical Institute he worked as an agronomist in Skvyra county (1917) and was appointed its commissioner. Under the Hetman government he was imprisoned by the Germans, but he escaped and took part in the overthrow of the hetman. Under the UNR Directory he served as deputy director of the agrarian reform department in the Ministry of Agriculture. In 1922 he emigrated to Czechoslovakia, where he completed a degree in agronomy (1927). He then worked as an auditor in the Audit Union of Ukrainian Co-operatives (RSUK) in Volhynia. In 1930 he was appointed auditor, and in 1937, inspector, of dairy unions at the head office in Lviv. During the Second World War he continued to work in RSUK in Cracow and Lviv. In 1944 he left Ukraine; eventually he emigrated to Australia.

**Zyblikevych, Yevhen** [Zyblikevyč, Jevhen] (Ziblykevych, Evhen; pseud: K. Porokhivsky), b 20 November 1895 in Staryi Sambir, Galicia, d 16 September 1987 in Philadelphia. Galician and émigré journalist and political figure. A veteran officer of the Ukrainian Sich Riflemen, in the 1920s he was a member of the Ukrainian Military Organization and directed its activities in the Peremyshl region. He was arrested for his political activities, and spent several years in a Polish prison. After his release he edited the Peremyshl newspapers *Ukraïns'kyi holos* (1926–9) and *Beskyd* (1930–3), and the sports magazine *Zmah* (1937–9). A founding member of the OUN, he soon left it and became a leading member of the hetmanite movement in Galicia. A postwar émigré, in Philadelphia he edited the newspaper *Ameryka* (1953–62) and founded and directed (from 1964) the *Lypynsky East European Research Institute.

**Žygimantas** (Ukrainian: Zhyhmont Keistutovych; Polish: Zygmunt; Latin: Sigismundus), b ca 1365, d 1440. Grand duke of Lithuania; younger brother of *Vytautas. After Vytautas died, Žygimantas supported his cousin, *Švitrigaila, who ascended to the throne and cultivated alliances with the Belarusians and Ukrainians in order to maintain an independence from Poland. In 1431 Žygimantas made a bid for the throne and, with the backing of Polish nobles, captured Vilnius. In 1432 he proclaimed himself grand duke. At the same time he ceded Podilia to the Poles, and in 1438, after six years of civil war, he was forced to abandon Volhynia. During his rule Žygimantas recognized the equal rights of his Orthodox subjects and introduced *Magdeburg law in Vilnius. He was assassinated by conspirators loyal to Švitrigaila.

**Zygmunt.** See Sigismund.

**Zyla, Wolodymyr** [Žyla, Volodymyr], b 25 June 1919 in Zbarazh, Galicia. Émigré literary scholar and community figure; member of the Shevchenko Scientific Society. As a postwar refugee he organized the first Ukrainian DP camp in the British zone of Austria near Villach and founded and edited the short-lived paper *Ukraïns'ki visti*. After emigrating to São Paulo, Brazil, in 1948, he was a coeditor of the weekly *Nasha dumka*. In 1952 he emigrated to Canada. He graduated from the University of Manitoba (1962) and the Ukrainian Free University (PH D, 1967). From 1963 to 1986 he was a professor of Russian, German, and comparative literature at Texas Tech University in Lubbock. He has written articles and reviews in the fields of Ukrainian and comparative literature and onomastics in North American scholarly publications.

*Zymivnyk.* A winter homestead of the Zaporozhian Cossacks who lived outside the Sich by farming, fishing, and hunting. Many of those Cossacks were married, but some were elderly single men. There were many such homesteads along the Samara River. In 1775 there were 763 *zymivnyky*, with 8,700 Cossack settlers, on the right bank of the Dnieper River alone.

**Zymne.** III-5. A village (1970 pop 1,100) on the Luh River in Volodomyr-Volynskyi raion, Volhynia oblast. Archeologists have discovered evidence of settlement dating back to the 3rd millennium BC. There was a village at the site in the period of Kievan Rus'. Zymne was first mentioned in a document in 1450. The village and its old Orthodox monastery were granted to the Basilian order in 1682. In the 1890s the monastery was restored and turned into an Orthodox convent. During the First World War it was destroyed. The ruins of the fortifications from the 15th century, the Church of the Holy Trinity (1465–75), the Dormition Church (1495), and the catacombs of the monastery have been preserved.

The Zymne Monastery

**Zymne Monastery.** Probably the oldest monastery in Volhynia, located in the village of Zymne, 5 km south of Volodymyr-Volynskyi. Because it was built on a steep promontory atop ancient caves on the Luh River, it also had the names *sviatohirskyi* 'holy hill' and *pecherskyi* 'cave.' According to medieval sources, Grand Prince Volodymyr the Great had the monastery's Church of the Dormition built ca 1001; Hegumen Varlaam of the Kievan Cave Monastery died at the monastery in 1065; and the chronicler Nifont was its hegumen in the 12th century. In the 1460s Prince

O. Chartoryisky, the owner of Zymne, had parapets with five gates and corner towers built around the monastery, and in 1495 the Church of Dormition was rebuilt out of stone. In 1682 the Catholic Basilian monastic order was granted Zymne and the monastery. In the 1740s M. Czacki, the castellan of Volodymyr-Volynskyi and owner (from 1724) of Zymne, removed all of the monastery's valuables and brought about its demise. The monastery was revived by the Russian Orthodox church in the 19th century, and from 1893 it was inhabited by nuns. Extensive reconstruction of its buildings was begun in 1899, and a campanile and a subterranean church at the entrance to the caves were built. During the First World War the monastery was extensively damaged, and its library and archives vanished. It was renovated in the 1930s but again destroyed during the Second World War. Restoration of the monastery's main buildings was begun in 1975. Nothing remains of the burial crypts inside the Church of the Dormition, where many prominent Volhynian nobles were once buried.

A. Zhukovsky

**Zymny, Leonid** [Zymnyj] (pseud of Leonid Pysarevsky), b 18 February 1907 in Kostiantynohrad (now Krasnohrad), Poltava gubernia, d 22 May 1942. Poet. He began publishing in 1929 in *Nova generatsiia*. Published separately were his collections *Ne v dni iuvileïv* (Not on Anniversary Days, 1930) and *Pisennyk* (Songbook, 1937), the narrative poem *Shturm shakht* (The Storming of the [Mine] Shafts, 1931), and several booklets of poems and stories for children. He died in combat against the Germans during the Soviet-German War. A posthumous edition of his poems was published in Kiev in 1956.

**Zymohiria** [Zymohirja]. V-19, DB II-5. A city (1989 pop 12,500) on the Luhan River in Slovianoserbske raion, Luhanske oblast. It was settled in 1645–7 by Zaporozhian Cossacks invited by the Muscovite government to defend the southern frontier from the Tatars. A century later the government brought in Serbian colonists to man the defense line in the steppe. In 1764 the name of the settlement was changed from Cherkaskyi Brid to Cherkaske, and it was made a volost center in Slovianoserbske county of New Russia gubernia. In 1865 coal was discovered in the region, and small shafts were dug by the peasants. By the 1880s large mining enterprises had been set up. In 1961 the village was renamed Zymohiria and raised to city status. Today it is an industrial center with a coal mine and enrichment plant, a canning factory, and a building-materials plant.

**Zynoviev, Klymentii.** See Klymentii, Zinovii's son.

*Zyz* (Cross-eye). A semimonthly and then monthly magazine of satire and humor, published in Lviv in 1924–33. It was edited by L. Lepky and, later, E. Kozak, who was also the chief illustrator from 1926. Contributors included O. Babii, M. Vorony, V. Hirny, R. Holiian, T. Krushelnytsky, R. Kupchynsky, A. Kurdydyk, and M. Rudnytsky. Caricatures were supplied by P. Kovzhun, M. Butovych, O. Sorokhtei, P. Kholodny, Jr, R. Lisovsky, and R. Chornii. In 1930 it had a pressrun of 1,450.

**Zyzanii, Lavrentii** [Zyzanij, Lavrentij] (Tustanovsky), b 1550s or 1560s in Tustan, near Halych, or Potelych, near Zhovkva, Galicia, d after 1634, possibly in Korets, Volhynia. Orthodox priest, teacher, writer, translator, and

Lavrentii Zyzanii's Slavonic grammar (1596)

grammarian; brother of S. Zyzanii. He taught in Orthodox brotherhood schools in Lviv (to 1592), Berestia (from 1592), and Vilnius (from 1595). In 1596 he published in Vilnius a Slavonic grammar, compiled on the basis of *Adelphotes* (1591), and a Slavonic primer. The primer included a lexicon of 1,061 Church Slavonic words explained in the Ukrainian vernacular; in effect, it was the first printed Church Slavonic–Ukrainian dictionary. Zyzanii's translation from Greek of Andrew of Caesarea's commentary on the Book of Revelation was published in Kiev in 1625. In 1620 Zyzanii completed an Orthodox catechism in Ukrainian; it was printed in an altered Church Slavonic translation in Moscow in 1627, and was soon ordered burned by the Muscovite patriarch Filaret as heretical, but it was retained by the Old Believers, who reprinted it in Hrodna in 1783, 1787, and 1788 and in Moscow in 1874. Zyzanii's lexicon was reprinted by M. Vozniak in *Zapysky NTSh* (vol 102 [1911]) and in separate facsimile editions edited by V. Nimchuk (Kiev 1964) and J. Rudnyckyj (Ottawa 1986). A facsimile edition of his grammar was edited by V. Nimchuk and published in Kiev in 1980. M. Botvinnik's monograph about Zyzanii was published in Minsk in 1973.

**Zyzanii, Stepan** [Zyzanij], b ca 1570 in Potelych, near Zhovkva, Galicia, d before 1621. Orthodox teacher and polemical writer; brother of L. Zyzanii. From 1586 he taught at the Lviv Dormition Brotherhood School, and he became its rector in 1592. From 1593 he was a teacher and secular preacher with the Orthodox brotherhood in Vilnius, where he sermonized against Catholicism and the clerical supporters of church union with Rome. In 1595 and 1596 he published several anti-Catholic polemical works and a catechism in Vilnius. He was forbidden to preach by Metropolitan M. Rahoza, and in January 1596 he was condemned as a heretic for his inflammatory sermons and writings and excommunicated by the Orthodox sobor in Navahrudak. He was exonerated later that year by the Orthodox sobor in Berestia. In 1599 he entered the Trinity Monastery in Vilnius but soon he was forced to leave by the municipal government under pressure from the crown. His further fate is unknown. His popular 1596 book distorting St Cyril's homily about the anti-Christ – in which Zyzanii developed the Protestant idea of the pope as the anti-Christ – was translated from Ukrainian into Church Slavonic and published in Moscow in 1644.